$149.95 per copy (in United States).
Price subject to change without prior notice.

0018

The 2008 *Building Construction Cost Data, 66th Annual Edition*, and all of RSMeans Annual Cost Data Books for 2008, are dedicated to the memory of our respected colleague and friend, Senior Engineering Operations Manager, John Ferguson.

**2008**

**RSMeans**
*Construction Publishers & Consultants*
*63 Smiths Lane*
*Kingston, MA 02364-0800*
**(781) 422-5000**

# RSMeans
# Building Construction Cost Data

## 66th Annual Edition

**Senior Editor**
Phillip R. Waier, PE

**Contributing Editors**
Christopher Babbitt
Ted Baker
Barbara Balboni
Robert A. Bastoni
John H. Chiang, PE
Gary W. Christensen
David G. Drain, PE
Cheryl Elsmore
Robert J. Kuchta
Robert C. McNichols
Robert W. Mewis, CCC
Melville J. Mossman, PE
Jeannene D. Murphy
Stephen C. Plotner
Eugene R. Spencer
Marshall J. Stetson

**Senior Engineering Operations Manager**
John H. Ferguson, PE

**Senior Vice President & General Manager**
John Ware

**Vice President of Direct Response**
John M. Shea

**Director of Sales**
Brian Hare

**Director of Product Development**
Thomas J. Dion

**Production Manager**
Michael Kokernak

**Production Coordinator**
Wayne D. Anderson

**Technical Support**
Jonathan Forgit
Mary Lou Geary
Jill Goodman
Roger Hancock
Gary L. Hoitt
Genevieve Medeiros
Paula Reale-Camelio
Kathryn S. Rodriguez
Sheryl A. Rose

**Book & Cover Design**
Norman R. Forgit

 Reed Construction Data®

 This book is recyclable.

 This book is printed on recycled stock.

# Foreword

## Our Mission

Since 1942, RSMeans has been actively engaged in construction cost publishing and consulting throughout North America.

Today, over 60 years after RSMeans began, our primary objective remains the same: to provide you, the construction and facilities professional, with the most current and comprehensive construction cost data possible.

Whether you are a contractor, an owner, an architect, an engineer, a facilities manager, or anyone else who needs a reliable construction cost estimate, you'll find this publication to be a highly useful and necessary tool.

With the constant flow of new construction methods and materials today, it's difficult to find the time to look at and evaluate all the different construction cost possibilities. In addition, because labor and material costs keep changing, last year's cost information is not a reliable basis for today's estimate or budget.

That's why so many construction professionals turn to RSMeans. We keep track of the costs for you, along with a wide range of other key information, from city cost indexes . . . to productivity rates . . . to crew composition . . . to contractor's overhead and profit rates.

RSMeans performs these functions by collecting data from all facets of the industry and organizing it in a format that is instantly accessible to you. From the preliminary budget to the detailed unit price estimate, you'll find the data in this book useful for all phases of construction cost determination.

## The Staff, the Organization, and Our Services

When you purchase one of RSMeans' publications, you are, in effect, hiring the services of a full-time staff of construction and engineering professionals.

Our thoroughly experienced and highly qualified staff works daily at collecting, analyzing, and disseminating comprehensive cost information for your needs. These staff members have years of practical construction experience and engineering training prior to joining the firm. As a result, you can count on them not only for the cost figures, but also for additional background reference information that will help you create a realistic estimate.

The RSMeans organization is always prepared to help you solve construction problems through its four major divisions: Construction and Cost Data Publishing, Electronic Products and Services, Consulting and Business Solutions, and Professional Development Services.

Besides a full array of construction cost estimating books, RSMeans also publishes a number of other reference works for the construction industry. Subjects include construction estimating and project and business management; special topics such as HVAC, roofing, plumbing, and hazardous waste remediation; and a library of facility management references.

In addition, you can access all of our construction cost data electronically using *Means CostWorks®* CD or on the Web.

What's more, you can increase your knowledge and improve your construction estimating and management performance with an RSMeans Construction Seminar or In-House Training Program. These two-day seminar programs offer unparalleled opportunities for everyone in your organization to get updated on a wide variety of construction-related issues.

RSMeans is also a worldwide provider of construction cost management and analysis services for commercial and government owners.

In short, RSMeans can provide you with the tools and expertise for constructing accurate and dependable construction estimates and budgets in a variety of ways.

## Part of a Family of Companies Dedicated to the Construction Industry

RSMeans is owned by Reed Construction Data, a leader in providing information solutions to the construction industry. Headquartered near Atlanta, Georgia, Reed Construction Data is a subsidiary of Reed Business Information, North America's largest business-to-business information provider.

With more than 80 market-leading publications and 55 websites, Reed Business Information's wide range of services also includes research, business development, direct marketing lists, training and development programs, and technology solutions. Reed Business Information is a member of the Reed Elsevier PLC group (NYSE: RUK and ENL), a leading provider of global information-driven services and solutions in the science and medical, legal, education, and business-to-business industry sectors.

## Robert Snow Means Established a Tradition of Quality That Continues Today

Robert Snow Means spent years building RSMeans, making certain he always delivered a quality product.

Today, at RSMeans, we do more than talk about the quality of our data and the usefulness of our books. We stand behind all of our data, from historical cost indexes to construction materials and techniques to current costs.

If you have any questions about our products or services, please call us toll-free at 1-800-334-3509. Our customer service representatives will be happy to assist you. You can also visit our Web site at www.rsmeans.com.

# Table of Contents

# Related RSMeans Products and Services

Phillip R. Waier, P.E., Senior Editor of this cost data book, suggests the following RSMeans products and services as companion information resources to *RSMeans Building Construction Cost Data:*

## Construction Cost Data Books
Assemblies Cost Data 2008
Square Foot Costs 2008

## Reference Books
ADA Compliance Pricing Guide, 2nd Ed.
Building Security: Strategies & Costs
Designing & Building with the IBC, 2nd Ed.
Estimating Building Costs
Estimating Handbook, 2nd Ed.
Green Building: Project Planning & Estimating, 2nd Ed.
How to Estimate with Means Data and CostWorks, 3rd Ed.
Plan Reading & Material Takeoff
Project Scheduling & Management for Construction, 3rd Ed.
Repair & Remodeling Estimating Methods, 4th Ed.

## Seminars and In-House Training
Unit Price Estimating
*Means CostWorks®* Training
Means Data for Job Order Contracting (JOC)
Practical Project Management
Scheduling & Project Management
Mechanical & Electrical Estimating

## RSMeans on the Internet
Visit RSMeans at **www.rsmeans.com.** The site contains useful interactive cost and reference material. Request or download **FREE** estimating software demos. Visit our bookstore for convenient ordering and to learn more about new publications and companion products.

## RSMeans Electronic Data
Get the information found in RSMeans cost books electronically on *Means CostWorks®* CD or on the Web at meanscostworks.com.

## RSMeans Business Solutions
Cost Engineers and Analysts conduct facility life cycle and benchmark research studies, predictive cost modeling, as well as offer consultation services for conceptual estimating, real property management, and job order contracting. Research studies are designed with the application of proprietary cost and project data from RCD/RSMeans extensive North American databases. For building product manufacturers, analysts offer qualitative and quantitative market research, as well as time/motion studies for new products, and web-based dashboards for market opportunity analysis. Clients are from both the public and private sectors, including federal, state, and municipal agencies, corporations, institutions, construction management firms, hospitals, and associations.

## RSMeans for Job Order Contracting (JOC)
Best practice JOC tools for cost estimating and project management to help streamline delivery processes for renovation projects. Renovation is a $147 billion market in the U.S., and includes projects in school districts, municipalities, health care facilities, colleges and universities, and corporations.

- RSMeans Engineers consult in contracting methods and conduct JOC Facility Audits

- JOCWorks™ Software (Basic, Advanced, PRO levels)

- RSMeans Job Order Contracting Cost Data for the entire U.S.

## Construction Costs for Software Applications
Over 25 unit price and assemblies cost databases are available through a number of leading estimating and facilities management software providers (listed below). For more information see the "Other RSMeans Products" pages at the back of this publication.

MeansData™ is also available to federal, state, and local government agencies as multi-year, multi-seat licenses.

- 3D International
- 4Clicks-Solutions, LLC
- ArenaSoft Estimating
- Beck Technology
- BSD – Building Systems Design, Inc.
- Building Explorer LLC
- CMS – Construction Management Software
- Corecon Technologies, Inc.
- CorVet Systems
- Digital Alchemy
- Earth Tech
- Estimating Systems, Inc.
- Maximus Asset Solutions
- MC² – Management Computer Controls
- PrioSoft
- Sage Timberline Office
- SchoolDude.com
- US Cost, Inc.
- VFA – Vanderweil Facility Advisers
- WinEstimator, Inc.

# How the Book is Built: An Overview

The Construction Specifications Institute (CSI) and Construction Specifications Canada (CSC) have produced the 2004 edition of MasterFormat™, a new and updated system of titles and numbers used extensively to organize construction information.

All unit price data in the RSMeans cost data books is now arranged in the 50-division MasterFormat™ 2004 system.

## A Powerful Construction Tool

You have in your hands one of the most powerful construction tools available today. A successful project is built on the foundation of an accurate and dependable estimate. This book will enable you to construct just such an estimate.

For the casual user the book is designed to be:

- quickly and easily understood so you can get right to your estimate.
- filled with valuable information so you can understand the necessary factors that go into the cost estimate.

For the regular user, the book is designed to be:

- a handy desk reference that can be quickly referred to for key costs.
- a comprehensive, fully reliable source of current construction costs and productivity rates so you'll be prepared to estimate any project.
- a source book for preliminary project cost, product selections, and alternate materials and methods.

To meet all of these requirements we have organized the book into the following clearly defined sections.

## How To Use the Book: The Details

This section contains an in-depth explanation of how the book is arranged . . . and how you can use it to determine a reliable construction cost estimate. It includes information about how we develop our cost figures and how to completely prepare your estimate.

## Unit Price Section

All cost data has been divided into the 50 divisions according to the MasterFormat system of classification and numbering. For a listing of these divisions and an outline of their subdivisions, see the Unit Price Section Table of Contents.

*Estimating tips are included at the beginning of each division.*

## Reference Section

This section includes information on Equipment Rental Costs, Crew Listings, Historical Cost Indexes, City Cost Indexes, Location Factors, Reference Tables, Change Orders, Square Foot Costs, and a listing of Abbreviations.

**Equipment Rental Costs:** This section contains the average costs to rent and operate hundreds of pieces of construction equipment.

**Crew Listings:** This section lists all the crews referenced in the book. For the purposes of this book, a crew is composed of more than one trade classification and/or the addition of power equipment to any trade classification. Power equipment is included in the cost of the crew. Costs are shown both with the bare labor rates and with the installing contractor's overhead and profit added. For each, the total crew cost per eight-hour day and the composite cost per labor-hour are listed.

**Historical Cost Indexes:** These indexes provide you with data to adjust construction costs over time.

**City Cost Indexes:** All costs in this book are U.S. national averages. Costs vary because of the regional economy. You can adjust costs by CSI Division to over 700 locations throughout the U.S. and Canada by using the data in this section.

**Location Factors:** You can adjust total project costs to over 900 locations throughout the U.S. and Canada by using the data in this section.

**Reference Tables:** At the beginning of selected major classifications in the Unit Price section are reference numbers shown in a shaded box. These numbers refer you to related information in the Reference Section. In this section, you'll find reference tables, explanations, estimating information that support how we develop the unit price data, technical data, and estimating procedures.

**Change Orders:** This section includes information on the factors that influence the pricing of change orders.

**Square Foot Costs:** This section contains costs for 59 different building types that allow you to make a rough estimate for the overall cost of a project or its major components.

**Abbreviations:** A listing of abbreviations used throughout this book, along with the terms they represent, is included in this section.

## Index

A comprehensive listing of all terms and subjects in this book will help you quickly find what you need when you are not sure where it falls in MasterFormat.

## The Scope of This Book

This book is designed to be as comprehensive and as easy to use as possible. To that end we have made certain assumptions and limited its scope in two key ways:

1. We have established material prices based on a national average.
2. We have computed labor costs based on a 30-city national average of union wage rates.

For a more detailed explanation of how the cost data is developed, see "How To Use the Book: The Details".

## Project Size

This book is aimed primarily at commercial and industrial projects costing $1,000,000 and up, or large multi-family housing projects. Costs are primarily for new construction or major renovation of buildings rather than repairs or minor alterations.

*With reasonable exercise of judgment the figures can be used for any building work. However, for civil engineering structures such as bridges, dams, highways, or the like, please refer to RSMeans Heavy Construction Cost Data.*

# How to Use the Book: The Details

## What's Behind the Numbers? The Development of Cost Data

The staff at RSMeans continuously monitors developments in the construction industry in order to ensure reliable, thorough, and up-to-date cost information.

While *overall* construction costs may vary relative to general economic conditions, price fluctuations within the industry are dependent upon many factors. Individual price variations may, in fact, be opposite to overall economic trends. Therefore, costs are continually monitored and complete updates are published yearly. Also, new items are frequently added in response to changes in materials and methods.

## Costs—$ (U.S.)

All costs represent U.S. national averages and are given in U.S. dollars. The RSMeans City Cost Indexes can be used to adjust costs to a particular location. The City Cost Indexes for Canada can be used to adjust U.S. national averages to local costs in Canadian dollars. No exchange rate conversion is necessary.

## Material Costs

The RSMeans staff contacts manufacturers, dealers, distributors, and contractors all across the U.S. and Canada to determine national average material costs. If you have access to current material costs for your specific location, you may wish to make adjustments to reflect differences from the national average. Included within material costs are fasteners for a normal installation. RSMeans engineers use manufacturers' recommendations, written specifications, and/or standard construction practice for size and spacing of fasteners. Adjustments to material costs may be required for your specific application or location. Material costs do not include sales tax.

## Labor Costs

Labor costs are based on the average of wage rates from 30 major U.S. cities. Rates are determined from labor union agreements or prevailing wages for construction trades for the current year. Rates, along with overhead and profit markups, are listed on the inside back cover of this book.

- If wage rates in your area vary from those used in this book, or if rate increases are expected within a given year, labor costs should be adjusted accordingly.

Labor costs reflect productivity based on actual working conditions. In addition to actual installation, these figures include time spent during a normal workday on tasks such as material receiving and handling, mobilization at site, site movement, breaks, and cleanup.

Productivity data is developed over an extended period so as not to be influenced by abnormal variations and reflects a typical average.

## Equipment Costs

Equipment costs include not only rental, but also operating costs for equipment under normal use. The operating costs include parts and labor for routine servicing, such as repair and replacement of pumps, filters, and worn lines. Normal operating expendables, such as fuel, lubricants, tires, and electricity (where applicable), are also included. Extraordinary operating expendables with highly variable wear patterns, such as diamond bits and blades, are excluded. These costs are included under materials. Equipment rental rates are obtained from industry sources throughout North America—contractors, suppliers, dealers, manufacturers, and distributors.

**Crew Equipment Cost/Day**—The power equipment required for each crew is included in the crew cost. The daily cost for crew equipment is based on dividing the weekly bare rental rate by 5 (number of working days per week) and then adding the hourly operating cost times 8 (hours per day). This "Crew Equipment Cost/Day" is listed in the Reference Section.

**Mobilization/Demobilization**—The cost to move construction equipment from an equipment yard or rental company to the job site and back again is not included in equipment costs. Mobilization (to the site) and demobilization (from the site) costs can be found in the Unit Price section. If a piece of equipment is already at the job site, it is not appropriate to utilize mobil./demob. costs again in an estimate.

## Overhead and Profit

Total Cost including O&P for the *Installing Contractor* is shown in the last column on the Unit Price pages of this book. This figure is the sum of the bare material cost plus 10% for overhead and profit, the bare labor cost plus total overhead and profit, and the bare equipment cost plus 10% for overhead and profit. Details for the calculation of Overhead and Profit on labor are shown on the inside back cover of this book. (See the "How To Use the Unit Price Pages" for an example of this calculation.)

## General Conditions

General Conditions, or General Requirements, of the contract should also be added to the Total Cost including O&P when applicable. Costs for General Conditions are listed in Division 1 and the Reference Section of this book. General Conditions for the *Installing Contractor* may range from 0% to 10% of the Total Cost including O&P. For the *General or Prime Contractor*, costs for General Conditions may range from 5% to 15% of the Total Cost including O&P, with a figure of 10% as the most typical allowance.

# Factors Affecting Costs

Costs can vary depending upon a number of variables. Here's how we have handled the main factors affecting costs.

**Quality**—The prices for materials and the workmanship upon which productivity is based represent sound construction work. They are also in line with U.S. government specifications.

**Overtime**—We have made no allowance for overtime. If you anticipate premium time or work beyond normal working hours, be sure to make an appropriate adjustment to your labor costs.

**Productivity**—The productivity, daily output, and labor-hour figures for each line item are based on working an eight-hour day in daylight hours in moderate temperatures. For work that extends beyond normal work hours or is performed under adverse conditions, productivity may decrease. (See the section in "How To Use the Unit Price Pages" for more on productivity.)

**Size of Project**—The size, scope of work, and type of construction project will have a significant impact on cost. Economies of scale can reduce costs for large projects. Unit costs can often run higher for small projects. Costs in this book are intended for the size and type of project as previously described in "How the Book Is Built: An Overview." Costs for projects of a significantly different size or type should be adjusted accordingly.

**Location**—Material prices in this book are for metropolitan areas. However, in dense urban areas, traffic and site storage limitations may increase costs. Beyond a 20-mile radius of large cities, extra trucking or transportation charges may also increase the material costs slightly. On the other hand, lower wage rates may be in effect. Be sure to consider both of these factors when preparing an estimate, particularly if the job site is located in a central city or remote rural location.

In addition, highly specialized subcontract items may require travel and per-diem expenses for mechanics.

**Other Factors**—
- season of year
- contractor management
- weather conditions
- local union restrictions
- building code requirements
- availability of:
  - adequate energy
  - skilled labor
  - building materials
- owner's special requirements/restrictions
- safety requirements
- environmental considerations

**Unpredictable Factors**—General business conditions influence "in-place" costs of all items. Substitute materials and construction methods may have to be employed. These may affect the installed cost and/or life cycle costs. Such factors may be difficult to evaluate and cannot necessarily be predicted on the basis of the job's location in a particular section of the country. Thus, where these factors apply, you may find significant but unavoidable cost variations for which you will have to apply a measure of judgment to your estimate.

## Rounding of Costs

In general, all unit prices in excess of $5.00 have been rounded to make them easier to use and still maintain adequate precision of the results. The rounding rules we have chosen are in the following table.

| Prices from ... | Rounded to the nearest ... |
|---|---|
| $.01 to $5.00 | $.01 |
| $5.01 to $20.00 | $.05 |
| $20.01 to $100.00 | $.50 |
| $100.01 to $300.00 | $1.00 |
| $300.01 to $1,000.00 | $5.00 |
| $1,000.01 to $10,000.00 | $25.00 |
| $10,000.01 to $50,000.00 | $100.00 |
| $50,000.01 and above | $500.00 |

# Final Checklist

Estimating can be a straightforward process provided you remember the basics. Here's a checklist of some of the steps you should remember to complete before finalizing your estimate.

Did you remember to . . .

- factor in the City Cost Index for your locale
- take into consideration which items have been marked up and by how much?
- mark up the entire estimate sufficiently for your purposes?
- read the background information on techniques and technical matters that could impact your project time span and cost?
- include all components of your project in the final estimate?
- double check your figures for accuracy?
- call RSMeans if you have any questions about your estimate or the data you've found in our publications?

Remember, RSMeans stands behind its publications. If you have any questions about your estimate . . . about the costs you've used from our books . . . or even about the technical aspects of the job that may affect your estimate, feel free to call the RSMeans editors at 1-800-334-3509.

# Unit Price Section

## Table of Contents

# Unit Price Section

## Table of Contents

# Unit Price Section

## Table of Contents

# How to Use the Unit Price Pages

The following is a detailed explanation of a sample entry in the Unit Price Section. Next to each bold number below is the described item with the appropriate component of the sample entry following in parentheses. Some prices are listed as bare costs; others as costs that include overhead and profit of the installing contractor. In most cases, if the work is to be subcontracted, the general contractor will need to add an additional markup (RSMeans suggests using 10%) to the figures in the column "Total Incl. O&P."

## 1 Division Number/Title (03 30/Cast-In-Place Concrete)

Use the Unit Price Section Table of Contents to locate specific items. The sections are classified according to the CSI MasterFormat 2004 system.

## 2 Line Numbers (03 30 53.40 3920)

Each unit price line item has been assigned a unique 12-digit code based on the CSI MasterFormat classification.

- MasterFormat Division (03)
- MasterFormat Level 2 (03 30 00)
- MasterFormat Level 3

**03 30 53.40 3920**

- MasterFormat Level 4
- RSMeans 12-Digit Line Number

## 3 Description (Concrete In Place, etc.)

Each line item is described in detail. Sub-items and additional sizes are indented beneath the appropriate line items. The first line or two after the main item (in boldface) may contain descriptive information that pertains to all line items beneath this boldface listing.

Items which include the symbol **CN** are updated in The *RSMeans Quarterly Update Service* online. To obtain access to this service contact RSMeans customer service at 1-800-334-3509.

## 4 Reference Number Information

R033053 -50  You'll see reference numbers shown in shaded boxes at the beginning of some sections. These refer to related items in the Reference Section, visually identified by a vertical gray bar on the page edges.

The relation may be an estimating procedure that should be read before estimating, or technical information.

The "R" designates the Reference Section. The numbers refer to the MasterFormat 2004 classification system.

**It is strongly recommended that you review all reference numbers that appear within the section in which you are working.**

## 03 30 Cast-In-Place Concrete

### 03 30 53 – Miscellaneous Cast-In-Place Concrete

| 03 30 53.40 Concrete In Place | | Crew | Daily Output | Labor-Hours | Unit | Material | Labor | Equipment | Total | Total Incl O&P |
|---|---|---|---|---|---|---|---|---|---|---|
| 3590 | 10' x 10' x 12" thick | | 5 | 9.600 | | 560 | 365 | 4.99 | 929.99 | 1,100 |
| 3800 | Footings, spread under 1 C.Y. | C-14C | 28 | 4 | C.Y. | 173 | 146 | .88 | 319.88 | 415 |
| 3825 | 1 C.Y to 5 C.Y. | | 43 | 2.605 | | 192 | 95.50 | .57 | 288.07 | 360 |
| 3850 | Over 5 C.Y. | | 75 | 1.493 | | 176 | 54.50 | .33 | 230.83 | 280 |
| 3900 | Footings, strip, 18" x 9", unreinforced | C-14L | 40 | 2.400 | | 119 | 85.50 | .62 | 205.12 | 264 |
| 3920 | 18" x 9", reinforced | C-14C | 35 | 3.200 | | 142 | 117 | .70 | 259.70 | 340 |
| 3925 | 20" x 10", unreinforced | C-14L | 45 | 2.133 | | 117 | 76 | .55 | 193.55 | 246 |
| 3930 | 20" x 10", reinforced | C-14C | 40 | 2.800 | | 135 | 103 | .62 | 238.62 | 310 |
| 3935 | 24" x 12", unreinforced | C-14L | 55 | 1.745 | | 115 | 62 | .45 | 177.45 | 222 |
| 3940 | 24" x 12", reinforced | C-14C | 48 | 2.333 | | 133 | 85.50 | .51 | 219.01 | 282 |
| 3945 | 36" x 12", unreinforced | C-14L | 70 | 1.371 | | 112 | 49 | .36 | 161.36 | 199 |

*(Columns above: 2008 Bare Costs comprising Labor / Equipment; with Material and Total columns.)*

## 5 Crew (C-14C)

The "Crew" column designates the typical trade or crew used to install the item. If an installation can be accomplished by one trade and requires no power equipment, that trade and the number of workers are listed (for example, "2 Carpenters"). If an installation requires a composite crew, a crew code designation is listed (for example, "C-14C"). You'll find full details on all composite crews in the Crew Listings.

- For a complete list of all trades utilized in this book and their abbreviations, see the inside back cover.

### Crews

| Crew No. | Bare Costs | | Incl. Subs O & P | | Cost Per Labor-Hour | |
|---|---|---|---|---|---|---|
| Crew C-14C | Hr. | Daily | Hr. | Daily | Bare Costs | Incl. O&P |
| 1 Carpenter Foreman (out) | $40.10 | $320.80 | $62.40 | $499.20 | $36.62 | $57.27 |
| 6 Carpenters | 38.10 | 1828.80 | 59.30 | 2846.40 | | |
| 2 Rodmen (reinf.) | 43.00 | 688.00 | 70.55 | 1128.80 | | |
| 4 Laborers | 30.25 | 968.00 | 47.05 | 1505.60 | | |
| 1 Cement Finisher | 37.00 | 296.00 | 54.30 | 434.40 | | |
| 1 Gas Engine Vibrator | | 24.80 | | 27.28 | .22 | .24 |
| 112 L.H., Daily Totals | | $4126.40 | | $6441.68 | $36.84 | $57.52 |

## 6 Productivity: Daily Output (35.0)/ Labor-Hours (3.20)

The "Daily Output" represents the typical number of units the designated crew will install in a normal 8-hour day. To find out the number of days the given crew would require to complete the installation, divide your quantity by the daily output. For example:

| Quantity | ÷ | Daily Output | = | Duration |
|---|---|---|---|---|
| 100 C.Y. | ÷ | 35.0/ Crew Day | = | 2.86 Crew Days |

The "Labor-Hours" figure represents the number of labor-hours required to install one unit of work. To find out the number of labor-hours required for your particular task, multiply the quantity of the item times the number of labor-hours shown. For example:

| Quantity | x | Productivity Rate | = | Duration |
|---|---|---|---|---|
| 100 C.Y. | x | 3.20 Labor-Hours/ C.Y. | = | 320 Labor-Hours |

## 7 Unit (C.Y.)

The abbreviated designation indicates the unit of measure upon which the price, production, and crew are based (C.Y. = Cubic Yard). For a complete listing of abbreviations, refer to the Abbreviations Listing in the Reference Section of this book.

## 8 Bare Costs:

### Mat. (Bare Material Cost) (142)

The unit material cost is the "bare" material cost with no overhead or profit included. Costs shown reflect national average material prices for January of the current year and include delivery to the job site. No sales taxes are included.

### Labor (117)

The unit labor cost is derived by multiplying bare labor-hour costs for Crew C-14C by labor-hour units. The bare labor-hour cost is found in the Crew Section under C-14C. (If a trade is listed, the hourly labor cost—the wage rate—is found on the inside back cover.)

| Labor-Hour Cost Crew C-14C | x | Labor-Hour Units | = | Labor |
|---|---|---|---|---|
| $36.62 | x | 3.20 | = | $117.00 |

### Equip. (Equipment) (.70)

Equipment costs for each crew are listed in the description of each crew. Tools or equipment whose value justifies purchase or ownership by a contractor are considered overhead as shown on the inside back cover. The unit equipment cost is derived by multiplying the bare equipment hourly cost by the labor-hour units.

| Equipment Cost Crew C-14C | x | Labor-Hour Units | = | Equip. |
|---|---|---|---|---|
| $.22 | x | 3.20 | = | $.70 |

### Total (259.70)

The total of the bare costs is the arithmetic total of the three previous columns: mat., labor, and equip.

| Material | + | Labor | + | Equip. | = | Total |
|---|---|---|---|---|---|---|
| $142 | + | $117 | + | $.70 | = | $259.70 |

## 9 Total Costs Including O &P

This figure is the sum of the bare material cost plus 10% for profit; the bare labor cost plus total overhead and profit (per the inside back cover or, if a crew is listed, from the crew listings); and the bare equipment cost plus 10% for profit.

| | | |
|---|---|---|
| Material is Bare Material Cost + 10% = 147 + 14.20 | = | $156.20 |
| Labor for Crew C-14C = Labor-Hour Cost (57.27) x Labor-Hour Units (3.20) | = | $183.64 |
| Equip. is Bare Equip. Cost + 10% = .70 + .07 | = | $ .77 |
| Total (Rounded) | = | $ 340 |

# Estimating Tips

## 01 20 00 Price & Payment Procedures

When estimating historic preservation projects (depending on the condition of the existing structure and the owner's requirements), a 15%–20% contingency or allowance is recommended, regardless of the stage of the drawings.

## 01 30 00 Administrative Requirements

- Before determining a final cost estimate, it is a good practice to review all the items listed in Subdivision 01 03 00 to make final adjustments for items that may need customizing to specific job conditions.

- Requirements for initial and periodic submittals can represent a significant cost to the General Requirements of a job. Thoroughly check the submittal specifications when estimating a project to determine any costs that should be included.

## 01 40 00 Quality Requirements

- All projects will require some degree of Quality Control. This cost is not included in the unit cost of construction listed in each division. Depending upon the terms of the contract, the various costs of inspection and testing can be the responsibility of either the owner or the contractor. Be sure to include the required costs in your estimate.

## 01 50 00 Temporary Facilities and Controls

- Barricades, access roads, safety nets, scaffolding, security, and many more requirements for the execution of a safe project are elements of direct cost. These costs can easily be overlooked when preparing an estimate. When looking through the major classifications of this subdivision, determine which items apply to each division in your estimate.

## 01 70 00 Execution and Closeout Requirements

- When preparing an estimate, thoroughly read the specifications to determine the requirements for Contract Closeout. Final cleaning, record documentation, operation and maintenance data, warranties and bonds, and spare parts and maintenance materials can all be elements of cost for the completion of a contract. Do not overlook these in your estimate.

## Reference Numbers

Reference numbers are shown in shaded boxes at the beginning of some major classifications. These numbers refer to related items in the Reference Section. The reference information may be an estimating procedure, an alternate pricing method, or technical information.

*Note:* Not all subdivisions listed here necessarily appear in this publication.

**Division 1 - General Requirements**

# 01 11 Summary of Work

## 01 11 31.10 Architectural Fees

| 01 11 31.10 Architectural Fees | | Crew | Daily Output | Labor-Hours | Unit | Material | 2008 Bare Costs Labor | Equipment | Total | Total Incl O&P |
|---|---|---|---|---|---|---|---|---|---|---|
| 0010 | **ARCHITECTURAL FEES** R011110-10 | | | | | | | | | |
| 0020 | For new construction | | | | | | | | | |
| 0060 | Minimum | | | | Project | | | | | 4.90% |
| 0090 | Maximum | | | | | | | | | 16% |
| 0100 | For alteration work, to $500,000, add to new construction fee | | | | | | | | | 50% |
| 0150 | Over $500,000, add to new construction fee | | | | | | | | | 25% |

## 01 11 31.20 Construction Management Fees

| 01 11 31.20 Construction Management Fees | | Crew | Daily Output | Labor-Hours | Unit | Material | Labor | Equipment | Total | Total Incl O&P |
|---|---|---|---|---|---|---|---|---|---|---|
| 0010 | **CONSTRUCTION MANAGEMENT FEES** | | | | | | | | | |
| 0020 | $1,000,000 job, minimum | | | | Project | | | | | 4.50% |
| 0050 | Maximum | | | | | | | | | 7.50% |
| 0300 | $50,000,000 job, minimum | | | | | | | | | 2.50% |
| 0350 | Maximum | | | | | | | | | 4% |

## 01 11 31.30 Engineering Fees

| 01 11 31.30 Engineering Fees | | Crew | Daily Output | Labor-Hours | Unit | Material | Labor | Equipment | Total | Total Incl O&P |
|---|---|---|---|---|---|---|---|---|---|---|
| 0010 | **ENGINEERING FEES** R011110-30 | | | | | | | | | |
| 0020 | Educational planning consultant, minimum | | | | Project | | | | | .50% |
| 0100 | Maximum | | | | " | | | | | 2.50% |
| 0200 | Electrical, minimum | | | | Contrct | | | | | 4.10% |
| 0300 | Maximum | | | | | | | | | 10.10% |
| 0400 | Elevator & conveying systems, minimum | | | | | | | | | 2.50% |
| 0500 | Maximum | | | | | | | | | 5% |
| 0600 | Food service & kitchen equipment, minimum | | | | | | | | | 8% |
| 0700 | Maximum | | | | | | | | | 12% |
| 0800 | Landscaping & site development, minimum | | | | | | | | | 2.50% |
| 0900 | Maximum | | | | | | | | | 6% |
| 1000 | Mechanical (plumbing & HVAC), minimum | | | | | | | | | 4.10% |
| 1100 | Maximum | | | | | | | | | 10.10% |
| 1200 | Structural, minimum | | | | Project | | | | | 1% |
| 1300 | Maximum | | | | " | | | | | 2.50% |

## 01 11 31.50 Models

| 01 11 31.50 Models | | Crew | Daily Output | Labor-Hours | Unit | Material | Labor | Equipment | Total | Total Incl O&P |
|---|---|---|---|---|---|---|---|---|---|---|
| 0010 | **MODELS** | | | | | | | | | |
| 0020 | Cardboard & paper, 1 building, minimum | | | | Ea. | 695 | | | 695 | 765 |
| 0050 | Maximum | | | | | 1,575 | | | 1,575 | 1,750 |
| 0100 | 2 buildings, minimum | | | | | 930 | | | 930 | 1,025 |
| 0150 | Maximum | | | | | 2,100 | | | 2,100 | 2,300 |
| 0200 | Plexiglass and metal, basic layout | | | | SF Flr. | .06 | | | .06 | .07 |
| 0210 | Including equipment and personnel | | | | " | .31 | | | .31 | .34 |
| 0300 | Site plan layout, minimum | | | | Ea. | 1,325 | | | 1,325 | 1,450 |
| 0350 | Maximum | | | | " | 2,225 | | | 2,225 | 2,450 |

## 01 11 31.75 Renderings

| 01 11 31.75 Renderings | | Crew | Daily Output | Labor-Hours | Unit | Material | Labor | Equipment | Total | Total Incl O&P |
|---|---|---|---|---|---|---|---|---|---|---|
| 0010 | **RENDERINGS** Color, matted, 20" x 30", eye level, | | | | | | | | | |
| 0020 | 1 building, minimum | | | | Ea. | 1,900 | | | 1,900 | 2,100 |
| 0050 | Average | | | | | 2,725 | | | 2,725 | 3,000 |
| 0100 | Maximum | | | | | 4,375 | | | 4,375 | 4,800 |
| 1000 | 5 buildings, minimum | | | | | 3,825 | | | 3,825 | 4,200 |
| 1100 | Maximum | | | | | 7,650 | | | 7,650 | 8,425 |
| 2000 | Aerial perspective, color, 1 building, minimum | | | | | 2,725 | | | 2,725 | 3,000 |
| 2100 | Maximum | | | | | 7,650 | | | 7,650 | 8,425 |
| 3000 | 5 buildings, minimum | | | | | 5,500 | | | 5,500 | 6,050 |
| 3100 | Maximum | | | | | 10,900 | | | 10,900 | 12,000 |

# 01 21 Allowances

## 01 21 16 – Contingency Allowances

### 01 21 16.50 Contingencies

| | | Crew | Daily Output | Labor-Hours | Unit | Material | 2008 Bare Costs Labor | Equipment | Total | Total Incl O&P |
|---|---|---|---|---|---|---|---|---|---|---|
| 0010 | **CONTINGENCIES**, ADD TO ESTIMATE | | | | | | | | | |
| 0020 | Conceptual stage | | | | Project | | | | | 20% |
| 0050 | Schematic stage | | | | | | | | | 15% |
| 0100 | Preliminary working drawing stage (Design Dev.) | | | | | | | | | 10% |
| 0150 | Final working drawing stage | | | | | | | | | 3% |

## 01 21 55 – Job Conditions Allowance

### 01 21 55.50 Job Conditions

| | | Crew | Daily Output | Labor-Hours | Unit | Material | Labor | Equipment | Total | Total Incl O&P |
|---|---|---|---|---|---|---|---|---|---|---|
| 0010 | **JOB CONDITIONS** Modifications to applicable | | | | | | | | | |
| 0020 | cost summaries | | | | | | | | | |
| 0100 | Economic conditions, favorable, deduct | | | | Project | | | | 2% | 2% |
| 0200 | Unfavorable, add | | | | | | | | 5% | 5% |
| 0300 | Hoisting conditions, favorable, deduct | | | | | | | | 2% | 2% |
| 0400 | Unfavorable, add | | | | | | | | 5% | 5% |
| 0500 | General Contractor management, experienced, deduct | | | | | | | | 2% | 2% |
| 0600 | Inexperienced, add | | | | | | | | 10% | 10% |
| 0700 | Labor availability, surplus, deduct | | | | | | | | 1% | 1% |
| 0800 | Shortage, add | | | | | | | | 10% | 10% |
| 0900 | Material storage area, available, deduct | | | | | | | | 1% | 1% |
| 1000 | Not available, add | | | | | | | | 2% | 2% |
| 1100 | Subcontractor availability, surplus, deduct | | | | | | | | 5% | 5% |
| 1200 | Shortage, add | | | | | | | | 12% | 12% |
| 1300 | Work space, available, deduct | | | | | | | | 2% | 2% |
| 1400 | Not available, add | | | | | | | | 5% | 5% |

## 01 21 57 – Overtime Allowance

### 01 21 57.50 Overtime

| | | Crew | Daily Output | Labor-Hours | Unit | Material | Labor | Equipment | Total | Total Incl O&P |
|---|---|---|---|---|---|---|---|---|---|---|
| 0010 | **OVERTIME** for early completion of projects or where R012909-90 | | | | | | | | | |
| 0020 | labor shortages exist, add to usual labor, up to | | | | Costs | | 100% | | | |

## 01 21 61 – Cost Indexes

### 01 21 61.10 Construction Cost Index

| | | Crew | Daily Output | Labor-Hours | Unit | Material | Labor | Equipment | Total | Total Incl O&P |
|---|---|---|---|---|---|---|---|---|---|---|
| 0010 | **CONSTRUCTION COST INDEX** (Reference) over 930 zip code locations in | | | | | | | | | |
| 0020 | The U.S. and Canada, total bldg cost, min. (Guymon, OK) | | | | % | | | | | 68.70% |
| 0050 | Average | | | | | | | | | 100% |
| 0100 | Maximum (New York, NY) | | | | | | | | | 131.30% |

### 01 21 61.20 Historical Cost Indexes

| | | Crew | Daily Output | Labor-Hours | Unit | Material | Labor | Equipment | Total | Total Incl O&P |
|---|---|---|---|---|---|---|---|---|---|---|
| 0010 | **HISTORICAL COST INDEXES** (See Reference section) | | | | | | | | | |

### 01 21 61.30 Labor Index

| | | Crew | Daily Output | Labor-Hours | Unit | Material | Labor | Equipment | Total | Total Incl O&P |
|---|---|---|---|---|---|---|---|---|---|---|
| 0010 | **LABOR INDEX** (Reference) For over 930 zip code locations in | | | | | | | | | |
| 0020 | the U.S. and Canada, minimum (Del Rio, TX) | | | | % | | 31.20% | | | |
| 0050 | Average | | | | | | 100% | | | |
| 0100 | Maximum (New York, NY) | | | | | | 166% | | | |

### 01 21 61.50 Material Index

| | | Crew | Daily Output | Labor-Hours | Unit | Material | Labor | Equipment | Total | Total Incl O&P |
|---|---|---|---|---|---|---|---|---|---|---|
| 0010 | **MATERIAL INDEX** (Reference) For over 930 zip code locations in | | | | | | | | | |
| 0020 | the U.S. and Canada, minimum (Elizabethtown, KY) | | | | % | 90.70% | | | | |
| 0040 | Average | | | | | 100% | | | | |
| 0060 | Maximum (Ketchikan, AK) | | | | | 141.80% | | | | |

## 01 21 63 – Taxes

### 01 21 63.10 Taxes

| | | Crew | Daily Output | Labor-Hours | Unit | Material | Labor | Equipment | Total | Total Incl O&P |
|---|---|---|---|---|---|---|---|---|---|---|
| 0010 | **TAXES** R012909-80 | | | | | | | | | |
| 0020 | Sales tax, State, average | | | | % | 4.87% | | | | |
| 0050 | Maximum R012909-85 | | | | | 7.25% | | | | |

# 01 21 Allowances

## 01 21 63 – Taxes

| 01 21 63.10 Taxes | Crew | Daily Output | Labor-Hours | Unit | Material | 2008 Bare Costs Labor | Equipment | Total | Total Incl O&P |
|---|---|---|---|---|---|---|---|---|---|
| 0200 | Social Security, on first $97,500 of wages | | | | % | | 7.65% | | | |
| 0300 | Unemployment, combined Federal and State, minimum | | | | | | .80% | | | |
| 0350 | Average | | | | | | 6.20% | | | |
| 0400 | Maximum | | | | | | 11.76% | | | |

# 01 31 Project Management and Coordination

## 01 31 13 – Project Coordination

### 01 31 13.20 Field Personnel

| | | Crew | Daily Output | Labor-Hours | Unit | Material | 2008 Bare Costs Labor | Equipment | Total | Total Incl O&P |
|---|---|---|---|---|---|---|---|---|---|---|
| 0010 | **FIELD PERSONNEL** | | | | | | | | | |
| 0020 | Clerk, average | | | | Week | | 365 | | 365 | 570 |
| 0100 | Field engineer, minimum | | | | | | 865 | | 865 | 1,350 |
| 0120 | Average | | | | | | 1,125 | | 1,125 | 1,750 |
| 0140 | Maximum | | | | | | 1,300 | | 1,300 | 2,025 |
| 0160 | General purpose laborer, average | | | | | | 1,200 | | 1,200 | 1,875 |
| 0180 | Project manager, minimum | | | | | | 1,600 | | 1,600 | 2,500 |
| 0200 | Average | | | | | | 1,850 | | 1,850 | 2,875 |
| 0220 | Maximum | | | | | | 2,100 | | 2,100 | 3,275 |
| 0240 | Superintendent, minimum | | | | | | 1,550 | | 1,550 | 2,400 |
| 0260 | Average | | | | | | 1,700 | | 1,700 | 2,650 |
| 0280 | Maximum | | | | | | 1,950 | | 1,950 | 3,025 |
| 0290 | Timekeeper, average | | | | | | 1,005 | | 1,005 | 1,575 |

### 01 31 13.30 Insurance

| | | | Crew | Daily Output | Labor-Hours | Unit | Material | 2008 Bare Costs Labor | Equipment | Total | Total Incl O&P |
|---|---|---|---|---|---|---|---|---|---|---|---|
| 0010 | **INSURANCE** | R013113-40 | | | | | | | | | |
| 0020 | Builders risk, standard, minimum | | | | | Job | | | | | .24% |
| 0050 | Maximum | R013113-50 | | | | | | | | | .64% |
| 0200 | All-risk type, minimum | | | | | | | | | | .25% |
| 0250 | Maximum | R013113-60 | | | | | | | | | .62% |
| 0400 | Contractor's equipment floater, minimum | | | | | Value | | | | | .50% |
| 0450 | Maximum | | | | | " | | | | | 1.50% |
| 0600 | Public liability, average | | | | | Job | | | | | 2.02% |
| 0800 | Workers' compensation & employer's liability, average | | | | | | | | | | |
| 0850 | by trade, carpentry, general | | | | | Payroll | | 18.31% | | | |
| 0900 | Clerical | | | | | | | .68% | | | |
| 0950 | Concrete | | | | | | | 15.22% | | | |
| 1000 | Electrical | | | | | | | 6.66% | | | |
| 1050 | Excavation | | | | | | | 10.46% | | | |
| 1100 | Glazing | | | | | | | 14.15% | | | |
| 1150 | Insulation | | | | | | | 15.12% | | | |
| 1200 | Lathing | | | | | | | 11.04% | | | |
| 1250 | Masonry | | | | | | | 14.80% | | | |
| 1300 | Painting & decorating | | | | | | | 12.86% | | | |
| 1350 | Pile driving | | | | | | | 21.48% | | | |
| 1400 | Plastering | | | | | | | 14.39% | | | |
| 1450 | Plumbing | | | | | | | 8.11% | | | |
| 1500 | Roofing | | | | | | | 32.94% | | | |
| 1550 | Sheet metal work (HVAC) | | | | | | | 11.88% | | | |
| 1600 | Steel erection, structural | | | | | | | 40.12% | | | |
| 1650 | Tile work, interior ceramic | | | | | | | 9.47% | | | |
| 1700 | Waterproofing, brush or hand caulking | | | | | | | 7.07% | | | |
| 1800 | Wrecking | | | | | | | 36.28% | | | |
| 2000 | Range of 35 trades in 50 states, excl. wrecking, min. | | | | | | | 2.04% | | | |

# 01 31 Project Management and Coordination

## 01 31 13 – Project Coordination

| 01 31 13.30 Insurance | | Crew | Daily Output | Labor-Hours | Unit | Material | 2008 Bare Costs Labor | Equipment | Total | Total Incl O&P |
|---|---|---|---|---|---|---|---|---|---|---|
| 2100 | Average | | | | Payroll | | 16.20% | | | |
| 2200 | Maximum | | | | | | 197.85% | | | |

### 01 31 13.40 Main Office Expense

| | | | | | | | | | | |
|---|---|---|---|---|---|---|---|---|---|---|
| 0010 | **MAIN OFFICE EXPENSE** Average for General Contractors     R013113-50 | | | | | | | | | |
| 0020 | As a percentage of their annual volume | | | | | | | | | |
| 0125 | Annual volume under 1 million dollars | | | | % Vol. | | | | 13.60% | |
| 0145 | Up to 2.5 million dollars | | | | | | | | 8% | |
| 0150 | Up to 4.0 million dollars | | | | | | | | 6.80% | |
| 0200 | Up to 7.0 million dollars | | | | | | | | 5.60% | |
| 0250 | Up to 10 million dollars | | | | | | | | 5.10% | |
| 0300 | Over 10 million dollars | | | | | | | | 3.90% | |

### 01 31 13.50 General Contractor's Mark-Up

| | | | | | | | | | | |
|---|---|---|---|---|---|---|---|---|---|---|
| 0010 | **GENERAL CONTRACTOR'S MARK-UP** on Change Orders | | | | | | | | | |
| 0200 | Extra work, by subcontractors, add | | | | % | | | | | 10% |
| 0250 | By General Contractor, add | | | | | | | | | 15% |
| 0400 | Omitted work, by subcontractors, deduct all but | | | | | | | | | 5% |
| 0450 | By General Contractor, deduct all but | | | | | | | | | 7.50% |
| 0600 | Overtime work, by subcontractors, add | | | | | | | | | 15% |
| 0650 | By General Contractor, add | | | | | | | | | 10% |

### 01 31 13.60 Installing Contractor's Main Office Overhead

| | | | | | | | | | | |
|---|---|---|---|---|---|---|---|---|---|---|
| 0010 | **INSTALLING CONTRACTOR'S MAIN OFFICE OVERHEAD**     R013113-50 | | | | | | | | | |
| 0020 | As percent of direct costs, minimum | | | | % | | | | 5% | |
| 0050 | Average | | | | | | | | 13% | |
| 0100 | Maximum | | | | | | | | 30% | |

### 01 31 13.80 Overhead and Profit

| | | | | | | | | | | |
|---|---|---|---|---|---|---|---|---|---|---|
| 0010 | **OVERHEAD & PROFIT** Allowance to add to items in this | | | | | | | | | |
| 0020 | book that do not include Subs O&P, average | | | | % | | | | 25% | |
| 0100 | Allowance to add to items in this book that | | | | | | | | | |
| 0110 | do include Subs O&P, minimum | | | | % | | | | | 5% |
| 0150 | Average | | | | | | | | | 10% |
| 0200 | Maximum | | | | | | | | | 15% |
| 0300 | Typical, by size of project, under $100,000 | | | | | | | | 30% | |
| 0350 | $500,000 project | | | | | | | | 25% | |
| 0400 | $2,000,000 project | | | | | | | | 20% | |
| 0450 | Over $10,000,000 project | | | | | | | | 15% | |

### 01 31 13.90 Performance Bond

| | | | | | | | | | | |
|---|---|---|---|---|---|---|---|---|---|---|
| 0010 | **PERFORMANCE BOND**     R013113-80 | | | | | | | | | |
| 0020 | For buildings, minimum | | | | Job | | | | | .60% |
| 0100 | Maximum | | | | " | | | | | 2.50% |

# 01 32 Construction Progress Documentation

## 01 32 13 – Scheduling of work

| 01 32 13.50 Scheduling | Crew | Daily Output | Labor-Hours | Unit | Material | 2008 Bare Costs Labor | | Equipment | Total | Total Incl O&P |
|---|---|---|---|---|---|---|---|---|---|---|
| 0010 **SCHEDULING** | | | | | | | | | | |
| 0020 Critical path, as % of architectural fee, minimum | | | | % | | | | | | .50% |
| 0100 Maximum | | | | " | | | | | | 1% |
| 0300 Computer-update, micro, no plots, minimum | | | | Ea. | | | | | 455 | 500 |
| 0400 Including plots, maximum | | | | " | | | | | 1,455 | 1,600 |
| 0600 Rule of thumb, CPM scheduling, small job ($10 Million) | | | | Job | | | | | | .05% |
| 0650 Large job ($50 Million +) | | | | | | | | | | .03% |
| 0700 Including cost control, small job | | | | | | | | | | .08% |
| 0750 Large job | | | | | | | | | | .04% |

## 01 32 33 – Photographic Documentation

| 01 32 33.50 Photographs | Crew | Daily Output | Labor-Hours | Unit | Material | 2008 Bare Costs Labor | | Equipment | Total | Total Incl O&P |
|---|---|---|---|---|---|---|---|---|---|---|
| 0010 **PHOTOGRAPHS** | | | | | | | | | | |
| 0020 8" x 10", 4 shots, 2 prints ea., std. mounting | | | | Set | 475 | | | | 475 | 520 |
| 0100 Hinged linen mounts | | | | | 530 | | | | 530 | 580 |
| 0200 8" x 10", 4 shots, 2 prints each, in color | | | | | 415 | | | | 415 | 460 |
| 0300 For I.D. slugs, add to all above | | | | | 5.30 | | | | 5.30 | 5.85 |
| 0500 Aerial photos, initial fly-over, 6 shots, 1 print ea., 8" x 10" | | | | | 825 | | | | 825 | 905 |
| 0550 11" x 14" prints | | | | | 1,000 | | | | 1,000 | 1,100 |
| 0600 16" x 20" prints | | | | | 1,175 | | | | 1,175 | 1,300 |
| 0700 For full color prints, add | | | | | 40% | | | | | 40% |
| 0750 Add for traffic control area | | | | | 294 | | | | 294 | 325 |
| 0900 For over 30 miles from airport, add per | | | | Mile | 5.30 | | | | 5.30 | 5.85 |
| 1000 Vertical photography, 4 to 6 shots with | | | | | | | | | | |
| 1010 different scales, 1 print each | | | | Set | 1,100 | | | | 1,100 | 1,200 |
| 1500 Time lapse equipment, camera and projector, buy | | | | | 3,775 | | | | 3,775 | 4,175 |
| 1550 Rent per month | | | | | 565 | | | | 565 | 620 |
| 1700 Cameraman and film, including processing, B.&W. | | | | Day | 1,375 | | | | 1,375 | 1,525 |
| 1720 Color | | | | " | 1,375 | | | | 1,375 | 1,525 |

# 01 41 Regulatory Requirements

## 01 41 26 – Permits

| 01 41 26.50 Permits | Crew | Daily Output | Labor-Hours | Unit | Material | 2008 Bare Costs Labor | | Equipment | Total | Total Incl O&P |
|---|---|---|---|---|---|---|---|---|---|---|
| 0010 **PERMITS** | | | | | | | | | | |
| 0020 Rule of thumb, most cities, minimum | | | | Job | | | | | | .50% |
| 0100 Maximum | | | | " | | | | | | 2% |

# 01 45 Quality Control

## 01 45 23 – Testing and Inspecting Services

| 01 45 23.50 Testing | Crew | Daily Output | Labor-Hours | Unit | Material | 2008 Bare Costs Labor | | Equipment | Total | Total Incl O&P |
|---|---|---|---|---|---|---|---|---|---|---|
| 0010 **TESTING** and Inspecting Services | | | | | | | | | | |
| 0015 For concrete building costing $1,000,000, minimum | | | | Project | | | | | 4,725 | 5,200 |
| 0020 Maximum | | | | | | | | | 38,000 | 41,800 |
| 0050 Steel building, minimum | | | | | | | | | 4,727 | 5,200 |
| 0070 Maximum | | | | | | | | | 14,818 | 16,300 |
| 0100 For building costing, $10,000,000, minimum | | | | | | | | | 30,091 | 33,100 |
| 0150 Maximum | | | | | | | | | 48,182 | 53,000 |
| 0200 Asphalt testing, compressive strength Marshall stability, set of 3 | | | | Ea. | | | | | 145 | 165 |
| 0220 Density, set of 3 | | | | | | | | | 86 | 95 |
| 0250 Extraction, individual tests on sample | | | | | | | | | 136 | 150 |

## 01 45 23 - Testing and Inspecting Services

| 01 45 23.50 Testing | Crew | Daily Output | Labor-Hours | Unit | Material | 2008 Bare Costs Labor | Equipment | Total | Total Incl O&P |
|---|---|---|---|---|---|---|---|---|---|
| 0300 Penetration | | | | Ea. | | | | 41 | 45 |
| 0350 Mix design, 5 specimens | | | | | | | | 182 | 200 |
| 0360 Additional specimen | | | | | | | | 36 | 40 |
| 0400 Specific gravity | | | | | | | | 41 | 45 |
| 0420 Swell test | | | | | | | | 64 | 70 |
| 0450 Water effect and cohesion, set of 6 | | | | | | | | 182 | 200 |
| 0470 Water effect and plastic flow | | | | | | | | 64 | 70 |
| 0600 Concrete testing, aggregates, abrasion, ASTM C 131 | | | | | | | | 136 | 150 |
| 0650 Absorption, ASTM C 127 | | | | | | | | 42 | 46 |
| 0800 Petrographic analysis, ASTM C 295 | | | | | | | | 773 | 850 |
| 0900 Specific gravity, ASTM C 127 | | | | | | | | 50 | 55 |
| 1000 Sieve analysis, washed, ASTM C 136 | | | | | | | | 59 | 65 |
| 1050 Unwashed | | | | | | | | 59 | 65 |
| 1200 Sulfate soundness | | | | | | | | 114 | 125 |
| 1300 Weight per cubic foot | | | | | | | | 36 | 40 |
| 1500 Cement, physical tests, ASTM C 150 | | | | | | | | 318 | 350 |
| 1600 Chemical tests, ASTM C 150 | | | | | | | | 245 | 270 |
| 1800 Compressive test, cylinder, delivered to lab, ASTM C 39 | | | | | | | | 12 | 13 |
| 1900 Picked up by lab, minimum | | | | | | | | 14 | 15 |
| 1950 Average | | | | | | | | 18 | 20 |
| 2000 Maximum | | | | | | | | 27 | 30 |
| 2200 Compressive strength, cores (not incl. drilling), ASTM C 42 | | | | ▼ | | | | 36 | 40 |
| 2250 Core drilling, 4" diameter (plus technician) | | | | Inch | | | | 23 | 25 |
| 2260 Technician for core drilling | | | | Hr. | | | | 45 | 50 |
| 2300 Patching core holes | | | | Ea. | | | | 22 | 24 |
| 2400 Drying shrinkage at 28 days | | | | | | | | 236 | 260 |
| 2500 Flexural test beams, ASTM C 78 | | | | | | | | 59 | 65 |
| 2600 Mix design, one batch mix | | | | | | | | 259 | 285 |
| 2650 Added trial batches | | | | | | | | 120 | 132 |
| 2800 Modulus of elasticity, ASTM C 469 | | | | | | | | 164 | 180 |
| 2900 Tensile test, cylinders, ASTM C 496 | | | | | | | | 45 | 50 |
| 3000 Water-Cement ratio curve, 3 batches | | | | | | | | 141 | 155 |
| 3100 4 batches | | | | | | | | 186 | 205 |
| 3300 Masonry testing, absorption, per 5 brick, ASTM C 67 | | | | | | | | 45 | 50 |
| 3350 Chemical resistance, per 2 brick | | | | | | | | 50 | 55 |
| 3400 Compressive strength, per 5 brick, ASTM C 67 | | | | | | | | 68 | 75 |
| 3420 Efflorescence, per 5 brick, ASTM C 67 | | | | | | | | 68 | 75 |
| 3440 Imperviousness, per 5 brick | | | | | | | | 87 | 96 |
| 3470 Modulus of rupture, per 5 brick | | | | | | | | 86 | 95 |
| 3500 Moisture, block only | | | | | | | | 32 | 35 |
| 3550 Mortar, compressive strength, set of 3 | | | | | | | | 23 | 25 |
| 4100 Reinforcing steel, bend test | | | | | | | | 55 | 61 |
| 4200 Tensile test, up to #8 bar | | | | | | | | 36 | 40 |
| 4220 #9 to #11 bar | | | | | | | | 41 | 45 |
| 4240 #14 bar and larger | | | | | | | | 64 | 70 |
| 4400 Soil testing, Atterberg limits, liquid and plastic limits | | | | | | | | 59 | 65 |
| 4510 Hydrometer analysis | | | | | | | | 109 | 120 |
| 4530 Specific gravity, ASTM D 354 | | | | | | | | 44 | 48 |
| 4600 Sieve analysis, washed, ASTM D 422 | | | | | | | | 55 | 60 |
| 4700 Unwashed, ASTM D 422 | | | | | | | | 59 | 65 |
| 4710 Consolidation test (ASTM D2435), minimum | | | | | | | | 250 | 275 |
| 4715 Maximum | | | | | | | | 432 | 475 |
| 4720 Density and classification of undisturbed sample | | | | ▼ | | | | 73 | 80 |

# 01 45 Quality Control

## 01 45 23 – Testing and Inspecting Services

| 01 45 23.50 Testing | Crew | Daily Output | Labor-Hours | Unit | Material | 2008 Bare Costs Labor | Equipment | Total | Total Incl O&P |
|---|---|---|---|---|---|---|---|---|---|
| 4735 | Soil density, nuclear method, ASTM D2922 | | | | Ea. | | | | 35 | 38.67 |
| 4740 | Sand cone method ASTM D1556 | | | | | | | | 27 | 30.17 |
| 4750 | Moisture content, ASTM D 2216 | | | | | | | | 9 | 10 |
| 4780 | Permeability test, double ring infiltrometer | | | | | | | | 500 | 550 |
| 4800 | Permeability, var. or constant head, undist., ASTM D 2434 | | | | | | | | 227 | 250 |
| 4850 | Recompacted | | | | | | | | 250 | 275 |
| 4900 | Proctor compaction, 4" standard mold, ASTM D 698 | | | | | | | | 123 | 135 |
| 4950 | 6" modified mold | | | | | | | | 68 | 75 |
| 5100 | Shear tests, triaxial, minimum | | | | | | | | 409 | 450 |
| 5150 | Maximum | | | | | | | | 545 | 600 |
| 5300 | Direct shear, minimum, ASTM D 3080 | | | | | | | | 318 | 350 |
| 5350 | Maximum | | | | | | | | 409 | 450 |
| 5550 | Technician for inspection, per day, earthwork | | | | | | | | 210 | 231 |
| 5650 | Bolting | | | | | | | | 268 | 295 |
| 5750 | Roofing | | | | | | | | 244 | 256 |
| 5790 | Welding | | | | ↓ | | | | 257 | 283 |
| 5820 | Non-destructive metal testing, dye penetrant | | | | Day | | | | 310 | 341 |
| 5840 | Magnetic particle | | | | | | | | 310 | 341 |
| 5860 | Radiography | | | | | | | | 450 | 495 |
| 5880 | Ultrasonic | | | | ↓ | | | | 309 | 340 |
| 6000 | Welding certification, minimum | | | | Ea. | | | | 91 | 100 |
| 6100 | Maximum | | | | " | | | | 250 | 275 |
| 7000 | Underground storage tank | | | | | | | | | |
| 7500 | Volumetric tightness test ,<=12,000 gal | | | | Ea. | | | | 435 | 478 |
| 7510 | <=30,000 gal | | | | " | | | | 613 | 675 |
| 7600 | Vadose zone (soil gas) sampling, 10-40 samples, min. | | | | Day | | | | 1,364 | 1,500 |
| 7610 | Maximum | | | | " | | | | 2,273 | 2,500 |
| 7700 | Ground water monitoring incl. drilling 3 wells, min. | | | | Total | | | | 4,545 | 5,000 |
| 7710 | Maximum | | | | " | | | | 6,364 | 7,000 |
| 8000 | X-ray concrete slabs | | | | Ea. | | | | 182 | 200 |

# 01 51 Temporary Utilities

## 01 51 13 – Temporary Electricity

| 01 51 13.80 Temporary Utilities | Crew | Daily Output | Labor-Hours | Unit | Material | 2008 Bare Costs Labor | Equipment | Total | Total Incl O&P |
|---|---|---|---|---|---|---|---|---|---|
| 0010 | **TEMPORARY UTILITIES** | | | | | | | | | |
| 0100 | Heat, incl. fuel and operation, per week, 12 hrs. per day | 1 Skwk | 100 | .080 | CSF Flr | 10.35 | 3.15 | | 13.50 | 16.25 |
| 0200 | 24 hrs. per day | " | 60 | .133 | | 19.95 | 5.25 | | 25.20 | 30 |
| 0350 | Lighting, incl. service lamps, wiring & outlets, minimum | 1 Elec | 34 | .235 | | 2.63 | 10.70 | | 13.33 | 18.85 |
| 0360 | Maximum | " | 17 | .471 | | 5.70 | 21.50 | | 27.20 | 38.50 |
| 0400 | Power for temp lighting only, per month, min/month 6.6 KWH | | | | | | | | .75 | .83 |
| 0450 | Maximum/month 23.6 KWH | | | | | | | | 2.85 | 3.14 |
| 0600 | Power for job duration incl. elevator, etc., minimum | | | | | | | | 47 | 51.70 |
| 0650 | Maximum | | | | ↓ | | | | 110 | 121 |
| 1000 | Toilet, portable, see Equip. Rental 01 54 33 in Reference Section | | | | | | | | | |

# 01 52 Construction Facilities

## 01 52 13 – Field Offices and Sheds

| 01 52 13.20 Office and Storage Space | Crew | Daily Output | Labor-Hours | Unit | Material | 2008 Bare Costs Labor | Equipment | Total | Total Incl O&P |
|---|---|---|---|---|---|---|---|---|---|
| 0010 | **OFFICE AND STORAGE SPACE** | | | | | | | | | |
| 0020 | Trailer, furnished, no hookups, 20' x 8', buy | 2 Skwk | 1 | 16 | Ea. | 7,975 | 630 | | 8,605 | 9,725 |
| 0250 | Rent per month | | | | | 201 | | | 201 | 221 |
| 0300 | 32' x 8', buy | 2 Skwk | .70 | 22.857 | | 11,900 | 900 | | 12,800 | 14,400 |
| 0350 | Rent per month | | | | | 241 | | | 241 | 265 |
| 0400 | 50' x 10', buy | 2 Skwk | .60 | 26.667 | | 22,500 | 1,050 | | 23,550 | 26,400 |
| 0450 | Rent per month | | | | | 330 | | | 330 | 365 |
| 0500 | 50' x 12', buy | 2 Skwk | .50 | 32 | | 27,600 | 1,250 | | 28,850 | 32,300 |
| 0550 | Rent per month | | | | | 375 | | | 375 | 410 |
| 0700 | For air conditioning, rent per month, add | | | | | 41 | | | 41 | 45 |
| 0800 | For delivery, add per mile | | | | Mile | 4.50 | | | 4.50 | 4.95 |
| 1000 | Portable buildings, prefab, on skids, economy, 8' x 8' | 2 Carp | 265 | .060 | S.F. | 85 | 2.30 | | 87.30 | 97 |
| 1100 | Deluxe, 8' x 12' | " | 150 | .107 | " | 95 | 4.06 | | 99.06 | 111 |
| 1200 | Storage boxes, 20' x 8', buy | 2 Skwk | 1.80 | 8.889 | Ea. | 4,275 | 350 | | 4,625 | 5,250 |
| 1250 | Rent per month | | | | | 73.50 | | | 73.50 | 80.50 |
| 1300 | 40' x 8', buy | 2 Skwk | 1.40 | 11.429 | | 5,925 | 450 | | 6,375 | 7,200 |
| 1350 | Rent per month | | | | | 97.50 | | | 97.50 | 107 |
| 5000 | Air supported structures, see Div. 13 31 13.13 | | | | | | | | | |

## 01 52 13.40 Field Office Expense

| | | Crew | Daily Output | Labor-Hours | Unit | Material | Labor | Equipment | Total | Total Incl O&P |
|---|---|---|---|---|---|---|---|---|---|---|
| 0010 | **FIELD OFFICE EXPENSE** | | | | | | | | | |
| 0100 | Office equipment rental average | | | | Month | 150 | | | 150 | 165 |
| 0120 | Office supplies, average | | | | " | 95 | | | 95 | 105 |
| 0125 | Office trailer rental, see Div. 01 52 13.20 | | | | | | | | | |
| 0140 | Telephone bill; avg. bill/month incl. long dist. | | | | Month | 210 | | | 210 | 231 |
| 0160 | Lights & HVAC | | | | " | 110 | | | 110 | 121 |

# 01 54 Construction Aids

## 01 54 09 – Protection Equipment

### 01 54 09.50 Personnel Protective Equipment

| | | Crew | Daily Output | Labor-Hours | Unit | Material | Labor | Equipment | Total | Total Incl O&P |
|---|---|---|---|---|---|---|---|---|---|---|
| 0010 | **PERSONNEL PROTECTIVE EQUIPMENT** | | | | | | | | | |
| 0015 | Hazardous waste protection | | | | | | | | | |
| 0020 | Respirator mask only, full face, silicone | | | | Ea. | 219 | | | 219 | 241 |
| 0030 | Half face, silicone | | | | | 32 | | | 32 | 35.50 |
| 0040 | Respirator cartridges, 2 req'd/mask, dust or asbestos | | | | | 5.30 | | | 5.30 | 5.85 |
| 0050 | Chemical vapor | | | | | 4.55 | | | 4.55 | 5 |
| 0060 | Combination vapor and dust | | | | | 9.45 | | | 9.45 | 10.40 |
| 0100 | Emergency escape breathing apparatus, 5 min | | | | | 455 | | | 455 | 500 |
| 0110 | 10 min | | | | | 525 | | | 525 | 575 |
| 0150 | Self contained breathing apparatus with full face piece, 30 min | | | | | 1,900 | | | 1,900 | 2,075 |
| 0160 | 60 min | | | | | 3,025 | | | 3,025 | 3,325 |
| 0200 | Encapsulating suits, limited use, level A | | | | | 890 | | | 890 | 980 |
| 0210 | Level B | | | | | 209 | | | 209 | 230 |
| 0300 | Over boots, latex | | | | Pr. | 4.11 | | | 4.11 | 4.52 |
| 0310 | PVC | | | | | 14.40 | | | 14.40 | 15.85 |
| 0320 | Neoprene | | | | | 51 | | | 51 | 56.50 |
| 0400 | Gloves, nitrile/PVC | | | | | 5.70 | | | 5.70 | 6.25 |
| 0410 | Neoprene coated | | | | | 26.50 | | | 26.50 | 29 |

### 01 54 09.60 Safety Nets

| | | Crew | Daily Output | Labor-Hours | Unit | Material | Labor | Equipment | Total | Total Incl O&P |
|---|---|---|---|---|---|---|---|---|---|---|
| 0010 | **SAFETY NETS** | | | | | | | | | |
| 0020 | No supports, stock sizes, nylon, 4" mesh | | | | S.F. | 1.10 | | | 1.10 | 1.21 |

# 01 54 Construction Aids

## 01 54 09 – Protection Equipment

### 01 54 09.60 Safety Nets

| 01 54 09.60 Safety Nets | Crew | Daily Output | Labor-Hours | Unit | Material | 2008 Bare Costs Labor | Equipment | Total | Total Incl O&P |
|---|---|---|---|---|---|---|---|---|---|
| 0100 | Polypropylene, 6" mesh | | | | S.F. | 1.59 | | | 1.59 | 1.75 |
| 0200 | Small mesh debris nets, 1/4" & 3/4" mesh, stock sizes | | | | | .74 | | | .74 | .81 |
| 0220 | Combined 4" mesh and 1/4" mesh, stock sizes | | | | | 2.05 | | | 2.05 | 2.26 |
| 0300 | Monthly rental, 4" mesh, stock sizes, 1st month | | | | | .50 | | | .50 | .55 |
| 0320 | 2nd month rental | | | | | .25 | | | .25 | .28 |
| 0340 | Maximum rental/year | | | | | 1.15 | | | 1.15 | 1.27 |

## 01 54 16 – Temporary Hoists

### 01 54 16.50 Weekly Forklift Crew

| 01 54 16.50 Weekly Forklift Crew | Crew | Daily Output | Labor-Hours | Unit | Material | Labor | Equipment | Total | Total Incl O&P |
|---|---|---|---|---|---|---|---|---|---|
| 0010 | **WEEKLY FORKLIFT CREW** | | | | | | | | | |
| 0100 | All-terrain forklift, 45' lift, 35' reach, 9000 lb. capacity | A-3P | .20 | 40 | Month | | 1,500 | 2,175 | 3,675 | 4,675 |

## 01 54 19 – Temporary Cranes

### 01 54 19.50 Daily Crane Crews

| 01 54 19.50 Daily Crane Crews | Crew | Daily Output | Labor-Hours | Unit | Material | Labor | Equipment | Total | Total Incl O&P |
|---|---|---|---|---|---|---|---|---|---|
| 0010 | **DAILY CRANE CREWS** for small jobs, portal to portal | | | | | | | | | |
| 0100 | 12-ton truck-mounted hydraulic crane | A-3H | 1 | 8 | Day | | 330 | 965 | 1,295 | 1,575 |
| 0200 | 25-ton | A-3I | 1 | 8 | | | 330 | 990 | 1,320 | 1,575 |
| 0300 | 40-ton | A-3J | 1 | 8 | | | 330 | 990 | 1,320 | 1,575 |
| 0400 | 55-ton | A-3K | 1 | 16 | | | 610 | 1,525 | 2,135 | 2,600 |
| 0500 | 80-ton | A-3L | 1 | 16 | | | 610 | 1,700 | 2,310 | 2,800 |
| 0600 | 100-ton | A-3M | 1 | 16 | | | 610 | 3,375 | 3,985 | 4,625 |

### 01 54 19.60 Monthly Tower Crane Crew

| 01 54 19.60 Monthly Tower Crane Crew | Crew | Daily Output | Labor-Hours | Unit | Material | Labor | Equipment | Total | Total Incl O&P |
|---|---|---|---|---|---|---|---|---|---|
| 0010 | **MONTHLY TOWER CRANE CREW**, excludes concrete footing | | | | | | | | | |
| 0100 | Static tower crane, 130' high, 106' jib, 6200 lb. capaccity | A-3N | .05 | 176 | Month | | 7,200 | 21,600 | 28,800 | 34,700 |

## 01 54 23 – Temporary Scaffolding and Platforms

### 01 54 23.60 Pump Staging

| 01 54 23.60 Pump Staging | Crew | Daily Output | Labor-Hours | Unit | Material | Labor | Equipment | Total | Total Incl O&P |
|---|---|---|---|---|---|---|---|---|---|
| 0010 | **PUMP STAGING**, Aluminum    R015423-20 | | | | | | | | | |
| 0200 | 24' long pole section, buy | | | | Ea. | 395 | | | 395 | 435 |
| 0300 | 18' long pole section, buy | | | | | 310 | | | 310 | 340 |
| 0400 | 12' long pole section, buy | | | | | 208 | | | 208 | 228 |
| 0500 | 6' long pole section, buy | | | | | 109 | | | 109 | 120 |
| 0600 | 6' long splice joint section, buy | | | | | 81.50 | | | 81.50 | 89.50 |
| 0700 | Pump jack, buy | | | | | 132 | | | 132 | 146 |
| 0900 | Foldable brace, buy | | | | | 54 | | | 54 | 59.50 |
| 1000 | Workbench/back safety rail support, buy | | | | | 70 | | | 70 | 77 |
| 1100 | Scaffolding planks/workbench, 14" wide x 24' long, buy | | | | | 650 | | | 650 | 715 |
| 1200 | Plank end safety rail, buy | | | | | 315 | | | 315 | 350 |
| 1250 | Safety net, 22' long, buy | | | | | 292 | | | 292 | 320 |
| 1300 | System in place, 50' working height, per use based on 50 uses | 2 Carp | 84.80 | .189 | C.S.F. | 6 | 7.20 | | 13.20 | 17.80 |
| 1400 | 100 uses | | 84.80 | .189 | | 3 | 7.20 | | 10.20 | 14.50 |
| 1500 | 150 uses | | 84.80 | .189 | | 2.01 | 7.20 | | 9.21 | 13.40 |

### 01 54 23.70 Scaffolding

| 01 54 23.70 Scaffolding | Crew | Daily Output | Labor-Hours | Unit | Material | Labor | Equipment | Total | Total Incl O&P |
|---|---|---|---|---|---|---|---|---|---|
| 0010 | **SCAFFOLDING**    R015423-10 | | | | | | | | | |
| 0015 | Steel tube, regular, no plank, labor only to erect & dismantle | | | | | | | | | |
| 0090 | Building exterior, wall face, 1 to 5 stories, 6'-4" x 5' frames | 3 Carp | 8 | 3 | C.S.F. | | 114 | | 114 | 178 |
| 0200 | 6 to 12 stories | 4 Carp | 8 | 4 | | | 152 | | 152 | 237 |
| 0310 | 13 to 20 stories | 5 Carp | 8 | 5 | | | 191 | | 191 | 297 |
| 0460 | Building interior, wall face area, up to 16' high | 3 Carp | 12 | 2 | | | 76 | | 76 | 119 |
| 0560 | 16' to 40' high | | 10 | 2.400 | | | 91.50 | | 91.50 | 142 |
| 0800 | Building interior floor area, up to 30' high | | 150 | .160 | C.C.F. | | 6.10 | | 6.10 | 9.50 |
| 0900 | Over 30' high | 4 Carp | 160 | .200 | " | | 7.60 | | 7.60 | 11.85 |
| 0906 | Complete system for face of walls, no plank, material only rent/mo | | | | C.S.F. | 34.50 | | | 34.50 | 37.50 |

| 01 54 23.70 Scaffolding | Crew | Daily Output | Labor-Hours | Unit | Material | 2008 Bare Costs Labor | Equipment | Total | Total Incl O&P |
|---|---|---|---|---|---|---|---|---|---|
| 0908     Interior spaces, no plank, material only rent/mo | | | | C.C.F. | 3.30 | | | 3.30 | 3.63 |
| 0910  Steel tubular, heavy duty shoring, buy | | | | | | | | | |
| 0920     Frames 5' high 2' wide | | | | Ea. | 87 | | | 87 | 95.50 |
| 0925      5' high 4' wide | | | | | 98 | | | 98 | 108 |
| 0930      6' high 2' wide | | | | | 99 | | | 99 | 109 |
| 0935      6' high 4' wide | | | | | 116 | | | 116 | 128 |
| 0940     Accessories | | | | | | | | | |
| 0945       Cross braces | | | | Ea. | 16.80 | | | 16.80 | 18.50 |
| 0950       U-head, 8" x 8" | | | | | 20.50 | | | 20.50 | 22.50 |
| 0955       J-head, 4" x 8" | | | | | 14.80 | | | 14.80 | 16.30 |
| 0960       Base plate, 8" x 8" | | | | | 16.50 | | | 16.50 | 18.15 |
| 0965       Leveling jack | | | | | 35.50 | | | 35.50 | 39 |
| 1000  Steel tubular, regular, buy | | | | | | | | | |
| 1100     Frames 3' high 5' wide | | | | Ea. | 67 | | | 67 | 73.50 |
| 1150      5' high 5' wide | | | | | 77 | | | 77 | 84.50 |
| 1200      6'-4" high 5' wide | | | | | 97 | | | 97 | 107 |
| 1350      7'-6" high 6' wide | | | | | 164 | | | 164 | 180 |
| 1500     Accessories cross braces | | | | | 19.10 | | | 19.10 | 21 |
| 1550      Guardrail post | | | | | 17.30 | | | 17.30 | 19.05 |
| 1600      Guardrail 7' section | | | | | 9.20 | | | 9.20 | 10.10 |
| 1650      Screw jacks & plates | | | | | 25 | | | 25 | 27.50 |
| 1700      Sidearm brackets | | | | | 32.50 | | | 32.50 | 35.50 |
| 1750      8" casters | | | | | 33 | | | 33 | 36.50 |
| 1800      Plank 2" x 10" x 16'-0" | | | | | 49.50 | | | 49.50 | 54.50 |
| 1900      Stairway section | | | | | 305 | | | 305 | 335 |
| 1910      Stairway starter bar | | | | | 34 | | | 34 | 37.50 |
| 1920      Stairway inside handrail | | | | | 62 | | | 62 | 68 |
| 1930      Stairway outside handrail | | | | | 91 | | | 91 | 100 |
| 1940      Walk-thru frame guardrail | | | | | 42.50 | | | 42.50 | 47 |
| 2000  Steel tubular, regular, rent/mo. | | | | | | | | | |
| 2100     Frames 3' high 5' wide | | | | Ea. | 5 | | | 5 | 5.50 |
| 2150      5' high 5' wide | | | | | 5 | | | 5 | 5.50 |
| 2200      6'-4" high 5' wide | | | | | 4.50 | | | 4.50 | 4.95 |
| 2250      7'-6" high 6' wide | | | | | 7 | | | 7 | 7.70 |
| 2500     Accessories, cross braces | | | | | 1 | | | 1 | 1.10 |
| 2550      Guardrail post | | | | | 1 | | | 1 | 1.10 |
| 2600      Guardrail 7' section | | | | | 1 | | | 1 | 1.10 |
| 2650      Screw jacks & plates | | | | | 2 | | | 2 | 2.20 |
| 2700      Sidearm brackets | | | | | 2 | | | 2 | 2.20 |
| 2750      8" casters | | | | | 8 | | | 8 | 8.80 |
| 2800      Outrigger for rolling tower | | | | | 3 | | | 3 | 3.30 |
| 2850      Plank 2" x 10" x 16'-0" | | | | | 6 | | | 6 | 6.60 |
| 2900      Stairway section | | | | | 40 | | | 40 | 44 |
| 2940      Walk-thru frame guardrail | | | | | 2.50 | | | 2.50 | 2.75 |
| 3000  Steel tubular, heavy duty shoring, rent/mo. | | | | | | | | | |
| 3250      5' high 2' & 4' wide | | | | Ea. | 5 | | | 5 | 5.50 |
| 3300      6' high 2' & 4' wide | | | | | 5 | | | 5 | 5.50 |
| 3500     Accessories, cross braces | | | | | 1 | | | 1 | 1.10 |
| 3600      U - head, 8" x 8" | | | | | 1 | | | 1 | 1.10 |
| 3650      J - head, 4" x 8" | | | | | 1 | | | 1 | 1.10 |
| 3700      Base plate, 8" x 8" | | | | | 1 | | | 1 | 1.10 |
| 3750      Leveling jack | | | | | 2 | | | 2 | 2.20 |
| 5700  Planks, 2x10x16'-0", labor only to erect & remove to 50' H | 3 Carp | 72 | .333 | | | 12.70 | | 12.70 | 19.75 |

## 01 54 23 – Temporary Scaffolding and Platforms

| 01 54 23.70 **Scaffolding** | Crew | Daily Output | Labor-Hours | Unit | Material | 2008 Bare Costs Labor | Equipment | Total | Total Incl O&P |
|---|---|---|---|---|---|---|---|---|---|
| 5800 | Over 50' high | 4 Carp | 80 | .400 | Ea. | | 15.25 | | 15.25 | 23.50 |
| 6000 | Heavy duty shoring for elevated slab forms to 8'-2" high, floor area | | | | | | | | | |
| 6100 | Labor only to erect & dismantle | 4 Carp | 16 | 2 | C.S.F. | | 76 | | 76 | 119 |
| 6110 | Materials only, rent.mo | | | | " | 29.50 | | | 29.50 | 32.50 |
| 6500 | To 14'-8" high | | | | | | | | | |
| 6600 | Labor only to erect & dismantle | 4 Carp | 10 | 3.200 | C.S.F. | | 122 | | 122 | 190 |
| 6610 | Materials only, rent/mo | | | | " | 43 | | | 43 | 47.50 |

### 01 54 23.75 Scaffolding Specialties

| | | Crew | Daily Output | Labor-Hours | Unit | Material | 2008 Bare Costs Labor | Equipment | Total | Total Incl O&P |
|---|---|---|---|---|---|---|---|---|---|---|
| 0010 | **SCAFFOLDING SPECIALTIES** | | | | | | | | | |
| 1200 | Sidewalk bridge, heavy duty steel posts & beams, including | | | | | | | | | |
| 1210 | parapet protection & waterproofing | | | | | | | | | |
| 1220 | 8' to 10' wide, 2 posts | 3 Carp | 15 | 1.600 | L.F. | 33.50 | 61 | | 94.50 | 132 |
| 1230 | 3 posts | " | 10 | 2.400 | " | 51 | 91.50 | | 142.50 | 198 |
| 1500 | Sidewalk bridge using tubular steel | | | | | | | | | |
| 1510 | scaffold frames, including planking | 3 Carp | 45 | .533 | L.F. | 5.60 | 20.50 | | 26.10 | 37.50 |
| 1600 | For 2 uses per month, deduct from all above | | | | | 50% | | | | |
| 1700 | For 1 use every 2 months, add to all above | | | | | 100% | | | | |
| 1900 | Catwalks, 20" wide, no guardrails, 7' span, buy | | | | Ea. | 143 | | | 143 | 157 |
| 2000 | 10' span, buy | | | | | 207 | | | 207 | 228 |
| 3720 | Putlog, standard, 8' span, with hangers, buy | | | | | 70 | | | 70 | 77 |
| 3730 | Rent per month | | | | | 10 | | | 10 | 11 |
| 3750 | 12' span, buy | | | | | 106 | | | 106 | 117 |
| 3755 | Rent per month | | | | | 15 | | | 15 | 16.50 |
| 3760 | Trussed type, 16' span, buy | | | | | 243 | | | 243 | 267 |
| 3770 | Rent per month | | | | | 20 | | | 20 | 22 |
| 3790 | 22' span, buy | | | | | 291 | | | 291 | 320 |
| 3795 | Rent per month | | | | | 30 | | | 30 | 33 |
| 3800 | Rolling ladders with handrails, 30" wide, buy, 2 step | | | | | 189 | | | 189 | 208 |
| 4000 | 7 step | | | | | 605 | | | 605 | 665 |
| 4050 | 10 step | | | | | 830 | | | 830 | 915 |
| 4100 | Rolling towers, buy, 5' wide, 7' long, 10' high | | | | | 1,225 | | | 1,225 | 1,350 |
| 4200 | For 5' high added sections, to buy, add | | | | | 192 | | | 192 | 211 |
| 4300 | Complete incl. wheels, railings, outriggers, | | | | | | | | | |
| 4350 | 21' high, to buy | | | | Ea. | 2,050 | | | 2,050 | 2,275 |
| 4400 | Rent/month = 5% of purchase cost | | | | " | 99 | | | 99 | 109 |

### 01 54 23.80 Staging Aids

| | | Crew | Daily Output | Labor-Hours | Unit | Material | 2008 Bare Costs Labor | Equipment | Total | Total Incl O&P |
|---|---|---|---|---|---|---|---|---|---|---|
| 0010 | **STAGING AIDS** and fall protection equipment | | | | | | | | | |
| 0100 | Sidewall staging bracket, tubular, buy | | | | Ea. | 40.50 | | | 40.50 | 44.50 |
| 0110 | Cost each per day, based on 250 days use | | | | Day | .16 | | | .16 | .18 |
| 0200 | Guard post, buy | | | | Ea. | 21 | | | 21 | 23 |
| 0210 | Cost each per day, based on 250 days use | | | | Day | .08 | | | .08 | .09 |
| 0300 | End guard chains, buy per pair | | | | Pair | 29 | | | 29 | 32 |
| 0310 | Cost per set per day, based on 250 days use | | | | Day | .16 | | | .16 | .18 |
| 1000 | Roof shingling bracket, steel, buy | | | | Ea. | 7.90 | | | 7.90 | 8.65 |
| 1010 | Cost each per day, based on 250 days use | | | | Day | .03 | | | .03 | .03 |
| 1100 | Wood bracket, buy | | | | Ea. | 16.50 | | | 16.50 | 18.15 |
| 1110 | Cost each per day, based on 250 days use | | | | Day | .07 | | | .07 | .07 |
| 2000 | Ladder jack, aluminum, buy per pair | | | | Pair | 107 | | | 107 | 117 |
| 2010 | Cost per pair per day, based on 250 days use | | | | Day | .43 | | | .43 | .47 |
| 2100 | Steel siderail jack, buy per pair | | | | Pair | 84 | | | 84 | 92.50 |
| 2110 | Cost per pair per day, based on 250 days use | | | | Day | .34 | | | .34 | .37 |
| 3000 | Laminated wood plank, 2x10x16', buy | | | | Ea. | 49.50 | | | 49.50 | 54.50 |

# 01 54 Construction Aids

## 01 54 23 – Temporary Scaffolding and Platforms

| 01 54 23.80 Staging Aids | Crew | Daily Output | Labor-Hours | Unit | Material | 2008 Bare Costs Labor | Equipment | Total | Total Incl O&P |
|---|---|---|---|---|---|---|---|---|---|
| 3010      Cost each per day, based on 250 days use | | | | Day | .20 | | | .20 | .22 |
| 3100   Aluminum scaffolding plank, 20" wide x 24' long, buy | | | | Ea. | 785 | | | 785 | 865 |
| 3110      Cost each per day, based on 250 days use | | | | Day | 3.14 | | | 3.14 | 3.46 |
| 4000   Nylon full body harness, lanyard and rope grab | | | | Ea. | 206 | | | 206 | 226 |
| 4010      Cost each per day, based on 250 days use | | | | Day | .82 | | | .82 | .91 |
| 4100   Rope for safety line, 5/8" x 100' nylon, buy | | | | Ea. | 55 | | | 55 | 60.50 |
| 4110      Cost each per day, based on 250 days use | | | | Day | .22 | | | .22 | .24 |
| 4200   Permanent U-Bolt roof anchor, buy | | | | Ea. | 33.50 | | | 33.50 | 36.50 |
| 4300   Temporary (one use) roof ridge anchor, buy | | | | " | 27.50 | | | 27.50 | 30.50 |
| 5000   Installation (setup and removal) of staging aids | | | | | | | | | |
| 5010     Sidewall staging bracket | 2 Carp | 64 | .250 | Ea. | | 9.55 | | 9.55 | 14.85 |
| 5020       Guard post with 2 wood rails | " | 64 | .250 | | | 9.55 | | 9.55 | 14.85 |
| 5030     End guard chains, set | 1 Carp | 64 | .125 | | | 4.76 | | 4.76 | 7.40 |
| 5100     Roof shingling bracket | | 96 | .083 | | | 3.17 | | 3.17 | 4.94 |
| 5200     Ladder jack | | 64 | .125 | | | 4.76 | | 4.76 | 7.40 |
| 5300     Wood plank, 2x10x16' | 2 Carp | 80 | .200 | | | 7.60 | | 7.60 | 11.85 |
| 5310     Aluminum scaffold plank, 20" x 24' | " | 40 | .400 | | | 15.25 | | 15.25 | 23.50 |
| 5410     Safety rope | 1 Carp | 40 | .200 | | | 7.60 | | 7.60 | 11.85 |
| 5420     Permanent U-Bolt roof anchor (install only) | 2 Carp | 40 | .400 | | | 15.25 | | 15.25 | 23.50 |
| 5430     Temporary roof ridge anchor (install only) | 1 Carp | 64 | .125 | | | 4.76 | | 4.76 | 7.40 |

## 01 54 26 – Temporary Swing Staging

| 01 54 26.50 Swing Staging | Crew | Daily Output | Labor-Hours | Unit | Material | 2008 Bare Costs Labor | Equipment | Total | Total Incl O&P |
|---|---|---|---|---|---|---|---|---|---|
| 0010  **SWING STAGING**, 500 lb cap., 2' wide to 24' long, hand operated | | | | | | | | | |
| 0020     steel cable type, with 60' cables, buy | | | | Ea. | 5,100 | | | 5,100 | 5,625 |
| 0030      Rent per month | | | | " | 510 | | | 510 | 560 |
| 0600   Lightweight (not for masons) 24' long for 150' height, | | | | | | | | | |
| 0610      manual type, buy | | | | Ea. | 5,500 | | | 5,500 | 6,050 |
| 0620       Rent per month | | | | | 550 | | | 550 | 605 |
| 0700     Powered, electric or air, to 150' high, buy | | | | | 18,800 | | | 18,800 | 20,700 |
| 0710      Rent per month | | | | | 1,325 | | | 1,325 | 1,450 |
| 0780     To 300' high, buy | | | | | 24,500 | | | 24,500 | 27,000 |
| 0800      Rent per month | | | | | 1,725 | | | 1,725 | 1,900 |
| 1000   Bosun's chair or work basket 3' x 3.5', to 300' high, electric, buy | | | | | 8,400 | | | 8,400 | 9,225 |
| 1010      Rent per month | | | | | 585 | | | 585 | 645 |
| 2200  Move swing staging (setup and remove) | E-4 | 2 | 16 | Move | | 695 | 66 | 761 | 1,325 |

## 01 54 36 – Equipment Mobilization

| 01 54 36.50 Mobilization or Demob. | Crew | Daily Output | Labor-Hours | Unit | Material | 2008 Bare Costs Labor | Equipment | Total | Total Incl O&P |
|---|---|---|---|---|---|---|---|---|---|
| 0010  **MOBILIZATION OR DEMOB.** (One or the other, unless noted)   R015433-10 | | | | | | | | | |
| 0015  Up to 25 mi haul dist (50 mi RT for mob/demob crew) | | | | | | | | | |
| 0020  Dozer, loader, backhoe, excav., grader, paver, roller, 70 to 150 H.P. | B-34N | 4 | 2 | Ea. | | 61 | 110 | 171 | 217 |
| 0100     Above 150 HP | B-34K | 3 | 2.667 | | | 81.50 | 207 | 288.50 | 355 |
| 0300   Scraper, towed type (incl. tractor), 6 C.Y. capacity | | 3 | 2.667 | | | 81.50 | 207 | 288.50 | 355 |
| 0400     10 C.Y. | | 2.50 | 3.200 | | | 98 | 248 | 346 | 425 |
| 0600   Self-propelled scraper, 15 C.Y. | | 2.50 | 3.200 | | | 98 | 248 | 346 | 425 |
| 0700     24 C.Y. | | 2 | 4 | | | 122 | 310 | 432 | 530 |
| 0900   Shovel or dragline, 3/4 C.Y. | | 3.60 | 2.222 | | | 68 | 173 | 241 | 295 |
| 1000     1-1/2 C.Y. | | 3 | 2.667 | | | 81.50 | 207 | 288.50 | 355 |
| 1100  Small equipment, placed in rear of, or towed by pickup truck | A-3A | 8 | 1 | | | 29.50 | 15.20 | 44.70 | 62 |
| 1150     Equip up to 70 HP, on flatbed trailer behind pickup truck | A-3D | 4 | 2 | | | 59 | 54.50 | 113.50 | 151 |
| 2000  Mob & demob truck-mounted crane up to 75 ton, driver only | 1 Eqhv | 3.60 | 2.222 | | | 91 | | 91 | 137 |
| 2100  Crane, truck-mounted, over 75 ton | A-3E | 2.50 | 6.400 | | | 229 | 48.50 | 277.50 | 405 |
| 2200     Crawler-mounted, up to 75 ton | A-3F | 2 | 8 | | | 286 | 385 | 671 | 860 |

# 01 54 Construction Aids

## 01 54 36 – Equipment Mobilization

### 01 54 36.50 Mobilization or Demob.

| | | Crew | Daily Output | Labor-Hours | Unit | Material | 2008 Bare Costs Labor | 2008 Bare Costs Equipment | Total | Total Incl O&P |
|---|---|---|---|---|---|---|---|---|---|---|
| 2300 | Over 75 ton | A-3G | 1.50 | 10.667 | Ea. | | 380 | 495 | 875 | 1,125 |
| 2500 | For each additional 5 miles haul distance, add | | | | | | 10% | 10% | | |
| 3000 | For large pieces of equipment, allow for assembly/knockdown | | | | | | | | | |
| 3001 | For mob/demob of vibrofloatation equip, see Div. 31 45 13.10 | | | | | | | | | |
| 3100 | For mob/demob of micro-tunneling equip, see Div. 33 05 23.19 | | | | | | | | | |
| 3200 | For mob/demob of pile driving equip, see Div. 31 62 19.10 | | | | | | | | | |
| 3300 | For mob/demob of caisson drilling equip, see Div. 31 63 26.13 | | | | | | | | | |

## 01 54 39 – Construction Equipment

### 01 54 39.70 Small Tools

| | | | | | | | | | | |
|---|---|---|---|---|---|---|---|---|---|---|
| 0010 | **SMALL TOOLS** | R013113-50 | | | | | | | | |
| 0020 | As % of contractor's work, minimum | | | | Total | | | | .45% | .50% |
| 0100 | Maximum | | | | " | | | | 1.82% | 2% |

# 01 55 Vehicular Access and Parking

## 01 55 23 – Temporary Roads

### 01 55 23.50 Roads and Sidewalks

| | | Crew | Daily Output | Labor-Hours | Unit | Material | 2008 Bare Costs Labor | 2008 Bare Costs Equipment | Total | Total Incl O&P |
|---|---|---|---|---|---|---|---|---|---|---|
| 0010 | **ROADS AND SIDEWALKS** Temporary | | | | | | | | | |
| 0050 | Roads, gravel fill, no surfacing, 4" gravel depth | B-14 | 715 | .067 | S.Y. | 4.73 | 2.14 | .40 | 7.27 | 8.95 |
| 0100 | 8" gravel depth | " | 615 | .078 | " | 9.45 | 2.48 | .46 | 12.39 | 14.75 |
| 1000 | Ramp, 3/4" plywood on 2" x 6" joists, 16" O.C. | 2 Carp | 300 | .053 | S.F. | 1.42 | 2.03 | | 3.45 | 4.72 |
| 1100 | On 2" x 10" joists, 16" O.C. | " | 275 | .058 | " | 1.90 | 2.22 | | 4.12 | 5.55 |

# 01 56 Temporary Barriers and Enclosures

## 01 56 13 – Temporary Air Barriers

### 01 56 13.60 Tarpaulins

| | | Crew | Daily Output | Labor-Hours | Unit | Material | 2008 Bare Costs Labor | 2008 Bare Costs Equipment | Total | Total Incl O&P |
|---|---|---|---|---|---|---|---|---|---|---|
| 0010 | **TARPAULINS** | | | | | | | | | |
| 0020 | Cotton duck, 10 oz. to 13.13 oz. per S.Y., minimum | | | | S.F. | .51 | | | .51 | .56 |
| 0050 | Maximum | | | | | .53 | | | .53 | .58 |
| 0100 | Polyvinyl coated nylon, 14 oz. to 18 oz., minimum | | | | | .48 | | | .48 | .53 |
| 0150 | Maximum | | | | | .68 | | | .68 | .75 |
| 0200 | Reinforced polyethylene 3 mils thick, white | | | | | .15 | | | .15 | .17 |
| 0300 | 4 mils thick, white, clear or black | | | | | .20 | | | .20 | .22 |
| 0400 | 5.5 mils thick, clear | | | | | .26 | | | .26 | .29 |
| 0500 | White, fire retardant | | | | | .35 | | | .35 | .39 |
| 0600 | 7.5 mils, oil resistant, fire retardant | | | | | .40 | | | .40 | .44 |
| 0700 | 8.5 mils, black | | | | | .53 | | | .53 | .58 |
| 0710 | Woven polyethylene, 6 mils thick | | | | | .35 | | | .35 | .39 |
| 0730 | Polyester reinforced w/ integral fastening system 11 mils thick | | | | | 1.07 | | | 1.07 | 1.18 |
| 0740 | Mylar polyester, non-reinforced, 7 mils thick | | | | | 1.17 | | | 1.17 | 1.29 |

### 01 56 13.90 Winter Protection

| | | Crew | Daily Output | Labor-Hours | Unit | Material | 2008 Bare Costs Labor | 2008 Bare Costs Equipment | Total | Total Incl O&P |
|---|---|---|---|---|---|---|---|---|---|---|
| 0010 | **WINTER PROTECTION** | | | | | | | | | |
| 0100 | Framing to close openings | 2 Clab | 750 | .021 | S.F. | .39 | .65 | | 1.04 | 1.43 |
| 0200 | Tarpaulins hung over scaffolding, 8 uses, not incl. scaffolding | | 1500 | .011 | | .25 | .32 | | .57 | .78 |
| 0250 | Tarpaulin polyester reinf. w/ integral fastening system 11 mils thick | | 1600 | .010 | | .80 | .30 | | 1.10 | 1.35 |
| 0300 | Prefab fiberglass panels, steel frame, 8 uses | | 1200 | .013 | | .85 | .40 | | 1.25 | 1.57 |

## 01 56 23 – Temporary Barricades

### 01 56 23.10 Barricades

| | | | | | | | | | | |
|---|---|---|---|---|---|---|---|---|---|---|
| 0010 | **BARRICADES** | | | | | | | | | |

# 01 56 Temporary Barriers and Enclosures

## 01 56 23 – Temporary Barricades

| 01 56 23.10 Barricades | | Crew | Daily Output | Labor-Hours | Unit | Material | 2008 Bare Costs Labor | 2008 Bare Costs Equipment | Total | Total Incl O&P |
|---|---|---|---|---|---|---|---|---|---|---|
| 0020 | 5' high, 3 rail @ 2" x 8", fixed | 2 Carp | 20 | .800 | L.F. | 5.35 | 30.50 | | 35.85 | 53.50 |
| 0150 | Movable | " | 30 | .533 | " | 4.40 | 20.50 | | 24.90 | 36.50 |
| 0300 | Stock units, 6' high, 8' wide, plain, buy | | | | Ea. | 435 | | | 435 | 480 |
| 0350 | With reflective tape, buy | | | | " | 525 | | | 525 | 580 |
| 0400 | Break-a-way 3" PVC pipe barricade | | | | | | | | | |
| 0410 | with 3 ea. 1' x 4' reflectorized panels, buy | | | | Ea. | 305 | | | 305 | 335 |
| 0500 | Plywood with steel legs, 32" wide | | | | | 72 | | | 72 | 79 |
| 0600 | Telescoping Christmas tree, 9' high, 5 flags, buy | | | | | 122 | | | 122 | 134 |
| 0800 | Traffic cones, PVC, 18" high | | | | | 7.20 | | | 7.20 | 7.90 |
| 0850 | 28" high | | | | | 14.35 | | | 14.35 | 15.80 |
| 1000 | Guardrail, wooden, 3' high, 1" x 6", on 2" x 4" posts | 2 Carp | 200 | .080 | L.F. | 1.09 | 3.05 | | 4.14 | 5.95 |
| 1100 | 2" x 6", on 4" x 4" posts | " | 165 | .097 | | 2.29 | 3.69 | | 5.98 | 8.25 |
| 1200 | Portable metal with base pads, buy | | | | | 13.15 | | | 13.15 | 14.50 |
| 1250 | Typical installation, assume 10 reuses | 2 Carp | 600 | .027 | | 1.31 | 1.02 | | 2.33 | 3.02 |
| 1300 | Barricade tape, polyethelyne, 7 mil, 3" wide x 500' long roll | | | | Ea. | 25 | | | 25 | 27.50 |
| 5000 | Barricades, see Div. 01 54 33.40 | | | | | | | | | |

## 01 56 26 – Temporary Fencing

### 01 56 26.50 Temporary Fencing

| | | Crew | Daily Output | Labor-Hours | Unit | Material | 2008 Bare Costs Labor | 2008 Bare Costs Equipment | Total | Total Incl O&P |
|---|---|---|---|---|---|---|---|---|---|---|
| 0010 | **TEMPORARY FENCING** | | | | | | | | | |
| 0020 | Chain link, 11 ga, 5' high | 2 Clab | 400 | .040 | L.F. | 6.50 | 1.21 | | 7.71 | 9.05 |
| 0100 | 6' high | | 300 | .053 | | 7 | 1.61 | | 8.61 | 10.20 |
| 0200 | Rented chain link, 6' high, to 1000' (up to 12 mo.) | | 400 | .040 | | 1.79 | 1.21 | | 3 | 3.85 |
| 0250 | Over 1000' (up to 12 mo.) | | 300 | .053 | | 1.97 | 1.61 | | 3.58 | 4.68 |
| 0350 | Plywood, painted, 2" x 4" frame, 4' high | A-4 | 135 | .178 | | 5.30 | 6.50 | | 11.80 | 15.90 |
| 0400 | 4" x 4" frame, 8' high | " | 110 | .218 | | 10.70 | 8 | | 18.70 | 24 |
| 0500 | Wire mesh on 4" x 4" posts, 4' high | 2 Carp | 100 | .160 | | 10.20 | 6.10 | | 16.30 | 20.50 |
| 0550 | 8' high | " | 80 | .200 | | 15.45 | 7.60 | | 23.05 | 29 |

## 01 56 29 – Temporary Protective Walkways

### 01 56 29.50 Protection

| | | Crew | Daily Output | Labor-Hours | Unit | Material | 2008 Bare Costs Labor | 2008 Bare Costs Equipment | Total | Total Incl O&P |
|---|---|---|---|---|---|---|---|---|---|---|
| 0010 | **PROTECTION** | | | | | | | | | |
| 0020 | Stair tread, 2" x 12" planks, 1 use | 1 Carp | 75 | .107 | Tread | 3.73 | 4.06 | | 7.79 | 10.45 |
| 0100 | Exterior plywood, 1/2" thick, 1 use | | 65 | .123 | | 1.56 | 4.69 | | 6.25 | 9 |
| 0200 | 3/4" thick, 1 use | | 60 | .133 | | 2.61 | 5.10 | | 7.71 | 10.75 |
| 2200 | Sidewalks, 2" x 12" planks, 2 uses | | 350 | .023 | S.F. | .62 | .87 | | 1.49 | 2.04 |
| 2300 | Exterior plywood, 2 uses, 1/2" thick | | 750 | .011 | | .26 | .41 | | .67 | .92 |
| 2400 | 5/8" thick | | 650 | .012 | | .34 | .47 | | .81 | 1 10 |
| 2500 | 3/4" thick | | 600 | .013 | | .44 | .51 | | .95 | 1.27 |

## 01 56 32 – Temporary Security

### 01 56 32.50 Watchman

| | | Crew | Daily Output | Labor-Hours | Unit | Material | 2008 Bare Costs Labor | 2008 Bare Costs Equipment | Total | Total Incl O&P |
|---|---|---|---|---|---|---|---|---|---|---|
| 0010 | **WATCHMAN** | | | | | | | | | |
| 0020 | Service, monthly basis, uniformed person, minimum | | | | Hr. | | | | 25 | 27.50 |
| 0100 | Maximum | | | | | | | | 45.45 | 50 |
| 0200 | Person and command dog, minimum | | | | | | | | 31 | 34 |
| 0300 | Maximum | | | | | | | | 54.55 | 60 |
| 0500 | Sentry dog, leased, with job patrol (yard dog), 1 dog | | | | Week | | | | 290 | 319 |
| 0600 | 2 dogs | | | | " | | | | 390 | 429 |
| 0800 | Purchase, trained sentry dog, minimum | | | | Ea. | | | | 1,364 | 1,500 |
| 0900 | Maximum | | | | " | | | | 2,727 | 3,000 |

# 01 58 Project Identification

## 01 58 13 – Temporary Project Signage

| 01 58 13.50 Signs | Crew | Daily Output | Labor-Hours | Unit | Material | 2008 Bare Costs Labor | Equipment | Total | Total Incl O&P |
|---|---|---|---|---|---|---|---|---|---|
| 0010 **SIGNS** | | | | | | | | | |
| 0020 High intensity reflectorized, no posts, buy | | | | S.F. | 17.90 | | | 17.90 | 19.70 |

# 01 71 Examination and Preparation

## 01 71 23 – Field Engineering

### 01 71 23.13 Construction Layout

| | Crew | Daily Output | Labor-Hours | Unit | Material | 2008 Bare Costs Labor | Equipment | Total | Total Incl O&P |
|---|---|---|---|---|---|---|---|---|---|
| 0010 **CONSTRUCTION LAYOUT** | | | | | | | | | |
| 1100 Crew for layout of building, trenching or pipe laying, 2 person crew | A-6 | 1 | 16 | Day | | 615 | 69 | 684 | 1,025 |
| 1200 3 person crew | A-7 | 1 | 24 | ↓ | | 1,000 | 69 | 1,069 | 1,625 |
| 1400 Crew for roadway layout, 4 person crew | A-8 | 1 | 32 | ↓ | | 1,300 | 69 | 1,369 | 2,075 |

### 01 71 23.19 Surveyor Stakes

| | Crew | Daily Output | Labor-Hours | Unit | Material | 2008 Bare Costs Labor | Equipment | Total | Total Incl O&P |
|---|---|---|---|---|---|---|---|---|---|
| 0010 **SURVEYOR STAKES** | | | | | | | | | |
| 0020 Hardwood, 1" x 1" x 48" long | | | | C | 54 | | | 54 | 59.50 |
| 0100 2" x 2" x 18" long | | | | | 68.50 | | | 68.50 | 75 |
| 0150 2" x 2" x 24" long | | | | | 80 | | | 80 | 88 |
| 0200 2" x 2" x 30" long | | | | ↓ | 74 | | | 74 | 81.50 |

# 01 74 Cleaning and Waste Management

## 01 74 13 – Progress Cleaning

### 01 74 13.20 Cleaning Up

| | Crew | Daily Output | Labor-Hours | Unit | Material | 2008 Bare Costs Labor | Equipment | Total | Total Incl O&P |
|---|---|---|---|---|---|---|---|---|---|
| 0010 **CLEANING UP** | | | | | | | | | |
| 0020 After job completion, allow, minimum | | | | Job | | | | | .30% |
| 0040 Maximum | | | | " | | | | | 1% |
| 0050 Cleanup of floor area, continuous, per day, during const. | A-5 | 24 | .750 | M.S.F. | 1.70 | 22.50 | 1.87 | 26.07 | 39 |
| 0100 Final by GC at end of job | " | 11.50 | 1.565 | " | 2.71 | 47 | 3.90 | 53.61 | 81 |
| 0200 Rubbish removal, see Div. 02 41 19.23 | | | | | | | | | |

# 01 91 Commissioning

## 01 91 13 – General Commissioning Requirements

### 01 91 13.50 Commissioning

| | Crew | Daily Output | Labor-Hours | Unit | Material | 2008 Bare Costs Labor | Equipment | Total | Total Incl O&P |
|---|---|---|---|---|---|---|---|---|---|
| 0010 **COMMISSIONING** Including documentation of design intent | | | | | | | | | |
| 0100 performance verification, O&M, training, min | | | | Project | | | | | .50% |
| 0150 Maximum | | | | " | | | | | .75% |

# Estimating Tips

## 02 20 00 Assessment

- If possible, visit the site and take an inventory of the type, quantity, and size of the trees. Certain trees may have a landscape resale value or firewood value. Stump disposal can be very expensive, particularly if they cannot be buried at the site. Consider using a bulldozer in lieu of hand-cutting trees.

- Estimators should visit the site to determine the need for haul road access, storage of materials, and security considerations. When estimating for access roads on unstable soil, consider using a geotextile stabilization fabric. It can greatly reduce the quantity of crushed stone or gravel. Sites of limited size and access can cause cost overruns due to lost productivity. Theft and damage is another consideration if the location is isolated. A temporary fence or security guards may be required. Investigate the site thoroughly.

## 02 30 00 Subsurface Investigation

In preparing estimates on structures involving earthwork or foundations, all information concerning soil characteristics should be obtained. Look particularly for hazardous waste, evidence of prior dumping of debris, and previous stream beds.

## 02 40 00 Demolition and Structure Moving

The costs shown for selective demolition do not include rubbish handling or disposal. These items should be estimated separately using RSMeans data or other sources.

- Historic preservation often requires that the contractor remove materials from the existing structure, rehab them, and replace them. The estimator must be aware of any related measures and precautions that must be taken when doing selective demolition and cutting and patching. Requirements may include special handling and storage, as well as security.

- In addition to Section 02 41 00, you can find selective demolition items in each division. Example: Roofing demolition is in Division 7.

# Reference Numbers

Reference numbers are shown in shaded boxes at the beginning of some major classifications. These numbers refer to related items in the Reference Section. The reference information may be an estimating procedure, an alternate pricing method, or technical information.

*Note:* Not all subdivisions listed here necessarily appear in this publication.

## Division 2 - Existing Conditions

# 02 21 Surveys

## 02 21 13 – Site Surveys

| 02 21 13.09 Topographical Surveys | Crew | Daily Output | Labor-Hours | Unit | Material | 2008 Bare Costs Labor | Equipment | Total | Total Incl O&P |
|---|---|---|---|---|---|---|---|---|---|
| 0010 **TOPOGRAPHICAL SURVEYS** | | | | | | | | | |
| 0020 Topographical surveying, conventional, minimum | A-7 | 3.30 | 7.273 | Acre | 17 | 305 | 21 | 343 | 505 |
| 0100 Maximum | A-8 | .60 | 53.333 | " | 52 | 2,175 | 115 | 2,342 | 3,500 |

### 02 21 13.13 Boundary and Survey Markers

| | Crew | Daily Output | Labor-Hours | Unit | Material | Labor | Equipment | Total | Total Incl O&P |
|---|---|---|---|---|---|---|---|---|---|
| 0010 **BOUNDARY AND SURVEY MARKERS** | | | | | | | | | |
| 0300 Lot location and lines, large quantities, minimum | A-7 | 2 | 12 | Acre | 30 | 500 | 34.50 | 564.50 | 840 |
| 0320 Average | " | 1.25 | 19.200 | | 48 | 800 | 55 | 903 | 1,350 |
| 0400 Small quantities, maximum | A-8 | 1 | 32 | ↓ | 64 | 1,300 | 69 | 1,433 | 2,150 |
| 0600 Monuments, 3' long | A-7 | 10 | 2.400 | Ea. | 30 | 100 | 6.90 | 136.90 | 195 |
| 0800 Property lines, perimeter, cleared land | " | 1000 | .024 | L.F. | .03 | 1 | .07 | 1.10 | 1.65 |
| 0900 Wooded land | A-8 | 875 | .037 | " | .05 | 1.49 | .08 | 1.62 | 2.43 |

### 02 21 13.16 Aerial Surveys

| | Crew | Daily Output | Labor-Hours | Unit | Material | Labor | Equipment | Total | Total Incl O&P |
|---|---|---|---|---|---|---|---|---|---|
| 0010 **AERIAL SURVEYS** | | | | | | | | | |
| 1500 Aerial surveying, including ground control, minimum fee, 10 acres | | | | Total | | | | | 5,700 |
| 1510 100 acres | | | | | | | | | 9,500 |
| 1550 From existing photography, deduct | | | | ↓ | | | | | 1,370 |
| 1600 2' contours, 10 acres | | | | Acre | | | | | 460 |
| 1650 20 acres | | | | | | | | | 315 |
| 1800 50 acres | | | | | | | | | 95 |
| 1850 100 acres | | | | | | | | | 85 |
| 2000 1000 acres | | | | | | | | | 17.85 |
| 2050 10,000 acres | | | | ↓ | | | | | 11.50 |
| 2150 For 1' contours and | | | | | | | | | |
| 2160 dense urban areas, add to above | | | | Acre | | | | | 40% |
| 3000 Inertial guidance system for | | | | | | | | | |
| 3010 locating coordinates, rent per day | | | | Ea. | | | | | 4,000 |

# 02 32 Geotechnical Investigations

## 02 32 13 – Subsurface Drilling and Sampling

### 02 32 13.10 Boring and Exploratory Drilling

| | Crew | Daily Output | Labor-Hours | Unit | Material | Labor | Equipment | Total | Total Incl O&P |
|---|---|---|---|---|---|---|---|---|---|
| 0010 **BORING AND EXPLORATORY DRILLING** | | | | | | | | | |
| 0020 Borings, initial field stake out & determination of elevations | A-6 | 1 | 16 | Day | | 615 | 69 | 684 | 1,025 |
| 0100 Drawings showing boring details | | | | Total | | 233.10 | | 233.10 | 340.20 |
| 0200 Report and recommendations from P.E. | | | | | | 525 | | 525 | 766.50 |
| 0300 Mobilization and demobilization, minimum | B-55 | 4 | 6 | ↓ | | 180 | 231 | 411 | 535 |
| 0350 For over 100 miles, per added mile | | 450 | .053 | Mile | | 1.60 | 2.06 | 3.66 | 4.74 |
| 0600 Auger holes in earth, no samples, 2-1/2" diameter | | 78.60 | .305 | L.F. | | 9.15 | 11.80 | 20.95 | 27 |
| 0650 4" diameter | | 67.50 | .356 | | | 10.65 | 13.70 | 24.35 | 31.50 |
| 0800 Cased borings in earth, with samples, 2-1/2" diameter | | 55.50 | .432 | | 17.40 | 12.95 | 16.70 | 47.05 | 57.50 |
| 0850 4" diameter | ↓ | 32.60 | .736 | | 27.50 | 22 | 28.50 | 78 | 95.50 |
| 1000 Drilling in rock, "BX" core, no sampling | B-56 | 34.90 | .458 | | | 15.60 | 37 | 52.60 | 64.50 |
| 1050 With casing & sampling | | 31.70 | .505 | | 17.40 | 17.15 | 41 | 75.55 | 90.50 |
| 1200 "NX" core, no sampling | | 25.92 | .617 | | | 21 | 50 | 71 | 87 |
| 1250 With casing and sampling | ↓ | 25 | .640 | ↓ | 21 | 22 | 51.50 | 94.50 | 114 |
| 1400 Borings, earth, drill rig and crew with truck mounted auger | B-55 | 1 | 24 | Day | | 720 | 925 | 1,645 | 2,150 |
| 1450 Rock using crawler type drill | B-56 | 1 | 16 | " | | 545 | 1,300 | 1,845 | 2,250 |
| 1500 For inner city borings add, minimum | | | | | | | | | 10% |
| 1510 Maximum | | | | | | | | | 20% |

# 02 32 Geotechnical Investigations

## 02 32 19 – Exploratory Excavations

### 02 32 19.10 Test Pits

| | | Crew | Daily Output | Labor-Hours | Unit | Material | Labor | Equipment | Total | Total Incl O&P |
|---|---|---|---|---|---|---|---|---|---|---|
| | | | | | | | 2008 Bare Costs | | | |
| 0010 | **TEST PITS** | | | | | | | | | |
| 0020 | Hand digging, light soil | 1 Clab | 4.50 | 1.778 | C.Y. | | 54 | | 54 | 83.50 |
| 0100 | Heavy soil | " | 2.50 | 3.200 | | | 97 | | 97 | 151 |
| 0120 | Loader-backhoe, light soil | B-11M | 28 | .571 | | | 20 | 12.15 | 32.15 | 44 |
| 0130 | Heavy soil | " | 20 | .800 | ↓ | | 28 | 17.05 | 45.05 | 62 |
| 1000 | Subsurface exploration, mobilization | | | | Mile | | | | 7.50 | 8.63 |
| 1010 | Difficult access for rig, add | | | | Hr. | | | | 150 | 172.20 |
| 1020 | Auger borings, drill rig, incl. samples | | | | L.F. | | | | 17.27 | 19.87 |
| 1030 | Hand auger | | | | | | | | 25.52 | 29.36 |
| 1050 | Drill and sample every 5', split spoon | | | | ↓ | | | | 22.52 | 25.90 |
| 1060 | Extra samples | | | | Ea. | | | | 30.45 | 35.02 |

# 02 41 Demolition

## 02 41 13 – Selective Site Demolition

### 02 41 13.15 Hydrodemolition

| | | | Crew | Daily Output | Labor-Hours | Unit | Material | Labor | Equipment | Total | Total Incl O&P |
|---|---|---|---|---|---|---|---|---|---|---|---|
| 0010 | **HYDRODEMOLITION** | R024119-10 | | | | | | | | | |
| 0015 | Hydrodemolition, concrete pavement, 4000 PSI, 2" depth | | B-5 | 500 | .112 | S.F. | | 3.73 | 2.17 | 5.90 | 8.15 |
| 0120 | 4" depth | | | 450 | .124 | | | 4.14 | 2.41 | 6.55 | 9.05 |
| 0130 | 6" depth | | | 400 | .140 | | | 4.66 | 2.71 | 7.37 | 10.15 |
| 0410 | 6000 PSI, 2" depth | | | 410 | .137 | | | 4.55 | 2.65 | 7.20 | 9.90 |
| 0420 | 4" depth | | | 350 | .160 | | | 5.30 | 3.10 | 8.40 | 11.60 |
| 0430 | 6" depth | | | 300 | .187 | | | 6.20 | 3.62 | 9.82 | 13.55 |
| 0510 | 8000 PSI, 2" depth | | | 330 | .170 | | | 5.65 | 3.29 | 8.94 | 12.30 |
| 0520 | 4" depth | | | 280 | .200 | | | 6.65 | 3.88 | 10.53 | 14.50 |
| 0530 | 6" depth | | ↓ | 240 | .233 | ↓ | | 7.75 | 4.52 | 12.27 | 16.90 |

### 02 41 13.17 Demolish, Remove Pavement and Curb

| | | | Crew | Daily Output | Labor-Hours | Unit | Material | Labor | Equipment | Total | Total Incl O&P |
|---|---|---|---|---|---|---|---|---|---|---|---|
| 0010 | **DEMOLISH, REMOVE PAVEMENT AND CURB** | R024119-10 | | | | | | | | | |
| 5010 | Pavement removal, bituminous roads, 3" thick | | B-38 | 690 | .058 | S.Y. | | 1.98 | 1.45 | 3.43 | 4.63 |
| 5050 | 4" to 6" thick | | | 420 | .095 | | | 3.24 | 2.39 | 5.63 | 7.60 |
| 5100 | Bituminous driveways | | | 640 | .063 | | | 2.13 | 1.57 | 3.70 | 4.99 |
| 5200 | Concrete to 6" thick, hydraulic hammer, mesh reinforced | | | 255 | .157 | | | 5.35 | 3.93 | 9.28 | 12.50 |
| 5300 | Rod reinforced | | | 200 | .200 | ↓ | | 6.80 | 5 | 11.80 | 15.95 |
| 5400 | Concrete, 7" to 24" thick, plain | | | 33 | 1.212 | C.Y. | | 41.50 | 30.50 | 72 | 97 |
| 5500 | Reinforced | | ↓ | 24 | 1.667 | " | | 57 | 42 | 99 | 133 |
| 5600 | With hand held air equipment, bituminous, to 6" thick | | B-39 | 1900 | .025 | S.F. | | .80 | .10 | .90 | 1.35 |
| 5700 | Concrete to 6" thick, no reinforcing | | | 1600 | .030 | | | .95 | .12 | 1.07 | 1.61 |
| 5800 | Mesh reinforced | | | 1400 | .034 | | | 1.09 | .14 | 1.23 | 1.84 |
| 5900 | Rod reinforced | | ↓ | 765 | .063 | ↓ | | 2 | .25 | 2.25 | 3.37 |
| 6000 | Curbs, concrete, plain | | B-6 | 360 | .067 | L.F. | | 2.18 | .79 | 2.97 | 4.23 |
| 6100 | Reinforced | | | 275 | .087 | | | 2.86 | 1.04 | 3.90 | 5.55 |
| 6200 | Granite | | | 360 | .067 | | | 2.18 | .79 | 2.97 | 4.23 |
| 6300 | Bituminous | | ↓ | 528 | .045 | ↓ | | 1.49 | .54 | 2.03 | 2.88 |

### 02 41 13.33 Minor Site Demolition

| | | | Crew | Daily Output | Labor-Hours | Unit | Material | Labor | Equipment | Total | Total Incl O&P |
|---|---|---|---|---|---|---|---|---|---|---|---|
| 0010 | **MINOR SITE DEMOLITION** | R024119-10 | | | | | | | | | |
| 0015 | No hauling, abandon catch basin or manhole | | B-6 | 7 | 3.429 | Ea. | | 112 | 41 | 153 | 218 |
| 0020 | Remove existing catch basin or manhole, masonry | | | 4 | 6 | | | 197 | 71.50 | 268.50 | 380 |
| 0030 | Catch basin or manhole frames and covers, stored | | | 13 | 1.846 | | | 60.50 | 22 | 82.50 | 117 |
| 0040 | Remove and reset | | ↓ | 7 | 3.429 | | | 112 | 41 | 153 | 218 |
| 0100 | Roadside delineators, remove only | | B-80 | 175 | .183 | | | 5.95 | 3.58 | 9.53 | 13.10 |
| 0110 | Remove and reset | | " | 100 | .320 | ↓ | | 10.35 | 6.25 | 16.60 | 23 |

# 02 41 Demolition

## 02 41 13 – Selective Site Demolition

### 02 41 13.33 Minor Site Demolition

| | | Crew | Daily Output | Labor-Hours | Unit | Material | 2008 Bare Costs Labor | 2008 Bare Costs Equipment | Total | Total Incl O&P |
|---|---|---|---|---|---|---|---|---|---|---|
| 0800 | Guiderail, corrugated steel, remove only | B-80A | 100 | .240 | L.F. | | 7.25 | 2.24 | 9.49 | 13.75 |
| 0850 | Remove and reset | " | 40 | .600 | " | | 18.15 | 5.60 | 23.75 | 34 |
| 0860 | Guide posts, remove only | B-80B | 120 | .267 | Ea. | | 8.55 | 1.87 | 10.42 | 15.25 |
| 0870 | Remove and reset | B-55 | 50 | .480 | | | 14.40 | 18.50 | 32.90 | 43 |
| 0900 | Hydrants, fire, remove only | B-21A | 5 | 8 | | | 300 | 122 | 422 | 590 |
| 0950 | Remove and reset | " | 2 | 20 | | | 750 | 305 | 1,055 | 1,475 |
| 1000 | Masonry walls, block or tile, solid, remove | B-5 | 1800 | .031 | C.F. | | 1.04 | .60 | 1.64 | 2.25 |
| 1100 | Cavity wall | | 2200 | .025 | | | .85 | .49 | 1.34 | 1.84 |
| 1200 | Brick, solid | | 900 | .062 | | | 2.07 | 1.21 | 3.28 | 4.52 |
| 1300 | With block back-up | | 1130 | .050 | | | 1.65 | .96 | 2.61 | 3.60 |
| 1400 | Stone, with mortar | | 900 | .062 | | | 2.07 | 1.21 | 3.28 | 4.52 |
| 1500 | Dry set | | 1500 | .037 | | | 1.24 | .72 | 1.96 | 2.71 |
| 1600 | Median barrier, precast concrete, remove and store | B-3 | 430 | .112 | L.F. | | 3.61 | 4.42 | 8.03 | 10.40 |
| 1610 | Remove and reset | " | 390 | .123 | | | 3.98 | 4.87 | 8.85 | 11.50 |
| 2900 | Pipe removal, sewer/water, no excavation, 12" diameter | B-6 | 175 | .137 | | | 4.49 | 1.63 | 6.12 | 8.70 |
| 2930 | 15"-18" diameter | | 150 | .160 | | | 5.25 | 1.90 | 7.15 | 10.15 |
| 2960 | 21"-24" diameter | | 120 | .200 | | | 6.55 | 2.38 | 8.93 | 12.65 |
| 3000 | 27"-36" diameter | | 90 | .267 | | | 8.75 | 3.17 | 11.92 | 16.95 |
| 3200 | Steel, welded connections, 4" diameter | | 160 | .150 | | | 4.91 | 1.78 | 6.69 | 9.50 |
| 3300 | 10" diameter | | 80 | .300 | | | 9.85 | 3.57 | 13.42 | 19 |
| 3500 | Railroad track removal, ties and track | B-13 | 330 | .170 | | | 5.55 | 2.38 | 7.93 | 11.15 |
| 3600 | Ballast | B-14 | 500 | .096 | C.Y. | | 3.06 | .57 | 3.63 | 5.35 |
| 3700 | Remove and re-install, ties & track using new bolts & spikes | | 50 | .960 | L.F. | | 30.50 | 5.70 | 36.20 | 54 |
| 3800 | Turnouts using new bolts and spikes | | 1 | 48 | Ea. | | 1,525 | 286 | 1,811 | 2,700 |
| 4000 | Sidewalk removal, bituminous, 2-1/2" thick | B-6 | 325 | .074 | S.Y. | | 2.42 | .88 | 3.30 | 4.69 |
| 4050 | Brick, set in mortar | | 185 | .130 | | | 4.25 | 1.54 | 5.79 | 8.25 |
| 4100 | Concrete, plain, 4" | | 160 | .150 | | | 4.91 | 1.78 | 6.69 | 9.50 |
| 4200 | Mesh reinforced | | 150 | .160 | | | 5.25 | 1.90 | 7.15 | 10.15 |
| 4300 | Slab on grade removal, plain | B-5 | 45 | 1.244 | C.Y. | | 41.50 | 24 | 65.50 | 90.50 |
| 4310 | Mesh reinforced | | 33 | 1.697 | | | 56.50 | 33 | 89.50 | 123 |
| 4320 | Rod reinforced | | 25 | 2.240 | | | 74.50 | 43.50 | 118 | 163 |
| 4400 | For congested sites or small quantities, add up to | | | | | | | | 200% | 200% |
| 4450 | For disposal on site, add | B-11A | 232 | .069 | | | 2.42 | 4.62 | 7.04 | 8.80 |
| 4500 | To 5 miles, add | B-34D | 76 | .105 | | | 3.22 | 7.60 | 10.82 | 13.35 |

### 02 41 13.60 Selective Demolition Fencing

| | | Crew | Daily Output | Labor-Hours | Unit | Material | 2008 Bare Costs Labor | 2008 Bare Costs Equipment | Total | Total Incl O&P |
|---|---|---|---|---|---|---|---|---|---|---|
| 0010 | **SELECTIVE DEMOLITION FENCING** R024119-10 | | | | | | | | | |
| 1600 | Fencing, barbed wire, 3 strand | 2 Clab | 430 | .037 | L.F. | | 1.13 | | 1.13 | 1.75 |
| 1650 | 5 strand | " | 280 | .057 | | | 1.73 | | 1.73 | 2.69 |
| 1700 | Chain link, posts & fabric, 8' to 10' high, remove only | B-6 | 445 | .054 | | | 1.77 | .64 | 2.41 | 3.43 |
| 1750 | Remove and reset | " | 70 | .343 | | | 11.25 | 4.08 | 15.33 | 21.50 |

## 02 41 16 – Structure Demolition

### 02 41 16.13 Building Demolition

| | | Crew | Daily Output | Labor-Hours | Unit | Material | 2008 Bare Costs Labor | 2008 Bare Costs Equipment | Total | Total Incl O&P |
|---|---|---|---|---|---|---|---|---|---|---|
| 0010 | **BUILDING DEMOLITION** Large urban projects, incl. 20 mi. haul R024119-10 | | | | | | | | | |
| 0011 | No foundation or dump fees, C.F. is vol. of building standing | | | | | | | | | |
| 0020 | Steel | B-8 | 21500 | .003 | C.F. | | .10 | .13 | .23 | .29 |
| 0050 | Concrete | | 15300 | .004 | | | .14 | .18 | .32 | .41 |
| 0080 | Masonry | | 20100 | .003 | | | .11 | .13 | .24 | .31 |
| 0100 | Mixture of types, average | | 20100 | .003 | | | .11 | .13 | .24 | .31 |
| 0500 | Small bldgs, or single bldgs, no salvage included, steel | B-3 | 14800 | .003 | | | .10 | .13 | .23 | .30 |
| 0600 | Concrete | | 11300 | .004 | | | .14 | .17 | .31 | .40 |
| 0650 | Masonry | | 14800 | .003 | | | .10 | .13 | .23 | .30 |
| 0700 | Wood | | 14800 | .003 | | | .10 | .13 | .23 | .30 |

# 02 41 Demolition

## 02 41 16 – Structure Demolition

### 02 41 16.13 Building Demolition

| | | Crew | Daily Output | Labor-Hours | Unit | Material | 2008 Bare Costs Labor | Equipment | Total | Total Incl O&P |
|---|---|---|---|---|---|---|---|---|---|---|
| 1000 | Single family, one story house, wood, minimum | | | | Ea. | | | | 3,520 | 3,872 |
| 1020 | Maximum | | | | | | | | 6,050 | 6,655 |
| 1200 | Two family, two story house, wood, minimum | | | | | | | | 4,620 | 5,082 |
| 1220 | Maximum | | | | | | | | 8,800 | 9,680 |
| 1300 | Three family, three story house, wood, minimum | | | | | | | | 6,050 | 6,655 |
| 1320 | Maximum | | | | | | | | 10,670 | 11,737 |
| 5000 | For buildings with no interior walls, deduct | | | | | | | | 50% | |

### 02 41 16.15 Explosive/Implosive Demolition

| | | Crew | Daily Output | Labor-Hours | Unit | Material | 2008 Bare Costs Labor | Equipment | Total | Total Incl O&P |
|---|---|---|---|---|---|---|---|---|---|---|
| 0010 | **EXPLOSIVE/IMPLOSIVE DEMOLITION** R024119-10 | | | | | | | | | |
| 0011 | Large projects, | | | | | | | | | |
| 0020 | No disposal fee based on building volume, steel building | B-5B | 16900 | .003 | C.F. | | .10 | .12 | .22 | .29 |
| 0100 | Concrete building | | 16900 | .003 | | | .10 | .12 | .22 | .29 |
| 0200 | Masonry building | | 16900 | .003 | | | .10 | .12 | .22 | .29 |
| 0400 | Disposal of material, minimum | B-3 | 445 | .108 | C.Y. | | 3.48 | 4.27 | 7.75 | 10.10 |
| 0500 | Maximum | " | 365 | .132 | " | | 4.25 | 5.20 | 9.45 | 12.25 |

### 02 41 16.17 Building Demolition Footings and Foundations

| | | Crew | Daily Output | Labor-Hours | Unit | Material | 2008 Bare Costs Labor | Equipment | Total | Total Incl O&P |
|---|---|---|---|---|---|---|---|---|---|---|
| 0010 | **BUILDING DEMOLITION FOOTINGS AND FOUNDATIONS** R024119-10 | | | | | | | | | |
| 0200 | Floors, concrete slab on grade, | | | | | | | | | |
| 0240 | 4" thick, plain concrete | B-9C | 500 | .080 | S.F. | | 2.45 | .38 | 2.83 | 4.23 |
| 0280 | Reinforced, wire mesh | | 470 | .085 | | | 2.61 | .41 | 3.02 | 4.51 |
| 0300 | Rods | | 400 | .100 | | | 3.07 | .48 | 3.55 | 5.30 |
| 0400 | 6" thick, plain concrete | | 375 | .107 | | | 3.27 | .51 | 3.78 | 5.65 |
| 0420 | Reinforced, wire mesh | | 340 | .118 | | | 3.61 | .56 | 4.17 | 6.20 |
| 0440 | Rods | | 300 | .133 | | | 4.09 | .64 | 4.73 | 7.05 |
| 1000 | Footings, concrete, 1' thick, 2' wide | B-5 | 300 | .187 | L.F. | | 6.20 | 3.62 | 9.82 | 13.55 |
| 1080 | 1'-6" thick, 2' wide | | 250 | .224 | | | 7.45 | 4.34 | 11.79 | 16.25 |
| 1120 | 3' wide | | 200 | .280 | | | 9.30 | 5.45 | 14.75 | 20.50 |
| 1140 | 2' thick, 3' wide | | 175 | .320 | | | 10.65 | 6.20 | 16.85 | 23 |
| 1200 | Average reinforcing, add | | | | | | | | 10% | 10% |
| 1220 | Heavy reinforcing, add | | | | | | | | 20% | 20% |
| 2000 | Walls, block, 4" thick | 1 Clab | 180 | .044 | S.F. | | 1.34 | | 1.34 | 2.09 |
| 2040 | 6" thick | | 170 | .047 | | | 1.42 | | 1.42 | 2.21 |
| 2080 | 8" thick | | 150 | .053 | | | 1.61 | | 1.61 | 2.51 |
| 2100 | 12" thick | | 150 | .053 | | | 1.61 | | 1.61 | 2.51 |
| 2200 | For horizontal reinforcing, add | | | | | | | | 10% | 10% |
| 2220 | For vertical reinforcing, add | | | | | | | | 20% | 20% |
| 2400 | Concrete, plain concrete, 6" thick | B-9 | 160 | .250 | | | 7.65 | 1.20 | 8.85 | 13.20 |
| 2420 | 8" thick | | 140 | .286 | | | 8.75 | 1.37 | 10.12 | 15.10 |
| 2440 | 10" thick | | 120 | .333 | | | 10.20 | 1.60 | 11.80 | 17.65 |
| 2500 | 12" thick | | 100 | .400 | | | 12.25 | 1.92 | 14.17 | 21 |
| 2600 | For average reinforcing, add | | | | | | | | 10% | 10% |
| 2620 | For heavy reinforcing, add | | | | | | | | 20% | 20% |
| 4000 | For congested sites or small quantities, add up to | | | | | | | | 200% | 200% |
| 4200 | Add for disposal, on site | B-11A | 232 | .069 | C.Y. | | 2.42 | 4.62 | 7.04 | 8.80 |
| 4250 | To five miles | B-30 | 220 | .109 | " | | 3.67 | 8.35 | 12.02 | 14.85 |

## 02 41 19 – Selective Structure Demolition

### 02 41 19.13 Selective Building Demolition

| | | Crew | Daily Output | Labor-Hours | Unit | Material | 2008 Bare Costs Labor | Equipment | Total | Total Incl O&P |
|---|---|---|---|---|---|---|---|---|---|---|
| 0010 | **SELECTIVE BUILDING DEMOLITION** | | | | | | | | | |
| 0020 | Costs related to selective demolition of specific building components | | | | | | | | | |
| 0025 | are included under Common Work Results (XX 05 00) | | | | | | | | | |
| 0030 | in the component's appropriate division. | | | | | | | | | |

27

# 02 41 Demolition

## 02 41 19 – Selective Structure Demolition

### 02 41 19.16 Selective Demolition, Cutout

| | Crew | Daily Output | Labor-Hours | Unit | Material | 2008 Bare Costs Labor | 2008 Bare Costs Equipment | Total | Total Incl O&P |
|---|---|---|---|---|---|---|---|---|---|
| **0010 SELECTIVE DEMOLITION, CUTOUT** R024119-10 | | | | | | | | | |
| 0020 Concrete, elev. slab, light reinforcement, under 6 CF | B-9C | 65 | .615 | C.F. | | 18.85 | 2.95 | 21.80 | 32.50 |
| 0050 Light reinforcing, over 6 C.F. | " | 75 | .533 | " | | 16.35 | 2.55 | 18.90 | 28.50 |
| 0200 Slab on grade to 6" thick, not reinforced, under 8 S.F. | B-9 | 85 | .471 | S.F. | | 14.40 | 2.25 | 16.65 | 25 |
| 0250 8 - 16 S.F. | " | 175 | .229 | " | | 7 | 1.09 | 8.09 | 12.10 |
| 0255 For over 16 SF see line 02 41 16.17 0400 | | | | | | | | | |
| 0600 Walls, not reinforced, under 6 C.F. | B-9 | 60 | .667 | C.F. | | 20.50 | 3.19 | 23.69 | 35.50 |
| 0650 6 - 12 C.F. | " | 80 | .500 | " | | 15.35 | 2.40 | 17.75 | 26.50 |
| 0655 For over 12 CF see line 02 41 16.17 2500 | | | | | | | | | |
| 1000 Concrete, elevated slab, bar reinforced, under 6 C.F. | B-9C | 45 | .889 | C.F. | | 27 | 4.26 | 31.26 | 47 |
| 1050 Bar reinforced, over 6 C.F. | " | 50 | .800 | " | | 24.50 | 3.83 | 28.33 | 42 |
| 1200 Slab on grade to 6" thick, bar reinforced, under 8 S.F. | B-9 | 75 | .533 | S.F. | | 16.35 | 2.55 | 18.90 | 28.50 |
| 1250 8 - 16 S.F. | " | 150 | .267 | " | | 8.15 | 1.28 | 9.43 | 14.10 |
| 1255 For over 16 SF see line 02 41 16.17 0440 | | | | | | | | | |
| 1400 Walls, bar reinforced, under 6 C.F. | B-9C | 50 | .800 | C.F. | | 24.50 | 3.83 | 28.33 | 42 |
| 1450 6 - 12 CF | " | 70 | .571 | " | | 17.50 | 2.74 | 20.24 | 30.50 |
| 1455 For over 12 CF see lines 02 41 16.17 2500 and 2600 | | | | | | | | | |
| 2000 Brick, to 4 S.F. opening, not including toothing | | | | | | | | | |
| 2040 4" thick | B-9C | 30 | 1.333 | Ea. | | 41 | 6.40 | 47.40 | 70.50 |
| 2060 8" thick | | 18 | 2.222 | | | 68 | 10.65 | 78.65 | 118 |
| 2080 12" thick | | 10 | 4 | | | 123 | 19.15 | 142.15 | 212 |
| 2400 Concrete block, to 4 S.F. opening, 2" thick | | 35 | 1.143 | | | 35 | 5.45 | 40.45 | 60.50 |
| 2420 4" thick | | 30 | 1.333 | | | 41 | 6.40 | 47.40 | 70.50 |
| 2440 8" thick | | 27 | 1.481 | | | 45.50 | 7.10 | 52.60 | 78.50 |
| 2460 12" thick | ↓ | 24 | 1.667 | | | 51 | 8 | 59 | 88.50 |
| 2600 Gypsum block, to 4 S.F. opening, 2" thick | B-9 | 80 | .500 | | | 15.35 | 2.40 | 17.75 | 26.50 |
| 2620 4" thick | | 70 | .571 | | | 17.50 | 2.74 | 20.24 | 30.50 |
| 2640 8" thick | | 55 | .727 | | | 22.50 | 3.48 | 25.98 | 38.50 |
| 2800 Terra cotta, to 4 S.F. opening, 4" thick | | 70 | .571 | | | 17.50 | 2.74 | 20.24 | 30.50 |
| 2840 8" thick | | 65 | .615 | | | 18.85 | 2.95 | 21.80 | 32.50 |
| 2880 12" thick | ↓ | 50 | .800 | ↓ | | 24.50 | 3.83 | 28.33 | 42 |
| 3000 Toothing masonry cutouts, brick, soft old mortar | 1 Brhe | 40 | .200 | V.L.F. | | 6.10 | | 6.10 | 9.30 |
| 3100 Hard mortar | | 30 | .267 | | | 8.15 | | 8.15 | 12.40 |
| 3200 Block, soft old mortar | | 70 | .114 | | | 3.50 | | 3.50 | 5.30 |
| 3400 Hard mortar | ↓ | 50 | .160 | ↓ | | 4.90 | | 4.90 | 7.45 |
| 6000 Walls, interior, not including re-framing, | | | | | | | | | |
| 6010 openings to 5 S.F. | | | | | | | | | |
| 6100 Drywall to 5/8" thick | 1 Clab | 24 | .333 | Ea. | | 10.10 | | 10.10 | 15.70 |
| 6200 Paneling to 3/4" thick | | 20 | .400 | | | 12.10 | | 12.10 | 18.80 |
| 6300 Plaster, on gypsum lath | | 20 | .400 | | | 12.10 | | 12.10 | 18.80 |
| 6340 On wire lath | ↓ | 14 | .571 | ↓ | | 17.30 | | 17.30 | 27 |
| 7000 Wood frame, not including re-framing, openings to 5 S.F. | | | | | | | | | |
| 7200 Floors, sheathing and flooring to 2" thick | 1 Clab | 5 | 1.600 | Ea. | | 48.50 | | 48.50 | 75.50 |
| 7310 Roofs, sheathing to 1" thick, not including roofing | | 6 | 1.333 | | | 40.50 | | 40.50 | 62.50 |
| 7410 Walls, sheathing to 1" thick, not including siding | ↓ | 7 | 1.143 | ↓ | | 34.50 | | 34.50 | 54 |

### 02 41 19.18 Selective Demolition, Disposal Only

| | Crew | Daily Output | Labor-Hours | Unit | Material | 2008 Bare Costs Labor | 2008 Bare Costs Equipment | Total | Total Incl O&P |
|---|---|---|---|---|---|---|---|---|---|
| **0010 SELECTIVE DEMOLITION, DISPOSAL ONLY** R024119-10 | | | | | | | | | |
| 0015 Urban bldg w/salvage value allowed | | | | | | | | | |
| 0020 Including loading and 5 mile haul to dump | | | | | | | | | |
| 0200 Steel frame | B-3 | 430 | .112 | C.Y. | | 3.61 | 4.42 | 8.03 | 10.40 |
| 0300 Concrete frame | | 365 | .132 | | | 4.25 | 5.20 | 9.45 | 12.25 |
| 0400 Masonry construction | ↓ | 445 | .108 | ↓ | | 3.48 | 4.27 | 7.75 | 10.10 |

28

# 02 41 Demolition

## 02 41 19 - Selective Structure Demolition

### 02 41 19.18 Selective Demolition, Disposal Only

| | | Crew | Daily Output | Labor-Hours | Unit | Material | 2008 Bare Costs Labor | 2008 Bare Costs Equipment | Total | Total Incl O&P |
|---|---|---|---|---|---|---|---|---|---|---|
| 0500 | Wood frame | B-3 | 247 | .194 | C.Y. | | 6.30 | 7.70 | 14 | 18.15 |

### 02 41 19.19 Selective Demolition, Dump Charges

| | | | Crew | Daily Output | Labor-Hours | Unit | Material | Labor | Equipment | Total | Total Incl O&P |
|---|---|---|---|---|---|---|---|---|---|---|---|
| 0010 | **SELECTIVE DEMOLITION, DUMP CHARGES** | R024119-10 | | | | | | | | | |
| 0020 | Dump charges, typical urban city, tipping fees only | | | | | | | | | | |
| 0100 | Building construction materials | | | | | Ton | 95 | | | 95 | 104.50 |
| 0200 | Trees, brush, lumber | | | | | | 71.50 | | | 71.50 | 78.65 |
| 0300 | Rubbish only | | | | | | 86 | | | 86 | 94.60 |
| 0500 | Reclamation station, usual charge | | | | | | 95 | | | 95 | 104.50 |

### 02 41 19.21 Selective Demolition, Gutting

| | | | Crew | Daily Output | Labor-Hours | Unit | Material | Labor | Equipment | Total | Total Incl O&P |
|---|---|---|---|---|---|---|---|---|---|---|---|
| 0010 | **SELECTIVE DEMOLITION, GUTTING** | R024119-10 | | | | | | | | | |
| 0020 | Building interior, including disposal, dumpster fees not included | | | | | | | | | | |
| 0500 | Residential building | | | | | | | | | | |
| 0560 | Minimum | | B-16 | 400 | .080 | SF Flr. | | 2.47 | 1.26 | 3.73 | 5.20 |
| 0580 | Maximum | | " | 360 | .089 | " | | 2.74 | 1.40 | 4.14 | 5.80 |
| 0900 | Commercial building | | | | | | | | | | |
| 1000 | Minimum | | B-16 | 350 | .091 | SF Flr. | | 2.82 | 1.44 | 4.26 | 5.95 |
| 1020 | Maximum | | " | 250 | .128 | " | | 3.95 | 2.01 | 5.96 | 8.35 |

### 02 41 19.23 Selective Demolition, Rubbish Handling

| | | | Crew | Daily Output | Labor-Hours | Unit | Material | Labor | Equipment | Total | Total Incl O&P |
|---|---|---|---|---|---|---|---|---|---|---|---|
| 0010 | **SELECTIVE DEMOLITION, RUBBISH HANDLING** | R024119-10 | | | | | | | | | |
| 0020 | The following are to be added to the demolition prices | | | | | | | | | | |
| 0400 | Chute, circular, prefabricated steel, 18" diameter | | B-1 | 40 | .600 | L.F. | 45 | 18.55 | | 63.55 | 78.50 |
| 0440 | 30" diameter | | " | 30 | .800 | " | 46 | 24.50 | | 70.50 | 89.50 |
| 0725 | Dumpster, weekly rental, 1 dump/week, 20 C.Y. capacity (8 Tons) | R024119-20 | | | | Week | 690 | | | 690 | 759 |
| 0800 | 30 C.Y. capacity (10 Tons) | | | | | | 900 | | | 900 | 990 |
| 0840 | 40 C.Y. capacity (13 Tons) | | | | | | 1,160 | | | 1,160 | 1,276 |
| 1000 | Dust partition, 6 mil polyethylene, 1" x 3" frame | | 2 Carp | 2000 | .008 | S.F. | .28 | .30 | | .58 | .78 |
| 1080 | 2" x 4" frame | | " | 2000 | .008 | " | .31 | .30 | | .61 | .81 |
| 2000 | Load, haul, and dump, 50' haul | | 2 Clab | 24 | .667 | C.Y. | | 20 | | 20 | 31.50 |
| 2040 | 100' haul | | | 16.50 | .970 | | | 29.50 | | 29.50 | 45.50 |
| 2080 | Over 100' haul, add per 100 L.F. | | | 35.50 | .451 | | | 13.65 | | 13.65 | 21 |
| 2120 | In elevators, per 10 floors, add | | | 140 | .114 | | | 3.46 | | 3.46 | 5.40 |
| 3000 | Loading & trucking, including 2 mile haul, chute loaded | | B-16 | 45 | .711 | | | 22 | 11.15 | 33.15 | 46.50 |
| 3040 | Hand loading truck, 50' haul | | " | 48 | .667 | | | 20.50 | 10.45 | 30.95 | 43.50 |
| 3080 | Machine loading truck | | B-17 | 120 | .267 | | | 8.60 | 4.95 | 13.55 | 18.70 |
| 5000 | Haul, per mile, up to 8 C.Y. truck | | B-34B | 1165 | .007 | | | .21 | .43 | .64 | .81 |
| 5100 | Over 8 C.Y. truck | | " | 1550 | .005 | | | .16 | .32 | .48 | .60 |

### 02 41 19.25 Selective Demolition, Saw Cutting

| | | | Crew | Daily Output | Labor-Hours | Unit | Material | Labor | Equipment | Total | Total Incl O&P |
|---|---|---|---|---|---|---|---|---|---|---|---|
| 0010 | **SELECTIVE DEMOLITION, SAW CUTTING** | R024119-10 | | | | | | | | | |
| 0015 | Asphalt, up to 3" deep | | B-89 | 1050 | .015 | L.F. | .38 | .51 | .36 | 1.25 | 1.60 |
| 0020 | Each additional inch of depth | | " | 1800 | .009 | | .08 | .30 | .21 | .59 | .78 |
| 1200 | Masonry walls, hydraulic saw, brick, per inch of depth | | B-89B | 300 | .053 | | .40 | 1.79 | 2.22 | 4.41 | 5.60 |
| 1220 | Block walls, solid, per inch of depth | | " | 250 | .064 | | .40 | 2.15 | 2.66 | 5.21 | 6.65 |
| 2000 | Brick or masonry w/hand held saw, per inch of depth | | A-1 | 125 | .064 | | .32 | 1.94 | .48 | 2.74 | 3.89 |
| 5000 | Wood sheathing to 1" thick, on walls | | 1 Carp | 200 | .040 | | | 1.52 | | 1.52 | 2.37 |
| 5020 | On roof | | " | 250 | .032 | | | 1.22 | | 1.22 | 1.90 |

### 02 41 19.27 Selective Demolition, Torch Cutting

| | | | Crew | Daily Output | Labor-Hours | Unit | Material | Labor | Equipment | Total | Total Incl O&P |
|---|---|---|---|---|---|---|---|---|---|---|---|
| 0010 | **SELECTIVE DEMOLITION, TORCH CUTTING** | R024119-10 | | | | | | | | | |
| 0020 | Steel, 1" thick plate | | 1 Clab | 360 | .022 | L.F. | .21 | .67 | | .88 | 1.28 |
| 0040 | 1" diameter bar | | " | 210 | .038 | Ea. | | 1.15 | | 1.15 | 1.79 |
| 1000 | Oxygen lance cutting, reinforced concrete walls | | | | | | | | | | |
| 1040 | 12" to 16" thick walls | | 1 Clab | 10 | .800 | L.F. | | 24 | | 24 | 37.50 |

# 02 41 Demolition

## 02 41 19 – Selective Structure Demolition

| 02 41 19.27 Selective Demolition, Torch Cutting | | Crew | Daily Output | Labor-Hours | Unit | Material | 2008 Bare Costs Labor | Equipment | Total | Total Incl O&P |
|---|---|---|---|---|---|---|---|---|---|---|
| 1080 | 24" thick walls | 1 Clab | 6 | 1.333 | L.F. | | 40.50 | | 40.50 | 62.50 |

# 02 43 Structure Moving

## 02 43 13 – Structure Relocation

### 02 43 13.13 Building Relocation

| | | Crew | Daily Output | Labor-Hours | Unit | Material | 2008 Bare Costs Labor | Equipment | Total | Total Incl O&P |
|---|---|---|---|---|---|---|---|---|---|---|
| 0010 | **BUILDING RELOCATION** | | | | | | | | | |
| 0011 | One day move, up to 24' wide | | | | | | | | | |
| 0020 | Reset on new foundation, patch & hook-up, average move | | | | Total | | | | | 10,695 |
| 0040 | Wood or steel frame bldg., based on ground floor area | B-4 | 185 | .259 | S.F. | | 7.95 | 2.19 | 10.14 | 14.75 |
| 0060 | Masonry bldg., based on ground floor area | " | 137 | .350 | ↓ | | 10.75 | 2.96 | 13.71 | 19.95 |
| 0200 | For 24' to 42' wide, add | | | | | | | | | 15% |
| 0220 | For each additional day on road, add | B-4 | 1 | 48 | Day | | 1,475 | 405 | 1,880 | 2,725 |
| 0240 | Construct new basement, move building, 1 day | | | | | | | | | |
| 0300 | move, patch & hook-up, based on ground floor area | B-3 | 155 | .310 | S.F. | 8.50 | 10 | 12.25 | 30.75 | 38.50 |

# 02 58 Snow Control

## 02 58 13 – Snow Fencing

### 02 58 13.10 Snow Fencing System

| | | Crew | Daily Output | Labor-Hours | Unit | Material | 2008 Bare Costs Labor | Equipment | Total | Total Incl O&P |
|---|---|---|---|---|---|---|---|---|---|---|
| 0010 | **SNOW FENCING SYSTEM** | | | | | | | | | |
| 7001 | Snow fence on steel posts 10' O.C., 4' high | B-1 | 500 | .048 | L.F. | 2.70 | 1.48 | | 4.18 | 5.30 |

# 02 65 Underground Storage Tank Removal

## 02 65 10 – Underground tank & contaiminated soil removal

### 02 65 10.30 Removal of Underground Storage Tanks

| | | | Crew | Daily Output | Labor-Hours | Unit | Material | 2008 Bare Costs Labor | Equipment | Total | Total Incl O&P |
|---|---|---|---|---|---|---|---|---|---|---|---|
| 0010 | **REMOVAL OF UNDERGROUND STORAGE TANKS** | R026510-20 | | | | | | | | | |
| 0011 | Petroleum storage tanks, non-leaking | | | | | | | | | | |
| 0100 | Excavate & load onto trailer | | | | | | | | | | |
| 0110 | 3000 gal. to 5000 gal. tank | | B-14 | 4 | 12 | Ea. | | 380 | 71.50 | 451.50 | 670 |
| 0120 | 6000 gal to 8000 gal tank | | B-3A | 3 | 13.333 | | | 430 | 277 | 707 | 965 |
| 0130 | 9000 gal to 12000 gal tank | | " | 2 | 20 | ↓ | | 645 | 415 | 1,060 | 1,450 |
| 0190 | Known leaking tank add | | | | | % | | | | 100% | 100% |
| 0200 | Remove sludge, water and remaining product from tank bottom | | | | | | | | | | |
| 0201 | of tank with vacuum truck | | | | | | | | | | |
| 0300 | 3000 gal to 5000 gal tank | | A-13 | 5 | 1.600 | Ea. | | 60.50 | 142 | 202.50 | 247 |
| 0310 | 6000 gal to 8000 gal tank | | ↓ | 4 | 2 | ↓ | | 75.50 | 178 | 253.50 | 310 |
| 0320 | 9000 gal to 12000 gal tank | | ↓ | 3 | 2.667 | ↓ | | 101 | 237 | 338 | 415 |
| 0390 | Dispose of sludge off-site, average | | | | | Gal. | | | | 6 | 6.60 |
| 0400 | Insert inert solid $CO_2$ "dry ice" into tank | | | | | | | | | | |
| 0401 | For cleaning/transporting tanks (1.5 lbs./100 gal. cap) | | 1 Clab | 500 | .016 | Lb. | 1.61 | .48 | | 2.09 | 2.52 |
| 1020 | Haul tank to certified salvage dump, 100 miles round trip | | | | | | | | | | |
| 1023 | 3000 gal. to 5000 gal. tank | | | | | Ea. | | | | 660 | 726 |
| 1026 | 6000 gal. to 8000 gal. tank | | | | | ↓ | | | | 780 | 858 |
| 1029 | 9,000 gal. to 12,000 gal. tank | | | | | ↓ | | | | 1,050 | 1,155 |
| 1100 | Disposal of contaminated soil to landfill | | | | | | | | | | |
| 1110 | Minimum | | | | | C.Y. | | | | 118.80 | 132 |
| 1111 | Maximum | | | | | " | | | | 356.40 | 396 |
| 1120 | Disposal of contaminated soil to | | | | | | | | | | |

# 02 65 Underground Storage Tank Removal

## 02 65 10 – Underground tank & contaiminated soil removal

| 02 65 10.30 Removal of Underground Storage Tanks | Crew | Daily Output | Labor-Hours | Unit | Material | 2008 Bare Costs Labor | Equipment | Total | Total Incl O&P |
|---|---|---|---|---|---|---|---|---|---|
| 1121     bituminous concrete batch plant | | | | | | | | | |
| 1130       Minimum | | | | C.Y. | | | | 59.40 | 66 |
| 1131       Maximum | | | | " | | | | 118.80 | 132 |
| 2010     Decontamination of soil on site incl poly tarp on top/bottom | | | | | | | | | |
| 2011       Soil containment berm, and chemical treatment | | | | | | | | | |
| 2020       Minimum | B-11C | 100 | .160 | C.Y. | 6.60 | 5.60 | 2.85 | 15.05 | 18.95 |
| 2021       Maximum | " | 100 | .160 | | 8.55 | 5.60 | 2.85 | 17 | 21 |
| 2050     Disposal of decontaminated soil, minimum | | | | | | | | 71.10 | 79 |
| 2055       Maximum | | | | | | | | 145.80 | 162 |

# 02 81 Transportation and Disposal of Hazardous Materials

## 02 81 20 – Hazardous Waste Handling

### 02 81 20.10 Hazardous Waste Cleanup/Pickup/Disposal

| | | Crew | Daily Output | Labor-Hours | Unit | Material | Labor | Equipment | Total | Total Incl O&P |
|---|---|---|---|---|---|---|---|---|---|---|
| 0010 | HAZARDOUS WASTE CLEANUP/PICKUP/DISPOSAL | | | | | | | | | |
| 0100 | For contractor rental equipment, i.e. Dozer, | | | | | | | | | |
| 0110 | Front end loader, Dump truck, etc., see 01 54 33 Reference Section | | | | | | | | | |
| 1000 | Solid pickup | | | | | | | | | |
| 1100 | 55 gal. drums | | | | Ea. | | | | 217.80 | 242 |
| 1120 | Bulk material, minimum | | | | Ton | | | | 163.80 | 182 |
| 1130 | Maximum | | | | " | | | | 544.50 | 605 |
| 1200 | Transportation to disposal site | | | | | | | | | |
| 1220 | Truckload = 80 drums or 25 C.Y. or 18 tons | | | | | | | | | |
| 1260 | Minimum | | | | Mile | | | | 3.38 | 3.75 |
| 1270 | Maximum | | | | " | | | | 5.94 | 6.60 |
| 3000 | Liquid pickup, vacuum truck, stainless steel tank | | | | | | | | | |
| 3100 | Minimum charge, 4 hours | | | | | | | | | |
| 3110 | 1 compartment, 2200 gallon | | | | Hr. | | | | 118.80 | 132 |
| 3120 | 2 compartment, 5000 gallon | | | | " | | | | 118.80 | 132 |
| 3400 | Transportation in 6900 gallon bulk truck | | | | Mile | | | | 6.42 | 7.13 |
| 3410 | In teflon lined truck | | | | " | | | | 7.43 | 8.25 |
| 5000 | Heavy sludge or dry vacuumable material | | | | Hr. | | | | 118.80 | 132 |
| 6000 | Dumpsite disposal charge, minimum | | | | Ton | | | | 118.80 | 132 |
| 6020 | Maximum | | | | " | | | | 435.60 | 484 |

# 02 82 Asbestos Remediation

## 02 82 13 – Asbestos Abatement

### 02 82 13.41 Asbestos Abatement Equip.

| | | Crew | Daily Output | Labor-Hours | Unit | Material | Labor | Equipment | Total | Total Incl O&P |
|---|---|---|---|---|---|---|---|---|---|---|
| 0010 | ASBESTOS ABATEMENT EQUIP.    R028213-20 | | | | | | | | | |
| 0011 | Equipment and supplies, buy | | | | | | | | | |
| 0200 | Air filtration device, 2000 C.F.M. | | | | Ea. | 795 | | | 795 | 875 |
| 0250 | Large volume air sampling pump, minimum | | | | | 305 | | | 305 | 335 |
| 0260 | Maximum | | | | | 455 | | | 455 | 500 |
| 0300 | Airless sprayer unit, 2 gun | | | | | 3,125 | | | 3,125 | 3,425 |
| 0350 | Light stand, 500 watt | | | | | 72.50 | | | 72.50 | 80 |
| 0400 | Personal respirators | | | | | | | | | |
| 0410 | Negative pressure, 1/2 face, dual operation, min. | | | | Ea. | 25.50 | | | 25.50 | 28 |
| 0420 | Maximum | | | | | 31 | | | 31 | 34.50 |
| 0450 | P.A.P.R., full face, minimum | | | | | 124 | | | 124 | 137 |
| 0460 | Maximum | | | | | 150 | | | 150 | 165 |

# 02 82 Asbestos Remediation

## 02 82 13 – Asbestos Abatement

### 02 82 13.41 Asbestos Abatement Equip.

| | Crew | Daily Output | Labor-Hours | Unit | Material | 2008 Bare Costs Labor | Equipment | Total | Total Incl O&P |
|---|---|---|---|---|---|---|---|---|---|
| 0470 | Supplied air, full face, incl. air line, minimum | | | | Ea. | 157 | | | 157 | 172 |
| 0480 | Maximum | | | | | 239 | | | 239 | 263 |
| 0500 | Personnel sampling pump, minimum | | | | | 201 | | | 201 | 221 |
| 1500 | Power panel, 20 unit, incl. G.F.I. | | | | | 1,100 | | | 1,100 | 1,200 |
| 1600 | Shower unit, including pump and filters | | | | | 1,075 | | | 1,075 | 1,200 |
| 1700 | Supplied air system (type C) | | | | | 9,800 | | | 9,800 | 10,800 |
| 1750 | Vacuum cleaner, HEPA, 16 gal., stainless steel, wet/dry | | | | | 675 | | | 675 | 745 |
| 1760 | 55 gallon | | | | | 1,700 | | | 1,700 | 1,875 |
| 1800 | Vacuum loader, 9-18 ton/hr | | | | | 90,000 | | | 90,000 | 99,000 |
| 1900 | Water atomizer unit, including 55 gal. drum | | | | | 230 | | | 230 | 253 |
| 2000 | Worker protection, whole body, foot, head cover & gloves, plastic | | | | | 6.80 | | | 6.80 | 7.45 |
| 2500 | Respirator, single use | | | | | 10.90 | | | 10.90 | 12 |
| 2550 | Cartridge for respirator | | | | | 12.30 | | | 12.30 | 13.55 |
| 2570 | Glove bag, 7 mil, 50" x 64" | | | | | 9.20 | | | 9.20 | 10.10 |
| 2580 | 10 mil, 44" x 60" | | | | | 8.40 | | | 8.40 | 9.25 |
| 3000 | HEPA vacuum for work area, minimun | | | | | 1,050 | | | 1,050 | 1,150 |
| 3050 | Maximum | | | | | 3,100 | | | 3,100 | 3,425 |
| 6000 | Disposable polyethelene bags, 6 mil, 3 C.F. | | | | | 1.24 | | | 1.24 | 1.36 |
| 6300 | Disposable fiber drums, 3 C.F. | | | | | 6.50 | | | 6.50 | 7.15 |
| 6400 | Pressure sensitive caution lables, 3" x 5" | | | | | 1.19 | | | 1.19 | 1.31 |
| 6450 | 11" x 17" | | | | | 7.05 | | | 7.05 | 7.75 |
| 6500 | Negative air machine, 1800 C.F.M. | | | | | 770 | | | 770 | 845 |

### 02 82 13.42 Preparation of Asbestos Containment Area

| | Crew | Daily Output | Labor-Hours | Unit | Material | 2008 Bare Costs Labor | Equipment | Total | Total Incl O&P |
|---|---|---|---|---|---|---|---|---|---|
| 0010 | **PREPARATION OF ASBESTOS CONTAINMENT AREA** | | | | | | | | | |
| 0100 | Pre-cleaning, HEPA vacuum and wet wipe, flat surfaces | A-10 | 12000 | .005 | S.F. | .02 | .23 | | .25 | .38 |
| 0200 | Protect carpeted area, 2 layers 6 mil poly on 3/4" plywood | " | 1000 | .064 | | 1.50 | 2.76 | | 4.26 | 6 |
| 0300 | Separation barrier, 2" x 4" @ 16", 1/2" plywood ea. side, 8' high | 2 Carp | 400 | .040 | | 1.25 | 1.52 | | 2.77 | 3.75 |
| 0310 | 12' high | | 320 | .050 | | 1.40 | 1.91 | | 3.31 | 4.51 |
| 0320 | 16' high | | 200 | .080 | | 1.50 | 3.05 | | 4.55 | 6.40 |
| 0400 | Personnel decontam. chamber, 2" x 4" @ 16", 3/4" ply ea. side | | 280 | .057 | | 2.50 | 2.18 | | 4.68 | 6.15 |
| 0450 | Waste decontam. chamber, 2" x 4" studs @ 16", 3/4" ply ea. side | | 360 | .044 | | 3 | 1.69 | | 4.69 | 5.95 |
| 0500 | Cover surfaces with polyethelene sheeting | | | | | | | | | |
| 0501 | Including glue and tape | | | | | | | | | |
| 0550 | Floors, each layer, 6 mil | A-10 | 8000 | .008 | S.F. | .05 | .35 | | .40 | .59 |
| 0551 | 4 mil | | 9000 | .007 | | .03 | .31 | | .34 | .52 |
| 0560 | Walls, each layer, 6 mil | | 6000 | .011 | | .05 | .46 | | .51 | .78 |
| 0561 | 4 mil | | 7000 | .009 | | .03 | .39 | | .42 | .66 |
| 0570 | For heights above 12', add | | | | | | 20% | | | |
| 0575 | For heights above 20', add | | | | | | 30% | | | |
| 0580 | For fire retardant poly, add | | | | | 100% | | | | |
| 0590 | For large open areas, deduct | | | | | 10% | 20% | | | |
| 0600 | Seal floor penetrations with foam firestop to 36 Sq. In. | 2 Carp | 200 | .080 | Ea. | 40 | 3.05 | | 43.05 | 48.50 |
| 0610 | 36 Sq. In. to 72 Sq. In. | | 125 | .128 | | 79.50 | 4.88 | | 84.38 | 95 |
| 0615 | 72 Sq. In. to 144 Sq. In. | | 80 | .200 | | 159 | 7.60 | | 166.60 | 187 |
| 0620 | Wall penetrations, to 36 square inches | | 180 | .089 | | 40 | 3.39 | | 43.39 | 49.50 |
| 0630 | 36 Sq. In. to 72 Sq. In. | | 100 | .160 | | 79.50 | 6.10 | | 85.60 | 97 |
| 0640 | 72 Sq. In. to 144 Sq. In. | | 60 | .267 | | 159 | 10.15 | | 169.15 | 191 |
| 0800 | Caulk seams with latex | 1 Carp | 230 | .035 | L.F. | .15 | 1.33 | | 1.48 | 2.23 |
| 0900 | Set up neg. air machine, 1-2k C.F.M. /25 M.C.F. volume | 1 Asbe | 4.30 | 1.860 | Ea. | | 80 | | 80 | 126 |

### 02 82 13.43 Bulk Asbestos Removal

| | | | | | | | | | |
|---|---|---|---|---|---|---|---|---|---|
| 0010 | **BULK ASBESTOS REMOVAL** | | | | | | | | | |
| 0020 | Includes disposable tools and 2 suits and 1respirator filter/day/worker | | | | | | | | | |

# 02 82 Asbestos Remediation

## 02 82 13 – Asbestos Abatement

### 02 82 13.43 Bulk Asbestos Removal

| | 02 82 13.43 Bulk Asbestos Removal | Crew | Daily Output | Labor-Hours | Unit | Material | 2008 Bare Costs Labor | Equipment | Total | Total Incl O&P |
|---|---|---|---|---|---|---|---|---|---|---|
| 0100 | Beams, W 10 x 19 | A-9 | 235 | .272 | L.F. | .88 | 11.75 | | 12.63 | 19.45 |
| 0110 | W 12 x 22 | | 210 | .305 | | .99 | 13.15 | | 14.14 | 21.50 |
| 0120 | W 14 x 26 | | 180 | .356 | | 1.15 | 15.35 | | 16.50 | 25.50 |
| 0130 | W 16 x 31 | | 160 | .400 | | 1.29 | 17.25 | | 18.54 | 28.50 |
| 0140 | W 18 x 40 | | 140 | .457 | | 1.48 | 19.75 | | 21.23 | 32.50 |
| 0150 | W 24 x 55 | | 110 | .582 | | 1.88 | 25 | | 26.88 | 41.50 |
| 0160 | W 30 x 108 | | 85 | .753 | | 2.43 | 32.50 | | 34.93 | 53.50 |
| 0170 | W 36 x 150 | | 72 | .889 | | 2.87 | 38.50 | | 41.37 | 63.50 |
| 0200 | Boiler insulation | | 480 | .133 | S.F. | .49 | 5.75 | | 6.24 | 9.60 |
| 0210 | With metal lath add | | | | % | | | | 50% | |
| 0300 | Boiler breeching or flue insulation | A-9 | 520 | .123 | S.F. | .40 | 5.30 | | 5.70 | 8.80 |
| 0310 | For active boiler, add | | | | % | | | | 100% | |
| 0400 | Duct or AHU insulation | A-10B | 440 | .073 | S.F. | .24 | 3.14 | | 3.38 | 5.20 |
| 0500 | Duct vibration isolation joints, up to 24 Sq. In. duct | A-9 | 56 | 1.143 | Ea. | 3.69 | 49.50 | | 53.19 | 81.50 |
| 0520 | 25 Sq. In. to 48 Sq. In. duct | | 48 | 1.333 | | 4.31 | 57.50 | | 61.81 | 95 |
| 0530 | 49 Sq. In. to 76 Sq. In. duct | | 40 | 1.600 | | 5.15 | 69 | | 74.15 | 115 |
| 0600 | Pipe insulation, air cell type, up to 4" diameter pipe | | 900 | .071 | L.F. | .23 | 3.07 | | 3.30 | 5.10 |
| 0610 | 4" to 8" diameter pipe | | 800 | .080 | | .26 | 3.45 | | 3.71 | 5.75 |
| 0620 | 10" to 12" diameter pipe | | 700 | .091 | | .30 | 3.95 | | 4.25 | 6.55 |
| 0630 | 14" to 16" diameter pipe | | 550 | .116 | | .38 | 5 | | 5.38 | 8.30 |
| 0650 | Over 16" diameter pipe | | 650 | .098 | S.F. | .32 | 4.25 | | 4.57 | 7.05 |
| 0700 | With glove bag up to 3" diameter pipe | | 200 | .320 | L.F. | 2.08 | 13.80 | | 15.88 | 24 |
| 1000 | Pipe fitting insulation up to 4" diameter pipe | | 320 | .200 | Ea. | .65 | 8.65 | | 9.30 | 14.30 |
| 1100 | 6" to 8" diameter pipe | | 304 | .211 | | .68 | 9.10 | | 9.78 | 15.05 |
| 1110 | 10" to 12" diameter pipe | | 192 | .333 | | 1.08 | 14.40 | | 15.48 | 23.50 |
| 1120 | 14" to 16" diameter pipe | | 128 | .500 | | 1.62 | 21.50 | | 23.12 | 36 |
| 1130 | Over 16" diameter pipe | | 176 | .364 | S.F. | 1.18 | 15.70 | | 16.88 | 26 |
| 1200 | With glove bag, up to 8" diameter pipe | | 75 | .853 | L.F. | 6.55 | 37 | | 43.55 | 65 |
| 2000 | Scrape foam fireproofing from flat surface | | 2400 | .027 | S.F. | .09 | 1.15 | | 1.24 | 1.90 |
| 2100 | Irregular surfaces | | 1200 | .053 | | .17 | 2.30 | | 2.47 | 3.81 |
| 3000 | Remove cementitious material from flat surface | | 1800 | .036 | | .11 | 1.53 | | 1.64 | 2.55 |
| 3100 | Irregular surface | | 1000 | .064 | | .15 | 2.76 | | 2.91 | 4.51 |
| 4000 | Scrape acoustical coating/fireproofing, from ceiling | | 3200 | .020 | | .06 | .86 | | .92 | 1.43 |
| 5000 | Remove VAT from floor by hand | | 2400 | .027 | | .09 | 1.15 | | 1.24 | 1.90 |
| 5100 | By machine | A-11 | 4800 | .013 | | .04 | .58 | .01 | .63 | .97 |
| 5150 | For 2 layers, add | | | | % | | | | 50% | |
| 6000 | Remove contaminated soil from crawl space by hand | A-9 | 400 | .160 | C.F. | .52 | 6.90 | | 7.42 | 11.40 |
| 6100 | With large production vacuum loader | A-12 | 700 | .091 | " | .30 | 3.95 | 1.02 | 5.27 | 7.65 |
| 7000 | Radiator backing, not including radiator removal | A-9 | 1200 | .053 | S.F. | .17 | 2.30 | | 2.47 | 3.81 |
| 8000 | Cement-asbestos transite board | 2 Asbe | 1000 | .016 | | .14 | .69 | | .83 | 1.25 |
| 8100 | Transite shingle siding | A-10B | 750 | .043 | | .22 | 1.84 | | 2.06 | 3.14 |
| 8200 | Shingle roofing | " | 2000 | .016 | | .08 | .69 | | .77 | 1.18 |
| 8250 | Built-up, no gravel, non-friable | B-2 | 1400 | .029 | | .08 | .88 | | .96 | 1.45 |
| 8300 | Asbestos millboard | 2 Asbe | 1000 | .016 | | .08 | .69 | | .77 | 1.18 |
| 9000 | For type C (supplied air) respirator equipment, add | | | | % | | | | | 10% |

### 02 82 13.44 Demolition In Asbestos Contaminated Area

| | | Crew | Daily Output | Labor-Hours | Unit | Material | Labor | Equipment | Total | Total Incl O&P |
|---|---|---|---|---|---|---|---|---|---|---|
| 0010 | **DEMOLITION IN ASBESTOS CONTAMINATED AREA** | | | | | | | | | |
| 0200 | Ceiling, including suspension system, plaster and lath | A-9 | 2100 | .030 | S.F. | .10 | 1.32 | | 1.42 | 2.18 |
| 0210 | Finished plaster, leaving wire lath | | 585 | .109 | | .35 | 4.72 | | 5.07 | 7.85 |
| 0220 | Suspended acoustical tile | | 3500 | .018 | | .06 | .79 | | .85 | 1.31 |
| 0230 | Concealed tile grid system | | 3000 | .021 | | .07 | .92 | | .99 | 1.53 |
| 0240 | Metal pan grid system | | 1500 | .043 | | .14 | 1.84 | | 1.98 | 3.05 |

# 02 82 Asbestos Remediation

## 02 82 13 – Asbestos Abatement

### 02 82 13.44 Demolition In Asbestos Contaminated Area

| | | Crew | Daily Output | Labor-Hours | Unit | Material | 2008 Bare Costs Labor | Equipment | Total | Total Incl O&P |
|---|---|---|---|---|---|---|---|---|---|---|
| 0250 | Gypsum board | A-9 | 2500 | .026 | S.F. | .08 | 1.10 | | 1.18 | 1.83 |
| 0260 | Lighting fixtures up to 2' x 4' | ↓ | 72 | .889 | Ea. | 2.87 | 38.50 | | 41.37 | 63.50 |
| 0400 | Partitions, non load bearing | | | | | | | | | |
| 0410 | Plaster, lath, and studs | A-9 | 690 | .093 | S.F. | .87 | 4 | | 4.87 | 7.25 |
| 0450 | Gypsum board and studs | " | 1390 | .046 | " | .15 | 1.99 | | 2.14 | 3.29 |
| 9000 | For type C (supplied air) respirator equipment, add | | | | % | | | | | 10% |

### 02 82 13.45 OSHA Testing

| | | Crew | Daily Output | Labor-Hours | Unit | Material | 2008 Bare Costs Labor | Equipment | Total | Total Incl O&P |
|---|---|---|---|---|---|---|---|---|---|---|
| 0010 | **OSHA TESTING** | | | | | | | | | |
| 0100 | Certified technician, minimum | | | | Day | | | | 278.18 | 306 |
| 0110 | Maximum | | | | " | | | | 463.64 | 510 |
| 0200 | Personal sampling, PCM analysis, NIOSH 7400, minimum | 1 Asbe | 8 | 1 | Ea. | 2.75 | 43 | | 45.75 | 71 |
| 0210 | Maximum | " | 4 | 2 | " | 3 | 86 | | 89 | 139 |
| 0300 | Industrial hygienist, minimum | | | | Day | | | | 370.09 | 408 |
| 0310 | Maximum | | | | " | | | | 510 | 561 |
| 1000 | Cleaned area samples | 1 Asbe | 8 | 1 | Ea. | 2.63 | 43 | | 45.63 | 71 |
| 1100 | PCM air sample analysis, NIOSH 7400, minimum | ↓ | 8 | 1 | | 30.50 | 43 | | 73.50 | 102 |
| 1110 | Maximum | ↓ | 4 | 2 | | 3.20 | 86 | | 89.20 | 140 |
| 1200 | TEM air sample analysis, NIOSH 7402, minimum | | | | | | | | 102 | 127.50 |
| 1210 | Maximum | | | | ↓ | | | | 408 | 510 |

### 02 82 13.46 Decontamination of Asbestos Containment Area

| | | Crew | Daily Output | Labor-Hours | Unit | Material | 2008 Bare Costs Labor | Equipment | Total | Total Incl O&P |
|---|---|---|---|---|---|---|---|---|---|---|
| 0010 | **DECONTAMINATION OF ASBESTOS CONTAINMENT AREA** | | | | | | | | | |
| 0100 | Spray exposed substrate with surfactant (bridging) | | | | | | | | | |
| 0200 | Flat surfaces | A-9 | 6000 | .011 | S.F. | .36 | .46 | | .82 | 1.13 |
| 0250 | Irregular surfaces | | 4000 | .016 | " | .31 | .69 | | 1 | 1.43 |
| 0300 | Pipes, beams, and columns | | 2000 | .032 | L.F. | .56 | 1.38 | | 1.94 | 2.79 |
| 1000 | Spray encapsulate polyethelene sheeting | | 8000 | .008 | S.F. | .31 | .35 | | .66 | .88 |
| 1100 | Roll down polyethelene sheeting | | 8000 | .008 | " | | .35 | | .35 | .54 |
| 1500 | Bag polyethelene sheeting | | 400 | .160 | Ea. | .77 | 6.90 | | 7.67 | 11.70 |
| 2000 | Fine clean exposed substrate, with nylon brush | | 2400 | .027 | S.F. | | 1.15 | | 1.15 | 1.81 |
| 2500 | Wet wipe substrate | | 4800 | .013 | | | .58 | | .58 | .91 |
| 2600 | Vacuum surfaces, fine brush | ↓ | 6400 | .010 | ↓ | | .43 | | .43 | .68 |
| 3000 | Structural demolition | | | | | | | | | |
| 3100 | Wood stud walls | A-9 | 2800 | .023 | S.F. | | .99 | | .99 | 1.55 |
| 3500 | Window manifolds, not incl. window replacement | | 4200 | .015 | | | .66 | | .66 | 1.04 |
| 3600 | Plywood carpet protection | ↓ | 2000 | .032 | ↓ | | 1.38 | | 1.38 | 2.17 |
| 4000 | Remove custom decontamination facility | A-10A | 8 | 3 | Ea. | 15 | 130 | | 145 | 221 |
| 4100 | Remove portable decontamination facility | 3 Asbe | 12 | 2 | " | 12.75 | 86 | | 98.75 | 150 |
| 5000 | HEPA vacuum, shampoo carpeting | A-9 | 4800 | .013 | S.F. | .05 | .58 | | .63 | .97 |
| 9000 | Final cleaning of protected surfaces | A-10A | 8000 | .003 | " | | .13 | | .13 | .20 |

### 02 82 13.47 Asbestos Waste Packaging, Handling, and Disposal

| | | Crew | Daily Output | Labor-Hours | Unit | Material | 2008 Bare Costs Labor | Equipment | Total | Total Incl O&P |
|---|---|---|---|---|---|---|---|---|---|---|
| 0010 | **ASBESTOS WASTE PACKAGING, HANDLING, AND DISPOSAL** | | | | | | | | | |
| 0100 | Collect and bag bulk material, 3 C.F. bags, by hand | A-9 | 400 | .160 | Ea. | 1.24 | 6.90 | | 8.14 | 12.20 |
| 0200 | Large production vacuum loader | A-12 | 880 | .073 | | .80 | 3.14 | .81 | 4.75 | 6.70 |
| 1000 | Double bag and decontaminate | A-9 | 960 | .067 | | 1.24 | 2.88 | | 4.12 | 5.90 |
| 2000 | Containerize bagged material in drums, per 3 C.F. drum | " | 800 | .080 | ↓ | 6.50 | 3.45 | | 9.95 | 12.60 |
| 3000 | Cart bags 50' to dumpster | 2 Asbe | 400 | .040 | ↓ | | 1.72 | | 1.72 | 2.71 |
| 5000 | Disposal charges, not including haul, minimum | | | | C.Y. | | | | 47.28 | 52.02 |
| 5020 | Maximum | | | | " | | | | 165.24 | 181.56 |
| 5100 | Remove refrigerant from system | 1 Plum | 40 | .200 | Lb. | | 9.35 | | 9.35 | 14.05 |
| 9000 | For type C (supplied air) respirator equipment, add | | | | % | | | | | 10% |

### 02 82 13.48 Asbestos Encapsulation With Sealants

| | | Crew | Daily Output | Labor-Hours | Unit | Material | 2008 Bare Costs Labor | Equipment | Total | Total Incl O&P |
|---|---|---|---|---|---|---|---|---|---|---|
| 0010 | **ASBESTOS ENCAPSULATION WITH SEALANTS** | | | | | | | | | |

# 02 82 Asbestos Remediation

## 02 82 13 – Asbestos Abatement

| 02 82 13.48 Asbestos Encapsulation With Sealants | | Crew | Daily Output | Labor-Hours | Unit | Material | 2008 Bare Costs Labor | Equipment | Total | Total Incl O&P |
|---|---|---|---|---|---|---|---|---|---|---|
| 0100 | Ceilings and walls, minimum | A-9 | 21000 | .003 | S.F. | .27 | .13 | | .40 | .51 |
| 0110 | Maximum | | 10600 | .006 | | .42 | .26 | | .68 | .87 |
| 0200 | Columns and beams, minimum | | 13300 | .005 | | .27 | .21 | | .48 | .63 |
| 0210 | Maximum | | 5325 | .012 | | .47 | .52 | | .99 | 1.34 |
| 0300 | Pipes to 12" diameter including minor repairs, minimum | | 800 | .080 | L.F. | .37 | 3.45 | | 3.82 | 5.85 |
| 0310 | Maximum | | 400 | .160 | " | 1.04 | 6.90 | | 7.94 | 12 |

# 02 83 Lead Remediation

## 02 83 19 – Lead-Based Paint Remediation

### 02 83 19.23 Encapsulation of Lead-Based Paint

| | | Crew | Daily Output | Labor-Hours | Unit | Material | 2008 Bare Costs Labor | Equipment | Total | Total Incl O&P |
|---|---|---|---|---|---|---|---|---|---|---|
| 0010 | **ENCAPSULATION OF LEAD-BASED PAINT** | | | | | | | | | |
| 0020 | Interior, brushwork, trim, under 6" | 1 Pord | 240 | .033 | L.F. | 2.46 | 1.12 | | 3.58 | 4.40 |
| 0030 | 6" to 12" wide | | 180 | .044 | | 3.28 | 1.50 | | 4.78 | 5.85 |
| 0040 | Balustrades | | 300 | .027 | | 1.98 | .90 | | 2.88 | 3.53 |
| 0050 | Pipe to 4" diameter | | 500 | .016 | | 1.19 | .54 | | 1.73 | 2.12 |
| 0060 | To 8" diameter | | 375 | .021 | | 1.57 | .72 | | 2.29 | 2.81 |
| 0070 | To 12" diameter | | 250 | .032 | | 2.36 | 1.08 | | 3.44 | 4.22 |
| 0080 | To 16" diameter | | 170 | .047 | | 3.47 | 1.59 | | 5.06 | 6.20 |
| 0090 | Cabinets, ornate design | | 200 | .040 | S.F. | 2.97 | 1.35 | | 4.32 | 5.30 |
| 0100 | Simple design | | 250 | .032 | " | 2.36 | 1.08 | | 3.44 | 4.22 |
| 0110 | Doors, 3' x 7', both sides, incl. frame & trim | | | | | | | | | |
| 0120 | Flush | 1 Pord | 6 | 1.333 | Ea. | 30.50 | 45 | | 75.50 | 101 |
| 0130 | French, 10-15 lite | | 3 | 2.667 | | 6.05 | 90 | | 96.05 | 142 |
| 0140 | Panel | | 4 | 2 | | 36.50 | 67.50 | | 104 | 141 |
| 0150 | Louvered | | 2.75 | 2.909 | | 33.50 | 98 | | 131.50 | 184 |
| 0160 | Windows, per interior side, per 15 S.F. | | | | | | | | | |
| 0170 | 1 to 6 lite | 1 Pord | 14 | .571 | Ea. | 21 | 19.30 | | 40.30 | 52 |
| 0180 | 7 to 10 lite | | 7.50 | 1.067 | | 23 | 36 | | 59 | 79.50 |
| 0190 | 12 lite | | 5.75 | 1.391 | | 31 | 47 | | 78 | 105 |
| 0200 | Radiators | | 8 | 1 | | 73.50 | 34 | | 107.50 | 132 |
| 0210 | Grilles, vents | | 275 | .029 | S.F. | 2.15 | .98 | | 3.13 | 3.84 |
| 0220 | Walls, roller, drywall or plaster | | 1000 | .008 | | .59 | .27 | | .86 | 1.06 |
| 0230 | With spunbonded reinforcing fabric | | 720 | .011 | | .68 | .38 | | 1.06 | 1.31 |
| 0240 | Wood | | 800 | .010 | | .74 | .34 | | 1.08 | 1.32 |
| 0250 | Ceilings, roller, drywall or plaster | | 900 | .009 | | .68 | .30 | | .98 | 1.20 |
| 0260 | Wood | | 700 | .011 | | .84 | .39 | | 1.23 | 1.50 |
| 0270 | Exterior, brushwork, gutters and downspouts | | 300 | .027 | L.F. | 1.98 | .90 | | 2.88 | 3.53 |
| 0280 | Columns | | 400 | .020 | S.F. | 1.47 | .68 | | 2.15 | 2.63 |
| 0290 | Spray, siding | | 600 | .013 | " | .99 | .45 | | 1.44 | 1.77 |
| 0300 | Miscellaneous | | | | | | | | | |
| 0310 | Electrical conduit, brushwork, to 2" diameter | 1 Pord | 500 | .016 | L.F. | 1.19 | .54 | | 1.73 | 2.12 |
| 0320 | Brick, block or concrete, spray | | 500 | .016 | S.F. | 1.19 | .54 | | 1.73 | 2.12 |
| 0330 | Steel, flat surfaces and tanks to 12" | | 500 | .016 | | 1.19 | .54 | | 1.73 | 2.12 |
| 0340 | Beams, brushwork | | 400 | .020 | | 1.47 | .68 | | 2.15 | 2.63 |
| 0350 | Trusses | | 400 | .020 | | 1.47 | .68 | | 2.15 | 2.63 |

### 02 83 19.26 Removal of Lead-Based Paint

| | | Crew | Daily Output | Labor-Hours | Unit | Material | 2008 Bare Costs Labor | Equipment | Total | Total Incl O&P |
|---|---|---|---|---|---|---|---|---|---|---|
| 0010 | **REMOVAL OF LEAD-BASED PAINT** R028319-60 | | | | | | | | | |
| 0050 | Baseboard, to 6" wide | 1 Pord | 64 | .125 | L.F. | .66 | 4.22 | | 4.88 | 7.10 |
| 0070 | To 12" wide | | 32 | .250 | " | 1.32 | 8.45 | | 9.77 | 14.15 |
| 0200 | Balustrades, one side | | 28 | .286 | S.F. | 1.32 | 9.65 | | 10.97 | 15.95 |
| 1400 | Cabinets, simple design | | 32 | .250 | | 1.32 | 8.45 | | 9.77 | 14.15 |

# 02 83 Lead Remediation

## 02 83 19 – Lead-Based Paint Remediation

| 02 83 19.26 Removal of Lead-Based Paint | | Crew | Daily Output | Labor-Hours | Unit | Material | 2008 Bare Costs Labor | Equipment | Total | Total Incl O&P |
|---|---|---|---|---|---|---|---|---|---|---|
| 1420 | Ornate design | 1 Pord | 25 | .320 | S.F. | 1.32 | 10.80 | | 12.12 | 17.65 |
| 1600 | Cornice, simple design | | 60 | .133 | | 1.32 | 4.50 | | 5.82 | 8.20 |
| 1620 | Ornate design | | 20 | .400 | | 5.05 | 13.50 | | 18.55 | 26 |
| 2800 | Doors, one side, flush | | 84 | .095 | | 1.32 | 3.21 | | 4.53 | 6.30 |
| 2820 | Two panel | | 80 | .100 | | 1.32 | 3.38 | | 4.70 | 6.50 |
| 2840 | Four panel | | 45 | .178 | ↓ | 1.32 | 6 | | 7.32 | 10.45 |
| 2880 | For trim, one side, add | | 64 | .125 | L.F. | .66 | 4.22 | | 4.88 | 7.10 |
| 3000 | Fence, picket, one side | | 30 | .267 | S.F. | 1.32 | 9 | | 10.32 | 14.95 |
| 3200 | Grilles, one side, simple design | | 30 | .267 | | 1.32 | 9 | | 10.32 | 14.95 |
| 3220 | Ornate design | | 25 | .320 | ↓ | 1.32 | 10.80 | | 12.12 | 17.65 |
| 4400 | Pipes, to 4" diameter | | 90 | .089 | L.F. | 1.25 | 3 | | 4.25 | 5.90 |
| 4420 | To 8" diameter | | 50 | .160 | | 2.77 | 5.40 | | 8.17 | 11.15 |
| 4440 | To 12" diameter | | 36 | .222 | | 4.16 | 7.50 | | 11.66 | 15.85 |
| 4460 | To 16" diameter | | 20 | .400 | ↓ | 5.55 | 13.50 | | 19.05 | 26.50 |
| 4500 | For hangers, add | | 40 | .200 | Ea. | 2.54 | 6.75 | | 9.29 | 12.95 |
| 4800 | Siding | | 90 | .089 | S.F. | 1.17 | 3 | | 4.17 | 5.80 |
| 5000 | Trusses, open | | 55 | .145 | SF Face | 1.85 | 4.91 | | 6.76 | 9.40 |
| 6200 | Windows, one side only, double hung, 1/1 light, 24" x 48" high | | 4 | 2 | Ea. | 25.50 | 67.50 | | 93 | 129 |
| 6220 | 30" x 60" high | | 3 | 2.667 | | 34 | 90 | | 124 | 173 |
| 6240 | 36" x 72" high | | 2.50 | 3.200 | | 41 | 108 | | 149 | 207 |
| 6280 | 40" x 80" high | | 2 | 4 | | 51 | 135 | | 186 | 259 |
| 6400 | Colonial window, 6/6 light, 24" x 48" high | | 2 | 4 | | 51 | 135 | | 186 | 260 |
| 6420 | 30" x 60" high | | 1.50 | 5.333 | | 68 | 180 | | 248 | 345 |
| 6440 | 36" x 72" high | | 1 | 8 | | 102 | 270 | | 372 | 515 |
| 6480 | 40" x 80" high | | 1 | 8 | | 102 | 270 | | 372 | 515 |
| 6600 | 8/8 light, 24" x 48" high | | 2 | 4 | | 51 | 135 | | 186 | 260 |
| 6620 | 40" x 80" high | | 1 | 8 | | 102 | 270 | | 372 | 515 |
| 6800 | 12/12 light, 24" x 48" high | | 1 | 8 | | 102 | 270 | | 372 | 515 |
| 6820 | 40" x 80" high | ↓ | .75 | 10.667 | ↓ | 136 | 360 | | 496 | 690 |
| 6840 | Window frame & trim items, included in pricing above | | | | | | | | | |

# 02 85 Mold Remediation

## 02 85 16 – Mold Remediation Preparation and Containment

### 02 85 16.40 Mold Remediation Plans and Methods

| | | Crew | Daily Output | Labor-Hours | Unit | Material | 2008 Bare Costs Labor | Equipment | Total | Total Incl O&P |
|---|---|---|---|---|---|---|---|---|---|---|
| 0010 | **MOLD REMEDIATION PLANS AND METHODS** | | | | | | | | | |
| 0020 | Initial inspection, average 3 bedroom home | | | | Total | | | | 241.10 | 265 |
| 0030 | Average 5 bedroom home | | | | | | | | 333.80 | 367 |
| 0040 | Testing, air sample each | | | | | | | | 241.10 | 265 |
| 0050 | Swab sample | | | | | | | | 143.75 | 158 |
| 0060 | Tape sample | | | | | | | | 143.75 | 158 |
| 0070 | Post remediation air test | | | | | | | | 241.10 | 265 |
| 0080 | Mold abatement plan, average 3 bedroom home | | | | | | | | 1,182 | 1,300 |
| 0090 | Average 5 bedroom home | | | | | | | | 1,437 | 1,580 |
| 0100 | Packup & removal of contents, average 3 bedroom home, excl storage | | | | | | | | 9,550 | 10,500 |
| 0110 | Average 5 bedroom home, excl storage | | | | ↓ | | | | 23,925 | 26,300 |
| 0120 | For demolition in mold contaminated areas, see Div. 02 85 33.50 | | | | | | | | | |
| 0130 | For personal protection equipment, see Div. 02 82 13.41 | | | | | | | | | |

### 02 85 16.50 Preparation of Mold Containment Area

| | | Crew | Daily Output | Labor-Hours | Unit | Material | 2008 Bare Costs Labor | Equipment | Total | Total Incl O&P |
|---|---|---|---|---|---|---|---|---|---|---|
| 0010 | **PREPARATION OF MOLD CONTAINMENT AREA** | | | | | | | | | |
| 0100 | Pre-cleaning, HEPA vacuum and wet wipe, flat surfaces | A-10 | 12000 | .005 | S.F. | .02 | .23 | | .25 | .38 |
| 0300 | Separation barrier, 2" x 4" @ 16", 1/2" plywood ea. side, 8' high | 2 Carp | 400 | .040 | ↓ | 1.25 | 1.52 | | 2.77 | 3.75 |

# 02 85 Mold Remediation

## 02 85 16 – Mold Remediation Preparation and Containment

### 02 85 16.50 Preparation of Mold Containment Area

| | | Crew | Daily Output | Labor-Hours | Unit | Material | 2008 Bare Costs Labor | Equipment | Total | Total Incl O&P |
|---|---|---|---|---|---|---|---|---|---|---|
| 0310 | 12' high | 2 Carp | 320 | .050 | S.F. | 1.40 | 1.91 | | 3.31 | 4.51 |
| 0320 | 16' high | | 200 | .080 | | 1.50 | 3.05 | | 4.55 | 6.40 |
| 0400 | Personnel decontam. chamber, 2" x 4" @ 16", 3/4" ply ea. side | | 280 | .057 | | 2.50 | 2.18 | | 4.68 | 6.15 |
| 0450 | Waste decontam. chamber, 2" x 4" studs @ 16", 3/4" ply each side | | 360 | .044 | | 3 | 1.69 | | 4.69 | 5.95 |
| 0500 | Cover surfaces with polyethelene sheeting | | | | | | | | | |
| 0501 | Including glue and tape | | | | | | | | | |
| 0550 | Floors, each layer, 6 mil | A-10 | 8000 | .008 | S.F. | .09 | .35 | | .44 | .64 |
| 0551 | 4 mil | | 9000 | .007 | | .05 | .31 | | .36 | .54 |
| 0560 | Walls, each layer, 6 mil | | 6000 | .011 | | .09 | .46 | | .55 | .83 |
| 0561 | 4 mil | | 7000 | .009 | | .07 | .39 | | .46 | .70 |
| 0570 | For heights above 12', add | | | | | | 20% | | | |
| 0575 | For heights above 20', add | | | | | | 30% | | | |
| 0580 | For fire retardant poly, add | | | | | 100% | | | | |
| 0590 | For large open areas, deduct | | | | | 10% | 20% | | | |
| 0600 | Seal floor penetrations with foam firestop to 36 sq in | 2 Carp | 200 | .080 | Ea. | 40 | 3.05 | | 43.05 | 48.50 |
| 0610 | 36 sq in to 72 sq in | | 125 | .128 | | 79.50 | 4.88 | | 84.38 | 95 |
| 0615 | 72 sq in to 144 sq in | | 80 | .200 | | 159 | 7.60 | | 166.60 | 187 |
| 0620 | Wall penetrations, to 36 square inches | | 180 | .089 | | 40 | 3.39 | | 43.39 | 49.50 |
| 0630 | 36 sq. in. to 72 sq. in. | | 100 | .160 | | 79.50 | 6.10 | | 85.60 | 97 |
| 0640 | 72 Sq. in. to 144 sq. in. | | 60 | .267 | | 159 | 10.15 | | 169.15 | 191 |
| 0800 | Caulk seams with latex caulk | 1 Carp | 230 | .035 | L.F. | .15 | 1.33 | | 1.48 | 2.23 |
| 0900 | Set up neg. air machine, 1-2k C.F.M. /25 M.C.F. volume | 1 Asbe | 4.30 | 1.860 | Ea. | | 80 | | 80 | 126 |

## 02 85 33 – Removal and Disposal of Materials with Mold

### 02 85 33.50 Demolition In Mold Contaminated Area

| | | Crew | Daily Output | Labor-Hours | Unit | Material | 2008 Bare Costs Labor | Equipment | Total | Total Incl O&P |
|---|---|---|---|---|---|---|---|---|---|---|
| 0010 | **DEMOLITION IN MOLD CONTAMINATED AREA** | | | | | | | | | |
| 0200 | Ceiling, including suspension system, plaster and lath | A-9 | 2100 | .030 | S.F. | .10 | 1.32 | | 1.42 | 2.18 |
| 0210 | Finished plaster, leaving wire lath | | 585 | .109 | | .35 | 4.72 | | 5.07 | 7.85 |
| 0220 | Suspended acoustical tile | | 3500 | .018 | | .06 | .79 | | .85 | 1.31 |
| 0230 | Concealed tile grid system | | 3000 | .021 | | .07 | .92 | | .99 | 1.53 |
| 0240 | Metal pan grid system | | 1500 | .043 | | .14 | 1.84 | | 1.98 | 3.05 |
| 0250 | Gypsum board | | 2500 | .026 | | .08 | 1.10 | | 1.18 | 1.83 |
| 0255 | Plywood | | 2500 | .026 | | .08 | 1.10 | | 1.18 | 1.83 |
| 0260 | Lighting fixtures up to 2' x 4' | | 72 | .889 | Ea. | 2.87 | 38.50 | | 41.37 | 63.50 |
| 0400 | Partitions, non load bearing | | | | | | | | | |
| 0410 | Plaster, lath, and studs | A-9 | 690 | .093 | S.F. | .87 | 4 | | 4.87 | 7.25 |
| 0450 | Gypsum board and studs | | 1390 | .046 | | .15 | 1.99 | | 2.14 | 3.29 |
| 0465 | Carpet & pad | | 1390 | .046 | | .15 | 1.99 | | 2.14 | 3.29 |
| 0600 | Pipe insulation, air cell type, up to 4" diameter pipe | | 900 | .071 | L.F. | .23 | 3.07 | | 3.30 | 5.10 |
| 0610 | 4" to 8" diameter pipe | | 800 | .080 | | .26 | 3.45 | | 3.71 | 5.75 |
| 0620 | 10" to 12" diameter pipe | | 700 | .091 | | .30 | 3.95 | | 4.25 | 6.55 |
| 0630 | 14" to 16" diameter pipe | | 550 | .116 | | .38 | 5 | | 5.38 | 8.30 |
| 0650 | Over 16" diameter pipe | | 650 | .098 | S.F. | .32 | 4.25 | | 4.57 | 7.05 |
| 9000 | For type C (supplied air) respirator equipment, add | | | | % | | | | | 10% |

# Division Notes

| | | CREW | DAILY OUTPUT | LABOR-HOURS | UNIT | 2008 BARE COSTS | | | | TOTAL INCL O&P |
|---|---|---|---|---|---|---|---|---|---|---|
| | | | | | | MAT. | LABOR | EQUIP. | TOTAL | |
| | | | | | | | | | | |
| | | | | | | | | | | |
| | | | | | | | | | | |
| | | | | | | | | | | |
| | | | | | | | | | | |
| | | | | | | | | | | |
| | | | | | | | | | | |
| | | | | | | | | | | |
| | | | | | | | | | | |
| | | | | | | | | | | |
| | | | | | | | | | | |
| | | | | | | | | | | |
| | | | | | | | | | | |
| | | | | | | | | | | |
| | | | | | | | | | | |
| | | | | | | | | | | |
| | | | | | | | | | | |
| | | | | | | | | | | |
| | | | | | | | | | | |
| | | | | | | | | | | |

# Estimating Tips

## General

- Carefully check all the plans and specifications. Concrete often appears on drawings other than structural drawings, including mechanical and electrical drawings for equipment pads. The cost of cutting and patching is often difficult to estimate. See section 03 81 for Concrete Cutting, section 02 41 19.16 for Cutout Demolition, section 03 05 05.10 for Concrete Demolition, and section 02 41 19.23 for Rubbish Handling (handling, loading and hauling of debris).

- Always obtain concrete prices from suppliers near the job site. A volume discount can often be negotiated depending upon competition in the area. Remember to add for waste, particularly for slabs and footings on grade.

## 03 10 00 Concrete Forming and Accessories

- A primary cost for concrete construction is forming. Most jobs today are constructed with prefabricated forms. The selection of the forms best suited for the job and the total square feet of forms required for efficient concrete forming and placing are key elements in estimating concrete construction. Enough forms must be available for erection to make efficient use of the concrete placing equipment and crew.

- Concrete accessories for forming and placing depend upon the systems used. Study the plans and specifications to assure that all special accessory requirements have been included in the cost estimate, such as anchor bolts, inserts, and hangers.

- Included within costs for forms-in-place are all necessary bracing and shoring.

## 03 20 00 Concrete Reinforcing

- Ascertain that the reinforcing steel supplier has included all accessories, cutting, bending, and an allowance for lapping, splicing, and waste. A good rule of thumb is 10% for lapping, splicing, and waste. Also, 10% waste should be allowed for welded wire fabric.

- The unit price items in the section for Reinforcing In Place include the labor to install accessories such as beam and slab bolsters, high chairs, and bar ties and tie wire. The material cost for these accessories is not included; they may be obtained from the Accessories section.

## 03 30 00 Cast-in-Place Concrete

- When estimating structural concrete, pay particular attention to requirements for concrete additives, curing methods, and surface treatments. Special consideration for climate, hot or cold, must be included in your estimate. Be sure to include requirements for concrete placing equipment and concrete finishing.

- For accurate concrete estimating, the estimator must consider each of the following major components individually: forms, reinforcing steel, ready-mix concrete, placement of the concrete, and finishing of the top surface. For faster estimating, section 03 30 53.40 for Concrete-In-Place can be used; here, various items of concrete work are presented that include the costs of all five major components (unless specifically stated otherwise).

## 03 40 00 Precast Concrete
## 03 50 00 Cast Decks and Underlayment

- The cost of hauling precast concrete structural members is often an important factor. For this reason, it is important to get a quote from the nearest supplier. It may become economically feasible to set up precasting beds on the site if the hauling costs are prohibitive.

## Reference Numbers

Reference numbers are shown in shaded boxes at the beginning of some major classifications. These numbers refer to related items in the Reference Section. The reference information may be an estimating procedure, an alternate pricing method, or technical information.

*Note:* Not all subdivisions listed here necessarily appear in this publication.

Division 3 - Concrete

# 03 01 Maintenance of Concrete

## 03 01 30 – Maintenance of Cast-In-Place Concrete

### 03 01 30.62 Concrete Patching

| 03 01 30.62 Concrete Patching | | Crew | Daily Output | Labor-Hours | Unit | Material | 2008 Bare Costs Labor | Equipment | Total | Total Incl O&P |
|---|---|---|---|---|---|---|---|---|---|---|
| 0010 | CONCRETE PATCHING | | | | | | | | | |
| 0100 | Floors, 1/4" thick, small areas, regular grout | 1 Cefi | 170 | .047 | S.F. | 1.13 | 1.74 | | 2.87 | 3.80 |
| 0150 | Epoxy grout | " | 100 | .080 | " | 7.05 | 2.96 | | 10.01 | 12.10 |
| 2000 | Walls, including chipping, cleaning and epoxy grout | | | | | | | | | |
| 2100 | 1/4" deep | 1 Cefi | 65 | .123 | S.F. | 7.50 | 4.55 | | 12.05 | 14.95 |
| 2150 | 1/2" deep | | 50 | .160 | | 15.05 | 5.90 | | 20.95 | 25.50 |
| 2200 | 3/4" deep | ↓ | 40 | .200 | ↓ | 22.50 | 7.40 | | 29.90 | 36 |

# 03 05 Common Work Results for Concrete

## 03 05 05 – Selective Concrete Demolition

### 03 05 05.10 Selective Demolition, Concrete

| 03 05 05.10 Selective Demolition, Concrete | | Crew | Daily Output | Labor-Hours | Unit | Material | 2008 Bare Costs Labor | Equipment | Total | Total Incl O&P |
|---|---|---|---|---|---|---|---|---|---|---|
| 0010 | SELECTIVE DEMOLITION, CONCRETE  R024119-10 | | | | | | | | | |
| 0012 | Excludes saw cutting, torch cutting, loading or hauling | | | | | | | | | |
| 0050 | Break up into small pieces, minimum reinforcing | B-9 | 24 | 1.667 | C.Y. | | 51 | 8 | 59 | 88.50 |
| 0060 | Average reinforcing | | 16 | 2.500 | | | 76.50 | 12 | 88.50 | 132 |
| 0070 | Maximum reinforcing | ↓ | 8 | 5 | ↓ | | 153 | 24 | 177 | 265 |
| 0150 | Remove whole pieces, up to 2 tons per piece | E-18 | 36 | 1.111 | Ea. | | 47.50 | 28 | 75.50 | 114 |
| 0160 | 2 - 5 tons per piece | | 30 | 1.333 | | | 57 | 33.50 | 90.50 | 137 |
| 0170 | 5 - 10 tons per piece | | 24 | 1.667 | | | 71.50 | 42 | 113.50 | 171 |
| 0180 | 10 - 15 tons per piece | ↓ | 18 | 2.222 | | | 95 | 56 | 151 | 228 |
| 0250 | Precast unit embedded in masonry, up to 1 CF | D-1 | 16 | 1 | | | 35 | | 35 | 53 |
| 0260 | 1 - 2 CF | | 12 | 1.333 | | | 46.50 | | 46.50 | 70.50 |
| 0270 | 2 - 5 CF | | 10 | 1.600 | | | 56 | | 56 | 85 |
| 0280 | 5 - 10 CF | ↓ | 8 | 2 | ↓ | | 70 | | 70 | 106 |

## 03 05 13 – Basic Concrete Materials

### 03 05 13.20 Concrete Admixtures and Surface Treatments

| 03 05 13.20 Concrete Admixtures and Surface Treatments | | Crew | Daily Output | Labor-Hours | Unit | Material | 2008 Bare Costs Labor | Equipment | Total | Total Incl O&P |
|---|---|---|---|---|---|---|---|---|---|---|
| 0010 | CONCRETE ADMIXTURES AND SURFACE TREATMENTS | | | | | | | | | |
| 0040 | Abrasives, aluminum oxide, over 20 tons | | | | Lb. | 1.30 | | | 1.30 | 1.43 |
| 0050 | 1 to 20 tons | | | | | 1.34 | | | 1.34 | 1.48 |
| 0070 | Under 1 ton | | | | | 1.40 | | | 1.40 | 1.54 |
| 0100 | Silicon carbide, black, over 20 tons | | | | | 1.78 | | | 1.78 | 1.96 |
| 0110 | 1 to 20 tons | | | | | 1.87 | | | 1.87 | 2.06 |
| 0120 | Under 1 ton | | | | ↓ | 1.95 | | | 1.95 | 2.15 |
| 0200 | Air entraining agent, .7 to 1.5 oz. per bag, 55 gallon drum | | | | Gal. | 9.50 | | | 9.50 | 10.45 |
| 0220 | 5 gallon pail | | | | | 10 | | | 10 | 11 |
| 0300 | Bonding agent, acrylic latex, 250 S.F. per gallon, 5 gallon pail | | | | | 17.75 | | | 17.75 | 19.55 |
| 0320 | Epoxy resin, 80 S.F. per gallon, 3.5 gallon unit | | | | ↓ | 42.50 | | | 42.50 | 46.50 |
| 0400 | Calcium chloride, 50 lb. bags, TL lots | | | | Ton | 420 | | | 420 | 460 |
| 0420 | Less than truckload lots | | | | Bag | 15.15 | | | 15.15 | 16.65 |
| 0500 | Carbon black, liquid, 2 to 8 lbs. per bag of cement | | | | Lb. | 4.70 | | | 4.70 | 5.15 |
| 0600 | Colors, integral, 2 to 10 lb. per bag of cement, minimum | | | | | 2.41 | | | 2.41 | 2.65 |
| 0610 | Average | | | | | 3.27 | | | 3.27 | 3.60 |
| 0620 | Maximum | | | | ↓ | 5.40 | | | 5.40 | 5.95 |
| 0920 | Dustproofing compound, 250 SF/gal, 5 gallon pail | | | | Gal. | 6.60 | | | 6.60 | 7.25 |
| 1010 | Epoxy based, 125 SF/Gal, 5 gallon pail | | | | " | 82 | | | 82 | 90 |
| 1100 | Hardeners, metallic, 55 lb. bags, natural (grey) | | | | Lb. | .86 | | | .86 | .95 |
| 1200 | Colors | | | | | 1.25 | | | 1.25 | 1.38 |
| 1300 | Non-metallic, 55 lb. bags, natural grey | | | | | .32 | | | .32 | .36 |
| 1320 | Colors | | | | ↓ | .62 | | | .62 | .68 |
| 1550 | Release agent, for tilt slabs, 5 gallon pail | | | | Gal. | 14.35 | | | 14.35 | 15.75 |

# 03 05 Common Work Results for Concrete

## 03 05 13 – Basic Concrete Materials

| 03 05 13.20 Concrete Admixtures and Surface Treatments | | Crew | Daily Output | Labor-Hours | Unit | Material | 2008 Bare Costs | | Total | Total Incl O&P |
|---|---|---|---|---|---|---|---|---|---|---|
| | | | | | | | Labor | Equipment | | |
| 1570 | For forms, 5 gallon pail | | | | Gal. | 9.10 | | | 9.10 | 10 |
| 1600 | Sealer, hardener and dustproofer, epoxy-based, 125 SF/gal, 5 gallon, min | | | | | 82 | | | 82 | 90 |
| 1620 | 5 gallon pail, maximum | | | | | 90 | | | 90 | 99 |
| 1630 | Sealer, solvent-based, 250 SF/gal, 55 gallon drum | | | | | 14.65 | | | 14.65 | 16.10 |
| 1640 | 5 gallon pail | | | | | 16.60 | | | 16.60 | 18.30 |
| 1650 | Sealer, water based, 350 S.F., 55 gallon drum | | | | | 18.95 | | | 18.95 | 21 |
| 1660 | 5 gallon pail | | | | | 21 | | | 21 | 23 |
| 1900 | Set retarder, 100 SF/gallon, 5 gallon pail | | | | ↓ | 16.60 | | | 16.60 | 18.25 |
| 2000 | Waterproofing, integral 1 lb. per bag of cement | | | | Lb. | 1.10 | | | 1.10 | 1.21 |
| 2100 | Powdered metallic, 40 lbs. per 100 S.F., minimum | | | | | 1.30 | | | 1.30 | 1.43 |
| 2120 | Maximum | | | | ↓ | 2.70 | | | 2.70 | 2.97 |
| 3000 | For integral colors, 2500 psi (5 bag mix) | | | | | | | | | |
| 3100 | Red, yellow or brown, 1.8 lb. per bag, add | | | | C.Y. | 21.50 | | | 21.50 | 24 |
| 3200 | 9.4 lb. per bag, add | | | | | 113 | | | 113 | 125 |
| 3400 | Black, 1.8 lb. per bag, add | | | | | 29.50 | | | 29.50 | 32.50 |
| 3500 | 7.5 lb. per bag, add | | | | | 123 | | | 123 | 135 |
| 3700 | Green, 1.8 lb. per bag, add | | | | | 48.50 | | | 48.50 | 53.50 |
| 3800 | 7.5 lb. per bag, add | | | | ↓ | 203 | | | 203 | 223 |

## 03 05 13.25 Aggregate

| | | | | | | | | | | |
|---|---|---|---|---|---|---|---|---|---|---|
| 0010 | **AGGREGATE** | R033105-20 | | | | | | | | |
| 0020 | Expanded shale, C.L. lots, 52 lb. per C.F., minimum | | | | Ton | 36 | | | 36 | 39.50 |
| 0050 | Maximum | R033105-30 | | | " | 48 | | | 48 | 53 |
| 0100 | Lightweight vermiculite or perlite, 4 C.F. bag, C.L. lots | | | | Bag | 6.40 | | | 6.40 | 7 |
| 0150 | L.C.L. lots | R033105-40 | | | " | 7 | | | 7 | 7.70 |
| 0250 | Sand & stone, loaded at pit, crushed bank gravel | | | | Ton | 15.15 | | | 15.15 | 16.65 |
| 0350 | Sand, washed, for concrete | R033105-50 | | | | 15.15 | | | 15.15 | 16.65 |
| 0400 | For plaster or brick | | | | | 15.15 | | | 15.15 | 16.65 |
| 0450 | Stone, 3/4" to 1-1/2" | | | | | 31 | | | 31 | 34 |
| 0500 | 3/8" roofing stone & 1/2" pea stone | | | | | 16 | | | 16 | 17.60 |
| 0550 | For trucking 10 miles (5 mile R/T), add to the above | B-34B | 117 | .068 | | | 2.09 | 4.30 | 6.39 | 7.95 |
| 0600 | 30 miles (15 mi R/T), add to the above | " | 72 | .111 | ↓ | | 3.40 | 7 | 10.40 | 12.95 |
| 0850 | Sand & stone, loaded at pit, crushed bank gravel | | | | C.Y. | 21 | | | 21 | 23.50 |
| 0950 | Sand, washed, for concrete | | | | | 21 | | | 21 | 23 |
| 1000 | For plaster or brick | | | | | 21 | | | 21 | 23 |
| 1050 | Stone, 3/4" to 1-1/2" | | | | | 24.50 | | | 24.50 | 27 |
| 1100 | 3/8" roofing stone & 1/2" pea stone | | | | | 33.50 | | | 33.50 | 37 |
| 1150 | For trucking 10 miles (5 mi R/T), add to the above | B-34B | 78 | .103 | | | 3.14 | 6.45 | 9.59 | 11.95 |
| 1200 | 30 miles (15 mi R/T), add to the above | " | 48 | .167 | ↓ | | 5.10 | 10.50 | 15.60 | 19.40 |
| 1310 | Quartz chips, 50 lb. bags | | | | Cwt. | 18.70 | | | 18.70 | 20.50 |
| 1330 | Silica chips, 50 lb. bags | | | | | 10.25 | | | 10.25 | 11.30 |
| 1410 | White marble, 3/8" to 1/2", 50 lb. bags | | | | ↓ | 15.45 | | | 15.45 | 17 |
| 1430 | 3/4" | | | | Ton | 76 | | | 76 | 83.50 |

## 03 05 13.30 Cement

| | | | | | | | | | | |
|---|---|---|---|---|---|---|---|---|---|---|
| 0010 | **CEMENT** | R033105-20 | | | | | | | | |
| 0240 | Portland, Type I/II, TL lots, 94 lb bags | | | | Bag | 10 | | | 10 | 11 |
| 0250 | LTL/LCL lots | R033105-30 | | | " | 10.60 | | | 10.60 | 11.65 |
| 0300 | Trucked in bulk, per cwt | **CN** | | | Cwt. | 6.90 | | | 6.90 | 7.60 |
| 0400 | Type III, high early strength, TL lots, 94 lb bags **CN** | R033105-40 | | | Bag | 10.70 | | | 10.70 | 11.75 |
| 0420 | L.T.L. or L.C.L. lots | | | | | 11.45 | | | 11.45 | 12.60 |
| 0500 | White, type III, high early strength, T.L. or C.L. lots, bags | R033105-50 | | | | 22.50 | | | 22.50 | 24.50 |
| 0520 | L.T.L. or L.C.L. lots | | | | ↓ | 23.50 | | | 23.50 | 26 |
| 0600 | White, type I, T.L. or C.L. lots, bags | | | | ↓ | 21.50 | | | 21.50 | 23.50 |

# 03 05 Common Work Results for Concrete

## 03 05 13 – Basic Concrete Materials

### 03 05 13.30 Cement

| | Crew | Daily Output | Labor-Hours | Unit | Material | 2008 Bare Costs Labor | 2008 Bare Costs Equipment | Total | Total Incl O&P |
|---|---|---|---|---|---|---|---|---|---|
| 0620 | L.T.L. or L.C.L. lots | | | | Bag | 22.50 | | | 22.50 | 24.50 |

### 03 05 13.80 Waterproofing and Dampproofing

| | Crew | Daily Output | Labor-Hours | Unit | Material | Labor | Equipment | Total | Total Incl O&P |
|---|---|---|---|---|---|---|---|---|---|
| 0010 | **WATERPROOFING AND DAMPPROOFING** | | | | | | | | | |
| 0050 | Integral waterproofing, add to cost of regular concrete | | | | C.Y. | 6.60 | | | 6.60 | 7.25 |

### 03 05 13.85 Winter Protection

| | | Crew | Daily Output | Labor-Hours | Unit | Material | Labor | Equipment | Total | Total Incl O&P |
|---|---|---|---|---|---|---|---|---|---|---|
| 0010 | **WINTER PROTECTION** | | | | | | | | | |
| 0012 | For heated ready mix, add, minimum | | | | C.Y. | 6.25 | | | 6.25 | 6.90 |
| 0050 | Maximum | | | | " | 7.80 | | | 7.80 | 8.60 |
| 0100 | Temporary heat to protect concrete, 24 hours, minimum | 2 Clab | 50 | .320 | M.S.F. | 200 | 9.70 | | 209.70 | 235 |
| 0150 | Maximum | " | 25 | .640 | " | 260 | 19.35 | | 279.35 | 315 |
| 0200 | Temporary shelter for slab on grade, wood frame/polyethylene sheeting | | | | | | | | | |
| 0201 | Build or remove, minimum | 2 Carp | 10 | 1.600 | M.S.F. | 277 | 61 | | 338 | 400 |
| 0210 | Maximum | " | 3 | 5.333 | " | 330 | 203 | | 533 | 675 |
| 0500 | Electrically heated pads, 110 volts, 15 watts per S.F., buy | | | | S.F. | 5.90 | | | 5.90 | 6.50 |
| 0600 | 20 watts per S.F., buy | | | | | 7.85 | | | 7.85 | 8.65 |
| 0710 | Electrically, heated pads, 15 watts/S.F., 20 uses, minimum | | | | | .21 | | | .21 | .23 |
| 0800 | Maximum | | | | | .35 | | | .35 | .39 |

# 03 11 Concrete Forming

## 03 11 13 – Structural Cast-In-Place Concrete Forming

### 03 11 13.13 Concrete Slip Forming

| | | Crew | Daily Output | Labor-Hours | Unit | Material | Labor | Equipment | Total | Total Incl O&P |
|---|---|---|---|---|---|---|---|---|---|---|
| 0010 | **CONCRETE SLIP FORMING** R031113-30 | | | | | | | | | |
| 0020 | Silos, minimum | C-17E | 3885 | .021 | SFCA | 3.47 | .82 | .02 | 4.31 | 5.10 |
| 0050 | Maximum | | 1095 | .073 | | 4.99 | 2.91 | .08 | 7.98 | 10.10 |
| 1000 | Buildings, minimum | | 3660 | .022 | | 2.21 | .87 | .02 | 3.10 | 3.81 |
| 1050 | Maximum | | 875 | .091 | | 4.08 | 3.64 | .10 | 7.82 | 10.25 |

### 03 11 13.20 Forms In Place, Beams and Girders

| | | Crew | Daily Output | Labor-Hours | Unit | Material | Labor | Equipment | Total | Total Incl O&P |
|---|---|---|---|---|---|---|---|---|---|---|
| 0010 | **FORMS IN PLACE, BEAMS AND GIRDERS** R031113-40 | | | | | | | | | |
| 0500 | Exterior spandrel, job-built plywood, 12" wide, 1 use | C-2 | 225 | .213 | SFCA | 3.53 | 7.90 | | 11.43 | 16.25 |
| 0550 | 2 use R031113-60 | | 275 | .175 | | 1.87 | 6.50 | | 8.37 | 12.15 |
| 0600 | 3 use | | 295 | .163 | | 1.41 | 6.05 | | 7.46 | 10.95 |
| 0650 | 4 use | | 310 | .155 | | 1.15 | 5.75 | | 6.90 | 10.20 |
| 1000 | 18" wide, 1 use | | 250 | .192 | | 2.96 | 7.15 | | 10.11 | 14.35 |
| 1050 | 2 use | | 275 | .175 | | 1.63 | 6.50 | | 8.13 | 11.90 |
| 1100 | 3 use | | 305 | .157 | | 1.18 | 5.85 | | 7.03 | 10.40 |
| 1150 | 4 use | | 315 | .152 | | .97 | 5.65 | | 6.62 | 9.85 |
| 1500 | 24" wide, 1 use | | 265 | .181 | | 2.71 | 6.75 | | 9.46 | 13.45 |
| 1550 | 2 use | | 290 | .166 | | 1.52 | 6.15 | | 7.67 | 11.20 |
| 1600 | 3 use | | 315 | .152 | | 1.08 | 5.65 | | 6.73 | 10 |
| 1650 | 4 use | | 325 | .148 | | .88 | 5.50 | | 6.38 | 9.50 |
| 2000 | Interior beam, job-built plywood, 12" wide, 1 use | | 300 | .160 | | 4.19 | 5.95 | | 10.14 | 13.85 |
| 2050 | 2 use | | 340 | .141 | | 2.06 | 5.25 | | 7.31 | 10.40 |
| 2100 | 3 use | | 364 | .132 | | 1.68 | 4.90 | | 6.58 | 9.45 |
| 2150 | 4 use | | 377 | .127 | | 1.36 | 4.73 | | 6.09 | 8.85 |
| 2500 | 24" wide, 1 use | | 320 | .150 | | 2.76 | 5.55 | | 8.31 | 11.70 |
| 2550 | 2 use | | 365 | .132 | | 1.55 | 4.88 | | 6.43 | 9.30 |
| 2600 | 3 use | | 385 | .125 | | 1.10 | 4.63 | | 5.73 | 8.40 |
| 2650 | 4 use | | 395 | .122 | | .89 | 4.51 | | 5.40 | 8 |
| 3000 | Encasing steel beam, hung, job-built plywood, 1 use | | 325 | .148 | | 3.10 | 5.50 | | 8.60 | 11.95 |
| 3050 | 2 use | | 390 | .123 | | 1.71 | 4.57 | | 6.28 | 9 |

# 03 11 Concrete Forming

## 03 11 13 – Structural Cast-In-Place Concrete Forming

### 03 11 13.20 Forms In Place, Beams and Girders

| | | Crew | Daily Output | Labor-Hours | Unit | Material | 2008 Bare Costs Labor | Equipment | Total | Total Incl O&P |
|---|---|---|---|---|---|---|---|---|---|---|
| 3100 | 3 use | C-2 | 415 | .116 | SFCA | 1.24 | 4.29 | | 5.53 | 8.05 |
| 3150 | 4 use | | 430 | .112 | | 1.01 | 4.14 | | 5.15 | 7.55 |
| 3500 | Bottoms only, to 30" wide, job-built plywood, 1 use | | 230 | .209 | | 4.13 | 7.75 | | 11.88 | 16.60 |
| 3550 | 2 use | | 265 | .181 | | 2.31 | 6.75 | | 9.06 | 13 |
| 3600 | 3 use | | 280 | .171 | | 1.65 | 6.35 | | 8 | 11.70 |
| 3650 | 4 use | | 290 | .166 | | 1.34 | 6.15 | | 7.49 | 11.05 |
| 4000 | Sides only, vertical, 36" high, job-built plywood, 1 use | | 335 | .143 | | 6.80 | 5.30 | | 12.10 | 15.80 |
| 4050 | 2 use | | 405 | .119 | | 3.75 | 4.40 | | 8.15 | 11 |
| 4100 | 3 use | | 430 | .112 | | 2.73 | 4.14 | | 6.87 | 9.45 |
| 4150 | 4 use | | 445 | .108 | | 2.22 | 4.01 | | 6.23 | 8.70 |
| 4500 | Sloped sides, 36" high, 1 use | | 305 | .157 | | 6.30 | 5.85 | | 12.15 | 16.05 |
| 4550 | 2 use | | 370 | .130 | | 3.51 | 4.82 | | 8.33 | 11.35 |
| 4600 | 3 use | | 405 | .119 | | 2.53 | 4.40 | | 6.93 | 9.65 |
| 4650 | 4 use | | 425 | .113 | | 2.05 | 4.19 | | 6.24 | 8.80 |
| 5000 | Upstanding beams, 36" high, 1 use | | 225 | .213 | | 8.90 | 7.90 | | 16.80 | 22 |
| 5050 | 2 use | | 255 | .188 | | 4.93 | 7 | | 11.93 | 16.30 |
| 5100 | 3 use | | 275 | .175 | | 3.57 | 6.50 | | 10.07 | 14.05 |
| 5150 | 4 use | | 280 | .171 | | 2.90 | 6.35 | | 9.25 | 13.10 |

### 03 11 13.25 Forms In Place, Columns

| | | Crew | Daily Output | Labor-Hours | Unit | Material | 2008 Bare Costs Labor | Equipment | Total | Total Incl O&P |
|---|---|---|---|---|---|---|---|---|---|---|
| 0010 | **FORMS IN PLACE, COLUMNS** R031113-40 | | | | | | | | | |
| 0500 | Round fiberglass, 4 use per mo., rent, 12" diameter | C-1 | 160 | .200 | L.F. | 6.50 | 7.25 | | 13.75 | 18.40 |
| 0550 | 16" diameter R031113-60 | | 150 | .213 | | 7.80 | 7.70 | | 15.50 | 20.50 |
| 0600 | 18" diameter | | 140 | .229 | | 8.65 | 8.25 | | 16.90 | 22.50 |
| 0650 | 24" diameter | | 135 | .237 | | 10.80 | 8.55 | | 19.35 | 25 |
| 0700 | 28" diameter | | 130 | .246 | | 12.05 | 8.90 | | 20.95 | 27 |
| 0800 | 30" diameter | | 125 | .256 | | 12.60 | 9.25 | | 21.85 | 28.50 |
| 0850 | 36" diameter | | 120 | .267 | | 16.75 | 9.65 | | 26.40 | 33.50 |
| 1500 | Round fiber tube, 1 use, 8" diameter | | 155 | .206 | | 1.39 | 7.45 | | 8.84 | 13.15 |
| 1550 | 10" diameter | | 155 | .206 | | 1.98 | 7.45 | | 9.43 | 13.80 |
| 1600 | 12" diameter | | 150 | .213 | | 2.33 | 7.70 | | 10.03 | 14.55 |
| 1650 | 14" diameter | | 145 | .221 | | 3.21 | 8 | | 11.21 | 15.95 |
| 1700 | 16" diameter | | 140 | .229 | | 4 | 8.25 | | 12.25 | 17.25 |
| 1750 | 20" diameter | | 135 | .237 | | 6.05 | 8.55 | | 14.60 | 20 |
| 1800 | 24" diameter | | 130 | .246 | | 7.95 | 8.90 | | 16.85 | 22.50 |
| 1850 | 30" diameter | | 125 | .256 | | 11.65 | 9.25 | | 20.90 | 27 |
| 1900 | 36" diameter | | 115 | .278 | | 14.90 | 10.05 | | 24.95 | 32 |
| 1950 | 42" diameter | | 100 | .320 | | 35 | 11.55 | | 46.55 | 56.50 |
| 2000 | 48" diameter | | 85 | .376 | | 41.50 | 13.60 | | 55.10 | 67 |
| 2200 | For seamless type, add | | | | | 15% | | | | |
| 3000 | Round, steel, 4 use per mo., rent, regular duty, 12" diameter | C-1 | 145 | .221 | L.F. | 10.45 | 8 | | 18.45 | 24 |
| 3050 | 16" diameter | | 125 | .256 | | 11.75 | 9.25 | | 21 | 27.50 |
| 3100 | Heavy duty, 20" diameter | | 105 | .305 | | 12.90 | 11 | | 23.90 | 31.50 |
| 3150 | 24" diameter | | 85 | .376 | | 14.15 | 13.60 | | 27.75 | 36.50 |
| 3200 | 30" diameter | | 70 | .457 | | 16.25 | 16.50 | | 32.75 | 43.50 |
| 3250 | 36" diameter | | 60 | .533 | | 17.40 | 19.25 | | 36.65 | 49 |
| 3300 | 48" diameter | | 50 | .640 | | 24 | 23 | | 47 | 62.50 |
| 3350 | 60" diameter | | 45 | .711 | | 32 | 25.50 | | 57.50 | 75 |
| 4000 | Column capitals, steel, 4 uses/mo., 24" col, 4' cap diameter | | 12 | 2.667 | Ea. | 199 | 96.50 | | 295.50 | 370 |
| 4050 | 5' cap diameter | | 11 | 2.909 | | 228 | 105 | | 333 | 415 |
| 4100 | 6' cap diameter | | 10 | 3.200 | | 310 | 116 | | 426 | 520 |
| 4150 | 7' cap diameter | | 9 | 3.556 | | 380 | 129 | | 509 | 620 |
| 4500 | For second and succeeding months, deduct | | | | | 50% | | | | |

# 03 11 Concrete Forming

## 03 11 13 – Structural Cast-In-Place Concrete Forming

### 03 11 13.25 Forms In Place, Columns

| | | Crew | Daily Output | Labor-Hours | Unit | Material | 2008 Bare Costs Labor | Equipment | Total | Total Incl O&P |
|---|---|---|---|---|---|---|---|---|---|---|
| 5000 | Job-built plywood, 8" x 8" columns, 1 use | C-1 | 165 | .194 | SFCA | 2.30 | 7 | | 9.30 | 13.45 |
| 5050 | 2 use | | 195 | .164 | | 1.32 | 5.95 | | 7.27 | 10.70 |
| 5100 | 3 use | | 210 | .152 | | .92 | 5.50 | | 6.42 | 9.55 |
| 5150 | 4 use | | 215 | .149 | | .75 | 5.40 | | 6.15 | 9.20 |
| 5500 | 12" x 12" columns, 1 use | | 180 | .178 | | 2.29 | 6.45 | | 8.74 | 12.50 |
| 5550 | 2 use | | 210 | .152 | | 1.26 | 5.50 | | 6.76 | 9.95 |
| 5600 | 3 use | | 220 | .145 | | .92 | 5.25 | | 6.17 | 9.20 |
| 5650 | 4 use | | 225 | .142 | | .74 | 5.15 | | 5.89 | 8.80 |
| 6000 | 16" x 16" columns, 1 use | | 185 | .173 | | 2.32 | 6.25 | | 8.57 | 12.30 |
| 6050 | 2 use | | 215 | .149 | | 1.22 | 5.40 | | 6.62 | 9.70 |
| 6100 | 3 use | | 230 | .139 | | .93 | 5.05 | | 5.98 | 8.85 |
| 6150 | 4 use | | 235 | .136 | | .76 | 4.92 | | 5.68 | 8.50 |
| 6500 | 24" x 24" columns, 1 use | | 190 | .168 | | 2.64 | 6.10 | | 8.74 | 12.35 |
| 6550 | 2 use | | 216 | .148 | | 1.45 | 5.35 | | 6.80 | 9.95 |
| 6600 | 3 use | | 230 | .139 | | 1.06 | 5.05 | | 6.11 | 8.95 |
| 6650 | 4 use | | 238 | .134 | | .86 | 4.86 | | 5.72 | 8.50 |
| 7000 | 36" x 36" columns, 1 use | | 200 | .160 | | 1.95 | 5.80 | | 7.75 | 11.15 |
| 7050 | 2 use | | 230 | .139 | | 1.10 | 5.05 | | 6.15 | 9 |
| 7100 | 3 use | | 245 | .131 | | .78 | 4.72 | | 5.50 | 8.20 |
| 7150 | 4 use | | 250 | .128 | | .63 | 4.63 | | 5.26 | 7.90 |
| 7500 | Steel framed plywood, 4 use per mo., rent, 8" x 8" | | 340 | .094 | | 3.52 | 3.40 | | 6.92 | 9.15 |
| 7550 | 10" x 10" | | 350 | .091 | | 2.45 | 3.30 | | 5.75 | 7.85 |
| 7600 | 12" x 12" | | 370 | .086 | | 3.27 | 3.13 | | 6.40 | 8.45 |
| 7650 | 16" x 16" | | 400 | .080 | | 3.62 | 2.89 | | 6.51 | 8.50 |
| 7700 | 20" x 20" | | 420 | .076 | | 1.65 | 2.75 | | 4.40 | 6.10 |
| 7750 | 24" x 24" | | 440 | .073 | | 1.58 | 2.63 | | 4.21 | 5.85 |
| 7755 | 30" x 30" | | 440 | .073 | | 1.40 | 2.63 | | 4.03 | 5.65 |

### 03 11 13.30 Forms In Place, Culvert

| | | | Crew | Daily Output | Labor-Hours | Unit | Material | Labor | Equipment | Total | Total Incl O&P |
|---|---|---|---|---|---|---|---|---|---|---|---|
| 0010 | **FORMS IN PLACE, CULVERT** | R031113-40 | | | | | | | | | |
| 0015 | 5' to 8' square or rectangular, 1 use | | C-1 | 170 | .188 | SFCA | 5.30 | 6.80 | | 12.10 | 16.45 |
| 0050 | 2 use | R031113-60 | | 180 | .178 | | 3.27 | 6.45 | | 9.72 | 13.60 |
| 0100 | 3 use | | | 190 | .168 | | 2.59 | 6.10 | | 8.69 | 12.30 |
| 0150 | 4 use | | | 200 | .160 | | 2.25 | 5.80 | | 8.05 | 11.50 |

### 03 11 13.35 Forms In Place, Elevated Slabs

| | | | Crew | Daily Output | Labor-Hours | Unit | Material | Labor | Equipment | Total | Total Incl O&P |
|---|---|---|---|---|---|---|---|---|---|---|---|
| 0010 | **FORMS IN PLACE, ELEVATED SLABS** | R031113-40 | | | | | | | | | |
| 1000 | Flat plate, job-built plywood, to 15' high, 1 use | R031113-60 | C-2 | 470 | .102 | S.F. | 4.36 | 3.79 | | 8.15 | 10.70 |
| 1050 | 2 use | | | 520 | .092 | | 2.40 | 3.43 | | 5.83 | 8 |
| 1100 | 3 use | | | 545 | .088 | | 1.75 | 3.27 | | 5.02 | 7 |
| 1150 | 4 use | | | 560 | .086 | | 1.42 | 3.18 | | 4.60 | 6.50 |
| 1500 | 15' to 20' high ceilings, 4 use | | | 495 | .097 | | 1.55 | 3.60 | | 5.15 | 7.30 |
| 1600 | 21' to 35' high ceilings, 4 use | | | 450 | .107 | | 2.24 | 3.96 | | 6.20 | 8.60 |
| 2000 | Flat slab, drop panels, job-built plywood, to 15' high, 1 use | | | 449 | .107 | | 4.84 | 3.97 | | 8.81 | 11.55 |
| 2050 | 2 use | | | 509 | .094 | | 2.66 | 3.50 | | 6.16 | 8.40 |
| 2100 | 3 use | | | 532 | .090 | | 1.94 | 3.35 | | 5.29 | 7.35 |
| 2150 | 4 use | | | 544 | .088 | | 1.57 | 3.28 | | 4.85 | 6.85 |
| 2250 | 15' to 20' high ceilings, 4 use | | | 480 | .100 | | 4.30 | 3.71 | | 8.01 | 10.55 |
| 2350 | 20' to 35' high ceilings, 4 use | | | 435 | .110 | | 4.98 | 4.10 | | 9.08 | 11.90 |
| 3000 | Floor slab hung from steel beams, 1 use | | | 485 | .099 | | 2.80 | 3.67 | | 6.47 | 8.80 |
| 3050 | 2 use | | | 535 | .090 | | 2.27 | 3.33 | | 5.60 | 7.70 |
| 3100 | 3 use | | | 550 | .087 | | 2.09 | 3.24 | | 5.33 | 7.35 |
| 3150 | 4 use | | | 565 | .085 | | 2 | 3.15 | | 5.15 | 7.10 |
| 3500 | Floor slab, with 20" metal pans, 1 use | | | 415 | .116 | | 6.15 | 4.29 | | 10.44 | 13.50 |

# 03 11 Concrete Forming

## 03 11 13 – Structural Cast-In-Place Concrete Forming

### 03 11 13.35 Forms In Place, Elevated Slabs

| | | Crew | Daily Output | Labor-Hours | Unit | Material | 2008 Bare Costs Labor | Equipment | Total | Total Incl O&P |
|---|---|---|---|---|---|---|---|---|---|---|
| 3550 | 2 use | C-2 | 445 | .108 | S.F. | 3.98 | 4.01 | | 7.99 | 10.65 |
| 3600 | 3 use | | 475 | .101 | | 3.26 | 3.75 | | 7.01 | 9.45 |
| 3650 | 4 use | | 500 | .096 | | 2.89 | 3.56 | | 6.45 | 8.75 |
| 3700 | Floor slab with 30" pans, 1 use | | 418 | .115 | | 6.10 | 4.26 | | 10.36 | 13.35 |
| 3720 | 2 use | | 455 | .105 | | 3.89 | 3.92 | | 7.81 | 10.40 |
| 3740 | 3 use | | 470 | .102 | | 3.16 | 3.79 | | 6.95 | 9.40 |
| 3760 | 4 use | | 480 | .100 | | 2.80 | 3.71 | | 6.51 | 8.90 |
| 4000 | Floor slab with 19" metal domes, 1 use | | 405 | .119 | | 6.55 | 4.40 | | 10.95 | 14.05 |
| 4050 | 2 use | | 435 | .110 | | 4.34 | 4.10 | | 8.44 | 11.20 |
| 4100 | 3 use | | 465 | .103 | | 3.61 | 3.83 | | 7.44 | 9.95 |
| 4150 | 4 use | | 495 | .097 | | 3.25 | 3.60 | | 6.85 | 9.15 |
| 4500 | With 30" fiberglass domes, 1 use | | 405 | .119 | | 6.35 | 4.40 | | 10.75 | 13.85 |
| 4520 | 2 use | | 450 | .107 | | 4.18 | 3.96 | | 8.14 | 10.75 |
| 4530 | 3 use | | 460 | .104 | | 3.45 | 3.87 | | 7.32 | 9.85 |
| 4550 | 4 use | | 470 | .102 | | 3.08 | 3.79 | | 6.87 | 9.30 |
| 5000 | Box out for slab openings, over 16" deep, 1 use | | 190 | .253 | SFCA | 3.91 | 9.40 | | 13.31 | 18.90 |
| 5050 | 2 use | | 240 | .200 | " | 2.15 | 7.45 | | 9.60 | 13.90 |
| 5500 | Shallow slab box outs, to 10 S.F. | | 42 | 1.143 | Ea. | 10.15 | 42.50 | | 52.65 | 77 |
| 5550 | Over 10 S.F. (use perimeter) | | 600 | .080 | L.F. | 1.36 | 2.97 | | 4.33 | 6.10 |
| 6000 | Bulkhead forms for slab, with keyway, 1 use, 2 piece | | 500 | .096 | | 1.82 | 3.56 | | 5.38 | 7.55 |
| 6100 | 3 piece (see also edge forms) | | 460 | .104 | | 1.98 | 3.87 | | 5.85 | 8.25 |
| 6200 | Slab bulkhead form, 4-1/2" high, exp metal, w/ keyway & stakes | C-1 | 1200 | .027 | | .76 | .96 | | 1.72 | 2.34 |
| 6210 | 5-1/2" high | | 1100 | .029 | | .83 | 1.05 | | 1.88 | 2.55 |
| 6215 | 7-1/2" high | | 960 | .033 | | 1.02 | 1.20 | | 2.22 | 2.99 |
| 6220 | 9-1/2" high | | 840 | .038 | | 1.95 | 1.38 | | 3.33 | 4.29 |
| 6500 | Curb forms, wood, 6" to 12" high, on elevated slabs, 1 use | | 180 | .178 | SFCA | 1.33 | 6.45 | | 7.78 | 11.45 |
| 6550 | 2 use | | 205 | .156 | | .73 | 5.65 | | 6.38 | 9.60 |
| 6600 | 3 use | | 220 | .145 | | .53 | 5.25 | | 5.78 | 8.80 |
| 6650 | 4 use | | 225 | .142 | | .43 | 5.15 | | 5.58 | 8.45 |
| 7000 | Edge forms to 6" high, on elevated slab, 4 use | | 500 | .064 | L.F. | .18 | 2.31 | | 2.49 | 3.80 |
| 7500 | Depressed area forms to 12" high, 4 use | | 300 | .107 | | .87 | 3.86 | | 4.73 | 6.95 |
| 7550 | 12" to 24" high, 4 use | | 175 | .183 | | 1.19 | 6.60 | | 7.79 | 11.60 |
| 8000 | Perimeter deck and rail for elevated slabs, straight | | 90 | .356 | | 13.35 | 12.85 | | 26.20 | 34.50 |
| 8050 | Curved | | 65 | .492 | | 18.30 | 17.80 | | 36.10 | 47.50 |
| 8500 | Void forms, round fiber, 3" diameter | | 450 | .071 | | .68 | 2.57 | | 3.25 | 4.75 |
| 8550 | 4" diameter | | 425 | .075 | | .95 | 2.72 | | 3.67 | 5.30 |
| 8600 | 6" diameter | | 400 | .080 | | 1.41 | 2.89 | | 4.30 | 6.05 |
| 8650 | 8" diameter | | 375 | .085 | | 2.02 | 3.08 | | 5.10 | 7 |
| 8700 | 10" diameter | | 350 | .091 | | 2.36 | 3.30 | | 5.66 | 7.75 |
| 8750 | 12" diameter | | 300 | .107 | | 2.91 | 3.86 | | 6.77 | 9.20 |

### 03 11 13.40 Forms In Place, Equipment Foundations

| | | Crew | Daily Output | Labor-Hours | Unit | Material | 2008 Bare Costs Labor | Equipment | Total | Total Incl O&P |
|---|---|---|---|---|---|---|---|---|---|---|
| 0010 | **FORMS IN PLACE, EQUIPMENT FOUNDATIONS** R031113-40 | | | | | | | | | |
| 0020 | 1 use | C-2 | 160 | .300 | SFCA | 2.94 | 11.15 | | 14.09 | 20.50 |
| 0050 | 2 use R031113-60 | | 190 | .253 | | 1.62 | 9.40 | | 11.02 | 16.40 |
| 0100 | 3 use | | 200 | .240 | | 1.18 | 8.90 | | 10.08 | 15.15 |
| 0150 | 4 use | | 205 | .234 | | .96 | 8.70 | | 9.66 | 14.60 |

### 03 11 13.45 Forms In Place, Footings

| | | Crew | Daily Output | Labor-Hours | Unit | Material | 2008 Bare Costs Labor | Equipment | Total | Total Incl O&P |
|---|---|---|---|---|---|---|---|---|---|---|
| 0010 | **FORMS IN PLACE, FOOTINGS** R031113-40 | | | | | | | | | |
| 0020 | Continuous wall, plywood, 1 use | C-1 | 375 | .085 | SFCA | 5.25 | 3.08 | | 8.33 | 10.60 |
| 0050 | 2 use R031113-60 | | 440 | .073 | | 2.89 | 2.63 | | 5.52 | 7.25 |
| 0100 | 3 use | | 470 | .068 | | 2.10 | 2.46 | | 4.56 | 6.15 |
| 0150 | 4 use | | 485 | .066 | | 1.71 | 2.38 | | 4.09 | 5.60 |

# 03 11 Concrete Forming

## 03 11 13 – Structural Cast-In-Place Concrete Forming

### 03 11 13.45 Forms In Place, Footings

| | | Crew | Daily Output | Labor-Hours | Unit | Material | 2008 Bare Costs Labor | Equipment | Total | Total Incl O&P |
|---|---|---|---|---|---|---|---|---|---|---|
| 0500 | Dowel supports for footings or beams, 1 use | C-1 | 500 | .064 | L.F. | .79 | 2.31 | | 3.10 | 4.47 |
| 1000 | Integral starter wall, to 4" high, 1 use | ↓ | 400 | .080 | | .82 | 2.89 | | 3.71 | 5.40 |
| 1500 | Keyway, 4 use, tapered wood, 2" x 4" | 1 Carp | 530 | .015 | | .19 | .57 | | .76 | 1.10 |
| 1550 | 2" x 6" | | 500 | .016 | | .27 | .61 | | .88 | 1.25 |
| 2000 | Tapered plastic, 2" x 3" | | 530 | .015 | | .70 | .57 | | 1.27 | 1.66 |
| 2050 | 2" x 4" | | 500 | .016 | | .90 | .61 | | 1.51 | 1.94 |
| 2250 | For keyway hung from supports, add | ↓ | 150 | .053 | ↓ | .79 | 2.03 | | 2.82 | 4.03 |
| 3000 | Pile cap, square or rectangular, job-built plywood, 1 use | C-1 | 290 | .110 | SFCA | 2.65 | 3.99 | | 6.64 | 9.10 |
| 3050 | 2 use | | 346 | .092 | | 1.46 | 3.34 | | 4.80 | 6.80 |
| 3100 | 3 use | | 371 | .086 | | 1.06 | 3.12 | | 4.18 | 6 |
| 3150 | 4 use | | 383 | .084 | | .86 | 3.02 | | 3.88 | 5.65 |
| 4000 | Triangular or hexagonal, 1 use | | 225 | .142 | | 3.11 | 5.15 | | 8.26 | 11.40 |
| 4050 | 2 use | | 280 | .114 | | 1.71 | 4.13 | | 5.84 | 8.35 |
| 4100 | 3 use | | 305 | .105 | | 1.24 | 3.79 | | 5.03 | 7.25 |
| 4150 | 4 use | | 315 | .102 | | 1.01 | 3.67 | | 4.68 | 6.80 |
| 5000 | Spread footings, job-built lumber, 1 use | | 305 | .105 | | 1.95 | 3.79 | | 5.74 | 8.05 |
| 5050 | 2 use | | 371 | .086 | | 1.08 | 3.12 | | 4.20 | 6.05 |
| 5100 | 3 use | | 401 | .080 | | .78 | 2.88 | | 3.66 | 5.35 |
| 5150 | 4 use | | 414 | .077 | | .63 | 2.79 | | 3.42 | 5.05 |
| 6000 | Supports for dowels, plinths or templates, 2' x 2' footing | | 25 | 1.280 | Ea. | 5.90 | 46.50 | | 52.40 | 78.50 |
| 6050 | 4' x 4' footing | | 22 | 1.455 | | 11.80 | 52.50 | | 64.30 | 95 |
| 6100 | 8' x 8' footing | | 20 | 1.600 | | 23.50 | 58 | | 81.50 | 116 |
| 6150 | 12' x 12' footing | | 17 | 1.882 | ↓ | 28.50 | 68 | | 96.50 | 138 |
| 7000 | Plinths, job-built plywood, 1 use | | 250 | .128 | SFCA | 2.98 | 4.63 | | 7.61 | 10.50 |
| 7100 | 4 use | ↓ | 270 | .119 | " | .98 | 4.28 | | 5.26 | 7.75 |

### 03 11 13.47 Forms In Place, Gas Station Forms

| | | Crew | Daily Output | Labor-Hours | Unit | Material | 2008 Bare Costs Labor | Equipment | Total | Total Incl O&P |
|---|---|---|---|---|---|---|---|---|---|---|
| 0010 | **FORMS IN PLACE, GAS STATION FORMS** | | | | | | | | | |
| 0050 | Curb fascia, with template, 12 ga. steel, left in place, 9" high | 1 Carp | 50 | .160 | L.F. | 11.55 | 6.10 | | 17.65 | 22 |
| 1000 | Sign or light bases, 18" diameter, 9" high | | 9 | .889 | Ea. | 72.50 | 34 | | 106.50 | 133 |
| 1050 | 30" diameter, 13" high | ↓ | 8 | 1 | | 115 | 38 | | 153 | 187 |
| 2000 | Island forms, 10' long, 9" high, 3'- 6" wide | C-1 | 10 | 3.200 | | 320 | 116 | | 436 | 535 |
| 2050 | 4' wide | | 9 | 3.556 | | 335 | 129 | | 464 | 565 |
| 2500 | 20' long, 9" high, 4' wide | | 6 | 5.333 | | 535 | 193 | | 728 | 890 |
| 2550 | 5' wide | ↓ | 5 | 6.400 | ↓ | 555 | 231 | | 786 | 975 |

### 03 11 13.50 Forms In Place, Grade Beam

| | | Crew | Daily Output | Labor-Hours | Unit | Material | 2008 Bare Costs Labor | Equipment | Total | Total Incl O&P |
|---|---|---|---|---|---|---|---|---|---|---|
| 0010 | **FORMS IN PLACE, GRADE BEAM** | R031113-40 | | | | | | | | |
| 0020 | Job-built plywood, 1 use | C-2 | 530 | .091 | SFCA | 2.53 | 3.36 | | 5.89 | 8.05 |
| 0050 | 2 use | R031113-60 | 580 | .083 | | 1.39 | 3.07 | | 4.46 | 6.30 |
| 0100 | 3 use | | 600 | .080 | | 1.01 | 2.97 | | 3.98 | 5.75 |
| 0150 | 4 use | ↓ | 605 | .079 | ↓ | .82 | 2.95 | | 3.77 | 5.50 |

### 03 11 13.55 Forms In Place, Mat Foundation

| | | Crew | Daily Output | Labor-Hours | Unit | Material | 2008 Bare Costs Labor | Equipment | Total | Total Incl O&P |
|---|---|---|---|---|---|---|---|---|---|---|
| 0010 | **FORMS IN PLACE, MAT FOUNDATION** | R031113-40 | | | | | | | | |
| 0020 | Job-built plywood, 1 use | C-2 | 290 | .166 | SFCA | 2.82 | 6.15 | | 8.97 | 12.65 |
| 0050 | 2 use | R031113-60 | 310 | .155 | | 1.07 | 5.75 | | 6.82 | 10.15 |
| 0100 | 3 use | | 330 | .145 | | .71 | 5.40 | | 6.11 | 9.20 |
| 0120 | 4 use | ↓ | 350 | .137 | ↓ | .63 | 5.10 | | 5.73 | 8.60 |

### 03 11 13.65 Forms In Place, Slab On Grade

| | | Crew | Daily Output | Labor-Hours | Unit | Material | 2008 Bare Costs Labor | Equipment | Total | Total Incl O&P |
|---|---|---|---|---|---|---|---|---|---|---|
| 0010 | **FORMS IN PLACE, SLAB ON GRADE** | R031113-40 | | | | | | | | |
| 1000 | Bulkhead forms w/keyway, wood, 6" high, 1 use | C-1 | 510 | .063 | L.F. | .87 | 2.27 | | 3.14 | 4.49 |
| 1050 | 2 uses | R031113-60 | 400 | .080 | | .48 | 2.89 | | 3.37 | 5.05 |
| 1100 | 4 uses | | 350 | .091 | | .28 | 3.30 | | 3.58 | 5.45 |
| 1400 | Bulkhead form for slab, 4-1/2" high, exp metal, incl keyway & stakes | | 1200 | .027 | ↓ | .76 | .96 | | 1.72 | 2.34 |

# 03 11 Concrete Forming

## 03 11 13 – Structural Cast-In-Place Concrete Forming

### 03 11 13.65 Forms In Place, Slab On Grade

| | | Crew | Daily Output | Labor-Hours | Unit | Material | 2008 Bare Costs Labor | Equipment | Total | Total Incl O&P |
|---|---|---|---|---|---|---|---|---|---|---|
| 1410 | 5-1/2" high | C-1 | 1100 | .029 | L.F. | .83 | 1.05 | | 1.88 | 2.55 |
| 1420 | 7-1/2" high | | 960 | .033 | | 1.02 | 1.20 | | 2.22 | 2.99 |
| 1430 | 9-1/2" high | | 840 | .038 | ↓ | 1.95 | 1.38 | | 3.33 | 4.29 |
| 2000 | Curb forms, wood, 6" to 12" high, on grade, 1 use | | 215 | .149 | SFCA | 2.32 | 5.40 | | 7.72 | 10.90 |
| 2050 | 2 use | | 250 | .128 | | 1.28 | 4.63 | | 5.91 | 8.60 |
| 2100 | 3 use | | 265 | .121 | | .93 | 4.36 | | 5.29 | 7.80 |
| 2150 | 4 use | | 275 | .116 | ↓ | .75 | 4.21 | | 4.96 | 7.40 |
| 3000 | Edge forms, wood, 4 use, on grade, to 6" high | | 600 | .053 | L.F. | .32 | 1.93 | | 2.25 | 3.35 |
| 3050 | 7" to 12" high | | 435 | .074 | SFCA | .70 | 2.66 | | 3.36 | 4.91 |
| 3500 | For depressed slabs, 4 use, to 12" high | | 300 | .107 | L.F. | .60 | 3.86 | | 4.46 | 6.65 |
| 3550 | To 24" high | | 175 | .183 | | .77 | 6.60 | | 7.37 | 11.15 |
| 4000 | For slab blockouts, to 12" high, 1 use | | 200 | .160 | | .60 | 5.80 | | 6.40 | 9.65 |
| 4050 | To 24" high, 1 use | | 120 | .267 | | .75 | 9.65 | | 10.40 | 15.85 |
| 4100 | Plastic (extruded), to 6" high, multiple use, on grade | ↓ | 800 | .040 | ↓ | .40 | 1.45 | | 1.85 | 2.69 |
| 5000 | Screed, 24 ga. metal key joint, see Div. 03 15 05.25 | | | | | | | | | |
| 5020 | Wood, incl. wood stakes, 1" x 3" | C-1 | 900 | .036 | L.F. | .34 | 1.29 | | 1.63 | 2.38 |
| 5050 | 2" x 4" | | 900 | .036 | " | .52 | 1.29 | | 1.81 | 2.58 |
| 6000 | Trench forms in floor, wood, 1 use | | 160 | .200 | SFCA | 1.63 | 7.25 | | 8.88 | 13.05 |
| 6050 | 2 use | | 175 | .183 | | .89 | 6.60 | | 7.49 | 11.30 |
| 6100 | 3 use | | 180 | .178 | | .65 | 6.45 | | 7.10 | 10.70 |
| 6150 | 4 use | | 185 | .173 | ↓ | .53 | 6.25 | | 6.78 | 10.35 |
| 8760 | Void form, corrugated fiberboard, 6" x 12", 10' long | ↓ | 240 | .133 | S.F. | .91 | 4.82 | | 5.73 | 8.50 |

### 03 11 13.85 Forms In Place, Walls

| | | | Crew | Daily Output | Labor-Hours | Unit | Material | 2008 Bare Costs Labor | Equipment | Total | Total Incl O&P |
|---|---|---|---|---|---|---|---|---|---|---|---|
| 0010 | **FORMS IN PLACE, WALLS** | R031113-10 | | | | | | | | | |
| 0100 | Box out for wall openings, to 16" thick, to 10 S.F. | | C-2 | 24 | 2 | Ea. | 23 | 74.50 | | 97.50 | 142 |
| 0150 | Over 10 S.F. (use perimeter) | R031113-40 | " | 280 | .171 | L.F. | 1.98 | 6.35 | | 8.33 | 12.10 |
| 0250 | Brick shelf, 4" w, add to wall forms, use wall area abv shelf | | | | | | | | | | |
| 0260 | 1 use | R031113-60 | C-2 | 240 | .200 | SFCA | 2.13 | 7.45 | | 9.58 | 13.90 |
| 0300 | 2 use | | | 275 | .175 | | 1.17 | 6.50 | | 7.67 | 11.40 |
| 0350 | 4 use | | | 300 | .160 | ↓ | .85 | 5.95 | | 6.80 | 10.20 |
| 0500 | Bulkhead, with keyway, 1 use, 2 piece | | | 265 | .181 | L.F. | 3.49 | 6.75 | | 10.24 | 14.30 |
| 0550 | 3 piece | | ↓ | 175 | .274 | | 4.40 | 10.20 | | 14.60 | 20.50 |
| 0600 | Bulkhead forms with keyway, 1 piece expanded metal, 8" wall | | C-1 | 1000 | .032 | | 1.02 | 1.16 | | 2.18 | 2.92 |
| 0610 | 10" wall | | | 800 | .040 | | 1.95 | 1.45 | | 3.40 | 4.40 |
| 0620 | 12" wall | | ↓ | 525 | .061 | ↓ | 2.29 | 2.20 | | 4.49 | 5.95 |
| 0700 | Buttress, to 8' high, 1 use | | C-2 | 350 | .137 | SFCA | 5.40 | 5.10 | | 10.50 | 13.85 |
| 0750 | 2 use | | | 430 | .112 | | 2.96 | 4.14 | | 7.10 | 9.70 |
| 0800 | 3 use | | | 460 | .104 | | 2.16 | 3.87 | | 6.03 | 8.45 |
| 0850 | 4 use | | | 480 | .100 | ↓ | 1.78 | 3.71 | | 5.49 | 7.75 |
| 1000 | Corbel or haunch, to 12" wide, add to wall forms, 1 use | | | 150 | .320 | L.F. | 2.20 | 11.90 | | 14.10 | 21 |
| 1050 | 2 use | | | 170 | .282 | | 1.21 | 10.50 | | 11.71 | 17.65 |
| 1100 | 3 use | | | 175 | .274 | | .88 | 10.20 | | 11.08 | 16.80 |
| 1150 | 4 use | | | 180 | .267 | ↓ | .72 | 9.90 | | 10.62 | 16.20 |
| 2000 | Wall, job-built plywood, to 8' high, 1 use | | | 370 | .130 | SFCA | 2.70 | 4.82 | | 7.52 | 10.50 |
| 2050 | 2 use | | | 435 | .110 | | 1.69 | 4.10 | | 5.79 | 8.25 |
| 2100 | 3 use | | | 495 | .097 | | 1.23 | 3.60 | | 4.83 | 6.95 |
| 2150 | 4 use | | | 505 | .095 | | 1 | 3.53 | | 4.53 | 6.60 |
| 2400 | Over 8' to 16' high, 1 use | | | 280 | .171 | | 7.20 | 6.35 | | 13.55 | 17.80 |
| 2450 | 2 use | | | 345 | .139 | | 1.31 | 5.15 | | 6.46 | 9.50 |
| 2500 | 3 use | | | 375 | .128 | | .94 | 4.75 | | 5.69 | 8.45 |
| 2550 | 4 use | | | 395 | .122 | | .77 | 4.51 | | 5.28 | 7.85 |
| 2700 | Over 16' high, 1 use | | ↓ | 235 | .204 | ↓ | 2.66 | 7.60 | | 10.26 | 14.75 |

47

# 03 11 Concrete Forming

## 03 11 13 – Structural Cast-In-Place Concrete Forming

| 03 11 13.85 Forms In Place, Walls | | Crew | Daily Output | Labor-Hours | Unit | Material | 2008 Bare Costs Labor | Equipment | Total | Total Incl O&P |
|---|---|---|---|---|---|---|---|---|---|---|
| 2750 | 2 use | C-2 | 290 | .166 | SFCA | 1.46 | 6.15 | | 7.61 | 11.15 |
| 2800 | 3 use | | 315 | .152 | | 1.06 | 5.65 | | 6.71 | 9.95 |
| 2850 | 4 use | | 330 | .145 | | .86 | 5.40 | | 6.26 | 9.35 |
| 3000 | For architectural finish, add | | 1820 | .026 | | 3.18 | .98 | | 4.16 | 5 |
| 4000 | Radial, smooth curved, job-built plywood, 1 use | | 245 | .196 | | 2.52 | 7.25 | | 9.77 | 14.05 |
| 4050 | 2 use | | 300 | .160 | | 1.39 | 5.95 | | 7.34 | 10.75 |
| 4100 | 3 use | | 325 | .148 | | 1.01 | 5.50 | | 6.51 | 9.65 |
| 4150 | 4 use | | 335 | .143 | | .83 | 5.30 | | 6.13 | 9.20 |
| 4200 | Below grade, job-built plywood, 1 use | | 225 | .213 | | 3.79 | 7.90 | | 11.69 | 16.50 |
| 4210 | 2 use | | 225 | .213 | | 2.10 | 7.90 | | 10 | 14.65 |
| 4220 | 3 use | | 225 | .213 | | 1.65 | 7.90 | | 9.55 | 14.15 |
| 4230 | 4 use | | 225 | .213 | | 1.23 | 7.90 | | 9.13 | 13.70 |
| 4300 | Curved, 2' chords, job-built plywood, 1 use | | 290 | .166 | | 2.09 | 6.15 | | 8.24 | 11.85 |
| 4350 | 2 use | | 355 | .135 | | 1.15 | 5 | | 6.15 | 9.05 |
| 4400 | 3 use | | 385 | .125 | | .84 | 4.63 | | 5.47 | 8.10 |
| 4450 | 4 use | | 400 | .120 | | .68 | 4.46 | | 5.14 | 7.70 |
| 4500 | Over 8' high, 1 use | | 290 | .166 | | .87 | 6.15 | | 7.02 | 10.50 |
| 4525 | 2 use | | 355 | .135 | | .48 | 5 | | 5.48 | 8.35 |
| 4550 | 3 use | | 385 | .125 | | .35 | 4.63 | | 4.98 | 7.60 |
| 4575 | 4 use | | 400 | .120 | | .29 | 4.46 | | 4.75 | 7.25 |
| 4600 | Retaining wall, battered, job-built plyw'd, to 8' high, 1 use | | 300 | .160 | | 1.98 | 5.95 | | 7.93 | 11.45 |
| 4650 | 2 use | | 355 | .135 | | 1.09 | 5 | | 6.09 | 9 |
| 4700 | 3 use | | 375 | .128 | | .79 | 4.75 | | 5.54 | 8.25 |
| 4750 | 4 use | | 390 | .123 | | .55 | 4.57 | | 5.12 | 7.70 |
| 4900 | Over 8' to 16' high, 1 use | | 240 | .200 | | 2.14 | 7.45 | | 9.59 | 13.90 |
| 4950 | 2 use | | 295 | .163 | | 1.18 | 6.05 | | 7.23 | 10.70 |
| 5000 | 3 use | | 305 | .157 | | .86 | 5.85 | | 6.71 | 10.05 |
| 5050 | 4 use | ▼ | 320 | .150 | | .70 | 5.55 | | 6.25 | 9.40 |
| 5500 | For gang wall forming, 192 S.F. sections, deduct | | | | | 10% | 10% | | | |
| 5550 | 384 S.F. sections, deduct | | | | ▼ | 20% | 20% | | | |
| 5750 | Liners for forms (add to wall forms), A.B.S. plastic | | | | | | | | | |
| 5800 | Aged wood, 4" wide, 1 use | 1 Carp | 256 | .031 | SFCA | 3.04 | 1.19 | | 4.23 | 5.20 |
| 5820 | 2 use | | 256 | .031 | | 1.67 | 1.19 | | 2.86 | 3.69 |
| 5830 | 3 use | | 256 | .031 | | 1.22 | 1.19 | | 2.41 | 3.19 |
| 5840 | 4 use | | 256 | .031 | | .99 | 1.19 | | 2.18 | 2.94 |
| 5900 | Fractured rope rib, 1 use | | 192 | .042 | | 5.40 | 1.59 | | 6.99 | 8.40 |
| 5925 | 2 use | | 192 | .042 | | 2.98 | 1.59 | | 4.57 | 5.75 |
| 5950 | 3 use | | 192 | .042 | | 2.16 | 1.59 | | 3.75 | 4.85 |
| 6000 | 4 use | | 192 | .042 | | 1.76 | 1.59 | | 3.35 | 4.40 |
| 6100 | Ribbed, 3/4" deep x 1-1/2" O.C., 1 use | | 224 | .036 | | 3.18 | 1.36 | | 4.54 | 5.60 |
| 6125 | 2 use | | 224 | .036 | | 1.75 | 1.36 | | 3.11 | 4.04 |
| 6150 | 3 use | | 224 | .036 | | 1.27 | 1.36 | | 2.63 | 3.52 |
| 6200 | 4 use | | 224 | .036 | | 1.03 | 1.36 | | 2.39 | 3.26 |
| 6300 | Rustic brick pattern, 1 use | | 224 | .036 | | 3.42 | 1.36 | | 4.78 | 5.90 |
| 6325 | 2 use | | 224 | .036 | | 1.88 | 1.36 | | 3.24 | 4.19 |
| 6350 | 3 use | | 224 | .036 | | 1.37 | 1.36 | | 2.73 | 3.62 |
| 6400 | 4 use | | 224 | .036 | | 1.11 | 1.36 | | 2.47 | 3.34 |
| 6500 | 3/8" striated, random, 1 use | | 224 | .036 | | 2.90 | 1.36 | | 4.26 | 5.30 |
| 6525 | 2 use | | 224 | .036 | | 1.60 | 1.36 | | 2.96 | 3.87 |
| 6550 | 3 use | | 224 | .036 | | 1.16 | 1.36 | | 2.52 | 3.40 |
| 6600 | 4 use | | 224 | .036 | | .94 | 1.36 | | 2.30 | 3.16 |
| 6850 | Random vertical rustication, 1 use | | 384 | .021 | | 4.97 | .79 | | 5.76 | 6.70 |
| 6900 | 2 use | ▼ | 384 | .021 | ▼ | 2.73 | .79 | | 3.52 | 4.25 |

# 03 11 Concrete Forming

## 03 11 13 – Structural Cast-In-Place Concrete Forming

### 03 11 13.85 Forms In Place, Walls

| | | Crew | Daily Output | Labor-Hours | Unit | Material | 2008 Bare Costs Labor | Equipment | Total | Total Incl O&P |
|---|---|---|---|---|---|---|---|---|---|---|
| 6925 | 3 use | 1 Carp | 384 | .021 | SFCA | 1.99 | .79 | | 2.78 | 3.43 |
| 6950 | 4 use | | 384 | .021 | ↓ | 1.62 | .79 | | 2.41 | 3.02 |
| 7050 | Wood, beveled edge, 3/4" deep, 1 use | | 384 | .021 | L.F. | .08 | .79 | | .87 | 1.33 |
| 7100 | 1" deep, 1 use | | 384 | .021 | " | .13 | .79 | | .92 | 1.38 |
| 7200 | 4" wide aged cedar, 1 use | | 256 | .031 | SFCA | 3.04 | 1.19 | | 4.23 | 5.20 |
| 7300 | 4" variable depth rough cedar | | 224 | .036 | | 4.41 | 1.36 | | 5.77 | 6.95 |
| 7500 | Lintel or sill forms, 1 use | | 30 | .267 | | 2.97 | 10.15 | | 13.12 | 19.05 |
| 7520 | 2 use | | 34 | .235 | | 1.63 | 8.95 | | 10.58 | 15.75 |
| 7540 | 3 use | | 36 | .222 | | 1.19 | 8.45 | | 9.64 | 14.50 |
| 7560 | 4 use | ↓ | 37 | .216 | | .96 | 8.25 | | 9.21 | 13.85 |
| 7800 | Modular prefabricated plywood, to 8' high, 1 use | C-2 | 1180 | .041 | | 2.11 | 1.51 | | 3.62 | 4.67 |
| 7820 | 2 use | | 1200 | .040 | | 1.16 | 1.49 | | 2.65 | 3.59 |
| 7840 | 3 use | | 1240 | .039 | | .84 | 1.44 | | 2.28 | 3.17 |
| 7860 | 4 use | | 1260 | .038 | | .70 | 1.41 | | 2.11 | 2.97 |
| 8000 | To 16' high, 1 use | | 715 | .067 | | 2.78 | 2.49 | | 5.27 | 6.95 |
| 8020 | 2 use | | 740 | .065 | | 1.53 | 2.41 | | 3.94 | 5.45 |
| 8040 | 3 use | | 770 | .062 | | 1.11 | 2.31 | | 3.42 | 4.82 |
| 8060 | 4 use | | 790 | .061 | | .92 | 2.26 | | 3.18 | 4.52 |
| 8100 | Over 16' high, 1 use | | 715 | .067 | | 3.34 | 2.49 | | 5.83 | 7.55 |
| 8120 | 2 use | | 740 | .065 | | 1.83 | 2.41 | | 4.24 | 5.75 |
| 8140 | 3 use | | 770 | .062 | | 1.33 | 2.31 | | 3.64 | 5.05 |
| 8160 | 4 use | | 790 | .061 | | 1.11 | 2.26 | | 3.37 | 4.73 |
| 8600 | Pilasters, 1 use | | 270 | .178 | | 3.15 | 6.60 | | 9.75 | 13.70 |
| 8620 | 2 use | | 330 | .145 | | 1.73 | 5.40 | | 7.13 | 10.30 |
| 8640 | 3 use | | 370 | .130 | | 1.26 | 4.82 | | 6.08 | 8.90 |
| 8660 | 4 use | ↓ | 385 | .125 | ↓ | 1.02 | 4.63 | | 5.65 | 8.35 |
| 9010 | Steel framed plywood, based on 100 uses of purchased | | | | | | | | | |
| 9020 | forms, and 4 uses of bracing lumber | | | | | | | | | |
| 9060 | To 8' high | C-2 | 600 | .080 | SFCA | .37 | 2.97 | | 3.34 | 5 |
| 9260 | Over 8' to 16' high | | 450 | .107 | | .37 | 3.96 | | 4.33 | 6.55 |
| 9460 | Over 16' to 20' high | ↓ | 400 | .120 | ↓ | .37 | 4.46 | | 4.83 | 7.35 |
| 9475 | For elevated walls, add | | | | | | 10% | | | |
| 9480 | For battered walls, 1 side battered, add | | | | | 10% | 10% | | | |
| 9485 | For battered walls, 2 sides battered, add | | | | | 15% | 15% | | | |

## 03 11 19 – Insulating Concrete Forming

### 03 11 19.10 Insulating Forms, Left In Place

| | | Crew | Daily Output | Labor-Hours | Unit | Material | 2008 Bare Costs Labor | Equipment | Total | Total Incl O&P |
|---|---|---|---|---|---|---|---|---|---|---|
| 0010 | **INSULATING FORMS, LEFT IN PLACE** | | | | | | | | | |
| 0020 | Forms left in place, S.F. is for one face, but incl. forms for both faces | | | | | | | | | |
| 1000 | Panel system, flat cavity, minimum | 2 Carp | 960 | .017 | S.F. | 2.40 | .64 | | 3.04 | 3.63 |
| 1010 | Maximum | | 960 | .017 | | 3.60 | .64 | | 4.24 | 4.95 |
| 1020 | Grid cavity, minimum | | 960 | .017 | | 2.40 | .64 | | 3.04 | 3.63 |
| 1030 | Maximum | | 960 | .017 | | 3.60 | .64 | | 4.24 | 4.95 |
| 1040 | Post and beam cavity, minimum | | 960 | .017 | | 2.48 | .64 | | 3.12 | 3.72 |
| 1050 | Maximum | | 960 | .017 | | 3.72 | .64 | | 4.36 | 5.10 |
| 1060 | Plank system, flat cavity, minimum | | 1920 | .008 | | 2.80 | .32 | | 3.12 | 3.57 |
| 1070 | Maximum | | 1920 | .008 | | 4.20 | .32 | | 4.52 | 5.10 |
| 1120 | Block system, flat cavity, minimum | | 480 | .033 | | 2.72 | 1.27 | | 3.99 | 4.97 |
| 1130 | Maximum | | 480 | .033 | | 4.08 | 1.27 | | 5.35 | 6.45 |
| 1140 | Grid cavity, minimum | | 480 | .033 | | 2.68 | 1.27 | | 3.95 | 4.93 |
| 1150 | Maximum | | 480 | .033 | | 4.02 | 1.27 | | 5.29 | 6.40 |
| 1160 | Post and beam cavity, minimum | | 480 | .033 | | 2.68 | 1.27 | | 3.95 | 4.93 |
| 1170 | Maximum | ↓ | 480 | .033 | ↓ | 4.02 | 1.27 | | 5.29 | 6.40 |

# 03 11 Concrete Forming

## 03 11 19 – Insulating Concrete Forming

| 03 11 19.60 Roof Deck Form Boards | | Crew | Daily Output | Labor-Hours | Unit | Material | 2008 Bare Costs Labor | Equipment | Total | Total Incl O&P |
|---|---|---|---|---|---|---|---|---|---|---|
| 0010 | **ROOF DECK FORM BOARDS** R051223-50 | | | | | | | | | |
| 0050 | Non-asbestos fiber cement, 1/8" thick | C-13 | 2950 | .008 | S.F. | 2.33 | .34 | .04 | 2.71 | 3.19 |
| 0070 | 1/4" thick | | 2950 | .008 | | 2.67 | .34 | .04 | 3.05 | 3.56 |
| 0100 | Fiberglass, 1" thick, economy | | 2700 | .009 | | 2.88 | .37 | .05 | 3.30 | 3.85 |

## 03 11 23 – Permanent Stair Forming

### 03 11 23.75 Forms In Place, Stairs

| | | Crew | Daily Output | Labor-Hours | Unit | Material | 2008 Bare Costs Labor | Equipment | Total | Total Incl O&P |
|---|---|---|---|---|---|---|---|---|---|---|
| 0010 | **FORMS IN PLACE, STAIRS** R031113-40 | C-2 | 165 | .291 | S.F. | 5.30 | 10.80 | | 16.10 | 22.50 |
| 0015 | (Slant length x width), 1 use | | | | | | | | | |
| 0050 | 2 use R031113-60 | | 170 | .282 | | 3.16 | 10.50 | | 13.66 | 19.75 |
| 0100 | 3 use | | 180 | .267 | | 2.44 | 9.90 | | 12.34 | 18.10 |
| 0150 | 4 use | | 190 | .253 | | 2.08 | 9.40 | | 11.48 | 16.90 |
| 1000 | Alternate pricing method (1.0 L.F./S.F.), 1 use | | 100 | .480 | LF Rsr | 5.30 | 17.80 | | 23.10 | 33.50 |
| 1050 | 2 use | | 105 | .457 | | 3.16 | 16.95 | | 20.11 | 30 |
| 1100 | 3 use | | 110 | .436 | | 2.44 | 16.20 | | 18.64 | 27.50 |
| 1150 | 4 use | | 115 | .417 | | 2.08 | 15.50 | | 17.58 | 26.50 |
| 2000 | Stairs, cast on sloping ground (length x width), 1 use | | 220 | .218 | S.F. | 1.94 | 8.10 | | 10.04 | 14.75 |
| 2025 | 2 use | | 232 | .207 | | 1.06 | 7.70 | | 8.76 | 13.10 |
| 2050 | 3 use | | 244 | .197 | | .77 | 7.30 | | 8.07 | 12.20 |
| 2100 | 4 use | | 256 | .188 | | .63 | 6.95 | | 7.58 | 11.55 |

# 03 15 Concrete Accessories

## 03 15 05 – Concrete Forming Accessories

### 03 15 05.02 Anchor Bolts

| | | Crew | Daily Output | Labor-Hours | Unit | Material | 2008 Bare Costs Labor | Equipment | Total | Total Incl O&P |
|---|---|---|---|---|---|---|---|---|---|---|
| 0010 | **ANCHOR BOLTS** | | | | | | | | | |
| 0015 | J-type, plain, incl. nut and washer | | | | | | | | | |
| 0020 | 1/2" diameter, 6" long | 1 Carp | 90 | .089 | Ea. | 1.14 | 3.39 | | 4.53 | 6.50 |
| 0050 | 10" long | | 85 | .094 | | 1.30 | 3.59 | | 4.89 | 7.05 |
| 0100 | 12" long | | 85 | .094 | | 1.43 | 3.59 | | 5.02 | 7.15 |
| 0200 | 5/8" diameter, 12" long | | 80 | .100 | | 1.43 | 3.81 | | 5.24 | 7.55 |
| 0250 | 18" long | | 70 | .114 | | 1.69 | 4.35 | | 6.04 | 8.65 |
| 0300 | 24" long | | 60 | .133 | | 1.94 | 5.10 | | 7.04 | 10.05 |
| 0350 | 3/4" diameter, 8" long | | 80 | .100 | | 1.69 | 3.81 | | 5.50 | 7.80 |
| 0400 | 12" long | | 70 | .114 | | 2.11 | 4.35 | | 6.46 | 9.10 |
| 0450 | 18" long | | 60 | .133 | | 2.74 | 5.10 | | 7.84 | 10.90 |
| 0500 | 24" long | | 50 | .160 | | 3.59 | 6.10 | | 9.69 | 13.45 |
| 0600 | 7/8" diameter, 12" long | | 60 | .133 | | 2.79 | 5.10 | | 7.89 | 10.95 |
| 0650 | 18" long | | 50 | .160 | | 3.74 | 6.10 | | 9.84 | 13.60 |
| 0700 | 24" long | | 40 | .200 | | 3.85 | 7.60 | | 11.45 | 16.10 |
| 0800 | 1" diameter, 12" long | | 55 | .145 | | 4.03 | 5.55 | | 9.58 | 13.10 |
| 0850 | 18" long | | 45 | .178 | | 4.86 | 6.75 | | 11.61 | 15.90 |
| 0900 | 24" long | | 35 | .229 | | 5.95 | 8.70 | | 14.65 | 20 |
| 0950 | 36" long | | 25 | .320 | | 8.10 | 12.20 | | 20.30 | 28 |
| 1200 | 1-1/2" diameter, 18" long | | 22 | .364 | | 14.35 | 13.85 | | 28.20 | 37.50 |
| 1250 | 24" long | | 18 | .444 | | 17.10 | 16.95 | | 34.05 | 45.50 |
| 1300 | 36" long | | 12 | .667 | | 21.50 | 25.50 | | 47 | 63 |

### 03 15 05.12 Chamfer Strips

| | | Crew | Daily Output | Labor-Hours | Unit | Material | 2008 Bare Costs Labor | Equipment | Total | Total Incl O&P |
|---|---|---|---|---|---|---|---|---|---|---|
| 0010 | **CHAMFER STRIPS** | | | | | | | | | |
| 2000 | Polyvinyl chloride, 1/2" wide with leg | 1 Carp | 535 | .015 | L.F. | .29 | .57 | | .86 | 1.21 |
| 2200 | 3/4" wide with leg | | 525 | .015 | | .42 | .58 | | 1 | 1.36 |
| 2400 | 1" radius with leg | | 515 | .016 | | .49 | .59 | | 1.08 | 1.46 |

# 03 15 Concrete Accessories

## 03 15 05 – Concrete Forming Accessories

| 03 15 05.12 Chamfer Strips | | Crew | Daily Output | Labor-Hours | Unit | Material | 2008 Bare Costs Labor | Equipment | Total | Total Incl O&P |
|---|---|---|---|---|---|---|---|---|---|---|
| 2800 | 2" radius with leg | 1 Carp | 500 | .016 | L.F. | 2.30 | .61 | | 2.91 | 3.48 |
| 5000 | Wood, 1/2" wide | | 535 | .015 | | .07 | .57 | | .64 | .97 |
| 5200 | 3/4" wide | | 525 | .015 | | .08 | .58 | | .66 | .99 |
| 5400 | 1" wide | ↓ | 515 | .016 | ↓ | .13 | .59 | | .72 | 1.06 |

### 03 15 05.15 Column Form Accessories

| | | Crew | Daily Output | Labor-Hours | Unit | Material | 2008 Bare Costs Labor | Equipment | Total | Total Incl O&P |
|---|---|---|---|---|---|---|---|---|---|---|
| 0010 | **COLUMN FORM ACCESSORIES** | | | | | | | | | |
| 1000 | Column clamps, adjustable to 24" x 24", buy | | | | Set | 119 | | | 119 | 131 |
| 1100 | Rent per month | | | | | 8.55 | | | 8.55 | 9.40 |
| 1300 | For sizes to 30" x 30", buy | | | | | 142 | | | 142 | 156 |
| 1400 | Rent per month | | | | | 12.50 | | | 12.50 | 13.75 |
| 1600 | For sizes to 36" x 36", buy | | | | | 154 | | | 154 | 170 |
| 1700 | Rent per month | | | | | 18.50 | | | 18.50 | 20.50 |
| 2000 | Bull winch (band iron) 36" x 36", buy | | | | | 49 | | | 49 | 54 |
| 2100 | Rent per month | | | | | 5 | | | 5 | 5.50 |
| 2300 | 48" x 48", buy | | | | | 50 | | | 50 | 55 |
| 2400 | Rent per month | | | | | 6 | | | 6 | 6.60 |
| 3000 | Chain & wedge type 36" x 36", buy | | | | | 68 | | | 68 | 75 |
| 3100 | Rent per month | | | | | 7.65 | | | 7.65 | 8.40 |
| 3300 | 60" x 60", buy | | | | | 92 | | | 92 | 101 |
| 3400 | Rent per month | | | | | 11 | | | 11 | 12.10 |
| 4000 | Friction collars 2'-6" dia., buy | | | | | 695 | | | 695 | 765 |
| 4100 | Rent per month | | | | | 68 | | | 68 | 75 |
| 4300 | 4'-0" dia., buy | | | | | 795 | | | 795 | 875 |
| 4400 | Rent per month | ↓ | | | | 87.50 | | | 87.50 | 96.50 |

### 03 15 05.20 Dovetail Anchor System

| | | Crew | Daily Output | Labor-Hours | Unit | Material | 2008 Bare Costs Labor | Equipment | Total | Total Incl O&P |
|---|---|---|---|---|---|---|---|---|---|---|
| 0010 | **DOVETAIL ANCHOR SYSTEM** | | | | | | | | | |
| 0500 | Anchor slot, galv., filled, 24 ga. | 1 Carp | 425 | .019 | L.F. | .83 | .72 | | 1.55 | 2.03 |
| 0600 | 20 ga. | | 400 | .020 | | .84 | .76 | | 1.60 | 2.11 |
| 0625 | 12 ga. | | 400 | .020 | | 1.37 | .76 | | 2.13 | 2.70 |
| 0800 | 16 oz. copper, foam filled | | 375 | .021 | | 4 | .81 | | 4.81 | 5.65 |
| 0900 | 26 ga. stainless steel, foam filled | ↓ | 375 | .021 | ↓ | 1.33 | .81 | | 2.14 | 2.72 |
| 1200 | Brick anchor, corr., galv., 3-1/2" long, 16 ga. | 1 Bric | 10.50 | .762 | C | 29.50 | 30 | | 59.50 | 78 |
| 1300 | 12 ga. | | 10.50 | .762 | | 41 | 30 | | 71 | 90.50 |
| 1500 | Flat, galv., 3-1/2" long, 16 ga. | | 10.50 | .762 | | 34 | 30 | | 64 | 83 |
| 1600 | 12 ga. | | 10.50 | .762 | | 50 | 30 | | 80 | 101 |
| 2000 | Cavity wall, corr., galv., 5" long, 16 ga. | | 10.50 | .762 | | 35 | 30 | | 65 | 84 |
| 2100 | 12 ga. | | 10.50 | .762 | | 49.50 | 30 | | 79.50 | 100 |
| 3000 | Furring anchors, corr., galv., 1-1/2" long, 16 ga. | | 10.50 | .762 | | 13.90 | 30 | | 43.90 | 61 |
| 3100 | 12 ga. | | 10.50 | .762 | | 23.50 | 30 | | 53.50 | 71 |
| 6000 | Stone anchors, 3-1/2" long, galv., 1/8" x 1" wide | | 10.50 | .762 | | 108 | 30 | | 138 | 164 |
| 6100 | 1/4" x 1" wide | ↓ | 10.50 | .762 | ↓ | 107 | 30 | | 137 | 163 |

### 03 15 05.25 Expansion Joints

| | | Crew | Daily Output | Labor-Hours | Unit | Material | 2008 Bare Costs Labor | Equipment | Total | Total Incl O&P |
|---|---|---|---|---|---|---|---|---|---|---|
| 0010 | **EXPANSION JOINTS** | | | | | | | | | |
| 0020 | Keyed, cold, 24 ga, incl. stakes, 3-1/2" high | 1 Carp | 200 | .040 | L.F. | .66 | 1.52 | | 2.18 | 3.10 |
| 0050 | 4-1/2" high | | 200 | .040 | | .76 | 1.52 | | 2.28 | 3.21 |
| 0100 | 5-1/2" high | | 195 | .041 | | .83 | 1.56 | | 2.39 | 3.34 |
| 0150 | 7-1/2" high | ↓ | 190 | .042 | | 1.02 | 1.60 | | 2.62 | 3.62 |
| 0300 | Poured asphalt, plain, 1/2" x 1" | 1 Clab | 450 | .018 | | .44 | .54 | | .98 | 1.32 |
| 0350 | 1" x 2" | | 400 | .020 | | 1.74 | .61 | | 2.35 | 2.85 |
| 0500 | Neoprene, liquid, cold applied, 1/2" x 1" | | 450 | .018 | | 2.07 | .54 | | 2.61 | 3.12 |
| 0550 | 1" x 2" | | 400 | .020 | | 6.25 | .61 | | 6.86 | 7.85 |
| 0700 | Polyurethane, poured, 2 part, 1/2" x 1" | ↓ | 400 | .020 | ↓ | 1.34 | .61 | | 1.95 | 2.42 |

# 03 15 Concrete Accessories

## 03 15 05 – Concrete Forming Accessories

### 03 15 05.25 Expansion Joints

| | Crew | Daily Output | Labor-Hours | Unit | Material | 2008 Bare Costs Labor | Equipment | Total | Total Incl O&P |
|---|---|---|---|---|---|---|---|---|---|
| 0750 | 1" x 2" | 1 Clab | 350 | .023 | L.F. | 5.35 | .69 | | 6.04 | 7 |
| 0900 | Rubberized asphalt, hot or cold applied, 1/2" x 1" | | 450 | .018 | | .42 | .54 | | .96 | 1.30 |
| 0950 | 1" x 2" | | 400 | .020 | | 1.50 | .61 | | 2.11 | 2.59 |
| 1100 | Hot applied, fuel resistant, 1/2" x 1" | | 450 | .018 | | 1.16 | .54 | | 1.70 | 2.12 |
| 1150 | 1" x 2" | | 400 | .020 | | 2.24 | .61 | | 2.85 | 3.40 |
| 2000 | Premolded, bituminous fiber, 1/2" x 6" | 1 Carp | 375 | .021 | | .41 | .81 | | 1.22 | 1.71 |
| 2050 | 1" x 12" | | 300 | .027 | | 1.76 | 1.02 | | 2.78 | 3.52 |
| 2250 | Cork with resin binder, 1/2" x 6" | | 375 | .021 | | 1.84 | .81 | | 2.65 | 3.28 |
| 2300 | 1" x 12" | | 300 | .027 | | 6.60 | 1.02 | | 7.62 | 8.85 |
| 2500 | Neoprene sponge, closed cell, 1/2" x 6" | | 375 | .021 | | 1.56 | .81 | | 2.37 | 2.98 |
| 2550 | 1" x 12" | | 300 | .027 | | 7.15 | 1.02 | | 8.17 | 9.50 |
| 2750 | Polyethylene foam, 1/2" x 6" | | 375 | .021 | | .53 | .81 | | 1.34 | 1.84 |
| 2800 | 1" x 12" | | 300 | .027 | | 1.85 | 1.02 | | 2.87 | 3.62 |
| 3000 | Polyethylene backer rod, 3/8" diameter | | 460 | .017 | | .05 | .66 | | .71 | 1.08 |
| 3050 | 3/4" diameter | | 460 | .017 | | .08 | .66 | | .74 | 1.11 |
| 3100 | 1" diameter | | 460 | .017 | | .13 | .66 | | .79 | 1.17 |
| 3500 | Polyurethane foam, with polybutylene, 1/2" x 1/2" | | 475 | .017 | | .95 | .64 | | 1.59 | 2.05 |
| 3550 | 1" x 1" | | 450 | .018 | | 1.95 | .68 | | 2.63 | 3.20 |
| 3750 | Polyurethane foam, regular, closed cell, 1/2" x 6" | | 375 | .021 | | .70 | .81 | | 1.51 | 2.03 |
| 3800 | 1" x 12" | | 300 | .027 | | 1.30 | 1.02 | | 2.32 | 3.01 |
| 4000 | Polyvinyl chloride foam, closed cell, 1/2" x 6" | | 375 | .021 | | 2.37 | .81 | | 3.18 | 3.87 |
| 4050 | 1" x 12" | | 300 | .027 | | 7.05 | 1.02 | | 8.07 | 9.40 |
| 4250 | Rubber, gray sponge, 1/2" x 6" | | 375 | .021 | | 2.26 | .81 | | 3.07 | 3.75 |
| 4300 | 1" x 12" | | 300 | .027 | | 9.75 | 1.02 | | 10.77 | 12.35 |
| 4500 | Lead wool for joints, 1 ton lots | | | | Lb. | 3.10 | | | 3.10 | 3.41 |
| 5000 | For installation in walls, add | | | | | | 75% | | | |
| 5250 | For installation in boxouts, add | | | | | | 25% | | | |

### 03 15 05.30 Hangers

| | | Crew | Daily Output | Labor-Hours | Unit | Material | Labor | Equipment | Total | Total Incl O&P |
|---|---|---|---|---|---|---|---|---|---|---|
| 0010 | **HANGERS** | | | | | | | | | |
| 0020 | Slab and beam form | | | | | | | | | |
| 0500 | Banding iron, 3/4" x 22 ga, 14 L.F. per lb or | | | | | | | | | |
| 0550 | 1/2" x 14 ga, 7 L.F. per lb. | | | | Lb. | 1.25 | | | 1.25 | 1.38 |
| 1000 | Fascia ties, coil type, to 24" long | | | | C | 520 | | | 520 | 570 |
| 1500 | Frame ties to 8-1/8" | | | | | 610 | | | 610 | 675 |
| 1550 | 8-1/8" to 10-1/8" | | | | | 645 | | | 645 | 710 |
| 5000 | Snap tie hanger, to 30" overall length, 3000 # | | | | | 515 | | | 515 | 570 |
| 5050 | To 36" overall length | | | | | 565 | | | 565 | 620 |
| 5100 | To 48" overall length | | | | | 660 | | | 660 | 725 |
| 5500 | Steel beam hanger | | | | | | | | | |
| 5600 | Flange to 8-1/8" | | | | C | 610 | | | 610 | 675 |
| 5650 | 8-1/8" to 10-1/8" | | | | | 645 | | | 645 | 710 |
| 6000 | Tie hangers to 30" overall length, 4000 # | | | | | 590 | | | 590 | 645 |
| 6100 | To 36" overall length | | | | | 635 | | | 635 | 700 |
| 6500 | Tie back hanger, up to 12-1/8" flange | | | | | 1,650 | | | 1,650 | 1,800 |
| 8500 | Wire, black annealed, 9 ga | | | | Cwt. | 79.50 | | | 79.50 | 87.50 |
| 8600 | 16 ga | | | | " | 113 | | | 113 | 124 |

### 03 15 05.35 Inserts

| | | Crew | Daily Output | Labor-Hours | Unit | Material | Labor | Equipment | Total | Total Incl O&P |
|---|---|---|---|---|---|---|---|---|---|---|
| 0010 | **INSERTS** | | | | | | | | | |
| 1000 | Inserts, slotted nut type for 3/4" bolts, 4" long | 1 Carp | 84 | .095 | Ea. | 16.30 | 3.63 | | 19.93 | 23.50 |
| 2100 | 6" long | | 84 | .095 | | 18.20 | 3.63 | | 21.83 | 25.50 |
| 2150 | 8" long | | 84 | .095 | | 23 | 3.63 | | 26.63 | 30.50 |
| 2200 | Slotted, strap type, 4" long | | 84 | .095 | | 15.85 | 3.63 | | 19.48 | 23 |

# 03 15 Concrete Accessories

## 03 15 05 – Concrete Forming Accessories

### 03 15 05.35 Inserts

| | | Crew | Daily Output | Labor-Hours | Unit | Material | 2008 Bare Costs Labor | 2008 Bare Costs Equipment | Total | Total Incl O&P |
|---|---|---|---|---|---|---|---|---|---|---|
| 2250 | 6" long | 1 Carp | 84 | .095 | Ea. | 18.20 | 3.63 | | 21.83 | 25.50 |
| 2300 | 8" long | | 84 | .095 | | 23 | 3.63 | | 26.63 | 30.50 |
| 2350 | Strap for slotted insert, 4" long | | 84 | .095 | | 11.85 | 3.63 | | 15.48 | 18.65 |
| 4100 | 6" long | | 84 | .095 | | 11.70 | 3.63 | | 15.33 | 18.50 |
| 4150 | 8" long | | 84 | .095 | | 14 | 3.63 | | 17.63 | 21 |
| 4200 | 10" long | | 84 | .095 | | 16.30 | 3.63 | | 19.93 | 23.50 |
| 7000 | Loop ferrule type | | | | | | | | | |
| 7100 | 1/4" diameter bolt | 1 Carp | 84 | .095 | Ea. | 3.13 | 3.63 | | 6.76 | 9.10 |
| 7350 | 7/8" diameter bolt | " | 84 | .095 | " | 14.60 | 3.63 | | 18.23 | 21.50 |
| 9000 | Wedge type | | | | | | | | | |
| 9100 | For 3/4" diameter bolt | 1 Carp | 60 | .133 | Ea. | 13.95 | 5.10 | | 19.05 | 23.50 |
| 9800 | Cut washers, black | | | | | | | | | |
| 9950 | For galvanized inserts, add | | | | | 30% | | | | |

### 03 15 05.70 Shores

| | | Crew | Daily Output | Labor-Hours | Unit | Material | 2008 Bare Costs Labor | 2008 Bare Costs Equipment | Total | Total Incl O&P |
|---|---|---|---|---|---|---|---|---|---|---|
| 0010 | **SHORES** | | | | | | | | | |
| 0020 | Erect and strip, by hand, horizontal members | | | | | | | | | |
| 0500 | Aluminum joists and stringers | 2 Carp | 60 | .267 | Ea. | | 10.15 | | 10.15 | 15.80 |
| 0600 | Steel, adjustable beams | | 45 | .356 | | | 13.55 | | 13.55 | 21 |
| 0700 | Wood joists | | 50 | .320 | | | 12.20 | | 12.20 | 19 |
| 0800 | Wood stringers | | 30 | .533 | | | 20.50 | | 20.50 | 31.50 |
| 1000 | Vertical members to 10' high | | 55 | .291 | | | 11.10 | | 11.10 | 17.25 |
| 1050 | To 13' high | | 50 | .320 | | | 12.20 | | 12.20 | 19 |
| 1100 | To 16' high | | 45 | .356 | | | 13.55 | | 13.55 | 21 |
| 1500 | Reshoring | | 1400 | .011 | S.F. | .83 | .44 | | 1.27 | 1.60 |
| 1600 | Flying truss system | C-17D | 9600 | .009 | SFCA | | .35 | .07 | .42 | .61 |
| 1760 | Horizontal, aluminum joists, 6-1/4" high x 5' to 21' span, buy | | | | L.F. | 37.50 | | | 37.50 | 41.50 |
| 1770 | Beams, 7-1/4" high x 4' to 30' span | | | | " | 51.50 | | | 51.50 | 56.50 |
| 1810 | Horizontal, steel beam, adjustable, 4' to 7' span, buy | | | | Ea. | 595 | | | 595 | 655 |
| 1830 | 6' to 10' span | | | | | 760 | | | 760 | 835 |
| 1920 | 9' to 15' span | | | | | 965 | | | 965 | 1,050 |
| 1940 | 12' to 20' span | | | | | 990 | | | 990 | 1,100 |
| 1970 | Steel stringer, W8x10, 4' to 16' span, buy | | | | L.F. | 22 | | | 22 | 24 |
| 3000 | Rent for job duration, aluminum joist @ 2' O.C., per mo | | | | SF Flr. | .94 | | | .94 | 1.04 |
| 3050 | Steel W8x10 | | | | | .55 | | | .55 | .60 |
| 3060 | Steel adjustable | | | | | 1.90 | | | 1.90 | 2.09 |
| 3500 | #1 post shore, steel, 5'-7" to 9'-6" high, 10000# cap., buy | | | | Ea. | 395 | | | 395 | 435 |
| 3550 | #2 post shore, 7'-3" to 12'-10" high, 7800# capacity | | | | | 410 | | | 410 | 450 |
| 3600 | #3 post shore, 8'-10" to 16'-1" high, 3800# capacity | | | | | 425 | | | 425 | 470 |
| 5010 | Frame shoring systems, steel, 12000#/leg, buy | | | | | | | | | |
| 5040 | Frame, 2' wide x 6' high | | | | Ea. | 99 | | | 99 | 109 |
| 5250 | X-brace | | | | | 16.80 | | | 16.80 | 18.50 |
| 5550 | Base plate | | | | | 16.50 | | | 16.50 | 18.15 |
| 5600 | Screw jack | | | | | 35.50 | | | 35.50 | 39 |
| 5650 | U-head, 8" x 8" | | | | | 20.50 | | | 20.50 | 22.50 |

### 03 15 05.75 Sleeves and Chases

| | | Crew | Daily Output | Labor-Hours | Unit | Material | 2008 Bare Costs Labor | 2008 Bare Costs Equipment | Total | Total Incl O&P |
|---|---|---|---|---|---|---|---|---|---|---|
| 0010 | **SLEEVES AND CHASES** | | | | | | | | | |
| 0100 | Plastic, 1 use, 9" long, 2" diameter | 1 Carp | 100 | .080 | Ea. | .81 | 3.05 | | 3.86 | 5.65 |
| 0150 | 4" diameter | | 90 | .089 | | 4.14 | 3.39 | | 7.53 | 9.80 |
| 0200 | 6" diameter | | 75 | .107 | | 7.30 | 4.06 | | 11.36 | 14.40 |
| 0250 | 12" diameter | | 60 | .133 | | 21 | 5.10 | | 26.10 | 31 |

### 03 15 05.80 Snap Ties

| | | | | | | | | | | |
|---|---|---|---|---|---|---|---|---|---|---|
| 0010 | **SNAP TIES**, 8-1/4" L&W (Lumber and wedge) | | | | | | | | | |

# 03 15 Concrete Accessories

## 03 15 05 – Concrete Forming Accessories

### 03 15 05.80 Snap Ties

| | | Crew | Daily Output | Labor-Hours | Unit | Material | 2008 Bare Costs Labor | Equipment | Total | Total Incl O&P |
|---|---|---|---|---|---|---|---|---|---|---|
| 0100 | 2250 lb., w/ flat washer, 8" wall | | | | C | 165 | | | 165 | 181 |
| 0200 | 12" wall | | | | | 174 | | | 174 | 192 |
| 0250 | 16" wall | | | | | 195 | | | 195 | 215 |
| 0300 | 18" wall | | | | | 205 | | | 205 | 225 |
| 0500 | With plastic cone, 8" wall | | | | | 176 | | | 176 | 194 |
| 0600 | 12" wall | | | | | 191 | | | 191 | 210 |
| 0650 | 16" wall | | | | | 210 | | | 210 | 231 |
| 0700 | 18" wall | | | | | 219 | | | 219 | 241 |
| 1000 | 3350 lb., w/ flat washer, 8" wall | | | | | 274 | | | 274 | 300 |
| 1150 | 12" wall | | | | | 310 | | | 310 | 340 |
| 1200 | 16" wall | | | | | 350 | | | 350 | 385 |
| 1250 | 18" wall | | | | | 365 | | | 365 | 405 |
| 1500 | With plastic cone, 8" wall | | | | | 274 | | | 274 | 300 |
| 1600 | 12" wall | | | | | 310 | | | 310 | 340 |
| 1650 | 16" wall | | | | | 350 | | | 350 | 385 |
| 1700 | 18" wall | | | | | 365 | | | 365 | 405 |

### 03 15 05.85 Stair Tread Inserts

| | | Crew | Daily Output | Labor-Hours | Unit | Material | 2008 Bare Costs Labor | Equipment | Total | Total Incl O&P |
|---|---|---|---|---|---|---|---|---|---|---|
| 0010 | **STAIR TREAD INSERTS** | | | | | | | | | |
| 0015 | Cast iron, abrasive, 3" wide | 1 Carp | 90 | .089 | L.F. | 8.85 | 3.39 | | 12.24 | 15 |
| 0020 | 4" wide | | 80 | .100 | | 11.80 | 3.81 | | 15.61 | 18.95 |
| 0040 | 6" wide | | 75 | .107 | | 17.75 | 4.06 | | 21.81 | 26 |
| 0050 | 9" wide | | 70 | .114 | | 26.50 | 4.35 | | 30.85 | 36.50 |
| 0100 | 12" wide | | 65 | .123 | | 35.50 | 4.69 | | 40.19 | 46.50 |
| 0300 | Cast aluminum, compared to cast iron, deduct | | | | | 10% | | | | |
| 0500 | Extruded aluminum safety tread, 3" wide | 1 Carp | 75 | .107 | | 10.10 | 4.06 | | 14.16 | 17.45 |
| 0550 | 4" wide | | 75 | .107 | | 13.45 | 4.06 | | 17.51 | 21 |
| 0600 | 6" wide | | 75 | .107 | | 20 | 4.06 | | 24.06 | 28.50 |
| 0650 | 9" wide to resurface stairs | | 70 | .114 | | 30.50 | 4.35 | | 34.85 | 40.50 |
| 1700 | Cement fill for pan-type metal treads, plain | 1 Cefi | 115 | .070 | S.F. | 1.85 | 2.57 | | 4.42 | 5.80 |
| 1750 | Non-slip | " | 100 | .080 | " | 2.04 | 2.96 | | 5 | 6.60 |

### 03 15 05.95 Wall and Foundation Form Accessories

| | | Crew | Daily Output | Labor-Hours | Unit | Material | 2008 Bare Costs Labor | Equipment | Total | Total Incl O&P |
|---|---|---|---|---|---|---|---|---|---|---|
| 0010 | **WALL AND FOUNDATION FORM ACCESSORIES** | | | | | | | | | |
| 2000 | Footings, turnbuckle form aligner | | | | Ea. | 30 | | | 30 | 33.50 |
| 2050 | Spreaders for footer, adjustable | | | | " | 18.15 | | | 18.15 | 20 |
| 3000 | Form oil, coverage varies greatly, minimum | | | | Gal. | 7.85 | | | 7.85 | 8.60 |
| 3050 | Maximum | | | | " | 10.10 | | | 10.10 | 11.10 |
| 3500 | Form patches, 1-3/4" diameter | | | | C | 208 | | | 208 | 229 |
| 3550 | 2-3/4" diameter | | | | " | 350 | | | 350 | 385 |
| 4000 | Nail stakes, 3/4" diameter, 18" long | | | | Ea. | 3.41 | | | 3.41 | 3.75 |
| 4050 | 24" long | | | | | 4.04 | | | 4.04 | 4.44 |
| 4200 | 30" long | | | | | 5.10 | | | 5.10 | 5.60 |
| 4250 | 36" long | | | | | 5.70 | | | 5.70 | 6.30 |

## 03 15 13 – Waterstops

### 03 15 13.50 Waterstops

| | | Crew | Daily Output | Labor-Hours | Unit | Material | 2008 Bare Costs Labor | Equipment | Total | Total Incl O&P |
|---|---|---|---|---|---|---|---|---|---|---|
| 0010 | **WATERSTOPS**, PVC and Rubber | | | | | | | | | |
| 0020 | PVC, ribbed 3/16" thick, 4" wide | 1 Carp | 155 | .052 | L.F. | 1.07 | 1.97 | | 3.04 | 4.24 |
| 0050 | 6" wide | | 145 | .055 | | 1.88 | 2.10 | | 3.98 | 5.35 |
| 0500 | With center bulb, 6" wide, 3/16" thick | | 135 | .059 | | 1.49 | 2.26 | | 3.75 | 5.15 |
| 0550 | 3/8" thick | | 130 | .062 | | 2.62 | 2.34 | | 4.96 | 6.55 |
| 0800 | Dumbbell type, 6" wide, 3/16" thick | | 150 | .053 | | 1.47 | 2.03 | | 3.50 | 4.78 |
| 0850 | 3/8" thick | | 145 | .055 | | 2.81 | 2.10 | | 4.91 | 6.35 |
| 1000 | 9" wide, 3/8" thick, plain | | 130 | .062 | | 4.26 | 2.34 | | 6.60 | 8.35 |

# 03 15 Concrete Accessories

## 03 15 13 – Waterstops

| 03 15 13.50 Waterstops | | Crew | Daily Output | Labor-Hours | Unit | Material | Labor | Equipment | Total | Total Incl O&P |
|---|---|---|---|---|---|---|---|---|---|---|
| 1050 | Center bulb | 1 Carp | 130 | .062 | L.F. | 7.75 | 2.34 | | 10.09 | 12.15 |
| 1250 | Split, 3/8" thick, 6" wide | | 145 | .055 | | 3.62 | 2.10 | | 5.72 | 7.25 |
| 1300 | 9" wide | | 130 | .062 | | 3.71 | 2.34 | | 6.05 | 7.75 |
| 2000 | Rubber, flat dumbbell, 3/8" thick, 6" wide | | 145 | .055 | | 7.60 | 2.10 | | 9.70 | 11.60 |
| 2050 | 9" wide | | 135 | .059 | | 11.30 | 2.26 | | 13.56 | 15.95 |
| 2500 | Flat dumbbell split, 3/8" thick, 6" wide | | 145 | .055 | | 3.62 | 2.10 | | 5.72 | 7.25 |
| 2550 | 9" wide | | 135 | .059 | | 3.71 | 2.26 | | 5.97 | 7.60 |
| 3000 | Center bulb, 1/4" thick, 6" wide | | 145 | .055 | | 6.55 | 2.10 | | 8.65 | 10.45 |
| 3050 | 9" wide | | 135 | .059 | | 12.70 | 2.26 | | 14.96 | 17.50 |
| 3500 | Center bulb split, 3/8" thick, 6" wide | | 145 | .055 | | 8.05 | 2.10 | | 10.15 | 12.10 |
| 3550 | 9" wide | | 135 | .059 | | 13.70 | 2.26 | | 15.96 | 18.55 |
| 5000 | Waterstop fittings, rubber, flat | | | | | | | | | |
| 5010 | Dumbbell or center bulb, 3/8" thick, | | | | | | | | | |
| 5200 | Field union, 6" wide | 1 Carp | 50 | .160 | Ea. | 25.50 | 6.10 | | 31.60 | 37.50 |
| 5250 | 9" wide | | 50 | .160 | | 30 | 6.10 | | 36.10 | 42.50 |
| 5500 | Flat cross, 6" wide | | 30 | .267 | | 52.50 | 10.15 | | 62.65 | 74 |
| 5550 | 9" wide | | 30 | .267 | | 75.50 | 10.15 | | 85.65 | 99 |
| 6000 | Flat tee, 6" wide | | 30 | .267 | | 49 | 10.15 | | 59.15 | 69.50 |
| 6050 | 9" wide | | 30 | .267 | | 64.50 | 10.15 | | 74.65 | 86.50 |
| 6500 | Flat ell, 6" wide | | 40 | .200 | | 44 | 7.60 | | 51.60 | 60.50 |
| 6550 | 9" wide | | 40 | .200 | | 59.50 | 7.60 | | 67.10 | 77.50 |
| 7000 | Vertical tee, 6" wide | | 25 | .320 | | 42.50 | 12.20 | | 54.70 | 66 |
| 7050 | 9" wide | | 25 | .320 | | 54.50 | 12.20 | | 66.70 | 79 |
| 7500 | Vertical ell, 6" wide | | 35 | .229 | | 38 | 8.70 | | 46.70 | 55 |
| 7550 | 9" wide | | 35 | .229 | | 52.50 | 8.70 | | 61.20 | 71 |

# 03 21 Reinforcing Steel

## 03 21 05 – Reinforcing Steel Accessories

### 03 21 05.10 Rebar Accessories

| | | Crew | Daily Output | Labor-Hours | Unit | Material | Labor | Equipment | Total | Total Incl O&P |
|---|---|---|---|---|---|---|---|---|---|---|
| 0010 | **REBAR ACCESSORIES** | | | | | | | | | |
| 0100 | Beam bolsters (BB), lower, 1-1/2" high, plain steel | | | | C.L.F. | 65 | | | 65 | 71.50 |
| 0102 | Galvanized | | | | | 97 | | | 97 | 107 |
| 0104 | Stainless tipped legs | | | | | 183 | | | 183 | 201 |
| 0106 | Plastic tipped legs | | | | | 111 | | | 111 | 122 |
| 0108 | Epoxy dipped | | | | | 151 | | | 151 | 166 |
| 0110 | 2" high, plain | | | | | 82.50 | | | 82.50 | 90.50 |
| 0120 | Galvanized | | | | | 110 | | | 110 | 121 |
| 0140 | Stainless tipped legs | | | | | 251 | | | 251 | 276 |
| 0160 | Plastic tipped legs | | | | | 114 | | | 114 | 126 |
| 0162 | Epoxy dipped | | | | | 160 | | | 160 | 176 |
| 0200 | Upper (BBU), 1-1/2" high, plain steel | | | | | 182 | | | 182 | 200 |
| 0210 | 3" high | | | | | 330 | | | 330 | 360 |
| 0300 | Beam bolster with plate (BBP), 1-1/2" high, plain steel | | | | | 213 | | | 213 | 234 |
| 0310 | 3" high | | | | | 340 | | | 340 | 370 |
| 0500 | Slab bolsters, continuous (SB), 1" high, plain steel | | | | | 55 | | | 55 | 60.50 |
| 0502 | Galvanized | | | | | 62.50 | | | 62.50 | 68.50 |
| 0504 | Stainless tipped legs | | | | | 84 | | | 84 | 92.50 |
| 0506 | Plastic tipped legs | | | | | 76 | | | 76 | 83.50 |
| 0510 | 2" high, plain steel | | | | | 65 | | | 65 | 71.50 |
| 0515 | Galvanized | | | | | 76 | | | 76 | 83.50 |
| 0520 | Stainless tipped legs | | | | | 144 | | | 144 | 159 |

| 03 21 05.10 Rebar Accessories | Crew | Daily Output | Labor-Hours | Unit | Material | 2008 Bare Costs Labor | Equipment | Total | Total Incl O&P |
|---|---|---|---|---|---|---|---|---|---|
| 0525 | Plastic tipped legs | | | | C.L.F. | 85 | | | 85 | 93.50 |
| 0530 | For bolsters with wire runners (SBR), add | | | | | 96 | | | 96 | 106 |
| 0540 | For bolsters with plates (SBP), add | | | | ↓ | 180 | | | 180 | 198 |
| 0700 | Bag ties, 16 ga., plain, 4" long | | | | C | .88 | | | .88 | .97 |
| 0710 | 5" long | | | | | .96 | | | .96 | 1.06 |
| 0720 | 6" long | | | | | .96 | | | .96 | 1.06 |
| 0730 | 7" long | | | | | 1.04 | | | 1.04 | 1.14 |
| 1200 | High chairs, individual (HC), 3" high, plain steel | | | | | 77.50 | | | 77.50 | 85.50 |
| 1202 | Galvanized | | | | | 110 | | | 110 | 121 |
| 1204 | Stainless tipped legs | | | | | 550 | | | 550 | 605 |
| 1206 | Plastic tipped legs | | | | | 104 | | | 104 | 114 |
| 1210 | 5" high, plain | | | | | 120 | | | 120 | 132 |
| 1212 | Galvanized | | | | | 150 | | | 150 | 165 |
| 1214 | Stainless tipped legs | | | | | 590 | | | 590 | 645 |
| 1216 | Plastic tipped legs | | | | | 150 | | | 150 | 165 |
| 1220 | 8" high, plain | | | | | 259 | | | 259 | 285 |
| 1222 | Galvanized | | | | | 330 | | | 330 | 360 |
| 1224 | Stainless tipped legs | | | | | 525 | | | 525 | 575 |
| 1226 | Plastic tipped legs | | | | | 325 | | | 325 | 360 |
| 1230 | 12" high, plain | | | | | 540 | | | 540 | 595 |
| 1232 | Galvanized | | | | | 600 | | | 600 | 660 |
| 1234 | Stainless tipped legs | | | | | 805 | | | 805 | 885 |
| 1236 | Plastic tipped legs | | | | | 610 | | | 610 | 670 |
| 1400 | Individual high chairs, with plate (HCP), 5" high | | | | | 310 | | | 310 | 345 |
| 1410 | 8" high | | | | | 470 | | | 470 | 520 |
| 1500 | Bar chair (BC), 1-1/2" high, plain steel | | | | | 40 | | | 40 | 44 |
| 1520 | Galvanized | | | | | 46.50 | | | 46.50 | 51 |
| 1530 | Stainless tipped legs | | | | | 136 | | | 136 | 149 |
| 1540 | Plastic tipped legs | | | | | 81.50 | | | 81.50 | 90 |
| 1550 | Joist chair (JC), 3/4" x 5", plain steel | | | | | 54.50 | | | 54.50 | 60 |
| 1580 | Galvanized | | | | | 68 | | | 68 | 74.50 |
| 1600 | Stainless tipped legs | | | | | 97 | | | 97 | 106 |
| 1620 | Plastic tipped legs | | | | | 93 | | | 93 | 102 |
| 1630 | Epoxy dipped | | | | ↓ | 224 | | | 224 | 247 |
| 1700 | Continuous high chairs (CHC), legs 8" O.C., 4" high, plain steel | | | | C.L.F. | 104 | | | 104 | 114 |
| 1705 | Galvanized | | | | | 122 | | | 122 | 134 |
| 1710 | Stainless tipped legs | | | | | 272 | | | 272 | 299 |
| 1715 | Plastic tipped legs | | | | | 129 | | | 129 | 142 |
| 1718 | Epoxy dipped | | | | | 183 | | | 183 | 202 |
| 1720 | 6" high, plain | | | | | 150 | | | 150 | 165 |
| 1725 | Galvanized | | | | | 205 | | | 205 | 225 |
| 1730 | Stainless tipped legs | | | | | 315 | | | 315 | 345 |
| 1735 | Plastic tipped legs | | | | | 205 | | | 205 | 225 |
| 1738 | Epoxy dipped | | | | | 248 | | | 248 | 273 |
| 1740 | 8" high, plain | | | | | 218 | | | 218 | 239 |
| 1745 | Galvanized | | | | | 300 | | | 300 | 330 |
| 1750 | Stainless tipped legs | | | | | 375 | | | 375 | 415 |
| 1755 | Plastic tipped legs | | | | | 285 | | | 285 | 315 |
| 1758 | Epoxy dipped | | | | | 380 | | | 380 | 415 |
| 1900 | For continuous bottom wire runners, add | | | | | 112 | | | 112 | 123 |
| 1940 | For continuous bottom plate, add | | | | | 216 | | | 216 | 238 |
| 2100 | Paper tubing, 4' lengths, for #4 bar | | | | | 73.50 | | | 73.50 | 81 |
| 2120 | For #6 bar | | | | ↓ | 86.50 | | | 86.50 | 95 |

# 03 21 Reinforcing Steel

## 03 21 05 – Reinforcing Steel Accessories

### 03 21 05.10 Rebar Accessories

| | | Crew | Daily Output | Labor-Hours | Unit | Material | 2008 Bare Costs Labor | Equipment | Total | Total Incl O&P |
|---|---|---|---|---|---|---|---|---|---|---|
| 2200 | Screed chair base, 1/2" coil thread diam, 2-1/2" high, plain steel | | | | C | 257 | | | 257 | 282 |
| 2210 | Galvanized | | | | | 272 | | | 272 | 299 |
| 2220 | 5-1/2" high, plain | | | | | 310 | | | 310 | 345 |
| 2250 | Galvanized | | | | | 330 | | | 330 | 360 |
| 2300 | 3/4" coil thread diam, 2-1/2" high, plain steel | | | | | 325 | | | 325 | 360 |
| 2310 | Galvanized | | | | | 435 | | | 435 | 480 |
| 2320 | 5-1/2" high, plain steel | | | | | 400 | | | 400 | 440 |
| 2350 | Galvanized | | | | | 560 | | | 560 | 615 |
| 2400 | Screed holder, 1/2" coil thread diam for pipe screed, plain steel, 6" long | | | | | 272 | | | 272 | 299 |
| 2420 | 12" long | | | | | 450 | | | 450 | 495 |
| 2500 | 3/4" coil thread diam for pipe screed, plain steel, 6" long | | | | | 490 | | | 490 | 535 |
| 2520 | 12" long | | | | | 795 | | | 795 | 875 |
| 2700 | Screw anchor for bolts, plain steel, 3/4" diameter x 4" long | | | | | 305 | | | 305 | 340 |
| 2720 | 1" diameter x 6" long | | | | | 530 | | | 530 | 580 |
| 2740 | 1-1/2" diameter x 8" long | | | | | 885 | | | 885 | 970 |
| 2800 | Screw anchor eye bolts, 3/4" x 7" long | | | | | 3,950 | | | 3,950 | 4,350 |
| 2820 | 1" x 9" long | | | | | 7,825 | | | 7,825 | 8,600 |
| 2840 | 1-1/2" x 14" long | | | | | 19,800 | | | 19,800 | 21,800 |
| 2900 | Screw anchor bolts, 3/4" x 7" long | | | | | 1,375 | | | 1,375 | 1,525 |
| 2920 | 1" x 9" long | | | | | 2,675 | | | 2,675 | 2,925 |
| 3001 | Slab lifting inserts, single pickup, galv, 3/4" dia., 5" high | | | | | 1,300 | | | 1,300 | 1,425 |
| 3010 | 6" high | | | | | 1,400 | | | 1,400 | 1,550 |
| 3030 | 7" high | | | | | 1,500 | | | 1,500 | 1,625 |
| 3100 | 1" diameter, 5-1/2" high | | | | | 1,500 | | | 1,500 | 1,650 |
| 3120 | 7" high | | | | | 1,575 | | | 1,575 | 1,750 |
| 3200 | Double pickup lifting inserts, 1" diameter, 5-1/2" high | | | | | 3,075 | | | 3,075 | 3,375 |
| 3220 | 7" high | | | | | 3,350 | | | 3,350 | 3,700 |
| 3330 | 1-1/2" diameter, 5-1/2" high | | | | | 4,025 | | | 4,025 | 4,425 |
| 3800 | Subgrade chairs, #4 bar head, 3-1/2" high | | | | | 55 | | | 55 | 60.50 |
| 3850 | 12" high | | | | | 97 | | | 97 | 106 |
| 3900 | #6 bar head, 3-1/2" high | | | | | 55 | | | 55 | 60.50 |
| 3950 | 12" high | | | | | 97 | | | 97 | 106 |
| 4200 | Subgrade stakes, 3/4" diameter, 12" long | | | | | 238 | | | 238 | 261 |
| 4250 | 24" long | | | | | 365 | | | 365 | 405 |
| 4300 | 1" diameter, 12" long | | | | | 345 | | | 345 | 380 |
| 4350 | 24" long | | | | | 485 | | | 485 | 530 |
| 4500 | Tie wire, 16 ga. annealed steel | | | | Cwt. | 113 | | | 113 | 124 |
| 4550 | Tie wire holder, plastic case | | | | Ea. | 35 | | | 35 | 38.50 |
| 4600 | Aluminum case | | | | " | 54 | | | 54 | 59.50 |

### 03 21 05.75 Splicing Reinforcing Bars

| | | Crew | Daily Output | Labor-Hours | Unit | Material | 2008 Bare Costs Labor | Equipment | Total | Total Incl O&P |
|---|---|---|---|---|---|---|---|---|---|---|
| 0010 | **SPLICING REINFORCING BARS** R032110-70 | | | | | | | | | |
| 0020 | Including holding bars in place while splicing | | | | | | | | | |
| 0100 | Standard, self-aligning type, taper threaded, #4 bars | C-25 | 190 | .168 | Ea. | 4.29 | 5.70 | | 9.99 | 14.15 |
| 0105 | #5 bars | | 170 | .188 | | 5.25 | 6.35 | | 11.60 | 16.35 |
| 0110 | #6 bars | | 150 | .213 | | 6.05 | 7.20 | | 13.25 | 18.65 |
| 0120 | #7 bars | | 130 | .246 | | 7.05 | 8.30 | | 15.35 | 21.50 |
| 0300 | #8 bars | | 115 | .278 | | 12.20 | 9.40 | | 21.60 | 29 |
| 0305 | #9 bars | C-5 | 105 | .533 | | 13.30 | 22.50 | 7.50 | 43.30 | 59 |
| 0310 | #10 bars | | 95 | .589 | | 14.80 | 24.50 | 8.30 | 47.60 | 65 |
| 0320 | #11 bars | | 85 | .659 | | 15.75 | 27.50 | 9.25 | 52.50 | 72 |
| 0330 | #14 bars | | 65 | .862 | | 23.50 | 36 | 12.10 | 71.60 | 97.50 |
| 0340 | #18 bars | | 45 | 1.244 | | 36 | 52 | 17.45 | 105.45 | 142 |

# 03 21 Reinforcing Steel

## 03 21 05 – Reinforcing Steel Accessories

| 03 21 05.75 Splicing Reinforcing Bars | Crew | Daily Output | Labor-Hours | Unit | Material | 2008 Bare Costs Labor | Equipment | Total | Total Incl O&P |
|---|---|---|---|---|---|---|---|---|---|
| 0500 | Transition self-aligning, taper threaded, #18-14 | C-5 | 45 | 1.244 | Ea. | 38.50 | 52 | 17.45 | 107.95 | 145 |
| 0510 | #18-11 | | 45 | 1.244 | | 35 | 52 | 17.45 | 104.45 | 141 |
| 0520 | #14-11 | | 65 | .862 | | 28 | 36 | 12.10 | 76.10 | 102 |
| 0540 | #11-10 | | 85 | .659 | | 22.50 | 27.50 | 9.25 | 59.25 | 79 |
| 0550 | #10-9 | | 95 | .589 | | 20.50 | 24.50 | 8.30 | 53.30 | 71 |
| 0560 | #9-8 | C-25 | 105 | .305 | | 19.95 | 10.30 | | 30.25 | 39 |
| 0580 | #8-7 | | 115 | .278 | | 18.45 | 9.40 | | 27.85 | 36 |
| 0590 | #7-6 | | 130 | .246 | | 17.95 | 8.30 | | 26.25 | 33.50 |
| 0600 | Position coupler for curved bars, taper threaded, #4 bars | | 160 | .200 | | 23 | 6.75 | | 29.75 | 37 |
| 0610 | #5 bars | | 145 | .221 | | 25.50 | 7.45 | | 32.95 | 40.50 |
| 0620 | #6 bars | | 130 | .246 | | 34 | 8.30 | | 42.30 | 51.50 |
| 0630 | #7 bars | | 110 | .291 | | 36.50 | 9.85 | | 46.35 | 56.50 |
| 0640 | #8 bars | | 100 | .320 | | 37.50 | 10.80 | | 48.30 | 59.50 |
| 0650 | #9 bars | C-5 | 90 | .622 | | 41 | 26 | 8.75 | 75.75 | 97 |
| 0660 | #10 bars | | 80 | .700 | | 44.50 | 29.50 | 9.85 | 83.85 | 107 |
| 0670 | #11 bars | | 70 | .800 | | 46 | 33.50 | 11.25 | 90.75 | 117 |
| 0680 | #14 bars | | 55 | 1.018 | | 57.50 | 42.50 | 14.30 | 114.30 | 148 |
| 0690 | #18 bars | | 40 | 1.400 | | 83 | 58.50 | 19.65 | 161.15 | 207 |
| 0700 | Transition position coupler for curved bars, taper threaded, #18-14 | | 40 | 1.400 | | 93.50 | 58.50 | 19.65 | 171.65 | 219 |
| 0710 | #18-11 | | 40 | 1.400 | | 91 | 58.50 | 19.65 | 169.15 | 216 |
| 0720 | #14-11 | | 55 | 1.018 | | 62.50 | 42.50 | 14.30 | 119.30 | 153 |
| 0730 | #11-10 | | 70 | .800 | | 51.50 | 33.50 | 11.25 | 96.25 | 123 |
| 0740 | #10-9 | | 80 | .700 | | 49 | 29.50 | 9.85 | 88.35 | 112 |
| 0750 | #9-8 | C-25 | 90 | .356 | | 45 | 12 | | 57 | 69.50 |
| 0760 | #8-7 | | 100 | .320 | | 41.50 | 10.80 | | 52.30 | 63.50 |
| 0770 | #7-6 | | 110 | .291 | | 40 | 9.85 | | 49.85 | 60.50 |
| 0800 | Sleeve type w/ grout filler, for precast concrete, #6 bars | | 72 | .444 | | 22 | 15 | | 37 | 49 |
| 0802 | #7 bars | | 64 | .500 | | 24 | 16.90 | | 40.90 | 54 |
| 0805 | #8 bars | | 56 | .571 | | 27 | 19.30 | | 46.30 | 62 |
| 0807 | #9 bars | | 48 | .667 | | 29.50 | 22.50 | | 52 | 70 |
| 0810 | #10 bars | C-5 | 40 | 1.400 | | 38.50 | 58.50 | 19.65 | 116.65 | 158 |
| 0900 | #11 bars | | 32 | 1.750 | | 45.50 | 73.50 | 24.50 | 143.50 | 195 |
| 0920 | #14 bars | | 24 | 2.333 | | 74.50 | 97.50 | 33 | 205 | 275 |
| 1000 | Sleeve type w/ ferrous filler, for critical structures, #6 bars | C-25 | 72 | .444 | | 36.50 | 15 | | 51.50 | 65.50 |
| 1210 | #7 bars | | 64 | .500 | | 37 | 16.90 | | 53.90 | 69 |
| 1220 | #8 bars | | 56 | .571 | | 39 | 19.30 | | 58.30 | 75 |
| 1230 | #9 bars | C-5 | 48 | 1.167 | | 40.50 | 49 | 16.40 | 105.90 | 141 |
| 1240 | #10 bars | | 40 | 1.400 | | 43 | 58.50 | 19.65 | 121.15 | 163 |
| 1250 | #11 bars | | 32 | 1.750 | | 52 | 73.50 | 24.50 | 150 | 202 |
| 1260 | #14 bars | | 24 | 2.333 | | 65 | 97.50 | 33 | 195.50 | 265 |
| 1270 | #18 bars | | 16 | 3.500 | | 94 | 147 | 49 | 290 | 390 |
| 2000 | Weldable half coupler, taper threaded, #4 bars | E-16 | 120 | .133 | | 6.75 | 5.85 | 1.10 | 13.70 | 19.20 |
| 2100 | #5 bars | | 112 | .143 | | 7.90 | 6.30 | 1.18 | 15.38 | 21.50 |
| 2200 | #6 bars | | 104 | .154 | | 12.55 | 6.75 | 1.27 | 20.57 | 27.50 |
| 2300 | #7 bars | | 96 | .167 | | 14.65 | 7.35 | 1.38 | 23.38 | 31 |
| 2400 | #8 bars | | 88 | .182 | | 15.25 | 8 | 1.50 | 24.75 | 33 |
| 2500 | #9 bars | | 80 | .200 | | 16.80 | 8.80 | 1.65 | 27.25 | 36 |
| 2600 | #10 bars | | 72 | .222 | | 17.20 | 9.80 | 1.84 | 28.84 | 38.50 |
| 2700 | #11 bars | | 64 | .250 | | 18.35 | 11 | 2.07 | 31.42 | 42 |
| 2800 | #14 bars | | 56 | .286 | | 21 | 12.55 | 2.36 | 35.91 | 48 |
| 2900 | #18 bars | | 48 | .333 | | 34.50 | 14.65 | 2.75 | 51.90 | 67.50 |

## 03 21 10 – Uncoated Reinforcing Steel

| 03 21 10.60 Reinforcing In Place | | Crew | Daily Output | Labor-Hours | Unit | Material | 2008 Bare Costs Labor | 2008 Bare Costs Equipment | Total | Total Incl O&P |
|---|---|---|---|---|---|---|---|---|---|---|
| 0015 | **REINFORCING IN PLACE** A615 Grade 60, incl. access. labor | R032110-10 | | | | | | | | |
| 0100 | Beams & Girders, #3 to #7 | **CN** 4 Rodm | 1.60 | 20 | Ton | 935 | 860 | | 1,795 | 2,425 |
| 0150 | #8 to #18 | R032110-20 | 2.70 | 11.852 | | 935 | 510 | | 1,445 | 1,850 |
| 0200 | Columns, #3 to #7 | | 1.50 | 21.333 | | 935 | 915 | | 1,850 | 2,525 |
| 0250 | #8 to #18 | | 2.30 | 13.913 | | 935 | 600 | | 1,535 | 2,000 |
| 0300 | Spirals, hot rolled, 8" to 15" diameter | | 2.20 | 14.545 | | 1,225 | 625 | | 1,850 | 2,375 |
| 0320 | 15" to 24" diameter | R032110-40 | 2.20 | 14.545 | | 1,175 | 625 | | 1,800 | 2,300 |
| 0330 | 24" to 36" diameter | | 2.30 | 13.913 | | 1,100 | 600 | | 1,700 | 2,200 |
| 0340 | 36" to 48" diameter | R032110-50 | 2.40 | 13.333 | | 1,050 | 575 | | 1,625 | 2,100 |
| 0360 | 48" to 64" diameter | | 2.50 | 12.800 | | 1,175 | 550 | | 1,725 | 2,175 |
| 0380 | 64" to 84" diameter | R032110-70 | 2.60 | 12.308 | | 1,225 | 530 | | 1,755 | 2,225 |
| 0390 | 84" to 96" diameter | | 2.70 | 11.852 | | 1,275 | 510 | | 1,785 | 2,225 |
| 0400 | Elevated slabs, #4 to #7 | R032110-80 | 2.90 | 11.034 | | 990 | 475 | | 1,465 | 1,875 |
| 0500 | Footings, #4 to #7 | | 2.10 | 15.238 | | 890 | 655 | | 1,545 | 2,050 |
| 0550 | #8 to #18 | | 3.60 | 8.889 | | 840 | 380 | | 1,220 | 1,550 |
| 0600 | Slab on grade, #3 to #7 | | 2.30 | 13.913 | | 890 | 600 | | 1,490 | 1,950 |
| 0700 | Walls, #3 to #7 | | 3 | 10.667 | | 890 | 460 | | 1,350 | 1,725 |
| 0750 | #8 to #18 | | 4 | 8 | | 890 | 345 | | 1,235 | 1,550 |
| 0900 | Use the following for a rough estimate guide | | | | | | | | | |
| 1000 | Typical in place, average, under 10 ton job, #3 to #7 | 4 Rodm | 1.80 | 17.778 | Ton | 965 | 765 | | 1,730 | 2,325 |
| 1010 | #8 to #18 | | 2.70 | 11.852 | | 985 | 510 | | 1,495 | 1,900 |
| 1050 | 10 - 50 ton job, #3 to #7 | | 2.10 | 15.238 | | 950 | 655 | | 1,605 | 2,125 |
| 1060 | #8 to #18 | | 3 | 10.667 | | 970 | 460 | | 1,430 | 1,825 |
| 1100 | 50 - 100 ton job, #3 - #7 | | 2.20 | 14.545 | | 925 | 625 | | 1,550 | 2,050 |
| 1110 | #8 to #18 | | 3.10 | 10.323 | | 945 | 445 | | 1,390 | 1,775 |
| 1150 | Over 100 ton job, #3 - #7 | | 2.30 | 13.913 | | 915 | 600 | | 1,515 | 1,975 |
| 1160 | #8 - #18 | | 3.20 | 10 | | 935 | 430 | | 1,365 | 1,725 |
| 1200 | High strength steel, Grade 75, #14 bars only, add | | | | | 66.50 | | | 66.50 | 73.50 |
| 2000 | Unloading & sorting, add to above | C-5 | 100 | .560 | | | 23.50 | 7.85 | 31.35 | 46 |
| 2200 | Crane cost for handling, add to above, minimum | | 135 | .415 | | | 17.35 | 5.80 | 23.15 | 34.50 |
| 2210 | Average | | 92 | .609 | | | 25.50 | 8.55 | 34.05 | 50.50 |
| 2220 | Maximum | | 35 | 1.600 | | | 67 | 22.50 | 89.50 | 133 |
| 2400 | Dowels, 2 feet long, deformed, #3 | 2 Rodm | 520 | .031 | Ea. | .39 | 1.32 | | 1.71 | 2.60 |
| 2410 | #4 | | 480 | .033 | | .69 | 1.43 | | 2.12 | 3.11 |
| 2420 | #5 | | 435 | .037 | | 1.07 | 1.58 | | 2.65 | 3.77 |
| 2430 | #6 | | 360 | .044 | | 1.54 | 1.91 | | 3.45 | 4.84 |
| 2450 | Longer and heavier dowels, add | | 725 | .022 | Lb. | .51 | .95 | | 1.46 | 2.13 |
| 2500 | Smooth dowels, 12" long, 1/4" or 3/8" diameter | | 140 | .114 | Ea. | .73 | 4.91 | | 5.64 | 8.85 |
| 2520 | 5/8" diameter | | 125 | .128 | | 1.28 | 5.50 | | 6.78 | 10.45 |
| 2530 | 3/4" diameter | | 110 | .145 | | 1.58 | 6.25 | | 7.83 | 12 |
| 2600 | Dowel sleeves for CIP concrete, 2-part system | | | | | | | | | |
| 2610 | Sleeve base, plastic, for 5/8" smooth dowel sleeve, fasten to edge form | 1 Rodm | 200 | .040 | Ea. | .41 | 1.72 | | 2.13 | 3.27 |
| 2615 | Sleeve, plastic, 12" long, for 5/8" smooth dowel, snap onto base | | 400 | .020 | | 1.17 | .86 | | 2.03 | 2.70 |
| 2620 | Sleeve base, for 3/4" smooth dowel sleeve | | 175 | .046 | | .41 | 1.97 | | 2.38 | 3.67 |
| 2625 | Sleeve, 12" long, for 3/4" smooth dowel | | 350 | .023 | | 1.20 | .98 | | 2.18 | 2.93 |
| 2630 | Sleeve base, for 1" smooth dowel sleeve | | 150 | .053 | | .50 | 2.29 | | 2.79 | 4.31 |
| 2635 | Sleeve, 12" long, for 1" smooth dowel | | 300 | .027 | | 1.33 | 1.15 | | 2.48 | 3.34 |
| 2700 | Dowel caps, visual warning only, plastic, #3 to #8 | 2 Rodm | 800 | .020 | | .65 | .86 | | 1.51 | 2.12 |
| 2720 | #8 to #18 | | 750 | .021 | | 1.32 | .92 | | 2.24 | 2.96 |
| 2750 | Impalement protective, plastic, #4 to #9 | | 800 | .020 | | 2.43 | .86 | | 3.29 | 4.08 |

# 03 21 Reinforcing Steel

## 03 21 13 – Galvanized Reinforcing Steel

| 03 21 13.10 Galvanized Reinforcing | Crew | Daily Output | Labor-Hours | Unit | Material | 2008 Bare Costs Labor | Equipment | Total | Total Incl O&P |
|---|---|---|---|---|---|---|---|---|---|
| 0010 **GALVANIZED REINFORCING** | | | | | | | | | |
| 0150 Galvanized, #3 | | | | Ton | 750 | | | 750 | 825 |
| 0200 #4 | | | | | 750 | | | 750 | 825 |
| 0250 #5 | | | | | 735 | | | 735 | 810 |
| 0300 #6 or over | | | | | 735 | | | 735 | 810 |
| 1000 For over 20 tons, #6 or larger, minimum | | | | | 680 | | | 680 | 750 |
| 1500 Maximum | | | | | 815 | | | 815 | 900 |

## 03 21 16 – Epoxy-Coated Reinforcing Steel

### 03 21 16.10 Epoxy-Coated Reinforcing

| | Crew | Daily Output | Labor-Hours | Unit | Material | Labor | Equipment | Total | Total Incl O&P |
|---|---|---|---|---|---|---|---|---|---|
| 0010 **EPOXY-COATED REINFORCING** | | | | | | | | | |
| 0100 Epoxy coated, A775 | | | | Ton | 400 | | | 400 | 440 |

# 03 22 Welded Wire Fabric Reinforcing

## 03 22 05 – Uncoated Welded Wire Fabric

### 03 22 05.50 Welded Wire Fabric

| | | Crew | Daily Output | Labor-Hours | Unit | Material | Labor | Equipment | Total | Total Incl O&P |
|---|---|---|---|---|---|---|---|---|---|---|
| 0010 **WELDED WIRE FABRIC** ASTM A185 | R032205-30 | | | | | | | | | |
| 0050 Sheets | | | | | | | | | | |
| 0100 6 x 6 - W1.4 x W1.4 (10 x 10) 21 lb. per C.S.F. | CN | 2 Rodm | 35 | .457 | C.S.F. | 13.25 | 19.65 | | 32.90 | 47 |
| 0200 6 x 6 - W2.1 x W2.1 (8 x 8) 30 lb. per C.S.F. | | | 31 | .516 | | 15.65 | 22 | | 37.65 | 53.50 |
| 0300 6 x 6 - W2.9 x W2.9 (6 x 6) 42 lb. per C.S.F. | | | 29 | .552 | | 20 | 23.50 | | 43.50 | 61 |
| 0400 6 x 6 - W4 x W4 (4 x 4) 58 lb. per C.S.F. | | | 27 | .593 | | 29 | 25.50 | | 54.50 | 74 |
| 0500 4 x 4 - W1.4 x W1.4 (10 x 10) 31 lb. per C.S.F. | | | 31 | .516 | | 20 | 22 | | 42 | 59 |
| 0600 4 x 4 - W2.1 x W2.1 (8 x 8) 44 lb. per C.S.F. | | | 29 | .552 | | 26.50 | 23.50 | | 50 | 68 |
| 0650 4 x 4 - W2.9 x W2.9 (6 x 6) 61 lb. per C.S.F. | | | 27 | .593 | | 31.50 | 25.50 | | 57 | 76.50 |
| 0700 4 x 4 - W4 x W4 (4 x 4) 85 lb. per C.S.F. | | | 25 | .640 | | 47 | 27.50 | | 74.50 | 97 |
| 0750 Rolls | | | | | | | | | | |
| 0800 2 x 2 - #14 galv., 21 lb/C.S.F., beam & column wrap | | 2 Rodm | 6.50 | 2.462 | C.S.F. | 33 | 106 | | 139 | 211 |
| 0900 2 x 2 - #12 galv. for gunite reinforcing | | " | 6.50 | 2.462 | " | 39.50 | 106 | | 145.50 | 218 |

# 03 23 Stressing Tendons

## 03 23 05 – Prestressing Tendons

### 03 23 05.50 Prestressing Steel

| | | Crew | Daily Output | Labor-Hours | Unit | Material | Labor | Equipment | Total | Total Incl O&P |
|---|---|---|---|---|---|---|---|---|---|---|
| 0010 **PRESTRESSING STEEL** | R034136-90 | | | | | | | | | |
| 0100 Grouted strand, post-tensioned in field, 50' span, 100 kip | | C-3 | 1200 | .053 | Lb. | 2.08 | 2.10 | .08 | 4.26 | 5.75 |
| 0150 300 kip | | | 2700 | .024 | | .91 | .93 | .04 | 1.88 | 2.54 |
| 0300 100' span, 100 kip | | | 1700 | .038 | | 2.08 | 1.48 | .06 | 3.62 | 4.75 |
| 0350 300 kip | | | 3200 | .020 | | 1.79 | .79 | .03 | 2.61 | 3.27 |
| 0500 200' span, 100 kip | | | 2700 | .024 | | 2.08 | .93 | .04 | 3.05 | 3.83 |
| 0550 300 kip | | | 3500 | .018 | | 1.79 | .72 | .03 | 2.54 | 3.16 |
| 0800 Grouted bars, 50' span, 42 kip | | | 2600 | .025 | | .91 | .97 | .04 | 1.92 | 2.60 |
| 0850 143 kip | | | 3200 | .020 | | .87 | .79 | .03 | 1.69 | 2.26 |
| 1000 75' span, 42 kip | | | 3200 | .020 | | .92 | .79 | .03 | 1.74 | 2.31 |
| 1050 143 kip | | | 4200 | .015 | | .78 | .60 | .02 | 1.40 | 1.86 |
| 1200 Ungrouted strand, 50' span, 100 kip | | C-4 | 1275 | .025 | | .51 | 1.09 | .02 | 1.62 | 2.37 |
| 1250 300 kip | | | 1475 | .022 | | .51 | .94 | .02 | 1.47 | 2.13 |
| 1400 100' span, 100 kip | | | 1500 | .021 | | .51 | .93 | .02 | 1.46 | 2.10 |
| 1450 300 kip | | | 1650 | .019 | | .51 | .84 | .02 | 1.37 | 1.96 |
| 1600 200' span, 100 kip | | | 1500 | .021 | | .51 | .93 | .02 | 1.46 | 2.10 |

# 03 23 Stressing Tendons

## 03 23 05 – Prestressing Tendons

### 03 23 05.50 Prestressing Steel

| | 03 23 05.50 Prestressing Steel | Crew | Daily Output | Labor-Hours | Unit | Material | 2008 Bare Costs Labor | 2008 Bare Costs Equipment | Total | Total Incl O&P |
|---|---|---|---|---|---|---|---|---|---|---|
| 1650 | 300 kip | C-4 | 1700 | .019 | Lb. | .51 | .82 | .02 | 1.35 | 1.92 |
| 1800 | Ungrouted bars, 50' span, 42 kip | | 1400 | .023 | | .47 | .99 | .02 | 1.48 | 2.16 |
| 1850 | 143 kip | | 1700 | .019 | | .47 | .82 | .02 | 1.31 | 1.87 |
| 2000 | 75' span, 42 kip | | 1800 | .018 | | .47 | .77 | .01 | 1.25 | 1.80 |
| 2050 | 143 kip | | 2200 | .015 | | .47 | .63 | .01 | 1.11 | 1.56 |
| 2220 | Ungrouted single strand, 100' slab, 25 kip | | 1200 | .027 | | .51 | 1.16 | .02 | 1.69 | 2.48 |
| 2250 | 35 kip | | 1475 | .022 | | .51 | .94 | .02 | 1.47 | 2.13 |

# 03 24 Fibrous Reinforcing

## 03 24 05 – Reinforcing Fibers

### 03 24 05.30 Synthetic Fibers

| | 03 24 05.30 Synthetic Fibers | Crew | Daily Output | Labor-Hours | Unit | Material | 2008 Bare Costs Labor | 2008 Bare Costs Equipment | Total | Total Incl O&P |
|---|---|---|---|---|---|---|---|---|---|---|
| 0010 | **SYNTHETIC FIBERS** | | | | | | | | | |
| 0100 | Synthetic fibers, add to concrete | | | | Lb. | 3.98 | | | 3.98 | 4.38 |
| 0110 | 1-1/2 lb. per C.Y. | | | | C.Y. | 6.15 | | | 6.15 | 6.75 |

### 03 24 05.70 Steel Fibers

| | 03 24 05.70 Steel Fibers | Crew | Daily Output | Labor-Hours | Unit | Material | 2008 Bare Costs Labor | 2008 Bare Costs Equipment | Total | Total Incl O&P |
|---|---|---|---|---|---|---|---|---|---|---|
| 0010 | **STEEL FIBERS** | | | | | | | | | |
| 0150 | Steel fibers, add to concrete | | | | Lb. | .46 | | | .46 | .51 |
| 0155 | 25 lb. per C.Y. | | | | C.Y. | 11.50 | | | 11.50 | 12.65 |
| 0160 | 50 lb. per C.Y. | | | | | 23 | | | 23 | 25.50 |
| 0170 | 75 lb. per C.Y. | | | | | 35.50 | | | 35.50 | 39 |
| 0180 | 100 lb. per C.Y. | | | | | 46 | | | 46 | 50.50 |

# 03 30 Cast-In-Place Concrete

## 03 30 53 – Miscellaneous Cast-In-Place Concrete

### 03 30 53.40 Concrete In Place

| | 03 30 53.40 Concrete In Place | Crew | Daily Output | Labor-Hours | Unit | Material | 2008 Bare Costs Labor | 2008 Bare Costs Equipment | Total | Total Incl O&P |
|---|---|---|---|---|---|---|---|---|---|---|
| 0010 | **CONCRETE IN PLACE** | | | | | | | | | |
| 0020 | Including forms (4 uses), reinforcing steel, concrete, placement, | | | | | | | | | |
| 0050 | and finishing unless otherwise indicated    R033053-50 | | | | | | | | | |
| 0300 | Beams, 5 kip per L.F., 10' span | C-14A | 15.62 | 12.804 | C.Y. | 315 | 490 | 48.50 | 853.50 | 1,175 |
| 0350 | 25' span | " | 18.55 | 10.782 | | 325 | 415 | 40.50 | 780.50 | 1,050 |
| 0500 | Chimney foundations, industrial, minimum | C-14C | 32.22 | 3.476 | | 145 | 127 | .76 | 272.76 | 360 |
| 0510 | Maximum | " | 23.71 | 4.724 | | 172 | 173 | 1.04 | 346.04 | 460 |
| 0700 | Columns, square, 12" x 12", minimum reinforcing | C-14A | 11.96 | 16.722 | | 335 | 640 | 63 | 1,038 | 1,450 |
| 0720 | Average reinforcing    R033105-85 | | 10.13 | 19.743 | | 530 | 755 | 74.50 | 1,359.50 | 1,850 |
| 0740 | Maximum reinforcing | | 9.03 | 22.148 | | 795 | 850 | 83.50 | 1,728.50 | 2,300 |
| 0800 | 16" x 16", minimum reinforcing | | 16.22 | 12.330 | | 269 | 475 | 46.50 | 790.50 | 1,075 |
| 0820 | Average reinforcing | | 12.57 | 15.911 | | 455 | 610 | 60 | 1,125 | 1,525 |
| 0840 | Maximum reinforcing | | 10.25 | 19.512 | | 700 | 750 | 73.50 | 1,523.50 | 2,025 |
| 0900 | 24" x 24", minimum reinforcing | | 23.66 | 8.453 | | 231 | 325 | 32 | 588 | 800 |
| 0920 | Average reinforcing | | 17.71 | 11.293 | | 410 | 435 | 42.50 | 887.50 | 1,175 |
| 0940 | Maximum reinforcing | | 14.15 | 14.134 | | 645 | 540 | 53.50 | 1,238.50 | 1,625 |
| 1000 | 36" x 36", minimum reinforcing | | 33.69 | 5.936 | | 205 | 228 | 22.50 | 455.50 | 605 |
| 1020 | Average reinforcing | | 23.32 | 8.576 | | 360 | 330 | 32.50 | 722.50 | 945 |
| 1040 | Maximum reinforcing | | 17.82 | 11.223 | | 605 | 430 | 42.50 | 1,077.50 | 1,375 |
| 1100 | Columns, round, tied, 12" diameter, minimum reinforcing | | 20.97 | 9.537 | | 294 | 365 | 36 | 695 | 940 |
| 1120 | Average reinforcing | | 15.27 | 13.098 | | 485 | 500 | 49.50 | 1,034.50 | 1,375 |
| 1140 | Maximum reinforcing | | 12.11 | 16.515 | | 740 | 635 | 62.50 | 1,437.50 | 1,875 |
| 1200 | 16" diameter, minimum reinforcing | | 31.49 | 6.351 | | 268 | 244 | 24 | 536 | 700 |
| 1220 | Average reinforcing | | 19.12 | 10.460 | | 465 | 400 | 39.50 | 904.50 | 1,175 |

| 03 30 53.40 Concrete In Place | | Crew | Daily Output | Labor-Hours | Unit | Material | 2008 Bare Costs Labor | Equipment | Total | Total Incl O&P |
|---|---|---|---|---|---|---|---|---|---|---|
| 1240 | Maximum reinforcing | C-14A | 13.77 | 14.524 | C.Y. | 695 | 555 | 55 | 1,305 | 1,700 |
| 1300 | 20" diameter, minimum reinforcing | | 41.04 | 4.873 | | 265 | 187 | 18.35 | 470.35 | 605 |
| 1320 | Average reinforcing | | 24.05 | 8.316 | | 445 | 320 | 31.50 | 796.50 | 1,025 |
| 1340 | Maximum reinforcing | | 17.01 | 11.758 | | 695 | 450 | 44.50 | 1,189.50 | 1,525 |
| 1400 | 24" diameter, minimum reinforcing | | 51.85 | 3.857 | | 251 | 148 | 14.55 | 413.55 | 525 |
| 1420 | Average reinforcing | | 27.06 | 7.391 | | 445 | 284 | 28 | 757 | 965 |
| 1440 | Maximum reinforcing | | 18.29 | 10.935 | | 685 | 420 | 41 | 1,146 | 1,450 |
| 1500 | 36" diameter, minimum reinforcing | | 75.04 | 2.665 | | 254 | 102 | 10.05 | 366.05 | 450 |
| 1520 | Average reinforcing | | 37.49 | 5.335 | | 425 | 205 | 20 | 650 | 810 |
| 1540 | Maximum reinforcing | ▼ | 22.84 | 8.757 | | 665 | 335 | 33 | 1,033 | 1,300 |
| 1900 | Elevated slabs, flat slab with drops, 125 psf Sup. Load, 20' span | C-14B | 38.45 | 5.410 | | 263 | 207 | 19.60 | 489.60 | 635 |
| 1950 | 30' span | | 50.99 | 4.079 | | 275 | 156 | 14.75 | 445.75 | 560 |
| 2100 | Flat plate, 125 psf Sup. Load, 15' span | | 30.24 | 6.878 | | 242 | 264 | 25 | 531 | 705 |
| 2150 | 25' span | | 49.60 | 4.194 | | 249 | 161 | 15.20 | 425.20 | 540 |
| 2300 | Waffle const., 30" domes, 125 psf Sup. Load, 20' span | | 37.07 | 5.611 | | 375 | 215 | 20.50 | 610.50 | 770 |
| 2350 | 30' span | | 44.07 | 4.720 | | 335 | 181 | 17.10 | 533.10 | 665 |
| 2500 | One way joists, 30" pans, 125 psf Sup. Load, 15' span | | 27.38 | 7.597 | | 450 | 291 | 27.50 | 768.50 | 980 |
| 2550 | 25' span | | 31.15 | 6.677 | | 410 | 256 | 24 | 690 | 880 |
| 2700 | One way beam & slab, 125 psf Sup. Load, 15' span | | 20.59 | 10.102 | | 264 | 385 | 36.50 | 685.50 | 935 |
| 2750 | 25' span | | 28.36 | 7.334 | | 246 | 281 | 26.50 | 553.50 | 740 |
| 2900 | Two way beam & slab, 125 psf Sup. Load, 15' span | | 24.04 | 8.652 | | 253 | 330 | 31.50 | 614.50 | 835 |
| 2950 | 25' span | ▼ | 35.87 | 5.799 | ▼ | 216 | 222 | 21 | 459 | 605 |
| 3100 | Elevated slabs including finish, not | | | | | | | | | |
| 3110 | including forms or reinforcing | | | | | | | | | |
| 3150 | Regular concrete, 4" slab | C-8 | 2613 | .021 | S.F. | 1.36 | .73 | .28 | 2.37 | 2.91 |
| 3200 | 6" slab | | 2585 | .022 | | 2.02 | .73 | .28 | 3.03 | 3.64 |
| 3250 | 2-1/2" thick floor fill | | 2685 | .021 | | .87 | .71 | .27 | 1.85 | 2.33 |
| 3300 | Lightweight, 110# per C.F., 2-1/2" thick floor fill | | 2585 | .022 | | 1.19 | .73 | .28 | 2.20 | 2.73 |
| 3400 | Cellular concrete, 1-5/8" fill, under 5000 S.F. | | 2000 | .028 | | .79 | .95 | .36 | 2.10 | 2.71 |
| 3450 | Over 10,000 S.F. | | 2200 | .025 | | .76 | .86 | .33 | 1.95 | 2.50 |
| 3500 | Add per floor for 3 to 6 stories high | | 31800 | .002 | | | .06 | .02 | .08 | .12 |
| 3520 | For 7 to 20 stories high | ▼ | 21200 | .003 | ▼ | | .09 | .03 | .12 | .18 |
| 3540 | Equipment pad, 3' x 3' x 6" thick | C-14H | 45 | 1.067 | Ea. | 45.50 | 40.50 | .55 | 86.55 | 113 |
| 3550 | 4' x 4' x 6" thick | | 30 | 1.600 | | 67 | 60.50 | .83 | 128.33 | 168 |
| 3560 | 5' x 5' x 8" thick | | 18 | 2.667 | | 116 | 101 | 1.39 | 218.39 | 287 |
| 3570 | 6' x 6' x 8" thick | | 14 | 3.429 | | 157 | 129 | 1.78 | 287.78 | 375 |
| 3580 | 8' x 8' x 10" thick | | 8 | 6 | | 330 | 227 | 3.12 | 560.12 | 725 |
| 3590 | 10' x 10' x 12" thick | ▼ | 5 | 9.600 | ▼ | 560 | 365 | 4.99 | 929.99 | 1,175 |
| 3800 | Footings, spread under 1 C.Y. | C-14C | 28 | 4 | C.Y. | 173 | 146 | .88 | 319.88 | 420 |
| 3825 | 1 C.Y to 5 C.Y. | | 43 | 2.605 | | 192 | 95.50 | .57 | 288.07 | 360 |
| 3850 | Over 5 C.Y. | ▼ | 75 | 1.493 | | 176 | 54.50 | .33 | 230.83 | 280 |
| 3900 | Footings, strip, 18" x 9", unreinforced | C-14L | 40 | 2.400 | | 119 | 85.50 | .62 | 205.12 | 264 |
| 3920 | 18" x 9", reinforced | C-14C | 35 | 3.200 | | 142 | 117 | .70 | 259.70 | 340 |
| 3925 | 20" x 10", unreinforced | C-14L | 45 | 2.133 | | 117 | 76 | .55 | 193.55 | 246 |
| 3930 | 20" x 10", reinforced | C-14C | 40 | 2.800 | | 135 | 103 | .62 | 238.62 | 310 |
| 3935 | 24" x 12", unreinforced | C-14L | 55 | 1.745 | | 115 | 62 | .45 | 177.45 | 222 |
| 3940 | 24" x 12", reinforced | C-14C | 48 | 2.333 | | 133 | 85.50 | .51 | 219.01 | 282 |
| 3945 | 36" x 12", unreinforced | C-14L | 70 | 1.371 | | 112 | 49 | .36 | 161.36 | 199 |
| 3950 | 36" x 12", reinforced | C-14C | 60 | 1.867 | | 128 | 68.50 | .41 | 196.91 | 248 |
| 4000 | Foundation mat, under 10 C.Y. | | 38.67 | 2.896 | | 197 | 106 | .64 | 303.64 | 385 |
| 4050 | Over 20 C.Y. | ▼ | 56.40 | 1.986 | | 173 | 72.50 | .44 | 245.94 | 305 |
| 4200 | Grade walls, 8" thick, 8' high | C-14D | 45.83 | 4.364 | | 177 | 166 | 16.45 | 359.45 | 470 |
| 4250 | 14' high | ▼ | 27.26 | 7.337 | ▼ | 228 | 279 | 27.50 | 534.50 | 715 |

## 03 30 53 – Miscellaneous Cast-In-Place Concrete

| 03 30 53.40 Concrete In Place | Crew | Daily Output | Labor-Hours | Unit | Material | 2008 Bare Costs Labor | Equipment | Total | Total Incl O&P |
|---|---|---|---|---|---|---|---|---|---|
| 4260 | 12" thick, 8' high | C-14D | 64.32 | 3.109 | C.Y. | 158 | 118 | 11.70 | 287.70 | 370 |
| 4270 | 14' high | | 40.01 | 4.999 | | 179 | 190 | 18.85 | 387.85 | 515 |
| 4300 | 15" thick, 8' high | | 80.02 | 2.499 | | 149 | 95 | 9.40 | 253.40 | 320 |
| 4350 | 12' high | | 51.26 | 3.902 | | 158 | 148 | 14.70 | 320.70 | 420 |
| 4500 | 18' high | | 48.85 | 4.094 | | 175 | 155 | 15.45 | 345.45 | 450 |
| 4520 | Handicap access ramp, railing both sides, 3' wide | C-14H | 14.58 | 3.292 | L.F. | 251 | 124 | 1.71 | 376.71 | 470 |
| 4525 | 5' wide | | 12.22 | 3.928 | | 259 | 148 | 2.04 | 409.04 | 520 |
| 4530 | With 6" curb and rails both sides, 3' wide | | 8.55 | 5.614 | | 259 | 212 | 2.92 | 473.92 | 620 |
| 4535 | 5' wide | | 7.31 | 6.566 | | 264 | 248 | 3.41 | 515.41 | 680 |
| 4650 | Slab on grade, not including finish, 4" thick | C-14E | 60.75 | 1.449 | C.Y. | 122 | 55 | .41 | 177.41 | 221 |
| 4700 | 6" thick | " | 92 | .957 | " | 117 | 36 | .27 | 153.27 | 187 |
| 4751 | Slab on grade, incl. troweled finish, not incl. forms | | | | | | | | | |
| 4760 | or reinforcing, over 10,000 S.F., 4" thick | C-14F | 3425 | .021 | S.F. | 1.34 | .74 | .01 | 2.09 | 2.58 |
| 4820 | 6" thick | | 3350 | .021 | | 1.95 | .75 | .01 | 2.71 | 3.28 |
| 4840 | 8" thick | | 3184 | .023 | | 2.67 | .79 | .01 | 3.47 | 4.13 |
| 4900 | 12" thick | | 2734 | .026 | | 4.01 | .92 | .01 | 4.94 | 5.80 |
| 4950 | 15" thick | | 2505 | .029 | | 5.05 | 1.01 | .01 | 6.07 | 7.05 |
| 5000 | Slab on grade, incl. textured finish, not incl. forms | | | | | | | | | |
| 5001 | or reinforcing, 4" thick | C-14G | 2873 | .019 | S.F. | 1.30 | .67 | .01 | 1.98 | 2.45 |
| 5010 | 6" thick | | 2590 | .022 | | 2.03 | .74 | .01 | 2.78 | 3.37 |
| 5020 | 8" thick | | 2320 | .024 | | 2.65 | .83 | .01 | 3.49 | 4.18 |
| 5200 | Lift slab in place above the foundation, incl. forms, | | | | | | | | | |
| 5210 | reinforcing, concrete and columns, minimum | C-14B | 2113 | .098 | S.F. | 6.10 | 3.77 | .36 | 10.23 | 13.05 |
| 5250 | Average | | 1650 | .126 | | 6.65 | 4.83 | .46 | 11.94 | 15.35 |
| 5300 | Maximum | | 1500 | .139 | | 7.15 | 5.30 | .50 | 12.95 | 16.75 |
| 5500 | Lightweight, ready mix, including screed finish only, | | | | | | | | | |
| 5510 | not including forms or reinforcing | | | | | | | | | |
| 5550 | 1:4 for structural roof decks | C-14B | 260 | .800 | C.Y. | 142 | 30.50 | 2.90 | 175.40 | 207 |
| 5600 | 1:6 for ground slab with radiant heat | C-14F | 92 | .783 | | 146 | 27.50 | .27 | 173.77 | 202 |
| 5650 | 1:3:2 with sand aggregate, roof deck | C-14B | 260 | .800 | | 147 | 30.50 | 2.90 | 180.40 | 213 |
| 5700 | Ground slab | C-14F | 107 | .673 | | 147 | 23.50 | .23 | 170.73 | 197 |
| 5900 | Pile caps, incl. forms and reinf., sq. or rect., under 5 C.Y. | C-14C | 54.14 | 2.069 | | 160 | 76 | .46 | 236.46 | 295 |
| 5950 | Over 10 C.Y. | | 75 | 1.493 | | 151 | 54.50 | .33 | 205.83 | 252 |
| 6000 | Triangular or hexagonal, under 5 C.Y. | | 53 | 2.113 | | 120 | 77.50 | .46 | 197.96 | 254 |
| 6050 | Over 10 C.Y. | | 85 | 1.318 | | 135 | 48.50 | .29 | 183.79 | 225 |
| 6200 | Retaining walls, gravity, 4' high see Div. 32 32 13.10 | C-14D | 66.20 | 3.021 | | 141 | 115 | 11.40 | 267.40 | 345 |
| 6250 | 10' high | | 125 | 1.600 | | 133 | 61 | 6.05 | 200.05 | 247 |
| 6300 | Cantilever, level backfill loading, 8' high | | 70 | 2.857 | | 157 | 108 | 10.75 | 275.75 | 355 |
| 6350 | 16' high | | 91 | 2.198 | | 149 | 83.50 | 8.30 | 240.80 | 305 |
| 6800 | Stairs, not including safety treads, free standing, 3'-6" wide | C-14H | 83 | .578 | LF Nose | 5.55 | 22 | .30 | 27.85 | 40.50 |
| 6850 | Cast on ground | | 125 | .384 | " | 4.42 | 14.50 | .20 | 19.12 | 27.50 |
| 7000 | Stair landings, free standing | | 200 | .240 | S.F. | 4.56 | 9.05 | .12 | 13.73 | 19.25 |
| 7050 | Cast on ground | | 475 | .101 | " | 3.41 | 3.82 | .05 | 7.28 | 9.75 |

# 03 31 Structural Concrete

## 03 31 05 – Normal Weight Structural Concrete

### 03 31 05.30 Concrete, Field Mix

| | | Crew | Daily Output | Labor-Hours | Unit | Material | 2008 Bare Costs Labor | Equipment | Total | Total Incl O&P |
|---|---|---|---|---|---|---|---|---|---|---|
| 0010 | **CONCRETE, FIELD MIX** | R033105-65 | | | | | | | | |
| 0015 | FOB forms 2250 psi | | | | C.Y. | 90.50 | | | 90.50 | 99.50 |
| 0020 | 3000 psi | | | | " | 93 | | | 93 | 102 |

### 03 31 05.35 Normal Weight Concrete, Ready Mix

| | | Crew | Daily Output | Labor-Hours | Unit | Material | 2008 Bare Costs Labor | Equipment | Total | Total Incl O&P |
|---|---|---|---|---|---|---|---|---|---|---|
| 0010 | **NORMAL WEIGHT CONCRETE, READY MIX**, delivered | R033105-10 | | | | | | | | |
| 0012 | Includes local aggregate, sand, portland cement, and water | | | | | | | | | |
| 0015 | Excludes all additives and treatments | R033105-20 | | | | | | | | |
| 0020 | 2000 psi | | | | C.Y. | 97 | | | 97 | 107 |
| 0100 | 2500 psi | R033105-30 | | | | 98.50 | | | 98.50 | 108 |
| 0150 | 3000 psi | *CN* | | | | 100 | | | 100 | 110 |
| 0200 | 3500 psi | R033105-40 | | | | 103 | | | 103 | 113 |
| 0300 | 4000 psi | | | | | 106 | | | 106 | 117 |
| 0350 | 4500 psi | R033105-50 | | | | 109 | | | 109 | 120 |
| 0400 | 5000 psi | *CN* | | | | 109 | | | 109 | 120 |
| 0411 | 6000 psi | | | | | 124 | | | 124 | 137 |
| 0412 | 8000 psi | | | | | 203 | | | 203 | 223 |
| 0413 | 10,000 psi | | | | | 288 | | | 288 | 315 |
| 0414 | 12,000 psi | | | | | 350 | | | 350 | 380 |
| 1000 | For high early strength cement, add | | | | | 10% | | | | |
| 1010 | For structural lightweight with regular sand, add | | | | | 25% | | | | |
| 2000 | For all lightweight aggregate, add | | | | | 45% | | | | |

### 03 31 05.70 Placing Concrete

| | | Crew | Daily Output | Labor-Hours | Unit | Material | 2008 Bare Costs Labor | Equipment | Total | Total Incl O&P |
|---|---|---|---|---|---|---|---|---|---|---|
| 0010 | **PLACING CONCRETE** | R033105-70 | | | | | | | | |
| 0020 | Includes labor and equipment to place and vibrate | | | | | | | | | |
| 0050 | Beams, elevated, small beams, pumped | C-20 | 60 | 1.067 | C.Y. | | 34.50 | 12.95 | 47.45 | 68 |
| 0100 | With crane and bucket | C-7 | 45 | 1.600 | | | 52.50 | 26.50 | 79 | 110 |
| 0200 | Large beams, pumped | C-20 | 90 | .711 | | | 23 | 8.65 | 31.65 | 45 |
| 0250 | With crane and bucket | C-7 | 65 | 1.108 | | | 36.50 | 18.30 | 54.80 | 75.50 |
| 0400 | Columns, square or round, 12" thick, pumped | C-20 | 60 | 1.067 | | | 34.50 | 12.95 | 47.45 | 68 |
| 0450 | With crane and bucket | C-7 | 40 | 1.800 | | | 59 | 29.50 | 88.50 | 123 |
| 0600 | 18" thick, pumped | C-20 | 90 | .711 | | | 23 | 8.65 | 31.65 | 45 |
| 0650 | With crane and bucket | C-7 | 55 | 1.309 | | | 43 | 21.50 | 64.50 | 90 |
| 0800 | 24" thick, pumped | C-20 | 92 | .696 | | | 22.50 | 8.45 | 30.95 | 44.50 |
| 0850 | With crane and bucket | C-7 | 70 | 1.029 | | | 34 | 16.95 | 50.95 | 70.50 |
| 1000 | 36" thick, pumped | C-20 | 140 | .457 | | | 14.90 | 5.55 | 20.45 | 29 |
| 1050 | With crane and bucket | C-7 | 100 | .720 | | | 23.50 | 11.90 | 35.40 | 49 |
| 1400 | Elevated slabs, less than 6" thick, pumped | C-20 | 140 | .457 | | | 14.90 | 5.55 | 20.45 | 29 |
| 1450 | With crane and bucket | C-7 | 95 | .758 | | | 25 | 12.50 | 37.50 | 52 |
| 1500 | 6" to 10" thick, pumped | C-20 | 160 | .400 | | | 13 | 4.86 | 17.86 | 25.50 |
| 1550 | With crane and bucket | C-7 | 110 | .655 | | | 21.50 | 10.80 | 32.30 | 45 |
| 1600 | Slabs over 10" thick, pumped | C-20 | 180 | .356 | | | 11.55 | 4.32 | 15.87 | 22.50 |
| 1650 | With crane and bucket | C-7 | 130 | .554 | | | 18.20 | 9.15 | 27.35 | 38 |
| 1900 | Footings, continuous, shallow, direct chute | C-6 | 120 | .400 | | | 12.70 | .41 | 13.11 | 19.95 |
| 1950 | Pumped | C-20 | 150 | .427 | | | 13.90 | 5.20 | 19.10 | 27 |
| 2000 | With crane and bucket | C-7 | 90 | .800 | | | 26.50 | 13.20 | 39.70 | 55 |
| 2100 | Footings, continuous, deep, direct chute | C-6 | 140 | .343 | | | 10.85 | .35 | 11.20 | 17.10 |
| 2150 | Pumped | C-20 | 160 | .400 | | | 13 | 4.86 | 17.86 | 25.50 |
| 2200 | With crane and bucket | C-7 | 110 | .655 | | | 21.50 | 10.80 | 32.30 | 45 |
| 2400 | Footings, spread, under 1 C.Y., direct chute | C-6 | 55 | .873 | | | 27.50 | .90 | 28.40 | 43.50 |
| 2450 | Pumped | C-20 | 65 | .985 | | | 32 | 11.95 | 43.95 | 62 |
| 2500 | With crane and bucket | C-7 | 45 | 1.600 | | | 52.50 | 26.50 | 79 | 110 |
| 2600 | Over 5 C.Y., direct chute | C-6 | 120 | .400 | | | 12.70 | .41 | 13.11 | 19.95 |

# 03 31 Structural Concrete

## 03 31 05 – Normal Weight Structural Concrete

| 03 31 05.70 Placing Concrete | Crew | Daily Output | Labor-Hours | Unit | Material | 2008 Bare Costs Labor | Equipment | Total | Total Incl O&P |
|---|---|---|---|---|---|---|---|---|---|
| 2650      Pumped | C-20 | 150 | .427 | C.Y. | | 13.90 | 5.20 | 19.10 | 27 |
| 2700      With crane and bucket | C-7 | 100 | .720 | | | 23.50 | 11.90 | 35.40 | 49 |
| 2900 Foundation mats, over 20 C.Y., direct chute | C-6 | 350 | .137 | | | 4.35 | .14 | 4.49 | 6.85 |
| 2950      Pumped | C-20 | 400 | .160 | | | 5.20 | 1.94 | 7.14 | 10.15 |
| 3000      With crane and bucket | C-7 | 300 | .240 | | | 7.90 | 3.96 | 11.86 | 16.40 |
| 3200 Grade beams, direct chute | C-6 | 150 | .320 | | | 10.15 | .33 | 10.48 | 15.95 |
| 3250      Pumped | C-20 | 180 | .356 | | | 11.55 | 4.32 | 15.87 | 22.50 |
| 3300      With crane and bucket | C-7 | 120 | .600 | | | 19.70 | 9.90 | 29.60 | 41 |
| 3500 High rise, for more than 5 stories, pumped, add per story | C-20 | 2100 | .030 | | | .99 | .37 | 1.36 | 1.93 |
| 3510      With crane and bucket, add per story | C-7 | 2100 | .034 | | | 1.13 | .57 | 1.70 | 2.35 |
| 3700 Pile caps, under 5 C.Y., direct chute | C-6 | 90 | .533 | | | 16.90 | .55 | 17.45 | 26.50 |
| 3750      Pumped | C-20 | 110 | .582 | | | 18.95 | 7.05 | 26 | 37 |
| 3800      With crane and bucket | C-7 | 80 | .900 | | | 29.50 | 14.85 | 44.35 | 62 |
| 3850 Pile cap, 5 C.Y. to 10 C.Y., direct chute | C-6 | 175 | .274 | | | 8.70 | .28 | 8.98 | 13.70 |
| 3900      Pumped | C-20 | 200 | .320 | | | 10.40 | 3.89 | 14.29 | 20.50 |
| 3950      With crane and bucket | C-7 | 150 | .480 | | | 15.75 | 7.90 | 23.65 | 32.50 |
| 4000 Over 10 C.Y., direct chute | C-6 | 215 | .223 | | | 7.10 | .23 | 7.33 | 11.15 |
| 4050      Pumped | C-20 | 240 | .267 | | | 8.70 | 3.24 | 11.94 | 16.90 |
| 4100      With crane and bucket | C-7 | 185 | .389 | | | 12.80 | 6.40 | 19.20 | 26.50 |
| 4300 Slab on grade, up to 6" thick, direct chute | C-6 | 110 | .436 | | | 13.85 | .45 | 14.30 | 22 |
| 4350      Pumped | C-20 | 130 | .492 | | | 16 | 6 | 22 | 31 |
| 4400      With crane and bucket | C-7 | 110 | .655 | | | 21.50 | 10.80 | 32.30 | 45 |
| 4600 Over 6" thick, direct chute | C-6 | 165 | .291 | | | 9.20 | .30 | 9.50 | 14.55 |
| 4650      Pumped | C-20 | 185 | .346 | | | 11.25 | 4.20 | 15.45 | 22 |
| 4700      With crane and bucket | C-7 | 145 | .497 | | | 16.30 | 8.20 | 24.50 | 34 |
| 4900 Walls, 8" thick, direct chute | C-6 | 90 | .533 | | | 16.90 | .55 | 17.45 | 26.50 |
| 4950      Pumped | C-20 | 100 | .640 | | | 21 | 7.80 | 28.80 | 40.50 |
| 5000      With crane and bucket | C-7 | 80 | .900 | | | 29.50 | 14.85 | 44.35 | 62 |
| 5050 12" thick, direct chute | C-6 | 100 | .480 | | | 15.20 | .49 | 15.69 | 24 |
| 5100      Pumped | C-20 | 110 | .582 | | | 18.95 | 7.05 | 26 | 37 |
| 5200      With crane and bucket | C-7 | 90 | .800 | | | 26.50 | 13.20 | 39.70 | 55 |
| 5300 15" thick, direct chute | C-6 | 105 | .457 | | | 14.50 | .47 | 14.97 | 23 |
| 5350      Pumped | C-20 | 120 | .533 | | | 17.35 | 6.50 | 23.85 | 33.50 |
| 5400      With crane and bucket | C-7 | 95 | .758 | | | 25 | 12.50 | 37.50 | 52 |
| 5600 Wheeled concrete dumping, add to placing costs above | | | | | | | | | |
| 5610      Walking cart, 50' haul, add | C-18 | 32 | .281 | C.Y. | | 8.55 | 1.76 | 10.31 | 15.30 |
| 5620          150' haul, add | | 24 | .375 | | | 11.45 | 2.35 | 13.80 | 20.50 |
| 5700          250' haul, add | | 18 | .500 | | | 15.25 | 3.14 | 18.39 | 27 |
| 5800      Riding cart, 50' haul, add | C-19 | 80 | .113 | | | 3.43 | 1.06 | 4.49 | 6.50 |
| 5810          150' haul, add | | 60 | .150 | | | 4.57 | 1.41 | 5.98 | 8.65 |
| 5900          250' haul, add | | 45 | .200 | | | 6.10 | 1.88 | 7.98 | 11.55 |

# 03 35 Concrete Finishing

## 03 35 29 – Tooled Concrete Finishing

### 03 35 29.30 Finishing Floors

| | Crew | Daily Output | Labor-Hours | Unit | Material | 2008 Bare Costs Labor | Equipment | Total | Total Incl O&P |
|---|---|---|---|---|---|---|---|---|---|
| 0010 **FINISHING FLOORS** | | | | | | | | | |
| 0020 Manual screed finish | C-10 | 4800 | .005 | S.F. | | .17 | | .17 | .26 |
| 0100 Manual screed and bull float | | 4000 | .006 | | | .21 | | .21 | .31 |
| 0125 Manual screed, bull float, manual float | | 2000 | .012 | | | .42 | | .42 | .62 |
| 0150 Manual screed, bull float, manual float & broom finish | | 1850 | .013 | | | .45 | | .45 | .67 |
| 0200 Manual screed, bull float, manual float, manual steel trowel | | 1265 | .019 | | | .66 | | .66 | .98 |
| 0250 Manual screed, bull float, machine float & trowel (walk-behind) | C-10C | 1715 | .014 | | | .49 | .02 | .51 | .76 |
| 0300 Power screed, bull float, machine float & trowel (walk-behind) | C-10D | 2400 | .010 | | | .35 | .04 | .39 | .57 |
| 0350 Power screed, bull float, machine float & trowel (ride-on) | C-10E | 4000 | .006 | | | .21 | .06 | .27 | .37 |
| 0400 Integral topping and finish, using 1:1:2 mix, 3/16" thick | C-10B | 1000 | .040 | | .08 | 1.32 | .23 | 1.63 | 2.34 |
| 0450 1/2" thick | | 950 | .042 | | .21 | 1.39 | .24 | 1.84 | 2.60 |
| 0500 3/4" thick | | 850 | .047 | | .32 | 1.55 | .27 | 2.14 | 3 |
| 0600 1" thick | | 750 | .053 | | .43 | 1.76 | .31 | 2.50 | 3.47 |
| 0800 Granolithic topping, laid after, 1:1:1-1/2 mix, 1/2" thick | | 590 | .068 | | .24 | 2.23 | .39 | 2.86 | 4.08 |
| 0820 3/4" thick | | 580 | .069 | | .36 | 2.27 | .40 | 3.03 | 4.29 |
| 0850 1" thick | | 575 | .070 | | .48 | 2.29 | .40 | 3.17 | 4.45 |
| 0950 2" thick | | 500 | .080 | | .96 | 2.64 | .46 | 4.06 | 5.55 |
| 1200 Heavy duty, 1:1:2, 3/4" thick, preshrunk, gray, 20 MSF | | 320 | .125 | | .32 | 4.12 | .72 | 5.16 | 7.40 |
| 1300 100 MSF | | 380 | .105 | | .32 | 3.47 | .60 | 4.39 | 6.25 |
| 1600 Exposed local aggregate finish, minimum | 1 Cefi | 625 | .013 | | .21 | .47 | | .68 | .93 |
| 1650 Maximum | | 465 | .017 | | .31 | .64 | | .95 | 1.27 |
| 1800 Floor abrasives, .25 psf, aluminum oxide | | 850 | .009 | | .35 | .35 | | .70 | .90 |
| 1850 Silicon carbide | | 850 | .009 | | .49 | .35 | | .84 | 1.05 |
| 2000 Floor hardeners, metallic, light service, .50 psf, add | | 850 | .009 | | .48 | .35 | | .83 | 1.04 |
| 2050 Medium service, .75 psf | | 750 | .011 | | .72 | .39 | | 1.11 | 1.38 |
| 2100 Heavy service, 1.0 psf | | 650 | .012 | | .96 | .46 | | 1.42 | 1.73 |
| 2150 Extra heavy, 1.5 psf | | 575 | .014 | | 1.45 | .51 | | 1.96 | 2.35 |
| 2300 Non-metallic, light service, .50 psf | | 850 | .009 | | .17 | .35 | | .52 | .70 |
| 2350 Medium service, .75 psf | | 750 | .011 | | .26 | .39 | | .65 | .87 |
| 2400 Heavy service, 1.00 psf | | 650 | .012 | | .35 | .46 | | .81 | 1.05 |
| 2450 Extra heavy, 1.50 psf | | 575 | .014 | | .52 | .51 | | 1.03 | 1.33 |
| 2800 Trap rock wearing surface for monolithic floors | | | | | | | | | |
| 2810 2.0 psf | C-10B | 1250 | .032 | S.F. | .03 | 1.05 | .18 | 1.26 | 1.83 |
| 3000 Floor coloring, dusted on, minimum (0.6 psf), add to above | 1 Cefi | 1300 | .006 | | .39 | .23 | | .62 | .76 |
| 3050 Maximum (1.0 psf), add to above | " | 625 | .013 | | .65 | .47 | | 1.12 | 1.42 |
| 3100 Colored powder only | | | | Lb. | .65 | | | .65 | .72 |
| 3600 1/2" topping using 0.6 psf powdered color | C-10B | 590 | .068 | S.F. | 5.05 | 2.23 | .39 | 7.67 | 9.35 |
| 3650 1/2" topping using 1.0 psf powdered color | " | 590 | .068 | | 5.30 | 2.23 | .39 | 7.92 | 9.65 |
| 3800 Dustproofing, solvent-based, 1 coat | 1 Cefi | 1900 | .004 | | .16 | .16 | | .32 | .40 |
| 3850 2 coats | | 1300 | .006 | | .56 | .23 | | .79 | .95 |
| 4000 Epoxy-based, 1 coat | | 1500 | .005 | | .12 | .20 | | .32 | .42 |
| 4050 2 coats | | 1500 | .005 | | .25 | .20 | | .45 | .56 |
| 4400 Stair finish, float | | 275 | .029 | | | 1.08 | | 1.08 | 1.58 |
| 4500 Steel trowel finish | | 200 | .040 | | | 1.48 | | 1.48 | 2.17 |
| 4600 Silicon carbide finish, .25 psf | | 150 | .053 | | .35 | 1.97 | | 2.32 | 3.29 |

### 03 35 29.35 Control Joints, Saw Cut

| | Crew | Daily Output | Labor-Hours | Unit | Material | 2008 Bare Costs Labor | Equipment | Total | Total Incl O&P |
|---|---|---|---|---|---|---|---|---|---|
| 0010 **CONTROL JOINTS, SAW CUT** | | | | | | | | | |
| 0100 Sawcut in green concrete | | | | | | | | | |
| 0120 1" depth | C-27 | 2000 | .008 | L.F. | .06 | .30 | .07 | .43 | .57 |
| 0140 1-1/2" depth | | 1800 | .009 | | .10 | .33 | .08 | .51 | .67 |
| 0160 2" depth | | 1600 | .010 | | .13 | .37 | .08 | .58 | .77 |
| 0200 Clean out control joint of debris | C-28 | 6000 | .001 | | | .05 | | .05 | .07 |

# 03 35 Concrete Finishing

## 03 35 29 - Tooled Concrete Finishing

### 03 35 29.35 Control Joints, Saw Cut

| | 03 35 29.35 Control Joints, Saw Cut | Crew | Daily Output | Labor-Hours | Unit | Material | 2008 Bare Costs Labor | 2008 Bare Costs Equipment | Total | Total Incl O&P |
|---|---|---|---|---|---|---|---|---|---|---|
| 0300 | Joint sealant | | | | | | | | | |
| 0320 | Backer rod, polyethylene, 1/4" diameter | 1 Cefi | 460 | .017 | L.F. | .03 | .64 | | .67 | .98 |
| 0340 | Sealant, polyurethane | | | | | | | | | |
| 0360 | 1/4" x 1/4" (308 LF/Gal) | 1 Cefi | 270 | .030 | L.F. | .17 | 1.10 | | 1.27 | 1.79 |
| 0380 | 1/4" x 1/2" (154 LF/Gal) | " | 255 | .031 | " | .34 | 1.16 | | 1.50 | 2.07 |

### 03 35 29.60 Finishing Walls

| | 03 35 29.60 Finishing Walls | Crew | Daily Output | Labor-Hours | Unit | Material | 2008 Bare Costs Labor | 2008 Bare Costs Equipment | Total | Total Incl O&P |
|---|---|---|---|---|---|---|---|---|---|---|
| 0010 | **FINISHING WALLS** | | | | | | | | | |
| 0020 | Break ties and patch voids | 1 Cefi | 540 | .015 | S.F. | .03 | .55 | | .58 | .83 |
| 0050 | Burlap rub with grout | | 450 | .018 | | .03 | .66 | | .69 | 1 |
| 0100 | Carborundum rub, dry | | 270 | .030 | | | 1.10 | | 1.10 | 1.61 |
| 0150 | Wet rub | ↓ | 175 | .046 | | | 1.69 | | 1.69 | 2.48 |
| 0300 | Bush hammer, green concrete | B-39 | 1000 | .048 | | | 1.53 | .19 | 1.72 | 2.57 |
| 0350 | Cured concrete | " | 650 | .074 | | | 2.35 | .29 | 2.64 | 3.96 |
| 0600 | Float finish, 1/16" thick | 1 Cefi | 300 | .027 | | .28 | .99 | | 1.27 | 1.76 |
| 0700 | Sandblast, light penetration | E-11 | 1100 | .029 | | .27 | .99 | .17 | 1.43 | 2.14 |
| 0750 | Heavy penetration | " | 375 | .085 | ↓ | .53 | 2.92 | .51 | 3.96 | 6 |
| 0850 | Grind form fins flush | 1 Clab | 700 | .011 | L.F. | | .35 | | .35 | .54 |

## 03 35 33 - Stamped Concrete Finishing

### 03 35 33.50 Slab Texture Stamping

| | 03 35 33.50 Slab Texture Stamping | Crew | Daily Output | Labor-Hours | Unit | Material | 2008 Bare Costs Labor | 2008 Bare Costs Equipment | Total | Total Incl O&P |
|---|---|---|---|---|---|---|---|---|---|---|
| 0010 | **SLAB TEXTURE STAMPING** | | | | | | | | | |
| 0020 | Buy re-usable stamp, small (2 S.F.) | | | | Ea. | 75 | | | 75 | 82.50 |
| 0030 | Medium (4 S.F.) | | | | | 150 | | | 150 | 165 |
| 0120 | Large (8 S.F.) | | | | ↓ | 250 | | | 250 | 275 |
| 0200 | Commonly used chemicals for texture systems | | | | | | | | | |
| 0210 | Hardener, colored powder | | | | S.F. | .55 | | | .55 | .61 |
| 0220 | Release agent, colored powder | | | | | .09 | | | .09 | .10 |
| 0230 | Curing & sealing compound, solvent based | | | | | .05 | | | .05 | .06 |
| 0300 | Broadcasting hardener & release agent, stamping | 2 Cefi | 1000 | .016 | ↓ | | .59 | | .59 | .87 |

# 03 37 Specialty Placed Concrete

## 03 37 13 - Shotcrete

### 03 37 13.30 Gunite (Dry-Mix)

| | 03 37 13.30 Gunite (Dry-Mix) | Crew | Daily Output | Labor-Hours | Unit | Material | 2008 Bare Costs Labor | 2008 Bare Costs Equipment | Total | Total Incl O&P |
|---|---|---|---|---|---|---|---|---|---|---|
| 0010 | **GUNITE (DRY-MIX)** | | | | | | | | | |
| 0020 | Applied in 1" layers, no mesh included | C-8 | 2000 | .028 | S.F. | .32 | .95 | .36 | 1.63 | 2.20 |
| 0100 | Mesh for gunite 2 x 2, #12, to 3" thick | 2 Rodm | 800 | .020 | | .39 | .86 | | 1.25 | 1.84 |
| 0150 | Over 3" thick | " | 500 | .032 | | .39 | 1.38 | | 1.77 | 2.69 |
| 0300 | Typical in place, including mesh, 2" thick, minimum | C-16 | 1000 | .072 | | 1.04 | 2.58 | .73 | 4.35 | 5.95 |
| 0350 | Maximum | | 500 | .144 | | 1.04 | 5.15 | 1.46 | 7.65 | 10.75 |
| 0500 | 4" thick, minimum | | 750 | .096 | | 1.69 | 3.44 | .97 | 6.10 | 8.30 |
| 0550 | Maximum | ↓ | 350 | .206 | | 1.69 | 7.40 | 2.08 | 11.17 | 15.60 |
| 0900 | Prepare old walls, no scaffolding, minimum | C-10 | 1000 | .024 | | | .83 | | .83 | 1.25 |
| 0950 | Maximum | " | 275 | .087 | | | 3.03 | | 3.03 | 4.53 |
| 1100 | For high finish requirement or close tolerance, add, minimum | | | | | | 50% | | | |
| 1150 | Maximum | | | | ↓ | | 110% | | | |

# 03 39 Concrete Curing

## 03 39 13 – Water Concrete Curing

| 03 39 13.50 Water Curing | Crew | Daily Output | Labor-Hours | Unit | Material | 2008 Bare Costs Labor | Equipment | Total | Total Incl O&P |
|---|---|---|---|---|---|---|---|---|---|
| 0010 **WATER CURING** | | | | | | | | | |
| 0015   With burlap, 4 uses assumed, 7.5 oz. | 2 Clab | 55 | .291 | C.S.F. | 7.20 | 8.80 | | 16 | 21.50 |
| 0100     10 oz. | " | 55 | .291 | " | 13 | 8.80 | | 21.80 | 28 |
| 0400   Curing blankets, 1" to 2" thick, buy, minimum | | | | S.F. | .33 | | | .33 | .36 |
| 0450     Maximum | | | | " | .50 | | | .50 | .54 |

## 03 39 23 – Membrane Concrete Curing

### 03 39 23.13 Chemical Compound Membrane Concrete Curing

| | Crew | Daily Output | Labor-Hours | Unit | Material | 2008 Bare Costs Labor | Equipment | Total | Total Incl O&P |
|---|---|---|---|---|---|---|---|---|---|
| 0010 **CHEMICAL COMPOUND MEMBRANE CONCRETE CURING** | | | | | | | | | |
| 0300   Sprayed membrane curing compound | 2 Clab | 95 | .168 | C.S.F. | 4.79 | 5.10 | | 9.89 | 13.15 |
| 0700   Curing compound, solvent based, 400 S.F./gal, 55 gal. lots | | | | Gal. | 14.65 | | | 14.65 | 16.10 |
| 0720     5 gallon lots | | | | | 16.60 | | | 16.60 | 18.30 |
| 0800   Curing compound, water based, 250 S.F./gal, 55 gallon lots | | | | | 18.95 | | | 18.95 | 21 |
| 0820     5 gallon lots | | | | | 21 | | | 21 | 23 |

### 03 39 23.23 Sheet Membrane Concrete Curing

| | Crew | Daily Output | Labor-Hours | Unit | Material | 2008 Bare Costs Labor | Equipment | Total | Total Incl O&P |
|---|---|---|---|---|---|---|---|---|---|
| 0010 **SHEET MEMBRANE CONCRETE CURING** | | | | | | | | | |
| 0200   Curing blanket, burlap/poly, 2-ply | 2 Clab | 70 | .229 | C.S.F. | 16.95 | 6.90 | | 23.85 | 29.50 |

# 03 41 Precast Structural Concrete

## 03 41 05 – Precast Concrete Members

### 03 41 05.10 Precast Beams

| | Crew | Daily Output | Labor-Hours | Unit | Material | 2008 Bare Costs Labor | Equipment | Total | Total Incl O&P |
|---|---|---|---|---|---|---|---|---|---|
| 0010 **PRECAST BEAMS**   R034105-30 | | | | | | | | | |
| 0011   L-shaped, 20' span, 12" x 20" | C-11 | 32 | 2.250 | Ea. | 1,225 | 95 | 59 | 1,379 | 1,575 |
| 1000   Inverted tee beams, add to above, small beams | | | | | 15% | | | | |
| 1050     Large beams | | | | | 20% | | | | |
| 1200   Rectangular, 20' span, 12" x 20" | C-11 | 32 | 2.250 | | 915 | 95 | 59 | 1,069 | 1,225 |
| 1250     18" x 36" | | 24 | 3 | | 1,025 | 126 | 78.50 | 1,229.50 | 1,450 |
| 1300     24" x 44" | | 22 | 3.273 | | 1,300 | 138 | 85.50 | 1,523.50 | 1,750 |
| 1400     30' span, 12" x 36" | | 24 | 3 | | 1,400 | 126 | 78.50 | 1,604.50 | 1,850 |
| 1450     18" x 44" | | 20 | 3.600 | | 1,750 | 152 | 94.50 | 1,996.50 | 2,300 |
| 1500     24" x 52" | | 16 | 4.500 | | 2,275 | 190 | 118 | 2,583 | 2,950 |
| 1600     40' span, 12" x 52" | | 20 | 3.600 | | 2,600 | 152 | 94.50 | 2,846.50 | 3,225 |
| 1650     18" x 52" | | 16 | 4.500 | | 3,075 | 190 | 118 | 3,383 | 3,850 |
| 1700     24" x 52" | | 12 | 6 | | 3,400 | 253 | 157 | 3,810 | 4,350 |
| 2000   "T" shaped, 20' span, 12" x 20" | | 32 | 2.250 | | 1,550 | 95 | 59 | 1,704 | 1,925 |
| 2050     18" x 36" | | 24 | 3 | | 1,775 | 126 | 78.50 | 1,979.50 | 2,250 |
| 2100     24" x 44" | | 22 | 3.273 | | 2,200 | 138 | 85.50 | 2,423.50 | 2,750 |
| 2200     30' span, 12" x 36" | | 24 | 3 | | 2,375 | 126 | 78.50 | 2,579.50 | 2,925 |
| 2250     18" x 44" | | 20 | 3.600 | | 2,975 | 152 | 94.50 | 3,221.50 | 3,650 |
| 2300     24" x 52" | | 16 | 4.500 | | 3,850 | 190 | 118 | 4,158 | 4,675 |
| 2500     40' span, 12" x 52" | | 20 | 3.600 | | 4,400 | 152 | 94.50 | 4,646.50 | 5,225 |
| 2550     18" x 52" | | 16 | 4.500 | | 5,250 | 190 | 118 | 5,558 | 6,225 |
| 2600     24" x 52" | | 12 | 6 | | 5,750 | 253 | 157 | 6,160 | 6,975 |

### 03 41 05.15 Precast Columns

| | Crew | Daily Output | Labor-Hours | Unit | Material | 2008 Bare Costs Labor | Equipment | Total | Total Incl O&P |
|---|---|---|---|---|---|---|---|---|---|
| 0010 **PRECAST COLUMNS**   R034105-30 | | | | | | | | | |
| 0020   Rectangular to 12' high, small columns | C-11 | 120 | .600 | L.F. | 47 | 25.50 | 15.70 | 88.20 | 113 |
| 0050     Large columns | | 96 | .750 | | 82 | 31.50 | 19.65 | 133.15 | 167 |
| 0300     24' high, small columns | | 192 | .375 | | 47 | 15.80 | 9.80 | 72.60 | 90.50 |
| 0350     Large columns | | 144 | .500 | | 82 | 21 | 13.10 | 116.10 | 141 |

### 03 41 05.25 Precast Joists

| | Crew | Daily Output | Labor-Hours | Unit | Material | 2008 Bare Costs Labor | Equipment | Total | Total Incl O&P |
|---|---|---|---|---|---|---|---|---|---|
| 0010 **PRECAST JOISTS**   R034105-30 | | | | | | | | | |

# 03 41 Precast Structural Concrete

## 03 41 05 – Precast Concrete Members

| 03 41 05.25 Precast Joists | Crew | Daily Output | Labor-Hours | Unit | Material | 2008 Bare Costs Labor | Equipment | Total | Total Incl O&P |
|---|---|---|---|---|---|---|---|---|---|
| 0015 | 40 psf L.L., 6" deep for 12' spans | C-12 | 600 | .080 | L.F. | 7.85 | 3.01 | 1.28 | 12.14 | 14.70 |
| 0050 | 8" deep for 16' spans | | 575 | .083 | | 13.10 | 3.14 | 1.33 | 17.57 | 20.50 |
| 0100 | 10" deep for 20' spans | | 550 | .087 | | 23 | 3.28 | 1.39 | 27.67 | 31.50 |
| 0150 | 12" deep for 24' spans | | 525 | .091 | | 31.50 | 3.44 | 1.46 | 36.40 | 41.50 |

## 03 41 13 – Precast Concrete Hollow Core Planks

### 03 41 13.50 Precast Slab Planks

| | | Crew | Daily Output | Labor-Hours | Unit | Material | Labor | Equipment | Total | Total Incl O&P |
|---|---|---|---|---|---|---|---|---|---|---|
| 0010 | **PRECAST SLAB PLANKS** R034105-30 | | | | | | | | | |
| 0020 | Prestressed roof/floor members, grouted, solid, 4" thick | C-11 | 2400 | .030 | S.F. | 5.40 | 1.26 | .79 | 7.45 | 8.95 |
| 0050 | 6" thick | | 2800 | .026 | | 6.60 | 1.08 | .67 | 8.35 | 9.90 |
| 0100 | Hollow, 8" thick  *CN* | | 3200 | .023 | | 7.20 | .95 | .59 | 8.74 | 10.20 |
| 0150 | 10" thick | | 3600 | .020 | | 7.65 | .84 | .52 | 9.01 | 10.50 |
| 0200 | 12" thick | | 4000 | .018 | | 8.85 | .76 | .47 | 10.08 | 11.55 |

## 03 41 16 – Precast Concrete Slabs

### 03 41 16.20 Precast Concrete Channel Slabs

| | | Crew | Daily Output | Labor-Hours | Unit | Material | Labor | Equipment | Total | Total Incl O&P |
|---|---|---|---|---|---|---|---|---|---|---|
| 0010 | **PRECAST CONCRETE CHANNEL SLABS** | | | | | | | | | |
| 0020 | Lightweight channel slab, 2.75" or 3.5" thk, straight | C-12 | 1575 | .030 | S.F. | 5.50 | 1.15 | .49 | 7.14 | 8.35 |
| 0050 | Chopped up | | 785 | .061 | | 6.05 | 2.30 | .98 | 9.33 | 11.30 |
| 0200 | 6" thick, span to 20' | | 1300 | .037 | | 6.25 | 1.39 | .59 | 8.23 | 9.70 |
| 0300 | 8" thick, span to 24' | | 1100 | .044 | | 7.05 | 1.64 | .70 | 9.39 | 11.05 |

### 03 41 16.50 Precast Lightweight Concrete Plank

| | | Crew | Daily Output | Labor-Hours | Unit | Material | Labor | Equipment | Total | Total Incl O&P |
|---|---|---|---|---|---|---|---|---|---|---|
| 0010 | **PRECAST LIGHTWEIGHT CONCRETE PLANK** | | | | | | | | | |
| 0015 | Lightweight plank, nailable, T&G, 2" thick | C-12 | 1800 | .027 | S.F. | 3.90 | 1 | .43 | 5.33 | 6.30 |
| 0050 | 2-3/4" thick | | 1575 | .030 | | 3.70 | 1.15 | .49 | 5.34 | 6.40 |
| 0100 | 3-3/4" thick | | 1375 | .035 | | 5.15 | 1.31 | .56 | 7.02 | 8.35 |
| 0150 | For premium ceiling finish, add | | | | | 10% | | | | |
| 0200 | For sloping roofs, slope over 4 in 12, add | | | | | | 25% | | | |
| 0250 | Slope over 6 in 12, add | | | | | | 150% | | | |

## 03 41 23 – Precast Concrete Stairs

### 03 41 23.50 Precast Stairs

| | | Crew | Daily Output | Labor-Hours | Unit | Material | Labor | Equipment | Total | Total Incl O&P |
|---|---|---|---|---|---|---|---|---|---|---|
| 0010 | **PRECAST STAIRS** | | | | | | | | | |
| 0020 | Precast concrete treads on steel stringers, 3' wide | C-12 | 75 | .640 | Riser | 110 | 24 | 10.20 | 144.20 | 169 |
| 0300 | Front entrance, 5' wide with 48" platform, 2 risers | | 16 | 3 | Flight | 340 | 113 | 48 | 501 | 605 |
| 0350 | 5 risers | | 12 | 4 | | 535 | 150 | 64 | 749 | 895 |
| 0500 | 6' wide, 2 risers | | 15 | 3.200 | | 365 | 120 | 51 | 536 | 640 |
| 0550 | 5 risers | | 11 | 4.364 | | 550 | 164 | 69.50 | 783.50 | 935 |
| 0700 | 7' wide, 2 risers | | 14 | 3.429 | | 500 | 129 | 55 | 684 | 810 |
| 0750 | 5 risers | | 10 | 4.800 | | 855 | 180 | 76.50 | 1,111.50 | 1,300 |
| 1200 | Basement entrance stairs, steel bulkhead doors, minimum | B-51 | 22 | 2.182 | | 1,350 | 66.50 | 8.15 | 1,424.65 | 1,575 |
| 1250 | Maximum | " | 11 | 4.364 | | 2,175 | 133 | 16.30 | 2,324.30 | 2,625 |

## 03 41 33 – Precast Structural Pretensioned Concrete

### 03 41 33.60 Tees

| | | Crew | Daily Output | Labor-Hours | Unit | Material | Labor | Equipment | Total | Total Incl O&P |
|---|---|---|---|---|---|---|---|---|---|---|
| 0010 | **TEES** R034105-30 | | | | | | | | | |
| 0020 | Quad tee, short spans, roof | C-11 | 7200 | .010 | S.F. | 6.55 | .42 | .26 | 7.23 | 8.20 |
| 0050 | Floor | | 7200 | .010 | | 6.55 | .42 | .26 | 7.23 | 8.20 |
| 0200 | Double tee, floor members, 60' span | | 8400 | .009 | | 8.20 | .36 | .22 | 8.78 | 9.90 |
| 0250 | 80' span | | 8000 | .009 | | 9.60 | .38 | .24 | 10.22 | 11.45 |
| 0300 | Roof members, 30' span | | 4800 | .015 | | 6.95 | .63 | .39 | 7.97 | 9.20 |
| 0350 | 50' span | | 6400 | .011 | | 7.95 | .47 | .29 | 8.71 | 9.90 |
| 0400 | Wall members, up to 55' high | | 3600 | .020 | | 11.05 | .84 | .52 | 12.41 | 14.25 |
| 0500 | Single tee roof members, 40' span | | 3200 | .023 | | 8.80 | .95 | .59 | 10.34 | 11.95 |

# 03 41 Precast Structural Concrete

## 03 41 33 – Precast Structural Pretensioned Concrete

### 03 41 33.60 Tees

| | | Crew | Daily Output | Labor-Hours | Unit | Material | 2008 Bare Costs Labor | Equipment | Total | Total Incl O&P |
|---|---|---|---|---|---|---|---|---|---|---|
| 0550 | 80' span | C-11 | 5120 | .014 | S.F. | 10.75 | .59 | .37 | 11.71 | 13.30 |
| 0600 | 100' span | | 6000 | .012 | | 16.20 | .51 | .31 | 17.02 | 19.05 |
| 0650 | 120' span | | 6000 | .012 | | 17.65 | .51 | .31 | 18.47 | 20.50 |
| 1000 | Double tees, floor members | | | | | | | | | |
| 1100 | Lightweight, 20" x 8' wide, 45' span | C-11 | 20 | 3.600 | Ea. | 2,800 | 152 | 94.50 | 3,046.50 | 3,450 |
| 1150 | 24" x 8' wide, 50' span | | 18 | 4 | | 3,050 | 168 | 105 | 3,323 | 3,750 |
| 1200 | 32" x 10' wide, 60' span | | 16 | 4.500 | | 5,150 | 190 | 118 | 5,458 | 6,100 |
| 1250 | Standard weight, 12" x 8' wide, 20' span | | 22 | 3.273 | | 1,050 | 138 | 85.50 | 1,273.50 | 1,475 |
| 1300 | 16" x 8' wide, 25' span | | 20 | 3.600 | | 1,400 | 152 | 94.50 | 1,646.50 | 1,900 |
| 1350 | 18" x 8' wide, 30' span | CN | 20 | 3.600 | | 1,775 | 152 | 94.50 | 2,021.50 | 2,325 |
| 1400 | 20" x 8' wide, 45' span | | 18 | 4 | | 2,000 | 168 | 105 | 2,273 | 2,600 |
| 1450 | 24" x 8' wide, 50' span | | 16 | 4.500 | | 2,575 | 190 | 118 | 2,883 | 3,300 |
| 1500 | 32" x 10' wide, 60' span | | 14 | 5.143 | | 4,725 | 217 | 135 | 5,077 | 5,725 |
| 2000 | Roof members | | | | | | | | | |
| 2050 | Lightweight, 20" x 8' wide, 40' span | C-11 | 20 | 3.600 | Ea. | 2,350 | 152 | 94.50 | 2,596.50 | 2,975 |
| 2100 | 24" x 8' wide, 50' span | | 18 | 4 | | 3,150 | 168 | 105 | 3,423 | 3,875 |
| 2150 | 32" x 10' wide, 60' span | | 16 | 4.500 | | 5,200 | 190 | 118 | 5,508 | 6,175 |
| 2200 | Standard weight, 12" x 8' wide, 30' span | | 22 | 3.273 | | 1,575 | 138 | 85.50 | 1,798.50 | 2,050 |
| 2250 | 16" x 8' wide, 30' span | | 20 | 3.600 | | 1,650 | 152 | 94.50 | 1,896.50 | 2,200 |
| 2300 | 18" x 8' wide, 30' span | | 20 | 3.600 | | 1,850 | 152 | 94.50 | 2,096.50 | 2,400 |
| 2350 | 20" x 8' wide, 40' span | | 18 | 4 | | 1,900 | 168 | 105 | 2,173 | 2,475 |
| 2400 | 24" x 8' wide, 50' span | | 16 | 4.500 | | 2,525 | 190 | 118 | 2,833 | 3,225 |
| 2450 | 32" x 10' wide, 60' span | | 14 | 5.143 | | 4,400 | 217 | 135 | 4,752 | 5,375 |

## 03 41 36 – Precast Structural Post-Tensioned Concrete

### 03 41 36.50 Post-Tensioned Jobs

| | | | Crew | Daily Output | Labor-Hours | Unit | Material | 2008 Bare Costs Labor | Equipment | Total | Total Incl O&P |
|---|---|---|---|---|---|---|---|---|---|---|---|
| 0010 | POST-TENSIONED JOBS | R034105-30 | | | | | | | | | |
| 0100 | Post-tensioned in place, small job | R034136-90 | C-17B | 8.50 | 9.647 | C.Y. | 655 | 385 | 39 | 1,079 | 1,350 |
| 0200 | Large job | | " | 10 | 8.200 | " | 490 | 325 | 33 | 848 | 1,075 |

# 03 45 Precast Architectural Concrete

## 03 45 13 – Faced Architectural Precast Concrete

### 03 45 13.50 Precast Wall Panels

| | | | Crew | Daily Output | Labor-Hours | Unit | Material | 2008 Bare Costs Labor | Equipment | Total | Total Incl O&P |
|---|---|---|---|---|---|---|---|---|---|---|---|
| 0010 | PRECAST WALL PANELS | R034513-10 | | | | | | | | | |
| 0050 | Uninsulated 4" thick, smooth gray | | | | | | | | | | |
| 0150 | Low rise, 4' x 8' x 4" thick | | C-11 | 320 | .225 | S.F. | 14.40 | 9.50 | 5.90 | 29.80 | 39 |
| 0210 | 8' x 8', 4" thick | | | 576 | .125 | | 14.25 | 5.25 | 3.27 | 22.77 | 28.50 |
| 0220 | Exposed aggregate | | | 576 | .125 | | 19.15 | 5.25 | 3.27 | 27.67 | 34 |
| 0250 | 8' x 16' x 4" thick | | | 1024 | .070 | | 14.10 | 2.96 | 1.84 | 18.90 | 22.50 |
| 0600 | High rise, 4' x 8' x 4" thick | | | 288 | .250 | | 14.40 | 10.55 | 6.55 | 31.50 | 41.50 |
| 0650 | 8' x 8' x 4" thick | | | 512 | .141 | | 14.25 | 5.90 | 3.68 | 23.83 | 30 |
| 0700 | 8' x 16' x 4" thick | | | 768 | .094 | | 14.10 | 3.95 | 2.45 | 20.50 | 25 |
| 0750 | 20' x 10', 6" thick, smooth gray | CN | | 1400 | .051 | | 24 | 2.17 | 1.35 | 27.52 | 32 |
| 0760 | Exposed aggregate | | | 1800 | .040 | | 28.50 | 1.68 | 1.05 | 31.23 | 35.50 |
| 0800 | Insulated panel, 2" polystyrene, add | | | | | | 1.04 | | | 1.04 | 1.14 |
| 0850 | 2" urethane, add | | | | | | .87 | | | .87 | .96 |
| 1200 | Finishes, white, add | | | | | | 2.78 | | | 2.78 | 3.05 |
| 1250 | Exposed aggregate, add | | | | | | 1.27 | | | 1.27 | 1.40 |
| 1300 | Granite faced, domestic, add | | | | | | 27 | | | 27 | 29.50 |
| 2200 | Fiberglass reinforced cement with urethane core | | | | | | | | | | |
| 2210 | R20, 8' x 8', minimum | | E-2 | 750 | .075 | S.F. | 19.65 | 3.13 | 2.09 | 24.87 | 29 |

# 03 45 Precast Architectural Concrete

## 03 45 13 – Faced Architectural Precast Concrete

| 03 45 13.50 Precast Wall Panels | | Crew | Daily Output | Labor-Hours | Unit | Material | 2008 Bare Costs Labor | Equipment | Total | Total Incl O&P |
|---|---|---|---|---|---|---|---|---|---|---|
| 2220 | Maximum | E-2 | 600 | .093 | S.F. | 22 | 3.91 | 2.61 | 28.52 | 33.50 |

# 03 47 Site-Cast Concrete

## 03 47 13 – Tilt-Up Concrete

### 03 47 13.50 Tilt-Up Wall Panels

| | | | Crew | Daily Output | Labor-Hours | Unit | Material | 2008 Bare Costs Labor | Equipment | Total | Total Incl O&P |
|---|---|---|---|---|---|---|---|---|---|---|---|
| 0010 | **TILT-UP WALL PANELS** | R034713-20 | | | | | | | | | |
| 0015 | Wall panel construction, walls only, 5-1/2" thick | | C-14 | 1600 | .090 | S.F. | 6.65 | 3.37 | .81 | 10.83 | 13.50 |
| 0100 | 7-1/2" thick | | | 1550 | .093 | | 7.95 | 3.48 | .83 | 12.26 | 15.10 |
| 0500 | Walls and columns, 5-1/2" thick walls, 12" x 12" columns | | | 1565 | .092 | | 10.15 | 3.44 | .82 | 14.41 | 17.50 |
| 0550 | 7-1/2" thick wall, 12" x 12" columns | | | 1370 | .105 | | 11.90 | 3.93 | .94 | 16.77 | 20.50 |
| 0800 | Columns only, site precast, minimum | | | 200 | .720 | L.F. | 16.75 | 27 | 6.45 | 50.20 | 67.50 |
| 0850 | Maximum | | | 105 | 1.371 | " | 19.85 | 51.50 | 12.30 | 83.65 | 116 |

# 03 48 Precast Concrete Specialties

## 03 48 43 – Precast Concrete Trim

### 03 48 43.40 Precast Lintels

| | | Crew | Daily Output | Labor-Hours | Unit | Material | 2008 Bare Costs Labor | Equipment | Total | Total Incl O&P |
|---|---|---|---|---|---|---|---|---|---|---|
| 0010 | **PRECAST LINTELS** | | | | | | | | | |
| 0800 | Precast concrete, 4" wide, 8" high, to 5' long | D-10 | 28 | 1.143 | Ea. | 27 | 43.50 | 22 | 92.50 | 120 |
| 0850 | 5'-12' long | | 24 | 1.333 | | 82 | 50.50 | 25.50 | 158 | 195 |
| 1000 | 6" wide, 8" high, to 5' long | | 26 | 1.231 | | 38.50 | 46.50 | 23.50 | 108.50 | 140 |
| 1050 | 5'-12' long | | 22 | 1.455 | | 92.50 | 55 | 28 | 175.50 | 217 |
| 1200 | 8" wide, 8" high, to 5' long | | 24 | 1.333 | | 44.50 | 50.50 | 25.50 | 120.50 | 154 |
| 1250 | 5'-12' long | | 20 | 1.600 | | 122 | 60.50 | 30.50 | 213 | 261 |
| 1400 | 10" wide, 8" high U-Shape, to 14' long | | 18 | 1.778 | | 176 | 67.50 | 34 | 277.50 | 335 |
| 1450 | 12" wide, 8" high U-Shape, to 19' long | | 16 | 2 | | 230 | 76 | 38 | 344 | 410 |

### 03 48 43.90 Precast Window Sills

| | | Crew | Daily Output | Labor-Hours | Unit | Material | 2008 Bare Costs Labor | Equipment | Total | Total Incl O&P |
|---|---|---|---|---|---|---|---|---|---|---|
| 0010 | **PRECAST WINDOW SILLS** | | | | | | | | | |
| 0600 | Precast concrete, 4" tapers to 3", 9" wide | D-1 | 70 | .229 | L.F. | 11.75 | 7.95 | | 19.70 | 25 |
| 0650 | 11" wide | | 60 | .267 | | 15.10 | 9.30 | | 24.40 | 31 |
| 0700 | 13" wide, 3 1/2" tapers to 2 1/2", 12" wall | | 50 | .320 | | 15 | 11.15 | | 26.15 | 33.50 |

# 03 51 Cast Roof Decks

## 03 51 13 – Cementitious Wood Fiber Decks

### 03 51 13.50 Cementitious/Wood Fiber Planks

| | | Crew | Daily Output | Labor-Hours | Unit | Material | 2008 Bare Costs Labor | Equipment | Total | Total Incl O&P |
|---|---|---|---|---|---|---|---|---|---|---|
| 0010 | **CEMENTITIOUS/WOOD FIBER PLANKS** | R051223-50 | | | | | | | | |
| 0050 | Plank, beveled, 1" thick | 2 Carp | 1000 | .016 | S.F. | 2.09 | .61 | | 2.70 | 3.25 |
| 0100 | Plank, T & G, 1-1/2" thick | | 975 | .016 | | 2.28 | .63 | | 2.91 | 3.48 |
| 0150 | 2" thick | | 950 | .017 | | 2.84 | .64 | | 3.48 | 4.12 |
| 0200 | 2-1/2" thick | | 925 | .017 | | 3.16 | .66 | | 3.82 | 4.51 |
| 0250 | 3" thick | | 900 | .018 | | 3.68 | .68 | | 4.36 | 5.10 |
| 0300 | 3-1/2" thick | | 875 | .018 | | 4.73 | .70 | | 5.43 | 6.30 |
| 0350 | 4" thick | | 850 | .019 | | 5.10 | .72 | | 5.82 | 6.70 |
| 1000 | Bulb tee, sub-purlin and grout, 6' span, add | E-1 | 5000 | .005 | | 1.82 | .20 | .03 | 2.05 | 2.38 |
| 1100 | 8' span | " | 4200 | .006 | | 2.07 | .24 | .03 | 2.34 | 2.71 |

# 03 52 Lightweight Concrete Roof Insulation

## 03 52 16 – Lightweight Insulating Concrete

| 03 52 16.13 Lightweight Cellular Insulating Concrete | | Crew | Daily Output | Labor-Hours | Unit | Material | 2008 Bare Costs Labor | Equipment | Total | Total Incl O&P |
|---|---|---|---|---|---|---|---|---|---|---|
| 0010 | **LIGHTWEIGHT CELLULAR INSULATING CONCRETE** R035216-10 | | | | | | | | | |
| 0020 | Portland cement and foaming agent | C-8 | 50 | 1.120 | C.Y. | 105 | 38 | 14.55 | 157.55 | 190 |

### 03 52 16.16 Lightweight Aggregate Insulating Concrete

| 0010 | **LIGHTWEIGHT AGGREGATE INSULATING CONCRETE** R035216-10 | | | | | | | | | |
|---|---|---|---|---|---|---|---|---|---|---|
| 0100 | Poured vermiculite or perlite, field mix, | | | | | | | | | |
| 0110 | 1:6 field mix | C-8 | 50 | 1.120 | C.Y. | 98 | 38 | 14.55 | 150.55 | 182 |
| 0200 | Ready mix, 1:6 mix, roof fill, 2" thick | | 10000 | .006 | S.F. | .54 | .19 | .07 | .80 | .97 |
| 0250 | 3" thick | | 7700 | .007 | | .82 | .25 | .09 | 1.16 | 1.37 |
| 0400 | Expanded volcanic glass rock, with binder, minimum | 2 Carp | 1500 | .011 | | .35 | .41 | | .76 | 1.02 |
| 0450 | Maximum | " | 1200 | .013 | | 1.06 | .51 | | 1.57 | 1.96 |

# 03 54 Cast Underlayment

## 03 54 13 – Gypsum Cement Underlayment

### 03 54 13.50 Gypsum Underlayment

| 0010 | **GYPSUM UNDERLAYMENT** | | | | | | | | | |
|---|---|---|---|---|---|---|---|---|---|---|
| 1000 | Poured gypsum, 2" thick | C-8 | 6000 | .009 | S.F. | 1.67 | .32 | .12 | 2.11 | 2.45 |
| 1100 | 3" thick | " | 4800 | .012 | " | 2.50 | .39 | .15 | 3.04 | 3.52 |

## 03 54 16 – Hydraulic Cement Underlayment

### 03 54 16.50 Cement Underlayment

| 0010 | **CEMENT UNDERLAYMENT** | | | | | | | | | |
|---|---|---|---|---|---|---|---|---|---|---|
| 2510 | Underlayment, P.C. based self-leveling, 4100 psi, pumped, 1/4" | C-8 | 20000 | .003 | S.F. | 1.54 | .09 | .04 | 1.67 | 1.87 |
| 2520 | 1/2" | | 19000 | .003 | | 3.07 | .10 | .04 | 3.21 | 3.57 |
| 2530 | 3/4" | | 18000 | .003 | | 4.61 | .11 | .04 | 4.76 | 5.25 |
| 2540 | 1" | | 17000 | .003 | | 6.15 | .11 | .04 | 6.30 | 6.95 |
| 2550 | 1-1/2" | | 15000 | .004 | | 9.20 | .13 | .05 | 9.38 | 10.40 |
| 2560 | Hand mix, 1/2" | C-18 | 4000 | .002 | | 3.07 | .07 | .01 | 3.15 | 3.51 |
| 2610 | Topping, P.C. based self-level/dry 6100 psi, pumped, 1/4" | C-8 | 20000 | .003 | | 2.33 | .09 | .04 | 2.46 | 2.74 |
| 2620 | 1/2" | | 19000 | .003 | | 4.66 | .10 | .04 | 4.80 | 5.30 |
| 2630 | 3/4" | | 18000 | .003 | | 7 | .11 | .04 | 7.15 | 7.90 |
| 2660 | 1" | | 17000 | .003 | | 9.30 | .11 | .04 | 9.45 | 10.45 |
| 2670 | 1-1/2" | | 15000 | .004 | | 14 | .13 | .05 | 14.18 | 15.60 |
| 2680 | Hand mix, 1/2" | C-18 | 4000 | .002 | | 4.66 | .07 | .01 | 4.74 | 5.25 |

# 03 62 Non-Shrink Grouting

## 03 62 13 – Non-Metallic Non-Shrink Grouting

### 03 62 13.50 Grout, Non-Metallic Non-shrink

| 0010 | **GROUT, NON-METALLIC NON-SHRINK** | | | | | | | | | |
|---|---|---|---|---|---|---|---|---|---|---|
| 0300 | Non-shrink, non-metallic, 1" deep | 1 Cefi | 35 | .229 | S.F. | 7.05 | 8.45 | | 15.50 | 20 |
| 0350 | 2" deep | " | 25 | .320 | " | 14.10 | 11.85 | | 25.95 | 33 |

## 03 62 16 – Metallic Non-Shrink Grouting

### 03 62 16.50 Grout, Metallic Non-Shrink

| 0010 | **GROUT, METALLIC NON-SHRINK** | | | | | | | | | |
|---|---|---|---|---|---|---|---|---|---|---|
| 0020 | Column & machine bases, non-shrink, metallic, 1" deep | 1 Cefi | 35 | .229 | S.F. | 7.75 | 8.45 | | 16.20 | 21 |
| 0050 | 2" deep | " | 25 | .320 | " | 15.50 | 11.85 | | 27.35 | 34.50 |

# 03 63 Epoxy Grouting

## 03 63 05 – Grouting of Dowels and Fasteners

| 03 63 05.10 Epoxy Only | Crew | Daily Output | Labor-Hours | Unit | Material | 2008 Bare Costs Labor | Equipment | Total | Total Incl O&P |
|---|---|---|---|---|---|---|---|---|---|
| 0010 **EPOXY ONLY** | | | | | | | | | |
| 1500 Chemical anchoring, epoxy cartridge, excludes layout, drilling, fastener | | | | | | | | | |
| 1530 For fastener 3/4" dia x 6" embedment | 2 Skwk | 72 | .222 | Ea. | 5.85 | 8.75 | | 14.60 | 20 |
| 1535 1" dia x 8" embedment | | 66 | .242 | | 8.75 | 9.55 | | 18.30 | 24.50 |
| 1540 1-1/4" dia x 10" embedment | | 60 | .267 | | 17.50 | 10.50 | | 28 | 35.50 |
| 1545 1-3/4" dia x 12" embedment | | 54 | .296 | | 29 | 11.65 | | 40.65 | 50 |
| 1550 14" embedment | | 48 | .333 | | 35 | 13.15 | | 48.15 | 59 |
| 1555 2" dia x 12" embedment | | 42 | .381 | | 46.50 | 15 | | 61.50 | 75 |
| 1560 18" embedment | | 32 | .500 | | 58.50 | 19.70 | | 78.20 | 94.50 |

# 03 81 Concrete Cutting

## 03 81 13 – Flat Concrete Sawing

### 03 81 13.50 Concrete Floor/Slab Cutting

| | Crew | Daily Output | Labor-Hours | Unit | Material | 2008 Bare Costs Labor | Equipment | Total | Total Incl O&P |
|---|---|---|---|---|---|---|---|---|---|
| 0010 **CONCRETE FLOOR/SLAB CUTTING** | | | | | | | | | |
| 0400 Concrete slabs, mesh reinforcing, up to 3" deep | B-89 | 980 | .016 | L.F. | .47 | .55 | .39 | 1.41 | 1.78 |
| 0420 Each additional inch of depth | " | 1600 | .010 | " | .16 | .34 | .24 | .74 | .94 |

## 03 81 16 – Track Mounted Concrete Wall Sawing

### 03 81 16.50 Concrete Wall Cutting

| | Crew | Daily Output | Labor-Hours | Unit | Material | 2008 Bare Costs Labor | Equipment | Total | Total Incl O&P |
|---|---|---|---|---|---|---|---|---|---|
| 0010 **CONCRETE WALL CUTTING** | | | | | | | | | |
| 0800 Concrete walls, hydraulic saw, plain, per inch of depth | B-89B | 250 | .064 | L.F. | .42 | 2.15 | 2.66 | 5.23 | 6.65 |
| 0820 Rod reinforcing, per inch of depth | " | 150 | .107 | " | .59 | 3.58 | 4.44 | 8.61 | 11 |

# 03 82 Concrete Boring

## 03 82 13 – Concrete Core Drilling

### 03 82 13.10 Core Drilling

| | Crew | Daily Output | Labor-Hours | Unit | Material | 2008 Bare Costs Labor | Equipment | Total | Total Incl O&P |
|---|---|---|---|---|---|---|---|---|---|
| 0010 **CORE DRILLING** | | | | | | | | | |
| 0020 Reinf. conc slab, up to 6" thick, incl. bit, layout & set up | | | | | | | | | |
| 0100 1" diameter core | B-89A | 28 | .571 | Ea. | 3 | 19.90 | 3.91 | 26.81 | 38.50 |
| 0150 Each added inch thick, add | | 300 | .053 | | .55 | 1.86 | .36 | 2.77 | 3.90 |
| 0300 3" diameter core | | 23 | .696 | | 6.45 | 24 | 4.76 | 35.21 | 50 |
| 0350 Each added inch thick, add | | 186 | .086 | | 1.20 | 3 | .59 | 4.79 | 6.65 |
| 0500 4" diameter core | | 19 | .842 | | 6.45 | 29.50 | 5.75 | 41.70 | 59 |
| 0550 Each added inch thick, add | | 170 | .094 | | 1.57 | 3.28 | .64 | 5.49 | 7.55 |
| 0700 6" diameter core | | 14 | 1.143 | | 10.65 | 40 | 7.80 | 58.45 | 82.50 |
| 0750 Each added inch thick, add | | 140 | .114 | | 1.89 | 3.98 | .78 | 6.65 | 9.15 |
| 0900 8" diameter core | | 11 | 1.455 | | 14.50 | 50.50 | 9.95 | 74.95 | 106 |
| 0950 Each added inch thick, add | | 95 | .168 | | 2.50 | 5.85 | 1.15 | 9.50 | 13.10 |
| 1100 10" diameter core | | 10 | 1.600 | | 18.95 | 55.50 | 10.95 | 85.40 | 120 |
| 1150 Each added inch thick, add | | 80 | .200 | | 3.15 | 6.95 | 1.37 | 11.47 | 15.80 |
| 1300 12" diameter core | | 9 | 1.778 | | 23.50 | 62 | 12.15 | 97.65 | 136 |
| 1350 Each added inch thick, add | | 68 | .235 | | 3.78 | 8.20 | 1.61 | 13.59 | 18.70 |
| 1500 14" diameter core | | 7 | 2.286 | | 28.50 | 79.50 | 15.65 | 123.65 | 173 |
| 1550 Each added inch thick, add | | 55 | .291 | | 5.10 | 10.15 | 1.99 | 17.24 | 23.50 |
| 1700 18" diameter core | | 4 | 4 | | 37 | 139 | 27.50 | 203.50 | 288 |
| 1750 Each added inch thick, add | | 28 | .571 | | 6.60 | 19.90 | 3.91 | 30.41 | 42.50 |
| 1760 For horizontal holes, add to above | | | | | | | | 30% | 30% |
| 1770 Prestressed hollow core plank, 6" thick | | | | | | | | | |
| 1780 1" diameter core | B-89A | 52 | .308 | Ea. | 2 | 10.70 | 2.10 | 14.80 | 21 |
| 1790 Each added inch thick, add | | 350 | .046 | | .40 | 1.59 | .31 | 2.30 | 3.26 |

# 03 82 Concrete Boring

## 03 82 13 – Concrete Core Drilling

### 03 82 13.10 Core Drilling

| | | Crew | Daily Output | Labor-Hours | Unit | Material | 2008 Bare Costs Labor | 2008 Bare Costs Equipment | Total | Total Incl O&P |
|---|---|---|---|---|---|---|---|---|---|---|
| 1800 | 3" diameter core | B-89A | 50 | .320 | Ea. | 4.18 | 11.15 | 2.19 | 17.52 | 24.50 |
| 1810 | Each added inch thick, add | | 240 | .067 | | .72 | 2.32 | .46 | 3.50 | 4.90 |
| 1820 | 4" diameter core | | 48 | .333 | | 5.75 | 11.60 | 2.28 | 19.63 | 27 |
| 1830 | Each added inch thick, add | | 216 | .074 | | 1.05 | 2.58 | .51 | 4.14 | 5.75 |
| 1840 | 6" diameter core | | 44 | .364 | | 7.05 | 12.65 | 2.49 | 22.19 | 30 |
| 1850 | Each added inch thick, add | | 175 | .091 | | 1.20 | 3.18 | .63 | 5.01 | 6.95 |
| 1860 | 8" diameter core | | 32 | .500 | | 10 | 17.40 | 3.42 | 30.82 | 42 |
| 1870 | Each added inch thick, add | | 118 | .136 | | 1.68 | 4.72 | .93 | 7.33 | 10.20 |
| 1880 | 10" diameter core | | 28 | .571 | | 13.25 | 19.90 | 3.91 | 37.06 | 50 |
| 1890 | Each added inch thick, add | | 99 | .162 | | 1.75 | 5.65 | 1.11 | 8.51 | 11.90 |
| 1900 | 12" diameter core | | 22 | .727 | | 15.50 | 25.50 | 4.97 | 45.97 | 62 |
| 1910 | Each added inch thick, add | | 85 | .188 | | 2.80 | 6.55 | 1.29 | 10.64 | 14.70 |
| 1950 | Minimum charge for above, 3" diameter core | | 7 | 2.286 | Total | | 79.50 | 15.65 | 95.15 | 141 |
| 2000 | 4" diameter core | | 6.80 | 2.353 | | | 82 | 16.10 | 98.10 | 145 |
| 2050 | 6" diameter core | | 6 | 2.667 | | | 93 | 18.25 | 111.25 | 164 |
| 2100 | 8" diameter core | | 5.50 | 2.909 | | | 101 | 19.90 | 120.90 | 180 |
| 2150 | 10" diameter core | | 4.75 | 3.368 | | | 117 | 23 | 140 | 208 |
| 2200 | 12" diameter core | | 3.90 | 4.103 | | | 143 | 28 | 171 | 253 |
| 2250 | 14" diameter core | | 3.38 | 4.734 | | | 165 | 32.50 | 197.50 | 292 |
| 2300 | 18" diameter core | | 3.15 | 5.079 | | | 177 | 34.50 | 211.50 | 315 |
| 3010 | Bits for core drill, diamond, premium, 1" diameter | | | | Ea. | 102 | | | 102 | 112 |
| 3020 | 3" diameter | | | | | 250 | | | 250 | 275 |
| 3040 | 4" diameter | | | | | 278 | | | 278 | 305 |
| 3050 | 6" diameter | | | | | 445 | | | 445 | 490 |
| 3080 | 8" diameter | | | | | 615 | | | 615 | 675 |
| 3120 | 12" diameter | | | | | 910 | | | 910 | 1,000 |
| 3180 | 18" diameter | | | | | 1,650 | | | 1,650 | 1,825 |
| 3240 | 24" diameter | | | | | 2,275 | | | 2,275 | 2,500 |

## 03 82 16 – Concrete Drilling

### 03 82 16.10 Concrete Impact Drilling

| | | Crew | Daily Output | Labor-Hours | Unit | Material | 2008 Bare Costs Labor | 2008 Bare Costs Equipment | Total | Total Incl O&P |
|---|---|---|---|---|---|---|---|---|---|---|
| 0010 | **CONCRETE IMPACT DRILLING** | | | | | | | | | |
| 0050 | Up to 4" deep in conc/brick floor/wall, incl. bit & layout, no anchor | | | | | | | | | |
| 0100 | Holes, 1/4" diameter | 1 Carp | 75 | .107 | Ea. | .10 | 4.06 | | 4.16 | 6.45 |
| 0150 | For each additional inch of depth, add | | 430 | .019 | | .03 | .71 | | .74 | 1.13 |
| 0200 | 3/8" diameter | | 63 | .127 | | .09 | 4.84 | | 4.93 | 7.65 |
| 0250 | For each additional inch of depth, add | | 340 | .024 | | .02 | .90 | | .92 | 1.43 |
| 0300 | 1/2" diameter | | 50 | .160 | | .10 | 6.10 | | 6.20 | 9.60 |
| 0350 | For each additional inch of depth, add | | 250 | .032 | | .02 | 1.22 | | 1.24 | 1.93 |
| 0400 | 5/8" diameter | | 48 | .167 | | .18 | 6.35 | | 6.53 | 10.10 |
| 0450 | For each additional inch of depth, add | | 240 | .033 | | .04 | 1.27 | | 1.31 | 2.03 |
| 0500 | 3/4" diameter | | 45 | .178 | | .21 | 6.75 | | 6.96 | 10.80 |
| 0550 | For each additional inch of depth, add | | 220 | .036 | | .05 | 1.39 | | 1.44 | 2.22 |
| 0600 | 7/8" diameter | | 43 | .186 | | .26 | 7.10 | | 7.36 | 11.35 |
| 0650 | For each additional inch of depth, add | | 210 | .038 | | .06 | 1.45 | | 1.51 | 2.33 |
| 0700 | 1" diameter | | 40 | .200 | | .30 | 7.60 | | 7.90 | 12.20 |
| 0750 | For each additional inch of depth, add | | 190 | .042 | | .07 | 1.60 | | 1.67 | 2.58 |
| 0800 | 1-1/4" diameter | | 38 | .211 | | .42 | 8 | | 8.42 | 12.95 |
| 0850 | For each additional inch of depth, add | | 180 | .044 | | .10 | 1.69 | | 1.79 | 2.76 |
| 0900 | 1-1/2" diameter | | 35 | .229 | | .64 | 8.70 | | 9.34 | 14.25 |
| 0950 | For each additional inch of depth, add | | 165 | .048 | | .16 | 1.85 | | 2.01 | 3.05 |
| 1000 | For ceiling installations, add | | | | | | 40% | | | |

# Estimating Tips

## 04 05 00 Common Work Results for Masonry

- The terms *mortar* and *grout* are often used interchangeably, and incorrectly. Mortar is used to bed masonry units, seal the entry of air and moisture, provide architectural appearance, and allow for size variations in the units. Grout is used primarily in reinforced masonry construction and is used to bond the masonry to the reinforcing steel. Common mortar types are M(2500 psi), S(1800 psi), N(750 psi), and O(350 psi), and conform to ASTM C270. Grout is either fine or coarse and conforms to ASTM C476, and in-place strengths generally exceed 2500 psi. Mortar and grout are different components of masonry construction and are placed by entirely different methods. An estimator should be aware of their unique uses and costs.

- Waste, specifically the loss/ droppings of mortar and the breakage of brick and block, is included in all masonry assemblies in this division. A factor of 25% is added for mortar and 3% for brick and concrete masonry units.

- Scaffolding or staging is not included in any of the Division 4 costs. Refer to section 01 54 23 for scaffolding and staging costs.

## 04 20 00 Unit Masonry

- The most common types of unit masonry are brick and concrete masonry. The major classifications of brick are building brick (ASTM C62), facing brick (ASTM C216), glazed brick, fire brick, and pavers. Many varieties of texture and appearance can exist within these classifications, and the estimator would be wise to check local custom and availability within the project area. For repair and remodeling jobs, matching the existing brick may be the most important criteria.

- Brick and concrete block are priced by the piece and then converted into a price per square foot of wall. Openings less than two square feet are generally ignored by the estimator because any savings in units used is offset by the cutting and trimming required.

- It is often difficult and expensive to find and purchase small lots of historic brick. Costs can vary widely. Many design issues affect costs, selection of mortar mix, and repairs or replacement of masonry materials. Cleaning techniques must be reflected in the estimate.

- All masonry walls, whether interior or exterior, require bracing. The cost of bracing walls during construction should be included by the estimator, and this bracing must remain in place until permanent bracing is complete. Permanent bracing of masonry walls is accomplished by masonry itself, in the form of pilasters or abutting wall corners, or by anchoring the walls to the structural frame. Accessories in the form of anchors, anchor slots, and ties are used, but their supply and installation can be by different trades. For instance, anchor slots on spandrel beams and columns are supplied and welded in place by the steel fabricator, but the ties from the slots into the masonry are installed by the bricklayer. Regardless of the installation method, the estimator must be certain that these accessories are accounted for in pricing.

## Reference Numbers

Reference numbers are shown in shaded boxes at the beginning of some major classifications. These numbers refer to related items in the Reference Section. The reference information may be an estimating procedure, an alternate pricing method, or technical information.

*Note:* Not all subdivisions listed here necessarily appear in this publication.

## 04 01 20 – Maintenance of Unit Masonry

### 04 01 20.20 Pointing Masonry

| | | Crew | Daily Output | Labor-Hours | Unit | Material | 2008 Bare Costs Labor | Equipment | Total | Total Incl O&P |
|---|---|---|---|---|---|---|---|---|---|---|
| 0010 | **POINTING MASONRY** | | | | | | | | | |
| 0300 | Cut and repoint brick, hard mortar, running bond | 1 Bric | 80 | .100 | S.F. | .51 | 3.92 | | 4.43 | 6.50 |
| 0320 | Common bond | | 77 | .104 | | .51 | 4.07 | | 4.58 | 6.75 |
| 0360 | Flemish bond | | 70 | .114 | | .53 | 4.47 | | 5 | 7.40 |
| 0400 | English bond | | 65 | .123 | | .53 | 4.82 | | 5.35 | 7.95 |
| 0600 | Soft old mortar, running bond | | 100 | .080 | | .51 | 3.13 | | 3.64 | 5.30 |
| 0620 | Common bond | | 96 | .083 | | .51 | 3.26 | | 3.77 | 5.50 |
| 0640 | Flemish bond | | 90 | .089 | | .53 | 3.48 | | 4.01 | 5.90 |
| 0680 | English bond | | 82 | .098 | | .53 | 3.82 | | 4.35 | 6.40 |
| 0700 | Stonework, hard mortar | | 140 | .057 | L.F. | .67 | 2.24 | | 2.91 | 4.14 |
| 0720 | Soft old mortar | | 160 | .050 | " | .67 | 1.96 | | 2.63 | 3.72 |
| 1000 | Repoint, mask and grout method, running bond | | 95 | .084 | S.F. | .67 | 3.30 | | 3.97 | 5.75 |
| 1020 | Common bond | | 90 | .089 | | .67 | 3.48 | | 4.15 | 6.05 |
| 1040 | Flemish bond | | 86 | .093 | | .71 | 3.64 | | 4.35 | 6.35 |
| 1060 | English bond | | 77 | .104 | | .71 | 4.07 | | 4.78 | 7 |
| 2000 | Scrub coat, sand grout on walls, minimum | | 120 | .067 | | 2.42 | 2.61 | | 5.03 | 6.65 |
| 2020 | Maximum | | 98 | .082 | | 3.36 | 3.20 | | 6.56 | 8.55 |

### 04 01 20.40 Sawing Masonry

| | | Crew | Daily Output | Labor-Hours | Unit | Material | 2008 Bare Costs Labor | Equipment | Total | Total Incl O&P |
|---|---|---|---|---|---|---|---|---|---|---|
| 0010 | **SAWING MASONRY** | | | | | | | | | |
| 0050 | Brick or block by hand, per inch depth | A-1 | 125 | .064 | L.F. | | 1.94 | .48 | 2.42 | 3.54 |

## 04 01 30 – Unit Masonry Cleaning

### 04 01 30.20 Cleaning Masonry

| | | Crew | Daily Output | Labor-Hours | Unit | Material | 2008 Bare Costs Labor | Equipment | Total | Total Incl O&P |
|---|---|---|---|---|---|---|---|---|---|---|
| 0010 | **CLEANING MASONRY** | | | | | | | | | |
| 0200 | Chemical cleaning, new construction, brush and wash, minimum | D-1 | 1000 | .016 | S.F. | .05 | .56 | | .61 | .90 |
| 0220 | Average | | 800 | .020 | | .07 | .70 | | .77 | 1.14 |
| 0240 | Maximum | | 600 | .027 | | .09 | .93 | | 1.02 | 1.51 |
| 0260 | Light restoration, minimum | | 800 | .020 | | .07 | .70 | | .77 | 1.13 |
| 0270 | Average | | 400 | .040 | | .10 | 1.40 | | 1.50 | 2.23 |
| 0280 | Maximum | | 330 | .048 | | .13 | 1.69 | | 1.82 | 2.71 |
| 0300 | Heavy restoration, minimum | | 600 | .027 | | .09 | .93 | | 1.02 | 1.51 |
| 0310 | Average | | 400 | .040 | | .14 | 1.40 | | 1.54 | 2.28 |
| 0320 | Maximum | | 250 | .064 | | .19 | 2.23 | | 2.42 | 3.61 |
| 0400 | High pressure water only, minimum | B-9 | 2000 | .020 | | | .61 | .10 | .71 | 1.06 |
| 0420 | Average | | 1500 | .027 | | | .82 | .13 | .95 | 1.41 |
| 0440 | Maximum | | 1000 | .040 | | | 1.23 | .19 | 1.42 | 2.12 |
| 2000 | Steam cleaning, minimum | | 3000 | .013 | | | .41 | .06 | .47 | .71 |
| 2020 | Average | | 2500 | .016 | | | .49 | .08 | .57 | .84 |
| 2040 | Maximum | | 1500 | .027 | | | .82 | .13 | .95 | 1.41 |
| 4000 | Add for masking doors and windows | 1 Clab | 800 | .010 | | .06 | .30 | | .36 | .54 |
| 4200 | Add for pedestrian protection | | | | Job | | | | | 10% |

### 04 01 30.40 Masonry Building Cleaning

| | | Crew | Daily Output | Labor-Hours | Unit | Material | 2008 Bare Costs Labor | Equipment | Total | Total Incl O&P |
|---|---|---|---|---|---|---|---|---|---|---|
| 0010 | **MASONRY BUILDING CLEANING** | | | | | | | | | |
| 0020 | Steam clean building, not incl scaffolding, minimum | B-9 | 3000 | .013 | S.F. | | .41 | .06 | .47 | .71 |
| 0100 | Maximum | | 1500 | .027 | | | .82 | .13 | .95 | 1.41 |
| 0300 | Common face brick | | 1750 | .023 | | | .70 | .11 | .81 | 1.21 |
| 0400 | Wire cut face brick | | 1250 | .032 | | | .98 | .15 | 1.13 | 1.70 |

### 04 01 30.60 Brick Washing

| | | Crew | Daily Output | Labor-Hours | Unit | Material | 2008 Bare Costs Labor | Equipment | Total | Total Incl O&P |
|---|---|---|---|---|---|---|---|---|---|---|
| 0010 | **BRICK WASHING** R040130-10 | | | | | | | | | |
| 0012 | Acid cleanser, smooth brick surface | 1 Bric | 560 | .014 | S.F. | .04 | .56 | | .60 | .89 |
| 0050 | Rough brick | | 400 | .020 | | .05 | .78 | | .83 | 1.24 |
| 0060 | Stone, acid wash | | 600 | .013 | | .06 | .52 | | .58 | .85 |

# 04 01 Maintenance of Masonry

## 04 01 30 – Unit Masonry Cleaning

| 04 01 30.60 Brick Washing | Crew | Daily Output | Labor-Hours | Unit | Material | 2008 Bare Costs Labor | Equipment | Total | Total Incl O&P |
|---|---|---|---|---|---|---|---|---|---|
| 1000    Muriatic acid, price per gallon in 5 gallon lots | | | | Gal. | 7.35 | | | 7.35 | 8.05 |

# 04 05 Common Work Results for Masonry

## 04 05 05 – Selective Masonry Demolition

### 04 05 05.10 Selective Demolition

| | | Crew | Daily Output | Labor-Hours | Unit | Material | 2008 Bare Costs Labor | Equipment | Total | Total Incl O&P |
|---|---|---|---|---|---|---|---|---|---|---|
| 0010 | **SELECTIVE DEMOLITION**    R024119-10 | | | | | | | | | |
| 0300 | Concrete block walls, unreinforced, 2" thick | 2 Clab | 1200 | .013 | S.F. | | .40 | | .40 | .63 |
| 0310 | 4" thick | | 1150 | .014 | | | .42 | | .42 | .65 |
| 0320 | 6" thick | | 1100 | .015 | | | .44 | | .44 | .68 |
| 0330 | 8" thick | | 1050 | .015 | | | .46 | | .46 | .72 |
| 0340 | 10" thick | | 1000 | .016 | | | .48 | | .48 | .75 |
| 0360 | 12" thick | | 950 | .017 | | | .51 | | .51 | .79 |
| 0380 | Reinforced alternate courses, 2" thick | | 1130 | .014 | | | .43 | | .43 | .67 |
| 0390 | 4" thick | | 1080 | .015 | | | .45 | | .45 | .70 |
| 0400 | 6" thick | | 1035 | .015 | | | .47 | | .47 | .73 |
| 0410 | 8" thick | | 990 | .016 | | | .49 | | .49 | .76 |
| 0420 | 10" thick | | 940 | .017 | | | .51 | | .51 | .80 |
| 0430 | 12" thick | | 890 | .018 | | | .54 | | .54 | .85 |
| 0440 | Reinforced alternate courses & vertically 48" OC, 4" thick | | 900 | .018 | | | .54 | | .54 | .84 |
| 0450 | 6" thick | | 850 | .019 | | | .57 | | .57 | .89 |
| 0460 | 8" thick | | 800 | .020 | | | .61 | | .61 | .94 |
| 0480 | 10" thick | | 750 | .021 | | | .65 | | .65 | 1 |
| 0490 | 12" thick | | 700 | .023 | | | .69 | | .69 | 1.08 |
| 1000 | Chimney, 16" x 16", soft old mortar | 1 Clab | 55 | .145 | C.F. | | 4.40 | | 4.40 | 6.85 |
| 1020 | Hard mortar | | 40 | .200 | | | 6.05 | | 6.05 | 9.40 |
| 1030 | 16" x 20", soft old mortar | | 55 | .145 | | | 4.40 | | 4.40 | 6.85 |
| 1040 | Hard mortar | | 40 | .200 | | | 6.05 | | 6.05 | 9.40 |
| 1050 | 16" x 24", soft old mortar | | 55 | .145 | | | 4.40 | | 4.40 | 6.85 |
| 1060 | Hard mortar | | 40 | .200 | | | 6.05 | | 6.05 | 9.40 |
| 1080 | 20" x 20", soft old mortar | | 55 | .145 | | | 4.40 | | 4.40 | 6.85 |
| 1100 | Hard mortar | | 40 | .200 | | | 6.05 | | 6.05 | 9.40 |
| 1110 | 20" x 24", soft old mortar | | 55 | .145 | | | 4.40 | | 4.40 | 6.85 |
| 1120 | Hard mortar | | 40 | .200 | | | 6.05 | | 6.05 | 9.40 |
| 1140 | 20" x 32", soft old mortar | | 55 | .145 | | | 4.40 | | 4.40 | 6.85 |
| 1160 | Hard mortar | | 40 | .200 | | | 6.05 | | 6.05 | 9.40 |
| 1200 | 48" x 48", soft old mortar | | 55 | .145 | | | 4.40 | | 4.40 | 6.85 |
| 1220 | Hard mortar | | 40 | .200 | | | 6.05 | | 6.05 | 9.40 |
| 1250 | Metal, high temp steel jacket, 24" diameter | E-2 | 130 | .431 | V.L.F. | | 18.05 | 12.05 | 30.10 | 44.50 |
| 1260 | 60" diameter | " | 60 | .933 | | | 39 | 26 | 65 | 96 |
| 1280 | Flue lining, up to 12" x 12" | 1 Clab | 200 | .040 | | | 1.21 | | 1.21 | 1.88 |
| 1282 | Up to 24" x 24" | | 150 | .053 | | | 1.61 | | 1.61 | 2.51 |
| 2000 | Columns, 8" x 8", soft old mortar | | 48 | .167 | | | 5.05 | | 5.05 | 7.85 |
| 2020 | Hard mortar | | 40 | .200 | | | 6.05 | | 6.05 | 9.40 |
| 2060 | 16" x 16", soft old mortar | | 16 | .500 | | | 15.15 | | 15.15 | 23.50 |
| 2100 | Hard mortar | | 14 | .571 | | | 17.30 | | 17.30 | 27 |
| 2140 | 24" x 24", soft old mortar | | 8 | 1 | | | 30.50 | | 30.50 | 47 |
| 2160 | Hard mortar | | 6 | 1.333 | | | 40.50 | | 40.50 | 62.50 |
| 2200 | 36" x 36", soft old mortar | | 4 | 2 | | | 60.50 | | 60.50 | 94 |
| 2220 | Hard mortar | | 3 | 2.667 | | | 80.50 | | 80.50 | 125 |
| 2230 | Alternate pricing method, soft old mortar | | 30 | .267 | C.F. | | 8.05 | | 8.05 | 12.55 |
| 2240 | Hard mortar | | 23 | .348 | " | | 10.50 | | 10.50 | 16.35 |

## 04 05 05 – Selective Masonry Demolition

| 04 05 05.10 Selective Demolition | | Crew | Daily Output | Labor-Hours | Unit | Material | 2008 Bare Costs Labor | Equipment | Total | Total Incl O&P |
|---|---|---|---|---|---|---|---|---|---|---|
| 3000 | Copings, precast or masonry, to 8" wide | | | | | | | | | |
| 3020 | Soft old mortar | 1 Clab | 180 | .044 | L.F. | | 1.34 | | 1.34 | 2.09 |
| 3040 | Hard mortar | " | 160 | .050 | " | | 1.51 | | 1.51 | 2.35 |
| 3100 | To 12" wide | | | | | | | | | |
| 3120 | Soft old mortar | 1 Clab | 160 | .050 | L.F. | | 1.51 | | 1.51 | 2.35 |
| 3140 | Hard mortar | " | 140 | .057 | " | | 1.73 | | 1.73 | 2.69 |
| 4000 | Fireplace, brick, 30" x 24" opening | | | | | | | | | |
| 4020 | Soft old mortar | 1 Clab | 2 | 4 | Ea. | | 121 | | 121 | 188 |
| 4040 | Hard mortar | | 1.25 | 6.400 | | | 194 | | 194 | 300 |
| 4100 | Stone, soft old mortar | | 1.50 | 5.333 | | | 161 | | 161 | 251 |
| 4120 | Hard mortar | | 1 | 8 | | | 242 | | 242 | 375 |
| 5000 | Veneers, brick, soft old mortar | | 140 | .057 | S.F. | | 1.73 | | 1.73 | 2.69 |
| 5020 | Hard mortar | | 125 | .064 | | | 1.94 | | 1.94 | 3.01 |
| 5100 | Granite and marble, 2" thick | | 180 | .044 | | | 1.34 | | 1.34 | 2.09 |
| 5120 | 4" thick | | 170 | .047 | | | 1.42 | | 1.42 | 2.21 |
| 5140 | Stone, 4" thick | | 180 | .044 | | | 1.34 | | 1.34 | 2.09 |
| 5160 | 8" thick | | 175 | .046 | | | 1.38 | | 1.38 | 2.15 |
| 5400 | Alternate pricing method, stone, 4" thick | | 60 | .133 | C.F. | | 4.03 | | 4.03 | 6.25 |
| 5420 | 8" thick | | 85 | .094 | " | | 2.85 | | 2.85 | 4.43 |

## 04 05 13 – Masonry Mortaring

### 04 05 13.10 Cement

| 0010 | **CEMENT** | | | | | | | | | |
|---|---|---|---|---|---|---|---|---|---|---|
| 0100 | Masonry, 70 lb. bag, T.L. lots | CN | | | Bag | 9.05 | | | 9.05 | 9.95 |
| 0150 | L.T.L. lots | | | | | 9.60 | | | 9.60 | 10.55 |
| 0200 | White, 70 lb. bag, T.L. lots | | | | | 15.35 | | | 15.35 | 16.85 |
| 0250 | L.T.L. lots | | | | | 16.45 | | | 16.45 | 18.05 |

### 04 05 13.20 Lime

| 0010 | **LIME** | | | | | | | | | |
|---|---|---|---|---|---|---|---|---|---|---|
| 0020 | Masons, hydrated, 50 lb. bag, T.L. lots | CN | | | Bag | 7.55 | | | 7.55 | 8.30 |
| 0050 | L.T.L. lots | | | | | 8.70 | | | 8.70 | 9.55 |
| 0200 | Finish, double hydrated, 50 lb. bag, T.L. lots | | | | | 9.90 | | | 9.90 | 10.90 |
| 0250 | L.T.L. lots | | | | | 11 | | | 11 | 12.10 |

### 04 05 13.23 Surface Bonding Masonry Mortaring

| 0010 | **SURFACE BONDING MASONRY MORTARING** | | | | | | | | | |
|---|---|---|---|---|---|---|---|---|---|---|
| 0020 | Gray or white colors, not incl. block work | 1 Bric | 540 | .015 | S.F. | .12 | .58 | | .70 | 1.01 |

### 04 05 13.30 Mortar

| 0010 | **MORTAR** R040513-10 | | | | | | | | | |
|---|---|---|---|---|---|---|---|---|---|---|
| 0020 | With masonry cement | | | | | | | | | |
| 0100 | Type M, 1:1:6 mix | 1 Brhe | 143 | .056 | C.F. | 4.32 | 1.71 | | 6.03 | 7.35 |
| 0200 | Type N, 1:3 mix | " | 143 | .056 | " | 4.15 | 1.71 | | 5.86 | 7.15 |
| 2000 | With portland cement and lime | | | | | | | | | |
| 2100 | Type M, 1:1/4:3 mix | 1 Brhe | 143 | .056 | C.F. | 7.75 | 1.71 | | 9.46 | 11.10 |
| 2200 | Type N, 1:1:6 mix, 750 psi | | 143 | .056 | | 6.50 | 1.71 | | 8.21 | 9.75 |
| 2300 | Type O, 1:2:9 mix (Pointing Mortar) | | 143 | .056 | | 7.10 | 1.71 | | 8.81 | 10.40 |
| 2650 | Pre-mixed, type S or N | | | | | 4.81 | | | 4.81 | 5.30 |
| 2700 | Mortar for glass block | 1 Brhe | 143 | .056 | | 8.90 | 1.71 | | 10.61 | 12.40 |
| 2900 | Mortar for Fire Brick, 80 lb. bag, T.L. Lots | | | | Bag | 25.50 | | | 25.50 | 28 |

### 04 05 13.91 Masonry Restoration Mortaring

| 0010 | **MASONRY RESTORATION MORTARING** | | | | | | | | | |
|---|---|---|---|---|---|---|---|---|---|---|
| 0020 | Masonry restoration mix | | | | Lb. | 1.97 | | | 1.97 | 2.17 |
| 0050 | White | | | | " | 2.27 | | | 2.27 | 2.50 |

# 04 05 Common Work Results for Masonry

## 04 05 13 – Masonry Mortaring

### 04 05 13.93 Mortar Pigments

| | | Crew | Daily Output | Labor-Hours | Unit | Material | 2008 Bare Costs Labor | Equipment | Total | Total Incl O&P |
|---|---|---|---|---|---|---|---|---|---|---|
| 0010 | **MORTAR PIGMENTS**, 50 lb. bags (2 bags per M bricks)   R040513-10 | | | | | | | | | |
| 0020 | Color admixture, range 2 to 10 lb. per bag of cement, minimum | | | | Lb. | 6.20 | | | 6.20 | 6.85 |
| 0050 | Average | | | | | 8.20 | | | 8.20 | 9.05 |
| 0100 | Maximum | | | | | 16.25 | | | 16.25 | 17.90 |

### 04 05 13.95 Sand

| | | Crew | Daily Output | Labor-Hours | Unit | Material | 2008 Bare Costs Labor | Equipment | Total | Total Incl O&P |
|---|---|---|---|---|---|---|---|---|---|---|
| 0010 | **SAND**, screened and washed at pit | | | | | | | | | |
| 0020 | For mortar, per ton   CN | | | | Ton | 15.15 | | | 15.15 | 16.65 |
| 0050 | With 10 mile haul | | | | | 22 | | | 22 | 24.50 |
| 0100 | With 30 mile haul | | | | | 36 | | | 36 | 39.50 |
| 0200 | Screened and washed, at the pit | | | | C.Y. | 21 | | | 21 | 23 |
| 0250 | With 10 mile haul | | | | | 30.50 | | | 30.50 | 33.50 |
| 0300 | With 30 mile haul | | | | | 50 | | | 50 | 55 |

### 04 05 13.98 Mortar Admixtures

| | | Crew | Daily Output | Labor-Hours | Unit | Material | 2008 Bare Costs Labor | Equipment | Total | Total Incl O&P |
|---|---|---|---|---|---|---|---|---|---|---|
| 0010 | **MORTAR ADMIXTURES** | | | | | | | | | |
| 0020 | Waterproofing admixture, per quart (1 qt. to 2 bags of masonry cement) | | | | Qt. | 9.50 | | | 9.50 | 10.45 |

## 04 05 16 – Masonry Grouting

### 04 05 16.30 Grouting

| | | Crew | Daily Output | Labor-Hours | Unit | Material | 2008 Bare Costs Labor | Equipment | Total | Total Incl O&P |
|---|---|---|---|---|---|---|---|---|---|---|
| 0010 | **GROUTING**   R040513-10 | | | | | | | | | |
| 0011 | Bond beams & lintels, 8" deep, 6" thick, 0.15 C.F. per L.F. | D-4 | 1480 | .022 | L.F. | .66 | .75 | .09 | 1.50 | 1.94 |
| 0020 | 8" thick, 0.2 C.F. per L.F. | | 1400 | .023 | | .99 | .79 | .09 | 1.87 | 2.39 |
| 0050 | 10" thick, 0.25 C.F. per L.F. | | 1200 | .027 | | 1.09 | .92 | .11 | 2.12 | 2.72 |
| 0060 | 12" thick, 0.3 C.F. per L.F. | | 1040 | .031 | | 1.31 | 1.06 | .12 | 2.49 | 3.18 |
| 0200 | Concrete block cores, solid, 4" thk., by hand, 0.067 C.F./S.F. of wall | D-8 | 1100 | .036 | S.F. | .29 | 1.30 | | 1.59 | 2.30 |
| 0210 | 6" thick, pumped, 0.175 C.F. per S.F. | D-4 | 720 | .044 | | .76 | 1.53 | .18 | 2.47 | 3.36 |
| 0250 | 8" thick, pumped, 0.258 C.F. per S.F. | | 680 | .047 | | 1.13 | 1.63 | .19 | 2.95 | 3.91 |
| 0300 | 10" thick, pumped, 0.340 C.F. per S.F. | | 660 | .048 | | 1.49 | 1.67 | .19 | 3.35 | 4.38 |
| 0350 | 12" thick, pumped, 0.422 C.F. per S.F. | | 640 | .050 | | 1.84 | 1.73 | .20 | 3.77 | 4.87 |
| 0500 | Cavity walls, 2" space, pumped, 0.167 C.F./S.F. of wall | | 1700 | .019 | | .73 | .65 | .07 | 1.45 | 1.87 |
| 0550 | 3" space, 0.250 C.F./S.F. | | 1200 | .027 | | 1.09 | .92 | .11 | 2.12 | 2.72 |
| 0600 | 4" space, 0.333 C.F. per S.F. | | 1150 | .028 | | 1.46 | .96 | .11 | 2.53 | 3.18 |
| 0700 | 6" space, 0.500 C.F. per S.F. | | 800 | .040 | | 2.19 | 1.38 | .16 | 3.73 | 4.67 |
| 0800 | Door frames, 3' x 7' opening, 2.5 C.F. per opening | | 60 | .533 | Opng. | 10.95 | 18.40 | 2.11 | 31.46 | 42.50 |
| 0850 | 6' x 7' opening, 3.5 C.F. per opening | | 45 | .711 | " | 15.30 | 24.50 | 2.81 | 42.61 | 57.50 |
| 2000 | Grout, C476, for bond beams, lintels and CMU cores | | 350 | .091 | C.F. | 4.37 | 3.16 | .36 | 7.89 | 10 |

## 04 05 19 – Masonry Anchorage and Reinforcing

### 04 05 19.05 Anchor Bolts

| | | Crew | Daily Output | Labor-Hours | Unit | Material | 2008 Bare Costs Labor | Equipment | Total | Total Incl O&P |
|---|---|---|---|---|---|---|---|---|---|---|
| 0010 | **ANCHOR BOLTS** | | | | | | | | | |
| 0020 | Hooked, with nut and washer, 1/2" diam., 8" long | 1 Bric | 200 | .040 | Ea. | .74 | 1.57 | | 2.31 | 3.19 |
| 0030 | 12" long | | 190 | .042 | | 1.43 | 1.65 | | 3.08 | 4.08 |
| 0040 | 5/8" diameter, 8" long | | 180 | .044 | | 1.13 | 1.74 | | 2.87 | 3.89 |
| 0050 | 12" long | | 170 | .047 | | 1.24 | 1.84 | | 3.08 | 4.17 |
| 0060 | 3/4" diameter, 8" long | | 160 | .050 | | 1.69 | 1.96 | | 3.65 | 4.84 |
| 0070 | 12" long | | 150 | .053 | | 2.11 | 2.09 | | 4.20 | 5.50 |

### 04 05 19.16 Masonry Anchors

| | | Crew | Daily Output | Labor-Hours | Unit | Material | 2008 Bare Costs Labor | Equipment | Total | Total Incl O&P |
|---|---|---|---|---|---|---|---|---|---|---|
| 0010 | **MASONRY ANCHORS** | | | | | | | | | |
| 0020 | For brick veneer, galv., corrugated, 7/8" x 7", 22 Ga. | 1 Bric | 10.50 | .762 | C | 6.20 | 30 | | 36.20 | 52.50 |
| 0100 | 24 Ga. | | 10.50 | .762 | | 5.95 | 30 | | 35.95 | 52 |
| 0150 | 16 Ga. | | 10.50 | .762 | | 23 | 30 | | 53 | 70.50 |
| 0200 | Buck anchors, galv., corrugated, 16 gauge, 2" bend, 8" x 2" | | 10.50 | .762 | | 122 | 30 | | 152 | 180 |
| 0250 | 8" x 3" | | 10.50 | .762 | | 125 | 30 | | 155 | 183 |

## 04 05 19 – Masonry Anchorage and Reinforcing

### 04 05 19.16 Masonry Anchors

| | | Crew | Daily Output | Labor-Hours | Unit | Material | 2008 Bare Costs Labor | Equipment | Total | Total Incl O&P |
|---|---|---|---|---|---|---|---|---|---|---|
| 0670 | 3/16" diameter | 1 Bric | 10.50 | .762 | C | 18.10 | 30 | | 48.10 | 65.50 |
| 0680 | 1/4" diameter | | 10.50 | .762 | | 36.50 | 30 | | 66.50 | 85.50 |
| 0850 | 8" long, 3/16" diameter | | 10.50 | .762 | | 20 | 30 | | 50 | 67.50 |
| 0855 | 1/4" diameter | | 10.50 | .762 | | 43 | 30 | | 73 | 93 |
| 1000 | Rectangular type, galvanized, 1/4" diameter, 2" x 6" | | 10.50 | .762 | | 58.50 | 30 | | 88.50 | 110 |
| 1050 | 4" x 6" | | 10.50 | .762 | | 73 | 30 | | 103 | 126 |
| 1100 | 3/16" diameter, 2" x 6" | | 10.50 | .762 | | 34 | 30 | | 64 | 83 |
| 1150 | 4" x 6" | | 10.50 | .762 | | 35 | 30 | | 65 | 84 |
| 1500 | Rigid partition anchors, plain, 8" long, 1" x 1/8" | | 10.50 | .762 | | 79.50 | 30 | | 109.50 | 133 |
| 1550 | 1" x 1/4" | | 10.50 | .762 | | 131 | 30 | | 161 | 190 |
| 1580 | 1-1/2" x 1/8" | | 10.50 | .762 | | 106 | 30 | | 136 | 162 |
| 1600 | 1-1/2" x 1/4" | | 10.50 | .762 | | 215 | 30 | | 245 | 283 |
| 1650 | 2" x 1/8" | | 10.50 | .762 | | 137 | 30 | | 167 | 197 |
| 1700 | 2" x 1/4" | | 10.50 | .762 | | 252 | 30 | | 282 | 325 |

### 04 05 19.26 Masonry Reinforcing Bars

| | | Crew | Daily Output | Labor-Hours | Unit | Material | 2008 Bare Costs Labor | Equipment | Total | Total Incl O&P |
|---|---|---|---|---|---|---|---|---|---|---|
| 0010 | **MASONRY REINFORCING BARS**                R040519-50 | | | | | | | | | |
| 0015 | Steel bars A615, placed horiz., #3 & #4 bars | 1 Bric | 450 | .018 | Lb. | .47 | .70 | | 1.17 | 1.57 |
| 0020 | #5 & #6 bars | | 800 | .010 | | .47 | .39 | | .86 | 1.11 |
| 0050 | Placed vertical, #3 & #4 bars | | 350 | .023 | | .47 | .90 | | 1.37 | 1.87 |
| 0060 | #5 & #6 bars | | 650 | .012 | | .47 | .48 | | .95 | 1.24 |
| 0200 | Joint reinforcing, regular truss, to 6" wide, mill std galvanized | | 30 | .267 | C.L.F. | 12.15 | 10.45 | | 22.60 | 29.50 |
| 0250 | 12" wide | | 20 | .400 | | 13.30 | 15.65 | | 28.95 | 38.50 |
| 0400 | Cavity truss with drip section, to 6" wide | | 30 | .267 | | 13.45 | 10.45 | | 23.90 | 30.50 |
| 0450 | 12" wide | | 20 | .400 | | 13.80 | 15.65 | | 29.45 | 39 |

## 04 05 23 – Masonry Accessories

### 04 05 23.13 Control Joint

| | | Crew | Daily Output | Labor-Hours | Unit | Material | 2008 Bare Costs Labor | Equipment | Total | Total Incl O&P |
|---|---|---|---|---|---|---|---|---|---|---|
| 0010 | **CONTROL JOINT** | | | | | | | | | |
| 0020 | Rubber, 4" wall | 1 Bric | 400 | .020 | L.F. | 2.07 | .78 | | 2.85 | 3.47 |
| 0025 | 6" wall | | 320 | .025 | | 2.56 | .98 | | 3.54 | 4.31 |
| 0030 | 8" and wider wall | | 280 | .029 | | 3.08 | 1.12 | | 4.20 | 5.10 |
| 0050 | PVC, 4" wall | | 400 | .020 | | 1.08 | .78 | | 1.86 | 2.38 |
| 0120 | 6" wall | | 320 | .025 | | 1.81 | .98 | | 2.79 | 3.48 |
| 0160 | 8" wall | | 280 | .029 | | 2.20 | 1.12 | | 3.32 | 4.12 |
| 0180 | 12" wall | | 240 | .033 | | 3.33 | 1.30 | | 4.63 | 5.65 |

### 04 05 23.19 Vent Box

| | | Crew | Daily Output | Labor-Hours | Unit | Material | 2008 Bare Costs Labor | Equipment | Total | Total Incl O&P |
|---|---|---|---|---|---|---|---|---|---|---|
| 0010 | **VENT BOX** | | | | | | | | | |
| 0020 | Extruded aluminum, 4" deep, 2-3/8" x 8-1/8" | 1 Bric | 30 | .267 | Ea. | 30.50 | 10.45 | | 40.95 | 49.50 |
| 0050 | 5" x 8-1/8" | | 25 | .320 | | 39.50 | 12.55 | | 52.05 | 62.50 |
| 0100 | 2-1/4" x 25" | | 25 | .320 | | 68.50 | 12.55 | | 81.05 | 94.50 |
| 0150 | 5" x 16-1/2" | | 22 | .364 | | 57 | 14.25 | | 71.25 | 84 |
| 0200 | 6" x 16-1/2" | | 22 | .364 | | 79.50 | 14.25 | | 93.75 | 109 |
| 0250 | 7-3/4" x 16-1/2" | | 20 | .400 | | 68.50 | 15.65 | | 84.15 | 99.50 |
| 0400 | For baked enamel finish, add | | | | | 35% | | | | |
| 0500 | For cast aluminum, painted, add | | | | | 60% | | | | |
| 1000 | Stainless steel ventilators, 6" x 6" | 1 Bric | 25 | .320 | | 126 | 12.55 | | 138.55 | 157 |
| 1050 | 8" x 8" | | 24 | .333 | | 132 | 13.05 | | 145.05 | 166 |
| 1100 | 12" x 12" | | 23 | .348 | | 153 | 13.60 | | 166.60 | 189 |
| 1150 | 12" x 6" | | 24 | .333 | | 134 | 13.05 | | 147.05 | 167 |
| 1200 | Foundation block vent, galv., 1-1/4" thk, 8" high, 16" long, no damper | | 30 | .267 | | 24.50 | 10.45 | | 34.95 | 43 |
| 1250 | For damper, add | | | | | 8.20 | | | 8.20 | 9 |

# 04 05 Common Work Results for Masonry

## 04 05 23 – Masonry Accessories

| 04 05 23.95 Wall Plugs | | Crew | Daily Output | Labor-Hours | Unit | Material | 2008 Bare Costs Labor | Equipment | Total | Total Incl O&P |
|---|---|---|---|---|---|---|---|---|---|---|
| 0010 | **WALL PLUGS** (for nailing to brickwork) | | | | | | | | | |
| 0020 | 26 ga., galvanized, plain | 1 Bric | 10.50 | .762 | C | 31 | 30 | | 61 | 79.50 |
| 0050 | Wood filled | " | 10.50 | .762 | " | 104 | 30 | | 134 | 160 |

# 04 21 Clay Unit Masonry

## 04 21 13 – Brick Masonry

### 04 21 13.13 Brick Veneer Masonry

| | 04 21 13.13 Brick Veneer Masonry | | Crew | Daily Output | Labor-Hours | Unit | Material | 2008 Bare Costs Labor | Equipment | Total | Total Incl O&P |
|---|---|---|---|---|---|---|---|---|---|---|---|
| 0010 | **BRICK VENEER MASONRY**, T.L. lots, excl. scaffolding, grout & reinforcing | | | | | | | | | | |
| 0015 | Material costs incl. 3% brick and 25% mortar waste | R042110-20 | | | | | | | | | |
| 0020 | Standard, select common, 4" x 2-2/3" x 8" (6.75/S.F.) | | D-8 | 1.50 | 26.667 | M | 530 | 955 | | 1,485 | 2,025 |
| 0050 | Red, 4" x 2-2/3" x 8", running bond | | | 1.50 | 26.667 | | 810 | 955 | | 1,765 | 2,350 |
| 0100 | Full header every 6th course (7.88/S.F.) | R042110-50 | | 1.45 | 27.586 | | 805 | 985 | | 1,790 | 2,400 |
| 0150 | English, full header every 2nd course (10.13/S.F.) | | | 1.40 | 28.571 | | 805 | 1,025 | | 1,830 | 2,425 |
| 0200 | Flemish, alternate header every course (9.00/S.F.) | | | 1.40 | 28.571 | | 805 | 1,025 | | 1,830 | 2,425 |
| 0250 | Flemish, alt. header every 6th course (7.13/S.F.) | | | 1.45 | 27.586 | | 810 | 985 | | 1,795 | 2,400 |
| 0300 | Full headers throughout (13.50/S.F.) | | | 1.40 | 28.571 | | 805 | 1,025 | | 1,830 | 2,425 |
| 0350 | Rowlock course (13.50/S.F.) | | | 1.35 | 29.630 | | 805 | 1,050 | | 1,855 | 2,475 |
| 0400 | Rowlock stretcher (4.50/S.F.) | | | 1.40 | 28.571 | | 810 | 1,025 | | 1,835 | 2,450 |
| 0450 | Soldier course (6.75/S.F.) | | | 1.40 | 28.571 | | 810 | 1,025 | | 1,835 | 2,450 |
| 0500 | Sailor course (4.50/S.F.) | | | 1.30 | 30.769 | | 810 | 1,100 | | 1,910 | 2,575 |
| 0601 | Buff or gray face, running bond, (6.75/S.F.) | | | 1.50 | 26.667 | | 810 | 955 | | 1,765 | 2,350 |
| 0700 | Glazed face, 4" x 2-2/3" x 8", running bond | | | 1.40 | 28.571 | | 1,550 | 1,025 | | 2,575 | 3,250 |
| 0750 | Full header every 6th course (7.88/S.F.) | | | 1.35 | 29.630 | | 1,475 | 1,050 | | 2,525 | 3,225 |
| 1000 | Jumbo, 6" x 4" x 12",(3.00/S.F.) | | | 1.30 | 30.769 | | 1,650 | 1,100 | | 2,750 | 3,500 |
| 1051 | Norman, 4" x 2-2/3" x 12" (4.50/S.F.) | | | 1.45 | 27.586 | | 1,100 | 985 | | 2,085 | 2,725 |
| 1100 | Norwegian, 4" x 3-1/5" x 12" (3.75/S.F.) | | | 1.40 | 28.571 | | 1,000 | 1,025 | | 2,025 | 2,650 |
| 1150 | Economy, 4" x 4" x 8" (4.50 per S.F.) | | | 1.40 | 28.571 | | 925 | 1,025 | | 1,950 | 2,575 |
| 1201 | Engineer, 4" x 3-1/5" x 8", (5.63/S.F.) | | | 1.45 | 27.586 | | 600 | 985 | | 1,585 | 2,150 |
| 1251 | Roman, 4" x 2" x 12", (6.00/S.F.) | | | 1.50 | 26.667 | | 980 | 955 | | 1,935 | 2,525 |
| 1300 | S.C.R. 6" x 2-2/3" x 12" (4.50/S.F.) | | | 1.40 | 28.571 | | 1,175 | 1,025 | | 2,200 | 2,850 |
| 1350 | Utility, 4" x 4" x 12" (3.00/S.F.) | | | 1.35 | 29.630 | | 1,250 | 1,050 | | 2,300 | 2,975 |
| 1360 | For less than truck load lots, add | | | | | | 12 | | | 12 | 13.20 |
| 1400 | For battered walls, add | | | | | | | 30% | | | |
| 1450 | For corbels, add | | | | | | | 75% | | | |
| 1500 | For curved walls, add | | | | | | | 30% | | | |
| 1550 | For pits and trenches, deduct | | | | | | | 20% | | | |
| 1999 | Alternate method of figuring by square foot | | | | | | | | | | |
| 2000 | Standard, sel. common, 4" x 2-2/3" x 8", (6.75/S.F.) | | D-8 | 230 | .174 | S.F. | 3.59 | 6.20 | | 9.79 | 13.40 |
| 2020 | Standard, red, 4" x 2-2/3" x 8", running bond (6.75/SF) | | | 220 | .182 | | 5.45 | 6.50 | | 11.95 | 15.90 |
| 2050 | Full header every 6th course (7.88/S.F.) | | | 185 | .216 | | 6.35 | 7.75 | | 14.10 | 18.75 |
| 2100 | English, full header every 2nd course (10.13/S.F.) | | | 140 | .286 | | 8.15 | 10.20 | | 18.35 | 24.50 |
| 2150 | Flemish, alternate header every course (9.00/S.F.) | | | 150 | .267 | | 7.25 | 9.55 | | 16.80 | 22.50 |
| 2200 | Flemish, alt. header every 6th course (7.13/S.F.) | | | 205 | .195 | | 5.75 | 6.95 | | 12.70 | 16.95 |
| 2250 | Full headers throughout (13.50/S.F.) | | | 105 | .381 | | 10.85 | 13.60 | | 24.45 | 32.50 |
| 2300 | Rowlock course (13.50/S.F.) | | | 100 | .400 | | 10.85 | 14.30 | | 25.15 | 33.50 |
| 2350 | Rowlock stretcher (4.50/S.F.) | | | 310 | .129 | | 3.66 | 4.61 | | 8.27 | 11 |
| 2400 | Soldier course (6.75/S.F.) | | | 200 | .200 | | 5.45 | 7.15 | | 12.60 | 16.85 |
| 2450 | Sailor course (4.50/S.F.) | | | 290 | .138 | | 3.66 | 4.93 | | 8.59 | 11.50 |
| 2600 | Buff or gray face, running bond, (6.75/S.F.) | | | 220 | .182 | | 5.80 | 6.50 | | 12.30 | 16.25 |
| 2700 | Glazed face brick, running bond | | | 210 | .190 | | 9.95 | 6.80 | | 16.75 | 21.50 |

# 04 21 Clay Unit Masonry

## 04 21 13 – Brick Masonry

### 04 21 13.13 Brick Veneer Masonry

| | | Crew | Daily Output | Labor-Hours | Unit | Material | 2008 Bare Costs Labor | 2008 Bare Costs Equipment | Total | Total Incl O&P |
|---|---|---|---|---|---|---|---|---|---|---|
| 2750 | Full header every 6th course (7.88/S.F.) | D-8 | 170 | .235 | S.F. | 11.65 | 8.40 | | 20.05 | 25.50 |
| 3000 | Jumbo, 6" x 4" x 12" running bond (3.00/S.F.) | | 435 | .092 | | 4.54 | 3.29 | | 7.83 | 10 |
| 3050 | Norman, 4" x 2-2/3" x 12" running bond, (4.5/S.F.) | | 320 | .125 | | 5.80 | 4.47 | | 10.27 | 13.20 |
| 3100 | Norwegian, 4" x 3-1/5" x 12" (3.75/S.F.) | | 375 | .107 | | 3.64 | 3.81 | | 7.45 | 9.80 |
| 3150 | Economy, 4" x 4" x 8" (4.50/S.F.) | | 310 | .129 | | 4.12 | 4.61 | | 8.73 | 11.55 |
| 3200 | Engineer, 4" x 3-1/5" x 8" (5.63/S.F.) | | 260 | .154 | | 3.37 | 5.50 | | 8.87 | 12.05 |
| 3250 | Roman, 4" x 2" x 12" (6.00/S.F.) | | 250 | .160 | | 5.75 | 5.70 | | 11.45 | 15 |
| 3300 | SCR, 6" x 2-2/3" x 12" (4.50/S.F.) | | 310 | .129 | | 5.20 | 4.61 | | 9.81 | 12.75 |
| 3350 | Utility, 4" x 4" x 12" (3.00/S.F.) | | 450 | .089 | | 3.61 | 3.18 | | 6.79 | 8.80 |
| 3400 | For cavity wall construction, add | | | | | | 15% | | | |
| 3450 | For stacked bond, add | | | | | | 10% | | | |
| 3500 | For interior veneer construction, add | | | | | | 15% | | | |
| 3550 | For curved walls, add | | | | | | 30% | | | |

### 04 21 13.15 Chimney

| | | Crew | Daily Output | Labor-Hours | Unit | Material | 2008 Bare Costs Labor | 2008 Bare Costs Equipment | Total | Total Incl O&P |
|---|---|---|---|---|---|---|---|---|---|---|
| 0010 | **CHIMNEY**, excludes foundation, scaffolding, grout and reinforcing | | | | | | | | | |
| 0100 | Brick, 16" x 16", 8" flue | D-1 | 18.20 | .879 | V.L.F. | 20 | 30.50 | | 50.50 | 68.50 |
| 0150 | 16" x 20" with one 8" x 12" flue | | 16 | 1 | | 30.50 | 35 | | 65.50 | 86.50 |
| 0200 | 16" x 24" with two 8" x 8" flues | | 14 | 1.143 | | 43.50 | 40 | | 83.50 | 109 |
| 0250 | 20" x 20" with one 12" x 12" flue | | 13.70 | 1.168 | | 37 | 40.50 | | 77.50 | 103 |
| 0300 | 20" x 24" with two 8" x 12" flues | | 12 | 1.333 | | 50 | 46.50 | | 96.50 | 126 |
| 0350 | 20" x 32" with two 12" x 12" flues | | 10 | 1.600 | | 64.50 | 56 | | 120.50 | 156 |
| 1800 | Metal, high temp. steel jacket, factory lining, 24" diam. | E-2 | 65 | .862 | | 210 | 36 | 24 | 270 | 320 |
| 1900 | 60" diameter | " | 30 | 1.867 | | 765 | 78 | 52 | 895 | 1,025 |
| 2100 | Poured concrete, brick lining, 200' high x 10' diam. | | | | | 6,925 | | | 6,925 | 7,625 |
| 2800 | 500' x 20' diameter | | | | | 12,100 | | | 12,100 | 13,300 |

### 04 21 13.18 Columns

| | | Crew | Daily Output | Labor-Hours | Unit | Material | 2008 Bare Costs Labor | 2008 Bare Costs Equipment | Total | Total Incl O&P |
|---|---|---|---|---|---|---|---|---|---|---|
| 0010 | **COLUMNS**, solid, excludes scaffolding, grout and reinforcing    R042110-10 | | | | | | | | | |
| 0050 | Brick, 8" x 8", 9 brick per VLF | D-1 | 56 | .286 | V.L.F. | 7 | 9.95 | | 16.95 | 23 |
| 0100 | 12" x 8", 13.5 brick per VLF | | 37 | .432 | | 10.55 | 15.10 | | 25.65 | 34.50 |
| 0200 | 12" x 12", 20 brick per VLF | | 25 | .640 | | 15.60 | 22.50 | | 38.10 | 51 |
| 0300 | 16" x 12", 27 brick per VLF | | 19 | .842 | | 21 | 29.50 | | 50.50 | 67.50 |
| 0400 | 16" x 16", 36 brick per VLF | | 14 | 1.143 | | 28 | 40 | | 68 | 91.50 |
| 0500 | 20" x 16", 45 brick per VLF | | 11 | 1.455 | | 35 | 50.50 | | 85.50 | 116 |
| 0600 | 20" x 20", 56 brick per VLF | | 9 | 1.778 | | 43.50 | 62 | | 105.50 | 143 |
| 0700 | 24" x 20", 68 brick per VLF | | 7 | 2.286 | | 53 | 79.50 | | 132.50 | 180 |
| 0800 | 24" x 24", 81 brick per VLF | | 6 | 2.667 | | 63 | 93 | | 156 | 211 |
| 1000 | 36" x 36", 182 brick per VLF | | 3 | 5.333 | | 142 | 186 | | 328 | 440 |

### 04 21 13.30 Oversized Brick

| | | Crew | Daily Output | Labor-Hours | Unit | Material | 2008 Bare Costs Labor | 2008 Bare Costs Equipment | Total | Total Incl O&P |
|---|---|---|---|---|---|---|---|---|---|---|
| 0010 | **OVERSIZED BRICK**, excludes scaffolding, grout and reinforcing | | | | | | | | | |
| 0100 | Veneer, 4" x 2.25" x 16" | D-8 | 387 | .103 | S.F. | 4.81 | 3.69 | | 8.50 | 10.90 |
| 0105 | 4" x 2.75" x 16" | | 412 | .097 | | 4.36 | 3.47 | | 7.83 | 10.10 |
| 0110 | 4" x 4" x 16" | | 460 | .087 | | 4.29 | 3.11 | | 7.40 | 9.45 |
| 0120 | 4" x 8" x 16" | | 533 | .075 | | 5.25 | 2.68 | | 7.93 | 9.90 |
| 0125 | Loadbearing, 6" x 4" x 16", grouted and reinforced | | 387 | .103 | | 7.70 | 3.69 | | 11.39 | 14.05 |
| 0130 | 8" x 4" x 16", grouted and reinforced | | 327 | .122 | | 8.10 | 4.37 | | 12.47 | 15.60 |
| 0135 | 6" x 8" x 16", grouted and reinforced | | 440 | .091 | | 7.35 | 3.25 | | 10.60 | 13 |
| 0140 | 8" x 8" x 16", grouted and reinforced | | 400 | .100 | | 8.25 | 3.57 | | 11.82 | 14.50 |
| 0145 | Curtainwall / reinforced veneer, 6" x 4" x 16" | | 387 | .103 | | 12 | 3.69 | | 15.69 | 18.80 |
| 0150 | 8" x 4" x 16" | | 327 | .122 | | 14.60 | 4.37 | | 18.97 | 22.50 |
| 0155 | 6" x 8" x 16" | | 440 | .091 | | 12.15 | 3.25 | | 15.40 | 18.30 |
| 0160 | 8" x 8" x 16" | | 400 | .100 | | 14.70 | 3.57 | | 18.27 | 21.50 |
| 0200 | For 1 to 3 slots in face, add | | | | | 25% | | | | |

# 04 21 Clay Unit Masonry

## 04 21 13 – Brick Masonry

| | | Crew | Daily Output | Labor-Hours | Unit | Material | 2008 Bare Costs Labor | Equipment | Total | Total Incl O&P |
|---|---|---|---|---|---|---|---|---|---|---|
| **04 21 13.30 Oversized Brick** | | | | | | | | | | |
| 0210 | For 4 to 7 slots in face, add | | | | S.F. | 15% | | | | |
| 0220 | For bond beams, add | | | | | 20% | | | | |
| 0230 | For bullnose shapes, add | | | | | 20% | | | | |
| 0240 | For open end knockout, add | | | | | 10% | | | | |
| 0250 | For white or gray color group, add | | | | | 10% | | | | |
| 0260 | For 135 degree corner, add | | | | | 250% | | | | |
| **04 21 13.35 Common Building Brick** | | | | | | | | | | |
| 0010 | **COMMON BUILDING BRICK**, C62, TL lots, material only    R042110-20 | | | | | | | | | |
| 0020 | Standard, minimum | | | | M | 340 | | | 340 | 375 |
| 0050 | Average (select) | | | | " | 430 | | | 430 | 475 |
| **04 21 13.40 Structural Brick** | | | | | | | | | | |
| 0010 | **STRUCTURAL BRICK** C652, Grade SW, incl. mortar, scaffolding not incl. | | | | | | | | | |
| 0100 | Standard unit, 4-5/8" x 2-3/4" x 9-5/8" | D-8 | 245 | .163 | S.F. | 5.25 | 5.85 | | 11.10 | 14.65 |
| 0120 | Bond beam | | 225 | .178 | | 9.95 | 6.35 | | 16.30 | 20.50 |
| 0140 | V cut bond beam | | 225 | .178 | | 10.45 | 6.35 | | 16.80 | 21 |
| 0160 | Stretcher quoin, 5-5/8" x 2-3/4" x 9-5/8" | | 245 | .163 | | 10.10 | 5.85 | | 15.95 | 19.95 |
| 0180 | Corner quoin | | 245 | .163 | | 11.30 | 5.85 | | 17.15 | 21.50 |
| 0200 | Corner, 45 deg, 4-5/8" x 2-3/4" x 10-7/16" | | 235 | .170 | | 11.70 | 6.10 | | 17.80 | 22 |
| **04 21 13.45 Face Brick** | | | | | | | | | | |
| 0010 | **FACE BRICK** Material Only, C216, TL lots    R042110-20 | | | | | | | | | |
| 0300 | Standard modular, 4" x 2-2/3" x 8", minimum | | | | M | 700 | | | 700 | 770 |
| 0350 | Maximum    **CN** | | | | | 775 | | | 775 | 855 |
| 0450 | Economy, 4" x 4" x 8", minimum | | | | | 800 | | | 800 | 880 |
| 0500 | Maximum | | | | | 1,050 | | | 1,050 | 1,150 |
| 0510 | Economy, 4" x 4" x 12", minimum | | | | | 1,100 | | | 1,100 | 1,200 |
| 0520 | Maximum | | | | | 1,425 | | | 1,425 | 1,575 |
| 0550 | Jumbo, 6" x 4" x 12", minimum | | | | | 1,375 | | | 1,375 | 1,500 |
| 0600 | Maximum | | | | | 1,750 | | | 1,750 | 1,925 |
| 0610 | Jumbo, 8" x 4" x 12", minimum | | | | | 1,375 | | | 1,375 | 1,500 |
| 0620 | Maximum | | | | | 1,750 | | | 1,750 | 1,925 |
| 0650 | Norwegian, 4" x 3-1/5" x 12", minimum | | | | | 855 | | | 855 | 940 |
| 0700 | Maximum | | | | | 1,100 | | | 1,100 | 1,225 |
| 0710 | Norwegian, 6" x 3-1/5" x 12", minimum | | | | | 1,250 | | | 1,250 | 1,375 |
| 0720 | Maximum | | | | | 1,625 | | | 1,625 | 1,775 |
| 0850 | Standard glazed, plain colors, 4" x 2-2/3" x 8", minimum | | | | | 1,350 | | | 1,350 | 1,475 |
| 0900 | Maximum | | | | | 1,750 | | | 1,750 | 1,925 |
| 1000 | Deep trim shades, 4" x 2-2/3" x 8", minimum | | | | | 1,400 | | | 1,400 | 1,550 |
| 1050 | Maximum | | | | | 1,550 | | | 1,550 | 1,725 |
| 1080 | Jumbo utility, 4" x 4" x 12" | | | | | 1,075 | | | 1,075 | 1,175 |
| 1120 | 4" x 8" x 8" | | | | | 1,300 | | | 1,300 | 1,450 |
| 1140 | 4" x 8" x 16" | | | | | 2,750 | | | 2,750 | 3,025 |
| 1260 | Engineer, 4" x 3-1/5" x 8", minimum | | | | | 495 | | | 495 | 545 |
| 1270 | Maximum | | | | | 595 | | | 595 | 655 |
| 1350 | King, 4" x 2-3/4" x 10", minimum | | | | | 525 | | | 525 | 575 |
| 1360 | Maximum | | | | | 560 | | | 560 | 620 |
| 1400 | Norman, 4" x 2-3/4" x 12" | | | | | 525 | | | 525 | 575 |
| 1450 | Roman, 4" x 2" x 12" | | | | | 525 | | | 525 | 575 |
| 1500 | SCR, 6" x 2-2/3" x 12" | | | | | 525 | | | 525 | 575 |
| 1550 | Double, 4" x 5-1/3" x 8" | | | | | 525 | | | 525 | 575 |
| 1600 | Triple, 4" x 5-1/3" x 12" | | | | | 525 | | | 525 | 575 |
| 1770 | Standard modular, double glazed, 4" x 2-2/3" x 8" | | | | | 1,175 | | | 1,175 | 1,300 |
| 1850 | Jumbo, colored glazed ceramic, 6" x 4" x 12" | | | | | 1,750 | | | 1,750 | 1,925 |

# 04 21 Clay Unit Masonry

## 04 21 13 – Brick Masonry

| 04 21 13.45 Face Brick | | Crew | Daily Output | Labor-Hours | Unit | Material | 2008 Bare Costs Labor | Equipment | Total | Total Incl O&P |
|---|---|---|---|---|---|---|---|---|---|---|
| 2050 | Jumbo utility, glazed, 4" x 4" x 12" | | | | M | 1,300 | | | 1,300 | 1,450 |
| 2100 | 4" x 8" x 8" | | | | | 1,800 | | | 1,800 | 2,000 |
| 2150 | 4" x 16" x 8" | | | | | 3,125 | | | 3,125 | 3,425 |
| 2170 | For less than truck load lots, add | | | | | 12 | | | 12 | 13.20 |
| 2180 | For buff or gray brick, add | | | | | 16 | | | 16 | 17.60 |

## 04 21 26 – Glazed Structural Clay Tile Masonry

### 04 21 26.10 Structural Facing Tile

| | | Crew | Daily Output | Labor-Hours | Unit | Material | 2008 Bare Costs Labor | Equipment | Total | Total Incl O&P |
|---|---|---|---|---|---|---|---|---|---|---|
| 0010 | **STRUCTURAL FACING TILE**, std. colors, excl. scaffolding, grout & reinforcing | | | | | | | | | |
| 0020 | 6T series, 5-1/3" x 12", 2.3 pieces per S.F., glazed 1 side, 2" thick | D-8 | 225 | .178 | S.F. | 6.65 | 6.35 | | 13 | 16.95 |
| 0100 | 4" thick | | 220 | .182 | | 7.80 | 6.50 | | 14.30 | 18.50 |
| 0150 | Glazed 2 sides | | 195 | .205 | | 12.45 | 7.35 | | 19.80 | 25 |
| 0250 | 6" thick | | 210 | .190 | | 12.05 | 6.80 | | 18.85 | 23.50 |
| 0300 | Glazed 2 sides | | 185 | .216 | | 14.25 | 7.75 | | 22 | 27.50 |
| 0400 | 8" thick | | 180 | .222 | | 15.20 | 7.95 | | 23.15 | 29 |
| 0500 | Special shapes, group 1 | | 400 | .100 | Ea. | 6 | 3.57 | | 9.57 | 12.05 |
| 0550 | Group 2 | | 375 | .107 | | 9.10 | 3.81 | | 12.91 | 15.80 |
| 0600 | Group 3 | | 350 | .114 | | 11.30 | 4.08 | | 15.38 | 18.65 |
| 0650 | Group 4 | | 325 | .123 | | 19.55 | 4.40 | | 23.95 | 28 |
| 0700 | Group 5 | | 300 | .133 | | 25.50 | 4.76 | | 30.26 | 35.50 |
| 0750 | Group 6 | | 275 | .145 | | 31 | 5.20 | | 36.20 | 42 |
| 1000 | Fire rated, 4" thick, 1 hr. rating | | 210 | .190 | S.F. | 13.30 | 6.80 | | 20.10 | 25 |
| 1300 | Acoustic, 4" thick | | 210 | .190 | " | 34 | 6.80 | | 40.80 | 48 |
| 1400 | For designer colors, add | | | | | 25% | | | | |
| 2000 | 8W series, 8" x 16", 1.125 pieces per S.F. | | | | | | | | | |
| 2050 | 2" thick, glazed 1 side | D-8 | 360 | .111 | S.F. | 7.40 | 3.97 | | 11.37 | 14.20 |
| 2100 | 4" thick, glazed 1 side | | 345 | .116 | | 8.05 | 4.14 | | 12.19 | 15.15 |
| 2150 | Glazed 2 sides | | 325 | .123 | | 12 | 4.40 | | 16.40 | 19.90 |
| 2200 | 6" thick, glazed 1 side | | 330 | .121 | | 11.35 | 4.33 | | 15.68 | 19.10 |
| 2250 | 8" thick, glazed 1 side | | 310 | .129 | | 13.20 | 4.61 | | 17.81 | 21.50 |
| 2500 | Special shapes, group 1 | | 300 | .133 | Ea. | 9.85 | 4.76 | | 14.61 | 18.05 |
| 2550 | Group 2 | | 280 | .143 | | 12.95 | 5.10 | | 18.05 | 22 |
| 2600 | Group 3 | | 260 | .154 | | 13.60 | 5.50 | | 19.10 | 23.50 |
| 2650 | Group 4 | | 250 | .160 | | 30 | 5.70 | | 35.70 | 41.50 |
| 2700 | Group 5 | | 240 | .167 | | 43 | 5.95 | | 48.95 | 56 |
| 2750 | Group 6 | | 230 | .174 | | 57.50 | 6.20 | | 63.70 | 73 |
| 3000 | 4" thick, glazed 1 side | | 345 | .116 | S.F. | 9.60 | 4.14 | | 13.74 | 16.85 |
| 3100 | Acoustic, 4" thick | | 345 | .116 | " | 12.45 | 4.14 | | 16.59 | 20 |
| 3120 | 4W series, 8" x 8", 2.25 pieces per S.F. | | | | | | | | | |
| 3125 | 2" thick, glazed 1 side | D-8 | 360 | .111 | S.F. | 8.65 | 3.97 | | 12.62 | 15.55 |
| 3130 | 4" thick, glazed 1 side | | 345 | .116 | | 8.65 | 4.14 | | 12.79 | 15.80 |
| 3135 | Glazed 2 sides | | 325 | .123 | | 12.40 | 4.40 | | 16.80 | 20.50 |
| 3140 | 6" thick, glazed 1 side | | 330 | .121 | | 11.60 | 4.33 | | 15.93 | 19.35 |
| 3150 | 8" thick, glazed 1 side | | 310 | .129 | | 16.70 | 4.61 | | 21.31 | 25.50 |
| 3155 | Special shapes, group I | | 300 | .133 | Ea. | 6.10 | 4.76 | | 10.86 | 13.95 |
| 3160 | Group II | | 280 | .143 | " | 7.40 | 5.10 | | 12.50 | 15.90 |
| 3200 | For designer colors, add | | | | | 25% | | | | |
| 3300 | For epoxy mortar joints, add | | | | S.F. | 1.46 | | | 1.46 | 1.61 |

## 04 21 29 – Terra Cotta Masonry

### 04 21 29.10 Terra Cotta Masonry Components

| | | Crew | Daily Output | Labor-Hours | Unit | Material | 2008 Bare Costs Labor | Equipment | Total | Total Incl O&P |
|---|---|---|---|---|---|---|---|---|---|---|
| 0010 | **TERRA COTTA MASONRY COMPONENTS** | | | | | | | | | |
| 0020 | Coping, split type, not glazed, 9" wide | D-1 | 90 | .178 | L.F. | 9.80 | 6.20 | | 16 | 20 |
| 0100 | 13" wide | | 80 | .200 | | 14.80 | 7 | | 21.80 | 27 |

# 04 21 Clay Unit Masonry

## 04 21 29 – Terra Cotta Masonry

### 04 21 29.10 Terra Cotta Masonry Components

| | | Crew | Daily Output | Labor-Hours | Unit | Material | 2008 Bare Costs Labor | Equipment | Total | Total Incl O&P |
|---|---|---|---|---|---|---|---|---|---|---|
| 0200 | Coping, split type, glazed, 9" wide | D-1 | 90 | .178 | L.F. | 16.70 | 6.20 | | 22.90 | 28 |
| 0250 | 13" wide | ↓ | 80 | .200 | ↓ | 22 | 7 | | 29 | 34.50 |
| 0500 | Partition or back-up blocks, scored, in C.L. lots | | | | | | | | | |
| 0700 | Non-load bearing 12" x 12", 3" thick, special order | D-8 | 550 | .073 | S.F. | 17.90 | 2.60 | | 20.50 | 23.50 |
| 0750 | 4" thick, standard | | 500 | .080 | | 6.55 | 2.86 | | 9.41 | 11.60 |
| 0800 | 6" thick | | 450 | .089 | | 7.70 | 3.18 | | 10.88 | 13.35 |
| 0850 | 8" thick | | 400 | .100 | | 9.95 | 3.57 | | 13.52 | 16.35 |
| 1000 | Load bearing, 12" x 12", 4" thick, in walls | | 500 | .080 | | 6.40 | 2.86 | | 9.26 | 11.40 |
| 1050 | In floors | | 750 | .053 | | 6.40 | 1.91 | | 8.31 | 9.95 |
| 1200 | 6" thick, in walls | | 450 | .089 | | 7.70 | 3.18 | | 10.88 | 13.35 |
| 1250 | In floors | | 675 | .059 | | 7.70 | 2.12 | | 9.82 | 11.70 |
| 1400 | 8" thick, in walls | | 400 | .100 | | 9.95 | 3.57 | | 13.52 | 16.35 |
| 1450 | In floors | | 575 | .070 | | 9.95 | 2.49 | | 12.44 | 14.70 |
| 1600 | 10" thick, in walls, special order | | 350 | .114 | | 13.40 | 4.08 | | 17.48 | 21 |
| 1650 | In floors, special order | | 500 | .080 | | 13.40 | 2.86 | | 16.26 | 19.10 |
| 1800 | 12" thick, in walls, special order | | 300 | .133 | | 25.50 | 4.76 | | 30.26 | 36 |
| 1850 | In floors, special order | ↓ | 450 | .089 | | 25.50 | 3.18 | | 28.68 | 33.50 |
| 2000 | For reinforcing with steel rods, add to above | | | | | 15% | 5% | | | |
| 2100 | For smooth tile instead of scored, add | | | | | 3.32 | | | 3.32 | 3.65 |
| 2200 | For L.C.L. quantities, add | | | | ↓ | 10% | 10% | | | |

### 04 21 29.20 Terra Cotta Tile

| | | Crew | Daily Output | Labor-Hours | Unit | Material | 2008 Bare Costs Labor | Equipment | Total | Total Incl O&P |
|---|---|---|---|---|---|---|---|---|---|---|
| 0010 | **TERRA COTTA TILE,** on walls, dry set, 1/2" thick | | | | | | | | | |
| 0100 | Square, hexagonal or lattice shapes, unglazed | 1 Tilf | 135 | .059 | S.F. | 6.05 | 2.19 | | 8.24 | 9.85 |
| 0300 | Glazed, plain colors | ↓ | 130 | .062 | | 8.30 | 2.28 | | 10.58 | 12.50 |
| 0400 | Intense colors | ↓ | 125 | .064 | ↓ | 9.70 | 2.37 | | 12.07 | 14.15 |

# 04 22 Concrete Unit Masonry

## 04 22 10 – Concrete Masonry Units

### 04 22 10.11 Autoclave Aerated Concrete Block

| | | Crew | Daily Output | Labor-Hours | Unit | Material | 2008 Bare Costs Labor | Equipment | Total | Total Incl O&P |
|---|---|---|---|---|---|---|---|---|---|---|
| 0010 | **AUTOCLAVE AERATED CONCRETE BLOCK,** excl. scaffolding, grout & reinforcing | | | | | | | | | |
| 0050 | Solid, 4" x 12" x 24", incl mortar | D-8 | 600 | .067 | S.F. | 1.87 | 2.38 | | 4.25 | 5.70 |
| 0060 | 6" x 12" x 24" | | 600 | .067 | | 2.52 | 2.38 | | 4.90 | 6.40 |
| 0070 | 8" x 8" x 24" | | 575 | .070 | | 3.17 | 2.49 | | 5.66 | 7.25 |
| 0080 | 10" x 12" x 24" | | 575 | .070 | | 4.13 | 2.49 | | 6.62 | 8.30 |
| 0090 | 12" x 12" x 24" | ↓ | 550 | .073 | ↓ | 4.81 | 2.60 | | 7.41 | 9.25 |

### 04 22 10.12 Chimney Block

| | | Crew | Daily Output | Labor-Hours | Unit | Material | 2008 Bare Costs Labor | Equipment | Total | Total Incl O&P |
|---|---|---|---|---|---|---|---|---|---|---|
| 0010 | **CHIMNEY BLOCK,** excludes scaffolding, grout and reinforcing | | | | | | | | | |
| 0220 | 1 piece, with 8" x 8" flue, 16" x 16" | D-1 | 28 | .571 | V.L.F. | 12.55 | 19.95 | | 32.50 | 44.50 |
| 0230 | 2 piece, 16" x 16" | | 26 | .615 | | 13.55 | 21.50 | | 35.05 | 47.50 |
| 0240 | 2 piece, with 8" x 12" flue, 16" x 20" | ↓ | 24 | .667 | ↓ | 25 | 23.50 | | 48.50 | 63 |

### 04 22 10.14 Concrete Block, Back-Up

| | | Crew | Daily Output | Labor-Hours | Unit | Material | 2008 Bare Costs Labor | Equipment | Total | Total Incl O&P |
|---|---|---|---|---|---|---|---|---|---|---|
| 0010 | **CONCRETE BLOCK, BACK-UP,** C90, 2000 psi  R042210-20 | | | | | | | | | |
| 0020 | Normal weight, 8" x 16" units, tooled joint 1 side | | | | | | | | | |
| 0050 | Not-reinforced, 2000 psi, 2" thick | D-8 | 475 | .084 | S.F. | 1.25 | 3.01 | | 4.26 | 5.95 |
| 0200 | 4" thick | | 460 | .087 | | 1.39 | 3.11 | | 4.50 | 6.25 |
| 0300 | 6" thick | | 440 | .091 | | 1.99 | 3.25 | | 5.24 | 7.15 |
| 0350 | 8" thick | | 400 | .100 | | 2.16 | 3.57 | | 5.73 | 7.80 |
| 0400 | 10" thick | ↓ | 330 | .121 | | 2.93 | 4.33 | | 7.26 | 9.85 |
| 0450 | 12" thick | D-9 | 310 | .155 | | 3.17 | 5.40 | | 8.57 | 11.70 |
| 1000 | Reinforced, alternate courses, 4" thick | D-8 | 450 | .089 | ↓ | 1.50 | 3.18 | | 4.68 | 6.50 |

# 04 22 Concrete Unit Masonry

## 04 22 10 – Concrete Masonry Units

| | 04 22 10.14 Concrete Block, Back-Up | Crew | Daily Output | Labor-Hours | Unit | Material | 2008 Bare Costs Labor | Equipment | Total | Total Incl O&P |
|---|---|---|---|---|---|---|---|---|---|---|
| 1100 | 6" thick | D-8 | 430 | .093 | S.F. | 2.10 | 3.32 | | 5.42 | 7.35 |
| 1150 | 8" thick | | 395 | .101 | | 2.27 | 3.62 | | 5.89 | 8 |
| 1200 | 10" thick | | 320 | .125 | | 3.06 | 4.47 | | 7.53 | 10.15 |
| 1250 | 12" thick | D-9 | 300 | .160 | | 3.30 | 5.60 | | 8.90 | 12.10 |

## 04 22 10.16 Concrete Block, Bond Beam

| 0010 | **CONCRETE BLOCK, BOND BEAM**, C90, 2000 psi | | | | | | | | | |
|---|---|---|---|---|---|---|---|---|---|---|
| 0020 | Not including grout or reinforcing | | | | | | | | | |
| 0125 | Regular block, 6" thick | D-8 | 584 | .068 | L.F. | 2.12 | 2.45 | | 4.57 | 6.05 |
| 0130 | 8" high, 8" thick | " | 565 | .071 | | 2.36 | 2.53 | | 4.89 | 6.45 |
| 0150 | 12" thick | D-9 | 510 | .094 | | 3.29 | 3.28 | | 6.57 | 8.60 |
| 0525 | Lightweight, 6" thick | D-8 | 592 | .068 | | 2.41 | 2.41 | | 4.82 | 6.30 |
| 0530 | 8" high, 8" thick | " | 575 | .070 | | 2.89 | 2.49 | | 5.38 | 6.95 |
| 0550 | 12" thick | D-9 | 520 | .092 | | 3.95 | 3.22 | | 7.17 | 9.25 |
| 2000 | Including grout and 2 #5 bars | | | | | | | | | |
| 2100 | Regular block, 8" high, 8" thick | D-8 | 300 | .133 | L.F. | 4.38 | 4.76 | | 9.14 | 12.05 |
| 2150 | 12" thick | D-9 | 250 | .192 | | 5.85 | 6.70 | | 12.55 | 16.65 |
| 2500 | Lightweight, 8" high, 8" thick | D-8 | 305 | .131 | | 4.92 | 4.69 | | 9.61 | 12.55 |
| 2550 | 12" thick | D-9 | 255 | .188 | | 6.55 | 6.55 | | 13.10 | 17.20 |

## 04 22 10.18 Concrete Block, Column

| 0010 | **CONCRETE BLOCK, COLUMN** or pilaster | | | | | | | | | |
|---|---|---|---|---|---|---|---|---|---|---|
| 0050 | Including vertical reinforcing (4-#4 bars) and grout | | | | | | | | | |
| 0160 | 1 piece unit, 16" x 16" | D-1 | 26 | .615 | V.L.F. | 18.25 | 21.50 | | 39.75 | 52.50 |
| 0170 | 2 piece units, 16" x 20" | | 24 | .667 | | 24 | 23.50 | | 47.50 | 62 |
| 0180 | 20" x 20" | | 22 | .727 | | 35 | 25.50 | | 60.50 | 77 |
| 0190 | 22" x 24" | | 18 | .889 | | 49.50 | 31 | | 80.50 | 102 |
| 0200 | 20" x 32" | | 14 | 1.143 | | 54 | 40 | | 94 | 120 |

## 04 22 10.19 Concrete Block, Insulation Inserts

| 0010 | **CONCRETE BLOCK, INSULATION INSERTS** | | | | | | | | | |
|---|---|---|---|---|---|---|---|---|---|---|
| 0100 | Styrofoam, plant installed, add to block prices | | | | | | | | | |
| 0200 | 8" x 16" units, 6" thick | | | | S.F. | 1.81 | | | 1.81 | 1.99 |
| 0250 | 8" thick | | | | | 1.81 | | | 1.81 | 1.99 |
| 0300 | 10" thick | | | | | 2.13 | | | 2.13 | 2.34 |
| 0350 | 12" thick | | | | | 2.24 | | | 2.24 | 2.46 |
| 0500 | 8" x 8" units, 8" thick | | | | | 1.49 | | | 1.49 | 1.64 |
| 0550 | 12" thick | | | | | 1.81 | | | 1.81 | 1.99 |

## 04 22 10.23 Concrete Block, Decorative

| 0010 | **CONCRETE BLOCK, DECORATIVE**, C90, 2000 psi | | | | | | | | | |
|---|---|---|---|---|---|---|---|---|---|---|
| 0020 | Embossed, simulated brick face | | | | | | | | | |
| 0100 | 8" x 16" units, 4" thick | D-8 | 400 | .100 | S.F. | 3.31 | 3.57 | | 6.88 | 9.10 |
| 0200 | 8" thick | | 340 | .118 | | 4.56 | 4.20 | | 8.76 | 11.40 |
| 0250 | 12" thick | | 300 | .133 | | 6 | 4.76 | | 10.76 | 13.85 |
| 0400 | Embossed both sides | | | | | | | | | |
| 0500 | 8" thick | D-8 | 300 | .133 | S.F. | 5.10 | 4.76 | | 9.86 | 12.85 |
| 0550 | 12" thick | " | 275 | .145 | " | 6.45 | 5.20 | | 11.65 | 15 |
| 1000 | Fluted high strength | | | | | | | | | |
| 1100 | 8" x 16" x 4" thick, flutes 1 side, | D-8 | 345 | .116 | S.F. | 3.93 | 4.14 | | 8.07 | 10.60 |
| 1150 | Flutes 2 sides | | 335 | .119 | | 4.77 | 4.27 | | 9.04 | 11.75 |
| 1200 | 8" thick | | 300 | .133 | | 6.20 | 4.76 | | 10.96 | 14.05 |
| 1250 | For special colors, add | | | | | .38 | | | .38 | .42 |
| 1400 | Deep grooved, smooth face | | | | | | | | | |
| 1450 | 8" x 16" x 4" thick | D-8 | 345 | .116 | S.F. | 2.56 | 4.14 | | 6.70 | 9.10 |
| 1500 | 8" thick | " | 300 | .133 | " | 4.41 | 4.76 | | 9.17 | 12.10 |

# 04 22 Concrete Unit Masonry

## 04 22 10 – Concrete Masonry Units

| 04 22 10.23 Concrete Block, Decorative | Crew | Daily Output | Labor-Hours | Unit | Material | 2008 Bare Costs Labor | Equipment | Total | Total Incl O&P |
|---|---|---|---|---|---|---|---|---|---|
| 2000 | Formblock, incl. inserts & reinforcing | | | | | | | | | |
| 2100 | 8" x 16" x 8" thick | D-8 | 345 | .116 | S.F. | 4.48 | 4.14 | | 8.62 | 11.25 |
| 2150 | 12" thick | " | 310 | .129 | " | 5.60 | 4.61 | | 10.21 | 13.15 |
| 2500 | Ground face | | | | | | | | | |
| 2600 | 8" x 16" x 4" thick | D-8 | 345 | .116 | S.F. | 4.09 | 4.14 | | 8.23 | 10.80 |
| 2650 | 6" thick | ↓ | 325 | .123 | ↓ | 5.35 | 4.40 | | 9.75 | 12.55 |
| 2700 | 8" thick | ↓ | 300 | .133 | | 6.20 | 4.76 | | 10.96 | 14.05 |
| 2750 | 12" thick | D-9 | 265 | .181 | ↓ | 7.45 | 6.30 | | 13.75 | 17.80 |
| 2900 | For special colors, add, minimum | | | | | 15% | | | | |
| 2950 | For special colors, add, maximum | | | | | 45% | | | | |
| 4000 | Slump block | | | | | | | | | |
| 4100 | 4" face height x 16" x 4" thick | D-1 | 165 | .097 | S.F. | 4 | 3.38 | | 7.38 | 9.55 |
| 4150 | 6" thick | ↓ | 160 | .100 | | 5.55 | 3.49 | | 9.04 | 11.40 |
| 4200 | 8" thick | | 155 | .103 | | 6.15 | 3.60 | | 9.75 | 12.25 |
| 4250 | 10" thick | | 140 | .114 | | 11.25 | 3.99 | | 15.24 | 18.40 |
| 4300 | 12" thick | | 130 | .123 | | 11.70 | 4.29 | | 15.99 | 19.40 |
| 4400 | 6" face height x 16" x 6" thick | | 155 | .103 | | 4.86 | 3.60 | | 8.46 | 10.85 |
| 4450 | 8" thick | | 150 | .107 | | 6.70 | 3.72 | | 10.42 | 13.05 |
| 4500 | 10" thick | | 130 | .123 | | 9.55 | 4.29 | | 13.84 | 17.05 |
| 4550 | 12" thick | ↓ | 120 | .133 | ↓ | 10.70 | 4.65 | | 15.35 | 18.80 |
| 5000 | Split rib profile units, 1" deep ribs, 8 ribs | | | | | | | | | |
| 5100 | 8" x 16" x 4" thick | D-8 | 345 | .116 | S.F. | 2.91 | 4.14 | | 7.05 | 9.50 |
| 5150 | 6" thick | ↓ | 325 | .123 | | 3.37 | 4.40 | | 7.77 | 10.40 |
| 5200 | 8" thick | ↓ | 300 | .133 | | 3.87 | 4.76 | | 8.63 | 11.50 |
| 5250 | 12" thick | D-9 | 275 | .175 | | 4.63 | 6.10 | | 10.73 | 14.35 |
| 5400 | For special deeper colors, 4" thick, add | | | | | 1.12 | | | 1.12 | 1.23 |
| 5450 | 12" thick, add | | | | | .96 | | | .96 | 1.06 |
| 5600 | For white, 4" thick, add | | | | | 1.12 | | | 1.12 | 1.23 |
| 5650 | 6" thick, add | | | | | 1.12 | | | 1.12 | 1.23 |
| 5700 | 8" thick, add | | | | | 1.04 | | | 1.04 | 1.14 |
| 5750 | 12" thick, add | | | | ↓ | .96 | | | .96 | 1.06 |
| 6000 | Split face | | | | | | | | | |
| 6100 | 8" x 16" x 4" thick | D-8 | 350 | .114 | S.F. | 2.76 | 4.08 | | 6.84 | 9.25 |
| 6150 | 6" thick | ↓ | 325 | .123 | | 3.20 | 4.40 | | 7.60 | 10.20 |
| 6200 | 8" thick | ↓ | 300 | .133 | | 3.74 | 4.76 | | 8.50 | 11.35 |
| 6250 | 12" thick | D-9 | 270 | .178 | | 4.47 | 6.20 | | 10.67 | 14.35 |
| 6300 | For scored, add | | | | | .32 | | | .32 | .35 |
| 6400 | For special deeper colors, 4" thick, add | | | | | .64 | | | .64 | .71 |
| 6450 | 6" thick, add | | | | | .64 | | | .64 | .71 |
| 6500 | 8" thick, add | | | | | .58 | | | .58 | .63 |
| 6550 | 12" thick, add | | | | | .49 | | | .49 | .53 |
| 6650 | For white, 4" thick, add | | | | | 1.12 | | | 1.12 | 1.23 |
| 6700 | 6" thick, add | | | | | 1.12 | | | 1.12 | 1.23 |
| 6750 | 8" thick, add | | | | | 1.04 | | | 1.04 | 1.14 |
| 6800 | 12" thick, add | | | | ↓ | .96 | | | .96 | 1.06 |
| 7000 | Scored ground face, 2 to 5 scores | | | | | | | | | |
| 7100 | 8" x 16" x 4" thick | D-8 | 340 | .118 | S.F. | 4.88 | 4.20 | | 9.08 | 11.75 |
| 7150 | 6" thick | ↓ | 310 | .129 | | 5.60 | 4.61 | | 10.21 | 13.15 |
| 7200 | 8" thick | ↓ | 290 | .138 | | 6.55 | 4.93 | | 11.48 | 14.70 |
| 7250 | 12" thick | D-9 | 265 | .181 | ↓ | 8.15 | 6.30 | | 14.45 | 18.55 |
| 8000 | Hexagonal face profile units, 8" x 16" units | | | | | | | | | |
| 8100 | 4" thick, hollow | D-8 | 340 | .118 | S.F. | 3.07 | 4.20 | | 7.27 | 9.80 |
| 8200 | Solid | ↓ | 340 | .118 | ↓ | 3.86 | 4.20 | | 8.06 | 10.65 |

### 04 22 10.23 Concrete Block, Decorative

| | | Crew | Daily Output | Labor-Hours | Unit | Material | 2008 Bare Costs Labor | Equipment | Total | Total Incl O&P |
|---|---|---|---|---|---|---|---|---|---|---|
| 8300 | 6" thick, hollow | D-8 | 310 | .129 | S.F. | 3.28 | 4.61 | | 7.89 | 10.60 |
| 8350 | 8" thick, hollow | ↓ | 290 | .138 | ↓ | 4.46 | 4.93 | | 9.39 | 12.40 |
| 8500 | For stacked bond, add | | | | | | 26% | | | |
| 8550 | For high rise construction, add per story | D-8 | 67.80 | .590 | M.S.F. | | 21 | | 21 | 32 |
| 8600 | For scored block, add | | | | | 10% | | | | |
| 8650 | For honed or ground face, per face, add | | | | Ea. | .36 | | | .36 | .40 |
| 8700 | For honed or ground end, per end, add | | | | " | 2.81 | | | 2.81 | 3.10 |
| 8750 | For bullnose block, add | | | | | 10% | | | | |
| 8800 | For special color, add | | | | | 13% | | | | |

### 04 22 10.24 Concrete Block, Exterior

| | | Crew | Daily Output | Labor-Hours | Unit | Material | 2008 Bare Costs Labor | Equipment | Total | Total Incl O&P |
|---|---|---|---|---|---|---|---|---|---|---|
| 0010 | **CONCRETE BLOCK, EXTERIOR**, C90, 2000 psi | | | | | | | | | |
| 0020 | Reinforced alt courses, tooled joints 2 sides | | | | | | | | | |
| 0100 | Normal weight, 8" x 16" x 6" thick | D-8 | 395 | .101 | S.F. | 2.35 | 3.62 | | 5.97 | 8.10 |
| 0200 | 8" thick | | 360 | .111 | | 3.45 | 3.97 | | 7.42 | 9.85 |
| 0250 | 10" thick | ↓ | 290 | .138 | | 4.07 | 4.93 | | 9 | 12 |
| 0300 | 12" thick | D-9 | 250 | .192 | | 4.26 | 6.70 | | 10.96 | 14.90 |
| 0500 | Lightweight, 8" x 16" x 6" thick | D-8 | 450 | .089 | | 2.65 | 3.18 | | 5.83 | 7.75 |
| 0600 | 8" thick | ↓ | 430 | .093 | | 3.53 | 3.32 | | 6.85 | 8.95 |
| 0650 | 10" thick | ↓ | 395 | .101 | | 4.10 | 3.62 | | 7.72 | 10 |
| 0700 | 12" thick | D-9 | 350 | .137 | ↓ | 5.95 | 4.78 | | 10.73 | 13.85 |

### 04 22 10.26 Concrete Block Foundation Wall

| | | Crew | Daily Output | Labor-Hours | Unit | Material | 2008 Bare Costs Labor | Equipment | Total | Total Incl O&P |
|---|---|---|---|---|---|---|---|---|---|---|
| 0010 | **CONCRETE BLOCK FOUNDATION WALL**, C90 / C145 | | | | | | | | | |
| 0050 | Normal-weight, cut joints, horiz joint reinf, no vert reinf | | | | | | | | | |
| 0200 | Hollow, 8" x 16" x 6" thick | D-8 | 455 | .088 | S.F. | 2.42 | 3.14 | | 5.56 | 7.45 |
| 0250 | 8" thick | | 425 | .094 | | 2.61 | 3.36 | | 5.97 | 7.95 |
| 0300 | 10" thick | ↓ | 350 | .114 | | 3.40 | 4.08 | | 7.48 | 9.95 |
| 0350 | 12" thick | D-9 | 300 | .160 | | 3.65 | 5.60 | | 9.25 | 12.50 |
| 0500 | Solid, 8" x 16" block, 6" thick | D-8 | 440 | .091 | | 2.42 | 3.25 | | 5.67 | 7.60 |
| 0550 | 8" thick | " | 415 | .096 | | 3.59 | 3.44 | | 7.03 | 9.20 |
| 0600 | 12" thick | D-9 | 350 | .137 | ↓ | 5.35 | 4.78 | | 10.13 | 13.20 |

### 04 22 10.28 Concrete Block, High Strength

| | | Crew | Daily Output | Labor-Hours | Unit | Material | 2008 Bare Costs Labor | Equipment | Total | Total Incl O&P |
|---|---|---|---|---|---|---|---|---|---|---|
| 0010 | **CONCRETE BLOCK, HIGH STRENGTH** | | | | | | | | | |
| 0050 | Hollow, reinforced alternate courses, 8" x 16" units | | | | | | | | | |
| 0200 | 3500 psi, 4" thick | D-8 | 440 | .091 | S.F. | 1.85 | 3.25 | | 5.10 | 6.95 |
| 0250 | 6" thick | | 395 | .101 | | 2.27 | 3.62 | | 5.89 | 8 |
| 0300 | 8" thick | ↓ | 360 | .111 | | 3.37 | 3.97 | | 7.34 | 9.75 |
| 0350 | 12" thick | D-9 | 250 | .192 | | 4.16 | 6.70 | | 10.86 | 14.75 |
| 0500 | 5000 psi, 4" thick | D-8 | 440 | .091 | | 2.25 | 3.25 | | 5.50 | 7.40 |
| 0550 | 6" thick | | 395 | .101 | | 2.82 | 3.62 | | 6.44 | 8.60 |
| 0600 | 8" thick | ↓ | 360 | .111 | | 3.82 | 3.97 | | 7.79 | 10.25 |
| 0650 | 12" thick | D-9 | 300 | .160 | ↓ | 5.65 | 5.60 | | 11.25 | 14.75 |
| 1000 | For 75% solid block, add | | | | | 30% | | | | |
| 1050 | For 100% solid block, add | | | | | 50% | | | | |

### 04 22 10.30 Concrete Block, Interlocking

| | | Crew | Daily Output | Labor-Hours | Unit | Material | 2008 Bare Costs Labor | Equipment | Total | Total Incl O&P |
|---|---|---|---|---|---|---|---|---|---|---|
| 0010 | **CONCRETE BLOCK, INTERLOCKING** | | | | | | | | | |
| 0100 | Not including grout or reinforcing | | | | | | | | | |
| 0200 | 8" x 16" units, 2,000 psi, 8" thick | D-1 | 245 | .065 | S.F. | 2.66 | 2.28 | | 4.94 | 6.40 |
| 0300 | 12" thick | | 220 | .073 | | 3.94 | 2.54 | | 6.48 | 8.20 |
| 0350 | 16" thick | ↓ | 185 | .086 | | 5.95 | 3.02 | | 8.97 | 11.15 |
| 0400 | Including grout & reinforcing, 8" thick | D-4 | 245 | .131 | | 7.40 | 4.51 | .52 | 12.43 | 15.55 |
| 0450 | 12" thick | | 220 | .145 | | 8.90 | 5 | .57 | 14.47 | 18.05 |
| 0500 | 16" thick | ↓ | 185 | .173 | ↓ | 11.10 | 5.95 | .68 | 17.73 | 22 |

| 04 22 10.32 Concrete Block, Lintels | Crew | Daily Output | Labor-Hours | Unit | Material | 2008 Bare Costs Labor | Equipment | Total | Total Incl O&P |
|---|---|---|---|---|---|---|---|---|---|
| 0010 **CONCRETE BLOCK, LINTELS,** C90, normal weight | | | | | | | | | |
| 0100 Including grout and horizontal reinforcing | | | | | | | | | |
| 0200 8" x 8" x 8", 1 #4 bar | D-4 | 300 | .107 | L.F. | 4.56 | 3.68 | .42 | 8.66 | 11.05 |
| 0250 2 #4 bars | | 295 | .108 | | 4.77 | 3.75 | .43 | 8.95 | 11.40 |
| 0400 8" x 16" x 8", 1 #4 bar | | 275 | .116 | | 3.23 | 4.02 | .46 | 7.71 | 10.15 |
| 0450 2 #4 bars | | 270 | .119 | | 3.44 | 4.09 | .47 | 8 | 10.50 |
| 1000 12" x 8" x 8", 1 #4 bar | | 275 | .116 | | 6.40 | 4.02 | .46 | 10.88 | 13.65 |
| 1100 2 #4 bars | | 270 | .119 | | 6.60 | 4.09 | .47 | 11.16 | 13.95 |
| 1150 2 #5 bars | | 270 | .119 | | 6.85 | 4.09 | .47 | 11.41 | 14.20 |
| 1200 2 #6 bars | | 265 | .121 | | 7.10 | 4.17 | .48 | 11.75 | 14.75 |
| 1500 12" x 16" x 8", 1 #4 bar | | 250 | .128 | | 10.15 | 4.42 | .51 | 15.08 | 18.40 |
| 1600 2 #3 bars | | 245 | .131 | | 10.20 | 4.51 | .52 | 15.23 | 18.60 |
| 1650 2 #4 bars | | 245 | .131 | | 10.35 | 4.51 | .52 | 15.38 | 18.80 |
| 1700 2 #5 bars | ▼ | 240 | .133 | ▼ | 10.60 | 4.60 | .53 | 15.73 | 19.25 |

| 04 22 10.34 Concrete Block, Partitions | Crew | Daily Output | Labor-Hours | Unit | Material | 2008 Bare Costs Labor | Equipment | Total | Total Incl O&P |
|---|---|---|---|---|---|---|---|---|---|
| 0010 **CONCRETE BLOCK, PARTITIONS,** excludes scaffolding    R042210-20 | | | | | | | | | |
| 0100 Acoustical slotted block | | | | | | | | | |
| 0200 4" thick, type A-1 | D-8 | 315 | .127 | S.F. | 3.23 | 4.54 | | 7.77 | 10.45 |
| 0210 8" thick | | 275 | .145 | | 4.75 | 5.20 | | 9.95 | 13.15 |
| 0250 8" thick, type Q | | 275 | .145 | | 6.50 | 5.20 | | 11.70 | 15.05 |
| 0260 4" thick, type RSC | | 315 | .127 | | 4.75 | 4.54 | | 9.29 | 12.10 |
| 0270 6" thick | | 295 | .136 | | 4.75 | 4.84 | | 9.59 | 12.55 |
| 0280 8" thick | | 275 | .145 | | 4.75 | 5.20 | | 9.95 | 13.10 |
| 0290 12" thick | | 250 | .160 | | 4.75 | 5.70 | | 10.45 | 13.90 |
| 0300 8" thick, type RSR | | 275 | .145 | | 4.75 | 5.20 | | 9.95 | 13.10 |
| 0400 8" thick, type RSC/RF | | 275 | .145 | | 5.85 | 5.20 | | 11.05 | 14.35 |
| 0410 10" thick | | 260 | .154 | | 6.35 | 5.50 | | 11.85 | 15.35 |
| 0420 12" thick | | 250 | .160 | | 7 | 5.70 | | 12.70 | 16.40 |
| 0430 12" thick, type RSC/RF-4 | | 250 | .160 | | 8.15 | 5.70 | | 13.85 | 17.70 |
| 0500 NRC .60 type R, 8" thick | | 265 | .151 | | 5.65 | 5.40 | | 11.05 | 14.40 |
| 0600 NRC .65 type RR, 8" thick | | 265 | .151 | | 6.35 | 5.40 | | 11.75 | 15.20 |
| 0700 NRC .65 type 4R-RF, 8" thick | | 265 | .151 | | 7.15 | 5.40 | | 12.55 | 16.05 |
| 0710 NRC .70 type R, 12" thick | ▼ | 245 | .163 | ▼ | 8 | 5.85 | | 13.85 | 17.65 |
| 1000 Lightweight block, tooled joints, 2 sides, hollow | | | | | | | | | |
| 1100 Not reinforced, 8" x 16" x 4" thick | D-8 | 440 | .091 | S.F. | 1.59 | 3.25 | | 4.84 | 6.70 |
| 1150 6" thick | | 410 | .098 | | 2.16 | 3.49 | | 5.65 | 7.70 |
| 1200 8" thick | | 385 | .104 | | 2.67 | 3.71 | | 6.38 | 8.60 |
| 1250 10" thick | ▼ | 370 | .108 | | 3.43 | 3.86 | | 7.29 | 9.65 |
| 1300 12" thick | D-9 | 350 | .137 | | 3.95 | 4.78 | | 8.73 | 11.65 |
| 2000 Not reinforced, 8" x 24" x 4" thick, hollow | | 460 | .104 | | 1.16 | 3.64 | | 4.80 | 6.85 |
| 2100 6" thick | | 440 | .109 | | 1.56 | 3.81 | | 5.37 | 7.50 |
| 2150 8" thick | | 415 | .116 | | 1.97 | 4.03 | | 6 | 8.30 |
| 2200 10" thick | | 385 | .125 | | 2.51 | 4.35 | | 6.86 | 9.35 |
| 2250 12" thick | ▼ | 365 | .132 | | 2.90 | 4.59 | | 7.49 | 10.20 |
| 2800 Solid, not reinforced, 8" x 16" x 2" thick | D-8 | 440 | .091 | | 1.41 | 3.25 | | 4.66 | 6.50 |
| 2900 4" thick | | 420 | .095 | | 2.18 | 3.40 | | 5.58 | 7.60 |
| 2950 6" thick | | 390 | .103 | | 2.57 | 3.66 | | 6.23 | 8.40 |
| 3000 8" thick | | 365 | .110 | | 3.44 | 3.92 | | 7.36 | 9.75 |
| 3050 10" thick | ▼ | 350 | .114 | | 4.01 | 4.08 | | 8.09 | 10.60 |
| 3100 12" thick | D-9 | 330 | .145 | ▼ | 5.85 | 5.05 | | 10.90 | 14.15 |
| 4000 Regular block, tooled joints, 2 sides, hollow | | | | | | | | | |
| 4100 Not reinforced, 8" x 16" x 4" thick | D-8 | 430 | .093 | S.F. | 1.31 | 3.32 | | 4.63 | 6.50 |

## 04 22 10.34 Concrete Block, Partitions

| | | Crew | Daily Output | Labor-Hours | Unit | Material | 2008 Bare Costs Labor | Equipment | Total | Total Incl O&P |
|---|---|---|---|---|---|---|---|---|---|---|
| 4150 | 6" thick | D-8 | 400 | .100 | S.F. | 1.90 | 3.57 | | 5.47 | 7.55 |
| 4200 | 8" thick  *CN* | | 375 | .107 | | 2.07 | 3.81 | | 5.88 | 8.10 |
| 4250 | 10" thick | | 360 | .111 | | 2.85 | 3.97 | | 6.82 | 9.20 |
| 4300 | 12" thick | D-9 | 340 | .141 | | 3.08 | 4.92 | | 8 | 10.90 |
| 4500 | Reinforced alternate courses, 8" x 16" x 4" thick | D-8 | 425 | .094 | | 1.41 | 3.36 | | 4.77 | 6.65 |
| 4550 | 6" thick | | 395 | .101 | | 2.01 | 3.62 | | 5.63 | 7.70 |
| 4600 | 8" thick | | 370 | .108 | | 2.19 | 3.86 | | 6.05 | 8.30 |
| 4650 | 10" thick | | 355 | .113 | | 3.08 | 4.03 | | 7.11 | 9.50 |
| 4700 | 12" thick | D-9 | 335 | .143 | | 3.21 | 5 | | 8.21 | 11.15 |
| 4900 | Solid, not reinforced, 2" thick | D-8 | 435 | .092 | | 1.20 | 3.29 | | 4.49 | 6.30 |
| 5000 | 3" thick | | 430 | .093 | | 1.20 | 3.32 | | 4.52 | 6.35 |
| 5050 | 4" thick | | 415 | .096 | | 1.78 | 3.44 | | 5.22 | 7.20 |
| 5100 | 6" thick | | 385 | .104 | | 1.90 | 3.71 | | 5.61 | 7.75 |
| 5150 | 8" thick | | 360 | .111 | | 3.06 | 3.97 | | 7.03 | 9.40 |
| 5200 | 12" thick | D-9 | 325 | .148 | | 4.80 | 5.15 | | 9.95 | 13.15 |
| 5500 | Solid, reinforced alternate courses, 4" thick | D-8 | 420 | .095 | | 1.85 | 3.40 | | 5.25 | 7.25 |
| 5550 | 6" thick | | 380 | .105 | | 1.98 | 3.76 | | 5.74 | 7.90 |
| 5600 | 8" thick | | 355 | .113 | | 3.14 | 4.03 | | 7.17 | 9.55 |
| 5650 | 12" thick | D-9 | 320 | .150 | | 4.19 | 5.25 | | 9.44 | 12.55 |

## 04 22 10.38 Concrete Brick

| | | Crew | Daily Output | Labor-Hours | Unit | Material | 2008 Bare Costs Labor | Equipment | Total | Total Incl O&P |
|---|---|---|---|---|---|---|---|---|---|---|
| 0010 | **CONCRETE BRICK**, C55, grade N, type 1 | | | | | | | | | |
| 0100 | Regular, 4 x 2-1/4 x 8 | D-8 | 660 | .061 | Ea. | .38 | 2.17 | | 2.55 | 3.71 |
| 0125 | Rusticated, 4 x 2-1/4 x 8 | | 660 | .061 | | .43 | 2.17 | | 2.60 | 3.76 |
| 0150 | Frog, 4 x 2-1/4 x 8 | | 660 | .061 | | .41 | 2.17 | | 2.58 | 3.74 |
| 0200 | Double, 4 x 4-7/8 x 8 | | 535 | .075 | | .67 | 2.67 | | 3.34 | 4.79 |

## 04 22 10.42 Concrete Block, Screen Block

| | | Crew | Daily Output | Labor-Hours | Unit | Material | 2008 Bare Costs Labor | Equipment | Total | Total Incl O&P |
|---|---|---|---|---|---|---|---|---|---|---|
| 0010 | **CONCRETE BLOCK, SCREEN BLOCK** | | | | | | | | | |
| 0200 | 8" x 16", 4" thick | D-8 | 330 | .121 | S.F. | 1.95 | 4.33 | | 6.28 | 8.75 |
| 0300 | 8" thick | | 270 | .148 | | 2.96 | 5.30 | | 8.26 | 11.30 |
| 0350 | 12" x 12", 4" thick | | 290 | .138 | | 2.20 | 4.93 | | 7.13 | 9.90 |
| 0500 | 8" thick | | 250 | .160 | | 3.02 | 5.70 | | 8.72 | 12.05 |

## 04 22 10.44 Glazed Concrete Block

| | | Crew | Daily Output | Labor-Hours | Unit | Material | 2008 Bare Costs Labor | Equipment | Total | Total Incl O&P |
|---|---|---|---|---|---|---|---|---|---|---|
| 0010 | **GLAZED CONCRETE BLOCK** C744 | | | | | | | | | |
| 0100 | Single face, 8" x 16" units, 2" thick | D-8 | 360 | .111 | S.F. | 7.85 | 3.97 | | 11.82 | 14.70 |
| 0200 | 4" thick | | 345 | .116 | | 8 | 4.14 | | 12.14 | 15.05 |
| 0250 | 6" thick | | 330 | .121 | | 8.55 | 4.33 | | 12.88 | 16 |
| 0300 | 8" thick | | 310 | .129 | | 9.20 | 4.61 | | 13.81 | 17.10 |
| 0350 | 10" thick | | 295 | .136 | | 10.30 | 4.84 | | 15.14 | 18.65 |
| 0400 | 12" thick | D-9 | 280 | .171 | | 10.80 | 6 | | 16.80 | 21 |
| 0700 | Double face, 8" x 16" units, 4" thick | D-8 | 340 | .118 | | 12.15 | 4.20 | | 16.35 | 19.80 |
| 0750 | 6" thick | | 320 | .125 | | 13.70 | 4.47 | | 18.17 | 22 |
| 0800 | 8" thick | | 300 | .133 | | 14.30 | 4.76 | | 19.06 | 23 |
| 1000 | Jambs, bullnose or square, single face, 8" x 16", 2" thick | | 315 | .127 | Ea. | 14.60 | 4.54 | | 19.14 | 23 |
| 1050 | 4" thick | | 285 | .140 | " | 15.60 | 5 | | 20.60 | 25 |
| 1200 | Caps, bullnose or square, 8" x 16", 2" thick | | 420 | .095 | L.F. | 12.25 | 3.40 | | 15.65 | 18.65 |
| 1250 | 4" thick | | 380 | .105 | | 15.95 | 3.76 | | 19.71 | 23.50 |
| 1500 | Cove base, 8" x 16", 2" thick | | 315 | .127 | | 7.90 | 4.54 | | 12.44 | 15.60 |
| 1550 | 4" thick | | 285 | .140 | | 7.15 | 5 | | 12.15 | 15.50 |
| 1600 | 6" thick | | 265 | .151 | | 7.70 | 5.40 | | 13.10 | 16.65 |
| 1650 | 8" thick | | 245 | .163 | | 8.10 | 5.85 | | 13.95 | 17.75 |

# 04 23 Glass Unit Masonry

## 04 23 13 – Vertical Glass Unit Masonry

| 04 23 13.10 Glass Block | | Crew | Daily Output | Labor-Hours | Unit | Material | 2008 Bare Costs Labor | Equipment | Total | Total Incl O&P |
|---|---|---|---|---|---|---|---|---|---|---|
| 0010 | **GLASS BLOCK** | | | | | | | | | |
| 0100 | Plain, 4" thick, under 1,000 S.F., 6" x 6" | D-8 | 115 | .348 | S.F. | 18.90 | 12.45 | | 31.35 | 40 |
| 0150 | 8" x 8" | | 160 | .250 | | 13.85 | 8.95 | | 22.80 | 29 |
| 0160 | end block | | 160 | .250 | | 36.50 | 8.95 | | 45.45 | 53.50 |
| 0170 | 90 deg corner | | 160 | .250 | | 35.50 | 8.95 | | 44.45 | 52.50 |
| 0180 | 45 deg corner | | 160 | .250 | | 15.75 | 8.95 | | 24.70 | 31 |
| 0200 | 12" x 12" | | 175 | .229 | | 15.25 | 8.15 | | 23.40 | 29 |
| 0210 | 4" x 8" | | 160 | .250 | | 8.55 | 8.95 | | 17.50 | 23 |
| 0220 | 6" x 8" | | 160 | .250 | | 10.25 | 8.95 | | 19.20 | 25 |
| 0300 | 1,000 to 5,000 S.F., 6" x 6" | | 135 | .296 | | 18.50 | 10.60 | | 29.10 | 36.50 |
| 0350 | 8" x 8" | | 190 | .211 | | 13.55 | 7.50 | | 21.05 | 26.50 |
| 0400 | 12" x 12" | | 215 | .186 | | 14.95 | 6.65 | | 21.60 | 26.50 |
| 0410 | 4" x 8" | | 215 | .186 | | 4.17 | 6.65 | | 10.82 | 14.70 |
| 0420 | 6" x 8" | | 215 | .186 | | 4.55 | 6.65 | | 11.20 | 15.10 |
| 0500 | Over 5,000 S.F., 6" x 6" | | 145 | .276 | | 17.95 | 9.85 | | 27.80 | 35 |
| 0550 | 8" x 8" | | 215 | .186 | | 13.15 | 6.65 | | 19.80 | 24.50 |
| 0600 | 12" x 12" | | 240 | .167 | | 14.50 | 5.95 | | 20.45 | 25 |
| 0610 | 4" x 8" | | 240 | .167 | | 4.09 | 5.95 | | 10.04 | 13.55 |
| 0620 | 6" x 8" | ↓ | 240 | .167 | ↓ | 4.51 | 5.95 | | 10.46 | 14 |
| 0700 | For solar reflective blocks, add | | | | | 100% | | | | |
| 1000 | Thinline, plain, 3-1/8" thick, under 1,000 S.F., 6" x 6" | D-8 | 115 | .348 | S.F. | 15.15 | 12.45 | | 27.60 | 35.50 |
| 1050 | 8" x 8" | | 160 | .250 | | 9.45 | 8.95 | | 18.40 | 24 |
| 1200 | Over 5,000 S.F., 6" x 6" | | 145 | .276 | | 13.95 | 9.85 | | 23.80 | 30.50 |
| 1250 | 8" x 8" | | 215 | .186 | | 7.70 | 6.65 | | 14.35 | 18.60 |
| 1400 | For cleaning block after installation (both sides), add | ↓ | 1000 | .040 | ↓ | .11 | 1.43 | | 1.54 | 2.29 |
| 4000 | Accessories | | | | | | | | | |
| 4100 | Anchors, 20 ga. galv., 1-3/4" wide x 24" long | | | | Ea. | 3.12 | | | 3.12 | 3.43 |
| 4200 | Emulsion asphalt | | | | Gal. | 10.85 | | | 10.85 | 11.90 |
| 4300 | Expansion joint, fiberglass | | | | L.F. | .69 | | | .69 | .76 |
| 4400 | Steel mesh, double galvanized | | | | " | .76 | | | .76 | .84 |

# 04 24 Adobe Unit Masonry

## 04 24 16 – Manufactured Adobe Unit Masonry

| 04 24 16.06 Adobe Brick | | Crew | Daily Output | Labor-Hours | Unit | Material | 2008 Bare Costs Labor | Equipment | Total | Total Incl O&P |
|---|---|---|---|---|---|---|---|---|---|---|
| 0010 | **ADOBE BRICK**, Semi-stabilized, with cement mortar | | | | | | | | | |
| 0060 | Brick, 10" x 4" x 14", 2.6/S.F. | D-8 | 560 | .071 | S.F. | 2.90 | 2.55 | | 5.45 | 7.05 |
| 0080 | 12" x 4" x 16", 2.3/S.F. | | 580 | .069 | | 4.45 | 2.46 | | 6.91 | 8.65 |
| 0100 | 10" x 4" x 16", 2.3/S.F. | | 590 | .068 | | 4.23 | 2.42 | | 6.65 | 8.35 |
| 0120 | 8" x 4" x 16", 2.3/S.F. | | 560 | .071 | | 3.07 | 2.55 | | 5.62 | 7.25 |
| 0140 | 4" x 4" x 16", 2.3/S.F. | | 540 | .074 | | 2.53 | 2.65 | | 5.18 | 6.80 |
| 0160 | 6" x 4" x 16", 2.3/S.F. | | 540 | .074 | | 2.55 | 2.65 | | 5.20 | 6.85 |
| 0180 | 4" x 4" x 12", 3.0/S.F. | | 520 | .077 | | 2.28 | 2.75 | | 5.03 | 6.70 |
| 0200 | 8" x 4" x 12", 3.0/S.F. | ↓ | 520 | .077 | ↓ | 2.51 | 2.75 | | 5.26 | 6.95 |

# 04 25 Unit Masonry Panels

## 04 25 20 – Pre-Fabricated Masonry Panels

| 04 25 20.10 Brick and Epoxy Mortar Panels | Crew | Daily Output | Labor-Hours | Unit | Material | 2008 Bare Costs Labor | Equipment | Total | Total Incl O&P |
|---|---|---|---|---|---|---|---|---|---|
| 0010 **BRICK AND EPOXY MORTAR PANELS** | | | | | | | | | |
| 0020 Prefabricated brick & epoxy mortar, 4" thick, minimum | C-11 | 775 | .093 | S.F. | 9.55 | 3.91 | 2.43 | 15.89 | 20 |
| 0100 Maximum | " | 500 | .144 | | 12.55 | 6.05 | 3.77 | 22.37 | 28.50 |
| 0200 For 2" concrete back-up, add | | | | | 50% | | | | |
| 0300 For 1" urethane & 3" concrete back-up, add | | | | ↓ | 70% | | | | |

# 04 27 Multiple-Wythe Unit Masonry

## 04 27 10 – Multiple-Wythe Masonry

### 04 27 10.20 Cavity Walls

| | | Crew | Daily Output | Labor-Hours | Unit | Material | Labor | Equipment | Total | Total Incl O&P |
|---|---|---|---|---|---|---|---|---|---|---|
| 0010 | **CAVITY WALLS**, brick and CMU, includes joint reinforcing and ties | | | | | | | | | |
| 0200 | 4" face brick, 4" block | D-8 | 165 | .242 | S.F. | 6.85 | 8.65 | | 15.50 | 21 |
| 0400 | 6" block | | 145 | .276 | | 7.35 | 9.85 | | 17.20 | 23 |
| 0600 | 8" block | ↓ | 125 | .320 | ↓ | 7.40 | 11.45 | | 18.85 | 25.50 |

### 04 27 10.30 Brick Walls

| | | Crew | Daily Output | Labor-Hours | Unit | Material | Labor | Equipment | Total | Total Incl O&P |
|---|---|---|---|---|---|---|---|---|---|---|
| 0010 | **BRICK WALLS**, including mortar, excludes scaffolding    R042110-20 | | | | | | | | | |
| 0140 | 4" thick, facing, 4" x 2-2/3" x 8" | D-8 | 1.45 | 27.586 | M | 430 | 985 | | 1,415 | 1,975 |
| 0150 | 4" thick, as back-up, 6.75 bricks per S.F. | | 1.60 | 25 | | 430 | 895 | | 1,325 | 1,825 |
| 0204 | 8" thick, 13.50 bricks per S.F. | | 1.80 | 22.222 | | 445 | 795 | | 1,240 | 1,700 |
| 0250 | 12" thick, 20.25 bricks per S.F. | | 1.90 | 21.053 | | 450 | 750 | | 1,200 | 1,650 |
| 0304 | 16" thick, 27.00 bricks per S.F. | | 2 | 20 | | 455 | 715 | | 1,170 | 1,575 |
| 0500 | Reinforced, 4" wall, 4" x 2-2/3" x 8" | | 1.40 | 28.571 | | 525 | 1,025 | | 1,550 | 2,125 |
| 0550 | 8" thick, 13.50 bricks per S.F. | | 1.75 | 22.857 | | 540 | 815 | | 1,355 | 1,850 |
| 0600 | 12" thick, 20.25 bricks per S.F. | | 1.85 | 21.622 | | 545 | 775 | | 1,320 | 1,775 |
| 0650 | 16" thick, 27.00 bricks per S.F. | | 1.95 | 20.513 | | 550 | 735 | | 1,285 | 1,725 |
| 0660 | 4" thick, select common, face, 4" x 2-2/3" x 8" | ↓ | 1.45 | 27.586 | ↓ | 525 | 985 | | 1,510 | 2,075 |
| 0790 | Alternate method of figuring by square foot | | | | | | | | | |
| 0800 | 4" wall, face, 4" x 2-2/3" x 8" | D-8 | 215 | .186 | S.F. | 5.40 | 6.65 | | 12.05 | 16.05 |
| 0850 | 4" thick, as back up, 6.75 bricks per S.F. | | 240 | .167 | | 2.89 | 5.95 | | 8.84 | 12.25 |
| 0900 | 8" thick wall, 13.50 brick per S.F. | | 135 | .296 | | 6 | 10.60 | | 16.60 | 22.50 |
| 1000 | 12" thick wall, 20.25 bricks per S.F. | | 95 | .421 | | 9.10 | 15.05 | | 24.15 | 33 |
| 1050 | 16" thick wall, 27.00 bricks per S.F. | | 75 | .533 | | 12.30 | 19.05 | | 31.35 | 42.50 |
| 1200 | Reinforced, 4" x 2-2/3" x 8" , 4" wall | | 205 | .195 | | 2.89 | 6.95 | | 9.84 | 13.80 |
| 1250 | 8" thick wall, 13.50 brick per S.F. | | 130 | .308 | | 6 | 11 | | 17 | 23.50 |
| 1300 | 12" thick wall, 20.25 bricks per S.F. | | 90 | .444 | | 9.10 | 15.90 | | 25 | 34 |
| 1350 | 16" thick wall, 27.00 bricks per S.F. | ↓ | 70 | .571 | ↓ | 12.30 | 20.50 | | 32.80 | 44.50 |

### 04 27 10.40 Steps

| | | Crew | Daily Output | Labor-Hours | Unit | Material | Labor | Equipment | Total | Total Incl O&P |
|---|---|---|---|---|---|---|---|---|---|---|
| 0010 | **STEPS** | | | | | | | | | |
| 0012 | Entry steps, select common brick | D-1 | .30 | 53.333 | M | 430 | 1,850 | | 2,280 | 3,300 |

# 04 41 Dry-Placed Stone

## 04 41 10 – Dry Placed Stone

| 04 41 10.10 Rough Stone Wall | | Crew | Daily Output | Labor-Hours | Unit | Material | 2008 Bare Costs | | Total | Total Incl O&P |
|---|---|---|---|---|---|---|---|---|---|---|
| | | | | | | | Labor | Equipment | | |
| 0011 | **ROUGH STONE WALL**, Dry | | | | | | | | | |
| 0100 | Random fieldstone, under 18" thick | D-12 | 60 | .533 | C.F. | 11.25 | 18.85 | | 30.10 | 41 |
| 0150 | Over 18" thick | " | 63 | .508 | " | 13.50 | 17.95 | | 31.45 | 42.50 |

# 04 43 Stone Masonry

## 04 43 10 – Masonry with Natural and Processed Stone

### 04 43 10.05 Ashlar Veneer

| | | | Crew | Daily Output | Labor-Hours | Unit | Material | Labor | Equipment | Total | Total Incl O&P |
|---|---|---|---|---|---|---|---|---|---|---|---|
| 0011 | **ASHLAR VENEER** 4" + or - thk, random or random rectangular | | | | | | | | | | |
| 0150 | Sawn face, split joints, low priced stone | | D-8 | 140 | .286 | S.F. | 11.25 | 10.20 | | 21.45 | 28 |
| 0200 | Medium priced stone | | | 130 | .308 | | 13.80 | 11 | | 24.80 | 32 |
| 0300 | High priced stone | | | 120 | .333 | | 19.40 | 11.90 | | 31.30 | 39.50 |
| 0600 | Seam face, split joints, medium price stone | | | 125 | .320 | | 14.55 | 11.45 | | 26 | 33.50 |
| 0700 | High price stone | | | 120 | .333 | | 20.50 | 11.90 | | 32.40 | 40.50 |
| 1000 | Split or rock face, split joints, medium price stone | | | 125 | .320 | | 14.30 | 11.45 | | 25.75 | 33 |
| 1100 | High price stone | | | 120 | .333 | | 20.50 | 11.90 | | 32.40 | 40.50 |

### 04 43 10.10 Bluestone

| | | | Crew | Daily Output | Labor-Hours | Unit | Material | Labor | Equipment | Total | Total Incl O&P |
|---|---|---|---|---|---|---|---|---|---|---|---|
| 0010 | **BLUESTONE**, cut to size | | | | | | | | | | |
| 0500 | Sills, natural cleft, 10" wide to 6' long, 1-1/2" thick | | D-11 | 70 | .343 | L.F. | 13.35 | 12.70 | | 26.05 | 34 |
| 0550 | 2" thick | | " | 63 | .381 | | 15.15 | 14.10 | | 29.25 | 38 |
| 1000 | Stair treads, natural cleft, 12" wide, 6' long, 1-1/2" thick | | D-10 | 115 | .278 | | 19.70 | 10.55 | 5.30 | 35.55 | 43.50 |
| 1050 | 2" thick | | | 105 | .305 | | 20.50 | 11.55 | 5.80 | 37.85 | 47 |
| 1100 | Smooth finish, 1-1/2" thick | | | 115 | .278 | | 24 | 10.55 | 5.30 | 39.85 | 48 |
| 1300 | Thermal finish | | | 115 | .278 | | 29.50 | 10.55 | 5.30 | 45.35 | 54.50 |
| 1350 | 2" thick | | | 105 | .305 | | 33.50 | 11.55 | 5.80 | 50.85 | 61 |

### 04 43 10.45 Granite

| | | | Crew | Daily Output | Labor-Hours | Unit | Material | Labor | Equipment | Total | Total Incl O&P |
|---|---|---|---|---|---|---|---|---|---|---|---|
| 0010 | **GRANITE**, cut to size | | | | | | | | | | |
| 0050 | Veneer, polished face, 3/4" to 1-1/2" thick | | | | | | | | | | |
| 0150 | Low price, gray, light gray, etc. | CN | D-10 | 130 | .246 | S.F. | 24.50 | 9.35 | 4.70 | 38.55 | 46.50 |
| 0220 | High price, red, black, etc. | CN | " | 130 | .246 | " | 38.50 | 9.35 | 4.70 | 52.55 | 62 |
| 0300 | 1-1/2" to 2-1/2" thick, veneer | | | | | | | | | | |
| 0350 | Low price, gray, light gray, etc. | | D-10 | 130 | .246 | S.F. | 26 | 9.35 | 4.70 | 40.05 | 48.50 |
| 0550 | High price, red, black, etc. | | " | 130 | .246 | " | 47.50 | 9.35 | 4.70 | 61.55 | 72 |
| 0700 | 2-1/2" to 4" thick, veneer | | | | | | | | | | |
| 0750 | Low price, gray, light gray, etc. | | D-10 | 110 | .291 | S.F. | 35 | 11.05 | 5.55 | 51.60 | 61.50 |
| 0950 | High price, red, black, etc. | | " | 110 | .291 | | 57.50 | 11.05 | 5.55 | 74.10 | 86 |
| 1000 | For bush hammered finish, deduct | | | | | | 5% | | | | |
| 1050 | Coarse rubbed finish, deduct | | | | | | 10% | | | | |
| 1100 | Honed finish, deduct | | | | | | 5% | | | | |
| 1150 | Thermal finish, deduct | | | | | | 18% | | | | |
| 2450 | For radius under 5', add | | | | | L.F. | 100% | | | | |
| 2500 | Steps, copings, etc., finished on more than one surface | | | | | | | | | | |
| 2550 | Minimum | | D-10 | 50 | .640 | C.F. | 91 | 24.50 | 12.20 | 127.70 | 150 |
| 2600 | Maximum | | " | 50 | .640 | " | 146 | 24.50 | 12.20 | 182.70 | 210 |
| 2800 | Pavers, 4" x 4" x 4" blocks, split face and joints | | | | | | | | | | |
| 2850 | Minimum | | D-11 | 80 | .300 | S.F. | 13.40 | 11.10 | | 24.50 | 31.50 |
| 2900 | Maximum | | " | 80 | .300 | | 26.50 | 11.10 | | 37.60 | 46 |
| 4000 | Soffits, 2" thick, minimum | | D-13 | 35 | 1.371 | | 37.50 | 50.50 | 17.45 | 105.45 | 138 |
| 4100 | Maximum | | | 35 | 1.371 | | 83 | 50.50 | 17.45 | 150.95 | 187 |
| 4200 | 4" thick, minimum | | | 35 | 1.371 | | 57.50 | 50.50 | 17.45 | 125.45 | 159 |
| 4300 | Maximum | | | 35 | 1.371 | | 108 | 50.50 | 17.45 | 175.95 | 215 |

# 04 43 Stone Masonry

## 04 43 10 – Masonry with Natural and Processed Stone

| 04 43 10.50 Lightweight Natural Stone | Crew | Daily Output | Labor-Hours | Unit | Material | 2008 Bare Costs Labor | Equipment | Total | Total Incl O&P |
|---|---|---|---|---|---|---|---|---|---|
| 0011 **LIGHTWEIGHT NATURAL STONE** Lava type | | | | | | | | | |
| 0100 Veneer, rubble face, sawed back, irregular shapes | D-10 | 130 | .246 | S.F. | 6.30 | 9.35 | 4.70 | 20.35 | 26.50 |
| 0200 Sawed face and back, irregular shapes | " | 130 | .246 | " | 6.30 | 9.35 | 4.70 | 20.35 | 26.50 |

### 04 43 10.55 Limestone

| | Crew | Daily Output | Labor-Hours | Unit | Material | 2008 Bare Costs Labor | Equipment | Total | Total Incl O&P |
|---|---|---|---|---|---|---|---|---|---|
| 0010 **LIMESTONE,** cut to size | | | | | | | | | |
| 0020 Veneer facing panels | | | | | | | | | |
| 0500 Texture finish, light stick, 4-1/2" thick, 5' x 12' | D-4 | 300 | .107 | S.F. | 48 | 3.68 | .42 | 52.10 | 59 |
| 0750 5" thick, 5' x 14' panels | D-10 | 275 | .116 | | 52.50 | 4.42 | 2.22 | 59.14 | 66.50 |
| 1000 Sugarcube finish, 2" Thick, 3' x 5' panels | | 275 | .116 | | 35 | 4.42 | 2.22 | 41.64 | 47.50 |
| 1050 3" Thick, 4' x 9' panels | | 275 | .116 | | 37.50 | 4.42 | 2.22 | 44.14 | 50.50 |
| 1200 4" Thick, 5' x 11' panels | | 275 | .116 | | 41 | 4.42 | 2.22 | 47.64 | 54 |
| 1400 Sugarcube, textured finish, 4-1/2" thick, 5' x 12' | | 275 | .116 | | 45 | 4.42 | 2.22 | 51.64 | 58.50 |
| 1450 5" thick, 5' x 14' panels | | 275 | .116 | | 53.50 | 4.42 | 2.22 | 60.14 | 67.50 |
| 2000 Coping, sugarcube finish, top & 2 sides | | 30 | 1.067 | C.F. | 58.50 | 40.50 | 20.50 | 119.50 | 149 |
| 2100 Sills, lintels, jambs, trim, stops, sugarcube finish, average | | 20 | 1.600 | | 58.50 | 60.50 | 30.50 | 149.50 | 190 |
| 2150 Detailed | | 20 | 1.600 | | 58.50 | 60.50 | 30.50 | 149.50 | 190 |
| 2300 Steps, extra hard, 14" wide, 6" rise | | 50 | .640 | L.F. | 35 | 24.50 | 12.20 | 71.70 | 89 |
| 3000 Quoins, plain finish, 6"x12"x12" | D-12 | 25 | 1.280 | Ea. | 58.50 | 45.50 | | 104 | 134 |
| 3050 6"x16"x24" | " | 25 | 1.280 | " | 78 | 45.50 | | 123.50 | 155 |

### 04 43 10.60 Marble

| | Crew | Daily Output | Labor-Hours | Unit | Material | 2008 Bare Costs Labor | Equipment | Total | Total Incl O&P |
|---|---|---|---|---|---|---|---|---|---|
| 0011 **MARBLE**, ashlar, split face, 4" + or - thick, random | | | | | | | | | |
| 0040 Lengths 1' to 4' & heights 2" to 7-1/2", average | D-8 | 175 | .229 | S.F. | 14.70 | 8.15 | | 22.85 | 28.50 |
| 0100 Base, polished, 3/4" or 7/8" thick, polished, 6" high | D-10 | 65 | .492 | L.F. | 13.35 | 18.70 | 9.40 | 41.45 | 53.50 |
| 0300 Carvings or bas relief, from templates, average | | 80 | .400 | S.F. | 119 | 15.20 | 7.65 | 141.85 | 162 |
| 0350 Maximum | | 80 | .400 | " | 278 | 15.20 | 7.65 | 300.85 | 335 |
| 0600 Columns, cornices, mouldings, etc. | | | | | | | | | |
| 0650 Hand or special machine cut, average | D-10 | 35 | .914 | C.F. | 119 | 34.50 | 17.45 | 170.95 | 203 |
| 0700 Maximum | " | 35 | .914 | " | 256 | 34.50 | 17.45 | 307.95 | 355 |
| 1000 Facing, polished finish, cut to size, 3/4" to 7/8" thick | | | | | | | | | |
| 1050 Average | D-10 | 130 | .246 | S.F. | 19.60 | 9.35 | 4.70 | 33.65 | 41 |
| 1100 Maximum | | 130 | .246 | | 45.50 | 9.35 | 4.70 | 59.55 | 69.50 |
| 1300 1-1/4" thick, average | | 125 | .256 | | 28.50 | 9.70 | 4.89 | 43.09 | 51.50 |
| 1350 Maximum | | 125 | .256 | | 57 | 9.70 | 4.89 | 71.59 | 82.50 |
| 1500 2" thick, average | | 120 | .267 | | 33 | 10.10 | 5.10 | 48.20 | 57.50 |
| 1550 Maximum | | 120 | .267 | | 57 | 10.10 | 5.10 | 72.20 | 84 |
| 2200 Window sills, 6" x 3/4" thick | D-1 | 85 | .188 | L.F. | 7.40 | 6.55 | | 13.95 | 18.15 |
| 2500 Flooring, polished tiles, 12" x 12" x 3/8" thick | | | | | | | | | |
| 2510 Thin set, average | D-11 | 90 | .267 | S.F. | 9.85 | 9.85 | | 19.70 | 26 |
| 2600 Maximum | | 90 | .267 | | 152 | 9.85 | | 161.85 | 182 |
| 2700 Mortar bed, average | | 65 | .369 | | 10 | 13.65 | | 23.65 | 32 |
| 2740 Maximum | | 65 | .369 | | 152 | 13.65 | | 165.65 | 188 |
| 2780 Travertine, 3/8" thick, average | D-10 | 130 | .246 | | 12.55 | 9.35 | 4.70 | 26.60 | 33 |
| 2790 Maximum | " | 130 | .246 | | 30.50 | 9.35 | 4.70 | 44.55 | 53.50 |
| 2800 Patio tile, non-slip, 1/2" thick, flame finish | D-11 | 75 | .320 | | 12.80 | 11.85 | | 24.65 | 32 |
| 2900 Shower or toilet partitions, 7/8" thick partitions | | | | | | | | | |
| 3050 3/4" or 1-1/4" thick stiles, polished 2 sides, average | D-11 | 75 | .320 | S.F. | 38 | 11.85 | | 49.85 | 60 |
| 3201 Soffits, add to above prices | | | | " | 20% | 100% | | | |
| 3210 Stairs, risers, 7/8" thick x 6" high | D-10 | 115 | .278 | L.F. | 12.85 | 10.55 | 5.30 | 28.70 | 36 |
| 3360 Treads, 12" wide x 1-1/4" thick | " | 115 | .278 | " | 18.75 | 10.55 | 5.30 | 34.60 | 42.50 |
| 3500 Thresholds, 3' long, 7/8" thick, 4" to 5" wide, plain | D-12 | 24 | 1.333 | Ea. | 14.20 | 47 | | 61.20 | 87.50 |
| 3550 Beveled | | 24 | 1.333 | " | 16.50 | 47 | | 63.50 | 90 |
| 3700 Window stools, polished, 7/8" thick, 5" wide | | 85 | .376 | L.F. | 13.25 | 13.30 | | 26.55 | 35 |

# 04 43 Stone Masonry

## 04 43 10 – Masonry with Natural and Processed Stone

### 04 43 10.75 Sandstone or Brownstone

| | | Crew | Daily Output | Labor-Hours | Unit | Material | 2008 Bare Costs Labor | Equipment | Total | Total Incl O&P |
|---|---|---|---|---|---|---|---|---|---|---|
| 0011 | **SANDSTONE OR BROWNSTONE** | | | | | | | | | |
| 0100 | Sawed face veneer, 2-1/2" thick, to 2' x 4' panels | D-10 | 130 | .246 | S.F. | 17.25 | 9.35 | 4.70 | 31.30 | 38.50 |
| 0150 | 4" thick, to 3'-6" x 8'panels | | 100 | .320 | | 17.25 | 12.15 | 6.10 | 35.50 | 44 |
| 0300 | Split face, random sizes | ↓ | 100 | .320 | ↓ | 12.40 | 12.15 | 6.10 | 30.65 | 39 |
| 0350 | Cut stone trim (limestone) | | | | | | | | | |
| 0360 | Ribbon stone, 4" thick, 5' pieces | D-8 | 120 | .333 | Ea. | 152 | 11.90 | | 163.90 | 185 |
| 0370 | Cove stone, 4" thick, 5' pieces | | 105 | .381 | | 153 | 13.60 | | 166.60 | 189 |
| 0380 | Cornice stone, 10" to 12" wide | | 90 | .444 | | 189 | 15.90 | | 204.90 | 231 |
| 0390 | Band stone, 4" thick, 5' pieces | | 145 | .276 | | 97.50 | 9.85 | | 107.35 | 122 |
| 0410 | Window and door trim, 3" to 4" wide | | 160 | .250 | | 82.50 | 8.95 | | 91.45 | 105 |
| 0420 | Key stone, 18" long | ↓ | 60 | .667 | ↓ | 87 | 24 | | 111 | 132 |

### 04 43 10.80 Slate

| | | Crew | Daily Output | Labor-Hours | Unit | Material | 2008 Bare Costs Labor | Equipment | Total | Total Incl O&P |
|---|---|---|---|---|---|---|---|---|---|---|
| 0010 | **SLATE** | | | | | | | | | |
| 0050 | Vermont - unfading green, mottled green & purple, gray & purple | | | | | | | | | |
| 0100 | Virginia, blue black | | | | | | | | | |
| 0200 | Exterior paving, natural cleft, 1" thick | | | | | | | | | |
| 0500 | 24" x 24", Pennsylvania | D-12 | 120 | .267 | S.F. | 13 | 9.45 | | 22.45 | 28.50 |
| 0550 | Vermont | | 120 | .267 | | 16.10 | 9.45 | | 25.55 | 32 |
| 0600 | Virginia | ↓ | 120 | .267 | ↓ | 20.50 | 9.45 | | 29.95 | 37 |
| 1000 | Interior flooring, natural cleft, 1/2" thick | | | | | | | | | |
| 1300 | 24" x 24" Pennsylvania | D-12 | 120 | .267 | S.F. | 7.90 | 9.45 | | 17.35 | 23 |
| 1350 | Vermont | | 120 | .267 | | 14.15 | 9.45 | | 23.60 | 30 |
| 1400 | Virginia | ↓ | 120 | .267 | ↓ | 14.75 | 9.45 | | 24.20 | 30.50 |
| 2000 | Facing panels, 1-1/4" thick, to 4' x 4' panels | | | | | | | | | |
| 2100 | Natural cleft finish, Pennsylvania | D-10 | 180 | .178 | S.F. | 32 | 6.75 | 3.39 | 42.14 | 49.50 |
| 2110 | Vermont | | 180 | .178 | | 27 | 6.75 | 3.39 | 37.14 | 44 |
| 2120 | Virginia | ↓ | 180 | .178 | | 33 | 6.75 | 3.39 | 43.14 | 50.50 |
| 2150 | Sand rubbed finish, surface, add | | | | | 10.15 | | | 10.15 | 11.20 |
| 2200 | Honed finish, add | | | | | 7.35 | | | 7.35 | 8.10 |
| 2500 | Ribbon, natural cleft finish, 1" thick, to 9 S.F. | D-10 | 80 | .400 | | 13.10 | 15.20 | 7.65 | 35.95 | 46 |
| 2700 | 1-1/2" thick | | 78 | .410 | | 17.05 | 15.55 | 7.85 | 40.45 | 51 |
| 2850 | 2" thick | ↓ | 76 | .421 | ↓ | 20.50 | 16 | 8.05 | 44.55 | 56 |
| 3500 | Stair treads, sand finish, 1" thick x 12" wide | | | | | | | | | |
| 3600 | 3 L.F. to 6 L.F. | D-10 | 120 | .267 | L.F. | 22.50 | 10.10 | 5.10 | 37.70 | 45.50 |
| 3700 | Ribbon, sand finish, 1" thick x 12" wide | | | | | | | | | |
| 3750 | To 6 L.F. | D-10 | 120 | .267 | L.F. | 16.30 | 10.10 | 5.10 | 31.50 | 39 |
| 4000 | Stools or sills, sand finish, 1" thick, 6" wide | D-12 | 160 | .200 | | 10.90 | 7.10 | | 18 | 23 |
| 4200 | 10" wide | | 90 | .356 | | 16.65 | 12.60 | | 29.25 | 37.50 |
| 4400 | 2" thick, 6" wide | | 140 | .229 | | 18.45 | 8.10 | | 26.55 | 33 |
| 4600 | 10" wide | ↓ | 90 | .356 | | 27.50 | 12.60 | | 40.10 | 49.50 |
| 4800 | For lengths over 3', add | | | | ↓ | 25% | | | | |

### 04 43 10.85 Window Sill

| | | Crew | Daily Output | Labor-Hours | Unit | Material | 2008 Bare Costs Labor | Equipment | Total | Total Incl O&P |
|---|---|---|---|---|---|---|---|---|---|---|
| 0010 | **WINDOW SILL** | | | | | | | | | |
| 0020 | Bluestone, thermal top, 10" wide, 1-1/2" thick | D-1 | 85 | .188 | S.F. | 16.05 | 6.55 | | 22.60 | 27.50 |
| 0050 | 2" thick | | 75 | .213 | " | 18.75 | 7.45 | | 26.20 | 32 |
| 0100 | Cut stone, 5" x 8" plain | | 48 | .333 | L.F. | 11.90 | 11.65 | | 23.55 | 31 |
| 0200 | Face brick on edge, brick, 8" wide | | 80 | .200 | | 2.53 | 7 | | 9.53 | 13.40 |
| 0400 | Marble, 9" wide, 1" thick | | 85 | .188 | | 8.50 | 6.55 | | 15.05 | 19.35 |
| 0900 | Slate, colored, unfading, honed, 12" wide, 1" thick | | 85 | .188 | | 17.10 | 6.55 | | 23.65 | 29 |
| 0950 | 2" thick | ↓ | 70 | .229 | ↓ | 24 | 7.95 | | 31.95 | 38 |

# 04 51 Flue Liner Masonry

## 04 51 10 – Clay Flue Lining

| 04 51 10.10 Flue Lining | Crew | Daily Output | Labor-Hours | Unit | Material | 2008 Bare Costs Labor | Equipment | Total | Total Incl O&P |
|---|---|---|---|---|---|---|---|---|---|
| 0010 | **FLUE LINING**, including mortar | | | | | | | | | |
| 0020 | 8" x 8" | D-1 | 125 | .128 | V.L.F. | 4.07 | 4.46 | | 8.53 | 11.25 |
| 0100 | 8" x 12" | | 103 | .155 | | 6.05 | 5.40 | | 11.45 | 14.90 |
| 0200 | 12" x 12" | | 93 | .172 | | 7.90 | 6 | | 13.90 | 17.85 |
| 0300 | 12" x 18" | | 84 | .190 | | 13.85 | 6.65 | | 20.50 | 25.50 |
| 0400 | 18" x 18" | | 75 | .213 | | 19.80 | 7.45 | | 27.25 | 33.50 |
| 0500 | 20" x 20" | | 66 | .242 | | 32.50 | 8.45 | | 40.95 | 49 |
| 0600 | 24" x 24" | | 56 | .286 | | 41.50 | 9.95 | | 51.45 | 60.50 |
| 1000 | Round, 18" diameter | | 66 | .242 | | 29.50 | 8.45 | | 37.95 | 45.50 |
| 1100 | 24" diameter | | 47 | .340 | | 62 | 11.85 | | 73.85 | 86 |

# 04 54 Refractory Brick Masonry

## 04 54 10 – Refractory Brick Work

### 04 54 10.10 Fire Brick

| | | Crew | Daily Output | Labor-Hours | Unit | Material | Labor | Equipment | Total | Total Incl O&P |
|---|---|---|---|---|---|---|---|---|---|---|
| 0010 | **FIRE BRICK** | | | | | | | | | |
| 0012 | Low duty, 2000° F, 9" x 2-1/2" x 4-1/2" | D-1 | .60 | 26.667 | M | 1,200 | 930 | | 2,130 | 2,750 |
| 0050 | High duty, 3000° F | " | .60 | 26.667 | " | 2,000 | 930 | | 2,930 | 3,625 |

### 04 54 10.20 Fire Clay

| | | Crew | Daily Output | Labor-Hours | Unit | Material | Labor | Equipment | Total | Total Incl O&P |
|---|---|---|---|---|---|---|---|---|---|---|
| 0010 | **FIRE CLAY** | | | | | | | | | |
| 0020 | Gray, high duty, 100 lb. bag | | | | Bag | 56.50 | | | 56.50 | 62 |
| 0050 | 100 lb. drum, premixed (400 brick per drum) | | | | Drum | 69.50 | | | 69.50 | 76.50 |

# 04 57 Masonry Fireplaces

## 04 57 10 – Brick or Stone Fireplaces

### 04 57 10.10 Fireplace

| | | Crew | Daily Output | Labor-Hours | Unit | Material | Labor | Equipment | Total | Total Incl O&P |
|---|---|---|---|---|---|---|---|---|---|---|
| 0010 | **FIREPLACE** | | | | | | | | | |
| 0100 | Brick fireplace, not incl. foundations or chimneys | | | | | | | | | |
| 0110 | 30" x 29" opening, incl. chamber, plain brickwork | D-1 | .40 | 40 | Ea. | 510 | 1,400 | | 1,910 | 2,675 |
| 0200 | Fireplace box only (110 brick) | " | 2 | 8 | " | 168 | 279 | | 447 | 610 |
| 0300 | For elaborate brickwork and details, add | | | | | 35% | 35% | | | |
| 0400 | For hearth, brick & stone, add | D-1 | 2 | 8 | Ea. | 188 | 279 | | 467 | 630 |
| 0410 | For steel angle, damper, cleanouts, add | | 4 | 4 | | 131 | 140 | | 271 | 355 |
| 0600 | Plain brickwork, incl. metal circulator | | .50 | 32 | | 970 | 1,125 | | 2,095 | 2,775 |
| 0800 | Face brick only, standard size, 8" x 2-2/3" x 4" | | .30 | 53.333 | M | 510 | 1,850 | | 2,360 | 3,375 |

# 04 71 Manufactured Brick Masonry

## 04 71 10 – Simulated or Manufactured Brick

### 04 71 10.10 Simulated Brick

| | | Crew | Daily Output | Labor-Hours | Unit | Material | Labor | Equipment | Total | Total Incl O&P |
|---|---|---|---|---|---|---|---|---|---|---|
| 0010 | **SIMULATED BRICK** | | | | | | | | | |
| 0020 | Aluminum, baked on colors | 1 Carp | 200 | .040 | S.F. | 3.36 | 1.52 | | 4.88 | 6.05 |
| 0050 | Fiberglass panels | | 200 | .040 | | 3.69 | 1.52 | | 5.21 | 6.45 |
| 0100 | Urethane pieces cemented in mastic | | 150 | .053 | | 6.35 | 2.03 | | 8.38 | 10.15 |
| 0150 | Vinyl siding panels | | 200 | .040 | | 2.54 | 1.52 | | 4.06 | 5.15 |
| 0160 | Cement base, brick, incl. mastic | D-1 | 100 | .160 | | 4.02 | 5.60 | | 9.62 | 12.90 |
| 0170 | Corner | | 50 | .320 | V.L.F. | 10.05 | 11.15 | | 21.20 | 28 |
| 0180 | Stone face, incl. mastic | | 100 | .160 | S.F. | 9.70 | 5.60 | | 15.30 | 19.20 |
| 0190 | Corner | | 50 | .320 | V.L.F. | 10.75 | 11.15 | | 21.90 | 29 |

# 04 72 Cast Stone Masonry

## 04 72 10 – Cast Stone Masonry Features

### 04 72 10.10 Coping

| | | Crew | Daily Output | Labor-Hours | Unit | Material | 2008 Bare Costs Labor | Equipment | Total | Total Incl O&P |
|---|---|---|---|---|---|---|---|---|---|---|
| 0010 | **COPING**, stock units | | | | | | | | | |
| 0050 | Precast concrete, 10" wide, 4" tapers to 3-1/2", 8" wall | D-1 | 75 | .213 | L.F. | 17.95 | 7.45 | | 25.40 | 31 |
| 0100 | 12" wide, 3-1/2" tapers to 3", 10" wall | | 70 | .229 | | 17.95 | 7.95 | | 25.90 | 32 |
| 0110 | 14" wide, 4" tapers to 3-1/2", 12" wall | | 65 | .246 | | 20.50 | 8.60 | | 29.10 | 36 |
| 0150 | 16" wide, 4" tapers to 3-1/2", 14" wall | | 60 | .267 | | 16.15 | 9.30 | | 25.45 | 32 |
| 0250 | Precast concrete corners | | 40 | .400 | Ea. | 26.50 | 13.95 | | 40.45 | 50.50 |
| 0300 | Limestone for 12" wall, 4" thick | | 90 | .178 | L.F. | 14.50 | 6.20 | | 20.70 | 25.50 |
| 0350 | 6" thick | | 80 | .200 | | 22 | 7 | | 29 | 34.50 |
| 0500 | Marble, to 4" thick, no wash, 9" wide | | 90 | .178 | | 22 | 6.20 | | 28.20 | 33.50 |
| 0550 | 12" wide | | 80 | .200 | | 33 | 7 | | 40 | 46.50 |
| 0700 | Terra cotta, 9" wide | | 90 | .178 | | 5.30 | 6.20 | | 11.50 | 15.25 |
| 0750 | 12" wide | | 80 | .200 | | 8.70 | 7 | | 15.70 | 20 |
| 0800 | Aluminum, for 12" wall | | 80 | .200 | | 12.55 | 7 | | 19.55 | 24.50 |

## 04 72 20 – Cultured Stone Veneer

### 04 72 20.10 Cultured Stone Veneer Components

| | | Crew | Daily Output | Labor-Hours | Unit | Material | 2008 Bare Costs Labor | Equipment | Total | Total Incl O&P |
|---|---|---|---|---|---|---|---|---|---|---|
| 0010 | **CULTURED STONE VENEER COMPONENTS** | | | | | | | | | |
| 0110 | On wood frame and sheathing substrate, random sized cobbles, corner stones | D-8 | 70 | .571 | V.L.F. | 12.65 | 20.50 | | 33.15 | 45 |
| 0120 | Field stones | | 140 | .286 | S.F. | 9.10 | 10.20 | | 19.30 | 25.50 |
| 0130 | Random sized flats, corner stones | | 70 | .571 | V.L.F. | 11.65 | 20.50 | | 32.15 | 44 |
| 0140 | Field stones | | 140 | .286 | S.F. | 9.85 | 10.20 | | 20.05 | 26.50 |
| 0150 | Horizontal lined ledgestones, corner stones | | 75 | .533 | V.L.F. | 12.65 | 19.05 | | 31.70 | 43 |
| 0160 | Field stones | | 150 | .267 | S.F. | 9.10 | 9.55 | | 18.65 | 24.50 |
| 0170 | Random shaped flats, corner stones | | 65 | .615 | V.L.F. | 12.65 | 22 | | 34.65 | 47.50 |
| 0180 | Field stones | | 150 | .267 | S.F. | 9.10 | 9.55 | | 18.65 | 24.50 |
| 0190 | Random shaped / textured face, corner stones | | 65 | .615 | V.L.F. | 12.65 | 22 | | 34.65 | 47.50 |
| 0200 | Field stones | | 130 | .308 | S.F. | 9.10 | 11 | | 20.10 | 26.50 |
| 0210 | Random shaped river rock, corner stones | | 65 | .615 | V.L.F. | 12.65 | 22 | | 34.65 | 47.50 |
| 0220 | Field stones | | 130 | .308 | S.F. | 9.10 | 11 | | 20.10 | 26.50 |
| 0240 | On concrete or CMU substrate, random sized cobbles, corner stones | | 70 | .571 | V.L.F. | 12 | 20.50 | | 32.50 | 44 |
| 0250 | Field stones | | 140 | .286 | S.F. | 8.80 | 10.20 | | 19 | 25 |
| 0260 | Random sized flats, corner stones | | 70 | .571 | V.L.F. | 11 | 20.50 | | 31.50 | 43 |
| 0270 | Field stones | | 140 | .286 | S.F. | 9.50 | 10.20 | | 19.70 | 26 |
| 0280 | Horizontal lined ledgestones, corner stones | | 75 | .533 | V.L.F. | 12 | 19.05 | | 31.05 | 42 |
| 0290 | Field stones | | 150 | .267 | S.F. | 8.80 | 9.55 | | 18.35 | 24 |
| 0300 | Random shaped flats, corner stones | | 70 | .571 | V.L.F. | 12 | 20.50 | | 32.50 | 44 |
| 0310 | Field stones | | 140 | .286 | S.F. | 8.80 | 10.20 | | 19 | 25 |
| 0320 | Random shaped / textured face, corner stones | | 65 | .615 | V.L.F. | 12 | 22 | | 34 | 46.50 |
| 0330 | Field stones | | 130 | .308 | S.F. | 8.80 | 11 | | 19.80 | 26.50 |
| 0340 | Random shaped river rock, corner stones | | 65 | .615 | V.L.F. | 12 | 22 | | 34 | 46.50 |
| 0350 | Field stones | | 130 | .308 | S.F. | 8.80 | 11 | | 19.80 | 26.50 |
| 0360 | Cultured stone veneer, #15 felt weather resistant barrier | 1 Clab | 3700 | .002 | Sq. | 4.10 | .07 | | 4.17 | 4.61 |
| 0370 | #15 felt weather resistant barrier | 1 Lath | 85 | .094 | S.Y. | 2.86 | 3.28 | | 6.14 | 8 |
| 0390 | Water table or window sill, 18" long | 1 Bric | 80 | .100 | Ea. | 12.60 | 3.92 | | 16.52 | 19.80 |

# 04 73 Manufactured Stone Masonry

## 04 73 20 – Simulated or Manufactured Stone

| 04 73 20.10 Simulated Stone | Crew | Daily Output | Labor-Hours | Unit | Material | 2008 Bare Costs Labor | Equipment | Total | Total Incl O&P |
|---|---|---|---|---|---|---|---|---|---|
| 0010 **SIMULATED STONE** | | | | | | | | | |
| 0100 Insulated fiberglass panels, 5/8" ply backer | L-4 | 200 | .120 | S.F. | 11.40 | 4.32 | | 15.72 | 19.20 |

# Estimating Tips

## 05 05 00 Common Work Results for Metals

- Nuts, bolts, washers, connection angles, and plates can add a significant amount to both the tonnage of a structural steel job and the estimated cost. As a rule of thumb, add 10% to the total weight to account for these accessories.

- Type 2 steel construction, commonly referred to as "simple construction," consists generally of field-bolted connections with lateral bracing supplied by other elements of the building, such as masonry walls or x-bracing. The estimator should be aware, however, that shop connections may be accomplished by welding or bolting. The method may be particular to the fabrication shop and may have an impact on the estimated cost.

## 05 12 23 Structural Steel

- Steel items can be obtained from two sources: a fabrication shop or a metals service center. Fabrication shops can fabricate items under more controlled conditions than can crews in the field. They are also more efficient and can produce items more economically. Metal service centers serve as a source of long mill shapes to both fabrication shops and contractors.

- Most line items in this structural steel section, and most items in 05 50 00 Metal Fabrications, are indicated as being shop fabricated. The bare material cost for these shop fabricated items is the "Invoice Cost" from the shop and includes the mill base price of steel plus mill extras, transportation to the shop, shop drawings and detailing where warranted, shop fabrication and handling, sandblasting and a shop coat of primer paint, all necessary structural bolts, and delivery to the job site. The bare labor cost and bare equipment cost for these shop fabricated items is for field installation or erection.

- Line items in section 05 12 23.40 Lightweight Framing, and other items scattered in Division 5, are indicated as being field fabricated. The bare material cost for these field fabricated items is the "Invoice Cost" from the metals service center and includes the mill base price of steel plus mill extras, transportation to the metals service center, material handling, and delivery of long lengths of mill shapes to the job site. Material costs for structural bolts and welding rods should be added to the estimate. The bare labor cost and bare equipment cost for these items is for both field fabrication and field installation or erection, and include time for cutting, welding and drilling in the fabricated metal items. Drilling into concrete and fasteners to fasten field fabricated items to other work are not included and should be added to the estimate.

## 05 20 00 Metal Joists

- In any given project the total weight of open web steel joists is determined by the loads to be supported and the design. However, economies can be realized in minimizing the amount of labor used to place the joists. This is done by maximizing the joist spacing, and therefore minimizing the number of joists required to be installed on the job. Certain spacings and locations may be required by the design, but in other cases maximizing the spacing and keeping it as uniform as possible will keep the costs down.

## 05 30 00 Metal Decking

- The takeoff and estimating of metal deck involves more than simply the area of the floor or roof and the type of deck specified or shown on the drawings. Many different sizes and types of openings may exist. Small openings for individual pipes or conduits may be drilled after the floor/roof is installed, but larger openings may require special deck lengths as well as reinforcing or structural support. The estimator should determine who will be supplying this reinforcing. Additionally, some deck terminations are part of the deck package, such as screed angles and pour stops, and others will be part of the steel contract, such as angles attached to structural members and cast-in-place angles and plates. The estimator must ensure that all pieces are accounted for in the complete estimate.

## 05 50 00 Metal Fabrications

- The most economical steel stairs are those that use common materials, standard details, and most importantly, a uniform and relatively simple method of field assembly. Commonly available A36 channels and plates are very good choices for the main stringers of the stairs, as are angles and tees for the carrier members. Risers and treads are usually made by specialty shops, and it is most economical to use a typical detail in as many places as possible. The stairs should be pre-assembled and shipped directly to the site. The field connections should be simple and straightforward to be accomplished efficiently, and with minimum equipment and labor.

# Reference Numbers

Reference numbers are shown in shaded boxes at the beginning of some major classifications. These numbers refer to related items in the Reference Section. The reference information may be an estimating procedure, an alternate pricing method, or technical information.
*Note:* Not all subdivisions listed here necessarily appear in this publication.

# 05 01 Maintenance of Metals

## 05 01 10 – Maintenance of Structural Metal Framing

| 05 01 10.51 Cleaning of Structural Metal Framing | Crew | Daily Output | Labor-Hours | Unit | Material | 2008 Bare Costs Labor | Equipment | Total | Total Incl O&P |
|---|---|---|---|---|---|---|---|---|---|
| 0010 **CLEANING OF STRUCTURAL METAL FRAMING** | | | | | | | | | |
| 6125 Steel surface treatments, PDCA guidelines | | | | | | | | | |
| 6170 Wire brush, hand (SSPC-SP2) | 1 Psst | 400 | .020 | S.F. | .02 | .69 | | .71 | 1.27 |
| 6180 Power tool (SSPC-SP3) | " | 700 | .011 | | .05 | .39 | | .44 | .77 |
| 6215 Pressure washing, 2800-6000 S.F./day | 1 Pord | 10000 | .001 | | | .03 | | .03 | .04 |
| 6220 Steam cleaning, 2800-4000 S.F./day | | 2000 | .004 | | | .14 | | .14 | .20 |
| 6225 Water blasting | | 2500 | .003 | | | .11 | | .11 | .16 |
| 6230 Brush-off blast (SSPC-SP7) | E-11 | 1750 | .018 | | .09 | .63 | .11 | .83 | 1.26 |
| 6235 Com'l blast (SSPC-SP6), loose scale, fine pwder rust, 2.0 #/S.F. sand | | 1200 | .027 | | .18 | .91 | .16 | 1.25 | 1.90 |
| 6240 Tight mill scale, little/no rust, 3.0 #/S.F. sand | | 1000 | .032 | | .27 | 1.09 | .19 | 1.55 | 2.33 |
| 6245 Exist coat blistered/pitted, 4.0 #/S.F. sand | | 875 | .037 | | .36 | 1.25 | .22 | 1.83 | 2.72 |
| 6250 Exist coat badly pitted/nodules, 6.7 #/S.F. sand | | 825 | .039 | | .60 | 1.33 | .23 | 2.16 | 3.13 |
| 6255 Near white blast (SSPC-SP10), loose scale, fine rust, 5.6 #/S.F. sand | | 450 | .071 | | .50 | 2.43 | .43 | 3.36 | 5.10 |
| 6260 Tight mill scale, little/no rust, 6.9 #/S.F. sand | | 325 | .098 | | .61 | 3.37 | .59 | 4.57 | 6.95 |
| 6265 Exist coat blistered/pitted, 9.0 #/S.F. sand | | 225 | .142 | | .80 | 4.86 | .85 | 6.51 | 9.90 |
| 6270 Exist coat badly pitted/nodules, 11.3 #/S.F. sand | | 150 | .213 | | 1.01 | 7.30 | 1.28 | 9.59 | 14.70 |

# 05 05 Common Work Results for Metals

## 05 05 05 – Selective Metals Demolition

### 05 05 05.10 Selective Demolition, Concrete

| 05 05 05.10 Selective Demolition, Concrete | Crew | Daily Output | Labor-Hours | Unit | Material | 2008 Bare Costs Labor | Equipment | Total | Total Incl O&P |
|---|---|---|---|---|---|---|---|---|---|
| 0010 **SELECTIVE DEMOLITION, CONCRETE**  R024119-10 | | | | | | | | | |
| 0015 Excludes shores, bracing, cutting, loading, hauling, dumping | | | | | | | | | |
| 0020 Remove nuts only up to 3/4" diameter | 1 Sswk | 480 | .017 | Ea. | | .72 | | .72 | 1.29 |
| 0030 7/8" to 1-1/4" diameter | | 240 | .033 | | | 1.43 | | 1.43 | 2.58 |
| 0040 1-3/8" to 2" diameter | | 160 | .050 | | | 2.15 | | 2.15 | 3.88 |
| 0060 Unbolt and remove structural bolts up to 3/4" diameter | | 240 | .033 | | | 1.43 | | 1.43 | 2.58 |
| 0070 7/8" to 2" diameter | | 160 | .050 | | | 2.15 | | 2.15 | 3.88 |
| 0140 Light weight framing members, remove whole or cut up, up to 20 lb | | 240 | .033 | | | 1.43 | | 1.43 | 2.58 |
| 0150 21 - 40 lb | 2 Sswk | 210 | .076 | | | 3.28 | | 3.28 | 5.90 |
| 0160 41 - 80 lb | 3 Sswk | 180 | .133 | | | 5.75 | | 5.75 | 10.35 |
| 0170 81 - 120 lb | 4 Sswk | 150 | .213 | | | 9.15 | | 9.15 | 16.55 |
| 0230 Structural members, remove whole or cut up, up to 500 lb | E-19 | 48 | .500 | | | 21 | 21 | 42 | 59 |
| 0240 1/4 - 2 tons | E-18 | 36 | 1.111 | | | 47.50 | 28 | 75.50 | 114 |
| 0250 2 - 5 tons | E-24 | 30 | 1.067 | | | 45 | 26 | 71 | 107 |
| 0260 5 - 10 tons | E-20 | 24 | 2.667 | | | 112 | 51 | 163 | 251 |
| 0270 10 - 15 tons | E-2 | 18 | 3.111 | | | 130 | 87 | 217 | 320 |
| 0340 Fabricated item, remove whole or cut up, up to 20 lb | 1 Sswk | 96 | .083 | | | 3.58 | | 3.58 | 6.45 |
| 0350 21 - 40 lb | 2 Sswk | 84 | .190 | | | 8.20 | | 8.20 | 14.75 |
| 0360 41 - 80 lb | 3 Sswk | 72 | .333 | | | 14.35 | | 14.35 | 26 |
| 0370 81 - 120 lb | 4 Sswk | 60 | .533 | | | 23 | | 23 | 41.50 |
| 0380 121 - 500 lb | E-19 | 48 | .500 | | | 21 | 21 | 42 | 59 |
| 0390 501 - 1000 lb | " | 36 | .667 | | | 28 | 28 | 56 | 78.50 |

## 05 05 13 – Shop-Applied Coatings for Metal

### 05 05 13.50 Paints and Protective Coatings

| 05 05 13.50 Paints and Protective Coatings | Crew | Daily Output | Labor-Hours | Unit | Material | 2008 Bare Costs Labor | Equipment | Total | Total Incl O&P |
|---|---|---|---|---|---|---|---|---|---|
| 0010 **PAINTS AND PROTECTIVE COATINGS** | | | | | | | | | |
| 5900 Galvanizing structural steel in shop, under 1 ton | | | | Ton | 625 | | | 625 | 685 |
| 5950 1 ton to 20 tons | | | | | 515 | | | 515 | 570 |
| 6000 Over 20 tons | | | | | 455 | | | 455 | 500 |

## 05 05 21 – Fastening Methods for Metal

| 05 05 21.10 Cutting Steel | Crew | Daily Output | Labor-Hours | Unit | Material | 2008 Bare Costs Labor | Equipment | Total | Total Incl O&P |
|---|---|---|---|---|---|---|---|---|---|
| 0010 **CUTTING STEEL** | | | | | | | | | |
| 0020 Hand burning, incl. preparation, torch cutting & grinding, no staging | | | | | | | | | |
| 0100 Steel to 1/2" thick | E-25 | 320 | .025 | L.F. | | 1.13 | .28 | 1.41 | 2.34 |
| 0150 3/4" thick | | 260 | .031 | | | 1.38 | .34 | 1.72 | 2.88 |
| 0200 1" thick | ↓ | 200 | .040 | ↓ | | 1.80 | .45 | 2.25 | 3.74 |

### 05 05 21.15 Drilling Steel

| | Crew | Daily Output | Labor-Hours | Unit | Material | Labor | Equipment | Total | Total Incl O&P |
|---|---|---|---|---|---|---|---|---|---|
| 0010 **DRILLING STEEL** | | | | | | | | | |
| 1910 Drilling & layout for steel, up to 1/4" deep, no anchor | | | | | | | | | |
| 1920 Holes, 1/4" diameter | 1 Sswk | 112 | .071 | Ea. | .14 | 3.07 | | 3.21 | 5.70 |
| 1925 For each additional 1/4" depth, add | | 336 | .024 | | .14 | 1.02 | | 1.16 | 2 |
| 1930 3/8" diameter | | 104 | .077 | | .15 | 3.31 | | 3.46 | 6.10 |
| 1935 For each additional 1/4" depth, add | | 312 | .026 | | .15 | 1.10 | | 1.25 | 2.16 |
| 1940 1/2" diameter | | 96 | .083 | | .17 | 3.58 | | 3.75 | 6.65 |
| 1945 For each additional 1/4" depth, add | | 288 | .028 | | .17 | 1.19 | | 1.36 | 2.34 |
| 1950 5/8" diameter | | 88 | .091 | | .29 | 3.91 | | 4.20 | 7.35 |
| 1955 For each additional 1/4" depth, add | | 264 | .030 | | .29 | 1.30 | | 1.59 | 2.66 |
| 1960 3/4" diameter | | 80 | .100 | | .32 | 4.30 | | 4.62 | 8.10 |
| 1965 For each additional 1/4" depth, add | | 240 | .033 | | .32 | 1.43 | | 1.75 | 2.93 |
| 1970 7/8" diameter | | 72 | .111 | | .38 | 4.78 | | 5.16 | 9 |
| 1975 For each additional 1/4" depth, add | | 216 | .037 | | .38 | 1.59 | | 1.97 | 3.29 |
| 1980 1" diameter | | 64 | .125 | | .43 | 5.40 | | 5.83 | 10.15 |
| 1985 For each additional 1/4" depth, add | ↓ | 192 | .042 | | .43 | 1.79 | | 2.22 | 3.70 |
| 1990 For drilling up, add | | | | ↓ | | 40% | | | |

### 05 05 21.90 Welding Steel

| | Crew | Daily Output | Labor-Hours | Unit | Material | Labor | Equipment | Total | Total Incl O&P |
|---|---|---|---|---|---|---|---|---|---|
| 0010 **WELDING STEEL**, Structural R050521-20 | | | | | | | | | |
| 0020 Field welding, 1/8" E6011, cost per welder, no oper. engr | E-14 | 8 | 1 | Hr. | 4.17 | 45 | 16.55 | 65.72 | 104 |
| 0200 With 1/2 operating engineer | E-13 | 8 | 1.500 | | 4.17 | 64 | 16.55 | 84.72 | 133 |
| 0300 With 1 operating engineer | E-12 | 8 | 2 | ↓ | 4.17 | 83 | 16.50 | 103.67 | 161 |
| 0500 With no operating engineer, 2# weld rod per ton | E-14 | 8 | 1 | Ton | 4.17 | 45 | 16.55 | 65.72 | 104 |
| 0600 8# E6011 per ton | " | 2 | 4 | | 16.70 | 180 | 66 | 262.70 | 415 |
| 0800 With one operating engineer per welder, 2# E6011 per ton | E-12 | 8 | 2 | | 4.17 | 83 | 16.50 | 103.67 | 161 |
| 0900 8# E6011 per ton | " | 2 | 8 | ↓ | 16.70 | 330 | 66 | 412.70 | 645 |
| 1200 Continuous fillet, stick welding, incl. equipment | | | | | | | | | |
| 1300 Single pass, 1/8" thick, 0.1#/L.F. | E-14 | 150 | .053 | L.F. | .21 | 2.40 | .88 | 3.49 | 5.55 |
| 1400 3/16" thick, 0.2#/L.F. | | 75 | .107 | | .42 | 4.80 | 1.76 | 6.98 | 11.05 |
| 1500 1/4" thick, 0.3#/L.F. | | 50 | .160 | | .63 | 7.20 | 2.64 | 10.47 | 16.60 |
| 1610 5/16" thick, 0.4#/L.F. | | 38 | .211 | | .83 | 9.45 | 3.48 | 13.76 | 22 |
| 1800 3 passes, 3/8" thick, 0.5#/L.F. | | 30 | .267 | | 1.04 | 12 | 4.41 | 17.45 | 27.50 |
| 2010 4 passes, 1/2" thick, 0.7#/L.F. | | 22 | .364 | | 1.46 | 16.35 | 6 | 23.81 | 37.50 |
| 2200 5 to 6 passes, 3/4" thick, 1.3#/L.F. | | 12 | .667 | | 2.71 | 30 | 11 | 43.71 | 69 |
| 2400 8 to 11 passes, 1" thick, 2.4#/L.F. | ↓ | 6 | 1.333 | | 5 | 60 | 22 | 87 | 138 |
| 2600 For all position welding, add, minimum | | | | | | 20% | | | |
| 2700 Maximum | | | | | | 300% | | | |
| 2900 For semi-automatic welding, deduct, minimum | | | | | | 5% | | | |
| 3000 Maximum | | | | ↓ | | 15% | | | |
| 4000 Cleaning and welding plates, bars, or rods | | | | | | | | | |
| 4010 to existing beams, columns, or trusses | E-14 | 12 | .667 | L.F. | 1.04 | 30 | 11 | 42.04 | 67.50 |

## 05 05 23 – Metal Fastenings

### 05 05 23.05 Anchor Bolts

| | Crew | Daily Output | Labor-Hours | Unit | Material | Labor | Equipment | Total | Total Incl O&P |
|---|---|---|---|---|---|---|---|---|---|
| 0010 **ANCHOR BOLTS** | | | | | | | | | |
| 0100 J-type, incl. hex nut & washer, 1/2" diameter x 6" long | 2 Carp | 70 | .229 | Ea. | 1.14 | 8.70 | | 9.84 | 14.80 |

# 05 05 Common Work Results for Metals

## 05 05 23 – Metal Fastenings

| 05 05 23.05 Anchor Bolts | | Crew | Daily Output | Labor-Hours | Unit | Material | 2008 Bare Costs Labor | Equipment | Total | Total Incl O&P |
|---|---|---|---|---|---|---|---|---|---|---|
| 0110 | 12" long | 2 Carp | 65 | .246 | Ea. | 1.43 | 9.40 | | 10.83 | 16.15 |
| 0120 | 18" long | | 60 | .267 | | 1.86 | 10.15 | | 12.01 | 17.85 |
| 0130 | 3/4" diameter x 8" long | | 50 | .320 | | 1.69 | 12.20 | | 13.89 | 21 |
| 0140 | 12" long | | 45 | .356 | | 2.11 | 13.55 | | 15.66 | 23.50 |
| 0150 | 18" long | | 40 | .400 | | 2.74 | 15.25 | | 17.99 | 26.50 |
| 0160 | 1" diameter x 12" long | | 35 | .457 | | 4.03 | 17.40 | | 21.43 | 31.50 |
| 0170 | 18" long | | 30 | .533 | | 4.86 | 20.50 | | 25.36 | 37 |
| 0180 | 24" long | | 25 | .640 | | 5.95 | 24.50 | | 30.45 | 44.50 |
| 0190 | 36" long | | 20 | .800 | | 8.10 | 30.50 | | 38.60 | 56.50 |
| 0200 | 1-1/2" diameter x 18" long | | 22 | .727 | | 14.35 | 27.50 | | 41.85 | 59 |
| 0210 | 24" long | | 16 | 1 | | 17.10 | 38 | | 55.10 | 78.50 |
| 0300 | L-type, incl. hex nut & washer, 3/4" diameter x 12" long | | 45 | .356 | | 1.59 | 13.55 | | 15.14 | 23 |
| 0310 | 18" long | | 40 | .400 | | 2.03 | 15.25 | | 17.28 | 25.50 |
| 0320 | 24" long | | 35 | .457 | | 2.48 | 17.40 | | 19.88 | 29.50 |
| 0330 | 30" long | | 30 | .533 | | 3.15 | 20.50 | | 23.65 | 35 |
| 0340 | 36" long | | 25 | .640 | | 3.60 | 24.50 | | 28.10 | 42 |
| 0350 | 1" diameter x 12" long | | 35 | .457 | | 2.76 | 17.40 | | 20.16 | 30 |
| 0360 | 18" long | | 30 | .533 | | 3.44 | 20.50 | | 23.94 | 35.50 |
| 0370 | 24" long | | 25 | .640 | | 4.25 | 24.50 | | 28.75 | 42.50 |
| 0380 | 30" long | | 23 | .696 | | 5 | 26.50 | | 31.50 | 47 |
| 0390 | 36" long | | 20 | .800 | | 5.75 | 30.50 | | 36.25 | 54 |
| 0400 | 42" long | | 18 | .889 | | 6.95 | 34 | | 40.95 | 60 |
| 0410 | 48" long | | 15 | 1.067 | | 7.80 | 40.50 | | 48.30 | 72 |
| 0420 | 1-1/4" diameter x 18" long | | 25 | .640 | | 6.20 | 24.50 | | 30.70 | 45 |
| 0430 | 24" long | | 22 | .727 | | 7.35 | 27.50 | | 34.85 | 51 |
| 0440 | 30" long | | 20 | .800 | | 8.50 | 30.50 | | 39 | 57 |
| 0450 | 36" long | | 18 | .889 | | 9.70 | 34 | | 43.70 | 63 |
| 0460 | 42" long | | 16 | 1 | | 10.95 | 38 | | 48.95 | 71.50 |
| 0470 | 48" long | | 14 | 1.143 | | 12.50 | 43.50 | | 56 | 82 |
| 0480 | 54" long | | 12 | 1.333 | | 14.70 | 51 | | 65.70 | 95 |
| 0490 | 60" long | | 10 | 1.600 | | 16.15 | 61 | | 77.15 | 113 |
| 0500 | 1-1/2" diameter x 18" long | | 22 | .727 | | 9.55 | 27.50 | | 37.05 | 53.50 |
| 0510 | 24" long | | 19 | .842 | | 11.10 | 32 | | 43.10 | 62.50 |
| 0520 | 30" long | | 17 | .941 | | 12.55 | 36 | | 48.55 | 70 |
| 0530 | 36" long | | 16 | 1 | | 14.45 | 38 | | 52.45 | 75.50 |
| 0540 | 42" long | | 15 | 1.067 | | 16.45 | 40.50 | | 56.95 | 81.50 |
| 0550 | 48" long | | 13 | 1.231 | | 18.50 | 47 | | 65.50 | 93.50 |
| 0560 | 54" long | | 11 | 1.455 | | 22.50 | 55.50 | | 78 | 112 |
| 0570 | 60" long | | 9 | 1.778 | | 24.50 | 67.50 | | 92 | 132 |
| 0580 | 1-3/4" diameter x 18" long | | 20 | .800 | | 14.40 | 30.50 | | 44.90 | 63.50 |
| 0590 | 24" long | | 18 | .889 | | 16.85 | 34 | | 50.85 | 71 |
| 0600 | 30" long | | 17 | .941 | | 19.65 | 36 | | 55.65 | 77.50 |
| 0610 | 36" long | | 16 | 1 | | 22.50 | 38 | | 60.50 | 84 |
| 0620 | 42" long | | 14 | 1.143 | | 25 | 43.50 | | 68.50 | 95.50 |
| 0630 | 48" long | | 12 | 1.333 | | 27.50 | 51 | | 78.50 | 110 |
| 0640 | 54" long | | 10 | 1.600 | | 34.50 | 61 | | 95.50 | 133 |
| 0650 | 60" long | | 8 | 2 | | 37 | 76 | | 113 | 160 |
| 0660 | 2" diameter x 24" long | | 17 | .941 | | 21.50 | 36 | | 57.50 | 79.50 |
| 0670 | 30" long | | 15 | 1.067 | | 24 | 40.50 | | 64.50 | 90 |
| 0680 | 36" long | | 13 | 1.231 | | 26.50 | 47 | | 73.50 | 103 |
| 0690 | 42" long | | 11 | 1.455 | | 29.50 | 55.50 | | 85 | 119 |
| 0700 | 48" long | | 10 | 1.600 | | 34 | 61 | | 95 | 133 |
| 0710 | 54" long | | 9 | 1.778 | | 40.50 | 67.50 | | 108 | 150 |

103

# 05 05 Common Work Results for Metals

## 05 05 23 – Metal Fastenings

### 05 05 23.05 Anchor Bolts

| | | Crew | Daily Output | Labor-Hours | Unit | Material | 2008 Bare Costs Labor | Equipment | Total | Total Incl O&P |
|---|---|---|---|---|---|---|---|---|---|---|
| 0720 | 60" long | 2 Carp | 8 | 2 | Ea. | 43.50 | 76 | | 119.50 | 167 |
| 0730 | 66" long | | 7 | 2.286 | | 47 | 87 | | 134 | 188 |
| 0740 | 72" long | ↓ | 6 | 2.667 | | 51 | 102 | | 153 | 215 |
| 0990 | For galvanized, add | | | | ↓ | 75% | | | | |

### 05 05 23.10 Bolts and Hex Nuts

| | | Crew | Daily Output | Labor-Hours | Unit | Material | 2008 Bare Costs Labor | Equipment | Total | Total Incl O&P |
|---|---|---|---|---|---|---|---|---|---|---|
| 0010 | **BOLTS & HEX NUTS**, Steel, A307 | | | | | | | | | |
| 0100 | 1/4" diameter, 1/2" long | 1 Sswk | 140 | .057 | Ea. | .08 | 2.46 | | 2.54 | 4.52 |
| 0200 | 1" long | | 140 | .057 | | .09 | 2.46 | | 2.55 | 4.53 |
| 0300 | 2" long | | 130 | .062 | | .12 | 2.65 | | 2.77 | 4.90 |
| 0400 | 3" long | | 130 | .062 | | .17 | 2.65 | | 2.82 | 4.96 |
| 0500 | 4" long | | 120 | .067 | | .19 | 2.87 | | 3.06 | 5.35 |
| 0600 | 3/8" diameter, 1" long | | 130 | .062 | | .12 | 2.65 | | 2.77 | 4.91 |
| 0700 | 2" long | | 130 | .062 | | .16 | 2.65 | | 2.81 | 4.94 |
| 0800 | 3" long | | 120 | .067 | | .21 | 2.87 | | 3.08 | 5.40 |
| 0900 | 4" long | | 120 | .067 | | .27 | 2.87 | | 3.14 | 5.45 |
| 1000 | 5" long | | 115 | .070 | | .33 | 2.99 | | 3.32 | 5.75 |
| 1100 | 1/2" diameter, 1-1/2" long | | 120 | .067 | | .24 | 2.87 | | 3.11 | 5.40 |
| 1200 | 2" long | | 120 | .067 | | .27 | 2.87 | | 3.14 | 5.45 |
| 1300 | 4" long | | 115 | .070 | | .42 | 2.99 | | 3.41 | 5.85 |
| 1400 | 6" long | | 110 | .073 | | .57 | 3.13 | | 3.70 | 6.30 |
| 1500 | 8" long | | 105 | .076 | | .75 | 3.28 | | 4.03 | 6.70 |
| 1600 | 5/8" diameter, 1-1/2" long | | 120 | .067 | | .49 | 2.87 | | 3.36 | 5.70 |
| 1700 | 2" long | | 120 | .067 | | .53 | 2.87 | | 3.40 | 5.75 |
| 1800 | 4" long | | 115 | .070 | | .74 | 2.99 | | 3.73 | 6.20 |
| 1900 | 6" long | | 110 | .073 | | .93 | 3.13 | | 4.06 | 6.65 |
| 2000 | 8" long | | 105 | .076 | | 1.35 | 3.28 | | 4.63 | 7.40 |
| 2100 | 10" long | | 100 | .080 | | 1.68 | 3.44 | | 5.12 | 8.05 |
| 2200 | 3/4" diameter, 2" long | | 120 | .067 | | .77 | 2.87 | | 3.64 | 6 |
| 2300 | 4" long | | 110 | .073 | | 1.07 | 3.13 | | 4.20 | 6.85 |
| 2400 | 6" long | | 105 | .076 | | 1.35 | 3.28 | | 4.63 | 7.40 |
| 2500 | 8" long | | 95 | .084 | | 2.01 | 3.62 | | 5.63 | 8.75 |
| 2600 | 10" long | | 85 | .094 | | 2.61 | 4.05 | | 6.66 | 10.20 |
| 2700 | 12" long | | 80 | .100 | | 3.05 | 4.30 | | 7.35 | 11.10 |
| 2800 | 1" diameter, 3" long | | 105 | .076 | | 1.99 | 3.28 | | 5.27 | 8.10 |
| 2900 | 6" long | | 90 | .089 | | 3.07 | 3.82 | | 6.89 | 10.30 |
| 3000 | 12" long | ↓ | 75 | .107 | | 5.80 | 4.59 | | 10.39 | 14.60 |
| 3100 | For galvanized, add | | | | | 75% | | | | |
| 3200 | For stainless, add | | | | ↓ | 350% | | | | |

### 05 05 23.15 Chemical Anchors

| | | Crew | Daily Output | Labor-Hours | Unit | Material | 2008 Bare Costs Labor | Equipment | Total | Total Incl O&P |
|---|---|---|---|---|---|---|---|---|---|---|
| 0010 | **CHEMICAL ANCHORS** | | | | | | | | | |
| 0020 | Includes layout & drilling | | | | | | | | | |
| 1430 | Chemical anchor, w/rod & epoxy cartridge, 3/4" diam. x 9-1/2" long | B-89A | 27 | .593 | Ea. | 14.40 | 20.50 | 4.05 | 38.95 | 52.50 |
| 1435 | 1" diameter x 11-3/4" long | | 24 | .667 | | 28 | 23 | 4.56 | 55.56 | 71.50 |
| 1440 | 1-1/4" diameter x 14" long | | 21 | .762 | | 53 | 26.50 | 5.20 | 84.70 | 105 |
| 1445 | 1-3/4" diameter x 15" long | | 20 | .800 | | 100 | 28 | 5.45 | 133.45 | 160 |
| 1450 | 18" long | | 17 | .941 | | 120 | 33 | 6.45 | 159.45 | 190 |
| 1455 | 2" diameter x 18" long | | 16 | 1 | | 153 | 35 | 6.85 | 194.85 | 230 |
| 1460 | 24" long | ↓ | 15 | 1.067 | ↓ | 200 | 37 | 7.30 | 244.30 | 286 |

### 05 05 23.20 Expansion Anchors

| | | Crew | Daily Output | Labor-Hours | Unit | Material | 2008 Bare Costs Labor | Equipment | Total | Total Incl O&P |
|---|---|---|---|---|---|---|---|---|---|---|
| 0010 | **EXPANSION ANCHORS** | | | | | | | | | |
| 0100 | Anchors for concrete, brick or stone, no layout and drilling | | | | | | | | | |
| 0200 | Expansion shields, zinc, 1/4" diameter, 1-5/16" long, single | 1 Carp | 90 | .089 | Ea. | 1.17 | 3.39 | | 4.56 | 6.55 |

| 05 05 23.20 Expansion Anchors | | Crew | Daily Output | Labor-Hours | Unit | Material | 2008 Bare Costs Labor | Equipment | Total | Total Incl O&P |
|---|---|---|---|---|---|---|---|---|---|---|
| 0300 | 1-3/8" long, double | 1 Carp | 85 | .094 | Ea. | 1.28 | 3.59 | | 4.87 | 7 |
| 0400 | 3/8" diameter, 1-1/2" long, single | | 85 | .094 | | 1.92 | 3.59 | | 5.51 | 7.70 |
| 0500 | 2" long, double | | 80 | .100 | | 2.37 | 3.81 | | 6.18 | 8.55 |
| 0600 | 1/2" diameter, 2-1/16" long, single | | 80 | .100 | | 3.18 | 3.81 | | 6.99 | 9.45 |
| 0700 | 2-1/2" long, double | | 75 | .107 | | 3.07 | 4.06 | | 7.13 | 9.75 |
| 0800 | 5/8" diameter, 2-5/8" long, single | | 75 | .107 | | 4.54 | 4.06 | | 8.60 | 11.35 |
| 0900 | 2-3/4" long, double | | 70 | .114 | | 4.54 | 4.35 | | 8.89 | 11.80 |
| 1000 | 3/4" diameter, 2-3/4" long, single | | 70 | .114 | | 6.75 | 4.35 | | 11.10 | 14.25 |
| 1100 | 3-15/16" long, double | | 65 | .123 | | 9 | 4.69 | | 13.69 | 17.20 |
| 1500 | Self drilling anchor, snap-off, for 1/4" diameter bolt | | 26 | .308 | | 1 | 11.70 | | 12.70 | 19.35 |
| 1600 | 3/8" diameter bolt | | 23 | .348 | | 1.46 | 13.25 | | 14.71 | 22 |
| 1700 | 1/2" diameter bolt | | 20 | .400 | | 2.24 | 15.25 | | 17.49 | 26 |
| 1800 | 5/8" diameter bolt | | 18 | .444 | | 3.74 | 16.95 | | 20.69 | 30.50 |
| 1900 | 3/4" diameter bolt | | 16 | .500 | | 6.30 | 19.05 | | 25.35 | 36.50 |
| 2100 | Hollow wall anchors for gypsum wall board, plaster or tile | | | | | | | | | |
| 2300 | 1/8" diameter, short | 1 Carp | 160 | .050 | Ea. | .32 | 1.91 | | 2.23 | 3.32 |
| 2400 | Long | | 150 | .053 | | .37 | 2.03 | | 2.40 | 3.57 |
| 2500 | 3/16" diameter, short | | 150 | .053 | | .67 | 2.03 | | 2.70 | 3.90 |
| 2600 | Long | | 140 | .057 | | .72 | 2.18 | | 2.90 | 4.18 |
| 2700 | 1/4" diameter, short | | 140 | .057 | | .82 | 2.18 | | 3 | 4.29 |
| 2800 | Long | | 130 | .062 | | .92 | 2.34 | | 3.26 | 4.66 |
| 3000 | Toggle bolts, bright steel, 1/8" diameter, 2" long | | 85 | .094 | | .30 | 3.59 | | 3.89 | 5.95 |
| 3100 | 4" long | | 80 | .100 | | .45 | 3.81 | | 4.26 | 6.45 |
| 3200 | 3/16" diameter, 3" long | | 80 | .100 | | .51 | 3.81 | | 4.32 | 6.50 |
| 3300 | 6" long | | 75 | .107 | | .70 | 4.06 | | 4.76 | 7.10 |
| 3400 | 1/4" diameter, 3" long | | 75 | .107 | | .57 | 4.06 | | 4.63 | 7 |
| 3500 | 6" long | | 70 | .114 | | .80 | 4.35 | | 5.15 | 7.70 |
| 3600 | 3/8" diameter, 3" long | | 70 | .114 | | 1.09 | 4.35 | | 5.44 | 8 |
| 3700 | 6" long | | 60 | .133 | | 1.91 | 5.10 | | 7.01 | 10 |
| 3800 | 1/2" diameter, 4" long | | 60 | .133 | | 2.83 | 5.10 | | 7.93 | 11 |
| 3900 | 6" long | | 50 | .160 | | 4.67 | 6.10 | | 10.77 | 14.65 |
| 4000 | Nailing anchors | | | | | | | | | |
| 4100 | Nylon nailing anchor, 1/4" diameter, 1" long | 1 Carp | 3.20 | 2.500 | C | 22 | 95.50 | | 117.50 | 172 |
| 4200 | 1-1/2" long | | 2.80 | 2.857 | | 28 | 109 | | 137 | 200 |
| 4300 | 2" long | | 2.40 | 3.333 | | 46.50 | 127 | | 173.50 | 250 |
| 4400 | Metal nailing anchor, 1/4" diameter, 1" long | | 3.20 | 2.500 | | 33.50 | 95.50 | | 129 | 185 |
| 4500 | 1-1/2" long | | 2.80 | 2.857 | | 45.50 | 109 | | 154.50 | 219 |
| 4600 | 2" long | | 2.40 | 3.333 | | 58 | 127 | | 185 | 262 |
| 5000 | Screw anchors for concrete, masonry, | | | | | | | | | |
| 5100 | stone & tile, no layout or drilling included | | | | | | | | | |
| 5200 | Jute fiber, #6, #8, & #10, 1" long | 1 Carp | 240 | .033 | Ea. | .28 | 1.27 | | 1.55 | 2.29 |
| 5300 | #12, 1-1/2" long | | 200 | .040 | | .40 | 1.52 | | 1.92 | 2.81 |
| 5400 | #14, 2" long | | 160 | .050 | | .63 | 1.91 | | 2.54 | 3.66 |
| 5500 | #16, 2" long | | 150 | .053 | | .66 | 2.03 | | 2.69 | 3.89 |
| 5600 | #20, 2" long | | 140 | .057 | | 1.06 | 2.18 | | 3.24 | 4.56 |
| 5700 | Lag screw shields, 1/4" diameter, short | | 90 | .089 | | .51 | 3.39 | | 3.90 | 5.80 |
| 5800 | Long | | 85 | .094 | | .59 | 3.59 | | 4.18 | 6.25 |
| 5900 | 3/8" diameter, short | | 85 | .094 | | .93 | 3.59 | | 4.52 | 6.60 |
| 6000 | Long | | 80 | .100 | | 1.09 | 3.81 | | 4.90 | 7.15 |
| 6100 | 1/2" diameter, short | | 80 | .100 | | 1.29 | 3.81 | | 5.10 | 7.35 |
| 6200 | Long | | 75 | .107 | | 1.61 | 4.06 | | 5.67 | 8.10 |
| 6300 | 3/4" diameter, short | | 70 | .114 | | 3.61 | 4.35 | | 7.96 | 10.75 |
| 6400 | Long | | 65 | .123 | | 4.37 | 4.69 | | 9.06 | 12.10 |

### 05 05 23.20 Expansion Anchors

| | | Crew | Daily Output | Labor-Hours | Unit | Material | 2008 Bare Costs Labor | Equipment | Total | Total Incl O&P |
|---|---|---|---|---|---|---|---|---|---|---|
| 6600 | Lead, #6 & #8, 3/4" long | 1 Carp | 260 | .031 | Ea. | .18 | 1.17 | | 1.35 | 2.02 |
| 6700 | #10 - #14, 1-1/2" long | | 200 | .040 | | .27 | 1.52 | | 1.79 | 2.67 |
| 6800 | #16 & #18, 1-1/2" long | | 160 | .050 | | .36 | 1.91 | | 2.27 | 3.37 |
| 6900 | Plastic, #6 & #8, 3/4" long | | 260 | .031 | | .12 | 1.17 | | 1.29 | 1.95 |
| 7000 | #8 & #10, 7/8" long | | 240 | .033 | | .05 | 1.27 | | 1.32 | 2.04 |
| 7100 | #10 & #12, 1" long | | 220 | .036 | | .17 | 1.39 | | 1.56 | 2.35 |
| 7200 | #14 & #16, 1-1/2" long | | 160 | .050 | | .09 | 1.91 | | 2 | 3.07 |
| 8000 | Wedge anchors, not including layout or drilling | | | | | | | | | |
| 8050 | Carbon steel, 1/4" diameter, 1-3/4" long | 1 Carp | 150 | .053 | Ea. | .51 | 2.03 | | 2.54 | 3.72 |
| 8100 | 3 1/4" long | | 140 | .057 | | .67 | 2.18 | | 2.85 | 4.13 |
| 8150 | 3/8" diameter, 2-1/4" long | | 145 | .055 | | .76 | 2.10 | | 2.86 | 4.11 |
| 8200 | 5" long | | 140 | .057 | | 1.34 | 2.18 | | 3.52 | 4.86 |
| 8250 | 1/2" diameter, 2-3/4" long | | 140 | .057 | | 1.17 | 2.18 | | 3.35 | 4.67 |
| 8300 | 7" long | | 125 | .064 | | 1.99 | 2.44 | | 4.43 | 6 |
| 8350 | 5/8" diameter, 3-1/2" long | | 130 | .062 | | 2.31 | 2.34 | | 4.65 | 6.20 |
| 8400 | 8-1/2" long | | 115 | .070 | | 4.91 | 2.65 | | 7.56 | 9.55 |
| 8450 | 3/4" diameter, 4-1/4" long | | 115 | .070 | | 2.78 | 2.65 | | 5.43 | 7.20 |
| 8500 | 10" long | | 95 | .084 | | 6.30 | 3.21 | | 9.51 | 11.95 |
| 8550 | 1" diameter, 6" long | | 100 | .080 | | 9.30 | 3.05 | | 12.35 | 15 |
| 8575 | 9" long | | 85 | .094 | | 12.10 | 3.59 | | 15.69 | 18.90 |
| 8600 | 12" long | | 75 | .107 | | 13.05 | 4.06 | | 17.11 | 20.50 |
| 8650 | 1-1/4" diameter, 9" long | | 70 | .114 | | 16.95 | 4.35 | | 21.30 | 25.50 |
| 8700 | 12" long | | 60 | .133 | | 21.50 | 5.10 | | 26.60 | 32 |
| 8750 | For type 303 stainless steel, add | | | | | 350% | | | | |
| 8800 | For type 316 stainless steel, add | | | | | 450% | | | | |
| 8950 | Self-drilling concrete screw, hex washer head, 3/16" dia x 1-3/4" long | 1 Carp | 300 | .027 | Ea. | .39 | 1.02 | | 1.41 | 2.01 |
| 8960 | 2-1/4" long | | 250 | .032 | | .59 | 1.22 | | 1.81 | 2.55 |
| 8970 | Phillips flat head, 3/16" dia x 1-3/4" long | | 300 | .027 | | .40 | 1.02 | | 1.42 | 2.02 |
| 8980 | 2-1/4" long | | 250 | .032 | | .59 | 1.22 | | 1.81 | 2.55 |

### 05 05 23.25 High Strength Bolts

| | | Crew | Daily Output | Labor-Hours | Unit | Material | 2008 Bare Costs Labor | Equipment | Total | Total Incl O&P |
|---|---|---|---|---|---|---|---|---|---|---|
| 0010 | **HIGH STRENGTH BOLTS** R050523-10 | | | | | | | | | |
| 0020 | A325 Type 1, structural steel, bolt-nut-washer set | | | | | | | | | |
| 0100 | 1/2" diameter x 1-1/2" long | 1 Sswk | 130 | .062 | Ea. | .39 | 2.65 | | 3.04 | 5.20 |
| 0120 | 2" long | | 125 | .064 | | .41 | 2.75 | | 3.16 | 5.40 |
| 0150 | 3" long | | 120 | .067 | | .53 | 2.87 | | 3.40 | 5.75 |
| 0170 | 5/8" diameter x 1-1/2" long | | 125 | .064 | | .61 | 2.75 | | 3.36 | 5.65 |
| 0180 | 2" long | | 120 | .067 | | .64 | 2.87 | | 3.51 | 5.85 |
| 0190 | 3" long | | 115 | .070 | | .75 | 2.99 | | 3.74 | 6.20 |
| 0200 | 3/4" diameter x 2" long | | 120 | .067 | | .91 | 2.87 | | 3.78 | 6.15 |
| 0220 | 3" long | | 115 | .070 | | 1.04 | 2.99 | | 4.03 | 6.55 |
| 0250 | 4" long | | 110 | .073 | | 1.22 | 3.13 | | 4.35 | 7 |
| 0300 | 6" long | | 105 | .076 | | 1.52 | 3.28 | | 4.80 | 7.55 |
| 0350 | 8" long | | 95 | .084 | | 2.77 | 3.62 | | 6.39 | 9.60 |
| 0360 | 7/8" diameter x 2" long | | 115 | .070 | | 1.33 | 2.99 | | 4.32 | 6.85 |
| 0365 | 3" long | | 110 | .073 | | 1.52 | 3.13 | | 4.65 | 7.30 |
| 0370 | 4" long | | 105 | .076 | | 1.77 | 3.28 | | 5.05 | 7.85 |
| 0380 | 6" long | | 100 | .080 | | 2.17 | 3.44 | | 5.61 | 8.60 |
| 0390 | 8" long | | 90 | .089 | | 3.27 | 3.82 | | 7.09 | 10.50 |
| 0400 | 1" diameter x 2" long | | 105 | .076 | | 1.85 | 3.28 | | 5.13 | 7.95 |
| 0420 | 3" long | | 100 | .080 | | 2.02 | 3.44 | | 5.46 | 8.45 |
| 0450 | 4" long | | 95 | .084 | | 2.23 | 3.62 | | 5.85 | 9 |
| 0500 | 6" long | | 90 | .089 | | 2.81 | 3.82 | | 6.63 | 10 |

# 05 05 Common Work Results for Metals

## 05 05 23 – Metal Fastenings

### 05 05 23.25 High Strength Bolts

| | Crew | Daily Output | Labor-Hours | Unit | Material | 2008 Bare Costs Labor | Equipment | Total | Total Incl O&P |
|---|---|---|---|---|---|---|---|---|---|
| 0550 | 8" long | 1 Sswk | 85 | .094 | Ea. | 4.52 | 4.05 | | 8.57 | 12.30 |
| 0600 | 1-1/4" diameter x 3" long | | 85 | .094 | | 4.20 | 4.05 | | 8.25 | 11.90 |
| 0650 | 4" long | | 80 | .100 | | 1.90 | 4.30 | | 6.20 | 9.85 |
| 0700 | 6" long | | 75 | .107 | | 5.45 | 4.59 | | 10.04 | 14.25 |
| 0750 | 8" long | | 70 | .114 | | 6.65 | 4.91 | | 11.56 | 16.20 |
| 1020 | A490, bolt-nut-washer set | | | | | | | | | |
| 1170 | 5/8" diameter x 1-1/2" long | 1 Sswk | 125 | .064 | Ea. | .88 | 2.75 | | 3.63 | 5.95 |
| 1180 | 2" long | | 120 | .067 | | 1 | 2.87 | | 3.87 | 6.25 |
| 1190 | 3" long | | 115 | .070 | | 1.17 | 2.99 | | 4.16 | 6.70 |
| 1200 | 3/4" diameter x 2" long | | 120 | .067 | | 1.15 | 2.87 | | 4.02 | 6.40 |
| 1220 | 3" long | | 115 | .070 | | 1.31 | 2.99 | | 4.30 | 6.85 |
| 1250 | 4" long | | 110 | .073 | | 1.48 | 3.13 | | 4.61 | 7.30 |
| 1300 | 6" long | | 105 | .076 | | 2.04 | 3.28 | | 5.32 | 8.15 |
| 1350 | 8" long | | 95 | .084 | | 3.27 | 3.62 | | 6.89 | 10.15 |
| 1360 | 7/8" diameter x 2" long | | 115 | .070 | | 1.58 | 2.99 | | 4.57 | 7.15 |
| 1365 | 3" long | | 110 | .073 | | 1.79 | 3.13 | | 4.92 | 7.60 |
| 1370 | 4" long | | 105 | .076 | | 2.12 | 3.28 | | 5.40 | 8.25 |
| 1380 | 6" long | | 100 | .080 | | 2.82 | 3.44 | | 6.26 | 9.30 |
| 1390 | 8" long | | 90 | .089 | | 3.91 | 3.82 | | 7.73 | 11.20 |
| 1400 | 1" diameter x 2" long | | 105 | .076 | | 2.13 | 3.28 | | 5.41 | 8.25 |
| 1420 | 3" long | | 100 | .080 | | 2.44 | 3.44 | | 5.88 | 8.90 |
| 1450 | 4" long | | 95 | .084 | | 2.71 | 3.62 | | 6.33 | 9.55 |
| 1500 | 6" long | | 90 | .089 | | 3.41 | 3.82 | | 7.23 | 10.65 |
| 1550 | 8" long | | 85 | .094 | | 5.05 | 4.05 | | 9.10 | 12.85 |
| 1600 | 1-1/4" diameter x 3" long | | 85 | .094 | | 4.90 | 4.05 | | 8.95 | 12.70 |
| 1650 | 4" long | | 80 | .100 | | 5.45 | 4.30 | | 9.75 | 13.70 |
| 1700 | 6" long | | 75 | .107 | | 6.95 | 4.59 | | 11.54 | 15.90 |
| 1750 | 8" long | | 70 | .114 | | 8.65 | 4.91 | | 13.56 | 18.40 |

### 05 05 23.30 Lag Screws

| | Crew | Daily Output | Labor-Hours | Unit | Material | 2008 Bare Costs Labor | Equipment | Total | Total Incl O&P |
|---|---|---|---|---|---|---|---|---|---|
| 0010 | **LAG SCREWS** | | | | | | | | | |
| 0020 | Steel, 1/4" diameter, 2" long | 1 Carp | 200 | .040 | Ea. | .10 | 1.52 | | 1.62 | 2.48 |
| 0100 | 3/8" diameter, 3" long | | 150 | .053 | | .28 | 2.03 | | 2.31 | 3.47 |
| 0200 | 1/2" diameter, 3" long | | 130 | .062 | | .46 | 2.34 | | 2.80 | 4.16 |
| 0300 | 5/8" diameter, 3" long | | 120 | .067 | | .91 | 2.54 | | 3.45 | 4.95 |

### 05 05 23.35 Machine Screws

| | Crew | Daily Output | Labor-Hours | Unit | Material | 2008 Bare Costs Labor | Equipment | Total | Total Incl O&P |
|---|---|---|---|---|---|---|---|---|---|
| 0010 | **MACHINE SCREWS** | | | | | | | | | |
| 0020 | Steel, round head, #8 x 1" long | 1 Carp | 4.80 | 1.667 | C | 2.77 | 63.50 | | 66.27 | 102 |
| 0110 | #8 x 2" long | | 2.40 | 3.333 | | 6 | 127 | | 133 | 205 |
| 0200 | #10 x 1" long | | 4 | 2 | | 3.94 | 76 | | 79.94 | 123 |
| 0300 | #10 x 2" long | | 2 | 4 | | 7.35 | 152 | | 159.35 | 245 |

### 05 05 23.40 Machinery Anchors

| | Crew | Daily Output | Labor-Hours | Unit | Material | 2008 Bare Costs Labor | Equipment | Total | Total Incl O&P |
|---|---|---|---|---|---|---|---|---|---|
| 0010 | **MACHINERY ANCHORS**, heavy duty, incl. sleeve, floating base nut, | | | | | | | | | |
| 0020 | lower stud & coupling nut, fiber plug, connecting stud, washer & nut. | | | | | | | | | |
| 0030 | For flush mounted embedment in poured concrete heavy equip. pads. | | | | | | | | | |
| 0200 | Stud & bolt, 1/2" diameter | E-16 | 40 | .400 | Ea. | 64 | 17.60 | 3.30 | 84.90 | 106 |
| 0300 | 5/8" diameter | | 35 | .457 | | 71 | 20 | 3.78 | 94.78 | 119 |
| 0500 | 3/4" diameter | | 30 | .533 | | 81.50 | 23.50 | 4.41 | 109.41 | 137 |
| 0600 | 7/8" diameter | | 25 | .640 | | 89 | 28 | 5.30 | 122.30 | 155 |
| 0800 | 1" diameter | | 20 | .800 | | 93.50 | 35 | 6.60 | 135.10 | 174 |
| 0900 | 1-1/4" diameter | | 15 | 1.067 | | 125 | 47 | 8.80 | 180.80 | 231 |

### 05 05 23.50 Powder Actuated Tools and Fasteners

| | | | | | | | | | |
|---|---|---|---|---|---|---|---|---|---|
| 0010 | **POWDER ACTUATED TOOLS & FASTENERS** | | | | | | | | | |

# 05 05 Common Work Results for Metals

## 05 05 23 – Metal Fastenings

### 05 05 23.50 Powder Actuated Tools and Fasteners

| | | Crew | Daily Output | Labor-Hours | Unit | Material | 2008 Bare Costs Labor | Equipment | Total | Total Incl O&P |
|---|---|---|---|---|---|---|---|---|---|---|
| 0020 | Stud driver, .22 caliber, buy, minimum | | | | Ea. | 375 | | | 375 | 410 |
| 0100 | Maximum | | | | " | 600 | | | 600 | 660 |
| 0300 | Powder charges for above, low velocity | | | | C | 19.20 | | | 19.20 | 21 |
| 0400 | Standard velocity | | | | | 27.50 | | | 27.50 | 30 |
| 0600 | Drive pins & studs, 1/4" & 3/8" diam., to 3" long, minimum | 1 Carp | 4.80 | 1.667 | | 14.40 | 63.50 | | 77.90 | 115 |
| 0700 | Maximum | " | 4 | 2 | | 56 | 76 | | 132 | 181 |
| 0800 | Pneumatic stud driver for 1/8" diameter studs | | | | Ea. | 2,600 | | | 2,600 | 2,850 |
| 0900 | Drive pins for above, 1/2" to 3/4" long | 1 Carp | 1 | 8 | M | 595 | 305 | | 900 | 1,125 |

### 05 05 23.55 Rivets

| | | Crew | Daily Output | Labor-Hours | Unit | Material | 2008 Bare Costs Labor | Equipment | Total | Total Incl O&P |
|---|---|---|---|---|---|---|---|---|---|---|
| 0010 | **RIVETS** | | | | | | | | | |
| 0100 | Aluminum rivet & mandrel, 1/2" grip length x 1/8" diameter | 1 Carp | 4.80 | 1.667 | C | 5.80 | 63.50 | | 69.30 | 105 |
| 0200 | 3/16" diameter | | 4 | 2 | | 8.90 | 76 | | 84.90 | 129 |
| 0300 | Aluminum rivet, steel mandrel, 1/8" diameter | | 4.80 | 1.667 | | 8.85 | 63.50 | | 72.35 | 109 |
| 0400 | 3/16" diameter | | 4 | 2 | | 8.10 | 76 | | 84.10 | 128 |
| 0500 | Copper rivet, steel mandrel, 1/8" diameter | | 4.80 | 1.667 | | 9.95 | 63.50 | | 73.45 | 110 |
| 0600 | Monel rivet, steel mandrel, 1/8" diameter | | 4.80 | 1.667 | | 28.50 | 63.50 | | 92 | 131 |
| 0700 | 3/16" diameter | | 4 | 2 | | 82.50 | 76 | | 158.50 | 210 |
| 0800 | Stainless rivet & mandrel, 1/8" diameter | | 4.80 | 1.667 | | 15.10 | 63.50 | | 78.60 | 116 |
| 0900 | 3/16" diameter | | 4 | 2 | | 28.50 | 76 | | 104.50 | 150 |
| 1000 | Stainless rivet, steel mandrel, 1/8" diameter | | 4.80 | 1.667 | | 11.75 | 63.50 | | 75.25 | 112 |
| 1100 | 3/16" diameter | | 4 | 2 | | 21.50 | 76 | | 97.50 | 143 |
| 1200 | Steel rivet and mandrel, 1/8" diameter | | 4.80 | 1.667 | | 6.95 | 63.50 | | 70.45 | 107 |
| 1300 | 3/16" diameter | | 4 | 2 | Ea. | 10.45 | 76 | | 86.45 | 131 |
| 1400 | Hand riveting tool, minimum | | | | Ea. | 135 | | | 135 | 148 |
| 1500 | Maximum | | | | | 257 | | | 257 | 283 |
| 1600 | Power riveting tool, minimum | | | | | 970 | | | 970 | 1,075 |
| 1700 | Maximum | | | | | 2,450 | | | 2,450 | 2,700 |

### 05 05 23.80 Vibration and Bearing Pads

| | | Crew | Daily Output | Labor-Hours | Unit | Material | 2008 Bare Costs Labor | Equipment | Total | Total Incl O&P |
|---|---|---|---|---|---|---|---|---|---|---|
| 0010 | **VIBRATION & BEARING PADS** | | | | | | | | | |
| 0300 | Laminated synthetic rubber impregnated cotton duck, 1/2" thick | 2 Sswk | 24 | .667 | S.F. | 68 | 28.50 | | 96.50 | 127 |
| 0400 | 1" thick | | 20 | .800 | | 137 | 34.50 | | 171.50 | 213 |
| 0600 | Neoprene bearing pads, 1/2" thick | | 24 | .667 | | 25.50 | 28.50 | | 54 | 80 |
| 0700 | 1" thick | | 20 | .800 | | 52.50 | 34.50 | | 87 | 120 |
| 0900 | Fabric reinforced neoprene, 5000 psi, 1/2" thick | | 24 | .667 | | 11.55 | 28.50 | | 40.05 | 64 |
| 1000 | 1" thick | | 20 | .800 | | 23 | 34.50 | | 57.50 | 87.50 |
| 1200 | Felt surfaced vinyl pads, cork and sisal, 5/8" thick | | 24 | .667 | | 29.50 | 28.50 | | 58 | 84 |
| 1300 | 1" thick | | 20 | .800 | | 54.50 | 34.50 | | 89 | 122 |
| 1500 | Teflon bonded to 10 ga. carbon steel, 1/32" layer | | 24 | .667 | | 51 | 28.50 | | 79.50 | 108 |
| 1600 | 3/32" layer | | 24 | .667 | | 77 | 28.50 | | 105.50 | 136 |
| 1800 | Bonded to 10 ga. stainless steel, 1/32" layer | | 24 | .667 | | 91 | 28.50 | | 119.50 | 152 |
| 1900 | 3/32" layer | | 24 | .667 | | 118 | 28.50 | | 146.50 | 182 |
| 2100 | Circular machine leveling pad & stud | | | | Kip | 7.45 | | | 7.45 | 8.20 |

### 05 05 23.85 Weld Shear Connectors

| | | Crew | Daily Output | Labor-Hours | Unit | Material | 2008 Bare Costs Labor | Equipment | Total | Total Incl O&P |
|---|---|---|---|---|---|---|---|---|---|---|
| 0010 | **WELD SHEAR CONNECTORS** | | | | | | | | | |
| 0020 | 3/4" diameter, 3-3/16" long | E-10 | 960 | .017 | Ea. | .46 | .73 | .37 | 1.56 | 2.23 |
| 0030 | 3-3/8" long | | 950 | .017 | | .48 | .74 | .37 | 1.59 | 2.27 |
| 0200 | 3-7/8" long | | 945 | .017 | | .51 | .74 | .38 | 1.63 | 2.31 |
| 0300 | 4-3/16" long | | 935 | .017 | | .54 | .75 | .38 | 1.67 | 2.37 |
| 0500 | 4-7/8" long | | 930 | .017 | | .60 | .76 | .38 | 1.74 | 2.45 |
| 0600 | 5-3/16" long | | 920 | .017 | | .62 | .77 | .39 | 1.78 | 2.50 |
| 0800 | 5-3/8" long | | 910 | .018 | | .63 | .77 | .39 | 1.79 | 2.52 |
| 0900 | 6-3/16" long | | 905 | .018 | | .69 | .78 | .39 | 1.86 | 2.59 |

# 05 05 Common Work Results for Metals

## 05 05 23 – Metal Fastenings

| | 05 05 23.85 Weld Shear Connectors | Crew | Daily Output | Labor-Hours | Unit | Material | 2008 Bare Costs Labor | Equipment | Total | Total Incl O&P |
|---|---|---|---|---|---|---|---|---|---|---|
| 1000 | 7-3/16" long | E-10 | 895 | .018 | Ea. | .86 | .79 | .40 | 2.05 | 2.81 |
| 1100 | 8-3/16" long | | 890 | .018 | | .94 | .79 | .40 | 2.13 | 2.90 |
| 1500 | 7/8" diameter, 3-11/16" long | | 920 | .017 | | .73 | .77 | .39 | 1.89 | 2.62 |
| 1600 | 4-3/16" long | | 910 | .018 | | .78 | .77 | .39 | 1.94 | 2.69 |
| 1700 | 5-3/16" long | | 905 | .018 | | .89 | .78 | .39 | 2.06 | 2.81 |
| 1800 | 6-3/16" long | | 895 | .018 | | 1 | .79 | .40 | 2.19 | 2.96 |
| 1900 | 7-3/16" long | | 890 | .018 | | 1.11 | .79 | .40 | 2.30 | 3.09 |
| 2000 | 8-3/16" long | ↓ | 880 | .018 | ↓ | 1.21 | .80 | .40 | 2.41 | 3.22 |

### 05 05 23.87 Weld Studs

| | | Crew | Daily Output | Labor-Hours | Unit | Material | 2008 Bare Costs Labor | Equipment | Total | Total Incl O&P |
|---|---|---|---|---|---|---|---|---|---|---|
| 0010 | **WELD STUDS** | | | | | | | | | |
| 0020 | 1/4" diameter, 2-11/16" long | E-10 | 1120 | .014 | Ea. | .29 | .63 | .32 | 1.24 | 1.80 |
| 0100 | 4-1/8" long | | 1080 | .015 | | .27 | .65 | .33 | 1.25 | 1.84 |
| 0200 | 3/8" diameter, 4-1/8" long | | 1080 | .015 | | .32 | .65 | .33 | 1.30 | 1.89 |
| 0300 | 6-1/8" long | | 1040 | .015 | | .42 | .68 | .34 | 1.44 | 2.06 |
| 0400 | 1/2" diameter, 2-1/8" long | | 1040 | .015 | | .30 | .68 | .34 | 1.32 | 1.93 |
| 0500 | 3-1/8" long | | 1025 | .016 | | .37 | .69 | .35 | 1.41 | 2.02 |
| 0600 | 4-1/8" long | | 1010 | .016 | | .43 | .70 | .35 | 1.48 | 2.12 |
| 0700 | 5-5/16" long | | 990 | .016 | | .53 | .71 | .36 | 1.60 | 2.26 |
| 0800 | 6-1/8" long | | 975 | .016 | | .57 | .72 | .37 | 1.66 | 2.33 |
| 0900 | 8-1/8" long | | 960 | .017 | | .81 | .73 | .37 | 1.91 | 2.62 |
| 1000 | 5/8" diameter, 2-11/16" long | | 1000 | .016 | | .52 | .70 | .36 | 1.58 | 2.23 |
| 1010 | 4-3/16" long | | 990 | .016 | | .64 | .71 | .36 | 1.71 | 2.39 |
| 1100 | 6-9/16" long | | 975 | .016 | | .84 | .72 | .37 | 1.93 | 2.62 |
| 1200 | 8-3/16" long | ↓ | 960 | .017 | ↓ | 1.13 | .73 | .37 | 2.23 | 2.97 |

### 05 05 23.90 Welding Rod

| | | Crew | Daily Output | Labor-Hours | Unit | Material | 2008 Bare Costs Labor | Equipment | Total | Total Incl O&P |
|---|---|---|---|---|---|---|---|---|---|---|
| 0010 | **WELDING ROD** | | | | | | | | | |
| 0020 | Steel, type 6011, 1/8" dia, less than 500# | | | | Lb. | 2.09 | | | 2.09 | 2.30 |
| 0100 | 500# to 2,000# | | | | | 1.88 | | | 1.88 | 2.07 |
| 0200 | 2,000# to 5,000# | | | | | 1.77 | | | 1.77 | 1.94 |
| 0300 | 5/32" diameter, less than 500# | | | | | 2.01 | | | 2.01 | 2.21 |
| 0310 | 500# to 2,000# | | | | | 1.81 | | | 1.81 | 1.99 |
| 0320 | 2,000# to 5,000# | | | | | 1.70 | | | 1.70 | 1.87 |
| 0400 | 3/16" dia, less than 500# | | | | | 2.02 | | | 2.02 | 2.22 |
| 0500 | 500# to 2,000# | | | | | 1.82 | | | 1.82 | 2 |
| 0600 | 2,000# to 5,000# | | | | | 1.71 | | | 1.71 | 1.88 |
| 0620 | Steel, type 6010, 1/8" dia, less than 500# | | | | | 2.30 | | | 2.30 | 2.53 |
| 0630 | 500# to 2,000# | | | | | 2.07 | | | 2.07 | 2.28 |
| 0640 | 2,000# to 5,000# | | | | | 1.95 | | | 1.95 | 2.14 |
| 0650 | Steel, type 7018 Low Hydrogen, 1/8" dia, less than 500# | | | | | 1.99 | | | 1.99 | 2.19 |
| 0660 | 500# to 2,000# | CN | | | | 1.79 | | | 1.79 | 1.97 |
| 0670 | 2,000# to 5,000# | | | | | 1.68 | | | 1.68 | 1.85 |
| 0700 | Steel, type 7024 Jet Weld, 1/8" dia, less than 500# | | | | | 2.09 | | | 2.09 | 2.30 |
| 0710 | 500# to 2,000# | | | | | 1.88 | | | 1.88 | 2.07 |
| 0720 | 2,000# to 5,000# | | | | | 1.77 | | | 1.77 | 1.94 |
| 1550 | Aluminum, type 4043 TIG, 1/8" dia, less than 10# | | | | | 7.20 | | | 7.20 | 7.90 |
| 1560 | 10# to 60# | | | | | 6.50 | | | 6.50 | 7.15 |
| 1570 | Over 60# | | | | | 6.10 | | | 6.10 | 6.70 |
| 1600 | Aluminum, type 5356 TIG, 1/8" dia, less than 10# | | | | | 8 | | | 8 | 8.80 |
| 1610 | 10# to 60# | | | | | 7.20 | | | 7.20 | 7.95 |
| 1620 | Over 60# | | | | | 6.80 | | | 6.80 | 7.45 |
| 1900 | Cast iron, type 8 Nickel, 1/8" dia, less than 500# | | | | | 24.50 | | | 24.50 | 27 |
| 1910 | 500# to 1,000# | | | | ↓ | 22.50 | | | 22.50 | 24.50 |

# 05 05 Common Work Results for Metals

## 05 05 23 – Metal Fastenings

| 05 05 23.90 Welding Rod | Crew | Daily Output | Labor-Hours | Unit | Material | 2008 Bare Costs Labor | Equipment | Total | Total Incl O&P |
|---|---|---|---|---|---|---|---|---|---|
| 1920 | Over 1,000# | | | | Lb. | 21 | | | 21 | 23 |
| 2000 | Stainless steel, type 316/316L, 1/8" dia, less than 500# | | | | | 11.40 | | | 11.40 | 12.50 |
| 2100 | 500# to 1000# | | | | | 10.25 | | | 10.25 | 11.30 |
| 2220 | Over 1000# | | | | | 9.65 | | | 9.65 | 10.60 |

# 05 12 Structural Steel Framing

## 05 12 23 – Structural Steel for Buildings

### 05 12 23.05 Canopy Framing

| | | Crew | Daily Output | Labor-Hours | Unit | Material | Labor | Equipment | Total | Total Incl O&P |
|---|---|---|---|---|---|---|---|---|---|---|
| 0010 | **CANOPY FRAMING** | | | | | | | | | |
| 0020 | 6" and 8" members, shop fabricated | E-4 | 3000 | .011 | Lb. | 1.32 | .46 | .04 | 1.82 | 2.34 |

### 05 12 23.10 Ceiling Supports

| | | Crew | Daily Output | Labor-Hours | Unit | Material | Labor | Equipment | Total | Total Incl O&P |
|---|---|---|---|---|---|---|---|---|---|---|
| 0010 | **CEILING SUPPORTS** | | | | | | | | | |
| 1000 | Entrance door/folding partition supports, shop fabricated | E-4 | 60 | .533 | L.F. | 22 | 23 | 2.20 | 47.20 | 68.50 |
| 1100 | Linear accelerator door supports | | 14 | 2.286 | | 100 | 99.50 | 9.45 | 208.95 | 299 |
| 1200 | Lintels or shelf angles, hung, exterior hot dipped galv. | | 267 | .120 | | 15 | 5.20 | .50 | 20.70 | 26.50 |
| 1250 | Two coats primer paint instead of galv. | | 267 | .120 | | 13 | 5.20 | .50 | 18.70 | 24 |
| 1400 | Monitor support, ceiling hung, expansion bolted | | 4 | 8 | Ea. | 350 | 350 | 33 | 733 | 1,050 |
| 1450 | Hung from pre-set inserts | | 6 | 5.333 | | 375 | 232 | 22 | 629 | 860 |
| 1600 | Motor supports for overhead doors | | 4 | 8 | | 177 | 350 | 33 | 560 | 860 |
| 1700 | Partition support for heavy folding partitions, without pocket | | 24 | 1.333 | L.F. | 50 | 58 | 5.50 | 113.50 | 166 |
| 1750 | Supports at pocket only | | 12 | 2.667 | | 100 | 116 | 11 | 227 | 330 |
| 2000 | Rolling grilles & fire door supports | | 34 | .941 | | 43 | 41 | 3.89 | 87.89 | 125 |
| 2100 | Spider-leg light supports, expansion bolted to ceiling slab | | 8 | 4 | Ea. | 143 | 174 | 16.50 | 333.50 | 490 |
| 2150 | Hung from pre-set inserts | | 12 | 2.667 | " | 154 | 116 | 11 | 281 | 390 |
| 2400 | Toilet partition support | | 36 | .889 | L.F. | 50 | 38.50 | 3.67 | 92.17 | 129 |
| 2500 | X-ray travel gantry support | | 12 | 2.667 | " | 172 | 116 | 11 | 299 | 410 |

### 05 12 23.15 Columns, Lightweight

| | | Crew | Daily Output | Labor-Hours | Unit | Material | Labor | Equipment | Total | Total Incl O&P |
|---|---|---|---|---|---|---|---|---|---|---|
| 0010 | **COLUMNS, LIGHTWEIGHT** | | | | | | | | | |
| 1000 | Lightweight units (lally), 3-1/2" diameter | E-2 | 780 | .072 | L.F. | 3.29 | 3.01 | 2.01 | 8.31 | 11.05 |
| 1050 | 4" diameter | " | 900 | .062 | " | 4.85 | 2.60 | 1.74 | 9.19 | 11.75 |
| 5800 | Adjustable jack post, 8' maximum height, 2-3/4" diameter | | | | Ea. | 26 | | | 26 | 29 |
| 5850 | 4" diameter | | | | " | 42 | | | 42 | 46 |

### 05 12 23.17 Columns, Structural

| | | Crew | Daily Output | Labor-Hours | Unit | Material | Labor | Equipment | Total | Total Incl O&P |
|---|---|---|---|---|---|---|---|---|---|---|
| 0010 | **COLUMNS, STRUCTURAL**    R051223-10 | | | | | | | | | |
| 0020 | Shop fab'd for 100-ton, 1-2 story project, bolted connections | | | | | | | | | |
| 0800 | Steel, concrete filled, extra strong pipe, 3-1/2" diameter | E-2 | 660 | .085 | L.F. | 36.50 | 3.55 | 2.37 | 42.42 | 49 |
| 0830 | 4" diameter | | 780 | .072 | | 40.50 | 3.01 | 2.01 | 45.52 | 52 |
| 0890 | 5" diameter | | 1020 | .055 | | 48 | 2.30 | 1.54 | 51.84 | 58.50 |
| 0930 | 6" diameter | | 1200 | .047 | | 64 | 1.95 | 1.31 | 67.26 | 75 |
| 0940 | 8" diameter | | 1100 | .051 | | 64 | 2.13 | 1.42 | 67.55 | 75.50 |
| 1100 | For galvanizing, add | | | | Lb. | .26 | | | .26 | .28 |
| 1300 | For web ties, angles, etc., add per added lb. | 1 Sswk | 945 | .008 | | 1.10 | .36 | | 1.46 | 1.87 |
| 1500 | Steel pipe, extra strong, no concrete, 3" to 5" diameter | E-2 | 16000 | .004 | | 1.10 | .15 | .10 | 1.35 | 1.57 |
| 1600 | 6" to 12" diameter | | 14000 | .004 | | 1.10 | .17 | .11 | 1.38 | 1.62 |
| 1700 | Steel pipe, extra strong, no concrete, 3" diameter x 12'-0" | | 60 | .933 | Ea. | 135 | 39 | 26 | 200 | 245 |
| 1750 | 4" diameter x 12'-0" | | 58 | .966 | | 198 | 40.50 | 27 | 265.50 | 320 |
| 1800 | 6" diameter x 12'-0" | | 54 | 1.037 | | 375 | 43.50 | 29 | 447.50 | 520 |
| 1850 | 8" diameter x 14'-0" | | 50 | 1.120 | | 670 | 47 | 31.50 | 748.50 | 850 |
| 1900 | 10" diameter x 16'-0" | | 48 | 1.167 | | 965 | 49 | 32.50 | 1,046.50 | 1,175 |
| 1950 | 12" diameter x 18'-0" | | 45 | 1.244 | | 1,300 | 52 | 35 | 1,387 | 1,550 |

# 05 12 Structural Steel Framing

## 05 12 23 – Structural Steel for Buildings

### 05 12 23.17 Columns, Structural

| | | Crew | Daily Output | Labor-Hours | Unit | Material | 2008 Bare Costs Labor | Equipment | Total | Total Incl O&P |
|---|---|---|---|---|---|---|---|---|---|---|
| 3300 | Structural tubing, square, A500GrB, 4" to 6" square, light section | E-2 | 11270 | .005 | Lb. | 1.10 | .21 | .14 | 1.45 | 1.72 |
| 3600 | Heavy section | ↓ | 32000 | .002 | " | 1.10 | .07 | .05 | 1.22 | 1.39 |
| 4000 | Concrete filled, add | | | | L.F. | 4.16 | | | 4.16 | 4.57 |
| 4500 | Structural tubing, sq, 4" x 4" x 1/4" x 12'-0" | E-2 | 58 | .966 | Ea. | 182 | 40.50 | 27 | 249.50 | 300 |
| 4550 | 6" x 6" x 1/4" x 12'-0" | | 54 | 1.037 | | 297 | 43.50 | 29 | 369.50 | 430 |
| 4600 | 8" x 8" x 3/8" x 14'-0" | | 50 | 1.120 | | 645 | 47 | 31.50 | 723.50 | 825 |
| 4650 | 10" x 10" x 1/2" x 16'-0" | | 48 | 1.167 | ↓ | 1,200 | 49 | 32.50 | 1,281.50 | 1,450 |
| 5100 | Structural tubing, rect, 5" to 6" wide, light section | | 8000 | .007 | Lb. | 1.10 | .29 | .20 | 1.59 | 1.94 |
| 5200 | Heavy section | | 12000 | .005 | | 1.10 | .20 | .13 | 1.43 | 1.69 |
| 5300 | 7" to 10" wide, light section | | 15000 | .004 | | 1.10 | .16 | .10 | 1.36 | 1.59 |
| 5400 | Heavy section | | 18000 | .003 | ↓ | 1.10 | .13 | .09 | 1.32 | 1.53 |
| 5500 | Structural tubing, rect, 5" x 3" x 1/4" x 12'-0" | | 58 | .966 | Ea. | 176 | 40.50 | 27 | 243.50 | 294 |
| 5550 | 6" x 4" x 5/16" x 12'-0" | | 54 | 1.037 | | 275 | 43.50 | 29 | 347.50 | 410 |
| 5600 | 8" x 4" x 3/8" x 12'-0" | | 54 | 1.037 | | 400 | 43.50 | 29 | 472.50 | 545 |
| 5650 | 10" x 6" x 3/8" x 14'-0" | | 50 | 1.120 | | 645 | 47 | 31.50 | 723.50 | 825 |
| 5700 | 12" x 8" x 1/2" x 16'-0" | | 48 | 1.167 | ↓ | 1,200 | 49 | 32.50 | 1,281.50 | 1,425 |
| 6800 | W Shape, A992 steel, 2 tier, W8 x 24 | | 1080 | .052 | L.F. | 29 | 2.17 | 1.45 | 32.62 | 37.50 |
| 6850 | W8 x 31 | | 1080 | .052 | | 37.50 | 2.17 | 1.45 | 41.12 | 47 |
| 6900 | W8 x 48 | | 1032 | .054 | | 58 | 2.27 | 1.52 | 61.79 | 69.50 |
| 6950 | W8 x 67 | | 984 | .057 | | 81 | 2.38 | 1.59 | 84.97 | 95 |
| 7000 | W10 x 45 | | 1032 | .054 | | 54.50 | 2.27 | 1.52 | 58.29 | 65.50 |
| 7050 | W10 x 68 | | 984 | .057 | | 82.50 | 2.38 | 1.59 | 86.47 | 96.50 |
| 7100 | W10 x 112 | | 960 | .058 | | 136 | 2.44 | 1.63 | 140.07 | 155 |
| 7150 | W12 x 50 | | 1032 | .054 | | 60.50 | 2.27 | 1.52 | 64.29 | 72 |
| 7200 | W12 x 87 | | 984 | .057 | | 105 | 2.38 | 1.59 | 108.97 | 122 |
| 7250 | W12 x 120 | | 960 | .058 | | 145 | 2.44 | 1.63 | 149.07 | 166 |
| 7300 | W12 x 190 | | 912 | .061 | | 230 | 2.57 | 1.72 | 234.29 | 259 |
| 7350 | W14 x 74 | | 984 | .057 | | 89.50 | 2.38 | 1.59 | 93.47 | 104 |
| 7400 | W14 x 120 | | 960 | .058 | | 145 | 2.44 | 1.63 | 149.07 | 166 |
| 7450 | W14 x 176 | ↓ | 912 | .061 | ↓ | 213 | 2.57 | 1.72 | 217.29 | 240 |
| 8090 | For projects 75 to 99 tons, add | | | | All | 10% | | | | |
| 8092 | 50 to 74 tons, add | | | | | 20% | | | | |
| 8094 | 25 to 49 tons, add | | | | | 30% | 10% | | | |
| 8096 | 10 to 24 tons, add | | | | | 50% | 25% | | | |
| 8098 | 2 to 9 tons, add | | | | | 75% | 50% | | | |
| 8099 | Less than 2 tons, add | | | | ↓ | 100% | 100% | | | |

### 05 12 23.20 Curb Edging

| | | Crew | Daily Output | Labor-Hours | Unit | Material | 2008 Bare Costs Labor | Equipment | Total | Total Incl O&P |
|---|---|---|---|---|---|---|---|---|---|---|
| 0010 | **CURB EDGING** | | | | | | | | | |
| 0020 | Steel angle w/anchors, shop fabricated, on forms, 1" x 1", 0.8#/L.F. | E-4 | 350 | .091 | L.F. | 1.84 | 3.98 | .38 | 6.20 | 9.60 |
| 0100 | 2" x 2" angles, 3.92#/L.F. | | 330 | .097 | | 5.95 | 4.22 | .40 | 10.57 | 14.60 |
| 0200 | 3" x 3" angles, 6.1#/L.F. | | 300 | .107 | | 9.40 | 4.64 | .44 | 14.48 | 19.20 |
| 0300 | 4" x 4" angles, 8.2#/L.F. | | 275 | .116 | | 12.15 | 5.05 | .48 | 17.68 | 23 |
| 1000 | 6" x 4" angles, 12.3#/L.F. | | 250 | .128 | | 17.60 | 5.55 | .53 | 23.68 | 30 |
| 1050 | Steel channels with anchors, on forms, 3" channel, 5#/L.F. | | 290 | .110 | | 7.40 | 4.80 | .46 | 12.66 | 17.25 |
| 1100 | 4" channel, 5.4#/L.F. | | 270 | .119 | | 7.90 | 5.15 | .49 | 13.54 | 18.55 |
| 1200 | 6" channel, 8.2#/L.F. | | 255 | .125 | | 12.15 | 5.45 | .52 | 18.12 | 24 |
| 1300 | 8" channel, 11.5#/L.F. | | 225 | .142 | | 16.50 | 6.20 | .59 | 23.29 | 30 |
| 1400 | 10" channel, 15.3#/L.F. | | 180 | .178 | | 21.50 | 7.75 | .73 | 29.98 | 38.50 |
| 1500 | 12" channel, 20.7#/L.F. | ↓ | 140 | .229 | | 28.50 | 9.95 | .94 | 39.39 | 50.50 |
| 2000 | For curved edging, add | | | | ↓ | 35% | 10% | | | |

### 05 12 23.40 Lightweight Framing

| | | | | | | | | | | | |
|---|---|---|---|---|---|---|---|---|---|---|---|
| 0010 | **LIGHTWEIGHT FRAMING** | R051223-35 | | | | | | | | | |

# 05 12 Structural Steel Framing

## 05 12 23 – Structural Steel for Buildings

### 05 12 23.40 Lightweight Framing

| | | Crew | Daily Output | Labor-Hours | Unit | Material | 2008 Bare Costs Labor | Equipment | Total | Total Incl O&P |
|---|---|---|---|---|---|---|---|---|---|---|
| 0200 | For load-bearing steel studs see Div. 05 41 13.30 | | | | | | | | | |
| 0400 | Angle framing, field fabricated, 4" and larger    R051223-45 | E-3 | 440 | .055 | Lb. | .64 | 2.38 | .30 | 3.32 | 5.35 |
| 0450 | Less than 4" angles | | 265 | .091 | " | .66 | 3.96 | .50 | 5.12 | 8.45 |
| 0460 | 1/2" x 1/2" x 1/8" | | 200 | .120 | L.F. | .13 | 5.25 | .66 | 6.04 | 10.35 |
| 0462 | 3/4" x 3/4" x 1/8" | | 160 | .150 | | .37 | 6.55 | .83 | 7.75 | 13.10 |
| 0464 | 1" x 1" x 1/8" | | 135 | .178 | | .53 | 7.75 | .98 | 9.26 | 15.65 |
| 0466 | 1-1/4" x 1-1/4" x 3/16" | | 115 | .209 | | .98 | 9.10 | 1.15 | 11.23 | 18.80 |
| 0468 | 1-1/2" x 1-1/2" x 3/16" | | 100 | .240 | | 1.19 | 10.50 | 1.32 | 13.01 | 21.50 |
| 0470 | 2" x 2" x 1/4" | | 90 | .267 | | 2.11 | 11.65 | 1.47 | 15.23 | 25 |
| 0472 | 2-1/2" x 2-1/2" x 1/4" | | 72 | .333 | | 2.71 | 14.55 | 1.84 | 19.10 | 31.50 |
| 0474 | 3" x 2" x 3/8" | | 65 | .369 | | 3.89 | 16.10 | 2.03 | 22.02 | 35.50 |
| 0476 | 3" x 3" x 3/8" | | 57 | .421 | ▼ | 4.75 | 18.40 | 2.32 | 25.47 | 41 |
| 0600 | Channel framing, field fabricated, 8" and larger | | 500 | .048 | Lb. | .66 | 2.10 | .26 | 3.02 | 4.80 |
| 0650 | Less than 8" channels | | 335 | .072 | " | .66 | 3.13 | .39 | 4.18 | 6.80 |
| 0660 | C2 x 1.78 | | 115 | .209 | L.F. | 1.17 | 9.10 | 1.15 | 11.42 | 19 |
| 0662 | C3 x 4.1 | | 80 | .300 | | 2.71 | 13.10 | 1.65 | 17.46 | 28.50 |
| 0664 | C4 x 5.4 | | 66 | .364 | | 3.56 | 15.90 | 2 | 21.46 | 34.50 |
| 0666 | C5 x 6.7 | | 57 | .421 | | 4.42 | 18.40 | 2.32 | 25.14 | 40.50 |
| 0668 | C6 x 8.2 | | 55 | .436 | | 5.25 | 19.05 | 2.40 | 26.70 | 43 |
| 0670 | C7 x 9.8 | | 40 | .600 | | 6.45 | 26 | 3.31 | 35.76 | 58 |
| 0672 | C8 x 11.5 | | 36 | .667 | | 7.60 | 29 | 3.67 | 40.27 | 65 |
| 0710 | Structural bar tee, field fabricated, 3/4" x 3/4" x 1/8" | | 160 | .150 | | .37 | 6.55 | .83 | 7.75 | 13.10 |
| 0712 | 1" x 1" x 1/8" | | 135 | .178 | | .53 | 7.75 | .98 | 9.26 | 15.65 |
| 0714 | 1-1/2" x 1-1/2" x 1/4" | | 114 | .211 | | 1.54 | 9.20 | 1.16 | 11.90 | 19.60 |
| 0716 | 2" x 2" x 1/4" | | 89 | .270 | | 2.11 | 11.80 | 1.49 | 15.40 | 25 |
| 0718 | 2-1/2" x 2-1/2" x 3/8" | | 72 | .333 | | 3.89 | 14.55 | 1.84 | 20.28 | 33 |
| 0720 | 3" x 3" x 3/8" | | 57 | .421 | | 4.75 | 18.40 | 2.32 | 25.47 | 41 |
| 0730 | Structural zee, field fabricated, 1-1/4" x 1-3/4" x 1-3/4" | | 114 | .211 | | .50 | 9.20 | 1.16 | 10.86 | 18.45 |
| 0732 | 2-11/16" x 3" x 2-11/16" | | 114 | .211 | | 1.17 | 9.20 | 1.16 | 11.53 | 19.15 |
| 0734 | 3-1/16" x 4" x 3-1/16" | | 133 | .180 | | 1.78 | 7.90 | .99 | 10.67 | 17.25 |
| 0736 | 3-1/4" x 5" x 3-1/4" | | 133 | .180 | | 2.42 | 7.90 | .99 | 11.31 | 17.95 |
| 0738 | 3-1/2" x 6" x 3-1/2" | | 160 | .150 | | 3.65 | 6.55 | .83 | 11.03 | 16.70 |
| 0740 | Junior beam, field fabricated, 3" | | 80 | .300 | | 3.76 | 13.10 | 1.65 | 18.51 | 29.50 |
| 0742 | 4" | | 72 | .333 | | 5.10 | 14.55 | 1.84 | 21.49 | 34 |
| 0744 | 5" | | 67 | .358 | | 6.60 | 15.65 | 1.97 | 24.22 | 37.50 |
| 0746 | 6" | | 62 | .387 | | 8.25 | 16.90 | 2.13 | 27.28 | 42 |
| 0748 | 7" | | 57 | .421 | | 10.10 | 18.40 | 2.32 | 30.82 | 46.50 |
| 0750 | 8" | ▼ | 53 | .453 | ▼ | 12.15 | 19.80 | 2.50 | 34.45 | 51.50 |
| 1000 | Continuous slotted channel framing system, shop fab, min | 2 Sswk | 2400 | .007 | Lb. | 3.41 | .29 | | 3.70 | 4.27 |
| 1200 | Maximum | " | 1600 | .010 | | 3.85 | .43 | | 4.28 | 5 |
| 1300 | Cross bracing, rods, shop fabricated, 3/4" diameter | E-3 | 700 | .034 | | 1.32 | 1.50 | .19 | 3.01 | 4.36 |
| 1310 | 7/8" diameter | | 850 | .028 | | 1.32 | 1.23 | .16 | 2.71 | 3.84 |
| 1320 | 1" diameter | | 1000 | .024 | | 1.32 | 1.05 | .13 | 2.50 | 3.49 |
| 1330 | Angle, 5" x 5" x 3/8" | | 2800 | .009 | | 1.32 | .37 | .05 | 1.74 | 2.18 |
| 1350 | Hanging lintels, shop fabricated, average | ▼ | 850 | .028 | | 1.32 | 1.23 | .16 | 2.71 | 3.84 |
| 1380 | Roof frames, shop fabricated, 3'-0" square, 5' span | E-2 | 4200 | .013 | | 1.32 | .56 | .37 | 2.25 | 2.82 |
| 1400 | Tie rod, not upset, 1-1/2" to 4" diameter, with turnbuckle | 2 Sswk | 800 | .020 | | 1.43 | .86 | | 2.29 | 3.12 |
| 1420 | No turnbuckle | | 700 | .023 | | 1.38 | .98 | | 2.36 | 3.28 |
| 1500 | Upset, 1-3/4" to 4" diameter, with turnbuckle | | 800 | .020 | | 1.43 | .86 | | 2.29 | 3.12 |
| 1520 | No turnbuckle | ▼ | 700 | .023 | ▼ | 1.38 | .98 | | 2.36 | 3.28 |

### 05 12 23.45 Lintels

| 0010 | **LINTELS** | | | | | | | | | |
|---|---|---|---|---|---|---|---|---|---|---|

## 05 12 23 – Structural Steel for Buildings

| 05 12 23.45 Lintels | | Crew | Daily Output | Labor-Hours | Unit | Material | 2008 Bare Costs Labor | Equipment | Total | Total Incl O&P |
|---|---|---|---|---|---|---|---|---|---|---|
| 0020 | Plain steel angles, shop fabricated, under 500 lb. | 1 Bric | 550 | .015 | Lb. | .85 | .57 | | 1.42 | 1.80 |
| 0100 | 500 to 1000 lb. **CN** | | 640 | .013 | | .83 | .49 | | 1.32 | 1.65 |
| 0200 | 1,000 to 2,000 lb. | | 640 | .013 | | .80 | .49 | | 1.29 | 1.62 |
| 0300 | 2,000 to 4,000 lb. | | 640 | .013 | | .78 | .49 | | 1.27 | 1.60 |
| 0500 | For built-up angles and plates, add to above | | | | | .28 | | | .28 | .30 |
| 0700 | For engineering, add to above | | | | | .11 | | | .11 | .12 |
| 0900 | For galvanizing, add to above, under 500 lb. | | | | | .34 | | | .34 | .38 |
| 0950 | 500 to 2,000 lb. | | | | | .31 | | | .31 | .34 |
| 1000 | Over 2,000 lb. | | | | | .26 | | | .26 | .28 |
| 2000 | Steel angles, 3-1/2" x 3", 1/4" thick, 2'-6" long | 1 Bric | 47 | .170 | Ea. | 11.90 | 6.65 | | 18.55 | 23 |
| 2100 | 4'-6" long | | 26 | .308 | | 21.50 | 12.05 | | 33.55 | 42 |
| 2600 | 4" x 3-1/2", 1/4" thick, 5'-0" long | | 21 | .381 | | 27.50 | 14.90 | | 42.40 | 52.50 |
| 2700 | 9'-0" long | | 12 | .667 | | 49 | 26 | | 75 | 93.50 |

| 05 12 23.60 Pipe Support Framing | | Crew | Daily Output | Labor-Hours | Unit | Material | 2008 Bare Costs Labor | Equipment | Total | Total Incl O&P |
|---|---|---|---|---|---|---|---|---|---|---|
| 0010 | **PIPE SUPPORT FRAMING** | | | | | | | | | |
| 0020 | Under 10#/L.F., shop fabricated | E-4 | 3900 | .008 | Lb. | 1.47 | .36 | .03 | 1.86 | 2.30 |
| 0200 | 10.1 to 15#/L.F. | | 4300 | .007 | | 1.45 | .32 | .03 | 1.80 | 2.21 |
| 0400 | 15.1 to 20#/L.F. | | 4800 | .007 | | 1.43 | .29 | .03 | 1.75 | 2.12 |
| 0600 | Over 20#/L.F. | | 5400 | .006 | | 1.41 | .26 | .02 | 1.69 | 2.05 |

| 05 12 23.65 Plates | | Crew | Daily Output | Labor-Hours | Unit | Material | 2008 Bare Costs Labor | Equipment | Total | Total Incl O&P |
|---|---|---|---|---|---|---|---|---|---|---|
| 0010 | **PLATES**           R051223-80 | | | | | | | | | |
| 0020 | For connections & stiffener plates, shop fabricated | | | | | | | | | |
| 0050 | 1/8" thick (5.1 Lb./S.F.) | | | | S.F. | 5.60 | | | 5.60 | 6.15 |
| 0100 | 1/4" thick (10.2 Lb./S.F.) | | | | | 11.20 | | | 11.20 | 12.35 |
| 0300 | 3/8" thick (15.3 Lb./S.F.) | | | | | 16.85 | | | 16.85 | 18.50 |
| 0400 | 1/2" thick (20.4 Lb./S.F.) | | | | | 22.50 | | | 22.50 | 24.50 |
| 0450 | 3/4" thick (30.6 Lb./S.F.) | | | | | 33.50 | | | 33.50 | 37 |
| 0500 | 1" thick (40.8 Lb.S.F.) | | | | | 45 | | | 45 | 49.50 |
| 2000 | Steel plate, warehouse prices, no shop fabrication | | | | | | | | | |
| 2100 | 1/4" thick (10.2 Lb./S.F.) | | | | S.F. | 4.26 | | | 4.26 | 4.69 |

| 05 12 23.70 Stressed Skin Steel Roof and Ceiling System | | Crew | Daily Output | Labor-Hours | Unit | Material | 2008 Bare Costs Labor | Equipment | Total | Total Incl O&P |
|---|---|---|---|---|---|---|---|---|---|---|
| 0010 | **STRESSED SKIN STEEL ROOF & CEILING SYSTEM** | | | | | | | | | |
| 0020 | Double panel flat roof, spans to 100' | E-2 | 1150 | .049 | S.F. | 8.80 | 2.04 | 1.36 | 12.20 | 14.70 |
| 0100 | Double panel convex roof, spans to 200' | | 960 | .058 | | 14.30 | 2.44 | 1.63 | 18.37 | 22 |
| 0200 | Double panel arched roof, spans to 300' | | 760 | .074 | | 22 | 3.08 | 2.06 | 27.14 | 31.50 |

| 05 12 23.75 Structural Steel Members | | Crew | Daily Output | Labor-Hours | Unit | Material | 2008 Bare Costs Labor | Equipment | Total | Total Incl O&P |
|---|---|---|---|---|---|---|---|---|---|---|
| 0010 | **STRUCTURAL STEEL MEMBERS**           R051223-10 | | | | | | | | | |
| 0020 | Shop fab'd for 100-ton, 1-2 story project, bolted connections | | | | | | | | | |
| 0100 | W 6 x 9 | E-2 | 600 | .093 | L.F. | 10.90 | 3.91 | 2.61 | 17.42 | 21.50 |
| 0120 | x 16 | | 600 | .093 | | 19.35 | 3.91 | 2.61 | 25.87 | 31 |
| 0140 | x 20 | | 600 | .093 | | 24 | 3.91 | 2.61 | 30.52 | 36 |
| 0300 | W 8 x 10 | | 600 | .093 | | 12.10 | 3.91 | 2.61 | 18.62 | 23 |
| 0320 | x 15 | | 600 | .093 | | 18.15 | 3.91 | 2.61 | 24.67 | 29.50 |
| 0350 | x 21 | | 600 | .093 | | 25.50 | 3.91 | 2.61 | 32.02 | 37.50 |
| 0360 | x 24 | | 550 | .102 | | 29 | 4.26 | 2.85 | 36.11 | 42.50 |
| 0370 | x 28 | | 550 | .102 | | 34 | 4.26 | 2.85 | 41.11 | 48 |
| 0500 | x 31 | | 550 | .102 | | 37.50 | 4.26 | 2.85 | 44.61 | 52 |
| 0520 | x 35 | | 550 | .102 | | 42.50 | 4.26 | 2.85 | 49.61 | 57 |
| 0540 | x 48 | | 550 | .102 | | 58 | 4.26 | 2.85 | 65.11 | 74.50 |
| 0600 | W 10 x 12 | | 600 | .093 | | 14.50 | 3.91 | 2.61 | 21.02 | 25.50 |
| 0620 | x 15 | | 600 | .093 | | 18.15 | 3.91 | 2.61 | 24.67 | 29.50 |
| 0700 | x 22 | | 600 | .093 | | 26.50 | 3.91 | 2.61 | 33.02 | 39 |

| 05 12 23.75 Structural Steel Members | | Crew | Daily Output | Labor-Hours | Unit | Material | 2008 Bare Costs Labor | Equipment | Total | Total Incl O&P |
|---|---|---|---|---|---|---|---|---|---|---|
| 0720 | x 26 | E-2 | 600 | .093 | L.F. | 31.50 | 3.91 | 2.61 | 38.02 | 44 |
| 0740 | x 33 | | 550 | .102 | | 40 | 4.26 | 2.85 | 47.11 | 54.50 |
| 0900 | x 49 | | 550 | .102 | | 59.50 | 4.26 | 2.85 | 66.61 | 75.50 |
| 1100 | W 12 x 14 | | 880 | .064 | | 16.95 | 2.66 | 1.78 | 21.39 | 25 |
| 1300 | x 22 | | 880 | .064 | | 26.50 | 2.66 | 1.78 | 30.94 | 36 |
| 1500 | x 26 | | 880 | .064 | | 31.50 | 2.66 | 1.78 | 35.94 | 41 |
| 1520 | x 35 | | 810 | .069 | | 42.50 | 2.89 | 1.93 | 47.32 | 53.50 |
| 1560 | x 50 | | 750 | .075 | | 60.50 | 3.13 | 2.09 | 65.72 | 74 |
| 1580 | x 58 | | 750 | .075 | | 70 | 3.13 | 2.09 | 75.22 | 84.50 |
| 1700 | x 72 | | 640 | .088 | | 87 | 3.66 | 2.45 | 93.11 | 105 |
| 1740 | x 87 | | 640 | .088 | | 105 | 3.66 | 2.45 | 111.11 | 125 |
| 1900 | W 14 x 26 | | 990 | .057 | | 31.50 | 2.37 | 1.58 | 35.45 | 40.50 |
| 2100 | x 30 | | 900 | .062 | | 36.50 | 2.60 | 1.74 | 40.84 | 46.50 |
| 2300 | x 34 | | 810 | .069 | | 41 | 2.89 | 1.93 | 45.82 | 52.50 |
| 2320 | x 43 | | 810 | .069 | | 52 | 2.89 | 1.93 | 56.82 | 64 |
| 2340 | x 53 | | 800 | .070 | | 64 | 2.93 | 1.96 | 68.89 | 77.50 |
| 2360 | x 74 | | 760 | .074 | | 89.50 | 3.08 | 2.06 | 94.64 | 106 |
| 2380 | x 90 | | 740 | .076 | | 109 | 3.17 | 2.12 | 114.29 | 128 |
| 2500 | x 120 | | 720 | .078 | | 145 | 3.26 | 2.18 | 150.44 | 168 |
| 2700 | W 16 x 26 | | 1000 | .056 | | 31.50 | 2.34 | 1.57 | 35.41 | 40.50 |
| 2900 | x 31 | | 900 | .062 | | 37.50 | 2.60 | 1.74 | 41.84 | 48 |
| 3100 | x 40 | | 800 | .070 | | 48.50 | 2.93 | 1.96 | 53.39 | 60 |
| 3120 | x 50 | | 800 | .070 | | 60.50 | 2.93 | 1.96 | 65.39 | 73.50 |
| 3140 | x 67 | | 760 | .074 | | 81 | 3.08 | 2.06 | 86.14 | 96.50 |
| 3300 | W 18 x 35 | E-5 | 960 | .083 | | 42.50 | 3.53 | 1.77 | 47.80 | 54.50 |
| 3500 | x 40 | | 960 | .083 | | 48.50 | 3.53 | 1.77 | 53.80 | 61 |
| 3520 | x 46 | | 960 | .083 | | 55.50 | 3.53 | 1.77 | 60.80 | 69 |
| 3700 | x 50 | | 912 | .088 | | 60.50 | 3.72 | 1.86 | 66.08 | 75 |
| 3900 | x 55 | | 912 | .088 | | 66.50 | 3.72 | 1.86 | 72.08 | 81.50 |
| 3920 | x 65 | | 900 | .089 | | 78.50 | 3.77 | 1.89 | 84.16 | 95 |
| 3940 | x 76 | | 900 | .089 | | 92 | 3.77 | 1.89 | 97.66 | 110 |
| 3960 | x 86 | | 900 | .089 | | 104 | 3.77 | 1.89 | 109.66 | 123 |
| 3980 | x 106 | | 900 | .089 | | 128 | 3.77 | 1.89 | 133.66 | 150 |
| 4100 | W 21 x 44 | | 1064 | .075 | | 53 | 3.19 | 1.60 | 57.79 | 66 |
| 4300 | x 50 | | 1064 | .075 | | 60.50 | 3.19 | 1.60 | 65.29 | 74 |
| 4500 | x 62 | | 1036 | .077 | | 75 | 3.27 | 1.64 | 79.91 | 90 |
| 4700 | x 68 | | 1036 | .077 | | 82.50 | 3.27 | 1.64 | 87.41 | 98 |
| 4720 | x 83 | | 1000 | .080 | | 100 | 3.39 | 1.70 | 105.09 | 118 |
| 4740 | x 93 | | 1000 | .080 | | 113 | 3.39 | 1.70 | 118.09 | 132 |
| 4760 | x 101 | | 1000 | .080 | | 122 | 3.39 | 1.70 | 127.09 | 142 |
| 4780 | x 122 | | 1000 | .080 | | 148 | 3.39 | 1.70 | 153.09 | 170 |
| 4900 | W 24 x 55 | | 1110 | .072 | | 66.50 | 3.06 | 1.53 | 71.09 | 80 |
| 5100 | x 62 | | 1110 | .072 | | 75 | 3.06 | 1.53 | 79.59 | 89.50 |
| 5300 | x 68 | | 1110 | .072 | | 82.50 | 3.06 | 1.53 | 87.09 | 97.50 |
| 5500 | x 76 | | 1110 | .072 | | 92 | 3.06 | 1.53 | 96.59 | 108 |
| 5700 | x 84 | | 1080 | .074 | | 102 | 3.14 | 1.57 | 106.71 | 119 |
| 5720 | x 94 | | 1080 | .074 | | 114 | 3.14 | 1.57 | 118.71 | 132 |
| 5740 | x 104 | | 1050 | .076 | | 126 | 3.23 | 1.62 | 130.85 | 145 |
| 5760 | x 117 | | 1050 | .076 | | 142 | 3.23 | 1.62 | 146.85 | 163 |
| 5780 | x 146 | | 1050 | .076 | | 177 | 3.23 | 1.62 | 181.85 | 201 |
| 5800 | W 27 x 84 | | 1190 | .067 | | 102 | 2.85 | 1.43 | 106.28 | 119 |
| 5900 | x 94 | | 1190 | .067 | | 114 | 2.85 | 1.43 | 118.28 | 132 |
| 5920 | x 114 | | 1150 | .070 | | 138 | 2.95 | 1.48 | 142.43 | 159 |

# 05 12 Structural Steel Framing

## 05 12 23 — Structural Steel for Buildings

### 05 12 23.75 Structural Steel Members

| | | Crew | Daily Output | Labor-Hours | Unit | Material | 2008 Bare Costs Labor | Equipment | Total | Total Incl O&P |
|---|---|---|---|---|---|---|---|---|---|---|
| 5940 | x 146 | E-5 | 1150 | .070 | L.F. | 177 | 2.95 | 1.48 | 181.43 | 201 |
| 5960 | x 161 | | 1150 | .070 | | 195 | 2.95 | 1.48 | 199.43 | 221 |
| 6100 | W 30 x 99 | | 1200 | .067 | | 120 | 2.83 | 1.42 | 124.25 | 139 |
| 6300 | x 108 | | 1200 | .067 | | 131 | 2.83 | 1.42 | 135.25 | 151 |
| 6500 | x 116 | | 1160 | .069 | | 140 | 2.93 | 1.46 | 144.39 | 161 |
| 6520 | x 132 | | 1160 | .069 | | 160 | 2.93 | 1.46 | 164.39 | 183 |
| 6540 | x 148 | | 1160 | .069 | | 179 | 2.93 | 1.46 | 183.39 | 204 |
| 6560 | x 173 | | 1120 | .071 | | 209 | 3.03 | 1.52 | 213.55 | 237 |
| 6580 | x 191 | | 1120 | .071 | | 231 | 3.03 | 1.52 | 235.55 | 261 |
| 6700 | W 33 x 118 | | 1176 | .068 | | 143 | 2.89 | 1.45 | 147.34 | 164 |
| 6900 | x 130 | | 1134 | .071 | | 157 | 2.99 | 1.50 | 161.49 | 180 |
| 7100 | x 141 | | 1134 | .071 | | 171 | 2.99 | 1.50 | 175.49 | 195 |
| 7120 | x 169 | | 1100 | .073 | | 204 | 3.08 | 1.54 | 208.62 | 232 |
| 7140 | x 201 | | 1100 | .073 | | 243 | 3.08 | 1.54 | 247.62 | 275 |
| 7300 | W 36 x 135 | | 1170 | .068 | | 163 | 2.90 | 1.45 | 167.35 | 187 |
| 7500 | x 150 | | 1170 | .068 | | 182 | 2.90 | 1.45 | 186.35 | 207 |
| 7600 | x 170 | | 1150 | .070 | | 206 | 2.95 | 1.48 | 210.43 | 233 |
| 7700 | x 194 | | 1125 | .071 | | 235 | 3.02 | 1.51 | 239.53 | 265 |
| 7900 | x 230 | | 1125 | .071 | | 278 | 3.02 | 1.51 | 282.53 | 310 |
| 7920 | x 260 | | 1035 | .077 | | 315 | 3.28 | 1.64 | 319.92 | 355 |
| 8100 | x 300 | ▼ | 1035 | .077 | | 365 | 3.28 | 1.64 | 369.92 | 410 |
| 8490 | For projects 75 to 99 tons, add | | | | | 10% | | | | |
| 8492 | 50 to 74 tons, add | | | | | 20% | | | | |
| 8494 | 25 to 49 tons, add | | | | | 30% | 10% | | | |
| 8496 | 10 to 24 tons, add | | | | | 50% | 25% | | | |
| 8498 | 2 to 9 tons, add | | | | | 75% | 50% | | | |
| 8499 | Less than 2 tons, add | | | | | 100% | 100% | | | |

### 05 12 23.77 Structural Steel Projects

| | | | Crew | Daily Output | Labor-Hours | Unit | Material | 2008 Bare Costs Labor | Equipment | Total | Total Incl O&P |
|---|---|---|---|---|---|---|---|---|---|---|---|
| 0010 | **STRUCTURAL STEEL PROJECTS** | R050516-30 | | | | | | | | | |
| 0020 | Shop fab'd for 100-ton, 1-2 story project, bolted connections | | | | | | | | | | |
| 0200 | Apartments, nursing homes, etc., 1 to 2 stories | R050523-10 | E-5 | 10.30 | 7.767 | Ton | 2,200 | 330 | 165 | 2,695 | 3,175 |
| 0300 | 3 to 6 stories | | " | 10.10 | 7.921 | | 2,250 | 335 | 168 | 2,753 | 3,250 |
| 0400 | 7 to 15 stories | R051223-10 | E-6 | 14.20 | 9.014 | | 2,300 | 380 | 132 | 2,812 | 3,350 |
| 0500 | Over 15 stories | | " | 13.90 | 9.209 | | 2,375 | 390 | 134 | 2,899 | 3,450 |
| 0700 | Offices, hospitals, etc., steel bearing, 1 to 2 stories  **CN** | R051223-20 | E-5 | 10.30 | 7.767 | | 2,200 | 330 | 165 | 2,695 | 3,175 |
| 0800 | 3 to 6 stories | | E-6 | 14.40 | 8.889 | | 2,250 | 375 | 130 | 2,755 | 3,275 |
| 0900 | 7 to 15 stories | R051223-25 | | 14.20 | 9.014 | | 2,300 | 380 | 132 | 2,812 | 3,350 |
| 1000 | Over 15 stories | | ▼ | 13.90 | 9.209 | | 2,375 | 390 | 134 | 2,899 | 3,450 |
| 1100 | For multi-story masonry wall bearing construction, add | R051223-30 | | | | | | 30% | | | |
| 1300 | Industrial bldgs., 1 story, beams & girders, steel bearing | | E-5 | 12.90 | 6.202 | | 2,200 | 263 | 132 | 2,595 | 3,025 |
| 1400 | Masonry bearing | | " | 10 | 8 | ▼ | 2,200 | 340 | 170 | 2,710 | 3,200 |
| 1500 | Industrial bldgs., 1 story, under 10 tons, | | | | | | | | | | |
| 1510 | steel from warehouse, trucked | | E-2 | 7.50 | 7.467 | Ton | 2,650 | 315 | 209 | 3,174 | 3,675 |
| 1600 | 1 story with roof trusses, steel bearing | | E-5 | 10.60 | 7.547 | | 2,600 | 320 | 160 | 3,080 | 3,575 |
| 1700 | Masonry bearing | | " | 8.30 | 9.639 | | 2,600 | 410 | 205 | 3,215 | 3,800 |
| 1900 | Monumental structures, banks, stores, etc., minimum | | E-6 | 13 | 9.846 | | 2,200 | 420 | 144 | 2,764 | 3,325 |
| 2000 | Maximum | | " | 9 | 14.222 | | 3,650 | 605 | 208 | 4,463 | 5,300 |
| 2200 | Churches, minimum | | E-5 | 11.60 | 6.897 | | 2,050 | 292 | 146 | 2,488 | 2,925 |
| 2300 | Maximum | | " | 5.20 | 15.385 | | 2,725 | 650 | 325 | 3,700 | 4,500 |
| 2800 | Power stations, fossil fuels, minimum | | E-6 | 11 | 11.636 | | 2,200 | 495 | 170 | 2,865 | 3,475 |
| 2900 | Maximum | | ▼ | 5.70 | 22.456 | | 3,300 | 955 | 330 | 4,585 | 5,650 |
| 2950 | Nuclear fuels, non-safety steel, minimum | | | 7 | 18.286 | ▼ | 2,200 | 775 | 267 | 3,242 | 4,075 |

# 05 12 Structural Steel Framing

## 05 12 23 – Structural Steel for Buildings

### 05 12 23.77 Structural Steel Projects

| | | Crew | Daily Output | Labor-Hours | Unit | Material | 2008 Bare Costs Labor | Equipment | Total | Total Incl O&P |
|---|---|---|---|---|---|---|---|---|---|---|
| 3000 | Maximum | E-6 | 5.50 | 23.273 | Ton | 3,300 | 985 | 340 | 4,625 | 5,725 |
| 3040 | Safety steel, minimum | | 2.50 | 51.200 | | 3,200 | 2,175 | 745 | 6,120 | 8,150 |
| 3070 | Maximum | ↓ | 1.50 | 85.333 | | 4,225 | 3,625 | 1,250 | 9,100 | 12,400 |
| 3100 | Roof trusses, minimum | E-5 | 13 | 6.154 | | 3,075 | 261 | 131 | 3,467 | 4,000 |
| 3200 | Maximum | | 8.30 | 9.639 | | 3,750 | 410 | 205 | 4,365 | 5,075 |
| 3210 | Schools, minimum | | 14.50 | 5.517 | | 2,200 | 234 | 117 | 2,551 | 2,975 |
| 3220 | Maximum | ↓ | 8.30 | 9.639 | | 3,200 | 410 | 205 | 3,815 | 4,475 |
| 3400 | Welded construction, simple commercial bldgs., 1 to 2 stories | E-7 | 7.60 | 10.526 | | 2,250 | 445 | 241 | 2,936 | 3,525 |
| 3500 | 7 to 15 stories | E-9 | 8.30 | 15.422 | ↓ | 2,600 | 655 | 268 | 3,523 | 4,300 |
| 3700 | Welded rigid frame, 1 story, minimum | E-7 | 15.80 | 5.063 | | 2,300 | 215 | 116 | 2,631 | 3,025 |
| 3800 | Maximum | " | 5.50 | 14.545 | | 2,975 | 615 | 335 | 3,925 | 4,725 |
| 3810 | Fabrication shop costs (included in project material cost, above) | | | | | | | | | |
| 3820 | Mini mill base price, A992 | | | | Ton | 725 | | | 725 | 800 |
| 3830 | Mill extra for delivery to shop | | | | | 220 | | | 220 | 242 |
| 3840 | Shop extra for shop drawings and detailing | | | | | 240 | | | 240 | 264 |
| 3850 | Shop fabricating and handling | | | | | 800 | | | 800 | 880 |
| 3860 | Shop sandblasting and primer coat of paint | | | | | 125 | | | 125 | 138 |
| 3870 | Shop delivery to the job site | | | | | 90 | | | 90 | 99 |
| 3880 | Total material cost, shop fabricated, primed, delivered | | | | ↓ | 2,200 | | | 2,200 | 2,425 |
| 3900 | High strength steel mill spec extras: A242, A441, | | | | | | | | | |
| 3950 | A529, A572 (42 ksi) and A992: same as A36 steel | | | | | | | | | |
| 4000 | Add to A992 price for A572 (50, 60, 65 ksi) | | | | Ton | 100 | | | 100 | 110 |
| 4100 | A588 Weathering | | | | " | 92.50 | | | 92.50 | 102 |
| 4200 | Mill size extras for W-Shapes: 0 to 30 plf: no extra charge | | | | | | | | | |
| 4210 | Member sizes 31 to 65 plf, add | | | | Ton | .10 | | | .10 | .11 |
| 4220 | Member sizes 66 to 100 plf, add | | | | | .10 | | | .10 | .11 |
| 4230 | Member sizes 101 to 387 plf, add | | | | ↓ | 56 | | | 56 | 61.50 |
| 4300 | Column base plates, light, up to 150 lb | 2 Sswk | 2000 | .008 | Lb. | 1.21 | .34 | | 1.55 | 1.95 |
| 4400 | Heavy, over 150 lb | E-2 | 7500 | .007 | " | 1.27 | .31 | .21 | 1.79 | 2.16 |
| 4600 | Castellated beams, light sections, to 50#/L.F., minimum | | 10.70 | 5.234 | Ton | 2,300 | 219 | 146 | 2,665 | 3,100 |
| 4700 | Maximum | | 7 | 8 | | 2,525 | 335 | 224 | 3,084 | 3,600 |
| 4900 | Heavy sections, over 50# per L.F., minimum | | 11.70 | 4.786 | | 2,425 | 200 | 134 | 2,759 | 3,150 |
| 5000 | Maximum | ↓ | 7.80 | 7.179 | | 2,650 | 300 | 201 | 3,151 | 3,650 |
| 5390 | For projects 75 to 99 tons, add | | | | | 10% | | | | |
| 5392 | 50 to 74 tons, add | | | | | 20% | | | | |
| 5394 | 25 to 49 tons, add | | | | | 30% | 10% | | | |
| 5396 | 10 to 24 tons, add | | | | | 50% | 25% | | | |
| 5398 | 2 to 9 tons, add | | | | | 75% | 50% | | | |
| 5399 | Less than 2 tons, add | | | | ↓ | 100% | 100% | | | |

### 05 12 23.80 Subpurlins

| | | | Crew | Daily Output | Labor-Hours | Unit | Material | Labor | Equipment | Total | Total Incl O&P |
|---|---|---|---|---|---|---|---|---|---|---|---|
| 0010 | **SUBPURLINS** | R051223-50 | | | | | | | | | |
| 0020 | Bulb tees, shop fabricated, painted, 32-5/8" O.C., 40 psf L.L. | | | | | | | | | | |
| 0100 | Type 178, max 8'-9" span, 2.15 plf, 2" high x 1-5/8" wide | | E-1 | 4200 | .006 | S.F. | 1.53 | .24 | .03 | 1.80 | 2.12 |
| 0200 | Type 218, max 10'-2" span, 3.19 plf, 2-1/8" high x 2-1/8" wide | | " | 3100 | .008 | | 1.77 | .32 | .04 | 2.13 | 2.56 |
| 1420 | For 24-5/8" spacing, add | | | | | | 33% | 33% | | | |
| 1430 | For 48-5/8" spacing, deduct | | | | | ↓ | 50% | 50% | | | |

# 05 14 Structural Aluminum Framing

## 05 14 23 – Non-Exposed Structural Aluminum Framing

| 05 14 23.05 Aluminum Shapes | | Crew | Daily Output | Labor-Hours | Unit | Material | 2008 Bare Costs Labor | Equipment | Total | Total Incl O&P |
|---|---|---|---|---|---|---|---|---|---|---|
| 0010 | **ALUMINUM SHAPES** | | | | | | | | | |
| 0020 | Structural shapes, 1" to 10" members, under 1 ton | E-2 | 1050 | .053 | Lb. | 2.66 | 2.23 | 1.49 | 6.38 | 8.45 |
| 0050 | 1 to 5 tons | | 1330 | .042 | | 2.54 | 1.76 | 1.18 | 5.48 | 7.15 |
| 0100 | Over 5 tons      **CN** | | 1330 | .042 | | 2.45 | 1.76 | 1.18 | 5.39 | 7.05 |
| 0300 | Extrusions, over 5 tons, stock shapes | | 1330 | .042 | | 2.65 | 1.76 | 1.18 | 5.59 | 7.25 |
| 0400 | Custom shapes | | 1330 | .042 | | 2.70 | 1.76 | 1.18 | 5.64 | 7.30 |

# 05 15 Wire Rope Assemblies

## 05 15 16 – Steel Wire Rope Assemblies

### 05 15 16.05 Accessories for Steel Wire Rope

| | | Crew | Daily Output | Labor-Hours | Unit | Material | Labor | Equipment | Total | Total Incl O&P |
|---|---|---|---|---|---|---|---|---|---|---|
| 0010 | **ACCESSORIES FOR STEEL WIRE ROPE** | | | | | | | | | |
| 1500 | Thimbles, heavy duty, 1/4" | E-17 | 160 | .100 | Ea. | .60 | 4.40 | | 5 | 8.60 |
| 1510 | 1/2" | | 160 | .100 | | 2.64 | 4.40 | | 7.04 | 10.85 |
| 1520 | 3/4" | | 105 | .152 | | 6 | 6.70 | | 12.70 | 18.70 |
| 1530 | 1" | | 52 | .308 | | 12 | 13.55 | | 25.55 | 37.50 |
| 1540 | 1-1/4" | | 38 | .421 | | 18.45 | 18.55 | | 37 | 54 |
| 1550 | 1-1/2" | | 13 | 1.231 | | 52 | 54 | | 106 | 155 |
| 1560 | 1-3/4" | | 8 | 2 | | 107 | 88 | | 195 | 277 |
| 1570 | 2" | | 6 | 2.667 | | 156 | 117 | | 273 | 385 |
| 1580 | 2-1/4" | | 4 | 4 | | 211 | 176 | | 387 | 550 |
| 1600 | Clips, 1/4" diameter | | 160 | .100 | | 2.70 | 4.40 | | 7.10 | 10.90 |
| 1610 | 3/8" diameter | | 160 | .100 | | 2.96 | 4.40 | | 7.36 | 11.20 |
| 1620 | 1/2" diameter | | 160 | .100 | | 4.76 | 4.40 | | 9.16 | 13.20 |
| 1630 | 3/4" diameter | | 102 | .157 | | 7.70 | 6.90 | | 14.60 | 21 |
| 1640 | 1" diameter | | 64 | .250 | | 12.85 | 11 | | 23.85 | 34 |
| 1650 | 1-1/4" diameter | | 35 | .457 | | 21 | 20 | | 41 | 59.50 |
| 1670 | 1-1/2" diameter | | 26 | .615 | | 28.50 | 27 | | 55.50 | 80.50 |
| 1680 | 1-3/4" diameter | | 16 | 1 | | 66 | 44 | | 110 | 153 |
| 1690 | 2" diameter | | 12 | 1.333 | | 73.50 | 58.50 | | 132 | 187 |
| 1700 | 2-1/4" diameter | | 10 | 1.600 | | 108 | 70.50 | | 178.50 | 246 |
| 2200 | Jaw & jaw turnbuckles, 1/4" x 4" | | 160 | .100 | | 21.50 | 4.40 | | 25.90 | 31.50 |
| 2250 | 1/2" x 6" | | 96 | .167 | | 27 | 7.35 | | 34.35 | 43.50 |
| 2260 | 1/2" x 9" | | 77 | .208 | | 36 | 9.15 | | 45.15 | 56.50 |
| 2270 | 1/2" x 12" | | 66 | .242 | | 40.50 | 10.65 | | 51.15 | 64.50 |
| 2300 | 3/4" x 6" | | 38 | .421 | | 53 | 18.55 | | 71.55 | 92 |
| 2310 | 3/4" x 9" | | 30 | .533 | | 59 | 23.50 | | 82.50 | 107 |
| 2320 | 3/4" x 12" | | 28 | .571 | | 75.50 | 25 | | 100.50 | 129 |
| 2330 | 3/4" x 18" | | 23 | .696 | | 90.50 | 30.50 | | 121 | 155 |
| 2350 | 1" x 6" | | 17 | .941 | | 103 | 41.50 | | 144.50 | 188 |
| 2360 | 1" x 12" | | 13 | 1.231 | | 113 | 54 | | 167 | 222 |
| 2370 | 1" x 18" | | 10 | 1.600 | | 170 | 70.50 | | 240.50 | 315 |
| 2380 | 1" x 24" | | 9 | 1.778 | | 187 | 78 | | 265 | 345 |
| 2400 | 1-1/4" x 12" | | 7 | 2.286 | | 190 | 101 | | 291 | 390 |
| 2410 | 1-1/4" x 18" | | 6.50 | 2.462 | | 235 | 108 | | 343 | 455 |
| 2420 | 1-1/4" x 24" | | 5.60 | 2.857 | | 315 | 126 | | 441 | 575 |
| 2450 | 1-1/2" x 12" | | 5.20 | 3.077 | | 320 | 135 | | 455 | 595 |
| 2460 | 1-1/2" x 18" | | 4 | 4 | | 340 | 176 | | 516 | 695 |
| 2470 | 1-1/2" x 24" | | 3.20 | 5 | | 455 | 220 | | 675 | 895 |
| 2500 | 1-3/4" x 18" | | 3.20 | 5 | | 690 | 220 | | 910 | 1,150 |
| 2510 | 1-3/4" x 24" | | 2.80 | 5.714 | | 785 | 251 | | 1,036 | 1,325 |
| 2550 | 2" x 24" | | 1.60 | 10 | | 1,050 | 440 | | 1,490 | 1,975 |

# 05 15 Wire Rope Assemblies

## 05 15 16 – Steel Wire Rope Assemblies

| 05 15 16.50 Steel Wire Rope | Crew | Daily Output | Labor-Hours | Unit | Material | 2008 Bare Costs Labor | Equipment | Total | Total Incl O&P |
|---|---|---|---|---|---|---|---|---|---|
| 0010 **STEEL WIRE ROPE** | | | | | | | | | |
| 0020   6 x 19, bright, fiber core, 5000' rolls, 1/2" diameter | | | | L.F. | .93 | | | .93 | 1.02 |
| 0050     Steel core | | | | | 1.23 | | | 1.23 | 1.35 |
| 0100     Fiber core, 1" diameter | | | | | 3.14 | | | 3.14 | 3.45 |
| 0150     Steel core | | | | | 3.58 | | | 3.58 | 3.93 |
| 0300   6 x 19, galvanized, fiber core, 1/2" diameter | | | | | 1.37 | | | 1.37 | 1.51 |
| 0350     Steel core | | | | | 1.57 | | | 1.57 | 1.72 |
| 0400     Fiber core, 1" diameter | | | | | 4.02 | | | 4.02 | 4.42 |
| 0450     Steel core | | | | | 4.21 | | | 4.21 | 4.64 |
| 0500   6 x 7, bright, IPS, fiber core, <500 L.F. w/acc., 1/4" diameter | E-17 | 6400 | .003 | | .69 | .11 | | .80 | .96 |
| 0510     1/2" diameter | | 2100 | .008 | | 1.69 | .34 | | 2.03 | 2.46 |
| 0520     3/4" diameter | | 960 | .017 | | 3.06 | .73 | | 3.79 | 4.68 |
| 0550   6 x 19, bright, IPS, IWRC, <500 L.F. w/acc., 1/4" diameter | | 5760 | .003 | | 1.03 | .12 | | 1.15 | 1.35 |
| 0560     1/2" diameter | | 1730 | .009 | | 1.67 | .41 | | 2.08 | 2.56 |
| 0570     3/4" diameter | | 770 | .021 | | 2.89 | .91 | | 3.80 | 4.83 |
| 0580     1" diameter | | 420 | .038 | | 4.90 | 1.68 | | 6.58 | 8.40 |
| 0590     1-1/4" diameter | | 290 | .055 | | 8.15 | 2.43 | | 10.58 | 13.35 |
| 0600     1-1/2" diameter | | 192 | .083 | | 10 | 3.67 | | 13.67 | 17.60 |
| 0610     1-3/4" diameter | E-18 | 240 | .167 | | 15.95 | 7.15 | 4.19 | 27.29 | 34.50 |
| 0620     2" diameter | | 160 | .250 | | 20.50 | 10.70 | 6.30 | 37.50 | 48 |
| 0630     2-1/4" diameter | | 160 | .250 | | 27.50 | 10.70 | 6.30 | 44.50 | 55.50 |
| 0650   6 x 37, bright, IPS, IWRC, <500 L.F. w/acc., 1/4" diameter | E-17 | 6400 | .003 | | 1.30 | .11 | | 1.41 | 1.63 |
| 0660     1/2" diameter | | 1730 | .009 | | 2.21 | .41 | | 2.62 | 3.16 |
| 0670     3/4" diameter | | 770 | .021 | | 3.57 | .91 | | 4.48 | 5.60 |
| 0680     1" diameter | | 430 | .037 | | 5.65 | 1.64 | | 7.29 | 9.20 |
| 0690     1-1/4" diameter | | 290 | .055 | | 8.55 | 2.43 | | 10.98 | 13.80 |
| 0700     1-1/2" diameter | | 190 | .084 | | 12.25 | 3.71 | | 15.96 | 20 |
| 0710     1-3/4" diameter | E-18 | 260 | .154 | | 19.45 | 6.60 | 3.87 | 29.92 | 37.50 |
| 0720     2" diameter | | 200 | .200 | | 25 | 8.55 | 5.05 | 38.60 | 48.50 |
| 0730     2-1/4" diameter | | 160 | .250 | | 33.50 | 10.70 | 6.30 | 50.50 | 62 |
| 0800   6 x 19 & 6 x 37, swaged, 1/2" diameter | E-17 | 1220 | .013 | | 3.97 | .58 | | 4.55 | 5.40 |
| 0810     9/16" diameter | | 1120 | .014 | | 4.61 | .63 | | 5.24 | 6.20 |
| 0820     5/8" diameter | | 930 | .017 | | 5.45 | .76 | | 6.21 | 7.35 |
| 0830     3/4" diameter | | 640 | .025 | | 6.95 | 1.10 | | 8.05 | 9.65 |
| 0840     7/8" diameter | | 480 | .033 | | 8.80 | 1.47 | | 10.27 | 12.30 |
| 0850     1" diameter | | 350 | .046 | | 10.70 | 2.01 | | 12.71 | 15.45 |
| 0860     1-1/8" diameter | | 288 | .056 | | 13.20 | 2.44 | | 15.64 | 18.90 |
| 0870     1-1/4" diameter | | 230 | .070 | | 15.95 | 3.06 | | 19.01 | 23 |
| 0880     1-3/8" diameter | | 192 | .083 | | 18.45 | 3.67 | | 22.12 | 27 |
| 0890     1-1/2" diameter | E-18 | 300 | .133 | | 22.50 | 5.70 | 3.35 | 31.55 | 38 |

## 05 15 16.70 Temporary Cable Safety Railing

| | Crew | Daily Output | Labor-Hours | Unit | Material | 2008 Bare Costs Labor | Equipment | Total | Total Incl O&P |
|---|---|---|---|---|---|---|---|---|---|
| 0010 **TEMPORARY CABLE SAFETY RAILING**, Each 100' strand incl. | | | | | | | | | |
| 0020   2 eyebolts, 1 turnbuckle, 100' cable, 2 thimbles, 6 clips | | | | | | | | | |
| 0100     One strand using 1/4" cable & accessories | 2 Sswk | 4 | 4 | C.L.F. | 136 | 172 | | 308 | 460 |
| 0200     1/2" cable & accessories | " | 2 | 8 | " | 252 | 345 | | 597 | 895 |

# 05 21 Steel Joist Framing

## 05 21 13 – Deep Longspan Steel Joist Framing

| 05 21 13.50 Deep Longspan Joists | Crew | Daily Output | Labor-Hours | Unit | Material | 2008 Bare Costs Labor | Equipment | Total | Total Incl O&P |
|---|---|---|---|---|---|---|---|---|---|
| 0010 **DEEP LONGSPAN JOISTS** | | | | | | | | | |
| 3010 DLH series, 40-ton job lots, bolted cross bridging, shop primer | | | | | | | | | |
| 3020 Spans to 144' (shipped in 2 pieces), minimum | E-7 | 16 | 5 | Ton | 1,650 | 212 | 114 | 1,976 | 2,325 |
| 3040 Average | | 13 | 6.154 | | 1,775 | 261 | 141 | 2,177 | 2,550 |
| 3100 Maximum | | 11 | 7.273 | | 2,150 | 310 | 166 | 2,626 | 3,100 |
| 3200 52DLH11, 26 Lb/LF | | 2000 | .040 | L.F. | 22 | 1.70 | .92 | 24.62 | 28.50 |
| 3220 52DLH16, 45 Lb/LF | | 2000 | .040 | | 40 | 1.70 | .92 | 42.62 | 48 |
| 3240 56DLH11, 26 Lb/LF | | 2000 | .040 | | 23 | 1.70 | .92 | 25.62 | 29.50 |
| 3260 56DLH16, 46 Lb/LF | | 2000 | .040 | | 41 | 1.70 | .92 | 43.62 | 49 |
| 3280 60DLH12, 29 Lb/LF | | 2000 | .040 | | 26 | 1.70 | .92 | 28.62 | 32.50 |
| 3300 60DLH17, 52 Lb/LF | | 2000 | .040 | | 46.50 | 1.70 | .92 | 49.12 | 55 |
| 3320 64DLH12, 31 Lb/LF | | 2200 | .036 | | 27.50 | 1.54 | .83 | 29.87 | 34 |
| 3340 64DLH17, 52 Lb/LF | | 2200 | .036 | | 46.50 | 1.54 | .83 | 48.87 | 54.50 |
| 3360 68DLH13, 37 Lb/LF | | 2200 | .036 | | 33 | 1.54 | .83 | 35.37 | 39.50 |
| 3380 68DLH18, 61 Lb/LF | | 2200 | .036 | | 54.50 | 1.54 | .83 | 56.87 | 63 |
| 3400 72DLH14, 41 Lb/LF | | 2200 | .036 | | 36.50 | 1.54 | .83 | 38.87 | 43.50 |
| 3420 72DLH19, 70 Lb/LF | | 2200 | .036 | | 62.50 | 1.54 | .83 | 64.87 | 72 |
| 3500 For less than 40-ton job lots | | | | | | | | | |
| 3502 For 30 to 39 tons, add | | | | | 10% | | | | |
| 3504 20 to 29 tons, add | | | | | 20% | | | | |
| 3506 10 to 19 tons, add | | | | | 30% | | | | |
| 3507 5 to 9 tons, add | | | | | 50% | 25% | | | |
| 3508 1 to 4 tons, add | | | | | 75% | 50% | | | |
| 3509 Less than 1 ton, add | | | | | 100% | 100% | | | |
| 4010 SLH series, 40-ton job lots, bolted cross bridging, shop primer | | | | | | | | | |
| 4020 Spans to 200' (shipped in 3 pieces), minimum | E-7 | 16 | 5 | Ton | 1,625 | 212 | 114 | 1,951 | 2,300 |
| 4040 Average | | 13 | 6.154 | | 1,825 | 261 | 141 | 2,227 | 2,600 |
| 4060 Maximum | | 11 | 7.273 | | 2,175 | 310 | 166 | 2,651 | 3,125 |
| 4200 80SLH15, 40 Lb/LF | | 1500 | .053 | L.F. | 36.50 | 2.26 | 1.22 | 39.98 | 45.50 |
| 4220 80SLH20, 75 Lb/LF | | 1500 | .053 | | 68.50 | 2.26 | 1.22 | 71.98 | 81 |
| 4240 88SLH16, 46 Lb/LF | | 1500 | .053 | | 42 | 2.26 | 1.22 | 45.48 | 52 |
| 4260 88SLH21, 89 Lb/LF | | 1500 | .053 | | 81.50 | 2.26 | 1.22 | 84.98 | 95 |
| 4280 96SLH17, 52 Lb/LF | | 1500 | .053 | | 47.50 | 2.26 | 1.22 | 50.98 | 58 |
| 4300 96SLH22, 102 Lb/LF | | 1500 | .053 | | 93.50 | 2.26 | 1.22 | 96.98 | 108 |
| 4320 104SLH18, 59 Lb/LF | | 1800 | .044 | | 54 | 1.88 | 1.02 | 56.90 | 64 |
| 4340 104SLH23, 109 Lb/LF | | 1800 | .044 | | 99.50 | 1.88 | 1.02 | 102.40 | 114 |
| 4360 112SLH19, 67 Lb/LF | | 1800 | .044 | | 61.50 | 1.88 | 1.02 | 64.40 | 72 |
| 4380 112SLH24, 131 Lb/LF | | 1800 | .044 | | 120 | 1.88 | 1.02 | 122.90 | 136 |
| 4400 120SLH20, 77 Lb/LF | | 1800 | .044 | | 70.50 | 1.88 | 1.02 | 73.40 | 82 |
| 4420 120SLH25, 152 Lb/LF | | 1800 | .044 | | 139 | 1.88 | 1.02 | 141.90 | 157 |
| 6100 For less than 40-ton job lots | | | | | | | | | |
| 6102 For 30 to 39 tons, add | | | | | 10% | | | | |
| 6104 20 to 29 tons, add | | | | | 20% | | | | |
| 6106 10 to 19 tons, add | | | | | 30% | | | | |
| 6107 5 to 9 tons, add | | | | | 50% | 25% | | | |
| 6108 1 to 4 tons, add | | | | | 75% | 50% | | | |
| 6109 Less than 1 ton, add | | | | | 100% | 100% | | | |

## 05 21 16 – Longspan Steel Joist Framing

### 05 21 16.50 Longspan Joists

| | Crew | Daily Output | Labor-Hours | Unit | Material | Labor | Equipment | Total | Total Incl O&P |
|---|---|---|---|---|---|---|---|---|---|
| 0010 **LONGSPAN JOISTS** | | | | | | | | | |
| 2000 LH series, 40-ton job lots, bolted cross bridging, shop primer | | | | | | | | | |
| 2020 Spans to 96', minimum | E-7 | 16 | 5 | Ton | 1,525 | 212 | 114 | 1,851 | 2,175 |

# 05 21 Steel Joist Framing

## 05 21 16 – Longspan Steel Joist Framing

| 05 21 16.50 Longspan Joists | Crew | Daily Output | Labor-Hours | Unit | Material | 2008 Bare Costs Labor | Equipment | Total | Total Incl O&P |
|---|---|---|---|---|---|---|---|---|---|
| 2040     Average | E-7 | 13 | 6.154 | Ton | 1,675 | 261 | 141 | 2,077 | 2,450 |
| 2080     Maximum | | 11 | 7.273 | ↓ | 1,975 | 310 | 166 | 2,451 | 2,900 |
| 2200     18LH04, 12 Lb/LF | | 1400 | .057 | L.F. | 10.05 | 2.42 | 1.31 | 13.78 | 16.75 |
| 2220     18LH08, 19 Lb/LF | | 1400 | .057 | | 15.90 | 2.42 | 1.31 | 19.63 | 23 |
| 2240     20LH04, 12 Lb/LF | | 1400 | .057 | | 10.05 | 2.42 | 1.31 | 13.78 | 16.75 |
| 2260     20LH08, 19 Lb/LF | | 1400 | .057 | | 15.90 | 2.42 | 1.31 | 19.63 | 23 |
| 2280     24LH05, 13 Lb/LF | | 1400 | .057 | | 10.85 | 2.42 | 1.31 | 14.58 | 17.65 |
| 2300     24LH10, 23 Lb/LF | | 1400 | .057 | | 19.25 | 2.42 | 1.31 | 22.98 | 26.50 |
| 2320     28LH06, 16 Lb/LF | | 1800 | .044 | | 13.40 | 1.88 | 1.02 | 16.30 | 19.10 |
| 2340     28LH11, 25 Lb/LF | | 1800 | .044 | | 21 | 1.88 | 1.02 | 23.90 | 27.50 |
| 2360     32LH08, 17 Lb/LF | | 1800 | .044 | | 14.20 | 1.88 | 1.02 | 17.10 | 20 |
| 2380     32LH13, 30 Lb/LF | | 1800 | .044 | | 25 | 1.88 | 1.02 | 27.90 | 32 |
| 2400     36LH09, 21 Lb/LF | | 1800 | .044 | | 17.55 | 1.88 | 1.02 | 20.45 | 23.50 |
| 2420     36LH14, 36 Lb/LF | | 1800 | .044 | | 30 | 1.88 | 1.02 | 32.90 | 37.50 |
| 2440     40LH10, 21 Lb/LF | | 2200 | .036 | | 17.55 | 1.54 | .83 | 19.92 | 23 |
| 2460     40LH15, 36 Lb/LF | | 2200 | .036 | | 30 | 1.54 | .83 | 32.37 | 36.50 |
| 2480     44LH11, 22 Lb/LF | | 2200 | .036 | | 18.40 | 1.54 | .83 | 20.77 | 23.50 |
| 2500     44LH16, 42 Lb/LF | | 2200 | .036 | | 35 | 1.54 | .83 | 37.37 | 42 |
| 2520     48LH11, 22 Lb/LF | | 2200 | .036 | | 18.40 | 1.54 | .83 | 20.77 | 23.50 |
| 2540     48LH16, 42 Lb/LF | ↓ | 2200 | .036 | ↓ | 35 | 1.54 | .83 | 37.37 | 42 |
| 2600 For less than 40-ton job lots | | | | | | | | | |
| 2602     For 30 to 39 tons, add | | | | | 10% | | | | |
| 2604     20 to 29 tons, add | | | | | 20% | | | | |
| 2606     10 to 19 tons, add | | | | | 30% | | | | |
| 2607     5 to 9 tons, add | | | | | 50% | 25% | | | |
| 2608     1 to 4 tons, add | | | | | 75% | 50% | | | |
| 2609     Less than 1 ton, add | | | | | 100% | 100% | | | |
| 6000 For welded cross bridging, add | | | | | | 30% | | | |

## 05 21 19 – Open Web Steel Joist Framing

| 05 21 19.10 Open Web Joists | Crew | Daily Output | Labor-Hours | Unit | Material | 2008 Bare Costs Labor | Equipment | Total | Total Incl O&P |
|---|---|---|---|---|---|---|---|---|---|
| 0010 **OPEN WEB JOISTS** | | | | | | | | | |
| 0020 K series, 40-ton lots, horiz. bridging, spans to 30', shop primer, minimum | E-7 | 15 | 5.333 | Ton | 1,350 | 226 | 122 | 1,698 | 2,000 |
| 0050     Average | | 12 | 6.667 | ↓ | 1,500 | 283 | 153 | 1,936 | 2,325 |
| 0080     Maximum | | 9 | 8.889 | ↓ | 1,825 | 375 | 203 | 2,403 | 2,875 |
| 0130     8K1, 5.1 Lb/LF | | 1200 | .067 | L.F. | 3.85 | 2.83 | 1.53 | 8.21 | 10.85 |
| 0140     10K1, 5.0 Lb/LF | | 1200 | .067 | | 3.78 | 2.83 | 1.53 | 8.14 | 10.80 |
| 0160     12K3, 5.7 Lb/LF | | 1500 | .053 | | 4.31 | 2.26 | 1.22 | 7.79 | 10.05 |
| 0180     14K3, 6.0 Lb/LF | | 1500 | .053 | | 4.53 | 2.26 | 1.22 | 8.01 | 10.30 |
| 0200     16K3, 6.3 Lb/LF | | 1800 | .044 | | 4.76 | 1.88 | 1.02 | 7.66 | 9.65 |
| 0220     16K6, 8.1 Lb/LF | | 1800 | .044 | | 6.10 | 1.88 | 1.02 | 9 | 11.15 |
| 0240     18K5, 7.7 Lb/LF | | 2000 | .040 | | 5.80 | 1.70 | .92 | 8.42 | 10.40 |
| 0260     18K9, 10.2 Lb/LF | | 2000 | .040 | ↓ | 7.70 | 1.70 | .92 | 10.32 | 12.45 |
| 0410     Span 30' to 50', minimum | | 17 | 4.706 | Ton | 1,325 | 200 | 108 | 1,633 | 1,925 |
| 0440     Average | CN | 17 | 4.706 | | 1,475 | 200 | 108 | 1,783 | 2,100 |
| 0460     Maximum | | 10 | 8 | ↓ | 1,575 | 340 | 183 | 2,098 | 2,525 |
| 0500     20K5, 8.2 Lb/LF | | 2000 | .040 | L.F. | 6.10 | 1.70 | .92 | 8.72 | 10.70 |
| 0520     20K9, 10.8 Lb/LF | | 2000 | .040 | | 8 | 1.70 | .92 | 10.62 | 12.80 |
| 0540     22K5, 8.8 Lb/LF | | 2000 | .040 | | 6.55 | 1.70 | .92 | 9.17 | 11.20 |
| 0560     22K9, 11.3 Lb/LF | | 2000 | .040 | | 8.40 | 1.70 | .92 | 11.02 | 13.20 |
| 0580     24K6, 9.7 Lb/LF | | 2200 | .036 | | 7.20 | 1.54 | .83 | 9.57 | 11.50 |
| 0600     24K10, 13.1 Lb/LF | | 2200 | .036 | | 9.70 | 1.54 | .83 | 12.07 | 14.30 |
| 0620     26K6, 10.6 Lb/LF | ↓ | 2200 | .036 | ↓ | 7.85 | 1.54 | .83 | 10.22 | 12.25 |

# 05 21 Steel Joist Framing

## 05 21 19 – Open Web Steel Joist Framing

### 05 21 19.10 Open Web Joists

| | | Crew | Daily Output | Labor-Hours | Unit | Material | 2008 Bare Costs Labor | Equipment | Total | Total Incl O&P |
|---|---|---|---|---|---|---|---|---|---|---|
| 0640 | 26K10, 13.8 Lb/LF | E-7 | 2200 | .036 | L.F. | 10.25 | 1.54 | .83 | 12.62 | 14.85 |
| 0660 | 28K8, 12.7 Lb/LF | | 2400 | .033 | | 9.40 | 1.41 | .76 | 11.57 | 13.65 |
| 0680 | 28K12, 17.1 Lb/LF | | 2400 | .033 | | 12.70 | 1.41 | .76 | 14.87 | 17.25 |
| 0700 | 30K8, 13.2 Lb/LF | | 2400 | .033 | | 9.80 | 1.41 | .76 | 11.97 | 14.05 |
| 0720 | 30K12, 17.6 Lb/LF | | 2400 | .033 | | 13.05 | 1.41 | .76 | 15.22 | 17.65 |
| 0800 | For less than 40-ton job lots | | | | | | | | | |
| 0802 | For 30 to 39 tons, add | | | | | 10% | | | | |
| 0804 | 20 to 29 tons, add | | | | | 20% | | | | |
| 0806 | 10 to 19 tons, add | | | | | 30% | | | | |
| 0807 | 5 to 9 tons, add | | | | | 50% | 25% | | | |
| 0808 | 1 to 4 tons, add | | | | | 75% | 50% | | | |
| 0809 | Less than 1 ton, add | | | | | 100% | 100% | | | |
| 1010 | CS series, 40-ton job lots, horizontal bridging, shop primer | | | | | | | | | |
| 1020 | Spans to 30', minimum | E-7 | 15 | 5.333 | Ton | 1,400 | 226 | 122 | 1,748 | 2,050 |
| 1040 | Average | | 12 | 6.667 | | 1,550 | 283 | 153 | 1,986 | 2,375 |
| 1060 | Maximum | | 9 | 8.889 | | 1,825 | 375 | 203 | 2,403 | 2,875 |
| 1100 | 10CS2, 7.5 Lb/LF | | 1200 | .067 | L.F. | 5.80 | 2.83 | 1.53 | 10.16 | 13.05 |
| 1120 | 12CS2, 8.0 Lb/LF | | 1500 | .053 | | 6.20 | 2.26 | 1.22 | 9.68 | 12.10 |
| 1140 | 14CS2, 8.0Lb/LF | | 1500 | .053 | | 6.20 | 2.26 | 1.22 | 9.68 | 12.10 |
| 1160 | 16CS2, 8.5 Lb/LF | | 1800 | .044 | | 6.60 | 1.88 | 1.02 | 9.50 | 11.65 |
| 1180 | 16CS4, 14.5 Lb/LF | | 1800 | .044 | | 11.25 | 1.88 | 1.02 | 14.15 | 16.75 |
| 1200 | 18CS2, 9.0 Lb/LF | | 2000 | .040 | | 7 | 1.70 | .92 | 9.62 | 11.65 |
| 1220 | 18CS4, 15.0 Lb/LF | | 2000 | .040 | | 11.65 | 1.70 | .92 | 14.27 | 16.80 |
| 1240 | 20CS2, 9.5 Lb/LF | | 2000 | .040 | | 7.35 | 1.70 | .92 | 9.97 | 12.10 |
| 1260 | 20CS4, 16.5 Lb/LF | | 2000 | .040 | | 12.80 | 1.70 | .92 | 15.42 | 18.05 |
| 1280 | 22CS2, 10.0 Lb/LF | | 2000 | .040 | | 7.75 | 1.70 | .92 | 10.37 | 12.55 |
| 1300 | 22CS4, 16.5 Lb/LF | | 2000 | .040 | | 12.80 | 1.70 | .92 | 15.42 | 18.05 |
| 1320 | 24CS2, 10.0 Lb/LF | | 2200 | .036 | | 7.75 | 1.54 | .83 | 10.12 | 12.15 |
| 1340 | 24CS4, 16.5 Lb/LF | | 2200 | .036 | | 12.80 | 1.54 | .83 | 15.17 | 17.65 |
| 1360 | 26CS2, 10.0 Lb/LF | | 2200 | .036 | | 7.75 | 1.54 | .83 | 10.12 | 12.15 |
| 1380 | 26CS4, 16.5 Lb/LF | | 2200 | .036 | | 12.80 | 1.54 | .83 | 15.17 | 17.65 |
| 1400 | 28CS2, 10.5 Lb/LF | | 2400 | .033 | | 8.15 | 1.41 | .76 | 10.32 | 12.25 |
| 1420 | 28CS4, 16.5 Lb/LF | | 2400 | .033 | | 12.80 | 1.41 | .76 | 14.97 | 17.35 |
| 1440 | 30CS2, 11.0 Lb/LF | | 2400 | .033 | | 8.55 | 1.41 | .76 | 10.72 | 12.70 |
| 1460 | 30CS4, 16.5 Lb/LF | | 2400 | .033 | | 12.80 | 1.41 | .76 | 14.97 | 17.35 |
| 1500 | For less than 40-ton job lots | | | | | | | | | |
| 1502 | For 30 to 39 tons, add | | | | | 10% | | | | |
| 1504 | 20 to 29 tons, add | | | | | 20% | | | | |
| 1506 | 10 to 19 tons, add | | | | | 30% | | | | |
| 1507 | 5 to 9 tons, add | | | | | 50% | 25% | | | |
| 1508 | 1 to 4 tons, add | | | | | 75% | 50% | | | |
| 1509 | Less than 1 ton, add | | | | | 100% | 100% | | | |
| 6200 | For shop prime paint other than mfrs. standard, add | | | | | 20% | | | | |
| 6300 | For bottom chord extensions, add per chord | | | | Ea. | 33 | | | 33 | 36 |
| 6400 | Individual steel bearing plate, 6" x 6" x 1/4" with J-hook | 1 Bric | 160 | .050 | " | 6.60 | 1.96 | | 8.56 | 10.25 |

## 05 21 23 – Steel Joist Girder Framing

### 05 21 23.50 Joist Girders

| | | Crew | Daily Output | Labor-Hours | Unit | Material | 2008 Bare Costs Labor | Equipment | Total | Total Incl O&P |
|---|---|---|---|---|---|---|---|---|---|---|
| 0010 | **JOIST GIRDERS** | | | | | | | | | |
| 7000 | Joist girders, 40-ton job lots, shop primer, minimum | E-5 | 15 | 5.333 | Ton | 1,375 | 226 | 113 | 1,714 | 2,025 |
| 7020 | Average | | 13 | 6.154 | | 1,500 | 261 | 131 | 1,892 | 2,250 |
| 7040 | Maximum | | 11 | 7.273 | | 1,575 | 310 | 154 | 2,039 | 2,450 |
| 7100 | For less than 40-ton job lots | | | | | | | | | |

# 05 21 Steel Joist Framing

## 05 21 23 – Steel Joist Girder Framing

| 05 21 23.50 Joist Girders | | Crew | Daily Output | Labor-Hours | Unit | Material | 2008 Bare Costs Labor | Equipment | Total | Total Incl O&P |
|---|---|---|---|---|---|---|---|---|---|---|
| 7104 | 20 to 29 tons, add | | | | | 20% | | | | |
| 7106 | 10 to 19 tons, add | | | | | 30% | | | | |
| 7107 | 5 to 9 tons, add | | | | | 50% | 25% | | | |
| 7108 | 1 to 4 tons, add | | | | | 75% | 50% | | | |
| 7109 | Less than 1 ton, add | | | | | 100% | 100% | | | |
| 8000 | Trusses, 40-ton job lots, shop fabricated WT chords, shop primer, average | E-5 | 11 | 7.273 | Ton | 4,950 | 310 | 154 | 5,414 | 6,150 |
| 8100 | For less than 40-ton job lots | | | | | | | | | |
| 8102 | For 30 to 39 tons, add | | | | | 10% | | | | |
| 8104 | 20 to 29 tons, add | | | | | 20% | | | | |
| 8106 | 10 to 19 tons, add | | | | | 30% | | | | |
| 8107 | 5 to 9 tons, add | | | | | 50% | 25% | | | |
| 8108 | 1 to 4 tons, add | | | | | 75% | 50% | | | |
| 8109 | Less than 1 ton, add | | | | | 100% | 100% | | | |

# 05 31 Steel Decking

## 05 31 13 – Steel Floor Decking

### 05 31 13.50 Floor Decking

| | | Crew | Daily Output | Labor-Hours | Unit | Material | 2008 Bare Costs Labor | Equipment | Total | Total Incl O&P |
|---|---|---|---|---|---|---|---|---|---|---|
| 0010 | **FLOOR DECKING**          R053100-10 | | | | | | | | | |
| 3200 | Open decking, 3" deep, wide rib, 22 gauge, galvanized, under 50 squares | E-4 | 3600 | .009 | S.F. | 2.21 | .39 | .04 | 2.64 | 3.18 |
| 3250 | 50-500 squares | | 3800 | .008 | | 1.77 | .37 | .03 | 2.17 | 2.65 |
| 3260 | over 500 squares | | 4000 | .008 | | 1.59 | .35 | .03 | 1.97 | 2.42 |
| 3300 | 20 gauge, under 50 squares | | 3400 | .009 | | 2.58 | .41 | .04 | 3.03 | 3.61 |
| 3350 | 50-500 squares | | 3600 | .009 | | 2.06 | .39 | .04 | 2.49 | 3.01 |
| 3360 | over 500 squares | | 3800 | .008 | | 1.85 | .37 | .03 | 2.25 | 2.74 |
| 3400 | 18 gauge, under 50 squares | | 3200 | .010 | | 3.32 | .44 | .04 | 3.80 | 4.48 |
| 3450 | 50-500 squares | | 3400 | .009 | | 2.66 | .41 | .04 | 3.11 | 3.70 |
| 3460 | over 500 squares | | 3600 | .009 | | 2.39 | .39 | .04 | 2.82 | 3.37 |
| 3500 | 16 gauge, under 50 squares | | 3000 | .011 | | 4.39 | .46 | .04 | 4.89 | 5.70 |
| 3550 | 50-500 squares | | 3200 | .010 | | 3.51 | .44 | .04 | 3.99 | 4.69 |
| 3560 | over 500 squares | | 3400 | .009 | | 3.16 | .41 | .04 | 3.61 | 4.26 |
| 3700 | 4-1/2" deep, long span roof, over 50 squares, 20 gauge | | 2700 | .012 | | 4.13 | .52 | .05 | 4.70 | 5.50 |
| 3800 | 18 gauge | | 2460 | .013 | | 5.30 | .57 | .05 | 5.92 | 6.95 |
| 3900 | 16 gauge | | 2350 | .014 | | 3.98 | .59 | .06 | 4.63 | 5.50 |
| 4100 | 6" deep, long span, 18 gauge | | 2000 | .016 | | 7.60 | .70 | .07 | 8.37 | 9.70 |
| 4200 | 16 gauge | | 1930 | .017 | | 5.70 | .72 | .07 | 6.49 | 7.65 |
| 4300 | 14 gauge | | 1860 | .017 | | 7.30 | .75 | .07 | 8.12 | 9.50 |
| 4500 | 7-1/2" deep, long span, 18 gauge | | 1690 | .019 | | 8.35 | .82 | .08 | 9.25 | 10.80 |
| 4600 | 16 gauge | | 1590 | .020 | | 6.25 | .88 | .08 | 7.21 | 8.50 |
| 4700 | 14 gauge | | 1490 | .021 | | 8.05 | .93 | .09 | 9.07 | 10.65 |
| 4800 | For painted instead of galvanized, deduct | | | | | 2% | | | | |
| 5000 | For acoustical perforated, with fiberglass, add | | | | S.F. | 1.09 | | | 1.09 | 1.20 |
| 5200 | Non-cellular composite deck, galv., 2" deep, 22 gauge | E-4 | 3860 | .008 | | 1.53 | .36 | .03 | 1.92 | 2.37 |
| 5300 | 20 gauge | | 3600 | .009 | | 1.69 | .39 | .04 | 2.12 | 2.60 |
| 5400 | 18 gauge | | 3380 | .009 | | 2.15 | .41 | .04 | 2.60 | 3.15 |
| 5500 | 16 gauge | | 3200 | .010 | | 2.69 | .44 | .04 | 3.17 | 3.79 |
| 5700 | 3" deep, galv., 22 gauge | | 3200 | .010 | | 1.67 | .44 | .04 | 2.15 | 2.66 |
| 5800 | 20 gauge | | 3000 | .011 | | 1.86 | .46 | .04 | 2.36 | 2.93 |
| 5900 | 18 gauge          *CN* | | 2850 | .011 | | 2.29 | .49 | .05 | 2.83 | 3.45 |
| 6000 | 16 gauge | | 2700 | .012 | | 3.06 | .52 | .05 | 3.63 | 4.35 |

# 05 31 Steel Decking

## 05 31 23 – Steel Roof Decking

| 05 31 23.50 Roof Decking | | Crew | Daily Output | Labor-Hours | Unit | Material | 2008 Bare Costs Labor | Equipment | Total | Total Incl O&P |
|---|---|---|---|---|---|---|---|---|---|---|
| 0010 | **ROOF DECKING** | | | | | | | | | |
| 2100 | Open type, galv., 1-1/2" deep wide rib, 22 gauge, under 50 squares | E-4 | 4500 | .007 | S.F. | 1.61 | .31 | .03 | 1.95 | 2.36 |
| 2200 | 50-500 squares   *CN* | | 4900 | .007 | | 1.25 | .28 | .03 | 1.56 | 1.92 |
| 2400 | Over 500 squares | | 5100 | .006 | | 1.16 | .27 | .03 | 1.46 | 1.79 |
| 2600 | 20 gauge, under 50 squares | | 3865 | .008 | | 1.89 | .36 | .03 | 2.28 | 2.77 |
| 2650 | 50-500 squares | | 4170 | .008 | | 1.51 | .33 | .03 | 1.87 | 2.30 |
| 2700 | Over 500 squares | | 4300 | .007 | | 1.36 | .32 | .03 | 1.71 | 2.11 |
| 2900 | 18 gauge, under 50 squares | | 3800 | .008 | | 2.45 | .37 | .03 | 2.85 | 3.39 |
| 2950 | 50-500 squares | | 4100 | .008 | | 1.96 | .34 | .03 | 2.33 | 2.80 |
| 3000 | Over 500 squares | | 4300 | .007 | | 1.76 | .32 | .03 | 2.11 | 2.55 |
| 3050 | 16 gauge, under 50 squares | | 3700 | .009 | | 3.30 | .38 | .04 | 3.72 | 4.35 |
| 3060 | 50-500 squares | | 4000 | .008 | | 2.64 | .35 | .03 | 3.02 | 3.57 |
| 3100 | Over 500 squares | ▼ | 4200 | .008 | | 2.37 | .33 | .03 | 2.73 | 3.24 |
| 3150 | For intermediate rib instead of wide rib, deduct | | | | | .03 | | | .03 | .03 |
| 3160 | For narrow rib instead of wide rib, add | | | | ▼ | .49 | | | .49 | .54 |

## 05 31 33 – Steel Form Decking

| 05 31 33.50 Form Decking | | Crew | Daily Output | Labor-Hours | Unit | Material | 2008 Bare Costs Labor | Equipment | Total | Total Incl O&P |
|---|---|---|---|---|---|---|---|---|---|---|
| 0010 | **FORM DECKING** | | | | | | | | | |
| 6100 | Slab form, steel, 28 gauge, 9/16" deep, uncoated | E-4 | 4000 | .008 | S.F. | 1.07 | .35 | .03 | 1.45 | 1.85 |
| 6200 | Galvanized | | 4000 | .008 | | .95 | .35 | .03 | 1.33 | 1.72 |
| 6220 | 24 gauge, 1" deep, uncoated | | 3900 | .008 | | 1.17 | .36 | .03 | 1.56 | 1.97 |
| 6240 | Galvanized | | 3900 | .008 | | 1.38 | .36 | .03 | 1.77 | 2.20 |
| 6300 | 24 gauge, 1-5/16" deep, uncoated | | 3800 | .008 | | 1.25 | .37 | .03 | 1.65 | 2.07 |
| 6400 | Galvanized | | 3800 | .008 | | 1.47 | .37 | .03 | 1.87 | 2.32 |
| 6500 | 22 gauge, 1-5/16" deep, uncoated | | 3700 | .009 | | 1.57 | .38 | .04 | 1.99 | 2.44 |
| 6600 | Galvanized | | 3700 | .009 | | 1.60 | .38 | .04 | 2.02 | 2.48 |
| 6700 | 22 gauge, 2" deep uncoated | | 3600 | .009 | | 2.05 | .39 | .04 | 2.48 | 3 |
| 6800 | Galvanized | ▼ | 3600 | .009 | ▼ | 2.01 | .39 | .04 | 2.44 | 2.95 |
| 7000 | Sheet metal edge closure form, 12" wide with 2 bends, galv | | | | | | | | | |
| 7100 | 18 gauge | E-14 | 360 | .022 | L.F. | 3.32 | 1 | .37 | 4.69 | 5.85 |
| 7200 | 16 gauge | " | 360 | .022 | " | 4.50 | 1 | .37 | 5.87 | 7.15 |

# 05 35 Raceway Decking Assemblies

## 05 35 13 – Steel Cellular Decking

| 05 35 13.50 Cellular Decking | | Crew | Daily Output | Labor-Hours | Unit | Material | 2008 Bare Costs Labor | Equipment | Total | Total Incl O&P |
|---|---|---|---|---|---|---|---|---|---|---|
| 0010 | **CELLULAR DECKING** | | | | | | | | | |
| 0200 | Cellular units, galv, 2" deep, 20-20 gauge, over 15 squares | E-4 | 1460 | .022 | S.F. | 6.40 | .95 | .09 | 7.44 | 8.85 |
| 0250 | 18-20 gauge | | 1420 | .023 | | 7.25 | .98 | .09 | 8.32 | 9.85 |
| 0300 | 18-18 gauge | | 1390 | .023 | | 7.45 | 1 | .10 | 8.55 | 10.10 |
| 0320 | 16-18 gauge | | 1360 | .024 | | 8.85 | 1.02 | .10 | 9.97 | 11.70 |
| 0340 | 16-16 gauge | | 1330 | .024 | | 9.90 | 1.05 | .10 | 11.05 | 12.90 |
| 0400 | 3" deep, galvanized, 20-20 gauge | | 1375 | .023 | | 7.05 | 1.01 | .10 | 8.16 | 9.70 |
| 0500 | 18-20 gauge | | 1350 | .024 | | 8.50 | 1.03 | .10 | 9.63 | 11.30 |
| 0600 | 18-18 gauge | | 1290 | .025 | | 8.50 | 1.08 | .10 | 9.68 | 11.40 |
| 0700 | 16-18 gauge | | 1230 | .026 | | 9.55 | 1.13 | .11 | 10.79 | 12.65 |
| 0800 | 16-16 gauge | | 1150 | .028 | | 10.40 | 1.21 | .11 | 11.72 | 13.75 |
| 1000 | 4-1/2" deep, galvanized, 20-18 gauge | | 1100 | .029 | | 9.80 | 1.27 | .12 | 11.19 | 13.20 |
| 1100 | 18-18 gauge | | 1040 | .031 | | 9.75 | 1.34 | .13 | 11.22 | 13.30 |
| 1200 | 16-18 gauge | | 980 | .033 | | 10.95 | 1.42 | .13 | 12.50 | 14.75 |
| 1300 | 16-16 gauge | ▼ | 935 | .034 | ▼ | 11.95 | 1.49 | .14 | 13.58 | 16 |

# 05 35 Raceway Decking Assemblies

## 05 35 13 – Steel Cellular Decking

| 05 35 13.50 Cellular Decking | Crew | Daily Output | Labor-Hours | Unit | Material | 2008 Bare Costs Labor | 2008 Bare Costs Equipment | Total | Total Incl O&P |
|---|---|---|---|---|---|---|---|---|---|
| 1500 | For acoustical deck, add | | | | | 15% | | | | |
| 1700 | For cells used for ventilation, add | | | | | 15% | | | | |
| 1900 | For multi-story or congested site, add | | | | | | 50% | | | |
| 8000 | Metal deck and trench, 2" thick, 20 gauge, combination | | | | | | | | | |
| 8010 | 60% cellular, 40% non-cellular, inserts and trench | R-4 | 1100 | .036 | S.F. | 12.80 | 1.60 | .12 | 14.52 | 16.95 |

# 05 41 Structural Metal Stud Framing

## 05 41 13 – Load-Bearing Metal Stud Framing

### 05 41 13.05 Bracing

| | | Crew | Daily Output | Labor-Hours | Unit | Material | Labor | Equipment | Total | Total Incl O&P |
|---|---|---|---|---|---|---|---|---|---|---|
| 0010 | **BRACING**, shear wall X-bracing, per 10' x 10' bay, one face | | | | | | | | | |
| 0120 | Metal strap, 20 ga x 4" wide | 2 Carp | 18 | .889 | Ea. | 22.50 | 34 | | 56.50 | 77.50 |
| 0130 | 6" wide | | 18 | .889 | | 35 | 34 | | 69 | 91 |
| 0160 | 18 ga x 4" wide | | 16 | 1 | | 32.50 | 38 | | 70.50 | 95 |
| 0170 | 6" wide | | 16 | 1 | | 47.50 | 38 | | 85.50 | 112 |
| 0410 | Continuous strap bracing, per horizontal row on both faces | | | | | | | | | |
| 0420 | Metal strap, 20 ga x 2" wide, studs 12" O.C. | 1 Carp | 7 | 1.143 | C.L.F. | 57 | 43.50 | | 100.50 | 131 |
| 0430 | 16" O.C. | | 8 | 1 | | 57 | 38 | | 95 | 123 |
| 0440 | 24" O.C. | | 10 | .800 | | 57 | 30.50 | | 87.50 | 111 |
| 0450 | 18 ga x 2" wide, studs 12" O.C. | | 6 | 1.333 | | 79 | 51 | | 130 | 166 |
| 0460 | 16" O.C. | | 7 | 1.143 | | 79 | 43.50 | | 122.50 | 155 |
| 0470 | 24" O.C. | | 8 | 1 | | 79 | 38 | | 117 | 147 |

### 05 41 13.10 Bridging

| | | Crew | Daily Output | Labor-Hours | Unit | Material | Labor | Equipment | Total | Total Incl O&P |
|---|---|---|---|---|---|---|---|---|---|---|
| 0010 | **BRIDGING**, solid between studs w/ 1-1/4" leg track, per stud bay | | | | | | | | | |
| 0200 | Studs 12" O.C., 18 ga x 2-1/2" wide | 1 Carp | 125 | .064 | Ea. | .97 | 2.44 | | 3.41 | 4.86 |
| 0210 | 3-5/8" wide | | 120 | .067 | | 1.16 | 2.54 | | 3.70 | 5.20 |
| 0220 | 4" wide | | 120 | .067 | | 1.24 | 2.54 | | 3.78 | 5.30 |
| 0230 | 6" wide | | 115 | .070 | | 1.61 | 2.65 | | 4.26 | 5.90 |
| 0240 | 8" wide | | 110 | .073 | | 2.03 | 2.77 | | 4.80 | 6.55 |
| 0300 | 16 ga x 2-1/2" wide | | 115 | .070 | | 1.21 | 2.65 | | 3.86 | 5.45 |
| 0310 | 3-5/8" wide | | 110 | .073 | | 1.47 | 2.77 | | 4.24 | 5.90 |
| 0320 | 4" wide | | 110 | .073 | | 1.57 | 2.77 | | 4.34 | 6.05 |
| 0330 | 6" wide | | 105 | .076 | | 2.01 | 2.90 | | 4.91 | 6.75 |
| 0340 | 8" wide | | 100 | .080 | | 2.56 | 3.05 | | 5.61 | 7.55 |
| 1200 | Studs 16" O.C., 18 ga x 2-1/2" wide | | 125 | .064 | | 1.24 | 2.44 | | 3.68 | 5.15 |
| 1210 | 3-5/8" wide | | 120 | .067 | | 1.49 | 2.54 | | 4.03 | 5.60 |
| 1220 | 4" wide | | 120 | .067 | | 1.58 | 2.54 | | 4.12 | 5.70 |
| 1230 | 6" wide | | 115 | .070 | | 2.06 | 2.65 | | 4.71 | 6.40 |
| 1240 | 8" wide | | 110 | .073 | | 2.61 | 2.77 | | 5.38 | 7.20 |
| 1300 | 16 ga x 2-1/2" wide | | 115 | .070 | | 1.55 | 2.65 | | 4.20 | 5.85 |
| 1310 | 3-5/8" wide | | 110 | .073 | | 1.88 | 2.77 | | 4.65 | 6.40 |
| 1320 | 4" wide | | 110 | .073 | | 2.01 | 2.77 | | 4.78 | 6.50 |
| 1330 | 6" wide | | 105 | .076 | | 2.57 | 2.90 | | 5.47 | 7.35 |
| 1340 | 8" wide | | 100 | .080 | | 3.28 | 3.05 | | 6.33 | 8.35 |
| 2200 | Studs 24" O.C., 18 ga x 2-1/2" wide | | 125 | .064 | | 1.79 | 2.44 | | 4.23 | 5.75 |
| 2210 | 3-5/8" wide | | 120 | .067 | | 2.15 | 2.54 | | 4.69 | 6.30 |
| 2220 | 4" wide | | 120 | .067 | | 2.29 | 2.54 | | 4.83 | 6.45 |
| 2230 | 6" wide | | 115 | .070 | | 2.98 | 2.65 | | 5.63 | 7.40 |
| 2240 | 8" wide | | 110 | .073 | | 3.77 | 2.77 | | 6.54 | 8.45 |
| 2300 | 16 ga x 2-1/2" wide | | 115 | .070 | | 2.24 | 2.65 | | 4.89 | 6.60 |
| 2310 | 3-5/8" wide | | 110 | .073 | | 2.72 | 2.77 | | 5.49 | 7.30 |
| 2320 | 4" wide | | 110 | .073 | | 2.91 | 2.77 | | 5.68 | 7.50 |

# 05 41 Structural Metal Stud Framing

## 05 41 13 – Load-Bearing Metal Stud Framing

| 05 41 13.10 Bridging | | Crew | Daily Output | Labor-Hours | Unit | Material | 2008 Bare Costs Labor | Equipment | Total | Total Incl O&P |
|---|---|---|---|---|---|---|---|---|---|---|
| 2330 | 6" wide | 1 Carp | 105 | .076 | Ea. | 3.72 | 2.90 | | 6.62 | 8.60 |
| 2340 | 8" wide | ↓ | 100 | .080 | ↓ | 4.75 | 3.05 | | 7.80 | 10 |
| 3000 | Continuous bridging, per row | | | | | | | | | |
| 3100 | 16 ga x 1-1/2" channel thru studs 12" O.C. | 1 Carp | 6 | 1.333 | C.L.F. | 54 | 51 | | 105 | 139 |
| 3110 | 16" O.C. | | 7 | 1.143 | | 54 | 43.50 | | 97.50 | 128 |
| 3120 | 24" O.C. | | 8.80 | .909 | | 54 | 34.50 | | 88.50 | 114 |
| 4100 | 2" x 2" angle x 18 ga, studs 12" O.C. | | 7 | 1.143 | | 79 | 43.50 | | 122.50 | 155 |
| 4110 | 16" O.C. | | 9 | .889 | | 79 | 34 | | 113 | 140 |
| 4120 | 24" O.C. | | 12 | .667 | | 79 | 25.50 | | 104.50 | 127 |
| 4200 | 16 ga, studs 12" O.C. | | 5 | 1.600 | | 100 | 61 | | 161 | 205 |
| 4210 | 16" O.C. | | 7 | 1.143 | | 100 | 43.50 | | 143.50 | 178 |
| 4220 | 24" O.C. | ↓ | 10 | .800 | ↓ | 100 | 30.50 | | 130.50 | 158 |

## 05 41 13.25 Framing, Boxed Headers/Beams

| | | Crew | Daily Output | Labor-Hours | Unit | Material | Labor | Equipment | Total | Total Incl O&P |
|---|---|---|---|---|---|---|---|---|---|---|
| 0010 | **FRAMING, BOXED HEADERS/BEAMS** | | | | | | | | | |
| 0200 | Double, 18 ga x 6" deep | 2 Carp | 220 | .073 | L.F. | 5.60 | 2.77 | | 8.37 | 10.45 |
| 0210 | 8" deep | | 210 | .076 | | 6.20 | 2.90 | | 9.10 | 11.35 |
| 0220 | 10" deep | | 200 | .080 | | 7.55 | 3.05 | | 10.60 | 13.05 |
| 0230 | 12" deep | | 190 | .084 | | 8.25 | 3.21 | | 11.46 | 14.10 |
| 0300 | 16 ga x 8" deep | | 180 | .089 | | 7.15 | 3.39 | | 10.54 | 13.10 |
| 0310 | 10" deep | | 170 | .094 | | 8.55 | 3.59 | | 12.14 | 15 |
| 0320 | 12" deep | | 160 | .100 | | 9.35 | 3.81 | | 13.16 | 16.20 |
| 0400 | 14 ga x 10" deep | | 140 | .114 | | 9.95 | 4.35 | | 14.30 | 17.75 |
| 0410 | 12" deep | | 130 | .123 | | 10.95 | 4.69 | | 15.64 | 19.35 |
| 1210 | Triple, 18 ga x 8" deep | | 170 | .094 | | 9 | 3.59 | | 12.59 | 15.50 |
| 1220 | 10" deep | | 165 | .097 | | 10.80 | 3.69 | | 14.49 | 17.65 |
| 1230 | 12" deep | | 160 | .100 | | 11.90 | 3.81 | | 15.71 | 19.05 |
| 1300 | 16 ga x 8" deep | | 145 | .110 | | 10.40 | 4.20 | | 14.60 | 17.95 |
| 1310 | 10" deep | | 140 | .114 | | 12.35 | 4.35 | | 16.70 | 20.50 |
| 1320 | 12" deep | | 135 | .119 | | 13.50 | 4.52 | | 18.02 | 22 |
| 1400 | 14 ga x 10" deep | | 115 | .139 | | 13.60 | 5.30 | | 18.90 | 23 |
| 1410 | 12" deep | ↓ | 110 | .145 | ↓ | 15.10 | 5.55 | | 20.65 | 25.50 |

## 05 41 13.30 Framing, Stud Walls

| | | Crew | Daily Output | Labor-Hours | Unit | Material | Labor | Equipment | Total | Total Incl O&P |
|---|---|---|---|---|---|---|---|---|---|---|
| 0010 | **FRAMING, STUD WALLS** w/ top & bottom track, no openings, | | | | | | | | | |
| 0020 | Headers, beams, bridging or bracing | | | | | | | | | |
| 4100 | 8' high walls, 18 ga x 2-1/2" wide, studs 12" O.C. | 2 Carp | 54 | .296 | L.F. | 9.35 | 11.30 | | 20.65 | 28 |
| 4110 | 16" O.C. | | 77 | .208 | | 7.50 | 7.90 | | 15.40 | 20.50 |
| 4120 | 24" O.C. | | 107 | .150 | | 5.60 | 5.70 | | 11.30 | 15 |
| 4130 | 3-5/8" wide, studs 12" O.C. | | 53 | .302 | | 11.15 | 11.50 | | 22.65 | 30 |
| 4140 | 16" O.C. | | 76 | .211 | | 8.95 | 8 | | 16.95 | 22.50 |
| 4150 | 24" O.C. | | 105 | .152 | | 6.70 | 5.80 | | 12.50 | 16.40 |
| 4160 | 4" wide, studs 12" O.C. | | 52 | .308 | | 11.70 | 11.70 | | 23.40 | 31 |
| 4170 | 16" O.C. | | 74 | .216 | | 9.35 | 8.25 | | 17.60 | 23 |
| 4180 | 24" O.C. | | 103 | .155 | | 7.05 | 5.90 | | 12.95 | 16.95 |
| 4190 | 6" wide, studs 12" O.C. | | 51 | .314 | | 14.80 | 11.95 | | 26.75 | 35 |
| 4200 | 16" O.C. | | 73 | .219 | | 11.90 | 8.35 | | 20.25 | 26 |
| 4210 | 24" O.C. | | 101 | .158 | | 8.95 | 6.05 | | 15 | 19.25 |
| 4220 | 8" wide, studs 12" O.C. | | 50 | .320 | | 18.20 | 12.20 | | 30.40 | 39 |
| 4230 | 16" O.C. | | 72 | .222 | | 14.60 | 8.45 | | 23.05 | 29.50 |
| 4240 | 24" O.C. | | 100 | .160 | | 11.05 | 6.10 | | 17.15 | 21.50 |
| 4300 | 16 ga x 2-1/2" wide, studs 12" O.C. | | 47 | .340 | | 11.05 | 12.95 | | 24 | 32 |
| 4310 | 16" O.C. | | 68 | .235 | | 8.75 | 8.95 | | 17.70 | 23.50 |
| 4320 | 24" O.C. | ↓ | 94 | .170 | ↓ | 6.45 | 6.50 | | 12.95 | 17.20 |

## 05 41 13 – Load-Bearing Metal Stud Framing

| 05 41 13.30 Framing, Stud Walls | Crew | Daily Output | Labor-Hours | Unit | Material | 2008 Bare Costs Labor | Equipment | Total | Total Incl O&P |
|---|---|---|---|---|---|---|---|---|---|
| 4330 | 3-5/8" wide, studs 12" O.C. | 2 Carp | 46 | .348 | L.F. | 13.25 | 13.25 | | 26.50 | 35 |
| 4340 | 16" O.C. | | 66 | .242 | | 10.50 | 9.25 | | 19.75 | 26 |
| 4350 | 24" O.C. | | 92 | .174 | | 7.75 | 6.65 | | 14.40 | 18.80 |
| 4360 | 4" wide, studs 12" O.C. | | 45 | .356 | | 13.95 | 13.55 | | 27.50 | 36.50 |
| 4370 | 16" O.C. | | 65 | .246 | | 11.05 | 9.40 | | 20.45 | 27 |
| 4380 | 24" O.C. | | 90 | .178 | | 8.15 | 6.75 | | 14.90 | 19.50 |
| 4390 | 6" wide, studs 12" O.C. | | 44 | .364 | | 17.55 | 13.85 | | 31.40 | 41 |
| 4400 | 16" O.C. | | 64 | .250 | | 13.90 | 9.55 | | 23.45 | 30 |
| 4410 | 24" O.C. | | 88 | .182 | | 10.30 | 6.95 | | 17.25 | 22 |
| 4420 | 8" wide, studs 12" O.C. | | 43 | .372 | | 21.50 | 14.20 | | 35.70 | 45.50 |
| 4430 | 16" O.C. | | 63 | .254 | | 17.15 | 9.70 | | 26.85 | 34 |
| 4440 | 24" O.C. | | 86 | .186 | | 12.70 | 7.10 | | 19.80 | 25 |
| 5100 | 10' high walls, 18 ga x 2-1/2" wide, studs 12" O.C. | | 54 | .296 | | 11.25 | 11.30 | | 22.55 | 30 |
| 5110 | 16" O.C. | | 77 | .208 | | 8.90 | 7.90 | | 16.80 | 22 |
| 5120 | 24" O.C. | | 107 | .150 | | 6.55 | 5.70 | | 12.25 | 16.05 |
| 5130 | 3-5/8" wide, studs 12" O.C. | | 53 | .302 | | 13.40 | 11.50 | | 24.90 | 32.50 |
| 5140 | 16" O.C. | | 76 | .211 | | 10.60 | 8 | | 18.60 | 24 |
| 5150 | 24" O.C. | | 105 | .152 | | 7.80 | 5.80 | | 13.60 | 17.65 |
| 5160 | 4" wide, studs 12" O.C. | | 52 | .308 | | 14.05 | 11.70 | | 25.75 | 33.50 |
| 5170 | 16" O.C. | | 74 | .216 | | 11.15 | 8.25 | | 19.40 | 25 |
| 5180 | 24" O.C. | | 103 | .155 | | 8.20 | 5.90 | | 14.10 | 18.20 |
| 5190 | 6" wide, studs 12" O.C. | | 51 | .314 | | 17.75 | 11.95 | | 29.70 | 38 |
| 5200 | 16" O.C. | | 73 | .219 | | 14.10 | 8.35 | | 22.45 | 28.50 |
| 5210 | 24" O.C. | | 101 | .158 | | 10.40 | 6.05 | | 16.45 | 21 |
| 5220 | 8" wide, studs 12" O.C. | | 50 | .320 | | 22 | 12.20 | | 34.20 | 43 |
| 5230 | 16" O.C. | | 72 | .222 | | 17.30 | 8.45 | | 25.75 | 32.50 |
| 5240 | 24" O.C. | | 100 | .160 | | 12.80 | 6.10 | | 18.90 | 23.50 |
| 5300 | 16 ga x 2-1/2" wide, studs 12" O.C. | | 47 | .340 | | 13.35 | 12.95 | | 26.30 | 34.50 |
| 5310 | 16" O.C. | | 68 | .235 | | 10.45 | 8.95 | | 19.40 | 25.50 |
| 5320 | 24" O.C. | | 94 | .170 | | 7.60 | 6.50 | | 14.10 | 18.45 |
| 5330 | 3-5/8" wide, studs 12" O.C. | | 46 | .348 | | 16 | 13.25 | | 29.25 | 38 |
| 5340 | 16" O.C. | | 66 | .242 | | 12.55 | 9.25 | | 21.80 | 28 |
| 5350 | 24" O.C. | | 92 | .174 | | 9.10 | 6.65 | | 15.75 | 20.50 |
| 5360 | 4" wide, studs 12" O.C. | | 45 | .356 | | 16.85 | 13.55 | | 30.40 | 39.50 |
| 5370 | 16" O.C. | | 65 | .246 | | 13.25 | 9.40 | | 22.65 | 29 |
| 5380 | 24" O.C. | | 90 | .178 | | 9.60 | 6.75 | | 16.35 | 21 |
| 5390 | 6" wide, studs 12" O.C. | | 44 | .364 | | 21 | 13.85 | | 34.85 | 45 |
| 5400 | 16" O.C. | | 64 | .250 | | 16.65 | 9.55 | | 26.20 | 33 |
| 5410 | 24" O.C. | | 88 | .182 | | 12.10 | 6.95 | | 19.05 | 24 |
| 5420 | 8" wide, studs 12" O.C. | | 43 | .372 | | 26 | 14.20 | | 40.20 | 50.50 |
| 5430 | 16" O.C. | | 63 | .254 | | 20.50 | 9.70 | | 30.20 | 37.50 |
| 5440 | 24" O.C. | | 86 | .186 | | 14.90 | 7.10 | | 22 | 27.50 |
| 6190 | 12' high walls, 18 ga x 6" wide, studs 12" O.C. | | 41 | .390 | | 20.50 | 14.85 | | 35.35 | 46 |
| 6200 | 16" O.C. | | 58 | .276 | | 16.30 | 10.50 | | 26.80 | 34.50 |
| 6210 | 24" O.C. | | 81 | .198 | | 11.90 | 7.55 | | 19.45 | 25 |
| 6220 | 8" wide, studs 12" O.C. | | 40 | .400 | | 25.50 | 15.25 | | 40.75 | 51.50 |
| 6230 | 16" O.C. | | 57 | .281 | | 20 | 10.70 | | 30.70 | 38.50 |
| 6240 | 24" O.C. | | 80 | .200 | | 14.60 | 7.60 | | 22.20 | 28 |
| 6390 | 16 ga x 6" wide, studs 12" O.C. | | 35 | .457 | | 25 | 17.40 | | 42.40 | 54.50 |
| 6400 | 16" O.C. | | 51 | .314 | | 19.35 | 11.95 | | 31.30 | 40 |
| 6410 | 24" O.C. | | 70 | .229 | | 13.90 | 8.70 | | 22.60 | 29 |
| 6420 | 8" wide, studs 12" O.C. | | 34 | .471 | | 30.50 | 17.95 | | 48.45 | 61.50 |
| 6430 | 16" O.C. | | 50 | .320 | | 24 | 12.20 | | 36.20 | 45 |

| 05 41 13.30 Framing, Stud Walls | Crew | Daily Output | Labor-Hours | Unit | Material | 2008 Bare Costs Labor | Equipment | Total | Total Incl O&P |
|---|---|---|---|---|---|---|---|---|---|
| 6440 | 24" O.C. | 2 Carp | 69 | .232 | L.F. | 17.15 | 8.85 | | 26 | 32.50 |
| 6530 | 14 ga x 3-5/8" wide, studs 12" O.C. | | 34 | .471 | | 23.50 | 17.95 | | 41.45 | 54 |
| 6540 | 16" O.C. | | 48 | .333 | | 18.35 | 12.70 | | 31.05 | 40 |
| 6550 | 24" O.C. | | 65 | .246 | | 13.15 | 9.40 | | 22.55 | 29 |
| 6560 | 4" wide, studs 12" O.C. | | 33 | .485 | | 25 | 18.45 | | 43.45 | 56.50 |
| 6570 | 16" O.C. | | 47 | .340 | | 19.35 | 12.95 | | 32.30 | 41.50 |
| 6580 | 24" O.C. | | 64 | .250 | | 13.90 | 9.55 | | 23.45 | 30 |
| 6730 | 12 ga x 3-5/8" wide, studs 12" O.C. | | 31 | .516 | | 32.50 | 19.65 | | 52.15 | 66.50 |
| 6740 | 16" O.C. | | 43 | .372 | | 25 | 14.20 | | 39.20 | 49.50 |
| 6750 | 24" O.C. | | 59 | .271 | | 17.65 | 10.35 | | 28 | 35.50 |
| 6760 | 4" wide, studs 12" O.C. | | 30 | .533 | | 35 | 20.50 | | 55.50 | 70 |
| 6770 | 16" O.C. | | 42 | .381 | | 27 | 14.50 | | 41.50 | 52 |
| 6780 | 24" O.C. | | 58 | .276 | | 18.90 | 10.50 | | 29.40 | 37.50 |
| 7390 | 16' high walls, 16 ga x 6" wide, studs 12" O.C. | | 33 | .485 | | 32 | 18.45 | | 50.45 | 64 |
| 7400 | 16" O.C. | | 48 | .333 | | 25 | 12.70 | | 37.70 | 47.50 |
| 7410 | 24" O.C. | | 67 | .239 | | 17.55 | 9.10 | | 26.65 | 33.50 |
| 7420 | 8" wide, studs 12" O.C. | | 32 | .500 | | 39 | 19.05 | | 58.05 | 72.50 |
| 7430 | 16" O.C. | | 47 | .340 | | 30.50 | 12.95 | | 43.45 | 53.50 |
| 7440 | 24" O.C. | | 66 | .242 | | 21.50 | 9.25 | | 30.75 | 38 |
| 7560 | 14 ga x 4" wide, studs 12" O.C. | | 31 | .516 | | 32 | 19.65 | | 51.65 | 66 |
| 7570 | 16" O.C. | | 45 | .356 | | 25 | 13.55 | | 38.55 | 48.50 |
| 7580 | 24" O.C. | | 61 | .262 | | 17.55 | 10 | | 27.55 | 35 |
| 7590 | 6" wide, studs 12" O.C. | | 30 | .533 | | 40.50 | 20.50 | | 61 | 76 |
| 7600 | 16" O.C. | | 44 | .364 | | 31.50 | 13.85 | | 45.35 | 56 |
| 7610 | 24" O.C. | | 60 | .267 | | 22 | 10.15 | | 32.15 | 40.50 |
| 7760 | 12 ga x 4" wide, studs 12" O.C. | | 29 | .552 | | 45.50 | 21 | | 66.50 | 82.50 |
| 7770 | 16" O.C. | | 40 | .400 | | 35 | 15.25 | | 50.25 | 62 |
| 7780 | 24" O.C. | | 55 | .291 | | 24 | 11.10 | | 35.10 | 44 |
| 7790 | 6" wide, studs 12" O.C. | | 28 | .571 | | 57.50 | 22 | | 79.50 | 97 |
| 7800 | 16" O.C. | | 39 | .410 | | 44 | 15.65 | | 59.65 | 73 |
| 7810 | 24" O.C. | | 54 | .296 | | 30.50 | 11.30 | | 41.80 | 51 |
| 8590 | 20' high walls, 14 ga x 6" wide, studs 12" O.C. | | 29 | .552 | | 49.50 | 21 | | 70.50 | 87 |
| 8600 | 16" O.C. | | 42 | .381 | | 38 | 14.50 | | 52.50 | 64.50 |
| 8610 | 24" O.C. | | 57 | .281 | | 26.50 | 10.70 | | 37.20 | 46 |
| 8620 | 8" wide, studs 12" O.C. | | 28 | .571 | | 60.50 | 22 | | 82.50 | 101 |
| 8630 | 16" O.C. | | 41 | .390 | | 46.50 | 14.85 | | 61.35 | 74.50 |
| 8640 | 24" O.C. | | 56 | .286 | | 33 | 10.90 | | 43.90 | 53 |
| 8790 | 12 ga x 6" wide, studs 12" O.C. | | 27 | .593 | | 71 | 22.50 | | 93.50 | 113 |
| 8800 | 16" O.C. | | 37 | .432 | | 54 | 16.50 | | 70.50 | 85 |
| 8810 | 24" O.C. | | 51 | .314 | | 37.50 | 11.95 | | 49.45 | 59.50 |
| 8820 | 8" wide, studs 12" O.C. | | 26 | .615 | | 86.50 | 23.50 | | 110 | 132 |
| 8830 | 16" O.C. | | 36 | .444 | | 66 | 16.95 | | 82.95 | 99 |
| 8840 | 24" O.C. | ▼ | 50 | .320 | ▼ | 45.50 | 12.20 | | 57.70 | 69 |

# 05 42 Cold-Formed Metal Joist Framing

## 05 42 13 – Cold-Formed Metal Floor Joist Framing

### 05 42 13.05 Bracing

| | | Crew | Daily Output | Labor-Hours | Unit | Material | 2008 Bare Costs Labor | Equipment | Total | Total Incl O&P |
|---|---|---|---|---|---|---|---|---|---|---|
| 0010 | **BRACING**, continuous, per row, top & bottom | | | | | | | | | |
| 0120 | Flat strap, 20 ga x 2" wide, joists at 12" O.C. | 1 Carp | 4.67 | 1.713 | C.L.F. | 60 | 65.50 | | 125.50 | 168 |
| 0130 | 16" O.C. | | 5.33 | 1.501 | | 57.50 | 57 | | 114.50 | 153 |
| 0140 | 24" O.C. | | 6.66 | 1.201 | | 55.50 | 46 | | 101.50 | 132 |
| 0150 | 18 ga x 2" wide, joists at 12" O.C. | | 4 | 2 | | 78.50 | 76 | | 154.50 | 206 |
| 0160 | 16" O.C. | | 4.67 | 1.713 | | 77 | 65.50 | | 142.50 | 187 |
| 0170 | 24" O.C. | | 5.33 | 1.501 | | 75.50 | 57 | | 132.50 | 172 |

### 05 42 13.10 Bridging

| | | Crew | Daily Output | Labor-Hours | Unit | Material | 2008 Bare Costs Labor | Equipment | Total | Total Incl O&P |
|---|---|---|---|---|---|---|---|---|---|---|
| 0010 | **BRIDGING**, solid between joists w/ 1-1/4" leg track, per joist bay | | | | | | | | | |
| 0230 | Joists 12" O.C., 18 ga track x 6" wide | 1 Carp | 80 | .100 | Ea. | 1.61 | 3.81 | | 5.42 | 7.70 |
| 0240 | 8" wide | | 75 | .107 | | 2.03 | 4.06 | | 6.09 | 8.60 |
| 0250 | 10" wide | | 70 | .114 | | 2.51 | 4.35 | | 6.86 | 9.55 |
| 0260 | 12" wide | | 65 | .123 | | 2.91 | 4.69 | | 7.60 | 10.50 |
| 0330 | 16 ga track x 6" wide | | 70 | .114 | | 2.01 | 4.35 | | 6.36 | 9 |
| 0340 | 8" wide | | 65 | .123 | | 2.56 | 4.69 | | 7.25 | 10.10 |
| 0350 | 10" wide | | 60 | .133 | | 3.15 | 5.10 | | 8.25 | 11.35 |
| 0360 | 12" wide | | 55 | .145 | | 3.64 | 5.55 | | 9.19 | 12.65 |
| 0440 | 14 ga track x 8" wide | | 60 | .133 | | 3.23 | 5.10 | | 8.33 | 11.45 |
| 0450 | 10" wide | | 55 | .145 | | 3.98 | 5.55 | | 9.53 | 13 |
| 0460 | 12" wide | | 50 | .160 | | 4.59 | 6.10 | | 10.69 | 14.55 |
| 0550 | 12 ga track x 10" wide | | 45 | .178 | | 5.85 | 6.75 | | 12.60 | 17 |
| 0560 | 12" wide | | 40 | .200 | | 6.60 | 7.60 | | 14.20 | 19.10 |
| 1230 | 16" O.C., 18 ga track x 6" wide | | 80 | .100 | | 2.06 | 3.81 | | 5.87 | 8.20 |
| 1240 | 8" wide | | 75 | .107 | | 2.61 | 4.06 | | 6.67 | 9.20 |
| 1250 | 10" wide | | 70 | .114 | | 3.22 | 4.35 | | 7.57 | 10.35 |
| 1260 | 12" wide | | 65 | .123 | | 3.73 | 4.69 | | 8.42 | 11.40 |
| 1330 | 16 ga track x 6" wide | | 70 | .114 | | 2.57 | 4.35 | | 6.92 | 9.65 |
| 1340 | 8" wide | | 65 | .123 | | 3.28 | 4.69 | | 7.97 | 10.90 |
| 1350 | 10" wide | | 60 | .133 | | 4.04 | 5.10 | | 9.14 | 12.35 |
| 1360 | 12" wide | | 55 | .145 | | 4.67 | 5.55 | | 10.22 | 13.80 |
| 1440 | 14 ga track x 8" wide | | 60 | .133 | | 4.14 | 5.10 | | 9.24 | 12.45 |
| 1450 | 10" wide | | 55 | .145 | | 5.10 | 5.55 | | 10.65 | 14.25 |
| 1460 | 12" wide | | 50 | .160 | | 5.90 | 6.10 | | 12 | 16 |
| 1550 | 12 ga track x 10" wide | | 45 | .178 | | 7.50 | 6.75 | | 14.25 | 18.80 |
| 1560 | 12" wide | | 40 | .200 | | 8.45 | 7.60 | | 16.05 | 21 |
| 2230 | 24" O.C., 18 ga track x 6" wide | | 80 | .100 | | 2.98 | 3.81 | | 6.79 | 9.25 |
| 2240 | 8" wide | | 75 | .107 | | 3.77 | 4.06 | | 7.83 | 10.50 |
| 2250 | 10" wide | | 70 | .114 | | 4.65 | 4.35 | | 9 | 11.90 |
| 2260 | 12" wide | | 65 | .123 | | 5.40 | 4.69 | | 10.09 | 13.25 |
| 2330 | 16 ga track x 6" wide | | 70 | .114 | | 3.72 | 4.35 | | 8.07 | 10.90 |
| 2340 | 8" wide | | 65 | .123 | | 4.75 | 4.69 | | 9.44 | 12.55 |
| 2350 | 10" wide | | 60 | .133 | | 5.85 | 5.10 | | 10.95 | 14.35 |
| 2360 | 12" wide | | 55 | .145 | | 6.75 | 5.55 | | 12.30 | 16.10 |
| 2440 | 14 ga track x 8" wide | | 60 | .133 | | 6 | 5.10 | | 11.10 | 14.50 |
| 2450 | 10" wide | | 55 | .145 | | 7.40 | 5.55 | | 12.95 | 16.75 |
| 2460 | 12" wide | | 50 | .160 | | 8.50 | 6.10 | | 14.60 | 18.85 |
| 2550 | 12 ga track x 10" wide | | 45 | .178 | | 10.85 | 6.75 | | 17.60 | 22.50 |
| 2560 | 12" wide | | 40 | .200 | | 12.25 | 7.60 | | 19.85 | 25.50 |

### 05 42 13.25 Framing, Band Joist

| | | Crew | Daily Output | Labor-Hours | Unit | Material | 2008 Bare Costs Labor | Equipment | Total | Total Incl O&P |
|---|---|---|---|---|---|---|---|---|---|---|
| 0010 | **FRAMING, BAND JOIST** (track) fastened to bearing wall | | | | | | | | | |
| 0220 | 18 ga track x 6" deep | 2 Carp | 1000 | .016 | L.F. | 1.31 | .61 | | 1.92 | 2.39 |
| 0230 | 8" deep | | 920 | .017 | | 1.66 | .66 | | 2.32 | 2.85 |

# 05 42 Cold-Formed Metal Joist Framing

## 05 42 13 – Cold-Formed Metal Floor Joist Framing

### 05 42 13.25 Framing, Band Joist

| | | Crew | Daily Output | Labor-Hours | Unit | Material | 2008 Bare Costs Labor | 2008 Bare Costs Equipment | Total | Total Incl O&P |
|---|---|---|---|---|---|---|---|---|---|---|
| 0240 | 10" deep | 2 Carp | 860 | .019 | L.F. | 2.05 | .71 | | 2.76 | 3.35 |
| 0320 | 16 ga track x 6" deep | | 900 | .018 | | 1.64 | .68 | | 2.32 | 2.85 |
| 0330 | 8" deep | | 840 | .019 | | 2.09 | .73 | | 2.82 | 3.43 |
| 0340 | 10" deep | | 780 | .021 | | 2.57 | .78 | | 3.35 | 4.05 |
| 0350 | 12" deep | | 740 | .022 | | 2.97 | .82 | | 3.79 | 4.55 |
| 0430 | 14 ga track x 8" deep | | 750 | .021 | | 2.64 | .81 | | 3.45 | 4.16 |
| 0440 | 10" deep | | 720 | .022 | | 3.24 | .85 | | 4.09 | 4.89 |
| 0450 | 12" deep | | 700 | .023 | | 3.75 | .87 | | 4.62 | 5.50 |
| 0540 | 12 ga track x 10" deep | | 670 | .024 | | 4.77 | .91 | | 5.68 | 6.65 |
| 0550 | 12" deep | ▼ | 650 | .025 | ▼ | 5.40 | .94 | | 6.34 | 7.40 |

### 05 42 13.30 Framing, Boxed Headers/Beams

| | | Crew | Daily Output | Labor-Hours | Unit | Material | 2008 Bare Costs Labor | 2008 Bare Costs Equipment | Total | Total Incl O&P |
|---|---|---|---|---|---|---|---|---|---|---|
| 0010 | **FRAMING, BOXED HEADERS/BEAMS** | | | | | | | | | |
| 0200 | Double, 18 ga x 6" deep | 2 Carp | 220 | .073 | L.F. | 5.60 | 2.77 | | 8.37 | 10.45 |
| 0210 | 8" deep | | 210 | .076 | | 6.20 | 2.90 | | 9.10 | 11.35 |
| 0220 | 10" deep | | 200 | .080 | | 7.55 | 3.05 | | 10.60 | 13.05 |
| 0230 | 12" deep | | 190 | .084 | | 8.25 | 3.21 | | 11.46 | 14.10 |
| 0300 | 16 ga x 8" deep | | 180 | .089 | | 7.15 | 3.39 | | 10.54 | 13.10 |
| 0310 | 10" deep | | 170 | .094 | | 8.55 | 3.59 | | 12.14 | 15 |
| 0320 | 12" deep | | 160 | .100 | | 9.35 | 3.81 | | 13.16 | 16.20 |
| 0400 | 14 ga x 10" deep | | 140 | .114 | | 9.95 | 4.35 | | 14.30 | 17.75 |
| 0410 | 12" deep | | 130 | .123 | | 10.95 | 4.69 | | 15.64 | 19.35 |
| 0500 | 12 ga x 10" deep | | 110 | .145 | | 13.20 | 5.55 | | 18.75 | 23 |
| 0510 | 12" deep | | 100 | .160 | | 14.60 | 6.10 | | 20.70 | 25.50 |
| 1210 | Triple, 18 ga x 8" deep | | 170 | .094 | | 9 | 3.59 | | 12.59 | 15.50 |
| 1220 | 10" deep | | 165 | .097 | | 10.80 | 3.69 | | 14.49 | 17.65 |
| 1230 | 12" deep | | 160 | .100 | | 11.90 | 3.81 | | 15.71 | 19.05 |
| 1300 | 16 ga x 8" deep | | 145 | .110 | | 10.40 | 4.20 | | 14.60 | 17.95 |
| 1310 | 10" deep | | 140 | .114 | | 12.35 | 4.35 | | 16.70 | 20.50 |
| 1320 | 12" deep | | 135 | .119 | | 13.50 | 4.52 | | 18.02 | 22 |
| 1400 | 14 ga x 10" deep | | 115 | .139 | | 14.45 | 5.30 | | 19.75 | 24 |
| 1410 | 12" deep | | 110 | .145 | | 15.95 | 5.55 | | 21.50 | 26 |
| 1500 | 12 ga x 10" deep | | 90 | .178 | | 19.30 | 6.75 | | 26.05 | 31.50 |
| 1510 | 12" deep | ▼ | 85 | .188 | ▼ | 21.50 | 7.15 | | 28.65 | 34.50 |

### 05 42 13.40 Framing, Joists

| | | Crew | Daily Output | Labor-Hours | Unit | Material | 2008 Bare Costs Labor | 2008 Bare Costs Equipment | Total | Total Incl O&P |
|---|---|---|---|---|---|---|---|---|---|---|
| 0010 | **FRAMING, JOISTS**, no band joists (track), web stiffeners, headers, | | | | | | | | | |
| 0020 | Beams, bridging or bracing | | | | | | | | | |
| 0030 | Joists (2" flange) and fasteners, materials only | | | | | | | | | |
| 0220 | 18 ga x 6" deep | | | | L.F. | 1.73 | | | 1.73 | 1.91 |
| 0230 | 8" deep | | | | | 2.06 | | | 2.06 | 2.26 |
| 0240 | 10" deep | | | | | 2.42 | | | 2.42 | 2.66 |
| 0320 | 16 ga x 6" deep | | | | | 2.12 | | | 2.12 | 2.33 |
| 0330 | 8" deep | | | | | 2.54 | | | 2.54 | 2.80 |
| 0340 | 10" deep | | | | | 2.96 | | | 2.96 | 3.26 |
| 0350 | 12" deep | | | | | 3.36 | | | 3.36 | 3.70 |
| 0430 | 14 ga x 8" deep | | | | | 3.20 | | | 3.20 | 3.52 |
| 0440 | 10" deep | | | | | 3.70 | | | 3.70 | 4.07 |
| 0450 | 12" deep | | | | | 4.21 | | | 4.21 | 4.63 |
| 0540 | 12 ga x 10" deep | | | | | 5.40 | | | 5.40 | 5.95 |
| 0550 | 12" deep | | | | ▼ | 6.15 | | | 6.15 | 6.75 |
| 1010 | Installation of joists to band joists, beams & headers, labor only | | | | | | | | | |
| 1220 | 18 ga x 6" deep | 2 Carp | 110 | .145 | Ea. | | 5.55 | | 5.55 | 8.65 |
| 1230 | 8" deep | ▼ | 90 | .178 | ▼ | | 6.75 | | 6.75 | 10.55 |

129

# 05 42 Cold-Formed Metal Joist Framing

## 05 42 13 – Cold-Formed Metal Floor Joist Framing

| | | Crew | Daily Output | Labor-Hours | Unit | Material | 2008 Bare Costs Labor | Equipment | Total | Total Incl O&P |
|---|---|---|---|---|---|---|---|---|---|---|
| **05 42 13.40 Framing, Joists** | | | | | | | | | | |
| 1240 | 10" deep | 2 Carp | 80 | .200 | Ea. | | 7.60 | | 7.60 | 11.85 |
| 1320 | 16 ga x 6" deep | | 95 | .168 | | | 6.40 | | 6.40 | 10 |
| 1330 | 8" deep | | 70 | .229 | | | 8.70 | | 8.70 | 13.55 |
| 1340 | 10" deep | | 60 | .267 | | | 10.15 | | 10.15 | 15.80 |
| 1350 | 12" deep | | 55 | .291 | | | 11.10 | | 11.10 | 17.25 |
| 1430 | 14 ga x 8" deep | | 65 | .246 | | | 9.40 | | 9.40 | 14.60 |
| 1440 | 10" deep | | 45 | .356 | | | 13.55 | | 13.55 | 21 |
| 1450 | 12" deep | | 35 | .457 | | | 17.40 | | 17.40 | 27 |
| 1540 | 12 ga x 10" deep | | 40 | .400 | | | 15.25 | | 15.25 | 23.50 |
| 1550 | 12" deep | | 30 | .533 | | | 20.50 | | 20.50 | 31.50 |
| **05 42 13.45 Framing, Web Stiffeners** | | | | | | | | | | |
| 0010 | **FRAMING, WEB STIFFENERS** at joist bearing, fabricated from | | | | | | | | | |
| 0020 | Stud piece (1-5/8" flange) to stiffen joist (2" flange) | | | | | | | | | |
| 2120 | For 6" deep joist, with 18 ga x 2-1/2" stud | 1 Carp | 120 | .067 | Ea. | 2.07 | 2.54 | | 4.61 | 6.20 |
| 2130 | 3-5/8" stud | | 110 | .073 | | 2.30 | 2.77 | | 5.07 | 6.85 |
| 2140 | 4" stud | | 105 | .076 | | 2.22 | 2.90 | | 5.12 | 6.95 |
| 2150 | 6" stud | | 100 | .080 | | 2.43 | 3.05 | | 5.48 | 7.40 |
| 2160 | 8" stud | | 95 | .084 | | 2.51 | 3.21 | | 5.72 | 7.75 |
| 2220 | 8" deep joist, with 2-1/2" stud | | 120 | .067 | | 2.27 | 2.54 | | 4.81 | 6.45 |
| 2230 | 3-5/8" stud | | 110 | .073 | | 2.48 | 2.77 | | 5.25 | 7.05 |
| 2240 | 4" stud | | 105 | .076 | | 2.43 | 2.90 | | 5.33 | 7.20 |
| 2250 | 6" stud | | 100 | .080 | | 2.66 | 3.05 | | 5.71 | 7.65 |
| 2260 | 8" stud | | 95 | .084 | | 2.88 | 3.21 | | 6.09 | 8.15 |
| 2320 | 10" deep joist, with 2-1/2" stud | | 110 | .073 | | 3.20 | 2.77 | | 5.97 | 7.85 |
| 2330 | 3-5/8" stud | | 100 | .080 | | 3.53 | 3.05 | | 6.58 | 8.65 |
| 2340 | 4" stud | | 95 | .084 | | 3.50 | 3.21 | | 6.71 | 8.85 |
| 2350 | 6" stud | | 90 | .089 | | 3.78 | 3.39 | | 7.17 | 9.40 |
| 2360 | 8" stud | | 85 | .094 | | 3.86 | 3.59 | | 7.45 | 9.85 |
| 2420 | 12" deep joist, with 2-1/2" stud | | 110 | .073 | | 3.38 | 2.77 | | 6.15 | 8.05 |
| 2430 | 3-5/8" stud | | 100 | .080 | | 3.70 | 3.05 | | 6.75 | 8.80 |
| 2440 | 4" stud | | 95 | .084 | | 3.63 | 3.21 | | 6.84 | 9 |
| 2450 | 6" stud | | 90 | .089 | | 3.97 | 3.39 | | 7.36 | 9.60 |
| 2460 | 8" stud | | 85 | .094 | | 4.30 | 3.59 | | 7.89 | 10.35 |
| 3130 | For 6" deep joist, with 16 ga x 3-5/8" stud | | 100 | .080 | | 2.42 | 3.05 | | 5.47 | 7.40 |
| 3140 | 4" stud | | 95 | .084 | | 2.39 | 3.21 | | 5.60 | 7.60 |
| 3150 | 6" stud | | 90 | .089 | | 2.62 | 3.39 | | 6.01 | 8.15 |
| 3160 | 8" stud | | 85 | .094 | | 2.76 | 3.59 | | 6.35 | 8.65 |
| 3230 | 8" deep joist, with 3-5/8" stud | | 100 | .080 | | 2.68 | 3.05 | | 5.73 | 7.70 |
| 3240 | 4" stud | | 95 | .084 | | 2.62 | 3.21 | | 5.83 | 7.90 |
| 3250 | 6" stud | | 90 | .089 | | 2.91 | 3.39 | | 6.30 | 8.45 |
| 3260 | 8" stud | | 85 | .094 | | 3.11 | 3.59 | | 6.70 | 9 |
| 3330 | 10" deep joist, with 3-5/8" stud | | 85 | .094 | | 3.67 | 3.59 | | 7.26 | 9.65 |
| 3340 | 4" stud | | 80 | .100 | | 3.73 | 3.81 | | 7.54 | 10.05 |
| 3350 | 6" stud | | 75 | .107 | | 4.06 | 4.06 | | 8.12 | 10.80 |
| 3360 | 8" stud | | 70 | .114 | | 4.22 | 4.35 | | 8.57 | 11.45 |
| 3430 | 12" deep joist, with 3-5/8" stud | | 85 | .094 | | 4 | 3.59 | | 7.59 | 10 |
| 3440 | 4" stud | | 80 | .100 | | 3.92 | 3.81 | | 7.73 | 10.25 |
| 3450 | 6" stud | | 75 | .107 | | 4.34 | 4.06 | | 8.40 | 11.15 |
| 3460 | 8" stud | | 70 | .114 | | 4.64 | 4.35 | | 8.99 | 11.90 |
| 4230 | For 8" deep joist, with 14 ga x 3-5/8" stud | | 90 | .089 | | 3.48 | 3.39 | | 6.87 | 9.10 |
| 4240 | 4" stud | | 85 | .094 | | 3.54 | 3.59 | | 7.13 | 9.50 |
| 4250 | 6" stud | | 80 | .100 | | 3.84 | 3.81 | | 7.65 | 10.15 |

## 05 42 13 – Cold-Formed Metal Floor Joist Framing

### 05 42 13.45 Framing, Web Stiffeners

| | | Crew | Daily Output | Labor-Hours | Unit | Material | 2008 Bare Costs Labor | Equipment | Total | Total Incl O&P |
|---|---|---|---|---|---|---|---|---|---|---|
| 4260 | 8" stud | 1 Carp | 75 | .107 | Ea. | 4.11 | 4.06 | | 8.17 | 10.85 |
| 4330 | 10" deep joist, with 3-5/8" stud | | 75 | .107 | | 4.88 | 4.06 | | 8.94 | 11.70 |
| 4340 | 4" stud | | 70 | .114 | | 4.83 | 4.35 | | 9.18 | 12.10 |
| 4350 | 6" stud | | 65 | .123 | | 5.30 | 4.69 | | 9.99 | 13.15 |
| 4360 | 8" stud | | 60 | .133 | | 5.55 | 5.10 | | 10.65 | 14 |
| 4430 | 12" deep joist, with 3-5/8" stud | | 75 | .107 | | 5.20 | 4.06 | | 9.26 | 12.05 |
| 4440 | 4" stud | | 70 | .114 | | 5.30 | 4.35 | | 9.65 | 12.60 |
| 4450 | 6" stud | | 65 | .123 | | 5.75 | 4.69 | | 10.44 | 13.60 |
| 4460 | 8" stud | | 60 | .133 | | 6.15 | 5.10 | | 11.25 | 14.65 |
| 5330 | For 10" deep joist, with 12 ga x 3-5/8" stud | | 65 | .123 | | 5.15 | 4.69 | | 9.84 | 12.95 |
| 5340 | 4" stud | | 60 | .133 | | 5.30 | 5.10 | | 10.40 | 13.70 |
| 5350 | 6" stud | | 55 | .145 | | 5.85 | 5.55 | | 11.40 | 15.05 |
| 5360 | 8" stud | | 50 | .160 | | 6.40 | 6.10 | | 12.50 | 16.55 |
| 5430 | 12" deep joist, with 3-5/8" stud | | 65 | .123 | | 5.70 | 4.69 | | 10.39 | 13.55 |
| 5440 | 4" stud | | 60 | .133 | | 5.55 | 5.10 | | 10.65 | 14 |
| 5450 | 6" stud | | 55 | .145 | | 6.35 | 5.55 | | 11.90 | 15.65 |
| 5460 | 8" stud | | 50 | .160 | | 7.35 | 6.10 | | 13.45 | 17.55 |

## 05 42 23 – Cold-Formed Metal Roof Joist Framing

### 05 42 23.05 Framing, Bracing

| | | Crew | Daily Output | Labor-Hours | Unit | Material | 2008 Bare Costs Labor | Equipment | Total | Total Incl O&P |
|---|---|---|---|---|---|---|---|---|---|---|
| 0010 | **FRAMING, BRACING** | | | | | | | | | |
| 0020 | Continuous bracing, per row | | | | | | | | | |
| 0100 | 16 ga x 1-1/2" channel thru rafters/trusses @ 16" O.C. | 1 Carp | 4.50 | 1.778 | C.L.F. | 54 | 67.50 | | 121.50 | 165 |
| 0120 | 24" O.C. | | 6 | 1.333 | | 54 | 51 | | 105 | 139 |
| 0300 | 2" x 2" angle x 18 ga, rafters/trusses @ 16" O.C. | | 6 | 1.333 | | 79 | 51 | | 130 | 166 |
| 0320 | 24" O.C. | | 8 | 1 | | 79 | 38 | | 117 | 147 |
| 0400 | 16 ga, rafters/trusses @ 16" O.C. | | 4.50 | 1.778 | | 100 | 67.50 | | 167.50 | 215 |
| 0420 | 24" O.C. | | 6.50 | 1.231 | | 100 | 47 | | 147 | 183 |

### 05 42 23.10 Framing, Bridging

| | | Crew | Daily Output | Labor-Hours | Unit | Material | 2008 Bare Costs Labor | Equipment | Total | Total Incl O&P |
|---|---|---|---|---|---|---|---|---|---|---|
| 0010 | **FRAMING, BRIDGING** | | | | | | | | | |
| 0020 | Solid, between rafters w/ 1-1/4" leg track, per rafter bay | | | | | | | | | |
| 1200 | Rafters 16" O.C., 18 ga x 4" deep | 1 Carp | 60 | .133 | Ea. | 1.58 | 5.10 | | 6.68 | 9.65 |
| 1210 | 6" deep | | 57 | .140 | | 2.06 | 5.35 | | 7.41 | 10.55 |
| 1220 | 8" deep | | 55 | .145 | | 2.61 | 5.55 | | 8.16 | 11.50 |
| 1230 | 10" deep | | 52 | .154 | | 3.22 | 5.85 | | 9.07 | 12.65 |
| 1240 | 12" deep | | 50 | .160 | | 3.73 | 6.10 | | 9.83 | 13.60 |
| 2200 | 24" O.C., 18 ga x 4" deep | | 60 | .133 | | 2.29 | 5.10 | | 7.39 | 10.40 |
| 2210 | 6" deep | | 57 | .140 | | 2.98 | 5.35 | | 8.33 | 11.60 |
| 2220 | 8" deep | | 55 | .145 | | 3.77 | 5.55 | | 9.32 | 12.80 |
| 2230 | 10" deep | | 52 | .154 | | 4.65 | 5.85 | | 10.50 | 14.20 |
| 2240 | 12" deep | | 50 | .160 | | 5.40 | 6.10 | | 11.50 | 15.45 |

### 05 42 23.50 Framing, Parapets

| | | Crew | Daily Output | Labor-Hours | Unit | Material | 2008 Bare Costs Labor | Equipment | Total | Total Incl O&P |
|---|---|---|---|---|---|---|---|---|---|---|
| 0010 | **FRAMING, PARAPETS** | | | | | | | | | |
| 0100 | 3' high installed on 1st story, 18 ga x 4" wide studs, 12" O.C. | 2 Carp | 100 | .160 | L.F. | 5.85 | 6.10 | | 11.95 | 15.95 |
| 0110 | 16" O.C. | | 150 | .107 | | 4.98 | 4.06 | | 9.04 | 11.85 |
| 0120 | 24" O.C. | | 200 | .080 | | 4.11 | 3.05 | | 7.16 | 9.25 |
| 0200 | 6" wide studs, 12" O.C. | | 100 | .160 | | 7.45 | 6.10 | | 13.55 | 17.70 |
| 0210 | 16" O.C. | | 150 | .107 | | 6.35 | 4.06 | | 10.41 | 13.35 |
| 0220 | 24" O.C. | | 200 | .080 | | 5.25 | 3.05 | | 8.30 | 10.55 |
| 1100 | Installed on 2nd story, 18 ga x 4" wide studs, 12" O.C. | | 95 | .168 | | 5.85 | 6.40 | | 12.25 | 16.45 |
| 1110 | 16" O.C. | | 145 | .110 | | 4.98 | 4.20 | | 9.18 | 12.05 |
| 1120 | 24" O.C. | | 190 | .084 | | 4.11 | 3.21 | | 7.32 | 9.50 |
| 1200 | 6" wide studs, 12" O.C. | | 95 | .168 | | 7.45 | 6.40 | | 13.85 | 18.20 |

# 05 42 Cold-Formed Metal Joist Framing

## 05 42 23 – Cold-Formed Metal Roof Joist Framing

### 05 42 23.50 Framing, Parapets

| | | Crew | Daily Output | Labor-Hours | Unit | Material | 2008 Bare Costs Labor | Equipment | Total | Total Incl O&P |
|---|---|---|---|---|---|---|---|---|---|---|
| 1210 | 16" O.C. | 2 Carp | 145 | .110 | L.F. | 6.35 | 4.20 | | 10.55 | 13.55 |
| 1220 | 24" O.C. | | 190 | .084 | | 5.25 | 3.21 | | 8.46 | 10.80 |
| 2100 | Installed on gable, 18 ga x 4" wide studs, 12" O.C. | | 85 | .188 | | 5.85 | 7.15 | | 13 | 17.60 |
| 2110 | 16" O.C. | | 130 | .123 | | 4.98 | 4.69 | | 9.67 | 12.80 |
| 2120 | 24" O.C. | | 170 | .094 | | 4.11 | 3.59 | | 7.70 | 10.10 |
| 2200 | 6" wide studs, 12" O.C. | | 85 | .188 | | 7.45 | 7.15 | | 14.60 | 19.35 |
| 2210 | 16" O.C. | | 130 | .123 | | 6.35 | 4.69 | | 11.04 | 14.30 |
| 2220 | 24" O.C. | | 170 | .094 | | 5.25 | 3.59 | | 8.84 | 11.40 |

### 05 42 23.60 Framing, Roof Rafters

| | | Crew | Daily Output | Labor-Hours | Unit | Material | 2008 Bare Costs Labor | Equipment | Total | Total Incl O&P |
|---|---|---|---|---|---|---|---|---|---|---|
| 0010 | **FRAMING, ROOF RAFTERS** | | | | | | | | | |
| 0100 | Boxed ridge beam, double, 18 ga x 6" deep | 2 Carp | 160 | .100 | L.F. | 5.60 | 3.81 | | 9.41 | 12.10 |
| 0110 | 8" deep | | 150 | .107 | | 6.20 | 4.06 | | 10.26 | 13.20 |
| 0120 | 10" deep | | 140 | .114 | | 7.55 | 4.35 | | 11.90 | 15.10 |
| 0130 | 12" deep | | 130 | .123 | | 8.25 | 4.69 | | 12.94 | 16.40 |
| 0200 | 16 ga x 6" deep | | 150 | .107 | | 6.35 | 4.06 | | 10.41 | 13.35 |
| 0210 | 8" deep | | 140 | .114 | | 7.15 | 4.35 | | 11.50 | 14.65 |
| 0220 | 10" deep | | 130 | .123 | | 8.55 | 4.69 | | 13.24 | 16.70 |
| 0230 | 12" deep | | 120 | .133 | | 9.35 | 5.10 | | 14.45 | 18.15 |
| 1100 | Rafters, 2" flange, material only, 18 ga x 6" deep | | | | | 1.73 | | | 1.73 | 1.91 |
| 1110 | 8" deep | | | | | 2.06 | | | 2.06 | 2.26 |
| 1120 | 10" deep | | | | | 2.42 | | | 2.42 | 2.66 |
| 1130 | 12" deep | | | | | 2.80 | | | 2.80 | 3.08 |
| 1200 | 16 ga x 6" deep | | | | | 2.12 | | | 2.12 | 2.33 |
| 1210 | 8" deep | | | | | 2.54 | | | 2.54 | 2.80 |
| 1220 | 10" deep | | | | | 2.96 | | | 2.96 | 3.26 |
| 1230 | 12" deep | | | | | 3.36 | | | 3.36 | 3.70 |
| 2100 | Installation only, ordinary rafter to 4:12 pitch, 18 ga x 6" deep | 2 Carp | 35 | .457 | Ea. | | 17.40 | | 17.40 | 27 |
| 2110 | 8" deep | | 30 | .533 | | | 20.50 | | 20.50 | 31.50 |
| 2120 | 10" deep | | 25 | .640 | | | 24.50 | | 24.50 | 38 |
| 2130 | 12" deep | | 20 | .800 | | | 30.50 | | 30.50 | 47.50 |
| 2200 | 16 ga x 6" deep | | 30 | .533 | | | 20.50 | | 20.50 | 31.50 |
| 2210 | 8" deep | | 25 | .640 | | | 24.50 | | 24.50 | 38 |
| 2220 | 10" deep | | 20 | .800 | | | 30.50 | | 30.50 | 47.50 |
| 2230 | 12" deep | | 15 | 1.067 | | | 40.50 | | 40.50 | 63.50 |
| 8100 | Add to labor, ordinary rafters on steep roofs | | | | | | 25% | | | |
| 8110 | Dormers & complex roofs | | | | | | 50% | | | |
| 8200 | Hip & valley rafters to 4:12 pitch | | | | | | 25% | | | |
| 8210 | Steep roofs | | | | | | 50% | | | |
| 8220 | Dormers & complex roofs | | | | | | 75% | | | |
| 8300 | Hip & valley jack rafters to 4:12 pitch | | | | | | 50% | | | |
| 8310 | Steep roofs | | | | | | 75% | | | |
| 8320 | Dormers & complex roofs | | | | | | 100% | | | |

### 05 42 23.70 Framing, Soffits and Canopies

| | | Crew | Daily Output | Labor-Hours | Unit | Material | 2008 Bare Costs Labor | Equipment | Total | Total Incl O&P |
|---|---|---|---|---|---|---|---|---|---|---|
| 0010 | **FRAMING, SOFFITS & CANOPIES** | | | | | | | | | |
| 0130 | Continuous ledger track @ wall, studs @ 16" O.C., 18 ga x 4" wide | 2 Carp | 535 | .030 | L.F. | 1.06 | 1.14 | | 2.20 | 2.93 |
| 0140 | 6" wide | | 500 | .032 | | 1.38 | 1.22 | | 2.60 | 3.41 |
| 0150 | 8" wide | | 465 | .034 | | 1.74 | 1.31 | | 3.05 | 3.95 |
| 0160 | 10" wide | | 430 | .037 | | 2.15 | 1.42 | | 3.57 | 4.57 |
| 0230 | Studs @ 24" O.C., 18 ga x 4" wide | | 800 | .020 | | 1.01 | .76 | | 1.77 | 2.30 |
| 0240 | 6" wide | | 750 | .021 | | 1.31 | .81 | | 2.12 | 2.70 |
| 0250 | 8" wide | | 700 | .023 | | 1.66 | .87 | | 2.53 | 3.18 |
| 0260 | 10" wide | | 650 | .025 | | 2.05 | .94 | | 2.99 | 3.71 |

# 05 42 Cold-Formed Metal Joist Framing

## 05 42 23 – Cold-Formed Metal Roof Joist Framing

| 05 42 23.70 Framing, Soffits and Canopies | | Crew | Daily Output | Labor-Hours | Unit | Material | 2008 Bare Costs Labor | Equipment | Total | Total Incl O&P |
|---|---|---|---|---|---|---|---|---|---|---|
| 1000 | Horizontal soffit and canopy members, material only | | | | | | | | | |
| 1030 | 1-5/8" flange studs, 18 ga x 4" deep | | | | L.F. | 1.40 | | | 1.40 | 1.54 |
| 1040 | 6" deep | | | | | 1.76 | | | 1.76 | 1.94 |
| 1050 | 8" deep | | | | | 2.15 | | | 2.15 | 2.36 |
| 1140 | 2" flange joists, 18 ga x 6" deep | | | | | 1.98 | | | 1.98 | 2.18 |
| 1150 | 8" deep | | | | | 2.35 | | | 2.35 | 2.59 |
| 1160 | 10" deep | | | | | 2.76 | | | 2.76 | 3.04 |
| 4030 | Installation only, 18 ga, 1-5/8" flange x 4" deep | 2 Carp | 130 | .123 | Ea. | | 4.69 | | 4.69 | 7.30 |
| 4040 | 6" deep | | 110 | .145 | | | 5.55 | | 5.55 | 8.65 |
| 4050 | 8" deep | | 90 | .178 | | | 6.75 | | 6.75 | 10.55 |
| 4140 | 2" flange, 18 ga x 6" deep | | 110 | .145 | | | 5.55 | | 5.55 | 8.65 |
| 4150 | 8" deep | | 90 | .178 | | | 6.75 | | 6.75 | 10.55 |
| 4160 | 10" deep | | 80 | .200 | | | 7.60 | | 7.60 | 11.85 |
| 6010 | Clips to attach facia to rafter tails, 2" x 2" x 18 ga angle | 1 Carp | 120 | .067 | | .94 | 2.54 | | 3.48 | 4.98 |
| 6020 | 16 ga angle | " | 100 | .080 | | 1.18 | 3.05 | | 4.23 | 6.05 |

# 05 44 Cold-Formed Metal Trusses

## 05 44 13 – Cold-Formed Metal Roof Trusses

| 05 44 13.60 Framing, Roof Trusses | | Crew | Daily Output | Labor-Hours | Unit | Material | 2008 Bare Costs Labor | Equipment | Total | Total Incl O&P |
|---|---|---|---|---|---|---|---|---|---|---|
| 0010 | **FRAMING, ROOF TRUSSES** | | | | | | | | | |
| 0020 | Fabrication of trusses on ground, Fink (W) or King Post, to 4:12 pitch | | | | | | | | | |
| 0120 | 18 ga x 4" chords, 16' span | 2 Carp | 12 | 1.333 | Ea. | 65.50 | 51 | | 116.50 | 151 |
| 0130 | 20' span | | 11 | 1.455 | | 82 | 55.50 | | 137.50 | 177 |
| 0140 | 24' span | | 11 | 1.455 | | 98.50 | 55.50 | | 154 | 195 |
| 0150 | 28' span | | 10 | 1.600 | | 115 | 61 | | 176 | 221 |
| 0160 | 32' span | | 10 | 1.600 | | 131 | 61 | | 192 | 239 |
| 0250 | 6" chords, 28' span | | 9 | 1.778 | | 144 | 67.50 | | 211.50 | 263 |
| 0260 | 32' span | | 9 | 1.778 | | 165 | 67.50 | | 232.50 | 286 |
| 0270 | 36' span | | 8 | 2 | | 185 | 76 | | 261 | 325 |
| 0280 | 40' span | | 8 | 2 | | 206 | 76 | | 282 | 345 |
| 1120 | 5:12 to 8:12 pitch, 18 ga x 4" chords, 16' span | | 10 | 1.600 | | 75 | 61 | | 136 | 178 |
| 1130 | 20' span | | 9 | 1.778 | | 93.50 | 67.50 | | 161 | 208 |
| 1140 | 24' span | | 9 | 1.778 | | 112 | 67.50 | | 179.50 | 229 |
| 1150 | 28' span | | 8 | 2 | | 131 | 76 | | 207 | 263 |
| 1160 | 32' span | | 8 | 2 | | 150 | 76 | | 226 | 284 |
| 1250 | 6" chords, 28' span | | 7 | 2.286 | | 165 | 87 | | 252 | 315 |
| 1260 | 32' span | | 7 | 2.286 | | 188 | 87 | | 275 | 345 |
| 1270 | 36' span | | 6 | 2.667 | | 212 | 102 | | 314 | 390 |
| 1280 | 40' span | | 6 | 2.667 | | 235 | 102 | | 337 | 415 |
| 2120 | 9:12 to 12:12 pitch, 18 ga x 4" chords, 16' span | | 8 | 2 | | 93.50 | 76 | | 169.50 | 222 |
| 2130 | 20' span | | 7 | 2.286 | | 117 | 87 | | 204 | 265 |
| 2140 | 24' span | | 7 | 2.286 | | 140 | 87 | | 227 | 290 |
| 2150 | 28' span | | 6 | 2.667 | | 164 | 102 | | 266 | 340 |
| 2160 | 32' span | | 6 | 2.667 | | 187 | 102 | | 289 | 365 |
| 2250 | 6" chords, 28' span | | 5 | 3.200 | | 206 | 122 | | 328 | 415 |
| 2260 | 32' span | | 5 | 3.200 | | 235 | 122 | | 357 | 450 |
| 2270 | 36' span | | 4 | 4 | | 265 | 152 | | 417 | 530 |
| 2280 | 40' span | | 4 | 4 | | 294 | 152 | | 446 | 560 |
| 5120 | Erection only of roof trusses, to 4:12 pitch, 16' span | F-6 | 48 | .833 | | | 29.50 | 15.95 | 45.45 | 63 |
| 5130 | 20' span | | 46 | .870 | | | 31 | 16.65 | 47.65 | 66 |
| 5140 | 24' span | | 44 | .909 | | | 32.50 | 17.40 | 49.90 | 69 |

133

# 05 44 Cold-Formed Metal Trusses

## 05 44 13 – Cold-Formed Metal Roof Trusses

### 05 44 13.60 Framing, Roof Trusses

| | | Crew | Daily Output | Labor-Hours | Unit | Material | 2008 Bare Costs Labor | Equipment | Total | Total Incl O&P |
|---|---|---|---|---|---|---|---|---|---|---|
| 5150 | 28' span | F-6 | 42 | .952 | Ea. | | 34 | 18.25 | 52.25 | 72.50 |
| 5160 | 32' span | | 40 | 1 | | | 35.50 | 19.15 | 54.65 | 76 |
| 5170 | 36' span | | 38 | 1.053 | | | 37.50 | 20 | 57.50 | 80 |
| 5180 | 40' span | | 36 | 1.111 | | | 39.50 | 21.50 | 61 | 84.50 |
| 5220 | 5:12 to 8:12 pitch, 16' span | | 42 | .952 | | | 34 | 18.25 | 52.25 | 72.50 |
| 5230 | 20' span | | 40 | 1 | | | 35.50 | 19.15 | 54.65 | 76 |
| 5240 | 24' span | | 38 | 1.053 | | | 37.50 | 20 | 57.50 | 80 |
| 5250 | 28' span | | 36 | 1.111 | | | 39.50 | 21.50 | 61 | 84.50 |
| 5260 | 32' span | | 34 | 1.176 | | | 42 | 22.50 | 64.50 | 89.50 |
| 5270 | 36' span | | 32 | 1.250 | | | 44.50 | 24 | 68.50 | 95 |
| 5280 | 40' span | | 30 | 1.333 | | | 47.50 | 25.50 | 73 | 101 |
| 5320 | 9:12 to 12:12 pitch, 16' span | | 36 | 1.111 | | | 39.50 | 21.50 | 61 | 84.50 |
| 5330 | 20' span | | 34 | 1.176 | | | 42 | 22.50 | 64.50 | 89.50 |
| 5340 | 24' span | | 32 | 1.250 | | | 44.50 | 24 | 68.50 | 95 |
| 5350 | 28' span | | 30 | 1.333 | | | 47.50 | 25.50 | 73 | 101 |
| 5360 | 32' span | | 28 | 1.429 | | | 51 | 27.50 | 78.50 | 109 |
| 5370 | 36' span | | 26 | 1.538 | | | 54.50 | 29.50 | 84 | 117 |
| 5380 | 40' span | ↓ | 24 | 1.667 | ↓ | | 59 | 32 | 91 | 127 |

# 05 51 Metal Stairs

## 05 51 13 – Metal Pan Stairs

### 05 51 13.50 Pan Stairs

| | | | Crew | Daily Output | Labor-Hours | Unit | Material | 2008 Bare Costs Labor | Equipment | Total | Total Incl O&P |
|---|---|---|---|---|---|---|---|---|---|---|---|
| 0010 | **PAN STAIRS**, shop fabricated, steel stringers | | | | | | | | | | |
| 0200 | Cement fill metal pan, picket rail, 3'-6" wide | | E-4 | 35 | .914 | Riser | 410 | 40 | 3.78 | 453.78 | 530 |
| 0300 | 4'-0" wide | | | 30 | 1.067 | | 465 | 46.50 | 4.41 | 515.91 | 605 |
| 0350 | Wall rail, both sides, 3'-6" wide | CN | | 53 | .604 | ↓ | 315 | 26.50 | 2.49 | 343.99 | 395 |
| 1500 | Landing, steel pan, conventional | | | 160 | .200 | S.F. | 55 | 8.70 | .83 | 64.53 | 77 |
| 1600 | Pre-erected | | ↓ | 255 | .125 | " | 96 | 5.45 | .52 | 101.97 | 116 |
| 1700 | Pre-erected, steel pan tread, 3'-6" wide, 2 line pipe rail | | E-2 | 87 | .644 | Riser | 455 | 27 | 18 | 500 | 565 |

## 05 51 16 – Metal Floor Plate Stairs

### 05 51 16.50 Floor Plate Stairs

| | | Crew | Daily Output | Labor-Hours | Unit | Material | 2008 Bare Costs Labor | Equipment | Total | Total Incl O&P |
|---|---|---|---|---|---|---|---|---|---|---|
| 0010 | **FLOOR PLATE STAIRS**, shop fabricated, steel stringers | | | | | | | | | |
| 0400 | Cast iron tread and pipe rail, 3'-6" wide | E-4 | 35 | .914 | Riser | 440 | 40 | 3.78 | 483.78 | 560 |
| 0500 | Checkered plate tread, industrial, 3'-6" wide | | 28 | 1.143 | | 274 | 49.50 | 4.72 | 328.22 | 395 |
| 0550 | Circular, for tanks, 3'-0" wide | ↓ | 33 | .970 | | 300 | 42 | 4 | 346 | 410 |
| 0600 | For isolated stairs, add | | | | | | 100% | | | |
| 0800 | Custom steel stairs, 3'-6" wide, minimum | E-4 | 35 | .914 | | 410 | 40 | 3.78 | 453.78 | 530 |
| 0810 | Average | | 30 | 1.067 | | 550 | 46.50 | 4.41 | 600.91 | 695 |
| 0900 | Maximum | ↓ | 20 | 1.600 | | 685 | 69.50 | 6.60 | 761.10 | 890 |
| 1100 | For 4' wide stairs, add | | | | | 5% | 5% | | | |
| 1300 | For 5' wide stairs, add | | | | ↓ | 10% | 10% | | | |

## 05 51 19 – Metal Grating Stairs

### 05 51 19.50 Grating Stairs

| | | Crew | Daily Output | Labor-Hours | Unit | Material | 2008 Bare Costs Labor | Equipment | Total | Total Incl O&P |
|---|---|---|---|---|---|---|---|---|---|---|
| 0010 | **GRATING STAIRS**, shop fabricated, steel stringers, safety nosing on treads | | | | | | | | | |
| 0020 | Grating tread and pipe railing, 3'-6" wide | E-4 | 35 | .914 | Riser | 274 | 40 | 3.78 | 317.78 | 375 |
| 0100 | 4'-0" wide | " | 30 | 1.067 | " | 355 | 46.50 | 4.41 | 405.91 | 485 |

## 05 51 23 – Metal Fire Escapes

### 05 51 23.25 Fire Escapes

| | | | | | | | | | | |
|---|---|---|---|---|---|---|---|---|---|---|
| 0010 | **FIRE ESCAPES**, shop fabricated | | | | | | | | | |

# 05 51 Metal Stairs

## 05 51 23 – Metal Fire Escapes

### 05 51 23.25 Fire Escapes

| | | Crew | Daily Output | Labor-Hours | Unit | Material | 2008 Bare Costs Labor | Equipment | Total | Total Incl O&P |
|---|---|---|---|---|---|---|---|---|---|---|
| 0200 | 2' wide balcony, 1" x 1/4" bars 1-1/2" O.C. | 1 Sswk | 5 | 1.600 | L.F. | 50.50 | 69 | | 119.50 | 180 |
| 0400 | 1st story cantilevered stair, standard | | .09 | 88.889 | Ea. | 2,100 | 3,825 | | 5,925 | 9,200 |
| 0700 | Platform & fixed stair, 36" x 40" | | .17 | 47.059 | Flight | 930 | 2,025 | | 2,955 | 4,675 |
| 0900 | For 3'-6" wide escapes, add to above | | | | | 100% | 150% | | | |

### 05 51 23.50 Fire Escape Stairs

| | | Crew | Daily Output | Labor-Hours | Unit | Material | 2008 Bare Costs Labor | Equipment | Total | Total Incl O&P |
|---|---|---|---|---|---|---|---|---|---|---|
| 0010 | **FIRE ESCAPE STAIRS**, shop fabricated | | | | | | | | | |
| 0020 | One story, disappearing, stainless steel | 2 Sswk | 20 | .800 | V.L.F. | 202 | 34.50 | | 236.50 | 285 |
| 0100 | Portable ladder | | | | Ea. | 61.50 | | | 61.50 | 67.50 |
| 1100 | Fire escape, galvanized steel, 8'-0" to 10'-4" ceiling | 2 Carp | 1 | 16 | | 1,450 | 610 | | 2,060 | 2,550 |
| 1110 | 10'-6" to 13'-6" ceiling | " | 1 | 16 | | 1,825 | 610 | | 2,435 | 2,950 |

## 05 51 33 – Metal Ladders

### 05 51 33.13 Vertical Metal Ladders

| | | Crew | Daily Output | Labor-Hours | Unit | Material | 2008 Bare Costs Labor | Equipment | Total | Total Incl O&P |
|---|---|---|---|---|---|---|---|---|---|---|
| 0010 | **VERTICAL METAL LADDERS**, shop fabricated | | | | | | | | | |
| 0020 | Steel, 20" wide, bolted to concrete, with cage | E-4 | 50 | .640 | V.L.F. | 75 | 28 | 2.64 | 105.64 | 135 |
| 0100 | Without cage | | 85 | .376 | | 35 | 16.40 | 1.55 | 52.95 | 69.50 |
| 0300 | Aluminum, bolted to concrete, with cage | | 50 | .640 | | 101 | 28 | 2.64 | 131.64 | 164 |
| 0400 | Without cage | | 85 | .376 | | 58.50 | 16.40 | 1.55 | 76.45 | 95.50 |

### 05 51 33.16 Inclined Metal Ladders

| | | Crew | Daily Output | Labor-Hours | Unit | Material | 2008 Bare Costs Labor | Equipment | Total | Total Incl O&P |
|---|---|---|---|---|---|---|---|---|---|---|
| 0010 | **INCLINED METAL LADDERS**, shop fabricated | | | | | | | | | |
| 3900 | Industrial ships ladder, 3' W, grating treads, 2 line pipe rail | E-4 | 30 | 1.067 | Riser | 156 | 46.50 | 4.41 | 206.91 | 260 |
| 4000 | Aluminum | " | 30 | 1.067 | " | 240 | 46.50 | 4.41 | 290.91 | 350 |

### 05 51 33.23 Alternating Tread Ladders

| | | Crew | Daily Output | Labor-Hours | Unit | Material | 2008 Bare Costs Labor | Equipment | Total | Total Incl O&P |
|---|---|---|---|---|---|---|---|---|---|---|
| 0010 | **ALTERNATING TREAD LADDERS**, shop fabricated | | | | | | | | | |
| 1350 | Alternating tread stair, 56/68°, steel, standard paint color | 2 Sswk | 50 | .320 | V.L.F. | 163 | 13.75 | | 176.75 | 204 |
| 1360 | Non-standard paint color | | 50 | .320 | | 185 | 13.75 | | 198.75 | 228 |
| 1370 | Galvanized steel | | 50 | .320 | | 190 | 13.75 | | 203.75 | 234 |
| 1380 | Stainless steel | | 50 | .320 | | 274 | 13.75 | | 287.75 | 325 |
| 1390 | 68°, aluminum | | 50 | .320 | | 200 | 13.75 | | 213.75 | 245 |

# 05 52 Metal Railings

## 05 52 13 – Pipe and Tube Railings

### 05 52 13.50 Railings, Pipe

| | | Crew | Daily Output | Labor-Hours | Unit | Material | 2008 Bare Costs Labor | Equipment | Total | Total Incl O&P |
|---|---|---|---|---|---|---|---|---|---|---|
| 0010 | **RAILINGS, PIPE**, shop fabricated | | | | | | | | | |
| 0020 | Aluminum, 2 rail, satin finish, 1-1/4" diameter | E-4 | 160 | .200 | L.F. | 25 | 8.70 | .83 | 34.53 | 44 |
| 0030 | Clear anodized | | 160 | .200 | | 31 | 8.70 | .83 | 40.53 | 50.50 |
| 0040 | Dark anodized | | 160 | .200 | | 34.50 | 8.70 | .83 | 44.03 | 54.50 |
| 0080 | 1-1/2" diameter, satin finish | | 160 | .200 | | 30 | 8.70 | .83 | 39.53 | 49 |
| 0090 | Clear anodized | | 160 | .200 | | 33 | 8.70 | .83 | 42.53 | 53 |
| 0100 | Dark anodized | | 160 | .200 | | 37 | 8.70 | .83 | 46.53 | 57 |
| 0140 | Aluminum, 3 rail, 1-1/4" diam., satin finish | | 137 | .234 | | 38 | 10.15 | .96 | 49.11 | 61.50 |
| 0150 | Clear anodized | | 137 | .234 | | 47.50 | 10.15 | .96 | 58.61 | 72 |
| 0160 | Dark anodized | | 137 | .234 | | 53 | 10.15 | .96 | 64.11 | 77.50 |
| 0200 | 1-1/2" diameter, satin finish | | 137 | .234 | | 45.50 | 10.15 | .96 | 56.61 | 70 |
| 0210 | Clear anodized | | 137 | .234 | | 52 | 10.15 | .96 | 63.11 | 76.50 |
| 0220 | Dark anodized | | 137 | .234 | | 57 | 10.15 | .96 | 68.11 | 82 |
| 0500 | Steel, 2 rail, on stairs, primed, 1-1/4" diameter | | 160 | .200 | | 20.50 | 8.70 | .83 | 30.03 | 39 |
| 0520 | 1-1/2" diameter | | 160 | .200 | | 22.50 | 8.70 | .83 | 32.03 | 41 |
| 0540 | Galvanized, 1-1/4" diameter | | 160 | .200 | | 28.50 | 8.70 | .83 | 38.03 | 47.50 |
| 0560 | 1-1/2" diameter | | 160 | .200 | | 31.50 | 8.70 | .83 | 41.03 | 51.50 |
| 0580 | Steel, 3 rail, primed, 1-1/4" diameter | | 137 | .234 | | 30.50 | 10.15 | .96 | 41.61 | 53 |

# 05 52 Metal Railings

## 05 52 13 – Pipe and Tube Railings

### 05 52 13.50 Railings, Pipe

| | | Crew | Daily Output | Labor-Hours | Unit | Material | 2008 Bare Costs Labor | Equipment | Total | Total Incl O&P |
|---|---|---|---|---|---|---|---|---|---|---|
| 0600 | 1-1/2" diameter | E-4 | 137 | .234 | L.F. | 32.50 | 10.15 | .96 | 43.61 | 55 |
| 0620 | Galvanized, 1-1/4" diameter | | 137 | .234 | | 42.50 | 10.15 | .96 | 53.61 | 66.50 |
| 0640 | 1-1/2" diameter **CN** | | 137 | .234 | | 50.50 | 10.15 | .96 | 61.61 | 75 |
| 0700 | Stainless steel, 2 rail, 1-1/4" diam. #4 finish | | 137 | .234 | | 73.50 | 10.15 | .96 | 84.61 | 100 |
| 0720 | High polish | | 137 | .234 | | 118 | 10.15 | .96 | 129.11 | 149 |
| 0740 | Mirror polish | | 137 | .234 | | 148 | 10.15 | .96 | 159.11 | 182 |
| 0760 | Stainless steel, 3 rail, 1-1/2" diam., #4 finish | | 120 | .267 | | 111 | 11.60 | 1.10 | 123.70 | 144 |
| 0770 | High polish | | 120 | .267 | | 183 | 11.60 | 1.10 | 195.70 | 224 |
| 0780 | Mirror finish | | 120 | .267 | | 223 | 11.60 | 1.10 | 235.70 | 268 |
| 0900 | Wall rail, alum. pipe, 1-1/4" diam., satin finish | | 213 | .150 | | 14.25 | 6.55 | .62 | 21.42 | 28 |
| 0905 | Clear anodized | | 213 | .150 | | 17.35 | 6.55 | .62 | 24.52 | 31.50 |
| 0910 | Dark anodized | | 213 | .150 | | 21 | 6.55 | .62 | 28.17 | 35.50 |
| 0915 | 1-1/2" diameter, satin finish | | 213 | .150 | | 15.75 | 6.55 | .62 | 22.92 | 30 |
| 0920 | Clear anodized | | 213 | .150 | | 19.80 | 6.55 | .62 | 26.97 | 34.50 |
| 0925 | Dark anodized | | 213 | .150 | | 24.50 | 6.55 | .62 | 31.67 | 39.50 |
| 0930 | Steel pipe, 1-1/4" diameter, primed | | 213 | .150 | | 12.40 | 6.55 | .62 | 19.57 | 26 |
| 0935 | Galvanized | | 213 | .150 | | 17.95 | 6.55 | .62 | 25.12 | 32 |
| 0940 | 1-1/2" diameter | | 176 | .182 | | 12.75 | 7.90 | .75 | 21.40 | 29 |
| 0945 | Galvanized | | 213 | .150 | | 18.05 | 6.55 | .62 | 25.22 | 32.50 |
| 0955 | Stainless steel pipe, 1-1/2" diam., #4 finish | | 107 | .299 | | 58.50 | 13 | 1.24 | 72.74 | 89.50 |
| 0960 | High polish | | 107 | .299 | | 120 | 13 | 1.24 | 134.24 | 157 |
| 0965 | Mirror polish | | 107 | .299 | | 141 | 13 | 1.24 | 155.24 | 180 |
| 2000 | Aluminum pipe & picket railing, double top rail, pickets @ 4-1/2" OC | | | | | | | | | |
| 2010 | 36" high, straight & level | 2 Sswk | 80 | .200 | L.F. | 73.50 | 8.60 | | 82.10 | 96 |
| 2020 | Curved & level | | 60 | .267 | | 103 | 11.45 | | 114.45 | 135 |
| 2030 | Straight & sloped | | 40 | .400 | | 84 | 17.20 | | 101.20 | 124 |

## 05 52 16 – Industrial Railings

### 05 52 16.50 Railings, Industrial

| | | Crew | Daily Output | Labor-Hours | Unit | Material | 2008 Bare Costs Labor | Equipment | Total | Total Incl O&P |
|---|---|---|---|---|---|---|---|---|---|---|
| 0010 | **RAILINGS, INDUSTRIAL**, shop fabricated | | | | | | | | | |
| 0020 | 2 rail, 3'-6" high, 1-1/2" pipe | E-4 | 255 | .125 | L.F. | 23.50 | 5.45 | .52 | 29.47 | 36.50 |
| 0100 | 2" angle rail | " | 255 | .125 | | 21.50 | 5.45 | .52 | 27.47 | 34.50 |
| 0200 | For 4" high kick plate, 10 gauge, add | | | | | 4.94 | | | 4.94 | 5.45 |
| 0300 | 1/4" thick, add | | | | | 6.35 | | | 6.35 | 7 |
| 0500 | For curved rails, add | | | | | 30% | 30% | | | |

# 05 53 Metal Gratings

## 05 53 13 – Floor Grating Frame

### 05 53 13.50 Grating Frame

| | | Crew | Daily Output | Labor-Hours | Unit | Material | 2008 Bare Costs Labor | Equipment | Total | Total Incl O&P |
|---|---|---|---|---|---|---|---|---|---|---|
| 0010 | **GRATING FRAME**, field fabricated | | | | | | | | | |
| 0020 | Aluminum, for gratings 1" to 1-1/2" deep | 1 Sswk | 70 | .114 | L.F. | 8.20 | 4.91 | | 13.11 | 17.85 |
| 0100 | For each corner, add | | | | Ea. | 6.45 | | | 6.45 | 7.10 |

## 05 53 16 – Floor Grating Planks

### 05 53 16.50 Grating Planks

| | | Crew | Daily Output | Labor-Hours | Unit | Material | 2008 Bare Costs Labor | Equipment | Total | Total Incl O&P |
|---|---|---|---|---|---|---|---|---|---|---|
| 0010 | **GRATING PLANKS**, field fabricated from planks | | | | | | | | | |
| 0020 | Aluminum, 9-1/2" wide, 14 ga., 2" rib | E-4 | 950 | .034 | L.F. | 15.50 | 1.47 | .14 | 17.11 | 19.85 |
| 0200 | Galvanized steel, 9-1/2" wide, 14 ga., 2-1/2" rib | | 950 | .034 | | 10.05 | 1.47 | .14 | 11.66 | 13.85 |
| 0300 | 4" rib | | 950 | .034 | | 12.05 | 1.47 | .14 | 13.66 | 16.05 |
| 0500 | 12 gauge, 2-1/2" rib | | 950 | .034 | | 13.35 | 1.47 | .14 | 14.96 | 17.45 |
| 0600 | 3" rib | | 950 | .034 | | 15.60 | 1.47 | .14 | 17.21 | 19.95 |
| 0800 | Stainless steel, type 304, 16 ga., 2" rib | | 950 | .034 | | 27 | 1.47 | .14 | 28.61 | 32.50 |

# 05 53 Metal Gratings

## 05 53 16 – Floor Grating Planks

| 05 53 16.50 Grating Planks | Crew | Daily Output | Labor-Hours | Unit | Material | 2008 Bare Costs Labor | Equipment | Total | Total Incl O&P |
|---|---|---|---|---|---|---|---|---|---|
| 0900 Type 316 | E-4 | 950 | .034 | L.F. | 32.50 | 1.47 | .14 | 34.11 | 39 |

## 05 53 19 – Aluminum Floor Grating

### 05 53 19.50 Floor Grating, Aluminum

| | Crew | Daily Output | Labor-Hours | Unit | Material | 2008 Bare Costs Labor | Equipment | Total | Total Incl O&P |
|---|---|---|---|---|---|---|---|---|---|
| 0010 **FLOOR GRATING, ALUMINUM**, field fabricated from panels | | | | | | | | | |
| 0110 Bearing bars @ 1-3/16" O.C., cross bars @ 4" O.C., | | | | | | | | | |
| 0111 Up to 300 S.F., 1" x 1/8" bar | E-4 | 900 | .036 | S.F. | 10.75 | 1.55 | .15 | 12.45 | 14.75 |
| 0112 Over 300 S.F. | | 850 | .038 | | 9.75 | 1.64 | .16 | 11.55 | 13.85 |
| 0113 1-1/4" x 1/8" bar, up to 300 S.F. | | 800 | .040 | | 12.20 | 1.74 | .17 | 14.11 | 16.70 |
| 0114 Over 300 S.F. | | 1000 | .032 | | 11.05 | 1.39 | .13 | 12.57 | 14.85 |
| 0122 1-1/4" x 3/16" bar, up to 300 S.F. | | 750 | .043 | | 15.60 | 1.86 | .18 | 17.64 | 20.50 |
| 0124 Over 300 S.F. | | 1000 | .032 | | 14.20 | 1.39 | .13 | 15.72 | 18.25 |
| 0132 1-1/2" x 1/8" bar, up to 300 S.F. | | 700 | .046 | | 9.75 | 1.99 | .19 | 11.93 | 14.55 |
| 0134 Over 300 S.F. | | 1000 | .032 | | 8.85 | 1.39 | .13 | 10.37 | 12.40 |
| 0136 1-3/4" x 3/16" bar, up to 300 S.F. | | 500 | .064 | | 21 | 2.78 | .26 | 24.04 | 28.50 |
| 0138 Over 300 S.F. | | 1000 | .032 | | 19.05 | 1.39 | .13 | 20.57 | 23.50 |
| 0146 2-1/4" x 3/16" bar, up to 300 S.F. | | 600 | .053 | | 24.50 | 2.32 | .22 | 27.04 | 31.50 |
| 0148 Over 300 S.F. | | 1000 | .032 | | 22.50 | 1.39 | .13 | 24.02 | 27 |
| 0162 Cross bars @ 2" O.C., 1" x 1/8", up to 300 S.F. | | 600 | .053 | | 13.50 | 2.32 | .22 | 16.04 | 19.25 |
| 0164 Over 300 S.F. | | 1000 | .032 | | 12.25 | 1.39 | .13 | 13.77 | 16.15 |
| 0172 1-1/4" x 3/16" bar, up to 300 S.F. | | 600 | .053 | | 18.70 | 2.32 | .22 | 21.24 | 25 |
| 0174 Over 300 S.F. | | 1000 | .032 | | 17 | 1.39 | .13 | 18.52 | 21.50 |
| 0182 1-1/2" x 1/8" bar, up to 300 S.F. | | 600 | .053 | | 13.40 | 2.32 | .22 | 15.94 | 19.15 |
| 0184 Over 300 S.F. | | 1000 | .032 | | 12.20 | 1.39 | .13 | 13.72 | 16.05 |
| 0186 1-3/4" x 3/16" bar, up to 300 S.F. | | 600 | .053 | | 19.45 | 2.32 | .22 | 21.99 | 26 |
| 0188 Over 300 S.F. | | 1000 | .032 | | 17.70 | 1.39 | .13 | 19.22 | 22 |
| 0200 For straight cuts, add | | | | L.F. | 2.65 | | | 2.65 | 2.92 |
| 0300 For curved cuts, add | | | | | 3.61 | | | 3.61 | 3.97 |
| 0400 For straight banding, add | | | | | 3.25 | | | 3.25 | 3.58 |
| 0500 For curved banding, add | | | | | 4.51 | | | 4.51 | 4.96 |
| 0600 For aluminum checkered plate nosings, add | | | | | 4.44 | | | 4.44 | 4.88 |
| 0700 For straight toe plate, add | | | | | 8.05 | | | 8.05 | 8.90 |
| 0800 For curved toe plate, add | | | | | 10.10 | | | 10.10 | 11.10 |
| 1000 For cast aluminum abrasive nosings, add | | | | | 5.40 | | | 5.40 | 5.95 |
| 1200 Expanded aluminum, .65# per S.F. | E-4 | 1050 | .030 | S.F. | 4.70 | 1.33 | .13 | 6.16 | 7.70 |
| 1400 Extruded I bars are 10% less than 3/16" bars | | | | | | | | | |
| 1600 Heavy duty, all extruded plank, 3/4" deep, 1.8 # per S.F. | E-4 | 1100 | .029 | S.F. | 13.20 | 1.27 | .12 | 14.59 | 16.90 |
| 1700 1-1/4" deep, 2.9# per S.F. | | 1000 | .032 | | 14.05 | 1.39 | .13 | 15.57 | 18.10 |
| 1800 1-3/4" deep, 4.2# per S.F. | | 925 | .035 | | 16.75 | 1.50 | .14 | 18.39 | 21.50 |
| 1900 2-1/4" deep, 5.0# per S.F. | | 875 | .037 | | 19.20 | 1.59 | .15 | 20.94 | 24 |
| 2100 For safety serrated surface, add | | | | | 15% | | | | |

## 05 53 21 – Steel Floor Grating

### 05 53 21.50 Floor Grating, Steel

| | Crew | Daily Output | Labor-Hours | Unit | Material | 2008 Bare Costs Labor | Equipment | Total | Total Incl O&P |
|---|---|---|---|---|---|---|---|---|---|
| 0010 **FLOOR GRATING, STEEL**, field fabricated from panels | | | | | | | | | |
| 0050 Labor for installing, from ground/floor | E-4 | 845 | .038 | S.F. | | 1.65 | .16 | 1.81 | 3.14 |
| 0100 Elevated | | 460 | .070 | " | | 3.03 | .29 | 3.32 | 5.75 |
| 0300 Platforms, to 12' high, rectangular | | 3150 | .010 | Lb. | 1.54 | .44 | .04 | 2.02 | 2.54 |
| 0400 Circular | | 2300 | .014 | " | 1.69 | .61 | .06 | 2.36 | 3.01 |
| 0410 Painted bearing bars @ 1-3/16" | | | | | | | | | |
| 0412 Cross bars @ 4" O.C., 3/4" x 1/8" bar, up to 300 S.F. | E-2 | 500 | .112 | S.F. | 6.45 | 4.69 | 3.13 | 14.27 | 18.65 |
| 0414 Over 300 S.F. | | 750 | .075 | | 5.85 | 3.13 | 2.09 | 11.07 | 14.15 |
| 0422 1-1/4" x 3/16", up to 300 S.F. | | 400 | .140 | | 8.70 | 5.85 | 3.92 | 18.47 | 24 |
| 0424 Over 300 S.F. | | 600 | .093 | | 7.90 | 3.91 | 2.61 | 14.42 | 18.30 |

137

| 05 53 21.50 Floor Grating, Steel | | Crew | Daily Output | Labor-Hours | Unit | Material | 2008 Bare Costs Labor | Equipment | Total | Total Incl O&P |
|---|---|---|---|---|---|---|---|---|---|---|
| 0432 | 1-1/2" x 1/8", up to 300 S.F. | E-2 | 400 | .140 | S.F. | 7.80 | 5.85 | 3.92 | 17.57 | 23 |
| 0434 | Over 300 S.F. | | 600 | .093 | | 7.10 | 3.91 | 2.61 | 13.62 | 17.40 |
| 0436 | 1-3/4" x 3/16", up to 300 S.F. | | 400 | .140 | | 11.35 | 5.85 | 3.92 | 21.12 | 27 |
| 0438 | Over 300 S.F. | | 600 | .093 | | 10.30 | 3.91 | 2.61 | 16.82 | 21 |
| 0452 | 2-1/4" x 3/16", up to 300 S.F. | | 300 | .187 | | 13.45 | 7.80 | 5.20 | 26.45 | 34 |
| 0454 | Over 300 S.F. | | 450 | .124 | | 12.20 | 5.20 | 3.48 | 20.88 | 26.50 |
| 0462 | Cross bars @ 2" O.C., 3/4" x 1/8", up to 300 S.F. | | 500 | .112 | | 12.45 | 4.69 | 3.13 | 20.27 | 25.50 |
| 0464 | Over 300 S.F. | | 750 | .075 | | 10.35 | 3.13 | 2.09 | 15.57 | 19.10 |
| 0472 | 1-1/4" x 3/16", up to 300 S.F. | | 400 | .140 | | 18.65 | 5.85 | 3.92 | 28.42 | 35 |
| 0474 | Over 300 S.F. | | 600 | .093 | | 15.55 | 3.91 | 2.61 | 22.07 | 26.50 |
| 0482 | 1-1/2" x 1/8", up to 300 S.F. | | 400 | .140 | | 14.40 | 5.85 | 3.92 | 24.17 | 30.50 |
| 0484 | Over 300 S.F. | | 600 | .093 | | 12 | 3.91 | 2.61 | 18.52 | 23 |
| 0486 | 1-3/4" x 3/16", up to 300 S.F. | | 400 | .140 | | 19.45 | 5.85 | 3.92 | 29.22 | 36 |
| 0488 | Over 300 S.F. | | 600 | .093 | | 16.20 | 3.91 | 2.61 | 22.72 | 27.50 |
| 0502 | 2-1/4" x 3/16", up to 300 S.F. | | 300 | .187 | | 23 | 7.80 | 5.20 | 36 | 45 |
| 0504 | Over 300 S.F. | ▼ | 450 | .124 | | 19.30 | 5.20 | 3.48 | 27.98 | 34.50 |
| 0690 | For galvanized grating, add | | | | ▼ | 25% | | | | |
| 0800 | For straight cuts, add | | | | L.F. | 2.82 | | | 2.82 | 3.10 |
| 0900 | For curved cuts, add | | | | | 3.88 | | | 3.88 | 4.27 |
| 1000 | For straight banding, add | | | | | 3.29 | | | 3.29 | 3.62 |
| 1100 | For curved banding, add | | | | | 5.10 | | | 5.10 | 5.60 |
| 1200 | For checkered plate nosings, add | | | | | 5.80 | | | 5.80 | 6.40 |
| 1300 | For straight toe or kick plate, add | | | | | 8.20 | | | 8.20 | 9 |
| 1400 | For curved toe or kick plate, add | | | | | 9.95 | | | 9.95 | 10.95 |
| 1500 | For abrasive nosings, add | | | | ▼ | 6 | | | 6 | 6.60 |
| 1510 | For stair treads, see Div. 05 55 13.50 | | | | | | | | | |
| 1600 | For safety serrated surface, minimum, add | | | | | 15% | | | | |
| 1700 | Maximum, add | | | | | 25% | | | | |
| 2000 | Stainless steel gratings, close spaced, 1" x 1/8" bars, up to 300 S.F. | E-4 | 450 | .071 | S.F. | 38.50 | 3.09 | .29 | 41.88 | 48 |
| 2100 | Standard spacing, 3/4" x 1/8" bars | | 500 | .064 | | 30 | 2.78 | .26 | 33.04 | 38.50 |
| 2200 | 1-1/4" x 3/16" bars | | 400 | .080 | | 47.50 | 3.48 | .33 | 51.31 | 59 |
| 2400 | Expanded steel grating, at ground, 3.0# per S.F. | | 900 | .036 | | 3.59 | 1.55 | .15 | 5.29 | 6.90 |
| 2500 | 3.14# per S.F. | | 900 | .036 | | 3.81 | 1.55 | .15 | 5.51 | 7.15 |
| 2600 | 4.0# per S.F. | | 850 | .038 | | 4.70 | 1.64 | .16 | 6.50 | 8.25 |
| 2650 | 4.27# per S.F. | | 850 | .038 | | 5.10 | 1.64 | .16 | 6.90 | 8.70 |
| 2700 | 5.0# per S.F. | | 800 | .040 | | 6.05 | 1.74 | .17 | 7.96 | 9.95 |
| 2800 | 6.25# per S.F. | | 750 | .043 | | 7.65 | 1.86 | .18 | 9.69 | 11.95 |
| 2900 | 7.0# per S.F. | ▼ | 700 | .046 | | 8.60 | 1.99 | .19 | 10.78 | 13.25 |
| 3100 | For flattened expanded steel grating, add | | | | | 8% | | | | |
| 3300 | For elevated installation above 15', add | | | | ▼ | | 15% | | | |

# 05 54 Metal Floor Plates

## 05 54 13 – Floor Plates

| 05 54 13.20 Checkered Plates | Crew | Daily Output | Labor-Hours | Unit | Material | 2008 Bare Costs Labor | Equipment | Total | Total Incl O&P |
|---|---|---|---|---|---|---|---|---|---|
| 0010 **CHECKERED PLATES**, steel, field fabricated | | | | | | | | | |
| 0020 1/4" & 3/8", 2000 to 5000 S.F., bolted | E-4 | 2900 | .011 | Lb. | .88 | .48 | .05 | 1.41 | 1.89 |
| 0100 Welded | | 4400 | .007 | " | .83 | .32 | .03 | 1.18 | 1.51 |
| 0300 Pit or trench cover and frame, 1/4" plate, 2' to 3' wide | | 100 | .320 | S.F. | 23 | 13.90 | 1.32 | 38.22 | 52 |
| 0400 For galvanizing, add | | | | Lb. | .47 | | | .47 | .52 |
| 0500 Platforms, 1/4" plate, no handrails included, rectangular | E-4 | 4200 | .008 | | 1.40 | .33 | .03 | 1.76 | 2.17 |
| 0600 Circular | " | 2500 | .013 | | 1.95 | .56 | .05 | 2.56 | 3.21 |

### 05 54 13.70 Trench Covers

| | Crew | Daily Output | Labor-Hours | Unit | Material | 2008 Bare Costs Labor | Equipment | Total | Total Incl O&P |
|---|---|---|---|---|---|---|---|---|---|
| 0010 **TRENCH COVERS**, field fabricated | | | | | | | | | |
| 0020 Cast iron grating with bar stops and angle frame, to 18" wide | 1 Sswk | 20 | .400 | L.F. | 61.50 | 17.20 | | 78.70 | 99 |
| 0100 Frame only (both sides of trench), 1" grating | | 45 | .178 | | 13.45 | 7.65 | | 21.10 | 28.50 |
| 0150 2" grating | | 35 | .229 | | 21 | 9.85 | | 30.85 | 41 |
| 0200 Aluminum, stock units, including frames and | | | | | | | | | |
| 0210 3/8" plain cover plate, 4" opening | E-4 | 205 | .156 | L.F. | 39 | 6.80 | .64 | 46.44 | 55.50 |
| 0300 6" opening | | 185 | .173 | | 48 | 7.50 | .71 | 56.21 | 67 |
| 0400 10" opening | | 170 | .188 | | 66 | 8.20 | .78 | 74.98 | 88 |
| 0500 16" opening | | 155 | .206 | | 90.50 | 9 | .85 | 100.35 | 117 |
| 0700 Add per inch for additional widths to 24" | | | | | 3.60 | | | 3.60 | 3.96 |
| 0900 For custom fabrication, add | | | | | 50% | | | | |
| 1100 For 1/4" plain cover plate, deduct | | | | | 12% | | | | |
| 1500 For cover recessed for tile, 1/4" thick, deduct | | | | | 12% | | | | |
| 1600 3/8" thick, add | | | | | 5% | | | | |
| 1800 For checkered plate cover, 1/4" thick, deduct | | | | | 12% | | | | |
| 1900 3/8" thick, add | | | | | 2% | | | | |
| 2100 For slotted or round holes in cover, 1/4" thick, add | | | | | 3% | | | | |
| 2200 3/8" thick, add | | | | | 4% | | | | |
| 2300 For abrasive cover, add | | | | | 12% | | | | |

# 05 55 Metal Stair Treads and Nosings

## 05 55 13 – Metal Stair Treads

### 05 55 13.50 Stair Treads

| | Crew | Daily Output | Labor-Hours | Unit | Material | 2008 Bare Costs Labor | Equipment | Total | Total Incl O&P |
|---|---|---|---|---|---|---|---|---|---|
| 0010 **STAIR TREADS** | | | | | | | | | |
| 0020 Aluminum grating, 3' long, 1-1/2" x 3/16" rect. bars, 6" wide | 1 Sswk | 24 | .333 | Ea. | 54.50 | 14.35 | | 68.85 | 86 |
| 0100 12" wide | | 22 | .364 | | 80.50 | 15.65 | | 96.15 | 117 |
| 0200 1-1/2" x 3/16" I-bars, 6" wide | | 24 | .333 | | 46 | 14.35 | | 60.35 | 76.50 |
| 0300 12" wide | | 22 | .364 | | 74 | 15.65 | | 89.65 | 110 |
| 0400 For abrasive nosings, add | | | | | 14.30 | | | 14.30 | 15.70 |
| 0500 For narrow mesh, add | | | | | 60% | | | | |
| 0600 Stair treads, not incl. stringers, see also Div. 03 15 05.85 | | | | | | | | | |
| 0700 Cast aluminum, abrasive, 3' long x 12" wide, 5/16" thick | 1 Sswk | 15 | .533 | Ea. | 121 | 23 | | 144 | 175 |
| 0800 3/8" thick | | 15 | .533 | | 129 | 23 | | 152 | 183 |
| 0900 1/2" thick | | 15 | .533 | | 141 | 23 | | 164 | 197 |
| 1000 Cast bronze, abrasive, 3/8" thick | | 8 | 1 | | 550 | 43 | | 593 | 685 |
| 1100 1/2" thick | | 8 | 1 | | 720 | 43 | | 763 | 875 |
| 1200 Cast iron, abrasive, 3' long x 12" wide, 3/8" thick | | 15 | .533 | | 106 | 23 | | 129 | 159 |
| 1300 1/2" thick | | 15 | .533 | | 123 | 23 | | 146 | 177 |
| 1400 Fiberglass reinforced plastic with safety nosing, | | | | | | | | | |
| 1500 1-1/2" thick, 12" wide, 24" long | 1 Sswk | 22 | .364 | Ea. | 120 | 15.65 | | 135.65 | 160 |
| 1600 30" long | | 22 | .364 | | 126 | 15.65 | | 141.65 | 167 |
| 1700 36" long | | 22 | .364 | | 138 | 15.65 | | 153.65 | 179 |
| 2000 Steel grating, painted, 3' long, 1-1/4" x 3/16" bars, 6" wide | | 20 | .400 | | 46 | 17.20 | | 63.20 | 82 |

## 05 55 13 – Metal Stair Treads

| 05 55 13.50 Stair Treads | | Crew | Daily Output | Labor-Hours | Unit | Material | 2008 Bare Costs Labor | Equipment | Total | Total Incl O&P |
|---|---|---|---|---|---|---|---|---|---|---|
| 2010 | 12" wide | 1 Sswk | 18 | .444 | Ea. | 53.50 | 19.10 | | 72.60 | 93.50 |
| 2100 | Add for abrasive nosing, 3' long, painted | | | | | 14.45 | | | 14.45 | 15.90 |
| 2200 | Galvanized | | | | | 19.40 | | | 19.40 | 21.50 |
| 2300 | Painting 3' treads, in shop, nonstandard paint | | | | | 2.55 | | | 2.55 | 2.81 |
| 2400 | Added coats, standard paint | | | | | 1.09 | | | 1.09 | 1.20 |
| 2500 | Expanded steel, 2-1/2" deep, 9" x 3' long, 18 gauge | 1 Sswk | 20 | .400 | | 25.50 | 17.20 | | 42.70 | 59 |
| 2600 | 14 gauge | " | 20 | .400 | | 31.50 | 17.20 | | 48.70 | 65.50 |

# 05 56 Metal Castings

## 05 56 13 – Metal Construction Castings

### 05 56 13.50 Construction Castings

| | | Crew | Daily Output | Labor-Hours | Unit | Material | 2008 Bare Costs Labor | Equipment | Total | Total Incl O&P |
|---|---|---|---|---|---|---|---|---|---|---|
| 0010 | **CONSTRUCTION CASTINGS** | | | | | | | | | |
| 0020 | Manhole covers and frames see Div. 33 44 13.13 | | | | | | | | | |
| 0100 | Column bases, cast iron, 16" x 16", approx. 65 lbs. | E-4 | 46 | .696 | Ea. | 118 | 30.50 | 2.87 | 151.37 | 188 |
| 0200 | 32" x 32", approx. 256 lbs. | " | 23 | 1.391 | | 440 | 60.50 | 5.75 | 506.25 | 600 |
| 0400 | Cast aluminum for wood columns, 8" x 8" | 1 Carp | 32 | .250 | | 38 | 9.55 | | 47.55 | 57 |
| 0500 | 12" x 12" | " | 32 | .250 | | 82 | 9.55 | | 91.55 | 105 |
| 0600 | Miscellaneous C.I. castings, light sections, less than 150 lbs | E-4 | 3200 | .010 | Lb. | 1.83 | .44 | .04 | 2.31 | 2.84 |
| 1100 | Heavy sections, more than 150 lb | | 4200 | .008 | | .89 | .33 | .03 | 1.25 | 1.61 |
| 1300 | Special low volume items | | 3200 | .010 | | 3.18 | .44 | .04 | 3.66 | 4.33 |
| 1500 | For ductile iron, add | | | | | 100% | | | | |

# 05 58 Formed Metal Fabrications

## 05 58 21 – Formed Chain

### 05 58 21.05 Alloy Steel Chain

| | | Crew | Daily Output | Labor-Hours | Unit | Material | 2008 Bare Costs Labor | Equipment | Total | Total Incl O&P |
|---|---|---|---|---|---|---|---|---|---|---|
| 0010 | **ALLOY STEEL CHAIN**, Grade 80 | | | | | | | | | |
| 0015 | Self-colored, cut lengths, w/accessories, 1/4" | E-17 | 4 | 4 | C.L.F. | 520 | 176 | | 696 | 890 |
| 0020 | 3/8" | | 2 | 8 | | 670 | 350 | | 1,020 | 1,375 |
| 0030 | 1/2" | | 1.20 | 13.333 | | 1,050 | 585 | | 1,635 | 2,200 |
| 0040 | 5/8" | | .72 | 22.222 | | 1,650 | 980 | | 2,630 | 3,600 |
| 0050 | 3/4" | E-18 | .48 | 83.333 | | 2,425 | 3,575 | 2,100 | 8,100 | 11,200 |
| 0060 | 7/8" | | .40 | 100 | | 3,550 | 4,275 | 2,525 | 10,350 | 14,200 |
| 0070 | 1" | | .35 | 114 | | 5,850 | 4,900 | 2,875 | 13,625 | 18,200 |
| 0080 | 1-1/4" | | .24 | 166 | | 10,900 | 7,125 | 4,200 | 22,225 | 29,100 |
| 0110 | Clevis slip hook, 1/4" | | | | Ea. | 15 | | | 15 | 16.50 |
| 0120 | 3/8" | | | | | 22.50 | | | 22.50 | 24.50 |
| 0130 | 1/2" | | | | | 38 | | | 38 | 41.50 |
| 0140 | 5/8" | | | | | 57 | | | 57 | 62.50 |
| 0150 | 3/4" | | | | | 119 | | | 119 | 131 |
| 0160 | Eye/sling hook w/ hammerlock coupling, 7/8" | | | | | 335 | | | 335 | 370 |
| 0170 | 1" | | | | | 470 | | | 470 | 520 |
| 0180 | 1-1/4" | | | | | 710 | | | 710 | 780 |

## 05 58 23 – Formed Columns

### 05 58 23.10 Aluminum Columns

| | | Crew | Daily Output | Labor-Hours | Unit | Material | 2008 Bare Costs Labor | Equipment | Total | Total Incl O&P |
|---|---|---|---|---|---|---|---|---|---|---|
| 0010 | **ALUMINUM COLUMNS** | | | | | | | | | |
| 0020 | Aluminum, extruded, stock units, no cap or base, 6" diameter | E-4 | 240 | .133 | L.F. | 11.65 | 5.80 | .55 | 18 | 24 |
| 0100 | 8" diameter | | 170 | .188 | | 15 | 8.20 | .78 | 23.98 | 32 |
| 0200 | 10" diameter | | 150 | .213 | | 20.50 | 9.30 | .88 | 30.68 | 40 |
| 0300 | 12" diameter | | 140 | .229 | | 37 | 9.95 | .94 | 47.89 | 59.50 |

# 05 58 Formed Metal Fabrications

## 05 58 23 – Formed Columns

| 05 58 23.10 Aluminum Columns | | Crew | Daily Output | Labor-Hours | Unit | Material | 2008 Bare Costs Labor | Equipment | Total | Total Incl O&P |
|---|---|---|---|---|---|---|---|---|---|---|
| 0400 | 15" diameter | E-4 | 120 | .267 | L.F. | 44 | 11.60 | 1.10 | 56.70 | 70.50 |
| 0410 | Caps and bases, plain, 6" diameter | | | | Set | 22 | | | 22 | 24 |
| 0420 | 8" diameter | | | | | 29 | | | 29 | 31.50 |
| 0430 | 10" diameter | | | | | 37 | | | 37 | 40.50 |
| 0440 | 12" diameter | | | | | 50 | | | 50 | 55 |
| 0450 | 15" diameter | | | | | 90 | | | 90 | 99 |
| 0460 | Caps, ornamental, minimum | | | | | 242 | | | 242 | 266 |
| 0470 | Maximum | | | | ↓ | 1,075 | | | 1,075 | 1,200 |
| 0500 | For square columns, add to column prices above | | | | L.F. | 50% | | | | |
| 0700 | Residential, flat, 8' high, plain | E-4 | 20 | 1.600 | Ea. | 88 | 69.50 | 6.60 | 164.10 | 230 |
| 0720 | Fancy | | 20 | 1.600 | | 167 | 69.50 | 6.60 | 243.10 | 315 |
| 0740 | Corner type, plain | | 20 | 1.600 | | 148 | 69.50 | 6.60 | 224.10 | 296 |
| 0760 | Fancy | ↓ | 20 | 1.600 | ↓ | 293 | 69.50 | 6.60 | 369.10 | 455 |

## 05 58 25 – Formed Lamp Posts

| 05 58 25.40 Lamp Posts | | Crew | Daily Output | Labor-Hours | Unit | Material | 2008 Bare Costs Labor | Equipment | Total | Total Incl O&P |
|---|---|---|---|---|---|---|---|---|---|---|
| 0010 | **LAMP POSTS** | | | | | | | | | |
| 0020 | Aluminum, 7' high, stock units, post only | 1 Carp | 16 | .500 | Ea. | 28 | 19.05 | | 47.05 | 60.50 |
| 0100 | Mild steel, plain | " | 16 | .500 | " | 23 | 19.05 | | 42.05 | 55 |

## 05 58 27 – Formed Guards

| 05 58 27.90 Window Guards | | Crew | Daily Output | Labor-Hours | Unit | Material | 2008 Bare Costs Labor | Equipment | Total | Total Incl O&P |
|---|---|---|---|---|---|---|---|---|---|---|
| 0010 | **WINDOW GUARDS**, shop fabricated | | | | | | | | | |
| 0015 | Expanded metal, steel angle frame, permanent | E-4 | 350 | .091 | S.F. | 21.50 | 3.98 | .38 | 25.86 | 31.50 |
| 0025 | Steel bars, 1/2" x 1/2", spaced 5" O.C. | " | 290 | .110 | " | 15 | 4.80 | .46 | 20.26 | 25.50 |
| 0030 | Hinge mounted, add | | | | Opng. | 43.50 | | | 43.50 | 47.50 |
| 0040 | Removable type, add | | | | " | 27.50 | | | 27.50 | 30.50 |
| 0050 | For galvanized guards, add | | | | S.F. | 35% | | | | |
| 0070 | For pivoted or projected type, add | | | | | 105% | 40% | | | |
| 0100 | Mild steel, stock units, economy | E-4 | 405 | .079 | | 5.90 | 3.44 | .33 | 9.67 | 13 |
| 0200 | Deluxe | | 405 | .079 | ↓ | 12.10 | 3.44 | .33 | 15.87 | 19.85 |
| 0400 | Woven wire, stock units, 3/8" channel frame, 3' x 5' opening | | 40 | .800 | Opng. | 159 | 35 | 3.30 | 197.30 | 242 |
| 0500 | 4' x 6' opening | ↓ | 38 | .842 | | 254 | 36.50 | 3.48 | 293.98 | 350 |
| 0800 | Basket guards for above, add | | | | | 218 | | | 218 | 239 |
| 1000 | Swinging guards for above, add | | | | ↓ | 74.50 | | | 74.50 | 82 |

# 05 59 Metal Specialties

## 05 59 63 – Detention Enclosures

| 05 59 63.13 Enclosures, Detention | | Crew | Daily Output | Labor-Hours | Unit | Material | 2008 Bare Costs Labor | Equipment | Total | Total Incl O&P |
|---|---|---|---|---|---|---|---|---|---|---|
| 0010 | **ENCLOSURES, DETENTION** | | | | | | | | | |
| 0500 | Bar front, rolling, 7/8" bars, 4" O.C., 7' high, 5' wide, with hardware | E-4 | 2 | 16 | Ea. | 5,075 | 695 | 66 | 5,836 | 6,900 |

# 05 71 Decorative Metal Stairs

## 05 71 13 – Fabricated Metal Spiral Stairs

### 05 71 13.50 Spiral Stairs

| | | Crew | Daily Output | Labor-Hours | Unit | Material | 2008 Bare Costs Labor | Equipment | Total | Total Incl O&P |
|---|---|---|---|---|---|---|---|---|---|---|
| 0010 | **SPIRAL STAIRS**, shop fabricated | | | | | | | | | |
| 1810 | Spiral aluminum, 5'-0" diameter, stock units | E-4 | 45 | .711 | Riser | 500 | 31 | 2.94 | 533.94 | 610 |
| 1820 | Custom units | | 45 | .711 | | 940 | 31 | 2.94 | 973.94 | 1,075 |
| 1900 | Spiral, cast iron, 4'-0" diameter, ornamental, minimum | | 45 | .711 | | 445 | 31 | 2.94 | 478.94 | 550 |
| 1920 | Maximum | | 25 | 1.280 | | 605 | 55.50 | 5.30 | 665.80 | 770 |
| 2000 | Spiral, steel, industrial checkered plate, 4' diameter | | 45 | .711 | | 445 | 31 | 2.94 | 478.94 | 550 |
| 2200 | Stock units, 6'-0" diameter | | 40 | .800 | | 540 | 35 | 3.30 | 578.30 | 655 |
| 3110 | Spiral steel, stock units, primed, flat metal tread, 3'-6" dia | 2 Carp | 1.60 | 10 | Flight | 1,175 | 380 | | 1,555 | 1,875 |
| 3120 | 4'-0" dia | | 1.45 | 11.034 | | 1,350 | 420 | | 1,770 | 2,125 |
| 3130 | 4'-6" dia | | 1.35 | 11.852 | | 1,475 | 450 | | 1,925 | 2,325 |
| 3140 | 5'-0" dia | | 1.25 | 12.800 | | 1,600 | 490 | | 2,090 | 2,525 |
| 3210 | Galvanized, 3'-6" dia | | 1.60 | 10 | | 2,050 | 380 | | 2,430 | 2,850 |
| 3220 | 4'-0" dia | | 1.45 | 11.034 | | 2,300 | 420 | | 2,720 | 3,175 |
| 3230 | 4'-6" dia | | 1.35 | 11.852 | | 2,500 | 450 | | 2,950 | 3,450 |
| 3240 | 5'-0" dia | | 1.25 | 12.800 | | 2,700 | 490 | | 3,190 | 3,725 |
| 3310 | Checkered plate tread, 3'-6" dia | | 1.45 | 11.034 | | 1,450 | 420 | | 1,870 | 2,225 |
| 3320 | 4'-0" dia | | 1.35 | 11.852 | | 1,625 | 450 | | 2,075 | 2,500 |
| 3330 | 4'-6" dia | | 1.25 | 12.800 | | 1,775 | 490 | | 2,265 | 2,700 |
| 3340 | 5'-0" dia | | 1.15 | 13.913 | | 1,925 | 530 | | 2,455 | 2,925 |
| 3410 | Galvanized, 3'-6" dia | | 1.45 | 11.034 | | 2,325 | 420 | | 2,745 | 3,225 |
| 3420 | 4'-0" dia | | 1.35 | 11.852 | | 2,625 | 450 | | 3,075 | 3,575 |
| 3430 | 4'-6" dia | | 1.25 | 12.800 | | 2,850 | 490 | | 3,340 | 3,875 |
| 3440 | 5'-0" dia | | 1.15 | 13.913 | | 3,075 | 530 | | 3,605 | 4,200 |
| 3510 | Red oak tread on flat metal, 3'-6" dia | | 1.35 | 11.852 | | 1,950 | 450 | | 2,400 | 2,850 |
| 3520 | 4'-0" dia | | 1.25 | 12.800 | | 2,175 | 490 | | 2,665 | 3,125 |
| 3530 | 4'-6" dia | | 1.15 | 13.913 | | 2,350 | 530 | | 2,880 | 3,425 |
| 3540 | 5'-0" dia | | 1.05 | 15.238 | | 2,525 | 580 | | 3,105 | 3,675 |

# 05 73 Decorative Metal Railings

## 05 73 16 – Wire Rope Decorative Metal Railings

### 05 73 16.10 Cable Railings

| | | Crew | Daily Output | Labor-Hours | Unit | Material | 2008 Bare Costs Labor | Equipment | Total | Total Incl O&P |
|---|---|---|---|---|---|---|---|---|---|---|
| 0010 | **CABLE RAILINGS**, with 316 stainless steel 1 x 19 cable, 3/16" diameter | | | | | | | | | |
| 0100 | 1-3/4" daimeter stainless steel posts x 42" high, cables 4" OC | 2 Sswk | 25 | .640 | L.F. | 39 | 27.50 | | 66.50 | 92.50 |

## 05 73 23 – Ornamental Railings

### 05 73 23.50 Railings, Ornamental

| | | Crew | Daily Output | Labor-Hours | Unit | Material | 2008 Bare Costs Labor | Equipment | Total | Total Incl O&P |
|---|---|---|---|---|---|---|---|---|---|---|
| 0010 | **RAILINGS, ORNAMENTAL**, shop fabricated | | | | | | | | | |
| 0020 | Aluminum, bronze or stainless, minimum | 1 Sswk | 24 | .333 | L.F. | 30.50 | 14.35 | | 44.85 | 59.50 |
| 0100 | Maximum | | 9 | .889 | | 300 | 38 | | 338 | 400 |
| 0200 | Aluminum ornamental rail, minimum | | 15 | .533 | | 30.50 | 23 | | 53.50 | 75 |
| 0300 | Maximum | | 8 | 1 | | 91 | 43 | | 134 | 178 |
| 0400 | Hand-forged wrought iron, minimum | | 12 | .667 | | 94.50 | 28.50 | | 123 | 156 |
| 0500 | Maximum | | 8 | 1 | | 284 | 43 | | 327 | 390 |
| 0550 | Steel, minimum | | 12 | .667 | | 29.50 | 28.50 | | 58 | 84 |
| 0560 | Maximum | | 8 | 1 | | 88 | 43 | | 131 | 175 |
| 0600 | Composite metal/wood/glass, minimum | | 6 | 1.333 | | 182 | 57.50 | | 239.50 | 305 |
| 0700 | Maximum | | 5 | 1.600 | | 365 | 69 | | 434 | 525 |

# 05 75 Decorative Formed Metal

## 05 75 13 – Columns

| 05 75 13.20 Columns, Ornamental | | Crew | Daily Output | Labor-Hours | Unit | Material | 2008 Bare Costs | | Total | Total Incl O&P |
|---|---|---|---|---|---|---|---|---|---|---|
| | | | | | | | Labor | Equipment | | |
| 0010 | **COLUMNS, ORNAMENTAL**, shop fabricated | R051223-10 | | | | | | | | |
| 6400 | Mild steel, flat, 9" wide, stock units, painted, plain | E-4 | 160 | .200 | L.F. | 8.25 | 8.70 | .83 | 17.78 | 25.50 |
| 6450 | Fancy | | 160 | .200 | | 15.65 | 8.70 | .83 | 25.18 | 34 |
| 6500 | Corner columns, painted, plain | | 160 | .200 | | 13.90 | 8.70 | .83 | 23.43 | 32 |
| 6550 | Fancy | | 160 | .200 | | 27.50 | 8.70 | .83 | 37.03 | 46.50 |

# Division Notes

| | CREW | DAILY OUTPUT | LABOR-HOURS | UNIT | 2008 BARE COSTS | | | | TOTAL INCL O&P |
|---|---|---|---|---|---|---|---|---|---|
| | | | | | MAT. | LABOR | EQUIP. | TOTAL | |
| | | | | | | | | | |
| | | | | | | | | | |
| | | | | | | | | | |
| | | | | | | | | | |
| | | | | | | | | | |
| | | | | | | | | | |
| | | | | | | | | | |
| | | | | | | | | | |
| | | | | | | | | | |
| | | | | | | | | | |
| | | | | | | | | | |
| | | | | | | | | | |
| | | | | | | | | | |
| | | | | | | | | | |
| | | | | | | | | | |
| | | | | | | | | | |
| | | | | | | | | | |
| | | | | | | | | | |
| | | | | | | | | | |

# Estimating Tips

## 06 05 00 Common Work Results for Wood, Plastics, and Composites

- Common to any wood-framed structure are the accessory connector items such as screws, nails, adhesives, hangers, connector plates, straps, angles, and hold-downs. For typical wood-framed buildings, such as residential projects, the aggregate total for these items can be significant, especially in areas where seismic loading is a concern. For floor and wall framing, the material cost is based on 10 to 25 lbs. per MBF. Hold-downs, hangers, and other connectors should be taken off by the piece.

## 06 10 00 Carpentry

- Lumber is a traded commodity and therefore sensitive to supply and demand in the marketplace. Even in "budgetary" estimating of wood-framed projects, it is advisable to call local suppliers for the latest market pricing.
- Common quantity units for wood-framed projects are "thousand board feet" (MBF). A board foot is a volume of wood, 1" x 1' x 1', or 144 cubic inches. Board-foot quantities are generally calculated using nominal material dimensions—dressed sizes are ignored. Board foot per lineal foot of any stick of lumber can be calculated by dividing the nominal cross-sectional area by 12. As an example, 2,000 lineal feet of 2 x 12 equates to 4 MBF by dividing the nominal area, 2 x 12, by 12, which equals 2, and multiplying by 2,000 to give 4,000 board feet. This simple rule applies to all nominal dimensioned lumber.
- Waste is an issue of concern at the quantity takeoff for any area of construction. Framing lumber is sold in even foot lengths, i.e., 10', 12', 14', 16', and depending on spans, wall heights and the grade of lumber, waste is inevitable. A rule of thumb for lumber waste is 5% to 10% depending on material quality and the complexity of the framing.
- Wood in various forms and shapes is used in many projects, even where the main structural framing is steel, concrete, or masonry. Plywood as a back-up partition material and 2x boards used as blocking and cant strips around roof edges are two common examples. The estimator should ensure that the costs of all wood materials are included in the final estimate.

## 06 20 00 Finish Carpentry

- It is necessary to consider the grade of workmanship when estimating labor costs for erecting millwork and interior finish. In practice, there are three grades: premium, custom, and economy. The RSMeans daily output for base and case moldings is in the range of 200 to 250 L.F. per carpenter per day. This is appropriate for most average custom-grade projects. For premium projects, an adjustment to productivity of 25% to 50% should be made depending on the complexity of the job.

## Reference Numbers

Reference numbers are shown in shaded boxes at the beginning of some major classifications. These numbers refer to related items in the Reference Section. The reference information may be an estimating procedure, an alternate pricing method, or technical information.

*Note:* Not all subdivisions listed here necessarily appear in this publication.

## 06 05 05 – Selective Wood and Plastics Demolition

| 06 05 05.10 Selective Demolition Wood Framing | Crew | Daily Output | Labor-Hours | Unit | Material | 2008 Bare Costs Labor | Equipment | Total | Total Incl O&P |
|---|---|---|---|---|---|---|---|---|---|
| 0010 **SELECTIVE DEMOLITION WOOD FRAMING** R024119-10 | | | | | | | | | |
| 0100 Timber connector, nailed, small | 1 Clab | 96 | .083 | Ea. | | 2.52 | | 2.52 | 3.92 |
| 0110　Medium | | 60 | .133 | | | 4.03 | | 4.03 | 6.25 |
| 0120　Large | | 48 | .167 | | | 5.05 | | 5.05 | 7.85 |
| 0130　Bolted, small | | 48 | .167 | | | 5.05 | | 5.05 | 7.85 |
| 0140　Medium | | 32 | .250 | | | 7.55 | | 7.55 | 11.75 |
| 0150　Large | | 24 | .333 | | | 10.10 | | 10.10 | 15.70 |
| 2958 Beams, 2" x 6" | 2 Clab | 1100 | .015 | L.F. | | .44 | | .44 | .68 |
| 2960　2" x 8" | | 825 | .019 | | | .59 | | .59 | .91 |
| 2965　2" x 10" | | 665 | .024 | | | .73 | | .73 | 1.13 |
| 2970　2" x 12" | | 550 | .029 | | | .88 | | .88 | 1.37 |
| 2972　2" x 14" | | 470 | .034 | | | 1.03 | | 1.03 | 1.60 |
| 2975　4" x 8" | B-1 | 413 | .058 | | | 1.80 | | 1.80 | 2.80 |
| 2980　4" x 10" | | 330 | .073 | | | 2.25 | | 2.25 | 3.50 |
| 2985　4" x 12" | | 275 | .087 | | | 2.70 | | 2.70 | 4.20 |
| 3000　6" x 8" | | 275 | .087 | | | 2.70 | | 2.70 | 4.20 |
| 3040　6" x 10" | | 220 | .109 | | | 3.37 | | 3.37 | 5.25 |
| 3080　6" x 12" | | 185 | .130 | | | 4.01 | | 4.01 | 6.25 |
| 3120　8" x 12" | | 140 | .171 | | | 5.30 | | 5.30 | 8.25 |
| 3160　10" x 12" | | 110 | .218 | | | 6.75 | | 6.75 | 10.50 |
| 3162　Alternate pricing method | | 1.10 | 21.818 | M.B.F. | | 675 | | 675 | 1,050 |
| 3170 Blocking, in 16" OC wall framing, 2" x 4" | 1 Clab | 600 | .013 | L.F. | | .40 | | .40 | .63 |
| 3172　2" x 6" | | 400 | .020 | | | .61 | | .61 | .94 |
| 3174　In 24" OC wall framing, 2" x 4" | | 600 | .013 | | | .40 | | .40 | .63 |
| 3176　2" x 6" | | 400 | .020 | | | .61 | | .61 | .94 |
| 3178　Alt method, wood blocking removal from wood framing | | .40 | 20 | M.B.F. | | 605 | | 605 | 940 |
| 3179　Wood blocking removal from steel framing | | .36 | 22.222 | " | | 670 | | 670 | 1,050 |
| 3180 Bracing, let in, 1" x 3", studs 16" OC | | 1050 | .008 | L.F. | | .23 | | .23 | .36 |
| 3181　Studs 24" OC | | 1080 | .007 | | | .22 | | .22 | .35 |
| 3182　1" x 4", studs 16" OC | | 1050 | .008 | | | .23 | | .23 | .36 |
| 3183　Studs 24" OC | | 1080 | .007 | | | .22 | | .22 | .35 |
| 3184　1" x 6", studs 16" OC | | 1050 | .008 | | | .23 | | .23 | .36 |
| 3185　Studs 24" OC | | 1080 | .007 | | | .22 | | .22 | .35 |
| 3186　2" x 3", studs 16" OC | | 800 | .010 | | | .30 | | .30 | .47 |
| 3187　Studs 24" OC | | 830 | .010 | | | .29 | | .29 | .45 |
| 3188　2" x 4", studs 16" OC | | 800 | .010 | | | .30 | | .30 | .47 |
| 3189　Studs 24" OC | | 830 | .010 | | | .29 | | .29 | .45 |
| 3190　2" x 6", studs 16" OC | | 800 | .010 | | | .30 | | .30 | .47 |
| 3191　Studs 24" OC | | 830 | .010 | | | .29 | | .29 | .45 |
| 3192　2" x 8", studs 16" OC | | 800 | .010 | | | .30 | | .30 | .47 |
| 3193　Studs 24" OC | | 830 | .010 | | | .29 | | .29 | .45 |
| 3194　"T" shaped metal bracing, studs at 16" OC | | 1060 | .008 | | | .23 | | .23 | .36 |
| 3195　Studs at 24" OC | | 1200 | .007 | | | .20 | | .20 | .31 |
| 3196　Metal straps, studs at 16" OC | | 1200 | .007 | | | .20 | | .20 | .31 |
| 3197　Studs at 24" OC | | 1240 | .006 | | | .20 | | .20 | .30 |
| 3200 Columns, round, 8' to 14' tall | | 40 | .200 | Ea. | | 6.05 | | 6.05 | 9.40 |
| 3202　Dimensional lumber sizes | 2 Clab | 1.10 | 14.545 | M.B.F. | | 440 | | 440 | 685 |
| 3250 Blocking, between joists | 1 Clab | 320 | .025 | Ea. | | .76 | | .76 | 1.18 |
| 3252 Bridging, metal strap, between joists | | 320 | .025 | Pr. | | .76 | | .76 | 1.18 |
| 3254　Wood, between joists | | 320 | .025 | " | | .76 | | .76 | 1.18 |
| 3260 Door buck, studs, header & access., 8' high 2" x 4" wall, 3' wide | | 32 | .250 | Ea. | | 7.55 | | 7.55 | 11.75 |
| 3261　4' wide | | 32 | .250 | | | 7.55 | | 7.55 | 11.75 |
| 3262　5' wide | | 32 | .250 | | | 7.55 | | 7.55 | 11.75 |

| 06 05 05.10 Selective Demolition Wood Framing | Crew | Daily Output | Labor-Hours | Unit | Material | 2008 Bare Costs Labor | Equipment | Total | Total Incl O&P |
|---|---|---|---|---|---|---|---|---|---|
| 3263 | 6' wide | 1 Clab | 32 | .250 | Ea. | | 7.55 | | 7.55 | 11.75 |
| 3264 | 8' wide | | 30 | .267 | | | 8.05 | | 8.05 | 12.55 |
| 3265 | 10' wide | | 30 | .267 | | | 8.05 | | 8.05 | 12.55 |
| 3266 | 12' wide | | 30 | .267 | | | 8.05 | | 8.05 | 12.55 |
| 3267 | 2" x 6" wall, 3' wide | | 32 | .250 | | | 7.55 | | 7.55 | 11.75 |
| 3268 | 4' wide | | 32 | .250 | | | 7.55 | | 7.55 | 11.75 |
| 3269 | 5' wide | | 32 | .250 | | | 7.55 | | 7.55 | 11.75 |
| 3270 | 6' wide | | 32 | .250 | | | 7.55 | | 7.55 | 11.75 |
| 3271 | 8' wide | | 30 | .267 | | | 8.05 | | 8.05 | 12.55 |
| 3272 | 10' wide | | 30 | .267 | | | 8.05 | | 8.05 | 12.55 |
| 3273 | 12' wide | | 30 | .267 | | | 8.05 | | 8.05 | 12.55 |
| 3274 | Window buck, studs, header & access, 8' high 2" x 4" wall, 2' wide | | 24 | .333 | | | 10.10 | | 10.10 | 15.70 |
| 3275 | 3' wide | | 24 | .333 | | | 10.10 | | 10.10 | 15.70 |
| 3276 | 4' wide | | 24 | .333 | | | 10.10 | | 10.10 | 15.70 |
| 3277 | 5' wide | | 24 | .333 | | | 10.10 | | 10.10 | 15.70 |
| 3278 | 6' wide | | 24 | .333 | | | 10.10 | | 10.10 | 15.70 |
| 3279 | 7' wide | | 24 | .333 | | | 10.10 | | 10.10 | 15.70 |
| 3280 | 8' wide | | 22 | .364 | | | 11 | | 11 | 17.10 |
| 3281 | 10' wide | | 22 | .364 | | | 11 | | 11 | 17.10 |
| 3282 | 12' wide | | 22 | .364 | | | 11 | | 11 | 17.10 |
| 3283 | 2" x 6" wall, 2' wide | | 24 | .333 | | | 10.10 | | 10.10 | 15.70 |
| 3284 | 3' wide | | 24 | .333 | | | 10.10 | | 10.10 | 15.70 |
| 3285 | 4' wide | | 24 | .333 | | | 10.10 | | 10.10 | 15.70 |
| 3286 | 5' wide | | 24 | .333 | | | 10.10 | | 10.10 | 15.70 |
| 3287 | 6' wide | | 24 | .333 | | | 10.10 | | 10.10 | 15.70 |
| 3288 | 7' wide | | 24 | .333 | | | 10.10 | | 10.10 | 15.70 |
| 3289 | 8' wide | | 22 | .364 | | | 11 | | 11 | 17.10 |
| 3290 | 10' wide | | 22 | .364 | | | 11 | | 11 | 17.10 |
| 3291 | 12' wide | | 22 | .364 | ↓ | | 11 | | 11 | 17.10 |
| 3400 | Fascia boards, 1" x 6" | | 500 | .016 | L.F. | | .48 | | .48 | .75 |
| 3440 | 1" x 8" | | 450 | .018 | | | .54 | | .54 | .84 |
| 3480 | 1" x 10" | | 400 | .020 | | | .61 | | .61 | .94 |
| 3490 | 2" x 6" | | 450 | .018 | | | .54 | | .54 | .84 |
| 3500 | 2" x 8" | | 400 | .020 | | | .61 | | .61 | .94 |
| 3510 | 2" x 10" | | 350 | .023 | ↓ | | .69 | | .69 | 1.08 |
| 3610 | Furring, on wood walls or ceiling | | 4000 | .002 | S.F. | | .06 | | .06 | .09 |
| 3620 | On masonry or concrete walls or ceiling | | 1200 | .007 | " | | .20 | | .20 | .31 |
| 3800 | Headers over openings, 2 @ 2" x 6" | | 110 | .073 | L.F. | | 2.20 | | 2.20 | 3.42 |
| 3840 | 2 @ 2" x 8" | | 100 | .080 | | | 2.42 | | 2.42 | 3.76 |
| 3880 | 2 @ 2" x 10" | | 90 | .089 | ↓ | | 2.69 | | 2.69 | 4.18 |
| 3885 | Alternate pricing method | | .26 | 30.651 | M.B.F. | | 925 | | 925 | 1,450 |
| 3920 | Joists, 1" x 4" | | 1250 | .006 | L.F. | | .19 | | .19 | .30 |
| 3930 | 1" x 6" | | 1135 | .007 | | | .21 | | .21 | .33 |
| 3940 | 1" x 8" | | 1000 | .008 | | | .24 | | .24 | .38 |
| 3950 | 1" x 10" | | 895 | .009 | | | .27 | | .27 | .42 |
| 3960 | 1" x 12" | | 765 | .010 | | | .32 | | .32 | .49 |
| 4200 | 2" x 4" | 2 Clab | 1000 | .016 | | | .48 | | .48 | .75 |
| 4230 | 2" x 6" | | 970 | .016 | | | .50 | | .50 | .78 |
| 4240 | 2" x 8" | | 940 | .017 | | | .51 | | .51 | .80 |
| 4250 | 2" x 10" | | 910 | .018 | | | .53 | | .53 | .83 |
| 4280 | 2" x 12" | | 880 | .018 | | | .55 | | .55 | .86 |
| 4281 | 2" x 14" | | 850 | .019 | | | .57 | | .57 | .89 |
| 4282 | Composite joists, 9-1/2" | ↓ | 960 | .017 | ↓ | | .50 | | .50 | .78 |

## 06 05 05 – Selective Wood and Plastics Demolition

| 06 05 05.10 Selective Demolition Wood Framing | | Crew | Daily Output | Labor-Hours | Unit | Material | 2008 Bare Costs Labor | Equipment | Total | Total Incl O&P |
|---|---|---|---|---|---|---|---|---|---|---|
| 4283 | 11-7/8" | 2 Clab | 930 | .017 | L.F. | | .52 | | .52 | .81 |
| 4284 | 14" | | 897 | .018 | | | .54 | | .54 | .84 |
| 4285 | 16" | | 865 | .019 | | | .56 | | .56 | .87 |
| 4290 | Wood joists, alternate pricing method | | 1.50 | 10.667 | M.B.F. | | 325 | | 325 | 500 |
| 4500 | Open web joist, 12" deep | | 500 | .032 | L.F. | | .97 | | .97 | 1.51 |
| 4505 | 14" deep | | 475 | .034 | | | 1.02 | | 1.02 | 1.58 |
| 4510 | 16" deep | | 450 | .036 | | | 1.08 | | 1.08 | 1.67 |
| 4520 | 18" deep | | 425 | .038 | | | 1.14 | | 1.14 | 1.77 |
| 4530 | 24" deep | | 400 | .040 | | | 1.21 | | 1.21 | 1.88 |
| 4550 | Ledger strips, 1" x 2" | 1 Clab | 1200 | .007 | | | .20 | | .20 | .31 |
| 4560 | 1" x 3" | | 1200 | .007 | | | .20 | | .20 | .31 |
| 4570 | 1" x 4" | | 1200 | .007 | | | .20 | | .20 | .31 |
| 4580 | 2" x 2" | | 1100 | .007 | | | .22 | | .22 | .34 |
| 4590 | 2" x 4" | | 1000 | .008 | | | .24 | | .24 | .38 |
| 4600 | 2" x 6" | | 1000 | .008 | | | .24 | | .24 | .38 |
| 4601 | 2" x 8" or 2" x 10" | | 800 | .010 | | | .30 | | .30 | .47 |
| 4602 | 4" x 6" | | 600 | .013 | | | .40 | | .40 | .63 |
| 4604 | 4" x 8" | | 450 | .018 | | | .54 | | .54 | .84 |
| 5400 | Posts, 4" x 4" | 2 Clab | 800 | .020 | | | .61 | | .61 | .94 |
| 5405 | 4" x 6" | | 550 | .029 | | | .88 | | .88 | 1.37 |
| 5410 | 4" x 8" | | 440 | .036 | | | 1.10 | | 1.10 | 1.71 |
| 5425 | 4" x 10" | | 390 | .041 | | | 1.24 | | 1.24 | 1.93 |
| 5430 | 4" x 12" | | 350 | .046 | | | 1.38 | | 1.38 | 2.15 |
| 5440 | 6" x 6" | | 400 | .040 | | | 1.21 | | 1.21 | 1.88 |
| 5445 | 6" x 8" | | 350 | .046 | | | 1.38 | | 1.38 | 2.15 |
| 5450 | 6" x 10" | | 320 | .050 | | | 1.51 | | 1.51 | 2.35 |
| 5455 | 6" x 12" | | 290 | .055 | | | 1.67 | | 1.67 | 2.60 |
| 5480 | 8" x 8" | | 300 | .053 | | | 1.61 | | 1.61 | 2.51 |
| 5500 | 10" x 10" | | 240 | .067 | | | 2.02 | | 2.02 | 3.14 |
| 5660 | Tongue and groove floor planks | | 2 | 8 | M.B.F. | | 242 | | 242 | 375 |
| 5750 | Rafters, ordinary, 16" OC, 2" x 4" | | 880 | .018 | S.F. | | .55 | | .55 | .86 |
| 5755 | 2" x 6" | | 840 | .019 | | | .58 | | .58 | .90 |
| 5760 | 2" x 8" | | 820 | .020 | | | .59 | | .59 | .92 |
| 5770 | 2" x 10" | | 820 | .020 | | | .59 | | .59 | .92 |
| 5780 | 2" x 12" | | 810 | .020 | | | .60 | | .60 | .93 |
| 5785 | 24" OC, 2" x 4" | | 1170 | .014 | | | .41 | | .41 | .64 |
| 5786 | 2" x 6" | | 1117 | .014 | | | .43 | | .43 | .67 |
| 5787 | 2" x 8" | | 1091 | .015 | | | .44 | | .44 | .69 |
| 5788 | 2" x 10" | | 1091 | .015 | | | .44 | | .44 | .69 |
| 5789 | 2" x 12" | | 1077 | .015 | | | .45 | | .45 | .70 |
| 5795 | Rafters, ordinary, 2" x 4" (alternate method) | | 862 | .019 | L.F. | | .56 | | .56 | .87 |
| 5800 | 2" x 6" (alternate method) | | 850 | .019 | | | .57 | | .57 | .89 |
| 5840 | 2" x 8" (alternate method) | | 837 | .019 | | | .58 | | .58 | .90 |
| 5855 | 2" x 10" (alternate method) | | 825 | .019 | | | .59 | | .59 | .91 |
| 5865 | 2" x 12" (alternate method) | | 812 | .020 | | | .60 | | .60 | .93 |
| 5870 | Sill plate, 2" x 4" | 1 Clab | 1170 | .007 | | | .21 | | .21 | .32 |
| 5871 | 2" x 6" | | 780 | .010 | | | .31 | | .31 | .48 |
| 5872 | 2" x 8" | | 586 | .014 | | | .41 | | .41 | .64 |
| 5873 | Alternate pricing method | | .78 | 10.256 | M.B.F. | | 310 | | 310 | 485 |
| 5885 | Ridge board, 1" x 4" | 2 Clab | 900 | .018 | L.F. | | .54 | | .54 | .84 |
| 5886 | 1" x 6" | | 875 | .018 | | | .55 | | .55 | .86 |
| 5887 | 1" x 8" | | 850 | .019 | | | .57 | | .57 | .89 |
| 5888 | 1" x 10" | | 825 | .019 | | | .59 | | .59 | .91 |

| 06 05 05.10 Selective Demolition Wood Framing | | Crew | Daily Output | Labor-Hours | Unit | Material | 2008 Bare Costs Labor | Equipment | Total | Total Incl O&P |
|---|---|---|---|---|---|---|---|---|---|---|
| 5889 | 1" x 12" | 2 Clab | 800 | .020 | L.F. | | .61 | | .61 | .94 |
| 5890 | 2" x 4" | | 900 | .018 | | | .54 | | .54 | .84 |
| 5892 | 2" x 6" | | 875 | .018 | | | .55 | | .55 | .86 |
| 5894 | 2" x 8" | | 850 | .019 | | | .57 | | .57 | .89 |
| 5896 | 2" x 10" | | 825 | .019 | | | .59 | | .59 | .91 |
| 5898 | 2" x 12" | | 800 | .020 | | | .61 | | .61 | .94 |
| 6050 | Rafter tie, 1" x 4" | | 1250 | .013 | | | .39 | | .39 | .60 |
| 6052 | 1" x 6" | | 1135 | .014 | | | .43 | | .43 | .66 |
| 6054 | 2" x 4" | | 1000 | .016 | | | .48 | | .48 | .75 |
| 6056 | 2" x 6" | ↓ | 970 | .016 | | | .50 | | .50 | .78 |
| 6070 | Sleepers, on concrete, 1" x 2" | 1 Clab | 4700 | .002 | | | .05 | | .05 | .08 |
| 6075 | 1" x 3" | | 4000 | .002 | | | .06 | | .06 | .09 |
| 6080 | 2" x 4" | | 3000 | .003 | | | .08 | | .08 | .13 |
| 6085 | 2" x 6" | ↓ | 2600 | .003 | ↓ | | .09 | | .09 | .14 |
| 6086 | Sheathing from roof, 5/16" | 2 Clab | 1600 | .010 | S.F. | | .30 | | .30 | .47 |
| 6088 | 3/8" | | 1525 | .010 | | | .32 | | .32 | .49 |
| 6090 | 1/2" | | 1400 | .011 | | | .35 | | .35 | .54 |
| 6092 | 5/8" | | 1300 | .012 | | | .37 | | .37 | .58 |
| 6094 | 3/4" | | 1200 | .013 | | | .40 | | .40 | .63 |
| 6096 | Board sheathing from roof | | 1400 | .011 | | | .35 | | .35 | .54 |
| 6100 | Sheathing, from walls, 1/4" | | 1200 | .013 | | | .40 | | .40 | .63 |
| 6110 | 5/16" | | 1175 | .014 | | | .41 | | .41 | .64 |
| 6120 | 3/8" | | 1150 | .014 | | | .42 | | .42 | .65 |
| 6130 | 1/2" | | 1125 | .014 | | | .43 | | .43 | .67 |
| 6140 | 5/8" | | 1100 | .015 | | | .44 | | .44 | .68 |
| 6150 | 3/4" | | 1075 | .015 | | | .45 | | .45 | .70 |
| 6152 | Board sheathing from walls | | 1500 | .011 | | | .32 | | .32 | .50 |
| 6158 | Subfloor, with boards | | 1050 | .015 | | | .46 | | .46 | .72 |
| 6160 | Plywood, 1/2" thick | | 768 | .021 | | | .63 | | .63 | .98 |
| 6162 | 5/8" thick | | 760 | .021 | | | .64 | | .64 | .99 |
| 6164 | 3/4"thick | | 750 | .021 | | | .65 | | .65 | 1 |
| 6165 | 1-1/8" thick | ↓ | 720 | .022 | | | .67 | | .67 | 1.05 |
| 6166 | Underlayment, particle board, 3/8" thick | 1 Clab | 780 | .010 | | | .31 | | .31 | .48 |
| 6168 | 1/2" thick | | 768 | .010 | | | .32 | | .32 | .49 |
| 6170 | 5/8" thick | | 760 | .011 | | | .32 | | .32 | .50 |
| 6172 | 3/4" thick | ↓ | 750 | .011 | | | .32 | | .32 | .50 |
| 6200 | Stairs and stringers, minimum | 2 Clab | 40 | .400 | Riser | | 12.10 | | 12.10 | 18.80 |
| 6240 | Maximum | " | 26 | .615 | " | | 18.60 | | 18.60 | 29 |
| 6300 | Components, tread | 1 Clab | 110 | .073 | Ea. | | 2.20 | | 2.20 | 3.42 |
| 6320 | Riser | | 80 | .100 | " | | 3.03 | | 3.03 | 4.71 |
| 6390 | Stringer, 2" x 10" | | 260 | .031 | L.F. | | .93 | | .93 | 1.45 |
| 6400 | 2" x 12" | | 260 | .031 | | | .93 | | .93 | 1.45 |
| 6410 | 3" x 10" | | 250 | .032 | | | .97 | | .97 | 1.51 |
| 6420 | 3" x 12" | ↓ | 250 | .032 | | | .97 | | .97 | 1.51 |
| 6590 | Wood studs, 2" x 3" | 2 Clab | 3076 | .005 | | | .16 | | .16 | .24 |
| 6600 | 2" x 4" | | 2000 | .008 | | | .24 | | .24 | .38 |
| 6640 | 2" x 6" | ↓ | 1600 | .010 | ↓ | | .30 | | .30 | .47 |
| 6720 | Wall framing, including studs plates and blocking, 2" x 4" | 1 Clab | 600 | .013 | S.F. | | .40 | | .40 | .63 |
| 6740 | 2" x 6" | | 480 | .017 | " | | .50 | | .50 | .78 |
| 6750 | Headers, 2" x 4" | | 1125 | .007 | L.F. | | .22 | | .22 | .33 |
| 6755 | 2" x 6" | | 1125 | .007 | | | .22 | | .22 | .33 |
| 6760 | 2" x 8" | | 1050 | .008 | | | .23 | | .23 | .36 |
| 6765 | 2" x 10" | ↓ | 1050 | .008 | ↓ | | .23 | | .23 | .36 |

# 06 05 Common Work Results for Wood, Plastics and Composites

## 06 05 05 – Selective Wood and Plastics Demolition

### 06 05 05.10 Selective Demolition Wood Framing

| | | Crew | Daily Output | Labor-Hours | Unit | Material | 2008 Bare Costs Labor | 2008 Bare Costs Equipment | Total | Total Incl O&P |
|---|---|---|---|---|---|---|---|---|---|---|
| 6770 | 2" x 12" | 1 Clab | 1000 | .008 | L.F. | | .24 | | .24 | .38 |
| 6780 | 4" x 10" | | 525 | .015 | | | .46 | | .46 | .72 |
| 6785 | 4" x 12" | | 500 | .016 | | | .48 | | .48 | .75 |
| 6790 | 6" x 8" | | 560 | .014 | | | .43 | | .43 | .67 |
| 6795 | 6" x 10" | | 525 | .015 | | | .46 | | .46 | .72 |
| 6797 | 6" x 12" | | 500 | .016 | | | .48 | | .48 | .75 |
| 8000 | Soffit, T & G wood | | 520 | .015 | S.F. | | .47 | | .47 | .72 |
| 8010 | Hardboard, vinyl or aluminum | | 640 | .013 | | | .38 | | .38 | .59 |
| 8030 | Plywood | 2 Carp | 315 | .051 | | | 1.94 | | 1.94 | 3.01 |
| 9500 | See Div. 02 41 19.23 for rubbish handling | | | | | | | | | |

### 06 05 05.20 Selective Demolition Millwork and Trim

| | | Crew | Daily Output | Labor-Hours | Unit | Material | 2008 Bare Costs Labor | 2008 Bare Costs Equipment | Total | Total Incl O&P |
|---|---|---|---|---|---|---|---|---|---|---|
| 0010 | SELECTIVE DEMOLITION MILLWORK AND TRIM   R024119-10 | | | | | | | | | |
| 1000 | Cabinets, wood, base cabinets, per L.F. | 2 Clab | 80 | .200 | L.F. | | 6.05 | | 6.05 | 9.40 |
| 1020 | Wall cabinets, per L.F. | " | 80 | .200 | " | | 6.05 | | 6.05 | 9.40 |
| 1060 | Remove and reset, base cabinets | 2 Carp | 18 | .889 | Ea. | | 34 | | 34 | 52.50 |
| 1070 | Wall cabinets | " | 20 | .800 | " | | 30.50 | | 30.50 | 47.50 |
| 1100 | Steel, painted, base cabinets | 2 Clab | 60 | .267 | L.F. | | 8.05 | | 8.05 | 12.55 |
| 1120 | Wall cabinets | " | 60 | .267 | " | | 8.05 | | 8.05 | 12.55 |
| 1200 | Casework, large area | | 320 | .050 | S.F. | | 1.51 | | 1.51 | 2.35 |
| 1220 | Selective | | 200 | .080 | " | | 2.42 | | 2.42 | 3.76 |
| 1500 | Counter top, minimum | | 200 | .080 | L.F. | | 2.42 | | 2.42 | 3.76 |
| 1510 | Maximum | | 120 | .133 | | | 4.03 | | 4.03 | 6.25 |
| 1550 | Remove and reset, minimum | 2 Carp | 50 | .320 | | | 12.20 | | 12.20 | 19 |
| 1560 | Maximum | " | 40 | .400 | | | 15.25 | | 15.25 | 23.50 |
| 2000 | Paneling, 4' x 8' sheets | 2 Clab | 2000 | .008 | S.F. | | .24 | | .24 | .38 |
| 2100 | Boards, 1" x 4" | | 700 | .023 | | | .69 | | .69 | 1.08 |
| 2120 | 1" x 6" | | 750 | .021 | | | .65 | | .65 | 1 |
| 2140 | 1" x 8" | | 800 | .020 | | | .61 | | .61 | .94 |
| 3000 | Trim, baseboard, to 6" wide | | 1200 | .013 | L.F. | | .40 | | .40 | .63 |
| 3040 | Greater than 6" and up to 12" wide | | 1000 | .016 | | | .48 | | .48 | .75 |
| 3080 | Remove and reset, minimum | 2 Carp | 400 | .040 | | | 1.52 | | 1.52 | 2.37 |
| 3090 | Maximum | " | 300 | .053 | | | 2.03 | | 2.03 | 3.16 |
| 3100 | Ceiling trim | 2 Clab | 1000 | .016 | | | .48 | | .48 | .75 |
| 3120 | Chair rail | | 1200 | .013 | | | .40 | | .40 | .63 |
| 3140 | Railings with balusters | | 240 | .067 | | | 2.02 | | 2.02 | 3.14 |
| 3160 | Wainscoting | | 700 | .023 | S.F. | | .69 | | .69 | 1.08 |

## 06 05 23 – Wood, Plastic, and Composite Fastenings

### 06 05 23.10 Nails

| | | Crew | Daily Output | Labor-Hours | Unit | Material | 2008 Bare Costs Labor | 2008 Bare Costs Equipment | Total | Total Incl O&P |
|---|---|---|---|---|---|---|---|---|---|---|
| 0010 | NAILS, material only, based upon 50# box purchase | | | | | | | | | |
| 0020 | Copper nails, plain | | | | Lb. | 10.20 | | | 10.20 | 11.20 |
| 0400 | Stainless steel, plain | | | | | 6.65 | | | 6.65 | 7.30 |
| 0500 | Box, 3d to 20d, bright | | | | | .76 | | | .76 | .84 |
| 0520 | Galvanized | | | | | .89 | | | .89 | .98 |
| 0600 | Common, 3d to 60d, plain | | | | | .83 | | | .83 | .91 |
| 0700 | Galvanized | | | | | 1.06 | | | 1.06 | 1.17 |
| 0800 | Aluminum | | | | | 4.45 | | | 4.45 | 4.90 |
| 1000 | Annular or spiral thread, 4d to 60d, plain | | | | | 1.79 | | | 1.79 | 1.97 |
| 1200 | Galvanized | | | | | 1.95 | | | 1.95 | 2.15 |
| 1400 | Drywall nails, plain | | | | | .79 | | | .79 | .87 |
| 1600 | Galvanized | | | | | 1.59 | | | 1.59 | 1.75 |
| 1800 | Finish nails, 4d to 10d, plain | | | | | 1.11 | | | 1.11 | 1.22 |
| 2000 | Galvanized | | | | | 1.51 | | | 1.51 | 1.66 |

### 06 05 23.10 Nails

| | | Crew | Daily Output | Labor-Hours | Unit | Material | 2008 Bare Costs Labor | Equipment | Total | Total Incl O&P |
|---|---|---|---|---|---|---|---|---|---|---|
| 2100 | Aluminum | | | | Lb. | 4.10 | | | 4.10 | 4.51 |
| 2300 | Flooring nails, hardened steel, 2d to 10d, plain | | | | | 1.61 | | | 1.61 | 1.77 |
| 2400 | Galvanized | | | | | 2.25 | | | 2.25 | 2.48 |
| 2500 | Gypsum lath nails, 1-1/8", 13 ga. flathead, blued | | | | | 1.54 | | | 1.54 | 1.69 |
| 2600 | Masonry nails, hardened steel, 3/4" to 3" long, plain | | | | | 1.61 | | | 1.61 | 1.77 |
| 2700 | Galvanized | | | | | 2 | | | 2 | 2.20 |
| 2900 | Roofing nails, threaded, galvanized | | | | | 1.05 | | | 1.05 | 1.16 |
| 3100 | Aluminum | | | | | 4.80 | | | 4.80 | 5.30 |
| 3300 | Compressed lead head, threaded, galvanized | | | | | 1.50 | | | 1.50 | 1.65 |
| 3600 | Siding nails, plain shank, galvanized | | | | | 1.20 | | | 1.20 | 1.32 |
| 3800 | Aluminum | | | | | 4.11 | | | 4.11 | 4.52 |
| 5000 | Add to prices above for cement coating | | | | | .10 | | | .10 | .11 |
| 5200 | Zinc or tin plating | | | | | .13 | | | .13 | .14 |
| 5500 | Vinyl coated sinkers, 8d to 16d | | | | | .57 | | | .57 | .63 |

### 06 05 23.20 Pneumatic Nails

| | | Crew | Daily Output | Labor-Hours | Unit | Material | 2008 Bare Costs Labor | Equipment | Total | Total Incl O&P |
|---|---|---|---|---|---|---|---|---|---|---|
| 0010 | **PNEUMATIC NAILS** | | | | | | | | | |
| 0020 | Framing, per carton of 5000, 2" | | | | Ea. | 37 | | | 37 | 41 |
| 0100 | 2-3/8" | | | | | 42.50 | | | 42.50 | 46.50 |
| 0200 | Per carton of 4000, 3" | | | | | 37.50 | | | 37.50 | 41.50 |
| 0300 | 3-1/4" | | | | | 40 | | | 40 | 44 |
| 0400 | Per carton of 5000, 2-3/8", galv. | | | | | 57.50 | | | 57.50 | 63.50 |
| 0500 | Per carton of 4000, 3", galv. | | | | | 65 | | | 65 | 71.50 |
| 0600 | 3-1/4", galv. | | | | | 80.50 | | | 80.50 | 88.50 |
| 0700 | Roofing, per carton of 7200, 1" | | | | | 34 | | | 34 | 37 |
| 0800 | 1-1/4" | | | | | 31.50 | | | 31.50 | 34.50 |
| 0900 | 1-1/2" | | | | | 36.50 | | | 36.50 | 40 |
| 1000 | 1-3/4" | | | | | 45.50 | | | 45.50 | 50 |

### 06 05 23.40 Sheet Metal Screws

| | | Crew | Daily Output | Labor-Hours | Unit | Material | 2008 Bare Costs Labor | Equipment | Total | Total Incl O&P |
|---|---|---|---|---|---|---|---|---|---|---|
| 0010 | **SHEET METAL SCREWS** | | | | | | | | | |
| 0020 | Steel, standard, #8 x 3/4", plain | | | | C | 3.29 | | | 3.29 | 3.62 |
| 0100 | Galvanized | | | | | 3.44 | | | 3.44 | 3.78 |
| 0300 | #10 x 1", plain | | | | | 4.49 | | | 4.49 | 4.94 |
| 0400 | Galvanized | | | | | 4.60 | | | 4.60 | 5.05 |
| 0600 | With washers, #14 x 1", plain | | | | | 10.20 | | | 10.20 | 11.20 |
| 0700 | Galvanized | | | | | 10.50 | | | 10.50 | 11.55 |
| 0900 | #14 x 2", plain | | | | | 18 | | | 18 | 19.80 |
| 1000 | Galvanized | | | | | 18.15 | | | 18.15 | 19.95 |
| 1500 | Self-drilling, with washers, (pinch point) #8 x 3/4", plain | | | | | 7.10 | | | 7.10 | 7.80 |
| 1600 | Galvanized | | | | | 7.20 | | | 7.20 | 7.90 |
| 1800 | #10 x 3/4", plain | | | | | 9.30 | | | 9.30 | 10.20 |
| 1900 | Galvanized | | | | | 9.40 | | | 9.40 | 10.35 |
| 3000 | Stainless steel w/aluminum or neoprene washers, #14 x 1", plain | | | | | 18.35 | | | 18.35 | 20 |
| 3100 | #14 x 2", plain | | | | | 25 | | | 25 | 27.50 |

### 06 05 23.50 Wood Screws

| | | Crew | Daily Output | Labor-Hours | Unit | Material | 2008 Bare Costs Labor | Equipment | Total | Total Incl O&P |
|---|---|---|---|---|---|---|---|---|---|---|
| 0010 | **WOOD SCREWS** | | | | | | | | | |
| 0020 | #8 x 1" long, steel | | | | C | 5.10 | | | 5.10 | 5.60 |
| 0100 | Brass | | | | | 11.50 | | | 11.50 | 12.65 |
| 0200 | #8, 2" long, steel | | | | | 5.60 | | | 5.60 | 6.15 |
| 0300 | Brass | | | | | 19.50 | | | 19.50 | 21.50 |
| 0400 | #10, 1" long, steel | | | | | 3.99 | | | 3.99 | 4.39 |
| 0500 | Brass | | | | | 14 | | | 14 | 15.40 |
| 0600 | #10, 2" long, steel | | | | | 6.30 | | | 6.30 | 6.90 |

## 06 05 23.50 Wood Screws

| | | Crew | Daily Output | Labor-Hours | Unit | Material | 2008 Bare Costs Labor | Equipment | Total | Total Incl O&P |
|---|---|---|---|---|---|---|---|---|---|---|
| 0700 | Brass | | | | C | 23 | | | 23 | 25.50 |
| 0800 | #10, 3" long, steel | | | | | 10.50 | | | 10.50 | 11.55 |
| 1000 | #12, 2" long, steel | | | | | 7.50 | | | 7.50 | 8.25 |
| 1100 | Brass | | | | | 30 | | | 30 | 33 |
| 1500 | #12, 3" long, steel | | | | | 11.50 | | | 11.50 | 12.65 |
| 2000 | #12, 4" long, steel | | | | ↓ | 16 | | | 16 | 17.60 |

## 06 05 23.60 Timber Connectors

| | | Crew | Daily Output | Labor-Hours | Unit | Material | 2008 Bare Costs Labor | Equipment | Total | Total Incl O&P |
|---|---|---|---|---|---|---|---|---|---|---|
| 0010 | **TIMBER CONNECTORS** | | | | | | | | | |
| 0020 | Add up cost of each part for total cost of connection | | | | | | | | | |
| 0100 | Connector plates, steel, with bolts, straight | 2 Carp | 75 | .213 | Ea. | 25 | 8.15 | | 33.15 | 40 |
| 0110 | Tee, 7 gauge | | 50 | .320 | | 29 | 12.20 | | 41.20 | 51 |
| 0120 | T- Strap, 14 gauge, 12" x 8" x 2" | | 50 | .320 | | 29 | 12.20 | | 41.20 | 51 |
| 0150 | Anchor plates, 7 ga, 9" x 7" | ↓ | 75 | .213 | | 25 | 8.15 | | 33.15 | 40 |
| 0200 | Bolts, machine, sq. hd. with nut & washer, 1/2" diameter, 4" long | 1 Carp | 140 | .057 | | .42 | 2.18 | | 2.60 | 3.85 |
| 0300 | 7-1/2" long | | 130 | .062 | | .74 | 2.34 | | 3.08 | 4.46 |
| 0500 | 3/4" diameter, 7-1/2" long | | 130 | .062 | | 2.01 | 2.34 | | 4.35 | 5.85 |
| 0610 | Machine bolts, w/ nut, washer, 3/4" dia, 15" L, HD's & beam hangers | | 95 | .084 | ↓ | 3.69 | 3.21 | | 6.90 | 9.05 |
| 0800 | Drilling bolt holes in timber, 1/2" diameter | | 450 | .018 | Inch | | .68 | | .68 | 1.05 |
| 0900 | 1" diameter | | 350 | .023 | " | | .87 | | .87 | 1.36 |
| 1100 | Framing anchor, angle, 3" x 3" x 1-1/2", 12 ga | | 175 | .046 | Ea. | 2.06 | 1.74 | | 3.80 | 4.98 |
| 1150 | Framing anchors, 18 gauge, 4 1/2" x 2 3/4" | | 175 | .046 | | 2.06 | 1.74 | | 3.80 | 4.98 |
| 1160 | Framing anchors, 18 gauge, 4 1/2" x 3" | | 175 | .046 | | 2.06 | 1.74 | | 3.80 | 4.98 |
| 1170 | Clip anchors plates, 18 gauge, 12" x 1 1/8" | | 175 | .046 | | 2.06 | 1.74 | | 3.80 | 4.98 |
| 1250 | Holdowns, 3 gauge base, 10 gauge body | | 8 | 1 | | 19.60 | 38 | | 57.60 | 81 |
| 1260 | Holdowns, 7 gauge 11 1/16" x 3 1/4" | | 8 | 1 | | 19.60 | 38 | | 57.60 | 81 |
| 1270 | Holdowns, 7 gauge 14 3/8" x 3 1/8" | | 8 | 1 | | 19.60 | 38 | | 57.60 | 81 |
| 1275 | Holdowns, 12 gauge 8" x 2 1/2" | | 8 | 1 | | 19.60 | 38 | | 57.60 | 81 |
| 1300 | Joist and beam hangers, 18 ga. galv., for 2" x 4" joist | | 175 | .046 | | .57 | 1.74 | | 2.31 | 3.34 |
| 1400 | 2" x 6" to 2" x 10" joist | | 165 | .048 | | .98 | 1.85 | | 2.83 | 3.95 |
| 1600 | 16 ga. galv., 3" x 6" to 3" x 10" joist | | 160 | .050 | | 2.33 | 1.91 | | 4.24 | 5.55 |
| 1700 | 3" x 10" to 3" x 14" joist | | 160 | .050 | | 3.87 | 1.91 | | 5.78 | 7.25 |
| 1800 | 4" x 6" to 4" x 10" joist | | 155 | .052 | | 2.41 | 1.97 | | 4.38 | 5.70 |
| 1900 | 4" x 10" to 4" x 14" joist | | 155 | .052 | | 3.95 | 1.97 | | 5.92 | 7.40 |
| 2000 | Two-2" x 6" to two-2" x 10" joists | | 150 | .053 | | 3.29 | 2.03 | | 5.32 | 6.80 |
| 2100 | Two-2" x 10" to two-2" x 14" joists | | 150 | .053 | | 3.68 | 2.03 | | 5.71 | 7.20 |
| 2300 | 3/16" thick, 6" x 8" joist | | 145 | .055 | | 51 | 2.10 | | 53.10 | 59.50 |
| 2400 | 6" x 10" joist | | 140 | .057 | | 53 | 2.18 | | 55.18 | 62 |
| 2500 | 6" x 12" joist | | 135 | .059 | | 55.50 | 2.26 | | 57.76 | 64.50 |
| 2700 | 1/4" thick, 6" x 14" joist | ↓ | 130 | .062 | | 57.50 | 2.34 | | 59.84 | 67 |
| 2900 | Plywood clips, extruded aluminum H clip, for 3/4" panels | | | | | .18 | | | .18 | .20 |
| 3000 | Galvanized 18 ga. back-up clip | | | | | .15 | | | .15 | .17 |
| 3200 | Post framing, 16 ga. galv. for 4" x 4" base, 2 piece | 1 Carp | 130 | .062 | | 12.90 | 2.34 | | 15.24 | 17.85 |
| 3300 | Cap | | 130 | .062 | | 17.90 | 2.34 | | 20.24 | 23.50 |
| 3500 | Rafter anchors, 18 ga. galv., 1-1/2" wide, 5-1/4" long | | 145 | .055 | | .38 | 2.10 | | 2.48 | 3.69 |
| 3600 | 10-3/4" long | | 145 | .055 | | 1.15 | 2.10 | | 3.25 | 4.54 |
| 3800 | Shear plates, 2-5/8" diameter | | 120 | .067 | | 1.98 | 2.54 | | 4.52 | 6.15 |
| 3900 | 4" diameter | | 115 | .070 | | 4.55 | 2.65 | | 7.20 | 9.15 |
| 4000 | Sill anchors, embedded in concrete or block, 25-1/2" long | | 115 | .070 | | 10 | 2.65 | | 12.65 | 15.15 |
| 4100 | Spike grids, 3" x 6" | | 120 | .067 | | .80 | 2.54 | | 3.34 | 4.83 |
| 4400 | Split rings, 2-1/2" diameter | | 120 | .067 | | 1.60 | 2.54 | | 4.14 | 5.70 |
| 4500 | 4" diameter | | 110 | .073 | | 2.47 | 2.77 | | 5.24 | 7.05 |
| 4550 | Tie plate, 20 gauge, 7" x 3 1/8" | ↓ | 110 | .073 | ↓ | 2.47 | 2.77 | | 5.24 | 7.05 |

| 06 05 23.60 Timber Connectors | Crew | Daily Output | Labor-Hours | Unit | Material | 2008 Bare Costs Labor | Equipment | Total | Total Incl O&P |
|---|---|---|---|---|---|---|---|---|---|
| 4560 Tie plate, 20 gauge, 5" x 4 1/8" | 1 Carp | 110 | .073 | Ea. | 2.47 | 2.77 | | 5.24 | 7.05 |
| 4575 Twist straps, 18 gauge, 12" x 1 1/4" | | 110 | .073 | | 2.47 | 2.77 | | 5.24 | 7.05 |
| 4580 Twist straps, 18 gauge, 16" x 1 1/4" | | 110 | .073 | | 2.47 | 2.77 | | 5.24 | 7.05 |
| 4600 Strap ties, 20 ga., 2-1/16" wide, 12 13/16" long | | 180 | .044 | | .75 | 1.69 | | 2.44 | 3.47 |
| 4700 Strap ties, 16 ga., 1-3/8" wide, 12" long | | 180 | .044 | | .75 | 1.69 | | 2.44 | 3.47 |
| 4800 21-5/8" x 1-1/4" | | 160 | .050 | | 2.33 | 1.91 | | 4.24 | 5.55 |
| 5000 Toothed rings, 2-5/8" or 4" diameter | | 90 | .089 | | 1.36 | 3.39 | | 4.75 | 6.75 |
| 5200 Truss plates, nailed, 20 gauge, up to 32' span | | 17 | .471 | Truss | 9.85 | 17.95 | | 27.80 | 39 |
| 5400 Washers, 2" x 2" x 1/8" | | | | Ea. | .31 | | | .31 | .34 |
| 5500 3" x 3" x 3/16" | | | | " | .81 | | | .81 | .89 |
| 6101 Beam hangers, polymer painted | | | | | | | | | |
| 6102 Bolted, 3 ga., (W x H x L) | | | | | | | | | |
| 6104 3-1/4" x 9" x 12" top flange | 1 Carp | 1 | 8 | C | 15,400 | 305 | | 15,705 | 17,500 |
| 6106 5-1/4" x 9" x 12" top flange | | 1 | 8 | | 16,100 | 305 | | 16,405 | 18,200 |
| 6108 5-1/4" x 11" x 11-3/4" top flange | | 1 | 8 | | 18,100 | 305 | | 18,405 | 20,400 |
| 6110 6-7/8" x 9" x 12" top flange | | 1 | 8 | | 16,700 | 305 | | 17,005 | 18,800 |
| 6112 6-7/8" x 11" x 13-1/2" top flange | | 1 | 8 | | 19,000 | 305 | | 19,305 | 21,400 |
| 6114 8-7/8" x 11" x 15-1/2" top flange | | 1 | 8 | | 20,400 | 305 | | 20,705 | 22,900 |
| 6116 Nailed, 3 ga., (W x H x L) | | | | | | | | | |
| 6118 3-1/4" x 10-1/2" x 10" top flange | 1 Carp | 1.80 | 4.444 | C | 15,900 | 169 | | 16,069 | 17,800 |
| 6120 3-1/4" x 10-1/2" x 12" top flange | | 1.80 | 4.444 | | 15,900 | 169 | | 16,069 | 17,800 |
| 6122 5-1/4" x 9-1/2" x 10" top flange | | 1.80 | 4.444 | | 16,300 | 169 | | 16,469 | 18,200 |
| 6124 5-1/4" x 9-1/2" x 12" top flange | | 1.80 | 4.444 | | 16,300 | 169 | | 16,469 | 18,200 |
| 6128 6-7/8" x 8-1/2" x 12" top flange | | 1.80 | 4.444 | | 16,700 | 169 | | 16,869 | 18,600 |
| 6201 Beam and purlin hangers, galvanized, 12 ga. | | | | | | | | | |
| 6202 Purlin or joist size, 3" x 8" | 1 Carp | 1.70 | 4.706 | C | 1,600 | 179 | | 1,779 | 2,025 |
| 6204 3" x 10" | | 1.70 | 4.706 | | 1,725 | 179 | | 1,904 | 2,175 |
| 6206 3" x 12" | | 1.65 | 4.848 | | 1,975 | 185 | | 2,160 | 2,475 |
| 6208 3" x 14" | | 1.65 | 4.848 | | 2,100 | 185 | | 2,285 | 2,600 |
| 6210 3" x 16" | | 1.65 | 4.848 | | 2,225 | 185 | | 2,410 | 2,750 |
| 6212 4" x 8" | | 1.65 | 4.848 | | 1,600 | 185 | | 1,785 | 2,050 |
| 6214 4" x 10" | | 1.65 | 4.848 | | 1,725 | 185 | | 1,910 | 2,200 |
| 6216 4" x 12" | | 1.60 | 5 | | 2,050 | 191 | | 2,241 | 2,550 |
| 6218 4" x 14" | | 1.60 | 5 | | 2,175 | 191 | | 2,366 | 2,675 |
| 6220 4" x 16" | | 1.60 | 5 | | 2,300 | 191 | | 2,491 | 2,825 |
| 6224 6" x 10" | | 1.55 | 5.161 | | 1,975 | 197 | | 2,172 | 2,475 |
| 6226 6" x 12" | | 1.55 | 5.161 | | 3,850 | 197 | | 4,047 | 4,550 |
| 6228 6" x 14" | | 1.50 | 5.333 | | 4,075 | 203 | | 4,278 | 4,800 |
| 6230 6" x 16" | | 1.50 | 5.333 | | 4,275 | 203 | | 4,478 | 5,050 |
| 6300 Column bases | | | | | | | | | |
| 6302 4 x 4, 16 ga. | 1 Carp | 1.80 | 4.444 | C | 610 | 169 | | 779 | 940 |
| 6306 7 ga. | | 1.80 | 4.444 | | 2,250 | 169 | | 2,419 | 2,750 |
| 6314 6 x 6, 16 ga. | | 1.75 | 4.571 | | 1,625 | 174 | | 1,799 | 2,050 |
| 6318 7 ga. | | 1.75 | 4.571 | | 2,750 | 174 | | 2,924 | 3,300 |
| 6326 8 x 8, 7 ga. | | 1.65 | 4.848 | | 4,875 | 185 | | 5,060 | 5,675 |
| 6330 8 x 10, 7 ga. | | 1.65 | 4.848 | | 5,850 | 185 | | 6,035 | 6,725 |
| 6590 Joist hangers, heavy duty 12 ga., galvanized | | | | | | | | | |
| 6592 2" x 4" | 1 Carp | 1.75 | 4.571 | C | 1,000 | 174 | | 1,174 | 1,375 |
| 6594 2" x 6" | | 1.65 | 4.848 | | 1,100 | 185 | | 1,285 | 1,500 |
| 6595 2" x 6", 16 gauge | | 1.65 | 4.848 | | 1,100 | 185 | | 1,285 | 1,500 |
| 6596 2" x 8" | | 1.65 | 4.848 | | 1,650 | 185 | | 1,835 | 2,125 |
| 6597 2" x 8", 16 gauge | | 1.65 | 4.848 | | 1,650 | 185 | | 1,835 | 2,125 |
| 6598 2" x 10" | | 1.65 | 4.848 | | 1,700 | 185 | | 1,885 | 2,175 |

## 06 05 23 – Wood, Plastic, and Composite Fastenings

### 06 05 23.60 Timber Connectors

| | | Crew | Daily Output | Labor-Hours | Unit | Material | 2008 Bare Costs Labor | Equipment | Total | Total Incl O&P |
|---|---|---|---|---|---|---|---|---|---|---|
| 6600 | 2" x 12" | 1 Carp | 1.65 | 4.848 | C | 2,100 | 185 | | 2,285 | 2,600 |
| 6622 | (2) 2" x 6" | | 1.60 | 5 | | 1,950 | 191 | | 2,141 | 2,450 |
| 6624 | (2) 2" x 8" | | 1.60 | 5 | | 2,000 | 191 | | 2,191 | 2,500 |
| 6626 | (2) 2" x 10" | | 1.55 | 5.161 | | 2,175 | 197 | | 2,372 | 2,700 |
| 6628 | (2) 2" x 12" | | 1.55 | 5.161 | | 2,775 | 197 | | 2,972 | 3,350 |
| 6890 | Purlin hangers, painted | | | | | | | | | |
| 6892 | 12 ga., 2" x 6" | 1 Carp | 1.80 | 4.444 | C | 1,450 | 169 | | 1,619 | 1,875 |
| 6894 | 2" x 8" | | 1.80 | 4.444 | | 1,575 | 169 | | 1,744 | 2,025 |
| 6896 | 2" x 10" | | 1.80 | 4.444 | | 1,700 | 169 | | 1,869 | 2,150 |
| 6898 | 2" x 12" | | 1.75 | 4.571 | | 1,825 | 174 | | 1,999 | 2,300 |
| 6934 | double 2" x 6" | | 1.70 | 4.706 | | 1,600 | 179 | | 1,779 | 2,025 |
| 6936 | double 2" x 8" | | 1.70 | 4.706 | | 1,725 | 179 | | 1,904 | 2,175 |
| 6938 | double 2" x 10" | | 1.70 | 4.706 | | 1,850 | 179 | | 2,029 | 2,300 |
| 6940 | double 2" x 12" | | 1.65 | 4.848 | | 1,975 | 185 | | 2,160 | 2,475 |

### 06 05 23.70 Rough Hardware

| | | Crew | Daily Output | Labor-Hours | Unit | Material | 2008 Bare Costs Labor | Equipment | Total | Total Incl O&P |
|---|---|---|---|---|---|---|---|---|---|---|
| 0010 | **ROUGH HARDWARE**, average percent of carpentry material | | | | | | | | | |
| 0020 | Minimum | | | | | .50% | | | | |
| 0200 | Maximum | | | | | 1.50% | | | | |
| 0210 | In seismic or hurricane areas, up to | | | | | 10% | | | | |

### 06 05 23.80 Metal Bracing

| | | Crew | Daily Output | Labor-Hours | Unit | Material | 2008 Bare Costs Labor | Equipment | Total | Total Incl O&P |
|---|---|---|---|---|---|---|---|---|---|---|
| 0010 | **METAL BRACING** | | | | | | | | | |
| 0300 | Let-in, "T" shaped, 22 ga. galv. steel, studs at 16" O.C. | 1 Carp | 5.80 | 1.379 | C.L.F. | 53 | 52.50 | | 105.50 | 141 |
| 0400 | Studs at 24" O.C. | | 6 | 1.333 | | 53 | 51 | | 104 | 138 |
| 0500 | 16 ga. galv. steel straps, studs at 16" O.C. | | 6 | 1.333 | | 80 | 51 | | 131 | 167 |
| 0600 | Studs at 24" O.C. | | 6.20 | 1.290 | | 80 | 49 | | 129 | 165 |

## 06 05 73 – Wood Treatment

### 06 05 73.10 Lumber Treatment

| | | Crew | Daily Output | Labor-Hours | Unit | Material | 2008 Bare Costs Labor | Equipment | Total | Total Incl O&P |
|---|---|---|---|---|---|---|---|---|---|---|
| 0011 | **LUMBER TREATMENT** | | | | | | | | | |
| 0400 | Fire retardant, wet | | | | M.B.F. | 330 | | | 330 | 365 |
| 0500 | KDAT | | | | | 315 | | | 315 | 345 |
| 0700 | Salt treated, water borne, .40 lb. retention | | | | | 150 | | | 150 | 166 |
| 0800 | Oil borne, 8 lb. retention | | | | | 176 | | | 176 | 194 |
| 1000 | Kiln dried lumber, 1" & 2" thick, softwoods | | | | | 101 | | | 101 | 111 |
| 1100 | Hardwoods | | | | | 107 | | | 107 | 118 |
| 1500 | For small size 1" stock, add | | | | | 13.60 | | | 13.60 | 14.95 |
| 1700 | For full size rough lumber, add | | | | | 20% | | | | |

### 06 05 73.20 Plywood Treatment

| | | Crew | Daily Output | Labor-Hours | Unit | Material | 2008 Bare Costs Labor | Equipment | Total | Total Incl O&P |
|---|---|---|---|---|---|---|---|---|---|---|
| 0010 | **PLYWOOD TREATMENT** | | | | | | | | | |
| 0020 | Fire retardant, 1/4" thick | | | | M.S.F. | 252 | | | 252 | 277 |
| 0030 | 3/8" thick | | | | | 276 | | | 276 | 305 |
| 0050 | 1/2" thick | | | | | 296 | | | 296 | 325 |
| 0070 | 5/8" thick | | | | | 315 | | | 315 | 345 |
| 0100 | 3/4" thick | | | | | 345 | | | 345 | 380 |
| 0200 | For KDAT, add | | | | | 75 | | | 75 | 83 |
| 0500 | Salt treated water borne, .25 lb., wet, 1/4" thick | | | | | 138 | | | 138 | 152 |
| 0530 | 3/8" thick | | | | | 144 | | | 144 | 159 |
| 0550 | 1/2" thick | | | | | 150 | | | 150 | 166 |
| 0570 | 5/8" thick | | | | | 164 | | | 164 | 180 |
| 0600 | 3/4" thick | | | | | 170 | | | 170 | 187 |
| 0800 | For KDAT add | | | | | 75 | | | 75 | 83 |
| 0900 | For .40 lb., per C.F. retention, add | | | | | 63 | | | 63 | 69 |

# 06 05 Common Work Results for Wood, Plastics and Composites

## 06 05 73 – Wood Treatment

| 06 05 73.20 Plywood Treatment | | Crew | Daily Output | Labor-Hours | Unit | Material | 2008 Bare Costs Labor | Equipment | Total | Total Incl O&P |
|---|---|---|---|---|---|---|---|---|---|---|
| 1000 | For certification stamp, add | | | | M.S.F. | 37 | | | 37 | 40.50 |

# 06 11 Wood Framing

## 06 11 10 – Framing with Dimensional, Engineered or Composite Lumber

### 06 11 10.02 Blocking

| | | Crew | Daily Output | Labor-Hours | Unit | Material | 2008 Bare Costs Labor | Equipment | Total | Total Incl O&P |
|---|---|---|---|---|---|---|---|---|---|---|
| 0010 | **BLOCKING** | | | | | | | | | |
| 2600 | Miscellaneous, to wood construction | | | | | | | | | |
| 2620 | 2" x 4" | 1 Carp | .17 | 47.059 | M.B.F. | 530 | 1,800 | | 2,330 | 3,375 |
| 2625 | Pneumatic nailed | | .21 | 38.095 | | 530 | 1,450 | | 1,980 | 2,825 |
| 2660 | 2" x 8" | | .27 | 29.630 | | 570 | 1,125 | | 1,695 | 2,375 |
| 2665 | Pneumatic nailed | | .33 | 24.242 | | 570 | 925 | | 1,495 | 2,075 |
| 2720 | To steel construction | | | | | | | | | |
| 2740 | 2" x 4" | 1 Carp | .14 | 57.143 | M.B.F. | 530 | 2,175 | | 2,705 | 3,975 |
| 2780 | 2" x 8" | " | .21 | 38.095 | " | 570 | 1,450 | | 2,020 | 2,875 |

### 06 11 10.04 Wood Bracing

| | | Crew | Daily Output | Labor-Hours | Unit | Material | 2008 Bare Costs Labor | Equipment | Total | Total Incl O&P |
|---|---|---|---|---|---|---|---|---|---|---|
| 0010 | **WOOD BRACING** | | | | | | | | | |
| 0011 | Let-in, with 1" x 6" boards, studs 16" OC | 1 Carp | 1.50 | 5.333 | C.L.F. | 62.50 | 203 | | 265.50 | 385 |
| 0200 | Studs @ 24" O.C. | " | 2.30 | 3.478 | " | 62.50 | 133 | | 195.50 | 275 |

### 06 11 10.06 Bridging

| | | Crew | Daily Output | Labor-Hours | Unit | Material | 2008 Bare Costs Labor | Equipment | Total | Total Incl O&P |
|---|---|---|---|---|---|---|---|---|---|---|
| 0010 | **BRIDGING** | | | | | | | | | |
| 0011 | Wood, for joists 16" OC, 1" x 3" | 1 Carp | 1.30 | 6.154 | C.Pr. | 25.50 | 234 | | 259.50 | 395 |
| 0015 | Pneumatic nailed | | 1.70 | 4.706 | | 25.50 | 179 | | 204.50 | 310 |
| 0100 | 2" x 3" bridging | | 1.30 | 6.154 | | 49 | 234 | | 283 | 420 |
| 0105 | Pneumatic nailed | | 1.70 | 4.706 | | 49 | 179 | | 228 | 335 |
| 0300 | Steel, galvanized, 18 ga., for 2" x 10" joists at 12" O.C. | | 1.30 | 6.154 | | 125 | 234 | | 359 | 500 |
| 0400 | 24" O.C. | | 1.40 | 5.714 | | 155 | 218 | | 373 | 510 |
| 0600 | For 2" x 14" joists at 16" O.C. | | 1.30 | 6.154 | | 153 | 234 | | 387 | 535 |
| 0700 | 24" O.C. | | 1.40 | 5.714 | | 239 | 218 | | 457 | 600 |
| 0900 | Compression type, 16" O.C., 2" x 8" joists | | 2 | 4 | | 150 | 152 | | 302 | 400 |
| 1000 | 2" x 12" joists | | 2 | 4 | | 150 | 152 | | 302 | 400 |

### 06 11 10.10 Beam and Girder Framing

| | | | Crew | Daily Output | Labor-Hours | Unit | Material | 2008 Bare Costs Labor | Equipment | Total | Total Incl O&P |
|---|---|---|---|---|---|---|---|---|---|---|---|
| 0010 | **BEAM AND GIRDER FRAMING** | R061110-30 | | | | | | | | | |
| 3500 | Single, 2" x 6" | | 2 Carp | .70 | 22.857 | M.B.F. | 550 | 870 | | 1,420 | 1,950 |
| 3505 | Pneumatic nailed | | | .81 | 19.704 | | 550 | 750 | | 1,300 | 1,775 |
| 3520 | 2" x 8" | | | .86 | 18.605 | | 570 | 710 | | 1,280 | 1,725 |
| 3525 | Pneumatic nailed | | | 1 | 16.048 | | 570 | 610 | | 1,180 | 1,575 |
| 3540 | 2" x 10" | | | 1 | 16 | | 620 | 610 | | 1,230 | 1,625 |
| 3545 | Pneumatic nailed | | | 1.16 | 13.793 | | 620 | 525 | | 1,145 | 1,500 |
| 3560 | 2" x 12" | | | 1.10 | 14.545 | | 620 | 555 | | 1,175 | 1,550 |
| 3565 | Pneumatic nailed | | | 1.28 | 12.539 | | 620 | 480 | | 1,100 | 1,425 |
| 3580 | 2" x 14" | | | 1.17 | 13.675 | | 935 | 520 | | 1,455 | 1,825 |
| 3585 | Pneumatic nailed | | | 1.36 | 11.791 | | 935 | 450 | | 1,385 | 1,725 |
| 3600 | 3" x 8" | | | 1.10 | 14.545 | | 1,200 | 555 | | 1,755 | 2,200 |
| 3620 | 3" x 10" | | | 1.25 | 12.800 | | 1,200 | 490 | | 1,690 | 2,075 |
| 3640 | 3" x 12" | | | 1.35 | 11.852 | | 1,200 | 450 | | 1,650 | 2,025 |
| 3660 | 3" x 14" | | | 1.40 | 11.429 | | 1,350 | 435 | | 1,785 | 2,150 |
| 3680 | 4" x 8" | | F-3 | 2.66 | 15.038 | | 1,600 | 580 | 288 | 2,468 | 3,000 |
| 3700 | 4" x 10" | | | 3.16 | 12.658 | | 1,675 | 490 | 243 | 2,408 | 2,875 |
| 3720 | 4" x 12" | | | 3.60 | 11.111 | | 1,650 | 430 | 213 | 2,293 | 2,725 |
| 3740 | 4" x 14" | | | 3.96 | 10.101 | | 1,675 | 390 | 194 | 2,259 | 2,675 |

# 06 11 Wood Framing

## 06 11 10 – Framing with Dimensional, Engineered or Composite Lumber

### 06 11 10.10 Beam and Girder Framing

| | | Crew | Daily Output | Labor-Hours | Unit | Material | 2008 Bare Costs Labor | Equipment | Total | Total Incl O&P |
|---|---|---|---|---|---|---|---|---|---|---|
| 4000 | Double, 2" x 6" | 2 Carp | 1.25 | 12.800 | M.B.F. | 550 | 490 | | 1,040 | 1,375 |
| 4005 | Pneumatic nailed | | 1.45 | 11.034 | | 550 | 420 | | 970 | 1,250 |
| 4020 | 2" x 8" | | 1.60 | 10 | | 570 | 380 | | 950 | 1,225 |
| 4025 | Pneumatic nailed | | 1.86 | 8.621 | | 570 | 330 | | 900 | 1,125 |
| 4040 | 2" x 10" | | 1.92 | 8.333 | | 620 | 320 | | 940 | 1,175 |
| 4045 | Pneumatic nailed | | 2.23 | 7.185 | | 620 | 274 | | 894 | 1,100 |
| 4060 | 2" x 12" | | 2.20 | 7.273 | | 620 | 277 | | 897 | 1,125 |
| 4065 | Pneumatic nailed | | 2.55 | 6.275 | | 620 | 239 | | 859 | 1,050 |
| 4080 | 2" x 14" | | 2.45 | 6.531 | | 935 | 249 | | 1,184 | 1,400 |
| 4085 | Pneumatic nailed | | 2.84 | 5.634 | | 935 | 215 | | 1,150 | 1,350 |
| 5000 | Triple, 2" x 6" | | 1.65 | 9.697 | | 550 | 370 | | 920 | 1,175 |
| 5005 | Pneumatic nailed | | 1.91 | 8.377 | | 550 | 320 | | 870 | 1,100 |
| 5020 | 2" x 8" | | 2.10 | 7.619 | | 570 | 290 | | 860 | 1,075 |
| 5025 | Pneumatic nailed | | 2.44 | 6.568 | | 570 | 250 | | 820 | 1,025 |
| 5040 | 2" x 10" | | 2.50 | 6.400 | | 620 | 244 | | 864 | 1,050 |
| 5045 | Pneumatic nailed | | 2.90 | 5.517 | | 620 | 210 | | 830 | 1,000 |
| 5060 | 2" x 12" | | 2.85 | 5.614 | | 620 | 214 | | 834 | 1,025 |
| 5065 | Pneumatic nailed | | 3.31 | 4.840 | | 620 | 184 | | 804 | 970 |
| 5080 | 2" x 14" | | 3.15 | 5.079 | | 935 | 194 | | 1,129 | 1,325 |
| 5085 | Pneumatic nailed | | 3.35 | 4.770 | | 935 | 182 | | 1,117 | 1,300 |

### 06 11 10.12 Ceiling Framing

| | | Crew | Daily Output | Labor-Hours | Unit | Material | 2008 Bare Costs Labor | Equipment | Total | Total Incl O&P |
|---|---|---|---|---|---|---|---|---|---|---|
| 0010 | **CEILING FRAMING** | | | | | | | | | |
| 6400 | Suspended, 2" x 3" | 2 Carp | .50 | 32 | M.B.F. | 650 | 1,225 | | 1,875 | 2,625 |
| 6450 | 2" x 4" | | .59 | 27.119 | | 530 | 1,025 | | 1,555 | 2,175 |
| 6500 | 2" x 6" | | .80 | 20 | | 550 | 760 | | 1,310 | 1,775 |
| 6550 | 2" x 8" | | .86 | 18.605 | | 570 | 710 | | 1,280 | 1,725 |

### 06 11 10.14 Posts and Columns

| | | Crew | Daily Output | Labor-Hours | Unit | Material | 2008 Bare Costs Labor | Equipment | Total | Total Incl O&P |
|---|---|---|---|---|---|---|---|---|---|---|
| 0010 | **POSTS AND COLUMNS** | | | | | | | | | |
| 0400 | 4" x 4" | 2 Carp | .52 | 30.769 | M.B.F. | 1,250 | 1,175 | | 2,425 | 3,200 |
| 0420 | 4" x 6" | | .55 | 29.091 | | 1,175 | 1,100 | | 2,275 | 3,025 |
| 0440 | 4" x 8" | | .59 | 27.119 | | 1,600 | 1,025 | | 2,625 | 3,375 |
| 0460 | 6" x 6" | | .65 | 24.615 | | 1,625 | 940 | | 2,565 | 3,250 |
| 0480 | 6" x 8" | | .70 | 22.857 | | 1,900 | 870 | | 2,770 | 3,425 |
| 0500 | 6" x 10" | | .75 | 21.333 | | 2,175 | 815 | | 2,990 | 3,675 |

### 06 11 10.18 Joist Framing

| | | Crew | Daily Output | Labor-Hours | Unit | Material | 2008 Bare Costs Labor | Equipment | Total | Total Incl O&P |
|---|---|---|---|---|---|---|---|---|---|---|
| 0010 | **JOIST FRAMING**　R061110-30 | | | | | | | | | |
| 2650 | Joists, 2" x 4" | 2 Carp | .83 | 19.277 | M.B.F. | 530 | 735 | | 1,265 | 1,725 |
| 2655 | Pneumatic nailed | | .96 | 16.667 | | 530 | 635 | | 1,165 | 1,575 |
| 2680 | 2" x 6" | | 1.25 | 12.800 | | 550 | 490 | | 1,040 | 1,375 |
| 2685 | Pneumatic nailed | | 1.44 | 11.111 | | 550 | 425 | | 975 | 1,275 |
| 2700 | 2" x 8" | | 1.46 | 10.959 | | 570 | 420 | | 990 | 1,275 |
| 2705 | Pneumatic nailed | | 1.68 | 9.524 | | 570 | 365 | | 935 | 1,200 |
| 2720 | 2" x 10" | | 1.49 | 10.738 | | 620 | 410 | | 1,030 | 1,325 |
| 2725 | Pneumatic nailed | | 1.71 | 9.357 | | 620 | 355 | | 975 | 1,225 |
| 2740 | 2" x 12" | | 1.75 | 9.143 | | 620 | 350 | | 970 | 1,225 |
| 2745 | Pneumatic nailed | | 2.01 | 7.960 | | 620 | 305 | | 925 | 1,150 |
| 2760 | 2" x 14" | | 1.79 | 8.939 | | 935 | 340 | | 1,275 | 1,550 |
| 2765 | Pneumatic nailed | | 2.06 | 7.767 | | 935 | 296 | | 1,231 | 1,475 |
| 2780 | 3" x 6" | | 1.39 | 11.511 | | 1,150 | 440 | | 1,590 | 1,950 |
| 2790 | 3" x 8" | | 1.90 | 8.421 | | 1,200 | 320 | | 1,520 | 1,825 |
| 2800 | 3" x 10" | | 1.95 | 8.205 | | 1,200 | 315 | | 1,515 | 1,800 |
| 2820 | 3" x 12" | | 1.80 | 8.889 | | 1,200 | 340 | | 1,540 | 1,850 |

# 06 11 Wood Framing

## 06 11 10 - Framing with Dimensional, Engineered or Composite Lumber

### 06 11 10.18 Joist Framing

| | | Crew | Daily Output | Labor-Hours | Unit | Material | 2008 Bare Costs Labor | Equipment | Total | Total Incl O&P |
|---|---|---|---|---|---|---|---|---|---|---|
| 2840 | 4" x 6" | 2 Carp | 1.60 | 10 | M.B.F. | 1,175 | 380 | | 1,555 | 1,900 |
| 2850 | 4" x 8" | | 4.15 | 3.855 | | 1,600 | 147 | | 1,747 | 2,000 |
| 2860 | 4" x 10" | | 2 | 8 | | 1,675 | 305 | | 1,980 | 2,325 |
| 2880 | 4" x 12" | | 1.80 | 8.889 | ▼ | 1,650 | 340 | | 1,990 | 2,350 |
| 3000 | Composite wood joist 9-1/2" deep | | .90 | 17.778 | M.L.F. | 2,025 | 675 | | 2,700 | 3,275 |
| 3010 | 11-1/2" deep | | .88 | 18.182 | | 2,150 | 695 | | 2,845 | 3,450 |
| 3020 | 14" deep | | .82 | 19.512 | | 2,550 | 745 | | 3,295 | 3,975 |
| 3030 | 16" deep | | .78 | 20.513 | | 2,825 | 780 | | 3,605 | 4,350 |
| 4000 | Open web joist 12" deep | | .88 | 18.182 | | 2,325 | 695 | | 3,020 | 3,650 |
| 4010 | 14" deep | | .82 | 19.512 | | 2,625 | 745 | | 3,370 | 4,050 |
| 4020 | 16" deep | | .78 | 20.513 | | 2,750 | 780 | | 3,530 | 4,250 |
| 4030 | 18" deep | | .74 | 21.622 | | 2,075 | 825 | | 2,900 | 3,575 |
| 6000 | Composite rim joist, 1-1/4" x 9-1/2" | | 90 | .178 | | 2,875 | 6.75 | | 2,881.75 | 3,150 |
| 6010 | 1-1/4" x 11-1/2" | | .88 | 18.182 | | 2,750 | 695 | | 3,445 | 4,100 |
| 6020 | 1-1/4" x 14-1/2" | | .82 | 19.512 | | 3,650 | 745 | | 4,395 | 5,150 |
| 6030 | 1-1/4" x 16-1/2" | ▼ | .78 | 20.513 | ▼ | 3,600 | 780 | | 4,380 | 5,175 |

### 06 11 10.24 Miscellaneous Framing

| | | Crew | Daily Output | Labor-Hours | Unit | Material | 2008 Bare Costs Labor | Equipment | Total | Total Incl O&P |
|---|---|---|---|---|---|---|---|---|---|---|
| 0010 | **MISCELLANEOUS FRAMING** | | | | | | | | | |
| 8500 | Firestops, 2" x 4" | 2 Carp | .51 | 31.373 | M.B.F. | 530 | 1,200 | | 1,730 | 2,425 |
| 8505 | Pneumatic nailed | | .62 | 25.806 | | 530 | 985 | | 1,515 | 2,100 |
| 8520 | 2" x 6" | | .60 | 26.667 | | 550 | 1,025 | | 1,575 | 2,175 |
| 8525 | Pneumatic nailed | | .73 | 21.858 | | 550 | 835 | | 1,385 | 1,900 |
| 8540 | 2" x 8" | | .60 | 26.667 | | 570 | 1,025 | | 1,595 | 2,200 |
| 8560 | 2" x 12" | | .70 | 22.857 | | 620 | 870 | | 1,490 | 2,025 |
| 8600 | Nailers, treated, wood construction, 2" x 4" | | .53 | 30.189 | | 885 | 1,150 | | 2,035 | 2,775 |
| 8605 | Pneumatic nailed | | .64 | 25.157 | | 885 | 960 | | 1,845 | 2,475 |
| 8620 | 2" x 6" | | .75 | 21.333 | | 805 | 815 | | 1,620 | 2,150 |
| 8625 | Pneumatic nailed | | .90 | 17.778 | | 805 | 675 | | 1,480 | 1,925 |
| 8640 | 2" x 8" | | .93 | 17.204 | | 790 | 655 | | 1,445 | 1,900 |
| 8645 | Pneumatic nailed | | 1.12 | 14.337 | | 790 | 545 | | 1,335 | 1,725 |
| 8660 | Steel construction, 2" x 4" | | .50 | 32 | | 885 | 1,225 | | 2,110 | 2,875 |
| 8680 | 2" x 6" | | .70 | 22.857 | | 805 | 870 | | 1,675 | 2,225 |
| 8700 | 2" x 8" | | .87 | 18.391 | | 790 | 700 | | 1,490 | 1,975 |
| 8760 | Rough bucks, treated, for doors or windows, 2" x 6" | | .40 | 40 | | 805 | 1,525 | | 2,330 | 3,250 |
| 8765 | Pneumatic nailed | | .48 | 33.333 | | 805 | 1,275 | | 2,080 | 2,850 |
| 8780 | 2" x 8" | | .51 | 31.373 | | 790 | 1,200 | | 1,990 | 2,725 |
| 8785 | Pneumatic nailed | | .61 | 26.144 | | 790 | 995 | | 1,785 | 2,425 |
| 8800 | Stair stringers, 2" x 10" | | .22 | 72.727 | | 620 | 2,775 | | 3,395 | 5,000 |
| 8820 | 2" x 12" | | .26 | 61.538 | | 620 | 2,350 | | 2,970 | 4,325 |
| 8840 | 3" x 10" | | .31 | 51.613 | | 1,200 | 1,975 | | 3,175 | 4,375 |
| 8860 | 3" x 12" | | .38 | 42.105 | ▼ | 1,200 | 1,600 | | 2,800 | 3,825 |
| 8870 | Laminated structural lumber, 1-1/4" x 11-1/2" | | 130 | .123 | L.F. | 2.75 | 4.69 | | 7.44 | 10.30 |
| 8880 | 1-1/4" x 14-1/2" | ▼ | 130 | .123 | " | 3.65 | 4.69 | | 8.34 | 11.30 |

### 06 11 10.26 Partitions

| | | Crew | Daily Output | Labor-Hours | Unit | Material | 2008 Bare Costs Labor | Equipment | Total | Total Incl O&P |
|---|---|---|---|---|---|---|---|---|---|---|
| 0010 | **PARTITIONS** | | | | | | | | | |
| 0020 | Single bottom and double top plate, no waste, std. & better lumber | | | | | | | | | |
| 0180 | 2" x 4" studs, 8' high, studs 12" O.C. | 2 Carp | 80 | .200 | L.F. | 3.87 | 7.60 | | 11.47 | 16.10 |
| 0185 | 12" O.C., pneumatic nailed | | 96 | .167 | | 3.87 | 6.35 | | 10.22 | 14.15 |
| 0200 | 16" O.C. | | 100 | .160 | | 3.17 | 6.10 | | 9.27 | 13 |
| 0205 | 16" O.C., pneumatic nailed | | 120 | .133 | | 3.17 | 5.10 | | 8.27 | 11.40 |
| 0300 | 24" O.C. | | 125 | .128 | | 2.46 | 4.88 | | 7.34 | 10.30 |
| 0305 | 24" O.C., pneumatic nailed | ▼ | 150 | .107 | ▼ | 2.46 | 4.06 | | 6.52 | 9.05 |

### 06 11 10.26 Partitions

| | | Crew | Daily Output | Labor-Hours | Unit | Material | 2008 Bare Costs Labor | Equipment | Total | Total Incl O&P |
|---|---|---|---|---|---|---|---|---|---|---|
| 0380 | 10' high, studs 12" O.C. | 2 Carp | 80 | .200 | L.F. | 4.58 | 7.60 | | 12.18 | 16.90 |
| 0385 | 12" O.C., pneumatic nailed | | 96 | .167 | | 4.58 | 6.35 | | 10.93 | 14.95 |
| 0400 | 16" O.C. | | 100 | .160 | | 3.70 | 6.10 | | 9.80 | 13.55 |
| 0405 | 16" O.C., pneumatic nailed | | 120 | .133 | | 3.70 | 5.10 | | 8.80 | 11.95 |
| 0500 | 24" O.C. | | 125 | .128 | | 2.82 | 4.88 | | 7.70 | 10.70 |
| 0505 | 24" O.C., pneumatic nailed | | 150 | .107 | | 2.82 | 4.06 | | 6.88 | 9.45 |
| 0580 | 12' high, studs 12" O.C. | | 65 | .246 | | 5.30 | 9.40 | | 14.70 | 20.50 |
| 0585 | 12" O.C., pneumatic nailed | | 78 | .205 | | 5.30 | 7.80 | | 13.10 | 17.95 |
| 0600 | 16" O.C. | | 80 | .200 | | 4.22 | 7.60 | | 11.82 | 16.50 |
| 0605 | 16" O.C., pneumatic nailed | | 96 | .167 | | 4.22 | 6.35 | | 10.57 | 14.55 |
| 0700 | 24" O.C. | | 100 | .160 | | 3.17 | 6.10 | | 9.27 | 13 |
| 0705 | 24" O.C., pneumatic nailed | | 120 | .133 | | 3.17 | 5.10 | | 8.27 | 11.40 |
| 0780 | 2" x 6" studs, 8' high, studs 12" O.C. | | 70 | .229 | | 6.05 | 8.70 | | 14.75 | 20 |
| 0785 | 12" O.C., pneumatic nailed | | 84 | .190 | | 6.05 | 7.25 | | 13.30 | 17.95 |
| 0800 | 16" O.C. | | 90 | .178 | | 4.94 | 6.75 | | 11.69 | 16 |
| 0805 | 16" O.C., pneumatic nailed | | 108 | .148 | | 4.94 | 5.65 | | 10.59 | 14.25 |
| 0900 | 24" O.C. | | 115 | .139 | | 3.84 | 5.30 | | 9.14 | 12.50 |
| 0905 | 24" O.C., pneumatic nailed | | 138 | .116 | | 3.84 | 4.42 | | 8.26 | 11.15 |
| 0980 | 10' high, studs 12" O.C. | | 70 | .229 | | 7.15 | 8.70 | | 15.85 | 21.50 |
| 0985 | 12" O.C., pneumatic nailed | | 84 | .190 | | 7.15 | 7.25 | | 14.40 | 19.15 |
| 1000 | 16" O.C. | | 90 | .178 | | 5.75 | 6.75 | | 12.50 | 16.90 |
| 1005 | 16" O.C., pneumatic nailed | | 108 | .148 | | 5.75 | 5.65 | | 11.40 | 15.15 |
| 1100 | 24" O.C. | | 115 | .139 | | 4.39 | 5.30 | | 9.69 | 13.10 |
| 1105 | 24" O.C., pneumatic nailed | | 138 | .116 | | 4.39 | 4.42 | | 8.81 | 11.75 |
| 1180 | 12' high, studs 12" O.C. | | 55 | .291 | | 8.25 | 11.10 | | 19.35 | 26.50 |
| 1185 | 12" O.C., pneumatic nailed | | 66 | .242 | | 8.25 | 9.25 | | 17.50 | 23.50 |
| 1200 | 16" O.C. | | 70 | .229 | | 6.60 | 8.70 | | 15.30 | 21 |
| 1205 | 16" O.C., pneumatic nailed | | 84 | .190 | | 6.60 | 7.25 | | 13.85 | 18.55 |
| 1300 | 24" O.C. | | 90 | .178 | | 4.94 | 6.75 | | 11.69 | 16 |
| 1305 | 24" O.C., pneumatic nailed | | 108 | .148 | | 4.94 | 5.65 | | 10.59 | 14.25 |
| 1400 | For horizontal blocking, 2" x 4", add | | 600 | .027 | | .35 | 1.02 | | 1.37 | 1.97 |
| 1500 | 2" x 6", add | | 600 | .027 | | .55 | 1.02 | | 1.57 | 2.18 |
| 1600 | For openings, add | | 250 | .064 | | | 2.44 | | 2.44 | 3.80 |
| 1700 | Headers for above openings, material only, add | | | | M.B.F. | 570 | | | 570 | 625 |

### 06 11 10.28 Porch or Deck Framing

| | | Crew | Daily Output | Labor-Hours | Unit | Material | 2008 Bare Costs Labor | Equipment | Total | Total Incl O&P |
|---|---|---|---|---|---|---|---|---|---|---|
| 0010 | **PORCH OR DECK FRAMING** | | | | | | | | | |
| 0100 | Treated lumber, posts or columns, 4" x 4" | 2 Carp | 390 | .041 | L.F. | 1.51 | 1.56 | | 3.07 | 4.09 |
| 0110 | 4" x 6" | | 275 | .058 | | 1.92 | 2.22 | | 4.14 | 5.55 |
| 0120 | 4" x 8" | | 220 | .073 | | 3.33 | 2.77 | | 6.10 | 7.95 |
| 0130 | Girder, single, 4" x 4" | | 675 | .024 | | 1.51 | .90 | | 2.41 | 3.07 |
| 0140 | 4" x 6" | | 600 | .027 | | 1.92 | 1.02 | | 2.94 | 3.70 |
| 0150 | 4" x 8" | | 525 | .030 | | 3.33 | 1.16 | | 4.49 | 5.45 |
| 0160 | Double, 2" x 4" | | 625 | .026 | | 1.20 | .98 | | 2.18 | 2.84 |
| 0170 | 2" x 6" | | 600 | .027 | | 1.64 | 1.02 | | 2.66 | 3.38 |
| 0180 | 2" x 8" | | 575 | .028 | | 2.15 | 1.06 | | 3.21 | 4.01 |
| 0190 | 2" x 10" | | 550 | .029 | | 2.64 | 1.11 | | 3.75 | 4.64 |
| 0200 | 2" x 12" | | 525 | .030 | | 4.22 | 1.16 | | 5.38 | 6.45 |
| 0210 | Triple, 2" x 4" | | 575 | .028 | | 1.80 | 1.06 | | 2.86 | 3.63 |
| 0220 | 2" x 6" | | 550 | .029 | | 2.46 | 1.11 | | 3.57 | 4.43 |
| 0230 | 2" x 8" | | 525 | .030 | | 3.22 | 1.16 | | 4.38 | 5.35 |
| 0240 | 2" x 10" | | 500 | .032 | | 3.97 | 1.22 | | 5.19 | 6.25 |
| 0250 | 2" x 12" | | 475 | .034 | | 6.35 | 1.28 | | 7.63 | 8.95 |

# 06 11 Wood Framing

## 06 11 10 – Framing with Dimensional, Engineered or Composite Lumber

| 06 11 10.28 Porch or Deck Framing | | Crew | Daily Output | Labor-Hours | Unit | Material | 2008 Bare Costs Labor | Equipment | Total | Total Incl O&P |
|---|---|---|---|---|---|---|---|---|---|---|
| 0260 | Ledger, bolted 4' O.C., 2" x 4" | 2 Carp | 400 | .040 | L.F. | .71 | 1.52 | | 2.23 | 3.15 |
| 0270 | 2" x 6" | | 395 | .041 | | .92 | 1.54 | | 2.46 | 3.41 |
| 0280 | 2" x 8" | | 390 | .041 | | 1.17 | 1.56 | | 2.73 | 3.71 |
| 0300 | 2" x 12" | | 380 | .042 | | 2.19 | 1.60 | | 3.79 | 4.91 |
| 0310 | Joists, 2" x 4" | | 1250 | .013 | | .60 | .49 | | 1.09 | 1.42 |
| 0320 | 2" x 6" | | 1250 | .013 | | .82 | .49 | | 1.31 | 1.66 |
| 0330 | 2" x 8" | | 1100 | .015 | | 1.07 | .55 | | 1.62 | 2.04 |
| 0340 | 2" x 10" | | 900 | .018 | | 1.32 | .68 | | 2 | 2.50 |
| 0350 | 2" x 12" | | 875 | .018 | | 1.58 | .70 | | 2.28 | 2.82 |
| 0360 | Railings and trim , 1" x 4" | 1 Carp | 300 | .027 | | .49 | 1.02 | | 1.51 | 2.12 |
| 0370 | 2" x 2" | | 300 | .027 | | .33 | 1.02 | | 1.35 | 1.94 |
| 0380 | 2" x 4" | | 300 | .027 | | .59 | 1.02 | | 1.61 | 2.23 |
| 0390 | 2" x 6" | | 300 | .027 | | .80 | 1.02 | | 1.82 | 2.46 |
| 0400 | Decking, 1" x 4" | | 275 | .029 | S.F. | 1.35 | 1.11 | | 2.46 | 3.22 |
| 0410 | 2" x 4" | | 300 | .027 | | 2.02 | 1.02 | | 3.04 | 3.80 |
| 0420 | 2" x 6" | | 320 | .025 | | 1.75 | .95 | | 2.70 | 3.41 |
| 0430 | 5/4" x 6" | | 320 | .025 | | 1.17 | .95 | | 2.12 | 2.76 |
| 0440 | Balusters, square, 2" x 2" | 2 Carp | 660 | .024 | L.F. | .33 | .92 | | 1.25 | 1.81 |
| 0450 | Turned, 2" x 2" | | 420 | .038 | | .44 | 1.45 | | 1.89 | 2.75 |
| 0460 | Stair stringer, 2" x 10" | | 130 | .123 | | 1.32 | 4.69 | | 6.01 | 8.75 |
| 0470 | 2" x 12" | | 130 | .123 | | 1.58 | 4.69 | | 6.27 | 9.05 |
| 0480 | Stair treads, 1" x 4" | | 140 | .114 | | .45 | 4.35 | | 4.80 | 7.30 |
| 0490 | 2" x 4" | | 140 | .114 | | .60 | 4.35 | | 4.95 | 7.45 |
| 0500 | 2" x 6" | | 160 | .100 | | .90 | 3.81 | | 4.71 | 6.95 |
| 0510 | 5/4" x 6" | | 160 | .100 | | .54 | 3.81 | | 4.35 | 6.55 |
| 0520 | Turned handrail post, 4" x 4" | | 64 | .250 | Ea. | 13.80 | 9.55 | | 23.35 | 30 |
| 0530 | Lattice panel, 4' x 8' | | 1600 | .010 | S.F. | .68 | .38 | | 1.06 | 1.33 |
| 0540 | Cedar, posts or columns, 4" x 4" | | 390 | .041 | L.F. | 3.02 | 1.56 | | 4.58 | 5.75 |
| 0550 | 4" x 6" | | 275 | .058 | | 4.59 | 2.22 | | 6.81 | 8.50 |
| 0560 | 4" x 8" | | 220 | .073 | | 6.90 | 2.77 | | 9.67 | 11.85 |
| 0800 | Decking, 1" x 4" | | 550 | .029 | | 1.61 | 1.11 | | 2.72 | 3.50 |
| 0810 | 2" x 4" | | 600 | .027 | | 3.14 | 1.02 | | 4.16 | 5.05 |
| 0820 | 2" x 6" | | 640 | .025 | | 4.52 | .95 | | 5.47 | 6.45 |
| 0830 | 5/4" x 6" | | 640 | .025 | | 3.29 | .95 | | 4.24 | 5.10 |
| 0840 | Railings and trim, 1" x 4" | | 600 | .027 | | 1.61 | 1.02 | | 2.63 | 3.35 |
| 0860 | 2" x 4" | | 600 | .027 | | 3.14 | 1.02 | | 4.16 | 5.05 |
| 0870 | 2" x 6" | | 600 | .027 | | 4.52 | 1.02 | | 5.54 | 6.55 |
| 0920 | Stair treads, 1" x 4" | | 140 | .114 | | 1.61 | 4.35 | | 5.96 | 8.55 |
| 0930 | 2" x 4" | | 140 | .114 | | 3.14 | 4.35 | | 7.49 | 10.25 |
| 0940 | 2" x 6" | | 160 | .100 | | 4.52 | 3.81 | | 8.33 | 10.90 |
| 0950 | 5/4" x 6" | | 160 | .100 | | 3.29 | 3.81 | | 7.10 | 9.55 |
| 0980 | Redwood, posts or columns, 4" x 4" | | 390 | .041 | | 8.40 | 1.56 | | 9.96 | 11.70 |
| 0990 | 4" x 6" | | 275 | .058 | | 10.85 | 2.22 | | 13.07 | 15.40 |
| 1000 | 4" x 8" | | 220 | .073 | | 23 | 2.77 | | 25.77 | 30 |
| 1240 | Redwood decking, 1" x 4" | 1 Carp | 275 | .029 | S.F. | 5.70 | 1.11 | | 6.81 | 8 |
| 1260 | 2" x 6" | | 340 | .024 | | 10.70 | .90 | | 11.60 | 13.15 |
| 1270 | 5/4" x 6" | | 320 | .025 | | 8.25 | .95 | | 9.20 | 10.60 |
| 1280 | Railings and trim, 1" x 4" | 2 Carp | 600 | .027 | L.F. | 1.67 | 1.02 | | 2.69 | 3.42 |
| 1310 | 2" x 6" | | 600 | .027 | | 4.92 | 1.02 | | 5.94 | 7 |
| 1420 | Alternative decking, wood / plastic composite, 5/4" x 6" | | 640 | .025 | | 2.03 | .95 | | 2.98 | 3.71 |
| 1430 | Vinyl, 1-1/2" x 5-1/2" | | 640 | .025 | | 3.73 | .95 | | 4.68 | 5.60 |
| 1440 | 1" x 4" square edge fir | | 550 | .029 | | 1.47 | 1.11 | | 2.58 | 3.34 |
| 1450 | 1" x 4" tongue and groove fir | | 450 | .036 | | 1.41 | 1.35 | | 2.76 | 3.66 |

# 06 11 Wood Framing

## 06 11 10 – Framing with Dimensional, Engineered or Composite Lumber

### 06 11 10.28 Porch or Deck Framing

| | | Crew | Daily Output | Labor-Hours | Unit | Material | 2008 Bare Costs Labor | Equipment | Total | Total Incl O&P |
|---|---|---|---|---|---|---|---|---|---|---|
| 1460 | 1" x 4" mahogany | 2 Carp | 550 | .029 | L.F. | 1.42 | 1.11 | | 2.53 | 3.29 |
| 1470 | Accessories, joist hangers, 2" x 4" | 1 Carp | 160 | .050 | Ea. | .57 | 1.91 | | 2.48 | 3.60 |
| 1480 | 2" x 6" through 2" x 12" | " | 150 | .053 | | .98 | 2.03 | | 3.01 | 4.24 |
| 1530 | Post footing, incl excav, backfill, tube form & concrete, 4' deep, 8" dia | F-7 | 12 | 2.667 | | 10.55 | 91 | | 101.55 | 154 |
| 1540 | 10" diameter | | 11 | 2.909 | | 15.90 | 99.50 | | 115.40 | 173 |
| 1550 | 12" diameter | | 10 | 3.200 | | 21.50 | 109 | | 130.50 | 194 |

### 06 11 10.30 Roof Framing

| | | Crew | Daily Output | Labor-Hours | Unit | Material | 2008 Bare Costs Labor | Equipment | Total | Total Incl O&P |
|---|---|---|---|---|---|---|---|---|---|---|
| 0010 | **ROOF FRAMING** | | | | | | | | | |
| 5250 | Composite rafter, 9-1/2" deep | 2 Carp | 575 | .028 | L.F. | 2.02 | 1.06 | | 3.08 | 3.88 |
| 5260 | 11-1/2" deep | | 575 | .028 | " | 2.16 | 1.06 | | 3.22 | 4.03 |
| 6070 | Fascia boards, 2" x 8" | | .30 | 53.333 | M.B.F. | 570 | 2,025 | | 2,595 | 3,800 |
| 6080 | 2" x 10" | | .30 | 53.333 | | 620 | 2,025 | | 2,645 | 3,850 |
| 7000 | Rafters, to 4 in 12 pitch, 2" x 6" | | 1 | 16 | | 550 | 610 | | 1,160 | 1,550 |
| 7060 | 2" x 8" | | 1.26 | 12.698 | | 570 | 485 | | 1,055 | 1,375 |
| 7300 | Hip and valley rafters, 2" x 6" | | .76 | 21.053 | | 550 | 800 | | 1,350 | 1,850 |
| 7360 | 2" x 8" | | .96 | 16.667 | | 570 | 635 | | 1,205 | 1,625 |
| 7540 | Hip and valley jacks, 2" x 6" | | .60 | 26.667 | | 550 | 1,025 | | 1,575 | 2,175 |
| 7600 | 2" x 8" | | .65 | 24.615 | | 570 | 940 | | 1,510 | 2,075 |
| 7780 | For slopes steeper than 4 in 12, add | | | | | | 30% | | | |
| 7790 | For dormers or complex roofs, add | | | | | | 50% | | | |
| 7800 | Rafter tie, 1" x 4", #3 | 2 Carp | .27 | 59.259 | M.B.F. | 1,150 | 2,250 | | 3,400 | 4,800 |
| 7820 | Ridge board, #2 or better, 1" x 6"          **CN** | | .30 | 53.333 | | 1,250 | 2,025 | | 3,275 | 4,550 |
| 7840 | 1" x 8" | | .37 | 43.243 | | 1,275 | 1,650 | | 2,925 | 3,975 |
| 7860 | 1" x 10" | | .42 | 38.095 | | 1,575 | 1,450 | | 3,025 | 3,975 |
| 7880 | 2" x 6" | | .50 | 32 | | 550 | 1,225 | | 1,775 | 2,500 |
| 7900 | 2" x 8" | | .60 | 26.667 | | 570 | 1,025 | | 1,595 | 2,200 |
| 7920 | 2" x 10" | | .66 | 24.242 | | 620 | 925 | | 1,545 | 2,125 |
| 7940 | Roof cants, split, 4" x 4" | | .86 | 18.605 | | 1,250 | 710 | | 1,960 | 2,475 |
| 7960 | 6" x 6" | | 1.80 | 8.889 | | 1,625 | 340 | | 1,965 | 2,325 |
| 7980 | Roof curbs, untreated, 2" x 6" | | .52 | 30.769 | | 550 | 1,175 | | 1,725 | 2,425 |
| 8000 | 2" x 12" | | .80 | 20 | | 620 | 760 | | 1,380 | 1,850 |

### 06 11 10.32 Sill and Ledger Framing

| | | Crew | Daily Output | Labor-Hours | Unit | Material | 2008 Bare Costs Labor | Equipment | Total | Total Incl O&P |
|---|---|---|---|---|---|---|---|---|---|---|
| 0010 | **SILL AND LEDGER FRAMING** | | | | | | | | | |
| 4482 | Ledgers, nailed, 2" x 4" | 2 Carp | .50 | 32 | M.B.F. | 530 | 1,225 | | 1,755 | 2,475 |
| 4484 | 2" x 6" | | .60 | 26.667 | | 550 | 1,025 | | 1,575 | 2,175 |
| 4486 | Bolted, not including bolts, 3" x 8" | | .65 | 24.615 | | 1,200 | 940 | | 2,140 | 2,775 |
| 4488 | 3" x 12" | | .70 | 22.857 | | 1,200 | 870 | | 2,070 | 2,675 |
| 4490 | Mud sills, redwood, construction grade, 2" x 4" | | .59 | 27.119 | | 4,900 | 1,025 | | 5,925 | 7,000 |
| 4492 | 2" x 6" | | .78 | 20.513 | | 4,900 | 780 | | 5,680 | 6,625 |
| 4500 | Sills, 2" x 4" | | .40 | 40 | | 530 | 1,525 | | 2,055 | 2,950 |
| 4520 | 2" x 6" | | .55 | 29.091 | | 550 | 1,100 | | 1,650 | 2,325 |
| 4540 | 2" x 8" | | .67 | 23.881 | | 570 | 910 | | 1,480 | 2,050 |
| 4600 | Treated, 2" x 4" | | .36 | 44.444 | | 885 | 1,700 | | 2,585 | 3,600 |
| 4620 | 2" x 6" | | .50 | 32 | | 805 | 1,225 | | 2,030 | 2,775 |
| 4640 | 2" x 8" | | .60 | 26.667 | | 790 | 1,025 | | 1,815 | 2,450 |
| 4700 | 4" x 4" | | .60 | 26.667 | | 1,125 | 1,025 | | 2,150 | 2,800 |
| 4720 | 4" x 6" | | .70 | 22.857 | | 945 | 870 | | 1,815 | 2,400 |
| 4740 | 4" x 8" | | .80 | 20 | | 1,225 | 760 | | 1,985 | 2,525 |
| 4760 | 4" x 10" | | .87 | 18.391 | | 1,225 | 700 | | 1,925 | 2,450 |

### 06 11 10.34 Sleepers

| | | Crew | Daily Output | Labor-Hours | Unit | Material | 2008 Bare Costs Labor | Equipment | Total | Total Incl O&P |
|---|---|---|---|---|---|---|---|---|---|---|
| 0010 | **SLEEPERS** | | | | | | | | | |
| 0300 | On concrete, treated, 1" x 2" | 2 Carp | .39 | 41.026 | M.B.F. | 1,225 | 1,575 | | 2,800 | 3,775 |

# 06 11 Wood Framing

## 06 11 10 – Framing with Dimensional, Engineered or Composite Lumber

| 06 11 10.34 Sleepers | | Crew | Daily Output | Labor-Hours | Unit | Material | 2008 Bare Costs Labor | Equipment | Total | Total Incl O&P |
|---|---|---|---|---|---|---|---|---|---|---|
| 0320 | 1" x 3" | 2 Carp | .50 | 32 | M.B.F. | 1,250 | 1,225 | | 2,475 | 3,275 |
| 0340 | 2" x 4" | | .99 | 16.162 | | 885 | 615 | | 1,500 | 1,925 |
| 0360 | 2" x 6" | ↓ | 1.30 | 12.308 | ↓ | 805 | 470 | | 1,275 | 1,625 |

### 06 11 10.36 Soffit and Canopy Framing

| | | Crew | Daily Output | Labor-Hours | Unit | Material | Labor | Equipment | Total | Total Incl O&P |
|---|---|---|---|---|---|---|---|---|---|---|
| 0010 | **SOFFIT AND CANOPY FRAMING** | | | | | | | | | |
| 1300 | Canopy or soffit framing, 1" x 4" | 2 Carp | .30 | 53.333 | M.B.F. | 1,150 | 2,025 | | 3,175 | 4,450 |
| 1340 | 1" x 8" | | .50 | 32 | | 1,275 | 1,225 | | 2,500 | 3,300 |
| 1360 | 2" x 4" | | .41 | 39.024 | | 530 | 1,475 | | 2,005 | 2,900 |
| 1400 | 2" x 8" | | .67 | 23.881 | | 570 | 910 | | 1,480 | 2,050 |
| 1420 | 3" x 4" | | .50 | 32 | | 930 | 1,225 | | 2,155 | 2,925 |
| 1460 | 3" x 8" | ↓ | .60 | 26.667 | ↓ | 1,200 | 1,025 | | 2,225 | 2,900 |

### 06 11 10.38 Treated Lumber Framing Material

| | | Crew | Daily Output | Labor-Hours | Unit | Material | Labor | Equipment | Total | Total Incl O&P |
|---|---|---|---|---|---|---|---|---|---|---|
| 0010 | **TREATED LUMBER FRAMING MATERIAL** | | | | | | | | | |
| 0100 | 2" x 4" | | | | M.B.F. | 885 | | | 885 | 975 |
| 0110 | 2" x 6" | | | | | 805 | | | 805 | 885 |
| 0120 | 2" x 8" | | | | | 790 | | | 790 | 870 |
| 0130 | 2" x 10" | | | | | 780 | | | 780 | 855 |
| 0140 | 2" x 12" | | | | | 1,050 | | | 1,050 | 1,150 |
| 0200 | 4" x 4" | | | | | 1,125 | | | 1,125 | 1,225 |
| 0210 | 4" x 6" | | | | | 1,225 | | | 1,225 | 1,350 |
| 0220 | 4" x 8" | | | | ↓ | 1,225 | | | 1,225 | 1,350 |

### 06 11 10.40 Wall Framing

| | | Crew | Daily Output | Labor-Hours | Unit | Material | Labor | Equipment | Total | Total Incl O&P |
|---|---|---|---|---|---|---|---|---|---|---|
| 0010 | **WALL FRAMING** R061110-30 | | | | | | | | | |
| 5860 | Headers over openings, 2" x 6" | 2 Carp | .36 | 44.444 | M.B.F. | 550 | 1,700 | | 2,250 | 3,225 |
| 5865 | 2" x 6", pneumatic nailed | | .43 | 37.209 | | 550 | 1,425 | | 1,975 | 2,800 |
| 5880 | 2" x 8" | | .45 | 35.556 | | 570 | 1,350 | | 1,920 | 2,725 |
| 5885 | 2" x 8", pneumatic nailed | | .54 | 29.630 | | 570 | 1,125 | | 1,695 | 2,375 |
| 5900 | 2" x 10" | | .53 | 30.189 | | 620 | 1,150 | | 1,770 | 2,475 |
| 5905 | 2" x 10", pneumatic nailed | | .67 | 23.881 | | 620 | 910 | | 1,530 | 2,100 |
| 5920 | 2" x 12" | | .60 | 26.667 | | 620 | 1,025 | | 1,645 | 2,250 |
| 5925 | 2" x 12", pneumatic nailed | | .72 | 22.222 | | 620 | 845 | | 1,465 | 2,000 |
| 5940 | 4" x 12" | | .76 | 21.053 | | 1,650 | 800 | | 2,450 | 3,075 |
| 5945 | 4" x 12", pneumatic nailed | | .92 | 17.391 | | 1,650 | 665 | | 2,315 | 2,850 |
| 5960 | 6" x 12" | | .84 | 19.048 | | 1,525 | 725 | | 2,250 | 2,800 |
| 5965 | 6" x 12", pneumatic nailed | | 1.01 | 15.873 | | 1,525 | 605 | | 2,130 | 2,625 |
| 6000 | Plates, untreated, 2" x 3" | | .43 | 37.209 | | 650 | 1,425 | | 2,075 | 2,925 |
| 6005 | 2" x 3", pneumatic nailed | | .52 | 30.769 | | 650 | 1,175 | | 1,825 | 2,550 |
| 6020 | 2" x 4" CN | | .53 | 30.189 | | 530 | 1,150 | | 1,680 | 2,375 |
| 6025 | 2" x 4", pneumatic nailed | | .67 | 23.881 | | 530 | 910 | | 1,440 | 2,000 |
| 6040 | 2" x 6" | | .75 | 21.333 | | 550 | 815 | | 1,365 | 1,875 |
| 6045 | 2" x 6", pneumatic nailed | | .90 | 17.778 | | 550 | 675 | | 1,225 | 1,650 |
| 6120 | Studs, 8' high wall, 2" x 3" | | .60 | 26.667 | | 650 | 1,025 | | 1,675 | 2,300 |
| 6125 | 2" x 3", pneumatic nailed | | .72 | 22.222 | | 650 | 845 | | 1,495 | 2,050 |
| 6140 | 2" x 4" | | .92 | 17.391 | | 530 | 665 | | 1,195 | 1,600 |
| 6145 | 2" x 4", pneumatic nailed | | 1.10 | 14.493 | | 530 | 550 | | 1,080 | 1,450 |
| 6160 | 2" x 6" | | 1 | 16 | | 550 | 610 | | 1,160 | 1,550 |
| 6165 | 2" x 6", pneumatic nailed | | 1.20 | 13.333 | | 550 | 510 | | 1,060 | 1,400 |
| 6180 | 3" x 4" | | .80 | 20 | | 930 | 760 | | 1,690 | 2,200 |
| 6185 | 3" x 4", pneumatic nailed | ↓ | .96 | 16.667 | ↓ | 930 | 635 | | 1,565 | 2,025 |
| 8200 | For 12' high walls, deduct | | | | | | 5% | | | |
| 8220 | For stub wall, 6' high, add | | | | | | 20% | | | |
| 8240 | 3' high, add | | | | | | 40% | | | |

# 06 11 Wood Framing

## 06 11 10 – Framing with Dimensional, Engineered or Composite Lumber

### 06 11 10.40 Wall Framing

| | | Crew | Daily Output | Labor-Hours | Unit | Material | 2008 Bare Costs Labor | Equipment | Total | Total Incl O&P |
|---|---|---|---|---|---|---|---|---|---|---|
| 8250 | For second story & above, add | | | | | | 5% | | | |
| 8300 | For dormer & gable, add | | | | | | 15% | | | |

### 06 11 10.42 Furring

| | | Crew | Daily Output | Labor-Hours | Unit | Material | 2008 Bare Costs Labor | Equipment | Total | Total Incl O&P |
|---|---|---|---|---|---|---|---|---|---|---|
| 0010 | **FURRING** | | | | | | | | | |
| 0012 | Wood strips, 1" x 2", on walls, on wood | 1 Carp | 550 | .015 | L.F. | .12 | .55 | | .67 | .99 |
| 0015 | On wood, pneumatic nailed | | 710 | .011 | | .12 | .43 | | .55 | .80 |
| 0300 | On masonry | | 495 | .016 | | .12 | .62 | | .74 | 1.09 |
| 0400 | On concrete | | 260 | .031 | | .12 | 1.17 | | 1.29 | 1.95 |
| 0600 | 1" x 3", on walls, on wood | | 550 | .015 | | .17 | .55 | | .72 | 1.05 |
| 0605 | On wood, pneumatic nailed | | 710 | .011 | | .17 | .43 | | .60 | .86 |
| 0700 | On masonry | | 495 | .016 | | .17 | .62 | | .79 | 1.15 |
| 0800 | On concrete | | 260 | .031 | | .17 | 1.17 | | 1.34 | 2.01 |
| 0850 | On ceilings, on wood | | 350 | .023 | | .17 | .87 | | 1.04 | 1.55 |
| 0855 | On wood, pneumatic nailed | | 450 | .018 | | .17 | .68 | | .85 | 1.24 |
| 0900 | On masonry | | 320 | .025 | | .17 | .95 | | 1.12 | 1.67 |
| 0950 | On concrete | | 210 | .038 | | .17 | 1.45 | | 1.62 | 2.45 |

### 06 11 10.44 Grounds

| | | Crew | Daily Output | Labor-Hours | Unit | Material | 2008 Bare Costs Labor | Equipment | Total | Total Incl O&P |
|---|---|---|---|---|---|---|---|---|---|---|
| 0010 | **GROUNDS** | | | | | | | | | |
| 0020 | For casework, 1" x 2" wood strips, on wood | 1 Carp | 330 | .024 | L.F. | .12 | .92 | | 1.04 | 1.57 |
| 0100 | On masonry | | 285 | .028 | | .12 | 1.07 | | 1.19 | 1.79 |
| 0200 | On concrete | | 250 | .032 | | .12 | 1.22 | | 1.34 | 2.03 |
| 0400 | For plaster, 3/4" deep, on wood | | 450 | .018 | | .12 | .68 | | .80 | 1.18 |
| 0500 | On masonry | | 225 | .036 | | .12 | 1.35 | | 1.47 | 2.24 |
| 0600 | On concrete | | 175 | .046 | | .12 | 1.74 | | 1.86 | 2.84 |
| 0700 | On metal lath | | 200 | .040 | | .12 | 1.52 | | 1.64 | 2.50 |

# 06 12 Structural Panels

## 06 12 10 – Structural Insulated Panels

### 06 12 10.10 OSB Faced Panels

| | | Crew | Daily Output | Labor-Hours | Unit | Material | 2008 Bare Costs Labor | Equipment | Total | Total Incl O&P |
|---|---|---|---|---|---|---|---|---|---|---|
| 0010 | **OSB FACED PANELS** | | | | | | | | | |
| 0100 | Structural insul. panels, 7/16" OSB both faces, EPS insul, 3-5/8" T | F-3 | 2075 | .019 | S.F. | 2.84 | .75 | .37 | 3.96 | 4.68 |
| 0110 | 5-5/8" thick | | 1725 | .023 | | 3.37 | .90 | .44 | 4.71 | 5.60 |
| 0120 | 7-3/8" thick | | 1425 | .028 | | 3.84 | 1.09 | .54 | 5.47 | 6.50 |
| 0130 | 9-3/8" thick | | 1125 | .036 | | 4.40 | 1.38 | .68 | 6.46 | 7.70 |
| 0140 | 7/16" OSB one face, EPS insul, 3-5/8" thick | | 2175 | .018 | | 1.65 | .71 | .35 | 2.71 | 3.31 |
| 0150 | 5-5/8" thick | | 1825 | .022 | | 2.06 | .85 | .42 | 3.33 | 4.04 |
| 0160 | 7-3/8" thick | | 1525 | .026 | | 2.40 | 1.01 | .50 | 3.91 | 4.76 |
| 0170 | 9-3/8" thick | | 1225 | .033 | | 2.81 | 1.26 | .63 | 4.70 | 5.75 |
| 0190 | 7/16" OSB - 1/2" GWB faces , EPS insul, 3-5/8" T | | 2075 | .019 | | 3.03 | .75 | .37 | 4.15 | 4.89 |
| 0200 | 5-5/8" thick | | 1725 | .023 | | 3.34 | .90 | .44 | 4.68 | 5.55 |
| 0210 | 7-3/8" thick | | 1425 | .028 | | 3.65 | 1.09 | .54 | 5.28 | 6.30 |
| 0220 | 9-3/8" thick | | 1125 | .036 | | 4 | 1.38 | .68 | 6.06 | 7.30 |
| 0240 | 7/16" OSB - 1/2" MRGWB faces , EPS insul, 3-5/8" T | | 2075 | .019 | | 3.03 | .75 | .37 | 4.15 | 4.89 |
| 0250 | 5-5/8" thick | | 1725 | .023 | | 3.34 | .90 | .44 | 4.68 | 5.55 |
| 0260 | 7-3/8" thick | | 1425 | .028 | | 3.65 | 1.09 | .54 | 5.28 | 6.30 |
| 0270 | 9-3/8" thick | | 1125 | .036 | | 4 | 1.38 | .68 | 6.06 | 7.30 |
| 0300 | For 1/2" GWB added to OSB skin, add | | | | | .60 | | | .60 | .66 |
| 0310 | For 1/2" MRGWB added to OSB skin, add | | | | | .75 | | | .75 | .83 |
| 0320 | For one T1-11 skin, add to OSB-OSB | | | | | .74 | | | .74 | .81 |
| 0330 | For one 19/32" CDX skin, add to OSB-OSB | | | | | .69 | | | .69 | .76 |

# 06 12 Structural Panels

## 06 12 10 – Structural Insulated Panels

### 06 12 10.10 Osb Faced Panels

| | | Crew | Daily Output | Labor-Hours | Unit | Material | 2008 Bare Costs Labor | Equipment | Total | Total Incl O&P |
|---|---|---|---|---|---|---|---|---|---|---|
| 0500 | Structural insulated panel, 7/16" OSB both sides, straw core | | | | | | | | | |
| 0510 | 4-3/8" T, walls (w/sill, splines, plates) | F-6 | 2400 | .017 | S.F. | 7.60 | .59 | .32 | 8.51 | 9.60 |
| 0520 | Floors (w/ splines) | | 2400 | .017 | | 7.60 | .59 | .32 | 8.51 | 9.60 |
| 0530 | Roof (w/ splines) | | 2400 | .017 | | 7.60 | .59 | .32 | 8.51 | 9.60 |
| 0550 | 7-7/8" T, walls (w/sill, splines, plates) | | 2400 | .017 | | 10.95 | .59 | .32 | 11.86 | 13.30 |
| 0560 | Floors (w/ splines) | | 2400 | .017 | | 10.95 | .59 | .32 | 11.86 | 13.30 |
| 0570 | Roof (w/ splines) | | 2400 | .017 | | 10.95 | .59 | .32 | 11.86 | 13.30 |

# 06 13 Heavy Timber

## 06 13 23 – Heavy Timber Construction

### 06 13 23.10 Heavy Framing

| | | Crew | Daily Output | Labor-Hours | Unit | Material | 2008 Bare Costs Labor | Equipment | Total | Total Incl O&P |
|---|---|---|---|---|---|---|---|---|---|---|
| 0010 | **HEAVY FRAMING** | | | | | | | | | |
| 0020 | Beams, single 6" x 10" | 2 Carp | 1.10 | 14.545 | M.B.F. | 2,125 | 555 | | 2,680 | 3,225 |
| 0100 | Single 8" x 16" | | 1.20 | 13.333 | | 2,675 | 510 | | 3,185 | 3,750 |
| 0200 | Built from 2" lumber, multiple 2" x 14" | | .90 | 17.778 | | 935 | 675 | | 1,610 | 2,075 |
| 0210 | Built from 3" lumber, multiple 3" x 6" | | .70 | 22.857 | | 1,150 | 870 | | 2,020 | 2,625 |
| 0220 | Multiple 3" x 8" | | .80 | 20 | | 1,200 | 760 | | 1,960 | 2,500 |
| 0230 | Multiple 3" x 10" | | .90 | 17.778 | | 1,200 | 675 | | 1,875 | 2,375 |
| 0240 | Multiple 3" x 12" | | 1 | 16 | | 1,200 | 610 | | 1,810 | 2,275 |
| 0250 | Built from 4" lumber, multiple 4" x 6" | | .80 | 20 | | 1,175 | 760 | | 1,935 | 2,475 |
| 0260 | Multiple 4" x 8" | | .90 | 17.778 | | 1,600 | 675 | | 2,275 | 2,825 |
| 0270 | Multiple 4" x 10" | | 1 | 16 | | 1,675 | 610 | | 2,285 | 2,800 |
| 0280 | Multiple 4" x 12" | | 1.10 | 14.545 | | 1,650 | 555 | | 2,205 | 2,700 |
| 0290 | Columns, structural grade, 1500f, 4" x 4" | | .60 | 26.667 | | 1,675 | 1,025 | | 2,700 | 3,400 |
| 0300 | 6" x 6" | | .65 | 24.615 | | 1,425 | 940 | | 2,365 | 3,025 |
| 0400 | 8" x 8" | | .70 | 22.857 | | 2,250 | 870 | | 3,120 | 3,825 |
| 0500 | 10" x 10" | | .75 | 21.333 | | 2,125 | 815 | | 2,940 | 3,625 |
| 0600 | 12" x 12" | | .80 | 20 | | 2,150 | 760 | | 2,910 | 3,525 |
| 0800 | Floor planks, 2" thick, T & G, 2" x 6" | | 1.05 | 15.238 | | 1,850 | 580 | | 2,430 | 2,950 |
| 0900 | 2" x 10" | | 1.10 | 14.545 | | 1,875 | 555 | | 2,430 | 2,925 |
| 1100 | 3" thick, 3" x 6" | | 1.05 | 15.238 | | 1,325 | 580 | | 1,905 | 2,375 |
| 1200 | 3" x 10" | | 1.10 | 14.545 | | 1,325 | 555 | | 1,880 | 2,350 |
| 1400 | Girders, structural grade, 12" x 12" | | .80 | 20 | | 2,025 | 760 | | 2,785 | 3,400 |
| 1500 | 10" x 16" | | 1 | 16 | | 1,975 | 610 | | 2,585 | 3,100 |
| 2300 | Roof purlins, 4" thick, structural grade | | 1.05 | 15.238 | | 1,375 | 580 | | 1,955 | 2,400 |
| 2500 | Roof trusses, add timber connectors, See Div 06 05 23.60 | | .45 | 35.556 | | 1,350 | 1,350 | | 2,700 | 3,575 |

# 06 15 Wood Decking

## 06 15 16 – Wood Roof Decking

### 06 15 16.10 Solid Wood Roof Decking

| | | Crew | Daily Output | Labor-Hours | Unit | Material | 2008 Bare Costs Labor | Equipment | Total | Total Incl O&P |
|---|---|---|---|---|---|---|---|---|---|---|
| 0010 | **SOLID WOOD ROOF DECKING** | | | | | | | | | |
| 0400 | Cedar planks, 3" thick | 2 Carp | 320 | .050 | S.F. | 6.35 | 1.91 | | 8.26 | 9.90 |
| 0500 | 4" thick | | 250 | .064 | | 8.55 | 2.44 | | 10.99 | 13.20 |
| 0700 | Douglas fir, 3" thick | | 320 | .050 | | 2.38 | 1.91 | | 4.29 | 5.60 |
| 0800 | 4" thick | | 250 | .064 | | 3.18 | 2.44 | | 5.62 | 7.30 |
| 1000 | Hemlock, 3" thick | | 320 | .050 | | 2.38 | 1.91 | | 4.29 | 5.60 |
| 1100 | 4" thick | | 250 | .064 | | 3.17 | 2.44 | | 5.61 | 7.30 |
| 1300 | Western white spruce, 3" thick | | 320 | .050 | | 2.29 | 1.91 | | 4.20 | 5.50 |
| 1400 | 4" thick | | 250 | .064 | | 3.05 | 2.44 | | 5.49 | 7.15 |

# 06 15 Wood Decking

## 06 15 23 – Laminated Wood Decking

| 06 15 23.10 Laminated Roof Deck | | Crew | Daily Output | Labor-Hours | Unit | Material | 2008 Bare Costs Labor | Equipment | Total | Total Incl O&P |
|---|---|---|---|---|---|---|---|---|---|---|
| 0010 | **LAMINATED ROOF DECK** | | | | | | | | | |
| 0020 | Pine or hemlock, 3" thick | 2 Carp | 425 | .038 | S.F. | 3.36 | 1.43 | | 4.79 | 5.95 |
| 0100 | 4" thick | | 325 | .049 | | 4.47 | 1.88 | | 6.35 | 7.85 |
| 0300 | Cedar, 3" thick | | 425 | .038 | | 4.11 | 1.43 | | 5.54 | 6.75 |
| 0400 | 4" thick | | 325 | .049 | | 5.25 | 1.88 | | 7.13 | 8.65 |
| 0600 | Fir, 3" thick | | 425 | .038 | | 3.43 | 1.43 | | 4.86 | 6 |
| 0700 | 4" thick | | 325 | .049 | | 4.29 | 1.88 | | 6.17 | 7.65 |

# 06 16 Sheathing

## 06 16 23 – Subflooring

### 06 16 23.10 Subfloor

| | | Crew | Daily Output | Labor-Hours | Unit | Material | Labor | Equipment | Total | Total Incl O&P |
|---|---|---|---|---|---|---|---|---|---|---|
| 0010 | **SUBFLOOR** R061636-20 | | | | | | | | | |
| 0011 | Plywood, CDX, 1/2" thick | 2 Carp | 1500 | .011 | SF Flr. | .52 | .41 | | .93 | 1.20 |
| 0015 | Pneumatic nailed | | 1860 | .009 | | .52 | .33 | | .85 | 1.08 |
| 0100 | 5/8" thick | | 1350 | .012 | | .68 | .45 | | 1.13 | 1.45 |
| 0105 | Pneumatic nailed | | 1674 | .010 | | .68 | .36 | | 1.04 | 1.32 |
| 0200 | 3/4" thick | | 1250 | .013 | | .87 | .49 | | 1.36 | 1.72 |
| 0205 | Pneumatic nailed | | 1550 | .010 | | .87 | .39 | | 1.26 | 1.57 |
| 0300 | 1-1/8" thick, 2-4-1 including underlayment | | 1050 | .015 | | 1.63 | .58 | | 2.21 | 2.69 |
| 0450 | 1" x 8", laid regular | | 1000 | .016 | | 1.36 | .61 | | 1.97 | 2.45 |
| 0460 | Laid diagonal | | 850 | .019 | | 1.36 | .72 | | 2.08 | 2.62 |
| 0500 | 1" x 10", laid regular | | 1100 | .015 | | 1.65 | .55 | | 2.20 | 2.68 |
| 0600 | Laid diagonal | | 900 | .018 | | 1.65 | .68 | | 2.33 | 2.87 |
| 8990 | Subfloor adhesive, 3/8" bead | 1 Carp | 2300 | .003 | L.F. | .12 | .13 | | .25 | .34 |

## 06 16 26 – Underlayment

### 06 16 26.10 Wood Product Underlayment

| | | Crew | Daily Output | Labor-Hours | Unit | Material | Labor | Equipment | Total | Total Incl O&P |
|---|---|---|---|---|---|---|---|---|---|---|
| 0010 | **WOOD PRODUCT UNDERLAYMENT** R061636-20 | | | | | | | | | |
| 0030 | Plywood, underlayment grade, 3/8" thick | 2 Carp | 1500 | .011 | SF Flr. | .81 | .41 | | 1.22 | 1.52 |
| 0070 | Pneumatic nailed | | 1860 | .009 | | .81 | .33 | | 1.14 | 1.40 |
| 0100 | 1/2" thick | | 1450 | .011 | | .90 | .42 | | 1.32 | 1.64 |
| 0105 | Pneumatic nailed | | 1798 | .009 | | .90 | .34 | | 1.24 | 1.52 |
| 0200 | 5/8" thick | | 1400 | .011 | | 1.09 | .44 | | 1.53 | 1.88 |
| 0205 | Pneumatic nailed | | 1736 | .009 | | 1.09 | .35 | | 1.44 | 1.75 |
| 0300 | 3/4" thick | | 1300 | .012 | | 1.11 | .47 | | 1.58 | 1.95 |
| 0305 | Pneumatic nailed | | 1612 | .010 | | 1.11 | .38 | | 1.49 | 1.81 |
| 0500 | Particle board, 3/8" thick | | 1500 | .011 | | .33 | .41 | | .74 | .99 |
| 0505 | Pneumatic nailed | | 1860 | .009 | | .33 | .33 | | .66 | .87 |
| 0600 | 1/2" thick | | 1450 | .011 | | .37 | .42 | | .79 | 1.06 |
| 0605 | Pneumatic nailed | | 1798 | .009 | | .37 | .34 | | .71 | .94 |
| 0800 | 5/8" thick | | 1400 | .011 | | .41 | .44 | | .85 | 1.13 |
| 0805 | Pneumatic nailed | | 1736 | .009 | | .41 | .35 | | .76 | 1 |
| 0900 | 3/4" thick | | 1300 | .012 | | .69 | .47 | | 1.16 | 1.49 |
| 0905 | Pneumatic nailed | | 1612 | .010 | | .69 | .38 | | 1.07 | 1.35 |
| 1100 | Hardboard, underlayment grade, 4' x 4', .215" thick | | 1500 | .011 | | .50 | .41 | | .91 | 1.18 |

## 06 16 36 – Wood Panel Product Sheathing

### 06 16 36.10 Sheathing

| | | Crew | Daily Output | Labor-Hours | Unit | Material | Labor | Equipment | Total | Total Incl O&P |
|---|---|---|---|---|---|---|---|---|---|---|
| 0010 | **SHEATHING**, plywood on roofs R061636-20 | | | | | | | | | |
| 0012 | Plywood on roofs, CDX | | | | | | | | | |
| 0030 | 5/16" thick | 2 Carp | 1600 | .010 | S.F. | .62 | .38 | | 1 | 1.27 |

# 06 16 Sheathing

## 06 16 36 – Wood Panel Product Sheathing

| 06 16 36.10 Sheathing | | Crew | Daily Output | Labor-Hours | Unit | Material | 2008 Bare Costs Labor | Equipment | Total | Total Incl O&P |
|---|---|---|---|---|---|---|---|---|---|---|
| 0035 | Pneumatic nailed R061110-30 | 2 Carp | 1952 | .008 | S.F. | .62 | .31 | | .93 | 1.17 |
| 0050 | 3/8" thick | | 1525 | .010 | | .46 | .40 | | .86 | 1.13 |
| 0055 | Pneumatic nailed | | 1860 | .009 | | .46 | .33 | | .79 | 1.02 |
| 0100 | 1/2" thick                      CN | | 1400 | .011 | | .52 | .44 | | .96 | 1.25 |
| 0105 | Pneumatic nailed | | 1708 | .009 | | .52 | .36 | | .88 | 1.13 |
| 0200 | 5/8" thick | | 1300 | .012 | | .68 | .47 | | 1.15 | 1.48 |
| 0205 | Pneumatic nailed | | 1586 | .010 | | .68 | .38 | | 1.06 | 1.35 |
| 0300 | 3/4" thick | | 1200 | .013 | | .87 | .51 | | 1.38 | 1.75 |
| 0305 | Pneumatic nailed | | 1464 | .011 | | .87 | .42 | | 1.29 | 1.61 |
| 0500 | Plywood on walls with exterior CDX, 3/8" thick | | 1200 | .013 | | .46 | .51 | | .97 | 1.30 |
| 0505 | Pneumatic nailed | | 1488 | .011 | | .46 | .41 | | .87 | 1.15 |
| 0600 | 1/2" thick | | 1125 | .014 | | .52 | .54 | | 1.06 | 1.41 |
| 0605 | Pneumatic nailed | | 1395 | .011 | | .52 | .44 | | .96 | 1.25 |
| 0700 | 5/8" thick | | 1050 | .015 | | .68 | .58 | | 1.26 | 1.65 |
| 0705 | Pneumatic nailed | | 1302 | .012 | | .68 | .47 | | 1.15 | 1.48 |
| 0800 | 3/4" thick | | 975 | .016 | | .87 | .63 | | 1.50 | 1.93 |
| 0805 | Pneumatic nailed | | 1209 | .013 | | .87 | .50 | | 1.37 | 1.74 |
| 1000 | For shear wall construction, add | | | | | | 20% | | | |
| 1200 | For structural 1 exterior plywood, add | | | | S.F. | 10% | | | | |
| 1400 | With boards, on roof 1" x 6" boards, laid horizontal | 2 Carp | 725 | .022 | | 1.36 | .84 | | 2.20 | 2.81 |
| 1500 | Laid diagonal | | 650 | .025 | | 1.36 | .94 | | 2.30 | 2.96 |
| 1700 | 1" x 8" boards, laid horizontal | | 875 | .018 | | 1.36 | .70 | | 2.06 | 2.58 |
| 1800 | Laid diagonal | | 725 | .022 | | 1.36 | .84 | | 2.20 | 2.81 |
| 2000 | For steep roofs, add | | | | | | 40% | | | |
| 2200 | For dormers, hips and valleys, add | | | | | 5% | 50% | | | |
| 2400 | Boards on walls, 1" x 6" boards, laid regular | 2 Carp | 650 | .025 | | 1.36 | .94 | | 2.30 | 2.96 |
| 2500 | Laid diagonal | | 585 | .027 | | 1.36 | 1.04 | | 2.40 | 3.12 |
| 2700 | 1" x 8" boards, laid regular | | 765 | .021 | | 1.36 | .80 | | 2.16 | 2.74 |
| 2800 | Laid diagonal | | 650 | .025 | | 1.36 | .94 | | 2.30 | 2.96 |
| 2850 | Gypsum, weatherproof, 1/2" thick | | 1125 | .014 | | .62 | .54 | | 1.16 | 1.52 |
| 2900 | With embedded glass mats | | 1100 | .015 | | .52 | .55 | | 1.07 | 1.43 |
| 3000 | Wood fiber, regular, no vapor barrier, 1/2" thick | | 1200 | .013 | | .55 | .51 | | 1.06 | 1.40 |
| 3100 | 5/8" thick | | 1200 | .013 | | .72 | .51 | | 1.23 | 1.58 |
| 3300 | No vapor barrier, in colors, 1/2" thick | | 1200 | .013 | | .78 | .51 | | 1.29 | 1.65 |
| 3400 | 5/8" thick | | 1200 | .013 | | .96 | .51 | | 1.47 | 1.85 |
| 3600 | With vapor barrier one side, white, 1/2" thick | | 1200 | .013 | | .55 | .51 | | 1.06 | 1.40 |
| 3700 | Vapor barrier 2 sides, 1/2" thick | | 1200 | .013 | | .77 | .51 | | 1.28 | 1.64 |
| 3800 | Asphalt impregnated, 25/32" thick | | 1200 | .013 | | .28 | .51 | | .79 | 1.10 |
| 3850 | Intermediate, 1/2" thick | | 1200 | .013 | | .18 | .51 | | .69 | .99 |

# 06 17 Shop-Fabricated Structural Wood

## 06 17 33 – Wood I-Joists

### 06 17 33.10 Wood and Composite I-Joists

| | | Crew | Daily Output | Labor-Hours | Unit | Material | 2008 Bare Costs Labor | Equipment | Total | Total Incl O&P |
|---|---|---|---|---|---|---|---|---|---|---|
| 0010 | **WOOD AND COMPOSITE I-JOISTS** | | | | | | | | | |
| 0100 | Plywood webs, incl. bridging & blocking, panels 24" O.C. | | | | | | | | | |
| 1200 | 15' to 24' span, 50 psf live load | F-5 | 2400 | .013 | SF Flr. | 2.31 | .51 | | 2.82 | 3.34 |
| 1300 | 55 psf live load | | 2250 | .014 | | 2.46 | .55 | | 3.01 | 3.56 |
| 1400 | 24' to 30' span, 45 psf live load | | 2600 | .012 | | 2.92 | .48 | | 3.40 | 3.95 |
| 1500 | 55 psf live load | | 2400 | .013 | | 3.23 | .51 | | 3.74 | 4.35 |
| 1600 | Tubular steel open webs, 45 psf, 24" O.C., 40' span | F-3 | 6250 | .006 | | 2.24 | .25 | .12 | 2.61 | 2.97 |
| 1700 | 55' span | | 7750 | .005 | | 2.17 | .20 | .10 | 2.47 | 2.81 |

# 06 17 Shop-Fabricated Structural Wood

## 06 17 33 – Wood I-Joists

### 06 17 33.10 Wood and Composite I-Joists

| | | Crew | Daily Output | Labor-Hours | Unit | Material | 2008 Bare Costs Labor | Equipment | Total | Total Incl O&P |
|---|---|---|---|---|---|---|---|---|---|---|
| 1800 | 70' span | F-3 | 9250 | .004 | SF Flr. | 2.82 | .17 | .08 | 3.07 | 3.45 |
| 1900 | 85 psf live load, 26' span | ↓ | 2300 | .017 | ↓ | 2.63 | .67 | .33 | 3.63 | 4.30 |

## 06 17 53 – Shop-Fabricated Wood Trusses

### 06 17 53.10 Roof Trusses

| | | Crew | Daily Output | Labor-Hours | Unit | Material | 2008 Bare Costs Labor | Equipment | Total | Total Incl O&P |
|---|---|---|---|---|---|---|---|---|---|---|
| 0010 | **ROOF TRUSSES** | | | | | | | | | |
| 0100 | Fink (W) or King post type, 2'-0" O.C. | | | | | | | | | |
| 0200 | Metal plate connected, 4 in 12 slope | | | | | | | | | |
| 0210 | 24' to 29' span | F-3 | 3000 | .013 | SF Flr. | 2.06 | .52 | .26 | 2.84 | 3.35 |
| 0300 | 30' to 43' span | ↓ | 3000 | .013 | | 2.28 | .52 | .26 | 3.06 | 3.59 |
| 0400 | 44' to 60' span | ↓ | 3000 | .013 | | 2.52 | .52 | .26 | 3.30 | 3.85 |
| 0700 | Glued and nailed, add | | | | ↓ | 50% | | | | |

# 06 18 Glued-Laminated Construction

## 06 18 13 – Glued-Laminated Beams

### 06 18 13.20 Laminated Framing

| | | Crew | Daily Output | Labor-Hours | Unit | Material | 2008 Bare Costs Labor | Equipment | Total | Total Incl O&P |
|---|---|---|---|---|---|---|---|---|---|---|
| 0010 | **LAMINATED FRAMING** | | | | | | | | | |
| 0020 | 30 lb., short term live load, 15 lb. dead load | | | | | | | | | |
| 0200 | Straight roof beams, 20' clear span, beams 8' O.C. | F-3 | 2560 | .016 | SF Flr. | 1.98 | .60 | .30 | 2.88 | 3.44 |
| 0300 | Beams 16' O.C. | ↓ | 3200 | .013 | | 1.43 | .48 | .24 | 2.15 | 2.58 |
| 0500 | 40' clear span, beams 8' O.C. | | 3200 | .013 | | 3.78 | .48 | .24 | 4.50 | 5.15 |
| 0600 | Beams 16' O.C. | ↓ | 3840 | .010 | | 3.09 | .40 | .20 | 3.69 | 4.24 |
| 0800 | 60' clear span, beams 8' O.C. | F-4 | 2880 | .017 | | 6.50 | .63 | .39 | 7.52 | 8.55 |
| 0900 | Beams 16' O.C. | " | 3840 | .013 | | 4.84 | .48 | .29 | 5.61 | 6.35 |
| 1100 | Tudor arches, 30' to 40' clear span, frames 8' O.C. | F-3 | 1680 | .024 | | 8.45 | .92 | .46 | 9.83 | 11.20 |
| 1200 | Frames 16' O.C. | " | 2240 | .018 | | 6.65 | .69 | .34 | 7.68 | 8.75 |
| 1400 | 50' to 60' clear span, frames 8' O.C. | F-4 | 2200 | .022 | | 9.15 | .83 | .51 | 10.49 | 11.90 |
| 1500 | Frames 16' O.C. | | 2640 | .018 | | 7.80 | .69 | .42 | 8.91 | 10.10 |
| 1700 | Radial arches, 60' clear span, frames 8' O.C. | | 1920 | .025 | | 8.55 | .95 | .58 | 10.08 | 11.50 |
| 1800 | Frames 16' O.C. | | 2880 | .017 | | 6.55 | .63 | .39 | 7.57 | 8.65 |
| 2000 | 100' clear span, frames 8' O.C. | | 1600 | .030 | | 8.85 | 1.14 | .70 | 10.69 | 12.30 |
| 2100 | Frames 16' O.C. | | 2400 | .020 | | 7.80 | .76 | .47 | 9.03 | 10.25 |
| 2300 | 120' clear span, frames 8' O.C. | | 1440 | .033 | | 11.75 | 1.27 | .78 | 13.80 | 15.75 |
| 2400 | Frames 16' O.C. | ↓ | 1920 | .025 | | 10.75 | .95 | .58 | 12.28 | 13.90 |
| 2600 | Bowstring trusses, 20' O.C., 40' clear span | F-3 | 2400 | .017 | | 5.30 | .64 | .32 | 6.26 | 7.20 |
| 2700 | 60' clear span | F-4 | 3600 | .013 | | 4.76 | .51 | .31 | 5.58 | 6.35 |
| 2800 | 100' clear span | | 4000 | .012 | | 6.75 | .46 | .28 | 7.49 | 8.40 |
| 2900 | 120' clear span | ↓ | 3600 | .013 | | 7.25 | .51 | .31 | 8.07 | 9.05 |
| 3000 | For less than 1000 B.F., add | | | | | 20% | | | | |
| 3050 | For over 5000 B.F., deduct | | | | | 10% | | | | |
| 3100 | For premium appearance, add to S.F. prices | | | | | 5% | | | | |
| 3300 | For industrial type, deduct | | | | | 15% | | | | |
| 3500 | For stain and varnish, add | | | | | 5% | | | | |
| 3900 | For 3/4" laminations, add to straight | | | | | 25% | | | | |
| 4100 | Add to curved | | | | ↓ | 15% | | | | |
| 4300 | Alternate pricing method: (use nominal footage of | | | | | | | | | |
| 4310 | components). Straight beams, camber less than 6" | F-3 | 3.50 | 11.429 | M.B.F. | 2,925 | 440 | 219 | 3,584 | 4,150 |
| 4400 | Columns, including hardware | | 2 | 20 | | 3,150 | 775 | 385 | 4,310 | 5,100 |
| 4600 | Curved members, radius over 32' | | 2.50 | 16 | | 3,225 | 620 | 305 | 4,150 | 4,850 |
| 4700 | Radius 10' to 32' | ↓ | 3 | 13.333 | | 3,200 | 515 | 255 | 3,970 | 4,600 |
| 4900 | For complicated shapes, add maximum | | | | ↓ | 100% | | | | |

# 06 18 Glued-Laminated Construction

## 06 18 13 – Glued-Laminated Beams

| 06 18 13.20 Laminated Framing | Crew | Daily Output | Labor-Hours | Unit | Material | 2008 Bare Costs Labor | Equipment | Total | Total Incl O&P |
|---|---|---|---|---|---|---|---|---|---|
| 5100    For pressure treating, add to straight | | | | M.B.F. | 35% | | | | |
| 5200      Add to curved | | | | ↓ | 45% | | | | |
| 6000   Laminated veneer members, southern pine or western species | | | | | | | | | |
| 6050      1-3/4" wide x 5-1/2" deep | 2 Carp | 480 | .033 | L.F. | 3.36 | 1.27 | | 4.63 | 5.70 |
| 6100          9-1/2" deep | | 480 | .033 | | 4.79 | 1.27 | | 6.06 | 7.25 |
| 6150          14" deep | | 450 | .036 | | 7.55 | 1.35 | | 8.90 | 10.40 |
| 6200          18" deep | | 450 | .036 | | 10.15 | 1.35 | | 11.50 | 13.30 |
| 6300   Parallel strand members, southern pine or western species | | | | | | | | | |
| 6350      1-3/4" wide x 9-1/4" deep | 2 Carp | 480 | .033 | L.F. | 4.46 | 1.27 | | 5.73 | 6.90 |
| 6400          11-1/4" deep | | 450 | .036 | | 5.45 | 1.35 | | 6.80 | 8.10 |
| 6450          14" deep | | 400 | .040 | | 6.55 | 1.52 | | 8.07 | 9.55 |
| 6500      3-1/2" wide x 9-1/4" deep | | 480 | .033 | | 10.50 | 1.27 | | 11.77 | 13.55 |
| 6550          11-1/4" deep | | 450 | .036 | | 13.15 | 1.35 | | 14.50 | 16.55 |
| 6600          14" deep | | 400 | .040 | | 15.95 | 1.52 | | 17.47 | 19.90 |
| 6650      7" wide x 9-1/4" deep | | 450 | .036 | | 22 | 1.35 | | 23.35 | 26.50 |
| 6700          11-1/4" deep | | 420 | .038 | | 26.50 | 1.45 | | 27.95 | 31.50 |
| 6750          14" deep | | 400 | .040 | | 28.50 | 1.52 | | 30.02 | 33.50 |

# 06 22 Millwork

## 06 22 13 – Standard Pattern Wood Trim

### 06 22 13.15 Moldings, Base

| | | Crew | Daily Output | Labor-Hours | Unit | Material | 2008 Bare Costs Labor | Equipment | Total | Total Incl O&P |
|---|---|---|---|---|---|---|---|---|---|---|
| 0010 | **MOLDINGS, BASE** | | | | | | | | | |
| 0500 | Base, stock pine, 9/16" x 3-1/2" | 1 Carp | 240 | .033 | L.F. | 2.21 | 1.27 | | 3.48 | 4.41 |
| 0550 |    9/16" x 4-1/2" | | 200 | .040 | | 2.40 | 1.52 | | 3.92 | 5 |
| 0561 | Base shoe, oak, 3/4" x 1" | | 240 | .033 | | 1.13 | 1.27 | | 2.40 | 3.22 |

### 06 22 13.30 Moldings, Casings

| | | Crew | Daily Output | Labor-Hours | Unit | Material | 2008 Bare Costs Labor | Equipment | Total | Total Incl O&P |
|---|---|---|---|---|---|---|---|---|---|---|
| 0010 | **MOLDINGS, CASINGS** | | | | | | | | | |
| 0090 | Apron, stock pine, 5/8" x 2" | 1 Carp | 250 | .032 | L.F. | 1.18 | 1.22 | | 2.40 | 3.20 |
| 0110 |    5/8" x 3-1/2" | | 220 | .036 | | 1.78 | 1.39 | | 3.17 | 4.12 |
| 0300 | Band, stock pine, 11/16" x 1-1/8" | | 270 | .030 | | .77 | 1.13 | | 1.90 | 2.61 |
| 0350 |    11/16" x 1-3/4" | | 250 | .032 | | 1.03 | 1.22 | | 2.25 | 3.03 |
| 0700 | Casing, stock pine, 11/16" x 2-1/2" | | 240 | .033 | | 1.26 | 1.27 | | 2.53 | 3.37 |
| 0750 |    11/16" x 3-1/2" | | 215 | .037 | | 1.78 | 1.42 | | 3.20 | 4.17 |

### 06 22 13.35 Moldings, Ceilings

| | | Crew | Daily Output | Labor-Hours | Unit | Material | 2008 Bare Costs Labor | Equipment | Total | Total Incl O&P |
|---|---|---|---|---|---|---|---|---|---|---|
| 0010 | **MOLDINGS, CEILINGS** | | | | | | | | | |
| 0600 | Bed, stock pine, 9/16" x 1-3/4" | 1 Carp | 270 | .030 | L.F. | .92 | 1.13 | | 2.05 | 2.77 |
| 0650 |    9/16" x 2" | | 240 | .033 | | 1.16 | 1.27 | | 2.43 | 3.26 |
| 1200 | Cornice molding, stock pine, 9/16" x 1-3/4" | | 330 | .024 | | .96 | .92 | | 1.88 | 2.50 |
| 1300 |    9/16" x 2-1/4" | | 300 | .027 | | 1.18 | 1.02 | | 2.20 | 2.88 |
| 2400 | Cove scotia, stock pine, 9/16" x 1-3/4" | | 270 | .030 | | .98 | 1.13 | | 2.11 | 2.84 |
| 2500 |    11/16" x 2-3/4" | | 255 | .031 | | 1.30 | 1.20 | | 2.50 | 3.29 |
| 2600 | Crown, stock pine, 9/16" x 3-5/8" | | 250 | .032 | | 1.79 | 1.22 | | 3.01 | 3.87 |
| 2700 |    11/16" x 4-5/8" | | 220 | .036 | | 3.04 | 1.39 | | 4.43 | 5.50 |

### 06 22 13.40 Moldings, Exterior

| | | Crew | Daily Output | Labor-Hours | Unit | Material | 2008 Bare Costs Labor | Equipment | Total | Total Incl O&P |
|---|---|---|---|---|---|---|---|---|---|---|
| 0010 | **MOLDINGS, EXTERIOR** | | | | | | | | | |
| 1500 | Cornice, boards, pine, 1" x 2" | 1 Carp | 330 | .024 | L.F. | .32 | .92 | | 1.24 | 1.79 |
| 1700 |    1" x 6" | | 250 | .032 | | 1.03 | 1.22 | | 2.25 | 3.03 |
| 2000 |    1" x 12" | | 180 | .044 | | 2.31 | 1.69 | | 4 | 5.20 |
| 2200 |    Three piece, built-up, pine, minimum | | 80 | .100 | | 2.01 | 3.81 | | 5.82 | 8.15 |
| 2300 |      Maximum | | 65 | .123 | | 5.45 | 4.69 | | 10.14 | 13.30 |

## 06 22 13 – Standard Pattern Wood Trim

### 06 22 13.40 Moldings, Exterior

| | | Crew | Daily Output | Labor-Hours | Unit | Material | 2008 Bare Costs Labor | Equipment | Total | Total Incl O&P |
|---|---|---|---|---|---|---|---|---|---|---|
| 3000 | Corner board, sterling pine, 1" x 4" | 1 Carp | 200 | .040 | L.F. | .69 | 1.52 | | 2.21 | 3.13 |
| 3100 | 1" x 6" | | 200 | .040 | | 1.05 | 1.52 | | 2.57 | 3.53 |
| 3350 | Fascia, sterling pine, 1" x 6" | | 250 | .032 | | 1.05 | 1.22 | | 2.27 | 3.06 |
| 3370 | 1" x 8" | | 225 | .036 | | 1.43 | 1.35 | | 2.78 | 3.68 |
| 3400 | Trim, back band, 11/16" x 1-1/16" | | 250 | .032 | | .78 | 1.22 | | 2 | 2.76 |
| 3500 | Casing, 11/16" x 4-1/4" | | 250 | .032 | | 2.57 | 1.22 | | 3.79 | 4.73 |
| 3600 | Crown, 11/16" x 4-1/4" | | 250 | .032 | | 3.37 | 1.22 | | 4.59 | 5.60 |
| 3700 | 1" x 4" and 1" x 6" railing w/ balusters 4" O.C. | | 22 | .364 | | 38.50 | 13.85 | | 52.35 | 64 |
| 3800 | Insect screen framing stock, 1-1/16" x 1-3/4" | | 395 | .020 | | 1.91 | .77 | | 2.68 | 3.30 |
| 4100 | Verge board, sterling pine, 1" x 4" | | 200 | .040 | | .69 | 1.52 | | 2.21 | 3.13 |
| 4200 | 1" x 6" | | 200 | .040 | | 1.05 | 1.52 | | 2.57 | 3.53 |
| 4300 | 2" x 6" | | 165 | .048 | | 1.98 | 1.85 | | 3.83 | 5.05 |
| 4400 | 2" x 8" | ▼ | 165 | .048 | ▼ | 2.63 | 1.85 | | 4.48 | 5.75 |
| 4700 | For redwood trim, add | | | | | 200% | | | | |

### 06 22 13.45 Moldings, Trim

| | | Crew | Daily Output | Labor-Hours | Unit | Material | 2008 Bare Costs Labor | Equipment | Total | Total Incl O&P |
|---|---|---|---|---|---|---|---|---|---|---|
| 0010 | **MOLDINGS, TRIM** | | | | | | | | | |
| 0200 | Astragal, stock pine, 11/16" x 1-3/4" | 1 Carp | 255 | .031 | L.F. | 1.13 | 1.20 | | 2.33 | 3.10 |
| 0250 | 1-5/16" x 2-3/16" | | 240 | .033 | | 2.43 | 1.27 | | 3.70 | 4.65 |
| 0800 | Chair rail, stock pine, 5/8" x 2-1/2" | | 270 | .030 | | 1.40 | 1.13 | | 2.53 | 3.30 |
| 0900 | 5/8" x 3-1/2" | | 240 | .033 | | 2.15 | 1.27 | | 3.42 | 4.35 |
| 1000 | Closet pole, stock pine, 1-1/8" diameter | | 200 | .040 | | 1 | 1.52 | | 2.52 | 3.47 |
| 1100 | Fir, 1-5/8" diameter | | 200 | .040 | | 1.72 | 1.52 | | 3.24 | 4.26 |
| 3300 | Half round, stock pine, 1/4" x 1/2" | | 270 | .030 | | .23 | 1.13 | | 1.36 | 2.01 |
| 3350 | 1/2" x 1" | ▼ | 255 | .031 | ▼ | .59 | 1.20 | | 1.79 | 2.51 |
| 3400 | Handrail, fir, single piece, stock, hardware not included | | | | | | | | | |
| 3450 | 1-1/2" x 1-3/4" | 1 Carp | 80 | .100 | L.F. | 1.80 | 3.81 | | 5.61 | 7.95 |
| 3470 | Pine, 1-1/2" x 1-3/4" | | 80 | .100 | | 1.80 | 3.81 | | 5.61 | 7.95 |
| 3500 | 1-1/2" x 2-1/2" | | 76 | .105 | | 2.05 | 4.01 | | 6.06 | 8.50 |
| 3600 | Lattice, stock pine, 1/4" x 1-1/8" | | 270 | .030 | | .41 | 1.13 | | 1.54 | 2.21 |
| 3700 | 1/4" x 1-3/4" | | 250 | .032 | | .63 | 1.22 | | 1.85 | 2.59 |
| 3800 | Miscellaneous, custom, pine, 1" x 1" | | 270 | .030 | | .34 | 1.13 | | 1.47 | 2.13 |
| 3900 | 1" x 3" | | 240 | .033 | | .69 | 1.27 | | 1.96 | 2.74 |
| 4100 | Birch or oak, nominal 1" x 1" | | 240 | .033 | | .53 | 1.27 | | 1.80 | 2.56 |
| 4200 | Nominal 1" x 3" | | 215 | .037 | | 1.81 | 1.42 | | 3.23 | 4.20 |
| 4400 | Walnut, nominal 1" x 1" | | 215 | .037 | | .87 | 1.42 | | 2.29 | 3.17 |
| 4500 | Nominal 1" x 3" | | 200 | .040 | | 2.61 | 1.52 | | 4.13 | 5.25 |
| 4700 | Teak, nominal 1" x 1" | | 215 | .037 | | 1.23 | 1.42 | | 2.65 | 3.56 |
| 4800 | Nominal 1" x 3" | | 200 | .040 | | 3.52 | 1.52 | | 5.04 | 6.25 |
| 4900 | Quarter round, stock pine, 1/4" x 1/4" | | 275 | .029 | | .22 | 1.11 | | 1.33 | 1.97 |
| 4950 | 3/4" x 3/4" | | 255 | .031 | | .59 | 1.20 | | 1.79 | 2.51 |
| 5600 | Wainscot moldings, 1-1/8" x 9/16", 2' high, minimum | | 76 | .105 | S.F. | 10.75 | 4.01 | | 14.76 | 18.05 |
| 5700 | Maximum | ▼ | 65 | .123 | " | 20 | 4.69 | | 24.69 | 29.50 |

### 06 22 13.50 Moldings, Window and Door

| | | Crew | Daily Output | Labor-Hours | Unit | Material | 2008 Bare Costs Labor | Equipment | Total | Total Incl O&P |
|---|---|---|---|---|---|---|---|---|---|---|
| 0010 | **MOLDINGS, WINDOW AND DOOR** | | | | | | | | | |
| 2800 | Door moldings, stock, decorative, 1-1/8" wide, plain | 1 Carp | 17 | .471 | Set | 43 | 17.95 | | 60.95 | 75 |
| 2900 | Detailed | | 17 | .471 | " | 87.50 | 17.95 | | 105.45 | 125 |
| 2960 | Clear pine door jamb, no stops, 11/16" x 4-9/16" | | 240 | .033 | L.F. | 4 | 1.27 | | 5.27 | 6.40 |
| 3150 | Door trim set, 1 head and 2 sides, pine, 2-1/2 wide | | 5.90 | 1.356 | Opng. | 21.50 | 51.50 | | 73 | 104 |
| 3170 | 3-1/2" wide | | 5.30 | 1.509 | " | 30.50 | 57.50 | | 88 | 123 |
| 3250 | Glass beads, stock pine, 3/8" x 1/2" | | 275 | .029 | L.F. | .30 | 1.11 | | 1.41 | 2.06 |
| 3270 | 3/8" x 7/8" | | 270 | .030 | | .40 | 1.13 | | 1.53 | 2.20 |
| 4850 | Parting bead, stock pine, 3/8" x 3/4" | ▼ | 275 | .029 | ▼ | .34 | 1.11 | | 1.45 | 2.10 |

# 06 22 Millwork

## 06 22 13 – Standard Pattern Wood Trim

### 06 22 13.50 Moldings, Window and Door

| | | Crew | Daily Output | Labor-Hours | Unit | Material | 2008 Bare Costs Labor | Equipment | Total | Total Incl O&P |
|---|---|---|---|---|---|---|---|---|---|---|
| 4870 | 1/2" x 3/4" | 1 Carp | 255 | .031 | L.F. | .43 | 1.20 | | 1.63 | 2.33 |
| 5000 | Stool caps, stock pine, 11/16" x 3-1/2" | | 200 | .040 | | 2.14 | 1.52 | | 3.66 | 4.72 |
| 5100 | 1-1/16" x 3-1/4" | | 150 | .053 | | 3.38 | 2.03 | | 5.41 | 6.90 |
| 5300 | Threshold, oak, 3' long, inside, 5/8" x 3-5/8" | | 32 | .250 | Ea. | 9 | 9.55 | | 18.55 | 25 |
| 5400 | Outside, 1-1/2" x 7-5/8" | | 16 | .500 | " | 37 | 19.05 | | 56.05 | 70 |
| 5900 | Window trim sets, including casings, header, stops, | | | | | | | | | |
| 5910 | stool and apron, 2-1/2" wide, minimum | 1 Carp | 13 | .615 | Opng. | 29 | 23.50 | | 52.50 | 68.50 |
| 5950 | Average | | 10 | .800 | | 34.50 | 30.50 | | 65 | 85 |
| 6000 | Maximum | | 6 | 1.333 | | 62.50 | 51 | | 113.50 | 148 |

### 06 22 13.60 Moldings, Soffits

| | | Crew | Daily Output | Labor-Hours | Unit | Material | 2008 Bare Costs Labor | Equipment | Total | Total Incl O&P |
|---|---|---|---|---|---|---|---|---|---|---|
| 0010 | **MOLDINGS, SOFFITS** | | | | | | | | | |
| 0200 | Soffits, pine, 1" x 4" | 2 Carp | 420 | .038 | L.F. | .39 | 1.45 | | 1.84 | 2.68 |
| 0210 | 1" x 6" | | 420 | .038 | | .63 | 1.45 | | 2.08 | 2.95 |
| 0220 | 1" x 8" | | 420 | .038 | | .85 | 1.45 | | 2.30 | 3.20 |
| 0230 | 1" x 10" | | 400 | .040 | | 1.31 | 1.52 | | 2.83 | 3.81 |
| 0240 | 1" x 12" | | 400 | .040 | | 1.69 | 1.52 | | 3.21 | 4.23 |
| 0250 | STK cedar, 1" x 4" | | 420 | .038 | | .59 | 1.45 | | 2.04 | 2.91 |
| 0260 | 1" x 6" | | 420 | .038 | | 1.07 | 1.45 | | 2.52 | 3.44 |
| 0270 | 1" x 8" | | 420 | .038 | | 1.39 | 1.45 | | 2.84 | 3.79 |
| 0280 | 1" x 10" | | 400 | .040 | | 1.77 | 1.52 | | 3.29 | 4.32 |
| 0290 | 1" x 12" | | 400 | .040 | | 2.14 | 1.52 | | 3.66 | 4.72 |
| 1000 | Exterior AC plywood, 1/4" thick | | 420 | .038 | S.F. | .77 | 1.45 | | 2.22 | 3.11 |
| 1050 | 3/8" thick | | 420 | .038 | | .81 | 1.45 | | 2.26 | 3.15 |
| 1100 | 1/2" thick | | 420 | .038 | | .90 | 1.45 | | 2.35 | 3.25 |
| 1150 | Polyvinyl chloride, white, solid | 1 Carp | 230 | .035 | | .95 | 1.33 | | 2.28 | 3.11 |
| 1160 | Perforated | " | 230 | .035 | | .95 | 1.33 | | 2.28 | 3.11 |

# 06 25 Prefinished Paneling

## 06 25 13 – Prefinished Hardboard Paneling

### 06 25 13.10 Paneling, Hardboard

| | | Crew | Daily Output | Labor-Hours | Unit | Material | 2008 Bare Costs Labor | Equipment | Total | Total Incl O&P |
|---|---|---|---|---|---|---|---|---|---|---|
| 0010 | **PANELING, HARDBOARD** | | | | | | | | | |
| 0050 | Not incl. furring or trim, hardboard, tempered, 1/8" thick | 2 Carp | 500 | .032 | S.F. | .38 | 1.22 | | 1.60 | 2.32 |
| 0100 | 1/4" thick | | 500 | .032 | | .53 | 1.22 | | 1.75 | 2.48 |
| 0300 | Tempered pegboard, 1/8" thick | | 500 | .032 | | .47 | 1.22 | | 1.69 | 2.42 |
| 0400 | 1/4" thick | | 500 | .032 | | .65 | 1.22 | | 1.87 | 2.62 |
| 0600 | Untempered hardboard, natural finish, 1/8" thick | | 500 | .032 | | .39 | 1.22 | | 1.61 | 2.33 |
| 0700 | 1/4" thick | | 500 | .032 | | .42 | 1.22 | | 1.64 | 2.36 |
| 0900 | Untempered pegboard, 1/8" thick | | 500 | .032 | | .38 | 1.22 | | 1.60 | 2.32 |
| 1000 | 1/4" thick | | 500 | .032 | | .42 | 1.22 | | 1.64 | 2.36 |
| 1200 | Plastic faced hardboard, 1/8" thick | | 500 | .032 | | .64 | 1.22 | | 1.86 | 2.60 |
| 1300 | 1/4" thick | | 500 | .032 | | .85 | 1.22 | | 2.07 | 2.84 |
| 1500 | Plastic faced pegboard, 1/8" thick | | 500 | .032 | | .61 | 1.22 | | 1.83 | 2.57 |
| 1600 | 1/4" thick | | 500 | .032 | | .75 | 1.22 | | 1.97 | 2.73 |
| 1800 | Wood grained, plain or grooved, 1/4" thick, minimum | | 500 | .032 | | .57 | 1.22 | | 1.79 | 2.53 |
| 1900 | Maximum | | 425 | .038 | | 1.19 | 1.43 | | 2.62 | 3.54 |
| 2100 | Moldings for hardboard, wood or aluminum, minimum | | 500 | .032 | L.F. | .38 | 1.22 | | 1.60 | 2.32 |
| 2200 | Maximum | | 425 | .038 | " | 1.08 | 1.43 | | 2.51 | 3.42 |

## 06 25 16 – Prefinished Plywood Paneling

### 06 25 16.10 Paneling, Plywood

| | | | | | | | | | | |
|---|---|---|---|---|---|---|---|---|---|---|
| 0010 | **PANELING, PLYWOOD** | R061636-20 | | | | | | | | |

## 06 25 16 – Prefinished Plywood Paneling

| 06 25 16.10 Paneling, Plywood | Crew | Daily Output | Labor-Hours | Unit | Material | 2008 Bare Costs Labor | Equipment | Total | Total Incl O&P |
|---|---|---|---|---|---|---|---|---|---|
| 2400 | Plywood, prefinished, 1/4" thick, 4' x 8' sheets | | | | | | | | | |
| 2410 | with vertical grooves. Birch faced, minimum | 2 Carp | 500 | .032 | S.F. | .87 | 1.22 | | 2.09 | 2.86 |
| 2420 | Average | | 420 | .038 | | 1.32 | 1.45 | | 2.77 | 3.71 |
| 2430 | Maximum | | 350 | .046 | | 1.93 | 1.74 | | 3.67 | 4.83 |
| 2600 | Mahogany, African | | 400 | .040 | | 2.46 | 1.52 | | 3.98 | 5.10 |
| 2700 | Philippine (Lauan) | | 500 | .032 | | 1.06 | 1.22 | | 2.28 | 3.07 |
| 2900 | Oak or Cherry, minimum | | 500 | .032 | | 2.06 | 1.22 | | 3.28 | 4.17 |
| 3000 | Maximum | | 400 | .040 | | 3.16 | 1.52 | | 4.68 | 5.85 |
| 3200 | Rosewood | | 320 | .050 | | 4.49 | 1.91 | | 6.40 | 7.90 |
| 3400 | Teak | | 400 | .040 | | 3.16 | 1.52 | | 4.68 | 5.85 |
| 3600 | Chestnut | | 375 | .043 | | 4.68 | 1.63 | | 6.31 | 7.70 |
| 3800 | Pecan | | 400 | .040 | | 2.02 | 1.52 | | 3.54 | 4.59 |
| 3900 | Walnut, minimum | | 500 | .032 | | 2.70 | 1.22 | | 3.92 | 4.87 |
| 3950 | Maximum | | 400 | .040 | | 5.10 | 1.52 | | 6.62 | 7.95 |
| 4000 | Plywood, prefinished, 3/4" thick, stock grades, minimum | | 320 | .050 | | 1.22 | 1.91 | | 3.13 | 4.31 |
| 4100 | Maximum | | 224 | .071 | | 5.25 | 2.72 | | 7.97 | 10.05 |
| 4300 | Architectural grade, minimum | | 224 | .071 | | 3.90 | 2.72 | | 6.62 | 8.55 |
| 4400 | Maximum | | 160 | .100 | | 5.95 | 3.81 | | 9.76 | 12.50 |
| 4600 | Plywood, "A" face, birch, V.C., 1/2" thick, natural | | 450 | .036 | | 1.85 | 1.35 | | 3.20 | 4.15 |
| 4700 | Select | | 450 | .036 | | 2.02 | 1.35 | | 3.37 | 4.33 |
| 4900 | Veneer core, 3/4" thick, natural | | 320 | .050 | | 1.95 | 1.91 | | 3.86 | 5.10 |
| 5000 | Select | | 320 | .050 | | 2.19 | 1.91 | | 4.10 | 5.40 |
| 5200 | Lumber core, 3/4" thick, natural | | 320 | .050 | | 2.93 | 1.91 | | 4.84 | 6.20 |
| 5500 | Plywood, knotty pine, 1/4" thick, A2 grade | | 450 | .036 | | 1.60 | 1.35 | | 2.95 | 3.87 |
| 5600 | A3 grade | | 450 | .036 | | 2.02 | 1.35 | | 3.37 | 4.33 |
| 5800 | 3/4" thick, veneer core, A2 grade | | 320 | .050 | | 2.07 | 1.91 | | 3.98 | 5.25 |
| 5900 | A3 grade | | 320 | .050 | | 2.33 | 1.91 | | 4.24 | 5.55 |
| 6100 | Aromatic cedar, 1/4" thick, plywood | | 400 | .040 | | 2.04 | 1.52 | | 3.56 | 4.61 |
| 6200 | 1/4" thick, particle board | | 400 | .040 | | .99 | 1.52 | | 2.51 | 3.46 |

## 06 25 26 – Panel System

### 06 25 26.10 Panel Systems

| 06 25 26.10 Panel Systems | Crew | Daily Output | Labor-Hours | Unit | Material | 2008 Bare Costs Labor | Equipment | Total | Total Incl O&P |
|---|---|---|---|---|---|---|---|---|---|
| 0010 | **PANEL SYSTEMS** | | | | | | | | | |
| 0100 | Raised panel, eng. wood core w/ wood veneer, std., paint grade | 2 Carp | 300 | .053 | S.F. | 11.55 | 2.03 | | 13.58 | 15.85 |
| 0110 | Oak veneer | | 300 | .053 | | 19.15 | 2.03 | | 21.18 | 24 |
| 0120 | Maple veneer | | 300 | .053 | | 24.50 | 2.03 | | 26.53 | 30 |
| 0130 | Cherry veneer | | 300 | .053 | | 31 | 2.03 | | 33.03 | 37 |
| 0300 | Class I fire rated, paint grade | | 300 | .053 | | 13.80 | 2.03 | | 15.83 | 18.35 |
| 0310 | Oak veneer | | 300 | .053 | | 23 | 2.03 | | 25.03 | 28.50 |
| 0320 | Maple veneer | | 300 | .053 | | 29 | 2.03 | | 31.03 | 35 |
| 0330 | Cherry veneer | | 300 | .053 | | 37 | 2.03 | | 39.03 | 44 |
| 0510 | Beadboard, 5/8" MDF, standard, primed | | 300 | .053 | | 8.15 | 2.03 | | 10.18 | 12.15 |
| 0520 | Oak veneer, unfinished | | 300 | .053 | | 14.15 | 2.03 | | 16.18 | 18.75 |
| 0530 | Maple veneer, unfinished | | 300 | .053 | | 16.75 | 2.03 | | 18.78 | 21.50 |
| 0610 | Rustic paneling, 5/8" MDF, standard, maple veneer, unfinished | | 300 | .053 | | 21.50 | 2.03 | | 23.53 | 26.50 |

# 06 26 Board Paneling

## 06 26 13 – Profile Board Paneling

| 06 26 13.10 Paneling, Boards | Crew | Daily Output | Labor-Hours | Unit | Material | 2008 Bare Costs Labor | Equipment | Total | Total Incl O&P |
|---|---|---|---|---|---|---|---|---|---|
| 0010 **PANELING, BOARDS** | | | | | | | | | |
| 6400 Wood board paneling, 3/4" thick, knotty pine | 2 Carp | 300 | .053 | S.F. | 1.41 | 2.03 | | 3.44 | 4.71 |
| 6500 Rough sawn cedar | | 300 | .053 | | 1.81 | 2.03 | | 3.84 | 5.15 |
| 6700 Redwood, clear, 1" x 4" boards | | 300 | .053 | | 4.22 | 2.03 | | 6.25 | 7.80 |
| 6900 Aromatic cedar, closet lining, boards | ↓ | 275 | .058 | ↓ | 3.25 | 2.22 | | 5.47 | 7.05 |

# 06 43 Wood Stairs and Railings

## 06 43 13 – Wood Stairs

### 06 43 13.20 Prefabricated Wood Stairs

| | | Crew | Daily Output | Labor-Hours | Unit | Material | Labor | Equipment | Total | Total Incl O&P |
|---|---|---|---|---|---|---|---|---|---|---|
| 0010 | **PREFABRICATED WOOD STAIRS** | | | | | | | | | |
| 0100 | Box stairs, prefabricated, 3'-0" wide | | | | | | | | | |
| 0110 | Oak treads, up to 14 risers | 2 Carp | 39 | .410 | Riser | 75.50 | 15.65 | | 91.15 | 108 |
| 0600 | With pine treads for carpet, up to 14 risers | " | 39 | .410 | " | 49 | 15.65 | | 64.65 | 78.50 |
| 1100 | For 4' wide stairs, add | | | | Flight | 25% | | | | |
| 1550 | Stairs, prefabricated stair handrail with balusters | 1 Carp | 30 | .267 | L.F. | 65.50 | 10.15 | | 75.65 | 88 |
| 1700 | Basement stairs, prefabricated, pine treads | | | | | | | | | |
| 1710 | Pine risers, 3' wide, up to 14 risers | 2 Carp | 52 | .308 | Riser | 49 | 11.70 | | 60.70 | 72.50 |
| 4000 | Residential, wood, oak treads, prefabricated | | 1.50 | 10.667 | Flight | 985 | 405 | | 1,390 | 1,700 |
| 4200 | Built in place | ↓ | .44 | 36.364 | " | 1,450 | 1,375 | | 2,825 | 3,750 |
| 4400 | Spiral, oak, 4'-6" diameter, unfinished, prefabricated, | | | | | | | | | |
| 4500 | incl. railing, 9' high | 2 Carp | 1.50 | 10.667 | Flight | 4,675 | 405 | | 5,080 | 5,750 |

### 06 43 13.40 Wood Stair Parts

| | | Crew | Daily Output | Labor-Hours | Unit | Material | Labor | Equipment | Total | Total Incl O&P |
|---|---|---|---|---|---|---|---|---|---|---|
| 0010 | **WOOD STAIR PARTS** | | | | | | | | | |
| 0020 | Pin top balusters, 1-1/4", oak, 34" | 1 Carp | 96 | .083 | Ea. | 8.30 | 3.17 | | 11.47 | 14.10 |
| 0030 | 36" | | 96 | .083 | | 8.75 | 3.17 | | 11.92 | 14.55 |
| 0040 | 42" | | 96 | .083 | | 10.60 | 3.17 | | 13.77 | 16.60 |
| 0050 | Poplar, 34" | | 96 | .083 | | 5.55 | 3.17 | | 8.72 | 11.05 |
| 0060 | 36" | | 96 | .083 | | 5.90 | 3.17 | | 9.07 | 11.45 |
| 0070 | 42" | | 96 | .083 | | 12.90 | 3.17 | | 16.07 | 19.15 |
| 0080 | Maple, 31" | | 96 | .083 | | 10.55 | 3.17 | | 13.72 | 16.60 |
| 0090 | 34" | | 96 | .083 | | 11.80 | 3.17 | | 14.97 | 17.90 |
| 0100 | 36" | | 96 | .083 | | 12.25 | 3.17 | | 15.42 | 18.45 |
| 0110 | 39" | | 96 | .083 | | 14.05 | 3.17 | | 17.22 | 20.50 |
| 0120 | 41" | | 96 | .083 | | 15.80 | 3.17 | | 18.97 | 22.50 |
| 0130 | Primed, 31" | | 96 | .083 | | 3.66 | 3.17 | | 6.83 | 8.95 |
| 0140 | 34" | | 96 | .083 | | 3.94 | 3.17 | | 7.11 | 9.25 |
| 0150 | 36" | | 96 | .083 | | 4.10 | 3.17 | | 7.27 | 9.45 |
| 0160 | 39" | | 96 | .083 | | 4.60 | 3.17 | | 7.77 | 10 |
| 0170 | 41" | | 96 | .083 | | 5.05 | 3.17 | | 8.22 | 10.50 |
| 0180 | Box top balusters, 1-1/4", oak, 34" | | 60 | .133 | | 8.55 | 5.10 | | 13.65 | 17.30 |
| 0190 | 36" | | 60 | .133 | | 9.30 | 5.10 | | 14.40 | 18.15 |
| 0200 | 42" | | 60 | .133 | | 10.40 | 5.10 | | 15.50 | 19.35 |
| 0210 | Poplar, 34" | | 60 | .133 | | 5.45 | 5.10 | | 10.55 | 13.90 |
| 0220 | 36" | | 60 | .133 | | 6.15 | 5.10 | | 11.25 | 14.65 |
| 0230 | 42" | | 60 | .133 | | 6.80 | 5.10 | | 11.90 | 15.40 |
| 0240 | Maple, 31" | | 60 | .133 | | 12.25 | 5.10 | | 17.35 | 21.50 |
| 0250 | 34" | | 60 | .133 | | 12.85 | 5.10 | | 17.95 | 22 |
| 0260 | 36" | | 60 | .133 | | 14.85 | 5.10 | | 19.95 | 24.50 |
| 0270 | 39" | | 60 | .133 | | 15.10 | 5.10 | | 20.20 | 24.50 |
| 0280 | 41" | | 60 | .133 | | 15.60 | 5.10 | | 20.70 | 25 |
| 0290 | Primed, 31" | ↓ | 60 | .133 | ↓ | 4.05 | 5.10 | | 9.15 | 12.35 |

171

## 06 43 13 – Wood Stairs

| 06 43 13.40 Wood Stair Parts | Crew | Daily Output | Labor-Hours | Unit | Material | 2008 Bare Costs Labor | Equipment | Total | Total Incl O&P |
|---|---|---|---|---|---|---|---|---|---|
| 0300 | 34" | 1 Carp | 60 | .133 | Ea. | 4.35 | 5.10 | | 9.45 | 12.70 |
| 0310 | 36" | | 60 | .133 | | 4.52 | 5.10 | | 9.62 | 12.85 |
| 0320 | 39" | | 60 | .133 | | 5.10 | 5.10 | | 10.20 | 13.50 |
| 0330 | 41" | | 60 | .133 | | 5.70 | 5.10 | | 10.80 | 14.15 |
| 0340 | Square balusters, cut from lineal stock, pine, 1-1/16" x 1-1/16" | | 180 | .044 | L.F. | 1.20 | 1.69 | | 2.89 | 3.96 |
| 0350 | 1-5/16" x 1-5/16" | | 180 | .044 | | 1.68 | 1.69 | | 3.37 | 4.49 |
| 0360 | 1-5/8" x 1-5/8" | | 180 | .044 | | 2.75 | 1.69 | | 4.44 | 5.65 |
| 0370 | Turned newel, oak, 3-1/2" square, 50" high | | 8 | 1 | Ea. | 105 | 38 | | 143 | 176 |
| 0380 | 65" high | | 8 | 1 | | 125 | 38 | | 163 | 198 |
| 0390 | Poplar, 3-1/2" square, 50" high | | 8 | 1 | | 95 | 38 | | 133 | 165 |
| 0400 | 65" high | | 8 | 1 | | 105 | 38 | | 143 | 176 |
| 0410 | Maple, 3-1/2" square, 50" high | | 8 | 1 | | 125 | 38 | | 163 | 198 |
| 0420 | 65" high | | 8 | 1 | | 145 | 38 | | 183 | 220 |
| 0430 | Square newel, oak, 3-1/2" square, 50" high | | 8 | 1 | | 205 | 38 | | 243 | 286 |
| 0440 | 65" high | | 8 | 1 | | 220 | 38 | | 258 | 300 |
| 0450 | Poplar, 3-1/2" square, 50" high | | 8 | 1 | | 195 | 38 | | 233 | 275 |
| 0460 | 65" high | | 8 | 1 | | 200 | 38 | | 238 | 280 |
| 0470 | Maple, 3" square, 50" high | | 8 | 1 | | 221 | 38 | | 259 | 305 |
| 0480 | 65" high | | 8 | 1 | | 241 | 38 | | 279 | 325 |
| 0490 | Railings, oak, minimum | | 96 | .083 | L.F. | 6.80 | 3.17 | | 9.97 | 12.45 |
| 0500 | Average | | 96 | .083 | | 8.35 | 3.17 | | 11.52 | 14.15 |
| 0510 | Maximum | | 96 | .083 | | 8.50 | 3.17 | | 11.67 | 14.30 |
| 0520 | Maple, minimum | | 96 | .083 | | 8 | 3.17 | | 11.17 | 13.75 |
| 0530 | Average | | 96 | .083 | | 10 | 3.17 | | 13.17 | 15.95 |
| 0540 | Maximum | | 96 | .083 | | 12 | 3.17 | | 15.17 | 18.15 |
| 0550 | Oak, for bending rail, minimum | | 48 | .167 | | 19.20 | 6.35 | | 25.55 | 31 |
| 0560 | Average | | 48 | .167 | | 27 | 6.35 | | 33.35 | 40 |
| 0570 | Maximum | | 48 | .167 | | 29 | 6.35 | | 35.35 | 42 |
| 0580 | Maple, for bending rail, minimum | | 48 | .167 | | 29 | 6.35 | | 35.35 | 42 |
| 0590 | Average | | 48 | .167 | | 32 | 6.35 | | 38.35 | 45 |
| 0600 | Maximum | | 48 | .167 | | 34 | 6.35 | | 40.35 | 47.50 |
| 0610 | Risers, oak, 3/4" x 8", 36" long | | 80 | .100 | Ea. | 19.95 | 3.81 | | 23.76 | 28 |
| 0620 | 42" long | | 80 | .100 | | 23.50 | 3.81 | | 27.31 | 31.50 |
| 0630 | 48" long | | 80 | .100 | | 26.50 | 3.81 | | 30.31 | 35.50 |
| 0640 | 54" long | | 80 | .100 | | 30 | 3.81 | | 33.81 | 39 |
| 0650 | 60" long | | 80 | .100 | | 33.50 | 3.81 | | 37.31 | 42.50 |
| 0660 | 72" long | | 80 | .100 | | 40 | 3.81 | | 43.81 | 50 |
| 0670 | Poplar, 3/4" x 8", 36" long | | 80 | .100 | | 13.05 | 3.81 | | 16.86 | 20.50 |
| 0680 | 42" long | | 80 | .100 | | 15.25 | 3.81 | | 19.06 | 22.50 |
| 0690 | 48" long | | 80 | .100 | | 17.40 | 3.81 | | 21.21 | 25 |
| 0700 | 54" long | | 80 | .100 | | 19.60 | 3.81 | | 23.41 | 27.50 |
| 0710 | 60" long | | 80 | .100 | | 22 | 3.81 | | 25.81 | 30 |
| 0720 | 72" long | | 80 | .100 | | 26 | 3.81 | | 29.81 | 34.50 |
| 0730 | Pine, 1" x 8", 36" long | | 80 | .100 | | 3,825 | 3.81 | | 3,828.81 | 4,200 |
| 0740 | 42" long | | 80 | .100 | | 4,475 | 3.81 | | 4,478.81 | 4,900 |
| 0750 | 48" long | | 80 | .100 | | 5,100 | 3.81 | | 5,103.81 | 5,600 |
| 0760 | 54" long | | 80 | .100 | | 5,750 | 3.81 | | 5,753.81 | 6,300 |
| 0770 | 60" long | | 80 | .100 | | 6,375 | 3.81 | | 6,378.81 | 7,025 |
| 0780 | 72" long | | 80 | .100 | | 7,650 | 3.81 | | 7,653.81 | 8,425 |
| 0790 | Treads, oak, no returns, 1-1/32" x 11-1/2" x 36" long | | 32 | .250 | | 39.50 | 9.55 | | 49.05 | 58.50 |
| 0800 | 42" long | | 32 | .250 | | 46 | 9.55 | | 55.55 | 65.50 |
| 0810 | 48" long | | 32 | .250 | | 52.50 | 9.55 | | 62.05 | 73 |
| 0820 | 54" long | | 32 | .250 | | 59 | 9.55 | | 68.55 | 80 |

# 06 43 Wood Stairs and Railings

## 06 43 13 – Wood Stairs

### 06 43 13.40 Wood Stair Parts

| | | Crew | Daily Output | Labor-Hours | Unit | Material | 2008 Bare Costs Labor | 2008 Bare Costs Equipment | Total | Total Incl O&P |
|---|---|---|---|---|---|---|---|---|---|---|
| 0830 | 60" long | 1 Carp | 32 | .250 | Ea. | 66 | 9.55 | | 75.55 | 87.50 |
| 0840 | 72" long | | 32 | .250 | | 79 | 9.55 | | 88.55 | 102 |
| 0850 | Mitred return one end, 1-1/32" x 11-1/2" x 36" long | | 24 | .333 | | 59 | 12.70 | | 71.70 | 85 |
| 0860 | 42" long | | 24 | .333 | | 69 | 12.70 | | 81.70 | 96 |
| 0870 | 48" long | | 24 | .333 | | 79 | 12.70 | | 91.70 | 106 |
| 0880 | 54" long | | 24 | .333 | | 88.50 | 12.70 | | 101.20 | 117 |
| 0890 | 60" long | | 24 | .333 | | 98.50 | 12.70 | | 111.20 | 128 |
| 0900 | 72" long | | 24 | .333 | | 118 | 12.70 | | 130.70 | 150 |
| 0910 | Mitred return two ends, 1-1/32" x 11-1/2" x 36" long | | 12 | .667 | | 74 | 25.50 | | 99.50 | 121 |
| 0920 | 42" long | | 12 | .667 | | 86 | 25.50 | | 111.50 | 135 |
| 0930 | 48" long | | 12 | .667 | | 98.50 | 25.50 | | 124 | 148 |
| 0940 | 54" long | | 12 | .667 | | 111 | 25.50 | | 136.50 | 162 |
| 0950 | 60" long | | 12 | .667 | | 123 | 25.50 | | 148.50 | 175 |
| 0960 | 72" long | | 12 | .667 | | 148 | 25.50 | | 173.50 | 202 |
| 0970 | Starting step, oak, 48", bullnose | | 8 | 1 | | 149 | 38 | | 187 | 223 |
| 0980 | Double end bullnose | | 8 | 1 | | 175 | 38 | | 213 | 253 |
| 0990 | Half circle | | 8 | 1 | | 196 | 38 | | 234 | 276 |
| 1010 | Double end half circle | | 8 | 1 | | 260 | 38 | | 298 | 345 |
| 1030 | Skirt board, pine, 1" x 10" | | 55 | .145 | L.F. | 1,575 | 5.55 | | 1,580.55 | 1,725 |
| 1040 | 1" x 12" | | 52 | .154 | " | 1,700 | 5.85 | | 1,705.85 | 1,850 |
| 1050 | Oak landing tread, 1-1/16" thick | | 54 | .148 | S.F. | 7.50 | 5.65 | | 13.15 | 17.05 |
| 1060 | Oak cove molding | | 96 | .083 | L.F. | 2.50 | 3.17 | | 5.67 | 7.70 |
| 1070 | Oak stringer molding | | 96 | .083 | | 2.50 | 3.17 | | 5.67 | 7.70 |
| 1080 | Oak shoe molding | | 96 | .083 | | 2.50 | 3.17 | | 5.67 | 7.70 |
| 1090 | Rail bolt, 5/16" x 3-1/2" | | 48 | .167 | Ea. | 1.50 | 6.35 | | 7.85 | 11.55 |
| 1100 | 5/16" x 4-1/2" | | 48 | .167 | | 2 | 6.35 | | 8.35 | 12.10 |
| 1120 | Newel post anchor | | 16 | .500 | | 25 | 19.05 | | 44.05 | 57 |
| 1130 | Tapered plug, 1/2" | | 240 | .033 | | .25 | 1.27 | | 1.52 | 2.26 |
| 1140 | 1" | | 240 | .033 | | .35 | 1.27 | | 1.62 | 2.37 |
| 1150 | Rail bolt kit | | 24 | .333 | | 10 | 12.70 | | 22.70 | 31 |

## 06 43 16 – Wood Railings

### 06 43 16.10 Wood Handrails and Railings

| | | Crew | Daily Output | Labor-Hours | Unit | Material | 2008 Bare Costs Labor | 2008 Bare Costs Equipment | Total | Total Incl O&P |
|---|---|---|---|---|---|---|---|---|---|---|
| 0010 | **WOOD HANDRAILS AND RAILINGS** | | | | | | | | | |
| 0020 | Custom design, architectural grade, hardwood, minimum | 1 Carp | 38 | .211 | L.F. | 8.35 | 8 | | 16.35 | 21.50 |
| 0100 | Maximum | | 30 | .267 | | 45 | 10.15 | | 55.15 | 65.50 |
| 0300 | Stock interior railing with spindles 4" O.C., 4' long | | 40 | .200 | | 31.50 | 7.60 | | 39.10 | 47 |
| 0400 | 8' long | | 48 | .167 | | 31.50 | 6.35 | | 37.85 | 45 |

# 06 44 Ornamental Woodwork

## 06 44 19 – Wood Grilles

### 06 44 19.10 Grilles

| | | Crew | Daily Output | Labor-Hours | Unit | Material | 2008 Bare Costs Labor | 2008 Bare Costs Equipment | Total | Total Incl O&P |
|---|---|---|---|---|---|---|---|---|---|---|
| 0010 | **GRILLES** and panels, hardwood, sanded | | | | | | | | | |
| 0020 | 2' x 4' to 4' x 8', custom designs, unfinished, minimum | 1 Carp | 38 | .211 | S.F. | 12.85 | 8 | | 20.85 | 26.50 |
| 0050 | Average | | 30 | .267 | | 28 | 10.15 | | 38.15 | 46.50 |
| 0100 | Maximum | | 19 | .421 | | 43 | 16.05 | | 59.05 | 72 |
| 0300 | As above, but prefinished, minimum | | 38 | .211 | | 12.85 | 8 | | 20.85 | 26.50 |
| 0400 | Maximum | | 19 | .421 | | 48 | 16.05 | | 64.05 | 78 |

## 06 44 33 – Wood Mantels

### 06 44 33.10 Fireplace Mantels

| | | | | | | | | | | |
|---|---|---|---|---|---|---|---|---|---|---|
| 0010 | **FIREPLACE MANTELS** | | | | | | | | | |

# 06 44 Ornamental Woodwork

## 06 44 33 – Wood Mantels

### 06 44 33.10 Fireplace Mantels

| | | Crew | Daily Output | Labor-Hours | Unit | Material | 2008 Bare Costs Labor | Equipment | Total | Total Incl O&P |
|---|---|---|---|---|---|---|---|---|---|---|
| 0015 | 6" molding, 6' x 3'-6" opening, minimum | 1 Carp | 5 | 1.600 | Opng. | 147 | 61 | | 208 | 257 |
| 0100 | Maximum | | 5 | 1.600 | | 183 | 61 | | 244 | 297 |
| 0300 | Prefabricated pine, colonial type, stock, deluxe | | 2 | 4 | | 2,300 | 152 | | 2,452 | 2,775 |
| 0400 | Economy | | 3 | 2.667 | | 395 | 102 | | 497 | 595 |

### 06 44 33.20 Fireplace Mantel Beam

| | | Crew | Daily Output | Labor-Hours | Unit | Material | 2008 Bare Costs Labor | Equipment | Total | Total Incl O&P |
|---|---|---|---|---|---|---|---|---|---|---|
| 0010 | **FIREPLACE MANTEL BEAM** | | | | | | | | | |
| 0020 | Rough texture wood, 4" x 8" | 1 Carp | 36 | .222 | L.F. | 5.45 | 8.45 | | 13.90 | 19.20 |
| 0100 | 4" x 10" | | 35 | .229 | " | 6.55 | 8.70 | | 15.25 | 21 |
| 0300 | Laminated hardwood, 2-1/4" x 10-1/2" wide, 6' long | | 5 | 1.600 | Ea. | 104 | 61 | | 165 | 210 |
| 0400 | 8' long | | 5 | 1.600 | " | 145 | 61 | | 206 | 254 |
| 0600 | Brackets for above, rough sawn | | 12 | .667 | Pr. | 9.60 | 25.50 | | 35.10 | 50 |
| 0700 | Laminated | | 12 | .667 | " | 14.50 | 25.50 | | 40 | 55.50 |

## 06 44 39 – Wood Posts and Columns

### 06 44 39.10 Decorative Beams

| | | Crew | Daily Output | Labor-Hours | Unit | Material | 2008 Bare Costs Labor | Equipment | Total | Total Incl O&P |
|---|---|---|---|---|---|---|---|---|---|---|
| 0010 | **DECORATIVE BEAMS** | | | | | | | | | |
| 0020 | Rough sawn cedar, non-load bearing, 4" x 4" | 2 Carp | 180 | .089 | L.F. | 1.47 | 3.39 | | 4.86 | 6.85 |
| 0100 | 4" x 6" | | 170 | .094 | | 2.21 | 3.59 | | 5.80 | 8.05 |
| 0200 | 4" x 8" | | 160 | .100 | | 2.95 | 3.81 | | 6.76 | 9.20 |
| 0300 | 4" x 10" | | 150 | .107 | | 3.68 | 4.06 | | 7.74 | 10.40 |
| 0400 | 4" x 12" | | 140 | .114 | | 4.42 | 4.35 | | 8.77 | 11.65 |
| 0500 | 8" x 8" | | 130 | .123 | | 7.50 | 4.69 | | 12.19 | 15.55 |

### 06 44 39.20 Columns

| | | Crew | Daily Output | Labor-Hours | Unit | Material | 2008 Bare Costs Labor | Equipment | Total | Total Incl O&P |
|---|---|---|---|---|---|---|---|---|---|---|
| 0010 | **COLUMNS** | | | | | | | | | |
| 0050 | Aluminum, round colonial, 6" diameter | 2 Carp | 80 | .200 | V.L.F. | 16 | 7.60 | | 23.60 | 29.50 |
| 0100 | 8" diameter | | 62.25 | .257 | | 17 | 9.80 | | 26.80 | 34 |
| 0200 | 10" diameter | | 55 | .291 | | 19.10 | 11.10 | | 30.20 | 38.50 |
| 0250 | Fir, stock units, hollow round, 6" diameter | | 80 | .200 | | 17.20 | 7.60 | | 24.80 | 31 |
| 0300 | 8" diameter | | 80 | .200 | | 20.50 | 7.60 | | 28.10 | 34.50 |
| 0350 | 10" diameter | | 70 | .229 | | 25.50 | 8.70 | | 34.20 | 42 |
| 0400 | Solid turned, to 8' high, 3-1/2" diameter | | 80 | .200 | | 8.40 | 7.60 | | 16 | 21 |
| 0500 | 4-1/2" diameter | | 75 | .213 | | 12.80 | 8.15 | | 20.95 | 27 |
| 0600 | 5-1/2" diameter | | 70 | .229 | | 16.40 | 8.70 | | 25.10 | 31.50 |
| 0800 | Square columns, built-up, 5" x 5" | | 65 | .246 | | 10.20 | 9.40 | | 19.60 | 26 |
| 0900 | Solid, 3-1/2" x 3-1/2" | | 130 | .123 | | 6.70 | 4.69 | | 11.39 | 14.65 |
| 1600 | Hemlock, tapered, T & G, 12" diam, 10' high | | 100 | .160 | | 31.50 | 6.10 | | 37.60 | 44 |
| 1700 | 16' high | | 65 | .246 | | 46.50 | 9.40 | | 55.90 | 65.50 |
| 1900 | 10' high, 14" diameter | | 100 | .160 | | 78.50 | 6.10 | | 84.60 | 96 |
| 2000 | 18' high | | 65 | .246 | | 63.50 | 9.40 | | 72.90 | 84.50 |
| 2200 | 18" diameter, 12' high | | 65 | .246 | | 114 | 9.40 | | 123.40 | 141 |
| 2300 | 20' high | | 50 | .320 | | 80 | 12.20 | | 92.20 | 107 |
| 2500 | 20" diameter, 14' high | | 40 | .400 | | 129 | 15.25 | | 144.25 | 166 |
| 2600 | 20' high | | 35 | .457 | | 120 | 17.40 | | 137.40 | 159 |
| 2800 | For flat pilasters, deduct | | | | | 33% | | | | |
| 3000 | For splitting into halves, add | | | | Ea. | 116 | | | 116 | 128 |
| 4000 | Rough sawn cedar posts, 4" x 4" | 2 Carp | 250 | .064 | V.L.F. | 3.70 | 2.44 | | 6.14 | 7.85 |
| 4100 | 4" x 6" | | 235 | .068 | | 6.70 | 2.59 | | 9.29 | 11.40 |
| 4200 | 6" x 6" | | 220 | .073 | | 12.50 | 2.77 | | 15.27 | 18.05 |
| 4300 | 8" x 8" | | 200 | .080 | | 28.50 | 3.05 | | 31.55 | 36 |

# 06 48 Wood Frames

## 06 48 13 – Exterior Wood Door Frames

| 06 48 13.10 Exterior Wood Door Frames and Accessories | Crew | Daily Output | Labor-Hours | Unit | Material | 2008 Bare Costs Labor | Equipment | Total | Total Incl O&P |
|---|---|---|---|---|---|---|---|---|---|
| 0010 **EXTERIOR WOOD DOOR FRAMES AND ACCESSORIES** | | | | | | | | | |
| 0400 Exterior frame, incl. ext. trim, pine, 5/4 x 4-9/16" deep | 2 Carp | 375 | .043 | L.F. | 5.40 | 1.63 | | 7.03 | 8.50 |
| 0420     5-3/16" deep | | 375 | .043 | | 11 | 1.63 | | 12.63 | 14.65 |
| 0440     6-9/16" deep | | 375 | .043 | | 8.35 | 1.63 | | 9.98 | 11.75 |
| 0600   Oak, 5/4 x 4-9/16" deep | | 350 | .046 | | 10.65 | 1.74 | | 12.39 | 14.45 |
| 0620     5-3/16" deep | | 350 | .046 | | 12.80 | 1.74 | | 14.54 | 16.75 |
| 0640     6-9/16" deep | | 350 | .046 | | 14.60 | 1.74 | | 16.34 | 18.80 |
| 0800   Walnut, 5/4 x 4-9/16" deep | | 350 | .046 | | 12.20 | 1.74 | | 13.94 | 16.10 |
| 0820     5-3/16" deep | | 350 | .046 | | 16.75 | 1.74 | | 18.49 | 21 |
| 0840     6-9/16" deep | | 350 | .046 | | 19.50 | 1.74 | | 21.24 | 24 |
| 1000   Sills, 8/4 x 8" deep, oak, no horns | | 100 | .160 | | 18.25 | 6.10 | | 24.35 | 29.50 |
| 1020     2" horns | | 100 | .160 | | 18.50 | 6.10 | | 24.60 | 30 |
| 1040     3" horns | | 100 | .160 | | 18.50 | 6.10 | | 24.60 | 30 |
| 1100     8/4 x 10" deep, oak, no horns | | 90 | .178 | | 23.50 | 6.75 | | 30.25 | 36 |
| 1120     2" horns | | 90 | .178 | | 21.50 | 6.75 | | 28.25 | 34 |
| 1140     3" horns | | 90 | .178 | | 21.50 | 6.75 | | 28.25 | 34 |
| 2000   Exterior, colonial, frame & trim, 3' opng., in-swing, minimum | | 22 | .727 | Ea. | 315 | 27.50 | | 342.50 | 390 |
| 2010     Average | | 21 | .762 | | 470 | 29 | | 499 | 560 |
| 2020     Maximum | | 20 | .800 | | 1,075 | 30.50 | | 1,105.50 | 1,225 |
| 2100   5'-4" opening, in-swing, minimum | | 17 | .941 | | 360 | 36 | | 396 | 450 |
| 2120     Maximum | | 15 | 1.067 | | 1,075 | 40.50 | | 1,115.50 | 1,250 |
| 2140   Out-swing, minimum | | 17 | .941 | | 365 | 36 | | 401 | 460 |
| 2160     Maximum | | 15 | 1.067 | | 1,100 | 40.50 | | 1,140.50 | 1,300 |
| 2400   6'-0" opening, in-swing, minimum | | 16 | 1 | | 345 | 38 | | 383 | 435 |
| 2420     Maximum | | 10 | 1.600 | | 1,100 | 61 | | 1,161 | 1,325 |
| 2460   Out-swing, minimum | | 16 | 1 | | 370 | 38 | | 408 | 470 |
| 2480     Maximum | | 10 | 1.600 | | 1,300 | 61 | | 1,361 | 1,525 |
| 2600   For two sidelights, add, minimum | | 30 | .533 | Opng. | 350 | 20.50 | | 370.50 | 420 |
| 2620     Maximum | | 20 | .800 | " | 1,125 | 30.50 | | 1,155.50 | 1,300 |
| 2700   Custom birch frame, 3'-0" opening | | 16 | 1 | Ea. | 202 | 38 | | 240 | 282 |
| 2750     6'-0" opening | | 16 | 1 | | 305 | 38 | | 343 | 395 |
| 2900   Exterior, modern, plain trim, 3' opng., in-swing, minimum | | 26 | .615 | | 34 | 23.50 | | 57.50 | 74 |
| 2920     Average | | 24 | .667 | | 40.50 | 25.50 | | 66 | 84 |
| 2940     Maximum | | 22 | .727 | | 49.50 | 27.50 | | 77 | 97.50 |

## 06 48 16 – Interior Wood Door Frames

### 06 48 16.10 Interior Wood Door Jamb and Frames

| | Crew | Daily Output | Labor-Hours | Unit | Material | 2008 Bare Costs Labor | Equipment | Total | Total Incl O&P |
|---|---|---|---|---|---|---|---|---|---|
| 0010 **INTERIOR WOOD DOOR JAMB AND FRAMES** | | | | | | | | | |
| 3000 Interior frame, pine, 11/16" x 3-5/8" deep | 2 Carp | 375 | .043 | L.F. | 5.20 | 1.63 | | 6.83 | 8.25 |
| 3020     4-9/16" deep | | 375 | .043 | | 6.30 | 1.63 | | 7.93 | 9.50 |
| 3200   Oak, 11/16" x 3-5/8" deep | | 350 | .046 | | 4.06 | 1.74 | | 5.80 | 7.20 |
| 3220     4-9/16" deep | | 350 | .046 | | 4.38 | 1.74 | | 6.12 | 7.55 |
| 3240     5-3/16" deep | | 350 | .046 | | 4.54 | 1.74 | | 6.28 | 7.70 |
| 3400   Walnut, 11/16" x 3-5/8" deep | | 350 | .046 | | 6.85 | 1.74 | | 8.59 | 10.25 |
| 3420     4-9/16" deep | | 350 | .046 | | 7.20 | 1.74 | | 8.94 | 10.65 |
| 3440     5-3/16" deep | | 350 | .046 | | 7.50 | 1.74 | | 9.24 | 10.95 |
| 3600   Pocket door frame | | 16 | 1 | Ea. | 64.50 | 38 | | 102.50 | 131 |
| 3800   Threshold, oak, 5/8" x 3-5/8" deep | | 200 | .080 | L.F. | 3.81 | 3.05 | | 6.86 | 8.95 |
| 3820     4-5/8" deep | | 190 | .084 | | 4.57 | 3.21 | | 7.78 | 10.05 |
| 3840     5-5/8" deep | | 180 | .089 | | 7.55 | 3.39 | | 10.94 | 13.55 |

# 06 49 Wood Screens and Exterior Wood Shutters

## 06 49 19 – Exterior Wood Shutters

| 06 49 19.10 Shutters, Exterior | | Crew | Daily Output | Labor-Hours | Unit | Material | 2008 Bare Costs Labor | Equipment | Total | Total Incl O&P |
|---|---|---|---|---|---|---|---|---|---|---|
| 0010 | **SHUTTERS, EXTERIOR** | | | | | | | | | |
| 0012 | Aluminum, louvered, 1'-4" wide, 3'-0" long | 1 Carp | 10 | .800 | Pr. | 48.50 | 30.50 | | 79 | 101 |
| 0400 | 6'-8" long | | 9 | .889 | | 97.50 | 34 | | 131.50 | 160 |
| 1000 | Pine, louvered, primed, each 1'-2" wide, 3'-3" long | | 10 | .800 | | 92 | 30.50 | | 122.50 | 149 |
| 1100 | 4'-7" long | | 10 | .800 | | 124 | 30.50 | | 154.50 | 185 |
| 1500 | Each 1'-6" wide, 3'-3" long | | 10 | .800 | | 97.50 | 30.50 | | 128 | 155 |
| 1600 | 4'-7" long | | 10 | .800 | | 137 | 30.50 | | 167.50 | 199 |
| 1620 | Hemlock, louvered, 1'-2" wide, 5'-7" long | | 10 | .800 | | 150 | 30.50 | | 180.50 | 213 |
| 1630 | Each 1'-4" wide, 2'-2" long | | 10 | .800 | | 94 | 30.50 | | 124.50 | 151 |
| 1670 | 4'-3" long | | 10 | .800 | | 112 | 30.50 | | 142.50 | 171 |
| 1690 | 5'-11" long | | 10 | .800 | | 158 | 30.50 | | 188.50 | 222 |
| 1700 | Door blinds, 6'-9" long, each 1'-3" wide | | 9 | .889 | | 159 | 34 | | 193 | 228 |
| 1710 | 1'-6" wide | | 9 | .889 | | 171 | 34 | | 205 | 241 |
| 1720 | Hemlock, solid raised panel, each 1'-4" wide, 3'-3" long | | 10 | .800 | | 152 | 30.50 | | 182.50 | 215 |
| 1740 | 4'-3" long | | 10 | .800 | | 192 | 30.50 | | 222.50 | 259 |
| 1770 | 5'-11" long | | 10 | .800 | | 257 | 30.50 | | 287.50 | 330 |
| 1800 | Door blinds, 6'-9" long, each 1'-3" wide | | 9 | .889 | | 289 | 34 | | 323 | 375 |
| 1900 | 1'-6" wide | | 9 | .889 | | 315 | 34 | | 349 | 400 |
| 2500 | Polystyrene, solid raised panel, each 1'-4" wide, 3'-3" long | | 10 | .800 | | 40.50 | 30.50 | | 71 | 92 |
| 2700 | 4'-7" long | | 10 | .800 | | 51 | 30.50 | | 81.50 | 104 |
| 4500 | Polystyrene, louvered, each 1'-2" wide, 3'-3" long | | 10 | .800 | | 27.50 | 30.50 | | 58 | 78 |
| 4750 | 5'-3" long | | 10 | .800 | | 39 | 30.50 | | 69.50 | 90.50 |
| 6000 | Vinyl, louvered, each 1'-2" x 4'-7" long | | 10 | .800 | | 34 | 30.50 | | 64.50 | 85 |
| 6200 | Each 1'-4" x 6'-8" long | | 9 | .889 | | 47.50 | 34 | | 81.50 | 105 |

# 06 52 Plastic Structural Assemblies

## 06 52 10 – Fiberglass Structural Assemblies

| 06 52 10.10 Castings, Fiberglass | | Crew | Daily Output | Labor-Hours | Unit | Material | 2008 Bare Costs Labor | Equipment | Total | Total Incl O&P |
|---|---|---|---|---|---|---|---|---|---|---|
| 0010 | **CASTINGS, FIBERGLASS** | | | | | | | | | |
| 0100 | Angle, 1" x 1" x 1/8" thick | 2 Sswk | 240 | .067 | L.F. | 1.31 | 2.87 | | 4.18 | 6.60 |
| 0120 | 3" x 3" x 1/4" thick | | 200 | .080 | | 5.45 | 3.44 | | 8.89 | 12.20 |
| 0140 | 4" x 4" x 1/4" thick | | 200 | .080 | | 7 | 3.44 | | 10.44 | 13.90 |
| 0160 | 4" x 4" x 3/8" thick | | 200 | .080 | | 10.80 | 3.44 | | 14.24 | 18.05 |
| 0180 | 6" x 6" x 1/2" thick | | 160 | .100 | | 21.50 | 4.30 | | 25.80 | 31.50 |
| 1000 | Flat sheet, 1/8" thick | | 140 | .114 | S.F. | 4.60 | 4.91 | | 9.51 | 13.90 |
| 1020 | 1/4" thick | | 120 | .133 | | 9 | 5.75 | | 14.75 | 20.50 |
| 1040 | 3/8" thick | | 100 | .160 | | 15.30 | 6.90 | | 22.20 | 29.50 |
| 1060 | 1/2" thick | | 80 | .200 | | 20 | 8.60 | | 28.60 | 37.50 |
| 2000 | Handrail, 42" high, 2" diam. rails pickets 5' O.C. | | 32 | .500 | L.F. | 46.50 | 21.50 | | 68 | 90 |
| 3000 | Round bar, 1/4" diam. | | 240 | .067 | | .53 | 2.87 | | 3.40 | 5.75 |
| 3020 | 1/2" diam. | | 200 | .080 | | .92 | 3.44 | | 4.36 | 7.20 |
| 3040 | 3/4" diam. | | 200 | .080 | | 1.87 | 3.44 | | 5.31 | 8.25 |
| 3060 | 1" diam. | | 160 | .100 | | 3.29 | 4.30 | | 7.59 | 11.35 |
| 3080 | 1-1/4" diam. | | 160 | .100 | | 3.75 | 4.30 | | 8.05 | 11.90 |
| 3100 | 1-1/2" diam. | | 140 | .114 | | 4.59 | 4.91 | | 9.50 | 13.90 |
| 3500 | Round tube, 1" diam. x 1/8" thick | | 240 | .067 | | 1.79 | 2.87 | | 4.66 | 7.10 |
| 3520 | 2" diam. x 1/4" thick | | 200 | .080 | | 5.75 | 3.44 | | 9.19 | 12.55 |
| 3540 | 3" diam. x 1/4" thick | | 160 | .100 | | 9.20 | 4.30 | | 13.50 | 17.85 |
| 4000 | Square bar, 1/2" square | | 240 | .067 | | 3.62 | 2.87 | | 6.49 | 9.15 |
| 4020 | 1" square | | 200 | .080 | | 4.64 | 3.44 | | 8.08 | 11.30 |
| 4040 | 1-1/2" square | | 160 | .100 | | 9.45 | 4.30 | | 13.75 | 18.15 |

# 06 52 Plastic Structural Assemblies

## 06 52 10 – Fiberglass Structural Assemblies

### 06 52 10.10 Castings, Fiberglass

| | | Crew | Daily Output | Labor-Hours | Unit | Material | 2008 Bare Costs Labor | 2008 Bare Costs Equipment | Total | Total Incl O&P |
|---|---|---|---|---|---|---|---|---|---|---|
| 4500 | Square tube, 1" x 1" x 1/8" thick | 2 Sswk | 240 | .067 | L.F. | 2.04 | 2.87 | | 4.91 | 7.40 |
| 4520 | 2" x 2" x 1/8" thick | | 200 | .080 | | 3.95 | 3.44 | | 7.39 | 10.55 |
| 4540 | 3" x 3" x 1/4" thick | | 160 | .100 | | 10.75 | 4.30 | | 15.05 | 19.60 |
| 5000 | Threaded rod, 3/8" diam. | | 320 | .050 | | 3.14 | 2.15 | | 5.29 | 7.35 |
| 5020 | 1/2" diam. | | 320 | .050 | | 3.69 | 2.15 | | 5.84 | 7.95 |
| 5040 | 5/8" diam. | | 280 | .057 | | 4.08 | 2.46 | | 6.54 | 8.90 |
| 5060 | 3/4" diam. | | 280 | .057 | | 4.64 | 2.46 | | 7.10 | 9.55 |
| 6000 | Wide flange beam, 4" x 4" x 1/4" thick | | 120 | .133 | | 9.55 | 5.75 | | 15.30 | 21 |
| 6020 | 6" x 6" x 1/4" thick | | 100 | .160 | | 18.15 | 6.90 | | 25.05 | 32.50 |
| 6040 | 8" x 8" x 3/8" thick | ▼ | 80 | .200 | ▼ | 32 | 8.60 | | 40.60 | 50.50 |

### 06 52 10.20 Fiberglass Stair Treads

| | | Crew | Daily Output | Labor-Hours | Unit | Material | 2008 Bare Costs Labor | 2008 Bare Costs Equipment | Total | Total Incl O&P |
|---|---|---|---|---|---|---|---|---|---|---|
| 0010 | **FIBERGLASS STAIR TREADS** | | | | | | | | | |
| 0100 | 24" wide | 2 Sswk | 52 | .308 | Ea. | 36 | 13.25 | | 49.25 | 63.50 |
| 0140 | 30" wide | | 52 | .308 | | 43 | 13.25 | | 56.25 | 71 |
| 0180 | 36" wide | | 52 | .308 | | 50.50 | 13.25 | | 63.75 | 79.50 |
| 0220 | 42" wide | ▼ | 52 | .308 | ▼ | 59.50 | 13.25 | | 72.75 | 89.50 |

### 06 52 10.30 Fiberglass Grating

| | | Crew | Daily Output | Labor-Hours | Unit | Material | 2008 Bare Costs Labor | 2008 Bare Costs Equipment | Total | Total Incl O&P |
|---|---|---|---|---|---|---|---|---|---|---|
| 0010 | **FIBERGLASS GRATING** | | | | | | | | | |
| 0100 | Molded, green (for mod. corrosive environment) | | | | | | | | | |
| 0140 | 1" x 4" mesh, 1" thick | 2 Sswk | 400 | .040 | S.F. | 11.15 | 1.72 | | 12.87 | 15.40 |
| 0180 | 1-1/2" square mesh, 1" thick | | 400 | .040 | | 16.60 | 1.72 | | 18.32 | 21.50 |
| 0220 | 1-1/4" thick | | 400 | .040 | | 13.25 | 1.72 | | 14.97 | 17.70 |
| 0260 | 1-1/2" thick | | 400 | .040 | | 24 | 1.72 | | 25.72 | 29.50 |
| 0300 | 2" square mesh, 2" thick | ▼ | 320 | .050 | ▼ | 22.50 | 2.15 | | 24.65 | 29 |
| 1000 | Orange (for highly corrosive environment) | | | | | | | | | |
| 1040 | 1" x 4" mesh, 1" thick | 2 Sswk | 400 | .040 | S.F. | 14.05 | 1.72 | | 15.77 | 18.55 |
| 1080 | 1-1/2" square mesh, 1" thick | | 400 | .040 | | 18.60 | 1.72 | | 20.32 | 23.50 |
| 1120 | 1-1/4" thick | | 400 | .040 | | 19.30 | 1.72 | | 21.02 | 24.50 |
| 1160 | 1-1/2" thick | | 400 | .040 | | 21 | 1.72 | | 22.72 | 26 |
| 1200 | 2" square mesh, 2" thick | ▼ | 320 | .050 | ▼ | 25 | 2.15 | | 27.15 | 31.50 |
| 3000 | Pultruded, green (for mod. corrosive environment) | | | | | | | | | |
| 3040 | 1" O.C. bar spacing, 1" thick | 2 Sswk | 400 | .040 | S.F. | 16.65 | 1.72 | | 18.37 | 21.50 |
| 3080 | 1-1/2" thick | | 320 | .050 | | 18.50 | 2.15 | | 20.65 | 24.50 |
| 3120 | 1-1/2" O.C. bar spacing, 1" thick | | 400 | .040 | | 13.50 | 1.72 | | 15.22 | 17.95 |
| 3160 | 1-1/2" thick | ▼ | 400 | .040 | ▼ | 15.15 | 1.72 | | 16.87 | 19.75 |
| 4000 | Grating support legs, fixed height, no base | | | | Ea. | 43.50 | | | 43.50 | 48 |
| 4040 | With base | | | | | 39 | | | 39 | 43 |
| 4080 | Adjustable to 60" | | | | ▼ | 59 | | | 59 | 65 |

### 06 52 10.40 Fiberglass Floor Grating

| | | Crew | Daily Output | Labor-Hours | Unit | Material | 2008 Bare Costs Labor | 2008 Bare Costs Equipment | Total | Total Incl O&P |
|---|---|---|---|---|---|---|---|---|---|---|
| 0010 | **FIBERGLASS FLOOR GRATING** | | | | | | | | | |
| 0100 | Reinforced polyester, fire retardant, 1" x 4" grid, 1" thick | E-4 | 510 | .063 | S.F. | 14.25 | 2.73 | .26 | 17.24 | 21 |
| 0200 | 1-1/2" x 6" mesh, 1-1/2" thick | | 500 | .064 | | 16.65 | 2.78 | .26 | 19.69 | 23.50 |
| 0300 | With grit surface, 1-1/2" x 6" grid, 1-1/2" thick | ▼ | 500 | .064 | ▼ | 17 | 2.78 | .26 | 20.04 | 24 |

# 06 65 Plastic Simulated Wood Trim

## 06 65 10 – PVC Trim

| | 06 65 10.10 PVC Trim, Exterior | Crew | Daily Output | Labor-Hours | Unit | Material | 2008 Bare Costs Labor | Equipment | Total | Total Incl O&P |
|---|---|---|---|---|---|---|---|---|---|---|
| 0010 | **PVC TRIM, EXTERIOR** | | | | | | | | | |
| 0100 | Cornerboards, 5/4" x 6" x 6" | 1 Carp | 240 | .033 | L.F. | 6.60 | 1.27 | | 7.87 | 9.25 |
| 0110 | Door / window casing, 1" x 4" | | 200 | .040 | | 1.40 | 1.52 | | 2.92 | 3.91 |
| 0120 | 1" x 6" | | 200 | .040 | | 2.18 | 1.52 | | 3.70 | 4.77 |
| 0130 | 1" x 8" | | 195 | .041 | | 2.87 | 1.56 | | 4.43 | 5.60 |
| 0140 | 1" x 10" | | 195 | .041 | | 3.65 | 1.56 | | 5.21 | 6.45 |
| 0150 | 1" x 12" | | 190 | .042 | | 4.45 | 1.60 | | 6.05 | 7.40 |
| 0160 | 5/4" x 4" | | 195 | .041 | | 1.78 | 1.56 | | 3.34 | 4.39 |
| 0170 | 5/4" x 6" | | 195 | .041 | | 2.79 | 1.56 | | 4.35 | 5.50 |
| 0180 | 5/4" x 8" | | 190 | .042 | | 3.69 | 1.60 | | 5.29 | 6.55 |
| 0190 | 5/4" x 10" | | 190 | .042 | | 4.70 | 1.60 | | 6.30 | 7.65 |
| 0200 | 5/4" x 12" | | 185 | .043 | | 5.70 | 1.65 | | 7.35 | 8.85 |
| 0210 | Fascia, 1" x 4" | | 250 | .032 | | 1.40 | 1.22 | | 2.62 | 3.44 |
| 0220 | 1" x 6" | | 250 | .032 | | 2.18 | 1.22 | | 3.40 | 4.30 |
| 0230 | 1" x 8" | | 225 | .036 | | 2.87 | 1.35 | | 4.22 | 5.25 |
| 0240 | 1" x 10" | | 225 | .036 | | 3.65 | 1.35 | | 5 | 6.15 |
| 0250 | 1" x 12" | | 200 | .040 | | 4.45 | 1.52 | | 5.97 | 7.25 |
| 0260 | 5/4" x 4" | | 240 | .033 | | 1.78 | 1.27 | | 3.05 | 3.94 |
| 0270 | 5/4" x 6" | | 240 | .033 | | 2.79 | 1.27 | | 4.06 | 5.05 |
| 0280 | 5/4" x 8" | | 215 | .037 | | 3.69 | 1.42 | | 5.11 | 6.25 |
| 0290 | 5/4" x 10" | | 215 | .037 | | 4.70 | 1.42 | | 6.12 | 7.35 |
| 0300 | 5/4" x 12" | | 190 | .042 | | 5.70 | 1.60 | | 7.30 | 8.80 |
| 0310 | Frieze, 1" x 4" | | 250 | .032 | | 1.40 | 1.22 | | 2.62 | 3.44 |
| 0320 | 1" x 6" | | 250 | .032 | | 2.18 | 1.22 | | 3.40 | 4.30 |
| 0330 | 1" x 8" | | 225 | .036 | | 2.87 | 1.35 | | 4.22 | 5.25 |
| 0340 | 1" x 10" | | 225 | .036 | | 3.65 | 1.35 | | 5 | 6.15 |
| 0350 | 1" x 12" | | 200 | .040 | | 4.45 | 1.52 | | 5.97 | 7.25 |
| 0360 | 5/4" x 4" | | 240 | .033 | | 1.78 | 1.27 | | 3.05 | 3.94 |
| 0370 | 5/4" x 6" | | 240 | .033 | | 2.79 | 1.27 | | 4.06 | 5.05 |
| 0380 | 5/4" x 8" | | 215 | .037 | | 3.69 | 1.42 | | 5.11 | 6.25 |
| 0390 | 5/4" x 10" | | 215 | .037 | | 4.70 | 1.42 | | 6.12 | 7.35 |
| 0400 | 5/4" x 12" | | 190 | .042 | | 5.70 | 1.60 | | 7.30 | 8.80 |
| 0410 | Rake, 1" x 4" | | 200 | .040 | | 1.40 | 1.52 | | 2.92 | 3.91 |
| 0420 | 1" x 6" | | 200 | .040 | | 2.18 | 1.52 | | 3.70 | 4.77 |
| 0430 | 1" x 8" | | 190 | .042 | | 2.87 | 1.60 | | 4.47 | 5.65 |
| 0440 | 1" x 10" | | 190 | .042 | | 3.65 | 1.60 | | 5.25 | 6.50 |
| 0450 | 1" x 12" | | 180 | .044 | | 4.45 | 1.69 | | 6.14 | 7.55 |
| 0460 | 5/4" x 4" | | 195 | .041 | | 1.78 | 1.56 | | 3.34 | 4.39 |
| 0470 | 5/4" x 6" | | 195 | .041 | | 2.79 | 1.56 | | 4.35 | 5.50 |
| 0480 | 5/4" x 8" | | 185 | .043 | | 3.69 | 1.65 | | 5.34 | 6.60 |
| 0490 | 5/4" x 10" | | 185 | .043 | | 4.70 | 1.65 | | 6.35 | 7.70 |
| 0500 | 5/4" x 12" | | 175 | .046 | | 5.70 | 1.74 | | 7.44 | 9 |
| 0510 | Rake trim, 1" x 4" | | 225 | .036 | | 1.40 | 1.35 | | 2.75 | 3.65 |
| 0520 | 1" x 6" | | 225 | .036 | | 2.18 | 1.35 | | 3.53 | 4.51 |
| 0560 | 5/4" x 4" | | 220 | .036 | | 1.78 | 1.39 | | 3.17 | 4.12 |
| 0570 | 5/4" x 6" | | 220 | .036 | | 2.79 | 1.39 | | 4.18 | 5.25 |
| 0610 | Soffit, 1" x 4" | 2 Carp | 420 | .038 | | 1.40 | 1.45 | | 2.85 | 3.80 |
| 0620 | 1" x 6" | | 420 | .038 | | 2.18 | 1.45 | | 3.63 | 4.66 |
| 0630 | 1" x 8" | | 420 | .038 | | 2.87 | 1.45 | | 4.32 | 5.40 |
| 0640 | 1" x 10" | | 400 | .040 | | 3.65 | 1.52 | | 5.17 | 6.40 |
| 0650 | 1" x 12" | | 400 | .040 | | 4.45 | 1.52 | | 5.97 | 7.25 |
| 0660 | 5/4" x 4" | | 410 | .039 | | 1.78 | 1.49 | | 3.27 | 4.27 |
| 0670 | 5/4" x 6" | | 410 | .039 | | 2.79 | 1.49 | | 4.28 | 5.40 |

| 06 65 10.10 PVC Trim, Exterior | | Crew | Daily Output | Labor-Hours | Unit | Material | 2008 Bare Costs Labor | Equipment | Total | Total Incl O&P |
|---|---|---|---|---|---|---|---|---|---|---|
| 0680 | 5/4" x 8" | 2 Carp | 410 | .039 | L.F. | 3.69 | 1.49 | | 5.18 | 6.35 |
| 0690 | 5/4" x 10" | | 390 | .041 | | 4.70 | 1.56 | | 6.26 | 7.60 |
| 0700 | 5/4" x 12" | | 390 | .041 | | 5.70 | 1.56 | | 7.26 | 8.75 |

# Division Notes

| | CREW | DAILY OUTPUT | LABOR-HOURS | UNIT | 2008 BARE COSTS | | | | TOTAL INCL O&P |
|---|---|---|---|---|---|---|---|---|---|
| | | | | | MAT. | LABOR | EQUIP. | TOTAL | |
| | | | | | | | | | |
| | | | | | | | | | |
| | | | | | | | | | |
| | | | | | | | | | |
| | | | | | | | | | |
| | | | | | | | | | |
| | | | | | | | | | |
| | | | | | | | | | |
| | | | | | | | | | |
| | | | | | | | | | |
| | | | | | | | | | |
| | | | | | | | | | |
| | | | | | | | | | |
| | | | | | | | | | |
| | | | | | | | | | |
| | | | | | | | | | |
| | | | | | | | | | |
| | | | | | | | | | |
| | | | | | | | | | |
| | | | | | | | | | |

# Estimating Tips

## 07 10 00 Dampproofing and Waterproofing

- Be sure of the job specifications before pricing this subdivision. The difference in cost between waterproofing and dampproofing can be great. Waterproofing will hold back standing water. Dampproofing prevents the transmission of water vapor. Also included in this section are vapor retarding membranes.

## 07 20 00 Thermal Protection

- Insulation and fireproofing products are measured by area, thickness, volume or R value. Specifications may give only what the specific R value should be in a certain situation. The estimator may need to choose the type of insulation to meet that R value.

## 07 30 00 Steep Slope Roofing
## 07 40 00 Roofing and Siding Panels

- Many roofing and siding products are bought and sold by the square. One square is equal to an area that measures 100 square feet.

This simple change in unit of measure could create a large error if the estimator is not observant. Accessories necessary for a complete installation must be figured into any calculations for both material and labor.

## 07 50 00 Membrane Roofing
## 07 60 00 Flashing and Sheet Metal
## 07 70 00 Roofing and Wall Specialties and Accessories

- The items in these subdivisions compose a roofing system. No one component completes the installation, and all must be estimated. Built-up or single-ply membrane roofing systems are made up of many products and installation trades. Wood blocking at roof perimeters or penetrations, parapet coverings, reglets, roof drains, gutters, downspouts, sheet metal flashing, skylights, smoke vents, and roof hatches all need to be considered along with the roofing material. Several different installation trades will need to work together on the roofing system. Inherent difficulties in the scheduling and coordination of various trades must be accounted for when estimating labor costs.

## 07 90 00 Joint Protection

- To complete the weather-tight shell, the sealants and caulkings must be estimated. Where different materials meet—at expansion joints, at flashing penetrations, and at hundreds of other locations throughout a construction project—they provide another line of defense against water penetration. Often, an entire system is based on the proper location and placement of caulking or sealants. The detailed drawings that are included as part of a set of architectural plans show typical locations for these materials. When caulking or sealants are shown at typical locations, this means the estimator must include them for all the locations where this detail is applicable. Be careful to keep different types of sealants separate, and remember to consider backer rods and primers if necessary.

## Reference Numbers

Reference numbers are shown in shaded boxes at the beginning of some major classifications. These numbers refer to related items in the Reference Section. The reference information may be an estimating procedure, an alternate pricing method, or technical information.

*Note:* Not all subdivisions listed here necessarily appear in this publication.

## 07 01 50 – Maintenance of Membrane Roofing

### 07 01 50.10 Roof Coatings

| | Crew | Daily Output | Labor-Hours | Unit | Material | 2008 Bare Costs Labor | Equipment | Total | Total Incl O&P |
|---|---|---|---|---|---|---|---|---|---|
| 0010 **ROOF COATINGS** | | | | | | | | | |
| 0012 Asphalt, brush grade, material only | CN | | | Gal. | 7.50 | | | 7.50 | 8.25 |
| 0200 Asphalt base, fibered aluminum coating | | | | | 10.05 | | | 10.05 | 11.05 |
| 0300 Asphalt primer, 5 gallon | | | | | 5.50 | | | 5.50 | 6.05 |
| 0600 Coal tar pitch, 200 lb. barrels | | | | Ton | 725 | | | 725 | 800 |
| 0700 Tar roof cement, 5 gal. lots | | | | Gal. | 7.25 | | | 7.25 | 7.95 |
| 0800 Glass fibered roof & patching cement, 5 gallon | | | | " | 6.60 | | | 6.60 | 7.30 |
| 0900 Reinforcing glass membrane, 450 S.F./roll | | | | Ea. | 48.50 | | | 48.50 | 53 |
| 1000 Neoprene roof coating, 5 gal, 2 gal/sq | | | | Gal. | 24.50 | | | 24.50 | 26.50 |
| 1100 Roof patch & flashing cement, 5 gallon | | | | | 11.70 | | | 11.70 | 12.85 |
| 1200 Roof resaturant, glass fibered, 3 gal/sq | | | | | 7.75 | | | 7.75 | 8.55 |
| 1300 Mineral rubber, 3 gal/sq | | | | | 4.99 | | | 4.99 | 5.50 |

## 07 05 05 – Selective Demolition

### 07 05 05.10 Selective Demolition, Roofing and Siding

| | Crew | Daily Output | Labor-Hours | Unit | Material | 2008 Bare Costs Labor | Equipment | Total | Total Incl O&P |
|---|---|---|---|---|---|---|---|---|---|
| 0010 **SELECTIVE DEMOLITION, ROOFING AND SIDING** R024119-10 | | | | | | | | | |
| 0200 Waterproofing demo., scrape off vertical waterproofing, to 1/2" thick | 2 Clab | 2000 | .008 | S.F. | | .24 | | .24 | .38 |
| 0210 Over 1/2" thick | | 1750 | .009 | " | | .28 | | .28 | .43 |
| 0250 Protection / drain board | | 3900 | .004 | B.F. | | .12 | | .12 | .19 |
| 1000 Deck, roof, concrete plank | B-13 | 1680 | .033 | S.F. | | 1.09 | .47 | 1.56 | 2.19 |
| 1100 Gypsum plank | | 3900 | .014 | | | .47 | .20 | .67 | .94 |
| 1150 Metal decking | | 3500 | .016 | | | .52 | .22 | .74 | 1.06 |
| 1200 Wood, boards, tongue and groove, 2" x 6" | 2 Clab | 960 | .017 | | | .50 | | .50 | .78 |
| 1220 2" x 10" | | 1040 | .015 | | | .47 | | .47 | .72 |
| 1280 Standard planks, 1" x 6" | | 1080 | .015 | | | .45 | | .45 | .70 |
| 1320 1" x 8" | | 1160 | .014 | | | .42 | | .42 | .65 |
| 1340 1" x 12" | | 1200 | .013 | | | .40 | | .40 | .63 |
| 1350 Plywood, to 1" thick | | 2000 | .008 | | | .24 | | .24 | .38 |
| 2000 Gutters, aluminum or wood, edge hung | 1 Clab | 240 | .033 | L.F. | | 1.01 | | 1.01 | 1.57 |
| 2100 Built-in | | 100 | .080 | " | | 2.42 | | 2.42 | 3.76 |
| 2200 Insulation removal, loose fitting | | 3000 | .003 | C.F. | | .08 | | .08 | .13 |
| 2250 Air barrier | | 3500 | .002 | S.F. | | .07 | | .07 | .11 |
| 2300 Batts or blankets | | 1400 | .006 | C.F. | | .17 | | .17 | .27 |
| 2350 Rigid board | | 3450 | .002 | B.F. | | .07 | | .07 | .11 |
| 2500 Roof accessories, plumbing vent flashing | | 14 | .571 | Ea. | | 17.30 | | 17.30 | 27 |
| 2600 Adjustable metal chimney flashing | | 9 | .889 | " | | 27 | | 27 | 42 |
| 2650 Coping, sheet metal, up to 12" wide | | 240 | .033 | L.F. | | 1.01 | | 1.01 | 1.57 |
| 2660 Concrete, up to 12" wide | 2 Clab | 160 | .100 | " | | 3.03 | | 3.03 | 4.71 |
| 3000 Roofing, built-up, 5 ply roof, no gravel | B-2 | 1600 | .025 | S.F. | | .77 | | .77 | 1.19 |
| 3001 Including gravel | | 890 | .045 | | | 1.38 | | 1.38 | 2.14 |
| 3100 Gravel removal, minimum | | 5000 | .008 | | | .25 | | .25 | .38 |
| 3120 Maximum | | 2000 | .020 | | | .61 | | .61 | .95 |
| 3400 Roof insulation board, up to 2" thick | | 3900 | .010 | | | .31 | | .31 | .49 |
| 3405 Over 2" thick | | 7800 | .005 | B.F. | | .16 | | .16 | .24 |
| 3450 Roll roofing, cold adhesive | 1 Clab | 12 | .667 | Sq. | | 20 | | 20 | 31.50 |
| 4000 Shingles, asphalt strip, 1 layer | B-2 | 3500 | .011 | S.F. | | .35 | | .35 | .55 |
| 4100 Slate | | 2500 | .016 | | | .49 | | .49 | .76 |
| 4300 Wood | | 2200 | .018 | | | .56 | | .56 | .87 |
| 4500 Skylight to 10 S.F. | 1 Clab | 8 | 1 | Ea. | | 30.50 | | 30.50 | 47 |
| 5000 Siding, metal, horizontal | | 444 | .018 | S.F. | | .55 | | .55 | .85 |

# 07 05 Common Work Results for Thermal and Moisture Protection

## 07 05 05 – Selective Demolition

| 07 05 05.10 Selective Demolition, Roofing and Siding | Crew | Daily Output | Labor-Hours | Unit | Material | 2008 Bare Costs Labor | Equipment | Total | Total Incl O&P |
|---|---|---|---|---|---|---|---|---|---|
| 5020 | Vertical | 1 Clab | 400 | .020 | S.F. | | .61 | | .61 | .94 |
| 5200 | Wood, boards, vertical | | 400 | .020 | | | .61 | | .61 | .94 |
| 5220 | Clapboards, horizontal | | 380 | .021 | | | .64 | | .64 | .99 |
| 5240 | Shingles | | 350 | .023 | | | .69 | | .69 | 1.08 |
| 5260 | Textured plywood | ↓ | 725 | .011 | ↓ | | .33 | | .33 | .52 |

# 07 11 Dampproofing

## 07 11 13 – Bituminous Damppoofing

### 07 11 13.10 Bituminous Asphalt Coating

| | 07 11 13.10 Bituminous Asphalt Coating | Crew | Daily Output | Labor-Hours | Unit | Material | 2008 Bare Costs Labor | Equipment | Total | Total Incl O&P |
|---|---|---|---|---|---|---|---|---|---|---|
| 0010 | **BITUMINOUS ASPHALT COATING** | | | | | | | | | |
| 0030 | Brushed on, below grade, 1 coat | 1 Rofc | 665 | .012 | S.F. | .13 | .40 | | .53 | .82 |
| 0100 | 2 coat | | 500 | .016 | | .25 | .53 | | .78 | 1.18 |
| 0300 | Sprayed on, below grade, 1 coat, 25.6 S.F./gal. | | 830 | .010 | | .13 | .32 | | .45 | .68 |
| 0400 | 2 coat, 20.5 S.F./gal. | ↓ | 500 | .016 | ↓ | .25 | .53 | | .78 | 1.17 |
| 0500 | Asphalt coating, with fibers | | | | Gal. | 6.35 | | | 6.35 | 7 |
| 0600 | Troweled on, asphalt with fibers, 1/16" thick | 1 Rofc | 500 | .016 | S.F. | .28 | .53 | | .81 | 1.20 |
| 0700 | 1/8" thick | | 400 | .020 | | .49 | .66 | | 1.15 | 1.66 |
| 1000 | 1/2" thick | ↓ | 350 | .023 | ↓ | 1.59 | .75 | | 2.34 | 3.03 |

## 07 11 16 – Cementitious Dampproofing

### 07 11 16.20 Cementitious Parging

| | 07 11 16.20 Cementitious Parging | Crew | Daily Output | Labor-Hours | Unit | Material | 2008 Bare Costs Labor | Equipment | Total | Total Incl O&P |
|---|---|---|---|---|---|---|---|---|---|---|
| 0010 | **CEMENTITIOUS PARGING** | | | | | | | | | |
| 0020 | Portland cement, 2 coats, 1/2" thick | D-1 | 250 | .064 | S.F. | .25 | 2.23 | | 2.48 | 3.67 |
| 0100 | Waterproofed Portland cement | " | 250 | .064 | " | 2.12 | 2.23 | | 4.35 | 5.75 |

# 07 12 Built-up Bituminous Waterproofing

## 07 12 13 – Built-Up Asphalt Waterproofing

### 07 12 13.20 Membrane Waterproofing

| | 07 12 13.20 Membrane Waterproofing | Crew | Daily Output | Labor-Hours | Unit | Material | 2008 Bare Costs Labor | Equipment | Total | Total Incl O&P |
|---|---|---|---|---|---|---|---|---|---|---|
| 0010 | **MEMBRANE WATERPROOFING** | | | | | | | | | |
| 0012 | On slabs, 1 ply, felt, mopped | G-1 | 3000 | .019 | S.F. | .27 | .58 | .14 | .99 | 1.42 |
| 0300 | On slabs, 2 ply, felt, mopped | | 2500 | .022 | | .53 | .69 | .16 | 1.38 | 1.95 |
| 0400 | On slabs, 2 ply, glass fiber fabric, mopped | | 1650 | .034 | | .62 | 1.05 | .25 | 1.92 | 2.74 |
| 0600 | On slabs, 3 ply, felt, mopped | | 2100 | .027 | | .80 | .82 | .20 | 1.82 | 2.50 |
| 0700 | On slabs, 3 ply, glass fiber fabric, mopped | ↓ | 1550 | .036 | | .83 | 1.12 | .27 | 2.22 | 3.10 |
| 0710 | Asphaltic hardboard protection board, 1/8" thick | 2 Rofc | 500 | .032 | | .33 | 1.06 | | 1.39 | 2.16 |
| 1000 | 1/4" EPS membrane protection board | | 3500 | .005 | | .20 | .15 | | .35 | .48 |
| 1050 | 3/8" thick | | 3500 | .005 | | .22 | .15 | | .37 | .50 |
| 1060 | 1/2" thick, add | | 3500 | .005 | ↓ | .25 | .15 | | .40 | .54 |
| 1070 | Fiberglass fabric, black, 20/10 mesh | | 116 | .138 | Sq. | 12 | 4.55 | | 16.55 | 21 |
| 1080 | White, 20/10 mesh | ↓ | 116 | .138 | " | 12 | 4.55 | | 16.55 | 21 |

# 07 13 Sheet Waterproofing

## 07 13 53 – Elastomeric Sheet Waterproofing

| 07 13 53.10 Elastomeric Sheet Waterproofing and Access. | Crew | Daily Output | Labor-Hours | Unit | Material | 2008 Bare Costs Labor | Equipment | Total | Total Incl O&P |
|---|---|---|---|---|---|---|---|---|---|
| 0010 **ELASTOMERIC SHEET WATERPROOFING AND ACCESS.** | | | | | | | | | |
| 0090 EPDM, plain, 45 mils thick | 2 Rofc | 580 | .028 | S.F. | 1.12 | .91 | | 2.03 | 2.79 |
| 0100 60 mils thick | | 570 | .028 | | 1.21 | .93 | | 2.14 | 2.91 |
| 0300 Nylon reinforced sheets, 45 mils thick | | 580 | .028 | | 1.10 | .91 | | 2.01 | 2.76 |
| 0400 60 mils thick | ↓ | 570 | .028 | ↓ | 1.40 | .93 | | 2.33 | 3.12 |
| 0600 Vulcanizing splicing tape for above, 2" wide | | | | C.L.F. | 39 | | | 39 | 42.50 |
| 0700 4" wide | | | | " | 89.50 | | | 89.50 | 98.50 |
| 0900 Adhesive, bonding, 60 SF per gal | | | | Gal. | 15.20 | | | 15.20 | 16.70 |
| 1000 Splicing, 75 SF per gal | | | | " | 25 | | | 25 | 27.50 |
| 1200 Neoprene sheets, plain, 45 mils thick | 2 Rofc | 580 | .028 | S.F. | 1.50 | .91 | | 2.41 | 3.20 |
| 1300 60 mils thick | | 570 | .028 | | 2.55 | .93 | | 3.48 | 4.39 |
| 1500 Nylon reinforced, 45 mils thick | | 580 | .028 | | 1.56 | .91 | | 2.47 | 3.27 |
| 1600 60 mils thick | | 570 | .028 | ↓ | 2.20 | .93 | | 3.13 | 4 |
| 1800 120 mils thick | ↓ | 500 | .032 | ↓ | 3.58 | 1.06 | | 4.64 | 5.75 |
| 1900 Adhesive, splicing, 150 S.F. per gal. per coat | | | | Gal. | 19 | | | 19 | 21 |
| 2100 Fiberglass reinforced, fluid applied, 1/8" thick | 2 Rofc | 500 | .032 | S.F. | 1.65 | 1.06 | | 2.71 | 3.62 |
| 2200 Polyethylene and rubberized asphalt sheets, 1/8" thick | | 550 | .029 | | .55 | .96 | | 1.51 | 2.24 |
| 2210 Asphaltic hardboard protection board, 1/8" thick | | 500 | .032 | | .33 | 1.06 | | 1.39 | 2.16 |
| 2220 1/4" thick | | 450 | .036 | | .57 | 1.17 | | 1.74 | 2.63 |
| 2400 Polyvinyl chloride sheets, plain, 10 mils thick | | 580 | .028 | | .17 | .91 | | 1.08 | 1.74 |
| 2500 20 mils thick | | 570 | .028 | ↓ | .28 | .93 | | 1.21 | 1.89 |
| 2700 30 mils thick | ↓ | 560 | .029 | | .39 | .94 | | 1.33 | 2.03 |
| 3000 Adhesives, trowel grade, 40-100 SF per gal | | | | Gal. | 25.50 | | | 25.50 | 28 |
| 3100 Brush grade, 100-250 SF per gal. | | | | " | 25.50 | | | 25.50 | 28 |
| 3300 Bitumen modified polyurethane, fluid applied, 55 mils thick | 2 Rofc | 665 | .024 | S.F. | .69 | .79 | | 1.48 | 2.11 |
| 3600 Vinyl plastic, sprayed on, 25 to 40 mils thick | " | 475 | .034 | " | 1.11 | 1.11 | | 2.22 | 3.11 |

# 07 16 Cementitious and Reactive Waterproofing

## 07 16 16 – Crystalline Waterproofing

| 07 16 16.20 Cementitious Waterproofing | Crew | Daily Output | Labor-Hours | Unit | Material | 2008 Bare Costs Labor | Equipment | Total | Total Incl O&P |
|---|---|---|---|---|---|---|---|---|---|
| 0010 **CEMENTITIOUS WATERPROOFING** | | | | | | | | | |
| 0020 1/8" application, sprayed on | G-2A | 1000 | .024 | S.F. | 1.62 | .70 | .60 | 2.92 | 3.60 |
| 0030 2 coat, cementitious/metallic slurry, troweled, 1/4" thick | 1 Cefi | 2.48 | 3.226 | C.S.F. | 24 | 119 | | 143 | 202 |
| 0040 3 coat, 3/8" thick | ↓ | 1.84 | 4.348 | | 42.50 | 161 | | 203.50 | 283 |
| 0050 4 coat, 1/2" thick | ↓ | 1.20 | 6.667 | ↓ | 56.50 | 247 | | 303.50 | 420 |

# 07 17 Bentonite Waterproofing

## 07 17 13 – Bentonite Panel Waterproofing

| 07 17 13.10 Bentonite | Crew | Daily Output | Labor-Hours | Unit | Material | 2008 Bare Costs Labor | Equipment | Total | Total Incl O&P |
|---|---|---|---|---|---|---|---|---|---|
| 0010 **BENTONITE** | | | | | | | | | |
| 0020 Panels, 4' x 4', 3/16" thick | 1 Rofc | 625 | .013 | S.F. | .83 | .42 | | 1.25 | 1.63 |
| 0100 Rolls, 3/8" thick, with geotextile fabric both sides | " | 550 | .015 | " | 1.02 | .48 | | 1.50 | 1.94 |
| 0300 Granular bentonite, 50 lb. bags (.625 C.F.) | | | | Bag | 19.90 | | | 19.90 | 22 |
| 0400 3/8" thick, troweled on | 1 Rofc | 475 | .017 | S.F. | .99 | .56 | | 1.55 | 2.04 |
| 0500 Drain board, expanded polystyrene, binder encapsulated, 1-1/2" thick | 1 Rohe | 1600 | .005 | | 1.16 | .12 | | 1.28 | 1.49 |
| 0510 2" thick | | 1600 | .005 | | 1.56 | .12 | | 1.68 | 1.93 |
| 0520 3" thick | | 1600 | .005 | | 2.33 | .12 | | 2.45 | 2.77 |
| 0530 4" thick | | 1600 | .005 | | 3.09 | .12 | | 3.21 | 3.61 |
| 0600 With filter fabric, 1-1/2" thick | ↓ | 1600 | .005 | ↓ | 1.41 | .12 | | 1.53 | 1.76 |

# 07 17 Bentonite Waterproofing

## 07 17 13 – Bentonite Panel Waterproofing

| 07 17 13.10 Bentonite | | Crew | Daily Output | Labor-Hours | Unit | Material | 2008 Bare Costs Labor | Equipment | Total | Total Incl O&P |
|---|---|---|---|---|---|---|---|---|---|---|
| 0625 | 2" thick | 1 Rohe | 1600 | .005 | S.F. | 1.85 | .12 | | 1.97 | 2.25 |
| 0650 | 3" thick | | 1600 | .005 | | 2.63 | .12 | | 2.75 | 3.10 |
| 0675 | 4" thick | | 1600 | .005 | | 3.41 | .12 | | 3.53 | 3.96 |

# 07 19 Water Repellents

## 07 19 19 – Silicone Water Repellents

### 07 19 19.10 Silicone Based Water Repellents

| | | Crew | Daily Output | Labor-Hours | Unit | Material | 2008 Bare Costs Labor | Equipment | Total | Total Incl O&P |
|---|---|---|---|---|---|---|---|---|---|---|
| 0010 | **SILICONE BASED WATER REPELLENTS** | | | | | | | | | |
| 0020 | Water base liquid, roller applied | 2 Rofc | 7000 | .002 | S.F. | .60 | .08 | | .68 | .79 |
| 0200 | Silicone or stearate, sprayed on CMU, 1 coat | 1 Rofc | 4000 | .002 | | .34 | .07 | | .41 | .48 |
| 0300 | 2 coats | " | 3000 | .003 | | .68 | .09 | | .77 | .89 |

# 07 21 Thermal Insulation

## 07 21 13 – Board Insulation

### 07 21 13.10 Rigid Insulation

| | | Crew | Daily Output | Labor-Hours | Unit | Material | 2008 Bare Costs Labor | Equipment | Total | Total Incl O&P |
|---|---|---|---|---|---|---|---|---|---|---|
| 0010 | **RIGID INSULATION** | | | | | | | | | |
| 0040 | Fiberglass, 1.5#/CF, unfaced, 1" thick, R4.1 | 1 Carp | 1000 | .008 | S.F. | .44 | .30 | | .74 | .95 |
| 0060 | 1-1/2" thick, R6.2 | | 1000 | .008 | | .64 | .30 | | .94 | 1.17 |
| 0080 | 2" thick, R8.3 | | 1000 | .008 | | .69 | .30 | | .99 | 1.23 |
| 0120 | 3" thick, R12.4 | | 800 | .010 | | .80 | .38 | | 1.18 | 1.47 |
| 0370 | 3#/CF, unfaced, 1" thick, R4.3 | | 1000 | .008 | | .49 | .30 | | .79 | 1.01 |
| 0390 | 1-1/2" thick, R6.5 | | 1000 | .008 | | .95 | .30 | | 1.25 | 1.52 |
| 0400 | 2" thick, R8.7 | | 890 | .009 | | 1.15 | .34 | | 1.49 | 1.80 |
| 0420 | 2-1/2" thick, R10.9 | | 800 | .010 | | 1.01 | .38 | | 1.39 | 1.70 |
| 0440 | 3" thick, R13 | | 800 | .010 | | 1.01 | .38 | | 1.39 | 1.70 |
| 0520 | Foil faced, 1" thick, R4.3 | | 1000 | .008 | | .92 | .30 | | 1.22 | 1.48 |
| 0540 | 1-1/2" thick, R6.5 | | 1000 | .008 | | 1.36 | .30 | | 1.66 | 1.97 |
| 0560 | 2" thick, R8.7 | | 890 | .009 | | 1.71 | .34 | | 2.05 | 2.41 |
| 0580 | 2-1/2" thick, R10.9 | | 800 | .010 | | 2.02 | .38 | | 2.40 | 2.81 |
| 0600 | 3" thick, R13 | | 800 | .010 | | 2.19 | .38 | | 2.57 | 3 |
| 0670 | 6#/CF, unfaced, 1" thick, R4.3 | | 1000 | .008 | | .98 | .30 | | 1.28 | 1.55 |
| 0690 | 1-1/2" thick, R6.5 | | 890 | .009 | | 1.50 | .34 | | 1.84 | 2.18 |
| 0700 | 2" thick, R8.7 | | 800 | .010 | | 2.12 | .38 | | 2.50 | 2.92 |
| 0721 | 2-1/2" thick, R10.9 | | 800 | .010 | | 2.32 | .38 | | 2.70 | 3.14 |
| 0741 | 3" thick, R13 | | 730 | .011 | | 2.78 | .42 | | 3.20 | 3.71 |
| 0821 | Foil faced, 1" thick, R4.3 | | 1000 | .008 | | 1.38 | .30 | | 1.68 | 1.99 |
| 0840 | 1-1/2" thick, R6.5 | | 890 | .009 | | 1.98 | .34 | | 2.32 | 2.71 |
| 0850 | 2" thick, R8.7 | | 800 | .010 | | 2.59 | .38 | | 2.97 | 3.44 |
| 0880 | 2-1/2" thick, R10.9 | | 800 | .010 | | 3.11 | .38 | | 3.49 | 4.01 |
| 0900 | 3" thick, R13 | | 730 | .011 | | 3.72 | .42 | | 4.14 | 4.74 |
| 1500 | Foamglass, 1-1/2" thick, R4.5 | | 800 | .010 | | 1.33 | .38 | | 1.71 | 2.05 |
| 1550 | 3" thick, R9 | | 730 | .011 | | 3.19 | .42 | | 3.61 | 4.16 |
| 1600 | Isocyanurate, 4' x 8' sheet, foil faced, both sides | | | | | | | | | |
| 1610 | 1/2" thick, R3.9 | 1 Carp | 800 | .010 | S.F. | .30 | .38 | | .68 | .92 |
| 1620 | 5/8" thick, R4.5 | | 800 | .010 | | .51 | .38 | | .89 | 1.15 |
| 1630 | 3/4" thick, R5.4 | | 800 | .010 | | .35 | .38 | | .73 | .98 |
| 1640 | 1" thick, R7.2 | | 800 | .010 | | .55 | .38 | | .93 | 1.20 |
| 1650 | 1-1/2" thick, R10.8 | | 730 | .011 | | .64 | .42 | | 1.06 | 1.35 |
| 1660 | 2" thick, R14.4 **CN** | | 730 | .011 | | .87 | .42 | | 1.29 | 1.61 |

# 07 21 Thermal Insulation

## 07 21 13 – Board Insulation

### 07 21 13.10 Rigid Insulation

| | | Crew | Daily Output | Labor-Hours | Unit | Material | 2008 Bare Costs Labor | Equipment | Total | Total Incl O&P |
|---|---|---|---|---|---|---|---|---|---|---|
| 1670 | 3" thick, R21.6 | 1 Carp | 730 | .011 | S.F. | 1.90 | .42 | | 2.32 | 2.74 |
| 1680 | 4" thick, R28.8 | | 730 | .011 | | 2.14 | .42 | | 2.56 | 3 |
| 1700 | Perlite, 1" thick, R2.77 | | 800 | .010 | | .30 | .38 | | .68 | .92 |
| 1750 | 2" thick, R5.55 | | 730 | .011 | | .60 | .42 | | 1.02 | 1.31 |
| 1900 | Extruded polystyrene, 25 PSI compressive strength, 1" thick, R5 | | 800 | .010 | | .51 | .38 | | .89 | 1.15 |
| 1940 | 2" thick R10 | | 730 | .011 | | 1.04 | .42 | | 1.46 | 1.79 |
| 1960 | 3" thick, R15 | | 730 | .011 | | 1.40 | .42 | | 1.82 | 2.19 |
| 2100 | Expanded polystyrene, 1" thick, R3.85 | | 800 | .010 | | .24 | .38 | | .62 | .85 |
| 2120 | 2" thick, R7.69 | | 730 | .011 | | .61 | .42 | | 1.03 | 1.32 |
| 2140 | 3" thick, R11.49 | | 730 | .011 | | .78 | .42 | | 1.20 | 1.51 |

### 07 21 13.13 Foam Board Insulation

| | | Crew | Daily Output | Labor-Hours | Unit | Material | 2008 Bare Costs Labor | Equipment | Total | Total Incl O&P |
|---|---|---|---|---|---|---|---|---|---|---|
| 0010 | **FOAM BOARD INSULATION** | | | | | | | | | |
| 0600 | Polystyrene, expanded, 1" thick, R4 | 1 Carp | 680 | .012 | S.F. | .31 | .45 | | .76 | 1.04 |
| 0700 | 2" thick, R8 | " | 675 | .012 | " | .62 | .45 | | 1.07 | 1.38 |

## 07 21 16 – Blanket Insulation

### 07 21 16.20 Blanket Insulation for Walls

| | | Crew | Daily Output | Labor-Hours | Unit | Material | 2008 Bare Costs Labor | Equipment | Total | Total Incl O&P |
|---|---|---|---|---|---|---|---|---|---|---|
| 0010 | **BLANKET INSULATION FOR WALLS** | | | | | | | | | |
| 0020 | Kraft faced fiberglass, 3-1/2" thick, R11, 15" wide | 1 Carp | 1350 | .006 | S.F. | .36 | .23 | | .59 | .75 |
| 0030 | 23" wide | | 1600 | .005 | | .36 | .19 | | .55 | .70 |
| 0060 | R13, 11" wide | | 1150 | .007 | | .37 | .27 | | .64 | .82 |
| 0080 | 15" wide | *CN* | 1350 | .006 | | .37 | .23 | | .60 | .76 |
| 0100 | 23" wide | | 1600 | .005 | | .37 | .19 | | .56 | .71 |
| 0110 | R-15, 11" wide | | 1150 | .007 | | .33 | .27 | | .60 | .77 |
| 0120 | 15" wide | | 1350 | .006 | | .33 | .23 | | .56 | .71 |
| 0130 | 23" wide | | 1600 | .005 | | .33 | .19 | | .52 | .66 |
| 0140 | 6" thick, R19, 11" wide | | 1150 | .007 | | .43 | .27 | | .70 | .88 |
| 0160 | 15" wide | | 1350 | .006 | | .43 | .23 | | .66 | .82 |
| 0180 | 23" wide | | 1600 | .005 | | .43 | .19 | | .62 | .77 |
| 0182 | R21, 11" wide | | 1150 | .007 | | .63 | .27 | | .90 | 1.10 |
| 0184 | 15" wide | | 1350 | .006 | | .63 | .23 | | .86 | 1.04 |
| 0186 | 23" wide | | 1600 | .005 | | .63 | .19 | | .82 | .99 |
| 0188 | 9" thick, R-30, 11" wide | | 985 | .008 | | .80 | .31 | | 1.11 | 1.36 |
| 0200 | 15" wide | | 1150 | .007 | | .80 | .27 | | 1.07 | 1.29 |
| 0220 | 23" wide | | 1350 | .006 | | .80 | .23 | | 1.03 | 1.23 |
| 0230 | 12" thick, R38, 11" wide | | 985 | .008 | | 1 | .31 | | 1.31 | 1.58 |
| 0240 | 15" wide | | 1150 | .007 | | 1 | .27 | | 1.27 | 1.51 |
| 0260 | 23" wide | | 1350 | .006 | | 1 | .23 | | 1.23 | 1.45 |
| 0410 | Foil faced fiberglass, 3-1/2" thick, R13, 11" wide | | 1150 | .007 | | .55 | .27 | | .82 | 1.02 |
| 0420 | 15" wide | | 1350 | .006 | | .55 | .23 | | .78 | .96 |
| 0440 | 23" wide | | 1600 | .005 | | .55 | .19 | | .74 | .91 |
| 0442 | R15, 11" wide | | 1150 | .007 | | .52 | .27 | | .79 | .98 |
| 0444 | 15" wide | | 1350 | .006 | | .52 | .23 | | .75 | .92 |
| 0446 | 23" wide | | 1600 | .005 | | .52 | .19 | | .71 | .87 |
| 0448 | 6" thick, R19, 11" wide | | 1150 | .007 | | .54 | .27 | | .81 | 1 |
| 0460 | 15" wide | | 1350 | .006 | | .54 | .23 | | .77 | .94 |
| 0480 | 23" wide | | 1600 | .005 | | .54 | .19 | | .73 | .89 |
| 0482 | R-21, 11" wide | | 1150 | .007 | | .57 | .27 | | .84 | 1.04 |
| 0484 | 15" wide | | 1350 | .006 | | .57 | .23 | | .80 | .98 |
| 0486 | 23" wide | | 1600 | .005 | | .57 | .19 | | .76 | .93 |
| 0488 | 9" thick, R-30, 11" wide | | 985 | .008 | | .84 | .31 | | 1.15 | 1.40 |
| 0500 | 9" thick, R30, 15" wide | | 1150 | .007 | | .84 | .27 | | 1.11 | 1.33 |
| 0550 | 23" wide | | 1350 | .006 | | .84 | .23 | | 1.07 | 1.27 |

# 07 21 Thermal Insulation

## 07 21 16 – Blanket Insulation

### 07 21 16.20 Blanket Insulation for Walls

| | | Crew | Daily Output | Labor-Hours | Unit | Material | 2008 Bare Costs Labor | Equipment | Total | Total Incl O&P |
|---|---|---|---|---|---|---|---|---|---|---|
| 0560 | 12" thick, R-38, 11" wide | 1 Carp | 985 | .008 | S.F. | .84 | .31 | | 1.15 | 1.40 |
| 0570 | 15" wide | | 1150 | .007 | | .84 | .27 | | 1.11 | 1.33 |
| 0580 | 23" wide | | 1350 | .006 | | .84 | .23 | | 1.07 | 1.27 |
| 0620 | Unfaced fiberglass, 3-1/2" thick, R-13, 11" wide | | 1150 | .007 | | .36 | .27 | | .63 | .81 |
| 0820 | 15" wide | | 1350 | .006 | | .36 | .23 | | .59 | .75 |
| 0830 | 23" wide | | 1600 | .005 | | .36 | .19 | | .55 | .70 |
| 0832 | R15, 11" wide | | 1150 | .007 | | .32 | .27 | | .59 | .76 |
| 0834 | 15" wide | | 1350 | .006 | | .32 | .23 | | .55 | .70 |
| 0836 | 23" wide | | 1600 | .005 | | .32 | .19 | | .51 | .65 |
| 0838 | 6" thick, R19, 11" wide | | 1150 | .007 | | .58 | .27 | | .85 | 1.05 |
| 0860 | 15" wide | | 1150 | .007 | | .58 | .27 | | .85 | 1.05 |
| 0880 | 23" wide | | 1350 | .006 | | .58 | .23 | | .81 | .99 |
| 0882 | R-21, 11" wide | | 1150 | .007 | | .67 | .27 | | .94 | 1.15 |
| 0886 | 15" wide | | 1350 | .006 | | .67 | .23 | | .90 | 1.09 |
| 0888 | 23" wide | | 1600 | .005 | | .67 | .19 | | .86 | 1.04 |
| 0890 | 9" thick, R30, 11" wide | | 985 | .008 | | .84 | .31 | | 1.15 | 1.40 |
| 0900 | 15" wide | | 1150 | .007 | | .84 | .27 | | 1.11 | 1.33 |
| 0920 | 23" wide | | 1350 | .006 | | .84 | .23 | | 1.07 | 1.27 |
| 0930 | 12" thick, R38, 11" wide | | 985 | .008 | | .90 | .31 | | 1.21 | 1.47 |
| 0940 | 15" wide | | 1000 | .008 | | .90 | .30 | | 1.20 | 1.46 |
| 0960 | 23" wide | | 1150 | .007 | | .90 | .27 | | 1.17 | 1.40 |
| 1300 | Mineral fiber batts, kraft faced | | | | | | | | | |
| 1320 | 3-1/2" thick, R12 | 1 Carp | 1600 | .005 | S.F. | .38 | .19 | | .57 | .72 |
| 1340 | 6" thick, R19 | | 1600 | .005 | | .51 | .19 | | .70 | .86 |
| 1380 | 10" thick, R30 | | 1350 | .006 | | .75 | .23 | | .98 | 1.18 |
| 1850 | Friction fit wire insulation supports, 16" O.C. | | 960 | .008 | Ea. | .08 | .32 | | .40 | .58 |

## 07 21 23 – Loose-Fill Insulation

### 07 21 23.10 Poured Loose-Fill Insulation

| | | Crew | Daily Output | Labor-Hours | Unit | Material | 2008 Bare Costs Labor | Equipment | Total | Total Incl O&P |
|---|---|---|---|---|---|---|---|---|---|---|
| 0010 | **POURED LOOSE-FILL INSULATION** | | | | | | | | | |
| 0020 | Cellulose fiber, R3.8 per inch | 1 Carp | 200 | .040 | C.F. | .64 | 1.52 | | 2.16 | 3.07 |
| 0040 | Ceramic type (perlite), R3.2 per inch | | 200 | .040 | | 1.72 | 1.52 | | 3.24 | 4.26 |
| 0080 | Fiberglass wool, R4 per inch | | 200 | .040 | | .51 | 1.52 | | 2.03 | 2.93 |
| 0100 | Mineral wool, R3 per inch | | 200 | .040 | | .39 | 1.52 | | 1.91 | 2.80 |
| 0300 | Polystyrene, R4 per inch | | 200 | .040 | | 3.09 | 1.52 | | 4.61 | 5.75 |
| 0400 | Vermiculite or perlite, R2.7 per inch | | 200 | .040 | | 1.72 | 1.52 | | 3.24 | 4.26 |
| 0700 | Wood fiber, R3.85 per inch | | 200 | .040 | | .70 | 1.52 | | 2.22 | 3.14 |

### 07 21 23.20 Masonry Loose-Fill Insulation

| | | Crew | Daily Output | Labor-Hours | Unit | Material | 2008 Bare Costs Labor | Equipment | Total | Total Incl O&P |
|---|---|---|---|---|---|---|---|---|---|---|
| 0010 | **MASONRY LOOSE-FILL INSULATION**, vermiculite or perlite | | | | | | | | | |
| 0100 | In cores of concrete block, 4" thick wall, .115 CF/SF | D-1 | 4800 | .003 | S.F. | .20 | .12 | | .32 | .40 |
| 0200 | 6" thick wall, .175 CF/SF | | 3000 | .005 | | .30 | .19 | | .49 | .61 |
| 0300 | 8" thick wall, .258 CF/SF | | 2400 | .007 | | .44 | .23 | | .67 | .84 |
| 0400 | 10" thick wall, .340 CF/SF | | 1850 | .009 | | .58 | .30 | | .88 | 1.10 |
| 0500 | 12" thick wall, .422 CF/SF | | 1200 | .013 | | .73 | .47 | | 1.20 | 1.51 |
| 0550 | For sand fill, deduct from above | | | | | 70% | | | | |
| 0600 | Poured cavity wall, vermiculite or perlite, water repellant | D-1 | 250 | .064 | C.F. | 1.72 | 2.23 | | 3.95 | 5.30 |
| 0700 | Foamed in place, urethane in 2-5/8" cavity | G-2A | 1035 | .023 | S.F. | .41 | .68 | .58 | 1.67 | 2.21 |
| 0800 | For each 1" added thickness, add | " | 2372 | .010 | " | .12 | .30 | .25 | .67 | .90 |

## 07 21 26 – Blown Insulation

### 07 21 26.10 Blown Insulation

| | | Crew | Daily Output | Labor-Hours | Unit | Material | 2008 Bare Costs Labor | Equipment | Total | Total Incl O&P |
|---|---|---|---|---|---|---|---|---|---|---|
| 0010 | **BLOWN INSULATION** Ceilings, with open access | | | | | | | | | |
| 0020 | Cellulose, 3-1/2" thick, R13 | G-4 | 5000 | .005 | S.F. | .21 | .15 | .06 | .42 | .53 |

# 07 21 Thermal Insulation

## 07 21 26 – Blown Insulation

| 07 21 26.10 Blown Insulation | Crew | Daily Output | Labor-Hours | Unit | Material | 2008 Bare Costs Labor | Equipment | Total | Total Incl O&P |
|---|---|---|---|---|---|---|---|---|---|
| 0030 | 5-3/16" thick, R19 | G-4 | 3800 | .006 | S.F. | .31 | .20 | .08 | .59 | .73 |
| 0050 | 6-1/2" thick, R22 | | 3000 | .008 | | .40 | .25 | .11 | .76 | .94 |
| 0100 | 8-11/16" thick, R30 | | 2600 | .009 | | .54 | .29 | .12 | .95 | 1.16 |
| 0120 | 10-7/8" thick, R38 | | 1800 | .013 | | .69 | .41 | .18 | 1.28 | 1.59 |
| 1000 | Fiberglass, 5.5" thick, R11 | | 3800 | .006 | | .21 | .20 | .08 | .49 | .62 |
| 1050 | 6" thick, R12 | | 3000 | .008 | | .25 | .25 | .11 | .61 | .78 |
| 1100 | 8.8" thick, R19 | | 2200 | .011 | | .36 | .34 | .14 | .84 | 1.07 |
| 1200 | 10" thick, R22 | | 1800 | .013 | | .42 | .41 | .18 | 1.01 | 1.29 |
| 1300 | 11.5" thick, R26 | | 1500 | .016 | | .50 | .49 | .21 | 1.20 | 1.55 |
| 1350 | 13" thick, R30 | | 1400 | .017 | | .54 | .53 | .23 | 1.30 | 1.67 |
| 1450 | 16" thick, R38 | | 1145 | .021 | | .67 | .65 | .28 | 1.60 | 2.04 |
| 1500 | 20" thick, R49 | | 920 | .026 | | .83 | .81 | .34 | 1.98 | 2.55 |
| 2000 | Mineral wool, 4" thick, R12 | | 3500 | .007 | | .23 | .21 | .09 | .53 | .68 |
| 2050 | 6" thick, R17 | | 2500 | .010 | | .26 | .30 | .13 | .69 | .89 |
| 2100 | 9" thick, R23 | ▼ | 1750 | .014 | ▼ | .34 | .42 | .18 | .94 | 1.23 |
| 2500 | Wall installation, incl. drilling & patching from outside, two 1" | | | | | | | | | |
| 2510 | diam. holes @ 16" O.C., top & mid-point of wall, add to above | | | | | | | | | |
| 2700 | For masonry | G-4 | 415 | .058 | S.F. | .06 | 1.79 | .76 | 2.61 | 3.69 |
| 2800 | For wood siding | | 840 | .029 | | .06 | .88 | .38 | 1.32 | 1.85 |
| 2900 | For stucco/plaster | ▼ | 665 | .036 | ▼ | .06 | 1.12 | .48 | 1.66 | 2.33 |

## 07 21 27 – Reflective Insulation

| 07 21 27.10 Reflective Insulation Options | Crew | Daily Output | Labor-Hours | Unit | Material | 2008 Bare Costs Labor | Equipment | Total | Total Incl O&P |
|---|---|---|---|---|---|---|---|---|---|
| 0010 | **REFLECTIVE INSULATION OPTIONS** | | | | | | | | | |
| 0020 | Aluminum foil on reinforced scrim | 1 Carp | 19 | .421 | C.S.F. | 14.05 | 16.05 | | 30.10 | 40.50 |
| 0100 | Reinforced with woven polyolefin | | 19 | .421 | | 17.15 | 16.05 | | 33.20 | 44 |
| 0500 | With single bubble air space, R8.8 | | 15 | .533 | | 25.50 | 20.50 | | 46 | 59.50 |
| 0600 | With double bubble air space, R9.8 | ▼ | 15 | .533 | ▼ | 26.50 | 20.50 | | 47 | 60.50 |

## 07 21 29 – Sprayed Insulation

| 07 21 29.10 Sprayed-On Insulation | Crew | Daily Output | Labor-Hours | Unit | Material | 2008 Bare Costs Labor | Equipment | Total | Total Incl O&P |
|---|---|---|---|---|---|---|---|---|---|
| 0010 | **SPRAYED-ON INSULATION** | | | | | | | | | |
| 0020 | Fibrous/cementitious, finished wall, 1" thick, R3.7 | G-2 | 2050 | .012 | S.F. | .24 | .38 | .06 | .68 | .90 |
| 0100 | Attic, 5.2" thick, R19 | " | 1550 | .015 | " | .39 | .50 | .08 | .97 | 1.28 |
| 0300 | Foam type, incl. preparation | | | | | | | | | |
| 0600 | 3 #/CF, 1" thick, R3.8 | G-2A | 770 | .031 | S.F. | .51 | .91 | .78 | 2.20 | 2.93 |
| 0700 | 2" thick, R7.5 | " | 475 | .051 | " | 1.03 | 1.48 | 1.27 | 3.78 | 4.97 |

# 07 22 Roof and Deck Insulation

## 07 22 16 – Roof Board Insulation

| 07 22 16.10 Roof Deck Insulation | Crew | Daily Output | Labor-Hours | Unit | Material | 2008 Bare Costs Labor | Equipment | Total | Total Incl O&P |
|---|---|---|---|---|---|---|---|---|---|
| 0010 | **ROOF DECK INSULATION** | | | | | | | | | |
| 0020 | Fiberboard low density, 1/2" thick R1.39 | 1 Rofc | 1000 | .008 | S.F. | .24 | .26 | | .50 | .71 |
| 0030 | 1" thick R2.78 | | 800 | .010 | | .42 | .33 | | .75 | 1.02 |
| 0080 | 1 1/2" thick R4.17 | | 800 | .010 | | .64 | .33 | | .97 | 1.26 |
| 0100 | 2" thick R5.56 | | 800 | .010 | | .85 | .33 | | 1.18 | 1.50 |
| 0110 | Fiberboard high density, 1/2" thick R1.3 | | 1000 | .008 | | .22 | .26 | | .48 | .69 |
| 0120 | 1" thick R2.5 | | 800 | .010 | | .44 | .33 | | .77 | 1.04 |
| 0130 | 1-1/2" thick R3.8 | | 800 | .010 | | .66 | .33 | | .99 | 1.29 |
| 0200 | Fiberglass, 3/4" thick R2.78 | | 1000 | .008 | | .56 | .26 | | .82 | 1.07 |
| 0400 | 15/16" thick R3.70 | | 1000 | .008 | | .74 | .26 | | 1 | 1.26 |
| 0460 | 1-1/16" thick R4.17 | | 1000 | .008 | | .93 | .26 | | 1.19 | 1.47 |

# 07 22 Roof and Deck Insulation

## 07 22 16 – Roof Board Insulation

| 07 22 16.10 Roof Deck Insulation | Crew | Daily Output | Labor-Hours | Unit | Material | 2008 Bare Costs Labor | Equipment | Total | Total Incl O&P |
|---|---|---|---|---|---|---|---|---|---|
| 0600 | 1-5/16" thick R5.26 | 1 Rofc | 1000 | .008 | S.F. | 1.26 | .26 | | 1.52 | 1.84 |
| 0650 | 2-1/16" thick R8.33 | | 800 | .010 | | 1.35 | .33 | | 1.68 | 2.05 |
| 0700 | 2-7/16" thick R10 | | 800 | .010 | | 1.55 | .33 | | 1.88 | 2.27 |
| 1500 | Foamglass, 1-1/2" thick R4.5 | | 800 | .010 | | 1.31 | .33 | | 1.64 | 2 |
| 1530 | 3" thick R9 | | 700 | .011 | ▼ | 2.67 | .38 | | 3.05 | 3.58 |
| 1600 | Tapered for drainage | | 600 | .013 | B.F. | 1.14 | .44 | | 1.58 | 2 |
| 1650 | Perlite, 1/2" thick R1.32 | | 1050 | .008 | S.F. | .33 | .25 | | .58 | .79 |
| 1655 | 3/4" thick R2.08 | | 800 | .010 | | .36 | .33 | | .69 | .96 |
| 1660 | 1" thick R2.78 | | 800 | .010 | | .45 | .33 | | .78 | 1.06 |
| 1670 | 1-1/2" thick R4.17 | | 800 | .010 | | .47 | .33 | | .80 | 1.08 |
| 1680 | 2" thick R5.56 | | 700 | .011 | | .79 | .38 | | 1.17 | 1.51 |
| 1685 | 2-1/2" thick R6.67 | | 700 | .011 | ▼ | .93 | .38 | | 1.31 | 1.66 |
| 1690 | Tapered for drainage | | 800 | .010 | B.F. | .72 | .33 | | 1.05 | 1.35 |
| 1700 | Polyisocyanurate, 2#/CF density, 3/4" thick, R5.1 | | 1500 | .005 | S.F. | .44 | .18 | | .62 | .78 |
| 1705 | 1" thick R7.14 | | 1400 | .006 | | .50 | .19 | | .69 | .87 |
| 1715 | 1-1/2" thick R10.87 | | 1250 | .006 | | .63 | .21 | | .84 | 1.05 |
| 1725 | 2" thick R14.29 | | 1100 | .007 | | .83 | .24 | | 1.07 | 1.32 |
| 1735 | 2-1/2" thick R16.67 | | 1050 | .008 | | 1.01 | .25 | | 1.26 | 1.54 |
| 1745 | 3" thick R21.74 | | 1000 | .008 | | 1.26 | .26 | | 1.52 | 1.84 |
| 1755 | 3-1/2" thick R25 | | 1000 | .008 | ▼ | 1.93 | .26 | | 2.19 | 2.57 |
| 1765 | Tapered for drainage | ▼ | 1400 | .006 | B.F. | 1.93 | .19 | | 2.12 | 2.44 |
| 1900 | Extruded Polystyrene | | | | | | | | | |
| 1910 | 15 PSI compressive strength, 1" thick, R5 | 1 Rofc | 1500 | .005 | S.F. | .49 | .18 | | .67 | .84 |
| 1920 | 2" thick, R10 | | 1250 | .006 | | .62 | .21 | | .83 | 1.04 |
| 1930 | 3" thick R15 | | 1000 | .008 | | 1.27 | .26 | | 1.53 | 1.85 |
| 1932 | 4" thick R20 | | 1000 | .008 | ▼ | 1.64 | .26 | | 1.90 | 2.25 |
| 1934 | Tapered for drainage | | 1500 | .005 | B.F. | .53 | .18 | | .71 | .88 |
| 1940 | 25 PSI compressive strength, 1" thick R5 | | 1500 | .005 | S.F. | .67 | .18 | | .85 | 1.04 |
| 1942 | 2" thick R10 | | 1250 | .006 | | 1.27 | .21 | | 1.48 | 1.76 |
| 1944 | 3" thick R15 | | 1000 | .008 | | 1.93 | .26 | | 2.19 | 2.57 |
| 1946 | 4" thick R20 | | 1000 | .008 | ▼ | 2.72 | .26 | | 2.98 | 3.44 |
| 1948 | Tapered for drainage | | 1500 | .005 | B.F. | .56 | .18 | | .74 | .92 |
| 1950 | 40 psi compressive strength, 1" thick R5 | | 1500 | .005 | S.F. | .51 | .18 | | .69 | .86 |
| 1952 | 2" thick R10 | | 1250 | .006 | | .96 | .21 | | 1.17 | 1.42 |
| 1954 | 3" thick R15 | | 1000 | .008 | | 1.40 | .26 | | 1.66 | 1.99 |
| 1956 | 4" thick R20 | | 1000 | .008 | ▼ | 1.88 | .26 | | 2.14 | 2.52 |
| 1958 | Tapered for drainage | | 1400 | .006 | B.F. | .71 | .19 | | .90 | 1.10 |
| 1960 | 60 PSI compressive strength, 1" thick R5 | | 1450 | .006 | S.F. | .59 | .18 | | .77 | .96 |
| 1962 | 2" thick R10 | | 1200 | .007 | | 1.05 | .22 | | 1.27 | 1.53 |
| 1964 | 3" thick R15 | | 975 | .008 | | 1.55 | .27 | | 1.82 | 2.17 |
| 1966 | 4" thick R20 | | 950 | .008 | ▼ | 2.17 | .28 | | 2.45 | 2.86 |
| 1968 | Tapered for drainage | | 1400 | .006 | B.F. | .85 | .19 | | 1.04 | 1.26 |
| 2010 | Expanded polystyrene, 1#/CF density, 3/4" thick R2.89 | | 1500 | .005 | S.F. | .31 | .18 | | .49 | .64 |
| 2020 | 1" thick R3.85 | | 1500 | .005 | | .31 | .18 | | .49 | .64 |
| 2100 | 2" thick R7.69 | | 1250 | .006 | | .62 | .21 | | .83 | 1.04 |
| 2110 | 3" thick R11.49 | | 1250 | .006 | | .91 | .21 | | 1.12 | 1.36 |
| 2120 | 4" thick R15.38 | | 1200 | .007 | | .83 | .22 | | 1.05 | 1.28 |
| 2130 | 5" thick R19.23 | | 1150 | .007 | | 1.05 | .23 | | 1.28 | 1.55 |
| 2140 | 6" thick R23.26 | | 1150 | .007 | ▼ | 1.23 | .23 | | 1.46 | 1.74 |
| 2150 | Tapered for drainage | ▼ | 1500 | .005 | B.F. | .49 | .18 | | .67 | .84 |
| 2400 | Composites with 2" EPS | | | | | | | | | |
| 2410 | 1" fiberboard | 1 Rofc | 950 | .008 | S.F. | 1.05 | .28 | | 1.33 | 1.63 |
| 2420 | 7/16" oriented strand board | ▼ | 800 | .010 | ▼ | 1.24 | .33 | | 1.57 | 1.92 |

189

# 07 22 Roof and Deck Insulation

## 07 22 16 – Roof Board Insulation

| 07 22 16.10 Roof Deck Insulation | Crew | Daily Output | Labor-Hours | Unit | Material | 2008 Bare Costs Labor | Equipment | Total | Total Incl O&P |
|---|---|---|---|---|---|---|---|---|---|
| 2430 | 1/2" plywood | 1 Rofc | 800 | .010 | S.F. | 1.34 | .33 | | 1.67 | 2.03 |
| 2440 | 1" perlite | ↓ | 800 | .010 | ↓ | 1.10 | .33 | | 1.43 | 1.77 |
| 2450 | Composites with 1-1/2" polyisocyanurate | | | | | | | | | |
| 2460 | 1" fiberboard | 1 Rofc | 800 | .010 | S.F. | 1.43 | .33 | | 1.76 | 2.13 |
| 2470 | 1" perlite | ↓ | 850 | .009 | ↓ | 1.50 | .31 | | 1.81 | 2.18 |
| 2480 | 7/16" oriented strand board | ↓ | 800 | .010 | ↓ | 1.74 | .33 | | 2.07 | 2.47 |

# 07 24 Exterior Insulation and Finish Systems

## 07 24 13 – Polymer Based Exterior Insulation and Finish Systems

### 07 24 13.10 Exterior Insulation and Finish Systems

| | | Crew | Daily Output | Labor-Hours | Unit | Material | 2008 Bare Costs Labor | Equipment | Total | Total Incl O&P |
|---|---|---|---|---|---|---|---|---|---|---|
| 0010 | **EXTERIOR INSULATION AND FINISH SYSTEMS** | | | | | | | | | |
| 0095 | Field applied, 1" EPS insulation | J-1 | 295 | .136 | S.F. | 2.18 | 4.53 | .41 | 7.12 | 9.70 |
| 0100 | With 1/2" cement board sheathing | | 220 | .182 | | 2.90 | 6.05 | .55 | 9.50 | 13 |
| 0105 | 2" EPS insulation | | 295 | .136 | | 2.55 | 4.53 | .41 | 7.49 | 10.10 |
| 0110 | With 1/2" cement board sheathing | | 220 | .182 | | 3.27 | 6.05 | .55 | 9.87 | 13.40 |
| 0115 | 3" EPS insulation | | 295 | .136 | | 2.72 | 4.53 | .41 | 7.66 | 10.30 |
| 0120 | With 1/2" cement board sheathing | | 220 | .182 | | 3.44 | 6.05 | .55 | 10.04 | 13.60 |
| 0125 | 4" EPS insulation | | 295 | .136 | | 3.16 | 4.53 | .41 | 8.10 | 10.80 |
| 0130 | With 1/2" cement board sheathing | | 220 | .182 | | 4.60 | 6.05 | .55 | 11.20 | 14.85 |
| 0140 | Premium finish add | | 1265 | .032 | | .31 | 1.06 | .10 | 1.47 | 2.05 |
| 0150 | Heavy duty reinforcement add | ↓ | 914 | .044 | ↓ | 1.08 | 1.46 | .13 | 2.67 | 3.56 |
| 0160 | 2.5#/S.Y. metal lath substrate add | 1 Lath | 75 | .107 | S.Y. | 2.37 | 3.71 | | 6.08 | 8.10 |
| 0170 | 3.4#/S.Y. metal lath substrate add | " | 75 | .107 | " | 2.58 | 3.71 | | 6.29 | 8.35 |
| 0180 | Color or texture change, | J-1 | 1265 | .032 | S.F. | .83 | 1.06 | .10 | 1.99 | 2.62 |
| 0190 | With substrate leveling base coat | 1 Plas | 530 | .015 | | .83 | .53 | | 1.36 | 1.71 |
| 0210 | With substrate sealing base coat | 1 Pord | 1224 | .007 | ↓ | .08 | .22 | | .30 | .42 |
| 0370 | V groove shape in panel face | | | | L.F. | .60 | | | .60 | .66 |
| 0380 | U groove shape in panel face | | | | " | .79 | | | .79 | .87 |
| 0440 | For higher than one story, add | | | | | | 25% | | | |

# 07 26 Vapor Retarders

## 07 26 10 – Vapor Retarders made of Natural and Synthetic Materials

### 07 26 10.10 Vapor Retarders

| | | Crew | Daily Output | Labor-Hours | Unit | Material | 2008 Bare Costs Labor | Equipment | Total | Total Incl O&P |
|---|---|---|---|---|---|---|---|---|---|---|
| 0010 | **VAPOR RETARDERS** | | | | | | | | | |
| 0020 | Aluminum and kraft laminated, foil 1 side | 1 Carp | 37 | .216 | Sq. | 5.15 | 8.25 | | 13.40 | 18.50 |
| 0100 | Foil 2 sides | ↓ | 37 | .216 | ↓ | 8.15 | 8.25 | | 16.40 | 22 |
| 0400 | Asphalt felt sheathing paper, 15# | ↓ | 37 | .216 | ↓ | 4.10 | 8.25 | | 12.35 | 17.30 |
| 0450 | Housewrap, exterior, spun bonded polypropylene | | | | | | | | | |
| 0470 | Small roll | 1 Carp | 3800 | .002 | S.F. | .24 | .08 | | .32 | .40 |
| 0480 | Large roll | " | 4000 | .002 | " | .13 | .08 | | .21 | .26 |
| 0500 | Material only, 3' x 111.1' roll | | | | Ea. | 81 | | | 81 | 89 |
| 0520 | 9' x 111.1' roll | | | | " | 131 | | | 131 | 144 |
| 0600 | Polyethylene vapor barrier, standard, .002" thick | 1 Carp | 37 | .216 | Sq. | 1.09 | 8.25 | | 9.34 | 14 |
| 0700 | .004" thick | | 37 | .216 | | 3.06 | 8.25 | | 11.31 | 16.15 |
| 0900 | .006" thick | | 37 | .216 | | 4.72 | 8.25 | | 12.97 | 18 |
| 1200 | .010" thick | | 37 | .216 | | 5.40 | 8.25 | | 13.65 | 18.75 |
| 1300 | Clear reinforced, fire retardant, .008" thick | | 37 | .216 | | 9.85 | 8.25 | | 18.10 | 23.50 |
| 1350 | Cross laminated type, .003" thick | | 37 | .216 | | 6.90 | 8.25 | | 15.15 | 20.50 |
| 1400 | .004" thick | ↓ | 37 | .216 | ↓ | 7.60 | 8.25 | | 15.85 | 21 |

# 07 26 Vapor Retarders

## 07 26 10 – Vapor Retarders made of Natural and Synthetic Materials

| 07 26 10.10 Vapor Retarders | | Crew | Daily Output | Labor-Hours | Unit | Material | 2008 Bare Costs Labor | Equipment | Total | Total Incl O&P |
|---|---|---|---|---|---|---|---|---|---|---|
| 1500 | Red rosin paper, 5 sq rolls, 4 lb per square | 1 Carp | 37 | .216 | Sq. | 2.11 | 8.25 | | 10.36 | 15.10 |
| 1600 | 5 lbs. per square | | 37 | .216 | | 2.83 | 8.25 | | 11.08 | 15.90 |
| 1800 | Reinf. waterproof, .002" polyethylene backing, 1 side | | 37 | .216 | | 5.15 | 8.25 | | 13.40 | 18.45 |
| 1900 | 2 sides | | 37 | .216 | | 6.75 | 8.25 | | 15 | 20.50 |
| 2100 | Asphalt felt roof deck vapor barrier, class 1 metal decks | 1 Rofc | 37 | .216 | | 15.10 | 7.15 | | 22.25 | 29 |
| 2200 | For all other decks | " | 37 | .216 | | 11 | 7.15 | | 18.15 | 24.50 |
| 2400 | Waterproofed kraft with sisal or fiberglass fibers, minimum | 1 Carp | 37 | .216 | | 5.55 | 8.25 | | 13.80 | 18.90 |
| 2500 | Maximum | " | 37 | .216 | | 13.75 | 8.25 | | 22 | 28 |

# 07 31 Shingles and Shakes

## 07 31 13 – Asphalt Shingles

### 07 31 13.10 Asphalt Roof Shingles

| | | | Crew | Daily Output | Labor-Hours | Unit | Material | 2008 Bare Costs Labor | Equipment | Total | Total Incl O&P |
|---|---|---|---|---|---|---|---|---|---|---|---|
| 0010 | **ASPHALT ROOF SHINGLES** | | | | | | | | | | |
| 0100 | Standard strip shingles | | | | | | | | | | |
| 0150 | Inorganic, class A, 210-235 lb/sq | CN | 1 Rofc | 5.50 | 1.455 | Sq. | 43 | 48 | | 91 | 129 |
| 0155 | Pneumatic nailed | | | 7 | 1.143 | | 43 | 37.50 | | 80.50 | 111 |
| 0200 | Organic, class C, 235-240 lb/sq | | | 5 | 1.600 | | 45.50 | 53 | | 98.50 | 141 |
| 0205 | Pneumatic nailed | | | 6.25 | 1.280 | | 45.50 | 42 | | 87.50 | 123 |
| 0250 | Standard, laminated multi-layered shingles | | | | | | | | | | |
| 0300 | Class A, 240-260 lb/sq | | 1 Rofc | 4.50 | 1.778 | Sq. | 53.50 | 58.50 | | 112 | 159 |
| 0305 | Pneumatic nailed | | | 5.63 | 1.422 | | 53.50 | 47 | | 100.50 | 139 |
| 0350 | Class C, 260-300 lb/square, 4 bundles/square | | | 4 | 2 | | 53 | 66 | | 119 | 171 |
| 0355 | Pneumatic nailed | | | 5 | 1.600 | | 53 | 53 | | 106 | 149 |
| 0400 | Premium, laminated multi-layered shingles | | | | | | | | | | |
| 0450 | Class A, 260-300 lb, 4 bundles/sq | | 1 Rofc | 3.50 | 2.286 | Sq. | 69.50 | 75.50 | | 145 | 205 |
| 0455 | Pneumatic nailed | | | 4.37 | 1.831 | | 69.50 | 60.50 | | 130 | 180 |
| 0500 | Class C, 300-385 lb/square, 5 bundles/square | | | 3 | 2.667 | | 78 | 88 | | 166 | 236 |
| 0505 | Pneumatic nailed | | | 3.75 | 2.133 | | 78 | 70.50 | | 148.50 | 206 |
| 0800 | #15 felt underlayment | | | 64 | .125 | | 4.10 | 4.13 | | 8.23 | 11.50 |
| 0825 | #30 felt underlayment | | | 58 | .138 | | 4.09 | 4.55 | | 8.64 | 12.25 |
| 0850 | Self adhering polyethylene and rubberized asphalt underlayment | | | 22 | .364 | | 51 | 12 | | 63 | 77 |
| 0900 | Ridge shingles | | | 330 | .024 | L.F. | 1.48 | .80 | | 2.28 | 2.99 |
| 0905 | Pneumatic nailed | | | 412.50 | .019 | " | 1.48 | .64 | | 2.12 | 2.72 |
| 1000 | For steep roofs (7 to 12 pitch or greater), add | | | | | | | 50% | | | |

## 07 31 16 – Metal Shingles

### 07 31 16.10 Aluminum Shingles

| | | | Crew | Daily Output | Labor-Hours | Unit | Material | 2008 Bare Costs Labor | Equipment | Total | Total Incl O&P |
|---|---|---|---|---|---|---|---|---|---|---|---|
| 0010 | **ALUMINUM SHINGLES** | | | | | | | | | | |
| 0020 | Mill finish, .019 thick | | 1 Carp | 5 | 1.600 | Sq. | 214 | 61 | | 275 | 330 |
| 0100 | .020" thick | | " | 5 | 1.600 | | 208 | 61 | | 269 | 325 |
| 0300 | For colors, add | | | | | | 16 | | | 16 | 17.60 |
| 0600 | Ridge cap, .024" thick | | 1 Carp | 170 | .047 | L.F. | 2.42 | 1.79 | | 4.21 | 5.45 |
| 0700 | End wall flashing, .024" thick | | | 170 | .047 | | 1.87 | 1.79 | | 3.66 | 4.85 |
| 0900 | Valley section, .024" thick | | | 170 | .047 | | 2.92 | 1.79 | | 4.71 | 6 |
| 1000 | Starter strip, .024" thick | | | 400 | .020 | | 1.61 | .76 | | 2.37 | 2.96 |
| 1200 | Side wall flashing, .024" thick | | | 170 | .047 | | 1.87 | 1.79 | | 3.66 | 4.85 |
| 1500 | Gable flashing, .024" thick | | | 400 | .020 | | 1.77 | .76 | | 2.53 | 3.14 |

### 07 31 16.20 Steel Shingles

| | | | Crew | Daily Output | Labor-Hours | Unit | Material | 2008 Bare Costs Labor | Equipment | Total | Total Incl O&P |
|---|---|---|---|---|---|---|---|---|---|---|---|
| 0010 | **STEEL SHINGLES** | | | | | | | | | | |
| 0012 | Galvanized, 26 gauge | | 1 Rots | 2.20 | 3.636 | Sq. | 194 | 120 | | 314 | 415 |
| 0200 | 24 gauge | | " | 2.20 | 3.636 | | 203 | 120 | | 323 | 430 |

# 07 31 Shingles and Shakes

## 07 31 16 – Metal Shingles

| 07 31 16.20 Steel Shingles | Crew | Daily Output | Labor-Hours | Unit | Material | 2008 Bare Costs Labor | Equipment | Total | Total Incl O&P |
|---|---|---|---|---|---|---|---|---|---|
| 0300 | For colored galvanized shingles, add | | | | Sq. | 53 | | | 53 | 58.50 |
| 0500 | For 1" factory applied polystyrene insulation, add | | | | ↓ | 39 | | | 39 | 43 |

## 07 31 19 – Mineral-Fiber Cement Shingles

### 07 31 19.10 Fiber Cement Shingles

| | | Crew | Daily Output | Labor-Hours | Unit | Material | Labor | Equipment | Total | Total Incl O&P |
|---|---|---|---|---|---|---|---|---|---|---|
| 0010 | **FIBER CEMENT SHINGLES** | | | | | | | | | |
| 0012 | Field shingles, 16" x 9.35", 500 lb per square | 1 Rofc | 2.20 | 3.636 | Sq. | 335 | 120 | | 455 | 575 |
| 0110 | Starters, 16" x 9.35" | | 3 | 2.667 | C.L.F. | 114 | 88 | | 202 | 275 |
| 0120 | Hip & ridge, 4.75" x 14" | | 1 | 8 | " | 825 | 264 | | 1,089 | 1,350 |
| 0200 | Shakes, 16" x 9.35", 550 lb per square | | 2.20 | 3.636 | Sq. | 305 | 120 | | 425 | 540 |
| 0300 | Hip & ridge, 4.75 x 14" | | 1 | 8 | C.L.F. | 825 | 264 | | 1,089 | 1,350 |
| 0400 | Hexagonal, 16" x 16" | | 3 | 2.667 | Sq. | 227 | 88 | | 315 | 400 |
| 0500 | Square, 16" x 16" | | 3 | 2.667 | " | 203 | 88 | | 291 | 375 |

## 07 31 26 – Slate Shingles

### 07 31 26.10 Slate Roof Shingles

| | | Crew | Daily Output | Labor-Hours | Unit | Material | Labor | Equipment | Total | Total Incl O&P |
|---|---|---|---|---|---|---|---|---|---|---|
| 0010 | **SLATE ROOF SHINGLES** R073126-20 | | | | | | | | | |
| 0100 | Buckingham Virginia black, 3/16" - 1/4" thick | 1 Rots | 1.75 | 4.571 | Sq. | 405 | 151 | | 556 | 705 |
| 0200 | 1/4" thick | | 1.75 | 4.571 | | 420 | 151 | | 571 | 720 |
| 0900 | Pennsylvania black, Bangor, #1 clear | | 1.75 | 4.571 | | 490 | 151 | | 641 | 795 |
| 1200 | Vermont, unfading, green, mottled green | | 1.75 | 4.571 | | 450 | 151 | | 601 | 750 |
| 1300 | Semi-weathering green & gray | | 1.75 | 4.571 | | 355 | 151 | | 506 | 645 |
| 1400 | Purple | | 1.75 | 4.571 | | 405 | 151 | | 556 | 700 |
| 1500 | Black or gray | | 1.75 | 4.571 | | 460 | 151 | | 611 | 760 |
| 1600 | Red | | 1.75 | 4.571 | | 1,150 | 151 | | 1,301 | 1,525 |
| 1700 | Variegated purple | | 1.75 | 4.571 | | 420 | 151 | | 571 | 720 |

## 07 31 29 – Wood Shingles and Shakes

### 07 31 29.13 Wood Shingles

| | | Crew | Daily Output | Labor-Hours | Unit | Material | Labor | Equipment | Total | Total Incl O&P |
|---|---|---|---|---|---|---|---|---|---|---|
| 0010 | **WOOD SHINGLES** | | | | | | | | | |
| 0012 | 16" No. 1 red cedar shingles, 5" exposure, on roof | 1 Carp | 2.50 | 3.200 | Sq. | 231 | 122 | | 353 | 445 |
| 0015 | Pneumatic nailed | | 3.25 | 2.462 | | 231 | 94 | | 325 | 400 |
| 0200 | 7-1/2" exposure, on walls | | 2.05 | 3.902 | | 154 | 149 | | 303 | 400 |
| 0205 | Pneumatic nailed | | 2.67 | 2.996 | | 154 | 114 | | 268 | 345 |
| 0300 | 18" No. 1 red cedar perfections, 5-1/2" exposure, on roof | | 2.75 | 2.909 | | 266 | 111 | | 377 | 465 |
| 0305 | Pneumatic nailed | | 3.57 | 2.241 | | 266 | 85.50 | | 351.50 | 425 |
| 0500 | 7-1/2" exposure, on walls | | 2.25 | 3.556 | | 196 | 135 | | 331 | 425 |
| 0505 | Pneumatic nailed | | 2.92 | 2.740 | | 196 | 104 | | 300 | 375 |
| 0600 | Resquared, and rebutted, 5-1/2" exposure, on roof | | 3 | 2.667 | | 320 | 102 | | 422 | 515 |
| 0605 | Pneumatic nailed | | 3.90 | 2.051 | | 320 | 78 | | 398 | 475 |
| 0900 | 7-1/2" exposure, on walls | | 2.45 | 3.265 | | 237 | 124 | | 361 | 455 |
| 0905 | Pneumatic nailed | | 3.18 | 2.516 | | 237 | 96 | | 333 | 410 |
| 1000 | Add to above for fire retardant shingles, 16" long | | | | | 42 | | | 42 | 46 |
| 1050 | 18" long | | | | ↓ | 42 | | | 42 | 46 |
| 1060 | Preformed ridge shingles | 1 Carp | 400 | .020 | L.F. | 1.75 | .76 | | 2.51 | 3.12 |
| 2000 | White cedar shingles, 16" long, extras, 5" exposure, on roof | | 2.40 | 3.333 | Sq. | 178 | 127 | | 305 | 395 |
| 2005 | Pneumatic nailed | | 3.12 | 2.564 | | 178 | 97.50 | | 275.50 | 350 |
| 2050 | 5" exposure on walls | | 2 | 4 | | 178 | 152 | | 330 | 435 |
| 2055 | Pneumatic nailed | | 2.60 | 3.077 | | 178 | 117 | | 295 | 380 |
| 2100 | 7-1/2" exposure, on walls | | 2 | 4 | | 127 | 152 | | 279 | 375 |
| 2105 | Pneumatic nailed | | 2.60 | 3.077 | | 127 | 117 | | 244 | 320 |
| 2150 | "B" grade, 5" exposure on walls | | 2 | 4 | | 150 | 152 | | 302 | 400 |
| 2155 | Pneumatic nailed | | 2.60 | 3.077 | | 150 | 117 | | 267 | 345 |
| 2300 | For 15# organic felt underlayment on roof, 1 layer, add | | 64 | .125 | | 4.10 | 4.76 | | 8.36 | 11.90 |

# 07 31 Shingles and Shakes

## 07 31 29 – Wood Shingles and Shakes

### 07 31 29.13 Wood Shingles

| | | Crew | Daily Output | Labor-Hours | Unit | Material | 2008 Bare Costs Labor | Equipment | Total | Total Incl O&P |
|---|---|---|---|---|---|---|---|---|---|---|
| 2400 | 2 layers, add | 1 Carp | 32 | .250 | Sq. | 8.20 | 9.55 | | 17.75 | 24 |
| 2600 | For steep roofs (7/12 pitch or greater), add to above | | | | ↓ | | 50% | | | |
| 2700 | Panelized systems, No.1 cedar shingles on 5/16" CDX plywood | | | | | | | | | |
| 2800 | On walls, 8' strips, 7" or 14" exposure | 2 Carp | 700 | .023 | S.F. | 4 | .87 | | 4.87 | 5.75 |
| 3500 | On roofs, 8' strips, 7" or 14" exposure | 1 Carp | 3 | 2.667 | Sq. | 365 | 102 | | 467 | 560 |
| 3505 | Pneumatic nailed | " | 4 | 2 | " | 365 | 76 | | 441 | 520 |

### 07 31 29.16 Wood Shakes

| | | Crew | Daily Output | Labor-Hours | Unit | Material | 2008 Bare Costs Labor | Equipment | Total | Total Incl O&P |
|---|---|---|---|---|---|---|---|---|---|---|
| 0010 | **WOOD SHAKES** | | | | | | | | | |
| 1100 | Hand-split red cedar shakes, 1/2" thick x 24" long, 10" exp. on roof | 1 Carp | 2.50 | 3.200 | Sq. | 228 | 122 | | 350 | 440 |
| 1105 | Pneumatic nailed | | 3.25 | 2.462 | | 228 | 94 | | 322 | 395 |
| 1110 | 3/4" thick x 24" long, 10" exp. on roof | | 2.25 | 3.556 | | 228 | 135 | | 363 | 460 |
| 1115 | Pneumatic nailed | | 2.92 | 2.740 | | 228 | 104 | | 332 | 415 |
| 1200 | 1/2" thick, 18" long, 8-1/2" exp. on roof | | 2 | 4 | | 192 | 152 | | 344 | 450 |
| 1205 | Pneumatic nailed | | 2.60 | 3.077 | | 192 | 117 | | 309 | 395 |
| 1210 | 3/4" thick x 18" long, 8 1/2" exp. on roof | | 1.80 | 4.444 | | 192 | 169 | | 361 | 475 |
| 1215 | Pneumatic nailed | | 2.34 | 3.419 | | 192 | 130 | | 322 | 415 |
| 1255 | 10" exp. on walls | | 2 | 4 | | 186 | 152 | | 338 | 440 |
| 1260 | 10" exposure on walls, pneumatic nailed | ↓ | 2.60 | 3.077 | | 186 | 117 | | 303 | 385 |
| 1700 | Add to above for fire retardant shakes, 24" long | | | | | 42 | | | 42 | 46 |
| 1800 | 18" long | | | | ↓ | 42 | | | 42 | 46 |
| 1810 | Ridge shakes | 1 Carp | 350 | .023 | L.F. | 3 | .87 | | 3.87 | 4.66 |

# 07 32 Roof Tiles

## 07 32 13 – Clay Roof Tiles

### 07 32 13.10 Clay Tiles

| | | Crew | Daily Output | Labor-Hours | Unit | Material | 2008 Bare Costs Labor | Equipment | Total | Total Incl O&P |
|---|---|---|---|---|---|---|---|---|---|---|
| 0010 | **CLAY TILES** | | | | | | | | | |
| 0200 | Lanai tile or Classic tile, 158 pc per sq | 1 Rots | 1.65 | 4.848 | Sq. | 500 | 160 | | 660 | 820 |
| 0300 | Americana, 158 pc per sq, most colors | | 1.65 | 4.848 | | 645 | 160 | | 805 | 980 |
| 0350 | Green, gray or brown | | 1.65 | 4.848 | | 625 | 160 | | 785 | 955 |
| 0400 | Blue | | 1.65 | 4.848 | | 625 | 160 | | 785 | 955 |
| 0600 | Spanish tile, 171 pc per sq, red | | 1.80 | 4.444 | | 315 | 147 | | 462 | 595 |
| 0800 | Blend | | 1.80 | 4.444 | | 600 | 147 | | 747 | 910 |
| 0900 | Glazed white | | 1.80 | 4.444 | | 665 | 147 | | 812 | 980 |
| 1100 | Mission tile, 192 pc per sq, machine scored finish, red | | 1.15 | 6.957 | | 740 | 230 | | 970 | 1,200 |
| 1700 | French tile, 133 pc per sq, smooth finish, red | | 1.35 | 5.926 | | 675 | 196 | | 871 | 1,075 |
| 1750 | Blue or green | | 1.35 | 5.926 | | 870 | 196 | | 1,066 | 1,300 |
| 1800 | Norman black 317 pc per sq | | 1 | 8 | | 990 | 264 | | 1,254 | 1,525 |
| 2200 | Williamsburg tile, 158 pc per sq, aged cedar | | 1.35 | 5.926 | | 595 | 196 | | 791 | 990 |
| 2250 | Gray or green | | 1.35 | 5.926 | | 595 | 196 | | 791 | 990 |
| 2510 | One piece mission tile, natural red, 75 pc per square | | 1.65 | 4.848 | | 231 | 160 | | 391 | 525 |
| 2530 | Mission Tile, 134 pc per square | ↓ | 1.15 | 6.957 | ↓ | 263 | 230 | | 493 | 680 |

## 07 32 16 – Concrete Roof Tiles

### 07 32 16.10 Concrete Tiles

| | | Crew | Daily Output | Labor-Hours | Unit | Material | 2008 Bare Costs Labor | Equipment | Total | Total Incl O&P |
|---|---|---|---|---|---|---|---|---|---|---|
| 0010 | **CONCRETE TILES** | | | | | | | | | |
| 0020 | Corrugated, 13" x 16-1/2", 90 per sq, 950 lb per sq | | | | | | | | | |
| 0050 | Earthtone colors, nailed to wood deck | 1 Rots | 1.35 | 5.926 | Sq. | 96.50 | 196 | | 292.50 | 440 |
| 0150 | Blues | | 1.35 | 5.926 | | 97.50 | 196 | | 293.50 | 440 |
| 0200 | Greens | | 1.35 | 5.926 | ↓ | 97.50 | 196 | | 293.50 | 440 |
| 0250 | Premium colors | ↓ | 1.35 | 5.926 | | 214 | 196 | | 410 | 570 |
| 0500 | Shakes, 13" x 16-1/2", 90 per sq, 950 lb per sq | | | | | | | | | |

# 07 32 Roof Tiles

## 07 32 16 – Concrete Roof Tiles

| 07 32 16.10 Concrete Tiles | Crew | Daily Output | Labor-Hours | Unit | Material | 2008 Bare Costs Labor | Equipment | Total | Total Incl O&P |
|---|---|---|---|---|---|---|---|---|---|
| 0600 | All colors, nailed to wood deck | 1 Rots | 1.50 | 5.333 | Sq. | 252 | 176 | | 428 | 575 |
| 1500 | Accessory pieces, ridge & hip, 10" x 16-1/2", 8 lbs. each | | | | Ea. | 3.40 | | | 3.40 | 3.74 |
| 1700 | Rake, 6-1/2" x 16-3/4", 9 lbs. each | | | | | 3.40 | | | 3.40 | 3.74 |
| 1800 | Mansard hip, 10" x 16-1/2", 9.2 lbs. each | | | | | 3.40 | | | 3.40 | 3.74 |
| 1900 | Hip starter, 10" x 16-1/2", 10.5 lbs. each | | | | | 10.70 | | | 10.70 | 11.80 |
| 2000 | 3 or 4 way apex, 10" each side, 11.5 lbs. each | | | | | 12.35 | | | 12.35 | 13.60 |

## 07 32 19 – Metal Roof Tiles

### 07 32 19.10 Aluminum Roof Tiles

| | | Crew | Daily Output | Labor-Hours | Unit | Material | Labor | Equipment | Total | Total Incl O&P |
|---|---|---|---|---|---|---|---|---|---|---|
| 0010 | **ALUMINUM ROOF TILES** | | | | | | | | | |
| 0020 | Accessories included, .032" thick, mission tile | 1 Carp | 2.50 | 3.200 | Sq. | 725 | 122 | | 847 | 990 |
| 0200 | Spanish tiles | " | 3 | 2.667 | " | 500 | 102 | | 602 | 710 |

# 07 41 Roof Panels

## 07 41 13 – Metal Roof Panels

### 07 41 13.10 Aluminum Roof Panels

| | | Crew | Daily Output | Labor-Hours | Unit | Material | Labor | Equipment | Total | Total Incl O&P |
|---|---|---|---|---|---|---|---|---|---|---|
| 0010 | **ALUMINUM ROOF PANELS** | | | | | | | | | |
| 0020 | Corrugated or ribbed, .0155" thick, natural | G-3 | 1200 | .027 | S.F. | .76 | 1.01 | | 1.77 | 2.40 |
| 0300 | Painted | | 1200 | .027 | | 1.10 | 1.01 | | 2.11 | 2.77 |
| 0400 | Corrugated, .018" thick, on steel frame, natural finish | | 1200 | .027 | | 1 | 1.01 | | 2.01 | 2.66 |
| 0600 | Painted | | 1200 | .027 | | 1.23 | 1.01 | | 2.24 | 2.91 |
| 0700 | Corrugated, on steel frame, natural, .024" thick | | 1200 | .027 | | 1.43 | 1.01 | | 2.44 | 3.13 |
| 0800 | Painted | | 1200 | .027 | | 1.73 | 1.01 | | 2.74 | 3.46 |
| 0900 | .032" thick, natural | | 1200 | .027 | | 1.83 | 1.01 | | 2.84 | 3.57 |
| 1200 | Painted | | 1200 | .027 | | 2.35 | 1.01 | | 3.36 | 4.15 |
| 1300 | V-Beam, on steel frame construction, .032" thick, natural | | 1200 | .027 | | 1.94 | 1.01 | | 2.95 | 3.69 |
| 1500 | Painted | | 1200 | .027 | | 2.38 | 1.01 | | 3.39 | 4.18 |
| 1600 | .040" thick, natural | | 1200 | .027 | | 2.36 | 1.01 | | 3.37 | 4.16 |
| 1800 | Painted | | 1200 | .027 | | 2.84 | 1.01 | | 3.85 | 4.68 |
| 1900 | .050" thick, natural | | 1200 | .027 | | 2.83 | 1.01 | | 3.84 | 4.67 |
| 2100 | Painted | | 1200 | .027 | | 3.42 | 1.01 | | 4.43 | 5.30 |
| 2200 | For roofing on wood frame, deduct | | 4600 | .007 | | .06 | .26 | | .32 | .48 |
| 2400 | Ridge cap, .032" thick, natural | | 800 | .040 | L.F. | 2.24 | 1.51 | | 3.75 | 4.80 |

### 07 41 13.20 Steel Roofing Panels

| | | Crew | Daily Output | Labor-Hours | Unit | Material | Labor | Equipment | Total | Total Incl O&P |
|---|---|---|---|---|---|---|---|---|---|---|
| 0010 | **STEEL ROOFING PANELS** | | | | | | | | | |
| 0012 | Corrugated or ribbed, on steel framing, 30 ga galv | G-3 | 1100 | .029 | S.F. | 1.50 | 1.10 | | 2.60 | 3.35 |
| 0100 | 28 ga | | 1050 | .030 | | 1.60 | 1.15 | | 2.75 | 3.54 |
| 0300 | 26 ga | | 1000 | .032 | | 1.12 | 1.21 | | 2.33 | 3.10 |
| 0400 | 24 ga | | 950 | .034 | | 2.60 | 1.27 | | 3.87 | 4.83 |
| 0600 | Colored, 28 ga | | 1050 | .030 | | 1.50 | 1.15 | | 2.65 | 3.43 |
| 0700 | 26 ga | | 1000 | .032 | | 1.78 | 1.21 | | 2.99 | 3.83 |
| 0710 | Flat profile, 1-3/4" standing seams, 10" wide, standard finish, 26 ga | | 1000 | .032 | | 3.47 | 1.21 | | 4.68 | 5.70 |
| 0715 | 24 ga | | 950 | .034 | | 4.03 | 1.27 | | 5.30 | 6.40 |
| 0720 | 22 ga | | 900 | .036 | | 4.97 | 1.34 | | 6.31 | 7.55 |
| 0725 | Zinc aluminum alloy finish, 26 ga | | 1000 | .032 | | 2.72 | 1.21 | | 3.93 | 4.86 |
| 0730 | 24 ga | | 950 | .034 | | 3.25 | 1.27 | | 4.52 | 5.55 |
| 0735 | 22 ga | | 900 | .036 | | 3.72 | 1.34 | | 5.06 | 6.15 |
| 0740 | 12" wide, standard finish, 26 ga | | 1000 | .032 | | 3.46 | 1.21 | | 4.67 | 5.70 |
| 0745 | 24 ga | | 950 | .034 | | 4.55 | 1.27 | | 5.82 | 6.95 |
| 0750 | Zinc aluminum alloy finish, 26 ga | | 1000 | .032 | | 3.94 | 1.21 | | 5.15 | 6.20 |
| 0755 | 24 ga | | 950 | .034 | | 3.24 | 1.27 | | 4.51 | 5.55 |

# 07 41 Roof Panels

## 07 41 13 – Metal Roof Panels

### 07 41 13.20 Steel Roofing Panels

| | | Crew | Daily Output | Labor-Hours | Unit | Material | 2008 Bare Costs Labor | Equipment | Total | Total Incl O&P |
|---|---|---|---|---|---|---|---|---|---|---|
| 0840 | Flat profile, 1" x 3/8" batten, 12" wide, standard finish, 26 ga | G-3 | 1000 | .032 | S.F. | 3.05 | 1.21 | | 4.26 | 5.25 |
| 0845 | 24 ga | | 950 | .034 | | 3.58 | 1.27 | | 4.85 | 5.90 |
| 0850 | 22 ga | | 900 | .036 | | 4.29 | 1.34 | | 5.63 | 6.80 |
| 0855 | Zinc aluminum alloy finish, 26 ga | | 1000 | .032 | | 2.93 | 1.21 | | 4.14 | 5.10 |
| 0860 | 24 ga | | 950 | .034 | | 3.27 | 1.27 | | 4.54 | 5.55 |
| 0865 | 22 ga | | 900 | .036 | | 3.78 | 1.34 | | 5.12 | 6.25 |
| 0870 | 16-1/2" wide, standard finish, 24 ga | | 950 | .034 | | 3.53 | 1.27 | | 4.80 | 5.85 |
| 0875 | 22 ga | | 900 | .036 | | 3.95 | 1.34 | | 5.29 | 6.45 |
| 0880 | Zinc aluminum alloy finish, 24 ga | | 950 | .034 | | 3.08 | 1.27 | | 4.35 | 5.35 |
| 0885 | 22 ga | | 900 | .036 | | 3.44 | 1.34 | | 4.78 | 5.85 |
| 0890 | Flat profile, 2" x 2" batten, 12" wide, standard finish, 26 ga | | 1000 | .032 | | 3.51 | 1.21 | | 4.72 | 5.75 |
| 0895 | 24 ga | | 950 | .034 | | 4.19 | 1.27 | | 5.46 | 6.60 |
| 0900 | 22 ga | | 900 | .036 | | 5.15 | 1.34 | | 6.49 | 7.75 |
| 0905 | Zinc aluminum alloy finish, 26 ga | | 1000 | .032 | | 3.27 | 1.21 | | 4.48 | 5.45 |
| 0910 | 24 ga | | 950 | .034 | | 3.73 | 1.27 | | 5 | 6.05 |
| 0915 | 22 ga | | 900 | .036 | | 4.35 | 1.34 | | 5.69 | 6.85 |
| 0920 | 16-1/2" wide, standard finish, 24 ga | | 950 | .034 | | 3.86 | 1.27 | | 5.13 | 6.20 |
| 0925 | 22 ga | | 900 | .036 | | 4.51 | 1.34 | | 5.85 | 7.05 |
| 0930 | Zinc aluminum alloy finish, 24 ga | | 950 | .034 | | 3.49 | 1.27 | | 4.76 | 5.80 |
| 0935 | 22 ga | | 900 | .036 | | 3.97 | 1.34 | | 5.31 | 6.45 |
| 1200 | Ridge, galvanized, 10" wide | | 800 | .040 | L.F. | 2.84 | 1.51 | | 4.35 | 5.45 |
| 1210 | 20" wide | | 750 | .043 | " | 4.40 | 1.61 | | 6.01 | 7.35 |

## 07 41 33 – Plastic Roof Panels

### 07 41 33.10 Fiberglass Panels

| | | Crew | Daily Output | Labor-Hours | Unit | Material | 2008 Bare Costs Labor | Equipment | Total | Total Incl O&P |
|---|---|---|---|---|---|---|---|---|---|---|
| 0010 | **FIBERGLASS PANELS** | | | | | | | | | |
| 0012 | Corrugated panels, roofing, 8 oz per SF | G-3 | 1000 | .032 | S.F. | 1.58 | 1.21 | | 2.79 | 3.61 |
| 0100 | 12 oz per SF | | 1000 | .032 | | 3.43 | 1.21 | | 4.64 | 5.65 |
| 0300 | Corrugated siding, 6 oz per SF | | 880 | .036 | | 1.58 | 1.37 | | 2.95 | 3.87 |
| 0400 | 8 oz per SF | | 880 | .036 | | 1.58 | 1.37 | | 2.95 | 3.87 |
| 0500 | Fire retardant | | 880 | .036 | | 3.21 | 1.37 | | 4.58 | 5.65 |
| 0600 | 12 oz. siding, textured | | 880 | .036 | | 3.32 | 1.37 | | 4.69 | 5.80 |
| 0700 | Fire retardant | | 880 | .036 | | 4.39 | 1.37 | | 5.76 | 6.95 |
| 0900 | Flat panels, 6 oz per SF, clear or colors | | 880 | .036 | | 1.83 | 1.37 | | 3.20 | 4.14 |
| 1100 | Fire retardant, class A | | 880 | .036 | | 3.18 | 1.37 | | 4.55 | 5.65 |
| 1300 | 8 oz per SF, clear or colors | | 880 | .036 | | 2.38 | 1.37 | | 3.75 | 4.75 |
| 1700 | Sandwich panels, fiberglass, 1-9/16" thick, panels to 20 SF | | 180 | .178 | | 23 | 6.70 | | 29.70 | 36 |
| 1900 | As above, but 2-3/4" thick, panels to 100 SF | | 265 | .121 | | 17.05 | 4.56 | | 21.61 | 26 |

# 07 42 Wall Panels

## 07 42 13 – Metal Wall Panels

### 07 42 13.10 Mansard Panels

| | | Crew | Daily Output | Labor-Hours | Unit | Material | 2008 Bare Costs Labor | Equipment | Total | Total Incl O&P |
|---|---|---|---|---|---|---|---|---|---|---|
| 0010 | **MANSARD PANELS** | | | | | | | | | |
| 0600 | Aluminum, stock units, straight surfaces | 1 Shee | 115 | .070 | S.F. | 2.64 | 3.15 | | 5.79 | 7.75 |
| 0700 | Concave or convex surfaces | | 75 | .107 | " | 2.90 | 4.83 | | 7.73 | 10.65 |
| 0800 | For framing, to 5' high, add | | 115 | .070 | L.F. | 2.90 | 3.15 | | 6.05 | 8.05 |
| 0900 | Soffits, to 1' wide | | 125 | .064 | S.F. | 1.44 | 2.90 | | 4.34 | 6.05 |

### 07 42 13.20 Aluminum Siding Panels

| | | Crew | Daily Output | Labor-Hours | Unit | Material | 2008 Bare Costs Labor | Equipment | Total | Total Incl O&P |
|---|---|---|---|---|---|---|---|---|---|---|
| 0010 | **ALUMINUM SIDING PANELS** | | | | | | | | | |
| 0012 | Corrugated, on steel framing, .019 thick, natural finish | G-3 | 775 | .041 | S.F. | 1.17 | 1.56 | | 2.73 | 3.70 |
| 0100 | Painted | | 775 | .041 | | 1.26 | 1.56 | | 2.82 | 3.80 |

# 07 42 Wall Panels

## 07 42 13 – Metal Wall Panels

| 07 42 13.20 Aluminum Siding Panels | Crew | Daily Output | Labor-Hours | Unit | Material | 2008 Bare Costs Labor | Equipment | Total | Total Incl O&P |
|---|---|---|---|---|---|---|---|---|---|
| 0400 | Farm type, .021" thick on steel frame, natural | G-3 | 775 | .041 | S.F. | 1.18 | 1.56 | | 2.74 | 3.71 |
| 0600 | Painted | | 775 | .041 | | 1.26 | 1.56 | | 2.82 | 3.80 |
| 0700 | Industrial type, corrugated, on steel, .024" thick, mill | | 775 | .041 | | 1.64 | 1.56 | | 3.20 | 4.21 |
| 0900 | Painted | | 775 | .041 | | 1.77 | 1.56 | | 3.33 | 4.36 |
| 1000 | .032" thick, mill | | 775 | .041 | | 1.89 | 1.56 | | 3.45 | 4.49 |
| 1200 | Painted | | 775 | .041 | | 2.31 | 1.56 | | 3.87 | 4.95 |
| 1300 | V-Beam, on steel frame, .032" thick, mill | | 775 | .041 | | 2.13 | 1.56 | | 3.69 | 4.75 |
| 1500 | Painted | | 775 | .041 | | 2.44 | 1.56 | | 4 | 5.10 |
| 1600 | .040" thick, mill | | 775 | .041 | | 2.59 | 1.56 | | 4.15 | 5.25 |
| 1800 | Painted | | 775 | .041 | | 3.03 | 1.56 | | 4.59 | 5.75 |
| 1900 | .050" thick, mill | | 775 | .041 | | 3.06 | 1.56 | | 4.62 | 5.80 |
| 2100 | Painted | | 775 | .041 | | 3.65 | 1.56 | | 5.21 | 6.45 |
| 2200 | Ribbed, 3" profile, on steel frame, .032" thick, natural | | 775 | .041 | | 1.84 | 1.56 | | 3.40 | 4.43 |
| 2400 | Painted | | 775 | .041 | | 2.34 | 1.56 | | 3.90 | 4.98 |
| 2500 | .040" thick, natural | | 775 | .041 | | 2.10 | 1.56 | | 3.66 | 4.72 |
| 2700 | Painted | | 775 | .041 | | 2.46 | 1.56 | | 4.02 | 5.10 |
| 2750 | .050" thick, natural | | 775 | .041 | | 2.43 | 1.56 | | 3.99 | 5.10 |
| 2760 | Painted | | 775 | .041 | | 2.78 | 1.56 | | 4.34 | 5.45 |
| 3300 | For siding on wood frame, deduct from above | | 2800 | .011 | | .07 | .43 | | .50 | .75 |
| 3400 | Screw fasteners, aluminum, self tapping, neoprene washer, 1" | | | | M | 159 | | | 159 | 175 |
| 3600 | Stitch screws, self tapping, with neoprene washer, 5/8" | | | | " | 120 | | | 120 | 131 |
| 3630 | Flashing, sidewall, .032" thick | G-3 | 800 | .040 | L.F. | 2.21 | 1.51 | | 3.72 | 4.77 |
| 3650 | End wall, .040" thick | | 800 | .040 | | 2.58 | 1.51 | | 4.09 | 5.20 |
| 3670 | Closure strips, corrugated, .032" thick | | 800 | .040 | | .65 | 1.51 | | 2.16 | 3.06 |
| 3680 | Ribbed, 4" or 8", .032" thick | | 800 | .040 | | .65 | 1.51 | | 2.16 | 3.06 |
| 3690 | V-beam, .040" thick | | 800 | .040 | | .89 | 1.51 | | 2.40 | 3.32 |
| 3800 | Horizontal, colored clapboard, 8" wide, plain | 2 Carp | 515 | .031 | S.F. | 1.36 | 1.18 | | 2.54 | 3.34 |
| 3810 | Insulated | | 515 | .031 | | 1.34 | 1.18 | | 2.52 | 3.31 |
| 4000 | Vertical board & batten, colored, non-insulated | | 515 | .031 | | 1.33 | 1.18 | | 2.51 | 3.30 |
| 4200 | For simulated wood design, add | | | | | .09 | | | .09 | .10 |
| 4300 | Corners for above, outside | 2 Carp | 515 | .031 | V.L.F. | 2.05 | 1.18 | | 3.23 | 4.10 |
| 4500 | Inside corners | " | 515 | .031 | " | 1.21 | 1.18 | | 2.39 | 3.17 |
| 4600 | Sandwich panels, 1" insulation, single story | G-3 | 395 | .081 | S.F. | 5.95 | 3.06 | | 9.01 | 11.30 |
| 4900 | Multi-story | " | 345 | .093 | | 8.35 | 3.50 | | 11.85 | 14.60 |
| 5100 | For baked enamel finish 1 side, add | | | | | .32 | | | .32 | .35 |

## 07 42 13.30 Steel Siding

| | | Crew | Daily Output | Labor-Hours | Unit | Material | 2008 Bare Costs Labor | Equipment | Total | Total Incl O&P |
|---|---|---|---|---|---|---|---|---|---|---|
| 0010 | **STEEL SIDING** | | | | | | | | | |
| 0020 | Beveled, vinyl coated, 8" wide | 1 Carp | 265 | .030 | S.F. | 1.62 | 1.15 | | 2.77 | 3.57 |
| 0050 | 10" wide | " | 275 | .029 | | 1.73 | 1.11 | | 2.84 | 3.63 |
| 0080 | Galv, corrugated or ribbed, on steel frame, 30 gauge | G-3 | 800 | .040 | | 1.08 | 1.51 | | 2.59 | 3.53 |
| 0100 | 28 gauge | | 795 | .040 | | 1.13 | 1.52 | | 2.65 | 3.59 |
| 0300 | 26 gauge | | 790 | .041 | | 1.59 | 1.53 | | 3.12 | 4.12 |
| 0400 | 24 gauge | | 785 | .041 | | 1.60 | 1.54 | | 3.14 | 4.14 |
| 0600 | 22 gauge | | 770 | .042 | | 1.84 | 1.57 | | 3.41 | 4.45 |
| 0700 | Colored, corrugated/ribbed, on steel frame, 10 yr fnsh, 28 ga. | | 800 | .040 | | 1.68 | 1.51 | | 3.19 | 4.19 |
| 0900 | 26 gauge | | 795 | .040 | | 1.76 | 1.52 | | 3.28 | 4.29 |
| 1000 | 24 gauge | | 790 | .041 | | 2.04 | 1.53 | | 3.57 | 4.61 |
| 1020 | 20 gauge | | 785 | .041 | | 2.59 | 1.54 | | 4.13 | 5.25 |
| 1200 | Factory sandwich panel, 26 ga., 1" insulation, galvanized | | 380 | .084 | | 4.31 | 3.18 | | 7.49 | 9.65 |
| 1300 | Colored 1 side | | 380 | .084 | | 5.25 | 3.18 | | 8.43 | 10.70 |
| 1500 | Galvanized 2 sides | | 380 | .084 | | 6.55 | 3.18 | | 9.73 | 12.10 |
| 1600 | Colored 2 sides | | 380 | .084 | | 6.80 | 3.18 | | 9.98 | 12.35 |

# 07 42 Wall Panels

## 07 42 13 - Metal Wall Panels

### 07 42 13.30 Steel Siding

| | 07 42 13.30 Steel Siding | Crew | Daily Output | Labor-Hours | Unit | Material | 2008 Bare Costs Labor | Equipment | Total | Total Incl O&P |
|---|---|---|---|---|---|---|---|---|---|---|
| 1800 | Acrylic paint face, regular paint liner | G-3 | 380 | .084 | S.F. | 5.10 | 3.18 | | 8.28 | 10.50 |
| 1900 | For 2" thick polystyrene, add | | | | | .79 | | | .79 | .87 |
| 2000 | 22 ga, galv, 2" insulation, baked enamel exterior | G-3 | 360 | .089 | | 10 | 3.36 | | 13.36 | 16.20 |
| 2100 | Polyvinylidene exterior finish | " | 360 | .089 | | 10.55 | 3.36 | | 13.91 | 16.80 |

# 07 44 Faced Panels

## 07 44 13 - Aggregate Coated Panels

### 07 44 13.10 Exposed Aggregate Panels

| | | Crew | Daily Output | Labor-Hours | Unit | Material | 2008 Bare Costs Labor | Equipment | Total | Total Incl O&P |
|---|---|---|---|---|---|---|---|---|---|---|
| 0010 | **EXPOSED AGGREGATE PANELS** | | | | | | | | | |
| 1400 | Fiberglass polymer back-up, | | | | | | | | | |
| 1500 | Small size aggregate | F-3 | 445 | .090 | S.F. | 5.05 | 3.48 | 1.72 | 10.25 | 12.80 |
| 1600 | Medium size aggregate | | 445 | .090 | | 5.70 | 3.48 | 1.72 | 10.90 | 13.50 |
| 1700 | Large size aggregate | | 445 | .090 | | 5.85 | 3.48 | 1.72 | 11.05 | 13.70 |

## 07 44 73 - Metal Faced Panels

### 07 44 73.10 Metal Faced Panels and Accessories

| | | Crew | Daily Output | Labor-Hours | Unit | Material | 2008 Bare Costs Labor | Equipment | Total | Total Incl O&P |
|---|---|---|---|---|---|---|---|---|---|---|
| 0010 | **METAL FACED PANELS AND ACCESSORIES** | | | | | | | | | |
| 0400 | Textured aluminum, 4' x 8' x 5/16" plywood backing, single face | 2 Shee | 375 | .043 | S.F. | 3.24 | 1.93 | | 5.17 | 6.55 |
| 0600 | Double face | | 375 | .043 | | 3.86 | 1.93 | | 5.79 | 7.25 |
| 0700 | 4' x 10' x 5/16" plywood backing, single face | | 375 | .043 | | 3.62 | 1.93 | | 5.55 | 6.95 |
| 0900 | Double face | | 375 | .043 | | 5.10 | 1.93 | | 7.03 | 8.60 |
| 1000 | 4' x 12' x 5/16" plywood backing, single face | | 375 | .043 | | 5.15 | 1.93 | | 7.08 | 8.65 |
| 1300 | Smooth aluminum, 1/4" plywood panel, fluoropolymer finish, double face | | 375 | .043 | | 5.05 | 1.93 | | 6.98 | 8.55 |
| 1350 | Clear anodized finish, double face | | 375 | .043 | | 7.95 | 1.93 | | 9.88 | 11.75 |
| 1400 | Double face textured aluminum, structural panel, 1" EPS insulation | | 375 | .043 | | 4.40 | 1.93 | | 6.33 | 7.80 |
| 1500 | Accessories, outside corner | 1 Shee | 175 | .046 | L.F. | 1.65 | 2.07 | | 3.72 | 5 |
| 1600 | Inside corner | | 175 | .046 | | 1.16 | 2.07 | | 3.23 | 4.47 |
| 1800 | Batten mounting clip | | 200 | .040 | | .43 | 1.81 | | 2.24 | 3.26 |
| 1900 | Low profile batten | | 480 | .017 | | .53 | .76 | | 1.29 | 1.74 |
| 2100 | High profile batten | | 480 | .017 | | 1.23 | .76 | | 1.99 | 2.51 |
| 2200 | Water table | | 200 | .040 | | 1.84 | 1.81 | | 3.65 | 4.81 |
| 2400 | Horizontal joint connector | | 200 | .040 | | 1.45 | 1.81 | | 3.26 | 4.39 |
| 2500 | Corner cap | | 200 | .040 | | 1.60 | 1.81 | | 3.41 | 4.55 |
| 2700 | H - moulding | | 480 | .017 | | 1.09 | .76 | | 1.85 | 2.36 |

# 07 46 Siding

## 07 46 23 - Wood Siding

### 07 46 23.10 Wood Board Siding

| | | Crew | Daily Output | Labor-Hours | Unit | Material | 2008 Bare Costs Labor | Equipment | Total | Total Incl O&P |
|---|---|---|---|---|---|---|---|---|---|---|
| 0010 | **WOOD BOARD SIDING** | | | | | | | | | |
| 3200 | Wood, cedar bevel, A grade, 1/2" x 6" | 1 Carp | 295 | .027 | S.F. | 3.30 | 1.03 | | 4.33 | 5.25 |
| 3300 | 1/2" x 8" | | 330 | .024 | | 3.96 | .92 | | 4.88 | 5.80 |
| 3500 | 3/4" x 10", clear grade | | 375 | .021 | | 5.70 | .81 | | 6.51 | 7.50 |
| 3600 | "B" grade | | 375 | .021 | | 6.25 | .81 | | 7.06 | 8.15 |
| 3800 | Cedar, rough sawn, 1" x 4", A grade, natural | | 220 | .036 | | 1.79 | 1.39 | | 3.18 | 4.13 |
| 3900 | Stained | | 220 | .036 | | 2.10 | 1.39 | | 3.49 | 4.47 |
| 4100 | 1" x 12", board & batten, #3 & Btr., natural | | 420 | .019 | | 1.10 | .73 | | 1.83 | 2.34 |
| 4200 | Stained | | 420 | .019 | | 1.18 | .73 | | 1.91 | 2.43 |
| 4400 | 1" x 8" channel siding, #3 & Btr., natural | | 330 | .024 | | 2.20 | .92 | | 3.12 | 3.86 |
| 4500 | Stained | | 330 | .024 | | 2.50 | .92 | | 3.42 | 4.19 |
| 4700 | Redwood, clear, beveled, vertical grain, 1/2" x 4" | | 220 | .036 | | 3.56 | 1.39 | | 4.95 | 6.10 |

# 07 46 Siding

## 07 46 23 – Wood Siding

### 07 46 23.10 Wood Board Siding

| | | Crew | Daily Output | Labor-Hours | Unit | Material | 2008 Bare Costs Labor | Equipment | Total | Total Incl O&P |
|---|---|---|---|---|---|---|---|---|---|---|
| 4750 | 1/2" x 6" | 1 Carp | 295 | .027 | S.F. | 2.95 | 1.03 | | 3.98 | 4.86 |
| 4800 | 1/2" x 8" | | 330 | .024 | | 2.38 | .92 | | 3.30 | 4.06 |
| 5000 | 3/4" x 10" | | 375 | .021 | | 3.91 | .81 | | 4.72 | 5.55 |
| 5200 | Channel siding, 1" x 10", B grade | | 375 | .021 | | 2.58 | .81 | | 3.39 | 4.10 |
| 5250 | Redwood, T&G boards, B grade, 1" x 4" | | 220 | .036 | | 2.99 | 1.39 | | 4.38 | 5.45 |
| 5270 | 1" x 8" | | 330 | .024 | | 2.68 | .92 | | 3.60 | 4.39 |
| 5400 | White pine, rough sawn, 1" x 8", natural | | 330 | .024 | | 1.10 | .92 | | 2.02 | 2.65 |
| 5500 | Stained | | 330 | .024 | | 1.18 | .92 | | 2.10 | 2.74 |

## 07 46 29 – Plywood Siding

### 07 46 29.10 Plywood Siding Options

| | | Crew | Daily Output | Labor-Hours | Unit | Material | 2008 Bare Costs Labor | Equipment | Total | Total Incl O&P |
|---|---|---|---|---|---|---|---|---|---|---|
| 0010 | **PLYWOOD SIDING OPTIONS** | | | | | | | | | |
| 0900 | Plywood, medium density overlaid, 3/8" thick | 2 Carp | 750 | .021 | S.F. | .87 | .81 | | 1.68 | 2.22 |
| 1000 | 1/2" thick | | 700 | .023 | | 1.09 | .87 | | 1.96 | 2.56 |
| 1100 | 3/4" thick | | 650 | .025 | | 1.31 | .94 | | 2.25 | 2.90 |
| 1600 | Texture 1-11, cedar, 5/8" thick, natural | | 675 | .024 | | 2.45 | .90 | | 3.35 | 4.11 |
| 1700 | Factory stained | | 675 | .024 | | 1.96 | .90 | | 2.86 | 3.57 |
| 1900 | Texture 1-11, fir, 5/8" thick, natural | | 675 | .024 | | 1.13 | .90 | | 2.03 | 2.65 |
| 2000 | Factory stained | | 675 | .024 | | 1.73 | .90 | | 2.63 | 3.31 |
| 2050 | Texture 1-11, S.Y.P., 5/8" thick, natural | | 675 | .024 | | 1.21 | .90 | | 2.11 | 2.74 |
| 2100 | Factory stained | | 675 | .024 | | 1.25 | .90 | | 2.15 | 2.79 |
| 2200 | Rough sawn cedar, 3/8" thick, natural | | 675 | .024 | | 1.21 | .90 | | 2.11 | 2.74 |
| 2300 | Factory stained | | 675 | .024 | | .97 | .90 | | 1.87 | 2.48 |
| 2500 | Rough sawn fir, 3/8" thick, natural | | 675 | .024 | | .77 | .90 | | 1.67 | 2.26 |
| 2600 | Factory stained | | 675 | .024 | | .97 | .90 | | 1.87 | 2.48 |
| 2800 | Redwood, textured siding, 5/8" thick | | 675 | .024 | | 1.94 | .90 | | 2.84 | 3.54 |
| 3000 | Polyvinyl chloride coated, 3/8" thick | | 750 | .021 | | 1.12 | .81 | | 1.93 | 2.49 |

## 07 46 33 – Plastic Siding

### 07 46 33.10 Vinyl Siding

| | | Crew | Daily Output | Labor-Hours | Unit | Material | 2008 Bare Costs Labor | Equipment | Total | Total Incl O&P |
|---|---|---|---|---|---|---|---|---|---|---|
| 0010 | **VINYL SIDING** | | | | | | | | | |
| 3995 | Clapboard profile, woodgrain texture, .048 thick, double 4 | 2 Carp | 495 | .032 | S.F. | .80 | 1.23 | | 2.03 | 2.80 |
| 4000 | Double 5 | | 550 | .029 | | .80 | 1.11 | | 1.91 | 2.61 |
| 4005 | Single 8 | | 495 | .032 | | .84 | 1.23 | | 2.07 | 2.84 |
| 4010 | Single 10 | | 550 | .029 | | 1.01 | 1.11 | | 2.12 | 2.84 |
| 4015 | .044 thick, double 4 | | 495 | .032 | | .73 | 1.23 | | 1.96 | 2.72 |
| 4020 | Double 5 | | 550 | .029 | | .73 | 1.11 | | 1.84 | 2.53 |
| 4025 | .042 thick, double 4 | | 495 | .032 | | .73 | 1.23 | | 1.96 | 2.72 |
| 4030 | Double 5 | | 550 | .029 | | .73 | 1.11 | | 1.84 | 2.53 |
| 4035 | Cross sawn texture, .040 thick, double 4 | | 495 | .032 | | .57 | 1.23 | | 1.80 | 2.55 |
| 4040 | Double 5 | | 550 | .029 | | .57 | 1.11 | | 1.68 | 2.36 |
| 4045 | Smooth texture, .042 thick, double 4 | | 495 | .032 | | .65 | 1.23 | | 1.88 | 2.64 |
| 4050 | Double 5 | | 550 | .029 | | .65 | 1.11 | | 1.76 | 2.45 |
| 4055 | Single 8 | | 495 | .032 | | .83 | 1.23 | | 2.06 | 2.83 |
| 4060 | Cedar texture, .044 thick, double 4 | | 495 | .032 | | .80 | 1.23 | | 2.03 | 2.80 |
| 4065 | Double 6 | | 600 | .027 | | .80 | 1.02 | | 1.82 | 2.46 |
| 4070 | Dutch lap profile, woodgrain texture, .048 thick, double 5 | | 550 | .029 | | .80 | 1.11 | | 1.91 | 2.61 |
| 4075 | .044 thick, double 4.5 | | 525 | .030 | | .80 | 1.16 | | 1.96 | 2.69 |
| 4080 | .042 thick, double 4.5 | | 525 | .030 | | .66 | 1.16 | | 1.82 | 2.54 |
| 4085 | .040 thick, double 4.5 | | 525 | .030 | | .57 | 1.16 | | 1.73 | 2.44 |
| 4090 | Shingle profile, random grooves, double 7 | | 400 | .040 | | 2.24 | 1.52 | | 3.76 | 4.83 |
| 4095 | Triple 5 | | 400 | .040 | | 2.24 | 1.52 | | 3.76 | 4.83 |
| 4100 | Shake profile, 10" wide | | 400 | .040 | | 1.91 | 1.52 | | 3.43 | 4.47 |
| 4105 | Vertical pattern, .046 thick, double 5 | | 550 | .029 | | .96 | 1.11 | | 2.07 | 2.79 |

# 07 46 Siding

## 07 46 33 – Plastic Siding

### 07 46 33.10 Vinyl Siding

| | | Crew | Daily Output | Labor-Hours | Unit | Material | 2008 Bare Costs Labor | Equipment | Total | Total Incl O&P |
|---|---|---|---|---|---|---|---|---|---|---|
| 4110 | .044 thick, triple 3 | 2 Carp | 550 | .029 | S.F. | .98 | 1.11 | | 2.09 | 2.81 |
| 4115 | .040 thick, triple 4 | | 550 | .029 | | .99 | 1.11 | | 2.10 | 2.82 |
| 4120 | .040 thick, triple 2.66 | | 550 | .029 | | 1.20 | 1.11 | | 2.31 | 3.05 |
| 4125 | Insulation, fan folded extruded polystyrene, 1/4" | | 2000 | .008 | | .22 | .30 | | .52 | .71 |
| 4130 | 3/8" | | 2000 | .008 | ▼ | .24 | .30 | | .54 | .74 |
| 4135 | Accessories, J channel, 5/8" pocket | | 700 | .023 | L.F. | .35 | .87 | | 1.22 | 1.74 |
| 4140 | 3/4" pocket | | 695 | .023 | | .39 | .88 | | 1.27 | 1.79 |
| 4145 | 1-1/4" pocket | | 680 | .024 | | .43 | .90 | | 1.33 | 1.87 |
| 4150 | Flexible, 3/4" pocket | | 600 | .027 | | 1.22 | 1.02 | | 2.24 | 2.92 |
| 4155 | Under sill finish trim | | 500 | .032 | | .37 | 1.22 | | 1.59 | 2.30 |
| 4160 | Vinyl starter strip | | 700 | .023 | | .25 | .87 | | 1.12 | 1.63 |
| 4165 | Aluminum starter strip | | 700 | .023 | | .19 | .87 | | 1.06 | 1.56 |
| 4170 | Window casing, 2-1/2" wide, 3/4" pocket | | 510 | .031 | | .77 | 1.20 | | 1.97 | 2.70 |
| 4175 | Outside corner, woodgrain finish, 4" face, 3/4" pocket | | 700 | .023 | | 1.45 | .87 | | 2.32 | 2.96 |
| 4180 | 5/8" pocket | | 700 | .023 | | 1.30 | .87 | | 2.17 | 2.79 |
| 4185 | Smooth finish, 4" face, 3/4" pocket | | 700 | .023 | | 1.52 | .87 | | 2.39 | 3.03 |
| 4190 | 7/8" pocket | | 690 | .023 | | 1.45 | .88 | | 2.33 | 2.98 |
| 4195 | 1-1/4" pocket | | 700 | .023 | | .94 | .87 | | 1.81 | 2.39 |
| 4200 | Soffit and fascia, 1' overhang, solid | | 120 | .133 | | 2.69 | 5.10 | | 7.79 | 10.85 |
| 4205 | Vented | | 120 | .133 | | 2.69 | 5.10 | | 7.79 | 10.85 |
| 4210 | 2' overhang, solid | | 110 | .145 | | 3.64 | 5.55 | | 9.19 | 12.65 |
| 4215 | Vented | ▼ | 110 | .145 | ▼ | 3.64 | 5.55 | | 9.19 | 12.65 |
| 4220 | Colors for siding and soffts, add | | | | S.F. | .16 | | | .16 | .18 |
| 4225 | Colors for accessories and trim, add | | | | L.F. | .32 | | | .32 | .35 |

## 07 46 46 – Mineral-Fiber Cement Siding

### 07 46 46.10 Fiber Cement Siding

| | | Crew | Daily Output | Labor-Hours | Unit | Material | 2008 Bare Costs Labor | Equipment | Total | Total Incl O&P |
|---|---|---|---|---|---|---|---|---|---|---|
| 0010 | **FIBER CEMENT SIDING** | | | | | | | | | |
| 0020 | Lap siding, 5/16" thick, 6" wide, 4-3/4" exposure, smooth texture | 2 Carp | 415 | .039 | S.F. | 1.36 | 1.47 | | 2.83 | 3.79 |
| 0025 | Woodgrain texture | | 415 | .039 | | 1.36 | 1.47 | | 2.83 | 3.79 |
| 0030 | 7-1/2" wide, 6-1/4" exposure, smooth texture | | 425 | .038 | | 1.25 | 1.43 | | 2.68 | 3.60 |
| 0035 | Woodgrain texture | | 425 | .038 | | 1.25 | 1.43 | | 2.68 | 3.60 |
| 0040 | 8" wide, 6-3/4" exposure, smooth texture | | 425 | .038 | | 1.21 | 1.43 | | 2.64 | 3.56 |
| 0045 | Roughsawn texture | | 425 | .038 | | 1.21 | 1.43 | | 2.64 | 3.56 |
| 0050 | 9-1/2" wide, 8-1/4" exposure, smooth texture | | 440 | .036 | | 1.22 | 1.39 | | 2.61 | 3.50 |
| 0055 | Woodgrain texture | | 440 | .036 | | 1.22 | 1.39 | | 2.61 | 3.50 |
| 0060 | 12" wide, 10-3/8" exposure, smooth texture | | 455 | .035 | | 1.22 | 1.34 | | 2.56 | 3.43 |
| 0065 | Woodgrain texture | | 455 | .035 | | 1.22 | 1.34 | | 2.56 | 3.43 |
| 0070 | Panel siding, 5/16" thick, smooth texture | | 750 | .021 | | 1.05 | .81 | | 1.86 | 2.41 |
| 0075 | Stucco texture | | 750 | .021 | | 1.05 | .81 | | 1.86 | 2.41 |
| 0080 | Grooved woodgrain texture | | 750 | .021 | | 1.05 | .81 | | 1.86 | 2.41 |
| 0085 | V - grooved woodgrain texture | | 750 | .021 | ▼ | 1.05 | .81 | | 1.86 | 2.41 |
| 0090 | Wood starter strip | ▼ | 400 | .040 | L.F. | .31 | 1.52 | | 1.83 | 2.71 |

## 07 46 73 – Soffit

### 07 46 73.10 Soffit Options

| | | Crew | Daily Output | Labor-Hours | Unit | Material | 2008 Bare Costs Labor | Equipment | Total | Total Incl O&P |
|---|---|---|---|---|---|---|---|---|---|---|
| 0010 | **SOFFIT OPTIONS** | | | | | | | | | |
| 0012 | Aluminum, residential, .020" thick | 1 Carp | 210 | .038 | S.F. | 1.41 | 1.45 | | 2.86 | 3.81 |
| 0100 | Baked enamel on steel, 16 or 18 gauge | | 105 | .076 | | 4.98 | 2.90 | | 7.88 | 10 |
| 0300 | Polyvinyl chloride, white, solid | | 230 | .035 | | .95 | 1.33 | | 2.28 | 3.11 |
| 0400 | Perforated | ▼ | 230 | .035 | | .95 | 1.33 | | 2.28 | 3.11 |
| 0500 | For colors, add | | | | ▼ | .11 | | | .11 | .12 |

# 07 51 Built-Up Bituminous Roofing

## 07 51 13 – Built-Up Asphalt Roofing

### 07 51 13.10 Built-Up Roofing Components

| | | Crew | Daily Output | Labor-Hours | Unit | Material | 2008 Bare Costs Labor | Equipment | Total | Total Incl O&P |
|---|---|---|---|---|---|---|---|---|---|---|
| 0010 | **BUILT-UP ROOFING COMPONENTS** | | | | | | | | | |
| 0012 | Asphalt saturated felt, #30, 2 square per roll | 1 Rofc | 58 | .138 | Sq. | 4.09 | 4.55 | | 8.64 | 12.25 |
| 0200 | #15, 4 sq per roll, plain or perforated, not mopped | | 58 | .138 | | 4.10 | 4.55 | | 8.65 | 12.25 |
| 0300 | Roll roofing, smooth, #65 | | 15 | .533 | | 7.35 | 17.60 | | 24.95 | 38 |
| 0500 | #90 | | 15 | .533 | | 23 | 17.60 | | 40.60 | 55 |
| 0520 | Mineralized | | 15 | .533 | | 18.05 | 17.60 | | 35.65 | 50 |
| 0540 | D.C. (Double coverage), 19" selvage edge | | 10 | .800 | | 39 | 26.50 | | 65.50 | 88 |
| 0580 | Adhesive (lap cement) | | | | Gal. | 4.37 | | | 4.37 | 4.81 |
| 0600 | Steep, flat or dead level asphalt, 10 ton lots, bulk | | | | Ton | 340 | | | 340 | 370 |
| 0800 | Packaged | | | | " | 575 | | | 575 | 635 |

### 07 51 13.13 Cold-Applied Built-Up Asphalt Roofing

| | | Crew | Daily Output | Labor-Hours | Unit | Material | 2008 Bare Costs Labor | Equipment | Total | Total Incl O&P |
|---|---|---|---|---|---|---|---|---|---|---|
| 0010 | **COLD-APPLIED BUILT-UP ASPHALT ROOFING** | | | | | | | | | |
| 0020 | 3 ply system, installation only (components listed below) | G-5 | 50 | .800 | Sq. | | 24 | 3.31 | 27.31 | 44.50 |
| 0100 | Spunbond poly. fabric, 1.35 oz/SY, 36"W, 10.8 Sq/roll | | | | Ea. | 155 | | | 155 | 171 |
| 0200 | 49" wide, 14.6 Sq./roll | | | | | 214 | | | 214 | 236 |
| 0300 | 2.10 oz./S.Y., 36" wide, 10.8 Sq./roll | | | | | 234 | | | 234 | 257 |
| 0400 | 49" wide, 14.6 Sq./roll | | | | | 315 | | | 315 | 350 |
| 0500 | Base & finish coat, 3 gal./Sq., 5 gal./can | | | | Gal. | 4.12 | | | 4.12 | 4.53 |
| 0600 | Coating, ceramic granules, 1/2 Sq./bag | | | | Ea. | 14.55 | | | 14.55 | 16.05 |
| 0700 | Aluminum, 2 gal./Sq. | | | | Gal. | 11.70 | | | 11.70 | 12.90 |
| 0800 | Emulsion, fibered or non-fibered, 4 gal./Sq. | | | | " | 5.40 | | | 5.40 | 5.95 |

### 07 51 13.20 Built-Up Roofing Systems

| | | Crew | Daily Output | Labor-Hours | Unit | Material | 2008 Bare Costs Labor | Equipment | Total | Total Incl O&P |
|---|---|---|---|---|---|---|---|---|---|---|
| 0010 | **BUILT-UP ROOFING SYSTEMS** R075113-20 | | | | | | | | | |
| 0120 | Asphalt flood coat with gravel/slag surfacing, not including | | | | | | | | | |
| 0140 | Insulation, flashing or wood nailers | | | | | | | | | |
| 0200 | Asphalt base sheet, 3 plies #15 asphalt felt, mopped | G-1 | 22 | 2.545 | Sq. | 66.50 | 78.50 | 18.75 | 163.75 | 228 |
| 0350 | On nailable decks | | 21 | 2.667 | | 71 | 82.50 | 19.65 | 173.15 | 240 |
| 0500 | 4 plies #15 asphalt felt, mopped | | 20 | 2.800 | | 93 | 86.50 | 20.50 | 200 | 272 |
| 0550 | On nailable decks | | 19 | 2.947 | | 83 | 91 | 21.50 | 195.50 | 271 |
| 0700 | Coated glass base sheet, 2 plies glass (type IV), mopped | | 22 | 2.545 | | 68.50 | 78.50 | 18.75 | 165.75 | 230 |
| 0850 | 3 plies glass, mopped | | 20 | 2.800 | | 81.50 | 86.50 | 20.50 | 188.50 | 260 |
| 0950 | On nailable decks | | 19 | 2.947 | | 77 | 91 | 21.50 | 189.50 | 264 |
| 1100 | 4 plies glass fiber felt (type IV), mopped | | 20 | 2.800 | | 100 | 86.50 | 20.50 | 207 | 280 |
| 1150 | On nailable decks | | 19 | 2.947 | | 90 | 91 | 21.50 | 202.50 | 278 |
| 1200 | Coated & saturated base sheet, 3 plies #15 asph. felt, mopped | | 20 | 2.800 | | 74.50 | 86.50 | 20.50 | 181.50 | 252 |
| 1250 | On nailable decks | | 19 | 2.947 | | 70 | 91 | 21.50 | 182.50 | 256 |
| 1300 | 4 plies #15 asphalt felt, mopped | | 22 | 2.545 | | 87 | 78.50 | 18.75 | 184.25 | 250 |
| 2000 | Asphalt flood coat, smooth surface | | | | | | | | | |
| 2200 | Asphalt base sheet & 3 plies #15 asphalt felt, mopped | G-1 | 24 | 2.333 | Sq. | 70.50 | 72 | 17.15 | 159.65 | 220 |
| 2400 | On nailable decks | | 23 | 2.435 | | 66 | 75 | 17.90 | 158.90 | 220 |
| 2600 | 4 plies #15 asphalt felt, mopped | | 24 | 2.333 | | 83 | 72 | 17.15 | 172.15 | 233 |
| 2700 | On nailable decks | | 23 | 2.435 | | 78 | 75 | 17.90 | 170.90 | 233 |
| 2900 | Coated glass fiber base sheet, mopped, and 2 plies of | | | | | | | | | |
| 2910 | glass fiber felt (type IV) | G-1 | 25 | 2.240 | Sq. | 63.50 | 69 | 16.50 | 149 | 206 |
| 3100 | On nailable decks | | 24 | 2.333 | | 59.50 | 72 | 17.15 | 148.65 | 207 |
| 3200 | 3 plies, mopped | | 23 | 2.435 | | 76.50 | 75 | 17.90 | 169.40 | 232 |
| 3300 | On nailable decks | | 22 | 2.545 | | 71.50 | 78.50 | 18.75 | 168.75 | 233 |
| 3800 | 4 plies glass fiber felt (type IV), mopped | | 23 | 2.435 | | 89.50 | 75 | 17.90 | 182.40 | 246 |
| 3900 | On nailable decks | | 22 | 2.545 | | 84.50 | 78.50 | 18.75 | 181.75 | 248 |
| 4000 | Coated & saturated base sheet, 3 plies #15 asph. felt, mopped | | 24 | 2.333 | | 69.50 | 72 | 17.15 | 158.65 | 218 |
| 4200 | On nailable decks | | 23 | 2.435 | | 64.50 | 75 | 17.90 | 157.40 | 219 |
| 4300 | 4 plies #15 organic felt, mopped | | 22 | 2.545 | | 81.50 | 78.50 | 18.75 | 178.75 | 245 |

# 07 51 Built-Up Bituminous Roofing

## 07 51 13 – Built-Up Asphalt Roofing

| | 07 51 13.20 Built-Up Roofing Systems | Crew | Daily Output | Labor-Hours | Unit | Material | 2008 Bare Costs Labor | Equipment | Total | Total Incl O&P |
|---|---|---|---|---|---|---|---|---|---|---|
| 4500 | Coal tar pitch with gravel/slag surfacing | | | | | | | | | |
| 4600 | 4 plies #15 tarred felt, mopped | G-1 | 21 | 2.667 | Sq. | 135 | 82.50 | 19.65 | 237.15 | 310 |
| 4800 | 3 plies glass fiber felt (type IV), mopped | " | 19 | 2.947 | " | 111 | 91 | 21.50 | 223.50 | 300 |
| 5000 | Coated glass fiber base sheet, and 2 plies of | | | | | | | | | |
| 5010 | glass fiber felt, (type IV), mopped | G-1 | 19 | 2.947 | Sq. | 110 | 91 | 21.50 | 222.50 | 300 |
| 5300 | On nailable decks | | 18 | 3.111 | | 98 | 96 | 23 | 217 | 296 |
| 5600 | 4 plies glass fiber felt (type IV), mopped | | 21 | 2.667 | | 153 | 82.50 | 19.65 | 255.15 | 330 |
| 5800 | On nailable decks | | 20 | 2.800 | | 141 | 86.50 | 20.50 | 248 | 325 |

## 07 51 13.30 Cants

| | CANTS | Crew | Daily Output | Labor-Hours | Unit | Material | Labor | Equipment | Total | Total Incl O&P |
|---|---|---|---|---|---|---|---|---|---|---|
| 0010 | CANTS | | | | | | | | | |
| 0012 | Lumber, treated, 4" x 4" cut diagonally | 1 Rofc | 325 | .025 | L.F. | 1.40 | .81 | | 2.21 | 2.92 |
| 0100 | Foamglass | | 325 | .025 | | 2.23 | .81 | | 3.04 | 3.83 |
| 0300 | Mineral or fiber, trapezoidal, 1"x 4" x 48" | | 325 | .025 | | .19 | .81 | | 1 | 1.59 |
| 0400 | 1-1/2" x 5-5/8" x 48" | | 325 | .025 | | .31 | .81 | | 1.12 | 1.72 |

## 07 51 13.40 Felts

| | FELTS | Crew | Daily Output | Labor-Hours | Unit | Material | Labor | Equipment | Total | Total Incl O&P |
|---|---|---|---|---|---|---|---|---|---|---|
| 0010 | FELTS | | | | | | | | | |
| 0012 | Glass fibered roofing felt, #15, not mopped | 1 Rofc | 58 | .138 | Sq. | 5.15 | 4.55 | | 9.70 | 13.45 |
| 0300 | Base sheet, #45, channel vented | | 58 | .138 | | 22 | 4.55 | | 26.55 | 32 |
| 0400 | #50, coated | | 58 | .138 | | 11.90 | 4.55 | | 16.45 | 21 |
| 0500 | Cap, mineral surfaced | | 58 | .138 | | 22 | 4.55 | | 26.55 | 32 |
| 0600 | Flashing membrane, #65 | | 16 | .500 | | 33.50 | 16.50 | | 50 | 65 |
| 0800 | Coal tar fibered, #15, no mopping | | 58 | .138 | | 10 | 4.55 | | 14.55 | 18.75 |
| 0900 | Asphalt felt, #15, 4 sq per roll, no mopping  CN | | 58 | .138 | | 4.10 | 4.55 | | 8.65 | 12.25 |
| 1100 | #30, 2 sq per roll | | 58 | .138 | | 4.09 | 4.55 | | 8.64 | 12.25 |
| 1200 | Double coated, #33 | | 58 | .138 | | 8.15 | 4.55 | | 12.70 | 16.75 |
| 1400 | #40, base sheet | | 58 | .138 | | 9.30 | 4.55 | | 13.85 | 18 |
| 1450 | Coated and saturated | | 58 | .138 | | 8.15 | 4.55 | | 12.70 | 16.70 |
| 1500 | Tarred felt, organic, #15, 4 sq rolls | | 58 | .138 | | 12 | 4.55 | | 16.55 | 21 |
| 1550 | #30, 2 sq roll | | 58 | .138 | | 21 | 4.55 | | 25.55 | 31 |
| 1700 | Add for mopping above felts, per ply, asphalt, 24 lb per sq | G-1 | 192 | .292 | | 6.90 | 9 | 2.15 | 18.05 | 25.50 |
| 1800 | Coal tar mopping, 30 lb per sq | | 186 | .301 | | 10.90 | 9.30 | 2.22 | 22.42 | 30 |
| 1900 | Flood coat, with asphalt, 60 lb per sq | | 60 | .933 | | 17.25 | 29 | 6.85 | 53.10 | 75.50 |
| 2000 | With coal tar, 75 lb per sq | | 56 | 1 | | 27 | 31 | 7.35 | 65.35 | 90.50 |

## 07 51 13.50 Walkways for Built-Up Roofs

| | WALKWAYS FOR BUILT-UP ROOFS | Crew | Daily Output | Labor-Hours | Unit | Material | Labor | Equipment | Total | Total Incl O&P |
|---|---|---|---|---|---|---|---|---|---|---|
| 0010 | WALKWAYS FOR BUILT-UP ROOFS | | | | | | | | | |
| 0020 | Asphalt impregnated, 3' x 6' x 1/2" thick | 1 Rofc | 400 | .020 | S.F. | 1.36 | .66 | | 2.02 | 2.62 |
| 0100 | 3' x 3' x 3/4" thick | " | 400 | .020 | | 2.57 | .66 | | 3.23 | 3.95 |
| 0300 | Concrete patio blocks, 2" thick, natural | 1 Clab | 115 | .070 | | 1.47 | 2.10 | | 3.57 | 4.89 |
| 0400 | Colors | " | 115 | .070 | | 1.86 | 2.10 | | 3.96 | 5.30 |

# 07 52 Modified Bituminous Membrane Roofing

## 07 52 13 – Atactic-Polypropylene-Modified Bituminous Membrane Roofing

### 07 52 13.10 APP Modified Bituminous Membrane

| | APP MODIFIED BITUMINOUS MEMBRANE   R075213-30 | Crew | Daily Output | Labor-Hours | Unit | Material | Labor | Equipment | Total | Total Incl O&P |
|---|---|---|---|---|---|---|---|---|---|---|
| 0010 | APP MODIFIED BITUMINOUS MEMBRANE | | | | | | | | | |
| 0020 | Base sheet, #15 glass fiber felt, nailed to deck | 1 Rofc | 58 | .138 | Sq. | 5.75 | 4.55 | | 10.30 | 14.10 |
| 0030 | Spot mopped to deck | G-1 | 295 | .190 | | 8.60 | 5.85 | 1.40 | 15.85 | 21 |
| 0040 | Fully mopped to deck | " | 192 | .292 | | 12.05 | 9 | 2.15 | 23.20 | 31 |
| 0050 | #15 organic felt, nailed to deck | 1 Rofc | 58 | .138 | | 4.69 | 4.55 | | 9.24 | 12.90 |
| 0060 | Spot mopped to deck | G-1 | 295 | .190 | | 7.55 | 5.85 | 1.40 | 14.80 | 19.85 |
| 0070 | Fully mopped to deck | " | 192 | .292 | | 11 | 9 | 2.15 | 22.15 | 30 |

# 07 52 Modified Bituminous Membrane Roofing

## 07 52 13 – Atactic-Polypropylene-Modified Bituminous Membrane Roofing

| | 07 52 13.10 APP Modified Bituminous Membrane | Crew | Daily Output | Labor-Hours | Unit | Material | 2008 Bare Costs Labor | Equipment | Total | Total Incl O&P |
|---|---|---|---|---|---|---|---|---|---|---|
| 2100 | APP mod., smooth surf. cap sheet, poly. reinf., torched, 160 mils | G-5 | 2100 | .019 | S.F. | .47 | .57 | .08 | 1.12 | 1.58 |
| 2150 | 170 mils | | 2100 | .019 | | .54 | .57 | .08 | 1.19 | 1.65 |
| 2200 | Granule surface cap sheet, poly. reinf., torched, 180 mils | | 2000 | .020 | | .58 | .60 | .08 | 1.26 | 1.75 |
| 2250 | Smooth surface flashing, torched, 160 mils | | 1260 | .032 | | .47 | .95 | .13 | 1.55 | 2.28 |
| 2300 | 170 mils | | 1260 | .032 | | .54 | .95 | .13 | 1.62 | 2.35 |
| 2350 | Granule surface flashing, torched, 180 mils | ↓ | 1260 | .032 | | .58 | .95 | .13 | 1.66 | 2.40 |
| 2400 | Fibrated aluminum coating | 1 Rofc | 3800 | .002 | ↓ | .10 | .07 | | .17 | .23 |

## 07 52 16 – Styrene-Butadiene-Styrene Modified Bituminous Membrane Roofing

### 07 52 16.10 SBS Modified Bituminous Membrane

| | | Crew | Daily Output | Labor-Hours | Unit | Material | 2008 Bare Costs Labor | Equipment | Total | Total Incl O&P |
|---|---|---|---|---|---|---|---|---|---|---|
| 0010 | **SBS MODIFIED BITUMINOUS MEMBRANE** | | | | | | | | | |
| 0080 | SBS modified, granule surf cap sheet, polyester rein., mopped | | | | | | | | | |
| 0600 | 150 mils | G-1 | 2000 | .028 | S.F. | .52 | .86 | .21 | 1.59 | 2.27 |
| 1100 | 160 mils | | 2000 | .028 | | .76 | .86 | .21 | 1.83 | 2.54 |
| 1500 | Glass fiber reinforced, mopped, 160 mils | | 2000 | .028 | | .48 | .86 | .21 | 1.55 | 2.23 |
| 1600 | Smooth surface cap sheet, mopped, 145 mils | | 2100 | .027 | | .48 | .82 | .20 | 1.50 | 2.15 |
| 1700 | Smooth surface flashing, 145 mils | | 1260 | .044 | | .48 | 1.37 | .33 | 2.18 | 3.23 |
| 1800 | 150 mils | | 1260 | .044 | | .47 | 1.37 | .33 | 2.17 | 3.22 |
| 1900 | Granular surface flashing, 150 mils | | 1260 | .044 | | .52 | 1.37 | .33 | 2.22 | 3.27 |
| 2000 | 160 mils | ↓ | 1260 | .044 | ↓ | .76 | 1.37 | .33 | 2.46 | 3.54 |

# 07 53 Elastomeric Membrane Roofing

## 07 53 16 – Chlorosulfonate-Polyethylene Roofing

### 07 53 16.10 Chlorosulfonated Polyehtylene Roofing

| | | Crew | Daily Output | Labor-Hours | Unit | Material | 2008 Bare Costs Labor | Equipment | Total | Total Incl O&P |
|---|---|---|---|---|---|---|---|---|---|---|
| 0010 | **CHLOROSULFONATED POLYEHTYLENE ROOFING** | | | | | | | | | |
| 0800 | Chlorosulfonated polyethylene-hypalon (CSPE), 45 mils, | | | | | | | | | |
| 0900 | 0.29 P.S.F., fully adhered | G-5 | 26 | 1.538 | Sq. | 141 | 46 | 6.35 | 193.35 | 241 |
| 1100 | Loose-laid & ballasted with stone (10 P.S.F.) | | 51 | .784 | | 149 | 23.50 | 3.25 | 175.75 | 208 |
| 1200 | Mechanically attached | | 35 | 1.143 | | 143 | 34.50 | 4.73 | 182.23 | 222 |
| 1300 | Plates with adhesive attachment | ↓ | 35 | 1.143 | ↓ | 141 | 34.50 | 4.73 | 180.23 | 219 |

## 07 53 23 – Ethylene-Propylene-Diene-Monomer Roofing

### 07 53 23.20 Ethylene-Propylene-Diene-Monomer Roofing (E.P.D.M.)

| | | Crew | Daily Output | Labor-Hours | Unit | Material | 2008 Bare Costs Labor | Equipment | Total | Total Incl O&P |
|---|---|---|---|---|---|---|---|---|---|---|
| 0010 | **ETHYLENE-PROPYLENE-DIENE-MONOMER ROOFING (E.P.D.M.)** | | | | | | | | | |
| 3500 | Ethylene propylene diene monomer (EPDM), 45 mils, 0.28 P.S.F. | | | | | | | | | |
| 3600 | Loose-laid & ballasted with stone (10 P.S.F.) | G-5 | 51 | .784 | Sq. | 68.50 | 23.50 | 3.25 | 95.25 | 119 |
| 3700 | Mechanically attached | | 35 | 1.143 | | 59 | 34.50 | 4.73 | 98.23 | 129 |
| 3800 | Fully adhered with adhesive | ↓ | 26 | 1.538 | ↓ | 86 | 46 | 6.35 | 138.35 | 180 |
| 4500 | 60 mils, 0.40 P.S.F. | | | | | | | | | |
| 4600 | Loose-laid & ballasted with stone (10 P.S.F.) | G-5 | 51 | .784 | Sq. | 86.50 | 23.50 | 3.25 | 113.25 | 139 |
| 4700 | Mechanically attached | | 35 | 1.143 | | 76 | 34.50 | 4.73 | 115.23 | 147 |
| 4800 | Fully adhered with adhesive | ↓ | 26 | 1.538 | | 102 | 46 | 6.35 | 154.35 | 199 |
| 4810 | 45 mil, .28 PSF, membrane only | CN | | | | 34 | | | 34 | 37.50 |
| 4820 | 60 mil, .40 PSF, membrane only | | | | ↓ | 49.50 | | | 49.50 | 54 |
| 4850 | Seam tape for membrane, 3" x 100' roll | | | | Ea. | 46.50 | | | 46.50 | 51.50 |
| 4900 | Batten strips, 10' sections | | | | | 3.38 | | | 3.38 | 3.72 |
| 4910 | Cover tape for batten strips, 6" x 100' roll | | | | ↓ | 172 | | | 172 | 189 |
| 4930 | Plate anchors | | | | M | 61 | | | 61 | 67 |
| 4970 | Adhesive for fully adhered systems, 60 S.F./gal. | | | | Gal. | 16.55 | | | 16.55 | 18.20 |

# 07 53 Elastomeric Membrane Roofing

## 07 53 29 – Polyisobutylene Roofing

### 07 53 29.10 Polyisobutylene Roofing

| | 07 53 29.10 Polyisobutylene Roofing | Crew | Daily Output | Labor-Hours | Unit | Material | 2008 Bare Costs Labor | Equipment | Total | Total Incl O&P |
|---|---|---|---|---|---|---|---|---|---|---|
| 0010 | **POLYISOBUTYLENE ROOFING** | | | | | | | | | |
| 7500 | Polyisobutylene (PIB), 100 mils, 0.57 P.S.F. | | | | | | | | | |
| 7600 | Loose-laid & ballasted with stone/gravel (10 P.S.F.) | G-5 | 51 | .784 | Sq. | 145 | 23.50 | 3.25 | 171.75 | 204 |
| 7700 | Partially adhered with adhesive | | 35 | 1.143 | | 182 | 34.50 | 4.73 | 221.23 | 264 |
| 7800 | Hot asphalt attachment | | 35 | 1.143 | | 173 | 34.50 | 4.73 | 212.23 | 255 |
| 7900 | Fully adhered with contact cement | | 26 | 1.538 | | 188 | 46 | 6.35 | 240.35 | 292 |

# 07 54 Thermoplastic Membrane Roofing

## 07 54 19 – Polyvinyl-Chloride Roofing

### 07 54 19.10 Polyvinyl-Chloride Roofing (P.V.C.)

| | 07 54 19.10 Polyvinyl-Chloride Roofing (P.V.C.) | Crew | Daily Output | Labor-Hours | Unit | Material | 2008 Bare Costs Labor | Equipment | Total | Total Incl O&P |
|---|---|---|---|---|---|---|---|---|---|---|
| 0010 | **POLYVINYL-CHLORIDE ROOFING (P.V.C.)** | | | | | | | | | |
| 8200 | Heat welded seams | | | | | | | | | |
| 8700 | Reinforced, 48 mils, 0.33 P.S.F. | | | | | | | | | |
| 8750 | Loose-laid & ballasted with stone/gravel (12 P.S.F.) | G-5 | 51 | .784 | Sq. | 116 | 23.50 | 3.25 | 142.75 | 172 |
| 8800 | Mechanically attached | | 35 | 1.143 | | 106 | 34.50 | 4.73 | 145.23 | 181 |
| 8850 | Fully adhered with adhesive | | 26 | 1.538 | | 155 | 46 | 6.35 | 207.35 | 257 |
| 8860 | Reinforced, 60 mils, .40 P.S.F. | | | | | | | | | |
| 8870 | Loose-laid & ballasted with stone/gravel (12 P.S.F.) | G-5 | 51 | .784 | Sq. | 118 | 23.50 | 3.25 | 144.75 | 174 |
| 8880 | Mechanically attached | | 35 | 1.143 | | 108 | 34.50 | 4.73 | 147.23 | 183 |
| 8890 | Fully adhered with adhesive | | 26 | 1.538 | | 157 | 46 | 6.35 | 209.35 | 259 |

## 07 54 23 – Thermoplastic Polyolefin Roofing

### 07 54 23.10 Thermoplastic Polyolefin Roofing (T.P.O)

| | 07 54 23.10 Thermoplastic Polyolefin Roofing (T.P.O) | Crew | Daily Output | Labor-Hours | Unit | Material | 2008 Bare Costs Labor | Equipment | Total | Total Incl O&P |
|---|---|---|---|---|---|---|---|---|---|---|
| 0010 | **THERMOPLASTIC POLYOLEFIN ROOFING (T.P.O.)** | | | | | | | | | |
| 0100 | 45 mils, loose laid & ballasted with stone(1/2 ton/sq.) | G-5 | 51 | .784 | Sq. | 90 | 23.50 | 3.25 | 116.75 | 143 |
| 0120 | Fully adhered | | 25 | 1.600 | | 129 | 48 | 6.60 | 183.60 | 231 |
| 0140 | Mechanically attached | | 34 | 1.176 | | 65.50 | 35.50 | 4.87 | 105.87 | 137 |
| 0160 | Self adhered | | 35 | 1.143 | | 74.50 | 34.50 | 4.73 | 113.73 | 145 |
| 0180 | 60 mil membrane, heat welded seams, ballasted | | 50 | .800 | | 106 | 24 | 3.31 | 133.31 | 162 |
| 0200 | Fully adhered | | 25 | 1.600 | | 145 | 48 | 6.60 | 199.60 | 248 |
| 0220 | Mechanically attached | | 34 | 1.176 | | 96 | 35.50 | 4.87 | 136.37 | 171 |
| 0240 | Self adhered | | 35 | 1.143 | | 90.50 | 34.50 | 4.73 | 129.73 | 163 |

# 07 56 Fluid-Applied Roofing

## 07 56 10 – Fluid-Applied Roofing Elastomers

### 07 56 10.10 Elastomeric Roofing

| | 07 56 10.10 Elastomeric Roofing | Crew | Daily Output | Labor-Hours | Unit | Material | 2008 Bare Costs Labor | Equipment | Total | Total Incl O&P |
|---|---|---|---|---|---|---|---|---|---|---|
| 0010 | **ELASTOMERIC ROOFING** | | | | | | | | | |
| 0110 | Acrylic rubber, fluid applied, 20 mils thick | G-5 | 2000 | .020 | S.F. | 2.06 | .60 | .08 | 2.74 | 3.38 |
| 0120 | 50 mils, reinforced | | 1200 | .033 | | 3.20 | 1 | .14 | 4.34 | 5.35 |
| 0130 | For walking surface, add | | 900 | .044 | | .97 | 1.34 | .18 | 2.49 | 3.54 |
| 0300 | Hypalon neoprene, fluid applied, 20 mil thick, not-reinforced | G-1 | 1135 | .049 | | 2.34 | 1.52 | .36 | 4.22 | 5.55 |
| 0600 | Non-woven polyester, reinforced | | 960 | .058 | | 2.37 | 1.80 | .43 | 4.60 | 6.15 |
| 0700 | 5 coat neoprene deck, 60 mil thick, under 10,000 SF | | 325 | .172 | | 5.20 | 5.30 | 1.27 | 11.77 | 16.20 |
| 0900 | Over 10,000 SF | | 625 | .090 | | 4.86 | 2.77 | .66 | 8.29 | 10.80 |
| 1300 | Vinyl plastic traffic deck, sprayed, 2 to 4 mils thick | | 625 | .090 | | 1.53 | 2.77 | .66 | 4.96 | 7.10 |
| 1500 | Vinyl and neoprene membrane traffic deck | | 1550 | .036 | | 1.61 | 1.12 | .27 | 3 | 3.96 |

203

# 07 57 Coated Foamed Roofing

## 07 57 13 – Sprayed Polyurethane Foam Roofing

| 07 57 13.10 Sprayed Polyurethane Foam Roofing (S.P.F.) | Crew | Daily Output | Labor-Hours | Unit | Material | 2008 Bare Costs Labor | Equipment | Total | Total Incl O&P |
|---|---|---|---|---|---|---|---|---|---|
| 0010 **SPRAYED POLYURETHANE FOAM ROOFING (S.P.F.)** | | | | | | | | | |
| 1600 Polyurethane spray-on with 20 mil silicone rubber coating applied | | | | | | | | | |
| 1700 1" thick, R7, minimum | G-2A | 875 | .027 | S.F. | 1.54 | .80 | .69 | 3.03 | 3.78 |
| 1800 Maximim | | 805 | .030 | | 2.06 | .87 | .75 | 3.68 | 4.53 |
| 1900 2" thick, R14, minimum | | 685 | .035 | | 2.18 | 1.03 | .88 | 4.09 | 5.05 |
| 2000 Maximum | | 575 | .042 | | 2.76 | 1.22 | 1.05 | 5.03 | 6.20 |
| 2100 3" thick, R21, minimum | | 500 | .048 | | 3.72 | 1.41 | 1.20 | 6.33 | 7.75 |
| 2200 Maximum | | 440 | .055 | | 4.76 | 1.60 | 1.37 | 7.73 | 9.40 |

# 07 58 Roll Roofing

## 07 58 10 – Asphalt Roll Roofing

### 07 58 10.10 Roll Roofing

| | Crew | Daily Output | Labor-Hours | Unit | Material | 2008 Bare Costs Labor | Equipment | Total | Total Incl O&P |
|---|---|---|---|---|---|---|---|---|---|
| 0010 **ROLL ROOFING** | | | | | | | | | |
| 0100 Asphalt, mineral surface | | | | | | | | | |
| 0200 1 ply #15 organic felt, 1 ply mineral surfaced | | | | | | | | | |
| 0300 Selvage roofing, lap 19", nailed & mopped | G-1 | 27 | 2.074 | Sq. | 53 | 64 | 15.25 | 132.25 | 184 |
| 0400 3 plies glass fiber felt (type IV), 1 ply mineral surfaced | | | | | | | | | |
| 0500 Selvage roofing, lapped 19", mopped | G-1 | 25 | 2.240 | Sq. | 82.50 | 69 | 16.50 | 168 | 227 |
| 0600 Coated glass fiber base sheet, 2 plies of glass fiber | | | | | | | | | |
| 0700 Felt (type IV), 1 ply mineral surfaced selvage | | | | | | | | | |
| 0800 Roofing, lapped 19", mopped | G-1 | 25 | 2.240 | Sq. | 89 | 69 | 16.50 | 174.50 | 234 |
| 0900 On nailable decks | " | 24 | 2.333 | " | 82 | 72 | 17.15 | 171.15 | 232 |
| 1000 3 plies glass fiber felt (type III), 1 ply mineral surfaced | | | | | | | | | |
| 1100 Selvage roofing, lapped 19", mopped | G-1 | 25 | 2.240 | Sq. | 82.50 | 69 | 16.50 | 168 | 227 |

# 07 61 Sheet Metal Roofing

## 07 61 13 – Standing Seam Sheet Metal Roofing

### 07 61 13.10 Standing Seam Sheet Metal Roofing, Field Fabricated

| | Crew | Daily Output | Labor-Hours | Unit | Material | 2008 Bare Costs Labor | Equipment | Total | Total Incl O&P |
|---|---|---|---|---|---|---|---|---|---|
| 0010 **STANDING SEAM SHEET METAL ROOFING, FIELD FABRICATED** | | | | | | | | | |
| 0400 Copper standing seam roofing, over 10 squares, 16 oz, 125 lb per sq | 1 Shee | 1.30 | 6.154 | Sq. | 915 | 279 | | 1,194 | 1,425 |
| 0600 18 oz, 140 lb per sq | | 1.20 | 6.667 | | 1,025 | 300 | | 1,325 | 1,600 |
| 0700 20 oz, 150 lb per sq | | 1.10 | 7.273 | | 1,100 | 330 | | 1,430 | 1,700 |
| 1200 For abnormal conditions or small areas, add | | | | | 25% | 100% | | | |
| 1300 For lead-coated copper, add | | | | | 25% | | | | |

## 07 61 16 – Batten Seam Sheet Metal Roofing

### 07 61 16.10 Batten Seam Sheet Metal Roofing, Field Fabricated

| | Crew | Daily Output | Labor-Hours | Unit | Material | 2008 Bare Costs Labor | Equipment | Total | Total Incl O&P |
|---|---|---|---|---|---|---|---|---|---|
| 0010 **BATTEN SEAM SHEET METAL ROOFING, FIELD FABRICATED** | | | | | | | | | |
| 0012 Copper batten seam roofing, over 10 sq, 16 oz, 130 lb per sq | 1 Shee | 1.10 | 7.273 | Sq. | 950 | 330 | | 1,280 | 1,550 |
| 0020 Lead batten seam roofing, 5 lb. per SF | | 1.20 | 6.667 | | 475 | 300 | | 775 | 985 |
| 0100 Zinc / copper alloy batten seam roofing, .020 thick | | 1.20 | 6.667 | | 1,200 | 300 | | 1,500 | 1,775 |
| 0200 Copper roofing, batten seam, over 10 sq, 18 oz, 145 lb per sq | | 1 | 8 | | 1,050 | 360 | | 1,410 | 1,725 |
| 0300 20 oz, 160 lb per sq | | 1 | 8 | | 1,175 | 360 | | 1,535 | 1,850 |
| 0500 Stainless steel batten seam roofing, type 304, 28 gauge | | 1.20 | 6.667 | | 595 | 300 | | 895 | 1,125 |
| 0600 26 gauge | | 1.15 | 6.957 | | 745 | 315 | | 1,060 | 1,300 |
| 0800 Zinc, copper alloy roofing, batten seam, .027" thick | | 1.15 | 6.957 | | 1,400 | 315 | | 1,715 | 2,025 |
| 0900 .032" thick | | 1.10 | 7.273 | | 1,625 | 330 | | 1,955 | 2,275 |
| 1000 .040" thick | | 1.05 | 7.619 | | 1,950 | 345 | | 2,295 | 2,675 |

# 07 61 Sheet Metal Roofing

## 07 61 19 – Flat Seam Sheet Metal Roofing

| 07 61 19.10 Flat Seam Sheet Metal Roofing, Field Fabricated | Crew | Daily Output | Labor-Hours | Unit | Material | 2008 Bare Costs Labor | Equipment | Total | Total Incl O&P |
|---|---|---|---|---|---|---|---|---|---|
| 0010 **FLAT SEAM SHEET METAL ROOFING, FIELD FABRICATED** | | | | | | | | | |
| 0900 Copper flat seam roofing, over 10 squares, 16 oz, 115 lb per sq | 1 Shee | 1.20 | 6.667 | Sq. | 840 | 300 | | 1,140 | 1,400 |
| 1000     20 oz, 145 lb per sq | | 1.10 | 7.273 | | 1,050 | 330 | | 1,380 | 1,675 |
| 1100 Lead flat seam roofing, 5 lb per SF | ↓ | 1.30 | 6.154 | ↓ | 475 | 279 | | 754 | 950 |

# 07 65 Flexible Flashing

## 07 65 10 – Sheet Metal Flashing

### 07 65 10.10 Sheet Metal Flashing and Counter Flashing

| | Crew | Daily Output | Labor-Hours | Unit | Material | 2008 Bare Costs Labor | Equipment | Total | Total Incl O&P |
|---|---|---|---|---|---|---|---|---|---|
| 0010 **SHEET METAL FLASHING AND COUNTER FLASHING** | | | | | | | | | |
| 0011   Including up to 4 bends | | | | | | | | | |
| 0020   Aluminum, mill finish, .013" thick | 1 Rofc | 145 | .055 | S.F. | .47 | 1.82 | | 2.29 | 3.62 |
| 0030     .016" thick | | 145 | .055 | | .69 | 1.82 | | 2.51 | 3.86 |
| 0060     .019" thick | | 145 | .055 | | .89 | 1.82 | | 2.71 | 4.08 |
| 0100     .032" thick | | 145 | .055 | | 1.29 | 1.82 | | 3.11 | 4.52 |
| 0200     .040" thick | | 145 | .055 | | 1.93 | 1.82 | | 3.75 | 5.20 |
| 0300     .050" thick | | 145 | .055 | ↓ | 2.19 | 1.82 | | 4.01 | 5.50 |
| 0325   Mill finish 5" x 7" step flashing, .016" thick | | 1920 | .004 | Ea. | .14 | .14 | | .28 | .38 |
| 0350   Mill finish 12" x 12" step flashing, .016" thick | ↓ | 1600 | .005 | " | .53 | .17 | | .70 | .86 |
| 0400     Painted finish, add | | | | S.F. | .32 | | | .32 | .35 |
| 1000   Mastic-coated 2 sides, .005" thick | 1 Rofc | 330 | .024 | | 1.45 | .80 | | 2.25 | 2.96 |
| 1100     .016" thick | | 330 | .024 | | 1.60 | .80 | | 2.40 | 3.12 |
| 1600   Copper, 16 oz, sheets, under 1000 lbs. | | 115 | .070 | | 6.10 | 2.30 | | 8.40 | 10.65 |
| 1700     Over 4000 lbs. | | 155 | .052 | | 7.20 | 1.70 | | 8.90 | 10.85 |
| 1900     20 oz sheets, under 1000 lbs. | | 110 | .073 | | 7.10 | 2.40 | | 9.50 | 11.90 |
| 2000     Over 4000 lbs. | | 145 | .055 | | 7.20 | 1.82 | | 9.02 | 11.05 |
| 2200     24 oz sheets, under 1000 lbs. | | 105 | .076 | | 8.65 | 2.51 | | 11.16 | 13.85 |
| 2300     Over 4000 lbs. | | 135 | .059 | | 8.75 | 1.96 | | 10.71 | 13 |
| 2500     32 oz sheets, under 1000 lbs. | | 100 | .080 | | 11.55 | 2.64 | | 14.19 | 17.20 |
| 2600     Over 4000 lbs. | | 130 | .062 | ↓ | 18.20 | 2.03 | | 20.23 | 23.50 |
| 2700     W shape for valleys, 16 oz, 24" wide | | 100 | .080 | L.F. | 13.20 | 2.64 | | 15.84 | 19 |
| 5800   Lead, 2.5 lb. per SF, up to 12" wide | | 135 | .059 | S.F. | 3.63 | 1.96 | | 5.59 | 7.30 |
| 5900     Over 12" wide | | 135 | .059 | | 3.63 | 1.96 | | 5.59 | 7.30 |
| 8650     Copper, 16 oz | | 100 | .080 | | 4.68 | 2.64 | | 7.32 | 9.65 |
| 8900   Stainless steel sheets, 32 ga, .010" thick | | 155 | .052 | | 3.38 | 1.70 | | 5.08 | 6.60 |
| 9000     28 ga, .015" thick | | 155 | .052 | | 4.20 | 1.70 | | 5.90 | 7.50 |
| 9100     26 ga, .018" thick | | 155 | .052 | | 5.10 | 1.70 | | 6.80 | 8.50 |
| 9200     24 ga, .025" thick | ↓ | 155 | .052 | ↓ | 6.60 | 1.70 | | 8.30 | 10.15 |
| 9290     For mechanically keyed flashing, add | | | | | 40% | | | | |
| 9320   Steel sheets, galvanized, 20 gauge | 1 Rofc | 130 | .062 | S.F. | 1.06 | 2.03 | | 3.09 | 4.63 |
| 9340     30 gauge | | 160 | .050 | | .45 | 1.65 | | 2.10 | 3.31 |
| 9400   Terne coated stainless steel, .015" thick, 28 ga | | 155 | .052 | | 6.55 | 1.70 | | 8.25 | 10.10 |
| 9500     .018" thick, 26 ga | | 155 | .052 | | 7.40 | 1.70 | | 9.10 | 11.05 |
| 9600   Zinc and copper alloy (brass), .020" thick | | 155 | .052 | | 4.60 | 1.70 | | 6.30 | 7.95 |
| 9700     .027" thick | | 155 | .052 | | 6.15 | 1.70 | | 7.85 | 9.70 |
| 9800     .032" thick | | 155 | .052 | | 7.20 | 1.70 | | 8.90 | 10.80 |
| 9900     .040" thick | ↓ | 155 | .052 | ↓ | 8.80 | 1.70 | | 10.50 | 12.55 |

## 07 65 12 – Fabric and Mastic Flashings

### 07 65 12.10 Fabric and Mastic Flashing and Counter Flashing

| | Crew | Daily Output | Labor-Hours | Unit | Material | 2008 Bare Costs Labor | Equipment | Total | Total Incl O&P |
|---|---|---|---|---|---|---|---|---|---|
| 0010 **FABRIC AND MASTIC FLASHING AND COUNTER FLASHING** | | | | | | | | | |
| 1300   Asphalt flashing cement, 5 gallon | | | | Gal. | 5.10 | | | 5.10 | 5.60 |

# 07 65 Flexible Flashing

## 07 65 12 – Fabric and Mastic Flashings

| 07 65 12.10 Fabric and Mastic Flashing and Counter Flashing | Crew | Daily Output | Labor-Hours | Unit | Material | 2008 Bare Costs Labor | Equipment | Total | Total Incl O&P |
|---|---|---|---|---|---|---|---|---|---|
| 4900 | Fabric, asphalt-saturated cotton, specification grade | 1 Rofc | 35 | .229 | S.Y. | 2.12 | 7.55 | | 9.67 | 15.20 |
| 5000 | Utility grade | | 35 | .229 | | 1.34 | 7.55 | | 8.89 | 14.30 |
| 5200 | Open-mesh fabric, saturated, 40 oz per S.Y. | | 35 | .229 | | 1.49 | 7.55 | | 9.04 | 14.50 |
| 5300 | Close-mesh fabric, saturated, 17 oz per S.Y. | | 35 | .229 | | 1.56 | 7.55 | | 9.11 | 14.55 |
| 5500 | Fiberglass, resin-coated | | 35 | .229 | | 1.28 | 7.55 | | 8.83 | 14.25 |
| 5600 | Asphalt-coated, 40 oz per S.Y. | | 35 | .229 | | 8.70 | 7.55 | | 16.25 | 22.50 |
| 8500 | Shower pan, bituminous membrane, 7 oz | | 155 | .052 | S.F. | 1.63 | 1.70 | | 3.33 | 4.69 |

## 07 65 13 – Laminated Sheet Flashing

### 07 65 13.10 Laminated Sheet Flashing

| | | Crew | Daily Output | Labor-Hours | Unit | Material | 2008 Bare Costs Labor | Equipment | Total | Total Incl O&P |
|---|---|---|---|---|---|---|---|---|---|---|
| 0010 | **LAMINATED SHEET FLASHING**, Including up to 4 bends | | | | | | | | | |
| 0500 | Fabric-backed 2 sides, .004" thick | 1 Rofc | 330 | .024 | S.F. | 1.23 | .80 | | 2.03 | 2.71 |
| 0700 | .005" thick | | 330 | .024 | | 1.45 | .80 | | 2.25 | 2.96 |
| 0750 | Mastic-backed, self adhesive | | 460 | .017 | | 3.01 | .57 | | 3.58 | 4.29 |
| 0800 | Mastic-coated 2 sides, .004" thick | | 330 | .024 | | 1.23 | .80 | | 2.03 | 2.71 |
| 2800 | Copper, paperbacked 1 side, 2 oz | | 330 | .024 | | 1.28 | .80 | | 2.08 | 2.77 |
| 2900 | 3 oz | | 330 | .024 | | 1.67 | .80 | | 2.47 | 3.20 |
| 3100 | Paperbacked 2 sides, 2 oz | | 330 | .024 | | 1.28 | .80 | | 2.08 | 2.77 |
| 3150 | 3 oz | | 330 | .024 | | 1.66 | .80 | | 2.46 | 3.19 |
| 3200 | 5 oz | | 330 | .024 | | 2.48 | .80 | | 3.28 | 4.09 |
| 3250 | 7 oz | | 330 | .024 | | 4.05 | .80 | | 4.85 | 5.80 |
| 3400 | Mastic-backed 2 sides, copper, 2 oz | | 330 | .024 | | 1.52 | .80 | | 2.32 | 3.03 |
| 3500 | 3 oz | | 330 | .024 | | 1.87 | .80 | | 2.67 | 3.42 |
| 3700 | 5 oz | | 330 | .024 | | 2.75 | .80 | | 3.55 | 4.39 |
| 3800 | Fabric-backed 2 sides, copper, 2 oz | | 330 | .024 | | 1.61 | .80 | | 2.41 | 3.13 |
| 4000 | 3 oz | | 330 | .024 | | 2.08 | .80 | | 2.88 | 3.65 |
| 4100 | 5 oz | | 330 | .024 | | 2.83 | .80 | | 3.63 | 4.47 |
| 4300 | Copper-clad stainless steel, .015" thick, under 500 lbs. | | 115 | .070 | | 4.71 | 2.30 | | 7.01 | 9.10 |
| 4400 | Over 2000 lbs. | | 155 | .052 | | 4.53 | 1.70 | | 6.23 | 7.90 |
| 4600 | .018" thick, under 500 lbs. | | 100 | .080 | | 6.20 | 2.64 | | 8.84 | 11.35 |
| 4700 | Over 2000 lbs. | | 145 | .055 | | 4.55 | 1.82 | | 6.37 | 8.10 |
| 6100 | Lead-coated copper, fabric-backed, 2 oz | | 330 | .024 | | 2.18 | .80 | | 2.98 | 3.76 |
| 6200 | 5 oz | | 330 | .024 | | 2.51 | .80 | | 3.31 | 4.12 |
| 6400 | Mastic-backed 2 sides, 2 oz | | 330 | .024 | | 1.70 | .80 | | 2.50 | 3.23 |
| 6500 | 5 oz | | 330 | .024 | | 2.11 | .80 | | 2.91 | 3.68 |
| 6700 | Paperbacked 1 side, 2 oz | | 330 | .024 | | 1.47 | .80 | | 2.27 | 2.98 |
| 6800 | 3 oz | | 330 | .024 | | 1.73 | .80 | | 2.53 | 3.26 |
| 7000 | Paperbacked 2 sides, 2 oz | | 330 | .024 | | 1.52 | .80 | | 2.32 | 3.03 |
| 7100 | 5 oz | | 330 | .024 | | 2.48 | .80 | | 3.28 | 4.09 |
| 8550 | 3 ply copper and fabric, 3 oz | | 155 | .052 | | 2.44 | 1.70 | | 4.14 | 5.60 |
| 8600 | 7 oz | | 155 | .052 | | 5.05 | 1.70 | | 6.75 | 8.50 |
| 8700 | Lead on copper and fabric, 5 oz | | 155 | .052 | | 2.51 | 1.70 | | 4.21 | 5.65 |
| 8800 | 7 oz | | 155 | .052 | | 4.41 | 1.70 | | 6.11 | 7.75 |
| 9300 | Stainless steel, paperbacked 2 sides, .005" thick | | 330 | .024 | | 2.98 | .80 | | 3.78 | 4.64 |

## 07 65 19 – Plastic Sheet Flashing

### 07 65 19.10 Plastic Sheet Flashing and Counter Flashing

| | | Crew | Daily Output | Labor-Hours | Unit | Material | 2008 Bare Costs Labor | Equipment | Total | Total Incl O&P |
|---|---|---|---|---|---|---|---|---|---|---|
| 0010 | **PLASTIC SHEET FLASHING AND COUNTER FLASHING** | | | | | | | | | |
| 7300 | Polyvinyl chloride, black, .010" thick | 1 Rofc | 285 | .028 | S.F. | .22 | .93 | | 1.15 | 1.82 |
| 7400 | .020" thick | | 285 | .028 | | .31 | .93 | | 1.24 | 1.92 |
| 7600 | .030" thick | | 285 | .028 | | .41 | .93 | | 1.34 | 2.03 |
| 7700 | .056" thick | | 285 | .028 | | .98 | .93 | | 1.91 | 2.66 |
| 7900 | Black or white for exposed roofs, .060" thick | | 285 | .028 | | 2.15 | .93 | | 3.08 | 3.95 |
| 8060 | PVC tape, 5" x 45 mils, for joint covers, 100 L.F./roll | | | | Ea. | 105 | | | 105 | 116 |

# 07 65 Flexible Flashing

## 07 65 19 – Plastic Sheet Flashing

| 07 65 19.10 Plastic Sheet Flashing and Counter Flashing | Crew | Daily Output | Labor-Hours | Unit | Material | 2008 Bare Costs Labor | Equipment | Total | Total Incl O&P |
|---|---|---|---|---|---|---|---|---|---|
| 8850  Polyvinyl chloride, .030" thick | 1 Rofc | 160 | .050 | S.F. | .38 | 1.65 | | 2.03 | 3.23 |

## 07 65 23 – Rubber Sheet Flashing

### 07 65 23.10 Rubber Sheet Flashing and Counterflashing

| | Crew | Daily Output | Labor-Hours | Unit | Material | Labor | Equipment | Total | Total Incl O&P |
|---|---|---|---|---|---|---|---|---|---|
| 0010  **RUBBER SHEET FLASHING AND COUNTERFLASHING** | | | | | | | | | |
| 8100  Rubber, butyl, 1/32" thick | 1 Rofc | 285 | .028 | S.F. | .93 | .93 | | 1.86 | 2.60 |
| 8200  1/16" thick | | 285 | .028 | | 1.39 | .93 | | 2.32 | 3.11 |
| 8300  Neoprene, cured, 1/16" thick | | 285 | .028 | | 1.97 | .93 | | 2.90 | 3.75 |
| 8400  1/8" thick | | 285 | .028 | | 3.97 | .93 | | 4.90 | 5.95 |

# 07 71 Roof Specialties

## 07 71 19 – Manufactured Gravel Stops and Fascias

### 07 71 19.10 Gravel Stop

| | Crew | Daily Output | Labor-Hours | Unit | Material | Labor | Equipment | Total | Total Incl O&P |
|---|---|---|---|---|---|---|---|---|---|
| 0010  **GRAVEL STOP** | | | | | | | | | |
| 0020  Aluminum, .050" thick, 4" face height, mill finish | 1 Shee | 145 | .055 | L.F. | 5.05 | 2.50 | | 7.55 | 9.40 |
| 0080  Duranodic finish | | 145 | .055 | | 4.86 | 2.50 | | 7.36 | 9.20 |
| 0100  Painted | | 145 | .055 | | 5.60 | 2.50 | | 8.10 | 10.05 |
| 0300  6" face height | | 135 | .059 | | 5.40 | 2.68 | | 8.08 | 10.10 |
| 0350  Duranodic finish | | 135 | .059 | | 5.75 | 2.68 | | 8.43 | 10.45 |
| 0400  Painted | | 135 | .059 | | 6.65 | 2.68 | | 9.33 | 11.50 |
| 0600  8" face height | | 125 | .064 | | 6.75 | 2.90 | | 9.65 | 11.90 |
| 0650  Duranodic finish | | 125 | .064 | | 6.55 | 2.90 | | 9.45 | 11.70 |
| 0700  Painted | | 125 | .064 | | 6.70 | 2.90 | | 9.60 | 11.80 |
| 0900  12" face height, .080 thick, 2 piece | | 100 | .080 | | 9 | 3.62 | | 12.62 | 15.50 |
| 0950  Duranodic finish | | 100 | .080 | | 8.30 | 3.62 | | 11.92 | 14.70 |
| 1000  Painted | | 100 | .080 | | 9.80 | 3.62 | | 13.42 | 16.35 |
| 1350  Galv steel, 24 ga., 4" leg, plain, with continuous cleat, 4" face | | 145 | .055 | | 1.98 | 2.50 | | 4.48 | 6.05 |
| 1360  6" face height | | 145 | .055 | | 2.99 | 2.50 | | 5.49 | 7.15 |
| 1500  Polyvinyl chloride, 6" face height | | 135 | .059 | | 4.32 | 2.68 | | 7 | 8.90 |
| 1600  9" face height | | 125 | .064 | | 5.10 | 2.90 | | 8 | 10.05 |
| 1800  Stainless steel, 24 ga., 6" face height | | 135 | .059 | | 9.45 | 2.68 | | 12.13 | 14.50 |
| 1900  12" face height | | 100 | .080 | | 19.75 | 3.62 | | 23.37 | 27.50 |
| 2100  20 ga., 6" face height | | 135 | .059 | | 10.70 | 2.68 | | 13.38 | 15.90 |
| 2200  12" face height | | 100 | .080 | | 22.50 | 3.62 | | 26.12 | 30.50 |

### 07 71 19.30 Fascia

| | Crew | Daily Output | Labor-Hours | Unit | Material | Labor | Equipment | Total | Total Incl O&P |
|---|---|---|---|---|---|---|---|---|---|
| 0010  **FASCIA** | | | | | | | | | |
| 0100  Aluminum, reverse board and batten, .032" thick, colored, no furring incl | 1 Shee | 145 | .055 | S.F. | 4.95 | 2.50 | | 7.45 | 9.30 |
| 0300  Steel, galv and enameled, stock, no furring, long panels | | 145 | .055 | | 3.24 | 2.50 | | 5.74 | 7.40 |
| 0600  Short panels | | 115 | .070 | | 4.32 | 3.15 | | 7.47 | 9.60 |

## 07 71 23 – Manufactured Gutters and Downspouts

### 07 71 23.10 Downspouts

| | Crew | Daily Output | Labor-Hours | Unit | Material | Labor | Equipment | Total | Total Incl O&P |
|---|---|---|---|---|---|---|---|---|---|
| 0010  **DOWNSPOUTS** | | | | | | | | | |
| 0020  Aluminum 2" x 3", .020" thick, embossed | 1 Shee | 190 | .042 | L.F. | .94 | 1.91 | | 2.85 | 3.97 |
| 0100  Enameled | | 190 | .042 | | 1.59 | 1.91 | | 3.50 | 4.69 |
| 0300  Enameled, .024" thick, 2" x 3" | | 180 | .044 | | 1.66 | 2.01 | | 3.67 | 4.93 |
| 0400  3" x 4" | | 140 | .057 | | 2.50 | 2.59 | | 5.09 | 6.75 |
| 0600  Round, corrugated aluminum, 3" diameter, .020" thick | | 190 | .042 | | 1.42 | 1.91 | | 3.33 | 4.50 |
| 0700  4" diameter, .025" thick | | 140 | .057 | | 1.92 | 2.59 | | 4.51 | 6.10 |
| 0900  Wire strainer, round, 2" diameter | | 155 | .052 | Ea. | 3.32 | 2.34 | | 5.66 | 7.25 |
| 1000  4" diameter | | 155 | .052 | | 6.10 | 2.34 | | 8.44 | 10.35 |
| 1200  Rectangular, perforated, 2" x 3" | | 145 | .055 | | 2.30 | 2.50 | | 4.80 | 6.40 |

## 07 71 23 – Manufactured Gutters and Downspouts

| 07 71 23.10 Downspouts | | Crew | Daily Output | Labor-Hours | Unit | Material | 2008 Bare Costs Labor | Equipment | Total | Total Incl O&P |
|---|---|---|---|---|---|---|---|---|---|---|
| 1300 | 3" x 4" | 1 Shee | 145 | .055 | Ea. | 3.32 | 2.50 | | 5.82 | 7.50 |
| 1500 | Copper, round, 16 oz., stock, 2" diameter | | 190 | .042 | L.F. | 9 | 1.91 | | 10.91 | 12.85 |
| 1600 | 3" diameter | | 190 | .042 | | 7.85 | 1.91 | | 9.76 | 11.60 |
| 1800 | 4" diameter | | 145 | .055 | | 9 | 2.50 | | 11.50 | 13.75 |
| 1900 | 5" diameter | | 130 | .062 | | 14.70 | 2.79 | | 17.49 | 20.50 |
| 2100 | Rectangular, corrugated copper, stock, 2" x 3" | | 190 | .042 | | 6.70 | 1.91 | | 8.61 | 10.35 |
| 2200 | 3" x 4" | | 145 | .055 | | 8.25 | 2.50 | | 10.75 | 12.95 |
| 2400 | Rectangular, plain copper, stock, 2" x 3" | | 190 | .042 | | 7 | 1.91 | | 8.91 | 10.65 |
| 2500 | 3" x 4" | | 145 | .055 | ↓ | 9.10 | 2.50 | | 11.60 | 13.85 |
| 2700 | Wire strainers, rectangular, 2" x 3" | | 145 | .055 | Ea. | 5.50 | 2.50 | | 8 | 9.90 |
| 2800 | 3" x 4" | | 145 | .055 | | 6.60 | 2.50 | | 9.10 | 11.10 |
| 3000 | Round, 2" diameter | | 145 | .055 | | 4.40 | 2.50 | | 6.90 | 8.70 |
| 3100 | 3" diameter | | 145 | .055 | | 6.10 | 2.50 | | 8.60 | 10.60 |
| 3300 | 4" diameter | | 145 | .055 | | 11.30 | 2.50 | | 13.80 | 16.25 |
| 3400 | 5" diameter | | 115 | .070 | ↓ | 16.60 | 3.15 | | 19.75 | 23 |
| 3600 | Lead-coated copper, round, stock, 2" diameter | | 190 | .042 | L.F. | 6.90 | 1.91 | | 8.81 | 10.55 |
| 3700 | 3" diameter | | 190 | .042 | | 12.60 | 1.91 | | 14.51 | 16.80 |
| 3900 | 4" diameter | | 145 | .055 | | 9.60 | 2.50 | | 12.10 | 14.40 |
| 4200 | 6" diameter, corrugated | | 105 | .076 | | 24 | 3.45 | | 27.45 | 32 |
| 4300 | Rectangular, corrugated, stock, 2" x 3" | | 190 | .042 | | 12.75 | 1.91 | | 14.66 | 17 |
| 4500 | Plain, stock, 2" x 3" | | 190 | .042 | | 9.75 | 1.91 | | 11.66 | 13.70 |
| 4600 | 3" x 4" | | 145 | .055 | | 10 | 2.50 | | 12.50 | 14.85 |
| 4800 | Steel, galvanized, round, corrugated, 2" or 3" diam, 28 ga | | 190 | .042 | | 1.56 | 1.91 | | 3.47 | 4.66 |
| 4900 | 4" diameter, 28 gauge | | 145 | .055 | | 2.21 | 2.50 | | 4.71 | 6.30 |
| 5100 | 5" diameter, 28 gauge | | 130 | .062 | | 3.28 | 2.79 | | 6.07 | 7.90 |
| 5200 | 26 gauge | | 130 | .062 | | 2.65 | 2.79 | | 5.44 | 7.20 |
| 5400 | 6" diameter, 28 gauge | | 105 | .076 | | 4.31 | 3.45 | | 7.76 | 10.05 |
| 5500 | 26 gauge | | 105 | .076 | | 5.45 | 3.45 | | 8.90 | 11.30 |
| 5700 | Rectangular, corrugated, 28 gauge, 2" x 3" | | 190 | .042 | | 1.43 | 1.91 | | 3.34 | 4.51 |
| 5800 | 3" x 4" | | 145 | .055 | | 1.43 | 2.50 | | 3.93 | 5.40 |
| 6000 | Rectangular, plain, 28 gauge, galvanized, 2" x 3" | | 190 | .042 | | 1.55 | 1.91 | | 3.46 | 4.65 |
| 6100 | 3" x 4" | | 145 | .055 | | 2.24 | 2.50 | | 4.74 | 6.30 |
| 6300 | Epoxy painted, 24 gauge, corrugated, 2" x 3" | | 190 | .042 | | 1.70 | 1.91 | | 3.61 | 4.81 |
| 6400 | 3" x 4" | | 145 | .055 | ↓ | 1.89 | 2.50 | | 4.39 | 5.95 |
| 6600 | Wire strainers, rectangular, 2" x 3" | | 145 | .055 | Ea. | 5.30 | 2.50 | | 7.80 | 9.65 |
| 6700 | 3" x 4" | | 145 | .055 | | 10.50 | 2.50 | | 13 | 15.40 |
| 6900 | Round strainers, 2" or 3" diameter | | 145 | .055 | | 5.30 | 2.50 | | 7.80 | 9.65 |
| 7000 | 4" diameter | | 145 | .055 | | 10.50 | 2.50 | | 13 | 15.40 |
| 7200 | 5" diameter | | 145 | .055 | | 2.38 | 2.50 | | 4.88 | 6.45 |
| 7300 | 6" diameter | | 115 | .070 | ↓ | 2.84 | 3.15 | | 5.99 | 8 |
| 7500 | Steel pipe, black, extra heavy, 4" diameter | | 20 | .400 | L.F. | 20.50 | 18.10 | | 38.60 | 50.50 |
| 7600 | 6" diameter | | 18 | .444 | | 30 | 20 | | 50 | 64 |
| 7800 | Stainless steel tubing, schedule 5, 2" x 3" or 3" diameter | | 190 | .042 | | 45 | 1.91 | | 46.91 | 52.50 |
| 7900 | 3" x 4" or 4" diameter | | 145 | .055 | | 57 | 2.50 | | 59.50 | 66.50 |
| 8100 | 4" x 5" or 5" diameter | | 135 | .059 | | 118 | 2.68 | | 120.68 | 133 |
| 8200 | Vinyl, rectangular, 2" x 3" | | 210 | .038 | | .75 | 1.73 | | 2.48 | 3.49 |
| 8300 | Round, 2-1/2" | ↓ | 220 | .036 | ↓ | .75 | 1.65 | | 2.40 | 3.37 |

## 07 71 23.20 Downspout Elbows

| | | Crew | Daily Output | Labor-Hours | Unit | Material | 2008 Bare Costs Labor | Equipment | Total | Total Incl O&P |
|---|---|---|---|---|---|---|---|---|---|---|
| 0010 | **DOWNSPOUT ELBOWS** | | | | | | | | | |
| 0020 | Aluminum, 2" x 3", embossed | 1 Shee | 100 | .080 | Ea. | 1.17 | 3.62 | | 4.79 | 6.90 |
| 0100 | Enameled | | 100 | .080 | | 1.17 | 3.62 | | 4.79 | 6.90 |
| 0200 | 3" x 4", .025" thick, embossed | ↓ | 100 | .080 | ↓ | 3.96 | 3.62 | | 7.58 | 9.95 |

# 07 71 Roof Specialties

## 07 71 23 – Manufactured Gutters and Downspouts

| 07 71 23.20 Downspout Elbows | Crew | Daily Output | Labor-Hours | Unit | Material | 2008 Bare Costs Labor | Equipment | Total | Total Incl O&P |
|---|---|---|---|---|---|---|---|---|---|
| 0300 | Enameled | 1 Shee | 100 | .080 | Ea. | 3.84 | 3.62 | | 7.46 | 9.80 |
| 0400 | Round corrugated, 3", embossed, .020" thick | | 100 | .080 | | 2.38 | 3.62 | | 6 | 8.20 |
| 0500 | 4", .025" thick | | 100 | .080 | | 6.50 | 3.62 | | 10.12 | 12.75 |
| 0600 | Copper, 16 oz. round, 2" diameter | | 100 | .080 | | 13.40 | 3.62 | | 17.02 | 20.50 |
| 0700 | 3" diameter | | 100 | .080 | | 9.75 | 3.62 | | 13.37 | 16.30 |
| 0800 | 4" diameter | | 100 | .080 | | 13.50 | 3.62 | | 17.12 | 20.50 |
| 1000 | 2" x 3" corrugated | | 100 | .080 | | 8.70 | 3.62 | | 12.32 | 15.15 |
| 1100 | 3" x 4" corrugated | | 100 | .080 | | 14.75 | 3.62 | | 18.37 | 22 |
| 1300 | Vinyl, 2-1/2" diameter, 45° or 75° | | 100 | .080 | | 3 | 3.62 | | 6.62 | 8.90 |
| 1400 | Tee Y junction | | 75 | .107 | | 11 | 4.83 | | 15.83 | 19.55 |

| 07 71 23.30 Gutters | Crew | Daily Output | Labor-Hours | Unit | Material | 2008 Bare Costs Labor | Equipment | Total | Total Incl O&P |
|---|---|---|---|---|---|---|---|---|---|
| 0010 | **GUTTERS** | | | | | | | | | |
| 0012 | Aluminum, stock units, 5" K type, .027" thick, plain | 1 Shee | 120 | .067 | L.F. | 1.99 | 3.02 | | 5.01 | 6.85 |
| 0100 | Enameled | | 120 | .067 | | 1.85 | 3.02 | | 4.87 | 6.70 |
| 0300 | 5" K type type, .032" thick, plain | | 120 | .067 | | 3.17 | 3.02 | | 6.19 | 8.15 |
| 0400 | Enameled | | 120 | .067 | | 2.60 | 3.02 | | 5.62 | 7.50 |
| 0700 | Copper, half round, 16 oz, stock units, 4" wide | | 120 | .067 | | 5.75 | 3.02 | | 8.77 | 10.95 |
| 0900 | 5" wide | | 120 | .067 | | 6.50 | 3.02 | | 9.52 | 11.80 |
| 1000 | 6" wide | | 115 | .070 | | 9.15 | 3.15 | | 12.30 | 14.95 |
| 1200 | K type, 16 oz, stock, 4" wide | | 120 | .067 | | 7.35 | 3.02 | | 10.37 | 12.70 |
| 1300 | 5" wide | | 120 | .067 | | 7.10 | 3.02 | | 10.12 | 12.45 |
| 1500 | Lead coated copper, half round, stock, 4" wide | | 120 | .067 | | 10.50 | 3.02 | | 13.52 | 16.20 |
| 1600 | 6" wide | | 115 | .070 | | 14.25 | 3.15 | | 17.40 | 20.50 |
| 1800 | K type, stock, 4" wide | | 120 | .067 | | 11.35 | 3.02 | | 14.37 | 17.15 |
| 1900 | 5" wide | | 120 | .067 | | 14.25 | 3.02 | | 17.27 | 20.50 |
| 2100 | Stainless steel, half round or box, stock, 4" wide | | 120 | .067 | | 5.25 | 3.02 | | 8.27 | 10.45 |
| 2200 | 5" wide | | 120 | .067 | | 5.65 | 3.02 | | 8.67 | 10.85 |
| 2400 | Steel, galv, half round or box, 28 ga, 5" wide, plain | | 120 | .067 | | 1.30 | 3.02 | | 4.32 | 6.10 |
| 2500 | Enameled | | 120 | .067 | | 1.35 | 3.02 | | 4.37 | 6.15 |
| 2700 | 26 ga, stock, 5" wide | | 120 | .067 | | 1.42 | 3.02 | | 4.44 | 6.20 |
| 2800 | 6" wide | | 120 | .067 | | 2.06 | 3.02 | | 5.08 | 6.95 |
| 3000 | Vinyl, O.G., 4" wide | 1 Carp | 110 | .073 | | 1 | 2.77 | | 3.77 | 5.40 |
| 3100 | 5" wide | | 110 | .073 | | 1.18 | 2.77 | | 3.95 | 5.60 |
| 3200 | 4" half round, stock units | | 110 | .073 | | .80 | 2.77 | | 3.57 | 5.20 |
| 3250 | Joint connectors | | | | Ea. | 1.60 | | | 1.60 | 1.76 |
| 3300 | Wood, clear treated cedar, fir or hemlock, 3" x 4" | 1 Carp | 100 | .080 | L.F. | 7 | 3.05 | | 10.05 | 12.45 |
| 3400 | 4" x 5" | " | 100 | .080 | " | 8 | 3.05 | | 11.05 | 13.55 |

| 07 71 23.35 Gutter Guard | Crew | Daily Output | Labor-Hours | Unit | Material | 2008 Bare Costs Labor | Equipment | Total | Total Incl O&P |
|---|---|---|---|---|---|---|---|---|---|
| 0010 | **GUTTER GUARD** | | | | | | | | | |
| 0020 | 6" wide strip, aluminum mesh | 1 Carp | 500 | .016 | L.F. | .42 | .61 | | 1.03 | 1.41 |
| 0100 | Vinyl mesh | " | 500 | .016 | " | .43 | .61 | | 1.04 | 1.42 |

## 07 71 26 – Reglets

| 07 71 26.10 Reglets and Accessories | Crew | Daily Output | Labor-Hours | Unit | Material | 2008 Bare Costs Labor | Equipment | Total | Total Incl O&P |
|---|---|---|---|---|---|---|---|---|---|
| 0010 | **REGLETS AND ACCESSORIES** | | | | | | | | | |
| 0020 | Aluminum, .025" thick, in concrete parapet | 1 Carp | 225 | .036 | L.F. | 1.18 | 1.35 | | 2.53 | 3.41 |
| 0100 | Copper, 10 oz. | | 225 | .036 | | 2.41 | 1.35 | | 3.76 | 4.76 |
| 0300 | 16 oz. | | 225 | .036 | | 4.71 | 1.35 | | 6.06 | 7.30 |
| 0400 | Galvanized steel, 24 gauge | | 225 | .036 | | .86 | 1.35 | | 2.21 | 3.06 |
| 0600 | Stainless steel, .020" thick | | 225 | .036 | | 1.93 | 1.35 | | 3.28 | 4.23 |
| 0700 | Zinc and copper alloy, 20 oz. | | 225 | .036 | | 2.41 | 1.35 | | 3.76 | 4.76 |
| 0900 | Counter flashing for above, 12" wide, .032" aluminum | 1 Shee | 150 | .053 | | 1.50 | 2.42 | | 3.92 | 5.40 |
| 1000 | Copper, 10 oz. | | 150 | .053 | | 4.55 | 2.42 | | 6.97 | 8.75 |

# 07 71 Roof Specialties

## 07 71 26 – Reglets

| 07 71 26.10 Reglets and Accessories | Crew | Daily Output | Labor-Hours | Unit | Material | 2008 Bare Costs Labor | Equipment | Total | Total Incl O&P |
|---|---|---|---|---|---|---|---|---|---|
| 1200 | 16 oz. | 1 Shee | 150 | .053 | L.F. | 5.25 | 2.42 | | 7.67 | 9.50 |
| 1300 | Galvanized steel, .020" thick | | 150 | .053 | | .85 | 2.42 | | 3.27 | 4.67 |
| 1500 | Stainless steel, .020" thick | | 150 | .053 | | 3.42 | 2.42 | | 5.84 | 7.50 |
| 1600 | Zinc and copper alloy, 20 oz. | | 150 | .053 | | 4.39 | 2.42 | | 6.81 | 8.55 |

## 07 71 29 – Manufactured Roof Expansion Joints

### 07 71 29.10 Expansion Joints

| | | Crew | Daily Output | Labor-Hours | Unit | Material | Labor | Equipment | Total | Total Incl O&P |
|---|---|---|---|---|---|---|---|---|---|---|
| 0010 | **EXPANSION JOINTS** | | | | | | | | | |
| 0300 | Butyl or neoprene center with foam insulation, metal flanges | | | | | | | | | |
| 0400 | Aluminum, .032" thick for openings to 2-1/2" | 1 Rofc | 165 | .048 | L.F. | 9.40 | 1.60 | | 11 | 13.05 |
| 0600 | For joint openings to 3-1/2" | | 165 | .048 | | 11 | 1.60 | | 12.60 | 14.80 |
| 0610 | For joint openings to 5" | | 165 | .048 | | 13.25 | 1.60 | | 14.85 | 17.30 |
| 0620 | For joint openings to 8" | | 165 | .048 | | 21 | 1.60 | | 22.60 | 25.50 |
| 0700 | Copper, 16 oz. for openings to 2-1/2" | | 165 | .048 | | 15.35 | 1.60 | | 16.95 | 19.55 |
| 0900 | For joint openings to 3-1/2" | | 165 | .048 | | 17.60 | 1.60 | | 19.20 | 22 |
| 0910 | For joint openings to 5" | | 165 | .048 | | 20.50 | 1.60 | | 22.10 | 25 |
| 0920 | For joint openings to 8" | | 165 | .048 | | 31 | 1.60 | | 32.60 | 36.50 |
| 1000 | Galvanized steel, 26 ga. for openings to 2-1/2" | | 165 | .048 | | 7.75 | 1.60 | | 9.35 | 11.20 |
| 1200 | For joint openings to 3-1/2" | | 165 | .048 | | 9.15 | 1.60 | | 10.75 | 12.80 |
| 1210 | For joint openings to 5" | | 165 | .048 | | 11.45 | 1.60 | | 13.05 | 15.30 |
| 1220 | For joint openings to 8" | | 165 | .048 | | 19.50 | 1.60 | | 21.10 | 24 |
| 1300 | Lead-coated copper, 16 oz. for openings to 2-1/2" | | 165 | .048 | | 27.50 | 1.60 | | 29.10 | 32.50 |
| 1500 | For joint openings to 3-1/2" | | 165 | .048 | | 32.50 | 1.60 | | 34.10 | 38 |
| 1600 | Stainless steel, .018", for openings to 2-1/2" | | 165 | .048 | | 11.80 | 1.60 | | 13.40 | 15.65 |
| 1800 | For joint openings to 3-1/2" | | 165 | .048 | | 13.45 | 1.60 | | 15.05 | 17.45 |
| 1810 | For joint openings to 5" | | 165 | .048 | | 16.60 | 1.60 | | 18.20 | 21 |
| 1820 | For joint openings to 8" | | 165 | .048 | | 25.50 | 1.60 | | 27.10 | 30.50 |
| 1900 | Neoprene, double-seal type with thick center, 4-1/2" wide | | 125 | .064 | | 11 | 2.11 | | 13.11 | 15.70 |
| 1950 | Polyethylene bellows, with galv steel flat flanges | | 100 | .080 | | 4.27 | 2.64 | | 6.91 | 9.20 |
| 1960 | With galvanized angle flanges | | 100 | .080 | | 4.71 | 2.64 | | 7.35 | 9.70 |
| 2000 | Roof joint with extruded aluminum cover, 2" | 1 Shee | 115 | .070 | | 29.50 | 3.15 | | 32.65 | 37.50 |
| 2100 | Roof joint, plastic curbs, foam center, standard | 1 Rofc | 100 | .080 | | 10.75 | 2.64 | | 13.39 | 16.35 |
| 2200 | Large | | 100 | .080 | | 14.35 | 2.64 | | 16.99 | 20.50 |
| 2300 | Transitions, regular, minimum | | 10 | .800 | Ea. | 93 | 26.50 | | 119.50 | 147 |
| 2350 | Maximum | | 4 | 2 | | 118 | 66 | | 184 | 242 |
| 2400 | Large, minimum | | 9 | .889 | | 136 | 29.50 | | 165.50 | 200 |
| 2450 | Maximum | | 3 | 2.667 | | 142 | 88 | | 230 | 305 |
| 2500 | Roof to wall joint with extruded aluminum cover | 1 Shee | 115 | .070 | L.F. | 25 | 3.15 | | 28.15 | 32.50 |
| 2700 | Wall joint, closed cell foam on PVC cover, 9" wide | 1 Rofc | 125 | .064 | | 3.83 | 2.11 | | 5.94 | 7.80 |
| 2800 | 12" wide | " | 115 | .070 | | 4.33 | 2.30 | | 6.63 | 8.65 |

## 07 71 43 – Drip Edge

### 07 71 43.10 Drip Edge, Rake Edge, Ice Belts

| | | Crew | Daily Output | Labor-Hours | Unit | Material | Labor | Equipment | Total | Total Incl O&P |
|---|---|---|---|---|---|---|---|---|---|---|
| 0010 | **DRIP EDGE, RAKE EDGE, ICE BELTS** | | | | | | | | | |
| 0020 | Aluminum, .016" thick, 5" wide, mill finish | 1 Carp | 400 | .020 | L.F. | .42 | .76 | | 1.18 | 1.65 |
| 0100 | White finish | | 400 | .020 | | .46 | .76 | | 1.22 | 1.70 |
| 0200 | 8" wide, mill finish | | 400 | .020 | | .56 | .76 | | 1.32 | 1.81 |
| 0300 | Ice belt, 28" wide, mill finish | | 100 | .080 | | 3.80 | 3.05 | | 6.85 | 8.90 |
| 0310 | Vented, mill finish | | 400 | .020 | | 2.29 | .76 | | 3.05 | 3.71 |
| 0320 | Painted finish | | 400 | .020 | | 2.42 | .76 | | 3.18 | 3.85 |
| 0400 | Galvanized, 5" wide | | 400 | .020 | | .52 | .76 | | 1.28 | 1.76 |
| 0500 | 8" wide, mill finish | | 400 | .020 | | .63 | .76 | | 1.39 | 1.88 |
| 0510 | Rake edge, aluminum, 1-1/2" x 1-1/2" | | 400 | .020 | | .24 | .76 | | 1 | 1.45 |
| 0520 | 3-1/2" x 1-1/2" | | 400 | .020 | | .46 | .76 | | 1.22 | 1.70 |

# 07 72 Roof Accessories

## 07 72 23 – Relief Vents

| 07 72 23.10 Roof Vents | Crew | Daily Output | Labor-Hours | Unit | Material | 2008 Bare Costs Labor | Equipment | Total | Total Incl O&P |
|---|---|---|---|---|---|---|---|---|---|
| 0010 **ROOF VENTS** | | | | | | | | | |
| 0020 Mushroom shape, for built-up roofs, aluminum | 1 Rofc | 30 | .267 | Ea. | 68.50 | 8.80 | | 77.30 | 90.50 |
| 0100 PVC, 6" high | " | 30 | .267 | " | 28.50 | 8.80 | | 37.30 | 46.50 |

## 07 72 26 – Ridge Vents

| 07 72 26.10 Ridge Vents and Accessories | Crew | Daily Output | Labor-Hours | Unit | Material | 2008 Bare Costs Labor | Equipment | Total | Total Incl O&P |
|---|---|---|---|---|---|---|---|---|---|
| 0010 **RIDGE VENTS AND ACCESSORIES** | | | | | | | | | |
| 0100 Aluminum strips, mill finish | 1 Rofc | 160 | .050 | L.F. | 2.50 | 1.65 | | 4.15 | 5.55 |
| 0150 Painted finish | | 160 | .050 | " | 3.61 | 1.65 | | 5.26 | 6.80 |
| 0200 Connectors | | 48 | .167 | Ea. | 3.50 | 5.50 | | 9 | 13.20 |
| 0300 End caps | | 48 | .167 | " | 1.30 | 5.50 | | 6.80 | 10.80 |
| 0400 Galvanized strips | | 160 | .050 | L.F. | 2.14 | 1.65 | | 3.79 | 5.15 |
| 0430 Molded polyethylene, shingles not included | | 160 | .050 | " | 3.05 | 1.65 | | 4.70 | 6.15 |
| 0440 End plugs | | 48 | .167 | Ea. | 1.30 | 5.50 | | 6.80 | 10.80 |
| 0450 Flexible roll, shingles not included | ↓ | 160 | .050 | L.F. | 2.25 | 1.65 | | 3.90 | 5.30 |
| 2300 Ridge vent strip, mill finish | 1 Shee | 155 | .052 | " | 2.68 | 2.34 | | 5.02 | 6.55 |

## 07 72 33 – Roof Hatches

| 07 72 33.10 Roof Hatch Options | Crew | Daily Output | Labor-Hours | Unit | Material | 2008 Bare Costs Labor | Equipment | Total | Total Incl O&P |
|---|---|---|---|---|---|---|---|---|---|
| 0010 **ROOF HATCH OPTIONS** | | | | | | | | | |
| 0500 2'-6" x 3', aluminum curb and cover | G-3 | 10 | 3.200 | Ea. | 720 | 121 | | 841 | 980 |
| 0520 Galvanized steel curb and aluminum cover *CN* | | 10 | 3.200 | | 695 | 121 | | 816 | 950 |
| 0540 Galvanized steel curb and cover | | 10 | 3.200 | | 565 | 121 | | 686 | 805 |
| 0600 2'-6" x 4'-6", aluminum curb and cover | | 9 | 3.556 | | 880 | 134 | | 1,014 | 1,175 |
| 0800 Galvanized steel curb and aluminum cover | | 9 | 3.556 | | 600 | 134 | | 734 | 870 |
| 0900 Galvanized steel curb and cover | | 9 | 3.556 | | 790 | 134 | | 924 | 1,075 |
| 1100 4' x 4' aluminum curb and cover | | 8 | 4 | | 1,475 | 151 | | 1,626 | 1,825 |
| 1120 Galvanized steel curb and aluminum cover | | 8 | 4 | | 600 | 151 | | 751 | 895 |
| 1140 Galvanized steel curb and cover | | 8 | 4 | | 1,425 | 151 | | 1,576 | 1,775 |
| 1200 2'-6" x 8'-0", aluminum curb and cover | | 6.60 | 4.848 | | 1,425 | 183 | | 1,608 | 1,850 |
| 1400 Galvanized steel curb and aluminum cover | | 6.60 | 4.848 | | 1,150 | 183 | | 1,333 | 1,550 |
| 1500 Galvanized steel curb and cover | ↓ | 6.60 | 4.848 | | 1,200 | 183 | | 1,383 | 1,600 |
| 1800 For plexiglass panels, 2'-6" x 3'-0", add to above | | | | ↓ | 400 | | | 400 | 440 |

## 07 72 36 – Smoke Vents

| 07 72 36.10 Smoke Hatches | Crew | Daily Output | Labor-Hours | Unit | Material | 2008 Bare Costs Labor | Equipment | Total | Total Incl O&P |
|---|---|---|---|---|---|---|---|---|---|
| 0010 **SMOKE HATCHES** | | | | | | | | | |
| 0200 For 3'-0" long, add to roof hatches from division 07 72 33.10 | | | | Ea. | 25% | 5% | | | |
| 0250 For 4'-0" long, add to roof hatches from division 07 72 33.10 | | | | | 20% | 5% | | | |
| 0300 For 8'-0" long, add to roof hatches from division 07 72 33.10 | | | | ↓ | 10% | 5% | | | |

| 07 72 36.20 Smoke Vent Options | Crew | Daily Output | Labor-Hours | Unit | Material | 2008 Bare Costs Labor | Equipment | Total | Total Incl O&P |
|---|---|---|---|---|---|---|---|---|---|
| 0010 **SMOKE VENT OPTIONS** | | | | | | | | | |
| 0100 4' x 4' aluminum cover and frame | G-3 | 13 | 2.462 | Ea. | 1,675 | 93 | | 1,768 | 2,000 |
| 0200 Galvanized steel cover and frame | | 13 | 2.462 | | 1,475 | 93 | | 1,568 | 1,775 |
| 0300 4' x 8' aluminum cover and frame | | 8 | 4 | | 2,300 | 151 | | 2,451 | 2,750 |
| 0400 Galvanized steel cover and frame | ↓ | 8 | 4 | ↓ | 1,950 | 151 | | 2,101 | 2,350 |

## 07 72 53 – Snow Guards

| 07 72 53.10 Snow Guard Options | Crew | Daily Output | Labor-Hours | Unit | Material | 2008 Bare Costs Labor | Equipment | Total | Total Incl O&P |
|---|---|---|---|---|---|---|---|---|---|
| 0010 **SNOW GUARD OPTIONS** | | | | | | | | | |
| 0100 Slate & asphalt shingle roofs | 1 Rofc | 160 | .050 | Ea. | 9.10 | 1.65 | | 10.75 | 12.80 |
| 0200 Standing seam metal roofs | | 48 | .167 | | 13.85 | 5.50 | | 19.35 | 24.50 |
| 0300 Surface mount for metal roofs | | 48 | .167 | ↓ | 7.70 | 5.50 | | 13.20 | 17.80 |
| 0400 Double rail pipe type, including pipe | ↓ | 130 | .062 | L.F. | 20 | 2.03 | | 22.03 | 25.50 |

# 07 72 Roof Accessories

## 07 72 73 – Pitch Pockets

| 07 72 73.10 Pitch Pockets, Variable Sizes | Crew | Daily Output | Labor-Hours | Unit | Material | 2008 Bare Costs Labor | 2008 Bare Costs Equipment | Total | Total Incl O&P |
|---|---|---|---|---|---|---|---|---|---|
| 0010 **PITCH POCKETS, VARIABLE SIZES** | | | | | | | | | |
| 0100 Adjustable, 4" to 7", welded corners, 4" deep | 1 Rofc | 48 | .167 | Ea. | 11 | 5.50 | | 16.50 | 21.50 |
| 0200 Side extenders, 6" | " | 240 | .033 | " | 1.97 | 1.10 | | 3.07 | 4.04 |

## 07 72 80 – Vents

### 07 72 80.30 Vent Options

| | Crew | Daily Output | Labor-Hours | Unit | Material | 2008 Bare Costs Labor | 2008 Bare Costs Equipment | Total | Total Incl O&P |
|---|---|---|---|---|---|---|---|---|---|
| 0010 **VENT OPTIONS** | | | | | | | | | |
| 0020 Plastic, for insulated decks, 1 per M.S.F., minimum | 1 Rofc | 40 | .200 | Ea. | 13.50 | 6.60 | | 20.10 | 26 |
| 0100 Maximum | ↓ | 20 | .400 | | 31 | 13.20 | | 44.20 | 57 |
| 0300 Aluminum | | 30 | .267 | | 13.50 | 8.80 | | 22.30 | 30 |
| 0800 Polystyrene baffles, 12" wide for 16" O.C. rafter spacing | 1 Carp | 90 | .089 | | .40 | 3.39 | | 3.79 | 5.70 |
| 0900 For 24" O.C. rafter spacing | " | 110 | .073 | ↓ | .60 | 2.77 | | 3.37 | 4.97 |

# 07 81 Applied Fireproofing

## 07 81 16 – Cementitious Fireproofing

### 07 81 16.10 Sprayed Cementitous Fireproofing

| | Crew | Daily Output | Labor-Hours | Unit | Material | 2008 Bare Costs Labor | 2008 Bare Costs Equipment | Total | Total Incl O&P |
|---|---|---|---|---|---|---|---|---|---|
| 0010 **SPRAYED CEMENTITOUS FIREPROOFING** | | | | | | | | | |
| 0050 Not incl tamping or canvas protection | | | | | | | | | |
| 0100 1" thick, on flat plate steel | G-2 | 3000 | .008 | S.F. | .47 | .26 | .04 | .77 | .96 |
| 0200 Flat decking | | 2400 | .010 | | .47 | .32 | .05 | .84 | 1.07 |
| 0400 Beams | | 1500 | .016 | | .47 | .51 | .08 | 1.06 | 1.39 |
| 0500 Corrugated or fluted decks | | 1250 | .019 | | .71 | .62 | .10 | 1.43 | 1.83 |
| 0700 Columns, 1-1/8" thick | | 1100 | .022 | | .53 | .70 | .12 | 1.35 | 1.78 |
| 0800 2-3/16" thick | ↓ | 700 | .034 | ↓ | 1.01 | 1.10 | .18 | 2.29 | 2.99 |
| 0850 For tamping, add | | | | | | 10% | | | |
| 0900 For canvas protection, add | G-2 | 5000 | .005 | S.F. | .06 | .15 | .03 | .24 | .34 |
| 1000 Acoustical sprayed, 1" thick, finished, straight work, minimum | | 520 | .046 | | .49 | 1.48 | .24 | 2.21 | 3.07 |
| 1100 Maximum | | 200 | .120 | | .53 | 3.85 | .63 | 5.01 | 7.15 |
| 1300 Difficult access, minimum | | 225 | .107 | | .53 | 3.42 | .56 | 4.51 | 6.45 |
| 1400 Maximum | ↓ | 130 | .185 | ↓ | .59 | 5.90 | .97 | 7.46 | 10.75 |
| 1500 Intumescent epoxy fireproofing on wire mesh, 3/16" thick | | | | | | | | | |
| 1550 1 hour rating, exterior use | G-2 | 136 | .176 | S.F. | 6.15 | 5.65 | .93 | 12.73 | 16.40 |
| 1600 Magnesium oxychloride, 35# to 40# density, 1/4" thick | | 3000 | .008 | | 1.29 | .26 | .04 | 1.59 | 1.86 |
| 1650 1/2" thick | | 2000 | .012 | | 2.59 | .38 | .06 | 3.03 | 3.51 |
| 1700 60# to 70# density, 1/4" thick | | 3000 | .008 | | 1.71 | .26 | .04 | 2.01 | 2.32 |
| 1750 1/2" thick | | 2000 | .012 | | 3.44 | .38 | .06 | 3.88 | 4.44 |
| 2000 Vermiculite cement, troweled or sprayed, 1/4" thick | | 3000 | .008 | | 1.17 | .26 | .04 | 1.47 | 1.73 |
| 2050 1/2" thick | ↓ | 2000 | .012 | ↓ | 2.32 | .38 | .06 | 2.76 | 3.21 |

# 07 84 Firestopping

## 07 84 13 – Penetration Firestopping

| 07 84 13.10 Firestopping | | Crew | Daily Output | Labor-Hours | Unit | Material | Labor | Equipment | Total | Total Incl O&P |
|---|---|---|---|---|---|---|---|---|---|---|
| 0010 | **FIRESTOPPING** | R078413-30 | | | | | | | | |
| 0100 | Metallic piping, non insulated | | | | | | | | | |
| 0110 | Through walls, 2" diameter | 1 Carp | 16 | .500 | Ea. | 11.30 | 19.05 | | 30.35 | 42 |
| 0120 | 4" diameter | | 14 | .571 | | 17.25 | 22 | | 39.25 | 53 |
| 0130 | 6" diameter | | 12 | .667 | | 23 | 25.50 | | 48.50 | 65 |
| 0140 | 12" diameter | | 10 | .800 | | 41 | 30.50 | | 71.50 | 92.50 |
| 0150 | Through floors, 2" diameter | | 32 | .250 | | 6.85 | 9.55 | | 16.40 | 22.50 |
| 0160 | 4" diameter | | 28 | .286 | | 9.85 | 10.90 | | 20.75 | 28 |
| 0170 | 6" diameter | | 24 | .333 | | 12.95 | 12.70 | | 25.65 | 34 |
| 0180 | 12" diameter | | 20 | .400 | | 22 | 15.25 | | 37.25 | 47.50 |
| 0190 | Metallic piping, insulated | | | | | | | | | |
| 0200 | Through walls, 2" diameter | 1 Carp | 16 | .500 | Ea. | 16 | 19.05 | | 35.05 | 47 |
| 0210 | 4" diameter | | 14 | .571 | | 22 | 22 | | 44 | 58 |
| 0220 | 6" diameter | | 12 | .667 | | 28 | 25.50 | | 53.50 | 70 |
| 0230 | 12" diameter | | 10 | .800 | | 46 | 30.50 | | 76.50 | 98 |
| 0240 | Through floors, 2" diameter | | 32 | .250 | | 11.60 | 9.55 | | 21.15 | 27.50 |
| 0250 | 4" diameter | | 28 | .286 | | 14.55 | 10.90 | | 25.45 | 33 |
| 0260 | 6" diameter | | 24 | .333 | | 17.70 | 12.70 | | 30.40 | 39 |
| 0270 | 12" diameter | | 20 | .400 | | 22 | 15.25 | | 37.25 | 47.50 |
| 0280 | Non metallic piping, non insulated | | | | | | | | | |
| 0290 | Through walls, 2" diameter | 1 Carp | 12 | .667 | Ea. | 46.50 | 25.50 | | 72 | 91 |
| 0300 | 4" diameter | | 10 | .800 | | 58.50 | 30.50 | | 89 | 112 |
| 0310 | 6" diameter | | 8 | 1 | | 81.50 | 38 | | 119.50 | 149 |
| 0330 | Through floors, 2" diameter | | 16 | .500 | | 36.50 | 19.05 | | 55.55 | 69.50 |
| 0340 | 4" diameter | | 6 | 1.333 | | 45 | 51 | | 96 | 129 |
| 0350 | 6" diameter | | 6 | 1.333 | | 54.50 | 51 | | 105.50 | 139 |
| 0370 | Ductwork, insulated & non insulated, round | | | | | | | | | |
| 0380 | Through walls, 6" diameter | 1 Carp | 12 | .667 | Ea. | 23.50 | 25.50 | | 49 | 65.50 |
| 0390 | 12" diameter | | 10 | .800 | | 47 | 30.50 | | 77.50 | 99.50 |
| 0400 | 18" diameter | | 8 | 1 | | 76.50 | 38 | | 114.50 | 144 |
| 0410 | Through floors, 6" diameter | | 16 | .500 | | 13 | 19.05 | | 32.05 | 44 |
| 0420 | 12" diameter | | 14 | .571 | | 23.50 | 22 | | 45.50 | 60 |
| 0430 | 18" diameter | | 12 | .667 | | 41.50 | 25.50 | | 67 | 85 |
| 0440 | Ductwork, insulated & non insulated, rectangular | | | | | | | | | |
| 0450 | With stiffener/closure angle, through walls, 6" x 12" | 1 Carp | 8 | 1 | Ea. | 19.65 | 38 | | 57.65 | 81 |
| 0460 | 12" x 24" | | 6 | 1.333 | | 26 | 51 | | 77 | 108 |
| 0470 | 24" x 48" | | 4 | 2 | | 74.50 | 76 | | 150.50 | 201 |
| 0480 | With stiffener/closure angle, through floors, 6" x 12" | | 10 | .800 | | 10.60 | 30.50 | | 41.10 | 59 |
| 0490 | 12" x 24" | | 8 | 1 | | 19.15 | 38 | | 57.15 | 80.50 |
| 0500 | 24" x 48" | | 6 | 1.333 | | 37.50 | 51 | | 88.50 | 121 |
| 0510 | Multi trade openings | | | | | | | | | |
| 0520 | Through walls, 6" x 12" | 1 Carp | 2 | 4 | Ea. | 41.50 | 152 | | 193.50 | 283 |
| 0530 | 12" x 24" | " | 1 | 8 | | 166 | 305 | | 471 | 660 |
| 0540 | 24" x 48" | 2 Carp | 1 | 16 | | 665 | 610 | | 1,275 | 1,675 |
| 0550 | 48" x 96" | " | .75 | 21.333 | | 2,675 | 815 | | 3,490 | 4,225 |
| 0560 | Through floors, 6" x 12" | 1 Carp | 2 | 4 | | 41.50 | 152 | | 193.50 | 283 |
| 0570 | 12" x 24" | " | 1 | 8 | | 166 | 305 | | 471 | 660 |
| 0580 | 24" x 48" | 2 Carp | .75 | 21.333 | | 665 | 815 | | 1,480 | 2,000 |
| 0590 | 48" x 96" | " | .50 | 32 | | 2,675 | 1,225 | | 3,900 | 4,850 |
| 0600 | Structural penetrations, through walls | | | | | | | | | |
| 0610 | Steel beams, W8 x 10 | 1 Carp | 8 | 1 | Ea. | 26 | 38 | | 64 | 88 |
| 0620 | W12 x 14 | | 6 | 1.333 | | 41.50 | 51 | | 92.50 | 125 |
| 0630 | W21 x 44 | | 5 | 1.600 | | 82.50 | 61 | | 143.50 | 186 |

# 07 84 Firestopping

## 07 84 13 – Penetration Firestopping

| 07 84 13.10 Firestopping | | Crew | Daily Output | Labor-Hours | Unit | Material | 2008 Bare Costs Labor | 2008 Bare Costs Equipment | Total | Total Incl O&P |
|---|---|---|---|---|---|---|---|---|---|---|
| 0640 | W36 x 135 | 1 Carp | 3 | 2.667 | Ea. | 201 | 102 | | 303 | 380 |
| 0650 | Bar joists, 18" deep | | 6 | 1.333 | | 38 | 51 | | 89 | 121 |
| 0660 | 24" deep | | 6 | 1.333 | | 47 | 51 | | 98 | 131 |
| 0670 | 36" deep | | 5 | 1.600 | | 71 | 61 | | 132 | 173 |
| 0680 | 48" deep | | 4 | 2 | | 82.50 | 76 | | 158.50 | 210 |
| 0690 | Construction joints, floor slab at exterior wall | | | | | | | | | |
| 0700 | Precast, brick, block or drywall exterior | | | | | | | | | |
| 0710 | 2" wide joint | 1 Carp | 125 | .064 | L.F. | 5.90 | 2.44 | | 8.34 | 10.30 |
| 0720 | 4" wide joint | " | 75 | .107 | " | 11.80 | 4.06 | | 15.86 | 19.30 |
| 0730 | Metal panel, glass or curtain wall exterior | | | | | | | | | |
| 0740 | 2" wide joint | 1 Carp | 40 | .200 | L.F. | 13.95 | 7.60 | | 21.55 | 27 |
| 0750 | 4" wide joint | " | 25 | .320 | " | 19.10 | 12.20 | | 31.30 | 40 |
| 0760 | Floor slab to drywall partition | | | | | | | | | |
| 0770 | Flat joint | 1 Carp | 100 | .080 | L.F. | 5.80 | 3.05 | | 8.85 | 11.10 |
| 0780 | Fluted joint | | 50 | .160 | | 11.80 | 6.10 | | 17.90 | 22.50 |
| 0790 | Etched fluted joint | | 75 | .107 | | 7.65 | 4.06 | | 11.71 | 14.80 |
| 0800 | Floor slab to concrete/masonry partition | | | | | | | | | |
| 0810 | Flat joint | 1 Carp | 75 | .107 | L.F. | 13 | 4.06 | | 17.06 | 20.50 |
| 0820 | Fluted joint | " | 50 | .160 | " | 15.35 | 6.10 | | 21.45 | 26.50 |
| 0830 | Concrete/CMU wall joints | | | | | | | | | |
| 0840 | 1" wide | 1 Carp | 100 | .080 | L.F. | 7.10 | 3.05 | | 10.15 | 12.55 |
| 0850 | 2" wide | | 75 | .107 | | 13 | 4.06 | | 17.06 | 20.50 |
| 0860 | 4" wide | | 50 | .160 | | 25 | 6.10 | | 31.10 | 37 |
| 0870 | Concrete/CMU floor joints | | | | | | | | | |
| 0880 | 1" wide | 1 Carp | 200 | .040 | L.F. | 3.54 | 1.52 | | 5.06 | 6.25 |
| 0890 | 2" wide | | 150 | .053 | | 6.50 | 2.03 | | 8.53 | 10.30 |
| 0900 | 4" wide | | 100 | .080 | | 12.40 | 3.05 | | 15.45 | 18.35 |

# 07 92 Joint Sealants

## 07 92 10 – Caulking and Sealants

| 07 92 10.10 Caulking and Sealant Options | | Crew | Daily Output | Labor-Hours | Unit | Material | 2008 Bare Costs Labor | 2008 Bare Costs Equipment | Total | Total Incl O&P |
|---|---|---|---|---|---|---|---|---|---|---|
| 0010 | **CAULKING AND SEALANT OPTIONS** | | | | | | | | | |
| 0020 | Acoustical sealant, elastomeric, cartridges | | | | Ea. | 4.60 | | | 4.60 | 5.05 |
| 0030 | Backer rod, polyethylene, 1/4" diameter | 1 Bric | 4.60 | 1.739 | C.L.F. | 3.29 | 68 | | 71.29 | 108 |
| 0050 | 1/2" diameter | | 4.60 | 1.739 | | 6 | 68 | | 74 | 111 |
| 0070 | 3/4" diameter | | 4.60 | 1.739 | | 7.50 | 68 | | 75.50 | 112 |
| 0090 | 1" diameter | | 4.60 | 1.739 | | 12.90 | 68 | | 80.90 | 118 |
| 0100 | Acrylic latex caulk, white | | | | | | | | | |
| 0200 | 11 fl. oz cartridge | | | | Ea. | 2.31 | | | 2.31 | 2.54 |
| 0500 | 1/4" x 1/2" | 1 Bric | 248 | .032 | L.F. | .19 | 1.26 | | 1.45 | 2.13 |
| 0600 | 1/2" x 1/2" | | 250 | .032 | | .38 | 1.25 | | 1.63 | 2.32 |
| 0800 | 3/4" x 3/4" | | 230 | .035 | | .85 | 1.36 | | 2.21 | 3 |
| 0900 | 3/4" x 1" | | 200 | .040 | | 1.13 | 1.57 | | 2.70 | 3.63 |
| 1000 | 1" x 1" | | 180 | .044 | | 1.42 | 1.74 | | 3.16 | 4.21 |
| 1400 | Butyl based, bulk | | | | Gal. | 24 | | | 24 | 26.50 |
| 1500 | Cartridges | | | | " | 29 | | | 29 | 32 |
| 1700 | Bulk, in place 1/4" x 1/2", 154 L.F./gal. | 1 Bric | 230 | .035 | L.F. | .16 | 1.36 | | 1.52 | 2.24 |
| 1800 | 1/2" x 1/2", 77 L.F./gal. | " | 180 | .044 | " | .31 | 1.74 | | 2.05 | 2.99 |
| 2000 | Latex acrylic based, bulk | | | | Gal. | 25 | | | 25 | 27.50 |
| 2100 | Cartridges | | | | | 31 | | | 31 | 34 |
| 2300 | Polysulfide compounds, 1 component, bulk | | | | | 47.50 | | | 47.50 | 52 |

# 07 92 Joint Sealants

## 07 92 10 – Caulking and Sealants

| 07 92 10.10 Caulking and Sealant Options | Crew | Daily Output | Labor-Hours | Unit | Material | 2008 Bare Costs Labor | Equipment | Total | Total Incl O&P |
|---|---|---|---|---|---|---|---|---|---|
| 2600     1 or 2 component, in place, 1/4" x 1/4", 308 L.F./gal. | 1 Bric | 145 | .055 | L.F. | .15 | 2.16 | | 2.31 | 3.46 |
| 2700     1/2" x 1/4", 154 L.F./gal. | | 135 | .059 | | .31 | 2.32 | | 2.63 | 3.87 |
| 2900     3/4" x 3/8", 68 L.F./gal. | | 130 | .062 | | .70 | 2.41 | | 3.11 | 4.43 |
| 3000     1" x 1/2", 38 L.F./gal. | | 130 | .062 | | 1.25 | 2.41 | | 3.66 | 5.05 |
| 3200   Polyurethane, 1 or 2 component | | | | Gal. | 51.50 | | | 51.50 | 57 |
| 3500     Bulk, in place, 1/4" x 1/4" | 1 Bric | 150 | .053 | L.F. | .17 | 2.09 | | 2.26 | 3.36 |
| 3600     1/2" x 1/4" | | 145 | .055 | | .34 | 2.16 | | 2.50 | 3.66 |
| 3800     3/4" x 3/8", 68 L.F./gal. | | 130 | .062 | | .76 | 2.41 | | 3.17 | 4.50 |
| 3900     1" x 1/2" | | 110 | .073 | | 1.34 | 2.85 | | 4.19 | 5.80 |
| 4100   Silicone rubber, bulk | | | | Gal. | 38 | | | 38 | 42 |
| 4200     Cartridges | | | | " | 38 | | | 38 | 41.50 |
| 4400   Neoprene gaskets, closed cell, adhesive, 1/8" x 3/8" | 1 Bric | 240 | .033 | L.F. | .24 | 1.30 | | 1.54 | 2.24 |
| 4500     1/4" x 3/4" | | 215 | .037 | | .54 | 1.46 | | 2 | 2.81 |
| 4700     1/2" x 1" | | 200 | .040 | | 1.20 | 1.57 | | 2.77 | 3.70 |
| 4800     3/4" x 1-1/2" | | 165 | .048 | | 1.33 | 1.90 | | 3.23 | 4.35 |
| 5500   Resin epoxy coating, 2 component, heavy duty | | | | Gal. | 28.50 | | | 28.50 | 31 |
| 5800   Tapes, sealant, P.V.C. foam adhesive, 1/16" x 1/4" | | | | C.L.F. | 5.25 | | | 5.25 | 5.75 |
| 5900     1/16" x 1/2" | | | | | 7.75 | | | 7.75 | 8.50 |
| 5950     1/16" x 1" | | | | | 12.85 | | | 12.85 | 14.10 |
| 6000     1/8" x 1/2" | | | | | 8.70 | | | 8.70 | 9.55 |
| 6200   Urethane foam, 2 component, handy pack, 1 C.F. | | | | Ea. | 31.50 | | | 31.50 | 34.50 |
| 6300     50.0 C.F. pack | | | | C.F. | 15.95 | | | 15.95 | 17.55 |

# 07 95 Expansion Control

## 07 95 13 – Expansion Joint Cover Assemblies

### 07 95 13.50 Expansion Joint Assemblies

| | Crew | Daily Output | Labor-Hours | Unit | Material | 2008 Bare Costs Labor | Equipment | Total | Total Incl O&P |
|---|---|---|---|---|---|---|---|---|---|
| 0010 **EXPANSION JOINT ASSEMBLIES** | | | | | | | | | |
| 0200   Floor cover assemblies, 1" space, aluminum | 1 Sswk | 38 | .211 | L.F. | 17.90 | 9.05 | | 26.95 | 36 |
| 0300     Bronze | | 38 | .211 | | 36 | 9.05 | | 45.05 | 56.50 |
| 0500     2" space, aluminum | | 38 | .211 | | 21.50 | 9.05 | | 30.55 | 40.50 |
| 0600     Bronze | | 38 | .211 | | 39 | 9.05 | | 48.05 | 59.50 |
| 0800   Wall and ceiling assemblies, 1" space, aluminum | | 38 | .211 | | 10.65 | 9.05 | | 19.70 | 28 |
| 0900     Bronze | | 38 | .211 | | 34 | 9.05 | | 43.05 | 54 |
| 1100     2" space, aluminum | | 38 | .211 | | 18.10 | 9.05 | | 27.15 | 36.50 |
| 1200     Bronze | | 38 | .211 | | 41.50 | 9.05 | | 50.55 | 62.50 |
| 1400   Floor to wall assemblies, 1" space, aluminum | | 38 | .211 | | 16.30 | 9.05 | | 25.35 | 34.50 |
| 1500     Bronze or stainless | | 38 | .211 | | 41 | 9.05 | | 50.05 | 62 |
| 1700   Gym floor angle covers, aluminum, 3" x 3" angle | | 46 | .174 | | 14.10 | 7.50 | | 21.60 | 29 |
| 1800     3" x 4" angle | | 46 | .174 | | 16.60 | 7.50 | | 24.10 | 32 |
| 2000   Roof closures, aluminum, flat roof, low profile, 1" space | | 57 | .140 | | 32.50 | 6.05 | | 38.55 | 47 |
| 2100     High profile | | 57 | .140 | | 40 | 6.05 | | 46.05 | 55 |
| 2300   Roof to wall, low profile, 1" space | | 57 | .140 | | 18 | 6.05 | | 24.05 | 30.50 |
| 2400     High profile | | 57 | .140 | | 23 | 6.05 | | 29.05 | 36.50 |

# Division Notes

| | CREW | DAILY OUTPUT | LABOR-HOURS | UNIT | 2008 BARE COSTS | | | | TOTAL INCL O&P |
|---|---|---|---|---|---|---|---|---|---|
| | | | | | MAT. | LABOR | EQUIP. | TOTAL | |
| | | | | | | | | | |
| | | | | | | | | | |
| | | | | | | | | | |
| | | | | | | | | | |
| | | | | | | | | | |
| | | | | | | | | | |
| | | | | | | | | | |
| | | | | | | | | | |
| | | | | | | | | | |
| | | | | | | | | | |
| | | | | | | | | | |
| | | | | | | | | | |
| | | | | | | | | | |
| | | | | | | | | | |
| | | | | | | | | | |
| | | | | | | | | | |
| | | | | | | | | | |
| | | | | | | | | | |
| | | | | | | | | | |
| | | | | | | | | | |
| | | | | | | | | | |

# Estimating Tips

## 08 10 00 Doors and Frames

- Most metal doors and frames look alike, but there may be significant differences among them. When estimating these items be sure to choose the line item that most closely compares to the specification or door schedule requirements regarding:
  - type of metal
  - metal gauge
  - door core material
  - fire rating
  - finish
- Wood and plastic doors vary considerably in price. The primary determinant is the veneer material. Lauan, birch, and oak are the most common veneers. Other variables include the following:
  - hollow or solid core
  - fire rating
  - flush or raised panel
  - finish

## 08 30 00 Specialty Doors and Frames

- There are many varieties of special doors, and they are usually priced per each. Add frames, hardware, or operators required for a complete installation.

## 08 40 00 Entrances, Storefronts, and Curtain Walls

- Glazed curtain walls consist of the metal tube framing and the glazing material. The cost data in this subdivision is presented for the metal tube framing alone or the composite wall. If your estimate requires a detailed takeoff of the framing, be sure to add the glazing cost.

## 08 50 00 Windows

- Most metal windows are delivered preglazed. However, some metal windows are priced without glass. Refer to 08 80 00 Glazing for glass pricing. The grade C indicates commercial grade windows, usually ASTM C-35.
- All wood windows are priced preglazed. The two glazing options priced are single pane float glass and insulating glass 1/2" thick. Add the cost of screens and grills if required.

## 08 70 00 Hardware

- Hardware costs add considerably to the cost of a door. The most efficient method to determine the hardware requirements for a project is to review the door schedule.

- Door hinges are priced by the pair, with most doors requiring 1-1/2 pairs per door. The hinge prices do not include installation labor because it is included in door installation. Hinges are classified according to the frequency of use.

## 08 80 00 Glazing

- Different openings require different types of glass. The three most common types are:
  - float
  - tempered
  - insulating
- Most exterior windows are glazed with insulating glass. Entrance doors and window walls, where the glass is less than 18" from the floor, are generally glazed with tempered glass. Interior windows and some residential windows are glazed with float glass.

# Reference Numbers

Reference numbers are shown in shaded boxes at the beginning of some major classifications. These numbers refer to related items in the Reference Section. The reference information may be an estimating procedure, an alternate pricing method, or technical information.

*Note:* Not all subdivisions listed here necessarily appear in this publication.

**Division 8 - Openings**

# 08 05 Common Work Results for Openings

## 08 05 05 – Selective Windows and Doors Demolition

### 08 05 05.10 Selective Demolition Doors

| | | Crew | Daily Output | Labor-Hours | Unit | Material | 2008 Bare Costs Labor | Equipment | Total | Total Incl O&P |
|---|---|---|---|---|---|---|---|---|---|---|
| 0010 | **SELECTIVE DEMOLITION DOORS**  R024119-10 | | | | | | | | | |
| 0200 | Doors, exterior, 1-3/4" thick, single, 3' x 7' high | 1 Clab | 16 | .500 | Ea. | | 15.15 | | 15.15 | 23.50 |
| 0220 | Double, 6' x 7' high | | 12 | .667 | | | 20 | | 20 | 31.50 |
| 0500 | Interior, 1-3/8" thick, single, 3' x 7' high | | 20 | .400 | | | 12.10 | | 12.10 | 18.80 |
| 0520 | Double, 6' x 7' high | | 16 | .500 | | | 15.15 | | 15.15 | 23.50 |
| 0700 | Bi-folding, 3' x 6'-8" high | | 20 | .400 | | | 12.10 | | 12.10 | 18.80 |
| 0720 | 6' x 6'-8" high | | 18 | .444 | | | 13.45 | | 13.45 | 21 |
| 0900 | Bi-passing, 3' x 6'-8" high | | 16 | .500 | | | 15.15 | | 15.15 | 23.50 |
| 0940 | 6' x 6'-8" high | | 14 | .571 | | | 17.30 | | 17.30 | 27 |
| 1500 | Remove and reset, minimum | 1 Carp | 8 | 1 | | | 38 | | 38 | 59.50 |
| 1520 | Maximum | | 6 | 1.333 | | | 51 | | 51 | 79 |
| 2000 | Frames, including trim, metal | | 8 | 1 | | | 38 | | 38 | 59.50 |
| 2200 | Wood | 2 Carp | 32 | .500 | | | 19.05 | | 19.05 | 29.50 |
| 3000 | Special doors, counter doors | | 6 | 2.667 | | | 102 | | 102 | 158 |
| 3100 | Double acting | | 10 | 1.600 | | | 61 | | 61 | 95 |
| 3200 | Floor door (trap type), or access type | | 8 | 2 | | | 76 | | 76 | 119 |
| 3300 | Glass, sliding, including frames | | 12 | 1.333 | | | 51 | | 51 | 79 |
| 3400 | Overhead, commercial, 12' x 12' high | | 4 | 4 | | | 152 | | 152 | 237 |
| 3440 | up to 20' x 16' high | | 3 | 5.333 | | | 203 | | 203 | 315 |
| 3445 | up to 35' x 30' high | | 1 | 16 | | | 610 | | 610 | 950 |
| 3500 | Residential, 9' x 7' high | | 8 | 2 | | | 76 | | 76 | 119 |
| 3540 | 16' x 7' high | | 7 | 2.286 | | | 87 | | 87 | 136 |
| 3600 | Remove and reset, minimum | | 4 | 4 | | | 152 | | 152 | 237 |
| 3620 | Maximum | | 2.50 | 6.400 | | | 244 | | 244 | 380 |
| 3700 | Roll-up grille | | 5 | 3.200 | | | 122 | | 122 | 190 |
| 3800 | Revolving door | | 2 | 8 | | | 305 | | 305 | 475 |
| 3900 | Storefront swing door | | 3 | 5.333 | | | 203 | | 203 | 315 |
| 6600 | Demo flexible transparent strip entrance | 3 Shee | 115 | .209 | SF Surf | | 9.45 | | 9.45 | 14.60 |
| 7100 | Remove double swing pneumatic doors, openers and sensors | 2 Skwk | .50 | 32 | Opng. | | 1,250 | | 1,250 | 1,950 |
| 7110 | Remove automatic operators, industrial, sliding doors, to 12' wide | " | .40 | 40 | " | | 1,575 | | 1,575 | 2,450 |
| 7550 | Hangar door demo | 2 Sswk | 220 | .073 | S.F. | | 3.13 | | 3.13 | 5.65 |
| 7570 | Remove shock absorbing door | " | 1.90 | 8.421 | Opng. | | 360 | | 360 | 655 |

### 08 05 05.20 Selective Demolition of Windows

| | | Crew | Daily Output | Labor-Hours | Unit | Material | 2008 Bare Costs Labor | Equipment | Total | Total Incl O&P |
|---|---|---|---|---|---|---|---|---|---|---|
| 0010 | **SELECTIVE DEMOLITION OF WINDOWS**  R024119-10 | | | | | | | | | |
| 0200 | Aluminum, including trim, to 12 S.F. | 1 Clab | 16 | .500 | Ea. | | 15.15 | | 15.15 | 23.50 |
| 0240 | To 25 S.F. | | 11 | .727 | | | 22 | | 22 | 34 |
| 0280 | To 50 S.F. | | 5 | 1.600 | | | 48.50 | | 48.50 | 75.50 |
| 0320 | Storm windows/screens, to 12 S.F. | | 27 | .296 | | | 8.95 | | 8.95 | 13.95 |
| 0360 | To 25 S.F. | | 21 | .381 | | | 11.50 | | 11.50 | 17.90 |
| 0400 | To 50 S.F. | | 16 | .500 | | | 15.15 | | 15.15 | 23.50 |
| 0600 | Glass, minimum | | 200 | .040 | S.F. | | 1.21 | | 1.21 | 1.88 |
| 0620 | Maximum | | 150 | .053 | " | | 1.61 | | 1.61 | 2.51 |
| 1000 | Steel, including trim, to 12 S.F. | | 13 | .615 | Ea. | | 18.60 | | 18.60 | 29 |
| 1020 | To 25 S.F. | | 9 | .889 | | | 27 | | 27 | 42 |
| 1040 | To 50 S.F. | | 4 | 2 | | | 60.50 | | 60.50 | 94 |
| 2000 | Wood, including trim, to 12 S.F. | | 22 | .364 | | | 11 | | 11 | 17.10 |
| 2020 | To 25 S.F. | | 18 | .444 | | | 13.45 | | 13.45 | 21 |
| 2060 | To 50 S.F. | | 13 | .615 | | | 18.60 | | 18.60 | 29 |
| 2065 | To 180 S.F. | | 8 | 1 | | | 30.50 | | 30.50 | 47 |
| 4300 | Remove bay/bow window | 2 Carp | 6 | 2.667 | | | 102 | | 102 | 158 |
| 4410 | Remove skylight, plstc domes,flush/curb mtd | G-3 | 395 | .081 | S.F. | | 3.06 | | 3.06 | 4.74 |
| 5020 | Remove and reset window, minimum | 1 Carp | 6 | 1.333 | Ea. | | 51 | | 51 | 79 |

218

# 08 05 Common Work Results for Openings

## 08 05 05 – Selective Windows and Doors Demolition

| 08 05 05.20 Selective Demolition of Windows | Crew | Daily Output | Labor-Hours | Unit | Material | 2008 Bare Costs Labor | Equipment | Total | Total Incl O&P |
|---|---|---|---|---|---|---|---|---|---|
| 5040 | Average | 1 Carp | 4 | 2 | Ea. | | 76 | | 76 | 119 |
| 5080 | Maximum | ↓ | 2 | 4 | ↓ | | 152 | | 152 | 237 |

# 08 11 Metal Doors and Frames

## 08 11 16 – Aluminum Doors and Frames

### 08 11 16.10 Entrance Doors and Frames

| | | Crew | Daily Output | Labor-Hours | Unit | Material | 2008 Bare Costs Labor | Equipment | Total | Total Incl O&P |
|---|---|---|---|---|---|---|---|---|---|---|
| 0010 | **ENTRANCE DOORS AND FRAMES** Aluminum, narrow stile | | | | | | | | | |
| 0015 | Standard hardware, clear finish, not incl. glass, 2'-6" x 7'-0" opng. | 2 Sswk | 2 | 8 | Ea. | 835 | 345 | | 1,180 | 1,550 |
| 0020 | 3'-0" x 7'-0" opening | | 2 | 8 | | 665 | 345 | | 1,010 | 1,350 |
| 0030 | 3'-6" x 7'-0" opening | | 2 | 8 | | 650 | 345 | | 995 | 1,325 |
| 0100 | 3'-0" x 10'-0" opening, 3' high transom | | 1.80 | 8.889 | | 980 | 380 | | 1,360 | 1,775 |
| 0200 | 3'-6" x 10'-0" opening, 3' high transom | | 1.80 | 8.889 | | 975 | 380 | | 1,355 | 1,775 |
| 0280 | 5'-0" x 7'-0" opening | | 2 | 8 | | 1,050 | 345 | | 1,395 | 1,800 |
| 0300 | 6'-0" x 7'-0" opening | | 1.30 | 12.308 | ↓ | 1,025 | 530 | | 1,555 | 2,075 |
| 0400 | 6'-0" x 10'-0" opening, 3' high transom | | 1.10 | 14.545 | Pr. | 1,250 | 625 | | 1,875 | 2,500 |
| 0420 | 7'-0" x 7'-0" opening | | 1 | 16 | " | 1,050 | 690 | | 1,740 | 2,400 |
| 0500 | Wide stile, 2'-6" x 7'-0" opening | | 2 | 8 | Ea. | 885 | 345 | | 1,230 | 1,600 |
| 0520 | 3'-0" x 7'-0" opening | | 2 | 8 | | 870 | 345 | | 1,215 | 1,575 |
| 0540 | 3'-6" x 7'-0" opening | | 2 | 8 | | 945 | 345 | | 1,290 | 1,675 |
| 0560 | 5'-0" x 7'-0" opening | | 2 | 8 | ↓ | 1,375 | 345 | | 1,720 | 2,150 |
| 0580 | 6'-0" x 7'-0" opening | | 1.30 | 12.308 | Pr. | 1,425 | 530 | | 1,955 | 2,500 |
| 0600 | 7'-0" x 7'-0" opening | ↓ | 1 | 16 | " | 1,525 | 690 | | 2,215 | 2,925 |
| 1100 | For full vision doors, with 1/2" glass, add | | | | Leaf | 55% | | | | |
| 1200 | For non-standard size, add | | | | | 67% | | | | |
| 1300 | Light bronze finish, add | | | | | 36% | | | | |
| 1400 | Dark bronze finish, add | | | | | 18% | | | | |
| 1500 | For black finish, add | | | | | 36% | | | | |
| 1600 | Concealed panic device, add | | | | ↓ | 1,050 | | | 1,050 | 1,150 |
| 1700 | Electric striker release, add | | | | Opng. | 272 | | | 272 | 299 |
| 1800 | Floor check, add | | | | Leaf | 810 | | | 810 | 890 |
| 1900 | Concealed closer, add | | | | " | 535 | | | 535 | 590 |
| 2000 | Flush 3' x 7' Insulated, 12"x 12" lite, clear finish | 2 Sswk | 2 | 8 | Ea. | 1,075 | 345 | | 1,420 | 1,800 |

## 08 11 63 – Metal Screen and Storm Doors and Frames

### 08 11 63.23 Aluminum Screen and Storm Doors and Frames

| | | Crew | Daily Output | Labor-Hours | Unit | Material | 2008 Bare Costs Labor | Equipment | Total | Total Incl O&P |
|---|---|---|---|---|---|---|---|---|---|---|
| 0010 | **ALUMINUM SCREEN AND STORM DOORS AND FRAMES** | | | | | | | | | |
| 0020 | Combination storm and screen | | | | | | | | | |
| 0400 | Clear anodic coating, 6'-8" x 2'-6" wide | 2 Carp | 15 | 1.067 | Ea. | 168 | 40.50 | | 208.50 | 249 |
| 0420 | 2'-8" wide | | 14 | 1.143 | | 193 | 43.50 | | 236.50 | 281 |
| 0440 | 3'-0" wide | ↓ | 14 | 1.143 | ↓ | 193 | 43.50 | | 236.50 | 281 |
| 0500 | For 7' door height, add | | | | | 5% | | | | |
| 1000 | Mill finish, 6'-8" x 2'-6" wide | 2 Carp | 15 | 1.067 | Ea. | 223 | 40.50 | | 263.50 | 310 |
| 1020 | 2'-8" wide | | 14 | 1.143 | | 223 | 43.50 | | 266.50 | 315 |
| 1040 | 3'-0" wide | ↓ | 14 | 1.143 | | 242 | 43.50 | | 285.50 | 335 |
| 1100 | For 7'-0" door, add | | | | | 5% | | | | |
| 1500 | White painted, 6'-8" x 2'-6" wide | 2 Carp | 15 | 1.067 | Ea. | 267 | 40.50 | | 307.50 | 360 |
| 1520 | 2'-8" wide | | 14 | 1.143 | | 228 | 43.50 | | 271.50 | 320 |
| 1540 | 3'-0" wide | ↓ | 14 | 1.143 | | 263 | 43.50 | | 306.50 | 355 |
| 1600 | For 7'-0" door, add | | | | ↓ | 5% | | | | |
| 2000 | Wood door & screen, see Div. 08 14 33.20 | | | | | | | | | |

# 08 11 Metal Doors and Frames

## 08 11 74 – Sliding Metal Grilles

| 08 11 74.10 Rolling Grille Supports | Crew | Daily Output | Labor-Hours | Unit | Material | 2008 Bare Costs Labor | Equipment | Total | Total Incl O&P |
|---|---|---|---|---|---|---|---|---|---|
| 0010 **ROLLING GRILLE SUPPORTS** | | | | | | | | | |
| 0020 Rolling grille supports, overhead framed | E-4 | 36 | .889 | L.F. | 21 | 38.50 | 3.67 | 63.17 | 96.50 |

# 08 12 Metal Frames

## 08 12 13 – Hollow Metal Frames

### 08 12 13.13 Standard Hollow Metal Frames

| | Crew | Daily Output | Labor-Hours | Unit | Material | 2008 Bare Costs Labor | Equipment | Total | Total Incl O&P |
|---|---|---|---|---|---|---|---|---|---|
| 0010 **STANDARD HOLLOW METAL FRAMES** | | | | | | | | | |
| 0020 16 ga., up to 5-3/4" jamb depth | | | | | | | | | |
| 0025 6'-8" high, 3'-0" wide, single | 2 Carp | 16 | 1 | Ea. | 120 | 38 | | 158 | 192 |
| 0028 3'-6" wide, single | | 16 | 1 | | 112 | 38 | | 150 | 183 |
| 0030 4'-0" wide, single | | 16 | 1 | | 112 | 38 | | 150 | 183 |
| 0040 6'-0" wide, double | | 14 | 1.143 | | 148 | 43.50 | | 191.50 | 231 |
| 0045 8'-0" wide, double | | 14 | 1.143 | | 154 | 43.50 | | 197.50 | 238 |
| 0100 7'-0" high, 3'-0" wide, single | | 16 | 1 | | 123 | 38 | | 161 | 195 |
| 0110 3'-6" wide, single | | 16 | 1 | | 115 | 38 | | 153 | 186 |
| 0112 4'-0" wide, single | | 16 | 1 | | 147 | 38 | | 185 | 221 |
| 0140 6'-0" wide, double | | 14 | 1.143 | | 155 | 43.50 | | 198.50 | 238 |
| 0145 8'-0" wide, double | | 14 | 1.143 | | 145 | 43.50 | | 188.50 | 228 |
| 1000 16 ga., up to 4-7/8" deep, 7'-0" H, 3'-0" W, single **CN** | | 16 | 1 | | 127 | 38 | | 165 | 199 |
| 1140 6'-0" wide, double | | 14 | 1.143 | | 154 | 43.50 | | 197.50 | 237 |
| 2800 14 ga., up to 3-7/8" deep, 7'-0" high, 3'-0" wide, single | | 16 | 1 | | 131 | 38 | | 169 | 204 |
| 2840 6'-0" wide, double | | 14 | 1.143 | | 157 | 43.50 | | 200.50 | 241 |
| 3000 14 ga., up to 5-3/4" deep, 6'-8" high, 3'-0" wide, single | | 16 | 1 | | 137 | 38 | | 175 | 211 |
| 3002 3'-6" wide, single | | 16 | 1 | | 136 | 38 | | 174 | 210 |
| 3005 4'-0" wide, single | | 16 | 1 | | 136 | 38 | | 174 | 210 |
| 3600 up to 5-3/4" jamb depth, 7'-0" high, 4'-0" wide, single | | 15 | 1.067 | | 107 | 40.50 | | 147.50 | 182 |
| 3620 6'-0" wide, double | | 12 | 1.333 | | 168 | 51 | | 219 | 263 |
| 3640 8'-0" wide, double | | 12 | 1.333 | | 159 | 51 | | 210 | 254 |
| 3700 8'-0" high, 4'-0" wide, single | | 15 | 1.067 | | 141 | 40.50 | | 181.50 | 219 |
| 3740 8'-0" wide, double | | 12 | 1.333 | | 175 | 51 | | 226 | 272 |
| 4000 6-3/4" deep, 7'-0" high, 4'-0" wide, single | | 15 | 1.067 | | 167 | 40.50 | | 207.50 | 247 |
| 4020 6'-0" wide, double | | 12 | 1.333 | | 195 | 51 | | 246 | 293 |
| 4040 8'-0", wide double | | 12 | 1.333 | | 221 | 51 | | 272 | 320 |
| 4100 8'-0" high, 4'-0" wide, single | | 15 | 1.067 | | 168 | 40.50 | | 208.50 | 248 |
| 4140 8'-0" wide, double | | 12 | 1.333 | | 195 | 51 | | 246 | 294 |
| 4400 8-3/4" deep, 7'-0" high, 4'-0" wide, single | | 15 | 1.067 | | 157 | 40.50 | | 197.50 | 237 |
| 4440 8'-0" wide, double | | 12 | 1.333 | | 224 | 51 | | 275 | 325 |
| 4500 8'-0" high, 4'-0" wide, single | | 15 | 1.067 | | 168 | 40.50 | | 208.50 | 249 |
| 4540 8'-0" wide, double | ▼ | 12 | 1.333 | | 196 | 51 | | 247 | 295 |
| 4900 For welded frames, add | | | | | 46 | | | 46 | 50.50 |
| 5400 14 ga., "B" label, up to 5-3/4" deep, 7'-0" high, 4'-0" wide, single | 2 Carp | 15 | 1.067 | | 166 | 40.50 | | 206.50 | 246 |
| 5440 8'-0" wide, double | | 12 | 1.333 | | 202 | 51 | | 253 | 300 |
| 5800 6-3/4" deep, 7'-0" high, 4'-0" wide, single | | 15 | 1.067 | | 145 | 40.50 | | 185.50 | 224 |
| 5840 8'-0" wide, double | | 12 | 1.333 | | 243 | 51 | | 294 | 345 |
| 6200 8-3/4" deep, 7'-0" high, 4'-0" wide, single | | 15 | 1.067 | | 207 | 40.50 | | 247.50 | 292 |
| 6240 8'-0" wide, double | ▼ | 12 | 1.333 | ▼ | 243 | 51 | | 294 | 345 |
| 6300 For "A" label use same price as "B" label | | | | | | | | | |
| 6400 For baked enamel finish, add | | | | | 30% | 15% | | | |
| 6500 For galvanizing, add | | | | | 15% | | | | |
| 6600 For hospital stop, add | | | | Ea. | 272 | | | 272 | 299 |

# 08 12 Metal Frames

## 08 12 13 – Hollow Metal Frames

### 08 12 13.13 Standard Hollow Metal Frames

| | | Crew | Daily Output | Labor-Hours | Unit | Material | 2008 Bare Costs Labor | 2008 Bare Costs Equipment | Total | Total Incl O&P |
|---|---|---|---|---|---|---|---|---|---|---|
| 7900 | Transom lite frames, fixed, add | 2 Carp | 155 | .103 | S.F. | 44 | 3.93 | | 47.93 | 54.50 |
| 8000 | Movable, add | " | 130 | .123 | " | 53 | 4.69 | | 57.69 | 66 |

### 08 12 13.25 Channel Metal Frames

| | | Crew | Daily Output | Labor-Hours | Unit | Material | 2008 Bare Costs Labor | 2008 Bare Costs Equipment | Total | Total Incl O&P |
|---|---|---|---|---|---|---|---|---|---|---|
| 0010 | **CHANNEL METAL FRAMES** | | | | | | | | | |
| 0020 | Steel channels with anchors and bar stops | | | | | | | | | |
| 0100 | 6" channel @ 8.2#/L.F., 3' x 7' door, weighs 150# | E-4 | 13 | 2.462 | Ea. | 198 | 107 | 10.15 | 315.15 | 420 |
| 0200 | 8" channel @ 11.5#/L.F., 6' x 8' door, weighs 275# | | 9 | 3.556 | | 365 | 155 | 14.70 | 534.70 | 695 |
| 0300 | 8' x 12' door, weighs 400# | | 6.50 | 4.923 | | 530 | 214 | 20.50 | 764.50 | 990 |
| 0400 | 10" channel @ 15.3#/L.F., 10' x 10' door, weighs 500# *CN* | | 6 | 5.333 | | 660 | 232 | 22 | 914 | 1,175 |
| 0500 | 12' x 12' door, weighs 600# | | 5.50 | 5.818 | | 790 | 253 | 24 | 1,067 | 1,350 |
| 0600 | 12" channel @ 20.7#/L.F., 12' x 12' door, weighs 825# | | 4.50 | 7.111 | | 1,100 | 310 | 29.50 | 1,439.50 | 1,800 |
| 0700 | 12' x 16' door, weighs 1000# | | 4 | 8 | | 1,325 | 350 | 33 | 1,708 | 2,125 |
| 0800 | For frames without bar stops, light sections, deduct | | | | | 15% | | | | |
| 0900 | Heavy sections, deduct | | | | | 10% | | | | |

# 08 13 Metal Doors

## 08 13 13 – Hollow Metal Doors

### 08 13 13.13 Standard Hollow Metal Doors

| | | Crew | Daily Output | Labor-Hours | Unit | Material | 2008 Bare Costs Labor | 2008 Bare Costs Equipment | Total | Total Incl O&P |
|---|---|---|---|---|---|---|---|---|---|---|
| 0010 | **STANDARD HOLLOW METAL DOORS** R081313-20 | | | | | | | | | |
| 0015 | Flush, full panel, hollow core | | | | | | | | | |
| 0020 | 1-3/8" thick, 20 ga., 2'-0"x 6'-8" | 2 Carp | 20 | .800 | Ea. | 257 | 30.50 | | 287.50 | 330 |
| 0040 | 2'-8" x 6'-8" | | 18 | .889 | | 265 | 34 | | 299 | 345 |
| 0060 | 3'-0" x 6'-8" | | 17 | .941 | | 270 | 36 | | 306 | 355 |
| 0100 | 3'-0" x 7'-0" | | 17 | .941 | | 287 | 36 | | 323 | 370 |
| 0120 | For vision lite, add | | | | | 87 | | | 87 | 96 |
| 0140 | For narrow lite, add | | | | | 96 | | | 96 | 105 |
| 0320 | Half glass, 20 ga., 2'-0" x 6'-8" | 2 Carp | 20 | .800 | | 385 | 30.50 | | 415.50 | 470 |
| 0340 | 2'-8" x 6'-8" | | 18 | .889 | | 395 | 34 | | 429 | 485 |
| 0360 | 3'-0" x 6'-8" | | 17 | .941 | | 400 | 36 | | 436 | 490 |
| 0400 | 3'-0" x 7'-0" | | 17 | .941 | | 400 | 36 | | 436 | 495 |
| 0410 | 1-3/8" thick, 18 ga., 2'-0"x 6'-8" | | 20 | .800 | | 310 | 30.50 | | 340.50 | 390 |
| 0420 | 3'-0" x 6'-8" | | 17 | .941 | | 315 | 36 | | 351 | 400 |
| 0425 | 3'-0" x 7'-0" | | 17 | .941 | | 320 | 36 | | 356 | 410 |
| 0450 | For vision lite, add | | | | | 87 | | | 87 | 96 |
| 0452 | For narrow lite, add | | | | | 96 | | | 96 | 105 |
| 0460 | Half glass, 18 ga., 2'-0" x 6'-8" | 2 Carp | 20 | .800 | | 435 | 30.50 | | 465.50 | 530 |
| 0465 | 2'-8" x 6'-8" | | 18 | .889 | | 450 | 34 | | 484 | 550 |
| 0470 | 3'-0" x 6'-8" | | 17 | .941 | | 440 | 36 | | 476 | 540 |
| 0475 | 3'-0" x 7'-0" | | 17 | .941 | | 445 | 36 | | 481 | 545 |
| 0500 | Hollow core, 1-3/4" thick, full panel, 20 ga., 2'-8" x 6'-8" | | 18 | .889 | | 295 | 34 | | 329 | 380 |
| 0520 | 3'-0" x 6'-8" | | 17 | .941 | | 270 | 36 | | 306 | 355 |
| 0640 | 3'-0" x 7'-0" | | 17 | .941 | | 320 | 36 | | 356 | 405 |
| 0680 | 4'-0" x 7'-0" | | 15 | 1.067 | | 450 | 40.50 | | 490.50 | 560 |
| 0700 | 4'-0" x 8'-0" | | 13 | 1.231 | | 515 | 47 | | 562 | 640 |
| 1000 | 18 ga., 2'-8" x 6'-8" | | 17 | .941 | | 298 | 36 | | 334 | 385 |
| 1020 | 3'-0" x 6'-8" | | 16 | 1 | | 289 | 38 | | 327 | 380 |
| 1120 | 3'-0" x 7'-0" *CN* | | 17 | .941 | | 360 | 36 | | 396 | 450 |
| 1180 | 4'-0" x 7'-0" | | 14 | 1.143 | | 435 | 43.50 | | 478.50 | 550 |
| 1200 | 4'-0" x 8'-0" | | 17 | .941 | | 515 | 36 | | 551 | 620 |
| 1212 | For vision lite, add | | | | | 87 | | | 87 | 96 |
| 1214 | For narrow lite, add | | | | | 96 | | | 96 | 105 |

# 08 13 Metal Doors

## 08 13 13 – Hollow Metal Doors

### 08 13 13.13 Standard Hollow Metal Doors

| | | Crew | Daily Output | Labor-Hours | Unit | Material | 2008 Bare Costs Labor | Equipment | Total | Total Incl O&P |
|---|---|---|---|---|---|---|---|---|---|---|
| 1230 | Half glass, 20 ga., 2'-8" x 6'-8" | 2 Carp | 20 | .800 | Ea. | 415 | 30.50 | | 445.50 | 505 |
| 1240 | 3'-0" x 6'-8" | | 18 | .889 | | 405 | 34 | | 439 | 505 |
| 1260 | 3'-0" x 7'-0" | | 18 | .889 | | 410 | 34 | | 444 | 505 |
| 1320 | 18 ga., 2'-8" x 6'-8" | | 18 | .889 | | 445 | 34 | | 479 | 545 |
| 1340 | 3'-0" x 6'-8" | | 17 | .941 | | 440 | 36 | | 476 | 540 |
| 1360 | 3'-0" x 7'-0" | | 17 | .941 | | 450 | 36 | | 486 | 550 |
| 1380 | 4'-0" x 7'-0" | | 15 | 1.067 | | 560 | 40.50 | | 600.50 | 680 |
| 1400 | 4'-0" x 8'-0" | | 14 | 1.143 | | 640 | 43.50 | | 683.50 | 775 |
| 1720 | Insulated, 1-3/4" thick, full panel, 18 ga., 3'-0" x 6'-8" | | 15 | 1.067 | | 390 | 40.50 | | 430.50 | 495 |
| 1740 | 2'-8" x 7'-0" | | 16 | 1 | | 405 | 38 | | 443 | 505 |
| 1760 | 3'-0" x 7'-0" | | 15 | 1.067 | | 400 | 40.50 | | 440.50 | 505 |
| 1800 | 4'-0" x 8'-0" | ▼ | 13 | 1.231 | | 585 | 47 | | 632 | 715 |
| 1805 | For vision lite, add | | | | | 87 | | | 87 | 96 |
| 1810 | For narrow lite, add | | | | | 96 | | | 96 | 105 |
| 1820 | Half glass, 18 ga., 3'-0" x 6'-8" | 2 Carp | 16 | 1 | | 520 | 38 | | 558 | 630 |
| 1840 | 2'-8" x 7'-0" | | 17 | .941 | | 530 | 36 | | 566 | 635 |
| 1860 | 3'-0" x 7'-0" | | 16 | 1 | | 565 | 38 | | 603 | 680 |
| 1900 | 4'-0" x 8'-0" | ▼ | 14 | 1.143 | | 635 | 43.50 | | 678.50 | 765 |
| 2000 | For bottom louver, add | | | | ▼ | 154 | | | 154 | 169 |
| 2020 | For baked enamel finish, add | | | | | 30% | 15% | | | |
| 2040 | For galvanizing, add | | | | | 15% | | | | |

### 08 13 13.15 Metal Fire Doors

| | | Crew | Daily Output | Labor-Hours | Unit | Material | 2008 Bare Costs Labor | Equipment | Total | Total Incl O&P |
|---|---|---|---|---|---|---|---|---|---|---|
| 0010 | **METAL FIRE DOORS** R081313-20 | | | | | | | | | |
| 0015 | Steel, flush, "B" label, 90 minute | | | | | | | | | |
| 0020 | Full panel, 20 ga., 2'-0" x 6'-8" | 2 Carp | 20 | .800 | Ea. | 330 | 30.50 | | 360.50 | 410 |
| 0040 | 2'-8" x 6'-8" | | 18 | .889 | | 335 | 34 | | 369 | 420 |
| 0060 | 3'-0" x 6'-8" | | 17 | .941 | | 335 | 36 | | 371 | 425 |
| 0080 | 3'-0" x 7'-0" | | 17 | .941 | | 350 | 36 | | 386 | 440 |
| 0140 | 18 ga., 3'-0" x 6'-8" | | 16 | 1 | | 380 | 38 | | 418 | 480 |
| 0160 | 2'-8" x 7'-0" | | 17 | .941 | | 400 | 36 | | 436 | 495 |
| 0180 | 3'-0" x 7'-0" | | 16 | 1 | | 385 | 38 | | 423 | 480 |
| 0200 | 4'-0" x 7'-0" | ▼ | 15 | 1.067 | ▼ | 500 | 40.50 | | 540.50 | 615 |
| 0220 | For "A" label, 3 hour, 18 ga., use same price as "B" label | | | | | | | | | |
| 0240 | For vision lite, add | | | | Ea. | 109 | | | 109 | 120 |
| 0520 | Flush, "B" label 90 min., composite, 20 ga., 2'-0" x 6'-8" | 2 Carp | 18 | .889 | | 415 | 34 | | 449 | 515 |
| 0540 | 2'-8" x 6'-8" | | 17 | .941 | | 420 | 36 | | 456 | 520 |
| 0560 | 3'-0" x 6'-8" | | 16 | 1 | | 425 | 38 | | 463 | 525 |
| 0580 | 3'-0" x 7'-0" | | 16 | 1 | | 435 | 38 | | 473 | 535 |
| 0640 | Flush, "A" label 3 hour, composite, 18 ga., 3'-0" x 6'-8" | | 15 | 1.067 | | 480 | 40.50 | | 520.50 | 595 |
| 0660 | 2'-8" x 7'-0" | | 16 | 1 | | 500 | 38 | | 538 | 610 |
| 0680 | 3'-0" x 7'-0" | | 15 | 1.067 | | 490 | 40.50 | | 530.50 | 605 |
| 0700 | 4'-0" x 7'-0" | ▼ | 14 | 1.143 | ▼ | 590 | 43.50 | | 633.50 | 720 |

### 08 13 13.20 Residential Steel Doors

| | | Crew | Daily Output | Labor-Hours | Unit | Material | 2008 Bare Costs Labor | Equipment | Total | Total Incl O&P |
|---|---|---|---|---|---|---|---|---|---|---|
| 0010 | **RESIDENTIAL STEEL DOORS** | | | | | | | | | |
| 0020 | Prehung, insulated, exterior | | | | | | | | | |
| 0030 | Embossed, full panel, 2'-8" x 6'-8" | 2 Carp | 17 | .941 | Ea. | 274 | 36 | | 310 | 355 |
| 0040 | 3'-0" x 6'-8" | | 15 | 1.067 | | 246 | 40.50 | | 286.50 | 335 |
| 0060 | 3'-0" x 7'-0" | | 15 | 1.067 | | 291 | 40.50 | | 331.50 | 385 |
| 0070 | 5'-4" x 6'-8", double | | 8 | 2 | | 505 | 76 | | 581 | 675 |
| 0220 | Half glass, 2'-8" x 6'-8" | | 17 | .941 | | 274 | 36 | | 310 | 355 |
| 0240 | 3'-0" x 6'-8" | | 16 | 1 | | 274 | 38 | | 312 | 360 |
| 0260 | 3'-0" x 7'-0" | ▼ | 16 | 1 | ▼ | 330 | 38 | | 368 | 425 |

# 08 13 Metal Doors

## 08 13 13 – Hollow Metal Doors

### 08 13 13.20 Residential Steel Doors

| | | Crew | Daily Output | Labor-Hours | Unit | Material | 2008 Bare Costs Labor | Equipment | Total | Total Incl O&P |
|---|---|---|---|---|---|---|---|---|---|---|
| 0270 | 5'-4" x 6'-8", double | 2 Carp | 8 | 2 | Ea. | 570 | 76 | | 646 | 745 |
| 0720 | Raised plastic face, full panel, 2'-8" x 6'-8" | | 16 | 1 | | 277 | 38 | | 315 | 365 |
| 0740 | 3'-0" x 6'-8" | | 15 | 1.067 | | 280 | 40.50 | | 320.50 | 375 |
| 0760 | 3'-0" x 7'-0" | | 15 | 1.067 | | 282 | 40.50 | | 322.50 | 375 |
| 0780 | 5'-4" x 6'-8", double | | 8 | 2 | | 520 | 76 | | 596 | 695 |
| 0820 | Half glass, 2'-8" x 6'-8" | | 17 | .941 | | 310 | 36 | | 346 | 395 |
| 0840 | 3'-0" x 6'-8" | | 16 | 1 | | 315 | 38 | | 353 | 405 |
| 0860 | 3'-0" x 7'-0" | | 16 | 1 | | 345 | 38 | | 383 | 440 |
| 0880 | 5'-4" x 6'-8", double | | 8 | 2 | | 665 | 76 | | 741 | 855 |
| 1320 | Flush face, full panel, 2'-6" x 6'-8" | | 16 | 1 | | 225 | 38 | | 263 | 305 |
| 1340 | 3'-0" x 6'-8" | | 15 | 1.067 | | 225 | 40.50 | | 265.50 | 310 |
| 1360 | 3'-0" x 7'-0" | | 15 | 1.067 | | 290 | 40.50 | | 330.50 | 385 |
| 1380 | 5'-4" x 6'-8", double | | 8 | 2 | | 470 | 76 | | 546 | 635 |
| 1420 | Half glass, 2'-8" x 6'-8" | | 17 | .941 | | 283 | 36 | | 319 | 365 |
| 1440 | 3'-0" x 6'-8" | | 16 | 1 | | 287 | 38 | | 325 | 375 |
| 1460 | 3'-0" x 7'-0" | | 16 | 1 | | 330 | 38 | | 368 | 420 |
| 1480 | 5'-4" x 6'-8", double | | 8 | 2 | | 555 | 76 | | 631 | 730 |
| 1500 | Sidelight, full lite, 1'-0" x 6'-8"with grille | | | | | 217 | | | 217 | 238 |
| 1510 | 1'-0" x 6'-8", low e | | | | | 246 | | | 246 | 270 |
| 1520 | 1'-0" x 6'-8", half lite | | | | | 197 | | | 197 | 216 |
| 1530 | 1'-0" x 6'-8", half lite, low e | | | | | 236 | | | 236 | 260 |
| 2300 | Interior, residential, closet, bi-fold, 6'-8" x 2'-0" wide | 2 Carp | 16 | 1 | | 147 | 38 | | 185 | 222 |
| 2330 | 3'-0" wide | | 16 | 1 | | 165 | 38 | | 203 | 241 |
| 2360 | 4'-0" wide | | 15 | 1.067 | | 250 | 40.50 | | 290.50 | 340 |
| 2400 | 5'-0" wide | | 14 | 1.143 | | 290 | 43.50 | | 333.50 | 390 |
| 2420 | 6'-0" wide | | 13 | 1.231 | | 325 | 47 | | 372 | 435 |

## 08 13 16 – Aluminum Doors

### 08 13 16.10 Commercial Aluminum Doors

| | | Crew | Daily Output | Labor-Hours | Unit | Material | 2008 Bare Costs Labor | Equipment | Total | Total Incl O&P |
|---|---|---|---|---|---|---|---|---|---|---|
| 0010 | **COMMERCIAL ALUMINUM DOORS,** no glazing | | | | | | | | | |
| 0020 | Incl. hinges, push/pull, deadlock, cyl., threshold | | | | | | | | | |
| 0800 | Narrow stile, no glazing, standard hardware, pair of 2'-6" x 7'-0" | 2 Carp | 1.70 | 9.412 | Pr. | 935 | 360 | | 1,295 | 1,575 |
| 1000 | 3'-0" x 7'-0", single | | 3 | 5.333 | Ea. | 545 | 203 | | 748 | 915 |
| 1200 | Pair of 3'-0" x 7'-0" | | 1.70 | 9.412 | Pr. | 1,100 | 360 | | 1,460 | 1,750 |
| 1500 | 3'-6" x 7'-0", single | | 3 | 5.333 | Ea. | 570 | 203 | | 773 | 940 |
| 2000 | Medium stile, pair of 2'-6" x 7'-0" | | 1.70 | 9.412 | Pr. | 1,000 | 360 | | 1,360 | 1,650 |
| 2100 | 3'-0" x 7'-0", single | | 3 | 5.333 | Ea. | 695 | 203 | | 898 | 1,075 |
| 2200 | Pair of 3'-0" x 7'-0" | | 1.70 | 9.412 | Pr. | 1,375 | 360 | | 1,735 | 2,050 |
| 2300 | 3'-6" x 7'-0", single | | 5.33 | 3.002 | Ea. | 825 | 114 | | 939 | 1,075 |
| 5000 | Flush panel doors, pair of 2'-6" x 7'-0" | 2 Sswk | 2 | 8 | Pr. | 980 | 345 | | 1,325 | 1,700 |
| 5050 | 3'-0" x 7'-0", single | | 2.50 | 6.400 | Ea. | 490 | 275 | | 765 | 1,025 |
| 5100 | Pair of 3'-0" x 7'-0" | | 2 | 8 | Pr. | 980 | 345 | | 1,325 | 1,700 |
| 5150 | 3'-6" x 7'-0", single | | 2.50 | 6.400 | Ea. | 585 | 275 | | 860 | 1,125 |

## 08 13 73 – Sliding Metal Doors

### 08 13 73.10 Steel Sliding Doors

| | | Crew | Daily Output | Labor-Hours | Unit | Material | 2008 Bare Costs Labor | Equipment | Total | Total Incl O&P |
|---|---|---|---|---|---|---|---|---|---|---|
| 0010 | **STEEL SLIDING DOORS** | | | | | | | | | |
| 0020 | Up to 50' x 18', electric, standard duty, minimum | L-5 | 360 | .156 | S.F. | 24.50 | 6.70 | 2.18 | 33.38 | 41 |
| 0100 | Maximum | | 340 | .165 | | 41 | 7.10 | 2.31 | 50.41 | 60 |
| 0500 | Heavy duty, minimum | | 297 | .189 | | 33 | 8.10 | 2.65 | 43.75 | 53.50 |
| 0600 | Maximum | | 277 | .202 | | 87.50 | 8.70 | 2.84 | 99.04 | 114 |

# 08 14 Wood Doors

## 08 14 13 – Carved Wood Doors

### 08 14 13.10 Types of Wood Doors, Carved

| | | Crew | Daily Output | Labor-Hours | Unit | Material | 2008 Bare Costs Labor | Equipment | Total | Total Incl O&P |
|---|---|---|---|---|---|---|---|---|---|---|
| 0010 | **TYPES OF WOOD DOORS, CARVED** | | | | | | | | | |
| 3000 | Solid wood, 1-3/4" thick stile and rail | | | | | | | | | |
| 3020 | Mahogany, 3'-0" x 7'-0", minimum | 2 Carp | 14 | 1.143 | Ea. | 855 | 43.50 | | 898.50 | 1,000 |
| 3030 | Maximum | | 10 | 1.600 | | 1,350 | 61 | | 1,411 | 1,600 |
| 3040 | 3'-6" x 8'-0", minimum | | 10 | 1.600 | | 985 | 61 | | 1,046 | 1,175 |
| 3050 | Maximum | | 8 | 2 | | 1,800 | 76 | | 1,876 | 2,100 |
| 3100 | Pine, 3'-0" x 7'-0", minimum | | 14 | 1.143 | | 415 | 43.50 | | 458.50 | 525 |
| 3110 | Maximum | | 10 | 1.600 | | 705 | 61 | | 766 | 870 |
| 3120 | 3'-6" x 8'-0", minimum | | 10 | 1.600 | | 690 | 61 | | 751 | 855 |
| 3130 | Maximum | | 8 | 2 | | 1,150 | 76 | | 1,226 | 1,375 |
| 3200 | Red oak, 3'-0" x 7'-0", minimum | | 14 | 1.143 | | 1,600 | 43.50 | | 1,643.50 | 1,850 |
| 3210 | Maximum | | 10 | 1.600 | | 1,925 | 61 | | 1,986 | 2,225 |
| 3220 | 3'-6" x 8'-0", minimum | | 10 | 1.600 | | 1,775 | 61 | | 1,836 | 2,050 |
| 3230 | Maximum | ↓ | 8 | 2 | ↓ | 3,150 | 76 | | 3,226 | 3,600 |
| 4000 | Hand carved door, mahogany | | | | | | | | | |
| 4020 | 3'-0" x 7'-0", minimum | 2 Carp | 14 | 1.143 | Ea. | 1,600 | 43.50 | | 1,643.50 | 1,825 |
| 4030 | Maximum | | 11 | 1.455 | | 3,125 | 55.50 | | 3,180.50 | 3,525 |
| 4040 | 3'-6" x 8'-0", minimum | | 10 | 1.600 | | 2,000 | 61 | | 2,061 | 2,300 |
| 4050 | Maximum | | 8 | 2 | | 3,075 | 76 | | 3,151 | 3,500 |
| 4200 | Red oak, 3'-0" x 7'-0", minimum | | 14 | 1.143 | | 4,850 | 43.50 | | 4,893.50 | 5,425 |
| 4210 | Maximum | | 11 | 1.455 | | 13,300 | 55.50 | | 13,355.50 | 14,700 |
| 4220 | 3'-6" x 8'-0", minimum | ↓ | 10 | 1.600 | | 5,475 | 61 | | 5,536 | 6,125 |
| 4280 | For 6'-8" high door, deduct from 7'-0" door | | | | | 34.50 | | | 34.50 | 38 |
| 4400 | For custom finish, add | | | | | 370 | | | 370 | 405 |
| 4600 | Side light, mahogany, 7'-0" x 1'-6" wide, minimum | 2 Carp | 18 | .889 | | 895 | 34 | | 929 | 1,050 |
| 4610 | Maximum | | 14 | 1.143 | | 2,625 | 43.50 | | 2,668.50 | 2,975 |
| 4620 | 8'-0" x 1'-6" wide, minimum | | 14 | 1.143 | | 1,675 | 43.50 | | 1,718.50 | 1,925 |
| 4630 | Maximum | | 10 | 1.600 | | 1,900 | 61 | | 1,961 | 2,200 |
| 4640 | Side light, oak, 7'-0" x 1'-6" wide, minimum | | 18 | .889 | | 1,025 | 34 | | 1,059 | 1,175 |
| 4650 | Maximum | | 14 | 1.143 | | 1,825 | 43.50 | | 1,868.50 | 2,100 |
| 4660 | 8'-0" x 1-6" wide, minimum | | 14 | 1.143 | | 970 | 43.50 | | 1,013.50 | 1,150 |
| 4670 | Maximum | ↓ | 10 | 1.600 | ↓ | 1,825 | 61 | | 1,886 | 2,125 |

## 08 14 16 – Flush Wood Doors

### 08 14 16.09 Smooth Wood Doors

| | | Crew | Daily Output | Labor-Hours | Unit | Material | 2008 Bare Costs Labor | Equipment | Total | Total Incl O&P |
|---|---|---|---|---|---|---|---|---|---|---|
| 0010 | **SMOOTH WOOD DOORS** | | | | | | | | | |
| 0015 | Flush, int., 1-3/8", 7 ply, hollow core, | | | | | | | | | |
| 0020 | Lauan face, 2'-0" x 6'-8" | 2 Carp | 17 | .941 | Ea. | 31 | 36 | | 67 | 90 |
| 0080 | 3'-0" x 6'-8" | | 17 | .941 | | 48 | 36 | | 84 | 109 |
| 0100 | 4'-0" x 6'-8" | | 16 | 1 | | 73.50 | 38 | | 111.50 | 141 |
| 0120 | Birch face, 2'-0" x 6'-8" | | 17 | .941 | | 47.50 | 36 | | 83.50 | 108 |
| 0140 | 2'-6" x 6'-8" | | 17 | .941 | | 79 | 36 | | 115 | 143 |
| 0180 | 3'-0" x 6'-8" | | 17 | .941 | | 90.50 | 36 | | 126.50 | 156 |
| 0200 | 4'-0" x 6'-8" | | 16 | 1 | | 100 | 38 | | 138 | 170 |
| 0220 | Oak face, 2'-0" x 6'-8" | | 17 | .941 | | 76.50 | 36 | | 112.50 | 141 |
| 0240 | 2'-6" x 6'-8" | | 17 | .941 | | 81.50 | 36 | | 117.50 | 146 |
| 0280 | 3'-0" x 6'-8" | | 17 | .941 | | 87.50 | 36 | | 123.50 | 152 |
| 0300 | 4'-0" x 6'-8" | | 16 | 1 | | 111 | 38 | | 149 | 182 |
| 0320 | Walnut face, 2'-0" x 6'-8" | | 17 | .941 | | 155 | 36 | | 191 | 226 |
| 0340 | 2'-6" x 6'-8" | | 17 | .941 | | 158 | 36 | | 194 | 230 |
| 0380 | 3'-0" x 6'-8" | | 17 | .941 | | 164 | 36 | | 200 | 236 |
| 0400 | 4'-0" x 6'-8" | ↓ | 16 | 1 | | 186 | 38 | | 224 | 264 |
| 0430 | For 7'-0" high, add | | | | ↓ | 15.20 | | | 15.20 | 16.70 |

| 08 14 16.09 Smooth Wood Doors | Crew | Daily Output | Labor-Hours | Unit | Material | 2008 Bare Costs Labor | Equipment | Total | Total Incl O&P |
|---|---|---|---|---|---|---|---|---|---|
| 0440 | For 8'-0" high, add | | | | Ea. | 28 | | | 28 | 31 |
| 0480 | For prefinishing, clear, add | | | | | 34 | | | 34 | 37.50 |
| 0500 | For prefinishing, stain, add | | | | | 45 | | | 45 | 49.50 |
| 1320 | M.D. overlay on hardboard, 2'-0" x 6'-8" | 2 Carp | 17 | .941 | | 94 | 36 | | 130 | 159 |
| 1340 | 2'-6" x 6'-8" | | 17 | .941 | | 94 | 36 | | 130 | 159 |
| 1380 | 3'-0" x 6'-8" | | 17 | .941 | | 111 | 36 | | 147 | 178 |
| 1400 | 4'-0" x 6'-8" | | 16 | 1 | | 153 | 38 | | 191 | 228 |
| 1420 | For 7'-0" high, add | | | | | 8.35 | | | 8.35 | 9.15 |
| 1440 | For 8'-0" high, add | | | | | 22 | | | 22 | 24.50 |
| 1720 | H.P. plastic laminate, 2'-0" x 6'-8" | 2 Carp | 16 | 1 | | 223 | 38 | | 261 | 305 |
| 1740 | 2'-6" x 6'-8" | | 16 | 1 | | 223 | 38 | | 261 | 305 |
| 1780 | 3'-0" x 6'-8" | | 15 | 1.067 | | 261 | 40.50 | | 301.50 | 350 |
| 1800 | 4'-0" x 6'-8" | | 14 | 1.143 | | 355 | 43.50 | | 398.50 | 460 |
| 1820 | For 7'-0" high, add | | | | | 8.75 | | | 8.75 | 9.65 |
| 1840 | For 8'-0" high, add | | | | | 22.50 | | | 22.50 | 24.50 |
| 2020 | 5 ply particle core, lauan face, 2'-6" x 6'-8" | 2 Carp | 15 | 1.067 | | 78 | 40.50 | | 118.50 | 150 |
| 2040 | 3'-0" x 6'-8" | | 14 | 1.143 | | 81.50 | 43.50 | | 125 | 158 |
| 2080 | 3'-0" x 7'-0" | | 13 | 1.231 | | 90.50 | 47 | | 137.50 | 173 |
| 2100 | 4'-0" x 7'-0" | | 12 | 1.333 | | 105 | 51 | | 156 | 195 |
| 2120 | Birch face, 2'-6" x 6'-8" | | 15 | 1.067 | | 89 | 40.50 | | 129.50 | 162 |
| 2140 | 3'-0" x 6'-8" | | 14 | 1.143 | | 97.50 | 43.50 | | 141 | 175 |
| 2180 | 3'-0" x 7'-0" | | 13 | 1.231 | | 99.50 | 47 | | 146.50 | 183 |
| 2200 | 4'-0" x 7'-0" | | 12 | 1.333 | | 121 | 51 | | 172 | 213 |
| 2220 | Oak face, 2'-6" x 6'-8" | | 15 | 1.067 | | 98.50 | 40.50 | | 139 | 172 |
| 2240 | 3'-0" x 6'-8" | | 14 | 1.143 | | 108 | 43.50 | | 151.50 | 187 |
| 2280 | 3'-0" x 7'-0" | | 13 | 1.231 | | 111 | 47 | | 158 | 195 |
| 2300 | 4'-0" x 7'-0" | | 12 | 1.333 | | 136 | 51 | | 187 | 229 |
| 2320 | Walnut face, 2'-0" x 6'-8" | | 15 | 1.067 | | 109 | 40.50 | | 149.50 | 184 |
| 2340 | 2'-6" x 6'-8" | | 14 | 1.143 | | 125 | 43.50 | | 168.50 | 205 |
| 2380 | 3'-0" x 6'-8" | | 13 | 1.231 | | 140 | 47 | | 187 | 227 |
| 2400 | 4'-0" x 6'-8" | | 12 | 1.333 | | 183 | 51 | | 234 | 280 |
| 2440 | For 8'-0" high, add | | | | | 27 | | | 27 | 29.50 |
| 2460 | For 8'-0" high walnut, add | | | | | 14.65 | | | 14.65 | 16.10 |
| 2480 | For solid wood core, add | | | | | 32.50 | | | 32.50 | 36 |
| 2720 | For prefinishing, clear, add | | | | | 21.50 | | | 21.50 | 23.50 |
| 2740 | For prefinishing, stain, add | | | | | 47.50 | | | 47.50 | 52.50 |
| 3320 | M.D. overlay on hardboard, 2'-6" x 6'-8" | 2 Carp | 14 | 1.143 | | 94.50 | 43.50 | | 138 | 172 |
| 3340 | 3'-0" x 6'-8" | | 13 | 1.231 | | 98.50 | 47 | | 145.50 | 182 |
| 3380 | 3'-0" x 7'-0" | | 12 | 1.333 | | 101 | 51 | | 152 | 190 |
| 3400 | 4'-0" x 7'-0" | | 10 | 1.600 | | 123 | 61 | | 184 | 231 |
| 3440 | For 8'-0" height, add | | | | | 27.50 | | | 27.50 | 30.50 |
| 3460 | For solid wood core, add | | | | | 36 | | | 36 | 39.50 |
| 3720 | H.P. plastic laminate, 2'-6" x 6'-8" | 2 Carp | 13 | 1.231 | | 138 | 47 | | 185 | 225 |
| 3740 | 3'-0" x 6'-8" | | 12 | 1.333 | | 157 | 51 | | 208 | 251 |
| 3780 | 3'-0" x 7'-0" | | 11 | 1.455 | | 162 | 55.50 | | 217.50 | 266 |
| 3800 | 4'-0" x 7'-0" | | 8 | 2 | | 198 | 76 | | 274 | 335 |
| 3840 | For 8'-0" height, add | | | | | 27.50 | | | 27.50 | 30.50 |
| 3860 | For solid wood core, add | | | | | 33.50 | | | 33.50 | 37 |
| 4000 | Exterior, flush, solid wood stave core, birch, 1-3/4" x 7'-0" x 2'-6" | 2 Carp | 15 | 1.067 | | 162 | 40.50 | | 202.50 | 243 |
| 4020 | 2'-8" wide | | 15 | 1.067 | | 170 | 40.50 | | 210.50 | 251 |
| 4040 | 3'-0" wide | | 14 | 1.143 | | 186 | 43.50 | | 229.50 | 273 |
| 4100 | Oak faced 1-3/4" x 7'-0" x 2'-6" wide | | 15 | 1.067 | | 179 | 40.50 | | 219.50 | 261 |
| 4120 | 2'-8" wide | | 15 | 1.067 | | 191 | 40.50 | | 231.50 | 274 |

# 08 14 Wood Doors

## 08 14 16 – Flush Wood Doors

### 08 14 16.09 Smooth Wood Doors

| | | Crew | Daily Output | Labor-Hours | Unit | Material | 2008 Bare Costs Labor | Equipment | Total | Total Incl O&P |
|---|---|---|---|---|---|---|---|---|---|---|
| 4140 | 3'-0" wide | 2 Carp | 14 | 1.143 | Ea. | 204 | 43.50 | | 247.50 | 292 |
| 4200 | Walnut faced, 1-3/4" x 7'-0" x 2'-6" wide | | 15 | 1.067 | | 263 | 40.50 | | 303.50 | 355 |
| 4220 | 2'-8" wide | | 15 | 1.067 | | 275 | 40.50 | | 315.50 | 365 |
| 4240 | 3'-0" wide | | 14 | 1.143 | | 286 | 43.50 | | 329.50 | 385 |
| 4300 | For 6'-8" high door, deduct from 7'-0" door | | | | | 14.65 | | | 14.65 | 16.10 |

### 08 14 16.10 Wood Doors Decorator

| | | Crew | Daily Output | Labor-Hours | Unit | Material | 2008 Bare Costs Labor | Equipment | Total | Total Incl O&P |
|---|---|---|---|---|---|---|---|---|---|---|
| 0010 | **WOOD DOORS DECORATOR** | | | | | | | | | |
| 0040 | 7 ply hollow core lauan face, 2'-6" x 6'-8" | 2 Carp | 17 | .941 | Ea. | 35 | 36 | | 71 | 94.50 |

### 08 14 16.20 Wood Fire Doors

| | | Crew | Daily Output | Labor-Hours | Unit | Material | 2008 Bare Costs Labor | Equipment | Total | Total Incl O&P |
|---|---|---|---|---|---|---|---|---|---|---|
| 0010 | **WOOD FIRE DOORS** | | | | | | | | | |
| 0020 | Particle core, 7 face plys, "B" label, | | | | | | | | | |
| 0040 | 1 hour, birch face, 1-3/4" x 2'-6" x 6'-8" | 2 Carp | 14 | 1.143 | Ea. | 310 | 43.50 | | 353.50 | 415 |
| 0080 | 3'-0" x 6'-8" | | 13 | 1.231 | | 320 | 47 | | 367 | 430 |
| 0090 | 3'-0" x 7'-0" | | 12 | 1.333 | | 335 | 51 | | 386 | 450 |
| 0100 | 4'-0" x 7'-0" | | 12 | 1.333 | | 450 | 51 | | 501 | 570 |
| 0140 | Oak face, 2'-6" x 6'-8" | | 14 | 1.143 | | 310 | 43.50 | | 353.50 | 415 |
| 0180 | 3'-0" x 6'-8" | | 13 | 1.231 | | 325 | 47 | | 372 | 430 |
| 0190 | 3'-0" x 7'-0" | | 12 | 1.333 | | 335 | 51 | | 386 | 450 |
| 0200 | 4'-0" x 7'-0" | | 12 | 1.333 | | 440 | 51 | | 491 | 565 |
| 0240 | Walnut face, 2'-6" x 6'-8" | | 14 | 1.143 | | 410 | 43.50 | | 453.50 | 520 |
| 0280 | 3'-0" x 6'-8" | | 13 | 1.231 | | 420 | 47 | | 467 | 535 |
| 0290 | 3'-0" x 7'-0" | | 12 | 1.333 | | 440 | 51 | | 491 | 560 |
| 0300 | 4'-0" x 7'-0" | | 12 | 1.333 | | 590 | 51 | | 641 | 730 |
| 0440 | M.D. overlay on hardboard, 2'-6" x 6'-8" | | 15 | 1.067 | | 274 | 40.50 | | 314.50 | 365 |
| 0480 | 3'-0" x 6'-8" | | 14 | 1.143 | | 285 | 43.50 | | 328.50 | 385 |
| 0490 | 3'-0" x 7'-0" | | 13 | 1.231 | | 300 | 47 | | 347 | 405 |
| 0500 | 4'-0" x 7'-0" | | 12 | 1.333 | | 365 | 51 | | 416 | 485 |
| 0540 | H.P. plastic laminate, 2'-6" x 6'-8" | | 13 | 1.231 | | 365 | 47 | | 412 | 475 |
| 0580 | 3'-0" x 6'-8" | | 12 | 1.333 | | 385 | 51 | | 436 | 505 |
| 0590 | 3'-0" x 7'-0" | | 11 | 1.455 | | 390 | 55.50 | | 445.50 | 515 |
| 0600 | 4'-0" x 7'-0" | | 10 | 1.600 | | 495 | 61 | | 556 | 640 |
| 0740 | 90 minutes, birch face, 1-3/4" x 2'-6" x 6'-8" | | 14 | 1.143 | | 291 | 43.50 | | 334.50 | 390 |
| 0780 | 3'-0" x 6'-8" | | 13 | 1.231 | | 277 | 47 | | 324 | 380 |
| 0790 | 3'-0" x 7'-0" | | 12 | 1.333 | | 335 | 51 | | 386 | 450 |
| 0800 | 4'-0" x 7'-0" | | 12 | 1.333 | | 400 | 51 | | 451 | 520 |
| 0840 | Oak face, 2'-6" x 6'-8" | | 14 | 1.143 | | 281 | 43.50 | | 324.50 | 380 |
| 0880 | 3'-0" x 6'-8" | | 13 | 1.231 | | 292 | 47 | | 339 | 395 |
| 0890 | 3'-0" x 7'-0" | | 12 | 1.333 | | 305 | 51 | | 356 | 415 |
| 0900 | 4'-0" x 7'-0" | | 12 | 1.333 | | 425 | 51 | | 476 | 545 |
| 0940 | Walnut face, 2'-6" x 6'-8" | | 14 | 1.143 | | 385 | 43.50 | | 428.50 | 495 |
| 0980 | 3'-0" x 6'-8" | | 13 | 1.231 | | 395 | 47 | | 442 | 510 |
| 0990 | 3'-0" x 7'-0" | | 12 | 1.333 | | 415 | 51 | | 466 | 535 |
| 1000 | 4'-0" x 7'-0" | | 12 | 1.333 | | 595 | 51 | | 646 | 735 |
| 1140 | M.D. overlay on hardboard, 2'-6" x 6'-8" | | 15 | 1.067 | | 305 | 40.50 | | 345.50 | 400 |
| 1180 | 3'-0" x 6'-8" | | 14 | 1.143 | | 315 | 43.50 | | 358.50 | 415 |
| 1190 | 3'-0" x 7'-0" | | 13 | 1.231 | | 325 | 47 | | 372 | 435 |
| 1200 | 4'-0" x 7'-0" | | 12 | 1.333 | | 445 | 51 | | 496 | 570 |
| 1240 | For 8'-0" height, add | | | | | 56 | | | 56 | 61.50 |
| 1260 | For 8'-0" height walnut, add | | | | | 74 | | | 74 | 81.50 |
| 1340 | H.P. plastic laminate, 2'-6" x 6'-8" | 2 Carp | 13 | 1.231 | | 380 | 47 | | 427 | 495 |
| 1380 | 3'-0" x 6'-8" | | 12 | 1.333 | | 400 | 51 | | 451 | 520 |
| 1390 | 3'-0" x 7'-0" | | 11 | 1.455 | | 405 | 55.50 | | 460.50 | 530 |

# 08 14 Wood Doors

## 08 14 16 – Flush Wood Doors

### 08 14 16.20 Wood Fire Doors

| | | Crew | Daily Output | Labor-Hours | Unit | Material | 2008 Bare Costs Labor | Equipment | Total | Total Incl O&P |
|---|---|---|---|---|---|---|---|---|---|---|
| 1400 | 4'-0" x 7'-0" | 2 Carp | 10 | 1.600 | Ea. | 525 | 61 | | 586 | 670 |
| 2200 | Custom architectural "B" label, flush, 1-3/4" thick, birch, | | | | | | | | | |
| 2210 | Solid core | | | | | | | | | |
| 2220 | 2'-6" x 7'-0" | 2 Carp | 15 | 1.067 | Ea. | 289 | 40.50 | | 329.50 | 385 |
| 2260 | 3'-0" x 7'-0" | | 14 | 1.143 | | 300 | 43.50 | | 343.50 | 400 |
| 2300 | 4'-0" x 7'-0" | | 13 | 1.231 | | 395 | 47 | | 442 | 510 |
| 2420 | 4'-0" x 8'-0" | | 11 | 1.455 | | 370 | 55.50 | | 425.50 | 490 |
| 2480 | For oak veneer, add | | | | | 50% | | | | |
| 2500 | For walnut veneer, add | | | | | 75% | | | | |

## 08 14 23 – Clad Wood Doors

### 08 14 23.13 Metal-Faced Wood Doors

| | | Crew | Daily Output | Labor-Hours | Unit | Material | 2008 Bare Costs Labor | Equipment | Total | Total Incl O&P |
|---|---|---|---|---|---|---|---|---|---|---|
| 0010 | **METAL-FACED WOOD DOORS** | | | | | | | | | |
| 0020 | Interior, flush type, 3' x 7' | 2 Carp | 4.30 | 3.721 | Opng. | 194 | 142 | | 336 | 435 |

### 08 14 23.20 Tin Clad Wood Doors

| | | Crew | Daily Output | Labor-Hours | Unit | Material | 2008 Bare Costs Labor | Equipment | Total | Total Incl O&P |
|---|---|---|---|---|---|---|---|---|---|---|
| 0010 | **TIN CLAD WOOD DOORS** | | | | | | | | | |
| 0020 | 3 ply, 6' x 7', double sliding, doors only | 2 Carp | 1 | 16 | Opng. | 1,525 | 610 | | 2,135 | 2,625 |
| 1000 | For electric operator, add | 1 Elec | 2 | 4 | " | 2,700 | 182 | | 2,882 | 3,250 |

## 08 14 33 – Stile and Rail Wood Doors

### 08 14 33.10 Wood Doors Paneled

| | | Crew | Daily Output | Labor-Hours | Unit | Material | 2008 Bare Costs Labor | Equipment | Total | Total Incl O&P |
|---|---|---|---|---|---|---|---|---|---|---|
| 0010 | **WOOD DOORS PANELED** | | | | | | | | | |
| 0020 | Interior, six panel, hollow core, 1-3/8" thick | | | | | | | | | |
| 0040 | Molded hardboard, 2'-0" x 6'-8" | 2 Carp | 17 | .941 | Ea. | 50 | 36 | | 86 | 111 |
| 0060 | 2'-6" x 6'-8" | | 17 | .941 | | 54 | 36 | | 90 | 116 |
| 0070 | 2'-8" x 6'-8" | | 17 | .941 | | 56.50 | 36 | | 92.50 | 118 |
| 0080 | 3'-0" x 6'-8" | | 17 | .941 | | 59.50 | 36 | | 95.50 | 122 |
| 0140 | Embossed print, molded hardboard, 2'-0" x 6'-8" | | 17 | .941 | | 54 | 36 | | 90 | 116 |
| 0160 | 2'-6" x 6'-8" | | 17 | .941 | | 54 | 36 | | 90 | 116 |
| 0180 | 3'-0" x 6'-8" | | 17 | .941 | | 59.50 | 36 | | 95.50 | 122 |
| 0540 | Six panel, solid, 1-3/8" thick, pine, 2'-0" x 6'-8" | | 15 | 1.067 | | 131 | 40.50 | | 171.50 | 208 |
| 0560 | 2'-6" x 6'-8" | | 14 | 1.143 | | 147 | 43.50 | | 190.50 | 230 |
| 0580 | 3'-0" x 6'-8" | | 13 | 1.231 | | 169 | 47 | | 216 | 259 |
| 1020 | Two panel, bored rail, solid, 1-3/8" thick, pine, 1'-6" x 6'-8" | | 16 | 1 | | 239 | 38 | | 277 | 325 |
| 1040 | 2'-0" x 6'-8" | | 15 | 1.067 | | 315 | 40.50 | | 355.50 | 410 |
| 1060 | 2'-6" x 6'-8" | | 14 | 1.143 | | 360 | 43.50 | | 403.50 | 465 |
| 1340 | Two panel, solid, 1-3/8" thick, fir, 2'-0" x 6'-8" | | 15 | 1.067 | | 131 | 40.50 | | 171.50 | 208 |
| 1360 | 2'-6" x 6'-8" | | 14 | 1.143 | | 147 | 43.50 | | 190.50 | 230 |
| 1380 | 3'-0" x 6'-8" | | 13 | 1.231 | | 360 | 47 | | 407 | 470 |
| 1740 | Five panel, solid, 1-3/8" thick, fir, 2'-0" x 6'-8" | | 15 | 1.067 | | 234 | 40.50 | | 274.50 | 320 |
| 1760 | 2'-6" x 6'-8" | | 14 | 1.143 | | 375 | 43.50 | | 418.50 | 485 |
| 1780 | 3'-0" x 6'-8" | | 13 | 1.231 | | 375 | 47 | | 422 | 490 |

### 08 14 33.20 Wood Doors Residential

| | | Crew | Daily Output | Labor-Hours | Unit | Material | 2008 Bare Costs Labor | Equipment | Total | Total Incl O&P |
|---|---|---|---|---|---|---|---|---|---|---|
| 0010 | **WOOD DOORS RESIDENTIAL** | | | | | | | | | |
| 0200 | Exterior, combination storm & screen, pine | | | | | | | | | |
| 0260 | 2'-8" wide | 2 Carp | 10 | 1.600 | Ea. | 276 | 61 | | 337 | 400 |
| 0280 | 3'-0" wide | | 9 | 1.778 | | 282 | 67.50 | | 349.50 | 415 |
| 0300 | 7'-1" x 3'-0" wide | | 9 | 1.778 | | 315 | 67.50 | | 382.50 | 450 |
| 0400 | Full lite, 6'-9" x 2'-6" wide | | 11 | 1.455 | | 294 | 55.50 | | 349.50 | 410 |
| 0420 | 2'-8" wide | | 10 | 1.600 | | 294 | 61 | | 355 | 420 |
| 0440 | 3'-0" wide | | 9 | 1.778 | | 305 | 67.50 | | 372.50 | 440 |
| 0500 | 7'-1" x 3'-0" wide | | 9 | 1.778 | | 325 | 67.50 | | 392.50 | 465 |
| 0700 | Dutch door, pine, 1-3/4" x 6'-8" x 2'-8" wide, minimum | | 12 | 1.333 | | 685 | 51 | | 736 | 830 |

## 08 14 33 – Stile and Rail Wood Doors

| 08 14 33.20 Wood Doors Residential | Crew | Daily Output | Labor-Hours | Unit | Material | 2008 Bare Costs Labor | Equipment | Total | Total Incl O&P |
|---|---|---|---|---|---|---|---|---|---|
| 0720 | Maximum | 2 Carp | 10 | 1.600 | Ea. | 720 | 61 | | 781 | 890 |
| 0800 | 3'-0" wide, minimum | | 12 | 1.333 | | 695 | 51 | | 746 | 845 |
| 0820 | Maximum | | 10 | 1.600 | | 760 | 61 | | 821 | 935 |
| 1000 | Entrance door, colonial, 1-3/4" x 6'-8" x 2'-8" wide | | 16 | 1 | | 385 | 38 | | 423 | 485 |
| 1020 | 6 panel pine, 3'-0" wide | | 15 | 1.067 | | 405 | 40.50 | | 445.50 | 510 |
| 1100 | 8 panel pine, 2'-8" wide | | 16 | 1 | | 570 | 38 | | 608 | 685 |
| 1120 | 3'-0" wide | | 15 | 1.067 | | 550 | 40.50 | | 590.50 | 670 |
| 1200 | For tempered safety glass lites, (min of 2)add | | | | | 65.50 | | | 65.50 | 72 |
| 1300 | Flush, birch, solid core, 1-3/4" x 6'-8" x 2'-8" wide | 2 Carp | 16 | 1 | | 99 | 38 | | 137 | 169 |
| 1320 | 3'-0" wide | | 15 | 1.067 | | 103 | 40.50 | | 143.50 | 178 |
| 1350 | 7'-0" x 2'-8" wide | | 16 | 1 | | 108 | 38 | | 146 | 179 |
| 1360 | 3'-0" wide | | 15 | 1.067 | | 116 | 40.50 | | 156.50 | 191 |
| 1380 | For tempered safety glass lites, add | | | | | 97.50 | | | 97.50 | 107 |
| 2700 | Interior, closet, bi-fold, w/hardware, no frame or trim incl. | | | | | | | | | |
| 2720 | Flush, birch, 6'-6" or 6'-8" x 2'-6" wide | 2 Carp | 13 | 1.231 | Ea. | 49.50 | 47 | | 96.50 | 127 |
| 2740 | 3'-0" wide | | 13 | 1.231 | | 53.50 | 47 | | 100.50 | 132 |
| 2760 | 4'-0" wide | | 12 | 1.333 | | 97.50 | 51 | | 148.50 | 186 |
| 2780 | 5'-0" wide | | 11 | 1.455 | | 98.50 | 55.50 | | 154 | 195 |
| 2800 | 6'-0" wide | | 10 | 1.600 | | 106 | 61 | | 167 | 212 |
| 3000 | Raised panel pine, 6'-6" or 6'-8" x 2'-6" wide | | 13 | 1.231 | | 166 | 47 | | 213 | 255 |
| 3020 | 3'-0" wide | | 13 | 1.231 | | 213 | 47 | | 260 | 305 |
| 3040 | 4'-0" wide | | 12 | 1.333 | | 305 | 51 | | 356 | 415 |
| 3060 | 5'-0" wide | | 11 | 1.455 | | 365 | 55.50 | | 420.50 | 485 |
| 3080 | 6'-0" wide | | 10 | 1.600 | | 400 | 61 | | 461 | 535 |
| 3200 | Louvered, pine 6'-6" or 6'-8" x 2'-6" wide | | 13 | 1.231 | | 106 | 47 | | 153 | 190 |
| 3220 | 3'-0" wide | | 13 | 1.231 | | 164 | 47 | | 211 | 253 |
| 3240 | 4'-0" wide | | 12 | 1.333 | | 199 | 51 | | 250 | 298 |
| 3260 | 5'-0" wide | | 11 | 1.455 | | 226 | 55.50 | | 281.50 | 335 |
| 3280 | 6'-0" wide | | 10 | 1.600 | | 251 | 61 | | 312 | 370 |
| 4400 | Bi-passing closet, incl. hardware and frame, no trim incl. | | | | | | | | | |
| 4420 | Flush, lauan, 6'-8" x 4'-0" wide | 2 Carp | 12 | 1.333 | Opng. | 169 | 51 | | 220 | 265 |
| 4440 | 5'-0" wide | | 11 | 1.455 | | 185 | 55.50 | | 240.50 | 291 |
| 4460 | 6'-0" wide | | 10 | 1.600 | | 198 | 61 | | 259 | 315 |
| 4600 | Flush, birch, 6'-8" x 4'-0" wide | | 12 | 1.333 | | 210 | 51 | | 261 | 310 |
| 4620 | 5'-0" wide | | 11 | 1.455 | | 209 | 55.50 | | 264.50 | 315 |
| 4640 | 6'-0" wide | | 10 | 1.600 | | 252 | 61 | | 313 | 370 |
| 4800 | Louvered, pine, 6'-8" x 4'-0" wide | | 12 | 1.333 | | 415 | 51 | | 466 | 535 |
| 4820 | 5'-0" wide | | 11 | 1.455 | | 390 | 55.50 | | 445.50 | 510 |
| 4840 | 6'-0" wide | | 10 | 1.600 | | 510 | 61 | | 571 | 655 |
| 5000 | Paneled, pine, 6'-8" x 4'-0" wide | | 12 | 1.333 | | 490 | 51 | | 541 | 620 |
| 5020 | 5'-0" wide | | 11 | 1.455 | | 405 | 55.50 | | 460.50 | 530 |
| 5040 | 6'-0" wide | | 10 | 1.600 | | 585 | 61 | | 646 | 740 |
| 6100 | Folding accordion, closet, including track and frame | | | | | | | | | |
| 6120 | Vinyl, 2 layer, stock, see Div. 10 22 26.13 | 2 Carp | 10 | 1.600 | Ea. | 44 | 61 | | 105 | 144 |
| 6140 | Woven mahogany and vinyl, stock | | 10 | 1.600 | | 38.50 | 61 | | 99.50 | 138 |
| 6160 | Wood slats with vinyl overlay, stock | | 10 | 1.600 | | 126 | 61 | | 187 | 234 |
| 6180 | Economy vinyl, stock | | 10 | 1.600 | | 28 | 61 | | 89 | 126 |
| 6200 | Rigid PVC | | 10 | 1.600 | | 31.50 | 61 | | 92.50 | 130 |
| 6220 | For custom partition, add | | | | | 25% | 10% | | | |
| 7310 | Passage doors, flush, no frame included | | | | | | | | | |
| 7320 | Hardboard, hollow core, 1-3/8" x 6'-8" x 1'-6" wide | 2 Carp | 18 | .889 | Ea. | 41.50 | 34 | | 75.50 | 98.50 |
| 7330 | 2'-0" wide | | 18 | .889 | | 41 | 34 | | 75 | 97.50 |
| 7340 | 2'-6" wide | | 18 | .889 | | 45.50 | 34 | | 79.50 | 103 |

# 08 14 Wood Doors

## 08 14 33 – Stile and Rail Wood Doors

| | 08 14 33.20 Wood Doors Residential | Crew | Daily Output | Labor-Hours | Unit | Material | 2008 Bare Costs Labor | Equipment | Total | Total Incl O&P |
|---|---|---|---|---|---|---|---|---|---|---|
| 7350 | 2'-8" wide | 2 Carp | 18 | .889 | Ea. | 48 | 34 | | 82 | 105 |
| 7360 | 3'-0" wide | | 17 | .941 | | 50 | 36 | | 86 | 111 |
| 7420 | Lauan, hollow core, 1-3/8" x 6'-8" x 1'-6" wide | | 18 | .889 | | 29 | 34 | | 63 | 84.50 |
| 7440 | 2'-0" wide | | 18 | .889 | | 27.50 | 34 | | 61.50 | 83 |
| 7450 | 2'-4" wide | | 18 | .889 | | 31 | 34 | | 65 | 86.50 |
| 7460 | 2'-6" wide | | 18 | .889 | | 31 | 34 | | 65 | 86.50 |
| 7480 | 2'-8" wide | | 18 | .889 | | 32.50 | 34 | | 66.50 | 88.50 |
| 7500 | 3'-0" wide | | 17 | .941 | | 34 | 36 | | 70 | 93.50 |
| 7700 | Birch, hollow core, 1-3/8" x 6'-8" x 1'-6" wide | | 18 | .889 | | 37 | 34 | | 71 | 93 |
| 7720 | 2'-0" wide | | 18 | .889 | | 40.50 | 34 | | 74.50 | 97 |
| 7740 | 2'-6" wide | | 18 | .889 | | 45 | 34 | | 79 | 102 |
| 7760 | 2'-8" wide | | 18 | .889 | | 47 | 34 | | 81 | 104 |
| 7780 | 3'-0" wide     CN | | 17 | .941 | | 51 | 36 | | 87 | 112 |
| 8000 | Pine louvered, 1-3/8" x 6'-8" x 1'-6" wide | | 19 | .842 | | 101 | 32 | | 133 | 161 |
| 8020 | 2'-0" wide | | 18 | .889 | | 127 | 34 | | 161 | 193 |
| 8040 | 2'-6" wide | | 18 | .889 | | 139 | 34 | | 173 | 206 |
| 8060 | 2'-8" wide | | 18 | .889 | | 146 | 34 | | 180 | 214 |
| 8080 | 3'-0" wide | | 17 | .941 | | 156 | 36 | | 192 | 228 |
| 8300 | Pine paneled, 1-3/8" x 6'-8" x 1'-6" wide | | 19 | .842 | | 110 | 32 | | 142 | 171 |
| 8320 | 2'-0" wide | | 18 | .889 | | 127 | 34 | | 161 | 193 |
| 8330 | 2'-4" wide | | 18 | .889 | | 139 | 34 | | 173 | 206 |
| 8340 | 2'-6" wide | | 18 | .889 | | 142 | 34 | | 176 | 210 |
| 8360 | 2'-8" wide | | 18 | .889 | | 155 | 34 | | 189 | 223 |
| 8380 | 3'-0" wide | ↓ | 17 | .941 | ↓ | 163 | 36 | | 199 | 235 |
| 8550 | For over 20 doors, deduct | | | | | 15% | | | | |

## 08 14 40 – Interior Cafe Doors

| | 08 14 40.10 Cafe Style Doors | Crew | Daily Output | Labor-Hours | Unit | Material | 2008 Bare Costs Labor | Equipment | Total | Total Incl O&P |
|---|---|---|---|---|---|---|---|---|---|---|
| 0010 | **CAFE STYLE DOORS** | | | | | | | | | |
| 6520 | Interior cafe doors, 2'-6" opening, stock, panel pine | 2 Carp | 16 | 1 | Ea. | 191 | 38 | | 229 | 270 |
| 6540 | 3'-0" opening | " | 16 | 1 | " | 199 | 38 | | 237 | 278 |
| 6550 | Louvered pine | | | | | | | | | |
| 6560 | 2'-6" opening | 2 Carp | 16 | 1 | Ea. | 166 | 38 | | 204 | 243 |
| 8000 | 3'-0" opening | | 16 | 1 | | 178 | 38 | | 216 | 255 |
| 8010 | 2'-6" opening, hardwood | | 16 | 1 | | 286 | 38 | | 324 | 375 |
| 8020 | 3'-0" opening | ↓ | 16 | 1 | ↓ | 315 | 38 | | 353 | 410 |

# 08 16 Composite Doors

## 08 16 13 – Fiberglass Doors

### 08 16 13.10 Entrance Doors, Fiberous Glass

| | | Crew | Daily Output | Labor-Hours | Unit | Material | 2008 Bare Costs Labor | Equipment | Total | Total Incl O&P |
|---|---|---|---|---|---|---|---|---|---|---|
| 0010 | **ENTRANCE DOORS, FIBEROUS GLASS** | | | | | | | | | |
| 0020 | Exterior, fiberglass, door, 2'-8" wide x 6'-8" high | 2 Carp | 15 | 1.067 | Ea. | 320 | 40.50 | | 360.50 | 415 |
| 0040 | 3'-0" wide x 6'-8" high | | 15 | 1.067 | | 320 | 40.50 | | 360.50 | 415 |
| 0060 | 3'-0" wide x 7'-0" high | | 15 | 1.067 | | 390 | 40.50 | | 430.50 | 495 |
| 0080 | 3'-0" wide x 6'-8" high, with two lites | | 15 | 1.067 | | 390 | 40.50 | | 430.50 | 495 |
| 0100 | 3'-0" wide x 7'-0" high, with two lites | | 15 | 1.067 | | 460 | 40.50 | | 500.50 | 570 |
| 0110 | Half glass, 3'-0" wide x 6'-8" high | | 15 | 1.067 | | 425 | 40.50 | | 465.50 | 530 |
| 0120 | 3'-0" wide x 6'-8" high, low e | | 15 | 1.067 | | 455 | 40.50 | | 495.50 | 565 |
| 0130 | 3'-0" wide x 7'-0" high | | 15 | 1.067 | | 500 | 40.50 | | 540.50 | 615 |
| 0140 | 3'-0" wide x 7'-0" high, low e | | 15 | 1.067 | | 525 | 40.50 | | 565.50 | 645 |
| 0150 | Side lights, 1'-0" wide x 6'-8" high, | ↓ | | | ↓ | 281 | | | 281 | 310 |

# 08 16 Composite Doors

## 08 16 13 – Fiberglass Doors

| 08 16 13.10 Entrance Doors, Fiberous Glass | Crew | Daily Output | Labor-Hours | Unit | Material | 2008 Bare Costs Labor | Equipment | Total | Total Incl O&P |
|---|---|---|---|---|---|---|---|---|---|
| 0160 | 1'-0" wide x 6'-8" high, low e | | | | Ea. | 293 | | | 293 | 325 |
| 0180 | 1'-0" wide x 6'-8" high, full glass | | | | | 320 | | | 320 | 355 |
| 0190 | 1'-0" wide x 6'-8" high, low e | | | | ↓ | 345 | | | 345 | 380 |

# 08 17 Integrated Door Opening Assemblies

## 08 17 13 – Integrated Metal Door Opening Assemblies

### 08 17 13.20 Tubular Steel Swing Doors

| | | Crew | Daily Output | Labor-Hours | Unit | Material | 2008 Bare Costs Labor | Equipment | Total | Total Incl O&P |
|---|---|---|---|---|---|---|---|---|---|---|
| 0010 | **TUBULAR STEEL SWING DOORS** | | | | | | | | | |
| 0020 | Tubular steel, 7' high, single, 3'-4" opening | 2 Sswk | 2.50 | 6.400 | Ea. | 640 | 275 | | 915 | 1,200 |
| 0100 | Double, 6'-0" opening | " | 2 | 8 | Pr. | 810 | 345 | | 1,155 | 1,500 |

## 08 17 23 – Integrated Wood Door Opening Assemblies

### 08 17 23.10 Pre-Hung Doors

| | | Crew | Daily Output | Labor-Hours | Unit | Material | 2008 Bare Costs Labor | Equipment | Total | Total Incl O&P |
|---|---|---|---|---|---|---|---|---|---|---|
| 0010 | **PRE-HUNG DOORS** | | | | | | | | | |
| 0300 | Exterior, wood, comb. storm & screen, 6'-9" x 2'-6" wide | 2 Carp | 15 | 1.067 | Ea. | 287 | 40.50 | | 327.50 | 380 |
| 0320 | 2'-8" wide | | 15 | 1.067 | | 287 | 40.50 | | 327.50 | 380 |
| 0340 | 3'-0" wide | ↓ | 15 | 1.067 | | 296 | 40.50 | | 336.50 | 390 |
| 0360 | For 7'-0" high door, add | | | | ↓ | 26.50 | | | 26.50 | 29.50 |
| 1600 | Entrance door, flush, birch, solid core | | | | | | | | | |
| 1620 | 4-5/8" solid jamb, 1-3/4" x 6'-8" x 2'-8" wide | 2 Carp | 16 | 1 | Ea. | 285 | 38 | | 323 | 375 |
| 1640 | 3'-0" wide | | 16 | 1 | | 355 | 38 | | 393 | 450 |
| 1642 | 5-5/8" jamb | ↓ | 16 | 1 | | 320 | 38 | | 358 | 410 |
| 1680 | For 7'-0" high door, add | | | | ↓ | 18.75 | | | 18.75 | 20.50 |
| 2000 | Entrance door, colonial, 6 panel pine | | | | | | | | | |
| 2020 | 4-5/8" solid jamb, 1-3/4" x 6'-8" x 2'-8" wide | 2 Carp | 16 | 1 | Ea. | 525 | 38 | | 563 | 640 |
| 2040 | 3'-0" wide | " | 16 | 1 | | 525 | 38 | | 563 | 640 |
| 2060 | For 7'-0" high door, add | | | | | 49.50 | | | 49.50 | 54.50 |
| 2200 | For 5-5/8" solid jamb, add | | | | ↓ | 39 | | | 39 | 43 |
| 4000 | Interior, passage door, 4-5/8" solid jamb | | | | | | | | | |
| 4400 | Lauan, flush, solid core, 1-3/8" x 6'-8" x 2'-6" wide | 2 Carp | 20 | .800 | Ea. | 180 | 30.50 | | 210.50 | 246 |
| 4420 | 2'-8" wide | | 20 | .800 | | 180 | 30.50 | | 210.50 | 246 |
| 4440 | 3'-0" wide | | 19 | .842 | | 194 | 32 | | 226 | 263 |
| 4600 | Hollow core, 1-3/8" x 6'-8" x 2'-6" wide | | 20 | .800 | | 122 | 30.50 | | 152.50 | 182 |
| 4620 | 2'-8" wide | | 20 | .800 | | 122 | 30.50 | | 152.50 | 182 |
| 4640 | 3'-0" wide | ↓ | 19 | .842 | | 122 | 32 | | 154 | 185 |
| 4700 | For 7'-0" high door, add | | | | | 23.50 | | | 23.50 | 26 |
| 5000 | Birch, flush, solid core, 1-3/8" x 6'-8" x 2'-6" wide | 2 Carp | 20 | .800 | | 170 | 30.50 | | 200.50 | 235 |
| 5020 | 2'-8" wide | | 20 | .800 | | 193 | 30.50 | | 223.50 | 260 |
| 5040 | 3'-0" wide | | 19 | .842 | | 204 | 32 | | 236 | 275 |
| 5200 | Hollow core, 1-3/8" x 6'-8" x 2'-6" wide | | 20 | .800 | | 141 | 30.50 | | 171.50 | 203 |
| 5220 | 2'-8" wide | | 20 | .800 | | 147 | 30.50 | | 177.50 | 210 |
| 5240 | 3'-0" wide | ↓ | 19 | .842 | | 147 | 32 | | 179 | 211 |
| 5280 | For 7'-0" high door, add | | | | | 20.50 | | | 20.50 | 22.50 |
| 5500 | Hardboard paneled, 1-3/8" x 6'-8" x 2'-6" wide | 2 Carp | 20 | .800 | | 141 | 30.50 | | 171.50 | 203 |
| 5520 | 2'-8" wide | | 20 | .800 | | 148 | 30.50 | | 178.50 | 211 |
| 5540 | 3'-0" wide | | 19 | .842 | | 146 | 32 | | 178 | 211 |
| 6000 | Pine paneled, 1-3/8" x 6'-8" x 2'-6" wide | | 20 | .800 | | 246 | 30.50 | | 276.50 | 320 |
| 6020 | 2'-8" wide | | 20 | .800 | | 266 | 30.50 | | 296.50 | 340 |
| 6040 | 3'-0" wide | | 19 | .842 | | 272 | 32 | | 304 | 350 |
| 6500 | For 5-5/8" solid jamb, add | | | | | 14.25 | | | 14.25 | 15.70 |
| 6520 | For split jamb, deduct | | | | ↓ | 16.05 | | | 16.05 | 17.70 |

# 08 31 Access Doors and Panels

## 08 31 13 – Access Doors and Frames

### 08 31 13.10 Types of Framed Access Doors

| | | Crew | Daily Output | Labor-Hours | Unit | Material | 2008 Bare Costs Labor | 2008 Bare Costs Equipment | Total | Total Incl O&P |
|---|---|---|---|---|---|---|---|---|---|---|
| 0010 | **TYPES OF FRAMED ACCESS DOORS** | | | | | | | | | |
| 1000 | Fire rated door with lock | | | | | | | | | |
| 1100 | Metal, 12" x 12" | 1 Carp | 10 | .800 | Ea. | 157 | 30.50 | | 187.50 | 221 |
| 1150 | 18" x 18" | | 9 | .889 | | 205 | 34 | | 239 | 279 |
| 1200 | 24" x 24" | | 9 | .889 | | 248 | 34 | | 282 | 325 |
| 1250 | 24" x 36" | | 8 | 1 | | 335 | 38 | | 373 | 425 |
| 1300 | 24" x 48" | | 8 | 1 | | 410 | 38 | | 448 | 515 |
| 1350 | 36" x 36" | | 7.50 | 1.067 | | 495 | 40.50 | | 535.50 | 610 |
| 1400 | 48" x 48" | | 7.50 | 1.067 | | 635 | 40.50 | | 675.50 | 765 |
| 1600 | Stainless steel, 12" x 12" | | 10 | .800 | | 281 | 30.50 | | 311.50 | 360 |
| 1650 | 18" x 18" | | 9 | .889 | | 410 | 34 | | 444 | 505 |
| 1700 | 24" x 24" | | 9 | .889 | | 500 | 34 | | 534 | 605 |
| 1750 | 24" x 36" | | 8 | 1 | | 640 | 38 | | 678 | 765 |
| 2000 | Flush door for finishing | | | | | | | | | |
| 2100 | Metal 8" x 8" | 1 Carp | 10 | .800 | Ea. | 45.50 | 30.50 | | 76 | 97.50 |
| 2150 | 12" x 12" | " | 10 | .800 | " | 50.50 | 30.50 | | 81 | 103 |
| 3000 | Recessed door for acoustic tile | | | | | | | | | |
| 3100 | Metal, 12" x 12" | 1 Carp | 4.50 | 1.778 | Ea. | 69.50 | 67.50 | | 137 | 181 |
| 3150 | 12" x 24" | | 4.50 | 1.778 | | 90.50 | 67.50 | | 158 | 205 |
| 3200 | 24" x 24" | | 4 | 2 | | 121 | 76 | | 197 | 252 |
| 3250 | 24" x 36" | | 4 | 2 | | 156 | 76 | | 232 | 290 |
| 4000 | Recessed door for drywall | | | | | | | | | |
| 4100 | Metal 12" x 12" | 1 Carp | 6 | 1.333 | Ea. | 77.50 | 51 | | 128.50 | 164 |
| 4150 | 12" x 24" | | 5.50 | 1.455 | | 115 | 55.50 | | 170.50 | 213 |
| 4200 | 24" x 36" | | 5 | 1.600 | | 183 | 61 | | 244 | 296 |
| 6000 | Standard door | | | | | | | | | |
| 6100 | Metal, 8" x 8" | 1 Carp | 10 | .800 | Ea. | 40 | 30.50 | | 70.50 | 91.50 |
| 6150 | 12" x 12" | | 10 | .800 | | 45.50 | 30.50 | | 76 | 97.50 |
| 6200 | 18" x 18" | | 9 | .889 | | 62.50 | 34 | | 96.50 | 122 |
| 6250 | 24" x 24" | | 9 | .889 | | 81.50 | 34 | | 115.50 | 142 |
| 6300 | 24" x 36" | | 8 | 1 | | 120 | 38 | | 158 | 192 |
| 6350 | 36" x 36" | | 8 | 1 | | 147 | 38 | | 185 | 221 |
| 6500 | Stainless steel, 8" x 8" | | 10 | .800 | | 80 | 30.50 | | 110.50 | 136 |
| 6550 | 12" x 12" | | 10 | .800 | | 107 | 30.50 | | 137.50 | 165 |
| 6600 | 18" x 18" | | 9 | .889 | | 197 | 34 | | 231 | 270 |
| 6650 | 24" x 24" | | 9 | .889 | | 258 | 34 | | 292 | 335 |

### 08 31 13.20 Bulkhead/Cellar Doors

| | | Crew | Daily Output | Labor-Hours | Unit | Material | 2008 Bare Costs Labor | 2008 Bare Costs Equipment | Total | Total Incl O&P |
|---|---|---|---|---|---|---|---|---|---|---|
| 0010 | **BULKHEAD/CELLAR DOORS** | | | | | | | | | |
| 0020 | Steel, not incl. sides, 44" x 62" | 1 Carp | 5.50 | 1.455 | Ea. | 320 | 55.50 | | 375.50 | 440 |
| 0100 | 52" x 73" | | 5.10 | 1.569 | | 335 | 60 | | 395 | 460 |
| 0500 | With sides and foundation plates, 57" x 45" x 24" | | 4.70 | 1.702 | | 420 | 65 | | 485 | 560 |
| 0600 | 42" x 49" x 51" | | 4.30 | 1.860 | | 690 | 71 | | 761 | 870 |

### 08 31 13.30 Commercial Floor Doors

| | | Crew | Daily Output | Labor-Hours | Unit | Material | 2008 Bare Costs Labor | 2008 Bare Costs Equipment | Total | Total Incl O&P |
|---|---|---|---|---|---|---|---|---|---|---|
| 0010 | **COMMERCIAL FLOOR DOORS** | | | | | | | | | |
| 0020 | Aluminum tile, steel frame, one leaf, 2' x 2' opng. | 2 Sswk | 3.50 | 4.571 | Opng. | 400 | 197 | | 597 | 795 |
| 0050 | 3'-6" x 3'-6" opening | | 3.50 | 4.571 | | 720 | 197 | | 917 | 1,150 |
| 0500 | Double leaf, 4' x 4' opening | | 3 | 5.333 | | 1,075 | 229 | | 1,304 | 1,600 |
| 0550 | 5' x 5' opening | | 3 | 5.333 | | 1,575 | 229 | | 1,804 | 2,150 |

### 08 31 13.35 Industrial Floor Doors

| | | Crew | Daily Output | Labor-Hours | Unit | Material | 2008 Bare Costs Labor | 2008 Bare Costs Equipment | Total | Total Incl O&P |
|---|---|---|---|---|---|---|---|---|---|---|
| 0010 | **INDUSTRIAL FLOOR DOORS** | | | | | | | | | |
| 0020 | Steel 300 psf L.L., single leaf, 2' x 2', 175# | 2 Sswk | 6 | 2.667 | Opng. | 630 | 115 | | 745 | 900 |
| 0050 | 3' x 3' opening, 300# | | 5.50 | 2.909 | | 870 | 125 | | 995 | 1,175 |

# 08 31 Access Doors and Panels

## 08 31 13 – Access Doors and Frames

| 08 31 13.35 Industrial Floor Doors | | Crew | Daily Output | Labor-Hours | Unit | Material | 2008 Bare Costs Labor | Equipment | Total | Total Incl O&P |
|---|---|---|---|---|---|---|---|---|---|---|
| 0300 | Double leaf, 4' x 4' opening, 455# | 2 Sswk | 5 | 3.200 | Opng. | 1,300 | 138 | | 1,438 | 1,700 |
| 0350 | 5' x 5' opening, 645# | | 4.50 | 3.556 | | 1,725 | 153 | | 1,878 | 2,150 |
| 1000 | Aluminum, 300 psf L.L., single leaf, 2' x 2', 60# | | 6 | 2.667 | | 620 | 115 | | 735 | 890 |
| 1050 | 3' x 3' opening, 100# | | 5.50 | 2.909 | | 965 | 125 | | 1,090 | 1,300 |
| 1500 | Double leaf, 4' x 4' opening, 160# | | 5 | 3.200 | | 1,525 | 138 | | 1,663 | 1,925 |
| 1550 | 5' x 5' opening, 235# | | 4.50 | 3.556 | | 2,025 | 153 | | 2,178 | 2,500 |
| 2000 | Aluminum, 150 psf L.L., single leaf, 2' x 2', 60# | | 6 | 2.667 | | 570 | 115 | | 685 | 830 |
| 2050 | 3' x 3' opening, 95# | | 5.50 | 2.909 | | 840 | 125 | | 965 | 1,150 |
| 2500 | Double leaf, 4' x 4' opening, 150# | | 5 | 3.200 | | 1,350 | 138 | | 1,488 | 1,725 |
| 2550 | 5' x 5' opening, 230# | | 4.50 | 3.556 | | 1,825 | 153 | | 1,978 | 2,275 |

## 08 31 13.40 Kennel Doors

| 08 31 13.40 Kennel Doors | | Crew | Daily Output | Labor-Hours | Unit | Material | Labor | Equipment | Total | Total Incl O&P |
|---|---|---|---|---|---|---|---|---|---|---|
| 0010 | **KENNEL DOORS** | | | | | | | | | |
| 0020 | 2 way, swinging type, 13" x 19" opening | 2 Carp | 11 | 1.455 | Opng. | 207 | 55.50 | | 262.50 | 315 |
| 0100 | 17" x 29" opening | " | 11 | 1.455 | " | 223 | 55.50 | | 278.50 | 330 |

# 08 32 Sliding Glass Doors

## 08 32 19 – Sliding Wood-Framed Glass Doors

| 08 32 19.15 Sliding Glass Vinyl-Clad Wood Doors | | Crew | Daily Output | Labor-Hours | Unit | Material | Labor | Equipment | Total | Total Incl O&P |
|---|---|---|---|---|---|---|---|---|---|---|
| 0010 | **SLIDING GLASS VINYL-CLAD WOOD DOORS** | | | | | | | | | |
| 0012 | Vinyl clad, 1" insul. glass, 6'-0" x 6'-10" high | 2 Carp | 4 | 4 | Opng. | 1,350 | 152 | | 1,502 | 1,700 |
| 0030 | 6'-0" x 8'-0" high | | 4 | 4 | Ea. | 1,950 | 152 | | 2,102 | 2,350 |
| 0100 | 8'-0" x 6'-10" high | | 4 | 4 | Opng. | 2,000 | 152 | | 2,152 | 2,425 |
| 0500 | 3 leaf, 9'-0" x 6'-10" high | | 3 | 5.333 | | 2,350 | 203 | | 2,553 | 2,900 |
| 0600 | 12'-0" x 6'-10" high | | 3 | 5.333 | | 3,175 | 203 | | 3,378 | 3,800 |

# 08 33 Coiling Doors and Grilles

## 08 33 13 – Coiling Counter Doors

| 08 33 13.10 Counter Doors, Coiling Type | | Crew | Daily Output | Labor-Hours | Unit | Material | Labor | Equipment | Total | Total Incl O&P |
|---|---|---|---|---|---|---|---|---|---|---|
| 0010 | **COUNTER DOORS, COILING TYPE** | | | | | | | | | |
| 0020 | Manual, incl. frm and hdwe, galv. stl., 4' roll-up, 6' long | 2 Carp | 2 | 8 | Opng. | 930 | 305 | | 1,235 | 1,500 |
| 0300 | Galvanized steel, UL label | | 1.80 | 8.889 | | 1,200 | 340 | | 1,540 | 1,825 |
| 0600 | Stainless steel, 4' high roll-up, 6' long | | 2 | 8 | | 1,575 | 305 | | 1,880 | 2,200 |
| 0700 | 10' long | | 1.80 | 8.889 | | 2,400 | 340 | | 2,740 | 3,150 |
| 2000 | Aluminum, 4' high, 4' long | | 2.20 | 7.273 | | 1,150 | 277 | | 1,427 | 1,700 |
| 2020 | 6' long | | 2 | 8 | | 1,300 | 305 | | 1,605 | 1,900 |
| 2040 | 8' long | | 1.90 | 8.421 | | 1,475 | 320 | | 1,795 | 2,125 |
| 2060 | 10' long | | 1.80 | 8.889 | | 1,575 | 340 | | 1,915 | 2,250 |
| 2080 | 14' long | | 1.40 | 11.429 | | 2,300 | 435 | | 2,735 | 3,200 |
| 2100 | 6' high, 4' long | | 2 | 8 | | 1,300 | 305 | | 1,605 | 1,900 |
| 2120 | 6' long | | 1.60 | 10 | | 1,325 | 380 | | 1,705 | 2,075 |
| 2140 | 10' long | | 1.40 | 11.429 | | 1,825 | 435 | | 2,260 | 2,675 |

## 08 33 16 – Coiling Counter Grilles

| 08 33 16.10 Coiling Grilles | | Crew | Daily Output | Labor-Hours | Unit | Material | Labor | Equipment | Total | Total Incl O&P |
|---|---|---|---|---|---|---|---|---|---|---|
| 0010 | **COILING GRILLES** | | | | | | | | | |
| 0015 | Aluminum, manual, incl. frame, mill finish | | | | | | | | | |
| 0020 | Top coiling, 4' high, 4' long | 2 Sswk | 3.20 | 5 | Opng. | 1,325 | 215 | | 1,540 | 1,875 |
| 0030 | 6' long | | 3.20 | 5 | | 1,400 | 215 | | 1,615 | 1,950 |
| 0040 | 8' long | | 2.40 | 6.667 | | 1,600 | 287 | | 1,887 | 2,275 |

# Reed Construction Data ®

Reed Construction Data is your all-inclusive source of information encompassing all phases of the construction process. Our products and services are designed specifically to help industry professionals advance their businesses with timely, accurate and actionable project, product and cost data.

Reed Bulletin and Reed Connect™ deliver the most comprehensive, timely and reliable project information to support contractors, distributors and building product manufacturers in identifying, bidding, and tracking projects — private and public, general building and civil. Reed Construction Data also offers in-depth construction activity statistics and forecasts covering major project categories, many at the county and metropolitan level.

For more information about Reed Construction Data, please call **877-REED411** or visit our website at **www.reedconstructiondata.com**.

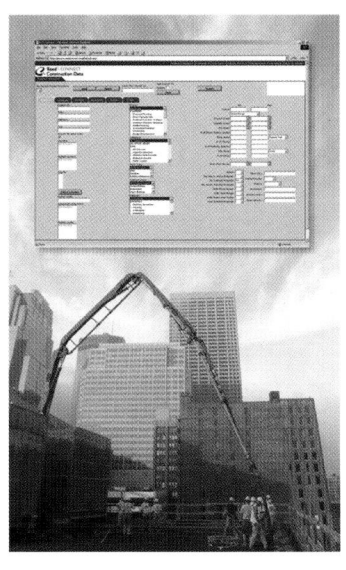

## Reed Connect

- Customized web-based project lead delivery service featuring advanced search capabilities.

- Manage and track actionable leads from planning to quote through winning the job.

- Competitive analysis tool to analyze lost sales opportunities.

- Potential integration with your CRM application.

## Reed Bulletin

- Project leads targeted by geographic region and formatted by construction stage — available online or in print.

- Locate those hard-to-find jobs that are more profitable to your business.

- Optional automatic e-mail updates sent whenever project details change.

- Download plans and specs online or order print copies.

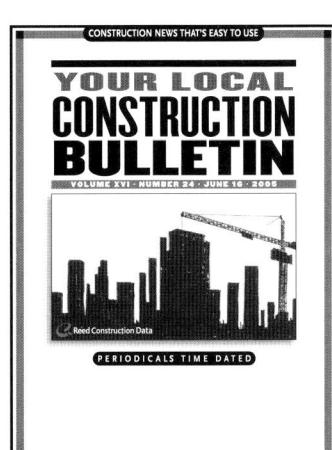

CONSTRUCTION NEWS THAT'S EASY TO USE

**YOUR LOCAL CONSTRUCTION BULLETIN**
VOLUME XVI · NUMBER 24 · JUNE 16 · 2005

Reed Construction Data

PERIODICALS TIME DATED

## Reed Research & Analytics

### Reed Construction Forecast
- Delivers timely construction industry activity combining historical data, current year projections and forecasts.

- Modeled at the individual MSA-level to capture changing local market conditions.

- Covers 21 major project categories.

### Reed Construction Starts
- Available in a monthly report or as an interactive database.

- Data provided in square footage and dollar value.

- Highly effective and efficient business planning tool.

### Market Fundamentals
- Metropolitan area-specific reporting.

- Five-year forecast of industry performance including major projects in development and underway.

- Property types include office, retail, hotel, warehouse and apartment.

# Reed Construction Data®

Reed Construction Data is a leading provider of information resources to the design community. Through our products and services we offer many ways for architects, engineers, designers, and contractors to better serve their clients and build their businesses.

For more information about Reed Construction Data, please call **877-REED411** or visit our website at **www.reedconstructiondata.com**.

## Reed Registry
### The Premier Source of Architectural Firms

The Reed Registry contains over 30,000 architecture firms and is used by industry professionals to find architects throughout the U.S. and Canada.

Architecture firms can add or update their listing, or enhance their listing to include logos, projects, and web links by visiting **www.reedregistry.com**.

## Reed First Source and Buildcore
### Leading Product Information Solutions for Design Professionals

Reed First Source and Buildcore are leading information solutions that allow design professionals to search, select, and specify building products throughout the design and construction cycle.

Covering both U.S. and Canadian markets, FirstSource and BuildCore provide access to over 11,000 commercial building manufacturers, all classified by MasterFormat™ 2004 categories. In addition, our specialists can create and publish SPEC-DATA 10-part format and MANU-SPEC three-part specifications for building product manufacturers.

Learn more at **www.reedfirstsource.com.**

## 08 33 16 – Coiling Counter Grilles

| 08 33 16.10 Coiling Grilles | | Crew | Daily Output | Labor-Hours | Unit | Material | 2008 Bare Costs Labor | Equipment | Total | Total Incl O&P |
|---|---|---|---|---|---|---|---|---|---|---|
| 0050 | 12' long | 2 Sswk | 2.40 | 6.667 | Opng. | 1,850 | 287 | | 2,137 | 2,575 |
| 0060 | 16' long | | 1.60 | 10 | | 2,300 | 430 | | 2,730 | 3,300 |
| 0070 | 6' high, 4' long | | 3.20 | 5 | | 1,425 | 215 | | 1,640 | 1,975 |
| 0080 | 6' long | | 3.20 | 5 | | 1,350 | 215 | | 1,565 | 1,900 |
| 0090 | 8' long | | 2.40 | 6.667 | | 1,525 | 287 | | 1,812 | 2,200 |
| 0100 | 12' long | | 1.60 | 10 | | 1,775 | 430 | | 2,205 | 2,725 |
| 0110 | 16' long | | 1.20 | 13.333 | | 2,275 | 575 | | 2,850 | 3,550 |
| 0200 | Side coiling, 8' high, 12' long | | .60 | 26.667 | | 2,025 | 1,150 | | 3,175 | 4,325 |
| 0220 | 18' long | | .50 | 32 | | 3,100 | 1,375 | | 4,475 | 5,900 |
| 0240 | 24' long | | .40 | 40 | | 3,275 | 1,725 | | 5,000 | 6,700 |
| 0260 | 12' high, 12' long | | .50 | 32 | | 2,950 | 1,375 | | 4,325 | 5,725 |
| 0280 | 18' long | | .40 | 40 | | 4,350 | 1,725 | | 6,075 | 7,900 |
| 0300 | 24' long | ▼ | .28 | 57.143 | ▼ | 5,825 | 2,450 | | 8,275 | 10,800 |

## 08 33 23 – Overhead Coiling Doors

### 08 33 23.10 Rolling Service Doors

| | | Crew | Daily Output | Labor-Hours | Unit | Material | 2008 Bare Costs Labor | Equipment | Total | Total Incl O&P |
|---|---|---|---|---|---|---|---|---|---|---|
| 0010 | **ROLLING SERVICE DOORS** Steel, manual, 20 ga., incl. hardware | | | | | | | | | |
| 0050 | 8' x 8' high | 2 Sswk | 1.60 | 10 | Ea. | 950 | 430 | | 1,380 | 1,825 |
| 0100 | 10' x 10' high | | 1.40 | 11.429 | | 1,675 | 490 | | 2,165 | 2,700 |
| 0200 | 20' x 10' high | | 1 | 16 | | 2,725 | 690 | | 3,415 | 4,250 |
| 0300 | 12' x 12' high | | 1.20 | 13.333 | | 1,725 | 575 | | 2,300 | 2,925 |
| 0400 | 20' x 12' high | | .90 | 17.778 | | 1,850 | 765 | | 2,615 | 3,425 |
| 0500 | 14' x 14' high | | .80 | 20 | | 2,800 | 860 | | 3,660 | 4,625 |
| 0600 | 20' x 16' high | | .60 | 26.667 | | 2,800 | 1,150 | | 3,950 | 5,150 |
| 0700 | 10' x 20' high | | .50 | 32 | | 2,000 | 1,375 | | 3,375 | 4,675 |
| 1000 | 12' x 12', crank operated, crank on door side | | .80 | 20 | | 1,350 | 860 | | 2,210 | 3,050 |
| 1100 | Crank thru wall | ▼ | .70 | 22.857 | ▼ | 1,525 | 985 | | 2,510 | 3,475 |
| 1300 | For vision panel, add | | | | | 267 | | | 267 | 294 |
| 1400 | For 22 ga., deduct | | | | S.F. | .99 | | | .99 | 1.09 |
| 1600 | 3' x 7' pass door within rolling steel door, new construction | | | | Ea. | 1,425 | | | 1,425 | 1,550 |
| 1700 | Existing construction | 2 Sswk | 2 | 8 | | 1,525 | 345 | | 1,870 | 2,300 |
| 2000 | Class A fire doors, manual, 20 ga., 8' x 8' high | | 1.40 | 11.429 | | 1,200 | 490 | | 1,690 | 2,200 |
| 2100 | 10' x 10' high | | 1.10 | 14.545 | | 1,650 | 625 | | 2,275 | 2,925 |
| 2200 | 20' x 10' high | | .80 | 20 | | 3,400 | 860 | | 4,260 | 5,275 |
| 2300 | 12' x 12' high | | 1 | 16 | | 2,575 | 690 | | 3,265 | 4,100 |
| 2400 | 20' x 12' high | | .80 | 20 | | 3,675 | 860 | | 4,535 | 5,600 |
| 2500 | 14' x 14' high | | .60 | 26.667 | | 2,850 | 1,150 | | 4,000 | 5,225 |
| 2600 | 20' x 16' high | | .50 | 32 | | 4,575 | 1,375 | | 5,950 | 7,525 |
| 2700 | 10' x 20' high | ▼ | .40 | 40 | ▼ | 3,550 | 1,725 | | 5,275 | 7,000 |
| 3000 | For 18 ga. doors, add | | | | S.F. | 1.10 | | | 1.10 | 1.21 |
| 3300 | For enamel finish, add | | | | " | 1.32 | | | 1.32 | 1.45 |
| 3600 | For safety edge bottom bar, pneumatic, add | | | | L.F. | 17.25 | | | 17.25 | 18.95 |
| 3700 | Electric, add | | | | | 32.50 | | | 32.50 | 35.50 |
| 4000 | For weatherstripping, extruded rubber, jambs, add | | | | | 11.15 | | | 11.15 | 12.25 |
| 4100 | Hood, add | | | | | 7.85 | | | 7.85 | 8.60 |
| 4200 | Sill, add | | | | ▼ | 4.46 | | | 4.46 | 4.91 |
| 4500 | Motor operators, to 14' x 14' opening | 2 Sswk | 5 | 3.200 | Ea. | 950 | 138 | | 1,088 | 1,300 |
| 4600 | Over 14' x 14', jack shaft type | " | 5 | 3.200 | | 940 | 138 | | 1,078 | 1,275 |
| 4700 | For fire door, additional fusible link, add | | | | ▼ | 20.50 | | | 20.50 | 22.50 |

# 08 34 Special Function Doors

## 08 34 13 – Cold Storage Doors

| 08 34 13.10 Doors for Cold Area Storage | Crew | Daily Output | Labor-Hours | Unit | Material | 2008 Bare Costs Labor | Equipment | Total | Total Incl O&P |
|---|---|---|---|---|---|---|---|---|---|
| 0010 | **DOORS FOR COLD AREA STORAGE** | | | | | | | | | |
| 0020 | Single, 20 ga. galvanized steel | | | | | | | | | |
| 0300 | Horizontal sliding, 5' x 7', manual operation, 3.5" thick | 2 Carp | 2 | 8 | Ea. | 2,900 | 305 | | 3,205 | 3,650 |
| 0400 | 4" thick | | 2 | 8 | | 3,525 | 305 | | 3,830 | 4,350 |
| 0500 | 6" thick | | 2 | 8 | | 2,975 | 305 | | 3,280 | 3,750 |
| 0800 | 5' x 7', power operation, 2" thick | | 1.90 | 8.421 | | 4,950 | 320 | | 5,270 | 5,925 |
| 0900 | 4" thick | | 1.90 | 8.421 | | 5,025 | 320 | | 5,345 | 6,025 |
| 1000 | 6" thick | | 1.90 | 8.421 | | 5,725 | 320 | | 6,045 | 6,775 |
| 1300 | 9' x 10', manual operation, 2" insulation | | 1.70 | 9.412 | | 4,000 | 360 | | 4,360 | 4,925 |
| 1400 | 4" insulation | | 1.70 | 9.412 | | 4,125 | 360 | | 4,485 | 5,075 |
| 1500 | 6" insulation | | 1.70 | 9.412 | | 4,950 | 360 | | 5,310 | 6,000 |
| 1800 | Power operation, 2" insulation | | 1.60 | 10 | | 6,875 | 380 | | 7,255 | 8,150 |
| 1900 | 4" insulation | | 1.60 | 10 | | 7,025 | 380 | | 7,405 | 8,325 |
| 2000 | 6" insulation | ↓ | 1.70 | 9.412 | ↓ | 7,975 | 360 | | 8,335 | 9,300 |
| 2300 | For stainless steel face, add | | | | | 20% | | | | |
| 3000 | Hinged, lightweight, 3' x 7'-0", galvanized 1 face, 2" thick | 2 Carp | 2 | 8 | Ea. | 1,300 | 305 | | 1,605 | 1,900 |
| 3050 | 4" thick | | 1.90 | 8.421 | | 1,525 | 320 | | 1,845 | 2,175 |
| 3300 | Aluminum doors, 3' x 7'-0", 4" thick | | 1.90 | 8.421 | | 1,175 | 320 | | 1,495 | 1,800 |
| 3350 | 6" thick | | 1.40 | 11.429 | | 2,100 | 435 | | 2,535 | 2,975 |
| 3600 | Stainless steel, 3' x 7'-0", 4" thick | | 1.90 | 8.421 | | 1,500 | 320 | | 1,820 | 2,150 |
| 3650 | 6" thick | | 1.40 | 11.429 | | 2,525 | 435 | | 2,960 | 3,475 |
| 3900 | Painted, 3' x 7'-0", 4" thick | | 1.90 | 8.421 | | 1,075 | 320 | | 1,395 | 1,700 |
| 3950 | 6" thick | ↓ | 1.40 | 11.429 | ↓ | 2,050 | 435 | | 2,485 | 2,950 |
| 5000 | Bi-parting, electric operated | | | | | | | | | |
| 5010 | 6' x 8' opening, galv. faces, 4" thick for cooler | 2 Carp | .80 | 20 | Opng. | 6,450 | 760 | | 7,210 | 8,275 |
| 5050 | For freezer, 4" thick | | .80 | 20 | | 7,100 | 760 | | 7,860 | 9,000 |
| 5300 | For door buck framing and door protection, add | | 2.50 | 6.400 | | 530 | 244 | | 774 | 960 |
| 6000 | Galvanized batten door, galvanized hinges, 4' x 7' | | 2 | 8 | | 1,600 | 305 | | 1,905 | 2,225 |
| 6050 | 6' x 8' | | 1.80 | 8.889 | | 2,175 | 340 | | 2,515 | 2,900 |
| 6500 | Fire door, 3 hr., 6' x 8', single slide | | .80 | 20 | | 7,450 | 760 | | 8,210 | 9,375 |
| 6550 | Double, bi-parting | ↓ | .70 | 22.857 | ↓ | 11,500 | 870 | | 12,370 | 14,000 |

## 08 34 16 – Hangar Doors

### 08 34 16.10 Aircraft Hangar Doors

| | | Crew | Daily Output | Labor-Hours | Unit | Material | Labor | Equipment | Total | Total Incl O&P |
|---|---|---|---|---|---|---|---|---|---|---|
| 0010 | **AIRCRAFT HANGAR DOORS** | | | | | | | | | |
| 0020 | Bi-fold, ovhd., 20 PSF wind load, incl. elec. oper. | | | | | | | | | |
| 0100 | Without sheeting, 12' high x 40' | 2 Sswk | 240 | .067 | S.F. | 13.70 | 2.87 | | 16.57 | 20 |
| 0200 | 16' high x 60' | | 230 | .070 | | 17.45 | 2.99 | | 20.44 | 24.50 |
| 0300 | 20' high x 80' | ↓ | 220 | .073 | ↓ | 17.75 | 3.13 | | 20.88 | 25 |

## 08 34 36 – Darkroom Doors

### 08 34 36.10 Various Types of Darkroom Doors

| | | Crew | Daily Output | Labor-Hours | Unit | Material | Labor | Equipment | Total | Total Incl O&P |
|---|---|---|---|---|---|---|---|---|---|---|
| 0010 | **VARIOUS TYPES OF DARKROOM DOORS** | | | | | | | | | |
| 0015 | Revolving, standard, 2 way, 36" diameter | 2 Carp | 3.10 | 5.161 | Opng. | 2,025 | 197 | | 2,222 | 2,525 |
| 0020 | 41" diameter | | 3.10 | 5.161 | | 2,175 | 197 | | 2,372 | 2,700 |
| 0050 | 3 way, 51" diameter | | 1.40 | 11.429 | | 2,700 | 435 | | 3,135 | 3,650 |
| 1000 | 4 way, 49" diameter | | 1.40 | 11.429 | | 3,200 | 435 | | 3,635 | 4,200 |
| 2000 | Hinged safety, 2 way, 41" diameter | | 2.30 | 6.957 | | 2,575 | 265 | | 2,840 | 3,250 |
| 2500 | 3 way, 51" diameter | | 1.40 | 11.429 | | 3,225 | 435 | | 3,660 | 4,225 |
| 3000 | Pop out safety, 2 way, 41" diameter | | 3.10 | 5.161 | | 3,175 | 197 | | 3,372 | 3,775 |
| 4000 | 3 way, 51" diameter | | 1.40 | 11.429 | | 3,150 | 435 | | 3,585 | 4,150 |
| 5000 | Wheelchair-type, pop out, 51" diameter | | 1.40 | 11.429 | | 3,225 | 435 | | 3,660 | 4,225 |
| 5020 | 72" diameter | ↓ | .90 | 17.778 | ↓ | 6,575 | 675 | | 7,250 | 8,275 |
| 9300 | For complete darkrooms, see Div. 13 21 53.50 | | | | | | | | | |

# 08 34 Special Function Doors

## 08 34 56 – Security Gates

| 08 34 56.10 For Information On Security Gates | Crew | Daily Output | Labor-Hours | Unit | Material | 2008 Bare Costs Labor | 2008 Bare Costs Equipment | Total | Total Incl O&P |
|---|---|---|---|---|---|---|---|---|---|
| 0010 **FOR INFORMATION ON SECURITY GATES,** see Div.10 22 16.10 | | | | | | | | | |

## 08 34 59 – Vault Doors and Day Gates

### 08 34 59.10 Secure Storage Doors

| | | Crew | Daily Output | Labor-Hours | Unit | Material | Labor | Equipment | Total | Total Incl O&P |
|---|---|---|---|---|---|---|---|---|---|---|
| 0010 | **SECURE STORAGE DOORS** | | | | | | | | | |
| 0020 | Door and frame, 32" x 78", clear opening | | | | | | | | | |
| 0100 | 1 hour test, 32" door, weighs 750 lbs. | 2 Sswk | 1.50 | 10.667 | Opng. | 3,725 | 460 | | 4,185 | 4,925 |
| 0200 | 2 hour test, 32" door, weighs 950 lbs. | | 1.30 | 12.308 | | 3,975 | 530 | | 4,505 | 5,325 |
| 0250 | 40" door, weighs 1130 lbs. | | 1 | 16 | | 4,525 | 690 | | 5,215 | 6,225 |
| 0300 | 4 hour test, 32" door, weighs 1025 lbs. | | 1.20 | 13.333 | | 4,325 | 575 | | 4,900 | 5,775 |
| 0350 | 40" door, weighs 1140 lbs. | | .90 | 17.778 | | 5,025 | 765 | | 5,790 | 6,900 |
| 0500 | For stainless steel front, including frame, add to above | | | | | 1,850 | | | 1,850 | 2,025 |
| 0550 | Back, add | | | | | 1,850 | | | 1,850 | 2,025 |
| 0600 | For time lock, two movement, add | 1 Elec | 2 | 4 | Ea. | 1,450 | 182 | | 1,632 | 1,850 |
| 0650 | Three movement, add | " | 2 | 4 | | 1,900 | 182 | | 2,082 | 2,375 |
| 0800 | Day gate, painted, steel, 32" wide | 2 Sswk | 1.50 | 10.667 | | 1,850 | 460 | | 2,310 | 2,875 |
| 0850 | 40" wide | | 1.40 | 11.429 | | 2,050 | 490 | | 2,540 | 3,125 |
| 0900 | Aluminum, 32" wide | | 1.50 | 10.667 | | 2,950 | 460 | | 3,410 | 4,075 |
| 0950 | 40" wide | | 1.40 | 11.429 | | 3,275 | 490 | | 3,765 | 4,475 |
| 2050 | Security vault door, class I, 3' wide, 3 1/2" thick | E-24 | .19 | 166 | Opng. | 14,600 | 7,025 | 4,100 | 25,725 | 32,700 |
| 2100 | Class II, 3' wide, 7" thick | | .19 | 166 | | 16,900 | 7,025 | 4,100 | 28,025 | 35,200 |
| 2150 | Class III, 9R, 3' wide, 10" thick, minimum | | .13 | 250 | | 21,000 | 10,600 | 6,150 | 37,750 | 48,200 |
| 2160 | Class V, type 1, 40" door | | 2.48 | 12.903 | Ea. | 6,050 | 545 | 315 | 6,910 | 7,950 |
| 2170 | Class V, type 2, 40" door | | 2.48 | 12.903 | | 6,025 | 545 | 315 | 6,885 | 7,925 |
| 2180 | Day gate for class V vault | 2 Sswk | 2 | 8 | | 1,250 | 345 | | 1,595 | 2,000 |

## 08 34 63 – Detention Doors and Frames

### 08 34 63.13 Steel Detention Doors and Frames

| | | Crew | Daily Output | Labor-Hours | Unit | Material | Labor | Equipment | Total | Total Incl O&P |
|---|---|---|---|---|---|---|---|---|---|---|
| 0010 | **STEEL DETENTION DOORS AND FRAMES** | | | | | | | | | |
| 1000 | Doors & frames, 3' x 7', complete, with hardware, single plate | E-4 | 4 | 8 | Ea. | 3,825 | 350 | 33 | 4,208 | 4,875 |
| 1650 | Double plate | " | 4 | 8 | " | 4,700 | 350 | 33 | 5,083 | 5,850 |

## 08 34 73 – Sound Control Door Assemblies

### 08 34 73.10 Accoustical Doors

| | | Crew | Daily Output | Labor-Hours | Unit | Material | Labor | Equipment | Total | Total Incl O&P |
|---|---|---|---|---|---|---|---|---|---|---|
| 0010 | **ACCOUSTICAL DOORS** | | | | | | | | | |
| 0020 | Including framed seals, 3' x 7', wood, 27 STC rating | 2 Carp | 1.50 | 10.667 | Ea. | 415 | 405 | | 820 | 1,100 |
| 0100 | Steel, 40 STC rating | | 1.50 | 10.667 | | 2,000 | 405 | | 2,405 | 2,825 |
| 0200 | 45 STC rating | | 1.50 | 10.667 | | 2,500 | 405 | | 2,905 | 3,375 |
| 0300 | 48 STC rating | | 1.50 | 10.667 | | 3,000 | 405 | | 3,405 | 3,925 |
| 0400 | 52 STC rating | | 1.50 | 10.667 | | 3,500 | 405 | | 3,905 | 4,475 |

# 08 36 Panel Doors

## 08 36 13 – Sectional Doors

### 08 36 13.10 Overhead Commercial Doors

| | | Crew | Daily Output | Labor-Hours | Unit | Material | Labor | Equipment | Total | Total Incl O&P |
|---|---|---|---|---|---|---|---|---|---|---|
| 0010 | **OVERHEAD COMMERCIAL DOORS** | | | | | | | | | |
| 1000 | Stock, sectional, heavy duty, wood, 1-3/4" thick, 8' x 8' high | 2 Carp | 2 | 8 | Ea. | 645 | 305 | | 950 | 1,175 |
| 1100 | 10' x 10' high | | 1.80 | 8.889 | | 970 | 340 | | 1,310 | 1,600 |
| 1200 | 12' x 12' high | | 1.50 | 10.667 | | 1,400 | 405 | | 1,805 | 2,175 |
| 1300 | Chain hoist, 14' x 14' high | | 1.30 | 12.308 | | 1,925 | 470 | | 2,395 | 2,850 |
| 1400 | 12' x 16' high | | 1 | 16 | | 1,875 | 610 | | 2,485 | 3,000 |
| 1500 | 20' x 8' high | | 1.30 | 12.270 | | 1,650 | 465 | | 2,115 | 2,550 |
| 1600 | 20' x 16' high | | .65 | 24.615 | | 4,950 | 940 | | 5,890 | 6,900 |

# 08 36 Panel Doors

## 08 36 13 – Sectional Doors

### 08 36 13.10 Overhead Commercial Doors

| | | Crew | Daily Output | Labor-Hours | Unit | Material | 2008 Bare Costs Labor | Equipment | Total | Total Incl O&P |
|---|---|---|---|---|---|---|---|---|---|---|
| 1800 | Center mullion openings, 8' high | 2 Carp | 4 | 4 | Ea. | 790 | 152 | | 942 | 1,100 |
| 1900 | 20' high | ↓ | 2 | 8 | ↓ | 1,400 | 305 | | 1,705 | 2,025 |
| 2100 | For medium duty custom door, deduct | | | | | 5% | 5% | | | |
| 2150 | For medium duty stock doors, deduct | | | | | 10% | 5% | | | |
| 2300 | Fiberglass and aluminum, heavy duty, sectional, 12' x 12' high | 2 Carp | 1.50 | 10.667 | Ea. | 2,050 | 405 | | 2,455 | 2,875 |
| 2450 | Chain hoist, 20' x 20' high | ↓ | .50 | 32 | | 5,150 | 1,225 | | 6,375 | 7,575 |
| 2600 | Steel, 24 ga. sectional, manual, 8' x 8' high | | 2 | 8 | | 615 | 305 | | 920 | 1,150 |
| 2650 | 10' x 10' high | | 1.80 | 8.889 | | 795 | 340 | | 1,135 | 1,400 |
| 2700 | 12' x 12' high | | 1.50 | 10.667 | | 1,000 | 405 | | 1,405 | 1,725 |
| 2800 | Chain hoist, 20' x 14' high | ↓ | .70 | 22.857 | ↓ | 2,900 | 870 | | 3,770 | 4,550 |
| 2850 | For 1-1/4" rigid insulation and 26 ga. galv. | | | | | | | | | |
| 2860 | back panel, add | | | | S.F. | 2.75 | | | 2.75 | 3.03 |
| 2900 | For electric trolley operator, 1/3 H.P., to 12' x 12', add | 1 Carp | 2 | 4 | Ea. | 820 | 152 | | 972 | 1,150 |
| 2950 | Over 12' x 12', 1/2 H.P., add | " | 1 | 8 | " | 965 | 305 | | 1,270 | 1,550 |

### 08 36 13.20 Residential Garage Doors

| | | Crew | Daily Output | Labor-Hours | Unit | Material | 2008 Bare Costs Labor | Equipment | Total | Total Incl O&P |
|---|---|---|---|---|---|---|---|---|---|---|
| 0010 | **RESIDENTIAL GARAGE DOORS** | | | | | | | | | |
| 0050 | Hinged, wood, custom, double door, 9' x 7' | 2 Carp | 4 | 4 | Ea. | 455 | 152 | | 607 | 735 |
| 0070 | 16' x 7' | | 3 | 5.333 | | 805 | 203 | | 1,008 | 1,200 |
| 0200 | Overhead, sectional, incl. hardware, fiberglass, 9' x 7', standard | | 5.28 | 3.030 | | 645 | 115 | | 760 | 890 |
| 0220 | Deluxe | | 5.28 | 3.030 | | 825 | 115 | | 940 | 1,075 |
| 0300 | 16' x 7', standard | | 6 | 2.667 | | 1,175 | 102 | | 1,277 | 1,450 |
| 0320 | Deluxe | | 6 | 2.667 | | 1,475 | 102 | | 1,577 | 1,775 |
| 0500 | Hardboard, 9' x 7', standard | | 8 | 2 | | 435 | 76 | | 511 | 600 |
| 0520 | Deluxe | | 8 | 2 | | 585 | 76 | | 661 | 765 |
| 0600 | 16' x 7', standard | | 6 | 2.667 | | 860 | 102 | | 962 | 1,100 |
| 0620 | Deluxe | | 6 | 2.667 | | 1,000 | 102 | | 1,102 | 1,250 |
| 0700 | Metal, 9' x 7', standard | | 5.28 | 3.030 | | 505 | 115 | | 620 | 740 |
| 0720 | Deluxe | | 8 | 2 | | 690 | 76 | | 766 | 875 |
| 0800 | 16' x 7', standard | | 3 | 5.333 | | 645 | 203 | | 848 | 1,025 |
| 0820 | Deluxe | | 6 | 2.667 | | 1,050 | 102 | | 1,152 | 1,300 |
| 0900 | Wood, 9' x 7', standard | | 8 | 2 | | 540 | 76 | | 616 | 715 |
| 0920 | Deluxe | | 8 | 2 | | 1,550 | 76 | | 1,626 | 1,825 |
| 1000 | 16' x 7', standard | | 6 | 2.667 | | 1,100 | 102 | | 1,202 | 1,350 |
| 1020 | Deluxe | ↓ | 6 | 2.667 | | 2,275 | 102 | | 2,377 | 2,650 |
| 1800 | Door hardware, sectional | 1 Carp | 4 | 2 | | 238 | 76 | | 314 | 380 |
| 1810 | Door tracks only | | 4 | 2 | | 110 | 76 | | 186 | 240 |
| 1820 | One side only | ↓ | 7 | 1.143 | | 77 | 43.50 | | 120.50 | 153 |
| 3000 | Swing-up, including hardware, fiberglass, 9' x 7', standard | 2 Carp | 8 | 2 | | 750 | 76 | | 826 | 945 |
| 3020 | Deluxe | | 8 | 2 | | 790 | 76 | | 866 | 990 |
| 3100 | 16' x 7', standard | | 6 | 2.667 | | 945 | 102 | | 1,047 | 1,200 |
| 3120 | Deluxe | | 6 | 2.667 | | 975 | 102 | | 1,077 | 1,225 |
| 3200 | Hardboard, 9' x 7', standard | | 8 | 2 | | 345 | 76 | | 421 | 500 |
| 3220 | Deluxe | | 8 | 2 | | 455 | 76 | | 531 | 620 |
| 3300 | 16' x 7', standard | | 6 | 2.667 | | 480 | 102 | | 582 | 690 |
| 3320 | Deluxe | | 6 | 2.667 | | 715 | 102 | | 817 | 945 |
| 3400 | Metal, 9' x 7', standard | | 8 | 2 | | 375 | 76 | | 451 | 535 |
| 3420 | Deluxe | | 8 | 2 | | 670 | 76 | | 746 | 855 |
| 3500 | 16' x 7', standard | | 6 | 2.667 | | 590 | 102 | | 692 | 810 |
| 3520 | Deluxe | | 6 | 2.667 | | 950 | 102 | | 1,052 | 1,200 |
| 3600 | Wood, 9' x 7', standard | | 8 | 2 | | 415 | 76 | | 491 | 575 |
| 3620 | Deluxe | | 8 | 2 | | 730 | 76 | | 806 | 920 |
| 3700 | 16' x 7', standard | ↓ | 6 | 2.667 | ↓ | 715 | 102 | | 817 | 950 |

# 08 36 Panel Doors

## 08 36 13 – Sectional Doors

### 08 36 13.20 Residential Garage Doors

| | | Crew | Daily Output | Labor-Hours | Unit | Material | 2008 Bare Costs Labor | 2008 Bare Costs Equipment | Total | Total Incl O&P |
|---|---|---|---|---|---|---|---|---|---|---|
| 3720 | Deluxe | 2 Carp | 6 | 2.667 | Ea. | 1,000 | 102 | | 1,102 | 1,250 |
| 3900 | Door hardware only, swing up | 1 Carp | 4 | 2 | | 119 | 76 | | 195 | 250 |
| 3920 | One side only | | 7 | 1.143 | | 67 | 43.50 | | 110.50 | 142 |
| 4000 | For electric operator, economy, add | | 8 | 1 | | 310 | 38 | | 348 | 405 |
| 4100 | Deluxe, including remote control | | 8 | 1 | | 455 | 38 | | 493 | 560 |
| 4500 | For transmitter/receiver control, add to operator | | | | Total | 94.50 | | | 94.50 | 104 |
| 4600 | Transmitters, additional | | | | " | 35 | | | 35 | 38.50 |

## 08 36 19 – Multi-Leaf Vertical Lift Doors

### 08 36 19.10 Sectional Vertical Lift Doors

| | | Crew | Daily Output | Labor-Hours | Unit | Material | 2008 Bare Costs Labor | 2008 Bare Costs Equipment | Total | Total Incl O&P |
|---|---|---|---|---|---|---|---|---|---|---|
| 0010 | **SECTIONAL VERTICAL LIFT DOORS** | | | | | | | | | |
| 0020 | Motorized, 14 ga. stl, incl., frm and ctrl pnl | | | | | | | | | |
| 0050 | 16' x 16' high | L-10 | .50 | 48 | Ea. | 19,300 | 2,075 | 1,525 | 22,900 | 26,400 |
| 0100 | 10' x 20' high | | 1.30 | 18.462 | | 27,900 | 795 | 590 | 29,285 | 32,700 |
| 0120 | 15' x 20' high | | 1.30 | 18.462 | | 34,100 | 795 | 590 | 35,485 | 39,500 |
| 0140 | 20' x 20' high | | 1 | 24 | | 39,900 | 1,025 | 765 | 41,690 | 46,500 |
| 0160 | 25' x 20' high | | 1 | 24 | | 44,100 | 1,025 | 765 | 45,890 | 51,000 |
| 0170 | 32' x 24' high | | .75 | 32 | | 42,200 | 1,375 | 1,025 | 44,600 | 49,900 |
| 0180 | 20' x 25' high | | 1 | 24 | | 45,700 | 1,025 | 765 | 47,490 | 52,500 |
| 0200 | 25' x 25' high | | .70 | 34.286 | | 51,500 | 1,475 | 1,100 | 54,075 | 60,000 |
| 0220 | 25' x 30' high | | .70 | 34.286 | | 60,000 | 1,475 | 1,100 | 62,575 | 69,500 |
| 0240 | 30' x 30' high | | .70 | 34.286 | | 69,000 | 1,475 | 1,100 | 71,575 | 79,500 |
| 0260 | 35' x 30' high | | .70 | 34.286 | | 75,500 | 1,475 | 1,100 | 78,075 | 86,500 |

## 08 36 23 – Telescoping Vertical Lift Doors

### 08 36 23.10 Telescoping Steel Doors

| | | Crew | Daily Output | Labor-Hours | Unit | Material | 2008 Bare Costs Labor | 2008 Bare Costs Equipment | Total | Total Incl O&P |
|---|---|---|---|---|---|---|---|---|---|---|
| 0010 | **TELESCOPING STEEL DOORS** | | | | | | | | | |
| 1000 | Overhead, .03" thick, electric operated, 10' x 10' | E-3 | .80 | 30 | Ea. | 11,800 | 1,300 | 165 | 13,265 | 15,500 |
| 2000 | 20' x 10' | | .60 | 40 | | 15,600 | 1,750 | 220 | 17,570 | 20,600 |
| 3000 | 20' x 16' | | .40 | 60 | | 17,900 | 2,625 | 330 | 20,855 | 24,700 |

# 08 38 Traffic Doors

## 08 38 13 – Flexible Strip Doors

### 08 38 13.10 Flexible Transparent Strip Doors

| | | Crew | Daily Output | Labor-Hours | Unit | Material | 2008 Bare Costs Labor | 2008 Bare Costs Equipment | Total | Total Incl O&P |
|---|---|---|---|---|---|---|---|---|---|---|
| 0010 | **FLEXIBLE TRANSPARENT STRIP DOORS** | | | | | | | | | |
| 0100 | 12" strip width, 2/3 overlap | 3 Shee | 135 | .178 | SF Surf | 5.65 | 8.05 | | 13.70 | 18.60 |
| 0200 | Full overlap | | 115 | .209 | | 5.90 | 9.45 | | 15.35 | 21 |
| 0220 | 8" strip width, 1/2 overlap | | 140 | .171 | | 5.50 | 7.75 | | 13.25 | 18 |
| 0240 | Full overlap | | 120 | .200 | | 7.25 | 9.05 | | 16.30 | 22 |
| 0300 | Add for suspension system, header mount | | | | L.F. | 8.35 | | | 8.35 | 9.15 |
| 0400 | Wall mount | | | | " | 8.40 | | | 8.40 | 9.25 |

## 08 38 19 – Rigid Traffic Doors

### 08 38 19.20 Double Acting Swing Doors

| | | Crew | Daily Output | Labor-Hours | Unit | Material | 2008 Bare Costs Labor | 2008 Bare Costs Equipment | Total | Total Incl O&P |
|---|---|---|---|---|---|---|---|---|---|---|
| 0010 | **DOUBLE ACTING SWING DOORS** | | | | | | | | | |
| 1000 | .063" aluminum, 7'-0" high, 4'-0" wide | 2 Carp | 4.20 | 3.810 | Pr. | 1,900 | 145 | | 2,045 | 2,325 |
| 1025 | 6'-0" wide | | 4 | 4 | | 2,300 | 152 | | 2,452 | 2,750 |
| 1050 | 6'-8" wide | | 4 | 4 | | 2,500 | 152 | | 2,652 | 2,975 |
| 2000 | Solid core wood, 3/4" thick, metal frame, stainless steel | | | | | | | | | |
| 2010 | base plate, 7' high opening, 4' wide | 2 Carp | 4 | 4 | Pr. | 2,200 | 152 | | 2,352 | 2,650 |
| 2050 | 7' wide | " | 3.80 | 4.211 | " | 2,500 | 160 | | 2,660 | 3,000 |

# 08 38 Traffic Doors

## 08 38 19 – Rigid Traffic Doors

| 08 38 19.30 Shock Absorbing Doors | Crew | Daily Output | Labor-Hours | Unit | Material | 2008 Bare Costs Labor | Equipment | Total | Total Incl O&P |
|---|---|---|---|---|---|---|---|---|---|
| 0010 **SHOCK ABSORBING DOORS** | | | | | | | | | |
| 0020 Rigid, no frame, 1-1/2" thick, 5' x 7' | 2 Sswk | 1.90 | 8.421 | Opng. | 1,400 | 360 | | 1,760 | 2,175 |
| 0100 8' x 8' | | 1.80 | 8.889 | | 1,950 | 380 | | 2,330 | 2,850 |
| 0500 Flexible, no frame, insulated, .16" thick, economy, 5' x 7' | | 2 | 8 | | 1,700 | 345 | | 2,045 | 2,500 |
| 0600 Deluxe | | 1.90 | 8.421 | | 2,575 | 360 | | 2,935 | 3,475 |
| 1000 8' x 8' opening, economy | | 2 | 8 | | 2,650 | 345 | | 2,995 | 3,550 |
| 1100 Deluxe | | 1.90 | 8.421 | | 3,400 | 360 | | 3,760 | 4,400 |

# 08 41 Entrances and Storefronts

## 08 41 13 – Aluminum-Framed Entrances and Storefronts

| 08 41 13.20 Tube Framing | Crew | Daily Output | Labor-Hours | Unit | Material | 2008 Bare Costs Labor | Equipment | Total | Total Incl O&P |
|---|---|---|---|---|---|---|---|---|---|
| 0010 **TUBE FRAMING**, For window walls and store fronts, aluminum stock | | | | | | | | | |
| 0050 Plain tube frame, mill finish, 1-3/4" x 1-3/4" | 2 Glaz | 103 | .155 | L.F. | 7.45 | 5.80 | | 13.25 | 17 |
| 0150 1-3/4" x 4" | | 98 | .163 | | 9.15 | 6.10 | | 15.25 | 19.25 |
| 0200 1-3/4" x 4-1/2" **CN** | | 95 | .168 | | 10.70 | 6.30 | | 17 | 21.50 |
| 0250 2" x 6" | | 89 | .180 | | 15.15 | 6.70 | | 21.85 | 27 |
| 0350 4" x 4" | | 87 | .184 | | 14.85 | 6.85 | | 21.70 | 27 |
| 0400 4-1/2" x 4-1/2" | | 85 | .188 | | 24 | 7 | | 31 | 37 |
| 0450 Glass bead | | 240 | .067 | | 1.99 | 2.49 | | 4.48 | 5.95 |
| 1000 Flush tube frame, mill finish, 1/4" glass, 1-3/4" x 4", open header | | 80 | .200 | | 8.90 | 7.45 | | 16.35 | 21 |
| 1050 Open sill | | 82 | .195 | | 7.80 | 7.30 | | 15.10 | 19.55 |
| 1100 Closed back header | | 83 | .193 | | 12.40 | 7.20 | | 19.60 | 24.50 |
| 1150 Closed back sill | | 85 | .188 | | 11.80 | 7 | | 18.80 | 23.50 |
| 1200 Vertical mullion, one piece | | 75 | .213 | | 13.15 | 7.95 | | 21.10 | 26.50 |
| 1250 Two piece | | 73 | .219 | | 14.05 | 8.20 | | 22.25 | 28 |
| 1300 90° or 180° vertical corner post | | 75 | .213 | | 21.50 | 7.95 | | 29.45 | 35.50 |
| 1400 1-3/4" x 4-1/2", open header | | 80 | .200 | | 10.85 | 7.45 | | 18.30 | 23 |
| 1450 Open sill | | 82 | .195 | | 9 | 7.30 | | 16.30 | 21 |
| 1500 Closed back header | | 83 | .193 | | 13.05 | 7.20 | | 20.25 | 25.50 |
| 1550 Closed back sill | | 85 | .188 | | 12.70 | 7 | | 19.70 | 24.50 |
| 1600 Vertical mullion, one piece | | 75 | .213 | | 14.20 | 7.95 | | 22.15 | 27.50 |
| 1650 Two piece | | 73 | .219 | | 15 | 8.20 | | 23.20 | 29 |
| 1700 90° or 180° vertical corner post | | 75 | .213 | | 15.30 | 7.95 | | 23.25 | 29 |
| 2000 Flush tube frame, mil fin.,ins. glass w/thml brk, 2" x 4-1/2", open header | | 75 | .213 | | 12.50 | 7.95 | | 20.45 | 26 |
| 2050 Open sill | | 77 | .208 | | 10.35 | 7.75 | | 18.10 | 23 |
| 2100 Closed back header | | 78 | .205 | | 11.60 | 7.65 | | 19.25 | 24.50 |
| 2150 Closed back sill | | 80 | .200 | | 12.55 | 7.45 | | 20 | 25 |
| 2200 Vertical mullion, one piece | | 70 | .229 | | 12.80 | 8.55 | | 21.35 | 27 |
| 2250 Two piece | | 68 | .235 | | 13.75 | 8.80 | | 22.55 | 28.50 |
| 2300 90° or 180° vertical corner post | | 70 | .229 | | 13.35 | 8.55 | | 21.90 | 27.50 |
| 5000 Flush tube frame, mill fin., thermal brk., 2-1/4"x 4-1/2", open header | | 74 | .216 | | 12.70 | 8.05 | | 20.75 | 26 |
| 5050 Open sill | | 75 | .213 | | 11.40 | 7.95 | | 19.35 | 24.50 |
| 5100 Vertical mullion, one piece | | 69 | .232 | | 13.90 | 8.65 | | 22.55 | 28.50 |
| 5150 Two piece | | 67 | .239 | | 16.35 | 8.90 | | 25.25 | 31.50 |
| 5200 90° or 180° vertical corner post | | 69 | .232 | | 14.30 | 8.65 | | 22.95 | 29 |
| 6980 Door stop (snap in) | | 380 | .042 | | 2.67 | 1.57 | | 4.24 | 5.30 |
| 7000 For joints, 90°, clip type, add | | | | Ea. | 19.50 | | | 19.50 | 21.50 |
| 7050 Screw spline joint, add | | | | | 15.90 | | | 15.90 | 17.50 |
| 7100 For joint other than 90°, add | | | | | 33 | | | 33 | 36.50 |
| 8000 For bronze anodized aluminum, add | | | | | 15% | | | | |

238

# 08 41 Entrances and Storefronts

## 08 41 13 – Aluminum-Framed Entrances and Storefronts

### 08 41 13.20 Tube Framing

| | | Crew | Daily Output | Labor-Hours | Unit | Material | 2008 Bare Costs Labor | Equipment | Total | Total Incl O&P |
|---|---|---|---|---|---|---|---|---|---|---|
| 8020 | For black finish, add | | | | | 27% | | | | |
| 8050 | For stainless steel materials, add | | | | | 350% | | | | |
| 8100 | For monumental grade, add | | | | | 50% | | | | |
| 8150 | For steel stiffener, add | 2 Glaz | 200 | .080 | L.F. | 8.10 | 2.98 | | 11.08 | 13.40 |
| 8200 | For 2 to 5 stories, add per story | | | | Story | | 5% | | | |

## 08 41 19 – Stainless-Steel-Framed Entrances and Storefronts

### 08 41 19.10 Stainless-Steel and Glass Entrance Unit

| | | Crew | Daily Output | Labor-Hours | Unit | Material | 2008 Bare Costs Labor | Equipment | Total | Total Incl O&P |
|---|---|---|---|---|---|---|---|---|---|---|
| 0010 | **STAINLESS-STEEL AND GLASS ENTRANCE UNIT**, narrow stiles | | | | | | | | | |
| 0020 | 3' x 7' opening, including hardware, minimum | 2 Sswk | 1.60 | 10 | Opng. | 5,475 | 430 | | 5,905 | 6,800 |
| 0050 | Average | | 1.40 | 11.429 | | 5,925 | 490 | | 6,415 | 7,400 |
| 0100 | Maximum | | 1.20 | 13.333 | | 6,350 | 575 | | 6,925 | 8,025 |
| 1000 | For solid bronze entrance units, statuary finish, add | | | | | 60% | | | | |
| 1100 | Without statuary finish, add | | | | | 45% | | | | |
| 2000 | Balanced doors, 3' x 7', economy | 2 Sswk | .90 | 17.778 | Ea. | 7,425 | 765 | | 8,190 | 9,525 |
| 2100 | Premium | " | .70 | 22.857 | " | 12,800 | 985 | | 13,785 | 15,900 |

## 08 41 26 – All-Glass Entrances and Storefronts

### 08 41 26.10 Window Walls Aluminum, Stock

| | | Crew | Daily Output | Labor-Hours | Unit | Material | 2008 Bare Costs Labor | Equipment | Total | Total Incl O&P |
|---|---|---|---|---|---|---|---|---|---|---|
| 0010 | **WINDOW WALLS ALUMINUM, STOCK,** including glazing | | | | | | | | | |
| 0020 | Minimum | H-2 | 160 | .150 | S.F. | 30.50 | 5.25 | | 35.75 | 41.50 |
| 0050 | Average | | 140 | .171 | | 42 | 6 | | 48 | 55 |
| 0100 | Maximum | | 110 | .218 | | 118 | 7.65 | | 125.65 | 142 |
| 0500 | For translucent sandwich wall systems, see Div. 07 41 33.10 | | | | | | | | | |
| 0850 | Cost of the above walls depends on material, | | | | | | | | | |
| 0860 | finish, repetition, and size of units. | | | | | | | | | |
| 0870 | The larger the opening, the lower the S.F. cost | | | | | | | | | |
| 1200 | Double glazed acoustical window wall for airports, | | | | | | | | | |
| 1220 | including 1" thick glass with 2" x 4-1/2" tube frame | H-2 | 40 | .600 | S.F. | 77 | 21 | | 98 | 117 |

# 08 42 Entrances

## 08 42 26 – All-Glass Entrances

### 08 42 26.10 Swinging Glass Doors

| | | Crew | Daily Output | Labor-Hours | Unit | Material | 2008 Bare Costs Labor | Equipment | Total | Total Incl O&P |
|---|---|---|---|---|---|---|---|---|---|---|
| 0010 | **SWINGING GLASS DOORS** | | | | | | | | | |
| 0020 | Including hardware, 1/2" thick, tempered, 3' x 7' opening | 2 Glaz | 2 | 8 | Opng. | 1,825 | 298 | | 2,123 | 2,450 |
| 0100 | 6' x 7' opening | | 1.40 | 11.429 | " | 3,650 | 425 | | 4,075 | 4,650 |
| 9000 | Minimum labor/equipment charge | | 2 | 8 | Job | | 298 | | 298 | 450 |

## 08 42 29 – Automatic Entrances

### 08 42 29.23 Sliding Automatic Entrances

| | | Crew | Daily Output | Labor-Hours | Unit | Material | 2008 Bare Costs Labor | Equipment | Total | Total Incl O&P |
|---|---|---|---|---|---|---|---|---|---|---|
| 0010 | **SLIDING AUTOMATIC ENTRANCES** 12' x 7'-6" opng., 5' x 7' door, 2 way traffic | | | | | | | | | |
| 0020 | Mat or electronic activated, panic pushout, incl. operator & hardware, | | | | | | | | | |
| 0030 | not including glass or glazing | 2 Glaz | .70 | 22.857 | Opng. | 7,025 | 855 | | 7,880 | 9,025 |
| 9000 | Minimum labor/equipment charge | " | .70 | 22.857 | Job | | 855 | | 855 | 1,300 |

## 08 42 33 – Revolving Door Entrances

### 08 42 33.10 Circular Rotating Entrance Doors

| | | Crew | Daily Output | Labor-Hours | Unit | Material | 2008 Bare Costs Labor | Equipment | Total | Total Incl O&P |
|---|---|---|---|---|---|---|---|---|---|---|
| 0010 | **CIRCULAR ROTATING ENTRANCE DOORS**, Aluminum | | | | | | | | | |
| 0020 | 6'-10" to 7' high, stock units, minimum | 4 Sswk | .75 | 42.667 | Opng. | 17,200 | 1,825 | | 19,025 | 22,200 |
| 0050 | Average | | .60 | 53.333 | | 21,200 | 2,300 | | 23,500 | 27,400 |
| 0100 | Maximum | | .45 | 71.111 | | 27,900 | 3,050 | | 30,950 | 36,200 |
| 1000 | Stainless steel | | .30 | 105 | | 34,300 | 4,550 | | 38,850 | 45,900 |
| 1100 | Solid bronze | | .15 | 213 | | 40,000 | 9,175 | | 49,175 | 60,500 |

# 08 42 Entrances

## 08 42 33 – Revolving Door Entrances

| 08 42 33.10 Circular Rotating Entrance Doors | Crew | Daily Output | Labor-Hours | Unit | Material | 2008 Bare Costs Labor | Equipment | Total | Total Incl O&P |
|---|---|---|---|---|---|---|---|---|---|
| 1500 | For automatic controls, add | 2 Elec | 2 | 8 | Opng. | 13,300 | 365 | | 13,665 | 15,100 |

## 08 42 36 – Balanced Door Entrances

### 08 42 36.10 Balanced Entrance Doors

| | | Crew | Daily Output | Labor-Hours | Unit | Material | Labor | Equipment | Total | Total Incl O&P |
|---|---|---|---|---|---|---|---|---|---|---|
| 0010 | **BALANCED ENTRANCE DOORS** | | | | | | | | | |
| 0020 | Hardware & frame, alum. & glass, 3' x 7', econ. | 2 Sswk | .90 | 17.778 | Ea. | 5,475 | 765 | | 6,240 | 7,375 |
| 0150 | Premium | " | .70 | 22.857 | " | 6,800 | 985 | | 7,785 | 9,250 |

# 08 43 Storefronts

## 08 43 13 – Aluminum-Framed Storefronts

### 08 43 13.10 Aluminum-Framed Entrance Doors (Frame Only)

| | | Crew | Daily Output | Labor-Hours | Unit | Material | Labor | Equipment | Total | Total Incl O&P |
|---|---|---|---|---|---|---|---|---|---|---|
| 0010 | **ALUMINUM-FRAMED Entrance doors (Frame Only)** | | | | | | | | | |
| 0020 | Entrance, 3' x 7' opening, clear anodized finish | 2 Sswk | 7 | 2.286 | Opng. | 415 | 98.50 | | 513.50 | 635 |
| 0040 | Bronze finish | | 7 | 2.286 | | 320 | 98.50 | | 418.50 | 530 |
| 0060 | Black finish | | 7 | 2.286 | | 415 | 98.50 | | 513.50 | 635 |
| 0500 | 6' x 7' opening, clear finish | | 6 | 2.667 | | 335 | 115 | | 450 | 570 |
| 0520 | Bronze finish | | 6 | 2.667 | | 555 | 115 | | 670 | 815 |
| 0540 | Black finish | | 6 | 2.667 | | 430 | 115 | | 545 | 675 |
| 1000 | With 3' high transoms, 3' x 10' opening, clear finish | | 6.50 | 2.462 | | 395 | 106 | | 501 | 625 |
| 1050 | Bronze finish | | 6.50 | 2.462 | | 435 | 106 | | 541 | 665 |
| 1100 | Black finish | | 6.50 | 2.462 | | 500 | 106 | | 606 | 740 |
| 1500 | With 3' high transoms, 6' x 10' opening, clear finish | | 5.50 | 2.909 | | 485 | 125 | | 610 | 760 |
| 1550 | Bronze finish | | 5.50 | 2.909 | | 525 | 125 | | 650 | 800 |
| 1600 | Black finish | | 5.50 | 2.909 | | 605 | 125 | | 730 | 890 |

### 08 43 13.20 Storefront Systems

| | | Crew | Daily Output | Labor-Hours | Unit | Material | Labor | Equipment | Total | Total Incl O&P |
|---|---|---|---|---|---|---|---|---|---|---|
| 0010 | **STOREFRONT SYSTEMS**, aluminum frame clear 3/8" plate glass | | | | | | | | | |
| 0020 | incl. 3' x 7' door with hardware (400 sq. ft. max. wall) | | | | | | | | | |
| 0500 | Wall height to 12' high, commercial grade | 2 Glaz | 150 | .107 | S.F. | 14.50 | 3.98 | | 18.48 | 22 |
| 0600 | Institutional grade | | 130 | .123 | | 18 | 4.59 | | 22.59 | 27 |
| 0700 | Monumental grade | | 115 | .139 | | 27.50 | 5.20 | | 32.70 | 38.50 |
| 1000 | 6' x 7' door with hardware, commercial grade | | 135 | .119 | | 14.70 | 4.42 | | 19.12 | 23 |
| 1100 | Institutional grade | | 115 | .139 | | 20 | 5.20 | | 25.20 | 30 |
| 1200 | Monumental grade | | 100 | .160 | | 37 | 5.95 | | 42.95 | 50 |
| 1500 | For bronze anodized finish, add | | | | | 15% | | | | |
| 1600 | For black anodized finish, add | | | | | 30% | | | | |
| 1700 | For stainless steel framing, add to monumental | | | | | 75% | | | | |

## 08 43 29 – Sliding Storefronts

### 08 43 29.10 Sliding Panels

| | | Crew | Daily Output | Labor-Hours | Unit | Material | Labor | Equipment | Total | Total Incl O&P |
|---|---|---|---|---|---|---|---|---|---|---|
| 0010 | **SLIDING PANELS** | | | | | | | | | |
| 0020 | Mall fronts, aluminum & glass, 15' x 9' high | 2 Glaz | 1.30 | 12.308 | Opng. | 2,750 | 460 | | 3,210 | 3,725 |
| 0100 | 24' x 9' high | | .70 | 22.857 | | 4,000 | 855 | | 4,855 | 5,700 |
| 0200 | 48' x 9' high, with fixed panels | | .90 | 17.778 | | 7,450 | 665 | | 8,115 | 9,200 |
| 0500 | For bronze finish, add | | | | | 17% | | | | |

# 08 44 Curtain Wall and Glazed Assemblies

## 08 44 13 – Glazed Aluminum Curtain Walls

| 08 44 13.10 Glazed Curtain Walls | Crew | Daily Output | Labor-Hours | Unit | Material | 2008 Bare Costs Labor | Equipment | Total | Total Incl O&P |
|---|---|---|---|---|---|---|---|---|---|
| 0010 **GLAZED CURTAIN WALLS**, aluminum, stock, including glazing | | | | | | | | | |
| 0020     Minimum | H-1 | 205 | .156 | S.F. | 24 | 6.25 | | 30.25 | 37 |
| 0050     Average, single glazed | | 195 | .164 | | 31.50 | 6.60 | | 38.10 | 45.50 |
| 0150     Average, double glazed | | 180 | .178 | | 44.50 | 7.15 | | 51.65 | 61 |
| 0200     Maximum | ↓ | 160 | .200 | ↓ | 122 | 8.05 | | 130.05 | 147 |

# 08 45 Translucent Wall and Roof Assemblies

## 08 45 10 – Translucent Roof Assemblies

### 08 45 10.10 Skyroofs

| | Crew | Daily Output | Labor-Hours | Unit | Material | 2008 Bare Costs Labor | Equipment | Total | Total Incl O&P |
|---|---|---|---|---|---|---|---|---|---|
| 0010 **SKYROOFS**, Translucent panels, 2-3/4" thick | | | | | | | | | |
| 0020     Under 500 S.F. | G-3 | 395 | .081 | SF Hor. | 29.50 | 3.06 | | 32.56 | 37 |
| 0100     Over 5000 S.F. | | 465 | .069 | | 28 | 2.60 | | 30.60 | 35 |
| 0300   Continuous vaulted, semi-circular, to 8' wide, double glazed | | 145 | .221 | | 47.50 | 8.35 | | 55.85 | 65 |
| 0400     Single glazed | | 160 | .200 | | 32 | 7.55 | | 39.55 | 47 |
| 0600   To 20' wide, single glazed | | 175 | .183 | | 36 | 6.90 | | 42.90 | 50 |
| 0700   Over 20' wide, single glazed | | 200 | .160 | | 41 | 6.05 | | 47.05 | 54.50 |
| 0900   Motorized opening type, single glazed, 1/3 opening | | 145 | .221 | | 42.50 | 8.35 | | 50.85 | 60 |
| 1000     Full opening | ↓ | 130 | .246 | ↓ | 48.50 | 9.30 | | 57.80 | 68 |
| 1200   Pyramid type units, self-supporting, to 30' clear opening, | | | | | | | | | |
| 1300     square or circular, single glazed, minimum | G-3 | 200 | .160 | SF Hor. | 24 | 6.05 | | 30.05 | 35.50 |
| 1310      Average | | 165 | .194 | | 33.50 | 7.35 | | 40.85 | 48.50 |
| 1400      Maximum | | 130 | .246 | | 48.50 | 9.30 | | 57.80 | 67.50 |
| 1500   Grid type, 4' to 10' modules, single glass glazed, minimum | | 200 | .160 | | 32 | 6.05 | | 38.05 | 44.50 |
| 1550     Maximum | | 128 | .250 | | 50.50 | 9.45 | | 59.95 | 70.50 |
| 1600   Preformed acrylic, minimum | | 300 | .107 | | 38 | 4.03 | | 42.03 | 48.50 |
| 1650     Maximum | ↓ | 175 | .183 | ↓ | 53 | 6.90 | | 59.90 | 69 |
| 1800   Skyroofs,dome type, self-supporting, to 100' clear opening, circular | | | | | | | | | |
| 1900     Rise to span ratio = 0.20 | | | | | | | | | |
| 1920      Minimum | G-3 | 197 | .162 | SF Hor. | 14.60 | 6.15 | | 20.75 | 25.50 |
| 1950      Maximum | | 113 | .283 | | 48.50 | 10.70 | | 59.20 | 70 |
| 2100     Rise to span ratio = 0.33, minimum | | 169 | .189 | | 29 | 7.15 | | 36.15 | 43 |
| 2150      Maximum | | 101 | .317 | | 57.50 | 11.95 | | 69.45 | 82 |
| 2200     Rise to span ratio = 0.50, minimum | | 148 | .216 | | 44 | 8.15 | | 52.15 | 61 |
| 2250      Maximum | | 87 | .368 | | 64 | 13.90 | | 77.90 | 92 |
| 2400   Ridge units, continuous, to 8' wide, double | | 130 | .246 | | 112 | 9.30 | | 121.30 | 137 |
| 2500     Single | | 200 | .160 | | 76.50 | 6.05 | | 82.55 | 94 |
| 2700   Ridge and furrow units, over 4' O.C., double, minimum | | 200 | .160 | | 24 | 6.05 | | 30.05 | 36 |
| 2750     Maximum | | 120 | .267 | | 44.50 | 10.05 | | 54.55 | 64.50 |
| 2800     Single, minimum | | 214 | .150 | | 20.50 | 5.65 | | 26.15 | 31.50 |
| 2850     Maximum | | 153 | .209 | ↓ | 43.50 | 7.90 | | 51.40 | 60 |
| 3000   Rolling roof, translucent panels, flat roof, mininum | | 253 | .126 | S.F. | 18.55 | 4.78 | | 23.33 | 28 |
| 3030     Maximum | | 160 | .200 | | 37 | 7.55 | | 44.55 | 52.50 |
| 3100   Lean-to skyroof, long span, double, minimum | | 197 | .162 | | 25 | 6.15 | | 31.15 | 37 |
| 3150     Maximum | | 101 | .317 | | 49.50 | 11.95 | | 61.45 | 73 |
| 3300     Single, minimum | | 321 | .100 | | 18.65 | 3.77 | | 22.42 | 26.50 |
| 3350     Maximum | ↓ | 160 | .200 | ↓ | 31 | 7.55 | | 38.55 | 45.50 |

## 08 51 13 – Aluminum Windows

| 08 51 13.10 Aluminum Sash | Crew | Daily Output | Labor-Hours | Unit | Material | 2008 Bare Costs Labor | Equipment | Total | Total Incl O&P |
|---|---|---|---|---|---|---|---|---|---|
| 0010 **ALUMINUM SASH** | | | | | | | | | |
| 0020 Stock, grade C, glaze & trim not incl., casement | 2 Sswk | 200 | .080 | S.F. | 31.50 | 3.44 | | 34.94 | 40.50 |
| 0050 Double hung | | 200 | .080 | | 32 | 3.44 | | 35.44 | 41 |
| 0100 Fixed casement | | 200 | .080 | | 12.60 | 3.44 | | 16.04 | 20 |
| 0150 Picture window | | 200 | .080 | | 13.55 | 3.44 | | 16.99 | 21 |
| 0200 Projected window | | 200 | .080 | | 29 | 3.44 | | 32.44 | 38 |
| 0250 Single hung | | 200 | .080 | | 14.65 | 3.44 | | 18.09 | 22.50 |
| 0300 Sliding | | 200 | .080 | | 18.95 | 3.44 | | 22.39 | 27 |
| 1000 Mullions for above, tubular | | 240 | .067 | L.F. | 4.95 | 2.87 | | 7.82 | 10.60 |
| 2000 Custom aluminum sash, grade HC, glazing not included, minimum | | 200 | .080 | S.F. | 35.50 | 3.44 | | 38.94 | 45 |
| 2100 Maximum | | 85 | .188 | " | 46 | 8.10 | | 54.10 | 65 |

### 08 51 13.20 Aluminum Windows

| | Crew | Daily Output | Labor-Hours | Unit | Material | 2008 Bare Costs Labor | Equipment | Total | Total Incl O&P |
|---|---|---|---|---|---|---|---|---|---|
| 0010 **ALUMINUM WINDOWS**, incl. frame and glazing, commercial grade | | | | | | | | | |
| 0020 See Div. 05 12 23.40 | | | | | | | | | |
| 1000 Stock units, casement, 3'-1" x 3'-2" opening | 2 Sswk | 10 | 1.600 | Ea. | 330 | 69 | | 399 | 485 |
| 1050 Add for storms | | | | | 106 | | | 106 | 117 |
| 1600 Projected, with screen, 3'-1" x 3'-2" opening | 2 Sswk | 10 | 1.600 | | 310 | 69 | | 379 | 470 |
| 1700 Add for storms | | | | | 104 | | | 104 | 114 |
| 2000 4'-5" x 5'-3" opening | 2 Sswk | 8 | 2 | | 355 | 86 | | 441 | 545 |
| 2100 Add for storms | | | | | 114 | | | 114 | 126 |
| 2500 Enamel finish windows, 3'-1" x 3'-2" | 2 Sswk | 10 | 1.600 | | 320 | 69 | | 389 | 480 |
| 2600 4'-5" x 5'-3" | | 8 | 2 | | 365 | 86 | | 451 | 555 |
| 3000 Single hung, 2' x 3' opening, enameled, standard glazed | | 10 | 1.600 | | 187 | 69 | | 256 | 330 |
| 3100 Insulating glass | | 10 | 1.600 | | 227 | 69 | | 296 | 375 |
| 3300 2'-8" x 6'-8" opening, standard glazed | | 8 | 2 | | 330 | 86 | | 416 | 515 |
| 3400 Insulating glass | | 8 | 2 | | 425 | 86 | | 511 | 620 |
| 3700 3'-4" x 5'-0" opening, standard glazed | | 9 | 1.778 | | 270 | 76.50 | | 346.50 | 435 |
| 3800 Insulating glass | | 9 | 1.778 | | 298 | 76.50 | | 374.50 | 470 |
| 3890 Awning type, 3' x 3' opening standard glass | | 14 | 1.143 | | 380 | 49 | | 429 | 510 |
| 3900 Insulating glass | | 14 | 1.143 | | 405 | 49 | | 454 | 535 |
| 3910 3' x 4' opening, standard glass | | 10 | 1.600 | | 445 | 69 | | 514 | 615 |
| 3920 Insulating glass | | 10 | 1.600 | | 510 | 69 | | 579 | 690 |
| 3930 3' x 5'-4" opening, standard glass | | 10 | 1.600 | | 535 | 69 | | 604 | 715 |
| 3940 Insulating glass | | 10 | 1.600 | | 635 | 69 | | 704 | 820 |
| 3950 4' x 5'-4" opening, standard glass | | 9 | 1.778 | | 590 | 76.50 | | 666.50 | 790 |
| 3960 Insulating glass | | 9 | 1.778 | | 705 | 76.50 | | 781.50 | 915 |
| 4000 Sliding aluminum, 3' x 2' opening, standard glazed | | 10 | 1.600 | | 198 | 69 | | 267 | 340 |
| 4100 Insulating glass | | 10 | 1.600 | | 212 | 69 | | 281 | 355 |
| 4300 5' x 3' opening, standard glazed | | 9 | 1.778 | | 300 | 76.50 | | 376.50 | 470 |
| 4400 Insulating glass | | 9 | 1.778 | | 350 | 76.50 | | 426.50 | 525 |
| 4600 8' x 4' opening, standard glazed | | 6 | 2.667 | | 320 | 115 | | 435 | 555 |
| 4700 Insulating glass | | 6 | 2.667 | | 510 | 115 | | 625 | 770 |
| 5000 9' x 5' opening, standard glazed | | 4 | 4 | | 480 | 172 | | 652 | 840 |
| 5100 Insulating glass | | 4 | 4 | | 770 | 172 | | 942 | 1,150 |
| 5500 Sliding, with thermal barrier and screen, 6' x 4', 2 track | | 8 | 2 | | 655 | 86 | | 741 | 880 |
| 5700 4 track | | 8 | 2 | | 830 | 86 | | 916 | 1,075 |
| 6000 For above units with bronze finish, add | | | | | 12% | | | | |
| 6200 For installation in concrete openings, add | | | | | 5% | | | | |

## 08 51 23 – Steel Windows

### 08 51 23.10 Steel Sash

| | Crew | Daily Output | Labor-Hours | Unit | Material | 2008 Bare Costs Labor | Equipment | Total | Total Incl O&P |
|---|---|---|---|---|---|---|---|---|---|
| 0010 **STEEL SASH** Custom units, glazing and trim not included    R085123-10 | | | | | | | | | |
| 0100 Casement, 100% vented | 2 Sswk | 200 | .080 | S.F. | 44 | 3.44 | | 47.44 | 54.50 |

# 08 51 Metal Windows

## 08 51 23 – Steel Windows

### 08 51 23.10 Steel Sash

| 08 51 23.10 Steel Sash | | Crew | Daily Output | Labor-Hours | Unit | Material | 2008 Bare Costs Labor | Equipment | Total | Total Incl O&P |
|---|---|---|---|---|---|---|---|---|---|---|
| 0200 | 50% vented | 2 Sswk | 200 | .080 | S.F. | 40 | 3.44 | | 43.44 | 50 |
| 0300 | Fixed | | 200 | .080 | | 27.50 | 3.44 | | 30.94 | 36.50 |
| 1000 | Projected, commercial, 40% vented | | 200 | .080 | | 46.50 | 3.44 | | 49.94 | 57 |
| 1100 | Intermediate, 50% vented | | 200 | .080 | | 51 | 3.44 | | 54.44 | 62.50 |
| 1500 | Industrial, horizontally pivoted | | 200 | .080 | | 48 | 3.44 | | 51.44 | 59 |
| 1600 | Fixed | | 200 | .080 | | 27.50 | 3.44 | | 30.94 | 36 |
| 2000 | Industrial security sash, 50% vented | | 200 | .080 | | 52 | 3.44 | | 55.44 | 63 |
| 2100 | Fixed | | 200 | .080 | | 42 | 3.44 | | 45.44 | 52.50 |
| 2500 | Picture window | | 200 | .080 | | 26.50 | 3.44 | | 29.94 | 35 |
| 3000 | Double hung | | 200 | .080 | | 50.50 | 3.44 | | 53.94 | 61.50 |
| 5000 | Mullions for above, open interior face | | 240 | .067 | L.F. | 9 | 2.87 | | 11.87 | 15.05 |
| 5100 | With interior cover | | 240 | .067 | " | 14.85 | 2.87 | | 17.72 | 21.50 |

### 08 51 23.20 Steel Windows

| 08 51 23.20 Steel Windows | | | Crew | Daily Output | Labor-Hours | Unit | Material | 2008 Bare Costs Labor | Equipment | Total | Total Incl O&P |
|---|---|---|---|---|---|---|---|---|---|---|---|
| 0010 | **STEEL WINDOWS** Stock, including frame, trim and insul. Glass | | | | | | | | | | |
| 0020 | See Div. 13 34 19.50 | | | | | | | | | | |
| 1000 | Custom units, double hung, 2'-8" x 4'-6" opening | R085123-10 | 2 Sswk | 12 | 1.333 | Ea. | 630 | 57.50 | | 687.50 | 800 |
| 1100 | 2'-4" x 3'-9" opening | | | 12 | 1.333 | | 520 | 57.50 | | 577.50 | 680 |
| 1500 | Commercial projected, 3'-9" x 5'-5" opening | | | 10 | 1.600 | | 1,100 | 69 | | 1,169 | 1,350 |
| 1600 | 6'-9" x 4'-1" opening | | | 7 | 2.286 | | 1,450 | 98.50 | | 1,548.50 | 1,775 |
| 2000 | Intermediate projected, 2'-9" x 4'-1" opening | | | 12 | 1.333 | | 620 | 57.50 | | 677.50 | 785 |
| 2100 | 4'-1" x 5'-5" opening | | | 10 | 1.600 | | 1,250 | 69 | | 1,319 | 1,500 |
| 9000 | Minimum labor/equipment charge | | 1 Sswk | 3 | 2.667 | Job | | 115 | | 115 | 207 |

## 08 51 66 – Metal Window Screens

### 08 51 66.10 Screens

| 08 51 66.10 Screens | | Crew | Daily Output | Labor-Hours | Unit | Material | 2008 Bare Costs Labor | Equipment | Total | Total Incl O&P |
|---|---|---|---|---|---|---|---|---|---|---|
| 0010 | **SCREENS** | | | | | | | | | |
| 0020 | For metal sash, aluminum or bronze mesh, flat screen | 2 Sswk | 1200 | .013 | S.F. | 3.80 | .57 | | 4.37 | 5.20 |
| 0500 | Wicket screen, inside window | | 1000 | .016 | | 5.75 | .69 | | 6.44 | 7.60 |
| 0800 | Security screen, aluminum frame with stainless steel cloth | | 1200 | .013 | | 20.50 | .57 | | 21.07 | 23.50 |
| 0900 | Steel grate, painted, on steel frame | | 1600 | .010 | | 11.45 | .43 | | 11.88 | 13.40 |
| 1000 | For solar louvers, add | | 160 | .100 | | 21.50 | 4.30 | | 25.80 | 31.50 |
| 4000 | See Div. 05 58 27.90 | | | | | | | | | |

# 08 52 Wood Windows

## 08 52 10 – Plain Wood Windows

### 08 52 10.20 Awning Window

| 08 52 10.20 Awning Window | | Crew | Daily Output | Labor-Hours | Unit | Material | 2008 Bare Costs Labor | Equipment | Total | Total Incl O&P |
|---|---|---|---|---|---|---|---|---|---|---|
| 0010 | **AWNING WINDOW**, Including frame, screens and grills | | | | | | | | | |
| 0100 | Average quality, builders model, 34" x 22", double insulated glass | 1 Carp | 10 | .800 | Ea. | 238 | 30.50 | | 268.50 | 310 |
| 0200 | Low E glass | | 10 | .800 | | 252 | 30.50 | | 282.50 | 325 |
| 0300 | 40" x 28", double insulated glass | | 9 | .889 | | 300 | 34 | | 334 | 385 |
| 0400 | Low E Glass | | 9 | .889 | | 320 | 34 | | 354 | 405 |
| 0500 | 48" x 36", double insulated glass | | 8 | 1 | | 440 | 38 | | 478 | 545 |
| 0600 | Low E glass | | 8 | 1 | | 465 | 38 | | 503 | 570 |
| 1000 | Vinyl clad, 34" x 22" | | 10 | .800 | | 254 | 30.50 | | 284.50 | 325 |
| 1100 | 40" x 22" | | 10 | .800 | | 277 | 30.50 | | 307.50 | 355 |
| 1200 | 36" x 28" | | 9 | .889 | | 295 | 34 | | 329 | 380 |
| 1300 | 36" x 36" | | 9 | .889 | | 330 | 34 | | 364 | 415 |
| 1400 | 48" x 28" | | 8 | 1 | | 355 | 38 | | 393 | 450 |
| 1500 | 60" x 36" | | 8 | 1 | | 510 | 38 | | 548 | 620 |
| 2200 | Metal clad, 36" x 25" | | 9 | .889 | | 259 | 34 | | 293 | 340 |
| 2300 | 40" x 30" | | 9 | .889 | | 325 | 34 | | 359 | 410 |

243

# 08 52 Wood Windows

## 08 52 10 – Plain Wood Windows

| 08 52 10.20 Awning Window | | Crew | Daily Output | Labor-Hours | Unit | Material | 2008 Bare Costs Labor | Equipment | Total | Total Incl O&P |
|---|---|---|---|---|---|---|---|---|---|---|
| 2400 | 48" x 28" | 1 Carp | 8 | 1 | Ea. | 330 | 38 | | 368 | 425 |
| 2500 | 60" x 36" | ↓ | 8 | 1 | ↓ | 350 | 38 | | 388 | 445 |

| 08 52 10.30 Wood Windows | | Crew | Daily Output | Labor-Hours | Unit | Material | Labor | Equipment | Total | Total Incl O&P |
|---|---|---|---|---|---|---|---|---|---|---|
| 0010 | **WOOD WINDOWS**, double hung | | | | | | | | | |
| 3200 | 20 S.F. and over | 1 Carp | 106 | .075 | S.F. | 15.90 | 2.88 | | 18.78 | 22 |
| 3800 | Triple glazing for above, add | | | | | 8 | | | 8 | 8.80 |
| 6000 | Replacement sash, double hung, double glazing, to 12 S.F. | 1 Carp | 64 | .125 | | 19.55 | 4.76 | | 24.31 | 29 |
| 6100 | 12 S.F. to 20 S.F. | | 94 | .085 | ↓ | 18.20 | 3.24 | | 21.44 | 25 |
| 7000 | Sash, single lite, 2'-0" x 2'-0" high | | 20 | .400 | Ea. | 41.50 | 15.25 | | 56.75 | 69 |
| 7050 | 2'-6" x 2'-0" high | | 19 | .421 | | 49 | 16.05 | | 65.05 | 78.50 |
| 7100 | 2'-6" x 2'-6" high | | 18 | .444 | | 52.50 | 16.95 | | 69.45 | 84.50 |
| 7150 | 3'-0" x 2'-0" high | ↓ | 17 | .471 | ↓ | 64 | 17.95 | | 81.95 | 98.50 |

| 08 52 10.40 Casement Window | | Crew | Daily Output | Labor-Hours | Unit | Material | Labor | Equipment | Total | Total Incl O&P |
|---|---|---|---|---|---|---|---|---|---|---|
| 0010 | **CASEMENT WINDOW**, including frame, screen and grills | | | | | | | | | |
| 0100 | Avg. quality, bldrs. model, 2'-0" x 3'-0" H, dbl. insulated glass | 1 Carp | 10 | .800 | Ea. | 272 | 30.50 | | 302.50 | 345 |
| 0150 | Low E glass _CN_ | | 10 | .800 | | 281 | 30.50 | | 311.50 | 360 |
| 0200 | 2'-0" x 4'-6" high, double insulated glass | | 9 | .889 | | 340 | 34 | | 374 | 430 |
| 0250 | Low E glass | | 9 | .889 | | 350 | 34 | | 384 | 440 |
| 0300 | 2'-4" x 6'-0" high, double insulated glass | | 8 | 1 | | 405 | 38 | | 443 | 505 |
| 0350 | Low E glass | | 8 | 1 | | 435 | 38 | | 473 | 535 |
| 0522 | Vinyl clad, premium, double insulated glass, 2'-0" x 3'-0" | | 10 | .800 | | 268 | 30.50 | | 298.50 | 345 |
| 0524 | 2'-0" x 4'-0" | | 9 | .889 | | 315 | 34 | | 349 | 400 |
| 0525 | 2'-0" x 5'-0" | | 8 | 1 | | 360 | 38 | | 398 | 455 |
| 0528 | 2'-0" x 6'-0" | ↓ | 8 | 1 | ↓ | 405 | 38 | | 443 | 505 |
| 2000 | Bay, casement units, 8' x 5', 30° angle, w/screens, dbl Insul glass | 2 Carp | 2.50 | 6.400 | Opng. | 1,450 | 244 | | 1,694 | 1,975 |
| 2100 | Low E glass | " | 2.50 | 6.400 | " | 1,525 | 244 | | 1,769 | 2,050 |
| 8100 | Metal clad, deluxe, dbl. insul. glass, 2'-0" x 3'-0" high | 1 Carp | 10 | .800 | Ea. | 210 | 30.50 | | 240.50 | 279 |
| 8120 | 2'-0" x 4'-0" high | | 9 | .889 | | 253 | 34 | | 287 | 330 |
| 8140 | 2'-0" x 5'-0" high | | 8 | 1 | | 288 | 38 | | 326 | 375 |
| 8160 | 2'-0" x 6'-0" high | ↓ | 8 | 1 | ↓ | 330 | 38 | | 368 | 425 |
| 8200 | For multiple leaf units, deduct for stationary sash | | | | | | | | | |
| 8220 | 2' high | | | | Ea. | 22 | | | 22 | 24 |
| 8240 | 4'-6" high | | | | | 25 | | | 25 | 28 |
| 8260 | 6' high | | | | | 33.50 | | | 33.50 | 37 |
| 8300 | For installation, add per leaf | | | | ↓ | | 15% | | | |

| 08 52 10.50 Double Hung | | Crew | Daily Output | Labor-Hours | Unit | Material | Labor | Equipment | Total | Total Incl O&P |
|---|---|---|---|---|---|---|---|---|---|---|
| 0010 | **DOUBLE HUNG**, Including frame, screens and grills  R085216-10 | | | | | | | | | |
| 0100 | Avg. quality, bldrs. model, 2'-0" x 3'-0" high, dbl insul. glass | 1 Carp | 10 | .800 | Ea. | 183 | 30.50 | | 213.50 | 250 |
| 0150 | Low E glass | | 10 | .800 | | 208 | 30.50 | | 238.50 | 277 |
| 0200 | 3'-0" x 4'-0" high, double insulated glass | | 9 | .889 | | 255 | 34 | | 289 | 335 |
| 0250 | Low E glass | | 9 | .889 | | 263 | 34 | | 297 | 345 |
| 0300 | 4'-0" x 4'-6" high, double insulated glass | | 8 | 1 | | 315 | 38 | | 353 | 405 |
| 0350 | Low E glass | | 8 | 1 | | 340 | 38 | | 378 | 435 |
| 1000 | Vinyl clad, premium, double insulated glass, 2'-6" x 3'-0" | | 10 | .800 | | 221 | 30.50 | | 251.50 | 291 |
| 1100 | 3'-0" x 3'-6" | | 10 | .800 | | 260 | 30.50 | | 290.50 | 335 |
| 1200 | 3'-0" x 4'-0" | | 9 | .889 | | 365 | 34 | | 399 | 455 |
| 1300 | 3'-0" x 4'-6" | | 9 | .889 | | 345 | 34 | | 379 | 435 |
| 1400 | 3'-0" x 5'-0" | | 8 | 1 | | 315 | 38 | | 353 | 405 |
| 1500 | 3'-6" x 6'-0" | | 8 | 1 | | 365 | 38 | | 403 | 465 |
| 2000 | Metal clad, deluxe, dbl. insul. glass, 2'-6" x 3'-0" high | | 10 | .800 | | 243 | 30.50 | | 273.50 | 315 |
| 2100 | 3'-0" x 3'-6" high | | 10 | .800 | | 277 | 30.50 | | 307.50 | 355 |
| 2200 | 3'-0" x 4'-0" high | ↓ | 9 | .889 | ↓ | 291 | 34 | | 325 | 375 |

# 08 52 Wood Windows

## 08 52 10 – Plain Wood Windows

### 08 52 10.50 Double Hung

| | | Crew | Daily Output | Labor-Hours | Unit | Material | 2008 Bare Costs Labor | Equipment | Total | Total Incl O&P |
|---|---|---|---|---|---|---|---|---|---|---|
| 2300 | 3'-0" x 4'-6" high | 1 Carp | 9 | .889 | Ea. | 305 | 34 | | 339 | 390 |
| 2400 | 3'-0" x 5'-0" high | | 8 | 1 | | 335 | 38 | | 373 | 425 |
| 2500 | 3'-6" x 6'-0" high | | 8 | 1 | | 400 | 38 | | 438 | 505 |

### 08 52 10.55 Picture Window

| | | Crew | Daily Output | Labor-Hours | Unit | Material | Labor | Equipment | Total | Total Incl O&P |
|---|---|---|---|---|---|---|---|---|---|---|
| 0010 | **PICTURE WINDOW**, Including frame and grills | | | | | | | | | |
| 0100 | Average quality, bldrs. model, 3'-6" x 4'-0" high, dbl insulated glass | 2 Carp | 12 | 1.333 | Ea. | 420 | 51 | | 471 | 545 |
| 0150 | Low E glass | | 12 | 1.333 | | 460 | 51 | | 511 | 590 |
| 0200 | 4'-0" x 4'-6" high, double insulated glass | | 11 | 1.455 | | 440 | 55.50 | | 495.50 | 570 |
| 0250 | Low E glass | | 11 | 1.455 | | 460 | 55.50 | | 515.50 | 590 |
| 0300 | 5'-0" x 4'-0" high, double insulated glass | | 11 | 1.455 | | 515 | 55.50 | | 570.50 | 650 |
| 0350 | Low E glass | | 11 | 1.455 | | 535 | 55.50 | | 590.50 | 675 |
| 0400 | 6'-0" x 4'-6" high, double insulated glass | | 10 | 1.600 | | 560 | 61 | | 621 | 710 |
| 0450 | Low E glass | | 10 | 1.600 | | 575 | 61 | | 636 | 730 |

### 08 52 10.65 Wood Sash

| | | Crew | Daily Output | Labor-Hours | Unit | Material | Labor | Equipment | Total | Total Incl O&P |
|---|---|---|---|---|---|---|---|---|---|---|
| 0010 | **WOOD SASH,** Including glazing but not trim | | | | | | | | | |
| 0050 | Custom, 5'-0" x 4'-0", 1" dbl. glazed, 3/16" thick lites | 2 Carp | 3.20 | 5 | Ea. | 166 | 191 | | 357 | 480 |
| 0100 | 1/4" thick lites | | 5 | 3.200 | | 171 | 122 | | 293 | 380 |
| 0200 | 1" thick, triple glazed | | 5 | 3.200 | | 390 | 122 | | 512 | 620 |
| 0300 | 7'-0" x 4'-6" high, 1" double glazed, 3/16" thick lites | | 4.30 | 3.721 | | 400 | 142 | | 542 | 660 |
| 0400 | 1/4" thick lites | | 4.30 | 3.721 | | 450 | 142 | | 592 | 715 |
| 0500 | 1" thick, triple glazed | | 4.30 | 3.721 | | 515 | 142 | | 657 | 785 |
| 0600 | 8'-6" x 5'-0" high, 1" double glazed, 3/16" thick lites | | 3.50 | 4.571 | | 540 | 174 | | 714 | 860 |
| 0700 | 1/4" thick lites | | 3.50 | 4.571 | | 590 | 174 | | 764 | 915 |
| 0800 | 1" thick, triple glazed | | 3.50 | 4.571 | | 595 | 174 | | 769 | 925 |
| 0900 | Window frames only, based on perimeter length | | | | L.F. | 3.65 | | | 3.65 | 4.02 |
| 1200 | Window sill, stock, per lineal foot | | | | | 7.60 | | | 7.60 | 8.35 |
| 1250 | Casing, stock | | | | | 3.05 | | | 3.05 | 3.36 |

### 08 52 10.70 Sliding Windows

| | | Crew | Daily Output | Labor-Hours | Unit | Material | Labor | Equipment | Total | Total Incl O&P |
|---|---|---|---|---|---|---|---|---|---|---|
| 0010 | **SLIDING WINDOWS** | | | | | | | | | |
| 0100 | Average quality, bldrs. model, 3'-0" x 3'-0" high, double insulated | 1 Carp | 10 | .800 | Ea. | 240 | 30.50 | | 270.50 | 310 |
| 0120 | Low E glass | | 10 | .800 | | 262 | 30.50 | | 292.50 | 335 |
| 0200 | 4'-0" x 3'-6" high, double insulated | | 9 | .889 | | 281 | 34 | | 315 | 365 |
| 0220 | Low E glass | | 9 | .889 | | 298 | 34 | | 332 | 385 |
| 0300 | 6'-0" x 5'-0" high, double insulated | | 8 | 1 | | 415 | 38 | | 453 | 515 |
| 0320 | Low E glass | | 8 | 1 | | 455 | 38 | | 493 | 560 |

## 08 52 13 – Metal-Clad Wood Windows

### 08 52 13.10 Awing Windows, Metal-Clad

| | | Crew | Daily Output | Labor-Hours | Unit | Material | Labor | Equipment | Total | Total Incl O&P |
|---|---|---|---|---|---|---|---|---|---|---|
| 0010 | **AWING WINDOWS, METAL-CLAD** | | | | | | | | | |
| 2000 | Metal clad, awning deluxe, double insulated glass, 34" x 22" | 1 Carp | 10 | .800 | Ea. | 237 | 30.50 | | 267.50 | 310 |
| 2100 | 40" x 22" | " | 10 | .800 | " | 278 | 30.50 | | 308.50 | 355 |

### 08 52 13.35 Picture and Sliding Windows Metal-Clad

| | | Crew | Daily Output | Labor-Hours | Unit | Material | Labor | Equipment | Total | Total Incl O&P |
|---|---|---|---|---|---|---|---|---|---|---|
| 0010 | **PICTURE AND SLIDING WINDOWS METAL-CLAD** | | | | | | | | | |
| 2000 | Metal clad, dlx picture, dbl. insul. glass, 4'-0" x 4'-0" high | 2 Carp | 12 | 1.333 | Ea. | 335 | 51 | | 386 | 450 |
| 2100 | 4'-0" x 6'-0" high | | 11 | 1.455 | | 495 | 55.50 | | 550.50 | 630 |
| 2200 | 5'-0" x 6'-0" high | | 10 | 1.600 | | 545 | 61 | | 606 | 695 |
| 2300 | 6'-0" x 6'-0" high | | 10 | 1.600 | | 625 | 61 | | 686 | 785 |
| 2400 | Metal clad, dlx sliding, double insulated glass, 3'-0" x 3'-0" high | 1 Carp | 10 | .800 | | 305 | 30.50 | | 335.50 | 390 |
| 2420 | 4'-0" x 3'-6" high | | 9 | .889 | | 380 | 34 | | 414 | 470 |
| 2440 | 5'-0" x 4'-0" high | | 9 | .889 | | 455 | 34 | | 489 | 555 |
| 2460 | 6'-0" x 5'-0" high | | 8 | 1 | | 680 | 38 | | 718 | 810 |

# 08 52 Wood Windows

## 08 52 16 – Plastic-Clad Wood Windows

### 08 52 16.10 Bow Window

| | | Crew | Daily Output | Labor-Hours | Unit | Material | 2008 Bare Costs Labor | Equipment | Total | Total Incl O&P |
|---|---|---|---|---|---|---|---|---|---|---|
| 0010 | **BOW WINDOW** Including frames, screens, and grilles | | | | | | | | | |
| 0020 | End panels operable | | | | | | | | | |
| 1000 | Bow type, casement, wood, bldrs mdl, 8' x 5' dbl insltd glass, 4 panel | 2 Carp | 10 | 1.600 | Ea. | 1,500 | 61 | | 1,561 | 1,750 |
| 1050 | Low E glass | | 10 | 1.600 | | 1,275 | 61 | | 1,336 | 1,500 |
| 1100 | 10'-0" x 5'-0", double insulated glass, 6 panels | | 6 | 2.667 | | 1,325 | 102 | | 1,427 | 1,625 |
| 1200 | Low E glass, 6 panels | | 6 | 2.667 | | 1,450 | 102 | | 1,552 | 1,750 |
| 1300 | Vinyl clad, bldrs model, double insulated glass, 6'-0" x 4'-0", 3 panel | | 10 | 1.600 | | 1,775 | 61 | | 1,836 | 2,075 |
| 1340 | 9'-0" x 4'-0", 4 panel | | 8 | 2 | | 1,450 | 76 | | 1,526 | 1,725 |
| 1380 | 10'-0" x 6'-0", 5 panels | | 7 | 2.286 | | 2,375 | 87 | | 2,462 | 2,725 |
| 1420 | 12'-0" x 6'-0", 6 panels | | 6 | 2.667 | | 3,000 | 102 | | 3,102 | 3,450 |
| 1600 | Metal clad, casement, bldrs mdl, 6'-0" x 4'-0", dbl insltd gls, 3 panels | | 10 | 1.600 | | 860 | 61 | | 921 | 1,050 |
| 1640 | 9'-0" x 4'-0", 4 panels | | 8 | 2 | | 1,200 | 76 | | 1,276 | 1,450 |
| 1680 | 10'-0" x 5'-0", 5 panels | | 7 | 2.286 | | 1,650 | 87 | | 1,737 | 1,950 |
| 1720 | 12'-0" x 6'-0", 6 panels | | 6 | 2.667 | | 2,300 | 102 | | 2,402 | 2,700 |
| 2000 | Bay window, casement, builders model, 8' x 5' dbl insul glass, 4 panels | | 10 | 1.600 | | 1,700 | 61 | | 1,761 | 1,975 |
| 2050 | Low E glass, | | 10 | 1.600 | | 2,050 | 61 | | 2,111 | 2,375 |
| 2100 | 12'-0" x 6'-0", double insulated glass, 6 panels | | 6 | 2.667 | | 2,125 | 102 | | 2,227 | 2,475 |
| 2200 | Low E glass | | 6 | 2.667 | | 2,175 | 102 | | 2,277 | 2,525 |
| 2280 | 6'-0" x 4'-0" | | 11 | 1.455 | | 1,100 | 55.50 | | 1,155.50 | 1,300 |
| 2300 | Vinyl clad, premium, double insulated glass, 8'-0" x 5'-0" | | 10 | 1.600 | | 1,300 | 61 | | 1,361 | 1,525 |
| 2340 | 10'-0" x 5'-0" | | 8 | 2 | | 1,850 | 76 | | 1,926 | 2,150 |
| 2380 | 10'-0" x 6'-0" | | 7 | 2.286 | | 1,925 | 87 | | 2,012 | 2,250 |
| 2420 | 12'-0" x 6'-0" | | 6 | 2.667 | | 2,300 | 102 | | 2,402 | 2,675 |
| 2600 | Metal clad, deluxe, dbl insul. glass, 8'-0" x 5'-0" high, 4 panels | | 10 | 1.600 | | 1,500 | 61 | | 1,561 | 1,750 |
| 2640 | 10'-0" x 5'-0" high, 5 panels | | 8 | 2 | | 1,625 | 76 | | 1,701 | 1,900 |
| 2680 | 10'-0" x 6'-0" high, 5 panels | | 7 | 2.286 | | 1,900 | 87 | | 1,987 | 2,225 |
| 2720 | 12'-0" x 6'-0" high, 6 panels | | 6 | 2.667 | | 2,650 | 102 | | 2,752 | 3,050 |
| 3000 | Double hung, bldrs. model, bay, 8' x 4' high, dbl insulated glass | | 10 | 1.600 | | 1,200 | 61 | | 1,261 | 1,425 |
| 3050 | Low E glass | | 10 | 1.600 | | 1,275 | 61 | | 1,336 | 1,525 |
| 3100 | 9'-0" x 5'-0" high, doublel insulated glass | | 6 | 2.667 | | 1,300 | 102 | | 1,402 | 1,575 |
| 3200 | Low E glass | | 6 | 2.667 | | 1,350 | 102 | | 1,452 | 1,650 |
| 3300 | Vinyl clad, premium, double insulated glass, 7'-0" x 4'-6" | | 10 | 1.600 | | 1,250 | 61 | | 1,311 | 1,450 |
| 3340 | 8'-0" x 4'-6" | | 8 | 2 | | 1,275 | 76 | | 1,351 | 1,525 |
| 3380 | 8'-0" x 5'-0" | | 7 | 2.286 | | 1,325 | 87 | | 1,412 | 1,575 |
| 3420 | 9'-0" x 5'-0" | | 6 | 2.667 | | 1,350 | 102 | | 1,452 | 1,650 |
| 3600 | Metal clad, deluxe, dbl insul. glass, 7'-0" x 4'-0" high | | 10 | 1.600 | | 1,150 | 61 | | 1,211 | 1,350 |
| 3640 | 8'-0" x 4'-0" high | | 8 | 2 | | 1,175 | 76 | | 1,251 | 1,425 |
| 3680 | 8'-0" x 5'-0" high | | 7 | 2.286 | | 1,225 | 87 | | 1,312 | 1,475 |
| 3720 | 9'-0" x 5'-0" high | | 6 | 2.667 | | 1,300 | 102 | | 1,402 | 1,575 |

### 08 52 16.30 Palladian Windows

| | | Crew | Daily Output | Labor-Hours | Unit | Material | 2008 Bare Costs Labor | Equipment | Total | Total Incl O&P |
|---|---|---|---|---|---|---|---|---|---|---|
| 0010 | **PALLADIAN WINDOWS** | | | | | | | | | |
| 0020 | Vinyl clad, double insulated glass, including frame and grills | | | | | | | | | |
| 0040 | 3'-2" x 2'-6" high | 2 Carp | 11 | 1.455 | Ea. | 1,150 | 55.50 | | 1,205.50 | 1,350 |
| 0060 | 3'-2" x 4'-10" | | 11 | 1.455 | | 1,475 | 55.50 | | 1,530.50 | 1,700 |
| 0080 | 3'-2" x 6'-4" | | 10 | 1.600 | | 1,675 | 61 | | 1,736 | 1,950 |
| 0100 | 4'-0" x 4'-0" | | 10 | 1.600 | | 1,450 | 61 | | 1,511 | 1,700 |
| 0120 | 4'-0" x 5'-4" | 3 Carp | 10 | 2.400 | | 1,750 | 91.50 | | 1,841.50 | 2,075 |
| 0140 | 4'-0" x 6'-0" | | 9 | 2.667 | | 1,950 | 102 | | 2,052 | 2,300 |
| 0160 | 4'-0" x 7'-4" | | 9 | 2.667 | | 1,950 | 102 | | 2,052 | 2,300 |
| 0180 | 5'-5" x 4'-10" | | 9 | 2.667 | | 2,050 | 102 | | 2,152 | 2,425 |
| 0200 | 5'-5" x 6'-10" | | 9 | 2.667 | | 2,375 | 102 | | 2,477 | 2,750 |
| 0220 | 5'-5" x 7'-9" | | 9 | 2.667 | | 2,575 | 102 | | 2,677 | 2,975 |

# 08 52 Wood Windows

## 08 52 16 – Plastic-Clad Wood Windows

### 08 52 16.30 Palladian Windows

| | | Crew | Daily Output | Labor-Hours | Unit | Material | 2008 Bare Costs Labor | Equipment | Total | Total Incl O&P |
|---|---|---|---|---|---|---|---|---|---|---|
| 0240 | 6'-0" x 7'-11" | 3 Carp | 8 | 3 | Ea. | 3,225 | 114 | | 3,339 | 3,725 |
| 0260 | 8'-0" x 6'-0" | ↓ | 8 | 3 | ↓ | 2,850 | 114 | | 2,964 | 3,325 |

### 08 52 16.40 Transom Windows

| | | Crew | Daily Output | Labor-Hours | Unit | Material | Labor | Equipment | Total | Total Incl O&P |
|---|---|---|---|---|---|---|---|---|---|---|
| 0010 | **TRANSOM WINDOWS** | | | | | | | | | |
| 1000 | Vinyl clad, premium, dbl. insul. glass, 4'-0" x 4'-0" | 2 Carp | 12 | 1.333 | Ea. | 480 | 51 | | 531 | 610 |
| 1100 | 4'-0" x 6'-0" | ↓ | 11 | 1.455 | | 910 | 55.50 | | 965.50 | 1,075 |
| 1200 | 5'-0" x 6'-0" | | 10 | 1.600 | | 1,000 | 61 | | 1,061 | 1,200 |
| 1300 | 6'-0" x 6'-0" | ↓ | 10 | 1.600 | ↓ | 1,025 | 61 | | 1,086 | 1,225 |

### 08 52 16.70 Vinyl Clad, Premium, DBL. Insulated Glass

| | | Crew | Daily Output | Labor-Hours | Unit | Material | Labor | Equipment | Total | Total Incl O&P |
|---|---|---|---|---|---|---|---|---|---|---|
| 0010 | **VINYL CLAD, PREMIUM, DBL. INSULATED GLASS** | | | | | | | | | |
| 1000 | Sliding, 3'-0" x 3'-0" | 1 Carp | 10 | .800 | Ea. | 565 | 30.50 | | 595.50 | 675 |
| 1050 | 4'-0" x 3'-6" | | 9 | .889 | | 665 | 34 | | 699 | 785 |
| 1100 | 5'-0" x 4'-0" | | 9 | .889 | | 850 | 34 | | 884 | 990 |
| 1150 | 6'-0" x 5'-0" | ↓ | 8 | 1 | ↓ | 1,075 | 38 | | 1,113 | 1,225 |

## 08 52 50 – Window Accessories

### 08 52 50.10 Window Grille or Muntin

| | | Crew | Daily Output | Labor-Hours | Unit | Material | Labor | Equipment | Total | Total Incl O&P |
|---|---|---|---|---|---|---|---|---|---|---|
| 0010 | **WINDOW GRILLE OR MUNTIN,** snap in type | | | | | | | | | |
| 0020 | Standard pattern interior grills | | | | | | | | | |
| 2000 | Wood, awning window, glass size 28" x 16" high | 1 Carp | 30 | .267 | Ea. | 22 | 10.15 | | 32.15 | 40.50 |
| 2060 | 44" x 24" high | | 32 | .250 | | 32 | 9.55 | | 41.55 | 50.50 |
| 2100 | Casement, glass size, 20" x 36" high | | 30 | .267 | | 27 | 10.15 | | 37.15 | 46 |
| 2180 | 20" x 56" high | | 32 | .250 | ↓ | 39 | 9.55 | | 48.55 | 58 |
| 2200 | Double hung, glass size, 16" x 24" high | | 24 | .333 | Set | 47.50 | 12.70 | | 60.20 | 72.50 |
| 2280 | 32" x 32" high | | 34 | .235 | " | 127 | 8.95 | | 135.95 | 154 |
| 2500 | Picture, glass size, 48" x 48" high | | 30 | .267 | Ea. | 145 | 10.15 | | 155.15 | 176 |
| 2580 | 60" x 68" high | | 28 | .286 | " | 109 | 10.90 | | 119.90 | 137 |
| 2600 | Sliding, glass size, 14" x 36" high | | 24 | .333 | Set | 25 | 12.70 | | 37.70 | 47.50 |
| 2680 | 36" x 36" high | ↓ | 22 | .364 | " | 39 | 13.85 | | 52.85 | 64.50 |

## 08 52 66 – Wood Window Screens

### 08 52 66.10 Wood Screens

| | | Crew | Daily Output | Labor-Hours | Unit | Material | Labor | Equipment | Total | Total Incl O&P |
|---|---|---|---|---|---|---|---|---|---|---|
| 0010 | **WOOD SCREENS** | | | | | | | | | |
| 0020 | Over 3 S.F., 3/4" frames | 2 Carp | 375 | .043 | S.F. | 4.25 | 1.63 | | 5.88 | 7.20 |
| 0100 | 1-1/8" frames | " | 375 | .043 | " | 7.30 | 1.63 | | 8.93 | 10.55 |

## 08 52 69 – Wood Storm Windows

### 08 52 69.10 Storm Windows

| | | Crew | Daily Output | Labor-Hours | Unit | Material | Labor | Equipment | Total | Total Incl O&P |
|---|---|---|---|---|---|---|---|---|---|---|
| 0010 | **STORM WINDOWS,** aluminum residential | | | | | | | | | |
| 0300 | Basement, mill finish, incl. fiberglass screen | | | | | | | | | |
| 0320 | 1'-10" x 1'-0" high | 2 Carp | 30 | .533 | Ea. | 30.50 | 20.50 | | 51 | 65 |
| 0340 | 2'-9" x 1'-6" high | " | 30 | .533 | " | 33.50 | 20.50 | | 54 | 68 |
| 1600 | Double-hung, combination, storm & screen | | | | | | | | | |
| 2000 | Average quality, clear anodic coating, 2'-0" x 3'-5" high | 2 Carp | 30 | .533 | Ea. | 80.50 | 20.50 | | 101 | 120 |
| 2020 | 2'-6" x 5'-0" high | | 28 | .571 | | 100 | 22 | | 122 | 144 |
| 2040 | 4'-0" x 6'-0" high | | 25 | .640 | | 119 | 24.50 | | 143.50 | 169 |
| 2400 | White painted, 2'-0" x 3'-5" high | | 30 | .533 | | 79 | 20.50 | | 99.50 | 119 |
| 2420 | 2'-6" x 5'-0" high | | 28 | .571 | | 87.50 | 22 | | 109.50 | 130 |
| 2440 | 4'-0" x 6'-0" high | | 25 | .640 | | 95.50 | 24.50 | | 120 | 143 |
| 2600 | Mill finish, 2'-0" x 3'-5" high | | 30 | .533 | | 72 | 20.50 | | 92.50 | 111 |
| 2620 | 2'-6" x 5'-0" high | | 28 | .571 | | 80.50 | 22 | | 102.50 | 123 |
| 2640 | 4'-0" x 6-8" high | ↓ | 25 | .640 | ↓ | 90 | 24.50 | | 114.50 | 137 |

# 08 53 Plastic Windows

## 08 53 13 – Vinyl Windows

| 08 53 13.20 Vinyl Single Hung Windows | Crew | Daily Output | Labor-Hours | Unit | Material | 2008 Bare Costs Labor | 2008 Bare Costs Equipment | Total | Total Incl O&P |
|---|---|---|---|---|---|---|---|---|---|
| 0010 **VINYL SINGLE HUNG WINDOWS** | | | | | | | | | |
| 0100   Grids, low E, J fin, ext. jambs, 21" x 53" | 2 Carp | 18 | .889 | Ea. | 151 | 34 | | 185 | 219 |
| 0110      21" x 57" | | 17 | .941 | | 155 | 36 | | 191 | 226 |
| 0120      21" x 65" | | 16 | 1 | | 161 | 38 | | 199 | 237 |
| 0130      25" x 41" | | 20 | .800 | | 142 | 30.50 | | 172.50 | 204 |
| 0140      25" x 49" | | 18 | .889 | | 157 | 34 | | 191 | 226 |
| 0150      25" x 57" | | 17 | .941 | | 161 | 36 | | 197 | 233 |
| 0160      25" x 65" | | 16 | 1 | | 168 | 38 | | 206 | 245 |
| 0170      29" x 41" | | 18 | .889 | | 151 | 34 | | 185 | 220 |
| 0180      29" x 53" | | 18 | .889 | | 162 | 34 | | 196 | 232 |
| 0190      29" x 57" | | 17 | .941 | | 166 | 36 | | 202 | 239 |
| 0200      29" x 65" | | 16 | 1 | | 173 | 38 | | 211 | 250 |
| 0210      33" x 41" | | 20 | .800 | | 157 | 30.50 | | 187.50 | 220 |
| 0220      33" x 53" | | 18 | .889 | | 169 | 34 | | 203 | 239 |
| 0230      33" x 57" | | 17 | .941 | | 173 | 36 | | 209 | 246 |
| 0240      33" x 65" | | 16 | 1 | | 180 | 38 | | 218 | 258 |
| 0250      37" x 41" | | 20 | .800 | | 165 | 30.50 | | 195.50 | 230 |
| 0260      37" x 53" | | 18 | .889 | | 178 | 34 | | 212 | 248 |
| 0270      37" x 57" | | 17 | .941 | | 181 | 36 | | 217 | 255 |
| 0280      37" x 65" | | 16 | 1 | | 189 | 38 | | 227 | 268 |

## 08 53 13.30 Vinyl Double Hung Windows

| | Crew | Daily Output | Labor-Hours | Unit | Material | 2008 Bare Costs Labor | 2008 Bare Costs Equipment | Total | Total Incl O&P |
|---|---|---|---|---|---|---|---|---|---|
| 0010 **VINYL DOUBLE HUNG WINDOWS** | | | | | | | | | |
| 0100   Grids, low E, J fin, ext. jambs, 21" x 53" | 2 Carp | 18 | .889 | Ea. | 173 | 34 | | 207 | 243 |
| 0102      21" x 37" | | 18 | .889 | | 154 | 34 | | 188 | 222 |
| 0104      21" x 41" | | 18 | .889 | | 157 | 34 | | 191 | 226 |
| 0106      21" x 49" | | 18 | .889 | | 165 | 34 | | 199 | 235 |
| 0110      21" x 57" | | 17 | .941 | | 176 | 36 | | 212 | 250 |
| 0120      21" x 65" | | 16 | 1 | | 184 | 38 | | 222 | 262 |
| 0128      25" x 37" | | 20 | .800 | | 162 | 30.50 | | 192.50 | 227 |
| 0130      25" x 41" | | 20 | .800 | | 166 | 30.50 | | 196.50 | 230 |
| 0140      25" x 49" | | 18 | .889 | | 171 | 34 | | 205 | 241 |
| 0145      25" x 53" | | 18 | .889 | | 178 | 34 | | 212 | 249 |
| 0150      25" x 57" | | 17 | .941 | | 179 | 36 | | 215 | 253 |
| 0160      25" x 65" | | 16 | 1 | | 190 | 38 | | 228 | 269 |
| 0162      25" x 69" | | 16 | 1 | | 198 | 38 | | 236 | 278 |
| 0164      25" x 77" | | 16 | 1 | | 209 | 38 | | 247 | 290 |
| 0168      29" x 37" | | 18 | .889 | | 168 | 34 | | 202 | 237 |
| 0170      29" x 41" | | 18 | .889 | | 171 | 34 | | 205 | 241 |
| 0172      29" x 49" | | 18 | .889 | | 180 | 34 | | 214 | 251 |
| 0180      29" x 53" | | 18 | .889 | | 184 | 34 | | 218 | 255 |
| 0190      29" x 57" | | 17 | .941 | | 188 | 36 | | 224 | 262 |
| 0200      29" x 65" | | 16 | 1 | | 195 | 38 | | 233 | 275 |
| 0202      29" x 69" | | 16 | 1 | | 202 | 38 | | 240 | 283 |
| 0205      29" x 77" | | 16 | 1 | | 214 | 38 | | 252 | 296 |
| 0208      33" x 37" | | 20 | .800 | | 172 | 30.50 | | 202.50 | 237 |
| 0210      33" x 41" | | 20 | .800 | | 176 | 30.50 | | 206.50 | 242 |
| 0215      33" x 49" | | 20 | .800 | | 186 | 30.50 | | 216.50 | 252 |
| 0220      33" x 53" | | 18 | .889 | | 190 | 34 | | 224 | 262 |
| 0230      33" x 57" | | 17 | .941 | | 194 | 36 | | 230 | 269 |
| 0240      33" x 65" | | 16 | 1 | | 199 | 38 | | 237 | 279 |
| 0242      33" x 69" | | 16 | 1 | | 211 | 38 | | 249 | 292 |
| 0246      33" x 77" | | 16 | 1 | | 222 | 38 | | 260 | 305 |

# 08 53 Plastic Windows

## 08 53 13 – Vinyl Windows

| 08 53 13.30 Vinyl Double Hung Windows | | Crew | Daily Output | Labor-Hours | Unit | Material | 2008 Bare Costs Labor | Equipment | Total | Total Incl O&P |
|---|---|---|---|---|---|---|---|---|---|---|
| 0250 | 37" x 41" | 2 Carp | 20 | .800 | Ea. | 180 | 30.50 | | 210.50 | 246 |
| 0255 | 37" x 49" | | 20 | .800 | | 190 | 30.50 | | 220.50 | 257 |
| 0260 | 37" x 53" | | 18 | .889 | | 197 | 34 | | 231 | 270 |
| 0270 | 37" x 57" | | 17 | .941 | | 202 | 36 | | 238 | 278 |
| 0280 | 37" x 65" | | 16 | 1 | | 207 | 38 | | 245 | 288 |
| 0282 | 37" x 69" | | 16 | 1 | | 262 | 38 | | 300 | 350 |
| 0286 | 37" x 77" | | 16 | 1 | | 274 | 38 | | 312 | 360 |
| 0300 | Solid vinyl, average quality, double insulated glass, 2'-0" x 3'-0" | 1 Carp | 10 | .800 | | 260 | 30.50 | | 290.50 | 335 |
| 0310 | 3'-0" x 4'-0" | | 9 | .889 | | 167 | 34 | | 201 | 237 |
| 0320 | 4'-0" x 4'-6" | | 8 | 1 | | 269 | 38 | | 307 | 355 |
| 0330 | Premium, double insulated glass, 2'-6" x 3'-0" | | 10 | .800 | | 191 | 30.50 | | 221.50 | 258 |
| 0340 | 3'-0" x 3'-6" | | 9 | .889 | | 222 | 34 | | 256 | 298 |
| 0350 | 3'-0" x 4"-0" | | 9 | .889 | | 235 | 34 | | 269 | 310 |
| 0360 | 3'-0" x 4'-6" | | 9 | .889 | | 239 | 34 | | 273 | 315 |
| 0370 | 3'-0" x 5'-0" | | 8 | 1 | | 257 | 38 | | 295 | 345 |
| 0380 | 3'-6" x 6"-0" | | 8 | 1 | | 296 | 38 | | 334 | 385 |

## 08 53 13.40 Vinyl Casement Windows

| | | Crew | Daily Output | Labor-Hours | Unit | Material | 2008 Bare Costs Labor | Equipment | Total | Total Incl O&P |
|---|---|---|---|---|---|---|---|---|---|---|
| 0010 | **VINYL CASEMENT WINDOWS** | | | | | | | | | |
| 0100 | Grids, low E, J fin, ext. jambs, 1 lt, 21" x 41" | 2 Carp | 20 | .800 | Ea. | 225 | 30.50 | | 255.50 | 296 |
| 0110 | 21" x 47" | | 20 | .800 | | 245 | 30.50 | | 275.50 | 320 |
| 0120 | 21" x 53" | | 20 | .800 | | 265 | 30.50 | | 295.50 | 340 |
| 0128 | 24" x 35" | | 19 | .842 | | 216 | 32 | | 248 | 288 |
| 0130 | 24" x 41" | | 19 | .842 | | 235 | 32 | | 267 | 310 |
| 0140 | 24" x 47" | | 19 | .842 | | 255 | 32 | | 287 | 330 |
| 0150 | 24" x 53" | | 19 | .842 | | 275 | 32 | | 307 | 350 |
| 0158 | 28" x 35" | | 19 | .842 | | 230 | 32 | | 262 | 305 |
| 0160 | 28" x 41" | | 19 | .842 | | 249 | 32 | | 281 | 325 |
| 0170 | 28" x 47" | | 19 | .842 | | 269 | 32 | | 301 | 345 |
| 0180 | 28" x 53" | | 19 | .842 | | 297 | 32 | | 329 | 375 |
| 0184 | 28" x 59" | | 19 | .842 | | 300 | 32 | | 332 | 385 |
| 0188 | Two lites, 33" x 35" | | 18 | .889 | | 370 | 34 | | 404 | 460 |
| 0190 | 33" x 41" | | 18 | .889 | | 395 | 34 | | 429 | 490 |
| 0200 | 33" x 47" | | 18 | .889 | | 425 | 34 | | 459 | 525 |
| 0210 | 33" x 53" | | 18 | .889 | | 455 | 34 | | 489 | 555 |
| 0212 | 33" x 59" | | 18 | .889 | | 485 | 34 | | 519 | 585 |
| 0215 | 33" x 72" | | 18 | .889 | | 500 | 34 | | 534 | 605 |
| 0220 | 41" x 41" | | 18 | .889 | | 435 | 34 | | 469 | 530 |
| 0230 | 41" x 47" | | 18 | .889 | | 465 | 34 | | 499 | 565 |
| 0240 | 41" x 53" | | 17 | .941 | | 490 | 36 | | 526 | 595 |
| 0242 | 41" x 59" | | 17 | .941 | | 520 | 36 | | 556 | 625 |
| 0246 | 41" x 72" | | 17 | .941 | | 545 | 36 | | 581 | 650 |
| 0250 | 47" x 41" | | 17 | .941 | | 440 | 36 | | 476 | 535 |
| 0260 | 47" x 47" | | 17 | .941 | | 465 | 36 | | 501 | 570 |
| 0270 | 47" x 53" | | 17 | .941 | | 495 | 36 | | 531 | 600 |
| 0272 | 47" x 59" | | 17 | .941 | | 540 | 36 | | 576 | 650 |
| 0280 | 56" x 41" | | 15 | 1.067 | | 470 | 40.50 | | 510.50 | 580 |
| 0290 | 56" x 47" | | 15 | 1.067 | | 495 | 40.50 | | 535.50 | 610 |
| 0300 | 56" x 53" | | 15 | 1.067 | | 540 | 40.50 | | 580.50 | 660 |
| 0302 | 56" x 59" | | 15 | 1.067 | | 565 | 40.50 | | 605.50 | 685 |
| 0310 | 56" x 72" | | 15 | 1.067 | | 610 | 40.50 | | 650.50 | 740 |
| 0340 | Solid vinyl, premium, double insulated glass, 2'-0" x 3'-0" high | 1 Carp | 10 | .800 | | 240 | 30.50 | | 270.50 | 310 |
| 0360 | 2'-0" x 4'-0" high | | 9 | .889 | | 275 | 34 | | 309 | 360 |

# 08 53 Plastic Windows

## 08 53 13 – Vinyl Windows

| 08 53 13.40 Vinyl Casement Windows | Crew | Daily Output | Labor-Hours | Unit | Material | 2008 Bare Costs Labor | Equipment | Total | Total Incl O&P |
|---|---|---|---|---|---|---|---|---|---|
| 0380 | 2'-0" x 5'-0" high | 1 Carp | 8 | 1 | Ea. | 271 | 38 | | 309 | 360 |

### 08 53 13.50 Vinyl Picture Windows

| | 08 53 13.50 Vinyl Picture Windows | Crew | Daily Output | Labor-Hours | Unit | Material | 2008 Bare Costs Labor | Equipment | Total | Total Incl O&P |
|---|---|---|---|---|---|---|---|---|---|---|
| 0010 | **VINYL PICTURE WINDOWS** | | | | | | | | | |
| 0100 | Grids, low E, J fin, ext. jambs, 33" x 47" | 2 Carp | 12 | 1.333 | Ea. | 221 | 51 | | 272 | 325 |
| 0110 | 35" x 71" | | 12 | 1.333 | | 230 | 51 | | 281 | 330 |
| 0120 | 41" x 47" | | 12 | 1.333 | | 252 | 51 | | 303 | 355 |
| 0130 | 41" x 71" | | 12 | 1.333 | | 273 | 51 | | 324 | 380 |
| 0140 | 47" x 47" | | 12 | 1.333 | | 285 | 51 | | 336 | 395 |
| 0150 | 47" x 71" | | 11 | 1.455 | | 299 | 55.50 | | 354.50 | 415 |
| 0160 | 53" x 47" | | 11 | 1.455 | | 280 | 55.50 | | 335.50 | 395 |
| 0170 | 53" x 71" | | 11 | 1.455 | | 293 | 55.50 | | 348.50 | 410 |
| 0180 | 59" x 47" | | 11 | 1.455 | | 320 | 55.50 | | 375.50 | 435 |
| 0190 | 59" x 71" | | 11 | 1.455 | | 340 | 55.50 | | 395.50 | 460 |
| 0200 | 71" x 47" | | 10 | 1.600 | | 350 | 61 | | 411 | 485 |
| 0210 | 71" x 71" | | 10 | 1.600 | | 370 | 61 | | 431 | 505 |

# 08 56 Special Function Windows

## 08 56 63 – Detention Windows

### 08 56 63.13 Visitor Cubicle Windows

| | 08 56 63.13 Visitor Cubicle Windows | Crew | Daily Output | Labor-Hours | Unit | Material | 2008 Bare Costs Labor | Equipment | Total | Total Incl O&P |
|---|---|---|---|---|---|---|---|---|---|---|
| 0010 | **VISITOR CUBICLE WINDOWS** | | | | | | | | | |
| 4000 | Visitor cubicle, vision panel, no intercom | E-4 | 2 | 16 | Ea. | 2,750 | 695 | 66 | 3,511 | 4,350 |

# 08 62 Unit Skylights

## 08 62 13 – Domed Unit Skylights

### 08 62 13.20 Skylights

| | 08 62 13.20 Skylights | Crew | Daily Output | Labor-Hours | Unit | Material | 2008 Bare Costs Labor | Equipment | Total | Total Incl O&P |
|---|---|---|---|---|---|---|---|---|---|---|
| 0010 | **SKYLIGHTS**, Plastic domes, flush or curb mounted ten or | | | | | | | | | |
| 0100 | more units, curb not included | | | | | | | | | |
| 0300 | Nominal size under 10 S.F., double | G-3 | 130 | .246 | S.F. | 23 | 9.30 | | 32.30 | 40 |
| 0400 | Single | | 160 | .200 | | 20 | 7.55 | | 27.55 | 33.50 |
| 0600 | 10 S.F. to 20 S.F., double | | 315 | .102 | | 19.40 | 3.84 | | 23.24 | 27.50 |
| 0700 | Single | | 395 | .081 | | 18.35 | 3.06 | | 21.41 | 24.50 |
| 0900 | 20 S.F. to 30 S.F., double | | 395 | .081 | | 17.15 | 3.06 | | 20.21 | 23.50 |
| 1000 | Single | | 465 | .069 | | 15.95 | 2.60 | | 18.55 | 21.50 |
| 1200 | 30 S.F. to 65 S.F., double | | 465 | .069 | | 15.45 | 2.60 | | 18.05 | 21 |
| 1300 | Single | | 610 | .052 | | 16.15 | 1.98 | | 18.13 | 21 |
| 1500 | For insulated 4" curbs, double, add | | | | | 25% | | | | |
| 1600 | Single, add | | | | | 30% | | | | |
| 1800 | For integral insulated 9" curbs, double, add | | | | | 30% | | | | |
| 1900 | Single, add | | | | | 40% | | | | |
| 2120 | Ventilating insulated plexiglass dome with | | | | | | | | | |
| 2130 | curb mounting, 36" x 36" | G-3 | 12 | 2.667 | Ea. | 380 | 101 | | 481 | 575 |
| 2150 | 52" x 52" | | 12 | 2.667 | | 570 | 101 | | 671 | 780 |
| 2160 | 28" x 52" | | 10 | 3.200 | | 445 | 121 | | 566 | 675 |
| 2170 | 36" x 52" | | 10 | 3.200 | | 480 | 121 | | 601 | 715 |
| 2180 | For electric opening system, add | | | | | 285 | | | 285 | 315 |
| 2200 | Field fabricated, factory type, aluminum and wire glass | G-3 | 120 | .267 | S.F. | 14.70 | 10.05 | | 24.75 | 32 |
| 2300 | Insulated safety glass with aluminum frame | | 160 | .200 | | 85.50 | 7.55 | | 93.05 | 106 |
| 2400 | Sandwich panels, fiberglass, for walls, 1-9/16" thick, to 250 SF | | 200 | .160 | | 15.55 | 6.05 | | 21.60 | 26.50 |
| 2500 | 250 SF and up | | 265 | .121 | | 13.95 | 4.56 | | 18.51 | 22.50 |

# 08 62 Unit Skylights

## 08 62 13 – Domed Unit Skylights

| 08 62 13.20 Skylights | | Crew | Daily Output | Labor-Hours | Unit | Material | 2008 Bare Costs Labor | Equipment | Total | Total Incl O&P |
|---|---|---|---|---|---|---|---|---|---|---|
| 2700 | As above, but for roofs, 2-3/4" thick, to 250 SF | G-3 | 295 | .108 | S.F. | 22.50 | 4.10 | | 26.60 | 31 |
| 2800 | 250 SF and up | ↓ | 330 | .097 | ↓ | 18.35 | 3.66 | | 22.01 | 25.50 |

# 08 63 Metal-Framed Skylights

## 08 63 23 – Ridge Metal-Framed Skylights

### 08 63 23.10 Prefabricated

| | | Crew | Daily Output | Labor-Hours | Unit | Material | 2008 Bare Costs Labor | Equipment | Total | Total Incl O&P |
|---|---|---|---|---|---|---|---|---|---|---|
| 0010 | **PREFABRICATED** glass block with metal frame | | | | | | | | | |
| 0020 | Minimum | G-3 | 265 | .121 | S.F. | 43.50 | 4.56 | | 48.06 | 54.50 |
| 0100 | Maximum | " | 160 | .200 | " | 86.50 | 7.55 | | 94.05 | 107 |

# 08 71 Door Hardware

## 08 71 13 – Automatic Door Operators

### 08 71 13.10 Automatic Openers Commercial

| | | Crew | Daily Output | Labor-Hours | Unit | Material | 2008 Bare Costs Labor | Equipment | Total | Total Incl O&P |
|---|---|---|---|---|---|---|---|---|---|---|
| 0010 | **AUTOMATIC OPENERS COMMERCIAL** | | | | | | | | | |
| 0020 | Pneumatic, incl opener, motion sens, control box, tubing, compressor | | | | | | | | | |
| 0050 | For single swing door, per opening | 2 Skwk | .80 | 20 | Ea. | 3,925 | 790 | | 4,715 | 5,550 |
| 0100 | Pair, per opening | | .50 | 32 | Opng. | 6,550 | 1,250 | | 7,800 | 9,150 |
| 1000 | For single sliding door, per opening | | .60 | 26.667 | | 4,350 | 1,050 | | 5,400 | 6,400 |
| 1300 | Bi-parting pair | ↓ | .50 | 32 | ↓ | 6,575 | 1,250 | | 7,825 | 9,175 |
| 1420 | Electronic door opener incl motion sens, 12V control box, motor | | | | | | | | | |
| 1450 | For single swing door, per opening | 2 Skwk | .80 | 20 | Opng. | 3,300 | 790 | | 4,090 | 4,850 |
| 1500 | Pair, per opening | | .50 | 32 | | 5,375 | 1,250 | | 6,625 | 7,875 |
| 1600 | For single sliding door, per opening | | .60 | 26.667 | | 3,575 | 1,050 | | 4,625 | 5,550 |
| 1700 | Bi-parting pair | | .50 | 32 | | 5,475 | 1,250 | | 6,725 | 7,975 |
| 1750 | Handicap actuator buttons, 2, including 12V DC wiring, add | 1 Carp | 1.50 | 5.333 | Pr. | 395 | 203 | | 598 | 750 |

### 08 71 13.20 Automatic Openers Industrial

| | | Crew | Daily Output | Labor-Hours | Unit | Material | 2008 Bare Costs Labor | Equipment | Total | Total Incl O&P |
|---|---|---|---|---|---|---|---|---|---|---|
| 0010 | **AUTOMATIC OPENERS INDUSTRIAL** | | | | | | | | | |
| 0015 | Sliding doors up to 6' wide | 2 Skwk | .60 | 26.667 | Opng. | 5,125 | 1,050 | | 6,175 | 7,275 |
| 0200 | To 12' wide | " | .40 | 40 | " | 6,275 | 1,575 | | 7,850 | 9,350 |
| 0400 | Over 12' wide, add per L.F. of excess | | | | L.F. | 685 | | | 685 | 755 |
| 1000 | Swing doors, to 5' wide | 2 Skwk | .80 | 20 | Ea. | 3,000 | 790 | | 3,790 | 4,525 |
| 1860 | Add for controls, wall pushbutton, 3 button | | 4 | 4 | | 183 | 158 | | 341 | 445 |
| 1870 | Ceiling pull cord | ↓ | 4.30 | 3.721 | ↓ | 157 | 147 | | 304 | 400 |

## 08 71 20 – Hardware

### 08 71 20.10 Bolts, Flush

| | | Crew | Daily Output | Labor-Hours | Unit | Material | 2008 Bare Costs Labor | Equipment | Total | Total Incl O&P |
|---|---|---|---|---|---|---|---|---|---|---|
| 0010 | **BOLTS, FLUSH** | | | | | | | | | |
| 0020 | Standard, concealed | 1 Carp | 7 | 1.143 | Ea. | 21 | 43.50 | | 64.50 | 91 |
| 0800 | Automatic fire exit | " | 5 | 1.600 | | 277 | 61 | | 338 | 400 |
| 1600 | For electric release, add | 1 Elec | 3 | 2.667 | | 115 | 121 | | 236 | 305 |
| 3000 | Barrel, brass, 2" long | 1 Carp | 40 | .200 | | 4.77 | 7.60 | | 12.37 | 17.10 |
| 3020 | 4" long | | 40 | .200 | | 3.35 | 7.60 | | 10.95 | 15.55 |
| 3060 | 6" long | ↓ | 40 | .200 | ↓ | 9.15 | 7.60 | | 16.75 | 22 |

### 08 71 20.15 Hardware

| | | Crew | Daily Output | Labor-Hours | Unit | Material | 2008 Bare Costs Labor | Equipment | Total | Total Incl O&P |
|---|---|---|---|---|---|---|---|---|---|---|
| 0009 | **HARDWARE** | | | | | | | | | |
| 0010 | Average percentage for hardware, total job cost | | | | | | | | | |
| 0025 | Minimum | | | | | | | | | .75% |
| 0050 | Maximum | | | | | | | | | 3.50% |
| 0500 | Total hardware for building, average distribution | | | | | 85% | 15% | | | |

# 08 71 Door Hardware

## 08 71 20 – Hardware

| 08 71 20.15 Hardware | | Crew | Daily Output | Labor-Hours | Unit | Material | 2008 Bare Costs Labor | Equipment | Total | Total Incl O&P |
|---|---|---|---|---|---|---|---|---|---|---|
| 1000 | Door hardware, apartment, interior | | | | Door | 133 | | | 133 | 146 |
| 1500 | Hospital bedroom, minimum | | | | | 297 | | | 297 | 325 |
| 2000 | Maximum | | | | | 650 | | | 650 | 715 |
| 2100 | Pocket door | | | | Ea. | 133 | | | 133 | 146 |
| 2250 | School, single exterior, incl. lever, not incl. panic device | | | | Door | 440 | | | 440 | 485 |
| 2500 | Single interior, regular use, no lever included | | | | | 293 | | | 293 | 320 |
| 2550 | Including handicap lever | | | | | 400 | | | 400 | 440 |
| 2600 | Heavy use, incl. lever and closer | | | | | 510 | | | 510 | 565 |
| 2850 | Stairway, single interior | | | | | 730 | | | 730 | 805 |
| 3100 | Double exterior, with panic device | | | | Pr. | 1,025 | | | 1,025 | 1,125 |
| 3600 | Toilet, public, single interior | | | | Door | 161 | | | 161 | 177 |

### 08 71 20.20 Door Protectors

| | | Crew | Daily Output | Labor-Hours | Unit | Material | Labor | Equipment | Total | Total Incl O&P |
|---|---|---|---|---|---|---|---|---|---|---|
| 0010 | **DOOR PROTECTORS** | | | | | | | | | |
| 0020 | 1-3/4" x 3/4" U channel | 2 Carp | 80 | .200 | L.F. | 18.75 | 7.60 | | 26.35 | 32.50 |
| 0021 | 1-3/4" x 1-1/4" U channel | | 80 | .200 | " | 10.10 | 7.60 | | 17.70 | 23 |
| 1000 | Tear drop, spring-stl, 8" high x 19" long | | 15 | 1.067 | Ea. | 87 | 40.50 | | 127.50 | 159 |
| 1010 | Tear drop, spring-stl, 8" high x 32" long | | 15 | 1.067 | | 108 | 40.50 | | 148.50 | 183 |
| 1100 | 8" high x19" long | | 15 | 1.067 | | 210 | 40.50 | | 250.50 | 295 |
| 1200 | 8" high x 32" long | | 15 | 1.067 | | 260 | 40.50 | | 300.50 | 350 |

### 08 71 20.30 Door Closers

| | | Crew | Daily Output | Labor-Hours | Unit | Material | Labor | Equipment | Total | Total Incl O&P |
|---|---|---|---|---|---|---|---|---|---|---|
| 0010 | **DOOR CLOSERS** | | | | | | | | | |
| 0020 | Adjustable backcheck, 3 way mount, all sizes, regular arm | 1 Carp | 6 | 1.333 | Ea. | 150 | 51 | | 201 | 244 |
| 0040 | Hold open arm | | 6 | 1.333 | | 164 | 51 | | 215 | 259 |
| 0100 | Fusible link | | 6.50 | 1.231 | | 128 | 47 | | 175 | 213 |
| 0200 | Non sized, regular arm | | 6 | 1.333 | | 142 | 51 | | 193 | 236 |
| 0240 | Hold open arm | | 6 | 1.333 | | 177 | 51 | | 228 | 274 |
| 0400 | 4 way mount, non sized, regular arm | | 6 | 1.333 | | 195 | 51 | | 246 | 294 |
| 0440 | Hold open arm | | 6 | 1.333 | | 210 | 51 | | 261 | 310 |
| 2000 | Backcheck and adjustable power, hinge face mount | | | | | | | | | |
| 2010 | All sizes, regular arm | 1 Carp | 6.50 | 1.231 | Ea. | 180 | 47 | | 227 | 271 |
| 2040 | Hold open arm | | 6.50 | 1.231 | | 193 | 47 | | 240 | 286 |
| 2400 | Top jamb mount, all sizes, regular arm | | 6 | 1.333 | | 180 | 51 | | 231 | 277 |
| 2440 | Hold open arm | | 6 | 1.333 | | 193 | 51 | | 244 | 292 |
| 2800 | Top face mount, all sizes, regular arm | | 6.50 | 1.231 | | 180 | 47 | | 227 | 271 |
| 2840 | Hold open arm | | 6.50 | 1.231 | | 193 | 47 | | 240 | 285 |
| 4000 | Backcheck, overhead concealed, all sizes, regular arm | | 5.50 | 1.455 | | 190 | 55.50 | | 245.50 | 296 |
| 4040 | Concealed arm | | 5 | 1.600 | | 203 | 61 | | 264 | 320 |
| 4400 | Compact overhead, concealed, all sizes, regular arm | | 5.50 | 1.455 | | 345 | 55.50 | | 400.50 | 465 |
| 4440 | Concealed arm | | 5 | 1.600 | | 360 | 61 | | 421 | 495 |
| 4800 | Concealed in door, all sizes, regular arm | | 5.50 | 1.455 | | 128 | 55.50 | | 183.50 | 228 |
| 4840 | Concealed arm | | 5 | 1.600 | | 138 | 61 | | 199 | 247 |
| 4900 | Floor concealed, all sizes, single acting | | 2.20 | 3.636 | | 163 | 139 | | 302 | 395 |
| 4940 | Double acting | | 2.20 | 3.636 | | 210 | 139 | | 349 | 445 |
| 5000 | For cast aluminum cylinder, deduct | | | | | 17.25 | | | 17.25 | 19 |
| 5040 | For delayed action, add | | | | | 30 | | | 30 | 33 |
| 5080 | For fusible link arm, add | | | | | 12.50 | | | 12.50 | 13.75 |
| 5120 | For shock absorbing arm, add | | | | | 37.50 | | | 37.50 | 41 |
| 5160 | For spring power adjustment, add | | | | | 29 | | | 29 | 31.50 |
| 6000 | Closer-holder, hinge face mount, all sizes, exposed arm | 1 Carp | 6.50 | 1.231 | | 132 | 47 | | 179 | 219 |
| 7000 | Electronic closer-holder, hinge facemount, concealed arm | | 5 | 1.600 | | 201 | 61 | | 262 | 315 |
| 7400 | With built-in detector | | 5 | 1.600 | | 605 | 61 | | 666 | 760 |
| 8000 | Surface mounted, stand. duty, parallel arm, primed, traditional | | 6 | 1.333 | | 138 | 51 | | 189 | 230 |

# 08 71 Door Hardware

## 08 71 20 – Hardware

### 08 71 20.30 Door Closers

| | | Crew | Daily Output | Labor-Hours | Unit | Material | 2008 Bare Costs Labor | Equipment | Total | Total Incl O&P |
|---|---|---|---|---|---|---|---|---|---|---|
| 8030 | Light duty | 1 Carp | 6 | 1.333 | Ea. | 82 | 51 | | 133 | 170 |
| 8050 | Heavy duty | | 6 | 1.333 | | 165 | 51 | | 216 | 260 |
| 8100 | Standard duty, parallel arm, modern | | 6 | 1.333 | | 154 | 51 | | 205 | 249 |
| 8150 | Heavy duty | | 6 | 1.333 | | 174 | 51 | | 225 | 270 |

### 08 71 20.31 Door Closers

| | | Crew | Daily Output | Labor-Hours | Unit | Material | 2008 Bare Costs Labor | Equipment | Total | Total Incl O&P |
|---|---|---|---|---|---|---|---|---|---|---|
| 0010 | **DOOR CLOSERS** | | | | | | | | | |
| 0015 | Door closer, rack and pinion | 1 Carp | 6.50 | 1.231 | Ea. | 136 | 47 | | 183 | 223 |
| 1520 | Door, single acting, standard arm | | 1 | 8 | | 188 | 305 | | 493 | 680 |
| 1526 | Frame, single acting, standard arm | | 1 | 8 | | 330 | 305 | | 635 | 835 |
| 1530 | Hold open arm | | 1 | 8 | | 345 | 305 | | 650 | 855 |
| 1534 | Double acting, standard arm | | 1 | 8 | | 440 | 305 | | 745 | 960 |
| 1536 | Hold open arm | | 1 | 8 | | 450 | 305 | | 755 | 970 |
| 1540 | Hold open arm | | 1 | 8 | | 202 | 305 | | 507 | 695 |
| 1554 | Floor, center hung, single acting, bottom arm | | 1 | 8 | | 275 | 305 | | 580 | 780 |
| 1558 | Double acting | | 1 | 8 | | 300 | 305 | | 605 | 805 |
| 1560 | Offset hung, single acting, bottom arm | | 1 | 8 | | 320 | 305 | | 625 | 825 |
| 6500 | Electro magnetic closer/holder | | | | | | | | | |
| 6510 | Single point, no detector | 1 Carp | 1 | 8 | Ea. | 360 | 305 | | 665 | 870 |
| 6515 | Including detector | | 1 | 8 | | 655 | 305 | | 960 | 1,200 |
| 6520 | Multi-point, no detector | | 1 | 8 | | 655 | 305 | | 960 | 1,200 |
| 6524 | Including detector | | 1 | 8 | | 755 | 305 | | 1,060 | 1,300 |
| 6550 | Electric automatic operators | | | | | | | | | |
| 6555 | Operator | 1 Carp | 1 | 8 | Ea. | 2,350 | 305 | | 2,655 | 3,050 |
| 6570 | Wall plate actuator | | 1 | 8 | | 187 | 305 | | 492 | 680 |
| 8010 | Light duty, regular arm | | 1 | 8 | | 103 | 305 | | 408 | 590 |
| 8032 | Parallel arm | | 1 | 8 | | 106 | 305 | | 411 | 590 |
| 8034 | Hold open arm | | 1 | 8 | | 114 | 305 | | 419 | 600 |
| 8036 | Fusible link arm | | 1 | 8 | | 167 | 305 | | 472 | 660 |
| 8040 | Medium duty, regular arm | | 1 | 8 | | 131 | 305 | | 436 | 620 |
| 8042 | Extra duty, parallel arm | | 1 | 8 | | 141 | 305 | | 446 | 630 |
| 8044 | Hold open arm | | 1 | 8 | | 150 | 305 | | 455 | 640 |
| 8046 | Positive stop arm | | 1 | 8 | | 154 | 305 | | 459 | 645 |
| 8052 | Heavy duty, regular arm | | 1 | 8 | | 158 | 305 | | 463 | 650 |
| 8054 | Top jamb mount | | 1 | 8 | | 158 | 305 | | 463 | 650 |
| 8056 | Extra duty parallel arm | | 1 | 8 | | 158 | 305 | | 463 | 650 |
| 8058 | Hold open arm | | 1 | 8 | | 173 | 305 | | 478 | 665 |
| 8060 | Positive stop arm | | 1 | 8 | | 172 | 305 | | 477 | 665 |
| 8062 | Fusible link arm | | 1 | 8 | | 206 | 305 | | 511 | 700 |
| 8080 | Universal heavy duty, regular arm | | 1 | 8 | | 171 | 305 | | 476 | 665 |
| 8084 | Parallel arm | | 1 | 8 | | 171 | 305 | | 476 | 665 |
| 8088 | Extra duty, parallel arm | | 1 | 8 | | 178 | 305 | | 483 | 670 |
| 8090 | Hold open arm | | 1 | 8 | | 183 | 305 | | 488 | 675 |
| 8094 | Positive stop arm | | 1 | 8 | | 188 | 305 | | 493 | 680 |
| 8098 | For delayed action add | | 1 | 8 | | 23 | 305 | | 328 | 500 |

### 08 71 20.35 Panic Devices

| | | Crew | Daily Output | Labor-Hours | Unit | Material | 2008 Bare Costs Labor | Equipment | Total | Total Incl O&P |
|---|---|---|---|---|---|---|---|---|---|---|
| 0010 | **PANIC DEVICES** | | | | | | | | | |
| 0015 | For rim locks, single door exit only | 1 Carp | 6 | 1.333 | Ea. | 385 | 51 | | 436 | 500 |
| 0020 | Outside key and pull | | 5 | 1.600 | | 435 | 61 | | 496 | 575 |
| 0200 | Bar and vertical rod, exit only | | 5 | 1.600 | | 555 | 61 | | 616 | 705 |
| 0210 | Outside key and pull | | 4 | 2 | | 665 | 76 | | 741 | 850 |
| 0400 | Bar and concealed rod | | 4 | 2 | | 560 | 76 | | 636 | 735 |
| 0600 | Touch bar, exit only | | 6 | 1.333 | | 445 | 51 | | 496 | 570 |

253

# 08 71 Door Hardware

## 08 71 20 – Hardware

### 08 71 20.35 Panic Devices

| | | Crew | Daily Output | Labor-Hours | Unit | Material | 2008 Bare Costs Labor | 2008 Bare Costs Equipment | Total | Total Incl O&P |
|---|---|---|---|---|---|---|---|---|---|---|
| 0610 | Outside key and pull | 1 Carp | 5 | 1.600 | Ea. | 535 | 61 | | 596 | 685 |
| 0700 | Touch bar and vertical rod, exit only | | 5 | 1.600 | | 605 | 61 | | 666 | 760 |
| 0710 | Outside key and pull | | 4 | 2 | | 705 | 76 | | 781 | 895 |
| 1000 | Mortise, bar, exit only | | 4 | 2 | | 500 | 76 | | 576 | 665 |
| 1600 | Touch bar, exit only | | 4 | 2 | | 570 | 76 | | 646 | 745 |
| 2000 | Narrow stile, rim mounted, bar, exit only | | 6 | 1.333 | | 600 | 51 | | 651 | 740 |
| 2010 | Outside key and pull | | 5 | 1.600 | | 650 | 61 | | 711 | 810 |
| 2200 | Bar and vertical rod, exit only | | 5 | 1.600 | | 615 | 61 | | 676 | 775 |
| 2210 | Outside key and pull | | 4 | 2 | | 615 | 76 | | 691 | 800 |
| 2400 | Bar and concealed rod, exit only | | 3 | 2.667 | | 715 | 102 | | 817 | 950 |
| 3000 | Mortise, bar, exit only | | 4 | 2 | | 530 | 76 | | 606 | 700 |
| 3600 | Touch bar, exit only | | 4 | 2 | | 770 | 76 | | 846 | 965 |

### 08 71 20.40 Lockset

| | | Crew | Daily Output | Labor-Hours | Unit | Material | 2008 Bare Costs Labor | 2008 Bare Costs Equipment | Total | Total Incl O&P |
|---|---|---|---|---|---|---|---|---|---|---|
| 0010 | **LOCKSET**, Standard duty | | | | | | | | | |
| 0020 | Non-keyed, passage | 1 Carp | 12 | .667 | Ea. | 44 | 25.50 | | 69.50 | 87.50 |
| 0100 | Privacy | | 12 | .667 | | 55.50 | 25.50 | | 81 | 101 |
| 0400 | Keyed, single cylinder function    CN | | 10 | .800 | | 77 | 30.50 | | 107.50 | 132 |
| 0420 | Hotel | | 8 | 1 | | 111 | 38 | | 149 | 182 |
| 0500 | Lever handled, keyed, single cylinder function | | 10 | .800 | | 136 | 30.50 | | 166.50 | 198 |
| 1000 | Heavy duty with sectional trim, non-keyed, passages | | 12 | .667 | | 129 | 25.50 | | 154.50 | 182 |
| 1100 | Privacy | | 12 | .667 | | 163 | 25.50 | | 188.50 | 219 |
| 1400 | Keyed, single cylinder function | | 10 | .800 | | 193 | 30.50 | | 223.50 | 260 |
| 1420 | Hotel | | 8 | 1 | | 287 | 38 | | 325 | 375 |
| 1600 | Communicating | | 10 | .800 | | 228 | 30.50 | | 258.50 | 298 |
| 1690 | For re-core cylinder, add | | | | | 32.50 | | | 32.50 | 35.50 |
| 1700 | Residential, interior door, minimum | 1 Carp | 16 | .500 | | 15.55 | 19.05 | | 34.60 | 46.50 |
| 1720 | Maximum | | 8 | 1 | | 41.50 | 38 | | 79.50 | 105 |
| 1800 | Exterior, minimum | | 14 | .571 | | 34.50 | 22 | | 56.50 | 72 |
| 1810 | Average | | 8 | 1 | | 65 | 38 | | 103 | 131 |
| 1820 | Maximum | | 8 | 1 | | 146 | 38 | | 184 | 220 |

### 08 71 20.41 Dead Locks

| | | Crew | Daily Output | Labor-Hours | Unit | Material | 2008 Bare Costs Labor | 2008 Bare Costs Equipment | Total | Total Incl O&P |
|---|---|---|---|---|---|---|---|---|---|---|
| 0010 | **DEAD LOCKS** | | | | | | | | | |
| 0011 | Mortise heavy duty outside key (security item) | 1 Carp | 9 | .889 | Ea. | 137 | 34 | | 171 | 203 |
| 0020 | Double cylinder | | 9 | .889 | | 151 | 34 | | 185 | 219 |
| 0100 | Medium duty, outside key | | 10 | .800 | | 106 | 30.50 | | 136.50 | 165 |
| 0110 | Double cylinder | | 10 | .800 | | 133 | 30.50 | | 163.50 | 194 |
| 1000 | Tubular, standard duty, outside key | | 10 | .800 | | 57 | 30.50 | | 87.50 | 111 |
| 1010 | Double cylinder | | 10 | .800 | | 73.50 | 30.50 | | 104 | 129 |
| 1200 | Night latch, outside key | | 10 | .800 | | 72 | 30.50 | | 102.50 | 127 |

### 08 71 20.42 Mortise Locksets

| | | Crew | Daily Output | Labor-Hours | Unit | Material | 2008 Bare Costs Labor | 2008 Bare Costs Equipment | Total | Total Incl O&P |
|---|---|---|---|---|---|---|---|---|---|---|
| 0010 | **MORTISE LOCKSETS**, Comm., wrought knobs & full escutcheon trim | | | | | | | | | |
| 0020 | Non-keyed, passage, minimum | 1 Carp | 9 | .889 | Ea. | 167 | 34 | | 201 | 236 |
| 0030 | Maximum | | 8 | 1 | | 269 | 38 | | 307 | 355 |
| 0040 | Privacy, minimum | | 9 | .889 | | 177 | 34 | | 211 | 248 |
| 0050 | Maximum | | 8 | 1 | | 291 | 38 | | 329 | 380 |
| 0100 | Keyed, office/entrance/apartment, minimum | | 8 | 1 | | 204 | 38 | | 242 | 284 |
| 0110 | Maximum | | 7 | 1.143 | | 350 | 43.50 | | 393.50 | 455 |
| 0120 | Single cylinder, typical, minimum | | 8 | 1 | | 174 | 38 | | 212 | 252 |
| 0130 | Maximum | | 7 | 1.143 | | 325 | 43.50 | | 368.50 | 425 |
| 0200 | Hotel, minimum | | 7 | 1.143 | | 210 | 43.50 | | 253.50 | 299 |
| 0210 | Maximum | | 6 | 1.333 | | 340 | 51 | | 391 | 455 |
| 0300 | Communication, double cylinder, minimum | | 8 | 1 | | 210 | 38 | | 248 | 291 |

## 08 71 20.42 Mortise Locksets

| | | Crew | Daily Output | Labor-Hours | Unit | Material | 2008 Bare Costs Labor | Equipment | Total | Total Incl O&P |
|---|---|---|---|---|---|---|---|---|---|---|
| 0310 | Maximum | 1 Carp | 7 | 1.143 | Ea. | 272 | 43.50 | | 315.50 | 365 |
| 1000 | Wrought knobs and sectional trim, non-keyed, passage, minimum | | 10 | .800 | | 110 | 30.50 | | 140.50 | 169 |
| 1010 | Maximum | | 9 | .889 | | 218 | 34 | | 252 | 293 |
| 1040 | Privacy, minimum | | 10 | .800 | | 129 | 30.50 | | 159.50 | 190 |
| 1050 | Maximum | | 9 | .889 | | 233 | 34 | | 267 | 310 |
| 1100 | Keyed, entrance, office/apartment, minimum | | 9 | .889 | | 192 | 34 | | 226 | 264 |
| 1110 | Maximum | | 8 | 1 | | 277 | 38 | | 315 | 365 |
| 1120 | Single cylinder, typical, minimum | | 9 | .889 | | 184 | 34 | | 218 | 256 |
| 1130 | Maximum | | 8 | 1 | | 268 | 38 | | 306 | 355 |
| 2000 | Cast knobs and full escutcheon trim | | | | | | | | | |
| 2010 | Non-keyed, passage, minimum | 1 Carp | 9 | .889 | Ea. | 235 | 34 | | 269 | 310 |
| 2020 | Maximum | | 8 | 1 | | 380 | 38 | | 418 | 480 |
| 2040 | Privacy, minimum | | 9 | .889 | | 283 | 34 | | 317 | 365 |
| 2050 | Maximum | | 8 | 1 | | 410 | 38 | | 448 | 510 |
| 2120 | Keyed, single cylinder, typical, minimum | | 8 | 1 | | 283 | 38 | | 321 | 370 |
| 2130 | Maximum | | 7 | 1.143 | | 445 | 43.50 | | 488.50 | 560 |
| 2200 | Hotel, minimum | | 7 | 1.143 | | 310 | 43.50 | | 353.50 | 410 |
| 2210 | Maximum | | 6 | 1.333 | | 550 | 51 | | 601 | 685 |
| 3000 | Cast knob and sectional trim, non-keyed, passage, minimum | | 10 | .800 | | 183 | 30.50 | | 213.50 | 249 |
| 3010 | Maximum | | 10 | .800 | | 365 | 30.50 | | 395.50 | 450 |
| 3040 | Privacy, minimum | | 10 | .800 | | 208 | 30.50 | | 238.50 | 276 |
| 3050 | Maximum | | 10 | .800 | | 365 | 30.50 | | 395.50 | 450 |
| 3100 | Keyed, office/entrance/apartment, minimum | | 9 | .889 | | 236 | 34 | | 270 | 310 |
| 3110 | Maximum | | 9 | .889 | | 370 | 34 | | 404 | 465 |
| 3120 | Single cylinder, typical, minimum | | 9 | .889 | | 236 | 34 | | 270 | 310 |
| 3130 | Maximum | | 9 | .889 | | 455 | 34 | | 489 | 560 |
| 3190 | For re-core cylinder, add | | | | | 32 | | | 32 | 35 |
| 3800 | Cipher lockset (security item) | 1 Carp | 13 | .615 | | 735 | 23.50 | | 758.50 | 840 |
| 3900 | Keyless, pushbutton type | | | | | | | | | |
| 4000 | Residential/light commercial, deadbolt, standard | 1 Carp | 9 | .889 | Ea. | 107 | 34 | | 141 | 170 |
| 4010 | Heavy duty | | 9 | .889 | | 127 | 34 | | 161 | 192 |
| 4020 | Industrial, heavy duty, with deadbolt | | 9 | .889 | | 252 | 34 | | 286 | 330 |
| 4030 | Key override | | 9 | .889 | | 284 | 34 | | 318 | 365 |
| 4040 | Lever activated handle | | 9 | .889 | | 300 | 34 | | 334 | 390 |
| 4050 | Key override | | 9 | .889 | | 335 | 34 | | 369 | 420 |
| 4060 | Double sided pushbutton type | | 8 | 1 | | 615 | 38 | | 653 | 740 |
| 4070 | Key override | | 8 | 1 | | 610 | 38 | | 648 | 730 |

## 08 71 20.45 Peepholes

| | | Crew | Daily Output | Labor-Hours | Unit | Material | 2008 Bare Costs Labor | Equipment | Total | Total Incl O&P |
|---|---|---|---|---|---|---|---|---|---|---|
| 0010 | **PEEPHOLES** | | | | | | | | | |
| 2010 | Peephole | 1 Carp | 32 | .250 | Ea. | 14.75 | 9.55 | | 24.30 | 31 |

## 08 71 20.50 Door Stops

| | | Crew | Daily Output | Labor-Hours | Unit | Material | 2008 Bare Costs Labor | Equipment | Total | Total Incl O&P |
|---|---|---|---|---|---|---|---|---|---|---|
| 0010 | **DOOR STOPS** | | | | | | | | | |
| 0020 | Holder & bumper, floor or wall | 1 Carp | 32 | .250 | Ea. | 32.50 | 9.55 | | 42.05 | 50.50 |
| 1300 | Wall bumper, 4" diameter, with rubber pad, aluminum | | 32 | .250 | | 9.85 | 9.55 | | 19.40 | 25.50 |
| 1600 | Door bumper, floor type, aluminum | | 32 | .250 | | 5.70 | 9.55 | | 15.25 | 21 |
| 1900 | Plunger type, door mounted | | 32 | .250 | | 26 | 9.55 | | 35.55 | 43.50 |

## 08 71 20.55 Push-Pull Plates

| | | Crew | Daily Output | Labor-Hours | Unit | Material | 2008 Bare Costs Labor | Equipment | Total | Total Incl O&P |
|---|---|---|---|---|---|---|---|---|---|---|
| 0010 | **PUSH-PULL PLATES** | | | | | | | | | |
| 0100 | Push plate, .050 thick, 4" x 16", aluminum | 1 Carp | 12 | .667 | Ea. | 7.45 | 25.50 | | 32.95 | 47.50 |
| 0500 | Bronze | | 12 | .667 | | 18.45 | 25.50 | | 43.95 | 60 |
| 1500 | Pull handle and push bar, aluminum | | 11 | .727 | | 124 | 27.50 | | 151.50 | 180 |
| 2000 | Bronze | | 10 | .800 | | 161 | 30.50 | | 191.50 | 225 |

# 08 71 Door Hardware

## 08 71 20 – Hardware

| 08 71 20.55 Push-Pull Plates | | Crew | Daily Output | Labor-Hours | Unit | Material | 2008 Bare Costs Labor | Equipment | Total | Total Incl O&P |
|---|---|---|---|---|---|---|---|---|---|---|
| 3000 | Push plate both sides, aluminum | 1 Carp | 14 | .571 | Ea. | 15.45 | 22 | | 37.45 | 51 |
| 3500 | Bronze | | 13 | .615 | | 38 | 23.50 | | 61.50 | 78.50 |
| 4000 | Door pull, designer style, cast aluminum, minimum | | 12 | .667 | | 66 | 25.50 | | 91.50 | 113 |
| 5000 | Maximum | | 8 | 1 | | 340 | 38 | | 378 | 435 |
| 6000 | Cast bronze, minimum | | 12 | .667 | | 79 | 25.50 | | 104.50 | 127 |
| 7000 | Maximum | | 8 | 1 | | 370 | 38 | | 408 | 465 |
| 8000 | Walnut, minimum | | 12 | .667 | | 60.50 | 25.50 | | 86 | 106 |
| 9000 | Maximum | | 8 | 1 | | 340 | 38 | | 378 | 435 |

| 08 71 20.60 Entrance Locks | | | | | | | | | | |
|---|---|---|---|---|---|---|---|---|---|---|
| 0010 | **ENTRANCE LOCKS** | | | | | | | | | |
| 0015 | Cylinder, grip handle deadlocking latch | 1 Carp | 9 | .889 | Ea. | 125 | 34 | | 159 | 191 |
| 0020 | Deadbolt | | 8 | 1 | | 152 | 38 | | 190 | 228 |
| 0100 | Push and pull plate, dead bolt | | 8 | 1 | | 145 | 38 | | 183 | 219 |
| 0900 | For handicapped lever, add | | | | | 158 | | | 158 | 174 |

| 08 71 20.65 Thresholds | | | | | | | | | | |
|---|---|---|---|---|---|---|---|---|---|---|
| 0010 | **THRESHOLDS** | | | | | | | | | |
| 0011 | Threshold 3' long saddles aluminum | 1 Carp | 48 | .167 | L.F. | 3.87 | 6.35 | | 10.22 | 14.15 |
| 0100 | Aluminum, 8" wide, 1/2" thick | | 12 | .667 | Ea. | 35.50 | 25.50 | | 61 | 78.50 |
| 0500 | Bronze | | 60 | .133 | L.F. | 33 | 5.10 | | 38.10 | 44.50 |
| 0600 | Bronze, panic threshold, 5" wide, 1/2" thick | | 12 | .667 | Ea. | 61 | 25.50 | | 86.50 | 107 |
| 0700 | Rubber, 1/2" thick, 5-1/2" wide | | 20 | .400 | | 35 | 15.25 | | 50.25 | 62 |
| 0800 | 2-3/4" wide | | 20 | .400 | | 15 | 15.25 | | 30.25 | 40 |

| 08 71 20.70 Floor Checks | | | | | | | | | | |
|---|---|---|---|---|---|---|---|---|---|---|
| 0010 | **FLOOR CHECKS** | | | | | | | | | |
| 0020 | For over 3' wide doors single acting | 1 Carp | 2.50 | 3.200 | Ea. | 480 | 122 | | 602 | 720 |
| 0500 | Double acting | " | 2.50 | 3.200 | " | 610 | 122 | | 732 | 865 |

| 08 71 20.75 Door Hardware Accessories | | | | | | | | | | |
|---|---|---|---|---|---|---|---|---|---|---|
| 0010 | **DOOR HARDWARE ACCESSORIES** | | | | | | | | | |
| 0050 | Door closing coordinator, 36" (for paired openings up to 56") | 1 Carp | 8 | 1 | Ea. | 89.50 | 38 | | 127.50 | 158 |
| 0060 | 48" (for paired openings up to 84") | | 8 | 1 | | 96 | 38 | | 134 | 165 |
| 0070 | 56" (for paired openings up to 96") | | 8 | 1 | | 105 | 38 | | 143 | 176 |

| 08 71 20.80 Hasps | | | | | | | | | | |
|---|---|---|---|---|---|---|---|---|---|---|
| 0010 | **HASPS**, steel assembly | | | | | | | | | |
| 0015 | 3" | 1 Carp | 26 | .308 | Ea. | 3.10 | 11.70 | | 14.80 | 21.50 |
| 0020 | 4-1/2" | | 13 | .615 | | 3.67 | 23.50 | | 27.17 | 40.50 |
| 0040 | 6" | | 12.50 | .640 | | 5.90 | 24.50 | | 30.40 | 44.50 |

| 08 71 20.90 Hinges | | | | | | | | | | |
|---|---|---|---|---|---|---|---|---|---|---|
| 0010 | **HINGES** R087120-10 | | | | | | | | | |
| 0012 | Full mortise, avg. freq., steel base, USP, 4-1/2" x 4-1/2" | | | | Pr. | 22 | | | 22 | 24 |
| 0100 | 5" x 5", USP | | | | | 36.50 | | | 36.50 | 40 |
| 0200 | 6" x 6", USP | | | | | 78 | | | 78 | 85.50 |
| 0400 | Brass base, 4-1/2" x 4-1/2", US10 | | | | | 45 | | | 45 | 49.50 |
| 0500 | 5" x 5", US10 | | | | | 66 | | | 66 | 72.50 |
| 0600 | 6" x 6", US10 | | | | | 112 | | | 112 | 123 |
| 0800 | Stainless steel base, 4-1/2" x 4-1/2", US32 | | | | | 67.50 | | | 67.50 | 74.50 |
| 0900 | For non removable pin, add (security item) | | | | Ea. | 3.86 | | | 3.86 | 4.25 |
| 0910 | For floating pin, driven tips, add | | | | | 2.81 | | | 2.81 | 3.09 |
| 0930 | For hospital type tip on pin, add | | | | | 12.15 | | | 12.15 | 13.35 |
| 0940 | For steeple type tip on pin, add | | | | | 10.65 | | | 10.65 | 11.70 |
| 0950 | Full mortise, high frequency, steel base, 3-1/2" x 3-1/2", US26D | | | | Pr. | 23.50 | | | 23.50 | 26 |
| 1000 | 4-1/2" x 4-1/2", USP | | | | | 52.50 | | | 52.50 | 58 |

# 08 71 Door Hardware

## 08 71 20 – Hardware

### 08 71 20.90 Hinges

| | | Crew | Daily Output | Labor-Hours | Unit | Material | 2008 Bare Costs Labor | Equipment | Total | Total Incl O&P |
|---|---|---|---|---|---|---|---|---|---|---|
| 1100 | 5" x 5", USP | | | | Pr. | 49.50 | | | 49.50 | 54.50 |
| 1200 | 6" x 6", USP | | | | | 120 | | | 120 | 132 |
| 1400 | Brass base, 3-1/2" x 3-1/2", US4 | | | | | 41.50 | | | 41.50 | 45.50 |
| 1430 | 4-1/2" x 4-1/2", US10 | | | | | 71 | | | 71 | 78 |
| 1500 | 5" x 5", US10 | | | | | 106 | | | 106 | 117 |
| 1600 | 6" x 6", US10 | | | | | 153 | | | 153 | 169 |
| 1800 | Stainless steel base, 4-1/2" x 4-1/2", US32 | | | | | 115 | | | 115 | 126 |
| 1810 | 5" x 4-1/2", US32 | | | | ↓ | 159 | | | 159 | 175 |
| 1930 | For hospital type tip on pin, add | | | | Ea. | 10.60 | | | 10.60 | 11.65 |
| 1950 | Full mortise, low frequency, steel base, 3-1/2" x 3-1/2", US26D | | | | Pr. | 9.50 | | | 9.50 | 10.45 |
| 2000 | 4-1/2" x 4-1/2", USP | | | | | 10.85 | | | 10.85 | 11.90 |
| 2100 | 5" x 5", USP | | | | | 27 | | | 27 | 29.50 |
| 2200 | 6" x 6", USP | | | | | 53.50 | | | 53.50 | 59 |
| 2300 | 4-1/2" x 4-1/2", US3 | | | | | 15.70 | | | 15.70 | 17.25 |
| 2310 | 5" x 5", US3 | | | | | 39 | | | 39 | 42.50 |
| 2400 | Brass bass, 4-1/2" x 4-1/2", US10 | | | | | 37.50 | | | 37.50 | 41.50 |
| 2500 | 5" x 5", US10 | | | | | 57.50 | | | 57.50 | 63 |
| 2800 | Stainless steel base, 4-1/2" x 4-1/2", US32 | | | | ↓ | 65 | | | 65 | 71.50 |

### 08 71 20.91 Special Hinges

| | | Crew | Daily Output | Labor-Hours | Unit | Material | 2008 Bare Costs Labor | Equipment | Total | Total Incl O&P |
|---|---|---|---|---|---|---|---|---|---|---|
| 0010 | **SPECIAL HINGES** | | | | | | | | | |
| 0015 | Paumelle, high frequency | | | | | | | | | |
| 0020 | Steel base, 6" x 4-1/2", US10 | | | | Pr. | 139 | | | 139 | 153 |
| 0100 | Bronze base, 5" x 4-1/2", US10 | | | | | 174 | | | 174 | 192 |
| 0200 | Paumelle, average frequency, steel base, 4-1/2" x 3-1/2", US10 | | | | | 94 | | | 94 | 104 |
| 0400 | Olive knuckle, low frequency, brass base, 6" x 4-1/2", US10 | | | | ↓ | 159 | | | 159 | 175 |
| 1000 | Electric hinge with concealed conductor, average frequency | | | | | | | | | |
| 1010 | Steel base, 4-1/2" x 4-1/2", US26D | | | | Pr. | 296 | | | 296 | 325 |
| 1100 | Bronze base, 4-1/2" x 4-1/2", US26D | | | | " | 310 | | | 310 | 340 |
| 1200 | Electric hinge with concealed conductor, high frequency | | | | | | | | | |
| 1210 | Steel base, 4-1/2" x 4-1/2", US26D | | | | Pr. | 221 | | | 221 | 243 |
| 1600 | Double weight, 800 lb., steel base, removable pin, 5" x 6", USP | | | | | 128 | | | 128 | 140 |
| 1700 | Steel base-welded pin, 5" x 6", USP | | | | | 144 | | | 144 | 158 |
| 1800 | Triple weight, 2000 lb., steel base, welded pin, 5" x 6", USP | | | | | 147 | | | 147 | 162 |
| 2000 | Pivot reinf., high frequency, steel base, 7-3/4" door plate, USP | | | | | 172 | | | 172 | 190 |
| 2200 | Bronze base, 7-3/4" door plate, US10 | | | | ↓ | 202 | | | 202 | 222 |
| 3000 | Swing clear, full mortise, full or half surface, high frequency, | | | | | | | | | |
| 3010 | Steel base, 5" high, USP | | | | Pr. | 148 | | | 148 | 163 |
| 3200 | Swing clear, full mortise, average frequency | | | | | | | | | |
| 3210 | Steel base, 4-1/2" high, USP | | | | Pr. | 118 | | | 118 | 129 |
| 4000 | Wide throw, average frequency, steel base, 4-1/2" x 6", USP | | | | | 90 | | | 90 | 99 |
| 4200 | High frequency, steel base, 4-1/2" x 6", USP | | | | ↓ | 137 | | | 137 | 151 |
| 4600 | Spring hinge, single acting, 6" flange, steel | | | | Ea. | 50.50 | | | 50.50 | 55.50 |
| 4700 | Brass | | | | | 88.50 | | | 88.50 | 97.50 |
| 4900 | Double acting, 6" flange, steel | | | | | 88 | | | 88 | 97 |
| 4950 | Brass | | | | ↓ | 144 | | | 144 | 159 |
| 9000 | Continuous hinge, steel, full mortise, heavy duty | 2 Carp | 64 | .250 | L.F. | 11.35 | 9.55 | | 20.90 | 27.50 |

### 08 71 20.95 Kick Plates

| | | Crew | Daily Output | Labor-Hours | Unit | Material | 2008 Bare Costs Labor | Equipment | Total | Total Incl O&P |
|---|---|---|---|---|---|---|---|---|---|---|
| 0010 | **KICK PLATES** | | | | | | | | | |
| 0020 | Stainless steel, 6" high, for 3' door | 1 Carp | 15 | .533 | Ea. | 29.50 | 20.50 | | 50 | 64 |
| 0500 | Bronze 6" high, for 3' door | | 15 | .533 | | 36.50 | 20.50 | | 57 | 71.50 |
| 2000 | Aluminum, .050, with 3 beveled edges, 10" x 28" | | 15 | .533 | | 21 | 20.50 | | 41.50 | 54.50 |
| 2010 | 10" x 30" | ↓ | 15 | .533 | ↓ | 23 | 20.50 | | 43.50 | 56.50 |

## 08 71 20 – Hardware

| 08 71 20.95 Kick Plates | Crew | Daily Output | Labor-Hours | Unit | Material | 2008 Bare Costs Labor | 2008 Bare Costs Equipment | Total | Total Incl O&P |
|---|---|---|---|---|---|---|---|---|---|
| 2020      10" x 34" | 1 Carp | 15 | .533 | Ea. | 24 | 20.50 | | 44.50 | 58 |
| 2040      10" x 38" | ↓ | 15 | .533 | ↓ | 26 | 20.50 | | 46.50 | 60 |

## 08 71 21 – Astragals

### 08 71 21.10 Exterior Mouldings, Astragals

| | Crew | Daily Output | Labor-Hours | Unit | Material | Labor | Equipment | Total | Total Incl O&P |
|---|---|---|---|---|---|---|---|---|---|
| 0010 **EXTERIOR MOULDINGS, ASTRAGALS** | | | | | | | | | |
| 0400   One piece, overlapping cadmium plated steel, flat, 3/16" x 2" | 1 Carp | 90 | .089 | L.F. | 3.19 | 3.39 | | 6.58 | 8.75 |
| 0600    Prime coated steel, flat, 1/8" x 3" | | 90 | .089 | | 4.44 | 3.39 | | 7.83 | 10.15 |
| 0800    Stainless steel, flat, 3/32" x 1-5/8" | | 90 | .089 | | 16.65 | 3.39 | | 20.04 | 23.50 |
| 1000    Aluminum, flat, 1/8" x 2" | | 90 | .089 | | 3.20 | 3.39 | | 6.59 | 8.75 |
| 1200     Nail on, "T" extrusion | | 120 | .067 | | .71 | 2.54 | | 3.25 | 4.73 |
| 1300      Vinyl bulb insert | | 105 | .076 | | 1.15 | 2.90 | | 4.05 | 5.80 |
| 1600     Screw on, "T" extrusion | | 90 | .089 | | 4.67 | 3.39 | | 8.06 | 10.40 |
| 1700      Vinyl insert | | 75 | .107 | | 3.15 | 4.06 | | 7.21 | 9.80 |
| 2000     "L" extrusion, neoprene bulbs | | 75 | .107 | | 1.81 | 4.06 | | 5.87 | 8.35 |
| 2100      Neoprene sponge insert | | 75 | .107 | | 5.55 | 4.06 | | 9.61 | 12.45 |
| 2200      Magnetic | | 75 | .107 | | 9.10 | 4.06 | | 13.16 | 16.35 |
| 2400     Spring hinged security seal, with cam | | 75 | .107 | | 5.85 | 4.06 | | 9.91 | 12.80 |
| 2600     Spring loaded locking bolt, vinyl insert | | 45 | .178 | | 8 | 6.75 | | 14.75 | 19.35 |
| 2800    Neoprene sponge strip, "Z" shaped, aluminum | | 60 | .133 | | 3.79 | 5.10 | | 8.89 | 12.05 |
| 2900    Solid neoprene strip, nail on aluminum strip | ↓ | 90 | .089 | ↓ | 3.18 | 3.39 | | 6.57 | 8.75 |
| 3000   One piece stile protection | | | | | | | | | |
| 3020    Neoprene fabric loop, nail on aluminum strips | 1 Carp | 60 | .133 | L.F. | .57 | 5.10 | | 5.67 | 8.55 |
| 3110     Flush mounted aluminum extrusion, 1/2" x 1-1/4" | | 60 | .133 | | 3.02 | 5.10 | | 8.12 | 11.20 |
| 3140      3/4" x 1-3/8" | | 60 | .133 | | 3.83 | 5.10 | | 8.93 | 12.10 |
| 3160      1-1/8" x 1-3/4" | | 60 | .133 | | 6.10 | 5.10 | | 11.20 | 14.65 |
| 3300     Mortise, 9/16" x 3/4" | | 60 | .133 | | 3.24 | 5.10 | | 8.34 | 11.45 |
| 3320      13/16" x 1-3/8" | | 60 | .133 | | 3.52 | 5.10 | | 8.62 | 11.75 |
| 3600    Spring bronze strip, nail on type | | 105 | .076 | | 2.77 | 2.90 | | 5.67 | 7.55 |
| 3620     Screw on, with retainer | | 75 | .107 | | 2.27 | 4.06 | | 6.33 | 8.85 |
| 3800    Flexible stainless steel housing, pile insert, 1/2" door | | 105 | .076 | | 6.25 | 2.90 | | 9.15 | 11.40 |
| 3820      3/4" door | | 105 | .076 | | 7.05 | 2.90 | | 9.95 | 12.25 |
| 4000    Extruded aluminum retainer, flush mount, pile insert | | 105 | .076 | | 2.19 | 2.90 | | 5.09 | 6.95 |
| 4080     Mortise, felt insert | | 90 | .089 | | 3.90 | 3.39 | | 7.29 | 9.55 |
| 4160     Mortise with spring, pile insert | | 90 | .089 | | 3.05 | 3.39 | | 6.44 | 8.60 |
| 4400    Rigid vinyl retainer, mortise, pile insert | | 105 | .076 | | 2.18 | 2.90 | | 5.08 | 6.90 |
| 4600    Wool pile filler strip, aluminum backing | ↓ | 105 | .076 | ↓ | 2.19 | 2.90 | | 5.09 | 6.95 |
| 5000   Two piece overlapping astragal, extruded aluminum retainer | | | | | | | | | |
| 5010      Pile insert | 1 Carp | 60 | .133 | L.F. | 2.84 | 5.10 | | 7.94 | 11 |
| 5020      Vinyl bulb insert | | 60 | .133 | | 1.83 | 5.10 | | 6.93 | 9.90 |
| 5040      Vinyl flap insert | | 60 | .133 | | 5.70 | 5.10 | | 10.80 | 14.20 |
| 5060      Solid neoprene flap insert | | 60 | .133 | | 5.65 | 5.10 | | 10.75 | 14.10 |
| 5080      Hypalon rubber flap insert | | 60 | .133 | | 5.80 | 5.10 | | 10.90 | 14.25 |
| 5090      Snap on cover, pile insert | | 60 | .133 | | 6.60 | 5.10 | | 11.70 | 15.15 |
| 5400     Magnetic aluminum, surface mounted | | 60 | .133 | | 22.50 | 5.10 | | 27.60 | 32.50 |
| 5500     Interlocking aluminum, 5/8" x 1" neoprene bulb insert | | 45 | .178 | | 3.54 | 6.75 | | 10.29 | 14.45 |
| 5600     Adjustable aluminum, 9/16" x 21/32", pile insert | ↓ | 45 | .178 | | 16.80 | 6.75 | | 23.55 | 29 |
| 5790      For vinyl bulb, deduct | | | | | .43 | | | .43 | .47 |
| 5800     Magnetic, adjustable, 9/16" x 21/32" | 1 Carp | 45 | .178 | ↓ | 21.50 | 6.75 | | 28.25 | 34.50 |
| 6000   Two piece stile protection | | | | | | | | | |
| 6010     Cloth backed rubber loop, 1" gap, nail on aluminum strips | 1 Carp | 45 | .178 | L.F. | 3.63 | 6.75 | | 10.38 | 14.55 |
| 6040      Screw on aluminum strips | | 45 | .178 | | 5.65 | 6.75 | | 12.40 | 16.75 |
| 6100      1-1/2" gap, screw on aluminum extrusion | ↓ | 45 | .178 | ↓ | 5.10 | 6.75 | | 11.85 | 16.15 |

# 08 71 Door Hardware

## 08 71 21 – Astragals

### 08 71 21.10 Exterior Mouldings, Astragals

| | | Crew | Daily Output | Labor-Hours | Unit | Material | 2008 Bare Costs Labor | Equipment | Total | Total Incl O&P |
|---|---|---|---|---|---|---|---|---|---|---|
| 6240 | Vinyl fabric loop, slotted aluminum extrusion, 1" gap | 1 Carp | 45 | .178 | L.F. | 1.79 | 6.75 | | 8.54 | 12.50 |
| 6300 | 1-1/4" gap | ↓ | 45 | .178 | ↓ | 5.35 | 6.75 | | 12.10 | 16.45 |

## 08 71 25 – Weatherstripping

### 08 71 25.10 Mechanical Seals, Weatherstripping

| | | Crew | Daily Output | Labor-Hours | Unit | Material | 2008 Bare Costs Labor | Equipment | Total | Total Incl O&P |
|---|---|---|---|---|---|---|---|---|---|---|
| 0010 | **MECHANICAL SEALS, WEATHERSTRIPPING** | | | | | | | | | |
| 1000 | Doors, wood frame, interlocking, for 3' x 7' door, zinc | 1 Carp | 3 | 2.667 | Opng. | 14.35 | 102 | | 116.35 | 174 |
| 1100 | Bronze | | 3 | 2.667 | | 22.50 | 102 | | 124.50 | 183 |
| 1300 | 6' x 7' opening, zinc | | 2 | 4 | | 15.70 | 152 | | 167.70 | 254 |
| 1400 | Bronze | ↓ | 2 | 4 | ↓ | 29.50 | 152 | | 181.50 | 270 |
| 1700 | Wood frame, spring type, bronze | | | | | | | | | |
| 1800 | 3' x 7' door | 1 Carp | 7.60 | 1.053 | Opng. | 18.85 | 40 | | 58.85 | 83 |
| 1900 | 6' x 7' door | " | 7 | 1.143 | " | 22.50 | 43.50 | | 66 | 93 |
| 2200 | Metal frame, spring type, bronze | | | | | | | | | |
| 2300 | 3' x 7' door | 1 Carp | 3 | 2.667 | Opng. | 32 | 102 | | 134 | 193 |
| 2400 | 6' x 7' door | " | 2.50 | 3.200 | " | 43 | 122 | | 165 | 237 |
| 2500 | For stainless steel, spring type, add | | | | | 133% | | | | |
| 2700 | Metal frame, extruded sections, 3' x 7' door, aluminum | 1 Carp | 2 | 4 | Opng. | 41.50 | 152 | | 193.50 | 283 |
| 2800 | Bronze | | 2 | 4 | | 105 | 152 | | 257 | 355 |
| 3100 | 6' x 7' door, aluminum | | 1.20 | 6.667 | | 53 | 254 | | 307 | 455 |
| 3200 | Bronze | ↓ | 1.20 | 6.667 | ↓ | 124 | 254 | | 378 | 530 |
| 3500 | Threshold weatherstripping | | | | | | | | | |
| 3650 | Door sweep, flush mounted, aluminum | 1 Carp | 25 | .320 | Ea. | 12.35 | 12.20 | | 24.55 | 32.50 |
| 3700 | Vinyl | | 25 | .320 | | 14.60 | 12.20 | | 26.80 | 35 |
| 5000 | Garage door bottom weatherstrip, 12' aluminum, clear | | 14 | .571 | | 19.75 | 22 | | 41.75 | 55.50 |
| 5010 | Bronze | | 14 | .571 | | 75.50 | 22 | | 97.50 | 117 |
| 5050 | Bottom protection, 12' aluminum, clear | | 14 | .571 | | 21.50 | 22 | | 43.50 | 57.50 |
| 5100 | Bronze | ↓ | 14 | .571 | ↓ | 85 | 22 | | 107 | 128 |

# 08 74 Access Control Hardware

## 08 74 13 – Card Key Access Control Hardware

### 08 74 13.50 Card Key Access

| | | Crew | Daily Output | Labor-Hours | Unit | Material | 2008 Bare Costs Labor | Equipment | Total | Total Incl O&P |
|---|---|---|---|---|---|---|---|---|---|---|
| 0010 | **CARD KEY ACCESS** | | | | | | | | | |
| 0020 | Card type, 1 time zone, minimum | | | | Ea. | 330 | | | 330 | 360 |
| 0040 | Maximum | | | | | 1,075 | | | 1,075 | 1,175 |
| 0060 | 3 time zones, minimum | | | | | 795 | | | 795 | 875 |
| 0080 | Maximum | | | | ↓ | 1,850 | | | 1,850 | 2,050 |
| 0100 | System with printer, and control console, 3 zones | | | | Total | 9,075 | | | 9,075 | 9,975 |
| 0120 | 6 zones | | | | " | 11,900 | | | 11,900 | 13,100 |
| 0140 | For each door, minimum, add | | | | Ea. | 1,325 | | | 1,325 | 1,475 |
| 0160 | Maximum, add | | | | " | 1,975 | | | 1,975 | 2,175 |

## 08 74 19 – Biometric Identity Access Control Hardware

### 08 74 19.50 Biometric Identity Access

| | | Crew | Daily Output | Labor-Hours | Unit | Material | 2008 Bare Costs Labor | Equipment | Total | Total Incl O&P |
|---|---|---|---|---|---|---|---|---|---|---|
| 0010 | **BIOMETRIC IDENTITY ACCESS** | | | | | | | | | |
| 0220 | Hand geometry scanner, mem of 512 users, excl striker/powr | 1 Elec | 3 | 2.667 | Ea. | 1,800 | 121 | | 1,921 | 2,150 |
| 0230 | Memory upgrade for, adds 9,700 user profiles | | 8 | 1 | | 232 | 45.50 | | 277.50 | 325 |
| 0240 | Adds 32,500 user profiles | | 8 | 1 | | 540 | 45.50 | | 585.50 | 665 |
| 0250 | Prison type, memory of 256 users, excl striker, power | | 3 | 2.667 | | 2,300 | 121 | | 2,421 | 2,700 |
| 0260 | Memory upgrade for, adds 3,300 user profiles | | 8 | 1 | | 186 | 45.50 | | 231.50 | 273 |
| 0270 | Adds 9,700 user profiles | | 8 | 1 | | 370 | 45.50 | | 415.50 | 480 |
| 0280 | Adds 27,900 user profiles | ↓ | 8 | 1 | ↓ | 520 | 45.50 | | 565.50 | 645 |

# 08 74 Access Control Hardware

## 08 74 19 – Biometric Identity Access Control Hardware

| 08 74 19.50 Biometric Identity Access | | Crew | Daily Output | Labor-Hours | Unit | Material | 2008 Bare Costs Labor | Equipment | Total | Total Incl O&P |
|---|---|---|---|---|---|---|---|---|---|---|
| 0290 | All weather, mem of 512 users, excl striker/pwr | 1 Elec | 3 | 2.667 | Ea. | 3,600 | 121 | | 3,721 | 4,125 |
| 0300 | Facial & fingerprint scanner, combination unit, excl striker/power | | 3 | 2.667 | | 4,200 | 121 | | 4,321 | 4,800 |
| 0310 | Access for, for initial setup, excl striker/power | | 3 | 2.667 | | 1,000 | 121 | | 1,121 | 1,275 |

# 08 75 Window Hardware

## 08 75 30 – Weatherstripping

### 08 75 30.10 Mechanical Weather Seals

| 08 75 30.10 Mechanical Weather Seals | | Crew | Daily Output | Labor-Hours | Unit | Material | 2008 Bare Costs Labor | Equipment | Total | Total Incl O&P |
|---|---|---|---|---|---|---|---|---|---|---|
| 0010 | **MECHANICAL WEATHER SEALS**, Window, double hung, 3' X 5' | | | | | | | | | |
| 0020 | Zinc | 1 Carp | 7.20 | 1.111 | Opng. | 12.25 | 42.50 | | 54.75 | 79.50 |
| 0100 | Bronze | | 7.20 | 1.111 | | 24.50 | 42.50 | | 67 | 93 |
| 0500 | As above but heavy duty, zinc | | 4.60 | 1.739 | | 16 | 66.50 | | 82.50 | 121 |
| 0600 | Bronze | | 4.60 | 1.739 | | 28 | 66.50 | | 94.50 | 134 |
| 9000 | Minimum labor/equipment charge | 1 Clab | 4.60 | 1.739 | Job | | 52.50 | | 52.50 | 82 |

# 08 79 Hardware Accessories

## 08 79 13 – Key Storage Equipment

### 08 79 13.10 Key Cabinets

| 08 79 13.10 Key Cabinets | | Crew | Daily Output | Labor-Hours | Unit | Material | 2008 Bare Costs Labor | Equipment | Total | Total Incl O&P |
|---|---|---|---|---|---|---|---|---|---|---|
| 0010 | **KEY CABINETS** | | | | | | | | | |
| 0020 | Wall mounted, 60 key capacity | 1 Carp | 20 | .400 | Ea. | 69 | 15.25 | | 84.25 | 99.50 |
| 0200 | Drawer type, 600 key capacity | 1 Clab | 15 | .533 | | 725 | 16.15 | | 741.15 | 825 |
| 0300 | 2,400 key capacity | | 20 | .400 | | 2,600 | 12.10 | | 2,612.10 | 2,875 |
| 0400 | Tray type, 20 key capacity | | 50 | .160 | | 40 | 4.84 | | 44.84 | 51.50 |
| 0500 | 50 key capacity | | 40 | .200 | | 72.50 | 6.05 | | 78.55 | 89.50 |

## 08 79 20 – Door Accessories

### 08 79 20.10 Door Hardware Accessories

| 08 79 20.10 Door Hardware Accessories | | Crew | Daily Output | Labor-Hours | Unit | Material | 2008 Bare Costs Labor | Equipment | Total | Total Incl O&P |
|---|---|---|---|---|---|---|---|---|---|---|
| 0010 | **DOOR HARDWARE ACCESSORIES** | | | | | | | | | |
| 0140 | Door bolt, surface, 4" | 1 Carp | 32 | .250 | Ea. | 8.65 | 9.55 | | 18.20 | 24.50 |
| 0160 | Door latch | " | 12 | .667 | " | 7.35 | 25.50 | | 32.85 | 47.50 |
| 0200 | Sliding closet door | | | | | | | | | |
| 0220 | Track and hanger, single | 1 Carp | 10 | .800 | Ea. | 49.50 | 30.50 | | 80 | 102 |
| 0240 | Double | | 8 | 1 | | 67 | 38 | | 105 | 133 |
| 0260 | Door guide, single | | 48 | .167 | | 22 | 6.35 | | 28.35 | 34 |
| 0280 | Double | | 48 | .167 | | 30 | 6.35 | | 36.35 | 43 |
| 0600 | Deadbolt and lock cover plate, brass or stainless steel | | 30 | .267 | | 24.50 | 10.15 | | 34.65 | 43 |
| 0620 | Hole cover plate, brass or chrome | | 35 | .229 | | 6.40 | 8.70 | | 15.10 | 20.50 |
| 2240 | Mortise lockset, passage, lever handle | | 9 | .889 | | 179 | 34 | | 213 | 250 |
| 4000 | Security chain, standard | | 18 | .444 | | 7.40 | 16.95 | | 24.35 | 34.50 |

# 08 81 Glass Glazing

## 08 81 10 – Float Glass

### 08 81 10.10 Various Types and Thickness of Float Glass

| | | Crew | Daily Output | Labor-Hours | Unit | Material | 2008 Bare Costs Labor | Equipment | Total | Total Incl O&P |
|---|---|---|---|---|---|---|---|---|---|---|
| 0010 | **VARIOUS TYPES AND THICKNESS OF FLOAT GLASS** R088110-10 | | | | | | | | | |
| 0020 | 3/16" Plain | 2 Glaz | 130 | .123 | S.F. | 4.51 | 4.59 | | 9.10 | 11.90 |
| 0200 | Tempered, clear | | 130 | .123 | | 5.25 | 4.59 | | 9.84 | 12.75 |
| 0300 | Tinted | | 130 | .123 | | 6.65 | 4.59 | | 11.24 | 14.30 |
| 0600 | 1/4" thick, clear, plain *CN* | | 120 | .133 | | 4.86 | 4.97 | | 9.83 | 12.90 |
| 0700 | Tinted | | 120 | .133 | | 5.60 | 4.97 | | 10.57 | 13.70 |
| 0800 | Tempered, clear | | 120 | .133 | | 6.45 | 4.97 | | 11.42 | 14.65 |
| 0900 | Tinted | | 120 | .133 | | 8.95 | 4.97 | | 13.92 | 17.35 |
| 1600 | 3/8" thick, clear, plain | | 75 | .213 | | 8.40 | 7.95 | | 16.35 | 21.50 |
| 1700 | Tinted | | 75 | .213 | | 11.20 | 7.95 | | 19.15 | 24.50 |
| 1800 | Tempered, clear | | 75 | .213 | | 12.95 | 7.95 | | 20.90 | 26.50 |
| 1900 | Tinted | | 75 | .213 | | 15.60 | 7.95 | | 23.55 | 29 |
| 2200 | 1/2" thick, clear, plain | | 55 | .291 | | 16.60 | 10.85 | | 27.45 | 34.50 |
| 2300 | Tinted | | 55 | .291 | | 19.65 | 10.85 | | 30.50 | 38 |
| 2400 | Tempered, clear | | 55 | .291 | | 19.30 | 10.85 | | 30.15 | 37.50 |
| 2500 | Tinted | | 55 | .291 | | 24 | 10.85 | | 34.85 | 43 |
| 2800 | 5/8" thick, clear, plain | | 45 | .356 | | 19.65 | 13.25 | | 32.90 | 41.50 |
| 2900 | Tempered, clear | | 45 | .356 | | 22.50 | 13.25 | | 35.75 | 44.50 |
| 3200 | 3/4" thick, clear, plain | | 35 | .457 | | 25.50 | 17.05 | | 42.55 | 54 |
| 3300 | Tempered, clear | | 35 | .457 | | 29.50 | 17.05 | | 46.55 | 58.50 |
| 3600 | 1" thick, clear, plain | | 30 | .533 | | 42 | 19.90 | | 61.90 | 76.50 |
| 8900 | For low emissivity coating for 3/16" & 1/4" only, add to above | | | | | 15% | | | | |

## 08 81 13 – Decorative Glass Glazing

### 08 81 13.10 Beveled Glass

| | | Crew | Daily Output | Labor-Hours | Unit | Material | 2008 Bare Costs Labor | Equipment | Total | Total Incl O&P |
|---|---|---|---|---|---|---|---|---|---|---|
| 0010 | **BEVELED GLASS**, with design patterns | | | | | | | | | |
| 0020 | Minimum | 2 Glaz | 150 | .107 | S.F. | 41.50 | 3.98 | | 45.48 | 52 |
| 0050 | Average | | 125 | .128 | | 98 | 4.77 | | 102.77 | 115 |
| 0100 | Maximum | | 100 | .160 | | 173 | 5.95 | | 178.95 | 199 |

### 08 81 13.20 Faceted Glass

| | | Crew | Daily Output | Labor-Hours | Unit | Material | 2008 Bare Costs Labor | Equipment | Total | Total Incl O&P |
|---|---|---|---|---|---|---|---|---|---|---|
| 0010 | **FACETED GLASS**, Color tinted 3/4" thick | | | | | | | | | |
| 0020 | Minimum | 2 Glaz | 95 | .168 | S.F. | 35.50 | 6.30 | | 41.80 | 48.50 |
| 0100 | Maximum | " | 75 | .213 | " | 61.50 | 7.95 | | 69.45 | 80 |

### 08 81 13.30 Sandblasted Glass

| | | Crew | Daily Output | Labor-Hours | Unit | Material | 2008 Bare Costs Labor | Equipment | Total | Total Incl O&P |
|---|---|---|---|---|---|---|---|---|---|---|
| 0010 | **SANDBLASTED GLASS**, float glass | | | | | | | | | |
| 0020 | 1/8" thick | 2 Glaz | 160 | .100 | S.F. | 7.80 | 3.73 | | 11.53 | 14.20 |
| 0100 | 3/16" thick | | 130 | .123 | | 8.60 | 4.59 | | 13.19 | 16.45 |
| 0500 | 1/4" thick | | 120 | .133 | | 8.95 | 4.97 | | 13.92 | 17.40 |
| 0600 | 3/8" thick | | 75 | .213 | | 9.75 | 7.95 | | 17.70 | 23 |

## 08 81 20 – Vision Panels

### 08 81 20.10 Full Vision

| | | Crew | Daily Output | Labor-Hours | Unit | Material | 2008 Bare Costs Labor | Equipment | Total | Total Incl O&P |
|---|---|---|---|---|---|---|---|---|---|---|
| 0010 | **FULL VISION**, window system with 3/4" glass mullions | | | | | | | | | |
| 0020 | Up to 10' high | H-2 | 130 | .185 | S.F. | 53 | 6.45 | | 59.45 | 68 |
| 0100 | 10' to 20' high, minimum | | 110 | .218 | | 56 | 7.65 | | 63.65 | 73 |
| 0150 | Average | | 100 | .240 | | 60.50 | 8.40 | | 68.90 | 79.50 |
| 0200 | Maximum | | 80 | .300 | | 68 | 10.50 | | 78.50 | 91 |

## 08 81 25 – Glazing Variables

### 08 81 25.10 Applications of Glazing

| | | Crew | Daily Output | Labor-Hours | Unit | Material | 2008 Bare Costs Labor | Equipment | Total | Total Incl O&P |
|---|---|---|---|---|---|---|---|---|---|---|
| 0010 | **APPLICATIONS OF GLAZING** R088110-10 | | | | | | | | | |
| 0500 | For high rise glazing, exterior, add per S.F. per story | | | | S.F. | | | | | .17 |
| 0600 | For glass replacement, add | | | | " | | 100% | | | |

# 08 81 Glass Glazing

## 08 81 25 – Glazing Variables

### 08 81 25.10 Applications of Glazing

| | | Crew | Daily Output | Labor-Hours | Unit | Material | 2008 Bare Costs Labor | Equipment | Total | Total Incl O&P |
|---|---|---|---|---|---|---|---|---|---|---|
| 0700 | For gasket settings, add | | | | L.F. | 4.20 | | | 4.20 | 4.62 |
| 0900 | For sloped glazing, add | | | | S.F. | | 25% | | | |
| 2000 | Fabrication, polished edges, 1/4" thick | | | | Inch | .36 | | | .36 | .40 |
| 2100 | 1/2" thick | | | | | .92 | | | .92 | 1.01 |
| 2500 | Mitered edges, 1/4" thick | | | | | .92 | | | .92 | 1.01 |
| 2600 | 1/2" thick | | | | | 1.48 | | | 1.48 | 1.63 |

## 08 81 30 – Insulating Glass

### 08 81 30.10 Reduce Heat Transfer Glass

| | | | Crew | Daily Output | Labor-Hours | Unit | Material | 2008 Bare Costs Labor | Equipment | Total | Total Incl O&P |
|---|---|---|---|---|---|---|---|---|---|---|---|
| 0010 | **REDUCE HEAT TRANSFER GLASS**, 2 lites 1/8" float, 1/2" thk under 15 S.F. | | | | | | | | | | |
| 0020 | Clear | R088110-10 | 2 Glaz | 95 | .168 | S.F. | 8.30 | 6.30 | | 14.60 | 18.65 |
| 0100 | Tinted | | | 95 | .168 | | 11.55 | 6.30 | | 17.85 | 22 |
| 0200 | 2 lites 3/16" float, for 5/8" thk unit, 15 to 30 S.F., clear | | | 90 | .178 | | 9.80 | 6.65 | | 16.45 | 21 |
| 0300 | Tinted | | | 90 | .178 | | 10.10 | 6.65 | | 16.75 | 21 |
| 0400 | 1" thk, dbl. glazed, 1/4" float, 30-70 S.F., clear | CN | | 75 | .213 | | 13.95 | 7.95 | | 21.90 | 27.50 |
| 0500 | Tinted | | | 75 | .213 | | 16.85 | 7.95 | | 24.80 | 30.50 |
| 0600 | 1" thick double glazed, 1/4" float, 1/4" wire | | | 75 | .213 | | 19.50 | 7.95 | | 27.45 | 33.50 |
| 0700 | 1/4" float, 1/4" tempered | | | 75 | .213 | | 19.05 | 7.95 | | 27 | 33 |
| 0800 | 1/4" wire, 1/4" tempered | | | 75 | .213 | | 26.50 | 7.95 | | 34.45 | 41 |
| 0900 | Both lites, 1/4" wire | | | 75 | .213 | | 26.50 | 7.95 | | 34.45 | 41.50 |
| 2000 | Both lites, light & heat reflective | | | 85 | .188 | | 22.50 | 7 | | 29.50 | 35 |
| 2500 | Heat reflective, film inside, 1" thick unit, clear | | | 85 | .188 | | 19.65 | 7 | | 26.65 | 32 |
| 2600 | Tinted | | | 85 | .188 | | 21 | 7 | | 28 | 34 |
| 3000 | Film on weatherside, clear, 1/2" thick unit | | | 95 | .168 | | 14.05 | 6.30 | | 20.35 | 25 |
| 3100 | 5/8" thick unit | | | 90 | .178 | | 17 | 6.65 | | 23.65 | 29 |
| 3200 | 1" thick unit | | | 85 | .188 | | 19.35 | 7 | | 26.35 | 32 |

## 08 81 35 – Translucent Glass

### 08 81 35.10 Obscure Glass

| | | Crew | Daily Output | Labor-Hours | Unit | Material | 2008 Bare Costs Labor | Equipment | Total | Total Incl O&P |
|---|---|---|---|---|---|---|---|---|---|---|
| 0010 | **OBSCURE GLASS**, 1/8" thick | | | | | | | | | |
| 0020 | Minimum | 2 Glaz | 140 | .114 | S.F. | 7.90 | 4.26 | | 12.16 | 15.15 |
| 0100 | Maximum | | 125 | .128 | | 9.50 | 4.77 | | 14.27 | 17.70 |
| 0300 | 7/32" thick, minimum | | 120 | .133 | | 8.80 | 4.97 | | 13.77 | 17.25 |
| 0400 | Maximum | | 105 | .152 | | 11.20 | 5.70 | | 16.90 | 21 |

### 08 81 35.20 Patterned Glass

| | | Crew | Daily Output | Labor-Hours | Unit | Material | 2008 Bare Costs Labor | Equipment | Total | Total Incl O&P |
|---|---|---|---|---|---|---|---|---|---|---|
| 0010 | **PATTERNED GLASS**, colored, 1/8" thick | | | | | | | | | |
| 0020 | Minimum | 2 Glaz | 140 | .114 | S.F. | 8.05 | 4.26 | | 12.31 | 15.35 |
| 0100 | Maximum | | 125 | .128 | | 10.90 | 4.77 | | 15.67 | 19.25 |
| 0300 | 7/32" thick, minimum | | 120 | .133 | | 10.05 | 4.97 | | 15.02 | 18.60 |
| 0400 | Maximum | | 105 | .152 | | 11.70 | 5.70 | | 17.40 | 21.50 |

## 08 81 45 – Sheet Glass

### 08 81 45.10 Window Glass, Sheet

| | | Crew | Daily Output | Labor-Hours | Unit | Material | 2008 Bare Costs Labor | Equipment | Total | Total Incl O&P |
|---|---|---|---|---|---|---|---|---|---|---|
| 0010 | **WINDOW GLASS, SHEET** gray | | | | | | | | | |
| 0020 | 1/8" thick | 2 Glaz | 160 | .100 | S.F. | 4.82 | 3.73 | | 8.55 | 10.95 |
| 0200 | 1/4" thick | " | 130 | .123 | " | 6 | 4.59 | | 10.59 | 13.55 |

## 08 81 50 – Spandrel Glass

### 08 81 50.10 Glass for Non Vision Areas

| | | Crew | Daily Output | Labor-Hours | Unit | Material | 2008 Bare Costs Labor | Equipment | Total | Total Incl O&P |
|---|---|---|---|---|---|---|---|---|---|---|
| 0010 | **GLASS FOR NON VISION AREAS**, 1/4" thick standard colors | | | | | | | | | |
| 0020 | Up to 100 S.F. | 2 Glaz | 110 | .145 | S.F. | 14 | 5.45 | | 19.45 | 23.50 |
| 0200 | 1,000 to 2,000 S.F. | " | 120 | .133 | " | 13.15 | 4.97 | | 18.12 | 22 |
| 0300 | For custom colors, add | | | | Total | 10% | | | | |

# 08 81 Glass Glazing

## 08 81 50 – Spandrel Glass

### 08 81 50.10 Glass for Non Vision Areas

| | | Crew | Daily Output | Labor-Hours | Unit | Material | 2008 Bare Costs Labor | Equipment | Total | Total Incl O&P |
|---|---|---|---|---|---|---|---|---|---|---|
| 0500 | For 3/8" thick, add | | | | S.F. | 8.05 | | | 8.05 | 8.85 |
| 1000 | For double coated, 1/4" thick, add | | | | | 3.01 | | | 3.01 | 3.31 |
| 1200 | For insulation on panels, add | | | | | 4.97 | | | 4.97 | 5.45 |
| 2000 | Panels, insulated, with aluminum backed fiberglass, 1" thick | 2 Glaz | 120 | .133 | | 12 | 4.97 | | 16.97 | 21 |
| 2100 | 2" thick | " | 120 | .133 | | 13.95 | 4.97 | | 18.92 | 23 |
| 2500 | With galvanized steel backing, add | | | | ↓ | 4.15 | | | 4.15 | 4.57 |

## 08 81 55 – Window Glass

### 08 81 55.10 Sheet Glass

| | | Crew | Daily Output | Labor-Hours | Unit | Material | 2008 Bare Costs Labor | Equipment | Total | Total Incl O&P |
|---|---|---|---|---|---|---|---|---|---|---|
| 0010 | **SHEET GLASS** (window), clear float, stops, putty bed | | | | | | | | | |
| 0015 | 1/8" thick, clear float | 2 Glaz | 480 | .033 | S.F. | 3.63 | 1.24 | | 4.87 | 5.85 |
| 0500 | 3/16" thick, clear | | 480 | .033 | | 4.47 | 1.24 | | 5.71 | 6.80 |
| 0600 | Tinted | | 480 | .033 | | 5.40 | 1.24 | | 6.64 | 7.85 |
| 0700 | Tempered | ↓ | 480 | .033 | ↓ | 6.55 | 1.24 | | 7.79 | 9.10 |

## 08 81 65 – Wire Glass

### 08 81 65.10 Glass Reinforced With Wire

| | | Crew | Daily Output | Labor-Hours | Unit | Material | 2008 Bare Costs Labor | Equipment | Total | Total Incl O&P |
|---|---|---|---|---|---|---|---|---|---|---|
| 0010 | **GLASS REINFORCED WITH WIRE** | | | | | | | | | |
| 0012 | 1/4" thick rough obscure | 2 Glaz | 135 | .119 | S.F. | 13.15 | 4.42 | | 17.57 | 21 |
| 1000 | Polished wire, 1/4" thick, diamond, clear | | 135 | .119 | | 17.05 | 4.42 | | 21.47 | 25.50 |
| 1500 | Pinstripe, obscure | ↓ | 135 | .119 | ↓ | 15.95 | 4.42 | | 20.37 | 24.50 |

# 08 83 Mirrors

## 08 83 13 – Mirrored Glass Glazing

### 08 83 13.10 Mirrors

| | | Crew | Daily Output | Labor-Hours | Unit | Material | 2008 Bare Costs Labor | Equipment | Total | Total Incl O&P |
|---|---|---|---|---|---|---|---|---|---|---|
| 0010 | **MIRRORS**, No frames, wall type, 1/4" plate glass, polished edge | | | | | | | | | |
| 0100 | Up to 5 S.F. | 2 Glaz | 125 | .128 | S.F. | 6.90 | 4.77 | | 11.67 | 14.80 |
| 0200 | Over 5 S.F. | | 160 | .100 | | 6.65 | 3.73 | | 10.38 | 13 |
| 0500 | Door type, 1/4" plate glass, up to 12 S.F. | | 160 | .100 | | 6.60 | 3.73 | | 10.33 | 12.90 |
| 1000 | Float glass, up to 10 S.F., 1/8" thick | | 160 | .100 | | 4.34 | 3.73 | | 8.07 | 10.40 |
| 1100 | 3/16" thick | | 150 | .107 | | 5.40 | 3.98 | | 9.38 | 12 |
| 1500 | 12" x 12" wall tiles, square edge, clear | | 195 | .082 | | 1.66 | 3.06 | | 4.72 | 6.45 |
| 1600 | Veined | | 195 | .082 | | 4.41 | 3.06 | | 7.47 | 9.50 |
| 2000 | 1/4" thick, stock sizes, one way transparent | | 125 | .128 | | 16.55 | 4.77 | | 21.32 | 25.50 |
| 2010 | Bathroom, unframed, laminated | ↓ | 160 | .100 | ↓ | 12.50 | 3.73 | | 16.23 | 19.40 |

### 08 83 13.15 Reflective Glass

| | | Crew | Daily Output | Labor-Hours | Unit | Material | 2008 Bare Costs Labor | Equipment | Total | Total Incl O&P |
|---|---|---|---|---|---|---|---|---|---|---|
| 0010 | **REFLECTIVE GLASS** | | | | | | | | | |
| 0100 | 1/4" float with fused metallic oxide fixed | 2 Glaz | 115 | .139 | S.F. | 11.70 | 5.20 | | 16.90 | 20.50 |
| 0500 | 1/4" float glass with reflective applied coating | " | 115 | .139 | " | 9.75 | 5.20 | | 14.95 | 18.55 |

# 08 84 Plastic Glazing

## 08 84 10 – Plexiglass Glazing

| 08 84 10.10 Plexiglass Acrylic | Crew | Daily Output | Labor-Hours | Unit | Material | 2008 Bare Costs Labor | Equipment | Total | Total Incl O&P |
|---|---|---|---|---|---|---|---|---|---|
| 0010 **PLEXIGLASS ACRYLIC**, clear, masked, | | | | | | | | | |
| 0020   1/8" thick, cut sheets | 2 Glaz | 170 | .094 | S.F. | 3.55 | 3.51 | | 7.06 | 9.20 |
| 0200      Full sheets | | 195 | .082 | | 1.85 | 3.06 | | 4.91 | 6.70 |
| 0500   1/4" thick, cut sheets | | 165 | .097 | | 6.25 | 3.62 | | 9.87 | 12.40 |
| 0600      Full sheets | | 185 | .086 | | 3.41 | 3.23 | | 6.64 | 8.65 |
| 0900   3/8" thick, cut sheets | | 155 | .103 | | 11.50 | 3.85 | | 15.35 | 18.50 |
| 1000      Full sheets | | 180 | .089 | | 6.20 | 3.32 | | 9.52 | 11.80 |
| 1300   1/2" thick, cut sheets | | 135 | .119 | | 13.25 | 4.42 | | 17.67 | 21.50 |
| 1400      Full sheets | | 150 | .107 | | 12.80 | 3.98 | | 16.78 | 20 |
| 1700   3/4" thick, cut sheets | | 115 | .139 | | 47 | 5.20 | | 52.20 | 59.50 |
| 1800      Full sheets | | 130 | .123 | | 27 | 4.59 | | 31.59 | 37 |
| 2100   1" thick, cut sheets | | 105 | .152 | | 53 | 5.70 | | 58.70 | 66.50 |
| 2200      Full sheets | | 125 | .128 | | 32.50 | 4.77 | | 37.27 | 43.50 |
| 3000   Colored, 1/8" thick, cut sheets | | 170 | .094 | | 10.90 | 3.51 | | 14.41 | 17.30 |
| 3200      Full sheets | | 195 | .082 | | 7.05 | 3.06 | | 10.11 | 12.40 |
| 3500   1/4" thick, cut sheets | | 165 | .097 | | 12.20 | 3.62 | | 15.82 | 18.95 |
| 3600      Full sheets | | 185 | .086 | | 8.35 | 3.23 | | 11.58 | 14.05 |
| 4000   Mirrors, untinted, cut sheets, 1/8" thick | | 185 | .086 | | 5.15 | 3.23 | | 8.38 | 10.55 |
| 4200      1/4" thick | | 180 | .089 | | 8.25 | 3.32 | | 11.57 | 14.10 |

## 08 84 20 – Polycarbonate

| 08 84 20.10 Thermoplastic | Crew | Daily Output | Labor-Hours | Unit | Material | Labor | Equipment | Total | Total Incl O&P |
|---|---|---|---|---|---|---|---|---|---|
| 0010 **THERMOPLASTIC**, clear, masked, cut sheets | | | | | | | | | |
| 0020   1/8" thick | 2 Glaz | 170 | .094 | S.F. | 7 | 3.51 | | 10.51 | 13 |
| 0500   3/16" thick | | 165 | .097 | | 8 | 3.62 | | 11.62 | 14.30 |
| 1000   1/4" thick | | 155 | .103 | | 9 | 3.85 | | 12.85 | 15.75 |
| 1500   3/8" thick | | 150 | .107 | | 16 | 3.98 | | 19.98 | 23.50 |

## 08 84 30 – Vinyl Glass

| 08 84 30.10 Vinyl Sheets | Crew | Daily Output | Labor-Hours | Unit | Material | Labor | Equipment | Total | Total Incl O&P |
|---|---|---|---|---|---|---|---|---|---|
| 0010 **VINYL SHEETS**, Steel mesh reinforced, stock sizes | | | | | | | | | |
| 0020   .090" thick | 2 Glaz | 170 | .094 | S.F. | 9 | 3.51 | | 12.51 | 15.20 |
| 0500   .120" thick | | 170 | .094 | | 11 | 3.51 | | 14.51 | 17.40 |
| 1000   .250" thick | | 155 | .103 | | 15 | 3.85 | | 18.85 | 22.50 |
| 1500   For non-standard sizes, add | | | | | 15% | | | | |

# 08 87 Glazing Surface Films

## 08 87 13 – Solar Control Films

| 08 87 13.10 Solar Films On Glass | Crew | Daily Output | Labor-Hours | Unit | Material | Labor | Equipment | Total | Total Incl O&P |
|---|---|---|---|---|---|---|---|---|---|
| 0010 **SOLAR FILMS ON GLASS** (glass not included) | | | | | | | | | |
| 2000   Minimum | 2 Glaz | 180 | .089 | S.F. | 4.71 | 3.32 | | 8.03 | 10.20 |
| 2050   Maximum | " | 225 | .071 | " | 10.90 | 2.65 | | 13.55 | 16 |

## 08 87 16 – Safety Films

| 08 87 16.10 Window Protection Film | Crew | Daily Output | Labor-Hours | Unit | Material | Labor | Equipment | Total | Total Incl O&P |
|---|---|---|---|---|---|---|---|---|---|
| 0010 **WINDOW PROTECTION FILM** | | | | | | | | | |
| 2010   Window protection film, controls blast damage | 2 Glaz | 80 | .200 | S.F. | 4.71 | 7.45 | | 12.16 | 16.50 |

## 08 87 53 – Security Films

| 08 87 53.10 Security Film | Crew | Daily Output | Labor-Hours | Unit | Material | Labor | Equipment | Total | Total Incl O&P |
|---|---|---|---|---|---|---|---|---|---|
| 0010 **SECURITY FILM**, clear, 32000psi tensile strength, adhered to glass | | | | | | | | | |
| 0100   .002" thick, daylight installation | H-2 | 950 | .025 | S.F. | 1.40 | .88 | | 2.28 | 2.89 |
| 0150   .004" thick, daylight installation   R088110-10 | | 800 | .030 | | 1.50 | 1.05 | | 2.55 | 3.25 |

# 08 87 Glazing Surface Films

## 08 87 53 – Security Films

| 08 87 53.10 Security Film | | Crew | Daily Output | Labor-Hours | Unit | Material | 2008 Bare Costs Labor | Equipment | Total | Total Incl O&P |
|---|---|---|---|---|---|---|---|---|---|---|
| 0200 | .006" thick, daylight installation | H-2 | 700 | .034 | S.F. | 1.60 | 1.20 | | 2.80 | 3.59 |
| 0210 | Install for anchorage | | 600 | .040 | | 1.78 | 1.40 | | 3.18 | 4.09 |
| 0400 | .007" thick, daylight istallation | | 600 | .040 | | 1.70 | 1.40 | | 3.10 | 4 |
| 0410 | Install for anchorage | | 500 | .048 | | 1.89 | 1.68 | | 3.57 | 4.64 |
| 0500 | .008" thick, daylight installation | | 500 | .048 | | 2 | 1.68 | | 3.68 | 4.76 |
| 0510 | Install for anchorage | | 500 | .048 | | 2.22 | 1.68 | | 3.90 | 5 |
| 0600 | .015" thick, daylight installation | | 400 | .060 | | 3.10 | 2.10 | | 5.20 | 6.60 |
| 0610 | Install for anchorage | | 400 | .060 | | 2.22 | 2.10 | | 4.32 | 5.65 |
| 0900 | Security film anchorage, mechanical attachment and cover plate | H-3 | 370 | .043 | L.F. | 7.45 | 1.44 | | 8.89 | 10.40 |
| 0950 | Security film anchorage, wet glaze structural caulking | 1 Glaz | 225 | .036 | " | .77 | 1.33 | | 2.10 | 2.85 |
| 1000 | Adhered security film removal | 1 Clab | 275 | .029 | S.F. | | .88 | | .88 | 1.37 |

# 08 88 Special Function Glazing

## 08 88 40 – Acoustical Glass Units

### 08 88 40.10 Sound Reducion Units

| | | Crew | Daily Output | Labor-Hours | Unit | Material | Labor | Equipment | Total | Total Incl O&P |
|---|---|---|---|---|---|---|---|---|---|---|
| 0010 | **SOUND REDUCION UNITS,** 1 lite at 3/8", 1 lite at 3/16" | | | | | | | | | |
| 0020 | For 1" thick | 2 Glaz | 100 | .160 | S.F. | 24.50 | 5.95 | | 30.45 | 36 |
| 0100 | For 4" thick | " | 80 | .200 | " | 41.50 | 7.45 | | 48.95 | 57.50 |

## 08 88 56 – Ballistics-Resistant Glazing

### 08 88 56.10 Laminated Glass

| | | Crew | Daily Output | Labor-Hours | Unit | Material | Labor | Equipment | Total | Total Incl O&P |
|---|---|---|---|---|---|---|---|---|---|---|
| 0010 | **LAMINATED GLASS** | | | | | | | | | |
| 0020 | Clear float .03" vinyl 1/4" | 2 Glaz | 90 | .178 | S.F. | 10.30 | 6.65 | | 16.95 | 21.50 |
| 0100 | 3/8" thick | | 78 | .205 | | 15.35 | 7.65 | | 23 | 28.50 |
| 0200 | .06" vinyl, 1/2" thick | | 65 | .246 | | 17.95 | 9.20 | | 27.15 | 33.50 |
| 1000 | 5/8" thick | | 90 | .178 | | 21 | 6.65 | | 27.65 | 33 |
| 2000 | Bullet-resisting, 1-3/16" thick, to 15 S.F. | | 16 | 1 | | 65 | 37.50 | | 102.50 | 128 |
| 2100 | Over 15 S.F. | | 16 | 1 | | 82.50 | 37.50 | | 120 | 147 |
| 2500 | 2-1/4" thick, to 15 S.F. | | 12 | 1.333 | | 69 | 49.50 | | 118.50 | 152 |
| 2600 | Over 15 S.F. | | 12 | 1.333 | | 61 | 49.50 | | 110.50 | 143 |

# 08 91 Louvers

## 08 91 19 – Fixed Louvers

### 08 91 19.10 Aluminum Louvers

| | | Crew | Daily Output | Labor-Hours | Unit | Material | Labor | Equipment | Total | Total Incl O&P |
|---|---|---|---|---|---|---|---|---|---|---|
| 0010 | **ALUMINUM LOUVERS** | | | | | | | | | |
| 0020 | Aluminum with screen, residential, 8" x 8" | 1 Carp | 38 | .211 | Ea. | 10.20 | 8 | | 18.20 | 24 |
| 0100 | 12" x 12" | | 38 | .211 | | 11.50 | 8 | | 19.50 | 25 |
| 0200 | 12" x 18" | | 35 | .229 | | 13.15 | 8.70 | | 21.85 | 28 |
| 0250 | 14" x 24" | | 30 | .267 | | 16.50 | 10.15 | | 26.65 | 34 |
| 0300 | 18" x 24" | | 27 | .296 | | 24 | 11.30 | | 35.30 | 44 |
| 0500 | 24" x 30" | | 24 | .333 | | 33 | 12.70 | | 45.70 | 56.50 |
| 0700 | Triangle, adjustable, small | | 20 | .400 | | 28.50 | 15.25 | | 43.75 | 54.50 |
| 0800 | Large | | 15 | .533 | | 49 | 20.50 | | 69.50 | 85 |
| 1200 | Extruded aluminum, see Div. 23 37 15.40 | | | | | | | | | |
| 2100 | Midget, aluminum, 3/4" deep, 1" diameter | 1 Carp | 85 | .094 | Ea. | .76 | 3.59 | | 4.35 | 6.45 |
| 2150 | 3" diameter | | 60 | .133 | | 1.59 | 5.10 | | 6.69 | 9.65 |
| 2200 | 4" diameter | | 50 | .160 | | 2.98 | 6.10 | | 9.08 | 12.80 |
| 2250 | 6" diameter | | 30 | .267 | | 3.52 | 10.15 | | 13.67 | 19.65 |

# 08 95 Vents

## 08 95 13 – Soffit Vents

| 08 95 13.10 Wall Louvers | Crew | Daily Output | Labor-Hours | Unit | Material | Labor | Equipment | Total | Total Incl O&P |
|---|---|---|---|---|---|---|---|---|---|
| 0010 **WALL LOUVERS** | | | | | | | | | |
| 2330  Soffit vent, continuous, 3" wide, aluminum, mill finish | 1 Carp | 200 | .040 | L.F. | .51 | 1.52 | | 2.03 | 2.93 |
| 2340    Baked enamel finish | | 200 | .040 | " | .46 | 1.52 | | 1.98 | 2.88 |
| 2400  Under eaves vent, aluminum, mill finish, 16" x 4" | | 48 | .167 | Ea. | 1.25 | 6.35 | | 7.60 | 11.30 |
| 2500    16" x 8" | | 48 | .167 | " | 1.45 | 6.35 | | 7.80 | 11.50 |

## 08 95 16 – Wall Vents

| 08 95 16.10 Louvers | Crew | Daily Output | Labor-Hours | Unit | Material | Labor | Equipment | Total | Total Incl O&P |
|---|---|---|---|---|---|---|---|---|---|
| 0010 **LOUVERS** | | | | | | | | | |
| 0020  Redwood, 2'-0" diameter, full circle | 1 Carp | 16 | .500 | Ea. | 144 | 19.05 | | 163.05 | 189 |
| 0100    Half circle | | 16 | .500 | | 138 | 19.05 | | 157.05 | 182 |
| 0200    Octagonal | | 16 | .500 | | 110 | 19.05 | | 129.05 | 151 |
| 0300    Triangular, 5/12 pitch, 5'-0" at base | | 16 | .500 | | 233 | 19.05 | | 252.05 | 287 |
| 7000  Vinyl gable vent, 8" x 8" | | 38 | .211 | | 10.90 | 8 | | 18.90 | 24.50 |
| 7020    12" x 12" | | 38 | .211 | | 22.50 | 8 | | 30.50 | 37.50 |
| 7080    12" x 18" | | 35 | .229 | | 29 | 8.70 | | 37.70 | 45.50 |
| 7200    18" x 24" | | 30 | .267 | | 35.50 | 10.15 | | 45.65 | 55 |

# Estimating Tips

## General

- Room Finish Schedule: A complete set of plans should contain a room finish schedule. If one is not available, it would be well worth the time and effort to obtain one.

## 09 20 00 Plaster and Gypsum Board

- Lath is estimated by the square yard plus a 5% allowance for waste. Furring, channels, and accessories are measured by the linear foot. An extra foot should be allowed for each accessory miter or stop.

- Plaster is also estimated by the square yard. Deductions for openings vary by preference, from zero deduction to 50% of all openings over 2 feet in width. The estimator should allow one extra square foot for each linear foot of horizontal interior or exterior angle located below the ceiling level. Also, double the areas of small radius work.

- Drywall accessories, studs, track, and acoustical caulking are all measured by the linear foot. Drywall taping is figured by the square foot. Gypsum wallboard is estimated by the square foot. No material deductions should be made for door or window openings under 32 S.F.

## 09 60 00 Flooring

- Tile and terrazzo areas are taken off on a square foot basis. Trim and base materials are measured by the linear foot. Accent tiles are listed per each. Two basic methods of installation are used. Mud set is approximately 30% more expensive than thin set. In terrazzo work, be sure to include the linear footage of embedded decorative strips, grounds, machine rubbing, and power cleanup.

- Wood flooring is available in strip, parquet, or block configuration. The latter two types are set in adhesives with quantities estimated by the square foot. The laying pattern will influence labor costs and material waste. In addition to the material and labor for laying wood floors, the estimator must make allowances for sanding and finishing these areas unless the flooring is prefinished.

- Sheet flooring is measured by the square yard. Roll widths vary, so consideration should be given to use the most economical width, as waste must be figured into the total quantity. Consider also the installation methods available, direct glue down or stretched.

## 09 70 00 Wall Finishes

- Wall coverings are estimated by the square foot. The area to be covered is measured, length by height of wall above baseboards, to calculate the square footage of each wall. This figure is divided by the number of square feet in the single roll which is being used. Deduct, in full, the areas of openings such as doors and windows. Where a pattern match is required allow 25%-30% waste.

## 09 80 00 Acoustic Treatment

- Acoustical systems fall into several categories. The takeoff of these materials should be by the square foot of area with a 5% allowance for waste. Do not forget about scaffolding, if applicable, when estimating these systems.

## 09 90 00 Painting and Coating

- A major portion of the work in painting involves surface preparation. Be sure to include cleaning, sanding, filling, and masking costs in the estimate.

- Protection of adjacent surfaces is not included in painting costs. When considering the method of paint application, an important factor is the amount of protection and masking required. These must be estimated separately and may be the determining factor in choosing the method of application.

## Reference Numbers

Reference numbers are shown in shaded boxes at the beginning of some major classifications. These numbers refer to related items in the Reference Section. The reference information may be an estimating procedure, an alternate pricing method, or technical information.
*Note:* Not all subdivisions listed here necessarily appear in this publication.

# 09 01 Maintenance of Finishes

## 09 01 60 – Maintenance of Flooring

### 09 01 60.10 Carpet Maintenance

| | | Crew | Daily Output | Labor-Hours | Unit | Material | 2008 Bare Costs Labor | Equipment | Total | Total Incl O&P |
|---|---|---|---|---|---|---|---|---|---|---|
| 0010 | **CARPET MAINTENANCE** | | | | | | | | | |
| 0020 | Steam clean, per cleaning, minimum | 1 Clab | 3000 | .003 | S.F. | .07 | .08 | | .15 | .21 |
| 0500 | Maximum | " | 2000 | .004 | " | .12 | .12 | | .24 | .32 |

## 09 01 70 – Maintenance of Wall Finishes

### 09 01 70.10 Gypsum Wallboard Repairs

| | | Crew | Daily Output | Labor-Hours | Unit | Material | 2008 Bare Costs Labor | Equipment | Total | Total Incl O&P |
|---|---|---|---|---|---|---|---|---|---|---|
| 0010 | **GYPSUM WALLBOARD REPAIRS** | | | | | | | | | |
| 0100 | Fill and sand, pin / nail holes | 1 Carp | 960 | .008 | Ea. | | .32 | | .32 | .49 |
| 0110 | Screw head pops | | 480 | .017 | | | .64 | | .64 | .99 |
| 0120 | Dents, up to 2" square | | 48 | .167 | | .01 | 6.35 | | 6.36 | 9.90 |
| 0130 | 2" to 4" square | | 24 | .333 | | .03 | 12.70 | | 12.73 | 19.80 |
| 0140 | Cut square, patch, sand and finish, holes, up to 2" square | | 12 | .667 | | .03 | 25.50 | | 25.53 | 39.50 |
| 0150 | 2" to 4" square | | 11 | .727 | | .09 | 27.50 | | 27.59 | 43 |
| 0160 | 4" to 8" square | | 10 | .800 | | .22 | 30.50 | | 30.72 | 47.50 |
| 0170 | 8" to 12" square | | 8 | 1 | | .42 | 38 | | 38.42 | 60 |
| 0180 | 12" to 32" square | | 6 | 1.333 | | 2.59 | 51 | | 53.59 | 82 |
| 0210 | 16" by 48" | | 5 | 1.600 | | 1.98 | 61 | | 62.98 | 97 |
| 0220 | 32" by 48" | | 4 | 2 | | 3.43 | 76 | | 79.43 | 123 |
| 0230 | 48" square | | 3.50 | 2.286 | | 4.83 | 87 | | 91.83 | 141 |
| 0240 | 60" square | | 3.20 | 2.500 | | 8.25 | 95.50 | | 103.75 | 157 |
| 0500 | Skim coat surface with joint compound | | 1600 | .005 | S.F. | .03 | .19 | | .22 | .33 |

# 09 05 Common Work Results for Finishes

## 09 05 05 – Selective Finishes Demolition

### 09 05 05.10 Selective Demolition, Ceilings

| | | Crew | Daily Output | Labor-Hours | Unit | Material | 2008 Bare Costs Labor | Equipment | Total | Total Incl O&P |
|---|---|---|---|---|---|---|---|---|---|---|
| 0010 | **SELECTIVE DEMOLITION, CEILINGS** R024119-10 | | | | | | | | | |
| 0200 | Ceiling, drywall, furred and nailed or screwed | 2 Clab | 800 | .020 | S.F. | | .61 | | .61 | .94 |
| 0220 | On metal frame | | 760 | .021 | | | .64 | | .64 | .99 |
| 0240 | On suspension system, including system | | 720 | .022 | | | .67 | | .67 | 1.05 |
| 1000 | Plaster, lime and horse hair, on wood lath, incl. lath | | 700 | .023 | | | .69 | | .69 | 1.08 |
| 1020 | On metal lath | | 570 | .028 | | | .85 | | .85 | 1.32 |
| 1100 | Gypsum, on gypsum lath | | 720 | .022 | | | .67 | | .67 | 1.05 |
| 1120 | On metal lath | | 500 | .032 | | | .97 | | .97 | 1.51 |
| 1200 | Suspended ceiling, mineral fiber, 2' x 2' or 2' x 4' | | 1500 | .011 | | | .32 | | .32 | .50 |
| 1250 | On suspension system, incl. system | | 1200 | .013 | | | .40 | | .40 | .63 |
| 1500 | Tile, wood fiber, 12" x 12", glued | | 900 | .018 | | | .54 | | .54 | .84 |
| 1540 | Stapled | | 1500 | .011 | | | .32 | | .32 | .50 |
| 1580 | On suspension system, incl. system | | 760 | .021 | | | .64 | | .64 | .99 |
| 2000 | Wood, tongue and groove, 1" x 4" | | 1000 | .016 | | | .48 | | .48 | .75 |
| 2040 | 1" x 8" | | 1100 | .015 | | | .44 | | .44 | .68 |
| 2400 | Plywood or wood fiberboard, 4' x 8' sheets | | 1200 | .013 | | | .40 | | .40 | .63 |

### 09 05 05.20 Selective Demolition, Flooring

| | | Crew | Daily Output | Labor-Hours | Unit | Material | 2008 Bare Costs Labor | Equipment | Total | Total Incl O&P |
|---|---|---|---|---|---|---|---|---|---|---|
| 0010 | **SELECTIVE DEMOLITION, FLOORING** R024119-10 | | | | | | | | | |
| 0200 | Brick with mortar | 2 Clab | 475 | .034 | S.F. | | 1.02 | | 1.02 | 1.58 |
| 0400 | Carpet, bonded, including surface scraping | | 2000 | .008 | | | .24 | | .24 | .38 |
| 0440 | Scrim applied | | 8000 | .002 | | | .06 | | .06 | .09 |
| 0480 | Tackless | | 9000 | .002 | | | .05 | | .05 | .08 |
| 0550 | Carpet tile, releasable adhesive | | 5000 | .003 | | | .10 | | .10 | .15 |
| 0560 | Permanent adhesive | | 1850 | .009 | | | .26 | | .26 | .41 |
| 0600 | Composition, acrylic or epoxy | | 400 | .040 | | | 1.21 | | 1.21 | 1.88 |
| 0700 | Concrete, scarify skin | A-1A | 225 | .036 | | | 1.40 | 1.18 | 2.58 | 3.47 |

# 09 05 Common Work Results for Finishes

## 09 05 05 – Selective Finishes Demolition

### 09 05 05.20 Selective Demolition, Flooring

| | | Crew | Daily Output | Labor-Hours | Unit | Material | Labor | Equipment | Total | Total Incl O&P |
|---|---|---|---|---|---|---|---|---|---|---|
| 0800 | Resilient, sheet goods | 2 Clab | 1400 | .011 | S.F. | | .35 | | .35 | .54 |
| 0820 | For gym floors | " | 900 | .018 | ↓ | | .54 | | .54 | .84 |
| 0850 | Vinyl or rubber cove base | 1 Clab | 1000 | .008 | L.F. | | .24 | | .24 | .38 |
| 0860 | Vinyl or rubber cove base, molded corner | " | 1000 | .008 | Ea. | | .24 | | .24 | .38 |
| 0900 | Vinyl composition tile, 12" x 12" | 2 Clab | 1000 | .016 | S.F. | | .48 | | .48 | .75 |
| 2000 | Tile, ceramic, thin set | | 675 | .024 | | | .72 | | .72 | 1.12 |
| 2020 | Mud set | | 625 | .026 | | | .77 | | .77 | 1.20 |
| 2200 | Marble, slate, thin set | | 675 | .024 | | | .72 | | .72 | 1.12 |
| 2220 | Mud set | | 625 | .026 | | | .77 | | .77 | 1.20 |
| 2600 | Terrazzo, thin set | | 450 | .036 | | | 1.08 | | 1.08 | 1.67 |
| 2620 | Mud set | | 425 | .038 | | | 1.14 | | 1.14 | 1.77 |
| 2640 | Cast in place | ↓ | 300 | .053 | | | 1.61 | | 1.61 | 2.51 |
| 3000 | Wood, block, on end | 1 Carp | 400 | .020 | | | .76 | | .76 | 1.19 |
| 3200 | Parquet | | 450 | .018 | | | .68 | | .68 | 1.05 |
| 3400 | Strip flooring, interior, 2-1/4" x 25/32" thick | | 325 | .025 | | | .94 | | .94 | 1.46 |
| 3500 | Exterior, porch flooring, 1" x 4" | | 220 | .036 | | | 1.39 | | 1.39 | 2.16 |
| 3800 | Subfloor, tongue and groove, 1" x 6" | | 325 | .025 | | | .94 | | .94 | 1.46 |
| 3820 | 1" x 8" | | 430 | .019 | | | .71 | | .71 | 1.10 |
| 3840 | 1" x 10" | | 520 | .015 | | | .59 | | .59 | .91 |
| 4000 | Plywood, nailed | | 600 | .013 | | | .51 | | .51 | .79 |
| 4100 | Glued and nailed | ↓ | 400 | .020 | | | .76 | | .76 | 1.19 |
| 8000 | Remove flooring, bead blast, minimum | A-1A | 1000 | .008 | | | .32 | .26 | .58 | .78 |
| 8100 | Maximum | | 400 | .020 | | | .79 | .66 | 1.45 | 1.96 |
| 8150 | Mastic only | ↓ | 1500 | .005 | ↓ | | .21 | .18 | .39 | .52 |

### 09 05 05.30 Selective Demolition, Walls and Partitions

| | | Crew | Daily Output | Labor-Hours | Unit | Material | Labor | Equipment | Total | Total Incl O&P |
|---|---|---|---|---|---|---|---|---|---|---|
| 0010 | **SELECTIVE DEMOLITION, WALLS AND PARTITIONS**  R024119-10 | | | | | | | | | |
| 0100 | Brick, 4" to 12" thick | B-9C | 220 | .182 | C.F. | | 5.55 | .87 | 6.42 | 9.60 |
| 0200 | Concrete block, 4" thick | | 1000 | .040 | S.F. | | 1.23 | .19 | 1.42 | 2.12 |
| 0280 | 8" thick | ↓ | 810 | .049 | | | 1.51 | .24 | 1.75 | 2.61 |
| 0300 | Exterior stucco 1" thick over mesh | B-9 | 3200 | .013 | | | .38 | .06 | .44 | .67 |
| 1000 | Drywall, nailed or screwed | 1 Clab | 1000 | .008 | | | .24 | | .24 | .38 |
| 1020 | Glued and nailed | | 900 | .009 | | | .27 | | .27 | .42 |
| 1500 | Fiberboard, nailed | | 900 | .009 | | | .27 | | .27 | .42 |
| 1520 | Glued and nailed | | 800 | .010 | | | .30 | | .30 | .47 |
| 1568 | Plenum barrier, sheet lead | | 300 | .027 | | | .81 | | .81 | 1.25 |
| 2000 | Movable walls, metal, 5' high | | 300 | .027 | | | .81 | | .81 | 1.25 |
| 2020 | 8' high | ↓ | 400 | .020 | | | .61 | | .61 | .94 |
| 2200 | Metal or wood studs, finish 2 sides, fiberboard | B-1 | 520 | .046 | | | 1.43 | | 1.43 | 2.22 |
| 2250 | Lath and plaster | | 260 | .092 | | | 2.85 | | 2.85 | 4.44 |
| 2300 | Plasterboard (drywall) | | 520 | .046 | | | 1.43 | | 1.43 | 2.22 |
| 2350 | Plywood | ↓ | 450 | .053 | | | 1.65 | | 1.65 | 2.57 |
| 3000 | Plaster, lime and horsehair, on wood lath | 1 Clab | 400 | .020 | | | .61 | | .61 | .94 |
| 3020 | On metal lath | | 335 | .024 | | | .72 | | .72 | 1.12 |
| 3400 | Gypsum or perlite, on gypsum lath | | 410 | .020 | | | .59 | | .59 | .92 |
| 3420 | On metal lath | ↓ | 300 | .027 | | | .81 | | .81 | 1.25 |
| 3600 | Plywood, one side | B-1 | 1500 | .016 | ↓ | | .49 | | .49 | .77 |
| 3750 | Terra cotta block and plaster, to 6" thick | " | 175 | .137 | | | 4.24 | | 4.24 | 6.60 |
| 3800 | Toilet partitions, slate or marble | 1 Clab | 5 | 1.600 | Ea. | | 48.50 | | 48.50 | 75.50 |
| 3820 | Hollow metal | " | 8 | 1 | " | | 30.50 | | 30.50 | 47 |
| 5000 | Wallcovering, vinyl | 1 Pape | 700 | .011 | S.F. | | .39 | | .39 | .58 |
| 5040 | Designer | " | 480 | .017 | " | | .56 | | .56 | .85 |

269

# 09 21 Plaster and Gypsum Board Assemblies

## 09 21 13 – Plaster Assemblies

| 09 21 13.10 Plaster Partition Wall | Crew | Daily Output | Labor-Hours | Unit | Material | 2008 Bare Costs Labor | Equipment | Total | Total Incl O&P |
|---|---|---|---|---|---|---|---|---|---|
| 0010 **PLASTER PARTITION WALL** | | | | | | | | | |
| 0400 Stud walls, 3.4 lb. metal lath, 3 coat gypsum plaster, 2 sides | | | | | | | | | |
| 0600 2" x 4" wood studs, 16" O.C. | J-2 | 315 | .152 | S.F. | 3.21 | 5.10 | .38 | 8.69 | 11.70 |
| 0700 2-1/2" metal studs, 25 ga., 12" O.C. | | 325 | .148 | | 2.97 | 4.97 | .37 | 8.31 | 11.20 |
| 0800 3-5/8" metal studs, 25 ga., 16" O.C. | ↓ | 320 | .150 | ↓ | 2.99 | 5.05 | .38 | 8.42 | 11.30 |
| 0900 Gypsum lath, 2 coat vermiculite plaster, 2 sides | | | | | | | | | |
| 1000 2" x 4" wood studs, 16" O.C. | J-2 | 355 | .135 | S.F. | 3.58 | 4.55 | .34 | 8.47 | 11.15 |
| 1200 2-1/2" metal studs, 25 ga., 12" O.C. | | 365 | .132 | | 3.17 | 4.42 | .33 | 7.92 | 10.55 |
| 1300 3-5/8" metal studs, 25 ga., 16" O.C. | ↓ | 360 | .133 | ↓ | 3.26 | 4.48 | .34 | 8.08 | 10.70 |

## 09 21 16 – Gypsum Board Assemblies

### 09 21 16.23 Gypsum Board Shaft Wall Assemblies

| 09 21 16.23 Gypsum Board Shaft Wall Assemblies | Crew | Daily Output | Labor-Hours | Unit | Material | 2008 Bare Costs Labor | Equipment | Total | Total Incl O&P |
|---|---|---|---|---|---|---|---|---|---|
| 0010 **GYPSUM BOARD SHAFT WALL ASSEMBLIES** | | | | | | | | | |
| 0030 1" thick coreboard wall liner on shaft side | | | | | | | | | |
| 0040 2-hour assembly with double layer | | | | | | | | | |
| 0060 5/8" fire rated gypsum board on room side | 2 Carp | 220 | .073 | S.F. | 1.18 | 2.77 | | 3.95 | 5.60 |
| 0100 3-hour assembly with triple layer | | | | | | | | | |
| 0300 5/8" fire rated gypsum board on room side | 2 Carp | 180 | .089 | S.F. | 1.46 | 3.39 | | 4.85 | 6.85 |
| 0400 4-hour assembly, 1" coreboard, 5/8" fire rated gypsum board | | | | | | | | | |
| 0600 and 3/4" galv. metal furring channels, 24" O.C., with | | | | | | | | | |
| 0700 Double layer 5/8" fire rated gypsum board on room side | 2 Carp | 110 | .145 | S.F. | 1.35 | 5.55 | | 6.90 | 10.15 |
| 0900 For taping & finishing, add per side | 1 Carp | 1050 | .008 | " | .04 | .29 | | .33 | .50 |
| 1000 For insulation, see Div. 07 21 | | | | | | | | | |
| 5200 For work over 8' high, add | 2 Carp | 3060 | .005 | S.F. | | .20 | | .20 | .31 |
| 5300 For distribution cost over 3 stories high, add per story | " | 6100 | .003 | " | | .10 | | .10 | .16 |

### 09 21 16.33 Partition Wall

| 09 21 16.33 Partition Wall | Crew | Daily Output | Labor-Hours | Unit | Material | 2008 Bare Costs Labor | Equipment | Total | Total Incl O&P |
|---|---|---|---|---|---|---|---|---|---|
| 0010 **PARTITION WALL** Stud wall, 8' to 12' high | | | | | | | | | |
| 0050 1/2", interior, gypsum board, std, tape & finish 2 sides | | | | | | | | | |
| 0500 Installed on and incl. 2" x 4" wood studs, 16" O.C. | 2 Carp | 310 | .052 | S.F. | .98 | 1.97 | | 2.95 | 4.14 |
| 1000 Metal studs, NLB, 25 ga., 16" O.C., 3-5/8" wide | | 350 | .046 | | .94 | 1.74 | | 2.68 | 3.74 |
| 1200 6" wide | | 330 | .048 | | 1.12 | 1.85 | | 2.97 | 4.10 |
| 1400 Water resistant, on 2" x 4" wood studs, 16" O.C. | | 310 | .052 | | 1.18 | 1.97 | | 3.15 | 4.36 |
| 1600 Metal studs, NLB, 25 ga., 16" O.C., 3-5/8" wide | | 350 | .046 | | 1.14 | 1.74 | | 2.88 | 3.96 |
| 1800 6" wide | | 330 | .048 | | 1.32 | 1.85 | | 3.17 | 4.32 |
| 2000 Fire res., 2 layers, 1-1/2 hr., on 2" x 4" wood studs, 16" O.C. | | 210 | .076 | | 1.52 | 2.90 | | 4.42 | 6.20 |
| 2200 Metal studs, NLB, 25 ga., 16" O.C., 3-5/8" wide | | 250 | .064 | | 1.48 | 2.44 | | 3.92 | 5.45 |
| 2400 6" wide | | 230 | .070 | | 1.66 | 2.65 | | 4.31 | 5.95 |
| 2600 Fire & water res., 2 layers, 1-1/2 hr., 2" x 4" studs, 16" O.C. | | 210 | .076 | | 1.52 | 2.90 | | 4.42 | 6.20 |
| 2800 Metal studs, NLB, 25 ga., 16" O.C., 3-5/8" wide | | 250 | .064 | | 1.48 | 2.44 | | 3.92 | 5.45 |
| 3000 6" wide | ↓ | 230 | .070 | ↓ | 1.66 | 2.65 | | 4.31 | 5.95 |
| 3200 5/8", interior, gypsum board, std, tape & finish 2 sides | | | | | | | | | |
| 3400 Installed on and including 2" x 4" wood studs, 16" O.C. | 2 Carp | 300 | .053 | S.F. | 1.04 | 2.03 | | 3.07 | 4.30 |
| 3600 24" O.C. | | 330 | .048 | | .95 | 1.85 | | 2.80 | 3.92 |
| 3800 Metal studs, NLB, 25 ga., 16" O.C., 3-5/8" wide | | 340 | .047 | | 1 | 1.79 | | 2.79 | 3.89 |
| 4000 6" wide | | 320 | .050 | | 1.18 | 1.91 | | 3.09 | 4.27 |
| 4200 24" O.C., 3-5/8" wide | | 360 | .044 | | .91 | 1.69 | | 2.60 | 3.64 |
| 4400 6" wide | | 340 | .047 | | 1.04 | 1.79 | | 2.83 | 3.93 |
| 4800 Water resistant, on 2" x 4" wood studs, 16" O.C. | | 300 | .053 | | 1.16 | 2.03 | | 3.19 | 4.43 |
| 5000 24" O.C. | | 330 | .048 | | 1.07 | 1.85 | | 2.92 | 4.05 |
| 5200 Metal studs, NLB, 25 ga. 16" O.C., 3-5/8" wide | | 340 | .047 | | 1.12 | 1.79 | | 2.91 | 4.02 |
| 5400 6" wide | | 320 | .050 | | 1.30 | 1.91 | | 3.21 | 4.40 |
| 5600 24" O.C., 3-5/8" wide | | 360 | .044 | | 1.03 | 1.69 | | 2.72 | 3.77 |
| 5800 6" wide | ↓ | 340 | .047 | ↓ | 1.16 | 1.79 | | 2.95 | 4.07 |

# 09 21 Plaster and Gypsum Board Assemblies

## 09 21 16 – Gypsum Board Assemblies

### 09 21 16.33 Partition Wall

| | | Crew | Daily Output | Labor-Hours | Unit | Material | 2008 Bare Costs Labor | Equipment | Total | Total Incl O&P |
|---|---|---|---|---|---|---|---|---|---|---|
| 6000 | Fire resistant, 2 layers, 2 hr., on 2" x 4" wood studs, 16" O.C. | 2 Carp | 205 | .078 | S.F. | 1.59 | 2.97 | | 4.56 | 6.40 |
| 6200 | 24" O.C. | | 235 | .068 | | 1.59 | 2.59 | | 4.18 | 5.80 |
| 6400 | Metal studs, NLB, 25 ga., 16" O.C., 3-5/8" wide | | 245 | .065 | | 1.67 | 2.49 | | 4.16 | 5.70 |
| 6600 | 6" wide | | 225 | .071 | | 1.82 | 2.71 | | 4.53 | 6.20 |
| 6800 | 24" O.C., 3-5/8" wide | | 265 | .060 | | 1.55 | 2.30 | | 3.85 | 5.30 |
| 7000 | 6" wide | | 245 | .065 | | 1.68 | 2.49 | | 4.17 | 5.70 |
| 7200 | Fire & water resistant, 2 layers, 2 hr., 2" x 4" studs, 16" O.C. | | 205 | .078 | | 1.68 | 2.97 | | 4.65 | 6.50 |
| 7400 | 24" O.C. | | 235 | .068 | | 1.59 | 2.59 | | 4.18 | 5.80 |
| 7600 | Metal studs, NLB, 25 ga., 16" O.C., 3-5/8" wide | | 245 | .065 | | 1.64 | 2.49 | | 4.13 | 5.65 |
| 7800 | 6" wide | | 225 | .071 | | 1.82 | 2.71 | | 4.53 | 6.20 |
| 8000 | 24" O.C., 3-5/8" wide | | 265 | .060 | | 1.55 | 2.30 | | 3.85 | 5.30 |
| 8200 | 6" wide | ↓ | 245 | .065 | ↓ | 1.68 | 2.49 | | 4.17 | 5.70 |
| 8600 | 1/2" blueboard, mesh tape both sides | | | | | | | | | |
| 8620 | Installed on and including 2" x 4" wood studs, 16" O.C. | 2 Carp | 300 | .053 | S.F. | 1.04 | 2.03 | | 3.07 | 4.30 |
| 8640 | Metal studs, NLB, 25 ga., 16" O.C., 3-5/8" wide | | 340 | .047 | | 1 | 1.79 | | 2.79 | 3.89 |
| 8660 | 6" wide | ↓ | 320 | .050 | ↓ | 1.18 | 1.91 | | 3.09 | 4.27 |
| 9000 | Exterior, 1/2" gypsum sheathing, 1/2" gypsum finished, interior, | | | | | | | | | |
| 9100 | including foil faced insulation, metal studs, 20 ga. | | | | | | | | | |
| 9200 | 16" O.C., 3-5/8" wide | 2 Carp | 290 | .055 | S.F. | 1.98 | 2.10 | | 4.08 | 5.45 |
| 9400 | 6" wide | " | 270 | .059 | " | 2.18 | 2.26 | | 4.44 | 5.90 |

# 09 22 Supports for Plaster and Gypsum Board

## 09 22 03 – Fastening Methods for Finishes

### 09 22 03.20 Drilling Plaster/Drywall

| | | Crew | Daily Output | Labor-Hours | Unit | Material | 2008 Bare Costs Labor | Equipment | Total | Total Incl O&P |
|---|---|---|---|---|---|---|---|---|---|---|
| 0010 | **DRILLING PLASTER/DRYWALL** | | | | | | | | | |
| 1100 | Drilling & layout for drywall/plaster walls, up to 1" deep, no anchor | | | | | | | | | |
| 1200 | Holes, 1/4" diameter | 1 Carp | 150 | .053 | Ea. | .01 | 2.03 | | 2.04 | 3.17 |
| 1300 | 3/8" diameter | | 140 | .057 | | .01 | 2.18 | | 2.19 | 3.40 |
| 1400 | 1/2" diameter | | 130 | .062 | | .01 | 2.34 | | 2.35 | 3.66 |
| 1500 | 3/4" diameter | | 120 | .067 | | .03 | 2.54 | | 2.57 | 3.98 |
| 1600 | 1" diameter | | 110 | .073 | | .04 | 2.77 | | 2.81 | 4.35 |
| 1700 | 1-1/4" diameter | | 100 | .080 | | .05 | 3.05 | | 3.10 | 4.80 |
| 1800 | 1-1/2" diameter | ↓ | 90 | .089 | | .08 | 3.39 | | 3.47 | 5.35 |
| 1900 | For ceiling installations, add | | | | ↓ | | 40% | | | |

## 09 22 13 – Metal Furring

### 09 22 13.13 Metal Channel Furring

| | | Crew | Daily Output | Labor-Hours | Unit | Material | 2008 Bare Costs Labor | Equipment | Total | Total Incl O&P |
|---|---|---|---|---|---|---|---|---|---|---|
| 0010 | **METAL CHANNEL FURRING** | | | | | | | | | |
| 0030 | Beams and columns, 7/8" channels, galvanized, 12" O.C. | 1 Lath | 155 | .052 | S.F. | .30 | 1.80 | | 2.10 | 2.99 |
| 0050 | 16" O.C. | | 170 | .047 | | .25 | 1.64 | | 1.89 | 2.70 |
| 0070 | 24" O.C. | | 185 | .043 | | .16 | 1.50 | | 1.66 | 2.41 |
| 0100 | Ceilings, on steel, 7/8" channels, galvanized, 12" O.C. | | 210 | .038 | | .27 | 1.33 | | 1.60 | 2.27 |
| 0300 | 16" O.C. | | 290 | .028 | | .25 | .96 | | 1.21 | 1.69 |
| 0400 | 24" O.C. | | 420 | .019 | | .16 | .66 | | .82 | 1.16 |
| 0600 | 1-5/8" channels, galvanized, 12" O.C. | | 190 | .042 | | .41 | 1.47 | | 1.88 | 2.62 |
| 0700 | 16" O.C. | | 260 | .031 | | .37 | 1.07 | | 1.44 | 2 |
| 0900 | 24" O.C. | | 390 | .021 | | .25 | .71 | | .96 | 1.33 |
| 0930 | 7/8" channels with sound isolation clips, 12" O.C. | | 120 | .067 | | 1.30 | 2.32 | | 3.62 | 4.87 |
| 0940 | 16" O.C. | | 100 | .080 | | 1.82 | 2.78 | | 4.60 | 6.15 |
| 0950 | 24" O.C. | | 165 | .048 | | 1.19 | 1.69 | | 2.88 | 3.81 |
| 0960 | 1-5/8" channels, galvanized, 12" O.C. | ↓ | 110 | .073 | ↓ | 1.44 | 2.53 | | 3.97 | 5.35 |

## 09 22 13 – Metal Furring

### 09 22 13.13 Metal Channel Furring

| | | Crew | Daily Output | Labor-Hours | Unit | Material | 2008 Bare Costs Labor | Equipment | Total | Total Incl O&P |
|---|---|---|---|---|---|---|---|---|---|---|
| 0970 | 16" O.C. | 1 Lath | 100 | .080 | S.F. | 1.94 | 2.78 | | 4.72 | 6.25 |
| 0980 | 24" O.C. | | 155 | .052 | | 1.27 | 1.80 | | 3.07 | 4.06 |
| 1000 | Walls, 7/8" channels, galvanized, 12" O.C. | | 235 | .034 | | .27 | 1.18 | | 1.45 | 2.06 |
| 1200 | 16" O.C. | | 265 | .030 | | .25 | 1.05 | | 1.30 | 1.83 |
| 1300 | 24" O.C. | | 350 | .023 | | .16 | .80 | | .96 | 1.36 |
| 1500 | 1-5/8" channels, galvanized, 12" O.C. | | 210 | .038 | | .41 | 1.33 | | 1.74 | 2.42 |
| 1600 | 16" O.C. | | 240 | .033 | | .37 | 1.16 | | 1.53 | 2.13 |
| 1800 | 24" O.C. | | 305 | .026 | | .25 | .91 | | 1.16 | 1.62 |
| 1920 | 7/8" channels with sound isolation clips, 12" O.C. | | 125 | .064 | | 1.30 | 2.23 | | 3.53 | 4.73 |
| 1940 | 16" O.C. | | 100 | .080 | | 1.82 | 2.78 | | 4.60 | 6.15 |
| 1950 | 24" O.C. | | 150 | .053 | | 1.19 | 1.86 | | 3.05 | 4.06 |
| 1960 | 1-5/8" channels, galvanized, 12" O.C. | | 115 | .070 | | 1.44 | 2.42 | | 3.86 | 5.15 |
| 1970 | 16" O.C. | | 95 | .084 | | 1.94 | 2.93 | | 4.87 | 6.50 |
| 1980 | 24" O.C. | | 140 | .057 | | 1.27 | 1.99 | | 3.26 | 4.35 |

## 09 22 16 – Non-Structural Metal Framing

### 09 22 16.13 Metal Studs and Track

| | | Crew | Daily Output | Labor-Hours | Unit | Material | 2008 Bare Costs Labor | Equipment | Total | Total Incl O&P |
|---|---|---|---|---|---|---|---|---|---|---|
| 0010 | **METAL STUDS AND TRACK** | | | | | | | | | |
| 1600 | Non-load bearing, galv, 8' high, 25 ga. 1-5/8" wide, 16" O.C. | 1 Carp | 619 | .013 | S.F. | .27 | .49 | | .76 | 1.07 |
| 1610 | 24" O.C. | | 950 | .008 | | .21 | .32 | | .53 | .73 |
| 1620 | 2-1/2" wide, 16" O.C. | | 613 | .013 | | .33 | .50 | | .83 | 1.14 |
| 1630 | 24" O.C. | | 938 | .009 | | .25 | .33 | | .58 | .79 |
| 1640 | 3-5/8" wide, 16" O.C. | | 600 | .013 | | .38 | .51 | | .89 | 1.21 |
| 1650 | 24" O.C. | | 925 | .009 | | .28 | .33 | | .61 | .82 |
| 1660 | 4" wide, 16" O.C. | | 594 | .013 | | .41 | .51 | | .92 | 1.25 |
| 1670 | 24" O.C. | | 925 | .009 | | .31 | .33 | | .64 | .85 |
| 1680 | 6" wide, 16" O.C. | | 588 | .014 | | .57 | .52 | | 1.09 | 1.44 |
| 1690 | 24" O.C. | | 906 | .009 | | .43 | .34 | | .77 | .99 |
| 1700 | 20 ga. studs, 1-5/8" wide, 16" O.C. | | 494 | .016 | | .42 | .62 | | 1.04 | 1.42 |
| 1710 | 24" O.C. | | 763 | .010 | | .31 | .40 | | .71 | .96 |
| 1720 | 2-1/2" wide, 16" O.C. | | 488 | .016 | | .48 | .62 | | 1.10 | 1.50 |
| 1730 | 24" O.C. | | 750 | .011 | | .37 | .41 | | .78 | 1.03 |
| 1740 | 3-5/8" wide, 16" O.C. | | 481 | .017 | | .54 | .63 | | 1.17 | 1.59 |
| 1750 | 24" O.C. | | 738 | .011 | | .41 | .41 | | .82 | 1.09 |
| 1760 | 4" wide, 16" O.C. | | 475 | .017 | | .64 | .64 | | 1.28 | 1.71 |
| 1770 | 24" O.C. | | 738 | .011 | | .48 | .41 | | .89 | 1.17 |
| 1780 | 6" wide, 16" O.C. | | 469 | .017 | | .76 | .65 | | 1.41 | 1.84 |
| 1790 | 24" O.C. | | 725 | .011 | | .57 | .42 | | .99 | 1.27 |
| 2000 | Non-load bearing, galv, 10' high, 25 ga. 1-5/8" wide, 16" O.C. | | 495 | .016 | | .26 | .62 | | .88 | 1.25 |
| 2100 | 24" O.C. | | 760 | .011 | | .19 | .40 | | .59 | .83 |
| 2200 | 2-1/2" wide, 16" O.C. | | 490 | .016 | | .31 | .62 | | .93 | 1.32 |
| 2250 | 24" O.C. | | 750 | .011 | | .23 | .41 | | .64 | .89 |
| 2300 | 3-5/8" wide, 16" O.C. | | 480 | .017 | | .36 | .64 | | 1 | 1.38 |
| 2350 | 24" O.C. | | 740 | .011 | | .26 | .41 | | .67 | .93 |
| 2400 | 4" wide, 16" O.C. | | 475 | .017 | | .39 | .64 | | 1.03 | 1.43 |
| 2450 | 24" O.C. | | 740 | .011 | | .29 | .41 | | .70 | .96 |
| 2500 | 6" wide, 16" O.C. | | 470 | .017 | | .54 | .65 | | 1.19 | 1.60 |
| 2550 | 24" O.C. | | 725 | .011 | | .40 | .42 | | .82 | 1.09 |
| 2600 | 20 ga. studs, 1-5/8" wide, 16" O.C. | | 395 | .020 | | .39 | .77 | | 1.16 | 1.63 |
| 2650 | 24" O.C. | | 610 | .013 | | .29 | .50 | | .79 | 1.10 |
| 2700 | 2-1/2" wide, 16" O.C. | | 390 | .021 | | .46 | .78 | | 1.24 | 1.72 |
| 2750 | 24" O.C. | | 600 | .013 | | .34 | .51 | | .85 | 1.16 |
| 2800 | 3-5/8" wide, 16" O.C. CN | | 385 | .021 | | .52 | .79 | | 1.31 | 1.80 |

# 09 22 Supports for Plaster and Gypsum Board

## 09 22 16 – Non-Structural Metal Framing

### 09 22 16.13 Metal Studs and Track

| | | Crew | Daily Output | Labor-Hours | Unit | Material | 2008 Bare Costs Labor | Equipment | Total | Total Incl O&P |
|---|---|---|---|---|---|---|---|---|---|---|
| 2850 | 24" O.C. | 1 Carp | 590 | .014 | S.F. | .38 | .52 | | .90 | 1.22 |
| 2900 | 4" wide, 16" O.C. | | 380 | .021 | | .61 | .80 | | 1.41 | 1.92 |
| 2950 | 24" O.C. | | 590 | .014 | | .45 | .52 | | .97 | 1.30 |
| 3000 | 6" wide, 16" O.C. | | 375 | .021 | | .72 | .81 | | 1.53 | 2.05 |
| 3050 | 24" O.C. | | 580 | .014 | | .53 | .53 | | 1.06 | 1.40 |
| 3060 | Non-load bearing, galv, 12' high, 25 ga. 1-5/8" wide, 16" O.C. | | 413 | .019 | | .25 | .74 | | .99 | 1.42 |
| 3070 | 24" O.C. | | 633 | .013 | | .18 | .48 | | .66 | .95 |
| 3080 | 2-1/2" wide, 16" O.C. | | 408 | .020 | | .30 | .75 | | 1.05 | 1.49 |
| 3090 | 24" O.C. | | 625 | .013 | | .22 | .49 | | .71 | 1 |
| 3100 | 3-5/8" wide, 16" O.C. | | 400 | .020 | | .34 | .76 | | 1.10 | 1.57 |
| 3110 | 24" O.C. | | 617 | .013 | | .25 | .49 | | .74 | 1.04 |
| 3120 | 4" wide, 16" O.C. | | 396 | .020 | | .37 | .77 | | 1.14 | 1.61 |
| 3130 | 24" O.C. | | 617 | .013 | | .27 | .49 | | .76 | 1.07 |
| 3140 | 6" wide, 16" O.C. | | 392 | .020 | | .51 | .78 | | 1.29 | 1.78 |
| 3150 | 24" O.C. | | 604 | .013 | | .38 | .50 | | .88 | 1.20 |
| 3160 | 20 ga. studs, 1-5/8" wide, 16" O.C. | | 329 | .024 | | .38 | .93 | | 1.31 | 1.85 |
| 3170 | 24" O.C. | | 508 | .016 | | .27 | .60 | | .87 | 1.23 |
| 3180 | 2-1/2" wide, 16" O.C. | | 325 | .025 | | .44 | .94 | | 1.38 | 1.94 |
| 3190 | 24" O.C. | | 500 | .016 | | .32 | .61 | | .93 | 1.30 |
| 3200 | 3-5/8" wide, 16" O.C. | | 321 | .025 | | .49 | .95 | | 1.44 | 2.02 |
| 3210 | 24" O.C. | | 492 | .016 | | .36 | .62 | | .98 | 1.36 |
| 3220 | 4" wide, 16" O.C. | | 317 | .025 | | .58 | .96 | | 1.54 | 2.14 |
| 3230 | 24" O.C. | | 492 | .016 | | .43 | .62 | | 1.05 | 1.43 |
| 3240 | 6" wide, 16" O.C. | | 313 | .026 | | .68 | .97 | | 1.65 | 2.27 |
| 3250 | 24" O.C. | ▼ | 483 | .017 | ▼ | .50 | .63 | | 1.13 | 1.53 |
| 5000 | Load bearing studs, see Div. 05 41 13.30 | | | | | | | | | |

## 09 22 26 – Suspension Systems

### 09 22 26.13 Ceiling Suspension Systems

| | | Crew | Daily Output | Labor-Hours | Unit | Material | 2008 Bare Costs Labor | Equipment | Total | Total Incl O&P |
|---|---|---|---|---|---|---|---|---|---|---|
| 0010 | **CEILING SUSPENSION SYSTEMS** For gypsum board or plaster | | | | | | | | | |
| 8000 | Suspended ceilings, including carriers | | | | | | | | | |
| 8200 | 1-1/2" carriers, 24" O.C. with: | | | | | | | | | |
| 8300 | 7/8" channels, 16" O.C. | 1 Lath | 165 | .048 | S.F. | .48 | 1.69 | | 2.17 | 3.02 |
| 8320 | 24" O.C. | | 200 | .040 | | .39 | 1.39 | | 1.78 | 2.49 |
| 8400 | 1-5/8" channels, 16" O.C. | | 155 | .052 | | .60 | 1.80 | | 2.40 | 3.32 |
| 8420 | 24" O.C. | ▼ | 190 | .042 | ▼ | .48 | 1.47 | | 1.95 | 2.69 |
| 8600 | 2" carriers, 24" O.C. with: | | | | | | | | | |
| 8700 | 7/8" channels, 16" O.C. | 1 Lath | 155 | .052 | S.F. | .49 | 1.80 | | 2.29 | 3.19 |
| 8720 | 24" O.C. | | 190 | .042 | | .40 | 1.47 | | 1.87 | 2.61 |
| 8800 | 1-5/8" channels, 16" O.C. | | 145 | .055 | | .61 | 1.92 | | 2.53 | 3.52 |
| 8820 | 24" O.C. | ▼ | 180 | .044 | ▼ | .49 | 1.55 | | 2.04 | 2.82 |

## 09 22 36 – Lath

### 09 22 36.13 Gypsum Lath

| | | | Crew | Daily Output | Labor-Hours | Unit | Material | 2008 Bare Costs Labor | Equipment | Total | Total Incl O&P |
|---|---|---|---|---|---|---|---|---|---|---|---|
| 0010 | **GYPSUM LATH** | R092000-50 | | | | | | | | | |
| 0020 | Plain or perforated, nailed, 3/8" thick | | 1 Lath | 85 | .094 | S.Y. | 4.95 | 3.28 | | 8.23 | 10.30 |
| 0100 | 1/2" thick | | | 80 | .100 | | 5.60 | 3.48 | | 9.08 | 11.30 |
| 0300 | Clipped to steel studs, 3/8" thick | | | 75 | .107 | | 4.95 | 3.71 | | 8.66 | 10.95 |
| 0400 | 1/2" thick | | | 70 | .114 | | 5.60 | 3.98 | | 9.58 | 12.05 |
| 1500 | For ceiling installations, add | | | 216 | .037 | | | 1.29 | | 1.29 | 1.91 |
| 1600 | For columns and beams, add | | ▼ | 170 | .047 | ▼ | | 1.64 | | 1.64 | 2.43 |

### 09 22 36.23 Metal Lath

| | | | |
|---|---|---|---|
| 0010 | **METAL LATH** | R092000-50 | |

## 09 22 36 – Lath

| 09 22 36.23 Metal Lath | | Crew | Daily Output | Labor-Hours | Unit | Material | 2008 Bare Costs Labor | Equipment | Total | Total Incl O&P |
|---|---|---|---|---|---|---|---|---|---|---|
| 0020 | Diamond, expanded, 2.5 lb. per S.Y., painted | | | | S.Y. | 3.32 | | | 3.32 | 3.65 |
| 0100 | Galvanized | | | | | 2.86 | | | 2.86 | 3.15 |
| 0300 | 3.4 lb. per S.Y., painted | | | | | 3.47 | | | 3.47 | 3.82 |
| 0400 | Galvanized | | | | | 3.62 | | | 3.62 | 3.98 |
| 0600 | For 15# asphalt sheathing paper, add | | | | | .37 | | | .37 | .41 |
| 0900 | Flat rib, 1/8" high, 2.75 lb., painted | | | | | 3.02 | | | 3.02 | 3.32 |
| 1000 | Foil backed | | | | | 3.26 | | | 3.26 | 3.59 |
| 1200 | 3.4 lb. per S.Y., painted | | | | | 3.84 | | | 3.84 | 4.22 |
| 1300 | Galvanized | | | | | 3.91 | | | 3.91 | 4.30 |
| 1500 | For 15# asphalt sheathing paper, add | | | | | .37 | | | .37 | .41 |
| 1800 | High rib, 3/8" high, 3.4 lb. per S.Y., painted | | | | | 4.64 | | | 4.64 | 5.10 |
| 1900 | Galvanized | | | | | 4.64 | | | 4.64 | 5.10 |
| 2400 | 3/4" high, painted, .60 lb. per S.F. | | | | S.F. | .48 | | | .48 | .53 |
| 2500 | .75 lb. per S.F. | | | | " | 1.04 | | | 1.04 | 1.14 |
| 2800 | Stucco mesh, painted, 3.6 lb. | | | | S.Y. | 3.37 | | | 3.37 | 3.71 |
| 3000 | K-lath, perforated, absorbent paper, regular | | | | | 3.69 | | | 3.69 | 4.06 |
| 3100 | Heavy duty | | | | | 4.36 | | | 4.36 | 4.80 |
| 3300 | Waterproof, heavy duty, grade B backing | | | | | 4.27 | | | 4.27 | 4.70 |
| 3400 | Fire resistant backing | | | | | 4.72 | | | 4.72 | 5.20 |
| 3600 | 2.5 lb. diamond painted, on wood framing, on walls | 1 Lath | 85 | .094 | | 3.32 | 3.28 | | 6.60 | 8.50 |
| 3700 | On ceilings | | 75 | .107 | | 3.32 | 3.71 | | 7.03 | 9.15 |
| 3900 | 3.4 lb. diamond painted, on wood framing, on walls | | 80 | .100 | | 3.84 | 3.48 | | 7.32 | 9.35 |
| 4000 | On ceilings | | 70 | .114 | | 3.84 | 3.98 | | 7.82 | 10.10 |
| 4200 | 3.4 lb. diamond painted, wired to steel framing | | 75 | .107 | | 3.84 | 3.71 | | 7.55 | 9.70 |
| 4300 | On ceilings | | 60 | .133 | | 3.84 | 4.64 | | 8.48 | 11.10 |
| 4500 | Columns and beams, wired to steel | | 40 | .200 | | 3.84 | 6.95 | | 10.79 | 14.50 |
| 4600 | Cornices, wired to steel | | 35 | .229 | | 3.84 | 7.95 | | 11.79 | 16 |
| 4800 | Screwed to steel studs, 2.5 lb. | | 80 | .100 | | 3.32 | 3.48 | | 6.80 | 8.80 |
| 4900 | 3.4 lb. | | 75 | .107 | | 3.47 | 3.71 | | 7.18 | 9.30 |
| 5100 | Rib lath, painted, wired to steel, on walls, 2.5 lb. | | 75 | .107 | | 3.02 | 3.71 | | 6.73 | 8.80 |
| 5200 | 3.4 lb. | | 70 | .114 | | 4.64 | 3.98 | | 8.62 | 11 |
| 5400 | 4.0 lb. | | 65 | .123 | | 5.20 | 4.28 | | 9.48 | 12.05 |
| 5500 | For self-furring lath, add | | | | | .09 | | | .09 | .10 |
| 5700 | Suspended ceiling system, incl. 3.4 lb. diamond lath, painted | 1 Lath | 15 | .533 | | 3.85 | 18.55 | | 22.40 | 31.50 |
| 5800 | Galvanized | " | 15 | .533 | | 7.25 | 18.55 | | 25.80 | 35.50 |
| 6000 | Hollow metal stud partitions, 3.4 lb. painted lath both sides | | | | | | | | | |
| 6010 | Non-load bearing, 25 ga., w/rib lath 2-1/2" studs, 12" O.C. | 1 Lath | 20.30 | .394 | S.Y. | 12.85 | 13.70 | | 26.55 | 34.50 |
| 6300 | 16" O.C. | | 21.10 | .379 | | 12.05 | 13.20 | | 25.25 | 33 |
| 6350 | 24" O.C. | | 22.70 | .352 | | 11.35 | 12.25 | | 23.60 | 30.50 |
| 6400 | 3-5/8" studs, 16" O.C. | | 19.50 | .410 | | 12.50 | 14.30 | | 26.80 | 35 |
| 6600 | 24" O.C. | | 20.40 | .392 | | 11.65 | 13.65 | | 25.30 | 33 |
| 6700 | 4" studs, 16" O.C. | | 20.40 | .392 | | 12.80 | 13.65 | | 26.45 | 34 |
| 6900 | 24" O.C. | | 21.60 | .370 | | 11.90 | 12.90 | | 24.80 | 32 |
| 7000 | 6" studs, 16" O.C. | | 19.50 | .410 | | 14.15 | 14.30 | | 28.45 | 36.50 |
| 7100 | 24" O.C. | | 21.10 | .379 | | 12.85 | 13.20 | | 26.05 | 33.50 |
| 7200 | L.B. partitions, 16 ga., w/rib lath, 2-1/2" studs, 16" O.C. | | 20 | .400 | | 14.20 | 13.90 | | 28.10 | 36 |
| 7300 | 3-5/8" studs, 16 ga. | | 19.70 | .406 | | 16.10 | 14.15 | | 30.25 | 38.50 |
| 7500 | 4" studs, 16 ga. | | 19.50 | .410 | | 16.70 | 14.30 | | 31 | 39.50 |
| 7600 | 6" studs, 16 ga. | | 18.70 | .428 | | 19.75 | 14.90 | | 34.65 | 43.50 |

## 09 22 36.43 Security Mesh

| | | Crew | Daily Output | Labor-Hours | Unit | Material | Labor | Equipment | Total | Total Incl O&P |
|---|---|---|---|---|---|---|---|---|---|---|
| 0010 | **SECURITY MESH**, expanded metal, flat, screwed to framing | | | | | | | | | |
| 0100 | On walls, 3/4", 1.76 lb/S.F. | 2 Carp | 1500 | .011 | S.F. | 1.37 | .41 | | 1.78 | 2.14 |

# 09 22 Supports for Plaster and Gypsum Board

## 09 22 36 – Lath

| 09 22 36.43 Security Mesh | Crew | Daily Output | Labor-Hours | Unit | Material | 2008 Bare Costs Labor | Equipment | Total | Total Incl O&P |
|---|---|---|---|---|---|---|---|---|---|
| 0110 | 1-1/2", 1.14 lb/S.F. | 2 Carp | 1600 | .010 | S.F. | 1.08 | .38 | | 1.46 | 1.78 |
| 0200 | On ceilings, 3/4", 1.76 lb/S.F. | | 1350 | .012 | | 1.37 | .45 | | 1.82 | 2.21 |
| 0210 | 1-1/2", 1.14 lb/S.F. | ↓ | 1450 | .011 | ↓ | 1.08 | .42 | | 1.50 | 1.84 |

| 09 22 36.83 Accessories, Plaster | Crew | Daily Output | Labor-Hours | Unit | Material | 2008 Bare Costs Labor | Equipment | Total | Total Incl O&P |
|---|---|---|---|---|---|---|---|---|---|
| 0010 | **ACCESSORIES, PLASTER** | | | | | | | | | |
| 0020 | Casing bead, expanded flange, galvanized | 1 Lath | 2.70 | 2.963 | C.L.F. | 41 | 103 | | 144 | 198 |
| 0900 | Channels, cold rolled, 16 ga., 3/4" deep, galvanized | | | | | 27.50 | | | 27.50 | 30 |
| 1200 | 1-1/2" deep, 16 ga., galvanized | | | | | 41 | | | 41 | 45 |
| 1620 | Corner bead, expanded bullnose, 3/4" radius, #10, galvanized | 1 Lath | 2.60 | 3.077 | | 31 | 107 | | 138 | 194 |
| 1650 | #1, galvanized | | 2.55 | 3.137 | | 50 | 109 | | 159 | 217 |
| 1670 | Expanded wing, 2-3/4" wide, #1, galvanized | | 2.65 | 3.019 | | 30 | 105 | | 135 | 189 |
| 1700 | Inside corner, (corner rite) 3" x 3", painted | | 2.60 | 3.077 | | 25.50 | 107 | | 132.50 | 187 |
| 1750 | Strip-ex, 4" wide, painted | | 2.55 | 3.137 | | 25.50 | 109 | | 134.50 | 190 |
| 1800 | Expansion joint, 3/4" grounds, limited expansion, galv., 1 piece | | 2.70 | 2.963 | | 95 | 103 | | 198 | 257 |
| 2100 | Extreme expansion, galvanized, 2 piece | ↓ | 2.60 | 3.077 | ↓ | 150 | 107 | | 257 | 325 |

# 09 23 Gypsum Plastering

## 09 23 13 – Acoustical Gypsum Plastering

### 09 23 13.10 Perlite or Vermiculite Plaster

| | | Crew | Daily Output | Labor-Hours | Unit | Material | 2008 Bare Costs Labor | Equipment | Total | Total Incl O&P |
|---|---|---|---|---|---|---|---|---|---|---|
| 0010 | **PERLITE OR VERMICULITE PLASTER**    R092000-50 | | | | | | | | | |
| 0020 | In 100 lb. bags, under 200 bags | | | | Bag | 14.25 | | | 14.25 | 15.65 |
| 0100 | Over 200 bags | | | | " | 12.95 | | | 12.95 | 14.20 |
| 0300 | 2 coats, no lath included, on walls | J-1 | 92 | .435 | S.Y. | 3.60 | 14.50 | 1.32 | 19.42 | 27.50 |
| 0400 | On ceilings | " | 79 | .506 | | 3.60 | 16.90 | 1.53 | 22.03 | 31 |
| 0600 | On and incl. 3/8" gypsum lath, on metal studs | J-2 | 84 | .571 | | 8.25 | 19.20 | 1.44 | 28.89 | 39.50 |
| 0700 | On ceilings | " | 70 | .686 | | 8.25 | 23 | 1.73 | 32.98 | 46 |
| 0900 | 3 coats, no lath included, on walls | J-1 | 74 | .541 | | 6.10 | 18.05 | 1.64 | 25.79 | 36 |
| 1000 | On ceilings | " | 63 | .635 | | 6.10 | 21 | 1.92 | 29.02 | 41 |
| 1200 | On and incl. painted metal lath, on metal studs | J-2 | 72 | .667 | | 10.75 | 22.50 | 1.68 | 34.93 | 47.50 |
| 1300 | On ceilings | | 61 | .787 | | 10.75 | 26.50 | 1.98 | 39.23 | 54 |
| 1500 | On and incl. suspended metal lath ceiling | ↓ | 37 | 1.297 | | 9.95 | 43.50 | 3.27 | 56.72 | 80.50 |
| 1700 | For irregular or curved surfaces, add to above | | | | | | 30% | | | |
| 1800 | For columns and beams, add to above | | | | | | 50% | | | |
| 1900 | For soffits, add to ceiling prices | | | | ↓ | | 40% | | | |

## 09 23 20 – Gypsum Plaster

### 09 23 20.10 Gypsum Plaster On Walls and Ceilings

| | | Crew | Daily Output | Labor-Hours | Unit | Material | 2008 Bare Costs Labor | Equipment | Total | Total Incl O&P |
|---|---|---|---|---|---|---|---|---|---|---|
| 0010 | **GYPSUM PLASTER ON WALLS AND CEILINGS**    R092000-50 | | | | | | | | | |
| 0020 | 80# bag, less than 1 ton | | | | Bag | 14.45 | | | 14.45 | 15.90 |
| 0100 | Over 1 ton | | | | " | 14.20 | | | 14.20 | 15.65 |
| 0300 | 2 coats, no lath included, on walls | J-1 | 105 | .381 | S.Y. | 3.63 | 12.70 | 1.15 | 17.48 | 24.50 |
| 0400 | On ceilings | " | 92 | .435 | | 3.63 | 14.50 | 1.32 | 19.45 | 27.50 |
| 0600 | On and incl. 3/8" gypsum lath on steel, on walls | J-2 | 97 | .495 | | 8.60 | 16.65 | 1.25 | 26.50 | 36 |
| 0700 | On ceilings | " | 83 | .578 | | 8.60 | 19.45 | 1.46 | 29.51 | 40.50 |
| 0900 | 3 coats, no lath included, on walls | J-1 | 87 | .460 | | 5.15 | 15.35 | 1.39 | 21.89 | 30.50 |
| 1000 | On ceilings | " | 78 | .513 | | 5.15 | 17.10 | 1.55 | 23.80 | 33.50 |
| 1200 | On and including painted metal lath, on wood studs | J-2 | 86 | .558 | | 9.65 | 18.75 | 1.41 | 29.81 | 40.50 |
| 1300 | On ceilings | " | 76.50 | .627 | ↓ | 9.65 | 21 | 1.58 | 32.23 | 44.50 |
| 1600 | For irregular or curved surfaces, add | | | | | | 30% | | | |
| 1800 | For columns & beams, add | | | | | | 50% | | | |

# 09 23 Gypsum Plastering

## 09 23 20 – Gypsum Plaster

| 09 23 20.20 Gauging Plaster | | Crew | Daily Output | Labor-Hours | Unit | Material | 2008 Bare Costs Labor | Equipment | Total | Total Incl O&P |
|---|---|---|---|---|---|---|---|---|---|---|
| 0010 | **GAUGING PLASTER** R092000-50 | | | | | | | | | |
| 0020 | 100 lb. bags, less than 1 ton | | | | Bag | 18.85 | | | 18.85 | 20.50 |
| 0100 | Over 1 ton | | | | " | 16.45 | | | 16.45 | 18.10 |

### 09 23 20.30 Keenes Cement

| | | Crew | Daily Output | Labor-Hours | Unit | Material | Labor | Equipment | Total | Total Incl O&P |
|---|---|---|---|---|---|---|---|---|---|---|
| 0010 | **KEENES CEMENT** R092000-50 | | | | | | | | | |
| 0020 | In 100 lb. bags, less than 1 ton | | | | Bag | 27 | | | 27 | 29.50 |
| 0100 | Over 1 ton | | | | " | 25.50 | | | 25.50 | 28 |
| 0300 | Finish only, add to plaster prices, standard | J-1 | 215 | .186 | S.Y. | 2.46 | 6.20 | .56 | 9.22 | 12.70 |
| 0400 | High quality | " | 144 | .278 | " | 2.48 | 9.25 | .84 | 12.57 | 17.70 |

# 09 24 Portland Cement Plastering

## 09 24 23 – Portland Cement Stucco

### 09 24 23.40 Stucco

| | | Crew | Daily Output | Labor-Hours | Unit | Material | Labor | Equipment | Total | Total Incl O&P |
|---|---|---|---|---|---|---|---|---|---|---|
| 0010 | **STUCCO** R092000-50 | | | | | | | | | |
| 0015 | 3 coats 1" thick, float finish, with mesh, on wood frame | J-2 | 63 | .762 | S.Y. | 5.50 | 25.50 | 1.92 | 32.92 | 46.50 |
| 0100 | On masonry construction, no mesh incl. | J-1 | 67 | .597 | | 2.15 | 19.95 | 1.81 | 23.91 | 34.50 |
| 0300 | For trowel finish, add | 1 Plas | 170 | .047 | | | 1.65 | | 1.65 | 2.50 |
| 0400 | For 3/4" thick, on masonry, deduct | J-1 | 880 | .045 | | .60 | 1.52 | .14 | 2.26 | 3.11 |
| 0600 | For coloring and special finish, add, minimum | | 685 | .058 | | .39 | 1.95 | .18 | 2.52 | 3.58 |
| 0700 | Maximum | | 200 | .200 | | 1.35 | 6.70 | .61 | 8.66 | 12.30 |
| 0900 | For soffits, add | J-2 | 155 | .310 | | 2.09 | 10.40 | .78 | 13.27 | 18.90 |
| 1000 | Exterior stucco, with bonding agent, 3 coats, on walls, no mesh incl. | J-1 | 200 | .200 | | 3.50 | 6.70 | .61 | 10.81 | 14.65 |
| 1200 | Ceilings | | 180 | .222 | | 3.50 | 7.40 | .67 | 11.57 | 15.85 |
| 1300 | Beams | | 80 | .500 | | 3.50 | 16.70 | 1.52 | 21.72 | 31 |
| 1500 | Columns | | 100 | .400 | | 3.50 | 13.35 | 1.21 | 18.06 | 25.50 |
| 1600 | Mesh, painted, nailed to wood, 1.8 lb. | 1 Lath | 60 | .133 | | 4.80 | 4.64 | | 9.44 | 12.20 |
| 1800 | 3.6 lb. | | 55 | .145 | | 3.37 | 5.05 | | 8.42 | 11.20 |
| 1900 | Wired to steel, painted, 1.8 lb. | | 53 | .151 | | 4.80 | 5.25 | | 10.05 | 13.10 |
| 2100 | 3.6 lb. | | 50 | .160 | | 3.37 | 5.55 | | 8.92 | 11.95 |

# 09 26 Veneer Plastering

## 09 26 13 – Gypsum Veneer Plastering

### 09 26 13.20 Blueboard

| | | Crew | Daily Output | Labor-Hours | Unit | Material | Labor | Equipment | Total | Total Incl O&P |
|---|---|---|---|---|---|---|---|---|---|---|
| 0010 | **BLUEBOARD** For use with thin coat | | | | | | | | | |
| 0100 | plaster application (see Div. 09 26 13.80) | | | | | | | | | |
| 1000 | 3/8" thick, on walls or ceilings, standard, no finish included | 2 Carp | 1900 | .008 | S.F. | .23 | .32 | | .55 | .75 |
| 1100 | With thin coat plaster finish | | 875 | .018 | | .31 | .70 | | 1.01 | 1.42 |
| 1400 | On beams, columns, or soffits, standard, no finish included | | 675 | .024 | | .26 | .90 | | 1.16 | 1.70 |
| 1450 | With thin coat plaster finish | | 475 | .034 | | .34 | 1.28 | | 1.62 | 2.38 |
| 3000 | 1/2" thick, on walls or ceilings, standard, no finish included | | 1900 | .008 | | .24 | .32 | | .56 | .76 |
| 3100 | With thin coat plaster finish | | 875 | .018 | | .32 | .70 | | 1.02 | 1.43 |
| 3300 | Fire resistant, no finish included | | 1900 | .008 | | .24 | .32 | | .56 | .76 |
| 3400 | With thin coat plaster finish | | 875 | .018 | | .32 | .70 | | 1.02 | 1.43 |
| 3450 | On beams, columns, or soffits, standard, no finish included | | 675 | .024 | | .28 | .90 | | 1.18 | 1.71 |
| 3500 | With thin coat plaster finish | | 475 | .034 | | .36 | 1.28 | | 1.64 | 2.39 |
| 3700 | Fire resistant, no finish included | | 675 | .024 | | .28 | .90 | | 1.18 | 1.71 |
| 3800 | With thin coat plaster finish | | 475 | .034 | | .36 | 1.28 | | 1.64 | 2.39 |
| 5000 | 5/8" thick, on walls or ceilings, fire resistant, no finish included | | 1900 | .008 | | .24 | .32 | | .56 | .76 |

# 09 26 Veneer Plastering

## 09 26 13 – Gypsum Veneer Plastering

| 09 26 13.20 Blueboard | | Crew | Daily Output | Labor-Hours | Unit | Material | 2008 Bare Costs Labor | Equipment | Total | Total Incl O&P |
|---|---|---|---|---|---|---|---|---|---|---|
| 5100 | With thin coat plaster finish | 2 Carp | 875 | .018 | S.F. | .32 | .70 | | 1.02 | 1.43 |
| 5500 | On beams, columns, or soffits, no finish included | | 675 | .024 | | .28 | .90 | | 1.18 | 1.71 |
| 5600 | With thin coat plaster finish | | 475 | .034 | | .36 | 1.28 | | 1.64 | 2.39 |
| 6000 | For high ceilings, over 8' high, add | | 3060 | .005 | | | .20 | | .20 | .31 |
| 6500 | For over 3 stories high, add per story | ▼ | 6100 | .003 | ▼ | | .10 | | .10 | .16 |

| 09 26 13.80 Thin Coat Plaster | | | | | | | | | | |
|---|---|---|---|---|---|---|---|---|---|---|
| 0010 | **THIN COAT PLASTER** | | | | | | | | | |
| 0012 | 1 coat veneer, not incl. lath | J-1 | 3600 | .011 | S.F. | .08 | .37 | .03 | .48 | .69 |
| 1000 | In 50 lb. bags | | | | Bag | 10.80 | | | 10.80 | 11.85 |

# 09 28 Backing Boards and Underlayments

## 09 28 13 – Cementitious Backing Boards

| 09 28 13.10 Cementitious Backerboard | | Crew | Daily Output | Labor-Hours | Unit | Material | 2008 Bare Costs Labor | Equipment | Total | Total Incl O&P |
|---|---|---|---|---|---|---|---|---|---|---|
| 0010 | **CEMENTITIOUS BACKERBOARD** | | | | | | | | | |
| 0070 | Cementitious backerboard, on floor, 3' x 4'x 1/2" sheets | 2 Carp | 525 | .030 | S.F. | .79 | 1.16 | | 1.95 | 2.67 |
| 0080 | 3' x 5' x 1/2" sheets | | 525 | .030 | | .78 | 1.16 | | 1.94 | 2.66 |
| 0090 | 3' x 6' x 1/2" sheets | | 525 | .030 | | .72 | 1.16 | | 1.88 | 2.60 |
| 0100 | 3' x 4'x 5/8" sheets | | 525 | .030 | | 1.04 | 1.16 | | 2.20 | 2.95 |
| 0110 | 3' x 5' x 5/8" sheets | | 525 | .030 | | 1.03 | 1.16 | | 2.19 | 2.94 |
| 0120 | 3' x 6' x 5/8" sheets | | 525 | .030 | | .96 | 1.16 | | 2.12 | 2.87 |
| 0150 | On wall, 3' x 4'x 1/2" sheets | | 350 | .046 | | .79 | 1.74 | | 2.53 | 3.57 |
| 0160 | 3' x 5' x 1/2" sheets | | 350 | .046 | | .78 | 1.74 | | 2.52 | 3.56 |
| 0170 | 3' x 6' x 1/2" sheets | | 350 | .046 | | .72 | 1.74 | | 2.46 | 3.50 |
| 0180 | 3' x 4'x 5/8" sheets | | 350 | .046 | | 1.04 | 1.74 | | 2.78 | 3.85 |
| 0190 | 3' x 5' x 5/8" sheets | | 350 | .046 | | 1.03 | 1.74 | | 2.77 | 3.84 |
| 0200 | 3' x 6' x 5/8" sheets | | 350 | .046 | | .96 | 1.74 | | 2.70 | 3.77 |
| 0250 | On counter, 3' x 4'x 1/2" sheets | | 180 | .089 | | .79 | 3.39 | | 4.18 | 6.10 |
| 0260 | 3' x 5' x 1/2" sheets | | 180 | .089 | | .78 | 3.39 | | 4.17 | 6.10 |
| 0270 | 3' x 6' x 1/2" sheets | | 180 | .089 | | .72 | 3.39 | | 4.11 | 6.05 |
| 0300 | 3' x 4'x 5/8" sheets | | 180 | .089 | | 1.04 | 3.39 | | 4.43 | 6.40 |
| 0310 | 3' x 5' x 5/8" sheets | | 180 | .089 | | 1.03 | 3.39 | | 4.42 | 6.40 |
| 0320 | 3' x 6' x 5/8" sheets | ▼ | 180 | .089 | ▼ | .96 | 3.39 | | 4.35 | 6.30 |

# 09 29 Gypsum Board

## 09 29 10 – Gypsum Board Panels

| 09 29 10.10 Gypsum Board Ceilings | | Crew | Daily Output | Labor-Hours | Unit | Material | 2008 Bare Costs Labor | Equipment | Total | Total Incl O&P |
|---|---|---|---|---|---|---|---|---|---|---|
| 0010 | **GYPSUM BOARD CEILINGS**, fire rated, finished | | | | | | | | | |
| 0100 | Screwed to grid, channel or joists, 1/2" thick | 2 Carp | 765 | .021 | S.F. | .26 | .80 | | 1.06 | 1.53 |
| 0150 | Mold resistant | | 765 | .021 | | .42 | .80 | | 1.22 | 1.70 |
| 0200 | 5/8" thick | | 765 | .021 | | .30 | .80 | | 1.10 | 1.57 |
| 0250 | Mold resistant | | 765 | .021 | | .51 | .80 | | 1.31 | 1.80 |
| 0300 | Over 8' high, 1/2" thick | | 615 | .026 | | .26 | .99 | | 1.25 | 1.83 |
| 0350 | Mold resistant | | 615 | .026 | | .42 | .99 | | 1.41 | 2 |
| 0400 | 5/8" thick | | 615 | .026 | | .30 | .99 | | 1.29 | 1.87 |
| 0450 | Mold resistant | ▼ | 615 | .026 | ▼ | .51 | .99 | | 1.50 | 2.10 |
| 0600 | Grid suspension system, direct hung | | | | | | | | | |
| 0700 | 1-1/2" C.R.C., with 7/8" hi hat furring channel, 16" O.C. | 2 Carp | 600 | .027 | S.F. | 1.15 | 1.02 | | 2.17 | 2.85 |
| 0800 | 24" O.C. | | 900 | .018 | | 1.05 | .68 | | 1.73 | 2.21 |
| 0900 | 3-5/8" C.R.C., with 7/8" hi hat furring channel, 16" O.C. | ▼ | 600 | .027 | ▼ | 1.22 | 1.02 | | 2.24 | 2.92 |

# 09 29 Gypsum Board

## 09 29 10 – Gypsum Board Panels

| 09 29 10.10 Gypsum Board Ceilings | Crew | Daily Output | Labor-Hours | Unit | Material | 2008 Bare Costs Labor | Equipment | Total | Total Incl O&P |
|---|---|---|---|---|---|---|---|---|---|
| 1000 | 24" O.C. | 2 Carp | 900 | .018 | S.F. | 1.06 | .68 | | 1.74 | 2.22 |

### 09 29 10.30 Gypsum Board

| | | Crew | Daily Output | Labor-Hours | Unit | Material | Labor | Equipment | Total | Total Incl O&P |
|---|---|---|---|---|---|---|---|---|---|---|
| 0010 | **GYPSUM BOARD** on walls & ceilings  R092910-10 | | | | | | | | | |
| 0100 | Nailed or screwed to studs unless otherwise noted | | | | | | | | | |
| 0150 | 3/8" thick, on walls, standard, no finish included | 2 Carp | 2000 | .008 | S.F. | .22 | .30 | | .52 | .71 |
| 0200 | On ceilings, standard, no finish included | | 1800 | .009 | | .22 | .34 | | .56 | .77 |
| 0250 | On beams, columns, or soffits, no finish included | | 675 | .024 | | .22 | .90 | | 1.12 | 1.65 |
| 0300 | 1/2" thick, on walls, standard, no finish included  *CN* | | 2000 | .008 | | .25 | .30 | | .55 | .75 |
| 0350 | Taped and finished (level 4 finish) | | 965 | .017 | | .29 | .63 | | .92 | 1.30 |
| 0390 | With compound skim coat (level 5 finish) | | 775 | .021 | | .33 | .79 | | 1.12 | 1.59 |
| 0400 | Fire resistant, no finish included | | 2000 | .008 | | .26 | .30 | | .56 | .76 |
| 0450 | Taped and finished (level 4 finish) | | 965 | .017 | | .30 | .63 | | .93 | 1.31 |
| 0490 | With compound skim coat (level 5 finish) | | 775 | .021 | | .34 | .79 | | 1.13 | 1.60 |
| 0500 | Water resistant, no finish included | | 2000 | .008 | | .35 | .30 | | .65 | .86 |
| 0550 | Taped and finished (level 4 finish) | | 965 | .017 | | .39 | .63 | | 1.02 | 1.41 |
| 0590 | With compound skim coat (level 5 finish) | | 775 | .021 | | .43 | .79 | | 1.22 | 1.70 |
| 0600 | Prefinished, vinyl, clipped to studs | | 900 | .018 | | .64 | .68 | | 1.32 | 1.75 |
| 0700 | Mold resistant, no finish included | | 2000 | .008 | | .38 | .30 | | .68 | .89 |
| 0710 | Taped and finished (level 4 finish) | | 965 | .017 | | .42 | .63 | | 1.05 | 1.44 |
| 0720 | With compound skim coat (level 5 finish) | | 775 | .021 | | .46 | .79 | | 1.25 | 1.73 |
| 1000 | On ceilings, standard, no finish included | | 1800 | .009 | | .25 | .34 | | .59 | .81 |
| 1050 | Taped and finished (level 4 finish) | | 765 | .021 | | .29 | .80 | | 1.09 | 1.56 |
| 1090 | With compound skim coat (level 5 finish) | | 610 | .026 | | .33 | 1 | | 1.33 | 1.93 |
| 1100 | Fire resistant, no finish included | | 1800 | .009 | | .26 | .34 | | .60 | .82 |
| 1150 | Taped and finished (level 4 finish) | | 765 | .021 | | .30 | .80 | | 1.10 | 1.57 |
| 1195 | With compound skim coat (level 5 finish) | | 610 | .026 | | .34 | 1 | | 1.34 | 1.94 |
| 1200 | Water resistant, no finish included | | 1800 | .009 | | .35 | .34 | | .69 | .92 |
| 1250 | Taped and finished (level 4 finish) | | 765 | .021 | | .39 | .80 | | 1.19 | 1.67 |
| 1290 | With compound skim coat (level 5 finish) | | 610 | .026 | | .43 | 1 | | 1.43 | 2.04 |
| 1310 | Mold resistant, no finish included | | 1800 | .009 | | .38 | .34 | | .72 | .95 |
| 1320 | Taped and finished (level 4 finish) | | 765 | .021 | | .42 | .80 | | 1.22 | 1.70 |
| 1330 | With compound skim coat (level 5 finish) | | 610 | .026 | | .46 | 1 | | 1.46 | 2.07 |
| 1500 | On beams, columns, or soffits, standard, no finish included | | 675 | .024 | | .29 | .90 | | 1.19 | 1.73 |
| 1550 | Taped and finished (level 4 finish) | | 475 | .034 | | .29 | 1.28 | | 1.57 | 2.32 |
| 1590 | With compound skim coat (level 5 finish) | | 540 | .030 | | .33 | 1.13 | | 1.46 | 2.13 |
| 1600 | Fire resistant, no finish included | | 675 | .024 | | .26 | .90 | | 1.16 | 1.70 |
| 1650 | Taped and finished (level 4 finish) | | 475 | .034 | | .30 | 1.28 | | 1.58 | 2.33 |
| 1690 | With compound skim coat (level 5 finish) | | 540 | .030 | | .34 | 1.13 | | 1.47 | 2.14 |
| 1700 | Water resistant, no finish included | | 675 | .024 | | .40 | .90 | | 1.30 | 1.85 |
| 1750 | Taped and finished (level 4 finish) | | 475 | .034 | | .39 | 1.28 | | 1.67 | 2.43 |
| 1790 | With compound skim coat (level 5 finish) | | 540 | .030 | | .43 | 1.13 | | 1.56 | 2.24 |
| 1800 | Mold resistant, no finish included | | 675 | .024 | | .44 | .90 | | 1.34 | 1.89 |
| 1810 | Taped and finished (level 4 finish) | | 475 | .034 | | .42 | 1.28 | | 1.70 | 2.46 |
| 1820 | With compound skim coat (level 5 finish) | | 540 | .030 | | .46 | 1.13 | | 1.59 | 2.27 |
| 2000 | 5/8" thick, on walls, standard, no finish included | | 2000 | .008 | | .28 | .30 | | .58 | .78 |
| 2050 | Taped and finished (level 4 finish) | | 965 | .017 | | .32 | .63 | | .95 | 1.33 |
| 2090 | With compound skim coat (level 5 finish) | | 775 | .021 | | .36 | .79 | | 1.15 | 1.62 |
| 2100 | Fire resistant, no finish included | | 2000 | .008 | | .30 | .30 | | .60 | .80 |
| 2150 | Taped and finished (level 4 finish) | | 965 | .017 | | .34 | .63 | | .97 | 1.36 |
| 2195 | With compound skim coat (level 5 finish) | | 775 | .021 | | .38 | .79 | | 1.17 | 1.64 |
| 2200 | Water resistant, no finish included | | 2000 | .008 | | .34 | .30 | | .64 | .84 |
| 2250 | Taped and finished (level 4 finish) | | 965 | .017 | | .38 | .63 | | 1.01 | 1.40 |

### 09 29 10.30 Gypsum Board

| | | Crew | Daily Output | Labor-Hours | Unit | Material | 2008 Bare Costs Labor | 2008 Bare Costs Equipment | Total | Total Incl O&P |
|---|---|---|---|---|---|---|---|---|---|---|
| 2290 | With compound skim coat (level 5 finish) | 2 Carp | 775 | .021 | S.F. | .42 | .79 | | 1.21 | 1.69 |
| 2300 | Prefinished, vinyl, clipped to studs | | 900 | .018 | | .78 | .68 | | 1.46 | 1.91 |
| 2510 | Mold resistant, no finish included | | 2000 | .008 | | .46 | .30 | | .76 | .98 |
| 2520 | Taped and finished (level 4 finish) | | 965 | .017 | | .50 | .63 | | 1.13 | 1.53 |
| 2530 | With compound skim coat (level 5 finish) | | 775 | .021 | | .54 | .79 | | 1.33 | 1.82 |
| 3000 | On ceilings, standard, no finish included | | 1800 | .009 | | .28 | .34 | | .62 | .84 |
| 3050 | Taped and finished (level 4 finish) | | 765 | .021 | | .32 | .80 | | 1.12 | 1.59 |
| 3090 | With compound skim coat (level 5 finish) | | 615 | .026 | | .36 | .99 | | 1.35 | 1.94 |
| 3100 | Fire resistant, no finish included | | 1800 | .009 | | .30 | .34 | | .64 | .86 |
| 3150 | Taped and finished (level 4 finish) | | 765 | .021 | | .34 | .80 | | 1.14 | 1.62 |
| 3190 | With compound skim coat (level 5 finish) | | 615 | .026 | | .38 | .99 | | 1.37 | 1.96 |
| 3200 | Water resistant, no finish included | | 1800 | .009 | | .34 | .34 | | .68 | .90 |
| 3250 | Taped and finished (level 4 finish) | | 765 | .021 | | .38 | .80 | | 1.18 | 1.66 |
| 3290 | With compound skim coat (level 5 finish) | | 615 | .026 | | .42 | .99 | | 1.41 | 2.01 |
| 3300 | Mold resistant, no finish included | | 1800 | .009 | | .46 | .34 | | .80 | 1.04 |
| 3310 | Taped and finished (level 4 finish) | | 765 | .021 | | .50 | .80 | | 1.30 | 1.79 |
| 3320 | With compound skim coat (level 5 finish) | | 615 | .026 | | .54 | .99 | | 1.53 | 2.14 |
| 3500 | On beams, columns, or soffits, no finish included | | 675 | .024 | | .32 | .90 | | 1.22 | 1.76 |
| 3550 | Taped and finished (level 4 finish) | | 475 | .034 | | .37 | 1.28 | | 1.65 | 2.41 |
| 3590 | With compound skim coat (level 5 finish) | | 380 | .042 | | .42 | 1.60 | | 2.02 | 2.96 |
| 3600 | Fire resistant, no finish included | | 675 | .024 | | .35 | .90 | | 1.25 | 1.79 |
| 3650 | Taped and finished (level 4 finish) | | 475 | .034 | | .39 | 1.28 | | 1.67 | 2.43 |
| 3690 | With compound skim coat (level 5 finish) | | 380 | .042 | | .38 | 1.60 | | 1.98 | 2.92 |
| 3700 | Water resistant, no finish included | | 675 | .024 | | .39 | .90 | | 1.29 | 1.84 |
| 3750 | Taped and finished (level 4 finish) | | 475 | .034 | | .44 | 1.28 | | 1.72 | 2.48 |
| 3790 | With compound skim coat (level 5 finish) | | 380 | .042 | | .42 | 1.60 | | 2.02 | 2.97 |
| 3800 | Mold resistant, no finish included | | 675 | .024 | | .53 | .90 | | 1.43 | 1.99 |
| 3810 | Taped and finished (level 4 finish) | | 475 | .034 | | .58 | 1.28 | | 1.86 | 2.63 |
| 3820 | With compound skim coat (level 5 finish) | | 380 | .042 | | .54 | 1.60 | | 2.14 | 3.10 |
| 4000 | Fireproofing, beams or columns, 2 layers, 1/2" thick, incl finish | | 330 | .048 | | .56 | 1.85 | | 2.41 | 3.49 |
| 4010 | Mold resistant | | 330 | .048 | | .80 | 1.85 | | 2.65 | 3.75 |
| 4050 | 5/8" thick | | 300 | .053 | | .68 | 2.03 | | 2.71 | 3.91 |
| 4060 | Mold resistant | | 300 | .053 | | 1 | 2.03 | | 3.03 | 4.26 |
| 4100 | 3 layers, 1/2" thick | | 225 | .071 | | .82 | 2.71 | | 3.53 | 5.10 |
| 4110 | Mold resistant | | 225 | .071 | | 1.18 | 2.71 | | 3.89 | 5.50 |
| 4150 | 5/8" thick | | 210 | .076 | | 1.02 | 2.90 | | 3.92 | 5.65 |
| 4160 | Mold resistant | | 210 | .076 | | 1.50 | 2.90 | | 4.40 | 6.15 |
| 5050 | For 1" thick coreboard on columns | | 480 | .033 | | .62 | 1.27 | | 1.89 | 2.66 |
| 5100 | For foil-backed board, add | | | | | .10 | | | .10 | .11 |
| 5200 | For work over 8' high, add | 2 Carp | 3060 | .005 | | | .20 | | .20 | .31 |
| 5270 | For textured spray, add | 2 Lath | 1600 | .010 | | .05 | .35 | | .40 | .58 |
| 5300 | For distribution cost over 3 stories high, add per story | 2 Carp | 6100 | .003 | | | .10 | | .10 | .16 |
| 5350 | For finishing inner corners, add | | 950 | .017 | L.F. | .09 | .64 | | .73 | 1.10 |
| 5355 | For finishing outer corners, add | | 1250 | .013 | | .18 | .49 | | .67 | .96 |
| 5500 | For acoustical sealant, add per bead | 1 Carp | 500 | .016 | | .03 | .61 | | .64 | .99 |
| 5550 | Sealant, 1 quart tube | | | | Ea. | 5.30 | | | 5.30 | 5.80 |
| 5600 | Sound deadening board, 1/4" gypsum | 2 Carp | 1800 | .009 | S.F. | .26 | .34 | | .60 | .82 |
| 5650 | 1/2" wood fiber | " | 1800 | .009 | " | .19 | .34 | | .53 | .74 |

### 09 29 10.50 High Abuse Gypsum Board

| | | Crew | Daily Output | Labor-Hours | Unit | Material | 2008 Bare Costs Labor | 2008 Bare Costs Equipment | Total | Total Incl O&P |
|---|---|---|---|---|---|---|---|---|---|---|
| 0010 | **HIGH ABUSE GYPSUM BOARD**, fiber reinforced, nailed or | | | | | | | | | |
| 0100 | screwed to studs unless otherwise noted | | | | | | | | | |
| 0110 | 1/2" thick, on walls, no finish included | 2 Carp | 1800 | .009 | S.F. | .65 | .34 | | .99 | 1.25 |

# 09 29 Gypsum Board

## 09 29 10 – Gypsum Board Panels

| | 09 29 10.50 High Abuse Gypsum Board | Crew | Daily Output | Labor-Hours | Unit | Material | 2008 Bare Costs Labor | Equipment | Total | Total Incl O&P |
|---|---|---|---|---|---|---|---|---|---|---|
| 0120 | Taped and finished (level 4 finish) | 2 Carp | 870 | .018 | S.F. | .69 | .70 | | 1.39 | 1.85 |
| 0130 | With compound skim coat (level 5 finish) | | 700 | .023 | | .73 | .87 | | 1.60 | 2.17 |
| 0150 | On ceilings, no finish included | | 1620 | .010 | | .65 | .38 | | 1.03 | 1.31 |
| 0160 | Taped and finished (level 4 finish) | | 690 | .023 | | .69 | .88 | | 1.57 | 2.14 |
| 0170 | With compound skim coat (level 5 finish) | | 550 | .029 | | .73 | 1.11 | | 1.84 | 2.54 |
| 0210 | 5/8" thick, on walls, no finish included | | 1800 | .009 | | .68 | .34 | | 1.02 | 1.28 |
| 0220 | Taped and finished (level 4 finish) | | 870 | .018 | | .72 | .70 | | 1.42 | 1.88 |
| 0230 | With compound skim coat (level 5 finish) | | 700 | .023 | | .76 | .87 | | 1.63 | 2.20 |
| 0250 | On ceilings, no finish included | | 1620 | .010 | | .68 | .38 | | 1.06 | 1.34 |
| 0260 | Taped and finished (level 4 finish) | | 690 | .023 | | .72 | .88 | | 1.60 | 2.17 |
| 0270 | With compound skim coat (level 5 finish) | | 550 | .029 | | .76 | 1.11 | | 1.87 | 2.57 |
| 0310 | 5/8" thick, on walls, very high impact, no finish included | | 1800 | .009 | | .67 | .34 | | 1.01 | 1.27 |
| 0320 | Taped and finished (level 4 finish) | | 870 | .018 | | .71 | .70 | | 1.41 | 1.87 |
| 0330 | With compound skim coat (level 5 finish) | | 700 | .023 | | .75 | .87 | | 1.62 | 2.19 |
| 0350 | On ceilings, no finish included | | 1620 | .010 | | .67 | .38 | | 1.05 | 1.33 |
| 0360 | Taped and finished (level 4 finish) | | 690 | .023 | | .71 | .88 | | 1.59 | 2.16 |
| 0370 | With compound skim coat (level 5 finish) | ▼ | 550 | .029 | ▼ | .75 | 1.11 | | 1.86 | 2.56 |
| 0400 | High abuse, gypsum core, paper face | | | | | | | | | |
| 0410 | 1/2" thick, on walls, no finish included | 2 Carp | 1800 | .009 | S.F. | .56 | .34 | | .90 | 1.15 |
| 0420 | Taped and finished (level 4 finish) | | 870 | .018 | | .60 | .70 | | 1.30 | 1.75 |
| 0430 | With compound skim coat (level 5 finish) | | 700 | .023 | | .64 | .87 | | 1.51 | 2.07 |
| 0450 | On ceilings, no finish included | | 1620 | .010 | | .56 | .38 | | .94 | 1.21 |
| 0460 | Taped and finished (level 4 finish) | | 690 | .023 | | .60 | .88 | | 1.48 | 2.04 |
| 0470 | With compound skim coat (level 5 finish) | | 550 | .029 | | .64 | 1.11 | | 1.75 | 2.44 |
| 0510 | 5/8" thick, on walls, no finish included | | 1800 | .009 | | .57 | .34 | | .91 | 1.16 |
| 0520 | Taped and finished (level 4 finish) | | 870 | .018 | | .61 | .70 | | 1.31 | 1.76 |
| 0530 | With compound skim coat (level 5 finish) | | 700 | .023 | | .65 | .87 | | 1.52 | 2.08 |
| 0550 | On ceilings, no finish included | | 1620 | .010 | | .57 | .38 | | .95 | 1.22 |
| 0560 | Taped and finished (level 4 finish) | | 690 | .023 | | .61 | .88 | | 1.49 | 2.05 |
| 0570 | With compound skim coat (level 5 finish) | | 550 | .029 | | .65 | 1.11 | | 1.76 | 2.45 |
| 1000 | For high ceilings, over 8' high, add | | 2750 | .006 | | | .22 | | .22 | .35 |
| 1010 | For distribution cost over 3 stories high, add per story | ▼ | 5500 | .003 | ▼ | | .11 | | .11 | .17 |

## 09 29 15 – Gypsum Board Accessories

### 09 29 15.10 Accessories, Gypsum Board

| | | Crew | Daily Output | Labor-Hours | Unit | Material | 2008 Bare Costs Labor | Equipment | Total | Total Incl O&P |
|---|---|---|---|---|---|---|---|---|---|---|
| 0010 | **ACCESSORIES, GYPSUM BOARD** | | | | | | | | | |
| 0020 | Casing bead, galvanized steel | 1 Carp | 2.90 | 2.759 | C.L.F. | 20.50 | 105 | | 125.50 | 187 |
| 0100 | Vinyl | | 3 | 2.667 | | 22 | 102 | | 124 | 182 |
| 0300 | Corner bead, galvanized steel, 1" x 1" | | 4 | 2 | | 11.95 | 76 | | 87.95 | 132 |
| 0400 | 1-1/4" x 1-1/4" | | 3.50 | 2.286 | | 15.30 | 87 | | 102.30 | 153 |
| 0600 | Vinyl | | 4 | 2 | | 16.35 | 76 | | 92.35 | 137 |
| 0900 | Furring channel, galv. steel, 7/8" deep, standard | | 2.60 | 3.077 | | 24.50 | 117 | | 141.50 | 209 |
| 1000 | Resilient | | 2.55 | 3.137 | | 24 | 120 | | 144 | 212 |
| 1100 | J trim, galvanized steel, 1/2" wide | | 3 | 2.667 | | 19.75 | 102 | | 121.75 | 180 |
| 1120 | 5/8" wide | | 2.95 | 2.712 | | 21 | 103 | | 124 | 184 |
| 1140 | L trim, galvanized | | 3 | 2.667 | | 16.90 | 102 | | 118.90 | 177 |
| 1150 | U trim, galvanized | ▼ | 2.95 | 2.712 | ▼ | 17.50 | 103 | | 120.50 | 180 |
| 1160 | Screws #6 x 1" A | | | | M | 6 | | | 6 | 6.60 |
| 1170 | #6 x 1-5/8" A | | | | " | 8.80 | | | 8.80 | 9.70 |
| 1200 | For stud partitions, see Div. 05 41 13.30 and 09 22 16.13 | | | | | | | | | |
| 1500 | Z stud, galvanized steel, 1-1/2" wide | 1 Carp | 2.60 | 3.077 | C.L.F. | 33.50 | 117 | | 150.50 | 219 |
| 1600 | 2" wide | " | 2.55 | 3.137 | " | 48.50 | 120 | | 168.50 | 239 |

| 09 30 13.10 Ceramic Tile | Crew | Daily Output | Labor-Hours | Unit | Material | 2008 Bare Costs Labor | Equipment | Total | Total Incl O&P |
|---|---|---|---|---|---|---|---|---|---|
| 0010 | **CERAMIC TILE** | | | | | | | | |
| 0050 | Base, using 1' x 4" high pc. with 1" x 1" tiles, mud set | D-7 | 82 | .195 | L.F. | 4.48 | 6.45 | | 10.93 | 14.40 |
| 0100 | Thin set | " | 128 | .125 | | 4.26 | 4.14 | | 8.40 | 10.75 |
| 0300 | For 6" high base, 1" x 1" tile face, add | | | | | .70 | | | .70 | .77 |
| 0400 | For 2" x 2" tile face, add to above | | | | | .37 | | | .37 | .41 |
| 0600 | Cove base, 4-1/4" x 4-1/4" high, mud set | D-7 | 91 | .176 | | 3.54 | 5.80 | | 9.34 | 12.45 |
| 0700 | Thin set | | 128 | .125 | | 3.56 | 4.14 | | 7.70 | 9.95 |
| 0900 | 6" x 4-1/4" high, mud set | | 100 | .160 | | 3.23 | 5.30 | | 8.53 | 11.30 |
| 1000 | Thin set | | 137 | .117 | | 3.23 | 3.86 | | 7.09 | 9.20 |
| 1200 | Sanitary cove base, 6" x 4-1/4" high, mud set | | 93 | .172 | | 3.61 | 5.70 | | 9.31 | 12.30 |
| 1300 | Thin set | | 124 | .129 | | 4.11 | 4.27 | | 8.38 | 10.75 |
| 1500 | 6" x 6" high, mud set | | 84 | .190 | | 4.47 | 6.30 | | 10.77 | 14.15 |
| 1600 | Thin set | | 117 | .137 | | 4.47 | 4.52 | | 8.99 | 11.55 |
| 1800 | Bathroom accessories, average | | 82 | .195 | Ea. | 10.35 | 6.45 | | 16.80 | 21 |
| 1900 | Bathtub, 5', rec. 4-1/4" x 4-1/4" tile wainscot, adhesive set 6' high | | 2.90 | 5.517 | | 156 | 183 | | 339 | 440 |
| 2100 | 7' high wainscot | | 2.50 | 6.400 | | 179 | 212 | | 391 | 505 |
| 2200 | 8' high wainscot | | 2.20 | 7.273 | | 190 | 241 | | 431 | 565 |
| 2400 | Bullnose trim, 4-1/4" x 4-1/4", mud set | | 82 | .195 | L.F. | 3.35 | 6.45 | | 9.80 | 13.15 |
| 2500 | Thin set | | 128 | .125 | | 3.12 | 4.14 | | 7.26 | 9.50 |
| 2700 | 6" x 4-1/4" bullnose trim, mud set | | 84 | .190 | | 2.54 | 6.30 | | 8.84 | 12.05 |
| 2800 | Thin set | | 124 | .129 | | 2.54 | 4.27 | | 6.81 | 9.05 |
| 3000 | Floors, natural clay, random or uniform, thin set, color group 1 | | 183 | .087 | S.F. | 3.95 | 2.89 | | 6.84 | 8.60 |
| 3100 | Color group 2 | | 183 | .087 | | 4.26 | 2.89 | | 7.15 | 8.95 |
| 3255 | Floors, glazed, thin set, 6" x 6", color group 1 | | 200 | .080 | | 3.36 | 2.65 | | 6.01 | 7.60 |
| 3260 | 8" x 8" tile | | 250 | .064 | | 3.36 | 2.12 | | 5.48 | 6.80 |
| 3270 | 12" x 12" tile | | 325 | .049 | | 4.22 | 1.63 | | 5.85 | 7.05 |
| 3280 | 16" x 16" tile | | 550 | .029 | | 6.05 | .96 | | 7.01 | 8.05 |
| 3285 | Border, 6" x 12" tile | | 275 | .058 | | 11.10 | 1.92 | | 13.02 | 15 |
| 3290 | 3" x 12" tile | | 200 | .080 | | 32.50 | 2.65 | | 35.15 | 40 |
| 3300 | Porcelain type, 1 color, color group 2, 1" x 1" | | 183 | .087 | | 4.57 | 2.89 | | 7.46 | 9.30 |
| 3310 | 2" x 2" or 2" x 1", thin set | | 190 | .084 | | 5.05 | 2.79 | | 7.84 | 9.65 |
| 3350 | For random blend, 2 colors, add | | | | | .85 | | | .85 | .94 |
| 3360 | 4 colors, add | | | | | 1.20 | | | 1.20 | 1.32 |
| 3370 | For color group 3, add | | | | | .49 | | | .49 | .54 |
| 3380 | For abrasive non-slip tile, add | | | | | .48 | | | .48 | .53 |
| 4300 | Specialty tile, 4-1/4" x 4-1/4" x 1/2", decorator finish | D-7 | 183 | .087 | | 10 | 2.89 | | 12.89 | 15.25 |
| 4500 | Add for epoxy grout, 1/16" joint, 1" x 1" tile | | 800 | .020 | | .60 | .66 | | 1.26 | 1.63 |
| 4600 | 2" x 2" tile | | 820 | .020 | | .54 | .65 | | 1.19 | 1.54 |
| 4800 | Pregrouted sheets, walls, 4-1/4" x 4-1/4", 6" x 4-1/4" | | | | | | | | | |
| 4810 | and 8-1/2" x 4-1/4", 4 S.F. sheets, silicone grout | D-7 | 240 | .067 | S.F. | 4.59 | 2.21 | | 6.80 | 8.30 |
| 5100 | Floors, unglazed, 2 S.F. sheets, | | | | | | | | | |
| 5110 | Urethane adhesive | D-7 | 180 | .089 | S.F. | 4.57 | 2.94 | | 7.51 | 9.35 |
| 5400 | Walls, interior, thin set, 4-1/4" x 4-1/4" tile    **CN** | | 190 | .084 | | 2.22 | 2.79 | | 5.01 | 6.55 |
| 5500 | 6" x 4-1/4" tile | | 190 | .084 | | 2.51 | 2.79 | | 5.30 | 6.85 |
| 5700 | 8-1/2" x 4-1/4" tile | | 190 | .084 | | 3.55 | 2.79 | | 6.34 | 8 |
| 5800 | 6" x 6" tile | | 200 | .080 | | 3.03 | 2.65 | | 5.68 | 7.20 |
| 5810 | 8" x 8" tile | | 225 | .071 | | 4.04 | 2.35 | | 6.39 | 7.90 |
| 5820 | 12" x 12" tile | | 300 | .053 | | 3.25 | 1.76 | | 5.01 | 6.15 |
| 5830 | 16" x 16" tile | | 500 | .032 | | 3.52 | 1.06 | | 4.58 | 5.40 |
| 6000 | Decorated wall tile, 4-1/4" x 4-1/4", minimum | | 270 | .059 | | 3.34 | 1.96 | | 5.30 | 6.55 |
| 6100 | Maximum | | 180 | .089 | | 42.50 | 2.94 | | 45.44 | 51 |
| 6300 | Exterior walls, frostproof, mud set, 4-1/4" x 4-1/4" | | 102 | .157 | | 6 | 5.20 | | 11.20 | 14.20 |
| 6400 | 1-3/8" x 1-3/8" | | 93 | .172 | | 4.13 | 5.70 | | 9.83 | 12.90 |

## 09 30 13 – Ceramic Tiling

### 09 30 13.10 Ceramic Tile

| | | Crew | Daily Output | Labor-Hours | Unit | Material | 2008 Bare Costs Labor | Equipment | Total | Total Incl O&P |
|---|---|---|---|---|---|---|---|---|---|---|
| 6600 | Crystalline glazed, 4-1/4" x 4-1/4", mud set, plain | D-7 | 100 | .160 | S.F. | 3.66 | 5.30 | | 8.96 | 11.80 |
| 6700 | 4-1/4" x 4-1/4", scored tile | | 100 | .160 | | 4.42 | 5.30 | | 9.72 | 12.60 |
| 6900 | 6"x 6" plain | | 93 | .172 | | 4.82 | 5.70 | | 10.52 | 13.65 |
| 7000 | For epoxy grout, 1/16" joints, 4-1/4" tile, add | | 800 | .020 | | .35 | .66 | | 1.01 | 1.36 |
| 7200 | For tile set in dry mortar, add | | 1735 | .009 | | | .31 | | .31 | .45 |
| 7300 | For tile set in portland cement mortar, add | | 290 | .055 | | | 1.83 | | 1.83 | 2.68 |
| 9000 | Regrout tile 4-1/2 x 4-1/2, or larger, wall | 1 Tilf | 100 | .080 | | .14 | 2.96 | | 3.10 | 4.49 |
| 9220 | Floor | " | 125 | .064 | | .15 | 2.37 | | 2.52 | 3.65 |

### 09 30 13.30 Ceramic Tile Panels

| | | Crew | Daily Output | Labor-Hours | Unit | Material | 2008 Bare Costs Labor | Equipment | Total | Total Incl O&P |
|---|---|---|---|---|---|---|---|---|---|---|
| 0010 | **CERAMIC TILE PANELS** | | | | | | | | | |
| 0020 | Insulated, over 1000 S.F., 1-1/2" thick | D-7 | 220 | .073 | S.F. | 9.30 | 2.41 | | 11.71 | 13.75 |
| 0100 | 2-1/2" thick | " | 220 | .073 | " | 9.95 | 2.41 | | 12.36 | 14.50 |

## 09 30 16 – Quarry Tiling

### 09 30 16.10 Quarry Tile

| | | Crew | Daily Output | Labor-Hours | Unit | Material | 2008 Bare Costs Labor | Equipment | Total | Total Incl O&P |
|---|---|---|---|---|---|---|---|---|---|---|
| 0010 | **QUARRY TILE** | | | | | | | | | |
| 0100 | Base, cove or sanitary, mud set, to 5" high, 1/2" thick | D-7 | 110 | .145 | L.F. | 4.79 | 4.81 | | 9.60 | 12.30 |
| 0300 | Bullnose trim, red, mud set, 6" x 6" x 1/2" thick | | 120 | .133 | | 4.02 | 4.41 | | 8.43 | 10.85 |
| 0400 | 4" x 4" x 1/2" thick | | 110 | .145 | | 4.53 | 4.81 | | 9.34 | 12.05 |
| 0600 | 4" x 8" x 1/2" thick, using 8" as edge | | 130 | .123 | | 3.99 | 4.07 | | 8.06 | 10.40 |
| 0700 | Floors, mud set, 1,000 S.F. lots, red, 4" x 4" x 1/2" thick | | 120 | .133 | S.F. | 4.08 | 4.41 | | 8.49 | 10.95 |
| 0900 | 6" x 6" x 1/2" thick | | 140 | .114 | | 3.36 | 3.78 | | 7.14 | 9.25 |
| 1000 | 4" x 8" x 1/2" thick | | 130 | .123 | | 4.08 | 4.07 | | 8.15 | 10.50 |
| 1300 | For waxed coating, add | | | | | .65 | | | .65 | .72 |
| 1500 | For non-standard colors, add | | | | | .39 | | | .39 | .43 |
| 1600 | For abrasive surface, add | | | | | .46 | | | .46 | .51 |
| 1800 | Brown tile, imported, 6" x 6" x 3/4" | D-7 | 120 | .133 | | 4.85 | 4.41 | | 9.26 | 11.80 |
| 1900 | 8" x 8" x 1" | | 110 | .145 | | 5.50 | 4.81 | | 10.31 | 13.10 |
| 2100 | For thin set mortar application, deduct | | 700 | .023 | | | .76 | | .76 | 1.11 |
| 2200 | For epoxy grout & mortar, 6" x 6" x 1/2", add | | 350 | .046 | | 1.78 | 1.51 | | 3.29 | 4.18 |
| 2700 | Stair tread, 6" x 6" x 3/4", plain | | 50 | .320 | | 5.10 | 10.60 | | 15.70 | 21 |
| 2800 | Abrasive | | 47 | .340 | | 5.15 | 11.25 | | 16.40 | 22.50 |
| 3000 | Wainscot, 6" x 6" x 1/2", thin set, red | | 105 | .152 | | 3.85 | 5.05 | | 8.90 | 11.65 |
| 3100 | Non-standard colors | | 105 | .152 | | 4.29 | 5.05 | | 9.34 | 12.10 |
| 3300 | Window sill, 6" wide, 3/4" thick | | 90 | .178 | L.F. | 4.94 | 5.90 | | 10.84 | 14.10 |
| 3400 | Corners | | 80 | .200 | Ea. | 5.40 | 6.60 | | 12 | 15.65 |

## 09 30 23 – Glass Mosaic Tiling

### 09 30 23.10 Glass Mosaics

| | | Crew | Daily Output | Labor-Hours | Unit | Material | 2008 Bare Costs Labor | Equipment | Total | Total Incl O&P |
|---|---|---|---|---|---|---|---|---|---|---|
| 0010 | **GLASS MOSAICS** 3/4" tile on 12" sheets, standard grout | | | | | | | | | |
| 0300 | Color group 1 & 2 | D-7 | 73 | .219 | S.F. | 16.85 | 7.25 | | 24.10 | 29 |
| 0350 | Color group 3 | | 73 | .219 | | 17.70 | 7.25 | | 24.95 | 30 |
| 0400 | Color group 4 | | 73 | .219 | | 24 | 7.25 | | 31.25 | 37 |
| 0450 | Color group 5 | | 73 | .219 | | 27 | 7.25 | | 34.25 | 40.50 |
| 0500 | Color group 6 | | 73 | .219 | | 33 | 7.25 | | 40.25 | 46.50 |
| 0600 | Color group 7 | | 73 | .219 | | 38 | 7.25 | | 45.25 | 52.50 |
| 0700 | Color group 8, golds, silvers & specialties | | 64 | .250 | | 55 | 8.25 | | 63.25 | 72.50 |

## 09 30 29 – Metal Tiling

### 09 30 29.10 Metal Tile

| | | Crew | Daily Output | Labor-Hours | Unit | Material | 2008 Bare Costs Labor | Equipment | Total | Total Incl O&P |
|---|---|---|---|---|---|---|---|---|---|---|
| 0010 | **METAL TILE** 4' x 4' sheet, 24 ga., tile pattern, nailed | | | | | | | | | |
| 0200 | Stainless steel | 2 Carp | 512 | .031 | S.F. | 24.50 | 1.19 | | 25.69 | 29 |
| 0400 | Aluminized steel | " | 512 | .031 | " | 13.15 | 1.19 | | 14.34 | 16.30 |

# 09 51 Acoustical Ceilings

## 09 51 23 - Acoustical Tile Ceilings

### 09 51 23.10 Suspended Acoustic Ceiling Tiles

| | 09 51 23.10 Suspended Acoustic Ceiling Tiles | Crew | Daily Output | Labor-Hours | Unit | Material | 2008 Bare Costs Labor | Equipment | Total | Total Incl O&P |
|---|---|---|---|---|---|---|---|---|---|---|
| 0010 | **SUSPENDED ACOUSTIC CEILING TILES**, Not including | | | | | | | | | |
| 0100 | suspension system | | | | | | | | | |
| 0300 | Fiberglass boards, film faced, 2' x 2' or 2' x 4', 5/8" thick | 1 Carp | 625 | .013 | S.F. | .61 | .49 | | 1.10 | 1.43 |
| 0400 | 3/4" thick | | 600 | .013 | | 1.39 | .51 | | 1.90 | 2.32 |
| 0500 | 3" thick, thermal, R11 | | 450 | .018 | | 1.46 | .68 | | 2.14 | 2.66 |
| 0600 | Glass cloth faced fiberglass, 3/4" thick | | 500 | .016 | | 1.74 | .61 | | 2.35 | 2.86 |
| 0700 | 1" thick | | 485 | .016 | | 1.93 | .63 | | 2.56 | 3.10 |
| 0820 | 1-1/2" thick, nubby face | | 475 | .017 | | 2.53 | .64 | | 3.17 | 3.78 |
| 1110 | Mineral fiber tile, lay-in, 2' x 2' or 2' x 4', 5/8" thick, fine texture | | 625 | .013 | | .52 | .49 | | 1.01 | 1.33 |
| 1115 | Rough textured | | 625 | .013 | | 1.17 | .49 | | 1.66 | 2.05 |
| 1125 | 3/4" thick, fine textured | | 600 | .013 | | 1.33 | .51 | | 1.84 | 2.25 |
| 1130 | Rough textured | | 600 | .013 | | 1.67 | .51 | | 2.18 | 2.63 |
| 1135 | Fissured | | 600 | .013 | | 2.13 | .51 | | 2.64 | 3.13 |
| 1150 | Tegular, 5/8" thick, fine textured | | 470 | .017 | | 1.26 | .65 | | 1.91 | 2.40 |
| 1155 | Rough textured | | 470 | .017 | | 1.65 | .65 | | 2.30 | 2.83 |
| 1165 | 3/4" thick, fine textured | | 450 | .018 | | 1.81 | .68 | | 2.49 | 3.04 |
| 1170 | Rough textured | | 450 | .018 | | 2.04 | .68 | | 2.72 | 3.29 |
| 1175 | Fissured | | 450 | .018 | | 3.16 | .68 | | 3.84 | 4.53 |
| 1180 | For aluminum face, add | | | | | 5.25 | | | 5.25 | 5.80 |
| 1185 | For plastic film face, add | | | | | .82 | | | .82 | .90 |
| 1190 | For fire rating, add | | | | | .39 | | | .39 | .43 |
| 1300 | Mirror faced panels, 15/16" thick, 2' x 2' | 1 Carp | 500 | .016 | | 10 | .61 | | 10.61 | 11.95 |
| 1900 | Eggcrate, acrylic, 1/2" x 1/2" x 1/2" cubes | | 500 | .016 | | 1.58 | .61 | | 2.19 | 2.69 |
| 2100 | Polystyrene eggcrate, 3/8" x 3/8" x 1/2" cubes | | 510 | .016 | | 1.33 | .60 | | 1.93 | 2.39 |
| 2200 | 1/2" x 1/2" x 1/2" cubes | | 500 | .016 | | 1.77 | .61 | | 2.38 | 2.90 |
| 2400 | Luminous panels, prismatic, acrylic | | 400 | .020 | | 1.93 | .76 | | 2.69 | 3.31 |
| 2500 | Polystyrene | | 400 | .020 | | .99 | .76 | | 1.75 | 2.28 |
| 2700 | Flat white acrylic | | 400 | .020 | | 3.36 | .76 | | 4.12 | 4.89 |
| 2800 | Polystyrene | | 400 | .020 | | 2.30 | .76 | | 3.06 | 3.72 |
| 3000 | Drop pan, white, acrylic | | 400 | .020 | | 4.92 | .76 | | 5.68 | 6.60 |
| 3100 | Polystyrene | | 400 | .020 | | 4.11 | .76 | | 4.87 | 5.70 |
| 3600 | Perforated aluminum sheets, .024" thick, corrugated, painted | | 490 | .016 | | 1.96 | .62 | | 2.58 | 3.13 |
| 3700 | Plain | | 500 | .016 | | 3.27 | .61 | | 3.88 | 4.55 |
| 3720 | Mineral fiber, 24" x 24" or 48", reveal edge, painted, 5/8" thick | | 600 | .013 | | 1.20 | .51 | | 1.71 | 2.11 |
| 3740 | 3/4" thick | | 575 | .014 | | 1.95 | .53 | | 2.48 | 2.97 |

### 09 51 23.30 Suspended Ceilings, Complete

| | 09 51 23.30 Suspended Ceilings, Complete | Crew | Daily Output | Labor-Hours | Unit | Material | 2008 Bare Costs Labor | Equipment | Total | Total Incl O&P |
|---|---|---|---|---|---|---|---|---|---|---|
| 0010 | **SUSPENDED CEILINGS, COMPLETE** Including standard | | | | | | | | | |
| 0100 | suspension system but not incl. 1-1/2" carrier channels | | | | | | | | | |
| 0600 | Fiberglass ceiling board, 2' x 4' x 5/8", plain faced | 1 Carp | 500 | .016 | S.F. | 1.14 | .61 | | 1.75 | 2.20 |
| 0700 | Offices, 2' x 4' x 3/4" | | 380 | .021 | | 1.92 | .80 | | 2.72 | 3.36 |
| 0800 | Mineral fiber, on 15/16" T bar susp. 2' x 2' x 3/4" lay-in board | | 345 | .023 | | 1.99 | .88 | | 2.87 | 3.57 |
| 0810 | 2' x 4' x 5/8" tile | | 380 | .021 | | 1.05 | .80 | | 1.85 | 2.41 |
| 0820 | Tegular, 2' x 2' x 5/8" tile on 9/16" grid | | 250 | .032 | | 2.08 | 1.22 | | 3.30 | 4.18 |
| 0830 | 2' x 4' x 3/4" tile | | 275 | .029 | | 2.50 | 1.11 | | 3.61 | 4.48 |
| 0900 | Luminous panels, prismatic, acrylic | | 255 | .031 | | 2.46 | 1.20 | | 3.66 | 4.57 |
| 1200 | Metal pan with acoustic pad, steel | | 75 | .107 | | 3.60 | 4.06 | | 7.66 | 10.30 |
| 1300 | Painted aluminum | | 75 | .107 | | 2.49 | 4.06 | | 6.55 | 9.10 |
| 1500 | Aluminum, degreased finish | | 75 | .107 | | 4.16 | 4.06 | | 8.22 | 10.95 |
| 1600 | Stainless steel | | 75 | .107 | | 7.85 | 4.06 | | 11.91 | 14.95 |
| 1800 | Tile, Z bar suspension, 5/8" mineral fiber tile | | 150 | .053 | | 1.88 | 2.03 | | 3.91 | 5.25 |
| 1900 | 3/4" mineral fiber tile | | 150 | .053 | | 2.01 | 2.03 | | 4.04 | 5.35 |
| 2400 | For strip lighting, see Div. 26 51 13.50 | | | | | | | | | |

# 09 51 Acoustical Ceilings

## 09 51 23 – Acoustical Tile Ceilings

| 09 51 23.30 Suspended Ceilings, Complete | Crew | Daily Output | Labor-Hours | Unit | Material | 2008 Bare Costs Labor | Equipment | Total | Total Incl O&P |
|---|---|---|---|---|---|---|---|---|---|
| 2500 | For rooms under 500 S.F., add | | | | S.F. | | 25% | | | |

## 09 51 53 – Direct-Applied Acoustical Ceilings

### 09 51 53.10 Ceiling Tile

| | 09 51 53.10 Ceiling Tile | | Crew | Daily Output | Labor-Hours | Unit | Material | Labor | Equipment | Total | Total Incl O&P |
|---|---|---|---|---|---|---|---|---|---|---|---|
| 0010 | **CEILING TILE**, Stapled or cemented | | | | | | | | | | |
| 0100 | 12" x 12" or 12" x 24", not including furring | | | | | | | | | | |
| 0600 | Mineral fiber, vinyl coated, 5/8" thick | CN | 1 Carp | 300 | .027 | S.F. | 1.65 | 1.02 | | 2.67 | 3.40 |
| 0700 | 3/4" thick | | | 300 | .027 | | 1.57 | 1.02 | | 2.59 | 3.31 |
| 0900 | Fire rated, 3/4" thick, plain faced | | | 300 | .027 | | 1.35 | 1.02 | | 2.37 | 3.07 |
| 1000 | Plastic coated face | | | 300 | .027 | | 1.15 | 1.02 | | 2.17 | 2.85 |
| 1200 | Aluminum faced, 5/8" thick, plain | | | 300 | .027 | | 1.31 | 1.02 | | 2.33 | 3.02 |
| 3700 | Wall application of above, add | | | 1000 | .008 | | | .30 | | .30 | .47 |
| 3900 | For ceiling primer, add | | | | | | .13 | | | .13 | .14 |
| 4000 | For ceiling cement, add | | | | | | .36 | | | .36 | .40 |

# 09 53 Acoustical Ceiling Suspension Assemblies

## 09 53 23 – Metal Acoustical Ceiling Suspension Assemblies

### 09 53 23.30 Ceiling Suspension Systems

| | 09 53 23.30 Ceiling Suspension Systems | | Crew | Daily Output | Labor-Hours | Unit | Material | Labor | Equipment | Total | Total Incl O&P |
|---|---|---|---|---|---|---|---|---|---|---|---|
| 0010 | **CEILING SUSPENSION SYSTEMS** for boards and tile | | | | | | | | | | |
| 0050 | Class A suspension system, 15/16" T bar, 2' x 4' grid | CN | 1 Carp | 800 | .010 | S.F. | .53 | .38 | | .91 | 1.17 |
| 0300 | 2' x 2' grid | | " | 650 | .012 | | .66 | .47 | | 1.13 | 1.45 |
| 0350 | For 9/16" grid, add | | | | | | .16 | | | .16 | .18 |
| 0360 | For fire rated grid, add | | | | | | .09 | | | .09 | .10 |
| 0370 | For colored grid, add | | | | | | .20 | | | .20 | .22 |
| 0400 | Concealed Z bar suspension system, 12" module | | 1 Carp | 520 | .015 | | .62 | .59 | | 1.21 | 1.59 |
| 0600 | 1-1/2" carrier channels, 4' O.C., add | | " | 470 | .017 | | .13 | .65 | | .78 | 1.15 |
| 0700 | Carrier channels for ceilings with | | | | | | | | | | |
| 0900 | recessed lighting fixtures, add | | 1 Carp | 460 | .017 | S.F. | .23 | .66 | | .89 | 1.28 |
| 1040 | Hanging wire, 12 ga., 4' long | | | 65 | .123 | C.S.F. | 6.75 | 4.69 | | 11.44 | 14.75 |
| 1080 | 8' long | | | 65 | .123 | " | 13.50 | 4.69 | | 18.19 | 22 |
| 1200 | Seismic bracing, 2-1/2" compression post with four bracing wires | | | 50 | .160 | Ea. | 2.74 | 6.10 | | 8.84 | 12.50 |

# 09 63 Masonry Flooring

## 09 63 13 – Brick Flooring

### 09 63 13.10 Miscellaneous Brick Flooring

| | 09 63 13.10 Miscellaneous Brick Flooring | Crew | Daily Output | Labor-Hours | Unit | Material | Labor | Equipment | Total | Total Incl O&P |
|---|---|---|---|---|---|---|---|---|---|---|
| 0010 | **MISCELLANEOUS BRICK FLOORING** | | | | | | | | | |
| 0020 | Acid proof shales, red, 8" x 3-3/4" x 1-1/4" thick | D-7 | .43 | 37.209 | M | 765 | 1,225 | | 1,990 | 2,650 |
| 0050 | 2-1/4" thick | D-1 | .40 | 40 | | 890 | 1,400 | | 2,290 | 3,100 |
| 0200 | Acid proof clay brick, 8" x 3-3/4" x 2-1/4" thick | " | .40 | 40 | | 840 | 1,400 | | 2,240 | 3,050 |
| 0260 | Cast ceramic, pressed, 4" x 8" x 1/2", unglazed | D-7 | 100 | .160 | S.F. | 5.55 | 5.30 | | 10.85 | 13.85 |
| 0270 | Glazed | | 100 | .160 | | 7.40 | 5.30 | | 12.70 | 15.90 |
| 0280 | Hand molded flooring, 4" x 8" x 3/4", unglazed | | 95 | .168 | | 7.35 | 5.55 | | 12.90 | 16.30 |
| 0290 | Glazed | | 95 | .168 | | 9.20 | 5.55 | | 14.75 | 18.35 |
| 0300 | 8" hexagonal, 3/4" thick, unglazed | | 85 | .188 | | 8.05 | 6.25 | | 14.30 | 18 |
| 0310 | Glazed | | 85 | .188 | | 14.55 | 6.25 | | 20.80 | 25 |
| 0400 | Heavy duty industrial, cement mortar bed, 2" thick, not incl. brick | D-1 | 80 | .200 | | .74 | 7 | | 7.74 | 11.40 |
| 0450 | Acid proof joints, 1/4" wide | " | 65 | .246 | | 1.28 | 8.60 | | 9.88 | 14.45 |
| 0500 | Pavers, 8" x 4", 1" to 1-1/4" thick, red | D-7 | 95 | .168 | | 3.24 | 5.55 | | 8.79 | 11.75 |
| 0510 | Ironspot | " | 95 | .168 | | 4.57 | 5.55 | | 10.12 | 13.25 |
| 0540 | 1-3/8" to 1-3/4" thick, red | D-1 | 95 | .168 | | 3.12 | 5.85 | | 8.97 | 12.40 |

# 09 63 Masonry Flooring

## 09 63 13 - Brick Flooring

### 09 63 13.10 Miscellaneous Brick Flooring

| | | Crew | Daily Output | Labor-Hours | Unit | Material | 2008 Bare Costs Labor | Equipment | Total | Total Incl O&P |
|---|---|---|---|---|---|---|---|---|---|---|
| 0560 | Ironspot | D-1 | 95 | .168 | S.F. | 4.52 | 5.85 | | 10.37 | 13.90 |
| 0580 | 2-1/4" thick, red | | 90 | .178 | | 3.18 | 6.20 | | 9.38 | 12.95 |
| 0590 | Ironspot | | 90 | .178 | | 4.93 | 6.20 | | 11.13 | 14.85 |
| 0870 | For epoxy joints, add | | 600 | .027 | | 2.42 | .93 | | 3.35 | 4.07 |
| 0880 | For Furan underlayment, add | | 600 | .027 | | 2 | .93 | | 2.93 | 3.61 |
| 0890 | For waxed surface, steam cleaned, add | A-1H | 1000 | .008 | | .18 | .24 | .06 | .48 | .65 |

## 09 63 40 - Stone Flooring

### 09 63 40.10 Marble

| | | Crew | Daily Output | Labor-Hours | Unit | Material | 2008 Bare Costs Labor | Equipment | Total | Total Incl O&P |
|---|---|---|---|---|---|---|---|---|---|---|
| 0010 | **MARBLE** | | | | | | | | | |
| 0020 | Thin gauge tile, 12" x 6", 3/8", white Carara | D-7 | 60 | .267 | S.F. | 11.15 | 8.80 | | 19.95 | 25.50 |
| 0100 | Travertine | | 60 | .267 | | 12.20 | 8.80 | | 21 | 26.50 |
| 0200 | 12" x 12" x 3/8", thin set, floors | | 60 | .267 | | 6.05 | 8.80 | | 14.85 | 19.60 |
| 0300 | On walls | | 52 | .308 | | 9.35 | 10.20 | | 19.55 | 25.50 |
| 1000 | Marble threshold, 4" wide x 36" long x 5/8" thick, white | | 60 | .267 | Ea. | 6.05 | 8.80 | | 14.85 | 19.60 |

### 09 63 40.20 Slate Tile

| | | Crew | Daily Output | Labor-Hours | Unit | Material | 2008 Bare Costs Labor | Equipment | Total | Total Incl O&P |
|---|---|---|---|---|---|---|---|---|---|---|
| 0010 | **SLATE TILE** | | | | | | | | | |
| 0020 | Vermont, 6" x 6" x 1/4" thick, thin set | D-7 | 180 | .089 | S.F. | 6.80 | 2.94 | | 9.74 | 11.75 |
| 0200 | See also Div. 32 14 40.10 | | | | | | | | | |

# 09 64 Wood Flooring

## 09 64 16 - Wood Block Flooring

### 09 64 16.10 End Grain Block Flooring

| | | Crew | Daily Output | Labor-Hours | Unit | Material | 2008 Bare Costs Labor | Equipment | Total | Total Incl O&P |
|---|---|---|---|---|---|---|---|---|---|---|
| 0010 | **END GRAIN BLOCK FLOORING** | | | | | | | | | |
| 0020 | End grain flooring, coated, 2" thick | 1 Carp | 295 | .027 | S.F. | 3.19 | 1.03 | | 4.22 | 5.10 |
| 0400 | Natural finish, 1" thick, fir | | 125 | .064 | | 3.30 | 2.44 | | 5.74 | 7.45 |
| 0600 | 1-1/2" thick, pine | | 125 | .064 | | 3.24 | 2.44 | | 5.68 | 7.35 |
| 0700 | 2" thick, pine | | 125 | .064 | | 4.60 | 2.44 | | 7.04 | 8.85 |

## 09 64 19 - Wood Composition Flooring

### 09 64 19.10 Wood Composition

| | | Crew | Daily Output | Labor-Hours | Unit | Material | 2008 Bare Costs Labor | Equipment | Total | Total Incl O&P |
|---|---|---|---|---|---|---|---|---|---|---|
| 0010 | **WOOD COMPOSITION** Gym floors | | | | | | | | | |
| 0100 | 2-1/4" x 6-7/8" x 3/8", on 2" grout setting bed | D-7 | 150 | .107 | S.F. | 5.70 | 3.53 | | 9.23 | 11.45 |
| 0200 | Thin set, on concrete | " | 250 | .064 | | 5.20 | 2.12 | | 7.32 | 8.80 |
| 0300 | Sanding and finishing, add | 1 Carp | 200 | .040 | | .77 | 1.52 | | 2.29 | 3.22 |

## 09 64 23 - Wood Parquet Flooring

### 09 64 23.10 Wood Parquet

| | | Crew | Daily Output | Labor-Hours | Unit | Material | 2008 Bare Costs Labor | Equipment | Total | Total Incl O&P |
|---|---|---|---|---|---|---|---|---|---|---|
| 0010 | **WOOD PARQUET** flooring | | | | | | | | | |
| 5200 | Parquetry, standard, 5/16" thick, not incl. finish, oak, minimum | 1 Carp | 160 | .050 | S.F. | 4.18 | 1.91 | | 6.09 | 7.55 |
| 5300 | Maximum | | 100 | .080 | | 4.95 | 3.05 | | 8 | 10.20 |
| 5500 | Teak, minimum | | 160 | .050 | | 4.79 | 1.91 | | 6.70 | 8.20 |
| 5600 | Maximum | | 100 | .080 | | 8.35 | 3.05 | | 11.40 | 13.95 |
| 5650 | 13/16" thick, select grade oak, minimum | | 160 | .050 | | 9.20 | 1.91 | | 11.11 | 13.10 |
| 5700 | Maximum | | 100 | .080 | | 14 | 3.05 | | 17.05 | 20 |
| 5800 | Custom parquetry, including finish, minimum | | 100 | .080 | | 15.45 | 3.05 | | 18.50 | 21.50 |
| 5900 | Maximum | | 50 | .160 | | 20.50 | 6.10 | | 26.60 | 32 |
| 6700 | Parquetry, prefinished white oak, 5/16" thick, minimum | | 160 | .050 | | 3.61 | 1.91 | | 5.52 | 6.95 |
| 6800 | Maximum | | 100 | .080 | | 7.30 | 3.05 | | 10.35 | 12.80 |
| 7000 | Walnut or teak, parquetry, minimum | | 160 | .050 | | 5.35 | 1.91 | | 7.26 | 8.85 |
| 7100 | Maximum | | 100 | .080 | | 9.35 | 3.05 | | 12.40 | 15.05 |
| 7200 | Acrylic wood parquet blocks, 12" x 12" x 5/16", | | | | | | | | | |

# 09 64 Wood Flooring

## 09 64 23 – Wood Parquet Flooring

| 09 64 23.10 Wood Parquet | | Crew | Daily Output | Labor-Hours | Unit | Material | 2008 Bare Costs Labor | Equipment | Total | Total Incl O&P |
|---|---|---|---|---|---|---|---|---|---|---|
| 7210 | Irradiated, set in epoxy | 1 Carp | 160 | .050 | S.F. | 7.80 | 1.91 | | 9.71 | 11.55 |

## 09 64 29 – Wood Strip and Plank Flooring

### 09 64 29.10 Wood

| | | Crew | Daily Output | Labor-Hours | Unit | Material | 2008 Bare Costs Labor | Equipment | Total | Total Incl O&P |
|---|---|---|---|---|---|---|---|---|---|---|
| 0010 | **WOOD** | | | | | | | | | |
| 0020 | Fir, vertical grain, 1" x 4", not incl. finish, grade B & better | 1 Carp | 255 | .031 | S.F. | 2.74 | 1.20 | | 3.94 | 4.87 |
| 0100 | C grade & better | | 255 | .031 | | 2.58 | 1.20 | | 3.78 | 4.70 |
| 4000 | Maple, strip, 25/32" x 2-1/4", not incl. finish, select | | 170 | .047 | | 5.15 | 1.79 | | 6.94 | 8.50 |
| 4100 | #2 & better | | 170 | .047 | | 3.22 | 1.79 | | 5.01 | 6.35 |
| 4300 | 33/32" x 3-1/4", not incl. finish, #1 grade | | 170 | .047 | | 4.07 | 1.79 | | 5.86 | 7.25 |
| 4400 | #2 & better | | 170 | .047 | | 3.62 | 1.79 | | 5.41 | 6.75 |
| 4600 | Oak, white or red, 25/32" x 2-1/4", not incl. finish | | | | | | | | | |
| 4700 | #1 common                            CN | 1 Carp | 170 | .047 | S.F. | 3.09 | 1.79 | | 4.88 | 6.20 |
| 4900 | Select quartered, 2-1/4" wide | | 170 | .047 | | 2.85 | 1.79 | | 4.64 | 5.95 |
| 5000 | Clear | | 170 | .047 | | 3.81 | 1.79 | | 5.60 | 7 |
| 6100 | Prefinished, white oak, prime grade, 2-1/4" wide | | 170 | .047 | | 6.40 | 1.79 | | 8.19 | 9.85 |
| 6200 | 3-1/4" wide | | 185 | .043 | | 8.20 | 1.65 | | 9.85 | 11.55 |
| 6400 | Ranch plank | | 145 | .055 | | 7.90 | 2.10 | | 10 | 11.95 |
| 6500 | Hardwood blocks, 9" x 9", 25/32" thick | | 160 | .050 | | 5.75 | 1.91 | | 7.66 | 9.30 |
| 7400 | Yellow pine, 3/4" x 3-1/8", T & G, C & better, not incl. finish | | 200 | .040 | | 2.35 | 1.52 | | 3.87 | 4.96 |
| 7500 | Refinish wood floor, sand, 2 cts poly, wax, soft wood, min. | 1 Clab | 400 | .020 | | .78 | .61 | | 1.39 | 1.80 |
| 7600 | Hard wood, max | | 130 | .062 | | 1.16 | 1.86 | | 3.02 | 4.18 |
| 7800 | Sanding and finishing, 2 coats polyurethane | | 295 | .027 | | .78 | .82 | | 1.60 | 2.14 |
| 7900 | Subfloor and underlayment, see Div. 06 16 | | | | | | | | | |
| 8015 | Transition molding, 2 1/4" wide, 5' long | 1 Carp | 19.20 | .417 | Ea. | 15 | 15.90 | | 30.90 | 41 |
| 8300 | Floating floor, wood composition strip, complete. | 1 Clab | 133 | .060 | S.F. | 4.23 | 1.82 | | 6.05 | 7.50 |
| 8310 | Components, T & G wood composite strips | | | | | 3.66 | | | 3.66 | 4.03 |
| 8320 | Film | | | | | .15 | | | .15 | .16 |
| 8330 | Foam | | | | | .30 | | | .30 | .33 |
| 8340 | Adhesive | | | | | .17 | | | .17 | .18 |
| 8350 | Installation kit | | | | | .17 | | | .17 | .19 |
| 8360 | Trim, 2" wide x 3' long | | | | L.F. | 2.49 | | | 2.49 | 2.74 |
| 8370 | Reducer moulding | | | | " | 4.29 | | | 4.29 | 4.72 |

## 09 64 66 – Wood Athletic Flooring

### 09 64 66.10 Gymnasium Flooring

| | | Crew | Daily Output | Labor-Hours | Unit | Material | 2008 Bare Costs Labor | Equipment | Total | Total Incl O&P |
|---|---|---|---|---|---|---|---|---|---|---|
| 0010 | **GYMNASIUM FLOORING** | | | | | | | | | |
| 0600 | Gym floor, in mastic, over 2 ply felt, #2 & better | | | | | | | | | |
| 0700 | 25/32" thick maple | 1 Carp | 100 | .080 | S.F. | 3.83 | 3.05 | | 6.88 | 8.95 |
| 0900 | 33/32" thick maple | | 98 | .082 | | 4.42 | 3.11 | | 7.53 | 9.70 |
| 1000 | For 1/2" corkboard underlayment, add | | 750 | .011 | | .87 | .41 | | 1.28 | 1.59 |
| 1300 | For #1 grade maple, add | | | | | .46 | | | .46 | .51 |
| 1600 | Maple flooring, over sleepers, #2 & better | | | | | | | | | |
| 1700 | 25/32" thick | 1 Carp | 85 | .094 | S.F. | 4.19 | 3.59 | | 7.78 | 10.20 |
| 1900 | 33/32" thick | " | 83 | .096 | | 4.88 | 3.67 | | 8.55 | 11.05 |
| 2000 | For #1 grade, add | | | | | .49 | | | .49 | .54 |
| 2200 | For 3/4" subfloor, add | 1 Carp | 350 | .023 | | 1.09 | .87 | | 1.96 | 2.56 |
| 2300 | With two 1/2" subfloors, 25/32" thick | " | 69 | .116 | | 5.25 | 4.42 | | 9.67 | 12.70 |
| 2500 | Maple, incl. finish, #2 & btr., 25/32" thick, on rubber | | | | | | | | | |
| 2600 | Sleepers, with two 1/2" subfloors | 1 Carp | 76 | .105 | S.F. | 5.65 | 4.01 | | 9.66 | 12.45 |
| 2800 | With steel spline, double connection to channels | " | 73 | .110 | | 6 | 4.18 | | 10.18 | 13.10 |
| 2900 | For 33/32" maple, add | | | | | .65 | | | .65 | .72 |
| 3100 | For #1 grade maple, add | | | | | .49 | | | .49 | .54 |
| 3500 | For termite proofing all of the above, add | | | | | .26 | | | .26 | .29 |

286

# 09 64 Wood Flooring

## 09 64 66 – Wood Athletic Flooring

### 09 64 66.10 Gymnasium Flooring

| | | Crew | Daily Output | Labor-Hours | Unit | Material | 2008 Bare Costs Labor | Equipment | Total | Total Incl O&P |
|---|---|---|---|---|---|---|---|---|---|---|
| 3700 | Portable hardwood, prefinished panels | 1 Carp | 83 | .096 | S.F. | 7.50 | 3.67 | | 11.17 | 13.95 |
| 3720 | Insulated with polystyrene, 1" thick, add | | 165 | .048 | | .65 | 1.85 | | 2.50 | 3.59 |
| 3750 | Running tracks, Sitka spruce surface, 25/32" x 2-1/4" | | 62 | .129 | | 13.75 | 4.92 | | 18.67 | 23 |
| 3770 | 3/4" plywood surface, finished | ↓ | 100 | .080 | ↓ | 3.26 | 3.05 | | 6.31 | 8.35 |

# 09 65 Resilient Flooring

## 09 65 10 – Resilient Tile Underlayment

### 09 65 10.10 Latex Underlayment

| | | Crew | Daily Output | Labor-Hours | Unit | Material | 2008 Bare Costs Labor | Equipment | Total | Total Incl O&P |
|---|---|---|---|---|---|---|---|---|---|---|
| 0010 | **LATEX UNDERLAYMENT** | | | | | | | | | |
| 3600 | Latex underlayment, 1/8" thk., cementitious for resilient flooring | 1 Tilf | 160 | .050 | S.F. | 1.56 | 1.85 | | 3.41 | 4.44 |
| 4000 | Liquid, fortified | | | | Gal. | 35 | | | 35 | 38.50 |

## 09 65 13 – Resilient Base and Accessories

### 09 65 13.13 Resilient Base

| | | Crew | Daily Output | Labor-Hours | Unit | Material | 2008 Bare Costs Labor | Equipment | Total | Total Incl O&P |
|---|---|---|---|---|---|---|---|---|---|---|
| 0010 | **RESILIENT BASE** | | | | | | | | | |
| 0800 | Base, cove, rubber or vinyl | | | | | | | | | |
| 1100 | Standard colors, 0.080" thick, 2-1/2" high | 1 Tilf | 315 | .025 | L.F. | .70 | .94 | | 1.64 | 2.15 |
| 1150 | 4" high | | 315 | .025 | | .72 | .94 | | 1.66 | 2.17 |
| 1200 | 6" high | | 315 | .025 | | 1.15 | .94 | | 2.09 | 2.65 |
| 1450 | 1/8" thick, 2-1/2" high | | 315 | .025 | | .80 | .94 | | 1.74 | 2.26 |
| 1500 | 4" high | CN | 315 | .025 | ↓ | .65 | .94 | | 1.59 | 2.10 |
| 1600 | Corners, 2-1/2" high | | 315 | .025 | Ea. | 1.45 | .94 | | 2.39 | 2.98 |
| 1630 | 4" high | | 315 | .025 | | 2.50 | .94 | | 3.44 | 4.13 |
| 1660 | 6" high | ↓ | 315 | .025 | ↓ | 2.65 | .94 | | 3.59 | 4.30 |

### 09 65 13.23 Resilient Stair Treads and Risers

| | | Crew | Daily Output | Labor-Hours | Unit | Material | 2008 Bare Costs Labor | Equipment | Total | Total Incl O&P |
|---|---|---|---|---|---|---|---|---|---|---|
| 0010 | **RESILIENT STAIR TREADS AND RISERS** | | | | | | | | | |
| 0300 | Rubber, molded tread, 12" wide, 5/16" thick, black | 1 Tilf | 115 | .070 | L.F. | 10.95 | 2.57 | | 13.52 | 15.85 |
| 0400 | Colors | | 115 | .070 | | 11.45 | 2.57 | | 14.02 | 16.40 |
| 0600 | 1/4" thick, black | | 115 | .070 | | 10.75 | 2.57 | | 13.32 | 15.65 |
| 0700 | Colors | | 115 | .070 | | 11.25 | 2.57 | | 13.82 | 16.20 |
| 0900 | Grip strip safety tread, colors, 5/16" thick | | 115 | .070 | | 15.65 | 2.57 | | 18.22 | 21 |
| 1000 | 3/16" thick | | 120 | .067 | ↓ | 9.65 | 2.47 | | 12.12 | 14.25 |
| 1200 | Landings, smooth sheet rubber, 1/8" thick | | 120 | .067 | S.F. | 5.25 | 2.47 | | 7.72 | 9.40 |
| 1300 | 3/16" thick | | 120 | .067 | " | 6.75 | 2.47 | | 9.22 | 11.05 |
| 1500 | Nosings, 3" wide, 3/16" thick, black | | 140 | .057 | L.F. | 3.15 | 2.11 | | 5.26 | 6.55 |
| 1600 | Colors | | 140 | .057 | | 3.12 | 2.11 | | 5.23 | 6.55 |
| 1800 | Risers, 7" high, 1/8" thick, flat | | 250 | .032 | | 4.89 | 1.18 | | 6.07 | 7.15 |
| 1900 | Coved | | 250 | .032 | | 3.59 | 1.18 | | 4.77 | 5.70 |
| 2100 | Vinyl, molded tread, 12" wide, colors, 1/8" thick | | 115 | .070 | | 5.25 | 2.57 | | 7.82 | 9.60 |
| 2200 | 1/4" thick | | 115 | .070 | ↓ | 7 | 2.57 | | 9.57 | 11.50 |
| 2300 | Landing material, 1/8" thick | | 200 | .040 | S.F. | 5.25 | 1.48 | | 6.73 | 7.95 |
| 2400 | Riser, 7" high, 1/8" thick, coved | | 175 | .046 | L.F. | 3 | 1.69 | | 4.69 | 5.80 |
| 2500 | Tread and riser combined, 1/8" thick | ↓ | 80 | .100 | " | 8.25 | 3.70 | | 11.95 | 14.55 |

## 09 65 16 – Resilient Sheet Flooring

### 09 65 16.10 Rubber and Vinyl Sheet Flooring

| | | Crew | Daily Output | Labor-Hours | Unit | Material | 2008 Bare Costs Labor | Equipment | Total | Total Incl O&P |
|---|---|---|---|---|---|---|---|---|---|---|
| 0010 | **RUBBER AND VINYL SHEET FLOORING** | | | | | | | | | |
| 5900 | Rubber, sheet goods, 36" wide, 1/8" thick | 1 Tilf | 120 | .067 | S.F. | 5.75 | 2.47 | | 8.22 | 9.95 |
| 5950 | 3/16" thick | | 100 | .080 | | 8 | 2.96 | | 10.96 | 13.15 |
| 6000 | 1/4" thick | | 90 | .089 | | 9.50 | 3.29 | | 12.79 | 15.30 |
| 8000 | Vinyl sheet goods, backed, .065" thick, minimum | | 250 | .032 | | 3.25 | 1.18 | | 4.43 | 5.30 |
| 8050 | Maximum | ↓ | 200 | .040 | ↓ | 3.10 | 1.48 | | 4.58 | 5.60 |

## 09 65 16 – Resilient Sheet Flooring

| 09 65 16.10 Rubber and Vinyl Sheet Flooring | | Crew | Daily Output | Labor-Hours | Unit | Material | 2008 Bare Costs Labor | Equipment | Total | Total Incl O&P |
|---|---|---|---|---|---|---|---|---|---|---|
| 8100 | .080" thick, minimum | 1 Tilf | 230 | .035 | S.F. | 3.25 | 1.29 | | 4.54 | 5.45 |
| 8150 | Maximum | | 200 | .040 | | 4.50 | 1.48 | | 5.98 | 7.10 |
| 8200 | .125" thick, minimum | | 230 | .035 | | 3.75 | 1.29 | | 5.04 | 6 |
| 8250 | Maximum | | 200 | .040 | | 5.50 | 1.48 | | 6.98 | 8.20 |
| 8700 | Adhesive cement, 1 gallon does 200 to 300 S.F. | | | | Gal. | 22.50 | | | 22.50 | 25 |
| 8800 | Asphalt primer, 1 gallon per 300 S.F. | | | | | 10.80 | | | 10.80 | 11.90 |
| 8900 | Emulsion, 1 gallon per 140 S.F. | | | | | 13.75 | | | 13.75 | 15.15 |

## 09 65 19 – Resilient Tile Flooring

### 09 65 19.10 Miscellaneous Resilient Tile Flooring

| | | Crew | Daily Output | Labor-Hours | Unit | Material | Labor | Equipment | Total | Total Incl O&P |
|---|---|---|---|---|---|---|---|---|---|---|
| 0010 | **MISCELLANEOUS RESILIENT TILE FLOORING** | | | | | | | | | |
| 2200 | Cork tile, standard finish, 1/8" thick | 1 Tilf | 315 | .025 | S.F. | 5.05 | .94 | | 5.99 | 6.95 |
| 2250 | 3/16" thick | | 315 | .025 | | 5.40 | .94 | | 6.34 | 7.35 |
| 2300 | 5/16" thick | | 315 | .025 | | 6.40 | .94 | | 7.34 | 8.45 |
| 2350 | 1/2" thick | | 315 | .025 | | 7.80 | .94 | | 8.74 | 9.95 |
| 2500 | Urethane finish, 1/8" thick | | 315 | .025 | | 6.30 | .94 | | 7.24 | 8.35 |
| 2550 | 3/16" thick | | 315 | .025 | | 6.70 | .94 | | 7.64 | 8.75 |
| 2600 | 5/16" thick | | 315 | .025 | | 8.50 | .94 | | 9.44 | 10.75 |
| 2650 | 1/2" thick | | 315 | .025 | | 11.50 | .94 | | 12.44 | 14.05 |
| 6050 | Rubber tile, marbleized colors, 12" x 12", 1/8" thick | | 400 | .020 | | 5.75 | .74 | | 6.49 | 7.45 |
| 6100 | 3/16" thick | | 400 | .020 | | 8.75 | .74 | | 9.49 | 10.75 |
| 6300 | Special tile, plain colors, 1/8" thick | | 400 | .020 | | 6.95 | .74 | | 7.69 | 8.75 |
| 6350 | 3/16" thick | | 400 | .020 | | 8.85 | .74 | | 9.59 | 10.85 |
| 6410 | Raised, radial or square, minimum | | 400 | .020 | | 10.70 | .74 | | 11.44 | 12.85 |
| 6430 | Maximum | | 400 | .020 | | 10.70 | .74 | | 11.44 | 12.85 |
| 6450 | For golf course, skating rink, etc., 1/4" thick | | 275 | .029 | | 10.70 | 1.08 | | 11.78 | 13.35 |
| 6700 | Synthetic turf, 3/8" thick | | 90 | .089 | | 5.25 | 3.29 | | 8.54 | 10.65 |
| 6750 | Interlocking 2' x 2' squares, 1/2" thick, not | | | | | | | | | |
| 6810 | cemented, for playgrounds, minimum | 1 Tilf | 210 | .038 | S.F. | 4.20 | 1.41 | | 5.61 | 6.70 |
| 6850 | Maximum | | 190 | .042 | | 10.50 | 1.56 | | 12.06 | 13.85 |
| 7000 | Vinyl composition tile, 12" x 12", 1/16" thick | | 500 | .016 | | .79 | .59 | | 1.38 | 1.74 |
| 7050 | Embossed | | 500 | .016 | | 1.88 | .59 | | 2.47 | 2.94 |
| 7100 | Marbleized | | 500 | .016 | | 1.88 | .59 | | 2.47 | 2.94 |
| 7150 | Solid | | 500 | .016 | | 2.42 | .59 | | 3.01 | 3.53 |
| 7200 | 3/32" thick, embossed | | 500 | .016 | | 1.18 | .59 | | 1.77 | 2.17 |
| 7250 | Marbleized | | 500 | .016 | | 2.15 | .59 | | 2.74 | 3.24 |
| 7300 | Solid | | 500 | .016 | | 2 | .59 | | 2.59 | 3.07 |
| 7350 | 1/8" thick, marbleized *CN* | | 500 | .016 | | 1.55 | .59 | | 2.14 | 2.58 |
| 7400 | Solid | | 500 | .016 | | 1.98 | .59 | | 2.57 | 3.05 |
| 7450 | Conductive | | 500 | .016 | | 4.92 | .59 | | 5.51 | 6.25 |
| 7500 | Vinyl tile, 12" x 12", .050" thick, minimum | | 500 | .016 | | 2.75 | .59 | | 3.34 | 3.90 |
| 7550 | Maximum | | 500 | .016 | | 5.50 | .59 | | 6.09 | 6.90 |
| 7600 | 1/8" thick, minimum | | 500 | .016 | | 3.85 | .59 | | 4.44 | 5.10 |
| 7650 | Solid colors | | 500 | .016 | | 5.35 | .59 | | 5.94 | 6.70 |
| 7700 | Marbleized or Travertine pattern | | 500 | .016 | | 5.15 | .59 | | 5.74 | 6.50 |
| 7750 | Florentine pattern | | 500 | .016 | | 5.20 | .59 | | 5.79 | 6.55 |
| 7800 | Maximum | | 500 | .016 | | 11.50 | .59 | | 12.09 | 13.50 |

## 09 65 33 – Conductive Resilient Flooring

### 09 65 33.10 Conductive Rubber and Vinyl Flooring

| | | Crew | Daily Output | Labor-Hours | Unit | Material | Labor | Equipment | Total | Total Incl O&P |
|---|---|---|---|---|---|---|---|---|---|---|
| 0010 | **CONDUCTIVE RUBBER AND VINYL FLOORING** | | | | | | | | | |
| 1700 | Conductive flooring, rubber tile, 1/8" thick | 1 Tilf | 315 | .025 | S.F. | 4.70 | .94 | | 5.64 | 6.55 |
| 1800 | Homogeneous vinyl tile, 1/8" thick | " | 315 | .025 | " | 5.95 | .94 | | 6.89 | 7.95 |

# 09 66 Terrazzo Flooring

## 09 66 13 – Portland Cement Terrazzo Flooring

| 09 66 13.10 Portland Cement Terrazzo | | Crew | Daily Output | Labor-Hours | Unit | Material | 2008 Bare Costs Labor | Equipment | Total | Total Incl O&P |
|---|---|---|---|---|---|---|---|---|---|---|
| 0010 | **PORTLAND CEMENT TERRAZZO**, cast-in-place      R096613-10 | | | | | | | | | |
| 0020 | Cove base, 6" high, 16ga. zinc | 1 Mstz | 20 | .400 | L.F. | 3.26 | 14.70 | | 17.96 | 25 |
| 0100 | Curb, 6" high and 6" wide | | 6 | 1.333 | | 5.25 | 49 | | 54.25 | 78 |
| 0300 | Divider strip for floors, 14 ga., 1-1/4" deep, zinc | | 375 | .021 | | 1.19 | .78 | | 1.97 | 2.46 |
| 0400 | Brass | | 375 | .021 | | 2.18 | .78 | | 2.96 | 3.55 |
| 0600 | Heavy top strip 1/4" thick, 1-1/4" deep, zinc | | 300 | .027 | | 1.71 | .98 | | 2.69 | 3.32 |
| 0900 | Galv. bottoms, brass | | 300 | .027 | | 2.95 | .98 | | 3.93 | 4.69 |
| 1200 | For thin set floors, 16 ga., 1/2" x 1/2", zinc | | 350 | .023 | | .72 | .84 | | 1.56 | 2.02 |
| 1300 | Brass | | 350 | .023 | | 1.43 | .84 | | 2.27 | 2.80 |
| 1500 | Floor, bonded to concrete, 1-3/4" thick, gray cement | J-3 | 75 | .213 | S.F. | 2.80 | 7.15 | 3.30 | 13.25 | 17.20 |
| 1600 | White cement, mud set | | 75 | .213 | | 3.19 | 7.15 | 3.30 | 13.64 | 17.65 |
| 1800 | Not bonded, 3" total thickness, gray cement | | 70 | .229 | | 3.50 | 7.65 | 3.54 | 14.69 | 19 |
| 1900 | White cement, mud set | | 70 | .229 | | 3.82 | 7.65 | 3.54 | 15.01 | 19.35 |
| 2100 | For Venetian terrazzo, 1" topping, add | | | | | 50% | 50% | | | |
| 2200 | For heavy duty abrasive terrazzo, add | | | | | 50% | 50% | | | |
| 2700 | Monolithic terrazzo, 1/2" thick | | | | | | | | | |
| 2710 | 10' panels | J-3 | 125 | .128 | S.F. | 2.55 | 4.29 | 1.98 | 8.82 | 11.30 |
| 3000 | Stairs, cast in place, pan filled treads | | 30 | .533 | L.F. | 2.53 | 17.85 | 8.25 | 28.63 | 38 |
| 3100 | Treads and risers | | 14 | 1.143 | " | 5.25 | 38.50 | 17.70 | 61.45 | 81.50 |
| 3300 | For stair landings, add to floor prices | | | | | | 50% | | | |
| 3400 | Stair stringers and fascia | J-3 | 30 | .533 | S.F. | 4.26 | 17.85 | 8.25 | 30.36 | 40 |
| 3600 | For abrasive metal nosings on stairs, add | | 150 | .107 | L.F. | 7.50 | 3.57 | 1.65 | 12.72 | 15.30 |
| 3700 | For abrasive surface finish, add | | 600 | .027 | S.F. | 1 | .89 | .41 | 2.30 | 2.86 |
| 3900 | For raised abrasive strips, add | | 150 | .107 | L.F. | .95 | 3.57 | 1.65 | 6.17 | 8.10 |
| 4000 | Wainscot, bonded, 1-1/2" thick | | 30 | .533 | S.F. | 3.22 | 17.85 | 8.25 | 29.32 | 38.50 |
| 4200 | Epoxy terrazzo, 1/4" thick | | 40 | .400 | " | 4.76 | 13.40 | 6.20 | 24.36 | 31.50 |
| 4300 | Stone chips, onyx gemstone, per 50 lb. bag | | | | Bag | 15.55 | | | 15.55 | 17.10 |

## 09 66 13.30 Terrazzo, Precast

| | | Crew | Daily Output | Labor-Hours | Unit | Material | 2008 Bare Costs Labor | Equipment | Total | Total Incl O&P |
|---|---|---|---|---|---|---|---|---|---|---|
| 0010 | **TERRAZZO, PRECAST** | | | | | | | | | |
| 0020 | Base, 6" high, straight | 1 Mstz | 70 | .114 | L.F. | 10.15 | 4.21 | | 14.36 | 17.35 |
| 0100 | Cove | | 60 | .133 | | 11.55 | 4.91 | | 16.46 | 19.90 |
| 0300 | 8" high, straight | | 60 | .133 | | 10.30 | 4.91 | | 15.21 | 18.55 |
| 0400 | Cove | | 50 | .160 | | 15.20 | 5.90 | | 21.10 | 25.50 |
| 0600 | For white cement, add | | | | | .41 | | | .41 | .45 |
| 0700 | For 16 ga. zinc toe strip, add | | | | | 1.52 | | | 1.52 | 1.67 |
| 0900 | Curbs, 4" x 4" high | 1 Mstz | 40 | .200 | | 29 | 7.35 | | 36.35 | 43 |
| 1000 | 8" x 8" high | " | 30 | .267 | | 33.50 | 9.80 | | 43.30 | 51 |
| 1200 | Floor tiles, non-slip, 1" thick, 12" x 12" | D-1 | 60 | .267 | S.F. | 17.10 | 9.30 | | 26.40 | 33 |
| 1300 | 1-1/4" thick, 12" x 12" | | 60 | .267 | | 19 | 9.30 | | 28.30 | 35 |
| 1500 | 16" x 16" | | 50 | .320 | | 20.50 | 11.15 | | 31.65 | 39.50 |
| 1600 | 1-1/2" thick, 16" x 16" | | 45 | .356 | | 18.90 | 12.40 | | 31.30 | 40 |
| 1800 | For Venetian terrazzo, add | | | | | 5.65 | | | 5.65 | 6.25 |
| 1900 | For white cement, add | | | | | .53 | | | .53 | .58 |
| 2400 | Stair treads, 1-1/2" thick, non-slip, three line pattern | 2 Mstz | 70 | .229 | L.F. | 38 | 8.40 | | 46.40 | 54.50 |
| 2500 | Nosing and two lines | | 70 | .229 | | 38 | 8.40 | | 46.40 | 54.50 |
| 2700 | 2" thick treads, straight | | 60 | .267 | | 41 | 9.80 | | 50.80 | 59.50 |
| 2800 | Curved | | 50 | .320 | | 53.50 | 11.80 | | 65.30 | 76 |
| 3000 | Stair risers, 1" thick, to 6" high, straight sections | | 60 | .267 | | 9.30 | 9.80 | | 19.10 | 24.50 |
| 3100 | Cove | | 50 | .320 | | 13.55 | 11.80 | | 25.35 | 32 |
| 3300 | Curved, 1" thick, to 6" high, vertical | | 48 | .333 | | 18.50 | 12.25 | | 30.75 | 38.50 |
| 3400 | Cove | | 38 | .421 | | 35 | 15.50 | | 50.50 | 61 |
| 3600 | Stair tread and riser, single piece, straight, minimum | | 60 | .267 | | 48.50 | 9.80 | | 58.30 | 68 |

# 09 66 Terrazzo Flooring

## 09 66 13 – Portland Cement Terrazzo Flooring

| 09 66 13.30 Terrazzo, Precast | | Crew | Daily Output | Labor-Hours | Unit | Material | 2008 Bare Costs Labor | Equipment | Total | Total Incl O&P |
|---|---|---|---|---|---|---|---|---|---|---|
| 3700 | Maximum | 2 Mstz | 40 | .400 | L.F. | 63 | 14.70 | | 77.70 | 90.50 |
| 3900 | Curved tread and riser, minimum | | 40 | .400 | | 68 | 14.70 | | 82.70 | 96.50 |
| 4000 | Maximum | | 32 | .500 | | 85.50 | 18.40 | | 103.90 | 122 |
| 4200 | Stair stringers, notched, 1" thick | | 25 | .640 | | 28 | 23.50 | | 51.50 | 65 |
| 4300 | 2" thick | | 22 | .727 | | 33 | 27 | | 60 | 75.50 |
| 4500 | Stair landings, structural, non-slip, 1-1/2" thick | | 85 | .188 | S.F. | 30.50 | 6.95 | | 37.45 | 43.50 |
| 4600 | 3" thick | | 75 | .213 | | 43 | 7.85 | | 50.85 | 59 |
| 4800 | Wainscot, 12" x 12" x 1" tiles | 1 Mstz | 12 | .667 | | 6.20 | 24.50 | | 30.70 | 43 |
| 4900 | 16" x 16" x 1-1/2" tiles | " | 8 | 1 | | 13.30 | 37 | | 50.30 | 68.50 |

## 09 66 16 – Terrazzo Floor Tile

| 09 66 16.10 Tile or Terrazzo Base | | Crew | Daily Output | Labor-Hours | Unit | Material | 2008 Bare Costs Labor | Equipment | Total | Total Incl O&P |
|---|---|---|---|---|---|---|---|---|---|---|
| 0010 | **TILE OR TERRAZZO BASE** | | | | | | | | | |
| 0020 | Scratch coat only | 1 Mstz | 150 | .053 | S.F. | .40 | 1.96 | | 2.36 | 3.32 |
| 0500 | Scratch and brown coat only | " | 75 | .107 | " | .76 | 3.93 | | 4.69 | 6.60 |

## 09 66 33 – Conductive Terrazzo Flooring

| 09 66 33.10 Conductive Terrazzo | | Crew | Daily Output | Labor-Hours | Unit | Material | 2008 Bare Costs Labor | Equipment | Total | Total Incl O&P |
|---|---|---|---|---|---|---|---|---|---|---|
| 0010 | **CONDUCTIVE TERRAZZO** | | | | | | | | | |
| 2400 | Bonded conductive floor for hospitals | J-3 | 90 | .178 | S.F. | 3.82 | 5.95 | 2.75 | 12.52 | 16 |
| 2500 | Epoxy terrazzo, 1/4" thick, minimum | | 100 | .160 | | 4.33 | 5.35 | 2.48 | 12.16 | 15.35 |
| 2550 | Average | | 75 | .213 | | 4.77 | 7.15 | 3.30 | 15.22 | 19.40 |
| 2600 | Maximum | | 60 | .267 | | 5.25 | 8.95 | 4.13 | 18.33 | 23.50 |

# 09 67 Fluid-Applied Flooring

## 09 67 20 – Epoxy-Marble Chip Flooring

| 09 67 20.13 Elastomeric Liquid Flooring | | Crew | Daily Output | Labor-Hours | Unit | Material | 2008 Bare Costs Labor | Equipment | Total | Total Incl O&P |
|---|---|---|---|---|---|---|---|---|---|---|
| 0010 | **ELASTOMERIC LIQUID FLOORING** | | | | | | | | | |
| 0020 | Cementitous acrylic, 1/4" thick | C-6 | 520 | .092 | S.F. | 1.43 | 2.93 | .10 | 4.46 | 6.20 |
| 0100 | 3/8" thick | " | 450 | .107 | | 1.80 | 3.38 | .11 | 5.29 | 7.30 |
| 0200 | Methyl methacrylate, 1/4" thick | C-8A | 3000 | .016 | | 5.15 | .53 | | 5.68 | 6.45 |
| 0210 | 1/8" thick | " | 3000 | .016 | | 2.83 | .53 | | 3.36 | 3.91 |
| 0300 | Cupric oxychloride, on bond coat, minimum | C-6 | 480 | .100 | | 3.06 | 3.17 | .10 | 6.33 | 8.35 |
| 0400 | Maximum | | 420 | .114 | | 5.10 | 3.62 | .12 | 8.84 | 11.35 |
| 2400 | Mastic, hot laid, 2 coat, 1-1/2" thick, standard, minimum | | 690 | .070 | | 3.54 | 2.21 | .07 | 5.82 | 7.35 |
| 2500 | Maximum | | 520 | .092 | | 4.55 | 2.93 | .10 | 7.58 | 9.60 |
| 2700 | Acidproof, minimum | | 605 | .079 | | 4.55 | 2.52 | .08 | 7.15 | 8.95 |
| 2800 | Maximum | | 350 | .137 | | 6.30 | 4.35 | .14 | 10.79 | 13.80 |
| 3000 | Neoprene, trowelled on, 1/4" thick, minimum | | 545 | .088 | | 3.49 | 2.79 | .09 | 6.37 | 8.25 |
| 3100 | Maximum | | 430 | .112 | | 4.80 | 3.54 | .12 | 8.46 | 10.90 |
| 4300 | Polyurethane, with suspended vinyl chips, minimum | | 1065 | .045 | | 6.80 | 1.43 | .05 | 8.28 | 9.70 |
| 4500 | Maximum | | 860 | .056 | | 9.80 | 1.77 | .06 | 11.63 | 13.55 |

| 09 67 20.16 Epoxy Terrazzo | | Crew | Daily Output | Labor-Hours | Unit | Material | 2008 Bare Costs Labor | Equipment | Total | Total Incl O&P |
|---|---|---|---|---|---|---|---|---|---|---|
| 0010 | **EPOXY TERRAZZO** | | | | | | | | | |
| 1800 | Epoxy terrazzo, 1/4" thick, chemical resistant, minimum | J-3 | 200 | .080 | S.F. | 5.15 | 2.68 | 1.24 | 9.07 | 10.95 |
| 1900 | Maximum | | 150 | .107 | | 7.50 | 3.57 | 1.65 | 12.72 | 15.30 |
| 2100 | Conductive, minimum | | 210 | .076 | | 6.75 | 2.55 | 1.18 | 10.48 | 12.45 |
| 2200 | Maximum | | 160 | .100 | | 8.75 | 3.35 | 1.55 | 13.65 | 16.20 |

| 09 67 20.19 Polyacrylate Terrazzo | | Crew | Daily Output | Labor-Hours | Unit | Material | 2008 Bare Costs Labor | Equipment | Total | Total Incl O&P |
|---|---|---|---|---|---|---|---|---|---|---|
| 0010 | **POLYACRYLATE TERRAZZO** | | | | | | | | | |
| 3150 | Polyacrylate, 1/4" thick, minimum | C-6 | 735 | .065 | S.F. | 2.91 | 2.07 | .07 | 5.05 | 6.45 |

# 09 67 Fluid-Applied Flooring

## 09 67 20 – Epoxy-Marble Chip Flooring

| 09 67 20.19 Polyacrylate Terrazzo | | Crew | Daily Output | Labor-Hours | Unit | Material | 2008 Bare Costs Labor | Equipment | Total | Total Incl O&P |
|---|---|---|---|---|---|---|---|---|---|---|
| 3170 | Maximum | C-6 | 480 | .100 | S.F. | 3.59 | 3.17 | .10 | 6.86 | 8.95 |
| 3200 | 3/8" thick, minimum | | 620 | .077 | | 3.80 | 2.46 | .08 | 6.34 | 8.05 |
| 3220 | Maximum | | 480 | .100 | | 5.05 | 3.17 | .10 | 8.32 | 10.55 |
| 3300 | Conductive, 1/4" thick, minimum | | 450 | .107 | | 6.10 | 3.38 | .11 | 9.59 | 12 |
| 3330 | Maximum | | 305 | .157 | | 7.55 | 4.99 | .16 | 12.70 | 16.20 |
| 3350 | 3/8" thick, minimum | | 365 | .132 | | 8 | 4.17 | .14 | 12.31 | 15.35 |
| 3370 | Maximum | | 255 | .188 | | 9.45 | 5.95 | .19 | 15.59 | 19.80 |
| 3450 | Granite, conductive, 1/4" thick, minimum | | 695 | .069 | | 7.80 | 2.19 | .07 | 10.06 | 12 |
| 3470 | Maximum | | 420 | .114 | | 10.05 | 3.62 | .12 | 13.79 | 16.80 |
| 3500 | 3/8" thick, minimum | | 695 | .069 | | 11.40 | 2.19 | .07 | 13.66 | 15.95 |
| 3520 | Maximum | ▼ | 380 | .126 | ▼ | 13.75 | 4.01 | .13 | 17.89 | 21.50 |

### 09 67 20.26 Quartz Flooring

| | | Crew | Daily Output | Labor-Hours | Unit | Material | Labor | Equipment | Total | Total Incl O&P |
|---|---|---|---|---|---|---|---|---|---|---|
| 0010 | **QUARTZ FLOORING** | | | | | | | | | |
| 0600 | Epoxy, with colored quartz chips, broadcast, minimum | C-6 | 675 | .071 | S.F. | 2.42 | 2.25 | .07 | 4.74 | 6.20 |
| 0700 | Maximum | | 490 | .098 | | 2.93 | 3.11 | .10 | 6.14 | 8.10 |
| 0900 | Trowelled, minimum | | 560 | .086 | | 3.12 | 2.72 | .09 | 5.93 | 7.70 |
| 1000 | Maximum | ▼ | 480 | .100 | ▼ | 4.55 | 3.17 | .10 | 7.82 | 10 |
| 1200 | Heavy duty epoxy topping, 1/4" thick, | | | | | | | | | |
| 1300 | 500 to 1,000 S.F. | C-6 | 420 | .114 | S.F. | 4.59 | 3.62 | .12 | 8.33 | 10.80 |
| 1500 | 1,000 to 2,000 S.F. | | 450 | .107 | | 3.80 | 3.38 | .11 | 7.29 | 9.50 |
| 1600 | Over 10,000 S.F. | | 480 | .100 | | 3.57 | 3.17 | .10 | 6.84 | 8.90 |
| 3600 | Polyester, with colored quartz chips, 1/16" thick, minimum | | 1065 | .045 | | 2.63 | 1.43 | .05 | 4.11 | 5.15 |
| 3700 | Maximum | | 560 | .086 | | 3.58 | 2.72 | .09 | 6.39 | 8.20 |
| 3900 | 1/8" thick, minimum | | 810 | .059 | | 3.07 | 1.88 | .06 | 5.01 | 6.35 |
| 4000 | Maximum | | 675 | .071 | | 4.15 | 2.25 | .07 | 6.47 | 8.10 |
| 4200 | Polyester, heavy duty, compared to epoxy, add | ▼ | 2590 | .019 | ▼ | 1.27 | .59 | .02 | 1.88 | 2.32 |

# 09 68 Carpeting

## 09 68 05 – Carpet Accessories

### 09 68 05.11 Flooring Transition Strip

| | | Crew | Daily Output | Labor-Hours | Unit | Material | Labor | Equipment | Total | Total Incl O&P |
|---|---|---|---|---|---|---|---|---|---|---|
| 0010 | **FLOORING TRANSITION STRIP** | | | | | | | | | |
| 0107 | Clamp down brass divider, 12' strip, vinyl to carpet | 1 Tilf | 31.25 | .256 | Ea. | 25.50 | 9.45 | | 34.95 | 42.50 |
| 0117 | Vinyl to hard surface | " | 31.25 | .256 | " | 25.50 | 9.45 | | 34.95 | 42.50 |

## 09 68 10 – Carpet Pad

### 09 68 10.10 Commercial Grade Carpet Pad

| | | Crew | Daily Output | Labor-Hours | Unit | Material | Labor | Equipment | Total | Total Incl O&P |
|---|---|---|---|---|---|---|---|---|---|---|
| 0010 | **COMMERCIAL GRADE CARPET PAD** | | | | | | | | | |
| 9000 | Sponge rubber pad, minimum | 1 Tilf | 150 | .053 | S.Y. | 3.94 | 1.97 | | 5.91 | 7.25 |
| 9100 | Maximum | | 150 | .053 | | 9.10 | 1.97 | | 11.07 | 12.90 |
| 9200 | Felt pad, minimum | | 150 | .053 | | 3.95 | 1.97 | | 5.92 | 7.25 |
| 9300 | Maximum | | 150 | .053 | | 7.05 | 1.97 | | 9.02 | 10.65 |
| 9400 | Bonded urethane pad, minimum | | 150 | .053 | | 4.15 | 1.97 | | 6.12 | 7.45 |
| 9500 | Maximum | | 150 | .053 | | 7.10 | 1.97 | | 9.07 | 10.70 |
| 9600 | Prime urethane pad, minimum | | 150 | .053 | | 2.38 | 1.97 | | 4.35 | 5.50 |
| 9700 | Maximum | ▼ | 150 | .053 | ▼ | 4.40 | 1.97 | | 6.37 | 7.75 |

## 09 68 13 – Tile Carpeting

### 09 68 13.10 Carpet Tile

| | | Crew | Daily Output | Labor-Hours | Unit | Material | Labor | Equipment | Total | Total Incl O&P |
|---|---|---|---|---|---|---|---|---|---|---|
| 0010 | **CARPET TILE** | | | | | | | | | |
| 0100 | Tufted nylon, 18" x 18", hard back, 20 oz. | 1 Tilf | 150 | .053 | S.Y. | 22 | 1.97 | | 23.97 | 27.50 |
| 0110 | 26 oz. | | 150 | .053 | | 38 | 1.97 | | 39.97 | 44.50 |
| 0200 | Cushion back, 20 oz. | ▼ | 150 | .053 | ▼ | 28 | 1.97 | | 29.97 | 33.50 |

# 09 68 Carpeting

## 09 68 13 – Tile Carpeting

| 09 68 13.10 Carpet Tile | | Crew | Daily Output | Labor-Hours | Unit | Material | 2008 Bare Costs Labor | Equipment | Total | Total Incl O&P |
|---|---|---|---|---|---|---|---|---|---|---|
| 0210 | 26 oz. | 1 Tilf | 150 | .053 | S.Y. | 43.50 | 1.97 | | 45.47 | 51 |

## 09 68 16 – Sheet Carpeting

### 09 68 16.10 Sheet Carpet

| | | | Crew | Daily Output | Labor-Hours | Unit | Material | 2008 Bare Costs Labor | Equipment | Total | Total Incl O&P |
|---|---|---|---|---|---|---|---|---|---|---|---|
| 0010 | **SHEET CARPET** | | | | | | | | | | |
| 0700 | Nylon, level loop, 26 oz., light to medium traffic | CN | 1 Tilf | 75 | .107 | S.Y. | 24 | 3.95 | | 27.95 | 32.50 |
| 0720 | 28 oz., light to medium traffic | | | 75 | .107 | | 25 | 3.95 | | 28.95 | 33.50 |
| 0900 | 32 oz., medium traffic | | | 75 | .107 | | 30 | 3.95 | | 33.95 | 39 |
| 1100 | 40 oz., medium to heavy traffic | | | 75 | .107 | | 44.50 | 3.95 | | 48.45 | 55 |
| 2920 | Nylon plush, 30 oz., medium traffic | | | 57 | .140 | | 22 | 5.20 | | 27.20 | 31.50 |
| 3000 | 36 oz., medium traffic | | | 75 | .107 | | 29 | 3.95 | | 32.95 | 38 |
| 3100 | 42 oz., medium to heavy traffic | | | 70 | .114 | | 33.50 | 4.23 | | 37.73 | 43 |
| 3200 | 46 oz., medium to heavy traffic | | | 70 | .114 | | 38.50 | 4.23 | | 42.73 | 48.50 |
| 3300 | 54 oz., heavy traffic | | | 70 | .114 | | 42 | 4.23 | | 46.23 | 52 |
| 3340 | 60 oz., heavy traffic | | | 70 | .114 | | 59 | 4.23 | | 63.23 | 71 |
| 3665 | Olefin, 24 oz., light to medium traffic | | | 75 | .107 | | 13.45 | 3.95 | | 17.40 | 20.50 |
| 3670 | 26 oz., medium traffic | | | 75 | .107 | | 14.25 | 3.95 | | 18.20 | 21.50 |
| 3680 | 28 oz., medium to heavy traffic | | | 75 | .107 | | 15.85 | 3.95 | | 19.80 | 23.50 |
| 3700 | 32 oz., medium to heavy traffic | | | 75 | .107 | | 20 | 3.95 | | 23.95 | 28 |
| 3730 | 42 oz., heavy traffic | | | 70 | .114 | | 26 | 4.23 | | 30.23 | 34.50 |
| 4110 | Wool, level loop, 40 oz., medium traffic | | | 75 | .107 | | 99 | 3.95 | | 102.95 | 115 |
| 4500 | 50 oz., medium to heavy traffic | | | 75 | .107 | | 102 | 3.95 | | 105.95 | 118 |
| 4700 | Patterned, 32 oz., medium to heavy traffic | | | 70 | .114 | | 101 | 4.23 | | 105.23 | 117 |
| 4900 | 48 oz., heavy traffic | | | 70 | .114 | | 103 | 4.23 | | 107.23 | 119 |
| 5000 | For less than full roll, add | | | | | | 25% | | | | |
| 5100 | For small rooms, less than 12' wide, add | | | | | | | 25% | | | |
| 5200 | For large open areas (no cuts), deduct | | | | | | | 25% | | | |
| 5600 | For bound carpet baseboard, add | | 1 Tilf | 300 | .027 | L.F. | 1.75 | .99 | | 2.74 | 3.38 |
| 5610 | For stairs, not incl. price of carpet, add | | " | 30 | .267 | Riser | | 9.85 | | 9.85 | 14.50 |
| 5620 | For borders and patterns, add to labor | | | | | | | 18% | | | |
| 8950 | For tackless, stretched installation, add padding to above | | | | | | | | | | |
| 9850 | For "branded" fiber, add | | | | | S.Y. | 25% | | | | |

## 09 68 20 – Athletic Carpet

### 09 68 20.10 Indoor Athletic Carpet

| | | | Crew | Daily Output | Labor-Hours | Unit | Material | 2008 Bare Costs Labor | Equipment | Total | Total Incl O&P |
|---|---|---|---|---|---|---|---|---|---|---|---|
| 0010 | **INDOOR ATHLETIC CARPET** | | | | | | | | | | |
| 3700 | Polyethylene, in rolls, no base incl., landscape surfaces | | 1 Tilf | 275 | .029 | S.F. | 2.90 | 1.08 | | 3.98 | 4.77 |
| 3800 | Nylon action surface, 1/8" thick | | | 275 | .029 | | 3.05 | 1.08 | | 4.13 | 4.94 |
| 3900 | 1/4" thick | | | 275 | .029 | | 4.39 | 1.08 | | 5.47 | 6.40 |
| 4000 | 3/8" thick | | | 275 | .029 | | 5.50 | 1.08 | | 6.58 | 7.65 |
| 4100 | Golf tee surface with foam back | | | 235 | .034 | | 5.45 | 1.26 | | 6.71 | 7.85 |
| 4200 | Practice putting, knitted nylon surface | | | 235 | .034 | | 4.63 | 1.26 | | 5.89 | 6.95 |
| 4400 | Polyurethane, thermoset, prefabricated in place, indoor | | | | | | | | | | |
| 4500 | 3/8" thick for basketball, gyms, etc. | | 1 Tilf | 100 | .080 | S.F. | 4.36 | 2.96 | | 7.32 | 9.15 |
| 4600 | 1/2" thick for professional sports | | | 95 | .084 | | 5.85 | 3.12 | | 8.97 | 11 |
| 4700 | Outdoor, 1/4" thick, smooth, for tennis | | | 100 | .080 | | 4.53 | 2.96 | | 7.49 | 9.30 |
| 4800 | Rough, for track, 3/8" thick | | | 95 | .084 | | 5.25 | 3.12 | | 8.37 | 10.30 |
| 5000 | Poured in place, indoor, with finish, 1/4" thick | | | 80 | .100 | | 3.22 | 3.70 | | 6.92 | 9 |
| 5050 | 3/8" thick | | | 65 | .123 | | 3.91 | 4.55 | | 8.46 | 11 |
| 5100 | 1/2" thick | | | 50 | .160 | | 5.25 | 5.90 | | 11.15 | 14.50 |
| 5500 | Polyvinyl chloride, sheet goods for gyms, 1/4" thick | | | 80 | .100 | | 7 | 3.70 | | 10.70 | 13.15 |
| 5600 | 3/8" thick | | | 60 | .133 | | 7.85 | 4.93 | | 12.78 | 15.90 |

# 09 69 Access Flooring

## 09 69 13 – Rigid-Grid Access Flooring

### 09 69 13.10 Access Floors

| 09 69 13.10 Access Floors | | Crew | Daily Output | Labor-Hours | Unit | Material | 2008 Bare Costs Labor | Equipment | Total | Total Incl O&P |
|---|---|---|---|---|---|---|---|---|---|---|
| 0010 | **ACCESS FLOORS** | | | | | | | | | |
| 0015 | Access floor package including panel, pedestal, stringers & laminate cover | | | | | | | | | |
| 0100 | Computer room, greater than 6,000 S.F. | 4 Carp | 750 | .043 | S.F. | 8.40 | 1.63 | | 10.03 | 11.80 |
| 0110 | Less than 6,000 S.F. | 2 Carp | 375 | .043 | | 9.70 | 1.63 | | 11.33 | 13.20 |
| 0120 | Office, greater than 6,000 S.F. | 4 Carp | 1050 | .030 | | 4.43 | 1.16 | | 5.59 | 6.70 |
| 0250 | Panels, particle board or steel, 1250# load, no covering, under 6,000 S.F. | 2 Carp | 600 | .027 | | 4.12 | 1.02 | | 5.14 | 6.10 |
| 0300 | Over 6,000 S.F. | | 640 | .025 | | 3.61 | .95 | | 4.56 | 5.45 |
| 0400 | Aluminum, 24" panels | | 500 | .032 | | 30.50 | 1.22 | | 31.72 | 35.50 |
| 0600 | For carpet covering, add | | | | | 8.30 | | | 8.30 | 9.15 |
| 0700 | For vinyl floor covering, add | | | | | 6.50 | | | 6.50 | 7.15 |
| 0900 | For high pressure laminate covering, add | | | | | 5.30 | | | 5.30 | 5.80 |
| 0910 | For snap on stringer system, add | 2 Carp | 1000 | .016 | | 1.40 | .61 | | 2.01 | 2.49 |
| 0950 | Office applications, steel or concrete panels, | | | | | | | | | |
| 0960 | no covering, over 6,000 S.F. | 2 Carp | 960 | .017 | S.F. | 9.80 | .64 | | 10.44 | 11.80 |
| 1000 | Machine cutouts after initial installation | 1 Carp | 50 | .160 | Ea. | 4.90 | 6.10 | | 11 | 14.90 |
| 1050 | Pedestals, 6" to 12" | 2 Carp | 85 | .188 | | 7.70 | 7.15 | | 14.85 | 19.65 |
| 1100 | Air conditioning grilles, 4" x 12" | 1 Carp | 17 | .471 | | 64 | 17.95 | | 81.95 | 98.50 |
| 1150 | 4" x 18" | " | 14 | .571 | | 87.50 | 22 | | 109.50 | 131 |
| 1200 | Approach ramps, minimum | 2 Carp | 60 | .267 | S.F. | 24.50 | 10.15 | | 34.65 | 43 |
| 1300 | Maximum | " | 40 | .400 | " | 32.50 | 15.25 | | 47.75 | 59 |
| 1500 | Handrail, 2 rail, aluminum | 1 Carp | 15 | .533 | L.F. | 96.50 | 20.50 | | 117 | 138 |

# 09 72 Wall Coverings

## 09 72 23 – Wallpapering

### 09 72 23.10 Wallpaper

| 09 72 23.10 Wallpaper | | Crew | Daily Output | Labor-Hours | Unit | Material | 2008 Bare Costs Labor | Equipment | Total | Total Incl O&P |
|---|---|---|---|---|---|---|---|---|---|---|
| 0010 | **WALLPAPER** including sizing; add 10-30 percent waste @ takeoff  R097223-10 | | | | | | | | | |
| 0050 | Aluminum foil | 1 Pape | 275 | .029 | S.F. | .94 | .98 | | 1.92 | 2.50 |
| 0100 | Copper sheets, .025" thick, vinyl backing | | 240 | .033 | | 5.05 | 1.12 | | 6.17 | 7.25 |
| 0300 | Phenolic backing | | 240 | .033 | | 6.55 | 1.12 | | 7.67 | 8.90 |
| 0600 | Cork tiles, light or dark, 12" x 12" x 3/16" | | 240 | .033 | | 4.05 | 1.12 | | 5.17 | 6.15 |
| 0700 | 5/16" thick | | 235 | .034 | | 3.45 | 1.15 | | 4.60 | 5.55 |
| 0900 | 1/4" basketweave | | 240 | .033 | | 5.30 | 1.12 | | 6.42 | 7.55 |
| 1000 | 1/2" natural, non-directional pattern | | 240 | .033 | | 6.65 | 1.12 | | 7.77 | 9.05 |
| 1100 | 3/4" natural, non-directional pattern | | 240 | .033 | | 10.15 | 1.12 | | 11.27 | 12.90 |
| 1200 | Granular surface, 12" x 36", 1/2" thick | | 385 | .021 | | 1.14 | .70 | | 1.84 | 2.30 |
| 1300 | 1" thick | | 370 | .022 | | 1.48 | .73 | | 2.21 | 2.73 |
| 1500 | Polyurethane coated, 12" x 12" x 3/16" thick | | 240 | .033 | | 3.58 | 1.12 | | 4.70 | 5.65 |
| 1600 | 5/16" thick | | 235 | .034 | | 5.10 | 1.15 | | 6.25 | 7.35 |
| 1800 | Cork wallpaper, paperbacked, natural | | 480 | .017 | | 1.91 | .56 | | 2.47 | 2.95 |
| 1900 | Colors | | 480 | .017 | | 2.52 | .56 | | 3.08 | 3.62 |
| 2100 | Flexible wood veneer, 1/32" thick, plain woods | | 100 | .080 | | 2.14 | 2.70 | | 4.84 | 6.40 |
| 2200 | Exotic woods | | 95 | .084 | | 3.25 | 2.84 | | 6.09 | 7.85 |
| 2400 | Gypsum-based, fabric-backed, fire | | | | | | | | | |
| 2500 | resistant for masonry walls, minimum, 21 oz./S.Y. | 1 Pape | 800 | .010 | S.F. | .74 | .34 | | 1.08 | 1.32 |
| 2700 | Maximum, (small quantities) | " | 640 | .013 | | 1.24 | .42 | | 1.66 | 1.99 |
| 2750 | Acrylic, modified, semi-rigid PVC, .028" thick | 2 Carp | 330 | .048 | | 1.03 | 1.85 | | 2.88 | 4 |
| 2800 | .040" thick | " | 320 | .050 | | 1.35 | 1.91 | | 3.26 | 4.46 |
| 3000 | Vinyl wall covering, fabric-backed, lightweight, (12-15 oz./S.Y.) | 1 Pape | 640 | .013 | | .62 | .42 | | 1.04 | 1.31 |
| 3300 | Medium weight, type 2, (20-24 oz./S.Y.) | | 480 | .017 | | .74 | .56 | | 1.30 | 1.66 |
| 3400 | Heavy weight, type 3, (28 oz./S.Y.) | | 435 | .018 | | 1.51 | .62 | | 2.13 | 2.59 |
| 3600 | Adhesive, 5 gal. lots, (18SY/Gal.) | | | | Gal. | 9.65 | | | 9.65 | 10.65 |

# 09 72 Wall Coverings

## 09 72 23 – Wallpapering

| 09 72 23.10 Wallpaper | Crew | Daily Output | Labor-Hours | Unit | Material | 2008 Bare Costs Labor | Equipment | Total | Total Incl O&P |
|---|---|---|---|---|---|---|---|---|---|
| 3700 | Wallpaper, average workmanship, solid pattern, low cost paper | 1 Pape | 640 | .013 | S.F. | .33 | .42 | | .75 | .99 |
| 3900 | basic patterns (matching required), avg. cost paper | | 535 | .015 | | .58 | .50 | | 1.08 | 1.40 |
| 4000 | Paper at $85 per double roll, quality workmanship | ↓ | 435 | .018 | ↓ | 2.24 | .62 | | 2.86 | 3.39 |
| 4100 | Linen wall covering, paper backed | | | | | | | | | |
| 4150 | Flame treatment, minimum | | | | S.F. | .82 | | | .82 | .90 |
| 4180 | Maximum | | | | | 1.41 | | | 1.41 | 1.55 |
| 4200 | Grass cloths with lining paper, minimum | 1 Pape | 400 | .020 | | .70 | .68 | | 1.38 | 1.78 |
| 4300 | Maximum | " | 350 | .023 | ↓ | 2.26 | .77 | | 3.03 | 3.65 |

# 09 77 Special Wall Surfacing

## 09 77 33 – Fiberglass Reinforced Panels

| 09 77 33.10 Fiberglass Reinforced Plastic | Crew | Daily Output | Labor-Hours | Unit | Material | 2008 Bare Costs Labor | Equipment | Total | Total Incl O&P |
|---|---|---|---|---|---|---|---|---|---|
| 0010 | **FIBERGLASS REINFORCED PLASTIC** panels, .090" thick | | | | | | | | | |
| 0020 | On walls, adhesive mounted, embossed surface | 2 Carp | 640 | .025 | S.F. | 1.23 | .95 | | 2.18 | 2.83 |
| 0030 | Smooth surface | | 640 | .025 | | 1.51 | .95 | | 2.46 | 3.14 |
| 0040 | Fire rated, embossed surface | | 640 | .025 | | 2.19 | .95 | | 3.14 | 3.89 |
| 0050 | Nylon rivet mounted, on drywall, embossed surface | | 480 | .033 | | 1.15 | 1.27 | | 2.42 | 3.25 |
| 0060 | Smooth surface | | 480 | .033 | | 1.43 | 1.27 | | 2.70 | 3.55 |
| 0070 | Fire rated, embossed surface | | 480 | .033 | | 2.11 | 1.27 | | 3.38 | 4.30 |
| 0080 | On masonry, embossed surface | | 320 | .050 | | 1.15 | 1.91 | | 3.06 | 4.24 |
| 0090 | Smooth surface | | 320 | .050 | | 1.43 | 1.91 | | 3.34 | 4.54 |
| 0100 | Fire rated, embossed surface | | 320 | .050 | | 2.11 | 1.91 | | 4.02 | 5.30 |
| 0110 | Nylon rivet and adhesive mounted, on drywall, embossed surface | | 240 | .067 | | 1.30 | 2.54 | | 3.84 | 5.40 |
| 0120 | Smooth surface | | 240 | .067 | | 1.58 | 2.54 | | 4.12 | 5.70 |
| 0130 | Fire rated, embossed surface | | 240 | .067 | | 2.26 | 2.54 | | 4.80 | 6.45 |
| 0140 | On masonry, embossed surface | | 190 | .084 | | 1.30 | 3.21 | | 4.51 | 6.40 |
| 0150 | Smooth surface | | 190 | .084 | | 1.58 | 3.21 | | 4.79 | 6.75 |
| 0160 | Fire rated, embossed surface | ↓ | 190 | .084 | ↓ | 2.26 | 3.21 | | 5.47 | 7.50 |
| 0170 | For moldings add | 1 Carp | 250 | .032 | L.F. | .28 | 1.22 | | 1.50 | 2.21 |
| 0180 | On ceilings, for lay in grid system, embossed surface | | 400 | .020 | S.F. | 1.23 | .76 | | 1.99 | 2.54 |
| 0190 | Smooth surface | | 400 | .020 | | 1.51 | .76 | | 2.27 | 2.85 |
| 0200 | Fire rated, embossed surface | ↓ | 400 | .020 | ↓ | 2.19 | .76 | | 2.95 | 3.60 |

## 09 77 43 – Panel Systems

| 09 77 43.20 Slatwall Panels and Accessories | Crew | Daily Output | Labor-Hours | Unit | Material | 2008 Bare Costs Labor | Equipment | Total | Total Incl O&P |
|---|---|---|---|---|---|---|---|---|---|
| 0010 | **SLATWALL PANELS AND ACCESSORIES** | | | | | | | | | |
| 0100 | Slatwall panel, 4' x 8' x 3/4" T, MDF, paint grade | 1 Carp | 500 | .016 | S.F. | 1.54 | .61 | | 2.15 | 2.64 |
| 0110 | Melamine finish | | 500 | .016 | | 2.22 | .61 | | 2.83 | 3.39 |
| 0120 | High pressure plastic laminate finish | ↓ | 500 | .016 | | 3.53 | .61 | | 4.14 | 4.83 |
| 0130 | Aluminum channel inserts, add | | | | ↓ | 3.42 | | | 3.42 | 3.76 |
| 0200 | Accessories, corner forms, 8' L | | | | L.F. | 4.70 | | | 4.70 | 5.15 |
| 0210 | T-connector, 8' L | | | | | 5.70 | | | 5.70 | 6.30 |
| 0220 | J-mold, 8' L | | | | | 1.35 | | | 1.35 | 1.49 |
| 0230 | Edge cap, 8' L | | | | | 1.01 | | | 1.01 | 1.11 |
| 0240 | Finish end cap, 8' L | | | | ↓ | 3.53 | | | 3.53 | 3.88 |
| 0300 | Display hook, metal, 4" L | | | | Ea. | 1.07 | | | 1.07 | 1.18 |
| 0310 | 6" L | | | | | 1.17 | | | 1.17 | 1.29 |
| 0320 | 8" L | | | | | 1.24 | | | 1.24 | 1.36 |
| 0330 | 10" L | | | | | 1.41 | | | 1.41 | 1.55 |
| 0340 | 12" L | | | | | 1.55 | | | 1.55 | 1.71 |
| 0350 | Acrylic, 4" L | | | | ↓ | .88 | | | .88 | .97 |

# 09 77 Special Wall Surfacing

## 09 77 43 – Panel Systems

| 09 77 43.20 Slatwall Panels and Accessories | Crew | Daily Output | Labor-Hours | Unit | Material | 2008 Bare Costs Labor | Equipment | Total | Total Incl O&P |
|---|---|---|---|---|---|---|---|---|---|
| 0360 | 6" L | | | | Ea. | 1.02 | | | 1.02 | 1.12 |
| 0370 | 8" L | | | | | 1.07 | | | 1.07 | 1.18 |
| 0380 | 10" L | | | | | 1.18 | | | 1.18 | 1.30 |
| 0400 | Waterfall hanger, metal, 12" - 16" | | | | | 6.20 | | | 6.20 | 6.80 |
| 0410 | Acrylic | | | | | 10.20 | | | 10.20 | 11.20 |
| 0500 | Shelf bracket, metal, 8" | | | | | 6.30 | | | 6.30 | 6.90 |
| 0510 | 10" | | | | | 6.50 | | | 6.50 | 7.15 |
| 0520 | 12" | | | | | 6.75 | | | 6.75 | 7.40 |
| 0530 | 14" | | | | | 5.65 | | | 5.65 | 6.20 |
| 0540 | 16" | | | | | 6.25 | | | 6.25 | 6.85 |
| 0550 | Acrylic, 8" | | | | | 3.31 | | | 3.31 | 3.64 |
| 0560 | 10" | | | | | 3.71 | | | 3.71 | 4.08 |
| 0570 | 12" | | | | | 4.11 | | | 4.11 | 4.52 |
| 0580 | 14" | | | | | 4.65 | | | 4.65 | 5.10 |
| 0600 | Shelf, acrylic, 12" x 16" x 1/4" | | | | | 26 | | | 26 | 29 |
| 0610 | 12" x 24" x 1/4" | | | | | 44 | | | 44 | 48.50 |

# 09 81 Acoustic Insulation

## 09 81 16 – Acoustic Blanket Insulation

### 09 81 16.10 Sound Attenuation Blanket

| | | Crew | Daily Output | Labor-Hours | Unit | Material | 2008 Bare Costs Labor | Equipment | Total | Total Incl O&P |
|---|---|---|---|---|---|---|---|---|---|---|
| 0010 | **SOUND ATTENUATION BLANKET** | | | | | | | | | |
| 0020 | Blanket, 1" thick | 1 Carp | 925 | .009 | S.F. | .23 | .33 | | .56 | .76 |
| 0500 | 1-1/2" thick | | 920 | .009 | | .23 | .33 | | .56 | .77 |
| 1000 | 2" thick | | 915 | .009 | | .32 | .33 | | .65 | .87 |
| 1500 | 3" thick | | 910 | .009 | | .47 | .33 | | .80 | 1.04 |
| 3000 | Thermal or acoustical batt above ceiling, 2" thick | | 900 | .009 | | .48 | .34 | | .82 | 1.06 |
| 3100 | 3" thick | | 900 | .009 | | .72 | .34 | | 1.06 | 1.32 |
| 3200 | 4" thick | | 900 | .009 | | .89 | .34 | | 1.23 | 1.51 |
| 3400 | Urethane plastic foam, open cell, on wall, 2" thick | 2 Carp | 2050 | .008 | | 2.96 | .30 | | 3.26 | 3.72 |
| 3500 | 3" thick | | 1550 | .010 | | 3.93 | .39 | | 4.32 | 4.93 |
| 3600 | 4" thick | | 1050 | .015 | | 5.50 | .58 | | 6.08 | 6.95 |
| 3700 | On ceiling, 2" thick | | 1700 | .009 | | 2.95 | .36 | | 3.31 | 3.81 |
| 3800 | 3" thick | | 1300 | .012 | | 3.93 | .47 | | 4.40 | 5.05 |
| 3900 | 4" thick | | 900 | .018 | | 5.50 | .68 | | 6.18 | 7.10 |
| 4000 | Nylon matting 0.4" thick, with carbon black spinerette | | | | | | | | | |
| 4010 | plus polyester fabric, on floor | J-4 | 4000 | .004 | S.F. | 2.19 | .13 | | 2.32 | 2.60 |
| 4200 | Fiberglass reinf. backer board underlayment, 7/16" thick, on floor | " | 800 | .020 | " | 1.84 | .66 | | 2.50 | 2.99 |

# 09 84 Acoustic Room Components

## 09 84 13 – Fixed Sound-Absorptive Panels

### 09 84 13.10 Fixed Panels

| | | Crew | Daily Output | Labor-Hours | Unit | Material | 2008 Bare Costs Labor | Equipment | Total | Total Incl O&P |
|---|---|---|---|---|---|---|---|---|---|---|
| 0010 | **FIXED PANELS** Perforated steel facing, painted with | | | | | | | | | |
| 0100 | Fiberglass or mineral filler, no backs, 2-1/4" thick, modular | | | | | | | | | |
| 0200 | space units, ceiling or wall hung, white or colored | 1 Carp | 100 | .080 | S.F. | 10 | 3.05 | | 13.05 | 15.75 |
| 0300 | Fiberboard sound deadening panels, 1/2" thick | " | 600 | .013 | " | .32 | .51 | | .83 | 1.14 |
| 0500 | Fiberglass panels, 4' x 8' x 1" thick, with | | | | | | | | | |
| 0600 | glass cloth face for walls, cemented | 1 Carp | 155 | .052 | S.F. | 7 | 1.97 | | 8.97 | 10.75 |
| 0700 | 1-1/2" thick, dacron covered, inner aluminum frame, | | | | | | | | | |
| 0710 | wall mounted | 1 Carp | 300 | .027 | S.F. | 8.75 | 1.02 | | 9.77 | 11.20 |

# 09 84 Acoustic Room Components

## 09 84 13 – Fixed Sound-Absorptive Panels

| 09 84 13.10 Fixed Panels | Crew | Daily Output | Labor-Hours | Unit | Material | 2008 Bare Costs Labor | Equipment | Total | Total Incl O&P |
|---|---|---|---|---|---|---|---|---|---|
| 0900 | Mineral fiberboard panels, fabric covered, 30"x 108", | | | | | | | | | |
| 1000 | 3/4" thick, concealed spline, wall mounted | 1 Carp | 150 | .053 | S.F. | 6.25 | 2.03 | | 8.28 | 10.05 |

## 09 84 36 – Sound-Absorbing Ceiling Units

### 09 84 36.10 Barriers

| | | Crew | Daily Output | Labor-Hours | Unit | Material | 2008 Bare Costs Labor | Equipment | Total | Total Incl O&P |
|---|---|---|---|---|---|---|---|---|---|---|
| 0010 | **BARRIERS** Plenum | | | | | | | | | |
| 0600 | Aluminum foil, fiberglass reinf., parallel with joists | 1 Carp | 275 | .029 | S.F. | .82 | 1.11 | | 1.93 | 2.63 |
| 0700 | Perpendicular to joists | | 180 | .044 | | .82 | 1.69 | | 2.51 | 3.54 |
| 0900 | Aluminum mesh, kraft paperbacked | | 275 | .029 | | .75 | 1.11 | | 1.86 | 2.56 |
| 0970 | Fiberglass batts, kraft faced, 3-1/2" thick | | 1400 | .006 | | .35 | .22 | | .57 | .73 |
| 0980 | 6" thick | | 1300 | .006 | | .63 | .23 | | .86 | 1.05 |
| 1000 | Sheet lead, 1 lb., 1/64" thick, perpendicular to joists | | 150 | .053 | | 8.15 | 2.03 | | 10.18 | 12.10 |
| 1100 | Vinyl foam reinforced, 1/8" thick, 1.0 lb. per S.F. | | 150 | .053 | | 9.50 | 2.03 | | 11.53 | 13.60 |

# 09 91 Painting

## 09 91 03 – Paint Restoration

### 09 91 03.20 Sanding

| | | Crew | Daily Output | Labor-Hours | Unit | Material | 2008 Bare Costs Labor | Equipment | Total | Total Incl O&P |
|---|---|---|---|---|---|---|---|---|---|---|
| 0010 | **SANDING** and puttying interior trim, compared to    R099100-10 | | | | | | | | | |
| 0100 | Painting 1 coat, on quality work | | | | L.F. | | 100% | | | |
| 0300 | Medium work | | | | | | 50% | | | |
| 0400 | Industrial grade | | | | | | 25% | | | |
| 0500 | Surface protection, placement and removal | | | | | | | | | |
| 0510 | Basic drop cloths | 1 Pord | 6400 | .001 | S.F. | | .04 | | .04 | .06 |
| 0520 | Masking with paper | | 800 | .010 | | .06 | .34 | | .40 | .58 |
| 0530 | Volume cover up (using plastic sheathing, or building paper) | | 16000 | .001 | | | .02 | | .02 | .03 |

### 09 91 03.30 Exterior Surface Preparation

| | | Crew | Daily Output | Labor-Hours | Unit | Material | 2008 Bare Costs Labor | Equipment | Total | Total Incl O&P |
|---|---|---|---|---|---|---|---|---|---|---|
| 0010 | **EXTERIOR SURFACE PREPARATION**    R099100-10 | | | | | | | | | |
| 0015 | Doors, per side, not incl. frames or trim | | | | | | | | | |
| 0020 | Scrape & sand | | | | | | | | | |
| 0030 | Wood, flush | 1 Pord | 616 | .013 | S.F. | | .44 | | .44 | .66 |
| 0040 | Wood, detail | | 496 | .016 | | | .54 | | .54 | .82 |
| 0050 | Wood, louvered | | 280 | .029 | | | .96 | | .96 | 1.45 |
| 0060 | Wood, overhead | | 616 | .013 | | | .44 | | .44 | .66 |
| 0070 | Wire brush | | | | | | | | | |
| 0080 | Metal, flush | 1 Pord | 640 | .013 | S.F. | | .42 | | .42 | .63 |
| 0090 | Metal, detail | | 520 | .015 | | | .52 | | .52 | .78 |
| 0100 | Metal, louvered | | 360 | .022 | | | .75 | | .75 | 1.13 |
| 0110 | Metal or fibr., overhead | | 640 | .013 | | | .42 | | .42 | .63 |
| 0120 | Metal, roll up | | 560 | .014 | | | .48 | | .48 | .72 |
| 0130 | Metal, bulkhead | | 640 | .013 | | | .42 | | .42 | .63 |
| 0140 | Power wash, based on 2500 lb. operating pressure | | | | | | | | | |
| 0150 | Metal, flush | A-1H | 2240 | .004 | S.F. | | .11 | .03 | .14 | .20 |
| 0160 | Metal, detail | | 2120 | .004 | | | .11 | .03 | .14 | .21 |
| 0170 | Metal, louvered | | 2000 | .004 | | | .12 | .03 | .15 | .22 |
| 0180 | Metal or fibr., overhead | | 2400 | .003 | | | .10 | .03 | .13 | .19 |
| 0190 | Metal, roll up | | 2400 | .003 | | | .10 | .03 | .13 | .19 |
| 0200 | Metal, bulkhead | | 2200 | .004 | | | .11 | .03 | .14 | .20 |
| 0400 | Windows, per side, not incl. trim | | | | | | | | | |
| 0410 | Scrape & sand | | | | | | | | | |
| 0420 | Wood, 1-2 lite | 1 Pord | 320 | .025 | S.F. | | .84 | | .84 | 1.27 |
| 0430 | Wood, 3-6 lite | | 280 | .029 | | | .96 | | .96 | 1.45 |

# 09 91 Painting

## 09 91 03 – Paint Restoration

### 09 91 03.30 Exterior Surface Preparation

| | | Crew | Daily Output | Labor-Hours | Unit | Material | 2008 Bare Costs Labor | Equipment | Total | Total Incl O&P |
|---|---|---|---|---|---|---|---|---|---|---|
| 0440 | Wood, 7-10 lite | 1 Pord | 240 | .033 | S.F. | | 1.12 | | 1.12 | 1.69 |
| 0450 | Wood, 12 lite | | 200 | .040 | | | 1.35 | | 1.35 | 2.03 |
| 0460 | Wood, Bay / Bow | ↓ | 320 | .025 | ↓ | | .84 | | .84 | 1.27 |
| 0470 | Wire brush | | | | | | | | | |
| 0480 | Metal, 1-2 lite | 1 Pord | 480 | .017 | S.F. | | .56 | | .56 | .85 |
| 0490 | Metal, 3-6 lite | | 400 | .020 | | | .68 | | .68 | 1.01 |
| 0500 | Metal, Bay / Bow | ↓ | 480 | .017 | ↓ | | .56 | | .56 | .85 |
| 0510 | Power wash, based on 2500 lb. operating pressure | | | | | | | | | |
| 0520 | 1-2 lite | A-1H | 4400 | .002 | S.F. | | .06 | .01 | .07 | .11 |
| 0530 | 3-6 lite | | 4320 | .002 | | | .06 | .01 | .07 | .11 |
| 0540 | 7-10 lite | | 4240 | .002 | | | .06 | .01 | .07 | .11 |
| 0550 | 12 lite | | 4160 | .002 | | | .06 | .02 | .08 | .11 |
| 0560 | Bay / Bow | ↓ | 4400 | .002 | ↓ | | .06 | .01 | .07 | .11 |
| 0600 | Siding, scrape and sand, light=10-30%, med.=30-70% | | | | | | | | | |
| 0610 | Heavy=70-100%, % of surface to sand | | | | | | | | | |
| 0650 | Texture 1-11, light | 1 Pord | 480 | .017 | S.F. | | .56 | | .56 | .85 |
| 0660 | Med. | | 440 | .018 | | | .61 | | .61 | .92 |
| 0670 | Heavy | | 360 | .022 | | | .75 | | .75 | 1.13 |
| 0680 | Wood shingles, shakes, light | | 440 | .018 | | | .61 | | .61 | .92 |
| 0690 | Med. | | 360 | .022 | | | .75 | | .75 | 1.13 |
| 0700 | Heavy | | 280 | .029 | | | .96 | | .96 | 1.45 |
| 0710 | Clapboard, light | | 520 | .015 | | | .52 | | .52 | .78 |
| 0720 | Med. | | 480 | .017 | | | .56 | | .56 | .85 |
| 0730 | Heavy | ↓ | 400 | .020 | ↓ | | .68 | | .68 | 1.01 |
| 0740 | Wire brush | | | | | | | | | |
| 0750 | Aluminum, light | 1 Pord | 600 | .013 | S.F. | | .45 | | .45 | .68 |
| 0760 | Med. | | 520 | .015 | | | .52 | | .52 | .78 |
| 0770 | Heavy | ↓ | 440 | .018 | | | .61 | | .61 | .92 |
| 0780 | Pressure wash, based on 2500 lb. operating pressure | | | | | | | | | |
| 0790 | Stucco | A-1H | 3080 | .003 | S.F. | | .08 | .02 | .10 | .14 |
| 0800 | Aluminum or vinyl | | 3200 | .003 | | | .08 | .02 | .10 | .14 |
| 0810 | Siding, masonry, brick & block | ↓ | 2400 | .003 | ↓ | | .10 | .03 | .13 | .19 |
| 1300 | Miscellaneous, wire brush | | | | | | | | | |
| 1310 | Metal, pedestrian gate | 1 Pord | 100 | .080 | S.F. | | 2.70 | | 2.70 | 4.06 |
| 8000 | For Chemical Washing, see Div. 04 01 30.20 | | | | | | | | | |
| 8010 | For Steam Cleaning, see Div. 04 01 30.20 | | | | | | | | | |
| 8020 | For Sand Blasting, see Div. 05 01 10.51 and 03 35 29.60 | | | | | | | | | |

### 09 91 03.40 Interior Surface Preparation

| | | Crew | Daily Output | Labor-Hours | Unit | Material | 2008 Bare Costs Labor | Equipment | Total | Total Incl O&P |
|---|---|---|---|---|---|---|---|---|---|---|
| 0010 | **INTERIOR SURFACE PREPARATION** R099100-10 | | | | | | | | | |
| 0020 | Doors, per side, not incl. frames or trim | | | | | | | | | |
| 0030 | Scrape & sand | | | | | | | | | |
| 0040 | Wood, flush | 1 Pord | 616 | .013 | S.F. | | .44 | | .44 | .66 |
| 0050 | Wood, detail | | 496 | .016 | | | .54 | | .54 | .82 |
| 0060 | Wood, louvered | ↓ | 280 | .029 | ↓ | | .96 | | .96 | 1.45 |
| 0070 | Wire brush | | | | | | | | | |
| 0080 | Metal, flush | 1 Pord | 640 | .013 | S.F. | | .42 | | .42 | .63 |
| 0090 | Metal, detail | | 520 | .015 | | | .52 | | .52 | .78 |
| 0100 | Metal, louvered | ↓ | 360 | .022 | ↓ | | .75 | | .75 | 1.13 |
| 0110 | Hand wash | | | | | | | | | |
| 0120 | Wood, flush | 1 Pord | 2160 | .004 | S.F. | | .12 | | .12 | .19 |
| 0130 | Wood, detailed | | 2000 | .004 | | | .14 | | .14 | .20 |
| 0140 | Wood, louvered | ↓ | 1360 | .006 | ↓ | | .20 | | .20 | .30 |

# 09 91 Painting

## 09 91 03 – Paint Restoration

### 09 91 03.40 Interior Surface Preparation

| | | Crew | Daily Output | Labor-Hours | Unit | Material | 2008 Bare Costs Labor | Equipment | Total | Total Incl O&P |
|---|---|---|---|---|---|---|---|---|---|---|
| 0150 | Metal, flush | 1 Pord | 2160 | .004 | S.F. | | .12 | | .12 | .19 |
| 0160 | Metal, detail | | 2000 | .004 | | | .14 | | .14 | .20 |
| 0170 | Metal, louvered | ↓ | 1360 | .006 | ↓ | | .20 | | .20 | .30 |
| 0400 | Windows, per side, not incl. trim | | | | | | | | | |
| 0410 | Scrape & sand | | | | | | | | | |
| 0420 | Wood, 1-2 lite | 1 Pord | 360 | .022 | S.F. | | .75 | | .75 | 1.13 |
| 0430 | Wood, 3-6 lite | | 320 | .025 | | | .84 | | .84 | 1.27 |
| 0440 | Wood, 7-10 lite | | 280 | .029 | | | .96 | | .96 | 1.45 |
| 0450 | Wood, 12 lite | | 240 | .033 | | | 1.12 | | 1.12 | 1.69 |
| 0460 | Wood, Bay / Bow | ↓ | 360 | .022 | ↓ | | .75 | | .75 | 1.13 |
| 0470 | Wire brush | | | | | | | | | |
| 0480 | Metal, 1-2 lite | 1 Pord | 520 | .015 | S.F. | | .52 | | .52 | .78 |
| 0490 | Metal, 3-6 lite | | 440 | .018 | | | .61 | | .61 | .92 |
| 0500 | Metal, Bay / Bow | ↓ | 520 | .015 | | | .52 | | .52 | .78 |
| 0600 | Walls, sanding, light=10-30% | | | | | | | | | |
| 0610 | Med.=30-70%, heavy=70-100%, % of surface to sand | | | | | | | | | |
| 0650 | Walls, sand | | | | | | | | | |
| 0660 | Drywall, gypsum, plaster, light | 1 Pord | 3077 | .003 | S.F. | | .09 | | .09 | .13 |
| 0670 | Drywall, gypsum, plaster, med. | | 2160 | .004 | | | .12 | | .12 | .19 |
| 0680 | Drywall, gypsum, plaster, heavy | | 923 | .009 | | | .29 | | .29 | .44 |
| 0690 | Wood, T&G, light | | 2400 | .003 | | | .11 | | .11 | .17 |
| 0700 | Wood, T&G, med. | | 1600 | .005 | | | .17 | | .17 | .25 |
| 0710 | Wood, T&G, heavy | ↓ | 800 | .010 | ↓ | | .34 | | .34 | .51 |
| 0720 | Walls, wash | | | | | | | | | |
| 0730 | Drywall, gypsum, plaster | 1 Pord | 3200 | .003 | S.F. | | .08 | | .08 | .13 |
| 0740 | Wood, T&G | | 3200 | .003 | | | .08 | | .08 | .13 |
| 0750 | Masonry, brick & block, smooth | | 2800 | .003 | | | .10 | | .10 | .15 |
| 0760 | Masonry, brick & block, coarse | ↓ | 2000 | .004 | ↓ | | .14 | | .14 | .20 |
| 8000 | For Chemical Washing, see Div. 04 01 30.20 | | | | | | | | | |
| 8010 | For Steam Cleaning, see Div. 04 01 30.20 | | | | | | | | | |
| 8020 | For Sand Blasting, see Div. 03 35 29.60 and 05 01 10.51 | | | | | | | | | |

## 09 91 13 – Exterior Painting

### 09 91 13.30 Fences

| | | Crew | Daily Output | Labor-Hours | Unit | Material | 2008 Bare Costs Labor | Equipment | Total | Total Incl O&P |
|---|---|---|---|---|---|---|---|---|---|---|
| 0010 | **FENCES**          R099100-20 | | | | | | | | | |
| 0100 | Chain link or wire metal, one side, water base | | | | | | | | | |
| 0110 | Roll & brush, first coat | 1 Pord | 960 | .008 | S.F. | .06 | .28 | | .34 | .49 |
| 0120 | Second coat | | 1280 | .006 | | .06 | .21 | | .27 | .38 |
| 0130 | Spray, first coat | | 2275 | .004 | | .06 | .12 | | .18 | .25 |
| 0140 | Second coat | ↓ | 2600 | .003 | ↓ | .06 | .10 | | .16 | .23 |
| 0150 | Picket, water base | | | | | | | | | |
| 0160 | Roll & brush, first coat | 1 Pord | 865 | .009 | S.F. | .07 | .31 | | .38 | .54 |
| 0170 | Second coat | | 1050 | .008 | | .07 | .26 | | .33 | .46 |
| 0180 | Spray, first coat | | 2275 | .004 | | .07 | .12 | | .19 | .25 |
| 0190 | Second coat | ↓ | 2600 | .003 | ↓ | .07 | .10 | | .17 | .23 |
| 0200 | Stockade, water base | | | | | | | | | |
| 0210 | Roll & brush, first coat | 1 Pord | 1040 | .008 | S.F. | .07 | .26 | | .33 | .46 |
| 0220 | Second coat | | 1200 | .007 | | .07 | .23 | | .30 | .41 |
| 0230 | Spray, first coat | | 2275 | .004 | | .07 | .12 | | .19 | .25 |
| 0240 | Second coat | | 2600 | .003 | ↓ | .07 | .10 | | .17 | .23 |

### 09 91 13.42 Miscellaneous, Exterior

| | | Crew | Daily Output | Labor-Hours | Unit | Material | 2008 Bare Costs Labor | Equipment | Total | Total Incl O&P |
|---|---|---|---|---|---|---|---|---|---|---|
| 0010 | **MISCELLANEOUS, EXTERIOR**          R099100-20 | | | | | | | | | |
| 0015 | For painting metals, see Div. 09 97 13.23 | | | | | | | | | |

# 09 91 Painting

## 09 91 13 – Exterior Painting

### 09 91 13.42 Miscellaneous, Exterior

| | | Crew | Daily Output | Labor-Hours | Unit | Material | 2008 Bare Costs Labor | 2008 Bare Costs Equipment | Total | Total Incl O&P |
|---|---|---|---|---|---|---|---|---|---|---|
| 0100 | Railing, ext., decorative wood, incl. cap & baluster | | | | | | | | | |
| 0110 | Newels & spindles @ 12" O.C. | | | | | | | | | |
| 0120 | Brushwork, stain, sand, seal & varnish | | | | | | | | | |
| 0130 | First coat | 1 Pord | 90 | .089 | L.F. | .57 | 3 | | 3.57 | 5.15 |
| 0140 | Second coat | " | 120 | .067 | " | .57 | 2.25 | | 2.82 | 4 |
| 0150 | Rough sawn wood, 42" high, 2" x 2" verticals, 6" O.C. | | | | | | | | | |
| 0160 | Brushwork, stain, each coat | 1 Pord | 90 | .089 | L.F. | .17 | 3 | | 3.17 | 4.70 |
| 0170 | Wrought iron, 1" rail, 1/2" sq. verticals | | | | | | | | | |
| 0180 | Brushwork, zinc chromate, 60" high, bars 6" O.C. | | | | | | | | | |
| 0190 | Primer | 1 Pord | 130 | .062 | L.F. | .52 | 2.08 | | 2.60 | 3.69 |
| 0200 | Finish coat | | 130 | .062 | | .16 | 2.08 | | 2.24 | 3.30 |
| 0210 | Additional coat | ↓ | 190 | .042 | ↓ | .19 | 1.42 | | 1.61 | 2.35 |
| 0220 | Shutters or blinds, single panel, 2' x 4', paint all sides | | | | | | | | | |
| 0230 | Brushwork, primer | 1 Pord | 20 | .400 | Ea. | .57 | 13.50 | | 14.07 | 21 |
| 0240 | Finish coat, exterior latex | | 20 | .400 | | .49 | 13.50 | | 13.99 | 21 |
| 0250 | Primer & 1 coat, exterior latex | | 13 | .615 | | .94 | 21 | | 21.94 | 32 |
| 0260 | Spray, primer | | 35 | .229 | | .83 | 7.70 | | 8.53 | 12.50 |
| 0270 | Finish coat, exterior latex | | 35 | .229 | | 1.05 | 7.70 | | 8.75 | 12.75 |
| 0280 | Primer & 1 coat, exterior latex | ↓ | 20 | .400 | ↓ | .90 | 13.50 | | 14.40 | 21.50 |
| 0290 | For louvered shutters, add | | | | S.F. | 10% | | | | |
| 0300 | Stair stringers, exterior, metal | | | | | | | | | |
| 0310 | Roll & brush, zinc chromate, to 14", each coat | 1 Pord | 320 | .025 | L.F. | .05 | .84 | | .89 | 1.33 |
| 0320 | Rough sawn wood, 4" x 12" | | | | | | | | | |
| 0330 | Roll & brush, exterior latex, each coat | 1 Pord | 215 | .037 | L.F. | .07 | 1.26 | | 1.33 | 1.97 |
| 0340 | Trellis/lattice, 2" x 2" @ 3" O.C. with 2" x 8" supports | | | | | | | | | |
| 0350 | Spray, latex, per side, each coat | 1 Pord | 475 | .017 | S.F. | .07 | .57 | | .64 | .93 |
| 0450 | Decking, ext., sealer, alkyd, brushwork, sealer coat | | 1140 | .007 | | .08 | .24 | | .32 | .45 |
| 0460 | 1st coat | | 1140 | .007 | | .07 | .24 | | .31 | .43 |
| 0470 | 2nd coat | | 1300 | .006 | | .05 | .21 | | .26 | .36 |
| 0500 | Paint, alkyd, brushwork, primer coat | | 1140 | .007 | | .07 | .24 | | .31 | .43 |
| 0510 | 1st coat | | 1140 | .007 | | .07 | .24 | | .31 | .44 |
| 0520 | 2nd coat | | 1300 | .006 | | .05 | .21 | | .26 | .37 |
| 0600 | Sand paint, alkyd, brushwork, 1 coat | ↓ | 150 | .053 | ↓ | .09 | 1.80 | | 1.89 | 2.80 |

### 09 91 13.60 Siding Exterior

| | | Crew | Daily Output | Labor-Hours | Unit | Material | 2008 Bare Costs Labor | 2008 Bare Costs Equipment | Total | Total Incl O&P |
|---|---|---|---|---|---|---|---|---|---|---|
| 0010 | **SIDING EXTERIOR**, Alkyd (oil base) R099100-10 | | | | | | | | | |
| 0450 | Steel siding, oil base, paint 1 coat, brushwork | 2 Pord | 2015 | .008 | S.F. | .06 | .27 | | .33 | .46 |
| 0500 | Spray R099100-20 | | 4550 | .004 | | .09 | .12 | | .21 | .27 |
| 0800 | Paint 2 coats, brushwork | | 1300 | .012 | | .11 | .42 | | .53 | .74 |
| 1000 | Spray | | 2750 | .006 | | .15 | .20 | | .35 | .47 |
| 1200 | Stucco, rough, oil base, paint 2 coats, brushwork | | 1300 | .012 | | .11 | .42 | | .53 | .74 |
| 1400 | Roller | | 1625 | .010 | | .12 | .33 | | .45 | .63 |
| 1600 | Spray | | 2925 | .005 | | .13 | .18 | | .31 | .42 |
| 1800 | Texture 1-11 or clapboard, oil base, primer coat, brushwork | | 1300 | .012 | | .09 | .42 | | .51 | .72 |
| 2000 | Spray | | 4550 | .004 | | .09 | .12 | | .21 | .28 |
| 2400 | Paint 2 coats, brushwork | | 810 | .020 | | .16 | .67 | | .83 | 1.18 |
| 2600 | Spray | | 2600 | .006 | | .18 | .21 | | .39 | .51 |
| 3400 | Stain 2 coats, brushwork | | 950 | .017 | | .12 | .57 | | .69 | .98 |
| 4000 | Spray | | 3050 | .005 | | .13 | .18 | | .31 | .41 |
| 4200 | Wood shingles, oil base primer coat, brushwork | | 1300 | .012 | | .08 | .42 | | .50 | .71 |
| 4400 | Spray | | 3900 | .004 | | .08 | .14 | | .22 | .29 |
| 5000 | Paint 2 coats, brushwork | | 810 | .020 | | .14 | .67 | | .81 | 1.15 |
| 5200 | Spray | ↓ | 2275 | .007 | ↓ | .13 | .24 | | .37 | .50 |

# 09 91 Painting

## 09 91 13 – Exterior Painting

### 09 91 13.60 Siding Exterior

| | | Crew | Daily Output | Labor-Hours | Unit | Material | 2008 Bare Costs Labor | Equipment | Total | Total Incl O&P |
|---|---|---|---|---|---|---|---|---|---|---|
| 6500 | Stain 2 coats, brushwork | 2 Pord | 950 | .017 | S.F. | .12 | .57 | | .69 | .98 |
| 7000 | Spray | ↓ | 2660 | .006 | | .16 | .20 | | .36 | .48 |
| 8000 | For latex paint, deduct | | | | | 10% | | | | |
| 8100 | For work over 12' H, from pipe scaffolding, add | | | | | | 15% | | | |
| 8200 | For work over 12' H, from extension ladder, add | | | | | | 25% | | | |
| 8300 | For work over 12' H, from swing staging, add | | | | | | 35% | | | |

### 09 91 13.62 Siding, Misc.

| | | Crew | Daily Output | Labor-Hours | Unit | Material | 2008 Bare Costs Labor | Equipment | Total | Total Incl O&P |
|---|---|---|---|---|---|---|---|---|---|---|
| 0010 | **SIDING, MISC.,** latex paint    R099100-10 | | | | | | | | | |
| 0100 | Aluminum siding | | | | | | | | | |
| 0110 | Brushwork, primer    R099100-20 | 2 Pord | 2275 | .007 | S.F. | .05 | .24 | | .29 | .42 |
| 0120 | Finish coat, exterior latex | | 2275 | .007 | | .04 | .24 | | .28 | .41 |
| 0130 | Primer & 1 coat exterior latex | | 1300 | .012 | | .10 | .42 | | .52 | .73 |
| 0140 | Primer & 2 coats exterior latex | ↓ | 975 | .016 | ↓ | .15 | .55 | | .70 | .99 |
| 0150 | Mineral Fiber shingles | | | | | | | | | |
| 0160 | Brushwork, primer | 2 Pord | 1495 | .011 | S.F. | .09 | .36 | | .45 | .64 |
| 0170 | Finish coat, industrial enamel | | 1495 | .011 | | .11 | .36 | | .47 | .67 |
| 0180 | Primer & 1 coat enamel | | 810 | .020 | | .20 | .67 | | .87 | 1.22 |
| 0190 | Primer & 2 coats enamel | | 540 | .030 | | .32 | 1 | | 1.32 | 1.85 |
| 0200 | Roll, primer | | 1625 | .010 | | .10 | .33 | | .43 | .61 |
| 0210 | Finish coat, industrial enamel | | 1625 | .010 | | .12 | .33 | | .45 | .64 |
| 0220 | Primer & 1 coat enamel | | 975 | .016 | | .22 | .55 | | .77 | 1.07 |
| 0230 | Primer & 2 coats enamel | | 650 | .025 | | .34 | .83 | | 1.17 | 1.63 |
| 0240 | Spray, primer | | 3900 | .004 | | .08 | .14 | | .22 | .29 |
| 0250 | Finish coat, industrial enamel | | 3900 | .004 | | .10 | .14 | | .24 | .32 |
| 0260 | Primer & 1 coat enamel | | 2275 | .007 | | .18 | .24 | | .42 | .56 |
| 0270 | Primer & 2 coats enamel | | 1625 | .010 | | .28 | .33 | | .61 | .81 |
| 0280 | Waterproof sealer, first coat | | 4485 | .004 | | .07 | .12 | | .19 | .26 |
| 0290 | Second coat | ↓ | 5235 | .003 | ↓ | .07 | .10 | | .17 | .23 |
| 0300 | Rough wood incl. shingles, shakes or rough sawn siding | | | | | | | | | |
| 0310 | Brushwork, primer | 2 Pord | 1280 | .013 | S.F. | .12 | .42 | | .54 | .76 |
| 0320 | Finish coat, exterior latex | | 1280 | .013 | | .08 | .42 | | .50 | .72 |
| 0330 | Primer & 1 coat exterior latex | | 960 | .017 | | .19 | .56 | | .75 | 1.06 |
| 0340 | Primer & 2 coats exterior latex | | 700 | .023 | | .27 | .77 | | 1.04 | 1.46 |
| 0350 | Roll, primer | | 2925 | .005 | | .15 | .18 | | .33 | .45 |
| 0360 | Finish coat, exterior latex | | 2925 | .005 | | .09 | .18 | | .27 | .38 |
| 0370 | Primer & 1 coat exterior latex | | 1790 | .009 | | .25 | .30 | | .55 | .72 |
| 0380 | Primer & 2 coats exterior latex | | 1300 | .012 | | .34 | .42 | | .76 | .99 |
| 0390 | Spray, primer | | 3900 | .004 | | .13 | .14 | | .27 | .35 |
| 0400 | Finish coat, exterior latex | | 3900 | .004 | | .07 | .14 | | .21 | .29 |
| 0410 | Primer & 1 coat exterior latex | | 2600 | .006 | | .20 | .21 | | .41 | .53 |
| 0420 | Primer & 2 coats exterior latex | | 2080 | .008 | | .27 | .26 | | .53 | .69 |
| 0430 | Waterproof sealer, first coat | | 4485 | .004 | | .12 | .12 | | .24 | .32 |
| 0440 | Second coat | ↓ | 4485 | .004 | ↓ | .07 | .12 | | .19 | .26 |
| 0450 | Smooth wood incl. butt, T&G, beveled, drop or B&B siding | | | | | | | | | |
| 0460 | Brushwork, primer | 2 Pord | 2325 | .007 | S.F. | .08 | .23 | | .31 | .44 |
| 0470 | Finish coat, exterior latex | | 1280 | .013 | | .08 | .42 | | .50 | .72 |
| 0480 | Primer & 1 coat exterior latex | | 800 | .020 | | .16 | .68 | | .84 | 1.19 |
| 0490 | Primer & 2 coats exterior latex | | 630 | .025 | | .24 | .86 | | 1.10 | 1.55 |
| 0500 | Roll, primer | | 2275 | .007 | | .09 | .24 | | .33 | .46 |
| 0510 | Finish coat, exterior latex | | 2275 | .007 | | .08 | .24 | | .32 | .45 |
| 0520 | Primer & 1 coat exterior latex | | 1300 | .012 | | .18 | .42 | | .60 | .81 |
| 0530 | Primer & 2 coats exterior latex | ↓ | 975 | .016 | ↓ | .26 | .55 | | .81 | 1.12 |

# 09 91 Painting

## 09 91 13 – Exterior Painting

### 09 91 13.62 Siding, Misc.

| | | Crew | Daily Output | Labor-Hours | Unit | Material | 2008 Bare Costs Labor | Equipment | Total | Total Incl O&P |
|---|---|---|---|---|---|---|---|---|---|---|
| 0540 | Spray, primer | 2 Pord | 4550 | .004 | S.F. | .07 | .12 | | .19 | .26 |
| 0550 | Finish coat, exterior latex | | 4550 | .004 | | .07 | .12 | | .19 | .26 |
| 0560 | Primer & 1 coat exterior latex | | 2600 | .006 | | .14 | .21 | | .35 | .47 |
| 0570 | Primer & 2 coats exterior latex | | 1950 | .008 | | .22 | .28 | | .50 | .66 |
| 0580 | Waterproof sealer, first coat | | 5230 | .003 | | .07 | .10 | | .17 | .24 |
| 0590 | Second coat | ↓ | 5980 | .003 | | .07 | .09 | | .16 | .22 |
| 0600 | For oil base paint, add | | | | ↓ | 10% | | | | |

### 09 91 13.70 Doors and Windows, Exterior

| | | Crew | Daily Output | Labor-Hours | Unit | Material | 2008 Bare Costs Labor | Equipment | Total | Total Incl O&P |
|---|---|---|---|---|---|---|---|---|---|---|
| 0010 | **DOORS AND WINDOWS, EXTERIOR**  R099100-10 | | | | | | | | | |
| 0100 | Door frames & trim, only | | | | | | | | | |
| 0110 | Brushwork, primer  R099100-20 | 1 Pord | 512 | .016 | L.F. | .05 | .53 | | .58 | .85 |
| 0120 | Finish coat, exterior latex | | 512 | .016 | | .06 | .53 | | .59 | .86 |
| 0130 | Primer & 1 coat, exterior latex | | 300 | .027 | | .11 | .90 | | 1.01 | 1.47 |
| 0140 | Primer & 2 coats, exterior latex | ↓ | 265 | .030 | ↓ | .17 | 1.02 | | 1.19 | 1.72 |
| 0150 | Doors, flush, both sides, incl. frame & trim | | | | | | | | | |
| 0160 | Roll & brush, primer | 1 Pord | 10 | .800 | Ea. | 3.94 | 27 | | 30.94 | 45 |
| 0170 | Finish coat, exterior latex | | 10 | .800 | | 4.68 | 27 | | 31.68 | 45.50 |
| 0180 | Primer & 1 coat, exterior latex | | 7 | 1.143 | | 8.60 | 38.50 | | 47.10 | 67.50 |
| 0190 | Primer & 2 coats, exterior latex | | 5 | 1.600 | | 13.30 | 54 | | 67.30 | 95.50 |
| 0200 | Brushwork, stain, sealer & 2 coats polyurethane | ↓ | 4 | 2 | ↓ | 19.60 | 67.50 | | 87.10 | 123 |
| 0210 | Doors, French, both sides, 10-15 lite, incl. frame & trim | | | | | | | | | |
| 0220 | Brushwork, primer | 1 Pord | 6 | 1.333 | Ea. | 1.97 | 45 | | 46.97 | 69.50 |
| 0230 | Finish coat, exterior latex | | 6 | 1.333 | | 2.34 | 45 | | 47.34 | 70 |
| 0240 | Primer & 1 coat, exterior latex | | 3 | 2.667 | | 4.31 | 90 | | 94.31 | 140 |
| 0250 | Primer & 2 coats, exterior latex | | 2 | 4 | | 6.50 | 135 | | 141.50 | 210 |
| 0260 | Brushwork, stain, sealer & 2 coats polyurethane | ↓ | 2.50 | 3.200 | ↓ | 7.20 | 108 | | 115.20 | 170 |
| 0270 | Doors, louvered, both sides, incl. frame & trim | | | | | | | | | |
| 0280 | Brushwork, primer | 1 Pord | 7 | 1.143 | Ea. | 3.94 | 38.50 | | 42.44 | 62.50 |
| 0290 | Finish coat, exterior latex | | 7 | 1.143 | | 4.68 | 38.50 | | 43.18 | 63 |
| 0300 | Primer & 1 coat, exterior latex | | 4 | 2 | | 8.60 | 67.50 | | 76.10 | 111 |
| 0310 | Primer & 2 coats, exterior latex | | 3 | 2.667 | | 13.05 | 90 | | 103.05 | 149 |
| 0320 | Brushwork, stain, sealer & 2 coats polyurethane | ↓ | 4.50 | 1.778 | ↓ | 19.60 | 60 | | 79.60 | 112 |
| 0330 | Doors, panel, both sides, incl. frame & trim | | | | | | | | | |
| 0340 | Roll & brush, primer | 1 Pord | 6 | 1.333 | Ea. | 3.94 | 45 | | 48.94 | 72 |
| 0350 | Finish coat, exterior latex | | 6 | 1.333 | | 4.68 | 45 | | 49.68 | 72.50 |
| 0360 | Primer & 1 coat, exterior latex | | 3 | 2.667 | | 8.60 | 90 | | 98.60 | 145 |
| 0370 | Primer & 2 coats, exterior latex | | 2.50 | 3.200 | | 13.05 | 108 | | 121.05 | 176 |
| 0380 | Brushwork, stain, sealer & 2 coats polyurethane | ↓ | 3 | 2.667 | ↓ | 19.60 | 90 | | 109.60 | 157 |
| 0400 | Windows, per ext. side, based on 15 SF | | | | | | | | | |
| 0410 | 1 to 6 lite | | | | | | | | | |
| 0420 | Brushwork, primer | 1 Pord | 13 | .615 | Ea. | .78 | 21 | | 21.78 | 32 |
| 0430 | Finish coat, exterior latex | | 13 | .615 | | .92 | 21 | | 21.92 | 32 |
| 0440 | Primer & 1 coat, exterior latex | | 8 | 1 | | 1.70 | 34 | | 35.70 | 52.50 |
| 0450 | Primer & 2 coats, exterior latex | | 6 | 1.333 | | 2.57 | 45 | | 47.57 | 70.50 |
| 0460 | Stain, sealer & 1 coat varnish | ↓ | 7 | 1.143 | ↓ | 2.84 | 38.50 | | 41.34 | 61 |
| 0470 | 7 to 10 lite | | | | | | | | | |
| 0480 | Brushwork, primer | 1 Pord | 11 | .727 | Ea. | .78 | 24.50 | | 25.28 | 38 |
| 0490 | Finish coat, exterior latex | | 11 | .727 | | .92 | 24.50 | | 25.42 | 38 |
| 0500 | Primer & 1 coat, exterior latex | | 7 | 1.143 | | 1.70 | 38.50 | | 40.20 | 60 |
| 0510 | Primer & 2 coats, exterior latex | | 5 | 1.600 | | 2.57 | 54 | | 56.57 | 84 |
| 0520 | Stain, sealer & 1 coat varnish | ↓ | 6 | 1.333 | ↓ | 2.84 | 45 | | 47.84 | 70.50 |
| 0530 | 12 lite | | | | | | | | | |

# 09 91 Painting

## 09 91 13 – Exterior Painting

### 09 91 13.70 Doors and Windows, Exterior

| | | Crew | Daily Output | Labor-Hours | Unit | Material | 2008 Bare Costs Labor | Equipment | Total | Total Incl O&P |
|---|---|---|---|---|---|---|---|---|---|---|
| 0540 | Brushwork, primer | 1 Pord | 10 | .800 | Ea. | .78 | 27 | | 27.78 | 41.50 |
| 0550 | Finish coat, exterior latex | | 10 | .800 | | .92 | 27 | | 27.92 | 41.50 |
| 0560 | Primer & 1 coat, exterior latex | | 6 | 1.333 | | 1.70 | 45 | | 46.70 | 69.50 |
| 0570 | Primer & 2 coats, exterior latex | | 5 | 1.600 | | 2.57 | 54 | | 56.57 | 84 |
| 0580 | Stain, sealer & 1 coat varnish | | 6 | 1.333 | | 2.80 | 45 | | 47.80 | 70.50 |
| 0590 | For oil base paint, add | | | | | 10% | | | | |

### 09 91 13.80 Trim, Exterior

| | | Crew | Daily Output | Labor-Hours | Unit | Material | 2008 Bare Costs Labor | Equipment | Total | Total Incl O&P |
|---|---|---|---|---|---|---|---|---|---|---|
| 0010 | **TRIM, EXTERIOR** R099100-10 | | | | | | | | | |
| 0100 | Door frames & trim (see Doors, interior or exterior) | | | | | | | | | |
| 0110 | Fascia, latex paint, one coat coverage R099100-20 | | | | | | | | | |
| 0120 | 1" x 4", brushwork | 1 Pord | 640 | .013 | L.F. | .02 | .42 | | .44 | .65 |
| 0130 | Roll | | 1280 | .006 | | .02 | .21 | | .23 | .34 |
| 0140 | Spray | | 2080 | .004 | | .02 | .13 | | .15 | .22 |
| 0150 | 1" x 6" to 1" x 10", brushwork | | 640 | .013 | | .07 | .42 | | .49 | .70 |
| 0160 | Roll | | 1230 | .007 | | .07 | .22 | | .29 | .41 |
| 0170 | Spray | | 2100 | .004 | | .05 | .13 | | .18 | .25 |
| 0180 | 1" x 12", brushwork | | 640 | .013 | | .07 | .42 | | .49 | .70 |
| 0190 | Roll | | 1050 | .008 | | .07 | .26 | | .33 | .47 |
| 0200 | Spray | | 2200 | .004 | | .05 | .12 | | .17 | .24 |
| 0210 | Gutters & downspouts, metal, zinc chromate paint | | | | | | | | | |
| 0220 | Brushwork, gutters, 5", first coat | 1 Pord | 640 | .013 | L.F. | .06 | .42 | | .48 | .69 |
| 0230 | Second coat | | 960 | .008 | | .05 | .28 | | .33 | .48 |
| 0240 | Third coat | | 1280 | .006 | | .04 | .21 | | .25 | .37 |
| 0250 | Downspouts, 4", first coat | | 640 | .013 | | .06 | .42 | | .48 | .69 |
| 0260 | Second coat | | 960 | .008 | | .05 | .28 | | .33 | .48 |
| 0270 | Third coat | | 1280 | .006 | | .04 | .21 | | .25 | .37 |
| 0280 | Gutters & downspouts, wood | | | | | | | | | |
| 0290 | Brushwork, gutters, 5", primer | 1 Pord | 640 | .013 | L.F. | .05 | .42 | | .47 | .69 |
| 0300 | Finish coat, exterior latex | | 640 | .013 | | .06 | .42 | | .48 | .69 |
| 0310 | Primer & 1 coat exterior latex | | 400 | .020 | | .11 | .68 | | .79 | 1.13 |
| 0320 | Primer & 2 coats exterior latex | | 325 | .025 | | .17 | .83 | | 1 | 1.44 |
| 0330 | Downspouts, 4", primer | | 640 | .013 | | .05 | .42 | | .47 | .69 |
| 0340 | Finish coat, exterior latex | | 640 | .013 | | .06 | .42 | | .48 | .69 |
| 0350 | Primer & 1 coat exterior latex | | 400 | .020 | | .11 | .68 | | .79 | 1.13 |
| 0360 | Primer & 2 coats exterior latex | | 325 | .025 | | .09 | .83 | | .92 | 1.35 |
| 0370 | Molding, exterior, up to 14" wide | | | | | | | | | |
| 0380 | Brushwork, primer | 1 Pord | 640 | .013 | L.F. | .06 | .42 | | .48 | .70 |
| 0390 | Finish coat, exterior latex | | 640 | .013 | | .07 | .42 | | .49 | .70 |
| 0400 | Primer & 1 coat exterior latex | | 400 | .020 | | .14 | .68 | | .82 | 1.16 |
| 0410 | Primer & 2 coats exterior latex | | 315 | .025 | | .14 | .86 | | 1 | 1.44 |
| 0420 | Stain & fill | | 1050 | .008 | | .07 | .26 | | .33 | .47 |
| 0430 | Shellac | | 1850 | .004 | | .08 | .15 | | .23 | .30 |
| 0440 | Varnish | | 1275 | .006 | | .08 | .21 | | .29 | .41 |

### 09 91 13.90 Walls, Masonry (CMU), Exterior

| | | Crew | Daily Output | Labor-Hours | Unit | Material | 2008 Bare Costs Labor | Equipment | Total | Total Incl O&P |
|---|---|---|---|---|---|---|---|---|---|---|
| 0350 | **WALLS, MASONRY (CMU), EXTERIOR** R099100-10 | | | | | | | | | |
| 0360 | Concrete masonry units (CMU), smooth surface | | | | | | | | | |
| 0370 | Brushwork, latex, first coat | 1 Pord | 640 | .013 | S.F. | .05 | .42 | | .47 | .69 |
| 0380 | Second coat | | 960 | .008 | | .04 | .28 | | .32 | .47 |
| 0390 | Waterproof sealer, first coat | | 736 | .011 | | .21 | .37 | | .58 | .78 |
| 0400 | Second coat | | 1104 | .007 | | .21 | .24 | | .45 | .60 |
| 0410 | Roll, latex, paint, first coat | | 1465 | .005 | | .06 | .18 | | .24 | .35 |
| 0420 | Second coat | | 1790 | .004 | | .05 | .15 | | .20 | .28 |

# 09 91 Painting

## 09 91 13 – Exterior Painting

### 09 91 13.90 Walls, Masonry (CMU), Exterior

| | | Crew | Daily Output | Labor-Hours | Unit | Material | 2008 Bare Costs Labor | Equipment | Total | Total Incl O&P |
|---|---|---|---|---|---|---|---|---|---|---|
| 0430 | Waterproof sealer, first coat | 1 Pord | 1680 | .005 | S.F. | .21 | .16 | | .37 | .47 |
| 0440 | Second coat | | 2060 | .004 | | .21 | .13 | | .34 | .43 |
| 0450 | Spray, latex, paint, first coat | | 1950 | .004 | | .05 | .14 | | .19 | .27 |
| 0460 | Second coat | | 2600 | .003 | | .04 | .10 | | .14 | .20 |
| 0470 | Waterproof sealer, first coat | | 2245 | .004 | | .21 | .12 | | .33 | .41 |
| 0480 | Second coat | | 2990 | .003 | | .21 | .09 | | .30 | .37 |
| 0490 | Concrete masonry unit (CMU), porous | | | | | | | | | |
| 0500 | Brushwork, latex, first coat | 1 Pord | 640 | .013 | S.F. | .11 | .42 | | .53 | .75 |
| 0510 | Second coat | | 960 | .008 | | .05 | .28 | | .33 | .48 |
| 0520 | Waterproof sealer, first coat | | 736 | .011 | | .21 | .37 | | .58 | .78 |
| 0530 | Second coat | | 1104 | .007 | | .21 | .24 | | .45 | .60 |
| 0540 | Roll latex, first coat | | 1465 | .005 | | .08 | .18 | | .26 | .37 |
| 0550 | Second coat | | 1790 | .004 | | .05 | .15 | | .20 | .29 |
| 0560 | Waterproof sealer, first coat | | 1680 | .005 | | .21 | .16 | | .37 | .47 |
| 0570 | Second coat | | 2060 | .004 | | .21 | .13 | | .34 | .43 |
| 0580 | Spray latex, first coat | | 1950 | .004 | | .06 | .14 | | .20 | .27 |
| 0590 | Second coat | | 2600 | .003 | | .04 | .10 | | .14 | .20 |
| 0600 | Waterproof sealer, first coat | | 2245 | .004 | | .21 | .12 | | .33 | .41 |
| 0610 | Second coat | | 2990 | .003 | | .21 | .09 | | .30 | .37 |

## 09 91 23 – Interior Painting

### 09 91 23.20 Cabinets and Casework

| | | | Crew | Daily Output | Labor-Hours | Unit | Material | 2008 Bare Costs Labor | Equipment | Total | Total Incl O&P |
|---|---|---|---|---|---|---|---|---|---|---|---|
| 0010 | **CABINETS AND CASEWORK** | R099100-10 | | | | | | | | | |
| 1000 | Primer coat, oil base, brushwork | | 1 Pord | 650 | .012 | S.F. | .05 | .42 | | .47 | .68 |
| 2000 | Paint, oil base, brushwork, 1 coat | R099100-20 | | 650 | .012 | | .06 | .42 | | .48 | .69 |
| 3000 | Stain, brushwork, wipe off | | | 650 | .012 | | .06 | .42 | | .48 | .68 |
| 4000 | Shellac, 1 coat, brushwork | | | 650 | .012 | | .06 | .42 | | .48 | .69 |
| 4500 | Varnish, 3 coats, brushwork, sand after 1st coat | | | 325 | .025 | | .20 | .83 | | 1.03 | 1.47 |
| 5000 | For latex paint, deduct | | | | | | 10% | | | | |

### 09 91 23.33 Doors and Windows, Interior Alkyd (Oil Base)

| | | | Crew | Daily Output | Labor-Hours | Unit | Material | 2008 Bare Costs Labor | Equipment | Total | Total Incl O&P |
|---|---|---|---|---|---|---|---|---|---|---|---|
| 0010 | **DOORS AND WINDOWS, INTERIOR ALKYD (OIL BASE)** | R099100-10 | | | | | | | | | |
| 0500 | Flush door & frame, 3' x 7', oil, primer, brushwork | | 1 Pord | 10 | .800 | Ea. | 2.21 | 27 | | 29.21 | 43 |
| 1000 | Paint, 1 coat | R099100-20 | | 10 | .800 | | 2.26 | 27 | | 29.26 | 43 |
| 1400 | Stain, brushwork, wipe off | | | 18 | .444 | | 1.21 | 15 | | 16.21 | 24 |
| 1600 | Shellac, 1 coat, brushwork | | | 25 | .320 | | 1.33 | 10.80 | | 12.13 | 17.65 |
| 1800 | Varnish, 3 coats, brushwork, sand after 1st coat | | | 9 | .889 | | 4.19 | 30 | | 34.19 | 49.50 |
| 2000 | Panel door & frame, 3' x 7', oil, primer, brushwork | | | 6 | 1.333 | | 2.06 | 45 | | 47.06 | 70 |
| 2200 | Paint, 1 coat | | | 6 | 1.333 | | 2.26 | 45 | | 47.26 | 70 |
| 2600 | Stain, brushwork, panel door, 3' x 7', not incl. frame | | | 16 | .500 | | 1.21 | 16.90 | | 18.11 | 27 |
| 2800 | Shellac, 1 coat, brushwork | | | 22 | .364 | | 1.33 | 12.25 | | 13.58 | 19.90 |
| 3000 | Varnish, 3 coats, brushwork, sand after 1st coat | | | 7.50 | 1.067 | | 4.19 | 36 | | 40.19 | 58.50 |
| 4400 | Windows, including frame and trim, per side | | | | | | | | | | |
| 4600 | Colonial type, 6/6 lites, 2' x 3', oil, primer, brushwork | | 1 Pord | 14 | .571 | Ea. | .33 | 19.30 | | 19.63 | 29.50 |
| 5800 | Paint, 1 coat | | | 14 | .571 | | .36 | 19.30 | | 19.66 | 29.50 |
| 6200 | 3' x 5' opening, 6/6 lites, primer coat, brushwork | | | 12 | .667 | | .81 | 22.50 | | 23.31 | 35 |
| 6400 | Paint, 1 coat | | | 12 | .667 | | .89 | 22.50 | | 23.39 | 35 |
| 6800 | 4' x 8' opening, 6/6 lites, primer coat, brushwork | | | 8 | 1 | | 1.74 | 34 | | 35.74 | 52.50 |
| 7000 | Paint, 1 coat | | | 8 | 1 | | 1.90 | 34 | | 35.90 | 52.50 |
| 8000 | Single lite type, 2' x 3', oil base, primer coat, brushwork | | | 33 | .242 | | .33 | 8.20 | | 8.53 | 12.65 |
| 8200 | Paint, 1 coat | | | 33 | .242 | | .36 | 8.20 | | 8.56 | 12.70 |
| 8600 | 3' x 5' opening, primer coat, brushwork | | | 20 | .400 | | .81 | 13.50 | | 14.31 | 21.50 |
| 8800 | Paint, 1 coat | | | 20 | .400 | | .89 | 13.50 | | 14.39 | 21.50 |
| 9200 | 4' x 8' opening, primer coat, brushwork | | | 14 | .571 | | 1.74 | 19.30 | | 21.04 | 31 |

## 09 91 23.33 Doors and Windows, Interior Alkyd (Oil Base)

| | | Crew | Daily Output | Labor-Hours | Unit | Material | 2008 Bare Costs Labor | 2008 Bare Costs Equipment | Total | Total Incl O&P |
|---|---|---|---|---|---|---|---|---|---|---|
| 9400 | Paint, 1 coat | 1 Pord | 14 | .571 | Ea. | 1.90 | 19.30 | | 21.20 | 31 |

## 09 91 23.35 Doors and Windows, Interior Latex

| | | Crew | Daily Output | Labor-Hours | Unit | Material | 2008 Bare Costs Labor | 2008 Bare Costs Equipment | Total | Total Incl O&P |
|---|---|---|---|---|---|---|---|---|---|---|
| 0010 | **DOORS & WINDOWS, INTERIOR LATEX**  R099100-10 | | | | | | | | | |
| 0100 | Doors, flush, both sides, incl. frame & trim | | | | | | | | | |
| 0110 | Roll & brush, primer  R099100-20 | 1 Pord | 10 | .800 | Ea. | 3.72 | 27 | | 30.72 | 44.50 |
| 0120 | Finish coat, latex | | 10 | .800 | | 4.74 | 27 | | 31.74 | 45.50 |
| 0130 | Primer & 1 coat latex | | 7 | 1.143 | | 8.45 | 38.50 | | 46.95 | 67.50 |
| 0140 | Primer & 2 coats latex | | 5 | 1.600 | | 12.95 | 54 | | 66.95 | 95 |
| 0160 | Spray, both sides, primer | | 20 | .400 | | 3.92 | 13.50 | | 17.42 | 25 |
| 0170 | Finish coat, latex | | 20 | .400 | | 4.97 | 13.50 | | 18.47 | 26 |
| 0180 | Primer & 1 coat latex | | 11 | .727 | | 8.95 | 24.50 | | 33.45 | 47 |
| 0190 | Primer & 2 coats latex | | 8 | 1 | | 13.70 | 34 | | 47.70 | 65.50 |
| 0200 | Doors, French, both sides, 10-15 lite, incl. frame & trim | | | | | | | | | |
| 0210 | Roll & brush, primer | 1 Pord | 6 | 1.333 | Ea. | 1.86 | 45 | | 46.86 | 69.50 |
| 0220 | Finish coat, latex | | 6 | 1.333 | | 2.37 | 45 | | 47.37 | 70 |
| 0230 | Primer & 1 coat latex | | 3 | 2.667 | | 4.23 | 90 | | 94.23 | 140 |
| 0240 | Primer & 2 coats latex | | 2 | 4 | | 6.45 | 135 | | 141.45 | 210 |
| 0260 | Doors, louvered, both sides, incl. frame & trim | | | | | | | | | |
| 0270 | Roll & brush, primer | 1 Pord | 7 | 1.143 | Ea. | 3.72 | 38.50 | | 42.22 | 62 |
| 0280 | Finish coat, latex | | 7 | 1.143 | | 4.74 | 38.50 | | 43.24 | 63 |
| 0290 | Primer & 1 coat, latex | | 4 | 2 | | 8.25 | 67.50 | | 75.75 | 110 |
| 0300 | Primer & 2 coats, latex | | 3 | 2.667 | | 13.20 | 90 | | 103.20 | 150 |
| 0320 | Spray, both sides, primer | | 20 | .400 | | 3.92 | 13.50 | | 17.42 | 25 |
| 0330 | Finish coat, latex | | 20 | .400 | | 4.97 | 13.50 | | 18.47 | 26 |
| 0340 | Primer & 1 coat, latex | | 11 | .727 | | 8.95 | 24.50 | | 33.45 | 47 |
| 0350 | Primer & 2 coats, latex | | 8 | 1 | | 14 | 34 | | 48 | 66 |
| 0360 | Doors, panel, both sides, incl. frame & trim | | | | | | | | | |
| 0370 | Roll & brush, primer | 1 Pord | 6 | 1.333 | Ea. | 3.92 | 45 | | 48.92 | 72 |
| 0380 | Finish coat, latex | | 6 | 1.333 | | 4.74 | 45 | | 49.74 | 72.50 |
| 0390 | Primer & 1 coat, latex | | 3 | 2.667 | | 8.45 | 90 | | 98.45 | 144 |
| 0400 | Primer & 2 coats, latex | | 2.50 | 3.200 | | 13.20 | 108 | | 121.20 | 177 |
| 0420 | Spray, both sides, primer | | 10 | .800 | | 3.92 | 27 | | 30.92 | 45 |
| 0430 | Finish coat, latex | | 10 | .800 | | 4.97 | 27 | | 31.97 | 46 |
| 0440 | Primer & 1 coat, latex | | 5 | 1.600 | | 8.95 | 54 | | 62.95 | 91 |
| 0450 | Primer & 2 coats, latex | | 4 | 2 | | 14 | 67.50 | | 81.50 | 116 |
| 0460 | Windows, per interior side, based on 15 SF | | | | | | | | | |
| 0470 | 1 to 6 lite | | | | | | | | | |
| 0480 | Brushwork, primer | 1 Pord | 13 | .615 | Ea. | .73 | 21 | | 21.73 | 32 |
| 0490 | Finish coat, enamel | | 13 | .615 | | .94 | 21 | | 21.94 | 32 |
| 0500 | Primer & 1 coat enamel | | 8 | 1 | | 1.67 | 34 | | 35.67 | 52.50 |
| 0510 | Primer & 2 coats enamel | | 6 | 1.333 | | 2.61 | 45 | | 47.61 | 70.50 |
| 0530 | 7 to 10 lite | | | | | | | | | |
| 0540 | Brushwork, primer | 1 Pord | 11 | .727 | Ea. | .73 | 24.50 | | 25.23 | 38 |
| 0550 | Finish coat, enamel | | 11 | .727 | | .94 | 24.50 | | 25.44 | 38 |
| 0560 | Primer & 1 coat enamel | | 7 | 1.143 | | 1.67 | 38.50 | | 40.17 | 60 |
| 0570 | Primer & 2 coats enamel | | 5 | 1.600 | | 2.61 | 54 | | 56.61 | 84 |
| 0590 | 12 lite | | | | | | | | | |
| 0600 | Brushwork, primer | 1 Pord | 10 | .800 | Ea. | .73 | 27 | | 27.73 | 41.50 |
| 0610 | Finish coat, enamel | | 10 | .800 | | .94 | 27 | | 27.94 | 41.50 |
| 0620 | Primer & 1 coat enamel | | 6 | 1.333 | | 1.67 | 45 | | 46.67 | 69.50 |
| 0630 | Primer & 2 coats enamel | | 5 | 1.600 | | 2.61 | 54 | | 56.61 | 84 |
| 0650 | For oil base paint, add | | | | | 10% | | | | |

## 09 91 23 – Interior Painting

| 09 91 23.40 Floors, Interior | | Crew | Daily Output | Labor-Hours | Unit | Material | 2008 Bare Costs Labor | Equipment | Total | Total Incl O&P |
|---|---|---|---|---|---|---|---|---|---|---|
| 0010 | **FLOORS, INTERIOR** R099100-10 | | | | | | | | | |
| 0100 | Concrete paint | | | | | | | | | |
| 0110 | Brushwork, latex, block filler | | | | | | | | | |
| 0120 | 1st coat | 1 Pord | 975 | .008 | S.F. | .13 | .28 | | .41 | .57 |
| 0130 | 2nd coat | | 1150 | .007 | | .09 | .23 | | .32 | .45 |
| 0140 | 3rd coat | | 1300 | .006 | | .07 | .21 | | .28 | .39 |
| 0150 | Roll, latex, block filler | | | | | | | | | |
| 0160 | 1st coat | 1 Pord | 2600 | .003 | S.F. | .18 | .10 | | .28 | .35 |
| 0170 | 2nd coat | | 3250 | .002 | | .11 | .08 | | .19 | .24 |
| 0180 | 3rd coat | | 3900 | .002 | | .08 | .07 | | .15 | .19 |
| 0190 | Spray, latex, block filler | | | | | | | | | |
| 0200 | 1st coat | 1 Pord | 2600 | .003 | S.F. | .15 | .10 | | .25 | .33 |
| 0210 | 2nd coat | | 3250 | .002 | | .08 | .08 | | .16 | .21 |
| 0220 | 3rd coat | | 3900 | .002 | | .07 | .07 | | .14 | .17 |
| 0300 | Acid stain and sealer | | | | | | | | | |
| 0310 | Stain, one coat | 1 Pord | 650 | .012 | S.F. | .11 | .42 | | .53 | .74 |
| 0320 | Two coats | | 570 | .014 | | .22 | .47 | | .69 | .95 |
| 0330 | Acrylic sealer, one coat | | 2600 | .003 | | .15 | .10 | | .25 | .33 |
| 0340 | Two coats | | 1400 | .006 | | .30 | .19 | | .49 | .62 |

### 09 91 23.52 Miscellaneous, Interior

| | | Crew | Daily Output | Labor-Hours | Unit | Material | Labor | Equipment | Total | Total Incl O&P |
|---|---|---|---|---|---|---|---|---|---|---|
| 0010 | **MISCELLANEOUS, INTERIOR** R099100-10 | | | | | | | | | |
| 2400 | Floors, conc./wood, oil base, primer/sealer coat, brushwork | 2 Pord | 1950 | .008 | S.F. | .05 | .28 | | .33 | .48 |
| 2450 | Roller | | 5200 | .003 | | .06 | .10 | | .16 | .22 |
| 2600 | Spray | | 6000 | .003 | | .06 | .09 | | .15 | .20 |
| 2650 | Paint 1 coat, brushwork | | 1950 | .008 | | .07 | .28 | | .35 | .50 |
| 2800 | Roller | | 5200 | .003 | | .08 | .10 | | .18 | .25 |
| 2850 | Spray | | 6000 | .003 | | .08 | .09 | | .17 | .23 |
| 3000 | Stain, wood floor, brushwork, 1 coat | | 4550 | .004 | | .06 | .12 | | .18 | .24 |
| 3200 | Roller | | 5200 | .003 | | .06 | .10 | | .16 | .23 |
| 3250 | Spray | | 6000 | .003 | | .06 | .09 | | .15 | .21 |
| 3400 | Varnish, wood floor, brushwork | | 4550 | .004 | | .07 | .12 | | .19 | .25 |
| 3450 | Roller | | 5200 | .003 | | .07 | .10 | | .17 | .24 |
| 3600 | Spray | | 6000 | .003 | | .07 | .09 | | .16 | .22 |
| 3650 | For dust proofing or anti skid, see Div. 03 35 29.30 | | | | | | | | | |
| 3800 | Grilles, per side, oil base, primer coat, brushwork | 1 Pord | 520 | .015 | S.F. | .11 | .52 | | .63 | .90 |
| 3850 | Spray | | 1140 | .007 | | .11 | .24 | | .35 | .48 |
| 3920 | Paint 2 coats, brushwork | | 325 | .025 | | .23 | .83 | | 1.06 | 1.50 |
| 3940 | Spray | | 650 | .012 | | .26 | .42 | | .68 | .91 |
| 5000 | Pipe, thru 4" diameter, primer or sealer coat, oil base, brushwork | 2 Pord | 1250 | .013 | L.F. | .06 | .43 | | .49 | .71 |
| 5100 | Spray | | 2165 | .007 | | .05 | .25 | | .30 | .43 |
| 5350 | Paint 2 coats, brushwork | | 775 | .021 | | .11 | .70 | | .81 | 1.17 |
| 5400 | Spray | | 1240 | .013 | | .12 | .44 | | .56 | .78 |
| 6300 | Thru 16" diameter, primer or sealer coat, brushwork | | 310 | .052 | | .23 | 1.74 | | 1.97 | 2.87 |
| 6350 | Spray | | 540 | .030 | | .26 | 1 | | 1.26 | 1.78 |
| 6500 | Paint 2 coats, brushwork | | 195 | .082 | | .44 | 2.77 | | 3.21 | 4.64 |
| 6550 | Spray | | 310 | .052 | | .49 | 1.74 | | 2.23 | 3.15 |
| 7000 | Trim, wood, incl. puttying, under 6" wide | | | | | | | | | |
| 7200 | Primer coat, oil base, brushwork | 1 Pord | 650 | .012 | L.F. | .03 | .42 | | .45 | .65 |
| 7250 | Paint, 1 coat, brushwork | | 650 | .012 | | .03 | .42 | | .45 | .65 |
| 7450 | 3 coats | | 325 | .025 | | .09 | .83 | | .92 | 1.34 |
| 7500 | Over 6" wide, primer coat, brushwork | | 650 | .012 | | .05 | .42 | | .47 | .68 |
| 7550 | Paint, 1 coat, brushwork | | 650 | .012 | | .06 | .42 | | .48 | .69 |

# 09 91 Painting

## 09 91 23 – Interior Painting

### 09 91 23.52 Miscellaneous, Interior

| | | Crew | Daily Output | Labor-Hours | Unit | Material | 2008 Bare Costs Labor | 2008 Bare Costs Equipment | Total | Total Incl O&P |
|---|---|---|---|---|---|---|---|---|---|---|
| 7650 | 3 coats | 1 Pord | 325 | .025 | L.F. | .17 | .83 | | 1 | 1.44 |
| 8000 | Cornice, simple design, primer coat, oil base, brushwork | | 650 | .012 | S.F. | .05 | .42 | | .47 | .68 |
| 8250 | Paint, 1 coat | | 650 | .012 | | .06 | .42 | | .48 | .69 |
| 8350 | Ornate design, primer coat | | 350 | .023 | | .05 | .77 | | .82 | 1.22 |
| 8400 | Paint, 1 coat | | 350 | .023 | | .06 | .77 | | .83 | 1.23 |
| 8600 | Balustrades, primer coat, oil base, brushwork | | 520 | .015 | | .05 | .52 | | .57 | .84 |
| 8650 | Paint, 1 coat | | 520 | .015 | | .06 | .52 | | .58 | .85 |
| 8900 | Trusses and wood frames, primer coat, oil base, brushwork | | 800 | .010 | | .05 | .34 | | .39 | .57 |
| 8950 | Spray | | 1200 | .007 | | .06 | .23 | | .29 | .40 |
| 9220 | Paint 2 coats, brushwork | | 500 | .016 | | .12 | .54 | | .66 | .94 |
| 9240 | Spray | | 600 | .013 | | .13 | .45 | | .58 | .82 |
| 9260 | Stain, brushwork, wipe off | | 600 | .013 | | .06 | .45 | | .51 | .74 |
| 9280 | Varnish, 3 coats, brushwork | ↓ | 275 | .029 | | .20 | .98 | | 1.18 | 1.69 |
| 9350 | For latex paint, deduct | | | | ↓ | 10% | | | | |

### 09 91 23.72 Walls and Ceilings, Interior

| | | Crew | Daily Output | Labor-Hours | Unit | Material | 2008 Bare Costs Labor | 2008 Bare Costs Equipment | Total | Total Incl O&P |
|---|---|---|---|---|---|---|---|---|---|---|
| 0010 | **WALLS AND CEILINGS, INTERIOR** R099100-10 | | | | | | | | | |
| 0100 | Concrete, drywall or plaster, oil base, primer or sealer coat R099100-20 | | | | | | | | | |
| 0200 | Smooth finish, brushwork | 1 Pord | 1150 | .007 | S.F. | .05 | .23 | | .28 | .41 |
| 0240 | Roller | | 1350 | .006 | | .05 | .20 | | .25 | .36 |
| 0280 | Spray | | 2750 | .003 | | .04 | .10 | | .14 | .19 |
| 0300 | Sand finish, brushwork | | 975 | .008 | | .05 | .28 | | .33 | .48 |
| 0340 | Roller | | 1150 | .007 | | .06 | .23 | | .29 | .41 |
| 0380 | Spray | | 2275 | .004 | | .04 | .12 | | .16 | .23 |
| 0800 | Paint 2 coats, smooth finish, brushwork | | 680 | .012 | | .12 | .40 | | .52 | .74 |
| 0840 | Roller | | 800 | .010 | | .13 | .34 | | .47 | .65 |
| 0880 | Spray | | 1625 | .005 | | .11 | .17 | | .28 | .37 |
| 0900 | Sand finish, brushwork | | 605 | .013 | | .12 | .45 | | .57 | .80 |
| 0940 | Roller | | 1020 | .008 | | .13 | .26 | | .39 | .54 |
| 0980 | Spray | | 1700 | .005 | | .11 | .16 | | .27 | .36 |
| 1200 | Paint 3 coats, smooth finish, brushwork | | 510 | .016 | | .18 | .53 | | .71 | 1 |
| 1240 | Roller | | 650 | .012 | | .19 | .42 | | .61 | .83 |
| 1280 | Spray | | 1625 | .005 | | .16 | .17 | | .33 | .43 |
| 1600 | Glaze coating, 2 coats, spray, clear | | 1200 | .007 | | .42 | .23 | | .65 | .80 |
| 1640 | Multicolor | ↓ | 1200 | .007 | | .87 | .23 | | 1.10 | 1.29 |
| 1700 | For latex paint, deduct | | | | ↓ | 10% | | | | |
| 1800 | For ceiling installations, add | | | | ↓ | | 25% | | | |
| 2000 | Masonry or concrete block, oil base, primer or sealer coat | | | | | | | | | |
| 2100 | Smooth finish, brushwork | 1 Pord | 1224 | .007 | S.F. | .05 | .22 | | .27 | .39 |
| 2180 | Spray | | 2400 | .003 | | .08 | .11 | | .19 | .26 |
| 2200 | Sand finish, brushwork | | 1089 | .007 | | .09 | .25 | | .34 | .47 |
| 2280 | Spray | | 2400 | .003 | | .08 | .11 | | .19 | .26 |
| 2800 | Paint 2 coats, smooth finish, brushwork | | 756 | .011 | | .18 | .36 | | .54 | .73 |
| 2880 | Spray | | 1360 | .006 | | .16 | .20 | | .36 | .48 |
| 2900 | Sand finish, brushwork | | 672 | .012 | | .18 | .40 | | .58 | .79 |
| 2980 | Spray | | 1360 | .006 | | .16 | .20 | | .36 | .48 |
| 3600 | Glaze coating, 3 coats, spray, clear | | 900 | .009 | | .60 | .30 | | .90 | 1.11 |
| 3620 | Multicolor | | 900 | .009 | | 1 | .30 | | 1.30 | 1.55 |
| 4000 | Block filler, 1 coat, brushwork | | 425 | .019 | | .12 | .64 | | .76 | 1.08 |
| 4100 | Silicone, water repellent, 2 coats, spray | ↓ | 2000 | .004 | | .27 | .14 | | .41 | .49 |
| 4120 | For latex paint, deduct | | | | | 10% | | | | |
| 8200 | For work 8 - 15' H, add | | | | | | 10% | | | |
| 8300 | For work over 15' H, add | | | | ↓ | | 20% | | | |

# 09 91 Painting

## 09 91 23 – Interior Painting

### 09 91 23.75 Dry Fall Painting

| | | Crew | Daily Output | Labor-Hours | Unit | Material | 2008 Bare Costs Labor | Equipment | Total | Total Incl O&P |
|---|---|---|---|---|---|---|---|---|---|---|
| 0010 | **DRY FALL PAINTING** R099100-10 | | | | | | | | | |
| 0100 | Walls | | | | | | | | | |
| 0200 | Wallboard and smooth plaster, one coat, brush R099100-20 | 1 Pord | 910 | .009 | S.F. | .04 | .30 | | .34 | .50 |
| 0210 | Roll | | 1560 | .005 | | .04 | .17 | | .21 | .31 |
| 0220 | Spray | | 2600 | .003 | | .04 | .10 | | .14 | .21 |
| 0230 | Two coats, brush | | 520 | .015 | | .09 | .52 | | .61 | .88 |
| 0240 | Roll | | 877 | .009 | | .09 | .31 | | .40 | .56 |
| 0250 | Spray | | 1560 | .005 | | .09 | .17 | | .26 | .36 |
| 0260 | Concrete or textured plaster, one coat, brush | | 747 | .011 | | .04 | .36 | | .40 | .59 |
| 0270 | Roll | | 1300 | .006 | | .04 | .21 | | .25 | .36 |
| 0280 | Spray | | 1560 | .005 | | .04 | .17 | | .21 | .31 |
| 0290 | Two coats, brush | | 422 | .019 | | .09 | .64 | | .73 | 1.06 |
| 0300 | Roll | | 747 | .011 | | .09 | .36 | | .45 | .64 |
| 0310 | Spray | | 1300 | .006 | | .09 | .21 | | .30 | .41 |
| 0320 | Concrete block, one coat, brush | | 747 | .011 | | .04 | .36 | | .40 | .59 |
| 0330 | Roll | | 1300 | .006 | | .04 | .21 | | .25 | .36 |
| 0340 | Spray | | 1560 | .005 | | .04 | .17 | | .21 | .31 |
| 0350 | Two coats, brush | | 422 | .019 | | .09 | .64 | | .73 | 1.06 |
| 0360 | Roll | | 747 | .011 | | .09 | .36 | | .45 | .64 |
| 0370 | Spray | | 1300 | .006 | | .09 | .21 | | .30 | .41 |
| 0380 | Wood, one coat, brush | | 747 | .011 | | .04 | .36 | | .40 | .59 |
| 0390 | Roll | | 1300 | .006 | | .04 | .21 | | .25 | .36 |
| 0400 | Spray | | 877 | .009 | | .04 | .31 | | .35 | .51 |
| 0410 | Two coats, brush | | 487 | .016 | | .09 | .55 | | .64 | .93 |
| 0420 | Roll | | 747 | .011 | | .09 | .36 | | .45 | .64 |
| 0430 | Spray | ↓ | 650 | .012 | ↓ | .09 | .42 | | .51 | .72 |
| 0440 | Ceilings | | | | | | | | | |
| 0450 | Wallboard and smooth plaster, one coat, brush | 1 Pord | 600 | .013 | S.F. | .04 | .45 | | .49 | .73 |
| 0460 | Roll | | 1040 | .008 | | .04 | .26 | | .30 | .44 |
| 0470 | Spray | | 1560 | .005 | | .04 | .17 | | .21 | .31 |
| 0480 | Two coats, brush | | 341 | .023 | | .09 | .79 | | .88 | 1.29 |
| 0490 | Roll | | 650 | .012 | | .09 | .42 | | .51 | .72 |
| 0500 | Spray | | 1300 | .006 | | .09 | .21 | | .30 | .41 |
| 0510 | Concrete or textured plaster, one coat, brush | | 487 | .016 | | .04 | .55 | | .59 | .88 |
| 0520 | Roll | | 877 | .009 | | .04 | .31 | | .35 | .51 |
| 0530 | Spray | | 1560 | .005 | | .04 | .17 | | .21 | .31 |
| 0540 | Two coats, brush | | 276 | .029 | | .09 | .98 | | 1.07 | 1.57 |
| 0550 | Roll | | 520 | .015 | | .09 | .52 | | .61 | .88 |
| 0560 | Spray | | 1300 | .006 | | .09 | .21 | | .30 | .41 |
| 0570 | Structural steel, bar joists or metal deck, one coat, spray | | 1560 | .005 | | .04 | .17 | | .21 | .31 |
| 0580 | Two coats, spray | ↓ | 1040 | .008 | ↓ | .09 | .26 | | .35 | .49 |

# 09 93 Staining and Transparent Finishing

## 09 93 23 – Interior Staining and Finishing

| 09 93 23.10 Varnish | Crew | Daily Output | Labor-Hours | Unit | Material | 2008 Bare Costs Labor | Equipment | Total | Total Incl O&P |
|---|---|---|---|---|---|---|---|---|---|
| 0010 **VARNISH** | | | | | | | | | |
| 0012   1 coat + sealer, on wood trim, brush, no sanding included | 1 Pord | 400 | .020 | S.F. | .07 | .68 | | .75 | 1.09 |
| 0100   Hardwood floors, 2 coats, no sanding included, roller | " | 1890 | .004 | " | .14 | .14 | | .28 | .36 |

# 09 96 High-Performance Coatings

## 09 96 56 – Epoxy Coatings

### 09 96 56.20 Wall Coatings

| | Crew | Daily Output | Labor-Hours | Unit | Material | 2008 Bare Costs Labor | Equipment | Total | Total Incl O&P |
|---|---|---|---|---|---|---|---|---|---|
| 0010 **WALL COATINGS** | | | | | | | | | |
| 0100   Acrylic glazed coatings, minimum | 1 Pord | 525 | .015 | S.F. | .27 | .51 | | .78 | 1.07 |
| 0200       Maximum | | 305 | .026 | | .57 | .89 | | 1.46 | 1.96 |
| 0300   Epoxy coatings, minimum | | 525 | .015 | | .35 | .51 | | .86 | 1.16 |
| 0400       Maximum | | 170 | .047 | | 1.07 | 1.59 | | 2.66 | 3.57 |
| 0600   Exposed aggregate, troweled on, 1/16" to 1/4", minimum | | 235 | .034 | | .53 | 1.15 | | 1.68 | 2.31 |
| 0700       Maximum (epoxy or polyacrylate) | | 130 | .062 | | 1.14 | 2.08 | | 3.22 | 4.37 |
| 0900       1/2" to 5/8" aggregate, minimum | | 130 | .062 | | 1.06 | 2.08 | | 3.14 | 4.29 |
| 1000       Maximum | | 80 | .100 | | 1.81 | 3.38 | | 5.19 | 7.05 |
| 1500   Exposed aggregate, sprayed on, 1/8" aggregate, minimum | | 295 | .027 | | .49 | .92 | | 1.41 | 1.92 |
| 1600       Maximum | | 145 | .055 | | .91 | 1.86 | | 2.77 | 3.80 |
| 1800   High build epoxy, 50 mil, minimum | | 390 | .021 | | .59 | .69 | | 1.28 | 1.69 |
| 1900       Maximum | | 95 | .084 | | 1.01 | 2.84 | | 3.85 | 5.40 |
| 2100   Laminated epoxy with fiberglass, minimum | | 295 | .027 | | .64 | .92 | | 1.56 | 2.08 |
| 2200       Maximum | | 145 | .055 | | 1.13 | 1.86 | | 2.99 | 4.04 |
| 2400   Sprayed perlite or vermiculite, 1/16" thick, minimum | | 2935 | .003 | | .23 | .09 | | .32 | .39 |
| 2500       Maximum | | 640 | .013 | | .65 | .42 | | 1.07 | 1.35 |
| 2700   Vinyl plastic wall coating, minimum | | 735 | .011 | | .29 | .37 | | .66 | .87 |
| 2800       Maximum | | 240 | .033 | | .71 | 1.12 | | 1.83 | 2.47 |
| 3000   Urethane on smooth surface, 2 coats, minimum | | 1135 | .007 | | .22 | .24 | | .46 | .60 |
| 3100       Maximum | | 665 | .012 | | .48 | .41 | | .89 | 1.14 |
| 3600   Ceramic-like glazed coating, cementitious, minimum | | 440 | .018 | | .42 | .61 | | 1.03 | 1.38 |
| 3700       Maximum | | 345 | .023 | | .70 | .78 | | 1.48 | 1.95 |
| 3900       Resin base, minimum | | 640 | .013 | | .29 | .42 | | .71 | .95 |
| 4000       Maximum | | 330 | .024 | | .47 | .82 | | 1.29 | 1.75 |

# 09 97 Special Coatings

## 09 97 13 – Steel Coatings

### 09 97 13.23 Exterior Steel Coatings

| | Crew | Daily Output | Labor-Hours | Unit | Material | 2008 Bare Costs Labor | Equipment | Total | Total Incl O&P |
|---|---|---|---|---|---|---|---|---|---|
| 0010 **EXTERIOR STEEL COATINGS** R050516-30 | | | | | | | | | |
| 6100   Cold galvanizing, brush in field | 1 Psst | 1100 | .007 | S.F. | .07 | .25 | | .32 | .52 |
| 6510   Paints & protective coatings, sprayed in field | | | | | | | | | |
| 6520       Alkyds, primer | 2 Psst | 3600 | .004 | S.F. | .05 | .15 | | .20 | .34 |
| 6540           Gloss topcoats | | 3200 | .005 | | .05 | .17 | | .22 | .36 |
| 6560           Silicone alkyd | | 3200 | .005 | | .10 | .17 | | .27 | .42 |
| 6610       Epoxy, primer | | 3000 | .005 | | .21 | .18 | | .39 | .56 |
| 6630           Intermediate or topcoat | | 2800 | .006 | | .19 | .20 | | .39 | .55 |
| 6650           Enamel coat | | 2800 | .006 | | .23 | .20 | | .43 | .61 |
| 6700       Epoxy ester, primer | | 2800 | .006 | | .47 | .20 | | .67 | .86 |
| 6720           Topcoats | | 2800 | .006 | | .16 | .20 | | .36 | .52 |
| 6810       Latex primer | | 3600 | .004 | | .05 | .15 | | .20 | .34 |
| 6830           Topcoats | | 3200 | .005 | | .07 | .17 | | .24 | .38 |

# 09 97 Special Coatings

## 09 97 13 – Steel Coatings

| 09 97 13.23 Exterior Steel Coatings | Crew | Daily Output | Labor-Hours | Unit | Material | 2008 Bare Costs Labor | Equipment | Total | Total Incl O&P |
|---|---|---|---|---|---|---|---|---|---|
| 6910 | Universal primers, one part, phenolic, modified alkyd | 2 Psst | 2000 | .008 | S.F. | .09 | .28 | | .37 | .60 |
| 6940 | Two part, epoxy spray | | 2000 | .008 | | .20 | .28 | | .48 | .72 |
| 7000 | Zinc rich primers, self cure, spray, inorganic | | 1800 | .009 | | .52 | .31 | | .83 | 1.12 |
| 7010 | Epoxy, spray, organic | ↓ | 1800 | .009 | ↓ | .19 | .31 | | .50 | .75 |
| 7020 | Above one story, spray painting simple structures, add | | | | | | 25% | | | |
| 7030 | Intricate structures, add | | | | | | 50% | | | |

# Division Notes

| | | CREW | DAILY OUTPUT | LABOR-HOURS | UNIT | 2008 BARE COSTS | | | | TOTAL INCL O&P |
| --- | --- | --- | --- | --- | --- | --- | --- | --- | --- | --- |
| | | | | | | MAT. | LABOR | EQUIP. | TOTAL | |
| | | | | | | | | | | |
| | | | | | | | | | | |
| | | | | | | | | | | |
| | | | | | | | | | | |
| | | | | | | | | | | |
| | | | | | | | | | | |
| | | | | | | | | | | |
| | | | | | | | | | | |
| | | | | | | | | | | |
| | | | | | | | | | | |
| | | | | | | | | | | |
| | | | | | | | | | | |
| | | | | | | | | | | |
| | | | | | | | | | | |
| | | | | | | | | | | |
| | | | | | | | | | | |
| | | | | | | | | | | |
| | | | | | | | | | | |
| | | | | | | | | | | |
| | | | | | | | | | | |

# Estimating Tips

## General

- The items in this division are usually priced per square foot or each.
- Many items in Division 10 require some type of support system or special anchors that are not usually furnished with the item. The required anchors must be added to the estimate in the appropriate division.
- Some items in Division 10, such as lockers, may require assembly before installation. Verify the amount of assembly required. Assembly can often exceed installation time.

## 10 20 00 Interior Specialties

- Support angles and blocking are not included in the installation of toilet compartments, shower/dressing compartments, or cubicles. Appropriate line items from Divisions 5 or 6 may need to be added to support the installations.
- Toilet partitions are priced by the stall. A stall consists of a side wall, pilaster, and door with hardware. Toilet tissue holders and grab bars are extra.
- The required acoustical rating of a folding partition can have a significant impact on costs. Verify the sound transmission coefficient rating of the panel priced to the specification requirements.

- Grab bar installation does not include supplemental blocking or backing to support the required load. When grab bars are installed at an existing facility, provisions must be made to attach the grab bars to solid structure.

# Reference Numbers

Reference numbers are shown in shaded boxes at the beginning of some major classifications. These numbers refer to related items in the Reference Section. The reference information may be an estimating procedure, an alternate pricing method, or technical information.

*Note:* Not all subdivisions listed here necessarily appear in this publication.

# 10 05 Common Work Results for Specialties

## 10 05 05 – Selective Specialities Demolition

| 10 05 05.10 Selective Demolition, Specialties | | Crew | Daily Output | Labor-Hours | Unit | Material | 2008 Bare Costs Labor | Equipment | Total | Total Incl O&P |
|---|---|---|---|---|---|---|---|---|---|---|
| 0010 | **SELECTIVE DEMOLITION, SPECIALTIES** | | | | | | | | | |
| 1100 | Boards and panels, wall mounted | 2 Clab | 15 | 1.067 | Ea. | | 32.50 | | 32.50 | 50 |
| 1200 | Cases, for directory and/or bulletin boards, incl doors | | 24 | .667 | | | 20 | | 20 | 31.50 |
| 1850 | Shower partitons, cabinet or stall, incl base and door | ↓ | 8 | 2 | | | 60.50 | | 60.50 | 94 |
| 1855 | Shower receptor, terrazo or concrete | 1 Clab | 14 | .571 | ↓ | | 17.30 | | 17.30 | 27 |
| 1900 | Curtain track or rod, hospital type, ceiling mounted or suspended | " | 220 | .036 | L.F. | | 1.10 | | 1.10 | 1.71 |
| 1910 | Toilet Cubicles, remove | 2 Clab | 8 | 2 | Ea. | | 60.50 | | 60.50 | 94 |
| 2650 | Wall guard, misc. wall or corner protection | 1 Clab | 320 | .025 | L.F. | | .76 | | .76 | 1.18 |
| 2750 | Access floor, metal panel system, incl pedestals, covering | 2 Clab | 850 | .019 | S.F. | | .57 | | .57 | .89 |
| 3050 | Fireplace, prefab, freestanding or wall hung, incl hood and screen | 1 Clab | 2 | 4 | Ea. | | 121 | | 121 | 188 |
| 3054 | Chimney top, simulated brick, 4' high | " | 15 | .533 | | | 16.15 | | 16.15 | 25 |
| 3200 | Stove, woodburning, cast iron | 2 Clab | 2 | 8 | | | 242 | | 242 | 375 |
| 3440 | Weathervane, residential | 1 Clab | 12 | .667 | | | 20 | | 20 | 31.50 |
| 3500 | Flagpole, groundset, to 70' high, excl base/fndn | K-1 | 1 | 16 | | | 540 | 224 | 764 | 1,075 |
| 3555 | To 30' high | " | 2.50 | 6.400 | | | 216 | 89.50 | 305.50 | 435 |
| 4300 | Letter, signs or plaques, exterior on wall | 1 Clab | 20 | .400 | | | 12.10 | | 12.10 | 18.80 |
| 4310 | Signs, street, reflective aluminum, incl post and bracket | ↓ | 60 | .133 | | | 4.03 | | 4.03 | 6.25 |
| 4320 | Door signs interior on door 6" x 6", selective demolition | ↓ | 20 | .400 | | | 12.10 | | 12.10 | 18.80 |
| 4550 | Turnstiles, manual or electric | 2 Clab | 2 | 8 | ↓ | | 242 | | 242 | 375 |
| 5050 | Lockers | " | 15 | 1.067 | Opng. | | 32.50 | | 32.50 | 50 |
| 5250 | Cabinets, recessed | Q-12 | 12 | 1.333 | Ea. | | 56 | | 56 | 84.50 |
| 5260 | Mail boxes, Horiz., Key Lock, front loading, Remove | 1 Carp | 34 | .235 | " | | 8.95 | | 8.95 | 13.95 |
| 5350 | Awning, fabric, including frame | 2 Clab | 100 | .160 | S.F. | | 4.84 | | 4.84 | 7.55 |
| 6050 | Partition, woven wire | ↓ | 1400 | .011 | | | .35 | | .35 | .54 |
| 6100 | Folding gate, security, door or window | | 500 | .032 | | | .97 | | .97 | 1.51 |
| 6580 | Acoustic air wall | | 650 | .025 | ↓ | | .74 | | .74 | 1.16 |
| 7550 | Telephone enclosure, exterior, post mounted | | 3 | 5.333 | Ea. | | 161 | | 161 | 251 |
| 8850 | Scale, platform, excludes foundation or pit | ↓ | .25 | 64 | " | | 1,925 | | 1,925 | 3,000 |

# 10 11 Visual Display Surfaces

## 10 11 13 – Chalkboards

### 10 11 13.13 Fixed Chalkboards

| 10 11 13.13 Fixed Chalkboards | | Crew | Daily Output | Labor-Hours | Unit | Material | 2008 Bare Costs Labor | Equipment | Total | Total Incl O&P |
|---|---|---|---|---|---|---|---|---|---|---|
| 0010 | **FIXED CHALKBOARDS** Porcelain enamel steel | | | | | | | | | |
| 3900 | Wall hung | | | | | | | | | |
| 4000 | Aluminum frame and chalktrough | | | | | | | | | |
| 4200 | 3' x 4' | 2 Carp | 16 | 1 | Ea. | 167 | 38 | | 205 | 244 |
| 4300 | 3' x 5' | ↓ | 15 | 1.067 | ↓ | 228 | 40.50 | | 268.50 | 315 |
| 4500 | 4' x 8' | | 14 | 1.143 | | 325 | 43.50 | | 368.50 | 430 |
| 4600 | 4' x 12' | ↓ | 13 | 1.231 | ↓ | 480 | 47 | | 527 | 600 |
| 4700 | Wood frame and chalktrough | | | | | | | | | |
| 4800 | 3' x 4' | 2 Carp | 16 | 1 | Ea. | 158 | 38 | | 196 | 233 |
| 5000 | 3' x 5' | | 15 | 1.067 | | 234 | 40.50 | | 274.50 | 320 |
| 5100 | 4' x 5' | | 14 | 1.143 | | 235 | 43.50 | | 278.50 | 325 |
| 5300 | 4' x 8' | ↓ | 13 | 1.231 | ↓ | 320 | 47 | | 367 | 425 |
| 5400 | Liquid chalk, white porcelain enamel, wall hung | | | | | | | | | |
| 5420 | Deluxe units, aluminum trim and chalktrough | | | | | | | | | |
| 5450 | 4' x 4' | 2 Carp | 16 | 1 | Ea. | 202 | 38 | | 240 | 282 |
| 5500 | 4' x 8' | | 14 | 1.143 | | 325 | 43.50 | | 368.50 | 425 |
| 5550 | 4' x 12' | ↓ | 12 | 1.333 | ↓ | 460 | 51 | | 511 | 585 |
| 5700 | Wood trim and chalktrough | | | | | | | | | |
| 5900 | 4' x 4' | 2 Carp | 16 | 1 | Ea. | 475 | 38 | | 513 | 580 |

# 10 11 Visual Display Surfaces

## 10 11 13 — Chalkboards

### 10 11 13.13 Fixed Chalkboards

| | | Crew | Daily Output | Labor-Hours | Unit | Material | 2008 Bare Costs Labor | 2008 Bare Costs Equipment | Total | Total Incl O&P |
|---|---|---|---|---|---|---|---|---|---|---|
| 6000 | 4' x 6' | 2 Carp | 15 | 1.067 | Ea. | 570 | 40.50 | | 610.50 | 690 |
| 6200 | 4' x 8' | ↓ | 14 | 1.143 | ↓ | 665 | 43.50 | | 708.50 | 805 |
| 6300 | Liquid chalk, felt tip markers | | | | | 1.70 | | | 1.70 | 1.87 |
| 6500 | Erasers | | | | | 1.38 | | | 1.38 | 1.52 |
| 6600 | Board cleaner, 8 oz. bottle | | | | ↓ | 4.22 | | | 4.22 | 4.64 |

### 10 11 13.23 Modular-Support-Mounted Chalkboards

| | | Crew | Daily Output | Labor-Hours | Unit | Material | 2008 Bare Costs Labor | 2008 Bare Costs Equipment | Total | Total Incl O&P |
|---|---|---|---|---|---|---|---|---|---|---|
| 0010 | **MODULAR-SUPPORT-MOUNTED CHALKBOARDS** | | | | | | | | | |
| 0400 | Sliding chalkboards | | | | | | | | | |
| 0450 | Vertical, one sliding board with back panel, wall mounted | | | | | | | | | |
| 0500 | 8' x 4' | 2 Carp | 8 | 2 | Ea. | 1,650 | 76 | | 1,726 | 1,950 |
| 0520 | 8' x 8' | ↓ | 7.50 | 2.133 | ↓ | 2,325 | 81.50 | | 2,406.50 | 2,675 |
| 0540 | 8' x 12' | ↓ | 7 | 2.286 | ↓ | 2,925 | 87 | | 3,012 | 3,325 |
| 0600 | Two sliding boards, with back panel | | | | | | | | | |
| 0620 | 8' x 4' | 2 Carp | 8 | 2 | Ea. | 2,500 | 76 | | 2,576 | 2,875 |
| 0640 | 8' x 8' | ↓ | 7.50 | 2.133 | | 3,500 | 81.50 | | 3,581.50 | 3,975 |
| 0660 | 8' x 12' | ↓ | 7 | 2.286 | ↓ | 4,375 | 87 | | 4,462 | 4,950 |
| 0700 | Horizontal, two track | | | | | | | | | |
| 0800 | 4' x 8', 2 sliding panels | 2 Carp | 8 | 2 | Ea. | 1,700 | 76 | | 1,776 | 2,000 |
| 0820 | 4' x 12', 2 sliding panels | ↓ | 7.50 | 2.133 | ↓ | 2,175 | 81.50 | | 2,256.50 | 2,525 |
| 0840 | 4' x 16', 4 sliding panels | ↓ | 7 | 2.286 | ↓ | 2,925 | 87 | | 3,012 | 3,350 |
| 0900 | Four track, four sliding panels | | | | | | | | | |
| 0920 | 4' x 8' | 2 Carp | 8 | 2 | Ea. | 2,725 | 76 | | 2,801 | 3,125 |
| 0940 | 4' x 12' | ↓ | 7.50 | 2.133 | ↓ | 2,175 | 81.50 | | 2,256.50 | 2,525 |
| 0960 | 4' x 16' | ↓ | 7 | 2.286 | ↓ | 4,425 | 87 | | 4,512 | 5,000 |
| 1200 | Vertical, motor operated | | | | | | | | | |
| 1400 | One sliding panel with back panel | | | | | | | | | |
| 1450 | 10' x 4' | 2 Carp | 4 | 4 | Ea. | 6,125 | 152 | | 6,277 | 6,975 |
| 1500 | 10' x 10' | ↓ | 3.75 | 4.267 | | 7,175 | 163 | | 7,338 | 8,125 |
| 1550 | 10' x 16' | ↓ | 3.50 | 4.571 | ↓ | 8,225 | 174 | | 8,399 | 9,325 |
| 1700 | Two sliding panels with back panel | | | | | | | | | |
| 1750 | 10' x 4' | 2 Carp | 4 | 4 | Ea. | 9,825 | 152 | | 9,977 | 11,000 |
| 1800 | 10' x 10' | ↓ | 3.75 | 4.267 | | 11,200 | 163 | | 11,363 | 12,600 |
| 1850 | 10' x 16' | ↓ | 3.50 | 4.571 | ↓ | 12,700 | 174 | | 12,874 | 14,200 |
| 2000 | Three sliding panels with back panel | | | | | | | | | |
| 2100 | 10' x 4' | 2 Carp | 4 | 4 | Ea. | 12,800 | 152 | | 12,952 | 14,300 |
| 2150 | 10' x 10' | ↓ | 3.75 | 4.267 | | 14,900 | 163 | | 15,063 | 16,700 |
| 2200 | 10' x 16' | ↓ | 3.50 | 4.571 | ↓ | 17,000 | 174 | | 17,174 | 19,000 |
| 2400 | For projection screen, glass beaded, add | | | | S.F. | 10.35 | | | 10.35 | 11.40 |
| 2500 | For remote control, 1 panel control, add | | | | Ea. | 480 | | | 480 | 525 |
| 2600 | 2 panel control, add | | | | " | 825 | | | 825 | 905 |
| 2800 | For units without back panels, deduct | | | | S.F. | 5.95 | | | 5.95 | 6.55 |
| 2850 | For liquid chalk porcelain panels, add | | | | " | 6.50 | | | 6.50 | 7.15 |
| 3000 | Swing leaf, any comb. of chalkboard & cork, aluminum frame | | | | | | | | | |
| 3100 | Floor style, 6 panels | | | | | | | | | |
| 3150 | 30" x 40" panels | | | | Ea. | 955 | | | 955 | 1,050 |
| 3200 | 48" x 40" panels | | | | " | 2,025 | | | 2,025 | 2,250 |
| 3300 | Wall mounted, 6 panels | | | | | | | | | |
| 3400 | 30" x 40" panels | 2 Carp | 16 | 1 | Ea. | 850 | 38 | | 888 | 995 |
| 3450 | 48" x 40" panels | " | 16 | 1 | " | 1,700 | 38 | | 1,738 | 1,925 |
| 3600 | Extra panels for swing leaf units | | | | | | | | | |
| 3700 | 30" x 40" panels | | | | Ea. | 276 | | | 276 | 305 |
| 3750 | 48" x 40" panels | | | | " | 330 | | | 330 | 360 |

# 10 11 Visual Display Surfaces

## 10 11 13 – Chalkboards

### 10 11 13.43 Portable Chalkboards

| | | Crew | Daily Output | Labor-Hours | Unit | Material | 2008 Bare Costs Labor | Equipment | Total | Total Incl O&P |
|---|---|---|---|---|---|---|---|---|---|---|
| 0010 | **PORTABLE CHALKBOARDS** | | | | | | | | | |
| 0100 | Freestanding, reversible | | | | | | | | | |
| 0120 | Economy, wood frame, 4' x 6' | | | | | | | | | |
| 0140 | Chalkboard both sides | | | | Ea. | 535 | | | 535 | 590 |
| 0160 | Chalkboard one side, cork other side | | | | " | 465 | | | 465 | 515 |
| 0200 | Standard, lightweight satin finished aluminum, 4' x 6' | | | | | | | | | |
| 0220 | Chalkboard both sides | | | | Ea. | 610 | | | 610 | 670 |
| 0240 | Chalkboard one side, cork other side | | | | " | 555 | | | 555 | 610 |
| 0300 | Deluxe, heavy duty extruded aluminum, 4' x 6' | | | | | | | | | |
| 0320 | Chalkboard both sides | | | | Ea. | 1,025 | | | 1,025 | 1,125 |
| 0340 | Chalkboard one side, cork other side | | | | " | 935 | | | 935 | 1,025 |

## 10 11 23 – Tackboards

### 10 11 23.10 Fixed Tackboards

| | | Crew | Daily Output | Labor-Hours | Unit | Material | 2008 Bare Costs Labor | Equipment | Total | Total Incl O&P |
|---|---|---|---|---|---|---|---|---|---|---|
| 0010 | **FIXED TACKBOARDS** | | | | | | | | | |
| 0020 | Cork sheets, unbacked, no frame, 1/4" thick | 2 Carp | 290 | .055 | S.F. | 3.60 | 2.10 | | 5.70 | 7.25 |
| 0100 | 1/2" thick | | 290 | .055 | | 6.15 | 2.10 | | 8.25 | 10 |
| 0300 | Fabric-face, no frame, on 7/32" cork underlay | | 290 | .055 | | 5.35 | 2.10 | | 7.45 | 9.10 |
| 0400 | On 1/4" cork on 1/4" hardboard | | 290 | .055 | | 7.30 | 2.10 | | 9.40 | 11.30 |
| 0600 | With edges wrapped | | 290 | .055 | | 7.65 | 2.10 | | 9.75 | 11.70 |
| 0700 | On 7/16" fire retardant core | | 290 | .055 | | 6.95 | 2.10 | | 9.05 | 10.85 |
| 0900 | With edges wrapped | | 290 | .055 | | 9.80 | 2.10 | | 11.90 | 14.05 |
| 1000 | Designer fabric only, cut to size | | | | | 2 | | | 2 | 2.20 |
| 1200 | 1/4" vinyl cork, on 1/4" hardboard, no frame | 2 Carp | 290 | .055 | | 7.80 | 2.10 | | 9.90 | 11.85 |
| 1300 | On 1/4" coreboard | | 290 | .055 | | 7.70 | 2.10 | | 9.80 | 11.75 |
| 2000 | For map and display rail, economy, add | | 385 | .042 | L.F. | 2.20 | 1.58 | | 3.78 | 4.88 |
| 2100 | Deluxe, add | | 350 | .046 | " | 3.21 | 1.74 | | 4.95 | 6.25 |
| 2120 | Prefabricated, 1/4" cork, 3' x 5' with aluminum frame | | 16 | 1 | Ea. | 107 | 38 | | 145 | 178 |
| 2140 | Wood frame | | 16 | 1 | | 128 | 38 | | 166 | 200 |
| 2160 | 4' x 4' with aluminum frame | | 16 | 1 | | 93 | 38 | | 131 | 162 |
| 2180 | Wood frame | | 16 | 1 | | 117 | 38 | | 155 | 189 |
| 2200 | 4' x 8' with aluminum frame | | 14 | 1.143 | | 163 | 43.50 | | 206.50 | 247 |
| 2210 | With wood frame | | 14 | 1.143 | | 114 | 43.50 | | 157.50 | 193 |
| 2220 | 4' x 12' with aluminum frame | | 12 | 1.333 | | 236 | 51 | | 287 | 340 |
| 2230 | Bulletin board case, single glass door, with lock | | | | | | | | | |
| 2240 | 36" x 24", economy | 2 Carp | 12 | 1.333 | Ea. | 260 | 51 | | 311 | 365 |
| 2250 | Deluxe | | 12 | 1.333 | | 385 | 51 | | 436 | 505 |
| 2260 | 42" x 30", economy | | 12 | 1.333 | | 257 | 51 | | 308 | 360 |
| 2270 | Deluxe | | 12 | 1.333 | | 420 | 51 | | 471 | 540 |
| 2300 | Glass enclosed cabinets, alum., cork panel, hinged doors | | | | | | | | | |
| 2400 | 3' x 3', 1 door | 2 Carp | 12 | 1.333 | Ea. | 535 | 51 | | 586 | 670 |
| 2500 | 4' x 4', 2 door | | 11 | 1.455 | | 895 | 55.50 | | 950.50 | 1,075 |
| 2600 | 4' x 7', 3 door | | 10 | 1.600 | | 1,500 | 61 | | 1,561 | 1,750 |
| 2800 | 4' x 10', 4 door | | 8 | 2 | | 1,950 | 76 | | 2,026 | 2,275 |
| 2900 | For lights, add per door opening | 1 Elec | 13 | .615 | | 164 | 28 | | 192 | 222 |
| 3100 | Horizontal sliding units, 4 doors, 4' x 8', 8' x 4' | 2 Carp | 9 | 1.778 | | 1,700 | 67.50 | | 1,767.50 | 1,975 |
| 3200 | 4' x 12' | | 7 | 2.286 | | 2,175 | 87 | | 2,262 | 2,525 |
| 3400 | 8 doors, 4' x 16' | | 5 | 3.200 | | 2,825 | 122 | | 2,947 | 3,300 |
| 3500 | 4' x 24' | | 4 | 4 | | 3,775 | 152 | | 3,927 | 4,400 |

### 10 11 23.20 Control Boards

| | | Crew | Daily Output | Labor-Hours | Unit | Material | 2008 Bare Costs Labor | Equipment | Total | Total Incl O&P |
|---|---|---|---|---|---|---|---|---|---|---|
| 0010 | **CONTROL BOARDS** | | | | | | | | | |
| 0020 | Magnetic, porcelain finish, 18" x 24", framed | 2 Carp | 8 | 2 | Ea. | 199 | 76 | | 275 | 340 |

# 10 11 Visual Display Surfaces

## 10 11 23 – Tackboards

| 10 11 23.20 Control Boards | | Crew | Daily Output | Labor-Hours | Unit | Material | 2008 Bare Costs Labor | 2008 Bare Costs Equipment | Total | Total Incl O&P |
|---|---|---|---|---|---|---|---|---|---|---|
| 0100 | 24" x 36" | 2 Carp | 7.50 | 2.133 | Ea. | 295 | 81.50 | | 376.50 | 450 |
| 0200 | 36" x 48" | | 7 | 2.286 | | 390 | 87 | | 477 | 565 |
| 0300 | 48" x 72" | | 6 | 2.667 | | 860 | 102 | | 962 | 1,100 |
| 0400 | 48" x 96" | | 5 | 3.200 | | 1,075 | 122 | | 1,197 | 1,375 |

# 10 13 Directories

## 10 13 10 – Building Directories

### 10 13 10.10 Directory Boards

| | | Crew | Daily Output | Labor-Hours | Unit | Material | 2008 Bare Costs Labor | 2008 Bare Costs Equipment | Total | Total Incl O&P |
|---|---|---|---|---|---|---|---|---|---|---|
| 0010 | **DIRECTORY BOARDS** | | | | | | | | | |
| 0050 | Plastic, glass covered, 30" x 20" | 2 Carp | 3 | 5.333 | Ea. | 242 | 203 | | 445 | 580 |
| 0100 | 36" x 48" | | 2 | 8 | | 875 | 305 | | 1,180 | 1,450 |
| 0300 | Grooved cork, 30" x 20" | | 3 | 5.333 | | 375 | 203 | | 578 | 725 |
| 0400 | 36" x 48" | | 2 | 8 | | 264 | 305 | | 569 | 765 |
| 0600 | Black felt, 30" x 20" | | 3 | 5.333 | | 178 | 203 | | 381 | 510 |
| 0700 | 36" x 48" | | 2 | 8 | | 355 | 305 | | 660 | 865 |
| 0900 | Outdoor, weatherproof, black plastic, 36" x 24" | | 2 | 8 | | 720 | 305 | | 1,025 | 1,275 |
| 1000 | 36" x 36" | | 1.50 | 10.667 | | 830 | 405 | | 1,235 | 1,550 |
| 1800 | Indoor, economy, open face, 18" x 24" | | 7 | 2.286 | | 126 | 87 | | 213 | 275 |
| 1900 | 24" x 36" | | 7 | 2.286 | | 144 | 87 | | 231 | 294 |
| 2000 | 36" x 24" | | 6 | 2.667 | | 164 | 102 | | 266 | 340 |
| 2100 | 36" x 48" | | 6 | 2.667 | | 245 | 102 | | 347 | 430 |
| 2400 | Building directory, alum., black felt panels, 1 door, 24" x 18" | | 4 | 4 | | 305 | 152 | | 457 | 570 |
| 2500 | 36" x 24" | | 3.50 | 4.571 | | 335 | 174 | | 509 | 635 |
| 2600 | 48" x 32" | | 3 | 5.333 | | 555 | 203 | | 758 | 925 |
| 2700 | 2 door, 36" x 48" | | 2.50 | 6.400 | | 595 | 244 | | 839 | 1,025 |
| 2800 | 36" x 60" | | 2 | 8 | | 895 | 305 | | 1,200 | 1,450 |
| 2900 | 48" x 60" | | 1 | 16 | | 900 | 610 | | 1,510 | 1,950 |
| 3100 | For bronze enamel finish, add | | | | | 15% | | | | |
| 3200 | For bronze anodized finish, add | | | | | 25% | | | | |
| 3400 | For illuminated directory, single door unit, add | | | | | 164 | | | 164 | 180 |
| 3500 | For 6" header panel, 6 letters per foot, add | | | | L.F. | 28.50 | | | 28.50 | 31.50 |

# 10 14 Signage

## 10 14 19 – Dimensional Letter Signage

### 10 14 19.10 Exterior Signs

| | | Crew | Daily Output | Labor-Hours | Unit | Material | 2008 Bare Costs Labor | 2008 Bare Costs Equipment | Total | Total Incl O&P |
|---|---|---|---|---|---|---|---|---|---|---|
| 0010 | **EXTERIOR SIGNS** | | | | | | | | | |
| 0020 | Letters, 2" high, 3/8" deep, cast bronze | 1 Carp | 24 | .333 | Ea. | 23 | 12.70 | | 35.70 | 45 |
| 0140 | 1/2" deep, cast aluminum | | 18 | .444 | | 23 | 16.95 | | 39.95 | 51.50 |
| 0160 | Cast bronze | | 32 | .250 | | 28.50 | 9.55 | | 38.05 | 46.50 |
| 0300 | 6" high, 5/8" deep, cast aluminum | | 24 | .333 | | 27 | 12.70 | | 39.70 | 49.50 |
| 0400 | Cast bronze | | 24 | .333 | | 54.50 | 12.70 | | 67.20 | 80 |
| 0600 | 8" high, 3/4" deep, cast aluminum | | 14 | .571 | | 32.50 | 22 | | 54.50 | 70 |
| 0700 | Cast bronze | | 20 | .400 | | 78 | 15.25 | | 93.25 | 109 |
| 0900 | 10" high, 1" deep, cast aluminum | | 18 | .444 | | 48 | 16.95 | | 64.95 | 79.50 |
| 1000 | Bronze | | 18 | .444 | | 102 | 16.95 | | 118.95 | 140 |
| 1200 | 12" high, 1-1/4" deep, cast aluminum | | 12 | .667 | | 51 | 25.50 | | 76.50 | 95.50 |
| 1500 | Cast bronze | | 18 | .444 | | 120 | 16.95 | | 136.95 | 159 |
| 1600 | 14" high, 2-5/16" deep, cast aluminum | | 12 | .667 | | 73 | 25.50 | | 98.50 | 120 |
| 1800 | Fabricated stainless steel, 6" high, 2" deep | | 20 | .400 | | 48 | 15.25 | | 63.25 | 76.50 |

315

# 10 14 Signage

## 10 14 19 – Dimensional Letter Signage

### 10 14 19.10 Exterior Signs

| | | Crew | Daily Output | Labor-Hours | Unit | Material | 2008 Bare Costs Labor | Equipment | Total | Total Incl O&P |
|---|---|---|---|---|---|---|---|---|---|---|
| 1900 | 12" high, 3" deep | 1 Carp | 18 | .444 | Ea. | 107 | 16.95 | | 123.95 | 145 |
| 2100 | 18" high, 3" deep | | 12 | .667 | | 207 | 25.50 | | 232.50 | 268 |
| 2200 | 24" high, 4" deep | | 10 | .800 | | 350 | 30.50 | | 380.50 | 435 |
| 2700 | Acrylic, on high density foam, 12" high, 2" deep | | 20 | .400 | | 19.75 | 15.25 | | 35 | 45 |
| 2800 | 18" high, 2" deep | | 18 | .444 | | 49.50 | 16.95 | | 66.45 | 80.50 |
| 3900 | Plaques, custom, 20" x 30", for up to 450 letters, cast aluminum | 2 Carp | 4 | 4 | | 1,000 | 152 | | 1,152 | 1,325 |
| 4000 | Cast bronze | | 4 | 4 | | 1,450 | 152 | | 1,602 | 1,825 |
| 4200 | 30" x 36", up to 900 letters cast aluminum | | 3 | 5.333 | | 1,825 | 203 | | 2,028 | 2,325 |
| 4300 | Cast bronze | | 3 | 5.333 | | 3,375 | 203 | | 3,578 | 4,025 |
| 4500 | 36" x 48", for up to 1300 letters, cast bronze | | 2 | 8 | | 3,925 | 305 | | 4,230 | 4,800 |
| 4800 | Signs, reflective alum. directional signs, dbl. face, 2-way, w/bracket | | 30 | .533 | | 78 | 20.50 | | 98.50 | 118 |
| 4900 | 4-way | | 30 | .533 | | 126 | 20.50 | | 146.50 | 170 |
| 5100 | Exit signs, 24 ga. alum., 14" x 12" surface mounted | 1 Carp | 30 | .267 | | 36.50 | 10.15 | | 46.65 | 56 |
| 5200 | 10" x 7" | | 20 | .400 | | 27.50 | 15.25 | | 42.75 | 54 |
| 5400 | Bracket mounted, double face, 12" x 10" | | 30 | .267 | | 36.50 | 10.15 | | 46.65 | 56 |
| 5500 | Sticky back, stock decals, 14" x 10" | 1 Clab | 50 | .160 | | 9.40 | 4.84 | | 14.24 | 17.90 |
| 6000 | Interior elec., wall mount, fiberglass panels, 2 lamps, 6" | 1 Elec | 8 | 1 | | 106 | 45.50 | | 151.50 | 185 |
| 6100 | 8" | " | 8 | 1 | | 85 | 45.50 | | 130.50 | 162 |
| 6400 | Replacement sign faces, 6" or 8" | 1 Clab | 50 | .160 | | 47 | 4.84 | | 51.84 | 59 |

## 10 14 23 – Panel Signage

### 10 14 23.13 Engraved Interior Panel Signage

| | | Crew | Daily Output | Labor-Hours | Unit | Material | 2008 Bare Costs Labor | Equipment | Total | Total Incl O&P |
|---|---|---|---|---|---|---|---|---|---|---|
| 0010 | **ENGRAVED INTERIOR PANEL SIGNAGE** | | | | | | | | | |
| 1010 | Flexible door sign, adhesive back, w/Braille, 5/8" letters, 4" x 4" | 1 Clab | 32 | .250 | Ea. | 26.50 | 7.55 | | 34.05 | 41.50 |
| 1050 | 6" x 6" | | 32 | .250 | | 39.50 | 7.55 | | 47.05 | 55.50 |
| 1100 | 8" x 2" | | 32 | .250 | | 27.50 | 7.55 | | 35.05 | 42 |
| 1150 | 8" x 4" | | 32 | .250 | | 34.50 | 7.55 | | 42.05 | 50 |
| 1200 | 8" x 8" | | 32 | .250 | | 48 | 7.55 | | 55.55 | 65 |
| 1250 | 12" x 2" | | 32 | .250 | | 35 | 7.55 | | 42.55 | 50.50 |
| 1300 | 12" x 6" | | 32 | .250 | | 49.50 | 7.55 | | 57.05 | 66.50 |
| 1350 | 12" x 12" | | 32 | .250 | | 99 | 7.55 | | 106.55 | 121 |
| 1500 | Graphic symbols, 2" x 2" | | 32 | .250 | | 12.20 | 7.55 | | 19.75 | 25 |
| 1550 | 6" x 6" | | 32 | .250 | | 31 | 7.55 | | 38.55 | 46 |
| 1600 | 8" x 8" | | 32 | .250 | | 31 | 7.55 | | 38.55 | 46 |

## 10 14 53 – Traffic Signage

### 10 14 53.20 Traffic Signs

| | | Crew | Daily Output | Labor-Hours | Unit | Material | 2008 Bare Costs Labor | Equipment | Total | Total Incl O&P |
|---|---|---|---|---|---|---|---|---|---|---|
| 0010 | **TRAFFIC SIGNS** | | | | | | | | | |
| 0012 | Stock, 24" x 24", no posts, .080" alum. reflectorized | B-80 | 70 | .457 | Ea. | 68.50 | 14.80 | 8.95 | 92.25 | 108 |
| 0100 | High intensity | | 70 | .457 | | 68.50 | 14.80 | 8.95 | 92.25 | 108 |
| 0300 | 30" x 30", reflectorized | | 70 | .457 | | 139 | 14.80 | 8.95 | 162.75 | 185 |
| 0400 | High intensity | | 70 | .457 | | 139 | 14.80 | 8.95 | 162.75 | 185 |
| 0600 | Guide and directional signs, 12" x 18", reflectorized | | 70 | .457 | | 44.50 | 14.80 | 8.95 | 68.25 | 82 |
| 0700 | High intensity | | 70 | .457 | | 42.50 | 14.80 | 8.95 | 66.25 | 79.50 |
| 0900 | 18" x 24", stock signs, reflectorized | | 70 | .457 | | 49.50 | 14.80 | 8.95 | 73.25 | 87.50 |
| 1000 | High intensity | | 70 | .457 | | 49.50 | 14.80 | 8.95 | 73.25 | 87.50 |
| 1200 | 24" x 24", stock signs, reflectorized | | 70 | .457 | | 61.50 | 14.80 | 8.95 | 85.25 | 101 |
| 1300 | High intensity | | 70 | .457 | | 61.50 | 14.80 | 8.95 | 85.25 | 101 |
| 1500 | Add to above for steel posts, galvanized, 10'-0" upright, bolted | | 200 | .160 | | 22 | 5.20 | 3.13 | 30.33 | 36 |
| 1600 | 12'-0" upright, bolted | | 140 | .229 | | 29.50 | 7.40 | 4.48 | 41.38 | 49 |
| 1800 | Highway road signs, aluminum, over 20 S. F., reflectorized | | 350 | .091 | S.F. | 28.50 | 2.96 | 1.79 | 33.25 | 37.50 |
| 2000 | High intensity | | 350 | .091 | | 28.50 | 2.96 | 1.79 | 33.25 | 37.50 |
| 2200 | Highway, suspended over road, 80 S.F. min., reflectorized | | 165 | .194 | | 28.50 | 6.30 | 3.80 | 38.60 | 45 |
| 2300 | High intensity | | 165 | .194 | | 28.50 | 6.30 | 3.80 | 38.60 | 45 |

# 10 17 Telephone Specialties

## 10 17 16 – Telephone Enclosures

| 10 17 16.10 Commercial Telephone Enclosures | | Crew | Daily Output | Labor-Hours | Unit | Material | 2008 Bare Costs Labor | Equipment | Total | Total Incl O&P |
|---|---|---|---|---|---|---|---|---|---|---|
| 0010 | **COMMERCIAL TELEPHONE ENCLOSURES** | | | | | | | | | |
| 0300 | Shelf type, wall hung, minimum | 2 Carp | 5 | 3.200 | Ea. | 1,250 | 122 | | 1,372 | 1,575 |
| 0400 | Maximum | | 5 | 3.200 | | 2,625 | 122 | | 2,747 | 3,100 |
| 0600 | Booth type, painted steel, indoor or outdoor, minimum | | 1.50 | 10.667 | | 3,375 | 405 | | 3,780 | 4,325 |
| 0700 | Maximum (stainless steel) | | 1.50 | 10.667 | | 11,200 | 405 | | 11,605 | 13,000 |
| 1300 | Outdoor, acoustical, on post | | 3 | 5.333 | | 1,475 | 203 | | 1,678 | 1,950 |
| 1400 | Phone carousel, pedestal mounted with dividers | | .60 | 26.667 | | 5,625 | 1,025 | | 6,650 | 7,775 |
| 1900 | Outdoor, drive-up type, wall mounted | | 4 | 4 | | 905 | 152 | | 1,057 | 1,225 |
| 2000 | Post mounted, stainless steel posts | ↓ | 3 | 5.333 | ↓ | 1,400 | 203 | | 1,603 | 1,850 |
| 2200 | Directory shelf, wall mounted, stainless steel | | | | | | | | | |
| 2300 | 3 binders | 2 Carp | 8 | 2 | Ea. | 1,075 | 76 | | 1,151 | 1,300 |
| 2500 | 4 binders | | 7 | 2.286 | | 1,225 | 87 | | 1,312 | 1,475 |
| 2600 | 5 binders | | 6 | 2.667 | | 1,575 | 102 | | 1,677 | 1,875 |
| 2800 | Table type, stainless steel, 4 binders | | 8 | 2 | | 1,275 | 76 | | 1,351 | 1,525 |
| 2900 | 7 binders | ↓ | 7 | 2.286 | ↓ | 1,575 | 87 | | 1,662 | 1,850 |

# 10 21 Compartments and Cubicles

## 10 21 13 – Toilet Compartments

### 10 21 13.13 Metal Toilet Compartments

| | 10 21 13.13 Metal Toilet Compartments | | Crew | Daily Output | Labor-Hours | Unit | Material | Labor | Equipment | Total | Total Incl O&P |
|---|---|---|---|---|---|---|---|---|---|---|---|
| 0010 | **METAL TOILET COMPARTMENTS** | | | | | | | | | | |
| 0110 | Cubicles, ceiling hung | | | | | | | | | | |
| 0200 | Painted metal | | 2 Carp | 4 | 4 | Ea. | 430 | 152 | | 582 | 710 |
| 0500 | Stainless steel | | " | 4 | 4 | | 1,250 | 152 | | 1,402 | 1,600 |
| 0600 | For handicap units, incl. 52" grab bars, add | ♿ | | | | ↓ | 420 | | | 420 | 460 |
| 0900 | Floor and ceiling anchored | | | | | | | | | | |
| 1000 | Painted metal | | 2 Carp | 5 | 3.200 | Ea. | 485 | 122 | | 607 | 725 |
| 1300 | Stainless steel | | " | 5 | 3.200 | | 1,450 | 122 | | 1,572 | 1,800 |
| 1400 | For handicap units, incl. 52" grab bars, add | ♿ | | | | ↓ | 251 | | | 251 | 276 |
| 1610 | Floor mounted | | | | | | | | | | |
| 1700 | Painted metal | | 2 Carp | 7 | 2.286 | Ea. | 515 | 87 | | 602 | 705 |
| 2000 | Stainless steel | | " | 7 | 2.286 | | 1,450 | 87 | | 1,537 | 1,725 |
| 2100 | For handicap units, incl. 52" grab bars, add | ♿ | | | . | | 251 | | | 251 | 276 |
| 2200 | For juvenile units, deduct | | | | | ↓ | 39.50 | | | 39.50 | 43.50 |
| 2450 | Floor mounted, headrail braced | | | | | | | | | | |
| 2500 | Painted metal | | 2 Carp | 6 | 2.667 | Ea. | 435 | 102 | | 537 | 635 |
| 2800 | Stainless steel | ♿ | " | 6 | 2.667 | | 1,075 | 102 | | 1,177 | 1,325 |
| 2900 | For handicap units, incl. 52" grab bars, add | | | | | | 320 | | | 320 | 355 |
| 3000 | Wall hung partitions, painted metal | | 2 Carp | 7 | 2.286 | | 595 | 87 | | 682 | 790 |
| 3300 | Stainless steel | ♿ | " | 7 | 2.286 | | 1,425 | 87 | | 1,512 | 1,675 |
| 3400 | For handicap units, incl. 52" grab bars, add | | | | | ↓ | 320 | | | 320 | 355 |
| 4000 | Screens, entrance, floor mounted, 58" high, 48" wide | | | | | | | | | | |
| 4200 | Painted metal | | 2 Carp | 15 | 1.067 | Ea. | 232 | 40.50 | | 272.50 | 320 |
| 4500 | Stainless steel | | " | 15 | 1.067 | " | 765 | 40.50 | | 805.50 | 910 |
| 4650 | Urinal screen, 18" wide | | | | | | | | | | |
| 4700 | Painted metal | | 2 Carp | 8 | 2 | Ea. | 200 | 76 | | 276 | 340 |
| 5000 | Stainless steel | | " | 8 | 2 | " | 610 | 76 | | 686 | 790 |
| 5100 | Floor mounted, head rail braced | | | | | | | | | | |
| 5300 | Painted metal | | 2 Carp | 8 | 2 | Ea. | 203 | 76 | | 279 | 340 |
| 5600 | Stainless steel | | " | 8 | 2 | " | 550 | 76 | | 626 | 725 |
| 5750 | Pilaster, flush | | | | | | | | | | |
| 5800 | Painted metal | | 2 Carp | 10 | 1.600 | Ea. | 269 | 61 | | 330 | 390 |

317

# 10 21 Compartments and Cubicles

## 10 21 13 – Toilet Compartments

### 10 21 13.13 Metal Toilet Compartments

| | | Crew | Daily Output | Labor-Hours | Unit | Material | 2008 Bare Costs Labor | Equipment | Total | Total Incl O&P |
|---|---|---|---|---|---|---|---|---|---|---|
| 6100 | Stainless steel | 2 Carp | 10 | 1.600 | Ea. | 615 | 61 | | 676 | 770 |
| 6300 | Post braced, painted metal | | 10 | 1.600 | | 168 | 61 | | 229 | 280 |
| 6600 | Stainless steel | ↓ | 10 | 1.600 | ↓ | 470 | 61 | | 531 | 610 |
| 6700 | Wall hung, bracket supported | | | | | | | | | |
| 6800 | Painted metal | 2 Carp | 10 | 1.600 | Ea. | 281 | 61 | | 342 | 405 |
| 7100 | Stainless steel | | 10 | 1.600 | | 275 | 61 | | 336 | 400 |
| 7400 | Flange supported, painted metal | | 10 | 1.600 | | 92 | 61 | | 153 | 196 |
| 7700 | Stainless steel | | 10 | 1.600 | | 268 | 61 | | 329 | 390 |
| 7800 | Wedge type, painted metal | | 10 | 1.600 | | 134 | 61 | | 195 | 243 |
| 8100 | Stainless steel | ↓ | 10 | 1.600 | ↓ | 525 | 61 | | 586 | 670 |

### 10 21 13.16 Plastic-Laminate-Clad Toilet Compartments

| | | Crew | Daily Output | Labor-Hours | Unit | Material | 2008 Bare Costs Labor | Equipment | Total | Total Incl O&P |
|---|---|---|---|---|---|---|---|---|---|---|
| 0010 | **PLASTIC-LAMINATE-CLAD TOILET COMPARTMENTS** | | | | | | | | | |
| 0110 | Cubicles, ceiling hung | | | | | | | | | |
| 0300 | Plastic laminate on particle board | 2 Carp | 4 | 4 | Ea. | 585 | 152 | | 737 | 880 |
| 0600 | For handicap units, incl. 52" grab bars, add | | | | " | 420 | | | 420 | 460 |
| 0900 | Floor and ceiling anchored | | | | | | | | | |
| 1100 | Plastic laminate on particle board | 2 Carp | 5 | 3.200 | Ea. | 620 | 122 | | 742 | 870 |
| 1400 | For handicap units, incl. 52" grab bars, add | | | | " | 251 | | | 251 | 276 |
| 1610 | Floor mounted | | | | | | | | | |
| 1800 | Plastic laminate on particle board | 2 Carp | 7 | 2.286 | Ea. | 555 | 87 | | 642 | 745 |
| 2450 | Floor mounted, headrail braced | | | | | | | | | |
| 2600 | Plastic laminate on particle board  CN | 2 Carp | 6 | 2.667 | Ea. | 555 | 102 | | 657 | 770 |
| 3400 | For handicap units, incl. 52" grab bars, add | | | | | 320 | | | 320 | 355 |
| 4300 | Entrance screen, floor mtd., plas. lam., 58" high, 48" wide | 2 Carp | 15 | 1.067 | | 465 | 40.50 | | 505.50 | 580 |
| 4800 | Urinal screen, 18" wide, ceiling braced, plastic laminate | | 8 | 2 | | 241 | 76 | | 317 | 385 |
| 5400 | Floor mounted, headrail braced | | 8 | 2 | | 340 | 76 | | 416 | 495 |
| 5900 | Pilaster, flush, plastic laminate | | 10 | 1.600 | | 390 | 61 | | 451 | 525 |
| 6400 | Post braced, plastic laminate | ↓ | 10 | 1.600 | ↓ | 273 | 61 | | 334 | 395 |
| 6700 | Wall hung, bracket supported | | | | | | | | | |
| 6900 | Plastic laminate on particle board | 2 Carp | 10 | 1.600 | Ea. | 112 | 61 | | 173 | 219 |
| 7450 | Flange supported | | | | | | | | | |
| 7500 | Plastic laminate on particle board | 2 Carp | 10 | 1.600 | Ea. | 198 | 61 | | 259 | 315 |

### 10 21 13.19 Plastic Toilet Compartments

| | | Crew | Daily Output | Labor-Hours | Unit | Material | 2008 Bare Costs Labor | Equipment | Total | Total Incl O&P |
|---|---|---|---|---|---|---|---|---|---|---|
| 0010 | **PLASTIC TOILET COMPARTMENTS** | | | | | | | | | |
| 0110 | Cubicles, ceiling hung | | | | | | | | | |
| 0250 | Phenolic | 2 Carp | 4 | 4 | Ea. | 825 | 152 | | 977 | 1,150 |
| 0600 | For handicap units, incl. 52" grab bars, add | | | | " | 420 | | | 420 | 460 |
| 0900 | Floor and ceiling anchored | | | | | | | | | |
| 1050 | Phenolic | 2 Carp | 5 | 3.200 | Ea. | 740 | 122 | | 862 | 1,000 |
| 1400 | For handicap units, incl. 52" grab bars, add | | | | " | 251 | | | 251 | 276 |
| 1610 | Floor mounted | | | | | | | | | |
| 1750 | Phenolic | 2 Carp | 7 | 2.286 | Ea. | 1,200 | 87 | | 1,287 | 1,425 |
| 2100 | For handicap units, incl. 52" grab bars, add | | | | ↓ | 251 | | | 251 | 276 |
| 2200 | For juvenile units, deduct | | | | ↓ | 39.50 | | | 39.50 | 43.50 |
| 2450 | Floor mounted, headrail braced | | | | | | | | | |
| 2550 | Phenolic | 2 Carp | 6 | 2.667 | Ea. | 740 | 102 | | 842 | 975 |

### 10 21 13.40 Stone Toilet Compartments

| | | Crew | Daily Output | Labor-Hours | Unit | Material | 2008 Bare Costs Labor | Equipment | Total | Total Incl O&P |
|---|---|---|---|---|---|---|---|---|---|---|
| 0010 | **STONE TOILET COMPARTMENTS** | | | | | | | | | |
| 0100 | Cubicles, ceiling hung, marble | 2 Marb | 2 | 8 | Ea. | 1,625 | 299 | | 1,924 | 2,225 |
| 0600 | For handicap units, incl. 52" grab bars, add | | | | | 420 | | | 420 | 460 |
| 0800 | Floor & ceiling anchored, marble | 2 Marb | 2.50 | 6.400 | | 1,775 | 239 | | 2,014 | 2,325 |
| 1400 | For handicap units, incl. 52" grab bars, add | | | | ↓ | 251 | | | 251 | 276 |

# 10 21 Compartments and Cubicles

## 10 21 13 – Toilet Compartments

### 10 21 13.40 Stone Toilet Compartments

| | | Crew | Daily Output | Labor-Hours | Unit | Material | 2008 Bare Costs Labor | Equipment | Total | Total Incl O&P |
|---|---|---|---|---|---|---|---|---|---|---|
| 1600 | Floor mounted, marble | 2 Marb | 3 | 5.333 | Ea. | 1,050 | 199 | | 1,249 | 1,450 |
| 2400 | Floor mounted, headrail braced, marble | " | 3 | 5.333 | | 995 | 199 | | 1,194 | 1,400 |
| 2900 | For handicap units, incl. 52" grab bars, add | | | | | 320 | | | 320 | 355 |
| 4100 | Entrance screen, floor mounted marble, 58" high, 48" wide | 2 Marb | 9 | 1.778 | | 655 | 66.50 | | 721.50 | 820 |
| 4600 | Urinal screen, 18" wide, ceiling braced, marble | D-1 | 6 | 2.667 | | 655 | 93 | | 748 | 860 |
| 5100 | Floor mounted, head rail braced | | | | | | | | | |
| 5200 | Marble | D-1 | 6 | 2.667 | Ea. | 575 | 93 | | 668 | 770 |
| 5700 | Pilaster, flush, marble | | 9 | 1.778 | | 730 | 62 | | 792 | 900 |
| 6200 | Post braced, marble | | 9 | 1.778 | | 725 | 62 | | 787 | 890 |

## 10 21 16 – Shower and Dressing Compartments

### 10 21 16.10 Partitions, Shower

| | | Crew | Daily Output | Labor-Hours | Unit | Material | 2008 Bare Costs Labor | Equipment | Total | Total Incl O&P |
|---|---|---|---|---|---|---|---|---|---|---|
| 0010 | **PARTITIONS, SHOWER** Floor mounted, no plumbing | | | | | | | | | |
| 0100 | Cabinet, incl. base, no door, painted steel, 1" thick walls | 2 Shee | 5 | 3.200 | Ea. | 880 | 145 | | 1,025 | 1,200 |
| 0300 | With door, fiberglass | | 4.50 | 3.556 | | 685 | 161 | | 846 | 1,000 |
| 0600 | Galvanized and painted steel, 1" thick walls | | 5 | 3.200 | | 930 | 145 | | 1,075 | 1,250 |
| 0800 | Stall, 1" thick wall, no base, enameled steel | | 5 | 3.200 | | 970 | 145 | | 1,115 | 1,300 |
| 1200 | Stainless steel | | 5 | 3.200 | | 1,650 | 145 | | 1,795 | 2,050 |
| 1400 | For double entry type, no doors, deduct | | | | | 10% | | | | |
| 1500 | Circular fiberglass, cabinet 36" diameter, | 2 Shee | 4 | 4 | | 705 | 181 | | 886 | 1,050 |
| 1700 | One piece, 36" diameter, less door | | 4 | 4 | | 595 | 181 | | 776 | 930 |
| 1800 | With door | | 3.50 | 4.571 | | 975 | 207 | | 1,182 | 1,400 |
| 2000 | Curved shell shower, no door needed | | 3 | 5.333 | | 850 | 242 | | 1,092 | 1,300 |
| 2300 | For fiberglass seat, add to both above | | | | | 120 | | | 120 | 132 |
| 2400 | Glass stalls, with doors, no receptors, chrome on brass | 2 Shee | 3 | 5.333 | | 1,425 | 242 | | 1,667 | 1,950 |
| 2700 | Anodized aluminum | " | 4 | 4 | | 990 | 181 | | 1,171 | 1,375 |
| 2900 | Marble shower stall, stock design, with shower door | 2 Marb | 1.20 | 13.333 | | 2,150 | 500 | | 2,650 | 3,100 |
| 3000 | With curtain | | 1.30 | 12.308 | | 1,900 | 460 | | 2,360 | 2,775 |
| 3200 | Receptors, precast terrazzo, 32" x 32" | | 14 | 1.143 | | 235 | 42.50 | | 277.50 | 325 |
| 3300 | 48" x 34" | | 9.50 | 1.684 | | 320 | 63 | | 383 | 445 |
| 3500 | Plastic, simulated terrazzo receptor, 32" x 32" | | 14 | 1.143 | | 97.50 | 42.50 | | 140 | 172 |
| 3600 | 32" x 48" | | 12 | 1.333 | | 185 | 50 | | 235 | 279 |
| 3800 | Precast concrete, colors, 32" x 32" | | 14 | 1.143 | | 181 | 42.50 | | 223.50 | 265 |
| 3900 | 48" x 48" | | 8 | 2 | | 380 | 74.50 | | 454.50 | 530 |
| 4100 | Shower doors, economy plastic, 24" wide | 1 Shee | 9 | .889 | | 124 | 40.50 | | 164.50 | 198 |
| 4200 | Tempered glass door, economy | | 8 | 1 | | 164 | 45.50 | | 209.50 | 251 |
| 4400 | Folding, tempered glass, aluminum frame | | 6 | 1.333 | | 375 | 60.50 | | 435.50 | 505 |
| 4500 | Sliding, tempered glass, 48" opening | | 6 | 1.333 | | 248 | 60.50 | | 308.50 | 365 |
| 4700 | Deluxe, tempered glass, chrome on brass frame, minimum | | 8 | 1 | | 216 | 45.50 | | 261.50 | 310 |
| 4800 | Maximum | | 1 | 8 | | 855 | 360 | | 1,215 | 1,500 |
| 4850 | On anodized aluminum frame, minimum | | 2 | 4 | | 140 | 181 | | 321 | 435 |
| 4900 | Maximum | | 1 | 8 | | 505 | 360 | | 865 | 1,125 |
| 5100 | Shower enclosure, tempered glass, anodized alum. frame | | | | | | | | | |
| 5120 | 2 panel & door, corner unit, 32" x 32" | 1 Shee | 2 | 4 | Ea. | 490 | 181 | | 671 | 820 |
| 5140 | Neo-angle corner unit, 16" x 24" x 16" | " | 2 | 4 | | 905 | 181 | | 1,086 | 1,275 |
| 5200 | Shower surround, 3 wall, polypropylene, 32" x 32" | 1 Carp | 4 | 2 | | 267 | 76 | | 343 | 415 |
| 5220 | PVC, 32" x 32" | | 4 | 2 | | 330 | 76 | | 406 | 485 |
| 5240 | Fiberglass | | 4 | 2 | | 360 | 76 | | 436 | 515 |
| 5250 | 2 wall, polypropylene, 32" x 32" | | 4 | 2 | | 274 | 76 | | 350 | 420 |
| 5270 | PVC | | 4 | 2 | | 340 | 76 | | 416 | 495 |
| 5290 | Fiberglass | | 4 | 2 | | 345 | 76 | | 421 | 500 |
| 5300 | Tub doors, tempered glass & frame, minimum | 1 Shee | 8 | 1 | | 198 | 45.50 | | 243.50 | 288 |
| 5400 | Maximum | | 6 | 1.333 | | 465 | 60.50 | | 525.50 | 605 |

# 10 21 Compartments and Cubicles

## 10 21 16 - Shower and Dressing Compartments

### 10 21 16.10 Partitions, Shower

| | | Crew | Daily Output | Labor-Hours | Unit | Material | 2008 Bare Costs Labor | Equipment | Total | Total Incl O&P |
|---|---|---|---|---|---|---|---|---|---|---|
| 5600 | Chrome plated, brass frame, minimum | 1 Shee | 8 | 1 | Ea. | 262 | 45.50 | | 307.50 | 360 |
| 5700 | Maximum | | 6 | 1.333 | | 640 | 60.50 | | 700.50 | 800 |
| 5900 | Tub/shower enclosure, temp. glass, alum. frame, minimum | | 2 | 4 | | 355 | 181 | | 536 | 670 |
| 6200 | Maximum | | 1.50 | 5.333 | | 740 | 242 | | 982 | 1,200 |
| 6500 | On chrome-plated brass frame, minimum | | 2 | 4 | | 490 | 181 | | 671 | 820 |
| 6600 | Maximum | | 1.50 | 5.333 | | 1,050 | 242 | | 1,292 | 1,525 |
| 6800 | Tub surround, 3 wall, polypropylene | 1 Carp | 4 | 2 | | 221 | 76 | | 297 | 360 |
| 6900 | PVC | | 4 | 2 | | 335 | 76 | | 411 | 490 |
| 7000 | Fiberglass, minimum | | 4 | 2 | | 345 | 76 | | 421 | 500 |
| 7100 | Maximum | | 3 | 2.667 | | 590 | 102 | | 692 | 805 |

## 10 21 23 - Cubicles

### 10 21 23.16 Cubicle Track and Hardware

| | | Crew | Daily Output | Labor-Hours | Unit | Material | 2008 Bare Costs Labor | Equipment | Total | Total Incl O&P |
|---|---|---|---|---|---|---|---|---|---|---|
| 0010 | **CUBICLE TRACK AND HARDWARE** | | | | | | | | | |
| 0020 | Curtain track, box channel, ceiling mounted | 1 Carp | 135 | .059 | L.F. | 5.60 | 2.26 | | 7.86 | 9.65 |
| 0100 | Suspended | " | 100 | .080 | " | 6.75 | 3.05 | | 9.80 | 12.20 |
| 0300 | Curtains, nylon mesh tops, fire resistant, 11 oz. per lineal yard | | | | | | | | | |
| 0310 | Polyester oxford cloth, 9' ceiling height | 1 Carp | 425 | .019 | L.F. | 11.30 | .72 | | 12.02 | 13.50 |
| 0500 | 8' ceiling height | | 425 | .019 | | 9.55 | .72 | | 10.27 | 11.60 |
| 0700 | Designer oxford cloth | | 425 | .019 | | 24 | .72 | | 24.72 | 27.50 |
| 0800 | I.V. track systems | | | | | | | | | |
| 0820 | I.V. track, oval | 1 Carp | 135 | .059 | L.F. | 4.96 | 2.26 | | 7.22 | 8.95 |
| 0830 | I.V. trolley | | 32 | .250 | Ea. | 34 | 9.55 | | 43.55 | 52.50 |
| 0840 | I.V. pendent, (tree, 5 hook) | | 32 | .250 | " | 122 | 9.55 | | 131.55 | 149 |

# 10 22 Partitions

## 10 22 13 - Wire Mesh Partitions

### 10 22 13.10 Partitions, Woven Wire

| | | Crew | Daily Output | Labor-Hours | Unit | Material | 2008 Bare Costs Labor | Equipment | Total | Total Incl O&P |
|---|---|---|---|---|---|---|---|---|---|---|
| 0010 | **PARTITIONS, WOVEN WIRE** For tool or stockroom enclosures | | | | | | | | | |
| 0100 | Channel frame, 1-1/2" diamond mesh, 10 ga. wire, painted | | | | | | | | | |
| 0300 | Wall panels, 4'-0" wide, 7' high | 2 Carp | 25 | .640 | Ea. | 120 | 24.50 | | 144.50 | 170 |
| 0400 | 8' high | | 23 | .696 | | 125 | 26.50 | | 151.50 | 180 |
| 0600 | 10' high | | 18 | .889 | | 153 | 34 | | 187 | 221 |
| 0700 | For 5' wide panels, add | | | | | 5% | | | | |
| 0900 | Ceiling panels, 10' long, 2' wide | 2 Carp | 25 | .640 | | 91.50 | 24.50 | | 116 | 138 |
| 1000 | 4' wide | | 15 | 1.067 | | 131 | 40.50 | | 171.50 | 208 |
| 1200 | Panel with service window & shelf, 5' wide, 7' high | | 20 | .800 | | 282 | 30.50 | | 312.50 | 360 |
| 1300 | 8' high | | 15 | 1.067 | | 290 | 40.50 | | 330.50 | 385 |
| 1500 | Sliding doors, full height, 3' wide, 7' high | | 6 | 2.667 | | 305 | 102 | | 407 | 495 |
| 1600 | 10' high | | 5 | 3.200 | | 400 | 122 | | 522 | 630 |
| 1800 | 6' wide sliding door, 7' full height | | 5 | 3.200 | | 455 | 122 | | 577 | 690 |
| 1900 | 10' high | | 4 | 4 | | 550 | 152 | | 702 | 840 |
| 2100 | Swinging doors, 3' wide, 7' high, no transom | | 6 | 2.667 | | 243 | 102 | | 345 | 425 |
| 2200 | 7' high, 3' transom | | 5 | 3.200 | | 283 | 122 | | 405 | 500 |

## 10 22 16 - Folding Gates

### 10 22 16.10 Security Gates

| | | Crew | Daily Output | Labor-Hours | Unit | Material | 2008 Bare Costs Labor | Equipment | Total | Total Incl O&P |
|---|---|---|---|---|---|---|---|---|---|---|
| 0010 | **SECURITY GATES** For roll up type, see Div. 08 33 13.10 | | | | | | | | | |
| 0300 | Scissors type folding gate, ptd. steel, single, 6-1/2' high, 5-1/2' wide | 2 Sswk | 4 | 4 | Opng. | 172 | 172 | | 344 | 500 |
| 0350 | 6-1/2' wide | | 4 | 4 | | 172 | 172 | | 344 | 500 |
| 0400 | 7-1/2' wide | | 4 | 4 | | 182 | 172 | | 354 | 510 |
| 0600 | Double gate, 8' high, 8' wide | | 2.50 | 6.400 | | 269 | 275 | | 544 | 790 |

# 10 22 Partitions

## 10 22 16 – Folding Gates

### 10 22 16.10 Security Gates

| | | Crew | Daily Output | Labor-Hours | Unit | Material | 2008 Bare Costs Labor | Equipment | Total | Total Incl O&P |
|---|---|---|---|---|---|---|---|---|---|---|
| 0650 | 10' wide | 2 Sswk | 2.50 | 6.400 | Opng. | 283 | 275 | | 558 | 805 |
| 0700 | 12' wide | | 2 | 8 | | 420 | 345 | | 765 | 1,075 |
| 0750 | 14' wide | | 2 | 8 | | 530 | 345 | | 875 | 1,200 |
| 0900 | Door gate, folding steel, 4' wide, 61" high | | 4 | 4 | | 85.50 | 172 | | 257.50 | 405 |
| 1000 | 71" high | | 4 | 4 | | 88.50 | 172 | | 260.50 | 405 |
| 1200 | 81" high | | 4 | 4 | | 96 | 172 | | 268 | 415 |
| 1300 | Window gates, 2' to 4' wide, 31" high | | 4 | 4 | | 56 | 172 | | 228 | 370 |
| 1500 | 55" high | | 3.75 | 4.267 | | 92 | 183 | | 275 | 430 |
| 1600 | 79" high | ↓ | 3.50 | 4.571 | ↓ | 90 | 197 | | 287 | 455 |

## 10 22 19 – Demountable Partitions

### 10 22 19.43 Demountable Composite Partitions

| | | | Crew | Daily Output | Labor-Hours | Unit | Material | 2008 Bare Costs Labor | Equipment | Total | Total Incl O&P |
|---|---|---|---|---|---|---|---|---|---|---|---|
| 0010 | **DEMOUNTABLE COMPOSITE PARTITIONS**, add for doors | | | | | | | | | | |
| 0100 | Do not deduct door openings from total L.F. | | | | | | | | | | |
| 0900 | Demountable gypsum system on 2" to 2-1/2" | | | | | | | | | | |
| 1000 | steel studs, 9' high, 3" to 3-3/4" thick | | | | | | | | | | |
| 1200 | Vinyl clad gypsum | CN | 2 Carp | 48 | .333 | L.F. | 56.50 | 12.70 | | 69.20 | 82.50 |
| 1300 | Fabric clad gypsum | | | 44 | .364 | | 141 | 13.85 | | 154.85 | 177 |
| 1500 | Steel clad gypsum | | ↓ | 40 | .400 | ↓ | 153 | 15.25 | | 168.25 | 192 |
| 1600 | 1.75 system, aluminum framing, vinyl clad hardboard, | | | | | | | | | | |
| 1800 | paper honeycomb core panel, 1-3/4" to 2-1/2" thick | | | | | | | | | | |
| 1900 | 9' high | | 2 Carp | 48 | .333 | L.F. | 95 | 12.70 | | 107.70 | 125 |
| 2100 | 7' high | | | 60 | .267 | | 85.50 | 10.15 | | 95.65 | 110 |
| 2200 | 5' high | | ↓ | 80 | .200 | ↓ | 72 | 7.60 | | 79.60 | 91.50 |
| 2250 | Unitized gypsum system | | | | | | | | | | |
| 2300 | Unitized panel, 9' high, 2" to 2-1/2" thick | | | | | | | | | | |
| 2350 | Vinyl clad gypsum | | 2 Carp | 48 | .333 | L.F. | 123 | 12.70 | | 135.70 | 155 |
| 2400 | Fabric clad gypsum | | " | 44 | .364 | " | 202 | 13.85 | | 215.85 | 244 |
| 2500 | Unitized mineral fiber system | | | | | | | | | | |
| 2510 | Unitized panel, 9' high, 2-1/4" thick, aluminum frame | | | | | | | | | | |
| 2550 | Vinyl clad mineral fiber | | 2 Carp | 48 | .333 | L.F. | 122 | 12.70 | | 134.70 | 154 |
| 2600 | Fabric clad mineral fiber | | " | 44 | .364 | " | 181 | 13.85 | | 194.85 | 222 |
| 2800 | Movable steel walls, modular system | | | | | | | | | | |
| 2900 | Unitized panels, 9' high, 48" wide | | | | | | | | | | |
| 3100 | Baked enamel, pre-finished | | 2 Carp | 60 | .267 | L.F. | 138 | 10.15 | | 148.15 | 168 |
| 3200 | Fabric clad steel | | | 56 | .286 | " | 199 | 10.90 | | 209.90 | 236 |
| 5310 | Trackless wall, cork finish, semi-acoustic, 1-5/8" thick, minimum | | | 325 | .049 | S.F. | 38.50 | 1.88 | | 40.38 | 45.50 |
| 5320 | Maximum | | | 190 | .084 | | 36.50 | 3.21 | | 39.71 | 45 |
| 5330 | Acoustic, 2" thick, minimum | | | 305 | .052 | | 31 | 2 | | 33 | 37 |
| 5340 | Maximum | | ↓ | 225 | .071 | | 53.50 | 2.71 | | 56.21 | 63 |
| 5500 | For acoustical partitions, add, minimum | | | | | | 2.22 | | | 2.22 | 2.44 |
| 5550 | Maximum | | | | | ↓ | 10.35 | | | 10.35 | 11.40 |
| 5700 | For doors, see Div. 08 11 & 08 16 | | | | | | | | | | |
| 5800 | For door hardware, see Div. 08 71 | | | | | | | | | | |
| 6100 | In-plant modular office system, w/prehung hollow core door | | | | | | | | | | |
| 6200 | 3" thick polystyrene core panels | | | | | | | | | | |
| 6250 | 12' x 12', 2 wall | | 2 Clab | 3.80 | 4.211 | Ea. | 2,875 | 127 | | 3,002 | 3,350 |
| 6300 | 4 wall | | | 1.90 | 8.421 | | 4,100 | 255 | | 4,355 | 4,900 |
| 6350 | 16' x 16', 2 wall | | | 3.60 | 4.444 | | 4,475 | 134 | | 4,609 | 5,100 |
| 6400 | 4 wall | | ↓ | 1.80 | 8.889 | ↓ | 5,875 | 269 | | 6,144 | 6,900 |

## 10 22 23 – Portable Partitions, Screens, and Panels

### 10 22 23.13 Wall Screens

| | | | | | | | | | | | |
|---|---|---|---|---|---|---|---|---|---|---|---|
| 0010 | **WALL SCREENS**, divider panels, free standing, fiber core | | | | | | | | | | |

# 10 22 Partitions

## 10 22 23 – Portable Partitions, Screens, and Panels

### 10 22 23.13 Wall Screens

| | | Crew | Daily Output | Labor-Hours | Unit | Material | 2008 Bare Costs Labor | Equipment | Total | Total Incl O&P |
|---|---|---|---|---|---|---|---|---|---|---|
| 0020 | Fabric face straight | | | | | | | | | |
| 0100 | 3'-0" long, 4'-0" high | 2 Carp | 100 | .160 | L.F. | 106 | 6.10 | | 112.10 | 126 |
| 0200 | 5'-0" high | | 90 | .178 | | 111 | 6.75 | | 117.75 | 133 |
| 0500 | 6'-0" high | | 75 | .213 | | 114 | 8.15 | | 122.15 | 138 |
| 0900 | 5'-0" long, 4'-0" high | | 175 | .091 | | 76.50 | 3.48 | | 79.98 | 90 |
| 1000 | 5'-0" high | | 150 | .107 | | 88 | 4.06 | | 92.06 | 103 |
| 1500 | 6"-0" high | | 125 | .128 | | 91 | 4.88 | | 95.88 | 108 |
| 1600 | 6'-0" long, 5'-0" high | | 162 | .099 | | 76 | 3.76 | | 79.76 | 89.50 |
| 3200 | Economical panels, fabric face, 4'-0" long, 5'-0" high | | 132 | .121 | | 45.50 | 4.62 | | 50.12 | 57 |
| 3250 | 6'-0" high | | 112 | .143 | | 45.50 | 5.45 | | 50.95 | 58.50 |
| 3300 | 5'-0" long, 5'-0" high | | 150 | .107 | | 32.50 | 4.06 | | 36.56 | 42 |
| 3350 | 6'-0" high | | 125 | .128 | | 39 | 4.88 | | 43.88 | 50.50 |
| 3450 | Acoustical panels, 60 to 90 NRC, 3'-0" long, 5'-0" high | | 90 | .178 | | 69.50 | 6.75 | | 76.25 | 87 |
| 3550 | 6'-0" high | | 75 | .213 | | 73 | 8.15 | | 81.15 | 93 |
| 3600 | 5'-0" long, 5'-0" high | | 150 | .107 | | 42.50 | 4.06 | | 46.56 | 53 |
| 3650 | 6'-0" high | | 125 | .128 | | 47 | 4.88 | | 51.88 | 59 |
| 3700 | 6'-0" long, 5'-0" high | | 162 | .099 | | 37 | 3.76 | | 40.76 | 47 |
| 3750 | 6'-0" high | | 138 | .116 | | 71.50 | 4.42 | | 75.92 | 85.50 |
| 3800 | Economy acoustical panels, 40 N.R.C., 4'-0" long, 5'-0" high | | 132 | .121 | | 45.50 | 4.62 | | 50.12 | 57 |
| 3850 | 6'-0" high | | 112 | .143 | | 45.50 | 5.45 | | 50.95 | 58.50 |
| 3900 | 5'-0" long, 6'-0" high | | 125 | .128 | | 39 | 4.88 | | 43.88 | 50.50 |
| 3950 | 6'-0" long, 5'-0" high | | 162 | .099 | | 29.50 | 3.76 | | 33.26 | 38.50 |
| 4000 | Metal chalkboard, 6'-6" high, chalkboard, 1 side | | 125 | .128 | | 98 | 4.88 | | 102.88 | 116 |
| 4100 | Metal chalkboard, 2 sides | | 120 | .133 | | 112 | 5.10 | | 117.10 | 131 |
| 4300 | Tackboard, both sides | | 123 | .130 | | 88.50 | 4.96 | | 93.46 | 105 |

## 10 22 26 – Operable Partitions

### 10 22 26.13 Accordion Folding Partitions

| | | Crew | Daily Output | Labor-Hours | Unit | Material | 2008 Bare Costs Labor | Equipment | Total | Total Incl O&P |
|---|---|---|---|---|---|---|---|---|---|---|
| 0010 | **ACCORDION FOLDING PARTITIONS** | | | | | | | | | |
| 0100 | Vinyl covered, over 150 S.F., frame not included | | | | | | | | | |
| 0300 | Residential, 1.25 lb. per S.F., 8' maximum height | 2 Carp | 300 | .053 | S.F. | 18.80 | 2.03 | | 20.83 | 23.50 |
| 0400 | Commercial, 1.75 lb. per S.F., 8' maximum height | | 225 | .071 | | 21.50 | 2.71 | | 24.21 | 27.50 |
| 0600 | 2 lb. per S.F., 17' maximum height | | 150 | .107 | | 22 | 4.06 | | 26.06 | 31 |
| 0700 | Industrial, 4 lb. per S.F., 20' maximum height | | 75 | .213 | | 32 | 8.15 | | 40.15 | 47.50 |
| 0900 | Acoustical, 3 lb. per S.F., 17' maximum height | | 100 | .160 | | 25 | 6.10 | | 31.10 | 37 |
| 1200 | 5 lb. per S.F., 20' maximum height | | 95 | .168 | | 34.50 | 6.40 | | 40.90 | 48 |
| 1300 | 5.5 lb. per S.F., 17' maximum height | | 90 | .178 | | 40.50 | 6.75 | | 47.25 | 55 |
| 1400 | Fire rated, 4.5 psf, 20' maximum height | | 160 | .100 | | 40.50 | 3.81 | | 44.31 | 50.50 |
| 1500 | Vinyl clad wood or steel, electric operation, 5.0 psf | | 160 | .100 | | 47 | 3.81 | | 50.81 | 57.50 |
| 1900 | Wood, non-acoustic, birch or mahogany, to 10' high | | 300 | .053 | | 25.50 | 2.03 | | 27.53 | 31 |

### 10 22 26.33 Folding Panel Partitions

| | | Crew | Daily Output | Labor-Hours | Unit | Material | 2008 Bare Costs Labor | Equipment | Total | Total Incl O&P |
|---|---|---|---|---|---|---|---|---|---|---|
| 0010 | **FOLDING PANEL PARTITIONS**, acoustic, wood | | | | | | | | | |
| 0100 | Vinyl faced, to 18' high, 6 psf, minimum | 2 Carp | 60 | .267 | S.F. | 47.50 | 10.15 | | 57.65 | 68.50 |
| 0150 | Average | | 45 | .356 | | 57 | 13.55 | | 70.55 | 83.50 |
| 0200 | Maximum | | 30 | .533 | | 73.50 | 20.50 | | 94 | 113 |
| 0400 | Formica or hardwood finish, minimum | | 60 | .267 | | 49 | 10.15 | | 59.15 | 70 |
| 0500 | Maximum | | 30 | .533 | | 52.50 | 20.50 | | 73 | 89 |
| 0600 | Wood, low acoustical type, 4.5 psf, to 14' high | | 50 | .320 | | 35.50 | 12.20 | | 47.70 | 58.50 |
| 1100 | Steel, acoustical, 9 to 12 lb. per S.F., vinyl faced, minimum | | 60 | .267 | | 50.50 | 10.15 | | 60.65 | 72 |
| 1200 | Maximum | | 30 | .533 | | 62 | 20.50 | | 82.50 | 99.50 |
| 1700 | Aluminum framed, acoustical, to 12' high, 5.5 psf, minimum | | 60 | .267 | | 34 | 10.15 | | 44.15 | 53.50 |
| 1800 | Maximum | | 30 | .533 | | 41.50 | 20.50 | | 62 | 77 |
| 2000 | 6.5 lb. per S.F., minimum | | 60 | .267 | | 36 | 10.15 | | 46.15 | 55.50 |

# 10 22 Partitions

## 10 22 26 – Operable Partitions

| 10 22 26.33 Folding Panel Partitions | | Crew | Daily Output | Labor-Hours | Unit | Material | 2008 Bare Costs Labor | Equipment | Total | Total Incl O&P |
|---|---|---|---|---|---|---|---|---|---|---|
| 2100 | Maximum | 2 Carp | 30 | .533 | S.F. | 44.50 | 20.50 | | 65 | 80.50 |

### 10 22 26.43 Sliding Partitions

| | | Crew | Daily Output | Labor-Hours | Unit | Material | Labor | Equipment | Total | Total Incl O&P |
|---|---|---|---|---|---|---|---|---|---|---|
| 0010 | **SLIDING PARTITIONS** | | | | | | | | | |
| 0020 | Acoustic air wall, 1-5/8" thick, minimum | 2 Carp | 375 | .043 | S.F. | 29 | 1.63 | | 30.63 | 34.50 |
| 0100 | Maximum | | 365 | .044 | | 50 | 1.67 | | 51.67 | 57.50 |
| 0300 | 2-1/4" thick, minimum | | 360 | .044 | | 32.50 | 1.69 | | 34.19 | 38.50 |
| 0400 | Maximum | | 330 | .048 | | 57 | 1.85 | | 58.85 | 66 |
| 0600 | For track type, add to above | | | | L.F. | 106 | | | 106 | 117 |
| 0700 | Overhead track type, acoustical, 3" thick, 11 psf, minimum | 2 Carp | 350 | .046 | S.F. | 73.50 | 1.74 | | 75.24 | 83 |
| 0800 | Maximum | " | 300 | .053 | " | 88.50 | 2.03 | | 90.53 | 100 |

# 10 26 Wall and Door Protection

## 10 26 13 – Corner Guards

### 10 26 13.10 Metal Corner Guards

| | | Crew | Daily Output | Labor-Hours | Unit | Material | Labor | Equipment | Total | Total Incl O&P |
|---|---|---|---|---|---|---|---|---|---|---|
| 0010 | **METAL CORNER GUARDS** | | | | | | | | | |
| 0020 | Steel angle w/anchors, 1" x 1" x 1/4", 1.5#/L.F. | 2 Carp | 160 | .100 | L.F. | 5.75 | 3.81 | | 9.56 | 12.30 |
| 0100 | 2" x 2" x 1/4" angles, 3.2#/L.F. | | 150 | .107 | | 10.45 | 4.06 | | 14.51 | 17.85 |
| 0200 | 3" x 3" x 5/16" angles, 6.1#/L.F. | | 140 | .114 | | 15.55 | 4.35 | | 19.90 | 24 |
| 0300 | 4" x 4" x 5/16" angles, 8.2#/L.F. | | 120 | .133 | | 18.95 | 5.10 | | 24.05 | 29 |
| 0350 | For angles drilled and anchored to masonry, add | | | | | 15% | 120% | | | |
| 0370 | Drilled and anchored to concrete, add | | | | | 20% | 170% | | | |
| 0400 | For galvanized angles, add | | | | | 35% | | | | |
| 0450 | For stainless steel angles, add | | | | | 100% | | | | |
| 0500 | Steel door track/wheel guards, 4' - 0" high | E-4 | 22 | 1.455 | Ea. | 156 | 63.50 | 6 | 225.50 | 292 |
| 0800 | Pipe bumper for truck doors, 8' long, 6" diameter, filled | | 20 | 1.600 | | 365 | 69.50 | 6.60 | 441.10 | 535 |
| 0900 | 8" diameter | | 20 | 1.600 | | 560 | 69.50 | 6.60 | 636.10 | 750 |

### 10 26 13.20 Corner Protection

| | | Crew | Daily Output | Labor-Hours | Unit | Material | Labor | Equipment | Total | Total Incl O&P |
|---|---|---|---|---|---|---|---|---|---|---|
| 0010 | **CORNER PROTECTION** | | | | | | | | | |
| 0100 | Stainless steel, 16 ga., adhesive mount, 3-1/2" leg | 1 Sswk | 80 | .100 | L.F. | 18.05 | 4.30 | | 22.35 | 27.50 |
| 0200 | 12 ga. stainless, adhesive mount | " | 80 | .100 | | 21 | 4.30 | | 25.30 | 31 |
| 0300 | For screw mount, add | | | | | | 10% | | | |
| 0500 | Vinyl acrylic, adhesive mount, 3" leg | 1 Carp | 128 | .063 | | 7.20 | 2.38 | | 9.58 | 11.60 |
| 0550 | 1-1/2" leg | | 160 | .050 | | 4.51 | 1.91 | | 6.42 | 7.95 |
| 0600 | Screw mounted, 3" leg | | 80 | .100 | | 7.75 | 3.81 | | 11.56 | 14.50 |
| 0650 | 1-1/2" leg | | 100 | .080 | | 4 | 3.05 | | 7.05 | 9.15 |
| 0700 | Clear plastic, screw mounted, 2-1/2" | | 60 | .133 | | 3.61 | 5.10 | | 8.71 | 11.85 |
| 1000 | Vinyl cover, alum. retainer, surface mount, 3" x 3" | | 48 | .167 | | 8.65 | 6.35 | | 15 | 19.40 |
| 1050 | 2" x 2" | | 48 | .167 | | 9.30 | 6.35 | | 15.65 | 20 |
| 1100 | Flush mounted, 3" x 3" | | 32 | .250 | | 19.25 | 9.55 | | 28.80 | 36 |
| 1150 | 2" x 2" | | 32 | .250 | | 15.65 | 9.55 | | 25.20 | 32 |

## 10 26 16 – Bumper Guards

### 10 26 16.10 Wallguard

| | | Crew | Daily Output | Labor-Hours | Unit | Material | Labor | Equipment | Total | Total Incl O&P |
|---|---|---|---|---|---|---|---|---|---|---|
| 0010 | **WALLGUARD** | | | | | | | | | |
| 0400 | Rub rail, vinyl, adhesive mounted | 1 Carp | 185 | .043 | L.F. | 7.70 | 1.65 | | 9.35 | 11 |
| 0500 | Neoprene, aluminum backing, 1-1/2" x 2" | | 110 | .073 | | 8.65 | 2.77 | | 11.42 | 13.80 |
| 1000 | Trolley rail, PVC, clipped to wall, 5" high | | 185 | .043 | | 7.65 | 1.65 | | 9.30 | 10.95 |
| 1050 | 8" high | | 180 | .044 | | 10.25 | 1.69 | | 11.94 | 13.90 |
| 1200 | Bed bumper, vinyl acrylic, alum. retainer, 21" long | | 10 | .800 | Ea. | 39.50 | 30.50 | | 70 | 91 |
| 1300 | 53" long with aligner | | 9 | .889 | " | 100 | 34 | | 134 | 163 |
| 1400 | Bumper, vinyl cover, alum. retain., cush. mnt., 1-1/2" x 2-3/4" | | 80 | .100 | L.F. | 13.95 | 3.81 | | 17.76 | 21.50 |

# 10 26 Wall and Door Protection

## 10 26 16 – Bumper Guards

| 10 26 16.10 Wallguard | | Crew | Daily Output | Labor-Hours | Unit | Material | 2008 Bare Costs Labor | Equipment | Total | Total Incl O&P |
|---|---|---|---|---|---|---|---|---|---|---|
| 1500 | 2" x 4-1/4" | 1 Carp | 80 | .100 | L.F. | 20.50 | 3.81 | | 24.31 | 28.50 |
| 1600 | Surface mounted, 1-3/4" x 3-5/8" | | 80 | .100 | | 11.70 | 3.81 | | 15.51 | 18.85 |
| 2000 | Crash rail, vinyl cover, alum. retainer, 1" x 4" | | 110 | .073 | | 10.80 | 2.77 | | 13.57 | 16.20 |
| 2100 | 1" x 8" | | 90 | .089 | | 16.90 | 3.39 | | 20.29 | 24 |
| 2150 | Vinyl inserts, aluminum plate, 1" x 2-1/2" | | 110 | .073 | | 14.60 | 2.77 | | 17.37 | 20.50 |
| 2200 | 1" x 5" | | 90 | .089 | | 22.50 | 3.39 | | 25.89 | 30.50 |
| 3000 | Handrail/bumper, vinyl cover, alum. retainer | | | | | | | | | |
| 3010 | Bracket mounted, flat rail, 5-1/2" | 1 Carp | 80 | .100 | L.F. | 17.55 | 3.81 | | 21.36 | 25.50 |
| 3100 | 6-1/2" | | 80 | .100 | | 22 | 3.81 | | 25.81 | 30 |
| 3200 | Bronze bracket, 1-3/4" diam. rail | | 80 | .100 | | 15.85 | 3.81 | | 19.66 | 23.50 |

# 10 28 Toilet, Bath, and Laundry Accessories

## 10 28 13 – Toilet Accessories

### 10 28 13.13 Commercial Toilet Accessories

| | | Crew | Daily Output | Labor-Hours | Unit | Material | 2008 Bare Costs Labor | Equipment | Total | Total Incl O&P |
|---|---|---|---|---|---|---|---|---|---|---|
| 0010 | **COMMERCIAL TOILET ACCESSORIES** | | | | | | | | | |
| 0200 | Curtain rod, stainless steel, 5' long, 1" diameter | 1 Carp | 13 | .615 | Ea. | 33 | 23.50 | | 56.50 | 73 |
| 0300 | 1-1/4" diameter | | 13 | .615 | | 31 | 23.50 | | 54.50 | 70.50 |
| 0400 | Diaper changing station, horizontal, wall mounted, plastic | | 10 | .800 | | 248 | 30.50 | | 278.50 | 320 |
| 0500 | Dispenser units, combined soap & towel dispensers, | | | | | | | | | |
| 0510 | mirror and shelf, flush mounted | 1 Carp | 10 | .800 | Ea. | 295 | 30.50 | | 325.50 | 375 |
| 0600 | Towel dispenser and waste receptacle, | | | | | | | | | |
| 0610 | 18 gallon capacity | 1 Carp | 10 | .800 | Ea. | 450 | 30.50 | | 480.50 | 545 |
| 0800 | Grab bar, straight, 1-1/4" diameter, stainless steel, 18" long | | 24 | .333 | | 26 | 12.70 | | 38.70 | 49 |
| 0900 | 24" long | | 23 | .348 | | 29.50 | 13.25 | | 42.75 | 53 |
| 1000 | 30" long | | 22 | .364 | | 30 | 13.85 | | 43.85 | 54.50 |
| 1100 | 36" long | | 20 | .400 | | 29.50 | 15.25 | | 44.75 | 56 |
| 1105 | 42" long | | 20 | .400 | | 37 | 15.25 | | 52.25 | 64 |
| 1200 | 1-1/2" diameter, 24" long | | 23 | .348 | | 30 | 13.25 | | 43.25 | 53.50 |
| 1300 | 36" long | | 20 | .400 | | 32 | 15.25 | | 47.25 | 59 |
| 1310 | 42" long | | 18 | .444 | | 38.50 | 16.95 | | 55.45 | 68.50 |
| 1500 | Tub bar, 1-1/4" diameter, 24" x 36" | | 14 | .571 | | 109 | 22 | | 131 | 153 |
| 1600 | Plus vertical arm | | 12 | .667 | | 95 | 25.50 | | 120.50 | 145 |
| 1900 | End tub bar, 1" diameter, 90° angle, 16" x 32" | | 12 | .667 | | 130 | 25.50 | | 155.50 | 183 |
| 2010 | Tub/shower/toilet, 2-wall, 36" x 24" | | 12 | .667 | | 118 | 25.50 | | 143.50 | 169 |
| 2300 | Hand dryer, surface mounted, electric, 115 volt, 20 amp | | 4 | 2 | | 380 | 76 | | 456 | 535 |
| 2400 | 230 volt, 10 amp | | 4 | 2 | | 535 | 76 | | 611 | 705 |
| 2600 | Hat and coat strip, stainless steel, 4 hook, 36" long | | 24 | .333 | | 43 | 12.70 | | 55.70 | 67.50 |
| 2700 | 6 hook, 60" long | | 20 | .400 | | 54 | 15.25 | | 69.25 | 83 |
| 3000 | Mirror, with stainless steel 3/4" square frame, 18" x 24" | | 20 | .400 | | 47 | 15.25 | | 62.25 | 75 |
| 3100 | 36" x 24" | | 15 | .533 | | 132 | 20.50 | | 152.50 | 177 |
| 3200 | 48" x 24" | | 10 | .800 | | 172 | 30.50 | | 202.50 | 238 |
| 3300 | 72" x 24" | | 6 | 1.333 | | 330 | 51 | | 381 | 445 |
| 3500 | With 5" stainless steel shelf, 18" x 24" | | 20 | .400 | | 227 | 15.25 | | 242.25 | 273 |
| 3600 | 36" x 24" | | 15 | .533 | | 300 | 20.50 | | 320.50 | 360 |
| 3700 | 48" x 24" | | 10 | .800 | | 189 | 30.50 | | 219.50 | 256 |
| 3800 | 72" x 24" | | 6 | 1.333 | | 360 | 51 | | 411 | 475 |
| 4100 | Mop holder strip, stainless steel, 5 holders, 48" long | | 20 | .400 | | 84 | 15.25 | | 99.25 | 116 |
| 4200 | Napkin/tampon dispenser, recessed | | 15 | .533 | | 820 | 20.50 | | 840.50 | 935 |
| 4300 | Robe hook, single, regular | | 36 | .222 | | 15.60 | 8.45 | | 24.05 | 30.50 |
| 4400 | Heavy duty, concealed mounting | | 36 | .222 | | 15.35 | 8.45 | | 23.80 | 30 |
| 4600 | Soap dispenser, chrome, surface mounted, liquid | | 20 | .400 | | 47 | 15.25 | | 62.25 | 75.50 |

# 10 28 Toilet, Bath, and Laundry Accessories

## 10 28 13 – Toilet Accessories

### 10 28 13.13 Commercial Toilet Accessories

| | 10 28 13.13 Commercial Toilet Accessories | Crew | Daily Output | Labor-Hours | Unit | Material | 2008 Bare Costs Labor | Equipment | Total | Total Incl O&P |
|---|---|---|---|---|---|---|---|---|---|---|
| 4700 | Powder | 1 Carp | 20 | .400 | Ea. | 46.50 | 15.25 | | 61.75 | 75 |
| 5000 | Recessed stainless steel, liquid | | 10 | .800 | | 164 | 30.50 | | 194.50 | 228 |
| 5100 | Powder | | 10 | .800 | | 213 | 30.50 | | 243.50 | 282 |
| 5300 | Soap tank, stainless steel, 1 gallon | | 10 | .800 | | 185 | 30.50 | | 215.50 | 251 |
| 5400 | 5 gallon | | 5 | 1.600 | | 254 | 61 | | 315 | 375 |
| 5600 | Shelf, stainless steel, 5" wide, 18 ga., 24" long | | 24 | .333 | | 62.50 | 12.70 | | 75.20 | 89 |
| 5700 | 48" long | | 16 | .500 | | 100 | 19.05 | | 119.05 | 140 |
| 5800 | 8" wide shelf, 18 ga., 24" long | | 22 | .364 | | 75 | 13.85 | | 88.85 | 104 |
| 5900 | 48" long | | 14 | .571 | | 124 | 22 | | 146 | 170 |
| 6000 | Toilet seat cover dispenser, stainless steel, recessed | | 20 | .400 | | 142 | 15.25 | | 157.25 | 180 |
| 6050 | Surface mounted | | 15 | .533 | | 34.50 | 20.50 | | 55 | 69 |
| 6100 | Toilet tissue dispenser, surface mounted, SS, single roll | | 30 | .267 | | 16.90 | 10.15 | | 27.05 | 34.50 |
| 6200 | Double roll | | 24 | .333 | | 21.50 | 12.70 | | 34.20 | 43.50 |
| 6400 | Towel bar, stainless steel, 18" long | | 23 | .348 | | 36.50 | 13.25 | | 49.75 | 60.50 |
| 6500 | 30" long | | 21 | .381 | | 101 | 14.50 | | 115.50 | 134 |
| 6700 | Towel dispenser, stainless steel, surface mounted | | 16 | .500 | | 41.50 | 19.05 | | 60.55 | 75.50 |
| 6800 | Flush mounted, recessed | | 10 | .800 | | 290 | 30.50 | | 320.50 | 370 |
| 7000 | Towel holder, hotel type, 2 guest size | | 20 | .400 | | 54.50 | 15.25 | | 69.75 | 83.50 |
| 7200 | Towel shelf, stainless steel, 24" long, 8" wide | | 20 | .400 | | 96 | 15.25 | | 111.25 | 129 |
| 7400 | Tumbler holder, tumbler only | | 30 | .267 | | 37.50 | 10.15 | | 47.65 | 57.50 |
| 7500 | Soap, tumbler & toothbrush | | 30 | .267 | | 25 | 10.15 | | 35.15 | 43.50 |
| 7700 | Wall urn ash receiver, surface mount, 11" long | | 12 | .667 | | 132 | 25.50 | | 157.50 | 186 |
| 7800 | 7-1/2", long | | 18 | .444 | | 131 | 16.95 | | 147.95 | 171 |
| 8000 | Waste receptacles, stainless steel, with top, 13 gallon | | 10 | .800 | | 330 | 30.50 | | 360.50 | 410 |
| 8100 | 36 gallon | ↓ | 8 | 1 | ↓ | 515 | 38 | | 553 | 625 |

## 10 28 16 – Bath Accessories

### 10 28 16.20 Medicine Cabinets

| | 10 28 16.20 Medicine Cabinets | Crew | Daily Output | Labor-Hours | Unit | Material | 2008 Bare Costs Labor | Equipment | Total | Total Incl O&P |
|---|---|---|---|---|---|---|---|---|---|---|
| 0010 | **MEDICINE CABINETS** | | | | | | | | | |
| 0020 | With mirror, st. st. frame, 16" x 22", unlighted | 1 Carp | 14 | .571 | Ea. | 79 | 22 | | 101 | 121 |
| 0100 | Wood frame | | 14 | .571 | | 110 | 22 | | 132 | 154 |
| 0300 | Sliding mirror doors, 20" x 16" x 4-3/4", unlighted | | 7 | 1.143 | | 98 | 43.50 | | 141.50 | 176 |
| 0400 | 24" x 19" x 8-1/2", lighted | | 5 | 1.600 | | 154 | 61 | | 215 | 265 |
| 0600 | Triple door, 30" x 32", unlighted, plywood body | | 7 | 1.143 | | 232 | 43.50 | | 275.50 | 325 |
| 0700 | Steel body | | 7 | 1.143 | | 305 | 43.50 | | 348.50 | 405 |
| 0900 | Oak door, wood body, beveled mirror, single door | | 7 | 1.143 | | 149 | 43.50 | | 192.50 | 232 |
| 1000 | Double door | | 6 | 1.333 | | 360 | 51 | | 411 | 480 |
| 1200 | Hotel cabinets, stainless, with lower shelf, unlighted | | 10 | .800 | | 196 | 30.50 | | 226.50 | 263 |
| 1300 | Lighted | ↓ | 5 | 1.600 | ↓ | 291 | 61 | | 352 | 415 |

## 10 28 23 – Laundry Accessories

### 10 28 23.13 Built-In Ironing Boards

| | 10 28 23.13 Built-In Ironing Boards | Crew | Daily Output | Labor-Hours | Unit | Material | 2008 Bare Costs Labor | Equipment | Total | Total Incl O&P |
|---|---|---|---|---|---|---|---|---|---|---|
| 0010 | **BUILT-IN IRONING BOARDS** | | | | | | | | | |
| 0020 | Including cabinet, board & light, minimum | 1 Carp | 2 | 4 | Ea. | 325 | 152 | | 477 | 595 |
| 0100 | Maximum, see also Div. 11 23 13.13 | " | 1.50 | 5.333 | " | 535 | 203 | | 738 | 900 |

# 10 31 Manufactured Fireplaces

## 10 31 13 – Manufactured Fireplace Chimneys

### 10 31 13.10 Fireplace Chimneys

| | | Crew | Daily Output | Labor-Hours | Unit | Material | 2008 Bare Costs Labor | 2008 Bare Costs Equipment | Total | Total Incl O&P |
|---|---|---|---|---|---|---|---|---|---|---|
| 0010 | **FIREPLACE CHIMNEYS** | | | | | | | | | |
| 0500 | Chimney dbl. wall, all stainless, over 8'-6", 7" diam., add to fireplace | 1 Carp | 33 | .242 | V.L.F. | 68 | 9.25 | | 77.25 | 89 |
| 0600 | 10" diameter, add to fireplace | | 32 | .250 | | 90 | 9.55 | | 99.55 | 114 |
| 0700 | 12" diameter, add to fireplace | | 31 | .258 | | 108 | 9.85 | | 117.85 | 133 |
| 0800 | 14" diameter, add to fireplace | | 30 | .267 | | 175 | 10.15 | | 185.15 | 208 |
| 1000 | Simulated brick chimney top, 4' high, 16" x 16" | | 10 | .800 | Ea. | 237 | 30.50 | | 267.50 | 310 |
| 1100 | 24" x 24" | | 7 | 1.143 | " | 445 | 43.50 | | 488.50 | 555 |

### 10 31 13.20 Chimney Accessories

| | | Crew | Daily Output | Labor-Hours | Unit | Material | 2008 Bare Costs Labor | 2008 Bare Costs Equipment | Total | Total Incl O&P |
|---|---|---|---|---|---|---|---|---|---|---|
| 0010 | **CHIMNEY ACCESSORIES** | | | | | | | | | |
| 0020 | Chimney screens, galv., 13" x 13" flue | 1 Bric | 8 | 1 | Ea. | 50.50 | 39 | | 89.50 | 116 |
| 0050 | 24" x 24" flue | | 5 | 1.600 | | 117 | 62.50 | | 179.50 | 225 |
| 0200 | Stainless steel, 13" x 13" flue | | 8 | 1 | | 310 | 39 | | 349 | 400 |
| 0250 | 20" x 20" flue | | 5 | 1.600 | | 420 | 62.50 | | 482.50 | 560 |
| 2400 | Squirrel and bird screens, galvanized, 8" x 8" flue | | 16 | .500 | | 44 | 19.60 | | 63.60 | 78.50 |
| 2450 | 13" x 13" flue | | 12 | .667 | | 47.50 | 26 | | 73.50 | 92 |

## 10 31 16 – Manufactured Fireplace Forms

### 10 31 16.10 Fireplace Forms

| | | Crew | Daily Output | Labor-Hours | Unit | Material | 2008 Bare Costs Labor | 2008 Bare Costs Equipment | Total | Total Incl O&P |
|---|---|---|---|---|---|---|---|---|---|---|
| 0010 | **FIREPLACE FORMS** | | | | | | | | | |
| 1800 | Fireplace forms, no accessories, 32" opening | 1 Bric | 3 | 2.667 | Ea. | 600 | 104 | | 704 | 820 |
| 1900 | 36" opening | | 2.50 | 3.200 | | 765 | 125 | | 890 | 1,025 |
| 2000 | 40" opening | | 2 | 4 | | 1,025 | 157 | | 1,182 | 1,375 |
| 2100 | 78" opening | | 1.50 | 5.333 | | 1,475 | 209 | | 1,684 | 1,950 |

## 10 31 23 – Prefabricated Fireplaces

### 10 31 23.10 Fireplace, Prefabricated

| | | Crew | Daily Output | Labor-Hours | Unit | Material | 2008 Bare Costs Labor | 2008 Bare Costs Equipment | Total | Total Incl O&P |
|---|---|---|---|---|---|---|---|---|---|---|
| 0010 | **FIREPLACE, PREFABRICATED**, free standing or wall hung | | | | | | | | | |
| 0100 | With hood & screen, minimum | 1 Carp | 1.30 | 6.154 | Ea. | 1,125 | 234 | | 1,359 | 1,625 |
| 0150 | Average | | 1 | 8 | | 1,575 | 305 | | 1,880 | 2,225 |
| 0200 | Maximum | | .90 | 8.889 | | 3,025 | 340 | | 3,365 | 3,850 |
| 1500 | Simulated logs, gas fired, 40,000 BTU, 2' long, minimum | | 7 | 1.143 | Set | 390 | 43.50 | | 433.50 | 495 |
| 1600 | Maximum | | 6 | 1.333 | | 915 | 51 | | 966 | 1,075 |
| 1700 | Electric, 1,500 BTU, 1'-6" long, minimum | | 7 | 1.143 | | 161 | 43.50 | | 204.50 | 245 |
| 1800 | 11,500 BTU, maximum | | 6 | 1.333 | | 360 | 51 | | 411 | 480 |
| 2000 | Fireplace, built-in, 36" hearth, radiant | | 1.30 | 6.154 | Ea. | 545 | 234 | | 779 | 965 |
| 2100 | Recirculating, small fan | | 1 | 8 | | 850 | 305 | | 1,155 | 1,400 |
| 2150 | Large fan | | .90 | 8.889 | | 1,775 | 340 | | 2,115 | 2,475 |
| 2200 | 42" hearth, radiant | | 1.20 | 6.667 | | 765 | 254 | | 1,019 | 1,250 |
| 2300 | Recirculating, small fan | | .90 | 8.889 | | 995 | 340 | | 1,335 | 1,625 |
| 2350 | Large fan | | .80 | 10 | | 1,775 | 380 | | 2,155 | 2,550 |
| 2400 | 48" hearth, radiant | | 1.10 | 7.273 | | 1,650 | 277 | | 1,927 | 2,225 |
| 2500 | Recirculating, small fan | | .80 | 10 | | 2,050 | 380 | | 2,430 | 2,875 |
| 2550 | Large fan | | .70 | 11.429 | | 3,175 | 435 | | 3,610 | 4,175 |
| 3000 | See through, including doors | | .80 | 10 | | 2,700 | 380 | | 3,080 | 3,550 |
| 3200 | Corner (2 wall) | | 1 | 8 | | 2,700 | 305 | | 3,005 | 3,450 |

# 10 32 Fireplace Specialties

## 10 32 13 – Fireplace Dampers

| 10 32 13.10  Dampers | Crew | Daily Output | Labor-Hours | Unit | Material | 2008 Bare Costs Labor | Equipment | Total | Total Incl O&P |
|---|---|---|---|---|---|---|---|---|---|
| 0010 | **DAMPERS** | | | | | | | | | |
| 0800 | Damper, rotary control, steel, 30" opening | 1 Bric | 6 | 1.333 | Ea. | 75 | 52 | | 127 | 162 |
| 0850 | Cast iron, 30" opening | | 6 | 1.333 | | 83.50 | 52 | | 135.50 | 172 |
| 0880 | 36" opening | | 6 | 1.333 | | 90.50 | 52 | | 142.50 | 180 |
| 0900 | 48" opening | | 6 | 1.333 | | 130 | 52 | | 182 | 222 |
| 0920 | 60" opening | | 6 | 1.333 | | 290 | 52 | | 342 | 400 |
| 0950 | 72" opening | | 5 | 1.600 | | 350 | 62.50 | | 412.50 | 480 |
| 1000 | 84" opening, special order | | 5 | 1.600 | | 745 | 62.50 | | 807.50 | 915 |
| 1050 | 96" opening, special order | | 4 | 2 | | 760 | 78.50 | | 838.50 | 955 |
| 1200 | Steel plate, poker control, 60" opening | | 8 | 1 | | 265 | 39 | | 304 | 350 |
| 1250 | 84" opening, special order | | 5 | 1.600 | | 485 | 62.50 | | 547.50 | 625 |
| 1400 | "Universal" type, chain operated, 32" x 20" opening | | 8 | 1 | | 206 | 39 | | 245 | 286 |
| 1450 | 48" x 24" opening | | 5 | 1.600 | | 305 | 62.50 | | 367.50 | 435 |

## 10 32 23 – Fireplace Doors

| 10 32 23.10  Doors | Crew | Daily Output | Labor-Hours | Unit | Material | 2008 Bare Costs Labor | Equipment | Total | Total Incl O&P |
|---|---|---|---|---|---|---|---|---|---|
| 0010 | **DOORS** | | | | | | | | | |
| 0400 | Cleanout doors and frames, cast iron, 8" x 8" | 1 Bric | 12 | .667 | Ea. | 35 | 26 | | 61 | 78 |
| 0450 | 12" x 12" | | 10 | .800 | | 43 | 31.50 | | 74.50 | 94.50 |
| 0500 | 18" x 24" | | 8 | 1 | | 123 | 39 | | 162 | 196 |
| 0550 | Cast iron frame, steel door, 24" x 30" | | 5 | 1.600 | | 267 | 62.50 | | 329.50 | 390 |
| 1600 | Dutch Oven door and frame, cast iron, 12" x 15" opening | | 13 | .615 | | 108 | 24 | | 132 | 156 |
| 1650 | Copper plated, 12" x 15" opening | | 13 | .615 | | 211 | 24 | | 235 | 269 |

# 10 35 Stoves

## 10 35 13 – Heating Stoves

| 10 35 13.10  Woodburning Stoves | Crew | Daily Output | Labor-Hours | Unit | Material | 2008 Bare Costs Labor | Equipment | Total | Total Incl O&P |
|---|---|---|---|---|---|---|---|---|---|
| 0010 | **WOODBURNING STOVES** | | | | | | | | | |
| 0015 | Cast iron, minimum | 2 Carp | 1.30 | 12.308 | Ea. | 1,100 | 470 | | 1,570 | 1,925 |
| 0020 | Average | | 1 | 16 | | 1,475 | 610 | | 2,085 | 2,575 |
| 0030 | Maximum | | .80 | 20 | | 2,675 | 760 | | 3,435 | 4,100 |
| 0050 | For gas log lighter, add | | | | | 36.50 | | | 36.50 | 40 |

# 10 44 Fire Protection Specialties

## 10 44 13 – Fire Extinguisher Cabinets

| 10 44 13.53  Fire Equipment Cabinets | Crew | Daily Output | Labor-Hours | Unit | Material | 2008 Bare Costs Labor | Equipment | Total | Total Incl O&P |
|---|---|---|---|---|---|---|---|---|---|
| 0010 | **FIRE EQUIPMENT CABINETS,** not equipped, 20 ga. steel box | | | | | | | | | |
| 0040 | recessed, D.S. glass in door, box size given | | | | | | | | | |
| 1000 | Portable extinguisher, single, 8" x 12" x 27", alum. door & frame | Q-12 | 8 | 2 | Ea. | 107 | 84 | | 191 | 244 |
| 1100 | Steel door and frame | " | 8 | 2 | " | 77 | 84 | | 161 | 211 |
| 3000 | Hose rack assy., 1-1/2" valve & 100' hose, 24" x 40" x 5-1/2" | | | | | | | | | |
| 3100 | Aluminum door and frame | Q-12 | 6 | 2.667 | Ea. | 263 | 112 | | 375 | 460 |
| 3200 | Steel door and frame | | 6 | 2.667 | | 263 | 112 | | 375 | 460 |
| 3300 | Stainless steel door and frame | | 6 | 2.667 | | 425 | 112 | | 537 | 640 |
| 4000 | Hose rack assy., 2-1/2" x 1-1/2" valve, 100' hose, 24" x 40" x 8" | | | | | | | | | |
| 4100 | Aluminum door and frame | Q-12 | 6 | 2.667 | Ea. | 266 | 112 | | 378 | 460 |
| 4200 | Steel door and frame | | 6 | 2.667 | | 180 | 112 | | 292 | 365 |
| 4300 | Stainless steel door and frame | | 6 | 2.667 | | 355 | 112 | | 467 | 560 |
| 5000 | Hose rack assy., 2-1/2" x 1-1/2" valve, 100' hose | | | | | | | | | |
| 5010 | and extinguisher, 30" x 40" x 8" | | | | | | | | | |

## 10 44 13 – Fire Extinguisher Cabinets

| 10 44 13.53 Fire Equipment Cabinets | Crew | Daily Output | Labor-Hours | Unit | Material | 2008 Bare Costs Labor | Equipment | Total | Total Incl O&P |
|---|---|---|---|---|---|---|---|---|---|
| 5100 | Aluminum door and frame | Q-12 | 5 | 3.200 | Ea. | 340 | 134 | | 474 | 570 |
| 5200 | Steel door and frame | | 5 | 3.200 | | 183 | 134 | | 317 | 405 |
| 5300 | Stainless steel door and frame | ↓ | 5 | 3.200 | ↓ | 570 | 134 | | 704 | 830 |
| 8000 | Valve cabinet for 2-1/2" FD angle valve, 18" x 18" x 8" | | | | | | | | | |
| 8100 | Aluminum door and frame | Q-12 | 12 | 1.333 | Ea. | 117 | 56 | | 173 | 214 |
| 8200 | Steel door and frame | | 12 | 1.333 | | 96.50 | 56 | | 152.50 | 191 |
| 8300 | Stainless steel door and frame | ↓ | 12 | 1.333 | ↓ | 157 | 56 | | 213 | 258 |

## 10 44 16 – Fire Extinguishers

### 10 44 16.13 Portable Fire Extinguishers

| | | Crew | Daily Output | Labor-Hours | Unit | Material | 2008 Bare Costs Labor | Equipment | Total | Total Incl O&P |
|---|---|---|---|---|---|---|---|---|---|---|
| 0010 | **PORTABLE FIRE EXTINGUISHERS** | | | | | | | | | |
| 0120 | $CO_2$, portable with swivel horn, 5 lb. | | | | Ea. | 130 | | | 130 | 143 |
| 0140 | With hose and "H" horn, 10 lb. | | | | | 160 | | | 160 | 176 |
| 0160 | 15 lb. | | | | | 190 | | | 190 | 209 |
| 0180 | 20 lb. | | | | ↓ | 220 | | | 220 | 242 |
| 1000 | Dry chemical, pressurized | | | | | | | | | |
| 1040 | Standard type, portable, painted, 2-1/2 lb. | | | | Ea. | 27.50 | | | 27.50 | 30.50 |
| 1060 | 5 lb. | | | | | 60 | | | 60 | 66 |
| 1080 | 10 lb. | | | | | 80 | | | 80 | 88 |
| 1100 | 20 lb. | | | | | 110 | | | 110 | 121 |
| 1120 | 30 lb. | | | | | 238 | | | 238 | 262 |
| 1300 | Standard type, wheeled, 150 lb. | | | | | 1,600 | | | 1,600 | 1,750 |
| 2000 | ABC all purpose type, portable, 2-1/2 lb. | | | | | 30 | | | 30 | 33 |
| 2060 | 5 lb. | | | | | 45 | | | 45 | 49.50 |
| 2080 | 9-1/2 lb. | | | | | 68 | | | 68 | 75 |
| 2100 | 20 lb. | | | | | 98 | | | 98 | 108 |
| 3000 | Dry chemical, outside cartridge to -65° F, painted, 9 lb. | | | | | 200 | | | 200 | 220 |
| 3060 | 26 lb. | | | | | 250 | | | 250 | 275 |
| 5000 | Pressurized water, 2-1/2 gallon, stainless steel | | | | | 85 | | | 85 | 93.50 |
| 5060 | With anti-freeze | | | | | 135 | | | 135 | 149 |
| 9400 | Installation of extinguishers, 12 or more, on wood | 1 Carp | 30 | .267 | | | 10.15 | | 10.15 | 15.80 |
| 9420 | On masonry or concrete | " | 15 | .533 | ↓ | | 20.50 | | 20.50 | 31.50 |

### 10 44 16.16 Wheeled Fire Extinguisher Units

| | | Crew | Daily Output | Labor-Hours | Unit | Material | 2008 Bare Costs Labor | Equipment | Total | Total Incl O&P |
|---|---|---|---|---|---|---|---|---|---|---|
| 0010 | **WHEELED FIRE EXTINGUISHER UNITS** | | | | | | | | | |
| 0350 | $CO_2$, portable, with swivel horn | | | | | | | | | |
| 0360 | Wheeled type, cart mounted, 50 lb. | | | | Ea. | 1,200 | | | 1,200 | 1,325 |
| 0400 | 100 lb. | | | | " | 2,600 | | | 2,600 | 2,875 |
| 2200 | ABC all purpose type | | | | | | | | | |
| 2300 | Wheeled, 45 lb. | | | | Ea. | 650 | | | 650 | 715 |
| 2360 | 150 lb. | | | | " | 1,600 | | | 1,600 | 1,750 |

# 10 51 Lockers

## 10 51 13 – Metal Lockers

### 10 51 13.10 Lockers

| | | Crew | Daily Output | Labor-Hours | Unit | Material | 2008 Bare Costs Labor | 2008 Bare Costs Equipment | Total | Total Incl O&P |
|---|---|---|---|---|---|---|---|---|---|---|
| 0011 | **LOCKERS** Steel, baked enamel | | | | | | | | | |
| 0110 | Single tier box locker, 12" x 15" x 72" | 1 Shee | 8 | 1 | Ea. | 178 | 45.50 | | 223.50 | 266 |
| 0120 | 18" x 15" x 72" | | 8 | 1 | | 199 | 45.50 | | 244.50 | 289 |
| 0130 | 12" x 18" x 72" | | 8 | 1 | | 189 | 45.50 | | 234.50 | 278 |
| 0140 | 18" x 18" x 72" | | 8 | 1 | | 205 | 45.50 | | 250.50 | 296 |
| 0410 | Double tier, 12" x 15" x 36" | | 21 | .381 | | 200 | 17.25 | | 217.25 | 247 |
| 0420 | 18" x 15" x 36" | | 21 | .381 | | 243 | 17.25 | | 260.25 | 295 |
| 0430 | 12" x 18" x 36" | | 21 | .381 | | 215 | 17.25 | | 232.25 | 264 |
| 0440 | 18" x 18" x 36" | | 21 | .381 | | 255 | 17.25 | | 272.25 | 305 |
| 0500 | Two person, 18" x 15" x 72" | | 8 | 1 | | 256 | 45.50 | | 301.50 | 350 |
| 0510 | 18" x 18" x 72" | | 8 | 1 | | 265 | 45.50 | | 310.50 | 360 |
| 0520 | Duplex, 15" x 15" x 72" | | 8 | 1 | | 290 | 45.50 | | 335.50 | 390 |
| 0530 | 15" x 21" x 72" | | 8 | 1 | | 315 | 45.50 | | 360.50 | 415 |
| 0600 | 5 tier box lockers, minimum | | 30 | .267 | Opng. | 36 | 12.10 | | 48.10 | 58 |
| 0700 | Maximum | | 24 | .333 | | 50.50 | 15.10 | | 65.60 | 79 |
| 0900 | 6 tier box lockers, minimum | | 36 | .222 | | 36.50 | 10.05 | | 46.55 | 55.50 |
| 1000 | Maximum | | 30 | .267 | | 42.50 | 12.10 | | 54.60 | 65.50 |
| 1100 | Wire meshed wardrobe, floor. mtd., open front varsity type | | 7.50 | 1.067 | Ea. | 205 | 48.50 | | 253.50 | 300 |
| 2400 | 16-person locker unit with clothing rack | | | | | | | | | |
| 2500 | 72 wide x 15" deep x 72" high | 1 Shee | 8 | 1 | Ea. | 500 | 45.50 | | 545.50 | 620 |
| 2550 | 18" deep | " | 8 | 1 | " | 525 | 45.50 | | 570.50 | 650 |
| 3000 | Wall mounted lockers, 4 person, with coat bar | | | | | | | | | |
| 3100 | 48" wide x 18" deep x 12" high | 1 Shee | 8 | 1 | Ea. | 270 | 45.50 | | 315.50 | 365 |
| 3250 | Rack w/ 24 wire mesh baskets | | 1.50 | 5.333 | Set | 335 | 242 | | 577 | 745 |
| 3260 | 30 baskets | | 1.25 | 6.400 | | 259 | 290 | | 549 | 730 |
| 3270 | 36 baskets | | .95 | 8.421 | | 340 | 380 | | 720 | 960 |
| 3280 | 42 baskets | | .80 | 10 | | 375 | 455 | | 830 | 1,100 |
| 3300 | For built-in lock with 2 keys, add | | | | Ea. | 6.95 | | | 6.95 | 7.65 |
| 3600 | For hanger rods, add | | | | " | 1.86 | | | 1.86 | 2.05 |

## 10 51 26 – Plastic Lockers

### 10 51 26.13 Lockers

| | | Crew | Daily Output | Labor-Hours | Unit | Material | 2008 Bare Costs Labor | 2008 Bare Costs Equipment | Total | Total Incl O&P |
|---|---|---|---|---|---|---|---|---|---|---|
| 0011 | **LOCKERS** Plastic, 30% recycled | | | | | | | | | |
| 0110 | Single tier box locker, 12" x 12" x 72" | 1 Shee | 8 | 1 | Ea. | 370 | 45.50 | | 415.50 | 475 |
| 0120 | 12" x 15" x 72" | | 8 | 1 | | 390 | 45.50 | | 435.50 | 500 |
| 0130 | 12" x 18" x 72" | | 8 | 1 | | 400 | 45.50 | | 445.50 | 510 |
| 0410 | Double tier, 12" x 12" x 72" | | 21 | .381 | | 370 | 17.25 | | 387.25 | 430 |
| 0420 | 12" x 15" x 72" | | 21 | .381 | | 370 | 17.25 | | 387.25 | 430 |
| 0430 | 12" x 18" x 72" | | 21 | .381 | | 390 | 17.25 | | 407.25 | 455 |

## 10 51 53 – Locker Room Benches

### 10 51 53.10 Benches

| | | Crew | Daily Output | Labor-Hours | Unit | Material | 2008 Bare Costs Labor | 2008 Bare Costs Equipment | Total | Total Incl O&P |
|---|---|---|---|---|---|---|---|---|---|---|
| 0010 | **BENCHES** | | | | | | | | | |
| 2100 | Locker bench, laminated maple, top only | 1 Shee | 100 | .080 | L.F. | 13.35 | 3.62 | | 16.97 | 20.50 |
| 2200 | Pedestals, steel pipe | " | 25 | .320 | Ea. | 36 | 14.50 | | 50.50 | 62 |

# 10 55 Postal Specialties

## 10 55 23 – Mail Boxes

| 10 55 23.10 Commercial Mail Boxes | | Crew | Daily Output | Labor-Hours | Unit | Material | 2008 Bare Costs Labor | Equipment | Total | Total Incl O&P |
|---|---|---|---|---|---|---|---|---|---|---|
| 0010 | **COMMERCIAL MAIL BOXES** | | | | | | | | | |
| 0020 | Horiz., key lock, 5"H x 6"W x 15"D, alum., rear load | 1 Carp | 34 | .235 | Ea. | 35 | 8.95 | | 43.95 | 52.50 |
| 0100 | Front loading | | 34 | .235 | | 36 | 8.95 | | 44.95 | 53.50 |
| 0200 | Double, 5"H x 12"W x 15"D, rear loading | | 26 | .308 | | 71.50 | 11.70 | | 83.20 | 97.50 |
| 0300 | Front loading | | 26 | .308 | | 66 | 11.70 | | 77.70 | 91 |
| 0500 | Quadruple, 10"H x 12"W x 15"D, rear loading | | 20 | .400 | | 91 | 15.25 | | 106.25 | 124 |
| 0600 | Front loading | | 20 | .400 | | 108 | 15.25 | | 123.25 | 143 |
| 0800 | Vertical, front load, 15"H x 5"W x 6"D, alum., per compartment | | 34 | .235 | | 30 | 8.95 | | 38.95 | 47 |
| 0900 | Bronze, duranodic finish | | 34 | .235 | | 40 | 8.95 | | 48.95 | 58 |
| 1000 | Steel, enameled | | 34 | .235 | | 34 | 8.95 | | 42.95 | 51.50 |
| 1700 | Alphabetical directories, 120 names | | 10 | .800 | | 122 | 30.50 | | 152.50 | 182 |
| 1800 | Letter collection box | | 6 | 1.333 | | 705 | 51 | | 756 | 855 |
| 1830 | Lobby collection boxes, aluminum | 2 Shee | 5 | 3.200 | | 2,025 | 145 | | 2,170 | 2,450 |
| 1840 | Bronze or stainless | " | 4.50 | 3.556 | | 2,500 | 161 | | 2,661 | 3,000 |
| 1900 | Letter slot, residential | 1 Carp | 20 | .400 | | 83 | 15.25 | | 98.25 | 115 |
| 2000 | Post office type | | 8 | 1 | | 110 | 38 | | 148 | 181 |
| 2200 | Post office counter window, with grille | | 2 | 4 | | 550 | 152 | | 702 | 840 |
| 2250 | Key keeper, single key, aluminum | | 26 | .308 | | 35.50 | 11.70 | | 47.20 | 57.50 |
| 2300 | Steel, enameled | | 26 | .308 | | 107 | 11.70 | | 118.70 | 136 |

## 10 55 91 – Mail Chutes

### 10 55 91.10 Commercial Mail Chutes

| | | Crew | Daily Output | Labor-Hours | Unit | Material | Labor | Equipment | Total | Total Incl O&P |
|---|---|---|---|---|---|---|---|---|---|---|
| 0010 | **COMMERCIAL MAIL CHUTES** | | | | | | | | | |
| 0020 | Aluminum & glass, 14-1/4" wide, 4-5/8" deep | 2 Shee | 4 | 4 | Floor | 705 | 181 | | 886 | 1,050 |
| 0100 | 8-5/8" deep | | 3.80 | 4.211 | | 855 | 191 | | 1,046 | 1,225 |
| 0300 | 8-3/4" x 3-1/2", aluminum | | 5 | 3.200 | | 650 | 145 | | 795 | 940 |
| 0400 | Bronze or stainless | | 4.50 | 3.556 | | 1,000 | 161 | | 1,161 | 1,350 |

# 10 56 Storage Assemblies

## 10 56 13 – Metal Storage Shelving

### 10 56 13.10 Shelving

| | | Crew | Daily Output | Labor-Hours | Unit | Material | Labor | Equipment | Total | Total Incl O&P |
|---|---|---|---|---|---|---|---|---|---|---|
| 0010 | **SHELVING** | | | | | | | | | |
| 0020 | Metal, industrial, cross-braced, 3' wide, 12" deep | 1 Sswk | 175 | .046 | SF Shlf | 6.30 | 1.97 | | 8.27 | 10.50 |
| 0100 | 24" deep | | 330 | .024 | | 4.26 | 1.04 | | 5.30 | 6.55 |
| 0300 | 4' wide, 12" deep | | 185 | .043 | | 5.75 | 1.86 | | 7.61 | 9.65 |
| 0400 | 24" deep | | 380 | .021 | | 4.74 | .91 | | 5.65 | 6.85 |
| 1200 | Enclosed sides, cross-braced back, 3' wide, 12" deep | | 175 | .046 | | 10.75 | 1.97 | | 12.72 | 15.35 |
| 1300 | 24" deep | | 290 | .028 | | 9.20 | 1.19 | | 10.39 | 12.25 |
| 1500 | Fully enclosed, sides and back, 3' wide, 12" deep | | 150 | .053 | | 11.65 | 2.29 | | 13.94 | 16.95 |
| 1600 | 24" deep | | 255 | .031 | | 7.70 | 1.35 | | 9.05 | 10.95 |
| 1800 | 4' wide, 12" deep | | 150 | .053 | | 9.15 | 2.29 | | 11.44 | 14.20 |
| 1900 | 24" deep | | 290 | .028 | | 6.55 | 1.19 | | 7.74 | 9.35 |
| 2200 | Wide span, 1600 lb. capacity per shelf, 6' wide, 24" deep | | 380 | .021 | | 8.65 | .91 | | 9.56 | 11.20 |
| 2400 | 36" deep | | 440 | .018 | | 7.55 | .78 | | 8.33 | 9.70 |
| 2600 | 8' wide, 24" deep | | 440 | .018 | | 7.80 | .78 | | 8.58 | 10 |
| 2800 | 36" deep | | 520 | .015 | | 7 | .66 | | 7.66 | 8.90 |
| 4000 | Pallet racks, steel frame 5,000 lb. capacity, 8' long, 36" deep | 2 Sswk | 450 | .036 | | 8.35 | 1.53 | | 9.88 | 11.90 |
| 4200 | 42" deep | | 500 | .032 | | 7.35 | 1.38 | | 8.73 | 10.60 |
| 4400 | 48" deep | | 520 | .031 | | 7.25 | 1.32 | | 8.57 | 10.35 |

### 10 56 13.20 Parts Bins

| | | | | | | | | | | |
|---|---|---|---|---|---|---|---|---|---|---|
| 0010 | **PARTS BINS** Metal, gray baked enamel finish | | | | | | | | | |

# 10 56 Storage Assemblies

## 10 56 13 – Metal Storage Shelving

| 10 56 13.20 Parts Bins | Crew | Daily Output | Labor-Hours | Unit | Material | 2008 Bare Costs Labor | Equipment | Total | Total Incl O&P |
|---|---|---|---|---|---|---|---|---|---|
| 0100 | 6'-3" high, 3' wide | | | | | | | | | |
| 0300 | 12 bins, 18" wide x 12" high, 12" deep | 2 Clab | 10 | 1.600 | Ea. | 275 | 48.50 | | 323.50 | 375 |
| 0400 | 24" deep | | 10 | 1.600 | | 345 | 48.50 | | 393.50 | 455 |
| 0600 | 72 bins, 6" wide x 6" high, 12" deep | | 8 | 2 | | 400 | 60.50 | | 460.50 | 530 |
| 0700 | 18" deep | | 8 | 2 | | 625 | 60.50 | | 685.50 | 785 |
| 1000 | 7'-3" high, 3' wide | | | | | | | | | |
| 1200 | 14 bins, 18" wide x 12" high, 12" deep | 2 Clab | 10 | 1.600 | Ea. | 266 | 48.50 | | 314.50 | 370 |
| 1300 | 24" deep | | 10 | 1.600 | | 350 | 48.50 | | 398.50 | 460 |
| 1500 | 84 bins, 6" wide x 6" high, 12" deep | | 8 | 2 | | 630 | 60.50 | | 690.50 | 790 |
| 1600 | 24" deep | | 8 | 2 | | 790 | 60.50 | | 850.50 | 965 |

# 10 57 Wardrobe and Closet Specialties

## 10 57 13 – Hat and Coat Racks

### 10 57 13.10 Coat Racks and Wardrobes

| | | Crew | Daily Output | Labor-Hours | Unit | Material | Labor | Equipment | Total | Total Incl O&P |
|---|---|---|---|---|---|---|---|---|---|---|
| 0010 | COAT RACKS AND WARDROBES | | | | | | | | | |
| 0020 | Hat & coat rack, floor model, 6 hangers | | | | | | | | | |
| 0050 | Standing, beech wood, 21" x 21" x 72", chrome | | | | Ea. | 230 | | | 230 | 253 |
| 0100 | 18 gauge tubular steel, 21" x 21" x 69", wood walnut | | | | " | 245 | | | 245 | 269 |
| 0500 | 16 gauge steel frame, 22 gauge steel shelves | | | | | | | | | |
| 0650 | Single pedestal, 30" x 18" x 63" | | | | Ea. | 175 | | | 175 | 193 |
| 0800 | Single face rack, 29" x 18-1/2" x 62" | | | | | 206 | | | 206 | 226 |
| 0900 | 51" x 18-1/2" x 70" | | | | | 340 | | | 340 | 375 |
| 0910 | Double face rack, 39" x 26" x 70" | | | | | 285 | | | 285 | 315 |
| 0920 | 63" x 26" x 70" | | | | | 380 | | | 380 | 420 |
| 0940 | For 2" ball casters, add | | | | Set | 83 | | | 83 | 91.50 |
| 1400 | Utility hook strips, 3/8" x 2-1/2" x 18", 6 hooks | 1 Carp | 48 | .167 | Ea. | 49 | 6.35 | | 55.35 | 64 |
| 1500 | 34" long, 12 hooks | " | 48 | .167 | " | 51 | 6.35 | | 57.35 | 66 |
| 1650 | Wall mounted racks, 16 gauge steel frame, 22 gauge steel shelves | | | | | | | | | |
| 1850 | 12" x 15" x 26", 6 hangers | 1 Carp | 32 | .250 | Ea. | 139 | 9.55 | | 148.55 | 168 |
| 2000 | 12" x 15" x 50", 12 hangers | " | 32 | .250 | " | 162 | 9.55 | | 171.55 | 194 |
| 2150 | Wardrobe cabinet, steel, baked enamel finish | | | | | | | | | |
| 2300 | 36" x 21" x 78", incl. top shelf & hanger rod | | | | Ea. | 280 | | | 280 | 310 |

## 10 57 23 – Closet and Utility Shelving

### 10 57 23.19 Wood Closet and Utility Shelving

| | | Crew | Daily Output | Labor-Hours | Unit | Material | Labor | Equipment | Total | Total Incl O&P |
|---|---|---|---|---|---|---|---|---|---|---|
| 0010 | WOOD CLOSET AND UTILITY SHELVING | | | | | | | | | |
| 0020 | Pine, clear grade, no edge band, 1" x 8" | 1 Carp | 115 | .070 | L.F. | 2.02 | 2.65 | | 4.67 | 6.35 |
| 0100 | 1" x 10" | | 110 | .073 | | 2.27 | 2.77 | | 5.04 | 6.80 |
| 0200 | 1" x 12" | | 105 | .076 | | 2.69 | 2.90 | | 5.59 | 7.50 |
| 0600 | Plywood, 3/4" thick with lumber edge, 12" wide | | 75 | .107 | | 1.45 | 4.06 | | 5.51 | 7.95 |
| 0700 | 24" wide | | 70 | .114 | | 2.56 | 4.35 | | 6.91 | 9.60 |
| 0900 | Bookcase, clear grade pine, shelves 12" O.C., 8" deep, /SF shelf | | 70 | .114 | S.F. | 6.55 | 4.35 | | 10.90 | 14 |
| 1000 | 12" deep shelves | | 65 | .123 | " | 8.75 | 4.69 | | 13.44 | 16.90 |
| 1200 | Adjustable closet rod and shelf, 12" wide, 3' long | | 20 | .400 | Ea. | 8.35 | 15.25 | | 23.60 | 32.50 |
| 1300 | 8' long | | 15 | .533 | " | 24 | 20.50 | | 44.50 | 57.50 |
| 1500 | Prefinished shelves with supports, stock, 8" wide | | 75 | .107 | L.F. | 3.87 | 4.06 | | 7.93 | 10.60 |
| 1600 | 10" wide | | 70 | .114 | " | 4.30 | 4.35 | | 8.65 | 11.55 |

# 10 73 Protective Covers

## 10 73 13 – Awnings

### 10 73 13.10 Awnings, Fabric

| | 10 73 13.10 Awnings, Fabric | Crew | Daily Output | Labor-Hours | Unit | Material | 2008 Bare Costs Labor | Equipment | Total | Total Incl O&P |
|---|---|---|---|---|---|---|---|---|---|---|
| 0010 | **AWNINGS, FABRIC** | | | | | | | | | |
| 0020 | Including acrylic canvas and frame, standard design | | | | | | | | | |
| 0100 | Door and window, slope, 3' high, 4' wide | 1 Carp | 4.50 | 1.778 | Ea. | 670 | 67.50 | | 737.50 | 845 |
| 0110 | 6' wide | | 3.50 | 2.286 | | 865 | 87 | | 952 | 1,075 |
| 0120 | 8' wide | | 3 | 2.667 | | 1,050 | 102 | | 1,152 | 1,300 |
| 0200 | Quarter round convex, 4' wide | | 3 | 2.667 | | 1,050 | 102 | | 1,152 | 1,300 |
| 0210 | 6' wide | | 2.25 | 3.556 | | 1,350 | 135 | | 1,485 | 1,700 |
| 0220 | 8' wide | | 1.80 | 4.444 | | 1,650 | 169 | | 1,819 | 2,100 |
| 0300 | Dome, 4' wide | | 7.50 | 1.067 | | 405 | 40.50 | | 445.50 | 510 |
| 0310 | 6' wide | | 3.50 | 2.286 | | 905 | 87 | | 992 | 1,125 |
| 0320 | 8' wide | | 2 | 4 | | 1,600 | 152 | | 1,752 | 2,000 |
| 0350 | Elongated dome, 4' wide | | 1.33 | 6.015 | | 1,500 | 229 | | 1,729 | 2,000 |
| 0360 | 6' wide | | 1.11 | 7.207 | | 1,800 | 275 | | 2,075 | 2,425 |
| 0370 | 8' wide | | 1 | 8 | | 2,100 | 305 | | 2,405 | 2,800 |
| 1000 | Entry or walkway, peak, 12' long, 4' wide | 2 Carp | .90 | 17.778 | | 4,775 | 675 | | 5,450 | 6,300 |
| 1010 | 6' wide | | .60 | 26.667 | | 7,350 | 1,025 | | 8,375 | 9,675 |
| 1020 | 8' wide | | .40 | 40 | | 10,200 | 1,525 | | 11,725 | 13,600 |
| 1100 | Radius with dome end, 4' wide | | 1.10 | 14.545 | | 3,625 | 555 | | 4,180 | 4,850 |
| 1110 | 6' wide | | .70 | 22.857 | | 5,825 | 870 | | 6,695 | 7,750 |
| 1120 | 8' wide | | .50 | 32 | | 8,275 | 1,225 | | 9,500 | 11,000 |
| 2000 | Retractable lateral arm awning, manual | | | | | | | | | |
| 2010 | To 12' wide, 8' - 6" projection | 2 Carp | 1.70 | 9.412 | Ea. | 1,075 | 360 | | 1,435 | 1,725 |
| 2020 | To 14' wide, 8' - 6" projection | | 1.10 | 14.545 | | 1,250 | 555 | | 1,805 | 2,250 |
| 2030 | To 19' wide, 8' - 6" projection | | .85 | 18.824 | | 1,700 | 715 | | 2,415 | 3,000 |
| 2040 | To 24' wide, 8' - 6" projection | | .67 | 23.881 | | 2,150 | 910 | | 3,060 | 3,800 |
| 2050 | Motor for above, add | 1 Carp | 2.67 | 3 | | 925 | 114 | | 1,039 | 1,200 |
| 3000 | Patio/deck canopy with frame | | | | | | | | | |
| 3010 | 12' wide, 12' projection | 2 Carp | 2 | 8 | Ea. | 1,525 | 305 | | 1,830 | 2,150 |
| 3020 | 16' wide, 14' projection | " | 1.20 | 13.333 | | 2,375 | 510 | | 2,885 | 3,400 |
| 9000 | For fire retardant canvas, add | | | | | 7% | | | | |
| 9010 | For lettering or graphics, add | | | | | 35% | | | | |
| 9020 | For painted or coated acrylic canvas, deduct | | | | | 8% | | | | |
| 9030 | For translucent or opaque vinyl canvas, add | | | | | 10% | | | | |
| 9040 | For 6 or more units, deduct | | | | | 20% | 15% | | | |

## 10 73 16 – Canopies

### 10 73 16.20 Metal Canopies

| | 10 73 16.20 Metal Canopies | Crew | Daily Output | Labor-Hours | Unit | Material | 2008 Bare Costs Labor | Equipment | Total | Total Incl O&P |
|---|---|---|---|---|---|---|---|---|---|---|
| 0010 | **METAL CANOPIES** | | | | | | | | | |
| 0020 | Wall hung, .032", aluminum, prefinished, 8' x 10' | K-2 | 1.30 | 18.462 | Ea. | 2,075 | 720 | 172 | 2,967 | 3,725 |
| 0300 | 8' x 20' | | 1.10 | 21.818 | | 4,150 | 855 | 204 | 5,209 | 6,275 |
| 0500 | 10' x 10' | | 1.30 | 18.462 | | 2,325 | 720 | 172 | 3,217 | 4,000 |
| 0700 | 10' x 20' | | 1.10 | 21.818 | | 4,325 | 855 | 204 | 5,384 | 6,450 |
| 1000 | 12' x 20' | | 1 | 24 | | 5,325 | 940 | 224 | 6,489 | 7,725 |
| 1360 | 12' x 30' | | .80 | 30 | | 7,800 | 1,175 | 280 | 9,255 | 11,000 |
| 1700 | 12' x 40' | | .60 | 40 | | 9,525 | 1,575 | 375 | 11,475 | 13,600 |
| 1900 | For free standing units, add | | | | | 20% | 10% | | | |
| 2300 | Aluminum entrance canopies, flat soffit, .032" | | | | | | | | | |
| 2500 | 3'-6" x 4'-0", clear anodized | 2 Carp | 4 | 4 | Ea. | 875 | 152 | | 1,027 | 1,200 |
| 2700 | Bronze anodized | | 4 | 4 | | 1,525 | 152 | | 1,677 | 1,925 |
| 3000 | Polyurethane painted | | 4 | 4 | | 1,250 | 152 | | 1,402 | 1,600 |
| 3300 | 4'-6" x 10'-0", clear anodized | | 2 | 8 | | 2,400 | 305 | | 2,705 | 3,125 |
| 3500 | Bronze anodized | | 2 | 8 | | 3,075 | 305 | | 3,380 | 3,850 |
| 3700 | Polyurethane painted | | 2 | 8 | | 2,575 | 305 | | 2,880 | 3,300 |

# 10 73 Protective Covers

## 10 73 16 – Canopies

| 10 73 16.20 Metal Canopies | | Crew | Daily Output | Labor-Hours | Unit | Material | 2008 Bare Costs Labor | 2008 Bare Costs Equipment | Total | Total Incl O&P |
|---|---|---|---|---|---|---|---|---|---|---|
| 4000 | Wall downspout, 10 L.F., clear anodized | 1 Carp | 7 | 1.143 | Ea. | 150 | 43.50 | | 193.50 | 233 |
| 4300 | Bronze anodized | | 7 | 1.143 | | 261 | 43.50 | | 304.50 | 355 |
| 4500 | Polyurethane painted | | 7 | 1.143 | | 224 | 43.50 | | 267.50 | 315 |
| 7000 | Carport, baked vinyl finish, .032", 20' x 10', no foundations, min. | K-2 | 4 | 6 | Car | 3,750 | 235 | 56 | 4,041 | 4,600 |
| 7250 | Maximum | | 2 | 12 | " | 6,800 | 470 | 112 | 7,382 | 8,425 |
| 7500 | Walkway cover, to 12' wide, stl., vinyl finish, .032",no fndtns., min. | | 250 | .096 | S.F. | 22 | 3.76 | .90 | 26.66 | 31.50 |
| 7750 | Maximum | | 200 | .120 | " | 24 | 4.70 | 1.12 | 29.82 | 35.50 |

# 10 74 Manufactured Exterior Specialties

## 10 74 23 – Cupolas

| 10 74 23.10 Wood Cupolas | | Crew | Daily Output | Labor-Hours | Unit | Material | 2008 Bare Costs Labor | 2008 Bare Costs Equipment | Total | Total Incl O&P |
|---|---|---|---|---|---|---|---|---|---|---|
| 0010 | **WOOD CUPOLAS** | | | | | | | | | |
| 0020 | Stock units, pine, painted, 18" sq., 28" high, alum. roof | 1 Carp | 4.10 | 1.951 | Ea. | 158 | 74.50 | | 232.50 | 289 |
| 0100 | Copper roof | | 3.80 | 2.105 | | 184 | 80 | | 264 | 325 |
| 0300 | 23" square, 33" high, aluminum roof | | 3.70 | 2.162 | | 345 | 82.50 | | 427.50 | 510 |
| 0400 | Copper roof | | 3.30 | 2.424 | | 465 | 92.50 | | 557.50 | 655 |
| 0600 | 30" square, 37" high, aluminum roof | | 3.70 | 2.162 | | 485 | 82.50 | | 567.50 | 660 |
| 0700 | Copper roof | | 3.30 | 2.424 | | 520 | 92.50 | | 612.50 | 715 |
| 0900 | Hexagonal, 31" wide, 46" high, copper roof | | 4 | 2 | | 640 | 76 | | 716 | 825 |
| 1000 | 36" wide, 50" high, copper roof | | 3.50 | 2.286 | | 1,125 | 87 | | 1,212 | 1,375 |
| 1200 | For deluxe stock units, add to above | | | | | 25% | | | | |
| 1400 | For custom built units, add to above | | | | | 50% | 50% | | | |

## 10 74 29 – Steeples

| 10 74 29.10 Prefabricated Steeples | | Crew | Daily Output | Labor-Hours | Unit | Material | 2008 Bare Costs Labor | 2008 Bare Costs Equipment | Total | Total Incl O&P |
|---|---|---|---|---|---|---|---|---|---|---|
| 0010 | **PREFABRICATED STEEPLES** | | | | | | | | | |
| 4000 | Steeples, translucent fiberglass, 30" square, 15' high | F-3 | 2 | 20 | Ea. | 4,550 | 775 | 385 | 5,710 | 6,625 |
| 4150 | 25' high | | 1.80 | 22.222 | | 5,300 | 860 | 425 | 6,585 | 7,625 |
| 4350 | Opaque fiberglass, 24" square, 14' high | | 2 | 20 | | 3,775 | 775 | 385 | 4,935 | 5,775 |
| 4500 | 28' high | | 1.80 | 22.222 | | 4,300 | 860 | 425 | 5,585 | 6,525 |
| 4600 | Aluminum, baked finish, 16" square, 14' high | | | | | 3,750 | | | 3,750 | 4,100 |
| 4620 | 20' high, 3'-6" base | | | | | 6,325 | | | 6,325 | 6,950 |
| 4640 | 35' high, 8' base | | | | | 24,500 | | | 24,500 | 27,000 |
| 4660 | 60' high, 14' base | | | | | 53,500 | | | 53,500 | 59,000 |
| 4680 | 152' high, custom | | | | | 453,000 | | | 453,000 | 498,500 |
| 4700 | Porcelain enamel steeples, custom, 40' high | F-3 | .50 | 80 | | 14,100 | 3,100 | 1,525 | 18,725 | 22,100 |
| 4800 | 60' high | " | .30 | 133 | | 24,500 | 5,150 | 2,550 | 32,200 | 37,800 |

## 10 74 46 – Window Wells

| 10 74 46.10 Area Window Wells | | Crew | Daily Output | Labor-Hours | Unit | Material | 2008 Bare Costs Labor | 2008 Bare Costs Equipment | Total | Total Incl O&P |
|---|---|---|---|---|---|---|---|---|---|---|
| 0010 | **AREA WINDOW WELLS**, Galvanized steel | | | | | | | | | |
| 0020 | 20 ga., 3'-2" wide, 1' deep | 1 Sswk | 29 | .276 | Ea. | 14 | 11.85 | | 25.85 | 37 |
| 0100 | 2' deep | | 23 | .348 | | 25 | 14.95 | | 39.95 | 54.50 |
| 0300 | 16 ga., 3'-2" wide, 1' deep | | 29 | .276 | | 20 | 11.85 | | 31.85 | 43.50 |
| 0400 | 3' deep | | 23 | .348 | | 39 | 14.95 | | 53.95 | 70 |
| 0600 | Welded grating for above, 15 lbs., painted | | 45 | .178 | | 44 | 7.65 | | 51.65 | 62.50 |
| 0700 | Galvanized | | 45 | .178 | | 86 | 7.65 | | 93.65 | 108 |
| 0900 | Translucent plastic cap for above | | 60 | .133 | | 15 | 5.75 | | 20.75 | 27 |

# 10 75 Flagpoles

## 10 75 16 – Ground-Set Flagpoles

### 10 75 16.10 Flagpoles

| | Crew | Daily Output | Labor-Hours | Unit | Material | 2008 Bare Costs Labor | Equipment | Total | Total Incl O&P |
|---|---|---|---|---|---|---|---|---|---|
| 0010 **FLAGPOLES**, Ground set | | | | | | | | | |
| 0050 Not including base or foundation | | | | | | | | | |
| 0100 Aluminum, tapered, ground set 20' high | K-1 | 2 | 8 | Ea. | 805 | 270 | 112 | 1,187 | 1,425 |
| 0200 25' high | | 1.70 | 9.412 | | 1,050 | 320 | 132 | 1,502 | 1,800 |
| 0300 30' high | | 1.50 | 10.667 | | 1,150 | 360 | 149 | 1,659 | 2,000 |
| 0400 35' high | | 1.40 | 11.429 | | 1,500 | 385 | 160 | 2,045 | 2,425 |
| 0500 40' high | | 1.20 | 13.333 | | 2,100 | 450 | 187 | 2,737 | 3,200 |
| 0600 50' high | | 1 | 16 | | 2,725 | 540 | 224 | 3,489 | 4,075 |
| 0700 60' high | | .90 | 17.778 | | 4,450 | 600 | 249 | 5,299 | 6,075 |
| 0800 70' high | | .80 | 20 | | 7,825 | 675 | 280 | 8,780 | 9,975 |
| 1100 Counterbalanced, internal halyard, 20' high | | 1.80 | 8.889 | | 2,125 | 300 | 124 | 2,549 | 2,950 |
| 1200 30' high | | 1.50 | 10.667 | | 2,350 | 360 | 149 | 2,859 | 3,325 |
| 1300 40' high | | 1.30 | 12.308 | | 4,650 | 415 | 172 | 5,237 | 5,950 |
| 1400 50' high | | 1 | 16 | | 7,250 | 540 | 224 | 8,014 | 9,050 |
| 2820 Aluminum, electronically operated, 30' high | | 1.40 | 11.429 | | 4,175 | 385 | 160 | 4,720 | 5,375 |
| 2840 35' high | | 1.30 | 12.308 | | 4,500 | 415 | 172 | 5,087 | 5,775 |
| 2860 39' high | | 1.10 | 14.545 | | 4,900 | 490 | 204 | 5,594 | 6,375 |
| 2880 45' high | | 1 | 16 | | 6,275 | 540 | 224 | 7,039 | 7,975 |
| 2900 50' high | | .90 | 17.778 | | 6,675 | 600 | 249 | 7,524 | 8,525 |
| 3000 Fiberglass, tapered, ground set, 23' high | | 2 | 8 | | 1,050 | 270 | 112 | 1,432 | 1,725 |
| 3100 29'-7" high | | 1.50 | 10.667 | | 1,325 | 360 | 149 | 1,834 | 2,200 |
| 3200 36'-1" high | | 1.40 | 11.429 | | 1,775 | 385 | 160 | 2,320 | 2,725 |
| 3300 39'-5" high | | 1.20 | 13.333 | | 2,150 | 450 | 187 | 2,787 | 3,250 |
| 3400 49'-2" high | | 1 | 16 | | 4,575 | 540 | 224 | 5,339 | 6,100 |
| 3500 59' high | | .90 | 17.778 | | 6,350 | 600 | 249 | 7,199 | 8,200 |
| 4300 Steel, direct imbedded installation | | | | | | | | | |
| 4400 Internal halyard, 20' high | K-1 | 2.50 | 6.400 | Ea. | 1,425 | 216 | 89.50 | 1,730.50 | 1,975 |
| 4500 25' high | | 2.50 | 6.400 | | 1,575 | 216 | 89.50 | 1,880.50 | 2,175 |
| 4600 30' high | | 2.30 | 6.957 | | 1,875 | 235 | 97.50 | 2,207.50 | 2,525 |
| 4700 40' high | | 2.10 | 7.619 | | 2,775 | 257 | 107 | 3,139 | 3,575 |
| 4800 50' high | | 1.90 | 8.421 | | 4,075 | 284 | 118 | 4,477 | 5,075 |
| 5000 60' high | | 1.80 | 8.889 | | 6,175 | 300 | 124 | 6,599 | 7,400 |
| 5100 70' high | | 1.60 | 10 | | 7,550 | 340 | 140 | 8,030 | 8,975 |
| 5200 80' high | | 1.40 | 11.429 | | 9,950 | 385 | 160 | 10,495 | 11,700 |
| 5300 90' high | | 1.20 | 13.333 | | 13,600 | 450 | 187 | 14,237 | 15,900 |
| 5500 100' high | | 1 | 16 | | 14,100 | 540 | 224 | 14,864 | 16,600 |
| 6400 Wood poles, tapered, clear vertical grain fir with tilting | | | | | | | | | |
| 6410 base, not incl. foundation, 4" butt, 25' high | K-1 | 1.90 | 8.421 | Ea. | 1,375 | 284 | 118 | 1,777 | 2,100 |
| 6800 6" butt, 30' high | " | 1.30 | 12.308 | " | 1,925 | 415 | 172 | 2,512 | 2,950 |
| 7300 Foundations for flagpoles, including | | | | | | | | | |
| 7400 excavation and concrete, to 35' high poles | C-1 | 10 | 3.200 | Ea. | 525 | 116 | | 641 | 760 |
| 7600 40' to 50' high | | 3.50 | 9.143 | | 955 | 330 | | 1,285 | 1,575 |
| 7700 Over 60' high | | 2 | 16 | | 1,075 | 580 | | 1,655 | 2,075 |

## 10 75 23 – Wall-Mounted Flagpoles

### 10 75 23.10 Flagpoles

| | Crew | Daily Output | Labor-Hours | Unit | Material | 2008 Bare Costs Labor | Equipment | Total | Total Incl O&P |
|---|---|---|---|---|---|---|---|---|---|
| 0010 **FLAGPOLES**, Structure mounted | | | | | | | | | |
| 0100 Fiberglass, vertical wall set, 19'-8" long | K-1 | 1.50 | 10.667 | Ea. | 1,225 | 360 | 149 | 1,734 | 2,075 |
| 0200 23' long | | 1.40 | 11.429 | | 1,300 | 385 | 160 | 1,845 | 2,200 |
| 0300 26'-3" long | | 1.30 | 12.308 | | 1,675 | 415 | 172 | 2,262 | 2,675 |
| 0800 19'-8" long outrigger | | 1.30 | 12.308 | | 1,275 | 415 | 172 | 1,862 | 2,225 |
| 1300 Aluminum, vertical wall set, tapered, with base, 20' high | | 1.20 | 13.333 | | 960 | 450 | 187 | 1,597 | 1,950 |
| 1400 29'-6" high | | 1 | 16 | | 2,225 | 540 | 224 | 2,989 | 3,525 |

# 10 75 Flagpoles

## 10 75 23 – Wall-Mounted Flagpoles

| 10 75 23.10 Flagpoles | Crew | Daily Output | Labor-Hours | Unit | Material | 2008 Bare Costs Labor | Equipment | Total | Total Incl O&P |
|---|---|---|---|---|---|---|---|---|---|
| 2400 | Outrigger poles with base, 12' long | K-1 | 1.30 | 12.308 | Ea. | 880 | 415 | 172 | 1,467 | 1,800 |
| 2500 | 14' long | ↓ | 1 | 16 | ↓ | 1,375 | 540 | 224 | 2,139 | 2,600 |

# 10 81 Pest Control Devices

## 10 81 13 – Bird Control Devices

### 10 81 13.10 Bird Control Netting

| | | Crew | Daily Output | Labor-Hours | Unit | Material | 2008 Bare Costs Labor | Equipment | Total | Total Incl O&P |
|---|---|---|---|---|---|---|---|---|---|---|
| 0010 | **BIRD CONTROL NETTING** | | | | | | | | | |
| 0020 | 1/8" square mesh | 4 Clab | 4000 | .008 | S.F. | .04 | .24 | | .28 | .42 |
| 0100 | 1/4" square mesh | | 4000 | .008 | | .05 | .24 | | .29 | .44 |
| 0120 | 1/2" square mesh | | 4000 | .008 | | .05 | .24 | | .29 | .44 |
| 0140 | 5/8" x 3/4" mesh | | 4000 | .008 | | .05 | .24 | | .29 | .44 |
| 0160 | 1-1/4" x 1-1/2" mesh | | 4000 | .008 | | .06 | .24 | | .30 | .45 |
| 0200 | 4" square mesh | ↓ | 4000 | .008 | ↓ | .07 | .24 | | .31 | .46 |
| 1000 | Poly clips | | | | Ea. | .01 | | | .01 | .01 |

# 10 88 Scales

## 10 88 05 – Commercial Scales

### 10 88 05.10 Scales

| | | Crew | Daily Output | Labor-Hours | Unit | Material | 2008 Bare Costs Labor | Equipment | Total | Total Incl O&P |
|---|---|---|---|---|---|---|---|---|---|---|
| 0010 | **SCALES** Built-in floor scale, not incl. foundations | | | | | | | | | |
| 0100 | Dial type, 5 ton capacity, 8' x 6' platform | 3 Carp | .50 | 48 | Ea. | 7,075 | 1,825 | | 8,900 | 10,600 |
| 0300 | 9' x 7' platform | | .40 | 60 | | 9,175 | 2,275 | | 11,450 | 13,700 |
| 0400 | 10 ton capacity, steel, 8' x 6' platform | | .40 | 60 | | 11,100 | 2,275 | | 13,375 | 15,800 |
| 0600 | 9' x 7' platform | ↓ | .35 | 68.571 | ↓ | 10,400 | 2,625 | | 13,025 | 15,600 |
| 0700 | Truck scales, incl. steel weigh bridge, | | | | | | | | | |
| 0800 | not including foundation, pits | | | | | | | | | |
| 1550 | Digital, electronic, 100 ton capacity, steel deck 12' x 10' platform | 3 Carp | .20 | 120 | Ea. | 11,700 | 4,575 | | 16,275 | 20,000 |
| 1600 | 40' x 10' platform | | .14 | 171 | | 23,900 | 6,525 | | 30,425 | 36,500 |
| 1640 | 60' x 10' platform | | .13 | 184 | | 29,600 | 7,025 | | 36,625 | 43,400 |
| 1680 | 70' x 10' platform | ↓ | .12 | 200 | | 33,000 | 7,625 | | 40,625 | 48,200 |
| 2000 | For standard automatic printing device, add | | | | | 2,375 | | | 2,375 | 2,625 |
| 2100 | For remote reading electronic system, add | | | | | 2,150 | | | 2,150 | 2,375 |
| 2300 | Concrete foundation pits for above, 8' x 6', 5 C.Y. required | C-1 | .50 | 64 | | 900 | 2,325 | | 3,225 | 4,600 |
| 2400 | 14' x 6' platform, 10 C.Y. required | | .35 | 91.429 | | 1,325 | 3,300 | | 4,625 | 6,600 |
| 2600 | 50' x 10' platform, 30 C.Y. required | | .25 | 128 | | 1,775 | 4,625 | | 6,400 | 9,150 |
| 2700 | 70' x 10' platform, 40 C.Y. required | ↓ | .15 | 213 | | 3,875 | 7,700 | | 11,575 | 16,300 |
| 2750 | Crane scales, dial, 1 ton capacity | | | | | 955 | | | 955 | 1,050 |
| 2780 | 5 ton capacity | | | | | 1,125 | | | 1,125 | 1,225 |
| 2800 | Digital, 1 ton capacity | | | | | 2,000 | | | 2,000 | 2,200 |
| 2850 | 10 ton capacity | | | | ↓ | 4,025 | | | 4,025 | 4,425 |
| 2900 | Low profile electronic warehouse scale, | | | | | | | | | |
| 3000 | not incl. printer, 4' x 4' platform, 10,000 lb. capacity | 2 Carp | .30 | 53.333 | Ea. | 1,950 | 2,025 | | 3,975 | 5,325 |
| 3300 | 5' x 7' platform, 10,000 lb. capacity | | .25 | 64 | | 3,875 | 2,450 | | 6,325 | 8,075 |
| 3400 | 20,000 lb. capacity | ↓ | .20 | 80 | | 5,000 | 3,050 | | 8,050 | 10,300 |
| 3500 | For printers, incl. time, date & numbering, add | | | | | 1,250 | | | 1,250 | 1,375 |
| 3800 | Portable, beam type, capacity 1000#, platform 18" x 24" | | | | | 725 | | | 725 | 795 |
| 3900 | Dial type, capacity 2000#, platform 24" x 24" | | | | | 1,250 | | | 1,250 | 1,375 |
| 4000 | Digital type, capacity 1000#, platform 24" x 30" | | | | | 2,000 | | | 2,000 | 2,200 |
| 4100 | Portable contractor truck scales, 50 ton cap., 40' x 10' platform | | | | | 31,100 | | | 31,100 | 34,200 |
| 4200 | 60' x 10' platform | | | | ↓ | 27,800 | | | 27,800 | 30,600 |

# Division Notes

| | CREW | DAILY OUTPUT | LABOR-HOURS | UNIT | 2008 BARE COSTS | | | | TOTAL INCL O&P |
|---|---|---|---|---|---|---|---|---|---|
| | | | | | MAT. | LABOR | EQUIP. | TOTAL | |
| | | | | | | | | | |
| | | | | | | | | | |
| | | | | | | | | | |
| | | | | | | | | | |
| | | | | | | | | | |
| | | | | | | | | | |
| | | | | | | | | | |
| | | | | | | | | | |
| | | | | | | | | | |
| | | | | | | | | | |
| | | | | | | | | | |
| | | | | | | | | | |
| | | | | | | | | | |
| | | | | | | | | | |
| | | | | | | | | | |
| | | | | | | | | | |
| | | | | | | | | | |
| | | | | | | | | | |
| | | | | | | | | | |
| | | | | | | | | | |

# Estimating Tips

## General

- The items in this division are usually priced per square foot or each. Many of these items are purchased by the owner for installation by the contractor. Check the specifications for responsibilities and include time for receiving, storage, installation, and mechanical and electrical hook-ups in the appropriate divisions.

- Many items in Division 11 require some type of support system that is not usually furnished with the item. Examples of these systems include blocking for the attachment of casework and support angles for ceiling-hung projection screens. The required blocking or supports must be added to the estimate in the appropriate division.

- Some items in Division 11 may require assembly or electrical hookups. Verify the amount of assembly required or the need for a hard electrical connection and add the appropriate costs.

# Reference Numbers

Reference numbers are shown in shaded boxes at the beginning of some major classifications. These numbers refer to related items in the Reference Section. The reference information may be an estimating procedure, an alternate pricing method, or technical information.

*Note:* Not all subdivisions listed here necessarily appear in this publication.

# 11 05 Common Work Results for Equipment

## 11 05 05 – Selective Equipment Demolition

| 11 05 05.10 Selective Demolition | Crew | Daily Output | Labor-Hours | Unit | Material | 2008 Bare Costs Labor | 2008 Bare Costs Equipment | Total | Total Incl O&P |
|---|---|---|---|---|---|---|---|---|---|
| **0010** | **SELECTIVE DEMOLITION** | | | | | | | | |
| 0130 | Central vacuum, motor unit, residential or commercial | 1 Clab | 2 | 4 | Ea. | 680 | 121 | | 801 | 935 |
| 0210 | Vault door and frame | 2 Skwk | 2 | 8 | | 680 | 315 | | 995 | 1,225 |
| 0215 | Day gate, for vault | " | 3 | 5.333 | | 680 | 210 | | 890 | 1,075 |
| 0380 | Bank equipment, teller window, bullet resistant | 1 Clab | 1.20 | 6.667 | ↓ | | 202 | | 202 | 315 |
| 0381 | Counter | 2 Clab | 1.50 | 10.667 | Station | | 325 | | 325 | 500 |
| 0382 | Drive-up window, including drawer and glass | | 1.50 | 10.667 | " | | 325 | | 325 | 500 |
| 0383 | Thru-wall boxes and chests, selective demolition | | 2.50 | 6.400 | Ea. | | 194 | | 194 | 300 |
| 0384 | Bullet resistant partitions | ↓ | 20 | .800 | L.F. | | 24 | | 24 | 37.50 |
| 0385 | Pneumatic tube system, 2 lane drive-up | L-3 | .45 | 35.556 | Ea. | | 1,475 | | 1,475 | 2,275 |
| 0386 | Safety deposit box | 1 Clab | 50 | .160 | Opng. | | 4.84 | | 4.84 | 7.55 |
| 0387 | Surveillance system, video, complete | 2 Elec | 2 | 8 | Ea. | | 365 | | 365 | 545 |
| 0410 | Church equipment, misc moveable fixtures | 2 Clab | 1 | 16 | | | 485 | | 485 | 755 |
| 0412 | Steeple, to 28' high | F-3 | 3 | 13.333 | | | 515 | 255 | 770 | 1,075 |
| 0414 | 40' to 60' high | " | .80 | 50 | ↓ | | 1,925 | 960 | 2,885 | 4,050 |
| 0510 | Library equipment, bookshelves, wood, to 90" high | 1 Clab | 20 | .400 | L.F. | | 12.10 | | 12.10 | 18.80 |
| 0515 | Carrels, hardwood, 36" x 24" | " | 9 | .889 | Ea. | | 27 | | 27 | 42 |
| 0630 | Stage equipment, light control panel | 1 Elec | 1 | 8 | " | | 365 | | 365 | 545 |
| 0632 | Border lights | | 40 | .200 | L.F. | | 9.10 | | 9.10 | 13.55 |
| 0634 | Spotlights | ↓ | 8 | 1 | Ea. | | 45.50 | | 45.50 | 68 |
| 0636 | Telescoping platforms and risers | 2 Clab | 175 | .091 | SF Stg. | | 2.77 | | 2.77 | 4.30 |
| 1020 | Barber equipment, hydraulic chair | 1 Clab | 40 | .200 | Ea. | | 6.05 | | 6.05 | 9.40 |
| 1030 | Checkout counter, supermarket or warehouse conveyor | 2 Clab | 18 | .889 | | | 27 | | 27 | 42 |
| 1040 | Food cases, refrigerated or frozen | Q-5 | 6 | 2.667 | | | 113 | | 113 | 170 |
| 1190 | Laundry equipment, commercial | L-6 | 3 | 4 | | | 185 | | 185 | 278 |
| 1360 | Movie equipment, lamphouse, to 4000 watt, incl rectifier | 1 Elec | 4 | 2 | | | 91 | | 91 | 136 |
| 1365 | Sound system, incl amplifier | " | 1.25 | 6.400 | | | 292 | | 292 | 435 |
| 1410 | Air compressor, to 5 H.P. | 2 Clab | 2.50 | 6.400 | ↓ | | 194 | | 194 | 300 |
| 1412 | Lubrication equipment, automotive, 3 reel type, incl pump, excl piping | L-4 | 1 | 24 | Set | | 865 | | 865 | 1,350 |
| 1414 | Booth, spray paint, complete, to 26' long | " | .80 | 30 | " | | 1,075 | | 1,075 | 1,675 |
| 1560 | Parking equipment, cashier booth | B-22 | 2 | 15 | Ea. | | 530 | 97 | 627 | 925 |
| 1600 | Loading dock equipment, dock bumpers, rubber | 1 Clab | 50 | .160 | " | | 4.84 | | 4.84 | 7.55 |
| 1610 | Door seal for door perimeter | " | 50 | .160 | L.F. | | 4.84 | | 4.84 | 7.55 |
| 1620 | Platform lifter, fixed, 6' x 8', 5000 lb capacity | E-16 | 1.50 | 10.667 | Ea. | | 470 | 88 | 558 | 940 |
| 1630 | Dock leveller | " | 2 | 8 | | | 350 | 66 | 416 | 710 |
| 1640 | Lights, single or double arm | 1 Elec | 8 | 1 | | | 45.50 | | 45.50 | 68 |
| 1650 | Shelter, fabric, truck or train | 1 Clab | 1.50 | 5.333 | | | 161 | | 161 | 251 |
| 1790 | Waste handling equipment, commercial compactor | L-4 | 2 | 12 | | | 430 | | 430 | 670 |
| 1792 | Commercial or municipal incinerator, gas | " | 2 | 12 | | | 430 | | 430 | 670 |
| 1795 | Crematory, excluding building | Q-3 | .25 | 128 | | | 5,700 | | 5,700 | 8,575 |
| 1910 | Detection equipment, cell bar front | E-4 | 4 | 8 | | | 350 | 33 | 383 | 665 |
| 1912 | Cell door and frame | | 8 | 4 | | | 174 | 16.50 | 190.50 | 335 |
| 1914 | Prefab cell, 4' to 5' wide, 7' to 8' high, 7' deep | | 8 | 4 | | | 174 | 16.50 | 190.50 | 335 |
| 1916 | Cot, bolted, single | | 40 | .800 | | | 35 | 3.30 | 38.30 | 66.50 |
| 1918 | Visitor cubicle | ↓ | 4 | 8 | | | 350 | 33 | 383 | 665 |
| 2850 | Hydraulic gates, canal, flap, knife, slide or sluice, to 18" diameter | L-5A | 8 | 4 | | | 172 | 87.50 | 259.50 | 395 |
| 2852 | 19" to 36" diameter | | 6 | 5.333 | | | 229 | 117 | 346 | 525 |
| 2854 | 37" to 48" diameter | | 2 | 16 | | | 690 | 350 | 1,040 | 1,575 |
| 2856 | 49" to 60" diameter | | 1 | 32 | | | 1,375 | 700 | 2,075 | 3,150 |
| 2858 | Over 60" diameter | ↓ | .30 | 106 | | | 4,575 | 2,350 | 6,925 | 10,500 |
| 3100 | Sewage pumping system, prefabricated, to 1000 GPM | C-17D | .20 | 420 | | | 16,700 | 3,225 | 19,925 | 29,600 |
| 3110 | Sewage treatment, holding tank for recirc chemical water closet | 1 Plum | 8 | 1 | | | 46.50 | | 46.50 | 70.50 |
| 3900 | Wastewater treatment system, to 1500 gallons | B-21 | 2 | 14 | ↓ | | 490 | 64.50 | 554.50 | 830 |

# 11 05 Common Work Results for Equipment

## 11 05 05 – Selective Equipment Demolition

### 11 05 05.10 Selective Demolition

| | | Crew | Daily Output | Labor-Hours | Unit | Material | 2008 Bare Costs Labor | 2008 Bare Costs Equipment | Total | Total Incl O&P |
|---|---|---|---|---|---|---|---|---|---|---|
| 4050 | Food storage equipment, walk-in refrigerator/freezer | 2 Clab | 64 | .250 | S.F. | | 7.55 | | 7.55 | 11.75 |
| 4052 | Shelving, stainless steel, 4 tier or dunnage rack | 1 Clab | 12 | .667 | Ea. | | 20 | | 20 | 31.50 |
| 4100 | Food preparation equipment, small countertop | | 18 | .444 | | | 13.45 | | 13.45 | 21 |
| 4150 | Food delivery carts, heated cabinets | ↓ | 18 | .444 | | | 13.45 | | 13.45 | 21 |
| 4200 | Cooking equipment, commercial range | Q-1 | 12 | 1.333 | | | 56 | | 56 | 84.50 |
| 4250 | Hood and ventilation equipment, kitchen exhaust hood, excl fire prot | 1 Clab | 3 | 2.667 | | | 80.50 | | 80.50 | 125 |
| 4255 | Fire protection system | Q-1 | 3 | 5.333 | | | 224 | | 224 | 335 |
| 4300 | Food dispensing equipment, countertop items | 1 Clab | 15 | .533 | ↓ | | 16.15 | | 16.15 | 25 |
| 4310 | Serving counter | " | 65 | .123 | L.F. | | 3.72 | | 3.72 | 5.80 |
| 4350 | Ice machine, ice cube maker, flakers and storage bins, to 2000 lb/day | Q-1 | 1.60 | 10 | Ea. | | 420 | | 420 | 630 |
| 4400 | Cleaning and disposal, dishwasher, commercial, rack type | L-6 | 1 | 12 | | | 555 | | 555 | 835 |
| 4410 | Dishwasher hood | 2 Clab | 5 | 3.200 | | | 97 | | 97 | 151 |
| 4420 | Garbage disposal, commercial, to 5 H.P. | L-1 | 8 | 2 | | | 92.50 | | 92.50 | 138 |
| 4540 | Water heater, residential, to 80 gal/day | " | 5 | 3.200 | | | 148 | | 148 | 221 |
| 4542 | Water softener, automatic | 2 Plum | 10 | 1.600 | | | 74.50 | | 74.50 | 112 |
| 4544 | Disappearing stairway, to 15' floor height | 2 Clab | 6 | 2.667 | | | 80.50 | | 80.50 | 125 |
| 4710 | Darkroom equipment, light | L-7 | 10 | 2.800 | | | 103 | | 103 | 160 |
| 4712 | Heavy | " | 1.50 | 18.667 | ↓ | | 690 | | 690 | 1,075 |
| 4720 | Doors | 2 Clab | 3.50 | 4.571 | Opng. | | 138 | | 138 | 215 |
| 4830 | Bowling alley, complete, incl pinsetter, scorer, counters, misc supplies | 4 Clab | .40 | 80 | Lane | | 2,425 | | 2,425 | 3,775 |
| 4840 | Health club equipment, circuit training apparatus | 2 Clab | 2 | 8 | Set | | 242 | | 242 | 375 |
| 4842 | Squat racks | " | 10 | 1.600 | Ea. | | 48.50 | | 48.50 | 75.50 |
| 4860 | School equipment, basketball backstop | L-2 | 2 | 8 | | | 269 | | 269 | 420 |
| 4862 | Table and benches, folding, in wall, 14' long | L-4 | 4 | 6 | ↓ | | 216 | | 216 | 335 |
| 4864 | Bleachers, telescoping, to 30 tier | F-5 | 120 | .267 | Seat | | 10.30 | | 10.30 | 16 |
| 4866 | Boxing ring, elevated | L-4 | .20 | 120 | Ea. | | 4,325 | | 4,325 | 6,700 |
| 4867 | Boxing ring, floor level | " | 2 | 12 | | | 430 | | 430 | 670 |
| 4868 | Exercise equipment | 1 Clab | 6 | 1.333 | ↓ | | 40.50 | | 40.50 | 62.50 |
| 4870 | Gym divider | L-4 | 1000 | .024 | S.F. | | .86 | | .86 | 1.34 |
| 4875 | Scoreboard | R-3 | 2 | 10 | Ea. | | 450 | 64.50 | 514.50 | 740 |
| 4880 | Shooting range, incl bullet traps, targets, excl structure | L-9 | 1 | 36 | Point | | 1,250 | | 1,250 | 2,025 |
| 5200 | Vocational shop equipment | 2 Clab | 8 | 2 | Ea. | | 60.50 | | 60.50 | 94 |
| 6200 | Fume hood, incl countertop, excl HVAC | " | 6 | 2.667 | L.F. | | 80.50 | | 80.50 | 125 |
| 7100 | Medical sterilizing, distiller, water, steam heated, 50 gal capacity | 1 Plum | 2.80 | 2.857 | Ea. | | 133 | | 133 | 201 |
| 7200 | Medical equipment, surgery table, minor | 1 Clab | 1 | 8 | | | 242 | | 242 | 375 |
| 7210 | Surgical lights, doctors office, single or double arm | 2 Elec | 3 | 5.333 | | | 243 | | 243 | 360 |
| 7300 | Physical therapy, table | 2 Clab | 4 | 4 | | | 121 | | 121 | 188 |
| 7310 | Whirlpool bath, fixed, incl mixing valves | 1 Plum | 4 | 2 | | | 93.50 | | 93.50 | 141 |
| 7400 | Dental equipment, chair, electric or hydraulic | 1 Clab | .75 | 10.667 | | | 325 | | 325 | 500 |
| 7410 | Central suction system | 1 Plum | 2 | 4 | | | 187 | | 187 | 281 |
| 7420 | Drill console with accessories | 1 Clab | 3.20 | 2.500 | | | 75.50 | | 75.50 | 118 |
| 7430 | X-ray unit | " | 4 | 2 | | | 60.50 | | 60.50 | 94 |
| 7440 | X-ray developer | 1 Plum | 10 | .800 | ↓ | | 37.50 | | 37.50 | 56 |

## 11 05 10 – Equipment Installation

### 11 05 10.10 Industrial Equipment Installation

| | | Crew | Daily Output | Labor-Hours | Unit | Material | 2008 Bare Costs Labor | 2008 Bare Costs Equipment | Total | Total Incl O&P |
|---|---|---|---|---|---|---|---|---|---|---|
| 0010 | **INDUSTRIAL EQUIPMENT INSTALLATION** | | | | | | | | | |
| 0020 | Industrial equipment, minimum | E-2 | 12 | 4.667 | Ton | | 195 | 131 | 326 | 480 |
| 0200 | Maximum | " | 2 | 28 | " | | 1,175 | 785 | 1,960 | 2,875 |

# 11 11 Vehicle Service Equipment

## 11 11 13 – Compressed-Air Vehicle Service Equipment

| 11 11 13.10 Compressed Air Equipment | Crew | Daily Output | Labor-Hours | Unit | Material | 2008 Bare Costs Labor | Equipment | Total | Total Incl O&P |
|---|---|---|---|---|---|---|---|---|---|
| 0010 **COMPRESSED AIR EQUIPMENT** | | | | | | | | | |
| 0030 Compressors, electric, 1-1/2 H.P., standard controls | L-4 | 1.50 | 16 | Ea. | 279 | 575 | | 854 | 1,200 |
| 0550 Dual controls | | 1.50 | 16 | | 495 | 575 | | 1,070 | 1,450 |
| 0600 5 H.P., 115/230 volt, standard controls | | 1 | 24 | | 1,800 | 865 | | 2,665 | 3,325 |
| 0650 Dual controls | ↓ | 1 | 24 | ↓ | 1,925 | 865 | | 2,790 | 3,450 |

## 11 11 19 – Vehicle Lubrication Equipment

### 11 11 19.10 Lubrication Equipment

| | Crew | Daily Output | Labor-Hours | Unit | Material | Labor | Equipment | Total | Total Incl O&P |
|---|---|---|---|---|---|---|---|---|---|
| 0010 **LUBRICATION EQUIPMENT** | | | | | | | | | |
| 3000 Lube equipment, 3 reel type, with pumps, not including piping | L-4 | .50 | 48 | Set | 7,525 | 1,725 | | 9,250 | 11,000 |

## 11 11 33 – Vehicle Spray Painting Equipment

### 11 11 33.10 Spray Painting Equipment

| | Crew | Daily Output | Labor-Hours | Unit | Material | Labor | Equipment | Total | Total Incl O&P |
|---|---|---|---|---|---|---|---|---|---|
| 0010 **SPRAY PAINTING EQUIPMENT** | | | | | | | | | |
| 4000 Spray painting booth, 26' long, complete | L-4 | .40 | 60 | Ea. | 14,400 | 2,150 | | 16,550 | 19,200 |

# 11 12 Parking Control Equipment

## 11 12 13 – Parking Key and Card Control Units

### 11 12 13.10 Parking Control Units

| | Crew | Daily Output | Labor-Hours | Unit | Material | Labor | Equipment | Total | Total Incl O&P |
|---|---|---|---|---|---|---|---|---|---|
| 0010 **PARKING CONTROL UNITS** | | | | | | | | | |
| 5100 Card reader | 1 Elec | 2 | 4 | Ea. | 1,800 | 182 | | 1,982 | 2,250 |
| 5120 Proximity with customer display | 2 Elec | 1 | 16 | | 5,500 | 730 | | 6,230 | 7,125 |
| 6000 Parking control software, minimum | 1 Elec | .50 | 16 | | 21,900 | 730 | | 22,630 | 25,200 |
| 6020 Maximum | " | .20 | 40 | ↓ | 91,000 | 1,825 | | 92,825 | 103,000 |

## 11 12 16 – Parking Ticket Dispensers

### 11 12 16.10 Ticket Dispensers

| | Crew | Daily Output | Labor-Hours | Unit | Material | Labor | Equipment | Total | Total Incl O&P |
|---|---|---|---|---|---|---|---|---|---|
| 0010 **TICKET DISPENSERS** | | | | | | | | | |
| 5900 Ticket spitter with time/date stamp, standard | 2 Elec | 2 | 8 | Ea. | 6,275 | 365 | | 6,640 | 7,450 |
| 5920 Mag stripe encoding | " | 2 | 8 | " | 18,600 | 365 | | 18,965 | 20,900 |

## 11 12 26 – Parking Fee Collection Equipment

### 11 12 26.13 Parking Fee Coin Collection Equipment

| | Crew | Daily Output | Labor-Hours | Unit | Material | Labor | Equipment | Total | Total Incl O&P |
|---|---|---|---|---|---|---|---|---|---|
| 0010 **PARKING FEE COIN COLLECTION EQUIPMENT** | | | | | | | | | |
| 5200 Cashier booth, average | B-22 | 1 | 30 | Ea. | 9,450 | 1,050 | 194 | 10,694 | 12,300 |
| 5300 Collector station, pay on foot | 2 Elec | .20 | 80 | | 109,500 | 3,650 | | 113,150 | 126,000 |
| 5320 Credit card only | " | .50 | 32 | ↓ | 20,200 | 1,450 | | 21,650 | 24,500 |

### 11 12 26.23 Fee Equipment

| | Crew | Daily Output | Labor-Hours | Unit | Material | Labor | Equipment | Total | Total Incl O&P |
|---|---|---|---|---|---|---|---|---|---|
| 0010 **FEE EQUIPMENT** | | | | | | | | | |
| 5600 Fee computer | 1 Elec | 1.50 | 5.333 | Ea. | 13,200 | 243 | | 13,443 | 14,900 |

## 11 12 33 – Parking Gates

### 11 12 33.13 Parking Gate Equipment

| | Crew | Daily Output | Labor-Hours | Unit | Material | Labor | Equipment | Total | Total Incl O&P |
|---|---|---|---|---|---|---|---|---|---|
| 0010 **PARKING GATE EQUIPMENT** | | | | | | | | | |
| 5000 Barrier gate with programmable controller | 2 Elec | 3 | 5.333 | Ea. | 3,275 | 243 | | 3,518 | 3,950 |
| 5020 Industrial | | 3 | 5.333 | | 4,425 | 243 | | 4,668 | 5,225 |
| 5500 Exit verifier | ↓ | 1 | 16 | | 17,400 | 730 | | 18,130 | 20,300 |
| 5700 Full sign, 4" letters | 1 Elec | 2 | 4 | | 1,225 | 182 | | 1,407 | 1,600 |
| 5800 Inductive loop | 2 Elec | 4 | 4 | | 169 | 182 | | 351 | 455 |
| 5950 Vehicle detector, microprocessor based | 1 Elec | 3 | 2.667 | ↓ | 385 | 121 | | 506 | 605 |

# 11 13 Loading Dock Equipment

## 11 13 13 – Loading Dock Bumpers

### 11 13 13.10 Dock Bumpers

| | | Crew | Daily Output | Labor-Hours | Unit | Material | 2008 Bare Costs Labor | Equipment | Total | Total Incl O&P |
|---|---|---|---|---|---|---|---|---|---|---|
| 0010 | **DOCK BUMPERS** Bolts not included | | | | | | | | | |
| 0020 | 2" x 6" to 4" x 8", average | 1 Carp | .30 | 26.667 | M.B.F. | 1,200 | 1,025 | | 2,225 | 2,900 |
| 0050 | Bumpers, rubber blocks 4-1/2" thick, 10" high, 14" long | | 26 | .308 | Ea. | 44 | 11.70 | | 55.70 | 67 |
| 0200 | 24" long | | 22 | .364 | | 86.50 | 13.85 | | 100.35 | 117 |
| 0300 | 36" long | | 17 | .471 | | 79.50 | 17.95 | | 97.45 | 116 |
| 0500 | 12" high, 14" long | | 25 | .320 | | 91 | 12.20 | | 103.20 | 119 |
| 0550 | 24" long | | 20 | .400 | | 101 | 15.25 | | 116.25 | 135 |
| 0600 | 36" long | | 15 | .533 | | 112 | 20.50 | | 132.50 | 155 |
| 0800 | Rubber blocks 6" thick, 10" high, 14" long | | 22 | .364 | | 82.50 | 13.85 | | 96.35 | 113 |
| 0850 | 24" long | | 18 | .444 | | 110 | 16.95 | | 126.95 | 148 |
| 0900 | 36" long | | 13 | .615 | | 131 | 23.50 | | 154.50 | 181 |
| 0910 | 20" high, 11" long | | 13 | .615 | | 133 | 23.50 | | 156.50 | 184 |
| 0920 | Extruded rubber bumpers, T section, 22" x 22" x 3" thick | | 41 | .195 | | 49 | 7.45 | | 56.45 | 65.50 |
| 0940 | Molded rubber bumpers, 24" x 12" x 3" thick | | 20 | .400 | | 47.50 | 15.25 | | 62.75 | 75.50 |
| 1000 | Welded installation of above bumpers | E-14 | 8 | 1 | | 3.40 | 45 | 16.55 | 64.95 | 103 |
| 1100 | For drilled anchors, add per anchor | 1 Carp | 36 | .222 | | 6.10 | 8.45 | | 14.55 | 19.90 |
| 1300 | Steel bumpers, see Div. 10 26 13.10 | | | | | | | | | |

## 11 13 16 – Loading Dock Seals and Shelters

### 11 13 16.10 Dock Seals and Shelters

| | | Crew | Daily Output | Labor-Hours | Unit | Material | 2008 Bare Costs Labor | Equipment | Total | Total Incl O&P |
|---|---|---|---|---|---|---|---|---|---|---|
| 0010 | **DOCK SEALS AND SHELTERS** | | | | | | | | | |
| 3600 | Door seal for door perimeter, 12" x 12", vinyl covered | 1 Carp | 26 | .308 | L.F. | 26 | 11.70 | | 37.70 | 47 |
| 3900 | Folding gates, see Div. 10 22 16.10 | | | | | | | | | |
| 6200 | Shelters, fabric, for truck or train, scissor arms, minimum | 1 Carp | 1 | 8 | Ea. | 1,400 | 305 | | 1,705 | 2,025 |
| 6300 | Maximum | " | .50 | 16 | " | 1,825 | 610 | | 2,435 | 2,950 |

## 11 13 19 – Stationary Loading Dock Equipment

### 11 13 19.10 Dock Equipment

| | | Crew | Daily Output | Labor-Hours | Unit | Material | 2008 Bare Costs Labor | Equipment | Total | Total Incl O&P |
|---|---|---|---|---|---|---|---|---|---|---|
| 0010 | **DOCK EQUIPMENT** | | | | | | | | | |
| 2200 | Dock boards, heavy duty, 60" x 60", aluminum, 5,000 lb. capacity | | | | Ea. | 1,000 | | | 1,000 | 1,100 |
| 2700 | 9,000 lb. capacity | | | | | 1,225 | | | 1,225 | 1,325 |
| 3200 | 15,000 lb. capacity | | | | | 1,375 | | | 1,375 | 1,500 |
| 4200 | Platform lifter, 6' x 6', portable, 3,000 lb. capacity | | | | | 8,300 | | | 8,300 | 9,150 |
| 4250 | 4,000 lb. capacity | | | | | 10,200 | | | 10,200 | 11,300 |
| 4400 | Fixed, 6' x 8', 5,000 lb. capacity | E-16 | .70 | 22.857 | | 8,950 | 1,000 | 189 | 10,139 | 11,900 |
| 4500 | Levelers, hinged for trucks, 10 ton capacity, 6' x 8' | | 1.08 | 14.815 | | 4,525 | 650 | 122 | 5,297 | 6,275 |
| 4650 | 7' x 8' | | 1.08 | 14.815 | | 4,525 | 650 | 122 | 5,297 | 6,275 |
| 4670 | Air bag power operated, 10 ton cap., 6'x8' | | 1.08 | 14.815 | | 5,250 | 650 | 122 | 6,022 | 7,075 |
| 4680 | 7' x 8' | | 1.08 | 14.815 | | 5,275 | 650 | 122 | 6,047 | 7,100 |
| 4700 | Hydraulic, 10 ton capacity, 6' x 8'    *CN* | | 1.08 | 14.815 | | 7,875 | 650 | 122 | 8,647 | 9,950 |
| 4800 | 7' x 8' | | 1.08 | 14.815 | | 8,475 | 650 | 122 | 9,247 | 10,600 |
| 5800 | Loading dock safety restraints, manual style | | 1.08 | 14.815 | | 2,875 | 650 | 122 | 3,647 | 4,475 |
| 5900 | Automatic style | | 1.08 | 14.815 | | 4,850 | 650 | 122 | 5,622 | 6,625 |

## 11 13 26 – Loading Dock Lights

### 11 13 26.10 Dock Lights

| | | Crew | Daily Output | Labor-Hours | Unit | Material | 2008 Bare Costs Labor | Equipment | Total | Total Incl O&P |
|---|---|---|---|---|---|---|---|---|---|---|
| 0010 | **DOCK LIGHTS** | | | | | | | | | |
| 5000 | Lights for loading docks, single arm, 24" long | 1 Elec | 3.80 | 2.105 | Ea. | 137 | 96 | | 233 | 293 |
| 5700 | Double arm, 60" long | " | 3.80 | 2.105 | " | 160 | 96 | | 256 | 320 |

341

# 11 14 Pedestrian Control Equipment

## 11 14 13 – Pedestrian Gates

### 11 14 13.13 Portable Posts and Railings

| | | Crew | Daily Output | Labor-Hours | Unit | Material | 2008 Bare Costs Labor | Equipment | Total | Total Incl O&P |
|---|---|---|---|---|---|---|---|---|---|---|
| 0010 | **PORTABLE POSTS AND RAILINGS** | | | | | | | | | |
| 0020 | Portable for pedestrian traffic control, standard, minimum | | | | Ea. | 111 | | | 111 | 122 |
| 0100 | Maximum | | | | | 172 | | | 172 | 189 |
| 0300 | Deluxe posts, minimum | | | | | 154 | | | 154 | 170 |
| 0400 | Maximum | | | | | 299 | | | 299 | 330 |
| 0600 | Ropes for above posts, plastic covered, 1-1/2" diameter | | | | L.F. | 9.85 | | | 9.85 | 10.80 |
| 0700 | Chain core | | | | " | 10.05 | | | 10.05 | 11.10 |
| 1500 | Portable security or safety barrier, black with 7' yellow strap | | | | Ea. | 215 | | | 215 | 236 |
| 1510 | 12' yellow strap | | | | | 250 | | | 250 | 275 |
| 1550 | Sign holder, standard design | | | | | 54 | | | 54 | 59.50 |

### 11 14 13.19 Turnstiles

| | | Crew | Daily Output | Labor-Hours | Unit | Material | 2008 Bare Costs Labor | Equipment | Total | Total Incl O&P |
|---|---|---|---|---|---|---|---|---|---|---|
| 0010 | **TURNSTILES** | | | | | | | | | |
| 0020 | One way, 4 arm, 46" diameter, economy, manual | 2 Carp | 5 | 3.200 | Ea. | 740 | 122 | | 862 | 1,000 |
| 0100 | Electric | | 1.20 | 13.333 | | 1,200 | 510 | | 1,710 | 2,125 |
| 0300 | High security, galv., 5'-5" diameter, 7' high, manual | | 1 | 16 | | 3,675 | 610 | | 4,285 | 5,000 |
| 0350 | Electric | | .60 | 26.667 | | 4,150 | 1,025 | | 5,175 | 6,150 |
| 0420 | Three arm, 24" opening, light duty, manual | | 2 | 8 | | 1,175 | 305 | | 1,480 | 1,750 |
| 0450 | Heavy duty | | 1.50 | 10.667 | | 2,900 | 405 | | 3,305 | 3,800 |
| 0460 | Manual, with registering & controls, light duty | | 2 | 8 | | 2,525 | 305 | | 2,830 | 3,250 |
| 0470 | Heavy duty | | 1.50 | 10.667 | | 3,050 | 405 | | 3,455 | 3,975 |
| 0480 | Electric, heavy duty | | 1.10 | 14.545 | | 3,525 | 555 | | 4,080 | 4,750 |
| 0500 | For coin or token operating, add | | | | | 565 | | | 565 | 620 |
| 1200 | One way gate with horizontal bars, 5'-5" diameter | | | | | | | | | |
| 1300 | 7' high, recreation or transit type | 2 Carp | .80 | 20 | Ea. | 4,075 | 760 | | 4,835 | 5,675 |
| 1500 | For electronic counter, add | | | | " | 195 | | | 195 | 214 |

# 11 16 Vault Equipment

## 11 16 16 – Safes

### 11 16 16.10 Commercial Safes

| | | Crew | Daily Output | Labor-Hours | Unit | Material | 2008 Bare Costs Labor | Equipment | Total | Total Incl O&P |
|---|---|---|---|---|---|---|---|---|---|---|
| 0010 | **COMMERCIAL SAFES** | | | | | | | | | |
| 0200 | Office, 1 hr. rating, 30" x 18" x 18" | | | | Ea. | 2,050 | | | 2,050 | 2,250 |
| 0250 | 40" x 18" x 18" | | | | | 3,800 | | | 3,800 | 4,175 |
| 0300 | 60" x 36" x 18", double door | | | | | 7,525 | | | 7,525 | 8,275 |
| 0600 | 1 hr. rating, 27" x 19" x 16" | | | | | 7,025 | | | 7,025 | 7,725 |
| 0700 | 63" x 34" x 16" | | | | | 13,400 | | | 13,400 | 14,700 |
| 0750 | Diskette, 1 hr., 14" x 12" x 11", inside | | | | | 3,650 | | | 3,650 | 4,025 |
| 0800 | Money, "B" label, 9" x 14" x 14" | | | | | 495 | | | 495 | 545 |
| 0900 | Tool resistive, 24" x 24" x 20" | | | | | 3,375 | | | 3,375 | 3,700 |
| 1050 | Tool and torch resistive, 24" x 24" x 20" | | | | | 8,625 | | | 8,625 | 9,500 |
| 1150 | Jewelers, 23" x 20" x 18" | | | | | 11,000 | | | 11,000 | 12,100 |
| 1200 | 63" x 25" x 18" | | | | | 20,900 | | | 20,900 | 23,000 |
| 1300 | For handling into building, add, minimum | A-2 | 8.50 | 2.824 | | | 84.50 | 21 | 105.50 | 154 |
| 1400 | Maximum | " | .78 | 30.769 | | | 920 | 230 | 1,150 | 1,675 |

# 11 17 Teller and Service Equipment

## 11 17 13 – Teller Equipment Systems

| 11 17 13.10 Bank Equipment | Crew | Daily Output | Labor-Hours | Unit | Material | 2008 Bare Costs Labor | Equipment | Total | Total Incl O&P |
|---|---|---|---|---|---|---|---|---|---|
| **0010** **BANK EQUIPMENT** | | | | | | | | | |
| 0020 | Alarm system, police | 2 Elec | 1.60 | 10 | Ea. | 4,450 | 455 | | 4,905 | 5,575 |
| 0100 | With vault alarm | " | .40 | 40 | | 17,700 | 1,825 | | 19,525 | 22,100 |
| 0400 | Bullet resistant teller window, 44" x 60" | 1 Glaz | .60 | 13.333 | | 3,000 | 495 | | 3,495 | 4,050 |
| 0500 | 48" x 60" | " | .60 | 13.333 | | 3,725 | 495 | | 4,220 | 4,850 |
| 3000 | Counters for banks, frontal only | 2 Carp | 1 | 16 | Station | 1,650 | 610 | | 2,260 | 2,775 |
| 3100 | Complete with steel undercounter | " | .50 | 32 | " | 3,250 | 1,225 | | 4,475 | 5,475 |
| 4600 | Door and frame, bullet-resistant, with vision panel, minimum | 2 Sswk | 1.10 | 14.545 | Ea. | 3,800 | 625 | | 4,425 | 5,300 |
| 4700 | Maximum | | 1.10 | 14.545 | | 5,150 | 625 | | 5,775 | 6,775 |
| 4800 | Drive-up window, drawer & mike, not incl. glass, minimum | | 1 | 16 | | 5,000 | 690 | | 5,690 | 6,750 |
| 4900 | Maximum | | .50 | 32 | | 8,450 | 1,375 | | 9,825 | 11,800 |
| 5000 | Night depository, with chest, minimum | | 1 | 16 | | 6,900 | 690 | | 7,590 | 8,850 |
| 5100 | Maximum | | .50 | 32 | | 9,800 | 1,375 | | 11,175 | 13,300 |
| 5200 | Package receiver, painted | | 3.20 | 5 | | 1,250 | 215 | | 1,465 | 1,775 |
| 5300 | Stainless steel | | 3.20 | 5 | | 2,100 | 215 | | 2,315 | 2,725 |
| 5400 | Partitions, bullet-resistant, 1-3/16" glass, 8' high | 2 Carp | 10 | 1.600 | L.F. | 180 | 61 | | 241 | 293 |
| 5450 | Acrylic | " | 10 | 1.600 | " | 340 | 61 | | 401 | 470 |
| 5500 | Pneumatic tube systems, 2 lane drive-up, complete | L-3 | .25 | 64 | Total | 23,400 | 2,675 | | 26,075 | 29,900 |
| 5550 | With T.V. viewer | " | .20 | 80 | " | 45,400 | 3,350 | | 48,750 | 55,000 |
| 5570 | Safety deposit boxes, minimum | 1 Sswk | 44 | .182 | Opng. | 52 | 7.80 | | 59.80 | 71.50 |
| 5580 | Maximum, 10" x 15" opening | | 19 | .421 | | 110 | 18.10 | | 128.10 | 154 |
| 5590 | Teller locker, average | | 15 | .533 | | 1,425 | 23 | | 1,448 | 1,625 |
| 5600 | Pass thru, bullet-res. window, painted steel, 24" x 36" | 2 Sswk | 1.60 | 10 | Ea. | 2,075 | 430 | | 2,505 | 3,050 |
| 5700 | 48" x 48" | | 1.20 | 13.333 | | 2,425 | 575 | | 3,000 | 3,675 |
| 5800 | 72" x 40" | | .80 | 20 | | 3,050 | 860 | | 3,910 | 4,925 |
| 5900 | For stainless steel frames, add | | | | | 20% | | | | |
| 6100 | Surveillance system, video camera, complete | 2 Elec | 1 | 16 | Ea. | 13,800 | 730 | | 14,530 | 16,300 |
| 6110 | For each additional camera, add | | | | " | 900 | | | 900 | 990 |
| 6120 | CCTV system, see Div. 27 41 19.10 | | | | | | | | | |
| 6200 | Twenty-four hour teller, single unit, | | | | | | | | | |
| 6300 | automated deposit, cash and memo | L-3 | .25 | 64 | Ea. | 41,600 | 2,675 | | 44,275 | 49,900 |
| 7000 | Vault front, see Div. 08 34 59.10 | | | | | | | | | |

# 11 19 Detention Equipment

## 11 19 30 – Detention Cell Equipment

### 11 19 30.10 Cell Equipment

| | | Crew | Daily Output | Labor-Hours | Unit | Material | Labor | Equipment | Total | Total Incl O&P |
|---|---|---|---|---|---|---|---|---|---|---|
| **0010** **CELL EQUIPMENT** | | | | | | | | | | |
| 3000 | Toilet apparatus including wash basin, average | L-8 | 1.50 | 13.333 | Ea. | 3,150 | 530 | | 3,680 | 4,275 |

# 11 21 Mercantile and Service Equipment

## 11 21 13 – Cash Registers and Checking Equipment

### 11 21 13.10 Checkout Counter

| | | Crew | Daily Output | Labor-Hours | Unit | Material | Labor | Equipment | Total | Total Incl O&P |
|---|---|---|---|---|---|---|---|---|---|---|
| **0010** **CHECKOUT COUNTER** | | | | | | | | | | |
| 0020 | Supermarket conveyor, single belt | 2 Clab | 10 | 1.600 | Ea. | 2,475 | 48.50 | | 2,523.50 | 2,800 |
| 0100 | Double belt, power take-away | | 9 | 1.778 | | 4,175 | 54 | | 4,229 | 4,675 |
| 0400 | Double belt, power take-away, incl. side scanning | | 7 | 2.286 | | 5,200 | 69 | | 5,269 | 5,800 |
| 0800 | Warehouse or bulk type | | 6 | 2.667 | | 6,075 | 80.50 | | 6,155.50 | 6,800 |
| 1000 | Scanning system, 2 lanes, w/registers, scan gun & memory | | | | System | 15,200 | | | 15,200 | 16,700 |
| 1100 | 10 lanes, single processor, full scan, with scales | | | | " | 144,500 | | | 144,500 | 158,500 |

# 11 21 Mercantile and Service Equipment

## 11 21 13 – Cash Registers and Checking Equipment

| 11 21 13.10 Checkout Counter | Crew | Daily Output | Labor-Hours | Unit | Material | 2008 Bare Costs Labor | Equipment | Total | Total Incl O&P |
|---|---|---|---|---|---|---|---|---|---|
| 2000 | Register, restaurant, minimum | | | | Ea. | 615 | | | 615 | 675 |
| 2100 | Maximum | | | | | 2,700 | | | 2,700 | 2,975 |
| 2150 | Store, minimum | | | | | 615 | | | 615 | 675 |
| 2200 | Maximum | | | | | 2,700 | | | 2,700 | 2,975 |

## 11 21 53 – Barber and Beauty Shop Equipment

### 11 21 53.10 Barber Equipment

| | | Crew | Daily Output | Labor-Hours | Unit | Material | Labor | Equipment | Total | Total Incl O&P |
|---|---|---|---|---|---|---|---|---|---|---|
| 0010 | **BARBER EQUIPMENT** | | | | | | | | | |
| 0020 | Chair, hydraulic, movable, minimum | 1 Carp | 24 | .333 | Ea. | 310 | 12.70 | | 322.70 | 365 |
| 0050 | Maximum | " | 16 | .500 | | 2,750 | 19.05 | | 2,769.05 | 3,050 |
| 0200 | Wall hung styling station with mirrors, minimum | L-2 | 8 | 2 | | 420 | 67 | | 487 | 570 |
| 0300 | Maximum | " | 4 | 4 | | 1,825 | 134 | | 1,959 | 2,225 |
| 0500 | Sink, hair washing basin, rough plumbing not incl. | 1 Plum | 8 | 1 | | 335 | 46.50 | | 381.50 | 435 |
| 1000 | Sterilizer, liquid solution for tools | | | | | 128 | | | 128 | 140 |
| 1100 | Total equipment, rule of thumb, per chair, minimum | L-8 | 1 | 20 | | 1,500 | 795 | | 2,295 | 2,875 |
| 1150 | Maximum | " | 1 | 20 | | 4,075 | 795 | | 4,870 | 5,725 |

# 11 23 Commercial Laundry and Dry Cleaning Equipment

## 11 23 13 – Dry Cleaning Equipment

### 11 23 13.13 Dry Cleaners

| | | Crew | Daily Output | Labor-Hours | Unit | Material | Labor | Equipment | Total | Total Incl O&P |
|---|---|---|---|---|---|---|---|---|---|---|
| 0010 | **DRY CLEANERS** Not incl. rough-in | | | | | | | | | |
| 2000 | Dry cleaners, electric, 20 lb. capacity | L-1 | .20 | 80 | Ea. | 32,800 | 3,700 | | 36,500 | 41,600 |
| 2050 | 25 lb. capacity | | .17 | 94.118 | | 44,200 | 4,350 | | 48,550 | 55,000 |
| 2100 | 30 lb. capacity | | .15 | 106 | | 46,600 | 4,925 | | 51,525 | 59,000 |
| 2150 | 60 lb. capacity | | .09 | 177 | | 72,000 | 8,200 | | 80,200 | 91,500 |

## 11 23 16 – Drying and Conditioning Equipment

### 11 23 16.13 Dryers

| | | Crew | Daily Output | Labor-Hours | Unit | Material | Labor | Equipment | Total | Total Incl O&P |
|---|---|---|---|---|---|---|---|---|---|---|
| 0010 | **DRYERS**, Not including rough-in | | | | | | | | | |
| 1500 | Industrial, 30 lb. capacity | 1 Plum | 2 | 4 | Ea. | 2,925 | 187 | | 3,112 | 3,500 |
| 1600 | 50 lb. capacity | " | 1.70 | 4.706 | | 3,125 | 220 | | 3,345 | 3,775 |
| 4700 | Lint collector, ductwork not included, 8,000 to 10,000 C.F.M. | Q-10 | .30 | 80 | | 8,400 | 3,375 | | 11,775 | 14,500 |

## 11 23 19 – Finishing Equipment

### 11 23 19.13 Folders and Spreaders

| | | Crew | Daily Output | Labor-Hours | Unit | Material | Labor | Equipment | Total | Total Incl O&P |
|---|---|---|---|---|---|---|---|---|---|---|
| 0010 | **FOLDERS AND SPREADERS** | | | | | | | | | |
| 3500 | Folders, blankets & sheets, minimum | 1 Elec | .17 | 47.059 | Ea. | 30,000 | 2,150 | | 32,150 | 36,200 |
| 3700 | King size with automatic stacker | | .10 | 80 | | 54,000 | 3,650 | | 57,650 | 65,000 |
| 3800 | For conveyor delivery, add | | .45 | 17.778 | | 6,000 | 810 | | 6,810 | 7,800 |
| 4900 | Spreader feeders, 240V, 2 station | L-6 | .70 | 17.143 | | 49,700 | 795 | | 50,495 | 55,500 |
| 4920 | 4 station | " | .35 | 34.286 | | 60,000 | 1,600 | | 61,600 | 68,500 |

## 11 23 23 – Commercial Ironing Equipment

### 11 23 23.13 Irons and Pressers

| | | Crew | Daily Output | Labor-Hours | Unit | Material | Labor | Equipment | Total | Total Incl O&P |
|---|---|---|---|---|---|---|---|---|---|---|
| 0010 | **IRONS AND PRESSERS** | | | | | | | | | |
| 4500 | Ironers, institutional, 110", single roll | 1 Elec | .20 | 40 | Ea. | 29,100 | 1,825 | | 30,925 | 34,700 |
| 4800 | Pressers, low capacity air operated | L-6 | 1.75 | 6.857 | | 8,600 | 320 | | 8,920 | 9,950 |
| 4820 | Hand operated | | 1.75 | 6.857 | | 7,925 | 320 | | 8,245 | 9,200 |
| 4840 | Ironer 48", 240V | | 3.50 | 3.429 | | 101,000 | 159 | | 101,159 | 111,500 |
| 6600 | Hand operated presser | | .70 | 17.143 | | 5,425 | 795 | | 6,220 | 7,150 |
| 6620 | Mushroom press 115V | | .70 | 17.143 | | 6,775 | 795 | | 7,570 | 8,650 |

# 11 23 Commercial Laundry and Dry Cleaning Equipment

## 11 23 26 – Commercial Washers and Extractors

| 11 23 26.13 Washers and Extractors | Crew | Daily Output | Labor-Hours | Unit | Material | 2008 Bare Costs Labor | 2008 Bare Costs Equipment | Total | Total Incl O&P |
|---|---|---|---|---|---|---|---|---|---|
| 0010 **WASHERS AND EXTRACTORS**, not including rough-in | | | | | | | | | |
| 6000 Combination washer/extractor, 20 lb. capacity | L-6 | 1.50 | 8 | Ea. | 5,225 | 370 | | 5,595 | 6,300 |
| 6100 30 lb. capacity | | .80 | 15 | | 8,325 | 695 | | 9,020 | 10,200 |
| 6200 50 lb. capacity | | .68 | 17.647 | | 9,700 | 815 | | 10,515 | 11,900 |
| 6300 75 lb. capacity | | .30 | 40 | | 18,200 | 1,850 | | 20,050 | 22,800 |
| 6350 125 lb. capacity | | .16 | 75 | | 24,400 | 3,475 | | 27,875 | 32,000 |
| 6380 Washer extractor/dryer, 110 lb., 240V | | 1 | 12 | | 8,025 | 555 | | 8,580 | 9,675 |
| 6400 Washer extractor, 135 lb, 240V | | 1 | 12 | | 23,100 | 555 | | 23,655 | 26,200 |
| 6450 Pass through | | 1 | 12 | | 63,000 | 555 | | 63,555 | 70,500 |
| 6500 200 lb. washer extractor | | 1 | 12 | | 66,000 | 555 | | 66,555 | 73,500 |
| 6550 Pass through | | 1 | 12 | | 68,500 | 555 | | 69,055 | 76,500 |
| 6600 Extractor, low capacity | | 1.75 | 6.857 | | 6,475 | 320 | | 6,795 | 7,600 |

## 11 23 33 – Coin-Operated Laundry Equipment

| 11 23 33.13 Coin Operated Washers and Dryers | Crew | Daily Output | Labor-Hours | Unit | Material | 2008 Bare Costs Labor | 2008 Bare Costs Equipment | Total | Total Incl O&P |
|---|---|---|---|---|---|---|---|---|---|
| 0010 **COIN OPERATED WASHERS AND DRYERS** | | | | | | | | | |
| 0990 Dryer, gas fired | | | | | | | | | |
| 1000 Commercial, 30 lb. capacity, coin operated, single | 1 Plum | 3 | 2.667 | Ea. | 3,050 | 125 | | 3,175 | 3,525 |
| 1100 Double stacked | " | 2 | 4 | | 6,050 | 187 | | 6,237 | 6,950 |
| 4860 Coin dry cleaner 20 lb. | L-6 | 1.75 | 6.857 | | 25,400 | 320 | | 25,720 | 28,400 |
| 5290 Clothes washer | | | | | | | | | |
| 5300 Commercial, coin operated, average | 1 Plum | 3 | 2.667 | Ea. | 1,100 | 125 | | 1,225 | 1,400 |

# 11 24 Maintenance Equipment

## 11 24 19 – Vacuum Cleaning Systems

| 11 24 19.10 Vacuum Cleaning | Crew | Daily Output | Labor-Hours | Unit | Material | 2008 Bare Costs Labor | 2008 Bare Costs Equipment | Total | Total Incl O&P |
|---|---|---|---|---|---|---|---|---|---|
| 0010 **VACUUM CLEANING** | | | | | | | | | |
| 0020 Central, 3 inlet, residential | 1 Skwk | .90 | 8.889 | Total | 680 | 350 | | 1,030 | 1,300 |
| 0200 Commercial | | .70 | 11.429 | | 1,275 | 450 | | 1,725 | 2,100 |
| 0400 5 inlet system, residential | | .50 | 16 | | 1,025 | 630 | | 1,655 | 2,100 |
| 0600 7 inlet system, commercial | | .40 | 20 | | 1,150 | 790 | | 1,940 | 2,500 |
| 0800 9 inlet system, residential | | .30 | 26.667 | | 1,450 | 1,050 | | 2,500 | 3,225 |
| 4010 Rule of thumb: First 1200 S.F., installed | | | | | | | | 1,125 | 1,240 |
| 4020 For each additional S.F., add | | | | S.F. | | | | | .20 |

# 11 26 Unit Kitchens

## 11 26 13 – Metal Unit Kitchens

| 11 26 13.10 Commercial Unit Kitchens | Crew | Daily Output | Labor-Hours | Unit | Material | 2008 Bare Costs Labor | 2008 Bare Costs Equipment | Total | Total Incl O&P |
|---|---|---|---|---|---|---|---|---|---|
| 0010 **COMMERCIAL UNIT KITCHENS** | | | | | | | | | |
| 1500 Combination range, refrigerator and sink, 30" wide, minimum | L-1 | 2 | 8 | Ea. | 900 | 370 | | 1,270 | 1,550 |
| 1550 Maximum | | 1 | 16 | | 2,675 | 740 | | 3,415 | 4,050 |
| 1570 60" wide, average | | 1.40 | 11.429 | | 2,225 | 525 | | 2,750 | 3,225 |
| 1590 72" wide, average | | 1.20 | 13.333 | | 3,200 | 615 | | 3,815 | 4,450 |
| 1600 Office model, 48" wide   *CN* | | 2 | 8 | | 2,250 | 370 | | 2,620 | 3,025 |
| 1620 Refrigerator and sink only | | 2.40 | 6.667 | | 1,725 | 310 | | 2,035 | 2,325 |
| 1640 Combination range, refrigerator, sink, microwave | | | | | | | | | |
| 1660 Oven and ice maker | L-1 | .80 | 20 | Ea. | 3,450 | 925 | | 4,375 | 5,175 |

# 11 27 Photographic Processing Equipment

## 11 27 13 – Darkroom Processing Equipment

| 11 27 13.10 Darkroom Equipment | Crew | Daily Output | Labor-Hours | Unit | Material | 2008 Bare Costs Labor | Equipment | Total | Total Incl O&P |
|---|---|---|---|---|---|---|---|---|---|
| 0010 **DARKROOM EQUIPMENT** | | | | | | | | | |
| 0020 Developing sink, 5" deep, 24" x 48" | Q-1 | 2 | 8 | Ea. | 4,875 | 335 | | 5,210 | 5,875 |
| 0050 48" x 52" | | 1.70 | 9.412 | | 4,950 | 395 | | 5,345 | 6,025 |
| 0200 10" deep, 24" x 48" | | 1.70 | 9.412 | | 6,275 | 395 | | 6,670 | 7,525 |
| 0250 24" x 108" | | 1.50 | 10.667 | | 8,275 | 450 | | 8,725 | 9,775 |
| 0500 Dryers, dehumidified filtered air, 36" x 25" x 68" high | L-7 | 6 | 4.667 | | 4,650 | 172 | | 4,822 | 5,400 |
| 0550 48" x 25" x 68" high | | 5 | 5.600 | | 8,750 | 207 | | 8,957 | 9,950 |
| 2000 Processors, automatic, color print, minimum | | 4 | 7 | | 12,700 | 258 | | 12,958 | 14,400 |
| 2050 Maximum | | .60 | 46.667 | | 12,600 | 1,725 | | 14,325 | 16,500 |
| 2300 Black and white print, minimum | | 2 | 14 | | 9,650 | 515 | | 10,165 | 11,400 |
| 2350 Maximum | | .80 | 35 | | 58,000 | 1,300 | | 59,300 | 65,500 |
| 2600 Manual processor, 16" x 20" maximum print size | | 2 | 14 | | 8,900 | 515 | | 9,415 | 10,600 |
| 2650 20" x 24" maximum print size | | 1 | 28 | | 8,475 | 1,025 | | 9,500 | 10,900 |
| 3000 Viewing lights, 20" x 24" | | 6 | 4.667 | | 365 | 172 | | 537 | 670 |
| 3100 20" x 24" with color correction | | 6 | 4.667 | | 520 | 172 | | 692 | 835 |
| 3500 Washers, round, minimum sheet 11" x 14" | Q-1 | 2 | 8 | | 2,975 | 335 | | 3,310 | 3,775 |
| 3550 Maximum sheet 20" x 24" | | 1 | 16 | | 3,375 | 670 | | 4,045 | 4,725 |
| 3800 Square, minimum sheet 20" x 24" | | 1 | 16 | | 3,025 | 670 | | 3,695 | 4,325 |
| 3900 Maximum sheet 50" x 56" | | .80 | 20 | | 4,700 | 840 | | 5,540 | 6,450 |
| 4500 Combination tank sink, tray sink, washers, with | | | | | | | | | |
| 4510 Dry side tables, average | Q-1 | .45 | 35.556 | Ea. | 9,325 | 1,500 | | 10,825 | 12,500 |

# 11 31 Residential Appliances

## 11 31 13 – Residential Kitchen Appliances

### 11 31 13.13 Cooking Equipment

| | Crew | Daily Output | Labor-Hours | Unit | Material | 2008 Bare Costs Labor | Equipment | Total | Total Incl O&P |
|---|---|---|---|---|---|---|---|---|---|
| 0010 **COOKING EQUIPMENT** | | | | | | | | | |
| 0020 Cooking range, 30" free standing, 1 oven, minimum | 2 Clab | 10 | 1.600 | Ea. | 270 | 48.50 | | 318.50 | 375 |
| 0050 Maximum | | 4 | 4 | | 1,775 | 121 | | 1,896 | 2,175 |
| 0150 2 oven, minimum | | 10 | 1.600 | | 1,525 | 48.50 | | 1,573.50 | 1,750 |
| 0200 Maximum | | 10 | 1.600 | | 1,775 | 48.50 | | 1,823.50 | 2,025 |
| 0350 Built-in, 30" wide, 1 oven, minimum | 1 Elec | 6 | 1.333 | | 480 | 60.50 | | 540.50 | 620 |
| 0400 Maximum | 2 Carp | 2 | 8 | | 1,475 | 305 | | 1,780 | 2,100 |
| 0500 2 oven, conventional, minimum | | 4 | 4 | | 1,350 | 152 | | 1,502 | 1,700 |
| 0550 1 conventional, 1 microwave, maximum | | 2 | 8 | | 1,650 | 305 | | 1,955 | 2,300 |
| 0700 Free-standing, 1 oven, 21" wide range, minimum | 2 Clab | 10 | 1.600 | | 325 | 48.50 | | 373.50 | 430 |
| 0750 21" wide, maximum | " | 4 | 4 | | 335 | 121 | | 456 | 555 |
| 0900 Countertop cooktops, 4 burner, standard, minimum | 1 Elec | 6 | 1.333 | | 219 | 60.50 | | 279.50 | 330 |
| 0950 Maximum | | 3 | 2.667 | | 615 | 121 | | 736 | 860 |
| 1050 As above, but with grill and griddle attachment, minimum | | 6 | 1.333 | | 825 | 60.50 | | 885.50 | 995 |
| 1100 Maximum | | 3 | 2.667 | | 1,350 | 121 | | 1,471 | 1,650 |
| 1200 Induction cooktop, 30" wide | | 3 | 2.667 | | 975 | 121 | | 1,096 | 1,250 |
| 1250 Microwave oven, minimum | | 4 | 2 | | 85.50 | 91 | | 176.50 | 230 |
| 1300 Maximum | | 2 | 4 | | 425 | 182 | | 607 | 740 |

### 11 31 13.23 Refrigeration Equipment

| | Crew | Daily Output | Labor-Hours | Unit | Material | 2008 Bare Costs Labor | Equipment | Total | Total Incl O&P |
|---|---|---|---|---|---|---|---|---|---|
| 0010 **REFRIGERATION EQUIPMENT** | | | | | | | | | |
| 2000 Deep freeze, 15 to 23 C.F., minimum | 2 Clab | 10 | 1.600 | Ea. | 500 | 48.50 | | 548.50 | 625 |
| 2050 Maximum | | 5 | 3.200 | | 575 | 97 | | 672 | 785 |
| 2200 30 C.F., minimum | | 8 | 2 | | 805 | 60.50 | | 865.50 | 980 |
| 2250 Maximum | | 3 | 5.333 | | 915 | 161 | | 1,076 | 1,250 |
| 5200 Icemaker, automatic, 20 lb. per day | 1 Plum | 7 | 1.143 | | 850 | 53.50 | | 903.50 | 1,025 |
| 5350 51 lb. per day | " | 2 | 4 | | 970 | 187 | | 1,157 | 1,350 |

# 11 31 Residential Appliances

## 11 31 13 – Residential Kitchen Appliances

### 11 31 13.23 Refrigeration Equipment

| | | Crew | Daily Output | Labor-Hours | Unit | Material | 2008 Bare Costs Labor | Equipment | Total | Total Incl O&P |
|---|---|---|---|---|---|---|---|---|---|---|
| 5500 | Refrigerator, no frost, 10 C.F. to 12 C.F. minimum | 2 Clab | 10 | 1.600 | Ea. | 485 | 48.50 | | 533.50 | 610 |
| 5600 | Maximum | | 6 | 2.667 | | 650 | 80.50 | | 730.50 | 840 |
| 5750 | 14 C.F. to 16 C.F., minimum | | 9 | 1.778 | | 515 | 54 | | 569 | 650 |
| 5800 | Maximum | | 5 | 3.200 | | 600 | 97 | | 697 | 810 |
| 5950 | 18 C.F. to 20 C.F., minimum | | 8 | 2 | | 610 | 60.50 | | 670.50 | 765 |
| 6000 | Maximum | | 4 | 4 | | 905 | 121 | | 1,026 | 1,175 |
| 6150 | 21 C.F. to 29 C.F., minimum | | 7 | 2.286 | | 765 | 69 | | 834 | 955 |
| 6200 | Maximum | ↓ | 3 | 5.333 | ↓ | 2,475 | 161 | | 2,636 | 2,975 |

### 11 31 13.33 Kitchen Cleaning Equipment

| | | Crew | Daily Output | Labor-Hours | Unit | Material | 2008 Bare Costs Labor | Equipment | Total | Total Incl O&P |
|---|---|---|---|---|---|---|---|---|---|---|
| 0010 | **KITCHEN CLEANING EQUIPMENT** | | | | | | | | | |
| 2750 | Dishwasher, built-in, 2 cycles, minimum | L-1 | 4 | 4 | Ea. | 269 | 185 | | 454 | 570 |
| 2800 | Maximum | | 2 | 8 | | 310 | 370 | | 680 | 890 |
| 2950 | 4 or more cycles, minimum | | 4 | 4 | | 295 | 185 | | 480 | 600 |
| 2960 | Average | | 4 | 4 | | 390 | 185 | | 575 | 705 |
| 3000 | Maximum | ↓ | 2 | 8 | ↓ | 685 | 370 | | 1,055 | 1,300 |

### 11 31 13.43 Waste Disposal Equipment

| | | Crew | Daily Output | Labor-Hours | Unit | Material | 2008 Bare Costs Labor | Equipment | Total | Total Incl O&P |
|---|---|---|---|---|---|---|---|---|---|---|
| 0010 | **WASTE DISPOSAL EQUIPMENT** | | | | | | | | | |
| 1750 | Compactor, residential size, 4 to 1 compaction, minimum | 1 Carp | 5 | 1.600 | Ea. | 475 | 61 | | 536 | 615 |
| 1800 | Maximum | " | 3 | 2.667 | | 560 | 102 | | 662 | 775 |
| 3300 | Garbage disposal, sink type, minimum | L-1 | 10 | 1.600 | | 62.50 | 74 | | 136.50 | 179 |
| 3350 | Maximum | " | 10 | 1.600 | | 195 | 74 | | 269 | 325 |

### 11 31 13.53 Kitchen Ventilation Equipment

| | | Crew | Daily Output | Labor-Hours | Unit | Material | 2008 Bare Costs Labor | Equipment | Total | Total Incl O&P |
|---|---|---|---|---|---|---|---|---|---|---|
| 0010 | **KITCHEN VENTILATION EQUIPMENT** | | | | | | | | | |
| 4150 | Hood for range, 2 speed, vented, 30" wide, minimum | L-3 | 5 | 3.200 | Ea. | 49 | 134 | | 183 | 259 |
| 4200 | Maximum | | 3 | 5.333 | | 905 | 223 | | 1,128 | 1,325 |
| 4300 | 42" wide, minimum | | 5 | 3.200 | | 250 | 134 | | 384 | 480 |
| 4330 | Custom | | 5 | 3.200 | | 1,400 | 134 | | 1,534 | 1,750 |
| 4350 | Maximum | ↓ | 3 | 5.333 | | 1,725 | 223 | | 1,948 | 2,225 |
| 4500 | For ventless hood, 2 speed, add | | | | | 16.55 | | | 16.55 | 18.20 |
| 4650 | For vented 1 speed, deduct from maximum | | | | ↓ | 44 | | | 44 | 48.50 |

## 11 31 23 – Residential Laundry Appliances

### 11 31 23.13 Washers

| | | Crew | Daily Output | Labor-Hours | Unit | Material | 2008 Bare Costs Labor | Equipment | Total | Total Incl O&P |
|---|---|---|---|---|---|---|---|---|---|---|
| 0010 | **WASHERS** | | | | | | | | | |
| 5000 | Residential, 4 cycle, average | 1 Plum | 3 | 2.667 | Ea. | 780 | 125 | | 905 | 1,050 |
| 6650 | Washing machine, automatic, minimum | | 3 | 2.667 | | 305 | 125 | | 430 | 525 |
| 6700 | Maximum | ↓ | 1 | 8 | ↓ | 1,150 | 375 | | 1,525 | 1,825 |

### 11 31 23.23 Dryers

| | | Crew | Daily Output | Labor-Hours | Unit | Material | 2008 Bare Costs Labor | Equipment | Total | Total Incl O&P |
|---|---|---|---|---|---|---|---|---|---|---|
| 0010 | **DRYERS** | | | | | | | | | |
| 0500 | Gas fired residential, 16 lb. capacity, average | 1 Plum | 3 | 2.667 | Ea. | 615 | 125 | | 740 | 860 |
| 3200 | Automatic, minimum | L-2 | 3 | 5.333 | | 298 | 179 | | 477 | 605 |
| 3250 | Maximum | " | 2 | 8 | | 1,225 | 269 | | 1,494 | 1,775 |
| 7450 | Vent kits for dryers | 1 Carp | 10 | .800 | ↓ | 33.50 | 30.50 | | 64 | 84 |

## 11 31 33 – Miscellaneous Residential Appliances

### 11 31 33.13 Sump Pumps

| | | Crew | Daily Output | Labor-Hours | Unit | Material | 2008 Bare Costs Labor | Equipment | Total | Total Incl O&P |
|---|---|---|---|---|---|---|---|---|---|---|
| 0010 | **SUMP PUMPS** | | | | | | | | | |
| 6400 | Cellar drainer, pedestal, 1/3 H.P., molded PVC base | 1 Plum | 3 | 2.667 | Ea. | 116 | 125 | | 241 | 315 |
| 6450 | Solid brass | " | 2 | 4 | " | 251 | 187 | | 438 | 555 |
| 6460 | Sump pump, see also Div. 22 14 29.16 | | | | | | | | | |

### 11 31 33.23 Water Heaters

| | | Crew | Daily Output | Labor-Hours | Unit | Material | 2008 Bare Costs Labor | Equipment | Total | Total Incl O&P |
|---|---|---|---|---|---|---|---|---|---|---|
| 0010 | **WATER HEATERS** | | | | | | | | | |

# 11 31 Residential Appliances

## 11 31 33 - Miscellaneous Residential Appliances

### 11 31 33.23 Water Heaters

| | | Crew | Daily Output | Labor-Hours | Unit | Material | 2008 Bare Costs Labor | 2008 Bare Costs Equipment | Total | Total Incl O&P |
|---|---|---|---|---|---|---|---|---|---|---|
| 6900 | Electric, glass lined, 30 gallon, minimum | L-1 | 5 | 3.200 | Ea. | 279 | 148 | | 427 | 525 |
| 6950 | Maximum | | 3 | 5.333 | | 385 | 246 | | 631 | 795 |
| 7100 | 80 gallon, minimum | | 2 | 8 | | 505 | 370 | | 875 | 1,100 |
| 7150 | Maximum | | 1 | 16 | | 700 | 740 | | 1,440 | 1,875 |
| 7180 | Gas, glass lined, 30 gallon, minimum | 2 Plum | 5 | 3.200 | | 540 | 149 | | 689 | 820 |
| 7220 | Maximum | | 3 | 5.333 | | 755 | 249 | | 1,004 | 1,200 |
| 7260 | 50 gallon, minimum | | 2.50 | 6.400 | | 845 | 299 | | 1,144 | 1,375 |
| 7300 | Maximum | | 1.50 | 10.667 | | 1,175 | 500 | | 1,675 | 2,025 |
| 7310 | Water heater, see also Div. 22 33 30.13 | | | | | | | | | |

### 11 31 33.43 Air Quality

| | | Crew | Daily Output | Labor-Hours | Unit | Material | 2008 Bare Costs Labor | 2008 Bare Costs Equipment | Total | Total Incl O&P |
|---|---|---|---|---|---|---|---|---|---|---|
| 0010 | **AIR QUALITY** | | | | | | | | | |
| 2450 | Dehumidifier, portable, automatic, 15 pint | | | | Ea. | 150 | | | 150 | 165 |
| 2550 | 40 pint | | | | | 183 | | | 183 | 202 |
| 3550 | Heater, electric, built-in, 1250 watt, ceiling type, minimum | 1 Elec | 4 | 2 | | 77.50 | 91 | | 168.50 | 222 |
| 3600 | Maximum | | 3 | 2.667 | | 127 | 121 | | 248 | 320 |
| 3700 | Wall type, minimum | | 4 | 2 | | 106 | 91 | | 197 | 252 |
| 3750 | Maximum | | 3 | 2.667 | | 146 | 121 | | 267 | 340 |
| 3900 | 1500 watt wall type, with blower | | 4 | 2 | | 136 | 91 | | 227 | 286 |
| 3950 | 3000 watt | | 3 | 2.667 | | 278 | 121 | | 399 | 485 |
| 4850 | Humidifier, portable, 8 gallons per day | | | | | 160 | | | 160 | 176 |
| 5000 | 15 gallons per day | | | | | 193 | | | 193 | 212 |

# 11 33 Retractable Stairs

## 11 33 10 - Disappearing Stairs

### 11 33 10.10 Disappearing Stairway

| | | Crew | Daily Output | Labor-Hours | Unit | Material | 2008 Bare Costs Labor | 2008 Bare Costs Equipment | Total | Total Incl O&P |
|---|---|---|---|---|---|---|---|---|---|---|
| 0010 | **DISAPPEARING STAIRWAY** No trim included | | | | | | | | | |
| 0100 | Custom grade, pine, 8'-6" ceiling, minimum | 1 Carp | 4 | 2 | Ea. | 213 | 76 | | 289 | 355 |
| 0150 | Average | | 3.50 | 2.286 | | 181 | 87 | | 268 | 335 |
| 0200 | Maximum | | 3 | 2.667 | | 275 | 102 | | 377 | 465 |
| 0500 | Heavy duty, pivoted, from 7'-7" to 12'-10" floor to floor | | 3 | 2.667 | | 650 | 102 | | 752 | 875 |
| 0600 | 16'-0" ceiling | | 2 | 4 | | 1,325 | 152 | | 1,477 | 1,675 |
| 0800 | Economy folding, pine, 8'-6" ceiling | | 4 | 2 | | 195 | 76 | | 271 | 335 |
| 0900 | 9'-6" ceiling | | 4 | 2 | | 225 | 76 | | 301 | 365 |
| 1100 | Automatic electric, aluminum, floor to floor height, 8' to 9' | 2 Carp | 1 | 16 | | 7,500 | 610 | | 8,110 | 9,200 |
| 1400 | 11' to 12' | | .90 | 17.778 | | 8,075 | 675 | | 8,750 | 9,925 |
| 1700 | 14' to 15' | | .70 | 22.857 | | 8,600 | 870 | | 9,470 | 10,800 |

# 11 41 Food Storage Equipment

## 11 41 13 - Refrigerated Food Storage Cases

### 11 41 13.10 Refrigerated Food Cases

| | | Crew | Daily Output | Labor-Hours | Unit | Material | 2008 Bare Costs Labor | 2008 Bare Costs Equipment | Total | Total Incl O&P |
|---|---|---|---|---|---|---|---|---|---|---|
| 0010 | **REFRIGERATED FOOD CASES** | | | | | | | | | |
| 0030 | Dairy, multi-deck, 12' long | Q-5 | 3 | 5.333 | Ea. | 9,025 | 226 | | 9,251 | 10,300 |
| 0100 | For rear sliding doors, add | | | | | 1,300 | | | 1,300 | 1,425 |
| 0200 | Delicatessen case, service deli, 12' long, single deck | Q-5 | 3.90 | 4.103 | | 6,075 | 174 | | 6,249 | 6,925 |
| 0300 | Multi-deck, 18 S.F. shelf display | | 3 | 5.333 | | 7,425 | 226 | | 7,651 | 8,525 |
| 0400 | Freezer, self-contained, chest-type, 30 C.F. | | 3.90 | 4.103 | | 4,425 | 174 | | 4,599 | 5,125 |
| 0500 | Glass door, upright, 78 C.F. | | 3.30 | 4.848 | | 8,450 | 206 | | 8,656 | 9,575 |
| 0600 | Frozen food, chest type, 12' long | | 3.30 | 4.848 | | 6,100 | 206 | | 6,306 | 7,000 |
| 0700 | Glass door, reach-in, 5 door | | 3 | 5.333 | | 11,700 | 226 | | 11,926 | 13,200 |

# 11 41 Food Storage Equipment

## 11 41 13 - Refrigerated Food Storage Cases

### 11 41 13.10 Refrigerated Food Cases

| | | Crew | Daily Output | Labor-Hours | Unit | Material | 2008 Bare Costs Labor | Equipment | Total | Total Incl O&P |
|---|---|---|---|---|---|---|---|---|---|---|
| 0800 | Island case, 12' long, single deck | Q-5 | 3.30 | 4.848 | Ea. | 6,900 | 206 | | 7,106 | 7,900 |
| 0900 | Multi-deck | | 3 | 5.333 | | 14,600 | 226 | | 14,826 | 16,400 |
| 1000 | Meat case, 12' long, single deck | | 3.30 | 4.848 | | 5,025 | 206 | | 5,231 | 5,825 |
| 1050 | Multi-deck | | 3.10 | 5.161 | | 8,625 | 219 | | 8,844 | 9,825 |
| 1100 | Produce, 12' long, single deck | | 3.30 | 4.848 | | 6,650 | 206 | | 6,856 | 7,600 |
| 1200 | Multi-deck | | 3.10 | 5.161 | | 7,250 | 219 | | 7,469 | 8,300 |

### 11 41 13.20 Refrigerated Food Storage Equipment

| | | Crew | Daily Output | Labor-Hours | Unit | Material | 2008 Bare Costs Labor | Equipment | Total | Total Incl O&P |
|---|---|---|---|---|---|---|---|---|---|---|
| 0010 | **REFRIGERATED FOOD STORAGE EQUIPMENT** | | | | | | | | | |
| 2350 | Cooler, reach-in, beverage, 6' long | Q-1 | 6 | 2.667 | Ea. | 3,925 | 112 | | 4,037 | 4,475 |
| 4300 | Freezers, reach-in, 44 C.F. | | 4 | 4 | | 7,175 | 168 | | 7,343 | 8,150 |
| 4500 | 68 C.F. | | 3 | 5.333 | | 6,700 | 224 | | 6,924 | 7,700 |
| 4600 | Freezer, pre-fab, 8' x 8' w/refrigeration | 2 Carp | .45 | 35.556 | | 9,225 | 1,350 | | 10,575 | 12,300 |
| 4620 | 8' x 12' | | .35 | 45.714 | | 11,000 | 1,750 | | 12,750 | 14,800 |
| 4640 | 8' x 16' | | .25 | 64 | | 13,700 | 2,450 | | 16,150 | 18,800 |
| 4660 | 8' x 20' | | .17 | 94.118 | | 16,400 | 3,575 | | 19,975 | 23,700 |
| 4680 | Reach-in, 1 compartment | Q-1 | 4 | 4 | | 1,475 | 168 | | 1,643 | 1,850 |
| 4700 | 2 compartment | | 3 | 5.333 | | 3,775 | 224 | | 3,999 | 4,475 |
| 8300 | Refrigerators, reach-in type, 44 C.F. | | 5 | 3.200 | | 5,650 | 135 | | 5,785 | 6,425 |
| 8310 | With glass doors, 68 C.F. | | 4 | 4 | | 6,100 | 168 | | 6,268 | 6,975 |
| 8320 | Refrigerator, reach-in, 1 compartment | R-18 | 7.80 | 3.333 | | 1,750 | 118 | | 1,868 | 2,100 |
| 8330 | 2 compartment | | 6.20 | 4.194 | | 2,375 | 149 | | 2,524 | 2,825 |
| 8340 | 3 compartment | | 5.60 | 4.643 | | 3,650 | 165 | | 3,815 | 4,250 |
| 8350 | Pre-fab, with refrigeration, 8' x 8' | 2 Carp | .45 | 35.556 | | 4,700 | 1,350 | | 6,050 | 7,275 |
| 8360 | 8' x 12' | | .35 | 45.714 | | 6,150 | 1,750 | | 7,900 | 9,450 |
| 8370 | 8' x 16' | | .25 | 64 | | 9,700 | 2,450 | | 12,150 | 14,500 |
| 8380 | 8' x 20' | | .17 | 94.118 | | 11,900 | 3,575 | | 15,475 | 18,700 |
| 8390 | Pass-thru/roll-in, 1 compartment | R-18 | 7.80 | 3.333 | | 3,275 | 118 | | 3,393 | 3,775 |
| 8400 | 2 compartment | | 6.24 | 4.167 | | 4,550 | 148 | | 4,698 | 5,225 |
| 8410 | 3 compartment | | 5.60 | 4.643 | | 5,550 | 165 | | 5,715 | 6,350 |
| 8420 | Walk-in, alum, door & floor only, no refrig, 6' x 6' x 7'-6" | 2 Carp | 1.40 | 11.429 | | 7,400 | 435 | | 7,835 | 8,825 |
| 8430 | 10' x 6' x 7'-6" | | .55 | 29.091 | | 10,600 | 1,100 | | 11,700 | 13,400 |
| 8440 | 12' x 14' x 7'-6" | | .25 | 64 | | 14,800 | 2,450 | | 17,250 | 20,100 |
| 8450 | 12' x 20' x 7'-6" | | .17 | 94.118 | | 18,200 | 3,575 | | 21,775 | 25,600 |
| 8460 | Refrigerated cabinets, mobile | | | | | 3,125 | | | 3,125 | 3,425 |
| 8470 | Refrigerator/freezer, reach-in, 1 compartment | R-18 | 5.60 | 4.643 | | 4,075 | 165 | | 4,240 | 4,725 |
| 8480 | 2 compartment | " | 4.80 | 5.417 | | 5,725 | 192 | | 5,917 | 6,600 |

### 11 41 13.30 Wine Cellar

| | | Crew | Daily Output | Labor-Hours | Unit | Material | 2008 Bare Costs Labor | Equipment | Total | Total Incl O&P |
|---|---|---|---|---|---|---|---|---|---|---|
| 0010 | **WINE CELLAR**, refrigerated, Redwood interior, carpeted, walk-in type | | | | | | | | | |
| 0020 | 6'-8" high, including racks | | | | | | | | | |
| 0200 | 80" W x 48" D for 900 bottles | 2 Carp | 1.50 | 10.667 | Ea. | 3,125 | 405 | | 3,530 | 4,050 |
| 0250 | 80" W x 72" D for 1300 bottles | | 1.33 | 12.030 | | 4,125 | 460 | | 4,585 | 5,275 |
| 0300 | 80" W x 94" D for 1900 bottles | | 1.17 | 13.675 | | 5,350 | 520 | | 5,870 | 6,700 |
| 0400 | 80" W x 124" D for 2500 bottles | | 1 | 16 | | 6,475 | 610 | | 7,085 | 8,075 |
| 0600 | Portable cabinets, red oak, reach-in temp.& humidity controlled | | | | | | | | | |
| 0650 | 26-5/8"W x 26-1/2"D x 68"H for 235 bottles | | | | Ea. | 2,000 | | | 2,000 | 2,200 |
| 0660 | 32"W x 21-1/2"D x 73-1/2"H for 144 bottles | | | | | 3,275 | | | 3,275 | 3,600 |
| 0670 | 32"W x 29-1/2"D x 73-1/2"H for 288 bottles | | | | | 2,275 | | | 2,275 | 2,500 |
| 0680 | 39-1/2"W x 29-1/2"D x 86-1/2"H for 440 bottles | | | | | 2,850 | | | 2,850 | 3,150 |
| 0690 | 52-1/2"W x 29-1/2"D x 73-1/2"H for 468 bottles | | | | | 3,400 | | | 3,400 | 3,750 |
| 0700 | 52-1/2"W x 29-1/2"D x 86-1/2"H for 572 bottles | | | | | 3,700 | | | 3,700 | 4,075 |
| 0730 | Portable, red oak, can be built-in with glass door | | | | | | | | | |
| 0750 | 23-7/8"W x 24"D x 34-1/2"H for 50 bottles | | | | Ea. | 900 | | | 900 | 990 |

# 11 41 Food Storage Equipment

## 11 41 33 – Food Storage Shelving

| 11 41 33.20 Metal Food Storage Shelving | Crew | Daily Output | Labor-Hours | Unit | Material | 2008 Bare Costs Labor | Equipment | Total | Total Incl O&P |
|---|---|---|---|---|---|---|---|---|---|
| 0010 **METAL FOOD STORAGE SHELVING** | | | | | | | | | |
| 8600 Stainless steel shelving, louvered 4-tier, 20" x 3' | 1 Clab | 6 | 1.333 | Ea. | 1,050 | 40.50 | | 1,090.50 | 1,250 |
| 8605     20" x 4' | | 6 | 1.333 | | 1,525 | 40.50 | | 1,565.50 | 1,750 |
| 8610     20" x 6' | | 6 | 1.333 | | 2,200 | 40.50 | | 2,240.50 | 2,500 |
| 8615     24" x 3' | | 6 | 1.333 | | 1,375 | 40.50 | | 1,415.50 | 1,600 |
| 8620     24" x 4' | | 6 | 1.333 | | 1,625 | 40.50 | | 1,665.50 | 1,850 |
| 8625     24" x 6' | | 6 | 1.333 | | 2,350 | 40.50 | | 2,390.50 | 2,650 |
| 8630    Flat 4-tier, 20" x 3' | | 6 | 1.333 | | 890 | 40.50 | | 930.50 | 1,050 |
| 8635     20" x 4' | | 6 | 1.333 | | 1,125 | 40.50 | | 1,165.50 | 1,300 |
| 8640     20" x 5' | | 6 | 1.333 | | 1,250 | 40.50 | | 1,290.50 | 1,425 |
| 8645     24" x 3' | | 6 | 1.333 | | 970 | 40.50 | | 1,010.50 | 1,150 |
| 8650     24" x 4' | | 6 | 1.333 | | 610 | 40.50 | | 650.50 | 740 |
| 8655     24" x 6' | | 6 | 1.333 | | 2,050 | 40.50 | | 2,090.50 | 2,325 |
| 8700   Galvanized shelving, louvered 4-tier, 20" x 3' | | 6 | 1.333 | | 540 | 40.50 | | 580.50 | 660 |
| 8705     20" x 4' | | 6 | 1.333 | | 600 | 40.50 | | 640.50 | 725 |
| 8710     20" x 6' | | 6 | 1.333 | | 635 | 40.50 | | 675.50 | 765 |
| 8715     24" x 3' | | 6 | 1.333 | | 475 | 40.50 | | 515.50 | 590 |
| 8720     24" x 4' | | 6 | 1.333 | | 645 | 40.50 | | 685.50 | 775 |
| 8725     24" x 6' | | 6 | 1.333 | | 925 | 40.50 | | 965.50 | 1,100 |
| 8730    Flat 4-tier, 20" x 3' | | 6 | 1.333 | | 390 | 40.50 | | 430.50 | 490 |
| 8735     20" x 4' | | 6 | 1.333 | | 440 | 40.50 | | 480.50 | 545 |
| 8740     20" x 6' | | 6 | 1.333 | | 760 | 40.50 | | 800.50 | 900 |
| 8745     24" x 3' | | 6 | 1.333 | | 390 | 40.50 | | 430.50 | 495 |
| 8750     24" x 4' | | 6 | 1.333 | | 560 | 40.50 | | 600.50 | 680 |
| 8755     24" x 6' | | 6 | 1.333 | | 785 | 40.50 | | 825.50 | 930 |
| 8760   Stainless steel dunnage rack, 24" x 3' | | 8 | 1 | | 435 | 30.50 | | 465.50 | 525 |
| 8765     24" x 4' | | 8 | 1 | | 705 | 30.50 | | 735.50 | 820 |
| 8770   Galvanized dunnage rack, 24" x 3' | | 8 | 1 | | 147 | 30.50 | | 177.50 | 209 |
| 8775     24" x 4' | | 8 | 1 | | 142 | 30.50 | | 172.50 | 203 |

# 11 42 Food Preparation Equipment

## 11 42 10 – Commercial Food Preparation Equipment

### 11 42 10.10 Choppers, Mixers and Misc. Equipment

| 11 42 10.10 Choppers, Mixers and Misc. Equipment | Crew | Daily Output | Labor-Hours | Unit | Material | Labor | Equipment | Total | Total Incl O&P |
|---|---|---|---|---|---|---|---|---|---|
| 0010 **CHOPPERS, MIXERS AND MISC. EQUIPMENT** | | | | | | | | | |
| 1700 Choppers, 5 pounds | R-18 | 7 | 3.714 | Ea. | 1,475 | 132 | | 1,607 | 1,825 |
| 1720    16 pounds | | 5 | 5.200 | | 1,825 | 184 | | 2,009 | 2,275 |
| 1740    35 to 40 pounds | | 4 | 6.500 | | 2,725 | 231 | | 2,956 | 3,325 |
| 1840 Coffee brewer, 5 burners | 1 Plum | 3 | 2.667 | | 1,100 | 125 | | 1,225 | 1,375 |
| 1850 Coffee urn, twin 6 gallon urns | | 2 | 4 | | 2,675 | 187 | | 2,862 | 3,225 |
| 1860    Single, 3 gallon | | 3 | 2.667 | | 1,700 | 125 | | 1,825 | 2,050 |
| 3000 Fast food equipment, total package, minimum | 6 Skwk | .08 | 600 | | 156,500 | 23,600 | | 180,100 | 209,000 |
| 3100    Maximum | " | .07 | 685 | | 213,500 | 27,000 | | 240,500 | 276,500 |
| 3800 Food mixers, 20 quarts | L-7 | 7 | 4 | | 2,600 | 148 | | 2,748 | 3,100 |
| 3850    40 quarts | | 5.40 | 5.185 | | 6,775 | 191 | | 6,966 | 7,750 |
| 3900    60 quarts | | 5 | 5.600 | | 9,300 | 207 | | 9,507 | 10,500 |
| 4040    80 quarts | | 3.90 | 7.179 | | 11,100 | 265 | | 11,365 | 12,600 |
| 4080    130 quarts | | 2.20 | 12.727 | | 16,000 | 470 | | 16,470 | 18,300 |
| 4100   Floor type, 20 quarts | | 15 | 1.867 | | 2,450 | 69 | | 2,519 | 2,800 |
| 4120    60 quarts | | 14 | 2 | | 7,450 | 74 | | 7,524 | 8,325 |
| 4140    80 quarts | | 12 | 2.333 | | 9,975 | 86 | | 10,061 | 11,100 |

# 11 42 Food Preparation Equipment

## 11 42 10 – Commercial Food Preparation Equipment

| 11 42 10.10 Choppers, Mixers and Misc. Equipment | Crew | Daily Output | Labor-Hours | Unit | Material | 2008 Bare Costs Labor | Equipment | Total | Total Incl O&P |
|---|---|---|---|---|---|---|---|---|---|
| 4160 | 140 quarts | L-7 | 8.60 | 3.256 | Ea. | 16,800 | 120 | | 16,920 | 18,700 |
| 6700 | Peelers, small | R-18 | 8 | 3.250 | | 1,325 | 115 | | 1,440 | 1,650 |
| 6720 | Large | " | 6 | 4.333 | | 4,000 | 154 | | 4,154 | 4,600 |
| 6800 | Pulper/extractor, close coupled, 5 HP | 1 Plum | 1.90 | 4.211 | | 2,775 | 197 | | 2,972 | 3,350 |
| 8580 | Slicer with table | R-18 | 9 | 2.889 | | 4,350 | 102 | | 4,452 | 4,925 |

# 11 43 Food Delivery Carts and Conveyors

## 11 43 13 – Food Delivery Carts

### 11 43 13.10 Mobile Carts, Racks and Trays

| | | Crew | Daily Output | Labor-Hours | Unit | Material | 2008 Bare Costs Labor | Equipment | Total | Total Incl O&P |
|---|---|---|---|---|---|---|---|---|---|---|
| 0010 | **MOBILE CARTS, RACKS AND TRAYS** | | | | | | | | | |
| 1650 | Cabinet, heated, 1 compartment, reach-in | R-18 | 5.60 | 4.643 | Ea. | 2,400 | 165 | | 2,565 | 2,900 |
| 1655 | Pass-thru roll-in | | 5.60 | 4.643 | | 4,275 | 165 | | 4,440 | 4,950 |
| 1660 | 2 compartment, reach-in | | 4.80 | 5.417 | | 4,575 | 192 | | 4,767 | 5,325 |
| 1670 | Mobile | | | | | 2,550 | | | 2,550 | 2,825 |
| 6850 | Mobile rack w/pan slide | | | | | 1,250 | | | 1,250 | 1,375 |
| 9180 | Tray and silver dispenser, mobile | 1 Clab | 16 | .500 | | 715 | 15.15 | | 730.15 | 815 |

# 11 44 Food Cooking Equipment

## 11 44 13 – Commercial Ranges

### 11 44 13.10 Cooking Equipment

| | | Crew | Daily Output | Labor-Hours | Unit | Material | 2008 Bare Costs Labor | Equipment | Total | Total Incl O&P |
|---|---|---|---|---|---|---|---|---|---|---|
| 0010 | **COOKING EQUIPMENT** | | | | | | | | | |
| 0020 | Bake oven, gas, one section | Q-1 | 8 | 2 | Ea. | 4,175 | 84 | | 4,259 | 4,725 |
| 0300 | Two sections | | 7 | 2.286 | | 9,025 | 96 | | 9,121 | 10,100 |
| 0600 | Three sections | | 6 | 2.667 | | 11,500 | 112 | | 11,612 | 12,800 |
| 0900 | Electric convection, single deck | L-7 | 4 | 7 | | 4,575 | 258 | | 4,833 | 5,425 |
| 1300 | Broiler, without oven, standard | Q-1 | 8 | 2 | | 2,975 | 84 | | 3,059 | 3,400 |
| 1550 | Infrared | L-7 | 4 | 7 | | 6,500 | 258 | | 6,758 | 7,550 |
| 4750 | Fryer, with twin baskets, modular model | Q-1 | 7 | 2.286 | | 1,400 | 96 | | 1,496 | 1,675 |
| 5000 | Floor model, on 6" legs | " | 5 | 3.200 | | 1,800 | 135 | | 1,935 | 2,175 |
| 5100 | Extra single basket, large | | | | | 81 | | | 81 | 89 |
| 5300 | Griddle, SS, 24" plate, w/4" legs, elec, 208V, 3 phase, 3' long | Q-1 | 7 | 2.286 | | 975 | 96 | | 1,071 | 1,225 |
| 5550 | 4' long | " | 6 | 2.667 | | 1,300 | 112 | | 1,412 | 1,600 |
| 6200 | Iced tea brewer | 1 Plum | 3.44 | 2.326 | | 630 | 109 | | 739 | 860 |
| 6350 | Kettle, w/steam jacket, tilting, w/positive lock, SS, 20 gallons | L-7 | 7 | 4 | | 5,525 | 148 | | 5,673 | 6,300 |
| 6600 | 60 gallons | " | 6 | 4.667 | | 7,875 | 172 | | 8,047 | 8,925 |
| 6900 | Range, restaurant type, 6 burners and 1 standard oven, 36" wide | Q-1 | 7 | 2.286 | | 1,950 | 96 | | 2,046 | 2,275 |
| 6950 | Convection | | 7 | 2.286 | | 4,700 | 96 | | 4,796 | 5,325 |
| 7150 | 2 standard ovens, 24" griddle, 60" wide | | 6 | 2.667 | | 3,725 | 112 | | 3,837 | 4,250 |
| 7200 | 1 standard, 1 convection oven | | 6 | 2.667 | | 6,250 | 112 | | 6,362 | 7,025 |
| 7450 | Heavy duty, single 34" standard oven, open top | | 5 | 3.200 | | 4,325 | 135 | | 4,460 | 4,950 |
| 7500 | Convection oven | | 5 | 3.200 | | 3,325 | 135 | | 3,460 | 3,850 |
| 7700 | Griddle top | | 6 | 2.667 | | 2,600 | 112 | | 2,712 | 3,025 |
| 7750 | Convection oven | | 6 | 2.667 | | 5,550 | 112 | | 5,662 | 6,275 |
| 8850 | Steamer, electric 27 KW | L-7 | 7 | 4 | | 6,650 | 148 | | 6,798 | 7,550 |
| 9100 | Electric, 10 KW or gas 100,000 BTU | " | 5 | 5.600 | | 4,850 | 207 | | 5,057 | 5,675 |
| 9150 | Toaster, conveyor type, 16-22 slices per minute | | | | | 1,150 | | | 1,150 | 1,250 |
| 9160 | Pop-up, 2 slot | | | | | 620 | | | 620 | 685 |
| 9200 | For deluxe models of above equipment, add | | | | | 75% | | | | |
| 9400 | Rule of thumb: Equipment cost based | | | | | | | | | |

# 11 44 Food Cooking Equipment

## 11 44 13 – Commercial Ranges

| 11 44 13.10 Cooking Equipment | Crew | Daily Output | Labor-Hours | Unit | Material | 2008 Bare Costs Labor | Equipment | Total | Total Incl O&P |
|---|---|---|---|---|---|---|---|---|---|
| 9410 | on kitchen work area | | | | | | | | | |
| 9420 | Office buildings, minimum | L-7 | 77 | .364 | S.F. | 69.50 | 13.45 | | 82.95 | 97 |
| 9450 | Maximum | | 58 | .483 | | 118 | 17.80 | | 135.80 | 157 |
| 9550 | Public eating facilities, minimum | | 77 | .364 | | 91.50 | 13.45 | | 104.95 | 121 |
| 9600 | Maximum | | 46 | .609 | | 148 | 22.50 | | 170.50 | 198 |
| 9750 | Hospitals, minimum | | 58 | .483 | | 94 | 17.80 | | 111.80 | 131 |
| 9800 | Maximum | | 39 | .718 | | 157 | 26.50 | | 183.50 | 214 |

# 11 46 Food Dispensing Equipment

## 11 46 16 – Service Line Equipment

### 11 46 16.10 Commercial Food Dispensing Equipment

| | | Crew | Daily Output | Labor-Hours | Unit | Material | Labor | Equipment | Total | Total Incl O&P |
|---|---|---|---|---|---|---|---|---|---|---|
| 0010 | **COMMERCIAL FOOD DISPENSING EQUIPMENT** | | | | | | | | | |
| 1050 | Butter pat dispenser | 1 Clab | 13 | .615 | Ea. | 835 | 18.60 | | 853.60 | 945 |
| 1100 | Bread dispenser, counter top | | 13 | .615 | | 795 | 18.60 | | 813.60 | 905 |
| 1900 | Cup and glass dispenser, drop in | | 4 | 2 | | 1,150 | 60.50 | | 1,210.50 | 1,350 |
| 1920 | Disposable cup, drop in | | 16 | .500 | | 365 | 15.15 | | 380.15 | 425 |
| 2650 | Dish dispenser, drop in, 12" | | 11 | .727 | | 1,300 | 22 | | 1,322 | 1,450 |
| 2660 | Mobile | | 10 | .800 | | 2,175 | 24 | | 2,199 | 2,450 |
| 3300 | Food warmer, counter, 1.2 KW | | | | | 570 | | | 570 | 630 |
| 3550 | 1.6 KW | | | | | 1,625 | | | 1,625 | 1,800 |
| 3600 | Well, hot food, built-in, rectangular, 12" x 20" | R-30 | 10 | 2.600 | | 765 | 94.50 | | 859.50 | 985 |
| 3610 | Circular, 7 qt | | 10 | 2.600 | | 298 | 94.50 | | 392.50 | 475 |
| 3620 | Refrigerated, 2 compartments | | 10 | 2.600 | | 1,975 | 94.50 | | 2,069.50 | 2,325 |
| 3630 | 3 compartments | | 9 | 2.889 | | 1,925 | 105 | | 2,030 | 2,250 |
| 3640 | 4 compartments | | 8 | 3.250 | | 2,525 | 118 | | 2,643 | 2,950 |
| 4720 | Frost cold plate | | 9 | 2.889 | | 7,900 | 105 | | 8,005 | 8,825 |
| 5700 | Hot chocolate dispenser | 1 Plum | 4 | 2 | | 885 | 93.50 | | 978.50 | 1,125 |
| 6250 | Jet spray dispenser | R-18 | 4.50 | 5.778 | | 2,850 | 205 | | 3,055 | 3,450 |
| 6300 | Juice dispenser, concentrate | " | 4.50 | 5.778 | | 1,350 | 205 | | 1,555 | 1,800 |
| 6690 | Milk dispenser, bulk, 2 flavor | R-30 | 8 | 3.250 | | 1,300 | 118 | | 1,418 | 1,600 |
| 6695 | 3 flavor | " | 8 | 3.250 | | 1,825 | 118 | | 1,943 | 2,200 |
| 8800 | Serving counter, straight | 1 Carp | 40 | .200 | L.F. | 680 | 7.60 | | 687.60 | 755 |
| 8820 | Curved section | " | 30 | .267 | " | 850 | 10.15 | | 860.15 | 950 |
| 8825 | Solid surface, see Div. 12 36 61.16 | | | | | | | | | |
| 8830 | Soft serve ice cream machine, medium | R-18 | 11 | 2.364 | Ea. | 8,950 | 84 | | 9,034 | 9,975 |
| 8840 | Large | " | 9 | 2.889 | " | 15,700 | 102 | | 15,802 | 17,500 |

# 11 47 Ice Machines

## 11 47 10 – Commercial Ice Machines

### 11 47 10.10 Commercial Ice Equipment

| | | Crew | Daily Output | Labor-Hours | Unit | Material | Labor | Equipment | Total | Total Incl O&P |
|---|---|---|---|---|---|---|---|---|---|---|
| 0010 | **COMMERCIAL ICE EQUIPMENT** | | | | | | | | | |
| 5800 | Ice cube maker, 50 pounds per day | Q-1 | 6 | 2.667 | Ea. | 1,325 | 112 | | 1,437 | 1,625 |
| 5900 | 250 pounds per day | | 1.20 | 13.333 | | 2,100 | 560 | | 2,660 | 3,150 |
| 6050 | 500 pounds per day | | 4 | 4 | | 2,800 | 168 | | 2,968 | 3,350 |
| 6060 | With bin | | 1.20 | 13.333 | | 2,500 | 560 | | 3,060 | 3,600 |
| 6090 | 1000 pounds per day, with bin | | 1 | 16 | | 4,400 | 670 | | 5,070 | 5,850 |
| 6100 | Ice flakers, 300 pounds per day | | 1.60 | 10 | | 2,800 | 420 | | 3,220 | 3,725 |
| 6120 | 600 pounds per day | | .95 | 16.842 | | 3,650 | 710 | | 4,360 | 5,100 |
| 6130 | 1000 pounds per day | | .75 | 21.333 | | 4,175 | 895 | | 5,070 | 5,950 |

# 11 47 Ice Machines

## 11 47 10 – Commercial Ice Machines

| 11 47 10.10 Commercial Ice Equipment | Crew | Daily Output | Labor-Hours | Unit | Material | 2008 Bare Costs Labor | Equipment | Total | Total Incl O&P |
|---|---|---|---|---|---|---|---|---|---|
| 6140 | 2000 pounds per day | Q-1 | .65 | 24.615 | Ea. | 16,600 | 1,025 | | 17,625 | 19,800 |
| 6160 | Ice storage bin, 500 pound capacity | Q-5 | 1 | 16 | | 955 | 680 | | 1,635 | 2,075 |
| 6180 | 1000 pound | " | .56 | 28.571 | | 1,700 | 1,200 | | 2,900 | 3,700 |

# 11 48 Cleaning and Disposal Equipment

## 11 48 13 – Commercial Dishwashers

### 11 48 13.10 Dishwashers

| | | Crew | Daily Output | Labor-Hours | Unit | Material | 2008 Bare Costs Labor | Equipment | Total | Total Incl O&P |
|---|---|---|---|---|---|---|---|---|---|---|
| 0010 | **DISHWASHERS** | | | | | | | | | |
| 2700 | Dishwasher, commercial, rack type | | | | | | | | | |
| 2720 | 10 to 12 racks per hour | Q-1 | 3.20 | 5 | Ea. | 3,675 | 210 | | 3,885 | 4,375 |
| 2750 | Semi-automatic 38 to 50 racks per hour | " | 1.30 | 12.308 | | 7,300 | 515 | | 7,815 | 8,800 |
| 2800 | Automatic, 190 to 230 racks per hour | L-6 | .35 | 34.286 | | 10,400 | 1,600 | | 12,000 | 13,900 |
| 2820 | 235 to 275 racks per hour | | .25 | 48 | | 24,700 | 2,225 | | 26,925 | 30,500 |
| 2840 | 8,750 to 12,500 dishes per hour | | .10 | 120 | | 44,900 | 5,550 | | 50,450 | 57,500 |
| 2950 | Dishwasher hood, canopy type | L-3A | 10 | 1.200 | L.F. | 485 | 50 | | 535 | 610 |
| 2960 | Pant leg type | " | 2.50 | 4.800 | Ea. | 7,025 | 201 | | 7,226 | 8,050 |
| 5200 | Garbage disposal 1.5 HP, 100 GPH | L-1 | 4.80 | 3.333 | | 1,450 | 154 | | 1,604 | 1,825 |
| 5210 | 3 HP, 120 GPH | | 4.60 | 3.478 | | 2,250 | 160 | | 2,410 | 2,725 |
| 5220 | 5 HP, 250 GPH | | 4.50 | 3.556 | | 3,225 | 164 | | 3,389 | 3,800 |
| 6750 | Pot sink, 3 compartment | 1 Plum | 7.25 | 1.103 | L.F. | 705 | 51.50 | | 756.50 | 855 |
| 6760 | Pot washer, small | | 1.60 | 5 | Ea. | 8,825 | 234 | | 9,059 | 10,100 |
| 6770 | Large | | 1.20 | 6.667 | | 12,800 | 310 | | 13,110 | 14,600 |
| 9170 | Trash compactor, small, up to 125 lb. compacted weight | L-4 | 4 | 6 | | 18,900 | 216 | | 19,116 | 21,100 |
| 9175 | Large, up to 175 lb. compacted weight | " | 3 | 8 | | 23,100 | 288 | | 23,388 | 25,800 |

# 11 52 Audio-Visual Equipment

## 11 52 13 – Projection Screens

### 11 52 13.10 Projection Screens, Wall or Ceiling Hung

| | | Crew | Daily Output | Labor-Hours | Unit | Material | 2008 Bare Costs Labor | Equipment | Total | Total Incl O&P |
|---|---|---|---|---|---|---|---|---|---|---|
| 0010 | **PROJECTION SCREENS, WALL OR CEILING HUNG**, matte white | | | | | | | | | |
| 0100 | Manually operated, economy | 2 Carp | 500 | .032 | S.F. | 5.55 | 1.22 | | 6.77 | 8.05 |
| 0300 | Intermediate | | 450 | .036 | | 6.50 | 1.35 | | 7.85 | 9.25 |
| 0400 | Deluxe | | 400 | .040 | | 9 | 1.52 | | 10.52 | 12.25 |
| 0600 | Electric operated, matte white, 25 S.F., economy | | 5 | 3.200 | Ea. | 815 | 122 | | 937 | 1,075 |
| 0700 | Deluxe | | 4 | 4 | | 1,700 | 152 | | 1,852 | 2,100 |
| 0900 | 50 S.F., economy | | 3 | 5.333 | | 885 | 203 | | 1,088 | 1,300 |
| 1000 | Deluxe | | 2 | 8 | | 1,900 | 305 | | 2,205 | 2,550 |
| 1200 | Heavy duty, electric operated, 200 S.F. | | 1.50 | 10.667 | | 3,725 | 405 | | 4,130 | 4,700 |
| 1300 | 400 S.F. | | 1 | 16 | | 4,575 | 610 | | 5,185 | 6,000 |
| 1500 | Rigid acrylic in wall, for rear projection, 1/4" thick | 2 Glaz | 30 | .533 | S.F. | 45 | 19.90 | | 64.90 | 79.50 |
| 1600 | 1/2" thick (maximum size 10' x 20') | " | 25 | .640 | " | 79.50 | 24 | | 103.50 | 124 |

## 11 52 16 – Projectors

### 11 52 16.10 Movie Equipment

| | | Crew | Daily Output | Labor-Hours | Unit | Material | 2008 Bare Costs Labor | Equipment | Total | Total Incl O&P |
|---|---|---|---|---|---|---|---|---|---|---|
| 0010 | **MOVIE EQUIPMENT** | | | | | | | | | |
| 0020 | Changeover, minimum | | | | Ea. | 445 | | | 445 | 485 |
| 0100 | Maximum | | | | | 860 | | | 860 | 945 |
| 0400 | Film transport, incl. platters and autowind, minimum | | | | | 4,775 | | | 4,775 | 5,275 |
| 0500 | Maximum | | | | | 13,600 | | | 13,600 | 15,000 |
| 0800 | Lamphouses, incl. rectifiers, xenon, 1,000 watt | 1 Elec | 2 | 4 | | 6,325 | 182 | | 6,507 | 7,250 |
| 0900 | 1,600 watt | | 2 | 4 | | 6,750 | 182 | | 6,932 | 7,700 |

## 11 52 16 – Projectors

| 11 52 16.10 Movie Equipment | Crew | Daily Output | Labor-Hours | Unit | Material | Labor | Equipment | Total | Total Incl O&P |
|---|---|---|---|---|---|---|---|---|---|
| | | | | | | 2008 Bare Costs | | | |
| 1000 | 2,000 watt | 1 Elec | 1.50 | 5.333 | Ea. | 7,250 | 243 | | 7,493 | 8,325 |
| 1100 | 4,000 watt | ↓ | 1.50 | 5.333 | | 8,975 | 243 | | 9,218 | 10,200 |
| 1400 | Lenses, anamorphic, minimum | | | | | 1,225 | | | 1,225 | 1,350 |
| 1500 | Maximum | | | | | 2,725 | | | 2,725 | 3,000 |
| 1800 | Flat 35 mm, minimum | | | | | 1,050 | | | 1,050 | 1,150 |
| 1900 | Maximum | | | | | 1,650 | | | 1,650 | 1,825 |
| 2200 | Pedestals, for projectors | | | | | 1,400 | | | 1,400 | 1,550 |
| 2300 | Console type | | | | | 10,200 | | | 10,200 | 11,200 |
| 2600 | Projector mechanisms, incl. soundhead, 35 mm, minimum | | | | | 10,500 | | | 10,500 | 11,600 |
| 2700 | Maximum | | | | ↓ | 14,500 | | | 14,500 | 15,900 |
| 3000 | Projection screens, rigid, in wall, acrylic, 1/4" thick | 2 Glaz | 195 | .082 | S.F. | 40 | 3.06 | | 43.06 | 48.50 |
| 3100 | 1/2" thick | " | 130 | .123 | " | 46 | 4.59 | | 50.59 | 58 |
| 3300 | Electric operated, heavy duty, 400 S.F. | 2 Carp | 1 | 16 | Ea. | 2,800 | 610 | | 3,410 | 4,050 |
| 3320 | Theatre projection screens, matte white, including frames | " | 200 | .080 | S.F. | 6.30 | 3.05 | | 9.35 | 11.70 |
| 3400 | Also see Div. 11 52 13.10 | | | | | | | | | |
| 3700 | Sound systems, incl. amplifier, mono, minimum | 1 Elec | .90 | 8.889 | Ea. | 3,150 | 405 | | 3,555 | 4,050 |
| 3800 | Dolby/Super Sound, maximum | | .40 | 20 | | 17,200 | 910 | | 18,110 | 20,300 |
| 4100 | Dual system, 2 channel, front surround, minimum | | .70 | 11.429 | | 4,400 | 520 | | 4,920 | 5,625 |
| 4200 | Dolby/Super Sound, 4 channel, maximum | ↓ | .40 | 20 | | 15,700 | 910 | | 16,610 | 18,700 |
| 4500 | Sound heads, 35 mm | | | | | 5,050 | | | 5,050 | 5,550 |
| 4900 | Splicer, tape system, minimum | | | | | 705 | | | 705 | 775 |
| 5000 | Tape type, maximum | | | | | 1,250 | | | 1,250 | 1,375 |
| 5300 | Speakers, recessed behind screen, minimum | 1 Elec | 2 | 4 | | 1,000 | 182 | | 1,182 | 1,375 |
| 5400 | Maximum | " | 1 | 8 | | 2,950 | 365 | | 3,315 | 3,775 |
| 5700 | Seating, painted steel, upholstered, minimum | 2 Carp | 35 | .457 | | 125 | 17.40 | | 142.40 | 165 |
| 5800 | Maximum | " | 28 | .571 | | 400 | 22 | | 422 | 475 |
| 6100 | Rewind tables, minimum | | | | | 2,525 | | | 2,525 | 2,775 |
| 6200 | Maximum | | | | ↓ | 4,500 | | | 4,500 | 4,925 |
| 7000 | For automation, varying sophistication, minimum | 1 Elec | 1 | 8 | System | 2,275 | 365 | | 2,640 | 3,050 |
| 7100 | Maximum | 2 Elec | .30 | 53.333 | " | 5,300 | 2,425 | | 7,725 | 9,450 |

# 11 53 Laboratory Equipment

## 11 53 03 – Laboratory Test Equipment

### 11 53 03.13 Test Equipment

| | | Crew | Daily Output | Labor-Hours | Unit | Material | Labor | Equipment | Total | Total Incl O&P |
|---|---|---|---|---|---|---|---|---|---|---|
| 0010 | **TEST EQUIPMENT** | | | | | | | | | |
| 1700 | Thermometer, electric, portable | | | | Ea. | 345 | | | 345 | 380 |
| 1800 | Titration unit, four 2000 ml reservoirs | | | | " | 5,500 | | | 5,500 | 6,050 |

## 11 53 13 – Laboratory Fume Hoods

### 11 53 13.13 Recirculating Laboratory Fume Hoods

| | | Crew | Daily Output | Labor-Hours | Unit | Material | Labor | Equipment | Total | Total Incl O&P |
|---|---|---|---|---|---|---|---|---|---|---|
| 0010 | **RECIRCULATING LABORATORY FUME HOODS** | | | | | | | | | |
| 0600 | Fume hood, with countertop & base, not including HVAC | | | | | | | | | |
| 0610 | Simple, minimum | 2 Carp | 5.40 | 2.963 | L.F. | 520 | 113 | | 633 | 745 |
| 0620 | Complex, including fixtures | | 2.40 | 6.667 | | 1,625 | 254 | | 1,879 | 2,200 |
| 0630 | Special, maximum | ↓ | 1.70 | 9.412 | ↓ | 1,825 | 360 | | 2,185 | 2,550 |
| 0670 | Service fixtures, average | | | | Ea. | 265 | | | 265 | 292 |
| 0680 | For sink assembly with hot and cold water, add | 1 Plum | 1.40 | 5.714 | | 685 | 267 | | 952 | 1,150 |
| 0750 | Glove box, fiberglass, bacteriological | | | | | 16,300 | | | 16,300 | 17,900 |
| 0760 | Controlled atmosphere | | | | | 16,900 | | | 16,900 | 18,600 |
| 0770 | Radioisotope | | | | | 16,300 | | | 16,300 | 17,900 |
| 0780 | Carcinogenic | | | | ↓ | 16,300 | | | 16,300 | 17,900 |

# 11 53 Laboratory Equipment

## 11 53 13 – Laboratory Fume Hoods

### 11 53 13.23 Exhaust Hoods

| 11 53 13.23 Exhaust Hoods | Crew | Daily Output | Labor-Hours | Unit | Material | 2008 Bare Costs Labor | Equipment | Total | Total Incl O&P |
|---|---|---|---|---|---|---|---|---|---|
| 0010 **EXHAUST HOODS** | | | | | | | | | |
| 0650 Ductwork, minimum | 2 Shee | 1 | 16 | Hood | 3,475 | 725 | | 4,200 | 4,925 |
| 0660 Maximum | " | .50 | 32 | " | 5,325 | 1,450 | | 6,775 | 8,100 |

## 11 53 16 – Laboratory Incubators

### 11 53 16.13 Incubators

| 11 53 16.13 Incubators | Crew | Daily Output | Labor-Hours | Unit | Material | 2008 Bare Costs Labor | Equipment | Total | Total Incl O&P |
|---|---|---|---|---|---|---|---|---|---|
| 0010 **INCUBATORS** | | | | | | | | | |
| 1000 Incubators, minimum | | | | Ea. | 3,100 | | | 3,100 | 3,425 |
| 1010 Maximum | | | | " | 18,600 | | | 18,600 | 20,500 |

## 11 53 19 – Laboratory Sterilizers

### 11 53 19.13 Sterilizers

| 11 53 19.13 Sterilizers | Crew | Daily Output | Labor-Hours | Unit | Material | 2008 Bare Costs Labor | Equipment | Total | Total Incl O&P |
|---|---|---|---|---|---|---|---|---|---|
| 0010 **STERILIZERS** | | | | | | | | | |
| 0700 Glassware washer, undercounter, minimum | L-1 | 1.80 | 8.889 | Ea. | 5,325 | 410 | | 5,735 | 6,475 |
| 0710 Maximum | " | 1 | 16 | | 10,900 | 740 | | 11,640 | 13,100 |
| 1850 Utensil washer-sanitizer | 1 Plum | 2 | 4 | | 10,100 | 187 | | 10,287 | 11,400 |

## 11 53 23 – Laboratory Refrigerators

### 11 53 23.13 Refrigerators

| 11 53 23.13 Refrigerators | Crew | Daily Output | Labor-Hours | Unit | Material | 2008 Bare Costs Labor | Equipment | Total | Total Incl O&P |
|---|---|---|---|---|---|---|---|---|---|
| 0010 **REFRIGERATORS** | | | | | | | | | |
| 1200 Blood bank, 28.6 C.F. emergency signal | | | | Ea. | 7,125 | | | 7,125 | 7,850 |
| 1210 Reach-in, 16.9 C.F. | | | | " | 7,150 | | | 7,150 | 7,875 |

## 11 53 33 – Emergency Safety Appliances

### 11 53 33.13 Emergency Equipment

| 11 53 33.13 Emergency Equipment | Crew | Daily Output | Labor-Hours | Unit | Material | 2008 Bare Costs Labor | Equipment | Total | Total Incl O&P |
|---|---|---|---|---|---|---|---|---|---|
| 0010 **EMERGENCY EQUIPMENT** | | | | | | | | | |
| 1400 Safety equipment, eye wash, hand held | | | | Ea. | 405 | | | 405 | 445 |
| 1450 Deluge shower | | | | " | 730 | | | 730 | 805 |

## 11 53 43 – Service Fittings and Accessories

### 11 53 43.13 Fittings

| 11 53 43.13 Fittings | Crew | Daily Output | Labor-Hours | Unit | Material | 2008 Bare Costs Labor | Equipment | Total | Total Incl O&P |
|---|---|---|---|---|---|---|---|---|---|
| 0010 **FITTINGS** | | | | | | | | | |
| 1600 Sink, one piece plastic, flask wash, hose, free standing | 1 Plum | 1.60 | 5 | Ea. | 1,725 | 234 | | 1,959 | 2,250 |
| 1610 Epoxy resin sink, 25" x 16" x 10" | " | 2 | 4 | " | 192 | 187 | | 379 | 490 |
| 1950 Utility table, acid resistant top with drawers | 2 Carp | 30 | .533 | L.F. | 142 | 20.50 | | 162.50 | 188 |
| 8000 Alternate pricing method: as percent of lab furniture | | | | | | | | | |
| 8050 Installation, not incl. plumbing & duct work | | | | % Furn. | | | | 20% | 22% |
| 8100 Plumbing, final connections, simple system | | | | | | | | 9.09% | 10% |
| 8110 Moderately complex system | | | | | | | | 13.64% | 15% |
| 8120 Complex system | | | | | | | | 18.18% | 20% |
| 8150 Electrical, simple system | | | | | | | | 9.09% | 10% |
| 8160 Moderately complex system | | | | | | | | 18.18% | 20% |
| 8170 Complex system | | | | | | | | 31.80% | 35% |

# 11 57 Vocational Shop Equipment

## 11 57 10 – Shop Equipment

| 11 57 10.10 Vocational School Shop Equipment | Crew | Daily Output | Labor-Hours | Unit | 2008 Bare Costs | | | Total | Total Incl O&P |
|---|---|---|---|---|---|---|---|---|---|
| | | | | | Material | Labor | Equipment | | |
| 0010 **VOCATIONAL SCHOOL SHOP EQUIPMENT** | | | | | | | | | |
| 0020 Benches, work, wood, average | 2 Carp | 5 | 3.200 | Ea. | 485 | 122 | | 607 | 720 |
| 0100 Metal, average | | 5 | 3.200 | | 385 | 122 | | 507 | 610 |
| 0400 Combination belt & disc sander, 6" | | 4 | 4 | | 1,225 | 152 | | 1,377 | 1,575 |
| 0700 Drill press, floor mounted, 12", 1/2 H.P. | | 4 | 4 | | 465 | 152 | | 617 | 745 |
| 0800 Dust collector, not incl. ductwork, 6" diameter | 1 Shee | 1.10 | 7.273 | | 2,900 | 330 | | 3,230 | 3,675 |
| 1000 Grinders, double wheel, 1/2 H.P. | 2 Carp | 5 | 3.200 | | 211 | 122 | | 333 | 420 |
| 1300 Jointer, 4", 3/4 H.P. | | 4 | 4 | | 1,250 | 152 | | 1,402 | 1,625 |
| 1600 Kilns, 16 C.F., to 2000° | | 4 | 4 | | 2,300 | 152 | | 2,452 | 2,750 |
| 1900 Lathe, woodworking, 10", 1/2 H.P. | | 4 | 4 | | 760 | 152 | | 912 | 1,075 |
| 2200 Planer, 13" x 6" | | 4 | 4 | | 1,200 | 152 | | 1,352 | 1,525 |
| 2500 Potter's wheel, motorized | | 4 | 4 | | 1,000 | 152 | | 1,152 | 1,325 |
| 2800 Saws, band, 14", 3/4 H.P. | | 4 | 4 | | 805 | 152 | | 957 | 1,125 |
| 3100 Metal cutting band saw, 14" | | 4 | 4 | | 1,900 | 152 | | 2,052 | 2,300 |
| 3400 Radial arm saw, 10", 2 H.P. | | 4 | 4 | | 945 | 152 | | 1,097 | 1,275 |
| 3700 Scroll saw, 24" | | 4 | 4 | | 1,525 | 152 | | 1,677 | 1,900 |
| 4000 Table saw, 10", 3 H.P. | | 4 | 4 | | 1,925 | 152 | | 2,077 | 2,350 |
| 4300 Welder AC arc, 30 amp capacity | | 4 | 4 | | 2,250 | 152 | | 2,402 | 2,700 |

# 11 61 Theater and Stage Equipment

## 11 61 23 – Folding and Portable Stages

### 11 61 23.10 Portable Stages

| | Crew | Daily Output | Labor-Hours | Unit | Material | Labor | Equipment | Total | Total Incl O&P |
|---|---|---|---|---|---|---|---|---|---|
| 0010 **PORTABLE STAGES** | | | | | | | | | |
| 1500 Flooring, portable oak parquet, 3' x 3' sections | | | | S.F. | 12.75 | | | 12.75 | 14 |
| 1600 Cart to carry 225 S.F. of flooring | | | | Ea. | 380 | | | 380 | 420 |
| 5000 Stages, portable with steps, folding legs, stock, 8" high | | | | SF Stg. | 24.50 | | | 24.50 | 27 |
| 5100 16" high | | | | | 22.50 | | | 22.50 | 25 |
| 5200 32" high | | | | | 33.50 | | | 33.50 | 37 |
| 5300 40" high | | | | | 56.50 | | | 56.50 | 62 |
| 6000 Telescoping platforms, extruded alum., straight, minimum | 4 Carp | 157 | .204 | | 26.50 | 7.75 | | 34.25 | 41 |
| 6100 Maximum | | 77 | .416 | | 36 | 15.85 | | 51.85 | 64 |
| 6500 Pie-shaped, minimum | | 150 | .213 | | 57.50 | 8.15 | | 65.65 | 75.50 |
| 6600 Maximum | | 70 | .457 | | 64 | 17.40 | | 81.40 | 97.50 |
| 6800 For 3/4" plywood covered deck, deduct | | | | | 3.67 | | | 3.67 | 4.04 |
| 7000 Band risers, steel frame, plywood deck, minimum | 4 Carp | 275 | .116 | | 29 | 4.43 | | 33.43 | 39 |
| 7100 Maximum | " | 138 | .232 | | 60.50 | 8.85 | | 69.35 | 80.50 |
| 7500 Chairs for above, self-storing, minimum | 2 Carp | 43 | .372 | Ea. | 94.50 | 14.20 | | 108.70 | 126 |
| 7600 Maximum | " | 40 | .400 | " | 164 | 15.25 | | 179.25 | 204 |

## 11 61 33 – Rigging Systems and Controls

### 11 61 33.10 Controls

| | Crew | Daily Output | Labor-Hours | Unit | Material | Labor | Equipment | Total | Total Incl O&P |
|---|---|---|---|---|---|---|---|---|---|
| 0010 **CONTROLS** | | | | | | | | | |
| 0050 Control boards with dimmers and breakers, minimum | 1 Elec | 1 | 8 | Ea. | 10,800 | 365 | | 11,165 | 12,400 |
| 0100 Average | | .50 | 16 | | 33,800 | 730 | | 34,530 | 38,300 |
| 0150 Maximum | | .20 | 40 | | 113,500 | 1,825 | | 115,325 | 127,500 |
| 8000 Rule of thumb: total stage equipment, minimum | 4 Carp | 100 | .320 | SF Stg. | 92.50 | 12.20 | | 104.70 | 121 |
| 8100 Maximum | " | 25 | 1.280 | " | 520 | 49 | | 569 | 650 |

## 11 61 43 – Stage Curtains

### 11 61 43.10 Curtains

| | Crew | Daily Output | Labor-Hours | Unit | Material | Labor | Equipment | Total | Total Incl O&P |
|---|---|---|---|---|---|---|---|---|---|
| 0010 **CURTAINS** | | | | | | | | | |
| 0500 Curtain track, straight, light duty | 2 Carp | 20 | .800 | L.F. | 24.50 | 30.50 | | 55 | 74.50 |

# 11 61 Theater and Stage Equipment

## 11 61 43 – Stage Curtains

### 11 61 43.10 Curtains

| | 11 61 43.10 Curtains | Crew | Daily Output | Labor-Hours | Unit | Material | 2008 Bare Costs Labor | Equipment | Total | Total Incl O&P |
|---|---|---|---|---|---|---|---|---|---|---|
| 0600 | Heavy duty | 2 Carp | 18 | .889 | L.F. | 56 | 34 | | 90 | 114 |
| 0700 | Curved sections | | 12 | 1.333 | ↓ | 156 | 51 | | 207 | 250 |
| 1000 | Curtains, velour, medium weight | | 600 | .027 | S.F. | 7.55 | 1.02 | | 8.57 | 9.90 |
| 1150 | Silica based yarn, inherently fire retardant | ↓ | 50 | .320 | " | 14.50 | 12.20 | | 26.70 | 35 |

# 11 62 Musical Equipment

## 11 62 16 – Carillons

### 11 62 16.10 Bell Tower Equipment

| | 11 62 16.10 Bell Tower Equipment | Crew | Daily Output | Labor-Hours | Unit | Material | 2008 Bare Costs Labor | Equipment | Total | Total Incl O&P |
|---|---|---|---|---|---|---|---|---|---|---|
| 0010 | **BELL TOWER EQUIPMENT** | | | | | | | | | |
| 0300 | 4 octave (48 bells), with keyboard | | | | System | 850,000 | | | 850,000 | 935,000 |
| 0320 | 2 octave (24 bells) | | | | | 400,000 | | | 400,000 | 440,000 |
| 0340 | 3 to 4 bell peal, minimum | | | | | 100,000 | | | 100,000 | 110,000 |
| 0360 | Maximum | | | | ↓ | 600,000 | | | 600,000 | 660,000 |
| 0380 | Cast bronze bell, average | | | | Ea. | 90,000 | | | 90,000 | 99,000 |
| 0400 | Electronic, digital, minimum | | | | | 15,000 | | | 15,000 | 16,500 |
| 0410 | With keyboard, maximum | | | | ↓ | 75,000 | | | 75,000 | 82,500 |

# 11 66 Athletic Equipment

## 11 66 13 – Exercise Equipment

### 11 66 13.10 Physical Training Equipment

| | 11 66 13.10 Physical Training Equipment | Crew | Daily Output | Labor-Hours | Unit | Material | 2008 Bare Costs Labor | Equipment | Total | Total Incl O&P |
|---|---|---|---|---|---|---|---|---|---|---|
| 0010 | **PHYSICAL TRAINING EQUIPMENT** | | | | | | | | | |
| 0020 | Abdominal rack, 2 board capacity | | | | Ea. | 455 | | | 455 | 500 |
| 0050 | Abdominal board, upholstered | | | | | 510 | | | 510 | 560 |
| 0200 | Bicycle trainer, minimum | | | | | 790 | | | 790 | 870 |
| 0300 | Deluxe, electric | | | | | 4,025 | | | 4,025 | 4,425 |
| 0400 | Barbell set, chrome plated steel, 25 lbs. | | | | | 237 | | | 237 | 261 |
| 0420 | 100 lbs. | | | | | 360 | | | 360 | 395 |
| 0450 | 200 lbs. | | | | ↓ | 695 | | | 695 | 765 |
| 0500 | Weight plates, cast iron, per lb. | | | | Lb. | 4.86 | | | 4.86 | 5.35 |
| 0520 | Storage rack, 10 station | | | | Ea. | 765 | | | 765 | 845 |
| 0600 | Circuit training apparatus, 12 machines minimum | 2 Clab | 1.25 | 12.800 | Set | 26,800 | 385 | | 27,185 | 30,000 |
| 0700 | Average | | 1 | 16 | | 32,900 | 485 | | 33,385 | 36,900 |
| 0800 | Maximum | ↓ | .75 | 21.333 | | 38,900 | 645 | | 39,545 | 43,800 |
| 0820 | Dumbbell set, cast iron, with rack and 5 pair | | | | ↓ | 570 | | | 570 | 630 |
| 0900 | Squat racks | 2 Clab | 5 | 3.200 | Ea. | 740 | 97 | | 837 | 965 |
| 1200 | Multi-station gym machine, 5 station | | | | | 7,725 | | | 7,725 | 8,500 |
| 1250 | 9 station | | | | | 10,800 | | | 10,800 | 11,900 |
| 1280 | Rowing machine, hydraulic | | | | | 1,425 | | | 1,425 | 1,575 |
| 1300 | Treadmill, manual | | | | | 1,400 | | | 1,400 | 1,550 |
| 1320 | Motorized | | | | | 3,500 | | | 3,500 | 3,850 |
| 1340 | Electronic | | | | | 5,300 | | | 5,300 | 5,825 |
| 1360 | Cardio-testing | | | | | 7,550 | | | 7,550 | 8,300 |
| 1400 | Treatment/massage tables, minimum | | | | | 535 | | | 535 | 590 |
| 1420 | Deluxe, with accessories | | | | | 665 | | | 665 | 735 |
| 4150 | Exercise equipment, bicycle trainer | | | | | 995 | | | 995 | 1,100 |
| 4180 | Chinning bar, adjustable, wall mounted | 1 Carp | 5 | 1.600 | | 295 | 61 | | 356 | 420 |
| 4200 | Exercise ladder, 16' x 1'-7", suspended | L-2 | 3 | 5.333 | | 1,125 | 179 | | 1,304 | 1,525 |
| 4210 | High bar, floor plate attached | 1 Carp | 4 | 2 | | 1,100 | 76 | | 1,176 | 1,350 |
| 4240 | Parallel bars, adjustable | ↓ | 4 | 2 | ↓ | 2,475 | 76 | | 2,551 | 2,825 |

# 11 66 Athletic Equipment

## 11 66 13 – Exercise Equipment

### 11 66 13.10 Physical Training Equipment

| 11 66 13.10 Physical Training Equipment | Crew | Daily Output | Labor-Hours | Unit | Material | 2008 Bare Costs Labor | Equipment | Total | Total Incl O&P |
|---|---|---|---|---|---|---|---|---|---|
| 4270 | Uneven parallel bars, adjustable | 1 Carp | 4 | 2 | Ea. | 2,675 | 76 | | 2,751 | 3,050 |
| 4280 | Wall mounted, adjustable | L-2 | 1.50 | 10.667 | Set | 835 | 360 | | 1,195 | 1,475 |
| 4300 | Rope, ceiling mounted, 18' long | 1 Carp | 3.66 | 2.186 | Ea. | 220 | 83.50 | | 303.50 | 370 |
| 4330 | Side horse, vaulting | | 5 | 1.600 | | 1,700 | 61 | | 1,761 | 1,975 |
| 4360 | Treadmill, motorized, deluxe, training type | | 5 | 1.600 | | 3,500 | 61 | | 3,561 | 3,950 |
| 4390 | Weight lifting multi-station, minimum | 2 Clab | 1 | 16 | | 395 | 485 | | 880 | 1,200 |
| 4450 | Maximum | " | .50 | 32 | | 14,700 | 970 | | 15,670 | 17,700 |

## 11 66 23 – Gymnasium Equipment

### 11 66 23.13 Basketball Equipment

| 0010 | BASKETBALL EQUIPMENT | | | | | | | | | |
|---|---|---|---|---|---|---|---|---|---|---|
| 1000 | Backstops, wall mtd., 6' extended, fixed, minimum | L-2 | 1 | 16 | Ea. | 1,100 | 540 | | 1,640 | 2,050 |
| 1100 | Maximum | | 1 | 16 | | 1,625 | 540 | | 2,165 | 2,625 |
| 1200 | Swing up, minimum | | 1 | 16 | | 1,325 | 540 | | 1,865 | 2,275 |
| 1250 | Maximum | | 1 | 16 | | 5,200 | 540 | | 5,740 | 6,550 |
| 1300 | Portable, manual, heavy duty, spring operated | | 1.90 | 8.421 | | 11,000 | 283 | | 11,283 | 12,600 |
| 1400 | Ceiling suspended, stationary, minimum | | .78 | 20.513 | | 1,975 | 690 | | 2,665 | 3,250 |
| 1450 | Fold up, with accessories, maximum | | .40 | 40 | | 5,925 | 1,350 | | 7,275 | 8,625 |
| 1600 | For electrically operated, add | 1 Elec | 1 | 8 | | 1,950 | 365 | | 2,315 | 2,675 |
| 5800 | Wall pads, 1-1/2" thick | 2 Carp | 640 | .025 | S.F. | 6.80 | .95 | | 7.75 | 9 |

### 11 66 23.19 Boxing Ring

| 0010 | BOXING RING | | | | | | | | | |
|---|---|---|---|---|---|---|---|---|---|---|
| 4100 | Elevated, 22' x 22' | L-4 | .10 | 240 | Ea. | 6,825 | 8,625 | | 15,450 | 20,900 |
| 4110 | For cellular plastic foam padding, add | | .10 | 240 | | 905 | 8,625 | | 9,530 | 14,400 |
| 4120 | Floor level, including posts and ropes only, 20' x 20' | | .80 | 30 | | 2,400 | 1,075 | | 3,475 | 4,325 |
| 4130 | Canvas, 30' x 30' | | 5 | 4.800 | | 1,075 | 173 | | 1,248 | 1,475 |

### 11 66 23.47 Gym Mats

| 0010 | GYM MATS | | | | | | | | | |
|---|---|---|---|---|---|---|---|---|---|---|
| 5500 | 2" thick, naugahyde covered | | | | S.F. | 3.59 | | | 3.59 | 3.95 |
| 5600 | Vinyl/nylon covered | | | | | 6.20 | | | 6.20 | 6.85 |
| 6000 | Wrestling mats, 1" thick, heavy duty | | | | | 5.50 | | | 5.50 | 6.05 |

## 11 66 43 – Interior Scoreboards

### 11 66 43.10 Scoreboards

| 0010 | SCOREBOARDS | | | | | | | | | |
|---|---|---|---|---|---|---|---|---|---|---|
| 7000 | Baseball, minimum | R-3 | 1.30 | 15.385 | Ea. | 3,125 | 690 | 99.50 | 3,914.50 | 4,575 |
| 7200 | Maximum | | .05 | 400 | | 15,200 | 17,900 | 2,600 | 35,700 | 46,400 |
| 7300 | Football, minimum | | .86 | 23.256 | | 3,875 | 1,050 | 150 | 5,075 | 5,975 |
| 7400 | Maximum | | .20 | 100 | | 12,300 | 4,475 | 645 | 17,420 | 20,900 |
| 7500 | Basketball (one side), minimum | | 2.07 | 9.662 | | 2,175 | 435 | 62.50 | 2,672.50 | 3,100 |
| 7600 | Maximum | | .30 | 66.667 | | 5,400 | 3,000 | 430 | 8,830 | 10,900 |
| 7700 | Hockey-basketball (four sides), minimum | | .25 | 80 | | 5,500 | 3,575 | 520 | 9,595 | 12,000 |
| 7800 | Maximum | | .15 | 133 | | 5,450 | 5,975 | 865 | 12,290 | 15,900 |

## 11 66 53 – Gymnasium Dividers

### 11 66 53.10 Divider Curtains

| 0010 | DIVIDER CURTAINS | | | | | | | | | |
|---|---|---|---|---|---|---|---|---|---|---|
| 4500 | Gym divider curtain, mesh top, vinyl bottom, manual | L-4 | 500 | .048 | S.F. | 8.05 | 1.73 | | 9.78 | 11.55 |
| 4700 | Electric roll up | L-7 | 400 | .070 | " | 11.75 | 2.58 | | 14.33 | 16.95 |

# 11 67 Recreational Equipment

## 11 67 13 – Bowling Alley Equipment

### 11 67 13.10 Bowling Alleys

| | | Crew | Daily Output | Labor-Hours | Unit | Material | 2008 Bare Costs Labor | Equipment | Total | Total Incl O&P |
|---|---|---|---|---|---|---|---|---|---|---|
| 0010 | **BOWLING ALLEYS** Including alley, pinsetter, scorer, | | | | | | | | | |
| 0020 | Counters and misc. supplies, minimum | 4 Carp | .20 | 160 | Lane | 36,800 | 6,100 | | 42,900 | 50,000 |
| 0150 | Average | | .19 | 168 | | 41,800 | 6,425 | | 48,225 | 56,000 |
| 0300 | Maximum | | .18 | 177 | | 48,000 | 6,775 | | 54,775 | 63,500 |
| 0400 | Combo table ball rack, add | | | | | 1,100 | | | 1,100 | 1,200 |
| 0600 | For automatic scorer, add, minimum | | | | | 7,900 | | | 7,900 | 8,700 |
| 0700 | Maximum | | | | | 9,500 | | | 9,500 | 10,500 |

## 11 67 23 – Shooting Range Equipment

### 11 67 23.10 Shooting Range

| | | Crew | Daily Output | Labor-Hours | Unit | Material | 2008 Bare Costs Labor | Equipment | Total | Total Incl O&P |
|---|---|---|---|---|---|---|---|---|---|---|
| 0010 | **SHOOTING RANGE** Incl. bullet traps, target provisions, controls, | | | | | | | | | |
| 0100 | Separators, ceiling system, etc. Not incl. structural shell | | | | | | | | | |
| 0200 | Commercial | L-9 | .64 | 56.250 | Point | 19,500 | 1,975 | | 21,475 | 24,700 |
| 0300 | Law enforcement | | .28 | 128 | | 23,000 | 4,475 | | 27,475 | 32,600 |
| 0400 | National Guard armories | | .71 | 50.704 | | 16,000 | 1,775 | | 17,775 | 20,500 |
| 0500 | Reserve training centers | | .71 | 50.704 | | 10,500 | 1,775 | | 12,275 | 14,500 |
| 0600 | Schools and colleges | | .32 | 112 | | 22,500 | 3,925 | | 26,425 | 31,100 |
| 0700 | Major acadamies | | .19 | 189 | | 35,900 | 6,600 | | 42,500 | 50,000 |
| 0800 | For acoustical treatment, add | | | | | 10% | 10% | | | |
| 0900 | For lighting, add | | | | | 28% | 25% | | | |
| 1000 | For plumbing, add | | | | | 5% | 5% | | | |
| 1100 | For ventilating system, add, minimum | | | | | 40% | 40% | | | |
| 1200 | Add, average | | | | | 25% | 25% | | | |
| 1300 | Add, maximum | | | | | 35% | 35% | | | |

# 11 68 Play Field Equipment and Structures

## 11 68 13 – Playground Equipment

### 11 68 13.10 Free-Standing Playground Equipment

| | | Crew | Daily Output | Labor-Hours | Unit | Material | 2008 Bare Costs Labor | Equipment | Total | Total Incl O&P |
|---|---|---|---|---|---|---|---|---|---|---|
| 0010 | **FREE-STANDING PLAYGROUND EQUIPMENT** See also individual items | | | | | | | | | |
| 0200 | Bike rack, 10' long, permanent | B-1 | 12 | 2 | Ea. | 605 | 62 | | 667 | 760 |
| 0400 | Horizontal monkey ladder, 14' long, 6' high | | 4 | 6 | | 925 | 186 | | 1,111 | 1,325 |
| 0590 | Parallel bars, 10' long | | 4 | 6 | | 310 | 186 | | 496 | 630 |
| 0600 | Posts, tether ball set, 2-3/8" O.D. | | 12 | 2 | | 258 | 62 | | 320 | 380 |
| 0800 | Poles, multiple purpose, 10'-6" long | | 12 | 2 | Pr. | 155 | 62 | | 217 | 266 |
| 1000 | Ground socket for movable posts, 2-3/8" post | | 10 | 2.400 | | 111 | 74 | | 185 | 237 |
| 1100 | 3-1/2" post | | 10 | 2.400 | | 155 | 74 | | 229 | 285 |
| 1300 | See-saw, spring, steel, 2 units | | 6 | 4 | Ea. | 925 | 124 | | 1,049 | 1,225 |
| 1400 | 4 units | | 4 | 6 | | 1,225 | 186 | | 1,411 | 1,650 |
| 1500 | 6 units | | 3 | 8 | | 1,550 | 247 | | 1,797 | 2,075 |
| 1700 | Shelter, fiberglass golf tee, 3 person | | 4.60 | 5.217 | | 3,275 | 161 | | 3,436 | 3,850 |
| 1900 | Slides, stainless steel bed, 12' long, 6' high | | 3 | 8 | | 4,325 | 247 | | 4,572 | 5,125 |
| 2000 | 20' long, 10' high | | 2 | 12 | | 2,475 | 370 | | 2,845 | 3,300 |
| 2200 | Swings, plain seats, 8' high, 4 seats | | 2 | 12 | | 1,225 | 370 | | 1,595 | 1,925 |
| 2300 | 8 seats | | 1.30 | 18.462 | | 2,050 | 570 | | 2,620 | 3,175 |
| 2500 | 12' high, 4 seats | | 2 | 12 | | 1,750 | 370 | | 2,120 | 2,500 |
| 2600 | 8 seats | | 1.30 | 18.462 | | 2,325 | 570 | | 2,895 | 3,475 |
| 2800 | Whirlers, 8' diameter | | 3 | 8 | | 3,100 | 247 | | 3,347 | 3,775 |
| 2900 | 10' diameter | | 3 | 8 | | 3,600 | 247 | | 3,847 | 4,350 |

### 11 68 13.20 Modular Playground

| | | Crew | Daily Output | Labor-Hours | Unit | Material | 2008 Bare Costs Labor | Equipment | Total | Total Incl O&P |
|---|---|---|---|---|---|---|---|---|---|---|
| 0010 | **MODULAR PLAYGROUND** Basic components | | | | | | | | | |
| 0100 | Deck, square, steel, 48" x 48" | B-1 | 1 | 24 | Ea. | 850 | 740 | | 1,590 | 2,075 |

# 11 68 Play Field Equipment and Structures

## 11 68 13 – Playground Equipment

### 11 68 13.20 Modular Playground

| | | Crew | Daily Output | Labor-Hours | Unit | Material | 2008 Bare Costs Labor | Equipment | Total | Total Incl O&P |
|---|---|---|---|---|---|---|---|---|---|---|
| 0110 | Recycled polyurethane | B-1 | 1 | 24 | Ea. | 850 | 740 | | 1,590 | 2,075 |
| 0120 | Triangular, steel, 48" side | | 1 | 24 | ↓ | 600 | 740 | | 1,340 | 1,800 |
| 0130 | Post, steel, 5" square | | 18 | 1.333 | L.F. | 25 | 41 | | 66 | 91.50 |
| 0140 | Aluminum, 2-3/8" square | | 20 | 1.200 | | 21 | 37 | | 58 | 80.50 |
| 0150 | 5" square | | 18 | 1.333 | ↓ | 30 | 41 | | 71 | 97 |
| 0160 | Roof, square poly, 54" side | | 18 | 1.333 | Ea. | 1,200 | 41 | | 1,241 | 1,400 |
| 0170 | Wheelchair transfer module, for 3' high deck | | 3 | 8 | " | 2,600 | 247 | | 2,847 | 3,225 |
| 0180 | Guardrail, pipe, 36" high | | 60 | .400 | L.F. | 120 | 12.35 | | 132.35 | 151 |
| 0190 | Steps, deck-to-deck, 3 - 8" steps | | 8 | 3 | Ea. | 1,200 | 93 | | 1,293 | 1,475 |
| 0200 | Activity panel, crawl through panel | | 2 | 12 | | 400 | 370 | | 770 | 1,025 |
| 0210 | Alphabet/spelling panel | | 2 | 12 | | 600 | 370 | | 970 | 1,225 |
| 0360 | With guardrails | | 3 | 8 | | 2,200 | 247 | | 2,447 | 2,800 |
| 0370 | Crawl tunnel, straight, 56" long | | 4 | 6 | | 1,200 | 186 | | 1,386 | 1,625 |
| 0380 | 90°, 4' long | | 4 | 6 | | 1,200 | 186 | | 1,386 | 1,625 |
| 1200 | Slide, tunnel, for 56" high deck | | 8 | 3 | | 1,800 | 93 | | 1,893 | 2,125 |
| 1210 | Straight, poly | | 8 | 3 | | 1,800 | 93 | | 1,893 | 2,125 |
| 1220 | Stainless steel, 54" high deck | | 6 | 4 | | 250 | 124 | | 374 | 465 |
| 1230 | Curved, poly, 40" high deck | | 6 | 4 | | 550 | 124 | | 674 | 795 |
| 1240 | Spiral slide, 56" - 72" high | | 5 | 4.800 | | 2,700 | 148 | | 2,848 | 3,200 |
| 1300 | Ladder, vertical, for 24" - 72" high deck | | 5 | 4.800 | | 600 | 148 | | 748 | 890 |
| 1310 | Horizontal, 8' long | | 5 | 4.800 | | 700 | 148 | | 848 | 1,000 |
| 1320 | Corkscrew climber, 6' high | | 3 | 8 | | 500 | 247 | | 747 | 935 |
| 1330 | Fire pole for 72" high deck | | 6 | 4 | | 550 | 124 | | 674 | 795 |
| 1340 | Bridge, ring climber, 8' long | | 4 | 6 | ↓ | 1,100 | 186 | | 1,286 | 1,500 |
| 1350 | Suspension | ↓ | 4 | 6 | L.F. | 500 | 186 | | 686 | 840 |

## 11 68 16 – Play Structures

### 11 68 16.10 Handball/Squash Court

| | | Crew | Daily Output | Labor-Hours | Unit | Material | 2008 Bare Costs Labor | Equipment | Total | Total Incl O&P |
|---|---|---|---|---|---|---|---|---|---|---|
| 0010 | **HANDBALL/SQUASH COURT**, outdoor | | | | | | | | | |
| 0900 | Handball or squash court, outdoor, wood | 2 Carp | .50 | 32 | Ea. | 4,400 | 1,225 | | 5,625 | 6,750 |
| 1000 | Masonry handball/squash court | D-1 | .30 | 53.333 | " | 23,900 | 1,850 | | 25,750 | 29,100 |

### 11 68 16.30 Platform/Paddle Tennis Court

| | | Crew | Daily Output | Labor-Hours | Unit | Material | 2008 Bare Costs Labor | Equipment | Total | Total Incl O&P |
|---|---|---|---|---|---|---|---|---|---|---|
| 0010 | **PLATFORM/PADDLE TENNIS COURT** Complete with lighting, etc. | | | | | | | | | |
| 0100 | Aluminum slat deck with aluminum frame | B-1 | .08 | 300 | Court | 50,500 | 9,275 | | 59,775 | 70,000 |
| 0500 | Aluminum slat deck with wood frame | C-1 | .12 | 266 | | 50,500 | 9,625 | | 60,125 | 70,500 |
| 0800 | Aluminum deck heater, add | B-1 | 1.18 | 20.339 | | 5,025 | 630 | | 5,655 | 6,500 |
| 0900 | Douglas fir planking with wood frame 2" x 6" x 30' | C-1 | .12 | 266 | | 47,600 | 9,625 | | 57,225 | 67,500 |
| 1000 | Plywood deck with steel frame | | .12 | 266 | | 47,600 | 9,625 | | 57,225 | 67,500 |
| 1100 | Steel slat deck with wood frame | ↓ | .12 | 266 | ↓ | 33,500 | 9,625 | | 43,125 | 52,000 |

## 11 68 33 – Athletic Field Equipment

### 11 68 33.13 Football Field Equipment

| | | Crew | Daily Output | Labor-Hours | Unit | Material | 2008 Bare Costs Labor | Equipment | Total | Total Incl O&P |
|---|---|---|---|---|---|---|---|---|---|---|
| 0010 | **FOOTBALL FIELD EQUIPMENT** | | | | | | | | | |
| 0020 | Goal posts, steel, football, double post | B-1 | 1.50 | 16 | Pr. | 1,950 | 495 | | 2,445 | 2,925 |
| 0100 | Deluxe, single post | | 1.50 | 16 | | 3,150 | 495 | | 3,645 | 4,225 |
| 0300 | Football, convertible to soccer | | 1.50 | 16 | | 3,125 | 495 | | 3,620 | 4,225 |
| 0500 | Soccer, regulation | ↓ | 2 | 12 | ↓ | 2,475 | 370 | | 2,845 | 3,300 |

# 11 71 Medical Sterilizing Equipment

## 11 71 10 – Medical Sterilizers & Distillers

### 11 71 10.10 Sterilizers and Distillers

| | 11 71 10.10 Sterilizers and Distillers | Crew | Daily Output | Labor-Hours | Unit | Material | 2008 Bare Costs Labor | Equipment | Total | Total Incl O&P |
|---|---|---|---|---|---|---|---|---|---|---|
| 0010 | **STERILIZERS AND DISTILLERS** | | | | | | | | | |
| 0700 | Distiller, water, steam heated, 50 gal. capacity | 1 Plum | 1.40 | 5.714 | Ea. | 17,100 | 267 | | 17,367 | 19,200 |
| 5600 | Sterilizers, floor loading, 26" x 62" x 42", single door, steam | | | | | 146,500 | | | 146,500 | 161,500 |
| 5650 | Double door, steam | | | | | 188,500 | | | 188,500 | 207,500 |
| 5800 | General purpose, 20" x 20" x 38", single door | | | | | 14,100 | | | 14,100 | 15,500 |
| 6000 | Portable, counter top, steam, minimum | | | | | 3,525 | | | 3,525 | 3,875 |
| 6020 | Maximum | | | | | 5,500 | | | 5,500 | 6,050 |
| 6050 | Portable, counter top, gas, 17" x 15" x 32-1/2" | | | | | 36,300 | | | 36,300 | 40,000 |
| 6150 | Manual washer/sterilizer, 16" x 16" x 26" | 1 Plum | 2 | 4 | ↓ | 49,800 | 187 | | 49,987 | 55,500 |
| 6200 | Steam generators, electric 10 kW to 180 kW, freestanding | | | | | | | | | |
| 6250 | Minimum | 1 Elec | 3 | 2.667 | Ea. | 7,400 | 121 | | 7,521 | 8,325 |
| 6300 | Maximum | " | .70 | 11.429 | | 26,600 | 520 | | 27,120 | 30,100 |
| 8200 | Bed pan washer-sanitizer | 1 Plum | 2 | 4 | ↓ | 6,600 | 187 | | 6,787 | 7,525 |

# 11 72 Examination and Treatment Equipment

## 11 72 13 – Examination Equipment

### 11 72 13.13 Examination Equipment

| | 11 72 13.13 Examination Equipment | Crew | Daily Output | Labor-Hours | Unit | Material | Labor | Equipment | Total | Total Incl O&P |
|---|---|---|---|---|---|---|---|---|---|---|
| 0010 | **EXAMINATION EQUIPMENT** | | | | | | | | | |
| 0300 | Blood pressure unit, mercurial, wall | | | | Ea. | 149 | | | 149 | 164 |
| 0400 | Diagnostic set, wall | | | | | 600 | | | 600 | 660 |
| 4400 | Scale, physician's, with height rod | | | | ↓ | 291 | | | 291 | 320 |

## 11 72 53 – Treatment Equipment

### 11 72 53.13 Medical Treatment Equipment

| | 11 72 53.13 Medical Treatment Equipment | Crew | Daily Output | Labor-Hours | Unit | Material | Labor | Equipment | Total | Total Incl O&P |
|---|---|---|---|---|---|---|---|---|---|---|
| 0010 | **MEDICAL TREATMENT EQUIPMENT** | | | | | | | | | |
| 6500 | Surgery table, minor minimum | 1 Sswk | .70 | 11.429 | Ea. | 12,800 | 490 | | 13,290 | 15,000 |
| 6520 | Maximum | " | .50 | 16 | | 24,100 | 690 | | 24,790 | 27,800 |
| 6700 | Surgical lights, doctor's office, single arm | 2 Elec | 2 | 8 | ↓ | 1,200 | 365 | | 1,565 | 1,850 |
| 6750 | Dual arm | " | 1 | 16 | | 5,375 | 730 | | 6,105 | 6,975 |

# 11 73 Patient Care Equipment

## 11 73 10 – Patient Treatment Equipment

### 11 73 10.10 Treatment Equipment

| | 11 73 10.10 Treatment Equipment | Crew | Daily Output | Labor-Hours | Unit | Material | Labor | Equipment | Total | Total Incl O&P |
|---|---|---|---|---|---|---|---|---|---|---|
| 0010 | **TREATMENT EQUIPMENT** | | | | | | | | | |
| 0750 | Exam room furnishings, average per room | | | | Ea. | 5,975 | | | 5,975 | 6,575 |
| 1800 | Heat therapy unit, humidified, 26" x 78" x 28" | | | | " | 3,150 | | | 3,150 | 3,450 |
| 2100 | Hubbard tank with accessories, stainless steel, | | | | | | | | | |
| 2110 | 125 GPM at 45 psi water pressure | | | | Ea. | 24,300 | | | 24,300 | 26,800 |
| 2150 | For electric overhead hoist, add | | | | | 2,650 | | | 2,650 | 2,925 |
| 2900 | K-Module for heat therapy, 20 oz. capacity, 75° to 110° F | | | | | 375 | | | 375 | 415 |
| 3600 | Paraffin bath, 126° F, auto controlled | | | | | 1,350 | | | 1,350 | 1,500 |
| 3900 | Parallel bars for walking training, 12'-0" | | | | | 1,125 | | | 1,125 | 1,225 |
| 4600 | Station, dietary, medium, with ice | | | | | 14,800 | | | 14,800 | 16,300 |
| 4700 | Medicine | | | | | 6,700 | | | 6,700 | 7,375 |
| 7000 | Tables, physical therapy, walk off, electric | 2 Carp | 3 | 5.333 | | 2,950 | 203 | | 3,153 | 3,575 |
| 7150 | Standard, vinyl top with base cabinets, minimum | | 3 | 5.333 | | 1,200 | 203 | | 1,403 | 1,650 |
| 7200 | Maximum | ↓ | 2 | 8 | | 3,575 | 305 | | 3,880 | 4,400 |
| 8400 | Whirlpool bath, mobile, sst, 18" x 24" x 60" | | | | | 4,150 | | | 4,150 | 4,575 |
| 8450 | Fixed, incl. mixing valves | 1 Plum | 2 | 4 | ↓ | 8,500 | 187 | | 8,687 | 9,650 |

# 11 74 Dental Equipment

## 11 74 10 – Dental Office Equipment

### 11 74 10.10 Diagnostic and Treatment Equipment

| | 11 74 10.10 Diagnostic and Treatment Equipment | Crew | Daily Output | Labor-Hours | Unit | Material | 2008 Bare Costs Labor | Equipment | Total | Total Incl O&P |
|---|---|---|---|---|---|---|---|---|---|---|
| 0010 | **DIAGNOSTIC AND TREATMENT EQUIPMENT** | | | | | | | | | |
| 0020 | Central suction system, minimum | 1 Plum | 1.20 | 6.667 | Ea. | 1,025 | 310 | | 1,335 | 1,625 |
| 0100 | Maximum | " | .90 | 8.889 | | 4,575 | 415 | | 4,990 | 5,650 |
| 0300 | Air compressor, minimum | 1 Skwk | .80 | 10 | | 2,200 | 395 | | 2,595 | 3,025 |
| 0400 | Maximum | | .50 | 16 | | 6,650 | 630 | | 7,280 | 8,300 |
| 0600 | Chair, electric or hydraulic, minimum | | .50 | 16 | | 3,700 | 630 | | 4,330 | 5,050 |
| 0700 | Maximum | | .25 | 32 | | 13,300 | 1,250 | | 14,550 | 16,700 |
| 0800 | Doctor's/assistant's stool, minimum | | | | | 189 | | | 189 | 208 |
| 0850 | Maximum | | | | | 750 | | | 750 | 825 |
| 1000 | Drill console with accessories, minimum | 1 Skwk | 1.60 | 5 | | 1,450 | 197 | | 1,647 | 1,900 |
| 1100 | Maximum | | 1.60 | 5 | | 4,675 | 197 | | 4,872 | 5,450 |
| 2000 | Light, ceiling mounted, minimum | | 8 | 1 | | 1,375 | 39.50 | | 1,414.50 | 1,550 |
| 2100 | Maximum | | 8 | 1 | | 1,625 | 39.50 | | 1,664.50 | 1,850 |
| 2200 | Unit light, minimum | 2 Skwk | 5.33 | 3.002 | | 560 | 118 | | 678 | 800 |
| 2210 | Maximum | | 5.33 | 3.002 | | 1,050 | 118 | | 1,168 | 1,350 |
| 2220 | Track light, minimum | | 3.20 | 5 | | 2,000 | 197 | | 2,197 | 2,500 |
| 2230 | Maximum | | 3.20 | 5 | | 3,425 | 197 | | 3,622 | 4,075 |
| 2300 | Sterilizers, steam portable, minimum | | | | | 1,175 | | | 1,175 | 1,300 |
| 2350 | Maximum | | | | | 9,600 | | | 9,600 | 10,600 |
| 2600 | Steam, institutional | | | | | 4,250 | | | 4,250 | 4,675 |
| 2650 | Dry heat, electric, portable, 3 trays | | | | | 1,125 | | | 1,125 | 1,225 |
| 2700 | Ultra-sonic cleaner, portable, minimum | | | | | 299 | | | 299 | 330 |
| 2750 | Maximum (institutional) | | | | | 1,400 | | | 1,400 | 1,550 |
| 3000 | X-ray unit, wall, minimum | 1 Skwk | 4 | 2 | | 2,150 | 79 | | 2,229 | 2,500 |
| 3010 | Maximum | | 4 | 2 | | 4,750 | 79 | | 4,829 | 5,350 |
| 3100 | Panoramic unit | | .60 | 13.333 | | 14,500 | 525 | | 15,025 | 16,700 |
| 3105 | Deluxe, minimum | 2 Skwk | 1.60 | 10 | | 16,100 | 395 | | 16,495 | 18,300 |
| 3110 | Maximum | " | 1.60 | 10 | | 50,000 | 395 | | 50,395 | 55,500 |
| 3500 | Developers, X-ray, average | 1 Plum | 5.33 | 1.501 | | 4,575 | 70 | | 4,645 | 5,125 |
| 3600 | Maximum | " | 5.33 | 1.501 | | 7,475 | 70 | | 7,545 | 8,325 |

# 11 76 Operating Room Equipment

## 11 76 10 – Operating Room Equipment

### 11 76 10.10 Surgical Equipment

| | 11 76 10.10 Surgical Equipment | Crew | Daily Output | Labor-Hours | Unit | Material | 2008 Bare Costs Labor | Equipment | Total | Total Incl O&P |
|---|---|---|---|---|---|---|---|---|---|---|
| 0010 | **SURGICAL EQUIPMENT** | | | | | | | | | |
| 5000 | Scrub, surgical, stainless steel, single station, minimum | 1 Plum | 3 | 2.667 | Ea. | 3,775 | 125 | | 3,900 | 4,325 |
| 5100 | Maximum | | | | | 7,800 | | | 7,800 | 8,575 |
| 6550 | Major surgery table, minimum | 1 Sswk | .50 | 16 | | 29,100 | 690 | | 29,790 | 33,300 |
| 6570 | Maximum | " | .50 | 16 | | 96,000 | 690 | | 96,690 | 107,000 |
| 6800 | Surgical lights, major operating room, dual head, minimum | 2 Elec | 1 | 16 | | 16,100 | 730 | | 16,830 | 18,900 |
| 6850 | Maximum | " | 1 | 16 | | 26,900 | 730 | | 27,630 | 30,700 |

# 11 77 Radiology Equipment

## 11 77 10 – Radiology Equipment

| 11 77 10.10 X-Ray Equipment | Crew | Daily Output | Labor-Hours | Unit | Material | 2008 Bare Costs Labor | Equipment | Total | Total Incl O&P |
|---|---|---|---|---|---|---|---|---|---|
| 0010 **X-RAY EQUIPMENT** | | | | | | | | | |
| 8700 X-ray, mobile, minimum | | | | Ea. | 12,400 | | | 12,400 | 13,600 |
| 8750 Maximum | | | | | 69,500 | | | 69,500 | 76,500 |
| 8900 Stationary, minimum | | | | | 38,700 | | | 38,700 | 42,600 |
| 8950 Maximum | | | | | 201,000 | | | 201,000 | 221,500 |
| 9150 Developing processors, minimum | | | | | 10,800 | | | 10,800 | 11,800 |
| 9200 Maximum | | | | | 28,300 | | | 28,300 | 31,100 |

# 11 78 Mortuary Equipment

## 11 78 13 – Mortuary Refrigerators

### 11 78 13.10 Mortuary and Autopsy Equipment

| | Crew | Daily Output | Labor-Hours | Unit | Material | 2008 Bare Costs Labor | Equipment | Total | Total Incl O&P |
|---|---|---|---|---|---|---|---|---|---|
| 0010 **MORTUARY AND AUTOPSY EQUIPMENT** | | | | | | | | | |
| 0015 Autopsy table, standard | 1 Plum | 1 | 8 | Ea. | 8,200 | 375 | | 8,575 | 9,575 |
| 0020 Deluxe | " | .60 | 13.333 | | 15,600 | 625 | | 16,225 | 18,100 |
| 3200 Mortuary refrigerator, end operated, 2 capacity | | | | | 11,400 | | | 11,400 | 12,500 |
| 3300 6 capacity | | | | | 20,500 | | | 20,500 | 22,500 |

## 11 78 16 – Crematorium Equipment

### 11 78 16.10 Crematory

| | Crew | Daily Output | Labor-Hours | Unit | Material | 2008 Bare Costs Labor | Equipment | Total | Total Incl O&P |
|---|---|---|---|---|---|---|---|---|---|
| 0010 **CREMATORY** | | | | | | | | | |
| 1500 Crematory, not including building, 1 place | Q-3 | .20 | 160 | Ea. | 57,000 | 7,125 | | 64,125 | 73,000 |
| 1750 2 place | " | .10 | 320 | " | 81,000 | 14,200 | | 95,200 | 110,500 |

# 11 82 Solid Waste Handling Equipment

## 11 82 19 – Packaged Incinerators

### 11 82 19.10 Packaged Gas Fired Incinerators

| | Crew | Daily Output | Labor-Hours | Unit | Material | 2008 Bare Costs Labor | Equipment | Total | Total Incl O&P |
|---|---|---|---|---|---|---|---|---|---|
| 0010 **PACKAGED GAS FIRED INCINERATORS** | | | | | | | | | |
| 4400 Incinerator, gas, not incl. chimney, elec. or pipe, 50#/hr., minimum | Q-3 | .80 | 40 | Ea. | 11,200 | 1,775 | | 12,975 | 15,000 |
| 4420 Maximum | | .70 | 45.714 | | 35,000 | 2,025 | | 37,025 | 41,600 |
| 4440 200 lb. per hr., minimum (batch type) | | .60 | 53.333 | | 62,000 | 2,375 | | 64,375 | 71,500 |
| 4460 Maximum (with feeder) | | .50 | 64 | | 85,000 | 2,850 | | 87,850 | 98,000 |
| 4480 400 lb. per hr., minimum (batch type) | | .30 | 106 | | 68,500 | 4,750 | | 73,250 | 82,500 |
| 4500 Maximum (with feeder) | | .25 | 128 | | 90,000 | 5,700 | | 95,700 | 107,500 |
| 4520 800 lb. per hr., with feeder, minimum | | .20 | 160 | | 112,000 | 7,125 | | 119,125 | 133,500 |
| 4540 Maximum | | .17 | 188 | | 150,000 | 8,375 | | 158,375 | 177,500 |
| 4560 1,200 lb. per hr., with feeder, minimum | | .15 | 213 | | 179,500 | 9,500 | | 189,000 | 211,500 |
| 4580 Maximum | | .11 | 290 | | 146,000 | 12,900 | | 158,900 | 180,000 |
| 4600 2,000 lb. per hr., with feeder, minimum | | .10 | 320 | | 504,000 | 14,200 | | 518,200 | 576,000 |
| 4620 Maximum | | .05 | 640 | | 357,000 | 28,500 | | 385,500 | 435,500 |
| 4700 For heat recovery system, add, minimum | | .25 | 128 | | 69,000 | 5,700 | | 74,700 | 84,500 |
| 4710 Add, maximum | | .11 | 290 | | 220,500 | 12,900 | | 233,400 | 262,000 |
| 4720 For automatic ash conveyer, add | | .50 | 64 | | 29,000 | 2,850 | | 31,850 | 36,200 |
| 4750 Large municipal incinerators, incl. stack, minimum | | .25 | 128 | Ton/day | 17,600 | 5,700 | | 23,300 | 28,000 |
| 4850 Maximum | | .10 | 320 | " | 46,800 | 14,200 | | 61,000 | 73,000 |

## 11 82 26 – Waste Compactors and Destructors

### 11 82 26.10 Compactors

| | Crew | Daily Output | Labor-Hours | Unit | Material | 2008 Bare Costs Labor | Equipment | Total | Total Incl O&P |
|---|---|---|---|---|---|---|---|---|---|
| 0010 **COMPACTORS** | | | | | | | | | |
| 0020 Compactors, 115 volt, 250#/hr., chute fed | L-4 | 1 | 24 | Ea. | 10,400 | 865 | | 11,265 | 12,800 |
| 0100 Hand fed | | 2.40 | 10 | | 7,600 | 360 | | 7,960 | 8,900 |

# 11 82 Solid Waste Handling Equipment

## 11 82 26 – Waste Compactors and Destructors

| 11 82 26.10 Compactors | Crew | Daily Output | Labor-Hours | Unit | Material | 2008 Bare Costs Labor | 2008 Bare Costs Equipment | Total | Total Incl O&P |
|---|---|---|---|---|---|---|---|---|---|
| 0300 | Multi-bag, 230 volt, 600#/hr, chute fed | L-4 | 1 | 24 | Ea. | 9,425 | 865 | | 10,290 | 11,800 |
| 0400 | Hand fed | | 1 | 24 | | 8,100 | 865 | | 8,965 | 10,300 |
| 0500 | Containerized, hand fed, 2 to 6 C.Y. containers, 250#/hr. | | 1 | 24 | | 10,000 | 865 | | 10,865 | 12,400 |
| 0550 | For chute fed, add per floor | | 1 | 24 | | 1,150 | 865 | | 2,015 | 2,625 |
| 1000 | Heavy duty industrial compactor, 0.5 C.Y. capacity | | 1 | 24 | | 6,750 | 865 | | 7,615 | 8,775 |
| 1050 | 1.0 C.Y. capacity | | 1 | 24 | | 10,300 | 865 | | 11,165 | 12,700 |
| 1100 | 3 C.Y. capacity | | .50 | 48 | | 14,100 | 1,725 | | 15,825 | 18,200 |
| 1150 | 5.0 C.Y. capacity | | .50 | 48 | | 17,400 | 1,725 | | 19,125 | 21,800 |
| 1200 | Combination shredder/compactor (5,000 lbs./hr.) | | .50 | 48 | | 34,400 | 1,725 | | 36,125 | 40,500 |
| 1400 | For handling hazardous waste materials, 55 gallon drum packer, std. | | | | | 16,000 | | | 16,000 | 17,600 |
| 1410 | 55 gallon drum packer w/HEPA filter | | | | | 19,900 | | | 19,900 | 21,900 |
| 1420 | 55 gallon drum packer w/charcoal & HEPA filter | | | | | 26,600 | | | 26,600 | 29,300 |
| 1430 | All of the above made explosion proof, add | | | | | 12,100 | | | 12,100 | 13,400 |
| 5500 | Shredder, municipal use, 35 ton per hour | | | | | 262,000 | | | 262,000 | 288,500 |
| 5600 | 60 ton per hour | | | | | 558,500 | | | 558,500 | 614,500 |
| 5750 | Shredder & baler, 50 ton per day | | | | | 523,500 | | | 523,500 | 576,000 |
| 5800 | Shredder, industrial, minimum | | | | | 20,600 | | | 20,600 | 22,700 |
| 5850 | Maximum | | | | | 110,500 | | | 110,500 | 121,500 |
| 5900 | Baler, industrial, minimum | | | | | 8,250 | | | 8,250 | 9,075 |
| 5950 | Maximum | | | | | 482,500 | | | 482,500 | 531,000 |
| 6000 | Transfer station compactor, with power unit | | | | | | | | | |
| 6050 | and pedestal, not including pit, 50 ton per hour | | | | Ea. | 165,000 | | | 165,000 | 181,500 |

# 11 91 Religious Equipment

## 11 91 13 – Baptistries

### 11 91 13.10 Baptistry

| | | Crew | Daily Output | Labor-Hours | Unit | Material | Labor | Equipment | Total | Total Incl O&P |
|---|---|---|---|---|---|---|---|---|---|---|
| 0010 | **BAPTISTRY** | | | | | | | | | |
| 0150 | Fiberglass, 3'-6" deep, x 13'-7" long, | | | | | | | | | |
| 0160 | steps at both ends, incl. plumbing, minimum | L-8 | 1 | 20 | Ea. | 3,475 | 795 | | 4,270 | 5,050 |
| 0200 | Maximum | " | .70 | 28.571 | | 5,675 | 1,150 | | 6,825 | 8,000 |
| 0250 | Add for filter, heater and lights | | | | | 1,250 | | | 1,250 | 1,375 |

## 11 91 23 – Sanctuary Equipment

### 11 91 23.10 Sanctuary Furnishings

| | | Crew | Daily Output | Labor-Hours | Unit | Material | Labor | Equipment | Total | Total Incl O&P |
|---|---|---|---|---|---|---|---|---|---|---|
| 0010 | **SANCTUARY FURNISHINGS** | | | | | | | | | |
| 0020 | Altar, wood, custom design, plain | 1 Carp | 1.40 | 5.714 | Ea. | 1,925 | 218 | | 2,143 | 2,450 |
| 0050 | Deluxe | " | .20 | 40 | | 9,225 | 1,525 | | 10,750 | 12,600 |
| 0070 | Granite or marble, average | 2 Marb | .50 | 32 | | 8,525 | 1,200 | | 9,725 | 11,200 |
| 0090 | Deluxe | " | .20 | 80 | | 24,300 | 3,000 | | 27,300 | 31,300 |
| 0100 | Arks, prefabricated, plain | 2 Carp | .80 | 20 | | 7,300 | 760 | | 8,060 | 9,200 |
| 0130 | Deluxe, maximum | " | .20 | 80 | | 91,000 | 3,050 | | 94,050 | 105,000 |
| 0500 | Reconciliation room, wood, prefabricated, single, plain | 1 Carp | .60 | 13.333 | | 2,425 | 510 | | 2,935 | 3,475 |
| 0550 | Deluxe | | .40 | 20 | | 6,675 | 760 | | 7,435 | 8,525 |
| 0650 | Double, plain | | .40 | 20 | | 4,850 | 760 | | 5,610 | 6,525 |
| 0700 | Deluxe | | .20 | 40 | | 15,200 | 1,525 | | 16,725 | 19,100 |
| 1000 | Lecterns, wood, plain | | 5 | 1.600 | | 685 | 61 | | 746 | 850 |
| 1100 | Deluxe | | 2 | 4 | | 5,000 | 152 | | 5,152 | 5,725 |
| 2000 | Pulpits, hardwood, prefabricated, plain | | 2 | 4 | | 1,225 | 152 | | 1,377 | 1,575 |
| 2100 | Deluxe | | 1.60 | 5 | | 8,325 | 191 | | 8,516 | 9,450 |
| 2500 | Railing, hardwood, average | | 25 | .320 | L.F. | 151 | 12.20 | | 163.20 | 185 |
| 3000 | Seating, individual, oak, contour, laminated | | 21 | .381 | Person | 133 | 14.50 | | 147.50 | 170 |

| 11 91 23.10 Sanctuary Furnishings | Crew | Daily Output | Labor-Hours | Unit | Material | 2008 Bare Costs Labor | Equipment | Total | Total Incl O&P |
|---|---|---|---|---|---|---|---|---|---|
| 3100 Cushion seat | 1 Carp | 21 | .381 | Person | 121 | 14.50 | | 135.50 | 156 |
| 3200 Fully upholstered | | 21 | .381 | | 108 | 14.50 | | 122.50 | 142 |
| 3300 Combination, self-rising | | 21 | .381 | | 335 | 14.50 | | 349.50 | 390 |
| 3500 For cherry, add | | | | | 30% | | | | |
| 5000 Wall cross, aluminum, extruded, 2" x 2" section | 1 Carp | 34 | .235 | L.F. | 110 | 8.95 | | 118.95 | 135 |
| 5150     4" x 4" section | | 29 | .276 | | 158 | 10.50 | | 168.50 | 190 |
| 5300 Bronze, extruded, 1" x 2" section | | 31 | .258 | | 217 | 9.85 | | 226.85 | 253 |
| 5350     2-1/2" x 2-1/2" section | | 34 | .235 | | 330 | 8.95 | | 338.95 | 375 |
| 5450     Solid bar stock, 1/2" x 3" section | | 29 | .276 | | 430 | 10.50 | | 440.50 | 490 |
| 5600 Fiberglass, stock | | 34 | .235 | | 89 | 8.95 | | 97.95 | 112 |
| 5700 Stainless steel, 4" deep, channel section | | 29 | .276 | | 350 | 10.50 | | 360.50 | 400 |
| 5800     4" deep box section | | 29 | .276 | | 475 | 10.50 | | 485.50 | 535 |

# Division Notes

| | | CREW | DAILY OUTPUT | LABOR-HOURS | UNIT | 2008 BARE COSTS | | | | TOTAL INCL O&P |
|---|---|---|---|---|---|---|---|---|---|---|
| | | | | | | MAT. | LABOR | EQUIP. | TOTAL | |
| | | | | | | | | | | |
| | | | | | | | | | | |
| | | | | | | | | | | |
| | | | | | | | | | | |
| | | | | | | | | | | |
| | | | | | | | | | | |
| | | | | | | | | | | |
| | | | | | | | | | | |
| | | | | | | | | | | |
| | | | | | | | | | | |
| | | | | | | | | | | |
| | | | | | | | | | | |
| | | | | | | | | | | |
| | | | | | | | | | | |
| | | | | | | | | | | |
| | | | | | | | | | | |
| | | | | | | | | | | |
| | | | | | | | | | | |
| | | | | | | | | | | |
| | | | | | | | | | | |
| | | | | | | | | | | |

# Estimating Tips

## General

• The items in this division are usually priced per square foot or each. Most of these items are purchased by the owner and placed by the supplier.
Do not assume the items in Division 12 will be purchased and installed by the supplier. Check the specifications for responsibilities and include receiving, storage, installation, and mechanical and electrical hookups in the appropriate divisions.

• Some items in this division require some type of support system that is not usually furnished with the item. Examples of these systems include blocking for the attachment of casework and heavy drapery rods. The required blocking must be added to the estimate in the appropriate division.

# Reference Numbers

Reference numbers are shown in shaded boxes at the beginning of some major classifications. These numbers refer to related items in the Reference Section. The reference information may be an estimating procedure, an alternate pricing method, or technical information.

*Note:* Not all subdivisions listed here necessarily appear in this publication.

**Division 12 - Furnishings**

# 12 21 Window Blinds

## 12 21 13 – Horizontal Louver Blinds

### 12 21 13.13 Metal Horizontal Louver Blinds

| | | Crew | Daily Output | Labor-Hours | Unit | Material | 2008 Bare Costs | | Total | Total Incl O&P |
|---|---|---|---|---|---|---|---|---|---|---|
| | | | | | | | Labor | Equipment | | |
| 0010 | **METAL HORIZONTAL LOUVER BLINDS** | | | | | | | | | |
| 0020 | Horizontal, 1" aluminum slats, solid color, stock | 1 Carp | 590 | .014 | S.F. | 4.01 | .52 | | 4.53 | 5.20 |
| 0090 | Custom, minimum | | 590 | .014 | | 3.07 | .52 | | 3.59 | 4.18 |
| 0100 | Maximum | | 440 | .018 | | 5.55 | .69 | | 6.24 | 7.25 |
| 0250 | 2" aluminum slats, custom, minimum | | 590 | .014 | | 3.53 | .52 | | 4.05 | 4.68 |
| 0350 | Maximum | | 440 | .018 | | 5.85 | .69 | | 6.54 | 7.50 |
| 0450 | Stock, minimum | | 590 | .014 | | 4.72 | .52 | | 5.24 | 6 |
| 0500 | Maximum | | 440 | .018 | | 7.70 | .69 | | 8.39 | 9.55 |
| 0600 | 2" steel slats, stock, minimum | | 590 | .014 | | 1.79 | .52 | | 2.31 | 2.77 |
| 0630 | Maximum | | 440 | .018 | | 5 | .69 | | 5.69 | 6.60 |
| 0750 | Custom, minimum | | 590 | .014 | | 1.62 | .52 | | 2.14 | 2.58 |
| 0850 | Maximum | | 400 | .020 | | 8 | .76 | | 8.76 | 10 |

## 12 21 16 – Vertical Louver Blinds

### 12 21 16.13 Metal Vertical Louver Blinds

| | | | Crew | Daily Output | Labor-Hours | Unit | Material | Labor | Equipment | Total | Total Incl O&P |
|---|---|---|---|---|---|---|---|---|---|---|---|
| 0010 | **METAL VERTICAL LOUVER BLINDS** | | | | | | | | | | |
| 1500 | Vertical, 3" to 5" PVC or cloth strips, minimum | *CN* | 1 Carp | 460 | .017 | S.F. | 5.20 | .66 | | 5.86 | 6.75 |
| 1600 | Maximum | | | 400 | .020 | | 10.60 | .76 | | 11.36 | 12.85 |
| 1800 | 4" aluminum slats, minimum | | | 460 | .017 | | 7 | .66 | | 7.66 | 8.75 |
| 1900 | Maximum | | | 400 | .020 | | 8.85 | .76 | | 9.61 | 10.90 |
| 1950 | Mylar mirror-finish strips, to 8" wide, minimum | | | 460 | .017 | | 3.35 | .66 | | 4.01 | 4.72 |
| 1970 | Maximum | | | 400 | .020 | | 8.85 | .76 | | 9.61 | 10.95 |

# 12 22 Curtains and Drapes

## 12 22 16 – Drapery Track and Accessories

### 12 22 16.10 Drapery Hardware

| | | Crew | Daily Output | Labor-Hours | Unit | Material | Labor | Equipment | Total | Total Incl O&P |
|---|---|---|---|---|---|---|---|---|---|---|
| 0010 | **DRAPERY HARDWARE** | | | | | | | | | |
| 0030 | Standard traverse, per foot, minimum | 1 Carp | 59 | .136 | L.F. | 3.44 | 5.15 | | 8.59 | 11.85 |
| 0100 | Maximum | | 51 | .157 | " | 9.95 | 6 | | 15.95 | 20.50 |
| 4000 | Traverse rods, adjustable, 28" to 48" | | 22 | .364 | Ea. | 20.50 | 13.85 | | 34.35 | 44 |
| 4020 | 48" to 84" | | 20 | .400 | | 27.50 | 15.25 | | 42.75 | 54 |
| 4040 | 66" to 120" | | 18 | .444 | | 39.50 | 16.95 | | 56.45 | 70 |
| 4060 | 84" to 156" | | 16 | .500 | | 32.50 | 19.05 | | 51.55 | 65 |
| 4080 | 100" to 180" | | 14 | .571 | | 41.50 | 22 | | 63.50 | 79.50 |
| 4090 | 156" to 228" | | 13 | .615 | | 48.50 | 23.50 | | 72 | 90 |
| 4100 | 228" to 312" | | 13 | .615 | | 58.50 | 23.50 | | 82 | 101 |
| 4200 | Double rods, adjustable, 30" to 48" | | 9 | .889 | | 42 | 34 | | 76 | 99 |
| 4220 | 48" to 86" | | 9 | .889 | | 43.50 | 34 | | 77.50 | 101 |
| 4240 | 86" to 150" | | 8 | 1 | | 56.50 | 38 | | 94.50 | 122 |
| 4260 | 100" to 180" | | 7 | 1.143 | | 58 | 43.50 | | 101.50 | 132 |
| 4300 | Tray and curtain rod, adjustable, 30" to 48" | | 9 | .889 | | 23 | 34 | | 57 | 78 |
| 4320 | 48" to 86" | | 9 | .889 | | 38.50 | 34 | | 72.50 | 95 |
| 4340 | 86" to 150" | | 8 | 1 | | 39.50 | 38 | | 77.50 | 103 |
| 4360 | 100" to 180" | | 7 | 1.143 | | 45.50 | 43.50 | | 89 | 118 |
| 4600 | Valance, pinch pleated fabric, 12" deep, up to 54" long, minimum | | | | | 36 | | | 36 | 39.50 |
| 4610 | Maximum | | | | | 90 | | | 90 | 99 |
| 4620 | Up to 77" long, minimum | | | | | 55 | | | 55 | 60.50 |
| 4630 | Maximum | | | | | 145 | | | 145 | 160 |
| 5000 | Stationary rods, first 2' | | | | | 9.70 | | | 9.70 | 10.70 |
| 5020 | Each additional foot, add | | | | L.F. | 3.57 | | | 3.57 | 3.93 |

368

# 12 22 Curtains and Drapes

## 12 22 16 – Drapery Track and Accessories

| 12 22 16.20 Blast Curtains | Crew | Daily Output | Labor-Hours | Unit | Material | 2008 Bare Costs Labor | Equipment | Total | Total Incl O&P |
|---|---|---|---|---|---|---|---|---|---|
| 0010 **BLAST CURTAINS**, per LF horizontal opening width, off-white or gray fabric | | | | | | | | | |
| 0100 Blast curtains, drapery system, complete, including hardware, minimum | | | | L.F. | | | | 119 | 131 |
| 0120 Average | | | | | | | | 129 | 142 |
| 0140 Maximum | | | | ↓ | | | | 138 | 152 |

# 12 23 Interior Shutters

## 12 23 10 – Wood Interior Shutters

### 12 23 10.10 Wood Interior Shutters

| | | Crew | Daily Output | Labor-Hours | Unit | Material | Labor | Equipment | Total | Total Incl O&P |
|---|---|---|---|---|---|---|---|---|---|---|
| 0010 | **WOOD INTERIOR SHUTTERS**, louvered | | | | | | | | | |
| 0200 | Two panel, 27" wide, 36" high | 1 Carp | 5 | 1.600 | Set | 114 | 61 | | 175 | 220 |
| 0300 | 33" wide, 36" high | | 5 | 1.600 | | 149 | 61 | | 210 | 259 |
| 0500 | 47" wide, 36" high | | 5 | 1.600 | | 199 | 61 | | 260 | 315 |
| 1000 | Four panel, 27" wide, 36" high | | 5 | 1.600 | | 134 | 61 | | 195 | 243 |
| 1100 | 33" wide, 36" high | | 5 | 1.600 | | 165 | 61 | | 226 | 276 |
| 1300 | 47" wide, 36" high | ↓ | 5 | 1.600 | ↓ | 234 | 61 | | 295 | 355 |

### 12 23 10.13 Wood Panels

| | | Crew | Daily Output | Labor-Hours | Unit | Material | Labor | Equipment | Total | Total Incl O&P |
|---|---|---|---|---|---|---|---|---|---|---|
| 0010 | **WOOD PANELS** | | | | | | | | | |
| 3000 | Wood folding panels with movable louvers, 7" x 20" each | 1 Carp | 17 | .471 | Pr. | 49.50 | 17.95 | | 67.45 | 82.50 |
| 3300 | 8" x 28" each | | 17 | .471 | | 71.50 | 17.95 | | 89.45 | 107 |
| 3450 | 9" x 36" each | | 17 | .471 | | 85.50 | 17.95 | | 103.45 | 122 |
| 3600 | 10" x 40" each | | 17 | .471 | | 96.50 | 17.95 | | 114.45 | 134 |
| 4000 | Fixed louver type, stock units, 8" x 20" each | | 17 | .471 | | 74.50 | 17.95 | | 92.45 | 110 |
| 4150 | 10" x 28" each | | 17 | .471 | | 82.50 | 17.95 | | 100.45 | 119 |
| 4300 | 12" x 36" each | | 17 | .471 | | 99 | 17.95 | | 116.95 | 137 |
| 4450 | 18" x 40" each | | 17 | .471 | | 160 | 17.95 | | 177.95 | 204 |
| 5000 | Insert panel type, stock, 7" x 20" each | | 17 | .471 | | 18.35 | 17.95 | | 36.30 | 48 |
| 5150 | 8" x 28" each | | 17 | .471 | | 33.50 | 17.95 | | 51.45 | 65 |
| 5300 | 9" x 36" each | | 17 | .471 | | 43 | 17.95 | | 60.95 | 75 |
| 5450 | 10" x 40" each | | 17 | .471 | | 46 | 17.95 | | 63.95 | 78.50 |
| 5600 | Raised panel type, stock, 10" x 24" each | | 17 | .471 | | 197 | 17.95 | | 214.95 | 245 |
| 5650 | 12" x 26" each | | 17 | .471 | | 149 | 17.95 | | 166.95 | 192 |
| 5700 | 14" x 30" each | | 17 | .471 | | 168 | 17.95 | | 185.95 | 213 |
| 5750 | 16" x 36" each | ↓ | 17 | .471 | | 189 | 17.95 | | 206.95 | 235 |
| 6000 | For custom built pine, add | | | | | 22% | | | | |
| 6500 | For custom built hardwood blinds, add | | | | ↓ | 42% | | | | |

# 12 24 Window Shades

## 12 24 13 – Roller Window Shades

### 12 24 13.10 Shades

| | | Crew | Daily Output | Labor-Hours | Unit | Material | Labor | Equipment | Total | Total Incl O&P |
|---|---|---|---|---|---|---|---|---|---|---|
| 0010 | **SHADES** | | | | | | | | | |
| 0020 | Basswood, roll-up, stain finish, 3/8" slats | 1 Carp | 300 | .027 | S.F. | 11.15 | 1.02 | | 12.17 | 13.85 |
| 0200 | 7/8" slats | | 300 | .027 | | 10.55 | 1.02 | | 11.57 | 13.20 |
| 0300 | Vertical side slide, stain finish, 3/8" slats | | 300 | .027 | | 16.85 | 1.02 | | 17.87 | 20 |
| 0400 | 7/8" slats | ↓ | 300 | .027 | | 16.85 | 1.02 | | 17.87 | 20 |
| 0500 | For fire retardant finishes, add | | | | | 16% | | | | |
| 0600 | For "B" rated finishes, add | | | | | 20% | | | | |
| 0900 | Mylar, single layer, non-heat reflective | 1 Carp | 685 | .012 | | 6.60 | .45 | | 7.05 | 7.95 |
| 1000 | Double layered, heat reflective | ↓ | 685 | .012 | ↓ | 9.10 | .45 | | 9.55 | 10.70 |

# 12 24 Window Shades

## 12 24 13 – Roller Window Shades

### 12 24 13.10 Shades

| | 12 24 13.10 Shades | Crew | Daily Output | Labor-Hours | Unit | Material | 2008 Bare Costs Labor | Equipment | Total | Total Incl O&P |
|---|---|---|---|---|---|---|---|---|---|---|
| 1100 | Triple layered, heat reflective | 1 Carp | 685 | .012 | S.F. | 10.55 | .45 | | 11 | 12.35 |
| 1200 | For metal roller instead of wood, add per | | | | Shade | 3.92 | | | 3.92 | 4.31 |
| 1300 | Vinyl coated cotton, standard | 1 Carp | 685 | .012 | S.F. | 2.21 | .45 | | 2.66 | 3.12 |
| 1400 | Lightproof decorator shades | | 685 | .012 | | 2 | .45 | | 2.45 | 2.89 |
| 1500 | Vinyl, lightweight, 4 gauge | | 685 | .012 | | .52 | .45 | | .97 | 1.26 |
| 1600 | Heavyweight, 6 gauge | | 685 | .012 | | 1.59 | .45 | | 2.04 | 2.44 |
| 1700 | Vinyl laminated fiberglass, 6 ga., translucent | | 685 | .012 | | 2.25 | .45 | | 2.70 | 3.17 |
| 1800 | Lightproof | | 685 | .012 | | 3.65 | .45 | | 4.10 | 4.71 |
| 3000 | Woven aluminum, 3/8" thick, lightproof and fireproof | | 350 | .023 | | 5.10 | .87 | | 5.97 | 7 |

# 12 32 Manufactured Wood Casework

## 12 32 16 – Manufactured Plastic-Laminate-Clad Casework

### 12 32 16.20 Plastic Laminate Casework Doors

| | | Crew | Daily Output | Labor-Hours | Unit | Material | 2008 Bare Costs Labor | Equipment | Total | Total Incl O&P |
|---|---|---|---|---|---|---|---|---|---|---|
| 0010 | **PLASTIC LAMINATE CASEWORK DOORS** | | | | | | | | | |
| 1000 | For casework frames, see Div. 12 32 23.15 | | | | | | | | | |
| 1100 | For casework hardware, see Div. 12 32 23.35 | | | | | | | | | |
| 6000 | Plastic laminate on particle board | | | | | | | | | |
| 6100 | 12" wide, 18" high | 1 Carp | 25 | .320 | Ea. | 10.75 | 12.20 | | 22.95 | 31 |
| 6140 | 30" high | | 23 | .348 | | 17.95 | 13.25 | | 31.20 | 40.50 |
| 6500 | 18" wide, 18" high | | 24 | .333 | | 16.15 | 12.70 | | 28.85 | 37.50 |
| 6600 | 30" high | | 22 | .364 | | 27 | 13.85 | | 40.85 | 51 |

### 12 32 16.25 Plastic Laminate Drawer Fronts

| | | Crew | Daily Output | Labor-Hours | Unit | Material | 2008 Bare Costs Labor | Equipment | Total | Total Incl O&P |
|---|---|---|---|---|---|---|---|---|---|---|
| 0010 | **PLASTIC LAMINATE DRAWER FRONTS** | | | | | | | | | |
| 2800 | Plastic laminate on particle board front | | | | | | | | | |
| 3000 | 4" high, 12" wide | 1 Carp | 17 | .471 | Ea. | 4.57 | 17.95 | | 22.52 | 33 |
| 3200 | 18" wide | " | 16 | .500 | " | 6.85 | 19.05 | | 25.90 | 37 |

## 12 32 23 – Hardwood Casework

### 12 32 23.10 Manufactured Wood Casework, Stock Units

| | | Crew | Daily Output | Labor-Hours | Unit | Material | 2008 Bare Costs Labor | Equipment | Total | Total Incl O&P |
|---|---|---|---|---|---|---|---|---|---|---|
| 0010 | **MANUFACTURED WOOD CASEWORK, STOCK UNITS** | | | | | | | | | |
| 0300 | Built-in drawer units, pine, 18" deep, 32" high, unfinished | | | | | | | | | |
| 0400 | Minimum | 2 Carp | 53 | .302 | L.F. | 125 | 11.50 | | 136.50 | 155 |
| 0500 | Maximum | " | 40 | .400 | " | 152 | 15.25 | | 167.25 | 191 |
| 0700 | Kitchen base cabinets, hardwood, not incl. counter tops, | | | | | | | | | |
| 0710 | 24" deep, 35" high, prefinished | | | | | | | | | |
| 0800 | One top drawer, one door below, 12" wide | 2 Carp | 24.80 | .645 | Ea. | 202 | 24.50 | | 226.50 | 262 |
| 0840 | 18" wide | | 23.30 | .687 | | 232 | 26 | | 258 | 296 |
| 0880 | 24" wide | | 22.30 | .717 | | 276 | 27.50 | | 303.50 | 350 |
| 1000 | Four drawers, 12" wide | | 24.80 | .645 | | 365 | 24.50 | | 389.50 | 440 |
| 1040 | 18" wide | | 23.30 | .687 | | 330 | 26 | | 356 | 405 |
| 1060 | 24" wide | | 22.30 | .717 | | 360 | 27.50 | | 387.50 | 440 |
| 1200 | Two top drawers, two doors below, 27" wide | | 22 | .727 | | 305 | 27.50 | | 332.50 | 385 |
| 1260 | 36" wide | | 20.30 | .788 | | 380 | 30 | | 410 | 465 |
| 1300 | 48" wide | | 18.90 | .847 | | 425 | 32.50 | | 457.50 | 520 |
| 1500 | Range or sink base, two doors below, 30" wide | | 21.40 | .748 | | 300 | 28.50 | | 328.50 | 375 |
| 1540 | 36" wide | | 20.30 | .788 | | 335 | 30 | | 365 | 410 |
| 1580 | 48" wide | | 18.90 | .847 | | 370 | 32.50 | | 402.50 | 455 |
| 1800 | For sink front units, deduct | | | | | 58 | | | 58 | 64 |
| 2000 | Corner base cabinets, 36" wide, standard | 2 Carp | 18 | .889 | | 435 | 34 | | 469 | 535 |
| 2100 | Lazy Susan with revolving door | " | 16.50 | .970 | | 430 | 37 | | 467 | 535 |
| 4000 | Kitchen wall cabinets, hardwood, 12" deep with two doors | | | | | | | | | |

# 12 32 Manufactured Wood Casework

## 12 32 23 – Hardwood Casework

### 12 32 23.10 Manufactured Wood Casework, Stock Units

| | | Crew | Daily Output | Labor-Hours | Unit | Material | 2008 Bare Costs Labor | Equipment | Total | Total Incl O&P |
|---|---|---|---|---|---|---|---|---|---|---|
| 4050 | 12" high, 30" wide | 2 Carp | 24.80 | .645 | Ea. | 163 | 24.50 | | 187.50 | 218 |
| 4100 | 36" wide | | 24 | .667 | | 190 | 25.50 | | 215.50 | 249 |
| 4400 | 15" high, 30" wide | | 24 | .667 | | 174 | 25.50 | | 199.50 | 231 |
| 4440 | 36" wide | | 22.70 | .705 | | 196 | 27 | | 223 | 258 |
| 4700 | 24" high, 30" wide | | 23.30 | .687 | | 215 | 26 | | 241 | 278 |
| 4720 | 36" wide | | 22.70 | .705 | | 238 | 27 | | 265 | 305 |
| 5000 | 30" high, one door, 12" wide | | 22 | .727 | | 146 | 27.50 | | 173.50 | 203 |
| 5040 | 18" wide | | 20.90 | .766 | | 180 | 29 | | 209 | 244 |
| 5060 | 24" wide | | 20.30 | .788 | | 203 | 30 | | 233 | 270 |
| 5300 | Two doors, 27" wide | | 19.80 | .808 | | 243 | 31 | | 274 | 315 |
| 5340 | 36" wide | | 18.80 | .851 | | 278 | 32.50 | | 310.50 | 355 |
| 5380 | 48" wide | | 18.40 | .870 | | 340 | 33 | | 373 | 425 |
| 6000 | Corner wall, 30" high, 24" wide | | 18 | .889 | | 166 | 34 | | 200 | 235 |
| 6050 | 30" wide | | 17.20 | .930 | | 201 | 35.50 | | 236.50 | 276 |
| 6100 | 36" wide | | 16.50 | .970 | | 217 | 37 | | 254 | 297 |
| 6500 | Revolving Lazy Susan | | 15.20 | 1.053 | | 370 | 40 | | 410 | 470 |
| 7000 | Broom cabinet, 84" high, 24" deep, 18" wide | | 10 | 1.600 | | 445 | 61 | | 506 | 585 |
| 7500 | Oven cabinets, 84" high, 24" deep, 27" wide | | 8 | 2 | | 655 | 76 | | 731 | 840 |
| 7750 | Valance board trim | | 396 | .040 | L.F. | 9.35 | 1.54 | | 10.89 | 12.70 |
| 9000 | For deluxe models of all cabinets, add | | | | | 40% | | | | |
| 9500 | For custom built in place, add | | | | | 25% | 10% | | | |
| 9550 | Rule of thumb, kitchen cabinets not including | | | | | | | | | |
| 9560 | appliances & counter top, minimum | 2 Carp | 30 | .533 | L.F. | 108 | 20.50 | | 128.50 | 151 |
| 9600 | Maximum | " | 25 | .640 | " | 260 | 24.50 | | 284.50 | 325 |
| 9610 | For metal cabinets, see Div. 12 35 70.13 | | | | | | | | | |

### 12 32 23.15 Manufactured Wood Casework Frames

| | | Crew | Daily Output | Labor-Hours | Unit | Material | 2008 Bare Costs Labor | Equipment | Total | Total Incl O&P |
|---|---|---|---|---|---|---|---|---|---|---|
| 0010 | **MANUFACTURED WOOD CASEWORK FRAMES** | | | | | | | | | |
| 0050 | Base cabinets, counter storage, 36" high | | | | | | | | | |
| 0100 | One bay, 18" wide | 1 Carp | 2.70 | 2.963 | Ea. | 119 | 113 | | 232 | 305 |
| 0400 | Two bay, 36" wide | | 2.20 | 3.636 | | 182 | 139 | | 321 | 415 |
| 1100 | Three bay, 54" wide | | 1.50 | 5.333 | | 216 | 203 | | 419 | 555 |
| 2800 | Bookcases, one bay, 7' high, 18" wide | | 2.40 | 3.333 | | 140 | 127 | | 267 | 350 |
| 3500 | Two bay, 36" wide | | 1.60 | 5 | | 203 | 191 | | 394 | 520 |
| 4100 | Three bay, 54" wide | | 1.20 | 6.667 | | 335 | 254 | | 589 | 765 |
| 5100 | Coat racks, one bay, 7' high, 24" wide | | 4.50 | 1.778 | | 140 | 67.50 | | 207.50 | 259 |
| 5300 | Two bay, 48" wide | | 2.75 | 2.909 | | 195 | 111 | | 306 | 385 |
| 5800 | Three bay, 72" wide | | 2.10 | 3.810 | | 287 | 145 | | 432 | 540 |
| 6100 | Wall mounted cabinet, one bay, 24" high, 18" wide | | 3.60 | 2.222 | | 77 | 84.50 | | 161.50 | 217 |
| 6800 | Two bay, 36" wide | | 2.20 | 3.636 | | 113 | 139 | | 252 | 340 |
| 7400 | Three bay, 54" wide | | 1.70 | 4.706 | | 140 | 179 | | 319 | 435 |
| 8400 | 30" high, one bay, 18" wide | | 3.60 | 2.222 | | 84 | 84.50 | | 168.50 | 224 |
| 9000 | Two bay, 36" wide | | 2.15 | 3.721 | | 111 | 142 | | 253 | 345 |
| 9400 | Three bay, 54" wide | | 1.60 | 5 | | 139 | 191 | | 330 | 450 |
| 9800 | Wardrobe, 7' high, single, 24" wide | | 2.70 | 2.963 | | 154 | 113 | | 267 | 345 |
| 9880 | Partition & adjustable shelves, 48" wide | | 1.70 | 4.706 | | 196 | 179 | | 375 | 495 |
| 9950 | Partition, adjustable shelves & drawers, 48" wide | | 1.40 | 5.714 | | 294 | 218 | | 512 | 665 |

### 12 32 23.20 Manufactured Hardwood Casework Doors

| | | Crew | Daily Output | Labor-Hours | Unit | Material | 2008 Bare Costs Labor | Equipment | Total | Total Incl O&P |
|---|---|---|---|---|---|---|---|---|---|---|
| 0010 | **MANUFACTURED HARDWOOD CASEWORK DOORS** | | | | | | | | | |
| 2000 | Glass panel, hardwood frame | | | | | | | | | |
| 2200 | 12" wide, 18" high | 1 Carp | 34 | .235 | Ea. | 14.90 | 8.95 | | 23.85 | 30.50 |
| 2600 | 30" high | | 32 | .250 | | 25 | 9.55 | | 34.55 | 42.50 |
| 4450 | 18" wide, 18" high | | 32 | .250 | | 22.50 | 9.55 | | 32.05 | 39.50 |

# 12 32 Manufactured Wood Casework

## 12 32 23 – Hardwood Casework

| 12 32 23.20 Manufactured Hardwood Casework Doors | Crew | Daily Output | Labor-Hours | Unit | Material | 2008 Bare Costs Labor | Equipment | Total | Total Incl O&P |
|---|---|---|---|---|---|---|---|---|---|
| 4550 | 30" high | 1 Carp | 29 | .276 | Ea. | 27.50 | 10.50 | | 38 | 46.50 |
| 5000 | Hardwood, raised panel | | | | | | | | | |
| 5100 | 12" wide, 18" high | 1 Carp | 16 | .500 | Ea. | 25 | 19.05 | | 44.05 | 57 |
| 5200 | 30" high | | 15 | .533 | | 41.50 | 20.50 | | 62 | 77 |
| 5500 | 18" wide, 18" high | | 15 | .533 | | 37.50 | 20.50 | | 58 | 72.50 |
| 5600 | 30" high | | 14 | .571 | | 62 | 22 | | 84 | 103 |

### 12 32 23.25 Manufactured Wood Casework Drawer Fronts

| | | Crew | Daily Output | Labor-Hours | Unit | Material | Labor | Equipment | Total | Total Incl O&P |
|---|---|---|---|---|---|---|---|---|---|---|
| 0010 | **MANUFACTURED WOOD CASEWORK DRAWER FRONTS** | | | | | | | | | |
| 0100 | Solid hardwood front | | | | | | | | | |
| 1000 | 4" high, 12" wide | 1 Carp | 17 | .471 | Ea. | 3.64 | 17.95 | | 21.59 | 32 |
| 1200 | 18" wide | " | 16 | .500 | " | 5.25 | 19.05 | | 24.30 | 35.50 |

### 12 32 23.30 Manufactured Wood Casework Vanities

| | | Crew | Daily Output | Labor-Hours | Unit | Material | Labor | Equipment | Total | Total Incl O&P |
|---|---|---|---|---|---|---|---|---|---|---|
| 0010 | **MANUFACTURED WOOD CASEWORK VANITIES** | | | | | | | | | |
| 8000 | Vanity bases, 2 doors, 30" high, 21" deep, 24" wide | 2 Carp | 20 | .800 | Ea. | 205 | 30.50 | | 235.50 | 273 |
| 8050 | 30" wide | | 16 | 1 | | 235 | 38 | | 273 | 320 |
| 8100 | 36" wide | | 13.33 | 1.200 | | 315 | 45.50 | | 360.50 | 415 |
| 8150 | 48" wide | | 11.43 | 1.400 | | 375 | 53.50 | | 428.50 | 495 |
| 9000 | For deluxe models of all vanities, add to above | | | | | 40% | | | | |
| 9500 | For custom built in place, add to above | | | | | 25% | 10% | | | |

### 12 32 23.35 Manufactured Wood Casework Hardware

| | | Crew | Daily Output | Labor-Hours | Unit | Material | Labor | Equipment | Total | Total Incl O&P |
|---|---|---|---|---|---|---|---|---|---|---|
| 0010 | **MANUFACTURED WOOD CASEWORK HARDWARE** | | | | | | | | | |
| 1000 | Catches, minimum | 1 Carp | 235 | .034 | Ea. | .87 | 1.30 | | 2.17 | 2.98 |
| 1040 | Maximum | " | 80 | .100 | " | 5.45 | 3.81 | | 9.26 | 11.90 |
| 2000 | Door/drawer pulls, handles | | | | | | | | | |
| 2200 | Handles and pulls, projecting, metal, minimum | 1 Carp | 160 | .050 | Ea. | 3.85 | 1.91 | | 5.76 | 7.20 |
| 2240 | Maximum | | 68 | .118 | | 8.15 | 4.48 | | 12.63 | 16 |
| 2300 | Wood, minimum | | 160 | .050 | | 4.06 | 1.91 | | 5.97 | 7.45 |
| 2340 | Maximum | | 68 | .118 | | 7.45 | 4.48 | | 11.93 | 15.20 |
| 2600 | Flush, metal, minimum | | 160 | .050 | | 4.06 | 1.91 | | 5.97 | 7.45 |
| 2640 | Maximum | | 68 | .118 | | 7.45 | 4.48 | | 11.93 | 15.20 |
| 3000 | Drawer tracks/glides, minimum | | 48 | .167 | Pr. | 6.90 | 6.35 | | 13.25 | 17.45 |
| 3040 | Maximum | | 24 | .333 | | 20 | 12.70 | | 32.70 | 42 |
| 4000 | Cabinet hinges, minimum | | 160 | .050 | | 2.34 | 1.91 | | 4.25 | 5.55 |
| 4040 | Maximum | | 68 | .118 | | 8.85 | 4.48 | | 13.33 | 16.70 |

# 12 35 Specialty Casework

## 12 35 50 – Educational/Library Casework

### 12 35 50.13 Educational Casework

| | | Crew | Daily Output | Labor-Hours | Unit | Material | Labor | Equipment | Total | Total Incl O&P |
|---|---|---|---|---|---|---|---|---|---|---|
| 0010 | **EDUCATIONAL CASEWORK** | | | | | | | | | |
| 5000 | School, 24" deep, metal, 84" high units | 2 Carp | 15 | 1.067 | L.F. | 355 | 40.50 | | 395.50 | 455 |
| 5150 | Counter height units | | 20 | .800 | | 239 | 30.50 | | 269.50 | 310 |
| 5450 | Wood, custom fabricated, 32" high counter | | 20 | .800 | | 199 | 30.50 | | 229.50 | 267 |
| 5600 | Add for counter top | | 56 | .286 | | 21 | 10.90 | | 31.90 | 40.50 |
| 5800 | 84" high wall units | | 15 | 1.067 | | 385 | 40.50 | | 425.50 | 490 |
| 6000 | Laminated plastic finish is same price as wood | | | | | | | | | |

## 12 35 53 – Laboratory Casework

### 12 35 53.13 Metal Laboratory Casework

| | | Crew | Daily Output | Labor-Hours | Unit | Material | Labor | Equipment | Total | Total Incl O&P |
|---|---|---|---|---|---|---|---|---|---|---|
| 0010 | **METAL LABORATORY CASEWORK** | | | | | | | | | |
| 0020 | Cabinets, base, door units, metal | 2 Carp | 18 | .889 | L.F. | 172 | 34 | | 206 | 243 |
| 0300 | Drawer units | | 18 | .889 | | 385 | 34 | | 419 | 480 |

# 12 35 Specialty Casework

## 12 35 53 – Laboratory Casework

### 12 35 53.13 Metal Laboratory Casework

| | | Crew | Daily Output | Labor-Hours | Unit | Material | 2008 Bare Costs Labor | Equipment | Total | Total Incl O&P |
|---|---|---|---|---|---|---|---|---|---|---|
| 0700 | Tall storage cabinets, open, 7' high | 2 Carp | 20 | .800 | L.F. | 370 | 30.50 | | 400.50 | 455 |
| 0900 | With glazed doors | | 20 | .800 | | 585 | 30.50 | | 615.50 | 690 |
| 1300 | Wall cabinets, metal, 12-1/2" deep, open | | 20 | .800 | | 120 | 30.50 | | 150.50 | 180 |
| 1500 | With doors | | 20 | .800 | | 250 | 30.50 | | 280.50 | 325 |
| 6300 | Rule of thumb: lab furniture including installation & connection | | | | | | | | | |
| 6320 | High school | | | | S.F. | | | | 30.55 | 33.60 |
| 6340 | College | | | | | | | | 45 | 49.50 |
| 6360 | Clinical, health care | | | | | | | | 38.65 | 42.50 |
| 6380 | Industrial | | | | | | | | 62.50 | 68.50 |

## 12 35 59 – Display Casework

### 12 35 59.10 Display Cases

| | | Crew | Daily Output | Labor-Hours | Unit | Material | 2008 Bare Costs Labor | Equipment | Total | Total Incl O&P |
|---|---|---|---|---|---|---|---|---|---|---|
| 0010 | **DISPLAY CASES** Free standing, all glass | | | | | | | | | |
| 0020 | Aluminum frame, 42" high x 36" x 12" deep | 2 Carp | 8 | 2 | Ea. | 1,425 | 76 | | 1,501 | 1,700 |
| 0100 | 70" high x 48" x 18" deep | " | 6 | 2.667 | | 2,625 | 102 | | 2,727 | 3,050 |
| 0500 | For wood bases, add | | | | | 9% | | | | |
| 0600 | For hardwood frames, deduct | | | | | 8% | | | | |
| 0700 | For bronze, baked enamel finish, add | | | | | 10% | | | | |
| 2000 | Wall mounted, glass front, aluminum frame | | | | | | | | | |
| 2010 | Non-illuminated, one section 3' x 4' x 1'-4" | 2 Carp | 5 | 3.200 | Ea. | 2,125 | 122 | | 2,247 | 2,550 |
| 2100 | 5' x 4' x 1'-4" | | 5 | 3.200 | | 2,300 | 122 | | 2,422 | 2,750 |
| 2200 | 6' x 4' x 1'-4" | | 4 | 4 | | 2,725 | 152 | | 2,877 | 3,225 |
| 2500 | Two sections, 8' x 4' x 1'-4" | | 2 | 8 | | 1,750 | 305 | | 2,055 | 2,400 |
| 2600 | 10' x 4' x 1'-4" | | 2 | 8 | | 2,025 | 305 | | 2,330 | 2,700 |
| 3000 | Three sections, 16' x 4' x 1'-4" | | 1.50 | 10.667 | | 3,500 | 405 | | 3,905 | 4,475 |
| 3500 | For fluorescent lights, add | | | | Section | 269 | | | 269 | 296 |
| 4000 | Table exhibit cases, 2' wide, 3' high, 4' long, flat top | 2 Carp | 5 | 3.200 | Ea. | 790 | 122 | | 912 | 1,050 |
| 4100 | 3' wide, 3' high, 4' long, sloping top | " | 3 | 5.333 | " | 1,200 | 203 | | 1,403 | 1,650 |

## 12 35 70 – Healthcare Casework

### 12 35 70.13 Hospital Casework

| | | Crew | Daily Output | Labor-Hours | Unit | Material | 2008 Bare Costs Labor | Equipment | Total | Total Incl O&P |
|---|---|---|---|---|---|---|---|---|---|---|
| 0010 | **HOSPITAL CASEWORK** | | | | | | | | | |
| 0500 | Base cabinets, laminated plastic | 2 Carp | 10 | 1.600 | L.F. | 228 | 61 | | 289 | 345 |
| 1000 | Stainless steel | " | 10 | 1.600 | | 420 | 61 | | 481 | 555 |
| 1200 | For all drawers, add | | | | | 24 | | | 24 | 26 |
| 1300 | Cabinet base trim, 4" high, enameled steel | 2 Carp | 200 | .080 | | 38 | 3.05 | | 41.05 | 46.50 |
| 1400 | Stainless steel | | 200 | .080 | | 76.50 | 3.05 | | 79.55 | 88.50 |
| 1450 | Counter top, laminated plastic, no backsplash | | 40 | .400 | | 39.50 | 15.25 | | 54.75 | 66.50 |
| 1650 | With backsplash | | 40 | .400 | | 49 | 15.25 | | 64.25 | 77.50 |
| 1800 | For sink cutout, add | | 12.20 | 1.311 | Ea. | | 50 | | 50 | 78 |
| 1900 | Stainless steel counter top | | 40 | .400 | L.F. | 127 | 15.25 | | 142.25 | 164 |
| 2000 | For drop-in stainless 43" x 21" sink, add | | | | Ea. | 835 | | | 835 | 920 |
| 2500 | Wall cabinets, laminated plastic | 2 Carp | 15 | 1.067 | L.F. | 171 | 40.50 | | 211.50 | 252 |
| 2600 | Enameled steel | | 15 | 1.067 | | 210 | 40.50 | | 250.50 | 294 |
| 2700 | Stainless steel | | 15 | 1.067 | | 415 | 40.50 | | 455.50 | 525 |
| 2800 | For glass doors, add | | | | | 28.50 | | | 28.50 | 31.50 |

### 12 35 70.16 Nurse Station Casework

| | | Crew | Daily Output | Labor-Hours | Unit | Material | 2008 Bare Costs Labor | Equipment | Total | Total Incl O&P |
|---|---|---|---|---|---|---|---|---|---|---|
| 0010 | **NURSE STATION CASEWORK** | | | | | | | | | |
| 2100 | Door type, laminated plastic | 2 Carp | 10 | 1.600 | L.F. | 264 | 61 | | 325 | 385 |
| 2200 | Enameled steel | | 10 | 1.600 | | 252 | 61 | | 313 | 375 |
| 2300 | Stainless steel | | 10 | 1.600 | | 505 | 61 | | 566 | 650 |
| 2400 | For drawer type, add | | | | | 214 | | | 214 | 236 |

# 12 35 Specialty Casework

## 12 35 80 – Commercial Kitchen Casework

### 12 35 80.13 Metal Kitchen Casework

| | 12 35 80.13 Metal Kitchen Casework | Crew | Daily Output | Labor-Hours | Unit | Material | 2008 Bare Costs Labor | Equipment | Total | Total Incl O&P |
|---|---|---|---|---|---|---|---|---|---|---|
| 0010 | **METAL KITCHEN CASEWORK** | | | | | | | | | |
| 3500 | Base cabinets, metal, minimum | 2 Carp | 30 | .533 | L.F. | 61.50 | 20.50 | | 82 | 99 |
| 3600 | Maximum | | 25 | .640 | | 156 | 24.50 | | 180.50 | 210 |
| 3700 | Wall cabinets, metal, minimum | | 30 | .533 | | 61.50 | 20.50 | | 82 | 99 |
| 3800 | Maximum | ↓ | 25 | .640 | ↓ | 141 | 24.50 | | 165.50 | 193 |

# 12 36 Countertops

## 12 36 16 – Metal Countertops

### 12 36 16.10 Stainless Steel Countertops

| | | Crew | Daily Output | Labor-Hours | Unit | Material | Labor | Equipment | Total | Total Incl O&P |
|---|---|---|---|---|---|---|---|---|---|---|
| 0010 | **STAINLESS STEEL COUNTERTOPS** | | | | | | | | | |
| 3200 | Stainless steel, custom | 1 Carp | 24 | .333 | S.F. | 135 | 12.70 | | 147.70 | 168 |

## 12 36 19 – Wood Countertops

### 12 36 19.10 Maple Countertops

| | | Crew | Daily Output | Labor-Hours | Unit | Material | Labor | Equipment | Total | Total Incl O&P |
|---|---|---|---|---|---|---|---|---|---|---|
| 0010 | **MAPLE COUNTERTOPS** | | | | | | | | | |
| 2900 | Solid, laminated, 1-1/2" thick, no splash | 1 Carp | 28 | .286 | L.F. | 59 | 10.90 | | 69.90 | 81.50 |
| 3000 | With square splash | | 28 | .286 | " | 70 | 10.90 | | 80.90 | 94 |
| 3400 | Recessed cutting block with trim, 16" x 20" x 1" | ↓ | 8 | 1 | Ea. | 68.50 | 38 | | 106.50 | 135 |

## 12 36 23 – Plastic Countertops

### 12 36 23.13 Plastic-Laminate-Clad Countertops

| | | Crew | Daily Output | Labor-Hours | Unit | Material | Labor | Equipment | Total | Total Incl O&P |
|---|---|---|---|---|---|---|---|---|---|---|
| 0010 | **PLASTIC-LAMINATE-CLAD COUNTERTOPS** | | | | | | | | | |
| 0020 | Stock, 24" wide w/ backsplash, minimum | 1 Carp | 30 | .267 | L.F. | 9.85 | 10.15 | | 20 | 26.50 |
| 0100 | Maximum | | 25 | .320 | | 17.80 | 12.20 | | 30 | 38.50 |
| 0300 | Custom plastic, 7/8" thick, aluminum molding, no splash | | 30 | .267 | | 19.65 | 10.15 | | 29.80 | 37.50 |
| 0400 | Cove splash | | 30 | .267 | | 26 | 10.15 | | 36.15 | 44.50 |
| 0600 | 1-1/4" thick, no splash | | 28 | .286 | | 29.50 | 10.90 | | 40.40 | 49 |
| 0700 | Square splash | | 28 | .286 | | 28 | 10.90 | | 38.90 | 48 |
| 0900 | Square edge, plastic face, 7/8" thick, no splash | | 30 | .267 | | 24.50 | 10.15 | | 34.65 | 43 |
| 1000 | With splash | ↓ | 30 | .267 | | 31.50 | 10.15 | | 41.65 | 50.50 |
| 1200 | For stainless channel edge, 7/8" thick, add | | | | | 2.59 | | | 2.59 | 2.85 |
| 1300 | 1-1/4" thick, add | | | | | 3.04 | | | 3.04 | 3.34 |
| 1500 | For solid color suede finish, add | | | | ↓ | 2.52 | | | 2.52 | 2.77 |
| 1700 | For end splash, add | | | | Ea. | 16.85 | | | 16.85 | 18.55 |
| 1900 | For cut outs, standard, add, minimum | 1 Carp | 32 | .250 | | 3.37 | 9.55 | | 12.92 | 18.55 |
| 2000 | Maximum | | 8 | 1 | ↓ | 5.60 | 38 | | 43.60 | 65.50 |
| 2100 | Postformed, including backsplash and front edge | | 30 | .267 | L.F. | 10.10 | 10.15 | | 20.25 | 27 |
| 2110 | Mitred, add | | 12 | .667 | Ea. | | 25.50 | | 25.50 | 39.50 |
| 2200 | Built-in place, 25" wide, plastic laminate | ↓ | 25 | .320 | L.F. | 13.50 | 12.20 | | 25.70 | 34 |

## 12 36 33 – Tile Countertops

### 12 36 33.10 Ceramic Tile Countertops

| | | Crew | Daily Output | Labor-Hours | Unit | Material | Labor | Equipment | Total | Total Incl O&P |
|---|---|---|---|---|---|---|---|---|---|---|
| 0010 | **CERAMIC TILE COUNTERTOPS** | | | | | | | | | |
| 2300 | Ceramic tile mosaic | 1 Carp | 25 | .320 | L.F. | 29 | 12.20 | | 41.20 | 51 |

## 12 36 40 – Stone Countertops

### 12 36 40.10 Natural Stone Countertops

| | | Crew | Daily Output | Labor-Hours | Unit | Material | Labor | Equipment | Total | Total Incl O&P |
|---|---|---|---|---|---|---|---|---|---|---|
| 0010 | **NATURAL STONE COUNTERTOPS** | | | | | | | | | |
| 2500 | Marble, stock, with splash, 1/2" thick, minimum | 1 Bric | 17 | .471 | L.F. | 36 | 18.40 | | 54.40 | 67.50 |
| 2700 | 3/4" thick, maximum | " | 13 | .615 | " | 90 | 24 | | 114 | 136 |

# 12 36 Countertops

## 12 36 53 – Laboratory Countertops

| 12 36 53.10 Laboratory Countertops and Sinks | | Crew | Daily Output | Labor-Hours | Unit | Material | 2008 Bare Costs Labor | Equipment | Total | Total Incl O&P |
|---|---|---|---|---|---|---|---|---|---|---|
| 0010 | **LABORATORY COUNTERTOPS AND SINKS** | | | | | | | | | |
| 0020 | Countertops, not incl. base cabinets, acidproof, minimum | 2 Carp | 82 | .195 | S.F. | 29.50 | 7.45 | | 36.95 | 43.50 |
| 0030 | Maximum | | 70 | .229 | | 38.50 | 8.70 | | 47.20 | 56 |
| 0040 | Stainless steel | ↓ | 82 | .195 | ↓ | 91 | 7.45 | | 98.45 | 112 |

## 12 36 61 – Simulated Stone Countertops

### 12 36 61.16 Solid Surface Countertops

| | | Crew | Daily Output | Labor-Hours | Unit | Material | 2008 Bare Costs Labor | Equipment | Total | Total Incl O&P |
|---|---|---|---|---|---|---|---|---|---|---|
| 0010 | **SOLID SURFACE COUNTERTOPS**, Acrylic polymer | | | | | | | | | |
| 0020 | Pricing for orders of 100 L.F. or greater | | | | | | | | | |
| 0100 | 25" wide, solid colors | 2 Carp | 28 | .571 | L.F. | 44.50 | 22 | | 66.50 | 83 |
| 0200 | Patterned colors | | 28 | .571 | | 56.50 | 22 | | 78.50 | 96 |
| 0300 | Premium patterned colors | | 28 | .571 | | 70.50 | 22 | | 92.50 | 112 |
| 0400 | With silicone attached 4" backsplash, solid colors | | 27 | .593 | | 49 | 22.50 | | 71.50 | 89 |
| 0500 | Patterned colors | | 27 | .593 | | 62 | 22.50 | | 84.50 | 103 |
| 0600 | Premium patterned colors | | 27 | .593 | | 77 | 22.50 | | 99.50 | 120 |
| 0700 | With hard seam attached 4" backsplash, solid colors | | 23 | .696 | | 49 | 26.50 | | 75.50 | 95.50 |
| 0800 | Patterned colors | | 23 | .696 | | 62 | 26.50 | | 88.50 | 110 |
| 0900 | Premium patterned colors | ↓ | 23 | .696 | ↓ | 77 | 26.50 | | 103.50 | 127 |
| 1000 | Pricing for order of 51 - 99 L.F. | | | | | | | | | |
| 1100 | 25" wide, solid colors | 2 Carp | 24 | .667 | L.F. | 51.50 | 25.50 | | 77 | 96 |
| 1200 | Patterned colors | | 24 | .667 | | 65 | 25.50 | | 90.50 | 111 |
| 1300 | Premium patterned colors | | 24 | .667 | | 81.50 | 25.50 | | 107 | 129 |
| 1400 | With silicone attached 4" backsplash, solid colors | | 23 | .696 | | 56.50 | 26.50 | | 83 | 104 |
| 1500 | Patterned colors | | 23 | .696 | | 71.50 | 26.50 | | 98 | 120 |
| 1600 | Premium patterned colors | | 23 | .696 | | 89 | 26.50 | | 115.50 | 139 |
| 1700 | With hard seam attached 4" backsplash, solid colors | | 20 | .800 | | 56.50 | 30.50 | | 87 | 110 |
| 1800 | Patterned colors | | 20 | .800 | | 71.50 | 30.50 | | 102 | 126 |
| 1900 | Premium patterned colors | ↓ | 20 | .800 | ↓ | 89 | 30.50 | | 119.50 | 145 |
| 2000 | Pricing for order of 1 - 50 L.F. | | | | | | | | | |
| 2100 | 25" wide, solid colors | 2 Carp | 20 | .800 | L.F. | 60 | 30.50 | | 90.50 | 114 |
| 2200 | Patterned colors | | 20 | .800 | | 76.50 | 30.50 | | 107 | 132 |
| 2300 | Premium patterned colors | | 20 | .800 | | 95.50 | 30.50 | | 126 | 153 |
| 2400 | With silicone attached 4" backsplash, solid colors | | 19 | .842 | | 66 | 32 | | 98 | 123 |
| 2500 | Patterned colors | | 19 | .842 | | 83.50 | 32 | | 115.50 | 142 |
| 2600 | Premium patterned colors | | 19 | .842 | | 104 | 32 | | 136 | 165 |
| 2700 | With hard seam attached 4" backsplash, solid colors | | 15 | 1.067 | | 66 | 40.50 | | 106.50 | 136 |
| 2800 | Patterned colors | | 15 | 1.067 | | 83.50 | 40.50 | | 124 | 156 |
| 2900 | Premium patterned colors | ↓ | 15 | 1.067 | ↓ | 104 | 40.50 | | 144.50 | 179 |
| 3000 | Sinks, pricing for order of 100 or greater units | | | | | | | | | |
| 3100 | Single bowl, hard seamed, solid colors, 13" x 17" | 1 Carp | 3 | 2.667 | Ea. | 300 | 102 | | 402 | 490 |
| 3200 | 10" x 15" | | 7 | 1.143 | | 139 | 43.50 | | 182.50 | 221 |
| 3300 | Cutouts for sinks | ↓ | 8 | 1 | ↓ | | 38 | | 38 | 59.50 |
| 3400 | Sinks, pricing for order of 51 - 99 units | | | | | | | | | |
| 3500 | Single bowl, hard seamed, solid colors, 13" x 17" | 1 Carp | 2.55 | 3.137 | Ea. | 345 | 120 | | 465 | 565 |
| 3600 | 10" x 15" | | 6 | 1.333 | | 160 | 51 | | 211 | 255 |
| 3700 | Cutouts for sinks | ↓ | 7 | 1.143 | ↓ | | 43.50 | | 43.50 | 68 |
| 3800 | Sinks, pricing for order of 1 - 50 units | | | | | | | | | |
| 3900 | Single bowl, hard seamed, solid colors, 13" x 17" | 1 Carp | 2 | 4 | Ea. | 405 | 152 | | 557 | 680 |
| 4000 | 10" x 15" | | 4.55 | 1.758 | | 188 | 67 | | 255 | 310 |
| 4100 | Cutouts for sinks | | 5.25 | 1.524 | | | 58 | | 58 | 90.50 |
| 4200 | Cooktop cutouts, pricing for 100 or greater units | | 4 | 2 | | 22 | 76 | | 98 | 144 |
| 4300 | 51 - 99 units | | 3.40 | 2.353 | | 25.50 | 89.50 | | 115 | 168 |
| 4400 | 1 - 50 units | ↓ | 3 | 2.667 | ↓ | 30 | 102 | | 132 | 191 |

## 12 36 61 – Simulated Stone Countertops

### 12 36 61.17 Solid Surface Vanity Tops

| | | Crew | Daily Output | Labor-Hours | Unit | Material | 2008 Bare Costs Labor | Equipment | Total | Total Incl O&P |
|---|---|---|---|---|---|---|---|---|---|---|
| 0010 | **SOLID SURFACE VANITY TOPS** | | | | | | | | | |
| 0015 | Solid surface, center bowl, 17" x 19" | 1 Carp | 12 | .667 | Ea. | 184 | 25.50 | | 209.50 | 242 |
| 0020 | 19" x 25" | | 12 | .667 | | 223 | 25.50 | | 248.50 | 285 |
| 0030 | 19" x 31" | | 12 | .667 | | 270 | 25.50 | | 295.50 | 335 |
| 0040 | 19" x 37" | | 12 | .667 | | 315 | 25.50 | | 340.50 | 385 |
| 0050 | 22" x 25" | | 10 | .800 | | 196 | 30.50 | | 226.50 | 264 |
| 0060 | 22" x 31" | | 10 | .800 | | 229 | 30.50 | | 259.50 | 300 |
| 0070 | 22" x 37" | | 10 | .800 | | 266 | 30.50 | | 296.50 | 340 |
| 0080 | 22" x 43" | | 10 | .800 | | 305 | 30.50 | | 335.50 | 385 |
| 0090 | 22" x 49" | | 10 | .800 | | 335 | 30.50 | | 365.50 | 420 |
| 0110 | 22" x 55" | | 8 | 1 | | 380 | 38 | | 418 | 480 |
| 0120 | 22" x 61" | | 8 | 1 | | 435 | 38 | | 473 | 540 |
| 0220 | Double bowl, 22" x 61" | | 8 | 1 | | 495 | 38 | | 533 | 600 |
| 0230 | Double bowl, 22" x 73" | | 8 | 1 | | 685 | 38 | | 723 | 810 |
| 0240 | For aggregate colors, add | | | | | 35% | | | | |
| 0250 | For faucets and fittings, see Div. 22 41 39.10 | | | | | | | | | |

### 12 36 61.19 Engineered Stone Countertops

| | | Crew | Daily Output | Labor-Hours | Unit | Material | 2008 Bare Costs Labor | Equipment | Total | Total Incl O&P |
|---|---|---|---|---|---|---|---|---|---|---|
| 0010 | **ENGINEERED STONE COUNTERTOPS** | | | | | | | | | |
| 0100 | 25" wide, 4" backsplash, color group A, minimum | 2 Carp | 15 | 1.067 | L.F. | 16.15 | 40.50 | | 56.65 | 81.50 |
| 0110 | Maximum | | 15 | 1.067 | | 41.50 | 40.50 | | 82 | 109 |
| 0120 | Color group B, minimum | | 15 | 1.067 | | 21 | 40.50 | | 61.50 | 86.50 |
| 0130 | Maximum | | 15 | 1.067 | | 48.50 | 40.50 | | 89 | 117 |
| 0140 | Color group C, minimum | | 15 | 1.067 | | 29 | 40.50 | | 69.50 | 95.50 |
| 0150 | Maximum | | 15 | 1.067 | | 59.50 | 40.50 | | 100 | 129 |
| 0160 | Color group D, minimum | | 15 | 1.067 | | 36 | 40.50 | | 76.50 | 104 |
| 0170 | Maximum | | 15 | 1.067 | | 69.50 | 40.50 | | 110 | 140 |

# 12 46 Furnishing Accessories

## 12 46 13 – Ash Receptacles

### 12 46 13.10 Ash/Trash Receivers

| | | Crew | Daily Output | Labor-Hours | Unit | Material | 2008 Bare Costs Labor | Equipment | Total | Total Incl O&P |
|---|---|---|---|---|---|---|---|---|---|---|
| 0010 | **ASH/TRASH RECEIVERS** | | | | | | | | | |
| 1000 | Ash urn, cylindrical metal | | | | | | | | | |
| 1020 | 8" diameter, 20" high | 1 Clab | 60 | .133 | Ea. | 125 | 4.03 | | 129.03 | 143 |
| 1060 | 10" diameter, 26" high | " | 60 | .133 | " | 110 | 4.03 | | 114.03 | 127 |
| 2000 | Combination ash/trash urn, metal | | | | | | | | | |
| 2020 | 8" diameter, 20" high | 1 Clab | 60 | .133 | Ea. | 73 | 4.03 | | 77.03 | 87 |
| 2050 | 10" diameter, 26" high | " | 60 | .133 | " | 99 | 4.03 | | 103.03 | 115 |

## 12 46 19 – Clocks

### 12 46 19.50 Wall Clocks

| | | Crew | Daily Output | Labor-Hours | Unit | Material | 2008 Bare Costs Labor | Equipment | Total | Total Incl O&P |
|---|---|---|---|---|---|---|---|---|---|---|
| 0010 | **WALL CLOCKS** | | | | | | | | | |
| 0080 | 12" diameter, single face | 1 Elec | 8 | 1 | Ea. | 75.50 | 45.50 | | 121 | 151 |
| 0100 | Double face | " | 6.20 | 1.290 | " | 144 | 59 | | 203 | 246 |

## 12 46 33 – Waste Receptacles

### 12 46 33.13 Trash Receptacles

| | | Crew | Daily Output | Labor-Hours | Unit | Material | 2008 Bare Costs Labor | Equipment | Total | Total Incl O&P |
|---|---|---|---|---|---|---|---|---|---|---|
| 0010 | **TRASH RECEPTACLES** | | | | | | | | | |
| 4000 | Trash receptacle, metal | | | | | | | | | |
| 4020 | 8" diameter, 15" high | 1 Clab | 60 | .133 | Ea. | 67 | 4.03 | | 71.03 | 80 |
| 4040 | 10" diameter, 18" high | | 60 | .133 | | 108 | 4.03 | | 112.03 | 125 |
| 5040 | 16" x 8" x 14" high | | 60 | .133 | | 17 | 4.03 | | 21.03 | 25 |

# RSMeans Business Solutions

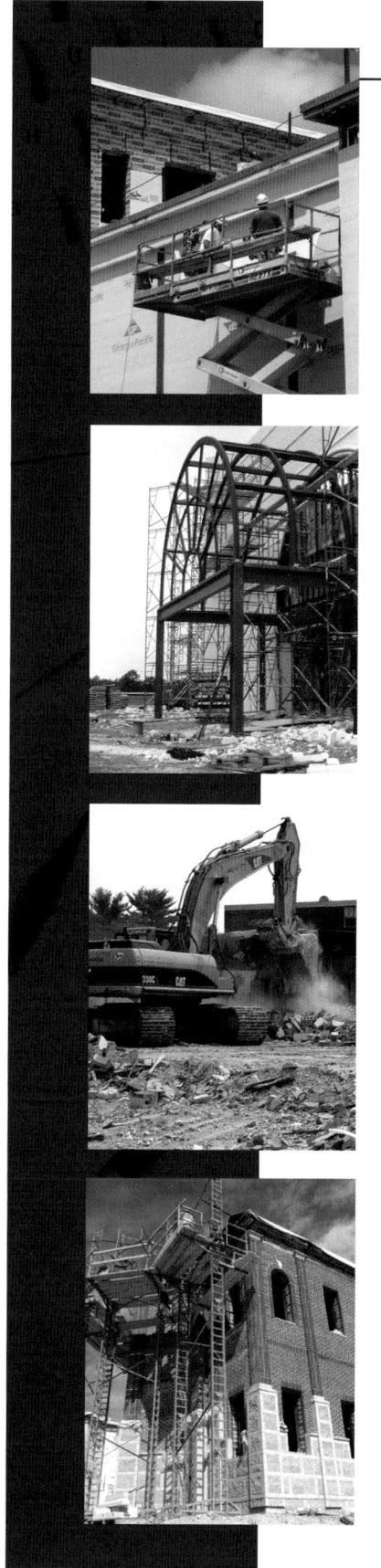

*Leaders in Cost Management Solutions for the Design, Construction, and Facilities Management Industry...*

**Our solutions target the cost management and operational challenges of concern to facility owners—from early planning through facility life cycle.**

*Research Studies and Third Party Validation* – RSMeans conducts benchmark studies from numerous perspectives, including escalation costs in local markets, labor demand analysis, market research and forecasting models and productivity studies for building product manufacturers. We are often called upon to produce "third party validation" cost analysis studies for owners, architects, and boards of directors.

*Predictive Cost Models for Construction and Facility Markets* – From early planning, cost modeling is driven by close attention to standards, codes, methods, and business processes that impact operational effectiveness. Predictive cost models offer cost management and standardization for facility owners, particularly in repetitive building environments. RSMeans custom models are based upon actual client plans and historical budgets, with cost data adjusted to regions anywhere in the U.S.

*Job Order Contracting and JOCWorks™* – A delivery method for construction renovation to reduce cycle times and overhead costs. RSMeans offers consulting in JOC management practices, JOCWorks™ software for renovation cost estimating and project management, and on-site training programs. JOC is available to government agencies, colleges and universities, school districts, municipalities, and health care systems.

*Analytic Databases and Web-Based Dashboards* – Applications of the RSMeans cost databases use the building blocks of construction cost engineering, including a standard code of accounts, activity descriptions, material, labor, and equipment costs. RSMeans has in-house technical expertise for rapid deployment of cost databases, online cost calculators, and Web-based interactive dashboards for client-specific requirements.

*Green Sustainability Practices and Life Cycle Costs* – RSMeans offers life cycle cost studies and sustainability audits to improve operational best practice for cost savings in the areas of building automation, security, energy, HVAC, lighting controls, water efficiency, and indoor air quality.

CORPORATE • HEALTH CARE • EDUCATION • GOVERNMENT • MUNICIPAL • RETAIL • ASSOCIATIONS • BUILDING PRODUCT MANUFACTURERS • HOSPITALITY

Visit our Web site at **www.rsmeans.com.** – Click on Business Solutions.
E-mail requests to **consulting@rsmeans.com**

# 12 46 Furnishing Accessories

## 12 46 33 – Waste Receptacles

### 12 46 33.13 Trash Receptacles

| | | Crew | Daily Output | Labor-Hours | Unit | Material | 2008 Bare Costs Labor | Equipment | Total | Total Incl O&P |
|---|---|---|---|---|---|---|---|---|---|---|
| 5500 | Plastic, with lid | | | | | | | | | |
| 5520 | 35 gallon | 1 Clab | 60 | .133 | Ea. | 211 | 4.03 | | 215.03 | 238 |
| 5540 | 45 gallon | | 60 | .133 | | 250 | 4.03 | | 254.03 | 281 |
| 5550 | Plastic recycling barrel, w/lid & wheels, 32 gal | | 60 | .133 | | 56 | 4.03 | | 60.03 | 68 |
| 5560 | 65 gal | | 60 | .133 | | 107 | 4.03 | | 111.03 | 124 |
| 5570 | 95 gal | | 60 | .133 | | 310 | 4.03 | | 314.03 | 345 |

# 12 48 Rugs and Mats

## 12 48 13 – Entrance Floor Mats and Frames

### 12 48 13.13 Entrance Floor Mats

| | | Crew | Daily Output | Labor-Hours | Unit | Material | 2008 Bare Costs Labor | Equipment | Total | Total Incl O&P |
|---|---|---|---|---|---|---|---|---|---|---|
| 0010 | **ENTRANCE FLOOR MATS** | | | | | | | | | |
| 0020 | Recessed, in-laid black rubber, 3/8" thick, solid | 1 Clab | 155 | .052 | S.F. | 16.40 | 1.56 | | 17.96 | 20.50 |
| 0050 | Perforated | | 155 | .052 | | 12.75 | 1.56 | | 14.31 | 16.50 |
| 0100 | 1/2" thick, solid | | 155 | .052 | | 15.35 | 1.56 | | 16.91 | 19.30 |
| 0150 | Perforated | | 155 | .052 | | 21 | 1.56 | | 22.56 | 25.50 |
| 0200 | In colors, 3/8" thick, solid | | 155 | .052 | | 16.55 | 1.56 | | 18.11 | 20.50 |
| 0250 | Perforated | | 155 | .052 | | 17.05 | 1.56 | | 18.61 | 21 |
| 0300 | 1/2" thick, solid | | 155 | .052 | | 21.50 | 1.56 | | 23.06 | 26 |
| 0350 | Perforated | | 155 | .052 | | 22 | 1.56 | | 23.56 | 26.50 |
| 0500 | Link mats, including nosings, aluminum, 3/8" thick **CN** | | 155 | .052 | | 19.80 | 1.56 | | 21.36 | 24.50 |
| 0550 | Black rubber with galvanized tie rods | | 155 | .052 | | 15.45 | 1.56 | | 17.01 | 19.45 |
| 0600 | Steel, galvanized, 3/8" thick | | 155 | .052 | | 8.55 | 1.56 | | 10.11 | 11.85 |
| 0650 | Vinyl, in colors | | 155 | .052 | | 19.85 | 1.56 | | 21.41 | 24.50 |
| 0750 | Add for nosings, rubber | | | | L.F. | 3.35 | | | 3.35 | 3.69 |
| 0850 | Recess frames for above mats, aluminum | 1 Carp | 100 | .080 | | 3.73 | 3.05 | | 6.78 | 8.85 |
| 0870 | Bronze | " | 100 | .080 | | 5.40 | 3.05 | | 8.45 | 10.70 |
| 0900 | Skate lock tile, 24" x 24" x 1/2" thick, rubber, black | 1 Clab | 125 | .064 | S.F. | 15.50 | 1.94 | | 17.44 | 20 |
| 0950 | Color | | 125 | .064 | " | 19.75 | 1.94 | | 21.69 | 25 |
| 1000 | 12" x 24" border, black | | 75 | .107 | L.F. | 17.05 | 3.23 | | 20.28 | 24 |
| 1100 | Color | | 75 | .107 | " | 23 | 3.23 | | 26.23 | 30 |
| 1150 | 12" x 12" outside corner, black | | 100 | .080 | S.F. | 14.65 | 2.42 | | 17.07 | 19.85 |
| 1200 | Color | | 100 | .080 | | 18.95 | 2.42 | | 21.37 | 25 |
| 1500 | Duckboard, aluminum slats | | 155 | .052 | | 16.40 | 1.56 | | 17.96 | 20.50 |
| 1700 | Hardwood strips on rubber base, to 54" wide | | 155 | .052 | | 13.40 | 1.56 | | 14.96 | 17.20 |
| 1800 | Assembled with brass rods and vinyl spacers, to 48" wide | | 155 | .052 | | 17.85 | 1.56 | | 19.41 | 22 |
| 1850 | Tire fabric, 3/4" thick | | 155 | .052 | | 11.60 | 1.56 | | 13.16 | 15.20 |
| 1900 | Vinyl, 36" wide, in colors, hollow top & bottoms | | 155 | .052 | | 9.35 | 1.56 | | 10.91 | 12.75 |
| 1950 | Solid top & bottom members | | 155 | .052 | | 9.35 | 1.56 | | 10.91 | 12.75 |

# 12 51 Office Furniture

## 12 51 16 – Case Goods

### 12 51 16.13 Metal Case Goods

| | | Crew | Daily Output | Labor-Hours | Unit | Material | 2008 Bare Costs Labor | Equipment | Total | Total Incl O&P |
|---|---|---|---|---|---|---|---|---|---|---|
| 0010 | **METAL CASE GOODS** | | | | | | | | | |
| 0020 | Desks, 29" high, double pedestal, 30" x 60", metal, minimum | | | | Ea. | 415 | | | 415 | 455 |
| 0030 | Maximum | | | | | 1,125 | | | 1,125 | 1,225 |
| 0600 | Desks, single pedestal, 30" x 60", metal, minimum | | | | | 385 | | | 385 | 425 |
| 0620 | Maximum | | | | | 905 | | | 905 | 995 |
| 0720 | Desks, secretarial, 30" x 60", metal, minimum | | | | | 355 | | | 355 | 390 |
| 0730 | Maximum | | | | | 600 | | | 600 | 660 |

# 12 51 Office Furniture

## 12 51 16 – Case Goods

### 12 51 16.13 Metal Case Goods

| | | Crew | Daily Output | Labor-Hours | Unit | Material | 2008 Bare Costs Labor | Equipment | Total | Total Incl O&P |
|---|---|---|---|---|---|---|---|---|---|---|
| 0740 | Return, 20" x 42", minimum | | | | Ea. | 263 | | | 263 | 290 |
| 0750 | Maximum | | | | | 405 | | | 405 | 445 |
| 0940 | 59" x 12" x 23" high, steel, minimum | | | | | 181 | | | 181 | 199 |
| 0960 | Maximum | | | | | 270 | | | 270 | 296 |

### 12 51 16.16 Wood Case Goods

| | | Crew | Daily Output | Labor-Hours | Unit | Material | 2008 Bare Costs Labor | Equipment | Total | Total Incl O&P |
|---|---|---|---|---|---|---|---|---|---|---|
| 0010 | **WOOD CASE GOODS** | | | | | | | | | |
| 0150 | Desk, 29" high, double pedestal, 30" x 60" | | | | | | | | | |
| 0160 | Wood, minimum | | | | Ea. | 400 | | | 400 | 440 |
| 0180 | Maximum | | | | " | 2,175 | | | 2,175 | 2,375 |
| 0630 | Single pedestal, 30" x 60" | | | | | | | | | |
| 0640 | Wood, minimum | | | | Ea. | 500 | | | 500 | 545 |
| 0650 | Maximum | | | | | 680 | | | 680 | 750 |
| 0670 | Executive return, 24" x 42", with box, file, wood, minimum | | | | | 330 | | | 330 | 365 |
| 0680 | Maximum | | | | | 680 | | | 680 | 750 |
| 0790 | Desk, 29" high, secretarial, 30" x 60" | | | | | | | | | |
| 0800 | Wood, minimum | | | | Ea. | 430 | | | 430 | 470 |
| 0810 | Maximum | | | | | 2,200 | | | 2,200 | 2,425 |
| 0820 | Return, 20" x 42", minimum | | | | | 266 | | | 266 | 292 |
| 0830 | Maximum | | | | | 835 | | | 835 | 915 |
| 0900 | Desktop organizer, 72" x 14" x 36" high, wood, minimum | | | | | 162 | | | 162 | 178 |
| 0920 | Maximum | | | | | 320 | | | 320 | 350 |
| 1110 | Furniture, credenza, 29" high, 18" to 22" x 60" to 72" | | | | | | | | | |
| 1120 | Wood, minimum | | | | Ea. | 585 | | | 585 | 640 |
| 1140 | Maximum | | | | " | 2,700 | | | 2,700 | 2,975 |

## 12 51 23 – Office Tables

### 12 51 23.33 Conference Tables

| | | Crew | Daily Output | Labor-Hours | Unit | Material | 2008 Bare Costs Labor | Equipment | Total | Total Incl O&P |
|---|---|---|---|---|---|---|---|---|---|---|
| 0010 | **CONFERENCE TABLES** | | | | | | | | | |
| 6050 | Boat, 96" x 42", minimum | | | | Ea. | 700 | | | 700 | 770 |
| 6150 | Maximum | | | | | 3,125 | | | 3,125 | 3,450 |
| 6720 | Rectangle, 96" x 42", minimum | | | | | 970 | | | 970 | 1,075 |
| 6740 | Maximum | | | | | 2,250 | | | 2,250 | 2,475 |

# 12 52 Seating

## 12 52 23 – Office Seating

### 12 52 23.13 Office Chairs

| | | Crew | Daily Output | Labor-Hours | Unit | Material | 2008 Bare Costs Labor | Equipment | Total | Total Incl O&P |
|---|---|---|---|---|---|---|---|---|---|---|
| 0010 | **OFFICE CHAIRS** | | | | | | | | | |
| 2000 | Standard office chair, executive, minimum | | | | Ea. | 248 | | | 248 | 272 |
| 2150 | Maximum | | | | | 1,750 | | | 1,750 | 1,925 |
| 2200 | Management, minimum | | | | | 178 | | | 178 | 196 |
| 2250 | Maximum | | | | | 2,000 | | | 2,000 | 2,200 |
| 2280 | Task, minimum | | | | | 114 | | | 114 | 126 |
| 2290 | Maximum | | | | | 645 | | | 645 | 710 |
| 2300 | Arm kit, minimum | | | | | 55.50 | | | 55.50 | 61 |
| 2320 | Maximum | | | | | 81 | | | 81 | 89 |

# 12 54 Hospitality Furniture

## 12 54 13 – Hotel and Motel Furniture

| 12 54 13.10 Hotel Furniture | Crew | Daily Output | Labor-Hours | Unit | Material | 2008 Bare Costs Labor | Equipment | Total | Total Incl O&P |
|---|---|---|---|---|---|---|---|---|---|
| 0010 **HOTEL FURNITURE** | | | | | | | | | |
| 0020 Standard quality set, minimum | | | | Room | 2,225 | | | 2,225 | 2,450 |
| 0200 Maximum | | | | " | 7,900 | | | 7,900 | 8,675 |

## 12 54 16 – Restaurant Furniture

### 12 54 16.10 Tables, Folding

| 12 54 16.10 Tables, Folding | Crew | Daily Output | Labor-Hours | Unit | Material | Labor | Equipment | Total | Total Incl O&P |
|---|---|---|---|---|---|---|---|---|---|
| 0010 **TABLES, FOLDING** Laminated plastic tops | | | | | | | | | |
| 1000 Tubular steel legs with glides | | | | | | | | | |
| 1020 18" x 60", minimum | | | | Ea. | 200 | | | 200 | 220 |
| 1040 Maximum | | | | | 950 | | | 950 | 1,050 |
| 1840 36" x 96", minimum | | | | | 243 | | | 243 | 268 |
| 1860 Maximum | | | | | 1,700 | | | 1,700 | 1,875 |
| 2000 Round, wood stained, plywood top, 60" diameter, minimum | | | | | 350 | | | 350 | 385 |
| 2020 Maximum | | | | | 2,050 | | | 2,050 | 2,250 |

### 12 54 16.20 Furniture, Restaurant

| 12 54 16.20 Furniture, Restaurant | Crew | Daily Output | Labor-Hours | Unit | Material | Labor | Equipment | Total | Total Incl O&P |
|---|---|---|---|---|---|---|---|---|---|
| 0010 **FURNITURE, RESTAURANT** | | | | | | | | | |
| 0020 Bars, built-in, front bar | 1 Carp | 5 | 1.600 | L.F. | 231 | 61 | | 292 | 350 |
| 0200 Back bar | " | 5 | 1.600 | " | 168 | 61 | | 229 | 280 |
| 0300 Booth seating, see Div. 12 54 16.70 | | | | | | | | | |
| 2000 Chair, bentwood side chair, metal, minimum | | | | Ea. | 78.50 | | | 78.50 | 86.50 |
| 2020 Maximum | | | | | 92 | | | 92 | 101 |
| 2600 Upholstered seat & back, arms, minimum | | | | | 158 | | | 158 | 174 |
| 2620 Maximum | | | | | 350 | | | 350 | 385 |

### 12 54 16.70 Booths

| 12 54 16.70 Booths | Crew | Daily Output | Labor-Hours | Unit | Material | Labor | Equipment | Total | Total Incl O&P |
|---|---|---|---|---|---|---|---|---|---|
| 0010 **BOOTHS** | | | | | | | | | |
| 1000 Banquet, upholstered seat and back, custom | | | | | | | | | |
| 1500 Straight, minimum | 2 Carp | 40 | .400 | L.F. | 153 | 15.25 | | 168.25 | 193 |
| 1520 Maximum | | 36 | .444 | | 298 | 16.95 | | 314.95 | 355 |
| 1600 "L" or "U" shape, minimum | | 35 | .457 | | 156 | 17.40 | | 173.40 | 199 |
| 1620 Maximum | | 30 | .533 | | 278 | 20.50 | | 298.50 | 335 |
| 1800 Upholstered outside finished backs for | | | | | | | | | |
| 1810 single booths and custom banquets | | | | | | | | | |
| 1820 Minimum | 2 Carp | 44 | .364 | L.F. | 17.70 | 13.85 | | 31.55 | 41 |
| 1840 Maximum | " | 40 | .400 | " | 53 | 15.25 | | 68.25 | 82 |
| 3000 Fixed seating, one piece plastic chair and | | | | | | | | | |
| 3010 plastic laminate table top | | | | | | | | | |
| 3100 Two seat, 24" x 24" table, minimum | F-7 | 30 | 1.067 | Ea. | 620 | 36.50 | | 656.50 | 735 |
| 3120 Maximum | | 26 | 1.231 | | 880 | 42 | | 922 | 1,025 |
| 3200 Four seat, 24" x 48" table, minimum | | 28 | 1.143 | | 615 | 39 | | 654 | 735 |
| 3220 Maximum | | 24 | 1.333 | | 1,050 | 45.50 | | 1,095.50 | 1,225 |
| 5000 Mount in floor, wood fiber core with | | | | | | | | | |
| 5010 plastic laminate face, single booth | | | | | | | | | |
| 5050 24" wide | F-7 | 30 | 1.067 | Ea. | 237 | 36.50 | | 273.50 | 320 |
| 5100 48" wide | " | 28 | 1.143 | " | 300 | 39 | | 339 | 390 |

# 12 55 Detention Furniture

## 12 55 13 - Detention Bunks

### 12 55 13.13 Cots

| | | Crew | Daily Output | Labor-Hours | Unit | Material | 2008 Bare Costs Labor | Equipment | Total | Total Incl O&P |
|---|---|---|---|---|---|---|---|---|---|---|
| 0010 | **COTS** | | | | | | | | | |
| 2500 | Bolted, single, painted steel | E-4 | 20 | 1.600 | Ea. | 315 | 69.50 | 6.60 | 391.10 | 485 |
| 2700 | Stainless steel | " | 20 | 1.600 | " | 875 | 69.50 | 6.60 | 951.10 | 1,100 |

# 12 56 Institutional Furniture

## 12 56 33 - Classroom Furniture

### 12 56 33.10 Furniture, School

| | | Crew | Daily Output | Labor-Hours | Unit | Material | 2008 Bare Costs Labor | Equipment | Total | Total Incl O&P |
|---|---|---|---|---|---|---|---|---|---|---|
| 0010 | **FURNITURE, SCHOOL** | | | | | | | | | |
| 0500 | Classroom, movable chair & desk type, minimum | | | | Set | | | | 70 | 77 |
| 0600 | Maximum | | | | " | | | | 128 | 141 |
| 1000 | Chair, molded plastic | | | | | | | | | |
| 1100 | Integral tablet arm, minimum | | | | Ea. | 68.50 | | | 68.50 | 75.50 |
| 1150 | Maximum | | | | | 191 | | | 191 | 211 |
| 2000 | Desk, single pedestal, top book compartment, minimum | | | | | 53.50 | | | 53.50 | 59 |
| 2020 | Maximum | | | | | 73.50 | | | 73.50 | 81 |
| 2200 | Flip top, minimum | | | | | 95.50 | | | 95.50 | 105 |
| 2220 | Maximum | | | | | 122 | | | 122 | 134 |

## 12 56 43 - Dormitory Furniture

### 12 56 43.10 Dormitory Furnishings

| | | Crew | Daily Output | Labor-Hours | Unit | Material | 2008 Bare Costs Labor | Equipment | Total | Total Incl O&P |
|---|---|---|---|---|---|---|---|---|---|---|
| 0010 | **DORMITORY FURNISHINGS** | | | | | | | | | |
| 1000 | Chest, four drawer, minimum | | | | Ea. | 420 | | | 420 | 460 |
| 1020 | Maximum | | | | " | 550 | | | 550 | 605 |
| 1050 | Built-in, minimum | 2 Carp | 13 | 1.231 | L.F. | 125 | 47 | | 172 | 210 |
| 1150 | Maximum | | 10 | 1.600 | | 231 | 61 | | 292 | 350 |
| 1200 | Desk top, built-in, laminated plastic, 24" deep, minimum | | 50 | .320 | | 36.50 | 12.20 | | 48.70 | 59 |
| 1300 | Maximum | | 40 | .400 | | 110 | 15.25 | | 125.25 | 145 |
| 1450 | 30" deep, minimum | | 50 | .320 | | 47 | 12.20 | | 59.20 | 70.50 |
| 1550 | Maximum | | 40 | .400 | | 205 | 15.25 | | 220.25 | 249 |
| 1750 | Dressing unit, built-in, minimum | | 12 | 1.333 | | 187 | 51 | | 238 | 285 |
| 1850 | Maximum | | 8 | 2 | | 560 | 76 | | 636 | 740 |
| 8000 | Rule of thumb: total cost for furniture, minimum | | | | Student | | | | 2,025 | 2,225 |
| 8050 | Maximum | | | | " | | | | 3,900 | 4,250 |

## 12 56 51 - Library Furniture

### 12 56 51.10 Library Furnishings

| | | Crew | Daily Output | Labor-Hours | Unit | Material | 2008 Bare Costs Labor | Equipment | Total | Total Incl O&P |
|---|---|---|---|---|---|---|---|---|---|---|
| 0010 | **LIBRARY FURNISHINGS** | | | | | | | | | |
| 0100 | Attendant desk, 36" x 62" x 29" high | 1 Carp | 16 | .500 | Ea. | 2,675 | 19.05 | | 2,694.05 | 2,975 |
| 0200 | Book display, "A" frame display, both sides, 42" x 42" x 60" high | | 16 | .500 | | 2,150 | 19.05 | | 2,169.05 | 2,400 |
| 0220 | Table with bulletin board, 42" x 24" x 49" high | | 16 | .500 | | 1,550 | 19.05 | | 1,569.05 | 1,725 |
| 0800 | Card catalogue, 30 tray unit | | 16 | .500 | | 3,025 | 19.05 | | 3,044.05 | 3,350 |
| 0840 | 60 tray unit | | 16 | .500 | | 5,350 | 19.05 | | 5,369.05 | 5,900 |
| 0880 | 72 tray unit | 2 Carp | 16 | 1 | | 6,175 | 38 | | 6,213 | 6,850 |
| 1000 | Carrels, single face, initial unit | 1 Carp | 16 | .500 | | 705 | 19.05 | | 724.05 | 805 |
| 1500 | Double face, initial unit | 2 Carp | 16 | 1 | | 1,050 | 38 | | 1,088 | 1,225 |
| 1710 | Carrels, hardwood, 36" x 24", minimum | 1 Carp | 5 | 1.600 | | 510 | 61 | | 571 | 655 |
| 1720 | Maximum | " | 4 | 2 | | 975 | 76 | | 1,051 | 1,200 |
| 2700 | Card catalog file, 60 trays, complete | | | | | 5,025 | | | 5,025 | 5,525 |
| 2720 | Alternate method: each tray | | | | | 83.50 | | | 83.50 | 92 |
| 3800 | Charging desk, built-in, with counter, plastic laminated top | 1 Carp | 7 | 1.143 | L.F. | 239 | 43.50 | | 282.50 | 330 |
| 4000 | Dictionary stand, stationary | | 16 | .500 | Ea. | 750 | 19.05 | | 769.05 | 855 |
| 4020 | Revolving | | 16 | .500 | | 299 | 19.05 | | 318.05 | 360 |

# 12 56 Institutional Furniture

## 12 56 51 – Library Furniture

| 12 56 51.10 Library Furnishings | | Crew | Daily Output | Labor-Hours | Unit | Material | 2008 Bare Costs Labor | Equipment | Total | Total Incl O&P |
|---|---|---|---|---|---|---|---|---|---|---|
| 4200 | Exhibit case, table style, 60" x 28" x 36" | 1 Carp | 11 | .727 | Ea. | 4,125 | 27.50 | | 4,152.50 | 4,600 |
| 6010 | Bookshelf, mtl, 90" high, 10" shelf, dbl face | | 11.50 | .696 | L.F. | 145 | 26.50 | | 171.50 | 201 |
| 6020 | Single face | | 12 | .667 | " | 96.50 | 25.50 | | 122 | 146 |
| 6050 | For 8" shelving, subtract from above | | | | | 10% | | | | |
| 6060 | For 12" shelving, add to above | | | | | 10% | | | | |
| 6070 | For 42" high with countertop, subtract from above | | | | | 20% | | | | |
| 6100 | Mobile compacted shelving, hand crank, 9'-0" high | | | | | | | | | |
| 6110 | Double face, including track, 3' section | | | | Ea. | 1,075 | | | 1,075 | 1,175 |
| 6150 | For electrical operation, add | | | | | 25% | | | | |
| 6200 | Magazine shelving, 82" high, 12" deep, single face | 1 Carp | 11.50 | .696 | L.F. | 189 | 26.50 | | 215.50 | 249 |
| 6210 | Double face | | 11.50 | .696 | " | 203 | 26.50 | | 229.50 | 265 |
| 7000 | Tables, card catalog reference, 24" x 60" x 42" | | 16 | .500 | Ea. | 935 | 19.05 | | 954.05 | 1,050 |
| 7200 | Reading table, laminated top, 60" x 36" | | | | " | 515 | | | 515 | 570 |

## 12 56 70 – Healthcare Furniture

### 12 56 70.10 Furniture, Hospital

| | | Crew | Daily Output | Labor-Hours | Unit | Material | Labor | Equipment | Total | Total Incl O&P |
|---|---|---|---|---|---|---|---|---|---|---|
| 0010 | **FURNITURE, HOSPITAL** | | | | | | | | | |
| 0020 | Beds, manual, minimum | | | | Ea. | 715 | | | 715 | 785 |
| 0100 | Maximum | | | | | 2,950 | | | 2,950 | 3,250 |
| 0300 | Manual and electric beds, minimum | | | | | 995 | | | 995 | 1,100 |
| 0400 | Maximum | | | | | 2,750 | | | 2,750 | 3,025 |
| 0600 | All electric hospital beds, minimum | | | | | 1,250 | | | 1,250 | 1,375 |
| 0700 | Maximum | | | | | 3,975 | | | 3,975 | 4,375 |
| 0900 | Manual, nursing home beds, minimum | | | | | 785 | | | 785 | 865 |
| 1000 | Maximum | | | | | 1,625 | | | 1,625 | 1,800 |
| 1020 | Overbed table, laminated top, minimum | | | | | 335 | | | 335 | 370 |
| 1040 | Maximum | | | | | 835 | | | 835 | 915 |
| 1100 | Patient wall systems, not incl. plumbing, minimum | | | | Room | 1,000 | | | 1,000 | 1,100 |
| 1200 | Maximum | | | | " | 1,850 | | | 1,850 | 2,025 |
| 2000 | Geriatric chairs, minimum | | | | Ea. | 505 | | | 505 | 555 |
| 2020 | Maximum | | | | " | 790 | | | 790 | 870 |

# 12 61 Fixed Audience Seating

## 12 61 13 – Upholstered Audience Seating

### 12 61 13.13 Auditorium Chairs

| | | Crew | Daily Output | Labor-Hours | Unit | Material | Labor | Equipment | Total | Total Incl O&P |
|---|---|---|---|---|---|---|---|---|---|---|
| 0010 | **AUDITORIUM CHAIRS** | | | | | | | | | |
| 2000 | All veneer construction | 2 Carp | 22 | .727 | Ea. | 159 | 27.50 | | 186.50 | 218 |
| 2200 | Veneer back, padded seat | | 22 | .727 | | 201 | 27.50 | | 228.50 | 264 |
| 2350 | Fully upholstered, spring seat | | 22 | .727 | | 201 | 27.50 | | 228.50 | 264 |
| 2450 | For tablet arms, add | | | | | 52.50 | | | 52.50 | 58 |
| 2500 | For fire retardancy, CATB-133, add | | | | | 22.50 | | | 22.50 | 25 |

### 12 61 13.23 Lecture Hall Seating

| | | Crew | Daily Output | Labor-Hours | Unit | Material | Labor | Equipment | Total | Total Incl O&P |
|---|---|---|---|---|---|---|---|---|---|---|
| 0010 | **LECTURE HALL SEATING** | | | | | | | | | |
| 1000 | Pedestal type, minimum | 2 Carp | 22 | .727 | Ea. | 150 | 27.50 | | 177.50 | 208 |
| 1200 | Maximum | " | 14.50 | 1.103 | " | 505 | 42 | | 547 | 620 |

# 12 63 Stadium and Arena Seating

## 12 63 13 – Stadium and Arena Bench Seating

### 12 63 13.13 Bleachers

| | | Crew | Daily Output | Labor-Hours | Unit | Material | 2008 Bare Costs Labor | Equipment | Total | Total Incl O&P |
|---|---|---|---|---|---|---|---|---|---|---|
| 0010 | **BLEACHERS** | | | | | | | | | |
| 3000 | Telescoping, manual to 15 tier, minimum | F-5 | 65 | .492 | Seat | 74 | 19 | | 93 | 111 |
| 3100 | Maximum | | 60 | .533 | | 111 | 20.50 | | 131.50 | 154 |
| 3300 | 16 to 20 tier, minimum | | 60 | .533 | | 177 | 20.50 | | 197.50 | 227 |
| 3400 | Maximum | | 55 | .582 | | 222 | 22.50 | | 244.50 | 279 |
| 3600 | 21 to 30 tier, minimum | | 50 | .640 | | 185 | 24.50 | | 209.50 | 242 |
| 3700 | Maximum | | 40 | .800 | | 222 | 31 | | 253 | 292 |
| 3900 | For integral power operation, add, minimum | 2 Elec | 300 | .053 | | 37 | 2.43 | | 39.43 | 44 |
| 4000 | Maximum | " | 250 | .064 | | 59 | 2.92 | | 61.92 | 69.50 |
| 5000 | Benches, folding, in wall, 14' table, 2 benches | L-4 | 2 | 12 | Set | 625 | 430 | | 1,055 | 1,350 |

# 12 67 Pews and Benches

## 12 67 13 – Pews

### 12 67 13.13 Sanctuary Pews

| | | Crew | Daily Output | Labor-Hours | Unit | Material | 2008 Bare Costs Labor | Equipment | Total | Total Incl O&P |
|---|---|---|---|---|---|---|---|---|---|---|
| 0010 | **SANCTUARY PEWS** | | | | | | | | | |
| 1500 | Bench type, hardwood, minimum | 1 Carp | 20 | .400 | L.F. | 67 | 15.25 | | 82.25 | 97.50 |
| 1550 | Maximum | " | 15 | .533 | | 133 | 20.50 | | 153.50 | 179 |
| 1570 | For kneeler, add | | | | | 16.50 | | | 16.50 | 18.15 |

# 12 92 Interior Planters and Artificial Plants

## 12 92 33 – Interior Planters

### 12 92 33.10 Planters

| | | Crew | Daily Output | Labor-Hours | Unit | Material | 2008 Bare Costs Labor | Equipment | Total | Total Incl O&P |
|---|---|---|---|---|---|---|---|---|---|---|
| 0010 | **PLANTERS** | | | | | | | | | |
| 1000 | Fiberglass, hanging, 12" diameter, 7" high | | | | Ea. | 66 | | | 66 | 72.50 |
| 1500 | Rectangular, 48" long, 16" high x 15" wide | | | | | 165 | | | 165 | 181 |
| 1650 | 60" long, 30" high, 28" wide | | | | | 310 | | | 310 | 340 |
| 2000 | Round, 12" diameter, 13" high | | | | | 48 | | | 48 | 53 |
| 2050 | 25" high | | | | | 53.50 | | | 53.50 | 59 |
| 5000 | Square, 10" side, 20" high | | | | | 115 | | | 115 | 127 |
| 5100 | 14" side, 15" high | | | | | 61.50 | | | 61.50 | 67.50 |
| 6000 | Metal bowl, 32" diameter, 8" high, minimum | | | | | 375 | | | 375 | 410 |
| 6050 | Maximum | | | | | 455 | | | 455 | 500 |
| 8750 | Wood, fiberglass liner, square | | | | | | | | | |
| 8780 | 14" square, 15" high, minimum | | | | Ea. | 221 | | | 221 | 243 |
| 8800 | Maximum | | | | | 272 | | | 272 | 299 |
| 9400 | Plastic cylinder, molded, 10" diameter, 10" high | | | | | 8.95 | | | 8.95 | 9.85 |
| 9500 | 11" diameter, 11" high | | | | | 28.50 | | | 28.50 | 31 |

# 12 93 Site Furnishings

## 12 93 23 – Trash and Litter Receptors

### 12 93 23.10 Trash Receptacles

| 12 93 23.10 Trash Receptacles | Crew | Daily Output | Labor-Hours | Unit | Material | 2008 Bare Costs Labor | 2008 Bare Costs Equipment | Total | Total Incl O&P |
|---|---|---|---|---|---|---|---|---|---|
| 0010 **TRASH RECEPTACLES** | | | | | | | | | |
| 0020 Fiberglass, 2' square, 18" high | 2 Clab | 30 | .533 | Ea. | 279 | 16.15 | | 295.15 | 330 |
| 0100     2' square, 2'-6" high | | 30 | .533 | | 390 | 16.15 | | 406.15 | 455 |
| 0300     Circular , 2' diameter, 18" high | | 30 | .533 | | 251 | 16.15 | | 267.15 | 300 |
| 0400     2' diameter, 2'-6" high | | 30 | .533 | | 335 | 16.15 | | 351.15 | 395 |

### 12 93 23.20 Trash Closure

| 12 93 23.20 Trash Closure | Crew | Daily Output | Labor-Hours | Unit | Material | 2008 Bare Costs Labor | 2008 Bare Costs Equipment | Total | Total Incl O&P |
|---|---|---|---|---|---|---|---|---|---|
| 0010 **TRASH CLOSURE** | | | | | | | | | |
| 0020 Steel with pullover cover, 2'-3" wide, 4'-7" high, 6'-2" long | 2 Clab | 5 | 3.200 | Ea. | 1,025 | 97 | | 1,122 | 1,275 |
| 0100     10'-1" long | | 4 | 4 | | 1,350 | 121 | | 1,471 | 1,700 |
| 0300 Wood, 10' wide, 6' high, 10' long | | 1.20 | 13.333 | | 1,075 | 405 | | 1,480 | 1,800 |

## 12 93 33 – Manufactured Planters

### 12 93 33.10 Planters

| 12 93 33.10 Planters | Crew | Daily Output | Labor-Hours | Unit | Material | 2008 Bare Costs Labor | 2008 Bare Costs Equipment | Total | Total Incl O&P |
|---|---|---|---|---|---|---|---|---|---|
| 0010 **PLANTERS** | | | | | | | | | |
| 0012 Concrete, sandblasted, precast, 48" diameter, 24" high | 2 Clab | 15 | 1.067 | Ea. | 615 | 32.50 | | 647.50 | 725 |
| 0100     Fluted, precast, 7' diameter, 36" high | | 10 | 1.600 | | 1,025 | 48.50 | | 1,073.50 | 1,225 |
| 0300 Fiberglass, circular, 36" diameter, 24" high | | 15 | 1.067 | | 450 | 32.50 | | 482.50 | 545 |
| 0320     36" diameter, 27" high | | 12 | 1.333 | | 355 | 40.50 | | 395.50 | 455 |
| 0330     33" high | | 15 | 1.067 | | 490 | 32.50 | | 522.50 | 590 |
| 0335     24" diameter, 36" high | | 15 | 1.067 | | 400 | 32.50 | | 432.50 | 490 |
| 0340     60" diameter, 39" high | | 8 | 2 | | 1,075 | 60.50 | | 1,135.50 | 1,275 |
| 0400     60" diameter, 24" high | | 10 | 1.600 | | 760 | 48.50 | | 808.50 | 910 |
| 0600     Square, 24" side, 36" high | | 15 | 1.067 | | 435 | 32.50 | | 467.50 | 530 |
| 0610     24" side, 27" high | | 12 | 1.333 | | 286 | 40.50 | | 326.50 | 380 |
| 0620     24" side, 16" high | | 20 | .800 | | 315 | 24 | | 339 | 390 |
| 0700     48" side, 36" high | | 15 | 1.067 | | 975 | 32.50 | | 1,007.50 | 1,125 |
| 0900     Planter/bench, 72" square, 36" high | | 5 | 3.200 | | 1,200 | 97 | | 1,297 | 1,475 |
| 1000     96" square, 27" high | | 5 | 3.200 | | 1,850 | 97 | | 1,947 | 2,200 |
| 1200 Wood, square, 48" side, 24" high | | 15 | 1.067 | | 950 | 32.50 | | 982.50 | 1,100 |
| 1300     Circular, 48" diameter, 30" high | | 10 | 1.600 | | 780 | 48.50 | | 828.50 | 935 |
| 1500     72" diameter, 30" high | | 10 | 1.600 | | 1,400 | 48.50 | | 1,448.50 | 1,600 |
| 1600     Planter/bench, 72" | | 5 | 3.200 | | 3,075 | 97 | | 3,172 | 3,525 |

## 12 93 43 – Site Seating and Tables

### 12 93 43.13 Site Seating

| 12 93 43.13 Site Seating | Crew | Daily Output | Labor-Hours | Unit | Material | 2008 Bare Costs Labor | 2008 Bare Costs Equipment | Total | Total Incl O&P |
|---|---|---|---|---|---|---|---|---|---|
| 0010 **SITE SEATING** | | | | | | | | | |
| 0012 Seating, benches, park, precast conc, w/backs, wood rails, 4' long | 2 Clab | 5 | 3.200 | Ea. | 350 | 97 | | 447 | 535 |
| 0100     8' long | | 4 | 4 | | 735 | 121 | | 856 | 1,000 |
| 0300     Fiberglass, without back, one piece, 4' long | | 10 | 1.600 | | 505 | 48.50 | | 553.50 | 630 |
| 0400     8' long | | 7 | 2.286 | | 1,050 | 69 | | 1,119 | 1,250 |
| 0500     Steel barstock pedestals w/backs, 2" x 3" wood rails, 4' long | | 10 | 1.600 | | 875 | 48.50 | | 923.50 | 1,025 |
| 0510     8' long | | 7 | 2.286 | | 1,025 | 69 | | 1,094 | 1,225 |
| 0520     3" x 8" wood plank, 4' long | | 10 | 1.600 | | 880 | 48.50 | | 928.50 | 1,050 |
| 0530     8' long | | 7 | 2.286 | | 920 | 69 | | 989 | 1,100 |
| 0540     Backless, 4" x 4" wood plank, 4' square | | 10 | 1.600 | | 855 | 48.50 | | 903.50 | 1,025 |
| 0550     8' long | | 7 | 2.286 | | 810 | 69 | | 879 | 1,000 |
| 0600     Aluminum pedestals, with backs, aluminum slats, 8' long | | 8 | 2 | | 266 | 60.50 | | 326.50 | 385 |
| 0610     15' long | | 5 | 3.200 | | 420 | 97 | | 517 | 610 |
| 0620     Portable, aluminum slats, 8' long | | 8 | 2 | | 370 | 60.50 | | 430.50 | 505 |
| 0630     15' long | | 5 | 3.200 | | 545 | 97 | | 642 | 750 |
| 0800     Cast iron pedestals, back & arms, wood slats, 4' long | | 8 | 2 | | 325 | 60.50 | | 385.50 | 450 |
| 0820     8' long | | 5 | 3.200 | | 940 | 97 | | 1,037 | 1,175 |
| 0840     Backless, wood slats, 4' long | | 8 | 2 | | 560 | 60.50 | | 620.50 | 710 |

# 12 93 Site Furnishings

## 12 93 43 – Site Seating and Tables

| 12 93 43.13 Site Seating | | Crew | Daily Output | Labor-Hours | Unit | Material | 2008 Bare Costs Labor | Equipment | Total | Total Incl O&P |
|---|---|---|---|---|---|---|---|---|---|---|
| 0860 | 8' long | 2 Clab | 5 | 3.200 | Ea. | 710 | 97 | | 807 | 930 |
| 1700 | Steel frame, fir seat, 10' long | ↓ | 10 | 1.600 | ↓ | 200 | 48.50 | | 248.50 | 295 |

# Estimating Tips

## General

- The items and systems in this division are usually estimated, purchased, supplied, and installed as a unit by one or more subcontractors. The estimator must ensure that all parties are operating from the same set of specifications and assumptions, and that all necessary items are estimated and will be provided. Many times the complex items and systems are covered, but the more common ones, such as excavation or a crane, are overlooked for the very reason that everyone assumes nobody could miss them.
The estimator should be the central focus and be able to ensure that all systems are complete.

- Another area where problems can develop in this division is at the interface between systems. The estimator must ensure, for instance, that anchor bolts, nuts, and washers are estimated and included for the air-supported structures and pre-engineered buildings to be bolted to their foundations. Utility supply is a common area where essential items or pieces of equipment can be missed or overlooked due to the fact that each subcontractor may feel it is another's responsibility. The estimator should also be aware of certain items which may be supplied as part of a package but installed by others, and ensure that the installing contractor's estimate includes the cost of installation. Conversely, the estimator must also ensure that items are not costed by two different subcontractors, resulting in an inflated overall estimate.

## 13 30 00 Special Structures

- The foundations and floor slab, as well as rough mechanical and electrical, should be estimated, as this work is required for the assembly and erection of the structure. Generally, as noted in the book, the pre-engineered building comes as a shell and additional features, such as windows and doors, must be included by the estimator. Here again, the estimator must have a clear understanding of the scope of each portion of the work and all the necessary interfaces.

## Reference Numbers

Reference numbers are shown in shaded boxes at the beginning of some major classifications. These numbers refer to related items in the Reference Section. The reference information may be an estimating procedure, an alternate pricing method, or technical information.

*Note:* Not all subdivisions listed here necessarily appear in this publication.

# 13 05 Common Work Results for Special Construction

## 13 05 05 – Selective Special Construction Demolition

| 13 05 05.10 Selective Demolition, Air Supported Structures | | Crew | Daily Output | Labor-Hours | Unit | Material | 2008 Bare Costs Labor | Equipment | Total | Total Incl O&P |
|---|---|---|---|---|---|---|---|---|---|---|
| 0010 | **SELECTIVE DEMOLITION, AIR SUPPORTED STRUCTURES** | | | | | | | | | |
| 0020 | Tank covers, scrim, dbl layer, vinyl poly w/ hdw, blower & controls | | | | | | | | | |
| 0050 | Round and rectangular      R024119-10 | B-2 | 9000 | .004 | S.F. | | .14 | | .14 | .21 |
| 0100 | Warehouse structures | | | | | | | | | |
| 0120 | Poly/vinyl fabric, 28 oz, incl tension cables & inflation system | 4 Clab | 9000 | .004 | SF Flr. | | .11 | | .11 | .17 |
| 0150 | Reinforced vinyl, 12 oz., 3000 S.F. | " | 5000 | .006 | | | .19 | | .19 | .30 |
| 0200 | 12,000 to 24,000 S.F. | 8 Clab | 20000 | .003 | | | .10 | | .10 | .15 |
| 0250 | Tedlar vinyl fabric, 28 oz. w/liner, to 3000 S.F. | 4 Clab | 5000 | .006 | | | .19 | | .19 | .30 |
| 0300 | 12,000 to 24,000 S.F. | 8 Clab | 20000 | .003 | ↓ | | .10 | | .10 | .15 |
| 0350 | Greenhouse/shelter, woven polyethylene with liner | | | | | | | | | |
| 0400 | 3000 S.F. | 4 Clab | 5000 | .006 | SF Flr. | | .19 | | .19 | .30 |
| 0450 | 12,000 to 24,000 S.F. | 8 Clab | 20000 | .003 | | | .10 | | .10 | .15 |
| 0500 | Tennis/gymnasium, poly/vinyl fabric, 28 oz., incl thermal liner | 4 Clab | 9000 | .004 | | | .11 | | .11 | .17 |
| 0600 | Stadium/convention center, teflon coated fiberglass, incl thermal liner | 9 Clab | 40000 | .002 | ↓ | | .05 | | .05 | .08 |
| 0700 | Doors, air lock, 15' long, 10' x 10' | 2 Carp | 1.50 | 10.667 | Ea. | | 405 | | 405 | 635 |
| 0720 | 15' x 15' | | .80 | 20 | | | 760 | | 760 | 1,175 |
| 0750 | Revolving personnel door, 6' dia. x 6'-6" high | ↓ | 1.50 | 10.667 | ↓ | | 405 | | 405 | 635 |

## 13 05 05.20 Selective Demolition, Garden Houses

| 13 05 05.20 Selective Demolition, Garden Houses | | Crew | Daily Output | Labor-Hours | Unit | Material | 2008 Bare Costs Labor | Equipment | Total | Total Incl O&P |
|---|---|---|---|---|---|---|---|---|---|---|
| 0010 | **SELECTIVE DEMOLITION, GARDEN HOUSES**      R024119-10 | | | | | | | | | |
| 0020 | Prefab, wood, excl foundation, average | 2 Clab | 400 | .040 | SF Flr. | | 1.21 | | 1.21 | 1.88 |

## 13 05 05.25 Selective Demolition, Geodesic Domes

| 13 05 05.25 Selective Demolition, Geodesic Domes | | Crew | Daily Output | Labor-Hours | Unit | Material | 2008 Bare Costs Labor | Equipment | Total | Total Incl O&P |
|---|---|---|---|---|---|---|---|---|---|---|
| 0010 | **SELECTIVE DEMOLITION, GEODESIC DOMES** | | | | | | | | | |
| 0050 | Shell only, interlocking plywood panels, 30' diameter | F-5 | 3.20 | 10 | Ea. | | 385 | | 385 | 600 |
| 0060 | 34' diameter | | 2.30 | 13.913 | | | 535 | | 535 | 835 |
| 0070 | 39' diameter | | 2 | 16 | | | 620 | | 620 | 960 |
| 0080 | 45' diameter | | 2.20 | 14.545 | | | 560 | | 560 | 875 |
| 0090 | 55' diameter | | 2 | 16 | | | 620 | | 620 | 960 |
| 0100 | 60' diameter | | 2 | 16 | | | 620 | | 620 | 960 |
| 0110 | 65' diameter | ↓ | 1.60 | 20 | ↓ | | 770 | | 770 | 1,200 |

## 13 05 05.30 Selective Demolition, Greenhouses

| 13 05 05.30 Selective Demolition, Greenhouses | | Crew | Daily Output | Labor-Hours | Unit | Material | 2008 Bare Costs Labor | Equipment | Total | Total Incl O&P |
|---|---|---|---|---|---|---|---|---|---|---|
| 0010 | **SELECTIVE DEMOLITION, GREENHOUSES**      R024119-10 | | | | | | | | | |
| 0020 | Resi-type, free standing, excl foundations, 9' long x 8' wide | 2 Clab | 160 | .100 | SF Flr. | | 3.03 | | 3.03 | 4.71 |
| 0030 | 9' long x 11' wide | | 170 | .094 | | | 2.85 | | 2.85 | 4.43 |
| 0040 | 9' long x 14' wide | | 220 | .073 | | | 2.20 | | 2.20 | 3.42 |
| 0050 | 9' long x 17' wide | | 320 | .050 | | | 1.51 | | 1.51 | 2.35 |
| 0060 | Lean-to type, 4' wide | | 64 | .250 | | | 7.55 | | 7.55 | 11.75 |
| 0070 | 7' wide | | 120 | .133 | ↓ | | 4.03 | | 4.03 | 6.25 |
| 0080 | Geodesic hemisphere, 1/8" plexiglass glazing, 8' dia | | 4 | 4 | Ea. | | 121 | | 121 | 188 |
| 0090 | 24' dia | | .80 | 20 | | | 605 | | 605 | 940 |
| 0100 | 48' dia | ↓ | .40 | 40 | ↓ | | 1,200 | | 1,200 | 1,875 |

## 13 05 05.35 Selective Demolition, Hangars

| 13 05 05.35 Selective Demolition, Hangars | | Crew | Daily Output | Labor-Hours | Unit | Material | 2008 Bare Costs Labor | Equipment | Total | Total Incl O&P |
|---|---|---|---|---|---|---|---|---|---|---|
| 0010 | **SELECTIVE DEMOLITION, HANGARS** | | | | | | | | | |
| 0020 | T type hangars, prefab, steel , galv roof & walls, incl doors, excl fndtn | E-2 | 2550 | .022 | SF Flr. | | .92 | .61 | 1.53 | 2.27 |
| 0030 | Circular type, prefab, steel frame, plastic skin, incl foundation, 80' dia | " | .50 | 112 | Total | | 4,700 | 3,125 | 7,825 | 11,600 |

## 13 05 05.45 Selective Demolition, Lightning Protection

| 13 05 05.45 Selective Demolition, Lightning Protection | | Crew | Daily Output | Labor-Hours | Unit | Material | 2008 Bare Costs Labor | Equipment | Total | Total Incl O&P |
|---|---|---|---|---|---|---|---|---|---|---|
| 0010 | **SELECTIVE DEMOLITION, LIGHTNING PROTECTION** | | | | | | | | | |
| 0020 | Air terminal & base, copper, 3/8" dia x 10", to 75' h | 1 Clab | 16 | .500 | Ea. | | 15.15 | | 15.15 | 23.50 |
| 0030 | 1/2" dia x 12", over 75' h | | 16 | .500 | | | 15.15 | | 15.15 | 23.50 |
| 0050 | Aluminum, 1/2" dia x 12", to 75' h | | 16 | .500 | | | 15.15 | | 15.15 | 23.50 |
| 0060 | 5/8" dia x 12", over 75' h | | 16 | .500 | ↓ | | 15.15 | | 15.15 | 23.50 |
| 0070 | Cable, copper, 220 lb per thousand feet, to 75' high | ↓ | 640 | .013 | L.F. | | .38 | | .38 | .59 |

# 13 05 Common Work Results for Special Construction

## 13 05 05 – Selective Special Construction Demolition

| 13 05 05.45 Selective Demolition, Lightning Protection | Crew | Daily Output | Labor-Hours | Unit | Material | 2008 Bare Costs Labor | Equipment | Total | Total Incl O&P |
|---|---|---|---|---|---|---|---|---|---|
| 0080 | 375 lb per thousand feet, over 75' high | 1 Clab | 460 | .017 | L.F. | | .53 | | .53 | .82 |
| 0090 | Aluminum, 101 lb per thousand feet, to 75' high | | 560 | .014 | | | .43 | | .43 | .67 |
| 0100 | 199 lb per thousand feet, over 75' high | | 480 | .017 | | | .50 | | .50 | .78 |
| 0110 | Arrester, 175 V AC, to ground | | 16 | .500 | Ea. | | 15.15 | | 15.15 | 23.50 |
| 0120 | 650 V AC, to ground | | 13 | .615 | " | | 18.60 | | 18.60 | 29 |

## 13 05 05.50 Selective Demolition, Pre-Engineered Steel Buildings

| | | Crew | Daily Output | Labor-Hours | Unit | Material | Labor | Equipment | Total | Total Incl O&P |
|---|---|---|---|---|---|---|---|---|---|---|
| 0010 | **SELECTIVE DEMOLITION, PRE-ENGINEERED STEEL BUILDINGS** | | | | | | | | | |
| 0500 | Pre-engd steel bldgs, rigid frame, clear span & multi post, excl salvage | | | | | | | | | |
| 0550 | 3,500 to 7,500 S.F | L-11 | 1350 | .024 | SF Flr. | | .82 | 1.27 | 2.09 | 2.73 |
| 0600 | 7,501 to 12,500 S.F | | 2000 | .016 | | | .56 | .86 | 1.42 | 1.83 |
| 0650 | 12,500 S.F or greater | | 2200 | .015 | | | .51 | .78 | 1.29 | 1.67 |
| 0700 | Pre-engd steel building components | | | | | | | | | |
| 0710 | Entrance canopy, including frame 4' x 4' | E-24 | 8 | 4 | Ea. | | 169 | 98 | 267 | 400 |
| 0720 | 4' x 8' | " | 7 | 4.571 | | | 193 | 112 | 305 | 460 |
| 0730 | H.M doors, self framing, single leaf | 2 Skwk | 8 | 2 | | | 79 | | 79 | 123 |
| 0740 | Double leaf | | 5 | 3.200 | | | 126 | | 126 | 196 |
| 0760 | Gutter, eave type | | 600 | .027 | L.F. | | 1.05 | | 1.05 | 1.63 |
| 0770 | Sash, single slide, double slide or fixed | | 24 | .667 | Ea. | | 26.50 | | 26.50 | 41 |
| 0780 | Skylight, fiberglass, to 30 S.F. | | 16 | 1 | | | 39.50 | | 39.50 | 61.50 |
| 0785 | Roof vents, circular, 12" to 24" diameter | | 12 | 1.333 | | | 52.50 | | 52.50 | 81.50 |
| 0790 | Continuous, 10' long | | 8 | 2 | | | 79 | | 79 | 123 |
| 0900 | Shelters, aluminum frame | | | | | | | | | |
| 0910 | Acrylic glazing, 3' x 9' x 8' high | 2 Skwk | 2 | 8 | Ea. | | 315 | | 315 | 490 |
| 0920 | 9' x 12' x 8' high | " | 1.50 | 10.667 | " | | 420 | | 420 | 655 |

## 13 05 05.60 Selective Demolition, Silos

| | | Crew | Daily Output | Labor-Hours | Unit | Material | Labor | Equipment | Total | Total Incl O&P |
|---|---|---|---|---|---|---|---|---|---|---|
| 0010 | **SELECTIVE DEMOLITION, SILOS** | | | | | | | | | |
| 0020 | Conc stave, indstrl, conical/sloping bott, excl fndtn, 12' dia, 35' h | D-8 | .22 | 181 | Ea. | | 6,500 | | 6,500 | 9,875 |
| 0030 | 16' dia, 45' h | | .16 | 250 | | | 8,925 | | 8,925 | 13,600 |
| 0040 | 25' dia, 75' h | | .10 | 400 | | | 14,300 | | 14,300 | 21,700 |
| 0050 | Steel, factory fabricated, 30,000 gal cap, painted or epoxy lined | L-5 | 2 | 28 | | | 1,200 | 395 | 1,595 | 2,550 |

## 13 05 05.65 Selective Demolition, Sound Control

| | | Crew | Daily Output | Labor-Hours | Unit | Material | Labor | Equipment | Total | Total Incl O&P |
|---|---|---|---|---|---|---|---|---|---|---|
| 0010 | **SELECTIVE DEMOLITION, SOUND CONTROL** R024119-10 | | | | | | | | | |
| 0120 | Acoustical enclosure, 4" thick walls & ceiling panels, 8 lbs/SF | 3 Carp | 144 | .167 | SF Surf | | 6.35 | | 6.35 | 9.90 |
| 0130 | 10.5 lbs/SF | | 128 | .188 | | | 7.15 | | 7.15 | 11.10 |
| 0140 | Reverb chamber, parallel walls, 4" thick | | 120 | .200 | | | 7.60 | | 7.60 | 11.85 |
| 0150 | Skewed walls, parallel roof, 4" thick | | 110 | .218 | | | 8.30 | | 8.30 | 12.95 |
| 0160 | Skewed walls/roof, 4" layer/air space | | 96 | .250 | | | 9.55 | | 9.55 | 14.85 |
| 0170 | Sound-absorbing panels, painted metal, 2'-6" x 8', under 1,000 SF | | 430 | .056 | | | 2.13 | | 2.13 | 3.31 |
| 0180 | Over 1,000 SF | | 480 | .050 | | | 1.91 | | 1.91 | 2.97 |
| 0190 | Flexible transparent curtain, clear | 3 Shee | 430 | .056 | | | 2.53 | | 2.53 | 3.90 |
| 0192 | 50% clear, 50% foam | | 430 | .056 | | | 2.53 | | 2.53 | 3.90 |
| 0194 | 25% clear, 75% foam | | 430 | .056 | | | 2.53 | | 2.53 | 3.90 |
| 0196 | 100% foam | | 430 | .056 | | | 2.53 | | 2.53 | 3.90 |
| 0200 | Audio-masking sys, incl speakers, amplfr, signal gnrtr, clng mntd, 5,000 SF | | | | | | | | | |
| 0205 | Ceiling mounted, 5,000 SF | 2 Elec | 4800 | .003 | S.F. | | .15 | | .15 | .23 |
| 0210 | 10,000 SF | | 5600 | .003 | | | .13 | | .13 | .19 |
| 0220 | Plenum mounted, 5,000 SF | | 7600 | .002 | | | .10 | | .10 | .14 |
| 0230 | 10,000 SF | | 8800 | .002 | | | .08 | | .08 | .12 |

## 13 05 05.70 Selective Demolition, Special Purpose Rooms

| | | Crew | Daily Output | Labor-Hours | Unit | Material | Labor | Equipment | Total | Total Incl O&P |
|---|---|---|---|---|---|---|---|---|---|---|
| 0010 | **SELECTIVE DEMOLITION, SPECIAL PURPOSE ROOMS** R024119-10 | | | | | | | | | |
| 0100 | Audiometric rooms, under 500 S.F. surface | 4 Carp | 200 | .160 | SF Surf | | 6.10 | | 6.10 | 9.50 |
| 0110 | Over 500 S.F. surface | " | 240 | .133 | " | | 5.10 | | 5.10 | 7.90 |

387

# 13 05 Common Work Results for Special Construction

## 13 05 05 – Selective Special Construction Demolition

| | 13 05 05.70 Selective Demolition, Special Purpose Rooms | Crew | Daily Output | Labor-Hours | Unit | Material | 2008 Bare Costs Labor | Equipment | Total | Total Incl O&P |
|---|---|---|---|---|---|---|---|---|---|---|
| 0200 | Clean rooms, 12' x 12' soft wall, class 100 | 1 Carp | .30 | 26.667 | Ea. | | 1,025 | | 1,025 | 1,575 |
| 0210 | Class 1000 | | .30 | 26.667 | | | 1,025 | | 1,025 | 1,575 |
| 0220 | Class 10,000 | | .35 | 22.857 | | | 870 | | 870 | 1,350 |
| 0230 | Class 100,000 | | .35 | 22.857 | | | 870 | | 870 | 1,350 |
| 0300 | Darkrooms, shell complete, 8' high | 2 Carp | 220 | .073 | SF Flr. | | 2.77 | | 2.77 | 4.31 |
| 0310 | 12' high | | 110 | .145 | " | | 5.55 | | 5.55 | 8.65 |
| 0350 | Darkrooms doors, mini-cylindrical, revolving | | 4 | 4 | Ea. | | 152 | | 152 | 237 |
| 0400 | Music room, practice modular | | 140 | .114 | SF Surf | | 4.35 | | 4.35 | 6.80 |
| 0500 | Refrigeration structures and finishes | | | | | | | | | |
| 0510 | Wall finish, 2 coat portland cement plaster, 1/2" thick | 1 Clab | 200 | .040 | S.F. | | 1.21 | | 1.21 | 1.88 |
| 0520 | Fiberglass panels, 1/8" thick | | 400 | .020 | | | .61 | | .61 | .94 |
| 0530 | Ceiling finish, polystyrene plastic, 1" to 2" thick | | 500 | .016 | | | .48 | | .48 | .75 |
| 0540 | 4" thick | | 450 | .018 | | | .54 | | .54 | .84 |
| 0550 | Refrigerator, prefab aluminum walk-in, 7'-6" high, 6' x 6' OD | 2 Carp | 100 | .160 | SF Flr. | | 6.10 | | 6.10 | 9.50 |
| 0560 | 10' x 10' OD | | 160 | .100 | | | 3.81 | | 3.81 | 5.95 |
| 0570 | Over 150 S.F. | | 200 | .080 | | | 3.05 | | 3.05 | 4.74 |
| 0600 | Sauna, prefabricated, including heater & controls, 7' high, to 30 S.F. | | 120 | .133 | | | 5.10 | | 5.10 | 7.90 |
| 0610 | To 40 S.F. | | 140 | .114 | | | 4.35 | | 4.35 | 6.80 |
| 0620 | To 60 S.F. | | 175 | .091 | | | 3.48 | | 3.48 | 5.40 |
| 0630 | To 100 S.F. | | 220 | .073 | | | 2.77 | | 2.77 | 4.31 |
| 0640 | To 130 S.F. | | 250 | .064 | | | 2.44 | | 2.44 | 3.80 |
| 0650 | Steam bath, heater, timer, head, single, to 140 CF | 1 Plum | 2.20 | 3.636 | Ea. | | 170 | | 170 | 255 |
| 0660 | To 300 CF | | 2.20 | 3.636 | | | 170 | | 170 | 255 |
| 0670 | Steam bath, comm. size, w/blow-down assembly, to 800 CF | | 1.80 | 4.444 | | | 208 | | 208 | 310 |
| 0680 | To 2500 CF | | 1.60 | 5 | | | 234 | | 234 | 350 |
| 0690 | Steam bath, comm. size, multiple, for motels, apts, 500 CF, 2 baths | | 2 | 4 | | | 187 | | 187 | 281 |
| 0700 | 1,000 CF, 4 baths | | 1.40 | 5.714 | | | 267 | | 267 | 400 |

## 13 05 05.75 Selective Demolition, Storage Tanks

| | | Crew | Daily Output | Labor-Hours | Unit | Material | Labor | Equipment | Total | Total Incl O&P |
|---|---|---|---|---|---|---|---|---|---|---|
| 0010 | **SELECTIVE DEMOLITION, STORAGE TANKS** | | | | | | | | | |
| 0500 | Steel tank, single wall, above ground, not incl fdn, pumps or piping | | | | | | | | | |
| 0510 | Single wall, 275 gallon    R024119-10 | Q-1 | 3 | 5.333 | Ea. | | 224 | | 224 | 335 |
| 0520 | 550 thru 2,000 gallon | B-34P | 2 | 12 | | | 465 | 255 | 720 | 985 |
| 0530 | 5,000 thru 10,000 gallon | B-34Q | 2 | 12 | | | 470 | 595 | 1,065 | 1,375 |
| 0540 | 15,000 thru 30,000 gallon | B-34N | 2 | 4 | | | 122 | 221 | 343 | 430 |
| 0600 | Steel tank, double wall, above ground not incl fdn, pumps & piping | | | | | | | | | |
| 0620 | 500 thru 2,000 gallon | B-34P | 2 | 12 | Ea. | | 465 | 255 | 720 | 985 |

## 13 05 05.85 Selective Demolition, Swimming Pool Equip

| | | Crew | Daily Output | Labor-Hours | Unit | Material | Labor | Equipment | Total | Total Incl O&P |
|---|---|---|---|---|---|---|---|---|---|---|
| 0010 | **SELECTIVE DEMOLITION, SWIMMING POOL EQUIP** | | | | | | | | | |
| 0020 | Diving stand, stainless steel, 3 meter | 2 Clab | 3 | 5.333 | Ea. | | 161 | | 161 | 251 |
| 0030 | 1 meter | | 5 | 3.200 | | | 97 | | 97 | 151 |
| 0040 | Diving board, 16' long, aluminum | | 5.40 | 2.963 | | | 89.50 | | 89.50 | 139 |
| 0050 | Fiberglass | | 5.40 | 2.963 | | | 89.50 | | 89.50 | 139 |
| 0070 | Ladders, heavy duty, stainless steel, 2 tread | | 14 | 1.143 | | | 34.50 | | 34.50 | 54 |
| 0080 | 4 tread | | 12 | 1.333 | | | 40.50 | | 40.50 | 62.50 |
| 0090 | Lifeguard chair, stainless steel, fixed | | 5 | 3.200 | | | 97 | | 97 | 151 |
| 0100 | Slide, tubular, fiberglass, aluminum handrails & ladder, 5', straight | | 4 | 4 | | | 121 | | 121 | 188 |
| 0110 | 8', curved | | 6 | 2.667 | | | 80.50 | | 80.50 | 125 |
| 0120 | 10', curved | | 3 | 5.333 | | | 161 | | 161 | 251 |
| 0130 | 12' straight, with platform | | 2.50 | 6.400 | | | 194 | | 194 | 300 |
| 0140 | Removable access ramp, stainless steel | | 4 | 4 | | | 121 | | 121 | 188 |
| 0150 | Removable stairs, stainless steel, collapsible | | 4 | 4 | | | 121 | | 121 | 188 |

# 13 05 Common Work Results for Special Construction

## 13 05 05 – Selective Special Construction Demolition

### 13 05 05.90 Selective Demolition, Tension Structures

| | | Crew | Daily Output | Labor-Hours | Unit | Material | 2008 Bare Costs Labor | 2008 Bare Costs Equipment | Total | Total Incl O&P |
|---|---|---|---|---|---|---|---|---|---|---|
| 0010 | **SELECTIVE DEMOLITION, TENSION STRUCTURES** | | | | | | | | | |
| 0020 | Tension structure, steel/alum frame, fabric shell, 60' clear span, 6,000 SF | B-41 | 2000 | .022 | SF Flr. | | .69 | .13 | .82 | 1.22 |
| 0030 | 12,000 SF | | 2200 | .020 | | | .63 | .12 | .75 | 1.10 |
| 0040 | 80' clear span, 20,800 SF | ↓ | 2440 | .018 | | | .56 | .11 | .67 | 1 |
| 0050 | 100' clear span, 10,000 SF | L-5 | 4350 | .013 | | | .55 | .18 | .73 | 1.18 |
| 0060 | 26,000 SF | " | 4600 | .012 | ↓ | | .52 | .17 | .69 | 1.11 |

### 13 05 05.95 Selective Demolition, X-Ray/Radio Freq Protection

| | | Crew | Daily Output | Labor-Hours | Unit | Material | 2008 Bare Costs Labor | 2008 Bare Costs Equipment | Total | Total Incl O&P |
|---|---|---|---|---|---|---|---|---|---|---|
| 0010 | **SELECTIVE DEMOLITION, X-RAY/RADIO FREQ PROTECTION** | | | | | | | | | |
| 0020 | Shielding lead, lined door frame, excl hdwe, 1/16" thick | 1 Clab | 4.80 | 1.667 | Ea. | | 50.50 | | 50.50 | 78.50 |
| 0030 | Lead sheets, 1/16" thick | R024119-10 | 2 Clab | 270 | .059 | S.F. | | 1.79 | | 1.79 | 2.79 |
| 0040 | 1/8" thick | | 240 | .067 | | | 2.02 | | 2.02 | 3.14 |
| 0050 | Lead shielding, 1/4" thick | | 270 | .059 | | | 1.79 | | 1.79 | 2.79 |
| 0060 | 1/2" thick | | 240 | .067 | ↓ | | 2.02 | | 2.02 | 3.14 |
| 0070 | Lead glass, 1/4" thick, 2.0 mm LE, 12" x 16" | 2 Glaz | 26 | .615 | Ea. | | 23 | | 23 | 35 |
| 0080 | 24" x 36" | | 16 | 1 | | | 37.50 | | 37.50 | 56.50 |
| 0090 | 36" x 60" | | 4 | 4 | | | 149 | | 149 | 226 |
| 0100 | Lead glass window frame, with 1/16" lead & voice passage, 36" x 60" | | 4 | 4 | | | 149 | | 149 | 226 |
| 0110 | Lead glass window frame, 24" x 36" | ↓ | 16 | 1 | ↓ | | 37.50 | | 37.50 | 56.50 |
| 0120 | Lead gypsum board, 5/8" thick with 1/16" lead | 2 Clab | 320 | .050 | S.F. | | 1.51 | | 1.51 | 2.35 |
| 0130 | 1/8" lead | | 280 | .057 | | | 1.73 | | 1.73 | 2.69 |
| 0140 | 1/32" lead | | 400 | .040 | ↓ | | 1.21 | | 1.21 | 1.88 |
| 0150 | Butt joints, 1/8" lead or thicker, 2" x 7' long batten strip | | 480 | .033 | Ea. | | 1.01 | | 1.01 | 1.57 |
| 0160 | X-ray protection, average radiography room, up to 300 SF, 1/16" lead, min | | .50 | 32 | Total | | 970 | | 970 | 1,500 |
| 0170 | Maximum | | .30 | 53.333 | | | 1,625 | | 1,625 | 2,500 |
| 0180 | Deep therapy X-ray room, 250 KV cap, up to 300 SF, 1/4" lead, min | | .20 | 80 | | | 2,425 | | 2,425 | 3,775 |
| 0190 | Max | | .12 | 133 | ↓ | | 4,025 | | 4,025 | 6,275 |
| 0880 | Radio frequency shielding, prefab or screen-type copper or steel, minimum | | 360 | .044 | SF Surf | | 1.34 | | 1.34 | 2.09 |
| 0890 | Average | | 310 | .052 | | | 1.56 | | 1.56 | 2.43 |
| 0895 | Maximum | ↓ | 290 | .055 | ↓ | | 1.67 | | 1.67 | 2.60 |

# 13 11 Swimming Pools

## 13 11 13 – Below-Grade Swimming Pools

### 13 11 13.50 Swimming Pools

| | | Crew | Daily Output | Labor-Hours | Unit | Material | 2008 Bare Costs Labor | 2008 Bare Costs Equipment | Total | Total Incl O&P |
|---|---|---|---|---|---|---|---|---|---|---|
| 0010 | **SWIMMING POOLS** Residential in-ground, vinyl lined, concrete | | | | | | | | | |
| 0020 | Sides including equipment, sand bottom | B-52 | 300 | .187 | SF Surf | 12.25 | 6.60 | 1.49 | 20.34 | 25.50 |
| 0100 | Metal or polystyrene sides | R131113-20 | B-14 | 410 | .117 | | 10.25 | 3.73 | .70 | 14.68 | 17.75 |
| 0200 | Add for vermiculite bottom | | | | ↓ | .79 | | | .79 | .87 |
| 0500 | Gunite bottom and sides, white plaster finish | | | | | | | | | |
| 0600 | 12' x 30' pool | B-52 | 145 | .386 | SF Surf | 23 | 13.65 | 3.08 | 39.73 | 49.50 |
| 0720 | 16' x 32' pool | | 155 | .361 | | 20.50 | 12.75 | 2.88 | 36.13 | 45.50 |
| 0750 | 20' x 40' pool | ↓ | 250 | .224 | ↓ | 18.35 | 7.90 | 1.79 | 28.04 | 34 |
| 0810 | Concrete bottom and sides, tile finish | | | | | | | | | |
| 0820 | 12' x 30' pool | B-52 | 80 | .700 | SF Surf | 23 | 24.50 | 5.60 | 53.10 | 70 |
| 0830 | 16' x 32' pool | | 95 | .589 | | 19.05 | 21 | 4.70 | 44.75 | 58 |
| 0840 | 20' x 40' pool | ↓ | 130 | .431 | ↓ | 15.15 | 15.20 | 3.44 | 33.79 | 44 |
| 1100 | Motel, gunite with plaster finish, incl. medium | | | | | | | | | |
| 1150 | capacity filtration & chlorination | B-52 | 115 | .487 | SF Surf | 28 | 17.20 | 3.89 | 49.09 | 62 |
| 1200 | Municipal, gunite with plaster finish, incl. high | | | | | | | | | |
| 1250 | capacity filtration & chlorination | B-52 | 100 | .560 | SF Surf | 36.50 | 19.80 | 4.47 | 60.77 | 75.50 |
| 1350 | Add for formed gutters | | | | L.F. | 53.50 | | | 53.50 | 59 |

# 13 11 Swimming Pools

## 13 11 13 – Below-Grade Swimming Pools

| 13 11 13.50 Swimming Pools | Crew | Daily Output | Labor-Hours | Unit | Material | 2008 Bare Costs Labor | Equipment | Total | Total Incl O&P |
|---|---|---|---|---|---|---|---|---|---|
| 1360 | Add for stainless steel gutters | | | | L.F. | 158 | | | 158 | 174 |
| 1600 | For water heating system, see Div. 23 52 28.10 | | | | | | | | | |
| 1700 | Filtration and deck equipment only, as % of total | | | | Total | | | | 20% | 20% |
| 1800 | Deck equipment, rule of thumb, 20' x 40' pool | | | | SF Pool | | | | 1.18 | 1.30 |
| 1900 | 5000 S.F. pool | | | | " | | | | 1.73 | 1.90 |
| 3000 | Painting pools, preparation + 3 coats, 20' x 40' pool, epoxy | 2 Pord | .33 | 48.485 | Total | 1,375 | 1,625 | | 3,000 | 3,950 |
| 3100 | Rubber base paint, 18 gallons | " | .33 | 48.485 | | 910 | 1,625 | | 2,535 | 3,450 |
| 3500 | 42' x 82' pool, 75 gallons, epoxy paint | 3 Pord | .14 | 171 | | 5,775 | 5,775 | | 11,550 | 15,100 |
| 3600 | Rubber base paint | " | .14 | 171 | | 3,750 | 5,775 | | 9,525 | 12,800 |

## 13 11 46 – Swimming Pool Accessories

### 13 11 46.50 Swimming Pool Equipment

| | | Crew | Daily Output | Labor-Hours | Unit | Material | 2008 Bare Costs Labor | Equipment | Total | Total Incl O&P |
|---|---|---|---|---|---|---|---|---|---|---|
| 0010 | **SWIMMING POOL EQUIPMENT** | | | | | | | | | |
| 0020 | Diving stand, stainless steel, 3 meter | 2 Carp | .40 | 40 | Ea. | 9,350 | 1,525 | | 10,875 | 12,700 |
| 0300 | 1 meter | | 2.70 | 5.926 | | 5,450 | 226 | | 5,676 | 6,350 |
| 0600 | Diving boards, 16' long, aluminum | | 2.70 | 5.926 | | 3,975 | 226 | | 4,201 | 4,725 |
| 0700 | Fiberglass | | 2.70 | 5.926 | | 2,525 | 226 | | 2,751 | 3,125 |
| 1100 | Gutter system, stainless steel, with grating, stock, | | | | | | | | | |
| 1110 | contains supply and drainage system | E-1 | 20 | 1.200 | L.F. | 205 | 50.50 | 6.60 | 262.10 | 320 |
| 1120 | Integral gutter and 5' high wall system, stainless steel | " | 10 | 2.400 | " | 310 | 101 | 13.20 | 424.20 | 530 |
| 1200 | Ladders, heavy duty, stainless steel, 2 tread | 2 Carp | 7 | 2.286 | Ea. | 485 | 87 | | 572 | 670 |
| 1500 | 4 tread | | 6 | 2.667 | | 650 | 102 | | 752 | 875 |
| 1800 | Lifeguard chair, stainless steel, fixed | | 2.70 | 5.926 | | 2,200 | 226 | | 2,426 | 2,775 |
| 1900 | Portable | | | | | 2,400 | | | 2,400 | 2,650 |
| 2100 | Lights, underwater, 12 volt, with transformer, 300 watt | 1 Elec | 1 | 8 | | 235 | 365 | | 600 | 805 |
| 2200 | 110 volt, 500 watt, standard | | 1 | 8 | | 197 | 365 | | 562 | 760 |
| 2400 | Low water cutoff type | | 1 | 8 | | 225 | 365 | | 590 | 790 |
| 2800 | Heaters, see Div. 23 52 28.10 | | | | | | | | | |
| 3000 | Pool covers, reinforced vinyl | 3 Clab | 1800 | .013 | S.F. | .36 | .40 | | .76 | 1.03 |
| 3050 | Automatic, electric | | | | | | | | 8.77 | 9.65 |
| 3100 | Vinyl water tube | 3 Clab | 3200 | .008 | | .46 | .23 | | .69 | .86 |
| 3200 | Maximum | " | 3000 | .008 | | .58 | .24 | | .82 | 1.02 |
| 3250 | Sealed air bubble polyethylene solar blanket | | | | | .27 | | | .27 | .30 |
| 3300 | Slides, tubular, fiberglass, aluminum handrails & ladder, 5'-0", straight | 2 Carp | 1.60 | 10 | Ea. | 3,625 | 380 | | 4,005 | 4,600 |
| 3320 | 8'-0", curved | | 3 | 5.333 | | 14,500 | 203 | | 14,703 | 16,300 |
| 3400 | 10'-0", curved | | 1 | 16 | | 20,800 | 610 | | 21,410 | 23,900 |
| 3420 | 12'-0", straight with platform | | 1.20 | 13.333 | | 5,100 | 510 | | 5,610 | 6,425 |
| 4500 | Hydraulic lift, movable pool bottom, single ram | | | | | | | | | |
| 4520 | Under 1,000 S.F. area | L-9 | .03 | 1200 | Ea. | 195,000 | 41,900 | | 236,900 | 282,000 |
| 4600 | Four ram lift, over 1,000 S.F. | " | .02 | 1800 | | 280,000 | 63,000 | | 343,000 | 409,500 |
| 5000 | Removable access ramp, stainless steel | 2 Clab | 2 | 8 | | 8,475 | 242 | | 8,717 | 9,700 |
| 5500 | Removable stairs, stainless steel, collapsible | " | 2 | 8 | | 4,025 | 242 | | 4,267 | 4,800 |

# 13 17 Tubs and Pools

## 13 17 23 – Therapeutic Pools

| 13 17 23.50 Therapeutic Pools | Crew | Daily Output | Labor-Hours | Unit | Material | 2008 Bare Costs Labor | Equipment | Total | Total Incl O&P |
|---|---|---|---|---|---|---|---|---|---|
| 0010 **THERAPEUTIC POOLS** See Div. 22 43 19.10 | | | | | | | | | |

## 13 17 33 – Whirlpool tubs

### 13 17 33.10 Whirlpool Bath

| | Crew | Daily Output | Labor-Hours | Unit | Material | Labor | Equipment | Total | Total Incl O&P |
|---|---|---|---|---|---|---|---|---|---|
| 0010 **WHIRLPOOL BATH** | | | | | | | | | |
| 6000 Whirlpool, bath with vented overflow, molded fiberglass | | | | | | | | | |
| 6100 66" x 48" x 24" | Q-1 | 1 | 16 | Ea. | 2,975 | 670 | | 3,645 | 4,275 |

# 13 18 Ice Rinks

## 13 18 13 – Ice Rink Floor Systems

### 13 18 13.50 Ice Skating

| | Crew | Daily Output | Labor-Hours | Unit | Material | Labor | Equipment | Total | Total Incl O&P |
|---|---|---|---|---|---|---|---|---|---|
| 0010 **ICE SKATING** Equipment incl. refrigeration, plumbing & cooling | | | | | | | | | |
| 0020 coils & concrete slab, 85' x 200' rink | | | | | | | | | |
| 0300 55° system, 5 mos., 100 ton | | | | Total | 496,000 | | | 496,000 | 545,500 |
| 0700 90° system, 12 mos., 135 ton | | | | " | 550,500 | | | 550,500 | 605,500 |
| 1200 Subsoil heating system (recycled from compressor), 85' x 200' | Q-7 | .27 | 118 | Ea. | 25,000 | 5,325 | | 30,325 | 35,500 |
| 1300 Subsoil insulation, 2 lb. polystyrene with vapor barrier, 85' x 200' | 2 Carp | .14 | 114 | " | 30,000 | 4,350 | | 34,350 | 39,800 |

## 13 18 16 – Ice Rink Dasher Boards

### 13 18 16.50 Ice Rink Dasher Boards

| | Crew | Daily Output | Labor-Hours | Unit | Material | Labor | Equipment | Total | Total Incl O&P |
|---|---|---|---|---|---|---|---|---|---|
| 0010 **ICE RINK DASHER BOARDS** | | | | | | | | | |
| 1000 Dasher boards, 1/2" H.D. polyethylene faced steel frame, 3' acrylic | | | | | | | | | |
| 1020 screen at sides, 5' acrylic ends, 85' x 200' | F-5 | .06 | 533 | Ea. | 120,000 | 20,600 | | 140,600 | 164,000 |
| 1100 Fiberglass & aluminum construction, same sides and ends | " | .06 | 533 | " | 130,000 | 20,600 | | 150,600 | 175,000 |

# 13 21 Controlled Environment Rooms

## 13 21 13 – Clean Rooms

### 13 21 13.50 Clean Rooms

| | Crew | Daily Output | Labor-Hours | Unit | Material | Labor | Equipment | Total | Total Incl O&P |
|---|---|---|---|---|---|---|---|---|---|
| 0010 **CLEAN ROOM COMPONENTS** | | | | | | | | | |
| 1100 Clean room, soft wall, 12' x 12', Class 100 | 1 Carp | .18 | 44.444 | Ea. | 13,600 | 1,700 | | 15,300 | 17,600 |
| 1110 Class 1,000 | | .18 | 44.444 | | 10,900 | 1,700 | | 12,600 | 14,600 |
| 1120 Class 10,000 | | .21 | 38.095 | | 9,525 | 1,450 | | 10,975 | 12,800 |
| 1130 Class 100,000 | | .21 | 38.095 | | 8,925 | 1,450 | | 10,375 | 12,100 |
| 2800 Ceiling grid support, slotted channel struts 4'-0" O.C., ea. way | | | | S.F. | | | | 5.91 | 6.50 |
| 3000 Ceiling panel, vinyl coated foil on mineral substrate | | | | | | | | | |
| 3020 Sealed, non-perforated | | | | S.F. | | | | 1.27 | 1.40 |
| 4000 Ceiling panel seal, silicone sealant, 150 L.F./gal. | 1 Carp | 150 | .053 | L.F. | .24 | 2.03 | | 2.27 | 3.42 |
| 4100 Two sided adhesive tape | " | 240 | .033 | " | .11 | 1.27 | | 1.38 | 2.10 |
| 4200 Clips, one per panel | | | | Ea. | .95 | | | .95 | 1.05 |
| 6000 HEPA filter, 2'x4', 99.97% eff., 3" dp beveled frame (silicone seal) | | | | | 315 | | | 315 | 345 |
| 6040 6" deep skirted frame (channel seal) | | | | | 335 | | | 335 | 365 |
| 6100 99.99% efficient, 3" deep beveled frame (silicone seal) | | | | | 330 | | | 330 | 360 |
| 6140 6" deep skirted frame (channel seal) | | | | | 350 | | | 350 | 380 |
| 6200 99.999% efficient, 3" deep beveled frame (silicone seal) | | | | | 345 | | | 345 | 375 |
| 6240 6" deep skirted frame (channel seal) | | | | | 365 | | | 365 | 400 |
| 7000 Wall panel systems, including channel strut framing | | | | | | | | | |
| 7020 Polyester coated aluminum, particle board | | | | S.F. | | | | 18.18 | 20 |
| 7100 Porcelain coated aluminum, particle board | | | | | | | | 31.82 | 35 |
| 7400 Wall panel support, slotted channel struts, to 12' high | | | | | | | | 16.36 | 18 |

# 13 21 Controlled Environment Rooms

## 13 21 26 – Cold Storage Rooms

| 13 21 26.50 Refrigeration | Crew | Daily Output | Labor-Hours | Unit | Material | 2008 Bare Costs Labor | Equipment | Total | Total Incl O&P |
|---|---|---|---|---|---|---|---|---|---|
| 0010 **REFRIGERATION** | | | | | | | | | |
| 0020 Curbs, 12" high, 4" thick, concrete | 2 Carp | 58 | .276 | L.F. | 3.83 | 10.50 | | 14.33 | 20.50 |
| 1000 Doors, see Div. 08 34 13.10 | | | | | | | | | |
| 2400 Finishes, 2 coat portland cement plaster, 1/2" thick | 1 Plas | 48 | .167 | S.F. | 1.06 | 5.85 | | 6.91 | 10 |
| 2500 For galvanized reinforcing mesh, add | 1 Lath | 335 | .024 | | .70 | .83 | | 1.53 | 2 |
| 2700 3/16" thick latex cement | 1 Plas | 88 | .091 | | 1.80 | 3.18 | | 4.98 | 6.80 |
| 2900 For glass cloth reinforced ceilings, add | " | 450 | .018 | | .43 | .62 | | 1.05 | 1.41 |
| 3100 Fiberglass panels, 1/8" thick | 1 Carp | 149.45 | .054 | | 2.38 | 2.04 | | 4.42 | 5.80 |
| 3200 Polystyrene, plastic finish ceiling, 1" thick | | 274 | .029 | | 2.19 | 1.11 | | 3.30 | 4.14 |
| 3400 2" thick | | 274 | .029 | | 2.50 | 1.11 | | 3.61 | 4.48 |
| 3500 4" thick | | 219 | .037 | | 2.78 | 1.39 | | 4.17 | 5.25 |
| 3800 Floors, concrete, 4" thick | 1 Cefi | 93 | .086 | | 1.05 | 3.18 | | 4.23 | 5.85 |
| 3900 6" thick | " | 85 | .094 | | 1.56 | 3.48 | | 5.04 | 6.80 |
| 4000 Insulation, 1" to 6" thick, cork | | | | B.F. | 1.02 | | | 1.02 | 1.12 |
| 4100 Urethane | | | | | 1 | | | 1 | 1.10 |
| 4300 Polystyrene, regular | | | | | .68 | | | .68 | .75 |
| 4400 Bead board | | | | | .51 | | | .51 | .56 |
| 4600 Installation of above, add per layer | 2 Carp | 657.60 | .024 | S.F. | .33 | .93 | | 1.26 | 1.80 |
| 4700 Wall and ceiling juncture | | 298.90 | .054 | L.F. | 1.64 | 2.04 | | 3.68 | 4.97 |
| 4900 Partitions, galvanized sandwich panels, 4" thick, stock | | 219.20 | .073 | S.F. | 6.90 | 2.78 | | 9.68 | 11.90 |
| 5000 Aluminum or fiberglass | | 219.20 | .073 | " | 7.50 | 2.78 | | 10.28 | 12.60 |
| 5200 Prefab walk-in, 7'-6" high, aluminum, incl. door & floors, | | | | | | | | | |
| 5210 not incl. partitions or refrigeration, 6' x 6' O.D. nominal | 2 Carp | 54.80 | .292 | SF Flr. | 123 | 11.10 | | 134.10 | 152 |
| 5500 10' x 10' O.D. nominal | | 82.20 | .195 | | 99 | 7.40 | | 106.40 | 121 |
| 5700 12' x 14' O.D. nominal | | 109.60 | .146 | | 88.50 | 5.55 | | 94.05 | 106 |
| 5800 12' x 20' O.D. nominal | | 109.60 | .146 | | 77.50 | 5.55 | | 83.05 | 93.50 |
| 6100 For 8'-6" high, add | | | | | 5% | | | | |
| 6300 Rule of thumb for complete units, w/o doors & refrigeration, cooler | 2 Carp | 146 | .110 | | 112 | 4.18 | | 116.18 | 130 |
| 6400 Freezer | | 109.60 | .146 | | 132 | 5.55 | | 137.55 | 154 |
| 6600 Shelving, plated or galvanized, steel wire type | | 360 | .044 | SF Hor. | 9.75 | 1.69 | | 11.44 | 13.40 |
| 6700 Slat shelf type | | 375 | .043 | | 12.05 | 1.63 | | 13.68 | 15.80 |
| 6900 For stainless steel shelving, add | | | | | 300% | | | | |
| 7000 Vapor barrier, on wood walls | 2 Carp | 1644 | .010 | S.F. | .14 | .37 | | .51 | .73 |
| 7200 On masonry walls | " | 1315 | .012 | " | .37 | .46 | | .83 | 1.13 |
| 7500 For air curtain doors, see Div. 23 34 33.10 | | | | | | | | | |

## 13 21 48 – Sound-Conditioned Rooms

### 13 21 48.10 Anechoic Chambers

| | Crew | Daily Output | Labor-Hours | Unit | Material | 2008 Bare Costs Labor | Equipment | Total | Total Incl O&P |
|---|---|---|---|---|---|---|---|---|---|
| 0010 **ANECHOIC CHAMBERS** Standard units, 7' ceiling heights | | | | | | | | | |
| 0100 Area for pricing is net inside dimensions | | | | | | | | | |
| 0300 200 cycles per second cutoff, 25 S.F. floor area | | | | SF Flr. | 1,500 | | | 1,500 | 1,650 |
| 0400 50 S.F. | | | | | | | | 1,045 | 1,150 |
| 0600 75 S.F. | | | | | | | | 1,000 | 1,100 |
| 0700 100 S.F. | | | | | 1,125 | | | 1,125 | 1,225 |
| 0900 For 150 cycles per second cutoff, add to 100 S.F. room | | | | | | | | | 30% |
| 1000 For 100 cycles per second cutoff, add to 100 S.F. room | | | | | | | | | 45% |

### 13 21 48.15 Audiometric Rooms

| | Crew | Daily Output | Labor-Hours | Unit | Material | 2008 Bare Costs Labor | Equipment | Total | Total Incl O&P |
|---|---|---|---|---|---|---|---|---|---|
| 0010 **AUDIOMETRIC ROOMS** | | | | | | | | | |
| 0020 Under 500 S.F. surface | 4 Carp | 98 | .327 | SF Surf | 48 | 12.45 | | 60.45 | 72.50 |
| 0100 Over 500 S.F. surface | " | 120 | .267 | " | 45.50 | 10.15 | | 55.65 | 66 |

# 13 21 Controlled Environment Rooms

## 13 21 53 – Darkrooms

### 13 21 53.50 Darkrooms

| | 13 21 53.50 Darkrooms | Crew | Daily Output | Labor-Hours | Unit | Material | 2008 Bare Costs Labor | Equipment | Total | Total Incl O&P |
|---|---|---|---|---|---|---|---|---|---|---|
| 0010 | **DARKROOMS** | | | | | | | | | |
| 0020 | Shell, complete except for door, 64 S.F., 8' high | 2 Carp | 128 | .125 | SF Flr. | 53.50 | 4.76 | | 58.26 | 66 |
| 0100 | 12' high | | 64 | .250 | | 67 | 9.55 | | 76.55 | 89 |
| 0500 | 120 S.F. floor, 8' high | | 120 | .133 | | 36.50 | 5.10 | | 41.60 | 48.50 |
| 0600 | 12' high | | 60 | .267 | | 50.50 | 10.15 | | 60.65 | 71.50 |
| 0800 | 240 S.F. floor, 8' high | | 120 | .133 | | 26.50 | 5.10 | | 31.60 | 37 |
| 0900 | 12' high | | 60 | .267 | | 37 | 10.15 | | 47.15 | 57 |
| 1200 | Mini-cylindrical, revolving, unlined, 4' diameter | | 3.50 | 4.571 | Ea. | 2,000 | 174 | | 2,174 | 2,475 |
| 1400 | 5'-6" diameter | | 2.50 | 6.400 | | 4,150 | 244 | | 4,394 | 4,950 |
| 1600 | Add for lead lining, inner cylinder, 1/32" thick | | | | | 1,475 | | | 1,475 | 1,625 |
| 1700 | 1/16" thick | | | | | 3,975 | | | 3,975 | 4,375 |
| 1800 | Add for lead lining, inner and outer cylinder, 1/32" thick | | | | | 2,725 | | | 2,725 | 3,000 |
| 1900 | 1/16" thick | | | | | 6,100 | | | 6,100 | 6,700 |
| 2000 | For darkroom door, see Div. 08 34 36.10 | | | | | | | | | |

## 13 21 56 – Music Rooms

### 13 21 56.50 Music Rooms

| | | Crew | Daily Output | Labor-Hours | Unit | Material | 2008 Bare Costs Labor | Equipment | Total | Total Incl O&P |
|---|---|---|---|---|---|---|---|---|---|---|
| 0010 | **MUSIC ROOMS** | | | | | | | | | |
| 0020 | Practice room, modular, perforated steel, under 500 S.F. | 2 Carp | 70 | .229 | SF Surf | 29.50 | 8.70 | | 38.20 | 46 |
| 0100 | Over 500 S.F. | " | 80 | .200 | " | 25 | 7.60 | | 32.60 | 39.50 |

# 13 24 Special Activity Rooms

## 13 24 16 – Saunas

### 13 24 16.50 Saunas

| | | Crew | Daily Output | Labor-Hours | Unit | Material | 2008 Bare Costs Labor | Equipment | Total | Total Incl O&P |
|---|---|---|---|---|---|---|---|---|---|---|
| 0010 | **SAUNAS AND HEATERS** | | | | | | | | | |
| 0020 | Prefabricated, incl. heater & controls, 7' high, 6' x 4', C/C | L-7 | 2.20 | 12.727 | Ea. | 4,175 | 470 | | 4,645 | 5,300 |
| 0050 | 6' x 4', C/P | | 2 | 14 | | 3,850 | 515 | | 4,365 | 5,050 |
| 0400 | 6' x 5', C/C | | 2 | 14 | | 4,650 | 515 | | 5,165 | 5,925 |
| 0450 | 6' x 5', C/P | | 2 | 14 | | 4,350 | 515 | | 4,865 | 5,600 |
| 0600 | 6' x 6', C/C | | 1.80 | 15.556 | | 4,975 | 575 | | 5,550 | 6,350 |
| 0650 | 6' x 6', C/P | | 1.80 | 15.556 | | 4,650 | 575 | | 5,225 | 5,975 |
| 0800 | 6' x 9', C/C | | 1.60 | 17.500 | | 6,225 | 645 | | 6,870 | 7,850 |
| 0850 | 6' x 9', C/P | | 1.60 | 17.500 | | 5,900 | 645 | | 6,545 | 7,500 |
| 1000 | 8' x 12', C/C | | 1.10 | 25.455 | | 9,650 | 940 | | 10,590 | 12,100 |
| 1050 | 8' x 12', C/P | | 1.10 | 25.455 | | 8,850 | 940 | | 9,790 | 11,200 |
| 1200 | 8' x 8', C/C | | 1.40 | 20 | | 7,350 | 740 | | 8,090 | 9,225 |
| 1250 | 8' x 8', C/P | | 1.40 | 20 | | 6,900 | 740 | | 7,640 | 8,750 |
| 1400 | 8' x 10', C/C | | 1.20 | 23.333 | | 8,150 | 860 | | 9,010 | 10,300 |
| 1450 | 8' x 10', C/P | | 1.20 | 23.333 | | 7,575 | 860 | | 8,435 | 9,650 |
| 1600 | 10' x 12', C/C | | 1 | 28 | | 10,200 | 1,025 | | 11,225 | 12,800 |
| 1650 | 10' x 12', C/P | | 1 | 28 | | 9,250 | 1,025 | | 10,275 | 11,800 |
| 1700 | Door only, cedar, 2'x6', with tempered insulated glass window | 2 Carp | 3.40 | 4.706 | | 545 | 179 | | 724 | 880 |
| 1800 | Prehung, incl. jambs, pulls & hardware | " | 12 | 1.333 | | 560 | 51 | | 611 | 695 |
| 2500 | Heaters only (incl. above), wall mounted, to 200 C.F. | | | | | 540 | | | 540 | 590 |
| 2750 | To 300 C.F. | | | | | 660 | | | 660 | 725 |
| 3000 | Floor standing, to 720 C.F., 10,000 watts, w/controls | 1 Elec | 3 | 2.667 | | 1,700 | 121 | | 1,821 | 2,025 |
| 3250 | To 1,000 C.F., 16,000 watts | " | 3 | 2.667 | | 1,825 | 121 | | 1,946 | 2,200 |

## 13 24 26 – Steam Baths

### 13 24 26.50 Steam Baths

| | | | | | | | | | | |
|---|---|---|---|---|---|---|---|---|---|---|
| 0010 | **STEAM BATHS AND COMPONENTS** | | | | | | | | | |

# 13 24 Special Activity Rooms

## 13 24 26 – Steam Baths

### 13 24 26.50 Steam Baths

| | | Crew | Daily Output | Labor-Hours | Unit | Material | 2008 Bare Costs Labor | Equipment | Total | Total Incl O&P |
|---|---|---|---|---|---|---|---|---|---|---|
| 0020 | Heater, timer & head, single, to 140 C.F. | 1 Plum | 1.20 | 6.667 | Ea. | 1,175 | 310 | | 1,485 | 1,775 |
| 0500 | To 300 C.F. | | 1.10 | 7.273 | | 1,325 | 340 | | 1,665 | 1,975 |
| 1000 | Commercial size, with blow-down assembly, to 800 C.F. | | .90 | 8.889 | | 4,600 | 415 | | 5,015 | 5,675 |
| 1500 | To 2500 C.F. | ↓ | .80 | 10 | | 7,250 | 465 | | 7,715 | 8,675 |
| 2000 | Multiple, motels, apts., 2 baths, w/ blow-down assm., 500 C.F. | Q-1 | 1.30 | 12.308 | | 4,550 | 515 | | 5,065 | 5,775 |
| 2500 | 4 baths | " | .70 | 22.857 | | 4,950 | 960 | | 5,910 | 6,900 |
| 2700 | Conversion unit for residential tub, including door | | | | ↓ | 3,725 | | | 3,725 | 4,100 |

# 13 28 Athletic and Recreational Special Construction

## 13 28 33 – Athletic and Recreational Court Walls

### 13 28 33.50 Sport Court

| | | Crew | Daily Output | Labor-Hours | Unit | Material | 2008 Bare Costs Labor | Equipment | Total | Total Incl O&P |
|---|---|---|---|---|---|---|---|---|---|---|
| 0010 | **SPORT COURT** | | | | | | | | | |
| 0020 | Floors, No. 2 & better maple, 25/32" thick | | | | SF Flr. | | | | 6.05 | 6.65 |
| 0100 | Walls, laminated plastic bonded to galv. steel studs | | | | SF Wall | | | | 7.68 | 8.45 |
| 0150 | Laminated fiberglass surfacing, minimum | | | | | | | | 1.91 | 2.10 |
| 0180 | Maximum | | | | ↓ | | | | 2.15 | 2.37 |
| 0300 | Squash, regulation court in existing building, minimum | | | | Court | 34,000 | | | 34,000 | 37,400 |
| 0400 | Maximum | | | | " | 38,000 | | | 38,000 | 41,800 |
| 0450 | Rule of thumb for components: | | | | | | | | | |
| 0470 | Walls | 3 Carp | .15 | 160 | Court | 8,500 | 6,100 | | 14,600 | 18,900 |
| 0500 | Floor | " | .25 | 96 | | 7,000 | 3,650 | | 10,650 | 13,400 |
| 0550 | Lighting | 2 Elec | .60 | 26.667 | | 2,000 | 1,225 | | 3,225 | 4,000 |
| 0600 | Handball, racquetball court in existing building, minimum | C-1 | .20 | 160 | | 33,000 | 5,775 | | 38,775 | 45,300 |
| 0800 | Maximum | " | .10 | 320 | | 40,000 | 11,600 | | 51,600 | 62,000 |
| 0900 | Rule of thumb for components: walls | 3 Carp | .12 | 200 | | 10,000 | 7,625 | | 17,625 | 22,900 |
| 1000 | Floor | | .25 | 96 | | 7,500 | 3,650 | | 11,150 | 14,000 |
| 1100 | Ceiling | ↓ | .33 | 72.727 | | 2,500 | 2,775 | | 5,275 | 7,075 |
| 1200 | Lighting | 2 Elec | .60 | 26.667 | ↓ | 2,100 | 1,225 | | 3,325 | 4,100 |

# 13 31 Fabric Structures

## 13 31 13 – Air-Supported Fabric Structures

### 13 31 13.09 Air Supported Tank Covers

| | | Crew | Daily Output | Labor-Hours | Unit | Material | 2008 Bare Costs Labor | Equipment | Total | Total Incl O&P |
|---|---|---|---|---|---|---|---|---|---|---|
| 0010 | **AIR SUPPORTED TANK COVERS**, vinyl polyester | | | | | | | | | |
| 0100 | scrim, double layer, with hardware, blower, standby & controls | | | | | | | | | |
| 0200 | Round, 75' diameter | B-2 | 4500 | .009 | S.F. | 8.70 | .27 | | 8.97 | 9.95 |
| 0300 | 100' diameter | | 5000 | .008 | | 7.90 | .25 | | 8.15 | 9.10 |
| 0400 | 150' diameter | | 5000 | .008 | | 6.25 | .25 | | 6.50 | 7.30 |
| 0500 | Rectangular, 20' x 20' | | 4500 | .009 | | 19.75 | .27 | | 20.02 | 22 |
| 0600 | 30' x 40' | | 4500 | .009 | | 19.75 | .27 | | 20.02 | 22 |
| 0700 | 50' x 60' | ↓ | 4500 | .009 | | 19.75 | .27 | | 20.02 | 22 |
| 0800 | For single wall construction, deduct, minimum | | | | | .67 | | | .67 | .74 |
| 0900 | Maximum | | | | | 1.98 | | | 1.98 | 2.18 |
| 1000 | For maximum resistance to atmosphere or cold, add | | | | ↓ | .97 | | | .97 | 1.07 |
| 1100 | For average shipping charges, add | | | | Total | 1,675 | | | 1,675 | 1,850 |

### 13 31 13.13 Single-Walled Air-Supported Structures

| | | Crew | Daily Output | Labor-Hours | Unit | Material | 2008 Bare Costs Labor | Equipment | Total | Total Incl O&P |
|---|---|---|---|---|---|---|---|---|---|---|
| 0010 | **SINGLE-WALLED AIR-SUPPORTED STRUCTURES** R133113-10 | | | | | | | | | |
| 0020 | Site preparation, incl. anchor placement and utilities | B-11B | 1000 | .016 | SF Flr. | .99 | .54 | .25 | 1.78 | 2.19 |
| 0030 | For concrete curb, see Div. 03 30 53.40 | | | | | | | | | |
| 0050 | Warehouse, polyester/vinyl fabric, 28 oz. over 10 yr. life, welded | | | | | | | | | |

| 13 31 13.13 Single-Walled Air-Supported Structures | Crew | Daily Output | Labor-Hours | Unit | Material | 2008 Bare Costs Labor | Equipment | Total | Total Incl O&P |
|---|---|---|---|---|---|---|---|---|---|
| 0060 Seams, tension cables, primary & auxiliary inflation system, | | | | | | | | | |
| 0070    airlock, personnel doors and liner | | | | | | | | | |
| 0100     5,000 S.F. | 4 Clab | 5000 | .006 | SF Flr. | 21.50 | .19 | | 21.69 | 24 |
| 0250     12,000 S.F. | " | 6000 | .005 | | 15.30 | .16 | | 15.46 | 17.05 |
| 0400     24,000 S.F. | 8 Clab | 12000 | .005 | | 10.75 | .16 | | 10.91 | 12.10 |
| 0500     50,000 S.F. | " | 12500 | .005 | ↓ | 9.95 | .15 | | 10.10 | 11.20 |
| 0700 12 oz. reinforced vinyl fabric, 5 yr. life, sewn seams, | | | | | | | | | |
| 0710    accordian door, including liner | | | | | | | | | |
| 0750     3000 S.F. | 4 Clab | 3000 | .011 | SF Flr. | 10.15 | .32 | | 10.47 | 11.70 |
| 0800     12,000 S.F. | " | 6000 | .005 | | 8.65 | .16 | | 8.81 | 9.75 |
| 0850     24,000 S.F. | 8 Clab | 12000 | .005 | | 7.30 | .16 | | 7.46 | 8.30 |
| 0950    Deduct for single layer | | | | | .87 | | | .87 | .96 |
| 1000    Add for welded seams | | | | | 1.01 | | | 1.01 | 1.11 |
| 1050    Add for double layer, welded seams included | | | | ↓ | 2.08 | | | 2.08 | 2.29 |
| 1250 Tedlar/vinyl fabric, 28 oz., with liner, over 10 yr. life, | | | | | | | | | |
| 1260    incl. overhead and personnel doors | | | | | | | | | |
| 1300     3000 S.F. | 4 Clab | 3000 | .011 | SF Flr. | 20.50 | .32 | | 20.82 | 23.50 |
| 1450     12,000 S.F. | " | 6000 | .005 | | 14.65 | .16 | | 14.81 | 16.35 |
| 1550     24,000 S.F. | 8 Clab | 12000 | .005 | | 11.30 | .16 | | 11.46 | 12.70 |
| 1700    Deduct for single layer | | | | ↓ | 1.44 | | | 1.44 | 1.58 |
| 2250 Greenhouse/shelter, woven polyethylene with liner, 2 yr. life, | | | | | | | | | |
| 2260    sewn seams, including doors | | | | | | | | | |
| 2300     3000 S.F. | 4 Clab | 3000 | .011 | SF Flr. | 6.60 | .32 | | 6.92 | 7.75 |
| 2350     12,000 S.F. | " | 6000 | .005 | | 6.70 | .16 | | 6.86 | 7.65 |
| 2450     24,000 S.F. | 8 Clab | 12000 | .005 | | 5.60 | .16 | | 5.76 | 6.40 |
| 2550    Deduct for single layer | | | | ↓ | .63 | | | .63 | .69 |
| 2600 Tennis/gymnasium, polyester/vinyl fabric, 28 oz., over 10 yr. life, | | | | | | | | | |
| 2610    including thermal liner, heat and lights | | | | | | | | | |
| 2650     7,200 S.F. | 4 Clab | 6000 | .005 | SF Flr. | 19.95 | .16 | | 20.11 | 22.50 |
| 2750     13,000 S.F. | " | 6500 | .005 | | 15.30 | .15 | | 15.45 | 17.05 |
| 2850     Over 24,000 S.F. | 8 Clab | 12000 | .005 | | 13.95 | .16 | | 14.11 | 15.60 |
| 2860 For low temperature conditions, add | | | | ↓ | .97 | | | .97 | 1.07 |
| 2870 For average shipping charges, add | | | | Total | 4,750 | | | 4,750 | 5,200 |
| 2900 Thermal liner, translucent reinforced vinyl | | | | SF Flr. | .97 | | | .97 | 1.07 |
| 2950    Metalized mylar fabric and mesh, double liner | | | | " | 1.98 | | | 1.98 | 2.18 |
| 3050 Stadium/convention center, teflon coated fiberglass, heavy weight, | | | | | | | | | |
| 3060    over 20 yr. life, incl. thermal liner and heating system | | | | | | | | | |
| 3100     Minimum | 9 Clab | 26000 | .003 | SF Flr. | 48.50 | .08 | | 48.58 | 53.50 |
| 3110     Maximum | " | 19000 | .004 | " | 58 | .11 | | 58.11 | 63.50 |
| 3400 Doors, air lock, 15' long, 10' x 10' | 2 Carp | .80 | 20 | Ea. | 18,300 | 760 | | 19,060 | 21,300 |
| 3600     15' x 15' | " | .50 | 32 | | 25,800 | 1,225 | | 27,025 | 30,300 |
| 3700    For each added 5' length, add | | | | | 4,600 | | | 4,600 | 5,075 |
| 3900    Revolving personnel door, 6' diameter, 6'-6" high | 2 Carp | .80 | 20 | ↓ | 12,900 | 760 | | 13,660 | 15,400 |
| 4200 Double wall, self supporting, shell only, minimum | | | | SF Flr. | | | | 19.09 | 21 |
| 4300    Maximum | | | | " | | | | 35.45 | 39 |

### 13 31 23.50 Tension Structures

| | Crew | Daily Output | Labor-Hours | Unit | Material | Labor | Equipment | Total | Total Incl O&P |
|---|---|---|---|---|---|---|---|---|---|
| 0010 **TENSION STRUCTURES** Rigid steel/alum. frame, vinyl coated poly | | | | | | | | | |
| 0100    fabric shell, 60' clear span, not incl. foundations or floors | | | | | | | | | |
| 0200     6,000 S.F. | B-41 | 1000 | .044 | SF Flr. | 11.55 | 1.38 | .26 | 13.19 | 15.15 |
| 0300     12,000 S.F. | ↓ | 1100 | .040 | | 10.10 | 1.25 | .24 | 11.59 | 13.35 |
| 0400     80' clear span, 20,800 S.F. | ↓ | 1220 | .036 | ↓ | 10.30 | 1.13 | .22 | 11.65 | 13.35 |

# 13 31 Fabric Structures

## 13 31 23 – Tensioned Fabric Structures

| 13 31 23.50 Tension Structures | | Crew | Daily Output | Labor-Hours | Unit | Material | 2008 Bare Costs Labor | Equipment | Total | Total Incl O&P |
|---|---|---|---|---|---|---|---|---|---|---|
| 0410 | 100' clear span, 10,000 S.F. | L-5 | 2175 | .026 | SF Flr. | 11.50 | 1.11 | .36 | 12.97 | 15 |
| 0430 | 26,000 S.F. | | 2300 | .024 | | 10.50 | 1.05 | .34 | 11.89 | 13.80 |
| 0450 | 36,000 S.F. | | 2500 | .022 | | 10.25 | .96 | .31 | 11.52 | 13.35 |
| 0460 | 120' clear span, 24,000 S.F. | | 3000 | .019 | | 12.40 | .80 | .26 | 13.46 | 15.35 |
| 0470 | 150' clear span, 30,000 S.F. | | 6000 | .009 | | 12.85 | .40 | .13 | 13.38 | 14.95 |
| 0480 | 200' clear span, 40,000 S.F. | E-6 | 8000 | .016 | | 15.65 | .68 | .23 | 16.56 | 18.65 |
| 0500 | For roll-up door, 12' x 14', add | L-2 | 1 | 16 | Ea. | 4,450 | 540 | | 4,990 | 5,725 |
| 0600 | For personnel doors, add, minimum | | | | SF Flr. | 5% | | | | |
| 0700 | Add, maximum | | | | | 15% | | | | |
| 0800 | For site work, simple foundation, etc., add, minimum | | | | | | | | 1.25 | 1.95 |
| 0900 | Add, maximum | | | | | | | | 2.75 | 3.05 |

# 13 34 Fabricated Engineered Structures

## 13 34 13 – Glazed Structures

### 13 34 13.13 Greenhouses

| | | Crew | Daily Output | Labor-Hours | Unit | Material | 2008 Bare Costs Labor | Equipment | Total | Total Incl O&P |
|---|---|---|---|---|---|---|---|---|---|---|
| 0010 | **GREENHOUSES**, Shell only, stock units, not incl. 2' stub walls, | | | | | | | | | |
| 0020 | foundation, floors, heat or compartments | | | | | | | | | |
| 0300 | Residential type, free standing, 8'-6" long x 7'-6" wide | 2 Carp | 59 | .271 | SF Flr. | 42 | 10.35 | | 52.35 | 62.50 |
| 0400 | 10'-6" wide | | 85 | .188 | | 35 | 7.15 | | 42.15 | 49.50 |
| 0600 | 13'-6" wide | | 108 | .148 | | 30 | 5.65 | | 35.65 | 42 |
| 0700 | 17'-0" wide | | 160 | .100 | | 31 | 3.81 | | 34.81 | 40 |
| 0900 | Lean-to type, 3'-10" wide | | 34 | .471 | | 38 | 17.95 | | 55.95 | 70 |
| 1000 | 6'-10" wide | | 58 | .276 | | 39.50 | 10.50 | | 50 | 59.50 |
| 1500 | Commercial, custom, truss frame, incl. equip., plumbing, elec., | | | | | | | | | |
| 1510 | benches and controls, under 2,000 S.F., minimum | | | | SF Flr. | | | | 27.27 | 30 |
| 1550 | Maximum | | | | | 30.50 | | | 30.50 | 33.50 |
| 1700 | Over 5,000 S.F., minimum | | | | | 20 | | | 20 | 22 |
| 1750 | Maximum | | | | | | | | 27.27 | 30 |
| 2000 | Institutional, custom, rigid frame, including compartments and | | | | | | | | | |
| 2010 | multi-controls, under 500 S.F., minimum | | | | SF Flr. | | | | 70 | 77 |
| 2050 | Maximum | | | | | 74 | | | 74 | 81 |
| 2150 | Over 2,000 S.F., minimum | | | | | 29.50 | | | 29.50 | 32.50 |
| 2200 | Maximum | | | | | | | | 59.09 | 65 |
| 2400 | Concealed rigid frame, under 500 S.F., minimum | | | | | | | | 81.82 | 90 |
| 2450 | Maximum | | | | | | | | 100 | 110 |
| 2550 | Over 2,000 S.F., minimum | | | | | | | | 61.82 | 68 |
| 2600 | Maximum | | | | | | | | 71.82 | 79 |
| 2800 | Lean-to type, under 500 S.F., minimum | | | | | | | | 72.73 | 80 |
| 2850 | Maximum | | | | | | | | 109.09 | 120 |
| 3000 | Over 2,000 S.F., minimum | | | | | | | | 40 | 44 |
| 3050 | Maximum | | | | | | | | 66.36 | 73 |
| 3600 | For 1/4" clear plate glass, add | | | | SF Surf | 1.86 | | | 1.86 | 2.05 |
| 3700 | For 1/4" tempered glass, add | | | | " | 4.21 | | | 4.21 | 4.63 |
| 3900 | For cooling, add, minimum | | | | SF Flr. | 2.81 | | | 2.81 | 3.09 |
| 4000 | Maximum | | | | | 6.95 | | | 6.95 | 7.65 |
| 4200 | For heaters, 13.6 MBH, add | | | | | 5.35 | | | 5.35 | 5.85 |
| 4300 | 60 MBH, add | | | | | 2 | | | 2 | 2.20 |
| 4500 | For benches, 2' x 3'-6", add | | | | SF Hor. | 24 | | | 24 | 26.50 |
| 4600 | 3' x 10', add | | | | S.F. | 12.95 | | | 12.95 | 14.25 |
| 4800 | For controls, add, minimum | | | | Total | 2,400 | | | 2,400 | 2,650 |
| 4900 | Maximum | | | | " | 14,300 | | | 14,300 | 15,700 |

# 13 34 Fabricated Engineered Structures

## 13 34 13 – Glazed Structures

### 13 34 13.13 Greenhouses

| | | Crew | Daily Output | Labor-Hours | Unit | Material | 2008 Bare Costs Labor | Equipment | Total | Total Incl O&P |
|---|---|---|---|---|---|---|---|---|---|---|
| 5100 | For humidification equipment, add | | | | M.C.F. | 6.15 | | | 6.15 | 6.75 |
| 5200 | For vinyl shading, add | | | | S.F. | 1.29 | | | 1.29 | 1.42 |
| 6000 | Geodesic hemisphere, 1/8" plexiglass glazing | | | | | | | | | |
| 6050 | 8' diameter | 2 Carp | 2 | 8 | Ea. | 2,700 | 305 | | 3,005 | 3,450 |
| 6150 | 24' diameter | | .35 | 45.714 | | 13,900 | 1,750 | | 15,650 | 18,000 |
| 6250 | 48' diameter | | .20 | 80 | | 37,600 | 3,050 | | 40,650 | 46,200 |

### 13 34 13.19 Swimming Pool Enclosures

| | | Crew | Daily Output | Labor-Hours | Unit | Material | 2008 Bare Costs Labor | Equipment | Total | Total Incl O&P |
|---|---|---|---|---|---|---|---|---|---|---|
| 0010 | **SWIMMING POOL ENCLOSURES** Translucent, free standing | | | | | | | | | |
| 0020 | not including foundations, heat or light | | | | | | | | | |
| 0200 | Economy, minimum | 2 Carp | 200 | .080 | SF Hor. | 12.85 | 3.05 | | 15.90 | 18.90 |
| 0300 | Maximum | | 100 | .160 | | 36 | 6.10 | | 42.10 | 49 |
| 0400 | Deluxe, minimum | | 100 | .160 | | 42.50 | 6.10 | | 48.60 | 56 |
| 0600 | Maximum | | 70 | .229 | | 196 | 8.70 | | 204.70 | 229 |
| 0700 | For motorized roof, 40% opening, solid roof, add | | | | | 6.95 | | | 6.95 | 7.60 |
| 0800 | Skylight type roof, add | | | | | 7.40 | | | 7.40 | 8.15 |
| 0900 | Air-inflated, including blowers and heaters, minimum | | | | | | | | 3.18 | 3.50 |
| 1000 | Maximum | | | | | | | | 6.09 | 6.70 |

## 13 34 16 – Grandstands and Bleachers

### 13 34 16.13 Grandstands

| | | Crew | Daily Output | Labor-Hours | Unit | Material | 2008 Bare Costs Labor | Equipment | Total | Total Incl O&P |
|---|---|---|---|---|---|---|---|---|---|---|
| 0010 | **GRANDSTANDS** Permanent, municipal, including foundation | | | | | | | | | |
| 0050 | Steel understructure w/aluminum closed deck, minimum | | | | Seat | | | | 118.18 | 130 |
| 0100 | Maximum | | | | | | | | 205 | 225 |
| 0300 | Steel, minimum | | | | | 50 | | | 50 | 55 |
| 0400 | Maximum | | | | | 100 | | | 100 | 110 |
| 0600 | Aluminum, extruded, stock design, minimum | | | | | | | | 63.64 | 70 |
| 0700 | Maximum | | | | | | | | 104.55 | 115 |
| 0900 | Composite, steel, wood and plastic, stock design, minimum | | | | | 125 | | | 125 | 138 |
| 1000 | Maximum | | | | | 250 | | | 250 | 275 |

### 13 34 16.53 Bleachers

| | | Crew | Daily Output | Labor-Hours | Unit | Material | 2008 Bare Costs Labor | Equipment | Total | Total Incl O&P |
|---|---|---|---|---|---|---|---|---|---|---|
| 0010 | **BLEACHERS** | | | | | | | | | |
| 0020 | Bleachers, outdoor, portable, 3 to 5 tiers, to 300' long, min | 2 Sswk | 120 | .133 | Seat | 41 | 5.75 | | 46.75 | 56 |
| 0100 | Maximum, less than 15' long, prefabricated | | 80 | .200 | | 54 | 8.60 | | 62.60 | 75 |
| 0200 | 6 to 20 tiers, minimum, up to 300' long | | 120 | .133 | | 49.50 | 5.75 | | 55.25 | 65 |
| 0300 | Max., under 15', (highly prefabricated, on wheels) | | 80 | .200 | | 72 | 8.60 | | 80.60 | 94.50 |
| 0500 | Permanent grandstands, wood seat, steel frame, 24" row | | | | | | | | | |
| 0600 | 3 to 15 tiers, minimum | 2 Sswk | 60 | .267 | Seat | 123 | 11.45 | | 134.45 | 156 |
| 0700 | Maximum | | 48 | .333 | | 135 | 14.35 | | 149.35 | 174 |
| 0900 | 16 to 30 tiers, minimum | | 60 | .267 | | 142 | 11.45 | | 153.45 | 177 |
| 0950 | Average | | 55 | .291 | | 177 | 12.50 | | 189.50 | 218 |
| 1000 | Maximum | | 48 | .333 | | 212 | 14.35 | | 226.35 | 260 |
| 1200 | Seat backs only, 30" row, fiberglass | | 160 | .100 | | 26.50 | 4.30 | | 30.80 | 37.50 |
| 1300 | Steel and wood | | 160 | .100 | | 31 | 4.30 | | 35.30 | 42 |
| 1400 | NOTE: average seating is 1.5' in width | | | | | | | | | |

## 13 34 19 – Metal Building Systems

### 13 34 19.50 Pre-Engineered Steel Buildings

| | | Crew | Daily Output | Labor-Hours | Unit | Material | 2008 Bare Costs Labor | Equipment | Total | Total Incl O&P |
|---|---|---|---|---|---|---|---|---|---|---|
| 0010 | **PRE-ENGINEERED STEEL BUILDINGS** R133419-10 | | | | | | | | | |
| 0100 | Clear span rigid frame, 26 ga. colored roofing and siding | | | | | | | | | |
| 0150 | 20 wide, 10' eave height | E-2 | 425 | .132 | SF Flr. | 8.30 | 5.50 | 3.69 | 17.49 | 23 |
| 0160 | 14' eave height | | 350 | .160 | | 8.80 | 6.70 | 4.48 | 19.98 | 26 |
| 0170 | 16' eave height | | 320 | .175 | | 9.30 | 7.35 | 4.90 | 21.55 | 28.50 |
| 0180 | 20' eave height | | 275 | .204 | | 10.25 | 8.50 | 5.70 | 24.45 | 32.50 |

# 13 34 Fabricated Engineered Structures

## 13 34 19 – Metal Building Systems

| 13 34 19.50 Pre-Engineered Steel Buildings | Crew | Daily Output | Labor-Hours | Unit | Material | 2008 Bare Costs Labor | Equipment | Total | Total Incl O&P |
|---|---|---|---|---|---|---|---|---|---|
| 0190 | 24' eave height | E-2 | 240 | .233 | SF Flr. | 11.65 | 9.75 | 6.55 | 27.95 | 37 |
| 0200 | 30' to 40' wide, 10' eave height | | 535 | .105 | | 6.85 | 4.38 | 2.93 | 14.16 | 18.30 |
| 0300 | 14' eave height | | 450 | .124 | | 7.25 | 5.20 | 3.48 | 15.93 | 21 |
| 0400 | 16' eave height | | 415 | .135 | | 7.65 | 5.65 | 3.78 | 17.08 | 22.50 |
| 0500 | 20' eave height | | 360 | .156 | | 8.35 | 6.50 | 4.35 | 19.20 | 25 |
| 0600 | 24' eave height | | 320 | .175 | | 9.40 | 7.35 | 4.90 | 21.65 | 28.50 |
| 0700 | 50' to 100' wide, 10' eave height | | 865 | .065 | | 5.90 | 2.71 | 1.81 | 10.42 | 13.15 |
| 0800 | 14' eave height | | 770 | .073 | | 6.30 | 3.04 | 2.04 | 11.38 | 14.40 |
| 0900 | 16' eave height | | 730 | .077 | | 6.65 | 3.21 | 2.15 | 12.01 | 15.25 |
| 1000 | 20' eave height | | 660 | .085 | | 7.15 | 3.55 | 2.37 | 13.07 | 16.65 |
| 1100 | 24' eave height | ▼ | 605 | .093 | ▼ | 7.85 | 3.87 | 2.59 | 14.31 | 18.20 |
| 1200 | Clear span tapered beam frame, 26 ga. colored roofing/siding | | | | | | | | | |
| 1300 | 30' wide, 10' eave height | E-2 | 535 | .105 | SF Flr. | 7.60 | 4.38 | 2.93 | 14.91 | 19.10 |
| 1400 | 14' eave height | | 450 | .124 | | 8.35 | 5.20 | 3.48 | 17.03 | 22 |
| 1500 | 16' eave height | | 415 | .135 | | 8.95 | 5.65 | 3.78 | 18.38 | 24 |
| 1600 | 20' eave height | | 360 | .156 | | 9.90 | 6.50 | 4.35 | 20.75 | 27 |
| 1700 | 40' wide, 10' eave height | | 600 | .093 | | 6.95 | 3.91 | 2.61 | 13.47 | 17.25 |
| 1800 | 14' eave height | | 510 | .110 | | 7.60 | 4.60 | 3.07 | 15.27 | 19.70 |
| 1900 | 16' eave height | | 475 | .118 | | 7.90 | 4.93 | 3.30 | 16.13 | 21 |
| 2000 | 20' eave height | | 415 | .135 | | 8.65 | 5.65 | 3.78 | 18.08 | 23.50 |
| 2100 | 50' to 80' wide, 10' eave height | | 770 | .073 | | 6.60 | 3.04 | 2.04 | 11.68 | 14.75 |
| 2200 | 14' eave height | | 675 | .083 | | 7.05 | 3.47 | 2.32 | 12.84 | 16.30 |
| 2300 | 16' eave height | | 635 | .088 | | 7.30 | 3.69 | 2.47 | 13.46 | 17.15 |
| 2400 | 20' eave height | ▼ | 565 | .099 | ▼ | 8.15 | 4.15 | 2.77 | 15.07 | 19.20 |
| 2500 | Single post 2-span frame, 26 ga. colored roofing and siding | | | | | | | | | |
| 2600 | 80' wide, 14' eave height | E-2 | 740 | .076 | SF Flr. | 5.65 | 3.17 | 2.12 | 10.94 | 14.05 |
| 2700 | 16' eave height | | 695 | .081 | | 6.05 | 3.37 | 2.25 | 11.67 | 15 |
| 2800 | 20' eave height | | 625 | .090 | | 6.60 | 3.75 | 2.51 | 12.86 | 16.50 |
| 2900 | 24' eave height | | 570 | .098 | | 7.10 | 4.11 | 2.75 | 13.96 | 17.90 |
| 3000 | 100' wide, 14' eave height | | 835 | .067 | | 5.50 | 2.81 | 1.88 | 10.19 | 12.95 |
| 3100 | 16' eave height | | 795 | .070 | | 5.40 | 2.95 | 1.97 | 10.32 | 13.20 |
| 3200 | 20' eave height | | 730 | .077 | | 6.35 | 3.21 | 2.15 | 11.71 | 14.85 |
| 3300 | 24' eave height | | 670 | .084 | | 6.85 | 3.50 | 2.34 | 12.69 | 16.15 |
| 3400 | 120' wide, 14' eave height | | 870 | .064 | | 5.45 | 2.69 | 1.80 | 9.94 | 12.65 |
| 3500 | 16' eave height | | 830 | .067 | | 5.70 | 2.82 | 1.89 | 10.41 | 13.20 |
| 3600 | 20' eave height | | 765 | .073 | | 6.15 | 3.06 | 2.05 | 11.26 | 14.30 |
| 3700 | 24' eave height | ▼ | 705 | .079 | ▼ | 6.70 | 3.32 | 2.22 | 12.24 | 15.60 |
| 3800 | Double post 3-span frame, 26 ga. colored roofing and siding | | | | | | | | | |
| 3900 | 150' wide, 14' eave height | E-2 | 925 | .061 | SF Flr. | 4.69 | 2.53 | 1.69 | 8.91 | 11.40 |
| 4000 | 16' eave height | | 890 | .063 | | 4.84 | 2.63 | 1.76 | 9.23 | 11.80 |
| 4100 | 20' eave height | | 820 | .068 | | 5.15 | 2.86 | 1.91 | 9.92 | 12.70 |
| 4200 | 24' eave height | ▼ | 765 | .073 | ▼ | 6.05 | 3.06 | 2.05 | 11.16 | 14.25 |
| 4300 | Triple post 4-span frame, 26 ga. colored roofing and siding | | | | | | | | | |
| 4400 | 160' wide, 14' eave height | E-2 | 970 | .058 | SF Flr. | 4.55 | 2.42 | 1.62 | 8.59 | 10.95 |
| 4500 | 16' eave height | | 930 | .060 | | 4.76 | 2.52 | 1.69 | 8.97 | 11.45 |
| 4600 | 20' eave height | | 870 | .064 | | 4.77 | 2.69 | 1.80 | 9.26 | 11.90 |
| 4700 | 24' eave height | | 815 | .069 | | 5.65 | 2.88 | 1.92 | 10.45 | 13.35 |
| 4800 | 200' wide, 14' eave height | | 1030 | .054 | | 4.37 | 2.28 | 1.52 | 8.17 | 10.40 |
| 4900 | 16' eave height | | 995 | .056 | | 4.48 | 2.36 | 1.57 | 8.41 | 10.75 |
| 5000 | 20' eave height | | 935 | .060 | | 4.86 | 2.51 | 1.68 | 9.05 | 11.50 |
| 5100 | 24' eave height | ▼ | 885 | .063 | ▼ | 5.70 | 2.65 | 1.77 | 10.12 | 12.80 |
| 5200 | Accessory items: add to the basic building cost above | | | | | | | | | |
| 5250 | Eave overhang, 2' wide, 26 ga., with soffit | E-2 | 360 | .156 | L.F. | 25 | 6.50 | 4.35 | 35.85 | 43.50 |

| 13 34 19.50 Pre-Engineered Steel Buildings | | Crew | Daily Output | Labor-Hours | Unit | Material | 2008 Bare Costs Labor | Equipment | Total | Total Incl O&P |
|---|---|---|---|---|---|---|---|---|---|---|
| 5300 | 4' wide, without soffit | E-2 | 300 | .187 | L.F. | 24 | 7.80 | 5.20 | 37 | 46 |
| 5350 | With soffit | | 250 | .224 | | 33.50 | 9.40 | 6.25 | 49.15 | 60 |
| 5400 | 6' wide, without soffit | | 250 | .224 | | 32.50 | 9.40 | 6.25 | 48.15 | 58.50 |
| 5450 | With soffit | | 200 | .280 | | 42.50 | 11.70 | 7.85 | 62.05 | 75 |
| 5500 | Entrance canopy, incl. frame, 4' x 4' | | 25 | 2.240 | Ea. | 330 | 94 | 62.50 | 486.50 | 590 |
| 5550 | 4' x 8' | | 19 | 2.947 | " | 445 | 123 | 82.50 | 650.50 | 795 |
| 5600 | End wall roof overhang, 4' wide, without soffit | | 850 | .066 | L.F. | 15.95 | 2.76 | 1.84 | 20.55 | 24.50 |
| 5650 | With soffit | | 500 | .112 | " | 23.50 | 4.69 | 3.13 | 31.32 | 37.50 |
| 5700 | Doors, H.M. self-framing, incl. butts, lockset and trim | | | | | | | | | |
| 5750 | Single leaf, 3070 (3' x 7'), economy | 2 Sswk | 5 | 3.200 | Opng. | 440 | 138 | | 578 | 735 |
| 5800 | Deluxe | | 4 | 4 | | 520 | 172 | | 692 | 885 |
| 5825 | Glazed | | 4 | 4 | | 535 | 172 | | 707 | 895 |
| 5850 | 3670 (3'-6" x 7') | | 4 | 4 | | 555 | 172 | | 727 | 925 |
| 5900 | 4070 (4' x 7') | | 3 | 5.333 | | 590 | 229 | | 819 | 1,075 |
| 5950 | Double leaf, 6070 (6' x 7') | | 2 | 8 | | 790 | 345 | | 1,135 | 1,500 |
| 6000 | Glazed | | 2 | 8 | | 975 | 345 | | 1,320 | 1,700 |
| 6050 | Framing only, for openings, 3' x 7' | E-2 | 25 | 2.240 | | 153 | 94 | 62.50 | 309.50 | 400 |
| 6100 | 10' x 10' | | 21 | 2.667 | | 505 | 112 | 74.50 | 691.50 | 830 |
| 6150 | For windows below, 2020 (2' x 2') | | 25 | 2.240 | | 162 | 94 | 62.50 | 318.50 | 410 |
| 6200 | 4030 (4' x 3') | | 22 | 2.545 | | 198 | 107 | 71 | 376 | 480 |
| 6250 | Flashings, 26 ga., corner or eave, painted | 2 Sswk | 240 | .067 | L.F. | 3.93 | 2.87 | | 6.80 | 9.45 |
| 6300 | Galvanized | | 240 | .067 | | 3.27 | 2.87 | | 6.14 | 8.75 |
| 6350 | Rake flashing, painted | | 240 | .067 | | 4.21 | 2.87 | | 7.08 | 9.80 |
| 6400 | Galvanized | | 240 | .067 | | 3.58 | 2.87 | | 6.45 | 9.10 |
| 6450 | Ridge flashing, 18" wide, painted | | 240 | .067 | | 5.25 | 2.87 | | 8.12 | 10.90 |
| 6500 | Galvanized | | 240 | .067 | | 4.69 | 2.87 | | 7.56 | 10.30 |
| 6550 | Gutter, eave type, 26 ga., painted | | 320 | .050 | | 5.45 | 2.15 | | 7.60 | 9.90 |
| 6600 | Galvanized | | 320 | .050 | | 3.08 | 2.15 | | 5.23 | 7.25 |
| 6650 | Valley type, between buildings, painted | | 120 | .133 | | 8.80 | 5.75 | | 14.55 | 20 |
| 6710 | Insulation, rated .6 lb density, unfaced 4" thick, R13 | 2 Carp | 2300 | .007 | S.F. | .31 | .27 | | .58 | .75 |
| 6720 | 6" thick, R-19 | | 2300 | .007 | | .40 | .27 | | .67 | .85 |
| 6730 | 10" thick, R-30 | | 2300 | .007 | | .74 | .27 | | 1.01 | 1.22 |
| 6750 | Insulation, rated .6 lb density, poly/scrim/foil (PSF) faced | | | | | | | | | |
| 6760 | 4" thick R-13 | 2 Carp | 2300 | .007 | S.F. | .43 | .27 | | .70 | .88 |
| 6770 | 6" thick, R-19 | | 2300 | .007 | | .57 | .27 | | .84 | 1.04 |
| 6780 | 10" thick, R-30 | | 2300 | .007 | | 1.06 | .27 | | 1.33 | 1.58 |
| 6800 | Insulation, rated .6 lb density, vinyl faced 1-1/2" thick, R5 | | 2300 | .007 | | .25 | .27 | | .52 | .69 |
| 6850 | 3" thick, R10 | | 2300 | .007 | | .34 | .27 | | .61 | .78 |
| 6900 | 4" thick, R13 | | 2300 | .007 | | .48 | .27 | | .75 | .94 |
| 6920 | 6" thick, R19 | | 2300 | .007 | | .67 | .27 | | .94 | 1.15 |
| 6930 | 10" thick, R30 | | 2300 | .007 | | .96 | .27 | | 1.23 | 1.47 |
| 6950 | Foil/scrim/kraft (FSK) faced, 1-1/2" thick, R5 | | 2300 | .007 | | .27 | .27 | | .54 | .71 |
| 7000 | 2" thick, R6 | | 2300 | .007 | | .34 | .27 | | .61 | .78 |
| 7050 | 3" thick, R10 | | 2300 | .007 | | .43 | .27 | | .70 | .88 |
| 7100 | 4" thick, R13 | | 2300 | .007 | | .54 | .27 | | .81 | 1 |
| 7110 | 6" thick, R19 | | 2300 | .007 | | .61 | .27 | | .88 | 1.08 |
| 7120 | 10" thick, R-30 | | 2300 | .007 | | 1.03 | .27 | | 1.30 | 1.54 |
| 7150 | Met polyester/scrim/kraft (PSK) facing, 1-1/2" thk, R5 | | 2300 | .007 | | .43 | .27 | | .70 | .88 |
| 7200 | 2" thick, R6 | | 2300 | .007 | | .50 | .27 | | .77 | .96 |
| 7250 | 3" thick, R11 | | 2300 | .007 | | .54 | .27 | | .81 | 1 |
| 7300 | 4" thick, R13 | | 2300 | .007 | | .66 | .27 | | .93 | 1.14 |
| 7310 | 6" thick, R19 | | 2300 | .007 | | .87 | .27 | | 1.14 | 1.37 |
| 7320 | 10" thick, R-30 | | 2300 | .007 | | 1.05 | .27 | | 1.32 | 1.57 |

## 13 34 19 – Metal Building Systems

| 13 34 19.50 Pre-Engineered Steel Buildings | | Crew | Daily Output | Labor-Hours | Unit | Material | 2008 Bare Costs Labor | Equipment | Total | Total Incl O&P |
|---|---|---|---|---|---|---|---|---|---|---|
| 7350 | Vinyl/scrim/foil (VSF), 1-1/2" thick, R5 | 2 Carp | 2300 | .007 | S.F. | .38 | .27 | | .65 | .83 |
| 7400 | 2" thick, R6 | | 2300 | .007 | | .48 | .27 | | .75 | .94 |
| 7450 | 3" thick, R10 | | 2300 | .007 | | .63 | .27 | | .90 | 1.10 |
| 7500 | 4" thick, R13 | | 2300 | .007 | | .73 | .27 | | 1 | 1.21 |
| 7510 | Vinyl/scrim/vinyl (VSV) 4" thick, R-13 | | 2300 | .007 | | .50 | .27 | | .77 | .96 |
| 7520 | 6" thick R-19 | | 2300 | .007 | | .63 | .27 | | .90 | 1.10 |
| 7530 | 10" thick, R-30 | | 2300 | .007 | | 1.01 | .27 | | 1.28 | 1.52 |
| 7540 | Polyprop/scrim/polyester (PSP), 4",R-13 | | 2300 | .007 | | .40 | .27 | | .67 | .85 |
| 7550 | 6" thick, R-19 | | 2300 | .007 | | .54 | .27 | | .81 | 1 |
| 7555 | 10" thick, R-30 | | 2300 | .007 | | .99 | .27 | | 1.26 | 1.50 |
| 7560 | Polyprop/scrim/kraft/polyester (PSKP), 4" thick, R-13 | | 2300 | .007 | | .42 | .27 | | .69 | .87 |
| 7570 | 6" thick, R-19 | | 2300 | .007 | | .55 | .27 | | .82 | 1.02 |
| 7580 | 10" thick, R-19 | | 2300 | .007 | | 1.05 | .27 | | 1.32 | 1.57 |
| 7585 | Vinyl/scrim/polyester (VSP), 4" thick, R-13 | | 2300 | .007 | | .44 | .27 | | .71 | .89 |
| 7590 | 6" thick, R-19 | | 2300 | .007 | | .60 | .27 | | .87 | 1.07 |
| 7600 | 10" thick, R-30 | | 2300 | .007 | | 1.08 | .27 | | 1.35 | 1.60 |
| 7635 | Insulation installation, over the purlin, second layer, up to 4" thick, add | | | | | | 90% | | | |
| 7640 | Insulation installation, between the purlins, up to 4" thick, add | | | | | | 100% | | | |
| 7650 | Sash, single slide, glazed, with screens, 2020 (2' x 2') | E-1 | 22 | 1.091 | Opng. | 91 | 45.50 | 6 | 142.50 | 185 |
| 7700 | 3030 (3' x 3') | | 14 | 1.714 | | 205 | 72 | 9.45 | 286.45 | 360 |
| 7750 | 4030 (4' x 3') | | 13 | 1.846 | | 274 | 77.50 | 10.15 | 361.65 | 445 |
| 7800 | 6040 (6' x 4') | | 12 | 2 | | 545 | 84 | 11 | 640 | 755 |
| 7850 | Double slide sash, 3030 (3' x 3') | | 14 | 1.714 | | 161 | 72 | 9.45 | 242.45 | 310 |
| 7900 | 6040 (6' x 4') | | 12 | 2 | | 430 | 84 | 11 | 525 | 625 |
| 7950 | Fixed glass, no screens, 3030 (3' x 3') | | 14 | 1.714 | | 206 | 72 | 9.45 | 287.45 | 360 |
| 8000 | 6040 (6' x 4') | | 12 | 2 | | 550 | 84 | 11 | 645 | 760 |
| 8050 | Prefinished storm sash, 3030 (3' x 3') | | 70 | .343 | | 67.50 | 14.35 | 1.89 | 83.74 | 101 |
| 8100 | Siding and roofing, see Div. 07 41 13.00 & 07 42 13.00 | | | | | | | | | |
| 8200 | Skylight, fiberglass panels, to 30 S.F. | E-1 | 10 | 2.400 | Ea. | 103 | 101 | 13.20 | 217.20 | 300 |
| 8250 | Larger sizes, add for excess over 30 S.F. | " | 300 | .080 | S.F. | 3.43 | 3.35 | .44 | 7.22 | 10 |
| 8300 | Roof vents, circular with damper, birdscreen | | | | | | | | | |
| 8350 | and operator hardware, painted | | | | | | | | | |
| 8400 | 26 ga., 12" diameter | 1 Sswk | 4 | 2 | Ea. | 65.50 | 86 | | 151.50 | 227 |
| 8450 | 20" diameter | | 3 | 2.667 | | 135 | 115 | | 250 | 355 |
| 8500 | 24 ga., 24" diameter | | 2 | 4 | | 267 | 172 | | 439 | 605 |
| 8550 | Galvanized | | 2 | 4 | | 224 | 172 | | 396 | 555 |
| 8600 | Continuous, 26 ga., 10' long, 9" wide | 2 Sswk | 4 | 4 | | 21.50 | 172 | | 193.50 | 335 |
| 8650 | 12" wide | " | 4 | 4 | | 25.50 | 172 | | 197.50 | 340 |

## 13 34 23 – Fabricated Structures

### 13 34 23.10 Comfort Stations

| | | Crew | Daily Output | Labor-Hours | Unit | Material | 2008 Bare Costs Labor | Equipment | Total | Total Incl O&P |
|---|---|---|---|---|---|---|---|---|---|---|
| 0010 | **COMFORT STATIONS** Prefab., stock, w/doors, windows & fixt. | | | | | | | | | |
| 0100 | Not incl. interior finish or electrical | | | | | | | | | |
| 0300 | Mobile, on steel frame, minimum | | | | S.F. | 36.50 | | | 36.50 | 40 |
| 0350 | Maximum | | | | | 57.50 | | | 57.50 | 63.50 |
| 0400 | Permanent, including concrete slab, minimum | B-12J | 50 | .320 | | 142 | 11.40 | 18.65 | 172.05 | 194 |
| 0500 | Maximum | " | 43 | .372 | | 206 | 13.25 | 21.50 | 240.75 | 271 |
| 0600 | Alternate pricing method, mobile, minimum | | | | Fixture | 1,775 | | | 1,775 | 1,950 |
| 0650 | Maximum | | | | | 2,650 | | | 2,650 | 2,925 |
| 0700 | Permanent, minimum | B-12J | .70 | 22.857 | | 10,200 | 815 | 1,325 | 12,340 | 13,900 |
| 0750 | Maximum | " | .50 | 32 | | 17,000 | 1,150 | 1,875 | 20,025 | 22,500 |

# 13 34 Fabricated Engineered Structures

## 13 34 23 – Fabricated Structures

| 13 34 23.15 Domes | Crew | Daily Output | Labor- Hours | Unit | Material | 2008 Bare Costs Labor | Equipment | Total | Total Incl O&P |
|---|---|---|---|---|---|---|---|---|---|
| 0010 **DOMES** | | | | | | | | | |
| 0020 Domes, rev alum, elec drive, for astronomy obsv shell only, stock units | | | | | | | | | |
| 0600 10'-0" diameter, 800#, dome | 2 Carp | .25 | 64 | Ea. | 11,000 | 2,450 | | 13,450 | 15,900 |
| 0700 Base | | .67 | 23.881 | | 3,800 | 910 | | 4,710 | 5,600 |
| 0900 18'-0" diameter, 2,500#, dome | | .17 | 94.118 | | 32,100 | 3,575 | | 35,675 | 40,900 |
| 1000 Base | | .33 | 48.485 | | 10,600 | 1,850 | | 12,450 | 14,600 |
| 1200 24'-0" diameter, 4,500#, dome | | .08 | 200 | | 59,500 | 7,625 | | 67,125 | 77,500 |
| 1300 Base | | .25 | 64 | | 19,200 | 2,450 | | 21,650 | 24,900 |
| 1500 Domes, bulk storage, shell only, dual radius hemisphere. arch, steel | | | | | | | | | |
| 1600 framing, corrugated steel covering, 150' diameter | E-2 | 550 | .102 | SF Flr. | 28 | 4.26 | 2.85 | 35.11 | 41 |
| 1700 400' diameter | " | 720 | .078 | | 22.50 | 3.26 | 2.18 | 27.94 | 33 |
| 1800 Wood framing, wood decking, to 400' diameter | F-4 | 400 | .120 | | 20.50 | 4.57 | 2.80 | 27.87 | 32.50 |
| 1900 Radial framed wood (2" x 6"), 1/2" thick | | | | | | | | | |
| 2000 plywood, asphalt shingles, 50' diameter | F-3 | 2000 | .020 | SF Flr. | 38.50 | .77 | .38 | 39.65 | 44 |
| 2100 60' diameter | | 1900 | .021 | | 29.50 | .81 | .40 | 30.71 | 34 |
| 2200 72' diameter | | 1800 | .022 | | 26.50 | .86 | .43 | 27.79 | 31 |
| 2300 116' diameter | | 1730 | .023 | | 23 | .89 | .44 | 24.33 | 27.50 |
| 2400 150' diameter | | 1500 | .027 | | 20 | 1.03 | .51 | 21.54 | 24 |

## 13 34 23.16 Fabricated Control Booths

| | Crew | Daily Output | Labor- Hours | Unit | Material | 2008 Bare Costs Labor | Equipment | Total | Total Incl O&P |
|---|---|---|---|---|---|---|---|---|---|
| 0010 **FABRICATED CONTROL BOOTHS** | | | | | | | | | |
| 0100 Guard House, prefab conc w/bullet resistant doors & windows, roof and wiring | | | | | | | | | |
| 0110 8' x 8', Level III | L-10 | 1 | 24 | Ea. | 20,000 | 1,025 | 765 | 21,790 | 24,600 |
| 0120 8' x 8', Level IV | " | 1 | 24 | " | 25,000 | 1,025 | 765 | 26,790 | 30,100 |

## 13 34 23.25 Garage Costs

| | Crew | Daily Output | Labor- Hours | Unit | Material | 2008 Bare Costs Labor | Equipment | Total | Total Incl O&P |
|---|---|---|---|---|---|---|---|---|---|
| 0010 **GARAGE COSTS** | | | | | | | | | |
| 0020 Public parking, average | | | | Car | | | | 15,500 | 17,100 |
| 0100 See also Square Foot Costs in Reference Section | | | | | | | | | |
| 0300 Residential, prefab shell, stock, wood, single car, minimum | 2 Carp | 1 | 16 | Total | 4,775 | 610 | | 5,385 | 6,200 |
| 0350 Maximum | | .67 | 23.881 | | 6,525 | 910 | | 7,435 | 8,600 |
| 0400 Two car, minimum | | .67 | 23.881 | | 7,275 | 910 | | 8,185 | 9,450 |
| 0450 Maximum | | .50 | 32 | | 10,400 | 1,225 | | 11,625 | 13,300 |

## 13 34 23.30 Garden House

| | Crew | Daily Output | Labor- Hours | Unit | Material | 2008 Bare Costs Labor | Equipment | Total | Total Incl O&P |
|---|---|---|---|---|---|---|---|---|---|
| 0010 **GARDEN HOUSE** Prefab wood, no floors or foundations | | | | | | | | | |
| 0100 32 to 200 S.F., minimum | 2 Carp | 200 | .080 | SF Flr. | 24 | 3.05 | | 27.05 | 31 |
| 0300 Maximum | " | 48 | .333 | " | 40 | 12.70 | | 52.70 | 64 |

## 13 34 23.35 Geodesic Domes

| | Crew | Daily Output | Labor- Hours | Unit | Material | 2008 Bare Costs Labor | Equipment | Total | Total Incl O&P |
|---|---|---|---|---|---|---|---|---|---|
| 0010 **GEODESIC DOMES** Shell only, interlocking plywood panels  R133423-30 | | | | | | | | | |
| 0400 30' diameter | F-5 | 1.60 | 20 | Ea. | 19,300 | 770 | | 20,070 | 22,400 |
| 0500 34' diameter | | 1.14 | 28.070 | | 22,800 | 1,075 | | 23,875 | 26,700 |
| 0600 39' diameter | | 1 | 32 | | 25,600 | 1,225 | | 26,825 | 30,100 |
| 0700 45' diameter | F-3 | 1.13 | 35.556 | | 31,500 | 1,375 | 680 | 33,555 | 37,600 |
| 0750 55' diameter | | 1 | 40 | | 45,200 | 1,550 | 765 | 47,515 | 53,000 |
| 0800 60' diameter | | 1 | 40 | | 58,500 | 1,550 | 765 | 60,815 | 67,500 |
| 0850 65' diameter | | .80 | 50 | | 71,500 | 1,925 | 960 | 74,385 | 83,000 |
| 1100 Aluminum panel, with 6" insulation | | | | | | | | | |
| 1200 100' diameter | | | | SF Flr. | 38 | | | 38 | 41.50 |
| 1300 500' diameter | | | | " | 32.50 | | | 32.50 | 35.50 |
| 1600 Aluminum framed, plexiglass closure panels | | | | | | | | | |
| 1700 40' diameter | | | | SF Flr. | 96 | | | 96 | 105 |
| 1800 200' diameter | | | | " | 76.50 | | | 76.50 | 84 |
| 2100 Aluminum framed, aluminum closure panels | | | | | | | | | |

# 13 34 Fabricated Engineered Structures

## 13 34 23 – Fabricated Structures

| 13 34 23.35 Geodesic Domes | Crew | Daily Output | Labor-Hours | Unit | Material | 2008 Bare Costs Labor | Equipment | Total | Total Incl O&P |
|---|---|---|---|---|---|---|---|---|---|
| 2200 | 40' diameter | | | | SF Flr. | 30 | | | 30 | 33.50 |
| 2300 | 100' diameter | | | | | 22.50 | | | 22.50 | 25 |
| 2400 | 200' diameter | | | | | 21.50 | | | 21.50 | 24 |
| 2500 | For VRP faced bonded fiberglass insulation, add | | | | ↓ | | | | | 10 |
| 2700 | Aluminum framed, fiberglass sandwich panel closure | | | | | | | | | |
| 2800 | 6' diameter | 2 Carp | 150 | .107 | SF Flr. | 33.50 | 4.06 | | 37.56 | 43.50 |
| 2900 | 28' diameter | " | 350 | .046 | " | 30.50 | 1.74 | | 32.24 | 36 |

### 13 34 23.45 Kiosks

| | | | | | | | | | |
|---|---|---|---|---|---|---|---|---|---|
| 0010 | **KIOSKS** | | | | | | | | | |
| 0020 | Round, 5' diameter, 8' high, 1/4" fiberglass wall | | | | Ea. | 5,600 | | | 5,600 | 6,175 |
| 0100 | 1" insulated double wall, fiberglass | | | | | 6,375 | | | 6,375 | 7,025 |
| 0500 | Rectangular, 5' x 9', 7'-6" high, 1/4" fiberglass wall | | | | | 8,150 | | | 8,150 | 8,975 |
| 0600 | 1" insulated double wall, fiberglass | | | | ↓ | 9,700 | | | 9,700 | 10,700 |

### 13 34 23.60 Portable Booths

| | | | | | | | | | |
|---|---|---|---|---|---|---|---|---|---|
| 0010 | **PORTABLE BOOTHS** Prefab aluminum with doors, windows, ext. roof | | | | | | | | | |
| 0100 | lights wiring & insulation, 15 S.F. building, O.D., painted, minimum | | | | S.F. | 290 | | | 290 | 320 |
| 0300 | 30 S.F. building, minimum | | | | | 198 | | | 198 | 218 |
| 0400 | 50 S.F. building, minimum | | | | | 147 | | | 147 | 162 |
| 0600 | 80 S.F. building, minimum | | | | | 120 | | | 120 | 132 |
| 0700 | 100 S.F. building, minimum | | | | ↓ | 112 | | | 112 | 123 |
| 0900 | Acoustical booth, 27 Db @ 1,000 Hz, 15 S.F. floor | | | | Ea. | 3,375 | | | 3,375 | 3,725 |
| 1000 | 7' x 7'-6", including light & ventilation | | | | | 6,950 | | | 6,950 | 7,625 |
| 1200 | Ticket booth, galv. steel, not incl. foundations., 4' x 4' | | | | | 5,550 | | | 5,550 | 6,100 |
| 1300 | 4' x 6' | | | | ↓ | 6,450 | | | 6,450 | 7,100 |

### 13 34 23.70 Shelters

| | | | | | | | | | |
|---|---|---|---|---|---|---|---|---|---|
| 0010 | **SHELTERS** | | | | | | | | | |
| 0020 | Aluminum frame, acrylic glazing, 3' x 9' x 8' high | 2 Sswk | 1.14 | 14.035 | Ea. | 2,750 | 605 | | 3,355 | 4,125 |
| 0100 | 9' x 12' x 8' high | " | .73 | 21.918 | " | 4,850 | 940 | | 5,790 | 7,050 |

## 13 34 43 – Aircraft Hangars

### 13 34 43.50 Hangars

| | | | | | | | | | |
|---|---|---|---|---|---|---|---|---|---|
| 0010 | **HANGARS** Prefabricated steel T hangars, Galv. steel roof & | | | | | | | | | |
| 0100 | walls, incl. electric bi-folding doors, 4 or more units, | | | | | | | | | |
| 0110 | not including floors or foundations, minimum | E-2 | 1275 | .044 | SF Flr. | 10.90 | 1.84 | 1.23 | 13.97 | 16.55 |
| 0130 | Maximum | | 1063 | .053 | | 11.90 | 2.21 | 1.47 | 15.58 | 18.55 |
| 0900 | With bottom rolling doors, minimum | | 1386 | .040 | | 10.75 | 1.69 | 1.13 | 13.57 | 16 |
| 1000 | Maximum | ↓ | 966 | .058 | ↓ | 12.10 | 2.43 | 1.62 | 16.15 | 19.25 |
| 1200 | Alternate pricing method: | | | | | | | | | |
| 1300 | Galv. roof and walls, electric bi-folding doors, minimum | E-2 | 1.06 | 52.830 | Plane | 14,500 | 2,200 | 1,475 | 18,175 | 21,400 |
| 1500 | Maximum | | .91 | 61.538 | | 17,200 | 2,575 | 1,725 | 21,500 | 25,400 |
| 1600 | With bottom rolling doors, minimum | | 1.25 | 44.800 | | 10,700 | 1,875 | 1,250 | 13,825 | 16,300 |
| 1800 | Maximum | ↓ | .97 | 57.732 | ↓ | 12,700 | 2,425 | 1,625 | 16,750 | 20,000 |
| 2000 | Circular type, prefab., steel frame, plastic skin, electric | | | | | | | | | |
| 2010 | door, including foundations, 80' diameter, | | | | | | | | | |
| 2020 | for up to 5 light planes, minimum | E-2 | .50 | 112 | Total | 63,000 | 4,700 | 3,125 | 70,825 | 81,000 |
| 2200 | Maximum | " | .25 | 224 | " | 70,500 | 9,375 | 6,275 | 86,150 | 100,500 |

## 13 34 53 – Agricultural Structures

### 13 34 53.50 Silos

| | | | | | | | | | |
|---|---|---|---|---|---|---|---|---|---|
| 0010 | **SILOS** Concrete stave industrial, conical or sloping bottom | | | | | | | | | |
| 0100 | excluding foundation, 12' diameter, 35' high | D-8 | .11 | 363 | Ea. | 40,000 | 13,000 | | 53,000 | 64,000 |
| 0200 | 16' diameter, 45' high | | .08 | 500 | | 65,000 | 17,900 | | 82,900 | 98,500 |
| 0400 | 25' diameter, 75' high | ↓ | .05 | 800 | ↓ | 150,000 | 28,600 | | 178,600 | 208,500 |

# 13 34 Fabricated Engineered Structures

## 13 34 53 – Agricultural Structures

### 13 34 53.50 Silos

| | | Crew | Daily Output | Labor-Hours | Unit | Material | 2008 Bare Costs Labor | Equipment | Total | Total Incl O&P |
|---|---|---|---|---|---|---|---|---|---|---|
| 0500 | Steel, factory fab., 30,000 gallon cap., painted, minimum | L-5 | 1 | 56 | Ea. | 17,200 | 2,400 | 785 | 20,385 | 24,100 |
| 0700 | Maximum | | .50 | 112 | | 27,400 | 4,825 | 1,575 | 33,800 | 40,400 |
| 0800 | Epoxy lined, minimum | | 1 | 56 | | 28,200 | 2,400 | 785 | 31,385 | 36,100 |
| 1000 | Maximum | | .50 | 112 | | 35,800 | 4,825 | 1,575 | 42,200 | 49,500 |

# 13 36 Towers

## 13 36 13 – Metal Towers

### 13 36 13.50 Control Towers

| | | Crew | Daily Output | Labor-Hours | Unit | Material | 2008 Bare Costs Labor | Equipment | Total | Total Incl O&P |
|---|---|---|---|---|---|---|---|---|---|---|
| 0010 | **CONTROL TOWERS** | | | | | | | | | |
| 0020 | Modular 12' x 10', incl. instruments, min. | | | | Ea. | 609,000 | | | 609,000 | 670,000 |
| 0100 | Maximum | | | | | | | | 927,273 | 1,020,000 |
| 0500 | With standard 40' tower, average | | | | | 850,000 | | | 850,000 | 935,000 |
| 1000 | Temporary portable control towers, 8' x 12', | | | | | | | | | |
| 1010 | complete with one position communications, minimum | | | | Ea. | | | | 266,000 | 293,000 |
| 2000 | For fixed facilities, depending on height, minimum | | | | | | | | 57,200 | 63,000 |
| 2010 | Maximum | | | | | | | | 115,000 | 127,000 |

# 13 42 Building Modules

## 13 42 63 – Detention Cell Modules

### 13 42 63.16 Steel Detention Cell Modules

| | | Crew | Daily Output | Labor-Hours | Unit | Material | 2008 Bare Costs Labor | Equipment | Total | Total Incl O&P |
|---|---|---|---|---|---|---|---|---|---|---|
| 0010 | **STEEL DETENTION CELL MODULES** | | | | | | | | | |
| 2000 | Cells, prefab., 5' to 6' wide, 7' to 8' high, 7' to 8' deep, | | | | | | | | | |
| 2010 | bar front, cot, not incl. plumbing | E-4 | 1.50 | 21.333 | Ea. | 8,400 | 930 | 88 | 9,418 | 11,000 |

# 13 48 Sound, Vibration, and Seismic Control

## 13 48 13 – Manufactured Sound and Vibration Control Components

### 13 48 13.50 Audio Masking

| | | Crew | Daily Output | Labor-Hours | Unit | Material | 2008 Bare Costs Labor | Equipment | Total | Total Incl O&P |
|---|---|---|---|---|---|---|---|---|---|---|
| 0010 | **AUDIO MASKING**, acoustical enclosure, 4" thick wall and ceiling | | | | | | | | | |
| 0020 | 8# per S.F., up to 12' span | 3 Carp | 72 | .333 | SF Surf | 30 | 12.70 | | 42.70 | 53 |
| 0300 | Better quality panels, 10.5# per S.F. | | 64 | .375 | | 34 | 14.30 | | 48.30 | 59.50 |
| 0400 | Reverb-chamber, 4" thick, parallel walls | | 60 | .400 | | 42.50 | 15.25 | | 57.75 | 70 |
| 0600 | Skewed wall, parallel roof, 4" thick panels | | 55 | .436 | | 48.50 | 16.65 | | 65.15 | 79.50 |
| 0700 | Skewed walls, skewed roof, 4" layers, 4" air space | | 48 | .500 | | 54.50 | 19.05 | | 73.55 | 89.50 |
| 0900 | Sound-absorbing panels, pntd mtl, 2'-6" x 8', under 1,000 S.F. | | 215 | .112 | | 11.30 | 4.25 | | 15.55 | 19 |
| 1100 | Over 1000 S.F. | | 240 | .100 | | 10.90 | 3.81 | | 14.71 | 17.90 |
| 1200 | Fabric faced | | 240 | .100 | | 8.80 | 3.81 | | 12.61 | 15.65 |
| 1500 | Flexible transparent curtain, clear | 3 Shee | 215 | .112 | | 6.80 | 5.05 | | 11.85 | 15.30 |
| 1600 | 50% foam | | 215 | .112 | | 9.50 | 5.05 | | 14.55 | 18.25 |
| 1700 | 75% foam | | 215 | .112 | | 9.50 | 5.05 | | 14.55 | 18.25 |
| 1800 | 100% foam | | 215 | .112 | | 9.50 | 5.05 | | 14.55 | 18.25 |
| 3100 | Audio masking system, including speakers, amplification | | | | | | | | | |
| 3110 | and signal generator | | | | | | | | | |
| 3200 | Ceiling mounted, 5,000 S.F. | 2 Elec | 2400 | .007 | S.F. | 1.21 | .30 | | 1.51 | 1.78 |
| 3300 | 10,000 S.F. | | 2800 | .006 | | .98 | .26 | | 1.24 | 1.47 |
| 3400 | Plenum mounted, 5,000 S.F. | | 3800 | .004 | | .99 | .19 | | 1.18 | 1.38 |
| 3500 | 10,000 S.F. | | 4400 | .004 | | .67 | .17 | | .84 | .99 |

# 13 49 Radiation Protection

## 13 49 13 – Lead Sheet

### 13 49 13.50 Lead Sheets

| | | Crew | Daily Output | Labor-Hours | Unit | Material | 2008 Bare Costs Labor | Equipment | Total | Total Incl O&P |
|---|---|---|---|---|---|---|---|---|---|---|
| 0010 | **LEAD SHEETS** | | | | | | | | | |
| 0300 | Lead sheets, 1/16" thick | 2 Lath | 135 | .119 | S.F. | 6.95 | 4.12 | | 11.07 | 13.75 |
| 0400 | 1/8" thick | | 120 | .133 | | 14.05 | 4.64 | | 18.69 | 22.50 |
| 0500 | Lead shielding, 1/4" thick | | 135 | .119 | | 33 | 4.12 | | 37.12 | 42.50 |
| 0550 | 1/2" thick | ↓ | 120 | .133 | ↓ | 58 | 4.64 | | 62.64 | 70.50 |
| 0950 | Lead headed nails (average 1 lb. per sheet) | | | | Lb. | 6.50 | | | 6.50 | 7.15 |
| 1000 | Butt joints in 1/8" lead or thicker, 2" batten strip x 7' long | 2 Lath | 240 | .067 | Ea. | 16.25 | 2.32 | | 18.57 | 21.50 |
| 1200 | X-ray protection, average radiography or fluoroscopy | | | | | | | | | |
| 1210 | room, up to 300 S.F. floor, 1/16" lead, minimum | 2 Lath | .25 | 64 | Total | 7,700 | 2,225 | | 9,925 | 11,800 |
| 1500 | Maximum, 7'-0" walls | " | .15 | 106 | " | 9,250 | 3,700 | | 12,950 | 15,700 |
| 1600 | Deep therapy X-ray room, 250 kV capacity, | | | | | | | | | |
| 1800 | up to 300 S.F. floor, 1/4" lead, minimum | 2 Lath | .08 | 200 | Total | 21,500 | 6,950 | | 28,450 | 33,900 |
| 1900 | Maximum, 7'-0" walls | " | .06 | 266 | " | 26,500 | 9,275 | | 35,775 | 43,000 |

## 13 49 19 – Lead-Lined Materials

### 13 49 19.50 Shielding Lead

| | | Crew | Daily Output | Labor-Hours | Unit | Material | 2008 Bare Costs Labor | Equipment | Total | Total Incl O&P |
|---|---|---|---|---|---|---|---|---|---|---|
| 0010 | **SHIELDING LEAD** | | | | | | | | | |
| 0100 | Laminated lead in wood doors, 1/16" thick, no hardware | | | | S.F. | 41 | | | 41 | 45 |
| 0200 | Lead lined door frame, not incl. hardware, | | | | | | | | | |
| 0210 | 1/16" thick lead, butt prepared for hardware | 1 Lath | 2.40 | 3.333 | Ea. | 530 | 116 | | 646 | 755 |
| 0850 | Window frame with 1/16" lead and voice passage, 36" x 60" | 2 Glaz | 2 | 8 | | 945 | 298 | | 1,243 | 1,500 |
| 0870 | 24" x 36" frame | | 8 | 2 | ↓ | 765 | 74.50 | | 839.50 | 955 |
| 0900 | Lead gypsum board, 5/8" thick with 1/16" lead | | 160 | .100 | S.F. | 6.90 | 3.73 | | 10.63 | 13.20 |
| 0910 | 1/8" lead | CN ↓ | 140 | .114 | | 12.95 | 4.26 | | 17.21 | 20.50 |
| 0930 | 1/32" lead | 2 Lath | 200 | .080 | ↓ | 4.11 | 2.78 | | 6.89 | 8.65 |

## 13 49 21 – Lead Glazing

### 13 49 21.50 Lead Glazing

| | | Crew | Daily Output | Labor-Hours | Unit | Material | 2008 Bare Costs Labor | Equipment | Total | Total Incl O&P |
|---|---|---|---|---|---|---|---|---|---|---|
| 0010 | **LEAD GLAZING** | | | | | | | | | |
| 0600 | Lead glass, 1/4" thick, 2.0 mm LE, 12" x 16" | 2 Glaz | 13 | 1.231 | Ea. | 245 | 46 | | 291 | 340 |
| 0700 | 24" x 36" | | 8 | 2 | | 910 | 74.50 | | 984.50 | 1,125 |
| 0800 | 36" x 60" | ↓ | 2 | 8 | ↓ | 3,325 | 298 | | 3,623 | 4,125 |
| 2000 | X-ray viewing panels, clear lead plastic | | | | | | | | | |
| 2010 | 7 mm thick, 0.3 mm LE, 2.3 lbs/S.F. | H-3 | 139 | .115 | S.F. | 119 | 3.82 | | 122.82 | 137 |
| 2020 | 12 mm thick, 0.5 mm LE, 3.9 lbs/S.F. | | 82 | .195 | | 161 | 6.50 | | 167.50 | 188 |
| 2030 | 18 mm thick, 0.8mm LE, 5.9 lbs/S.F. | | 54 | .296 | | 175 | 9.85 | | 184.85 | 208 |
| 2040 | 22 mm thick, 1.0 mm LE, 7.2 lbs/S.F. | | 44 | .364 | | 179 | 12.05 | | 191.05 | 216 |
| 2050 | 35 mm thick, 1.5 mm LE, 11.5 lbs/S.F. | | 28 | .571 | | 201 | 18.95 | | 219.95 | 250 |
| 2060 | 46 mm thick, 2.0 mm LE, 15.0 lbs/S.F. | ↓ | 21 | .762 | ↓ | 264 | 25.50 | | 289.50 | 330 |
| 2090 | For panels 12 S.F. to 48 S.F., add crating charge | | | | Ea. | | | | | 50 |

## 13 49 23 – Modular Shielding Partitions

### 13 49 23.50 Modular Shielding Partitions

| | | Crew | Daily Output | Labor-Hours | Unit | Material | 2008 Bare Costs Labor | Equipment | Total | Total Incl O&P |
|---|---|---|---|---|---|---|---|---|---|---|
| 0010 | **MODULAR SHIELDING PARTITIONS** | | | | | | | | | |
| 4000 | X-ray barriers, modular, panels mounted within framework for | | | | | | | | | |
| 4002 | attaching to floor, wall or ceiling, upper portion is clear lead | | | | | | | | | |
| 4005 | plastic window panels 48"H, lower portion is opaque leaded | | | | | | | | | |
| 4008 | steel panels 36"H, structural supports not incl. | | | | | | | | | |
| 4010 | 1-section barrier, 36"W x 84"H overall | | | | | | | | | |
| 4020 | 0.5 mm LE panels | H-3 | 6.40 | 2.500 | Ea. | 3,775 | 83 | | 3,858 | 4,275 |
| 4030 | 0.8 mm LE panels | | 6.40 | 2.500 | | 4,025 | 83 | | 4,108 | 4,550 |
| 4040 | 1.0 mm LE panels | | 5.33 | 3.002 | | 4,100 | 99.50 | | 4,199.50 | 4,650 |
| 4050 | 1.5 mm LE panels | ↓ | 5.33 | 3.002 | ↓ | 4,375 | 99.50 | | 4,474.50 | 4,950 |
| 4060 | 2-section barrier, 72"W x 84"H overall | | | | | | | | | |

# 13 49 Radiation Protection

## 13 49 23 – Modular Shielding Partitions

| 13 49 23.50 Modular Shielding Partitions | Crew | Daily Output | Labor-Hours | Unit | Material | 2008 Bare Costs Labor | Equipment | Total | Total Incl O&P |
|---|---|---|---|---|---|---|---|---|---|
| 4070 | 0.5 mm LE panels | H-3 | 4 | 4 | Ea. | 7,700 | 133 | | 7,833 | 8,675 |
| 4080 | 0.8 mm LE panels | | 4 | 4 | | 8,150 | 133 | | 8,283 | 9,175 |
| 4090 | 1.0 mm LE panels | | 3.56 | 4.494 | | 8,325 | 149 | | 8,474 | 9,375 |
| 5000 | 1.5 mm LE panels | | 3.20 | 5 | | 9,450 | 166 | | 9,616 | 10,700 |
| 5010 | 3-section barrier, 108"W x 84"H overall | | | | | | | | | |
| 5020 | 0.5 mm LE panels | H-3 | 3.20 | 5 | Ea. | 11,600 | 166 | | 11,766 | 13,000 |
| 5030 | 0.8 mm LE panels | | 3.20 | 5 | | 12,200 | 166 | | 12,366 | 13,700 |
| 5040 | 1.0 mm LE panels | | 2.67 | 5.993 | | 12,400 | 199 | | 12,599 | 14,000 |
| 5050 | 1.5 mm LE panels | | 2.46 | 6.504 | | 13,500 | 216 | | 13,716 | 15,100 |
| 7000 | X-ray barriers, mobile, mounted within framework w/casters on | | | | | | | | | |
| 7005 | bottom, clear lead plastic window panels on upper portion, | | | | | | | | | |
| 7010 | opaque on lower, 30"W x 75"H overall, incl. framework | | | | | | | | | |
| 7020 | 24"H upper w/0.5 mm LE, 48"H lower w/0.8 mm LE | 1 Carp | 16 | .500 | Ea. | 2,000 | 19.05 | | 2,019.05 | 2,225 |
| 7030 | 48"W x 75"H overall, incl. framework | | | | | | | | | |
| 7040 | 36"H upper w/0.5 mm LE, 36"H lower w/0.8 mm LE | 1 Carp | 16 | .500 | Ea. | 3,675 | 19.05 | | 3,694.05 | 4,075 |
| 7050 | 36"H upper w/1.0 mm LE, 36"H lower w/1.5 mm LE | " | 16 | .500 | " | 4,375 | 19.05 | | 4,394.05 | 4,825 |
| 7060 | 72"W x 75"H overall, incl. framework | | | | | | | | | |
| 7070 | 36"H upper w/0.5 mm LE, 36"H lower w/0.8 mm LE | 1 Carp | 16 | .500 | Ea. | 4,350 | 19.05 | | 4,369.05 | 4,825 |
| 7080 | 36"H upper w/1.0 mm LE, 36"H lower w/1.5 mm LE | " | 16 | .500 | " | 5,450 | 19.05 | | 5,469.05 | 6,025 |

## 13 49 33 – Radio Frequency Shielding

| 13 49 33.50 Shielding, Radio Frequency | Crew | Daily Output | Labor-Hours | Unit | Material | 2008 Bare Costs Labor | Equipment | Total | Total Incl O&P |
|---|---|---|---|---|---|---|---|---|---|
| 0010 | **SHIELDING, RADIO FREQUENCY** | | | | | | | | | |
| 0020 | Prefabricated or screen-type copper or steel, minimum | 2 Carp | 180 | .089 | SF Surf | 25 | 3.39 | | 28.39 | 33 |
| 0100 | Average | | 155 | .103 | | 27.50 | 3.93 | | 31.43 | 36 |
| 0150 | Maximum | | 145 | .110 | | 32.50 | 4.20 | | 36.70 | 42.50 |

# 13 53 Meteorological Instrumentation

## 13 53 09 – Weather Instrumentation

| 13 53 09.50 Weather Station | Crew | Daily Output | Labor-Hours | Unit | Material | 2008 Bare Costs Labor | Equipment | Total | Total Incl O&P |
|---|---|---|---|---|---|---|---|---|---|
| 0010 | **WEATHER STATION** | | | | | | | | | |
| 0020 | Remote recording, minimum | | | | Ea. | 3,000 | | | 3,000 | 3,300 |
| 0100 | Maximum | | | | " | 27,000 | | | 27,000 | 29,700 |

# Division Notes

| | CREW | DAILY OUTPUT | LABOR-HOURS | UNIT | 2008 BARE COSTS | | | | TOTAL INCL O&P |
|---|---|---|---|---|---|---|---|---|---|
| | | | | | MAT. | LABOR | EQUIP. | TOTAL | |
| | | | | | | | | | |
| | | | | | | | | | |
| | | | | | | | | | |
| | | | | | | | | | |
| | | | | | | | | | |
| | | | | | | | | | |
| | | | | | | | | | |
| | | | | | | | | | |
| | | | | | | | | | |
| | | | | | | | | | |
| | | | | | | | | | |
| | | | | | | | | | |
| | | | | | | | | | |
| | | | | | | | | | |
| | | | | | | | | | |
| | | | | | | | | | |
| | | | | | | | | | |
| | | | | | | | | | |
| | | | | | | | | | |
| | | | | | | | | | |
| | | | | | | | | | |

# Estimating Tips

## General

- Many products in Division 14 will require some type of support or blocking for installation not included with the item itself. Examples are supports for conveyors or tube systems, attachment points for lifts, and footings for hoists or cranes. Add these supports in the appropriate division.

## 14 10 00 Dumbwaiters
## 14 20 00 Elevators

- Dumbwaiters and elevators are estimated and purchased in a method similar to buying a car. The manufacturer has a base unit with standard features. Added to this base unit price will be whatever options the owner or specifications require. Increased load capacity, additional vertical travel, additional stops, higher speed, and cab finish options are items to be considered. When developing an estimate for dumbwaiters and elevators, remember that some items needed by the installers may have to be included as part of the general contract.

Examples are:
- shaftway
- rail support brackets
- machine room
- electrical supply
- sill angles
- electrical connections
- pits
- roof penthouses
- pit ladders

Check the job specifications and drawings before pricing.

- Installation of elevators and handicapped lifts in historic structures can require significant additional costs. The associated structural requirements may involve cutting into and repairing finishes, mouldings, flooring, etc. The estimator must account for these special conditions.

## 14 30 00 Escalators and Moving Walks

- Escalators and moving walks are specialty items installed by specialty contractors. There are numerous options associated with these items. For specific options contact a manufacturer or contractor.

  In a method similar to estimating dumbwaiters and elevators, you should verify the extent of general contract work and add items as necessary.

## 14 40 00 Lifts
## 14 90 00 Other Conveying Equipment

- Products such as correspondence lifts, conveyors, chutes, pneumatic tube systems, material handling cranes, and hoists, as well as other items specified in this subdivision, may require trained installers. The general contractor might not have any choice as to who will perform the installation or when it will be performed. Long lead times are often required for these products, making early decisions in scheduling necessary.

## Reference Numbers

Reference numbers are shown in shaded boxes at the beginning of some major classifications. These numbers refer to related items in the Reference Section. The reference information may be an estimating procedure, an alternate pricing method, or technical information.

*Note:* Not all subdivisions listed here necessarily appear in this publication.

# 14 11 Manual Dumbwaiters

## 14 11 10 – Hand Operated Dumbwaiters

| 14 11 10.20 Manual Dumbwaiters | Crew | Daily Output | Labor-Hours | Unit | Material | 2008 Bare Costs Labor | Equipment | Total | Total Incl O&P |
|---|---|---|---|---|---|---|---|---|---|
| 0010 **MANUAL DUMBWAITERS** | | | | | | | | | |
| 0020   2 stop, minimum | 2 Elev | .75 | 21.333 | Ea. | 2,650 | 1,175 | | 3,825 | 4,675 |
| 0100     Maximum | | .50 | 32 | " | 6,050 | 1,775 | | 7,825 | 9,275 |
| 0300   For each additional stop, add | ↓ | .75 | 21.333 | Stop | 960 | 1,175 | | 2,135 | 2,800 |

# 14 12 Electric Dumbwaiters

## 14 12 10 – Dumbwaiters

### 14 12 10.10 Electric Dumbwaiters

| | Crew | Daily Output | Labor-Hours | Unit | Material | 2008 Bare Costs Labor | Equipment | Total | Total Incl O&P |
|---|---|---|---|---|---|---|---|---|---|
| 0010 **ELECTRIC DUMBWAITERS** | | | | | | | | | |
| 0020   2 stop, minimum | 2 Elev | .13 | 123 | Ea. | 6,725 | 6,775 | | 13,500 | 17,500 |
| 0100     Maximum | | .11 | 145 | " | 20,100 | 8,025 | | 28,125 | 34,100 |
| 0600   For each additional stop, add | ↓ | .54 | 29.630 | Stop | 2,950 | 1,625 | | 4,575 | 5,675 |
| 0750   Correspondence lift, 1 floor, 2 stop, 45 lb capacity | 2 Elec | .20 | 80 | Ea. | 7,600 | 3,650 | | 11,250 | 13,800 |

# 14 21 Electric Traction Elevators

## 14 21 13 – Electric Traction Freight Elevators

### 14 21 13.10 Electric Traction Freight Elevators and Options

| | Crew | Daily Output | Labor-Hours | Unit | Material | 2008 Bare Costs Labor | Equipment | Total | Total Incl O&P |
|---|---|---|---|---|---|---|---|---|---|
| 0010 **ELECTRIC TRACTION FREIGHT ELEVATORS AND OPTIONS** R142000-10 | | | | | | | | | |
| 0425   Electric freight, base unit, 4000 lb, 200 fpm, 4 stop, std. fin. | 2 Elev | .05 | 320 | Ea. | 81,000 | 17,600 | | 98,600 | 115,500 |
| 0450     For 5000 lb capacity, add | | | | | 5,800 | | | 5,800 | 6,375 |
| 0500     For 6000 lb capacity, add | | | | | 10,200 | | | 10,200 | 11,200 |
| 0525     For 7000 lb capacity, add | | | | | 13,700 | | | 13,700 | 15,000 |
| 0550     For 8000 lb capacity, add | | | | | 18,800 | | | 18,800 | 20,700 |
| 0575     For 10000 lb capacity, add | | | | | 22,400 | | | 22,400 | 24,600 |
| 0600     For 12000 lb capacity, add | | | | | 27,300 | | | 27,300 | 30,100 |
| 0625     For 16000 lb capacity, add | | | | | 32,800 | | | 32,800 | 36,100 |
| 0650     For 20000 lb capacity, add | | | | | 36,200 | | | 36,200 | 39,800 |
| 0675     For increased speed, 250 fpm, add | | | | | 10,900 | | | 10,900 | 12,000 |
| 0700       300 fpm, geared electric, add | | | | | 13,600 | | | 13,600 | 14,900 |
| 0725       350 fpm, geared electric, add | | | | | 16,000 | | | 16,000 | 17,600 |
| 0750       400 fpm, geared electric, add | | | | | 18,100 | | | 18,100 | 19,900 |
| 0775       500 fpm, gearless electric, add | | | | | 23,100 | | | 23,100 | 25,400 |
| 0800       600 fpm, gearless electric, add | | | | | 25,500 | | | 25,500 | 28,100 |
| 0825       700 fpm, gearless electric, add | | | | | 29,800 | | | 29,800 | 32,700 |
| 0850       800 fpm, gearless electric, add | | | | | 33,100 | | | 33,100 | 36,400 |
| 0875   For class "B" loading, add | | | | | 1,950 | | | 1,950 | 2,150 |
| 0900   For class "C-1" loading, add | | | | | 4,850 | | | 4,850 | 5,350 |
| 0925   For class "C-2" loading, add | | | | | 5,800 | | | 5,800 | 6,375 |
| 0950   For class "C-3" loading, add | | | | | 7,950 | | | 7,950 | 8,750 |
| 0975   For travel over 40 V.L.F., add | 2 Elev | 7.25 | 2.207 | V.L.F. | 115 | 122 | | 237 | 310 |
| 1000   For number of stops over 4, add | " | .27 | 59.259 | Stop | 2,050 | 3,275 | | 5,325 | 7,100 |

## 14 21 23 – Electric Traction Passenger Elevators

### 14 21 23.10 Electric Traction Passenger Elevators and Options

| | Crew | Daily Output | Labor-Hours | Unit | Material | 2008 Bare Costs Labor | Equipment | Total | Total Incl O&P |
|---|---|---|---|---|---|---|---|---|---|
| 0010 **ELECTRIC TRACTION PASSENGER ELEVATORS AND OPTIONS** | | | | | | | | | |
| 1625   Electric pass., base unit, 2000 lb, 200 fpm, 4 stop, std. fin. | 2 Elev | .05 | 320 | Ea. | 75,500 | 17,600 | | 93,100 | 109,500 |
| 1650     For 2500 lb capacity, add | | | | | 3,100 | | | 3,100 | 3,400 |
| 1675     For 3000 lb capacity, add | | | | | 4,725 | | | 4,725 | 5,175 |
| 1700     For 3500 lb capacity, add | | | | | 6,700 | | | 6,700 | 7,375 |
| 1725     For 4000 lb capacity, add | | | | | 7,000 | | | 7,000 | 7,700 |

# 14 21 Electric Traction Elevators

## 14 21 23 – Electric Traction Passenger Elevators

| 14 21 23.10 Electric Traction Passenger Elevators and Options | Crew | Daily Output | Labor-Hours | Unit | Material | 2008 Bare Costs Labor | Equipment | Total | Total Incl O&P |
|---|---|---|---|---|---|---|---|---|---|
| 1750 | For 4500 lb capacity, add | | | | Ea. | 9,225 | | | 9,225 | 10,100 |
| 1775 | For 5000 lb capacity, add | | | | | 11,700 | | | 11,700 | 12,900 |
| 1800 | For increased speed, 250 fpm, geared electric, add | | | | | 2,600 | | | 2,600 | 2,850 |
| 1825 | 300 fpm, geared electric, add | | | | | 5,325 | | | 5,325 | 5,875 |
| 1850 | 350 fpm, geared electric, add | | | | | 6,325 | | | 6,325 | 6,950 |
| 1875 | 400 fpm, geared electric, add | | | | | 8,975 | | | 8,975 | 9,875 |
| 1900 | 500 fpm, gearless electric, add | | | | | 42,200 | | | 42,200 | 46,400 |
| 1925 | 600 fpm, gearless electric, add | | | | | 44,600 | | | 44,600 | 49,000 |
| 1950 | 700 fpm, gearless electric, add | | | | | 48,800 | | | 48,800 | 53,500 |
| 1975 | 800 fpm, gearless electric, add | | | | | 54,000 | | | 54,000 | 59,000 |
| 2000 | For travel over 40 V.L.F., add | 2 Elev | 7.25 | 2.207 | V.L.F. | 118 | 122 | | 240 | 310 |
| 2025 | For number of stops over 4, add | | .27 | 59.259 | Stop | 2,750 | 3,275 | | 6,025 | 7,875 |
| 2400 | Electric hospital, base unit, 4000 lb, 200 fpm, 4 stop, std fin. | | .05 | 320 | Ea. | 82,500 | 17,600 | | 100,100 | 117,500 |
| 2425 | For 4500 lb capacity, add | | | | | 5,700 | | | 5,700 | 6,275 |
| 2450 | For 5000 lb capacity, add | | | | | 7,450 | | | 7,450 | 8,200 |
| 2475 | For increased speed, 250 fpm, geared electric, add | | | | | 2,775 | | | 2,775 | 3,075 |
| 2500 | 300 fpm, geared electric, add | | | | | 5,300 | | | 5,300 | 5,825 |
| 2525 | 350 fpm, geared electric, add | | | | | 6,450 | | | 6,450 | 7,100 |
| 2550 | 400 fpm, geared electric, add | | | | | 9,000 | | | 9,000 | 9,900 |
| 2575 | 500 fpm, gearless electric, add | | | | | 40,400 | | | 40,400 | 44,400 |
| 2600 | 600 fpm, gearless electric, add | | | | | 44,600 | | | 44,600 | 49,000 |
| 2625 | 700 fpm, gearless electric, add | | | | | 48,700 | | | 48,700 | 53,500 |
| 2650 | 800 fpm, gearless electric, add | | | | | 54,000 | | | 54,000 | 59,000 |
| 2675 | For travel over 40 V.L.F., add | 2 Elev | 7.25 | 2.207 | V.L.F. | 118 | 122 | | 240 | 310 |
| 2700 | For number of stops over 4, add | " | .27 | 59.259 | Stop | 3,275 | 3,275 | | 6,550 | 8,450 |

## 14 21 33 – Electric Traction Residential Elevators

### 14 21 33.20 Residential Elevators

| | | Crew | Daily Output | Labor-Hours | Unit | Material | Labor | Equipment | Total | Total Incl O&P |
|---|---|---|---|---|---|---|---|---|---|---|
| 0010 | **RESIDENTIAL ELEVATORS** | | | | | | | | | |
| 7000 | Residential, cab type, 1 floor, 2 stop, minimum | 2 Elev | .20 | 80 | Ea. | 9,175 | 4,400 | | 13,575 | 16,700 |
| 7100 | Maximum | | .10 | 160 | | 15,500 | 8,825 | | 24,325 | 30,200 |
| 7200 | 2 floor, 3 stop, minimum | | .12 | 133 | | 13,600 | 7,350 | | 20,950 | 25,900 |
| 7300 | Maximum | | .06 | 266 | | 22,200 | 14,700 | | 36,900 | 46,400 |

# 14 24 Hydraulic Elevators

## 14 24 13 – Hydraulic Freight Elevators

### 14 24 13.10 Hydraulic Freight Elevators and Options

| | | Crew | Daily Output | Labor-Hours | Unit | Material | Labor | Equipment | Total | Total Incl O&P |
|---|---|---|---|---|---|---|---|---|---|---|
| 0010 | **HYDRAULIC FREIGHT ELEVATORS AND OPTIONS** | | | | | | | | | |
| 1025 | Hydraulic freight, base unit, 2000 lb, 50 fpm, 2 stop, std. fin. | 2 Elev | .10 | 160 | Ea. | 39,800 | 8,825 | | 48,625 | 57,000 |
| 1050 | For 2500 lb capacity, add | | | | | 3,100 | | | 3,100 | 3,400 |
| 1075 | For 3000 lb capacity, add | | | | | 4,875 | | | 4,875 | 5,375 |
| 1100 | For 3500 lb capacity, add | | | | | 7,375 | | | 7,375 | 8,125 |
| 1125 | For 4000 lb capacity, add | | | | | 7,900 | | | 7,900 | 8,675 |
| 1150 | For 4500 lb capacity, add | | | | | 8,500 | | | 8,500 | 9,350 |
| 1175 | For 5000 lb capacity, add | | | | | 11,600 | | | 11,600 | 12,800 |
| 1200 | For 6000 lb capacity, add | | | | | 12,200 | | | 12,200 | 13,500 |
| 1225 | For 7000 lb capacity, add | | | | | 18,700 | | | 18,700 | 20,600 |
| 1250 | For 8000 lb capacity, add | | | | | 21,000 | | | 21,000 | 23,100 |
| 1275 | For 10000 lb capacity, add | | | | | 22,300 | | | 22,300 | 24,500 |
| 1300 | For 12000 lb capacity, add | | | | | 26,900 | | | 26,900 | 29,600 |
| 1325 | For 16000 lb capacity, add | | | | | 35,100 | | | 35,100 | 38,600 |

# 14 24 Hydraulic Elevators

## 14 24 13 – Hydraulic Freight Elevators

| 14 24 13.10 Hydraulic Freight Elevators and Options | Crew | Daily Output | Labor-Hours | Unit | Material | 2008 Bare Costs Labor | Equipment | Total | Total Incl O&P |
|---|---|---|---|---|---|---|---|---|---|
| 1350 | For 20000 lb capacity, add | | | | Ea. | 38,900 | | | 38,900 | 42,800 |
| 1375 | For increased speed, 100 fpm, add | | | | | 835 | | | 835 | 915 |
| 1400 | 125 fpm, add | | | | | 1,700 | | | 1,700 | 1,875 |
| 1425 | 150 fpm, add | | | | | 3,225 | | | 3,225 | 3,525 |
| 1450 | 175 fpm, add | | | | | 4,575 | | | 4,575 | 5,050 |
| 1475 | For class "B" loading, add | | | | | 1,925 | | | 1,925 | 2,100 |
| 1500 | For class "C-1" loading, add | | | | | 4,800 | | | 4,800 | 5,275 |
| 1525 | For class "C-2" loading, add | | | | | 5,750 | | | 5,750 | 6,325 |
| 1550 | For class "C-3" loading, add | | | | | 7,900 | | | 7,900 | 8,700 |
| 1575 | For travel over 20 V.L.F., add | 2 Elev | 7.25 | 2.207 | V.L.F. | 420 | 122 | | 542 | 640 |
| 1600 | For number of stops over 2, add | " | .27 | 59.259 | Stop | 3,425 | 3,275 | | 6,700 | 8,625 |

## 14 24 23 – Hydraulic Passenger Elevators

| 14 24 23.10 Hydraulic Passenger Elevators and Options | | Crew | Daily Output | Labor-Hours | Unit | Material | 2008 Bare Costs Labor | Equipment | Total | Total Incl O&P |
|---|---|---|---|---|---|---|---|---|---|---|
| 0010 | **HYDRAULIC PASSENGER ELEVATORS AND OPTIONS** | | | | | | | | | |
| 2050 | Hyd. pass., base unit, 1500 lb, 100 fpm, 2 stop, std. fin. | CN | 2 Elev | .10 | 160 | Ea. | 33,800 | 8,825 | | 42,625 | 50,000 |
| 2075 | For 2000 lb capacity, add | | | | | | 1,175 | | | 1,175 | 1,300 |
| 2100 | For 2500 lb capacity, add | | | | | | 2,400 | | | 2,400 | 2,650 |
| 2125 | For 3000 lb capacity, add | | | | | | 4,300 | | | 4,300 | 4,725 |
| 2150 | For 3500 lb capacity, add | | | | | | 6,350 | | | 6,350 | 6,975 |
| 2175 | For 4000 lb capacity, add | | | | | | 7,650 | | | 7,650 | 8,425 |
| 2200 | For 4500 lb capacity, add | | | | | | 9,200 | | | 9,200 | 10,100 |
| 2225 | For 5000 lb capacity, add | | | | | | 14,000 | | | 14,000 | 15,400 |
| 2250 | For increased speed, 125 fpm, add | | | | | | 1,375 | | | 1,375 | 1,525 |
| 2275 | 150 fpm, add | | | | | | 2,725 | | | 2,725 | 3,000 |
| 2300 | 175 fpm, add | | | | | | 4,425 | | | 4,425 | 4,850 |
| 2325 | 200 fpm, add | | | | | | 6,400 | | | 6,400 | 7,050 |
| 2350 | For travel over 12 V.L.F., add | | 2 Elev | 7.25 | 2.207 | V.L.F. | 420 | 122 | | 542 | 645 |
| 2375 | For number of stops over 2, add | | | .27 | 59.259 | Stop | 3,775 | 3,275 | | 7,050 | 9,000 |
| 2725 | Hydraulic hospital, base unit, 4000 lb, 100 fpm, 2 stop, std. fin. | | | .10 | 160 | Ea. | 46,800 | 8,825 | | 55,625 | 64,500 |
| 2750 | For 4000 lb capacity, add | | | | | | 5,650 | | | 5,650 | 6,225 |
| 2775 | For 4500 lb capacity, add | | | | | | 6,625 | | | 6,625 | 7,300 |
| 2800 | For 5000 lb capacity, add | | | | | | 9,675 | | | 9,675 | 10,600 |
| 2825 | For increased speed, 125 fpm, add | | | | | | 1,575 | | | 1,575 | 1,725 |
| 2850 | 150 fpm, add | | | | | | 2,650 | | | 2,650 | 2,925 |
| 2875 | 175 fpm, add | | | | | | 4,250 | | | 4,250 | 4,700 |
| 2900 | 200 fpm, add | | | | | | 6,225 | | | 6,225 | 6,850 |
| 2925 | For travel over 12 V.L.F., add | | 2 Elev | 7.25 | 2.207 | V.L.F. | 258 | 122 | | 380 | 465 |
| 2950 | For number of stops over 2, add | | " | .27 | 59.259 | Stop | 3,250 | 3,275 | | 6,525 | 8,450 |

# 14 27 Custom Elevator Cabs

## 14 27 13 – Custom Elevator Cab Finishes

| 14 27 13.10 Cab Finishes | Crew | Daily Output | Labor-Hours | Unit | Material | 2008 Bare Costs Labor | Equipment | Total | Total Incl O&P |
|---|---|---|---|---|---|---|---|---|---|
| 0010 | **CAB FINISHES** | | | | | | | | | |
| 3325 | Passenger elevator cab finishes (based on 3500 lb cab size) | | | | | | | | | |
| 3350 | Acrylic panel ceiling | | | | Ea. | 485 | | | 485 | 535 |
| 3375 | Aluminum eggcrate ceiling | | | | | 560 | | | 560 | 620 |
| 3400 | Stainless steel doors | | | | | 2,950 | | | 2,950 | 3,250 |
| 3425 | Carpet flooring | | | | | 405 | | | 405 | 450 |
| 3450 | Epoxy flooring | | | | | 335 | | | 335 | 370 |
| 3475 | Quarry tile flooring | | | | | 515 | | | 515 | 570 |

# 14 27 Custom Elevator Cabs

## 14 27 13 – Custom Elevator Cab Finishes

| 14 27 13.10 Cab Finishes | Crew | Daily Output | Labor-Hours | Unit | Material | 2008 Bare Costs Labor | Equipment | Total | Total Incl O&P |
|---|---|---|---|---|---|---|---|---|---|
| 3500 | Slate flooring | | | | Ea. | 720 | | | 720 | 790 |
| 3525 | Textured rubber flooring | | | | | 132 | | | 132 | 145 |
| 3550 | Stainless steel walls | | | | | 2,925 | | | 2,925 | 3,225 |
| 3575 | Stainless steel returns at door | | | | | 615 | | | 615 | 680 |
| 4450 | Hospital elevator cab finishes (based on 3500 lb cab size) | | | | | | | | | |
| 4475 | Aluminum eggcrate ceiling | | | | Ea. | 560 | | | 560 | 620 |
| 4500 | Stainless steel doors | | | | | 1,800 | | | 1,800 | 1,975 |
| 4525 | Epoxy flooring | | | | | 335 | | | 335 | 370 |
| 4550 | Quarry tile flooring | | | | | 515 | | | 515 | 565 |
| 4575 | Textured rubber flooring | | | | | 132 | | | 132 | 145 |
| 4600 | Stainless steel walls | | | | | 2,925 | | | 2,925 | 3,225 |
| 4625 | Stainless steel returns at door | | | | | 615 | | | 615 | 680 |

# 14 28 Elevator Equipment and Controls

## 14 28 10 – Elevator Equipment and Control Options

### 14 28 10.10 Elevator Controls and Doors

| 14 28 10.10 | | Crew | Daily Output | Labor-Hours | Unit | Material | 2008 Bare Costs Labor | Equipment | Total | Total Incl O&P |
|---|---|---|---|---|---|---|---|---|---|---|
| 0010 | **ELEVATOR CONTROLS AND DOORS** | | | | | | | | | |
| 2975 | Passenger elevator options | | | | | | | | | |
| 3000 | 2 car group automatic controls | 2 Elev | .66 | 24.242 | Ea. | 2,675 | 1,325 | | 4,000 | 4,950 |
| 3025 | 3 car group automatic controls | | .44 | 36.364 | | 4,050 | 2,000 | | 6,050 | 7,425 |
| 3050 | 4 car group automatic controls | | .33 | 48.485 | | 6,700 | 2,675 | | 9,375 | 11,300 |
| 3075 | 5 car group automatic controls | | .26 | 61.538 | | 9,100 | 3,400 | | 12,500 | 15,100 |
| 3100 | 6 car group automatic controls | | .22 | 72.727 | | 13,800 | 4,000 | | 17,800 | 21,200 |
| 3125 | Intercom service | | 3 | 5.333 | | 355 | 294 | | 649 | 835 |
| 3150 | Duplex car selective collective | | .66 | 24.242 | | 2,975 | 1,325 | | 4,300 | 5,250 |
| 3175 | Center opening 1 speed doors | | 2 | 8 | | 1,550 | 440 | | 1,990 | 2,350 |
| 3200 | Center opening 2 speed doors | | 2 | 8 | | 1,825 | 440 | | 2,265 | 2,675 |
| 3225 | Rear opening doors (opposite front) | | 2 | 8 | | 4,275 | 440 | | 4,715 | 5,375 |
| 3250 | Side opening 2 speed doors | | 2 | 8 | | 4,075 | 440 | | 4,515 | 5,125 |
| 3275 | Automatic emergency power switching | | .66 | 24.242 | | 965 | 1,325 | | 2,290 | 3,050 |
| 3300 | Manual emergency power switching | | 8 | 2 | | 370 | 110 | | 480 | 570 |
| 3625 | Hall finishes, stainless steel doors | | | | | 1,025 | | | 1,025 | 1,125 |
| 3650 | Stainless steel frames | | | | | 1,025 | | | 1,025 | 1,125 |
| 3675 | 12 month maintenance contract | | | | | | | | 2,590 | 2,850 |
| 3700 | Signal devices, hall lanterns | 2 Elev | 8 | 2 | | 380 | 110 | | 490 | 580 |
| 3725 | Position indicators, up to 3 | | 9.40 | 1.702 | | 263 | 94 | | 357 | 430 |
| 3750 | Position indicators, per each over 3 | | 32 | .500 | | 72.50 | 27.50 | | 100 | 121 |
| 3775 | High speed heavy duty door opener | | | | | 1,850 | | | 1,850 | 2,025 |
| 3800 | Variable voltage, O.H. gearless machine, min. | 2 Elev | .16 | 100 | | 27,100 | 5,500 | | 32,600 | 38,100 |
| 3815 | Maximum | | .07 | 228 | | 60,000 | 12,600 | | 72,600 | 85,000 |
| 3825 | Basement installed geared machine | | .33 | 48.485 | | 13,400 | 2,675 | | 16,075 | 18,800 |
| 3850 | Freight elevator options | | | | | | | | | |
| 3875 | Doors, bi-parting | 2 Elev | .66 | 24.242 | Ea. | 4,625 | 1,325 | | 5,950 | 7,075 |
| 3900 | Power operated door and gate | " | .66 | 24.242 | | 18,600 | 1,325 | | 19,925 | 22,500 |
| 3925 | Finishes, steel plate floor | | | | | 810 | | | 810 | 890 |
| 3950 | 14 ga. 1/4" x 4' steel plate walls | | | | | 1,975 | | | 1,975 | 2,175 |
| 3975 | 12 month maintenance contract | | | | | | | | 1,955 | 2,150 |
| 4000 | Signal devices, hall lanterns | 2 Elev | 8 | 2 | | 380 | 110 | | 490 | 580 |
| 4025 | Position indicators, up to 3 | | 9.40 | 1.702 | | 263 | 94 | | 357 | 430 |
| 4050 | Position indicators, per each over 3 | | 32 | .500 | | 72.50 | 27.50 | | 100 | 121 |
| 4075 | Variable voltage basement installed geared machine | | .66 | 24.242 | | 15,000 | 1,325 | | 16,325 | 18,500 |

# 14 28 Elevator Equipment and Controls

## 14 28 10 – Elevator Equipment and Control Options

| 14 28 10.10 Elevator Controls and Doors | Crew | Daily Output | Labor-Hours | Unit | Material | 2008 Bare Costs Labor | Equipment | Total | Total Incl O&P |
|---|---|---|---|---|---|---|---|---|---|
| 4100 | Hospital elevator options | | | | | | | | | |
| 4125 | 2 car group automatic controls | 2 Elev | .66 | 24.242 | Ea. | 2,675 | 1,325 | | 4,000 | 4,950 |
| 4150 | 3 car group automatic controls | | .44 | 36.364 | | 4,050 | 2,000 | | 6,050 | 7,425 |
| 4175 | 4 car group automatic controls | | .33 | 48.485 | | 6,700 | 2,675 | | 9,375 | 11,400 |
| 4200 | 5 car group automatic controls | | .26 | 61.538 | | 9,150 | 3,400 | | 12,550 | 15,200 |
| 4225 | 6 car group automatic controls | | .22 | 72.727 | | 13,800 | 4,000 | | 17,800 | 21,200 |
| 4250 | Intercom service | | 3 | 5.333 | | 355 | 294 | | 649 | 835 |
| 4275 | Duplex car selective collective | | .66 | 24.242 | | 2,975 | 1,325 | | 4,300 | 5,250 |
| 4300 | Center opening 1 speed doors | | 2 | 8 | | 1,550 | 440 | | 1,990 | 2,350 |
| 4325 | Center opening 2 speed doors | | 2 | 8 | | 2,050 | 440 | | 2,490 | 2,900 |
| 4350 | Rear opening doors (opposite front) | | 2 | 8 | | 4,275 | 440 | | 4,715 | 5,375 |
| 4375 | Side opening 2 speed doors | | 2 | 8 | | 6,525 | 440 | | 6,965 | 7,825 |
| 4400 | Automatic emergency power switching | | .66 | 24.242 | | 965 | 1,325 | | 2,290 | 3,050 |
| 4425 | Manual emergency power switching | | 8 | 2 | | 370 | 110 | | 480 | 570 |
| 4675 | Hall finishes, stainless steel doors | | | | | 1,025 | | | 1,025 | 1,125 |
| 4700 | Stainless steel frames | | | | | 1,025 | | | 1,025 | 1,125 |
| 4725 | 12 month maintenance contract | | | | | | | | 3,910 | 4,300 |
| 4750 | Signal devices, hall lanterns | 2 Elev | 8 | 2 | | 380 | 110 | | 490 | 580 |
| 4775 | Position indicators, up to 3 | | 9.40 | 1.702 | | 263 | 94 | | 357 | 430 |
| 4800 | Position indicators, per each over 3 | | 32 | .500 | | 72.50 | 27.50 | | 100 | 121 |
| 4825 | High speed heavy duty door opener | | | | | 1,850 | | | 1,850 | 2,025 |
| 4850 | Variable voltage, O.H. gearless machine, min. | 2 Elev | .16 | 100 | | 27,100 | 5,500 | | 32,600 | 38,100 |
| 4865 | Maximum | | .07 | 228 | | 60,000 | 12,600 | | 72,600 | 85,000 |
| 4875 | Basement installed geared machine | | .33 | 48.485 | | 13,400 | 2,675 | | 16,075 | 18,800 |
| 5000 | Drilling for piston, casing included, 18" diameter | B-48 | 80 | .700 | V.L.F. | 41 | 23.50 | 35.50 | 100 | 121 |

# 14 31 Escalators

## 14 31 10 – Glass and Steel Escalators

### 14 31 10.10 Escalators

| 0010 | ESCALATORS | R143110-10 | | | | | | | | | |
|---|---|---|---|---|---|---|---|---|---|---|---|
| 1000 | Glass, 32" wide x 10' floor to floor height | | M-1 | .07 | 457 | Ea. | 70,500 | 23,900 | 715 | 95,115 | 114,000 |
| 1010 | 48" wide x 10' floor to floor height | | | .07 | 457 | | 77,500 | 23,900 | 715 | 102,115 | 122,000 |
| 1020 | 32" wide x 15' floor to floor height | CN | | .06 | 533 | | 74,000 | 27,900 | 830 | 102,730 | 124,000 |
| 1030 | 48" wide x 15' floor to floor height | | | .06 | 533 | | 78,500 | 27,900 | 830 | 107,230 | 128,500 |
| 1040 | 32" wide x 20' floor to floor height | | | .05 | 653 | | 76,500 | 34,200 | 1,025 | 111,725 | 136,000 |
| 1050 | 48" wide x 20' floor to floor height | | | .05 | 653 | | 81,500 | 34,200 | 1,025 | 116,725 | 141,500 |
| 1060 | 32" wide x 25' floor to floor height | | | .04 | 800 | | 82,000 | 41,900 | 1,250 | 125,150 | 154,500 |
| 1070 | 48" wide x 25' floor to floor height | | | .04 | 800 | | 88,000 | 41,900 | 1,250 | 131,150 | 160,500 |
| 1080 | Enameled steel, 32" wide x 10' floor to floor height | | | .07 | 457 | | 72,500 | 23,900 | 715 | 97,115 | 116,000 |
| 1090 | 48" wide x 10' floor to floor height | | | .07 | 457 | | 77,500 | 23,900 | 715 | 102,115 | 122,000 |
| 1110 | 32" wide x 15' floor to floor height | | | .06 | 533 | | 74,000 | 27,900 | 830 | 102,730 | 124,000 |
| 1120 | 48" wide x 15' floor to floor height | | | .06 | 533 | | 78,500 | 27,900 | 830 | 107,230 | 128,500 |
| 1130 | 32" wide x 20' floor to floor height | | | .05 | 653 | | 76,500 | 34,200 | 1,025 | 111,725 | 136,000 |
| 1140 | 48" wide x 20' floor to floor height | | | .05 | 653 | | 81,500 | 34,200 | 1,025 | 116,725 | 141,500 |
| 1150 | 32" wide x 25' floor to floor height | | | .04 | 800 | | 82,000 | 41,900 | 1,250 | 125,150 | 154,500 |
| 1160 | 48" wide x 25' floor to floor height | | | .04 | 800 | | 88,000 | 41,900 | 1,250 | 131,150 | 160,500 |
| 1170 | Stainless steel, 32" wide x 10' floor to floor height | | | .07 | 457 | | 79,500 | 23,900 | 715 | 104,115 | 124,000 |
| 1180 | 48" wide x 10' floor to floor height | | | .07 | 457 | | 83,000 | 23,900 | 715 | 107,615 | 128,000 |
| 1500 | 32" wide x 15' floor to floor height | | | .06 | 533 | | 80,500 | 27,900 | 830 | 109,230 | 131,500 |
| 1700 | 48" wide x 15' floor to floor height | | | .06 | 533 | | 84,500 | 27,900 | 830 | 113,230 | 135,500 |
| 2300 | 32" wide x 25' floor to floor height | | | .04 | 800 | | 91,500 | 41,900 | 1,250 | 134,650 | 164,500 |

# 14 31 Escalators

## 14 31 10 – Glass and Steel Escalators

| 14 31 10.10 Escalators | Crew | Daily Output | Labor-Hours | Unit | Material | 2008 Bare Costs Labor | Equipment | Total | Total Incl O&P |
|---|---|---|---|---|---|---|---|---|---|
| 2500 | 48" wide x 25' floor to floor height | M-1 | .04 | 800 | Ea. | 97,000 | 41,900 | 1,250 | 140,150 | 170,500 |

# 14 32 Moving Walks

## 14 32 10 – Moving Walkways

### 14 32 10.10 Moving Walks

| | | Crew | Daily Output | Labor-Hours | Unit | Material | 2008 Bare Costs Labor | Equipment | Total | Total Incl O&P |
|---|---|---|---|---|---|---|---|---|---|---|
| 0010 | **MOVING WALKS** R143210-20 | | | | | | | | | |
| 0020 | Walk, 27" tread width, minimum | M-1 | 6.50 | 4.923 | L.F. | 775 | 258 | 7.70 | 1,040.70 | 1,250 |
| 0100 | 300' to 500', maximum | | 4.43 | 7.223 | | 1,075 | 380 | 11.25 | 1,466.25 | 1,750 |
| 0300 | 48" tread width walk, minimum | | 4.43 | 7.223 | | 1,750 | 380 | 11.25 | 2,141.25 | 2,500 |
| 0400 | 100' to 350', maximum | | 3.82 | 8.377 | | 2,050 | 440 | 13.05 | 2,503.05 | 2,925 |
| 0600 | Ramp, 12° incline, 36" tread width, minimum | | 5.27 | 6.072 | | 1,425 | 320 | 9.45 | 1,754.45 | 2,050 |
| 0700 | 70' to 90' maximum | | 3.82 | 8.377 | | 2,050 | 440 | 13.05 | 2,503.05 | 2,925 |
| 0900 | 48" tread width, minimum | | 3.57 | 8.964 | | 2,100 | 470 | 14 | 2,584 | 3,025 |
| 1000 | 40' to 70', maximum | | 2.91 | 10.997 | | 2,650 | 575 | 17.15 | 3,242.15 | 3,775 |

# 14 42 Wheelchair Lifts

## 14 42 13 – Inclined Wheelchair Lifts

### 14 42 13.10 Inclined Wheelchair Lifts and Stairclimbers

| | | Crew | Daily Output | Labor-Hours | Unit | Material | 2008 Bare Costs Labor | Equipment | Total | Total Incl O&P |
|---|---|---|---|---|---|---|---|---|---|---|
| 0010 | **INCLINED WHEELCHAIR LIFTS AND STAIRCLIMBERS** | | | | | | | | | |
| 7700 | Stair climber (chair lift), single seat, minimum | 2 Elev | 1 | 16 | Ea. | 4,450 | 880 | | 5,330 | 6,225 |
| 7800 | Maximum | | .20 | 80 | | 6,125 | 4,400 | | 10,525 | 13,300 |
| 8700 | Stair lift, minimum | | 1 | 16 | | 12,100 | 880 | | 12,980 | 14,600 |
| 8900 | Maximum | | .20 | 80 | | 19,100 | 4,400 | | 23,500 | 27,600 |

## 14 42 16 – Vertical Wheelchair Lifts

### 14 42 16.10 Wheelchair Lifts

| | | Crew | Daily Output | Labor-Hours | Unit | Material | 2008 Bare Costs Labor | Equipment | Total | Total Incl O&P |
|---|---|---|---|---|---|---|---|---|---|---|
| 0010 | **WHEELCHAIR LIFTS** | | | | | | | | | |
| 8000 | Wheelchair lift, minimum | 2 Elev | 1 | 16 | Ea. | 6,100 | 880 | | 6,980 | 8,025 |
| 8500 | Maximum | " | .50 | 32 | " | 14,400 | 1,775 | | 16,175 | 18,500 |

# 14 45 Vehicle Lifts

## 14 45 10 – Hydraulic Vehicle Lifts

### 14 45 10.10 Hydraulic Lifts

| | | Crew | Daily Output | Labor-Hours | Unit | Material | 2008 Bare Costs Labor | Equipment | Total | Total Incl O&P |
|---|---|---|---|---|---|---|---|---|---|---|
| 0010 | **HYDRAULIC LIFTS** | | | | | | | | | |
| 0200 | Double post, 9000 lb frame | L-4 | 1.15 | 20.870 | Ea. | 5,300 | 750 | | 6,050 | 7,000 |
| 0400 | 26000 lb frame | | .22 | 109 | | 25,700 | 3,925 | | 29,625 | 34,300 |
| 2200 | Hoists, single post, 8,000# capacity, swivel arms | | .40 | 60 | | 4,750 | 2,150 | | 6,900 | 8,575 |
| 2400 | Two posts, adjustable frames, 11,000# capacity | | .25 | 96 | | 6,100 | 3,450 | | 9,550 | 12,100 |
| 2500 | 24,000# capacity | | .15 | 160 | | 8,125 | 5,750 | | 13,875 | 17,900 |
| 2700 | 7,500# capacity, frame supports | | .50 | 48 | | 6,775 | 1,725 | | 8,500 | 10,100 |
| 2800 | Four post, roll on ramp | | .50 | 48 | | 6,100 | 1,725 | | 7,825 | 9,400 |
| 2810 | Hydraulic lifts, above ground, 2 post, clear floor, 6000 lb cap | | 2.67 | 8.989 | | 6,700 | 325 | | 7,025 | 7,850 |
| 2815 | 9000 lb capacity | | 2.29 | 10.480 | | 15,900 | 375 | | 16,275 | 18,100 |
| 2820 | 15,000 lb capacity | | 2 | 12 | | 17,900 | 430 | | 18,330 | 20,400 |
| 2825 | 30,000 lb capacity | | 1.60 | 15 | | 39,700 | 540 | | 40,240 | 44,400 |
| 2830 | 4 post, ramp style, 25,000 lb capacity | | 2 | 12 | | 15,500 | 430 | | 15,930 | 17,800 |
| 2835 | 35,000 lb capacity | | 1 | 24 | | 72,500 | 865 | | 73,365 | 81,000 |
| 2840 | 50,000 lb capacity | | 1 | 24 | | 81,000 | 865 | | 81,865 | 90,500 |

413

# 14 45 Vehicle Lifts

## 14 45 10 – Hydraulic Vehicle Lifts

### 14 45 10.10 Hydraulic Lifts

| | | Crew | Daily Output | Labor-Hours | Unit | Material | 2008 Bare Costs Labor | Equipment | Total | Total Incl O&P |
|---|---|---|---|---|---|---|---|---|---|---|
| 2845 | 75,000 lb capacity | L-4 | 1 | 24 | Ea. | 94,000 | 865 | | 94,865 | 105,000 |
| 2850 | For drive thru tracks, add, minimum | | | | | 995 | | | 995 | 1,100 |
| 2855 | Maximum | | | | | 1,700 | | | 1,700 | 1,875 |
| 2860 | Ramp extensions, 3' (set of 2) | | | | | 820 | | | 820 | 900 |
| 2865 | Rolling jack platform | | | | | 2,850 | | | 2,850 | 3,125 |
| 2870 | Elec/hyd jacking beam | | | | | 7,625 | | | 7,625 | 8,375 |
| 2880 | Scissor lift, portable, 6000 lb capacity | | | | ↓ | 7,475 | | | 7,475 | 8,225 |

# 14 51 Correspondence and Parcel Lifts

## 14 51 10 – Electric Correspondence and Parcel Lifts

### 14 51 10.10 Correspondence Lifts

| | | Crew | Daily Output | Labor-Hours | Unit | Material | Labor | Equipment | Total | Total Incl O&P |
|---|---|---|---|---|---|---|---|---|---|---|
| 0010 | **CORRESPONDENCE LIFTS** | | | | | | | | | |
| 0020 | 1 floor, 2 stop, 25 lb capacity, electric | 2 Elev | .20 | 80 | Ea. | 5,425 | 4,400 | | 9,825 | 12,600 |
| 0100 | Hand, 5 lb capacity | " | .20 | 80 | " | 2,050 | 4,400 | | 6,450 | 8,825 |

### 14 51 10.20 Parcel Lifts

| | | Crew | Daily Output | Labor-Hours | Unit | Material | Labor | Equipment | Total | Total Incl O&P |
|---|---|---|---|---|---|---|---|---|---|---|
| 0010 | **PARCEL LIFTS** | | | | | | | | | |
| 0020 | 20" x 20", 100 lb capacity, electric, per floor | 2 Mill | .25 | 64 | Ea. | 8,500 | 2,550 | | 11,050 | 13,100 |

# 14 91 Facility Chutes

## 14 91 33 – Laundry and Linen Chutes

### 14 91 33.10 Chutes

| | | Crew | Daily Output | Labor-Hours | Unit | Material | Labor | Equipment | Total | Total Incl O&P |
|---|---|---|---|---|---|---|---|---|---|---|
| 0011 | **CHUTES**, linen, trash or refuse | | | | | | | | | |
| 0050 | Aluminized steel, 16 ga., 18" diameter | 2 Shee | 3.50 | 4.571 | Floor | 865 | 207 | | 1,072 | 1,275 |
| 0100 | 24" diameter | | 3.20 | 5 | | 910 | 227 | | 1,137 | 1,350 |
| 0200 | 30" diameter | | 3 | 5.333 | | 1,050 | 242 | | 1,292 | 1,525 |
| 0300 | 36" diameter | | 2.80 | 5.714 | | 1,175 | 259 | | 1,434 | 1,700 |
| 0400 | Galvanized steel, 16 ga., 18" diameter | | 3.50 | 4.571 | | 835 | 207 | | 1,042 | 1,225 |
| 0500 | 24" diameter | | 3.20 | 5 | | 940 | 227 | | 1,167 | 1,375 |
| 0600 | 30" diameter | | 3 | 5.333 | | 1,050 | 242 | | 1,292 | 1,525 |
| 0700 | 36" diameter | | 2.80 | 5.714 | | 1,250 | 259 | | 1,509 | 1,775 |
| 0800 | Stainless steel, 18" diameter | | 3.50 | 4.571 | | 1,900 | 207 | | 2,107 | 2,425 |
| 0900 | 24" diameter | | 3.20 | 5 | | 2,050 | 227 | | 2,277 | 2,625 |
| 1000 | 30" diameter | | 3 | 5.333 | | 2,425 | 242 | | 2,667 | 3,050 |
| 1005 | 36" diameter | | 2.80 | 5.714 | ↓ | 2,675 | 259 | | 2,934 | 3,350 |
| 1200 | Linen chute bottom collector, aluminized steel | | 4 | 4 | Ea. | 1,175 | 181 | | 1,356 | 1,550 |
| 1300 | Stainless steel | | 4 | 4 | | 1,425 | 181 | | 1,606 | 1,850 |
| 1500 | Refuse, bottom hopper, aluminized steel, 18" diameter | | 3 | 5.333 | | 700 | 242 | | 942 | 1,150 |
| 1600 | 24" diameter | | 3 | 5.333 | | 845 | 242 | | 1,087 | 1,300 |
| 1800 | 36" diameter | ↓ | 3 | 5.333 | ↓ | 1,425 | 242 | | 1,667 | 1,925 |

## 14 91 82 – Trash Chutes

### 14 91 82.10 Trash Chutes and Accessories

| | | Crew | Daily Output | Labor-Hours | Unit | Material | Labor | Equipment | Total | Total Incl O&P |
|---|---|---|---|---|---|---|---|---|---|---|
| 0010 | **TRASH CHUTES AND ACCESSORIES** | | | | | | | | | |
| 2900 | Package chutes, spiral type, minimum | 2 Shee | 4.50 | 3.556 | Floor | 2,025 | 161 | | 2,186 | 2,475 |
| 3000 | Maximum | " | 1.50 | 10.667 | " | 5,275 | 485 | | 5,760 | 6,550 |

# 14 92 Pneumatic Tube Systems

## 14 92 10 – Conventional, Automatic and Computer Controlled Pneumatic Tube Systems

| 14 92 10.10 Pneumatic Tube Systems | Crew | Daily Output | Labor-Hours | Unit | Material | 2008 Bare Costs Labor | Equipment | Total | Total Incl O&P |
|---|---|---|---|---|---|---|---|---|---|
| 0010 **PNEUMATIC TUBE SYSTEMS** | | | | | | | | | |
| 0020   100' long, single tube, 2 stations, stock | | | | | | | | | |
| 0100     3" diameter | 2 Stpi | .12 | 133 | Total | 5,500 | 6,275 | | 11,775 | 15,500 |
| 0300     4" diameter | " | .09 | 177 | " | 6,200 | 8,375 | | 14,575 | 19,400 |
| 0400   Twin tube, two stations or more, conventional system | | | | | | | | | |
| 0600     2-1/2" round | 2 Stpi | 62.50 | .256 | L.F. | 11.10 | 12.05 | | 23.15 | 30.50 |
| 0700     3" round | | 46 | .348 | | 12.70 | 16.40 | | 29.10 | 38.50 |
| 0900     4" round | | 49.60 | .323 | | 14.10 | 15.20 | | 29.30 | 38.50 |
| 1000     4" x 7" oval | | 37.60 | .426 | | 20.50 | 20 | | 40.50 | 52.50 |
| 1050     Add for blower | | 2 | 8 | System | 4,350 | 375 | | 4,725 | 5,350 |
| 1110       Plus for each round station, add | | 7.50 | 2.133 | Ea. | 490 | 100 | | 590 | 690 |
| 1150       Plus for each oval station, add | | 7.50 | 2.133 | " | 490 | 100 | | 590 | 690 |
| 1200   Alternate pricing method: base cost, minimum | | .75 | 21.333 | Total | 5,325 | 1,000 | | 6,325 | 7,350 |
| 1300     Maximum | | .25 | 64 | " | 10,600 | 3,025 | | 13,625 | 16,100 |
| 1500     Plus total system length, add, minimum | | 93.40 | .171 | L.F. | 6.85 | 8.05 | | 14.90 | 19.65 |
| 1600     Maximum | | 37.60 | .426 | " | 20 | 20 | | 40 | 52.50 |
| 1800   Completely automatic system, 4" round, 15 to 50 stations | | .29 | 55.172 | Station | 16,800 | 2,600 | | 19,400 | 22,300 |
| 2200     51 to 144 stations | | .32 | 50 | | 13,000 | 2,350 | | 15,350 | 17,900 |
| 2400   6" round or 4" x 7" oval, 15 to 50 stations | | .24 | 66.667 | | 21,000 | 3,150 | | 24,150 | 27,800 |
| 2800     51 to 144 stations | | .23 | 69.565 | | 17,600 | 3,275 | | 20,875 | 24,300 |

# Division Notes

| | CREW | DAILY OUTPUT | LABOR-HOURS | UNIT | 2008 BARE COSTS | | | | TOTAL INCL O&P |
|---|---|---|---|---|---|---|---|---|---|
| | | | | | MAT. | LABOR | EQUIP. | TOTAL | |
| | | | | | | | | | |
| | | | | | | | | | |
| | | | | | | | | | |
| | | | | | | | | | |
| | | | | | | | | | |
| | | | | | | | | | |
| | | | | | | | | | |
| | | | | | | | | | |
| | | | | | | | | | |
| | | | | | | | | | |
| | | | | | | | | | |
| | | | | | | | | | |
| | | | | | | | | | |
| | | | | | | | | | |
| | | | | | | | | | |
| | | | | | | | | | |
| | | | | | | | | | |
| | | | | | | | | | |
| | | | | | | | | | |
| | | | | | | | | | |
| | | | | | | | | | |
| | | | | | | | | | |

416

## Estimating Tips

Pipe for fire protection and all uses is located in Section 22 22 13.

When installing piping above 10' review Section 22 02 02.20 for percentage adds due to the elevated work.

Many, but not all, areas require backflow protection in the fire system. It is advisable to check local building codes for specific requirements.

For your reference, the following is a list of the most applicable Fire Codes and Standards which may be purchased from the NFPA, 1 Batterymarch Park, Quincy, MA 02169-7471.

NFPA 1: Uniform Fire Code
NFPA 10: Portable Fire Extinguishers
NFPA 11: Low-, Medium-, and High-Expansion Foam
NFPA 12: Carbon Dioxide Extinguishing Systems (Also companion 12A)
NFPA 13: Installation of Sprinkler Systems (Also companion 13D, 13E, and 13R)
NFPA 14: Installation of Standpipe and Hose Systems
NFPA 15: Water Spray Fixed Systems for Fire Protection
NFPA 16: Installation of Foam-Water Sprinkler and Foam-Water Spray Systems
NFPA 17: Dry Chemical Extinguishing Systems (Also companion 17A)
NFPA 18: Wetting Agents

NFPA 20: Installation of Stationary Pumps for Fire Protection
NFPA 22: Water Tanks for Private Fire Protection
NFPA 24: Installation of Private Fire Service Mains and their Appurtenances
NFPA 25: Inspection, Testing and Maintenance of Water-Based Fire Protection

## Reference Numbers

Reference numbers are shown in shaded boxes at the beginning of some major classifications. These numbers refer to related items in the Reference Section. The reference information may be an estimating procedure, an alternate pricing method, or technical information.

*Note:* Not all subdivisions listed here necessarily appear in this publication.

*Note:* **Trade Service,** *in part, has been used as a reference source for some of the material prices used in Division 21.*

# 21 05 Common Work Results for Fire Suppression

## 21 05 23 – General-Duty Valves for Water-Based Fire-Suppression Piping

| 21 05 23.50 General-Duty Valves for Water-Based Fire Supp. | Crew | Daily Output | Labor-Hours | Unit | Material | 2008 Bare Costs Labor | Equipment | Total | Total Incl O&P |
|---|---|---|---|---|---|---|---|---|---|
| 0010 **GENERAL-DUTY VALVES FOR WATER-BASED FIRE SUPPRESSION PIPING** | | | | | | | | | |
| 6200 Valves and components | | | | | | | | | |
| 6500 Check, swing, C.I. body, brass fittings, auto. ball drip | | | | | | | | | |
| 6520 4" size | Q-12 | 3 | 5.333 | Ea. | 220 | 224 | | 444 | 575 |
| 6800 Check, wafer, butterfly type, C.I. body, bronze fittings | | | | | | | | | |
| 6820 4" size | Q-12 | 4 | 4 | Ea. | 345 | 168 | | 513 | 635 |

# 21 11 Facility Fire-Suppression Water-Service Piping

## 21 11 16 – Facility Fire Hydrants

### 21 11 16.50 Fire Hydrants for Buildings

| | Crew | Daily Output | Labor-Hours | Unit | Material | 2008 Bare Costs Labor | Equipment | Total | Total Incl O&P |
|---|---|---|---|---|---|---|---|---|---|
| 0010 **FIRE HYDRANTS FOR BUILDINGS** | | | | | | | | | |
| 3750 Hydrants, wall, w/caps, single, flush, polished brass | | | | | | | | | |
| 3800 2-1/2" x 2-1/2" | Q-12 | 5 | 3.200 | Ea. | 152 | 134 | | 286 | 370 |
| 3840 2-1/2" x 3" | " | 5 | 3.200 | " | 203 | 134 | | 337 | 425 |
| 3950 Double, flush, polished brass | | | | | | | | | |
| 4000 2-1/2" x 2-1/2" x 4" | Q-12 | 5 | 3.200 | Ea. | 405 | 134 | | 539 | 650 |
| 4040 2-1/2" x 2-1/2" x 6" | " | 4.60 | 3.478 | ↓ | 585 | 146 | | 731 | 865 |
| 4200 For polished chrome, add | | | | | 10% | | | | |
| 4350 Double, projecting, polished brass | | | | | | | | | |
| 4400 2-1/2" x 2-1/2" x 4" | Q-12 | 5 | 3.200 | Ea. | 180 | 134 | | 314 | 400 |
| 4450 2-1/2" x 2-1/2" x 6" | " | 4.60 | 3.478 | " | 370 | 146 | | 516 | 625 |
| 4460 Valve control, dbl. flush/projecting hydrant, cap & | | | | | | | | | |
| 4470 chain, extension rod & cplg., escutcheon, polished brass | Q-12 | 8 | 2 | Ea. | 215 | 84 | | 299 | 365 |

## 21 11 19 – Fire-Department Connections

### 21 11 19.50 Connections for The Fire-Department

| | Crew | Daily Output | Labor-Hours | Unit | Material | 2008 Bare Costs Labor | Equipment | Total | Total Incl O&P |
|---|---|---|---|---|---|---|---|---|---|
| 0010 **CONNECTIONS FOR THE FIRE-DEPARTMENT** | | | | | | | | | |
| 7140 Standpipe connections, wall, w/plugs & chains | | | | | | | | | |
| 7160 Single, flush, brass, 2-1/2" x 2-1/2" | Q-12 | 5 | 3.200 | Ea. | 113 | 134 | | 247 | 325 |
| 7180 2-1/2" x 3" | " | 5 | 3.200 | " | 117 | 134 | | 251 | 330 |
| 7240 For polished chrome, add | | | | | 15% | | | | |
| 7280 Double, flush, polished brass | | | | | | | | | |
| 7300 2-1/2" x 2-1/2" x 4" | Q-12 | 5 | 3.200 | Ea. | 345 | 134 | | 479 | 580 |
| 7330 2-1/2" x 2-1/2" x 6" | " | 4.60 | 3.478 | " | 730 | 146 | | 876 | 1,025 |
| 7400 For polished chrome, add | | | | | 15% | | | | |
| 7440 For sill cock combination, add | | | | Ea. | 64 | | | 64 | 70.50 |
| 7900 Three way, flush, polished brass | | | | | | | | | |
| 7920 2-1/2" (3) x 4" | Q-12 | 4.80 | 3.333 | Ea. | 1,000 | 140 | | 1,140 | 1,300 |
| 7930 2-1/2" (3) x 6" | " | 4.80 | 3.333 | ↓ | 1,125 | 140 | | 1,265 | 1,450 |
| 8000 For polished chrome, add | | | | | 9% | | | | |
| 8020 Three way, projecting, polished brass | | | | | | | | | |
| 8040 2-1/2"(3) x 4" | Q-12 | 4.80 | 3.333 | Ea. | 850 | 140 | | 990 | 1,150 |

# 21 12 Fire-Suppression Standpipes

## 21 12 13 – Fire-Suppression Hoses and Nozzles

| 21 12 13.50 Fire Hoses and Nozzles | Crew | Daily Output | Labor-Hours | Unit | Material | 2008 Bare Costs Labor | Equipment | Total | Total Incl O&P |
|---|---|---|---|---|---|---|---|---|---|
| 0010 **FIRE HOSES AND NOZZLES** | | | | | | | | | |
| 0200 Adapters, rough brass, straight hose threads | | | | | | | | | |
| 0220 One piece, female to male, rocker lugs | | | | | | | | | |
| 0240 1" x 1" | | | | Ea. | 34 | | | 34 | 37.50 |
| 2200 Hose, less couplings | | | | | | | | | |
| 2260 Synthetic jacket, lined, 300 lb. test, 1-1/2" diameter | Q-12 | 2600 | .006 | L.F. | 2.07 | .26 | | 2.33 | 2.67 |
| 2280 2-1/2" diameter | | 2200 | .007 | | 3.44 | .31 | | 3.75 | 4.24 |
| 2360 High strength, 500 lb. test, 1-1/2" diameter | | 2600 | .006 | | 2.14 | .26 | | 2.40 | 2.74 |
| 2380 2-1/2" diameter | ↓ | 2200 | .007 | ↓ | 3.71 | .31 | | 4.02 | 4.54 |
| 5600 Nozzles, brass | | | | | | | | | |
| 5620 Adjustable fog, 3/4" booster line | | | | Ea. | 87 | | | 87 | 95.50 |
| 5630 1" booster line | | | | | 101 | | | 101 | 111 |
| 5640 1-1/2" leader line | | | | | 61 | | | 61 | 67.50 |
| 5660 2-1/2" direct connection | | | | ↓ | 206 | | | 206 | 227 |
| 5780 For chrome plated, add | | | | | 8% | | | | |
| 5850 Electrical fire, adjustable fog, no shock | | | | | | | | | |
| 5900 1-1/2" | | | | Ea. | 330 | | | 330 | 365 |
| 5920 2-1/2" | | | | ↓ | 445 | | | 445 | 490 |
| 5980 For polished chrome, add | | | | ↓ | 6% | | | | |
| 6200 Heavy duty, comb. adj. fog and str. stream, with handle | | | | | | | | | |
| 6210 1" booster line | | | | Ea. | 315 | | | 315 | 350 |

## 21 12 19 – Fire-Suppression Hose Racks

### 21 12 19.50 Fire Hose Racks

| | Crew | Daily Output | Labor-Hours | Unit | Material | Labor | Equipment | Total | Total Incl O&P |
|---|---|---|---|---|---|---|---|---|---|
| 0010 **FIRE HOSE RACKS** | | | | | | | | | |
| 2600 Hose rack, swinging, for 1-1/2" diameter hose, | | | | | | | | | |
| 2620 Enameled steel, 50' & 75' lengths of hose | Q-12 | 20 | .800 | Ea. | 27.50 | 33.50 | | 61 | 81 |
| 2640 100' and 125' lengths of hose | " | 20 | .800 | " | 27.50 | 33.50 | | 61 | 81 |

## 21 12 23 – Fire-Suppression Hose Valves

### 21 12 23.70 Fire Hose Valves

| | Crew | Daily Output | Labor-Hours | Unit | Material | Labor | Equipment | Total | Total Incl O&P |
|---|---|---|---|---|---|---|---|---|---|
| 0010 **FIRE HOSE VALVES** | | | | | | | | | |
| 0080 Wheel handle, 300 lb., 1-1/2" | 1 Spri | 12 | .667 | Ea. | 35.50 | 31 | | 66.50 | 86 |
| 0090 2-1/2" | " | 7 | 1.143 | " | 60 | 53.50 | | 113.50 | 147 |
| 0100 For polished brass, add | | | | | 35% | | | | |
| 0110 For polished chrome, add | | | | | 50% | | | | |

# 21 13 Fire-Suppression Sprinkler Systems

## 21 13 13 – Wet-Pipe Sprinkler Systems

### 21 13 13.50 Wet-Pipe Sprinkler System Components

| | Crew | Daily Output | Labor-Hours | Unit | Material | Labor | Equipment | Total | Total Incl O&P |
|---|---|---|---|---|---|---|---|---|---|
| 0010 **WET-PIPE SPRINKLER SYSTEM COMPONENTS** | | | | | | | | | |
| 2600 Sprinkler heads, not including supply piping | | | | | | | | | |
| 3700 Standard spray, pendent or upright, brass, 135° to 286° F | | | | | | | | | |
| 3730 1/2" NPT, 7/16" orifice | 1 Spri | 16 | .500 | Ea. | 9.80 | 23.50 | | 33.30 | 46 |
| 3740 1/2" NPT, 1/2" orifice **CN** | " | 16 | .500 | | 6.40 | 23.50 | | 29.90 | 42 |
| 3860 For wax and lead coating, add | | | | | 21.50 | | | 21.50 | 23.50 |
| 3880 For wax coating, add | | | | | 12.65 | | | 12.65 | 13.90 |
| 3900 For lead coating, add | | | | ↓ | 13.50 | | | 13.50 | 14.85 |
| 3920 For 360° F, same cost | | | | | | | | | |
| 3930 For 400° F, add | | | | Ea. | 34 | | | 34 | 37.50 |
| 3940 For 500° F, add | | | | " | 34 | | | 34 | 37.50 |
| 4500 Sidewall, horizontal, brass, 135° to 286° F | | | | | | | | | |

# 21 13 Fire-Suppression Sprinkler Systems

## 21 13 13 – Wet-Pipe Sprinkler Systems

### 21 13 13.50 Wet-Pipe Sprinkler System Components

| | | Crew | Daily Output | Labor-Hours | Unit | Material | 2008 Bare Costs Labor | 2008 Bare Costs Equipment | Total | Total Incl O&P |
|---|---|---|---|---|---|---|---|---|---|---|
| 4520 | 1/2" NPT, 1/2" orifice | 1 Spri | 16 | .500 | Ea. | 15 | 23.50 | | 38.50 | 51.50 |
| 4540 | For 360° F, same cost | | | | | | | | | |
| 4800 | Recessed pendent, brass, 135° to 286° F | | | | | | | | | |
| 4820 | 1/2" NPT, 3/8" orifice | 1 Spri | 10 | .800 | Ea. | 29 | 37.50 | | 66.50 | 87.50 |
| 4830 | 1/2" NPT, 7/16" orifice | | 10 | .800 | | 29 | 37.50 | | 66.50 | 87.50 |
| 4840 | 1/2" NPT, 1/2" orifice | | 10 | .800 | | 29 | 37.50 | | 66.50 | 87.50 |

## 21 13 16 – Dry-Pipe Sprinkler Systems

### 21 13 16.50 Dry-Pipe Sprinkler System Components

| | | Crew | Daily Output | Labor-Hours | Unit | Material | 2008 Bare Costs Labor | 2008 Bare Costs Equipment | Total | Total Incl O&P |
|---|---|---|---|---|---|---|---|---|---|---|
| 0010 | **DRY-PIPE SPRINKLER SYSTEM COMPONENTS** | | | | | | | | | |
| 0600 | Accelerator | 1 Spri | 8 | 1 | Ea. | 460 | 46.50 | | 506.50 | 575 |
| 2600 | Sprinkler heads, not including supply piping | | | | | | | | | |
| 2640 | Dry, pendent, 1/2" orifice, 3/4" or 1" NPT | | | | | | | | | |
| 2700 | 15-1/4" to 18" length | 1 Spri | 14 | .571 | Ea. | 93.50 | 26.50 | | 120 | 143 |
| 2710 | 18-1/4" to 21" length | | 13 | .615 | | 97 | 28.50 | | 125.50 | 149 |
| 2720 | 21-1/4" to 24" length | | 13 | .615 | | 101 | 28.50 | | 129.50 | 154 |
| 2730 | 24-1/4" to 27" length | | 13 | .615 | | 104 | 28.50 | | 132.50 | 158 |

## 21 13 26 – Deluge Fire-Suppression Sprinkler Systems

### 21 13 26.50 Deluge Fire-Suppression Sprinkler System Components

| | | Crew | Daily Output | Labor-Hours | Unit | Material | 2008 Bare Costs Labor | 2008 Bare Costs Equipment | Total | Total Incl O&P |
|---|---|---|---|---|---|---|---|---|---|---|
| 0010 | **DELUGE FIRE-SUPPRESSION SPRINKLER SYSTEM COMPONENTS** | | | | | | | | | |
| 6200 | Valves and components | | | | | | | | | |
| 7000 | Deluge, assembly, incl. trim, pressure | | | | | | | | | |
| 7020 | operated relief, emergency release, gauges | | | | | | | | | |
| 7040 | 2" size | Q-12 | 2 | 8 | Ea. | 1,700 | 335 | | 2,035 | 2,375 |
| 7060 | 3" size | " | 1.50 | 10.667 | " | 1,950 | 450 | | 2,400 | 2,825 |

## 21 13 39 – Foam-Water Systems

### 21 13 39.50 Foam-Water System Components

| | | Crew | Daily Output | Labor-Hours | Unit | Material | 2008 Bare Costs Labor | 2008 Bare Costs Equipment | Total | Total Incl O&P |
|---|---|---|---|---|---|---|---|---|---|---|
| 0010 | **FOAM-WATER SYSTEM COMPONENTS** | | | | | | | | | |
| 2600 | Sprinkler heads, not including supply piping | | | | | | | | | |
| 3600 | Foam-water, pendent or upright, 1/2" NPT | 1 Spri | 12 | .667 | Ea. | 112 | 31 | | 143 | 170 |

# 21 21 Carbon-Dioxide Fire-Extinguishing Systems

## 21 21 16 – Carbon-Dioxide Fire-Extinguishing Equipment

### 21 21 16.50 CO2 Fire Extinguishing System

| | | Crew | Daily Output | Labor-Hours | Unit | Material | 2008 Bare Costs Labor | 2008 Bare Costs Equipment | Total | Total Incl O&P |
|---|---|---|---|---|---|---|---|---|---|---|
| 0010 | **$CO_2$ FIRE EXTINGUISHING SYSTEM** | | | | | | | | | |
| 0042 | For detectors and control stations, see Div. 28 31 23.50 | | | | | | | | | |
| 1000 | Dispersion nozzle, $CO_2$, 3" x 5" | 1 Plum | 18 | .444 | Ea. | 52.50 | 21 | | 73.50 | 89 |
| 2000 | Extinguisher, $CO_2$ system, high pressure, 75 lb. cylinder | Q-1 | 6 | 2.667 | | 1,000 | 112 | | 1,112 | 1,275 |
| 3000 | Electro/mechanical release | L-1 | 4 | 4 | | 131 | 185 | | 316 | 420 |
| 3400 | Manual pull station | 1 Plum | 6 | 1.333 | | 47.50 | 62.50 | | 110 | 146 |

# 21 22 Clean-Agent Fire-Extinguishing Systems

## 21 22 16 – Clean-Agent Fire-Extinguishing Equipment

| 21 22 16.50 FM200 Fire Extinguishing System | Crew | Daily Output | Labor-Hours | Unit | Material | 2008 Bare Costs Labor | Equipment | Total | Total Incl O&P |
|---|---|---|---|---|---|---|---|---|---|
| 0010 **FM200 FIRE EXTINGUISHING SYSTEM** | | | | | | | | | |
| 1100    Dispersion nozzle FM200, 1-1/2" | 1 Plum | 14 | .571 | Ea. | 52.50 | 26.50 | | 79 | 98 |
| 2400    Extinguisher, FM 200 system, filled, with mounting bracket | | | | | | | | | |
| 2540       196 lb. container | Q-1 | 4 | 4 | Ea. | 6,100 | 168 | | 6,268 | 6,950 |
| 6000    Average FM200 system, minimum | | | | C.F. | 1.38 | | | 1.38 | 1.52 |
| 6020       Maximum | | | | " | 2.75 | | | 2.75 | 3.03 |

# 21 31 Centrifugal Fire Pumps

## 21 31 13 – Electric-Drive, Centrifugal Fire Pumps

### 21 31 13.50 Electric-Drive Fire Pumps

| | Crew | Daily Output | Labor-Hours | Unit | Material | 2008 Bare Costs Labor | Equipment | Total | Total Incl O&P |
|---|---|---|---|---|---|---|---|---|---|
| 0010 **ELECTRIC-DRIVE FIRE PUMPS** Including controller, fittings and relief valve | | | | | | | | | |
| 3100    250 GPM, 55 psi, 15 HP, 3,550 RPM, 2" pump | Q-13 | .70 | 45.714 | Ea. | 15,300 | 2,025 | | 17,325 | 19,900 |
| 3200    500 GPM, 50 psi, 27 HP, 1770 RPM, 4" pump | | .68 | 47.059 | | 18,900 | 2,100 | | 21,000 | 24,000 |
| 3350    750 GPM, 50 psi, 44 HP, 1,770 RPM, 5" pump | | .64 | 50 | | 27,700 | 2,225 | | 29,925 | 33,800 |
| 3400    750 GPM, 100 psi, 66 HP, 3550 RPM, 4" pump | ↓ | .58 | 55.172 | | 24,500 | 2,450 | | 26,950 | 30,700 |
| 5000    For jockey pump 1", 3 HP, with control, add | Q-12 | 2 | 8 | ↓ | 3,400 | 335 | | 3,735 | 4,250 |

## 21 31 16 – Diesel-Drive, Centrifugal Fire Pumps

### 21 31 16.50 Diesel-Drive Fire Pumps

| | Crew | Daily Output | Labor-Hours | Unit | Material | 2008 Bare Costs Labor | Equipment | Total | Total Incl O&P |
|---|---|---|---|---|---|---|---|---|---|
| 0010 **DIESEL-DRIVE FIRE PUMPS** Including controller, fittings and relief valve | | | | | | | | | |
| 0050    500 GPM, 50 psi, 27 HP, 4" pump | Q-13 | .64 | 50 | Ea. | 65,000 | 2,225 | | 67,225 | 75,000 |
| 0200    750 GPM, 50 psi, 44 HP, 5" pump | | .60 | 53.333 | | 69,500 | 2,375 | | 71,875 | 80,000 |
| 0400    1000 GPM, 100 psi, 89 HP, 4" pump | | .56 | 57.143 | | 74,500 | 2,550 | | 77,050 | 86,000 |
| 0700    2,000 GPM, 100 psi, 167 HP, 6" pump | | .34 | 94.118 | | 79,000 | 4,175 | | 83,175 | 93,500 |
| 0950    3500 GPM, 100 psi, 300 HP, 10" pump | ↓ | .24 | 133 | ↓ | 139,000 | 5,925 | | 144,925 | 161,500 |

# Division Notes

| | CREW | DAILY OUTPUT | LABOR-HOURS | UNIT | 2008 BARE COSTS | | | | TOTAL INCL O&P |
| --- | --- | --- | --- | --- | --- | --- | --- | --- | --- |
| | | | | | MAT. | LABOR | EQUIP. | TOTAL | |
| | | | | | | | | | |
| | | | | | | | | | |
| | | | | | | | | | |
| | | | | | | | | | |
| | | | | | | | | | |
| | | | | | | | | | |
| | | | | | | | | | |
| | | | | | | | | | |
| | | | | | | | | | |
| | | | | | | | | | |
| | | | | | | | | | |
| | | | | | | | | | |
| | | | | | | | | | |
| | | | | | | | | | |
| | | | | | | | | | |
| | | | | | | | | | |
| | | | | | | | | | |
| | | | | | | | | | |
| | | | | | | | | | |
| | | | | | | | | | |

# Estimating Tips

## 22 10 00 Plumbing Piping and Pumps

This subdivision is primarily basic pipe and related materials. The pipe may be used by any of the mechanical disciplines, i.e., plumbing, fire protection, heating, and air conditioning.

- The piping section lists the add to labor for elevated pipe installation. These adds apply to all elevated pipe, fittings, valves, insulation, etc., that are placed above 10' high. CAUTION: the correct percentage may vary for the same pipe. For example, the percentage add for the basic pipe installation should be based on the maximum height that the craftsman must install for that particular section. If the pipe is to be located 14' above the floor but it is suspended on threaded rod from beams, the bottom flange of which is 18' high (4' rods), then the height is actually 18' and the add is 20%. The pipe coverer, however, does not have to go above the 14', and so his or her add should be 10%.

- Most pipe is priced first as straight pipe with a joint (coupling, weld, etc.) every 10' and a hanger usually every 10'.

There are exceptions with hanger spacing such as for cast iron pipe (5') and plastic pipe (3 per 10'). Following each type of pipe there are several lines listing sizes and the amount to be subtracted to delete couplings and hangers. This is for pipe that is to be buried or supported together on trapeze hangers. The reason that the couplings are deleted is that these runs are usually long, and frequently longer lengths of pipe are used. By deleting the couplings, the estimator is expected to look up and add back the correct reduced number of couplings.

- When preparing an estimate it may be necessary to approximate the fittings. Fittings usually run between 25% and 50% of the cost of the pipe. The lower percentage is for simpler runs, and the higher number is for complex areas such as mechanical rooms.

- For historic restoration projects, the systems must be as invisible as possible, and pathways must be sought for pipes, conduit, and ductwork. While installations in accessible spaces (such as basements and attics) are relatively straightforward to estimate, labor costs may be more difficult to determine when delivery systems must be concealed.

## 22 40 00 Plumbing Fixtures

- Plumbing fixture costs usually require two lines: the fixture itself and its "rough-in, supply and waste."

- In the Assemblies Section (Plumbing D2010) for the desired fixture, the System Components Group at the center of the page shows the fixture on the first line. The rest of the list (fittings, pipe, tubing, etc.) will total up to what we refer to in the Unit Price section as "Rough-in, supply, waste and vent." Note that for most fixtures we allow a nominal 5' of tubing to reach from the fixture to a main or riser.

- Remember that gas- and oil-fired units need venting.

## Reference Numbers

Reference numbers are shown in shaded boxes at the beginning of some major classifications. These numbers refer to related items in the Reference Section. The reference information may be an estimating procedure, an alternate pricing method, or technical information.

*Note:* Not all subdivisions listed here necessarily appear in this publication.

*Note:* **Trade Service,** *in part, has been used as a reference source for some of the material prices used in Division 22.*

# 22 01 Operation and Maintenance of Plumbing

## 22 01 02 – Labor Adjustments

| 22 01 02.10 Boilers, General | Crew | Daily Output | Labor-Hours | Unit | Material | 2008 Bare Costs Labor | Equipment | Total | Total Incl O&P |
|---|---|---|---|---|---|---|---|---|---|
| 0010 **BOILERS, GENERAL**, Prices do not include flue piping, elec. wiring, | | | | | | | | | |
| 0020 gas or oil piping, boiler base, pad, or tankless unless noted | | | | | | | | | |
| 0100 Boiler H.P.: 10 KW = 34 lbs/steam/hr = 33,475 BTU/hr.   R235000-50 | | | | | | | | | |
| 0150 To convert SFR to BTU rating: Hot water, 150 x SFR; | | | | | | | | | |
| 0160 Forced hot water, 180 x SFR; steam, 240 x SFR | | | | | | | | | |

### 22 01 02.20 Labor Adjustment Factors

| | Crew | Daily Output | Labor-Hours | Unit | Material | 2008 Bare Costs Labor | Equipment | Total | Total Incl O&P |
|---|---|---|---|---|---|---|---|---|---|
| 0010 **LABOR ADJUSTMENT FACTORS** | | | | | | | | | |
| 1000 Add to labor for elevated installation (Above floor level) | | | | | | | | | |
| 1080 10' to 14.5' high | | | | | | 10% | | | |
| 1100 15' to 19.5' high | | | | | | 20% | | | |
| 1120 20' to 24.5' high | | | | | | 25% | | | |
| 1140 25' to 29.5' high | | | | | | 35% | | | |
| 1160 30' to 34.5' high | | | | | | 40% | | | |
| 1180 35' to 39.5' high | | | | | | 50% | | | |
| 1200 40' and higher | | | | | | 55% | | | |
| 2000 Add to labor for crawl space | | | | | | | | | |
| 2100 3' high | | | | | | 40% | | | |
| 2140 4' high | | | | | | 30% | | | |
| 3000 Add to labor for multi-story building | | | | | | | | | |
| 3100 Add per floor for floors 3 thru 19 | | | | | | 2% | | | |
| 3140 Add per floor for floors 20 and up | | | | | | 4% | | | |
| 4000 Add to labor for working in existing occupied buildings | | | | | | | | | |
| 4100 Hospital | | | | | | 35% | | | |
| 4140 Office building | | | | | | 25% | | | |
| 4180 School | | | | | | 20% | | | |
| 4220 Factory or warehouse | | | | | | 15% | | | |
| 4260 Multi dwelling | | | | | | 15% | | | |
| 5000 Add to labor, miscellaneous | | | | | | | | | |
| 5100 Cramped shaft | | | | | | 35% | | | |
| 5140 Congested area | | | | | | 15% | | | |
| 5180 Excessive heat or cold | | | | | | 30% | | | |
| 9000 Labor factors, The above are reasonable suggestions, however | | | | | | | | | |
| 9010 each project should be evaluated for its own peculiarities. | | | | | | | | | |
| 9100 Other factors to be considered are: | | | | | | | | | |
| 9140 Movement of material and equipment through finished areas | | | | | | | | | |
| 9180 Equipment room | | | | | | | | | |
| 9220 Attic space | | | | | | | | | |
| 9260 No service road | | | | | | | | | |
| 9300 Poor unloading/storage area | | | | | | | | | |
| 9340 Congested site area/heavy traffic | | | | | | | | | |

# 22 05 Common Work Results for Plumbing

## 22 05 05 – Selective Plumbing Demolition

### 22 05 05.10 Plumbing Demolition

| | | Crew | Daily Output | Labor-Hours | Unit | Material | 2008 Bare Costs Labor | Equipment | Total | Total Incl O&P |
|---|---|---|---|---|---|---|---|---|---|---|
| 0010 | **PLUMBING DEMOLITION** | | | | | | | | | |
| 1020 | Fixtures, including 10' piping | | | | | | | | | |
| 1100 | Bath tubs, cast iron | 1 Plum | 4 | 2 | Ea. | | 93.50 | | 93.50 | 141 |
| 1120 | Fiberglass | | 6 | 1.333 | | | 62.50 | | 62.50 | 93.50 |
| 1140 | Steel | | 5 | 1.600 | | | 74.50 | | 74.50 | 112 |
| 1200 | Lavatory, wall hung | | 10 | .800 | | | 37.50 | | 37.50 | 56 |
| 1220 | Counter top | | 8 | 1 | | | 46.50 | | 46.50 | 70.50 |
| 1300 | Sink, single compartment | | 8 | 1 | | | 46.50 | | 46.50 | 70.50 |
| 1320 | Double compartment | | 7 | 1.143 | | | 53.50 | | 53.50 | 80.50 |
| 1400 | Water closet, floor mounted | | 8 | 1 | | | 46.50 | | 46.50 | 70.50 |
| 1420 | Wall mounted | | 7 | 1.143 | | | 53.50 | | 53.50 | 80.50 |
| 1500 | Urinal, floor mounted | | 4 | 2 | | | 93.50 | | 93.50 | 141 |
| 1520 | Wall mounted | | 7 | 1.143 | | | 53.50 | | 53.50 | 80.50 |
| 1600 | Water fountains, free standing | | 8 | 1 | | | 46.50 | | 46.50 | 70.50 |
| 1620 | Wall or deck mounted | | 6 | 1.333 | | | 62.50 | | 62.50 | 93.50 |
| 2000 | Piping, metal, up thru 1-1/2" diameter | | 200 | .040 | L.F. | | 1.87 | | 1.87 | 2.81 |
| 2050 | 2" thru 3-1/2" diameter | | 150 | .053 | | | 2.49 | | 2.49 | 3.75 |
| 2100 | 4" thru 6" diameter | 2 Plum | 100 | .160 | | | 7.45 | | 7.45 | 11.25 |
| 2150 | 8" thru 14" diameter | " | 60 | .267 | | | 12.45 | | 12.45 | 18.75 |
| 2153 | 16" thru 20" diameter | Q-18 | 70 | .343 | | | 15.10 | .80 | 15.90 | 23.50 |
| 2155 | 24" thru 26" diameter | | 55 | .436 | | | 19.20 | 1.02 | 20.22 | 30 |
| 2156 | 30" thru 36" diameter | | 40 | .600 | | | 26.50 | 1.40 | 27.90 | 41 |
| 2212 | Deduct for salvage, aluminum scrap | | | | Ton | | | | 825 | 908 |
| 2214 | Brass scrap | | | | | | | | 748 | 823 |
| 2216 | Copper scrap | | | | | | | | 2,248 | 2,473 |
| 2218 | Lead scrap | | | | | | | | 709 | 780 |
| 2220 | Steel scrap | | | | | | | | 125 | 138 |
| 2250 | Water heater, 40 gal. | 1 Plum | 6 | 1.333 | Ea. | | 62.50 | | 62.50 | 93.50 |

## 22 05 23 – General-Duty Valves for Plumbing Piping

### 22 05 23.10 Valves, Brass

| | | Crew | Daily Output | Labor-Hours | Unit | Material | 2008 Bare Costs Labor | Equipment | Total | Total Incl O&P |
|---|---|---|---|---|---|---|---|---|---|---|
| 0010 | **VALVES, BRASS** | | | | | | | | | |
| 0500 | Gas cocks, threaded | | | | | | | | | |
| 0530 | 1/2" | 1 Plum | 24 | .333 | Ea. | 16.30 | 15.55 | | 31.85 | 41.50 |
| 0540 | 3/4" | | 22 | .364 | | 17.85 | 17 | | 34.85 | 45 |
| 0550 | 1" | | 19 | .421 | | 16 | 19.65 | | 35.65 | 47 |
| 0560 | 1-1/4" | | 15 | .533 | | 30.50 | 25 | | 55.50 | 71 |

### 22 05 23.20 Valves, Bronze

| | | Crew | Daily Output | Labor-Hours | Unit | Material | 2008 Bare Costs Labor | Equipment | Total | Total Incl O&P |
|---|---|---|---|---|---|---|---|---|---|---|
| 0010 | **VALVES, BRONZE** | | | | | | | | | |
| 1020 | Angle, 150 lb., rising stem, threaded | | | | | | | | | |
| 1030 | 1/8" | 1 Plum | 24 | .333 | Ea. | 78 | 15.55 | | 93.55 | 110 |
| 1040 | 1/4" | | 24 | .333 | | 80.50 | 15.55 | | 96.05 | 112 |
| 1050 | 3/8" | | 24 | .333 | | 80.50 | 15.55 | | 96.05 | 112 |
| 1060 | 1/2" | | 22 | .364 | | 80.50 | 17 | | 97.50 | 114 |
| 1070 | 3/4" | | 20 | .400 | | 110 | 18.70 | | 128.70 | 148 |
| 1080 | 1" | | 19 | .421 | | 158 | 19.65 | | 177.65 | 204 |
| 1100 | 1-1/2" | | 13 | .615 | | 264 | 28.50 | | 292.50 | 335 |
| 1110 | 2" | | 11 | .727 | | 365 | 34 | | 399 | 455 |
| 1380 | Ball, 150 psi, threaded | | | | | | | | | |
| 1400 | 1/4" | 1 Plum | 24 | .333 | Ea. | 10.30 | 15.55 | | 25.85 | 35 |
| 1430 | 3/8" | | 24 | .333 | | 10.30 | 15.55 | | 25.85 | 35 |
| 1450 | 1/2" | | 22 | .364 | | 10.30 | 17 | | 27.30 | 37 |
| 1460 | 3/4" | | 20 | .400 | | 16.95 | 18.70 | | 35.65 | 46.50 |

## 22 05 23 – General-Duty Valves for Plumbing Piping

| 22 05 23.20 Valves, Bronze | | Crew | Daily Output | Labor-Hours | Unit | Material | 2008 Bare Costs Labor | Equipment | Total | Total Incl O&P |
|---|---|---|---|---|---|---|---|---|---|---|
| 1470 | 1" | 1 Plum | 19 | .421 | Ea. | 21.50 | 19.65 | | 41.15 | 53 |
| 1480 | 1-1/4" | | 15 | .533 | | 32.50 | 25 | | 57.50 | 73.50 |
| 1490 | 1-1/2" | | 13 | .615 | | 42.50 | 28.50 | | 71 | 89.50 |
| 1500 | 2" | | 11 | .727 | | 51.50 | 34 | | 85.50 | 108 |
| 1750 | Check, swing, class 150, regrinding disc, threaded | | | | | | | | | |
| 1800 | 1/8" | 1 Plum | 24 | .333 | Ea. | 37.50 | 15.55 | | 53.05 | 65 |
| 1830 | 1/4" | | 24 | .333 | | 37.50 | 15.55 | | 53.05 | 65 |
| 1840 | 3/8" | | 24 | .333 | | 39 | 15.55 | | 54.55 | 66.50 |
| 1850 | 1/2" | | 24 | .333 | | 39 | 15.55 | | 54.55 | 66.50 |
| 1860 | 3/4" | | 20 | .400 | | 57 | 18.70 | | 75.70 | 90.50 |
| 1870 | 1" | | 19 | .421 | | 82 | 19.65 | | 101.65 | 120 |
| 1880 | 1-1/4" | | 15 | .533 | | 118 | 25 | | 143 | 168 |
| 1890 | 1-1/2" | | 13 | .615 | | 137 | 28.50 | | 165.50 | 194 |
| 1900 | 2" | | 11 | .727 | | 202 | 34 | | 236 | 273 |
| 1910 | 2-1/2" | Q-1 | 15 | 1.067 | | 405 | 45 | | 450 | 515 |
| 2000 | For 200 lb, add | | | | | 5% | 10% | | | |
| 2040 | For 300 lb, add | | | | | 15% | 15% | | | |
| 2850 | Gate, N.R.S., soldered, 125 psi | | | | | | | | | |
| 2900 | 3/8" | 1 Plum | 24 | .333 | Ea. | 32.50 | 15.55 | | 48.05 | 59 |
| 2920 | 1/2" | | 24 | .333 | | 27.50 | 15.55 | | 43.05 | 54 |
| 2940 | 3/4" | | 20 | .400 | | 31.50 | 18.70 | | 50.20 | 63 |
| 2950 | 1" | | 19 | .421 | | 45.50 | 19.65 | | 65.15 | 79.50 |
| 2960 | 1-1/4" | | 15 | .533 | | 72 | 25 | | 97 | 117 |
| 2970 | 1-1/2" | | 13 | .615 | | 77.50 | 28.50 | | 106 | 128 |
| 2980 | 2" | | 11 | .727 | | 109 | 34 | | 143 | 171 |
| 2990 | 2-1/2" | Q-1 | 15 | 1.067 | | 272 | 45 | | 317 | 365 |
| 3000 | 3" | " | 13 | 1.231 | | 355 | 51.50 | | 406.50 | 470 |
| 3850 | Rising stem, soldered, 300 psi | | | | | | | | | |
| 3950 | 1" | 1 Plum | 19 | .421 | Ea. | 111 | 19.65 | | 130.65 | 152 |
| 3980 | 2" | " | 11 | .727 | | 294 | 34 | | 328 | 375 |
| 4000 | 3" | Q-1 | 13 | 1.231 | | 930 | 51.50 | | 981.50 | 1,100 |
| 4250 | Threaded, class 150 | | | | | | | | | |
| 4310 | 1/4" | 1 Plum | 24 | .333 | Ea. | 42 | 15.55 | | 57.55 | 69.50 |
| 4320 | 3/8" | | 24 | .333 | | 42 | 15.55 | | 57.55 | 69.50 |
| 4330 | 1/2" | | 24 | .333 | | 39 | 15.55 | | 54.55 | 66.50 |
| 4340 | 3/4" | | 20 | .400 | | 46 | 18.70 | | 64.70 | 78.50 |
| 4350 | 1" | | 19 | .421 | | 61 | 19.65 | | 80.65 | 97 |
| 4360 | 1-1/4" | | 15 | .533 | | 82 | 25 | | 107 | 128 |
| 4370 | 1-1/2" | | 13 | .615 | | 104 | 28.50 | | 132.50 | 157 |
| 4380 | 2" | | 11 | .727 | | 141 | 34 | | 175 | 206 |
| 4390 | 2-1/2" | Q-1 | 15 | 1.067 | | 325 | 45 | | 370 | 430 |
| 4400 | 3" | " | 13 | 1.231 | | 455 | 51.50 | | 506.50 | 580 |
| 4500 | For 300 psi, threaded, add | | | | | 100% | 15% | | | |
| 4540 | For chain operated type, add | | | | | 15% | | | | |
| 4850 | Globe, class 150, rising stem, threaded | | | | | | | | | |
| 4920 | 1/4" | 1 Plum | 24 | .333 | Ea. | 60 | 15.55 | | 75.55 | 89.50 |
| 4940 | 3/8" size | | 24 | .333 | | 60 | 15.55 | | 75.55 | 89.50 |
| 4950 | 1/2" | | 24 | .333 | | 60 | 15.55 | | 75.55 | 89.50 |
| 4960 | 3/4" | | 20 | .400 | | 80.50 | 18.70 | | 99.20 | 117 |
| 4970 | 1" | | 19 | .421 | | 126 | 19.65 | | 145.65 | 169 |
| 4980 | 1-1/4" | | 15 | .533 | | 200 | 25 | | 225 | 258 |
| 4990 | 1-1/2" | | 13 | .615 | | 244 | 28.50 | | 272.50 | 310 |
| 5000 | 2" | | 11 | .727 | | 365 | 34 | | 399 | 450 |

# 22 05 Common Work Results for Plumbing

## 22 05 23 – General-Duty Valves for Plumbing Piping

| 22 05 23.20 Valves, Bronze | | Crew | Daily Output | Labor-Hours | Unit | Material | 2008 Bare Costs Labor | Equipment | Total | Total Incl O&P |
|---|---|---|---|---|---|---|---|---|---|---|
| 5010 | 2-1/2" | Q-1 | 15 | 1.067 | Ea. | 735 | 45 | | 780 | 880 |
| 5020 | 3" | " | 13 | 1.231 | ↓ | 1,050 | 51.50 | | 1,101.50 | 1,225 |
| 5120 | For 300 lb threaded, add | | | | | 50% | 15% | | | |
| 5600 | Relief, pressure & temperature, self-closing, ASME, threaded | | | | | | | | | |
| 5640 | 3/4" | 1 Plum | 28 | .286 | Ea. | 153 | 13.35 | | 166.35 | 188 |
| 5650 | 1" | | 24 | .333 | | 162 | 15.55 | | 177.55 | 202 |
| 5660 | 1-1/4" | | 20 | .400 | | 325 | 18.70 | | 343.70 | 385 |
| 5670 | 1-1/2" | | 18 | .444 | | 620 | 21 | | 641 | 710 |
| 5680 | 2" | ↓ | 16 | .500 | ↓ | 675 | 23.50 | | 698.50 | 780 |
| 5950 | Pressure, poppet type, threaded | | | | | | | | | |
| 6000 | 1/2" | 1 Plum | 30 | .267 | Ea. | 31 | 12.45 | | 43.45 | 53 |
| 6040 | 3/4" | " | 28 | .286 | " | 31 | 13.35 | | 44.35 | 54 |
| 6400 | Pressure, water, ASME, threaded | | | | | | | | | |
| 6440 | 3/4" | 1 Plum | 28 | .286 | Ea. | 66 | 13.35 | | 79.35 | 92.50 |
| 6450 | 1" | | 24 | .333 | | 140 | 15.55 | | 155.55 | 178 |
| 6460 | 1-1/4" | | 20 | .400 | | 222 | 18.70 | | 240.70 | 273 |
| 6470 | 1-1/2" | | 18 | .444 | | 230 | 21 | | 251 | 284 |
| 6480 | 2" | | 16 | .500 | | 355 | 23.50 | | 378.50 | 425 |
| 6490 | 2-1/2" | ↓ | 15 | .533 | ↓ | 2,075 | 25 | | 2,100 | 2,325 |
| 6900 | Reducing, water pressure | | | | | | | | | |
| 6920 | 300 psi to 25-75 psi, threaded or sweat | | | | | | | | | |
| 6940 | 1/2" | 1 Plum | 24 | .333 | Ea. | 196 | 15.55 | | 211.55 | 240 |
| 6950 | 3/4" | | 20 | .400 | | 196 | 18.70 | | 214.70 | 244 |
| 6960 | 1" | | 19 | .421 | | 305 | 19.65 | | 324.65 | 365 |
| 6970 | 1-1/4" | | 15 | .533 | | 560 | 25 | | 585 | 655 |
| 6980 | 1-1/2" | ↓ | 13 | .615 | ↓ | 820 | 28.50 | | 848.50 | 945 |
| 8350 | Tempering, water, sweat connections | | | | | | | | | |
| 8400 | 1/2" | 1 Plum | 24 | .333 | Ea. | 65 | 15.55 | | 80.55 | 95 |
| 8440 | 3/4" | " | 20 | .400 | " | 79.50 | 18.70 | | 98.20 | 116 |
| 8650 | Threaded connections | | | | | | | | | |
| 8700 | 1/2" | 1 Plum | 24 | .333 | Ea. | 79.50 | 15.55 | | 95.05 | 111 |
| 8740 | 3/4" | | 20 | .400 | | 340 | 18.70 | | 358.70 | 405 |
| 8750 | 1" | | 19 | .421 | | 375 | 19.65 | | 394.65 | 445 |
| 8760 | 1-1/4" | | 15 | .533 | | 595 | 25 | | 620 | 695 |
| 8770 | 1-1/2" | | 13 | .615 | | 650 | 28.50 | | 678.50 | 760 |
| 8780 | 2" | ↓ | 11 | .727 | ↓ | 975 | 34 | | 1,009 | 1,125 |

| 22 05 23.60 Valves, Plastic | | Crew | Daily Output | Labor-Hours | Unit | Material | 2008 Bare Costs Labor | Equipment | Total | Total Incl O&P |
|---|---|---|---|---|---|---|---|---|---|---|
| 0010 | **VALVES, PLASTIC** | | | | | | | | | |
| 1100 | Angle, PVC, threaded | | | | | | | | | |
| 1110 | 1/4" | 1 Plum | 26 | .308 | Ea. | 57 | 14.35 | | 71.35 | 84 |
| 1120 | 1/2" | | 26 | .308 | | 57 | 14.35 | | 71.35 | 84 |
| 1130 | 3/4" | | 25 | .320 | | 67.50 | 14.95 | | 82.45 | 96.50 |
| 1140 | 1" | ↓ | 23 | .348 | ↓ | 82 | 16.25 | | 98.25 | 115 |
| 1150 | Ball, PVC, socket or threaded, single union | | | | | | | | | |
| 1230 | 1/2" | 1 Plum | 26 | .308 | Ea. | 20.50 | 14.35 | | 34.85 | 44 |
| 1240 | 3/4" | | 25 | .320 | | 23.50 | 14.95 | | 38.45 | 48.50 |
| 1250 | 1" | | 23 | .348 | | 29.50 | 16.25 | | 45.75 | 57 |
| 1260 | 1-1/4" | | 21 | .381 | | 39.50 | 17.80 | | 57.30 | 70.50 |
| 1270 | 1-1/2" | | 20 | .400 | | 47 | 18.70 | | 65.70 | 80 |
| 1280 | 2" | ↓ | 17 | .471 | | 68.50 | 22 | | 90.50 | 108 |
| 1360 | For PVC, flanged, add | | | | | ↓ | 100% | 15% | | |
| 1650 | CPVC, socket or threaded, single union | | | | | | | | | |

427

## 22 05 23 – General-Duty Valves for Plumbing Piping

| 22 05 23.60 Valves, Plastic | | Crew | Daily Output | Labor-Hours | Unit | Material | 2008 Bare Costs Labor | Equipment | Total | Total Incl O&P |
|---|---|---|---|---|---|---|---|---|---|---|
| 1700 | 1/2" | 1 Plum | 26 | .308 | Ea. | 39 | 14.35 | | 53.35 | 64 |
| 1720 | 3/4" | | 25 | .320 | | 49 | 14.95 | | 63.95 | 76 |
| 1730 | 1" | | 23 | .348 | | 58 | 16.25 | | 74.25 | 88.50 |
| 1750 | 1-1/4" | | 21 | .381 | | 93 | 17.80 | | 110.80 | 129 |
| 1760 | 1-1/2" | | 20 | .400 | | 93 | 18.70 | | 111.70 | 130 |
| 1840 | For CPVC, flanged, add | | | | | 65% | 15% | | | |
| 1880 | For true union, socket or threaded, add | | | | | 50% | 5% | | | |
| 2050 | Polypropylene, threaded | | | | | | | | | |
| 2100 | 1/4" | 1 Plum | 26 | .308 | Ea. | 38.50 | 14.35 | | 52.85 | 63.50 |
| 2120 | 3/8" | | 26 | .308 | | 38.50 | 14.35 | | 52.85 | 63.50 |
| 2130 | 1/2" | | 26 | .308 | | 38.50 | 14.35 | | 52.85 | 63.50 |
| 2140 | 3/4" | | 25 | .320 | | 49 | 14.95 | | 63.95 | 76 |
| 2150 | 1" | | 23 | .348 | | 57.50 | 16.25 | | 73.75 | 88 |
| 2160 | 1-1/4" | | 21 | .381 | | 83 | 17.80 | | 100.80 | 119 |
| 2170 | 1-1/2" | | 20 | .400 | | 96 | 18.70 | | 114.70 | 134 |
| 2180 | 2" | | 17 | .471 | | 131 | 22 | | 153 | 177 |
| 4850 | Foot valve, PVC, socket or threaded | | | | | | | | | |
| 4900 | 1/2" | 1 Plum | 34 | .235 | Ea. | 57 | 11 | | 68 | 79 |
| 4930 | 3/4" | | 32 | .250 | | 64 | 11.70 | | 75.70 | 88 |
| 4940 | 1" | | 28 | .286 | | 85.50 | 13.35 | | 98.85 | 114 |
| 4950 | 1-1/4" | | 27 | .296 | | 160 | 13.85 | | 173.85 | 197 |
| 4960 | 1-1/2" | | 26 | .308 | | 160 | 14.35 | | 174.35 | 198 |
| 6350 | Y sediment strainer, PVC, socket or threaded | | | | | | | | | |
| 6400 | 1/2" | 1 Plum | 26 | .308 | Ea. | 38.50 | 14.35 | | 52.85 | 63.50 |
| 6440 | 3/4" | | 24 | .333 | | 41.50 | 15.55 | | 57.05 | 69.50 |
| 6450 | 1" | | 23 | .348 | | 50.50 | 16.25 | | 66.75 | 80 |
| 6460 | 1-1/4" | | 21 | .381 | | 83 | 17.80 | | 100.80 | 119 |
| 6470 | 1-1/2" | | 20 | .400 | | 83 | 18.70 | | 101.70 | 120 |

## 22 05 76 – Facility Drainage Piping Cleanouts

### 22 05 76.10 Cleanouts

| 22 05 76.10 Cleanouts | | Crew | Daily Output | Labor-Hours | Unit | Material | 2008 Bare Costs Labor | Equipment | Total | Total Incl O&P |
|---|---|---|---|---|---|---|---|---|---|---|
| 0010 | **CLEANOUTS** | | | | | | | | | |
| 0060 | Floor type | | | | | | | | | |
| 0080 | Round or square, scoriated nickel bronze top | | | | | | | | | |
| 0100 | 2" pipe size | 1 Plum | 10 | .800 | Ea. | 123 | 37.50 | | 160.50 | 192 |
| 0120 | 3" pipe size | | 8 | 1 | | 185 | 46.50 | | 231.50 | 274 |
| 0140 | 4" pipe size | | 6 | 1.333 | | 185 | 62.50 | | 247.50 | 297 |
| 0980 | Round top, recessed for terrazzo | | | | | | | | | |
| 1000 | 2" pipe size | 1 Plum | 9 | .889 | Ea. | 123 | 41.50 | | 164.50 | 199 |
| 1080 | 3" pipe size | | 6 | 1.333 | | 185 | 62.50 | | 247.50 | 297 |
| 1100 | 4" pipe size | | 4 | 2 | | 185 | 93.50 | | 278.50 | 345 |
| 1120 | 5" pipe size | Q-1 | 6 | 2.667 | | 235 | 112 | | 347 | 430 |

### 22 05 76.20 Cleanout Tees

| 22 05 76.20 Cleanout Tees | | Crew | Daily Output | Labor-Hours | Unit | Material | 2008 Bare Costs Labor | Equipment | Total | Total Incl O&P |
|---|---|---|---|---|---|---|---|---|---|---|
| 0010 | **CLEANOUT TEES** | | | | | | | | | |
| 0100 | Cast iron, B&S, with countersunk plug | | | | | | | | | |
| 0200 | 2" pipe size | 1 Plum | 4 | 2 | Ea. | 168 | 93.50 | | 261.50 | 325 |
| 0220 | 3" pipe size | | 3.60 | 2.222 | | 183 | 104 | | 287 | 360 |
| 0240 | 4" pipe size | | 3.30 | 2.424 | | 228 | 113 | | 341 | 420 |
| 0280 | 6" pipe size | Q-1 | 5 | 3.200 | | 615 | 135 | | 750 | 875 |
| 0500 | For round smooth access cover, same price | | | | | | | | | |
| 4000 | Plastic, tees and adapters. Add plugs | | | | | | | | | |
| 4010 | ABS, DWV | | | | | | | | | |
| 4020 | Cleanout tee, 1-1/2" pipe size | 1 Plum | 15 | .533 | Ea. | 5.30 | 25 | | 30.30 | 43.50 |

## 22 05 76 – Facility Drainage Piping Cleanouts

| 22 05 76.20 Cleanout Tees | | Crew | Daily Output | Labor-Hours | Unit | Material | 2008 Bare Costs Labor | Equipment | Total | Total Incl O&P |
|---|---|---|---|---|---|---|---|---|---|---|
| 4030 | 2" pipe size | Q-1 | 27 | .593 | Ea. | 6.20 | 25 | | 31.20 | 44.50 |
| 4040 | 3" pipe size | | 21 | .762 | | 12.45 | 32 | | 44.45 | 61.50 |
| 4050 | 4" pipe size | ↓ | 16 | 1 | | 21.50 | 42 | | 63.50 | 87 |
| 4100 | Cleanout plug, 1-1/2" pipe size | 1 Plum | 32 | .250 | | .97 | 11.70 | | 12.67 | 18.60 |
| 4110 | 2" pipe size | Q-1 | 56 | .286 | | 1.27 | 12 | | 13.27 | 19.45 |
| 4120 | 3" pipe size | | 36 | .444 | | 2.05 | 18.70 | | 20.75 | 30.50 |
| 4130 | 4" pipe size | ↓ | 30 | .533 | | 3.98 | 22.50 | | 26.48 | 38 |
| 4180 | Cleanout adapter fitting, 1-1/2" pipe size | 1 Plum | 32 | .250 | | 1.37 | 11.70 | | 13.07 | 19.05 |
| 4190 | 2" pipe size | Q-1 | 56 | .286 | | 1.93 | 12 | | 13.93 | 20 |
| 4200 | 3" pipe size | | 36 | .444 | | 5.40 | 18.70 | | 24.10 | 34 |
| 4210 | 4" pipe size | ↓ | 30 | .533 | ↓ | 8.70 | 22.50 | | 31.20 | 43 |
| 5000 | PVC, DWV | | | | | | | | | |
| 5010 | Cleanout tee, 1-1/2" pipe size | 1 Plum | 15 | .533 | Ea. | 3.89 | 25 | | 28.89 | 42 |
| 5020 | 2" pipe size | Q-1 | 27 | .593 | | 4.79 | 25 | | 29.79 | 43 |
| 5030 | 3" pipe size | | 21 | .762 | | 9.55 | 32 | | 41.55 | 58.50 |
| 5040 | 4" pipe size | ↓ | 16 | 1 | | 17.75 | 42 | | 59.75 | 82.50 |
| 5090 | Cleanout plug, 1-1/2" pipe size | 1 Plum | 32 | .250 | | 1.04 | 11.70 | | 12.74 | 18.70 |
| 5100 | 2" pipe size | Q-1 | 56 | .286 | | 1.07 | 12 | | 13.07 | 19.25 |
| 5110 | 3" pipe size | | 36 | .444 | | 2.07 | 18.70 | | 20.77 | 30.50 |
| 5120 | 4" pipe size | | 30 | .533 | | 3.06 | 22.50 | | 25.56 | 37 |
| 5130 | 6" pipe size | ↓ | 24 | .667 | | 10.15 | 28 | | 38.15 | 53 |
| 5170 | Cleanout adapter fitting, 1-1/2" pipe size | 1 Plum | 32 | .250 | | 1.27 | 11.70 | | 12.97 | 18.95 |
| 5180 | 2" pipe size | Q-1 | 56 | .286 | | 1.80 | 12 | | 13.80 | 20 |
| 5190 | 3" pipe size | | 36 | .444 | | 5.05 | 18.70 | | 23.75 | 33.50 |
| 5200 | 4" pipe size | | 30 | .533 | | 8.30 | 22.50 | | 30.80 | 42.50 |
| 5210 | 6" pipe size | ↓ | 24 | .667 | ↓ | 22.50 | 28 | | 50.50 | 66.50 |

# 22 07 Plumbing Insulation

## 22 07 19 – Plumbing Piping Insulation

### 22 07 19.10 Piping Insulation

| | | Crew | Daily Output | Labor-Hours | Unit | Material | 2008 Bare Costs Labor | Equipment | Total | Total Incl O&P |
|---|---|---|---|---|---|---|---|---|---|---|
| 0010 | **PIPING INSULATION** | | | | | | | | | |
| 0100 | Rule of thumb, as a percentage of total mechanical costs | | | | Job | | | | 10% | |
| 0110 | Insulation req'd is based on the surface size/area to be covered | | | | | | | | | |
| 4000 | Pipe covering (price copper tube one size less than IPS) | | | | | | | | | |
| 6600 | Fiberglass, with all service jacket | | | | | | | | | |
| 6840 | 1" wall, 1/2" iron pipe size | Q-14 | 240 | .067 | L.F. | .89 | 2.59 | | 3.48 | 5.05 |
| 6870 | 1" iron pipe size | | 220 | .073 | | 1.04 | 2.82 | | 3.86 | 5.60 |
| 6900 | 2" iron pipe size | | 200 | .080 | | 1.31 | 3.10 | | 4.41 | 6.35 |
| 6920 | 3" iron pipe size | | 180 | .089 | | 1.59 | 3.45 | | 5.04 | 7.20 |
| 6940 | 4" iron pipe size | | 150 | .107 | | 2.11 | 4.14 | | 6.25 | 8.80 |
| 7320 | 2" wall, 1/2" iron pipe size | | 220 | .073 | | 2.60 | 2.82 | | 5.42 | 7.30 |
| 7440 | 6" iron pipe size | | 100 | .160 | | 5.20 | 6.20 | | 11.40 | 15.50 |
| 7460 | 8" iron pipe size | | 80 | .200 | | 6.35 | 7.75 | | 14.10 | 19.15 |
| 7480 | 10" iron pipe size | | 70 | .229 | | 7.60 | 8.85 | | 16.45 | 22.50 |
| 7490 | 12" iron pipe size | ↓ | 65 | .246 | ↓ | 8.50 | 9.55 | | 18.05 | 24.50 |
| 7800 | For fiberglass with standard canvas jacket, deduct | | | | | 5% | | | | |
| 7802 | For fittings, add 3 L.F. for each fitting | | | | | | | | | |
| 7804 | plus 4 L.F. for each flange of the fitting | | | | | | | | | |
| 7810 | Finishes | | | | | | | | | |
| 7811 | Finishes, for .010" aluminum jacket, add | Q-14 | 200 | .080 | S.F. | .77 | 3.10 | | 3.87 | 5.75 |
| 7812 | For .016" aluminum jacket, add | ↓ | 200 | .080 | ↓ | 1.12 | 3.10 | | 4.22 | 6.10 |

| 22 07 19.10 Piping Insulation | Crew | Daily Output | Labor-Hours | Unit | Material | 2008 Bare Costs Labor | Equipment | Total | Total Incl O&P |
|---|---|---|---|---|---|---|---|---|---|
| 7813 | For .010" stainless steel, add | Q-14 | 160 | .100 | S.F. | 3.44 | 3.88 | | 7.32 | 9.90 |
| 7814 | For single layer of felt, add | | | | | 10% | 10% | | | |
| 7816 | For roofing paper, 45 lb to 55 lb, add | | | | | 25% | 10% | | | |
| 7879 | Rubber tubing, flexible closed cell foam | | | | | | | | | |
| 7880 | 3/8" wall, 1/4" iron pipe size | 1 Asbe | 120 | .067 | L.F. | .55 | 2.87 | | 3.42 | 5.15 |
| 7910 | 1/2" iron pipe size | | 115 | .070 | | .70 | 3 | | 3.70 | 5.50 |
| 7920 | 3/4" iron pipe size | | 115 | .070 | | .85 | 3 | | 3.85 | 5.65 |
| 7930 | 1" iron pipe size | | 110 | .073 | | .98 | 3.13 | | 4.11 | 6 |
| 7950 | 1-1/2" iron pipe size | | 110 | .073 | | 1.30 | 3.13 | | 4.43 | 6.35 |
| 8100 | 1/2" wall, 1/4" iron pipe size | | 90 | .089 | | .41 | 3.83 | | 4.24 | 6.50 |
| 8130 | 1/2" iron pipe size | | 89 | .090 | | .51 | 3.87 | | 4.38 | 6.65 |
| 8140 | 3/4" iron pipe size | | 89 | .090 | | .57 | 3.87 | | 4.44 | 6.75 |
| 8150 | 1" iron pipe size | | 88 | .091 | | .63 | 3.92 | | 4.55 | 6.85 |
| 8170 | 1-1/2" iron pipe size | | 87 | .092 | | .87 | 3.96 | | 4.83 | 7.20 |
| 8180 | 2" iron pipe size | | 86 | .093 | | 1.12 | 4.01 | | 5.13 | 7.55 |
| 8200 | 3" iron pipe size | | 85 | .094 | | 1.58 | 4.06 | | 5.64 | 8.15 |
| 8300 | 3/4" wall, 1/4" iron pipe size | | 90 | .089 | | .64 | 3.83 | | 4.47 | 6.75 |
| 8330 | 1/2" iron pipe size | | 89 | .090 | | .84 | 3.87 | | 4.71 | 7 |
| 8340 | 3/4" iron pipe size | | 89 | .090 | | 1.02 | 3.87 | | 4.89 | 7.20 |
| 8350 | 1" iron pipe size | | 88 | .091 | | 1.17 | 3.92 | | 5.09 | 7.45 |
| 8370 | 1-1/2" iron pipe size | | 87 | .092 | | 1.78 | 3.96 | | 5.74 | 8.20 |
| 8380 | 2" iron pipe size | | 86 | .093 | | 2.09 | 4.01 | | 6.10 | 8.60 |
| 8400 | 3" iron pipe size | | 85 | .094 | | 3.49 | 4.06 | | 7.55 | 10.25 |
| 8444 | 1" wall, 1/2" iron pipe size | | 86 | .093 | | 1.63 | 4.01 | | 5.64 | 8.10 |
| 8445 | 3/4" iron pipe size | | 84 | .095 | | 1.97 | 4.10 | | 6.07 | 8.60 |
| 8446 | 1" iron pipe size | | 84 | .095 | | 2.29 | 4.10 | | 6.39 | 8.95 |
| 8447 | 1-1/4" iron pipe size | | 82 | .098 | | 2.60 | 4.20 | | 6.80 | 9.45 |
| 8448 | 1-1/2" iron pipe size | | 82 | .098 | | 3.02 | 4.20 | | 7.22 | 9.90 |
| 8449 | 2" iron pipe size | | 80 | .100 | | 4.03 | 4.31 | | 8.34 | 11.25 |
| 8450 | 2-1/2" iron pipe size | | 80 | .100 | | 5.25 | 4.31 | | 9.56 | 12.60 |
| 8456 | Rubber insulation tape, 1/8" x 2" x 30' | | | | Ea. | 11.40 | | | 11.40 | 12.50 |

### 22 11 13.14 Pipe, Brass

| | | Crew | Daily Output | Labor-Hours | Unit | Material | Labor | Equipment | Total | Total Incl O&P |
|---|---|---|---|---|---|---|---|---|---|---|
| 0010 | **PIPE, BRASS**, Plain end | | | | | | | | | |
| 0900 | Field threaded, coupling & clevis hanger assembly 10' O.C. | | | | | | | | | |
| 0920 | Regular weight | | | | | | | | | |
| 1120 | 1/2" diameter | 1 Plum | 48 | .167 | L.F. | 4.58 | 7.80 | | 12.38 | 16.75 |
| 1140 | 3/4" diameter | | 46 | .174 | | 6.30 | 8.10 | | 14.40 | 19.10 |
| 1160 | 1" diameter | | 43 | .186 | | 9.25 | 8.70 | | 17.95 | 23.50 |
| 1180 | 1-1/4" diameter | Q-1 | 72 | .222 | | 14.25 | 9.35 | | 23.60 | 30 |
| 1200 | 1-1/2" diameter | | 65 | .246 | | 17.10 | 10.35 | | 27.45 | 34.50 |
| 1220 | 2" diameter | | 53 | .302 | | 24 | 12.70 | | 36.70 | 45.50 |

### 22 11 13.23 Pipe, Copper

| | | Crew | Daily Output | Labor-Hours | Unit | Material | Labor | Equipment | Total | Total Incl O&P |
|---|---|---|---|---|---|---|---|---|---|---|
| 0010 | **PIPE, COPPER**, Solder joints | | | | | | | | | |
| 1000 | Type K tubing, couplings & clevis hanger assemblies 10' O.C. | | | | | | | | | |
| 1100 | 1/4" diameter | 1 Plum | 84 | .095 | L.F. | 2.14 | 4.45 | | 6.59 | 9.05 |
| 1200 | 1" diameter | | 66 | .121 | | 6.70 | 5.65 | | 12.35 | 15.90 |
| 1260 | 2" diameter | | 40 | .200 | | 16.90 | 9.35 | | 26.25 | 32.50 |
| 2000 | Type L tubing, couplings & clevis hanger assemblies 10' O.C. | | | | | | | | | |

| 22 11 13.23 Pipe, Copper | | Crew | Daily Output | Labor-Hours | Unit | Material | 2008 Bare Costs Labor | Equipment | Total | Total Incl O&P |
|---|---|---|---|---|---|---|---|---|---|---|
| 2100 | 1/4" diameter | 1 Plum | 88 | .091 | L.F. | 1.29 | 4.25 | | 5.54 | 7.80 |
| 2120 | 3/8" diameter | | 84 | .095 | | 1.86 | 4.45 | | 6.31 | 8.75 |
| 2140 | 1/2" diameter        CN | | 81 | .099 | | 2.26 | 4.61 | | 6.87 | 9.45 |
| 2160 | 5/8" diameter | | 79 | .101 | | 3.22 | 4.73 | | 7.95 | 10.65 |
| 2180 | 3/4" diameter | | 76 | .105 | | 3.51 | 4.92 | | 8.43 | 11.25 |
| 2200 | 1" diameter | | 68 | .118 | | 5.10 | 5.50 | | 10.60 | 13.85 |
| 2220 | 1-1/4" diameter | | 58 | .138 | | 7.05 | 6.45 | | 13.50 | 17.45 |
| 2240 | 1-1/2" diameter | | 52 | .154 | | 9.05 | 7.20 | | 16.25 | 21 |
| 2260 | 2" diameter | | 42 | .190 | | 14.05 | 8.90 | | 22.95 | 29 |
| 2280 | 2-1/2" diameter | Q-1 | 62 | .258 | | 21.50 | 10.85 | | 32.35 | 40.50 |
| 2300 | 3" diameter | | 56 | .286 | | 29.50 | 12 | | 41.50 | 50 |
| 2320 | 3-1/2" diameter | | 43 | .372 | | 40.50 | 15.65 | | 56.15 | 68 |
| 2340 | 4" diameter | | 39 | .410 | | 50 | 17.25 | | 67.25 | 81 |
| 2360 | 5" diameter | | 34 | .471 | | 107 | 19.80 | | 126.80 | 147 |
| 2380 | 6" diameter | Q-2 | 40 | .600 | | 149 | 26 | | 175 | 204 |
| 2400 | 8" diameter | " | 36 | .667 | | 208 | 29 | | 237 | 272 |
| 2410 | For other than full hard temper, add | | | | | 21% | | | | |
| 2590 | For silver solder, add | | | | | | 15% | | | |
| 4000 | Type DWV tubing, couplings & clevis hanger assemblies 10' O.C. | | | | | | | | | |
| 4100 | 1-1/4" diameter | 1 Plum | 60 | .133 | L.F. | 6.15 | 6.25 | | 12.40 | 16.15 |
| 4120 | 1-1/2" diameter | | 54 | .148 | | 7.75 | 6.90 | | 14.65 | 18.95 |
| 4140 | 2" diameter | | 44 | .182 | | 10.45 | 8.50 | | 18.95 | 24.50 |
| 4160 | 3" diameter | Q-1 | 58 | .276 | | 19.05 | 11.60 | | 30.65 | 38.50 |
| 4180 | 4" diameter | | 40 | .400 | | 34 | 16.80 | | 50.80 | 62.50 |
| 4200 | 5" diameter | | 36 | .444 | | 95.50 | 18.70 | | 114.20 | 133 |
| 4220 | 6" diameter | Q-2 | 42 | .571 | | 137 | 25 | | 162 | 189 |

## 22 11 13.44 Pipe, Steel

| | | Crew | Daily Output | Labor-Hours | Unit | Material | 2008 Bare Costs Labor | Equipment | Total | Total Incl O&P |
|---|---|---|---|---|---|---|---|---|---|---|
| 0010 | **PIPE, STEEL** | | | | | | | | | |
| 0012 | The steel pipe in this section does not include fittings such as ells, tees | | | | | | | | | |
| 0014 | For fittings either add a % (usually 25 to 35%) or see | | | | | | | | | |
| 0015 | the Mechanical or Plumbing Cost Data | | | | | | | | | |
| 0020 | All pipe sizes are to Spec. A-53 unless noted otherwise       R221113-50 | | | | | | | | | |
| 0050 | Schedule 40, threaded, with couplings, and clevis hanger | | | | | | | | | |
| 0060 | assemblies sized for covering, 10' O.C. | | | | | | | | | |
| 0540 | Black, 1/4" diameter | 1 Plum | 66 | .121 | L.F. | 1.70 | 5.65 | | 7.35 | 10.35 |
| 0550 | 3/8" diameter | | 65 | .123 | | 1.93 | 5.75 | | 7.68 | 10.75 |
| 0560 | 1/2" diameter | | 63 | .127 | | 2.18 | 5.95 | | 8.13 | 11.30 |
| 0570 | 3/4" diameter | | 61 | .131 | | 2.58 | 6.10 | | 8.68 | 12.05 |
| 0580 | 1" diameter | | 53 | .151 | | 3.79 | 7.05 | | 10.84 | 14.75 |
| 0590 | 1-1/4" diameter | Q-1 | 89 | .180 | | 5 | 7.55 | | 12.55 | 16.85 |
| 0600 | 1-1/2" diameter | | 80 | .200 | | 5.95 | 8.40 | | 14.35 | 19.20 |
| 0610 | 2" diameter        CN | | 64 | .250 | | 7.90 | 10.50 | | 18.40 | 24.50 |
| 0620 | 2-1/2" diameter | | 50 | .320 | | 12.35 | 13.45 | | 25.80 | 33.50 |
| 0630 | 3" diameter | | 43 | .372 | | 15.90 | 15.65 | | 31.55 | 41 |
| 0640 | 3-1/2" diameter | | 40 | .400 | | 22 | 16.80 | | 38.80 | 49.50 |
| 0650 | 4" diameter | | 36 | .444 | | 23.50 | 18.70 | | 42.20 | 54 |
| 0660 | 5" diameter | | 26 | .615 | | 33 | 26 | | 59 | 75 |
| 0670 | 6" diameter | Q-2 | 31 | .774 | | 36.50 | 33.50 | | 70 | 91.50 |
| 1280 | All pipe sizes are to Spec. A-53 unless noted otherwise | | | | | | | | | |
| 1281 | Schedule 40, threaded, with couplings and clevis hanger | | | | | | | | | |
| 1282 | assemblies sized for covering, 10' O. C. | | | | | | | | | |
| 1290 | Galvanized, 1/4" diameter | 1 Plum | 66 | .121 | L.F. | 2.31 | 5.65 | | 7.96 | 11.05 |

431

### 22 11 13.44 Pipe, Steel

| | | Crew | Daily Output | Labor-Hours | Unit | Material | 2008 Bare Costs Labor | 2008 Bare Costs Equipment | Total | Total Incl O&P |
|---|---|---|---|---|---|---|---|---|---|---|
| 1300 | 3/8" diameter | 1 Plum | 65 | .123 | L.F. | 2.56 | 5.75 | | 8.31 | 11.45 |
| 1310 | 1/2" diameter | | 63 | .127 | | 3.10 | 5.95 | | 9.05 | 12.30 |
| 1320 | 3/4" diameter | | 61 | .131 | | 3.73 | 6.10 | | 9.83 | 13.30 |
| 1330 | 1" diameter | | 53 | .151 | | 5.10 | 7.05 | | 12.15 | 16.25 |
| 1340 | 1-1/4" diameter | Q-1 | 89 | .180 | | 6.85 | 7.55 | | 14.40 | 18.90 |
| 1350 | 1-1/2" diameter | | 80 | .200 | | 8.10 | 8.40 | | 16.50 | 21.50 |
| 1360 | 2" diameter | | 64 | .250 | | 10.85 | 10.50 | | 21.35 | 28 |
| 1370 | 2-1/2" diameter | | 50 | .320 | | 18.10 | 13.45 | | 31.55 | 40 |
| 1380 | 3" diameter | | 43 | .372 | | 23 | 15.65 | | 38.65 | 49 |
| 1390 | 3-1/2" diameter | | 40 | .400 | | 24 | 16.80 | | 40.80 | 52 |
| 1400 | 4" diameter | | 36 | .444 | | 33.50 | 18.70 | | 52.20 | 64.50 |
| 1410 | 5" diameter | | 26 | .615 | | 43.50 | 26 | | 69.50 | 86.50 |
| 1420 | 6" diameter | Q-2 | 31 | .774 | | 55 | 33.50 | | 88.50 | 112 |
| 1430 | 8" diameter | | 27 | .889 | | 85.50 | 38.50 | | 124 | 153 |
| 1440 | 10" diameter | | 23 | 1.043 | | 158 | 45.50 | | 203.50 | 243 |
| 1450 | 12" diameter | | 18 | 1.333 | | 219 | 58 | | 277 | 330 |
| 2000 | Welded, sch. 40, on yoke & roll hanger assys, sized for covering, 10' O.C. | | | | | | | | | |
| 2040 | Black, 1" diameter | Q-15 | 93 | .172 | L.F. | 3.70 | 7.25 | .60 | 11.55 | 15.60 |
| 2070 | 2" diameter | | 61 | .262 | | 7.40 | 11 | .92 | 19.32 | 26 |
| 2090 | 3" diameter | | 43 | .372 | | 12.50 | 15.65 | 1.31 | 29.46 | 38.50 |
| 2110 | 4" diameter | | 37 | .432 | | 16.50 | 18.20 | 1.52 | 36.22 | 47.50 |
| 2120 | 5" diameter | | 32 | .500 | | 24 | 21 | 1.76 | 46.76 | 59.50 |
| 2130 | 6" diameter | Q-16 | 36 | .667 | | 30 | 29 | 1.56 | 60.56 | 78 |
| 2140 | 8" diameter | | 29 | .828 | | 47 | 36 | 1.94 | 84.94 | 108 |
| 2150 | 10" diameter | | 24 | 1 | | 88 | 43.50 | 2.34 | 133.84 | 165 |
| 2160 | 12" diameter | | 19 | 1.263 | | 122 | 55 | 2.96 | 179.96 | 220 |

### 22 11 13.48 Pipe, Fittings and Valves, Steel, Grooved-Joint

| | | Crew | Daily Output | Labor-Hours | Unit | Material | 2008 Bare Costs Labor | 2008 Bare Costs Equipment | Total | Total Incl O&P |
|---|---|---|---|---|---|---|---|---|---|---|
| 0010 | **PIPE, FITTINGS AND VALVES, STEEL, GROOVED-JOINT** | | | | | | | | | |
| 0012 | Fittings are ductile iron. Steel fittings noted. | | | | | | | | | |
| 0020 | Pipe includes coupling & clevis type hanger assemblies, 10' O.C. | | | | | | | | | |
| 1000 | Schedule 40, black | | | | | | | | | |
| 1040 | 3/4" diameter | 1 Plum | 71 | .113 | L.F. | 3.27 | 5.25 | | 8.52 | 11.50 |
| 1050 | 1" diameter | | 63 | .127 | | 3.94 | 5.95 | | 9.89 | 13.25 |
| 1060 | 1-1/4" diameter | | 58 | .138 | | 5.25 | 6.45 | | 11.70 | 15.45 |
| 1070 | 1-1/2" diameter | | 51 | .157 | | 6.10 | 7.35 | | 13.45 | 17.70 |
| 1080 | 2" diameter | | 40 | .200 | | 7.90 | 9.35 | | 17.25 | 22.50 |
| 1090 | 2-1/2" diameter | Q-1 | 57 | .281 | | 10.65 | 11.80 | | 22.45 | 29.50 |
| 1100 | 3" diameter | | 50 | .320 | | 13.55 | 13.45 | | 27 | 35 |
| 1110 | 4" diameter | | 45 | .356 | | 17.95 | 14.95 | | 32.90 | 42.50 |
| 1120 | 5" diameter | | 37 | .432 | | 26 | 18.20 | | 44.20 | 56 |
| 1130 | 6" diameter | Q-2 | 42 | .571 | | 32.50 | 25 | | 57.50 | 73.50 |
| 1800 | Galvanized | | | | | | | | | |
| 1840 | 3/4" diameter | 1 Plum | 71 | .113 | L.F. | 4.40 | 5.25 | | 9.65 | 12.75 |
| 1850 | 1" diameter | | 63 | .127 | | 5.10 | 5.95 | | 11.05 | 14.50 |
| 1860 | 1-1/4" diameter | | 58 | .138 | | 6.85 | 6.45 | | 13.30 | 17.25 |
| 1870 | 1-1/2" diameter | | 51 | .157 | | 8 | 7.35 | | 15.35 | 19.80 |
| 1880 | 2" diameter | | 40 | .200 | | 10.35 | 9.35 | | 19.70 | 25.50 |
| 1890 | 2-1/2" diameter | Q-1 | 57 | .281 | | 15.75 | 11.80 | | 27.55 | 35 |
| 1900 | 3" diameter | | 50 | .320 | | 20 | 13.45 | | 33.45 | 42.50 |
| 1910 | 4" diameter | | 45 | .356 | | 28 | 14.95 | | 42.95 | 53.50 |
| 1920 | 5" diameter | | 37 | .432 | | 30 | 18.20 | | 48.20 | 60.50 |
| 1930 | 6" diameter | Q-2 | 42 | .571 | | 42.50 | 25 | | 67.50 | 84 |

| 22 11 13.48 Pipe, Fittings and Valves, Steel, Grooved-Joint | Crew | Daily Output | Labor-Hours | Unit | Material | 2008 Bare Costs Labor | Equipment | Total | Total Incl O&P |
|---|---|---|---|---|---|---|---|---|---|
| 3990 | Fittings: coupling material required at joints not incl. in fitting price. | | | | | | | | |
| 3994 | Add 1 selected coupling, material only, per joint for installed price. | | | | | | | | |
| 4000 | Elbow, 90° or 45°, painted | | | | | | | | |
| 4030 | 3/4" diameter | 1 Plum | 50 | .160 | Ea. | 29 | 7.45 | | 36.45 | 43.50 |
| 4040 | 1" diameter | | 50 | .160 | | 15.50 | 7.45 | | 22.95 | 28.50 |
| 4050 | 1-1/4" diameter | | 40 | .200 | | 15.50 | 9.35 | | 24.85 | 31 |
| 4060 | 1-1/2" diameter | | 33 | .242 | | 15.50 | 11.30 | | 26.80 | 34 |
| 4070 | 2" diameter | | 25 | .320 | | 15.50 | 14.95 | | 30.45 | 39.50 |
| 4080 | 2-1/2" diameter | Q-1 | 40 | .400 | | 15.50 | 16.80 | | 32.30 | 42.50 |
| 4090 | 3" diameter | | 33 | .485 | | 27.50 | 20.50 | | 48 | 60.50 |
| 4100 | 4" diameter | | 25 | .640 | | 30 | 27 | | 57 | 73.50 |
| 4110 | 5" diameter | | 20 | .800 | | 72 | 33.50 | | 105.50 | 130 |
| 4120 | 6" diameter | Q-2 | 25 | .960 | | 84.50 | 42 | | 126.50 | 156 |
| 4250 | For galvanized elbows, add | | | | | 26% | | | | |
| 4690 | Tee, painted | | | | | | | | | |
| 4700 | 3/4" diameter | 1 Plum | 38 | .211 | Ea. | 31.50 | 9.85 | | 41.35 | 49.50 |
| 4740 | 1" diameter | | 33 | .242 | | 24 | 11.30 | | 35.30 | 43.50 |
| 4750 | 1-1/4" diameter | | 27 | .296 | | 24 | 13.85 | | 37.85 | 47.50 |
| 4760 | 1-1/2" diameter | | 22 | .364 | | 24 | 17 | | 41 | 52 |
| 4770 | 2" diameter | | 17 | .471 | | 24 | 22 | | 46 | 59.50 |
| 4780 | 2-1/2" diameter | Q-1 | 27 | .593 | | 24 | 25 | | 49 | 64 |
| 4790 | 3" diameter | | 22 | .727 | | 33.50 | 30.50 | | 64 | 82.50 |
| 4800 | 4" diameter | | 17 | .941 | | 50.50 | 39.50 | | 90 | 116 |
| 4810 | 5" diameter | | 13 | 1.231 | | 119 | 51.50 | | 170.50 | 209 |
| 4820 | 6" diameter | Q-2 | 17 | 1.412 | | 137 | 61.50 | | 198.50 | 244 |
| 4900 | For galvanized tees, add | | | | | 24% | | | | |
| 4906 | Couplings, rigid style, painted | | | | | | | | | |
| 4908 | 1" diameter | 1 Plum | 100 | .080 | Ea. | 11.50 | 3.74 | | 15.24 | 18.25 |
| 4909 | 1-1/4" diameter | | 100 | .080 | | 11.50 | 3.74 | | 15.24 | 18.25 |
| 4910 | 1-1/2" diameter | | 67 | .119 | | 11.50 | 5.60 | | 17.10 | 21 |
| 4912 | 2" diameter | | 50 | .160 | | 11.80 | 7.45 | | 19.25 | 24.50 |
| 4914 | 2-1/2" diameter | Q-1 | 80 | .200 | | 13.50 | 8.40 | | 21.90 | 27.50 |
| 4916 | 3" diameter | | 67 | .239 | | 15.80 | 10.05 | | 25.85 | 32.50 |
| 4918 | 4" diameter | | 50 | .320 | | 22.50 | 13.45 | | 35.95 | 44.50 |
| 4920 | 5" diameter | | 40 | .400 | | 29 | 16.80 | | 45.80 | 57.50 |
| 4922 | 6" diameter | Q-2 | 50 | .480 | | 38.50 | 21 | | 59.50 | 74 |
| 4940 | Flexible, standard, painted | | | | | | | | | |
| 4950 | 3/4" diameter | 1 Plum | 100 | .080 | Ea. | 8.30 | 3.74 | | 12.04 | 14.75 |
| 4960 | 1" diameter | | 100 | .080 | | 8.30 | 3.74 | | 12.04 | 14.75 |
| 4970 | 1-1/4" diameter | | 80 | .100 | | 11 | 4.67 | | 15.67 | 19.15 |
| 4980 | 1-1/2" diameter | | 67 | .119 | | 12 | 5.60 | | 17.60 | 21.50 |
| 4990 | 2" diameter | | 50 | .160 | | 12.80 | 7.45 | | 20.25 | 25.50 |
| 5000 | 2-1/2" diameter | Q-1 | 80 | .200 | | 15.10 | 8.40 | | 23.50 | 29.50 |
| 5010 | 3" diameter | | 67 | .239 | | 16.70 | 10.05 | | 26.75 | 33.50 |
| 5020 | 3-1/2" diameter | | 57 | .281 | | 24.50 | 11.80 | | 36.30 | 44.50 |
| 5030 | 4" diameter | | 50 | .320 | | 24.50 | 13.45 | | 37.95 | 46.50 |
| 5040 | 5" diameter | | 40 | .400 | | 37 | 16.80 | | 53.80 | 66 |
| 5050 | 6" diameter | Q-2 | 50 | .480 | | 44 | 21 | | 65 | 79.50 |

## 22 11 13.64 Pipe, Stainless Steel

| | | | | | | | | | |
|---|---|---|---|---|---|---|---|---|---|
| 0010 | **PIPE, STAINLESS STEEL** | | | | | | | | | |
| 3500 | Threaded, couplings and clevis hanger assemblies, 10' O.C. | | | | | | | | | |
| 3520 | Schedule 40, type 304 | | | | | | | | | |

# 22 11 Facility Water Distribution

## 22 11 13 – Facility Water Distribution Piping

### 22 11 13.64 Pipe, Stainless Steel

| | | Crew | Daily Output | Labor-Hours | Unit | Material | 2008 Bare Costs Labor | Equipment | Total | Total Incl O&P |
|---|---|---|---|---|---|---|---|---|---|---|
| 3540 | 1/4" diameter | 1 Plum | 54 | .148 | L.F. | 5.10 | 6.90 | | 12 | 16.05 |
| 3550 | 3/8" diameter | | 53 | .151 | | 6.35 | 7.05 | | 13.40 | 17.60 |
| 3560 | 1/2" diameter | | 52 | .154 | | 5.60 | 7.20 | | 12.80 | 16.95 |
| 3580 | 1" diameter | | 45 | .178 | | 11.65 | 8.30 | | 19.95 | 25.50 |
| 3610 | 2" diameter | Q-1 | 57 | .281 | | 25 | 11.80 | | 36.80 | 45.50 |
| 3640 | 4" diameter | Q-2 | 51 | .471 | | 76 | 20.50 | | 96.50 | 115 |
| 3740 | For small quantities, add | | | | | 10% | | | | |
| 4250 | Schedule 40, type 316 | | | | | | | | | |
| 4290 | 1/4" diameter | 1 Plum | 54 | .148 | L.F. | 6.35 | 6.90 | | 13.25 | 17.40 |
| 4300 | 3/8" diameter | | 53 | .151 | | 7.25 | 7.05 | | 14.30 | 18.55 |
| 4310 | 1/2" diameter | | 52 | .154 | | 9.10 | 7.20 | | 16.30 | 21 |
| 4320 | 3/4" diameter | | 51 | .157 | | 11.95 | 7.35 | | 19.30 | 24 |
| 4330 | 1" diameter | | 45 | .178 | | 16.10 | 8.30 | | 24.40 | 30.50 |
| 4360 | 2" diameter | Q-1 | 57 | .281 | | 35.50 | 11.80 | | 47.30 | 57 |
| 4390 | 4" diameter | Q-2 | 51 | .471 | | 114 | 20.50 | | 134.50 | 156 |
| 4490 | For small quantities, add | | | | | 10% | | | | |

### 22 11 13.74 Pipe, Plastic

| | | Crew | Daily Output | Labor-Hours | Unit | Material | 2008 Bare Costs Labor | Equipment | Total | Total Incl O&P |
|---|---|---|---|---|---|---|---|---|---|---|
| 0010 | **PIPE, PLASTIC** | | | | | | | | | |
| 1800 | PVC, couplings 10' O.C., clevis hanger assy's, 3 per 10' | | | | | | | | | |
| 1820 | Schedule 40 | | | | | | | | | |
| 1860 | 1/2" diameter | 1 Plum | 54 | .148 | L.F. | 1.08 | 6.90 | | 7.98 | 11.60 |
| 1870 | 3/4" diameter | | 51 | .157 | | 1.25 | 7.35 | | 8.60 | 12.40 |
| 1880 | 1" diameter | | 46 | .174 | | 1.55 | 8.10 | | 9.65 | 13.90 |
| 1890 | 1-1/4" diameter | | 42 | .190 | | 1.95 | 8.90 | | 10.85 | 15.55 |
| 1900 | 1-1/2" diameter | | 36 | .222 | | 2.09 | 10.40 | | 12.49 | 17.90 |
| 1910 | 2" diameter   *CN* | Q-1 | 59 | .271 | | 2.07 | 11.40 | | 13.47 | 19.40 |
| 1920 | 2-1/2" diameter | | 56 | .286 | | 3.97 | 12 | | 15.97 | 22.50 |
| 1930 | 3" diameter | | 53 | .302 | | 4.57 | 12.70 | | 17.27 | 24 |
| 1940 | 4" diameter | | 48 | .333 | | 6.70 | 14 | | 20.70 | 28.50 |
| 1950 | 5" diameter | | 43 | .372 | | 9.10 | 15.65 | | 24.75 | 33.50 |
| 1960 | 6" diameter | | 39 | .410 | | 12.35 | 17.25 | | 29.60 | 39.50 |
| 4100 | DWV type, schedule 40, couplings 10' O.C., clevis hanger assy's, 3 per 10' | | | | | | | | | |
| 4120 | ABS | | | | | | | | | |
| 4140 | 1-1/4" diameter | 1 Plum | 42 | .190 | L.F. | 1.48 | 8.90 | | 10.38 | 15.05 |
| 4150 | 1-1/2" diameter | " | 36 | .222 | | 1.63 | 10.40 | | 12.03 | 17.40 |
| 4160 | 2" diameter | Q-1 | 59 | .271 | | 1.95 | 11.40 | | 13.35 | 19.30 |
| 4400 | PVC | | | | | | | | | |
| 4410 | 1-1/4" diameter | 1 Plum | 42 | .190 | L.F. | 1.72 | 8.90 | | 10.62 | 15.30 |
| 4420 | 1-1/2" diameter | " | 36 | .222 | | 1.72 | 10.40 | | 12.12 | 17.50 |
| 4460 | 2" diameter | Q-1 | 59 | .271 | | 2.07 | 11.40 | | 13.47 | 19.45 |
| 4470 | 3" diameter | | 53 | .302 | | 4.04 | 12.70 | | 16.74 | 23.50 |
| 4480 | 4" diameter | | 48 | .333 | | 5.50 | 14 | | 19.50 | 27 |
| 4490 | 6" diameter | | 39 | .410 | | 10.05 | 17.25 | | 27.30 | 37 |
| 5360 | CPVC, couplings 10' O.C., clevis hanger assy's, 3 per 10' | | | | | | | | | |
| 5380 | Schedule 40 | | | | | | | | | |
| 5460 | 1/2" diameter | 1 Plum | 54 | .148 | L.F. | 2.39 | 6.90 | | 9.29 | 13.05 |
| 5470 | 3/4" diameter | | 51 | .157 | | 3.26 | 7.35 | | 10.61 | 14.60 |
| 5480 | 1" diameter | | 46 | .174 | | 4.08 | 8.10 | | 12.18 | 16.70 |
| 5490 | 1-1/4" diameter | | 42 | .190 | | 4.77 | 8.90 | | 13.67 | 18.65 |
| 5500 | 1-1/2" diameter | | 36 | .222 | | 5.40 | 10.40 | | 15.80 | 21.50 |
| 5510 | 2" diameter | Q-1 | 59 | .271 | | 6.65 | 11.40 | | 18.05 | 24.50 |
| 5520 | 2-1/2" diameter | | 56 | .286 | | 11 | 12 | | 23 | 30 |

# 22 11 Facility Water Distribution

## 22 11 13 – Facility Water Distribution Piping

| 22 11 13.74 Pipe, Plastic | Crew | Daily Output | Labor-Hours | Unit | Material | 2008 Bare Costs Labor | Equipment | Total | Total Incl O&P |
|---|---|---|---|---|---|---|---|---|---|
| 5530      3" diameter | Q-1 | 53 | .302 | L.F. | 13.50 | 12.70 | | 26.20 | 34 |

## 22 11 19 – Domestic Water Piping Specialties

### 22 11 19.10 Flexible Connectors

| | | Crew | Daily Output | Labor-Hours | Unit | Material | Labor | Equipment | Total | Total Incl O&P |
|---|---|---|---|---|---|---|---|---|---|---|
| 0010 | **FLEXIBLE CONNECTORS**, Corrugated, 7/8" O.D., 1/2" I.D. | | | | | | | | | |
| 0050 | Gas, seamless brass, steel fittings | | | | | | | | | |
| 0200 |      12" long | 1 Plum | 36 | .222 | Ea. | 13.70 | 10.40 | | 24.10 | 30.50 |
| 0220 |      18" long | | 36 | .222 | | 17 | 10.40 | | 27.40 | 34.50 |
| 0240 |      24" long | | 34 | .235 | | 20 | 11 | | 31 | 38.50 |
| 0280 |      36" long | | 32 | .250 | | 24 | 11.70 | | 35.70 | 44 |
| 0340 |      60" long | | 30 | .267 | | 36 | 12.45 | | 48.45 | 59 |
| 2000 | Water, copper tubing, dielectric separators | | | | | | | | | |
| 2100 |      12" long | 1 Plum | 36 | .222 | Ea. | 14 | 10.40 | | 24.40 | 31 |
| 2260 |      24" long | " | 34 | .235 | " | 20.50 | 11 | | 31.50 | 39 |

### 22 11 19.14 Flexible Metal Hose

| | | Crew | Daily Output | Labor-Hours | Unit | Material | Labor | Equipment | Total | Total Incl O&P |
|---|---|---|---|---|---|---|---|---|---|---|
| 0010 | **FLEXIBLE METAL HOSE**, Connectors, standard lengths | | | | | | | | | |
| 0100 | Bronze braided, bronze ends | | | | | | | | | |
| 0120 |      3/8" diameter x 12" | 1 Stpi | 26 | .308 | Ea. | 16.95 | 14.50 | | 31.45 | 40.50 |
| 0160 |      3/4" diameter x 12" | | 20 | .400 | | 23.50 | 18.85 | | 42.35 | 54.50 |
| 0180 |      1" diameter x 18" | | 19 | .421 | | 30.50 | 19.85 | | 50.35 | 63.50 |
| 0200 |      1-1/2" diameter x 18" | | 13 | .615 | | 48.50 | 29 | | 77.50 | 96.50 |
| 0220 |      2" diameter x 18" | | 11 | .727 | | 58 | 34.50 | | 92.50 | 116 |

### 22 11 19.26 Pressure Regulators

| | | Crew | Daily Output | Labor-Hours | Unit | Material | Labor | Equipment | Total | Total Incl O&P |
|---|---|---|---|---|---|---|---|---|---|---|
| 0010 | **PRESSURE REGULATORS** | | | | | | | | | |
| 3000 | Steam, high capacity, bronze body, stainless steel trim | | | | | | | | | |
| 3020 |      Threaded, 1/2" diameter | 1 Stpi | 24 | .333 | Ea. | 1,200 | 15.70 | | 1,215.70 | 1,325 |
| 3030 |      3/4" diameter | | 24 | .333 | | 1,200 | 15.70 | | 1,215.70 | 1,325 |
| 3040 |      1" diameter | | 19 | .421 | | 1,325 | 19.85 | | 1,344.85 | 1,475 |
| 3060 |      1-1/4" diameter | | 15 | .533 | | 1,475 | 25 | | 1,500 | 1,675 |
| 3080 |      1-1/2" diameter | | 13 | .615 | | 1,675 | 29 | | 1,704 | 1,900 |
| 3100 |      2" diameter | | 11 | .727 | | 2,050 | 34.50 | | 2,084.50 | 2,325 |
| 3120 |      2-1/2" diameter | Q-5 | 12 | 1.333 | | 2,575 | 56.50 | | 2,631.50 | 2,900 |
| 3140 |      3" diameter | " | 11 | 1.455 | | 2,950 | 61.50 | | 3,011.50 | 3,325 |
| 3500 | Flanged connection, iron body, 125 lb. W.S.P. | | | | | | | | | |
| 3520 |      3" diameter | Q-5 | 11 | 1.455 | Ea. | 3,225 | 61.50 | | 3,286.50 | 3,650 |
| 3540 |      4" diameter | " | 5 | 3.200 | " | 4,050 | 136 | | 4,186 | 4,675 |

### 22 11 19.38 Water Supply Meters

| | | Crew | Daily Output | Labor-Hours | Unit | Material | Labor | Equipment | Total | Total Incl O&P |
|---|---|---|---|---|---|---|---|---|---|---|
| 0010 | **WATER SUPPLY METERS** | | | | | | | | | |
| 2000 | Domestic/commercial, bronze | | | | | | | | | |
| 2020 | Threaded | | | | | | | | | |
| 2060 |      5/8" diameter, to 20 GPM | 1 Plum | 16 | .500 | Ea. | 38.50 | 23.50 | | 62 | 77.50 |
| 2080 |      3/4" diameter, to 30 GPM | | 14 | .571 | | 71 | 26.50 | | 97.50 | 119 |
| 2100 |      1" diameter, to 50 GPM | | 12 | .667 | | 108 | 31 | | 139 | 165 |
| 2300 | Threaded/flanged | | | | | | | | | |
| 2340 |      1-1/2" diameter, to 100 GPM | 1 Plum | 8 | 1 | Ea. | 263 | 46.50 | | 309.50 | 360 |
| 2360 |      2" diameter, to 160 GPM | " | 6 | 1.333 | " | 355 | 62.50 | | 417.50 | 485 |
| 2600 | Flanged, compound | | | | | | | | | |
| 2640 |      3" diameter, 320 GPM | Q-1 | 3 | 5.333 | Ea. | 2,275 | 224 | | 2,499 | 2,825 |
| 2660 |      4" diameter, to 500 GPM | | 1.50 | 10.667 | | 3,650 | 450 | | 4,100 | 4,675 |
| 2680 |      6" diameter, to 1,000 GPM | | 1 | 16 | | 5,825 | 670 | | 6,495 | 7,400 |
| 2700 |      8" diameter, to 1,800 GPM | | .80 | 20 | | 9,125 | 840 | | 9,965 | 11,300 |

435

### 22 11 19.42 Backflow Preventers

| | | Crew | Daily Output | Labor-Hours | Unit | Material | 2008 Bare Costs Labor | Equipment | Total | Total Incl O&P |
|---|---|---|---|---|---|---|---|---|---|---|
| 0010 | **BACKFLOW PREVENTERS**, Includes valves | | | | | | | | | |
| 0020 | and four test cocks, corrosion resistant, automatic operation | | | | | | | | | |
| 4000 | Reduced pressure principle | | | | | | | | | |
| 4100 | Threaded, bronze, valves are ball | | | | | | | | | |
| 4120 | 3/4" pipe size | 1 Plum | 16 | .500 | Ea. | 286 | 23.50 | | 309.50 | 350 |
| 4140 | 1" pipe size | | 14 | .571 | | 310 | 26.50 | | 336.50 | 380 |
| 4150 | 1-1/4" pipe size | | 12 | .667 | | 530 | 31 | | 561 | 625 |
| 4160 | 1-1/2" pipe size | | 10 | .800 | | 580 | 37.50 | | 617.50 | 690 |
| 4180 | 2" pipe size | ↓ | 7 | 1.143 | ↓ | 650 | 53.50 | | 703.50 | 795 |
| 5000 | Flanged, bronze, valves are OS&Y | | | | | | | | | |
| 5060 | 2-1/2" pipe size | Q-1 | 5 | 3.200 | Ea. | 2,900 | 135 | | 3,035 | 3,400 |
| 5080 | 3" pipe size | | 4.50 | 3.556 | | 3,050 | 149 | | 3,199 | 3,575 |
| 5100 | 4" pipe size | ↓ | 3 | 5.333 | | 3,825 | 224 | | 4,049 | 4,550 |
| 5120 | 6" pipe size | Q-2 | 3 | 8 | ↓ | 5,550 | 350 | | 5,900 | 6,625 |
| 5600 | Flanged, iron, valves are OS&Y | | | | | | | | | |
| 5660 | 2-1/2" pipe size | Q-1 | 5 | 3.200 | Ea. | 2,325 | 135 | | 2,460 | 2,750 |
| 5680 | 3" pipe size | | 4.50 | 3.556 | | 2,450 | 149 | | 2,599 | 2,900 |
| 5700 | 4" pipe size | ↓ | 3 | 5.333 | | 3,075 | 224 | | 3,299 | 3,700 |
| 5720 | 6" pipe size | Q-2 | 3 | 8 | | 4,425 | 350 | | 4,775 | 5,400 |
| 5740 | 8" pipe size | | 2 | 12 | | 7,800 | 525 | | 8,325 | 9,350 |
| 5760 | 10" pipe size | ↓ | 1 | 24 | ↓ | 10,400 | 1,050 | | 11,450 | 13,100 |

### 22 11 19.46 Vacuum Breakers

| | | Crew | Daily Output | Labor-Hours | Unit | Material | 2008 Bare Costs Labor | Equipment | Total | Total Incl O&P |
|---|---|---|---|---|---|---|---|---|---|---|
| 0010 | **VACUUM BREAKERS**, Hot or cold water | | | | | | | | | |
| 1030 | Anti-siphon, brass | | | | | | | | | |
| 1040 | 1/4" size | 1 Plum | 24 | .333 | Ea. | 32 | 15.55 | | 47.55 | 58.50 |
| 1050 | 3/8" size | | 24 | .333 | | 32 | 15.55 | | 47.55 | 58.50 |
| 1060 | 1/2" size | | 24 | .333 | | 36 | 15.55 | | 51.55 | 63 |
| 1080 | 3/4" size | | 20 | .400 | | 42.50 | 18.70 | | 61.20 | 75 |
| 1100 | 1" size | | 19 | .421 | | 66.50 | 19.65 | | 86.15 | 103 |
| 1120 | 1-1/4" size | | 15 | .533 | | 112 | 25 | | 137 | 162 |
| 1140 | 1-1/2" size | | 13 | .615 | | 137 | 28.50 | | 165.50 | 194 |
| 1160 | 2" size | ↓ | 11 | .727 | ↓ | 214 | 34 | | 248 | 286 |
| 1300 | For polished chrome, (1/4" thru 1"), add | | | | | 50% | | | | |
| 1900 | Vacuum relief, water service, bronze | | | | | | | | | |
| 2000 | 1/2" size | 1 Plum | 30 | .267 | Ea. | 31.50 | 12.45 | | 43.95 | 54 |

### 22 11 19.54 Water Hammer Arresters/Shock Absorbers

| | | Crew | Daily Output | Labor-Hours | Unit | Material | 2008 Bare Costs Labor | Equipment | Total | Total Incl O&P |
|---|---|---|---|---|---|---|---|---|---|---|
| 0010 | **WATER HAMMER ARRESTERS/SHOCK ABSORBERS** | | | | | | | | | |
| 0490 | Copper | | | | | | | | | |
| 0500 | 3/4" male I.P.S. For 1 to 11 fixtures | 1 Plum | 12 | .667 | Ea. | 15.55 | 31 | | 46.55 | 64 |
| 0600 | 1" male I.P.S., For 12 to 32 fixtures | | 8 | 1 | | 39.50 | 46.50 | | 86 | 114 |
| 0700 | 1-1/4" male I.P.S. For 33 to 60 fixtures | | 8 | 1 | | 46 | 46.50 | | 92.50 | 121 |
| 0800 | 1-1/2" male I.P.S. For 61 to 113 fixtures | | 8 | 1 | | 62.50 | 46.50 | | 109 | 140 |
| 0900 | 2" male I.P.S. For 114 to 154 fixtures | | 8 | 1 | | 100 | 46.50 | | 146.50 | 181 |
| 1000 | 2-1/2" male I.P.S. For 155 to 330 fixtures | ↓ | 4 | 2 | ↓ | 285 | 93.50 | | 378.50 | 455 |

### 22 11 19.64 Hydrants

| | | Crew | Daily Output | Labor-Hours | Unit | Material | 2008 Bare Costs Labor | Equipment | Total | Total Incl O&P |
|---|---|---|---|---|---|---|---|---|---|---|
| 0010 | **HYDRANTS** | | | | | | | | | |
| 0050 | Wall type, moderate climate, bronze, encased | | | | | | | | | |
| 0200 | 3/4" IPS connection | 1 Plum | 16 | .500 | Ea. | 480 | 23.50 | | 503.50 | 560 |
| 0300 | 1" IPS connection | " | 14 | .571 | | 550 | 26.50 | | 576.50 | 645 |
| 0500 | Anti-siphon type, 3/4" connection | | | | ↓ | 415 | | | 415 | 455 |
| 1000 | Non-freeze, bronze, exposed | | | | | | | | | |

# 22 11 Facility Water Distribution

## 22 11 19 – Domestic Water Piping Specialties

### 22 11 19.64 Hydrants

| | Crew | Daily Output | Labor-Hours | Unit | Material | 2008 Bare Costs Labor | Equipment | Total | Total Incl O&P |
|---|---|---|---|---|---|---|---|---|---|
| 1100 | 3/4" IPS connection, 4" to 9" thick wall | 1 Plum | 14 | .571 | Ea. | 325 | 26.50 | | 351.50 | 395 |
| 1120 | 10" to 14" thick wall | | 12 | .667 | | 350 | 31 | | 381 | 430 |
| 1140 | 15" to 19" thick wall | | 12 | .667 | | 420 | 31 | | 451 | 505 |
| 1160 | 20" to 24" thick wall | | 10 | .800 | | 425 | 37.50 | | 462.50 | 520 |
| 1200 | For 1" IPS connection, add | | | | | 15% | 10% | | | |
| 1240 | For 3/4" adapter type vacuum breaker, add | | | | Ea. | 35 | | | 35 | 38.50 |
| 1280 | For anti-siphon type, add | | | | " | 79 | | | 79 | 87 |
| 2000 | Non-freeze bronze, encased, anti-siphon type | | | | | | | | | |
| 2100 | 3/4" IPS connection, 5" to 9" thick wall | 1 Plum | 14 | .571 | Ea. | 825 | 26.50 | | 851.50 | 950 |
| 2140 | 15" to 19" thick wall | " | 12 | .667 | " | 885 | 31 | | 916 | 1,025 |
| 3000 | Ground box type, bronze frame, 3/4" IPS connection | | | | | | | | | |
| 3080 | Non-freeze, all bronze, polished face, set flush | | | | | | | | | |
| 3100 | 2 feet depth of bury | 1 Plum | 8 | 1 | Ea. | 595 | 46.50 | | 641.50 | 725 |
| 3180 | 6 feet depth of bury | | 7 | 1.143 | | 780 | 53.50 | | 833.50 | 935 |
| 3220 | 8 feet depth of bury | | 5 | 1.600 | | 870 | 74.50 | | 944.50 | 1,075 |
| 3400 | For 1" IPS connection, add | | | | | 15% | 10% | | | |
| 3550 | For 2" connection, add | | | | | 445% | 24% | | | |
| 3600 | For tapped drain port in box, add | | | | | 55.50 | | | 55.50 | 61 |
| 5000 | Moderate climate, all bronze, polished face | | | | | | | | | |
| 5020 | and scoriated cover, set flush | | | | | | | | | |
| 5100 | 3/4" IPS connection | 1 Plum | 16 | .500 | Ea. | 425 | 23.50 | | 448.50 | 500 |
| 5120 | 1" IPS connection | " | 14 | .571 | | 520 | 26.50 | | 546.50 | 615 |
| 5200 | For tapped drain port in box, add | | | | | 55.50 | | | 55.50 | 61 |

## 22 11 23 – Domestic Water Pumps

### 22 11 23.10 General Utility Pumps

| | Crew | Daily Output | Labor-Hours | Unit | Material | 2008 Bare Costs Labor | Equipment | Total | Total Incl O&P |
|---|---|---|---|---|---|---|---|---|---|
| 0010 | **GENERAL UTILITY PUMPS** | | | | | | | | | |
| 2000 | Single stage | | | | | | | | | |
| 3000 | Double suction, | | | | | | | | | |
| 3190 | 75 HP, to 2500 GPM | Q-3 | .28 | 114 | Ea. | 14,500 | 5,075 | | 19,575 | 23,600 |
| 3220 | 100 HP, to 3000 GPM | | .26 | 123 | | 18,400 | 5,475 | | 23,875 | 28,500 |
| 3240 | 150 HP, to 4000 GPM | | .24 | 133 | | 29,200 | 5,925 | | 35,125 | 41,000 |

# 22 13 Facility Sanitary Sewerage

## 22 13 16 – Sanitary Waste and Vent Piping

### 22 13 16.20 Pipe, Cast Iron

| | Crew | Daily Output | Labor-Hours | Unit | Material | 2008 Bare Costs Labor | Equipment | Total | Total Incl O&P |
|---|---|---|---|---|---|---|---|---|---|
| 0010 | **PIPE, CAST IRON**, Soil, on clevis hanger assemblies, 5' O.C. | | | | | | | | | |
| 0020 | Single hub, service wt., lead & oakum joints 10' O.C. | | | | | | | | | |
| 2120 | 2" diameter | Q-1 | 63 | .254 | L.F. | 6.05 | 10.65 | | 16.70 | 22.50 |
| 2140 | 3" diameter | | 60 | .267 | | 8.50 | 11.20 | | 19.70 | 26 |
| 2160 | 4" diameter **CN** | | 55 | .291 | | 10.95 | 12.25 | | 23.20 | 30.50 |
| 2180 | 5" diameter | Q-2 | 76 | .316 | | 15.15 | 13.75 | | 28.90 | 37 |
| 2200 | 6" diameter | " | 73 | .329 | | 18.60 | 14.35 | | 32.95 | 42 |
| 2220 | 8" diameter | Q-3 | 59 | .542 | | 28.50 | 24 | | 52.50 | 68 |
| 2240 | 10" diameter | | 54 | .593 | | 47.50 | 26.50 | | 74 | 91.50 |
| 2260 | 12" diameter | | 48 | .667 | | 68 | 29.50 | | 97.50 | 119 |
| 2320 | For service weight, double hub, add | | | | | 10% | | | | |
| 2340 | For extra heavy, single hub, add | | | | | 48% | 4% | | | |
| 2360 | For extra heavy, double hub, add | | | | | 71% | 4% | | | |
| 2400 | Lead for caulking, (1#/dia in) | Q-1 | 160 | .100 | Lb. | 1.04 | 4.20 | | 5.24 | 7.45 |
| 2420 | Oakum for caulking, (1/8#/dia in) | " | 40 | .400 | " | 3.95 | 16.80 | | 20.75 | 30 |

437

# 22 13 Facility Sanitary Sewerage

## 22 13 16 – Sanitary Waste and Vent Piping

### 22 13 16.20 Pipe, Cast Iron

| | | Crew | Daily Output | Labor-Hours | Unit | Material | 2008 Bare Costs Labor | 2008 Bare Costs Equipment | Total | Total Incl O&P |
|---|---|---|---|---|---|---|---|---|---|---|
| 4000 | No hub, couplings 10' O.C. | | | | | | | | | |
| 4100 | 1-1/2" diameter | Q-1 | 71 | .225 | L.F. | 6.60 | 9.45 | | 16.05 | 21.50 |
| 4120 | 2" diameter | | 67 | .239 | | 6.85 | 10.05 | | 16.90 | 22.50 |
| 4160 | 4" diameter | | 58 | .276 | | 11.90 | 11.60 | | 23.50 | 30.50 |

### 22 13 16.50 Shower Drains

| | | Crew | Daily Output | Labor-Hours | Unit | Material | 2008 Bare Costs Labor | 2008 Bare Costs Equipment | Total | Total Incl O&P |
|---|---|---|---|---|---|---|---|---|---|---|
| 0010 | **SHOWER DRAINS** | | | | | | | | | |
| 2780 | Shower, with strainer, uniform diam. trap, bronze top | | | | | | | | | |
| 2800 | 2" and 3" pipe size | Q-1 | 8 | 2 | Ea. | 266 | 84 | | 350 | 420 |
| 2820 | 4" pipe size | " | 7 | 2.286 | | 294 | 96 | | 390 | 470 |
| 2840 | For galvanized body, add | | | | | 118 | | | 118 | 130 |

### 22 13 16.60 Traps

| | | Crew | Daily Output | Labor-Hours | Unit | Material | 2008 Bare Costs Labor | 2008 Bare Costs Equipment | Total | Total Incl O&P |
|---|---|---|---|---|---|---|---|---|---|---|
| 0010 | **TRAPS** | | | | | | | | | |
| 0030 | Cast iron, service weight | | | | | | | | | |
| 0050 | Running P trap, without vent | | | | | | | | | |
| 1100 | 2" | Q-1 | 16 | 1 | Ea. | 94.50 | 42 | | 136.50 | 167 |
| 1140 | 3" | | 14 | 1.143 | | 94.50 | 48 | | 142.50 | 176 |
| 1150 | 4" | | 13 | 1.231 | | 94.50 | 51.50 | | 146 | 182 |
| 1160 | 6" | Q-2 | 17 | 1.412 | | 415 | 61.50 | | 476.50 | 550 |
| 1180 | Running trap, single hub, with vent | | | | | | | | | |
| 2080 | 3" pipe size, 3" vent | Q-1 | 14 | 1.143 | Ea. | 75 | 48 | | 123 | 155 |
| 2120 | 4" pipe size, 4" vent | " | 13 | 1.231 | | 101 | 51.50 | | 152.50 | 189 |
| 2300 | For double hub, vent, add | | | | | 10% | 20% | | | |
| 3000 | P trap, B&S, 2" pipe size | Q-1 | 16 | 1 | | 22.50 | 42 | | 64.50 | 87.50 |
| 3040 | 3" pipe size | " | 14 | 1.143 | | 33.50 | 48 | | 81.50 | 109 |
| 3350 | Deep seal trap, B&S | | | | | | | | | |
| 3400 | 1-1/4" pipe size | Q-1 | 14 | 1.143 | Ea. | 38.50 | 48 | | 86.50 | 115 |
| 3410 | 1-1/2" pipe size | | 14 | 1.143 | | 38.50 | 48 | | 86.50 | 115 |
| 3420 | 2" pipe size | | 14 | 1.143 | | 30 | 48 | | 78 | 106 |
| 3440 | 3" pipe size | | 12 | 1.333 | | 41 | 56 | | 97 | 130 |
| 4700 | Copper, drainage, drum trap | | | | | | | | | |
| 4800 | 3" x 5" solid, 1-1/2" pipe size | 1 Plum | 16 | .500 | Ea. | 81.50 | 23.50 | | 105 | 125 |
| 4840 | 3" x 6" swivel, 1-1/2" pipe size | " | 16 | .500 | " | 129 | 23.50 | | 152.50 | 177 |
| 5100 | P trap, standard pattern | | | | | | | | | |
| 5200 | 1-1/4" pipe size | 1 Plum | 18 | .444 | Ea. | 61 | 21 | | 82 | 98 |
| 5240 | 1-1/2" pipe size | | 17 | .471 | | 58 | 22 | | 80 | 97 |
| 5260 | 2" pipe size | | 15 | .533 | | 99 | 25 | | 124 | 147 |
| 5280 | 3" pipe size | | 11 | .727 | | 216 | 34 | | 250 | 288 |
| 5340 | With cleanout and slip joint | | | | | | | | | |
| 5360 | 1-1/4" pipe size | 1 Plum | 18 | .444 | Ea. | 55.50 | 21 | | 76.50 | 92.50 |
| 5400 | 1-1/2" pipe size | " | 17 | .471 | " | 88.50 | 22 | | 110.50 | 131 |

### 22 13 16.80 Vent Flashing and Caps

| | | Crew | Daily Output | Labor-Hours | Unit | Material | 2008 Bare Costs Labor | 2008 Bare Costs Equipment | Total | Total Incl O&P |
|---|---|---|---|---|---|---|---|---|---|---|
| 0010 | **VENT FLASHING AND CAPS** | | | | | | | | | |
| 0120 | Vent caps | | | | | | | | | |
| 0140 | Cast iron | | | | | | | | | |
| 0180 | 2-1/2" - 3-5/8" pipe | 1 Plum | 21 | .381 | Ea. | 36.50 | 17.80 | | 54.30 | 67 |
| 0190 | 4" - 4-1/8" pipe | " | 19 | .421 | " | 44 | 19.65 | | 63.65 | 77.50 |
| 0900 | Vent flashing | | | | | | | | | |
| 1000 | Aluminum with lead ring | | | | | | | | | |
| 1020 | 1-1/4" pipe | 1 Plum | 20 | .400 | Ea. | 9 | 18.70 | | 27.70 | 38 |
| 1030 | 1-1/2" pipe | | 20 | .400 | | 9.65 | 18.70 | | 28.35 | 38.50 |
| 1040 | 2" pipe | | 18 | .444 | | 9.65 | 21 | | 30.65 | 41.50 |
| 1050 | 3" pipe | | 17 | .471 | | 10.65 | 22 | | 32.65 | 45 |

# 22 13 Facility Sanitary Sewerage

## 22 13 16 – Sanitary Waste and Vent Piping

### 22 13 16.80 Vent Flashing and Caps

| | | Crew | Daily Output | Labor-Hours | Unit | Material | 2008 Bare Costs Labor | Equipment | Total | Total Incl O&P |
|---|---|---|---|---|---|---|---|---|---|---|
| 1060 | 4" pipe | 1 Plum | 16 | .500 | Ea. | 12.85 | 23.50 | | 36.35 | 49 |
| 1350 | Copper with neoprene ring | | | | | | | | | |
| 1400 | 1-1/4" pipe | 1 Plum | 20 | .400 | Ea. | 19.95 | 18.70 | | 38.65 | 50 |
| 1430 | 1-1/2" pipe | | 20 | .400 | | 19.95 | 18.70 | | 38.65 | 50 |
| 1440 | 2" pipe | | 18 | .444 | | 21 | 21 | | 42 | 54 |
| 1450 | 3" pipe | | 17 | .471 | | 24.50 | 22 | | 46.50 | 60 |
| 1460 | 4" pipe | | 16 | .500 | | 27 | 23.50 | | 50.50 | 65 |

## 22 13 19 – Sanitary Waste Piping Specialties

### 22 13 19.13 Sanitary Drains

| | | Crew | Daily Output | Labor-Hours | Unit | Material | 2008 Bare Costs Labor | Equipment | Total | Total Incl O&P |
|---|---|---|---|---|---|---|---|---|---|---|
| 0010 | **SANITARY DRAINS** | | | | | | | | | |
| 0400 | Deck, auto park, C.I., 13" top | | | | | | | | | |
| 0440 | 3", 4", 5", and 6" pipe size | Q-1 | 8 | 2 | Ea. | 900 | 84 | | 984 | 1,125 |
| 0480 | For galvanized body, add | | | | " | 485 | | | 485 | 535 |
| 2000 | Floor, medium duty, C.I., deep flange, 7" dia top | | | | | | | | | |
| 2040 | 2" and 3" pipe size | Q-1 | 12 | 1.333 | Ea. | 126 | 56 | | 182 | 224 |
| 2080 | For galvanized body, add | | | | | 60 | | | 60 | 66 |
| 2120 | For polished bronze top, add | | | | | 70.50 | | | 70.50 | 78 |
| 2400 | Heavy duty, with sediment bucket, C.I., 12" dia. loose grate | | | | | | | | | |
| 2420 | 2", 3", 4", 5", and 6" pipe size | Q-1 | 9 | 1.778 | Ea. | 435 | 74.50 | | 509.50 | 585 |
| 2460 | For polished bronze top, add | | | | " | 179 | | | 179 | 197 |
| 2500 | Heavy duty, cleanout & trap w/bucket, C.I., 15" top | | | | | | | | | |
| 2540 | 2", 3", and 4" pipe size | Q-1 | 6 | 2.667 | Ea. | 4,025 | 112 | | 4,137 | 4,600 |
| 2560 | For galvanized body, add | | | | | 1,050 | | | 1,050 | 1,150 |
| 2580 | For polished bronze top, add | | | | | 445 | | | 445 | 485 |

## 22 13 23 – Sanitary Waste Interceptors

### 22 13 23.10 Interceptors

| | | Crew | Daily Output | Labor-Hours | Unit | Material | 2008 Bare Costs Labor | Equipment | Total | Total Incl O&P |
|---|---|---|---|---|---|---|---|---|---|---|
| 0010 | **INTERCEPTORS** | | | | | | | | | |
| 0150 | Grease, cast iron, 4 GPM, 8 lb. fat capacity | 1 Plum | 4 | 2 | Ea. | 745 | 93.50 | | 838.50 | 960 |
| 0200 | 7 GPM, 14 lb. fat capacity | | 4 | 2 | | 1,025 | 93.50 | | 1,118.50 | 1,300 |
| 1000 | 10 GPM, 20 lb. fat capacity | | 4 | 2 | | 1,225 | 93.50 | | 1,318.50 | 1,500 |
| 1040 | 15 GPM, 30 lb. fat capacity | | 4 | 2 | | 1,775 | 93.50 | | 1,868.50 | 2,100 |
| 1060 | 20 GPM, 40 lb. fat capacity | | 3 | 2.667 | | 2,200 | 125 | | 2,325 | 2,600 |
| 1120 | Fabricated steel, 50 GPM, 100 lb. fat capacity | Q-1 | 2 | 8 | | 4,050 | 335 | | 4,385 | 4,950 |
| 1160 | 100 GPM, 200 lb. fat capacity | " | 2 | 8 | | 9,200 | 335 | | 9,535 | 10,600 |
| 1580 | For seepage pan, add | | | | | 7% | | | | |
| 3000 | Hair, cast iron, 1-1/4" and 1-1/2" pipe connection | 1 Plum | 8 | 1 | Ea. | 279 | 46.50 | | 325.50 | 375 |
| 3100 | For chrome-plated cast iron, add | | | | | 172 | | | 172 | 189 |
| 4000 | Oil, fabricated steel, 10 GPM, 2" pipe size | 1 Plum | 4 | 2 | | 1,675 | 93.50 | | 1,768.50 | 1,975 |
| 4100 | 15 GPM, 2" or 3" pipe size | | 4 | 2 | | 2,300 | 93.50 | | 2,393.50 | 2,675 |
| 4120 | 20 GPM, 2" or 3" pipe size | | 3 | 2.667 | | 2,750 | 125 | | 2,875 | 3,200 |
| 4220 | 100 GPM, 3" pipe size | Q-1 | 2 | 8 | | 9,200 | 335 | | 9,535 | 10,600 |
| 6000 | Solids, precious metals recovery, C.I., 1-1/4" to 2" pipe | 1 Plum | 4 | 2 | | 420 | 93.50 | | 513.50 | 605 |
| 6100 | Dental Lab., large, C.I., 1-1/2" to 2" pipe | " | 3 | 2.667 | | 1,475 | 125 | | 1,600 | 1,800 |

## 22 13 29 – Sanitary Sewerage Pumps

### 22 13 29.13 Wet-Pit-Mounted, Vertical Sewerage Pumps

| | | Crew | Daily Output | Labor-Hours | Unit | Material | 2008 Bare Costs Labor | Equipment | Total | Total Incl O&P |
|---|---|---|---|---|---|---|---|---|---|---|
| 0010 | **WET-PIT-MOUNTED, VERTICAL SEWERAGE PUMPS** | | | | | | | | | |
| 0020 | Controls incl. alarm/disconnect panel w/wire. Excavation not included | | | | | | | | | |
| 0260 | Simplex, 9 GPM at 60 PSIG, 91 gal. tank | | | | Ea. | 2,725 | | | 2,725 | 3,000 |
| 0300 | Unit with manway, 26" I.D., 18" high | | | | | 3,125 | | | 3,125 | 3,450 |
| 0340 | 26" I.D., 36" high | | | | | 3,250 | | | 3,250 | 3,600 |
| 0380 | 43" I.D., 4' high | | | | | 3,325 | | | 3,325 | 3,650 |

# 22 13 Facility Sanitary Sewerage

## 22 13 29 – Sanitary Sewerage Pumps

### 22 13 29.14 Sewage Ejector Pumps

| | | Crew | Daily Output | Labor-Hours | Unit | Material | 2008 Bare Costs Labor | Equipment | Total | Total Incl O&P |
|---|---|---|---|---|---|---|---|---|---|---|
| 0010 | **SEWAGE EJECTOR PUMPS**, With operating and level controls | | | | | | | | | |
| 0100 | Simplex system incl. tank, cover, pump 15' head | | | | | | | | | |
| 0500 | 37 gal PE tank, 12 GPM, 1/2 HP, 2" discharge | Q-1 | 3.20 | 5 | Ea. | 425 | 210 | | 635 | 785 |
| 0510 | 3" discharge | | 3.10 | 5.161 | | 465 | 217 | | 682 | 835 |
| 0530 | 87 GPM, .7 HP, 2" discharge | | 3.20 | 5 | | 645 | 210 | | 855 | 1,025 |
| 0540 | 3" discharge | | 3.10 | 5.161 | | 700 | 217 | | 917 | 1,100 |
| 0600 | 45 gal. coated stl tank, 12 GPM, 1/2 HP, 2" discharge | | 3 | 5.333 | | 755 | 224 | | 979 | 1,175 |
| 0610 | 3" discharge | | 2.90 | 5.517 | | 785 | 232 | | 1,017 | 1,225 |
| 0630 | 87 GPM, .7 HP, 2" discharge | | 3 | 5.333 | | 965 | 224 | | 1,189 | 1,400 |
| 0640 | 3" discharge | | 2.90 | 5.517 | | 1,025 | 232 | | 1,257 | 1,475 |
| 0660 | 134 GPM, 1 HP, 2" discharge | | 2.80 | 5.714 | | 1,050 | 240 | | 1,290 | 1,500 |
| 0680 | 3" discharge | | 2.70 | 5.926 | | 1,100 | 249 | | 1,349 | 1,575 |
| 0700 | 70 gal. PE tank, 12 GPM, 1/2 HP, 2" discharge | | 2.60 | 6.154 | | 825 | 259 | | 1,084 | 1,300 |
| 0710 | 3" discharge | | 2.40 | 6.667 | | 880 | 280 | | 1,160 | 1,375 |
| 0730 | 87 GPM, 0.7 HP, 2" discharge | | 2.50 | 6.400 | | 1,050 | 269 | | 1,319 | 1,550 |
| 0740 | 3" discharge | | 2.30 | 6.957 | | 1,125 | 292 | | 1,417 | 1,675 |
| 0760 | 134 GPM, 1 HP, 2" discharge | | 2.20 | 7.273 | | 1,150 | 305 | | 1,455 | 1,725 |
| 0770 | 3" discharge | | 2 | 8 | | 1,225 | 335 | | 1,560 | 1,850 |

# 22 14 Facility Storm Drainage

## 22 14 23 – Storm Drainage Piping Specialties

### 22 14 23.33 Backwater Valves

| | | Crew | Daily Output | Labor-Hours | Unit | Material | 2008 Bare Costs Labor | Equipment | Total | Total Incl O&P |
|---|---|---|---|---|---|---|---|---|---|---|
| 0010 | **BACKWATER VALVES**, C.I. Body. | | | | | | | | | |
| 6980 | Bronze gate and automatic flapper valves | | | | | | | | | |
| 7000 | 3" and 4" pipe size | Q-1 | 13 | 1.231 | Ea. | 1,275 | 51.50 | | 1,326.50 | 1,475 |
| 7100 | 5" and 6" pipe size | " | 13 | 1.231 | " | 1,975 | 51.50 | | 2,026.50 | 2,225 |
| 7240 | Bronze flapper valve, bolted cover | | | | | | | | | |
| 7260 | 2" pipe size | Q-1 | 16 | 1 | Ea. | 375 | 42 | | 417 | 475 |
| 7300 | 4" pipe size | " | 13 | 1.231 | | 720 | 51.50 | | 771.50 | 875 |
| 7340 | 6" pipe size | Q-2 | 17 | 1.412 | | 1,025 | 61.50 | | 1,086.50 | 1,250 |

## 22 14 26 – Facility Storm Drains

### 22 14 26.13 Roof Drains

| | | Crew | Daily Output | Labor-Hours | Unit | Material | 2008 Bare Costs Labor | Equipment | Total | Total Incl O&P |
|---|---|---|---|---|---|---|---|---|---|---|
| 0010 | **ROOF DRAINS** | | | | | | | | | |
| 0140 | Cornice, C.I., 45° or 90° outlet | | | | | | | | | |
| 0200 | 3" and 4" pipe size | Q-1 | 12 | 1.333 | Ea. | 207 | 56 | | 263 | 310 |
| 0260 | For galvanized body, add | | | | | 47.50 | | | 47.50 | 52.50 |
| 0280 | For polished bronze dome, add | | | | | 35 | | | 35 | 38.50 |
| 3860 | Roof, flat metal deck, C.I. body, 12" C.I. dome | | | | | | | | | |
| 3890 | 3" pipe size | Q-1 | 14 | 1.143 | Ea. | 247 | 48 | | 295 | 345 |
| 3920 | 6" pipe size | " | 10 | 1.600 | " | 430 | 67.50 | | 497.50 | 570 |
| 4620 | Main, all aluminum, 12" low profile dome | | | | | | | | | |
| 4640 | 2", 3" and 4" pipe size | Q-1 | 14 | 1.143 | Ea. | 274 | 48 | | 322 | 370 |

### 22 14 26.16 Facility Area Drains

| | | Crew | Daily Output | Labor-Hours | Unit | Material | 2008 Bare Costs Labor | Equipment | Total | Total Incl O&P |
|---|---|---|---|---|---|---|---|---|---|---|
| 0010 | **FACILITY AREA DRAINS** | | | | | | | | | |
| 4980 | Scupper floor, oblique strainer, C.I. | | | | | | | | | |
| 5000 | 6" x 7" top, 2", 3" and 4" pipe size | Q-1 | 16 | 1 | Ea. | 178 | 42 | | 220 | 259 |
| 5100 | 8" x 12" top, 5" and 6" pipe size | " | 14 | 1.143 | | 345 | 48 | | 393 | 450 |
| 5160 | For galvanized body, add | | | | | 40% | | | | |
| 5200 | For polished bronze strainer, add | | | | | 85% | | | | |

# 22 14 Facility Storm Drainage

## 22 14 26 - Facility Storm Drains

### 22 14 26.19 Facility Trench Drains

| 22 14 26.19 Facility Trench Drains | Crew | Daily Output | Labor-Hours | Unit | Material | 2008 Bare Costs Labor | Equipment | Total | Total Incl O&P |
|---|---|---|---|---|---|---|---|---|---|
| 0010 **FACILITY TRENCH DRAINS** | | | | | | | | | |
| 5980 Trench, floor, hvy duty, modular, C.I., 12" x 12" top | | | | | | | | | |
| 6000     2", 3", 4", 5", & 6" pipe size | Q-1 | 8 | 2 | Ea. | 560 | 84 | | 644 | 745 |
| 6100     For unit with polished bronze top | | | | " | 840 | | | 840 | 920 |
| 6600 Trench, floor, for cement concrete encasement | | | | | | | | | |
| 6610   Not including trenching or concrete | | | | | | | | | |
| 6640     Polyester polymer concrete | | | | | | | | | |
| 6650       4" internal width, with grate | | | | | | | | | |
| 6660         Light duty steel grate | Q-1 | 120 | .133 | L.F. | 26.50 | 5.60 | | 32.10 | 37.50 |
| 6670         Medium duty steel grate | | 115 | .139 | | 32 | 5.85 | | 37.85 | 44.50 |
| 6680         Heavy duty iron grate | ↓ | 110 | .145 | ↓ | 48 | 6.10 | | 54.10 | 62 |
| 6700       12" internal width, with grate | | | | | | | | | |
| 6770         Heavy duty galvanized grate | Q-1 | 80 | .200 | L.F. | 120 | 8.40 | | 128.40 | 145 |
| 6800     Fiberglass | | | | | | | | | |
| 6810       8" internal width, with grate | | | | | | | | | |
| 6820         Medium duty galvanized grate | Q-1 | 115 | .139 | L.F. | 80 | 5.85 | | 85.85 | 96.50 |
| 6830         Heavy duty iron grate | " | 110 | .145 | " | 82.50 | 6.10 | | 88.60 | 99.50 |

## 22 14 29 - Sump Pumps

### 22 14 29.13 Wet-Pit-Mounted, Vertical Sump Pumps

| 22 14 29.13 Wet-Pit-Mounted, Vertical Sump Pumps | Crew | Daily Output | Labor-Hours | Unit | Material | 2008 Bare Costs Labor | Equipment | Total | Total Incl O&P |
|---|---|---|---|---|---|---|---|---|---|
| 0010 **WET-PIT-MOUNTED, VERTICAL SUMP PUMPS** | | | | | | | | | |
| 0400   Molded PVC base, 21 GPM at 15' head, 1/3 HP | 1 Plum | 5 | 1.600 | Ea. | 116 | 74.50 | | 190.50 | 239 |
| 0800   Iron base, 21 GPM at 15' head, 1/3 HP | | 5 | 1.600 | | 143 | 74.50 | | 217.50 | 269 |
| 1200   Solid brass, 21 GPM at 15' head, 1/3 HP | ↓ | 5 | 1.600 | ↓ | 251 | 74.50 | | 325.50 | 390 |

### 22 14 29.16 Submersible Sump Pumps

| 22 14 29.16 Submersible Sump Pumps | Crew | Daily Output | Labor-Hours | Unit | Material | 2008 Bare Costs Labor | Equipment | Total | Total Incl O&P |
|---|---|---|---|---|---|---|---|---|---|
| 0010 **SUBMERSIBLE SUMP PUMPS** | | | | | | | | | |
| 7000   Sump pump, automatic | | | | | | | | | |
| 7100     Plastic, 1-1/4" discharge, 1/4 HP | 1 Plum | 6 | 1.333 | Ea. | 131 | 62.50 | | 193.50 | 238 |
| 7140       1/3 HP | | 5 | 1.600 | | 158 | 74.50 | | 232.50 | 285 |
| 7160       1/2 HP | | 5 | 1.600 | | 194 | 74.50 | | 268.50 | 325 |
| 7180       1-1/2" discharge, 1/2 HP | | 4 | 2 | | 215 | 93.50 | | 308.50 | 380 |
| 7500     Cast iron, 1-1/4" discharge, 1/4 HP | | 6 | 1.333 | | 150 | 62.50 | | 212.50 | 259 |
| 7540       1/3 HP | | 6 | 1.333 | | 177 | 62.50 | | 239.50 | 289 |
| 7560       1/2 HP | ↓ | 5 | 1.600 | ↓ | 215 | 74.50 | | 289.50 | 350 |

# 22 31 Domestic Water Softeners

## 22 31 13 - Residential Domestic Water Softeners

### 22 31 13.10 Residential Water Softeners

| 22 31 13.10 Residential Water Softeners | Crew | Daily Output | Labor-Hours | Unit | Material | 2008 Bare Costs Labor | Equipment | Total | Total Incl O&P |
|---|---|---|---|---|---|---|---|---|---|
| 0010 **RESIDENTIAL WATER SOFTENERS** | | | | | | | | | |
| 7350   Water softener, automatic, to 30 grains per gallon | 2 Plum | 5 | 3.200 | Ea. | 480 | 149 | | 629 | 755 |
| 7400     To 100 grains per gallon | " | 4 | 4 | " | 700 | 187 | | 887 | 1,050 |

## 22 31 16 - Commercial Domestic Water Softeners

### 22 31 16.10 Water Softeners

| 22 31 16.10 Water Softeners | Crew | Daily Output | Labor-Hours | Unit | Material | 2008 Bare Costs Labor | Equipment | Total | Total Incl O&P |
|---|---|---|---|---|---|---|---|---|---|
| 0010 **WATER SOFTENERS** | | | | | | | | | |
| 5800   Softener systems, automatic, intermediate sizes | | | | | | | | | |
| 5820     available, may be used in multiples. | | | | | | | | | |
| 6000     Hardness capacity between regenerations and flow | | | | | | | | | |
| 6100       150,000 grains, 37 GPM cont., 51 GPM peak | Q-1 | 1.20 | 13.333 | Ea. | 3,250 | 560 | | 3,810 | 4,425 |
| 6200       300,000 grains, 81 GPM cont., 113 GPM peak | ↓ | 1 | 16 | ↓ | 7,350 | 670 | | 8,020 | 9,100 |
| 6300       750,000 grains, 160 GPM cont., 230 GPM peak | ↓ | .80 | 20 | ↓ | 9,600 | 840 | | 10,440 | 11,900 |

# 22 31 Domestic Water Softeners

## 22 31 16 – Commercial Domestic Water Softeners

| 22 31 16.10 Water Softeners | | Crew | Daily Output | Labor-Hours | Unit | Material | 2008 Bare Costs | | Total | Total Incl O&P |
|---|---|---|---|---|---|---|---|---|---|---|
| | | | | | | | Labor | Equipment | | |
| 6400 | 900,000 grains, 185 GPM cont., 270 GPM peak | Q-1 | .70 | 22.857 | Ea. | 15,400 | 960 | | 16,360 | 18,500 |

# 22 33 Electric Domestic Water Heaters

## 22 33 13 – Instantaneous Electric Domestic Water Heaters

### 22 33 13.10 Hot Water Dispensers

| | | Crew | Daily Output | Labor-Hours | Unit | Material | Labor | Equipment | Total | Total Incl O&P |
|---|---|---|---|---|---|---|---|---|---|---|
| 0010 | **HOT WATER DISPENSERS** | | | | | | | | | |
| 0160 | Commercial, 100 cup, 11.3 amp | 1 Plum | 14 | .571 | Ea. | 345 | 26.50 | | 371.50 | 420 |
| 3180 | Household, 60 cup | " | 14 | .571 | " | 173 | 26.50 | | 199.50 | 231 |

## 22 33 30 – Residential, Electric Domestic Water Heaters

### 22 33 30.13 Residential, Small-Capacity Elec. Domestic Wtr Heaters

| | | Crew | Daily Output | Labor-Hours | Unit | Material | Labor | Equipment | Total | Total Incl O&P |
|---|---|---|---|---|---|---|---|---|---|---|
| 0010 | **RESIDENTIAL, SMALL-CAPACITY ELECTRIC DOMESTIC WATER HEATERS** | | | | | | | | | |
| 1000 | Residential, electric, glass lined tank, 5 yr, 10 gal., single element | 1 Plum | 2.30 | 3.478 | Ea. | 315 | 162 | | 477 | 590 |
| 1040 | 20 gallon, single element | | 2.20 | 3.636 | | 360 | 170 | | 530 | 650 |
| 1060 | 30 gallon, double element | | 2.20 | 3.636 | | 310 | 170 | | 480 | 595 |
| 1080 | 40 gallon, double element | | 2 | 4 | | 330 | 187 | | 517 | 645 |
| 1100 | 52 gallon, double element | | 2 | 4 | | 370 | 187 | | 557 | 690 |
| 1180 | 120 gallon, double element | | 1.40 | 5.714 | | 790 | 267 | | 1,057 | 1,275 |

## 22 33 33 – Light-Commercial Electric Domestic Water Heaters

### 22 33 33.10 Commercial Electric Water Heaters

| | | Crew | Daily Output | Labor-Hours | Unit | Material | Labor | Equipment | Total | Total Incl O&P |
|---|---|---|---|---|---|---|---|---|---|---|
| 0010 | **COMMERCIAL ELECTRIC WATER HEATERS** | | | | | | | | | |
| 4000 | Commercial, 100° rise. NOTE: for each size tank, a range of | | | | | | | | | |
| 4010 | heaters between the ones shown are available | | | | | | | | | |
| 4020 | Electric | | | | | | | | | |
| 4100 | 5 gal., 3 kW, 12 GPH, 208V | 1 Plum | 2 | 4 | Ea. | 2,650 | 187 | | 2,837 | 3,200 |
| 4120 | 10 gal., 6 kW, 25 GPH, 208V | | 2 | 4 | | 2,950 | 187 | | 3,137 | 3,525 |
| 4140 | 50 gal., 9 kW, 37 GPH, 208V | | 1.80 | 4.444 | | 4,025 | 208 | | 4,233 | 4,750 |
| 4160 | 50 gal., 36 kW, 148 GPH, 208V | | 1.80 | 4.444 | | 6,275 | 208 | | 6,483 | 7,200 |
| 4300 | 200 gal., 15 kW, 61 GPH, 480V | Q-1 | 1.70 | 9.412 | | 19,500 | 395 | | 19,895 | 22,000 |
| 4320 | 200 gal., 120 kW , 490 GPH, 480V | | 1.70 | 9.412 | | 26,600 | 395 | | 26,995 | 29,800 |
| 4460 | 400 gal., 30 kW, 123 GPH, 480V | | 1 | 16 | | 26,800 | 670 | | 27,470 | 30,500 |
| 5400 | Modulating step control, 2-5 steps | 1 Elec | 5.30 | 1.509 | | 1,925 | 69 | | 1,994 | 2,225 |
| 5440 | 6-10 steps | | 3.20 | 2.500 | | 2,500 | 114 | | 2,614 | 2,925 |
| 5460 | 11-15 steps | | 2.70 | 2.963 | | 3,025 | 135 | | 3,160 | 3,525 |
| 5480 | 16-20 steps | | 1.60 | 5 | | 3,500 | 228 | | 3,728 | 4,200 |

# 22 34 Fuel-Fired Domestic Water Heaters

## 22 34 30 – Residential Gas Domestic Water Heaters

### 22 34 30.13 Residential, Atmos, Gas Domestic Wtr Heaters

| | | Crew | Daily Output | Labor-Hours | Unit | Material | Labor | Equipment | Total | Total Incl O&P |
|---|---|---|---|---|---|---|---|---|---|---|
| 0010 | **RESIDENTIAL, ATMOSPHERIC, GAS DOMESTIC WATER HEATERS** | | | | | | | | | |
| 2000 | Gas fired, foam lined tank, 10 yr, vent not incl., | | | | | | | | | |
| 2040 | 30 gallon | 1 Plum | 2 | 4 | Ea. | 600 | 187 | | 787 | 945 |
| 2100 | 75 gallon | | 1.50 | 5.333 | | 1,225 | 249 | | 1,474 | 1,725 |
| 2120 | 100 gallon | | 1.30 | 6.154 | | 1,525 | 287 | | 1,812 | 2,100 |

## 22 34 36 – Commercial Gas Domestic Water Heaters

### 22 34 36.13 Commercial, Atmos., Gas Domestic Water Htrs.

| | | Crew | Daily Output | Labor-Hours | Unit | Material | Labor | Equipment | Total | Total Incl O&P |
|---|---|---|---|---|---|---|---|---|---|---|
| 0010 | **COMMERCIAL, ATMOSPHERIC, GAS DOMESTIC WATER HEATERS** | | | | | | | | | |
| 6000 | Gas fired, flush jacket, std. controls, vent not incl. | | | | | | | | | |
| 6040 | 75 MBH input, 73 GPH | 1 Plum | 1.40 | 5.714 | Ea. | 1,575 | 267 | | 1,842 | 2,125 |

# 22 34 Fuel-Fired Domestic Water Heaters

## 22 34 36 – Commercial Gas Domestic Water Heaters

| 22 34 36.13 Commercial, Atmos., Gas Domestic Water Htrs. | Crew | Daily Output | Labor-Hours | Unit | Material | 2008 Bare Costs Labor | Equipment | Total | Total Incl O&P |
|---|---|---|---|---|---|---|---|---|---|
| 6060 | 98 MBH input, 95 GPH | 1 Plum | 1.40 | 5.714 | Ea. | 3,600 | 267 | | 3,867 | 4,350 |
| 6080 | 120 MBH input, 110 GPH **CN** | | 1.20 | 6.667 | | 4,125 | 310 | | 4,435 | 5,025 |
| 6180 | 200 MBH input, 192 GPH | | .60 | 13.333 | | 6,275 | 625 | | 6,900 | 7,850 |
| 6200 | 250 MBH input, 245 GPH | | .50 | 16 | | 6,700 | 745 | | 7,445 | 8,500 |
| 6900 | For low water cutoff, add | | 8 | 1 | | 263 | 46.50 | | 309.50 | 360 |
| 6960 | For bronze body hot water circulator, add | ▼ | 4 | 2 | ▼ | 1,475 | 93.50 | | 1,568.50 | 1,775 |

## 22 34 46 – Oil-Fired Domestic Water Heaters

### 22 34 46.10 Residential Oil-Fired Water Heaters

| | | Crew | Daily Output | Labor-Hours | Unit | Material | Labor | Equipment | Total | Total Incl O&P |
|---|---|---|---|---|---|---|---|---|---|---|
| 0010 | **RESIDENTIAL OIL-FIRED WATER HEATERS** | | | | | | | | | |
| 3000 | Oil fired, glass lined tank, 5 yr, vent not included, 30 gallon | 1 Plum | 2 | 4 | Ea. | 665 | 187 | | 852 | 1,000 |
| 3040 | 50 gallon | | 1.80 | 4.444 | | 1,375 | 208 | | 1,583 | 1,800 |
| 3060 | 70 gallon | | 1.50 | 5.333 | | 1,725 | 249 | | 1,974 | 2,275 |
| 3080 | 85 gallon | ▼ | 1.40 | 5.714 | ▼ | 4,750 | 267 | | 5,017 | 5,625 |

### 22 34 46.20 Commercial Oil-Fired Water Heaters

| | | Crew | Daily Output | Labor-Hours | Unit | Material | Labor | Equipment | Total | Total Incl O&P |
|---|---|---|---|---|---|---|---|---|---|---|
| 0010 | **COMMERCIAL OIL-FIRED WATER HEATERS** | | | | | | | | | |
| 8000 | Oil fired, glass lined, UL listed, std. controls, vent not incl. | | | | | | | | | |
| 8060 | 140 gal., 140 MBH input, 134 GPH | Q-1 | 2.13 | 7.512 | Ea. | 13,800 | 315 | | 14,115 | 15,700 |
| 8080 | 140 gal., 199 MBH input, 191 GPH | | 2 | 8 | | 14,300 | 335 | | 14,635 | 16,200 |
| 8100 | 140 gal., 255 MBH input, 247 GPH | | 1.60 | 10 | | 14,700 | 420 | | 15,120 | 16,800 |
| 8160 | 140 gal., 540 MBH input, 519 GPH | | .96 | 16.667 | | 19,500 | 700 | | 20,200 | 22,600 |
| 8180 | 140 gal., 720 MBH input, 691 GPH | ▼ | .92 | 17.391 | | 19,900 | 730 | | 20,630 | 23,000 |
| 8280 | 201 gal., 1250 MBH input, 1200 GPH | Q-2 | 1.22 | 19.672 | | 30,500 | 855 | | 31,355 | 34,900 |
| 8300 | 201 gal., 1500 MBH input, 1441 GPH | " | 1.16 | 20.690 | | 33,200 | 900 | | 34,100 | 37,900 |
| 8900 | For low water cutoff, add | 1 Plum | 8 | 1 | | 263 | 46.50 | | 309.50 | 360 |
| 8960 | For bronze body hot water circulator, add | " | 4 | 2 | ▼ | 555 | 93.50 | | 648.50 | 750 |

# 22 35 Domestic Water Heat Exchangers

## 22 35 30 – Water Heating by Steam

### 22 35 30.10 Water Heating Transfer Package

| | | Crew | Daily Output | Labor-Hours | Unit | Material | Labor | Equipment | Total | Total Incl O&P |
|---|---|---|---|---|---|---|---|---|---|---|
| 0010 | **WATER HEATING TRANSFER PACKAGE**, Complete controls | | | | | | | | | |
| 0020 | expansion tank, converter, air separator | | | | | | | | | |
| 1000 | Hot water, 180° F enter, 200° F leaving, 15# steam | | | | | | | | | |
| 1010 | One pump system, 28 GPM | Q-6 | .75 | 32 | Ea. | 14,900 | 1,400 | | 16,300 | 18,500 |
| 1020 | 35 GPM | | .70 | 34.286 | | 16,400 | 1,500 | | 17,900 | 20,300 |
| 1040 | 55 GPM | | .65 | 36.923 | | 18,600 | 1,625 | | 20,225 | 22,900 |
| 1060 | 130 GPM | | .55 | 43.636 | | 23,100 | 1,925 | | 25,025 | 28,300 |
| 1080 | 255 GPM | | .40 | 60 | | 31,300 | 2,650 | | 33,950 | 38,500 |
| 1100 | 550 GPM | ▼ | .30 | 80 | ▼ | 39,600 | 3,525 | | 43,125 | 48,900 |

# 22 41 Residential Plumbing Fixtures

## 22 41 06 - Plumbing Fixtures General

### 22 41 06.10 Plumbing Fixture Notes

| | | Crew | Daily Output | Labor-Hours | Unit | Material | 2008 Bare Costs Labor | Equipment | Total | Total Incl O&P |
|---|---|---|---|---|---|---|---|---|---|---|
| 0010 | **PLUMBING FIXTURE NOTES**, Incl. trim fittings unless otherwise noted R224000-40 | | | | | | | | | |
| 0080 | For rough-in, supply, waste, and vent, see add for each type | | | | | | | | | |
| 0122 | For electric water coolers, see Div. 22 47 16.10 | | | | | | | | | |
| 0160 | For color, unless otherwise noted, add | | | | Ea. | 20% | | | | |

## 22 41 13 - Residential Water Closets, Urinals, and Bidets

### 22 41 13.40 Water Closets

| | | Crew | Daily Output | Labor-Hours | Unit | Material | 2008 Bare Costs Labor | Equipment | Total | Total Incl O&P |
|---|---|---|---|---|---|---|---|---|---|---|
| 0010 | **WATER CLOSETS** R224000-40 | | | | | | | | | |
| 0032 | For automatic flush, see Div. 22 41 39.10 0972 | | | | | | | | | |
| 0150 | Tank type, vitreous china, incl. seat, supply pipe w/stop | | | | | | | | | |
| 0200 | Wall hung | | | | | | | | | |
| 0400 | Two piece, close coupled | Q-1 | 5.30 | 3.019 | Ea. | 550 | 127 | | 677 | 795 |
| 0960 | For rough-in, supply, waste, vent and carrier | | 2.73 | 5.861 | | 555 | 246 | | 801 | 980 |
| 1000 | Floor mounted, one piece | | 5.30 | 3.019 | | 530 | 127 | | 657 | 775 |
| 1100 | Two piece, close coupled **CN** | ↓ | 5.30 | 3.019 | ↓ | 183 | 127 | | 310 | 390 |
| 1960 | For color, add | | | | | 30% | | | | |
| 1980 | For rough-in, supply, waste and vent | Q-1 | 3.05 | 5.246 | Ea. | 258 | 220 | | 478 | 615 |

## 22 41 16 - Residential Lavatories and Sinks

### 22 41 16.10 Lavatories

| | | Crew | Daily Output | Labor-Hours | Unit | Material | 2008 Bare Costs Labor | Equipment | Total | Total Incl O&P |
|---|---|---|---|---|---|---|---|---|---|---|
| 0010 | **LAVATORIES**, With trim, white unless noted otherwise R224000-40 | | | | | | | | | |
| 0500 | Vanity top, porcelain enamel on cast iron | | | | | | | | | |
| 0600 | 20" x 18" | Q-1 | 6.40 | 2.500 | Ea. | 217 | 105 | | 322 | 395 |
| 0640 | 33" x 19" oval | | 6.40 | 2.500 | | 470 | 105 | | 575 | 680 |
| 0720 | 19" round | ↓ | 6.40 | 2.500 | ↓ | 204 | 105 | | 309 | 385 |
| 0860 | For color, add | | | | | 25% | | | | |
| 1000 | Cultured marble, 19" x 17", single bowl | Q-1 | 6.40 | 2.500 | Ea. | 166 | 105 | | 271 | 340 |
| 1040 | 25" x 19", single bowl | " | 6.40 | 2.500 | " | 178 | 105 | | 283 | 355 |
| 1580 | For color, same price | | | | | | | | | |
| 1900 | Stainless steel, self-rimming, 25" x 22", single bowl, ledge | Q-1 | 6.40 | 2.500 | Ea. | 272 | 105 | | 377 | 455 |
| 1960 | 17" x 22", single bowl | | 6.40 | 2.500 | | 265 | 105 | | 370 | 450 |
| 2600 | Steel, enameled, 20" x 17", single bowl | | 5.80 | 2.759 | | 142 | 116 | | 258 | 330 |
| 2660 | 19" round | | 5.80 | 2.759 | | 139 | 116 | | 255 | 325 |
| 2900 | Vitreous china, 20" x 16", single bowl | | 5.40 | 2.963 | | 262 | 125 | | 387 | 475 |
| 2960 | 20" x 17", single bowl | | 5.40 | 2.963 | | 158 | 125 | | 283 | 360 |
| 3020 | 19" round, single bowl | | 5.40 | 2.963 | | 156 | 125 | | 281 | 360 |
| 3200 | 22" x 13", single bowl | ↓ | 5.40 | 2.963 | ↓ | 244 | 125 | | 369 | 455 |
| 3560 | For color, add | | | | | 50% | | | | |
| 3580 | Rough-in, supply, waste and vent for all above lavatories | Q-1 | 2.30 | 6.957 | Ea. | 172 | 292 | | 464 | 630 |
| 4000 | Wall hung | | | | | | | | | |
| 4040 | Porcelain enamel on cast iron, 16" x 14", single bowl | Q-1 | 8 | 2 | Ea. | 365 | 84 | | 449 | 525 |
| 4180 | 20" x 18", single bowl | | 8 | 2 | | 283 | 84 | | 367 | 435 |
| 4240 | 22" x 19", single bowl | ↓ | 8 | 2 | ↓ | 485 | 84 | | 569 | 660 |
| 4580 | For color, add | | | | | 30% | | | | |
| 6000 | Vitreous china, 18" x 15", single bowl with backsplash | Q-1 | 7 | 2.286 | Ea. | 210 | 96 | | 306 | 375 |
| 6500 | For color, add | | | | | 30% | | | | |
| 6960 | Rough-in, supply, waste and vent for above lavatories | Q-1 | 1.66 | 9.639 | Ea. | 375 | 405 | | 780 | 1,025 |

### 22 41 16.30 Sinks

| | | Crew | Daily Output | Labor-Hours | Unit | Material | 2008 Bare Costs Labor | Equipment | Total | Total Incl O&P |
|---|---|---|---|---|---|---|---|---|---|---|
| 0010 | **SINKS**, With faucets and drain. R224000-40 | | | | | | | | | |
| 2000 | Kitchen, counter top style, P.E. on C.I., 24" x 21" single bowl | Q-1 | 5.60 | 2.857 | Ea. | 251 | 120 | | 371 | 455 |
| 2100 | 31" x 22" single bowl | | 5.60 | 2.857 | | 278 | 120 | | 398 | 485 |
| 2200 | 32" x 21" double bowl | | 4.80 | 3.333 | | 325 | 140 | | 465 | 570 |
| 2300 | 42" x 21" double bowl | ↓ | 4.80 | 3.333 | ↓ | 500 | 140 | | 640 | 760 |

## 22 41 16 – Residential Lavatories and Sinks

### 22 41 16.30 Sinks

| | | Crew | Daily Output | Labor-Hours | Unit | Material | 2008 Bare Costs Labor | 2008 Bare Costs Equipment | Total | Total Incl O&P |
|---|---|---|---|---|---|---|---|---|---|---|
| 3000 | Stainless steel, self rimming, 19" x 18" single bowl | Q-1 | 5.60 | 2.857 | Ea. | 430 | 120 | | 550 | 650 |
| 3100 | 25" x 22" single bowl | | 5.60 | 2.857 | | 475 | 120 | | 595 | 705 |
| 4000 | Steel, enameled, with ledge, 24" x 21" single bowl | | 5.60 | 2.857 | | 145 | 120 | | 265 | 340 |
| 4100 | 32" x 21" double bowl | | 4.80 | 3.333 | | 166 | 140 | | 306 | 395 |
| 4960 | For color sinks except stainless steel, add | | | | | 10% | | | | |
| 4980 | For rough-in, supply, waste and vent, counter top sinks | Q-1 | 2.14 | 7.477 | | 196 | 315 | | 511 | 690 |
| 5000 | Kitchen, raised deck, P.E. on C.I. | | | | | | | | | |
| 5100 | 32" x 21", dual level, double bowl | Q-1 | 2.60 | 6.154 | Ea. | 272 | 259 | | 531 | 690 |
| 5700 | For color, add | | | | | 20% | | | | |
| 5790 | For rough-in, supply, waste & vent, sinks | Q-1 | 1.85 | 8.649 | | 196 | 365 | | 561 | 760 |

## 22 41 19 – Residential Bathtubs

### 22 41 19.10 Baths

| | | Crew | Daily Output | Labor-Hours | Unit | Material | 2008 Bare Costs Labor | 2008 Bare Costs Equipment | Total | Total Incl O&P |
|---|---|---|---|---|---|---|---|---|---|---|
| 0010 | **BATHS** | | | | | | | | | |
| 0100 | Tubs, recessed porcelain enamel on cast iron, with trim | | | | | | | | | |
| 0180 | 48" x 42" | Q-1 | 4 | 4 | Ea. | 1,750 | 168 | | 1,918 | 2,175 |
| 0220 | 72" x 36" | | 3 | 5.333 | | 1,800 | 224 | | 2,024 | 2,300 |
| 2000 | Enameled formed steel, 4'-6" long | | 5.80 | 2.759 | | 365 | 116 | | 481 | 575 |
| 4000 | Soaking, acrylic with pop-up drain, 60" x 32" x 21" deep | | 5.50 | 2.909 | | 855 | 122 | | 977 | 1,125 |
| 4100 | 60" x 48" x 18-1/2" deep | | 5 | 3.200 | | 795 | 135 | | 930 | 1,075 |
| 9600 | Rough-in, supply, waste and vent, for all above tubs, add | | 2.07 | 7.729 | | 258 | 325 | | 583 | 775 |

## 22 41 23 – Residential Shower Receptors and Basins

### 22 41 23.20 Showers

| | | Crew | Daily Output | Labor-Hours | Unit | Material | 2008 Bare Costs Labor | 2008 Bare Costs Equipment | Total | Total Incl O&P |
|---|---|---|---|---|---|---|---|---|---|---|
| 0010 | **SHOWERS** | | | | | | | | | |
| 1500 | Stall, with drain only. Add for valve and door/curtain | | | | | | | | | |
| 3000 | Fiberglass, one piece, with 3 walls, 32" x 32" square | Q-1 | 5.50 | 2.909 | Ea. | 460 | 122 | | 582 | 695 |
| 3100 | 36" x 36" square | | 5.50 | 2.909 | | 525 | 122 | | 647 | 760 |
| 3250 | 64" x 65-3/4" x 81-1/2" fold. seat, whlchr. | | 3.80 | 4.211 | | 3,075 | 177 | | 3,252 | 3,650 |
| 4000 | Polypropylene, stall only, w/ molded-stone floor, 30" x 30" | | 2 | 8 | | 340 | 335 | | 675 | 875 |
| 4200 | Rough-in, supply, waste and vent for above showers | | 2.05 | 7.805 | | 305 | 330 | | 635 | 830 |

### 22 41 23.40 Shower System Components

| | | Crew | Daily Output | Labor-Hours | Unit | Material | 2008 Bare Costs Labor | 2008 Bare Costs Equipment | Total | Total Incl O&P |
|---|---|---|---|---|---|---|---|---|---|---|
| 0010 | **SHOWER SYSTEM COMPONENTS** | | | | | | | | | |
| 4520 | Showers, fiberglass receptor only | 1 Plum | 8 | 1 | Ea. | 187 | 46.50 | | 233.50 | 276 |
| 5000 | Built-in, head, arm, 2.5 GPM valve | | 4 | 2 | | 208 | 93.50 | | 301.50 | 370 |
| 5200 | Head, arm, by-pass, integral stops, handles | | 3.60 | 2.222 | | 207 | 104 | | 311 | 385 |

## 22 41 36 – Residential Laundry Trays

### 22 41 36.10 Laundry Sinks

| | | Crew | Daily Output | Labor-Hours | Unit | Material | 2008 Bare Costs Labor | 2008 Bare Costs Equipment | Total | Total Incl O&P |
|---|---|---|---|---|---|---|---|---|---|---|
| 0010 | **LAUNDRY SINKS**, With trim | | | | | | | | | |
| 0020 | Porcelain enamel on cast iron, black iron frame | | | | | | | | | |
| 0050 | 24" x 21", single compartment | Q-1 | 6 | 2.667 | Ea. | 365 | 112 | | 477 | 570 |
| 0100 | 26" x 21", single compartment | " | 6 | 2.667 | " | 375 | 112 | | 487 | 580 |
| 2000 | Molded stone, on wall hanger or legs | | | | | | | | | |
| 2020 | 22" x 23", single compartment | Q-1 | 6 | 2.667 | Ea. | 122 | 112 | | 234 | 305 |
| 2100 | 45" x 21", double compartment | " | 5 | 3.200 | " | 213 | 135 | | 348 | 435 |
| 3000 | Plastic, on wall hanger or legs | | | | | | | | | |
| 3020 | 18" x 23", single compartment | Q-1 | 6.50 | 2.462 | Ea. | 99 | 103 | | 202 | 265 |
| 3300 | 40" x 24", double compartment | | 5.50 | 2.909 | | 235 | 122 | | 357 | 445 |
| 5000 | Stainless steel, counter top, 22" x 17" single compartment | | 6 | 2.667 | | 57.50 | 112 | | 169.50 | 232 |
| 5200 | 33" x 22", double compartment | | 5 | 3.200 | | 69.50 | 135 | | 204.50 | 279 |
| 9600 | Rough-in, supply, waste and vent, for all laundry sinks | | 2.14 | 7.477 | | 196 | 315 | | 511 | 690 |

# 22 41 Residential Plumbing Fixtures

## 22 41 39 – Residential Faucets, Supplies and Trim

| 22 41 39.10 Faucets and Fittings | Crew | Daily Output | Labor-Hours | Unit | Material | 2008 Bare Costs Labor | 2008 Bare Costs Equipment | Total | Total Incl O&P |
|---|---|---|---|---|---|---|---|---|---|
| **0010** | **FAUCETS AND FITTINGS** | | | | | | | | | |
| 0150 | Bath, faucets, diverter spout combination, sweat | 1 Plum | 8 | 1 | Ea. | 104 | 46.50 | | 150.50 | 185 |
| 0200 | For integral stops, IPS unions, add | | | | | 109 | | | 109 | 120 |
| 0420 | Bath, press-bal mix valve w/diverter, spout, shower hd, arm/flange | 1 Plum | 8 | 1 | ↓ | 137 | 46.50 | | 183.50 | 222 |
| 0810 | Bidet | | | | | | | | | |
| 0812 | Fitting, over the rim, swivel spray/pop-up drain | 1 Plum | 8 | 1 | Ea. | 154 | 46.50 | | 200.50 | 240 |
| 1000 | Kitchen sink faucets, top mount, cast spout | | 10 | .800 | | 55 | 37.50 | | 92.50 | 117 |
| 1100 | For spray, add | ↓ | 24 | .333 | ↓ | 16.15 | 15.55 | | 31.70 | 41.50 |
| 1300 | Single control lever handle | | | | | | | | | |
| 1310 | With pull out spray | | | | | | | | | |
| 1320 | Polished chrome | 1 Plum | 10 | .800 | Ea. | 192 | 37.50 | | 229.50 | 267 |
| 1330 | Polished brass | | 10 | .800 | | 230 | 37.50 | | 267.50 | 310 |
| 1340 | White | ↓ | 10 | .800 | ↓ | 211 | 37.50 | | 248.50 | 288 |
| 1348 | With spray thru escutcheon | | | | | | | | | |
| 1350 | Polished chrome | 1 Plum | 10 | .800 | Ea. | 149 | 37.50 | | 186.50 | 219 |
| 1360 | Polished brass | | 10 | .800 | | 178 | 37.50 | | 215.50 | 252 |
| 1370 | White | | 10 | .800 | | 164 | 37.50 | | 201.50 | 236 |
| 2000 | Laundry faucets, shelf type, IPS or copper unions | | 12 | .667 | | 45 | 31 | | 76 | 96.50 |
| 2100 | Lavatory faucet, centerset, without drain | ↓ | 10 | .800 | ↓ | 36.50 | 37.50 | | 74 | 96 |
| 2210 | Porcelain cross handles and pop-up drain | | | | | | | | | |
| 2220 | Polished chrome | 1 Plum | 6.66 | 1.201 | Ea. | 119 | 56 | | 175 | 216 |
| 2230 | Polished brass | " | 6.66 | 1.201 | " | 178 | 56 | | 234 | 281 |
| 2260 | Single lever handle and pop-up drain | | | | | | | | | |
| 2270 | Black nickel | 1 Plum | 6.66 | 1.201 | Ea. | 220 | 56 | | 276 | 325 |
| 2280 | Polished brass | | 6.66 | 1.201 | | 220 | 56 | | 276 | 325 |
| 2290 | Polished chrome | | 6.66 | 1.201 | | 161 | 56 | | 217 | 262 |
| 2810 | Automatic sensor and operator, with faucet head | | 6.15 | 1.301 | | 355 | 61 | | 416 | 480 |
| 4000 | Shower by-pass valve with union | | 18 | .444 | | 54 | 21 | | 75 | 90.50 |
| 4200 | Shower thermostatic mixing valve, concealed | ↓ | 8 | 1 | ↓ | 320 | 46.50 | | 366.50 | 420 |
| 4220 | Shower pressure balancing mixing valve, | | | | | | | | | |
| 4230 | With shower head, arm, flange and diverter tub spout | | | | | | | | | |
| 4240 | Chrome | 1 Plum | 6.14 | 1.303 | Ea. | 192 | 61 | | 253 | 305 |
| 4250 | Polished brass | | 6.14 | 1.303 | | 228 | 61 | | 289 | 345 |
| 4260 | Satin | | 6.14 | 1.303 | | 228 | 61 | | 289 | 345 |
| 4270 | Polished chrome/brass | | 6.14 | 1.303 | | 187 | 61 | | 248 | 298 |
| 5000 | Sillcock, compact, brass, IPS or copper to hose | ↓ | 24 | .333 | ↓ | 7.65 | 15.55 | | 23.20 | 32 |

# 22 42 Commercial Plumbing Fixtures

## 22 42 13 – Commercial Water Closets, Urinals, and Bidets

### 22 42 13.30 Urinals

| | | Crew | Daily Output | Labor-Hours | Unit | Material | Labor | Equipment | Total | Total Incl O&P |
|---|---|---|---|---|---|---|---|---|---|---|
| **0010** | **URINALS** | | | | | | | | | |
| 3000 | Wall hung, vitreous china, with hanger & self-closing valve | | | | | | | | | |
| 3100 | Siphon jet type | Q-1 | 3 | 5.333 | Ea. | 340 | 224 | | 564 | 705 |
| 3120 | Blowout type | | 3 | 5.333 | | 380 | 224 | | 604 | 750 |
| 3300 | Rough-in, supply, waste & vent | | 2.83 | 5.654 | | 201 | 238 | | 439 | 575 |
| 5000 | Stall type, vitreous china, includes valve | | 2.50 | 6.400 | | 565 | 269 | | 834 | 1,025 |
| 6980 | Rough-in, supply, waste and vent | ↓ | 1.99 | 8.040 | | 300 | 340 | | 640 | 840 |

### 22 42 13.40 Water Closets

| | | | | | | | | | | |
|---|---|---|---|---|---|---|---|---|---|---|
| **0010** | **WATER CLOSETS** | | | | | | | | | |
| 3000 | Bowl only, with flush valve, seat | | | | | | | | | |

# 22 42 Commercial Plumbing Fixtures

## 22 42 13 – Commercial Water Closets, Urinals, and Bidets

### 22 42 13.40 Water Closets

| | | Crew | Daily Output | Labor-Hours | Unit | Material | 2008 Bare Costs Labor | Equipment | Total | Total Incl O&P |
|---|---|---|---|---|---|---|---|---|---|---|
| 3100 | Wall hung | Q-1 | 5.80 | 2.759 | Ea. | 330 | 116 | | 446 | 535 |
| 3200 | For rough-in, supply, waste and vent, single WC | | 2.56 | 6.250 | | 585 | 263 | | 848 | 1,050 |
| 3300 | Floor mounted | | 5.80 | 2.759 | | 390 | 116 | | 506 | 605 |
| 3350 | With wall outlet | | 5.80 | 2.759 | | 550 | 116 | | 666 | 780 |
| 3400 | For rough-in, supply, waste and vent, single WC | | 2.84 | 5.634 | | 288 | 237 | | 525 | 670 |

## 22 42 16 – Commercial Lavatories and Sinks

### 22 42 16.10 Handwasher-Dryer Module

| | | Crew | Daily Output | Labor-Hours | Unit | Material | 2008 Bare Costs Labor | Equipment | Total | Total Incl O&P |
|---|---|---|---|---|---|---|---|---|---|---|
| 0010 | **HANDWASHER-DRYER MODULE** | | | | | | | | | |
| 0030 | Wall mounted | | | | | | | | | |
| 0040 | With electric dryer | | | | | | | | | |
| 0050 | Sensor operated | Q-1 | 8 | 2 | Ea. | 3,075 | 84 | | 3,159 | 3,500 |
| 0110 | Sensor operated (ADA) | | 8 | 2 | | 3,075 | 84 | | 3,159 | 3,500 |
| 0140 | Sensor operated (ADA), surface mounted | | 8 | 2 | | 3,625 | 84 | | 3,709 | 4,125 |
| 0150 | With paper towels | | | | | | | | | |
| 0180 | Sensor operated | Q-1 | 8 | 2 | Ea. | 3,000 | 84 | | 3,084 | 3,425 |

### 22 42 16.40 Service Sinks

| | | Crew | Daily Output | Labor-Hours | Unit | Material | 2008 Bare Costs Labor | Equipment | Total | Total Incl O&P |
|---|---|---|---|---|---|---|---|---|---|---|
| 0010 | **SERVICE SINKS** | | | | | | | | | |
| 6650 | Service, floor, corner, P.E. on C.I., 28" x 28" | Q-1 | 4.40 | 3.636 | Ea. | 605 | 153 | | 758 | 895 |
| 6790 | For rough-in, supply, waste & vent, floor service sinks | | 1.64 | 9.756 | | 510 | 410 | | 920 | 1,175 |
| 7000 | Service, wall, P.E. on C.I., roll rim, 22" x 18" | | 4 | 4 | | 515 | 168 | | 683 | 820 |
| 7100 | 24" x 20" | | 4 | 4 | | 570 | 168 | | 738 | 880 |
| 8600 | Vitreous china, 22" x 20" | | 4 | 4 | | 425 | 168 | | 593 | 725 |
| 8960 | For stainless steel rim guard, front or side, add | | | | | 32.50 | | | 32.50 | 35.50 |
| 8980 | For rough-in, supply, waste & vent, wall service sinks | Q-1 | 1.30 | 12.308 | | 735 | 515 | | 1,250 | 1,600 |

## 22 42 23 – Commercial Shower Receptors and Basins

### 22 42 23.30 Group Showers

| | | Crew | Daily Output | Labor-Hours | Unit | Material | 2008 Bare Costs Labor | Equipment | Total | Total Incl O&P |
|---|---|---|---|---|---|---|---|---|---|---|
| 0010 | **GROUP SHOWERS** | | | | | | | | | |
| 6000 | Group, w/pressure balancing valve, rough-in and rigging not included | | | | | | | | | |
| 6800 | Column, 6 heads, no receptors, less partitions | Q-1 | 3 | 5.333 | Ea. | 2,925 | 224 | | 3,149 | 3,550 |
| 6900 | With stainless steel partitions | | 1 | 16 | | 8,975 | 670 | | 9,645 | 10,900 |
| 7600 | 5 heads, no receptors, less partitions | | 3 | 5.333 | | 2,400 | 224 | | 2,624 | 2,975 |
| 7620 | 4 heads (1 handicap) no receptors, less partitions | | 3 | 5.333 | | 3,850 | 224 | | 4,074 | 4,575 |
| 7700 | With stainless steel partitions | | 1 | 16 | | 7,375 | 670 | | 8,045 | 9,125 |
| 8000 | Wall, 2 heads, no receptors, less partitions | | 4 | 4 | | 1,350 | 168 | | 1,518 | 1,725 |
| 8100 | With stainless steel partitions | | 2 | 8 | | 3,125 | 335 | | 3,460 | 3,950 |

## 22 42 33 – Wash Fountains

### 22 42 33.20 Commercial Wash Fountains

| | | Crew | Daily Output | Labor-Hours | Unit | Material | 2008 Bare Costs Labor | Equipment | Total | Total Incl O&P |
|---|---|---|---|---|---|---|---|---|---|---|
| 0010 | **COMMERCIAL WASH FOUNTAINS** | | | | | | | | | |
| 1900 | Group, foot control | | | | | | | | | |
| 2000 | Precast terrazzo, circular, 36" diam., 5 or 6 persons | Q-2 | 3 | 8 | Ea. | 4,075 | 350 | | 4,425 | 5,000 |
| 2100 | 54" diameter for 8 or 10 persons | | 2.50 | 9.600 | | 5,050 | 420 | | 5,470 | 6,200 |
| 2400 | Semi-circular, 36" diam. for 3 persons | | 3 | 8 | | 3,750 | 350 | | 4,100 | 4,650 |
| 2500 | 54" diam. for 4 or 5 persons | | 2.50 | 9.600 | | 4,525 | 420 | | 4,945 | 5,600 |
| 2700 | Quarter circle (corner), 54" for 3 persons | | 3.50 | 6.857 | | 4,400 | 299 | | 4,699 | 5,275 |
| 3000 | Stainless steel, circular, 36" diameter | | 3.50 | 6.857 | | 3,975 | 299 | | 4,274 | 4,825 |
| 3100 | 54" diameter | | 2.80 | 8.571 | | 5,150 | 375 | | 5,525 | 6,225 |
| 3400 | Semi-circular, 36" diameter | | 3.50 | 6.857 | | 3,475 | 299 | | 3,774 | 4,275 |
| 3500 | 54" diameter | | 2.80 | 8.571 | | 4,450 | 375 | | 4,825 | 5,450 |
| 5610 | Group, infrared control, barrier free | | | | | | | | | |
| 5614 | Precast terrazzo | | | | | | | | | |
| 5620 | Semi-circular 36" diam. for 3 persons | Q-2 | 3 | 8 | Ea. | 5,725 | 350 | | 6,075 | 6,800 |

# 22 42 Commercial Plumbing Fixtures

## 22 42 33 – Wash Fountains

| 22 42 33.20 Commercial Wash Fountains | Crew | Daily Output | Labor-Hours | Unit | Material | 2008 Bare Costs Labor | Equipment | Total | Total Incl O&P |
|---|---|---|---|---|---|---|---|---|---|
| 5630 | 46" diam. for 4 persons | Q-2 | 2.80 | 8.571 | Ea. | 6,225 | 375 | | 6,600 | 7,400 |
| 5640 | Circular, 54" diam. for 8 persons, button control | ↓ | 2.50 | 9.600 | | 7,475 | 420 | | 7,895 | 8,850 |
| 5700 | Rough-in, supply, waste and vent for above wash fountains | Q-1 | 1.82 | 8.791 | | 281 | 370 | | 651 | 865 |
| 6200 | Duo for small washrooms, stainless steel | | 2 | 8 | | 2,625 | 335 | | 2,960 | 3,400 |
| 6500 | Rough-in, supply, waste & vent for duo fountains | ↓ | 2.02 | 7.921 | ↓ | 156 | 335 | | 491 | 670 |

## 22 42 39 – Commercial Faucets, Supplies, and Trim

### 22 42 39.10 Faucets and Fittings

| | | Crew | Daily Output | Labor-Hours | Unit | Material | 2008 Bare Costs Labor | Equipment | Total | Total Incl O&P |
|---|---|---|---|---|---|---|---|---|---|---|
| 0010 | **FAUCETS AND FITTINGS** | | | | | | | | | |
| 0840 | Flush valves, with vacuum breaker | | | | | | | | | |
| 0850 | Water closet | | | | | | | | | |
| 0860 | Exposed, rear spud | 1 Plum | 8 | 1 | Ea. | 130 | 46.50 | | 176.50 | 214 |
| 0870 | Top spud | | 8 | 1 | | 120 | 46.50 | | 166.50 | 203 |
| 0880 | Concealed, rear spud | | 8 | 1 | | 171 | 46.50 | | 217.50 | 260 |
| 0890 | Top spud | | 8 | 1 | | 141 | 46.50 | | 187.50 | 226 |
| 0900 | Wall hung | ↓ | 8 | 1 | ↓ | 151 | 46.50 | | 197.50 | 237 |
| 0920 | Urinal | | | | | | | | | |
| 0930 | Exposed, stall | 1 Plum | 8 | 1 | Ea. | 120 | 46.50 | | 166.50 | 203 |
| 0940 | Wall, (washout) | | 8 | 1 | | 120 | 46.50 | | 166.50 | 203 |
| 0950 | Pedestal, top spud | | 8 | 1 | | 122 | 46.50 | | 168.50 | 206 |
| 0960 | Concealed, stall | | 8 | 1 | | 138 | 46.50 | | 184.50 | 222 |
| 0970 | Wall (washout) | ↓ | 8 | 1 | | 148 | 46.50 | | 194.50 | 234 |
| 0971 | Automatic flush sensor and operator for | | | | | | | | | |
| 0972 | urinals or water closets | 1 Plum | 8 | 1 | Ea. | 405 | 46.50 | | 451.50 | 515 |
| 3000 | Service sink faucet, cast spout, pail hook, hose end | " | 14 | .571 | " | 76.50 | 26.50 | | 103 | 125 |

### 22 42 39.30 Carriers and Supports

| | | Crew | Daily Output | Labor-Hours | Unit | Material | 2008 Bare Costs Labor | Equipment | Total | Total Incl O&P |
|---|---|---|---|---|---|---|---|---|---|---|
| 0010 | **CARRIERS AND SUPPORTS**, For plumbing fixtures. | | | | | | | | | |
| 0500 | Drinking fountain, wall mounted | | | | | | | | | |
| 0600 | Plate type with studs, top back plate | 1 Plum | 7 | 1.143 | Ea. | 56 | 53.50 | | 109.50 | 142 |
| 0700 | Top front and back plate | | 7 | 1.143 | | 69.50 | 53.50 | | 123 | 157 |
| 0800 | Top & bottom, front & back plates, w/bearing jacks | ↓ | 7 | 1.143 | ↓ | 101 | 53.50 | | 154.50 | 192 |
| 3000 | Lavatory, concealed arm | | | | | | | | | |
| 3050 | Floor mounted, single | | | | | | | | | |
| 3100 | High back fixture | 1 Plum | 6 | 1.333 | Ea. | 315 | 62.50 | | 377.50 | 440 |
| 3200 | Flat slab fixture | | 6 | 1.333 | | 256 | 62.50 | | 318.50 | 375 |
| 3220 | Paraplegic | ↓ | 6 | 1.333 | | 350 | 62.50 | | 412.50 | 480 |
| 3250 | Floor mounted, back to back | | | | | | | | | |
| 3300 | High back fixtures | 1 Plum | 5 | 1.600 | Ea. | 445 | 74.50 | | 519.50 | 600 |
| 3400 | Flat slab fixtures | | 5 | 1.600 | | 550 | 74.50 | | 624.50 | 715 |
| 3430 | Paraplegic | ↓ | 5 | 1.600 | ↓ | 465 | 74.50 | | 539.50 | 620 |
| 3500 | Wall mounted, in stud or masonry | | | | | | | | | |
| 3600 | High back fixture | 1 Plum | 6 | 1.333 | Ea. | 185 | 62.50 | | 247.50 | 298 |
| 3700 | Flat slab fixture | " | 6 | 1.333 | " | 237 | 62.50 | | 299.50 | 355 |
| 4600 | Sink, floor mounted | | | | | | | | | |
| 4650 | Exposed arm system | | | | | | | | | |
| 4700 | Single heavy fixture | 1 Plum | 5 | 1.600 | Ea. | 525 | 74.50 | | 599.50 | 685 |
| 4750 | Single heavy sink with slab | | 5 | 1.600 | | 425 | 74.50 | | 499.50 | 575 |
| 4800 | Back to back, standard fixtures | | 5 | 1.600 | | 385 | 74.50 | | 459.50 | 535 |
| 4850 | Back to back, heavy fixtures | | 5 | 1.600 | | 545 | 74.50 | | 619.50 | 710 |
| 4900 | Back to back, heavy sink with slab | ↓ | 5 | 1.600 | ↓ | 545 | 74.50 | | 619.50 | 710 |
| 4950 | Exposed offset arm system | | | | | | | | | |
| 5000 | Single heavy deep fixture | 1 Plum | 5 | 1.600 | Ea. | 500 | 74.50 | | 574.50 | 660 |
| 5100 | Plate type system | | | | | | | | | |

# 22 42 Commercial Plumbing Fixtures

## 22 42 39 – Commercial Faucets, Supplies, and Trim

| 22 42 39.30 Carriers and Supports | | Crew | Daily Output | Labor-Hours | Unit | Material | 2008 Bare Costs Labor | Equipment | Total | Total Incl O&P |
|---|---|---|---|---|---|---|---|---|---|---|
| 5200 | With bearing jacks, single fixture | 1 Plum | 5 | 1.600 | Ea. | 525 | 74.50 | | 599.50 | 685 |
| 5300 | With exposed arms, single heavy fixture | | 5 | 1.600 | | 735 | 74.50 | | 809.50 | 920 |
| 5400 | Wall mounted, exposed arms, single heavy fixture | | 5 | 1.600 | | 267 | 74.50 | | 341.50 | 405 |
| 6000 | Urinal, floor mounted, 2" or 3" coupling, blowout type | | 6 | 1.333 | | 335 | 62.50 | | 397.50 | 460 |
| 6100 | With fixture or hanger bolts, blowout or washout | | 6 | 1.333 | | 238 | 62.50 | | 300.50 | 355 |
| 6200 | With bearing plate | | 6 | 1.333 | | 238 | 62.50 | | 300.50 | 355 |
| 6300 | Wall mounted, plate type system | ↓ | 6 | 1.333 | ↓ | 205 | 62.50 | | 267.50 | 320 |
| 6980 | Water closet, siphon jet | | | | | | | | | |
| 7000 | Horizontal, adjustable, caulk | | | | | | | | | |
| 7040 | Single, 4" pipe size | 1 Plum | 5.33 | 1.501 | Ea. | 435 | 70 | | 505 | 580 |
| 7050 | 4" pipe size, paraplegic | | 5.33 | 1.501 | | 435 | 70 | | 505 | 580 |
| 7060 | 5" pipe size | | 5.33 | 1.501 | | 575 | 70 | | 645 | 735 |
| 7100 | Double, 4" pipe size | | 5 | 1.600 | | 810 | 74.50 | | 884.50 | 1,000 |
| 7110 | 4" pipe size, paraplegic | | 5 | 1.600 | | 810 | 74.50 | | 884.50 | 1,000 |
| 7120 | 5" pipe size | ↓ | 5 | 1.600 | ↓ | 1,000 | 74.50 | | 1,074.50 | 1,200 |
| 7160 | Horizontal, adjustable, extended, caulk | | | | | | | | | |
| 7180 | Single, 4" pipe size | 1 Plum | 5.33 | 1.501 | Ea. | 585 | 70 | | 655 | 745 |
| 7200 | 5" pipe size | | 5.33 | 1.501 | | 775 | 70 | | 845 | 960 |
| 7240 | Double, 4" pipe size | | 5 | 1.600 | | 1,025 | 74.50 | | 1,099.50 | 1,225 |
| 7260 | 5" pipe size | ↓ | 5 | 1.600 | ↓ | 1,300 | 74.50 | | 1,374.50 | 1,525 |
| 7400 | Vertical, adjustable, caulk or thread | | | | | | | | | |
| 7440 | Single, 4" pipe size | 1 Plum | 5.33 | 1.501 | Ea. | 600 | 70 | | 670 | 765 |
| 7460 | 5" pipe size | | 5.33 | 1.501 | | 735 | 70 | | 805 | 915 |
| 7480 | 6" pipe size | | 5 | 1.600 | | 840 | 74.50 | | 914.50 | 1,025 |
| 7520 | Double, 4" pipe size | | 5 | 1.600 | | 890 | 74.50 | | 964.50 | 1,075 |
| 7540 | 5" pipe size | | 5 | 1.600 | | 1,025 | 74.50 | | 1,099.50 | 1,225 |
| 7560 | 6" pipe size | ↓ | 4 | 2 | ↓ | 1,275 | 93.50 | | 1,368.50 | 1,550 |
| 7600 | Vertical, adjustable, extended, caulk | | | | | | | | | |
| 7620 | Single, 4" pipe size | 1 Plum | 5.33 | 1.501 | Ea. | 595 | 70 | | 665 | 760 |
| 7640 | 5" pipe size | | 5.33 | 1.501 | | 735 | 70 | | 805 | 915 |
| 7680 | 6" pipe size | | 5 | 1.600 | | 840 | 74.50 | | 914.50 | 1,025 |
| 7720 | Double, 4" pipe size | | 5 | 1.600 | | 890 | 74.50 | | 964.50 | 1,075 |
| 7740 | 5" pipe size | | 5 | 1.600 | | 1,025 | 74.50 | | 1,099.50 | 1,225 |
| 7760 | 6" pipe size | ↓ | 4 | 2 | ↓ | 1,125 | 93.50 | | 1,218.50 | 1,400 |
| 7780 | Water closet, blow out | | | | | | | | | |
| 7800 | Vertical offset, caulk or thread | | | | | | | | | |
| 7820 | Single, 4" pipe size | 1 Plum | 5.33 | 1.501 | Ea. | 445 | 70 | | 515 | 595 |
| 7840 | Double, 4" pipe size | " | 5 | 1.600 | " | 775 | 74.50 | | 849.50 | 960 |
| 7880 | Vertical offset, extended, caulk | | | | | | | | | |
| 7900 | Single, 4" pipe size | 1 Plum | 5.33 | 1.501 | Ea. | 565 | 70 | | 635 | 730 |
| 7920 | Double, 4" pipe size | " | 5 | 1.600 | " | 885 | 74.50 | | 959.50 | 1,075 |
| 7960 | Vertical, for floor mounted back-outlet | | | | | | | | | |
| 7980 | Single, 4" thread, 2" vent | 1 Plum | 5.33 | 1.501 | Ea. | 400 | 70 | | 470 | 545 |
| 8000 | Double, 4" thread, 2" vent | " | 6 | 1.333 | " | 1,175 | 62.50 | | 1,237.50 | 1,375 |
| 8040 | Vertical, for floor mounted back-outlet, extended | | | | | | | | | |
| 8060 | Single, 4" caulk, 2" vent | 1 Plum | 6 | 1.333 | Ea. | 400 | 62.50 | | 462.50 | 535 |
| 8080 | Double, 4" caulk, 2" vent | " | 6 | 1.333 | " | 1,200 | 62.50 | | 1,262.50 | 1,400 |
| 8200 | Water closet, residential | | | | | | | | | |
| 8220 | Vertical centerline, floor mount | | | | | | | | | |
| 8240 | Single, 3" caulk, 2" or 3" vent | 1 Plum | 6 | 1.333 | Ea. | 360 | 62.50 | | 422.50 | 490 |
| 8260 | 4" caulk, 2" or 4" vent | | 6 | 1.333 | | 465 | 62.50 | | 527.50 | 605 |
| 8280 | 3" copper sweat, 3" vent | | 6 | 1.333 | | 325 | 62.50 | | 387.50 | 450 |
| 8300 | 4" copper sweat, 4" vent | ↓ | 6 | 1.333 | ↓ | 395 | 62.50 | | 457.50 | 525 |

449

# 22 42 Commercial Plumbing Fixtures

## 22 42 39 – Commercial Faucets, Supplies, and Trim

| 22 42 39.30 Carriers and Supports | Crew | Daily Output | Labor-Hours | Unit | Material | 2008 Bare Costs Labor | Equipment | Total | Total Incl O&P |
|---|---|---|---|---|---|---|---|---|---|
| 8400 | Vertical offset, floor mount | | | | | | | | | |
| 8420 | Single, 3" or 4" caulk, vent | 1 Plum | 4 | 2 | Ea. | 450 | 93.50 | | 543.50 | 635 |
| 8440 | 3" or 4" copper sweat, vent | | 5 | 1.600 | | 450 | 74.50 | | 524.50 | 605 |
| 8460 | Double, 3" or 4" caulk, vent | | 4 | 2 | | 805 | 93.50 | | 898.50 | 1,025 |
| 8480 | 3" or 4" copper sweat, vent | ↓ | 5 | 1.600 | ↓ | 805 | 74.50 | | 879.50 | 995 |
| 9000 | Water cooler (electric), floor mounted | | | | | | | | | |
| 9100 | Plate type with bearing plate, single | 1 Plum | 6 | 1.333 | Ea. | 228 | 62.50 | | 290.50 | 345 |

# 22 45 Emergency Plumbing Fixtures

## 22 45 13 – Emergency Showers

### 22 45 13.10 Emergency Showers

| | | Crew | Daily Output | Labor-Hours | Unit | Material | 2008 Bare Costs Labor | Equipment | Total | Total Incl O&P |
|---|---|---|---|---|---|---|---|---|---|---|
| 0010 | **EMERGENCY SHOWERS,** Rough-in not included | | | | | | | | | |
| 5000 | Shower, single head, drench, ball valve, pull, freestanding | Q-1 | 4 | 4 | Ea. | 294 | 168 | | 462 | 580 |
| 5200 | Horizontal or vertical supply | | 4 | 4 | | 275 | 168 | | 443 | 555 |
| 6000 | Multi-nozzle, eye/face wash combination | | 4 | 4 | | 555 | 168 | | 723 | 865 |
| 6400 | Multi-nozzle, 12 spray, shower only | | 4 | 4 | | 1,525 | 168 | | 1,693 | 1,925 |
| 6600 | For freeze-proof, add | ↓ | 6 | 2.667 | ↓ | 305 | 112 | | 417 | 505 |

## 22 45 16 – Eyewash Equipment

### 22 45 16.10 Eyewash Safety Equipment

| | | Crew | Daily Output | Labor-Hours | Unit | Material | 2008 Bare Costs Labor | Equipment | Total | Total Incl O&P |
|---|---|---|---|---|---|---|---|---|---|---|
| 0010 | **EYEWASH SAFETY EQUIPMENT,** Rough-in not included | | | | | | | | | |
| 1000 | Eye wash fountain | | | | | | | | | |
| 1400 | Plastic bowl, pedestal mounted | Q-1 | 4 | 4 | Ea. | 217 | 168 | | 385 | 490 |
| 1600 | Unmounted | | 4 | 4 | | 153 | 168 | | 321 | 420 |
| 1800 | Wall mounted | | 4 | 4 | | 156 | 168 | | 324 | 425 |
| 2000 | Stainless steel, pedestal mounted | | 4 | 4 | | 330 | 168 | | 498 | 620 |
| 2200 | Unmounted | | 4 | 4 | | 208 | 168 | | 376 | 480 |
| 2400 | Wall mounted | ↓ | 4 | 4 | ↓ | 198 | 168 | | 366 | 470 |

## 22 45 19 – Self-Contained Eyewash Equipment

### 22 45 19.10 Self-Contained Eyewash Safety Equipment

| | | Crew | Daily Output | Labor-Hours | Unit | Material | 2008 Bare Costs Labor | Equipment | Total | Total Incl O&P |
|---|---|---|---|---|---|---|---|---|---|---|
| 0010 | **SELF-CONTAINED EYEWASH SAFETY EQUIPMENT** | | | | | | | | | |
| 3000 | Eye wash, portable, self-contained | | | | Ea. | 435 | | | 435 | 475 |

## 22 45 26 – Eye/Face Wash Equipment

### 22 45 26.10 Eye/Face Wash Safety Equipment

| | | Crew | Daily Output | Labor-Hours | Unit | Material | 2008 Bare Costs Labor | Equipment | Total | Total Incl O&P |
|---|---|---|---|---|---|---|---|---|---|---|
| 0010 | **EYE/FACE WASH SAFETY EQUIPMENT,** Rough-in not included | | | | | | | | | |
| 4000 | Eye and face wash, combination fountain | | | | | | | | | |
| 4200 | Stainless steel, pedestal mounted | Q-1 | 4 | 4 | Ea. | 445 | 168 | | 613 | 745 |
| 4400 | Unmounted | | 4 | 4 | | 330 | 168 | | 498 | 620 |
| 4600 | Wall mounted | ↓ | 4 | 4 | ↓ | 335 | 168 | | 503 | 625 |

## 22 47 13 – Drinking Fountains

| 22 47 13.10 Drinking Water Fountains | | Crew | Daily Output | Labor-Hours | Unit | Material | 2008 Bare Costs Labor | Equipment | Total | Total Incl O&P |
|---|---|---|---|---|---|---|---|---|---|---|
| 0010 | **DRINKING WATER FOUNTAINS,** For connection to cold water supply R224000-40 | | | | | | | | | |
| 1000 | Wall mounted, non-recessed | | | | | | | | | |
| 1400 | Bronze, with no back | 1 Plum | 4 | 2 | Ea. | 1,175 | 93.50 | | 1,268.50 | 1,450 |
| 1800 | Cast aluminum, enameled, for correctional institutions | | 4 | 2 | | 725 | 93.50 | | 818.50 | 940 |
| 2000 | Fiberglass, 12" back, single bubbler unit | | 4 | 2 | | 650 | 93.50 | | 743.50 | 855 |
| 2040 | Dual bubbler | | 3.20 | 2.500 | | 940 | 117 | | 1,057 | 1,200 |
| 2400 | Precast stone, no back | | 4 | 2 | | 590 | 93.50 | | 683.50 | 785 |
| 2700 | Stainless steel, single bubbler, no back | | 4 | 2 | | 1,150 | 93.50 | | 1,243.50 | 1,425 |
| 2740 | With back | | 4 | 2 | | 1,900 | 93.50 | | 1,993.50 | 2,225 |
| 2780 | Dual handle & wheelchair projection type | | 4 | 2 | | 565 | 93.50 | | 658.50 | 765 |
| 2820 | Dual level for handicapped type | | 3.20 | 2.500 | | 1,150 | 117 | | 1,267 | 1,450 |
| 3300 | Vitreous china | | | | | | | | | |
| 3340 | 7" back | 1 Plum | 4 | 2 | Ea. | 485 | 93.50 | | 578.50 | 675 |
| 3940 | For vandal-resistant bottom plate, add | | | | | 57.50 | | | 57.50 | 63 |
| 3960 | For freeze-proof valve system, add | 1 Plum | 2 | 4 | | 470 | 187 | | 657 | 800 |
| 3980 | For rough-in, supply and waste, add | " | 2.21 | 3.620 | | 127 | 169 | | 296 | 395 |
| 4000 | Wall mounted, semi-recessed | | | | | | | | | |
| 4200 | Poly-marble, single bubbler | 1 Plum | 4 | 2 | Ea. | 745 | 93.50 | | 838.50 | 960 |
| 4600 | Stainless steel, satin finish, single bubbler | | 4 | 2 | | 865 | 93.50 | | 958.50 | 1,100 |
| 4900 | Vitreous china, single bubbler | | 4 | 2 | | 610 | 93.50 | | 703.50 | 810 |
| 5980 | For rough-in, supply and waste, add | | 1.83 | 4.372 | | 127 | 204 | | 331 | 445 |
| 6000 | Wall mounted, fully recessed | | | | | | | | | |
| 6400 | Poly-marble, single bubbler | 1 Plum | 4 | 2 | Ea. | 850 | 93.50 | | 943.50 | 1,075 |
| 6800 | Stainless steel, single bubbler | | 4 | 2 | | 830 | 93.50 | | 923.50 | 1,050 |
| 7560 | For freeze-proof valve system, add | | 2 | 4 | | 575 | 187 | | 762 | 915 |
| 7580 | For rough-in, supply and waste, add | | 1.83 | 4.372 | | 127 | 204 | | 331 | 445 |
| 7600 | Floor mounted, pedestal type | | | | | | | | | |
| 7700 | Aluminum, architectural style, C.I. base | 1 Plum | 2 | 4 | Ea. | 505 | 187 | | 692 | 835 |
| 7780 | Wheelchair handicap unit | | 2 | 4 | | 1,225 | 187 | | 1,412 | 1,600 |
| 8400 | Stainless steel, architectural style | | 2 | 4 | | 1,300 | 187 | | 1,487 | 1,700 |
| 8600 | Enameled iron, heavy duty service, 2 bubblers | | 2 | 4 | | 1,200 | 187 | | 1,387 | 1,600 |
| 8660 | 4 bubblers | | 2 | 4 | | 1,275 | 187 | | 1,462 | 1,700 |
| 8880 | For freeze-proof valve system, add | | 2 | 4 | | 370 | 187 | | 557 | 685 |
| 8900 | For rough-in, supply and waste, add | | 1.83 | 4.372 | | 127 | 204 | | 331 | 445 |
| 9100 | Deck mounted | | | | | | | | | |
| 9500 | Stainless steel, circular receptor | 1 Plum | 4 | 2 | Ea. | 330 | 93.50 | | 423.50 | 505 |
| 9760 | White enameled steel, 14" x 9" receptor | | 4 | 2 | | 287 | 93.50 | | 380.50 | 455 |
| 9860 | White enameled cast iron, 24" x 16" receptor | | 3 | 2.667 | | 287 | 125 | | 412 | 500 |
| 9980 | For rough-in, supply and waste, add | | 1.83 | 4.372 | | 127 | 204 | | 331 | 445 |

## 22 47 16 – Pressure Water Coolers

### 22 47 16.10 Electric Water Coolers

| 22 47 16.10 Electric Water Coolers | | Crew | Daily Output | Labor-Hours | Unit | Material | 2008 Bare Costs Labor | Equipment | Total | Total Incl O&P |
|---|---|---|---|---|---|---|---|---|---|---|
| 0010 | **ELECTRIC WATER COOLERS** R224000-50 | | | | | | | | | |
| 0100 | Wall mounted, non-recessed | | | | | | | | | |
| 0140 | 4 GPH | Q-1 | 4 | 4 | Ea. | 545 | 168 | | 713 | 855 |
| 0160 | 8 GPH, barrier free, sensor operated | | 4 | 4 | | 690 | 168 | | 858 | 1,025 |
| 0180 | 8.2 GPH | | 4 | 4 | | 615 | 168 | | 783 | 930 |
| 0600 | For hot and cold water, add | | | | | 158 | | | 158 | 174 |
| 0640 | For stainless steel cabinet, add | | | | | 80.50 | | | 80.50 | 88.50 |
| 1000 | Dual height, 8.2 GPH | Q-1 | 3.80 | 4.211 | | 885 | 177 | | 1,062 | 1,250 |
| 1040 | 14.3 GPH | " | 3.80 | 4.211 | | 935 | 177 | | 1,112 | 1,300 |
| 1240 | For stainless steel cabinet, add | | | | | 122 | | | 122 | 135 |
| 2600 | Wheelchair type, 8 GPH | Q-1 | 4 | 4 | | 1,550 | 168 | | 1,718 | 1,975 |

# 22 47 Drinking Fountains and Water Coolers

## 22 47 16 – Pressure Water Coolers

### 22 47 16.10 Electric Water Coolers

| | | Crew | Daily Output | Labor-Hours | Unit | Material | 2008 Bare Costs Labor | Equipment | Total | Total Incl O&P |
|---|---|---|---|---|---|---|---|---|---|---|
| 3300 | Semi-recessed, 8.1 GPH | Q-1 | 4 | 4 | Ea. | 920 | 168 | | 1,088 | 1,250 |
| 3320 | 12 GPH | ↓ | 4 | 4 | ↓ | 970 | 168 | | 1,138 | 1,325 |
| 4600 | Floor mounted, flush-to-wall | | | | | | | | | |
| 4640 | 4 GPH | 1 Plum | 3 | 2.667 | Ea. | 570 | 125 | | 695 | 815 |
| 4680 | 8.2 GPH | | 3 | 2.667 | | 660 | 125 | | 785 | 915 |
| 4720 | 14.3 GPH | | 3 | 2.667 | | 680 | 125 | | 805 | 935 |
| 4960 | 14 GPH hot and cold water | ↓ | 3 | 2.667 | | 950 | 125 | | 1,075 | 1,225 |
| 4980 | For stainless steel cabinet, add | | | | | 122 | | | 122 | 135 |
| 5000 | Dual height, 8.2 GPH | 1 Plum | 2 | 4 | | 955 | 187 | | 1,142 | 1,325 |
| 5040 | 14.3 GPH | " | 2 | 4 | | 990 | 187 | | 1,177 | 1,375 |
| 5120 | For stainless steel cabinet, add | | | | | 161 | | | 161 | 177 |
| 9800 | For supply, waste & vent, all coolers | 1 Plum | 2.21 | 3.620 | ↓ | 127 | 169 | | 296 | 395 |

# 22 51 Swimming Pool Plumbing Systems

## 22 51 19 – Swimming Pool Water Treatment Equipment

### 22 51 19.50 Swimming Pool Filtration Equipment

| | | Crew | Daily Output | Labor-Hours | Unit | Material | 2008 Bare Costs Labor | Equipment | Total | Total Incl O&P |
|---|---|---|---|---|---|---|---|---|---|---|
| 0010 | **SWIMMING POOL FILTRATION EQUIPMENT** | | | | | | | | | |
| 0900 | Filter system, sand or diatomite type, incl. pump, 6,000 gal./hr. | 2 Plum | 1.80 | 8.889 | Total | 1,025 | 415 | | 1,440 | 1,750 |
| 1020 | Add for chlorination system, 800 S.F. pool | ↓ | 3 | 5.333 | Ea. | 78.50 | 249 | | 327.50 | 460 |
| 1040 | 5,000 S.F. pool | ↓ | 3 | 5.333 | " | 1,950 | 249 | | 2,199 | 2,500 |

# 22 52 Fountain Plumbing Systems

## 22 52 16 – Fountain Pumps

### 22 52 16.10 Fountain Water Pumps

| | | Crew | Daily Output | Labor-Hours | Unit | Material | 2008 Bare Costs Labor | Equipment | Total | Total Incl O&P |
|---|---|---|---|---|---|---|---|---|---|---|
| 0010 | **FOUNTAIN WATER PUMPS** | | | | | | | | | |
| 0100 | Pump w/controls | | | | | | | | | |
| 0200 | Single phase, 100' cord, 1/2 H.P. pump | 2 Skwk | 4.40 | 3.636 | Ea. | 3,850 | 143 | | 3,993 | 4,450 |
| 0300 | 3/4 H.P. pump | | 4.30 | 3.721 | | 4,375 | 147 | | 4,522 | 5,025 |
| 0400 | 1 H.P. pump | | 4.20 | 3.810 | | 4,425 | 150 | | 4,575 | 5,075 |
| 0500 | 1-1/2 H.P. pump | | 4.10 | 3.902 | | 4,575 | 154 | | 4,729 | 5,275 |
| 0600 | 2 H.P. pump | | 4 | 4 | | 4,625 | 158 | | 4,783 | 5,350 |
| 0700 | Three phase, 200' cord, 5 H.P. pump | | 3.90 | 4.103 | | 11,200 | 162 | | 11,362 | 12,700 |
| 0800 | 7-1/2 H.P. pump | | 3.80 | 4.211 | | 12,700 | 166 | | 12,866 | 14,200 |
| 0900 | 10 H.P. pump | | 3.70 | 4.324 | | 14,200 | 170 | | 14,370 | 15,900 |
| 1000 | 15 H.P. pump | ↓ | 3.60 | 4.444 | ↓ | 16,800 | 175 | | 16,975 | 18,700 |

## 22 52 33 – Fountain Ancillary

### 22 52 33.10 Fountain Miscellaneous

| | | Crew | Daily Output | Labor-Hours | Unit | Material | 2008 Bare Costs Labor | Equipment | Total | Total Incl O&P |
|---|---|---|---|---|---|---|---|---|---|---|
| 0010 | **FOUNTAIN MISCELLANEOUS** | | | | | | | | | |
| 1100 | Nozzles, minimum | 2 Skwk | 8 | 2 | Ea. | 269 | 79 | | 348 | 420 |
| 1200 | Maximum | | 8 | 2 | | 355 | 79 | | 434 | 515 |
| 1300 | Lights w/mounting kits, 200 watt | | 18 | .889 | | 465 | 35 | | 500 | 565 |
| 1400 | 300 watt | | 18 | .889 | | 515 | 35 | | 550 | 620 |
| 1500 | 500 watt | | 18 | .889 | | 560 | 35 | | 595 | 675 |
| 1600 | Color blender | ↓ | 12 | 1.333 | ↓ | 440 | 52.50 | | 492.50 | 560 |

452

## 22 66 53 – Laboratory Chemical-Waste and Vent Piping

| 22 66 53.30 Glass Pipe | | Crew | Daily Output | Labor-Hours | Unit | Material | 2008 Bare Costs Labor | Equipment | Total | Total Incl O&P |
|---|---|---|---|---|---|---|---|---|---|---|
| 0010 | **GLASS PIPE**, Borosilicate, couplings & clevis hanger assemblies, 10' O.C. | | | | | | | | | |
| 0020 | Drainage | | | | | | | | | |
| 1100 | 1-1/2" diameter | Q-1 | 52 | .308 | L.F. | 12.05 | 12.95 | | 25 | 32.50 |
| 1120 | 2" diameter | | 44 | .364 | | 16 | 15.30 | | 31.30 | 40.50 |
| 1140 | 3" diameter | | 39 | .410 | | 21.50 | 17.25 | | 38.75 | 50 |
| 1160 | 4" diameter | | 30 | .533 | | 39 | 22.50 | | 61.50 | 76.50 |
| 1180 | 6" diameter | | 26 | .615 | | 71 | 26 | | 97 | 117 |

| 22 66 53.60 Corrosion Resistant Pipe | | Crew | Daily Output | Labor-Hours | Unit | Material | 2008 Bare Costs Labor | Equipment | Total | Total Incl O&P |
|---|---|---|---|---|---|---|---|---|---|---|
| 0010 | **CORROSION RESISTANT PIPE**, No couplings or hangers | | | | | | | | | |
| 0020 | Iron alloy, drain, mechanical joint | | | | | | | | | |
| 1000 | 1-1/2" diameter | Q-1 | 70 | .229 | L.F. | 34.50 | 9.60 | | 44.10 | 52.50 |
| 1100 | 2" diameter | | 66 | .242 | | 35.50 | 10.20 | | 45.70 | 54.50 |
| 1120 | 3" diameter | | 60 | .267 | | 45.50 | 11.20 | | 56.70 | 67 |
| 1140 | 4" diameter | | 52 | .308 | | 58.50 | 12.95 | | 71.45 | 84 |
| 2980 | Plastic, epoxy, fiberglass filament wound, B&S joint | | | | | | | | | |
| 3000 | 2" diameter | Q-1 | 62 | .258 | L.F. | 8.90 | 10.85 | | 19.75 | 26 |
| 3100 | 3" diameter | | 51 | .314 | | 10.55 | 13.20 | | 23.75 | 31.50 |
| 3120 | 4" diameter | | 45 | .356 | | 15.25 | 14.95 | | 30.20 | 39.50 |
| 3140 | 6" diameter | | 32 | .500 | | 21.50 | 21 | | 42.50 | 55.50 |
| 3980 | Polyester, fiberglass filament wound, B&S joint | | | | | | | | | |
| 4000 | 2" diameter | Q-1 | 62 | .258 | L.F. | 9.75 | 10.85 | | 20.60 | 27 |
| 4100 | 3" diameter | | 51 | .314 | | 13.30 | 13.20 | | 26.50 | 34.50 |
| 4120 | 4" diameter | | 45 | .356 | | 19 | 14.95 | | 33.95 | 43.50 |
| 4140 | 6" diameter | | 32 | .500 | | 28 | 21 | | 49 | 62 |
| 4980 | Polypropylene, acid resistant, fire retardant, schedule 40 | | | | | | | | | |
| 5000 | 1-1/2" diameter | Q-1 | 68 | .235 | L.F. | 4.26 | 9.90 | | 14.16 | 19.55 |
| 5100 | 2" diameter | | 62 | .258 | | 5.80 | 10.85 | | 16.65 | 22.50 |
| 5120 | 3" diameter | | 51 | .314 | | 11.85 | 13.20 | | 25.05 | 33 |
| 5140 | 4" diameter | | 45 | .356 | | 15.10 | 14.95 | | 30.05 | 39 |
| 5980 | Proxylene, fire retardant, Schedule 40 | | | | | | | | | |
| 6000 | 1-1/2" diameter | Q-1 | 68 | .235 | L.F. | 6.60 | 9.90 | | 16.50 | 22 |
| 6100 | 2" diameter | | 62 | .258 | | 9.10 | 10.85 | | 19.95 | 26.50 |
| 6120 | 3" diameter | | 51 | .314 | | 16.45 | 13.20 | | 29.65 | 38 |
| 6140 | 4" diameter | | 45 | .356 | | 23.50 | 14.95 | | 38.45 | 48 |

# Division Notes

| | | CREW | DAILY OUTPUT | LABOR-HOURS | UNIT | 2008 BARE COSTS | | | | TOTAL INCL O&P |
|---|---|---|---|---|---|---|---|---|---|---|
| | | | | | | MAT. | LABOR | EQUIP. | TOTAL | |
| | | | | | | | | | | |
| | | | | | | | | | | |
| | | | | | | | | | | |
| | | | | | | | | | | |
| | | | | | | | | | | |
| | | | | | | | | | | |
| | | | | | | | | | | |
| | | | | | | | | | | |
| | | | | | | | | | | |
| | | | | | | | | | | |
| | | | | | | | | | | |
| | | | | | | | | | | |
| | | | | | | | | | | |
| | | | | | | | | | | |
| | | | | | | | | | | |
| | | | | | | | | | | |
| | | | | | | | | | | |
| | | | | | | | | | | |
| | | | | | | | | | | |
| | | | | | | | | | | |

# Estimating Tips

## 23 10 00 Facility Fuel Systems

- The prices in this subdivision for above- and below-ground storage tanks do not include foundations or hold-down slabs. The estimator should refer to Divisions 3 and 31 for foundation system pricing. In addition to the foundations, required tank accessories, such as tank gauges, leak detection devices, and additional manholes and piping, must be added to the tank prices.

## 23 50 00 Central Heating Equipment

- When estimating the cost of an HVAC system, check to see who is responsible for providing and installing the temperature control system. It is possible to overlook controls, assuming that they would be included in the electrical estimate.
- When looking up a boiler, be careful on specified capacity. Some manufacturers rate their products on output while others use input.
- Include HVAC insulation for pipe, boiler, and duct (wrap and liner).
- Be careful when looking up mechanical items to get the correct pressure rating and connection type (thread, weld, flange).

## 23 70 00 Central HVAC Equipment

- Combination heating and cooling units are sized by the air conditioning requirements. (See Reference No. R236000-20 for preliminary sizing guide.)
- A ton of air conditioning is nominally 400 CFM.
- Rectangular duct is taken off by the linear foot for each size, but its cost is usually estimated by the pound. Remember that SMACNA standards now base duct on internal pressure.
- Prefabricated duct is estimated and purchased like pipe: straight sections and fittings.
- Note that cranes or other lifting equipment are not included on any lines in Division 23. For example, if a crane is required to lift a heavy piece of pipe into place high above a gym floor, or to put a rooftop unit on the roof of a four-story building, etc., it must be added. Due to the potential for extreme variation—from nothing additional required to a major crane or helicopter—we feel that including a nominal amount for "lifting contingency" would be useless and detract from the accuracy of the estimate. When using equipment rental from RSMeans do not forget to include the cost of the operator(s).

# Reference Numbers

Reference numbers are shown in shaded boxes at the beginning of some major classifications. These numbers refer to related items in the Reference Section. The reference information may be an estimating procedure, an alternate pricing method, or technical information.

*Note:* Not all subdivisions listed here necessarily appear in this publication.

*Note:* **Trade Service,** *in part, has been used as a reference source for some of the material prices used in Division 23.*

# 23 05 Common Work Results for HVAC

## 23 05 05 – Selective HVAC Demolition

### 23 05 05.10 HVAC Demolition

| | | Crew | Daily Output | Labor-Hours | Unit | Material | 2008 Bare Costs Labor | Equipment | Total | Total Incl O&P |
|---|---|---|---|---|---|---|---|---|---|---|
| 0010 | **HVAC DEMOLITION** | | | | | | | | | |
| 0100 | Air conditioner, split unit, 3 ton | Q-5 | 2 | 8 | Ea. | | 340 | | 340 | 510 |
| 0150 | Package unit, 3 ton | Q-6 | 3 | 8 | " | | 350 | | 350 | 530 |
| 0298 | Boilers | | | | | | | | | |
| 0300 | Electric, up thru 148 kW | Q-19 | 2 | 12 | Ea. | | 520 | | 520 | 780 |
| 0310 | 150 thru 518 kW | " | 1 | 24 | | | 1,050 | | 1,050 | 1,575 |
| 0320 | 550 thru 2000 kW | Q-21 | .40 | 80 | | | 3,550 | | 3,550 | 5,325 |
| 0330 | 2070 kW and up | " | .30 | 106 | | | 4,725 | | 4,725 | 7,100 |
| 0340 | Gas and/or oil, up thru 150 MBH | Q-7 | 2.20 | 14.545 | | | 655 | | 655 | 980 |
| 0350 | 160 thru 2000 MBH | | .80 | 40 | | | 1,800 | | 1,800 | 2,700 |
| 0360 | 2100 thru 4500 MBH | | .50 | 64 | | | 2,875 | | 2,875 | 4,325 |
| 0370 | 4600 thru 7000 MBH | | .30 | 106 | | | 4,775 | | 4,775 | 7,200 |
| 0380 | 7100 thru 12,000 MBH | | .16 | 200 | | | 8,975 | | 8,975 | 13,500 |
| 0390 | 12,200 thru 25,000 MBH | | .12 | 266 | | | 12,000 | | 12,000 | 18,000 |
| 1000 | Ductwork, 4" high, 8" wide | 1 Clab | 200 | .040 | L.F. | | 1.21 | | 1.21 | 1.88 |
| 1100 | 6" high, 8" wide | | 165 | .048 | | | 1.47 | | 1.47 | 2.28 |
| 1200 | 10" high, 12" wide | | 125 | .064 | | | 1.94 | | 1.94 | 3.01 |
| 1300 | 12"-14" high, 16"-18" wide | | 85 | .094 | | | 2.85 | | 2.85 | 4.43 |
| 1400 | 18" high, 24" wide | | 67 | .119 | | | 3.61 | | 3.61 | 5.60 |
| 1500 | 30" high, 36" wide | | 56 | .143 | | | 4.32 | | 4.32 | 6.70 |
| 1540 | 72" wide | | 50 | .160 | | | 4.84 | | 4.84 | 7.55 |
| 3000 | Mechanical equipment, light items. Unit is weight, not cooling. | Q-5 | .90 | 17.778 | Ton | | 755 | | 755 | 1,125 |
| 3600 | Heavy items | " | 1.10 | 14.545 | " | | 615 | | 615 | 930 |
| 3700 | Deduct for salvage (when applicable), minimum | | | | Job | | | | 59 | 65 |
| 3710 | Maximum | | | | " | | | | 455 | 490 |

## 23 05 23 – General-Duty Valves for HVAC Piping

### 23 05 23.30 Valves, Iron Body

| | | Crew | Daily Output | Labor-Hours | Unit | Material | 2008 Bare Costs Labor | Equipment | Total | Total Incl O&P |
|---|---|---|---|---|---|---|---|---|---|---|
| 0010 | **VALVES, IRON BODY** | | | | | | | | | |
| 1020 | Butterfly, wafer type, gear actuator, 200 lb. | | | | | | | | | |
| 1030 | 2" | 1 Plum | 14 | .571 | Ea. | 155 | 26.50 | | 181.50 | 210 |
| 1040 | 2-1/2" | Q-1 | 9 | 1.778 | | 159 | 74.50 | | 233.50 | 287 |
| 1050 | 3" | | 8 | 2 | | 165 | 84 | | 249 | 310 |
| 1060 | 4" | | 5 | 3.200 | | 188 | 135 | | 323 | 410 |
| 1070 | 5" | Q-2 | 5 | 4.800 | | 249 | 209 | | 458 | 590 |
| 1080 | 6" | " | 5 | 4.800 | | 281 | 209 | | 490 | 625 |
| 1650 | Gate, 125 lb., N.R.S. | | | | | | | | | |
| 2150 | Flanged | | | | | | | | | |
| 2200 | 2" | 1 Plum | 5 | 1.600 | Ea. | 410 | 74.50 | | 484.50 | 565 |
| 2240 | 2-1/2" | Q-1 | 5 | 3.200 | | 420 | 135 | | 555 | 665 |
| 2260 | 3" | | 4.50 | 3.556 | | 475 | 149 | | 624 | 745 |
| 2280 | 4" | | 3 | 5.333 | | 675 | 224 | | 899 | 1,075 |
| 2300 | 6" | Q-2 | 3 | 8 | | 1,150 | 350 | | 1,500 | 1,800 |
| 3550 | OS&Y, 125 lb., flanged | | | | | | | | | |
| 3600 | 2" | 1 Plum | 5 | 1.600 | Ea. | 269 | 74.50 | | 343.50 | 410 |
| 3660 | 3" | Q-1 | 4.50 | 3.556 | | 310 | 149 | | 459 | 570 |
| 3680 | 4" | " | 3 | 5.333 | | 445 | 224 | | 669 | 825 |
| 3700 | 6" | Q-2 | 3 | 8 | | 735 | 350 | | 1,085 | 1,325 |
| 3900 | For 175 lb, flanged, add | | | | | 200% | 10% | | | |
| 5450 | Swing check, 125 lb., threaded | | | | | | | | | |
| 5470 | 1" | 1 Plum | 13 | .615 | Ea. | 450 | 28.50 | | 478.50 | 540 |
| 5500 | 2" | " | 11 | .727 | | 525 | 34 | | 559 | 630 |
| 5540 | 2-1/2" | Q-1 | 15 | 1.067 | | 550 | 45 | | 595 | 675 |

# 23 05 Common Work Results for HVAC

## 23 05 23 – General-Duty Valves for HVAC Piping

### 23 05 23.30 Valves, Iron Body

| | | Crew | Daily Output | Labor-Hours | Unit | Material | 2008 Bare Costs Labor | 2008 Bare Costs Equipment | Total | Total Incl O&P |
|---|---|---|---|---|---|---|---|---|---|---|
| 5550 | 3" | Q-1 | 13 | 1.231 | Ea. | 610 | 51.50 | | 661.50 | 750 |
| 5560 | 4" | ↓ | 10 | 1.600 | ↓ | 1,050 | 67.50 | | 1,117.50 | 1,250 |
| 5950 | Flanged | | | | | | | | | |
| 6000 | 2" | 1 Plum | 5 | 1.600 | Ea. | 185 | 74.50 | | 259.50 | 315 |
| 6040 | 2-1/2" | Q-1 | 5 | 3.200 | | 225 | 135 | | 360 | 450 |
| 6050 | 3" | | 4.50 | 3.556 | | 241 | 149 | | 390 | 490 |
| 6060 | 4" | ↓ | 3 | 5.333 | | 380 | 224 | | 604 | 750 |
| 6070 | 6" | Q-2 | 3 | 8 | ↓ | 650 | 350 | | 1,000 | 1,250 |

### 23 05 23.80 Valves, Steel

| | | Crew | Daily Output | Labor-Hours | Unit | Material | 2008 Bare Costs Labor | 2008 Bare Costs Equipment | Total | Total Incl O&P |
|---|---|---|---|---|---|---|---|---|---|---|
| 0010 | **VALVES, STEEL** | | | | | | | | | |
| 0800 | Cast | | | | | | | | | |
| 1350 | Check valve, swing type, 150 lb., flanged | | | | | | | | | |
| 1370 | 1" | 1 Plum | 10 | .800 | Ea. | 510 | 37.50 | | 547.50 | 615 |
| 1400 | 2" | " | 8 | 1 | | 645 | 46.50 | | 691.50 | 780 |
| 1440 | 2-1/2" | Q-1 | 5 | 3.200 | | 745 | 135 | | 880 | 1,025 |
| 1450 | 3" | | 4.50 | 3.556 | | 745 | 149 | | 894 | 1,050 |
| 1460 | 4" | ↓ | 3 | 5.333 | | 1,100 | 224 | | 1,324 | 1,525 |
| 1540 | For 300 lb., flanged, add | | | | | 50% | 15% | | | |
| 1548 | For 600 lb., flanged, add | | | | ↓ | 110% | 20% | | | |
| 1950 | Gate valve, 150 lb., flanged | | | | | | | | | |
| 2000 | 2" | 1 Plum | 8 | 1 | Ea. | 695 | 46.50 | | 741.50 | 830 |
| 2040 | 2-1/2" | Q-1 | 5 | 3.200 | | 980 | 135 | | 1,115 | 1,275 |
| 2050 | 3" | | 4.50 | 3.556 | | 980 | 149 | | 1,129 | 1,300 |
| 2060 | 4" | ↓ | 3 | 5.333 | | 1,225 | 224 | | 1,449 | 1,675 |
| 2070 | 6" | Q-2 | 3 | 8 | ↓ | 1,900 | 350 | | 2,250 | 2,600 |
| 3650 | Globe valve, 150 lb., flanged | | | | | | | | | |
| 3700 | 2" | 1 Plum | 8 | 1 | Ea. | 870 | 46.50 | | 916.50 | 1,025 |
| 3740 | 2-1/2" | Q-1 | 5 | 3.200 | | 1,100 | 135 | | 1,235 | 1,425 |
| 3750 | 3" | | 4.50 | 3.556 | | 1,100 | 149 | | 1,249 | 1,450 |
| 3760 | 4" | ↓ | 3 | 5.333 | | 1,625 | 224 | | 1,849 | 2,100 |
| 3770 | 6" | Q-2 | 3 | 8 | ↓ | 2,550 | 350 | | 2,900 | 3,325 |
| 5150 | Forged | | | | | | | | | |
| 5650 | Check valve, class 800, horizontal, socket | | | | | | | | | |
| 5698 | Threaded | | | | | | | | | |
| 5700 | 1/4" | 1 Plum | 24 | .333 | Ea. | 72 | 15.55 | | 87.55 | 103 |
| 5720 | 3/8" | | 24 | .333 | | 72 | 15.55 | | 87.55 | 103 |
| 5730 | 1/2" | | 24 | .333 | | 72 | 15.55 | | 87.55 | 103 |
| 5740 | 3/4" | | 20 | .400 | | 78 | 18.70 | | 96.70 | 114 |
| 5750 | 1" | | 19 | .421 | | 90.50 | 19.65 | | 110.15 | 130 |
| 5760 | 1-1/4" | ↓ | 15 | .533 | ↓ | 179 | 25 | | 204 | 234 |

## 23 05 93 – Testing, Adjusting, and Balancing for HVAC

### 23 05 93.10 Balancing, Air

| | | Crew | Daily Output | Labor-Hours | Unit | Material | 2008 Bare Costs Labor | 2008 Bare Costs Equipment | Total | Total Incl O&P |
|---|---|---|---|---|---|---|---|---|---|---|
| 0010 | **BALANCING, AIR**, (Subcontractor's quote incl. material and labor.) | | | | | | | | | |
| 0900 | Heating and ventilating equipment | | | | | | | | | |
| 1000 | Centrifugal fans, utility sets | | | | Ea. | | | | 305.10 | 335 |
| 1100 | Heating and ventilating unit | | | | | | | | 457.70 | 503 |
| 1200 | In-line fan | | | | | | | | 457.70 | 503 |
| 1300 | Propeller and wall fan | | | | | | | | 86.45 | 95 |
| 1400 | Roof exhaust fan | | | | | | | | 203.40 | 223.50 |
| 2000 | Air conditioning equipment, central station | | | | | | | | 661.05 | 726.40 |
| 2100 | Built-up low pressure unit | | | | | | | | 610.20 | 670.60 |
| 2200 | Built-up high pressure unit | | | | ↓ | | | | 711.90 | 782.30 |

# 23 05 Common Work Results for HVAC

## 23 05 93 – Testing, Adjusting, and Balancing for HVAC

### 23 05 93.10 Balancing, Air

| | | Crew | Daily Output | Labor-Hours | Unit | Material | 2008 Bare Costs Labor | Equipment | Total | Total Incl O&P |
|---|---|---|---|---|---|---|---|---|---|---|
| 2500 | Multi-zone A.C. and heating unit | | | | Ea. | | | | 457.70 | 502.90 |
| 2600 | For each zone over one, add | | | | | | | | 101.70 | 111.80 |
| 2700 | Package A.C. unit | | | | | | | | 254.25 | 279.40 |
| 2800 | Rooftop heating and cooling unit | | | | | | | | 356 | 391.20 |
| 3000 | Supply, return, exhaust, registers & diffusers, avg. height ceiling | | | | | | | | 61 | 67.10 |
| 3100 | High ceiling | | | | | | | | 91.50 | 100.60 |
| 3200 | Floor height | | | | | | | | 50.90 | 55.90 |

### 23 05 93.20 Balancing, Water

| | | Crew | Daily Output | Labor-Hours | Unit | Material | 2008 Bare Costs Labor | Equipment | Total | Total Incl O&P |
|---|---|---|---|---|---|---|---|---|---|---|
| 0010 | **BALANCING, WATER,** (Subcontractor's quote incl. material and labor.) | | | | | | | | | |
| 0050 | Air cooled condenser | | | | Ea. | | | | 180.50 | 198.40 |
| 0080 | Boiler | | | | | | | | 363.10 | 399 |
| 0100 | Cabinet unit heater | | | | | | | | 61.90 | 68 |
| 0200 | Chiller | | | | | | | | 438.40 | 481.80 |
| 0300 | Convector | | | | | | | | 51.60 | 56.70 |
| 0500 | Cooling tower | | | | | | | | 335.30 | 368.40 |
| 0600 | Fan coil unit, unit ventilator | | | | | | | | 92.80 | 102 |
| 0700 | Fin tube and radiant panels | | | | | | | | 103.20 | 113.40 |
| 0800 | Main and duct re-heat coils | | | | | | | | 95.40 | 104.90 |
| 0810 | Heat exchanger | | | | | | | | 95.40 | 104.90 |
| 1000 | Pumps | | | | | | | | 227 | 249.40 |
| 1100 | Unit heater | | | | | | | | 72.20 | 79.40 |

# 23 07 HVAC Insulation

## 23 07 13 – Duct Insulation

### 23 07 13.10 Duct Thermal Insulation

| | | Crew | Daily Output | Labor-Hours | Unit | Material | 2008 Bare Costs Labor | Equipment | Total | Total Incl O&P |
|---|---|---|---|---|---|---|---|---|---|---|
| 0010 | **DUCT THERMAL INSULATION** | | | | | | | | | |
| 0100 | Rule of thumb, as a percentage of total mechanical costs | | | | Job | | | | 10% | |
| 0110 | Insulation req'd is based on the surface size/area to be covered | | | | | | | | | |
| 3000 | Ductwork | | | | | | | | | |
| 3020 | Blanket type, fiberglass, flexible | | | | | | | | | |
| 3140 | FSK vapor barrier wrap, .75 lb. density | | | | | | | | | |
| 3160 | 1" thick | Q-14 | 350 | .046 | S.F. | .15 | 1.77 | | 1.92 | 2.96 |
| 3170 | 1-1/2" thick | | 320 | .050 | | .19 | 1.94 | | 2.13 | 3.26 |
| 3180 | 2" thick | | 300 | .053 | | .25 | 2.07 | | 2.32 | 3.54 |
| 3190 | 3" thick | | 260 | .062 | | .38 | 2.39 | | 2.77 | 4.18 |
| 3200 | 4" thick | | 242 | .066 | | .99 | 2.57 | | 3.56 | 5.15 |
| 3210 | Vinyl jacket, same as FSK | | | | | | | | | |
| 3280 | Unfaced, 1 lb. density | | | | | | | | | |
| 3310 | 1" thick | Q-14 | 360 | .044 | S.F. | .41 | 1.72 | | 2.13 | 3.16 |
| 3320 | 1-1/2" thick | | 330 | .048 | | .57 | 1.88 | | 2.45 | 3.59 |
| 3330 | 2" thick | | 310 | .052 | | .64 | 2 | | 2.64 | 3.85 |
| 3795 | Finishes | | | | | | | | | |
| 3800 | 1/2" cement over 1" wire mesh, incl. corner bead | Q-14 | 100 | .160 | S.F. | 1.80 | 6.20 | | 8 | 11.75 |
| 3820 | Glass cloth, pasted on | | 170 | .094 | | 3.04 | 3.65 | | 6.69 | 9.10 |
| 3900 | Weatherproof, non-metallic, 2 lb. per S.F. | | 180 | .089 | | 2.98 | 3.45 | | 6.43 | 8.75 |
| 9600 | Minimum labor/equipment charge | 1 Stpi | 4 | 2 | Job | | 94 | | 94 | 142 |

## 23 07 16 – HVAC Equipment Insulation

### 23 07 16.10 HVAC Equipment Thermal In

| | | Crew | Daily Output | Labor-Hours | Unit | Material | 2008 Bare Costs Labor | Equipment | Total | Total Incl O&P |
|---|---|---|---|---|---|---|---|---|---|---|
| 0010 | **HVAC EQUIPMENT THERMAL INSULATION** | | | | | | | | | |
| 0100 | Rule of thumb, as a percentage of total mechanical costs | | | | Job | | | | 10% | |

# 23 07 HVAC Insulation

## 23 07 16 – HVAC Equipment Insulation

| 23 07 16.10 HVAC Equipment Thermal In | Crew | Daily Output | Labor-Hours | Unit | Material | 2008 Bare Costs Labor | Equipment | Total | Total Incl O&P |
|---|---|---|---|---|---|---|---|---|---|
| 0110 Insulation req'd is based on the surface size/area to be covered | | | | | | | | | |
| 1000 Boiler, 1-1/2" calcium silicate, 1/2" cement finish | Q-14 | 50 | .320 | S.F. | 3.98 | 12.40 | | 16.38 | 24 |
| 1020      2" fiberglass | " | 80 | .200 | " | 2.74 | 7.75 | | 10.49 | 15.20 |
| 2000 Breeching, 2" calcium silicate with 1/2" cement finish, no lath | | | | | | | | | |
| 2020      Rectangular | Q-14 | 42 | .381 | S.F. | 5.20 | 14.80 | | 20 | 29 |
| 2040      Round | " | 38.70 | .413 | " | 5.45 | 16.05 | | 21.50 | 31.50 |

# 23 09 Instrumentation and Control for HVAC

## 23 09 33 – Electric and Electronic Control System for HVAC

### 23 09 33.10 Electronic Control Systems

| | | | | | | | | | |
|---|---|---|---|---|---|---|---|---|---|
| 0010 **ELECTRONIC CONTROL SYSTEMS** | | | | | | | | | |
| 0020      For electronic costs, add to division 23 09 43.10 | | | | Ea. | | | | | 15% |

## 23 09 43 – Pneumatic Control System for HVAC

### 23 09 43.10 Pneumatic Control Systems

| | Crew | Daily Output | Labor-Hours | Unit | Material | 2008 Bare Costs Labor | Equipment | Total | Total Incl O&P |
|---|---|---|---|---|---|---|---|---|---|
| 0010 **PNEUMATIC CONTROL SYSTEMS** | | | | | | | | | |
| 0011      Including a nominal 50 Ft. of tubing. Add control panelboard if req'd. | | | | | | | | | |
| 0100      Heating and Ventilating, split system | | | | | | | | | |
| 0200        Mixed air control, economizer cycle, panel readout, tubing | | | | | | | | | |
| 0220          Up to 10 tons | Q-19 | .68 | 35.294 | Ea. | 3,250 | 1,525 | | 4,775 | 5,875 |
| 0240          For 10 to 20 tons | | .63 | 37.915 | | 3,475 | 1,650 | | 5,125 | 6,300 |
| 0260          For over 20 tons | | .58 | 41.096 | | 3,775 | 1,775 | | 5,550 | 6,825 |
| 0300      Heating coil, hot water, 3 way valve, | | | | | | | | | |
| 0320        Freezestat, limit control on discharge, readout | Q-5 | .69 | 23.088 | Ea. | 2,400 | 980 | | 3,380 | 4,125 |
| 0500      Cooling coil, chilled water, room | | | | | | | | | |
| 0520        Thermostat, 3 way valve | Q-5 | 2 | 8 | Ea. | 1,075 | 340 | | 1,415 | 1,675 |
| 0600      Cooling tower, fan cycle, damper control, | | | | | | | | | |
| 0620        Control system including water readout in/out at panel | Q-19 | .67 | 35.821 | Ea. | 4,275 | 1,550 | | 5,825 | 7,025 |
| 1000      Unit ventilator, day/night operation, | | | | | | | | | |
| 1100        freezestat, ASHRAE, cycle 2 | Q-19 | .91 | 26.374 | Ea. | 2,375 | 1,150 | | 3,525 | 4,325 |
| 2000      Compensated hot water from boiler, valve control, | | | | | | | | | |
| 2100        readout and reset at panel, up to 60 GPM | Q-19 | .55 | 43.956 | Ea. | 4,425 | 1,900 | | 6,325 | 7,750 |
| 2120          For 120 GPM | | .51 | 47.059 | | 4,725 | 2,050 | | 6,775 | 8,275 |
| 2140          For 240 GPM | | .49 | 49.180 | | 4,950 | 2,125 | | 7,075 | 8,650 |
| 3000      Boiler room combustion air, damper to 5 SF, controls | | 1.37 | 17.582 | | 2,125 | 765 | | 2,890 | 3,500 |
| 3500      Fan coil, heating and cooling valves, 4 pipe control system | | 3 | 8 | | 960 | 350 | | 1,310 | 1,575 |
| 3600      Heat exchanger system controls | | .86 | 27.907 | | 2,075 | 1,225 | | 3,300 | 4,100 |
| 4000      Pneumatic thermostat, including controlling room radiator valve | Q-5 | 2.43 | 6.593 | | 640 | 280 | | 920 | 1,125 |
| 4060      Pump control system | Q-19 | 3 | 8 | | 985 | 350 | | 1,335 | 1,600 |
| 4500      Air supply for pneumatic control system | | | | | | | | | |
| 4600        Tank mounted duplex compressor, starter, alternator, | | | | | | | | | |
| 4620        piping, dryer, PRV station and filter | | | | | | | | | |
| 4630          1/2 HP | Q-19 | .68 | 35.139 | Ea. | 7,925 | 1,525 | | 9,450 | 11,000 |
| 4660          1-1/2 HP | | .58 | 41.739 | | 9,675 | 1,825 | | 11,500 | 13,400 |
| 4690          5 HP | | .42 | 57.143 | | 23,000 | 2,475 | | 25,475 | 29,000 |

# 23 12 Facility Fuel Pumps

## 23 12 16 – Facility Gasoline Dispensing Pumps

| 23 12 16.20 Fuel Dispensing Equipment | Crew | Daily Output | Labor-Hours | Unit | Material | 2008 Bare Costs Labor | Equipment | Total | Total Incl O&P |
|---|---|---|---|---|---|---|---|---|---|
| 0010 **FUEL DISPENSING EQUIPMENT** | | | | | | | | | |
| 1100 Product dispenser with vapor recovery for 6 nozzles, installed, not | | | | | | | | | |
| 1110 including piping to storage tanks | | | | Ea. | 19,800 | | | 19,800 | 21,800 |

# 23 13 Facility Fuel-Storage Tanks

## 23 13 13 – Facility Underground Fuel-Oil, Storage Tanks

### 23 13 13.09 Single-Wall Steel Fuel-Oil Tanks

| | Crew | Daily Output | Labor-Hours | Unit | Material | 2008 Bare Costs Labor | Equipment | Total | Total Incl O&P |
|---|---|---|---|---|---|---|---|---|---|
| 0010 **SINGLE-WALL STEEL FUEL-OIL TANKS** | | | | | | | | | |
| 5000 Steel underground, sti-P3, set in place, not incl. hold-down bars. | | | | | | | | | |
| 5500 Excavation, pad, pumps and piping not included | | | | | | | | | |
| 5510 Single wall, 500 gallon capacity, 7 gauge shell | Q-5 | 2.70 | 5.926 | Ea. | 1,650 | 251 | | 1,901 | 2,200 |
| 5520 1,000 gallon capacity, 7 gauge shell | " | 2.50 | 6.400 | | 2,550 | 271 | | 2,821 | 3,200 |
| 5530 2,000 gallon capacity, 1/4" thick shell | Q-7 | 4.60 | 6.957 | | 4,125 | 310 | | 4,435 | 5,025 |
| 5535 2,500 gallon capacity, 7 gauge shell | Q-5 | 3 | 5.333 | | 4,550 | 226 | | 4,776 | 5,375 |
| 5540 5,000 gallon capacity, 1/4" thick shell | Q-7 | 3.20 | 10 | | 5,600 | 450 | | 6,050 | 6,825 |
| 5580 15,000 gallon capacity, 5/16" thick shell | | 1.70 | 18.824 | | 11,500 | 845 | | 12,345 | 14,000 |
| 5600 20,000 gallon capacity, 5/16" thick shell | | 1.50 | 21.333 | | 17,600 | 955 | | 18,555 | 20,900 |
| 5610 25,000 gallon capacity, 3/8" thick shell | | 1.30 | 24.615 | | 23,400 | 1,100 | | 24,500 | 27,400 |
| 5620 30,000 gallon capacity, 3/8" thick shell | | 1.10 | 29.091 | | 25,600 | 1,300 | | 26,900 | 30,100 |
| 5630 40,000 gallon capacity, 3/8" thick shell | | .90 | 35.556 | | 33,000 | 1,600 | | 34,600 | 38,700 |
| 5640 50,000 gallon capacity, 3/8" thick shell | | .80 | 40 | | 41,300 | 1,800 | | 43,100 | 48,100 |

### 23 13 13.23 Glass-Fiber-Reinfcd-Plastic, Fuel-Oil, Storage

| | Crew | Daily Output | Labor-Hours | Unit | Material | 2008 Bare Costs Labor | Equipment | Total | Total Incl O&P |
|---|---|---|---|---|---|---|---|---|---|
| 0010 **GLASS-FIBER-REINFCD-PLASTIC, UNDERGRND FUEL-OIL, STORAGE** | | | | | | | | | |
| 0210 Fiberglass, underground, single wall, U.L. listed, not including | | | | | | | | | |
| 0220 manway or hold-down strap | | | | | | | | | |
| 0240 2,000 gallon capacity | Q-7 | 4.57 | 7.002 | Ea. | 5,075 | 315 | | 5,390 | 6,075 |
| 0250 4,000 gallon capacity | | 3.55 | 9.014 | | 7,225 | 405 | | 7,630 | 8,550 |
| 0260 6,000 gallon capacity | | 2.67 | 11.985 | | 8,025 | 540 | | 8,565 | 9,625 |
| 0280 10,000 gallon capacity | | 2 | 16 | | 10,800 | 720 | | 11,520 | 13,000 |
| 0284 15,000 gallon capacity | | 1.68 | 19.048 | | 16,900 | 855 | | 17,755 | 19,900 |
| 0290 20,000 gallon capacity | | 1.45 | 22.069 | | 21,600 | 990 | | 22,590 | 25,200 |
| 0500 For manway, fittings and hold-downs, add | | | | | 20% | 15% | | | |
| 1020 Fiberglass, underground, double wall, U.L. listed | | | | | | | | | |
| 1030 includes manways, not incl. hold-down straps | | | | | | | | | |
| 1040 600 gallon capacity | Q-5 | 2.42 | 6.612 | Ea. | 5,900 | 280 | | 6,180 | 6,900 |
| 1050 1,000 gallon capacity | " | 2.25 | 7.111 | | 7,800 | 300 | | 8,100 | 9,025 |
| 1060 2,500 gallon capacity | Q-7 | 4.16 | 7.692 | | 10,900 | 345 | | 11,245 | 12,500 |
| 1070 3,000 gallon capacity | | 3.90 | 8.205 | | 11,800 | 370 | | 12,170 | 13,500 |
| 1080 4,000 gallon capacity | | 3.64 | 8.791 | | 13,700 | 395 | | 14,095 | 15,700 |
| 1090 6,000 gallon capacity | | 2.42 | 13.223 | | 15,700 | 595 | | 16,295 | 18,200 |
| 1100 8,000 gallon capacity | *CN* | 2.08 | 15.385 | | 17,900 | 690 | | 18,590 | 20,800 |
| 1110 10,000 gallon capacity | | 1.82 | 17.582 | | 20,600 | 790 | | 21,390 | 23,800 |
| 1120 12,000 gallon capacity | | 1.70 | 18.824 | | 25,300 | 845 | | 26,145 | 29,200 |
| 2210 Fiberglass, underground, single wall, U.L. listed, including | | | | | | | | | |
| 2220 hold-down straps, no manways | | | | | | | | | |
| 2240 2,000 gallon capacity | Q-7 | 3.55 | 9.014 | Ea. | 5,425 | 405 | | 5,830 | 6,550 |
| 2250 4,000 gallon capacity | | 2.90 | 11.034 | | 7,550 | 495 | | 8,045 | 9,075 |
| 2260 6,000 gallon capacity | | 2 | 16 | | 8,675 | 720 | | 9,395 | 10,600 |
| 2280 10,000 gallon capacity | | 1.60 | 20 | | 11,500 | 900 | | 12,400 | 14,000 |
| 2284 15,000 gallon capacity | | 1.39 | 23.022 | | 17,600 | 1,025 | | 18,625 | 20,900 |
| 2290 20,000 gallon capacity | | 1.14 | 28.070 | | 22,600 | 1,250 | | 23,850 | 26,700 |

# 23 13 Facility Fuel-Storage Tanks

## 23 13 13 – Facility Underground Fuel-Oil, Storage Tanks

### 23 13 13.23 Glass-Fiber-Reinfcd-Plastic, Fuel-Oil, Storage

| | | Crew | Daily Output | Labor-Hours | Unit | Material | 2008 Bare Costs Labor | 2008 Bare Costs Equipment | Total | Total Incl O&P |
|---|---|---|---|---|---|---|---|---|---|---|
| 3020 | Fiberglass, underground, double wall, U.L. listed | | | | | | | | | |
| 3030 | includes manways and hold-down straps | | | | | | | | | |
| 3040 | 600 gallon capacity | Q-5 | 1.86 | 8.602 | Ea. | 6,225 | 365 | | 6,590 | 7,400 |
| 3050 | 1,000 gallon capacity | " | 1.70 | 9.412 | | 8,125 | 400 | | 8,525 | 9,550 |
| 3060 | 2,500 gallon capacity | Q-7 | 3.29 | 9.726 | | 11,200 | 435 | | 11,635 | 13,000 |
| 3070 | 3,000 gallon capacity | | 3.13 | 10.224 | | 12,100 | 460 | | 12,560 | 14,000 |
| 3080 | 4,000 gallon capacity | | 2.93 | 10.922 | | 14,100 | 490 | | 14,590 | 16,200 |
| 3090 | 6,000 gallon capacity | | 1.86 | 17.204 | | 16,400 | 770 | | 17,170 | 19,200 |
| 3100 | 8,000 gallon capacity | | 1.65 | 19.394 | | 18,600 | 870 | | 19,470 | 21,700 |
| 3110 | 10,000 gallon capacity | | 1.48 | 21.622 | | 21,200 | 970 | | 22,170 | 24,900 |
| 3120 | 12,000 gallon capacity | | 1.40 | 22.857 | | 26,000 | 1,025 | | 27,025 | 30,200 |

## 23 13 23 – Facility Aboveground Fuel-Oil, Storage Tanks

### 23 13 23.13 Vertical, Steel, Aboveground Fuel-Oil, Storage Tanks

| | | Crew | Daily Output | Labor-Hours | Unit | Material | 2008 Bare Costs Labor | 2008 Bare Costs Equipment | Total | Total Incl O&P |
|---|---|---|---|---|---|---|---|---|---|---|
| 0010 | **VERTICAL, STEEL, ABOVEGROUND FUEL-OIL, STORAGE TANKS** | | | | | | | | | |
| 4000 | Fixed roof oil storage tanks, steel, (1 BBL=42 GAL w/ fdn 3'D x 1'W) | | | | | | | | | |
| 4200 | 5,000 barrels | | | | Ea. | | | | 157,273 | 173,000 |
| 4300 | 24,000 barrels | | | | | | | | 269,091 | 296,000 |
| 4500 | 56,000 barrels | | | | | | | | 535,000 | 588,500 |
| 4600 | 110,000 barrels | | | | | | | | 777,273 | 855,000 |
| 4800 | 143,000 barrels | | | | | | | | 996,818 | 1,096,500 |
| 4900 | 224,000 barrels | | | | | | | | 1,495,909 | 1,645,500 |
| 5100 | Floating roof gasoline tanks, steel, 5,000 barrels | | | | | | | | 172,727 | 190,000 |
| 5200 | 25,000 barrels | | | | | | | | 295,455 | 325,000 |
| 5400 | 55,000 barrels | | | | | | | | 590,909 | 650,000 |
| 5500 | 100,000 barrels | | | | | | | | 854,545 | 940,000 |
| 5700 | 150,000 barrels | | | | | | | | 1,095,455 | 1,205,000 |
| 5800 | 225,000 barrels | | | | | | | | 1,645,455 | 1,810,000 |

### 23 13 23.16 Horizontal, Stl, Abvgrd Fuel-Oil, Storage Tanks

| | | Crew | Daily Output | Labor-Hours | Unit | Material | 2008 Bare Costs Labor | 2008 Bare Costs Equipment | Total | Total Incl O&P |
|---|---|---|---|---|---|---|---|---|---|---|
| 0010 | **HORIZONTAL, STEEL, ABOVEGROUND FUEL-OIL, STORAGE TANKS** | | | | | | | | | |
| 3000 | Steel, storage, above ground, including cradles, coating, | | | | | | | | | |
| 3020 | fittings, not including fdn, pumps or piping | | | | | | | | | |
| 3040 | Single wall, interior, 275 gallon | Q-5 | 5 | 3.200 | Ea. | 325 | 136 | | 461 | 565 |
| 3060 | 550 gallon | " | 2.70 | 5.926 | | 2,075 | 251 | | 2,326 | 2,650 |
| 3080 | 1,000 gallon | Q-7 | 5 | 6.400 | | 2,550 | 287 | | 2,837 | 3,225 |
| 3100 | 1,500 gallon | | 4.75 | 6.737 | | 3,750 | 300 | | 4,050 | 4,575 |
| 3120 | 2,000 gallon | | 4.60 | 6.957 | | 4,300 | 310 | | 4,610 | 5,225 |
| 3140 | 5,000 gallon | | 3.20 | 10 | | 5,825 | 450 | | 6,275 | 7,075 |
| 3150 | 10,000 gallon | | 2 | 16 | | 16,800 | 720 | | 17,520 | 19,500 |
| 3160 | 15,000 gallon | | 1.70 | 18.824 | | 19,500 | 845 | | 20,345 | 22,700 |
| 3170 | 20,000 gallon | | 1.45 | 22.069 | | 24,400 | 990 | | 25,390 | 28,400 |
| 3180 | 25,000 gallon | | 1.30 | 24.615 | | 28,600 | 1,100 | | 29,700 | 33,200 |
| 3190 | 30,000 gallon | | 1.10 | 29.091 | | 33,500 | 1,300 | | 34,800 | 38,800 |
| 3320 | Double wall, 500 gallon capacity | Q-5 | 2.40 | 6.667 | | 1,825 | 283 | | 2,108 | 2,450 |
| 3330 | 2000 gallon capacity | Q-7 | 4.15 | 7.711 | | 6,650 | 345 | | 6,995 | 7,850 |
| 3340 | 4000 gallon capacity | | 3.60 | 8.889 | | 11,900 | 400 | | 12,300 | 13,700 |
| 3350 | 6000 gallon capacity | | 2.40 | 13.333 | | 14,000 | 600 | | 14,600 | 16,300 |
| 3360 | 8000 gallon capacity | | 2 | 16 | | 18,000 | 720 | | 18,720 | 20,900 |
| 3370 | 10000 gallon capacity | | 1.80 | 17.778 | | 20,100 | 800 | | 20,900 | 23,400 |
| 3380 | 15000 gallon capacity | | 1.50 | 21.333 | | 30,600 | 955 | | 31,555 | 35,200 |
| 3390 | 20000 gallon capacity | | 1.30 | 24.615 | | 34,800 | 1,100 | | 35,900 | 40,000 |
| 3400 | 25000 gallon capacity | | 1.15 | 27.826 | | 42,300 | 1,250 | | 43,550 | 48,500 |
| 3410 | 30000 gallon capacity | | 1 | 32 | | 46,400 | 1,425 | | 47,825 | 53,000 |

461

# 23 21 Hydronic Piping and Pumps

## 23 21 20 – Hydronic HVAC Piping Specialties

### 23 21 20.10 Air Control

| | | Crew | Daily Output | Labor-Hours | Unit | Material | 2008 Bare Costs Labor | Equipment | Total | Total Incl O&P |
|---|---|---|---|---|---|---|---|---|---|---|
| 0010 | **AIR CONTROL** | | | | | | | | | |
| 0030 | Air separator, with strainer | | | | | | | | | |
| 0040 | 2" diameter | Q-5 | 6 | 2.667 | Ea. | 725 | 113 | | 838 | 970 |
| 0080 | 2-1/2" diameter | | 5 | 3.200 | | 840 | 136 | | 976 | 1,125 |
| 0100 | 3" diameter | | 4 | 4 | | 1,250 | 170 | | 1,420 | 1,625 |
| 0120 | 4" diameter | | 3 | 5.333 | | 1,825 | 226 | | 2,051 | 2,350 |
| 0130 | 5" diameter | Q-6 | 3.60 | 6.667 | | 2,325 | 293 | | 2,618 | 3,000 |
| 0140 | 6" diameter | " | 3.40 | 7.059 | | 2,775 | 310 | | 3,085 | 3,525 |

### 23 21 20.18 Automatic Air Vent

| | | Crew | Daily Output | Labor-Hours | Unit | Material | 2008 Bare Costs Labor | Equipment | Total | Total Incl O&P |
|---|---|---|---|---|---|---|---|---|---|---|
| 0010 | **AUTOMATIC AIR VENT** | | | | | | | | | |
| 0020 | Cast iron body, stainless steel internals, float type | | | | | | | | | |
| 0060 | 1/2" NPT inlet, 300 psi | 1 Stpi | 12 | .667 | Ea. | 84.50 | 31.50 | | 116 | 140 |
| 0220 | 3/4" NPT inlet, 250 psi | " | 10 | .800 | | 271 | 37.50 | | 308.50 | 355 |
| 0340 | 1-1/2" NPT inlet, 250 psi | Q-5 | 12 | 1.333 | | 840 | 56.50 | | 896.50 | 1,000 |

### 23 21 20.42 Expansion Joints

| | | Crew | Daily Output | Labor-Hours | Unit | Material | 2008 Bare Costs Labor | Equipment | Total | Total Incl O&P |
|---|---|---|---|---|---|---|---|---|---|---|
| 0010 | **EXPANSION JOINTS** | | | | | | | | | |
| 0100 | Bellows type, neoprene cover, flanged spool | | | | | | | | | |
| 0140 | 6" face to face, 1-1/4" diameter | 1 Stpi | 11 | .727 | Ea. | 231 | 34.50 | | 265.50 | 305 |
| 0160 | 1-1/2" diameter | " | 10.60 | .755 | | 231 | 35.50 | | 266.50 | 310 |
| 0180 | 2" diameter | Q-5 | 13.30 | 1.203 | | 235 | 51 | | 286 | 335 |
| 0190 | 2-1/2" diameter | | 12.40 | 1.290 | | 244 | 54.50 | | 298.50 | 350 |
| 0200 | 3" diameter | | 11.40 | 1.404 | | 277 | 59.50 | | 336.50 | 395 |
| 0480 | 10" face to face, 2" diameter | | 13 | 1.231 | | 345 | 52 | | 397 | 460 |
| 0500 | 2-1/2" diameter | | 12 | 1.333 | | 365 | 56.50 | | 421.50 | 485 |
| 0520 | 3" diameter | | 11 | 1.455 | | 370 | 61.50 | | 431.50 | 500 |
| 0540 | 4" diameter | | 8 | 2 | | 415 | 85 | | 500 | 585 |
| 0560 | 5" diameter | | 7 | 2.286 | | 500 | 97 | | 597 | 695 |
| 0580 | 6" diameter | | 6 | 2.667 | | 515 | 113 | | 628 | 735 |

### 23 21 20.46 Expansion Tanks

| | | Crew | Daily Output | Labor-Hours | Unit | Material | 2008 Bare Costs Labor | Equipment | Total | Total Incl O&P |
|---|---|---|---|---|---|---|---|---|---|---|
| 0010 | **EXPANSION TANKS** | | | | | | | | | |
| 1507 | Fiberglass and steel single / double wall storage, see Div 23 13 13 | | | | | | | | | |
| 1512 | Tank leak detection systems, see Div 28 33 33.50 | | | | | | | | | |
| 2000 | Steel, liquid expansion, ASME, painted, 15 gallon capacity | Q-5 | 17 | .941 | Ea. | 420 | 40 | | 460 | 525 |
| 2020 | 24 gallon capacity | | 14 | 1.143 | | 450 | 48.50 | | 498.50 | 570 |
| 2040 | 30 gallon capacity | | 12 | 1.333 | | 470 | 56.50 | | 526.50 | 605 |
| 2060 | 40 gallon capacity | | 10 | 1.600 | | 550 | 68 | | 618 | 705 |
| 2080 | 60 gallon capacity | | 8 | 2 | | 660 | 85 | | 745 | 855 |
| 2100 | 80 gallon capacity | | 7 | 2.286 | | 710 | 97 | | 807 | 925 |
| 2120 | 100 gallon capacity | | 6 | 2.667 | | 960 | 113 | | 1,073 | 1,225 |
| 3000 | Steel ASME expansion, rubber diaphragm, 19 gal. cap. accept. | | 12 | 1.333 | | 1,875 | 56.50 | | 1,931.50 | 2,150 |
| 3020 | 31 gallon capacity | | 8 | 2 | | 1,950 | 85 | | 2,035 | 2,275 |
| 3040 | 61 gallon capacity | | 6 | 2.667 | | 2,925 | 113 | | 3,038 | 3,400 |
| 3080 | 119 gallon capacity | | 4 | 4 | | 3,150 | 170 | | 3,320 | 3,725 |
| 3100 | 158 gallon capacity | | 3.80 | 4.211 | | 4,400 | 179 | | 4,579 | 5,100 |
| 3140 | 317 gallon capacity | | 2.80 | 5.714 | | 6,625 | 242 | | 6,867 | 7,650 |
| 3180 | 528 gallon capacity | | 2.40 | 6.667 | | 10,800 | 283 | | 11,083 | 12,200 |

### 23 21 20.58 Hydronic Heating Control Valves

| | | Crew | Daily Output | Labor-Hours | Unit | Material | 2008 Bare Costs Labor | Equipment | Total | Total Incl O&P |
|---|---|---|---|---|---|---|---|---|---|---|
| 0010 | **HYDRONIC HEATING CONTROL VALVES** | | | | | | | | | |
| 0100 | Radiator supply, 1/2" diameter | 1 Stpi | 24 | .333 | Ea. | 65.50 | 15.70 | | 81.20 | 95.50 |
| 0120 | 3/4" diameter | | 20 | .400 | | 44 | 18.85 | | 62.85 | 77 |
| 0140 | 1" diameter | | 19 | .421 | | 54 | 19.85 | | 73.85 | 89.50 |
| 0160 | 1-1/4" diameter | | 15 | .533 | | 76 | 25 | | 101 | 122 |

# 23 21 Hydronic Piping and Pumps

## 23 21 20 – Hydronic HVAC Piping Specialties

### 23 21 20.58 Hydronic Heating Control Valves

| | | Crew | Daily Output | Labor-Hours | Unit | Material | 2008 Bare Costs Labor | Equipment | Total | Total Incl O&P |
|---|---|---|---|---|---|---|---|---|---|---|
| 0500 | For low pressure steam, add | | | | | 25% | | | | |

### 23 21 20.70 Steam Traps

| | | Crew | Daily Output | Labor-Hours | Unit | Material | 2008 Bare Costs Labor | Equipment | Total | Total Incl O&P |
|---|---|---|---|---|---|---|---|---|---|---|
| 0010 | **STEAM TRAPS** | | | | | | | | | |
| 0030 | Cast iron body, threaded | | | | | | | | | |
| 0040 | Inverted bucket | | | | | | | | | |
| 0050 | 1/2" pipe size | 1 Stpi | 12 | .667 | Ea. | 123 | 31.50 | | 154.50 | 182 |
| 0070 | 3/4" pipe size | | 10 | .800 | | 214 | 37.50 | | 251.50 | 293 |
| 0100 | 1" pipe size | | 9 | .889 | | 330 | 42 | | 372 | 430 |
| 0120 | 1-1/4" pipe size | | 8 | 1 | | 500 | 47 | | 547 | 620 |
| 1000 | Float & thermostatic, 15 psi | | | | | | | | | |
| 1010 | 3/4" pipe size | 1 Stpi | 16 | .500 | Ea. | 99.50 | 23.50 | | 123 | 146 |
| 1020 | 1" pipe size | | 15 | .533 | | 119 | 25 | | 144 | 169 |
| 1040 | 1-1/2" pipe size | | 9 | .889 | | 211 | 42 | | 253 | 295 |
| 1060 | 2" pipe size | | 6 | 1.333 | | 385 | 63 | | 448 | 520 |

### 23 21 20.76 Strainers, Y Type, Bronze Body

| | | Crew | Daily Output | Labor-Hours | Unit | Material | 2008 Bare Costs Labor | Equipment | Total | Total Incl O&P |
|---|---|---|---|---|---|---|---|---|---|---|
| 0010 | **STRAINERS, Y TYPE, BRONZE BODY** | | | | | | | | | |
| 0050 | Screwed, 150 lb., 1/4" pipe size | 1 Stpi | 24 | .333 | Ea. | 14.55 | 15.70 | | 30.25 | 39.50 |
| 0070 | 3/8" pipe size | | 24 | .333 | | 19.20 | 15.70 | | 34.90 | 44.50 |
| 0100 | 1/2" pipe size | | 20 | .400 | | 19.20 | 18.85 | | 38.05 | 49.50 |
| 0140 | 1" pipe size | | 17 | .471 | | 23 | 22 | | 45 | 58.50 |
| 0160 | 1-1/2" pipe size | | 14 | .571 | | 49.50 | 27 | | 76.50 | 95 |
| 0180 | 2" pipe size | | 13 | .615 | | 66 | 29 | | 95 | 116 |
| 0182 | 3" pipe size | | 12 | .667 | | 495 | 31.50 | | 526.50 | 585 |
| 0200 | 300 lb., 2-1/2" pipe size | Q-5 | 17 | .941 | | 350 | 40 | | 390 | 445 |
| 0220 | 3" pipe size | | 16 | 1 | | 695 | 42.50 | | 737.50 | 830 |
| 0240 | 4" pipe size | | 15 | 1.067 | | 1,575 | 45 | | 1,620 | 1,825 |
| 0500 | For 300 lb rating 1/4" thru 2", add | | | | | 15% | | | | |
| 1000 | Flanged, 150 lb., 1-1/2" pipe size | 1 Stpi | 11 | .727 | Ea. | 365 | 34.50 | | 399.50 | 450 |
| 1020 | 2" pipe size | " | 8 | 1 | | 440 | 47 | | 487 | 555 |
| 1030 | 2-1/2" pipe size | Q-5 | 5 | 3.200 | | 650 | 136 | | 786 | 920 |
| 1040 | 3" pipe size | | 4.50 | 3.556 | | 805 | 151 | | 956 | 1,100 |
| 1060 | 4" pipe size | | 3 | 5.333 | | 1,225 | 226 | | 1,451 | 1,700 |
| 1100 | 6" pipe size | Q-6 | 3 | 8 | | 2,325 | 350 | | 2,675 | 3,075 |
| 1106 | 8" pipe size | " | 2.60 | 9.231 | | 2,550 | 405 | | 2,955 | 3,425 |
| 1500 | For 300 lb rating, add | | | | | 40% | | | | |

### 23 21 20.78 Strainers, Y Type, Iron Body

| | | Crew | Daily Output | Labor-Hours | Unit | Material | 2008 Bare Costs Labor | Equipment | Total | Total Incl O&P |
|---|---|---|---|---|---|---|---|---|---|---|
| 0010 | **STRAINERS, Y TYPE, IRON BODY** | | | | | | | | | |
| 0050 | Screwed, 250 lb., 1/4" pipe size | 1 Stpi | 20 | .400 | Ea. | 7.75 | 18.85 | | 26.60 | 37 |
| 0070 | 3/8" pipe size | | 20 | .400 | | 7.75 | 18.85 | | 26.60 | 37 |
| 0100 | 1/2" pipe size | | 20 | .400 | | 7.75 | 18.85 | | 26.60 | 37 |
| 0140 | 1" pipe size | | 16 | .500 | | 12.90 | 23.50 | | 36.40 | 49.50 |
| 0160 | 1-1/2" pipe size | | 12 | .667 | | 21 | 31.50 | | 52.50 | 70 |
| 0180 | 2" pipe size | | 8 | 1 | | 32 | 47 | | 79 | 106 |
| 0220 | 3" pipe size | Q-5 | 11 | 1.455 | | 187 | 61.50 | | 248.50 | 299 |
| 0240 | 4" pipe size | " | 5 | 3.200 | | 315 | 136 | | 451 | 555 |
| 0500 | For galvanized body, add | | | | | 50% | | | | |
| 1000 | Flanged, 125 lb., 1-1/2" pipe size | 1 Stpi | 11 | .727 | Ea. | 101 | 34.50 | | 135.50 | 163 |
| 1020 | 2" pipe size | " | 8 | 1 | | 106 | 47 | | 153 | 187 |
| 1040 | 3" pipe size | Q-5 | 4.50 | 3.556 | | 142 | 151 | | 293 | 385 |
| 1060 | 4" pipe size | " | 3 | 5.333 | | 181 | 226 | | 407 | 540 |
| 1080 | 5" pipe size | Q-6 | 3.40 | 7.059 | | 283 | 310 | | 593 | 775 |
| 1100 | 6" pipe size | " | 3 | 8 | | 283 | 350 | | 633 | 840 |

# 23 21 Hydronic Piping and Pumps

## 23 21 20 – Hydronic HVAC Piping Specialties

### 23 21 20.78 Strainers, Y Type, Iron Body

| | | Crew | Daily Output | Labor-Hours | Unit | Material | 2008 Bare Costs Labor | Equipment | Total | Total Incl O&P |
|---|---|---|---|---|---|---|---|---|---|---|
| 1500 | For 250 lb rating, add | | | | | 20% | | | | |
| 2000 | For galvanized body, add | | | | | 50% | | | | |
| 2500 | For steel body, add | | | | | 40% | | | | |

### 23 21 20.88 Venturi Flow

| | | Crew | Daily Output | Labor-Hours | Unit | Material | 2008 Bare Costs Labor | Equipment | Total | Total Incl O&P |
|---|---|---|---|---|---|---|---|---|---|---|
| 0010 | **VENTURI FLOW**, Measuring device | | | | | | | | | |
| 0050 | 1/2" diameter | 1 Stpi | 24 | .333 | Ea. | 228 | 15.70 | | 243.70 | 275 |
| 0120 | 1" diameter | | 19 | .421 | | 225 | 19.85 | | 244.85 | 278 |
| 0140 | 1-1/4" diameter | | 15 | .533 | | 280 | 25 | | 305 | 350 |
| 0160 | 1-1/2" diameter | | 13 | .615 | | 293 | 29 | | 322 | 365 |
| 0180 | 2" diameter | | 11 | .727 | | 299 | 34.50 | | 333.50 | 380 |
| 0220 | 3" diameter | Q-5 | 14 | 1.143 | | 425 | 48.50 | | 473.50 | 540 |
| 0240 | 4" diameter | " | 11 | 1.455 | | 635 | 61.50 | | 696.50 | 790 |
| 0280 | 6" diameter | Q-6 | 3.50 | 6.857 | | 925 | 300 | | 1,225 | 1,475 |
| 0500 | For meter, add | | | | | 1,675 | | | 1,675 | 1,850 |

## 23 21 23 – Hydronic Pumps

### 23 21 23.13 In-Line Centrifugal Hydronic Pumps

| | | Crew | Daily Output | Labor-Hours | Unit | Material | 2008 Bare Costs Labor | Equipment | Total | Total Incl O&P |
|---|---|---|---|---|---|---|---|---|---|---|
| 0010 | **IN-LINE CENTRIFUGAL HYDRONIC PUMPS** | | | | | | | | | |
| 0600 | Bronze, sweat connections, 1/40 HP, in line | | | | | | | | | |
| 0640 | 3/4" size | Q-1 | 16 | 1 | Ea. | 163 | 42 | | 205 | 242 |
| 1000 | Flange connection, 3/4" to 1-1/2" size | | | | | | | | | |
| 1040 | 1/12 HP | Q-1 | 6 | 2.667 | Ea. | 420 | 112 | | 532 | 635 |
| 1060 | 1/8 HP | | 6 | 2.667 | | 725 | 112 | | 837 | 965 |
| 1100 | 1/3 HP | | 6 | 2.667 | | 810 | 112 | | 922 | 1,050 |
| 1140 | 2" size, 1/6 HP | | 5 | 3.200 | | 1,050 | 135 | | 1,185 | 1,350 |
| 1180 | 2-1/2" size, 1/4 HP | | 5 | 3.200 | | 1,325 | 135 | | 1,460 | 1,650 |
| 2000 | Cast iron, flange connection | | | | | | | | | |
| 2040 | 3/4" to 1-1/2" size, in line, 1/12 HP | Q-1 | 6 | 2.667 | Ea. | 272 | 112 | | 384 | 470 |
| 2100 | 1/3 HP | | 6 | 2.667 | | 505 | 112 | | 617 | 725 |
| 2140 | 2" size, 1/6 HP | | 5 | 3.200 | | 555 | 135 | | 690 | 810 |
| 2180 | 2-1/2" size, 1/4 HP | | 5 | 3.200 | | 705 | 135 | | 840 | 980 |
| 2220 | 3" size, 1/4 HP | | 4 | 4 | | 725 | 168 | | 893 | 1,050 |
| 2600 | For non-ferrous impeller, add | | | | | 3% | | | | |

# 23 22 Steam and Condensate Piping and Pumps

## 23 22 13 – Steam and Condensate Heating Piping

### 23 22 13.23 Aboveground Steam and Condensate Piping

| | | Crew | Daily Output | Labor-Hours | Unit | Material | 2008 Bare Costs Labor | Equipment | Total | Total Incl O&P |
|---|---|---|---|---|---|---|---|---|---|---|
| 0010 | **ABOVEGROUND STEAM AND CONDENSATE HEATING PIPING** | | | | | | | | | |
| 0020 | Condensate meter | | | | | | | | | |
| 0100 | 500 lb. per hour | 1 Stpi | 14 | .571 | Ea. | 2,300 | 27 | | 2,327 | 2,575 |
| 0140 | 1500 lb. per hour | " | 7 | 1.143 | " | 2,475 | 54 | | 2,529 | 2,800 |

## 23 22 23 – Steam Condensate Pumps

### 23 22 23.10 Condensate Return System

| | | Crew | Daily Output | Labor-Hours | Unit | Material | 2008 Bare Costs Labor | Equipment | Total | Total Incl O&P |
|---|---|---|---|---|---|---|---|---|---|---|
| 0010 | **CONDENSATE RETURN SYSTEM** | | | | | | | | | |
| 0200 | Simplex, 3/4 H.P. mtr, float switch, controls, 10 Gal. C.I. rcvr, 6-15GPM | Q-1 | 1 | 16 | Ea. | 2,275 | 670 | | 2,945 | 3,500 |
| 1000 | Duplex, 2 pumps, 3/4 H.P. motors, float switch, | | | | | | | | | |
| 1060 | alternator asssembly, 15 Gal. C.I. receiver | Q-1 | .50 | 32 | Ea. | 3,600 | 1,350 | | 4,950 | 6,000 |

# 23 31 HVAC Ducts and Casings

## 23 31 13 – Metal Ducts

### 23 31 13.13 Rectangular Metal Ducts

| 23 31 13.13 Rectangular Metal Ducts | | Crew | Daily Output | Labor-Hours | Unit | Material | 2008 Bare Costs Labor | 2008 Bare Costs Equipment | Total | Total Incl O&P |
|---|---|---|---|---|---|---|---|---|---|---|
| 0010 | **RECTANGULAR METAL DUCTS** R233100-20 | | | | | | | | | |
| 0020 | Fabricated rectangular, includes fittings, joints, supports, | | | | | | | | | |
| 0030 | allowance for flexible connections, no insulation | | | | | | | | | |
| 0031 | NOTE: Fabrication and installation are combined | | | | | | | | | |
| 0040 | as LABOR cost. Approx. 25% fittings assumed. | | | | | | | | | |
| 0050 | Add to labor for elevated installation | | | | | | | | | |
| 0051 | of fabricated ductwork | | | | | | | | | |
| 0052 | 10' to 15' high | | | | | | 6% | | | |
| 0053 | 15' to 20' high | | | | | | 12% | | | |
| 0054 | 20' to 25' high | | | | | | 15% | | | |
| 0055 | 25' to 30' high | | | | | | 21% | | | |
| 0056 | 30' to 35' high | | | | | | 24% | | | |
| 0057 | 35' to 40' high | | | | | | 30% | | | |
| 0058 | Over 40' high | | | | | | 33% | | | |
| 0072 | For duct insulation see Div. 23 07 13.10 3000 | | | | | | | | | |
| 0100 | Aluminum, alloy 3003-H14, under 100 lb. | Q-10 | 75 | .320 | Lb. | 3.87 | 13.55 | | 17.42 | 25.50 |
| 0110 | 100 to 500 lb. | | 80 | .300 | | 2.58 | 12.70 | | 15.28 | 22.50 |
| 0120 | 500 to 1,000 lb. | | 95 | .253 | | 2.42 | 10.70 | | 13.12 | 19.10 |
| 0140 | 1,000 to 2,000 lb. | | 120 | .200 | | 2.28 | 8.45 | | 10.73 | 15.55 |
| 0150 | 2,000 to 5,000 lb. **CN** | | 130 | .185 | | 2.28 | 7.80 | | 10.08 | 14.55 |
| 0160 | Over 5,000 lb. | | 145 | .166 | | 2.28 | 7 | | 9.28 | 13.30 |
| 0500 | Galvanized steel, under 200 lb. | | 235 | .102 | | .60 | 4.32 | | 4.92 | 7.30 |
| 0520 | 200 to 500 lb. | | 245 | .098 | | .60 | 4.14 | | 4.74 | 7.05 |
| 0540 | 500 to 1,000 lb. | | 255 | .094 | | .58 | 3.98 | | 4.56 | 6.80 |
| 0560 | 1,000 to 2,000 lb. | | 265 | .091 | | .58 | 3.83 | | 4.41 | 6.55 |
| 0570 | 2,000 to 5,000 lb. | | 275 | .087 | | .57 | 3.69 | | 4.26 | 6.35 |
| 0580 | Over 5,000 lb. **CN** | | 285 | .084 | | .57 | 3.56 | | 4.13 | 6.15 |
| 1000 | Stainless steel, type 304, under 100 lb. | | 165 | .145 | | 4.29 | 6.15 | | 10.44 | 14.20 |
| 1020 | 100 to 500 lb. | | 175 | .137 | | 3.96 | 5.80 | | 9.76 | 13.30 |
| 1030 | 500 to 1,000 lb. | | 190 | .126 | | 3.62 | 5.35 | | 8.97 | 12.25 |
| 1040 | 1,000 to 2,000 lb. | | 200 | .120 | | 3.55 | 5.05 | | 8.60 | 11.70 |
| 1050 | 2,000 to 5,000 lb. | | 225 | .107 | | 3.25 | 4.51 | | 7.76 | 10.55 |
| 1060 | Over 5,000 lb. | | 235 | .102 | | 3.18 | 4.32 | | 7.50 | 10.15 |
| 1100 | For medium pressure ductwork, add | | | | | | 15% | | | |
| 1200 | For high pressure ductwork, add | | | | | | 40% | | | |
| 1210 | For welded ductwork, add | | | | | | 85% | | | |
| 1220 | For 30% fittings, add | | | | | | 11% | | | |
| 1224 | For 40% fittings, add | | | | | | 34% | | | |
| 1228 | For 50% fittings, add | | | | | | 56% | | | |
| 1232 | For 60% fittings, add | | | | | | 79% | | | |
| 1236 | For 70% fittings, add | | | | | | 101% | | | |
| 1240 | For 80% fittings, add | | | | | | 124% | | | |
| 1244 | For 90% fittings, add | | | | | | 147% | | | |
| 1248 | For 100% fittings, add | | | | | | 169% | | | |
| 1252 | Note: Fittings add includes time for detailing and installation. | | | | | | | | | |

### 23 31 13.19 Metal Duct Fittings

| 23 31 13.19 Metal Duct Fittings | | Crew | Daily Output | Labor-Hours | Unit | Material | 2008 Bare Costs Labor | 2008 Bare Costs Equipment | Total | Total Incl O&P |
|---|---|---|---|---|---|---|---|---|---|---|
| 0010 | **METAL DUCT FITTINGS** | | | | | | | | | |
| 0050 | Air extractors, 12" x 4" | 1 Shee | 24 | .333 | Ea. | 13.95 | 15.10 | | 29.05 | 39 |
| 0100 | 8" x 6" | | 22 | .364 | | 13.95 | 16.45 | | 30.40 | 41 |
| 0200 | 20" x 8" | | 16 | .500 | | 31.50 | 22.50 | | 54 | 70 |
| 0280 | 24" x 12" | | 10 | .800 | | 43 | 36 | | 79 | 103 |
| 2000 | Fabrics for flexible connections, with metal edge | | 100 | .080 | L.F. | 1.97 | 3.62 | | 5.59 | 7.75 |

465

# 23 31 HVAC Ducts and Casings

## 23 31 13 – Metal Ducts

### 23 31 13.19 Metal Duct Fittings

| | | Crew | Daily Output | Labor-Hours | Unit | Material | 2008 Bare Costs Labor | 2008 Bare Costs Equipment | Total | Total Incl O&P |
|---|---|---|---|---|---|---|---|---|---|---|
| 2100 | Without metal edge | 1 Shee | 160 | .050 | L.F. | 1.42 | 2.27 | | 3.69 | 5.05 |

## 23 31 16 – Nonmetal Ducts

### 23 31 16.13 Fibrous-Glass Ducts

| | | | Crew | Daily Output | Labor-Hours | Unit | Material | Labor | Equipment | Total | Total Incl O&P |
|---|---|---|---|---|---|---|---|---|---|---|---|
| 0010 | **FIBROUS-GLASS DUCTS** | R233100-20 | | | | | | | | | |
| 3490 | Rigid fiberglass duct board, foil reinf. kraft facing | | | | | | | | | | |
| 3500 | Rectangular, 1" thick, alum. faced, (FRK), std. weight | | Q-10 | 350 | .069 | SF Surf | .73 | 2.90 | | 3.63 | 5.25 |

# 23 33 Air Duct Accessories

## 23 33 13 – Dampers

### 23 33 13.13 Volume-Control Dampers

| | | Crew | Daily Output | Labor-Hours | Unit | Material | Labor | Equipment | Total | Total Incl O&P |
|---|---|---|---|---|---|---|---|---|---|---|
| 0010 | **VOLUME-CONTROL DAMPERS** | | | | | | | | | |
| 5990 | Multi-blade dampers, opposed blade, 8" x 6" | 1 Shee | 24 | .333 | Ea. | 19.45 | 15.10 | | 34.55 | 45 |
| 5994 | 8" x 8" | | 22 | .364 | | 20 | 16.45 | | 36.45 | 47.50 |
| 5996 | 10" x 10" | | 21 | .381 | | 23 | 17.25 | | 40.25 | 52 |
| 6000 | 12" x 12" | | 21 | .381 | | 26 | 17.25 | | 43.25 | 55 |
| 6020 | 12" x 18" | | 18 | .444 | | 35.50 | 20 | | 55.50 | 70 |
| 6030 | 14" x 10" | | 20 | .400 | | 25 | 18.10 | | 43.10 | 55.50 |
| 6031 | 14" x 14" | | 17 | .471 | | 31 | 21.50 | | 52.50 | 67 |
| 6033 | 16" x 12" | | 17 | .471 | | 31 | 21.50 | | 52.50 | 67 |
| 6035 | 16" x 16" | | 16 | .500 | | 38 | 22.50 | | 60.50 | 77 |
| 6037 | 18" x 16" | | 15 | .533 | | 42.50 | 24 | | 66.50 | 84 |
| 6038 | 18" x 18" | | 15 | .533 | | 46 | 24 | | 70 | 88 |
| 6070 | 20" x 16" | | 14 | .571 | | 46 | 26 | | 72 | 90.50 |
| 6072 | 20" x 20" | | 13 | .615 | | 54.50 | 28 | | 82.50 | 103 |
| 6074 | 22" x 18" | | 14 | .571 | | 54.50 | 26 | | 80.50 | 100 |
| 6076 | 24" x 16" | | 11 | .727 | | 54 | 33 | | 87 | 111 |
| 6078 | 24" x 20" | | 8 | 1 | | 64 | 45.50 | | 109.50 | 141 |
| 6080 | 24" x 24" | | 8 | 1 | | 75 | 45.50 | | 120.50 | 153 |
| 6110 | 26" x 26" | | 6 | 1.333 | | 82 | 60.50 | | 142.50 | 184 |
| 6133 | 30" x 30" | Q-9 | 6.60 | 2.424 | | 118 | 99 | | 217 | 282 |
| 6135 | 32" x 32" | | 6.40 | 2.500 | | 137 | 102 | | 239 | 305 |
| 6180 | 48" x 36" | | 5.60 | 2.857 | | 225 | 117 | | 342 | 430 |
| 8000 | Multi-blade dampers, parallel blade | | | | | | | | | |
| 8100 | 8" x 8" | 1 Shee | 24 | .333 | Ea. | 65 | 15.10 | | 80.10 | 95 |
| 8140 | 16" x 10" | | 20 | .400 | | 86 | 18.10 | | 104.10 | 123 |
| 8200 | 24" x 16" | | 11 | .727 | | 110 | 33 | | 143 | 172 |
| 8260 | 30" x 18" | | 7 | 1.143 | | 140 | 52 | | 192 | 234 |

### 23 33 13.16 Fire Dampers

| | | Crew | Daily Output | Labor-Hours | Unit | Material | Labor | Equipment | Total | Total Incl O&P |
|---|---|---|---|---|---|---|---|---|---|---|
| 0010 | **FIRE DAMPERS** | | | | | | | | | |
| 3000 | Fire damper, curtain type, 1-1/2 hr rated, vertical, 6" x 6" | 1 Shee | 24 | .333 | Ea. | 19.80 | 15.10 | | 34.90 | 45.50 |
| 3020 | 8" x 6" | | 22 | .364 | | 12.80 | 16.45 | | 29.25 | 39.50 |
| 3240 | 16" x 14" | | 18 | .444 | | 27.50 | 20 | | 47.50 | 61.50 |
| 3400 | 24" x 20" | | 8 | 1 | | 38.50 | 45.50 | | 84 | 113 |

### 23 33 13.28 Splitter Damper Assembly

| | | Crew | Daily Output | Labor-Hours | Unit | Material | Labor | Equipment | Total | Total Incl O&P |
|---|---|---|---|---|---|---|---|---|---|---|
| 0009 | **SPLITTER DAMPER ASSEMBLY** | | | | | | | | | |
| 0010 | Self locking, 1' rod | 1 Shee | 24 | .333 | Ea. | 20 | 15.10 | | 35.10 | 45.50 |
| 7020 | 3' rod | | 22 | .364 | | 26 | 16.45 | | 42.45 | 54 |
| 7040 | 4' rod | | 20 | .400 | | 29 | 18.10 | | 47.10 | 60 |
| 7060 | 6' rod | | 18 | .444 | | 35.50 | 20 | | 55.50 | 70 |

# 23 33 Air Duct Accessories

## 23 33 19 – Duct Silencers

| 23 33 19.10 Duct Silencers | Crew | Daily Output | Labor-Hours | Unit | Material | 2008 Bare Costs Labor | Equipment | Total | Total Incl O&P |
|---|---|---|---|---|---|---|---|---|---|
| 0009 **DUCT SILENCERS** | | | | | | | | | |
| 0010 Silencers, noise control for air flow, duct | | | | MCFM | 49 | | | 49 | 54 |

## 23 33 33 – Duct-Mounting Access Doors

### 23 33 33.13 Duct Access Doors

| 23 33 33.13 Duct Access Doors | Crew | Daily Output | Labor-Hours | Unit | Material | 2008 Bare Costs Labor | Equipment | Total | Total Incl O&P |
|---|---|---|---|---|---|---|---|---|---|
| 0010 **DUCT ACCESS DOORS** | | | | | | | | | |
| 1000 Duct access door, insulated, 6" x 6" | 1 Shee | 14 | .571 | Ea. | 13.85 | 26 | | 39.85 | 55.50 |
| 1020 10" x 10" | | 11 | .727 | | 16.75 | 33 | | 49.75 | 69.50 |
| 1040 12" x 12" | | 10 | .800 | | 17.90 | 36 | | 53.90 | 75.50 |
| 1050 12" x 18" | | 9 | .889 | | 27.50 | 40.50 | | 68 | 92.50 |
| 1070 18" x 18" | | 8 | 1 | | 32 | 45.50 | | 77.50 | 105 |
| 1074 24" x 18" | | 8 | 1 | | 38 | 45.50 | | 83.50 | 112 |

## 23 33 46 – Flexible Ducts

### 23 33 46.10 Flexible Air Ducts

| 23 33 46.10 Flexible Air Ducts | Crew | Daily Output | Labor-Hours | Unit | Material | 2008 Bare Costs Labor | Equipment | Total | Total Incl O&P |
|---|---|---|---|---|---|---|---|---|---|
| 0010 **FLEXIBLE AIR DUCTS** R233100-20 | | | | | | | | | |
| 1280 Add to labor for elevated installation | | | | | | | | | |
| 1282 of prefabricated (purchased) ductwork | | | | | | | | | |
| 1283 10' to 15' high | | | | | | 10% | | | |
| 1284 15' to 20' high | | | | | | 20% | | | |
| 1285 20' to 25' high | | | | | | 25% | | | |
| 1286 25' to 30' high | | | | | | 35% | | | |
| 1287 30' to 35' high | | | | | | 40% | | | |
| 1288 35' to 40' high | | | | | | 50% | | | |
| 1289 Over 40' high | | | | | | 55% | | | |
| 1300 Flexible, coated fiberglass fabric on corr. resist. metal helix | | | | | | | | | |
| 1400 pressure to 12" (WG) UL-181 | | | | | | | | | |
| 1500 Non-insulated, 3" diameter | Q-9 | 400 | .040 | L.F. | .91 | 1.63 | | 2.54 | 3.52 |
| 1540 5" diameter | | 320 | .050 | | 1.14 | 2.04 | | 3.18 | 4.39 |
| 1560 6" diameter | | 280 | .057 | | 1.35 | 2.33 | | 3.68 | 5.10 |
| 1580 7" diameter | | 240 | .067 | | 1.61 | 2.72 | | 4.33 | 5.95 |
| 1600 8" diameter | | 200 | .080 | | 1.86 | 3.26 | | 5.12 | 7.10 |
| 1640 10" diameter | | 160 | .100 | | 2.34 | 4.08 | | 6.42 | 8.85 |
| 1660 12" diameter | | 120 | .133 | | 2.83 | 5.45 | | 8.28 | 11.50 |
| 1900 Insulated, 1" thick, PE jacket, 3" diameter | | 380 | .042 | | 1.88 | 1.72 | | 3.60 | 4.72 |
| 1910 4" diameter | | 340 | .047 | | 1.88 | 1.92 | | 3.80 | 5.05 |
| 1920 5" diameter | | 300 | .053 | | 2.02 | 2.17 | | 4.19 | 5.55 |
| 1940 6" diameter | | 260 | .062 | | 2.15 | 2.51 | | 4.66 | 6.25 |
| 1960 7" diameter | | 220 | .073 | | 2.50 | 2.97 | | 5.47 | 7.30 |
| 1980 8" diameter | | 180 | .089 | | 2.66 | 3.62 | | 6.28 | 8.55 |
| 2020 10" diameter | | 140 | .114 | | 3.14 | 4.66 | | 7.80 | 10.65 |
| 2040 12" diameter | | 100 | .160 | | 3.91 | 6.50 | | 10.41 | 14.35 |

## 23 33 53 – Duct Liners

### 23 33 53.10 Duct Liner Board

| 23 33 53.10 Duct Liner Board | Crew | Daily Output | Labor-Hours | Unit | Material | 2008 Bare Costs Labor | Equipment | Total | Total Incl O&P |
|---|---|---|---|---|---|---|---|---|---|
| 0010 **DUCT LINER BOARD** | | | | | | | | | |
| 3490 Board type, fiberglass liner, 3 lb. density | | | | | | | | | |
| 3500 Fire resistant, black pigmented, 1 side | | | | | | | | | |
| 3520 1" thick | Q-14 | 150 | .107 | S.F. | 1.82 | 4.14 | | 5.96 | 8.50 |
| 3540 1-1/2" thick | | 130 | .123 | | 2.24 | 4.78 | | 7.02 | 9.95 |
| 3560 2" thick | | 120 | .133 | | 2.69 | 5.15 | | 7.84 | 11.10 |
| 3600 FSK vapor barrier | | | | | | | | | |
| 3620 1" thick | Q-14 | 150 | .107 | S.F. | .73 | 4.14 | | 4.87 | 7.30 |

# 23 33 Air Duct Accessories

## 23 33 53 – Duct Liners

| 23 33 53.10 Duct Liner Board | | Crew | Daily Output | Labor-Hours | Unit | Material | 2008 Bare Costs Labor | Equipment | Total | Total Incl O&P |
|---|---|---|---|---|---|---|---|---|---|---|
| 3630 | 1-1/2" thick | Q-14 | 130 | .123 | S.F. | .92 | 4.78 | | 5.70 | 8.50 |
| 3640 | 2" thick | ↓ | 120 | .133 | ↓ | 1.12 | 5.15 | | 6.27 | 9.40 |
| 3680 | No finish | | | | | | | | | |
| 3700 | 1" thick | Q-14 | 170 | .094 | S.F. | .38 | 3.65 | | 4.03 | 6.15 |
| 3710 | 1-1/2" thick | ↓ | 140 | .114 | | .57 | 4.43 | | 5 | 7.65 |
| 3720 | 2" thick | ↓ | 130 | .123 | ↓ | .77 | 4.78 | | 5.55 | 8.35 |

# 23 34 HVAC Fans

## 23 34 13 – Axial HVAC Fans

### 23 34 13.10 Axial Flow HVAC Fans

| | | Crew | Daily Output | Labor-Hours | Unit | Material | 2008 Bare Costs Labor | Equipment | Total | Total Incl O&P |
|---|---|---|---|---|---|---|---|---|---|---|
| 0010 | **AXIAL FLOW HVAC FANS** R233400-10 | | | | | | | | | |
| 0020 | Air conditioning and process air handling | | | | | | | | | |
| 0030 | Axial flow, compact, low sound, 2.5" S.P. | | | | | | | | | |
| 0050 | 3,800 CFM, 5 HP | Q-20 | 3.40 | 5.882 | Ea. | 4,200 | 245 | | 4,445 | 5,000 |
| 0080 | 6,400 CFM, 5 HP | | 2.80 | 7.143 | | 4,700 | 298 | | 4,998 | 5,600 |
| 0100 | 10,500 CFM, 7-1/2 HP | | 2.40 | 8.333 | | 5,850 | 350 | | 6,200 | 6,950 |
| 0120 | 15,600 CFM, 10 HP | | 1.60 | 12.500 | | 7,350 | 520 | | 7,870 | 8,900 |
| 1500 | Vaneaxial, low pressure, 2000 CFM, 1/2 HP | | 3.60 | 5.556 | | 1,450 | 232 | | 1,682 | 1,950 |
| 1520 | 4,000 CFM, 1 HP | | 3.20 | 6.250 | | 1,675 | 261 | | 1,936 | 2,250 |
| 1540 | 8,000 CFM, 2 HP | ↓ | 2.80 | 7.143 | ↓ | 2,175 | 298 | | 2,473 | 2,850 |

## 23 34 14 – Blower HVAC Fans

### 23 34 14.10 Blower Type HVAC Fans

| | | Crew | Daily Output | Labor-Hours | Unit | Material | 2008 Bare Costs Labor | Equipment | Total | Total Incl O&P |
|---|---|---|---|---|---|---|---|---|---|---|
| 0010 | **BLOWER TYPE HVAC FANS** | | | | | | | | | |
| 2500 | Ceiling fan, right angle, extra quiet, 0.10" S.P. | | | | | | | | | |
| 2520 | 95 CFM | Q-20 | 20 | 1 | Ea. | 199 | 41.50 | | 240.50 | 282 |
| 2540 | 210 CFM | | 19 | 1.053 | | 235 | 44 | | 279 | 325 |
| 2560 | 385 CFM | | 18 | 1.111 | | 298 | 46.50 | | 344.50 | 400 |
| 2580 | 885 CFM | | 16 | 1.250 | | 585 | 52 | | 637 | 725 |
| 2600 | 1,650 CFM | | 13 | 1.538 | | 810 | 64 | | 874 | 995 |
| 2620 | 2,960 CFM | ↓ | 11 | 1.818 | | 1,075 | 76 | | 1,151 | 1,325 |
| 2640 | For wall or roof cap, add | 1 Shee | 16 | .500 | | 199 | 22.50 | | 221.50 | 253 |
| 2660 | For straight thru fan, add | | | | | 10% | | | | |
| 2680 | For speed control switch, add | 1 Elec | 16 | .500 | ↓ | 108 | 23 | | 131 | 153 |
| 7500 | Utility set, steel construction, pedestal, 1/4" S.P. | | | | | | | | | |
| 7520 | Direct drive, 150 CFM, 1/8 HP | Q-20 | 6.40 | 3.125 | Ea. | 705 | 130 | | 835 | 975 |
| 7540 | 485 CFM, 1/6 HP | | 5.80 | 3.448 | | 885 | 144 | | 1,029 | 1,200 |
| 7560 | 1950 CFM, 1/2 HP | | 4.80 | 4.167 | | 1,050 | 174 | | 1,224 | 1,425 |
| 7580 | 2410 CFM, 3/4 HP | | 4.40 | 4.545 | | 1,925 | 190 | | 2,115 | 2,400 |
| 7600 | 3328 CFM, 1-1/2 HP | ↓ | 3 | 6.667 | ↓ | 2,150 | 278 | | 2,428 | 2,775 |
| 7680 | V-belt drive, drive cover, 3 phase | | | | | | | | | |
| 7700 | 800 CFM, 1/4 HP | Q-20 | 6 | 3.333 | Ea. | 645 | 139 | | 784 | 920 |
| 7720 | 1,300 CFM, 1/3 HP | | 5 | 4 | | 675 | 167 | | 842 | 995 |
| 7740 | 2,000 CFM, 1 HP | | 4.60 | 4.348 | | 800 | 181 | | 981 | 1,150 |
| 7760 | 2,900 CFM, 3/4 HP | ↓ | 4.20 | 4.762 | ↓ | 1,075 | 199 | | 1,274 | 1,475 |

## 23 34 16 – Centrifugal HVAC Fans

### 23 34 16.10 Centrifugal Type HVAC Fans

| | | Crew | Daily Output | Labor-Hours | Unit | Material | 2008 Bare Costs Labor | Equipment | Total | Total Incl O&P |
|---|---|---|---|---|---|---|---|---|---|---|
| 0010 | **CENTRIFUGAL TYPE HVAC FANS** | | | | | | | | | |
| 0200 | In-line centrifugal, supply/exhaust booster | | | | | | | | | |
| 0220 | aluminum wheel/hub, disconnect switch, 1/4" S.P. | | | | | | | | | |
| 0240 | 500 CFM, 10" diameter connection | Q-20 | 3 | 6.667 | Ea. | 1,050 | 278 | | 1,328 | 1,575 |

| 23 34 16.10 Centrifugal Type HVAC Fans | | Crew | Daily Output | Labor-Hours | Unit | Material | 2008 Bare Costs Labor | Equipment | Total | Total Incl O&P |
|---|---|---|---|---|---|---|---|---|---|---|
| 0260 | 1,380 CFM, 12" diameter connection | Q-20 | 2 | 10 | Ea. | 1,100 | 415 | | 1,515 | 1,875 |
| 0280 | 1,520 CFM, 16" diameter connection | | 2 | 10 | | 1,200 | 415 | | 1,615 | 1,975 |
| 0300 | 2,560 CFM, 18" diameter connection | | 1 | 20 | | 1,300 | 835 | | 2,135 | 2,725 |
| 0320 | 3,480 CFM, 20" diameter connection | | .80 | 25 | | 1,550 | 1,050 | | 2,600 | 3,300 |
| 0326 | 5,080 CFM, 20" diameter connection | | .75 | 26.667 | | 1,700 | 1,125 | | 2,825 | 3,575 |
| 3500 | Centrifugal, airfoil, motor and drive, complete | | | | | | | | | |
| 3520 | 1000 CFM, 1/2 HP | Q-20 | 2.50 | 8 | Ea. | 1,250 | 335 | | 1,585 | 1,875 |
| 3540 | 2,000 CFM, 1 HP | | 2 | 10 | | 1,375 | 415 | | 1,790 | 2,175 |
| 3560 | 4,000 CFM, 3 HP | | 1.80 | 11.111 | | 1,675 | 465 | | 2,140 | 2,550 |
| 3580 | 8,000 CFM, 7-1/2 HP | | 1.40 | 14.286 | | 2,625 | 595 | | 3,220 | 3,775 |
| 3600 | 12,000 CFM, 10 HP | | 1 | 20 | | 3,225 | 835 | | 4,060 | 4,825 |
| 4500 | Corrosive fume resistant, plastic | | | | | | | | | |
| 4600 | roof ventilators, centrifugal, V belt drive, motor | | | | | | | | | |
| 4620 | 1/4" S.P., 250 CFM, 1/4 HP | Q-20 | 6 | 3.333 | Ea. | 2,575 | 139 | | 2,714 | 3,075 |
| 4640 | 895 CFM, 1/3 HP | | 5 | 4 | | 2,800 | 167 | | 2,967 | 3,350 |
| 4660 | 1630 CFM, 1/2 HP | | 4 | 5 | | 3,325 | 209 | | 3,534 | 3,975 |
| 4680 | 2240 CFM, 1 HP | | 3 | 6.667 | | 3,475 | 278 | | 3,753 | 4,225 |
| 5000 | Utility set, centrifugal, V belt drive, motor | | | | | | | | | |
| 5020 | 1/4" S.P., 1200 CFM, 1/4 HP | Q-20 | 6 | 3.333 | Ea. | 3,550 | 139 | | 3,689 | 4,125 |
| 5040 | 1520 CFM, 1/3 HP | | 5 | 4 | | 3,550 | 167 | | 3,717 | 4,150 |
| 5060 | 1850 CFM, 1/2 HP | | 4 | 5 | | 3,550 | 209 | | 3,759 | 4,250 |
| 5080 | 2180 CFM, 3/4 HP | | 3 | 6.667 | | 3,600 | 278 | | 3,878 | 4,375 |
| 5100 | 1/2" S.P., 3600 CFM, 1 HP | | 2 | 10 | | 5,225 | 415 | | 5,640 | 6,400 |
| 5120 | 4250 CFM, 1-1/2 HP | | 1.60 | 12.500 | | 5,300 | 520 | | 5,820 | 6,625 |
| 5140 | 4800 CFM, 2 HP | | 1.40 | 14.286 | | 5,350 | 595 | | 5,945 | 6,800 |
| 7000 | Roof exhauster, centrifugal, aluminum housing, 12" galvanized | | | | | | | | | |
| 7020 | curb, bird screen, back draft damper, 1/4" S.P. | | | | | | | | | |
| 7100 | Direct drive, 320 CFM, 11" sq. damper | Q-20 | 7 | 2.857 | Ea. | 445 | 119 | | 564 | 670 |
| 7120 | 600 CFM, 11" sq. damper | | 6 | 3.333 | | 450 | 139 | | 589 | 710 |
| 7140 | 815 CFM, 13" sq. damper | | 5 | 4 | | 450 | 167 | | 617 | 750 |
| 7160 | 1450 CFM, 13" sq. damper | | 4.20 | 4.762 | | 580 | 199 | | 779 | 940 |
| 7180 | 2050 CFM, 16" sq. damper | | 4 | 5 | | 580 | 209 | | 789 | 955 |
| 7200 | V-belt drive, 1650 CFM, 12" sq. damper | | 6 | 3.333 | | 890 | 139 | | 1,029 | 1,200 |
| 7220 | 2750 CFM, 21" sq. damper | | 5 | 4 | | 1,025 | 167 | | 1,192 | 1,375 |
| 7230 | 3500 CFM, 21" sq. damper | | 4.50 | 4.444 | | 1,125 | 185 | | 1,310 | 1,525 |
| 7240 | 4910 CFM, 23" sq. damper | | 4 | 5 | | 1,400 | 209 | | 1,609 | 1,875 |
| 7260 | 8525 CFM, 28" sq. damper | | 3 | 6.667 | | 1,750 | 278 | | 2,028 | 2,350 |
| 7280 | 13,760 CFM, 35" sq. damper | | 2 | 10 | | 2,425 | 415 | | 2,840 | 3,325 |
| 7300 | 20,558 CFM, 43" sq. damper | | 1 | 20 | | 5,150 | 835 | | 5,985 | 6,950 |
| 7320 | For 2 speed winding, add | | | | | 15% | | | | |
| 7340 | For explosionproof motor, add | | | | | 365 | | | 365 | 400 |
| 7360 | For belt driven, top discharge, add | | | | | 15% | | | | |
| 8500 | Wall exhausters, centrifugal, auto damper, 1/8" S.P. | | | | | | | | | |
| 8520 | Direct drive, 610 CFM, 1/20 HP | Q-20 | 14 | 1.429 | Ea. | 288 | 59.50 | | 347.50 | 405 |
| 8540 | 796 CFM, 1/12 HP | | 13 | 1.538 | | 298 | 64 | | 362 | 430 |
| 8560 | 822 CFM, 1/6 HP | | 12 | 1.667 | | 470 | 69.50 | | 539.50 | 620 |
| 8580 | 1,320 CFM, 1/4 HP | | 12 | 1.667 | | 475 | 69.50 | | 544.50 | 630 |
| 9500 | V-belt drive, 3 phase | | | | | | | | | |
| 9520 | 2,800 CFM, 1/4 HP | Q-20 | 9 | 2.222 | Ea. | 1,300 | 92.50 | | 1,392.50 | 1,600 |
| 9540 | 3,740 CFM, 1/2 HP | " | 8 | 2.500 | " | 1,350 | 104 | | 1,454 | 1,650 |

# 23 34 HVAC Fans

## 23 34 23 – HVAC Power Ventilators

| 23 34 23.10 HVAC Power Circulators and Ventilators | Crew | Daily Output | Labor-Hours | Unit | Material | 2008 Bare Costs Labor | Equipment | Total | Total Incl O&P |
|---|---|---|---|---|---|---|---|---|---|
| 0010 **HVAC POWER CIRCULATORS AND VENTILATORS** | | | | | | | | | |
| 3000 Paddle blade air circulator, 3 speed switch | | | | | | | | | |
| 3020 42", 5,000 CFM high, 3000 CFM low | 1 Elec | 2.40 | 3.333 | Ea. | 89 | 152 | | 241 | 325 |
| 3040 52", 6,500 CFM high, 4000 CFM low | " | 2.20 | 3.636 | " | 96.50 | 166 | | 262.50 | 355 |
| 3100 For antique white motor, same cost | | | | | | | | | |
| 3200 For brass plated motor, same cost | | | | | | | | | |
| 3300 For light adaptor kit, add | | | | Ea. | 29 | | | 29 | 31.50 |
| 6000 Propeller exhaust, wall shutter, 1/4" S.P. | | | | | | | | | |
| 6020 Direct drive, two speed | | | | | | | | | |
| 6100 375 CFM, 1/10 HP | Q-20 | 10 | 2 | Ea. | 355 | 83.50 | | 438.50 | 520 |
| 6120 730 CFM, 1/7 HP | | 9 | 2.222 | | 395 | 92.50 | | 487.50 | 575 |
| 6140 1000 CFM, 1/8 HP | | 8 | 2.500 | | 550 | 104 | | 654 | 770 |
| 6200 4720 CFM, 1 HP | | 5 | 4 | | 885 | 167 | | 1,052 | 1,225 |
| 6300 V-belt drive, 3 phase | | | | | | | | | |
| 6320 6175 CFM, 3/4 HP | Q-20 | 5 | 4 | Ea. | 740 | 167 | | 907 | 1,075 |
| 6340 7500 CFM, 3/4 HP | | 5 | 4 | | 780 | 167 | | 947 | 1,125 |
| 6360 10,100 CFM, 1 HP | | 4.50 | 4.444 | | 955 | 185 | | 1,140 | 1,325 |
| 6380 14,300 CFM, 1-1/2 HP | | 4 | 5 | | 1,125 | 209 | | 1,334 | 1,550 |
| 6650 Residential, bath exhaust, grille, back draft damper | | | | | | | | | |
| 6660 50 CFM | Q-20 | 24 | .833 | Ea. | 39.50 | 35 | | 74.50 | 96.50 |
| 6670 110 CFM | | 22 | .909 | | 63.50 | 38 | | 101.50 | 128 |
| 6680 Light combination, squirrel cage, 100 watt, 70 CFM | | 24 | .833 | | 71 | 35 | | 106 | 132 |
| 6700 Light/heater combination, ceiling mounted | | | | | | | | | |
| 6710 70 CFM, 1450 watt | Q-20 | 24 | .833 | Ea. | 86.50 | 35 | | 121.50 | 148 |
| 6800 Heater combination, recessed, 70 CFM | | 24 | .833 | | 41 | 35 | | 76 | 98 |
| 6820 With 2 infrared bulbs | | 23 | .870 | | 62 | 36.50 | | 98.50 | 124 |
| 6900 Kitchen exhaust, grille, complete, 160 CFM | | 22 | .909 | | 74 | 38 | | 112 | 140 |
| 6910 180 CFM | | 20 | 1 | | 66.50 | 41.50 | | 108 | 138 |
| 6920 270 CFM | | 18 | 1.111 | | 113 | 46.50 | | 159.50 | 196 |
| 6930 350 CFM | | 16 | 1.250 | | 88.50 | 52 | | 140.50 | 177 |
| 6940 Residential roof jacks and wall caps | | | | | | | | | |
| 6944 Wall cap with back draft damper | | | | | | | | | |
| 6946 3" & 4" dia. round duct | 1 Shee | 11 | .727 | Ea. | 15.65 | 33 | | 48.65 | 68.50 |
| 6948 6" dia. round duct | " | 11 | .727 | " | 38 | 33 | | 71 | 92.50 |
| 6958 Roof jack with bird screen and back draft damper | | | | | | | | | |
| 6960 3" & 4" dia. round duct | 1 Shee | 11 | .727 | Ea. | 15.05 | 33 | | 48.05 | 67.50 |
| 6962 3-1/4" x 10" rectangular duct | " | 10 | .800 | " | 27.50 | 36 | | 63.50 | 86.50 |
| 6980 Transition | | | | | | | | | |
| 6982 3-1/4" x 10" to 6" dia. round | 1 Shee | 20 | .400 | Ea. | 16.50 | 18.10 | | 34.60 | 46 |

## 23 34 33 – Air Curtains

### 23 34 33.10 Air Barrier Curtains

| | Crew | Daily Output | Labor-Hours | Unit | Material | 2008 Bare Costs Labor | Equipment | Total | Total Incl O&P |
|---|---|---|---|---|---|---|---|---|---|
| 0010 **AIR BARRIER CURTAINS**, Incl. motor starters, transformers, | | | | | | | | | |
| 0050 door switches & temperature controls | | | | | | | | | |
| 0100 Shipping and receiving doors, unheated, minimal wind stoppage | | | | | | | | | |
| 0150 8' high, multiples of 3' wide | 2 Shee | 6 | 2.667 | L.F. | 345 | 121 | | 466 | 565 |
| 0160 5' wide | | 10 | 1.600 | | 335 | 72.50 | | 407.50 | 480 |
| 0210 10' high, multiples of 4' wide | | 8 | 2 | | 330 | 90.50 | | 420.50 | 505 |
| 0250 12' high, 3'-6" wide | | 7 | 2.286 | | 360 | 104 | | 464 | 555 |
| 0260 12' wide | | 6 | 2.667 | | 330 | 121 | | 451 | 550 |
| 0350 16' high, 3'-6" wide | | 7 | 2.286 | | 345 | 104 | | 449 | 540 |
| 0360 12' wide | | 6 | 2.667 | | 385 | 121 | | 506 | 605 |
| 0500 Maximum wind stoppage | | | | | | | | | |

# 23 34 HVAC Fans

## 23 34 33 – Air Curtains

| 23 34 33.10 Air Barrier Curtains | | Crew | Daily Output | Labor-Hours | Unit | Material | 2008 Bare Costs Labor | Equipment | Total | Total Incl O&P |
|---|---|---|---|---|---|---|---|---|---|---|
| 0550 | 10' high, multiples of 4' wide | 2 Shee | 8 | 2 | L.F. | 266 | 90.50 | | 356.50 | 430 |
| 0650 | 14' high, multiples of 4' wide | | 8 | 2 | | 250 | 90.50 | | 340.50 | 415 |
| 0750 | 20' high, multiples of 8' wide | | 6 | 2.667 | | 865 | 121 | | 986 | 1,125 |
| 1100 | Heated, maximum wind stoppage, steam heat | | | | | | | | | |
| 1150 | 10' high, multiples of 4' wide | 2 Shee | 6 | 2.667 | L.F. | 435 | 121 | | 556 | 665 |
| 1250 | 14' high, multiples of 4' wide | | 6 | 2.667 | | 475 | 121 | | 596 | 710 |
| 1350 | 20' high, multiples of 8' wide | | 4 | 4 | | 1,325 | 181 | | 1,506 | 1,725 |
| 1500 | Customer entrance doors, unheated, minimal wind stoppage | | | | | | | | | |
| 1550 | 10' high, multiples of 3' wide | 2 Shee | 6 | 2.667 | L.F. | 305 | 121 | | 426 | 520 |
| 1560 | 5' wide | | 10 | 1.600 | | 330 | 72.50 | | 402.50 | 475 |
| 1650 | Maximum wind stoppage, 12' high, multiples of 4' wide | | 8 | 2 | | 233 | 90.50 | | 323.50 | 395 |
| 1700 | Heated, minimal wind stoppage, electric heat | | | | | | | | | |
| 1750 | 8' high, multiples of 3' wide | 2 Shee | 6 | 2.667 | L.F. | 610 | 121 | | 731 | 855 |
| 1760 | Multiples of 5' wide | | 10 | 1.600 | | 435 | 72.50 | | 507.50 | 590 |
| 1850 | 10' high, multiples of 3' wide | | 6 | 2.667 | | 490 | 121 | | 611 | 725 |
| 1860 | Multiples of 5' wide | | 10 | 1.600 | | 535 | 72.50 | | 607.50 | 695 |
| 1950 | Maximum wind stoppage, steam heat | | | | | | | | | |
| 1960 | 12' high, multiples of 4' wide | 2 Shee | 8 | 2 | L.F. | 525 | 90.50 | | 615.50 | 720 |
| 2000 | Walk-in coolers and freezers, ambient air, minimal wind stoppage | | | | | | | | | |
| 2050 | 8' high, multiples of 3' wide | 2 Shee | 6 | 2.667 | L.F. | 215 | 121 | | 336 | 425 |
| 2060 | Multiples of 5' wide | | 10 | 1.600 | | 234 | 72.50 | | 306.50 | 370 |
| 2250 | Maximum wind stoppage, 12' high, multiples of 3' wide | | 6 | 2.667 | | 249 | 121 | | 370 | 460 |
| 2450 | Conveyor openings or service windows, unheated, 5' high | | 5 | 3.200 | | 289 | 145 | | 434 | 545 |
| 2460 | Heated, electric, 5' high, 2'-6" wide | | 5 | 3.200 | | 260 | 145 | | 405 | 510 |

# 23 37 Air Outlets and Inlets

## 23 37 13 – Diffusers, Registers, and Grilles

### 23 37 13.10 Diffusers

| | | Crew | Daily Output | Labor-Hours | Unit | Material | 2008 Bare Costs Labor | Equipment | Total | Total Incl O&P |
|---|---|---|---|---|---|---|---|---|---|---|
| 0010 | **DIFFUSERS**, Aluminum, opposed blade damper unless noted | | | | | | | | | |
| 0100 | Ceiling, linear, also for sidewall | | | | | | | | | |
| 0500 | Perforated, 24" x 24" lay-in panel size, 6" x 6" | 1 Shee | 16 | .500 | Ea. | 70 | 22.50 | | 92.50 | 112 |
| 0520 | 8" x 8" | | 15 | .533 | | 72 | 24 | | 96 | 117 |
| 0530 | 9" x 9" | | 14 | .571 | | 75.50 | 26 | | 101.50 | 123 |
| 0540 | 10" x 10" | | 14 | .571 | | 77.50 | 26 | | 103.50 | 125 |
| 0560 | 12" x 12" | | 12 | .667 | | 80 | 30 | | 110 | 135 |
| 0590 | 16" x 16" | | 11 | .727 | | 107 | 33 | | 140 | 169 |
| 0600 | 18" x 18" | | 10 | .800 | | 115 | 36 | | 151 | 183 |
| 0610 | 20" x 20" | | 10 | .800 | | 131 | 36 | | 167 | 200 |
| 0620 | 24" x 24" | | 9 | .889 | | 151 | 40.50 | | 191.50 | 228 |
| 1000 | Rectangular, 1 to 4 way blow, 6" x 6" | | 16 | .500 | | 41.50 | 22.50 | | 64 | 80.50 |
| 1010 | 8" x 8" | | 15 | .533 | | 49.50 | 24 | | 73.50 | 91.50 |
| 1014 | 9" x 9" | | 15 | .533 | | 53.50 | 24 | | 77.50 | 96.50 |
| 1016 | 10" x 10" | | 15 | .533 | | 62.50 | 24 | | 86.50 | 106 |
| 1020 | 12" x 6" | | 15 | .533 | | 65.50 | 24 | | 89.50 | 110 |
| 1040 | 12" x 9" | | 14 | .571 | | 71.50 | 26 | | 97.50 | 119 |
| 1060 | 12" x 12" | | 12 | .667 | | 73 | 30 | | 103 | 127 |
| 1070 | 14" x 6" | | 13 | .615 | | 71 | 28 | | 99 | 121 |
| 1074 | 14" x 14" | | 12 | .667 | | 95.50 | 30 | | 125.50 | 152 |
| 1150 | 18" x 18" | | 9 | .889 | | 135 | 40.50 | | 175.50 | 210 |
| 1160 | 21" x 21" | | 8 | 1 | | 170 | 45.50 | | 215.50 | 257 |
| 1170 | 24" x 12" | | 10 | .800 | | 126 | 36 | | 162 | 195 |

# 23 37 Air Outlets and Inlets

## 23 37 13 – Diffusers, Registers, and Grilles

### 23 37 13.10 Diffusers

| | | Crew | Daily Output | Labor-Hours | Unit | Material | 2008 Bare Costs Labor | Equipment | Total | Total Incl O&P |
|---|---|---|---|---|---|---|---|---|---|---|
| 1500 | Round, butterfly damper, steel, 6" diameter | 1 Shee | 18 | .444 | Ea. | 19.20 | 20 | | 39.20 | 52 |
| 1520 | 8" diameter | | 16 | .500 | | 20.50 | 22.50 | | 43 | 58 |
| 1540 | 10" diameter | | 14 | .571 | | 25.50 | 26 | | 51.50 | 68 |
| 1560 | 12" diameter | | 12 | .667 | | 34 | 30 | | 64 | 83.50 |
| 1580 | 14" diameter | | 10 | .800 | | 43.50 | 36 | | 79.50 | 104 |
| 2000 | T bar mounting, 24" x 24" lay-in frame, 6" x 6" | | 16 | .500 | | 80 | 22.50 | | 102.50 | 123 |
| 2020 | 9" x 9" | | 14 | .571 | | 88.50 | 26 | | 114.50 | 138 |
| 2040 | 12" x 12" | | 12 | .667 | | 114 | 30 | | 144 | 172 |
| 2060 | 15" x 15" | | 11 | .727 | | 146 | 33 | | 179 | 212 |
| 2080 | 18" x 18" | | 10 | .800 | | 161 | 36 | | 197 | 233 |
| 6000 | For steel diffusers instead of aluminum, deduct | | | | | 10% | | | | |

### 23 37 13.30 Grilles

| | | Crew | Daily Output | Labor-Hours | Unit | Material | 2008 Bare Costs Labor | Equipment | Total | Total Incl O&P |
|---|---|---|---|---|---|---|---|---|---|---|
| 0010 | **GRILLES** | | | | | | | | | |
| 0020 | Aluminum | | | | | | | | | |
| 1000 | Air return, 6" x 6" | 1 Shee | 26 | .308 | Ea. | 12.10 | 13.95 | | 26.05 | 35 |
| 1020 | 10" x 6" | | 24 | .333 | | 14.30 | 15.10 | | 29.40 | 39.50 |
| 1080 | 16" x 8" | | 22 | .364 | | 21.50 | 16.45 | | 37.95 | 49 |
| 1100 | 12" x 12" | | 22 | .364 | | 21.50 | 16.45 | | 37.95 | 49 |
| 1120 | 24" x 12" | | 18 | .444 | | 38 | 20 | | 58 | 73 |
| 1220 | 24" x 18" | | 16 | .500 | | 42 | 22.50 | | 64.50 | 81 |
| 1280 | 36" x 24" | | 14 | .571 | | 83.50 | 26 | | 109.50 | 132 |
| 3000 | Filter grille with filter, 12" x 12" | | 24 | .333 | | 36 | 15.10 | | 51.10 | 63 |
| 3020 | 18" x 12" | | 20 | .400 | | 52.50 | 18.10 | | 70.60 | 85.50 |
| 3040 | 24" x 18" | | 18 | .444 | | 64 | 20 | | 84 | 101 |
| 3060 | 24" x 24" | | 16 | .500 | | 99.50 | 22.50 | | 122 | 145 |
| 6000 | For steel grilles instead of aluminum in above, deduct | | | | | 10% | | | | |

### 23 37 13.60 Registers

| | | Crew | Daily Output | Labor-Hours | Unit | Material | 2008 Bare Costs Labor | Equipment | Total | Total Incl O&P |
|---|---|---|---|---|---|---|---|---|---|---|
| 0010 | **REGISTERS** | | | | | | | | | |
| 0980 | Air supply | | | | | | | | | |
| 1000 | Ceiling/wall, O.B. damper, anodized aluminum | | | | | | | | | |
| 1010 | One or two way deflection, adj. curved face bars | | | | | | | | | |
| 1020 | 8" x 4" | 1 Shee | 26 | .308 | Ea. | 23.50 | 13.95 | | 37.45 | 47.50 |
| 1120 | 12" x 12" | | 18 | .444 | | 38.50 | 20 | | 58.50 | 73.50 |
| 1240 | 20" x 6" | | 18 | .444 | | 38.50 | 20 | | 58.50 | 73 |
| 1340 | 24" x 8" | | 13 | .615 | | 52 | 28 | | 80 | 100 |
| 1350 | 24" x 18" | | 12 | .667 | | 96 | 30 | | 126 | 153 |
| 2700 | Above registers in steel instead of aluminum, deduct | | | | | 10% | | | | |
| 4000 | Floor, toe operated damper, enameled steel | | | | | | | | | |
| 4020 | 4" x 8" | 1 Shee | 32 | .250 | Ea. | 20 | 11.35 | | 31.35 | 39.50 |
| 4100 | 8" x 10" | | 22 | .364 | | 24.50 | 16.45 | | 40.95 | 52.50 |
| 4140 | 10" x 10" | | 20 | .400 | | 29 | 18.10 | | 47.10 | 60 |
| 4220 | 14" x 14" | | 16 | .500 | | 103 | 22.50 | | 125.50 | 148 |
| 4240 | 14" x 20" | | 15 | .533 | | 137 | 24 | | 161 | 189 |
| 4980 | Air return | | | | | | | | | |
| 5000 | Ceiling or wall, fixed 45° face blades | | | | | | | | | |
| 5010 | Adjustable O.B. damper, anodized aluminum | | | | | | | | | |
| 5020 | 4" x 8" | 1 Shee | 26 | .308 | Ea. | 21.50 | 13.95 | | 35.45 | 45 |
| 5060 | 6" x 10" | | 19 | .421 | | 23.50 | 19.05 | | 42.55 | 55.50 |
| 5280 | 24" x 24" | | 11 | .727 | | 102 | 33 | | 135 | 163 |
| 5300 | 24" x 36" | | 8 | 1 | | 158 | 45.50 | | 203.50 | 244 |
| 6000 | For steel construction instead of aluminum, deduct | | | | | 10% | | | | |

# 23 37 Air Outlets and Inlets

## 23 37 15 – Louvers

| 23 37 15.40 HVAC Louvers | Crew | Daily Output | Labor-Hours | Unit | Material | 2008 Bare Costs Labor | Equipment | Total | Total Incl O&P |
|---|---|---|---|---|---|---|---|---|---|
| 0010 **HVAC LOUVERS** | | | | | | | | | |
| 0100 Aluminum, extruded, with screen, mill finish | | | | | | | | | |
| 1002 Brick vent, see also Div. 04 05 23.19 | | | | | | | | | |
| 1100 Standard, 4" deep, 8" wide, 5" high | 1 Shee | 24 | .333 | Ea. | 31 | 15.10 | | 46.10 | 58 |
| 1200 Modular, 4" deep, 7-3/4" wide, 5" high | | 24 | .333 | | 32.50 | 15.10 | | 47.60 | 59.50 |
| 1300 Speed brick, 4" deep, 11-5/8" wide, 3-7/8" high | | 24 | .333 | | 32.50 | 15.10 | | 47.60 | 59.50 |
| 1400 Fuel oil brick, 4" deep, 8" wide, 5" high | | 24 | .333 | | 56 | 15.10 | | 71.10 | 85 |
| 2000 Cooling tower and mechanical equip., screens, light weight | | 40 | .200 | S.F. | 14.05 | 9.05 | | 23.10 | 29.50 |
| 2020 Standard weight | | 35 | .229 | | 37.50 | 10.35 | | 47.85 | 57 |
| 2500 Dual combination, automatic, intake or exhaust | | 20 | .400 | | 51 | 18.10 | | 69.10 | 84 |
| 2520 Manual operation | | 20 | .400 | | 38 | 18.10 | | 56.10 | 69.50 |
| 2540 Electric or pneumatic operation | | 20 | .400 | | 38 | 18.10 | | 56.10 | 69.50 |
| 2560 Motor, for electric or pneumatic | | 14 | .571 | Ea. | 440 | 26 | | 466 | 520 |
| 3000 Fixed blade, continuous line | | | | | | | | | |
| 3100 Mullion type, stormproof | 1 Shee | 28 | .286 | S.F. | 38 | 12.95 | | 50.95 | 61.50 |
| 3200 Stormproof | | 28 | .286 | | 38 | 12.95 | | 50.95 | 61.50 |
| 3300 Vertical line | | 28 | .286 | | 45 | 12.95 | | 57.95 | 69.50 |
| 3500 For damper to use with above, add | | | | | 50% | 30% | | | |
| 3520 Motor, for damper, electric or pneumatic | 1 Shee | 14 | .571 | Ea. | 440 | 26 | | 466 | 520 |
| 4000 Operating, 45°, manual, electric or pneumatic | | 24 | .333 | S.F. | 38 | 15.10 | | 53.10 | 65 |
| 4100 Motor, for electric or pneumatic | | 14 | .571 | Ea. | 440 | 26 | | 466 | 520 |
| 4200 Penthouse, roof | | 56 | .143 | S.F. | 22.50 | 6.45 | | 28.95 | 34.50 |
| 4300 Walls | | 40 | .200 | | 52.50 | 9.05 | | 61.55 | 72 |
| 5000 Thinline, under 4" thick, fixed blade | | 40 | .200 | | 22 | 9.05 | | 31.05 | 38 |
| 5010 Finishes, applied by mfr. at additional cost, available in colors | | | | | | | | | |
| 5020 Prime coat only, add | | | | S.F. | 3.04 | | | 3.04 | 3.34 |
| 5040 Baked enamel finish coating, add | | | | | 5.60 | | | 5.60 | 6.15 |
| 5060 Anodized finish, add | | | | | 6.05 | | | 6.05 | 6.65 |
| 5080 Duranodic finish, add | | | | | 11 | | | 11 | 12.10 |
| 5100 Fluoropolymer finish coating, add | | | | | 17.20 | | | 17.20 | 18.90 |
| 9980 For small orders (under 10 pieces), add | | | | | 25% | | | | |

## 23 37 23 – HVAC Gravity Ventilators

### 23 37 23.10 HVAC Gravity Air Ventilators

| | Crew | Daily Output | Labor-Hours | Unit | Material | 2008 Bare Costs Labor | Equipment | Total | Total Incl O&P |
|---|---|---|---|---|---|---|---|---|---|
| 0010 **HVAC GRAVITY AIR VENTILATORS**, Incl. base and damper | | | | | | | | | |
| 1280 Rotary ventilators, wind driven, galvanized | | | | | | | | | |
| 1300 4" neck diameter | Q-9 | 20 | .800 | Ea. | 47.50 | 32.50 | | 80 | 103 |
| 1340 6" neck diameter | | 16 | 1 | | 53 | 41 | | 94 | 122 |
| 1400 12" neck diameter | | 10 | 1.600 | | 77 | 65.50 | | 142.50 | 186 |
| 1500 24" neck diameter, 3,100 CFM | | 8 | 2 | | 224 | 81.50 | | 305.50 | 375 |
| 1540 36" neck diameter, 5,500 CFM | | 6 | 2.667 | | 660 | 109 | | 769 | 895 |
| 2000 Stationary, gravity, syphon, galvanized | | | | | | | | | |
| 2160 6" neck diameter, 66 CFM | Q-9 | 16 | 1 | Ea. | 41 | 41 | | 82 | 108 |
| 2240 12" neck diameter, 160 CFM | | 10 | 1.600 | | 86 | 65.50 | | 151.50 | 196 |
| 2340 24" neck diameter, 900 CFM | | 8 | 2 | | 235 | 81.50 | | 316.50 | 385 |
| 2380 36" neck diameter, 2,000 CFM | | 6 | 2.667 | | 735 | 109 | | 844 | 980 |
| 4200 Stationary mushroom, aluminum, 16" orifice diameter | | 10 | 1.600 | | 445 | 65.50 | | 510.50 | 590 |
| 4220 26" orifice diameter | | 6.15 | 2.602 | | 655 | 106 | | 761 | 885 |
| 4230 30" orifice diameter | | 5.71 | 2.802 | | 960 | 114 | | 1,074 | 1,225 |
| 4240 38" orifice diameter | | 5 | 3.200 | | 1,375 | 131 | | 1,506 | 1,700 |
| 4250 42" orifice diameter | | 4.70 | 3.404 | | 1,825 | 139 | | 1,964 | 2,225 |
| 4260 50" orifice diameter | | 4.44 | 3.604 | | 2,175 | 147 | | 2,322 | 2,600 |
| 5000 Relief vent | | | | | | | | | |

# 23 37 Air Outlets and Inlets

## 23 37 23 – HVAC Gravity Ventilators

### 23 37 23.10 HVAC Gravity Air Ventilators

| | | Crew | Daily Output | Labor-Hours | Unit | Material | 2008 Bare Costs Labor | Equipment | Total | Total Incl O&P |
|---|---|---|---|---|---|---|---|---|---|---|
| 5500 | Rectangular, aluminum, galvanized curb | | | | | | | | | |
| 5510 | intake/exhaust, 0.05" SP | | | | | | | | | |
| 5600 | 500 CFM, 12" x 16" | Q-9 | 8 | 2 | Ea. | 430 | 81.50 | | 511.50 | 600 |
| 5640 | 1000 CFM, 12" x 24" | ↓ | 6.60 | 2.424 | | 510 | 99 | | 609 | 715 |
| 5680 | 3000 CFM, 20" x 42" | ↓ | 4 | 4 | ↓ | 885 | 163 | | 1,048 | 1,225 |

# 23 38 Ventilation Hoods

## 23 38 13 – Commercial-Kitchen Hoods

### 23 38 13.10 Hood and Ventilation Equipment

| | | Crew | Daily Output | Labor-Hours | Unit | Material | 2008 Bare Costs Labor | Equipment | Total | Total Incl O&P |
|---|---|---|---|---|---|---|---|---|---|---|
| 0010 | **HOOD AND VENTILATION EQUIPMENT** | | | | | | | | | |
| 2970 | Exhaust hood, sst, gutter on all sides, 4' x 4' x 2' | 1 Carp | 1.80 | 4.444 | Ea. | 3,525 | 169 | | 3,694 | 4,150 |
| 2980 | 4' x 4' x 7' | " | 1.60 | 5 | | 5,450 | 191 | | 5,641 | 6,300 |
| 7950 | Hood fire protection system, minimum | Q-1 | 3 | 5.333 | | 3,725 | 224 | | 3,949 | 4,425 |
| 8050 | Maximum | " | 1 | 16 | ↓ | 28,700 | 670 | | 29,370 | 32,600 |

# 23 41 Particulate Air Filtration

## 23 41 13 – Panel Air Filters

### 23 41 13.10 Panel Type Air Filters

| | | Crew | Daily Output | Labor-Hours | Unit | Material | 2008 Bare Costs Labor | Equipment | Total | Total Incl O&P |
|---|---|---|---|---|---|---|---|---|---|---|
| 0010 | **PANEL TYPE AIR FILTERS** | | | | | | | | | |
| 2950 | Mechanical media filtration units | | | | | | | | | |
| 3000 | High efficiency type, with frame, non-supported | | | | MCFM | 45 | | | 45 | 49.50 |
| 3100 | Supported type | | | | " | 60 | | | 60 | 66 |
| 5500 | Throwaway glass or paper media type | | | | Ea. | 3.54 | | | 3.54 | 3.89 |

## 23 41 16 – Renewable-Media Air Filters

### 23 41 16.10 Disposable Media Air Filters

| | | Crew | Daily Output | Labor-Hours | Unit | Material | 2008 Bare Costs Labor | Equipment | Total | Total Incl O&P |
|---|---|---|---|---|---|---|---|---|---|---|
| 0010 | **DISPOSABLE MEDIA AIR FILTERS** | | | | | | | | | |
| 5000 | Renewable disposable roll | | | | MCFM | 200 | | | 200 | 220 |

## 23 41 19 – Washable Air Filters

### 23 41 19.10 Permanent Air Filters

| | | Crew | Daily Output | Labor-Hours | Unit | Material | 2008 Bare Costs Labor | Equipment | Total | Total Incl O&P |
|---|---|---|---|---|---|---|---|---|---|---|
| 0010 | **PERMANENT AIR FILTERS** | | | | | | | | | |
| 4500 | Permanent washable | | | | MCFM | 20 | | | 20 | 22 |

## 23 41 23 – Extended Surface Filters

### 23 41 23.10 Expanded Surface Filters

| | | Crew | Daily Output | Labor-Hours | Unit | Material | 2008 Bare Costs Labor | Equipment | Total | Total Incl O&P |
|---|---|---|---|---|---|---|---|---|---|---|
| 0010 | **EXPANDED SURFACE FILTERS** | | | | | | | | | |
| 4000 | Medium efficiency, extended surface | | | | MCFM | 5.50 | | | 5.50 | 6.05 |

# 23 42 Gas-Phase Air Filtration

## 23 42 13 – Activated-Carbon Air Filtration

| 23 42 13.10 Charcoal Type Air Filtration | Crew | Daily Output | Labor-Hours | Unit | Material | 2008 Bare Costs Labor | Equipment | Total | Total Incl O&P |
|---|---|---|---|---|---|---|---|---|---|
| 0010 **CHARCOAL TYPE AIR FILTRATION** | | | | | | | | | |
| 0050 Activated charcoal type, full flow | | | | MCFM | 600 | | | 600 | 660 |
| 0060 full flow, impregnated media 12" deep | | | | | 225 | | | 225 | 248 |
| 0070 HEPA filter & frame for field erection | | | | | 250 | | | 250 | 275 |
| 0080 HEPA filter-diffuser, ceiling install. | | | | | 275 | | | 275 | 305 |

# 23 43 Electronic Air Cleaners

## 23 43 13 – Washable Electronic Air Cleaners

### 23 43 13.10 Electronic Air Cleaners

| | Crew | Daily Output | Labor-Hours | Unit | Material | 2008 Bare Costs Labor | Equipment | Total | Total Incl O&P |
|---|---|---|---|---|---|---|---|---|---|
| 0010 **ELECTRONIC AIR CLEANERS** | | | | | | | | | |
| 2000 Electronic air cleaner, duct mounted | | | | | | | | | |
| 2150 400 - 1000 CFM | 1 Shee | 2.30 | 3.478 | Ea. | 935 | 158 | | 1,093 | 1,275 |
| 2200 1000 - 1400 CFM | | 2.20 | 3.636 | | 1,225 | 165 | | 1,390 | 1,600 |
| 2250 1400 - 2000 CFM | | 2.10 | 3.810 | | 1,325 | 173 | | 1,498 | 1,725 |

# 23 51 Breechings, Chimneys, and Stacks

## 23 51 13 – Draft Control Devices

### 23 51 13.13 Draft-Induction Fans

| | Crew | Daily Output | Labor-Hours | Unit | Material | 2008 Bare Costs Labor | Equipment | Total | Total Incl O&P |
|---|---|---|---|---|---|---|---|---|---|
| 0010 **DRAFT-INDUCTION FANS** | | | | | | | | | |
| 1000 Breeching installation | | | | | | | | | |
| 1800 Hot gas, 600° F, variable pitch pulley and motor | | | | | | | | | |
| 1860 8" diam. inlet, 1/4 H.P., 1phase, 1120 CFM | Q-9 | 4 | 4 | Ea. | 2,200 | 163 | | 2,363 | 2,675 |
| 1900 12" diam. inlet, 3/4 H.P., 3 phase, 2960 CFM | | 3 | 5.333 | | 3,000 | 217 | | 3,217 | 3,625 |
| 1940 18" diam. inlet, 3 H.P., 3 phase, 9120 CFM | | 2 | 8 | | 4,650 | 325 | | 4,975 | 5,625 |
| 1980 24" diam. inlet, 7-1/2 H.P., 3 phase, 17,760 CFM | | .80 | 20 | | 7,300 | 815 | | 8,115 | 9,275 |
| 2300 For multi-blade damper at fan inlet, add | | | | | 20% | | | | |

## 23 51 23 – Gas Vents

### 23 51 23.10 Gas Chimney Vents

| | Crew | Daily Output | Labor-Hours | Unit | Material | 2008 Bare Costs Labor | Equipment | Total | Total Incl O&P |
|---|---|---|---|---|---|---|---|---|---|
| 0010 **GAS CHIMNEY VENTS,** Prefab metal, U.L. listed | | | | | | | | | |
| 0020 Gas, double wall, galvanized steel | | | | | | | | | |
| 0080 3" diameter | Q-9 | 72 | .222 | V.L.F. | 4.75 | 9.05 | | 13.80 | 19.20 |
| 0100 4" diameter | | 68 | .235 | | 5.95 | 9.60 | | 15.55 | 21.50 |
| 0120 5" diameter | | 64 | .250 | | 6.95 | 10.20 | | 17.15 | 23.50 |
| 0140 6" diameter | | 60 | .267 | | 8.05 | 10.85 | | 18.90 | 25.50 |
| 0160 7" diameter | | 56 | .286 | | 11.85 | 11.65 | | 23.50 | 31 |
| 0180 8" diameter | | 52 | .308 | | 13.20 | 12.55 | | 25.75 | 34 |
| 0200 10" diameter | | 48 | .333 | | 30 | 13.60 | | 43.60 | 54 |
| 0220 12" diameter | | 44 | .364 | | 40 | 14.85 | | 54.85 | 67 |
| 0260 16" diameter | | 40 | .400 | | 91.50 | 16.30 | | 107.80 | 126 |
| 0300 20" diameter | Q-10 | 36 | .667 | | 139 | 28 | | 167 | 197 |
| 0480 38" diameter | " | 24 | 1 | | 445 | 42.50 | | 487.50 | 555 |

## 23 51 26 – All-Fuel Vent Chimneys

### 23 51 26.30 All-Fuel Vent Chimneys, Double Wall, St. Stl.

| | Crew | Daily Output | Labor-Hours | Unit | Material | 2008 Bare Costs Labor | Equipment | Total | Total Incl O&P |
|---|---|---|---|---|---|---|---|---|---|
| 0010 **ALL-FUEL VENT CHIMNEYS, DOUBLE WALL, STAINLESS STEEL** | | | | | | | | | |
| 7800 All fuel, double wall, stainless steel, 6" diameter | Q-9 | 60 | .267 | V.L.F. | 34 | 10.85 | | 44.85 | 54 |
| 7802 7" diameter | | 56 | .286 | | 43.50 | 11.65 | | 55.15 | 66 |
| 7804 8" diameter | | 52 | .308 | | 51 | 12.55 | | 63.55 | 75.50 |
| 7806 10" diameter | | 48 | .333 | | 74.50 | 13.60 | | 88.10 | 103 |

# 23 51 Breechings, Chimneys, and Stacks

## 23 51 26 – All-Fuel Vent Chimneys

| 23 51 26.30 All-Fuel Vent Chimneys, Double Wall, St. Stl. | | Crew | Daily Output | Labor-Hours | Unit | Material | 2008 Bare Costs Labor | Equipment | Total | Total Incl O&P |
|---|---|---|---|---|---|---|---|---|---|---|
| 7808 | 12" diameter | Q-9 | 44 | .364 | V.L.F. | 100 | 14.85 | | 114.85 | 133 |
| 7810 | 14" diameter | ↓ | 42 | .381 | ↓ | 131 | 15.55 | | 146.55 | 168 |

## 23 51 33 – Insulated Sectional Chimneys

### 23 51 33.10 Prefabricated Insulated Sectional Chimneys

| | | Crew | Daily Output | Labor-Hours | Unit | Material | Labor | Equipment | Total | Total Incl O&P |
|---|---|---|---|---|---|---|---|---|---|---|
| 0010 | **PREFABRICATED INSULATED SECTIONAL CHIMNEYS** | | | | | | | | | |
| 9000 | High temp. (2000° F), steel jacket, acid resist. refractory lining | | | | | | | | | |
| 9010 | 11 ga. galvanized jacket, U.L. listed | | | | | | | | | |
| 9020 | Straight section, 48" long, 10" diameter | Q-10 | 13.30 | 1.805 | Ea. | 400 | 76.50 | | 476.50 | 560 |
| 9040 | 18" diameter | ↓ | 7.40 | 3.243 | | 615 | 137 | | 752 | 885 |
| 9070 | 36" diameter | ↓ | 2.70 | 8.889 | | 1,300 | 375 | | 1,675 | 2,025 |
| 9090 | 48" diameter | Q-11 | 2.70 | 11.852 | | 1,925 | 510 | | 2,435 | 2,900 |
| 9120 | Tee section, 10" diameter | Q-10 | 4.40 | 5.455 | | 850 | 231 | | 1,081 | 1,300 |
| 9140 | 18" diameter | | 2.40 | 10 | | 1,225 | 425 | | 1,650 | 2,000 |
| 9170 | 36" diameter | ↓ | .80 | 30 | | 3,975 | 1,275 | | 5,250 | 6,325 |
| 9190 | 48" diameter | Q-11 | .90 | 35.556 | | 6,775 | 1,525 | | 8,300 | 9,825 |
| 9220 | Cleanout pier section, 10" diameter | Q-10 | 3.50 | 6.857 | | 655 | 290 | | 945 | 1,175 |
| 9240 | 18" diameter | | 1.90 | 12.632 | | 885 | 535 | | 1,420 | 1,800 |
| 9270 | 36" diameter | ↓ | .75 | 32 | | 1,625 | 1,350 | | 2,975 | 3,850 |
| 9290 | 48" diameter | Q-11 | .75 | 42.667 | | 2,475 | 1,850 | | 4,325 | 5,575 |
| 9320 | For drain, add | | | | | 53% | | | | |
| 9330 | Elbow, 30° and 45°, 10" diameter | Q-10 | 6.60 | 3.636 | | 555 | 154 | | 709 | 850 |
| 9350 | 18" diameter | | 3.70 | 6.486 | | 900 | 274 | | 1,174 | 1,425 |
| 9380 | 36" diameter | ↓ | 1.30 | 18.462 | | 2,225 | 780 | | 3,005 | 3,650 |
| 9400 | 48" diameter | Q-11 | 1.35 | 23.704 | | 3,900 | 1,025 | | 4,925 | 5,850 |
| 9430 | For 60° and 90° elbow, add | | | | | 112% | | | | |
| 9440 | End cap, 10" diameter | Q-10 | 26 | .923 | | 955 | 39 | | 994 | 1,100 |
| 9460 | 18" diameter | | 15 | 1.600 | | 1,350 | 67.50 | | 1,417.50 | 1,575 |
| 9490 | 36" diameter | ↓ | 5 | 4.800 | | 2,350 | 203 | | 2,553 | 2,925 |
| 9510 | 48" diameter | Q-11 | 5.30 | 6.038 | | 3,475 | 261 | | 3,736 | 4,200 |
| 9540 | Increaser (1 diameter), 10" diameter | Q-10 | 6.60 | 3.636 | | 475 | 154 | | 629 | 755 |
| 9560 | 18" diameter | | 3.70 | 6.486 | | 740 | 274 | | 1,014 | 1,225 |
| 9590 | 36" diameter | ↓ | 1.30 | 18.462 | | 1,450 | 780 | | 2,230 | 2,800 |
| 9592 | 42" diameter | Q-11 | 1.60 | 20 | | 1,600 | 865 | | 2,465 | 3,075 |
| 9594 | 48" diameter | ↓ | 1.35 | 23.704 | | 1,925 | 1,025 | | 2,950 | 3,675 |
| 9596 | 54" diameter | ↓ | 1.10 | 29.091 | | 2,325 | 1,250 | | 3,575 | 4,475 |
| 9600 | For expansion joints, add to straight section | | | | | 7% | | | | |
| 9610 | For 1/4" hot rolled steel jacket, add | | | | | 157% | | | | |
| 9620 | For 2950° F very high temperature, add | | | | ↓ | 89% | | | | |
| 9630 | 26 ga. aluminized jacket, straight section, 48" long | | | | | | | | | |
| 9640 | 10" diameter | Q-10 | 15.30 | 1.569 | V.L.F. | 238 | 66.50 | | 304.50 | 365 |
| 9660 | 18" diameter | | 8.50 | 2.824 | | 365 | 119 | | 484 | 585 |
| 9690 | 36" diameter | ↓ | 3.10 | 7.742 | ↓ | 845 | 325 | | 1,170 | 1,425 |
| 9810 | Draw band, galv. stl., 11 gauge, 10" diameter | | 32 | .750 | Ea. | 64.50 | 31.50 | | 96 | 120 |
| 9820 | 12" diameter | | 30 | .800 | | 69 | 34 | | 103 | 128 |
| 9830 | 18" diameter | | 26 | .923 | | 86 | 39 | | 125 | 155 |
| 9860 | 36" diameter | ↓ | 18 | 1.333 | | 146 | 56.50 | | 202.50 | 247 |
| 9880 | 48" diameter | Q-11 | 20 | 1.600 | ↓ | 250 | 69 | | 319 | 380 |

# 23 52 Heating Boilers

## 23 52 13 – Electric Boilers

| 23 52 13.10 Electric Boilers, ASME | Crew | Daily Output | Labor-Hours | Unit | Material | 2008 Bare Costs Labor | Equipment | Total | Total Incl O&P |
|---|---|---|---|---|---|---|---|---|---|
| 0010 **ELECTRIC BOILERS, ASME**, Standard controls and trim. | | | | | | | | | |
| 1000     Steam, 6 KW, 20.5 MBH | Q-19 | 1.20 | 20 | Ea. | 3,000 | 870 | | 3,870 | 4,600 |
| 1160     60 KW, 205 MBH | | 1 | 24 | | 5,150 | 1,050 | | 6,200 | 7,250 |
| 1220     112 KW, 382 MBH | | .75 | 32 | | 7,075 | 1,400 | | 8,475 | 9,850 |
| 1280     222 KW, 758 MBH | | .55 | 43.636 | | 11,700 | 1,900 | | 13,600 | 15,800 |
| 1380     518 KW, 1768 MBH | Q-21 | .36 | 88.889 | | 19,800 | 3,950 | | 23,750 | 27,600 |
| 1480     814 KW, 2778 MBH | | .25 | 128 | | 27,700 | 5,675 | | 33,375 | 38,900 |
| 1600     2,340 KW, 7984 MBH | | .16 | 200 | | 56,500 | 8,875 | | 65,375 | 75,500 |
| 2000     Hot water, 7.5 KW, 25.6 MBH | Q-19 | 1.30 | 18.462 | | 3,225 | 800 | | 4,025 | 4,725 |
| 2100     90 KW, 307 MBH | | 1.10 | 21.818 | | 4,700 | 950 | | 5,650 | 6,600 |
| 2220     296 KW, 1010 MBH | | .55 | 43.636 | | 10,300 | 1,900 | | 12,200 | 14,300 |
| 2500     1,036 KW, 3536 MBH | Q-21 | .34 | 94.118 | | 24,000 | 4,175 | | 28,175 | 32,700 |
| 2680     2,400 KW, 8191 MBH | | .25 | 128 | | 50,000 | 5,675 | | 55,675 | 63,500 |
| 2820     3,600 KW, 12,283 MBH | | .16 | 200 | | 70,500 | 8,875 | | 79,375 | 91,000 |

## 23 52 23 – Cast-Iron Boilers

### 23 52 23.20 Gas-Fired Boilers

| | Crew | Daily Output | Labor-Hours | Unit | Material | Labor | Equipment | Total | Total Incl O&P |
|---|---|---|---|---|---|---|---|---|---|
| 0010 **GAS-FIRED BOILERS**, Natural or propane, standard controls, packaged. | | | | | | | | | |
| 1000     Cast iron, with insulated jacket | | | | | | | | | |
| 2000     Steam, gross output, 81 MBH | Q-7 | 1.40 | 22.857 | Ea. | 1,725 | 1,025 | | 2,750 | 3,450 |
| 2080     203 MBH | | .90 | 35.556 | | 2,700 | 1,600 | | 4,300 | 5,375 |
| 2180     400 MBH | | .56 | 56.838 | | 4,625 | 2,550 | | 7,175 | 8,925 |
| 2240     765 MBH | | .43 | 74.419 | | 9,175 | 3,350 | | 12,525 | 15,100 |
| 2320     1,875 MBH | | .30 | 106 | | 14,600 | 4,775 | | 19,375 | 23,300 |
| 2440     4,720 MBH | | .15 | 207 | | 26,800 | 9,325 | | 36,125 | 43,500 |
| 2480     6,100 MBH | | .13 | 246 | | 67,500 | 11,000 | | 78,500 | 90,500 |
| 2540     6,970 MBH | | .10 | 320 | | 75,500 | 14,400 | | 89,900 | 104,500 |
| 3000     Hot water, gross output, 80 MBH | | 1.46 | 21.918 | | 1,575 | 985 | | 2,560 | 3,225 |
| 3140     320 MBH     **CN** | | .80 | 40 | | 3,750 | 1,800 | | 5,550 | 6,825 |
| 3260     1,088 MBH | | .40 | 80 | | 11,100 | 3,600 | | 14,700 | 17,600 |
| 3360     2,856 MBH | | .20 | 160 | | 19,900 | 7,175 | | 27,075 | 32,700 |
| 3380     3,264 MBH | | .18 | 179 | | 21,000 | 8,075 | | 29,075 | 35,200 |
| 3480     6,100 MBH | | .13 | 250 | | 72,500 | 11,200 | | 83,700 | 97,000 |
| 3540     6,970 MBH | | .09 | 359 | | 79,500 | 16,100 | | 95,600 | 112,000 |
| 7000     For tankless water heater, add | | | | | 10% | | | | |

### 23 52 23.30 Gas/Oil Fired Boilers

| | Crew | Daily Output | Labor-Hours | Unit | Material | Labor | Equipment | Total | Total Incl O&P |
|---|---|---|---|---|---|---|---|---|---|
| 0010 **GAS/OIL FIRED BOILERS**, Combination with burners and controls, packaged. | | | | | | | | | |
| 1000     Cast iron with insulated jacket | | | | | | | | | |
| 2000     Steam, gross output, 720 MBH | Q-7 | .43 | 74.074 | Ea. | 10,900 | 3,325 | | 14,225 | 17,000 |
| 2080     1,600 MBH | | .30 | 107 | | 17,000 | 4,800 | | 21,800 | 25,900 |
| 2140     2,700 MBH | | .19 | 165 | | 23,100 | 7,450 | | 30,550 | 36,600 |
| 2280     5,520 MBH | | .14 | 235 | | 78,000 | 10,600 | | 88,600 | 101,500 |
| 2340     6,390 MBH | | .11 | 296 | | 83,500 | 13,300 | | 96,800 | 111,500 |
| 2380     6,970 MBH | | .09 | 372 | | 88,500 | 16,700 | | 105,200 | 122,000 |
| 2900     Hot water, gross output | | | | | | | | | |
| 2910     200 MBH | Q-6 | .62 | 39.024 | Ea. | 7,050 | 1,725 | | 8,775 | 10,300 |
| 2920     300 MBH | | .49 | 49.080 | | 7,050 | 2,150 | | 9,200 | 11,000 |
| 2930     400 MBH | | .41 | 57.971 | | 8,250 | 2,550 | | 10,800 | 12,900 |
| 2940     500 MBH | | .36 | 67.039 | | 8,900 | 2,950 | | 11,850 | 14,200 |
| 3000     584 MBH | Q-7 | .44 | 72.072 | | 9,950 | 3,225 | | 13,175 | 15,800 |
| 3060     1,460 MBH | | .28 | 113 | | 15,000 | 5,075 | | 20,075 | 24,100 |
| 3160     4,088 MBH | | .16 | 195 | | 41,300 | 8,750 | | 50,050 | 58,500 |
| 3300     13,500 MBH, 403.3 BHP | | .04 | 727 | | 127,500 | 32,600 | | 160,100 | 189,000 |

# 23 52 Heating Boilers

## 23 52 23 – Cast-Iron Boilers

| 23 52 23.40 Oil-Fired Boilers | | Crew | Daily Output | Labor-Hours | Unit | Material | 2008 Bare Costs Labor | Equipment | Total | Total Incl O&P |
|---|---|---|---|---|---|---|---|---|---|---|
| 0010 | **OIL-FIRED BOILERS,** Standard controls, flame retention burner, packaged. | | | | | | | | | |
| 1000 | Cast iron, with insulated flush jacket | | | | | | | | | |
| 2000 | Steam, gross output, 109 MBH | Q-7 | 1.20 | 26.667 | Ea. | 1,750 | 1,200 | | 2,950 | 3,725 |
| 2060 | 207 MBH | | .90 | 35.556 | | 2,400 | 1,600 | | 4,000 | 5,025 |
| 2180 | 1,084 MBH | | .38 | 85.106 | | 8,200 | 3,825 | | 12,025 | 14,800 |
| 2280 | 3,000 MBH | | .19 | 170 | | 19,200 | 7,650 | | 26,850 | 32,600 |
| 2380 | 5,520 MBH | | .14 | 235 | | 61,500 | 10,600 | | 72,100 | 83,500 |
| 2460 | 6,970 MBH | | .09 | 363 | | 78,500 | 16,300 | | 94,800 | 111,000 |
| 3000 | Hot water, same price as steam | | | | | | | | | |
| 4000 | For tankless coil in smaller sizes, add | | | | Ea. | 15% | | | | |

## 23 52 26 – Steel Boilers

| 23 52 26.40 Oil-Fired Boilers | | Crew | Daily Output | Labor-Hours | Unit | Material | 2008 Bare Costs Labor | Equipment | Total | Total Incl O&P |
|---|---|---|---|---|---|---|---|---|---|---|
| 0010 | **OIL-FIRED BOILERS,** Standard controls, flame retention burner | | | | | | | | | |
| 5000 | Steel, with insulated flush jacket | | | | | | | | | |
| 7000 | Hot water, gross output, 103 MBH | Q-6 | 1.60 | 15 | Ea. | 1,475 | 660 | | 2,135 | 2,625 |
| 7120 | 420 MBH | | .70 | 34.483 | | 6,975 | 1,525 | | 8,500 | 9,950 |
| 7320 | 3,150 MBH | | .13 | 184 | | 24,700 | 8,125 | | 32,825 | 39,400 |
| 7340 | For tankless coil in steam or hot water, add | | | | | 7% | | | | |

## 23 52 28 – Swimming Pool Boilers

| 23 52 28.10 Swimming Pool Heaters | | Crew | Daily Output | Labor-Hours | Unit | Material | 2008 Bare Costs Labor | Equipment | Total | Total Incl O&P |
|---|---|---|---|---|---|---|---|---|---|---|
| 0010 | **SWIMMING POOL HEATERS,** Not including wiring, external | | | | | | | | | |
| 0020 | piping, base or pad, | | | | | | | | | |
| 0160 | Gas fired, input, 155 MBH | Q-6 | 1.50 | 16 | Ea. | 1,575 | 705 | | 2,280 | 2,775 |
| 0200 | 199 MBH | | 1 | 24 | | 1,675 | 1,050 | | 2,725 | 3,425 |
| 0280 | 500 MBH | | .40 | 60 | | 6,775 | 2,650 | | 9,425 | 11,500 |
| 0400 | 1,800 MBH | | .14 | 171 | | 14,800 | 7,550 | | 22,350 | 27,500 |
| 2000 | Electric, 12 KW, 4,800 gallon pool | Q-19 | 3 | 8 | | 2,050 | 350 | | 2,400 | 2,775 |
| 2020 | 15 KW, 7,200 gallon pool | | 2.80 | 8.571 | | 2,075 | 370 | | 2,445 | 2,825 |
| 2040 | 24 KW, 9,600 gallon pool | | 2.40 | 10 | | 2,775 | 435 | | 3,210 | 3,700 |
| 2100 | 55 KW, 24,000 gallon pool | | 1.20 | 20 | | 3,950 | 870 | | 4,820 | 5,650 |

# 23 54 Furnaces

## 23 54 13 – Electric-Resistance Furnaces

| 23 54 13.10 Electric Furnaces | | Crew | Daily Output | Labor-Hours | Unit | Material | 2008 Bare Costs Labor | Equipment | Total | Total Incl O&P |
|---|---|---|---|---|---|---|---|---|---|---|
| 0010 | **ELECTRIC FURNACES,** Hot air, blowers, std. controls. | | | | | | | | | |
| 0011 | not including gas, oil or flue piping | | | | | | | | | |
| 1000 | Electric, UL listed | | | | | | | | | |
| 1020 | 10.2 MBH | Q-20 | 5 | 4 | Ea. | 345 | 167 | | 512 | 635 |
| 1040 | 17.1 MBH | | 4.80 | 4.167 | | 360 | 174 | | 534 | 665 |
| 1060 | 27.3 MBH | | 4.60 | 4.348 | | 435 | 181 | | 616 | 760 |
| 1100 | 34.1 MBH | | 4.40 | 4.545 | | 450 | 190 | | 640 | 785 |

## 23 54 16 – Fuel-Fired Furnaces

| 23 54 16.13 Gas-Fired Furnaces | | Crew | Daily Output | Labor-Hours | Unit | Material | 2008 Bare Costs Labor | Equipment | Total | Total Incl O&P |
|---|---|---|---|---|---|---|---|---|---|---|
| 0010 | **GAS-FIRED FURNACES** | | | | | | | | | |
| 3000 | Gas, AGA certified, upflow, direct drive models | | | | | | | | | |
| 3020 | 45 MBH input | Q-9 | 4 | 4 | Ea. | 550 | 163 | | 713 | 855 |
| 3040 | 60 MBH input | | 3.80 | 4.211 | | 585 | 172 | | 757 | 910 |
| 3060 | 75 MBH input | | 3.60 | 4.444 | | 650 | 181 | | 831 | 995 |
| 3100 | 100 MBH input | | 3.20 | 5 | | 655 | 204 | | 859 | 1,025 |

# 23 54 Furnaces

## 23 54 16 – Fuel-Fired Furnaces

| 23 54 16.16 Oil-Fired Furnaces | Crew | Daily Output | Labor-Hours | Unit | Material | 2008 Bare Costs Labor | Equipment | Total | Total Incl O&P |
|---|---|---|---|---|---|---|---|---|---|
| 0010 **OIL-FIRED FURNACES** | | | | | | | | | |
| 6000 Oil, UL listed, atomizing gun type burner | | | | | | | | | |
| 6020 56 MBH output | Q-9 | 3.60 | 4.444 | Ea. | 1,650 | 181 | | 1,831 | 2,100 |
| 6030 84 MBH output | | 3.50 | 4.571 | | 1,675 | 186 | | 1,861 | 2,125 |
| 6040 95 MBH output | | 3.40 | 4.706 | | 1,700 | 192 | | 1,892 | 2,175 |
| 6060 134 MBH output | | 3.20 | 5 | | 1,750 | 204 | | 1,954 | 2,275 |
| 6080 151 MBH output | | 3 | 5.333 | | 2,050 | 217 | | 2,267 | 2,575 |

# 23 55 Fuel-Fired Heaters

## 23 55 13 – Fuel-Fired Duct Heaters

### 23 55 13.16 Gas-Fired Duct Heaters

| | Crew | Daily Output | Labor-Hours | Unit | Material | 2008 Bare Costs Labor | Equipment | Total | Total Incl O&P |
|---|---|---|---|---|---|---|---|---|---|
| 0010 **GAS-FIRED DUCT HEATERS**, Includes burner, controls, stainless steel | | | | | | | | | |
| 0020 heat exchanger. Gas fired, electric ignition | | | | | | | | | |
| 0030 Indoor installation | | | | | | | | | |
| 0100 120 MBH output | Q-5 | 4 | 4 | Ea. | 1,675 | 170 | | 1,845 | 2,075 |
| 0130 200 MBH output | | 2.70 | 5.926 | | 1,750 | 251 | | 2,001 | 2,300 |
| 0140 240 MBH output | | 2.30 | 6.957 | | 2,325 | 295 | | 2,620 | 3,000 |
| 0180 320 MBH output | | 1.60 | 10 | | 2,800 | 425 | | 3,225 | 3,725 |
| 0300 For powered venter and adapter, add | | | | | 370 | | | 370 | 410 |
| 0502 For required flue pipe, see Div. 23 51 23.10 | | | | | | | | | |
| 1000 Outdoor installation, with vent cap | | | | | | | | | |
| 1020 75 MBH output | Q-5 | 4 | 4 | Ea. | 2,175 | 170 | | 2,345 | 2,650 |
| 1060 120 MBH output | | 4 | 4 | | 2,775 | 170 | | 2,945 | 3,300 |
| 1100 187 MBH output | | 3 | 5.333 | | 3,975 | 226 | | 4,201 | 4,725 |
| 1140 300 MBH output | | 1.80 | 8.889 | | 5,175 | 375 | | 5,550 | 6,275 |
| 1180 450 MBH output | | 1.40 | 11.429 | | 5,725 | 485 | | 6,210 | 7,025 |
| 1400 For powered venter, add | | | | | 10% | | | | |

## 23 55 33 – Fuel-Fired Unit Heaters

### 23 55 33.13 Oil-Fired Unit Heaters

| | Crew | Daily Output | Labor-Hours | Unit | Material | 2008 Bare Costs Labor | Equipment | Total | Total Incl O&P |
|---|---|---|---|---|---|---|---|---|---|
| 0010 **OIL-FIRED UNIT HEATERS**, Cabinet, grilles, fan, ctrl, burner, no piping | | | | | | | | | |
| 6000 Oil fired, suspension mounted, 94 MBH output | Q-5 | 4 | 4 | Ea. | 2,400 | 170 | | 2,570 | 2,900 |
| 6040 140 MBH output | | 3 | 5.333 | | 2,575 | 226 | | 2,801 | 3,175 |
| 6060 184 MBH output | | 3 | 5.333 | | 2,775 | 226 | | 3,001 | 3,400 |

### 23 55 33.16 Gas-Fired Unit Heaters

| | Crew | Daily Output | Labor-Hours | Unit | Material | 2008 Bare Costs Labor | Equipment | Total | Total Incl O&P |
|---|---|---|---|---|---|---|---|---|---|
| 0010 **GAS-FIRED UNIT HEATERS**, Cabinet, grilles, fan, ctrls., burner, no piping | | | | | | | | | |
| 0022 thermostat, no piping. For flue see Div. 23 51 23.10 | | | | | | | | | |
| 1000 Gas fired, floor mounted | | | | | | | | | |
| 1100 60 MBH output | Q-5 | 10 | 1.600 | Ea. | 665 | 68 | | 733 | 830 |
| 1140 100 MBH output | | 8 | 2 | | 735 | 85 | | 820 | 940 |
| 1180 180 MBH output | | 6 | 2.667 | | 1,050 | 113 | | 1,163 | 1,325 |
| 2000 Suspension mounted, propeller fan, 20 MBH output | | 8.50 | 1.882 | | 495 | 80 | | 575 | 660 |
| 2040 60 MBH output | | 7 | 2.286 | | 605 | 97 | | 702 | 810 |
| 2060 80 MBH output | | 6 | 2.667 | | 695 | 113 | | 808 | 935 |
| 2100 130 MBH output | | 5 | 3.200 | | 900 | 136 | | 1,036 | 1,200 |
| 2240 320 MBH output | | 2 | 8 | | 1,850 | 340 | | 2,190 | 2,550 |
| 2500 For powered venter and adapter, add | | | | | 315 | | | 315 | 350 |
| 5000 Wall furnace, 17.5 MBH output | Q-5 | 6 | 2.667 | | 615 | 113 | | 728 | 850 |
| 5020 24 MBH output | | 5 | 3.200 | | 640 | 136 | | 776 | 910 |
| 5040 35 MBH output | | 4 | 4 | | 770 | 170 | | 940 | 1,100 |

# 23 56 Solar Energy Heating Equipment

## 23 56 16 – Packaged Solar Heating Equipment

### 23 56 16.40 Solar Heating Systems

| | | Crew | Daily Output | Labor-Hours | Unit | Material | 2008 Bare Costs Labor | Equipment | Total | Total Incl O&P |
|---|---|---|---|---|---|---|---|---|---|---|
| 0010 | **SOLAR HEATING SYSTEMS** R235616-60 | | | | | | | | | |
| 0020 | System/Package prices, not including connecting | | | | | | | | | |
| 0030 | pipe, insulation, or special heating/plumbing fixtures | | | | | | | | | |
| 0500 | Hot water, standard package, low temperature | | | | | | | | | |
| 0540 | 1 collector, circulator, fittings, 65 gal. tank | Q-1 | .50 | 32 | Ea. | 2,125 | 1,350 | | 3,475 | 4,375 |
| 0580 | 2 collectors, circulator, fittings, 120 gal. tank | | .40 | 40 | | 3,200 | 1,675 | | 4,875 | 6,050 |
| 0620 | 3 collectors, circulator, fittings, 120 gal. tank | ↓ | .34 | 47.059 | ↓ | 4,150 | 1,975 | | 6,125 | 7,525 |
| 0700 | Medium temperature package | | | | | | | | | |
| 0720 | 1 collector, circulator, fittings, 80 gal. tank | Q-1 | .50 | 32 | Ea. | 1,850 | 1,350 | | 3,200 | 4,075 |
| 0740 | 2 collectors, circulator, fittings, 120 gal. tank | | .40 | 40 | | 2,700 | 1,675 | | 4,375 | 5,500 |
| 0780 | 3 collectors, circulator, fittings, 120 gal. tank | ↓ | .30 | 53.333 | | 3,650 | 2,250 | | 5,900 | 7,400 |
| 0980 | For each additional 120 gal. tank, add | | | | ↓ | 980 | | | 980 | 1,075 |

## 23 56 19 – Solar Heating Components

### 23 56 19.50 Solar Heating Ancillary

| | | Crew | Daily Output | Labor-Hours | Unit | Material | 2008 Bare Costs Labor | Equipment | Total | Total Incl O&P |
|---|---|---|---|---|---|---|---|---|---|---|
| 0010 | **SOLAR HEATING ANCILLARY** | | | | | | | | | |
| 2300 | Circulators, air | | | | | | | | | |
| 2310 | Blowers | | | | | | | | | |
| 2400 | Reversible fan, 20" diameter, 2 speed | Q-9 | 18 | .889 | Ea. | 108 | 36.50 | | 144.50 | 175 |
| 2520 | Space & DHW system, less duct work | " | .50 | 32 | | 1,475 | 1,300 | | 2,775 | 3,625 |
| 2870 | 1/12 HP, 30 GPM | Q-1 | 10 | 1.600 | ↓ | 330 | 67.50 | | 397.50 | 465 |
| 3000 | Collector panels, air with aluminum absorber plate | | | | | | | | | |
| 3010 | Wall or roof mount | | | | | | | | | |
| 3040 | Flat black, plastic glazing | | | | | | | | | |
| 3080 | 4' x 8' | Q-9 | 6 | 2.667 | Ea. | 635 | 109 | | 744 | 865 |
| 3200 | Flush roof mount, 10' to 16' x 22" wide | " | 96 | .167 | L.F. | 300 | 6.80 | | 306.80 | 340 |
| 3300 | Collector panels, liquid with copper absorber plate | | | | | | | | | |
| 3330 | Alum. frame, 4' x 8', 5/32" single glazing | Q-1 | 9.50 | 1.684 | Ea. | 680 | 71 | | 751 | 850 |
| 3390 | Alum. frame, 4' x 10', 5/32" single glazing | | 6 | 2.667 | | 810 | 112 | | 922 | 1,050 |
| 3450 | Flat black, alum. frame, 3.5' x 7.5' | | 9 | 1.778 | | 560 | 74.50 | | 634.50 | 730 |
| 3500 | 4' x 8' | | 5.50 | 2.909 | | 690 | 122 | | 812 | 940 |
| 3520 | 4' x 10' | | 10 | 1.600 | | 830 | 67.50 | | 897.50 | 1,025 |
| 3540 | 4' x 12.5' | | 5 | 3.200 | | 1,025 | 135 | | 1,160 | 1,325 |
| 3600 | Liquid, full wetted, plastic, alum. frame, 3' x 10' | | 5 | 3.200 | | 195 | 135 | | 330 | 415 |
| 3650 | Collector panel mounting, flat roof or ground rack | | 7 | 2.286 | ↓ | 212 | 96 | | 308 | 375 |
| 3670 | Roof clamps | ↓ | 70 | .229 | Set | 2.35 | 9.60 | | 11.95 | 17.05 |
| 3700 | Roof strap, teflon | 1 Plum | 205 | .039 | L.F. | 9.50 | 1.82 | | 11.32 | 13.20 |
| 3900 | Differential controller with two sensors | | | | | | | | | |
| 3930 | Thermostat, hard wired | 1 Plum | 8 | 1 | Ea. | 79.50 | 46.50 | | 126 | 158 |
| 4100 | Five station with digital read-out | " | 3 | 2.667 | " | 218 | 125 | | 343 | 425 |
| 4300 | Heat exchanger | | | | | | | | | |
| 4580 | Fluid to fluid package includes two circulating pumps | | | | | | | | | |
| 4590 | expansion tank, check valve, relief valve | | | | | | | | | |
| 4600 | controller, high temperature cutoff and sensors | Q-1 | 2.50 | 6.400 | Ea. | 695 | 269 | | 964 | 1,175 |
| 4650 | Heat transfer fluid | | | | | | | | | |
| 4700 | Propylene glycol, inhibited anti-freeze | 1 Plum | 28 | .286 | Gal. | 12.15 | 13.35 | | 25.50 | 33.50 |
| 8250 | Water storage tank with heat exchanger and electric element | | | | | | | | | |
| 8300 | 80 gal. with 2" x 2 lb. density insulation | 1 Plum | 1.60 | 5 | Ea. | 1,050 | 234 | | 1,284 | 1,500 |
| 8380 | 120 gal. with 2" x 2 lb. density insulation | | 1.40 | 5.714 | | 1,175 | 267 | | 1,442 | 1,675 |
| 8400 | 120 gal. with 2" x 2 lb. density insul., 40 S.F. heat coil | ↓ | 1.40 | 5.714 | | 1,500 | 267 | | 1,767 | 2,050 |

# 23 57 Heat Exchangers for HVAC

## 23 57 16 – Steam-to-Water Heat Exchangers

### 23 57 16.10 Shell & Tube Steam-to-Water Heat Exchangers

| 23 57 16.10 Shell & Tube Steam-to-Water Heat Exchangers | Crew | Daily Output | Labor-Hours | Unit | Material | 2008 Bare Costs Labor | Equipment | Total | Total Incl O&P |
|---|---|---|---|---|---|---|---|---|---|
| 0010 **SHELL AND TUBE TYPE STEAM-TO-WATER HEAT EXCHANGERS** | | | | | | | | | |
| 0016 Shell & tube type, 2 or 4 pass, 3/4" O.D. copper tubes, | | | | | | | | | |
| 0020 C.I. heads, C.I. tube sheet, steel shell | | | | | | | | | |
| 0100 Hot water 40° F to 180° F, by steam at 10 PSI | | | | | | | | | |
| 0120     8 GPM | Q-5 | 6 | 2.667 | Ea. | 1,475 | 113 | | 1,588 | 1,800 |
| 0140     10 GPM | | 5 | 3.200 | | 2,225 | 136 | | 2,361 | 2,650 |
| 0160     40 GPM | | 4 | 4 | | 3,450 | 170 | | 3,620 | 4,050 |
| 0180     64 GPM | | 2 | 8 | | 5,275 | 340 | | 5,615 | 6,325 |
| 0200     96 GPM | ↓ | 1 | 16 | | 7,075 | 680 | | 7,755 | 8,800 |
| 0220     120 GPM | Q-6 | 1.50 | 16 | ↓ | 9,275 | 705 | | 9,980 | 11,300 |

## 23 57 19 – Liquid-to-Liquid Heat Exchangers

### 23 57 19.13 Plate-Type, Liquid-to-Liquid Heat Exchangers

| | Crew | Daily Output | Labor-Hours | Unit | Material | 2008 Bare Costs Labor | Equipment | Total | Total Incl O&P |
|---|---|---|---|---|---|---|---|---|---|
| 0010 **PLATE-TYPE, LIQUID-TO-LIQUID HEAT EXCHANGERS** | | | | | | | | | |
| 3000 Plate type, | | | | | | | | | |
| 3100     400 GPM | Q-6 | .80 | 30 | Ea. | 29,900 | 1,325 | | 31,225 | 34,800 |
| 3120     800 GPM | " | .50 | 48 | | 51,500 | 2,100 | | 53,600 | 59,500 |
| 3140     1200 GPM | Q-7 | .34 | 94.118 | | 76,500 | 4,225 | | 80,725 | 90,500 |
| 3160     1800 GPM | " | .24 | 133 | ↓ | 101,500 | 5,975 | | 107,475 | 120,500 |

### 23 57 19.16 Shell-Type, Liquid-to-Liquid Heat Exchangers

| | Crew | Daily Output | Labor-Hours | Unit | Material | 2008 Bare Costs Labor | Equipment | Total | Total Incl O&P |
|---|---|---|---|---|---|---|---|---|---|
| 0010 **SHELL-TYPE, LIQUID-TO-LIQUID HEAT EXCHANGERS** | | | | | | | | | |
| 1000 Hot water 40° F to 140° F, by water at 200° F | | | | | | | | | |
| 1020     7 GPM | Q-5 | 6 | 2.667 | Ea. | 1,825 | 113 | | 1,938 | 2,175 |
| 1040     16 GPM | | 5 | 3.200 | | 2,575 | 136 | | 2,711 | 3,025 |
| 1060     34 GPM | | 4 | 4 | | 3,900 | 170 | | 4,070 | 4,525 |
| 1100     74 GPM | ↓ | 1.50 | 10.667 | ↓ | 7,050 | 450 | | 7,500 | 8,425 |

# 23 62 Packaged Compressor and Condenser Units

## 23 62 13 – Packaged Air-Cooled Refrigerant Compressor and Condenser Units

### 23 62 13.10 Packaged Air-Cooled Refrig. Condensing Units

| | Crew | Daily Output | Labor-Hours | Unit | Material | 2008 Bare Costs Labor | Equipment | Total | Total Incl O&P |
|---|---|---|---|---|---|---|---|---|---|
| 0010 **PACKAGED AIR-COOLED REFRIGERANT CONDENSING UNITS** | | | | | | | | | |
| 0020 Condensing unit | | | | | | | | | |
| 0030 Air cooled, compressor, standard controls | | | | | | | | | |
| 0050     1.5 ton | Q-5 | 2.50 | 6.400 | Ea. | 1,050 | 271 | | 1,321 | 1,575 |
| 0500     5 ton | | .60 | 26.667 | | 1,925 | 1,125 | | 3,050 | 3,825 |
| 0600     10 ton | ↓ | .50 | 32 | | 4,125 | 1,350 | | 5,475 | 6,600 |
| 0700     20 ton | Q-6 | .40 | 60 | ↓ | 9,400 | 2,650 | | 12,050 | 14,300 |

# 23 63 Refrigerant Condensers

## 23 63 13 – Air-Cooled Refrigerant Condensers

### 23 63 13.10 Air-Cooled Refrig. Condensers

| | Crew | Daily Output | Labor-Hours | Unit | Material | 2008 Bare Costs Labor | Equipment | Total | Total Incl O&P |
|---|---|---|---|---|---|---|---|---|---|
| 0010 **AIR-COOLED REFRIG. CONDENSERS**, Ratings for 30° F TD, R-22. | | | | | | | | | |
| 0080 Air cooled, belt drive, propeller fan | | | | | | | | | |
| 0240     50 ton | Q-6 | .69 | 34.985 | Ea. | 11,900 | 1,550 | | 13,450 | 15,400 |
| 0280     59 ton | | .58 | 41.308 | | 13,200 | 1,825 | | 15,025 | 17,300 |
| 0320     73 ton | | .47 | 51.173 | | 15,600 | 2,250 | | 17,850 | 20,600 |
| 0360     86 ton | | .40 | 60.302 | | 18,500 | 2,650 | | 21,150 | 24,300 |
| 0380     88 ton | ↓ | .39 | 61.697 | ↓ | 19,800 | 2,725 | | 22,525 | 25,900 |
| 1550 Air cooled, direct drive, propeller fan | | | | | | | | | |

# 23 63 Refrigerant Condensers

## 23 63 13 - Air-Cooled Refrigerant Condensers

| 23 63 13.10 Air-Cooled Refrig. Condensers | Crew | Daily Output | Labor-Hours | Unit | Material | 2008 Bare Costs Labor | 2008 Bare Costs Equipment | Total | Total Incl O&P |
|---|---|---|---|---|---|---|---|---|---|
| 1590 | 1 ton | Q-5 | 3.80 | 4.211 | Ea. | 660 | 179 | | 839 | 995 |
| 1600 | 1-1/2 ton | | 3.60 | 4.444 | | 785 | 188 | | 973 | 1,150 |
| 1620 | 2 ton | | 3.20 | 5 | | 865 | 212 | | 1,077 | 1,275 |
| 1640 | 5 ton | | 2 | 8 | | 1,750 | 340 | | 2,090 | 2,425 |
| 1660 | 10 ton | | 1.40 | 11.429 | | 2,725 | 485 | | 3,210 | 3,725 |
| 1690 | 16 ton | | 1.10 | 14.545 | | 3,825 | 615 | | 4,440 | 5,125 |
| 1720 | 26 ton | | .84 | 19.002 | | 4,950 | 805 | | 5,755 | 6,650 |
| 1760 | 41 ton | Q-6 | .77 | 31.008 | | 9,075 | 1,375 | | 10,450 | 12,000 |
| 1800 | 63 ton | " | .55 | 44.037 | | 14,300 | 1,925 | | 16,225 | 18,600 |

# 23 64 Packaged Water Chillers

## 23 64 13 - Absorption Water Chillers

### 23 64 13.16 Indirect-Fired Absorption Water Chillers

| | | Crew | Daily Output | Labor-Hours | Unit | Material | 2008 Bare Costs Labor | 2008 Bare Costs Equipment | Total | Total Incl O&P |
|---|---|---|---|---|---|---|---|---|---|---|
| 0010 | **INDIRECT-FIRED ABSORPTION WATER CHILLERS** | | | | | | | | | |
| 0020 | Steam or hot water, water cooled | | | | | | | | | |
| 0050 | 100 ton | Q-7 | .13 | 240 | Ea. | 125,000 | 10,800 | | 135,800 | 153,500 |
| 0400 | 420 ton | " | .10 | 323 | " | 301,000 | 14,500 | | 315,500 | 353,000 |

## 23 64 16 - Centrifugal Water Chillers

### 23 64 16.10 Centrifugal Type Water Chillers

| | | Crew | Daily Output | Labor-Hours | Unit | Material | 2008 Bare Costs Labor | 2008 Bare Costs Equipment | Total | Total Incl O&P |
|---|---|---|---|---|---|---|---|---|---|---|
| 0010 | **CENTRIFUGAL TYPE WATER CHILLERS**, With standard controls. | | | | | | | | | |
| 0020 | Centrifugal liquid chiller, water cooled | | | | | | | | | |
| 0030 | not including water tower | | | | | | | | | |
| 0100 | 2000 ton, (twin 1000 ton units) | Q-7 | .07 | 477 | Ea. | 762,000 | 21,400 | | 783,400 | 870,500 |

## 23 64 19 - Reciprocating Water Chillers

### 23 64 19.10 Reciprocating Type Water Chillers

| | | Crew | Daily Output | Labor-Hours | Unit | Material | 2008 Bare Costs Labor | 2008 Bare Costs Equipment | Total | Total Incl O&P |
|---|---|---|---|---|---|---|---|---|---|---|
| 0010 | **RECIPROCATING TYPE WATER CHILLERS**, With standard controls. | | | | | | | | | |
| 0494 | Water chillers, integral air cooled condenser | | | | | | | | | |
| 0600 | 100 ton cooling | Q-7 | .25 | 129 | Ea. | 65,000 | 5,800 | | 70,800 | 80,000 |
| 0980 | Water cooled, multiple compr., semi-hermetic, tower not incl. | | | | | | | | | |
| 1000 | 15 ton cooling | Q-6 | .36 | 65.934 | Ea. | 13,200 | 2,900 | | 16,100 | 18,900 |
| 1020 | 20 ton cooling | Q-7 | .41 | 78.049 | | 14,500 | 3,500 | | 18,000 | 21,300 |
| 1060 | 30 ton cooling | | .31 | 101 | | 17,100 | 4,575 | | 21,675 | 25,700 |
| 1100 | 50 ton cooling | | .28 | 113 | | 30,700 | 5,100 | | 35,800 | 41,500 |
| 1160 | 100 ton cooling | | .18 | 179 | | 55,000 | 8,075 | | 63,075 | 72,500 |
| 1180 | 120 ton cooling | | .16 | 196 | | 62,000 | 8,800 | | 70,800 | 81,500 |
| 1200 | 140 ton cooling | | .16 | 202 | | 73,000 | 9,100 | | 82,100 | 94,000 |
| 1451 | Water cooled, dual compressors, semi-hermetic, tower not incl. | | | | | | | | | |
| 1500 | 80 ton cooling | Q-7 | .14 | 222 | Ea. | 30,600 | 9,975 | | 40,575 | 48,700 |
| 1520 | 100 ton cooling | | .14 | 228 | | 37,500 | 10,300 | | 47,800 | 56,500 |
| 1540 | 120 ton cooling | | .14 | 231 | | 45,500 | 10,400 | | 55,900 | 65,500 |

## 23 64 23 - Scroll Water Chillers

### 23 64 23.10 Scroll Water Chillers

| | | Crew | Daily Output | Labor-Hours | Unit | Material | 2008 Bare Costs Labor | 2008 Bare Costs Equipment | Total | Total Incl O&P |
|---|---|---|---|---|---|---|---|---|---|---|
| 0010 | **SCROLL WATER CHILLERS**, With standard controls. | | | | | | | | | |
| 0490 | Packaged w/integral air cooled condenser, 15 ton cool | Q-7 | .37 | 86.486 | Ea. | 16,100 | 3,875 | | 19,975 | 23,600 |
| 0500 | 20 ton cooling | | .34 | 94.118 | | 21,300 | 4,225 | | 25,525 | 29,800 |
| 0520 | 40 ton cooling | | .30 | 108 | | 28,900 | 4,850 | | 33,750 | 39,100 |
| 0680 | Scroll water cooled, single compressor, hermetic, tower not incl. | | | | | | | | | |
| 0700 | 2 ton cooling | Q-5 | .57 | 28.070 | Ea. | 3,100 | 1,200 | | 4,300 | 5,200 |
| 0710 | 5 ton cooling | | .57 | 28.070 | | 3,775 | 1,200 | | 4,975 | 5,950 |

# 23 64 Packaged Water Chillers

## 23 64 23 – Scroll Water Chillers

| 23 64 23.10 Scroll Water Chillers | | Crew | Daily Output | Labor-Hours | Unit | Material | 2008 Bare Costs Labor | Equipment | Total | Total Incl O&P |
|---|---|---|---|---|---|---|---|---|---|---|
| 0740 | 8 ton cooling | Q-5 | .31 | 52.117 | Ea. | 5,450 | 2,200 | | 7,650 | 9,300 |
| 0760 | 10 ton cooling | Q-6 | .36 | 67.039 | | 5,875 | 2,950 | | 8,825 | 10,900 |
| 0800 | 20 ton cooling | Q-7 | .38 | 83.990 | | 10,400 | 3,775 | | 14,175 | 17,200 |
| 0820 | 30 ton cooling | " | .33 | 96.096 | | 11,700 | 4,325 | | 16,025 | 19,300 |

## 23 64 26 – Rotary-Screw Water Chillers

### 23 64 26.10 Rotary-Screw Type Water Chillers

| | | Crew | Daily Output | Labor-Hours | Unit | Material | Labor | Equipment | Total | Total Incl O&P |
|---|---|---|---|---|---|---|---|---|---|---|
| 0010 | **ROTARY-SCREW TYPE WATER CHILLERS**, With standard controls. | | | | | | | | | |
| 0110 | Screw, liquid chiller, air cooled, insulated evaporator | | | | | | | | | |
| 0120 | 130 ton | Q-7 | .14 | 228 | Ea. | 74,500 | 10,300 | | 84,800 | 97,500 |
| 0124 | 160 ton | | .13 | 246 | | 92,000 | 11,000 | | 103,000 | 117,500 |
| 0128 | 180 ton | | .13 | 250 | | 103,500 | 11,200 | | 114,700 | 130,500 |
| 0132 | 210 ton | | .12 | 258 | | 114,000 | 11,600 | | 125,600 | 143,000 |
| 0136 | 270 ton | | .12 | 266 | | 130,000 | 12,000 | | 142,000 | 161,000 |
| 0140 | 320 ton | | .12 | 275 | | 163,500 | 12,400 | | 175,900 | 198,000 |
| 0200 | Packaged unit, water cooled, not incl. tower | | | | | | | | | |
| 0210 | 80 ton | Q-7 | .14 | 223 | Ea. | 38,500 | 10,000 | | 48,500 | 57,500 |
| 0240 | 200 ton | | .13 | 251 | | 72,500 | 11,300 | | 83,800 | 97,000 |
| 0270 | 350 ton | | .12 | 275 | | 134,500 | 12,400 | | 146,900 | 166,500 |
| 1450 | Water cooled, tower not included | | | | | | | | | |
| 1580 | 150 ton cooling, screw compressors | Q-7 | .13 | 240 | Ea. | 63,500 | 10,800 | | 74,300 | 86,000 |
| 1620 | 200 ton cooling, screw compressors | | .13 | 250 | | 87,500 | 11,200 | | 98,700 | 113,500 |
| 1660 | 291 ton cooling, screw compressors | | .12 | 260 | | 91,500 | 11,700 | | 103,200 | 118,500 |

# 23 65 Cooling Towers

## 23 65 13 – Forced-Draft Cooling Towers

### 23 65 13.10 Forced-Draft Type Cooling Towers

| | | Crew | Daily Output | Labor-Hours | Unit | Material | Labor | Equipment | Total | Total Incl O&P |
|---|---|---|---|---|---|---|---|---|---|---|
| 0010 | **FORCED-DRAFT TYPE COOLING TOWERS**, Packaged units. | | | | | | | | | |
| 0070 | Galvanized steel | | | | | | | | | |
| 0080 | Induced draft, crossflow | | | | | | | | | |
| 0100 | Vertical, belt drive, 61 tons | Q-6 | 90 | .267 | TonAC | 96 | 11.75 | | 107.75 | 123 |
| 0150 | 100 ton | | 100 | .240 | | 76 | 10.55 | | 86.55 | 99.50 |
| 0200 | 115 ton | | 109 | .220 | | 74 | 9.70 | | 83.70 | 96 |
| 0250 | 131 ton | | 120 | .200 | | 65.50 | 8.80 | | 74.30 | 85.50 |
| 0260 | 162 ton | | 132 | .182 | | 55 | 8 | | 63 | 72.50 |
| 1500 | Induced air, double flow | | | | | | | | | |
| 1900 | Vertical, gear drive, 167 ton | Q-6 | 126 | .190 | TonAC | 102 | 8.40 | | 110.40 | 125 |
| 2000 | 297 ton | | 129 | .186 | | 73 | 8.20 | | 81.20 | 92.50 |
| 2100 | 582 ton | | 132 | .182 | | 60.50 | 8 | | 68.50 | 78.50 |
| 2150 | 849 ton | | 142 | .169 | | 59.50 | 7.45 | | 66.95 | 76.50 |
| 2200 | 1016 ton | | 150 | .160 | | 57 | 7.05 | | 64.05 | 73 |
| 3000 | For higher capacities, use multiples | | | | | | | | | |
| 3500 | For pumps and piping, add | Q-6 | 38 | .632 | TonAC | 48 | 28 | | 76 | 94.50 |
| 4000 | For absorption systems, add | | | | " | 75% | 75% | | | |
| 5000 | Fiberglass | | | | | | | | | |
| 5010 | Draw thru | | | | | | | | | |
| 5100 | 60 ton | Q-6 | 1.50 | 16 | Ea. | 3,450 | 705 | | 4,155 | 4,850 |
| 5120 | 125 ton | | .99 | 24.242 | | 7,050 | 1,075 | | 8,125 | 9,350 |
| 5140 | 300 ton | | .43 | 55.814 | | 16,500 | 2,450 | | 18,950 | 21,800 |
| 5160 | 600 ton | | .22 | 109 | | 29,600 | 4,800 | | 34,400 | 39,800 |
| 5180 | 1000 ton | | .15 | 160 | | 51,000 | 7,025 | | 58,025 | 66,500 |

# 23 65 Cooling Towers

## 23 65 13 – Forced-Draft Cooling Towers

### 23 65 13.10 Forced-Draft Type Cooling Towers

| 23 65 13.10 Forced-Draft Type Cooling Towers | | Crew | Daily Output | Labor-Hours | Unit | Material | 2008 Bare Costs Labor | 2008 Bare Costs Equipment | Total | Total Incl O&P |
|---|---|---|---|---|---|---|---|---|---|---|
| 6000 | Stainless steel | | | | | | | | | |
| 6010 | Induced draft, crossflow, horizontal, belt drive | | | | | | | | | |
| 6100 | 57 ton | Q-6 | 1.50 | 16 | Ea. | 9,675 | 705 | | 10,380 | 11,700 |
| 6120 | 91 ton | | .99 | 24.242 | | 13,900 | 1,075 | | 14,975 | 16,900 |
| 6140 | 111 ton | | .43 | 55.814 | | 16,400 | 2,450 | | 18,850 | 21,700 |
| 6160 | 126 ton | ↓ | .22 | 109 | ↓ | 17,800 | 4,800 | | 22,600 | 26,700 |

# 23 73 Indoor Central-Station Air-Handling Units

## 23 73 13 – Modular Indoor Central-Station Air-Handling Units

### 23 73 13.10 Air Handling Units

| 23 73 13.10 Air Handling Units | | Crew | Daily Output | Labor-Hours | Unit | Material | 2008 Bare Costs Labor | 2008 Bare Costs Equipment | Total | Total Incl O&P |
|---|---|---|---|---|---|---|---|---|---|---|
| 0010 | **AIR HANDLING UNITS**, Built-Up | | | | | | | | | |
| 0100 | With cooling/heating coil section, filters, mixing box | | | | | | | | | |
| 0880 | Single zone, horizontal / vertical | | | | | | | | | |
| 0890 | Constant volume | | | | | | | | | |
| 0900 | 1600 CFM | Q-5 | 1.20 | 13.333 | Ea. | 3,000 | 565 | | 3,565 | 4,150 |
| 0920 | 5000 CFM | Q-6 | 1.40 | 17.143 | | 7,825 | 755 | | 8,580 | 9,725 |
| 0940 | 11,500 CFM | | 1 | 24 | | 15,800 | 1,050 | | 16,850 | 19,000 |
| 0970 | 22,000 CFM | | .60 | 40 | | 30,300 | 1,750 | | 32,050 | 36,000 |
| 1000 | 40,000 CFM | ↓ | .30 | 80 | | 46,400 | 3,525 | | 49,925 | 56,500 |
| 1140 | 60,000 CFM | Q-7 | .18 | 177 | ↓ | 68,000 | 7,975 | | 75,975 | 86,500 |

## 23 73 39 – Indoor, Direct Gas-Fired Heating and Ventilating Units

### 23 73 39.10 Make-Up Air Unit

| 23 73 39.10 Make-Up Air Unit | | Crew | Daily Output | Labor-Hours | Unit | Material | 2008 Bare Costs Labor | 2008 Bare Costs Equipment | Total | Total Incl O&P |
|---|---|---|---|---|---|---|---|---|---|---|
| 0010 | **MAKE-UP AIR UNIT** | | | | | | | | | |
| 0020 | Indoor suspension, natural/LP gas, direct fired, | | | | | | | | | |
| 0032 | standard control. For flue see Div. 23 51 23.10 | | | | | | | | | |
| 0040 | 70° F temperature rise, MBH is input | | | | | | | | | |
| 0100 | 2000 CFM, 168 MBH | Q-6 | 3 | 8 | Ea. | 7,525 | 350 | | 7,875 | 8,800 |
| 0160 | 6000 CFM, 502 MBH | | 1.50 | 16 | | 9,500 | 705 | | 10,205 | 11,500 |
| 0220 | 12,000 CFM, 1005 MBH | ↓ | 1 | 24 | | 11,800 | 1,050 | | 12,850 | 14,600 |
| 0300 | 24,000 CFM, 2007 MBH | Q-7 | 1 | 32 | | 15,400 | 1,425 | | 16,825 | 19,100 |
| 0400 | 50,000 CFM, 4180 MBH | " | .80 | 40 | | 21,100 | 1,800 | | 22,900 | 25,900 |
| 0600 | For discharge louver assembly, add | | | | | 10% | | | | |
| 0700 | For filters, add | | | | | 20% | | | | |
| 0800 | For air shut-off damper section, add | | | | | 10% | | | | |
| 0900 | For vertical unit, add | | | | ↓ | 10% | | | | |

# 23 74 Packaged Outdoor HVAC Equipment

## 23 74 33 – Packaged, Outdoor, Heating and Cooling Makeup Air-Conditioners

### 23 74 33.10 Roof Top Air Conditioners

| 23 74 33.10 Roof Top Air Conditioners | | | Crew | Daily Output | Labor-Hours | Unit | Material | 2008 Bare Costs Labor | 2008 Bare Costs Equipment | Total | Total Incl O&P |
|---|---|---|---|---|---|---|---|---|---|---|---|
| 0010 | **ROOF TOP AIR CONDITIONERS**, Standard controls, curb, economizer. | | | | | | | | | | |
| 1000 | Single zone, electric cool, gas heat | | | | | | | | | | |
| 1090 | 2 ton cooling, 55 MBH heating | R236000-20 | Q-5 | .93 | 17.204 | Ea. | 2,900 | 730 | | 3,630 | 4,300 |
| 1100 | 3 ton cooling, 60 MBH heating | | | .70 | 22.857 | | 3,000 | 970 | | 3,970 | 4,750 |
| 1120 | 4 ton cooling, 95 MBH heating | | | .61 | 26.403 | | 3,550 | 1,125 | | 4,675 | 5,575 |
| 1140 | 5 ton cooling, 112 MBH heating | | | .56 | 28.521 | | 3,900 | 1,200 | | 5,100 | 6,125 |
| 1145 | 6 ton cooling, 140 MBH heating | | | .52 | 30.769 | | 4,600 | 1,300 | | 5,900 | 7,000 |
| 1150 | 7.5 ton cooling, 170 MBH heating | | ↓ | .50 | 32.258 | | 5,400 | 1,375 | | 6,775 | 8,000 |
| 1160 | 10 ton cooling, 200 MBH heating | | Q-6 | .67 | 35.982 | | 7,800 | 1,575 | | 9,375 | 11,000 |
| 1170 | 12.5 ton cooling, 230 MBH heating | | | .63 | 37.975 | ↓ | 8,850 | 1,675 | | 10,525 | 12,200 |

# 23 74 Packaged Outdoor HVAC Equipment

## 23 74 33 – Packaged, Outdoor, Heating and Cooling Makeup Air-Conditioners

| 23 74 33.10 Roof Top Air Conditioners | Crew | Daily Output | Labor-Hours | Unit | Material | 2008 Bare Costs Labor | Equipment | Total | Total Incl O&P |
|---|---|---|---|---|---|---|---|---|---|
| 1190 | 18 ton cooling, 330 MBH heating | Q-6 | .52 | 45.889 | Ea. | 14,500 | 2,025 | | 16,525 | 18,900 |
| 1200 | 20 ton cooling, 360 MBH heating | Q-7 | .67 | 47.976 | | 19,500 | 2,150 | | 21,650 | 24,800 |
| 1210 | 25 ton cooling, 450 MBH heating | | .56 | 57.554 | | 23,000 | 2,575 | | 25,575 | 29,100 |
| 1220 | 30 ton cooling, 540 MBH heating | | .47 | 68.376 | | 25,000 | 3,075 | | 28,075 | 32,100 |
| 1240 | 40 ton cooling, 675 MBH heating | | .35 | 91.168 | | 32,000 | 4,100 | | 36,100 | 41,300 |
| 2000 | Multizone, electric cool, gas heat, economizer | | | | | | | | | |
| 2100 | 15 ton cooling, 360 MBH heating | Q-7 | .61 | 52.545 | Ea. | 51,000 | 2,350 | | 53,350 | 59,500 |
| 2120 | 20 ton cooling, 360 MBH heating | CN | .53 | 60.038 | | 68,000 | 2,700 | | 70,700 | 79,000 |
| 2200 | 40 ton cooling, 540 MBH heating | | .28 | 113 | | 118,000 | 5,100 | | 123,100 | 137,000 |
| 2210 | 50 ton cooling, 540 MBH heating | | .23 | 142 | | 146,500 | 6,375 | | 152,875 | 170,500 |
| 2220 | 70 ton cooling, 1500 MBH heating | | .16 | 198 | | 159,000 | 8,925 | | 167,925 | 188,000 |
| 2240 | 80 ton cooling, 1500 MBH heating | | .14 | 228 | | 181,500 | 10,300 | | 191,800 | 215,000 |
| 2260 | 90 ton cooling, 1500 MBH heating | | .13 | 256 | | 193,000 | 11,500 | | 204,500 | 230,000 |
| 2280 | 105 ton cooling, 1500 MBH heating | | .11 | 290 | | 209,500 | 13,100 | | 222,600 | 250,000 |
| 2400 | For hot water heat coil, deduct | | | | | 5% | | | | |
| 2500 | For steam heat coil, deduct | | | | | 2% | | | | |
| 2600 | For electric heat, deduct | | | | | 3% | 5% | | | |

# 23 81 Decentralized Unitary HVAC Equipment

## 23 81 13 – Packaged Terminal Air-Conditioners

### 23 81 13.10 Packaged Cabinet Type Air-Conditioners

| | | Crew | Daily Output | Labor-Hours | Unit | Material | Labor | Equipment | Total | Total Incl O&P |
|---|---|---|---|---|---|---|---|---|---|---|
| 0010 | **PACKAGED CABINET TYPE AIR-CONDITIONERS**, Cabinet, wall sleeve, | | | | | | | | | |
| 0100 | louver, electric heat, thermostat, manual changeover, 208 V | | | | | | | | | |
| 0200 | 6,000 BTUH cooling, 8800 BTU heat | Q-5 | 6 | 2.667 | Ea. | 595 | 113 | | 708 | 825 |
| 0220 | 9,000 BTUH cooling, 13,900 BTU heat | | 5 | 3.200 | | 685 | 136 | | 821 | 960 |
| 0240 | 12,000 BTUH cooling, 13,900 BTU heat | | 4 | 4 | | 735 | 170 | | 905 | 1,075 |
| 0260 | 15,000 BTUH cooling, 13,900 BTU heat | | 3 | 5.333 | | 825 | 226 | | 1,051 | 1,250 |
| 0500 | For hot water coil, increase heat by 10%, add | | | | | 5% | 10% | | | |
| 1000 | For steam, increase heat output by 30%, add | | | | | 8% | 10% | | | |

## 23 81 19 – Self-Contained Air-Conditioners

### 23 81 19.20 Self-Contained Single Package

| | | Crew | Daily Output | Labor-Hours | Unit | Material | Labor | Equipment | Total | Total Incl O&P |
|---|---|---|---|---|---|---|---|---|---|---|
| 0010 | **SELF-CONTAINED SINGLE PACKAGE** | | | | | | | | | |
| 0100 | Air cooled, for free blow or duct, not incl. remote condenser | | | | | | | | | |
| 0200 | 3 ton cooling | Q-5 | 1 | 16 | Ea. | 3,125 | 680 | | 3,805 | 4,450 |
| 0220 | 5 ton cooling | Q-6 | 1.20 | 20 | | 3,700 | 880 | | 4,580 | 5,400 |
| 0240 | 10 ton cooling | Q-7 | 1 | 32 | | 6,400 | 1,425 | | 7,825 | 9,200 |
| 0260 | 20 ton cooling | | .90 | 35.556 | | 12,700 | 1,600 | | 14,300 | 16,300 |
| 0280 | 30 ton cooling | | .80 | 40 | | 18,500 | 1,800 | | 20,300 | 23,100 |
| 0340 | 60 ton cooling | Q-8 | .40 | 80 | | 45,800 | 3,600 | 141 | 49,541 | 56,000 |
| 0490 | For duct mounting no price change | | | | | | | | | |
| 0500 | For steam heating coils, add | | | | Ea. | 10% | 10% | | | |
| 1000 | Water cooled for free blow or duct, not including tower | | | | | | | | | |
| 1010 | Constant volume | | | | | | | | | |
| 1100 | 3 ton cooling | Q-6 | 1 | 24 | Ea. | 2,975 | 1,050 | | 4,025 | 4,850 |
| 1120 | 5 ton cooling | " | 1 | 24 | | 3,900 | 1,050 | | 4,950 | 5,875 |
| 1140 | 10 ton cooling | Q-7 | .90 | 35.556 | | 7,675 | 1,600 | | 9,275 | 10,900 |
| 1160 | 20 ton cooling | | .80 | 40 | | 25,000 | 1,800 | | 26,800 | 30,200 |
| 1180 | 30 ton cooling | | .70 | 45.714 | | 33,100 | 2,050 | | 35,150 | 39,500 |

# 23 81 Decentralized Unitary HVAC Equipment

## 23 81 23 – Computer-Room Air-Conditioners

### 23 81 23.10 Computer Room Units

| | | Crew | Daily Output | Labor-Hours | Unit | Material | 2008 Bare Costs Labor | Equipment | Total | Total Incl O&P |
|---|---|---|---|---|---|---|---|---|---|---|
| 0010 | **COMPUTER ROOM UNITS** | | | | | | | | | |
| 1000 | Air cooled, includes remote condenser but not | | | | | | | | | |
| 1020 | interconnecting tubing or refrigerant | | | | | | | | | |
| 1080 | 3 ton | Q-5 | .50 | 32 | Ea. | 15,300 | 1,350 | | 16,650 | 18,900 |
| 1120 | 5 ton | | .45 | 35.556 | | 16,300 | 1,500 | | 17,800 | 20,200 |
| 1160 | 6 ton | | .30 | 53.333 | | 27,100 | 2,250 | | 29,350 | 33,200 |
| 1200 | 8 ton | | .27 | 59.259 | | 28,500 | 2,525 | | 31,025 | 35,200 |
| 1240 | 10 ton | | .25 | 64 | | 29,800 | 2,725 | | 32,525 | 36,900 |
| 1280 | 15 ton | | .22 | 72.727 | | 32,700 | 3,075 | | 35,775 | 40,700 |
| 1290 | 18 ton | | .20 | 80 | | 36,500 | 3,400 | | 39,900 | 45,300 |
| 1300 | 20 ton | Q-6 | .26 | 92.308 | | 39,100 | 4,050 | | 43,150 | 49,100 |
| 1320 | 22 ton | | .24 | 100 | | 39,900 | 4,400 | | 44,300 | 50,500 |
| 1360 | 30 ton | | .21 | 114 | | 48,900 | 5,025 | | 53,925 | 61,500 |
| 2200 | Chilled water, for connection to | | | | | | | | | |
| 2220 | existing chiller system of adequate capacity | | | | | | | | | |
| 2260 | 5 ton | Q-5 | .74 | 21.622 | Ea. | 10,900 | 915 | | 11,815 | 13,400 |

## 23 81 43 – Air-Source Unitary Heat Pumps

### 23 81 43.10 Air-Source Heat Pumps

| | | Crew | Daily Output | Labor-Hours | Unit | Material | 2008 Bare Costs Labor | Equipment | Total | Total Incl O&P |
|---|---|---|---|---|---|---|---|---|---|---|
| 0010 | **AIR-SOURCE HEAT PUMPS**, Not including interconnecting tubing. | | | | | | | | | |
| 1000 | Air to air, split system, not including curbs, pads, fan coil and ductwork | | | | | | | | | |
| 1012 | Outside condensing unit only, for fan coil see Div. 23 82 19.10 | | | | | | | | | |
| 1020 | 2 ton cooling, 8.5 MBH heat @ 0° F | Q-5 | 2 | 8 | Ea. | 1,575 | 340 | | 1,915 | 2,225 |
| 1060 | 5 ton cooling, 27 MBH heat @ 0° F | | .50 | 32 | | 2,550 | 1,350 | | 3,900 | 4,850 |
| 1080 | 7.5 ton cooling, 33 MBH heat @ 0° F | | .45 | 35.556 | | 4,800 | 1,500 | | 6,300 | 7,550 |
| 1100 | 10 ton cooling, 50 MBH heat @ 0° F | Q-6 | .64 | 37.500 | | 6,700 | 1,650 | | 8,350 | 9,850 |
| 1120 | 15 ton cooling, 64 MBH heat @ 0° F | | .50 | 48 | | 9,700 | 2,100 | | 11,800 | 13,900 |
| 1130 | 20 ton cooling, 85 MBH heat @ 0° F | | .35 | 68.571 | | 14,600 | 3,025 | | 17,625 | 20,500 |
| 1140 | 25 ton cooling, 119 MBH heat @ 0° F | | .25 | 96 | | 17,600 | 4,225 | | 21,825 | 25,700 |
| 1500 | Single package, not including curbs, pads, or plenums | | | | | | | | | |
| 1520 | 2 ton cooling, 6.5 MBH heat @ 0° F | Q-5 | 1.50 | 10.667 | Ea. | 2,500 | 450 | | 2,950 | 3,425 |
| 1580 | 4 ton cooling, 13 MBH heat @ 0° F | | .96 | 16.667 | | 3,525 | 705 | | 4,230 | 4,950 |
| 1640 | 7.5 ton cooling, 35 MBH heat @ 0° F | | .40 | 40 | | 6,150 | 1,700 | | 7,850 | 9,325 |

## 23 81 46 – Water-Source Unitary Heat Pumps

### 23 81 46.10 Water Source Heat Pumps

| | | Crew | Daily Output | Labor-Hours | Unit | Material | 2008 Bare Costs Labor | Equipment | Total | Total Incl O&P |
|---|---|---|---|---|---|---|---|---|---|---|
| 0010 | **WATER SOURCE HEAT PUMPS**, Not incl. conn. tubing or wtr. source | | | | | | | | | |
| 2000 | Water source to air, single package | | | | | | | | | |
| 2100 | 1 ton cooling, 13 MBH heat @ 75° F | Q-5 | 2 | 8 | Ea. | 1,275 | 340 | | 1,615 | 1,900 |
| 2140 | 2 ton cooling, 19 MBH heat @ 75° F | | 1.70 | 9.412 | | 1,500 | 400 | | 1,900 | 2,250 |
| 2220 | 5 ton cooling, 29 MBH heat @ 75° F | | .90 | 17.778 | | 2,350 | 755 | | 3,105 | 3,725 |
| 3960 | For supplementary heat coil, add | | | | | 10% | | | | |
| 4000 | For increase in capacity thru use | | | | | | | | | |
| 4020 | of solar collector, size boiler at 60% | | | | | | | | | |

# 23 82 Convection Heating and Cooling Units

## 23 82 16 – Air Coils

| 23 82 16.10 Flanged Coils | | Crew | Daily Output | Labor-Hours | Unit | Material | 2008 Bare Costs Labor | Equipment | Total | Total Incl O&P |
|---|---|---|---|---|---|---|---|---|---|---|
| 0010 | **FLANGED COILS** | | | | | | | | | |
| 0500 | Chilled water cooling, 6 rows, 24" x 48" | Q-5 | 3.20 | 5 | Ea. | 3,425 | 212 | | 3,637 | 4,100 |
| 1000 | Direct expansion cooling, 6 rows, 24" x 48" | | 2.80 | 5.714 | | 3,725 | 242 | | 3,967 | 4,475 |
| 1500 | Hot water heating, 1 row, 24" x 48" | | 4 | 4 | | 1,375 | 170 | | 1,545 | 1,750 |
| 2000 | Steam heating, 1 row, 24" x 48" | ↓ | 3.06 | 5.229 | ↓ | 1,950 | 222 | | 2,172 | 2,450 |

### 23 82 16.20 Duct Heaters

| | | Crew | Daily Output | Labor-Hours | Unit | Material | 2008 Bare Costs Labor | Equipment | Total | Total Incl O&P |
|---|---|---|---|---|---|---|---|---|---|---|
| 0010 | **DUCT HEATERS**, Electric, 480 V, 3 Ph. | | | | | | | | | |
| 0020 | Finned tubular insert, 500 ° F | | | | | | | | | |
| 0100 | 8" wide x 6" high, 4.0 kW | Q-20 | 16 | 1.250 | Ea. | 670 | 52 | | 722 | 815 |
| 0120 | 12" high, 8.0 kW | | 15 | 1.333 | | 1,100 | 55.50 | | 1,155.50 | 1,300 |
| 0140 | 18" high, 12.0 kW | | 14 | 1.429 | | 1,550 | 59.50 | | 1,609.50 | 1,800 |
| 0160 | 24" high, 16.0 kW | | 13 | 1.538 | | 2,000 | 64 | | 2,064 | 2,300 |
| 0180 | 30" high, 20.0 kW | | 12 | 1.667 | | 2,450 | 69.50 | | 2,519.50 | 2,800 |
| 0300 | 12" wide x 6" high, 6.7 kW | | 15 | 1.333 | | 710 | 55.50 | | 765.50 | 865 |
| 0360 | 24" high, 26.7 kW | | 12 | 1.667 | | 2,075 | 69.50 | | 2,144.50 | 2,375 |
| 0700 | 24" wide x 6" high, 17.8 kW | | 13 | 1.538 | | 805 | 64 | | 869 | 985 |
| 0760 | 24" high, 71.1 kW | ↓ | 10 | 2 | ↓ | 2,575 | 83.50 | | 2,658.50 | 2,975 |
| 8000 | To obtain BTU multiply kW by 3413 | | | | | | | | | |

## 23 82 19 – Fan Coil Units

### 23 82 19.10 Fan Coil Air Conditioning

| | | Crew | Daily Output | Labor-Hours | Unit | Material | 2008 Bare Costs Labor | Equipment | Total | Total Incl O&P |
|---|---|---|---|---|---|---|---|---|---|---|
| 0010 | **FAN COIL AIR CONDITIONING** Cabinet mounted, filters, controls. | | | | | | | | | |
| 0100 | Chilled water, 1/2 ton cooling | Q-5 | 8 | 2 | Ea. | 650 | 85 | | 735 | 845 |
| 0120 | 1 ton cooling | | 6 | 2.667 | | 750 | 113 | | 863 | 995 |
| 0140 | 1.5 ton cooling | | 5.50 | 2.909 | | 850 | 123 | | 973 | 1,125 |
| 0150 | 2 ton cooling | | 5.25 | 3.048 | | 1,050 | 129 | | 1,179 | 1,350 |
| 0180 | 3 ton cooling | | 4 | 4 | | 1,600 | 170 | | 1,770 | 2,000 |
| 0190 | 7.5 ton cooling | ↓ | 2.70 | 5.926 | ↓ | 1,900 | 251 | | 2,151 | 2,450 |
| 0262 | For hot water coil, add | | | | | 40% | 10% | | | |
| 0940 | Direct expansion, for use w/air cooled condensing unit, 1.5 ton cooling | Q-5 | 5 | 3.200 | Ea. | 515 | 136 | | 651 | 770 |
| 1000 | 5 ton cooling | " | 3 | 5.333 | | 975 | 226 | | 1,201 | 1,425 |
| 1040 | 10 ton cooling | Q-6 | 2.60 | 9.231 | | 2,625 | 405 | | 3,030 | 3,500 |
| 1060 | 20 ton cooling | " | .70 | 34.286 | ↓ | 4,600 | 1,500 | | 6,100 | 7,325 |

### 23 82 19.20 Heating and Ventilating Units

| | | Crew | Daily Output | Labor-Hours | Unit | Material | 2008 Bare Costs Labor | Equipment | Total | Total Incl O&P |
|---|---|---|---|---|---|---|---|---|---|---|
| 0010 | **HEATING AND VENTILATING UNITS**, Classroom units | | | | | | | | | |
| 0020 | Includes filter, heating/cooling coils, standard controls | | | | | | | | | |
| 0080 | 750 CFM, 2 tons cooling | Q-6 | 2 | 12 | Ea. | 3,550 | 530 | | 4,080 | 4,700 |
| 0120 | 1250 CFM, 3 tons cooling | | 1.40 | 17.143 | | 4,325 | 755 | | 5,080 | 5,900 |
| 0140 | 1500 CFM, 4 tons cooling | ↓ | .80 | 30 | | 4,625 | 1,325 | | 5,950 | 7,075 |
| 0500 | For electric heat, add | | | | | 35% | | | | |
| 1000 | For no cooling, deduct | | | | ↓ | 25% | 10% | | | |

## 23 82 27 – Infrared Units

### 23 82 27.10 Infrared Type Heating Units

| | | Crew | Daily Output | Labor-Hours | Unit | Material | 2008 Bare Costs Labor | Equipment | Total | Total Incl O&P |
|---|---|---|---|---|---|---|---|---|---|---|
| 0010 | **INFRARED TYPE HEATING UNITS** | | | | | | | | | |
| 0020 | Gas fired, unvented, electric ignition, 100% shutoff. | | | | | | | | | |
| 0030 | Piping and wiring not included | | | | | | | | | |
| 0060 | Input, 15 MBH | Q-5 | 7 | 2.286 | Ea. | 420 | 97 | | 517 | 610 |
| 0120 | 45 MBH | | 5 | 3.200 | | 435 | 136 | | 571 | 685 |
| 0160 | 60 MBH | | 4 | 4 | | 515 | 170 | | 685 | 820 |
| 0240 | 120 MBH | ↓ | 2 | 8 | ↓ | 895 | 340 | | 1,235 | 1,500 |

## 23 82 29 – Radiators

| 23 82 29.10 Hydronic Heating | Crew | Daily Output | Labor-Hours | Unit | Material | 2008 Bare Costs Labor | Equipment | Total | Total Incl O&P |
|---|---|---|---|---|---|---|---|---|---|
| 0010 **HYDRONIC HEATING**, Terminal units, not incl. main supply pipe | | | | | | | | | |
| 1000 Radiation | | | | | | | | | |
| 1100 Panel, baseboard, C.I., including supports, no covers | Q-5 | 46 | .348 | L.F. | 30 | 14.75 | | 44.75 | 54.50 |
| 3000 Radiators, cast iron | | | | | | | | | |
| 3100 Free standing or wall hung, 6 tube, 25" high | Q-5 | 96 | .167 | Section | 28 | 7.05 | | 35.05 | 41.50 |
| 3200 4 tube, 19" high | " | 96 | .167 | " | 19.55 | 7.05 | | 26.60 | 32 |
| 3250 Adj. brackets, 2 per wall radiator up to 30 sections | 1 Stpi | 32 | .250 | Ea. | 21 | 11.80 | | 32.80 | 40.50 |
| 9500 To convert SFR to BTU rating: Hot water, 150 x SFR | | | | | | | | | |
| 9510 Forced hot water, 180 x SFR; steam, 240 x SFR | | | | | | | | | |

## 23 82 33 – Convectors

### 23 82 33.10 Convector Units

| | Crew | Daily Output | Labor-Hours | Unit | Material | 2008 Bare Costs Labor | Equipment | Total | Total Incl O&P |
|---|---|---|---|---|---|---|---|---|---|
| 0010 **CONVECTOR UNITS**, Terminal units, not incl. main supply pipe | | | | | | | | | |
| 2204 Convector, multifin, 2 pipe w/ cabinet | | | | | | | | | |
| 2210 17" H x 24" L | Q-5 | 10 | 1.600 | Ea. | 89 | 68 | | 157 | 200 |
| 2214 17" H x 36" L | | 8.60 | 1.860 | | 134 | 79 | | 213 | 266 |
| 2218 17" H x 48" L | | 7.40 | 2.162 | | 178 | 91.50 | | 269.50 | 335 |
| 2222 21" H x 24" L | | 9 | 1.778 | | 87.50 | 75.50 | | 163 | 210 |
| 2226 21" H x 36" L | | 8.20 | 1.951 | | 131 | 82.50 | | 213.50 | 268 |
| 2228 21" H x 48" L | | 6.80 | 2.353 | | 175 | 100 | | 275 | 345 |
| 2240 For knob operated damper, add | | | | | 140% | | | | |
| 2241 For metal trim strips, add | Q-5 | 64 | .250 | Ea. | 4.76 | 10.60 | | 15.36 | 21 |
| 2243 For snap-on inlet grille, add | | | | | 10% | 10% | | | |
| 2245 For hinged access door, add | Q-5 | 64 | .250 | Ea. | 16.95 | 10.60 | | 27.55 | 34.50 |
| 2246 For air chamber, auto-venting, add | " | 58 | .276 | " | 5.35 | 11.70 | | 17.05 | 23.50 |

## 23 82 36 – Finned-Tube Radiation Heaters

### 23 82 36.10 Finned Tube Radiation

| | Crew | Daily Output | Labor-Hours | Unit | Material | 2008 Bare Costs Labor | Equipment | Total | Total Incl O&P |
|---|---|---|---|---|---|---|---|---|---|
| 0010 **FINNED TUBE RADIATION**, Terminal units, not incl. main supply pipe | | | | | | | | | |
| 1150 Fin tube, wall hung, 14" slope top cover, with damper | | | | | | | | | |
| 1200 1-1/4" copper tube, 4-1/4" alum. fin | Q-5 | 38 | .421 | L.F. | 37 | 17.85 | | 54.85 | 67.50 |
| 1250 1-1/4" steel tube, 4-1/4" steel fin | " | 36 | .444 | " | 35 | 18.85 | | 53.85 | 67 |
| 1500 Note: fin tube may also require corners, caps, etc. | | | | | | | | | |

## 23 82 39 – Unit Heaters

### 23 82 39.16 Propeller Unit Heaters

| | Crew | Daily Output | Labor-Hours | Unit | Material | 2008 Bare Costs Labor | Equipment | Total | Total Incl O&P |
|---|---|---|---|---|---|---|---|---|---|
| 0010 **PROPELLER UNIT HEATERS** | | | | | | | | | |
| 3950 Unit heaters, propeller, 115 V 2 psi steam, 60° F entering air | | | | | | | | | |
| 4000 Horizontal, 12 MBH | Q-5 | 12 | 1.333 | Ea. | 298 | 56.50 | | 354.50 | 410 |
| 4060 43.9 MBH | | 8 | 2 | | 450 | 85 | | 535 | 625 |
| 4140 96.8 MBH | | 6 | 2.667 | | 620 | 113 | | 733 | 855 |
| 4180 157.6 MBH | | 4 | 4 | | 875 | 170 | | 1,045 | 1,225 |
| 4240 286.9 MBH | | 2 | 8 | | 1,350 | 340 | | 1,690 | 2,000 |
| 4250 326.0 MBH | | 1.90 | 8.421 | | 1,675 | 355 | | 2,030 | 2,375 |
| 4260 364 MBH | | 1.80 | 8.889 | | 1,700 | 375 | | 2,075 | 2,450 |
| 4270 404 MBH | | 1.60 | 10 | | 2,300 | 425 | | 2,725 | 3,175 |
| 4300 For vertical diffuser, add | | | | | 160 | | | 160 | 176 |
| 4310 Vertical flow, 40 MBH | Q-5 | 11 | 1.455 | | 400 | 61.50 | | 461.50 | 535 |
| 4314 58.5 MBH | | 8 | 2 | | 460 | 85 | | 545 | 635 |
| 4326 131.0 MBH | | 4 | 4 | | 695 | 170 | | 865 | 1,025 |
| 4346 297.0 MBH | | 1.80 | 8.889 | | 1,225 | 375 | | 1,600 | 1,925 |
| 4354 420 MBH, (460 V) | Q-6 | 1.80 | 13.333 | | 1,950 | 585 | | 2,535 | 3,025 |
| 4358 500 MBH, (460 V) | | 1.71 | 14.035 | | 2,600 | 615 | | 3,215 | 3,800 |

# 23 82 Convection Heating and Cooling Units

## 23 82 39 – Unit Heaters

| 23 82 39.16 Propeller Unit Heaters | Crew | Daily Output | Labor-Hours | Unit | Material | 2008 Bare Costs Labor | Equipment | Total | Total Incl O&P |
|---|---|---|---|---|---|---|---|---|---|
| 4362 | 570 MBH, (460 V) | Q-6 | 1.40 | 17.143 | Ea. | 3,425 | 755 | | 4,180 | 4,875 |
| 4366 | 620 MBH, (460 V) | | 1.30 | 18.462 | | 3,925 | 810 | | 4,735 | 5,525 |
| 4370 | 960 MBH, (460 V) | ↓ | 1.10 | 21.818 | ↓ | 6,775 | 960 | | 7,735 | 8,925 |

# 23 83 Radiant Heating Units

## 23 83 33 – Electric Radiant Heaters

### 23 83 33.10 Electric Heating

| | | Crew | Daily Output | Labor-Hours | Unit | Material | 2008 Bare Costs Labor | Equipment | Total | Total Incl O&P |
|---|---|---|---|---|---|---|---|---|---|---|
| 0010 | **ELECTRIC HEATING**, Not incl. conduit or feed wiring. | | | | | | | | | |
| 1100 | Rule of thumb: Baseboard units, including control | 1 Elec | 4.40 | 1.818 | kW | 88 | 83 | | 171 | 220 |
| 1300 | Baseboard heaters, 2' long, 375 watt | | 8 | 1 | Ea. | 36 | 45.50 | | 81.50 | 108 |
| 1400 | 3' long, 500 watt | | 8 | 1 | | 43 | 45.50 | | 88.50 | 116 |
| 1600 | 4' long, 750 watt | | 6.70 | 1.194 | | 51 | 54.50 | | 105.50 | 137 |
| 1800 | 5' long, 935 watt | | 5.70 | 1.404 | | 60 | 64 | | 124 | 161 |
| 2000 | 6' long, 1125 watt | | 5 | 1.600 | | 67 | 73 | | 140 | 183 |
| 2400 | 8' long, 1500 watt | ↓ | 4 | 2 | ↓ | 84 | 91 | | 175 | 229 |
| 2950 | Wall heaters with fan, 120 to 277 volt | | | | | | | | | |
| 3600 | Thermostats, integral | 1 Elec | 16 | .500 | Ea. | 20.50 | 23 | | 43.50 | 56.50 |
| 3800 | Line voltage, 1 pole | " | 8 | 1 | " | 18 | 45.50 | | 63.50 | 88 |

# 23 84 Humidity Control Equipment

## 23 84 13 – Humidifiers

### 23 84 13.10 Humidifier Units

| | | Crew | Daily Output | Labor-Hours | Unit | Material | 2008 Bare Costs Labor | Equipment | Total | Total Incl O&P |
|---|---|---|---|---|---|---|---|---|---|---|
| 0010 | **HUMIDIFIER UNITS** | | | | | | | | | |
| 0520 | Steam, room or duct, filter, regulators, auto. controls, 220 V | | | | | | | | | |
| 0540 | 11 lb. per hour | Q-5 | 6 | 2.667 | Ea. | 2,275 | 113 | | 2,388 | 2,675 |
| 0560 | 22 lb. per hour | | 5 | 3.200 | | 2,525 | 136 | | 2,661 | 2,975 |
| 0580 | 33 lb. per hour | | 4 | 4 | | 2,575 | 170 | | 2,745 | 3,100 |
| 0600 | 50 lb. per hour | | 4 | 4 | | 3,175 | 170 | | 3,345 | 3,725 |
| 0620 | 100 lb. per hour | ↓ | 3 | 5.333 | ↓ | 3,800 | 226 | | 4,026 | 4,525 |

# Division Notes

| | CREW | DAILY OUTPUT | LABOR-HOURS | UNIT | 2008 BARE COSTS | | | | TOTAL INCL O&P |
|---|---|---|---|---|---|---|---|---|---|
| | | | | | MAT. | LABOR | EQUIP. | TOTAL | |
| | | | | | | | | | |
| | | | | | | | | | |
| | | | | | | | | | |
| | | | | | | | | | |
| | | | | | | | | | |
| | | | | | | | | | |
| | | | | | | | | | |
| | | | | | | | | | |
| | | | | | | | | | |
| | | | | | | | | | |
| | | | | | | | | | |
| | | | | | | | | | |
| | | | | | | | | | |
| | | | | | | | | | |
| | | | | | | | | | |
| | | | | | | | | | |
| | | | | | | | | | |
| | | | | | | | | | |
| | | | | | | | | | |
| | | | | | | | | | |

# Estimating Tips

## 26 05 00 Common Work Results for Electrical

- Conduit should be taken off in three main categories–power distribution, branch power, and branch lighting–so the estimator can concentrate on systems and components, therefore making it easier to ensure all items have been accounted for.
- For cost modifications for elevated conduit installation, add the percentages to labor according to the height of installation, and only to the quantities exceeding the different height levels, not to the total conduit quantities.
- Remember that aluminum wiring of equal ampacity is larger in diameter than copper and may require larger conduit.
- If more than three wires at a time are being pulled, deduct percentages from the labor hours of that grouping of wires.

- The estimator should take the weights of materials into consideration when completing a takeoff. Topics to consider include: How will the materials be supported? What methods of support are available? How high will the support structure have to reach? Will the final support structure be able to withstand the total burden? Is the support material included or separate from the fixture, equipment, and material specified?
- Do not overlook the costs for equipment used in the installation. If scaffolding or highlifts are available in the field, contractors may use them in lieu of the proposed ladders and rolling staging.

## 26 20 00 Low-Voltage Electrical Transmission

- Supports and concrete pads may be shown on drawings for the larger equipment, or the support system may be only a piece of plywood for the back of a panelboard. In either case, it must be included in the costs.

## 26 40 00 Electrical and Cathodic Protection

- When taking off grounding system, identify separately the type and size of wire, and list each unique type of ground connection.

## 26 50 00 Lighting

- Fixtures should be taken off room by room, using the fixture schedule, specifications, and the ceiling plan. For large concentrations of lighting fixtures in the same area, deduct the percentages from labor hours.

## Reference Numbers

Reference numbers are shown in shaded boxes at the beginning of some major classifications. These numbers refer to related items in the Reference Section. The reference information may be an estimating procedure, an alternate pricing method, or technical information.

*Note:* Not all subdivisions listed here necessarily appear in this publication.

*Note:* **Trade Service,** *in part, has been used as a reference source for some of the material prices used in Division 26.*

| 26 05 05.10 Electrical Demolition | Crew | Daily Output | Labor-Hours | Unit | Material | 2008 Bare Costs Labor | Equipment | Total | Total Incl O&P |
|---|---|---|---|---|---|---|---|---|---|
| 0010 **ELECTRICAL DEMOLITION** | | | | | | | | | |
| 0020 Conduit to 15' high, including fittings & hangers | | | | | | | | | |
| 0100 Rigid galvanized steel, 1/2" to 1" diameter | 1 Elec | 242 | .033 | L.F. | | 1.51 | | 1.51 | 2.24 |
| 0120 1-1/4" to 2" | " | 200 | .040 | | | 1.82 | | 1.82 | 2.71 |
| 0140 2-1/2" to 3-1/2" | 2 Elec | 302 | .053 | | | 2.41 | | 2.41 | 3.59 |
| 0160 4" to 6" | " | 160 | .100 | | | 4.56 | | 4.56 | 6.80 |
| 0200 Electric metallic tubing (EMT), 1/2" to 1" | 1 Elec | 394 | .020 | | | .92 | | .92 | 1.38 |
| 0220 1-1/4" to 1-1/2" | " | 326 | .025 | | | 1.12 | | 1.12 | 1.67 |
| 0260 3-1/2" to 4" | 2 Elec | 310 | .052 | ↓ | | 2.35 | | 2.35 | 3.50 |
| 0270 Armored cable, (BX) avg. 50' runs | | | | | | | | | |
| 0280 #14, 2 wire | 1 Elec | 690 | .012 | L.F. | | .53 | | .53 | .79 |
| 0290 #14, 3 wire | | 571 | .014 | | | .64 | | .64 | .95 |
| 0300 #12, 2 wire | | 605 | .013 | | | .60 | | .60 | .90 |
| 0310 #12, 3 wire | | 514 | .016 | | | .71 | | .71 | 1.06 |
| 0320 #10, 2 wire | | 514 | .016 | | | .71 | | .71 | 1.06 |
| 0330 #10, 3 wire | | 425 | .019 | | | .86 | | .86 | 1.28 |
| 0340 #8, 3 wire | ↓ | 342 | .023 | ↓ | | 1.07 | | 1.07 | 1.59 |
| 0350 Non metallic sheathed cable (Romex) | | | | | | | | | |
| 0360 #14, 2 wire | 1 Elec | 720 | .011 | L.F. | | .51 | | .51 | .75 |
| 0370 #14, 3 wire | | 657 | .012 | | | .55 | | .55 | .83 |
| 0380 #12, 2 wire | | 629 | .013 | | | .58 | | .58 | .86 |
| 0390 #10, 3 wire | ↓ | 450 | .018 | ↓ | | .81 | | .81 | 1.21 |
| 0400 Wiremold raceway, including fittings & hangers | | | | | | | | | |
| 0420 No. 3000 | 1 Elec | 250 | .032 | L.F. | | 1.46 | | 1.46 | 2.17 |
| 0440 No. 4000 | | 217 | .037 | | | 1.68 | | 1.68 | 2.50 |
| 0460 No. 6000 | | 166 | .048 | ↓ | | 2.20 | | 2.20 | 3.27 |
| 0465 Telephone/power pole | | 12 | .667 | Ea. | | 30.50 | | 30.50 | 45 |
| 0470 Non-metallic, straight section | ↓ | 480 | .017 | L.F. | | .76 | | .76 | 1.13 |
| 0500 Channels, steel, including fittings & hangers | | | | | | | | | |
| 0520 3/4" x 1-1/2" | 1 Elec | 308 | .026 | L.F. | | 1.18 | | 1.18 | 1.76 |
| 0540 1-1/2" x 1-1/2" | | 269 | .030 | | | 1.35 | | 1.35 | 2.02 |
| 0560 1-1/2" x 1-7/8" | ↓ | 229 | .035 | ↓ | | 1.59 | | 1.59 | 2.37 |
| 0600 Copper bus duct, indoor, 3 phase | | | | | | | | | |
| 0610 Including hangers & supports | | | | | | | | | |
| 0620 225 amp | 2 Elec | 135 | .119 | L.F. | | 5.40 | | 5.40 | 8.05 |
| 0640 400 amp | | 106 | .151 | | | 6.90 | | 6.90 | 10.25 |
| 0660 600 amp | | 86 | .186 | | | 8.45 | | 8.45 | 12.60 |
| 0680 1000 amp | | 60 | .267 | | | 12.15 | | 12.15 | 18.10 |
| 0700 1600 amp | | 40 | .400 | | | 18.20 | | 18.20 | 27 |
| 0720 3000 amp | ↓ | 10 | 1.600 | ↓ | | 73 | | 73 | 109 |
| 1300 Transformer, dry type, 1 ph, incl. removal of | | | | | | | | | |
| 1320 supports, wire & conduit terminations | | | | | | | | | |
| 1340 1 kVA | 1 Elec | 7.70 | 1.039 | Ea. | | 47.50 | | 47.50 | 70.50 |
| 1420 75 kVA | 2 Elec | 2.50 | 6.400 | " | | 292 | | 292 | 435 |
| 1440 3 Phase to 600V, primary | | | | | | | | | |
| 1460 3 kVA | 1 Elec | 3.85 | 2.078 | Ea. | | 94.50 | | 94.50 | 141 |
| 1520 75 kVA | 2 Elec | 2.70 | 5.926 | ↓ | | 270 | | 270 | 400 |
| 1550 300 kVA | R-3 | 1.80 | 11.111 | | | 500 | 72 | 572 | 825 |
| 1570 750 kVA | " | 1.10 | 18.182 | ↓ | | 815 | 118 | 933 | 1,350 |
| 1800 Wire, THW-THWN-THHN, removed from | | | | | | | | | |
| 1810 in place conduit, to 15' high | | | | | | | | | |
| 1830 #14 | 1 Elec | 65 | .123 | C.L.F. | | 5.60 | | 5.60 | 8.35 |
| 1840 #12 | ↓ | 55 | .145 | ↓ | | 6.65 | | 6.65 | 9.85 |

## 26 05 05 – Selective Electrical Demolition

### 26 05 05.10 Electrical Demolition

| | | Crew | Daily Output | Labor-Hours | Unit | Material | 2008 Bare Costs Labor | Equipment | Total | Total Incl O&P |
|---|---|---|---|---|---|---|---|---|---|---|
| 1850 | #10 | 1 Elec | 45.50 | .176 | C.L.F. | | 8 | | 8 | 11.95 |
| 1860 | #8 | | 40.40 | .198 | | | 9 | | 9 | 13.45 |
| 1870 | #6 | | 32.60 | .245 | | | 11.20 | | 11.20 | 16.65 |
| 1880 | #4 | 2 Elec | 53 | .302 | | | 13.75 | | 13.75 | 20.50 |
| 1890 | #3 | | 50 | .320 | | | 14.60 | | 14.60 | 21.50 |
| 1900 | #2 | | 44.60 | .359 | | | 16.35 | | 16.35 | 24.50 |
| 1910 | 1/0 | | 33.20 | .482 | | | 22 | | 22 | 32.50 |
| 1920 | 2/0 | | 29.20 | .548 | | | 25 | | 25 | 37 |
| 1930 | 3/0 | | 25 | .640 | | | 29 | | 29 | 43.50 |
| 1940 | 4/0 | | 22 | .727 | | | 33 | | 33 | 49.50 |
| 1950 | 250 kcmil | | 20 | .800 | | | 36.50 | | 36.50 | 54.50 |
| 1960 | 300 kcmil | | 19 | .842 | | | 38.50 | | 38.50 | 57 |
| 1970 | 350 kcmil | | 18 | .889 | | | 40.50 | | 40.50 | 60.50 |
| 1980 | 400 kcmil | | 17 | .941 | | | 43 | | 43 | 64 |
| 1990 | 500 kcmil | | 16.20 | .988 | | | 45 | | 45 | 67 |
| 2000 | Interior fluorescent fixtures, incl. supports | | | | | | | | | |
| 2010 | & whips, to 15' high | | | | | | | | | |
| 2100 | Recessed drop-in 2' x 2', 2 lamp | 2 Elec | 35 | .457 | Ea. | | 21 | | 21 | 31 |
| 2120 | 2' x 4', 2 lamp | | 33 | .485 | | | 22 | | 22 | 33 |
| 2140 | 2' x 4', 4 lamp | | 30 | .533 | | | 24.50 | | 24.50 | 36 |
| 2160 | 4' x 4', 4 lamp | | 20 | .800 | | | 36.50 | | 36.50 | 54.50 |
| 2180 | Surface mount, acrylic lens & hinged frame | | | | | | | | | |
| 2200 | 1' x 4', 2 lamp | 2 Elec | 44 | .364 | Ea. | | 16.55 | | 16.55 | 24.50 |
| 2220 | 2' x 2', 2 lamp | | 44 | .364 | | | 16.55 | | 16.55 | 24.50 |
| 2260 | 2' x 4', 4 lamp | | 33 | .485 | | | 22 | | 22 | 33 |
| 2280 | 4' x 4', 4 lamp | | 23 | .696 | | | 31.50 | | 31.50 | 47 |
| 2300 | Strip fixtures, surface mount | | | | | | | | | |
| 2320 | 4' long, 1 lamp | 2 Elec | 53 | .302 | Ea. | | 13.75 | | 13.75 | 20.50 |
| 2340 | 4' long, 2 lamp | | 50 | .320 | | | 14.60 | | 14.60 | 21.50 |
| 2360 | 8' long, 1 lamp | | 42 | .381 | | | 17.35 | | 17.35 | 26 |
| 2380 | 8' long, 2 lamp | | 40 | .400 | | | 18.20 | | 18.20 | 27 |
| 2400 | Pendant mount, industrial, incl. removal | | | | | | | | | |
| 2410 | of chain or rod hangers, to 15' high | | | | | | | | | |
| 2420 | 4' long, 2 lamp | 2 Elec | 35 | .457 | Ea. | | 21 | | 21 | 31 |
| 2440 | 8' long, 2 lamp | " | 27 | .593 | " | | 27 | | 27 | 40 |

## 26 05 13 – Medium-Voltage Cables

### 26 05 13.16 Medium-Voltage, Single Cable

| | | Crew | Daily Output | Labor-Hours | Unit | Material | 2008 Bare Costs Labor | Equipment | Total | Total Incl O&P |
|---|---|---|---|---|---|---|---|---|---|---|
| 0010 | **MEDIUM-VOLTAGE, SINGLE CABLE** Splicing & terminations not included | | | | | | | | | |
| 0040 | Copper, XLP shielding, 5 kV, #6 | 2 Elec | 4.40 | 3.636 | C.L.F. | 164 | 166 | | 330 | 425 |
| 0050 | #4 | | 4.40 | 3.636 | | 213 | 166 | | 379 | 480 |
| 0100 | #2 | | 4 | 4 | | 252 | 182 | | 434 | 550 |
| 0200 | #1 | | 4 | 4 | | 289 | 182 | | 471 | 585 |
| 0400 | 1/0 | | 3.80 | 4.211 | | 320 | 192 | | 512 | 635 |
| 0600 | 2/0 | | 3.60 | 4.444 | | 400 | 202 | | 602 | 740 |
| 0800 | 4/0 | | 3.20 | 5 | | 520 | 228 | | 748 | 915 |
| 1000 | 250 kcmil | 3 Elec | 4.50 | 5.333 | | 645 | 243 | | 888 | 1,075 |
| 1200 | 350 kcmil | | 3.90 | 6.154 | | 830 | 280 | | 1,110 | 1,325 |
| 1400 | 500 kcmil | | 3.60 | 6.667 | | 1,025 | 305 | | 1,330 | 1,575 |
| 1600 | 15 kV, ungrounded neutral, #1 | 2 Elec | 4 | 4 | | 350 | 182 | | 532 | 655 |
| 1800 | 1/0 | | 3.80 | 4.211 | | 420 | 192 | | 612 | 745 |
| 2000 | 2/0 | | 3.60 | 4.444 | | 480 | 202 | | 682 | 825 |
| 2200 | 4/0 | | 3.20 | 5 | | 635 | 228 | | 863 | 1,025 |

# 26 05 Common Work Results for Electrical

## 26 05 13 – Medium-Voltage Cables

| 26 05 13.16 Medium-Voltage, Single Cable | Crew | Daily Output | Labor-Hours | Unit | Material | 2008 Bare Costs Labor | Equipment | Total | Total Incl O&P |
|---|---|---|---|---|---|---|---|---|---|
| 2400 | 250 kcmil | 3 Elec | 4.50 | 5.333 | C.L.F. | 700 | 243 | | 943 | 1,125 |
| 2600 | 350 kcmil | | 3.90 | 6.154 | | 885 | 280 | | 1,165 | 1,400 |
| 2800 | 500 kcmil | ↓ | 3.60 | 6.667 | ↓ | 1,100 | 305 | | 1,405 | 1,650 |

## 26 05 19 – Low-Voltage Electrical Power Conductors and Cables

### 26 05 19.20 Armored Cable

| | | Crew | Daily Output | Labor-Hours | Unit | Material | 2008 Bare Costs Labor | Equipment | Total | Total Incl O&P |
|---|---|---|---|---|---|---|---|---|---|---|
| 0010 | **ARMORED CABLE** | | | | | | | | | |
| 0050 | 600 volt, copper (BX), #14, 2 conductor, solid | 1 Elec | 2.40 | 3.333 | C.L.F. | 75.50 | 152 | | 227.50 | 310 |
| 0100 | 3 conductor, solid | | 2.20 | 3.636 | | 118 | 166 | | 284 | 375 |
| 0150 | #12, 2 conductor, solid | | 2.30 | 3.478 | | 77.50 | 158 | | 235.50 | 320 |
| 0200 | 3 conductor, solid | | 2 | 4 | | 125 | 182 | | 307 | 410 |
| 0250 | #10, 2 conductor, solid | | 2 | 4 | | 147 | 182 | | 329 | 430 |
| 0300 | 3 conductor, solid | | 1.60 | 5 | | 216 | 228 | | 444 | 580 |
| 0350 | #8, 3 conductor, solid | | 1.30 | 6.154 | | 440 | 280 | | 720 | 905 |
| 0400 | 3 conductor with PVC jacket, in cable tray, #6 | ↓ | 3.10 | 2.581 | | 405 | 118 | | 523 | 620 |
| 0450 | #4 | 2 Elec | 5.40 | 2.963 | | 520 | 135 | | 655 | 775 |
| 0500 | #2 | | 4.60 | 3.478 | | 695 | 158 | | 853 | 995 |
| 0550 | #1 | | 4 | 4 | | 940 | 182 | | 1,122 | 1,300 |
| 0600 | 1/0 | | 3.60 | 4.444 | | 1,100 | 202 | | 1,302 | 1,525 |
| 0650 | 2/0 | | 3.40 | 4.706 | | 1,350 | 214 | | 1,564 | 1,800 |
| 0700 | 3/0 | | 3.20 | 5 | | 1,575 | 228 | | 1,803 | 2,075 |
| 0750 | 4/0 | ↓ | 3 | 5.333 | | 1,800 | 243 | | 2,043 | 2,325 |
| 0800 | 250 kcmil | 3 Elec | 3.60 | 6.667 | | 2,025 | 305 | | 2,330 | 2,675 |
| 0850 | 350 kcmil | | 3.30 | 7.273 | | 2,700 | 330 | | 3,030 | 3,475 |
| 0900 | 500 kcmil | ↓ | 3 | 8 | ↓ | 3,500 | 365 | | 3,865 | 4,400 |
| 1050 | 5 kV, copper, 3 conductor with PVC jacket, | | | | | | | | | |
| 1060 | non-shielded, in cable tray, #4 | 2 Elec | 380 | .042 | L.F. | 8 | 1.92 | | 9.92 | 11.65 |
| 1100 | #2 | | 360 | .044 | | 10.35 | 2.02 | | 12.37 | 14.40 |
| 1200 | #1 | | 300 | .053 | | 13.20 | 2.43 | | 15.63 | 18.10 |
| 1400 | 1/0 | | 290 | .055 | | 15.25 | 2.51 | | 17.76 | 20.50 |
| 1600 | 2/0 | | 260 | .062 | | 17.60 | 2.80 | | 20.40 | 23.50 |
| 2000 | 4/0 | ↓ | 240 | .067 | | 23.50 | 3.04 | | 26.54 | 30.50 |
| 2100 | 250 kcmil | 3 Elec | 330 | .073 | | 32 | 3.31 | | 35.31 | 40.50 |
| 2150 | 350 kcmil | | 315 | .076 | | 39.50 | 3.47 | | 42.97 | 48.50 |
| 2200 | 500 kcmil | ↓ | 270 | .089 | ↓ | 53 | 4.05 | | 57.05 | 64 |
| 2400 | 15 kV, copper, 3 conductor with PVC jacket galv steel armored | | | | | | | | | |
| 2500 | grounded neutral, in cable tray, #2 | 2 Elec | 300 | .053 | L.F. | 16.75 | 2.43 | | 19.18 | 22 |
| 2600 | #1 | | 280 | .057 | | 17.85 | 2.60 | | 20.45 | 23.50 |
| 2800 | 1/0 | | 260 | .062 | | 20.50 | 2.80 | | 23.30 | 26.50 |
| 2900 | 2/0 | | 220 | .073 | | 27 | 3.31 | | 30.31 | 35 |
| 3000 | 4/0 | ↓ | 190 | .084 | | 30.50 | 3.84 | | 34.34 | 39.50 |
| 3100 | 250 kcmil | 3 Elec | 270 | .089 | | 34.50 | 4.05 | | 38.55 | 43.50 |
| 3150 | 350 kcmil | | 240 | .100 | | 40.50 | 4.56 | | 45.06 | 51.50 |
| 3200 | 500 kcmil | | 210 | .114 | ↓ | 54 | 5.20 | | 59.20 | 67.50 |
| 3400 | 15 kV, copper, 3 conductor with PVC jacket, | | | | | | | | | |
| 3450 | ungrounded neutral, in cable tray, #2 | 2 Elec | 260 | .062 | L.F. | 18.05 | 2.80 | | 20.85 | 24 |
| 3500 | #1 | | 230 | .070 | | 20 | 3.17 | | 23.17 | 26.50 |
| 3600 | 1/0 | | 200 | .080 | | 23 | 3.64 | | 26.64 | 30.50 |
| 3700 | 2/0 | | 190 | .084 | | 28 | 3.84 | | 31.84 | 36.50 |
| 3800 | 4/0 | ↓ | 160 | .100 | | 34 | 4.56 | | 38.56 | 44.50 |
| 4000 | 250 kcmil | 3 Elec | 210 | .114 | | 39.50 | 5.20 | | 44.70 | 51.50 |
| 4050 | 350 kcmil | | 195 | .123 | | 52 | 5.60 | | 57.60 | 66 |
| 4100 | 500 kcmil | ↓ | 180 | .133 | ↓ | 63.50 | 6.05 | | 69.55 | 78.50 |

## 26 05 19 – Low-Voltage Electrical Power Conductors and Cables

| 26 05 19.20 Armored Cable | | Crew | Daily Output | Labor-Hours | Unit | Material | 2008 Bare Costs Labor | Equipment | Total | Total Incl O&P |
|---|---|---|---|---|---|---|---|---|---|---|
| 9010 | 600 volt, copper (MC) steel clad, #14, 2 wire | 1 Elec | 2.40 | 3.333 | C.L.F. | 75.50 | 152 | | 227.50 | 310 |
| 9020 | 3 wire | | 2.20 | 3.636 | | 117 | 166 | | 283 | 375 |
| 9040 | #12, 2 wire | | 2.30 | 3.478 | | 77.50 | 158 | | 235.50 | 320 |
| 9050 | 3 wire | | 2 | 4 | | 125 | 182 | | 307 | 410 |
| 9070 | #10, 2 wire | | 2 | 4 | | 147 | 182 | | 329 | 430 |
| 9080 | 3 wire | | 1.60 | 5 | | 216 | 228 | | 444 | 580 |
| 9100 | #8, 2 wire, stranded | | 1.80 | 4.444 | | 299 | 202 | | 501 | 630 |
| 9110 | 3 wire, stranded | | 1.30 | 6.154 | | 445 | 280 | | 725 | 910 |
| 9200 | 600 volt, copper (MC) aluminum clad, #14, 2 wire | | 2.65 | 3.019 | | 75.50 | 138 | | 213.50 | 288 |
| 9210 | 3 wire | | 2.45 | 3.265 | | 117 | 149 | | 266 | 350 |
| 9220 | 4 wire | | 2.20 | 3.636 | | 158 | 166 | | 324 | 420 |
| 9230 | #12, 2 wire | | 2.55 | 3.137 | | 77.50 | 143 | | 220.50 | 298 |
| 9240 | 3 wire | | 2.20 | 3.636 | | 125 | 166 | | 291 | 385 |
| 9250 | 4 wire | | 2 | 4 | | 165 | 182 | | 347 | 450 |
| 9260 | #10, 2 wire | | 2.20 | 3.636 | | 147 | 166 | | 313 | 410 |
| 9270 | 3 wire | | 1.80 | 4.444 | | 216 | 202 | | 418 | 540 |
| 9280 | 4 wire | | 1.55 | 5.161 | | 340 | 235 | | 575 | 725 |

## 26 05 19.35 Cable Terminations

| 0010 | CABLE TERMINATIONS | Crew | Daily Output | Labor-Hours | Unit | Material | 2008 Bare Costs Labor | Equipment | Total | Total Incl O&P |
|---|---|---|---|---|---|---|---|---|---|---|
| 0015 | Wire connectors, screw type, #22 to #14 | 1 Elec | 260 | .031 | Ea. | .08 | 1.40 | | 1.48 | 2.18 |
| 0020 | #18 to #12 | | 240 | .033 | | .10 | 1.52 | | 1.62 | 2.37 |
| 0025 | #18 to #10 | | 240 | .033 | | .15 | 1.52 | | 1.67 | 2.43 |
| 0030 | Screw-on connectors, insulated, #18 to #12 | | 240 | .033 | | .10 | 1.52 | | 1.62 | 2.37 |
| 0035 | #16 to #10 | | 230 | .035 | | .14 | 1.58 | | 1.72 | 2.51 |
| 0040 | #14 to #8 | | 210 | .038 | | .29 | 1.74 | | 2.03 | 2.91 |
| 0045 | #12 to #6 | | 180 | .044 | | .49 | 2.02 | | 2.51 | 3.56 |
| 0050 | Terminal lugs, solderless, #16 to #10 | | 50 | .160 | | .53 | 7.30 | | 7.83 | 11.45 |
| 0100 | #8 to #4 | | 30 | .267 | | .82 | 12.15 | | 12.97 | 19 |
| 0150 | #2 to #1 | | 22 | .364 | | 1.11 | 16.55 | | 17.66 | 25.50 |
| 0200 | 1/0 to 2/0 | | 16 | .500 | | 2.22 | 23 | | 25.22 | 36.50 |
| 0250 | 3/0 | | 12 | .667 | | 3.80 | 30.50 | | 34.30 | 49 |
| 0300 | 4/0 | | 11 | .727 | | 3.80 | 33 | | 36.80 | 53.50 |
| 0350 | 250 kcmil | | 9 | .889 | | 3.80 | 40.50 | | 44.30 | 64.50 |
| 0400 | 350 kcmil | | 7 | 1.143 | | 4.90 | 52 | | 56.90 | 83 |
| 0450 | 500 kcmil | | 6 | 1.333 | | 9.55 | 60.50 | | 70.05 | 101 |
| 1600 | Crimp 1 hole lugs, copper or aluminum, 600 volt | | | | | | | | | |
| 1620 | #14 | 1 Elec | 60 | .133 | Ea. | .40 | 6.05 | | 6.45 | 9.50 |
| 1630 | #12 | | 50 | .160 | | .55 | 7.30 | | 7.85 | 11.45 |
| 1640 | #10 | | 45 | .178 | | .55 | 8.10 | | 8.65 | 12.65 |
| 1780 | #8 | | 36 | .222 | | 2.15 | 10.10 | | 12.25 | 17.45 |
| 1800 | #6 | | 30 | .267 | | 2.92 | 12.15 | | 15.07 | 21.50 |
| 2000 | #4 | | 27 | .296 | | 3.30 | 13.50 | | 16.80 | 23.50 |
| 2200 | #2 | | 24 | .333 | | 6.05 | 15.20 | | 21.25 | 29 |
| 2400 | #1 | | 20 | .400 | | 6.25 | 18.20 | | 24.45 | 34 |
| 2600 | 2/0 | | 15 | .533 | | 7.80 | 24.50 | | 32.30 | 44.50 |
| 2800 | 3/0 | | 12 | .667 | | 9.10 | 30.50 | | 39.60 | 55 |
| 3000 | 4/0 | | 11 | .727 | | 10.30 | 33 | | 43.30 | 61 |
| 3200 | 250 kcmil | | 9 | .889 | | 12.05 | 40.50 | | 52.55 | 74 |
| 3400 | 300 kcmil | | 8 | 1 | | 14.40 | 45.50 | | 59.90 | 84 |
| 3500 | 350 kcmil | | 7 | 1.143 | | 14.20 | 52 | | 66.20 | 93 |
| 3600 | 400 kcmil | | 6.50 | 1.231 | | 18 | 56 | | 74 | 103 |
| 3800 | 500 kcmil | | 6 | 1.333 | | 20 | 60.50 | | 80.50 | 113 |

### 26 05 19.50 Mineral Insulated Cable

| | | Crew | Daily Output | Labor-Hours | Unit | Material | 2008 Bare Costs Labor | Equipment | Total | Total Incl O&P |
|---|---|---|---|---|---|---|---|---|---|---|
| 0010 | **MINERAL INSULATED CABLE** 600 volt | | | | | | | | | |
| 0100 | 1 conductor, #12 | 1 Elec | 1.60 | 5 | C.L.F. | 291 | 228 | | 519 | 660 |
| 0200 | #10 | | 1.60 | 5 | | 380 | 228 | | 608 | 760 |
| 0400 | #8 | | 1.50 | 5.333 | | 445 | 243 | | 688 | 850 |
| 0500 | #6 | | 1.40 | 5.714 | | 500 | 260 | | 760 | 940 |
| 0600 | #4 | 2 Elec | 2.40 | 6.667 | | 695 | 305 | | 1,000 | 1,225 |
| 0800 | #2 | | 2.20 | 7.273 | | 925 | 330 | | 1,255 | 1,525 |
| 0900 | #1 | | 2.10 | 7.619 | | 1,050 | 345 | | 1,395 | 1,700 |
| 1000 | 1/0 | | 2 | 8 | | 1,225 | 365 | | 1,590 | 1,900 |
| 1100 | 2/0 | | 1.90 | 8.421 | | 1,450 | 385 | | 1,835 | 2,175 |
| 1200 | 3/0 | | 1.80 | 8.889 | | 1,725 | 405 | | 2,130 | 2,500 |
| 1400 | 4/0 | | 1.60 | 10 | | 1,975 | 455 | | 2,430 | 2,850 |
| 1410 | 250 kcmil | 3 Elec | 2.40 | 10 | | 2,250 | 455 | | 2,705 | 3,150 |
| 1420 | 350 kcmil | | 1.95 | 12.308 | | 2,500 | 560 | | 3,060 | 3,575 |
| 1430 | 500 kcmil | | 1.95 | 12.308 | | 3,150 | 560 | | 3,710 | 4,275 |

### 26 05 19.55 Non-Metallic Sheathed Cable

| | | Crew | Daily Output | Labor-Hours | Unit | Material | 2008 Bare Costs Labor | Equipment | Total | Total Incl O&P |
|---|---|---|---|---|---|---|---|---|---|---|
| 0010 | **NON-METALLIC SHEATHED CABLE** 600 volt | | | | | | | | | |
| 0100 | Copper with ground wire, (Romex) | | | | | | | | | |
| 0150 | #14, 2 conductor | 1 Elec | 2.70 | 2.963 | C.L.F. | 32.50 | 135 | | 167.50 | 237 |
| 0200 | 3 conductor | | 2.40 | 3.333 | | 50 | 152 | | 202 | 281 |
| 0250 | #12, 2 conductor | | 2.50 | 3.200 | | 50 | 146 | | 196 | 272 |
| 0300 | 3 conductor | | 2.20 | 3.636 | | 70 | 166 | | 236 | 325 |
| 0350 | #10, 2 conductor | | 2.20 | 3.636 | | 78 | 166 | | 244 | 335 |
| 0400 | 3 conductor | | 1.80 | 4.444 | | 111 | 202 | | 313 | 420 |
| 0450 | #8, 3 conductor | | 1.50 | 5.333 | | 185 | 243 | | 428 | 565 |
| 0500 | #6, 3 conductor | | 1.40 | 5.714 | | 300 | 260 | | 560 | 720 |
| 0550 | SE type SER aluminum cable, 3 RHW and | | | | | | | | | |
| 0600 | 1 bare neutral, 3 #8 & 1 #8 | 1 Elec | 1.60 | 5 | C.L.F. | 123 | 228 | | 351 | 475 |
| 0650 | 3 #6 & 1 #6 | " | 1.40 | 5.714 | | 139 | 260 | | 399 | 545 |
| 0700 | 3 #4 & 1 #6 | 2 Elec | 2.40 | 6.667 | | 156 | 305 | | 461 | 620 |
| 0750 | 3 #2 & 1 #4 | | 2.20 | 7.273 | | 230 | 330 | | 560 | 750 |
| 0800 | 3 #1/0 & 1 #2 | | 2 | 8 | | 350 | 365 | | 715 | 930 |
| 0850 | 3 #2/0 & 1 #1 | | 1.80 | 8.889 | | 410 | 405 | | 815 | 1,050 |
| 0900 | 3 #4/0 & 1 #2/0 | | 1.60 | 10 | | 585 | 455 | | 1,040 | 1,325 |

### 26 05 19.90 Wire

| | | | Crew | Daily Output | Labor-Hours | Unit | Material | 2008 Bare Costs Labor | Equipment | Total | Total Incl O&P |
|---|---|---|---|---|---|---|---|---|---|---|---|
| 0010 | **WIRE** | R260519-92 | | | | | | | | | |
| 0020 | 600 volt type THW, copper, solid, #14 | | 1 Elec | 13 | .615 | C.L.F. | 10 | 28 | | 38 | 53 |
| 0030 | #12 | | | 11 | .727 | | 14.90 | 33 | | 47.90 | 66 |
| 0040 | #10 | | | 10 | .800 | | 23 | 36.50 | | 59.50 | 80 |
| 0050 | Stranded, #14 | R260533-22 | | 13 | .615 | | 10.15 | 28 | | 38.15 | 53 |
| 0100 | #12 | | | 11 | .727 | | 15.70 | 33 | | 48.70 | 67 |
| 0120 | #10 | | | 10 | .800 | | 24 | 36.50 | | 60.50 | 81 |
| 0140 | #8 | | | 8 | 1 | | 40.50 | 45.50 | | 86 | 113 |
| 0160 | #6 | | | 6.50 | 1.231 | | 62 | 56 | | 118 | 152 |
| 0180 | #4 | | 2 Elec | 10.60 | 1.509 | | 97.50 | 69 | | 166.50 | 209 |
| 0200 | #3 | | | 10 | 1.600 | | 123 | 73 | | 196 | 244 |
| 0220 | #2 | | | 9 | 1.778 | | 154 | 81 | | 235 | 291 |
| 0240 | #1 | | | 8 | 2 | | 195 | 91 | | 286 | 350 |
| 0260 | 1/0 | | | 6.60 | 2.424 | | 234 | 110 | | 344 | 420 |
| 0280 | 2/0 | | | 5.80 | 2.759 | | 293 | 126 | | 419 | 505 |
| 0300 | 3/0 | | | 5 | 3.200 | | 370 | 146 | | 516 | 620 |
| 0350 | 4/0 | | | 4.40 | 3.636 | | 460 | 166 | | 626 | 755 |

# 26 05 Common Work Results for Electrical

## 26 05 19 – Low-Voltage Electrical Power Conductors and Cables

### 26 05 19.90 Wire

| | | Crew | Daily Output | Labor-Hours | Unit | Material | 2008 Bare Costs Labor | Equipment | Total | Total Incl O&P |
|---|---|---|---|---|---|---|---|---|---|---|
| 0400 | 250 kcmil | 3 Elec | 6 | 4 | C.L.F. | 565 | 182 | | 747 | 895 |
| 0420 | 300 kcmil | | 5.70 | 4.211 | | 655 | 192 | | 847 | 1,000 |
| 0450 | 350 kcmil | | 5.40 | 4.444 | | 765 | 202 | | 967 | 1,150 |
| 0480 | 400 kcmil | | 5.10 | 4.706 | | 870 | 214 | | 1,084 | 1,275 |
| 0490 | 500 kcmil | | 4.80 | 5 | | 1,075 | 228 | | 1,303 | 1,550 |
| 0540 | Aluminum, stranded, #6 | 1 Elec | 8 | 1 | | 27.50 | 45.50 | | 73 | 98 |
| 0560 | #4 | 2 Elec | 13 | 1.231 | | 34 | 56 | | 90 | 121 |
| 0580 | #2 | | 10.60 | 1.509 | | 46.50 | 69 | | 115.50 | 153 |
| 0600 | #1 | | 9 | 1.778 | | 68 | 81 | | 149 | 196 |
| 0620 | 1/0 | | 8 | 2 | | 81.50 | 91 | | 172.50 | 226 |
| 0640 | 2/0 | | 7.20 | 2.222 | | 96 | 101 | | 197 | 256 |
| 0680 | 3/0 | | 6.60 | 2.424 | | 119 | 110 | | 229 | 295 |
| 0700 | 4/0 | | 6.20 | 2.581 | | 133 | 118 | | 251 | 320 |
| 0720 | 250 kcmil | 3 Elec | 8.70 | 2.759 | | 162 | 126 | | 288 | 365 |
| 0740 | 300 kcmil | | 8.10 | 2.963 | | 224 | 135 | | 359 | 445 |
| 0760 | 350 kcmil | | 7.50 | 3.200 | | 227 | 146 | | 373 | 465 |
| 0780 | 400 kcmil | | 6.90 | 3.478 | | 266 | 158 | | 424 | 530 |
| 0800 | 500 kcmil | | 6 | 4 | | 293 | 182 | | 475 | 590 |
| 0850 | 600 kcmil | | 5.70 | 4.211 | | 370 | 192 | | 562 | 695 |
| 0880 | 700 kcmil | | 5.10 | 4.706 | | 430 | 214 | | 644 | 790 |
| 0900 | 750 kcmil | | 4.80 | 5 | | 435 | 228 | | 663 | 815 |
| 0920 | Type THWN-THHN, copper, solid, #14 | 1 Elec | 13 | .615 | | 10 | 28 | | 38 | 53 |
| 0940 | #12 | | 11 | .727 | | 14.90 | 33 | | 47.90 | 66 |
| 0960 | #10 | | 10 | .800 | | 23 | 36.50 | | 59.50 | 80 |
| 1000 | Stranded, #14 | | 13 | .615 | | 10.15 | 28 | | 38.15 | 53 |
| 1200 | #12 | | 11 | .727 | | 15.70 | 33 | | 48.70 | 67 |
| 1250 | #10 | CN | 10 | .800 | | 24 | 36.50 | | 60.50 | 81 |
| 1300 | #8 | | 8 | 1 | | 40.50 | 45.50 | | 86 | 113 |
| 1350 | #6 | | 6.50 | 1.231 | | 62 | 56 | | 118 | 152 |
| 1400 | #4 | 2 Elec | 10.60 | 1.509 | | 97.50 | 69 | | 166.50 | 209 |

## 26 05 23 – Control-Voltage Electrical Power Cables

### 26 05 23.10 Control Cable

| | | Crew | Daily Output | Labor-Hours | Unit | Material | 2008 Bare Costs Labor | Equipment | Total | Total Incl O&P |
|---|---|---|---|---|---|---|---|---|---|---|
| 0010 | **CONTROL CABLE** | | | | | | | | | |
| 0020 | 600 volt, copper, #14 THWN wire with PVC jacket, 2 wires | 1 Elec | 9 | .889 | C.L.F. | 22.50 | 40.50 | | 63 | 85 |
| 0100 | 4 wires | | 7 | 1.143 | | 39 | 52 | | 91 | 121 |
| 0200 | 6 wires | | 6 | 1.333 | | 57.50 | 60.50 | | 118 | 154 |
| 0300 | 8 wires | | 5.30 | 1.509 | | 69.50 | 69 | | 138.50 | 179 |
| 0400 | 10 wires | | 4.80 | 1.667 | | 102 | 76 | | 178 | 225 |
| 0500 | 12 wires | | 4.30 | 1.860 | | 117 | 84.50 | | 201.50 | 255 |
| 0600 | 14 wires | | 3.80 | 2.105 | | 140 | 96 | | 236 | 297 |
| 0700 | 16 wires | | 3.50 | 2.286 | | 143 | 104 | | 247 | 310 |
| 0800 | 18 wires | | 3.30 | 2.424 | | 161 | 110 | | 271 | 340 |
| 0900 | 20 wires | | 3 | 2.667 | | 186 | 121 | | 307 | 385 |
| 1000 | 22 wires | | 2.80 | 2.857 | | 193 | 130 | | 323 | 405 |

## 26 05 26 – Grounding and Bonding for Electrical Systems

### 26 05 26.80 Grounding

| | | Crew | Daily Output | Labor-Hours | Unit | Material | 2008 Bare Costs Labor | Equipment | Total | Total Incl O&P |
|---|---|---|---|---|---|---|---|---|---|---|
| 0010 | **GROUNDING** | | | | | | | | | |
| 0030 | Rod, copper clad, 8' long, 1/2" diameter | 1 Elec | 5.50 | 1.455 | Ea. | 14.80 | 66.50 | | 81.30 | 115 |
| 0050 | 3/4" diameter | | 5.30 | 1.509 | | 27 | 69 | | 96 | 132 |
| 0080 | 10' long, 1/2" diameter | | 4.80 | 1.667 | | 17.35 | 76 | | 93.35 | 132 |
| 0100 | 3/4" diameter | | 4.40 | 1.818 | | 32.50 | 83 | | 115.50 | 159 |
| 0130 | 15' long, 3/4" diameter | | 4 | 2 | | 92 | 91 | | 183 | 237 |

## 26 05 26 – Grounding and Bonding for Electrical Systems

| 26 05 26.80 Grounding | | Crew | Daily Output | Labor-Hours | Unit | Material | 2008 Bare Costs Labor | Equipment | Total | Total Incl O&P |
|---|---|---|---|---|---|---|---|---|---|---|
| 0390 | Bare copper wire, stranded, #8 | 1 Elec | 11 | .727 | C.L.F. | 36 | 33 | | 69 | 89 |
| 0400 | #6 | ↓ | 10 | .800 | | 56.50 | 36.50 | | 93 | 117 |
| 0600 | #2 | 2 Elec | 10 | 1.600 | | 143 | 73 | | 216 | 266 |
| 0800 | 3/0 | ↓ | 6.60 | 2.424 | | 335 | 110 | | 445 | 535 |
| 1000 | 4/0 | ↓ | 5.70 | 2.807 | | 425 | 128 | | 553 | 655 |
| 1200 | 250 kcmil | 3 Elec | 7.20 | 3.333 | ↓ | 500 | 152 | | 652 | 775 |
| 1800 | Water pipe ground clamps, heavy duty | | | | | | | | | |
| 2000 | Bronze, 1/2" to 1" diameter | 1 Elec | 8 | 1 | Ea. | 24.50 | 45.50 | | 70 | 95 |
| 2100 | 1-1/4" to 2" diameter | | 8 | 1 | | 32 | 45.50 | | 77.50 | 104 |
| 2200 | 2-1/2" to 3" diameter | | 6 | 1.333 | | 54 | 60.50 | | 114.50 | 150 |
| 2800 | Brazed connections, #6 wire | | 12 | .667 | | 12.90 | 30.50 | | 43.40 | 59 |
| 3000 | #2 wire | | 10 | .800 | | 17.30 | 36.50 | | 53.80 | 73.50 |
| 3100 | 3/0 wire | | 8 | 1 | | 26 | 45.50 | | 71.50 | 96.50 |
| 3200 | 4/0 wire | | 7 | 1.143 | | 29.50 | 52 | | 81.50 | 110 |
| 3400 | 250 kcmil wire | | 5 | 1.600 | | 34.50 | 73 | | 107.50 | 147 |
| 3600 | 500 kcmil wire | ↓ | 4 | 2 | ↓ | 42.50 | 91 | | 133.50 | 183 |

## 26 05 33 – Raceway and Boxes for Electrical Systems

| 26 05 33.05 Conduit | | Crew | Daily Output | Labor-Hours | Unit | Material | 2008 Bare Costs Labor | Equipment | Total | Total Incl O&P |
|---|---|---|---|---|---|---|---|---|---|---|
| 0010 | **CONDUIT** To 15' high, includes 2 terminations, 2 elbows,    R260533-22 | | | | | | | | | |
| 0020 | 11 beam clamps, and 11 couplings per 100 L.F. | | | | | | | | | |
| 0300 | Aluminum, 1/2" diameter | 1 Elec | 100 | .080 | L.F. | 2.17 | 3.64 | | 5.81 | 7.85 |
| 0500 | 3/4" diameter | | 90 | .089 | | 2.95 | 4.05 | | 7 | 9.30 |
| 0700 | 1" diameter | | 80 | .100 | | 3.88 | 4.56 | | 8.44 | 11.05 |
| 1000 | 1-1/4" diameter | | 70 | .114 | | 5.25 | 5.20 | | 10.45 | 13.50 |
| 1030 | 1-1/2" diameter | | 65 | .123 | | 6.30 | 5.60 | | 11.90 | 15.25 |
| 1050 | 2" diameter | | 60 | .133 | | 8.60 | 6.05 | | 14.65 | 18.50 |
| 1070 | 2-1/2" diameter | | 50 | .160 | | 14 | 7.30 | | 21.30 | 26.50 |
| 1100 | 3" diameter | 2 Elec | 90 | .178 | | 19.20 | 8.10 | | 27.30 | 33 |
| 1130 | 3-1/2" diameter | | 80 | .200 | | 25.50 | 9.10 | | 34.60 | 41.50 |
| 1140 | 4" diameter | ↓ | 70 | .229 | | 30.50 | 10.40 | | 40.90 | 49 |
| 1750 | Rigid galvanized steel, 1/2" diameter | 1 Elec | 90 | .089 | | 2.30 | 4.05 | | 6.35 | 8.60 |
| 1770 | 3/4" diameter | | 80 | .100 | | 2.54 | 4.56 | | 7.10 | 9.60 |
| 1800 | 1" diameter | | 65 | .123 | | 3.66 | 5.60 | | 9.26 | 12.40 |
| 1830 | 1-1/4" diameter | | 60 | .133 | | 5.15 | 6.05 | | 11.20 | 14.75 |
| 1850 | 1-1/2" diameter | | 55 | .145 | | 6 | 6.65 | | 12.65 | 16.45 |
| 1870 | 2" diameter | | 45 | .178 | | 7.55 | 8.10 | | 15.65 | 20.50 |
| 1900 | 2-1/2" diameter | ↓ | 35 | .229 | | 14.45 | 10.40 | | 24.85 | 31.50 |
| 1930 | 3" diameter | 2 Elec | 50 | .320 | | 17.85 | 14.60 | | 32.45 | 41 |
| 1950 | 3-1/2" diameter | | 44 | .364 | | 22.50 | 16.55 | | 39.05 | 49 |
| 1970 | 4" diameter | ↓ | 40 | .400 | | 25 | 18.20 | | 43.20 | 54.50 |
| 2500 | Steel, intermediate conduit (IMC), 1/2" diameter | 1 Elec | 100 | .080 | | 1.64 | 3.64 | | 5.28 | 7.25 |
| 2530 | 3/4" diameter | | 90 | .089 | | 2 | 4.05 | | 6.05 | 8.25 |
| 2550 | 1" diameter | | 70 | .114 | | 2.76 | 5.20 | | 7.96 | 10.80 |
| 2570 | 1-1/4" diameter | | 65 | .123 | | 3.72 | 5.60 | | 9.32 | 12.45 |
| 2600 | 1-1/2" diameter | | 60 | .133 | | 4.39 | 6.05 | | 10.44 | 13.90 |
| 2630 | 2" diameter | | 50 | .160 | | 5.60 | 7.30 | | 12.90 | 17 |
| 2650 | 2-1/2" diameter | ↓ | 40 | .200 | | 10.75 | 9.10 | | 19.85 | 25.50 |
| 2670 | 3" diameter | 2 Elec | 60 | .267 | | 14.35 | 12.15 | | 26.50 | 34 |
| 2700 | 3-1/2" diameter | | 54 | .296 | | 18.40 | 13.50 | | 31.90 | 40.50 |
| 2730 | 4" diameter | ↓ | 50 | .320 | | 20.50 | 14.60 | | 35.10 | 44.50 |
| 5000 | Electric metallic tubing (EMT), 1/2" diameter | 1 Elec | 170 | .047 | | .57 | 2.14 | | 2.71 | 3.82 |
| 5020 | 3/4" diameter    **CN** | ↓ | 130 | .062 | ↓ | .91 | 2.80 | | 3.71 | 5.20 |

### 26 05 33.05 Conduit

| | | Crew | Daily Output | Labor-Hours | Unit | Material | 2008 Bare Costs Labor | Equipment | Total | Total Incl O&P |
|---|---|---|---|---|---|---|---|---|---|---|
| 5040 | 1" diameter | 1 Elec | 115 | .070 | L.F. | 1.54 | 3.17 | | 4.71 | 6.40 |
| 5060 | 1-1/4" diameter | | 100 | .080 | | 2.50 | 3.64 | | 6.14 | 8.20 |
| 5080 | 1-1/2" diameter | | 90 | .089 | | 3.17 | 4.05 | | 7.22 | 9.55 |
| 5100 | 2" diameter | | 80 | .100 | | 4.07 | 4.56 | | 8.63 | 11.25 |
| 5120 | 2-1/2" diameter | | 60 | .133 | | 9.80 | 6.05 | | 15.85 | 19.85 |
| 5140 | 3" diameter | 2 Elec | 100 | .160 | | 11.55 | 7.30 | | 18.85 | 23.50 |
| 5160 | 3-1/2" diameter | | 90 | .178 | | 14.60 | 8.10 | | 22.70 | 28 |
| 5180 | 4" diameter | | 80 | .200 | | 15.85 | 9.10 | | 24.95 | 31 |
| 9900 | Add to labor for higher elevated installation | | | | | | | | | |
| 9910 | 15' to 20' high, add | | | | | | 10% | | | |
| 9920 | 20' to 25' high, add | | | | | | 20% | | | |
| 9930 | 25' to 30' high, add | | | | | | 25% | | | |
| 9940 | 30' to 35' high, add | | | | | | 30% | | | |
| 9950 | 35' to 40' high, add | | | | | | 35% | | | |
| 9960 | Over 40' high, add | | | | | | 40% | | | |
| 9980 | Allow. for cond. ftngs., 5% min.-20% max. | | | | | | | | | |

### 26 05 33.45 Wireway

| | | Crew | Daily Output | Labor-Hours | Unit | Material | 2008 Bare Costs Labor | Equipment | Total | Total Incl O&P |
|---|---|---|---|---|---|---|---|---|---|---|
| 0010 | **WIREWAY** to 15' high | | | | | | | | | |
| 0100 | Screw cover, NEMA 1 w/ fittings and supports, 2-1/2" x 2-1/2" | 1 Elec | 45 | .178 | L.F. | 11.45 | 8.10 | | 19.55 | 24.50 |
| 0200 | 4" x 4" | " | 40 | .200 | | 12.65 | 9.10 | | 21.75 | 27.50 |
| 0400 | 6" x 6" | 2 Elec | 60 | .267 | | 19.70 | 12.15 | | 31.85 | 39.50 |
| 0600 | 8" x 8" | " | 40 | .400 | | 33 | 18.20 | | 51.20 | 63.50 |
| 4475 | Screw cover, NEMA 3R w/ fittings and supports, 4" x 4" | 1 Elec | 36 | .222 | | 27 | 10.10 | | 37.10 | 44.50 |
| 4480 | 6" x 6" | 2 Elec | 55 | .291 | | 34 | 13.25 | | 47.25 | 57.50 |
| 4485 | 8" x 8" | | 36 | .444 | | 55 | 20 | | 75 | 90.50 |
| 4490 | 12" x 12" | | 18 | .889 | | 77 | 40.50 | | 117.50 | 145 |
| 9980 | Allow. for wireway ftngs., 5% min.-20% max. | | | | | | | | | |

### 26 05 33.50 Outlet Boxes

| | | Crew | Daily Output | Labor-Hours | Unit | Material | 2008 Bare Costs Labor | Equipment | Total | Total Incl O&P |
|---|---|---|---|---|---|---|---|---|---|---|
| 0010 | **OUTLET BOXES** | | | | | | | | | |
| 0020 | Pressed steel, octagon, 4" | 1 Elec | 20 | .400 | Ea. | 2.91 | 18.20 | | 21.11 | 30 |
| 0060 | Covers, blank | | 64 | .125 | | 1.21 | 5.70 | | 6.91 | 9.85 |
| 0100 | Extension rings | | 40 | .200 | | 4.80 | 9.10 | | 13.90 | 18.85 |
| 0150 | Square, 4" | | 20 | .400 | | 2.49 | 18.20 | | 20.69 | 29.50 |
| 0200 | Extension rings | | 40 | .200 | | 4.83 | 9.10 | | 13.93 | 18.85 |
| 0250 | Covers, blank | | 64 | .125 | | 1.37 | 5.70 | | 7.07 | 10 |
| 0300 | Plaster rings | | 64 | .125 | | 2.66 | 5.70 | | 8.36 | 11.45 |
| 0650 | Switchbox | | 27 | .296 | | 4.66 | 13.50 | | 18.16 | 25 |
| 1100 | Concrete, floor, 1 gang | | 5.30 | 1.509 | | 81 | 69 | | 150 | 191 |
| 2000 | Poke-thru fitting, fire rated, for 3-3/4" floor | | 6.80 | 1.176 | | 111 | 53.50 | | 164.50 | 203 |
| 2040 | For 7" floor | | 6.80 | 1.176 | | 111 | 53.50 | | 164.50 | 203 |
| 2100 | Pedestal, 15 amp, duplex receptacle & blank plate | | 5.25 | 1.524 | | 115 | 69.50 | | 184.50 | 230 |
| 2120 | Duplex receptacle and telephone plate | | 5.25 | 1.524 | | 116 | 69.50 | | 185.50 | 230 |
| 2140 | Pedestal, 20 amp, duplex recept. & phone plate | | 5 | 1.600 | | 116 | 73 | | 189 | 237 |
| 2200 | Abandonment plate | | 32 | .250 | | 34 | 11.40 | | 45.40 | 54.50 |

### 26 05 33.65 Pull Boxes

| | | Crew | Daily Output | Labor-Hours | Unit | Material | 2008 Bare Costs Labor | Equipment | Total | Total Incl O&P |
|---|---|---|---|---|---|---|---|---|---|---|
| 0010 | **PULL BOXES** | | | | | | | | | |
| 0100 | Sheet metal, pull box, NEMA 1, type SC, 6" W x 6" H x 4" D | 1 Elec | 8 | 1 | Ea. | 12.20 | 45.50 | | 57.70 | 81.50 |
| 0200 | 8" W x 8" H x 4" D | | 8 | 1 | | 16.70 | 45.50 | | 62.20 | 86.50 |
| 0300 | 10" W x 12" H x 6" D | | 5.30 | 1.509 | | 29.50 | 69 | | 98.50 | 135 |
| 0400 | 16" W x 20" H x 8" D | | 4 | 2 | | 111 | 91 | | 202 | 258 |
| 0500 | 20" W x 24" H x 8" D | | 3.20 | 2.500 | | 130 | 114 | | 244 | 315 |
| 0600 | 24" W x 36" H x 8" D | | 2.70 | 2.963 | | 184 | 135 | | 319 | 405 |

## 26 05 33 – Raceway and Boxes for Electrical Systems

### 26 05 33.65 Pull Boxes

| | | Crew | Daily Output | Labor-Hours | Unit | Material | 2008 Bare Costs Labor | Equipment | Total | Total Incl O&P |
|---|---|---|---|---|---|---|---|---|---|---|
| 0650 | Pull box, hinged , NEMA 1, 6" W x 6" H x 4" D | 1 Elec | 8 | 1 | Ea. | 12.40 | 45.50 | | 57.90 | 81.50 |
| 0800 | 12" W x 16" H x 6" D | | 4.70 | 1.702 | | 40.50 | 77.50 | | 118 | 160 |
| 1000 | 20" W x 20" H x 6" D | | 3.60 | 2.222 | | 81.50 | 101 | | 182.50 | 241 |
| 1200 | 20" W x 20" H x 8" D | | 3.20 | 2.500 | | 163 | 114 | | 277 | 350 |
| 1400 | 24" W x 36" H x 8" D | | 2.70 | 2.963 | | 262 | 135 | | 397 | 490 |
| 1600 | 24" W x 42" H x 8" D | | 2 | 4 | | 395 | 182 | | 577 | 705 |
| 2100 | Pull box, NEMA 3R, type SC, raintight & weatherproof | | | | | | | | | |
| 2150 | 6" L x 6" W x 6" D | 1 Elec | 10 | .800 | Ea. | 21 | 36.50 | | 57.50 | 77.50 |
| 2200 | 8" L x 6" W x 6" D | | 8 | 1 | | 26 | 45.50 | | 71.50 | 96.50 |
| 2250 | 10" L x 6" W x 6" D | | 7 | 1.143 | | 34.50 | 52 | | 86.50 | 116 |
| 2300 | 12" L x 12" W x 6" D | | 5 | 1.600 | | 49 | 73 | | 122 | 163 |
| 2350 | 16" L x 16" W x 6" D | | 4.50 | 1.778 | | 97.50 | 81 | | 178.50 | 228 |
| 2400 | 20" L x 20" W x 6" D | | 4 | 2 | | 133 | 91 | | 224 | 282 |
| 2450 | 24" L x 18" W x 8" D | | 3 | 2.667 | | 146 | 121 | | 267 | 340 |
| 2500 | 24" L x 24" W x 10" D | | 2.50 | 3.200 | | 196 | 146 | | 342 | 435 |
| 2550 | 30" L x 24" W x 12" D | | 2 | 4 | | 355 | 182 | | 537 | 660 |
| 2600 | 36" L x 36" W x 12" D | | 1.50 | 5.333 | | 470 | 243 | | 713 | 875 |
| 2800 | Cast iron, pull boxes for surface mounting | | | | | | | | | |
| 3000 | NEMA 4, watertight & dust tight | | | | | | | | | |
| 3050 | 6" L x 6" W x 6" D | 1 Elec | 4 | 2 | Ea. | 188 | 91 | | 279 | 345 |
| 3100 | 8" L x 6" W x 6" D | | 3.20 | 2.500 | | 232 | 114 | | 346 | 425 |
| 3150 | 10" L x 6" W x 6" D | | 2.50 | 3.200 | | 289 | 146 | | 435 | 535 |
| 3200 | 12" L x 12" W x 6" D | | 2.30 | 3.478 | | 495 | 158 | | 653 | 780 |
| 3250 | 16" L x 16" W x 6" D | | 1.30 | 6.154 | | 1,100 | 280 | | 1,380 | 1,625 |
| 3300 | 20" L x 20" W x 6" D | | .80 | 10 | | 2,050 | 455 | | 2,505 | 2,925 |
| 3350 | 24" L x 18" W x 8" D | | .70 | 11.429 | | 2,150 | 520 | | 2,670 | 3,150 |
| 3400 | 24" L x 24" W x 10" D | | .50 | 16 | | 3,300 | 730 | | 4,030 | 4,700 |
| 3450 | 30" L x 24" W x 12" D | | .40 | 20 | | 5,525 | 910 | | 6,435 | 7,425 |
| 3500 | 36" L x 36" W x 12" D | | .20 | 40 | | 6,825 | 1,825 | | 8,650 | 10,300 |
| 6000 | J.I.C. wiring boxes, NEMA 12, dust tight & drip tight | | | | | | | | | |
| 6050 | 6" L x 8" W x 4" D | 1 Elec | 10 | .800 | Ea. | 50 | 36.50 | | 86.50 | 110 |
| 6100 | 8" L x 10" W x 4" D | | 8 | 1 | | 62.50 | 45.50 | | 108 | 137 |
| 6150 | 12" L x 14" W x 6" D | | 5.30 | 1.509 | | 101 | 69 | | 170 | 213 |
| 6200 | 14" L x 16" W x 6" D | | 4.70 | 1.702 | | 121 | 77.50 | | 198.50 | 248 |
| 6250 | 16" L x 20" W x 6" D | | 4.40 | 1.818 | | 257 | 83 | | 340 | 405 |
| 6300 | 24" L x 30" W x 6" D | | 3.20 | 2.500 | | 380 | 114 | | 494 | 585 |
| 6350 | 24" L x 30" W x 8" D | | 2.90 | 2.759 | | 405 | 126 | | 531 | 630 |
| 6400 | 24" L x 36" W x 8" D | | 2.70 | 2.963 | | 450 | 135 | | 585 | 695 |
| 6450 | 24" L x 42" W x 8" D | | 2.30 | 3.478 | | 490 | 158 | | 648 | 775 |
| 6500 | 24" L x 48" W x 8" D | | 2 | 4 | | 535 | 182 | | 717 | 855 |

## 26 05 36 – Cable Trays for Electrical Systems

### 26 05 36.10 Cable Tray Ladder Type

| | | Crew | Daily Output | Labor-Hours | Unit | Material | 2008 Bare Costs Labor | Equipment | Total | Total Incl O&P |
|---|---|---|---|---|---|---|---|---|---|---|
| 0010 | **CABLE TRAY LADDER TYPE** w/ ftngs. & supports, 4" dp., to 15' elev. | | | | | | | | | |
| 0160 | Galvanized steel tray | | | | | | | | | |
| 0170 | 4" rung spacing, 6" wide | 2 Elec | 98 | .163 | L.F. | 11.05 | 7.45 | | 18.50 | 23.50 |
| 0200 | 12" wide | | 86 | .186 | | 13.25 | 8.45 | | 21.70 | 27 |
| 0400 | 18" wide | | 82 | .195 | | 15.40 | 8.90 | | 24.30 | 30 |
| 0600 | 24" wide | | 78 | .205 | | 17.75 | 9.35 | | 27.10 | 33.50 |
| 3200 | Aluminum tray, 4" deep, 6" rung spacing, 6" wide | | 134 | .119 | | 13.85 | 5.45 | | 19.30 | 23.50 |
| 3220 | 12" wide | | 124 | .129 | | 15.50 | 5.90 | | 21.40 | 26 |
| 3230 | 18" wide | | 114 | .140 | | 17.25 | 6.40 | | 23.65 | 28.50 |
| 3240 | 24" wide | | 106 | .151 | | 20 | 6.90 | | 26.90 | 32.50 |

# 26 05 Common Work Results for Electrical

## 26 05 36 – Cable Trays for Electrical Systems

| 26 05 36.10 Cable Tray Ladder Type | Crew | Daily Output | Labor-Hours | Unit | Material | 2008 Bare Costs Labor | Equipment | Total | Total Incl O&P |
|---|---|---|---|---|---|---|---|---|---|
| 9980 | Allow. for tray ftngs., 5% min.-20% max. | | | | | | | | |

## 26 05 39 – Underfloor Raceways for Electrical Systems

### 26 05 39.30 Conduit In Concrete Slab

| 26 05 39.30 Conduit In Concrete Slab | | Crew | Daily Output | Labor-Hours | Unit | Material | Labor | Equipment | Total | Total Incl O&P |
|---|---|---|---|---|---|---|---|---|---|---|
| 0010 | CONDUIT IN CONCRETE SLAB Including terminations, | | | | | | | | | |
| 0020 | fittings and supports | | | | | | | | | |
| 3230 | PVC, schedule 40, 1/2" diameter | 1 Elec | 270 | .030 | L.F. | .76 | 1.35 | | 2.11 | 2.84 |
| 3250 | 3/4" diameter | | 230 | .035 | | .94 | 1.58 | | 2.52 | 3.39 |
| 3270 | 1" diameter | | 200 | .040 | | 1.30 | 1.82 | | 3.12 | 4.14 |
| 3300 | 1-1/4" diameter | | 170 | .047 | | 1.81 | 2.14 | | 3.95 | 5.20 |
| 3330 | 1-1/2" diameter | | 140 | .057 | | 2.17 | 2.60 | | 4.77 | 6.25 |
| 3350 | 2" diameter | | 120 | .067 | | 2.81 | 3.04 | | 5.85 | 7.60 |
| 4350 | Rigid galvanized steel, 1/2" diameter | | 200 | .040 | | 1.97 | 1.82 | | 3.79 | 4.88 |
| 4400 | 3/4" diameter | | 170 | .047 | | 2.22 | 2.14 | | 4.36 | 5.65 |
| 4450 | 1" diameter | | 130 | .062 | | 3.34 | 2.80 | | 6.14 | 7.85 |
| 4500 | 1-1/4" diameter | | 110 | .073 | | 4.59 | 3.31 | | 7.90 | 10 |
| 4600 | 1-1/2" diameter | | 100 | .080 | | 5.40 | 3.64 | | 9.04 | 11.40 |
| 4800 | 2" diameter | | 90 | .089 | | 6.80 | 4.05 | | 10.85 | 13.50 |

### 26 05 39.40 Conduit In Trench

| 26 05 39.40 Conduit In Trench | | Crew | Daily Output | Labor-Hours | Unit | Material | Labor | Equipment | Total | Total Incl O&P |
|---|---|---|---|---|---|---|---|---|---|---|
| 0010 | CONDUIT IN TRENCH Includes terminations and fittings | | | | | | | | | |
| 0020 | Does not include excavation or backfill, see Div. 31 23 16.00 | | | | | | | | | |
| 0200 | Rigid galvanized steel, 2" diameter | 1 Elec | 150 | .053 | L.F. | 6.55 | 2.43 | | 8.98 | 10.80 |
| 0400 | 2-1/2" diameter | " | 100 | .080 | | 12.95 | 3.64 | | 16.59 | 19.70 |
| 0600 | 3" diameter | 2 Elec | 160 | .100 | | 16.30 | 4.56 | | 20.86 | 25 |
| 0800 | 3-1/2" diameter | | 140 | .114 | | 21 | 5.20 | | 26.20 | 31.50 |
| 1000 | 4" diameter | | 100 | .160 | | 22.50 | 7.30 | | 29.80 | 36 |
| 1200 | 5" diameter | | 80 | .200 | | 49 | 9.10 | | 58.10 | 67.50 |
| 1400 | 6" diameter | | 60 | .267 | | 72.50 | 12.15 | | 84.65 | 97.50 |

## 26 05 43 – Underground Ducts and Raceways for Electrical Systems

### 26 05 43.10 Trench Duct

| 26 05 43.10 Trench Duct | | Crew | Daily Output | Labor-Hours | Unit | Material | Labor | Equipment | Total | Total Incl O&P |
|---|---|---|---|---|---|---|---|---|---|---|
| 0010 | TRENCH DUCT Steel with cover | | | | | | | | | |
| 0020 | Standard adjustable, depths to 4" | | | | | | | | | |
| 0100 | Straight, single compartment, 9" wide | 2 Elec | 40 | .400 | L.F. | 82 | 18.20 | | 100.20 | 117 |
| 0200 | 12" wide | | 32 | .500 | | 93 | 23 | | 116 | 136 |
| 0400 | 18" wide | | 26 | .615 | | 124 | 28 | | 152 | 178 |
| 0600 | 24" wide | | 22 | .727 | | 159 | 33 | | 192 | 225 |
| 0800 | 30" wide | | 20 | .800 | | 192 | 36.50 | | 228.50 | 266 |
| 1000 | 36" wide | | 16 | 1 | | 231 | 45.50 | | 276.50 | 320 |
| 1200 | Horizontal elbow, 9" wide | | 5.40 | 2.963 | Ea. | 305 | 135 | | 440 | 535 |
| 1400 | 12" wide | | 4.60 | 3.478 | | 350 | 158 | | 508 | 620 |
| 1600 | 18" wide | | 4 | 4 | | 450 | 182 | | 632 | 765 |
| 1800 | 24" wide | | 3.20 | 5 | | 630 | 228 | | 858 | 1,025 |
| 2000 | 30" wide | | 2.60 | 6.154 | | 840 | 280 | | 1,120 | 1,350 |
| 2200 | 36" wide | | 2.40 | 6.667 | | 1,100 | 305 | | 1,405 | 1,650 |
| 2400 | Vertical elbow, 9" wide | | 5.40 | 2.963 | | 106 | 135 | | 241 | 320 |
| 2600 | 12" wide | | 4.60 | 3.478 | | 115 | 158 | | 273 | 365 |
| 2800 | 18" wide | | 4 | 4 | | 132 | 182 | | 314 | 415 |
| 3000 | 24" wide | | 3.20 | 5 | | 164 | 228 | | 392 | 520 |
| 3200 | 30" wide | | 2.60 | 6.154 | | 181 | 280 | | 461 | 620 |
| 3400 | 36" wide | | 2.40 | 6.667 | | 199 | 305 | | 504 | 670 |
| 3600 | Cross, 9" wide | | 4 | 4 | | 495 | 182 | | 677 | 815 |
| 3800 | 12" wide | | 3.20 | 5 | | 525 | 228 | | 753 | 920 |

# 26 05 Common Work Results for Electrical

## 26 05 43 – Underground Ducts and Raceways for Electrical Systems

| 26 05 43.10 Trench Duct | | Crew | Daily Output | Labor-Hours | Unit | Material | 2008 Bare Costs Labor | Equipment | Total | Total Incl O&P |
|---|---|---|---|---|---|---|---|---|---|---|
| 4000 | 18" wide | 2 Elec | 2.60 | 6.154 | Ea. | 630 | 280 | | 910 | 1,125 |
| 4200 | 24" wide | | 2.20 | 7.273 | | 800 | 330 | | 1,130 | 1,375 |
| 4400 | 30" wide | | 2 | 8 | | 1,025 | 365 | | 1,390 | 1,700 |
| 4600 | 36" wide | | 1.80 | 8.889 | | 1,300 | 405 | | 1,705 | 2,025 |
| 4800 | End closure, 9" wide | | 14.40 | 1.111 | | 31 | 50.50 | | 81.50 | 110 |
| 5000 | 12" wide | | 12 | 1.333 | | 35.50 | 60.50 | | 96 | 130 |
| 5200 | 18" wide | | 10 | 1.600 | | 54.50 | 73 | | 127.50 | 169 |
| 5400 | 24" wide | | 8 | 2 | | 72 | 91 | | 163 | 215 |
| 5600 | 30" wide | | 6.60 | 2.424 | | 90 | 110 | | 200 | 263 |
| 5800 | 36" wide | | 5.80 | 2.759 | | 107 | 126 | | 233 | 305 |
| 6000 | Tees, 9" wide | | 4 | 4 | | 300 | 182 | | 482 | 600 |
| 6200 | 12" wide | | 3.60 | 4.444 | | 350 | 202 | | 552 | 685 |
| 6400 | 18" wide | | 3.20 | 5 | | 450 | 228 | | 678 | 835 |
| 6600 | 24" wide | | 3 | 5.333 | | 645 | 243 | | 888 | 1,075 |
| 6800 | 30" wide | | 2.60 | 6.154 | | 840 | 280 | | 1,120 | 1,350 |
| 7000 | 36" wide | | 2 | 8 | | 1,100 | 365 | | 1,465 | 1,750 |
| 7200 | Riser, and cabinet connector, 9" wide | | 5.40 | 2.963 | | 132 | 135 | | 267 | 345 |
| 7400 | 12" wide | | 4.60 | 3.478 | | 154 | 158 | | 312 | 405 |
| 7600 | 18" wide | | 4 | 4 | | 189 | 182 | | 371 | 480 |
| 7800 | 24" wide | | 3.20 | 5 | | 229 | 228 | | 457 | 590 |
| 8000 | 30" wide | | 2.60 | 6.154 | | 263 | 280 | | 543 | 710 |
| 8200 | 36" wide | ▼ | 2 | 8 | | 305 | 365 | | 670 | 880 |
| 8400 | Insert assembly, cell to conduit adapter, 1-1/4" | 1 Elec | 16 | .500 | ▼ | 52.50 | 23 | | 75.50 | 91.50 |

| 26 05 43.20 Underfloor Duct | | Crew | Daily Output | Labor-Hours | Unit | Material | 2008 Bare Costs Labor | Equipment | Total | Total Incl O&P |
|---|---|---|---|---|---|---|---|---|---|---|
| 0010 | **UNDERFLOOR DUCT** | | | | | | | | | |
| 0100 | Duct, 1-3/8" x 3-1/8" blank, standard | 2 Elec | 160 | .100 | L.F. | 10 | 4.56 | | 14.56 | 17.80 |
| 0200 | 1-3/8" x 7-1/4" blank, super duct | | 120 | .133 | | 20 | 6.05 | | 26.05 | 31 |
| 0400 | 7/8" or 1-3/8" insert type, 24" O.C., 1-3/8" x 3-1/8", std. | | 140 | .114 | | 13.40 | 5.20 | | 18.60 | 22.50 |
| 0600 | 1-3/8" x 7-1/4", super duct | ▼ | 100 | .160 | ▼ | 23.50 | 7.30 | | 30.80 | 36.50 |
| 0800 | Junction box, single duct, 1 level, 3-1/8" | 1 Elec | 4 | 2 | Ea. | 300 | 91 | | 391 | 465 |
| 1000 | Junction box, single duct, 1 level, 7-1/4" | | 2.70 | 2.963 | | 350 | 135 | | 485 | 585 |
| 1200 | 1 level, 2 duct, 3-1/8" | | 3.20 | 2.500 | | 400 | 114 | | 514 | 610 |
| 1400 | Junction box, 1 level, 2 duct, 7-1/4" | | 2.30 | 3.478 | | 1,025 | 158 | | 1,183 | 1,350 |
| 1600 | Triple duct, 3-1/8" | | 2.30 | 3.478 | | 680 | 158 | | 838 | 985 |
| 1800 | Insert to conduit adapter, 3/4" & 1" | | 32 | .250 | | 24.50 | 11.40 | | 35.90 | 44 |
| 2000 | Support, single cell | | 27 | .296 | | 37 | 13.50 | | 50.50 | 60.50 |
| 2200 | Super duct | | 16 | .500 | | 37 | 23 | | 60 | 74.50 |
| 2400 | Double cell | | 16 | .500 | | 37 | 23 | | 60 | 74.50 |
| 2600 | Triple cell | | 11 | .727 | | 37 | 33 | | 70 | 90 |
| 2800 | Vertical elbow, standard duct | | 10 | .800 | | 66.50 | 36.50 | | 103 | 128 |
| 3000 | Super duct | | 8 | 1 | | 66.50 | 45.50 | | 112 | 141 |
| 3200 | Cabinet connector, standard duct | | 32 | .250 | | 50 | 11.40 | | 61.40 | 72 |
| 3400 | Super duct | | 27 | .296 | | 50 | 13.50 | | 63.50 | 75 |
| 3600 | Conduit adapter, 1" to 1-1/4" | | 32 | .250 | | 50 | 11.40 | | 61.40 | 72 |
| 3800 | 2" to 1-1/4" | | 27 | .296 | | 60 | 13.50 | | 73.50 | 86 |
| 4000 | Outlet, low tension (tele, computer, etc.) | | 8 | 1 | | 70 | 45.50 | | 115.50 | 145 |
| 4200 | High tension, receptacle (120 volt) | ▼ | 8 | 1 | ▼ | 70 | 45.50 | | 115.50 | 145 |

## 26 05 80 – Wiring Connections

| 26 05 80.10 Motor Connections | | Crew | Daily Output | Labor-Hours | Unit | Material | 2008 Bare Costs Labor | Equipment | Total | Total Incl O&P |
|---|---|---|---|---|---|---|---|---|---|---|
| 0010 | **MOTOR CONNECTIONS** | | | | | | | | | |
| 0020 | Flexible conduit and fittings, 115 volt, 1 phase, up to 1 HP motor | 1 Elec | 8 | 1 | Ea. | 8.95 | 45.50 | | 54.45 | 78 |
| 0120 | 230 volt, 10 HP motor, 3 phase | ▼ | 4.20 | 1.905 | ▼ | 15.10 | 87 | | 102.10 | 146 |

# 26 05 Common Work Results for Electrical

## 26 05 80 – Wiring Connections

### 26 05 80.10 Motor Connections

| | | Crew | Daily Output | Labor-Hours | Unit | Material | 2008 Bare Costs Labor | Equipment | Total | Total Incl O&P |
|---|---|---|---|---|---|---|---|---|---|---|
| 0200 | 25 HP motor | 1 Elec | 2.70 | 2.963 | Ea. | 30 | 135 | | 165 | 234 |
| 0400 | 50 HP motor | | 2.20 | 3.636 | | 76.50 | 166 | | 242.50 | 330 |
| 0600 | 100 HP motor | | 1.50 | 5.333 | | 188 | 243 | | 431 | 565 |

## 26 05 90 – Residential Applications

### 26 05 90.10 Residential Wiring

| | | Crew | Daily Output | Labor-Hours | Unit | Material | 2008 Bare Costs Labor | Equipment | Total | Total Incl O&P |
|---|---|---|---|---|---|---|---|---|---|---|
| 0010 | **RESIDENTIAL WIRING** | | | | | | | | | |
| 0020 | 20' avg. runs and #14/2 wiring incl. unless otherwise noted | | | | | | | | | |
| 1000 | Service & panel, includes 24' SE-AL cable, service eye, meter, | | | | | | | | | |
| 1010 | Socket, panel board, main bkr., ground rod, 15 or 20 amp | | | | | | | | | |
| 1020 | 1-pole circuit breakers, and misc. hardware | | | | | | | | | |
| 1100 | 100 amp, with 10 branch breakers | 1 Elec | 1.19 | 6.723 | Ea. | 530 | 305 | | 835 | 1,050 |
| 1110 | With PVC conduit and wire | | .92 | 8.696 | | 595 | 395 | | 990 | 1,250 |
| 1120 | With RGS conduit and wire | | .73 | 10.959 | | 750 | 500 | | 1,250 | 1,575 |
| 1150 | 150 amp, with 14 branch breakers | | 1.03 | 7.767 | | 825 | 355 | | 1,180 | 1,425 |
| 1170 | With PVC conduit and wire | | .82 | 9.756 | | 955 | 445 | | 1,400 | 1,700 |
| 1180 | With RGS conduit and wire | | .67 | 11.940 | | 1,250 | 545 | | 1,795 | 2,175 |
| 1200 | 200 amp, with 18 branch breakers | 2 Elec | 1.80 | 8.889 | | 1,075 | 405 | | 1,480 | 1,800 |
| 1220 | With PVC conduit and wire | | 1.46 | 10.959 | | 1,225 | 500 | | 1,725 | 2,100 |
| 1230 | With RGS conduit and wire | | 1.24 | 12.903 | | 1,625 | 590 | | 2,215 | 2,675 |
| 1800 | Lightning surge suppressor for above services, add | 1 Elec | 32 | .250 | | 46 | 11.40 | | 57.40 | 67.50 |
| 2000 | Switch devices | | | | | | | | | |
| 2100 | Single pole, 15 amp, Ivory, with a 1-gang box, cover plate, | | | | | | | | | |
| 2110 | Type NM (Romex) cable | 1 Elec | 17.10 | .468 | Ea. | 11.60 | 21.50 | | 33.10 | 44.50 |
| 2120 | Type MC (BX) cable | | 14.30 | .559 | | 27.50 | 25.50 | | 53 | 68 |
| 2130 | EMT & wire | | 5.71 | 1.401 | | 31 | 64 | | 95 | 129 |
| 2150 | 3-way, #14/3, type NM cable | | 14.55 | .550 | | 17 | 25 | | 42 | 56 |
| 2170 | Type MC cable | | 12.31 | .650 | | 37.50 | 29.50 | | 67 | 85.50 |
| 2180 | EMT & wire | | 5 | 1.600 | | 35 | 73 | | 108 | 147 |
| 2200 | 4-way, #14/3, type NM cable | | 14.55 | .550 | | 30.50 | 25 | | 55.50 | 71.50 |
| 2220 | Type MC cable | | 12.31 | .650 | | 51.50 | 29.50 | | 81 | 101 |
| 2230 | EMT & wire | | 5 | 1.600 | | 48.50 | 73 | | 121.50 | 163 |
| 2250 | S.P., 20 amp, #12/2, type NM cable | | 13.33 | .600 | | 19.60 | 27.50 | | 47.10 | 62 |
| 2270 | Type MC cable | | 11.43 | .700 | | 32 | 32 | | 64 | 83 |
| 2280 | EMT & wire | | 4.85 | 1.649 | | 40.50 | 75 | | 115.50 | 157 |
| 2290 | S.P. rotary dimmer, 600W, no wiring | | 17 | .471 | | 17.85 | 21.50 | | 39.35 | 51.50 |
| 2300 | S.P. rotary dimmer, 600W, type NM cable | | 14.55 | .550 | | 24.50 | 25 | | 49.50 | 64.50 |
| 2320 | Type MC cable | | 12.31 | .650 | | 40 | 29.50 | | 69.50 | 88 |
| 2330 | EMT & wire | | 5 | 1.600 | | 45.50 | 73 | | 118.50 | 159 |
| 2350 | 3-way rotary dimmer, type NM cable | | 13.33 | .600 | | 22 | 27.50 | | 49.50 | 65 |
| 2370 | Type MC cable | | 11.43 | .700 | | 38 | 32 | | 70 | 89 |
| 2380 | EMT & wire | | 4.85 | 1.649 | | 43.50 | 75 | | 118.50 | 160 |
| 2400 | Interval timer wall switch, 20 amp, 1-30 min., #12/2 | | | | | | | | | |
| 2410 | Type NM cable | 1 Elec | 14.55 | .550 | Ea. | 51 | 25 | | 76 | 93.50 |
| 2420 | Type MC cable | | 12.31 | .650 | | 57.50 | 29.50 | | 87 | 108 |
| 2430 | EMT & wire | | 5 | 1.600 | | 71.50 | 73 | | 144.50 | 188 |
| 2500 | Decorator style | | | | | | | | | |
| 2510 | S.P., 15 amp, type NM cable | 1 Elec | 17.10 | .468 | Ea. | 15.90 | 21.50 | | 37.40 | 49 |
| 2520 | Type MC cable | | 14.30 | .559 | | 31.50 | 25.50 | | 57 | 73 |
| 2530 | EMT & wire | | 5.71 | 1.401 | | 35 | 64 | | 99 | 134 |
| 2550 | 3-way, #14/3, type NM cable | | 14.55 | .550 | | 21.50 | 25 | | 46.50 | 61 |
| 2570 | Type MC cable | | 12.31 | .650 | | 42 | 29.50 | | 71.50 | 90 |
| 2580 | EMT & wire | | 5 | 1.600 | | 39 | 73 | | 112 | 152 |

| 26 05 90.10 Residential Wiring | Crew | Daily Output | Labor-Hours | Unit | Material | 2008 Bare Costs Labor | 2008 Bare Costs Equipment | Total | Total Incl O&P |
|---|---|---|---|---|---|---|---|---|---|
| 2600     4-way, #14/3, type NM cable | 1 Elec | 14.55 | .550 | Ea. | 35 | 25 | | 60 | 76 |
| 2620     Type MC cable | | 12.31 | .650 | | 55.50 | 29.50 | | 85 | 106 |
| 2630     EMT & wire | | 5 | 1.600 | | 52.50 | 73 | | 125.50 | 167 |
| 2650     S.P., 20 amp, #12/2, type NM cable | | 13.33 | .600 | | 24 | 27.50 | | 51.50 | 67 |
| 2670     Type MC cable | | 11.43 | .700 | | 36.50 | 32 | | 68.50 | 87.50 |
| 2680     EMT & wire | | 4.85 | 1.649 | | 44.50 | 75 | | 119.50 | 161 |
| 2700     S.P., slide dimmer, type NM cable | | 17.10 | .468 | | 30 | 21.50 | | 51.50 | 64.50 |
| 2720     Type MC cable | | 14.30 | .559 | | 46 | 25.50 | | 71.50 | 88.50 |
| 2730     EMT & wire | | 5.71 | 1.401 | | 51.50 | 64 | | 115.50 | 152 |
| 2750     S.P., touch dimmer, type NM cable | | 17.10 | .468 | | 27 | 21.50 | | 48.50 | 61.50 |
| 2770     Type MC cable | | 14.30 | .559 | | 43 | 25.50 | | 68.50 | 85 |
| 2780     EMT & wire | | 5.71 | 1.401 | | 48.50 | 64 | | 112.50 | 148 |
| 2800     3-way touch dimmer, type NM cable | | 13.33 | .600 | | 47 | 27.50 | | 74.50 | 92 |
| 2820     Type MC cable | | 11.43 | .700 | | 62.50 | 32 | | 94.50 | 117 |
| 2830     EMT & wire | ↓ | 4.85 | 1.649 | ↓ | 68 | 75 | | 143 | 187 |
| 3000   Combination devices | | | | | | | | | |
| 3100     S.P. switch/15 amp recpt., Ivory, 1-gang box, plate | | | | | | | | | |
| 3110     Type NM cable | 1 Elec | 11.43 | .700 | Ea. | 22 | 32 | | 54 | 71.50 |
| 3120     Type MC cable | | 10 | .800 | | 37.50 | 36.50 | | 74 | 96 |
| 3130     EMT & wire | | 4.40 | 1.818 | | 43 | 83 | | 126 | 171 |
| 3150     S.P. switch/pilot light, type NM cable | | 11.43 | .700 | | 22.50 | 32 | | 54.50 | 72.50 |
| 3170     Type MC cable | | 10 | .800 | | 38.50 | 36.50 | | 75 | 96.50 |
| 3180     EMT & wire | | 4.43 | 1.806 | | 44 | 82.50 | | 126.50 | 172 |
| 3190     2-S.P. switches, 2-#14/2, no wiring | | 14 | .571 | | 7.60 | 26 | | 33.60 | 47.50 |
| 3200     2-S.P. switches, 2-#14/2, type NM cables | | 10 | .800 | | 27.50 | 36.50 | | 64 | 84.50 |
| 3220     Type MC cable | | 8.89 | .900 | | 52 | 41 | | 93 | 118 |
| 3230     EMT & wire | | 4.10 | 1.951 | | 48 | 89 | | 137 | 185 |
| 3250     3-way switch/15 amp recpt., #14/3, type NM cable | | 10 | .800 | | 31 | 36.50 | | 67.50 | 88.50 |
| 3270     Type MC cable | | 8.89 | .900 | | 51.50 | 41 | | 92.50 | 118 |
| 3280     EMT & wire | | 4.10 | 1.951 | | 48.50 | 89 | | 137.50 | 186 |
| 3300     2-3 way switches, 2-#14/3, type NM cables | | 8.89 | .900 | | 43.50 | 41 | | 84.50 | 109 |
| 3320     Type MC cable | | 8 | 1 | | 77.50 | 45.50 | | 123 | 154 |
| 3330     EMT & wire | | 4 | 2 | | 57 | 91 | | 148 | 199 |
| 3350     S.P. switch/20 amp recpt., #12/2, type NM cable | | 10 | .800 | | 35 | 36.50 | | 71.50 | 93 |
| 3370     Type MC cable | | 8.89 | .900 | | 42 | 41 | | 83 | 107 |
| 3380     EMT & wire | ↓ | 4.10 | 1.951 | ↓ | 56 | 89 | | 145 | 194 |
| 3400   Decorator style | | | | | | | | | |
| 3410     S.P. switch/15 amp recpt., type NM cable | 1 Elec | 11.43 | .700 | Ea. | 26 | 32 | | 58 | 76.50 |
| 3420     Type MC cable | | 10 | .800 | | 42 | 36.50 | | 78.50 | 101 |
| 3430     EMT & wire | | 4.40 | 1.818 | | 47.50 | 83 | | 130.50 | 175 |
| 3450     S.P. switch/pilot light, type NM cable | | 11.43 | .700 | | 27 | 32 | | 59 | 77 |
| 3470     Type MC cable | | 10 | .800 | | 42.50 | 36.50 | | 79 | 102 |
| 3480     EMT & wire | | 4.40 | 1.818 | | 48 | 83 | | 131 | 176 |
| 3500     2-S.P. switches, 2-#14/2, type NM cables | | 10 | .800 | | 32 | 36.50 | | 68.50 | 89.50 |
| 3520     Type MC cable | | 8.89 | .900 | | 56 | 41 | | 97 | 123 |
| 3530     EMT & wire | | 4.10 | 1.951 | | 52.50 | 89 | | 141.50 | 190 |
| 3550     3-way/15 amp recpt., #14/3, type NM cable | | 10 | .800 | | 35 | 36.50 | | 71.50 | 93 |
| 3570     Type MC cable | | 8.89 | .900 | | 56 | 41 | | 97 | 123 |
| 3580     EMT & wire | | 4.10 | 1.951 | | 53 | 89 | | 142 | 190 |
| 3650     2-3 way switches, 2-#14/3, type NM cables | | 8.89 | .900 | | 47.50 | 41 | | 88.50 | 114 |
| 3670     Type MC cable | | 8 | 1 | | 82 | 45.50 | | 127.50 | 158 |
| 3680     EMT & wire | | 4 | 2 | | 61.50 | 91 | | 152.50 | 204 |
| 3700     S.P. switch/20 amp recpt., #12/2, type NM cable | ↓ | 10 | .800 | | 39.50 | 36.50 | | 76 | 98 |

| 26 05 90.10 Residential Wiring | Crew | Daily Output | Labor-Hours | Unit | Material | 2008 Bare Costs Labor | Equipment | Total | Total Incl O&P |
|---|---|---|---|---|---|---|---|---|---|
| 3720      Type MC cable | 1 Elec | 8.89 | .900 | Ea. | 46.50 | 41 | | 87.50 | 112 |
| 3730      EMT & wire | ↓ | 4.10 | 1.951 | ↓ | 60 | 89 | | 149 | 198 |
| 4000  Receptacle devices | | | | | | | | | |
| 4010     Duplex outlet, 15 amp recpt., Ivory, 1-gang box, plate | | | | | | | | | |
| 4015        Type NM cable | 1 Elec | 14.55 | .550 | Ea. | 10.05 | 25 | | 35.05 | 48.50 |
| 4020        Type MC cable | | 12.31 | .650 | | 26 | 29.50 | | 55.50 | 72.50 |
| 4030        EMT & wire | | 5.33 | 1.501 | | 29.50 | 68.50 | | 98 | 134 |
| 4050       With #12/2, type NM cable | | 12.31 | .650 | | 13.50 | 29.50 | | 43 | 59 |
| 4070        Type MC cable | | 10.67 | .750 | | 26 | 34 | | 60 | 79.50 |
| 4080        EMT & wire | | 4.71 | 1.699 | | 34 | 77.50 | | 111.50 | 153 |
| 4100       20 amp recpt., #12/2, type NM cable | | 12.31 | .650 | | 22 | 29.50 | | 51.50 | 68 |
| 4120        Type MC cable | | 10.67 | .750 | | 34.50 | 34 | | 68.50 | 89 |
| 4130        EMT & wire | ↓ | 4.71 | 1.699 | ↓ | 42.50 | 77.50 | | 120 | 162 |
| 4140       For GFI see Div. 26 05 90.10 line 4300 below | | | | | | | | | |
| 4150     Decorator style, 15 amp recpt., type NM cable | 1 Elec | 14.55 | .550 | Ea. | 14.35 | 25 | | 39.35 | 53.50 |
| 4170        Type MC cable | | 12.31 | .650 | | 30 | 29.50 | | 59.50 | 77 |
| 4180        EMT & wire | | 5.33 | 1.501 | | 33.50 | 68.50 | | 102 | 139 |
| 4200       With #12/2, type NM cable | | 12.31 | .650 | | 17.85 | 29.50 | | 47.35 | 63.50 |
| 4220        Type MC cable | | 10.67 | .750 | | 30.50 | 34 | | 64.50 | 84.50 |
| 4230        EMT & wire | | 4.71 | 1.699 | | 38.50 | 77.50 | | 116 | 158 |
| 4250       20 amp recpt. #12/2, type NM cable | | 12.31 | .650 | | 26.50 | 29.50 | | 56 | 73 |
| 4270        Type MC cable | | 10.67 | .750 | | 39 | 34 | | 73 | 94 |
| 4280        EMT & wire | | 4.71 | 1.699 | | 47 | 77.50 | | 124.50 | 167 |
| 4300       GFI, 15 amp recpt., type NM cable | | 12.31 | .650 | | 41.50 | 29.50 | | 71 | 89.50 |
| 4320        Type MC cable | | 10.67 | .750 | | 57 | 34 | | 91 | 114 |
| 4330        EMT & wire | | 4.71 | 1.699 | | 60.50 | 77.50 | | 138 | 182 |
| 4350       GFI with #12/2, type NM cable | | 10.67 | .750 | | 45 | 34 | | 79 | 100 |
| 4370        Type MC cable | | 9.20 | .870 | | 57.50 | 39.50 | | 97 | 122 |
| 4380        EMT & wire | | 4.21 | 1.900 | | 65.50 | 86.50 | | 152 | 201 |
| 4400       20 amp recpt., #12/2 type NM cable | | 10.67 | .750 | | 46.50 | 34 | | 80.50 | 102 |
| 4420        Type MC cable | | 9.20 | .870 | | 59 | 39.50 | | 98.50 | 124 |
| 4430        EMT & wire | | 4.21 | 1.900 | | 67.50 | 86.50 | | 154 | 203 |
| 4500     Weather-proof cover for above receptacles, add | ↓ | 32 | .250 | ↓ | 4.55 | 11.40 | | 15.95 | 22 |
| 4550     Air conditioner outlet, 20 amp-240 volt recpt. | | | | | | | | | |
| 4560       30' of #12/2, 2 pole circuit breaker | | | | | | | | | |
| 4570        Type NM cable | 1 Elec | 10 | .800 | Ea. | 60.50 | 36.50 | | 97 | 121 |
| 4580        Type MC cable | | 9 | .889 | | 76 | 40.50 | | 116.50 | 144 |
| 4590        EMT & wire | | 4 | 2 | | 81 | 91 | | 172 | 225 |
| 4600       Decorator style, type NM cable | | 10 | .800 | | 65 | 36.50 | | 101.50 | 126 |
| 4620        Type MC cable | | 9 | .889 | | 80.50 | 40.50 | | 121 | 149 |
| 4630        EMT & wire | ↓ | 4 | 2 | ↓ | 85.50 | 91 | | 176.50 | 230 |
| 4650     Dryer outlet, 30 amp-240 volt recpt., 20' of #10/3 | | | | | | | | | |
| 4660       2 pole circuit breaker | | | | | | | | | |
| 4670        Type NM cable | 1 Elec | 6.41 | 1.248 | Ea. | 73 | 57 | | 130 | 165 |
| 4680        Type MC cable | | 5.71 | 1.401 | | 80.50 | 64 | | 144.50 | 184 |
| 4690        EMT & wire | ↓ | 3.48 | 2.299 | ↓ | 81.50 | 105 | | 186.50 | 246 |
| 4700     Range outlet, 50 amp-240 volt recpt., 30' of #8/3 | | | | | | | | | |
| 4710        Type NM cable | 1 Elec | 4.21 | 1.900 | Ea. | 107 | 86.50 | | 193.50 | 247 |
| 4720        Type MC cable | | 4 | 2 | | 189 | 91 | | 280 | 345 |
| 4730        EMT & wire | | 2.96 | 2.703 | | 111 | 123 | | 234 | 305 |
| 4750     Central vacuum outlet, Type NM cable | | 6.40 | 1.250 | | 68 | 57 | | 125 | 160 |
| 4770        Type MC cable | | 5.71 | 1.401 | | 91 | 64 | | 155 | 195 |
| 4780        EMT & wire | ↓ | 3.48 | 2.299 | ↓ | 87.50 | 105 | | 192.50 | 253 |

| 26 05 90.10 Residential Wiring | Crew | Daily Output | Labor-Hours | Unit | Material | 2008 Bare Costs Labor | Equipment | Total | Total Incl O&P |
|---|---|---|---|---|---|---|---|---|---|
| 4800 | 30 amp-110 volt locking recpt., #10/2 circ. bkr. | | | | | | | | | |
| 4810 | Type NM cable | 1 Elec | 6.20 | 1.290 | Ea. | 78.50 | 59 | | 137.50 | 174 |
| 4820 | Type MC cable | | 5.40 | 1.481 | | 107 | 67.50 | | 174.50 | 219 |
| 4830 | EMT & wire | ↓ | 3.20 | 2.500 | ↓ | 101 | 114 | | 215 | 281 |
| 4900 | Low voltage outlets | | | | | | | | | |
| 4910 | Telephone recpt., 20' of 4/C phone wire | 1 Elec | 26 | .308 | Ea. | 10 | 14 | | 24 | 32 |
| 4920 | TV recpt., 20' of RG59U coax wire, F type connector | " | 16 | .500 | " | 18 | 23 | | 41 | 54 |
| 4950 | Door bell chime, transformer, 2 buttons, 60' of bellwire | | | | | | | | | |
| 4970 | Economy model | 1 Elec | 11.50 | .696 | Ea. | 64 | 31.50 | | 95.50 | 118 |
| 4980 | Custom model | ↓ | 11.50 | .696 | | 98 | 31.50 | | 129.50 | 155 |
| 4990 | Luxury model, 3 buttons | ↓ | 9.50 | .842 | ↓ | 254 | 38.50 | | 292.50 | 335 |
| 6000 | Lighting outlets | | | | | | | | | |
| 6050 | Wire only (for fixture), type NM cable | 1 Elec | 32 | .250 | Ea. | 8.40 | 11.40 | | 19.80 | 26 |
| 6070 | Type MC cable | | 24 | .333 | | 18.20 | 15.20 | | 33.40 | 42.50 |
| 6080 | EMT & wire | | 10 | .800 | | 20 | 36.50 | | 56.50 | 76.50 |
| 6100 | Box (4"), and wire (for fixture), type NM cable | | 25 | .320 | | 16.80 | 14.60 | | 31.40 | 40 |
| 6120 | Type MC cable | | 20 | .400 | | 26.50 | 18.20 | | 44.70 | 56.50 |
| 6130 | EMT & wire | ↓ | 11 | .727 | ↓ | 28.50 | 33 | | 61.50 | 81 |
| 6200 | Fixtures (use with lines 6050 or 6100 above) | | | | | | | | | |
| 6210 | Canopy style, economy grade | 1 Elec | 40 | .200 | Ea. | 28.50 | 9.10 | | 37.60 | 45 |
| 6220 | Custom grade | | 40 | .200 | | 50 | 9.10 | | 59.10 | 68.50 |
| 6250 | Dining room chandelier, economy grade | | 19 | .421 | | 81 | 19.20 | | 100.20 | 118 |
| 6260 | Custom grade | | 19 | .421 | | 239 | 19.20 | | 258.20 | 292 |
| 6270 | Luxury grade | | 15 | .533 | | 530 | 24.50 | | 554.50 | 620 |
| 6310 | Kitchen fixture (fluorescent), economy grade | | 30 | .267 | | 60 | 12.15 | | 72.15 | 84 |
| 6320 | Custom grade | | 25 | .320 | | 165 | 14.60 | | 179.60 | 204 |
| 6350 | Outdoor, wall mounted, economy grade | | 30 | .267 | | 29 | 12.15 | | 41.15 | 50 |
| 6360 | Custom grade | | 30 | .267 | | 106 | 12.15 | | 118.15 | 135 |
| 6370 | Luxury grade | | 25 | .320 | | 240 | 14.60 | | 254.60 | 286 |
| 6410 | Outdoor PAR floodlights, 1 lamp, 150 watt | | 20 | .400 | | 30 | 18.20 | | 48.20 | 60 |
| 6420 | 2 lamp, 150 watt each | | 20 | .400 | | 48 | 18.20 | | 66.20 | 80 |
| 6430 | For infrared security sensor, add | | 32 | .250 | | 92 | 11.40 | | 103.40 | 118 |
| 6450 | Outdoor, quartz-halogen, 300 watt flood | | 20 | .400 | | 40 | 18.20 | | 58.20 | 71 |
| 6600 | Recessed downlight, round, pre-wired, 50 or 75 watt trim | | 30 | .267 | | 39.50 | 12.15 | | 51.65 | 61.50 |
| 6610 | With shower light trim | | 30 | .267 | | 49 | 12.15 | | 61.15 | 72 |
| 6620 | With wall washer trim | | 28 | .286 | | 58.50 | 13 | | 71.50 | 84 |
| 6630 | With eye-ball trim | ↓ | 28 | .286 | | 58.50 | 13 | | 71.50 | 84 |
| 6640 | For direct contact with insulation, add | | | | | 2 | | | 2 | 2.20 |
| 6700 | Porcelain lamp holder | 1 Elec | 40 | .200 | | 3.95 | 9.10 | | 13.05 | 17.90 |
| 6710 | With pull switch | | 40 | .200 | | 4.53 | 9.10 | | 13.63 | 18.55 |
| 6750 | Fluorescent strip, 1-20 watt tube, wrap around diffuser, 24" | | 24 | .333 | | 53 | 15.20 | | 68.20 | 81 |
| 6760 | 1-40 watt tube, 48" | | 24 | .333 | | 65 | 15.20 | | 80.20 | 94 |
| 6770 | 2-40 watt tubes, 48" | | 20 | .400 | | 79 | 18.20 | | 97.20 | 114 |
| 6780 | With residential ballast | | 20 | .400 | | 89.50 | 18.20 | | 107.70 | 126 |
| 6800 | Bathroom heat lamp, 1-250 watt | | 28 | .286 | | 45 | 13 | | 58 | 69 |
| 6810 | 2-250 watt lamps | ↓ | 28 | .286 | ↓ | 70 | 13 | | 83 | 96.50 |
| 6820 | For timer switch, see Div. 26 05 90.10 line 2400 | | | | | | | | | |
| 6900 | Outdoor post lamp, incl. post, fixture, 35' of #14/2 | | | | | | | | | |
| 6910 | Type NMC cable | 1 Elec | 3.50 | 2.286 | Ea. | 202 | 104 | | 306 | 380 |
| 6920 | Photo-eye, add | | 27 | .296 | | 32 | 13.50 | | 45.50 | 55 |
| 6950 | Clock dial time switch, 24 hr., w/enclosure, type NM cable | | 11.43 | .700 | | 59.50 | 32 | | 91.50 | 113 |
| 6970 | Type MC cable | | 11 | .727 | | 75.50 | 33 | | 108.50 | 133 |
| 6980 | EMT & wire | ↓ | 4.85 | 1.649 | ↓ | 79 | 75 | | 154 | 199 |

| 26 05 90.10 Residential Wiring | | Crew | Daily Output | Labor-Hours | Unit | Material | 2008 Bare Costs Labor | Equipment | Total | Total Incl O&P |
|---|---|---|---|---|---|---|---|---|---|---|
| 7000 | Alarm systems | | | | | | | | | |
| 7050 | Smoke detectors, box, #14/3, type NM cable | 1 Elec | 14.55 | .550 | Ea. | 35 | 25 | | 60 | 76 |
| 7070 | Type MC cable | | 12.31 | .650 | | 50 | 29.50 | | 79.50 | 99 |
| 7080 | EMT & wire | | 5 | 1.600 | | 47 | 73 | | 120 | 161 |
| 7090 | For relay output to security system, add | | | | | 12.90 | | | 12.90 | 14.20 |
| 8000 | Residential equipment | | | | | | | | | |
| 8050 | Disposal hook-up, incl. switch, outlet box, 3' of flex | | | | | | | | | |
| 8060 | 20 amp-1 pole circ. bkr., and 25' of #12/2 | | | | | | | | | |
| 8070 | Type NM cable | 1 Elec | 10 | .800 | Ea. | 32.50 | 36.50 | | 69 | 90.50 |
| 8080 | Type MC cable | | 8 | 1 | | 46.50 | 45.50 | | 92 | 120 |
| 8090 | EMT & wire | | 5 | 1.600 | | 55.50 | 73 | | 128.50 | 170 |
| 8100 | Trash compactor or dishwasher hook-up, incl. outlet box, | | | | | | | | | |
| 8110 | 3' of flex, 15 amp-1 pole circ. bkr., and 25' of #14/2 | | | | | | | | | |
| 8120 | Type NM cable | 1 Elec | 10 | .800 | Ea. | 23.50 | 36.50 | | 60 | 80.50 |
| 8130 | Type MC cable | | 8 | 1 | | 42 | 45.50 | | 87.50 | 114 |
| 8140 | EMT & wire | | 5 | 1.600 | | 47 | 73 | | 120 | 161 |
| 8150 | Hot water sink dispenser hook-up, use line 8100 | | | | | | | | | |
| 8200 | Vent/exhaust fan hook-up, type NM cable | 1 Elec | 32 | .250 | Ea. | 8.40 | 11.40 | | 19.80 | 26 |
| 8220 | Type MC cable | | 24 | .333 | | 18.20 | 15.20 | | 33.40 | 42.50 |
| 8230 | EMT & wire | | 10 | .800 | | 20 | 36.50 | | 56.50 | 76.50 |
| 8250 | Bathroom vent fan, 50 CFM (use with above hook-up) | | | | | | | | | |
| 8260 | Economy model | 1 Elec | 15 | .533 | Ea. | 22.50 | 24.50 | | 47 | 61 |
| 8270 | Low noise model | | 15 | .533 | | 32 | 24.50 | | 56.50 | 71 |
| 8280 | Custom model | | 12 | .667 | | 117 | 30.50 | | 147.50 | 174 |
| 8300 | Bathroom or kitchen vent fan, 110 CFM | | | | | | | | | |
| 8310 | Economy model | 1 Elec | 15 | .533 | Ea. | 60.50 | 24.50 | | 85 | 103 |
| 8320 | Low noise model | " | 15 | .533 | " | 79 | 24.50 | | 103.50 | 123 |
| 8350 | Paddle fan, variable speed (w/o lights) | | | | | | | | | |
| 8360 | Economy model (AC motor) | 1 Elec | 10 | .800 | Ea. | 105 | 36.50 | | 141.50 | 171 |
| 8370 | Custom model (AC motor) | | 10 | .800 | | 182 | 36.50 | | 218.50 | 255 |
| 8380 | Luxury model (DC motor) | | 8 | 1 | | 360 | 45.50 | | 405.50 | 465 |
| 8390 | Remote speed switch for above, add | | 12 | .667 | | 26 | 30.50 | | 56.50 | 73.50 |
| 8500 | Whole house exhaust fan, ceiling mount, 36", variable speed | | | | | | | | | |
| 8510 | Remote switch, incl. shutters, 20 amp-1 pole circ. bkr. | | | | | | | | | |
| 8520 | 30' of #12/2, type NM cable | 1 Elec | 4 | 2 | Ea. | 860 | 91 | | 951 | 1,075 |
| 8530 | Type MC cable | | 3.50 | 2.286 | | 875 | 104 | | 979 | 1,125 |
| 8540 | EMT & wire | | 3 | 2.667 | | 885 | 121 | | 1,006 | 1,150 |
| 8600 | Whirlpool tub hook-up, incl. timer switch, outlet box | | | | | | | | | |
| 8610 | 3' of flex, 20 amp-1 pole GFI circ. bkr. | | | | | | | | | |
| 8620 | 30' of #12/2, type NM cable | 1 Elec | 5 | 1.600 | Ea. | 121 | 73 | | 194 | 242 |
| 8630 | Type MC cable | | 4.20 | 1.905 | | 129 | 87 | | 216 | 271 |
| 8640 | EMT & wire | | 3.40 | 2.353 | | 137 | 107 | | 244 | 310 |
| 8650 | Hot water heater hook-up, incl. 1-2 pole circ. bkr., box; | | | | | | | | | |
| 8660 | 3' of flex, 20' of #10/2, type NM cable | 1 Elec | 5 | 1.600 | Ea. | 35 | 73 | | 108 | 148 |
| 8670 | Type MC cable | | 4.20 | 1.905 | | 56 | 87 | | 143 | 191 |
| 8680 | EMT & wire | | 3.40 | 2.353 | | 50 | 107 | | 157 | 215 |
| 9000 | Heating/air conditioning | | | | | | | | | |
| 9050 | Furnace/boiler hook-up, incl. firestat, local on-off switch | | | | | | | | | |
| 9060 | Emergency switch, and 40' of type NM cable | 1 Elec | 4 | 2 | Ea. | 55.50 | 91 | | 146.50 | 197 |
| 9070 | Type MC cable | | 3.50 | 2.286 | | 80 | 104 | | 184 | 243 |
| 9080 | EMT & wire | | 1.50 | 5.333 | | 86.50 | 243 | | 329.50 | 455 |
| 9100 | Air conditioner hook-up, incl. local 60 amp disc. switch | | | | | | | | | |
| 9110 | 3' sealtite, 40 amp, 2 pole circuit breaker | | | | | | | | | |

# 26 05 Common Work Results for Electrical

## 26 05 90 – Residential Applications

### 26 05 90.10 Residential Wiring

| | | Crew | Daily Output | Labor-Hours | Unit | Material | 2008 Bare Costs Labor | Equipment | Total | Total Incl O&P |
|---|---|---|---|---|---|---|---|---|---|---|
| 9130 | 40' of #8/2, type NM cable | 1 Elec | 3.50 | 2.286 | Ea. | 216 | 104 | | 320 | 395 |
| 9140 | Type MC cable | | 3 | 2.667 | | 340 | 121 | | 461 | 555 |
| 9150 | EMT & wire | ↓ | 1.30 | 6.154 | ↓ | 244 | 280 | | 524 | 690 |
| 9200 | Heat pump hook-up, 1-40 & 1-100 amp 2 pole circ. bkr. | | | | | | | | | |
| 9210 | Local disconnect switch, 3' sealtite | | | | | | | | | |
| 9220 | 40' of #8/2 & 30' of #3/2 | | | | | | | | | |
| 9230 | Type NM cable | 1 Elec | 1.30 | 6.154 | Ea. | 575 | 280 | | 855 | 1,050 |
| 9240 | Type MC cable | | 1.08 | 7.407 | | 835 | 335 | | 1,170 | 1,425 |
| 9250 | EMT & wire | ↓ | .94 | 8.511 | ↓ | 615 | 390 | | 1,005 | 1,250 |
| 9500 | Thermostat hook-up, using low voltage wire | | | | | | | | | |
| 9520 | Heating only, 25' of #18-3 | 1 Elec | 24 | .333 | Ea. | 6.80 | 15.20 | | 22 | 30 |
| 9530 | Heating/cooling, 25' of #18-4 | " | 20 | .400 | " | 8.10 | 18.20 | | 26.30 | 36 |

# 26 09 Instrumentation and Control for Electrical Systems

## 26 09 13 – Electrical Power Monitoring and Control

### 26 09 13.10 Switchboard Instruments

| | | Crew | Daily Output | Labor-Hours | Unit | Material | 2008 Bare Costs Labor | Equipment | Total | Total Incl O&P |
|---|---|---|---|---|---|---|---|---|---|---|
| 0010 | **SWITCHBOARD INSTRUMENTS** 3 phase, 4 wire | | | | | | | | | |
| 0100 | AC indicating, ammeter & switch | 1 Elec | 8 | 1 | Ea. | 1,775 | 45.50 | | 1,820.50 | 2,050 |
| 0200 | Voltmeter & switch | | 8 | 1 | | 1,950 | 45.50 | | 1,995.50 | 2,225 |
| 0300 | Wattmeter | | 8 | 1 | | 3,875 | 45.50 | | 3,920.50 | 4,325 |
| 0400 | AC recording, ammeter | | 4 | 2 | | 6,900 | 91 | | 6,991 | 7,700 |
| 0500 | Voltmeter | | 4 | 2 | | 6,900 | 91 | | 6,991 | 7,700 |
| 0600 | Ground fault protection, zero sequence | | 2.70 | 2.963 | | 6,075 | 135 | | 6,210 | 6,900 |
| 0700 | Ground return path | | 2.70 | 2.963 | | 6,075 | 135 | | 6,210 | 6,900 |
| 0800 | 3 current transformers, 5 to 800 amp | | 2 | 4 | | 2,825 | 182 | | 3,007 | 3,400 |
| 0900 | 1000 to 1500 amp | | 1.30 | 6.154 | | 4,075 | 280 | | 4,355 | 4,900 |
| 1200 | 2000 to 4000 amp | | 1 | 8 | | 4,800 | 365 | | 5,165 | 5,825 |
| 1300 | Fused potential transformer, maximum 600 volt | ↓ | 8 | 1 | ↓ | 1,075 | 45.50 | | 1,120.50 | 1,250 |

# 26 12 Medium-Voltage Transformers

## 26 12 19 – Pad-Mounted, Liquid-Filled, Medium-Voltage Transformers

### 26 12 19.10 Transformer, Oil-Filled

| | | Crew | Daily Output | Labor-Hours | Unit | Material | 2008 Bare Costs Labor | Equipment | Total | Total Incl O&P |
|---|---|---|---|---|---|---|---|---|---|---|
| 0010 | **TRANSFORMER, OIL-FILLED** primary delta or Y, | | | | | | | | | |
| 0050 | Pad mounted 5 kV or 15 kV, with taps, 277/480 V secondary, 3 phase | | | | | | | | | |
| 0100 | 150 kVA | R-3 | .65 | 30.769 | Ea. | 8,575 | 1,375 | 199 | 10,149 | 11,700 |
| 0200 | 300 kVA | | .45 | 44.444 | | 11,200 | 2,000 | 288 | 13,488 | 15,600 |
| 0300 | 500 kVA | | .40 | 50 | | 17,200 | 2,250 | 325 | 19,775 | 22,600 |
| 0400 | 750 kVA | | .38 | 52.632 | | 20,400 | 2,350 | 340 | 23,090 | 26,400 |
| 0500 | 1000 kVA | | .26 | 76.923 | | 24,200 | 3,450 | 500 | 28,150 | 32,300 |
| 0600 | 1500 kVA | | .23 | 86.957 | | 28,800 | 3,900 | 565 | 33,265 | 38,000 |
| 0700 | 2000 kVA | | .20 | 100 | | 36,300 | 4,475 | 645 | 41,420 | 47,400 |
| 0800 | 3750 kVA | ↓ | .16 | 125 | ↓ | 68,000 | 5,600 | 810 | 74,410 | 84,500 |

# 26 22 Low-Voltage Transformers

## 26 22 13 – Low-Voltage Distribution Transformers

| 26 22 13.10 Transformer, Dry-Type | | Crew | Daily Output | Labor-Hours | Unit | Material | 2008 Bare Costs Labor | Equipment | Total | Total Incl O&P |
|---|---|---|---|---|---|---|---|---|---|---|
| 0010 | **TRANSFORMER, DRY-TYPE** | | | | | | | | | |
| 0050 | Single phase, 240/480 volt primary, 120/240 volt secondary | | | | | | | | | |
| 0100 | 1 kVA | 1 Elec | 2 | 4 | Ea. | 241 | 182 | | 423 | 535 |
| 0300 | 2 kVA | | 1.60 | 5 | | 360 | 228 | | 588 | 740 |
| 0500 | 3 kVA | | 1.40 | 5.714 | | 450 | 260 | | 710 | 885 |
| 0700 | 5 kVA | | 1.20 | 6.667 | | 620 | 305 | | 925 | 1,125 |
| 0900 | 7.5 kVA | 2 Elec | 2.20 | 7.273 | | 855 | 330 | | 1,185 | 1,450 |
| 1100 | 10 kVA | | 1.60 | 10 | | 1,100 | 455 | | 1,555 | 1,875 |
| 1300 | 15 kVA | | 1.20 | 13.333 | | 1,500 | 605 | | 2,105 | 2,550 |
| 1500 | 25 kVA | CN | 1 | 16 | | 2,050 | 730 | | 2,780 | 3,325 |
| 1700 | 37.5 kVA | | .80 | 20 | | 2,650 | 910 | | 3,560 | 4,275 |
| 1900 | 50 kVA | | .70 | 22.857 | | 3,150 | 1,050 | | 4,200 | 5,000 |
| 2100 | 75 kVA | | .65 | 24.615 | | 4,175 | 1,125 | | 5,300 | 6,250 |
| 2190 | 480V primary 120/240V secondary, nonvent., 15 kVA | | 1.20 | 13.333 | | 1,525 | 605 | | 2,130 | 2,575 |
| 2200 | 25 kVA | | .90 | 17.778 | | 2,225 | 810 | | 3,035 | 3,650 |
| 2210 | 37 kVA | | .75 | 21.333 | | 2,650 | 970 | | 3,620 | 4,375 |
| 2220 | 50 kVA | | .65 | 24.615 | | 3,150 | 1,125 | | 4,275 | 5,125 |
| 2300 | 3 phase, 480 volt primary 120/208 volt secondary | | | | | | | | | |
| 2310 | Ventilated, 3 kVA | 1 Elec | 1 | 8 | Ea. | 835 | 365 | | 1,200 | 1,450 |
| 2700 | 6 kVA | | .80 | 10 | | 1,150 | 455 | | 1,605 | 1,925 |
| 2900 | 9 kVA | | .70 | 11.429 | | 1,300 | 520 | | 1,820 | 2,200 |
| 3100 | 15 kVA | 2 Elec | 1.10 | 14.545 | | 1,725 | 665 | | 2,390 | 2,875 |
| 3300 | 30 kVA | | .90 | 17.778 | | 2,025 | 810 | | 2,835 | 3,425 |
| 3500 | 45 kVA | | .80 | 20 | | 2,450 | 910 | | 3,360 | 4,025 |
| 3700 | 75 kVA | | .70 | 22.857 | | 3,675 | 1,050 | | 4,725 | 5,575 |
| 3900 | 112.5 kVA | R-3 | .90 | 22.222 | | 4,875 | 995 | 144 | 6,014 | 7,000 |
| 4100 | 150 kVA | | .85 | 23.529 | | 6,350 | 1,050 | 152 | 7,552 | 8,750 |
| 4300 | 225 kVA | | .65 | 30.769 | | 8,625 | 1,375 | 199 | 10,199 | 11,800 |
| 4500 | 300 kVA | | .55 | 36.364 | | 10,900 | 1,625 | 235 | 12,760 | 14,700 |
| 4700 | 500 kVA | | .45 | 44.444 | | 18,000 | 2,000 | 288 | 20,288 | 23,200 |
| 4800 | 750 kVA | | .35 | 57.143 | | 31,700 | 2,550 | 370 | 34,620 | 39,000 |

# 26 24 Switchboards and Panelboards

## 26 24 13 – Switchboards

### 26 24 13.10 Incoming Switchboards

| | | Crew | Daily Output | Labor-Hours | Unit | Material | Labor | Equipment | Total | Total Incl O&P |
|---|---|---|---|---|---|---|---|---|---|---|
| 0010 | **INCOMING SWITCHBOARDS** main service section | | | | | | | | | |
| 0100 | Aluminum bus bars, not including CT's or PT's | | | | | | | | | |
| 0200 | No main disconnect, includes CT compartment | | | | | | | | | |
| 0300 | 120/208 volt, 4 wire, 600 amp | 2 Elec | 1 | 16 | Ea. | 3,925 | 730 | | 4,655 | 5,400 |
| 0400 | 800 amp | | .88 | 18.182 | | 3,925 | 830 | | 4,755 | 5,550 |
| 0500 | 1000 amp | | .80 | 20 | | 4,725 | 910 | | 5,635 | 6,525 |
| 0600 | 1200 amp | | .72 | 22.222 | | 4,725 | 1,000 | | 5,725 | 6,675 |
| 0700 | 1600 amp | | .66 | 24.242 | | 4,725 | 1,100 | | 5,825 | 6,825 |
| 0800 | 2000 amp | | .62 | 25.806 | | 5,075 | 1,175 | | 6,250 | 7,325 |
| 1000 | 3000 amp | | .56 | 28.571 | | 6,700 | 1,300 | | 8,000 | 9,325 |
| 2000 | Fused switch & CT compartment | | | | | | | | | |
| 2100 | 120/208 volt, 4 wire, 400 amp | 2 Elec | 1.12 | 14.286 | Ea. | 3,775 | 650 | | 4,425 | 5,125 |
| 2200 | 600 amp | | .94 | 17.021 | | 4,475 | 775 | | 5,250 | 6,050 |
| 2300 | 800 amp | | .84 | 19.048 | | 10,600 | 870 | | 11,470 | 13,000 |
| 2400 | 1200 amp | | .68 | 23.529 | | 13,800 | 1,075 | | 14,875 | 16,800 |
| 2900 | Pressure switch & CT compartment | | | | | | | | | |

# 26 24 Switchboards and Panelboards

## 26 24 13 – Switchboards

### 26 24 13.10 Incoming Switchboards

| | | Crew | Daily Output | Labor-Hours | Unit | Material | 2008 Bare Costs Labor | 2008 Bare Costs Equipment | Total | Total Incl O&P |
|---|---|---|---|---|---|---|---|---|---|---|
| 3000 | 120/208 volt, 4 wire, 800 amp | 2 Elec | .80 | 20 | Ea. | 9,525 | 910 | | 10,435 | 11,900 |
| 3100 | 1200 amp | | .66 | 24.242 | | 18,500 | 1,100 | | 19,600 | 22,000 |
| 3200 | 1600 amp | | .62 | 25.806 | | 19,600 | 1,175 | | 20,775 | 23,400 |
| 3300 | 2000 amp | | .56 | 28.571 | | 20,900 | 1,300 | | 22,200 | 24,900 |
| 4400 | Circuit breaker, molded case & CT compartment | | | | | | | | | |
| 4600 | 3 pole, 4 wire, 600 amp | 2 Elec | .94 | 17.021 | Ea. | 8,225 | 775 | | 9,000 | 10,200 |
| 4800 | 800 amp | | .84 | 19.048 | | 9,825 | 870 | | 10,695 | 12,100 |
| 5000 | 1200 amp | | .68 | 23.529 | | 13,400 | 1,075 | | 14,475 | 16,300 |
| 5100 | Copper bus bars, not incl. CT's or PT's, add, minimum | | | | | 15% | | | | |

### 26 24 13.30 Distribution Switchboards Section

| | | Crew | Daily Output | Labor-Hours | Unit | Material | 2008 Bare Costs Labor | 2008 Bare Costs Equipment | Total | Total Incl O&P |
|---|---|---|---|---|---|---|---|---|---|---|
| 0010 | **DISTRIBUTION SWITCHBOARDS SECTION** | | | | | | | | | |
| 0100 | Aluminum bus bars, not including breakers | | | | | | | | | |
| 0200 | 120/208 or 277/480 volt, 4 wire, 600 amp | 2 Elec | 1 | 16 | Ea. | 2,100 | 730 | | 2,830 | 3,375 |
| 0300 | 800 amp | | .88 | 18.182 | | 2,750 | 830 | | 3,580 | 4,250 |
| 0400 | 1000 amp | | .80 | 20 | | 2,750 | 910 | | 3,660 | 4,375 |
| 0500 | 1200 amp | | .72 | 22.222 | | 3,425 | 1,000 | | 4,425 | 5,275 |
| 0600 | 1600 amp | | .66 | 24.242 | | 3,925 | 1,100 | | 5,025 | 5,975 |
| 0700 | 2000 amp | | .62 | 25.806 | | 4,600 | 1,175 | | 5,775 | 6,800 |
| 0800 | 2500 amp | | .60 | 26.667 | | 5,200 | 1,225 | | 6,425 | 7,500 |
| 0900 | 3000 amp | | .56 | 28.571 | | 6,300 | 1,300 | | 7,600 | 8,875 |
| 0950 | 4000 amp | | .52 | 30.769 | | 9,200 | 1,400 | | 10,600 | 12,200 |

### 26 24 13.40 Switchboards Feeder Section

| | | Crew | Daily Output | Labor-Hours | Unit | Material | 2008 Bare Costs Labor | 2008 Bare Costs Equipment | Total | Total Incl O&P |
|---|---|---|---|---|---|---|---|---|---|---|
| 0010 | **SWITCHBOARDS FEEDER SECTION** group mounted devices | | | | | | | | | |
| 0030 | Circuit breakers | | | | | | | | | |
| 0160 | FA frame, 15 to 60 amp, 240 volt, 1 pole | 1 Elec | 8 | 1 | Ea. | 102 | 45.50 | | 147.50 | 181 |
| 0280 | FA frame, 70 to 100 amp, 240 volt, 1 pole | | 7 | 1.143 | | 135 | 52 | | 187 | 227 |
| 0420 | KA frame, 70 to 225 amp | | 3.20 | 2.500 | | 1,125 | 114 | | 1,239 | 1,425 |
| 0430 | LA frame, 125 to 400 amp | | 2.30 | 3.478 | | 2,550 | 158 | | 2,708 | 3,050 |
| 0460 | MA frame, 450 to 600 amp | | 1.60 | 5 | | 4,225 | 228 | | 4,453 | 5,000 |
| 0470 | 700 to 800 amp | | 1.30 | 6.154 | | 5,500 | 280 | | 5,780 | 6,450 |
| 0480 | MAL frame, 1000 amp | | 1 | 8 | | 5,700 | 365 | | 6,065 | 6,825 |
| 0490 | PA frame, 1200 amp | | .80 | 10 | | 11,600 | 455 | | 12,055 | 13,400 |
| 0500 | Branch circuit, fusible switch, 600 volt, double 30/30 amp | | 4 | 2 | | 1,125 | 91 | | 1,216 | 1,350 |
| 0550 | 60/60 amp | | 3.20 | 2.500 | | 1,125 | 114 | | 1,239 | 1,425 |
| 0600 | 100/100 amp | | 2.70 | 2.963 | | 1,575 | 135 | | 1,710 | 1,950 |
| 0650 | Single, 30 amp | | 5.30 | 1.509 | | 720 | 69 | | 789 | 890 |
| 0700 | 60 amp | | 4.70 | 1.702 | | 720 | 77.50 | | 797.50 | 905 |
| 0750 | 100 amp | | 4 | 2 | | 1,075 | 91 | | 1,166 | 1,300 |
| 0800 | 200 amp | | 2.70 | 2.963 | | 1,575 | 135 | | 1,710 | 1,925 |
| 0850 | 400 amp | | 2.30 | 3.478 | | 2,975 | 158 | | 3,133 | 3,500 |
| 0900 | 600 amp | | 1.80 | 4.444 | | 3,525 | 202 | | 3,727 | 4,175 |
| 0950 | 800 amp | | 1.30 | 6.154 | | 5,775 | 280 | | 6,055 | 6,775 |
| 1000 | 1200 amp | | .80 | 10 | | 6,875 | 455 | | 7,330 | 8,250 |

## 26 24 16 – Panelboards

### 26 24 16.20 Panelboard and Load Center Circuit Breakers

| | | Crew | Daily Output | Labor-Hours | Unit | Material | 2008 Bare Costs Labor | 2008 Bare Costs Equipment | Total | Total Incl O&P |
|---|---|---|---|---|---|---|---|---|---|---|
| 0010 | **PANELBOARD AND LOAD CENTER CIRCUIT BREAKERS** | | | | | | | | | |
| 0050 | Bolt-on, 10,000 amp IC, 120 volt, 1 pole | | | | | | | | | |
| 0100 | 15 to 50 amp | 1 Elec | 10 | .800 | Ea. | 15 | 36.50 | | 51.50 | 71 |
| 0200 | 60 amp | | 8 | 1 | | 15 | 45.50 | | 60.50 | 84.50 |
| 0300 | 70 amp | | 8 | 1 | | 28.50 | 45.50 | | 74 | 99.50 |
| 0350 | 240 volt, 2 pole | | | | | | | | | |
| 0400 | 15 to 50 amp | 1 Elec | 8 | 1 | Ea. | 33 | 45.50 | | 78.50 | 105 |

## 26 24 16 – Panelboards

| 26 24 16.20 Panelboard and Load Center Circuit Breakers | Crew | Daily Output | Labor-Hours | Unit | Material | 2008 Bare Costs Labor | Equipment | Total | Total Incl O&P |
|---|---|---|---|---|---|---|---|---|---|
| 0500 | 60 amp | 1 Elec | 7.50 | 1.067 | Ea. | 33 | 48.50 | | 81.50 | 109 |
| 0600 | 80 to 100 amp | | 5 | 1.600 | | 85 | 73 | | 158 | 202 |
| 0700 | 3 pole, 15 to 60 amp | | 6.20 | 1.290 | | 104 | 59 | | 163 | 203 |
| 0800 | 70 amp | | 5 | 1.600 | | 131 | 73 | | 204 | 253 |
| 0900 | 80 to 100 amp | | 3.60 | 2.222 | | 149 | 101 | | 250 | 315 |
| 1000 | 22,000 amp I.C., 240 volt, 2 pole, 70 - 225 amp | | 2.70 | 2.963 | | 640 | 135 | | 775 | 905 |
| 1100 | 3 pole, 70 - 225 amp | | 2.30 | 3.478 | | 715 | 158 | | 873 | 1,025 |
| 1200 | 14,000 amp I.C., 277 volts, 1 pole, 15 - 30 amp | | 8 | 1 | | 40 | 45.50 | | 85.50 | 112 |
| 1300 | 22,000 amp I.C., 480 volts, 2 pole, 70 - 225 amp | | 2.70 | 2.963 | | 640 | 135 | | 775 | 905 |
| 1400 | 3 pole, 70 - 225 amp | | 2.30 | 3.478 | | 795 | 158 | | 953 | 1,100 |

## 26 24 16.30 Panelboards Commercial Applications

| | 26 24 16.30 Panelboards Commercial Applications | Crew | Daily Output | Labor-Hours | Unit | Material | Labor | Equipment | Total | Total Incl O&P |
|---|---|---|---|---|---|---|---|---|---|---|
| 0010 | **PANELBOARDS COMMERCIAL APPLICATIONS** | | | | | | | | | |
| 0050 | NQOD, w/20 amp 1 pole bolt-on circuit breakers | | | | | | | | | |
| 0100 | 3 wire, 120/240 volts, 100 amp main lugs | | | | | | | | | |
| 0150 | 10 circuits | 1 Elec | 1 | 8 | Ea. | 470 | 365 | | 835 | 1,075 |
| 0200 | 14 circuits | | .88 | 9.091 | | 555 | 415 | | 970 | 1,225 |
| 0250 | 18 circuits | | .75 | 10.667 | | 605 | 485 | | 1,090 | 1,400 |
| 0300 | 20 circuits | | .65 | 12.308 | | 680 | 560 | | 1,240 | 1,575 |
| 0350 | 225 amp main lugs, 24 circuits | 2 Elec | 1.20 | 13.333 | | 775 | 605 | | 1,380 | 1,750 |
| 0400 | 30 circuits | | .90 | 17.778 | | 900 | 810 | | 1,710 | 2,200 |
| 0450 | 36 circuits | | .80 | 20 | | 1,025 | 910 | | 1,935 | 2,475 |
| 0500 | 38 circuits | | .72 | 22.222 | | 1,100 | 1,000 | | 2,100 | 2,725 |
| 0550 | 42 circuits | | .66 | 24.242 | | 1,150 | 1,100 | | 2,250 | 2,925 |
| 0600 | 4 wire, 120/208 volts, 100 amp main lugs, 12 circuits | 1 Elec | 1 | 8 | | 535 | 365 | | 900 | 1,125 |
| 0650 | 16 circuits | | .75 | 10.667 | | 615 | 485 | | 1,100 | 1,400 |
| 0700 | 20 circuits | | .65 | 12.308 | | 715 | 560 | | 1,275 | 1,625 |
| 0750 | 24 circuits | | .60 | 13.333 | | 775 | 605 | | 1,380 | 1,750 |
| 0800 | 30 circuits | | .53 | 15.094 | | 895 | 690 | | 1,585 | 2,000 |
| 0850 | 225 amp main lugs, 32 circuits | 2 Elec | .90 | 17.778 | | 1,000 | 810 | | 1,810 | 2,300 |
| 0900 | 34 circuits | | .84 | 19.048 | | 1,025 | 870 | | 1,895 | 2,425 |
| 0950 | 36 circuits | | .80 | 20 | | 1,050 | 910 | | 1,960 | 2,525 |
| 1000 | 42 circuits | | .68 | 23.529 | | 1,175 | 1,075 | | 2,250 | 2,900 |
| 1200 | NEHB, w/20 amp, 1 pole bolt-on circuit breakers | | | | | | | | | |
| 1250 | 4 wire, 277/480 volts, 100 amp main lugs, 12 circuits | 1 Elec | .88 | 9.091 | Ea. | 1,025 | 415 | | 1,440 | 1,750 |
| 1300 | 20 circuits | " | .60 | 13.333 | | 1,500 | 605 | | 2,105 | 2,550 |
| 1350 | 225 amp main lugs, 24 circuits | 2 Elec | .90 | 17.778 | | 1,750 | 810 | | 2,560 | 3,125 |
| 1400 | 30 circuits | | .80 | 20 | | 2,100 | 910 | | 3,010 | 3,650 |
| 1450 | 36 circuits | | .72 | 22.222 | | 2,450 | 1,000 | | 3,450 | 4,175 |
| 1600 | NQOD panel, w/20 amp, 1 pole, circuit breakers | | | | | | | | | |
| 1650 | 3 wire, 120/240 volt with main circuit breaker | | | | | | | | | |
| 1700 | 100 amp main, 12 circuits | 1 Elec | .80 | 10 | Ea. | 655 | 455 | | 1,110 | 1,400 |
| 1750 | 20 circuits | " | .60 | 13.333 | | 835 | 605 | | 1,440 | 1,825 |
| 1800 | 225 amp main, 30 circuits | 2 Elec | .68 | 23.529 | | 1,600 | 1,075 | | 2,675 | 3,375 |
| 1850 | 42 circuits | | .52 | 30.769 | | 1,850 | 1,400 | | 3,250 | 4,150 |
| 1900 | 400 amp main, 30 circuits | | .54 | 29.630 | | 2,225 | 1,350 | | 3,575 | 4,450 |
| 1950 | 42 circuits | | .50 | 32 | | 2,475 | 1,450 | | 3,925 | 4,900 |
| 2000 | 4 wire, 120/208 volts with main circuit breaker | | | | | | | | | |
| 2050 | 100 amp main, 24 circuits | 1 Elec | .47 | 17.021 | Ea. | 980 | 775 | | 1,755 | 2,225 |
| 2100 | 30 circuits | " | .40 | 20 | | 1,100 | 910 | | 2,010 | 2,575 |
| 2200 | 225 amp main, 32 circuits | 2 Elec | .72 | 22.222 | | 1,875 | 1,000 | | 2,875 | 3,550 |
| 2250 | 42 circuits | | .56 | 28.571 | | 2,050 | 1,300 | | 3,350 | 4,200 |
| 2300 | 400 amp main, 42 circuits | | .48 | 33.333 | | 2,750 | 1,525 | | 4,275 | 5,300 |

*CN*

# 26 24 Switchboards and Panelboards

## 26 24 16 – Panelboards

### 26 24 16.30 Panelboards Commercial Applications

| | | Crew | Daily Output | Labor-Hours | Unit | Material | 2008 Bare Costs Labor | Equipment | Total | Total Incl O&P |
|---|---|---|---|---|---|---|---|---|---|---|
| 2350 | 600 amp main, 42 circuits | 2 Elec | .40 | 40 | Ea. | 4,100 | 1,825 | | 5,925 | 7,225 |
| 2400 | NEHB, with 20 amp, 1 pole circuit breaker | | | | | | | | | |
| 2450 | 4 wire, 277/480 volts with main circuit breaker | | | | | | | | | |
| 2500 | 100 amp main, 24 circuits | 1 Elec | .42 | 19.048 | Ea. | 2,000 | 870 | | 2,870 | 3,500 |
| 2550 | 30 circuits | " | .38 | 21.053 | | 2,350 | 960 | | 3,310 | 4,025 |
| 2600 | 225 amp main, 30 circuits | 2 Elec | .72 | 22.222 | | 2,975 | 1,000 | | 3,975 | 4,775 |
| 2650 | 42 circuits | " | .56 | 28.571 | ↓ | 3,675 | 1,300 | | 4,975 | 5,975 |

## 26 24 19 – Motor-Control Centers

### 26 24 19.40 Motor Starters and Controls

| | | Crew | Daily Output | Labor-Hours | Unit | Material | 2008 Bare Costs Labor | Equipment | Total | Total Incl O&P |
|---|---|---|---|---|---|---|---|---|---|---|
| 0010 | **MOTOR STARTERS AND CONTROLS** | | | | | | | | | |
| 0050 | Magnetic, FVNR, with enclosure and heaters, 480 volt | | | | | | | | | |
| 0100 | 5 HP, size 0 | 1 Elec | 2.30 | 3.478 | Ea. | 238 | 158 | | 396 | 500 |
| 0200 | 10 HP, size 1 | " | 1.60 | 5 | | 268 | 228 | | 496 | 635 |
| 0300 | 25 HP, size 2 | 2 Elec | 2.20 | 7.273 | | 505 | 330 | | 835 | 1,050 |
| 0400 | 50 HP, size 3 | | 1.80 | 8.889 | | 820 | 405 | | 1,225 | 1,500 |
| 0500 | 100 HP, size 4 | | 1.20 | 13.333 | | 1,825 | 605 | | 2,430 | 2,900 |
| 0600 | 200 HP, size 5 | ↓ | .90 | 17.778 | | 4,250 | 810 | | 5,060 | 5,875 |
| 0700 | Combination, with motor circuit protectors, 5 HP, size 0 | 1 Elec | 1.80 | 4.444 | | 775 | 202 | | 977 | 1,150 |
| 0800 | 10 HP, size 1 | " | 1.30 | 6.154 | | 805 | 280 | | 1,085 | 1,300 |
| 0900 | 25 HP, size 2 | 2 Elec | 2 | 8 | | 1,125 | 365 | | 1,490 | 1,800 |
| 1000 | 50 HP, size 3 | | 1.32 | 12.121 | | 1,625 | 550 | | 2,175 | 2,625 |
| 1200 | 100 HP, size 4 | ↓ | .80 | 20 | | 3,525 | 910 | | 4,435 | 5,250 |
| 1400 | Combination, with fused switch, 5 HP, size 0 | 1 Elec | 1.80 | 4.444 | | 590 | 202 | | 792 | 950 |
| 1600 | 10 HP, size 1 | " | 1.30 | 6.154 | | 630 | 280 | | 910 | 1,125 |
| 1800 | 25 HP, size 2 | 2 Elec | 2 | 8 | | 1,025 | 365 | | 1,390 | 1,675 |
| 2000 | 50 HP, size 3 | | 1.32 | 12.121 | | 1,725 | 550 | | 2,275 | 2,725 |
| 2200 | 100 HP, size 4 | ↓ | .80 | 20 | ↓ | 3,025 | 910 | | 3,935 | 4,675 |

# 26 25 Enclosed Bus Assemblies

## 26 25 13 – Bus Duct/Busway and Fittings

### 26 25 13.40 Copper Bus Duct

| | | Crew | Daily Output | Labor-Hours | Unit | Material | 2008 Bare Costs Labor | Equipment | Total | Total Incl O&P |
|---|---|---|---|---|---|---|---|---|---|---|
| 0010 | **COPPER BUS DUCT** 10 ft. long | | | | | | | | | |
| 0050 | Indoor 3 pole 4 wire, plug-in, straight section, 225 amp | 2 Elec | 40 | .400 | L.F. | 182 | 18.20 | | 200.20 | 228 |
| 1000 | 400 amp | | 32 | .500 | | 182 | 23 | | 205 | 235 |
| 1500 | 600 amp | | 26 | .615 | | 182 | 28 | | 210 | 243 |
| 2400 | 800 amp | | 20 | .800 | | 217 | 36.50 | | 253.50 | 293 |
| 2450 | 1000 amp | | 18 | .889 | | 239 | 40.50 | | 279.50 | 325 |
| 2500 | 1350 amp | | 16 | 1 | | 340 | 45.50 | | 385.50 | 445 |
| 2510 | 1600 amp | | 12 | 1.333 | | 390 | 60.50 | | 450.50 | 515 |
| 2520 | 2000 amp | | 10 | 1.600 | | 490 | 73 | | 563 | 650 |
| 2550 | Feeder, 600 amp | | 28 | .571 | | 160 | 26 | | 186 | 215 |
| 2600 | 800 amp | | 22 | .727 | | 194 | 33 | | 227 | 263 |
| 2700 | 1000 amp | | 20 | .800 | | 217 | 36.50 | | 253.50 | 293 |
| 2800 | 1350 amp | | 18 | .889 | | 320 | 40.50 | | 360.50 | 410 |
| 2900 | 1600 amp | | 14 | 1.143 | | 365 | 52 | | 417 | 480 |
| 3000 | 2000 amp | | 12 | 1.333 | ↓ | 465 | 60.50 | | 525.50 | 605 |
| 3100 | Elbows, 225 amp | | 4 | 4 | Ea. | 1,075 | 182 | | 1,257 | 1,475 |
| 3200 | 400 amp | | 3.60 | 4.444 | | 1,075 | 202 | | 1,277 | 1,500 |
| 3300 | 600 amp | | 3.20 | 5 | | 1,075 | 228 | | 1,303 | 1,550 |
| 3400 | 800 amp | ↓ | 2.80 | 5.714 | | 1,175 | 260 | | 1,435 | 1,700 |

# 26 25 Enclosed Bus Assemblies

## 26 25 13 - Bus Duct/Busway and Fittings

| 26 25 13.40 Copper Bus Duct | | Crew | Daily Output | Labor-Hours | Unit | Material | 2008 Bare Costs | | | Total | Total Incl O&P |
|---|---|---|---|---|---|---|---|---|---|---|---|
| | | | | | | | Labor | Equipment | | | |
| 3500 | 1000 amp | 2 Elec | 2.60 | 6.154 | Ea. | 1,300 | 280 | | | 1,580 | 1,875 |
| 3600 | 1350 amp | | 2.40 | 6.667 | | 1,525 | 305 | | | 1,830 | 2,150 |
| 3700 | 1600 amp | | 2.20 | 7.273 | | 1,675 | 330 | | | 2,005 | 2,350 |
| 3800 | 2000 amp | | 1.80 | 8.889 | | 2,075 | 405 | | | 2,480 | 2,875 |
| 4000 | End box, 225 amp | | 34 | .471 | | 146 | 21.50 | | | 167.50 | 193 |
| 4100 | 400 amp | | 32 | .500 | | 146 | 23 | | | 169 | 195 |
| 4200 | 600 amp | | 28 | .571 | | 146 | 26 | | | 172 | 200 |
| 4300 | 800 amp | | 26 | .615 | | 146 | 28 | | | 174 | 203 |
| 4400 | 1000 amp | | 24 | .667 | | 146 | 30.50 | | | 176.50 | 206 |
| 4500 | 1350 amp | | 22 | .727 | | 146 | 33 | | | 179 | 211 |
| 4600 | 1600 amp | | 20 | .800 | | 146 | 36.50 | | | 182.50 | 216 |
| 4700 | 2000 amp | | 18 | .889 | | 179 | 40.50 | | | 219.50 | 258 |
| 4800 | Cable tap box end, 225 amp | | 3.20 | 5 | | 950 | 228 | | | 1,178 | 1,400 |
| 5000 | 400 amp | | 2.60 | 6.154 | | 950 | 280 | | | 1,230 | 1,475 |
| 5100 | 600 amp | | 2.20 | 7.273 | | 950 | 330 | | | 1,280 | 1,550 |
| 5200 | 800 amp | | 2 | 8 | | 1,075 | 365 | | | 1,440 | 1,725 |
| 5300 | 1000 amp | | 1.60 | 10 | | 1,175 | 455 | | | 1,630 | 1,975 |
| 5400 | 1350 amp | | 1.40 | 11.429 | | 1,400 | 520 | | | 1,920 | 2,325 |
| 5500 | 1600 amp | | 1.20 | 13.333 | | 1,575 | 605 | | | 2,180 | 2,625 |
| 5600 | 2000 amp | | 1 | 16 | | 1,800 | 730 | | | 2,530 | 3,050 |
| 5700 | Switchboard stub, 225 amp | | 5.40 | 2.963 | | 1,100 | 135 | | | 1,235 | 1,400 |
| 5800 | 400 amp | | 4.60 | 3.478 | | 1,100 | 158 | | | 1,258 | 1,425 |
| 5900 | 600 amp | | 4 | 4 | | 1,100 | 182 | | | 1,282 | 1,475 |
| 6000 | 800 amp | | 3.20 | 5 | | 1,325 | 228 | | | 1,553 | 1,800 |
| 6100 | 1000 amp | | 3 | 5.333 | | 1,525 | 243 | | | 1,768 | 2,050 |
| 6200 | 1350 amp | | 2.60 | 6.154 | | 1,975 | 280 | | | 2,255 | 2,600 |
| 6300 | 1600 amp | | 2.40 | 6.667 | | 2,225 | 305 | | | 2,530 | 2,900 |
| 6400 | 2000 amp | | 2 | 8 | | 2,700 | 365 | | | 3,065 | 3,525 |
| 6490 | Tee fittings, 225 amp | | 2.40 | 6.667 | | 1,475 | 305 | | | 1,780 | 2,075 |
| 6500 | 400 amp | | 2 | 8 | | 1,475 | 365 | | | 1,840 | 2,175 |
| 6600 | 600 amp | | 1.80 | 8.889 | | 1,475 | 405 | | | 1,880 | 2,225 |
| 6700 | 800 amp | | 1.60 | 10 | | 1,725 | 455 | | | 2,180 | 2,550 |
| 6800 | 1350 amp | | 1.20 | 13.333 | | 2,475 | 605 | | | 3,080 | 3,625 |
| 7000 | 1600 amp | | 1 | 16 | | 2,800 | 730 | | | 3,530 | 4,175 |
| 7100 | 2000 amp | | .80 | 20 | | 3,325 | 910 | | | 4,235 | 5,025 |
| 7200 | Plug-in fusible switches w/3 fuses, 600 volt, 3 pole, 30 amp | 1 Elec | 4 | 2 | | 650 | 91 | | | 741 | 850 |
| 7300 | 60 amp | | 3.60 | 2.222 | | 730 | 101 | | | 831 | 955 |
| 7400 | 100 amp | | 2.70 | 2.963 | | 1,125 | 135 | | | 1,260 | 1,425 |
| 7500 | 200 amp | 2 Elec | 3.20 | 5 | | 2,000 | 228 | | | 2,228 | 2,550 |
| 7600 | 400 amp | | 1.40 | 11.429 | | 5,825 | 520 | | | 6,345 | 7,175 |
| 7700 | 600 amp | | .90 | 17.778 | | 6,600 | 810 | | | 7,410 | 8,475 |
| 7800 | 800 amp | | .66 | 24.242 | | 8,975 | 1,100 | | | 10,075 | 11,500 |
| 7900 | 1200 amp | | .50 | 32 | | 16,800 | 1,450 | | | 18,250 | 20,700 |
| 8000 | Plug-in circuit breakers, molded case, 15 to 50 amp | 1 Elec | 4.40 | 1.818 | | 615 | 83 | | | 698 | 800 |
| 8100 | 70 to 100 amp | " | 3.10 | 2.581 | | 685 | 118 | | | 803 | 925 |
| 8200 | 150 to 225 amp | 2 Elec | 3.40 | 4.706 | | 1,850 | 214 | | | 2,064 | 2,375 |
| 8300 | 250 to 400 amp | | 1.40 | 11.429 | | 3,250 | 520 | | | 3,770 | 4,350 |
| 8400 | 500 to 600 amp | | 1 | 16 | | 4,400 | 730 | | | 5,130 | 5,900 |
| 8500 | 700 to 800 amp | | .64 | 25 | | 5,425 | 1,150 | | | 6,575 | 7,650 |
| 8600 | 900 to 1000 amp | | .56 | 28.571 | | 7,750 | 1,300 | | | 9,050 | 10,500 |
| 8700 | 1200 amp | | .44 | 36.364 | | 9,300 | 1,650 | | | 10,950 | 12,700 |

513

# 26 27 Low-Voltage Distribution Equipment

## 26 27 16 – Electrical Cabinets and Enclosures

### 26 27 16.10 Cabinets

| | | Crew | Daily Output | Labor-Hours | Unit | Material | 2008 Bare Costs Labor | Equipment | Total | Total Incl O&P |
|---|---|---|---|---|---|---|---|---|---|---|
| 0010 | **CABINETS** | | | | | | | | | |
| 7000 | Cabinets, current transformer | | | | | | | | | |
| 7050 | Single door, 24" H x 24" W x 10" D | 1 Elec | 1.60 | 5 | Ea. | 206 | 228 | | 434 | 565 |
| 7100 | 30" H x 24" W x 10" D | | 1.30 | 6.154 | | 210 | 280 | | 490 | 650 |
| 7150 | 36" H x 24" W x 10" D | | 1.10 | 7.273 | | 215 | 330 | | 545 | 730 |
| 7200 | 30" H x 30" W x 10" D | | 1 | 8 | | 225 | 365 | | 590 | 795 |
| 7250 | 36" H x 30" W x 10" D | | .90 | 8.889 | | 305 | 405 | | 710 | 940 |
| 7300 | 36" H x 36" W x 10" D | | .80 | 10 | | 325 | 455 | | 780 | 1,050 |
| 7500 | Double door, 48" H x 36" W x 10" D | | .60 | 13.333 | | 600 | 605 | | 1,205 | 1,575 |
| 7550 | 24" H x 24" W x 12" D | | 1 | 8 | | 263 | 365 | | 628 | 835 |

## 26 27 23 – Indoor Service Poles

### 26 27 23.40 Surface Raceway

| | | Crew | Daily Output | Labor-Hours | Unit | Material | 2008 Bare Costs Labor | Equipment | Total | Total Incl O&P |
|---|---|---|---|---|---|---|---|---|---|---|
| 0010 | **SURFACE RACEWAY** | | | | | | | | | |
| 0090 | Metal, straight section | | | | | | | | | |
| 0100 | No. 500 | 1 Elec | 100 | .080 | L.F. | .95 | 3.64 | | 4.59 | 6.50 |
| 0110 | No. 700 | | 100 | .080 | | 1.07 | 3.64 | | 4.71 | 6.65 |
| 0400 | No. 1500, small pancake | | 90 | .089 | | 1.93 | 4.05 | | 5.98 | 8.15 |
| 0600 | No. 2000, base & cover, blank | | 90 | .089 | | 1.98 | 4.05 | | 6.03 | 8.25 |
| 0800 | No. 3000, base & cover, blank | | 75 | .107 | | 3.80 | 4.86 | | 8.66 | 11.45 |
| 1000 | No. 4000, base & cover, blank | | 65 | .123 | | 6.20 | 5.60 | | 11.80 | 15.15 |
| 1200 | No. 6000, base & cover, blank | | 50 | .160 | | 10.30 | 7.30 | | 17.60 | 22 |
| 2400 | Fittings, elbows, No. 500 | | 40 | .200 | Ea. | 1.72 | 9.10 | | 10.82 | 15.45 |
| 2800 | Elbow cover, No. 2000 | | 40 | .200 | | 3.28 | 9.10 | | 12.38 | 17.15 |
| 2880 | Tee, No. 500 | | 42 | .190 | | 3.30 | 8.70 | | 12 | 16.55 |
| 2900 | No. 2000 | | 27 | .296 | | 10.85 | 13.50 | | 24.35 | 32 |
| 3000 | Switch box, No. 500 | | 16 | .500 | | 11.20 | 23 | | 34.20 | 46.50 |
| 3400 | Telephone outlet, No. 1500 | | 16 | .500 | | 13.40 | 23 | | 36.40 | 49 |
| 3600 | Junction box, No. 1500 | | 16 | .500 | | 9.05 | 23 | | 32.05 | 44 |
| 3800 | Plugmold wired sections, No. 2000 | | | | | | | | | |
| 4000 | 1 circuit, 6 outlets, 3 ft. long | 1 Elec | 8 | 1 | Ea. | 35.50 | 45.50 | | 81 | 108 |
| 4100 | 2 circuits, 8 outlets, 6 ft. long | " | 5.30 | 1.509 | " | 55.50 | 69 | | 124.50 | 163 |

## 26 27 26 – Wiring Devices

### 26 27 26.10 Low Voltage Switching

| | | Crew | Daily Output | Labor-Hours | Unit | Material | 2008 Bare Costs Labor | Equipment | Total | Total Incl O&P |
|---|---|---|---|---|---|---|---|---|---|---|
| 0010 | **LOW VOLTAGE SWITCHING** | | | | | | | | | |
| 3600 | Relays, 120 V or 277 V standard | 1 Elec | 12 | .667 | Ea. | 30 | 30.50 | | 60.50 | 78 |
| 3800 | Flush switch, standard | | 40 | .200 | | 10.35 | 9.10 | | 19.45 | 25 |
| 4000 | Interchangeable | | 40 | .200 | | 13.50 | 9.10 | | 22.60 | 28.50 |
| 4100 | Surface switch, standard | | 40 | .200 | | 7.60 | 9.10 | | 16.70 | 22 |
| 4200 | Transformer 115 V to 25 V | | 12 | .667 | | 106 | 30.50 | | 136.50 | 162 |
| 4400 | Master control, 12 circuit, manual | | 4 | 2 | | 108 | 91 | | 199 | 255 |
| 4500 | 25 circuit, motorized | | 4 | 2 | | 117 | 91 | | 208 | 265 |
| 4600 | Rectifier, silicon | | 12 | .667 | | 35 | 30.50 | | 65.50 | 83.50 |
| 4800 | Switchplates, 1 gang, 1, 2 or 3 switch, plastic | | 80 | .100 | | 3.45 | 4.56 | | 8.01 | 10.60 |
| 5000 | Stainless steel | | 80 | .100 | | 9.30 | 4.56 | | 13.86 | 17.05 |
| 5400 | 2 gang, 3 switch, stainless steel | | 53 | .151 | | 17.90 | 6.90 | | 24.80 | 30 |
| 5500 | 4 switch, plastic | | 53 | .151 | | 7.70 | 6.90 | | 14.60 | 18.70 |
| 5800 | 3 gang, 9 switch, stainless steel | | 32 | .250 | | 57.50 | 11.40 | | 68.90 | 80 |

### 26 27 26.20 Wiring Devices Elements

| | | | Crew | Daily Output | Labor-Hours | Unit | Material | 2008 Bare Costs Labor | Equipment | Total | Total Incl O&P |
|---|---|---|---|---|---|---|---|---|---|---|---|
| 0010 | **WIRING DEVICES ELEMENTS** | | | | | | | | | | |
| 0200 | Toggle switch, quiet type, single pole, 15 amp | CN | 1 Elec | 40 | .200 | Ea. | 5.30 | 9.10 | | 14.40 | 19.35 |
| 0600 | 3 way, 15 amp | | | 23 | .348 | | 7.65 | 15.85 | | 23.50 | 32 |

# 26 27 Low-Voltage Distribution Equipment

## 26 27 26 – Wiring Devices

| 26 27 26.20 Wiring Devices Elements | | Crew | Daily Output | Labor-Hours | Unit | Material | 2008 Bare Costs Labor | Equipment | Total | Total Incl O&P |
|---|---|---|---|---|---|---|---|---|---|---|
| 0900 | 4 way, 15 amp | 1 Elec | 15 | .533 | Ea. | 21.50 | 24.50 | | 46 | 60 |
| 1650 | Dimmer switch, 120 volt, incandescent, 600 watt, 1 pole | | 16 | .500 | | 11.25 | 23 | | 34.25 | 46.50 |
| 2460 | Receptacle, duplex, 120 volt, grounded, 15 amp | | 40 | .200 | | 1.30 | 9.10 | | 10.40 | 15 |
| 2470 | 20 amp | | 27 | .296 | | 9.75 | 13.50 | | 23.25 | 31 |
| 2490 | Dryer, 30 amp | | 15 | .533 | | 6.05 | 24.50 | | 30.55 | 42.50 |
| 2500 | Range, 50 amp | | 11 | .727 | | 12.70 | 33 | | 45.70 | 63.50 |
| 2600 | Wall plates, stainless steel, 1 gang | | 80 | .100 | | 2.26 | 4.56 | | 6.82 | 9.30 |
| 2800 | 2 gang | | 53 | .151 | | 4.10 | 6.90 | | 11 | 14.75 |
| 3200 | Lampholder, keyless | | 26 | .308 | | 11.90 | 14 | | 25.90 | 34 |
| 3400 | Pullchain with receptacle | ▼ | 22 | .364 | ▼ | 12.95 | 16.55 | | 29.50 | 39 |

## 26 27 73 – Door Chimes

### 26 27 73.10 Doorbell System

| | | Crew | Daily Output | Labor-Hours | Unit | Material | 2008 Bare Costs Labor | Equipment | Total | Total Incl O&P |
|---|---|---|---|---|---|---|---|---|---|---|
| 0010 | **DOORBELL SYSTEM**, incl. transformer, button & signal | | | | | | | | | |
| 0100 | 6" bell | 1 Elec | 4 | 2 | Ea. | 101 | 91 | | 192 | 247 |
| 0200 | Buzzer | " | 4 | 2 | " | 80 | 91 | | 171 | 224 |

# 26 28 Low-Voltage Circuit Protective Devices

## 26 28 16 – Enclosed Switches and Circuit Breakers

### 26 28 16.10 Circuit Breakers

| | | Crew | Daily Output | Labor-Hours | Unit | Material | 2008 Bare Costs Labor | Equipment | Total | Total Incl O&P |
|---|---|---|---|---|---|---|---|---|---|---|
| 0010 | **CIRCUIT BREAKERS** (in enclosure) | | | | | | | | | |
| 0100 | Enclosed (NEMA 1), 600 volt, 3 pole, 30 amp | 1 Elec | 3.20 | 2.500 | Ea. | 565 | 114 | | 679 | 790 |
| 0200 | 60 amp | | 2.80 | 2.857 | | 565 | 130 | | 695 | 815 |
| 0400 | 100 amp | | 2.30 | 3.478 | | 645 | 158 | | 803 | 945 |
| 0600 | 225 amp | ▼ | 1.50 | 5.333 | | 1,500 | 243 | | 1,743 | 2,000 |
| 0700 | 400 amp | 2 Elec | 1.60 | 10 | | 2,550 | 455 | | 3,005 | 3,475 |
| 0800 | 600 amp | | 1.20 | 13.333 | | 3,700 | 605 | | 4,305 | 4,950 |
| 1000 | 800 amp | ▼ | .94 | 17.021 | ▼ | 4,800 | 775 | | 5,575 | 6,425 |

### 26 28 16.20 Safety Switches

| | | Crew | Daily Output | Labor-Hours | Unit | Material | 2008 Bare Costs Labor | Equipment | Total | Total Incl O&P |
|---|---|---|---|---|---|---|---|---|---|---|
| 0010 | **SAFETY SWITCHES** | | | | | | | | | |
| 0100 | General duty 240 volt, 3 pole NEMA 1, fusible, 30 amp | 1 Elec | 3.20 | 2.500 | Ea. | 106 | 114 | | 220 | 286 |
| 0200 | 60 amp | | 2.30 | 3.478 | | 179 | 158 | | 337 | 435 |
| 0300 | 100 amp | | 1.90 | 4.211 | | 305 | 192 | | 497 | 625 |
| 0400 | 200 amp | ▼ | 1.30 | 6.154 | | 660 | 280 | | 940 | 1,150 |
| 0500 | 400 amp | 2 Elec | 1.80 | 8.889 | | 1,675 | 405 | | 2,080 | 2,425 |
| 0600 | 600 amp | " | 1.20 | 13.333 | ▼ | 3,100 | 605 | | 3,705 | 4,325 |
| 2900 | Heavy duty, 240 volt, 3 pole NEMA 1 fusible | | | | | | | | | |
| 2910 | 30 amp | 1 Elec | 3.20 | 2.500 | Ea. | 171 | 114 | | 285 | 360 |
| 3000 | 60 amp | | 2.30 | 3.478 | | 289 | 158 | | 447 | 555 |
| 3300 | 100 amp | | 1.90 | 4.211 | | 455 | 192 | | 647 | 785 |
| 3500 | 200 amp | ▼ | 1.30 | 6.154 | | 785 | 280 | | 1,065 | 1,275 |
| 3700 | 400 amp | 2 Elec | 1.80 | 8.889 | | 2,000 | 405 | | 2,405 | 2,800 |
| 3900 | 600 amp | " | 1.20 | 13.333 | ▼ | 3,450 | 605 | | 4,055 | 4,700 |

# 26 29 Low-Voltage Controllers

## 26 29 13 – Enclosed Controllers

| 26 29 13.20 Control Stations | | Crew | Daily Output | Labor-Hours | Unit | Material | 2008 Bare Costs Labor | 2008 Bare Costs Equipment | Total | Total Incl O&P |
|---|---|---|---|---|---|---|---|---|---|---|
| 0010 | **CONTROL STATIONS** | | | | | | | | | |
| 0050 | NEMA 1, heavy duty, stop/start | 1 Elec | 8 | 1 | Ea. | 132 | 45.50 | | 177.50 | 214 |
| 0100 | Stop/start, pilot light | | 6.20 | 1.290 | | 180 | 59 | | 239 | 287 |
| 0200 | Hand/off/automatic | | 6.20 | 1.290 | | 98 | 59 | | 157 | 196 |
| 0400 | Stop/start/reverse | | 5.30 | 1.509 | | 179 | 69 | | 248 | 298 |

# 26 32 Packaged Generator Assemblies

## 26 32 13 – Engine Generators

### 26 32 13.13 Diesel-Engine-Driven Generator Sets

| | | Crew | Daily Output | Labor-Hours | Unit | Material | Labor | Equipment | Total | Total Incl O&P |
|---|---|---|---|---|---|---|---|---|---|---|
| 0010 | **DIESEL-ENGINE-DRIVEN GENERATOR SETS** | | | | | | | | | |
| 2000 | Diesel engine, including battery, charger, | | | | | | | | | |
| 2010 | muffler, automatic transfer switch & day tank, 30 kW | R-3 | .55 | 36.364 | Ea. | 19,000 | 1,625 | 235 | 20,860 | 23,600 |
| 2100 | 50 kW | | .42 | 47.619 | | 23,400 | 2,125 | 310 | 25,835 | 29,200 |
| 2200 | 75 kW | | .35 | 57.143 | | 30,500 | 2,550 | 370 | 33,420 | 37,700 |
| 2300 | 100 kW | | .31 | 64.516 | | 33,800 | 2,900 | 415 | 37,115 | 42,000 |
| 2400 | 125 kW | | .29 | 68.966 | | 35,600 | 3,100 | 445 | 39,145 | 44,300 |
| 2500 | 150 kW | | .26 | 76.923 | | 40,900 | 3,450 | 500 | 44,850 | 50,500 |
| 2600 | 175 kW | | .25 | 80 | | 44,500 | 3,575 | 520 | 48,595 | 55,000 |
| 2700 | 200 kW | | .24 | 83.333 | | 45,900 | 3,725 | 540 | 50,165 | 56,500 |
| 2800 | 250 kW | | .23 | 86.957 | | 54,000 | 3,900 | 565 | 58,465 | 66,000 |
| 2900 | 300 kW | | .22 | 90.909 | | 58,500 | 4,075 | 590 | 63,165 | 71,000 |
| 3000 | 350 kW | | .20 | 100 | | 66,000 | 4,475 | 645 | 71,120 | 80,000 |
| 3100 | 400 kW | | .19 | 105 | | 81,500 | 4,725 | 680 | 86,905 | 98,000 |
| 3200 | 500 kW | | .18 | 111 | | 102,500 | 4,975 | 720 | 108,195 | 121,000 |

### 26 32 13.16 Gas-Engine-Driven Generator Sets

| | | Crew | Daily Output | Labor-Hours | Unit | Material | Labor | Equipment | Total | Total Incl O&P |
|---|---|---|---|---|---|---|---|---|---|---|
| 0010 | **GAS-ENGINE-DRIVEN GENERATOR SETS** | | | | | | | | | |
| 0020 | Gas or gasoline operated, includes battery, | | | | | | | | | |
| 0050 | charger, muffler & transfer switch | | | | | | | | | |
| 0200 | 3 phase 4 wire, 277/480 volt, 7.5 kW | R-3 | .83 | 24.096 | Ea. | 7,125 | 1,075 | 156 | 8,356 | 9,625 |
| 0300 | 11.5 kW | | .71 | 28.169 | | 10,100 | 1,275 | 182 | 11,557 | 13,200 |
| 0400 | 20 kW | | .63 | 31.746 | | 11,900 | 1,425 | 205 | 13,530 | 15,500 |
| 0500 | 35 kW | | .55 | 36.364 | | 14,200 | 1,625 | 235 | 16,060 | 18,400 |
| 0600 | 80 kW | | .40 | 50 | | 24,300 | 2,250 | 325 | 26,875 | 30,500 |
| 0700 | 100 kW | | .33 | 60.606 | | 26,700 | 2,725 | 390 | 29,815 | 33,900 |
| 0800 | 125 kW | | .28 | 71.429 | | 54,500 | 3,200 | 460 | 58,160 | 65,500 |
| 0900 | 185 kW | | .25 | 80 | | 72,000 | 3,575 | 520 | 76,095 | 85,500 |

# 26 35 Power Filters and Conditioners

## 26 35 13 – Capacitors

### 26 35 13.10 Capacitors Indoor

| | | Crew | Daily Output | Labor-Hours | Unit | Material | Labor | Equipment | Total | Total Incl O&P |
|---|---|---|---|---|---|---|---|---|---|---|
| 0010 | **CAPACITORS INDOOR** | | | | | | | | | |
| 0020 | 240 volts, single & 3 phase, 0.5 kVAR | 1 Elec | 2.70 | 2.963 | Ea. | 350 | 135 | | 485 | 585 |
| 0100 | 1.0 kVAR | | 2.70 | 2.963 | | 420 | 135 | | 555 | 665 |
| 0150 | 2.5 kVAR | | 2 | 4 | | 475 | 182 | | 657 | 790 |
| 0200 | 5.0 kVAR | | 1.80 | 4.444 | | 565 | 202 | | 767 | 925 |
| 0250 | 7.5 kVAR | | 1.60 | 5 | | 660 | 228 | | 888 | 1,075 |
| 0300 | 10 kVAR | | 1.50 | 5.333 | | 795 | 243 | | 1,038 | 1,225 |
| 0350 | 15 kVAR | | 1.30 | 6.154 | | 1,100 | 280 | | 1,380 | 1,625 |
| 0400 | 20 kVAR | | 1.10 | 7.273 | | 1,350 | 330 | | 1,680 | 2,000 |

# 26 35 Power Filters and Conditioners

## 26 35 13 – Capacitors

| 26 35 13.10 Capacitors Indoor | Crew | Daily Output | Labor-Hours | Unit | Material | 2008 Bare Costs Labor | Equipment | Total | Total Incl O&P |
|---|---|---|---|---|---|---|---|---|---|
| 0450 | 25 kVAR | 1 Elec | 1 | 8 | Ea. | 1,600 | 365 | | 1,965 | 2,325 |
| 1000 | 480 volts, single & 3 phase, 1 kVAR | | 2.70 | 2.963 | | 320 | 135 | | 455 | 550 |
| 1050 | 2 kVAR | | 2.70 | 2.963 | | 365 | 135 | | 500 | 605 |
| 1100 | 5 kVAR | | 2 | 4 | | 460 | 182 | | 642 | 780 |
| 1150 | 7.5 kVAR | | 2 | 4 | | 500 | 182 | | 682 | 820 |
| 1200 | 10 kVAR | | 2 | 4 | | 555 | 182 | | 737 | 885 |
| 1250 | 15 kVAR | | 2 | 4 | | 690 | 182 | | 872 | 1,025 |
| 1300 | 20 kVAR | | 1.60 | 5 | | 765 | 228 | | 993 | 1,175 |
| 1350 | 30 kVAR | | 1.50 | 5.333 | | 960 | 243 | | 1,203 | 1,400 |
| 1400 | 40 kVAR | | 1.20 | 6.667 | | 1,225 | 305 | | 1,530 | 1,800 |
| 1450 | 50 kVAR | ↓ | 1.10 | 7.273 | ↓ | 1,375 | 330 | | 1,705 | 2,025 |

# 26 42 Cathodic Protection

## 26 42 16 – Passive Cathodic Protection for Underground Storage Tank

### 26 42 16.50 Cathodic Protection Wiring Methods

| | | Crew | Daily Output | Labor-Hours | Unit | Material | Labor | Equipment | Total | Total Incl O&P |
|---|---|---|---|---|---|---|---|---|---|---|
| 0010 | **CATHODIC PROTECTION WIRING METHODS** | | | | | | | | | |
| 1000 | Anodes, magnesium type, 9 # | R-15 | 18.50 | 2.595 | Ea. | 24 | 115 | 17.25 | 156.25 | 217 |
| 1010 | 17 # | | 13 | 3.692 | | 41 | 164 | 24.50 | 229.50 | 315 |
| 1020 | 32 # | | 10 | 4.800 | | 73 | 213 | 32 | 318 | 435 |
| 1030 | 48 # | ↓ | 7.20 | 6.667 | | 109 | 296 | 44.50 | 449.50 | 610 |
| 1100 | Graphite type w/ epoxy cap, 3" x 60" (32 #) | R-22 | 8.40 | 4.438 | | 99 | 171 | | 270 | 365 |
| 1110 | 4" x 80" (68 #) | | 6 | 6.213 | | 186 | 240 | | 426 | 565 |
| 1120 | 6" x 72" (80 #) | | 5.20 | 7.169 | | 1,150 | 276 | | 1,426 | 1,675 |
| 1130 | 6" x 36" (45 #) | ↓ | 9.60 | 3.883 | | 575 | 150 | | 725 | 860 |
| 2000 | Rectifiers, silicon type, air cooled, 28 V/10 A | R-19 | 3.50 | 5.714 | | 1,775 | 261 | | 2,036 | 2,350 |
| 2010 | 20 V/20 A | | 3.50 | 5.714 | | 1,875 | 261 | | 2,136 | 2,450 |
| 2100 | Oil immersed, 28 V/10 A | | 3 | 6.667 | | 2,525 | 305 | | 2,830 | 3,225 |
| 2110 | 20 V/20 A | ↓ | 3 | 6.667 | ↓ | 2,725 | 305 | | 3,030 | 3,450 |
| 3000 | Anode backfill, coke breeze | R-22 | 3850 | .010 | Lb. | .13 | .37 | | .50 | .70 |
| 4000 | Cable, OR2, No. 8 | | 2.40 | 15.533 | M.L.F. | 300 | 600 | | 900 | 1,225 |
| 4010 | No. 6 | | 2.40 | 15.533 | | 450 | 600 | | 1,050 | 1,400 |
| 4020 | No. 4 | | 2.40 | 15.533 | | 655 | 600 | | 1,255 | 1,625 |
| 4030 | No. 2 | | 2.40 | 15.533 | | 1,050 | 600 | | 1,650 | 2,050 |
| 4040 | No. 1 | | 2.20 | 16.945 | | 1,375 | 655 | | 2,030 | 2,500 |
| 4050 | No. 1/0 | | 2.20 | 16.945 | | 1,700 | 655 | | 2,355 | 2,825 |
| 4060 | No. 2/0 | | 2.20 | 16.945 | | 2,050 | 655 | | 2,705 | 3,225 |
| 4070 | No. 4/0 | ↓ | 2 | 18.640 | ↓ | 4,325 | 720 | | 5,045 | 5,825 |
| 5000 | Test station, 7 terminal box, flush curb type w/lockable cover | R-19 | 12 | 1.667 | Ea. | 70 | 76 | | 146 | 190 |
| 5010 | Reference cell, 2" dia PVC conduit, cplg, plug, set flush | " | 4.80 | 4.167 | " | 33.50 | 190 | | 223.50 | 320 |

# 26 51 Interior Lighting

## 26 51 13 – Interior Lighting Fixtures, Lamps, and Ballasts

| 26 51 13.50 Interior Lighting Fixtures | | Crew | Daily Output | Labor-Hours | Unit | Material | 2008 Bare Costs Labor | Equipment | Total | Total Incl O&P |
|---|---|---|---|---|---|---|---|---|---|---|
| 0010 | **INTERIOR LIGHTING FIXTURES** Including lamps, mounting | | | | | | | | | |
| 0030 | hardware and connections | | | | | | | | | |
| 0100 | Fluorescent, C.W. lamps, troffer, recess mounted in grid, RS | | | | | | | | | |
| 0200 | Acrylic lens, 1'W x 4'L, two 40 watt | 1 Elec | 5.70 | 1.404 | Ea. | 52 | 64 | | 116 | 153 |
| 0210 | 1'W x 4'L, three 40 watt | | 5.40 | 1.481 | | 61 | 67.50 | | 128.50 | 168 |
| 0300 | 2'W x 2'L, two U40 watt | | 5.70 | 1.404 | | 55.50 | 64 | | 119.50 | 157 |
| 0400 | 2'W x 4'L, two 40 watt | | 5.30 | 1.509 | | 55.50 | 69 | | 124.50 | 164 |
| 0500 | 2'W x 4'L, three 40 watt | | 5 | 1.600 | | 59.50 | 73 | | 132.50 | 175 |
| 0600 | 2'W x 4'L, four 40 watt              CN | | 4.70 | 1.702 | | 63 | 77.50 | | 140.50 | 185 |
| 0700 | 4'W x 4'L, four 40 watt | 2 Elec | 6.40 | 2.500 | | 335 | 114 | | 449 | 535 |
| 0800 | 4'W x 4'L, six 40 watt | | 6.20 | 2.581 | | 345 | 118 | | 463 | 555 |
| 0900 | 4'W x 4'L, eight 40 watt | | 5.80 | 2.759 | | 355 | 126 | | 481 | 580 |
| 0910 | Acrylic lens, 1'W x 4'L, two 32 watt | 1 Elec | 5.70 | 1.404 | | 65.50 | 64 | | 129.50 | 167 |
| 0930 | 2'W x 2'L, two U32 watt | | 5.70 | 1.404 | | 80 | 64 | | 144 | 183 |
| 0940 | 2'W x 4'L, two 32 watt | | 5.30 | 1.509 | | 72 | 69 | | 141 | 182 |
| 0950 | 2'W x 4'L, three 32 watt | | 5 | 1.600 | | 76.50 | 73 | | 149.50 | 193 |
| 0960 | 2'W x 4'L, four 32 watt | | 4.70 | 1.702 | | 78.50 | 77.50 | | 156 | 202 |
| 1000 | Surface mounted, RS | | | | | | | | | |
| 1030 | Acrylic lens with hinged & latched door frame | | | | | | | | | |
| 1100 | 1'W x 4'L, two 40 watt | 1 Elec | 7 | 1.143 | Ea. | 73.50 | 52 | | 125.50 | 159 |
| 1110 | 1'W x 4'L, three 40 watt | | 6.70 | 1.194 | | 75.50 | 54.50 | | 130 | 164 |
| 1200 | 2'W x 2'L, two U40 watt | | 7 | 1.143 | | 79 | 52 | | 131 | 164 |
| 1300 | 2'W x 4'L, two 40 watt | | 6.20 | 1.290 | | 90.50 | 59 | | 149.50 | 187 |
| 1400 | 2'W x 4'L, three 40 watt | | 5.70 | 1.404 | | 91.50 | 64 | | 155.50 | 195 |
| 1500 | 2'W x 4'L, four 40 watt | | 5.30 | 1.509 | | 93.50 | 69 | | 162.50 | 205 |
| 1600 | 4'W x 4'L, four 40 watt | 2 Elec | 7.20 | 2.222 | | 465 | 101 | | 566 | 660 |
| 1700 | 4'W x 4'L, six 40 watt | | 6.60 | 2.424 | | 505 | 110 | | 615 | 720 |
| 1800 | 4'W x 4'L, eight 40 watt | | 6.20 | 2.581 | | 520 | 118 | | 638 | 750 |
| 1900 | 2'W x 8'L, four 40 watt | | 6.40 | 2.500 | | 181 | 114 | | 295 | 370 |
| 2000 | 2'W x 8'L, eight 40 watt | | 6.20 | 2.581 | | 194 | 118 | | 312 | 390 |
| 2100 | Strip fixture | | | | | | | | | |
| 2130 | Surface mounted | | | | | | | | | |
| 2200 | 4' long, one 40 watt RS | 1 Elec | 8.50 | .941 | Ea. | 30.50 | 43 | | 73.50 | 97.50 |
| 2300 | 4' long, two 40 watt RS | | 8 | 1 | | 33 | 45.50 | | 78.50 | 104 |
| 2400 | 4' long, one 40 watt, SL | | 8 | 1 | | 44.50 | 45.50 | | 90 | 117 |
| 2500 | 4' long, two 40 watt, SL | | 7 | 1.143 | | 61 | 52 | | 113 | 145 |
| 2600 | 8' long, one 75 watt, SL | 2 Elec | 13.40 | 1.194 | | 46 | 54.50 | | 100.50 | 132 |
| 2700 | 8' long, two 75 watt, SL | " | 12.40 | 1.290 | | 55 | 59 | | 114 | 148 |
| 2800 | 4' long, two 60 watt, HO | 1 Elec | 6.70 | 1.194 | | 89.50 | 54.50 | | 144 | 180 |
| 2900 | 8' long, two 110 watt, HO | 2 Elec | 10.60 | 1.509 | | 94 | 69 | | 163 | 205 |
| 2950 | High bay, 16" W x 4' L, four T5HO/54 watt, high output | | 8.90 | 1.798 | | 192 | 82 | | 274 | 335 |
| 2952 | 2' W x 4' L, six T5HO/54 watt | | 8.50 | 1.882 | | 282 | 85.50 | | 367.50 | 440 |
| 2954 | 2' W x 4' L, six T8/32 watt | | 8.50 | 1.882 | | 167 | 85.50 | | 252.50 | 310 |
| 3000 | Strip, pendent mounted, industrial, white porcelain enamel | | | | | | | | | |
| 3100 | 4' long, two 40 watt, RS | 1 Elec | 5.70 | 1.404 | Ea. | 50.50 | 64 | | 114.50 | 151 |
| 3200 | 4' long, two 60 watt, HO | " | 5 | 1.600 | | 80 | 73 | | 153 | 197 |
| 3300 | 8' long, two 75 watt, SL | 2 Elec | 8.80 | 1.818 | | 95 | 83 | | 178 | 228 |
| 3400 | 8' long, two 110 watt, HO | " | 8 | 2 | | 122 | 91 | | 213 | 270 |
| 3470 | Troffer, air handling, 2'W x 4'L with four 40 watt, RS | 1 Elec | 4 | 2 | | 92.50 | 91 | | 183.50 | 238 |
| 3480 | 2'W x 2'L with two U40 watt RS | | 5.50 | 1.455 | | 80.50 | 66.50 | | 147 | 187 |
| 3490 | Air connector insulated, 5" diameter | | 20 | .400 | | 63 | 18.20 | | 81.20 | 96.50 |
| 3500 | 6" diameter | | 20 | .400 | | 64 | 18.20 | | 82.20 | 97.50 |
| 3510 | Troffer parabolic lay-in, 1'W x 4'L with one 32 W | | 5.70 | 1.404 | | 106 | 64 | | 170 | 212 |

# 26 51 Interior Lighting

## 26 51 13 – Interior Lighting Fixtures, Lamps, and Ballasts

| 26 51 13.50 Interior Lighting Fixtures | | Crew | Daily Output | Labor-Hours | Unit | Material | 2008 Bare Costs Labor | Equipment | Total | Total Incl O&P |
|---|---|---|---|---|---|---|---|---|---|---|
| 3520 | 1'W x 4'L with two 32 W | 1 Elec | 5.30 | 1.509 | Ea. | 109 | 69 | | 178 | 222 |
| 3525 | 2'W x 2'L with two U32 W | | 5.70 | 1.404 | | 107 | 64 | | 171 | 213 |
| 3530 | 2'W x 4'L with three 32 W | ↓ | 5 | 1.600 | ↓ | 127 | 73 | | 200 | 249 |
| 4450 | Incandescent, high hat can, round alzak reflector, prewired | | | | | | | | | |
| 4470 | 100 watt | 1 Elec | 8 | 1 | Ea. | 66 | 45.50 | | 111.50 | 141 |
| 4480 | 150 watt | | 8 | 1 | | 97 | 45.50 | | 142.50 | 175 |
| 4500 | 300 watt | ↓ | 6.70 | 1.194 | ↓ | 228 | 54.50 | | 282.50 | 330 |
| 4600 | Square glass lens with metal trim, prewired | | | | | | | | | |
| 4630 | 100 watt | 1 Elec | 6.70 | 1.194 | Ea. | 50 | 54.50 | | 104.50 | 136 |
| 4700 | 200 watt | | 6.70 | 1.194 | | 92 | 54.50 | | 146.50 | 182 |
| 4800 | 300 watt | | 5.70 | 1.404 | | 131 | 64 | | 195 | 239 |
| 4900 | Ceiling/wall, surface mounted, metal cylinder, 75 watt | | 10 | .800 | | 51 | 36.50 | | 87.50 | 111 |
| 4920 | 150 watt | ↓ | 10 | .800 | ↓ | 73 | 36.50 | | 109.50 | 135 |
| 5200 | Ceiling, surface mounted, opal glass drum | | | | | | | | | |
| 5300 | 8", one 60 watt lamp | 1 Elec | 10 | .800 | Ea. | 42 | 36.50 | | 78.50 | 101 |
| 5400 | 10", two 60 watt lamps | | 8 | 1 | | 47 | 45.50 | | 92.50 | 120 |
| 5500 | 12", four 60 watt lamps | | 6.70 | 1.194 | | 63.50 | 54.50 | | 118 | 151 |
| 6010 | Vapor tight, incandescent, ceiling mounted, 200 watt | | 6.20 | 1.290 | | 64.50 | 59 | | 123.50 | 158 |
| 6100 | Fluorescent, surface mounted, 2 lamps, 4'L, RS, 40 watt | | 3.20 | 2.500 | | 108 | 114 | | 222 | 289 |
| 6850 | Vandalproof, surface mounted, fluorescent, two 40 watt | | 3.20 | 2.500 | | 228 | 114 | | 342 | 420 |
| 6860 | Incandescent, one 150 watt | ↓ | 8 | 1 | ↓ | 57.50 | 45.50 | | 103 | 132 |
| 7500 | Ballast replacement, by weight of ballast, to 15' high | | | | | | | | | |
| 7520 | Indoor fluorescent, less than 2 lbs. | 1 Elec | 10 | .800 | Ea. | 20 | 36.50 | | 56.50 | 76.50 |
| 7540 | Two 40W, watt reducer, 2 to 5 lbs. | | 9.40 | .851 | | 38 | 39 | | 77 | 99.50 |
| 7560 | Two F96 slimline, over 5 lbs. | | 8 | 1 | | 71.50 | 45.50 | | 117 | 147 |
| 7580 | Vaportite ballast, less than 2 lbs. | | 9.40 | .851 | | 20 | 39 | | 59 | 79.50 |
| 7600 | 2 lbs. to 5 lbs. | | 8.90 | .899 | | 38 | 41 | | 79 | 103 |
| 7620 | Over 5 lbs. | | 7.60 | 1.053 | | 71.50 | 48 | | 119.50 | 150 |
| 7630 | Electronic ballast for two tubes | | 8 | 1 | | 36.50 | 45.50 | | 82 | 108 |
| 7640 | Dimmable ballast one lamp | | 8 | 1 | | 79 | 45.50 | | 124.50 | 155 |
| 7650 | Dimmable ballast two-lamp | ↓ | 7.60 | 1.053 | | 129 | 48 | | 177 | 214 |

# 26 52 Emergency Lighting

## 26 52 13 – Emergency Lighting Equipments

### 26 52 13.10 Emergency Lighting and Battery Units

| | | Crew | Daily Output | Labor-Hours | Unit | Material | Labor | Equipment | Total | Total Incl O&P |
|---|---|---|---|---|---|---|---|---|---|---|
| 0010 | **EMERGENCY LIGHTING AND BATTERY UNITS** | | | | | | | | | |
| 0300 | Emergency light units, battery operated | | | | | | | | | |
| 0350 | Twin sealed beam light, 25 watt, 6 volt each | | | | | | | | | |
| 0500 | Lead battery operated | 1 Elec | 4 | 2 | Ea. | 129 | 91 | | 220 | 278 |
| 0700 | Nickel cadmium battery operated | | 4 | 2 | | 605 | 91 | | 696 | 800 |
| 0900 | Self-contained fluorescent lamp pack | ↓ | 10 | .800 | ↓ | 145 | 36.50 | | 181.50 | 215 |

# 26 53 Exit Signs

## 26 53 13 – Exit Lighting

| 26 53 13.10 Exit Lighting Fixtures | Crew | Daily Output | Labor-Hours | Unit | Material | 2008 Bare Costs Labor | Equipment | Total | Total Incl O&P |
|---|---|---|---|---|---|---|---|---|---|
| 0010 **EXIT LIGHTING FIXTURES** | | | | | | | | | |
| 0080 Exit light ceiling or wall mount, incandescent, single face | 1 Elec | 8 | 1 | Ea. | 42.50 | 45.50 | | 88 | 115 |
| 0100 Double face | | 6.70 | 1.194 | | 49 | 54.50 | | 103.50 | 135 |
| 0200 L.E.D. standard, single face | | 8 | 1 | | 65 | 45.50 | | 110.50 | 140 |
| 0220 Double face | | 6.70 | 1.194 | | 73 | 54.50 | | 127.50 | 161 |
| 0240 L.E.D. w/battery unit, single face | | 4.40 | 1.818 | | 125 | 83 | | 208 | 261 |
| 0260 Double face | | 4 | 2 | | 127 | 91 | | 218 | 276 |

# 26 54 Classified Location Lighting

## 26 54 13 – Classified Lighting

| 26 54 13.20 Explosionproof | Crew | Daily Output | Labor-Hours | Unit | Material | 2008 Bare Costs Labor | Equipment | Total | Total Incl O&P |
|---|---|---|---|---|---|---|---|---|---|
| 0010 **EXPLOSIONPROOF**, incl lamps, mounting hardware and connections | | | | | | | | | |
| 6510 Incandescent, ceiling mounted, 200 watt | 1 Elec | 4 | 2 | Ea. | 795 | 91 | | 886 | 1,000 |
| 6600 Fluorescent, RS, 4' long, ceiling mounted, two 40 watt | " | 2.70 | 2.963 | " | 1,900 | 135 | | 2,035 | 2,275 |

# 26 55 Special Purpose Lighting

## 26 55 61 – Theatrical Lighting

| 26 55 61.10 Lights | Crew | Daily Output | Labor-Hours | Unit | Material | 2008 Bare Costs Labor | Equipment | Total | Total Incl O&P |
|---|---|---|---|---|---|---|---|---|---|
| 0010 **LIGHTS** | | | | | | | | | |
| 2000 Lights, border, quartz, reflector, vented, | | | | | | | | | |
| 2100 colored or white | 1 Elec | 20 | .400 | L.F. | 164 | 18.20 | | 182.20 | 208 |
| 2500 Spotlight, follow spot, with transformer, 2,100 watt | " | 4 | 2 | Ea. | 2,925 | 91 | | 3,016 | 3,350 |
| 2600 For no transformer, deduct | | | | | 865 | | | 865 | 955 |
| 3000 Stationary spot, fresnel quartz, 6" lens | 1 Elec | 4 | 2 | | 125 | 91 | | 216 | 274 |
| 3100 8" lens | | 4 | 2 | | 220 | 91 | | 311 | 380 |
| 3500 Ellipsoidal quartz, 1,000W, 6" lens | | 4 | 2 | | 320 | 91 | | 411 | 485 |
| 3600 12" lens | | 4 | 2 | | 570 | 91 | | 661 | 760 |
| 4000 Strobe light, 1 to 15 flashes per second, quartz | | 3 | 2.667 | | 715 | 121 | | 836 | 970 |
| 4500 Color wheel, portable, five hole, motorized | | 4 | 2 | | 185 | 91 | | 276 | 340 |

# 26 56 Exterior Lighting

## 26 56 13 – Lighting Poles and Standards

| 26 56 13.10 Lighting Poles | Crew | Daily Output | Labor-Hours | Unit | Material | 2008 Bare Costs Labor | Equipment | Total | Total Incl O&P |
|---|---|---|---|---|---|---|---|---|---|
| 0010 **LIGHTING POLES** | | | | | | | | | |
| 2800 Light poles, anchor base | | | | | | | | | |
| 2820 not including concrete bases | | | | | | | | | |
| 2840 Aluminum pole, 8' high | 1 Elec | 4 | 2 | Ea. | 635 | 91 | | 726 | 835 |
| 3000 20' high | R-3 | 2.90 | 6.897 | | 830 | 310 | 44.50 | 1,184.50 | 1,425 |
| 3200 30' high | | 2.60 | 7.692 | | 1,625 | 345 | 50 | 2,020 | 2,350 |
| 3400 35' high | | 2.30 | 8.696 | | 1,750 | 390 | 56.50 | 2,196.50 | 2,575 |
| 3600 40' high | | 2 | 10 | | 2,000 | 450 | 64.50 | 2,514.50 | 2,950 |
| 3800 Bracket arms, 1 arm | 1 Elec | 8 | 1 | | 109 | 45.50 | | 154.50 | 188 |
| 4000 2 arms | | 8 | 1 | | 219 | 45.50 | | 264.50 | 310 |
| 4200 3 arms | | 5.30 | 1.509 | | 330 | 69 | | 399 | 460 |
| 4400 4 arms | | 5.30 | 1.509 | | 435 | 69 | | 504 | 580 |
| 4500 Steel pole, galvanized, 8' high | | 3.80 | 2.105 | | 555 | 96 | | 651 | 755 |
| 4600 20' high | R-3 | 2.60 | 7.692 | | 985 | 345 | 50 | 1,380 | 1,650 |

# 26 56 Exterior Lighting

## 26 56 13 − Lighting Poles and Standards

### 26 56 13.10 Lighting Poles

| | 26 56 13.10 Lighting Poles | Crew | Daily Output | Labor-Hours | Unit | Material | 2008 Bare Costs Labor | 2008 Bare Costs Equipment | Total | Total Incl O&P |
|---|---|---|---|---|---|---|---|---|---|---|
| 4800 | 30' high | R-3 | 2.30 | 8.696 | Ea. | 1,150 | 390 | 56.50 | 1,596.50 | 1,925 |
| 5000 | 35' high | | 2.20 | 9.091 | | 1,275 | 410 | 59 | 1,744 | 2,075 |
| 5200 | 40' high | | 1.70 | 11.765 | | 1,575 | 525 | 76 | 2,176 | 2,600 |
| 5400 | Bracket arms, 1 arm | 1 Elec | 8 | 1 | | 161 | 45.50 | | 206.50 | 245 |
| 5600 | 2 arms | | 8 | 1 | | 249 | 45.50 | | 294.50 | 340 |
| 5800 | 3 arms | | 5.30 | 1.509 | | 271 | 69 | | 340 | 400 |
| 6000 | 4 arms | | 5.30 | 1.509 | | 375 | 69 | | 444 | 515 |

## 26 56 19 − Roadway Lighting

### 26 56 19.20 Roadway Area Luminaire

| | 26 56 19.20 Roadway Area Luminaire | Crew | Daily Output | Labor-Hours | Unit | Material | Labor | Equipment | Total | Total Incl O&P |
|---|---|---|---|---|---|---|---|---|---|---|
| 0010 | **ROADWAY AREA LUMINAIRE** | | | | | | | | | |
| 2650 | Roadway area luminaire, low pressure sodium, 135 watt | 1 Elec | 2 | 4 | Ea. | 585 | 182 | | 767 | 910 |
| 2700 | 180 watt | " | 2 | 4 | | 615 | 182 | | 797 | 945 |
| 2750 | Metal halide, 400 watt | 2 Elec | 4.40 | 3.636 | | 465 | 166 | | 631 | 755 |
| 2760 | 1000 watt | | 4 | 4 | | 525 | 182 | | 707 | 850 |
| 2780 | High pressure sodium, 400 watt | | 4.40 | 3.636 | | 485 | 166 | | 651 | 775 |
| 2790 | 1000 watt | | 4 | 4 | | 550 | 182 | | 732 | 875 |

## 26 56 23 − Area Lighting

### 26 56 23.10 Exterior Fixtures

| | 26 56 23.10 Exterior Fixtures | Crew | Daily Output | Labor-Hours | Unit | Material | Labor | Equipment | Total | Total Incl O&P |
|---|---|---|---|---|---|---|---|---|---|---|
| 0010 | **EXTERIOR FIXTURES** With lamps | | | | | | | | | |
| 0200 | Wall mounted, incandescent, 100 watt | 1 Elec | 8 | 1 | Ea. | 30.50 | 45.50 | | 76 | 102 |
| 0400 | Quartz, 500 watt | | 5.30 | 1.509 | | 54 | 69 | | 123 | 162 |
| 1100 | Wall pack, low pressure sodium, 35 watt | | 4 | 2 | | 233 | 91 | | 324 | 395 |
| 1150 | 55 watt | | 4 | 2 | | 278 | 91 | | 369 | 440 |

## 26 56 36 − Flood Lighting

### 26 56 36.20 Floodlights

| | 26 56 36.20 Floodlights | Crew | Daily Output | Labor-Hours | Unit | Material | Labor | Equipment | Total | Total Incl O&P |
|---|---|---|---|---|---|---|---|---|---|---|
| 0010 | **FLOODLIGHTS** with ballast and lamp, | | | | | | | | | |
| 1400 | pole mounted, pole not included | | | | | | | | | |
| 1950 | Metal halide, 175 watt | 1 Elec | 2.70 | 2.963 | Ea. | 325 | 135 | | 460 | 560 |
| 2000 | 400 watt | 2 Elec | 4.40 | 3.636 | | 405 | 166 | | 571 | 690 |
| 2200 | 1000 watt | " | 4 | 4 | | 555 | 182 | | 737 | 880 |
| 2340 | High pressure sodium, 70 watt | 1 Elec | 2.70 | 2.963 | | 224 | 135 | | 359 | 445 |
| 2400 | 400 watt | 2 Elec | 4.40 | 3.636 | | 365 | 166 | | 531 | 645 |
| 2600 | 1000 watt | " | 4 | 4 | | 625 | 182 | | 807 | 960 |

# 26 61 Lighting Systems and Accessories

## 26 61 23 − Lamps Applications

### 26 61 23.10 Lamps

| | 26 61 23.10 Lamps | Crew | Daily Output | Labor-Hours | Unit | Material | Labor | Equipment | Total | Total Incl O&P |
|---|---|---|---|---|---|---|---|---|---|---|
| 0010 | **LAMPS** | | | | | | | | | |
| 0080 | Fluorescent, rapid start, cool white, 2' long, 20 watt | 1 Elec | 1 | 8 | C | 315 | 365 | | 680 | 890 |
| 0100 | 4' long, 40 watt | | .90 | 8.889 | | 350 | 405 | | 755 | 990 |
| 0200 | Slimline, 4' long, 40 watt | | .90 | 8.889 | | 825 | 405 | | 1,230 | 1,500 |
| 0210 | 4' long, 30 watt energy saver | | .90 | 8.889 | | 825 | 405 | | 1,230 | 1,500 |
| 0400 | High output, 4' long, 60 watt | | .90 | 8.889 | | 945 | 405 | | 1,350 | 1,625 |
| 0410 | 8' long, 95 watt energy saver | | .80 | 10 | | 960 | 455 | | 1,415 | 1,725 |
| 0500 | 8' long, 110 watt | | .80 | 10 | | 960 | 455 | | 1,415 | 1,725 |
| 0512 | 2' long, T5, 14 watt energy saver | | 1 | 8 | | 1,325 | 365 | | 1,690 | 2,000 |
| 0514 | 3' long, T5, 21 watt energy saver | | .90 | 8.889 | | 1,325 | 405 | | 1,730 | 2,050 |
| 0516 | 4' long, T5, 28 watt energy saver | | .90 | 8.889 | | 1,150 | 405 | | 1,555 | 1,850 |
| 0560 | Twin tube compact lamp | | .90 | 8.889 | | 560 | 405 | | 965 | 1,225 |

# 26 61 Lighting Systems and Accessories

## 26 61 23 – Lamps Applications

### 26 61 23.10 Lamps

| | | Crew | Daily Output | Labor-Hours | Unit | Material | 2008 Bare Costs Labor | Equipment | Total | Total Incl O&P |
|---|---|---|---|---|---|---|---|---|---|---|
| 0570 | Double twin tube compact lamp | 1 Elec | .80 | 10 | C | 1,425 | 455 | | 1,880 | 2,225 |
| 0600 | Mercury vapor, mogul base, deluxe white, 100 watt | | .30 | 26.667 | | 3,100 | 1,225 | | 4,325 | 5,225 |
| 0700 | 250 watt | | .30 | 26.667 | | 4,125 | 1,225 | | 5,350 | 6,325 |
| 0800 | 400 watt | | .30 | 26.667 | | 3,300 | 1,225 | | 4,525 | 5,450 |
| 0900 | 1000 watt | | .20 | 40 | | 7,725 | 1,825 | | 9,550 | 11,200 |
| 1000 | Metal halide, mogul base, 175 watt | | .30 | 26.667 | | 3,825 | 1,225 | | 5,050 | 6,000 |
| 1200 | 400 watt | | .30 | 26.667 | | 4,100 | 1,225 | | 5,325 | 6,300 |
| 1300 | 1000 watt | | .20 | 40 | | 9,900 | 1,825 | | 11,725 | 13,600 |
| 1350 | High pressure sodium, 70 watt | | .30 | 26.667 | | 4,450 | 1,225 | | 5,675 | 6,675 |
| 1380 | 250 watt | | .30 | 26.667 | | 5,050 | 1,225 | | 6,275 | 7,375 |
| 1400 | 400 watt | | .30 | 26.667 | | 5,200 | 1,225 | | 6,425 | 7,525 |
| 1450 | 1000 watt | | .20 | 40 | | 14,300 | 1,825 | | 16,125 | 18,400 |
| 3000 | Guards, fluorescent lamp, 4' long | | 1 | 8 | | 1,025 | 365 | | 1,390 | 1,675 |
| 3200 | 8' long | | .90 | 8.889 | | 2,050 | 405 | | 2,455 | 2,850 |

# 26 71 Electrical Machines

## 26 71 13 – Motors Applications

### 26 71 13.20 Motors

| | | Crew | Daily Output | Labor-Hours | Unit | Material | 2008 Bare Costs Labor | Equipment | Total | Total Incl O&P |
|---|---|---|---|---|---|---|---|---|---|---|
| 0010 | **MOTORS** 230/460 volts, 60 HZ | | | | | | | | | |
| 0050 | Dripproof, premium efficiency, 1.15 service factor | | | | | | | | | |
| 0060 | 1800 RPM, 1/4 HP | 1 Elec | 5.33 | 1.501 | Ea. | 158 | 68.50 | | 226.50 | 276 |
| 0070 | 1/3 HP | | 5.33 | 1.501 | | 173 | 68.50 | | 241.50 | 292 |
| 0080 | 1/2 HP | | 5.33 | 1.501 | | 204 | 68.50 | | 272.50 | 325 |
| 0090 | 3/4 HP | | 5.33 | 1.501 | | 228 | 68.50 | | 296.50 | 355 |
| 0100 | 1 HP | | 4.50 | 1.778 | | 239 | 81 | | 320 | 385 |
| 0250 | 5 HP | | 4.50 | 1.778 | | 370 | 81 | | 451 | 530 |
| 0350 | 10 HP | | 4 | 2 | | 635 | 91 | | 726 | 835 |
| 0450 | 20 HP **CN** | 2 Elec | 5.20 | 3.077 | | 1,050 | 140 | | 1,190 | 1,375 |

## Estimating Tips

*27 20 00 Data Communications*

*27 30 00 Voice Communications*

*27 40 00 Audio-Video Communications*

- When estimating material costs for special systems, it is always prudent to obtain manufacturers' quotations for equipment prices and special installation requirements which will affect the total costs.

## Reference Numbers

Reference numbers are shown in shaded boxes at the beginning of some major classifications. These numbers refer to related items in the Reference Section. The reference information may be an estimating procedure, an alternate pricing method, or technical information.

*Note:* Not all subdivisions listed here necessarily appear in this publication.

# 27 13 Communications Backbone Cabling

## 27 13 23 – Communications Optical Fiber Backbone Cabling

| 27 13 23.13 Communications Optical Fiber | Crew | Daily Output | Labor-Hours | Unit | Material | 2008 Bare Costs Labor | 2008 Bare Costs Equipment | Total | Total Incl O&P |
|---|---|---|---|---|---|---|---|---|---|
| 0010 **COMMUNICATIONS OPTICAL FIBER** | | | | | | | | | |
| 0040 Specialized tools & techniques cause installation costs to vary. | | | | | | | | | |
| 0070 Fiber optic, cable, bulk simplex, minimum | 1 Elec | 8 | 1 | C.L.F. | 23 | 45.50 | | 68.50 | 93.50 |
| 0080 Bulk plenum quad, maximum | " | 2.29 | 3.493 | " | 66 | 159 | | 225 | 310 |
| 0150 Jumper | | | | Ea. | 55.50 | | | 55.50 | 61 |
| 0200 Pigtail | | | | | 30 | | | 30 | 33 |
| 0300 Connector | 1 Elec | 24 | .333 | | 18.45 | 15.20 | | 33.65 | 43 |
| 0350 Finger splice | | 32 | .250 | | 32 | 11.40 | | 43.40 | 52 |
| 0400 Transceiver (low cost bi-directional) | | 8 | 1 | | 295 | 45.50 | | 340.50 | 395 |
| 0450 Rack housing, 4 rack spaces, 12 panels (144 fibers) | | 2 | 4 | | 450 | 182 | | 632 | 765 |
| 0500 Patch panel, 12 ports | ↓ | 6 | 1.333 | ↓ | 178 | 60.50 | | 238.50 | 287 |

# 27 41 Audio-Video Systems

## 27 41 19 – Portable Audio-Video Equipment

### 27 41 19.10 T.V. Systems

| | Crew | Daily Output | Labor-Hours | Unit | Material | 2008 Bare Costs Labor | 2008 Bare Costs Equipment | Total | Total Incl O&P |
|---|---|---|---|---|---|---|---|---|---|
| 0010 **T.V. SYSTEMS**, not including rough-in wires, cables & conduits | | | | | | | | | |
| 0100 Master TV antenna system | | | | | | | | | |
| 0200 VHF reception & distribution, 12 outlets | 1 Elec | 6 | 1.333 | Outlet | 189 | 60.50 | | 249.50 | 299 |
| 0400 30 outlets | | 10 | .800 | | 124 | 36.50 | | 160.50 | 192 |
| 0600 100 outlets | | 13 | .615 | | 125 | 28 | | 153 | 179 |
| 0800 VHF & UHF reception & distribution, 12 outlets | | 6 | 1.333 | | 188 | 60.50 | | 248.50 | 298 |
| 1000 30 outlets | | 10 | .800 | | 124 | 36.50 | | 160.50 | 192 |
| 1200 100 outlets | | 13 | .615 | | 127 | 28 | | 155 | 182 |
| 1400 School and deluxe systems, 12 outlets | | 2.40 | 3.333 | | 248 | 152 | | 400 | 500 |
| 1600 30 outlets | | 4 | 2 | | 217 | 91 | | 308 | 375 |
| 1800 80 outlets | ↓ | 5.30 | 1.509 | ↓ | 209 | 69 | | 278 | 330 |

# 27 51 Distributed Audio-Video Communications Systems

## 27 51 16 – Public Address and Mass Notification Systems

### 27 51 16.10 Public Address System

| | Crew | Daily Output | Labor-Hours | Unit | Material | 2008 Bare Costs Labor | 2008 Bare Costs Equipment | Total | Total Incl O&P |
|---|---|---|---|---|---|---|---|---|---|
| 0010 **PUBLIC ADDRESS SYSTEM** | | | | | | | | | |
| 0100 Conventional, office | 1 Elec | 5.33 | 1.501 | Speaker | 118 | 68.50 | | 186.50 | 232 |
| 0200 Industrial | " | 2.70 | 2.963 | " | 227 | 135 | | 362 | 450 |

## 27 51 19 – Sound Masking Systems

### 27 51 19.10 Sound System

| | Crew | Daily Output | Labor-Hours | Unit | Material | 2008 Bare Costs Labor | 2008 Bare Costs Equipment | Total | Total Incl O&P |
|---|---|---|---|---|---|---|---|---|---|
| 0010 **SOUND SYSTEM**, not including rough-in wires, cables & conduits | | | | | | | | | |
| 0100 Components, projector outlet | 1 Elec | 8 | 1 | Ea. | 54.50 | 45.50 | | 100 | 128 |
| 0200 Microphone | | 4 | 2 | | 60.50 | 91 | | 151.50 | 203 |
| 0400 Speakers, ceiling or wall | | 8 | 1 | | 103 | 45.50 | | 148.50 | 181 |
| 0600 Trumpets | | 4 | 2 | | 191 | 91 | | 282 | 345 |
| 0800 Privacy switch | | 8 | 1 | | 76 | 45.50 | | 121.50 | 152 |
| 1000 Monitor panel | | 4 | 2 | | 340 | 91 | | 431 | 510 |
| 1200 Antenna, AM/FM | | 4 | 2 | | 190 | 91 | | 281 | 345 |
| 1400 Volume control | | 8 | 1 | | 76 | 45.50 | | 121.50 | 152 |
| 1600 Amplifier, 250 watts | | 1 | 8 | | 1,525 | 365 | | 1,890 | 2,225 |
| 1800 Cabinets | | 1 | 8 | | 740 | 365 | | 1,105 | 1,350 |
| 2000 Intercom, 25 station capacity, master station | 2 Elec | 2 | 8 | | 1,775 | 365 | | 2,140 | 2,500 |
| 2200 Remote station | 1 Elec | 8 | 1 | | 143 | 45.50 | | 188.50 | 225 |
| 2400 Intercom outlets | ↓ | 8 | 1 | ↓ | 84 | 45.50 | | 129.50 | 160 |

# 27 51 Distributed Audio-Video Communications Systems

## 27 51 19 – Sound Masking Systems

### 27 51 19.10 Sound System

| | 27 51 19.10 Sound System | Crew | Daily Output | Labor-Hours | Unit | Material | 2008 Bare Costs Labor | Equipment | Total | Total Incl O&P |
|---|---|---|---|---|---|---|---|---|---|---|
| 2600 | Handset | 1 Elec | 4 | 2 | Ea. | 278 | 91 | | 369 | 440 |
| 2800 | Emergency call system, 12 zones, annunciator | | 1.30 | 6.154 | | 835 | 280 | | 1,115 | 1,350 |
| 3000 | Bell | | 5.30 | 1.509 | | 86.50 | 69 | | 155.50 | 197 |
| 3200 | Light or relay | | 8 | 1 | | 43 | 45.50 | | 88.50 | 116 |
| 3400 | Transformer | | 4 | 2 | | 190 | 91 | | 281 | 345 |
| 3600 | House telephone, talking station | | 1.60 | 5 | | 410 | 228 | | 638 | 790 |
| 3800 | Press to talk, release to listen | ↓ | 5.30 | 1.509 | | 95 | 69 | | 164 | 206 |
| 4000 | System-on button | | | | | 57 | | | 57 | 62.50 |
| 4200 | Door release | 1 Elec | 4 | 2 | | 102 | 91 | | 193 | 248 |
| 4400 | Combination speaker and microphone | | 8 | 1 | | 173 | 45.50 | | 218.50 | 258 |
| 4600 | Termination box | | 3.20 | 2.500 | | 54.50 | 114 | | 168.50 | 230 |
| 4800 | Amplifier or power supply | | 5.30 | 1.509 | ↓ | 625 | 69 | | 694 | 790 |
| 5000 | Vestibule door unit | | 16 | .500 | Name | 115 | 23 | | 138 | 160 |
| 5200 | Strip cabinet | | 27 | .296 | Ea. | 217 | 13.50 | | 230.50 | 259 |
| 5400 | Directory | ↓ | 16 | .500 | " | 102 | 23 | | 125 | 146 |

# 27 52 Healthcare Communications and Monitoring Systems

## 27 52 23 – Nurse Call/Code Blue Systems

### 27 52 23.10 Nurse Call Systems

| | | Crew | Daily Output | Labor-Hours | Unit | Material | 2008 Bare Costs Labor | Equipment | Total | Total Incl O&P |
|---|---|---|---|---|---|---|---|---|---|---|
| 0010 | **NURSE CALL SYSTEMS** | | | | | | | | | |
| 0100 | Single bedside call station | 1 Elec | 8 | 1 | Ea. | 210 | 45.50 | | 255.50 | 299 |
| 0200 | Ceiling speaker station | | 8 | 1 | | 61.50 | 45.50 | | 107 | 136 |
| 0400 | Emergency call station | | 8 | 1 | | 104 | 45.50 | | 149.50 | 182 |
| 0600 | Pillow speaker | | 8 | 1 | | 199 | 45.50 | | 244.50 | 286 |
| 0800 | Double bedside call station | | 4 | 2 | | 208 | 91 | | 299 | 365 |
| 1000 | Duty station | | 4 | 2 | | 159 | 91 | | 250 | 310 |
| 1200 | Standard call button | | 8 | 1 | | 80.50 | 45.50 | | 126 | 157 |
| 1400 | Lights, corridor, dome or zone indicator | ↓ | 8 | 1 | ↓ | 56 | 45.50 | | 101.50 | 130 |
| 1600 | Master control station for 20 stations | 2 Elec | .65 | 24.615 | Total | 3,725 | 1,125 | | 4,850 | 5,775 |

# 27 53 Distributed Systems

## 27 53 13 – Clock Systems

### 27 53 13.50 Clock Equipments

| | | Crew | Daily Output | Labor-Hours | Unit | Material | 2008 Bare Costs Labor | Equipment | Total | Total Incl O&P |
|---|---|---|---|---|---|---|---|---|---|---|
| 0010 | **CLOCK EQUIPMENTS**, not including wires & conduits | | | | | | | | | |
| 0100 | Time system components, master controller | 1 Elec | .33 | 24.242 | Ea. | 1,625 | 1,100 | | 2,725 | 3,450 |
| 0200 | Program bell | | 8 | 1 | | 53.50 | 45.50 | | 99 | 127 |
| 0400 | Combination clock & speaker | | 3.20 | 2.500 | | 189 | 114 | | 303 | 380 |
| 0600 | Frequency generator | | 2 | 4 | | 6,350 | 182 | | 6,532 | 7,250 |
| 0800 | Job time automatic stamp recorder, minimum | | 4 | 2 | | 445 | 91 | | 536 | 625 |
| 1000 | Maximum | ↓ | 4 | 2 | | 680 | 91 | | 771 | 885 |
| 1200 | Time stamp for correspondence, hand operated | | | | | 340 | | | 340 | 375 |
| 1400 | Fully automatic | | | | | 495 | | | 495 | 545 |
| 1600 | Master time clock system, clocks & bells, 20 room | 4 Elec | .20 | 160 | | 4,075 | 7,300 | | 11,375 | 15,400 |
| 1800 | 50 room | " | .08 | 400 | | 9,400 | 18,200 | | 27,600 | 37,400 |
| 2000 | Time clock, 100 cards in & out, 1 color | 1 Elec | 3.20 | 2.500 | | 950 | 114 | | 1,064 | 1,225 |
| 2200 | 2 colors | | 3.20 | 2.500 | | 1,025 | 114 | | 1,139 | 1,300 |
| 2400 | With 3 circuit program device, minimum | | 2 | 4 | | 375 | 182 | | 557 | 685 |
| 2600 | Maximum | | 2 | 4 | | 545 | 182 | | 727 | 870 |
| 2800 | Metal rack for 25 cards | ↓ | 7 | 1.143 | ↓ | 60 | 52 | | 112 | 144 |

# 27 53 Distributed Systems

## 27 53 13 – Clock Systems

| 27 53 13.50 Clock Equipments | Crew | Daily Output | Labor-Hours | Unit | Material | 2008 Bare Costs Labor | Equipment | Total | Total Incl O&P |
|---|---|---|---|---|---|---|---|---|---|
| 3000 | Watchman's tour station | 1 Elec | 8 | 1 | Ea. | 63 | 45.50 | | 108.50 | 138 |
| 3200 | Annunciator with zone indication | | 1 | 8 | | 230 | 365 | | 595 | 800 |
| 3400 | Time clock with tape | ↓ | 1 | 8 | ↓ | 610 | 365 | | 975 | 1,225 |

## Estimating Tips

- When estimating material costs for electronic safety and security systems, it is always prudent to obtain manufacturers' quotations for equipment prices and special installation requirements, which affect the total cost.

- Fire alarm systems consist of control panels, annunciator panels, battery with rack, charger, and fire alarm actuating and indicating devices. Some fire alarm systems include speakers, telephone lines, door closer controls, and other components. Be careful not to overlook the costs related to installation for these items.

Also be aware of costs for integrated automation instrumentation and terminal devices, control equipment, control wiring, and programming.

- Security equipment includes items such as CCTV, access control, and other detection and identification systems to perform alert and alarm functions. Be sure to consider the costs related to installation for this security equipment, such as for integrated automation instrumentation and terminal devices, control equipment, control wiring, and programming.

## Reference Numbers

Reference numbers are shown in shaded boxes at the beginning of some major classifications. These numbers refer to related items in the Reference Section. The reference information may be an estimating procedure, an alternate pricing method, or technical information.

*Note:* Not all subdivisions listed here necessarily appear in this publication.

**Division 28 – Electronic Safety and Security**

# 28 13 Access Control

## 28 13 53 – Security Access Detection

### 28 13 53.13 Security Access Metal Detectors

| | Crew | Daily Output | Labor-Hours | Unit | Material | 2008 Bare Costs Labor | Equipment | Total | Total Incl O&P |
|---|---|---|---|---|---|---|---|---|---|
| 0010 **SECURITY ACCESS METAL DETECTORS** | | | | | | | | | |
| 0240 Metal detector, hand-held, wand type, unit only | | | | Ea. | | | | 81.82 | 90 |
| 0250 Metal detector, walk through portal type, single zone | 1 Elec | 2 | 4 | | 4,000 | 182 | | 4,182 | 4,675 |
| 0260 Multi-zone | " | 2 | 4 | | 5,000 | 182 | | 5,182 | 5,775 |

### 28 13 53.16 Security Access X-Ray Equipment

| | Crew | Daily Output | Labor-Hours | Unit | Material | 2008 Bare Costs Labor | Equipment | Total | Total Incl O&P |
|---|---|---|---|---|---|---|---|---|---|
| 0010 **SECURITY ACCESS X-RAY EQUIPMENT** | | | | | | | | | |
| 0290 X-ray machine, desk top, for mail/small packages/letters | 1 Elec | 4 | 2 | Ea. | 3,000 | 91 | | 3,091 | 3,425 |
| 0300 Conveyor type, incl monitor, minimum | | 2 | 4 | | 14,000 | 182 | | 14,182 | 15,700 |
| 0310 Maximum | | 2 | 4 | | 25,000 | 182 | | 25,182 | 27,800 |
| 0320 X-ray machine, large unit, for airports, incl monitor, min | 2 Elec | 1 | 16 | | 35,000 | 730 | | 35,730 | 39,600 |
| 0330 Maximum | " | .50 | 32 | | 60,000 | 1,450 | | 61,450 | 68,000 |

### 28 13 53.23 Security Access Explosive Detection Equipment

| | Crew | Daily Output | Labor-Hours | Unit | Material | 2008 Bare Costs Labor | Equipment | Total | Total Incl O&P |
|---|---|---|---|---|---|---|---|---|---|
| 0010 **SECURITY ACCESS EXPLOSIVE DETECTION EQUIPMENT** | | | | | | | | | |
| 0270 Explosives detector, walk through portal type | 1 Elec | 2 | 4 | Ea. | 3,500 | 182 | | 3,682 | 4,125 |
| 0280 Hand-held, battery operated | | | | " | | | | 25,455 | 28,000 |

# 28 16 Intrusion Detection

## 28 16 16 – Intrusion Detection Systems Infrastructure

### 28 16 16.50 Intrusion Detection

| | Crew | Daily Output | Labor-Hours | Unit | Material | 2008 Bare Costs Labor | Equipment | Total | Total Incl O&P |
|---|---|---|---|---|---|---|---|---|---|
| 0010 **INTRUSION DETECTION**, not including wires & conduits | | | | | | | | | |
| 0100 Burglar alarm, battery operated, mechanical trigger | 1 Elec | 4 | 2 | Ea. | 254 | 91 | | 345 | 415 |
| 0200 Electrical trigger | | 4 | 2 | | 305 | 91 | | 396 | 470 |
| 0400 For outside key control, add | | 8 | 1 | | 72 | 45.50 | | 117.50 | 147 |
| 0600 For remote signaling circuitry, add | | 8 | 1 | | 114 | 45.50 | | 159.50 | 194 |
| 0800 Card reader, flush type, standard | | 2.70 | 2.963 | | 850 | 135 | | 985 | 1,125 |
| 1000 Multi-code | | 2.70 | 2.963 | | 1,100 | 135 | | 1,235 | 1,400 |
| 1200 Door switches, hinge switch | | 5.30 | 1.509 | | 53.50 | 69 | | 122.50 | 161 |
| 1400 Magnetic switch | | 5.30 | 1.509 | | 63 | 69 | | 132 | 172 |
| 1600 Exit control locks, horn alarm | | 4 | 2 | | 315 | 91 | | 406 | 485 |
| 1800 Flashing light alarm | | 4 | 2 | | 355 | 91 | | 446 | 530 |
| 2000 Indicating panels, 1 channel | | 2.70 | 2.963 | | 335 | 135 | | 470 | 570 |
| 2200 10 channel | 2 Elec | 3.20 | 5 | | 1,150 | 228 | | 1,378 | 1,600 |
| 2400 20 channel | | 2 | 8 | | 2,250 | 365 | | 2,615 | 3,025 |
| 2600 40 channel | | 1.14 | 14.035 | | 4,075 | 640 | | 4,715 | 5,450 |
| 2800 Ultrasonic motion detector, 12 volt | 1 Elec | 2.30 | 3.478 | | 210 | 158 | | 368 | 465 |
| 3000 Infrared photoelectric detector | " | 2.30 | 3.478 | | 173 | 158 | | 331 | 425 |

# 28 23 Video Surveillance

## 28 23 13 – Video Surveillance Control and Management Systems

### 28 23 13.10 Closed Circuit Television System

| | Crew | Daily Output | Labor-Hours | Unit | Material | 2008 Bare Costs Labor | Equipment | Total | Total Incl O&P |
|---|---|---|---|---|---|---|---|---|---|
| 0010 **CLOSED CIRCUIT TELEVISION SYSTEM** | | | | | | | | | |
| 2000 Surveillance, one station (camera & monitor) | 2 Elec | 2.60 | 6.154 | Total | 1,200 | 280 | | 1,480 | 1,750 |
| 2200 For additional camera stations, add | 1 Elec | 2.70 | 2.963 | Ea. | 670 | 135 | | 805 | 940 |
| 2400 Industrial quality, one station (camera & monitor) | 2 Elec | 2.60 | 6.154 | Total | 2,500 | 280 | | 2,780 | 3,175 |
| 2600 For additional camera stations, add | 1 Elec | 2.70 | 2.963 | Ea. | 1,525 | 135 | | 1,660 | 1,875 |
| 2610 For low light, add | | 2.70 | 2.963 | | 1,225 | 135 | | 1,360 | 1,550 |
| 2620 For very low light, add | | 2.70 | 2.963 | | 9,025 | 135 | | 9,160 | 10,100 |
| 2800 For weatherproof camera station, add | | 1.30 | 6.154 | | 940 | 280 | | 1,220 | 1,450 |
| 3000 For pan and tilt, add | | 1.30 | 6.154 | | 2,425 | 280 | | 2,705 | 3,100 |

# 28 23 Video Surveillance

## 28 23 13 – Video Surveillance Control and Management Systems

### 28 23 13.10 Closed Circuit Television System

| | | Crew | Daily Output | Labor-Hours | Unit | Material | 2008 Bare Costs Labor | Equipment | Total | Total Incl O&P |
|---|---|---|---|---|---|---|---|---|---|---|
| 3200 | For zoom lens - remote control, add, minimum | 1 Elec | 2 | 4 | Ea. | 2,250 | 182 | | 2,432 | 2,750 |
| 3400 | Maximum | | 2 | 4 | | 8,175 | 182 | | 8,357 | 9,275 |
| 3410 | For automatic iris for low light, add | | 2 | 4 | | 1,950 | 182 | | 2,132 | 2,425 |
| 3600 | Educational T.V. studio, basic 3 camera system, black & white, | | | | | | | | | |
| 3800 | electrical & electronic equip. only, minimum | 4 Elec | .80 | 40 | Total | 11,600 | 1,825 | | 13,425 | 15,500 |
| 4000 | Maximum (full console) | | .28 | 114 | | 49,500 | 5,200 | | 54,700 | 62,500 |
| 4100 | As above, but color system, minimum | | .28 | 114 | | 65,500 | 5,200 | | 70,700 | 80,000 |
| 4120 | Maximum | | .12 | 266 | | 285,000 | 12,100 | | 297,100 | 331,500 |
| 4200 | For film chain, black & white, add | 1 Elec | 1 | 8 | Ea. | 13,300 | 365 | | 13,665 | 15,100 |
| 4250 | Color, add | | .25 | 32 | | 16,200 | 1,450 | | 17,650 | 20,000 |
| 4400 | For video tape recorders, add, minimum | | 1 | 8 | | 2,800 | 365 | | 3,165 | 3,625 |
| 4600 | Maximum | 4 Elec | .40 | 80 | | 23,300 | 3,650 | | 26,950 | 31,000 |

## 28 23 23 – Video Surveillance Systems Infrastructure

### 28 23 23.50 Video Surveillance Equipments

| | | Crew | Daily Output | Labor-Hours | Unit | Material | 2008 Bare Costs Labor | Equipment | Total | Total Incl O&P |
|---|---|---|---|---|---|---|---|---|---|---|
| 0010 | **VIDEO SURVEILLANCE EQUIPMENTS** | | | | | | | | | |
| 0200 | Video cameras, wireless, hidden in exit signs, clocks, etc, incl receiver | 1 Elec | 3 | 2.667 | Ea. | 300 | 121 | | 421 | 510 |
| 0210 | Accessories for, VCR, single camera | | 3 | 2.667 | | 500 | 121 | | 621 | 730 |
| 0220 | For multiple cameras | | 3 | 2.667 | | 1,500 | 121 | | 1,621 | 1,825 |
| 0230 | Video cameras, wireless, for under vehicle searching, complete | | 2 | 4 | | 3,500 | 182 | | 3,682 | 4,125 |

# 28 31 Fire Detection and Alarm

## 28 31 23 – Fire Detection and Alarm Annunciation Panels and Fire Stations

### 28 31 23.50 Alarm Panels and Devices

| | | Crew | Daily Output | Labor-Hours | Unit | Material | 2008 Bare Costs Labor | Equipment | Total | Total Incl O&P |
|---|---|---|---|---|---|---|---|---|---|---|
| 0010 | **ALARM PANELS AND DEVICES**, not incluidng wires & conduits | | | | | | | | | |
| 3594 | Fire, alarm control panel | | | | | | | | | |
| 3600 | 4 zone | 2 Elec | 2 | 8 | Ea. | 940 | 365 | | 1,305 | 1,575 |
| 3800 | 8 zone | | 1 | 16 | | 1,400 | 730 | | 2,130 | 2,625 |
| 4000 | 12 zone | | .67 | 23.988 | | 1,825 | 1,100 | | 2,925 | 3,625 |
| 4020 | Alarm device | 1 Elec | 8 | 1 | | 122 | 45.50 | | 167.50 | 202 |
| 4050 | Actuating device | | 8 | 1 | | 292 | 45.50 | | 337.50 | 390 |
| 4200 | Battery and rack | | 4 | 2 | | 725 | 91 | | 816 | 935 |
| 4400 | Automatic charger | | 8 | 1 | | 445 | 45.50 | | 490.50 | 560 |
| 4600 | Signal bell | | 8 | 1 | | 52 | 45.50 | | 97.50 | 125 |
| 4800 | Trouble buzzer or manual station | | 8 | 1 | | 37 | 45.50 | | 82.50 | 109 |
| 5600 | Strobe and horn | | 5.30 | 1.509 | | 95 | 69 | | 164 | 207 |
| 5800 | Fire alarm horn | | 6.70 | 1.194 | | 36.50 | 54.50 | | 91 | 121 |
| 6000 | Door holder, electro-magnetic | | 4 | 2 | | 77.50 | 91 | | 168.50 | 222 |
| 6200 | Combination holder and closer | | 3.20 | 2.500 | | 430 | 114 | | 544 | 645 |
| 6400 | Code transmitter | | 4 | 2 | | 690 | 91 | | 781 | 895 |
| 6600 | Drill switch | | 8 | 1 | | 86.50 | 45.50 | | 132 | 163 |
| 6800 | Master box | | 2.70 | 2.963 | | 3,100 | 135 | | 3,235 | 3,600 |
| 7000 | Break glass station | | 8 | 1 | | 50 | 45.50 | | 95.50 | 123 |
| 7800 | Remote annunciator, 8 zone lamp | | 1.80 | 4.444 | | 201 | 202 | | 403 | 520 |
| 8000 | 12 zone lamp | 2 Elec | 2.60 | 6.154 | | 345 | 280 | | 625 | 800 |
| 8200 | 16 zone lamp | " | 2.20 | 7.273 | | 345 | 330 | | 675 | 875 |

## 28 31 43 – Fire Detection Sensors

### 28 31 43.50 Fire and Heat Detectors

| | | Crew | Daily Output | Labor-Hours | Unit | Material | 2008 Bare Costs Labor | Equipment | Total | Total Incl O&P |
|---|---|---|---|---|---|---|---|---|---|---|
| 0010 | **FIRE & HEAT DETECTORS** | | | | | | | | | |
| 5000 | Detector, rate of rise | 1 Elec | 8 | 1 | Ea. | 35 | 45.50 | | 80.50 | 107 |

# 28 31 Fire Detection and Alarm

## 28 31 46 – Smoke Detection Sensors

| 28 31 46.50 Smoke Detectors | Crew | Daily Output | Labor-Hours | Unit | Material | 2008 Bare Costs Labor | Equipment | Total | Total Incl O&P |
|---|---|---|---|---|---|---|---|---|---|
| **0010 SMOKE DETECTORS** | | | | | | | | | |
| 5200     Smoke detector, ceiling type | 1 Elec | 6.20 | 1.290 | Ea. | 79 | 59 | | 138 | 174 |
| 5400     Duct type | " | 3.20 | 2.500 | " | 250 | 114 | | 364 | 445 |

# 28 33 Fuel-Gas Detection and Alarm

## 28 33 33 – Fuel-Gas Detection Sensors

### 28 33 33.50 Tank Leak Detection Systems

| | | Crew | Daily Output | Labor-Hours | Unit | Material | Labor | Equipment | Total | Total Incl O&P |
|---|---|---|---|---|---|---|---|---|---|---|
| 0010 | **TANK LEAK DETECTION SYSTEMS** Liquid and vapor | | | | | | | | | |
| 0100 | For hydrocarbons and hazardous liquids/vapors | | | | | | | | | |
| 0120 | Controller, data acquisition, incl. printer, modem, RS232 port | | | | | | | | | |
| 0140 | 24 channel, for use with all probes | | | | Ea. | 2,175 | | | 2,175 | 2,400 |
| 0160 | 9 channel, for external monitoring | | | | " | 1,700 | | | 1,700 | 1,850 |
| 0200 | Probes | | | | | | | | | |
| 0210 | Well monitoring | | | | | | | | | |
| 0220 | Liquid phase detection | | | | Ea. | 760 | | | 760 | 835 |
| 0230 | Hydrocarbon vapor, fixed position | | | | | 700 | | | 700 | 770 |
| 0240 | Hydrocarbon vapor, float mounted | | | | | 645 | | | 645 | 710 |
| 0250 | Both liquid and vapor hydrocarbon | | | | ↓ | 940 | | | 940 | 1,025 |
| 0300 | Secondary containment, liquid phase | | | | | | | | | |
| 0310 | Pipe trench/manway sump | | | | Ea. | 340 | | | 340 | 375 |
| 0320 | Double wall pipe and manual sump | | | | | 330 | | | 330 | 365 |
| 0330 | Double wall fiberglass annular space | | | | | 305 | | | 305 | 335 |
| 0340 | Double wall steel tank annular space | | | | ↓ | 305 | | | 305 | 335 |
| 0500 | Accessories | | | | | | | | | |
| 0510 | Modem, non-dedicated phone line | | | | Ea. | 273 | | | 273 | 300 |
| 0600 | Monitoring, internal | | | | | | | | | |
| 0610 | Automatic tank gauge, incl. overfill | | | | Ea. | 1,100 | | | 1,100 | 1,200 |
| 0620 | Product line | | | | " | 1,175 | | | 1,175 | 1,300 |
| 0700 | Monitoring, special | | | | | | | | | |
| 0710 | Cathodic protection | | | | Ea. | 650 | | | 650 | 715 |
| 0720 | Annular space chemical monitor | | | | " | 885 | | | 885 | 975 |

## Estimating Tips

### 31 05 00 Common Work Results for Earthwork

- Estimating the actual cost of performing earthwork requires careful consideration of the variables involved. This includes items such as type of soil, whether water will be encountered, dewatering, whether banks need bracing, disposal of excavated earth, and length of haul to fill or spoil sites, etc. If the project has large quantities of cut or fill, consider raising or lowering the site to reduce costs, while paying close attention to the effect on site drainage and utilities.

- If the project has large quantities of fill, creating a borrow pit on the site can significantly lower the costs.

- It is very important to consider what time of year the project is scheduled for completion. Bad weather can create large cost overruns from dewatering, site repair, and lost productivity from cold weather.

## Reference Numbers

Reference numbers are shown in shaded boxes at the beginning of some major classifications. These numbers refer to related items in the Reference Section. The reference information may be an estimating procedure, an alternate pricing method, or technical information.

*Note:* Not all subdivisions listed here necessarily appear in this publication.

# 31 05 Common Work Results for Earthwork

## 31 05 13 – Soils for Earthwork

### 31 05 13.10 Borrow

| | | Crew | Daily Output | Labor-Hours | Unit | Material | 2008 Bare Costs Labor | Equipment | Total | Total Incl O&P |
|---|---|---|---|---|---|---|---|---|---|---|
| 0010 | **BORROW** R312316-40 | | | | | | | | | |
| 0020 | Spread, 200 H.P. dozer, no compaction, 2 mi. RT haul | | | | | | | | | |
| 0200 | Common borrow | B-15 | 600 | .047 | C.Y. | 7 | 1.55 | 3.46 | 12.01 | 13.90 |
| 0700 | Screened loam **CN** | | 600 | .047 | | 25 | 1.55 | 3.46 | 30.01 | 33.50 |
| 0800 | Topsoil, weed free | ↓ | 600 | .047 | | 22 | 1.55 | 3.46 | 27.01 | 30 |
| 0900 | For 5 mile haul, add | B-34B | 200 | .040 | ↓ | | 1.22 | 2.51 | 3.73 | 4.66 |

## 31 05 16 – Aggregates for Earthwork

### 31 05 16.10 Borrow

| | | Crew | Daily Output | Labor-Hours | Unit | Material | 2008 Bare Costs Labor | Equipment | Total | Total Incl O&P |
|---|---|---|---|---|---|---|---|---|---|---|
| 0010 | **BORROW** R312316-40 | | | | | | | | | |
| 0020 | Spread, with 200 H.P. dozer, no compaction, 2 mi RT haul | | | | | | | | | |
| 0100 | Bank run gravel **CN** | B-15 | 600 | .047 | C.Y. | 26 | 1.55 | 3.46 | 31.01 | 34.50 |
| 0300 | Crushed stone (1.40 tons per CY) , 1-1/2" | | 600 | .047 | | 46.50 | 1.55 | 3.46 | 51.51 | 57.50 |
| 0320 | 3/4" **CN** | | 600 | .047 | | 46.50 | 1.55 | 3.46 | 51.51 | 57.50 |
| 0340 | 1/2" | | 600 | .047 | | 35.50 | 1.55 | 3.46 | 40.51 | 45 |
| 0360 | 3/8" | | 600 | .047 | | 41 | 1.55 | 3.46 | 46.01 | 51 |
| 0400 | Sand, washed, concrete | | 600 | .047 | | 40.50 | 1.55 | 3.46 | 45.51 | 50.50 |
| 0500 | Dead or bank sand | | 600 | .047 | | 10 | 1.55 | 3.46 | 15.01 | 17.20 |
| 0600 | Select structural fill | ↓ | 600 | .047 | | 14.50 | 1.55 | 3.46 | 19.51 | 22 |
| 0900 | For 5 mile haul, add | B-34B | 200 | .040 | ↓ | | 1.22 | 2.51 | 3.73 | 4.66 |

## 31 05 23 – Cement and Concrete for Earthwork

### 31 05 23.30 Plant Mixed Bituminous Concrete

| | | Crew | Daily Output | Labor-Hours | Unit | Material | 2008 Bare Costs Labor | Equipment | Total | Total Incl O&P |
|---|---|---|---|---|---|---|---|---|---|---|
| 0010 | **PLANT MIXED BITUMINOUS CONCRETE** | | | | | | | | | |
| 0020 | Asphaltic concrete plant mix (145 LB per c.f.) **CN** | | | | Ton | 52 | | | 52 | 57 |
| 0040 | Asphaltic concrete less than 300 tons add trucking costs | | | | | | | | | |
| 0050 | See Div. 31 23 23.18 for hauling costs | | | | | | | | | |
| 0200 | All weather patching mix, hot | | | | | 55 | | | 55 | 60.50 |
| 0250 | Cold patch | | | | | 55 | | | 55 | 60.50 |
| 0300 | Berm mix | | | | ↓ | 55 | | | 55 | 60.50 |

# 31 06 Schedules for Earthwork

## 31 06 60 – Schedules for Special Foundations and Load Bearing Elements

### 31 06 60.14 Piling Special Costs

| | | Crew | Daily Output | Labor-Hours | Unit | Material | 2008 Bare Costs Labor | Equipment | Total | Total Incl O&P |
|---|---|---|---|---|---|---|---|---|---|---|
| 0010 | **PILING SPECIAL COSTS** | | | | | | | | | |
| 0011 | Piling special costs, pile caps, see Div. 03 30 53.40 | | | | | | | | | |
| 0500 | Cutoffs, concrete piles, plain | 1 Pile | 5.50 | 1.455 | Ea. | | 54 | | 54 | 88.50 |
| 0600 | With steel thin shell, add | | 38 | .211 | | | 7.80 | | 7.80 | 12.80 |
| 0700 | Steel pile or "H" piles | | 19 | .421 | | | 15.65 | | 15.65 | 25.50 |
| 0800 | Wood piles | ↓ | 38 | .211 | ↓ | | 7.80 | | 7.80 | 12.80 |
| 0900 | Pre-augering up to 30' deep, average soil, 24" diameter | B-43 | 180 | .267 | L.F. | | 8.85 | 14.05 | 22.90 | 29 |
| 0920 | 36" diameter | | 115 | .417 | | | 13.85 | 22 | 35.85 | 45.50 |
| 0960 | 48" diameter | | 70 | .686 | | | 23 | 36 | 59 | 75 |
| 0980 | 60" diameter | ↓ | 50 | .960 | ↓ | | 32 | 50.50 | 82.50 | 105 |
| 1000 | Testing, any type piles, test load is twice the design load | | | | | | | | | |
| 1050 | 50 ton design load, 100 ton test | | | | Ea. | | | | 16,695 | 17,864 |
| 1100 | 100 ton design load, 200 ton test | | | | | | | | 21,425 | 23,446 |
| 1150 | 150 ton design load, 300 ton test | | | | | | | | 27,835 | 29,683 |
| 1200 | 200 ton design load, 400 ton test | | | | | | | | 30,261 | 33,264 |
| 1250 | 400 ton design load, 800 ton test | | | | ↓ | | | | 34,996 | 38,923 |
| 1500 | Wet conditions, soft damp ground | | | | | | | | | |
| 1600 | Requiring mats for crane, add | | | | | | | | 40% | 40% |

# 31 06 Schedules for Earthwork

## 31 06 60 – Schedules for Special Foundations and Load Bearing Elements

### 31 06 60.14 Piling Special Costs

| | | Crew | Daily Output | Labor-Hours | Unit | Material | 2008 Bare Costs Labor | 2008 Bare Costs Equipment | Total | Total Incl O&P |
|---|---|---|---|---|---|---|---|---|---|---|
| 1700 | Barge mounted driving rig, add | | | | | | | | 30% | 30% |

### 31 06 60.15 Mobilization

| | | Crew | Daily Output | Labor-Hours | Unit | Material | Labor | Equipment | Total | Total Incl O&P |
|---|---|---|---|---|---|---|---|---|---|---|
| 0010 | **MOBILIZATION** | | | | | | | | | |
| 0020 | Set up & remove, air compressor, 600 C.F.M. | A-5 | 3.30 | 5.455 | Ea. | | 165 | 13.60 | 178.60 | 271 |
| 0100 | 1200 C.F.M. | " | 2.20 | 8.182 | | | 247 | 20.50 | 267.50 | 410 |
| 0200 | Crane, with pile leads and pile hammer, 75 ton | B-19 | .60 | 106 | | | 4,075 | 2,900 | 6,975 | 9,650 |
| 0300 | 150 ton | " | .36 | 177 | | | 6,775 | 4,850 | 11,625 | 16,100 |
| 0500 | Drill rig, for caissons, to 36", minimum | B-43 | 2 | 24 | | | 795 | 1,275 | 2,070 | 2,625 |
| 0600 | Up to 84" | " | 1 | 48 | | | 1,600 | 2,525 | 4,125 | 5,225 |
| 0800 | Auxiliary boiler, for steam small | A-5 | 1.66 | 10.843 | | | 325 | 27 | 352 | 540 |
| 0900 | Large | " | .83 | 21.687 | | | 655 | 54 | 709 | 1,075 |
| 1100 | Rule of thumb: complete pile driving set up, small | B-19 | .45 | 142 | | | 5,425 | 3,875 | 9,300 | 12,900 |
| 1200 | Large | " | .27 | 237 | | | 9,025 | 6,450 | 15,475 | 21,400 |

# 31 11 Clearing and Grubbing Land

## 31 11 10 – Clearing and Grubbing land

### 31 11 10.10 Clear and Grub Site

| | | Crew | Daily Output | Labor-Hours | Unit | Material | Labor | Equipment | Total | Total Incl O&P |
|---|---|---|---|---|---|---|---|---|---|---|
| 0010 | **CLEAR AND GRUB SITE** | | | | | | | | | |
| 0020 | Cut & chip light trees to 6" diam. | B-7 | 1 | 48 | Acre | | 1,550 | 1,175 | 2,725 | 3,700 |
| 0150 | Grub stumps and remove | B-30 | 2 | 12 | | | 405 | 920 | 1,325 | 1,625 |
| 0200 | Cut & chip medium, trees to 12" diam. | B-7 | .70 | 68.571 | | | 2,200 | 1,700 | 3,900 | 5,250 |
| 0250 | Grub stumps and remove | B-30 | 1 | 24 | | | 810 | 1,825 | 2,635 | 3,275 |
| 0300 | Cut & chip heavy, trees to 24" diam. | B-7 | .30 | 160 | | | 5,150 | 3,950 | 9,100 | 12,300 |
| 0350 | Grub stumps and remove | B-30 | .50 | 48 | | | 1,625 | 3,675 | 5,300 | 6,525 |
| 0400 | If burning is allowed, reduce cut & chip | | | | | | | | | 40% |
| 3000 | Chipping stumps, to 18" deep, 12" diam. | B-86 | 20 | .400 | Ea. | | 15.95 | 7.85 | 23.80 | 32.50 |
| 3040 | 18" diameter | | 16 | .500 | | | 19.95 | 9.80 | 29.75 | 41 |
| 3080 | 24" diameter | | 14 | .571 | | | 23 | 11.20 | 34.20 | 47 |
| 3100 | 30" diameter | | 12 | .667 | | | 26.50 | 13.05 | 39.55 | 54.50 |
| 3120 | 36" diameter | | 10 | .800 | | | 32 | 15.70 | 47.70 | 65.50 |
| 3160 | 48" diameter | | 8 | 1 | | | 40 | 19.60 | 59.60 | 81.50 |
| 5000 | Tree thinning, feller buncher, conifer | | | | | | | | | |
| 5080 | Up to 8" diameter | B-93 | 240 | .033 | Ea. | | 1.33 | 2.27 | 3.60 | 4.50 |
| 5120 | 12" diameter | | 160 | .050 | | | 1.99 | 3.40 | 5.39 | 6.75 |
| 5240 | Hardwood, up to 4" diameter | | 240 | .033 | | | 1.33 | 2.27 | 3.60 | 4.50 |
| 5280 | 8" diameter | | 180 | .044 | | | 1.77 | 3.02 | 4.79 | 6 |
| 5320 | 12" diameter | | 120 | .067 | | | 2.66 | 4.54 | 7.20 | 9 |
| 7000 | Tree removal, congested area, aerial lift truck | | | | | | | | | |
| 7040 | 8" diameter | B-85 | 7 | 5.714 | Ea. | | 184 | 120 | 304 | 415 |
| 7080 | 12" diameter | | 6 | 6.667 | | | 215 | 140 | 355 | 485 |
| 7120 | 18" diameter | | 5 | 8 | | | 258 | 168 | 426 | 585 |
| 7160 | 24" diameter | | 4 | 10 | | | 320 | 209 | 529 | 725 |
| 7240 | 36" diameter | | 3 | 13.333 | | | 430 | 279 | 709 | 970 |
| 7280 | 48" diameter | | 2 | 20 | | | 645 | 420 | 1,065 | 1,450 |

## 31 13 13 – Selective Tree and Shrub Removal

### 31 13 13.10 Selective Clearing

| | | Crew | Daily Output | Labor-Hours | Unit | Material | 2008 Bare Costs Labor | Equipment | Total | Total Incl O&P |
|---|---|---|---|---|---|---|---|---|---|---|
| 0010 | **SELECTIVE CLEARING** | | | | | | | | | |
| 0020 | Clearing brush with brush saw | A-1C | .25 | 32 | Acre | | 970 | 99 | 1,069 | 1,600 |
| 0100 | By hand | 1 Clab | .12 | 66.667 | | | 2,025 | | 2,025 | 3,125 |
| 0300 | With dozer, ball and chain, light clearing | B-11A | 2 | 8 | | | 280 | 535 | 815 | 1,025 |
| 0400 | Medium clearing | | 1.50 | 10.667 | | | 375 | 715 | 1,090 | 1,350 |
| 0500 | With dozer and brush rake, light | | 10 | 1.600 | | | 56 | 107 | 163 | 204 |
| 0550 | Medium brush to 4" diameter | | 8 | 2 | | | 70 | 134 | 204 | 254 |
| 0600 | Heavy brush to 4" diameter | | 6.40 | 2.500 | | | 87.50 | 167 | 254.50 | 320 |
| 1000 | Brush mowing, tractor w/rotary mower, no removal | | | | | | | | | |
| 1020 | Light density | B-84 | 2 | 4 | Acre | | 159 | 132 | 291 | 385 |
| 1040 | Medium density | | 1.50 | 5.333 | | | 213 | 176 | 389 | 515 |
| 1080 | Heavy density | | 1 | 8 | | | 320 | 265 | 585 | 770 |

### 31 13 13.20 Selective Tree Removal

| | | Crew | Daily Output | Labor-Hours | Unit | Material | 2008 Bare Costs Labor | Equipment | Total | Total Incl O&P |
|---|---|---|---|---|---|---|---|---|---|---|
| 0010 | **SELECTIVE TREE REMOVAL** | | | | | | | | | |
| 0011 | With tractor, large tract, firm | | | | | | | | | |
| 0020 | level terrain, no boulders, less than 12" diam. trees | | | | | | | | | |
| 0300 | 300 HP dozer, up to 400 trees/acre, 0 to 25% hardwoods | B-10M | .75 | 16 | Acre | | 585 | 1,850 | 2,435 | 2,925 |
| 0340 | 25% to 50% hardwoods | | .60 | 20 | | | 735 | 2,325 | 3,060 | 3,675 |
| 0370 | 75% to 100% hardwoods | | .45 | 26.667 | | | 975 | 3,075 | 4,050 | 4,875 |
| 0400 | 500 trees/acre, 0% to 25% hardwoods | | .60 | 20 | | | 735 | 2,325 | 3,060 | 3,675 |
| 0440 | 25% to 50% hardwoods | | .48 | 25 | | | 915 | 2,900 | 3,815 | 4,575 |
| 0470 | 75% to 100% hardwoods | | .36 | 33.333 | | | 1,225 | 3,850 | 5,075 | 6,100 |
| 0500 | More than 600 trees/acre, 0 to 25% hardwoods | | .52 | 23.077 | | | 845 | 2,675 | 3,520 | 4,200 |
| 0540 | 25% to 50% hardwoods | | .42 | 28.571 | | | 1,050 | 3,300 | 4,350 | 5,225 |
| 0570 | 75% to 100% hardwoods | | .31 | 38.710 | | | 1,425 | 4,475 | 5,900 | 7,075 |
| 0900 | Large tract clearing per tree | | | | | | | | | |
| 1500 | 300 HP dozer, to 12" diameter, softwood | B-10M | 320 | .038 | Ea. | | 1.37 | 4.34 | 5.71 | 6.85 |
| 1550 | Hardwood | | 100 | .120 | | | 4.40 | 13.90 | 18.30 | 22 |
| 1600 | 12" to 24" diameter, softwood | | 200 | .060 | | | 2.20 | 6.95 | 9.15 | 11 |
| 1650 | Hardwood | | 80 | .150 | | | 5.50 | 17.35 | 22.85 | 27.50 |
| 1700 | 24" to 36" diameter, softwood | | 100 | .120 | | | 4.40 | 13.90 | 18.30 | 22 |
| 1750 | Hardwood | | 50 | .240 | | | 8.80 | 28 | 36.80 | 44 |
| 1800 | 36" to 48" diameter, softwood | | 70 | .171 | | | 6.30 | 19.85 | 26.15 | 31.50 |
| 1850 | Hardwood | | 35 | .343 | | | 12.55 | 39.50 | 52.05 | 62.50 |
| 2000 | Stump removal on site by hydraulic backhoe, 1-1/2 C.Y. | | | | | | | | | |
| 2040 | 4" to 6" diameter | B-17 | 60 | .533 | Ea. | | 17.20 | 9.90 | 27.10 | 37.50 |
| 2050 | 8" to 12" diameter | B-30 | 33 | .727 | | | 24.50 | 55.50 | 80 | 98.50 |
| 2100 | 14" to 24" diameter | | 25 | .960 | | | 32.50 | 73.50 | 106 | 131 |
| 2150 | 26" to 36" diameter | | 16 | 1.500 | | | 50.50 | 115 | 165.50 | 204 |
| 3000 | Remove selective trees, on site using chain saws and chipper, | | | | | | | | | |
| 3050 | not incl. stumps, up to 6" diameter | B-7 | 18 | 2.667 | Ea. | | 86 | 65.50 | 151.50 | 206 |
| 3100 | 8" to 12" diameter | | 12 | 4 | | | 129 | 98.50 | 227.50 | 305 |
| 3150 | 14" to 24" diameter | | 10 | 4.800 | | | 154 | 118 | 272 | 370 |
| 3200 | 26" to 36" diameter | | 8 | 6 | | | 193 | 148 | 341 | 460 |
| 3300 | Machine load, 2 mile haul to dump, 12" diam. tree, add | | | | | | | | 208 | 312 |

# 31 14 Earth Stripping and Stockpiling

## 31 14 13 – Soil Stripping and Stockpiling

| 31 14 13.23 Topsoil Stripping and Stockpiling | Crew | Daily Output | Labor-Hours | Unit | Material | 2008 Bare Costs Labor | Equipment | Total | Total Incl O&P |
|---|---|---|---|---|---|---|---|---|---|
| 0010 **TOPSOIL STRIPPING AND STOCKPILING** | | | | | | | | | |
| 0020    200 H.P. dozer, ideal conditions | B-10B | 2300 | .005 | C.Y. | | .19 | .47 | .66 | .80 |
| 0100    Adverse conditions | " | 1150 | .010 | | | .38 | .93 | 1.31 | 1.60 |
| 0200    300 HP dozer, ideal conditions | B-10M | 3000 | .004 | | | .15 | .46 | .61 | .73 |
| 0300    Adverse conditions | " | 1650 | .007 | | | .27 | .84 | 1.11 | 1.34 |
| 0400    400 HP dozer, ideal conditions | B-10X | 3900 | .003 | | | .11 | .47 | .58 | .68 |
| 0500    Adverse conditions | " | 2000 | .006 | | | .22 | .91 | 1.13 | 1.33 |
| 0600    Clay, dry and soft, 200 HP dozer, ideal conditions | B-10B | 1600 | .008 | | | .27 | .67 | .94 | 1.16 |
| 0700    Adverse conditions | " | 800 | .015 | | | .55 | 1.34 | 1.89 | 2.31 |
| 1000    Medium hard, 300 HP dozer, ideal conditions | B-10M | 2000 | .006 | | | .22 | .69 | .91 | 1.09 |
| 1100    Adverse conditions | " | 1100 | .011 | | | .40 | 1.26 | 1.66 | 2 |
| 1200    Very hard, 400 HP dozer, ideal conditions | B-10X | 2600 | .005 | | | .17 | .70 | .87 | 1.03 |
| 1300    Adverse conditions | " | 1340 | .009 | ↓ | | .33 | 1.36 | 1.69 | 1.99 |
| 1400    Loam or topsoil, remove and stockpile on site | | | | | | | | | |
| 1420       6" deep, 200' haul | B-10B | 865 | .014 | C.Y. | | .51 | 1.24 | 1.75 | 2.13 |
| 1430          300' haul | | 520 | .023 | | | .85 | 2.06 | 2.91 | 3.56 |
| 1440          500' haul | | 225 | .053 | ↓ | | 1.95 | 4.76 | 6.71 | 8.20 |
| 1450    Alternate method: 6" deep, 200' haul | | 5090 | .002 | S.Y. | | .09 | .21 | .30 | .36 |
| 1460          500' haul | | 1325 | .009 | " | | .33 | .81 | 1.14 | 1.40 |

# 31 22 Grading

## 31 22 16 – Fine Grading

### 31 22 16.10 Finish Grading

| | Crew | Daily Output | Labor-Hours | Unit | Material | Labor | Equipment | Total | Total Incl O&P |
|---|---|---|---|---|---|---|---|---|---|
| 0010 **FINISH GRADING** | | | | | | | | | |
| 0012    Finish grading area to be paved with grader, small area | B-11L | 400 | .040 | S.Y. | | 1.40 | 1.34 | 2.74 | 3.61 |
| 0016    Finish grading lagoon bottoms | | 4 | 4 | M.S.F. | | 140 | 134 | 274 | 360 |
| 0100       Large area | | 2000 | .008 | S.Y. | | .28 | .27 | .55 | .72 |
| 1100    Fine grade for slab on grade, machine | ↓ | 1040 | .015 | | | .54 | .51 | 1.05 | 1.39 |
| 1150       Hand grading | B-18 | 700 | .034 | ↓ | | 1.06 | .05 | 1.11 | 1.71 |

# 31 23 Excavation and Fill

## 31 23 16 – Excavation

### 31 23 16.13 Excavating, Trench

| | Crew | Daily Output | Labor-Hours | Unit | Material | Labor | Equipment | Total | Total Incl O&P |
|---|---|---|---|---|---|---|---|---|---|
| 0010 **EXCAVATING, TRENCH** | | | | | | | | | |
| 0011    Or continuous footing | | | | | | | | | |
| 0020    Common earth with no sheeting or dewatering included | | | | | | | | | |
| 0050       1' to 4' deep, 3/8 C.Y. excavator | B-11C | 150 | .107 | B.C.Y. | | 3.74 | 1.90 | 5.64 | 7.80 |
| 0060          1/2 C.Y. excavator | B-11M | 200 | .080 | | | 2.80 | 1.70 | 4.50 | 6.15 |
| 0090       4' to 6' deep, 1/2 C.Y. excavator | " | 200 | .080 | | | 2.80 | 1.70 | 4.50 | 6.15 |
| 0100          5/8 C.Y. excavator | B-12Q | 250 | .064 | | | 2.28 | 1.99 | 4.27 | 5.65 |
| 0110          3/4 C.Y. excavator | B-12F | 300 | .053 | | | 1.90 | 1.83 | 3.73 | 4.91 |
| 0300          1/2 C.Y. excavator, truck mounted | B-12J | 200 | .080 | | | 2.85 | 4.66 | 7.51 | 9.50 |
| 0500       6' to 10' deep, 3/4 C.Y. excavator | B-12F | 225 | .071 | | | 2.53 | 2.44 | 4.97 | 6.55 |
| 0510          1 C.Y. excavator | B-12A | 400 | .040 | | | 1.42 | 1.62 | 3.04 | 3.96 |
| 0600          1 C.Y. excavator, truck mounted | B-12K | 400 | .040 | | | 1.42 | 2.72 | 4.14 | 5.15 |
| 0610          1-1/2 C.Y. excavator | B-12B | 600 | .027 | | | .95 | 1.38 | 2.33 | 2.97 |
| 0900       10' to 14' deep, 3/4 C.Y. excavator | B-12F | 200 | .080 | | | 2.85 | 2.75 | 5.60 | 7.35 |
| 0910          1 C.Y. excavator | B-12A | 360 | .044 | | | 1.58 | 1.80 | 3.38 | 4.40 |
| 1000          1-1/2 C.Y. excavator | B-12B | 540 | .030 | ↓ | | 1.05 | 1.54 | 2.59 | 3.30 |

| 31 23 16.13 Excavating, Trench | | Crew | Daily Output | Labor-Hours | Unit | Material | 2008 Bare Costs | | Total | Total Incl O&P |
|---|---|---|---|---|---|---|---|---|---|---|
| | | | | | | | Labor | Equipment | | |
| 1300 | 14' to 20' deep, 1 C.Y. excavator | B-12A | 320 | .050 | B.C.Y. | | 1.78 | 2.02 | 3.80 | 4.94 |
| 1310 | 1-1/2 C.Y. excavator | B-12B | 480 | .033 | | | 1.19 | 1.73 | 2.92 | 3.71 |
| 1320 | 2-1/2 C.Y. excavator | B-12S | 850 | .019 | | | .67 | 1.72 | 2.39 | 2.92 |
| 1340 | 20' to 24' deep, 1 C.Y. excavator | B-12A | 288 | .056 | | | 1.98 | 2.25 | 4.23 | 5.50 |
| 1342 | 1-1/2 C.Y. excavator | B-12B | 432 | .037 | | | 1.32 | 1.92 | 3.24 | 4.13 |
| 1344 | 2-1/2 C.Y. excavator | B-12S | 765 | .021 | | | .74 | 1.92 | 2.66 | 3.25 |
| 1352 | 4' to 6' deep, 1/2 C.Y. excavator w/ trench box | B-13H | 188 | .085 | | | 3.03 | 5.55 | 8.58 | 10.75 |
| 1354 | 5/8 C.Y. excavator | " | 235 | .068 | | | 2.42 | 4.45 | 6.87 | 8.60 |
| 1356 | 3/4 C.Y. excavator | B-13G | 282 | .057 | | | 2.02 | 2.35 | 4.37 | 5.70 |
| 1362 | 6' to 10' deep, 3/4 C.Y. excavator w/trench box | " | 212 | .075 | | | 2.69 | 3.13 | 5.82 | 7.55 |
| 1370 | 1 C.Y. excavator/ trench box | B-13D | 376 | .043 | | | 1.51 | 2.02 | 3.53 | 4.53 |
| 1371 | 1-1/2 C.Y. excavator/ trench box | B-13E | 564 | .028 | | | 1.01 | 1.67 | 2.68 | 3.38 |
| 1374 | 10' to 14' deep, 3/4 C.Y. excavator w/trench box | B-13G | 188 | .085 | | | 3.03 | 3.53 | 6.56 | 8.50 |
| 1375 | 1 C.Y. excavator/ trench box | B-13D | 338 | .047 | | | 1.69 | 2.25 | 3.94 | 5.05 |
| 1376 | 1-1/2 C.Y. excavator/ trench box | B-13E | 508 | .032 | | | 1.12 | 1.86 | 2.98 | 3.75 |
| 1381 | 14' to 20' deep, 1 C.Y. excavator w/trench box | B-13D | 301 | .053 | | | 1.89 | 2.53 | 4.42 | 5.65 |
| 1382 | 1-1/2 C.Y. excavator/ trench box | B-13E | 451 | .035 | | | 1.26 | 2.09 | 3.35 | 4.23 |
| 1383 | 2-1/2 C.Y. excavator/ trench box | B-13J | 799 | .020 | | | .71 | 1.98 | 2.69 | 3.26 |
| 1386 | 20' to 24' deep, 1 C.Y. excavator w/trench box | B-13D | 271 | .059 | | | 2.10 | 2.80 | 4.90 | 6.30 |
| 1387 | 1-1/2 C.Y. excavator/ trench box | B-13E | 406 | .039 | | | 1.40 | 2.32 | 3.72 | 4.70 |
| 1388 | 2-1/2 C.Y. excavator/ trench box | B-13J | 719 | .022 | | | .79 | 2.20 | 2.99 | 3.63 |
| 1391 | Shoring by SF/day trench wall protected loose matl, 4' W | B-6 | 3200 | .008 | SF Wall | .47 | .25 | .09 | .81 | .99 |
| 1392 | Rent shoring per week per SF wall protected, loose matl, 4' W | | | | | 1.29 | | | 1.29 | 1.42 |
| 1395 | Hydraulic shoring, SF trench wall protected stable matl, 4' W | 2 Clab | 2700 | .006 | | .15 | .18 | | .33 | .44 |
| 1397 | semi-stable material, 4' W | " | 2400 | .007 | | .21 | .20 | | .41 | .55 |
| 1398 | Rent hyraulic shoring per day/SF wall, stable matl. 4' W | | | | | .15 | | | .15 | .16 |
| 1399 | semi-stable material | | | | | .21 | | | .21 | .24 |
| 1400 | By hand with pick and shovel 2' to 6' deep, light soil | 1 Clab | 8 | 1 | B.C.Y. | | 30.50 | | 30.50 | 47 |
| 1500 | Heavy soil | " | 4 | 2 | " | | 60.50 | | 60.50 | 94 |
| 1700 | For tamping backfilled trenches, air tamp, add | A-1G | 100 | .080 | E.C.Y. | | 2.42 | .43 | 2.85 | 4.23 |
| 1900 | Vibrating plate, add | B-18 | 180 | .133 | " | | 4.12 | .21 | 4.33 | 6.65 |
| 2100 | Trim sides and bottom for concrete pours, common earth | | 1500 | .016 | S.F. | | .49 | .03 | .52 | .80 |
| 2300 | Hardpan | | 600 | .040 | " | | 1.24 | .06 | 1.30 | 1.99 |
| 2400 | Pier and spread footing excavation, add to above | | | | B.C.Y. | | | | 30% | 30% |
| 3000 | Backfill trench, F.E. loader, wheel mtd., 1 C.Y. bucket | | | | | | | | | |
| 3020 | Minimal haul | B-10R | 400 | .030 | L.C.Y. | | 1.10 | .57 | 1.67 | 2.29 |
| 3040 | 100' haul | " | 200 | .060 | | | 2.20 | 1.13 | 3.33 | 4.60 |
| 3080 | 2-1/4 C.Y. bucket, minimum haul | B-10T | 600 | .020 | | | .73 | .64 | 1.37 | 1.83 |
| 3090 | 100' haul | " | 300 | .040 | | | 1.47 | 1.29 | 2.76 | 3.65 |
| 5020 | Loam & Sandy clay with no sheeting or dewatering included | | | | | | | | | |
| 5050 | 1' to 4' deep, 3/8 C.Y. tractor loader/backhoe | B-11C | 162 | .099 | B.C.Y. | | 3.46 | 1.76 | 5.22 | 7.25 |
| 5060 | 1/2 C.Y. excavator | B-11M | 216 | .074 | | | 2.60 | 1.58 | 4.18 | 5.70 |
| 5080 | 4' to 6' deep, 1/2 C.Y. excavator | " | 216 | .074 | | | 2.60 | 1.58 | 4.18 | 5.70 |
| 5090 | 5/8 C.Y. excavator | B-12Q | 276 | .058 | | | 2.06 | 1.80 | 3.86 | 5.15 |
| 5100 | 3/4 C.Y. excavator | B-12F | 324 | .049 | | | 1.76 | 1.70 | 3.46 | 4.56 |
| 5130 | 1/2 C.Y. excavator, truck mounted | B-12J | 216 | .074 | | | 2.64 | 4.32 | 6.96 | 8.80 |
| 5140 | 6' to 10' deep, 3/4 C.Y. excavator | B-12F | 243 | .066 | | | 2.34 | 2.26 | 4.60 | 6.05 |
| 5150 | 1 C.Y. excavator | B-12A | 432 | .037 | | | 1.32 | 1.50 | 2.82 | 3.67 |
| 5160 | 1 C.Y. excavator, truck mounted | B-12K | 432 | .037 | | | 1.32 | 2.52 | 3.84 | 4.79 |
| 5170 | 1-1/2 C.Y. excavator | B-12B | 648 | .025 | | | .88 | 1.28 | 2.16 | 2.75 |
| 5190 | 10' to 14' deep, 3/4 C.Y. excavator | B-12F | 216 | .074 | | | 2.64 | 2.54 | 5.18 | 6.85 |
| 5200 | 1 C.Y. excavator | B-12A | 389 | .041 | | | 1.46 | 1.66 | 3.12 | 4.07 |
| 5210 | 1-1/2 C.Y. excavator | B-12B | 583 | .027 | | | .98 | 1.42 | 2.40 | 3.06 |

### 31 23 16.13 Excavating, Trench

| | | Crew | Daily Output | Labor-Hours | Unit | Material | 2008 Bare Costs | | Total | Total Incl O&P |
|---|---|---|---|---|---|---|---|---|---|---|
| | | | | | | | Labor | Equipment | | |
| 5250 | 14' to 20' deep, 1 C.Y. excavator | B-12A | 346 | .046 | B.C.Y. | | 1.65 | 1.87 | 3.52 | 4.58 |
| 5260 | 1-1/2 C.Y. excavator | B-12B | 518 | .031 | | | 1.10 | 1.60 | 2.70 | 3.44 |
| 5270 | 2-1/2 C.Y. excavator | B-12S | 918 | .017 | | | .62 | 1.60 | 2.22 | 2.71 |
| 5300 | 20' to 24' deep, 1 C.Y. excavator | B-12A | 311 | .051 | | | 1.83 | 2.08 | 3.91 | 5.10 |
| 5310 | 1-1/2 C.Y. excavator | B-12B | 467 | .034 | | | 1.22 | 1.78 | 3 | 3.81 |
| 5320 | 2-1/2 C.Y. excavator | B-12S | 826 | .019 | | | .69 | 1.77 | 2.46 | 3 |
| 5352 | 4' to 6' deep, 1/2 C.Y. excavator w/trench box | B-13H | 205 | .078 | | | 2.78 | 5.10 | 7.88 | 9.85 |
| 5354 | 5/8 C.Y. excavator w/trench box | " | 257 | .062 | | | 2.22 | 4.07 | 6.29 | 7.85 |
| 5356 | 3/4 C.Y. excavator/T-box | B-13G | 308 | .052 | | | 1.85 | 2.15 | 4 | 5.20 |
| 5362 | 6' to 10' deep, 3/4 C.Y. excavator w/ trench box | " | 231 | .069 | | | 2.47 | 2.87 | 5.34 | 6.95 |
| 5364 | 1 C.Y. excavator/T-box | B-13D | 410 | .039 | | | 1.39 | 1.85 | 3.24 | 4.16 |
| 5366 | 1-1/2 C.Y. excavator/T-box | B-13E | 616 | .026 | | | .92 | 1.53 | 2.45 | 3.09 |
| 5370 | 10' to 14' deep, 3/4 C.Y. excavator w/ trench box | B-13G | 205 | .078 | | | 2.78 | 3.23 | 6.01 | 7.80 |
| 5372 | 1 C.Y. excavator | B-13D | 370 | .043 | | | 1.54 | 2.05 | 3.59 | 4.61 |
| 5374 | 1-1/2 C.Y. excavator | B-13E | 554 | .029 | | | 1.03 | 1.70 | 2.73 | 3.44 |
| 5382 | 14' to 20' deep, 1 C.Y. excavator w/ trench box | B-13D | 329 | .049 | | | 1.73 | 2.31 | 4.04 | 5.20 |
| 5384 | 1-1/2 C.Y. excavator w/ trench box | B-13E | 492 | .033 | | | 1.16 | 1.92 | 3.08 | 3.88 |
| 5386 | 2-1/2 C.Y. excavator w/ trench box | B-13J | 872 | .018 | | | .65 | 1.81 | 2.46 | 2.99 |
| 5392 | 20' to 24' deep, 1 C.Y. excavator w/ trench box | B-13D | 295 | .054 | | | 1.93 | 2.58 | 4.51 | 5.80 |
| 5394 | 1-1/2 C.Y. excavator w/ trench box | B-13E | 444 | .036 | | | 1.28 | 2.12 | 3.40 | 4.30 |
| 5396 | 2-1/2 C.Y. excavator w/ trench box | B-13J | 785 | .020 | | | .73 | 2.01 | 2.74 | 3.32 |
| 6020 | Sand & gravel with no sheeting or dewatering included | | | | | | | | | |
| 6050 | 1' to 4' deep, 3/8 C.Y. excavator | B-11C | 165 | .097 | B.C.Y. | | 3.40 | 1.73 | 5.13 | 7.10 |
| 6060 | 1/2 C.Y. excavator | B-11M | 220 | .073 | | | 2.55 | 1.55 | 4.10 | 5.60 |
| 6080 | 4' to 6' deep, 1/2 C.Y. excavator | " | 220 | .073 | | | 2.55 | 1.55 | 4.10 | 5.60 |
| 6090 | 5/8 C.Y. excavator | B-12Q | 275 | .058 | | | 2.07 | 1.81 | 3.88 | 5.15 |
| 6100 | 3/4 C.Y. excavator | B-12F | 330 | .048 | | | 1.73 | 1.66 | 3.39 | 4.47 |
| 6130 | 1/2 C.Y. excavator, truck mounted | B-12J | 220 | .073 | | | 2.59 | 4.24 | 6.83 | 8.60 |
| 6140 | 6' to 10' deep, 3/4 C.Y. excavator | B-12F | 248 | .065 | | | 2.30 | 2.22 | 4.52 | 5.95 |
| 6150 | 1 C.Y. excavator | B-12A | 440 | .036 | | | 1.29 | 1.47 | 2.76 | 3.60 |
| 6160 | 1 C.Y. excavator, truck mounted | B-12K | 440 | .036 | | | 1.29 | 2.47 | 3.76 | 4.70 |
| 6170 | 1-1/2 C.Y. excavator | B-12B | 660 | .024 | | | .86 | 1.26 | 2.12 | 2.70 |
| 6190 | 10' to 14' deep, 3/4 C.Y. excavator | B-12F | 220 | .073 | | | 2.59 | 2.50 | 5.09 | 6.70 |
| 6200 | 1 C.Y. excavator | B-12A | 396 | .040 | | | 1.44 | 1.63 | 3.07 | 4 |
| 6210 | 1-1/2 C.Y. excavator | B-12B | 594 | .027 | | | .96 | 1.40 | 2.36 | 3.01 |
| 6250 | 14' to 20' deep, 1 C.Y. excavator | B-12A | 352 | .045 | | | 1.62 | 1.84 | 3.46 | 4.49 |
| 6260 | 1-1/2 C.Y. excavator | B-12B | 528 | .030 | | | 1.08 | 1.57 | 2.65 | 3.38 |
| 6270 | 2-1/2 C.Y. excavator | B-12S | 935 | .017 | | | .61 | 1.57 | 2.18 | 2.65 |
| 6300 | 20' to 24' deep, 1 C.Y. excavator | B-12A | 317 | .050 | | | 1.80 | 2.04 | 3.84 | 4.99 |
| 6310 | 1-1/2 C.Y. excavator | B-12B | 475 | .034 | | | 1.20 | 1.75 | 2.95 | 3.75 |
| 6320 | 2-1/2 C.Y. excavator | B-12S | 842 | .019 | | | .68 | 1.74 | 2.42 | 2.95 |
| 6352 | 4' to 6' deep, 1/2 C.Y. excavator w/ trench box | B-13H | 209 | .077 | | | 2.73 | 5 | 7.73 | 9.65 |
| 6354 | 5/8 C.Y. excavator w/ trench box | " | 261 | .061 | | | 2.18 | 4.01 | 6.19 | 7.75 |
| 6356 | 3/4 C.Y. excavator w/ trench box | B-13G | 314 | .051 | | | 1.81 | 2.11 | 3.92 | 5.10 |
| 6362 | 6' to 10' deep, 3/4 C.Y. excavator w/ trench box | " | 236 | .068 | | | 2.41 | 2.81 | 5.22 | 6.80 |
| 6364 | 1 C.Y. excavator w/ trench box | B-13D | 418 | .038 | | | 1.36 | 1.82 | 3.18 | 4.08 |
| 6366 | 1-1/2 C.Y. excavator w/ trench box | B-13E | 627 | .026 | | | .91 | 1.50 | 2.41 | 3.05 |
| 6370 | 10' to 14' deep, 3/4 C.Y. excavator w/ trench box | B-13G | 209 | .077 | | | 2.73 | 3.17 | 5.90 | 7.65 |
| 6372 | 1 C.Y. excavator w/ trench box | B-13D | 376 | .043 | | | 1.51 | 2.02 | 3.53 | 4.53 |
| 6374 | 1-1/2 C.Y. excavator w/ trench box | B-13E | 564 | .028 | | | 1.01 | 1.67 | 2.68 | 3.38 |
| 6382 | 14' to 20' deep, 1 C.Y. excavator w/ trench box | B-13D | 334 | .048 | | | 1.71 | 2.28 | 3.99 | 5.10 |
| 6384 | 1-1/2 C.Y. excavator w/ trench box | B-13E | 502 | .032 | | | 1.13 | 1.88 | 3.01 | 3.80 |
| 6386 | 2-1/2 C.Y. excavator w/ trench box | B-13J | 888 | .018 | | | .64 | 1.78 | 2.42 | 2.94 |

### 31 23 16.13 Excavating, Trench

| | | Crew | Daily Output | Labor-Hours | Unit | Material | 2008 Bare Costs Labor | Equipment | Total | Total Incl O&P |
|---|---|---|---|---|---|---|---|---|---|---|
| 6392 | 20' to 24' deep, 1 C.Y. excavator w/ trench box | B-13D | 301 | .053 | B.C.Y. | | 1.89 | 2.53 | 4.42 | 5.65 |
| 6394 | 1-1/2 C.Y. excavator w/ trench box | B-13E | 452 | .035 | | | 1.26 | 2.09 | 3.35 | 4.23 |
| 6396 | 2-1/2 C.Y. excavator w/ trench box | B-13J | 800 | .020 | ▼ | | .71 | 1.97 | 2.68 | 3.26 |
| 7020 | Dense hard clay with no sheeting or dewatering included | | | | | | | | | |
| 7050 | 1' to 4' deep, 3/8 C.Y. excavator | B-11C | 132 | .121 | B.C.Y. | | 4.25 | 2.16 | 6.41 | 8.90 |
| 7060 | 1/2 C.Y. excavator | B-11M | 176 | .091 | | | 3.19 | 1.94 | 5.13 | 7 |
| 7080 | 4' to 6' deep, 1/2 C.Y. excavator | " | 176 | .091 | | | 3.19 | 1.94 | 5.13 | 7 |
| 7090 | 5/8 C.Y. excavator | B-12Q | 220 | .073 | | | 2.59 | 2.26 | 4.85 | 6.45 |
| 7100 | 3/4 C.Y. excavator | B-12F | 264 | .061 | | | 2.16 | 2.08 | 4.24 | 5.60 |
| 7130 | 1/2 C.Y. excavator, truck mounted | B-12J | 176 | .091 | | | 3.24 | 5.30 | 8.54 | 10.80 |
| 7140 | 6' to 10' deep, 3/4 C.Y. excavator | B-12F | 198 | .081 | | | 2.88 | 2.78 | 5.66 | 7.45 |
| 7150 | 1 C.Y. excavator | B-12A | 352 | .045 | | | 1.62 | 1.84 | 3.46 | 4.49 |
| 7160 | 1 C.Y. excavator, truck mounted | B-12K | 352 | .045 | | | 1.62 | 3.09 | 4.71 | 5.85 |
| 7170 | 1-1/2 C.Y. excavator | B-12B | 528 | .030 | | | 1.08 | 1.57 | 2.65 | 3.38 |
| 7190 | 10' to 14' deep, 3/4 C.Y. excavator | B-12F | 176 | .091 | | | 3.24 | 3.12 | 6.36 | 8.40 |
| 7200 | 1 C.Y. excavator | B-12A | 317 | .050 | | | 1.80 | 2.04 | 3.84 | 4.99 |
| 7210 | 1-1/2 C.Y. excavator | B-12B | 475 | .034 | | | 1.20 | 1.75 | 2.95 | 3.75 |
| 7250 | 14' to 20' deep, 1 C.Y. excavator | B-12A | 282 | .057 | | | 2.02 | 2.29 | 4.31 | 5.60 |
| 7260 | 1-1/2 C.Y. excavator | B-12B | 422 | .038 | | | 1.35 | 1.97 | 3.32 | 4.22 |
| 7270 | 2-1/2 C.Y. excavator | B-12S | 748 | .021 | | | .76 | 1.96 | 2.72 | 3.32 |
| 7300 | 20' to 24' deep, 1 C.Y. excavator | B-12A | 254 | .063 | | | 2.24 | 2.55 | 4.79 | 6.25 |
| 7310 | 1-1/2 C.Y. excavator | B-12B | 380 | .042 | | | 1.50 | 2.18 | 3.68 | 4.69 |
| 7320 | 2-1/2 C.Y. excavator | B-12S | 673 | .024 | ▼ | | .85 | 2.18 | 3.03 | 3.69 |

### 31 23 16.14 Excavating, Utility Trench

| | | Crew | Daily Output | Labor-Hours | Unit | Material | 2008 Bare Costs Labor | Equipment | Total | Total Incl O&P |
|---|---|---|---|---|---|---|---|---|---|---|
| 0010 | **EXCAVATING, UTILITY TRENCH** | | | | | | | | | |
| 0011 | Common earth | | | | | | | | | |
| 0050 | Trenching with chain trencher, 12 H.P., operator walking | | | | | | | | | |
| 0100 | 4" wide trench, 12" deep | B-53 | 800 | .010 | L.F. | | .38 | .07 | .45 | .65 |
| 0150 | 18" deep | | 750 | .011 | | | .40 | .08 | .48 | .69 |
| 0200 | 24" deep | | 700 | .011 | | | .43 | .08 | .51 | .74 |
| 0300 | 6" wide trench, 12" deep | | 650 | .012 | | | .46 | .09 | .55 | .80 |
| 0350 | 18" deep | | 600 | .013 | | | .50 | .09 | .59 | .86 |
| 0400 | 24" deep | | 550 | .015 | | | .55 | .10 | .65 | .94 |
| 0450 | 36" deep | | 450 | .018 | | | .67 | .13 | .80 | 1.15 |
| 0600 | 8" wide trench, 12" deep | | 475 | .017 | | | .64 | .12 | .76 | 1.09 |
| 0650 | 18" deep | | 400 | .020 | | | .76 | .14 | .90 | 1.30 |
| 0700 | 24" deep | | 350 | .023 | | | .86 | .16 | 1.02 | 1.48 |
| 0750 | 36" deep | ▼ | 300 | .027 | ▼ | | 1.01 | .19 | 1.20 | 1.73 |
| 1000 | Backfill by hand including compaction, add | | | | | | | | | |
| 1050 | 4" wide trench, 12" deep | A-1G | 800 | .010 | L.F. | | .30 | .05 | .35 | .53 |
| 1100 | 18" deep | | 530 | .015 | | | .46 | .08 | .54 | .80 |
| 1150 | 24" deep | | 400 | .020 | | | .61 | .11 | .72 | 1.06 |
| 1300 | 6" wide trench, 12" deep | | 540 | .015 | | | .45 | .08 | .53 | .79 |
| 1350 | 18" deep | | 405 | .020 | | | .60 | .11 | .71 | 1.05 |
| 1400 | 24" deep | | 270 | .030 | | | .90 | .16 | 1.06 | 1.57 |
| 1450 | 36" deep | | 180 | .044 | | | 1.34 | .24 | 1.58 | 2.35 |
| 1600 | 8" wide trench, 12" deep | | 400 | .020 | | | .61 | .11 | .72 | 1.06 |
| 1650 | 18" deep | | 265 | .030 | | | .91 | .16 | 1.07 | 1.60 |
| 1700 | 24" deep | | 200 | .040 | | | 1.21 | .22 | 1.43 | 2.12 |
| 1750 | 36" deep | ▼ | 135 | .059 | ▼ | | 1.79 | .32 | 2.11 | 3.14 |
| 2000 | Chain trencher, 40 H.P. operator riding | | | | | | | | | |
| 2050 | 6" wide trench and backfill, 12" deep | B-54 | 1200 | .007 | L.F. | | .25 | .20 | .45 | .60 |

# 31 23 Excavation and Fill

## 31 23 16 - Excavation

### 31 23 16.14 Excavating, Utility Trench

| | | Crew | Daily Output | Labor-Hours | Unit | Material | 2008 Bare Costs Labor | 2008 Bare Costs Equipment | Total | Total Incl O&P |
|---|---|---|---|---|---|---|---|---|---|---|
| 2100 | 18" deep | B-54 | 1000 | .008 | L.F. | | .30 | .24 | .54 | .73 |
| 2150 | 24" deep | | 975 | .008 | | | .31 | .25 | .56 | .75 |
| 2200 | 36" deep | | 900 | .009 | | | .34 | .27 | .61 | .81 |
| 2250 | 48" deep | | 750 | .011 | | | .40 | .33 | .73 | .97 |
| 2300 | 60" deep | | 650 | .012 | | | .46 | .38 | .84 | 1.11 |
| 2400 | 8" wide trench and backfill, 12" deep | | 1000 | .008 | | | .30 | .24 | .54 | .73 |
| 2450 | 18" deep | | 950 | .008 | | | .32 | .26 | .58 | .76 |
| 2500 | 24" deep | | 900 | .009 | | | .34 | .27 | .61 | .81 |
| 2550 | 36" deep | | 800 | .010 | | | .38 | .31 | .69 | .91 |
| 2600 | 48" deep | | 650 | .012 | | | .46 | .38 | .84 | 1.11 |
| 2700 | 12" wide trench and backfill, 12" deep | | 975 | .008 | | | .31 | .25 | .56 | .75 |
| 2750 | 18" deep | | 860 | .009 | | | .35 | .28 | .63 | .84 |
| 2800 | 24" deep | | 800 | .010 | | | .38 | .31 | .69 | .91 |
| 2850 | 36" deep | | 725 | .011 | | | .42 | .34 | .76 | 1 |
| 3000 | 16" wide trench and backfill, 12" deep | | 835 | .010 | | | .36 | .29 | .65 | .87 |
| 3050 | 18" deep | | 750 | .011 | | | .40 | .33 | .73 | .97 |
| 3100 | 24" deep | ▼ | 700 | .011 | ▼ | | .43 | .35 | .78 | 1.03 |
| 3200 | Compaction with vibratory plate, add | | | | | | | | 50% | 50% |
| 5100 | Hand excavate and trim for pipe bells after trench excavation | | | | | | | | | |
| 5200 | 8" pipe | 1 Clab | 155 | .052 | L.F. | | 1.56 | | 1.56 | 2.43 |
| 5300 | 18" pipe | " | 130 | .062 | " | | 1.86 | | 1.86 | 2.90 |

### 31 23 16.16 Structural Excavation for Minor Structures

| | | Crew | Daily Output | Labor-Hours | Unit | Material | 2008 Bare Costs Labor | 2008 Bare Costs Equipment | Total | Total Incl O&P |
|---|---|---|---|---|---|---|---|---|---|---|
| 0010 | **STRUCTURAL EXCAVATION FOR MINOR STRUCTURES** R312316-40 | | | | | | | | | |
| 0015 | Hand, pits to 6' deep, sandy soil | 1 Clab | 8 | 1 | B.C.Y. | | 30.50 | | 30.50 | 47 |
| 0100 | Heavy soil or clay | | 4 | 2 | | | 60.50 | | 60.50 | 94 |
| 0300 | Pits 6' to 12' deep, sandy soil | | 5 | 1.600 | | | 48.50 | | 48.50 | 75.50 |
| 0500 | Heavy soil or clay | | 3 | 2.667 | | | 80.50 | | 80.50 | 125 |
| 0700 | Pits 12' to 18' deep, sandy soil | | 4 | 2 | | | 60.50 | | 60.50 | 94 |
| 0900 | Heavy soil or clay | | 2 | 4 | | | 121 | | 121 | 188 |
| 1100 | Hand loading trucks from stock pile, sandy soil | | 12 | .667 | | | 20 | | 20 | 31.50 |
| 1300 | Heavy soil or clay | ▼ | 8 | 1 | ▼ | | 30.50 | | 30.50 | 47 |
| 1500 | For wet or muck hand excavation, add to above | | | | % | | | | 50% | 50% |
| 6000 | Machine excavation, for spread and mat footings, elevator pits, | | | | | | | | | |
| 6001 | and small building foundations | | | | | | | | | |
| 6030 | Common earth, hydraulic backhoe, 1/2 C.Y. bucket | B-12E | 55 | .291 | B.C.Y. | | 10.35 | 6.95 | 17.30 | 23.50 |
| 6035 | 3/4 C.Y. bucket | B-12F | 90 | .178 | | | 6.35 | 6.10 | 12.45 | 16.35 |
| 6040 | 1 C.Y. bucket | B-12A | 108 | .148 | | | 5.25 | 6 | 11.25 | 14.65 |
| 6050 | 1-1/2 C.Y. bucket | B-12B | 144 | .111 | | | 3.96 | 5.75 | 9.71 | 12.40 |
| 6060 | 2 C.Y. bucket | B-12C | 200 | .080 | | | 2.85 | 5.30 | 8.15 | 10.20 |
| 6070 | Sand and gravel, 3/4 C.Y. bucket | B-12F | 100 | .160 | | | 5.70 | 5.50 | 11.20 | 14.75 |
| 6080 | 1 C.Y. bucket | B-12A | 120 | .133 | | | 4.75 | 5.40 | 10.15 | 13.20 |
| 6090 | 1-1/2 C.Y. bucket | B-12B | 160 | .100 | | | 3.56 | 5.20 | 8.76 | 11.15 |
| 6100 | 2 C.Y. bucket | B-12C | 220 | .073 | | | 2.59 | 4.82 | 7.41 | 9.25 |
| 6110 | Clay, till, or blasted rock, 3/4 C.Y. bucket | B-12F | 80 | .200 | | | 7.10 | 6.85 | 13.95 | 18.45 |
| 6120 | 1 C.Y. bucket | B-12A | 95 | .168 | | | 6 | 6.80 | 12.80 | 16.65 |
| 6130 | 1-1/2 C.Y. bucket | B-12B | 130 | .123 | | | 4.38 | 6.40 | 10.78 | 13.70 |
| 6140 | 2 C.Y. bucket | B-12C | 175 | .091 | | | 3.25 | 6.05 | 9.30 | 11.60 |
| 6230 | Sandy clay & loam, hydraulic backhoe, 1/2 C.Y. bucket | B-12E | 60 | .267 | | | 9.50 | 6.35 | 15.85 | 21.50 |
| 6235 | 3/4 C.Y. bucket | B-12F | 98 | .163 | | | 5.80 | 5.60 | 11.40 | 15.05 |
| 6240 | 1 C.Y. bucket | B-12A | 116 | .138 | | | 4.91 | 5.55 | 10.46 | 13.65 |
| 6250 | 1-1/2 C.Y. bucket | B-12B | 156 | .103 | ▼ | | 3.65 | 5.30 | 8.95 | 11.45 |
| 9010 | For mobilization or demobilization, see Div. 01 54 36.50 | | | | | | | | | |

## 31 23 16 – Excavation

| 31 23 16.16 Structural Excavation for Minor Structures | | Crew | Daily Output | Labor-Hours | Unit | Material | 2008 Bare Costs Labor | Equipment | Total | Total Incl O&P |
|---|---|---|---|---|---|---|---|---|---|---|
| 9020 | For dewatering, see Div. 31 23 19.20 | | | | | | | | | |
| 9022 | For larger structures, see Bulk Excavation, Div. 31 23 16.42 | | | | | | | | | |
| 9024 | For loading onto trucks, add | | | | | | | | 15% | |
| 9026 | For hauling, see Div. 31 23 23.18 | | | | | | | | | |
| 9030 | For sheeting or soldier bms/lagging, see Div. 31 52 16.10 & 31 62 13.13 | | | | | | | | | |
| 9040 | For trench excavation of strip ftgs, see Div. 31 23 16.13 | | | | | | | | | |

## 31 23 16.26 Rock Removal

| 0010 | **ROCK REMOVAL** R312316-40 | Crew | Daily Output | Labor-Hours | Unit | Material | Labor | Equipment | Total | Total Incl O&P |
|---|---|---|---|---|---|---|---|---|---|---|
| 0015 | Drilling only rock, 2" hole for rock bolts | B-47 | 316 | .076 | L.F. | | 2.54 | 4.14 | 6.68 | 8.45 |
| 0800 | 2-1/2" hole for pre-splitting | | 600 | .040 | | | 1.34 | 2.18 | 3.52 | 4.46 |
| 4600 | Quarry operations, 2-1/2" to 3-1/2" diameter | | 715 | .034 | | | 1.12 | 1.83 | 2.95 | 3.74 |

## 31 23 16.30 Drilling and Blasting Rock

| 0010 | **DRILLING AND BLASTING ROCK** | Crew | Daily Output | Labor-Hours | Unit | Material | Labor | Equipment | Total | Total Incl O&P |
|---|---|---|---|---|---|---|---|---|---|---|
| 0020 | Rock, open face, under 1500 CY | B-47 | 225 | .107 | B.C.Y. | 2.50 | 3.56 | 5.80 | 11.86 | 14.65 |
| 0100 | Over 1500 C.Y. | | 300 | .080 | | 2.50 | 2.67 | 4.36 | 9.53 | 11.65 |
| 0200 | Areas where blasting mats are required, under 1500 C.Y. | | 175 | .137 | | 2.50 | 4.58 | 7.50 | 14.58 | 18.05 |
| 0250 | Over 1500 C.Y. | | 250 | .096 | | 2.50 | 3.21 | 5.25 | 10.96 | 13.45 |
| 0300 | Bulk drilling and blasting, can vary greatly, average | | | | | | | | 9.90 | 11 |
| 0500 | Pits, average | | | | | | | | 39.60 | 44 |
| 1300 | Deep hole method, up to 1500 C.Y. | B-47 | 50 | .480 | | 2.50 | 16.05 | 26 | 44.55 | 56.50 |
| 1400 | Over 1500 C.Y. | | 66 | .364 | | 2.50 | 12.15 | 19.85 | 34.50 | 43.50 |
| 1900 | Restricted areas, up to 1500 C.Y. | | 13 | 1.846 | | 2.50 | 61.50 | 101 | 165 | 209 |
| 2000 | Over 1500 C.Y. | | 20 | 1.200 | | 2.50 | 40 | 65.50 | 108 | 136 |
| 2200 | Trenches, up to 1500 C.Y. | | 22 | 1.091 | | 7.25 | 36.50 | 59.50 | 103.25 | 130 |
| 2300 | Over 1500 C.Y. | | 26 | .923 | | 7.25 | 31 | 50.50 | 88.75 | 111 |
| 2500 | Pier holes, up to 1500 C.Y. | | 22 | 1.091 | | 2.50 | 36.50 | 59.50 | 98.50 | 124 |
| 2600 | Over 1500 C.Y. | | 31 | .774 | | 2.50 | 26 | 42 | 70.50 | 89.50 |
| 2800 | Boulders under 1/2 C.Y., loaded on truck, no hauling | B-100 | 80 | .150 | | | 5.50 | 7.95 | 13.45 | 17.10 |
| 2900 | Boulders, drilled, blasted | B-47 | 100 | .240 | | 2.50 | 8 | 13.10 | 23.60 | 29.50 |
| 3100 | Jackhammer operators with foreman compressor, air tools | B-9 | 1 | 40 | Day | | 1,225 | 192 | 1,417 | 2,100 |
| 3300 | Track drill, compressor, operator and foreman | B-47 | 1 | 24 | " | | 800 | 1,300 | 2,100 | 2,675 |
| 3500 | Blasting caps | | | | Ea. | 4.65 | | | 4.65 | 5.10 |
| 3700 | Explosives | | | | | .34 | | | .34 | .37 |
| 3900 | Blasting mats, rent, for first day | | | | | 109 | | | 109 | 120 |
| 4000 | Per added day | | | | | 36.50 | | | 36.50 | 40 |
| 4200 | Preblast survey for 6 room house, individual lot, minimum | A-6 | 2.40 | 6.667 | | | 256 | 28.50 | 284.50 | 425 |
| 4300 | Maximum | " | 1.35 | 11.852 | | | 455 | 51 | 506 | 755 |
| 4500 | City block within zone of influence, minimum | A-8 | 25200 | .001 | S.F. | | .05 | | .05 | .08 |
| 4600 | Maximum | " | 15100 | .002 | " | | .09 | | .09 | .14 |

## 31 23 16.42 Excavating, Bulk Bank Measure

| 0010 | **EXCAVATING, BULK BANK MEASURE** R312316-40 | Crew | Daily Output | Labor-Hours | Unit | Material | Labor | Equipment | Total | Total Incl O&P |
|---|---|---|---|---|---|---|---|---|---|---|
| 0011 | Common earth piled | | | | | | | | | |
| 0020 | For loading onto trucks, add | | | | | | | | 15% | 15% |
| 0050 | For mobilization and demobilization, see Div. 01 54 36.50 R312316-45 | | | | | | | | | |
| 0100 | For hauling, see Div. 31 23 23.18 | | | | | | | | | |
| 0200 | Excavator, hydraulic, crawler mtd., 1 C.Y. cap. = 100 C.Y./hr. | B-12A | 800 | .020 | B.C.Y. | | .71 | .81 | 1.52 | 1.98 |
| 0250 | 1-1/2 C.Y. cap. = 125 C.Y./hr. | B-12B | 1000 | .016 | | | .57 | .83 | 1.40 | 1.78 |
| 0260 | 2 C.Y. cap. = 165 C.Y./hr. | B-12C | 1320 | .012 | | | .43 | .80 | 1.23 | 1.54 |
| 0300 | 3 C.Y. cap. = 260 C.Y./hr. | B-12D | 2080 | .008 | | | .27 | 1.12 | 1.39 | 1.66 |
| 0305 | 3.5 C.Y. cap. = 300 C.Y./hr. | " | 2400 | .007 | | | .24 | .97 | 1.21 | 1.43 |
| 0310 | Wheel mounted, 1/2 C.Y. cap. = 40 C.Y./hr. | B-12E | 320 | .050 | | | 1.78 | 1.19 | 2.97 | 4.03 |
| 0360 | 3/4 C.Y. cap. = 60 C.Y./hr. | B-12F | 480 | .033 | | | 1.19 | 1.14 | 2.33 | 3.07 |

# 31 23 Excavation and Fill

## 31 23 16 – Excavation

### 31 23 16.42 Excavating, Bulk Bank Measure

| | | Crew | Daily Output | Labor-Hours | Unit | Material | 2008 Bare Costs Labor | 2008 Bare Costs Equipment | Total | Total Incl O&P |
|---|---|---|---|---|---|---|---|---|---|---|
| 0500 | Clamshell, 1/2 C.Y. cap. = 20 C.Y./hr. | B-12G | 160 | .100 | B.C.Y. | | 3.56 | 4.01 | 7.57 | 9.85 |
| 0550 | 1 C.Y. cap. = 35 C.Y./hr. | B-12H | 280 | .057 | | | 2.03 | 3.85 | 5.88 | 7.35 |
| 0950 | Dragline, 1/2 C.Y. cap. = 30 C.Y./hr. | B-12I | 240 | .067 | | | 2.37 | 3.31 | 5.68 | 7.25 |
| 1000 | 3/4 C.Y. cap. = 35 C.Y./hr. | " | 280 | .057 | | | 2.03 | 2.84 | 4.87 | 6.25 |
| 1050 | 1-1/2 C.Y. cap. = 65 C.Y./hr. | B-12P | 520 | .031 | | | 1.10 | 2.09 | 3.19 | 3.97 |
| 1200 | Front end loader, track mtd., 1-1/2 C.Y. cap. = 70 C.Y./hr. | B-10N | 560 | .021 | | | .79 | .64 | 1.43 | 1.89 |
| 1250 | 2-1/2 C.Y. cap. = 95 C.Y./hr. | B-10O | 760 | .016 | | | .58 | .84 | 1.42 | 1.80 |
| 1300 | 3 C.Y. cap. = 130 C.Y./hr. | B-10P | 1040 | .012 | | | .42 | .86 | 1.28 | 1.59 |
| 1350 | 5 C.Y. cap. = 160 C.Y./hr. | B-10Q | 1280 | .009 | | | .34 | .97 | 1.31 | 1.59 |
| 1500 | Wheel mounted, 3/4 C.Y. cap. = 45 C.Y./hr. | B-10R | 360 | .033 | | | 1.22 | .63 | 1.85 | 2.55 |
| 1550 | 1-1/2 C.Y. cap. = 80 C.Y./hr. | B-10S | 640 | .019 | | | .69 | .47 | 1.16 | 1.57 |
| 1600 | 2-1/4 C.Y. cap. = 100 C.Y./hr. | B-10T | 800 | .015 | | | .55 | .48 | 1.03 | 1.37 |
| 1650 | 5 C.Y. cap. = 185 C.Y./hr. | B-10U | 1480 | .008 | | | .30 | .56 | .86 | 1.06 |
| 1800 | Hydraulic excavator, truck mtd, 1/2 C.Y. = 30 C.Y./hr. | B-12J | 240 | .067 | | | 2.37 | 3.89 | 6.26 | 7.90 |
| 1850 | 48 inch bucket, 1 C.Y. = 45 C.Y./hr. | B-12K | 360 | .044 | | | 1.58 | 3.02 | 4.60 | 5.75 |
| 3700 | Shovel, 1/2 C.Y. capacity = 55 C.Y./hr. | B-12L | 440 | .036 | | | 1.29 | 1.49 | 2.78 | 3.62 |
| 3750 | 3/4 C.Y. capacity = 85 C.Y./hr. | B-12M | 680 | .024 | | | .84 | 1.22 | 2.06 | 2.63 |
| 3800 | 1 C.Y. capacity = 120 C.Y./hr. | B-12N | 960 | .017 | | | .59 | 1.14 | 1.73 | 2.17 |
| 3850 | 1-1/2 C.Y. capacity = 160 C.Y./hr. | B-12O | 1280 | .013 | | | .45 | .88 | 1.33 | 1.65 |
| 3900 | 3 C.Y. cap. = 250 C.Y./hr. | B-12T | 2000 | .008 | | | .28 | .79 | 1.07 | 1.31 |
| 4000 | For soft soil or sand, deduct | | | | | | | | 15% | 15% |
| 4100 | For heavy soil or stiff clay, add | | | | | | | | 60% | 60% |
| 4200 | For wet excavation with clamshell or dragline, add | | | | | | | | 100% | 100% |
| 4250 | All other equipment, add | | | | | | | | 50% | 50% |
| 4400 | Clamshell in sheeting or cofferdam, minimum | B-12H | 160 | .100 | | | 3.56 | 6.75 | 10.31 | 12.85 |
| 4450 | Maximum | " | 60 | .267 | | | 9.50 | 18 | 27.50 | 34.50 |
| 5000 | Excavating, bulk bank measure, sandy clay & loam piled | | | | | | | | | |
| 5020 | For loading onto trucks, add | | | | | | | | 15% | 15% |
| 5100 | Excavator, hydraulic, crawler mtd., 1 C.Y. cap. = 120 C.Y./hr. | B-12A | 960 | .017 | B.C.Y. | | .59 | .67 | 1.26 | 1.65 |
| 5150 | 1-1/2 C.Y. cap. = 150 C.Y./hr. | B-12B | 1200 | .013 | | | .47 | .69 | 1.16 | 1.49 |
| 5300 | 2 C.Y. cap. = 195 C.Y./hr. | B-12C | 1560 | .010 | | | .37 | .68 | 1.05 | 1.31 |
| 5400 | 3 C.Y. cap. = 300 C.Y./hr. | B-12D | 2400 | .007 | | | .24 | .97 | 1.21 | 1.43 |
| 5500 | 3.5 C.Y. cap. = 350 C.Y./hr. | " | 2800 | .006 | | | .20 | .83 | 1.03 | 1.23 |
| 5610 | Wheel mounted, 1/2 C.Y. cap. = 44 C.Y./hr. | B-12E | 352 | .045 | | | 1.62 | 1.09 | 2.71 | 3.66 |
| 5660 | 3/4 C.Y. cap. = 66 C.Y./hr. | B-12F | 528 | .030 | | | 1.08 | 1.04 | 2.12 | 2.79 |
| 8000 | For hauling excavated material, see Div. 31 23 23.18 | | | | | | | | | |

### 31 23 16.46 Excavating, Bulk, Dozer

| | | Crew | Daily Output | Labor-Hours | Unit | Material | 2008 Bare Costs Labor | 2008 Bare Costs Equipment | Total | Total Incl O&P |
|---|---|---|---|---|---|---|---|---|---|---|
| 0010 | **EXCAVATING, BULK, DOZER** | | | | | | | | | |
| 0011 | Open site | | | | | | | | | |
| 2000 | 80 H.P., 50' haul, sand & gravel | B-10L | 460 | .026 | B.C.Y. | | .96 | .83 | 1.79 | 2.36 |
| 2010 | Sandy clay & loam | | 440 | .027 | | | 1 | .86 | 1.86 | 2.47 |
| 2020 | Common earth | | 400 | .030 | | | 1.10 | .95 | 2.05 | 2.71 |
| 2040 | Clay | | 250 | .048 | | | 1.76 | 1.52 | 3.28 | 4.35 |
| 2200 | 150' haul, sand & gravel | | 230 | .052 | | | 1.91 | 1.65 | 3.56 | 4.72 |
| 2210 | Sandy clay & loam | | 220 | .055 | | | 2 | 1.72 | 3.72 | 4.94 |
| 2220 | Common earth | | 200 | .060 | | | 2.20 | 1.90 | 4.10 | 5.45 |
| 2240 | Clay | | 125 | .096 | | | 3.52 | 3.04 | 6.56 | 8.70 |
| 2400 | 300' haul, sand & gravel | | 120 | .100 | | | 3.67 | 3.16 | 6.83 | 9.10 |
| 2410 | Sandy clay & loam | | 115 | .104 | | | 3.82 | 3.30 | 7.12 | 9.45 |
| 2420 | Common earth | | 100 | .120 | | | 4.40 | 3.79 | 8.19 | 10.85 |
| 2440 | Clay | | 65 | .185 | | | 6.75 | 5.85 | 12.60 | 16.70 |
| 3000 | 105 H.P., 50' haul, sand & gravel | B-10W | 700 | .017 | | | .63 | .76 | 1.39 | 1.80 |

# 31 23 Excavation and Fill

## 31 23 16 – Excavation

### 31 23 16.46 Excavating, Bulk, Dozer

| | | Crew | Daily Output | Labor-Hours | Unit | Material | Labor | Equipment | Total | Total Incl O&P |
|---|---|---|---|---|---|---|---|---|---|---|
| | | | | | | | **2008 Bare Costs** | | | |
| 3010 | Sandy clay & loam | B-10W | 680 | .018 | B.C.Y. | | .65 | .78 | 1.43 | 1.84 |
| 3020 | Common earth | | 610 | .020 | | | .72 | .87 | 1.59 | 2.06 |
| 3040 | Clay | | 385 | .031 | | | 1.14 | 1.38 | 2.52 | 3.26 |
| 3200 | 150' haul, sand & gravel | | 310 | .039 | | | 1.42 | 1.72 | 3.14 | 4.05 |
| 3210 | Sandy clay & loam | | 300 | .040 | | | 1.47 | 1.77 | 3.24 | 4.18 |
| 3220 | Common earth | | 270 | .044 | | | 1.63 | 1.97 | 3.60 | 4.65 |
| 3240 | Clay | | 170 | .071 | | | 2.59 | 3.13 | 5.72 | 7.40 |
| 3300 | 300' haul, sand & gravel | | 140 | .086 | | | 3.14 | 3.80 | 6.94 | 8.95 |
| 3310 | Sandy clay & loam | | 135 | .089 | | | 3.26 | 3.94 | 7.20 | 9.30 |
| 3320 | Common earth | | 120 | .100 | | | 3.67 | 4.44 | 8.11 | 10.50 |
| 3340 | Clay | | 100 | .120 | | | 4.40 | 5.30 | 9.70 | 12.55 |
| 4000 | 200 H.P., 50' haul, sand & gravel | B-10B | 1400 | .009 | | | .31 | .76 | 1.07 | 1.32 |
| 4010 | Sandy clay & loam | | 1360 | .009 | | | .32 | .79 | 1.11 | 1.36 |
| 4020 | Common earth | | 1230 | .010 | | | .36 | .87 | 1.23 | 1.50 |
| 4040 | Clay | | 770 | .016 | | | .57 | 1.39 | 1.96 | 2.40 |
| 4200 | 150' haul, sand & gravel | | 595 | .020 | | | .74 | 1.80 | 2.54 | 3.10 |
| 4210 | Sandy clay & loam | | 580 | .021 | | | .76 | 1.85 | 2.61 | 3.18 |
| 4220 | Common earth | | 516 | .023 | | | .85 | 2.08 | 2.93 | 3.58 |
| 4240 | Clay | | 325 | .037 | | | 1.35 | 3.30 | 4.65 | 5.70 |
| 4400 | 300' haul, sand & gravel | | 310 | .039 | | | 1.42 | 3.45 | 4.87 | 5.95 |
| 4410 | Sandy clay & loam | | 300 | .040 | | | 1.47 | 3.57 | 5.04 | 6.15 |
| 4420 | Common earth | | 270 | .044 | | | 1.63 | 3.97 | 5.60 | 6.85 |
| 4440 | Clay | | 170 | .071 | | | 2.59 | 6.30 | 8.89 | 10.90 |
| 5000 | 300 H.P., 50' haul, sand & gravel | B-10M | 1900 | .006 | | | .23 | .73 | .96 | 1.15 |
| 5010 | Sandy clay & loam | | 1850 | .006 | | | .24 | .75 | .99 | 1.19 |
| 5020 | Common earth | | 1650 | .007 | | | .27 | .84 | 1.11 | 1.34 |
| 5040 | Clay | | 1025 | .012 | | | .43 | 1.35 | 1.78 | 2.14 |
| 5200 | 150' haul, sand & gravel | | 920 | .013 | | | .48 | 1.51 | 1.99 | 2.39 |
| 5210 | Sandy clay & loam | | 895 | .013 | | | .49 | 1.55 | 2.04 | 2.46 |
| 5220 | Common earth | | 800 | .015 | | | .55 | 1.74 | 2.29 | 2.75 |
| 5240 | Clay | | 500 | .024 | | | .88 | 2.78 | 3.66 | 4.39 |
| 5400 | 300' haul, sand & gravel | | 470 | .026 | | | .94 | 2.95 | 3.89 | 4.67 |
| 5410 | Sandy clay & loam | | 455 | .026 | | | .97 | 3.05 | 4.02 | 4.83 |
| 5420 | Common earth | | 410 | .029 | | | 1.07 | 3.39 | 4.46 | 5.35 |
| 5440 | Clay | | 250 | .048 | | | 1.76 | 5.55 | 7.31 | 8.80 |
| 5500 | 460 H.P., 50' haul, sand & gravel | B-10X | 1930 | .006 | | | .23 | .94 | 1.17 | 1.39 |
| 5506 | Sandy clay & loam | | 1880 | .006 | | | .23 | .97 | 1.20 | 1.42 |
| 5510 | Common earth | | 1680 | .007 | | | .26 | 1.08 | 1.34 | 1.59 |
| 5520 | Clay | | 1050 | .011 | | | .42 | 1.73 | 2.15 | 2.54 |
| 5530 | 150' haul, sand & gravel | | 1290 | .009 | | | .34 | 1.41 | 1.75 | 2.07 |
| 5535 | Sandy clay & loam | | 1250 | .010 | | | .35 | 1.45 | 1.80 | 2.14 |
| 5540 | Common earth | | 1120 | .011 | | | .39 | 1.62 | 2.01 | 2.38 |
| 5550 | Clay | | 700 | .017 | | | .63 | 2.60 | 3.23 | 3.81 |
| 5560 | 300' haul, sand & gravel | | 660 | .018 | | | .67 | 2.75 | 3.42 | 4.04 |
| 5565 | Sandy clay & loam | | 640 | .019 | | | .69 | 2.84 | 3.53 | 4.17 |
| 5570 | Common earth | | 575 | .021 | | | .76 | 3.16 | 3.92 | 4.64 |
| 5580 | Clay | | 350 | .034 | | | 1.26 | 5.20 | 6.46 | 7.60 |
| 6000 | 700 H.P., 50' haul, sand & gravel | B-10V | 3500 | .003 | | | .13 | 1.05 | 1.18 | 1.35 |
| 6006 | Sandy clay & loam | | 3400 | .004 | | | .13 | 1.08 | 1.21 | 1.39 |
| 6010 | Common earth | | 3035 | .004 | | | .14 | 1.21 | 1.35 | 1.55 |
| 6020 | Clay | | 1925 | .006 | | | .23 | 1.91 | 2.14 | 2.45 |
| 6030 | 150' haul, sand & gravel | | 2025 | .006 | | | .22 | 1.82 | 2.04 | 2.33 |
| 6035 | Sandy clay & loam | | 1960 | .006 | | | .22 | 1.88 | 2.10 | 2.41 |

# 31 23 Excavation and Fill

## 31 23 16 – Excavation

### 31 23 16.46 Excavating, Bulk, Dozer

| | | Crew | Daily Output | Labor-Hours | Unit | Material | 2008 Bare Costs Labor | Equipment | Total | Total Incl O&P |
|---|---|---|---|---|---|---|---|---|---|---|
| 6040 | Common earth | B-10V | 1750 | .007 | B.C.Y. | | .25 | 2.10 | 2.35 | 2.70 |
| 6050 | Clay | | 1100 | .011 | | | .40 | 3.35 | 3.75 | 4.29 |
| 6060 | 300' haul, sand & gravel | | 1030 | .012 | | | .43 | 3.57 | 4 | 4.58 |
| 6065 | Sandy clay & loam | | 1005 | .012 | | | .44 | 3.66 | 4.10 | 4.70 |
| 6070 | Common earth | | 900 | .013 | | | .49 | 4.09 | 4.58 | 5.25 |
| 6080 | Clay | | 550 | .022 | | | .80 | 6.70 | 7.50 | 8.55 |

### 31 23 16.50 Excavation, Bulk, Scrapers

| | | Crew | Daily Output | Labor-Hours | Unit | Material | 2008 Bare Costs Labor | Equipment | Total | Total Incl O&P |
|---|---|---|---|---|---|---|---|---|---|---|
| 0010 | **EXCAVATION, BULK, SCRAPERS**   R312316-40 | | | | | | | | | |
| 0100 | Elev. scraper 11 C.Y., sand & gravel 1500' haul, 1/4 dozer | B-33F | 690 | .020 | B.C.Y. | | .75 | 1.85 | 2.60 | 3.17 |
| 0150 | 3000' haul | | 610 | .023 | | | .85 | 2.09 | 2.94 | 3.59 |
| 0200 | 5000' haul | | 505 | .028 | | | 1.03 | 2.52 | 3.55 | 4.34 |
| 0300 | Common earth, 1500' haul | | 600 | .023 | | | .87 | 2.12 | 2.99 | 3.66 |
| 0350 | 3000' haul | | 530 | .026 | | | .98 | 2.41 | 3.39 | 4.14 |
| 0400 | 5000' haul | | 440 | .032 | | | 1.18 | 2.90 | 4.08 | 4.98 |
| 0410 | Sandy clay & loam, 1500' haul | | 648 | .022 | | | .80 | 1.97 | 2.77 | 3.38 |
| 0420 | 3000' haul | | 572 | .024 | | | .91 | 2.23 | 3.14 | 3.83 |
| 0430 | 5000' haul | | 475 | .029 | | | 1.09 | 2.68 | 3.77 | 4.61 |
| 0500 | Clay, 1500' haul | | 375 | .037 | | | 1.39 | 3.40 | 4.79 | 5.85 |
| 0550 | 3000' haul | | 330 | .042 | | | 1.57 | 3.86 | 5.43 | 6.65 |
| 0600 | 5000' haul | | 275 | .051 | | | 1.89 | 4.63 | 6.52 | 7.95 |
| 1000 | Self propelled scraper, 14 C.Y. 1/4 push dozer, sand | | | | | | | | | |
| 1050 | Sand and gravel, 1500' haul | B-33D | 920 | .015 | B.C.Y. | | .56 | 2.42 | 2.98 | 3.53 |
| 1100 | 3000' haul | | 805 | .017 | | | .65 | 2.77 | 3.42 | 4.03 |
| 1200 | 5000' haul | | 645 | .022 | | | .81 | 3.46 | 4.27 | 5 |
| 1300 | Common earth, 1500' haul | | 800 | .018 | | | .65 | 2.79 | 3.44 | 4.06 |
| 1350 | 3000' haul | | 700 | .020 | | | .74 | 3.18 | 3.92 | 4.63 |
| 1400 | 5000' haul | | 560 | .025 | | | .93 | 3.98 | 4.91 | 5.80 |
| 1420 | Sandy clay & loam, 1500' haul | | 864 | .016 | | | .60 | 2.58 | 3.18 | 3.75 |
| 1430 | 3000' haul | | 786 | .018 | | | .66 | 2.84 | 3.50 | 4.12 |
| 1440 | 5000' haul | | 605 | .023 | | | .86 | 3.68 | 4.54 | 5.35 |
| 1500 | Clay, 1500' haul | | 500 | .028 | | | 1.04 | 4.46 | 5.50 | 6.50 |
| 1550 | 3000' haul | | 440 | .032 | | | 1.18 | 5.05 | 6.23 | 7.35 |
| 1600 | 5000' haul | | 350 | .040 | | | 1.48 | 6.35 | 7.83 | 9.25 |
| 2000 | 21 C.Y., 1/4 push dozer, sand & gravel, 1500' haul | B-33E | 1180 | .012 | | | .44 | 2.69 | 3.13 | 3.63 |
| 2100 | 3000' haul | | 910 | .015 | | | .57 | 3.49 | 4.06 | 4.71 |
| 2200 | 5000' haul | | 750 | .019 | | | .69 | 4.24 | 4.93 | 5.70 |
| 2300 | Common earth, 1500' haul | | 1030 | .014 | | | .50 | 3.08 | 3.58 | 4.16 |
| 2350 | 3000' haul | | 790 | .018 | | | .66 | 4.02 | 4.68 | 5.40 |
| 2400 | 5000' haul | | 650 | .022 | | | .80 | 4.89 | 5.69 | 6.60 |
| 2420 | Sandy clay & loam, 1500' haul | | 1112 | .013 | | | .47 | 2.86 | 3.33 | 3.85 |
| 2430 | 3000' haul | | 854 | .016 | | | .61 | 3.72 | 4.33 | 5 |
| 2440 | 5000' haul | | 702 | .020 | | | .74 | 4.52 | 5.26 | 6.10 |
| 2500 | Clay, 1500' haul | | 645 | .022 | | | .81 | 4.93 | 5.74 | 6.60 |
| 2550 | 3000' haul | | 495 | .028 | | | 1.05 | 6.40 | 7.45 | 8.65 |
| 2600 | 5000' haul | | 405 | .035 | | | 1.28 | 7.85 | 9.13 | 10.60 |
| 2700 | Towed, 10 C.Y., 1/4 push dozer, sand & gravel, 1500' haul | B-33B | 560 | .025 | | | .93 | 3.39 | 4.32 | 5.15 |
| 2720 | 3000' haul | | 450 | .031 | | | 1.15 | 4.22 | 5.37 | 6.40 |
| 2730 | 5000' haul | | 365 | .038 | | | 1.42 | 5.20 | 6.62 | 7.85 |
| 2750 | Common earth, 1500' haul | | 420 | .033 | | | 1.24 | 4.52 | 5.76 | 6.85 |
| 2770 | 3000' haul | | 400 | .035 | | | 1.30 | 4.75 | 6.05 | 7.15 |
| 2780 | 5000' haul | | 310 | .045 | | | 1.68 | 6.10 | 7.78 | 9.30 |
| 2785 | Sandy clay & Loam, 1500' haul | | 454 | .031 | | | 1.14 | 4.18 | 5.32 | 6.35 |

543

## 31 23 16 – Excavation

### 31 23 16.50 Excavation, Bulk, Scrapers

| | | Crew | Daily Output | Labor-Hours | Unit | Material | 2008 Bare Costs Labor | 2008 Bare Costs Equipment | Total | Total Incl O&P |
|---|---|---|---|---|---|---|---|---|---|---|
| 2790 | 3000' haul | B-33B | 432 | .032 | B.C.Y. | | 1.20 | 4.39 | 5.59 | 6.65 |
| 2795 | 5000' haul | | 340 | .041 | | | 1.53 | 5.60 | 7.13 | 8.45 |
| 2800 | Clay, 1500' haul | | 315 | .044 | | | 1.65 | 6.05 | 7.70 | 9.15 |
| 2820 | 3000' haul | | 300 | .047 | | | 1.73 | 6.35 | 8.08 | 9.60 |
| 2840 | 5000' haul | | 225 | .062 | | | 2.31 | 8.45 | 10.76 | 12.80 |
| 2900 | 15 C.Y., 1/4 push dozer, sand & gravel, 1500' haul | B-33C | 800 | .018 | | | .65 | 2.37 | 3.02 | 3.60 |
| 2920 | 3000' haul | | 640 | .022 | | | .81 | 2.97 | 3.78 | 4.49 |
| 2940 | 5000' haul | | 520 | .027 | | | 1 | 3.65 | 4.65 | 5.55 |
| 2960 | Common earth, 1500' haul | | 600 | .023 | | | .87 | 3.16 | 4.03 | 4.80 |
| 2980 | 3000' haul | | 560 | .025 | | | .93 | 3.39 | 4.32 | 5.15 |
| 3000 | 5000' haul | | 440 | .032 | | | 1.18 | 4.31 | 5.49 | 6.55 |
| 3005 | Sandy clay & Loam, 1500' haul | | 648 | .022 | | | .80 | 2.93 | 3.73 | 4.44 |
| 3010 | 3000' haul | | 605 | .023 | | | .86 | 3.14 | 4 | 4.75 |
| 3015 | 5000' haul | | 475 | .029 | | | 1.09 | 4 | 5.09 | 6.05 |
| 3020 | Clay, 1500' haul | | 450 | .031 | | | 1.15 | 4.22 | 5.37 | 6.40 |
| 3040 | 3000' haul | | 420 | .033 | | | 1.24 | 4.52 | 5.76 | 6.85 |
| 3060 | 5000' haul | | 320 | .044 | | | 1.62 | 5.95 | 7.57 | 9 |

## 31 23 19 – Dewatering

### 31 23 19.20 Dewatering Systems

| | | Crew | Daily Output | Labor-Hours | Unit | Material | 2008 Bare Costs Labor | 2008 Bare Costs Equipment | Total | Total Incl O&P |
|---|---|---|---|---|---|---|---|---|---|---|
| 0010 | **DEWATERING SYSTEMS** | | | | | | | | | |
| 0020 | Excavate drainage trench, 2' wide, 2' deep | B-11C | 90 | .178 | C.Y. | | 6.25 | 3.17 | 9.42 | 13.05 |
| 0100 | 2' wide, 3' deep, with backhoe loader | " | 135 | .119 | | | 4.15 | 2.11 | 6.26 | 8.70 |
| 0200 | Excavate sump pits by hand, light soil | 1 Clab | 7.10 | 1.127 | | | 34 | | 34 | 53 |
| 0300 | Heavy soil | " | 3.50 | 2.286 | | | 69 | | 69 | 108 |
| 0500 | Pumping 8 hr., attended 2 hrs. per day, including 20 L.F. | | | | | | | | | |
| 0550 | of suction hose & 100 L.F. discharge hose | | | | | | | | | |
| 0600 | 2" diaphragm pump used for 8 hours | B-10H | 4 | 3 | Day | | 110 | 16.40 | 126.40 | 185 |
| 0650 | 4" diaphragm pump used for 8 hours | B-10I | 4 | 3 | | | 110 | 23 | 133 | 193 |
| 0800 | 8 hrs. attended, 2" diaphragm pump | B-10H | 1 | 12 | | | 440 | 65.50 | 505.50 | 740 |
| 0900 | 3" centrifugal pump | B-10J | 1 | 12 | | | 440 | 74 | 514 | 750 |
| 1000 | 4" diaphragm pump | B-10I | 1 | 12 | | | 440 | 92.50 | 532.50 | 770 |
| 1100 | 6" centrifugal pump | B-10K | 1 | 12 | | | 440 | 330 | 770 | 1,025 |
| 1300 | CMP, incl. excavation 3' deep, 12" diameter | B-6 | 115 | .209 | L.F. | 11.40 | 6.85 | 2.48 | 20.73 | 25.50 |
| 1400 | 18" diameter | | 100 | .240 | " | 14.15 | 7.85 | 2.85 | 24.85 | 31 |
| 1600 | Sump hole construction, incl. excavation and gravel, pit | | 1250 | .019 | C.F. | .91 | .63 | .23 | 1.77 | 2.22 |
| 1700 | With 12" gravel collar, 12" pipe, corrugated, 16 ga. | | 70 | .343 | L.F. | 18.75 | 11.25 | 4.08 | 34.08 | 42 |
| 1800 | 15" pipe, corrugated, 16 ga. | | 55 | .436 | | 24 | 14.30 | 5.20 | 43.50 | 54 |
| 1900 | 18" pipe, corrugated, 16 ga. | | 50 | .480 | | 28 | 15.70 | 5.70 | 49.40 | 61.50 |
| 2000 | 24" pipe, corrugated, 14 ga. | | 40 | .600 | | 33.50 | 19.65 | 7.15 | 60.30 | 75 |
| 2200 | Wood lining, up to 4' x 4', add | | 300 | .080 | SFCA | 15.90 | 2.62 | .95 | 19.47 | 22.50 |
| 9950 | See Div. 31 23 19.40 for wellpoints | | | | | | | | | |
| 9960 | See Div. 31 23 19.30 for deep well systems | | | | | | | | | |

### 31 23 19.30 Wells

| | | Crew | Daily Output | Labor-Hours | Unit | Material | 2008 Bare Costs Labor | 2008 Bare Costs Equipment | Total | Total Incl O&P |
|---|---|---|---|---|---|---|---|---|---|---|
| 0010 | **WELLS** | | | | | | | | | |
| 0011 | For dewatering 10' to 20' deep, 2' diameter | | | | | | | | | |
| 0020 | with steel casing, minimum | B-6 | 165 | .145 | V.L.F. | 39 | 4.76 | 1.73 | 45.49 | 52 |
| 0050 | Average | | 98 | .245 | | 39 | 8 | 2.91 | 49.91 | 58.50 |
| 0100 | Maximum | | 49 | .490 | | 39 | 16.05 | 5.80 | 60.85 | 74 |
| 0300 | For dewatering pumps see 01 54 33 in Reference Section | | | | | | | | | |
| 0500 | For domestic water wells, see Div. 33 21 13.10 | | | | | | | | | |

### 31 23 19.40 Wellpoints

| | | | | | | | | | | |
|---|---|---|---|---|---|---|---|---|---|---|
| 0010 | **WELLPOINTS** | R312319-90 | | | | | | | | |

# 31 23 Excavation and Fill

## 31 23 19 – Dewatering

### 31 23 19.40 Wellpoints

| | | Crew | Daily Output | Labor-Hours | Unit | Material | 2008 Bare Costs Labor | Equipment | Total | Total Incl O&P |
|---|---|---|---|---|---|---|---|---|---|---|
| 0011 | For equipment rental, see 01 54 33 in Reference Section | | | | | | | | | |
| 0100 | Installation and removal of single stage system | | | | | | | | | |
| 0110 | Labor only, .75 labor-hours per L.F., minimum | 1 Clab | 10.70 | .748 | LF Hdr | | 22.50 | | 22.50 | 35 |
| 0200 | 2.0 labor-hours per L.F., maximum | " | 4 | 2 | " | | 60.50 | | 60.50 | 94 |
| 0400 | Pump operation, 4 @ 6 hr. shifts | | | | | | | | | |
| 0410 | Per 24 hour day | 4 Eqlt | 1.27 | 25.197 | Day | | 950 | | 950 | 1,425 |
| 0500 | Per 168 hour week, 160 hr. straight, 8 hr. double time | | .18 | 177 | Week | | 6,700 | | 6,700 | 10,100 |
| 0550 | Per 4.3 week month | ↓ | .04 | 800 | Month | | 30,200 | | 30,200 | 45,600 |
| 0600 | Complete installation, operation, equipment rental, fuel & | | | | | | | | | |
| 0610 | removal of system with 2" wellpoints 5' O.C. | | | | | | | | | |
| 0700 | 100' long header, 6" diameter, first month | 4 Eqlt | 3.23 | 9.907 | LF Hdr | 148 | 375 | | 523 | 730 |
| 0800 | Thereafter, per month | | 4.13 | 7.748 | | 118 | 292 | | 410 | 570 |
| 1000 | 200' long header, 8" diameter, first month | | 6 | 5.333 | | 131 | 201 | | 332 | 450 |
| 1100 | Thereafter, per month | | 8.39 | 3.814 | | 66.50 | 144 | | 210.50 | 290 |
| 1300 | 500' long header, 8" diameter, first month | | 10.63 | 3.010 | | 52 | 114 | | 166 | 228 |
| 1400 | Thereafter, per month | | 20.91 | 1.530 | | 37 | 58 | | 95 | 128 |
| 1600 | 1,000' long header, 10" diameter, first month | | 11.62 | 2.754 | | 44.50 | 104 | | 148.50 | 206 |
| 1700 | Thereafter, per month | ↓ | 41.81 | .765 | ↓ | 22 | 29 | | 51 | 68 |
| 1900 | Note: above figures include pumping 168 hrs. per week | | | | | | | | | |
| 1910 | and include the pump operator and one stand-by pump. | | | | | | | | | |

## 31 23 23 – Fill

### 31 23 23.13 Backfill

| | | Crew | Daily Output | Labor-Hours | Unit | Material | 2008 Bare Costs Labor | Equipment | Total | Total Incl O&P |
|---|---|---|---|---|---|---|---|---|---|---|
| 0010 | **BACKFILL**                    R312323-30 | | | | | | | | | |
| 0015 | By hand, no compaction, light soil | 1 Clab | 14 | .571 | L.C.Y. | | 17.30 | | 17.30 | 27 |
| 0100 | Heavy soil | ↓ | 11 | .727 | " | | 22 | | 22 | 34 |
| 0300 | Compaction in 6" layers, hand tamp, add to above | | 20.60 | .388 | E.C.Y. | | 11.75 | | 11.75 | 18.25 |
| 0400 | Roller compaction operator walking, add | B-10A | 100 | .120 | | | 4.40 | 1.43 | 5.83 | 8.25 |
| 0500 | Air tamp, add | B-9D | 190 | .211 | | | 6.45 | 1.16 | 7.61 | 11.35 |
| 0600 | Vibrating plate, add | A-1D | 60 | .133 | | | 4.03 | .52 | 4.55 | 6.80 |
| 0800 | Compaction in 12" layers, hand tamp, add to above | 1 Clab | 34 | .235 | | | 7.10 | | 7.10 | 11.05 |
| 0900 | Roller compaction operator walking, add | B-10A | 150 | .080 | | | 2.93 | .95 | 3.88 | 5.50 |
| 1000 | Air tamp, add | B-9 | 285 | .140 | | | 4.30 | .67 | 4.97 | 7.45 |
| 1100 | Vibrating plate, add | A-1E | 90 | .089 | ↓ | | 2.69 | .43 | 3.12 | 4.65 |
| 1300 | Dozer backfilling, bulk, up to 300' haul, no compaction | B-10B | 1200 | .010 | L.C.Y. | | .37 | .89 | 1.26 | 1.54 |
| 1400 | Air tamped, add | B-11B | 80 | .200 | E.C.Y. | | 6.80 | 3.09 | 9.89 | 13.80 |
| 1600 | Compacting backfill, 6" to 12" lifts, vibrating roller | B-10C | 800 | .015 | | | .55 | 1.80 | 2.35 | 2.82 |
| 1700 | Sheepsfoot roller | B-10D | 750 | .016 | ↓ | | .59 | 1.96 | 2.55 | 3.04 |
| 1900 | Dozer backfilling, trench, up to 300' haul, no compaction | B-10B | 900 | .013 | L.C.Y. | | .49 | 1.19 | 1.68 | 2.05 |
| 2000 | Air tamped, add | B-11B | 80 | .200 | E.C.Y. | | 6.80 | 3.09 | 9.89 | 13.80 |
| 2200 | Compacting backfill, 6" to 12" lifts, vibrating roller | B-10C | 700 | .017 | | | .63 | 2.06 | 2.69 | 3.23 |
| 2300 | Sheepsfoot roller | B-10D | 650 | .018 | ↓ | | .68 | 2.26 | 2.94 | 3.52 |
| 2350 | Spreading in 8" layers, small dozer | B-10B | 1060 | .011 | L.C.Y. | | .41 | 1.01 | 1.42 | 1.74 |

### 31 23 23.14 Backfill, Structural

| | | Crew | Daily Output | Labor-Hours | Unit | Material | 2008 Bare Costs Labor | Equipment | Total | Total Incl O&P |
|---|---|---|---|---|---|---|---|---|---|---|
| 0010 | **BACKFILL, STRUCTURAL** | | | | | | | | | |
| 0011 | Dozer or F.E. loader | | | | | | | | | |
| 0020 | From existing stockpile, no compaction | | | | | | | | | |
| 2000 | 80 H.P., 50' haul, sand & gravel | B-10L | 1100 | .011 | L.C.Y. | | .40 | .35 | .75 | .99 |
| 2010 | Sandy clay & loam | | 1070 | .011 | | | .41 | .35 | .76 | 1.02 |
| 2020 | Common earth | | 975 | .012 | | | .45 | .39 | .84 | 1.12 |
| 2040 | Clay | | 850 | .014 | | | .52 | .45 | .97 | 1.28 |
| 2400 | 300' haul, sand & gravel | | 370 | .032 | | | 1.19 | 1.03 | 2.22 | 2.94 |
| 2410 | Sandy clay & loam | ↓ | 360 | .033 | ↓ | | 1.22 | 1.05 | 2.27 | 3.02 |

### 31 23 23.14 Backfill, Structural

| | | Crew | Daily Output | Labor-Hours | Unit | Material | 2008 Bare Costs Labor | Equipment | Total | Total Incl O&P |
|---|---|---|---|---|---|---|---|---|---|---|
| 2420 | Common earth | B-10L | 330 | .036 | L.C.Y. | | 1.33 | 1.15 | 2.48 | 3.29 |
| 2440 | Clay | ↓ | 290 | .041 | | | 1.52 | 1.31 | 2.83 | 3.75 |
| 3000 | 105 H.P., 50' haul, sand & gravel | B-10W | 1350 | .009 | | | .33 | .39 | .72 | .93 |
| 3010 | Sandy clay & loam | | 1325 | .009 | | | .33 | .40 | .73 | .95 |
| 3020 | Common earth | | 1225 | .010 | | | .36 | .43 | .79 | 1.03 |
| 3040 | Clay | | 1100 | .011 | | | .40 | .48 | .88 | 1.14 |
| 3300 | 300' haul, sand & gravel | | 465 | .026 | | | .95 | 1.15 | 2.10 | 2.70 |
| 3310 | Sandy clay & loam | | 455 | .026 | | | .97 | 1.17 | 2.14 | 2.76 |
| 3320 | Common earth | | 415 | .029 | | | 1.06 | 1.28 | 2.34 | 3.02 |
| 3340 | Clay | ↓ | 370 | .032 | | | 1.19 | 1.44 | 2.63 | 3.39 |
| 4000 | 200 H.P., 50' haul, sand & gravel | B-10B | 2500 | .005 | | | .18 | .43 | .61 | .74 |
| 4010 | Sandy clay & loam | | 2435 | .005 | | | .18 | .44 | .62 | .75 |
| 4020 | Common earth | | 2200 | .005 | | | .20 | .49 | .69 | .84 |
| 4040 | Clay | | 1950 | .006 | | | .23 | .55 | .78 | .94 |
| 4400 | 300' haul, sand & gravel | | 805 | .015 | | | .55 | 1.33 | 1.88 | 2.29 |
| 4410 | Sandy clay & loam | | 790 | .015 | | | .56 | 1.36 | 1.92 | 2.34 |
| 4420 | Common earth | | 735 | .016 | | | .60 | 1.46 | 2.06 | 2.51 |
| 4440 | Clay | ↓ | 660 | .018 | | | .67 | 1.62 | 2.29 | 2.79 |
| 5000 | 300 H.P., 50' haul, sand & gravel | B-10M | 3170 | .004 | | | .14 | .44 | .58 | .69 |
| 5010 | Sandy clay & loam | | 3110 | .004 | | | .14 | .45 | .59 | .71 |
| 5020 | Common earth | | 2900 | .004 | | | .15 | .48 | .63 | .76 |
| 5040 | Clay | | 2700 | .004 | | | .16 | .51 | .67 | .81 |
| 5400 | 300' haul, sand & gravel | | 1500 | .008 | | | .29 | .93 | 1.22 | 1.47 |
| 5410 | Sandy clay & loam | | 1470 | .008 | | | .30 | .94 | 1.24 | 1.49 |
| 5420 | Common earth | | 1350 | .009 | | | .33 | 1.03 | 1.36 | 1.63 |
| 5440 | Clay | ↓ | 1225 | .010 | ↓ | | .36 | 1.13 | 1.49 | 1.80 |
| 6010 | For trench backfill, see Div. 31 23 16.13 and 31 23 16.14 | | | | | | | | | |
| 6100 | For compaction, see Div. 31 23 23.24 | | | | | | | | | |

### 31 23 23.16 Fill By Borrow and Utility Bedding

| | | Crew | Daily Output | Labor-Hours | Unit | Material | 2008 Bare Costs Labor | Equipment | Total | Total Incl O&P |
|---|---|---|---|---|---|---|---|---|---|---|
| 0010 | **FILL BY BORROW AND UTILITY BEDDING** | | | | | | | | | |
| 0015 | Fill by borrow, load, 1 mile haul, spread with dozer | | | | | | | | | |
| 0020 | for embankments | B-15 | 1200 | .023 | L.C.Y. | 7 | .77 | 1.73 | 9.50 | 10.80 |
| 0035 | Select fill for shoulders & embankments | " | 1200 | .023 | " | 14.50 | .77 | 1.73 | 17 | 19.05 |
| 0040 | For hauling over 1 mile, add to above per C.Y., see Div. 31 23 23.18 | | | | Mile | | | | 1.50 | 1.50 |
| 0049 | Utility bedding, for pipe & conduit, not incl. compaction | | | | | | | | | |
| 0050 | Crushed or screened bank run gravel | B-6 | 150 | .160 | L.C.Y. | 29.50 | 5.25 | 1.90 | 36.65 | 42.50 |
| 0100 | Crushed stone 3/4" to 1/2" | | 150 | .160 | | 46.50 | 5.25 | 1.90 | 53.65 | 61.50 |
| 0200 | Sand, dead or bank | ↓ | 150 | .160 | ↓ | 10 | 5.25 | 1.90 | 17.15 | 21 |
| 0500 | Compacting bedding in trench | A-1D | 90 | .089 | E.C.Y. | | 2.69 | .34 | 3.03 | 4.56 |
| 0600 | If material source exceeds 2 miles, add for extra mileage. | | | | | | | | | |
| 0610 | See Div. 31 23 23 .18 for hauling mileage add. | | | | | | | | | |

### 31 23 23.17 General Fill

| | | Crew | Daily Output | Labor-Hours | Unit | Material | 2008 Bare Costs Labor | Equipment | Total | Total Incl O&P |
|---|---|---|---|---|---|---|---|---|---|---|
| 0010 | **GENERAL FILL** | | | | | | | | | |
| 0011 | Spread dumped material, no compaction | | | | | | | | | |
| 0020 | By dozer, no compaction | B-10B | 1000 | .012 | L.C.Y. | | .44 | 1.07 | 1.51 | 1.85 |
| 0100 | By hand | 1 Clab | 12 | .667 | " | | 20 | | 20 | 31.50 |
| 0500 | Gravel fill, compacted, under floor slabs, 4" deep | B-37 | 10000 | .005 | S.F. | .29 | .15 | .01 | .45 | .57 |
| 0600 | 6" deep | | 8600 | .006 | | .44 | .18 | .02 | .64 | .77 |
| 0700 | 9" deep | | 7200 | .007 | | .73 | .21 | .02 | .96 | 1.15 |
| 0800 | 12" deep | | 6000 | .008 | ↓ | 1.02 | .25 | .02 | 1.29 | 1.53 |
| 1000 | Alternate pricing method, 4" deep | | 120 | .400 | E.C.Y. | 22 | 12.75 | 1.08 | 35.83 | 45 |
| 1100 | 6" deep | ↓ | 160 | .300 | ↓ | 22 | 9.55 | .81 | 32.36 | 39.50 |

## 31 23 23 – Fill

| 31 23 23.17 General Fill | | Crew | Daily Output | Labor-Hours | Unit | Material | 2008 Bare Costs Labor | 2008 Bare Costs Equipment | Total | Total Incl O&P |
|---|---|---|---|---|---|---|---|---|---|---|
| 1200 | 9" deep | B-37 | 200 | .240 | E.C.Y. | 22 | 7.65 | .65 | 30.30 | 36.50 |
| 1300 | 12" deep | ↓ | 220 | .218 | ↓ | 22 | 6.95 | .59 | 29.54 | 35.50 |
| 1500 | For fill under exterior paving, see Div. 32 11 23.23 | | | | | | | | | |

### 31 23 23.18 Hauling

| | | Crew | Daily Output | Labor-Hours | Unit | Material | Labor | Equipment | Total | Total Incl O&P |
|---|---|---|---|---|---|---|---|---|---|---|
| 0010 | **HAULING**  R312316-40 | | | | | | | | | |
| 0011 | Excavated or borrow, loose cubic yards | | | | | | | | | |
| 0012 | no loading included, highway haulers | | | | | | | | | |
| 0020 | 8 C.Y. dump truck, 1/4 mile round trip, 5.0 loads/hr. | B-34A | 195 | .041 | L.C.Y. | | 1.26 | 1.58 | 2.84 | 3.68 |
| 0030 | 1/2 mile round trip, 4.1 loads/hr. | | 160 | .050 | | | 1.53 | 1.93 | 3.46 | 4.49 |
| 0040 | 1 mile round trip, 3.3 loads/hr. | | 130 | .062 | | | 1.88 | 2.37 | 4.25 | 5.50 |
| 0100 | 2 mile round trip, 2.6 loads/hr. | | 100 | .080 | | | 2.45 | 3.09 | 5.54 | 7.20 |
| 0150 | 3 mile round trip, 2.1 loads/hr. | | 80 | .100 | | | 3.06 | 3.86 | 6.92 | 9 |
| 0200 | 4 mile round trip, 1.8 loads/hr. | ↓ | 70 | .114 | | | 3.50 | 4.41 | 7.91 | 10.25 |
| 0310 | 12 C.Y. dump truck, 1/4 mile round trip 3.7 loads/hr. | B-34B | 288 | .028 | | | .85 | 1.75 | 2.60 | 3.24 |
| 0320 | 1/2 mile round trip, 3.2 loads/hr. | | 250 | .032 | | | .98 | 2.01 | 2.99 | 3.73 |
| 0330 | 1 mile round trip 2.7, loads/hr. | | 210 | .038 | | | 1.17 | 2.39 | 3.56 | 4.43 |
| 0400 | 2 mile round trip, 2.2 loads/hr. | | 180 | .044 | | | 1.36 | 2.79 | 4.15 | 5.15 |
| 0450 | 3 mile round trip, 1.9 loads/hr. | | 170 | .047 | | | 1.44 | 2.96 | 4.40 | 5.50 |
| 0500 | 4 mile round trip, 1.6 loads/hr. | | 125 | .064 | | | 1.96 | 4.02 | 5.98 | 7.45 |
| 0540 | 5 mile round trip, 1 load/hr. | | 78 | .103 | | | 3.14 | 6.45 | 9.59 | 11.95 |
| 0550 | 10 mile round trip, 0.60 load/hr. | | 58 | .138 | | | 4.22 | 8.65 | 12.87 | 16.10 |
| 0560 | 20 mile round trip, 0.4 load/hr. | ↓ | 39 | .205 | | | 6.30 | 12.90 | 19.20 | 24 |
| 0600 | 16.5 C.Y. dump trailer, 1 mile round trip, 2.6 loads/hr. | B-34C | 280 | .029 | | | .87 | 2.02 | 2.89 | 3.57 |
| 0700 | 2 mile round trip, 2.1 loads/hr. | | 225 | .036 | | | 1.09 | 2.51 | 3.60 | 4.44 |
| 1000 | 3 mile round trip, 1.8 loads/hr. | | 193 | .041 | | | 1.27 | 2.93 | 4.20 | 5.20 |
| 1100 | 4 mile round trip, 1.6 loads/hr. | | 172 | .047 | | | 1.42 | 3.28 | 4.70 | 5.80 |
| 1110 | 5 mile round trip, 1 load/hr. | | 108 | .074 | | | 2.27 | 5.25 | 7.52 | 9.25 |
| 1120 | 10 mile round trip, .60 load/hr. | | 80 | .100 | | | 3.06 | 7.05 | 10.11 | 12.50 |
| 1130 | 20 mile round trip, .4 load/hr. | ↓ | 54 | .148 | | | 4.53 | 10.45 | 14.98 | 18.50 |
| 1150 | 20 C.Y. dump trailer, 1 mile round trip, 2.5 loads/hr. | B-34D | 325 | .025 | | | .75 | 1.78 | 2.53 | 3.12 |
| 1200 | 2 mile round trip, 2 loads/hr. | | 260 | .031 | | | .94 | 2.22 | 3.16 | 3.90 |
| 1220 | 3 mile round trip, 1.7 loads/hr. | | 221 | .036 | | | 1.11 | 2.61 | 3.72 | 4.58 |
| 1240 | 4 mile round trip, 1.5 loads/hr. | | 195 | .041 | | | 1.26 | 2.96 | 4.22 | 5.20 |
| 1245 | 5 mile round trip, 1.1 load/hr. | | 143 | .056 | | | 1.71 | 4.04 | 5.75 | 7.10 |
| 1250 | 10 mile round trip, .75 load/hr. | | 110 | .073 | | | 2.23 | 5.25 | 7.48 | 9.20 |
| 1255 | 20 mile round trip, .5 load/hr. | ↓ | 78 | .103 | | | 3.14 | 7.40 | 10.54 | 13 |
| 1300 | Hauling in medium traffic, add | | | | | | | | 20% | 20% |
| 1400 | Heavy traffic, add | | | | | | | | 30% | 30% |
| 1600 | Grading at dump, or embankment if required, by dozer | B-10B | 1000 | .012 | ↓ | | .44 | 1.07 | 1.51 | 1.85 |
| 1800 | Spotter at fill or cut, if required | 1 Clab | 8 | 1 | Hr. | | 30.50 | | 30.50 | 47 |

### 31 23 23.20 Hauling

| | | Crew | Daily Output | Labor-Hours | Unit | Material | Labor | Equipment | Total | Total Incl O&P |
|---|---|---|---|---|---|---|---|---|---|---|
| 0010 | **HAULING** | | | | | | | | | |
| 0011 | Excavated or borrow, loose cubic yards | | | | | | | | | |
| 0012 | no loading equipment, including hauling, waiting, loading/dumping | | | | | | | | | |
| 0013 | time per cycle (wait, load, travel, unload or dump & return) | | | | | | | | | |
| 0014 | 8 CY truck, 15 MPH ave, cycle 0.5 miles, 10 min. wait/Ld./Uld. | B-34A | 320 | .025 | L.C.Y. | | .77 | .96 | 1.73 | 2.24 |
| 0016 | cycle 1 mile | | 272 | .029 | | | .90 | 1.13 | 2.03 | 2.64 |
| 0018 | cycle 2 miles | | 208 | .038 | | | 1.18 | 1.48 | 2.66 | 3.45 |
| 0020 | cycle 4 miles | | 144 | .056 | | | 1.70 | 2.14 | 3.84 | 4.99 |
| 0022 | cycle 6 miles | | 112 | .071 | | | 2.19 | 2.76 | 4.95 | 6.40 |
| 0024 | cycle 8 miles | | 88 | .091 | | | 2.78 | 3.51 | 6.29 | 8.15 |
| 0026 | 20 MPH ave, cycle 0.5 mile | ↓ | 336 | .024 | ↓ | | .73 | .92 | 1.65 | 2.14 |

| | 31 23 23.20 Hauling | Crew | Daily Output | Labor-Hours | Unit | Material | 2008 Bare Costs Labor | Equipment | Total | Total Incl O&P |
|---|---|---|---|---|---|---|---|---|---|---|
| 0028 | cycle 1 mile | B-34A | 296 | .027 | L.C.Y. | | .83 | 1.04 | 1.87 | 2.43 |
| 0030 | cycle 2 miles | | 240 | .033 | | | 1.02 | 1.29 | 2.31 | 2.99 |
| 0032 | cycle 4 miles | | 176 | .045 | | | 1.39 | 1.75 | 3.14 | 4.08 |
| 0034 | cycle 6 miles | | 136 | .059 | | | 1.80 | 2.27 | 4.07 | 5.30 |
| 0036 | cycle 8 miles | | 112 | .071 | | | 2.19 | 2.76 | 4.95 | 6.40 |
| 0044 | 25 MPH ave, cycle 4 miles | | 192 | .042 | | | 1.28 | 1.61 | 2.89 | 3.74 |
| 0046 | cycle 6 miles | | 160 | .050 | | | 1.53 | 1.93 | 3.46 | 4.49 |
| 0048 | cycle 8 miles | | 128 | .063 | | | 1.91 | 2.41 | 4.32 | 5.60 |
| 0050 | 30 MPH ave, cycle 4 miles | | 216 | .037 | | | 1.13 | 1.43 | 2.56 | 3.32 |
| 0052 | cycle 6 miles | | 176 | .045 | | | 1.39 | 1.75 | 3.14 | 4.08 |
| 0054 | cycle 8 miles | | 144 | .056 | | | 1.70 | 2.14 | 3.84 | 4.99 |
| 0114 | 15 MPH ave, cycle 0.5 mile, 15 min. wait/Ld./Uld. | | 224 | .036 | | | 1.09 | 1.38 | 2.47 | 3.21 |
| 0116 | cycle 1 mile | | 200 | .040 | | | 1.22 | 1.54 | 2.76 | 3.59 |
| 0118 | cycle 2 miles | | 168 | .048 | | | 1.46 | 1.84 | 3.30 | 4.27 |
| 0120 | cycle 4 miles | | 120 | .067 | | | 2.04 | 2.57 | 4.61 | 6 |
| 0122 | cycle 6 miles | | 96 | .083 | | | 2.55 | 3.21 | 5.76 | 7.50 |
| 0124 | cycle 8 miles | | 80 | .100 | | | 3.06 | 3.86 | 6.92 | 9 |
| 0126 | 20 MPH ave, cycle 0.5 mile | | 232 | .034 | | | 1.06 | 1.33 | 2.39 | 3.09 |
| 0128 | cycle 1 mile | | 208 | .038 | | | 1.18 | 1.48 | 2.66 | 3.45 |
| 0130 | cycle 2 miles | | 184 | .043 | | | 1.33 | 1.68 | 3.01 | 3.90 |
| 0132 | cycle 4 miles | | 144 | .056 | | | 1.70 | 2.14 | 3.84 | 4.99 |
| 0134 | cycle 6 miles | | 112 | .071 | | | 2.19 | 2.76 | 4.95 | 6.40 |
| 0136 | cycle 8 miles | | 96 | .083 | | | 2.55 | 3.21 | 5.76 | 7.50 |
| 0144 | 25 MPH ave, cycle 4 miles | | 152 | .053 | | | 1.61 | 2.03 | 3.64 | 4.72 |
| 0146 | cycle 6 miles | | 128 | .063 | | | 1.91 | 2.41 | 4.32 | 5.60 |
| 0148 | cycle 8 miles | | 112 | .071 | | | 2.19 | 2.76 | 4.95 | 6.40 |
| 0150 | 30 MPH ave, cycle 4 miles, 15 min. wait/Ld./Uld. | | 168 | .048 | | | 1.46 | 1.84 | 3.30 | 4.27 |
| 0152 | cycle 6 miles | | 144 | .056 | | | 1.70 | 2.14 | 3.84 | 4.99 |
| 0154 | cycle 8 miles | | 120 | .067 | | | 2.04 | 2.57 | 4.61 | 6 |
| 0214 | 15 MPH ave, cycle 0.5 mile, 20 min wait/Ld./Uld. | | 176 | .045 | | | 1.39 | 1.75 | 3.14 | 4.08 |
| 0216 | cycle 1 mile | | 160 | .050 | | | 1.53 | 1.93 | 3.46 | 4.49 |
| 0218 | cycle 2 miles | | 136 | .059 | | | 1.80 | 2.27 | 4.07 | 5.30 |
| 0220 | cycle 4 miles | | 104 | .077 | | | 2.35 | 2.97 | 5.32 | 6.90 |
| 0222 | cycle 6 miles | | 88 | .091 | | | 2.78 | 3.51 | 6.29 | 8.15 |
| 0224 | cycle 8 miles | | 72 | .111 | | | 3.40 | 4.29 | 7.69 | 9.95 |
| 0226 | 20 MPH ave, cycle 0.5 mile, 20 min. wait/Ld./Uld. | | 176 | .045 | | | 1.39 | 1.75 | 3.14 | 4.08 |
| 0228 | cycle 1 mile | | 168 | .048 | | | 1.46 | 1.84 | 3.30 | 4.27 |
| 0230 | cycle 2 miles | | 144 | .056 | | | 1.70 | 2.14 | 3.84 | 4.99 |
| 0232 | cycle 4 miles | | 120 | .067 | | | 2.04 | 2.57 | 4.61 | 6 |
| 0234 | cycle 6 miles | | 96 | .083 | | | 2.55 | 3.21 | 5.76 | 7.50 |
| 0236 | cycle 8 miles | | 88 | .091 | | | 2.78 | 3.51 | 6.29 | 8.15 |
| 0244 | 25 MPH ave, cycle 4 miles, 20 min. wait/Ld./Uld. | | 128 | .063 | | | 1.91 | 2.41 | 4.32 | 5.60 |
| 0246 | cycle 6 miles | | 112 | .071 | | | 2.19 | 2.76 | 4.95 | 6.40 |
| 0248 | cycle 8 miles | | 96 | .083 | | | 2.55 | 3.21 | 5.76 | 7.50 |
| 0250 | 30 MPH ave, cycle 0.5 mile, 20 min. wait/Ld./Uld. | | 136 | .059 | | | 1.80 | 2.27 | 4.07 | 5.30 |
| 0252 | cycle 6 miles | | 120 | .067 | | | 2.04 | 2.57 | 4.61 | 6 |
| 0254 | cycle 8 miles | | 104 | .077 | | | 2.35 | 2.97 | 5.32 | 6.90 |
| 0314 | 15 MPH ave, cycle 0.5 mile, 25 min wait/Ld./Uld., | | 144 | .056 | | | 1.70 | 2.14 | 3.84 | 4.99 |
| 0316 | cycle 1 mile | | 128 | .063 | | | 1.91 | 2.41 | 4.32 | 5.60 |
| 0318 | cycle 2 miles | | 112 | .071 | | | 2.19 | 2.76 | 4.95 | 6.40 |
| 0320 | cycle 4 miles | | 96 | .083 | | | 2.55 | 3.21 | 5.76 | 7.50 |
| 0322 | cycle 6 miles | | 80 | .100 | | | 3.06 | 3.86 | 6.92 | 9 |
| 0324 | cycle 8 miles | | 64 | .125 | | | 3.83 | 4.82 | 8.65 | 11.20 |

# 31 23 Excavation and Fill

## 31 23 23 – Fill

| 31 23 23.20 Hauling | | Crew | Daily Output | Labor-Hours | Unit | Material | 2008 Bare Costs Labor | 2008 Bare Costs Equipment | Total | Total Incl O&P |
|---|---|---|---|---|---|---|---|---|---|---|
| 0326 | 20 MPH ave, cycle 0.5 mile, 25 min. wait/Ld./Uld. | B-34A | 144 | .056 | L.C.Y. | | 1.70 | 2.14 | 3.84 | 4.99 |
| 0328 | cycle 1 mile | | 136 | .059 | | | 1.80 | 2.27 | 4.07 | 5.30 |
| 0330 | cycle 2 miles | | 120 | .067 | | | 2.04 | 2.57 | 4.61 | 6 |
| 0332 | cycle 4 miles | | 104 | .077 | | | 2.35 | 2.97 | 5.32 | 6.90 |
| 0334 | cycle 6 miles | | 88 | .091 | | | 2.78 | 3.51 | 6.29 | 8.15 |
| 0336 | cycle 8 miles | | 80 | .100 | | | 3.06 | 3.86 | 6.92 | 9 |
| 0344 | 25 MPH ave, cycle 4 miles, 25 min. wait/Ld./Uld. | | 112 | .071 | | | 2.19 | 2.76 | 4.95 | 6.40 |
| 0346 | cycle 6 miles | | 96 | .083 | | | 2.55 | 3.21 | 5.76 | 7.50 |
| 0348 | cycle 8 miles | | 88 | .091 | | | 2.78 | 3.51 | 6.29 | 8.15 |
| 0350 | 30 MPH ave, cycle 4 miles, 25 min. wait/Ld./Uld. | | 112 | .071 | | | 2.19 | 2.76 | 4.95 | 6.40 |
| 0352 | cycle 6 miles | | 104 | .077 | | | 2.35 | 2.97 | 5.32 | 6.90 |
| 0354 | cycle 8 miles | | 96 | .083 | | | 2.55 | 3.21 | 5.76 | 7.50 |
| 0414 | 15 MPH ave, cycle 0.5 mile, 30 min wait/Ld./Uld., | | 120 | .067 | | | 2.04 | 2.57 | 4.61 | 6 |
| 0416 | cycle 1 mile | | 112 | .071 | | | 2.19 | 2.76 | 4.95 | 6.40 |
| 0418 | cycle 2 miles | | 96 | .083 | | | 2.55 | 3.21 | 5.76 | 7.50 |
| 0420 | cycle 4 miles | | 80 | .100 | | | 3.06 | 3.86 | 6.92 | 9 |
| 0422 | cycle 6 miles | | 72 | .111 | | | 3.40 | 4.29 | 7.69 | 9.95 |
| 0424 | cycle 8 miles | | 64 | .125 | | | 3.83 | 4.82 | 8.65 | 11.20 |
| 0426 | 20 MPH ave, cycle 0.5 mile, 30 min. wait/Ld./Uld. | | 120 | .067 | | | 2.04 | 2.57 | 4.61 | 6 |
| 0428 | cycle 1 mile | | 112 | .071 | | | 2.19 | 2.76 | 4.95 | 6.40 |
| 0430 | cycle 2 miles | | 104 | .077 | | | 2.35 | 2.97 | 5.32 | 6.90 |
| 0432 | cycle 4 miles | | 88 | .091 | | | 2.78 | 3.51 | 6.29 | 8.15 |
| 0434 | cycle 6 miles | | 80 | .100 | | | 3.06 | 3.86 | 6.92 | 9 |
| 0436 | cycle 8 miles | | 72 | .111 | | | 3.40 | 4.29 | 7.69 | 9.95 |
| 0444 | 25 MPH ave, cycle 4 miles, 30 min. wait/Ld./Uld. | | 96 | .083 | | | 2.55 | 3.21 | 5.76 | 7.50 |
| 0446 | cycle 6 miles | | 88 | .091 | | | 2.78 | 3.51 | 6.29 | 8.15 |
| 0448 | cycle 8 miles | | 80 | .100 | | | 3.06 | 3.86 | 6.92 | 9 |
| 0450 | 30 MPH ave, cycle 4 miles, 30 min. wait/Ld./Uld. | | 96 | .083 | | | 2.55 | 3.21 | 5.76 | 7.50 |
| 0452 | cycle 6 miles | | 88 | .091 | | | 2.78 | 3.51 | 6.29 | 8.15 |
| 0454 | cycle 8 miles | | 80 | .100 | | | 3.06 | 3.86 | 6.92 | 9 |
| 0514 | 15 MPH ave, cycle 0.5 mile, 35 min wait/Ld./Uld., | | 104 | .077 | | | 2.35 | 2.97 | 5.32 | 6.90 |
| 0516 | cycle 1 mile | | 96 | .083 | | | 2.55 | 3.21 | 5.76 | 7.50 |
| 0518 | cycle 2 miles | | 88 | .091 | | | 2.78 | 3.51 | 6.29 | 8.15 |
| 0520 | cycle 4 miles | | 72 | .111 | | | 3.40 | 4.29 | 7.69 | 9.95 |
| 0522 | cycle 6 miles | | 64 | .125 | | | 3.83 | 4.82 | 8.65 | 11.20 |
| 0524 | cycle 8 miles | | 56 | .143 | | | 4.37 | 5.50 | 9.87 | 12.80 |
| 0526 | 20 MPH ave, cycle 0.5 mile, 35 min. wait/Ld./Uld. | | 104 | .077 | | | 2.35 | 2.97 | 5.32 | 6.90 |
| 0528 | cycle 1 mile | | 96 | .083 | | | 2.55 | 3.21 | 5.76 | 7.50 |
| 0530 | cycle 2 miles | | 96 | .083 | | | 2.55 | 3.21 | 5.76 | 7.50 |
| 0532 | cycle 4 miles | | 80 | .100 | | | 3.06 | 3.86 | 6.92 | 9 |
| 0534 | cycle 6 miles | | 72 | .111 | | | 3.40 | 4.29 | 7.69 | 9.95 |
| 0536 | cycle 8 miles | | 64 | .125 | | | 3.83 | 4.82 | 8.65 | 11.20 |
| 0544 | 25 MPH ave, cycle 4 miles, 35 min. wait/Ld./Uld. | | 88 | .091 | | | 2.78 | 3.51 | 6.29 | 8.15 |
| 0546 | cycle 6 miles | | 80 | .100 | | | 3.06 | 3.86 | 6.92 | 9 |
| 0548 | cycle 8 miles | | 72 | .111 | | | 3.40 | 4.29 | 7.69 | 9.95 |
| 0550 | 30 MPH ave, cycle 4 miles, 35 min. wait/Ld./Uld. | | 88 | .091 | | | 2.78 | 3.51 | 6.29 | 8.15 |
| 0552 | cycle 6 miles | | 80 | .100 | | | 3.06 | 3.86 | 6.92 | 9 |
| 0554 | cycle 8 miles | | 72 | .111 | | | 3.40 | 4.29 | 7.69 | 9.95 |
| 1014 | 12 CY truck, cycle 0.5 mile, 15 MPH ave, 15 min. wait/Ld./Uld. | B-34B | 336 | .024 | | | .73 | 1.50 | 2.23 | 2.78 |
| 1016 | cycle 1 mile | | 300 | .027 | | | .82 | 1.68 | 2.50 | 3.10 |
| 1018 | cycle 2 miles | | 252 | .032 | | | .97 | 2 | 2.97 | 3.70 |
| 1020 | cycle 4 miles | | 180 | .044 | | | 1.36 | 2.79 | 4.15 | 5.15 |
| 1022 | cycle 6 miles | | 144 | .056 | | | 1.70 | 3.49 | 5.19 | 6.45 |

| 31 23 23.20 Hauling | Crew | Daily Output | Labor-Hours | Unit | Material | 2008 Bare Costs Labor | 2008 Bare Costs Equipment | Total | Total Incl O&P |
|---|---|---|---|---|---|---|---|---|---|
| 1024 | cycle 8 miles | B-34B | 120 | .067 | L.C.Y. | | 2.04 | 4.19 | 6.23 | 7.75 |
| 1026 | 20 MPH ave, cycle 0.5 mile, 15 min. wait/Ld./Uld. | | 348 | .023 | | | .70 | 1.44 | 2.14 | 2.68 |
| 1028 | cycle 1 mile | | 312 | .026 | | | .78 | 1.61 | 2.39 | 2.98 |
| 1030 | cycle 2 miles | | 276 | .029 | | | .89 | 1.82 | 2.71 | 3.37 |
| 1032 | cycle 4 miles | | 216 | .037 | | | 1.13 | 2.33 | 3.46 | 4.31 |
| 1034 | cycle 6 miles | | 168 | .048 | | | 1.46 | 2.99 | 4.45 | 5.55 |
| 1036 | cycle 8 miles | | 144 | .056 | | | 1.70 | 3.49 | 5.19 | 6.45 |
| 1040 | 25 MPH ave, cycle 4 miles, 15 min. wait/Ld./Uld. | | 228 | .035 | | | 1.07 | 2.21 | 3.28 | 4.09 |
| 1042 | cycle 6 miles | | 192 | .042 | | | 1.28 | 2.62 | 3.90 | 4.85 |
| 1044 | cycle 8 miles | | 168 | .048 | | | 1.46 | 2.99 | 4.45 | 5.55 |
| 1050 | 30 MPH ave, cycle 4 miles, 15 min. wait/Ld./Uld. | | 252 | .032 | | | .97 | 2 | 2.97 | 3.70 |
| 1052 | cycle 6 miles | | 216 | .037 | | | 1.13 | 2.33 | 3.46 | 4.31 |
| 1054 | cycle 8 miles | | 180 | .044 | | | 1.36 | 2.79 | 4.15 | 5.15 |
| 1060 | 35 MPH ave, cycle 4 miles, 15 min. wait/Ld./Uld. | | 264 | .030 | | | .93 | 1.90 | 2.83 | 3.52 |
| 1062 | cycle 6 miles | | 228 | .035 | | | 1.07 | 2.21 | 3.28 | 4.09 |
| 1064 | cycle 8 miles | | 204 | .039 | | | 1.20 | 2.47 | 3.67 | 4.57 |
| 1066 | cycle 10 miles | | 180 | .044 | | | 1.36 | 2.79 | 4.15 | 5.15 |
| 1068 | cycle 20 miles | | 120 | .067 | | | 2.04 | 4.19 | 6.23 | 7.75 |
| 1070 | cycle 40 miles | | 72 | .111 | | | 3.40 | 7 | 10.40 | 12.95 |
| 1072 | 40 MPH ave, cycle 6 miles, 15 min. wait/Ld./Uld. | | 240 | .033 | | | 1.02 | 2.09 | 3.11 | 3.88 |
| 1074 | cycle 8 miles | | 216 | .037 | | | 1.13 | 2.33 | 3.46 | 4.31 |
| 1076 | cycle 10 miles | | 192 | .042 | | | 1.28 | 2.62 | 3.90 | 4.85 |
| 1078 | cycle 20 miles | | 120 | .067 | | | 2.04 | 4.19 | 6.23 | 7.75 |
| 1080 | cycle 30 miles | | 96 | .083 | | | 2.55 | 5.25 | 7.80 | 9.70 |
| 1082 | cycle 40 miles | | 72 | .111 | | | 3.40 | 7 | 10.40 | 12.95 |
| 1084 | cycle 50 miles | | 60 | .133 | | | 4.08 | 8.40 | 12.48 | 15.50 |
| 1094 | 45 MPH ave, cycle 8 miles, 15 min. wait/Ld./Uld. | | 216 | .037 | | | 1.13 | 2.33 | 3.46 | 4.31 |
| 1096 | cycle 10 miles | | 204 | .039 | | | 1.20 | 2.47 | 3.67 | 4.57 |
| 1098 | cycle 20 miles | | 132 | .061 | | | 1.85 | 3.81 | 5.66 | 7.05 |
| 1100 | cycle 30 miles | | 108 | .074 | | | 2.27 | 4.66 | 6.93 | 8.60 |
| 1102 | cycle 40 miles | | 84 | .095 | | | 2.91 | 6 | 8.91 | 11.10 |
| 1104 | cycle 50 miles | | 72 | .111 | | | 3.40 | 7 | 10.40 | 12.95 |
| 1106 | 50 MPH ave, cycle 10 miles, 15 min. wait/Ld./Uld. | | 216 | .037 | | | 1.13 | 2.33 | 3.46 | 4.31 |
| 1108 | cycle 20 miles | | 144 | .056 | | | 1.70 | 3.49 | 5.19 | 6.45 |
| 1110 | cycle 30 miles | | 108 | .074 | | | 2.27 | 4.66 | 6.93 | 8.60 |
| 1112 | cycle 40 miles | | 84 | .095 | | | 2.91 | 6 | 8.91 | 11.10 |
| 1114 | cycle 50 miles | | 72 | .111 | | | 3.40 | 7 | 10.40 | 12.95 |
| 1214 | 15 MPH ave, cycle 0.5 mile, 20 min. wait/Ld./Uld., | | 264 | .030 | | | .93 | 1.90 | 2.83 | 3.52 |
| 1216 | cycle 1 mile | | 240 | .033 | | | 1.02 | 2.09 | 3.11 | 3.88 |
| 1218 | cycle 2 miles | | 204 | .039 | | | 1.20 | 2.47 | 3.67 | 4.57 |
| 1220 | cycle 4 miles | | 156 | .051 | | | 1.57 | 3.22 | 4.79 | 6 |
| 1222 | cycle 6 miles | | 132 | .061 | | | 1.85 | 3.81 | 5.66 | 7.05 |
| 1224 | cycle 8 miles | | 108 | .074 | | | 2.27 | 4.66 | 6.93 | 8.60 |
| 1226 | 20 MPH ave, cycle 0.5 mile, 20 min. wait/Ld./Uld. | | 264 | .030 | | | .93 | 1.90 | 2.83 | 3.52 |
| 1228 | cycle 1 mile | | 252 | .032 | | | .97 | 2 | 2.97 | 3.70 |
| 1230 | cycle 2 miles | | 216 | .037 | | | 1.13 | 2.33 | 3.46 | 4.31 |
| 1232 | cycle 4 miles | | 180 | .044 | | | 1.36 | 2.79 | 4.15 | 5.15 |
| 1234 | cycle 6 miles | | 144 | .056 | | | 1.70 | 3.49 | 5.19 | 6.45 |
| 1236 | cycle 8 miles | | 132 | .061 | | | 1.85 | 3.81 | 5.66 | 7.05 |
| 1240 | 25 MPH ave, cycle 4 miles, 20 min. wait/Ld./Uld. | | 192 | .042 | | | 1.28 | 2.62 | 3.90 | 4.85 |
| 1242 | cycle 6 miles | | 168 | .048 | | | 1.46 | 2.99 | 4.45 | 5.55 |
| 1244 | cycle 8 miles | | 144 | .056 | | | 1.70 | 3.49 | 5.19 | 6.45 |
| 1250 | 30 MPH ave, cycle 4 miles, 20 min. wait/Ld./Uld. | | 204 | .039 | | | 1.20 | 2.47 | 3.67 | 4.57 |

# 31 23 Excavation and Fill

## 31 23 23 – Fill

| 31 23 23.20 Hauling | | Crew | Daily Output | Labor-Hours | Unit | Material | 2008 Bare Costs Labor | 2008 Bare Costs Equipment | Total | Total Incl O&P |
|---|---|---|---|---|---|---|---|---|---|---|
| 1252 | cycle 6 miles | B-34B | 188 | .043 | L.C.Y. | | 1.30 | 2.67 | 3.97 | 4.95 |
| 1254 | cycle 8 miles | | 156 | .051 | | | 1.57 | 3.22 | 4.79 | 6 |
| 1260 | 35 MPH ave, cycle 4 miles, 20 min. wait/Ld./Uld. | | 216 | .037 | | | 1.13 | 2.33 | 3.46 | 4.31 |
| 1262 | cycle 6 miles | | 192 | .042 | | | 1.28 | 2.62 | 3.90 | 4.85 |
| 1264 | cycle 8 miles | | 168 | .048 | | | 1.46 | 2.99 | 4.45 | 5.55 |
| 1266 | cycle 10 miles | | 156 | .051 | | | 1.57 | 3.22 | 4.79 | 6 |
| 1268 | cycle 20 miles | | 108 | .074 | | | 2.27 | 4.66 | 6.93 | 8.60 |
| 1270 | cycle 40 miles | | 60 | .133 | | | 4.08 | 8.40 | 12.48 | 15.50 |
| 1272 | 40 MPH ave, cycle 6 miles, 20 min. wait/Ld./Uld. | | 192 | .042 | | | 1.28 | 2.62 | 3.90 | 4.85 |
| 1274 | cycle 8 miles | | 180 | .044 | | | 1.36 | 2.79 | 4.15 | 5.15 |
| 1276 | cycle 10 miles | | 168 | .048 | | | 1.46 | 2.99 | 4.45 | 5.55 |
| 1278 | cycle 20 miles | | 108 | .074 | | | 2.27 | 4.66 | 6.93 | 8.60 |
| 1280 | cycle 30 miles | | 84 | .095 | | | 2.91 | 6 | 8.91 | 11.10 |
| 1282 | cycle 40 miles | | 72 | .111 | | | 3.40 | 7 | 10.40 | 12.95 |
| 1284 | cycle 50 miles | | 60 | .133 | | | 4.08 | 8.40 | 12.48 | 15.50 |
| 1294 | 45 MPH ave, cycle 8 miles, 20 min. wait/Ld./Uld. | | 180 | .044 | | | 1.36 | 2.79 | 4.15 | 5.15 |
| 1296 | cycle 10 miles | | 168 | .048 | | | 1.46 | 2.99 | 4.45 | 5.55 |
| 1298 | cycle 20 miles | | 120 | .067 | | | 2.04 | 4.19 | 6.23 | 7.75 |
| 1300 | cycle 30 miles | | 96 | .083 | | | 2.55 | 5.25 | 7.80 | 9.70 |
| 1302 | cycle 40 miles | | 72 | .111 | | | 3.40 | 7 | 10.40 | 12.95 |
| 1304 | cycle 50 miles | | 60 | .133 | | | 4.08 | 8.40 | 12.48 | 15.50 |
| 1306 | 50 MPH ave, cycle 10 miles, 20 min. wait/Ld./Uld. | | 180 | .044 | | | 1.36 | 2.79 | 4.15 | 5.15 |
| 1308 | cycle 20 miles | | 132 | .061 | | | 1.85 | 3.81 | 5.66 | 7.05 |
| 1310 | cycle 30 miles | | 108 | .074 | | | 2.27 | 4.66 | 6.93 | 8.60 |
| 1312 | cycle 40 miles | | 84 | .095 | | | 2.91 | 6 | 8.91 | 11.10 |
| 1314 | cycle 50 miles | | 72 | .111 | | | 3.40 | 7 | 10.40 | 12.95 |
| 1414 | 15 MPH ave, cycle 0.5 mile, 25 min. wait/Ld./Uld., | | 216 | .037 | | | 1.13 | 2.33 | 3.46 | 4.31 |
| 1416 | cycle 1 mile | | 192 | .042 | | | 1.28 | 2.62 | 3.90 | 4.85 |
| 1418 | cycle 2 miles | | 168 | .048 | | | 1.46 | 2.99 | 4.45 | 5.55 |
| 1420 | cycle 4 miles | | 144 | .056 | | | 1.70 | 3.49 | 5.19 | 6.45 |
| 1422 | cycle 6 miles | | 120 | .067 | | | 2.04 | 4.19 | 6.23 | 7.75 |
| 1424 | cycle 8 miles | | 96 | .083 | | | 2.55 | 5.25 | 7.80 | 9.70 |
| 1426 | 20 MPH ave, cycle 0.5 mile, 25 min. wait/Ld./Uld. | | 216 | .037 | | | 1.13 | 2.33 | 3.46 | 4.31 |
| 1428 | cycle 1 mile | | 204 | .039 | | | 1.20 | 2.47 | 3.67 | 4.57 |
| 1430 | cycle 2 miles | | 180 | .044 | | | 1.36 | 2.79 | 4.15 | 5.15 |
| 1432 | cycle 4 miles | | 156 | .051 | | | 1.57 | 3.22 | 4.79 | 6 |
| 1434 | cycle 6 miles | | 132 | .061 | | | 1.85 | 3.81 | 5.66 | 7.05 |
| 1436 | cycle 8 miles | | 120 | .067 | | | 2.04 | 4.19 | 6.23 | 7.75 |
| 1440 | 25 MPH ave, cycle 4 miles, 25 min. wait/Ld./Uld. | | 168 | .048 | | | 1.46 | 2.99 | 4.45 | 5.55 |
| 1442 | cycle 6 miles | | 144 | .056 | | | 1.70 | 3.49 | 5.19 | 6.45 |
| 1444 | cycle 8 miles | | 132 | .061 | | | 1.85 | 3.81 | 5.66 | 7.05 |
| 1450 | 30 MPH ave, cycle 4 miles, 25 min. wait/Ld./Uld. | | 168 | .048 | | | 1.46 | 2.99 | 4.45 | 5.55 |
| 1452 | cycle 6 miles | | 156 | .051 | | | 1.57 | 3.22 | 4.79 | 6 |
| 1454 | cycle 8 miles | | 144 | .056 | | | 1.70 | 3.49 | 5.19 | 6.45 |
| 1460 | 35 MPH ave, cycle 4 miles, 25 min. wait/Ld./Uld. | | 180 | .044 | | | 1.36 | 2.79 | 4.15 | 5.15 |
| 1462 | cycle 6 miles | | 156 | .051 | | | 1.57 | 3.22 | 4.79 | 6 |
| 1464 | cycle 8 miles | | 144 | .056 | | | 1.70 | 3.49 | 5.19 | 6.45 |
| 1466 | cycle 10 miles | | 132 | .061 | | | 1.85 | 3.81 | 5.66 | 7.05 |
| 1468 | cycle 20 miles | | 96 | .083 | | | 2.55 | 5.25 | 7.80 | 9.70 |
| 1470 | cycle 40 miles | | 60 | .133 | | | 4.08 | 8.40 | 12.48 | 15.50 |
| 1472 | 40 MPH ave, cycle 6 miles, 25 min. wait/Ld./Uld. | | 168 | .048 | | | 1.46 | 2.99 | 4.45 | 5.55 |
| 1474 | cycle 8 miles | | 156 | .051 | | | 1.57 | 3.22 | 4.79 | 6 |
| 1476 | cycle 10 miles | | 144 | .056 | | | 1.70 | 3.49 | 5.19 | 6.45 |

| 31 23 23.20 Hauling | Crew | Daily Output | Labor-Hours | Unit | Material | 2008 Bare Costs Labor | Equipment | Total | Total Incl O&P |
|---|---|---|---|---|---|---|---|---|---|
| 1478 | cycle 20 miles | B-34B | 108 | .074 | L.C.Y. | | 2.27 | 4.66 | 6.93 | 8.60 |
| 1480 | cycle 30 miles | | 84 | .095 | | | 2.91 | 6 | 8.91 | 11.10 |
| 1482 | cycle 40 miles | | 60 | .133 | | | 4.08 | 8.40 | 12.48 | 15.50 |
| 1484 | cycle 50 miles | | 60 | .133 | | | 4.08 | 8.40 | 12.48 | 15.50 |
| 1494 | 45 MPH ave, cycle 8 miles, 25 min. wait/Ld./Uld. | | 156 | .051 | | | 1.57 | 3.22 | 4.79 | 6 |
| 1496 | cycle 10 miles | | 144 | .056 | | | 1.70 | 3.49 | 5.19 | 6.45 |
| 1498 | cycle 20 miles | | 106 | .075 | | | 2.31 | 4.74 | 7.05 | 8.75 |
| 1500 | cycle 30 miles | | 84 | .095 | | | 2.91 | 6 | 8.91 | 11.10 |
| 1502 | cycle 40 miles | | 72 | .111 | | | 3.40 | 7 | 10.40 | 12.95 |
| 1504 | cycle 50 miles | | 60 | .133 | | | 4.08 | 8.40 | 12.48 | 15.50 |
| 1506 | 50 MPH ave, cycle 10 miles, 25 min. wait/Ld./Uld. | | 156 | .051 | | | 1.57 | 3.22 | 4.79 | 6 |
| 1508 | cycle 20 miles | | 120 | .067 | | | 2.04 | 4.19 | 6.23 | 7.75 |
| 1510 | cycle 30 miles | | 96 | .083 | | | 2.55 | 5.25 | 7.80 | 9.70 |
| 1512 | cycle 40 miles | | 72 | .111 | | | 3.40 | 7 | 10.40 | 12.95 |
| 1514 | cycle 50 miles | | 60 | .133 | | | 4.08 | 8.40 | 12.48 | 15.50 |
| 1614 | 15 MPH, cycle 0.5 mile, 30 min. wait/Ld./Uld., | | 180 | .044 | | | 1.36 | 2.79 | 4.15 | 5.15 |
| 1616 | cycle 1 mile | | 168 | .048 | | | 1.46 | 2.99 | 4.45 | 5.55 |
| 1618 | cycle 2 miles | | 168 | .048 | | | 1.46 | 2.99 | 4.45 | 5.55 |
| 1620 | cycle 4 miles | | 120 | .067 | | | 2.04 | 4.19 | 6.23 | 7.75 |
| 1622 | cycle 6 miles | | 108 | .074 | | | 2.27 | 4.66 | 6.93 | 8.60 |
| 1624 | cycle 8 miles | | 96 | .083 | | | 2.55 | 5.25 | 7.80 | 9.70 |
| 1626 | 20 MPH ave, cycle 0.5 mile, 30 min. wait/Ld./Uld. | | 180 | .044 | | | 1.36 | 2.79 | 4.15 | 5.15 |
| 1628 | cycle 1 mile | | 168 | .048 | | | 1.46 | 2.99 | 4.45 | 5.55 |
| 1630 | cycle 2 miles | | 156 | .051 | | | 1.57 | 3.22 | 4.79 | 6 |
| 1632 | cycle 4 miles | | 132 | .061 | | | 1.85 | 3.81 | 5.66 | 7.05 |
| 1634 | cycle 6 miles | | 120 | .067 | | | 2.04 | 4.19 | 6.23 | 7.75 |
| 1636 | cycle 8 miles | | 108 | .074 | | | 2.27 | 4.66 | 6.93 | 8.60 |
| 1640 | 25 MPH ave, cycle 4 miles, 30 min. wait/Ld./Uld. | | 144 | .056 | | | 1.70 | 3.49 | 5.19 | 6.45 |
| 1642 | cycle 6 miles | | 132 | .061 | | | 1.85 | 3.81 | 5.66 | 7.05 |
| 1644 | cycle 8 miles | | 120 | .067 | | | 2.04 | 4.19 | 6.23 | 7.75 |
| 1650 | 30 MPH ave, cycle 4 miles, 30 min. wait/Ld./Uld. | | 144 | .056 | | | 1.70 | 3.49 | 5.19 | 6.45 |
| 1652 | cycle 6 miles | | 132 | .061 | | | 1.85 | 3.81 | 5.66 | 7.05 |
| 1654 | cycle 8 miles | | 120 | .067 | | | 2.04 | 4.19 | 6.23 | 7.75 |
| 1660 | 35 MPH ave, cycle 4 miles, 30 min. wait/Ld./Uld. | | 156 | .051 | | | 1.57 | 3.22 | 4.79 | 6 |
| 1662 | cycle 6 miles | | 144 | .056 | | | 1.70 | 3.49 | 5.19 | 6.45 |
| 1664 | cycle 8 miles | | 132 | .061 | | | 1.85 | 3.81 | 5.66 | 7.05 |
| 1666 | cycle 10 miles | | 120 | .067 | | | 2.04 | 4.19 | 6.23 | 7.75 |
| 1668 | cycle 20 miles | | 84 | .095 | | | 2.91 | 6 | 8.91 | 11.10 |
| 1670 | cycle 40 miles | | 60 | .133 | | | 4.08 | 8.40 | 12.48 | 15.50 |
| 1672 | 40 MPH, cycle 6 miles, 30 min. wait/Ld./Uld. | | 144 | .056 | | | 1.70 | 3.49 | 5.19 | 6.45 |
| 1674 | cycle 8 miles | | 132 | .061 | | | 1.85 | 3.81 | 5.66 | 7.05 |
| 1676 | cycle 10 miles | | 120 | .067 | | | 2.04 | 4.19 | 6.23 | 7.75 |
| 1678 | cycle 20 miles | | 96 | .083 | | | 2.55 | 5.25 | 7.80 | 9.70 |
| 1680 | cycle 30 miles | | 72 | .111 | | | 3.40 | 7 | 10.40 | 12.95 |
| 1682 | cycle 40 miles | | 60 | .133 | | | 4.08 | 8.40 | 12.48 | 15.50 |
| 1684 | cycle 50 miles | | 60 | .133 | | | 4.08 | 8.40 | 12.48 | 15.50 |
| 1694 | 45 MPH ave, cycle 8 miles, 30 min. wait/Ld./Uld. | | 144 | .056 | | | 1.70 | 3.49 | 5.19 | 6.45 |
| 1696 | cycle 10 miles | | 132 | .061 | | | 1.85 | 3.81 | 5.66 | 7.05 |
| 1698 | cycle 20 miles | | 96 | .083 | | | 2.55 | 5.25 | 7.80 | 9.70 |
| 1700 | cycle 30 miles | | 84 | .095 | | | 2.91 | 6 | 8.91 | 11.10 |
| 1702 | cycle 40 miles | | 72 | .111 | | | 3.40 | 7 | 10.40 | 12.95 |
| 1704 | cycle 50 miles | | 60 | .133 | | | 4.08 | 8.40 | 12.48 | 15.50 |
| 1706 | 50 MPH ave, cycle 10 miles, 30 min. wait/Ld./Uld. | | 132 | .061 | | | 1.85 | 3.81 | 5.66 | 7.05 |

# 31 23 Excavation and Fill

## 31 23 23 – Fill

### 31 23 23.20 Hauling

| | | Crew | Daily Output | Labor-Hours | Unit | Material | 2008 Bare Costs Labor | Equipment | Total | Total Incl O&P |
|---|---|---|---|---|---|---|---|---|---|---|
| 1708 | cycle 20 miles | B-34B | 108 | .074 | L.C.Y. | | 2.27 | 4.66 | 6.93 | 8.60 |
| 1710 | cycle 30 miles | | 84 | .095 | | | 2.91 | 6 | 8.91 | 11.10 |
| 1712 | cycle 40 miles | | 72 | .111 | | | 3.40 | 7 | 10.40 | 12.95 |
| 1714 | cycle 50 miles | | 60 | .133 | | | 4.08 | 8.40 | 12.48 | 15.50 |
| 2000 | Hauling, 8 CY truck, small project cost per hour | B-34A | 8 | 1 | Hr. | | 30.50 | 38.50 | 69 | 90 |
| 2100 | 12 CY Truck | B-34B | 8 | 1 | " | | 30.50 | 63 | 93.50 | 117 |

### 31 23 23.24 Compaction, Structural

| | | Crew | Daily Output | Labor-Hours | Unit | Material | 2008 Bare Costs Labor | Equipment | Total | Total Incl O&P |
|---|---|---|---|---|---|---|---|---|---|---|
| 0010 | **COMPACTION, STRUCTURAL** R312323-30 | | | | | | | | | |
| 0020 | Steel wheel tandem roller, 5 tons | B-10E | 8 | 1.500 | Hr. | | 55 | 16.30 | 71.30 | 101 |
| 0100 | 10 tons | B-10F | 8 | 1.500 | " | | 55 | 27.50 | 82.50 | 114 |
| 0300 | Sheepsfoot or wobbly wheel roller, 8" lifts, common fill | B-10G | 1300 | .009 | E.C.Y. | | .34 | .77 | 1.11 | 1.36 |
| 0400 | Select fill | " | 1500 | .008 | | | .29 | .67 | .96 | 1.19 |
| 0600 | Vibratory plate, 8" lifts, common fill | A-1D | 200 | .040 | | | 1.21 | .16 | 1.37 | 2.05 |
| 0700 | Select fill | " | 216 | .037 | | | 1.12 | .14 | 1.26 | 1.90 |

# 31 25 Erosion and Sedimentation Controls

## 31 25 13 – Erosion Controls

### 31 25 13.10 Synthetic Erosion Control

| | | Crew | Daily Output | Labor-Hours | Unit | Material | 2008 Bare Costs Labor | Equipment | Total | Total Incl O&P |
|---|---|---|---|---|---|---|---|---|---|---|
| 0010 | **SYNTHETIC EROSION CONTROL** | | | | | | | | | |
| 0020 | Jute mesh, 100 SY per roll, 4' wide, stapled | B-80A | 2400 | .010 | S.Y. | .94 | .30 | .09 | 1.33 | 1.60 |
| 0100 | Plastic netting, stapled, 2" x 1" mesh, 20 mil | B-1 | 2500 | .010 | | .71 | .30 | | 1.01 | 1.24 |
| 0200 | Polypropylene mesh, stapled, 6.5 oz./S.Y. | | 2500 | .010 | | 1.47 | .30 | | 1.77 | 2.08 |
| 0300 | Tobacco netting, or jute mesh #2, stapled | | 2500 | .010 | | .08 | .30 | | .38 | .55 |
| 1000 | Silt fence, polypropylene, 3' high, ideal conditions | 2 Clab | 1600 | .010 | L.F. | .34 | .30 | | .64 | .84 |
| 1100 | Adverse conditions | " | 950 | .017 | " | .34 | .51 | | .85 | 1.16 |
| 1200 | Place and remove hay bales | A-2 | 3 | 8 | Ton | 151 | 240 | 60 | 451 | 600 |
| 1250 | Hay bales, staked | " | 2500 | .010 | L.F. | 6.05 | .29 | .07 | 6.41 | 7.20 |

# 31 31 Soil Treatment

## 31 31 16 – Termite Control

### 31 31 16.13 Chemical Termite Control

| | | Crew | Daily Output | Labor-Hours | Unit | Material | 2008 Bare Costs Labor | Equipment | Total | Total Incl O&P |
|---|---|---|---|---|---|---|---|---|---|---|
| 0010 | **CHEMICAL TERMITE CONTROL** | | | | | | | | | |
| 0020 | Slab and walls, residential | 1 Skwk | 1200 | .007 | SF Flr. | .29 | .26 | | .55 | .73 |
| 0100 | Commercial, minimum | | 2496 | .003 | | .31 | .13 | | .44 | .54 |
| 0200 | Maximum | | 1645 | .005 | | .47 | .19 | | .66 | .81 |
| 0400 | Insecticides for termite control, minimum | | 14.20 | .563 | Gal. | 11.85 | 22 | | 33.85 | 47.50 |
| 0500 | Maximum | | 11 | .727 | " | 20.50 | 28.50 | | 49 | 67 |

# 31 32 Soil Stabilization

## 31 32 13 – Soil Mixing Stabilization

### 31 32 13.30 Calcium Chloride

| | | Crew | Daily Output | Labor-Hours | Unit | Material | 2008 Bare Costs Labor | 2008 Bare Costs Equipment | Total | Total Incl O&P |
|---|---|---|---|---|---|---|---|---|---|---|
| 0010 | **CALCIUM CHLORIDE** | | | | | | | | | |
| 0020 | Calcium chloride delivered, 100 LB bags, truckload lots | | | | Ton | 535 | | | 535 | 590 |
| 0030 | Solution, 4 lb. flake per gallon, tank truck delivery | | | | Gal. | 1.14 | | | 1.14 | 1.25 |

# 31 33 Rock Stabilization

## 31 33 13 – Rock Bolting and Grouting

### 31 33 13.10 Rock Bolting

| | | Crew | Daily Output | Labor-Hours | Unit | Material | 2008 Bare Costs Labor | 2008 Bare Costs Equipment | Total | Total Incl O&P |
|---|---|---|---|---|---|---|---|---|---|---|
| 0010 | **ROCK BOLTING** | | | | | | | | | |
| 2020 | Hollow core, prestressable anchor, 1" diameter, 5' long | 2 Skwk | 32 | .500 | Ea. | 89 | 19.70 | | 108.70 | 129 |
| 2025 | 10' long | | 24 | .667 | | 178 | 26.50 | | 204.50 | 237 |
| 2060 | 2" diameter, 5' long | | 32 | .500 | | 335 | 19.70 | | 354.70 | 395 |
| 2065 | 10' long | | 24 | .667 | | 665 | 26.50 | | 691.50 | 775 |
| 2100 | Super high-tensile, 3/4" diameter, 5' long | | 32 | .500 | | 20 | 19.70 | | 39.70 | 53 |
| 2105 | 10' long | | 24 | .667 | | 40.50 | 26.50 | | 67 | 85.50 |
| 2160 | 2" diameter, 5' long | | 32 | .500 | | 180 | 19.70 | | 199.70 | 229 |
| 2165 | 10' long | | 24 | .667 | | 360 | 26.50 | | 386.50 | 435 |
| 4400 | Drill hole for rock bolt, 1-3/4" diam., 5' long (for 3/4" bolt) | B-56 | 17 | .941 | | | 32 | 76 | 108 | 133 |
| 4405 | 10' long | | 9 | 1.778 | | | 60.50 | 144 | 204.50 | 251 |
| 4420 | 2" diameter, 5' long (for 1" bolt) | | 13 | 1.231 | | | 42 | 99.50 | 141.50 | 173 |
| 4425 | 10' long | | 7 | 2.286 | | | 77.50 | 185 | 262.50 | 320 |
| 4460 | 3-1/2" diameter, 5' long (for 2" bolt) | | 10 | 1.600 | | | 54.50 | 129 | 183.50 | 225 |
| 4465 | 10' long | | 5 | 3.200 | | | 109 | 259 | 368 | 450 |

# 31 36 Gabions

## 31 36 13 – Gabion Boxes

### 31 36 13.10 Gabion Box Systems

| | | Crew | Daily Output | Labor-Hours | Unit | Material | 2008 Bare Costs Labor | 2008 Bare Costs Equipment | Total | Total Incl O&P |
|---|---|---|---|---|---|---|---|---|---|---|
| 0010 | **GABION BOX SYSTEMS** | | | | | | | | | |
| 0400 | Gabions, galvanized steel mesh mats or boxes, stone filled, 6" deep | B-13 | 200 | .280 | S.Y. | 21 | 9.15 | 3.93 | 34.08 | 41.50 |
| 0500 | 9" deep | | 163 | .344 | | 32.50 | 11.25 | 4.82 | 48.57 | 58 |
| 0600 | 12" deep | | 153 | .366 | | 36 | 12 | 5.15 | 53.15 | 63.50 |
| 0700 | 18" deep | | 102 | .549 | | 51 | 18 | 7.70 | 76.70 | 92 |
| 0800 | 36" deep | | 60 | .933 | | 73 | 30.50 | 13.10 | 116.60 | 141 |

# 31 37 Riprap

## 31 37 13 – Machined Riprap

### 31 37 13.10 Rip-Rap and Rock Lining

| | | Crew | Daily Output | Labor-Hours | Unit | Material | 2008 Bare Costs Labor | 2008 Bare Costs Equipment | Total | Total Incl O&P |
|---|---|---|---|---|---|---|---|---|---|---|
| 0010 | **RIP-RAP AND ROCK LINING** | | | | | | | | | |
| 0011 | Random, broken stone | | | | | | | | | |
| 0100 | Machine placed for slope protection | B-12G | 62 | .258 | L.C.Y. | 26.50 | 9.20 | 10.35 | 46.05 | 55 |
| 0110 | 3/8 to 1/4 C.Y. pieces, grouted | B-13 | 80 | .700 | S.Y. | 65.50 | 23 | 9.85 | 98.35 | 118 |
| 0200 | 18" minimum thickness, not grouted | " | 53 | 1.057 | " | 16.65 | 34.50 | 14.85 | 66 | 88 |
| 0300 | Dumped, 50 lb. average | B-11A | 800 | .020 | Ton | 24 | .70 | 1.34 | 26.04 | 29 |
| 0350 | 100 lb. average | | 700 | .023 | | 34.50 | .80 | 1.53 | 36.83 | 41 |
| 0370 | 300 lb. average | | 600 | .027 | | 40 | .93 | 1.79 | 42.72 | 48 |

# 31 41 Shoring

## 31 41 13 – Timber Shoring

| 31 41 13.10 Building Shoring | | Crew | Daily Output | Labor-Hours | Unit | Material | 2008 Bare Costs Labor | Equipment | Total | Total Incl O&P |
|---|---|---|---|---|---|---|---|---|---|---|
| 0010 | **BUILDING SHORING** | | | | | | | | | |
| 0020 | Shoring, existing building, with timber, no salvage allowance | B-51 | 2.20 | 21.818 | M.B.F. | 620 | 665 | 81.50 | 1,366.50 | 1,800 |
| 1000 | On cribbing with 35 ton screw jacks, per box and jack | " | 3.60 | 13.333 | Jack | 53 | 405 | 49.50 | 507.50 | 745 |

## 31 41 16 – Sheet Piling

### 31 41 16.10 Sheet Piling Systems

| | 31 41 16.10 Sheet Piling Systems | | Crew | Daily Output | Labor-Hours | Unit | Material | 2008 Bare Costs Labor | Equipment | Total | Total Incl O&P |
|---|---|---|---|---|---|---|---|---|---|---|---|
| 0010 | **SHEET PILING SYSTEMS** | | | | | | | | | | |
| 0020 | Sheet piling steel, not incl. wales, 22 psf, 15' excav., left in place | | B-40 | 10.81 | 5.920 | Ton | 1,025 | 226 | 299 | 1,550 | 1,825 |
| 0100 | Drive, extract & salvage | R314116-40 | | 6 | 10.667 | | 455 | 405 | 540 | 1,400 | 1,750 |
| 0300 | 20' deep excavation, 27 psf, left in place | | | 12.95 | 4.942 | | 1,025 | 188 | 250 | 1,463 | 1,700 |
| 0400 | Drive, extract & salvage | R314116-45 | | 6.55 | 9.771 | | 455 | 370 | 495 | 1,320 | 1,650 |
| 0600 | 25' deep excavation, 38 psf, left in place | | | 19 | 3.368 | | 1,025 | 128 | 170 | 1,323 | 1,525 |
| 0700 | Drive, extract & salvage | | | 10.50 | 6.095 | | 455 | 232 | 310 | 997 | 1,225 |
| 0900 | 40' deep excavation, 38 psf, left in place | CN | | 21.20 | 3.019 | | 1,025 | 115 | 152 | 1,292 | 1,475 |
| 1000 | Drive, extract & salvage | | | 12.25 | 5.224 | | 455 | 199 | 264 | 918 | 1,100 |
| 1200 | 15' deep excavation, 22 psf, left in place | | | 983 | .065 | S.F. | 11.95 | 2.48 | 3.29 | 17.72 | 20.50 |
| 1300 | Drive, extract & salvage | | | 545 | .117 | | 5.15 | 4.47 | 5.95 | 15.57 | 19.25 |
| 1500 | 20' deep excavation, 27 psf, left in place | | | 960 | .067 | | 15.05 | 2.54 | 3.37 | 20.96 | 24.50 |
| 1600 | Drive, extract & salvage | | | 485 | .132 | | 6.65 | 5.05 | 6.65 | 18.35 | 22.50 |
| 1800 | 25' deep excavation, 38 psf, left in place | | | 1000 | .064 | | 22 | 2.44 | 3.23 | 27.67 | 32 |
| 1900 | Drive, extract & salvage | | | 553 | .116 | | 9.15 | 4.41 | 5.85 | 19.41 | 23.50 |
| 2100 | Rent steel sheet piling and wales, first month | | | | | Ton | 245 | | | 245 | 269 |
| 2200 | Per added month | | | | | | 24.50 | | | 24.50 | 27 |
| 2300 | Rental piling left in place, add to rental | | | | | | 815 | | | 815 | 900 |
| 2500 | Wales, connections & struts, 2/3 salvage | | | | | | 250 | | | 250 | 275 |
| 2700 | High strength piling, 50,000 psi, add | | | | | | 55.50 | | | 55.50 | 61 |
| 2800 | 55,000 psi, add | | | | | | 59 | | | 59 | 65 |
| 3000 | Tie rod, not upset, 1-1/2" to 4" diameter with turnbuckle | | | | | | 1,825 | | | 1,825 | 2,000 |
| 3100 | No turnbuckle | | | | | | 1,400 | | | 1,400 | 1,550 |
| 3300 | Upset, 1-3/4" to 4" diameter with turnbuckle | | | | | | 2,050 | | | 2,050 | 2,250 |
| 3400 | No turnbuckle | | | | | | 1,775 | | | 1,775 | 1,950 |
| 3600 | Lightweight, 18" to 28" wide, 7 ga., 9.22 psf, and | | | | | | | | | | |
| 3610 | 9 ga., 8.6 psf, minimum | | | | | Lb. | .75 | | | .75 | .83 |
| 3700 | Average | | | | | | .82 | | | .82 | .90 |
| 3750 | Maximum | | | | | | .94 | | | .94 | 1.03 |
| 3900 | Wood, solid sheeting, incl. wales, braces and spacers, | R314116-40 | | | | | | | | | |
| 3910 | drive, extract & salvage, 8' deep excavation | | B-31 | 330 | .121 | S.F. | 1.58 | 3.91 | .55 | 6.04 | 8.45 |
| 4000 | 10' deep, 50 S.F./hr. in & 150 S.F./hr. out | | | 300 | .133 | | 1.62 | 4.30 | .60 | 6.52 | 9.15 |
| 4100 | 12' deep, 45 S.F./hr. in & 135 S.F./hr. out | | | 270 | .148 | | 1.67 | 4.77 | .67 | 7.11 | 10 |
| 4200 | 14' deep, 42 S.F./hr. in & 126 S.F./hr. out | | | 250 | .160 | | 1.72 | 5.15 | .72 | 7.59 | 10.70 |
| 4300 | 16' deep, 40 S.F./hr. in & 120 S.F./hr. out | | | 240 | .167 | | 1.78 | 5.35 | .75 | 7.88 | 11.15 |
| 4400 | 18' deep, 38 S.F./hr. in & 114 S.F./hr. out | | | 230 | .174 | | 1.83 | 5.60 | .78 | 8.21 | 11.60 |
| 4500 | 20' deep, 35 S.F./hr. in & 105 S.F./hr. out | | | 210 | .190 | | 1.89 | 6.15 | .86 | 8.90 | 12.55 |
| 4520 | Left in place, 8' deep, 55 S.F./hr. | | | 440 | .091 | | 2.84 | 2.93 | .41 | 6.18 | 8.15 |
| 4540 | 10' deep, 50 S.F./hr. | | | 400 | .100 | | 2.99 | 3.22 | .45 | 6.66 | 8.80 |
| 4560 | 12' deep, 45 S.F./hr. | | | 360 | .111 | | 3.16 | 3.58 | .50 | 7.24 | 9.55 |
| 4565 | 14' deep, 42 S.F./hr. | | | 335 | .119 | | 3.34 | 3.85 | .54 | 7.73 | 10.25 |
| 4570 | 16' deep, 40 S.F./hr. | | | 320 | .125 | | 3.55 | 4.03 | .56 | 8.14 | 10.80 |
| 4580 | 18' deep, 38 S.F./hr. | | | 305 | .131 | | 3.79 | 4.23 | .59 | 8.61 | 11.35 |
| 4590 | 20' deep, 35 S.F./hr. | | | 280 | .143 | | 4.06 | 4.60 | .64 | 9.30 | 12.30 |
| 4700 | Alternate pricing, left in place, 8' deep | | | 1.76 | 22.727 | M.B.F. | 640 | 730 | 102 | 1,472 | 1,975 |
| 4800 | Drive, extract and salvage, 8' deep | | | 1.32 | 30.303 | " | 570 | 975 | 136 | 1,681 | 2,300 |
| 5000 | For treated lumber add cost of treatment to lumber | | | | | | | | | | |

555

# 31 41 Shoring

## 31 41 16 – Sheet Piling

| 31 41 16.10 Sheet Piling Systems | Crew | Daily Output | Labor-Hours | Unit | Material | 2008 Bare Costs Labor | Equipment | Total | Total Incl O&P |
|---|---|---|---|---|---|---|---|---|---|
| 5010      See Div. 06 05 73.10 | | | | | | | | | |

# 31 43 Concrete Raising

## 31 43 13 – Pressure Grouting

### 31 43 13.13 Concrete Pressure Grouting

| | | Crew | Daily Output | Labor-Hours | Unit | Material | 2008 Bare Costs Labor | Equipment | Total | Total Incl O&P |
|---|---|---|---|---|---|---|---|---|---|---|
| 0010 | CONCRETE PRESSURE GROUTING | | | | | | | | | |
| 0020 | Grouting, pressure, cement & sand, 1:1 mix, minimum | B-61 | 124 | .323 | Bag | 10.70 | 10.35 | 2.60 | 23.65 | 30.50 |
| 0100 |      Maximum | | 51 | .784 | " | 10.70 | 25 | 6.30 | 42 | 57.50 |
| 0200 | Cement and sand, 1:1 mix, minimum | | 250 | .160 | C.F. | 21.50 | 5.15 | 1.29 | 27.94 | 33 |
| 0300 |      Maximum | | 100 | .400 | | 32 | 12.85 | 3.22 | 48.07 | 59 |
| 0400 | Epoxy cement grout, minimum | | 137 | .292 | | 104 | 9.40 | 2.35 | 115.75 | 131 |
| 0500 |      Maximum | | 57 | .702 | | 104 | 22.50 | 5.65 | 132.15 | 155 |
| 0600 | Structural epoxy grout | | | | Gal. | 64 | | | 64 | 70 |
| 0700 | Alternate pricing method: (Add for materials) | | | | | | | | | |
| 0710 |      5 person crew and equipment | B-61 | 1 | 40 | Day | | 1,275 | 320 | 1,595 | 2,325 |

# 31 45 Vibroflotation and Densification

## 31 45 13 – Vibroflotation

### 31 45 13.10 Vibroflotation Densification

| | | Crew | Daily Output | Labor-Hours | Unit | Material | 2008 Bare Costs Labor | Equipment | Total | Total Incl O&P |
|---|---|---|---|---|---|---|---|---|---|---|
| 0010 | VIBROFLOTATION DENSIFICATION     R314513-90 | | | | | | | | | |
| 0900 | Vibroflotation compacted sand cylinder, minimum | B-60 | 750 | .075 | V.L.F. | | 2.61 | 2.31 | 4.92 | 6.50 |
| 0950 |      Maximum | | 325 | .172 | | | 6 | 5.35 | 11.35 | 15.05 |
| 1100 | Vibro replacement compacted stone cylinder, minimum | | 500 | .112 | | | 3.91 | 3.47 | 7.38 | 9.75 |
| 1150 |      Maximum | | 250 | .224 | | | 7.80 | 6.95 | 14.75 | 19.60 |
| 1300 | Mobilization and demobilization, minimum | | .47 | 119 | Total | 4,150 | 3,700 | | 7,850 | 10,400 |
| 1400 |      Maximum | | .14 | 400 | " | 14,000 | 12,400 | | 26,400 | 34,900 |

# 31 46 Needle Beams

## 31 46 13 – Cantilever Needle Beams

### 31 46 13.10 Needle Beams

| | | Crew | Daily Output | Labor-Hours | Unit | Material | 2008 Bare Costs Labor | Equipment | Total | Total Incl O&P |
|---|---|---|---|---|---|---|---|---|---|---|
| 0010 | NEEDLE BEAMS | | | | | | | | | |
| 0011 | Incl. wood shoring 10' x 10' opening | | | | | | | | | |
| 0400 | Block, concrete, 8" thick | B-9 | 7.10 | 5.634 | Ea. | 48 | 173 | 27 | 248 | 350 |
| 0420 |      12" thick | | 6.70 | 5.970 | | 54.50 | 183 | 28.50 | 266 | 375 |
| 0800 | Brick, 4" thick with 8" backup block | | 5.70 | 7.018 | | 54.50 | 215 | 33.50 | 303 | 430 |
| 1000 | Brick, solid, 8" thick | | 6.20 | 6.452 | | 48 | 198 | 31 | 277 | 395 |
| 1040 |      12" thick | | 4.90 | 8.163 | | 54.50 | 250 | 39 | 343.50 | 495 |
| 1080 |      16" thick | | 4.50 | 8.889 | | 67.50 | 272 | 42.50 | 382 | 545 |
| 2000 | Add for additional floors of shoring | B-1 | 6 | 4 | | 48 | 124 | | 172 | 245 |

# 31 48 Underpinning

## 31 48 13 – Underpinning Piers

### 31 48 13.10 Underpinning Foundations

| | | Crew | Daily Output | Labor-Hours | Unit | Material | 2008 Bare Costs Labor | Equipment | Total | Total Incl O&P |
|---|---|---|---|---|---|---|---|---|---|---|
| 0010 | **UNDERPINNING FOUNDATIONS** | | | | | | | | | |
| 0011 | Including excavation, | | | | | | | | | |
| 0020 | forming, reinforcing, concrete and equipment | | | | | | | | | |
| 0100 | 5' to 16' below grade, 100 to 500 C.Y. | B-52 | 2.30 | 24.348 | C.Y. | 273 | 860 | 194 | 1,327 | 1,850 |
| 0200 | Over 500 C.Y. | | 2.50 | 22.400 | | 245 | 790 | 179 | 1,214 | 1,700 |
| 0400 | 16' to 25' below grade, 100 to 500 C.Y. | | 2 | 28 | | 300 | 990 | 223 | 1,513 | 2,100 |
| 0500 | Over 500 C.Y. | | 2.10 | 26.667 | | 283 | 940 | 213 | 1,436 | 2,000 |
| 0700 | 26' to 40' below grade, 100 to 500 C.Y. | | 1.60 | 35 | | 325 | 1,225 | 279 | 1,829 | 2,575 |
| 0800 | Over 500 C.Y. | | 1.80 | 31.111 | | 300 | 1,100 | 248 | 1,648 | 2,300 |
| 0900 | For under 50 C.Y., add | | | | | 10% | 40% | | | |
| 1000 | For 50 C.Y. to 100 C.Y., add | | | | | 5% | 20% | | | |

# 31 52 Cofferdams

## 31 52 16 – Timber Cofferdams

### 31 52 16.10 Cofferdams

| | | Crew | Daily Output | Labor-Hours | Unit | Material | 2008 Bare Costs Labor | Equipment | Total | Total Incl O&P |
|---|---|---|---|---|---|---|---|---|---|---|
| 0010 | **COFFERDAMS** | | | | | | | | | |
| 0011 | Incl. mobilization and temporary sheeting | | | | | | | | | |
| 0080 | Soldier beams & lagging H piles with 3" wood sheeting | | | | | | | | | |
| 0090 | horizontal between piles, including removal of wales & braces | | | | | | | | | |
| 0100 | No hydrostatic head, 15' deep, 1 line of braces, minimum | B-50 | 545 | .206 | S.F. | 6.20 | 7.45 | 3.59 | 17.24 | 22.50 |
| 0200 | Maximum | | 495 | .226 | | 6.90 | 8.20 | 3.95 | 19.05 | 25 |
| 0400 | 15' to 22' deep with 2 lines of braces, 10" H, minimum | | 360 | .311 | | 7.30 | 11.30 | 5.45 | 24.05 | 32 |
| 0500 | Maximum | | 330 | .339 | | 8.30 | 12.35 | 5.95 | 26.60 | 35.50 |
| 0700 | 23' to 35' deep with 3 lines of braces, 12" H, minimum | | 325 | .345 | | 9.55 | 12.55 | 6 | 28.10 | 37 |
| 0800 | Maximum | | 295 | .380 | | 10.35 | 13.80 | 6.65 | 30.80 | 40.50 |
| 1000 | 36' to 45' deep with 4 lines of braces, 14" H, minimum | | 290 | .386 | | 10.70 | 14.05 | 6.75 | 31.50 | 41.50 |
| 1100 | Maximum | | 265 | .423 | | 11.30 | 15.35 | 7.40 | 34.05 | 45 |
| 1300 | No hydrostatic head, left in place, 15' dp., 1 line of braces, min. | | 635 | .176 | | 8.30 | 6.40 | 3.08 | 17.78 | 22.50 |
| 1400 | Maximum | | 575 | .195 | | 8.90 | 7.10 | 3.40 | 19.40 | 25 |
| 1600 | 15' to 22' deep with 2 lines of braces, minimum | | 455 | .246 | | 12.45 | 8.95 | 4.30 | 25.70 | 32.50 |
| 1700 | Maximum | | 415 | .270 | | 13.80 | 9.80 | 4.71 | 28.31 | 36 |
| 1900 | 23' to 35' deep with 3 lines of braces, minimum | | 420 | .267 | | 14.80 | 9.70 | 4.66 | 29.16 | 37 |
| 2000 | Maximum | | 380 | .295 | | 16.35 | 10.70 | 5.15 | 32.20 | 40.50 |
| 2200 | 36' to 45' deep with 4 lines of braces, minimum | | 385 | .291 | | 17.75 | 10.55 | 5.10 | 33.40 | 42 |
| 2300 | Maximum | | 350 | .320 | | 20.50 | 11.65 | 5.60 | 37.75 | 47.50 |
| 2350 | Lagging only, 3" thick wood between piles 8' O.C., minimum | B-46 | 400 | .120 | | 1.38 | 4.08 | .09 | 5.55 | 8.15 |
| 2370 | Maximum | | 250 | .192 | | 2.07 | 6.55 | .15 | 8.77 | 12.90 |
| 2400 | Open sheeting no bracing, for trenches to 10' deep, min. | | 1736 | .028 | | .62 | .94 | .02 | 1.58 | 2.21 |
| 2450 | Maximum | | 1510 | .032 | | .69 | 1.08 | .02 | 1.79 | 2.52 |
| 2500 | Tie-back method, add to open sheeting, add, minimum | | | | | | | | 20% | 20% |
| 2550 | Maximum | | | | | | | | 60% | 60% |
| 2700 | Tie-backs only, based on tie-backs total length, minimum | B-46 | 86.80 | .553 | L.F. | 14.15 | 18.80 | .43 | 33.38 | 46 |
| 2750 | Maximum | | 38.50 | 1.247 | " | 25 | 42.50 | .96 | 68.46 | 96.50 |
| 3500 | Tie-backs only, typical average, 25' long | | 2 | 24 | Ea. | 625 | 815 | 18.50 | 1,458.50 | 2,000 |
| 3600 | 35' long | | 1.58 | 30.380 | " | 830 | 1,025 | 23.50 | 1,878.50 | 2,600 |

557

# 31 56 Slurry Walls

## 31 56 23 – Lean Concrete Slurry Walls

| 31 56 23.20 Slurry Trench | Crew | Daily Output | Labor-Hours | Unit | Material | 2008 Bare Costs Labor | Equipment | Total | Total Incl O&P |
|---|---|---|---|---|---|---|---|---|---|
| 0010 **SLURRY TRENCH** | | | | | | | | | |
| 0011 Excavated slurry trench in wet soils | | | | | | | | | |
| 0020 backfilled with 3000 PSI concrete, no reinforcing steel | | | | | | | | | |
| 0050     Minimum | C-7 | 333 | .216 | C.F. | 7.40 | 7.10 | 3.57 | 18.07 | 23 |
| 0100     Maximum | | 200 | .360 | " | 12.40 | 11.80 | 5.95 | 30.15 | 38.50 |
| 0200 Alternate pricing method, minimum | | 150 | .480 | S.F. | 14.80 | 15.75 | 7.90 | 38.45 | 49 |
| 0300     Maximum | | 120 | .600 | | 22 | 19.70 | 9.90 | 51.60 | 65.50 |
| 0500 Reinforced slurry trench, minimum | B-48 | 177 | .316 | | 11.10 | 10.70 | 16.10 | 37.90 | 46.50 |
| 0600     Maximum | " | 69 | .812 | | 37 | 27.50 | 41.50 | 106 | 128 |
| 0800 Haul for disposal, 2 mile haul, excavated material, add | B-34B | 99 | .081 | C.Y. | | 2.47 | 5.10 | 7.57 | 9.45 |
| 0900     Haul bentonite castings for disposal, add | " | 40 | .200 | " | | 6.10 | 12.55 | 18.65 | 23.50 |

# 31 62 Driven Piles

## 31 62 13 – Concrete Piles

| 31 62 13.23 Prestressed Concrete Piles | Crew | Daily Output | Labor-Hours | Unit | Material | 2008 Bare Costs Labor | Equipment | Total | Total Incl O&P |
|---|---|---|---|---|---|---|---|---|---|
| 0010 **PRESTRESSED CONCRETE PILES**, 200 piles | | | | | | | | | |
| 0020 unless specified otherwise, not incl. pile caps or mobilization | | | | | | | | | |
| 2200 Precast, prestressed, 50' long, 12" diam., 2-3/8" wall | B-19 | 720 | .089 | V.L.F. | 15.30 | 3.39 | 2.42 | 21.11 | 25 |
| 2300     14" diameter, 2-1/2" wall | | 680 | .094 | | 20 | 3.59 | 2.56 | 26.15 | 30.50 |
| 2500     16" diameter, 3" wall | | 640 | .100 | | 28 | 3.81 | 2.72 | 34.53 | 39.50 |
| 2600     18" diameter, 3" wall | B-19A | 600 | .107 | | 35 | 4.06 | 3.76 | 42.82 | 49 |
| 2800     20" diameter, 3-1/2" wall | | 560 | .114 | | 40.50 | 4.35 | 4.03 | 48.88 | 56 |
| 2900     24" diameter, 3-1/2" wall | | 520 | .123 | | 49.50 | 4.69 | 4.34 | 58.53 | 66.50 |
| 3100 Precast, prestressed, 40' long, 10" thick, square | B-19 | 700 | .091 | | 11.10 | 3.48 | 2.49 | 17.07 | 20.50 |
| 3200     12" thick, square | | 680 | .094 | | 13.95 | 3.59 | 2.56 | 20.10 | 24 |
| 3400     14" thick, square | | 600 | .107 | | 16.45 | 4.06 | 2.90 | 23.41 | 27.50 |
| 3500     Octagonal | | 640 | .100 | | 23 | 3.81 | 2.72 | 29.53 | 34 |
| 3700     16" thick, square | | 560 | .114 | | 26 | 4.35 | 3.11 | 33.46 | 39 |
| 3800     Octagonal | | 600 | .107 | | 27.50 | 4.06 | 2.90 | 34.46 | 39.50 |
| 4000     18" thick, square | B-19A | 520 | .123 | | 31.50 | 4.69 | 4.34 | 40.53 | 46.50 |
| 4100     Octagonal | B-19 | 560 | .114 | | 32.50 | 4.35 | 3.11 | 39.96 | 46 |
| 4300     20" thick, square | B-19A | 480 | .133 | | 38.50 | 5.10 | 4.70 | 48.30 | 55.50 |
| 4400     Octagonal | B-19 | 520 | .123 | | 36 | 4.69 | 3.35 | 44.04 | 50.50 |
| 4600     24" thick, square | B-19A | 440 | .145 | | 55 | 5.55 | 5.10 | 65.65 | 75.50 |
| 4700     Octagonal | B-19 | 480 | .133 | | 51.50 | 5.10 | 3.63 | 60.23 | 68.50 |
| 4730 Precast, prestressed, 60' long, 10" thick, square | | 700 | .091 | | 11.65 | 3.48 | 2.49 | 17.62 | 21 |
| 4740     12" thick, square ( 60' long) | | 680 | .094 | | 14.50 | 3.59 | 2.56 | 20.65 | 24.50 |
| 4750 Mobilization for 10,000 L.F. pile job, add | | 3300 | .019 | | | .74 | .53 | 1.27 | 1.75 |
| 4800     25,000 L.F. pile job, add | | 8500 | .008 | | | .29 | .21 | .50 | .69 |

## 31 62 16 – Steel Piles

| 31 62 16.13 Sheet Steel Piles | Crew | Daily Output | Labor-Hours | Unit | Material | 2008 Bare Costs Labor | Equipment | Total | Total Incl O&P |
|---|---|---|---|---|---|---|---|---|---|
| 0010 **SHEET STEEL PILES** | | | | | | | | | |
| 0100 Step tapered, round, concrete filled | | | | | | | | | |
| 0110     8" tip, 60 ton capacity, 30' depth | B-19 | 760 | .084 | V.L.F. | 8.45 | 3.21 | 2.29 | 13.95 | 16.90 |
| 0120     60' depth | | 740 | .086 | | 9.55 | 3.29 | 2.36 | 15.20 | 18.35 |
| 0130     80' depth | | 700 | .091 | | 9.85 | 3.48 | 2.49 | 15.82 | 19.15 |
| 0150     10" tip, 90 ton capacity, 30' depth | | 700 | .091 | | 10.40 | 3.48 | 2.49 | 16.37 | 19.70 |
| 0160     60' depth | | 690 | .093 | | 10.70 | 3.53 | 2.53 | 16.76 | 20 |
| 0170     80' depth | | 670 | .096 | | 11.50 | 3.64 | 2.60 | 17.74 | 21.50 |
| 0190     12" tip, 120 ton capacity, 30' depth | | 660 | .097 | | 14.30 | 3.69 | 2.64 | 20.63 | 24.50 |

# 31 62 Driven Piles

## 31 62 16 – Steel Piles

### 31 62 16.13 Sheet Steel Piles

| | | Crew | Daily Output | Labor-Hours | Unit | Material | 2008 Bare Costs Labor | Equipment | Total | Total Incl O&P |
|---|---|---|---|---|---|---|---|---|---|---|
| 0200 | 60' depth, 12" diameter | B-19 | 630 | .102 | V.L.F. | 14.35 | 3.87 | 2.77 | 20.99 | 25 |
| 0210 | 80' depth | | 590 | .108 | | 12.65 | 4.13 | 2.95 | 19.73 | 24 |
| 0250 | "H" Sections, 50' long, HP8 x 36 | | 640 | .100 | | 14.50 | 3.81 | 2.72 | 21.03 | 25 |
| 0400 | HP10 X 42 | | 610 | .105 | | 16.95 | 4 | 2.86 | 23.81 | 28 |
| 0500 | HP10 X 57 | | 610 | .105 | | 23 | 4 | 2.86 | 29.86 | 35 |
| 0700 | HP12 X 53 | | 590 | .108 | | 21.50 | 4.13 | 2.95 | 28.58 | 34 |
| 0800 | HP12 X 74 | B-19A | 590 | .108 | | 30.50 | 4.13 | 3.82 | 38.45 | 44.50 |
| 1000 | HP14 X 73 | | 540 | .119 | | 30 | 4.51 | 4.18 | 38.69 | 44.50 |
| 1100 | HP14 X 89 | | 540 | .119 | | 36.50 | 4.51 | 4.18 | 45.19 | 51.50 |
| 1300 | HP14 X 102 | | 510 | .125 | | 42 | 4.78 | 4.42 | 51.20 | 58.50 |
| 1400 | HP14 X 117 | | 510 | .125 | | 48 | 4.78 | 4.42 | 57.20 | 65.50 |
| 1600 | Splice on standard points, not in leads, 8" or 10" | 1 Sswl | 5 | 1.600 | Ea. | 95 | 69 | | 164 | 229 |
| 1700 | 12" or 14" | | 4 | 2 | | 138 | 86 | | 224 | 305 |
| 1900 | Heavy duty points, not in leads, 10" wide | | 4 | 2 | | 147 | 86 | | 233 | 315 |
| 2100 | 14" wide | | 3.50 | 2.286 | | 190 | 98.50 | | 288.50 | 385 |

## 31 62 19 – Timber Piles

### 31 62 19.10 Wood Piles

| | | Crew | Daily Output | Labor-Hours | Unit | Material | 2008 Bare Costs Labor | Equipment | Total | Total Incl O&P |
|---|---|---|---|---|---|---|---|---|---|---|
| 0010 | **WOOD PILES** | | | | | | | | | |
| 0011 | Friction or end bearing, not including | | | | | | | | | |
| 0050 | mobilization or demobilization | | | | | | | | | |
| 0100 | Untreated piles, up to 30' long, 12" butts, 8" points | B-19 | 625 | .102 | V.L.F. | 6.90 | 3.90 | 2.79 | 13.59 | 16.85 |
| 0200 | 30' to 39' long, 12" butts, 8" points | | 700 | .091 | | 6.90 | 3.48 | 2.49 | 12.87 | 15.90 |
| 0300 | 40' to 49' long, 12" butts, 7" points | | 720 | .089 | | 6.90 | 3.39 | 2.42 | 12.71 | 15.65 |
| 0400 | 50' to 59' long, 13"butts, 7" points | | 800 | .080 | | 6.95 | 3.05 | 2.18 | 12.18 | 14.90 |
| 0500 | 60' to 69' long, 13" butts, 7" points | | 840 | .076 | | 7.85 | 2.90 | 2.07 | 12.82 | 15.55 |
| 0600 | 70' to 80' long, 13" butts, 6" points | | 840 | .076 | | 8.70 | 2.90 | 2.07 | 13.67 | 16.50 |
| 0800 | Treated piles, 12 lb. per C.F., | | | | | | | | | |
| 0810 | friction or end bearing, ASTM class B | | | | | | | | | |
| 1000 | Up to 30' long, 12" butts, 8" points | B-19 | 625 | .102 | V.L.F. | 10.15 | 3.90 | 2.79 | 16.84 | 20.50 |
| 1100 | 30' to 39' long, 12" butts, 8" points | | 700 | .091 | | 9.95 | 3.48 | 2.49 | 15.92 | 19.25 |
| 1200 | 40' to 49' long, 12" butts, 7" points | | 720 | .089 | | 10.65 | 3.39 | 2.42 | 16.46 | 19.75 |
| 1300 | 50' to 59' long, 13" butts, 7" points | | 800 | .080 | | 11.75 | 3.05 | 2.18 | 16.98 | 20 |
| 1400 | 60' to 69' long, 13" butts, 6" points | B-19A | 840 | .076 | | 16.05 | 2.90 | 2.68 | 21.63 | 25 |
| 1500 | 70' to 80' long, 13" butts, 6" points | " | 840 | .076 | | 20 | 2.90 | 2.68 | 25.58 | 29.50 |
| 1600 | Treated piles, C.C.A. 2.5# per C.F. | | | | | | | | | |
| 1610 | 8" butts, 10' long | B-19 | 400 | .160 | V.L.F. | 7.40 | 6.10 | 4.36 | 17.86 | 22.50 |
| 1620 | 11' to 16' long | | 500 | .128 | | 7.40 | 4.88 | 3.49 | 15.77 | 19.75 |
| 1630 | 17' to 20' long | | 575 | .111 | | 7.40 | 4.24 | 3.03 | 14.67 | 18.25 |
| 1640 | 10" butts, 10' to 16' long | | 500 | .128 | | 8.45 | 4.88 | 3.49 | 16.82 | 21 |
| 1650 | 17' to 20' long | | 575 | .111 | | 8.45 | 4.24 | 3.03 | 15.72 | 19.40 |
| 1660 | 21' to 40' long | | 700 | .091 | | 8.45 | 3.48 | 2.49 | 14.42 | 17.60 |
| 1670 | 12" butts, 10' to 20' long | | 575 | .111 | | 9.10 | 4.24 | 3.03 | 16.37 | 20 |
| 1680 | 21' to 35' long | | 650 | .098 | | 9.10 | 3.75 | 2.68 | 15.53 | 18.95 |
| 1690 | 36' to 40' long | | 700 | .091 | | 9.10 | 3.48 | 2.49 | 15.07 | 18.35 |
| 1695 | 14" butts, to 40' long | | 700 | .091 | | 13.05 | 3.48 | 2.49 | 19.02 | 22.50 |
| 1700 | Boot for pile tip, minimum | 1 Pile | 27 | .296 | Ea. | 21 | 11 | | 32 | 41 |
| 1800 | Maximum | | 21 | .381 | | 62.50 | 14.15 | | 76.65 | 91.50 |
| 2000 | Point for pile tip, minimum | | 20 | .400 | | 21 | 14.85 | | 35.85 | 47.50 |
| 2100 | Maximum | | 15 | .533 | | 75 | 19.80 | | 94.80 | 115 |
| 2300 | Splice for piles over 50' long, minimum | B-46 | 35 | 1.371 | | 52 | 46.50 | 1.06 | 99.56 | 133 |
| 2400 | Maximum | | 20 | 2.400 | | 62.50 | 81.50 | 1.85 | 145.85 | 202 |
| 2600 | Concrete encasement with wire mesh and tube | | 331 | .145 | V.L.F. | 9.80 | 4.94 | .11 | 14.85 | 18.75 |

# 31 62 Driven Piles

## 31 62 19 – Timber Piles

| 31 62 19.10 Wood Piles | Crew | Daily Output | Labor-Hours | Unit | Material | 2008 Bare Costs Labor | Equipment | Total | Total Incl O&P |
|---|---|---|---|---|---|---|---|---|---|
| 2700 | Mobilization for 10,000 L.F. pile job, add | B-19 | 3300 | .019 | V.L.F. | | .74 | .53 | 1.27 | 1.75 |
| 2800 | 25,000 L.F. pile job, add | " | 8500 | .008 | ↓ | | .29 | .21 | .50 | .69 |

## 31 62 23 – Composite piles

### 31 62 23.13 Concrete Filled Steel Piles

| | 31 62 23.13 Concrete Filled Steel Piles | Crew | Daily Output | Labor-Hours | Unit | Material | 2008 Bare Costs Labor | Equipment | Total | Total Incl O&P |
|---|---|---|---|---|---|---|---|---|---|---|
| 0010 | **CONCRETE FILLED STEEL PILES** no mobilization or demobilization | | | | | | | | | |
| 2600 | Pipe piles, 50' lg. 8" diam., 29 lb. per L.F., no concrete | B-19 | 500 | .128 | V.L.F. | 15.70 | 4.88 | 3.49 | 24.07 | 29 |
| 2700 | Concrete filled | | 460 | .139 | | 16.70 | 5.30 | 3.79 | 25.79 | 31 |
| 2900 | 10" diameter, 34 lb. per L.F., no concrete | | 500 | .128 | | 19.55 | 4.88 | 3.49 | 27.92 | 33 |
| 3000 | Concrete filled | | 450 | .142 | | 21.50 | 5.40 | 3.87 | 30.77 | 36.50 |
| 3200 | 12" diameter, 44 lb. per L.F., no concrete | | 475 | .135 | | 24 | 5.15 | 3.67 | 32.82 | 38.50 |
| 3300 | Concrete filled | | 415 | .154 | | 25 | 5.85 | 4.20 | 35.05 | 41.50 |
| 3500 | 14" diameter, 46 lb. per L.F., no concrete | | 430 | .149 | | 26 | 5.65 | 4.05 | 35.70 | 42 |
| 3600 | Concrete filled | | 355 | .180 | | 28 | 6.85 | 4.91 | 39.76 | 47 |
| 3800 | 16" diameter, 52 lb. per L.F., no concrete | | 385 | .166 | | 29 | 6.35 | 4.53 | 39.88 | 46.50 |
| 3900 | Concrete filled | | 335 | .191 | | 32 | 7.30 | 5.20 | 44.50 | 52.50 |
| 4100 | 18" diameter, 59 lb. per L.F., no concrete | | 355 | .180 | | 38 | 6.85 | 4.91 | 49.76 | 58 |
| 4200 | Concrete filled | ↓ | 310 | .206 | ↓ | 37.50 | 7.85 | 5.60 | 50.95 | 60 |
| 4400 | Splices for pipe piles, not in leads, 8" diameter | 1 Sswl | 4.67 | 1.713 | Ea. | 70.50 | 73.50 | | 144 | 211 |
| 4500 | 14" diameter | | 3.79 | 2.111 | | 92 | 91 | | 183 | 265 |
| 4600 | 16" diameter | | 3.03 | 2.640 | | 114 | 114 | | 228 | 330 |
| 4800 | Points, standard, 8" diameter | | 4.61 | 1.735 | | 78.50 | 74.50 | | 153 | 222 |
| 4900 | 14" diameter | | 4.05 | 1.975 | | 109 | 85 | | 194 | 273 |
| 5000 | 16" diameter | | 3.37 | 2.374 | | 133 | 102 | | 235 | 330 |
| 5200 | Points, heavy duty, 10" diameter | | 2.89 | 2.768 | | 54.50 | 119 | | 173.50 | 275 |
| 5300 | 14" or 16" diameter | | 2.02 | 3.960 | ↓ | 87 | 170 | | 257 | 400 |
| 5500 | For reinforcing steel, add | ↓ | 1150 | .007 | Lb. | .65 | .30 | | .95 | 1.26 |
| 5700 | For thick wall sections, add | | | | " | .74 | | | .74 | .81 |

# 31 63 Bored Piles

## 31 63 26 – Drilled Caissons

### 31 63 26.13 Fixed End Cassion Piles

| | 31 63 26.13 Fixed End Cassion Piles | Crew | Daily Output | Labor-Hours | Unit | Material | 2008 Bare Costs Labor | Equipment | Total | Total Incl O&P |
|---|---|---|---|---|---|---|---|---|---|---|
| 0010 | **FIXED END CASSION PILES**     R316326-60 | | | | | | | | | |
| 0015 | including excavation, concrete, 50 lbs reinforcing | | | | | | | | | |
| 0020 | per C.Y., not incl. mobilization, boulder removal, disposal | | | | | | | | | |
| 0100 | Open style, machine drilled, to 50' deep, in stable ground, no | | | | | | | | | |
| 0110 | casings or ground water, 18" diam., 0.065 C.Y./L.F. | B-43 | 200 | .240 | V.L.F. | 8 | 7.95 | 12.65 | 28.60 | 35 |
| 0200 | 24" diameter, 0.116 C.Y./L.F. | | 190 | .253 | | 14.30 | 8.40 | 13.30 | 36 | 43.50 |
| 0300 | 30" diameter, 0.182 C.Y./L.F. | | 150 | .320 | | 22.50 | 10.60 | 16.85 | 49.95 | 59.50 |
| 0400 | 36" diameter, 0.262 C.Y./L.F. | | 125 | .384 | | 32.50 | 12.75 | 20 | 65.25 | 77.50 |
| 0500 | 48" diameter, 0.465 C.Y./L.F. | | 100 | .480 | | 57.50 | 15.95 | 25.50 | 98.95 | 116 |
| 0600 | 60" diameter, 0.727 C.Y./L.F. | | 90 | .533 | | 89.50 | 17.70 | 28 | 135.20 | 157 |
| 0700 | 72" diameter, 1.05 C.Y./L.F. | | 80 | .600 | | 130 | 19.90 | 31.50 | 181.40 | 209 |
| 0800 | 84" diameter, 1.43 C.Y./L.F. | ↓ | 75 | .640 | ↓ | 176 | 21 | 33.50 | 230.50 | 264 |
| 1000 | For bell excavation and concrete, add | | | | | | | | | |
| 1020 | 4' bell diameter, 24" shaft, 0.444 C.Y. | B-43 | 20 | 2.400 | Ea. | 44.50 | 79.50 | 127 | 251 | 310 |
| 1040 | 6' bell diameter, 30" shaft, 1.57 C.Y. | | 5.70 | 8.421 | | 157 | 279 | 445 | 881 | 1,100 |
| 1060 | 8' bell diameter, 36" shaft, 3.72 C.Y. | | 2.40 | 20 | | 370 | 665 | 1,050 | 2,085 | 2,575 |
| 1080 | 9' bell diameter, 48" shaft, 4.48 C.Y. | | 2 | 24 | | 450 | 795 | 1,275 | 2,520 | 3,125 |
| 1100 | 10' bell diameter, 60" shaft, 5.24 C.Y. | | 1.70 | 28.235 | | 525 | 935 | 1,500 | 2,960 | 3,650 |
| 1120 | 12' bell diameter, 72" shaft, 8.74 C.Y. | ↓ | 1 | 48 | ↓ | 875 | 1,600 | 2,525 | 5,000 | 6,175 |

# 31 63 Bored Piles

## 31 63 26 – Drilled Caissons

### 31 63 26.13 Fixed End Cassion Piles

| | Crew | Daily Output | Labor-Hours | Unit | Material | 2008 Bare Costs Labor | Equipment | Total | Total Incl O&P |
|---|---|---|---|---|---|---|---|---|---|
| 1140 14' bell diameter, 84" shaft, 13.6 C.Y. | B-43 | .70 | 68.571 | Ea. | 1,350 | 2,275 | 3,625 | 7,250 | 8,975 |
| 1200 Open style, machine drilled, to 50' deep, in wet ground, pulled | | | | | | | | | |
| 1300 casing and pumping, 18" diameter, 0.065 C.Y./L.F. | B-48 | 160 | .350 | V.L.F. | 8 | 11.85 | 17.85 | 37.70 | 46.50 |
| 1400 24" diameter, 0.116 C.Y./L.F. | | 125 | .448 | | 14.30 | 15.15 | 23 | 52.45 | 64 |
| 1500 30" diameter, 0.182 C.Y./L.F. | | 85 | .659 | | 22.50 | 22.50 | 33.50 | 78.50 | 95.50 |
| 1600 36" diameter, 0.262 C.Y./L.F. | | 60 | .933 | | 32.50 | 31.50 | 47.50 | 111.50 | 137 |
| 1700 48" diameter, 0.465 C.Y./L.F. | B-49 | 55 | 1.600 | | 57.50 | 56.50 | 66 | 180 | 223 |
| 1800 60" diameter, 0.727 C.Y./L.F. | | 35 | 2.514 | | 89.50 | 88.50 | 104 | 282 | 350 |
| 1900 72" diameter, 1.05 C.Y./L.F. | | 30 | 2.933 | | 130 | 103 | 121 | 354 | 435 |
| 2000 84" diameter, 1.43 C.Y./L.F. | | 25 | 3.520 | | 176 | 124 | 146 | 446 | 545 |
| 2100 For bell excavation and concrete, add | | | | | | | | | |
| 2120 4' bell diameter, 24" shaft, 0.444 C.Y. | B-48 | 19.80 | 2.828 | Ea. | 44.50 | 95.50 | 144 | 284 | 355 |
| 2140 6' bell diameter, 30" shaft, 1.57 C.Y. | | 5.70 | 9.825 | | 157 | 330 | 500 | 987 | 1,225 |
| 2160 8' bell diameter, 36" shaft, 3.72 C.Y. | | 2.40 | 23.333 | | 370 | 790 | 1,200 | 2,360 | 2,900 |
| 2180 9' bell diameter, 48" shaft, 4.48 C.Y. | B-49 | 3.30 | 26.667 | | 450 | 940 | 1,100 | 2,490 | 3,175 |
| 2200 10' bell diameter, 60" shaft, 5.24 C.Y. | | 2.80 | 31.429 | | 525 | 1,100 | 1,300 | 2,925 | 3,725 |
| 2220 12' bell diameter, 72" shaft, 8.74 C.Y. | | 1.60 | 55 | | 875 | 1,925 | 2,275 | 5,075 | 6,450 |
| 2240 14' bell diameter, 84" shaft, 13.6 C.Y. | | 1 | 88 | | 1,350 | 3,100 | 3,650 | 8,100 | 10,300 |
| 2300 Open style, machine drilled, to 50' deep, in soft rocks and | | | | | | | | | |
| 2400 medium hard shales, 18" diameter, 0.065 C.Y./L.F. | B-49 | 50 | 1.760 | V.L.F. | 8 | 62 | 73 | 143 | 185 |
| 2500 24" diameter, 0.116 C.Y./L.F. | | 30 | 2.933 | | 14.30 | 103 | 121 | 238.30 | 310 |
| 2600 30" diameter, 0.182 C.Y./L.F. | | 20 | 4.400 | | 22.50 | 155 | 182 | 359.50 | 465 |
| 2700 36" diameter, 0.262 C.Y./L.F. | | 15 | 5.867 | | 32.50 | 207 | 243 | 482.50 | 625 |
| 2800 48" diameter, 0.465 C.Y./L.F. | | 10 | 8.800 | | 57.50 | 310 | 365 | 732.50 | 945 |
| 2900 60" diameter, 0.727 C.Y./L.F. | | 7 | 12.571 | | 89.50 | 445 | 520 | 1,054.50 | 1,350 |
| 3000 72" diameter, 1.05 C.Y./L.F. | | 6 | 14.667 | | 130 | 515 | 605 | 1,250 | 1,600 |
| 3100 84" diameter, 1.43 C.Y./L.F. | | 5 | 17.600 | | 176 | 620 | 730 | 1,526 | 1,950 |
| 3200 For bell excavation and concrete, add | | | | | | | | | |
| 3220 4' bell diameter, 24" shaft, 0.444 C.Y. | B-49 | 10.90 | 8.073 | Ea. | 44.50 | 284 | 335 | 663.50 | 855 |
| 3240 6' bell diameter, 30" shaft, 1.57 C.Y. | | 3.10 | 28.387 | | 157 | 1,000 | 1,175 | 2,332 | 3,025 |
| 3260 8' bell diameter, 36" shaft, 3.72 C.Y. | | 1.30 | 67.692 | | 370 | 2,375 | 2,800 | 5,545 | 7,175 |
| 3280 9' bell diameter, 48" shaft, 4.48 C.Y. | | 1.10 | 80 | | 450 | 2,825 | 3,300 | 6,575 | 8,500 |
| 3300 10' bell diameter, 60" shaft, 5.24 C.Y. | | .90 | 97.778 | | 525 | 3,450 | 4,050 | 8,025 | 10,400 |
| 3320 12' bell diameter, 72" shaft, 8.74 C.Y. | | .60 | 146 | | 875 | 5,175 | 6,075 | 12,125 | 15,600 |
| 3340 14' bell diameter, 84" shaft, 13.6 C.Y. | | .40 | 220 | | 1,350 | 7,750 | 9,100 | 18,200 | 23,500 |
| 3600 For rock excavation, sockets, add, minimum | | 120 | .733 | C.F. | | 26 | 30.50 | 56.50 | 73.50 |
| 3650 Average | | 95 | .926 | | | 32.50 | 38.50 | 71 | 92.50 |
| 3700 Maximum | | 48 | 1.833 | | | 64.50 | 76 | 140.50 | 184 |
| 3900 For 50' to 100' deep, add | | | | V.L.F. | | | | 7% | 7% |
| 4000 For 100' to 150' deep, add | | | | | | | | 25% | 25% |
| 4100 For 150' to 200' deep, add | | | | | | | | 30% | 30% |
| 4200 For casings left in place, add | | | | Lb. | .87 | | | .87 | .96 |
| 4300 For other than 50 lb. reinf. per C.Y., add or deduct | | | | " | .92 | | | .92 | 1.01 |
| 4400 For steel "I" beam cores, add | B-49 | 8.30 | 10.602 | Ton | 1,750 | 375 | 440 | 2,565 | 2,975 |
| 4500 Load and haul excess excavation, 2 miles | B-34B | 178 | .045 | L.C.Y. | | 1.38 | 2.82 | 4.20 | 5.25 |
| 4600 For mobilization, 50 mile radius, rig to 36" | B-43 | 2 | 24 | Ea. | | 795 | 1,275 | 2,070 | 2,625 |
| 4650 Rig to 84" | B-48 | 1.75 | 32 | | | 1,075 | 1,625 | 2,700 | 3,450 |
| 4700 For low headroom, add | | | | | | | | 50% | |
| 5000 Bottom inspection | 1 Skwk | 1.20 | 6.667 | | | 263 | | 263 | 410 |

### 31 63 26.16 Concrete Caissons for Marine Construction

| | | | | | | | | | |
|---|---|---|---|---|---|---|---|---|---|
| 0010 **CONCRETE CAISSONS FOR MARINE CONSTRUCTION** | | | | | | | | | |
| 0100 Caissons, incl. mobilization and demobilization, up to 50 miles | | | | | | | | | |

561

# 31 63 Bored Piles

## 31 63 26 – Drilled Caissons

### 31 63 26.16 Concrete Caissons for Marine Construction

| | | Crew | Daily Output | Labor-Hours | Unit | Material | 2008 Bare Costs Labor | Equipment | Total | Total Incl O&P |
|---|---|---|---|---|---|---|---|---|---|---|
| 0200 | Uncased shafts, 30 to 80 tons cap., 17" diam., 10' depth | B-44 | 88 | .727 | V.L.F. | 20 | 27.50 | 16.45 | 63.95 | 83.50 |
| 0300 | 25' depth | | 165 | .388 | | 14.30 | 14.55 | 8.80 | 37.65 | 48.50 |
| 0400 | 80-150 ton capacity, 22" diameter, 10' depth | | 80 | .800 | | 25 | 30 | 18.10 | 73.10 | 95.50 |
| 0500 | 20' depth | | 130 | .492 | | 20 | 18.45 | 11.15 | 49.60 | 64 |
| 0700 | Cased shafts, 10 to 30 ton capacity, 10-5/8" diam., 20' depth | | 175 | .366 | | 14.30 | 13.70 | 8.30 | 36.30 | 47 |
| 0800 | 30' depth | | 240 | .267 | | 13.35 | 10 | 6.05 | 29.40 | 37.50 |
| 0850 | 30 to 60 ton capacity, 12" diameter, 20' depth | | 160 | .400 | | 20 | 15 | 9.05 | 44.05 | 56 |
| 0900 | 40' depth | | 230 | .278 | | 15.40 | 10.45 | 6.30 | 32.15 | 40.50 |
| 1000 | 80 to 100 ton capacity, 16" diameter, 20' depth | | 160 | .400 | | 28.50 | 15 | 9.05 | 52.55 | 65.50 |
| 1100 | 40' depth | | 230 | .278 | | 26.50 | 10.45 | 6.30 | 43.25 | 53 |
| 1200 | 110 to 140 ton capacity, 17-5/8" diameter, 20' depth | | 160 | .400 | | 31 | 15 | 9.05 | 55.05 | 68 |
| 1300 | 40' depth | | 230 | .278 | | 28.50 | 10.45 | 6.30 | 45.25 | 55 |
| 1400 | 140 to 175 ton capacity, 19" diameter, 20' depth | | 130 | .492 | | 33.50 | 18.45 | 11.15 | 63.10 | 78.50 |
| 1500 | 40' depth | ↓ | 210 | .305 | ↓ | 31 | 11.45 | 6.90 | 49.35 | 60 |
| 1700 | Over 30' long, L.F. cost tends to be lower | | | | | | | | | |
| 1900 | Maximum depth is about 90' | | | | | | | | | |

## 31 63 29 – Drilled Concrete Piers and Shafts

### 31 63 29.13 Uncased Drilled Concrete Piers

| | | Crew | Daily Output | Labor-Hours | Unit | Material | 2008 Bare Costs Labor | Equipment | Total | Total Incl O&P |
|---|---|---|---|---|---|---|---|---|---|---|
| 0010 | **UNCASED DRILLED CONCRETE PIERS** | | | | | | | | | |
| 0020 | Unless specified otherwise, not incl. pile caps or mobilization | | | | | | | | | |
| 0050 | Cast in place augered piles, no casing or reinforcing | | | | | | | | | |
| 0060 | 8" diameter | B-43 | 540 | .089 | V.L.F. | 3.80 | 2.95 | 4.69 | 11.44 | 13.85 |
| 0065 | 10" diameter | | 480 | .100 | | 6.05 | 3.32 | 5.25 | 14.62 | 17.55 |
| 0070 | 12" diameter | | 420 | .114 | | 8.50 | 3.79 | 6 | 18.29 | 22 |
| 0075 | 14" diameter | | 360 | .133 | | 11.50 | 4.42 | 7.05 | 22.97 | 27 |
| 0080 | 16" diameter | | 300 | .160 | | 15.45 | 5.30 | 8.45 | 29.20 | 34.50 |
| 0085 | 18" diameter | ↓ | 240 | .200 | ↓ | 19.15 | 6.65 | 10.55 | 36.35 | 43 |
| 0100 | Cast in place, thin wall shell pile, straight sided, | | | | | | | | | |
| 0110 | not incl. reinforcing, 8" diam., 16 ga., 5.8 lb./L.F. | B-19 | 700 | .091 | V.L.F. | 7.15 | 3.48 | 2.49 | 13.12 | 16.15 |
| 0200 | 10" diameter, 16 ga. corrugated, 7.3 lb./L.F. | | 650 | .098 | | 9.35 | 3.75 | 2.68 | 15.78 | 19.15 |
| 0300 | 12" diameter, 16 ga. corrugated, 8.7 lb./L.F. | | 600 | .107 | | 12.10 | 4.06 | 2.90 | 19.06 | 23 |
| 0400 | 14" diameter, 16 ga. corrugated, 10.0 lb./L.F. | | 550 | .116 | | 14.25 | 4.43 | 3.17 | 21.85 | 26 |
| 0500 | 16" diameter, 16 ga. corrugated, 11.6 lb./L.F. | ↓ | 500 | .128 | ↓ | 17.45 | 4.88 | 3.49 | 25.82 | 31 |
| 0800 | Cast in place friction pile, 50' long, fluted, | | | | | | | | | |
| 0810 | tapered steel, 4000 psi concrete, no reinforcing | | | | | | | | | |
| 0900 | 12" diameter, 7 ga. | B-19 | 600 | .107 | V.L.F. | 21.50 | 4.06 | 2.90 | 28.46 | 33 |
| 1000 | 14" diameter, 7 ga. | | 560 | .114 | | 23.50 | 4.35 | 3.11 | 30.96 | 36 |
| 1100 | 16" diameter, 7 ga. | | 520 | .123 | | 27.50 | 4.69 | 3.35 | 35.54 | 41 |
| 1200 | 18" diameter, 7 ga. | ↓ | 480 | .133 | ↓ | 32 | 5.10 | 3.63 | 40.73 | 47.50 |
| 1300 | End bearing, fluted, constant diameter, | | | | | | | | | |
| 1320 | 4000 psi concrete, no reinforcing | | | | | | | | | |
| 1340 | 12" diameter, 7 ga. | B-19 | 600 | .107 | V.L.F. | 22.50 | 4.06 | 2.90 | 29.46 | 34 |
| 1360 | 14" diameter, 7 ga. | | 560 | .114 | | 28 | 4.35 | 3.11 | 35.46 | 41 |
| 1380 | 16" diameter, 7 ga. | | 520 | .123 | | 32.50 | 4.69 | 3.35 | 40.54 | 46.50 |
| 1400 | 18" diameter, 7 ga. | ↓ | 480 | .133 | ↓ | 35.50 | 5.10 | 3.63 | 44.23 | 51.50 |

### 31 63 29.20 Cast In Place Piles, Adds

| | | Crew | Daily Output | Labor-Hours | Unit | Material | 2008 Bare Costs Labor | Equipment | Total | Total Incl O&P |
|---|---|---|---|---|---|---|---|---|---|---|
| 0010 | **CAST IN PLACE PILES, ADDS** | | | | | | | | | |
| 1500 | For reinforcing steel, add | | | | Lb. | .94 | | | .94 | 1.03 |
| 1700 | For ball or pedestal end, add | B-19 | 11 | 5.818 | C.Y. | 115 | 222 | 158 | 495 | 650 |
| 1900 | For lengths above 60', concrete, add | " | 11 | 5.818 | " | 120 | 222 | 158 | 500 | 655 |
| 2000 | For steel thin shell, pipe only | | | | Lb. | .81 | | | .81 | .89 |

# Estimating Tips

## 32 01 00 Operations and Maintenance of Exterior Improvements

- Recycling of asphalt pavement is becoming very popular and is an alternative to removal and replacement of asphalt pavement. It can be a good value engineering proposal if removed pavement can be recycled either at the site or another site that is reasonably close to the project site.

## 32 10 00 Bases, Ballasts, and Paving

- When estimating paving, keep in mind the project schedule. If an asphaltic paving project is in a colder climate and runs through to the spring, consider placing the base course in the autumn and then topping it in the spring just prior to completion. This could save considerable costs in spring repair. Keep in mind that prices for asphalt and concrete are generally higher in the cold seasons.

## 32 90 00 Planting

- The timing of planting and guarantee specifications often dictate the costs for establishing tree and shrub growth and a stand of grass or ground cover. Establish the work performance schedule to coincide with the local planting season. Maintenance and growth guarantees can add from 20% to 100% to the total landscaping cost. The cost to replace trees and shrubs can be as high as 5% of the total cost depending on the planting zone, soil conditions, and time of year.

# Reference Numbers

Reference numbers are shown in shaded boxes at the beginning of some major classifications. These numbers refer to related items in the Reference Section. The reference information may be an estimating procedure, an alternate pricing method, or technical information.

*Note:* Not all subdivisions listed here necessarily appear in this publication.

# 32 01 Operation and Maintenance of Exterior Improvements

## 32 01 13 – Flexible Paving Surface Treatment

### 32 01 13.61 Slurry Seal (Latex Modified)

| | | Crew | Daily Output | Labor-Hours | Unit | Material | 2008 Bare Costs Labor | 2008 Bare Costs Equipment | Total | Total Incl O&P |
|---|---|---|---|---|---|---|---|---|---|---|
| 0010 | **SLURRY SEAL (LATEX MODIFIED)** | | | | | | | | | |
| 3780 | Rubberized asphalt (latex) seal | B-45 | 5000 | .003 | S.Y. | 1.74 | .11 | .15 | 2 | 2.24 |

### 32 01 13.64 Sand Seal

| | | Crew | Daily Output | Labor-Hours | Unit | Material | 2008 Bare Costs Labor | 2008 Bare Costs Equipment | Total | Total Incl O&P |
|---|---|---|---|---|---|---|---|---|---|---|
| 0010 | **SAND SEAL** | | | | | | | | | |
| 2080 | Sand sealing, sharp sand, asphalt emulsion, small area | B-91 | 10000 | .006 | S.Y. | .95 | .23 | .21 | 1.39 | 1.63 |
| 2120 | Roadway or large area | " | 18000 | .004 | " | .82 | .13 | .12 | 1.07 | 1.22 |

### 32 01 13.66 Fog Seal

| | | Crew | Daily Output | Labor-Hours | Unit | Material | 2008 Bare Costs Labor | 2008 Bare Costs Equipment | Total | Total Incl O&P |
|---|---|---|---|---|---|---|---|---|---|---|
| 0010 | **FOG SEAL** | | | | | | | | | |
| 0012 | Sealcoating, 2 coat coal tar pitch emulsion over 10,000 SY | B-45 | 5000 | .003 | S.Y. | .77 | .11 | .15 | 1.03 | 1.18 |
| 0030 | 1000 to 10,000 S.Y. | " | 3000 | .005 | | .77 | .19 | .25 | 1.21 | 1.41 |
| 0100 | Under 1000 S.Y. | B-1 | 1050 | .023 | | .77 | .71 | | 1.48 | 1.95 |
| 0300 | Petroleum resistant, over 10,000 S.Y. | B-45 | 5000 | .003 | | .95 | .11 | .15 | 1.21 | 1.38 |
| 0320 | 1000 to 10,000 S.Y. | " | 3000 | .005 | | .95 | .19 | .25 | 1.39 | 1.61 |
| 0400 | Under 1000 S.Y. | B-1 | 1050 | .023 | | .95 | .71 | | 1.66 | 2.15 |
| 0600 | Non-skid pavement renewal, over 10,000 S.Y. | B-45 | 5000 | .003 | | 1.10 | .11 | .15 | 1.36 | 1.54 |
| 0620 | 1000 to 10,000 S.Y. | " | 3000 | .005 | | 1.10 | .19 | .25 | 1.54 | 1.77 |
| 0700 | Under 1000 S.Y. | B-1 | 1050 | .023 | | 1.10 | .71 | | 1.81 | 2.31 |
| 0800 | Prepare and clean surface for above | A-2 | 8545 | .003 | ↓ | | .08 | .02 | .10 | .15 |
| 1000 | Hand seal asphalt curbing | B-1 | 4420 | .005 | L.F. | .56 | .17 | | .73 | .88 |
| 1900 | Asphalt surface treatment, single course, small area | | | | | | | | | |
| 1901 | 0.30 gal/S.Y. asphalt material, 20#/S.Y. aggregate | B-91 | 5000 | .013 | S.Y. | 1.31 | .45 | .42 | 2.18 | 2.59 |
| 1910 | Roadway or large area | | 10000 | .006 | | 1.21 | .23 | .21 | 1.65 | 1.91 |
| 1950 | Asphalt surface treatment, dbl. course for small area | | 3000 | .021 | | 2.42 | .75 | .69 | 3.86 | 4.57 |
| 1960 | Roadway or large area | | 6000 | .011 | | 2.18 | .38 | .35 | 2.91 | 3.36 |
| 1980 | Asphalt surface treatment, single course, for shoulders | ↓ | 7500 | .009 | ↓ | 1.39 | .30 | .28 | 1.97 | 2.30 |

# 32 06 Schedules for Exterior Improvements

## 32 06 10 – Schedules for Bases, Ballasts, and Paving

### 32 06 10.10 Sidewalks, Driveways and Patios

| | | Crew | Daily Output | Labor-Hours | Unit | Material | 2008 Bare Costs Labor | 2008 Bare Costs Equipment | Total | Total Incl O&P |
|---|---|---|---|---|---|---|---|---|---|---|
| 0010 | **SIDEWALKS, DRIVEWAYS AND PATIOS** No base | | | | | | | | | |
| 0020 | Asphaltic concrete, 2" thick | B-37 | 720 | .067 | S.Y. | 5.50 | 2.12 | .18 | 7.80 | 9.55 |
| 0100 | 2-1/2" thick | " | 660 | .073 | " | 7 | 2.32 | .20 | 9.52 | 11.50 |
| 0300 | Concrete, 3000 psi, CIP, 6 x 6 - W1.4 x W1.4 mesh, | | | | | | | | | |
| 0310 | broomed finish, no base, 4" thick | B-24 | 600 | .040 | S.F. | 1.67 | 1.40 | | 3.07 | 3.97 |
| 0350 | 5" thick | | 545 | .044 | | 2.22 | 1.55 | | 3.77 | 4.80 |
| 0400 | 6" thick | | 510 | .047 | | 2.59 | 1.65 | | 4.24 | 5.35 |
| 0450 | For bank run gravel base, 4" thick, add | B-18 | 2500 | .010 | | .61 | .30 | .02 | .93 | 1.15 |
| 0520 | 8" thick, add | " | 1600 | .015 | | 1.22 | .46 | .02 | 1.70 | 2.10 |
| 0550 | Exposed aggregate finish, add to above, minimum | B-24 | 1875 | .013 | | .16 | .45 | | .61 | .87 |
| 0600 | Maximum | " | 455 | .053 | | .54 | 1.85 | | 2.39 | 3.41 |
| 1000 | Crushed stone, 1" thick, white marble | 2 Clab | 1700 | .009 | | .21 | .28 | | .49 | .67 |
| 1050 | Bluestone | " | 1700 | .009 | | .23 | .28 | | .51 | .69 |
| 1700 | Redwood, prefabricated, 4' x 4' sections | 2 Carp | 316 | .051 | | 8.25 | 1.93 | | 10.18 | 12.10 |
| 1750 | Redwood planks, 1" thick, on sleepers | " | 240 | .067 | ↓ | 5.80 | 2.54 | | 8.34 | 10.30 |
| 2250 | Stone dust, 4" thick | B-62 | 900 | .027 | S.Y. | 3.24 | .87 | .15 | 4.26 | 5.05 |

### 32 06 10.20 Steps

| | | Crew | Daily Output | Labor-Hours | Unit | Material | 2008 Bare Costs Labor | 2008 Bare Costs Equipment | Total | Total Incl O&P |
|---|---|---|---|---|---|---|---|---|---|---|
| 0010 | **STEPS** | | | | | | | | | |
| 0011 | Incl. excav., borrow & concrete base as required | | | | | | | | | |
| 0100 | Brick steps | B-24 | 35 | .686 | LF Riser | 11.40 | 24 | | 35.40 | 49 |
| 0200 | Railroad ties | 2 Clab | 25 | .640 | ↓ | 3.25 | 19.35 | | 22.60 | 33.50 |

# 32 06 Schedules for Exterior Improvements

## 32 06 10 – Schedules for Bases, Ballasts, and Paving

| 32 06 10.20 Steps | Crew | Daily Output | Labor-Hours | Unit | Material | 2008 Bare Costs Labor | Equipment | Total | Total Incl O&P |
|---|---|---|---|---|---|---|---|---|---|
| 0300 | Bluestone treads, 12" x 2" or 12" x 1-1/2" | B-24 | 30 | .800 | LF Riser | 26.50 | 28 | | 54.50 | 72 |
| 0500 | Concrete, cast in place, see Div. 03 30 53.40 | | | | | | | | | |
| 0600 | Precast concrete, see Div. 03 41 23.50 | | | | | | | | | |
| 4025 | Steel edge strips, incl. stakes, 1/4" x 5" | B-1 | 390 | .062 | L.F. | 4.02 | 1.90 | | 5.92 | 7.40 |
| 4050 | Edging, landscape timber or railroad ties, 6" x 8" | 2 Carp | 170 | .094 | " | 2.99 | 3.59 | | 6.58 | 8.90 |

# 32 11 Base Courses

## 32 11 23 – Aggregate Base Courses

### 32 11 23.23 Base Course Drainage Layers

| | | Crew | Daily Output | Labor-Hours | Unit | Material | 2008 Bare Costs Labor | Equipment | Total | Total Incl O&P |
|---|---|---|---|---|---|---|---|---|---|---|
| 0010 | **BASE COURSE DRAINAGE LAYERS** | | | | | | | | | |
| 0011 | For roadways and large areas | | | | | | | | | |
| 0050 | Crushed 3/4" stone base, compacted, 3" deep | B-36C | 5200 | .008 | S.Y. | 4.53 | .28 | .59 | 5.40 | 6.05 |
| 0100 | 6" deep | | 5000 | .008 | | 9.10 | .29 | .61 | 10 | 11.10 |
| 0200 | 9" deep | | 4600 | .009 | | 13.60 | .32 | .67 | 14.59 | 16.20 |
| 0300 | 12" deep | | 4200 | .010 | | 18.15 | .35 | .73 | 19.23 | 21.50 |
| 0301 | Crushed 1-1/2" stone base, compacted to 4" deep | B-36B | 6000 | .011 | | 6.50 | .38 | .59 | 7.47 | 8.30 |
| 0302 | 6" deep | | 5400 | .012 | | 9.70 | .42 | .65 | 10.77 | 12.05 |
| 0303 | 8" deep | | 4500 | .014 | | 12.95 | .50 | .78 | 14.23 | 15.90 |
| 0304 | 12" deep | | 3800 | .017 | | 19.45 | .60 | .92 | 20.97 | 23.50 |
| 0350 | Bank run gravel, spread and compacted | | | | | | | | | |
| 0370 | 6" deep | B-32 | 6000 | .005 | S.Y. | 5.05 | .20 | .30 | 5.55 | 6.25 |
| 0390 | 9" deep | | 4900 | .007 | | 7.60 | .24 | .37 | 8.21 | 9.15 |
| 0400 | 12" deep | | 4200 | .008 | | 10.15 | .29 | .43 | 10.87 | 12.05 |
| 6000 | Stabilization fabric, polypropylene, 6 oz./S.Y. | B-6 | 10000 | .002 | | 1.12 | .08 | .03 | 1.23 | 1.38 |
| 6900 | For small and irregular areas, add | | | | | | 50% | 50% | | |
| 7000 | Prepare and roll sub-base, small areas to 2500 S.Y. | B-32A | 1500 | .016 | S.Y. | | .59 | .75 | 1.34 | 1.72 |
| 8000 | Large areas over 2500 S.Y. | B-32 | 3700 | .009 | " | | .32 | .49 | .81 | 1.03 |

## 32 11 26 – Asphaltic Base Courses

### 32 11 26.19 Bituminous-Stabilized Base Courses

| | | Crew | Daily Output | Labor-Hours | Unit | Material | 2008 Bare Costs Labor | Equipment | Total | Total Incl O&P |
|---|---|---|---|---|---|---|---|---|---|---|
| 0010 | **BITUMINOUS-STABILIZED BASE COURSES** | | | | | | | | | |
| 0020 | and large paved areas | | | | | | | | | |
| 0700 | Liquid application to gravel base, asphalt emulsion | B-45 | 6000 | .003 | Gal. | 4.49 | .09 | .12 | 4.70 | 5.20 |
| 0800 | Prime and seal, cut back asphalt | | 6000 | .003 | " | 5.30 | .09 | .12 | 5.51 | 6.15 |
| 1000 | Macadam penetration crushed stone, 2 gal. per S.Y., 4" thick | | 6000 | .003 | S.Y. | 9 | .09 | .12 | 9.21 | 10.20 |
| 1100 | 6" thick, 3 gal. per S.Y. | | 4000 | .004 | | 13.45 | .14 | .19 | 13.78 | 15.20 |
| 1200 | 8" thick, 4 gal. per S.Y. | | 3000 | .005 | | 17.95 | .19 | .25 | 18.39 | 20.50 |
| 8900 | For small and irregular areas, add | | | | | | 50% | 50% | | |

# 32 12 Flexible Paving

## 32 12 16 – Asphalt Paving

### 32 12 16.13 Plant-Mix Asphalt Paving

| | | Crew | Daily Output | Labor-Hours | Unit | Material | 2008 Bare Costs Labor | Equipment | Total | Total Incl O&P |
|---|---|---|---|---|---|---|---|---|---|---|
| 0010 | **PLANT-MIX ASPHALT PAVING** | | | | | | | | | |
| 0020 | and large paved areas with no hauling included | | | | | | | | | |
| 0025 | See Div. 31 23 23.18 for hauling costs | | | | | | | | | |
| 0080 | Binder course, 1-1/2" thick | B-25 | 7725 | .011 | S.Y. | 4.25 | .38 | .31 | 4.94 | 5.60 |
| 0120 | 2" thick | | 6345 | .014 | | 5.65 | .46 | .37 | 6.48 | 7.30 |
| 0130 | 2-1/2" thick | | 5620 | .016 | | 7.05 | .52 | .42 | 7.99 | 9.05 |
| 0160 | 3" thick | | 4905 | .018 | | 8.50 | .59 | .48 | 9.57 | 10.80 |
| 0170 | 3-1/2 " thick | | 4520 | .019 | | 9.90 | .64 | .52 | 11.06 | 12.45 |

# 32 12 Flexible Paving

## 32 12 16 – Asphalt Paving

### 32 12 16.13 Plant-Mix Asphalt Paving

| | | Crew | Daily Output | Labor-Hours | Unit | Material | 2008 Bare Costs Labor | Equipment | Total | Total Incl O&P |
|---|---|---|---|---|---|---|---|---|---|---|
| 0200 | 4" thick | B-25 | 4140 | .021 | S.Y. | 11.30 | .70 | .57 | 12.57 | 14.15 |
| 0300 | Wearing course, 1" thick | B-25B | 10575 | .009 | | 2.81 | .31 | .24 | 3.36 | 3.83 |
| 0340 | 1-1/2" thick | | 7725 | .012 | | 4.71 | .42 | .33 | 5.46 | 6.20 |
| 0380 | 2" thick | | 6345 | .015 | | 6.35 | .51 | .41 | 7.27 | 8.20 |
| 0420 | 2-1/2" thick | | 5480 | .018 | | 7.80 | .59 | .47 | 8.86 | 10.05 |
| 0460 | 3" thick | | 4900 | .020 | | 9.30 | .66 | .53 | 10.49 | 11.85 |
| 0470 | 3-1/2" thick | | 4520 | .021 | | 10.95 | .71 | .57 | 12.23 | 13.75 |
| 0480 | 4 " thick | | 4140 | .023 | | 12.50 | .78 | .62 | 13.90 | 15.65 |
| 0500 | Open graded friction course | B-25C | 5000 | .010 | | 2.60 | .32 | .41 | 3.33 | 3.81 |
| 0800 | Alternate method of figuring paving costs | | | | | | | | | |
| 0810 | Binder course, 1-1/2" thick | B-25 | 630 | .140 | Ton | 52 | 4.62 | 3.75 | 60.37 | 68 |
| 0811 | 2" thick | | 690 | .128 | | 52 | 4.22 | 3.43 | 59.65 | 67.50 |
| 0812 | 3" thick | | 800 | .110 | | 52 | 3.64 | 2.95 | 58.59 | 66 |
| 0813 | 4" thick | | 900 | .098 | | 52 | 3.23 | 2.63 | 57.86 | 65 |
| 0850 | Wearing course, 1" thick | B-25B | 575 | .167 | | 55 | 5.60 | 4.49 | 65.09 | 74 |
| 0851 | 1-1/2" thick | | 630 | .152 | | 55 | 5.10 | 4.10 | 64.20 | 73 |
| 0852 | 2" thick | | 690 | .139 | | 55 | 4.68 | 3.74 | 63.42 | 72 |
| 0853 | 2-1/2" thick | | 765 | .125 | | 55 | 4.22 | 3.38 | 62.60 | 70.50 |
| 0854 | 3" thick | | 800 | .120 | | 55 | 4.03 | 3.23 | 62.26 | 70.50 |
| 1000 | Pavement replacement over trench, 2" thick | B-37 | 90 | .533 | S.Y. | 5.85 | 17 | 1.45 | 24.30 | 34.50 |
| 1050 | 4" thick | | 70 | .686 | | 11.55 | 22 | 1.86 | 35.41 | 48.50 |
| 1080 | 6" thick | | 55 | .873 | | 18.40 | 28 | 2.37 | 48.77 | 65.50 |

### 32 12 16.14 Asphaltic Concrete Paving, Parking Lots and Driveways

| | | Crew | Daily Output | Labor-Hours | Unit | Material | 2008 Bare Costs Labor | Equipment | Total | Total Incl O&P |
|---|---|---|---|---|---|---|---|---|---|---|
| 0011 | **ASPHALTIC CONCRETE PAVING, PARKING LOTS & DRIVEWAYS** | | | | | | | | | |
| 0020 | 6" stone base, 2" binder course, 1" topping | B-25C | 9000 | .005 | S.F. | 2.08 | .18 | .23 | 2.49 | 2.82 |
| 0300 | Binder course, 1-1/2" thick | | 35000 | .001 | | .47 | .05 | .06 | .58 | .65 |
| 0400 | 2" thick | | 25000 | .002 | | .61 | .06 | .08 | .75 | .86 |
| 0500 | 3" thick | | 15000 | .003 | | .95 | .11 | .14 | 1.20 | 1.36 |
| 0600 | 4" thick | | 10800 | .004 | | 1.24 | .15 | .19 | 1.58 | 1.80 |
| 0800 | Sand finish course, 3/4" thick | | 41000 | .001 | | .26 | .04 | .05 | .35 | .41 |
| 0900 | 1" thick | | 34000 | .001 | | .32 | .05 | .06 | .43 | .50 |
| 1000 | Fill pot holes, hot mix, 2" thick | B-16 | 4200 | .008 | | .68 | .24 | .12 | 1.04 | 1.25 |
| 1100 | 4" thick | | 3500 | .009 | | .99 | .28 | .14 | 1.41 | 1.69 |
| 1120 | 6" thick | | 3100 | .010 | | 1.33 | .32 | .16 | 1.81 | 2.14 |
| 1140 | Cold patch, 2" thick | B-51 | 3000 | .016 | | .69 | .49 | .06 | 1.24 | 1.59 |
| 1160 | 4" thick | | 2700 | .018 | | 1.31 | .54 | .07 | 1.92 | 2.35 |
| 1180 | 6" thick | | 1900 | .025 | | 2.04 | .77 | .09 | 2.90 | 3.54 |

# 32 13 Rigid Paving

## 32 13 13 – Concrete Paving

### 32 13 13.23 Concrete Paving Surface Treatment

| | | Crew | Daily Output | Labor-Hours | Unit | Material | 2008 Bare Costs Labor | Equipment | Total | Total Incl O&P |
|---|---|---|---|---|---|---|---|---|---|---|
| 0010 | **CONCRETE PAVING SURFACE TREATMENT** | | | | | | | | | |
| 0015 | Including joints, finishing and curing | | | | | | | | | |
| 0020 | Fixed form, 12' pass, unreinforced, 6" thick | B-26 | 3000 | .029 | S.Y. | 21.50 | 1 | .99 | 23.49 | 26.50 |
| 0100 | 8" thick | | 2750 | .032 | | 32 | 1.09 | 1.08 | 34.17 | 38 |
| 0110 | 8" thick, small area | | 1375 | .064 | | 32 | 2.17 | 2.17 | 36.34 | 41 |
| 0200 | 9" thick | | 2500 | .035 | | 36 | 1.20 | 1.19 | 38.39 | 42.50 |
| 0300 | 10" thick | | 2100 | .042 | | 39 | 1.42 | 1.42 | 41.84 | 47 |
| 0310 | 10" thick, small area | | 1050 | .084 | | 39 | 2.85 | 2.84 | 44.69 | 50.50 |
| 0400 | 12" thick | | 1800 | .049 | | 44.50 | 1.66 | 1.66 | 47.82 | 53.50 |
| 0410 | Conc pavement, w/jt,fnsh&curing,fix form,24' pass,unreinforced,6"T | | 6000 | .015 | | 19.95 | .50 | .50 | 20.95 | 23.50 |

# 32 13 Rigid Paving

## 32 13 13 – Concrete Paving

| 32 13 13.23 Concrete Paving Surface Treatment | | Crew | Daily Output | Labor-Hours | Unit | Material | 2008 Bare Costs Labor | Equipment | Total | Total Incl O&P |
|---|---|---|---|---|---|---|---|---|---|---|
| 0430 | 8" thick | B-26 | 5500 | .016 | S.Y. | 29 | .54 | .54 | 30.08 | 33 |
| 0440 | 9" thick | | 5000 | .018 | | 33 | .60 | .60 | 34.20 | 37.50 |
| 0450 | 10" thick | | 4200 | .021 | | 36 | .71 | .71 | 37.42 | 41.50 |
| 0460 | 12" thick | | 3600 | .024 | | 41.50 | .83 | .83 | 43.16 | 47.50 |
| 0470 | 15" thick | | 3000 | .029 | | 54.50 | 1 | .99 | 56.49 | 62.50 |
| 0500 | Fixed form 12' pass 15" thick | | 1500 | .059 | | 57.50 | 1.99 | 1.99 | 61.48 | 68.50 |
| 0510 | For small irregular areas, add | | | | % | | 100% | | | . |
| 0520 | Welded wire fabric, sheets for rigid paving 2.33 lbs/SY | 2 Rodm | 389 | .041 | S.Y. | 1.19 | 1.77 | | 2.96 | 4.21 |
| 0530 | Reinforcing steel for rigid paving 12 lbs/SY | | 666 | .024 | | 5.90 | 1.03 | | 6.93 | 8.20 |
| 0540 | Reinforcing steel for rigid paving 18 lbs/SY | | 444 | .036 | | 8.85 | 1.55 | | 10.40 | 12.30 |
| 0620 | Slip form, 12' pass, unreinforced, 6" thick | B-26A | 5600 | .016 | | 21 | .53 | .56 | 22.09 | 24.50 |
| 0624 | 8" thick | | 5300 | .017 | | 31 | .56 | .59 | 32.15 | 35.50 |
| 0626 | 9" thick | | 4820 | .018 | | 35 | .62 | .65 | 36.27 | 40 |
| 0628 | 10" thick | | 4050 | .022 | | 38 | .74 | .77 | 39.51 | 44 |
| 0630 | 12" thick | | 3470 | .025 | | 43.50 | .86 | .90 | 45.26 | 50.50 |
| 0632 | 15" thick | | 2890 | .030 | | 56 | 1.03 | 1.08 | 58.11 | 64.50 |
| 0640 | Slip form, 24' pass, unreinforced, 6" thick | | 11200 | .008 | | 20 | .27 | .28 | 20.55 | 22.50 |
| 0644 | 8" thick | | 10600 | .008 | | 28.50 | .28 | .29 | 29.07 | 32 |
| 0646 | 9" thick | | 9640 | .009 | | 32.50 | .31 | .32 | 33.13 | 36.50 |
| 0648 | 10" thick | | 8100 | .011 | | 35.50 | .37 | .38 | 36.25 | 40 |
| 0650 | 12" thick | | 6940 | .013 | | 41 | .43 | .45 | 41.88 | 46 |
| 0652 | 15" thick | | 5780 | .015 | | 52 | .52 | .54 | 53.06 | 59 |
| 0700 | Finishing, broom finish small areas | 2 Cefi | 120 | .133 | | | 4.93 | | 4.93 | 7.25 |
| 1000 | Curing, with sprayed membrane by hand | 2 Clab | 1500 | .011 | | .43 | .32 | | .75 | .97 |
| 1650 | For integral coloring, see Div. 03 31 05.35 | | | | | | | | | |

# 32 14 Unit Paving

## 32 14 13 – Precast Concrete Unit Paving

### 32 14 13.13 Interlocking Precast Concrete Unit Paving

| 0010 | **INTERLOCKING PRECAST CONCRETE UNIT PAVING** | | | | | | | | | |
|---|---|---|---|---|---|---|---|---|---|---|
| 0020 | "V" blocks for retaining soil | D-1 | 205 | .078 | S.F. | 7.80 | 2.72 | | 10.52 | 12.75 |

### 32 14 13.16 Precast Concrete Unit Paving Slabs

| 0010 | **PRECAST CONCRETE UNIT PAVING SLABS** | | | | | | | | | |
|---|---|---|---|---|---|---|---|---|---|---|
| 0710 | Precast concrete patio blocks, 2-3/8" thick, colors, 8" x 16" | D-1 | 265 | .060 | S.F. | 1.36 | 2.11 | | 3.47 | 4.70 |
| 0750 | Exposed local aggregate, natural | 2 Bric | 250 | .064 | | 5.85 | 2.51 | | 8.36 | 10.25 |
| 0800 | Colors | | 250 | .064 | | 6.40 | 2.51 | | 8.91 | 10.85 |
| 0850 | Exposed granite or limestone aggregate | | 250 | .064 | | 7.10 | 2.51 | | 9.61 | 11.60 |
| 0900 | Exposed white tumblestone aggregate | | 250 | .064 | | 4.18 | 2.51 | | 6.69 | 8.40 |

## 32 14 16 – Brick Unit Paving

### 32 14 16.10 Brick Paving

| 0010 | **BRICK PAVING** | | | | | | | | | |
|---|---|---|---|---|---|---|---|---|---|---|
| 0012 | 4" x 8" x 1-1/2", without joints (4.5 brick/S.F.) | D-1 | 110 | .145 | S.F. | 2.78 | 5.05 | | 7.83 | 10.75 |
| 0100 | Grouted, 3/8" joint (3.9 brick/S.F.) | | 90 | .178 | | 3.38 | 6.20 | | 9.58 | 13.15 |
| 0200 | 4" x 8" x 2-1/4", without joints (4.5 bricks/S.F.) | | 110 | .145 | | 3.74 | 5.05 | | 8.79 | 11.80 |
| 0300 | Grouted, 3/8" joint (3.9 brick/S.F.) | | 90 | .178 | | 3.45 | 6.20 | | 9.65 | 13.25 |
| 0500 | Bedding, asphalt, 3/4" thick | B-25 | 5130 | .017 | | .52 | .57 | .46 | 1.55 | 1.95 |
| 0540 | Course washed sand bed, 1" thick | B-18 | 5000 | .005 | | .26 | .15 | .01 | .42 | .53 |
| 0580 | Mortar, 1" thick | D-1 | 300 | .053 | | .64 | 1.86 | | 2.50 | 3.53 |
| 0620 | 2" thick | | 200 | .080 | | 1.27 | 2.79 | | 4.06 | 5.65 |
| 1500 | Brick on 1" thick sand bed laid flat, 4.5 per S.F. | | 100 | .160 | | 2.81 | 5.60 | | 8.41 | 11.60 |

# 32 14 Unit Paving

## 32 14 16 – Brick Unit Paving

### 32 14 16.10 Brick Paving

| | | Crew | Daily Output | Labor-Hours | Unit | Material | 2008 Bare Costs Labor | Equipment | Total | Total Incl O&P |
|---|---|---|---|---|---|---|---|---|---|---|
| 2000 | Brick pavers, laid on edge, 7.2 per S.F. | D-1 | 70 | .229 | S.F. | 2.70 | 7.95 | | 10.65 | 15.10 |
| 2500 | For 4" thick concrete bed and joints, add | ↓ | 595 | .027 | | 1.20 | .94 | | 2.14 | 2.74 |
| 2800 | For steam cleaning, add | A-1H | 950 | .008 | ↓ | .06 | .25 | .07 | .38 | .54 |

## 32 14 23 – Asphalt Unit Paving

### 32 14 23.10 Asphalt Blocks

| | | Crew | Daily Output | Labor-Hours | Unit | Material | 2008 Bare Costs Labor | Equipment | Total | Total Incl O&P |
|---|---|---|---|---|---|---|---|---|---|---|
| 0010 | **ASPHALT BLOCKS** | | | | | | | | | |
| 0020 | Rectangular, 6" x 12" x 1-1/4", w/bed & neopr. adhesive | D-1 | 135 | .119 | S.F. | 6.65 | 4.13 | | 10.78 | 13.65 |
| 0100 | 3" thick | | 130 | .123 | | 9.35 | 4.29 | | 13.64 | 16.80 |
| 0300 | Hexagonal tile, 8" wide, 1-1/4" thick | | 135 | .119 | | 6.65 | 4.13 | | 10.78 | 13.65 |
| 0400 | 2" thick | | 130 | .123 | | 9.35 | 4.29 | | 13.64 | 16.80 |
| 0500 | Square, 8" x 8", 1-1/4" thick | | 135 | .119 | | 6.65 | 4.13 | | 10.78 | 13.65 |
| 0600 | 2" thick | ↓ | 130 | .123 | | 9.35 | 4.29 | | 13.64 | 16.80 |
| 0900 | For exposed aggregate (ground finish) add | | | | | .46 | | | .46 | .51 |
| 0910 | For colors, add | | | | ↓ | .35 | | | .35 | .39 |

## 32 14 40 – Stone Paving

### 32 14 40.10 Stone Pavers

| | | Crew | Daily Output | Labor-Hours | Unit | Material | 2008 Bare Costs Labor | Equipment | Total | Total Incl O&P |
|---|---|---|---|---|---|---|---|---|---|---|
| 0010 | **STONE PAVERS** | | | | | | | | | |
| 1100 | Flagging, bluestone, irregular, 1" thick, | D-1 | 81 | .198 | S.F. | 5.95 | 6.90 | | 12.85 | 17.05 |
| 1150 | Snapped random rectangular, 1" thick | | 92 | .174 | | 9 | 6.05 | | 15.05 | 19.15 |
| 1200 | 1-1/2" thick | | 85 | .188 | | 10.80 | 6.55 | | 17.35 | 22 |
| 1250 | 2" thick | | 83 | .193 | | 12.60 | 6.70 | | 19.30 | 24 |
| 1300 | Slate, natural cleft, irregular, 3/4" thick | | 92 | .174 | | 6.65 | 6.05 | | 12.70 | 16.55 |
| 1350 | Random rectangular, gauged, 1/2" thick | | 105 | .152 | | 14.35 | 5.30 | | 19.65 | 24 |
| 1400 | Random rectangular, butt joint, gauged, 1/4" thick | ↓ | 150 | .107 | ↓ | 15.45 | 3.72 | | 19.17 | 22.50 |
| 1500 | For interior setting, add | | | | | | | | 25% | 25% |
| 1550 | Granite blocks, 3-1/2" x 3-1/2" x 3-1/2" | D-1 | 92 | .174 | S.F. | 8.05 | 6.05 | | 14.10 | 18.10 |
| 1600 | 4" to 12" long, 3" to 5" wide, 3" to 5" thick | | 98 | .163 | | 6.70 | 5.70 | | 12.40 | 16.05 |
| 1650 | 6" to 15" long, 3" to 6" wide, 3" to 5" thick | ↓ | 105 | .152 | | 3.58 | 5.30 | | 8.88 | 12.05 |

# 32 16 Curbs and Gutters

## 32 16 13 – Concrete Curbs and Gutters

### 32 16 13.13 Cast-in-Place Concrete Curbs and Gutters

| | | Crew | Daily Output | Labor-Hours | Unit | Material | 2008 Bare Costs Labor | Equipment | Total | Total Incl O&P |
|---|---|---|---|---|---|---|---|---|---|---|
| 0010 | **CAST-IN-PLACE CONCRETE CURBS AND GUTTERS** | | | | | | | | | |
| 0300 | Concrete, wood forms, 6" x 18", straight | C-2A | 500 | .096 | L.F. | 3.73 | 3.55 | | 7.28 | 9.55 |
| 0400 | 6" x 18", radius | | 200 | .240 | | 3.83 | 8.85 | | 12.68 | 17.85 |
| 0410 | Steel forms, 6" x 18", straight | | 700 | .069 | | 4.30 | 2.53 | | 6.83 | 8.65 |
| 0411 | 6" x 18", radius | ↓ | 400 | .120 | | 4.42 | 4.43 | | 8.85 | 11.70 |
| 0415 | Machine formed, 6" x 18", straight | B-69A | 2000 | .024 | | 3.87 | .80 | .37 | 5.04 | 5.90 |
| 0416 | 6" x 18", radius | " | 900 | .053 | ↓ | 4.04 | 1.78 | .82 | 6.64 | 8.05 |
| 0421 | Curb and gutter, straight | | | | | | | | | |
| 0422 | with 6" high curb and 6" thick gutter, wood forms | | | | | | | | | |
| 0430 | 24" wide, .055 C.Y. per L.F. | C-2A | 375 | .128 | L.F. | 15.30 | 4.73 | | 20.03 | 24 |
| 0435 | 30" wide, .066 C.Y. per L.F. | | 340 | .141 | | 16.75 | 5.20 | | 21.95 | 26.50 |
| 0440 | Steel forms, 24" wide, straight | | 700 | .069 | | 6.30 | 2.53 | | 8.83 | 10.85 |
| 0441 | Radius | | 300 | .160 | | 6.30 | 5.90 | | 12.20 | 16.05 |
| 0442 | 30" wide, straight | | 700 | .069 | | 7.60 | 2.53 | | 10.13 | 12.25 |
| 0443 | Radius | ↓ | 300 | .160 | | 7.60 | 5.90 | | 13.50 | 17.45 |
| 0445 | Machine formed, 24" wide, straight | B-69A | 2000 | .024 | | 6.30 | .80 | .37 | 7.47 | 8.55 |
| 0446 | Radius | | 900 | .053 | | 6.30 | 1.78 | .82 | 8.90 | 10.55 |
| 0447 | 30" wide, straight | ↓ | 2000 | .024 | ↓ | 7.60 | .80 | .37 | 8.77 | 9.95 |

# RSMEANS 2008
# Job Order Contracting (JOC)

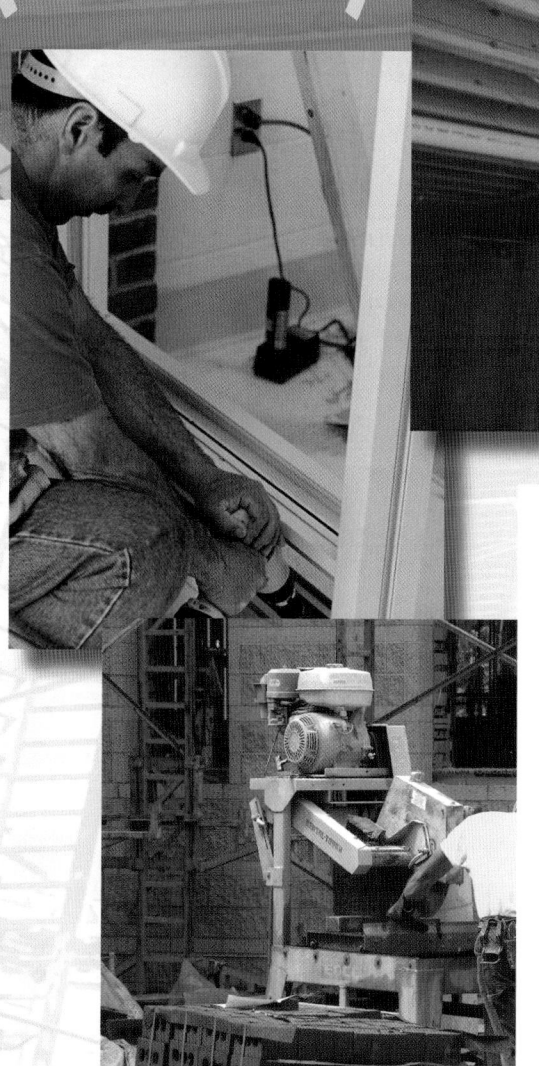

Job Order Contracting (JOC), used in the municipal, education, healthcare and federal sectors, is the preferred delivery method for quickly and effectively reducing the backlog of renovation projects. For organizations considering the productivity gains realized with JOC, RSMeans Business Solutions offers project management services, training and JOCWorks™ for renovation estimating. JOCWorks™ software improves productivity by developing estimates faster and tracking projects in one system.

**RSMeans** Business Solutions

Reed Construction Data®

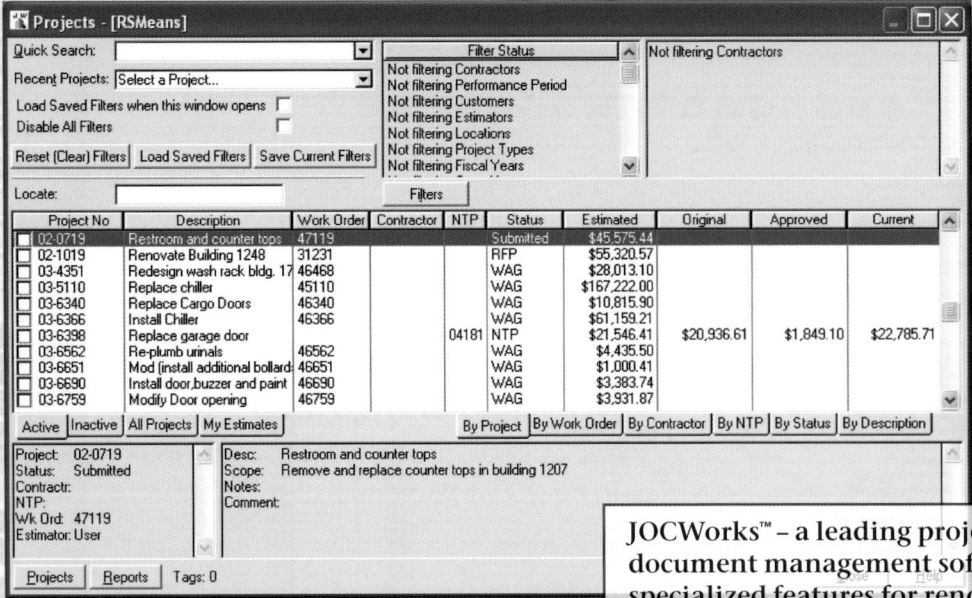

JOCWorks™ – a leading project management and document management software program with specialized features for renovation and repair projects.

# Facility-Owner Benefits of Adopting JOC

- Dramatically reduces the backlog of renovation projects

- Reduces administrative costs by accomplishing more projects with the same team

- Leverages purchasing and maintenance tasks

- Dramatically reduces change orders

- Decreases up-front design and administrative costs and time

- Eliminates multiple project solicitation

- Minimizes construction claims

- Dramatically increases facility productivity

## RSMeans services for developing a JOC System

*A JOC-Knowledgeable Staff:* Facility Management staffs must have knowledge of the JOC process, how to interact with JOC contractors, and the concept of partnering that is integral to successful JOCs. This requires familiarity with the master bidding document (i.e., Unit Price Book) and the development of JOC project specifications and contracts.

*The RSMeans Unit Price Book (UPB):* This customized document is the line-item listing of JOC tasks and the components of those tasks. When both the JOC client and contractor agree to this document, negotiations are reduced to project-specific peculiarities.

*Training Programs:* JOC-specific training programs to understand how to organize a JOC program, how to effectively use RSMeans Unit Price Book for JOC, and how to use JOCWorks™ Software.

**RSMeans** Business Solutions

℞ Reed Construction Data®

# 32 16 Curbs and Gutters

## 32 16 13 – Concrete Curbs and Gutters

| 32 16 13.13 Cast-in-Place Concrete Curbs and Gutters | Crew | Daily Output | Labor-Hours | Unit | Material | 2008 Bare Costs Labor | Equipment | Total | Total Incl O&P |
|---|---|---|---|---|---|---|---|---|---|
| 0448 Radius | B-69A | 900 | .053 | L.F. | 7.60 | 1.78 | .82 | 10.20 | 11.95 |

### 32 16 13.26 Precast Concrete Curbs

| | Crew | Daily Output | Labor-Hours | Unit | Material | Labor | Equipment | Total | Total Incl O&P |
|---|---|---|---|---|---|---|---|---|---|
| 0010 **PRECAST CONCRETE CURBS** | | | | | | | | | |
| 0550 Precast, 6" x 18", straight | B-29 | 700 | .080 | L.F. | 9.50 | 2.62 | 1.33 | 13.45 | 15.95 |
| 0600 6" x 18", radius | " | 325 | .172 | " | 10.90 | 5.65 | 2.87 | 19.42 | 24 |

## 32 16 19 – Asphalt Curbs

### 32 16 19.10 Bituminous Concrete Curbs

| | Crew | Daily Output | Labor-Hours | Unit | Material | Labor | Equipment | Total | Total Incl O&P |
|---|---|---|---|---|---|---|---|---|---|
| 0010 **BITUMINOUS CONCRETE CURBS** | | | | | | | | | |
| 0012 Curbs, asphaltic, machine formed, 8" wide, 6" high, 40 L.F./ton | B-27 | 1000 | .032 | L.F. | 1.10 | .98 | .26 | 2.34 | 3.03 |
| 0100 8" wide, 8" high, 30 L.F. per ton | | 900 | .036 | | 1.27 | 1.09 | .29 | 2.65 | 3.41 |
| 0150 Asphaltic berm, 12" W, 3"-6" H, 35 L.F./ton, before pavement | | 700 | .046 | | 1.27 | 1.41 | .38 | 3.06 | 3.99 |
| 0200 12" W, 1-1/2" to 4" H, 60 L.F. per ton, laid with pavement | B-2 | 1050 | .038 | | .77 | 1.17 | | 1.94 | 2.67 |

## 32 16 40 – Stone Curbs

### 32 16 40.13 Cut Stone Curbs

| | Crew | Daily Output | Labor-Hours | Unit | Material | Labor | Equipment | Total | Total Incl O&P |
|---|---|---|---|---|---|---|---|---|---|
| 0010 **CUT STONE CURBS** | | | | | | | | | |
| 1000 Granite, split face, straight, 5" x 16" | D-13 | 500 | .096 | L.F. | 11.15 | 3.53 | 1.22 | 15.90 | 19.05 |
| 1100 6" x 18" | " | 450 | .107 | | 14.65 | 3.92 | 1.36 | 19.93 | 23.50 |
| 1300 Radius curbing, 6" x 18", over 10' radius | B-29 | 260 | .215 | | 17.95 | 7.05 | 3.59 | 28.59 | 34.50 |
| 1400 Corners, 2' radius | | 80 | .700 | Ea. | 60.50 | 23 | 11.65 | 95.15 | 115 |
| 1600 Edging, 4-1/2" x 12", straight | | 300 | .187 | L.F. | 5.60 | 6.10 | 3.11 | 14.81 | 18.95 |
| 1800 Curb inlets, (guttermouth) straight | | 41 | 1.366 | Ea. | 134 | 45 | 22.50 | 201.50 | 241 |
| 2000 Indian granite (belgian block) | | | | | | | | | |
| 2100 Jumbo, 10-1/2" x 7-1/2" x 4", grey | D-1 | 150 | .107 | L.F. | 2.05 | 3.72 | | 5.77 | 7.90 |
| 2150 Pink | | 150 | .107 | | 2.66 | 3.72 | | 6.38 | 8.60 |
| 2200 Regular, 9" x 4-1/2" x 4-1/2", grey | | 160 | .100 | | 1.86 | 3.49 | | 5.35 | 7.35 |
| 2250 Pink | | 160 | .100 | | 2.55 | 3.49 | | 6.04 | 8.10 |
| 2300 Cubes, 4" x 4" x 4", grey | | 175 | .091 | | 1.77 | 3.19 | | 4.96 | 6.80 |
| 2350 Pink | | 175 | .091 | | 1.85 | 3.19 | | 5.04 | 6.90 |
| 2400 6" x 6" x 6", pink | | 155 | .103 | | 4.59 | 3.60 | | 8.19 | 10.55 |
| 2500 Alternate pricing method for indian granite | | | | | | | | | |
| 2550 Jumbo, 10-1/2" x 7-1/2" x 4" (30 lb), grey | | | | Ton | 117 | | | 117 | 128 |
| 2600 Pink | | | | | 155 | | | 155 | 170 |
| 2650 Regular, 9" x 4-1/2" x 4-1/2" (20 lb), grey | | | | | 131 | | | 131 | 144 |
| 2700 Pink | | | | | 179 | | | 179 | 196 |
| 2750 Cubes, 4" x 4" x 4" (5 lb), grey | | | | | 214 | | | 214 | 236 |
| 2800 Pink | | | | | 238 | | | 238 | 262 |
| 2850 6" x 6" x 6" (25 lb), pink | | | | | 179 | | | 179 | 196 |
| 2900 For pallets, add | | | | | 18.90 | | | 18.90 | 20.79 |

# 32 17 Paving Specialties

## 32 17 13 – Parking Bumpers

### 32 17 13.13 Metal Parking Bumpers

| | Crew | Daily Output | Labor-Hours | Unit | Material | Labor | Equipment | Total | Total Incl O&P |
|---|---|---|---|---|---|---|---|---|---|
| 0010 **METAL PARKING BUMPERS** | | | | | | | | | |
| 0015 Bumper rails for garages, 12 Ga. rail, 6" wide, with steel | | | | | | | | | |
| 0020 posts 12'-6" O.C., minimum | E-4 | 190 | .168 | L.F. | 14.90 | 7.35 | .70 | 22.95 | 30.50 |
| 0030 Average | | 165 | .194 | | 18.65 | 8.45 | .80 | 27.90 | 36.50 |
| 0100 Maximum | | 140 | .229 | | 22.50 | 9.95 | .94 | 33.39 | 43.50 |
| 0300 12" channel rail, minimum | | 160 | .200 | | 18.65 | 8.70 | .83 | 28.18 | 37 |
| 0400 Maximum | | 120 | .267 | | 28 | 11.60 | 1.10 | 40.70 | 52.50 |
| 1300 Pipe bollards, conc filled/paint, 8' L x 4' D hole, 6" diam. | B-6 | 20 | 1.200 | Ea. | 340 | 39.50 | 14.25 | 393.75 | 450 |

# 32 17 Paving Specialties

## 32 17 13 – Parking Bumpers

### 32 17 13.13 Metal Parking Bumpers

| | | Crew | Daily Output | Labor-Hours | Unit | Material | 2008 Bare Costs Labor | 2008 Bare Costs Equipment | Total | Total Incl O&P |
|---|---|---|---|---|---|---|---|---|---|---|
| 1400 | 8" diam. | B-6 | 15 | 1.600 | Ea. | 515 | 52.50 | 19 | 586.50 | 670 |
| 1500 | 12" diam. | | 12 | 2 | | 670 | 65.50 | 24 | 759.50 | 865 |
| 1592 | Bollards, steel, 3' H, retractable, incl hydraulic controls, min | | 4 | 6 | | 33,900 | 197 | 71.50 | 34,168.50 | 37,700 |
| 1594 | Max | | 2 | 12 | | 37,800 | 395 | 143 | 38,338 | 42,300 |
| 2030 | Folding with individual padlocks | B-2 | 50 | .800 | | 825 | 24.50 | | 849.50 | 950 |
| 8000 | Parking lot control, see Div. 11 12 13.10 | | | | | | | | | |

### 32 17 13.16 Plastic Parking Bumpers

| | | Crew | Daily Output | Labor-Hours | Unit | Material | 2008 Bare Costs Labor | 2008 Bare Costs Equipment | Total | Total Incl O&P |
|---|---|---|---|---|---|---|---|---|---|---|
| 0010 | **PLASTIC PARKING BUMPERS** | | | | | | | | | |
| 1200 | Thermoplastic, 6" x 10" x 6'-0" | B-2 | 120 | .333 | Ea. | 90 | 10.20 | | 100.20 | 115 |

### 32 17 13.19 Precast Concrete Parking Bumpers

| | | Crew | Daily Output | Labor-Hours | Unit | Material | 2008 Bare Costs Labor | 2008 Bare Costs Equipment | Total | Total Incl O&P |
|---|---|---|---|---|---|---|---|---|---|---|
| 0010 | **PRECAST CONCRETE PARKING BUMPERS** | | | | | | | | | |
| 1000 | Wheel stops, precast concrete incl. dowels, 6" x 10" x 6'-0" | B-2 | 120 | .333 | Ea. | 49 | 10.20 | | 59.20 | 69.50 |
| 1100 | 8" x 13" x 6'-0" | " | 120 | .333 | " | 56.50 | 10.20 | | 66.70 | 78 |

### 32 17 13.26 Wood Parking Bumpers

| | | Crew | Daily Output | Labor-Hours | Unit | Material | 2008 Bare Costs Labor | 2008 Bare Costs Equipment | Total | Total Incl O&P |
|---|---|---|---|---|---|---|---|---|---|---|
| 0010 | **WOOD PARKING BUMPERS** | | | | | | | | | |
| 0020 | Parking barriers, timber w/saddles, treated type | | | | | | | | | |
| 0100 | 4" x 4" for cars | B-2 | 520 | .077 | L.F. | 2.75 | 2.36 | | 5.11 | 6.70 |
| 0200 | 6" x 6" for trucks | | 520 | .077 | " | 5.70 | 2.36 | | 8.06 | 9.95 |
| 0600 | Flexible fixed stanchion, 2' high, 3" diameter | | 100 | .400 | Ea. | 29 | 12.25 | | 41.25 | 51 |

## 32 17 23 – Pavement Markings

### 32 17 23.13 Painted Pavement Markings

| | | Crew | Daily Output | Labor-Hours | Unit | Material | 2008 Bare Costs Labor | 2008 Bare Costs Equipment | Total | Total Incl O&P |
|---|---|---|---|---|---|---|---|---|---|---|
| 0010 | **PAINTED PAVEMENT MARKINGS** | | | | | | | | | |
| 0020 | Acrylic waterborne, white or yellow, 4" wide | B-78 | 20000 | .002 | L.F. | .15 | .07 | .02 | .24 | .31 |
| 0200 | 6" wide | | 11000 | .004 | | .14 | .13 | .04 | .31 | .41 |
| 0500 | 8" wide | | 10000 | .005 | | .20 | .15 | .05 | .40 | .49 |
| 0600 | 12" wide | | 4000 | .012 | | .36 | .37 | .12 | .85 | 1.10 |
| 0620 | Arrows or gore lines | | 2300 | .021 | S.F. | .58 | .64 | .21 | 1.43 | 1.86 |
| 0640 | Temporary paint, white or yellow | | 15000 | .003 | L.F. | .19 | .10 | .03 | .32 | .40 |
| 0660 | Removal | 1 Clab | 300 | .027 | | | .81 | | .81 | 1.25 |
| 0680 | Temporary tape | 2 Clab | 1500 | .011 | | 1.69 | .32 | | 2.01 | 2.36 |
| 0710 | Thermoplastic, white or yellow, 4" wide | B-79 | 15000 | .003 | | .68 | .08 | .07 | .83 | .96 |
| 0730 | 6" wide | | 14000 | .003 | | .99 | .09 | .08 | 1.16 | 1.31 |
| 0740 | 8" wide | | 12000 | .003 | | 1.33 | .10 | .09 | 1.52 | 1.72 |
| 0750 | 12" wide | | 6000 | .007 | | 1.97 | .20 | .19 | 2.36 | 2.69 |
| 0760 | Arrows | | 660 | .061 | S.F. | 1.78 | 1.85 | 1.69 | 5.32 | 6.70 |
| 0770 | Gore lines | | 2500 | .016 | | 1.18 | .49 | .45 | 2.12 | 2.55 |
| 0780 | Letters | | 660 | .061 | | 1.47 | 1.85 | 1.69 | 5.01 | 6.35 |
| 1000 | Airport painted markings | | | | | | | | | |
| 1100 | Painting, white or yellow, taxiway markings | B-79 | 4000 | .010 | S.F. | .15 | .30 | .28 | .73 | .95 |
| 1200 | Runway markings | | 3500 | .011 | | .15 | .35 | .32 | .82 | 1.06 |
| 1300 | Pavement location or direction signs | | 2500 | .016 | | .15 | .49 | .45 | 1.09 | 1.42 |
| 1350 | Mobilization airport pavement painting | | 4 | 10 | Ea. | | 305 | 278 | 583 | 780 |
| 1400 | Paint markings or pavement signs removal daytime | B-78B | 400 | .045 | S.F. | | 1.40 | .77 | 2.17 | 3.01 |
| 1500 | Removal nighttime | | 335 | .054 | " | | 1.67 | .91 | 2.58 | 3.59 |
| 1600 | Mobilization pavement paint removal | | 4 | 4.500 | Ea. | | 140 | 76.50 | 216.50 | 300 |

### 32 17 23.14 Pavement Parking Markings

| | | Crew | Daily Output | Labor-Hours | Unit | Material | 2008 Bare Costs Labor | 2008 Bare Costs Equipment | Total | Total Incl O&P |
|---|---|---|---|---|---|---|---|---|---|---|
| 0010 | **PAVEMENT PARKING MARKINGS** | | | | | | | | | |
| 0790 | Layout of pavement marking | A-2 | 25000 | .001 | L.F. | | .03 | .01 | .04 | .05 |
| 0800 | Lines on pvmt, parking stall, paint, white, 4" wide | B-78 | 440 | .109 | Stall | 3.09 | 3.32 | 1.08 | 7.49 | 9.75 |
| 1000 | Street letters and numbers | " | 1600 | .030 | S.F. | .59 | .91 | .30 | 1.80 | 2.40 |

# 32 18 Athletic and Recreational Surfacing

## 32 18 13 – Synthetic Grass Surfacing

### 32 18 13.10 Artificial Grass Surfacing

| 32 18 13.10 Artificial Grass Surfacing | Crew | Daily Output | Labor-Hours | Unit | Material | 2008 Bare Costs Labor | Equipment | Total | Total Incl O&P |
|---|---|---|---|---|---|---|---|---|---|
| 0010 **ARTIFICIAL GRASS SURFACING** | | | | | | | | | |
| 0015 Not including asphalt base or drainage, | | | | | | | | | |
| 0020 but including cushion pad, over 50,000 S.F. | | | | | | | | | |
| 0200 1/2" pile and 5/16" cushion pad, standard | C-17 | 3200 | .025 | S.F. | 8.95 | 1 | | 9.95 | 11.40 |
| 0300 Deluxe | | 2560 | .031 | | 10.60 | 1.24 | | 11.84 | 13.60 |
| 0500 1/2" pile and 5/8" cushion pad, standard | | 2844 | .028 | | 13.05 | 1.12 | | 14.17 | 16.10 |
| 0600 Deluxe | | 2327 | .034 | | 14.25 | 1.37 | | 15.62 | 17.85 |
| 0800 For asphaltic concrete base, 2-1/2" thick, | | | | | | | | | |
| 0900 with 6" crushed stone sub-base, add | B-25 | 12000 | .007 | S.F. | 1.88 | .24 | .20 | 2.32 | 2.66 |

## 32 18 23 – Athletic Surfacing

### 32 18 23.33 Running Track Surfacing

| 32 18 23.33 Running Track Surfacing | Crew | Daily Output | Labor-Hours | Unit | Material | Labor | Equipment | Total | Total Incl O&P |
|---|---|---|---|---|---|---|---|---|---|
| 0010 **RUNNING TRACK SURFACING** | | | | | | | | | |
| 0020 Running track, asphalt, incl base, 3" thick | B-37 | 300 | .160 | S.Y. | 19.05 | 5.10 | .43 | 24.58 | 29.50 |
| 0100 Surface, latex rubber system, 3/8" thick, black | B-20 | 125 | .192 | | 8.60 | 6.50 | | 15.10 | 19.60 |
| 0150 Colors | | 125 | .192 | | 15.25 | 6.50 | | 21.75 | 27 |
| 0300 Urethane rubber system, 3/8" thick, black | | 120 | .200 | | 23 | 6.80 | | 29.80 | 35.50 |
| 0400 Color coating | | 115 | .209 | | 27 | 7.10 | | 34.10 | 41 |

### 32 18 23.53 Tennis Court Surfacing

| 32 18 23.53 Tennis Court Surfacing | Crew | Daily Output | Labor-Hours | Unit | Material | Labor | Equipment | Total | Total Incl O&P |
|---|---|---|---|---|---|---|---|---|---|
| 0010 **TENNIS COURT SURFACING** | | | | | | | | | |
| 0020 Tennis court, asphalt, incl. base, 2-1/2" thick, one court | B-37 | 450 | .107 | S.Y. | 23 | 3.40 | .29 | 26.69 | 31 |
| 0200 Two courts | | 675 | .071 | | 10.45 | 2.26 | .19 | 12.90 | 15.20 |
| 0300 Clay courts | | 360 | .133 | | 34.50 | 4.24 | .36 | 39.10 | 45 |
| 0400 Pulverized natural greenstone with 4" base, fast dry | | 250 | .192 | | 33 | 6.10 | .52 | 39.62 | 46.50 |
| 0800 Rubber-acrylic base resilient pavement | | 600 | .080 | | 45.50 | 2.55 | .22 | 48.27 | 54.50 |
| 1000 Colored sealer, acrylic emulsion, 3 coats | 2 Clab | 800 | .020 | | 5.50 | .61 | | 6.11 | 7 |
| 1100 3 coat, 2 colors | " | 900 | .018 | | 7.65 | .54 | | 8.19 | 9.25 |
| 1200 For preparing old courts, add | 1 Clab | 825 | .010 | | | .29 | | .29 | .46 |
| 1400 Posts for nets, 3-1/2" diameter with eye bolts | B-1 | 3.40 | 7.059 | Pr. | 193 | 218 | | 411 | 550 |
| 1500 With pulley & reel | | 3.40 | 7.059 | " | 274 | 218 | | 492 | 640 |
| 1700 Net, 42' long, nylon thread with binder | | 50 | .480 | Ea. | 254 | 14.85 | | 268.85 | 305 |
| 1800 All metal | | 6.50 | 3.692 | " | 450 | 114 | | 564 | 675 |
| 2000 Paint markings on asphalt, 2 coats | 1 Pord | 1.78 | 4.494 | Court | 92 | 152 | | 244 | 330 |
| 2200 Complete court with fence, etc., asphaltic conc., minimum | B-37 | .20 | 240 | | 19,600 | 7,650 | 650 | 27,900 | 34,000 |
| 2300 Maximum | | .16 | 300 | | 24,300 | 9,550 | 815 | 34,665 | 42,400 |
| 2800 Clay courts, minimum | | .20 | 240 | | 21,100 | 7,650 | 650 | 29,400 | 35,800 |
| 2900 Maximum | | .16 | 300 | | 25,400 | 9,550 | 815 | 35,765 | 43,600 |

# 32 31 Fences and Gates

## 32 31 13 – Chain Link Fences and Gates

### 32 31 13.20 Fence, Chain Link Industrial

| 32 31 13.20 Fence, Chain Link Industrial | Crew | Daily Output | Labor-Hours | Unit | Material | Labor | Equipment | Total | Total Incl O&P |
|---|---|---|---|---|---|---|---|---|---|
| 0010 **FENCE, CHAIN LINK INDUSTRIAL** | | | | | | | | | |
| 0011 Schedule 40, including concrete | | | | | | | | | |
| 0020 3 strands barb wire, 2" post @ 10' O.C., set in concrete, 6' H | | | | | | | | | |
| 0200 9 ga. wire, galv. steel, in concrete | B-80C | 240 | .100 | L.F. | 14.60 | 3 | .78 | 18.38 | 21.50 |
| 0300 Aluminized steel | | 240 | .100 | | 18.70 | 3 | .78 | 22.48 | 26 |
| 0500 6 ga. wire, galv. steel | | 240 | .100 | | 23 | 3 | .78 | 26.78 | 30.50 |
| 0600 Aluminized steel | | 240 | .100 | | 26 | 3 | .78 | 29.78 | 34 |
| 0800 6 ga. wire, 6' high but omit barbed wire, galv. steel | | 250 | .096 | | 22 | 2.88 | .74 | 25.62 | 30 |
| 0900 Aluminized steel, in concrete | | 250 | .096 | | 31 | 2.88 | .74 | 34.62 | 39.50 |
| 0920 8' H, 6 ga. wire, 2-1/2" line post, galv. steel, in concrete | | 180 | .133 | | 35.50 | 4 | 1.03 | 40.53 | 46.50 |

# 32 31 Fences and Gates

## 32 31 13 – Chain Link Fences and Gates

### 32 31 13.20 Fence, Chain Link Industrial

| | | Crew | Daily Output | Labor-Hours | Unit | Material | 2008 Bare Costs Labor | Equipment | Total | Total Incl O&P |
|---|---|---|---|---|---|---|---|---|---|---|
| 0940 | Aluminized steel, in concrete | B-80C | 180 | .133 | L.F. | 43.50 | 4 | 1.03 | 48.53 | 55 |
| 1100 | Add for corner posts, 3" diam., galv. steel, in concrete | | 40 | .600 | Ea. | 103 | 18 | 4.65 | 125.65 | 146 |
| 1200 | Aluminized steel, in concrete | | 40 | .600 | | 123 | 18 | 4.65 | 145.65 | 168 |
| 1300 | Add for braces, galv. steel | | 80 | .300 | | 27.50 | 9 | 2.33 | 38.83 | 47 |
| 1350 | Aluminized steel | | 80 | .300 | | 37 | 9 | 2.33 | 48.33 | 57 |
| 1400 | Gate for 6' high fence, 1-5/8" frame, 3' wide, galv. steel | | 10 | 2.400 | | 163 | 72 | 18.60 | 253.60 | 310 |
| 1500 | Aluminized steel, in concrete | | 10 | 2.400 | | 201 | 72 | 18.60 | 291.60 | 355 |
| 2000 | 5'-0" high fence, 9 ga., no barbed wire, 2" line post, in concrete | | | | | | | | | |
| 2010 | 10' O.C., 1-5/8" top rail, in concrete | | | | | | | | | |
| 2100 | Galvanized steel, in concrete | B-80C | 300 | .080 | L.F. | 12.65 | 2.40 | .62 | 15.67 | 18.35 |
| 2200 | Aluminized steel, in concrete | | 300 | .080 | " | 15.20 | 2.40 | .62 | 18.22 | 21 |
| 2400 | Gate, 4' wide, 5' high, 2" frame, galv. steel, in concrete | | 10 | 2.400 | Ea. | 186 | 72 | 18.60 | 276.60 | 335 |
| 2500 | Aluminized steel, in concrete | | 10 | 2.400 | " | 208 | 72 | 18.60 | 298.60 | 360 |
| 3100 | Overhead slide gate, chain link, 6' high, to 18' wide, in concrete | | 38 | .632 | L.F. | 165 | 18.95 | 4.89 | 188.84 | 216 |
| 3110 | Cantilever type, in concrete | B-80 | 48 | .667 | | 72.50 | 21.50 | 13.05 | 107.05 | 128 |
| 3120 | 8' high, in concrete | | 24 | 1.333 | | 104 | 43 | 26 | 173 | 209 |
| 3130 | 10' high, in concrete | | 18 | 1.778 | | 122 | 57.50 | 35 | 214.50 | 263 |
| 5000 | Double swing gates, incl. posts & hardware, in concrete | | | | | | | | | |
| 5010 | 5' high, 12' opening, in concrete | B-80C | 3.40 | 7.059 | Opng. | 495 | 212 | 54.50 | 761.50 | 935 |
| 5020 | 20' opening, in concrete | | 2.80 | 8.571 | | 675 | 257 | 66.50 | 998.50 | 1,225 |
| 5060 | 6' high, 12' opening, in concrete | | 3.20 | 7.500 | | 835 | 225 | 58 | 1,118 | 1,325 |
| 5070 | 20' opening, in concrete | | 2.60 | 9.231 | | 1,150 | 277 | 71.50 | 1,498.50 | 1,775 |
| 5080 | 8' high, 12' opening, in concrete | B-80 | 2.13 | 15.002 | | 1,300 | 485 | 294 | 2,079 | 2,500 |
| 5090 | 20' opening, in concrete | | 1.45 | 22.069 | | 1,700 | 715 | 430 | 2,845 | 3,450 |
| 5100 | 10' high, 12' opening, in concrete | | 1.31 | 24.427 | | 1,475 | 790 | 480 | 2,745 | 3,375 |
| 5110 | 20' opening, in concrete | | 1.03 | 31.068 | | 2,225 | 1,000 | 610 | 3,835 | 4,675 |
| 5120 | 12' high, 12' opening, in concrete | | 1.05 | 30.476 | | 2,150 | 990 | 595 | 3,735 | 4,550 |
| 5130 | 20' opening, in concrete | | .85 | 37.647 | | 2,775 | 1,225 | 740 | 4,740 | 5,725 |
| 5190 | For aluminized steel add | | | | | 20% | | | | |

### 32 31 13.25 Fence, Chain Link Residential

| | | Crew | Daily Output | Labor-Hours | Unit | Material | 2008 Bare Costs Labor | Equipment | Total | Total Incl O&P |
|---|---|---|---|---|---|---|---|---|---|---|
| 0010 | **FENCE, CHAIN LINK RESIDENTIAL** | | | | | | | | | |
| 0011 | Schedule 20, 11 gauge wire, 1-5/8" post | | | | | | | | | |
| 0020 | 10' O.C., 1-3/8" top rail, 2" corner post, galv. stl. 3' high | B-80C | 500 | .048 | L.F. | 4.42 | 1.44 | .37 | 6.23 | 7.50 |
| 0050 | 4' high | | 400 | .060 | | 5 | 1.80 | .47 | 7.27 | 8.80 |
| 0100 | 6' high | | 200 | .120 | | 6.10 | 3.60 | .93 | 10.63 | 13.30 |
| 0150 | Add for gate 3' wide, 1-3/8" frame, 3' high | | 12 | 2 | Ea. | 65 | 60 | 15.50 | 140.50 | 182 |
| 0170 | 4' high | | 10 | 2.400 | | 75 | 72 | 18.60 | 165.60 | 215 |
| 0190 | 6' high | | 10 | 2.400 | | 102 | 72 | 18.60 | 192.60 | 246 |
| 0200 | Add for gate 4' wide, 1-3/8" frame, 3' high | | 9 | 2.667 | | 73 | 80 | 20.50 | 173.50 | 228 |
| 0220 | 4' high | | 9 | 2.667 | | 82.50 | 80 | 20.50 | 183 | 238 |
| 0240 | 6' high | | 8 | 3 | | 97 | 90 | 23.50 | 210.50 | 273 |
| 0350 | Aluminized steel, 11 ga. wire, 3' high | | 500 | .048 | L.F. | 5.75 | 1.44 | .37 | 7.56 | 9 |
| 0380 | 4' high | | 400 | .060 | | 7.35 | 1.80 | .47 | 9.62 | 11.40 |
| 0400 | 6' high | | 200 | .120 | | 10.40 | 3.60 | .93 | 14.93 | 18 |
| 0450 | Add for gate 3' wide, 1-3/8" frame, 3' high | | 12 | 2 | Ea. | 79.50 | 60 | 15.50 | 155 | 198 |
| 0470 | 4' high | | 10 | 2.400 | | 130 | 72 | 18.60 | 220.60 | 276 |
| 0490 | 6' high | | 10 | 2.400 | | 164 | 72 | 18.60 | 254.60 | 315 |
| 0500 | Add for gate 4' wide, 1-3/8" frame, 3' high | | 10 | 2.400 | | 90 | 72 | 18.60 | 180.60 | 232 |
| 0520 | 4' high | | 9 | 2.667 | | 100 | 80 | 20.50 | 200.50 | 257 |
| 0540 | 6' high | | 8 | 3 | | 115 | 90 | 23.50 | 228.50 | 293 |
| 0620 | Vinyl covered, 9 ga. wire, 3' high | | 500 | .048 | L.F. | 4.70 | 1.44 | .37 | 6.51 | 7.80 |
| 0640 | 4' high | | 400 | .060 | | 5.50 | 1.80 | .47 | 7.77 | 9.35 |

# 32 31 Fences and Gates

## 32 31 13 – Chain Link Fences and Gates

### 32 31 13.25 Fence, Chain Link Residential

| | | Crew | Daily Output | Labor-Hours | Unit | Material | 2008 Bare Costs Labor | Equipment | Total | Total Incl O&P |
|---|---|---|---|---|---|---|---|---|---|---|
| 0660 | 6' high | B-80C | 200 | .120 | L.F. | 6.95 | 3.60 | .93 | 11.48 | 14.25 |
| 0720 | Add for gate 3' wide, 1-3/8" frame, 3' high | | 12 | 2 | Ea. | 90.50 | 60 | 15.50 | 166 | 210 |
| 0740 | 4' high | | 10 | 2.400 | | 102 | 72 | 18.60 | 192.60 | 246 |
| 0760 | 6' high | | 10 | 2.400 | | 159 | 72 | 18.60 | 249.60 | 310 |
| 0780 | Add for gate 4' wide, 1-3/8" frame, 3' high | | 10 | 2.400 | | 104 | 72 | 18.60 | 194.60 | 247 |
| 0800 | 4' high | | 9 | 2.667 | | 113 | 80 | 20.50 | 213.50 | 272 |
| 0820 | 6' high | ↓ | 8 | 3 | ↓ | 128 | 90 | 23.50 | 241.50 | 305 |

### 32 31 13.26 Tennis Court Fences and Gates

| | | Crew | Daily Output | Labor-Hours | Unit | Material | 2008 Bare Costs Labor | Equipment | Total | Total Incl O&P |
|---|---|---|---|---|---|---|---|---|---|---|
| 0010 | **TENNIS COURT FENCES AND GATES** | | | | | | | | | |
| 0860 | Tennis courts, 11 ga. wire, 2-1/2" post set | | | | | | | | | |
| 0870 | in concrete, 10' O.C., 1-5/8" top rail | | | | | | | | | |
| 0900 | 10' high | B-80 | 190 | .168 | L.F. | 14.10 | 5.45 | 3.30 | 22.85 | 27.50 |
| 0920 | 12' high | | 170 | .188 | " | 16.65 | 6.10 | 3.69 | 26.44 | 32 |
| 1000 | Add for gate 4' wide, 1-5/8" frame 7' high | | 10 | 3.200 | Ea. | 133 | 104 | 62.50 | 299.50 | 375 |
| 1040 | Aluminized steel, 11 ga. wire 10' high | | 190 | .168 | L.F. | 17.15 | 5.45 | 3.30 | 25.90 | 31 |
| 1100 | 12' high | | 170 | .188 | " | 21 | 6.10 | 3.69 | 30.79 | 36.50 |
| 1140 | Add for gate 4' wide, 1-5/8" frame, 7' high | | 10 | 3.200 | Ea. | 155 | 104 | 62.50 | 321.50 | 400 |
| 1250 | Vinyl covered, 9 ga. wire, 10' high | | 190 | .168 | L.F. | 16.70 | 5.45 | 3.30 | 25.45 | 30.50 |
| 1300 | 12' high | | 170 | .188 | " | 28 | 6.10 | 3.69 | 37.79 | 44 |
| 1310 | Fence, CL, tennis ct, transom gate, single, galv, 4' x 7' x 3' | B-80A | 8.72 | 2.752 | Ea. | 293 | 83.50 | 25.50 | 402 | 480 |
| 1400 | Add for gate 4' wide, 1-5/8" frame, 7' high | B-80 | 10 | 3.200 | " | 155 | 104 | 62.50 | 321.50 | 400 |

### 32 31 13.33 Chain Link Backstops

| | | Crew | Daily Output | Labor-Hours | Unit | Material | 2008 Bare Costs Labor | Equipment | Total | Total Incl O&P |
|---|---|---|---|---|---|---|---|---|---|---|
| 0010 | **CHAIN LINK BACKSTOPS** | | | | | | | | | |
| 0015 | Backstops, baseball, prefabricated, 30' wide, 12' high & 1 overhang | B-1 | 1 | 24 | Ea. | 3,075 | 740 | | 3,815 | 4,525 |
| 0100 | 40' wide, 12' high & 2 overhangs | " | .75 | 32 | | 3,850 | 990 | | 4,840 | 5,775 |
| 0300 | Basketball, steel, single goal | B-13 | 3.04 | 18.421 | | 1,200 | 605 | 259 | 2,064 | 2,550 |
| 0400 | Double goal | " | 1.92 | 29.167 | ↓ | 730 | 955 | 410 | 2,095 | 2,725 |
| 0600 | Tennis, wire mesh with pair of ends | B-1 | 2.48 | 9.677 | Set | 1,875 | 299 | | 2,174 | 2,550 |
| 0700 | Enclosed court | " | 1.30 | 18.462 | Ea. | 5,350 | 570 | | 5,920 | 6,800 |

### 32 31 13.53 High-Security Chain Link Fences, Gates and Systems

| | | Crew | Daily Output | Labor-Hours | Unit | Material | 2008 Bare Costs Labor | Equipment | Total | Total Incl O&P |
|---|---|---|---|---|---|---|---|---|---|---|
| 0010 | **HIGH-SECURITY CHAIN LINK FENCES, GATES AND SYSTEMS** | | | | | | | | | |
| 0100 | Fence, chain link, security, 7' H, standard FE-7, incl excavation & posts | B-80C | 480 | .050 | L.F. | 49 | 1.50 | .39 | 50.89 | 57 |
| 0200 | Fence, barbed wire, security, 7' high, with 3 wire barbed wire arm | " | 400 | .060 | " | 6.75 | 1.80 | .47 | 9.02 | 10.70 |
| 0300 | Complete systems, including material and installation | | | | | | | | | |
| 0310 | Taunt wire fence detection system | | | | M.L.F. | | | | 19,800 | 21,780 |
| 0410 | Microwave fence detection system | | | | | | | | 33,000 | 36,300 |
| 0510 | Passive magnetic fence detection system | | | | | | | | 15,840 | 17,028 |
| 0610 | Infrared fence detection system | | | | | | | | 10,560 | 11,616 |
| 0710 | Strain relief fence detection system | | | | | | | | 19,800 | 21,780 |
| 0810 | Electro-shock fence detection system | | | | | | | | 29,040 | 31,944 |
| 0910 | Photo-electric fence detection system | | | | ↓ | | | | 13,200 | 14,520 |

## 32 31 19 – Decorative Metal Fences and Gates

### 32 31 19.10 Decorative Fence

| | | Crew | Daily Output | Labor-Hours | Unit | Material | 2008 Bare Costs Labor | Equipment | Total | Total Incl O&P |
|---|---|---|---|---|---|---|---|---|---|---|
| 0010 | **DECORATIVE FENCE** | | | | | | | | | |
| 5300 | Tubular picket, steel, 6' sections, 1-9/16" posts, 4' high | B-80C | 300 | .080 | L.F. | 28 | 2.40 | .62 | 31.02 | 35.50 |
| 5400 | 2" posts, 5' high | | 240 | .100 | | 39 | 3 | .78 | 42.78 | 48.50 |
| 5600 | 2" posts, 6' high | | 200 | .120 | | 44 | 3.60 | .93 | 48.53 | 55 |
| 5700 | Staggered picket 1-9/16" posts, 4' high | | 300 | .080 | | 25.50 | 2.40 | .62 | 28.52 | 32.50 |
| 5800 | 2" posts, 5' high | | 240 | .100 | | 41.50 | 3 | .78 | 45.28 | 51.50 |
| 5900 | 2" posts, 6' high | ↓ | 200 | .120 | ↓ | 43 | 3.60 | .93 | 47.53 | 54 |
| 6200 | Gates, 4' high, 3' wide | B-1 | 10 | 2.400 | Ea. | 244 | 74 | | 318 | 385 |

573

# 32 31 Fences and Gates

## 32 31 19 – Decorative Metal Fences and Gates

### 32 31 19.10 Decorative Fence

| | | Crew | Daily Output | Labor-Hours | Unit | Material | 2008 Bare Costs Labor | Equipment | Total | Total Incl O&P |
|---|---|---|---|---|---|---|---|---|---|---|
| 6300 | 5' high, 3' wide | B-1 | 10 | 2.400 | Ea. | 315 | 74 | | 389 | 465 |
| 6400 | 6' high, 3' wide | | 10 | 2.400 | | 325 | 74 | | 399 | 475 |
| 6500 | 4' wide | ↓ | 10 | 2.400 | ↓ | 380 | 74 | | 454 | 535 |

## 32 31 26 – Wire Fences and Gates

### 32 31 26.10 Fences, Misc. Metal

| | | Crew | Daily Output | Labor-Hours | Unit | Material | 2008 Bare Costs Labor | Equipment | Total | Total Incl O&P |
|---|---|---|---|---|---|---|---|---|---|---|
| 0010 | **FENCES, MISC. METAL** | | | | | | | | | |
| 0012 | Chicken wire, posts @ 4', 1" mesh, 4' high | B-80C | 410 | .059 | L.F. | 2 | 1.75 | .45 | 4.20 | 5.40 |
| 0100 | 2" mesh, 6' high | | 350 | .069 | | 1.81 | 2.06 | .53 | 4.40 | 5.75 |
| 0200 | Galv. steel, 12 ga., 2" x 4" mesh, posts 5' O.C., 3' high | | 300 | .080 | | 2.71 | 2.40 | .62 | 5.73 | 7.40 |
| 0300 | 5' high | | 300 | .080 | | 3.62 | 2.40 | .62 | 6.64 | 8.40 |
| 0400 | 14 ga., 1" x 2" mesh, 3' high | | 300 | .080 | | 2.88 | 2.40 | .62 | 5.90 | 7.55 |
| 0500 | 5' high | ↓ | 300 | .080 | ↓ | 3.98 | 2.40 | .62 | 7 | 8.80 |
| 1000 | Kennel fencing, 1-1/2" mesh, 6' long, 3'-6" wide, 6'-2" high | 2 Clab | 4 | 4 | Ea. | 450 | 121 | | 571 | 690 |
| 1050 | 12' long | | 4 | 4 | | 545 | 121 | | 666 | 785 |
| 1200 | Top covers, 1-1/2" mesh, 6' long | | 15 | 1.067 | | 92 | 32.50 | | 124.50 | 151 |
| 1250 | 12' long | ↓ | 12 | 1.333 | ↓ | 147 | 40.50 | | 187.50 | 225 |
| 1300 | For kennel doors, see Div. 08 31 13.40 | | | | | | | | | |
| 4500 | Security fence, prison grade, set in concrete, 12' high | B-80 | 25 | 1.280 | L.F. | 40 | 41.50 | 25 | 106.50 | 136 |
| 4600 | 16' high | " | 20 | 1.600 | " | 48 | 52 | 31.50 | 131.50 | 167 |

### 32 31 26.20 Wire Fencing, General

| | | Crew | Daily Output | Labor-Hours | Unit | Material | 2008 Bare Costs Labor | Equipment | Total | Total Incl O&P |
|---|---|---|---|---|---|---|---|---|---|---|
| 0010 | **WIRE FENCING, GENERAL** | | | | | | | | | |
| 0015 | Barbed wire, galvanized, domestic steel, hi-tensile 15-1/2 ga. | | | | M.L.F. | 33 | | | 33 | 36.50 |
| 0020 | Standard, 12-3/4 ga. | | | | | 44.50 | | | 44.50 | 49 |
| 0210 | Barbless wire, 2-strand galvanized, 12-1/2 ga. | | | | ↓ | 44.50 | | | 44.50 | 49 |
| 0500 | Helical razor ribbon, stainless steel, 18" dia x 18" spacing | | | | C.L.F. | 129 | | | 129 | 142 |
| 0600 | Hardware cloth galv., 1/4" mesh, 23 ga., 2' wide | | | | C.S.F. | 58 | | | 58 | 63.50 |
| 0700 | 3' wide | | | | | 56.50 | | | 56.50 | 62 |
| 0900 | 1/2" mesh, 19 ga., 2' wide | | | | | 51 | | | 51 | 56.50 |
| 1000 | 4' wide | | | | | 50 | | | 50 | 55 |
| 1200 | Chain link fabric, steel, 2" mesh, 6 ga, galvanized | | | | | 191 | | | 191 | 211 |
| 1300 | 9 ga, galvanized | | | | | 94.50 | | | 94.50 | 104 |
| 1350 | Vinyl coated | | | | | 79 | | | 79 | 87 |
| 1360 | Aluminized | | | | | 123 | | | 123 | 135 |
| 1400 | 2-1/4" mesh, 11.5 ga, galvanized | | | | | 64 | | | 64 | 70 |
| 1600 | 1-3/4" mesh (tennis courts), 11.5 ga (core), vinyl coated | | | | | 90.50 | | | 90.50 | 99.50 |
| 1700 | 9 ga, galvanized | | | | | 81.50 | | | 81.50 | 89.50 |
| 2100 | Welded wire fabric, galvanized, 1" x 2", 14 ga. | | | | | 54 | | | 54 | 59.50 |
| 2200 | 2" x 4", 12-1/2 ga. | | | | ↓ | 18.50 | | | 18.50 | 20.50 |

## 32 31 29 – Wood Fences and Gates

### 32 31 29.20 Fence, Wood Rail

| | | Crew | Daily Output | Labor-Hours | Unit | Material | 2008 Bare Costs Labor | Equipment | Total | Total Incl O&P |
|---|---|---|---|---|---|---|---|---|---|---|
| 0010 | **FENCE, WOOD RAIL** | | | | | | | | | |
| 0012 | Picket, No. 2 cedar, Gothic, 2 rail, 3' high | B-1 | 160 | .150 | L.F. | 5.70 | 4.64 | | 10.34 | 13.45 |
| 0050 | Gate, 3'-6" wide | B-80C | 9 | 2.667 | Ea. | 49 | 80 | 20.50 | 149.50 | 201 |
| 0400 | 3 rail, 4' high | | 150 | .160 | L.F. | 6.55 | 4.80 | 1.24 | 12.59 | 16 |
| 0500 | Gate, 3'-6" wide | | 9 | 2.667 | Ea. | 59 | 80 | 20.50 | 159.50 | 212 |
| 0600 | Open rail, rustic, No. 1 cedar, 2 rail, 3' high | | 160 | .150 | L.F. | 5.10 | 4.50 | 1.16 | 10.76 | 13.90 |
| 0650 | Gate, 3' wide | | 9 | 2.667 | Ea. | 56.50 | 80 | 20.50 | 157 | 210 |
| 0700 | 3 rail, 4' high | | 150 | .160 | L.F. | 5.80 | 4.80 | 1.24 | 11.84 | 15.20 |
| 0900 | Gate, 3' wide | | 9 | 2.667 | Ea. | 73 | 80 | 20.50 | 173.50 | 228 |
| 1200 | Stockade, No. 2 cedar, treated wood rails, 6' high | | 160 | .150 | L.F. | 7.10 | 4.50 | 1.16 | 12.76 | 16.10 |
| 1250 | Gate, 3' wide | ↓ | 9 | 2.667 | Ea. | 58 | 80 | 20.50 | 158.50 | 211 |

# 32 31 Fences and Gates

## 32 31 29 – Wood Fences and Gates

| 32 31 29.20 Fence, Wood Rail | | Crew | Daily Output | Labor-Hours | Unit | Material | 2008 Bare Costs Labor | Equipment | Total | Total Incl O&P |
|---|---|---|---|---|---|---|---|---|---|---|
| 1300 | No. 1 cedar, 3-1/4" cedar rails, 6' high | B-80C | 160 | .150 | L.F. | 17.80 | 4.50 | 1.16 | 23.46 | 28 |
| 1500 | Gate, 3' wide | | 9 | 2.667 | Ea. | 148 | 80 | 20.50 | 248.50 | 310 |
| 1520 | Open rail, split, No. 1 cedar, 2 rail, 3' high | | 160 | .150 | L.F. | 5.20 | 4.50 | 1.16 | 10.86 | 14 |
| 1540 | 3 rail, 4'-0" high | | 150 | .160 | | 6.75 | 4.80 | 1.24 | 12.79 | 16.20 |
| 3300 | Board, shadow box, 1" x 6", treated pine, 6' high | | 160 | .150 | | 10.50 | 4.50 | 1.16 | 16.16 | 19.85 |
| 3400 | No. 1 cedar, 6' high | | 150 | .160 | | 20.50 | 4.80 | 1.24 | 26.54 | 32 |
| 3900 | Basket weave, No. 1 cedar, 6' high | ↓ | 160 | .150 | ↓ | 20.50 | 4.50 | 1.16 | 26.16 | 31 |
| 3950 | Gate, 3'-6" wide | B-1 | 8 | 3 | Ea. | 140 | 93 | | 233 | 298 |
| 4000 | Treated pine, 6' high | | 150 | .160 | L.F. | 12.15 | 4.95 | | 17.10 | 21 |
| 4200 | Gate, 3'-6" wide | | 9 | 2.667 | Ea. | 65.50 | 82.50 | | 148 | 200 |
| 5000 | Fence rail, redwood, 2" x 4", merch grade 8' | | 2400 | .010 | L.F. | 1.11 | .31 | | 1.42 | 1.70 |
| 5050 | Select grade, 8' | | 2400 | .010 | " | 3.44 | .31 | | 3.75 | 4.26 |
| 6000 | Fence post, select redwood, earthpacked & treated, 4" x 4" x 6' | | 96 | .250 | Ea. | 11 | 7.75 | | 18.75 | 24 |
| 6010 | 4" x 4" x 8' | | 96 | .250 | | 13.10 | 7.75 | | 20.85 | 26.50 |
| 6020 | Set in concrete, 4" x 4" x 6' | | 50 | .480 | | 14.20 | 14.85 | | 29.05 | 38.50 |
| 6030 | 4" x 4" x 8' | | 50 | .480 | | 16.95 | 14.85 | | 31.80 | 41.50 |
| 6040 | Wood post, 4' high, set in concrete, incl. concrete | | 50 | .480 | | 8.25 | 14.85 | | 23.10 | 32 |
| 6050 | Earth packed | | 96 | .250 | | 5.65 | 7.75 | | 13.40 | 18.25 |
| 6060 | 6' high, set in concrete, incl. concrete | | 50 | .480 | | 10.60 | 14.85 | | 25.45 | 34.50 |
| 6070 | Earth packed | ↓ | 96 | .250 | ↓ | 7.70 | 7.75 | | 15.45 | 20.50 |

# 32 32 Retaining Walls

## 32 32 13 – Cast-in-place Concrete Retaining Walls

### 32 32 13.10 Retaining Walls, Cast Concrete

| | | Crew | Daily Output | Labor-Hours | Unit | Material | 2008 Bare Costs Labor | Equipment | Total | Total Incl O&P |
|---|---|---|---|---|---|---|---|---|---|---|
| 0010 | **RETAINING WALLS, CAST CONCRETE** | | | | | | | | | |
| 1800 | Concrete gravity wall with vertical face including excavation & backfill | | | | | | | | | |
| 1850 | No reinforcing | | | | | | | | | |
| 1900 | 6' high, level embankment | C-17C | 36 | 2.306 | L.F. | 74 | 92 | 13.45 | 179.45 | 239 |
| 2000 | 33° slope embankment | | 32 | 2.594 | | 66.50 | 103 | 15.10 | 184.60 | 251 |
| 2200 | 8' high, no surcharge | | 27 | 3.074 | | 91 | 122 | 17.90 | 230.90 | 310 |
| 2300 | 33° slope embankment | | 24 | 3.458 | | 110 | 138 | 20 | 268 | 355 |
| 2500 | 10' high, level embankment | | 19 | 4.368 | | 130 | 174 | 25.50 | 329.50 | 440 |
| 2600 | 33° slope embankment | ↓ | 18 | 4.611 | ↓ | 180 | 184 | 27 | 391 | 515 |
| 2800 | Reinforced concrete cantilever, incl. excavation, backfill & reinf. | | | | | | | | | |
| 2900 | 6' high, 33° slope embankment | C-17C | 35 | 2.371 | L.F. | 66.50 | 94.50 | 13.85 | 174.85 | 236 |
| 3000 | 8' high, 33° slope embankment | | 29 | 2.862 | | 77 | 114 | 16.70 | 207.70 | 280 |
| 3100 | 10' high, 33° slope embankment | | 20 | 4.150 | | 100 | 165 | 24 | 289 | 395 |
| 3200 | 20' high, 500 lb. per L.F. surcharge | ↓ | 7.50 | 11.067 | ↓ | 300 | 440 | 64.50 | 804.50 | 1,075 |
| 3500 | Concrete cribbing, incl. excavation and backfill | | | | | | | | | |
| 3700 | 12' high, open face | B-13 | 210 | .267 | S.F. | 33.50 | 8.75 | 3.74 | 45.99 | 54 |
| 3900 | Closed face | " | 210 | .267 | " | 31.50 | 8.75 | 3.74 | 43.99 | 52 |
| 4100 | Concrete filled slurry trench, see Div. 31 56 23.20 | | | | | | | | | |

## 32 32 23 – Segmental Retaining Walls

### 32 32 23.13 Segmental Conc. Unit Masonry Retaining Walls

| | | Crew | Daily Output | Labor-Hours | Unit | Material | 2008 Bare Costs Labor | Equipment | Total | Total Incl O&P |
|---|---|---|---|---|---|---|---|---|---|---|
| 0010 | **SEGMENTAL CONC. UNIT MASONRY RETAINING WALLS** | | | | | | | | | |
| 7100 | Segmental Retaining Wall system, incl pins, and void fill | | | | | | | | | |
| 7120 | base not included | | | | | | | | | |
| 7140 | Large unit, 8" high x 18" wide x 20" deep, 3 plane split | B-62 | 300 | .080 | S.F. | 9.35 | 2.62 | .46 | 12.43 | 14.85 |
| 7150 | Straight split | | 300 | .080 | | 9.35 | 2.62 | .46 | 12.43 | 14.85 |
| 7160 | Medium, ltwt, 8" high x 18" wide x 12" deep, 3 plane split | ↓ | 400 | .060 | ↓ | 10.45 | 1.97 | .35 | 12.77 | 14.90 |

# 32 32 Retaining Walls

## 32 32 23 – Segmental Retaining Walls

### 32 32 23.13 Segmental Conc. Unit Masonry Retaining Walls

| | | Crew | Daily Output | Labor-Hours | Unit | Material | 2008 Bare Costs Labor | Equipment | Total | Total Incl O&P |
|---|---|---|---|---|---|---|---|---|---|---|
| 7170 | Straight split | B-62 | 400 | .060 | S.F. | 7.85 | 1.97 | .35 | 10.17 | 12.05 |
| 7180 | Small unit, 4" x 18" x 10" deep, 3 plane split | | 400 | .060 | | 11.15 | 1.97 | .35 | 13.47 | 15.65 |
| 7190 | Straight split | | 400 | .060 | | 11.75 | 1.97 | .35 | 14.07 | 16.35 |
| 7200 | Cap unit, 3 plane split | | 300 | .080 | | 13.20 | 2.62 | .46 | 16.28 | 19.05 |
| 7210 | Cap unit, straight split | | 300 | .080 | | 13.20 | 2.62 | .46 | 16.28 | 19.05 |
| 7260 | For reinforcing, add | | | | | | | | 2.64 | 3.30 |
| 8000 | For higher walls, add components as necessary | | | | | | | | | |

## 32 32 26 – Metal Crib Retaining Walls

### 32 32 26.10 Metal Bin Retaining Walls

| | | Crew | Daily Output | Labor-Hours | Unit | Material | 2008 Bare Costs Labor | Equipment | Total | Total Incl O&P |
|---|---|---|---|---|---|---|---|---|---|---|
| 0010 | **METAL BIN RETAINING WALLS** | | | | | | | | | |
| 0011 | Aluminized steel bin, excavation | | | | | | | | | |
| 0020 | and backfill not included, 10' wide | | | | | | | | | |
| 0100 | 4' high, 5.5' deep | B-13 | 650 | .086 | S.F. | 19.40 | 2.82 | 1.21 | 23.43 | 27 |
| 0200 | 8' high, 5.5' deep | | 615 | .091 | | 22.50 | 2.98 | 1.28 | 26.76 | 30.50 |
| 0300 | 10' high, 7.7' deep | | 580 | .097 | | 23.50 | 3.16 | 1.36 | 28.02 | 32.50 |
| 0400 | 12' high, 7.7' deep | | 530 | .106 | | 25.50 | 3.46 | 1.48 | 30.44 | 35 |
| 0500 | 16' high, 7.7' deep | | 515 | .109 | | 26.50 | 3.56 | 1.53 | 31.59 | 36.50 |
| 0600 | 16' high, 9.9' deep | | 500 | .112 | | 28 | 3.67 | 1.57 | 33.24 | 38.50 |
| 0700 | 20' high, 9.9' deep | | 470 | .119 | | 31.50 | 3.90 | 1.67 | 37.07 | 43 |
| 0800 | 20' high, 12.1' deep | | 460 | .122 | | 34 | 3.99 | 1.71 | 39.70 | 45.50 |
| 0900 | 24' high, 12.1' deep | | 455 | .123 | | 36 | 4.03 | 1.73 | 41.76 | 47.50 |
| 1000 | 24' high, 14.3' deep | | 450 | .124 | | 37.50 | 4.08 | 1.75 | 43.33 | 49.50 |
| 1100 | 28' high, 14.3' deep | | 440 | .127 | | 39 | 4.17 | 1.79 | 44.96 | 51.50 |
| 1300 | For plain galvanized bin type walls, deduct | | | | | 10% | | | | |

## 32 32 36 – Gabion Retaining Walls

### 32 32 36.10 Stone Gabion Retaining Walls

| | | Crew | Daily Output | Labor-Hours | Unit | Material | 2008 Bare Costs Labor | Equipment | Total | Total Incl O&P |
|---|---|---|---|---|---|---|---|---|---|---|
| 0010 | **STONE GABION RETAINING WALLS** | | | | | | | | | |
| 4300 | Stone filled gabions, not incl. excavation, | | | | | | | | | |
| 4310 | Stone, delivered, 3' wide | | | | | | | | | |
| 4350 | Galvanized, 6' high, 33° slope embankment | B-13 | 49 | 1.143 | L.F. | 20.50 | 37.50 | 16.05 | 74.05 | 97.50 |
| 4500 | Highway surcharge | | 27 | 2.074 | | 43.50 | 68 | 29 | 140.50 | 185 |
| 4600 | 9' high, up to 33° slope embankment | | 24 | 2.333 | | 46 | 76.50 | 33 | 155.50 | 205 |
| 4700 | Highway surcharge | | 16 | 3.500 | | 76 | 115 | 49 | 240 | 315 |
| 4900 | 12' high, up to 33° slope embankment | | 14 | 4 | | 71.50 | 131 | 56 | 258.50 | 345 |
| 5000 | Highway surcharge | | 11 | 5.091 | | 108 | 167 | 71.50 | 346.50 | 455 |
| 5950 | For PVC coating, add | | | | | 20% | | | | |

## 32 32 60 – Stone Retaining Walls

### 32 32 60.10 Retaining Walls, Stone

| | | Crew | Daily Output | Labor-Hours | Unit | Material | 2008 Bare Costs Labor | Equipment | Total | Total Incl O&P |
|---|---|---|---|---|---|---|---|---|---|---|
| 0010 | **RETAINING WALLS, STONE** | | | | | | | | | |
| 0015 | Including excavation, concrete footing and | | | | | | | | | |
| 0020 | stone 3' below grade. Price is exposed face area. | | | | | | | | | |
| 0200 | Decorative random stone, to 6' high, 1'-6" thick, dry set | D-1 | 35 | .457 | S.F. | 43 | 15.95 | | 58.95 | 71.50 |
| 0300 | Mortar set | | 40 | .400 | | 43 | 13.95 | | 56.95 | 68 |
| 0500 | Cut stone, to 6' high, 1'-6" thick, dry set | | 35 | .457 | | 43 | 15.95 | | 58.95 | 71.50 |
| 0600 | Mortar set | | 40 | .400 | | 43 | 13.95 | | 56.95 | 68 |
| 0800 | Random stone, 6' to 10' high, 2' thick, dry set | | 45 | .356 | | 43 | 12.40 | | 55.40 | 66 |
| 0900 | Mortar set | | 50 | .320 | | 43 | 11.15 | | 54.15 | 64 |
| 1100 | Cut stone, 6' to 10' high, 2' thick, dry set | | 45 | .356 | | 43 | 12.40 | | 55.40 | 66 |
| 1200 | Mortar set | | 50 | .320 | | 43 | 11.15 | | 54.15 | 64 |

# 32 34 Fabricated Bridges

## 32 34 20 – Fabricated Pedestrian Bridges

| 32 34 20.10 Bridges, Pedestrian | Crew | Daily Output | Labor-Hours | Unit | Material | 2008 Bare Costs Labor | Equipment | Total | Total Incl O&P |
|---|---|---|---|---|---|---|---|---|---|
| 0010 **BRIDGES, PEDESTRIAN** | | | | | | | | | |
| 0011 Spans over streams, roadways, etc. | | | | | | | | | |
| 0020 including erection, not including foundations | | | | | | | | | |
| 0050 Precast concrete, complete in place, 8' wide, 60' span | E-2 | 215 | .260 | S.F. | 58.50 | 10.90 | 7.30 | 76.70 | 91.50 |
| 0100 100' span | | 185 | .303 | | 64.50 | 12.65 | 8.45 | 85.60 | 102 |
| 0150 120' span | | 160 | .350 | | 70 | 14.65 | 9.80 | 94.45 | 113 |
| 0200 150' span | | 145 | .386 | | 72.50 | 16.15 | 10.80 | 99.45 | 120 |
| 0300 Steel, trussed or arch spans, compl. in place, 8' wide, 40' span | | 320 | .175 | | 76.50 | 7.35 | 4.90 | 88.75 | 102 |
| 0400 50' span | | 395 | .142 | | 68.50 | 5.95 | 3.97 | 78.42 | 90 |
| 0500 60' span | | 465 | .120 | | 68.50 | 5.05 | 3.37 | 76.92 | 88 |
| 0600 80' span | | 570 | .098 | | 81.50 | 4.11 | 2.75 | 88.36 | 100 |
| 0700 100' span | | 465 | .120 | | 115 | 5.05 | 3.37 | 123.42 | 138 |
| 0800 120' span | | 365 | .153 | | 145 | 6.40 | 4.29 | 155.69 | 175 |
| 0900 150' span | | 310 | .181 | | 154 | 7.55 | 5.05 | 166.60 | 189 |
| 1000 160' span | | 255 | .220 | | 154 | 9.20 | 6.15 | 169.35 | 193 |
| 1100 10' wide, 80' span | | 640 | .088 | | 85 | 3.66 | 2.45 | 91.11 | 103 |
| 1200 120' span | | 415 | .135 | | 110 | 5.65 | 3.78 | 119.43 | 135 |
| 1300 150' span | | 445 | .126 | | 124 | 5.25 | 3.52 | 132.77 | 149 |
| 1400 200' span | ↓ | 205 | .273 | | 132 | 11.45 | 7.65 | 151.10 | 173 |
| 1600 Wood, laminated type, complete in place, 80' span | C-12 | 203 | .236 | | 50.50 | 8.90 | 3.78 | 63.18 | 73.50 |
| 1700 130' span | " | 153 | .314 | ↓ | 52.50 | 11.80 | 5 | 69.30 | 81.50 |

# 32 35 Screening Devices

## 32 35 16 – Sound Barriers

### 32 35 16.10 Traffic Barriers, Highway Sound Barriers

| | Crew | Daily Output | Labor-Hours | Unit | Material | 2008 Bare Costs Labor | Equipment | Total | Total Incl O&P |
|---|---|---|---|---|---|---|---|---|---|
| 0010 **TRAFFIC BARRIERS, HIGHWAY SOUND BARRIERS** | | | | | | | | | |
| 0020 Highway sound barriers, not including footing | | | | | | | | | |
| 0100 Precast concrete, concrete columns @ 30' OC, 8" T, 8' H | C-12 | 400 | .120 | L.F. | 108 | 4.51 | 1.92 | 114.43 | 128 |
| 0110 12' H | | 265 | .181 | | 162 | 6.80 | 2.89 | 171.69 | 192 |
| 0120 16' H | | 200 | .240 | | 216 | 9 | 3.83 | 228.83 | 256 |
| 0130 20' H | ↓ | 160 | .300 | | 270 | 11.30 | 4.79 | 286.09 | 320 |
| 0400 Lt. Wt. composite panel, cementitious face, St. posts @ 12' OC, 8' H | B-80B | 190 | .168 | | 124 | 5.40 | 1.18 | 130.58 | 146 |
| 0410 12' H | | 125 | .256 | | 186 | 8.25 | 1.80 | 196.05 | 219 |
| 0420 16' H | | 95 | .337 | | 248 | 10.80 | 2.36 | 261.16 | 292 |
| 0430 20' H | ↓ | 75 | .427 | ↓ | 310 | 13.70 | 3 | 326.70 | 365 |

# 32 84 Planting Irrigation

## 32 84 23 – Underground Sprinklers

### 32 84 23.10 Sprinkler Irrigation System

| | Crew | Daily Output | Labor-Hours | Unit | Material | 2008 Bare Costs Labor | Equipment | Total | Total Incl O&P |
|---|---|---|---|---|---|---|---|---|---|
| 0010 **SPRINKLER IRRIGATION SYSTEM** | | | | | | | | | |
| 0011 For lawns | | | | | | | | | |
| 0100 Golf course with fully automatic system | C-17 | .05 | 1600 | 9 holes | 95,000 | 63,500 | | 158,500 | 203,500 |
| 0200 24' diam. head at 15' O.C incl. piping, auto oper., minimum | B-20 | 70 | .343 | Head | 21 | 11.65 | | 32.65 | 41 |
| 0300 Maximum | | 40 | .600 | | 48 | 20.50 | | 68.50 | 84.50 |
| 0500 60' diam. head at 40' O.C. incl. piping, auto oper., minimum | | 28 | .857 | | 63 | 29 | | 92 | 115 |
| 0600 Maximum | | 23 | 1.043 | ↓ | 177 | 35.50 | | 212.50 | 250 |
| 0800 Residential system, custom, 1" supply | | 2000 | .012 | S.F. | .30 | .41 | | .71 | .96 |
| 0900 1-1/2" supply | ↓ | 1800 | .013 | " | .37 | .45 | | .82 | 1.11 |
| 1020 Pop up spray head w/risers, hi-pop, full circle pattern, 4" | 2 Skwk | 76 | .211 | Ea. | 3.59 | 8.30 | | 11.89 | 16.85 |

| 32 84 23.10 Sprinkler Irrigation System | Crew | Daily Output | Labor-Hours | Unit | Material | Labor | Equipment | Total | Total Incl O&P |
|---|---|---|---|---|---|---|---|---|---|
| 1030     1/2 circle pattern, 4" | 2 Skwk | 76 | .211 | Ea. | 3.67 | 8.30 | | 11.97 | 16.95 |
| 1040     6", full circle pattern | | 76 | .211 | | 9.20 | 8.30 | | 17.50 | 23 |
| 1050     1/2 circle pattern, 6" | | 76 | .211 | | 9.20 | 8.30 | | 17.50 | 23 |
| 1060     12", full circle pattern | | 76 | .211 | | 13.15 | 8.30 | | 21.45 | 27.50 |
| 1070     1/2 circle pattern, 12" | | 76 | .211 | | 13.20 | 8.30 | | 21.50 | 27.50 |
| 1080 Pop up bubbler head w/risers, hi-pop bubbler head, 4" | | 76 | .211 | | 3.75 | 8.30 | | 12.05 | 17.05 |
| 1090     6" | | 76 | .211 | | 9.20 | 8.30 | | 17.50 | 23 |
| 1100     12" | | 76 | .211 | | 13.15 | 8.30 | | 21.45 | 27.50 |
| 1110 Impact full/part circle sprinklers, 28'-54' 25-60 PSI | | 37 | .432 | | 12.25 | 17.05 | | 29.30 | 40 |
| 1120     Spaced 37'-49' @ 25-50 PSI | | 37 | .432 | | 27 | 17.05 | | 44.05 | 56 |
| 1130     Spaced 43'-61' @ 30-60 PSI | | 37 | .432 | | 48.50 | 17.05 | | 65.55 | 80 |
| 1140     Spaced 54'-78' @ 40-80 PSI | | 37 | .432 | | 112 | 17.05 | | 129.05 | 150 |
| 1145 Impact rotor pop-up full/part commercial circle sprinklers | | | | | | | | | |
| 1150     Spaced 42'-65' 35-80 PSI | 2 Skwk | 25 | .640 | Ea. | 24.50 | 25 | | 49.50 | 66 |
| 1160     Spaced 48'-76' 45-85 PSI | " | 25 | .640 | " | 10.20 | 25 | | 35.20 | 50.50 |
| 1165 Impact rotor pop-up part. circle comm., 53'-75', 55-100 PSI, w/ accessories | | | | | | | | | |
| 1170     Plastic case, metal cover | 2 Skwk | 25 | .640 | Ea. | 171 | 25 | | 196 | 228 |
| 1180     Rubber cover | | 25 | .640 | | 129 | 25 | | 154 | 181 |
| 1190     Iron case, metal cover | | 22 | .727 | | 157 | 28.50 | | 185.50 | 218 |
| 1200     Rubber cover | | 22 | .727 | | 170 | 28.50 | | 198.50 | 232 |
| 1250     Plastic case, 2 nozzle, metal cover | | 25 | .640 | | 149 | 25 | | 174 | 202 |
| 1260     Rubber cover | | 25 | .640 | | 158 | 25 | | 183 | 212 |
| 1270     Iron case, 2 nozzle, metal cover | | 22 | .727 | | 216 | 28.50 | | 244.50 | 283 |
| 1280     Rubber cover | | 22 | .727 | | 221 | 28.50 | | 249.50 | 288 |
| 1282 Impact rotor pop-up full circle commercial, 39'-99', 30-100 PSI | | | | | | | | | |
| 1284     Plastic case, metal cover | 2 Skwk | 25 | .640 | Ea. | 152 | 25 | | 177 | 206 |
| 1286     Rubber cover | | 25 | .640 | | 169 | 25 | | 194 | 224 |
| 1288     Iron case, metal cover | | 22 | .727 | | 219 | 28.50 | | 247.50 | 286 |
| 1290     Rubber cover | | 22 | .727 | | 230 | 28.50 | | 258.50 | 298 |
| 1292     Plastic case, 2 nozzle, metal cover | | 22 | .727 | | 164 | 28.50 | | 192.50 | 225 |
| 1294     Rubber cover | | 22 | .727 | | 170 | 28.50 | | 198.50 | 232 |
| 1296     Iron case, 2 nozzle, metal cover | | 20 | .800 | | 211 | 31.50 | | 242.50 | 281 |
| 1298     Rubber cover | | 20 | .800 | | 226 | 31.50 | | 257.50 | 297 |
| 1305 Electric remote control valve, plastic, 3/4" | | 18 | .889 | | 23 | 35 | | 58 | 80 |
| 1310     1" | | 18 | .889 | | 40.50 | 35 | | 75.50 | 99 |
| 1320     1-1/2" | | 18 | .889 | | 78 | 35 | | 113 | 141 |
| 1335 Quick coupling valves, brass, locking cover | | | | | | | | | |
| 1340     Inlet coupling valve, 3/4" | 2 Skwk | 18.75 | .853 | Ea. | 51 | 33.50 | | 84.50 | 109 |
| 1350     1" | | 18.75 | .853 | | 62 | 33.50 | | 95.50 | 121 |
| 1360 Controller valve boxes, 6" round boxes | | 18.75 | .853 | | 4.56 | 33.50 | | 38.06 | 57.50 |
| 1370     10" round boxes | | 14.25 | 1.123 | | 9.95 | 44 | | 53.95 | 80 |
| 1380     12" square box | | 9.75 | 1.641 | | 20 | 64.50 | | 84.50 | 123 |
| 1388 Electromech. control, 14 day 3-60 min, auto start to 23/day | | | | | | | | | |
| 1390     4 station | 2 Skwk | 1.04 | 15.385 | Ea. | 217 | 605 | | 822 | 1,175 |
| 1400     7 station | | .64 | 25 | | 280 | 985 | | 1,265 | 1,825 |
| 1410     12 station | | .40 | 40 | | 345 | 1,575 | | 1,920 | 2,825 |
| 1420     Dual programs, 18 station | | .24 | 66.667 | | 1,725 | 2,625 | | 4,350 | 5,950 |
| 1430     23 station | | .16 | 100 | | 2,250 | 3,950 | | 6,200 | 8,600 |
| 1435 Backflow preventer, bronze, 0-175 PSI, w/valves, test cocks | | | | | | | | | |
| 1440     3/4" | 2 Skwk | 2 | 8 | Ea. | 141 | 315 | | 456 | 645 |
| 1450     1" | | 2 | 8 | | 147 | 315 | | 462 | 650 |
| 1460     1-1/2" | | 2 | 8 | | 292 | 315 | | 607 | 810 |
| 1470     2" | | 2 | 8 | | 305 | 315 | | 620 | 825 |

# 32 84 Planting Irrigation

## 32 84 23 – Underground Sprinklers

### 32 84 23.10 Sprinkler Irrigation System

| 32 84 23.10 Sprinkler Irrigation System | Crew | Daily Output | Labor-Hours | Unit | Material | 2008 Bare Costs Labor | 2008 Bare Costs Equipment | Total | Total Incl O&P |
|---|---|---|---|---|---|---|---|---|---|
| 1475 | Pressure vacuum breaker, brass, 15-150 PSI | | | | | | | | |
| 1480 | 3/4" | 2 Skwk | 2 | 8 | Ea. | 85.50 | 315 | | 400.50 | 585 |
| 1490 | 1" | | 2 | 8 | | 111 | 315 | | 426 | 615 |
| 1500 | 1-1/2" | | 2 | 8 | | 220 | 315 | | 535 | 730 |
| 1510 | 2" | | 2 | 8 | | 204 | 315 | | 519 | 715 |

# 32 91 Planting Preparation

## 32 91 13 – Soil Preparation

### 32 91 13.16 Mulching

| 32 91 13.16 Mulching | Crew | Daily Output | Labor-Hours | Unit | Material | 2008 Bare Costs Labor | 2008 Bare Costs Equipment | Total | Total Incl O&P |
|---|---|---|---|---|---|---|---|---|---|
| 0010 | **MULCHING** | | | | | | | | | |
| 0100 | Aged barks, 3" deep, hand spread | 1 Clab | 100 | .080 | S.Y. | 2.55 | 2.42 | | 4.97 | 6.55 |
| 0150 | Skid steer loader | B-63 | 13.50 | 2.963 | M.S.F. | 283 | 94 | 10.20 | 387.20 | 465 |
| 0200 | Hay, 1" deep, hand spread | 1 Clab | 475 | .017 | S.Y. | .46 | .51 | | .97 | 1.30 |
| 0250 | Power mulcher, small | B-64 | 180 | .089 | M.S.F. | 51 | 2.65 | 1.72 | 55.37 | 62 |
| 0350 | Large | B-65 | 530 | .030 | " | 51 | .90 | .83 | 52.73 | 58.50 |
| 0400 | Humus peat, 1" deep, hand spread | 1 Clab | 700 | .011 | S.Y. | 4.20 | .35 | | 4.55 | 5.15 |
| 0450 | Push spreader | " | 2500 | .003 | " | 4.20 | .10 | | 4.30 | 4.77 |
| 0550 | Tractor spreader | B-66 | 700 | .011 | M.S.F. | 465 | .43 | .31 | 465.74 | 515 |
| 0600 | Oat straw, 1" deep, hand spread | 1 Clab | 475 | .017 | S.Y. | .44 | .51 | | .95 | 1.27 |
| 0650 | Power mulcher, small | B-64 | 180 | .089 | M.S.F. | 49 | 2.65 | 1.72 | 53.37 | 60 |
| 0700 | Large | B-65 | 530 | .030 | " | 49 | .90 | .83 | 50.73 | 56.50 |
| 0750 | Add for asphaltic emulsion | B-45 | 1770 | .009 | Gal. | 2.22 | .32 | .42 | 2.96 | 3.39 |
| 0800 | Peat moss, 1" deep, hand spread | 1 Clab | 900 | .009 | S.Y. | 1.80 | .27 | | 2.07 | 2.40 |
| 0850 | Push spreader | " | 2500 | .003 | " | 1.80 | .10 | | 1.90 | 2.13 |
| 0950 | Tractor spreader | B-66 | 700 | .011 | M.S.F. | 200 | .43 | .31 | 200.74 | 221 |
| 1000 | Polyethylene film, 6 mil. | 2 Clab | 2000 | .008 | S.Y. | .19 | .24 | | .43 | .59 |
| 1100 | Redwood nuggets, 3" deep, hand spread | 1 Clab | 150 | .053 | " | 4.61 | 1.61 | | 6.22 | 7.55 |
| 1150 | Skid steer loader | B-63 | 13.50 | 2.963 | M.S.F. | 510 | 94 | 10.20 | 614.20 | 720 |
| 1200 | Stone mulch, hand spread, ceramic chips, economy | 1 Clab | 125 | .064 | S.Y. | 6.90 | 1.94 | | 8.84 | 10.60 |
| 1250 | Deluxe | " | 95 | .084 | " | 10.55 | 2.55 | | 13.10 | 15.60 |
| 1300 | Granite chips | B-1 | 10 | 2.400 | C.Y. | 34.50 | 74 | | 108.50 | 153 |
| 1400 | Marble chips | | 10 | 2.400 | | 129 | 74 | | 203 | 257 |
| 1600 | Pea gravel | | 28 | .857 | | 58.50 | 26.50 | | 85 | 106 |
| 1700 | Quartz | | 10 | 2.400 | | 166 | 74 | | 240 | 297 |
| 1800 | Tar paper, 15 Lb. felt | 1 Clab | 800 | .010 | S.Y. | .37 | .30 | | .67 | .88 |
| 1900 | Wood chips, 2" deep, hand spread | " | 220 | .036 | " | 1.88 | 1.10 | | 2.98 | 3.78 |
| 1950 | Skid steer loader | B-63 | 20.30 | 1.970 | M.S.F. | 209 | 62.50 | 6.80 | 278.30 | 335 |

### 32 91 13.26 Planting Beds

| 32 91 13.26 Planting Beds | Crew | Daily Output | Labor-Hours | Unit | Material | 2008 Bare Costs Labor | 2008 Bare Costs Equipment | Total | Total Incl O&P |
|---|---|---|---|---|---|---|---|---|---|
| 0010 | **PLANTING BEDS** | | | | | | | | | |
| 0100 | Backfill planting pit, by hand, on site topsoil | 2 Clab | 18 | .889 | C.Y. | | 27 | | 27 | 42 |
| 0200 | Prepared planting mix, by hand | " | 24 | .667 | | | 20 | | 20 | 31.50 |
| 0300 | Skid steer loader, on site topsoil | B-62 | 340 | .071 | | | 2.31 | .41 | 2.72 | 4 |
| 0400 | Prepared planting mix | " | 410 | .059 | | | 1.92 | .34 | 2.26 | 3.32 |
| 1000 | Excavate planting pit, by hand, sandy soil | 2 Clab | 16 | 1 | | | 30.50 | | 30.50 | 47 |
| 1100 | Heavy soil or clay | " | 8 | 2 | | | 60.50 | | 60.50 | 94 |
| 1200 | 1/2 C.Y. backhoe, sandy soil | B-11C | 150 | .107 | | | 3.74 | 1.90 | 5.64 | 7.80 |
| 1300 | Heavy soil or clay | " | 115 | .139 | | | 4.88 | 2.48 | 7.36 | 10.20 |
| 2000 | Mix planting soil, incl. loam, manure, peat, by hand | 2 Clab | 60 | .267 | | 38 | 8.05 | | 46.05 | 54.50 |
| 2100 | Skid steer loader | B-62 | 150 | .160 | | 38 | 5.25 | .92 | 44.17 | 51 |
| 3000 | Pile sod, skid steer loader | " | 2800 | .009 | S.Y. | | .28 | .05 | .33 | .48 |
| 3100 | By hand | 2 Clab | 400 | .040 | | | 1.21 | | 1.21 | 1.88 |

# 32 91 Planting Preparation

## 32 91 13 – Soil Preparation

### 32 91 13.26 Planting Beds

| | | Crew | Daily Output | Labor-Hours | Unit | Material | 2008 Bare Costs Labor | 2008 Bare Costs Equipment | Total | Total Incl O&P |
|---|---|---|---|---|---|---|---|---|---|---|
| 4000 | Remove sod, F.E. loader | B-10S | 2000 | .006 | S.Y. | | .22 | .15 | .37 | .50 |
| 4100 | Sod cutter | B-12K | 3200 | .005 | | | .18 | .34 | .52 | .64 |
| 4200 | By hand | 2 Clab | 240 | .067 | ↓ | | 2.02 | | 2.02 | 3.14 |

## 32 91 19 – Landscape Grading

### 32 91 19.13 Topsoil Placement and Grading

| | | Crew | Daily Output | Labor-Hours | Unit | Material | 2008 Bare Costs Labor | 2008 Bare Costs Equipment | Total | Total Incl O&P |
|---|---|---|---|---|---|---|---|---|---|---|
| 0010 | **TOPSOIL PLACEMENT AND GRADING** | | | | | | | | | |
| 0400 | Spread from pile to rough finish grade, F.E. loader, 1.5 CY | B-10S | 200 | .060 | E.C.Y. | | 2.20 | 1.51 | 3.71 | 5 |
| 0500 | Up to 200' radius, by hand | 1 Clab | 14 | .571 | | | 17.30 | | 17.30 | 27 |
| 0600 | Top dress by hand, 1 C.Y. for 600 S.F. | " | 11.50 | .696 | ↓ | 25 | 21 | | 46 | 60 |
| 0700 | Furnish and place, truck dumped, screened, 4" deep | B-10S | 1300 | .009 | S.Y. | 3.15 | .34 | .23 | 3.72 | 4.24 |
| 0800 | 6" deep | " | 820 | .015 | " | 4.03 | .54 | .37 | 4.94 | 5.65 |

# 32 92 Turf and Grasses

## 32 92 19 – Seeding

### 32 92 19.13 Mechanical Seeding

| | | Crew | Daily Output | Labor-Hours | Unit | Material | 2008 Bare Costs Labor | 2008 Bare Costs Equipment | Total | Total Incl O&P |
|---|---|---|---|---|---|---|---|---|---|---|
| 0010 | **MECHANICAL SEEDING** R329219-50 | | | | | | | | | |
| 0020 | Mechanical seeding, 215 lb./acre | B-66 | 1.50 | 5.333 | Acre | 565 | 201 | 146 | 912 | 1,075 |
| 0100 | 44 lb./M.S.Y. | " | 2500 | .003 | S.Y. | .16 | .12 | .09 | .37 | .46 |
| 0300 | Fine grading and seeding incl. lime, fertilizer & seed, | | | | | | | | | |
| 0310 | with equipment | B-14 | 1000 | .048 | S.Y. | .18 | 1.53 | .29 | 2 | 2.87 |
| 0600 | Limestone hand push spreader, 50 lbs. per M.S.F. | 1 Clab | 180 | .044 | M.S.F. | 3.71 | 1.34 | | 5.05 | 6.15 |
| 0800 | Grass seed hand push spreader, 4.5 lbs. per M.S.F. | " | 180 | .044 | " | 17.80 | 1.34 | | 19.14 | 21.50 |
| 1000 | Hydro or air seeding for large areas, incl. seed and fertilizer | B-81 | 8900 | .003 | S.Y. | .16 | .09 | .06 | .31 | .39 |
| 1100 | With wood fiber mulch added | " | 8900 | .003 | " | .30 | .09 | .06 | .45 | .54 |
| 1300 | Seed only, over 100 lbs., field seed, minimum | | | | Lb. | 1.23 | | | 1.23 | 1.35 |
| 1400 | Maximum | | | | | 4.08 | | | 4.08 | 4.49 |
| 1500 | Lawn seed, minimum | | | | | 1.90 | | | 1.90 | 2.09 |
| 1600 | Maximum | | | | ↓ | 4.95 | | | 4.95 | 5.45 |
| 1800 | Aerial operations, seeding only, field seed | B-58 | 50 | .480 | Acre | 400 | 15.70 | 54.50 | 470.20 | 525 |
| 1900 | Lawn seed | | 50 | .480 | | 620 | 15.70 | 54.50 | 690.20 | 765 |
| 2100 | Seed and liquid fertilizer, field seed | | 50 | .480 | | 480 | 15.70 | 54.50 | 550.20 | 615 |
| 2200 | Lawn seed | ↓ | 50 | .480 | ↓ | 700 | 15.70 | 54.50 | 770.20 | 850 |

## 32 92 23 – Sodding

### 32 92 23.10 Sodding Systems

| | | Crew | Daily Output | Labor-Hours | Unit | Material | 2008 Bare Costs Labor | 2008 Bare Costs Equipment | Total | Total Incl O&P |
|---|---|---|---|---|---|---|---|---|---|---|
| 0010 | **SODDING SYSTEMS** | | | | | | | | | |
| 0020 | Sodding, 1" deep, bluegrass sod, on level ground, over 8 MSF | B-63 | 22 | 1.818 | M.S.F. | 241 | 57.50 | 6.25 | 304.75 | 360 |
| 0200 | 4 M.S.F. | | 17 | 2.353 | | 269 | 74.50 | 8.10 | 351.60 | 420 |
| 0300 | 1000 S.F. | | 13.50 | 2.963 | | 294 | 94 | 10.20 | 398.20 | 480 |
| 0500 | Sloped ground, over 8 M.S.F. | | 6 | 6.667 | | 241 | 212 | 23 | 476 | 615 |
| 0600 | 4 M.S.F. | | 5 | 8 | | 269 | 254 | 27.50 | 550.50 | 715 |
| 0700 | 1000 S.F. | | 4 | 10 | | 294 | 320 | 34.50 | 648.50 | 855 |
| 1000 | Bent grass sod, on level ground, over 6 M.S.F. | | 20 | 2 | | 540 | 63.50 | 6.90 | 610.40 | 700 |
| 1100 | 3 M.S.F. | | 18 | 2.222 | | 600 | 70.50 | 7.65 | 678.15 | 775 |
| 1200 | Sodding 1000 S.F. or less | | 14 | 2.857 | | 685 | 90.50 | 9.85 | 785.35 | 900 |
| 1500 | Sloped ground, over 6 M.S.F. | | 15 | 2.667 | | 540 | 84.50 | 9.20 | 633.70 | 735 |
| 1600 | 3 M.S.F. | | 13.50 | 2.963 | | 600 | 94 | 10.20 | 704.20 | 815 |
| 1700 | 1000 S.F. | ↓ | 12 | 3.333 | ↓ | 685 | 106 | 11.50 | 802.50 | 925 |

# 32 93 Plants

## 32 93 10 – General Planting Costs

| 32 93 10.12 Travel | | Crew | Daily Output | Labor-Hours | Unit | Material | 2008 Bare Costs Labor | Equipment | Total | Total Incl O&P |
|---|---|---|---|---|---|---|---|---|---|---|
| 0010 | **TRAVEL** to all nursery items, for 10 to 20 miles, add | | | | | | | | | |
| 0015 | 10 to 20 miles one way, add | | | | All | | | | | 5% |
| 0100 | 30 to 50 miles one way, add | | | | " | | | | | 10% |

## 32 93 13 – Ground Covers

### 32 93 13.10 Ground Cover Plants

| | | Crew | Daily Output | Labor-Hours | Unit | Material | 2008 Bare Costs Labor | Equipment | Total | Total Incl O&P |
|---|---|---|---|---|---|---|---|---|---|---|
| 0010 | **GROUND COVER PLANTS** | | | | | | | | | |
| 0012 | Plants, pachysandra, in prepared beds | B-1 | 15 | 1.600 | C | 26 | 49.50 | | 75.50 | 106 |
| 0200 | Vinca minor, 1 yr, bare root, in prepared beds | | 12 | 2 | " | 39 | 62 | | 101 | 139 |
| 0600 | Stone chips, in 50 lb. bags, Georgia marble | | 520 | .046 | Bag | 2.60 | 1.43 | | 4.03 | 5.10 |
| 0700 | Onyx gemstone | | 260 | .092 | | 18.55 | 2.85 | | 21.40 | 25 |
| 0800 | Quartz | | 260 | .092 | | 6.95 | 2.85 | | 9.80 | 12.05 |
| 0900 | Pea gravel, truckload lots | | 28 | .857 | Ton | 38 | 26.50 | | 64.50 | 82.50 |

## 32 93 33 – Shrubs

### 32 93 33.10 Shrubs and Trees

| | | Crew | Daily Output | Labor-Hours | Unit | Material | 2008 Bare Costs Labor | Equipment | Total | Total Incl O&P |
|---|---|---|---|---|---|---|---|---|---|---|
| 0010 | **SHRUBS AND TREES** | | | | | | | | | |
| 0011 | Evergreen, in prepared beds, B & B | | | | | | | | | |
| 0100 | Arborvitae pyramidal, 4'-5' | B-17 | 30 | 1.067 | Ea. | 46 | 34.50 | 19.80 | 100.30 | 126 |
| 0150 | Globe, 12"-15" | B-1 | 96 | .250 | | 12.95 | 7.75 | | 20.70 | 26.50 |
| 0300 | Cedar, blue, 8'-10' | B-17 | 18 | 1.778 | | 228 | 57.50 | 33 | 318.50 | 375 |
| 0500 | Hemlock, canadian, 2-1/2'-3' | B-1 | 36 | .667 | | 32 | 20.50 | | 52.50 | 67 |
| 0550 | Holly, Savannah, 8' - 10' H | | 9.68 | 2.479 | | 545 | 76.50 | | 621.50 | 720 |
| 0600 | Juniper, andorra, 18"-24" | | 80 | .300 | | 16.70 | 9.30 | | 26 | 33 |
| 0620 | Wiltoni, 15"-18" | | 80 | .300 | | 16.95 | 9.30 | | 26.25 | 33 |
| 0640 | Skyrocket, 4-1/2'-5' | B-17 | 55 | .582 | | 50.50 | 18.75 | 10.80 | 80.05 | 96.50 |
| 0660 | Blue pfitzer, 2'-2-1/2' | B-1 | 44 | .545 | | 25.50 | 16.85 | | 42.35 | 54 |
| 0680 | Ketleerie, 2-1/2'-3' | | 50 | .480 | | 33.50 | 14.85 | | 48.35 | 59.50 |
| 0700 | Pine, black, 2-1/2'-3' | | 50 | .480 | | 44.50 | 14.85 | | 59.35 | 72 |
| 0720 | Mugo, 18"-24" | | 60 | .400 | | 36 | 12.35 | | 48.35 | 59 |
| 0740 | White, 4'-5' | B-17 | 75 | .427 | | 55.50 | 13.75 | 7.90 | 77.15 | 90.50 |
| 0800 | Spruce, blue, 18"-24" | B-1 | 60 | .400 | | 43 | 12.35 | | 55.35 | 67 |
| 0840 | Norway, 4'-5' | B-17 | 75 | .427 | | 65 | 13.75 | 7.90 | 86.65 | 101 |
| 0900 | Yew, denisforma, 12"-15" | B-1 | 60 | .400 | | 24.50 | 12.35 | | 36.85 | 46.50 |
| 1000 | Capitata, 18"-24" | | 30 | .800 | | 20.50 | 24.50 | | 45 | 61 |
| 1100 | Hicksi, 2'-2-1/2' | | 30 | .800 | | 30 | 24.50 | | 54.50 | 71.50 |

### 32 93 33.20 Shrubs

| | | Crew | Daily Output | Labor-Hours | Unit | Material | 2008 Bare Costs Labor | Equipment | Total | Total Incl O&P |
|---|---|---|---|---|---|---|---|---|---|---|
| 0010 | **SHRUBS**, Broadleaf Evergreen | | | | | | | | | |
| 0011 | Planted in prepared beds | | | | | | | | | |
| 0100 | Andromeda, 15"-18", container | B-1 | 96 | .250 | Ea. | 26 | 7.75 | | 33.75 | 40.50 |
| 0200 | Azalea, 15" - 18", container | | 96 | .250 | | 32.50 | 7.75 | | 40.25 | 48 |
| 0300 | Barberry, 9"-12", container | | 130 | .185 | | 11.40 | 5.70 | | 17.10 | 21.50 |
| 0400 | Boxwood, 15"-18", B & B | | 96 | .250 | | 30.50 | 7.75 | | 38.25 | 45.50 |
| 0500 | Euonymus, emerald gaiety, 12" to 15", container | | 115 | .209 | | 20.50 | 6.45 | | 26.95 | 32.50 |
| 0600 | Holly, 15"-18", B & B | | 96 | .250 | | 16.70 | 7.75 | | 24.45 | 30.50 |
| 0900 | Mount laurel, 18" - 24", B & B | | 80 | .300 | | 56 | 9.30 | | 65.30 | 76 |
| 1000 | Paxistema, 9 - 12" high | | 130 | .185 | | 18.15 | 5.70 | | 23.85 | 29 |
| 1100 | Rhododendron, 18"-24", container | | 48 | .500 | | 31 | 15.45 | | 46.45 | 58.50 |
| 1200 | Rosemary, 1 gal container | | 600 | .040 | | 62 | 1.24 | | 63.24 | 70 |
| 2000 | Deciduous, amelanchier, 2'-3', B & B | | 57 | .421 | | 90 | 13 | | 103 | 120 |
| 2100 | Azalea, 15"-18", B & B | | 96 | .250 | | 24 | 7.75 | | 31.75 | 38.50 |
| 2300 | Bayberry, 2'-3', B & B | | 57 | .421 | | 27.50 | 13 | | 40.50 | 51 |
| 2600 | Cotoneaster, 15"-18", B & B | | 80 | .300 | | 16.45 | 9.30 | | 25.75 | 32.50 |

# 32 93 Plants

## 32 93 33 – Shrubs

### 32 93 33.20 Shrubs

| | | Crew | Daily Output | Labor-Hours | Unit | Material | 2008 Bare Costs Labor | Equipment | Total | Total Incl O&P |
|---|---|---|---|---|---|---|---|---|---|---|
| 2800 | Dogwood, 3'-4', B & B | B-17 | 40 | .800 | Ea. | 26 | 26 | 14.85 | 66.85 | 84.50 |
| 2900 | Euonymus, alatus compacta, 15" to 18", container | B-1 | 80 | .300 | | 21.50 | 9.30 | | 30.80 | 38.50 |
| 3200 | Forsythia, 2'-3', container | " | 60 | .400 | | 18.95 | 12.35 | | 31.30 | 40.50 |
| 3300 | Hibiscus, 3'-4', B & B | B-17 | 75 | .427 | | 13.70 | 13.75 | 7.90 | 35.35 | 45 |
| 3400 | Honeysuckle, 3'-4', B & B | B-1 | 60 | .400 | | 21 | 12.35 | | 33.35 | 43 |
| 3500 | Hydrangea, 2'-3', B & B | " | 57 | .421 | | 24.50 | 13 | | 37.50 | 47.50 |
| 3600 | Lilac, 3'-4', B & B | B-17 | 40 | .800 | | 26 | 26 | 14.85 | 66.85 | 84.50 |
| 3900 | Privet, bare root, 18"-24" | B-1 | 80 | .300 | | 13.15 | 9.30 | | 22.45 | 29 |
| 4100 | Quince, 2'-3', B & B | " | 57 | .421 | | 22 | 13 | | 35 | 44.50 |
| 4200 | Russian olive, 3'-4', B & B | B-17 | 75 | .427 | | 23.50 | 13.75 | 7.90 | 45.15 | 55.50 |
| 4400 | Spirea, 3'-4', B & B | B-1 | 70 | .343 | | 27 | 10.60 | | 37.60 | 46.50 |
| 4500 | Viburnum, 3'-4', B & B | B-17 | 40 | .800 | | 28.50 | 26 | 14.85 | 69.35 | 87 |

## 32 93 43 – Trees

### 32 93 43.20 Trees

| | | Crew | Daily Output | Labor-Hours | Unit | Material | 2008 Bare Costs Labor | Equipment | Total | Total Incl O&P |
|---|---|---|---|---|---|---|---|---|---|---|
| 0010 | **TREES** | | | | | | | | | |
| 0011 | Deciduous, in prep. beds, balled & burlapped (B&B) | | | | | | | | | |
| 0100 | Ash, 2" caliper | B-17 | 8 | 4 | Ea. | 114 | 129 | 74 | 317 | 405 |
| 0200 | Beech, 5'-6' | | 50 | .640 | | 222 | 20.50 | 11.90 | 254.40 | 289 |
| 0300 | Birch, 6'-8', 3 stems | | 20 | 1.600 | | 123 | 51.50 | 29.50 | 204 | 247 |
| 0500 | Crabapple, 6'-8' | | 20 | 1.600 | | 160 | 51.50 | 29.50 | 241 | 288 |
| 0600 | Dogwood, 4'-5' | | 40 | .800 | | 67 | 26 | 14.85 | 107.85 | 129 |
| 0700 | Eastern redbud 4'-5' | | 40 | .800 | | 131 | 26 | 14.85 | 171.85 | 200 |
| 0800 | Elm, 8'-10' | | 20 | 1.600 | | 119 | 51.50 | 29.50 | 200 | 243 |
| 0900 | Ginkgo, 6'-7' | | 24 | 1.333 | | 163 | 43 | 25 | 231 | 272 |
| 1000 | Hawthorn, 8'-10', 1" caliper | | 20 | 1.600 | | 136 | 51.50 | 29.50 | 217 | 262 |
| 1100 | Honeylocust, 10'-12', 1-1/2" caliper | | 10 | 3.200 | | 149 | 103 | 59.50 | 311.50 | 390 |
| 1300 | Larch, 8' | | 32 | 1 | | 95 | 32 | 18.55 | 145.55 | 175 |
| 1400 | Linden, 8'-10', 1" caliper | | 20 | 1.600 | | 107 | 51.50 | 29.50 | 188 | 230 |
| 1500 | Magnolia, 4'-5' | | 20 | 1.600 | | 80.50 | 51.50 | 29.50 | 161.50 | 201 |
| 1600 | Maple, red, 8'-10', 1-1/2" caliper | | 10 | 3.200 | | 171 | 103 | 59.50 | 333.50 | 415 |
| 1700 | Mountain ash, 8'-10', 1" caliper | | 16 | 2 | | 181 | 64.50 | 37 | 282.50 | 340 |
| 1800 | Oak, 2-1/2"-3" caliper | | 6 | 5.333 | | 256 | 172 | 99 | 527 | 655 |
| 2100 | Planetree, 9'-11', 1-1/4" caliper | | 10 | 3.200 | | 103 | 103 | 59.50 | 265.50 | 340 |
| 2200 | Plum, 6'-8', 1" caliper | | 20 | 1.600 | | 91 | 51.50 | 29.50 | 172 | 212 |
| 2300 | Poplar, 9'-11', 1-1/4" caliper | | 10 | 3.200 | | 47.50 | 103 | 59.50 | 210 | 277 |
| 2500 | Sumac, 2'-3' | | 75 | .427 | | 23 | 13.75 | 7.90 | 44.65 | 54.50 |
| 2700 | Tulip, 5'-6' | | 40 | .800 | | 49 | 26 | 14.85 | 89.85 | 109 |
| 2800 | Willow, 6'-8', 1" caliper | | 20 | 1.600 | | 61 | 51.50 | 29.50 | 142 | 179 |

# 32 94 Planting Accessories

## 32 94 13 – Landscape Edging

### 32 94 13.20 Edging

| | | Crew | Daily Output | Labor-Hours | Unit | Material | 2008 Bare Costs Labor | Equipment | Total | Total Incl O&P |
|---|---|---|---|---|---|---|---|---|---|---|
| 0010 | **EDGING** | | | | | | | | | |
| 0050 | Aluminum alloy, including stakes, 1/8" x 4", mill finish | B-1 | 390 | .062 | L.F. | 3 | 1.90 | | 4.90 | 6.25 |
| 0051 | Black paint | | 390 | .062 | | 3.48 | 1.90 | | 5.38 | 6.80 |
| 0052 | Black anodized | | 390 | .062 | | 4.02 | 1.90 | | 5.92 | 7.40 |
| 0100 | Brick, set horizontally, 1-1/2 bricks per L.F. | D-1 | 370 | .043 | | 1.55 | 1.51 | | 3.06 | 4 |
| 0150 | Set vertically, 3 bricks per L.F. | " | 135 | .119 | | 4 | 4.13 | | 8.13 | 10.70 |
| 0200 | Corrugated aluminum, roll, 4" wide | 1 Carp | 650 | .012 | | .65 | .47 | | 1.12 | 1.45 |
| 0250 | 6" wide | " | 550 | .015 | | .81 | .55 | | 1.36 | 1.75 |

# 32 94 Planting Accessories

## 32 94 13 – Landscape Edging

### 32 94 13.20 Edging

| | | Crew | Daily Output | Labor-Hours | Unit | Material | 2008 Bare Costs Labor | 2008 Bare Costs Equipment | Total | Total Incl O&P |
|---|---|---|---|---|---|---|---|---|---|---|
| 0600 | Railroad ties, 6" x 8" | 2 Carp | 170 | .094 | L.F. | 2.99 | 3.59 | | 6.58 | 8.90 |
| 0650 | 7" x 9" | | 136 | .118 | | 3.32 | 4.48 | | 7.80 | 10.65 |
| 0750 | 2" x 4" | | 330 | .048 | | 3.27 | 1.85 | | 5.12 | 6.45 |
| 0800 | Steel edge strips, incl. stakes, 1/4" x 5" | B-1 | 390 | .062 | | 4.02 | 1.90 | | 5.92 | 7.40 |
| 0850 | 3/16" x 4" | " | 390 | .062 | | 3.18 | 1.90 | | 5.08 | 6.45 |

## 32 94 50 – Tree Guying

### 32 94 50.10 Tree Guying Systems

| | | Crew | Daily Output | Labor-Hours | Unit | Material | 2008 Bare Costs Labor | 2008 Bare Costs Equipment | Total | Total Incl O&P |
|---|---|---|---|---|---|---|---|---|---|---|
| 0010 | **TREE GUYING SYSTEMS** | | | | | | | | | |
| 0015 | Tree guying Including stakes, guy wire and wrap | | | | | | | | | |
| 0100 | Less than 3" caliper, 2 stakes | 2 Clab | 35 | .457 | Ea. | 16.75 | 13.85 | | 30.60 | 40 |
| 0200 | 3" to 4" caliper, 3 stakes | " | 21 | .762 | " | 20 | 23 | | 43 | 58 |
| 1000 | Including arrowhead anchor, cable, turnbuckles and wrap | | | | | | | | | |
| 1100 | Less than 3" caliper, 3" anchors | 2 Clab | 20 | .800 | Ea. | 51 | 24 | | 75 | 93.50 |
| 1200 | 3" to 6" caliper, 4" anchors | | 15 | 1.067 | | 73.50 | 32.50 | | 106 | 131 |
| 1300 | 6" caliper, 6" anchors | | 12 | 1.333 | | 90.50 | 40.50 | | 131 | 162 |
| 1400 | 8" caliper, 8" anchors | | 9 | 1.778 | | 104 | 54 | | 158 | 198 |

# 32 96 Transplanting

## 32 96 23 – Plant and Bulb Transplanting

### 32 96 23.23 Planting

| | | Crew | Daily Output | Labor-Hours | Unit | Material | 2008 Bare Costs Labor | 2008 Bare Costs Equipment | Total | Total Incl O&P |
|---|---|---|---|---|---|---|---|---|---|---|
| 0010 | **PLANTING** | | | | | | | | | |
| 0012 | Moving shrubs on site, 12" ball | B-62 | 28 | .857 | Ea. | | 28 | 4.93 | 32.93 | 48.50 |
| 0100 | 24" ball | " | 22 | 1.091 | " | | 35.50 | 6.25 | 41.75 | 62 |

### 32 96 23.43 Moving Trees

| | | Crew | Daily Output | Labor-Hours | Unit | Material | 2008 Bare Costs Labor | 2008 Bare Costs Equipment | Total | Total Incl O&P |
|---|---|---|---|---|---|---|---|---|---|---|
| 0290 | **MOVING TREES**, On site | | | | | | | | | |
| 0300 | Moving trees on site, 36" ball | B-6 | 3.75 | 6.400 | Ea. | | 210 | 76 | 286 | 405 |
| 0400 | 60" ball | " | 1 | 24 | " | | 785 | 285 | 1,070 | 1,525 |

# Division Notes

| | | CREW | DAILY OUTPUT | LABOR-HOURS | UNIT | 2008 BARE COSTS | | | | TOTAL INCL O&P |
|---|---|---|---|---|---|---|---|---|---|---|
| | | | | | | MAT. | LABOR | EQUIP. | TOTAL | |
| | | | | | | | | | | |
| | | | | | | | | | | |
| | | | | | | | | | | |
| | | | | | | | | | | |
| | | | | | | | | | | |
| | | | | | | | | | | |
| | | | | | | | | | | |
| | | | | | | | | | | |
| | | | | | | | | | | |
| | | | | | | | | | | |
| | | | | | | | | | | |
| | | | | | | | | | | |
| | | | | | | | | | | |
| | | | | | | | | | | |
| | | | | | | | | | | |
| | | | | | | | | | | |
| | | | | | | | | | | |
| | | | | | | | | | | |
| | | | | | | | | | | |
| | | | | | | | | | | |
| | | | | | | | | | | |

## Estimating Tips

### 33 10 00 Water Utilities
### 33 30 00 Sanitary Sewerage Utilities
### 33 40 00 Storm Drainage Utilities

- Never assume that the water, sewer, and drainage lines will go in at the early stages of the project. Consider the site access needs before dividing the site in half with open trenches, loose pipe, and machinery obstructions. Always inspect the site to establish that the site drawings are complete. Check off all existing utilities on your drawings as you locate them. If you find any discrepancies, mark up the site plan for further research. Differing site conditions can be very costly if discovered later in the project.

- See also Section 33 01 00 for restoration of pipe where removal/replacement may be undesirable. Use of new types of piping materials can reduce the overall project cost. Owners/design engineers should consider the installing construction as a valuable source of current information on piping products that could lead to significant utility cost savings.

## Reference Numbers

Reference numbers are shown in shaded boxes at the beginning of some major classifications. These numbers refer to related items in the Reference Section. The reference information may be an estimating procedure, an alternate pricing method, or technical information.

*Note:* Not all subdivisions listed here necessarily appear in this publication.

## Division 33 - Utilities

*Note:* **Trade Service,** *in part, has been used as a reference source for some of the material prices used in Division 33.*

# 33 01 Operation and Maintenance of Utilities

## 33 01 10 – Operation and Maintenance of Water Utilities

### 33 01 10.10 Corrosion Resistance

| 33 01 10.10 Corrosion Resistance | Crew | Daily Output | Labor-Hours | Unit | Material | 2008 Bare Costs Labor | Equipment | Total | Total Incl O&P |
|---|---|---|---|---|---|---|---|---|---|
| 0010 **CORROSION RESISTANCE** | | | | | | | | | |
| 0012 Wrap & coat, add to pipe, 4" dia. | | | | L.F. | 1.90 | | | 1.90 | 2.09 |
| 0040 6" diameter | | | | | 1.98 | | | 1.98 | 2.18 |
| 0060 8" diameter | | | | | 3.07 | | | 3.07 | 3.38 |
| 0100 12" diameter | | | | | 4.58 | | | 4.58 | 5.05 |
| 0200 24" diameter | | | | | 8.70 | | | 8.70 | 9.55 |
| 0500 Coating, bituminous, per diameter inch, 1 coat, add | | | | | .35 | | | .35 | .39 |
| 0540 3 coat | | | | | .54 | | | .54 | .59 |
| 0560 Coal tar epoxy, per diameter inch, 1 coat, add | | | | | .20 | | | .20 | .22 |
| 0600 3 coat | | | | | .44 | | | .44 | .48 |

## 33 01 30 – Operation and Maintenance of Sewer Utilities

### 33 01 30.72 Relining Sewers

| 33 01 30.72 Relining Sewers | Crew | Daily Output | Labor-Hours | Unit | Material | 2008 Bare Costs Labor | Equipment | Total | Total Incl O&P |
|---|---|---|---|---|---|---|---|---|---|
| 0010 **RELINING SEWERS** | | | | | | | | | |
| 0011 with cement inc bypass & cleaning | | | | | | | | | |
| 0020 Less than 10,000 L.F., urban, 6" to 10" | C-17E | 130 | .615 | L.F. | 8.10 | 24.50 | .65 | 33.25 | 47.50 |
| 0200 24" to 36" | | 90 | .889 | | 12.90 | 35.50 | .93 | 49.33 | 70 |
| 0300 48" to 72" | | 80 | 1 | | 20.50 | 40 | 1.05 | 61.55 | 85.50 |

# 33 05 Common Work Results for Utilities

## 33 05 16 – Utility Structures

### 33 05 16.13 Utility Boxes

| 33 05 16.13 Utility Boxes | Crew | Daily Output | Labor-Hours | Unit | Material | 2008 Bare Costs Labor | Equipment | Total | Total Incl O&P |
|---|---|---|---|---|---|---|---|---|---|
| 0010 **UTILITY BOXES** Precast concrete, 6" thick | | | | | | | | | |
| 0050 5' x 10' x 6' high, I.D. | B-13 | 2 | 28 | Ea. | 1,725 | 915 | 395 | 3,035 | 3,725 |
| 0100 6' x 10' x 6' high, I.D. | | 2 | 28 | | 1,775 | 915 | 395 | 3,085 | 3,775 |
| 0150 5' x 12' x 6' high, I.D. | | 2 | 28 | | 1,875 | 915 | 395 | 3,185 | 3,900 |
| 0200 6' x 12' x 6' high, I.D. | | 1.80 | 31.111 | | 2,100 | 1,025 | 435 | 3,560 | 4,375 |
| 0250 6' x 13' x 6' high, I.D. | | 1.50 | 37.333 | | 2,775 | 1,225 | 525 | 4,525 | 5,500 |
| 0300 8' x 14' x 7' high, I.D. | | 1 | 56 | | 3,000 | 1,825 | 785 | 5,610 | 7,000 |
| 0350 Hand hole, precast concrete, 1-1/2" thick | | | | | | | | | |
| 0400 1'-0" x 2'-0" x 1'-9", I.D., light duty | B-1 | 4 | 6 | Ea. | 292 | 186 | | 478 | 610 |
| 0450 4'-6" x 3'-2" x 2'-0", O.D., heavy duty | B-6 | 3 | 8 | " | 895 | 262 | 95 | 1,252 | 1,500 |

## 33 05 23 – Trenchless Utility Installation

### 33 05 23.19 Microtunneling

| 33 05 23.19 Microtunneling | Crew | Daily Output | Labor-Hours | Unit | Material | 2008 Bare Costs Labor | Equipment | Total | Total Incl O&P |
|---|---|---|---|---|---|---|---|---|---|
| 0010 **MICROTUNNELING** | | | | | | | | | |
| 0011 Not including excavation, backfill, shoring, | | | | | | | | | |
| 0020 or dewatering, average 50'/day, slurry method | | | | | | | | | |
| 0100 24" to 48" outside diameter, minimum | | | | L.F. | | | | 793.80 | 882 |
| 0110 Adverse conditions, add | | | | % | | | | 50% | 50% |
| 1000 Rent microtunneling machine, average monthly lease | | | | Month | | | | 93,555 | 103,950 |
| 1010 Operating technician | | | | Day | | | | 694.58 | 771.75 |
| 1100 Mobilization and demobilization, minimum | | | | Job | | | | 46,588.50 | 51,765 |
| 1110 Maximum | | | | " | | | | 444,150 | 493,500 |

### 33 05 23.20 Horizontal Boring

| 33 05 23.20 Horizontal Boring | Crew | Daily Output | Labor-Hours | Unit | Material | 2008 Bare Costs Labor | Equipment | Total | Total Incl O&P |
|---|---|---|---|---|---|---|---|---|---|
| 0010 **HORIZONTAL BORING** | | | | | | | | | |
| 0011 Casing only, 100' minimum, | | | | | | | | | |
| 0020 not incl. jacking pits or dewatering | | | | | | | | | |
| 0100 Roadwork, 1/2" thick wall, 24" diameter casing | B-42 | 20 | 3.200 | L.F. | 90.50 | 109 | 68 | 267.50 | 345 |
| 0200 36" diameter | | 16 | 4 | | 144 | 136 | 85 | 365 | 465 |
| 0300 48" diameter | | 15 | 4.267 | | 211 | 145 | 90.50 | 446.50 | 560 |
| 0500 Railroad work, 24" diameter | | 15 | 4.267 | | 90.50 | 145 | 90.50 | 326 | 430 |

# 33 05 Common Work Results for Utilities

## 33 05 23 – Trenchless Utility Installation

### 33 05 23.20 Horizontal Boring

| | | Crew | Daily Output | Labor-Hours | Unit | Material | 2008 Bare Costs Labor | Equipment | Total | Total Incl O&P |
|---|---|---|---|---|---|---|---|---|---|---|
| 0600 | 36" diameter | B-42 | 14 | 4.571 | L.F. | 144 | 156 | 97 | 397 | 510 |
| 0700 | 48" diameter | ↓ | 12 | 5.333 | | 211 | 182 | 113 | 506 | 645 |
| 0900 | For ledge, add | | | | ↓ | | | | 195.30 | 239.40 |

## 33 05 26 – Utility Line Signs, Markers, and Flags

### 33 05 26.10 Utility Accessories

| | | Crew | Daily Output | Labor-Hours | Unit | Material | 2008 Bare Costs Labor | Equipment | Total | Total Incl O&P |
|---|---|---|---|---|---|---|---|---|---|---|
| 0010 | **UTILITY ACCESSORIES** | | | | | | | | | |
| 0400 | Underground tape, detectable, reinforced, alum. foil core, 2" | 1 Clab | 150 | .053 | C.L.F. | 2 | 1.61 | | 3.61 | 4.71 |
| 0500 | 6" | " | 140 | .057 | " | 5 | 1.73 | | 6.73 | 8.20 |

# 33 11 Water Utility Distribution Piping

## 33 11 13 – Public Water Utility Distribution Piping

### 33 11 13.15 Water Supply, Ductile Iron Pipe

| | | | Crew | Daily Output | Labor-Hours | Unit | Material | 2008 Bare Costs Labor | Equipment | Total | Total Incl O&P |
|---|---|---|---|---|---|---|---|---|---|---|---|
| 0010 | **WATER SUPPLY, DUCTILE IRON PIPE** | R331113-80 | | | | | | | | | |
| 0020 | Not including excavation or backfill | | | | | | | | | | |
| 2000 | Pipe, class 50 water piping, 18' lengths | | | | | | | | | | |
| 2020 | Mechanical joint, 4" diameter | | B-21A | 200 | .200 | L.F. | 14.60 | 7.50 | 3.06 | 25.16 | 31 |
| 2040 | 6" diameter | | | 160 | .250 | | 16.95 | 9.40 | 3.82 | 30.17 | 37 |
| 2060 | 8" diameter | | | 133.33 | .300 | | 18.75 | 11.25 | 4.58 | 34.58 | 42.50 |
| 2080 | 10" diameter | | | 114.29 | .350 | | 25.50 | 13.10 | 5.35 | 43.95 | 54 |
| 2100 | 12" diameter | | | 105.26 | .380 | | 31 | 14.25 | 5.80 | 51.05 | 62.50 |
| 2120 | 14" diameter | | | 100 | .400 | | 40 | 15 | 6.10 | 61.10 | 73.50 |
| 2140 | 16" diameter | | | 72.73 | .550 | | 43.50 | 20.50 | 8.40 | 72.40 | 89 |
| 2160 | 18" diameter | | | 68.97 | .580 | | 54.50 | 22 | 8.85 | 85.35 | 103 |
| 2170 | 20" diameter | | | 57.14 | .700 | | 64 | 26.50 | 10.70 | 101.20 | 122 |
| 2180 | 24" diameter | | | 47.06 | .850 | | 82 | 32 | 13 | 127 | 153 |
| 3000 | Tyton, push-on joint, 4" diameter | | | 400 | .100 | | 8.60 | 3.75 | 1.53 | 13.88 | 16.90 |
| 3020 | 6" diameter | | | 333.33 | .120 | | 11 | 4.50 | 1.83 | 17.33 | 21 |
| 3040 | 8" diameter | | | 200 | .200 | | 15.40 | 7.50 | 3.06 | 25.96 | 31.50 |
| 3060 | 10" diameter | | | 181.82 | .220 | | 21.50 | 8.25 | 3.36 | 33.11 | 40.50 |
| 3080 | 12" diameter | | | 160 | .250 | | 23 | 9.40 | 3.82 | 36.22 | 43.50 |
| 3100 | 14" diameter | | | 133.33 | .300 | | 25 | 11.25 | 4.58 | 40.83 | 49.50 |
| 3120 | 16" diameter | | | 114.29 | .350 | | 40.50 | 13.10 | 5.35 | 58.95 | 70.50 |
| 3140 | 18" diameter | | | 100 | .400 | | 45 | 15 | 6.10 | 66.10 | 79 |
| 3160 | 20" diameter | | | 88.89 | .450 | | 49.50 | 16.85 | 6.90 | 73.25 | 87.50 |
| 3180 | 24" diameter | | ↓ | 76.92 | .520 | ↓ | 68 | 19.50 | 7.95 | 95.45 | 113 |
| 8000 | Fittings, mechanical joint | | | | | | | | | | |
| 8006 | 90° bend, 4" diameter | | B-20A | 16 | 2 | Ea. | 186 | 73.50 | | 259.50 | 315 |
| 8020 | 6" diameter | | | 12.80 | 2.500 | | 254 | 91.50 | | 345.50 | 420 |
| 8040 | 8" diameter | | ↓ | 10.67 | 2.999 | | 370 | 110 | | 480 | 575 |
| 8060 | 10" diameter | | B-21A | 11.43 | 3.500 | | 405 | 131 | 53.50 | 589.50 | 705 |
| 8080 | 12" diameter | | | 10.53 | 3.799 | | 730 | 142 | 58 | 930 | 1,075 |
| 8100 | 14" diameter | | | 10 | 4 | | 1,100 | 150 | 61 | 1,311 | 1,525 |
| 8120 | 16" diameter | | | 7.27 | 5.502 | | 1,650 | 206 | 84 | 1,940 | 2,225 |
| 8140 | 18" diameter | | | 6.90 | 5.797 | | 1,650 | 217 | 88.50 | 1,955.50 | 2,225 |
| 8160 | 20" diameter | | | 5.71 | 7.005 | | 3,675 | 263 | 107 | 4,045 | 4,575 |
| 8180 | 24" diameter | | ↓ | 4.70 | 8.511 | | 4,075 | 320 | 130 | 4,525 | 5,100 |
| 8200 | Wye or tee, 4" diameter | | B-20A | 10.67 | 2.999 | | 281 | 110 | | 391 | 480 |
| 8220 | 6" diameter | | | 8.53 | 3.751 | | 375 | 137 | | 512 | 625 |
| 8240 | 8" diameter | | ↓ | 7.11 | 4.501 | | 540 | 165 | | 705 | 840 |
| 8260 | 10" diameter | | B-21A | 7.62 | 5.249 | ↓ | 1,100 | 197 | 80 | 1,377 | 1,625 |

# 33 11 Water Utility Distribution Piping

## 33 11 13 – Public Water Utility Distribution Piping

### 33 11 13.15 Water Supply, Ductile Iron Pipe

| | | Crew | Daily Output | Labor-Hours | Unit | Material | 2008 Bare Costs Labor | 2008 Bare Costs Equipment | Total | Total Incl O&P |
|---|---|---|---|---|---|---|---|---|---|---|
| 8280 | 12" diameter | B-21A | 7.02 | 5.698 | Ea. | 1,400 | 214 | 87 | 1,701 | 1,975 |
| 8300 | 14" diameter | | 6.67 | 5.997 | | 1,575 | 225 | 91.50 | 1,891.50 | 2,175 |
| 8320 | 16" diameter | | 4.85 | 8.247 | | 1,650 | 310 | 126 | 2,086 | 2,400 |
| 8340 | 18" diameter | | 4.60 | 8.696 | | 4,275 | 325 | 133 | 4,733 | 5,350 |
| 8360 | 20" diameter | | 3.81 | 10.499 | | 6,675 | 395 | 160 | 7,230 | 8,125 |
| 8380 | 24" diameter | | 3.14 | 12.739 | | 7,900 | 480 | 195 | 8,575 | 9,650 |
| 8450 | Decreaser, 6" x 4" diameter | B-20A | 14.22 | 2.250 | | 156 | 82.50 | | 238.50 | 298 |
| 8460 | 8" x 6" diameter | " | 11.64 | 2.749 | | 199 | 101 | | 300 | 375 |
| 8470 | 10" x 6 " diameter | B-21A | 13.33 | 3.001 | | 252 | 113 | 46 | 411 | 500 |
| 8480 | 12" x 6" diameter | | 12.70 | 3.150 | | 310 | 118 | 48 | 476 | 575 |
| 8490 | 16" x 6" diameter | | 10 | 4 | | 710 | 150 | 61 | 921 | 1,075 |
| 8500 | 20" x 6" diameter | | 8.42 | 4.751 | | 1,775 | 178 | 72.50 | 2,025.50 | 2,300 |
| 8550 | Butterfly valves with boxes, cast iron | | | | | | | | | |
| 8560 | 4" diameter | B-20 | 6 | 4 | Ea. | 745 | 136 | | 881 | 1,025 |
| 8570 | 6" diameter | " | 5 | 4.800 | | 1,125 | 163 | | 1,288 | 1,475 |
| 8580 | 8" diameter | B-21 | 4 | 7 | | 1,325 | 245 | 32.50 | 1,602.50 | 1,875 |
| 8590 | 10" diameter | | 3.50 | 8 | | 1,700 | 280 | 37 | 2,017 | 2,350 |
| 8600 | 12" diameter | | 3 | 9.333 | | 2,350 | 325 | 43 | 2,718 | 3,150 |
| 8610 | 14" diameter | | 2 | 14 | | 2,875 | 490 | 64.50 | 3,429.50 | 4,000 |
| 8620 | 16" diameter | | 2 | 14 | | 4,450 | 490 | 64.50 | 5,004.50 | 5,725 |

### 33 11 13.25 Water Supply, Polyvinyl Chloride Pipe

| | | Crew | Daily Output | Labor-Hours | Unit | Material | 2008 Bare Costs Labor | 2008 Bare Costs Equipment | Total | Total Incl O&P |
|---|---|---|---|---|---|---|---|---|---|---|
| 0010 | **WATER SUPPLY, POLYVINYL CHLORIDE PIPE** | | | | | | | | | |
| 0020 | Not including excavation or backfill, unless specified | | | | | | | | | |
| 2100 | AWWA Class 160, S.D.R. 26, 1-1/2" diameter | Q-1A | 750 | .013 | L.F. | .44 | .63 | | 1.07 | 1.42 |
| 2120 | 2" diameter | | 686 | .015 | | .87 | .69 | | 1.56 | 1.99 |
| 2140 | 2-1/2" diameter | | 500 | .020 | | 1.32 | .94 | | 2.26 | 2.87 |
| 2160 | 3" diameter | B-20 | 430 | .056 | | 1.89 | 1.90 | | 3.79 | 5.05 |
| 2180 | 4" diameter | | 375 | .064 | | 3.09 | 2.17 | | 5.26 | 6.80 |
| 2200 | 6" diameter | | 316 | .076 | | 6.65 | 2.58 | | 9.23 | 11.35 |
| 2210 | 8" diameter | | 260 | .092 | | 11.30 | 3.14 | | 14.44 | 17.30 |
| 3010 | AWWA C905, PR 100, DR 41 | | | | | | | | | |
| 3030 | 14" diameter | B-20A | 213 | .150 | L.F. | 18.80 | 5.50 | | 24.30 | 29 |
| 3040 | 16" diameter | | 200 | .160 | | 18.95 | 5.85 | | 24.80 | 30 |
| 3050 | 18" diameter | | 160 | .200 | | 31 | 7.35 | | 38.35 | 45 |
| 3060 | 20" diameter | | 133 | .241 | | 24 | 8.80 | | 32.80 | 39.50 |
| 3070 | 24" diameter | | 107 | .299 | | 34.50 | 10.95 | | 45.45 | 54 |
| 3080 | 30" diameter | | 80 | .400 | | 52.50 | 14.65 | | 67.15 | 80.50 |
| 3090 | 36" diameter | | 80 | .400 | | 75.50 | 14.65 | | 90.15 | 106 |
| 3100 | 42" diameter | | 60 | .533 | | 101 | 19.55 | | 120.55 | 141 |
| 3200 | 48" diameter | | 60 | .533 | | 132 | 19.55 | | 151.55 | 175 |
| 4520 | Pressure pipe Class 150, SDR 18, AWWA C900, 4" diameter | | 380 | .084 | | 2.32 | 3.09 | | 5.41 | 7.25 |
| 4540 | 8" diameter | | 264 | .121 | | 8.05 | 4.44 | | 12.49 | 15.65 |
| 4550 | 10" diameter | | 220 | .145 | | 12.20 | 5.35 | | 17.55 | 21.50 |
| 4560 | 12" diameter | | 186 | .172 | | 17.25 | 6.30 | | 23.55 | 28.50 |
| 8000 | Fittings with rubber gasket | | | | | | | | | |
| 8003 | Class 150, D.R. 18 | | | | | | | | | |
| 8006 | 90° Bend , 4" diameter | B-20 | 100 | .240 | Ea. | 50 | 8.15 | | 58.15 | 67.50 |
| 8020 | 6" diameter | | 90 | .267 | | 90 | 9.05 | | 99.05 | 113 |
| 8040 | 8" diameter | | 80 | .300 | | 171 | 10.20 | | 181.20 | 204 |
| 8060 | 10" diameter | | 50 | .480 | | 260 | 16.30 | | 276.30 | 310 |
| 8080 | 12" diameter | | 30 | .800 | | 395 | 27 | | 422 | 480 |
| 8100 | Tee, 4" diameter | | 90 | .267 | | 97.50 | 9.05 | | 106.55 | 122 |

# 33 11 Water Utility Distribution Piping

## 33 11 13 – Public Water Utility Distribution Piping

### 33 11 13.25 Water Supply, Polyvinyl Chloride Pipe

| | | Crew | Daily Output | Labor-Hours | Unit | Material | 2008 Bare Costs Labor | Equipment | Total | Total Incl O&P |
|---|---|---|---|---|---|---|---|---|---|---|
| 8120 | 6" diameter | B-20 | 80 | .300 | Ea. | 145 | 10.20 | | 155.20 | 175 |
| 8140 | 8" diameter | | 70 | .343 | | 249 | 11.65 | | 260.65 | 292 |
| 8160 | 10" diameter | | 40 | .600 | | 425 | 20.50 | | 445.50 | 500 |
| 8180 | 12" diameter | | 20 | 1.200 | | 600 | 41 | | 641 | 720 |
| 8200 | 45° Bend, 4" diameter | | 100 | .240 | | 50 | 8.15 | | 58.15 | 67.50 |
| 8220 | 6" diameter | | 90 | .267 | | 90 | 9.05 | | 99.05 | 113 |
| 8240 | 8" diameter | | 50 | .480 | | 171 | 16.30 | | 187.30 | 214 |
| 8260 | 10" diameter | | 50 | .480 | | 475 | 16.30 | | 491.30 | 545 |
| 8280 | 12" diameter | | 30 | .800 | | 625 | 27 | | 652 | 735 |
| 8300 | Reducing tee 6"x4" | | 100 | .240 | | 118 | 8.15 | | 126.15 | 143 |
| 8320 | 8" x 6" | | 90 | .267 | | 286 | 9.05 | | 295.05 | 330 |
| 8330 | 10" x 6" | | 90 | .267 | | 330 | 9.05 | | 339.05 | 380 |
| 8340 | 10"x8" | | 90 | .267 | | 355 | 9.05 | | 364.05 | 405 |
| 8350 | 12" x 6" | | 90 | .267 | | 445 | 9.05 | | 454.05 | 505 |
| 8360 | 12" x 8" | | 90 | .267 | | 495 | 9.05 | | 504.05 | 555 |
| 8400 | Tapped service tee (threaded type) 6" x 6" x 3/4 | | 100 | .240 | | 73.50 | 8.15 | | 81.65 | 93.50 |
| 8420 | 6" x 6" x 3/4" | | 90 | .267 | | 73.50 | 9.05 | | 82.55 | 95 |
| 8430 | 6" x 6" x 1" | | 90 | .267 | | 73.50 | 9.05 | | 82.55 | 95 |
| 8440 | 6" x 6" x 1 1/2" | | 90 | .267 | | 73.50 | 9.05 | | 82.55 | 95 |
| 8450 | 6" x 6" x 2" | | 90 | .267 | | 73.50 | 9.05 | | 82.55 | 95 |
| 8460 | 8" x 8" x 3/4" | | 90 | .267 | | 116 | 9.05 | | 125.05 | 142 |
| 8470 | 8" x 8" x 1" | | 90 | .267 | | 116 | 9.05 | | 125.05 | 142 |
| 8480 | 8" x 8" x 1 1/2" | | 90 | .267 | | 116 | 9.05 | | 125.05 | 142 |
| 8490 | 8" x 8" x 2" | | 90 | .267 | | 116 | 9.05 | | 125.05 | 142 |
| 8500 | Repair coupling 4" | | 100 | .240 | | 48 | 8.15 | | 56.15 | 65 |
| 8520 | 6" diameter | | 90 | .267 | | 65 | 9.05 | | 74.05 | 85.50 |
| 8540 | 8" diameter | | 50 | .480 | | 93.50 | 16.30 | | 109.80 | 129 |
| 8560 | 10" diameter | | 50 | .480 | | 148 | 16.30 | | 164.30 | 189 |
| 8580 | 12" diameter | | 50 | .480 | | 202 | 16.30 | | 218.30 | 248 |
| 8600 | Plug end 4" | | 100 | .240 | | 37 | 8.15 | | 45.15 | 53.50 |
| 8620 | 6" diameter | | 90 | .267 | | 72.50 | 9.05 | | 81.55 | 94 |
| 8640 | 8" diameter | | 50 | .480 | | 78 | 16.30 | | 94.30 | 112 |
| 8660 | 10" diameter | | 50 | .480 | | 125 | 16.30 | | 141.30 | 163 |
| 8680 | 12" diameter | | 50 | .480 | | 153 | 16.30 | | 169.30 | 194 |

# 33 12 Water Utility Distribution Equipment

## 33 12 19 – Water Utility Distribution Fire Hydrants

### 33 12 19.10 Fire Hydrants

| | | Crew | Daily Output | Labor-Hours | Unit | Material | 2008 Bare Costs Labor | Equipment | Total | Total Incl O&P |
|---|---|---|---|---|---|---|---|---|---|---|
| 0010 | **FIRE HYDRANTS** | | | | | | | | | |
| 0020 | Mechanical joints unless otherwise noted | | | | | | | | | |
| 1000 | Fire hydrants, two way; excavation and backfill not incl. | | | | | | | | | |
| 1100 | 4-1/2" valve size, depth 2'-0" | B-21 | 10 | 2.800 | Ea. | 1,400 | 98 | 12.95 | 1,510.95 | 1,725 |
| 1120 | 2'-6" | | 10 | 2.800 | | 1,500 | 98 | 12.95 | 1,610.95 | 1,825 |
| 1140 | 3'-0" | | 10 | 2.800 | | 1,550 | 98 | 12.95 | 1,660.95 | 1,875 |
| 1300 | 7'-0" | | 6 | 4.667 | | 1,875 | 163 | 21.50 | 2,059.50 | 2,325 |
| 2400 | Lower barrel extensions with stems, 1'-0" | B-20 | 14 | 1.714 | | 575 | 58 | | 633 | 720 |
| 2480 | 3'-0" | " | 12 | 2 | | 670 | 68 | | 738 | 845 |

# 33 16 Water Utility Storage Tanks

## 33 16 13 – Aboveground Water Utility Storage Tanks

### 33 16 13.13 Steel Water Storage Tanks

| | | Crew | Daily Output | Labor-Hours | Unit | Material | 2008 Bare Costs Labor | Equipment | Total | Total Incl O&P |
|---|---|---|---|---|---|---|---|---|---|---|
| 0010 | **STEEL WATER STORAGE TANKS** | | | | | | | | | |
| 0910 | Steel, ground level, ht/dia. less than 1, not incl. fdn., 100,000 gallons | | | | Ea. | | | | 144,000 | 158,000 |
| 1000 | 250,000 gallons | | | | | | | | 153,000 | 168,000 |
| 1200 | 500,000 gallons | | | | | | | | 233,000 | 256,000 |
| 1250 | 750,000 gallons | | | | | | | | 278,000 | 305,000 |
| 1300 | 1,000,000 gallons | | | | | | | | 424,000 | 467,000 |
| 1500 | 2,000,000 gallons | | | | | | | | 685,000 | 754,000 |
| 1600 | 4,000,000 gallons | | | | | | | | 1,064,000 | 1,170,000 |
| 1800 | 6,000,000 gallons | | | | | | | | 1,476,500 | 1,624,000 |
| 1850 | 8,000,000 gallons | | | | | | | | 1,933,000 | 2,126,500 |
| 1910 | 10,000,000 gallons | | | | ↓ | | | | 2,882,500 | 3,171,000 |
| 2100 | Steel standpipes, hgt/dia more than 1, 100' to overflow, no fdn | | | | | | | | | |
| 2200 | 500,000 gallons | | | | Ea. | | | | 306,500 | 337,000 |
| 2400 | 750,000 gallons | | | | | | | | 373,500 | 410,500 |
| 2500 | 1,000,000 gallons | | | | | | | | 454,500 | 500,100 |
| 2700 | 1,500,000 gallons | | | | | | | | 635,000 | 698,500 |
| 2800 | 2,000,000 gallons | | | | ↓ | | | | 780,000 | 858,000 |

### 33 16 13.16 Prestressed Conc. Aboveground Water Utility Storage

| | | Crew | Daily Output | Labor-Hours | Unit | Material | 2008 Bare Costs Labor | Equipment | Total | Total Incl O&P |
|---|---|---|---|---|---|---|---|---|---|---|
| 0010 | **PRESTRESSED CONC. ABOVEGROUND WATER UTILITY STORAGE** TANKS | | | | | | | | | |
| 0020 | Not including pipe or pumps, 250,000 gallons | | | | Ea. | | | | 258,500 | 284,000 |
| 0100 | 500,000 gallons | | | | | | | | 350,500 | 385,500 |
| 0300 | 1,000,000 gallons | | | | | | | | 498,500 | 548,000 |
| 0400 | 2,000,000 gallons | | | | | | | | 753,000 | 828,000 |
| 0600 | 4,000,000 gallons | | | | | | | | 1,190,500 | 1,309,500 |
| 0700 | 6,000,000 gallons | | | | | | | | 1,624,000 | 1,786,500 |
| 0750 | 8,000,000 gallons | | | | | | | | 2,067,000 | 2,273,500 |
| 0800 | 10,000,000 gallons | | | | ↓ | | | | 2,491,500 | 2,740,500 |

### 33 16 13.19 Wood Water Storage Tanks

| | | Crew | Daily Output | Labor-Hours | Unit | Material | 2008 Bare Costs Labor | Equipment | Total | Total Incl O&P |
|---|---|---|---|---|---|---|---|---|---|---|
| 0010 | **WOOD WATER STORAGE TANKS** | | | | | | | | | |
| 6000 | Wood tanks, ground level, 2" cypress, 3,000 gallons | C-1 | .19 | 168 | Ea. | 7,850 | 6,075 | | 13,925 | 18,100 |
| 6100 | 2-1/2" cypress, 10,000 gallons | | .12 | 266 | | 20,800 | 9,625 | | 30,425 | 37,900 |
| 6300 | 3" redwood or 3" fir, 20,000 gallons | | .10 | 320 | | 31,800 | 11,600 | | 43,400 | 53,000 |
| 6400 | 30,000 gallons | | .08 | 400 | | 39,300 | 14,500 | | 53,800 | 65,500 |
| 6600 | 45,000 gallons | ↓ | .07 | 457 | ↓ | 59,500 | 16,500 | | 76,000 | 91,000 |
| 6700 | Larger sizes, minimum | | | | Gal. | | | | .60 | .66 |
| 6900 | Maximum | | | | " | | | | .74 | .81 |

### 33 16 13.23 Plastic-Coated Fabric Pillow Water Tanks

| | | Crew | Daily Output | Labor-Hours | Unit | Material | 2008 Bare Costs Labor | Equipment | Total | Total Incl O&P |
|---|---|---|---|---|---|---|---|---|---|---|
| 0010 | **PLASTIC-COATED FABRIC PILLOW WATER TANKS** | | | | | | | | | |
| 7000 | Water tanks, vinyl coated fabric pillow tanks, freestanding, 5,000 gallons | 4 Clab | 4 | 8 | Ea. | 9,025 | 242 | | 9,267 | 10,300 |
| 7100 | Supporting embankment not included, 25,000 gallons | 6 Clab | 2 | 24 | | 14,000 | 725 | | 14,725 | 16,500 |
| 7200 | 50,000 gallons | 8 Clab | 1.50 | 42.667 | | 26,000 | 1,300 | | 27,300 | 30,600 |
| 7300 | 100,000 gallons | 9 Clab | .90 | 80 | | 56,000 | 2,425 | | 58,425 | 65,500 |
| 7400 | 150,000 gallons | | .50 | 144 | | 75,500 | 4,350 | | 79,850 | 90,500 |
| 7500 | 200,000 gallons | | .40 | 180 | | 92,000 | 5,450 | | 97,450 | 110,000 |
| 7600 | 250,000 gallons | ↓ | .30 | 240 | ↓ | 136,500 | 7,250 | | 143,750 | 161,500 |

## 33 16 19 – Elevated Water Utility Storage Tanks

### 33 16 19.50 Elevated Water Storage Tanks

| | | Crew | Daily Output | Labor-Hours | Unit | Material | 2008 Bare Costs Labor | Equipment | Total | Total Incl O&P |
|---|---|---|---|---|---|---|---|---|---|---|
| 0010 | **ELEVATED WATER STORAGE TANKS** | | | | | | | | | |
| 0011 | Not incl pipe, pumps or foundation | | | | | | | | | |
| 3000 | Elevated water tanks, 100' to bottom capacity line, incl painting | | | | | | | | | |
| 3010 | 50,000 gallons | | | | Ea. | | | | 185,000 | 203,500 |

# 33 16 Water Utility Storage Tanks

## 33 16 19 – Elevated Water Utility Storage Tanks

| 33 16 19.50 Elevated Water Storage Tanks | Crew | Daily Output | Labor-Hours | Unit | Material | 2008 Bare Costs Labor | Equipment | Total | Total Incl O&P |
|---|---|---|---|---|---|---|---|---|---|
| 3300 | 100,000 gallons | | | | Ea. | | | | 255,000 | 280,500 |
| 3400 | 250,000 gallons | | | | | | | | 352,000 | 387,500 |
| 3600 | 500,000 gallons | | | | | | | | 568,000 | 625,000 |
| 3700 | 750,000 gallons | | | | | | | | 783,500 | 861,500 |
| 3900 | 1,000,000 gallons | | | | | | | | 786,500 | 865,500 |

# 33 21 Water Supply Wells

## 33 21 13 – Public Water Supply Wells

### 33 21 13.10 Wells and Accessories

| | | Crew | Daily Output | Labor-Hours | Unit | Material | 2008 Bare Costs Labor | Equipment | Total | Total Incl O&P |
|---|---|---|---|---|---|---|---|---|---|---|
| 0010 | **WELLS & ACCESSORIES** | | | | | | | | | |
| 0011 | domestic | | | | | | | | | |
| 0100 | Drilled, 4" to 6" diameter | B-23 | 120 | .333 | L.F. | | 10.20 | 23 | 33.20 | 41.50 |
| 0200 | 8" diameter | " | 95.20 | .420 | " | | 12.90 | 29 | 41.90 | 52 |
| 0400 | Gravel pack well, 40' deep, incl. gravel & casing, complete | | | | | | | | | |
| 0500 | 24" diameter casing x 18" diameter screen | B-23 | .13 | 307 | Total | 28,400 | 9,425 | 21,200 | 59,025 | 69,000 |
| 0600 | 36" diameter casing x 18" diameter screen | | .12 | 333 | " | 30,500 | 10,200 | 23,000 | 63,700 | 74,500 |
| 0800 | Observation wells, 1-1/4" riser pipe | | 163 | .245 | V.L.F. | 15.60 | 7.50 | 16.90 | 40 | 47.50 |
| 0900 | For flush Buffalo roadway box, add | 1 Skwk | 16.60 | .482 | Ea. | 42.50 | 19 | | 61.50 | 76.50 |
| 1200 | Test well, 2-1/2" diameter, up to 50' deep (15 to 50 GPM) | B-23 | 1.51 | 26.490 | " | 640 | 810 | 1,825 | 3,275 | 3,975 |
| 1300 | Over 50' deep, add | " | 121.80 | .328 | L.F. | 17 | 10.05 | 22.50 | 49.55 | 59.50 |
| 1500 | Pumps, installed in wells to 100' deep, 4" submersible | | | | | | | | | |
| 1510 | 1/2 H.P. | Q-1 | 3.22 | 4.969 | Ea. | 400 | 209 | | 609 | 750 |
| 1520 | 3/4 H.P. | | 2.66 | 6.015 | | 460 | 253 | | 713 | 885 |
| 1600 | 1 H.P. | | 2.29 | 6.987 | | 470 | 294 | | 764 | 960 |
| 1700 | 1-1/2 H.P. | Q-22 | 1.60 | 10 | | 680 | 420 | 480 | 1,580 | 1,900 |
| 1800 | 2 H.P. | | 1.33 | 12.030 | | 1,475 | 505 | 575 | 2,555 | 3,000 |
| 1900 | 3 H.P. | | 1.14 | 14.035 | | 1,100 | 590 | 670 | 2,360 | 2,825 |
| 2000 | 5 H.P. | | 1.14 | 14.035 | | 1,475 | 590 | 670 | 2,735 | 3,250 |
| 3000 | Pump, 6" submersible, 25' to 150' deep, 25 H.P., 249 to 297 GPM | | .89 | 17.978 | | 5,250 | 755 | 860 | 6,865 | 7,850 |
| 3100 | 25' to 500' deep, 30 H.P., 100 to 300 GPM | | .73 | 21.918 | | 6,000 | 920 | 1,050 | 7,970 | 9,125 |
| 8000 | Steel well casing | B-23A | 3020 | .008 | Lb. | .72 | .27 | .87 | 1.86 | 2.17 |
| 9950 | See Div. 31 23 19.40 for wellpoints | | | | | | | | | |
| 9960 | See Div. 31 23 19.30 for drainage wells | | | | | | | | | |

### 33 21 13.20 Water Supply Wells, Pumps

| | | Crew | Daily Output | Labor-Hours | Unit | Material | 2008 Bare Costs Labor | Equipment | Total | Total Incl O&P |
|---|---|---|---|---|---|---|---|---|---|---|
| 0010 | **WATER SUPPLY WELLS, PUMPS** | | | | | | | | | |
| 0011 | with pressure control | | | | | | | | | |
| 1000 | Deep well, jet, 42 gal. galvanized tank | | | | | | | | | |
| 1040 | 3/4 HP | 1 Plum | .80 | 10 | Ea. | 650 | 465 | | 1,115 | 1,425 |
| 3000 | Shallow well, jet, 30 gal. galvanized tank | | | | | | | | | |
| 3040 | 1/2 HP | 1 Plum | 2 | 4 | Ea. | 470 | 187 | | 657 | 800 |

# 33 31 Sanitary Utility Sewerage Piping

## 33 31 13 – Public Sanitary Utility Sewerage Piping

### 33 31 13.15 Sewage Collection, Concrete Pipe

| | | Crew | Daily Output | Labor-Hours | Unit | Material | 2008 Bare Costs Labor | Equipment | Total | Total Incl O&P |
|---|---|---|---|---|---|---|---|---|---|---|
| 0010 | **SEWAGE COLLECTION, CONCRETE PIPE** | | | | | | | | | |
| 0020 | See Div. 33 41 13.60 for sewage/drainage collection, concrete pipe | | | | | | | | | |

### 33 31 13.25 Sewage Collection, Polyvinyl Chloride Pipe

| | | Crew | Daily Output | Labor-Hours | Unit | Material | 2008 Bare Costs Labor | Equipment | Total | Total Incl O&P |
|---|---|---|---|---|---|---|---|---|---|---|
| 0010 | **SEWAGE COLLECTION, POLYVINYL CHLORIDE PIPE** | | | | | | | | | |
| 0020 | Not including excavation or backfill | | | | | | | | | |
| 2000 | 20' lengths, S.D.R. 35, B&S, 4" diameter | B-20 | 375 | .064 | L.F. | 1.24 | 2.17 | | 3.41 | 4.74 |
| 2040 | 6" diameter | | 350 | .069 | | 2.28 | 2.33 | | 4.61 | 6.15 |
| 2080 | 13' lengths , S.D.R. 35, B&S, 8" diameter | | 335 | .072 | | 4.89 | 2.43 | | 7.32 | 9.20 |
| 2120 | 10" diameter | B-21 | 330 | .085 | | 8 | 2.97 | .39 | 11.36 | 13.75 |
| 2160 | 12" diameter | | 320 | .088 | | 9.15 | 3.06 | .40 | 12.61 | 15.20 |
| 2200 | 15" diameter | | 240 | .117 | | 8.90 | 4.08 | .54 | 13.52 | 16.70 |

# 33 36 Utility Septic Tanks

## 33 36 13 – Utility Septic Tank and Effluent Wet Wells

### 33 36 13.10 Septic Tanks

| | | Crew | Daily Output | Labor-Hours | Unit | Material | 2008 Bare Costs Labor | Equipment | Total | Total Incl O&P |
|---|---|---|---|---|---|---|---|---|---|---|
| 0010 | **SEPTIC TANKS** | | | | | | | | | |
| 0011 | Not including excavation or piping | | | | | | | | | |
| 0015 | Septic tanks, not incl exc or piping, precast, 1,000 gal | B-21 | 8 | 3.500 | Ea. | 670 | 122 | 16.15 | 808.15 | 945 |
| 0100 | 2,000 gallon | " | 5 | 5.600 | | 2,100 | 196 | 26 | 2,322 | 2,625 |
| 0200 | 5,000 gallon | B-13 | 3.50 | 16 | | 7,275 | 525 | 225 | 8,025 | 9,050 |
| 0300 | 15,000 gallon, 4 piece | B-13B | 1.70 | 32.941 | | 20,100 | 1,075 | 660 | 21,835 | 24,500 |
| 0400 | 25,000 gallon, 4 piece | | 1.10 | 50.909 | | 42,600 | 1,675 | 1,025 | 45,300 | 50,500 |
| 0500 | 40,000 gallon, 4 piece | | .80 | 70 | | 50,000 | 2,300 | 1,400 | 53,700 | 60,000 |
| 0520 | 50,000 gallon, 5 piece | B-13C | .60 | 93.333 | | 57,500 | 3,050 | 2,650 | 63,200 | 71,000 |
| 0540 | 75,000 gallon, cast in place | C-14C | .25 | 448 | | 70,000 | 16,400 | 98.50 | 86,498.50 | 103,000 |
| 0560 | 100,000 gallon | " | .15 | 746 | | 87,000 | 27,300 | 164 | 114,464 | 138,500 |
| 0600 | High density polyethylene, 1,000 gallon | B-21 | 6 | 4.667 | | 1,125 | 163 | 21.50 | 1,309.50 | 1,500 |
| 0700 | 1,500 gallon | " | 4 | 7 | | 1,450 | 245 | 32.50 | 1,727.50 | 2,000 |
| 1000 | Distribution boxes, concrete, 7 outlets | 2 Clab | 16 | 1 | | 124 | 30.50 | | 154.50 | 183 |
| 1100 | 9 outlets | " | 8 | 2 | | 460 | 60.50 | | 520.50 | 600 |
| 1150 | Leaching field chambers, 13' x 3'-7" x 1'-4", standard | B-13 | 16 | 3.500 | | 685 | 115 | 49 | 849 | 985 |
| 1200 | Heavy duty, 8' x 4' x 1'-6" | | 14 | 4 | | 435 | 131 | 56 | 622 | 745 |
| 1300 | 13' x 3'-9" x 1'-6" | | 12 | 4.667 | | 985 | 153 | 65.50 | 1,203.50 | 1,375 |
| 1350 | 20' x 4' x 1'-6" | | 5 | 11.200 | | 1,050 | 365 | 157 | 1,572 | 1,900 |
| 1400 | Leaching pit, precast concrete, 3' diameter, 3' deep | B-21 | 8 | 3.500 | | 615 | 122 | 16.15 | 753.15 | 880 |
| 1500 | 6' diameter, 3' section | | 4.70 | 5.957 | | 1,025 | 208 | 27.50 | 1,260.50 | 1,475 |
| 2000 | Velocity reducing pit, precast conc., 6' diameter, 3' deep | | 4.70 | 5.957 | | 1,225 | 208 | 27.50 | 1,460.50 | 1,700 |
| 2200 | Excavation for septic tank, 3/4 C.Y. backhoe | B-12F | 145 | .110 | C.Y. | | 3.93 | 3.79 | 7.72 | 10.15 |
| 2400 | 4' trench for disposal field, 3/4 C.Y. backhoe | " | 335 | .048 | L.F. | | 1.70 | 1.64 | 3.34 | 4.40 |
| 2600 | Gravel fill, run of bank | B-6 | 150 | .160 | C.Y. | 23.50 | 5.25 | 1.90 | 30.65 | 36 |
| 2800 | Crushed stone, 3/4" | " | 150 | .160 | " | 24.50 | 5.25 | 1.90 | 31.65 | 37 |

# 33 41 Storm Utility Drainage Piping

## 33 41 13 – Public Storm Utility Drainage Piping

### 33 41 13.40 Piping, Storm Drainage, Corrugated Metal

| | | Crew | Daily Output | Labor-Hours | Unit | Material | 2008 Bare Costs Labor | Equipment | Total | Total Incl O&P |
|---|---|---|---|---|---|---|---|---|---|---|
| 0010 | **PIPING, STORM DRAINAGE, CORRUGATED METAL** | | | | | | | | | |
| 0020 | Not including excavation or backfill | | | | | | | | | |
| 2000 | Corrugated metal pipe, galvanized | | | | | | | | | |
| 2020 | Bituminous coated with paved invert, 20' lengths | | | | | | | | | |
| 2040 | 8" diameter, 16 ga. | B-14 | 330 | .145 | L.F. | 10.55 | 4.63 | .87 | 16.05 | 19.70 |
| 2060 | 10" diameter, 16 ga. | | 260 | .185 | | 12.65 | 5.90 | 1.10 | 19.65 | 24.50 |
| 2080 | 12" diameter, 16 ga. | | 210 | .229 | | 15.15 | 7.30 | 1.36 | 23.81 | 29.50 |
| 2100 | 15" diameter, 16 ga. | | 200 | .240 | | 18.45 | 7.65 | 1.43 | 27.53 | 34 |
| 2120 | 18" diameter, 16 ga. | | 190 | .253 | | 23.50 | 8.05 | 1.50 | 33.05 | 40 |
| 2140 | 24" diameter, 14 ga. CN | | 160 | .300 | | 29 | 9.55 | 1.79 | 40.34 | 48.50 |
| 2160 | 30" diameter, 14 ga. | B-13 | 120 | .467 | | 38 | 15.30 | 6.55 | 59.85 | 72.50 |
| 2180 | 36" diameter, 12 ga. | | 120 | .467 | | 56 | 15.30 | 6.55 | 77.85 | 92 |
| 2200 | 48" diameter, 12 ga. | | 100 | .560 | | 85 | 18.35 | 7.85 | 111.20 | 131 |
| 2220 | 60" diameter, 10 ga. | B-13B | 75 | .747 | | 110 | 24.50 | 14.90 | 149.40 | 175 |
| 2240 | 72" diameter, 8 ga. | " | 45 | 1.244 | | 165 | 41 | 25 | 231 | 272 |
| 2500 | Galvanized, uncoated, 20' lengths | | | | | | | | | |
| 2520 | 8" diameter, 16 ga. | B-14 | 355 | .135 | L.F. | 8.65 | 4.30 | .80 | 13.75 | 17.05 |
| 2540 | 10" diameter, 16 ga. | | 280 | .171 | | 9.45 | 5.45 | 1.02 | 15.92 | 19.95 |
| 2560 | 12" diameter, 16 ga. | | 220 | .218 | | 10.80 | 6.95 | 1.30 | 19.05 | 24 |
| 2580 | 15" diameter, 16 ga. | | 220 | .218 | | 13.75 | 6.95 | 1.30 | 22 | 27.50 |
| 2600 | 18" diameter, 16 ga. | | 205 | .234 | | 18.20 | 7.45 | 1.39 | 27.04 | 33 |
| 2620 | 24" diameter, 14 ga. | | 175 | .274 | | 26.50 | 8.75 | 1.63 | 36.88 | 44.50 |
| 2640 | 30" diameter, 14 ga. | B-13 | 130 | .431 | | 33.50 | 14.10 | 6.05 | 53.65 | 65 |
| 2660 | 36" diameter, 12 ga. | | 130 | .431 | | 55 | 14.10 | 6.05 | 75.15 | 88.50 |
| 2680 | 48" diameter, 12 ga. | | 110 | .509 | | 73.50 | 16.70 | 7.15 | 97.35 | 114 |
| 2690 | 60" diameter, 10 ga. | B-13B | 78 | .718 | | 116 | 23.50 | 14.35 | 153.85 | 179 |
| 2780 | End sections, 8" diameter | B-14 | 24 | 2 | Ea. | 84 | 63.50 | 11.90 | 159.40 | 204 |
| 2785 | 10" diameter | | 22 | 2.182 | | 86.50 | 69.50 | 13 | 169 | 216 |
| 2790 | 12" diameter | | 35 | 1.371 | | 97.50 | 43.50 | 8.15 | 149.15 | 183 |
| 2800 | 18" diameter | | 30 | 1.600 | | 116 | 51 | 9.50 | 176.50 | 216 |
| 2810 | 24" diameter | B-13 | 25 | 2.240 | | 169 | 73.50 | 31.50 | 274 | 335 |
| 2820 | 30" diameter | | 25 | 2.240 | | 320 | 73.50 | 31.50 | 425 | 500 |
| 2825 | 36" diameter | | 20 | 2.800 | | 425 | 91.50 | 39.50 | 556 | 650 |
| 2830 | 48" diameter | | 10 | 5.600 | | 875 | 183 | 78.50 | 1,136.50 | 1,325 |
| 2835 | 60" diameter | B-13B | 5 | 11.200 | | 1,150 | 365 | 224 | 1,739 | 2,050 |
| 2840 | 72" diameter | " | 4 | 14 | | 2,050 | 460 | 280 | 2,790 | 3,300 |

### 33 41 13.60 Sewage/Drainage Collection, Concrete Pipe

| | | Crew | Daily Output | Labor-Hours | Unit | Material | 2008 Bare Costs Labor | Equipment | Total | Total Incl O&P |
|---|---|---|---|---|---|---|---|---|---|---|
| 0010 | **SEWAGE/DRAINAGE COLLECTION, CONCRETE PIPE** | | | | | | | | | |
| 0020 | Not including excavation or backfill | | | | | | | | | |
| 1000 | Non-reinforced pipe, extra strength, B&S or T&G joints | | | | | | | | | |
| 1010 | 6" diameter | B-14 | 265.04 | .181 | L.F. | 5.05 | 5.75 | 1.08 | 11.88 | 15.65 |
| 1020 | 8" diameter | | 224 | .214 | | 5.55 | 6.80 | 1.28 | 13.63 | 18.05 |
| 1030 | 10" diameter | | 216 | .222 | | 6.15 | 7.05 | 1.32 | 14.52 | 19.20 |
| 1040 | 12" diameter | | 200 | .240 | | 7.60 | 7.65 | 1.43 | 16.68 | 21.50 |
| 1050 | 15" diameter | | 180 | .267 | | 8.85 | 8.50 | 1.59 | 18.94 | 24.50 |
| 1060 | 18" diameter | | 144 | .333 | | 10.90 | 10.60 | 1.98 | 23.48 | 30.50 |
| 1070 | 21" diameter | | 112 | .429 | | 13.40 | 13.65 | 2.55 | 29.60 | 38.50 |
| 1080 | 24" diameter | | 100 | .480 | | 16.45 | 15.30 | 2.86 | 34.61 | 44.50 |
| 2000 | Reinforced culvert, class 3, no gaskets | | | | | | | | | |
| 2010 | 12" diameter | B-14 | 150 | .320 | L.F. | 13.40 | 10.20 | 1.90 | 25.50 | 32.50 |
| 2020 | 15" diameter | | 150 | .320 | | 12.45 | 10.20 | 1.90 | 24.55 | 31.50 |
| 2030 | 18" diameter | | 132 | .364 | | 14.55 | 11.55 | 2.16 | 28.26 | 36.50 |

# 33 41 Storm Utility Drainage Piping

## 33 41 13 – Public Storm Utility Drainage Piping

| 33 41 13.60 Sewage/Drainage Collection, Concrete Pipe | Crew | Daily Output | Labor-Hours | Unit | Material | 2008 Bare Costs Labor | Equipment | Total | Total Incl O&P |
|---|---|---|---|---|---|---|---|---|---|
| 2035 | 21" diameter | B-14 | 120 | .400 | L.F. | 18.10 | 12.75 | 2.38 | 33.23 | 42 |
| 2040 | 24" diameter | CN | 100 | .480 | | 27.50 | 15.30 | 2.86 | 45.66 | 56.50 |
| 2045 | 27" diameter | B-13 | 92 | .609 | | 34 | 19.95 | 8.55 | 62.50 | 77.50 |
| 2050 | 30" diameter | | 88 | .636 | | 34 | 21 | 8.95 | 63.95 | 79.50 |
| 2060 | 36" diameter | | 72 | .778 | | 44.50 | 25.50 | 10.90 | 80.90 | 100 |
| 2070 | 42" diameter | B-13B | 72 | .778 | | 64.50 | 25.50 | 15.55 | 105.55 | 127 |
| 2080 | 48" diameter | | 64 | .875 | | 94 | 28.50 | 17.50 | 140 | 166 |
| 2090 | 60" diameter | | 48 | 1.167 | | 168 | 38 | 23.50 | 229.50 | 270 |
| 2100 | 72" diameter | | 40 | 1.400 | | 187 | 46 | 28 | 261 | 310 |
| 2120 | 84" diameter | | 32 | 1.750 | | 335 | 57.50 | 35 | 427.50 | 495 |
| 2140 | 96" diameter | | 24 | 2.333 | | 405 | 76.50 | 46.50 | 528 | 615 |
| 2200 | With gaskets, class 3, 12" diameter | B-21 | 168 | .167 | | 11.75 | 5.85 | .77 | 18.37 | 23 |
| 2220 | 15" diameter | | 160 | .175 | | 14.10 | 6.10 | .81 | 21.01 | 26 |
| 2230 | 18" diameter | | 152 | .184 | | 17.60 | 6.45 | .85 | 24.90 | 30 |
| 2240 | 24" diameter | | 136 | .206 | | 26.50 | 7.20 | .95 | 34.65 | 41 |
| 2260 | 30" diameter | B-13 | 88 | .636 | | 35 | 21 | 8.95 | 64.95 | 80.50 |
| 2270 | 36" diameter | " | 72 | .778 | | 53 | 25.50 | 10.90 | 89.40 | 109 |
| 2290 | 48" diameter | B-13B | 64 | .875 | | 86.50 | 28.50 | 17.50 | 132.50 | 158 |
| 2310 | 72" diameter | " | 40 | 1.400 | | 223 | 46 | 28 | 297 | 345 |
| 2330 | Flared ends, 6'-1" long, 12" diameter | B-21 | 190 | .147 | | 43 | 5.15 | .68 | 48.83 | 55.50 |
| 2340 | 15" diameter | | 155 | .181 | | 49 | 6.30 | .83 | 56.13 | 64.50 |
| 2400 | 6'-2" long, 18" diameter | | 122 | .230 | | 51 | 8 | 1.06 | 60.06 | 69.50 |
| 2420 | 24" diameter | | 88 | .318 | | 59 | 11.10 | 1.47 | 71.57 | 83.50 |
| 2440 | 36" diameter | B-13 | 60 | .933 | | 107 | 30.50 | 13.10 | 150.60 | 179 |
| 3080 | Radius pipe, add to pipe prices, 12" to 60" diameter | | | | | 50% | | | | |
| 3090 | Over 60" diameter, add | | | | | 20% | | | | |
| 3500 | Reinforced elliptical, 8' lengths, C507 class 3 | | | | | | | | | |
| 3520 | 14" x 23" inside, round equivalent 18" diameter | B-21 | 82 | .341 | L.F. | 41.50 | 11.95 | 1.58 | 55.03 | 65.50 |
| 3530 | 24" x 38" inside, round equivalent 30" diameter | B-13 | 58 | .966 | | 61.50 | 31.50 | 13.55 | 106.55 | 131 |
| 3540 | 29" x 45" inside, round equivalent 36" diameter | | 52 | 1.077 | | 102 | 35.50 | 15.10 | 152.60 | 183 |
| 3550 | 38" x 60" inside, round equivalent 48" diameter | | 38 | 1.474 | | 174 | 48.50 | 20.50 | 243 | 290 |
| 3560 | 48" x 76" inside, round equivalent 60" diameter | | 26 | 2.154 | | 245 | 70.50 | 30 | 345.50 | 415 |
| 3570 | 58" x 91" inside, round equivalent 72" diameter | | 22 | 2.545 | | 340 | 83.50 | 35.50 | 459 | 545 |
| 3780 | Concrete slotted pipe, class 4 mortar joint | | | | | | | | | |
| 3800 | 12" diameter | B-21 | 168 | .167 | L.F. | 15.65 | 5.85 | .77 | 22.27 | 27 |
| 3840 | 18" diameter | " | 152 | .184 | " | 24 | 6.45 | .85 | 31.30 | 37.50 |
| 3900 | Class 4 O-ring | | | | | | | | | |
| 3940 | 12" diameter | B-21 | 168 | .167 | L.F. | 16.40 | 5.85 | .77 | 23.02 | 28 |
| 3960 | 18" diameter | " | 152 | .184 | " | 22 | 6.45 | .85 | 29.30 | 35 |

# 33 42 Culverts

## 33 42 16 – Concrete Culverts

### 33 42 16.15 Oval Arch Culverts

| | | Crew | Daily Output | Labor-Hours | Unit | Material | 2008 Bare Costs Labor | Equipment | Total | Total Incl O&P |
|---|---|---|---|---|---|---|---|---|---|---|
| 0010 | **OVAL ARCH CULVERTS** | | | | | | | | | |
| 3000 | Corrugated galvanized or aluminum, coated & paved | | | | | | | | | |
| 3020 | 17" x 13", 16 ga., 15" equivalent | B-14 | 200 | .240 | L.F. | 33 | 7.65 | 1.43 | 42.08 | 50 |
| 3040 | 21" x 15", 16 ga., 18" equivalent | | 150 | .320 | | 42.50 | 10.20 | 1.90 | 54.60 | 64.50 |
| 3060 | 28" x 20", 14 ga., 24" equivalent | | 125 | .384 | | 61 | 12.20 | 2.28 | 75.48 | 88.50 |
| 3080 | 35" x 24", 14 ga., 30" equivalent | | 100 | .480 | | 74 | 15.30 | 2.86 | 92.16 | 108 |
| 3100 | 42" x 29", 12 ga., 36" equivalent | B-13 | 100 | .560 | | 111 | 18.35 | 7.85 | 137.20 | 159 |
| 3120 | 49" x 33", 12 ga., 42" equivalent | | 90 | .622 | | 133 | 20.50 | 8.75 | 162.25 | 188 |

594

# 33 42 Culverts

## 33 42 16 – Concrete Culverts

| 33 42 16.15 Oval Arch Culverts | | Crew | Daily Output | Labor-Hours | Unit | Material | 2008 Bare Costs Labor | Equipment | Total | Total Incl O&P |
|---|---|---|---|---|---|---|---|---|---|---|
| 3140 | 57" x 38", 12 ga., 48" equivalent | B-13 | 75 | .747 | L.F. | 148 | 24.50 | 10.50 | 183 | 212 |
| 3160 | Steel, plain oval arch culverts, plain | | | | | | | | | |
| 3180 | 17" x 13", 16 ga., 15" equivalent | B-14 | 225 | .213 | L.F. | 17.85 | 6.80 | 1.27 | 25.92 | 31.50 |
| 3200 | 21" x 15", 16 ga., 18" equivalent | | 175 | .274 | | 21 | 8.75 | 1.63 | 31.38 | 38.50 |
| 3220 | 28" x 20", 14 ga., 24" equivalent | | 150 | .320 | | 34 | 10.20 | 1.90 | 46.10 | 55.50 |
| 3240 | 35" x 24", 14 ga., 30" equivalent | B-13 | 108 | .519 | | 42.50 | 17 | 7.30 | 66.80 | 81 |
| 3260 | 42" x 29", 12 ga., 36" equivalent | | 108 | .519 | | 70.50 | 17 | 7.30 | 94.80 | 112 |
| 3280 | 49" x 33", 12 ga., 42" equivalent | | 92 | .609 | | 83 | 19.95 | 8.55 | 111.50 | 131 |
| 3300 | 57" x 38", 12 ga., 48" equivalent | | 75 | .747 | | 73 | 24.50 | 10.50 | 108 | 130 |
| 3320 | End sections, 17" x 13" | | 22 | 2.545 | Ea. | 97.50 | 83.50 | 35.50 | 216.50 | 275 |
| 3340 | 42" x 29" | | 17 | 3.294 | " | 400 | 108 | 46.50 | 554.50 | 655 |
| 3360 | Multi-plate arch, steel | B-20 | 1690 | .014 | Lb. | 1.12 | .48 | | 1.60 | 1.98 |

# 33 44 Storm Utility Water Drains

## 33 44 13 – Utility Area Drains

### 33 44 13.13 Catchbasins

| | | Crew | Daily Output | Labor-Hours | Unit | Material | 2008 Bare Costs Labor | Equipment | Total | Total Incl O&P |
|---|---|---|---|---|---|---|---|---|---|---|
| 0010 | **CATCHBASINS** | | | | | | | | | |
| 0011 | Not including footing & excavation | | | | | | | | | |
| 1600 | Frames & covers, C.I., 24" square, 500 lb. | B-6 | 7.80 | 3.077 | Ea. | 249 | 101 | 36.50 | 386.50 | 470 |
| 1700 | 26" D shape, 600 lb. | | 7 | 3.429 | | 425 | 112 | 41 | 578 | 690 |
| 1800 | Light traffic, 18" diameter, 100 lb. | | 10 | 2.400 | | 139 | 78.50 | 28.50 | 246 | 305 |
| 1900 | 24" diameter, 300 lb. | | 8.70 | 2.759 | | 215 | 90.50 | 33 | 338.50 | 410 |
| 2000 | 36" diameter, 900 lb. | | 5.80 | 4.138 | | 430 | 136 | 49 | 615 | 735 |
| 2100 | Heavy traffic, 24" diameter, 400 lb. | | 7.80 | 3.077 | | 208 | 101 | 36.50 | 345.50 | 425 |
| 2200 | 36" diameter, 1150 lb. | | 3 | 8 | | 690 | 262 | 95 | 1,047 | 1,275 |
| 2300 | Mass. State standard, 26" diameter, 475 lb. | | 7 | 3.429 | | 520 | 112 | 41 | 673 | 795 |
| 2400 | 30" diameter, 620 lb. | | 7 | 3.429 | | 330 | 112 | 41 | 483 | 585 |
| 2500 | Watertight, 24" diameter, 350 lb. | | 7.80 | 3.077 | | 355 | 101 | 36.50 | 492.50 | 585 |
| 2600 | 26" diameter, 500 lb. | | 7 | 3.429 | | 335 | 112 | 41 | 488 | 590 |
| 2700 | 32" diameter, 575 lb. | | 6 | 4 | | 745 | 131 | 47.50 | 923.50 | 1,075 |
| 2800 | 3 piece cover & frame, 10" deep, | | | | | | | | | |
| 2900 | 1200 lbs., for heavy equipment | B-6 | 3 | 8 | Ea. | 1,075 | 262 | 95 | 1,432 | 1,675 |
| 3000 | Raised for paving 1-1/4" to 2" high, | | | | | | | | | |
| 3100 | 4 piece expansion ring | | | | | | | | | |
| 3200 | 20" to 26" diameter | 1 Clab | 3 | 2.667 | Ea. | 117 | 80.50 | | 197.50 | 253 |
| 3300 | 30" to 36" diameter | " | 3 | 2.667 | " | 162 | 80.50 | | 242.50 | 305 |
| 3320 | Frames and covers, existing, raised for paving, 2", including | | | | | | | | | |
| 3340 | row of brick, concrete collar, up to 12" wide frame | B-6 | 18 | 1.333 | Ea. | 36.50 | 43.50 | 15.85 | 95.85 | 124 |
| 3360 | 20" to 26" wide frame | | 11 | 2.182 | | 57.50 | 71.50 | 26 | 155 | 202 |
| 3380 | 30" to 36" wide frame | | 9 | 2.667 | | 71 | 87.50 | 31.50 | 190 | 248 |
| 3400 | Inverts, single channel brick | D-1 | 3 | 5.333 | | 80 | 186 | | 266 | 370 |
| 3500 | Concrete | | 5 | 3.200 | | 62.50 | 112 | | 174.50 | 239 |
| 3600 | Triple channel, brick | | 2 | 8 | | 121 | 279 | | 400 | 560 |
| 3700 | Concrete | | 3 | 5.333 | | 107 | 186 | | 293 | 400 |

# 33 46 Subdrainage

## 33 46 16 – Subdrainage Piping

### 33 46 16.20 Piping, Subdrainage, Concrete

| | | Crew | Daily Output | Labor-Hours | Unit | Material | 2008 Bare Costs Labor | Equipment | Total | Total Incl O&P |
|---|---|---|---|---|---|---|---|---|---|---|
| 0010 | **PIPING, SUBDRAINAGE, CONCRETE** | | | | | | | | | |
| 0021 | Not including excavation and backfill | | | | | | | | | |
| 3000 | Porous wall concrete underdrain, std. strength, 4" diameter | B-20 | 335 | .072 | L.F. | 3.02 | 2.43 | | 5.45 | 7.10 |
| 3020 | 6" diameter | " | 315 | .076 | | 3.93 | 2.59 | | 6.52 | 8.35 |
| 3040 | 8" diameter | B-21 | 310 | .090 | | 4.85 | 3.16 | .42 | 8.43 | 10.70 |
| 3060 | 12" diameter | | 285 | .098 | | 10.25 | 3.43 | .45 | 14.13 | 17.10 |
| 3080 | 15" diameter | | 230 | .122 | | 11.80 | 4.26 | .56 | 16.62 | 20 |
| 3100 | 18" diameter | | 165 | .170 | | 15.55 | 5.95 | .78 | 22.28 | 27 |
| 4000 | Extra strength, 6" diameter | B-20 | 315 | .076 | | 3.97 | 2.59 | | 6.56 | 8.40 |
| 4020 | 8" diameter | B-21 | 310 | .090 | | 5.95 | 3.16 | .42 | 9.53 | 11.90 |
| 4040 | 10" diameter | | 295 | .095 | | 11.90 | 3.32 | .44 | 15.66 | 18.75 |
| 4060 | 12" diameter | | 285 | .098 | | 12.90 | 3.43 | .45 | 16.78 | 20 |
| 4080 | 15" diameter | | 230 | .122 | | 14.30 | 4.26 | .56 | 19.12 | 23 |
| 4100 | 18" diameter | | 165 | .170 | | 21 | 5.95 | .78 | 27.73 | 33 |

### 33 46 16.25 Piping, Subdrainage, Corrugated Metal

| | | Crew | Daily Output | Labor-Hours | Unit | Material | Labor | Equipment | Total | Total Incl O&P |
|---|---|---|---|---|---|---|---|---|---|---|
| 0010 | **PIPING, SUBDRAINAGE, CORRUGATED METAL** | | | | | | | | | |
| 0021 | Not including excavation and backfill | | | | | | | | | |
| 2010 | Aluminum, perforated | | | | | | | | | |
| 2020 | 6" diameter, 18 ga. | B-14 | 380 | .126 | L.F. | 4.30 | 4.02 | .75 | 9.07 | 11.75 |
| 2200 | 8" diameter, 16 ga. | | 370 | .130 | | 6.15 | 4.13 | .77 | 11.05 | 14.05 |
| 2220 | 10" diameter, 16 ga. | | 360 | .133 | | 7.70 | 4.24 | .79 | 12.73 | 15.85 |
| 2240 | 12" diameter, 16 ga. | | 285 | .168 | | 8.60 | 5.35 | 1 | 14.95 | 18.90 |
| 2260 | 18" diameter, 16 ga. | | 205 | .234 | | 12.95 | 7.45 | 1.39 | 21.79 | 27.50 |
| 3000 | Uncoated galvanized, perforated | | | | | | | | | |
| 3020 | 6" diameter, 18 ga. | B-20 | 380 | .063 | L.F. | 6.85 | 2.15 | | 9 | 10.90 |
| 3200 | 8" diameter, 16 ga. | " | 370 | .065 | | 9.45 | 2.20 | | 11.65 | 13.85 |
| 3220 | 10" diameter, 16 ga. | B-21 | 360 | .078 | | 14.15 | 2.72 | .36 | 17.23 | 20 |
| 3240 | 12" diameter, 16 ga. | | 285 | .098 | | 14.80 | 3.43 | .45 | 18.68 | 22 |
| 3260 | 18" diameter, 16 ga. | | 205 | .137 | | 22.50 | 4.78 | .63 | 27.91 | 33 |
| 4000 | Steel, perforated, asphalt coated | | | | | | | | | |
| 4020 | 6" diameter 18 ga. | B-20 | 380 | .063 | L.F. | 5.50 | 2.15 | | 7.65 | 9.40 |
| 4030 | 8" diameter 18 ga | " | 370 | .065 | | 8.60 | 2.20 | | 10.80 | 12.90 |
| 4040 | 10" diameter 16 ga | B-21 | 360 | .078 | | 9.85 | 2.72 | .36 | 12.93 | 15.45 |
| 4050 | 12" diameter 16 ga | | 285 | .098 | | 11.30 | 3.43 | .45 | 15.18 | 18.25 |
| 4060 | 18" diameter 16 ga | | 205 | .137 | | 15.45 | 4.78 | .63 | 20.86 | 25 |

### 33 46 16.40 Piping, Subdrainage, Polyvinyl Chloride

| | | Crew | Daily Output | Labor-Hours | Unit | Material | Labor | Equipment | Total | Total Incl O&P |
|---|---|---|---|---|---|---|---|---|---|---|
| 0010 | **PIPING, SUBDRAINAGE, POLYVINYL CHLORIDE** | | | | | | | | | |
| 0020 | Perforated, price as solid pipe, Division 33 41 13.25 | | | | | | | | | |

# 33 49 Storm Drainage Structures

## 33 49 13 – Storm Drainage Manholes, Frames, and Covers

### 33 49 13.10 Storm Drainage Manholes, Frames and Covers

| | | Crew | Daily Output | Labor-Hours | Unit | Material | Labor | Equipment | Total | Total Incl O&P |
|---|---|---|---|---|---|---|---|---|---|---|
| 0010 | **STORM DRAINAGE MANHOLES, FRAMES & COVERS** | | | | | | | | | |
| 0020 | excludes footing, excavation, backfill (See line items for frame & cover) | | | | | | | | | |
| 0050 | Brick, 4' inside diameter, 4' deep | D-1 | 1 | 16 | Ea. | 395 | 560 | | 955 | 1,275 |
| 0100 | 6' deep | | .70 | 22.857 | | 555 | 795 | | 1,350 | 1,825 |
| 0150 | 8' deep | | .50 | 32 | | 710 | 1,125 | | 1,835 | 2,475 |
| 0200 | For depths over 8', add | | 4 | 4 | V.L.F. | 147 | 140 | | 287 | 375 |
| 0400 | Concrete blocks (radial), 4' I.D., 4' deep | | 1.50 | 10.667 | Ea. | 340 | 370 | | 710 | 940 |
| 0500 | 6' deep | | 1 | 16 | | 450 | 560 | | 1,010 | 1,350 |

# 33 49 Storm Drainage Structures

## 33 49 13 – Storm Drainage Manholes, Frames, and Covers

| 33 49 13.10 Storm Drainage Manholes, Frames and Covers | Crew | Daily Output | Labor-Hours | Unit | Material | 2008 Bare Costs Labor | Equipment | Total | Total Incl O&P |
|---|---|---|---|---|---|---|---|---|---|
| 0600 | 8' deep | D-1 | .70 | 22.857 | Ea. | 560 | 795 | | 1,355 | 1,850 |
| 0700 | For depths over 8', add | ↓ | 5.50 | 2.909 | V.L.F. | 57.50 | 101 | | 158.50 | 217 |
| 0800 | Concrete, cast in place, 4' x 4', 8" thick, 4' deep | C-14H | 2 | 24 | Ea. | 510 | 905 | 12.50 | 1,427.50 | 1,975 |
| 0900 | 6' deep | | 1.50 | 32 | | 740 | 1,200 | 16.65 | 1,956.65 | 2,700 |
| 1000 | 8' deep | | 1 | 48 | ↓ | 1,050 | 1,800 | 25 | 2,875 | 4,025 |
| 1100 | For depths over 8', add | ↓ | 8 | 6 | V.L.F. | 120 | 227 | 3.12 | 350.12 | 490 |
| 1110 | Precast, 4' I.D., 4' deep | B-22 | 4.10 | 7.317 | Ea. | 680 | 259 | 47.50 | 986.50 | 1,200 |
| 1120 | 6' deep | | 3 | 10 | | 850 | 355 | 64.50 | 1,269.50 | 1,550 |
| 1130 | 8' deep | | 2 | 15 | ↓ | 1,025 | 530 | 97 | 1,652 | 2,050 |
| 1140 | For depths over 8', add | ↓ | 16 | 1.875 | V.L.F. | 139 | 66.50 | 12.15 | 217.65 | 268 |
| 1150 | 5' I.D., 4' deep | B-6 | 3 | 8 | Ea. | 700 | 262 | 95 | 1,057 | 1,275 |
| 1160 | 6' deep | | 2 | 12 | | 945 | 395 | 143 | 1,483 | 1,800 |
| 1170 | 8' deep | | 1.50 | 16 | ↓ | 1,200 | 525 | 190 | 1,915 | 2,325 |
| 1180 | For depths over 8', add | | 12 | 2 | V.L.F. | 155 | 65.50 | 24 | 244.50 | 298 |
| 1190 | 6' I.D., 4' deep | | 2 | 12 | Ea. | 1,150 | 395 | 143 | 1,688 | 2,000 |
| 1200 | 6' deep | | 1.50 | 16 | | 1,500 | 525 | 190 | 2,215 | 2,650 |
| 1210 | 8' deep | | 1 | 24 | ↓ | 1,825 | 785 | 285 | 2,895 | 3,550 |
| 1220 | For depths over 8', add | ↓ | 8 | 3 | V.L.F. | 240 | 98.50 | 35.50 | 374 | 455 |
| 1250 | Slab tops, precast, 8" thick | | | | | | | | | |
| 1300 | 4' diameter manhole | B-6 | 8 | 3 | Ea. | 161 | 98.50 | 35.50 | 295 | 365 |
| 1400 | 5' diameter manhole | | 7.50 | 3.200 | | 315 | 105 | 38 | 458 | 555 |
| 1500 | 6' diameter manhole | ↓ | 7 | 3.429 | | 460 | 112 | 41 | 613 | 725 |
| 3800 | Steps, heavyweight cast iron, 7" x 9" | 1 Bric | 40 | .200 | | 12.95 | 7.85 | | 20.80 | 26 |
| 3900 | 8" x 9" | | 40 | .200 | | 19.45 | 7.85 | | 27.30 | 33.50 |
| 3928 | 12" x 10-1/2" | | 40 | .200 | | 18.40 | 7.85 | | 26.25 | 32 |
| 4000 | Standard sizes, galvanized steel | | 40 | .200 | | 15.60 | 7.85 | | 23.45 | 29 |
| 4100 | Aluminum | ↓ | 40 | .200 | ↓ | 21 | 7.85 | | 28.85 | 35.50 |

# 33 51 Natural-Gas Distribution

## 33 51 13 – Natural-Gas Piping

### 33 51 13.10 Piping, Gas Service and Distribution, Polyethylene

| | | Crew | Daily Output | Labor-Hours | Unit | Material | 2008 Bare Costs Labor | Equipment | Total | Total Incl O&P |
|---|---|---|---|---|---|---|---|---|---|---|
| 0010 | **PIPING, GAS SERVICE AND DISTRIBUTION, POLYETHYLENE** | | | | | | | | | |
| 0020 | not including excavation or backfill | | | | | | | | | |
| 1000 | 60 psi coils, compression coupling @ 100', 1/2" diameter, SDR 11 | B-20A | 608 | .053 | L.F. | 1.40 | 1.93 | | 3.33 | 4.48 |
| 1040 | 1-1/4" diameter, SDR 11 | | 544 | .059 | | 2.16 | 2.16 | | 4.32 | 5.65 |
| 1100 | 2" diameter, SDR 11 | | 488 | .066 | | 2.69 | 2.40 | | 5.09 | 6.60 |
| 1160 | 3" diameter, SDR 11 | ↓ | 408 | .078 | | 5.60 | 2.87 | | 8.47 | 10.55 |
| 1500 | 60 PSI 40' joints with coupling, 3" diameter, SDR 11 | B-21A | 408 | .098 | | 5.60 | 3.68 | 1.50 | 10.78 | 13.40 |
| 1540 | 4" diameter, SDR 11 | | 352 | .114 | | 12.80 | 4.26 | 1.74 | 18.80 | 22.50 |
| 1600 | 6" diameter, SDR 11 | | 328 | .122 | | 40 | 4.57 | 1.86 | 46.43 | 53 |
| 1640 | 8" diameter, SDR 11 | ↓ | 272 | .147 | ↓ | 54.50 | 5.50 | 2.25 | 62.25 | 71 |

597

# 33 52 Liquid Fuel Distribution

## 33 52 16 – Gasoline Distribution

| 33 52 16.13 Gasoline Piping | Crew | Daily Output | Labor-Hours | Unit | Material | 2008 Bare Costs Labor | Equipment | Total | Total Incl O&P |
|---|---|---|---|---|---|---|---|---|---|
| **0010** | **GASOLINE PIPING** | | | | | | | | |
| 0020 | Primary containment pipe, fiberglass-reinforced | | | | | | | | |
| 0030 | Plastic pipe 15' & 30' lengths | | | | | | | | |
| 0040 | 2" diameter | Q-6 | 425 | .056 | L.F. | 4.29 | 2.48 | | 6.77 | 8.45 |
| 0050 | 3" diameter | | 400 | .060 | | 5.60 | 2.64 | | 8.24 | 10.15 |
| 0060 | 4" diameter | ↓ | 375 | .064 | ↓ | 7.25 | 2.81 | | 10.06 | 12.25 |
| 0100 | Fittings | | | | | | | | |
| 0110 | Elbows, 90° & 45°, bell-ends, 2" | Q-6 | 24 | 1 | Ea. | 43.50 | 44 | | 87.50 | 114 |
| 0120 | 3" diameter | | 22 | 1.091 | | 45.50 | 48 | | 93.50 | 122 |
| 0130 | 4" diameter | | 20 | 1.200 | | 60.50 | 53 | | 113.50 | 146 |
| 0200 | Tees, bell ends, 2" | | 21 | 1.143 | | 52.50 | 50.50 | | 103 | 134 |
| 0210 | 3" diameter | | 18 | 1.333 | | 53 | 58.50 | | 111.50 | 147 |
| 0220 | 4" diameter | | 15 | 1.600 | | 73 | 70.50 | | 143.50 | 186 |
| 0230 | Flanges bell ends, 2" | | 24 | 1 | | 17.40 | 44 | | 61.40 | 85 |
| 0240 | 3" diameter | | 22 | 1.091 | | 22 | 48 | | 70 | 96 |
| 0250 | 4" diameter | | 20 | 1.200 | | 30 | 53 | | 83 | 113 |
| 0260 | Sleeve couplings, 2" | | 21 | 1.143 | | 11.10 | 50.50 | | 61.60 | 87.50 |
| 0270 | 3" diameter | | 18 | 1.333 | | 15.70 | 58.50 | | 74.20 | 105 |
| 0280 | 4" diameter | | 15 | 1.600 | | 21.50 | 70.50 | | 92 | 130 |
| 0290 | Threaded adapters 2" | | 21 | 1.143 | | 14.55 | 50.50 | | 65.05 | 91.50 |
| 0300 | 3" diameter | | 18 | 1.333 | | 25.50 | 58.50 | | 84 | 116 |
| 0310 | 4" diameter | | 15 | 1.600 | | 34.50 | 70.50 | | 105 | 144 |
| 0320 | Reducers, 2" | | 27 | .889 | | 19.35 | 39 | | 58.35 | 80.50 |
| 0330 | 3" diameter | | 22 | 1.091 | | 22.50 | 48 | | 70.50 | 96.50 |
| 0340 | 4" diameter | ↓ | 20 | 1.200 | ↓ | 29 | 53 | | 82 | 112 |
| 1010 | Gas station product line for secondary containment (double wall) | | | | | | | | |
| 1100 | Fiberglass reinforced plastic pipe 25' lengths | | | | | | | | |
| 1120 | Pipe, plain end, 3" diameter | Q-6 | 375 | .064 | L.F. | 7.35 | 2.81 | | 10.16 | 12.35 |
| 1130 | 4" diameter | | 350 | .069 | | 12.10 | 3.02 | | 15.12 | 17.85 |
| 1140 | 5" diameter | | 325 | .074 | | 15.70 | 3.25 | | 18.95 | 22 |
| 1150 | 6" diameter | ↓ | 300 | .080 | ↓ | 16.20 | 3.52 | | 19.72 | 23 |
| 1200 | Fittings | | | | | | | | |
| 1230 | Elbows, 90° & 45°, 3" diameter | Q-6 | 18 | 1.333 | Ea. | 53 | 58.50 | | 111.50 | 147 |
| 1240 | 4" diameter | | 16 | 1.500 | | 92.50 | 66 | | 158.50 | 201 |
| 1250 | 5" diameter | | 14 | 1.714 | | 215 | 75.50 | | 290.50 | 350 |
| 1260 | 6" diameter | | 12 | 2 | | 217 | 88 | | 305 | 370 |
| 1270 | Tees, 3" diameter | | 15 | 1.600 | | 78.50 | 70.50 | | 149 | 193 |
| 1280 | 4" diameter | | 12 | 2 | | 116 | 88 | | 204 | 259 |
| 1290 | 5" diameter | | 9 | 2.667 | | 234 | 117 | | 351 | 435 |
| 1300 | 6" diameter | | 6 | 4 | | 244 | 176 | | 420 | 535 |
| 1310 | Couplings, 3" diameter | | 18 | 1.333 | | 37.50 | 58.50 | | 96 | 129 |
| 1320 | 4" diameter | | 16 | 1.500 | | 96 | 66 | | 162 | 205 |
| 1330 | 5" diameter | | 14 | 1.714 | | 200 | 75.50 | | 275.50 | 335 |
| 1340 | 6" diameter | | 12 | 2 | | 207 | 88 | | 295 | 360 |
| 1350 | Cross-over nipples, 3" diameter | | 18 | 1.333 | | 8.50 | 58.50 | | 67 | 97.50 |
| 1360 | 4" diameter | | 16 | 1.500 | | 10 | 66 | | 76 | 110 |
| 1370 | 5" diameter | | 14 | 1.714 | | 14.80 | 75.50 | | 90.30 | 129 |
| 1380 | 6" diameter | | 12 | 2 | | 15.55 | 88 | | 103.55 | 149 |
| 1400 | Telescoping, reducers, concentric 4" x 3" | | 18 | 1.333 | | 28.50 | 58.50 | | 87 | 119 |
| 1410 | 5" x 4" | | 17 | 1.412 | | 74 | 62 | | 136 | 175 |
| 1420 | 6" x 5" | ↓ | 16 | 1.500 | ↓ | 178 | 66 | | 244 | 294 |

# 33 71 Electrical Utility Transmission and Distribution

## 33 71 16 – Electrical Utility Poles

| 33 71 16.33 Wood Electrical Utility Poles | | Crew | Daily Output | Labor-Hours | Unit | Material | 2008 Bare Costs Labor | Equipment | Total | Total Incl O&P |
|---|---|---|---|---|---|---|---|---|---|---|
| 0010 | **WOOD ELECTRICAL UTILITY POLES** | | | | | | | | | |
| 0011 | excludes excavation, backfill and cast-in-place concrete | | | | | | | | | |
| 6200 | Electric & tel sitework, 20' high, treated wd, see Div. 26 56 13.10 | R-3 | 3.10 | 6.452 | Ea. | 251 | 289 | 41.50 | 581.50 | 750 |
| 6400 | 25' high | | 2.90 | 6.897 | | 265 | 310 | 44.50 | 619.50 | 800 |
| 6600 | 30' high | | 2.60 | 7.692 | | 292 | 345 | 50 | 687 | 890 |
| 6800 | 35' high | | 2.40 | 8.333 | | 380 | 375 | 54 | 809 | 1,050 |
| 7000 | 40' high | | 2.30 | 8.696 | | 465 | 390 | 56.50 | 911.50 | 1,150 |
| 7200 | 45' high | | 1.70 | 11.765 | | 570 | 525 | 76 | 1,171 | 1,500 |
| 7400 | Cross arms with hardware & insulators, see Div. 26 56 13.10 | | | | | | | | | |
| 7600 | 4' long | 1 Elec | 2.50 | 3.200 | Ea. | 119 | 146 | | 265 | 350 |
| 7800 | 5' long | | 2.40 | 3.333 | | 138 | 152 | | 290 | 380 |
| 8000 | 6' long | | 2.20 | 3.636 | | 159 | 166 | | 325 | 420 |

## 33 71 19 – Electrical Underground Ducts and Manholes

### 33 71 19.17 Electric and Telephone Underground

| | | Crew | Daily Output | Labor-Hours | Unit | Material | 2008 Bare Costs Labor | Equipment | Total | Total Incl O&P |
|---|---|---|---|---|---|---|---|---|---|---|
| 0010 | **ELECTRIC AND TELEPHONE UNDERGROUND** | | | | | | | | | |
| 0011 | Not including excavation | | | | | | | | | |
| 0200 | backfill and cast in place concrete | | | | | | | | | |
| 0400 | Hand holes, precast concrete, with concrete cover | | | | | | | | | |
| 0600 | 2' x 2' x 3' deep | R-3 | 2.40 | 8.333 | Ea. | 295 | 375 | 54 | 724 | 945 |
| 0800 | 3' x 3' x 3' deep | | 1.90 | 10.526 | | 385 | 470 | 68 | 923 | 1,200 |
| 1000 | 4' x 4' x 4' deep | | 1.40 | 14.286 | | 765 | 640 | 92.50 | 1,497.50 | 1,900 |
| 1200 | Manholes, precast with iron racks & pulling irons, C.I. frame | | | | | | | | | |
| 1400 | and cover, 4' x 6' x 7' deep | B-13 | 2 | 28 | Ea. | 1,475 | 915 | 395 | 2,785 | 3,450 |
| 1600 | 6' x 8' x 7' deep | | 1.90 | 29.474 | | 1,800 | 965 | 415 | 3,180 | 3,900 |
| 1800 | 6' x 10' x 7' deep | | 1.80 | 31.111 | | 2,025 | 1,025 | 435 | 3,485 | 4,275 |
| 4200 | Underground duct, banks ready for concrete fill, min. of 7.5" | | | | | | | | | |
| 4400 | between conduits, center to center | | | | | | | | | |
| 4580 | PVC, type EB, 1 @ 2" diameter | 2 Elec | 480 | .033 | L.F. | .86 | 1.52 | | 2.38 | 3.20 |
| 4600 | 2 @ 2" diameter | | 240 | .067 | | 1.72 | 3.04 | | 4.76 | 6.40 |
| 4800 | 4 @ 2" diameter | | 120 | .133 | | 3.43 | 6.05 | | 9.48 | 12.85 |
| 5000 | 2 @ 3" diameter | | 200 | .080 | | 2.34 | 3.64 | | 5.98 | 8.05 |
| 5200 | 4 @ 3" diameter | | 100 | .160 | | 4.68 | 7.30 | | 11.98 | 16 |
| 5400 | 2 @ 4" diameter | | 160 | .100 | | 3.56 | 4.56 | | 8.12 | 10.70 |
| 5600 | 4 @ 4" diameter | | 80 | .200 | | 7.15 | 9.10 | | 16.25 | 21.50 |
| 5800 | 6 @ 4" diameter | | 54 | .296 | | 10.70 | 13.50 | | 24.20 | 32 |
| 6200 | Rigid galvanized steel, 2 @ 2" diameter | | 180 | .089 | | 13.25 | 4.05 | | 17.30 | 20.50 |
| 6400 | 4 @ 2" diameter | | 90 | .178 | | 26.50 | 8.10 | | 34.60 | 41 |
| 6800 | 2 @ 3" diameter | | 100 | .160 | | 32.50 | 7.30 | | 39.80 | 46.50 |
| 7000 | 4 @ 3" diameter | | 50 | .320 | | 64.50 | 14.60 | | 79.10 | 92.50 |
| 7200 | 2 @ 4" diameter | | 70 | .229 | | 44 | 10.40 | | 54.40 | 64 |
| 7400 | 4 @ 4" diameter | | 34 | .471 | | 88.50 | 21.50 | | 110 | 129 |
| 7600 | 6 @ 4" diameter | | 22 | .727 | | 132 | 33 | | 165 | 196 |

# 33 81 Communications Structures

## 33 81 13 – Communications Transmission Towers

| 33 81 13.10 Radio Towers | Crew | Daily Output | Labor-Hours | Unit | Material | 2008 Bare Costs Labor | Equipment | Total | Total Incl O&P |
|---|---|---|---|---|---|---|---|---|---|
| 0010 **RADIO TOWERS** | | | | | | | | | |
| 0020　Guyed, 50' H, 40 lb. sec., 70 MPH basic wind spd. | 2 Sswk | 1 | 16 | Ea. | 2,725 | 690 | | 3,415 | 4,250 |
| 0100　　Wind load 90 MPH basic wind speed | " | 1 | 16 | | 2,725 | 690 | | 3,415 | 4,250 |
| 0300　　190' high, 40 lb. section, wind load 70 MPH basic wind speed | K-2 | .33 | 72.727 | | 7,350 | 2,850 | 680 | 10,880 | 13,800 |
| 0400　　200' high, 70 lb. section, wind load 90 MPH basic wind speed | | .33 | 72.727 | | 14,800 | 2,850 | 680 | 18,330 | 22,000 |
| 0600　　300' high, 70 lb. section, wind load 70 MPH basic wind speed | | .20 | 120 | | 21,000 | 4,700 | 1,125 | 26,825 | 32,500 |
| 0700　　270' high, 90 lb. section, wind load 90 MPH basic wind speed | | .20 | 120 | | 24,300 | 4,700 | 1,125 | 30,125 | 36,100 |
| 0800　　400' high, 100 lb. section, wind load 70 MPH basic wind speed | | .14 | 171 | | 35,300 | 6,700 | 1,600 | 43,600 | 52,500 |
| 0900　Self-supporting, 60' high, wind load 70 MPH basic wind speed | | .80 | 30 | | 5,675 | 1,175 | 280 | 7,130 | 8,600 |
| 0910　　60' high, wind load 90 MPH basic wind speed | | .45 | 53.333 | | 10,200 | 2,075 | 500 | 12,775 | 15,400 |
| 1000　　120' high, wind load 70 MPH basic wind speed | | .40 | 60 | | 13,900 | 2,350 | 560 | 16,810 | 20,000 |
| 1200　　190' high, wind load 90 MPH basic wind speed | | .20 | 120 | | 33,800 | 4,700 | 1,125 | 39,625 | 46,600 |
| 2000　For states west of Rocky Mountains, add for shipping | | | | | 10% | | | | |

# Estimating Tips

## 34 11 00 Rail Tracks

This section includes items that may involve either repair of existing, or construction of new, railroad tracks. Additional preparation work, such as the roadbed earthwork, would be found in Division 31. Additional new construction siding and turnouts are found in Section 34 72. Maintenance of railroads is found under 34 01 23 Operation and Maintenance of Railways.

## 34 41 13 Traffic Signals

This section includes traffic signal systems. Other traffic control devices such as traffic signs are found in Section 10 14 53 Traffic Signage.

## 34 71 13 Vehicle Barriers

This section includes security vehicle barriers, guide and guard rails, crash barriers, and delineators. The actual maintenance and construction of concrete and asphalt pavement is found in Division 32.

# Reference Numbers

Reference numbers are shown in shaded boxes at the beginning of some major classifications. These numbers refer to related items in the Reference Section. The reference information may be an estimating procedure, an alternate pricing method, or technical information.

*Note:* Not all subdivisions listed here necessarily appear in this publication.

# 34 01 Operation and Maintenance of Transportation

## 34 01 23 – Operation and Maintenance of Railways

| 34 01 23.51 Maintenance of Railroads | Crew | Daily Output | Labor-Hours | Unit | Material | 2008 Bare Costs Labor | Equipment | Total | Total Incl O&P |
|---|---|---|---|---|---|---|---|---|---|
| 0010 **MAINTENANCE OF RAILROADS** | | | | | | | | | |
| 0400 Resurface and realign existing track | B-14 | 200 | .240 | L.F. | | 7.65 | 1.43 | 9.08 | 13.35 |
| 0600 For crushed stone ballast, add | " | 500 | .096 | " | 19.45 | 3.06 | .57 | 23.08 | 27 |

# 34 11 Rail Tracks

## 34 11 13 – Track Rails

### 34 11 13.23 Heavy Rail Track

| | Crew | Daily Output | Labor-Hours | Unit | Material | Labor | Equipment | Total | Total Incl O&P |
|---|---|---|---|---|---|---|---|---|---|
| 0010 **HEAVY RAIL TRACK** R347216-10 | | | | | | | | | |
| 1000 Rail, 100 lb. prime grade | | | | L.F. | 26 | | | 26 | 28.50 |
| 1500 Relay rail | | | | " | 13.05 | | | 13.05 | 14.35 |

## 34 11 33 – Track Cross Ties

### 34 11 33.13 Concrete Track Cross Ties

| | Crew | Daily Output | Labor-Hours | Unit | Material | Labor | Equipment | Total | Total Incl O&P |
|---|---|---|---|---|---|---|---|---|---|
| 0010 **CONCRETE TRACK CROSS TIES** | | | | | | | | | |
| 1400 Ties, concrete, 8'-6" long, 30" O.C. | B-14 | 80 | .600 | Ea. | 98.50 | 19.10 | 3.57 | 121.17 | 141 |

### 34 11 33.16 Timber Track Cross Ties

| | Crew | Daily Output | Labor-Hours | Unit | Material | Labor | Equipment | Total | Total Incl O&P |
|---|---|---|---|---|---|---|---|---|---|
| 0010 **TIMBER TRACK CROSS TIES** | | | | | | | | | |
| 1600 Wood, pressure treated, 6" x 8" x 8'-6", C.L. lots | B-14 | 90 | .533 | Ea. | 41 | 17 | 3.17 | 61.17 | 75.50 |
| 1700 L.C.L. lots | | 90 | .533 | | 43.50 | 17 | 3.17 | 63.67 | 77.50 |
| 1900 Heavy duty, 7" x 9" x 8'-6", C.L. lots | | 70 | .686 | | 45.50 | 22 | 4.08 | 71.58 | 88.50 |
| 2000 L.C.L. lots | | 70 | .686 | | 45.50 | 22 | 4.08 | 71.58 | 88.50 |

### 34 11 33.17 Timber Switch Ties

| | Crew | Daily Output | Labor-Hours | Unit | Material | Labor | Equipment | Total | Total Incl O&P |
|---|---|---|---|---|---|---|---|---|---|
| 0010 **TIMBER SWITCH TIES** | | | | | | | | | |
| 1200 Switch timber, for a #8 switch, pressure treated | B-14 | 3.70 | 12.973 | M.B.F. | 2,475 | 415 | 77 | 2,967 | 3,450 |
| 1300 Complete set of timbers, 3.7 M.B.F. for #8 switch | " | 1 | 48 | Total | 9,525 | 1,525 | 286 | 11,336 | 13,200 |

## 34 11 93 – Track Appurtenances and Accessories

### 34 11 93.50 Track Accessories

| | Crew | Daily Output | Labor-Hours | Unit | Material | Labor | Equipment | Total | Total Incl O&P |
|---|---|---|---|---|---|---|---|---|---|
| 0010 **TRACK ACCESSORIES** | | | | | | | | | |
| 0020 Car bumpers, test | B-14 | 2 | 24 | Ea. | 2,925 | 765 | 143 | 3,833 | 4,525 |
| 0100 Heavy duty R347216-20 | | 2 | 24 | | 5,525 | 765 | 143 | 6,433 | 7,400 |
| 0200 Derails hand throw (sliding) | | 10 | 4.800 | | 920 | 153 | 28.50 | 1,101.50 | 1,300 |
| 0300 Hand throw with standard timbers, open stand & target | | 8 | 6 | | 1,000 | 191 | 35.50 | 1,226.50 | 1,425 |
| 2400 Wheel stops, fixed | | 18 | 2.667 | Pr. | 655 | 85 | 15.85 | 755.85 | 870 |
| 2450 Hinged | | 14 | 3.429 | " | 885 | 109 | 20.50 | 1,014.50 | 1,150 |

### 34 11 93.60 Track Material

| | Crew | Daily Output | Labor-Hours | Unit | Material | Labor | Equipment | Total | Total Incl O&P |
|---|---|---|---|---|---|---|---|---|---|
| 0010 **TRACK MATERIAL** | | | | | | | | | |
| 0020 Track bolts | | | | Ea. | 2.30 | | | 2.30 | 2.53 |
| 0100 Joint bars | | | | Pr. | 69.50 | | | 69.50 | 76.50 |
| 0200 Spikes | | | | Ea. | .62 | | | .62 | .68 |
| 0300 Tie plates | | | | " | 11.60 | | | 11.60 | 12.75 |

# 34 41 Roadway Signaling and Control Equipment

## 34 41 13 – Traffic signals

### 34 41 13.10 Traffic Signals Systems

| | 34 41 13.10 Traffic Signals Systems | Crew | Daily Output | Labor-Hours | Unit | Material | 2008 Bare Costs Labor | Equipment | Total | Total Incl O&P |
|---|---|---|---|---|---|---|---|---|---|---|
| 0010 | **TRAFFIC SIGNALS SYSTEMS** | | | | | | | | | |
| 0020 | Mid block pedestrian crosswalk with pushbutton and mast arms | R-11 | .30 | 186 | Total | 70,500 | 7,975 | 3,100 | 81,575 | 93,000 |
| 0600 | Traffic signals, school flashing system, solar powered, remote controlled | " | 1 | 56 | Signal | 17,400 | 2,400 | 925 | 20,725 | 23,700 |
| 1000 | Intersection traffic signals, LED, mast, programmable, no lane control | | | | | | | | | |
| 1010 | Includes all labor, material and equip. for complete installation | R-11 | 1 | 56 | Signal | 181,000 | 2,400 | 925 | 184,325 | 203,500 |
| 1100 | Intersection traffic signals, LED, mast, programmable, R/L lane control | | | | | | | | | |
| 1110 | Includes all labor, material and equip. for complete installation | R-11 | 1 | 56 | Signal | 241,500 | 2,400 | 925 | 244,825 | 270,000 |
| 1200 | Add protective/permissive left turns to existing traffic light | | | | | | | | | |
| 1210 | Includes all labor, material and equip. for complete installation | R-11 | 1 | 56 | Signal | 72,500 | 2,400 | 925 | 75,825 | 84,000 |
| 1300 | Replace existing light heads with LED Heads wire hung | | | | | | | | | |
| 1310 | Includes all labor, material and equip. for complete installation | R-11 | 1 | 56 | Signal | 48,300 | 2,400 | 925 | 51,625 | 57,500 |
| 1400 | Replace existing light heads with LED Heads mast arm hung | | | | | | | | | |
| 1410 | Includes all labor, material and equip. for complete installation | R-11 | 1 | 56 | Signal | 96,500 | 2,400 | 925 | 99,825 | 111,000 |

# 34 71 Roadway Construction

## 34 71 13 – Vehicle Barriers

### 34 71 13.17 Security Vehicle Barriers

| | 34 71 13.17 Security Vehicle Barriers | Crew | Daily Output | Labor-Hours | Unit | Material | 2008 Bare Costs Labor | Equipment | Total | Total Incl O&P |
|---|---|---|---|---|---|---|---|---|---|---|
| 0010 | **SECURITY VEHICLE BARRIERS** | | | | | | | | | |
| 0020 | Security planters excludes filling material | | | | | | | | | |
| 0100 | Concrete security planter, exposed aggregate 36" dia x 30" high | B-11M | 8 | 2 | Ea. | 430 | 70 | 42.50 | 542.50 | 625 |
| 0200 | 48" dia x 36" high | | 8 | 2 | | 695 | 70 | 42.50 | 807.50 | 920 |
| 0300 | 53" dia x 18" high | | 8 | 2 | | 515 | 70 | 42.50 | 627.50 | 720 |
| 0400 | 72" dia x 18" high with seats | | 8 | 2 | | 1,100 | 70 | 42.50 | 1,212.50 | 1,350 |
| 0450 | 84" dia x 36" high | | 8 | 2 | | 935 | 70 | 42.50 | 1,047.50 | 1,175 |
| 0500 | 36" x 36" x 24" high square | | 8 | 2 | | 340 | 70 | 42.50 | 452.50 | 530 |
| 0600 | 36" x 36" x 30" high square | | 8 | 2 | | 370 | 70 | 42.50 | 482.50 | 565 |
| 0700 | 48" L x 24" W x 30" H rectangle | | 8 | 2 | | 330 | 70 | 42.50 | 442.50 | 520 |
| 0800 | 72" L x 24" W x 30" H rectangle | | 8 | 2 | | 545 | 70 | 42.50 | 657.50 | 755 |
| 0900 | 96" L x 24" W x 30" H rectangle | | 8 | 2 | | 540 | 70 | 42.50 | 652.50 | 750 |
| 0950 | Decorative geometric concrete barrier, 96" L x 24" W x 36" H | | 8 | 2 | | 845 | 70 | 42.50 | 957.50 | 1,075 |
| 1000 | Concrete security planter, filling with washed sand or gravel °1 CY | | 8 | 2 | | 38.50 | 70 | 42.50 | 151 | 197 |
| 1050 | Concrete security planter, filling with washed sand or gravel °2 CY | | 6 | 2.667 | | 77.50 | 93.50 | 57 | 228 | 291 |
| 1200 | Jersey concete barrier, 10' L x 2' by 0.5' W x 30" H | B-21B | 16 | 2.500 | | 330 | 82 | 48 | 460 | 545 |
| 1300 | 10' L x 2' by 0.5' W x 30" H, 10 or more same site | | 24 | 1.667 | | 330 | 54.50 | 32 | 416.50 | 485 |
| 1400 | Jersey concete barrier, 10' L x 2' by 0.5' W x 32" H | | 16 | 2.500 | | 330 | 82 | 48 | 460 | 545 |
| 1500 | 10' L x 2' by 6" W x 32" H, 10 or more same site | | 24 | 1.667 | | 330 | 54.50 | 32 | 416.50 | 485 |
| 1600 | Jersey concete barrier, 20' L x 2' by 0.5' W x 30" H | | 12 | 3.333 | | 820 | 109 | 64 | 993 | 1,150 |
| 1700 | 20' L x 2' by 0.5' W x 30" H, 10 or more same site | | 18 | 2.222 | | 820 | 73 | 42.50 | 935.50 | 1,050 |
| 1800 | Jersey concete barrier, 20' L x 2' by 0.5' W x 32" H | | 12 | 3.333 | | 820 | 109 | 64 | 993 | 1,150 |
| 1900 | 20' L x 2' by 0.5' W x 32" H, 10 or more same site | | 18 | 2.222 | | 820 | 73 | 42.50 | 935.50 | 1,050 |
| 2000 | GFRC decorative security barrier per 10 feet section including concrete | | 4 | 10 | | 2,175 | 330 | 192 | 2,697 | 3,100 |
| 2100 | GFRC decorative security barrier per 12 feet section including concrete | | 4 | 10 | | 2,600 | 330 | 192 | 3,122 | 3,575 |
| 2210 | GFRC decorative security barrier will stop 30 MPH, 4000 lb vehicle | | | | | | | | | |
| 2300 | High security barrier base prep per 12 feet section on bare ground | B-11C | 4 | 4 | Ea. | 42.50 | 140 | 71.50 | 254 | 340 |
| 2310 | GFRC barrier base prep does not include haul away of excavated matl | | | | | | | | | |
| 2400 | GFRC decorative high security barrier per 12 feet section w/concrete | B-21B | 3 | 13.333 | Ea. | 5,675 | 435 | 255 | 6,365 | 7,200 |
| 2410 | GFRC decorative high security barrier will stop 50 MPH, 15000 lb vehl | | | | | | | | | |
| 2500 | GFRC decorative impaler security barrier per 10 feet section w/prep | B-6 | 4 | 6 | Ea. | 2,150 | 197 | 71.50 | 2,418.50 | 2,750 |
| 2600 | GFRC decorative impaler security barrier per 12 feet section w/prep | " | 4 | 6 | " | 2,600 | 197 | 71.50 | 2,868.50 | 3,225 |
| 2610 | Impaler barrier should stop 50 MPH, 15000 lb vehl w/some penetr | | | | | | | | | |
| 2700 | Pipe bollards, steel, concrete filled/painted, 8' L x 4' D hole, 8" diam. | B-6 | 10 | 2.400 | Ea. | 815 | 78.50 | 28.50 | 922 | 1,050 |

# 34 71 Roadway Construction

## 34 71 13 – Vehicle Barriers

### 34 71 13.17 Security Vehicle Barriers

| | | Crew | Daily Output | Labor-Hours | Unit | Material | 2008 Bare Costs Labor | Equipment | Total | Total Incl O&P |
|---|---|---|---|---|---|---|---|---|---|---|
| 2710 | Schedule 80 concrete bollards will stop 4000 lb vehicle @ 30 MPH | | | | | | | | | |
| 2800 | GFRC decorative jersey barrier cover per 10 feet section excludes soil | B-6 | 8 | 3 | Ea. | 990 | 98.50 | 35.50 | 1,124 | 1,300 |
| 2900 | GFRC decorative jersey barrier cover per 12 feet section excludes soil | | 8 | 3 | | 1,200 | 98.50 | 35.50 | 1,334 | 1,500 |
| 3000 | GFRC decorative 8" diameter bollard cover | | 12 | 2 | | 495 | 65.50 | 24 | 584.50 | 670 |
| 3100 | GFRC decorative barrier face 10 foot section excludes earth backing | ↓ | 10 | 2.400 | ↓ | 925 | 78.50 | 28.50 | 1,032 | 1,175 |
| 3200 | Drop arm crash barrier, 20' width or less, 15000 lb vehl @ 50 MPH | | | | | | | | | |
| 3205 | Includes all material, labor for complete installation | | | | | | | | | |
| 3210 | Drop arm crash barrier, 20' width or less, 15,000lb vehl @ 50MPH | | | | Ea. | | | | 76,230 | 83,737.50 |
| 3310 | 24' width | | | | | | | | 82,585 | 90,668 |
| 3410 | Portable wedge crash barrier, 10' width | | | | | | | | 75,075 | 82,582 |
| 3510 | 12' width | | | | | | | | 82,582 | 90,667 |
| 3610 | Sliding crash barrier, 12' width | | | | | | | | 106,838 | 117,232 |
| 3710 | Sliding roller crash barrier, 20' width | | | | | | | | 76,230 | 83,738 |
| 3810 | Sliding cantilever crash barrier, 20' width | | | | ↓ | | | | 82,582 | 90,668 |
| 3890 | Note: Raised bollard crash barriers should be used w/tire shredders | | | | | | | | | |
| 3910 | Raised bollard crash barrier, 10' width | | | | Ea. | | | | 25,410 | 27,951 |
| 4010 | 12' width | | | | | | | | 29,222 | 32,109 |
| 4110 | Includes all labor, material and equip. for complete installation | | | | | | | | 32,340 | 35,574 |
| 4210 | 12' width | | | | | | | | 36,152 | 39,732 |
| 4310 | In ground tire shredder, 16' width | | | | ↓ | | | | 36,540 | 40,194 |

### 34 71 13.26 Vehicle Guide Rails

| | | Crew | Daily Output | Labor-Hours | Unit | Material | 2008 Bare Costs Labor | Equipment | Total | Total Incl O&P |
|---|---|---|---|---|---|---|---|---|---|---|
| 0010 | **VEHICLE GUIDE RAILS** | | | | | | | | | |
| 0012 | Corrugated stl, galv. stl posts, 6'-3" O.C. | B-80 | 850 | .038 | L.F. | 18.65 | 1.22 | .74 | 20.61 | 23 |
| 0200 | End sections, galvanized, flared | | 50 | .640 | Ea. | 77.50 | 20.50 | 12.55 | 110.55 | 131 |
| 0300 | Wrap around end | | 50 | .640 | " | 116 | 20.50 | 12.55 | 149.05 | 174 |
| 0400 | Timber guide rail, 4" x 8" with 6" x 8" wood posts, treated | | 960 | .033 | L.F. | 24.50 | 1.08 | .65 | 26.23 | 29.50 |
| 0600 | Cable guide rail, 3 at 3/4" cables, steel posts, single face | | 900 | .036 | | 8.25 | 1.15 | .70 | 10.10 | 11.60 |
| 0700 | Wood posts | | 950 | .034 | | 11.45 | 1.09 | .66 | 13.20 | 14.95 |
| 0900 | Guide rail, steel box beam, 6" x 6" | | 120 | .267 | | 28.50 | 8.65 | 5.20 | 42.35 | 50 |
| 1100 | Median barrier, steel box beam, 6" x 8" | ↓ | 215 | .149 | | 35 | 4.82 | 2.92 | 42.74 | 49 |
| 1400 | Resilient guide fence and light shield, 6' high | B-2 | 130 | .308 | ↓ | 27 | 9.45 | | 36.45 | 44.50 |
| 1500 | Concrete posts, individual, 6'-5", triangular | B-80 | 110 | .291 | Ea. | 57.50 | 9.45 | 5.70 | 72.65 | 84.50 |
| 1550 | Square | " | 110 | .291 | " | 62 | 9.45 | 5.70 | 77.15 | 89 |
| 2000 | Median, precast concrete, 3'-6" high, 2' wide, single face | B-29 | 380 | .147 | L.F. | 45 | 4.83 | 2.45 | 52.28 | 59.50 |
| 2200 | Double face | " | 340 | .165 | " | 51.50 | 5.40 | 2.74 | 59.64 | 68 |
| 2400 | Speed bumps, thermoplastic, 10-1/2" x 2-1/4" x 48" long | B-2 | 120 | .333 | Ea. | 117 | 10.20 | | 127.20 | 145 |
| 3030 | Impact barrier, UTMCD, barrel type | B-16 | 30 | 1.067 | " | 375 | 33 | 16.75 | 424.75 | 485 |

## 34 71 19 – Vehicle Delineators

### 34 71 19.13 Fixed Vehicle Delineators

| | | Crew | Daily Output | Labor-Hours | Unit | Material | 2008 Bare Costs Labor | Equipment | Total | Total Incl O&P |
|---|---|---|---|---|---|---|---|---|---|---|
| 0010 | **FIXED VEHICLE DELINEATORS** | | | | | | | | | |
| 0020 | Crash barriers | | | | | | | | | |
| 0100 | Traffic channelizing pavement markers, layout only | A-7 | 2000 | .012 | Ea. | | .50 | .03 | .53 | .81 |
| 0110 | 13" x 7-1/2" x 2-1/2" high, non-plowable install | 2 Clab | 96 | .167 | | 25 | 5.05 | | 30.05 | 35.50 |
| 0200 | 8" x 8"x 3-1/4" high, non-plowable, install | | 96 | .167 | | 23 | 5.05 | | 28.05 | 33 |
| 0230 | 4" x 4" x 3/4" high, non-plowable, install | ↓ | 120 | .133 | | 3.05 | 4.03 | | 7.08 | 9.60 |
| 0240 | 9-1/4" x 5-7/8" x 1/4" high, plowable, concrete pav't | A-2A | 70 | .343 | | 18.25 | 10.30 | 4.49 | 33.04 | 41 |
| 0250 | 9-1/4" x 5-7/8" x 1/4" high, plowable, asphalt pav't | " | 120 | .200 | | 3.49 | 6 | 2.62 | 12.11 | 16 |
| 0300 | Barrier and curb delineators,reflectorized, 2" x 4" | 2 Clab | 150 | .107 | ↓ | 1.99 | 3.23 | | 5.22 | 7.20 |
| 0310 | 3" x 5" | " | 150 | .107 | ↓ | 4.04 | 3.23 | | 7.27 | 9.45 |
| 0500 | Rumble strip, polycarbonate | | | | | | | | | |
| 0510 | 24" x 3-1/2" x 1/2" high | 2 Clab | 50 | .320 | Ea. | 7.60 | 9.70 | | 17.30 | 23.50 |

# 34 72 Railway Construction

## 34 72 16 – Railway Siding

| 34 72 16.50 Railroad Sidings | Crew | Daily Output | Labor-Hours | Unit | Material | 2008 Bare Costs Labor | Equipment | Total | Total Incl O&P |
|---|---|---|---|---|---|---|---|---|---|
| 0010 **RAILROAD SIDINGS** R347216-10 | | | | | | | | | |
| 0800     Siding, yard spur, level grade | | | | | | | | | |
| 0810         100 lb. rail, new material on wood ties | B-14 | 57 | .842 | L.F. | 108 | 27 | 5 | 140 | 165 |
| 1000       Steel ties in concrete w/100 lb new rail, fasteners & plates | " | 22 | 2.182 | " | 143 | 69.50 | 13 | 225.50 | 279 |

## 34 72 16.60 Railroad Turnouts

| | Crew | Daily Output | Labor-Hours | Unit | Material | 2008 Bare Costs Labor | Equipment | Total | Total Incl O&P |
|---|---|---|---|---|---|---|---|---|---|
| 0010 **RAILROAD TURNOUTS** | | | | | | | | | |
| 2200     Turnouts, #8, incl. 100 lb. rails, plates, bars, frog, switch pt. | | | | | | | | | |
| 2300       Timbers and ballast 6" below bottom of tie | B-14 | .50 | 96 | Ea. | 11,700 | 3,050 | 570 | 15,320 | 18,200 |

# Division Notes

| | CREW | DAILY OUTPUT | LABOR-HOURS | UNIT | 2008 BARE COSTS | | | | TOTAL INCL O&P |
|---|---|---|---|---|---|---|---|---|---|
| | | | | | MAT. | LABOR | EQUIP. | TOTAL | |
| | | | | | | | | | |
| | | | | | | | | | |
| | | | | | | | | | |
| | | | | | | | | | |
| | | | | | | | | | |
| | | | | | | | | | |
| | | | | | | | | | |
| | | | | | | | | | |
| | | | | | | | | | |
| | | | | | | | | | |
| | | | | | | | | | |
| | | | | | | | | | |
| | | | | | | | | | |
| | | | | | | | | | |
| | | | | | | | | | |
| | | | | | | | | | |
| | | | | | | | | | |
| | | | | | | | | | |
| | | | | | | | | | |
| | | | | | | | | | |
| | | | | | | | | | |

# Estimating Tips

## 35 20 16 Hydraulic Gates

This section includes various types of gates that are commonly used in waterway and canal construction. Various earthwork items and structural support is found in Division 31, and concrete work in Division 3.

## 35 20 23 Dredging

This section includes barge and shore dredging systems for rivers, canals, and channels.

## 35 31 00 Shoreline Protection

This section includes breakwaters, bulkheads, and revetments for ocean and river inlets. Additional earthwork may be required from Division 31, and concrete work from Division 3.

## 35 49 00 Waterway Structures

This section includes breakwaters and bulkheads for canals.

## 35 51 00 Floating Construction

This section includes floating piers, docks, and dock accessories. Fixed Pier Timber Construction is found in 06 13 33. Driven piles are found in Division 31, as well as sheet piling, cofferdams, and riprap.

# Reference Numbers

Reference numbers are shown in shaded boxes at the beginning of some major classifications. These numbers refer to related items in the Reference Section. The reference information may be an estimating procedure, an alternate pricing method, or technical information.

*Note:* Not all subdivisions listed here necessarily appear in this publication.

**Division 35 – Waterway and Marine**

# 35 20 Waterway and Marine Construction and Equipment

## 35 20 23 – Dredging

### 35 20 23.13 Mechanical Dredging

| | | Crew | Daily Output | Labor-Hours | Unit | Material | 2008 Bare Costs Labor | Equipment | Total | Total Incl O&P |
|---|---|---|---|---|---|---|---|---|---|---|
| 0010 | **MECHANICAL DREDGING** | | | | | | | | | |
| 0020 | Dredging mobilization and demobilization., add to below, minimum | B-8 | .53 | 120 | Total | | 4,050 | 5,075 | 9,125 | 11,800 |
| 0100 | Maximum | " | .10 | 640 | " | | 21,500 | 26,800 | 48,300 | 62,500 |
| 0300 | Barge mounted clamshell excavation into scows, | | | | | | | | | |
| 0310 | Dumped 20 miles at sea, minimum | B-57 | 310 | .155 | B.C.Y. | | 5.35 | 4.91 | 10.26 | 13.55 |
| 0400 | Maximum | " | 213 | .225 | " | | 7.75 | 7.15 | 14.90 | 19.70 |
| 0500 | Barge mounted dragline or clamshell, hopper dumped, | | | | | | | | | |
| 0510 | pumped 1000' to shore dump, minimum | B-57 | 340 | .141 | B.C.Y. | | 4.86 | 4.48 | 9.34 | 12.40 |
| 0525 | All pumping uses 2000 gallons of water per cubic yard | | | | | | | | | |
| 0600 | Maximum | B-57 | 243 | .198 | B.C.Y. | | 6.80 | 6.25 | 13.05 | 17.30 |

### 35 20 23.23 Hydraulic Dredging

| | | Crew | Daily Output | Labor-Hours | Unit | Material | 2008 Bare Costs Labor | Equipment | Total | Total Incl O&P |
|---|---|---|---|---|---|---|---|---|---|---|
| 0010 | **HYDRAULIC DREDGING** | | | | | | | | | |
| 1000 | Hydraulic method, pumped 1000' to shore dump, minimum | B-57 | 460 | .104 | B.C.Y. | | 3.59 | 3.31 | 6.90 | 9.15 |
| 1100 | Maximum | ↓ | 310 | .155 | | | 5.35 | 4.91 | 10.26 | 13.55 |
| 1400 | Into scows dumped 20 miles, minimum | | 425 | .113 | | | 3.89 | 3.58 | 7.47 | 9.90 |
| 1500 | Maximum | ↓ | 243 | .198 | ↓ | | 6.80 | 6.25 | 13.05 | 17.30 |
| 1600 | For inland rivers and canals in South, deduct | | | | | | | | 30% | 30% |

# 35 51 Floating Construction

## 35 51 13 – Floating Piers

### 35 51 13.23 Floating Wood Piers

| | | Crew | Daily Output | Labor-Hours | Unit | Material | 2008 Bare Costs Labor | Equipment | Total | Total Incl O&P |
|---|---|---|---|---|---|---|---|---|---|---|
| 0010 | **FLOATING WOOD PIERS** | | | | | | | | | |
| 0020 | Polyethylene encased polystyrene, no pilings included | F-3 | 330 | .121 | S.F. | 32 | 4.69 | 2.32 | 39.01 | 45 |
| 0200 | Pile supported, shore constructed, bare, 3" decking | ↓ | 130 | .308 | | 22 | 11.90 | 5.90 | 39.80 | 49 |
| 0250 | 4" decking | | 120 | .333 | | 21.50 | 12.90 | 6.40 | 40.80 | 50.50 |
| 0400 | Floating, small boat, prefab, no shore facilities, minimum | | 250 | .160 | | 11.10 | 6.20 | 3.07 | 20.37 | 25 |
| 0500 | Maximum | | 150 | .267 | ↓ | 36.50 | 10.30 | 5.10 | 51.90 | 62 |
| 0700 | Per slip, minimum (180 S.F. each) | | 1.59 | 25.157 | Ea. | 2,325 | 975 | 480 | 3,780 | 4,575 |
| 0800 | Maximum | ↓ | 1.40 | 28.571 | " | 6,900 | 1,100 | 545 | 8,545 | 9,900 |

608

## Estimating Tips

Products such as correspondence lifts, conveyors, chutes, pneumatic tube systems, material handling cranes and hoists, as well as other items specified in this division, may require trained installers. The general contractor may not have any choice as to who will perform the installation or when it will be performed. Long lead times are often required for these products, making early decisions in purchasing and scheduling necessary.

The installation of this type of equipment may require the embedment of mounting hardware during construction of floors, structural walls, or interior walls/partitions. Electrical connections will require coordination with the electrical contractor.

## Reference Numbers

Reference numbers are shown in shaded boxes at the beginning of some major classifications. These numbers refer to related items in the Reference Section. The reference information may be an estimating procedure, an alternate pricing method, or technical information.

*Note:* Not all subdivisions listed here necessarily appear in this publication.

# 41 21 Conveyors

## 41 21 23 – Piece Material Conveyors

| 41 21 23.16 Material Handling Conveyors | Crew | Daily Output | Labor-Hours | Unit | Material | 2008 Bare Costs Labor | Equipment | Total | Total Incl O&P |
|---|---|---|---|---|---|---|---|---|---|
| 0010 **MATERIAL HANDLING CONVEYORS** | | | | | | | | | |
| 0020 Gravity fed, 2" rollers, 3" O.C. | | | | | | | | | |
| 0050 10' sections with 2 supports, 600 lb. capacity, 18" wide | | | | Ea. | 405 | | | 405 | 450 |
| 0100 24" wide | | | | | 470 | | | 470 | 515 |
| 0150 1400 lb. capacity, 18" wide | | | | | 375 | | | 375 | 415 |
| 0200 24" wide | | | | | 415 | | | 415 | 460 |
| 0350 Horizontal belt, center drive and takeup, 60 fpm | | | | | | | | | |
| 0400 16" belt, 26.5' length | 2 Mill | .50 | 32 | Ea. | 2,875 | 1,275 | | 4,150 | 5,025 |
| 0450 24" belt, 41.5' length | | .40 | 40 | | 4,925 | 1,575 | | 6,500 | 7,750 |
| 0500 61.5' length | | .30 | 53.333 | | 6,175 | 2,125 | | 8,300 | 9,925 |
| 0600 Inclined belt, 10' rise with horizontal loader and | | | | | | | | | |
| 0620 End idler assembly, 27.5' length, 18" belt | 2 Mill | .30 | 53.333 | Ea. | 8,375 | 2,125 | | 10,500 | 12,300 |
| 0700 24" belt | " | .15 | 106 | " | 9,400 | 4,225 | | 13,625 | 16,500 |
| 3600 Monorail, overhead, manual, channel type | | | | | | | | | |
| 3700 125 lb. per L.F. | 1 Mill | 26 | .308 | L.F. | 9.30 | 12.20 | | 21.50 | 28 |
| 3900 500 lb. per L.F. | " | 21 | .381 | " | 8.45 | 15.10 | | 23.55 | 32 |
| 4000 Trolleys for above, 2 wheel, 125 lb. capacity | | | | Ea. | 69.50 | | | 69.50 | 76.50 |
| 4200 4 wheel, 250 lb. capacity | | | | | 176 | | | 176 | 194 |
| 4300 8 wheel, 1,000 lb. capacity | | | | | 340 | | | 340 | 370 |

# 41 22 Cranes and Hoists

## 41 22 13 – Cranes

### 41 22 13.10 Crane Rail

| | | Crew | Daily Output | Labor-Hours | Unit | Material | 2008 Bare Costs Labor | Equipment | Total | Total Incl O&P |
|---|---|---|---|---|---|---|---|---|---|---|
| 0010 | **CRANE RAIL** | | | | | | | | | |
| 0020 | Box beam bridge, no equipment included | E-4 | 3400 | .009 | Lb. | .99 | .41 | .04 | 1.44 | 1.87 |
| 0200 | Running track only, 104 lb per yard | " | 5600 | .006 | " | .52 | .25 | .02 | .79 | 1.05 |

### 41 22 13.13 Bridge Cranes

| | | Crew | Daily Output | Labor-Hours | Unit | Material | 2008 Bare Costs Labor | Equipment | Total | Total Incl O&P |
|---|---|---|---|---|---|---|---|---|---|---|
| 0010 | **BRIDGE CRANES** | | | | | | | | | |
| 0100 | 1 girder, 20' span, 3 ton | M-3 | 1 | 34 | Ea. | 20,700 | 1,500 | 171 | 22,371 | 25,200 |
| 0125 | 5 ton | | 1 | 34 | | 22,600 | 1,500 | 171 | 24,271 | 27,300 |
| 0150 | 7.5 ton | | 1 | 34 | | 27,000 | 1,500 | 171 | 28,671 | 32,000 |
| 0175 | 10 ton | | .80 | 42.500 | | 35,600 | 1,875 | 214 | 37,689 | 42,200 |
| 0200 | 15 ton | | .80 | 42.500 | | 45,800 | 1,875 | 214 | 47,889 | 53,500 |
| 0225 | 30' span, 3 ton | | 1 | 34 | | 21,500 | 1,500 | 171 | 23,171 | 26,100 |
| 0250 | 5 ton | | 1 | 34 | | 23,600 | 1,500 | 171 | 25,271 | 28,400 |
| 0275 | 7.5 ton | | 1 | 34 | | 28,300 | 1,500 | 171 | 29,971 | 33,600 |
| 0300 | 10 ton | | .80 | 42.500 | | 36,800 | 1,875 | 214 | 38,889 | 43,500 |
| 0325 | 15 ton | | .80 | 42.500 | | 47,800 | 1,875 | 214 | 49,889 | 55,500 |
| 0350 | 2 girder, 40' span, 3 ton | M-4 | .50 | 72 | | 35,500 | 3,125 | 460 | 39,085 | 44,300 |
| 0375 | 5 ton | | .50 | 72 | | 37,200 | 3,125 | 460 | 40,785 | 46,100 |
| 0400 | 7.5 ton | | .50 | 72 | | 40,800 | 3,125 | 460 | 44,385 | 50,000 |
| 0425 | 10 ton | | .40 | 90 | | 47,700 | 3,925 | 570 | 52,195 | 59,000 |
| 0450 | 15 ton | | .40 | 90 | | 65,000 | 3,925 | 570 | 69,495 | 78,000 |
| 0475 | 25 ton | | .30 | 120 | | 76,500 | 5,225 | 765 | 82,490 | 93,000 |
| 0500 | 50' span, 3 ton | | .50 | 72 | | 40,500 | 3,125 | 460 | 44,085 | 49,700 |
| 0525 | 5 ton | | .50 | 72 | | 42,100 | 3,125 | 460 | 45,685 | 51,500 |
| 0550 | 7.5 ton | | .50 | 72 | | 45,000 | 3,125 | 460 | 48,585 | 54,500 |
| 0575 | 10 ton | | .40 | 90 | | 52,000 | 3,925 | 570 | 56,495 | 63,500 |
| 0600 | 15 ton | | .40 | 90 | | 68,000 | 3,925 | 570 | 72,495 | 81,000 |
| 0625 | 25 ton | | .30 | 120 | | 80,500 | 5,225 | 765 | 86,490 | 97,000 |

# 41 22 Cranes and Hoists

## 41 22 23 – Hoists

| 41 22 23.10 Material Handling | Crew | Daily Output | Labor-Hours | Unit | Material | 2008 Bare Costs Labor | Equipment | Total | Total Incl O&P |
|---|---|---|---|---|---|---|---|---|---|
| 0010 **MATERIAL HANDLING**, cranes, hoists and lifts | | | | | | | | | |
| 1500     Cranes, portable hydraulic, floor type, 2,000 lb capacity | | | | Ea. | 2,050 | | | 2,050 | 2,250 |
| 1600         4,000 lb capacity | | | | | 3,450 | | | 3,450 | 3,800 |
| 1800         Movable gantry type, 12' to 15' range, 2,000 lb capacity | | | | | 3,000 | | | 3,000 | 3,300 |
| 1900         6,000 lb capacity | | | | | 4,350 | | | 4,350 | 4,800 |
| 2100     Hoists, electric overhead, chain, hook hung, 15' lift, 1 ton cap. | | | | | 1,850 | | | 1,850 | 2,025 |
| 2200         3 ton capacity | | | | | 2,100 | | | 2,100 | 2,300 |
| 2500         5 ton capacity | | | | | 5,525 | | | 5,525 | 6,075 |
| 2600         For hand-pushed trolley, add | | | | | 15% | | | | |
| 2700         For geared trolley, add | | | | | 30% | | | | |
| 2800         For motor trolley, add | | | | | 75% | | | | |
| 3000         For lifts over 15', 1 ton, add | | | | L.F. | 19.45 | | | 19.45 | 21.50 |
| 3100         5 ton, add | | | | " | 43.50 | | | 43.50 | 47.50 |
| 3300     Lifts, scissor type, portable, electric, 36" high, 2,000 lb | | | | Ea. | 3,575 | | | 3,575 | 3,925 |
| 3400         48" high, 4,000 lb | | | | " | 3,900 | | | 3,900 | 4,275 |

# Division Notes

| | CREW | DAILY OUTPUT | LABOR-HOURS | UNIT | 2008 BARE COSTS | | | | TOTAL INCL O&P |
|---|---|---|---|---|---|---|---|---|---|
| | | | | | MAT. | LABOR | EQUIP. | TOTAL | |
| | | | | | | | | | |
| | | | | | | | | | |
| | | | | | | | | | |
| | | | | | | | | | |
| | | | | | | | | | |
| | | | | | | | | | |
| | | | | | | | | | |
| | | | | | | | | | |
| | | | | | | | | | |
| | | | | | | | | | |
| | | | | | | | | | |
| | | | | | | | | | |
| | | | | | | | | | |
| | | | | | | | | | |
| | | | | | | | | | |
| | | | | | | | | | |
| | | | | | | | | | |
| | | | | | | | | | |
| | | | | | | | | | |
| | | | | | | | | | |

## Estimating Tips

There are four basic types of pollution: Air, Noise, Water, and Solid.

These systems may be interrelated and care must be taken that the complete systems are estimated. For example, Air Pollution Equipment may include dust and air-entrained particles that have to be collected. The vacuum systems could be noisy, requiring silencers to reduce noise pollution, and the collected solids have to be disposed of to prevent Solid Pollution.

Water Treatment may be accomplished as comparatively small packaged plants providing Chemical, Biological or Thermal Treatment. These are usually priced by GPH or GPD.

Large plants and municipal treatment facilities are sized MGD. These facilities are usually priced in two steps. First, the large concrete structures used as settling ponds, etc.; and second, the equipment required. Storm water does not need as much treatment as sanitary wastewater.

The total cost of the system is greatly affected by the level of purification required by specifications and codes before release.

An additional cost may be encountered if there is a possibility that the water being treated may contain petroleum products, which have to be isolated and disposed of in an environmentally acceptable manner.

## Reference Numbers

Reference numbers are shown in shaded boxes at the beginning of some major classifications. These numbers refer to related items in the Reference Section. The reference information may be an estimating procedure, an alternate pricing method, or technical information.

*Note:* Not all subdivisions listed here necessarily appear in this publication.

| 44 11 16.10 Dust Collection Systems | Crew | Daily Output | Labor-Hours | Unit | Material | 2008 Bare Costs Labor | 2008 Bare Costs Equipment | Total | Total Incl O&P |
|---|---|---|---|---|---|---|---|---|---|
| 0010 **DUST COLLECTION SYSTEMS** Commercial / industrial | | | | | | | | | |
| 0120 Central vacuum units | | | | | | | | | |
| 0130 Includes stand, filters and motorized shaker | | | | | | | | | |
| 0200 500 CFM, 10" inlet, 2 HP | Q-20 | 2.40 | 8.333 | Ea. | 3,725 | 350 | | 4,075 | 4,600 |
| 0220 1000 CFM, 10" inlet, 3 HP | | 2.20 | 9.091 | | 3,900 | 380 | | 4,280 | 4,850 |
| 0240 1500 CFM, 10" inlet, 5 HP | | 2 | 10 | | 3,975 | 415 | | 4,390 | 5,025 |
| 0260 3000 CFM, 13" inlet, 10 HP | | 1.50 | 13.333 | | 10,400 | 555 | | 10,955 | 12,300 |
| 0280 5000 CFM, 16" inlet, 2 @ 10 HP | | 1 | 20 | | 11,000 | 835 | | 11,835 | 13,400 |
| 1000 Vacuum tubing, galvanized | | | | | | | | | |
| 1100 2-1/8" OD, 16 ga. | Q-9 | 440 | .036 | L.F. | 2.29 | 1.48 | | 3.77 | 4.81 |
| 1110 2-1/2" OD, 16 ga. | | 420 | .038 | | 2.64 | 1.55 | | 4.19 | 5.30 |
| 1120 3" OD, 16 ga. | | 400 | .040 | | 3.02 | 1.63 | | 4.65 | 5.85 |
| 1130 3-1/2" OD, 16 ga. | | 380 | .042 | | 4.36 | 1.72 | | 6.08 | 7.45 |
| 1140 4" OD, 16 ga. | | 360 | .044 | | 4.89 | 1.81 | | 6.70 | 8.20 |
| 1150 5" OD, 14 ga. | | 320 | .050 | | 8.80 | 2.04 | | 10.84 | 12.85 |
| 1160 6" OD, 14 ga. | | 280 | .057 | | 10.15 | 2.33 | | 12.48 | 14.80 |
| 1170 8" OD, 14 ga. | | 200 | .080 | | 15.30 | 3.26 | | 18.56 | 22 |
| 1180 10" OD, 12 ga. | | 160 | .100 | | 15.30 | 4.08 | | 19.38 | 23 |
| 1190 12" OD, 12 ga. | | 120 | .133 | | 26.50 | 5.45 | | 31.95 | 38 |
| 1200 14" OD, 12 ga. | | 80 | .200 | | 32.50 | 8.15 | | 40.65 | 48 |
| 1940 Hose, flexible wire reinforced rubber | | | | | | | | | |
| 1956 3" dia. | Q-9 | 400 | .040 | L.F. | 6.15 | 1.63 | | 7.78 | 9.30 |
| 1960 4" dia. | | 360 | .044 | | 7 | 1.81 | | 8.81 | 10.50 |
| 1970 5" dia. | | 320 | .050 | | 7.95 | 2.04 | | 9.99 | 11.90 |
| 1980 6" dia. | | 280 | .057 | | 8.60 | 2.33 | | 10.93 | 13.05 |
| 2000 90° Elbow, slip fit | | | | | | | | | |
| 2110 2-1/8" dia. | Q-9 | 70 | .229 | Ea. | 9.55 | 9.30 | | 18.85 | 25 |
| 2120 2-1/2" dia. | | 65 | .246 | | 13.35 | 10.05 | | 23.40 | 30 |
| 2130 3" dia. | | 60 | .267 | | 18.10 | 10.85 | | 28.95 | 36.50 |
| 2140 3-1/2" dia. | | 55 | .291 | | 22.50 | 11.85 | | 34.35 | 43 |
| 2150 4" dia. | | 50 | .320 | | 28 | 13.05 | | 41.05 | 50.50 |
| 2160 5" dia. | | 45 | .356 | | 52.50 | 14.50 | | 67 | 80.50 |
| 2170 6" dia. | | 40 | .400 | | 72.50 | 16.30 | | 88.80 | 105 |
| 2180 8" dia. | | 30 | .533 | | 138 | 22 | | 160 | 186 |
| 2400 45° Elbow, slip fit | | | | | | | | | |
| 2410 2-1/8" dia. | Q-9 | 70 | .229 | Ea. | 8.35 | 9.30 | | 17.65 | 23.50 |
| 2420 2-1/2" dia. | | 65 | .246 | | 12.30 | 10.05 | | 22.35 | 29 |
| 2430 3" dia. | | 60 | .267 | | 14.90 | 10.85 | | 25.75 | 33 |
| 2440 3-1/2" dia. | | 55 | .291 | | 18.70 | 11.85 | | 30.55 | 39 |
| 2450 4" dia. | | 50 | .320 | | 24.50 | 13.05 | | 37.55 | 46.50 |
| 2460 5" dia. | | 45 | .356 | | 41 | 14.50 | | 55.50 | 67.50 |
| 2470 6" dia. | | 40 | .400 | | 55.50 | 16.30 | | 71.80 | 86 |
| 2480 8" dia. | | 35 | .457 | | 109 | 18.65 | | 127.65 | 148 |
| 2800 90° TY, slip fit thru 6" dia | | | | | | | | | |
| 2810 2-1/8" dia. | Q-9 | 42 | .381 | Ea. | 18.70 | 15.55 | | 34.25 | 44.50 |
| 2820 2-1/2" dia. | | 39 | .410 | | 24.50 | 16.75 | | 41.25 | 53 |
| 2830 3" dia. | | 36 | .444 | | 32 | 18.10 | | 50.10 | 63.50 |
| 2840 3-1/2" dia. | | 33 | .485 | | 41 | 19.75 | | 60.75 | 75.50 |
| 2850 4" dia. | | 30 | .533 | | 59 | 22 | | 81 | 98 |
| 2860 5" dia. | | 27 | .593 | | 112 | 24 | | 136 | 161 |
| 2870 6" dia. | | 24 | .667 | | 152 | 27 | | 179 | 210 |
| 2880 8" dia., butt end | | | | | 325 | | | 325 | 355 |
| 2890 10" dia., butt end | | | | | 585 | | | 585 | 640 |

# 44 11 Air Pollution Control Equipment

## 44 11 16 – Industrial Dust Collectors

### 44 11 16.10 Dust Collection Systems

| 44 11 16.10 Dust Collection Systems | Crew | Daily Output | Labor-Hours | Unit | Material | 2008 Bare Costs Labor | Equipment | Total | Total Incl O&P |
|---|---|---|---|---|---|---|---|---|---|
| 2900 | 12" dia., butt end | | | | Ea. | 585 | | | 585 | 640 |
| 2910 | 14" dia., butt end | | | | | 1,050 | | | 1,050 | 1,175 |
| 2920 | 6" x 4" dia., butt end | | | | | 93 | | | 93 | 102 |
| 2930 | 8" x 4" dia., butt end | | | | | 176 | | | 176 | 193 |
| 2940 | 10" x 4" dia., butt end | | | | | 230 | | | 230 | 254 |
| 2950 | 12" x 4" dia., butt end | | | | ↓ | 264 | | | 264 | 290 |
| 3100 | 90° Elbow, butt end segmented | | | | | | | | | |
| 3110 | 8" dia., butt end, segmented | | | | Ea. | 138 | | | 138 | 152 |
| 3120 | 10" dia., butt end, segmented | | | | | 345 | | | 345 | 375 |
| 3130 | 12" dia., butt end, segmented | | | | | 435 | | | 435 | 480 |
| 3140 | 14" dia., butt end, segmented | | | | ↓ | 545 | | | 545 | 600 |
| 3200 | 45° Elbow, butt end segmented | | | | | | | | | |
| 3210 | 8" dia., butt end, segmented | | | | Ea. | 109 | | | 109 | 119 |
| 3220 | 10" dia., butt end, segmented | | | | | 248 | | | 248 | 273 |
| 3230 | 12" dia., butt end, segmented | | | | | 254 | | | 254 | 279 |
| 3240 | 14" dia., butt end, segmented | | | | ↓ | 310 | | | 310 | 345 |
| 3400 | All butt end fittings require one coupling per joint. | | | | | | | | | |
| 3410 | Labor for fitting included with couplings. | | | | | | | | | |
| 3460 | Compression coupling, galvanized, neoprene gasket | | | | | | | | | |
| 3470 | 2-1/8" dia. | Q-9 | 44 | .364 | Ea. | 11.10 | 14.85 | | 25.95 | 35 |
| 3480 | 2-1/2" dia. | | 44 | .364 | | 11.10 | 14.85 | | 25.95 | 35 |
| 3490 | 3" dia. | | 38 | .421 | | 16 | 17.15 | | 33.15 | 44 |
| 3500 | 3-1/2" dia. | | 35 | .457 | | 18.10 | 18.65 | | 36.75 | 49 |
| 3510 | 4" dia. | | 33 | .485 | | 19.70 | 19.75 | | 39.45 | 52 |
| 3520 | 5" dia. | | 29 | .552 | | 22.50 | 22.50 | | 45 | 59 |
| 3530 | 6" dia. | | 26 | .615 | | 22.50 | 25 | | 47.50 | 63.50 |
| 3540 | 8" dia. | | 22 | .727 | | 47 | 29.50 | | 76.50 | 97 |
| 3550 | 10" dia. | | 20 | .800 | | 63.50 | 32.50 | | 96 | 120 |
| 3560 | 12" dia. | | 18 | .889 | | 78 | 36.50 | | 114.50 | 142 |
| 3570 | 14" dia. | ↓ | 16 | 1 | ↓ | 100 | 41 | | 141 | 173 |
| 3800 | Air gate valves, galvanized | | | | | | | | | |
| 3810 | 2-1/8" dia. | Q-9 | 30 | .533 | Ea. | 162 | 22 | | 184 | 212 |
| 3820 | 2-1/2" dia. | | 28 | .571 | | 179 | 23.50 | | 202.50 | 233 |
| 3830 | 3" dia. | | 26 | .615 | | 195 | 25 | | 220 | 254 |
| 3840 | 4" dia. | | 23 | .696 | | 246 | 28.50 | | 274.50 | 315 |
| 3850 | 6" dia. | ↓ | 18 | .889 | ↓ | 330 | 36.50 | | 366.50 | 420 |

# 44 41 Packaged Water Treatment

## 44 41 13 – Packaged Water Treatment Plants

### 44 41 13.16 Biological Packaged Water Treatment Plants

| | | Crew | Daily Output | Labor-Hours | Unit | Material | Labor | Equipment | Total | Total Incl O&P |
|---|---|---|---|---|---|---|---|---|---|---|
| 0010 | **BIOLOGICAL PACKAGED WATER TREATMENT PLANTS** | | | | | | | | | |
| 0011 | Not including fencing or external piping | | | | | | | | | |
| 0020 | Steel packaged, blown air aeration plants | | | | | | | | | |
| 0100 | 1,000 GPD | | | | Gal. | | | | 20.46 | 23.54 |
| 0200 | 5,000 GPD | | | | | | | | 12.39 | 14.25 |
| 0300 | 15,000 GPD | | | | | | | | 6.83 | 7.85 |
| 0400 | 30,000 GPD | | | | | | | | 6.45 | 7.40 |
| 0500 | 50,000 GPD | | | | | | | | 5.50 | 6.32 |
| 0600 | 100,000 GPD | | | | | | | | 4.80 | 5.50 |
| 0700 | 200,000 GPD | | | | | | | | 3.41 | 3.93 |
| 0800 | 500,000 GPD | | | | ↓ | | | | 3.33 | 3.83 |

# 44 41 Packaged Water Treatment

## 44 41 13 – Packaged Water Treatment Plants

| 44 41 13.16 Biological Packaged Water Treatment Plants | Crew | Daily Output | Labor-Hours | Unit | Material | 2008 Bare Costs Labor | Equipment | Total | Total Incl O&P |
|---|---|---|---|---|---|---|---|---|---|
| 1000 | Concrete, extended aeration, primary and secondary treatment | | | | | | | | |
| 1010 | 10,000 GPD | | | | Gal. | | | | 15.70 | 18.06 |
| 1100 | 30,000 GPD | | | | | | | 7.19 | 8.30 |
| 1200 | 50,000 GPD | | | | | | | 6.14 | 7.09 |
| 1400 | 100,000 GPD | | | | | | | 4.57 | 5.25 |
| 1500 | 500,000 GPD | | | | | | | 3.25 | 3.75 |
| 1700 | Municipal wastewater treatment facility | | | | | | | | |
| 1720 | 1.0 MGD | | | | Gal. | | | 5.62 | 6.45 |
| 1740 | 1.5 MGD | | | | | | | 5.53 | 6.35 |
| 1760 | 2.0 MGD | | | | | | | 4.75 | 5.46 |
| 1780 | 3.0 MGD | | | | | | | 3.71 | 4.26 |
| 1800 | 5.0 MGD | | | | | | | 3.38 | 3.88 |
| 2000 | Holding tank system, not incl. excavation or backfill | | | | | | | | |
| 2010 | Recirculating chemical water closet | 2 Plum | 4 | 4 | Ea. | 875 | 187 | | 1,062 | 1,250 |
| 2100 | For voltage converter, add | " | 16 | 1 | | 232 | 46.50 | | 278.50 | 325 |
| 2200 | For high level alarm, add | 1 Plum | 7.80 | 1.026 | | 133 | 48 | | 181 | 218 |

## 44 41 13.17 Wastewater Treatment System

| | | Crew | Daily Output | Labor-Hours | Unit | Material | 2008 Bare Costs Labor | Equipment | Total | Total Incl O&P |
|---|---|---|---|---|---|---|---|---|---|---|
| 0010 | **WASTEWATER TREATMENT SYSTEM** | | | | | | | | | |
| 0020 | Fiberglass, 1,000 gallon | B-21 | 1.29 | 21.705 | Ea. | 3,300 | 760 | 100 | 4,160 | 4,900 |
| 0100 | 1,500 gallon | B-21 | 1.03 | 27.184 | Ea. | 7,200 | 950 | 126 | 8,276 | 9,550 |

# Reference Section

All the reference information is in one section, making it easy to find what you need to know . . . and easy to use the book on a daily basis. This section is visually identified by a vertical gray bar on the page edges.

In this Reference Section, we've included Equipment Rental Costs, a listing of rental and operating costs; Crew Listings, a full listing of all crews and equipment, and their costs; Historical Cost Indexes for cost comparisons over time; City Cost Indexes and Location Factors for adjusting costs to the region you are in; Reference Tables, where you will find explanations, estimating information and procedures, or technical data; Change Orders, information on pricing changes to contract documents; Square Foot Costs that allow you to make a rough estimate for the overall cost of a project; and an explanation of all the Abbreviations in the book.

## Table of Contents

# Estimating Tips

- This section contains the average costs to rent and operate hundreds of pieces of construction equipment. This is useful information when estimating the time and material requirements of any particular operation in order to establish a unit or total cost. Equipment costs include not only rental, but also operating costs for equipment under normal use.

# Rental Costs

- Equipment rental rates are obtained from industry sources throughout North America–contractors, suppliers, dealers, manufacturers, and distributors.
- Rental rates vary throughout the country, with larger cities generally having lower rates. Lease plans for new equipment are available for periods in excess of six months, with a percentage of payments applying toward purchase.
- Monthly rental rates vary from 2% to 5% of the purchase price of the equipment depending on the anticipated life of the equipment and its wearing parts.
- Weekly rental rates are about 1/3 the monthly rates, and daily rental rates are about 1/3 the weekly rate.

# Operating Costs

- The operating costs include parts and labor for routine servicing, such as repair and replacement of pumps, filters and worn lines. Normal operating expendables, such as fuel, lubricants, tires and electricity (where applicable), are also included.
- Extraordinary operating expendables with highly variable wear patterns, such as diamond bits and blades, are excluded. These costs can be found as material costs in the Unit Price section.
- The hourly operating costs listed do not include the operator's wages.

# Crew Equipment Cost/Day

- Any power equipment required by a crew is shown in the Crew Listings with a daily cost.
- The daily cost of crew equipment is based on dividing the weekly rental rate by 5 (number of working days in the week), and then adding the hourly operating cost times 8 (the number of hours in a day). This "Crew Equipment Cost/ Day" is shown in the far right column of the Equipment Rental pages.
- If equipment is needed for only one or two days, it is best to develop your own cost by including components for daily rent and hourly operating cost. This is important when the listed Crew for a task does not contain the equipment needed, such as a crane for lifting mechanical heating/cooling equipment up onto a roof.

# Mobilization/ Demobilization

- The cost to move construction equipment from an equipment yard or rental company to the jobsite and back again is not included in equipment rental costs listed in the Reference section, nor in the bare equipment cost of any Unit Price line item, nor in any equipment costs shown in the Crew listings.
- Mobilization (to the site) and demobilization (from the site) costs can be found in the Unit Price section.
- If a piece of equipment is already at the jobsite, it is not appropriate to utilize mobil./ demob. costs again in an estimate.

**Equipment Rental Costs**

## 01 54 33 | Equipment Rental

| | | UNIT | HOURLY OPER. COST | RENT PER DAY | RENT PER WEEK | RENT PER MONTH | CREW EQUIPMENT COST/DAY | |
|---|---|---|---|---|---|---|---|---|
| 10 | 0010 | **CONCRETE EQUIPMENT RENTAL** without operators   R015433 -10 | | | | | | 10 |
| | 0150 | For batch plant, see Equipment Section 01 54 33.50 | | | | | | |
| | 0200 | Bucket, concrete lightweight, 1/2 C.Y. | Ea. | .65 | 19 | 57 | 171 | 16.60 |
| | 0300 | 1 C.Y. | | .70 | 23.50 | 70 | 210 | 19.60 |
| | 0400 | 1-1/2 C.Y. | | .90 | 31.50 | 95 | 285 | 26.20 |
| | 0500 | 2 C.Y. | | .95 | 38.50 | 115 | 345 | 30.60 |
| | 0580 | 8 C.Y. | | 5.25 | 250 | 750 | 2,250 | 192 |
| | 0600 | Cart, concrete, self propelled, operator walking, 10 C.F. | | 2.55 | 60 | 180 | 540 | 56.40 |
| | 0700 | Operator riding, 18 C.F. | | 4.05 | 86.50 | 260 | 780 | 84.40 |
| | 0800 | Conveyer for concrete, portable, gas, 16" wide, 26' long | | 9.35 | 122 | 365 | 1,100 | 147.80 |
| | 0900 | 46' long | | 9.70 | 147 | 440 | 1,325 | 165.60 |
| | 1000 | 56' long | | 9.85 | 157 | 470 | 1,400 | 172.80 |
| | 1100 | Core drill, electric, 2-1/2 H.P., 1" to 8" bit diameter | | 1.73 | 67 | 201 | 605 | 54.05 |
| | 1150 | 11 HP, 8" to 18" cores | | 5.05 | 115 | 345 | 1,025 | 109.40 |
| | 1200 | Finisher, concrete floor, gas, riding trowel, 96" wide | | 9.25 | 145 | 435 | 1,300 | 161 |
| | 1300 | Gas, walk-behind, 3 blade, 36" trowel | | 1.45 | 20.50 | 62 | 186 | 24 |
| | 1400 | 4 blade, 48" trowel | | 2.95 | 27 | 81 | 243 | 39.80 |
| | 1500 | Float, hand-operated (Bull float) 48" wide | | .08 | 13.35 | 40 | 120 | 8.65 |
| | 1570 | Curb builder, 14 H.P., gas, single screw | | 11.30 | 238 | 715 | 2,150 | 233.40 |
| | 1590 | Double screw | | 11.95 | 278 | 835 | 2,500 | 262.60 |
| | 1600 | Grinder, concrete and terrazzo, electric, floor | | 2.43 | 103 | 310 | 930 | 81.45 |
| | 1700 | Wall grinder | | 1.22 | 51.50 | 155 | 465 | 40.75 |
| | 1800 | Mixer, powered, mortar and concrete, gas, 6 C.F., 18 H.P. | | 6.50 | 115 | 345 | 1,025 | 121 |
| | 1900 | 10 C.F., 25 H.P. | | 8.10 | 142 | 425 | 1,275 | 149.80 |
| | 2000 | 16 C.F. | | 8.40 | 165 | 495 | 1,475 | 166.20 |
| | 2100 | Concrete, stationary, tilt drum, 2 C.Y. | | 5.90 | 228 | 685 | 2,050 | 184.20 |
| | 2120 | Pump, concrete, truck mounted 4" line 80' boom | | 22.40 | 915 | 2,745 | 8,225 | 728.20 |
| | 2140 | 5" line, 110' boom | | 29.20 | 1,225 | 3,660 | 11,000 | 965.60 |
| | 2160 | Mud jack, 50 C.F. per hr. | | 6.05 | 130 | 390 | 1,175 | 126.40 |
| | 2180 | 225 C.F. per hr. | | 7.85 | 147 | 440 | 1,325 | 150.80 |
| | 2190 | Shotcrete pump rig, 12 CY/hr | | 14.40 | 243 | 730 | 2,200 | 261.20 |
| | 2600 | Saw, concrete, manual, gas, 18 H.P. | | 4.80 | 36.50 | 110 | 330 | 60.40 |
| | 2650 | Self-propelled, gas, 30 H.P. | | 9.50 | 98.50 | 295 | 885 | 135 |
| | 2700 | Vibrators, concrete, electric, 60 cycle, 2 H.P. | | .43 | 8 | 24 | 72 | 8.25 |
| | 2800 | 3 H.P. | | .59 | 9.65 | 29 | 87 | 10.50 |
| | 2900 | Gas engine, 5 H.P. | | 1.30 | 14 | 42 | 126 | 18.80 |
| | 3000 | 8 H.P. | | 1.95 | 15.35 | 46 | 138 | 24.80 |
| | 3050 | Vibrating screed, gas engine, 8 H.P. | | 2.77 | 73 | 219 | 655 | 65.95 |
| | 3100 | Concrete transit mixer, hydraulic drive | | | | | | |
| | 3120 | 6 x 4, 250 H.P., 8 C.Y., rear discharge | | 44.70 | 565 | 1,695 | 5,075 | 696.60 |
| | 3200 | Front discharge | | 52.65 | 700 | 2,095 | 6,275 | 840.20 |
| | 3300 | 6 x 6, 285 H.P., 12 C.Y., rear discharge | | 51.75 | 660 | 1,975 | 5,925 | 809 |
| | 3400 | Front discharge | | 54.10 | 705 | 2,120 | 6,350 | 856.80 |
| 20 | 0010 | **EARTHWORK EQUIPMENT RENTAL** without operators   R015433 -10 | | | | | | 20 |
| | 0040 | Aggregate spreader, push type 8' to 12' wide | Ea. | 2.30 | 25.50 | 76 | 228 | 33.60 |
| | 0045 | Tailgate type, 8' wide | " | 2.20 | 33 | 99 | 297 | 37.40 |
| | 0050 | Augers for vertical drilling | | | | | | |
| | 0055 | Earth auger, truck-mounted, for fence & sign posts, utility poles | Ea. | 12.60 | 505 | 1,510 | 4,525 | 402.80 |
| | 0060 | For borings and monitoring wells | | 37.85 | 665 | 1,995 | 5,975 | 701.80 |
| | 0070 | Earth auger, portable, trailer mounted | | 2.60 | 24.50 | 74 | 222 | 35.60 |
| | 0075 | Earth auger, truck-mounted, for caissons, water wells | | 85.50 | 3,075 | 9,230 | 27,700 | 2,530 |
| | 0080 | Auger, horizontal boring machine, 12" to 36" diameter, 45 H.P. | | 19.90 | 200 | 600 | 1,800 | 279.20 |
| | 0090 | 12" to 48" diameter, 65 H.P. | | 28.40 | 355 | 1,070 | 3,200 | 441.20 |
| | 0095 | Auger, for fence posts, gas engine, hand held | | .45 | 5.35 | 16 | 48 | 6.80 |
| | 0100 | Excavator, diesel hydraulic, crawler mounted, 1/2 C.Y. cap. | | 19.75 | 375 | 1,120 | 3,350 | 382 |

## 01 54 33 | Equipment Rental

| | | UNIT | HOURLY OPER. COST | RENT PER DAY | RENT PER WEEK | RENT PER MONTH | CREW EQUIPMENT COST/DAY | |
|---|---|---|---|---|---|---|---|---|
| **20** | 0120 | 5/8 C.Y. capacity | Ea. | 24.05 | 510 | 1,525 | 4,575 | 497.40 | **20** |
| | 0140 | 3/4 C.Y. capacity | | 27.30 | 550 | 1,655 | 4,975 | 549.40 | |
| | 0150 | 1 C.Y. capacity | | 34.70 | 615 | 1,845 | 5,525 | 646.60 | |
| | 0200 | 1-1/2 C.Y. capacity | | 42.50 | 815 | 2,450 | 7,350 | 830 | |
| | 0300 | 2 C.Y. capacity | | 56.25 | 1,025 | 3,050 | 9,150 | 1,060 | |
| | 0320 | 2-1/2 C.Y. capacity | | 75.95 | 1,425 | 4,290 | 12,900 | 1,466 | |
| | 0340 | 3-1/2 C.Y. capacity | | 118.75 | 2,300 | 6,935 | 20,800 | 2,337 | |
| | 0341 | Attachments | | | | | | | |
| | 0342 | Bucket thumbs | | 2.60 | 215 | 645 | 1,925 | 149.80 | |
| | 0345 | Grapples | | 2.40 | 187 | 560 | 1,675 | 131.20 | |
| | 0350 | Gradall type, truck mounted, 3 ton @ 15' radius, 5/8 C.Y. | | 46.95 | 930 | 2,785 | 8,350 | 932.60 | |
| | 0370 | 1 C.Y. capacity | | 52.15 | 1,125 | 3,360 | 10,100 | 1,089 | |
| | 0400 | Backhoe-loader, 40 to 45 H.P., 5/8 C.Y. capacity | | 11.20 | 215 | 645 | 1,925 | 218.60 | |
| | 0450 | 45 H.P. to 60 H.P., 3/4 C.Y. capacity | | 15.05 | 275 | 825 | 2,475 | 285.40 | |
| | 0460 | 80 H.P., 1-1/4 C.Y. capacity | | 18.10 | 325 | 980 | 2,950 | 340.80 | |
| | 0470 | 112 H.P., 1-1/2 C.Y. capacity | | 24.30 | 465 | 1,390 | 4,175 | 472.40 | |
| | 0480 | Attachments | | | | | | | |
| | 0482 | Compactor, 20,000 lb | | 4.70 | 123 | 370 | 1,100 | 111.60 | |
| | 0485 | Hydraulic hammer, 750 ft-lbs | | 2.70 | 88.50 | 265 | 795 | 74.60 | |
| | 0486 | Hydraulic hammer, 1200 ft-lbs | | 3.60 | 162 | 485 | 1,450 | 125.80 | |
| | 0500 | Brush chipper, gas engine, 6" cutter head, 35 H.P. | | 8.40 | 107 | 320 | 960 | 131.20 | |
| | 0550 | 12" cutter head, 130 H.P. | | 13.95 | 173 | 520 | 1,550 | 215.60 | |
| | 0600 | 15" cutter head, 165 H.P. | | 20.90 | 218 | 655 | 1,975 | 298.20 | |
| | 0750 | Bucket, clamshell, general purpose, 3/8 C.Y. | | 1.05 | 36.50 | 110 | 330 | 30.40 | |
| | 0800 | 1/2 C.Y. | | 1.20 | 43.50 | 130 | 390 | 35.60 | |
| | 0850 | 3/4 C.Y. | | 1.35 | 53.50 | 160 | 480 | 42.80 | |
| | 0900 | 1 C.Y. | | 1.40 | 58.50 | 175 | 525 | 46.20 | |
| | 0950 | 1-1/2 C.Y. | | 2.20 | 78.50 | 235 | 705 | 64.60 | |
| | 1000 | 2 C.Y. | | 2.30 | 88.50 | 265 | 795 | 71.40 | |
| | 1010 | Bucket, dragline, medium duty, 1/2 C.Y. | | .60 | 23.50 | 70 | 210 | 18.80 | |
| | 1020 | 3/4 C.Y. | | .65 | 24.50 | 73 | 219 | 19.80 | |
| | 1030 | 1 C.Y. | | .65 | 26 | 78 | 234 | 20.80 | |
| | 1040 | 1-1/2 C.Y. | | 1.05 | 40 | 120 | 360 | 32.40 | |
| | 1050 | 2 C.Y. | | 1.10 | 45 | 135 | 405 | 35.80 | |
| | 1070 | 3 C.Y. | | 1.60 | 55 | 165 | 495 | 45.80 | |
| | 1200 | Compactor, manually guided 2-drum vibratory smooth roller, 7.5 H.P. | | 5.75 | 162 | 485 | 1,450 | 143 | |
| | 1250 | Rammer compactor, gas, 1000 lb. blow | | 2.25 | 41.50 | 125 | 375 | 43 | |
| | 1300 | Vibratory plate, gas, 18" plate, 3000 lb. blow | | 2.20 | 22.50 | 67 | 201 | 31 | |
| | 1350 | 21" plate, 5000 lb. blow | | 2.70 | 28 | 84 | 252 | 38.40 | |
| | 1370 | Curb builder/extruder, 14 H.P., gas, single screw | | 11.30 | 238 | 715 | 2,150 | 233.40 | |
| | 1390 | Double screw | | 11.95 | 278 | 835 | 2,500 | 262.60 | |
| | 1500 | Disc harrow attachment, for tractor | | .39 | 64.50 | 193 | 580 | 41.70 | |
| | 1750 | Extractor, piling, see lines 2500 to 2750 | | | | | | | |
| | 1810 | Feller buncher, shearing & accumulating trees, 100 H.P. | Ea. | 27.30 | 545 | 1,630 | 4,900 | 544.40 | |
| | 1860 | Grader, self-propelled, 25,000 lb. | | 23.65 | 445 | 1,340 | 4,025 | 457.20 | |
| | 1910 | 30,000 lb. | | 27.30 | 525 | 1,580 | 4,750 | 534.40 | |
| | 1920 | 40,000 lb. | | 38.60 | 810 | 2,425 | 7,275 | 793.80 | |
| | 1930 | 55,000 lb. | | 51.10 | 1,150 | 3,465 | 10,400 | 1,102 | |
| | 1950 | Hammer, pavement demo., hyd., gas, self-prop., 1000 to 1250 lb. | | 22.35 | 325 | 970 | 2,900 | 372.80 | |
| | 2000 | Diesel 1300 to 1500 lb. | | 33.53 | 645 | 1,940 | 5,825 | 656.25 | |
| | 2050 | Pile driving hammer, steam or air, 4150 ft.-lb. @ 225 BPM | | 7.00 | 283 | 850 | 2,550 | 226 | |
| | 2100 | 8750 ft.-lb. @ 145 BPM | | 8.55 | 425 | 1,275 | 3,825 | 323.40 | |
| | 2150 | 15,000 ft.-lb. @ 60 BPM | | 8.90 | 460 | 1,375 | 4,125 | 346.20 | |
| | 2200 | 24,450 ft.-lb. @ 111 BPM | | 12.35 | 545 | 1,635 | 4,900 | 425.80 | |
| | 2250 | Leads, 20' long for pile driving hammers up to 20,000 ft.-lb. | | .95 | 28.50 | 85 | 255 | 24.60 | |
| | 2300 | 30' long for hammers over 20,000 ft.-lb. | | 1.55 | 71.50 | 215 | 645 | 55.40 | |

R015433
-10

## 01 54 33 | Equipment Rental

| | | UNIT | HOURLY OPER. COST | RENT PER DAY | RENT PER WEEK | RENT PER MONTH | CREW EQUIPMENT COST/DAY | |
|---|---|---|---|---|---|---|---|---|
| **20** | 2350 | Diesel type hammer, 22,400 ft.-lb. | Ea. | 24.85 | 630 | 1,895 | 5,675 | 577.80 | **20** |
| | 2400 | 41,300 ft.-lb. | | 31.40 | 685 | 2,050 | 6,150 | 661.20 | |
| | 2450 | 141,000 ft.-lb. | | 47.65 | 1,175 | 3,525 | 10,600 | 1,086 | |
| | 2500 | Vib. elec. hammer/extractor, 200 KW diesel generator, 34 H.P. | | 38.80 | 660 | 1,975 | 5,925 | 705.40 | |
| | 2550 | 80 H.P. | | 69.40 | 965 | 2,895 | 8,675 | 1,134 | |
| | 2600 | 150 H.P. | | 130.95 | 1,875 | 5,650 | 17,000 | 2,178 | |
| | 2700 | Extractor, steam or air, 700 ft.-lb. | | 15.40 | 480 | 1,440 | 4,325 | 411.20 | |
| | 2750 | 1000 ft.-lb. | | 17.50 | 600 | 1,795 | 5,375 | 499 | |
| | 2800 | Log chipper, up to 22" diam, 600 H.P. | | 37.90 | 450 | 1,350 | 4,050 | 573.20 | |
| | 2850 | Logger, for skidding & stacking logs, 150 H.P. | | 42.80 | 875 | 2,620 | 7,850 | 866.40 | |
| | 2900 | Rake, spring tooth, with tractor | | 10.69 | 226 | 678 | 2,025 | 221.10 | |
| | 3000 | Roller, vibratory, tandem, smooth drum, 20 H.P. | | 6.65 | 128 | 385 | 1,150 | 130.20 | |
| | 3050 | 35 H.P. | | 9.25 | 242 | 725 | 2,175 | 219 | |
| | 3100 | Towed type vibratory compactor, smooth drum, 50 H.P. | | 21.20 | 335 | 1,010 | 3,025 | 371.60 | |
| | 3150 | Sheepsfoot, 50 H.P. | | 22.20 | 365 | 1,100 | 3,300 | 397.60 | |
| | 3170 | Landfill compactor, 220 HP | | 65.95 | 1,275 | 3,805 | 11,400 | 1,289 | |
| | 3200 | Pneumatic tire roller, 80 H.P. | | 13.10 | 340 | 1,015 | 3,050 | 307.80 | |
| | 3250 | 120 H.P. | | 20.00 | 610 | 1,825 | 5,475 | 525 | |
| | 3300 | Sheepsfoot vibratory roller, 200 H.P. | | 53.90 | 960 | 2,875 | 8,625 | 1,006 | |
| | 3320 | 340 H.P. | | 76.10 | 1,400 | 4,235 | 12,700 | 1,456 | |
| | 3350 | Smooth drum vibratory roller, 75 H.P. | | 19.55 | 525 | 1,570 | 4,700 | 470.40 | |
| | 3400 | 125 H.P. | | 25.60 | 650 | 1,945 | 5,825 | 593.80 | |
| | 3410 | Rotary mower, brush, 60", with tractor | | 14.45 | 248 | 745 | 2,225 | 264.60 | |
| | 3420 | Rototiller, 5 HP, walk-behind | | 2.09 | 62.50 | 188 | 565 | 54.30 | |
| | 3450 | Scrapers, towed type, 9 to 12 C.Y. capacity | | 5.95 | 170 | 510 | 1,525 | 149.60 | |
| | 3500 | 12 to 17 C.Y. capacity | | 6.55 | 185 | 555 | 1,675 | 163.40 | |
| | 3550 | Scrapers, self-propelled, 4 x 4 drive, 2 engine, 14 C.Y. capacity | | 113.05 | 1,625 | 4,890 | 14,700 | 1,882 | |
| | 3600 | 2 engine, 24 C.Y. capacity | | 157.55 | 2,625 | 7,845 | 23,500 | 2,829 | |
| | 3640 | 32 - 44 C.Y. capacity | | 184.65 | 3,175 | 9,495 | 28,500 | 3,376 | |
| | 3650 | Self-loading, 11 C.Y. capacity | | 49.30 | 890 | 2,665 | 8,000 | 927.40 | |
| | 3700 | 22 C.Y. capacity | | 93.80 | 1,875 | 5,610 | 16,800 | 1,872 | |
| | 3710 | Screening plant 110 H.P. w/ 5' x 10' screen | | 30.60 | 405 | 1,210 | 3,625 | 486.80 | |
| | 3720 | 5' x 16' screen | | 32.70 | 505 | 1,520 | 4,550 | 565.60 | |
| | 3850 | Shovels, see Cranes division 01590-600 | | | | | | | |
| | 3860 | Shovel/backhoe bucket, 1/2 C.Y. | Ea. | 2.00 | 58.50 | 175 | 525 | 51 | |
| | 3870 | 3/4 C.Y. | | 2.05 | 66.50 | 200 | 600 | 56.40 | |
| | 3880 | 1 C.Y. | | 2.15 | 75 | 225 | 675 | 62.20 | |
| | 3890 | 1-1/2 C.Y. | | 2.30 | 88.50 | 265 | 795 | 71.40 | |
| | 3910 | 3 C.Y. | | 2.60 | 123 | 370 | 1,100 | 94.80 | |
| | 3950 | Stump chipper, 18" deep, 30 H.P. | | 7.60 | 160 | 480 | 1,450 | 156.80 | |
| | 4110 | Tractor, crawler, with bulldozer, torque converter, diesel 80 H.P. | | 20.55 | 360 | 1,075 | 3,225 | 379.40 | |
| | 4150 | 105 H.P. | | 28.80 | 505 | 1,510 | 4,525 | 532.40 | |
| | 4200 | 140 H.P. | | 34.55 | 645 | 1,940 | 5,825 | 664.40 | |
| | 4260 | 200 H.P. | | 52.85 | 1,075 | 3,240 | 9,725 | 1,071 | |
| | 4310 | 300 H.P. | | 67.65 | 1,400 | 4,235 | 12,700 | 1,388 | |
| | 4360 | 410 H.P. | | 90.40 | 1,825 | 5,470 | 16,400 | 1,817 | |
| | 4370 | 500 H.P. | | 120.70 | 2,450 | 7,320 | 22,000 | 2,430 | |
| | 4380 | 700 H.P. | | 179.00 | 3,750 | 11,250 | 33,800 | 3,682 | |
| | 4400 | Loader, crawler, torque conv., diesel, 1-1/2 C.Y., 80 H.P. | | 18.90 | 345 | 1,030 | 3,100 | 357.20 | |
| | 4450 | 1-1/2 to 1-3/4 C.Y., 95 H.P. | | 22.20 | 435 | 1,305 | 3,925 | 438.60 | |
| | 4510 | 1-3/4 to 2-1/4 C.Y., 130 H.P. | | 29.90 | 660 | 1,980 | 5,950 | 635.20 | |
| | 4530 | 2-1/2 to 3-1/4 C.Y., 190 H.P. | | 42.80 | 920 | 2,755 | 8,275 | 893.40 | |
| | 4560 | 3-1/2 to 5 C.Y., 275 H.P. | | 59.85 | 1,275 | 3,815 | 11,400 | 1,242 | |
| | 4610 | Tractor loader, wheel, torque conv., 4 x 4, 1 to 1-1/4 C.Y., 65 H.P. | | 13.30 | 200 | 600 | 1,800 | 226.40 | |
| | 4620 | 1-1/2 to 1-3/4 C.Y., 80 H.P. | | 17.35 | 273 | 820 | 2,450 | 302.80 | |
| | 4650 | 1-3/4 to 2 C.Y., 100 H.P. | | 19.70 | 315 | 940 | 2,825 | 345.60 | |

R015433 -10

## 01 54 33 | Equipment Rental

| | | UNIT | HOURLY OPER. COST | RENT PER DAY | RENT PER WEEK | RENT PER MONTH | CREW EQUIPMENT COST/DAY | |
|---|---|---|---|---|---|---|---|---|
| **20** | 4710 | 2-1/2 to 3-1/2 C.Y., 130 H.P. [R015433 -10] | Ea. | 21.55 | 355 | 1,070 | 3,200 | 386.40 | **20** |
| | 4730 | 3 to 4-1/2 C.Y., 170 H.P. | | 28.00 | 520 | 1,560 | 4,675 | 536 | |
| | 4760 | 5-1/4 to 5-3/4 C.Y., 270 H.P. | | 45.35 | 775 | 2,320 | 6,950 | 826.80 | |
| | 4810 | 7 to 8 C.Y., 375 H.P. | | 77.35 | 1,450 | 4,340 | 13,000 | 1,487 | |
| | 4870 | 12-1/2 C.Y., 690 H.P. | | 106.25 | 2,225 | 6,655 | 20,000 | 2,181 | |
| | 4880 | Wheeled, skid steer, 10 C.F., 30 H.P. gas | | 7.50 | 130 | 390 | 1,175 | 138 | |
| | 4890 | 1 C.Y., 78 H.P., diesel | | 14.05 | 223 | 670 | 2,000 | 246.40 | |
| | 4891 | Attachments for all skid steer loaders | | | | | | | |
| | 4892 | Auger | Ea. | .52 | 87 | 261 | 785 | 56.35 | |
| | 4893 | Backhoe | | .69 | 116 | 347 | 1,050 | 74.90 | |
| | 4894 | Broom | | .71 | 118 | 355 | 1,075 | 76.70 | |
| | 4895 | Forks | | .24 | 40.50 | 121 | 365 | 26.10 | |
| | 4896 | Grapple | | .58 | 97.50 | 292 | 875 | 63.05 | |
| | 4897 | Concrete hammer | | 1.02 | 170 | 511 | 1,525 | 110.35 | |
| | 4898 | Tree spade | | .76 | 127 | 381 | 1,150 | 82.30 | |
| | 4899 | Trencher | | .89 | 148 | 443 | 1,325 | 95.70 | |
| | 4900 | Trencher, chain, boom type, gas, operator walking, 12 H.P. | | 3.55 | 46.50 | 140 | 420 | 56.40 | |
| | 4910 | Operator riding, 40 H.P. | | 11.15 | 258 | 775 | 2,325 | 244.20 | |
| | 5000 | Wheel type, diesel, 4' deep, 12" wide | | 61.55 | 790 | 2,375 | 7,125 | 967.40 | |
| | 5100 | Diesel, 6' deep, 20" wide | | 73.90 | 1,850 | 5,550 | 16,700 | 1,701 | |
| | 5150 | Chain type, diesel, 5' deep, 8" wide | | 27.45 | 575 | 1,725 | 5,175 | 564.60 | |
| | 5200 | Diesel, 8' deep, 16" wide | | 70.75 | 1,950 | 5,850 | 17,600 | 1,736 | |
| | 5210 | Tree spade, self-propelled | | 13.30 | 267 | 800 | 2,400 | 266.40 | |
| | 5250 | Truck, dump, 2-axle, 12 ton, 8 CY payload, 220 H.P. | | 22.95 | 208 | 625 | 1,875 | 308.60 | |
| | 5300 | Three axle dump, 16 ton, 12 CY payload, 400 H.P. | | 40.35 | 300 | 900 | 2,700 | 502.80 | |
| | 5350 | Dump trailer only, rear dump, 16-1/2 C.Y. | | 4.50 | 125 | 375 | 1,125 | 111 | |
| | 5400 | 20 C.Y. | | 4.85 | 142 | 425 | 1,275 | 123.80 | |
| | 5450 | Flatbed, single axle, 1-1/2 ton rating | | 17.65 | 63.50 | 190 | 570 | 179.20 | |
| | 5500 | 3 ton rating | | 21.25 | 90 | 270 | 810 | 224 | |
| | 5550 | Off highway rear dump, 25 ton capacity | | 52.25 | 1,075 | 3,240 | 9,725 | 1,066 | |
| | 5600 | 35 ton capacity | | 53.15 | 1,100 | 3,320 | 9,950 | 1,089 | |
| | 5610 | 50 ton capacity | | 69.20 | 1,450 | 4,360 | 13,100 | 1,426 | |
| | 5620 | 65 ton capacity | | 74.25 | 1,550 | 4,615 | 13,800 | 1,517 | |
| | 5630 | 100 ton capacity | | 95.45 | 1,975 | 5,960 | 17,900 | 1,956 | |
| | 6000 | Vibratory plow, 25 H.P., walking | | 6.20 | 60 | 180 | 540 | 85.60 | |
| **40** | 0010 | **GENERAL EQUIPMENT RENTAL** without operators [R015433 -10] | | | | | | | **40** |
| | 0150 | Aerial lift, scissor type, to 15' high, 1000 lb. cap., electric | Ea. | 2.60 | 55 | 165 | 495 | 53.80 | |
| | 0160 | To 25' high, 2000 lb. capacity | | 3.05 | 80 | 240 | 720 | 72.40 | |
| | 0170 | Telescoping boom to 40' high, 500 lb. capacity, gas | | 16.75 | 310 | 925 | 2,775 | 319 | |
| | 0180 | To 45' high, 500 lb. capacity | | 17.70 | 360 | 1,075 | 3,225 | 356.60 | |
| | 0190 | To 60' high, 600 lb. capacity | | 19.80 | 475 | 1,420 | 4,250 | 442.40 | |
| | 0195 | Air compressor, portable, 6.5 CFM, electric | | .44 | 12 | 36 | 108 | 10.70 | |
| | 0196 | Gasoline | | .73 | 18 | 54 | 162 | 16.65 | |
| | 0200 | Air compressor, portable, gas engine, 60 C.F.M. | | 11.55 | 46.50 | 140 | 420 | 120.40 | |
| | 0300 | 160 C.F.M. | | 13.45 | 50 | 150 | 450 | 137.60 | |
| | 0400 | Diesel engine, rotary screw, 250 C.F.M. | | 12.85 | 98.50 | 295 | 885 | 161.80 | |
| | 0500 | 365 C.F.M. | | 17.35 | 122 | 365 | 1,100 | 211.80 | |
| | 0550 | 450 C.F.M. | | 22.00 | 152 | 455 | 1,375 | 267 | |
| | 0600 | 600 C.F.M. | | 38.55 | 213 | 640 | 1,925 | 436.40 | |
| | 0700 | 750 C.F.M. | | 38.70 | 222 | 665 | 2,000 | 442.60 | |
| | 0800 | For silenced models, small sizes, add | | 3% | 5% | 5% | 5% | | |
| | 0900 | Large sizes, add | | 5% | 7% | 7% | 7% | | |
| | 0920 | Air tools and accessories | | | | | | | |
| | 0930 | Breaker, pavement, 60 lb. | Ea. | .40 | 9 | 27 | 81 | 8.60 | |
| | 0940 | 80 lb. | | .40 | 9.35 | 28 | 84 | 8.80 | |

## 01 54 33 | Equipment Rental

| | | | UNIT | HOURLY OPER. COST | RENT PER DAY | RENT PER WEEK | RENT PER MONTH | CREW EQUIPMENT COST/DAY | |
|---|---|---|---|---|---|---|---|---|---|
| **40** | 0950 | Drills, hand (jackhammer) 65 lb. | Ea. | .50 | 16 | 48 | 144 | 13.60 | **40** |
| | 0960 | Track or wagon, swing boom, 4" drifter | | 48.75 | 750 | 2,250 | 6,750 | 840 | |
| | 0970 | 5" drifter | | 59.70 | 810 | 2,435 | 7,300 | 964.60 | |
| | 0975 | Track mounted quarry drill, 6" diameter drill | | 81.60 | 1,250 | 3,740 | 11,200 | 1,401 | |
| | 0980 | Dust control per drill | | .93 | 18.65 | 56 | 168 | 18.65 | |
| | 0990 | Hammer, chipping, 12 lb. | | .45 | 21 | 63 | 189 | 16.20 | |
| | 1000 | Hose, air with couplings, 50' long, 3/4" diameter | | .03 | 4.33 | 13 | 39 | 2.85 | |
| | 1100 | 1" diameter | | .04 | 6 | 18 | 54 | 3.90 | |
| | 1200 | 1-1/2" diameter | | .06 | 9.65 | 29 | 87 | 6.30 | |
| | 1300 | 2" diameter | | .10 | 17 | 51 | 153 | 11 | |
| | 1400 | 2-1/2" diameter | | .12 | 19.65 | 59 | 177 | 12.75 | |
| | 1410 | 3" diameter | | .15 | 25 | 75 | 225 | 16.20 | |
| | 1450 | Drill, steel, 7/8" x 2' | | .06 | 9.35 | 28 | 84 | 6.10 | |
| | 1460 | 7/8" x 6' | | .07 | 11 | 33 | 99 | 7.15 | |
| | 1520 | Moil points | | .02 | 3.67 | 11 | 33 | 2.35 | |
| | 1525 | Pneumatic nailer w/accessories | | .45 | 30 | 90 | 270 | 21.60 | |
| | 1530 | Sheeting driver for 60 lb. breaker | | .04 | 6 | 18 | 54 | 3.90 | |
| | 1540 | For 90 lb. breaker | | .12 | 8 | 24 | 72 | 5.75 | |
| | 1550 | Spade, 25 lb. | | .40 | 7 | 21 | 63 | 7.40 | |
| | 1560 | Tamper, single, 35 lb. | | .48 | 32 | 96 | 288 | 23.05 | |
| | 1570 | Triple, 140 lb. | | .72 | 48 | 144 | 430 | 34.55 | |
| | 1580 | Wrenches, impact, air powered, up to 3/4" bolt | | .30 | 8.35 | 25 | 75 | 7.40 | |
| | 1590 | Up to 1-1/4" bolt | | .40 | 20 | 60 | 180 | 15.20 | |
| | 1600 | Barricades, barrels, reflectorized, 1 to 50 barrels | | .03 | 4.33 | 13 | 39 | 2.85 | |
| | 1610 | 100 to 200 barrels | | .02 | 3.33 | 10 | 30 | 2.15 | |
| | 1620 | Barrels with flashers, 1 to 50 barrels | | .03 | 5 | 15 | 45 | 3.25 | |
| | 1630 | 100 to 200 barrels | | .02 | 4 | 12 | 36 | 2.55 | |
| | 1640 | Barrels with steady burn type C lights | | .04 | 6.65 | 20 | 60 | 4.30 | |
| | 1650 | Illuminated board, trailer mounted, with generator | | .70 | 120 | 360 | 1,075 | 77.60 | |
| | 1670 | Portable barricade, stock, with flashers, 1 to 6 units | | .03 | 5 | 15 | 45 | 3.25 | |
| | 1680 | 25 to 50 units | | .03 | 4.67 | 14 | 42 | 3.05 | |
| | 1690 | Butt fusion machine, electric | | 21.20 | 147 | 440 | 1,325 | 257.60 | |
| | 1695 | Electro fusion machine | | 15.65 | 70 | 210 | 630 | 167.20 | |
| | 1700 | Carts, brick, hand powered, 1000 lb. capacity | | .36 | 60 | 180 | 540 | 38.90 | |
| | 1800 | Gas engine, 1500 lb., 7-1/2' lift | | 3.95 | 115 | 344 | 1,025 | 100.40 | |
| | 1822 | Dehumidifier, medium, 6 lb/hr, 150 CFM | | .79 | 48 | 144 | 430 | 35.10 | |
| | 1824 | Large, 18 lb/hr, 600 CFM | | 1.56 | 95.50 | 286 | 860 | 69.70 | |
| | 1830 | Distributor, asphalt, trailer mtd, 2000 gal., 38 H.P. diesel | | 8.75 | 330 | 990 | 2,975 | 268 | |
| | 1840 | 3000 gal., 38 H.P. diesel | | 10.00 | 355 | 1,070 | 3,200 | 294 | |
| | 1850 | Drill, rotary hammer, electric, 1-1/2" diameter | | .80 | 25.50 | 77 | 231 | 21.80 | |
| | 1860 | Carbide bit for above | | .04 | 7 | 21 | 63 | 4.50 | |
| | 1865 | Rotary, crawler, 250 H.P. | | 121.75 | 1,975 | 5,955 | 17,900 | 2,165 | |
| | 1870 | Emulsion sprayer, 65 gal., 5 H.P. gas engine | | 2.77 | 95 | 285 | 855 | 79.15 | |
| | 1880 | 200 gal., 5 H.P. engine | | 6.65 | 158 | 475 | 1,425 | 148.20 | |
| | 1920 | Floodlight, mercury vapor, or quartz, on tripod | Ea. | | | | | | |
| | 1930 | 1000 watt | | .32 | 12.65 | 38 | 114 | 10.15 | |
| | 1940 | 2000 watt | | .56 | 23.50 | 70 | 210 | 18.50 | |
| | 1950 | Floodlights, trailer mounted with generator, 1 - 300 watt light | | 2.90 | 68.50 | 205 | 615 | 64.20 | |
| | 1960 | 2 - 1000 watt lights | | 3.95 | 103 | 310 | 930 | 93.60 | |
| | 2000 | 4 - 300 watt lights | | 3.45 | 85 | 255 | 765 | 78.60 | |
| | 2005 | Foam spray rig, incl. box trailer, compressor, generator, proportioner | | 25.05 | 490 | 1,465 | 4,400 | 493.40 | |
| | 2020 | Forklift, straight mast, 12' lift, 5000 lb., 2 wheel drive, gas | | 21.65 | 193 | 580 | 1,750 | 289.20 | |
| | 2040 | 21' lift, 5000 lb., 4 wheel drive, diesel | | 16.60 | 242 | 725 | 2,175 | 277.80 | |
| | 2050 | For rough terrain, 42' lift, 35' reach, 9000 lb., 110 HP | | 22.20 | 430 | 1,285 | 3,850 | 434.60 | |
| | 2060 | For plant, 4 T. capacity, 80 H.P., 2 wheel drive, gas | | 13.30 | 95 | 285 | 855 | 163.40 | |
| | 2080 | 10 T. capacity, 120 H.P., 2 wheel drive, diesel | | 18.70 | 165 | 495 | 1,475 | 248.60 | |

Note: R015433 -10 (0950 reference)

## 01 54 33 | Equipment Rental

| | | UNIT | HOURLY OPER. COST | RENT PER DAY | RENT PER WEEK | RENT PER MONTH | CREW EQUIPMENT COST/DAY | |
|---|---|---|---|---|---|---|---|---|
| 40 | 2100 | Generator, electric, gas engine, 1.5 KW to 3 KW | Ea. | 3.00 | 10.35 | 31 | 93 | 30.20 | 40 |
| | 2200 | 5 KW | | 3.90 | 14 | 42 | 126 | 39.60 | |
| | 2300 | 10 KW | | 7.35 | 33.50 | 100 | 300 | 78.80 | |
| | 2400 | 25 KW | | 9.10 | 65 | 195 | 585 | 111.80 | |
| | 2500 | Diesel engine, 20 KW | | 9.25 | 71.50 | 215 | 645 | 117 | |
| | 2600 | 50 KW | | 16.70 | 96.50 | 290 | 870 | 191.60 | |
| | 2700 | 100 KW | | 32.35 | 123 | 370 | 1,100 | 332.80 | |
| | 2800 | 250 KW | | 63.80 | 230 | 690 | 2,075 | 648.40 | |
| | 2850 | Hammer, hydraulic, for mounting on boom, to 500 ft.-lb. | | 2.05 | 65 | 195 | 585 | 55.40 | |
| | 2860 | 1000 ft.-lb. | | 3.50 | 108 | 325 | 975 | 93 | |
| | 2900 | Heaters, space, oil or electric, 50 MBH | | 1.74 | 7.65 | 23 | 69 | 18.50 | |
| | 3000 | 100 MBH | | 3.15 | 11.35 | 34 | 102 | 32 | |
| | 3100 | 300 MBH | | 10.07 | 35 | 105 | 315 | 101.55 | |
| | 3150 | 500 MBH | | 20.32 | 50 | 150 | 450 | 192.55 | |
| | 3200 | Hose, water, suction with coupling, 20' long, 2" diameter | | .02 | 3 | 9 | 27 | 1.95 | |
| | 3210 | 3" diameter | | .03 | 4.67 | 14 | 42 | 3.05 | |
| | 3220 | 4" diameter | | .03 | 5.35 | 16 | 48 | 3.45 | |
| | 3230 | 6" diameter | | .11 | 18.35 | 55 | 165 | 11.90 | |
| | 3240 | 8" diameter | | .19 | 31.50 | 95 | 285 | 20.50 | |
| | 3250 | Discharge hose with coupling, 50' long, 2" diameter | | .01 | 1.67 | 5 | 15 | 1.10 | |
| | 3260 | 3" diameter | | .02 | 2.67 | 8 | 24 | 1.75 | |
| | 3270 | 4" diameter | | .02 | 3.67 | 11 | 33 | 2.35 | |
| | 3280 | 6" diameter | | .06 | 9.65 | 29 | 87 | 6.30 | |
| | 3290 | 8" diameter | | .19 | 31.50 | 95 | 285 | 20.50 | |
| | 3295 | Insulation blower | | .25 | 7.35 | 22 | 66 | 6.40 | |
| | 3300 | Ladders, extension type, 16' to 36' long | | .14 | 23 | 69 | 207 | 14.90 | |
| | 3400 | 40' to 60' long | | .20 | 33.50 | 100 | 300 | 21.60 | |
| | 3405 | Lance for cutting concrete | | 2.87 | 104 | 313 | 940 | 85.55 | |
| | 3407 | Lawn mower, rotary, 22", 5HP | | 2.14 | 65 | 195 | 585 | 56.10 | |
| | 3408 | 48" self propelled | | 3.18 | 92.50 | 278 | 835 | 81.05 | |
| | 3410 | Level, laser type, for pipe and sewer leveling | | 1.44 | 95.50 | 287 | 860 | 68.90 | |
| | 3430 | Electronic | | .75 | 50 | 150 | 450 | 36 | |
| | 3440 | Laser type, rotating beam for grade control | | 1.07 | 71.50 | 214 | 640 | 51.35 | |
| | 3460 | Builders level with tripod and rod | | .08 | 14 | 42 | 126 | 9.05 | |
| | 3500 | Light towers, towable, with diesel generator, 2000 watt | | 3.45 | 85 | 255 | 765 | 78.60 | |
| | 3600 | 4000 watt | | 3.95 | 103 | 310 | 930 | 93.60 | |
| | 3700 | Mixer, powered, plaster and mortar, 6 C.F., 7 H.P. | | 1.75 | 18.65 | 56 | 168 | 25.20 | |
| | 3800 | 10 C.F., 9 H.P. | | 2.10 | 30.50 | 91 | 273 | 35 | |
| | 3850 | Nailer, pneumatic | | .45 | 30 | 90 | 270 | 21.60 | |
| | 3900 | Paint sprayers complete, 8 CFM | | .70 | 46.50 | 140 | 420 | 33.60 | |
| | 4000 | 17 CFM | | 1.14 | 76 | 228 | 685 | 54.70 | |
| | 4020 | Pavers, bituminous, rubber tires, 8' wide, 50 H.P., diesel | | 34.70 | 1,025 | 3,075 | 9,225 | 892.60 | |
| | 4030 | 10' wide, 150 H.P. | | 74.05 | 1,625 | 4,895 | 14,700 | 1,571 | |
| | 4050 | Crawler, 8' wide, 100 H.P., diesel | | 73.85 | 1,700 | 5,125 | 15,400 | 1,616 | |
| | 4060 | 10' wide, 150 H.P. | | 83.15 | 2,050 | 6,160 | 18,500 | 1,897 | |
| | 4070 | Concrete paver, 12' to 24' wide, 250 H.P. | | 77.30 | 1,575 | 4,690 | 14,100 | 1,556 | |
| | 4080 | Placer-spreader-trimmer, 24' wide, 300 H.P. | | 111.95 | 2,575 | 7,755 | 23,300 | 2,447 | |
| | 4100 | Pump, centrifugal gas pump, 1-1/2" diam., 65 GPM | | 3.25 | 41.50 | 125 | 375 | 51 | |
| | 4200 | 2" diameter, 130 GPM | | 4.40 | 48.50 | 145 | 435 | 64.20 | |
| | 4300 | 3" diameter, 250 GPM | | 4.70 | 50 | 150 | 450 | 67.60 | |
| | 4400 | 6" diameter, 1500 GPM | | 25.15 | 173 | 520 | 1,550 | 305.20 | |
| | 4500 | Submersible electric pump, 1-1/4" diameter, 55 GPM | | .37 | 15.35 | 46 | 138 | 12.15 | |
| | 4600 | 1-1/2" diameter, 83 GPM | | .41 | 17.65 | 53 | 159 | 13.90 | |
| | 4700 | 2" diameter, 120 GPM | | 1.15 | 22 | 66 | 198 | 22.40 | |
| | 4800 | 3" diameter, 300 GPM | | 1.95 | 40 | 120 | 360 | 39.60 | |
| | 4900 | 4" diameter, 560 GPM | | 8.60 | 163 | 490 | 1,475 | 166.80 | |

R015433 -10

## 01 54 33 | Equipment Rental

| | | | UNIT | HOURLY OPER. COST | RENT PER DAY | RENT PER WEEK | RENT PER MONTH | CREW EQUIPMENT COST/DAY | |
|---|---|---|---|---|---|---|---|---|---|
| 40 | 5000 | 6" diameter, 1590 GPM | Ea. | 12.60 | 220 | 660 | 1,975 | 232.80 | 40 |
| | 5100 | Diaphragm pump, gas, single, 1-1/2" diameter | R015433 -10 | 1.05 | 44 | 132 | 395 | 34.80 | |
| | 5200 | 2" diameter | | 3.55 | 55 | 165 | 495 | 61.40 | |
| | 5300 | 3" diameter | | 3.55 | 55 | 165 | 495 | 61.40 | |
| | 5400 | Double, 4" diameter | | 4.80 | 76.50 | 230 | 690 | 84.40 | |
| | 5500 | Trash pump, self-priming, gas, 2" diameter | | 3.75 | 19.65 | 59 | 177 | 41.80 | |
| | 5600 | Diesel, 4" diameter | | 10.10 | 58.50 | 175 | 525 | 115.80 | |
| | 5650 | Diesel, 6" diameter | | 33.60 | 128 | 385 | 1,150 | 345.80 | |
| | 5655 | Grout Pump | | 12.55 | 85 | 255 | 765 | 151.40 | |
| | 5660 | Rollers, see division 01590-200 | | | | | | | |
| | 5700 | Salamanders, L.P. gas fired, 100,000 BTU | Ea. | 3.15 | 11.65 | 35 | 105 | 32.20 | |
| | 5705 | 50,000 BTU | | 2.36 | 8.35 | 25 | 75 | 23.90 | |
| | 5720 | Sandblaster, portable, open top, 3 C.F. capacity | | .40 | 24.50 | 74 | 222 | 18 | |
| | 5730 | 6 C.F. capacity | | .70 | 36.50 | 110 | 330 | 27.60 | |
| | 5740 | Accessories for above | | .12 | 19.35 | 58 | 174 | 12.55 | |
| | 5750 | Sander, floor | | .78 | 18.65 | 56 | 168 | 17.45 | |
| | 5760 | Edger | | .73 | 25.50 | 77 | 231 | 21.25 | |
| | 5800 | Saw, chain, gas engine, 18" long | | 1.85 | 16.65 | 50 | 150 | 24.80 | |
| | 5900 | 36" long | | .60 | 53.50 | 160 | 480 | 36.80 | |
| | 5950 | 60" long | | .60 | 53.50 | 160 | 480 | 36.80 | |
| | 6000 | Masonry, table mounted, 14" diameter, 5 H.P. | | 1.13 | 47.50 | 143 | 430 | 37.65 | |
| | 6050 | Portable cut-off, 8 H.P. | | 2.05 | 30 | 90 | 270 | 34.40 | |
| | 6100 | Circular, hand held, electric, 7-1/4" diameter | | .21 | 5.35 | 16 | 48 | 4.90 | |
| | 6200 | 12" diameter | | .28 | 8.65 | 26 | 78 | 7.45 | |
| | 6250 | Wall saw, w/hydraulic power, 10 H.P | | 6.90 | 58.50 | 175 | 525 | 90.20 | |
| | 6275 | Shot blaster, walk behind, 20" wide | | 7.21 | 345 | 1,035 | 3,100 | 264.70 | |
| | 6280 | Sidewalk broom, walk-behind | | 1.78 | 48 | 144 | 430 | 43.05 | |
| | 6300 | Steam cleaner, 100 gallons per hour | | 3.00 | 65 | 195 | 585 | 63 | |
| | 6310 | 200 gallons per hour | | 4.30 | 80 | 240 | 720 | 82.40 | |
| | 6340 | Tar Kettle/Pot, 400 gallon | | 4.76 | 80 | 240 | 720 | 86.10 | |
| | 6350 | Torch, cutting, acetylene-oxygen, 150' hose | | .50 | 21.50 | 65 | 195 | 17 | |
| | 6360 | Hourly operating cost includes tips and gas | | 9.00 | | | | 72 | |
| | 6410 | Toilet, portable chemical | | .11 | 18.65 | 56 | 168 | 12.10 | |
| | 6420 | Recycle flush type | | .14 | 22.50 | 68 | 204 | 14.70 | |
| | 6430 | Toilet, fresh water flush, garden hose, | | .15 | 25.50 | 77 | 231 | 16.60 | |
| | 6440 | Hoisted, non-flush, for high rise | | .13 | 22.50 | 67 | 201 | 14.45 | |
| | 6450 | Toilet, trailers, minimum | | .23 | 38.50 | 116 | 350 | 25.05 | |
| | 6460 | Maximum | | .70 | 117 | 351 | 1,050 | 75.80 | |
| | 6465 | Tractor, farm with attachment | | 13.60 | 253 | 760 | 2,275 | 260.80 | |
| | 6470 | Trailer, office, see division 01520-500 | | | | | | | |
| | 6500 | Trailers, platform, flush deck, 2 axle, 25 ton capacity | Ea. | 4.50 | 102 | 305 | 915 | 97 | |
| | 6600 | 40 ton capacity | | 5.90 | 143 | 430 | 1,300 | 133.20 | |
| | 6700 | 3 axle, 50 ton capacity | | 6.35 | 158 | 475 | 1,425 | 145.80 | |
| | 6800 | 75 ton capacity | | 7.95 | 208 | 625 | 1,875 | 188.60 | |
| | 6810 | Trailer mounted cable reel for H.V. line work | | 4.75 | 226 | 678 | 2,025 | 173.60 | |
| | 6820 | Trailer mounted cable tensioning rig | | 9.38 | 445 | 1,340 | 4,025 | 343.05 | |
| | 6830 | Cable pulling rig | | 63.70 | 2,525 | 7,560 | 22,700 | 2,022 | |
| | 6850 | Trailer, storage, see division 01520-500 | | | | | | | |
| | 6900 | Water tank, engine driven discharge, 5000 gallons | Ea. | 5.95 | 137 | 410 | 1,225 | 129.60 | |
| | 6925 | 10,000 gallons | | 8.20 | 192 | 575 | 1,725 | 180.60 | |
| | 6950 | Water truck, off highway, 6000 gallons | | 63.60 | 765 | 2,290 | 6,875 | 966.80 | |
| | 7010 | Tram car for H.V. line work, powered, 2 conductor | | 6.15 | 123 | 368 | 1,100 | 122.80 | |
| | 7020 | Transit (builder's level) with tripod | | .08 | 14 | 42 | 126 | 9.05 | |
| | 7030 | Trench box, 3000 lbs. 6'x8' | | .56 | 93 | 279 | 835 | 60.30 | |
| | 7040 | 7200 lbs. 6'x20' | | 1.05 | 175 | 525 | 1,575 | 113.40 | |
| | 7050 | 8000 lbs., 8' x 16' | | .95 | 158 | 475 | 1,425 | 102.60 | |

## 01 54 33 | Equipment Rental

| | | UNIT | HOURLY OPER. COST | RENT PER DAY | RENT PER WEEK | RENT PER MONTH | CREW EQUIPMENT COST/DAY | |
|---|---|---|---|---|---|---|---|---|
| **40** | 7060 | 9500 lbs., 8'x20' | Ea. | 1.16 | 194 | 581 | 1,750 | 125.50 | **40** |
| | 7065 | 11,000 lbs., 8'x24' | | 1.27 | 212 | 637 | 1,900 | 137.55 | |
| | 7070 | 12,000 lbs., 10' x 20' | | 1.71 | 285 | 855 | 2,575 | 184.70 | |
| | 7100 | Truck, pickup, 3/4 ton, 2 wheel drive | | 9.50 | 55 | 165 | 495 | 109 | |
| | 7200 | 4 wheel drive | | 9.80 | 71.50 | 215 | 645 | 121.40 | |
| | 7250 | Crew carrier, 9 passenger | | 13.55 | 86.50 | 260 | 780 | 160.40 | |
| | 7290 | Flat bed truck, 20,000 G.V.W. | | 14.50 | 117 | 350 | 1,050 | 186 | |
| | 7300 | Tractor, 4 x 2, 220 H.P. | | 20.35 | 182 | 545 | 1,625 | 271.80 | |
| | 7410 | 330 H.P. | | 30.00 | 252 | 755 | 2,275 | 391 | |
| | 7500 | 6 x 4, 380 H.P. | | 34.45 | 297 | 890 | 2,675 | 453.60 | |
| | 7600 | 450 H.P. | | 30.85 | 300 | 905 | 2,725 | 427.80 | |
| | 7620 | Vacuum truck, hazardous material, 2500 gallon | | 10.45 | 305 | 915 | 2,750 | 266.60 | |
| | 7625 | 5,000 gallon | | 13.15 | 425 | 1,280 | 3,850 | 361.20 | |
| | 7640 | Tractor, with A frame, boom and winch, 225 H.P. | | 22.80 | 257 | 770 | 2,300 | 336.40 | |
| | 7650 | Vacuum, H.E.P.A., 16 gal., wet/dry | | .92 | 22 | 66 | 198 | 20.55 | |
| | 7655 | 55 gal, wet/dry | | .89 | 33 | 99 | 297 | 26.90 | |
| | 7660 | Water tank, portable | | .17 | 28.50 | 85.50 | 257 | 18.45 | |
| | 7690 | Sewer/catch basin vacuum, 14 CY, 1500 Gallon | | 17.63 | 640 | 1,920 | 5,750 | 525.05 | |
| | 7700 | Welder, electric, 200 amp | | 3.39 | 24 | 72 | 216 | 41.50 | |
| | 7800 | 300 amp | | 5.00 | 27 | 81 | 243 | 56.20 | |
| | 7900 | Gas engine, 200 amp | | 12.70 | 25.50 | 77 | 231 | 117 | |
| | 8000 | 300 amp | | 14.50 | 27 | 81 | 243 | 132.20 | |
| | 8100 | Wheelbarrow, any size | | .07 | 11.65 | 35 | 105 | 7.55 | |
| | 8200 | Wrecking ball, 4000 lb. | | 2.05 | 71.50 | 215 | 645 | 59.40 | |
| **50** | 0010 | **HIGHWAY EQUIPMENT RENTAL** without operators | | | | | | | **50** |
| | 0050 | Asphalt batch plant, portable drum mixer, 100 ton/hr. | Ea. | 61.55 | 1,425 | 4,265 | 12,800 | 1,345 | |
| | 0060 | 200 ton/hr. | | 68.60 | 1,500 | 4,490 | 13,500 | 1,447 | |
| | 0070 | 300 ton/hr. | | 79.70 | 1,775 | 5,305 | 15,900 | 1,699 | |
| | 0100 | Backhoe attachment, long stick, up to 185 HP, 10.5' long | | .32 | 21 | 63 | 189 | 15.15 | |
| | 0140 | Up to 250 HP, 12' long | | .34 | 22.50 | 68 | 204 | 16.30 | |
| | 0180 | Over 250 HP, 15' long | | .46 | 30.50 | 91 | 273 | 21.90 | |
| | 0200 | Special dipper arm, up to 100 HP, 32' long | | .94 | 62.50 | 187 | 560 | 44.90 | |
| | 0240 | Over 100 HP, 33' long | | 1.17 | 77.50 | 233 | 700 | 55.95 | |
| | 0300 | Concrete batch plant, portable, electric, 200 CY/Hr | | 10.74 | 500 | 1,505 | 4,525 | 386.90 | |
| | 0500 | Grader/dozer attachment, ripper/scarifier, rear mounted | | | | | | | |
| | 0520 | Up to 135 HP | Ea. | 3.05 | 63.50 | 190 | 570 | 62.40 | |
| | 0540 | Up to 180 HP | | 3.60 | 81.50 | 245 | 735 | 77.80 | |
| | 0580 | Up to 250 HP | | 4.00 | 93.50 | 280 | 840 | 88 | |
| | 0700 | Pvmt. removal bucket, for hyd. excavator, up to 90 HP | | 1.55 | 46.50 | 140 | 420 | 40.40 | |
| | 0740 | Up to 200 HP | | 1.75 | 68.50 | 205 | 615 | 55 | |
| | 0780 | Over 200 HP | | 1.90 | 81.50 | 245 | 735 | 64.20 | |
| | 0900 | Aggregate spreader, self-propelled, 187 HP | | 51.10 | 665 | 2,000 | 6,000 | 808.80 | |
| | 1000 | Chemical spreader, 3 C.Y. | | 2.60 | 43.50 | 130 | 390 | 46.80 | |
| | 1900 | Hammermill, traveling, 250 HP | | 62.03 | 1,800 | 5,430 | 16,300 | 1,582 | |
| | 2000 | Horizontal borer, 3" diam, 13 HP gas driven | | 5.30 | 56.50 | 170 | 510 | 76.40 | |
| | 2150 | Horizontal directional drill, 20,000 lb. thrust, 78 H.P. diesel | | 25.50 | 665 | 1,995 | 5,975 | 603 | |
| | 2160 | Horizontal directional drill, 30,000 lb. thrust, 115 H.P. diesel | | 31.40 | 990 | 2,970 | 8,900 | 845.20 | |
| | 2170 | Horizontal directional drill, 50,000 lb. thrust, 170 H.P. diesel | | 44.55 | 1,275 | 3,805 | 11,400 | 1,117 | |
| | 2190 | Mud trailer for HDD, 1500 gallon, 175 H.P., gas | | 22.50 | 145 | 435 | 1,300 | 267 | |
| | 2200 | Hydromulchers, gas power, 3000 gal., for truck mounting | | 15.95 | 257 | 770 | 2,300 | 281.60 | |
| | 2400 | Joint & crack cleaner, walk behind, 25 HP | | 2.85 | 48.50 | 145 | 435 | 51.80 | |
| | 2500 | Filler, trailer mounted, 400 gal., 20 HP | | 7.60 | 215 | 645 | 1,925 | 189.80 | |
| | 3000 | Paint striper, self propelled, double line, 30 HP | | 6.00 | 160 | 480 | 1,450 | 144 | |
| | 3200 | Post drivers, 6" I-Beam frame, for truck mounting | | 12.45 | 435 | 1,300 | 3,900 | 359.60 | |
| | 3400 | Road sweeper, self propelled, 8' wide, 90 HP | | 30.40 | 565 | 1,695 | 5,075 | 582.20 | |
| | 4000 | Road mixer, self-propelled, 130 HP | | 37.35 | 715 | 2,140 | 6,425 | 726.80 | |

R015433 -10

## 01 54 33 | Equipment Rental

| | | | UNIT | HOURLY OPER. COST | RENT PER DAY | RENT PER WEEK | RENT PER MONTH | CREW EQUIPMENT COST/DAY | |
|---|---|---|---|---|---|---|---|---|---|
| **50** | 4100 | 310 HP | ▼ | 70.30 | 2,200 | 6,610 | 19,800 | 1,884 | **50** |
| | 4200 | Cold mix paver, incl pug mill and bitumen tank, R015433 -10 | Ea. | | | | | | |
| | 4220 | 165 HP | | 83.15 | 2,075 | 6,200 | 18,600 | 1,905 | |
| | 4250 | Paver, asphalt, wheel or crawler, 130 H.P., diesel | | 81.85 | 1,975 | 5,910 | 17,700 | 1,837 | |
| | 4300 | Paver, road widener, gas 1' to 6', 67 HP | | 39.20 | 810 | 2,430 | 7,300 | 799.60 | |
| | 4400 | Diesel, 2' to 14', 88 HP | | 51.65 | 1,050 | 3,135 | 9,400 | 1,040 | |
| | 4600 | Slipform pavers, curb and gutter, 2 track, 75 HP | | 35.15 | 755 | 2,270 | 6,800 | 735.20 | |
| | 4700 | 4 track, 165 HP | | 43.30 | 805 | 2,420 | 7,250 | 830.40 | |
| | 4800 | Median barrier, 215 HP | | 43.95 | 840 | 2,515 | 7,550 | 854.60 | |
| | 4901 | Trailer, low bed, 75 ton capacity | | 8.55 | 208 | 625 | 1,875 | 193.40 | |
| | 5000 | Road planer, walk behind, 10" cutting width, 10 HP | | 2.65 | 29 | 87 | 261 | 38.60 | |
| | 5100 | Self propelled, 12" cutting width, 64 HP | | 7.50 | 113 | 340 | 1,025 | 128 | |
| | 5200 | Pavement profiler, 4' to 6' wide, 450 HP | | 208.95 | 3,250 | 9,765 | 29,300 | 3,625 | |
| | 5300 | 8' to 10' wide, 750 HP | | 331.60 | 4,650 | 13,960 | 41,900 | 5,445 | |
| | 5400 | Roadway plate, steel, 1"x8'x20' | | .07 | 11 | 33 | 99 | 7.15 | |
| | 5600 | Stabilizer, self-propelled, 150 HP | | 39.10 | 600 | 1,805 | 5,425 | 673.80 | |
| | 5700 | 310 HP | | 66.50 | 1,350 | 4,025 | 12,100 | 1,337 | |
| | 5800 | Striper, thermal, truck mounted 120 gal. paint, 150 H.P. | | 46.20 | 500 | 1,505 | 4,525 | 670.60 | |
| | 6000 | Tar kettle, 330 gal., trailer mounted | | 4.34 | 60 | 180 | 540 | 70.70 | |
| | 7000 | Tunnel locomotive, diesel, 8 to 12 ton | | 26.25 | 580 | 1,735 | 5,200 | 557 | |
| | 7005 | Electric, 10 ton | | 22.55 | 660 | 1,980 | 5,950 | 576.40 | |
| | 7010 | Muck cars, 1/2 C.Y. capacity | | 1.70 | 22.50 | 67 | 201 | 27 | |
| | 7020 | 1 C.Y. capacity | | 1.90 | 30.50 | 92 | 276 | 33.60 | |
| | 7030 | 2 C.Y. capacity | | 2.00 | 36.50 | 110 | 330 | 38 | |
| | 7040 | Side dump, 2 C.Y. capacity | | 2.20 | 43.50 | 130 | 390 | 43.60 | |
| | 7050 | 3 C.Y. capacity | | 3.00 | 50 | 150 | 450 | 54 | |
| | 7060 | 5 C.Y. capacity | | 4.25 | 63.50 | 190 | 570 | 72 | |
| | 7100 | Ventilating blower for tunnel, 7-1/2 H.P. | | 1.31 | 51.50 | 155 | 465 | 41.50 | |
| | 7110 | 10 H.P. | | 1.52 | 53.50 | 160 | 480 | 44.15 | |
| | 7120 | 20 H.P. | | 2.47 | 69.50 | 208 | 625 | 61.35 | |
| | 7140 | 40 H.P. | | 4.31 | 96.50 | 290 | 870 | 92.50 | |
| | 7160 | 60 H.P. | | 6.57 | 152 | 455 | 1,375 | 143.55 | |
| | 7175 | 75 H.P. | | 8.40 | 202 | 607 | 1,825 | 188.60 | |
| | 7180 | 200 H.P. | | 18.85 | 305 | 910 | 2,725 | 332.80 | |
| | 7800 | Windrow loader, elevating | ▼ | 41.10 | 970 | 2,910 | 8,725 | 910.80 | |
| **60** | 0010 | **LIFTING AND HOISTING EQUIPMENT RENTAL** without operators R015433 -10 | | | | | | | **60** |
| | 0120 | Aerial lift truck, 2 person, to 80' | Ea. | 24.70 | 695 | 2,085 | 6,250 | 614.60 | |
| | 0140 | Boom work platform, 40' snorkel R015433 -15 | | 15.15 | 258 | 775 | 2,325 | 276.20 | |
| | 0150 | Crane, flatbed mntd, 3 ton cap. | | 13.45 | 195 | 585 | 1,750 | 224.60 | |
| | 0200 | Crane, climbing, 106' jib, 6000 lb. capacity, 410 FPM R312316 -45 | | 35.85 | 1,425 | 4,310 | 12,900 | 1,149 | |
| | 0300 | 101' jib, 10,250 lb. capacity, 270 FPM | | 41.65 | 1,825 | 5,470 | 16,400 | 1,427 | |
| | 0400 | Tower, static, 130' high, 106' jib, | | | | | | | |
| | 0500 | 6200 lb. capacity at 400 FPM | Ea. | 39.25 | 1,675 | 4,990 | 15,000 | 1,312 | |
| | 0600 | Crawler mounted, lattice boom, 1/2 C.Y., 15 tons at 12' radius | | 28.43 | 630 | 1,890 | 5,675 | 605.45 | |
| | 0700 | 3/4 C.Y., 20 tons at 12' radius | | 37.91 | 785 | 2,360 | 7,075 | 775.30 | |
| | 0800 | 1 C.Y., 25 tons at 12' radius | | 50.55 | 1,050 | 3,145 | 9,425 | 1,033 | |
| | 0900 | 1-1/2 C.Y., 40 tons at 12' radius | | 55.15 | 1,025 | 3,065 | 9,200 | 1,054 | |
| | 1000 | 2 C.Y., 50 tons at 12' radius | | 53.20 | 1,125 | 3,360 | 10,100 | 1,098 | |
| | 1100 | 3 C.Y., 75 tons at 12' radius | | 72.00 | 1,500 | 4,535 | 13,600 | 1,483 | |
| | 1200 | 100 ton capacity, 60' boom | | 71.10 | 1,700 | 5,085 | 15,300 | 1,586 | |
| | 1300 | 165 ton capacity, 60' boom | | 122.35 | 2,450 | 7,365 | 22,100 | 2,452 | |
| | 1400 | 200 ton capacity, 70' boom | | 110.65 | 2,325 | 6,980 | 20,900 | 2,281 | |
| | 1500 | 350 ton capacity, 80' boom | | 195.60 | 3,675 | 11,025 | 33,100 | 3,770 | |
| | 1600 | Truck mounted, lattice boom, 6 x 4, 20 tons at 10' radius | | 35.66 | 1,200 | 3,600 | 10,800 | 1,005 | |
| | 1700 | 25 tons at 10' radius | ▼ | 38.53 | 1,300 | 3,910 | 11,700 | 1,090 | |

## 01 54 33 | Equipment Rental

| | | | UNIT | HOURLY OPER. COST | RENT PER DAY | RENT PER WEEK | RENT PER MONTH | CREW EQUIPMENT COST/DAY |
|---|---|---|---|---|---|---|---|---|
| 1800 | 8 x 4, 30 tons at 10' radius | R015433 -10 | Ea. | 41.68 | 1,375 | 4,160 | 12,500 | 1,165 |
| 1900 | 40 tons at 12' radius | | | 44.40 | 1,450 | 4,350 | 13,100 | 1,225 |
| 2000 | 8 x 4, 60 tons at 15' radius | R015433 -15 | | 49.71 | 1,525 | 4,610 | 13,800 | 1,320 |
| 2050 | 82 tons at 15' radius | | | 55.37 | 1,650 | 4,920 | 14,800 | 1,427 |
| 2100 | 90 tons at 15' radius | R312316 -45 | | 61.93 | 1,775 | 5,360 | 16,100 | 1,567 |
| 2200 | 115 tons at 15' radius | | | 69.83 | 2,000 | 5,990 | 18,000 | 1,757 |
| 2300 | 150 tons at 18' radius | | | 77.85 | 2,100 | 6,310 | 18,900 | 1,885 |
| 2350 | 165 tons at 18' radius | | | 81.71 | 2,225 | 6,690 | 20,100 | 1,992 |
| 2400 | Truck mounted, hydraulic, 12 ton capacity | | | 49.05 | 625 | 1,870 | 5,600 | 766.40 |
| 2500 | 25 ton capacity | | | 49.25 | 655 | 1,960 | 5,875 | 786 |
| 2550 | 33 ton capacity | | | 50.30 | 690 | 2,065 | 6,200 | 815.40 |
| 2560 | 40 ton capacity | | | 48.45 | 665 | 2,000 | 6,000 | 787.60 |
| 2600 | 55 ton capacity | | | 72.20 | 900 | 2,705 | 8,125 | 1,119 |
| 2700 | 80 ton capacity | | | 85.40 | 1,000 | 3,035 | 9,100 | 1,290 |
| 2720 | 100 ton capacity | | | 104.40 | 1,550 | 4,650 | 14,000 | 1,765 |
| 2740 | 120 ton capacity | | | 82.85 | 1,925 | 5,810 | 17,400 | 1,825 |
| 2760 | 150 ton capacity | | | 88.74 | 2,125 | 6,405 | 19,200 | 1,991 |
| 2800 | Self-propelled, 4 x 4, with telescoping boom, 5 ton | | | 14.60 | 237 | 710 | 2,125 | 258.80 |
| 2900 | 12-1/2 ton capacity | | | 34.75 | 555 | 1,665 | 5,000 | 611 |
| 3000 | 15 ton capacity | | | 32.30 | 580 | 1,745 | 5,225 | 607.40 |
| 3050 | 20 ton capacity | | | 37.00 | 650 | 1,945 | 5,825 | 685 |
| 3100 | 25 ton capacity | | | 37.85 | 665 | 1,995 | 5,975 | 701.80 |
| 3150 | 40 ton capacity | | | 50.30 | 855 | 2,570 | 7,700 | 916.40 |
| 3200 | Derricks, guy, 20 ton capacity, 60' boom, 75' mast | | | 21.35 | 350 | 1,057 | 3,175 | 382.20 |
| 3300 | 100' boom, 115' mast | | | 33.60 | 605 | 1,810 | 5,425 | 630.80 |
| 3400 | Stiffleg, 20 ton capacity, 70' boom, 37' mast | | | 23.54 | 455 | 1,370 | 4,100 | 462.30 |
| 3500 | 100' boom, 47' mast | | | 36.33 | 735 | 2,200 | 6,600 | 730.65 |
| 3550 | Helicopter, small, lift to 1250 lbs. maximum, w/pilot | | | 90.58 | 2,850 | 8,540 | 25,600 | 2,433 |
| 3600 | Hoists, chain type, overhead, manual, 3/4 ton | | | .10 | .67 | 2 | 6 | 1.20 |
| 3900 | 10 ton | | | .65 | 8 | 24 | 72 | 10 |
| 4000 | Hoist and tower, 5000 lb. cap., portable electric, 40' high | | | 4.48 | 203 | 609 | 1,825 | 157.65 |
| 4100 | For each added 10' section, add | | | .10 | 16 | 48 | 144 | 10.40 |
| 4200 | Hoist and single tubular tower, 5000 lb. electric, 100' high | | | 6.04 | 283 | 850 | 2,550 | 218.30 |
| 4300 | For each added 6'-6" section, add | | | .16 | 27 | 81 | 243 | 17.50 |
| 4400 | Hoist and double tubular tower, 5000 lb., 100' high | | | 6.47 | 310 | 936 | 2,800 | 238.95 |
| 4500 | For each added 6'-6" section, add | | | .18 | 30.50 | 91 | 273 | 19.65 |
| 4550 | Hoist and tower, mast type, 6000 lb., 100' high | | | 7.00 | 325 | 971 | 2,925 | 250.20 |
| 4570 | For each added 10' section, add | | | .12 | 19.35 | 58 | 174 | 12.55 |
| 4600 | Hoist and tower, personnel, electric, 2000 lb., 100' @ 125 FPM | | | 14.38 | 865 | 2,590 | 7,775 | 633.05 |
| 4700 | 3000 lb., 100' @ 200 FPM | | | 16.44 | 975 | 2,930 | 8,800 | 717.50 |
| 4800 | 3000 lb., 150' @ 300 FPM | | | 18.14 | 1,100 | 3,270 | 9,800 | 799.10 |
| 4900 | 4000 lb., 100' @ 300 FPM | | | 18.85 | 1,125 | 3,340 | 10,000 | 818.80 |
| 5000 | 6000 lb., 100' @ 275 FPM | | | 20.41 | 1,175 | 3,510 | 10,500 | 865.30 |
| 5100 | For added heights up to 500', add | | L.F. | .01 | 1.67 | 5 | 15 | 1.10 |
| 5200 | Jacks, hydraulic, 20 ton | | Ea. | .05 | 3.33 | 10 | 30 | 2.40 |
| 5500 | 100 ton | | " | .30 | 10.35 | 31 | 93 | 8.60 |
| 6000 | Jacks, hydraulic, climbing with 50' jackrods | | | | | | | |
| 6010 | and control consoles, minimum 3 mo. rental | | | | | | | |
| 6100 | 30 ton capacity | | Ea. | 1.75 | 117 | 350 | 1,050 | 84 |
| 6150 | For each added 10' jackrod section, add | | | .05 | 3.33 | 10 | 30 | 2.40 |
| 6300 | 50 ton capacity | | | 2.82 | 188 | 563 | 1,700 | 135.15 |
| 6350 | For each added 10' jackrod section, add | | | .06 | 4 | 12 | 36 | 2.90 |
| 6500 | 125 ton capacity | | | 7.40 | 495 | 1,480 | 4,450 | 355.20 |
| 6550 | For each added 10' jackrod section, add | | | .51 | 33.50 | 101 | 305 | 24.30 |
| 6600 | Cable jack, 10 ton capacity with 200' cable | | | 1.47 | 97.50 | 293 | 880 | 70.35 |
| 6650 | For each added 50' of cable, add | | | .17 | 11 | 33 | 99 | 7.95 |

60

## 01 54 33 | Equipment Rental

| | | | | UNIT | HOURLY OPER. COST | RENT PER DAY | RENT PER WEEK | RENT PER MONTH | CREW EQUIPMENT COST/DAY | |
|---|---|---|---|---|---|---|---|---|---|---|
| 70 | 0010 | **WELLPOINT EQUIPMENT RENTAL** without operators | R015433 -10 | | | | | | | 70 |
| | 0020 | Based on 2 months rental | | | | | | | | |
| | 0100 | Combination jetting & wellpoint pump, 60 H.P. diesel | | Ea. | 14.44 | 289 | 867 | 2,600 | 288.90 | |
| | 0200 | High pressure gas jet pump, 200 H.P., 300 psi | | " | 33.09 | 247 | 741 | 2,225 | 412.90 | |
| | 0300 | Discharge pipe, 8" diameter | | L.F. | .01 | .47 | 1.41 | 4.23 | .35 | |
| | 0350 | 12" diameter | | | .01 | .69 | 2.08 | 6.25 | .50 | |
| | 0400 | Header pipe, flows up to 150 G.P.M., 4" diameter | | | .01 | .42 | 1.26 | 3.78 | .35 | |
| | 0500 | 400 G.P.M., 6" diameter | | | .01 | .50 | 1.51 | 4.53 | .40 | |
| | 0600 | 800 G.P.M., 8" diameter | | | .01 | .69 | 2.08 | 6.25 | .50 | |
| | 0700 | 1500 G.P.M., 10" diameter | | | .01 | .73 | 2.18 | 6.55 | .50 | |
| | 0800 | 2500 G.P.M., 12" diameter | | | .02 | 1.38 | 4.13 | 12.40 | 1 | |
| | 0900 | 4500 G.P.M., 16" diameter | | | .03 | 1.76 | 5.28 | 15.85 | 1.30 | |
| | 0950 | For quick coupling aluminum and plastic pipe, add | | ↓ | .03 | 1.82 | 5.47 | 16.40 | 1.35 | |
| | 1100 | Wellpoint, 25' long, with fittings & riser pipe, 1-1/2" or 2" diameter | | Ea. | .05 | 3.64 | 10.91 | 32.50 | 2.60 | |
| | 1200 | Wellpoint pump, diesel powered, 4" diameter, 20 H.P. | | | 6.29 | 167 | 500 | 1,500 | 150.30 | |
| | 1300 | 6" diameter, 30 H.P. | | | 8.53 | 207 | 620 | 1,850 | 192.25 | |
| | 1400 | 8" suction, 40 H.P. | | | 11.53 | 283 | 850 | 2,550 | 262.25 | |
| | 1500 | 10" suction, 75 H.P. | | | 17.41 | 330 | 993 | 2,975 | 337.90 | |
| | 1600 | 12" suction, 100 H.P. | | | 25.08 | 530 | 1,590 | 4,775 | 518.65 | |
| | 1700 | 12" suction, 175 H.P. | | ↓ | 36.59 | 580 | 1,740 | 5,225 | 640.70 | |
| 80 | 0010 | **MARINE EQUIPMENT RENTAL** without operators | R015433 -10 | | | | | | | 80 |
| | 0200 | Barge, 400 Ton, 30' wide x 90' long | | Ea. | 14.60 | 1,025 | 3,055 | 9,175 | 727.80 | |
| | 0240 | 800 Ton, 45' wide x 90' long | | | 17.65 | 1,225 | 3,680 | 11,000 | 877.20 | |
| | 2000 | Tugboat, diesel, 100 HP | | | 25.95 | 187 | 560 | 1,675 | 319.60 | |
| | 2040 | 250 HP | | | 52.25 | 345 | 1,030 | 3,100 | 624 | |
| | 2080 | 380 HP | | Ea. | 108.20 | 1,025 | 3,060 | 9,175 | 1,478 | |

| Crew No. | Bare Costs | | Incl. Subs O & P | | Cost Per Labor-Hour | |
|---|---|---|---|---|---|---|
| **Crew A-1** | Hr. | Daily | Hr. | Daily | Bare Costs | Incl. O&P |
| 1 Building Laborer | $30.25 | $242.00 | $47.05 | $376.40 | $30.25 | $47.05 |
| 1 Concrete saw, gas manual | | 60.40 | | 66.44 | 7.55 | 8.30 |
| 8 L.H., Daily Totals | | $302.40 | | $442.84 | $37.80 | $55.35 |

| **Crew A-1A** | Hr. | Daily | Hr. | Daily | Bare Costs | Incl. O&P |
|---|---|---|---|---|---|---|
| 1 Skilled Worker | $39.40 | $315.20 | $61.25 | $490.00 | $39.40 | $61.25 |
| 1 Shot Blaster, 20" | | 264.70 | | 291.17 | 33.09 | 36.40 |
| 8 L.H., Daily Totals | | $579.90 | | $781.17 | $72.49 | $97.65 |

| **Crew A-1B** | Hr. | Daily | Hr. | Daily | Bare Costs | Incl. O&P |
|---|---|---|---|---|---|---|
| 1 Building Laborer | $30.25 | $242.00 | $47.05 | $376.40 | $30.25 | $47.05 |
| 1 Concrete Saw | | 135.00 | | 148.50 | 16.88 | 18.56 |
| 8 L.H., Daily Totals | | $377.00 | | $524.90 | $47.13 | $65.61 |

| **Crew A-1C** | Hr. | Daily | Hr. | Daily | Bare Costs | Incl. O&P |
|---|---|---|---|---|---|---|
| 1 Building Laborer | $30.25 | $242.00 | $47.05 | $376.40 | $30.25 | $47.05 |
| 1 Chain saw, gas, 18" | | 24.80 | | 27.28 | 3.10 | 3.41 |
| 8 L.H., Daily Totals | | $266.80 | | $403.68 | $33.35 | $50.46 |

| **Crew A-1D** | Hr. | Daily | Hr. | Daily | Bare Costs | Incl. O&P |
|---|---|---|---|---|---|---|
| 1 Building Laborer | $30.25 | $242.00 | $47.05 | $376.40 | $30.25 | $47.05 |
| 1 Vibrating plate, gas, 18" | | 31.00 | | 34.10 | 3.88 | 4.26 |
| 8 L.H., Daily Totals | | $273.00 | | $410.50 | $34.13 | $51.31 |

| **Crew A-1E** | Hr. | Daily | Hr. | Daily | Bare Costs | Incl. O&P |
|---|---|---|---|---|---|---|
| 1 Building Laborer | $30.25 | $242.00 | $47.05 | $376.40 | $30.25 | $47.05 |
| 1 Vibratory Plate, Gas, 21" | | 38.40 | | 42.24 | 4.80 | 5.28 |
| 8 L.H., Daily Totals | | $280.40 | | $418.64 | $35.05 | $52.33 |

| **Crew A-1F** | Hr. | Daily | Hr. | Daily | Bare Costs | Incl. O&P |
|---|---|---|---|---|---|---|
| 1 Building Laborer | $30.25 | $242.00 | $47.05 | $376.40 | $30.25 | $47.05 |
| 1 Rammer/tamper, gas, 8" | | 43.00 | | 47.30 | 5.38 | 5.91 |
| 8 L.H., Daily Totals | | $285.00 | | $423.70 | $35.63 | $52.96 |

| **Crew A-1G** | Hr. | Daily | Hr. | Daily | Bare Costs | Incl. O&P |
|---|---|---|---|---|---|---|
| 1 Building Laborer | $30.25 | $242.00 | $47.05 | $376.40 | $30.25 | $47.05 |
| 1 Rammer/tamper, gas, 8" | | 43.00 | | 47.30 | 5.38 | 5.91 |
| 8 L.H., Daily Totals | | $285.00 | | $423.70 | $35.63 | $52.96 |

| **Crew A-1H** | Hr. | Daily | Hr. | Daily | Bare Costs | Incl. O&P |
|---|---|---|---|---|---|---|
| 1 Building Laborer | $30.25 | $242.00 | $47.05 | $376.40 | $30.25 | $47.05 |
| 1 Exterior Steam Cleaner | | 63.00 | | 69.30 | 7.88 | 8.66 |
| 8 L.H., Daily Totals | | $305.00 | | $445.70 | $38.13 | $55.71 |

| **Crew A-1J** | Hr. | Daily | Hr. | Daily | Bare Costs | Incl. O&P |
|---|---|---|---|---|---|---|
| 1 Building Laborer | $30.25 | $242.00 | $47.05 | $376.40 | $30.25 | $47.05 |
| 1 Cultivator, Walk-Behind | | 54.30 | | 59.73 | 6.79 | 7.47 |
| 8 L.H., Daily Totals | | $296.30 | | $436.13 | $37.04 | $54.52 |

| **Crew A-1K** | Hr. | Daily | Hr. | Daily | Bare Costs | Incl. O&P |
|---|---|---|---|---|---|---|
| 1 Building Laborer | $30.25 | $242.00 | $47.05 | $376.40 | $30.25 | $47.05 |
| 1 Cultivator, Walk-Behind | | 54.30 | | 59.73 | 6.79 | 7.47 |
| 8 L.H., Daily Totals | | $296.30 | | $436.13 | $37.04 | $54.52 |

| **Crew A-1M** | Hr. | Daily | Hr. | Daily | Bare Costs | Incl. O&P |
|---|---|---|---|---|---|---|
| 1 Building Laborer | $30.25 | $242.00 | $47.05 | $376.40 | $30.25 | $47.05 |
| 1 Snow Blower, Walk-Behind | | 43.05 | | 47.35 | 5.38 | 5.92 |
| 8 L.H., Daily Totals | | $285.05 | | $423.76 | $35.63 | $52.97 |

| Crew No. | Bare Costs | | Incl. Subs O & P | | Cost Per Labor-Hour | |
|---|---|---|---|---|---|---|
| **Crew A-2** | Hr. | Daily | Hr. | Daily | Bare Costs | Incl. O&P |
| 2 Laborers | $30.25 | $484.00 | $47.05 | $752.80 | $29.97 | $46.53 |
| 1 Truck Driver (light) | 29.40 | 235.20 | 45.50 | 364.00 | | |
| 1 Flatbed Truck, Gas, 1.5 Ton | | 179.20 | | 197.12 | 7.47 | 8.21 |
| 24 L.H., Daily Totals | | $898.40 | | $1313.92 | $37.43 | $54.75 |

| **Crew A-2A** | Hr. | Daily | Hr. | Daily | Bare Costs | Incl. O&P |
|---|---|---|---|---|---|---|
| 2 Laborers | $30.25 | $484.00 | $47.05 | $752.80 | $29.97 | $46.53 |
| 1 Truck Driver (light) | 29.40 | 235.20 | 45.50 | 364.00 | | |
| 1 Flatbed Truck, Gas, 1.5 Ton | | 179.20 | | 197.12 | | |
| 1 Concrete Saw | | 135.00 | | 148.50 | 13.09 | 14.40 |
| 24 L.H., Daily Totals | | $1033.40 | | $1462.42 | $43.06 | $60.93 |

| **Crew A-2B** | Hr. | Daily | Hr. | Daily | Bare Costs | Incl. O&P |
|---|---|---|---|---|---|---|
| 1 Truck Driver (light) | $29.40 | $235.20 | $45.50 | $364.00 | $29.40 | $45.50 |
| 1 Flatbed Truck, Gas, 1.5 Ton | | 179.20 | | 197.12 | 22.40 | 24.64 |
| 8 L.H., Daily Totals | | $414.40 | | $561.12 | $51.80 | $70.14 |

| **Crew A-3** | Hr. | Daily | Hr. | Daily | Bare Costs | Incl. O&P |
|---|---|---|---|---|---|---|
| 1 Truck Driver (heavy) | $30.60 | $244.80 | $47.35 | $378.80 | $30.60 | $47.35 |
| 1 Dump Truck, 8 C.Y., 220 H.P. | | 308.60 | | 339.46 | 38.58 | 42.43 |
| 8 L.H., Daily Totals | | $553.40 | | $718.26 | $69.17 | $89.78 |

| **Crew A-3A** | Hr. | Daily | Hr. | Daily | Bare Costs | Incl. O&P |
|---|---|---|---|---|---|---|
| 1 Truck Driver (light) | $29.40 | $235.20 | $45.50 | $364.00 | $29.40 | $45.50 |
| 1 Pickup truck, 4 x 4, 3/4 ton | | 121.40 | | 133.54 | 15.18 | 16.69 |
| 8 L.H., Daily Totals | | $356.60 | | $497.54 | $44.58 | $62.19 |

| **Crew A-3B** | Hr. | Daily | Hr. | Daily | Bare Costs | Incl. O&P |
|---|---|---|---|---|---|---|
| 1 Equip. Oper. (medium) | $39.85 | $318.80 | $60.10 | $480.80 | $35.23 | $53.73 |
| 1 Truck Driver (heavy) | 30.60 | 244.80 | 47.35 | 378.80 | | |
| 1 Dump Truck, 12 C.Y., 400 H.P. | | 502.80 | | 553.08 | | |
| 1 F.E. Loader, W.M., 2.5 C.Y. | | 386.40 | | 425.04 | 55.58 | 61.13 |
| 16 L.H., Daily Totals | | $1452.80 | | $1837.72 | $90.80 | $114.86 |

| **Crew A-3C** | Hr. | Daily | Hr. | Daily | Bare Costs | Incl. O&P |
|---|---|---|---|---|---|---|
| 1 Equip. Oper. (light) | $37.75 | $302.00 | $56.95 | $455.60 | $37.75 | $56.95 |
| 1 Loader, Skid Steer, 78 HP | | 246.40 | | 271.04 | 30.80 | 33.88 |
| 8 L.H., Daily Totals | | $548.40 | | $726.64 | $68.55 | $90.83 |

| **Crew A-3D** | Hr. | Daily | Hr. | Daily | Bare Costs | Incl. O&P |
|---|---|---|---|---|---|---|
| 1 Truck Driver, Light | $29.40 | $235.20 | $45.50 | $364.00 | $29.40 | $45.50 |
| 1 Pickup truck, 4 x 4, 3/4 ton | | 121.40 | | 133.54 | | |
| 1 Flatbed Trailer, 25 Ton | | 97.00 | | 106.70 | 27.30 | 30.03 |
| 8 L.H., Daily Totals | | $453.60 | | $604.24 | $56.70 | $75.53 |

| **Crew A-3E** | Hr. | Daily | Hr. | Daily | Bare Costs | Incl. O&P |
|---|---|---|---|---|---|---|
| 1 Equip. Oper. (crane) | $40.95 | $327.60 | $61.75 | $494.00 | $35.77 | $54.55 |
| 1 Truck Driver (heavy) | 30.60 | 244.80 | 47.35 | 378.80 | | |
| 1 Pickup truck, 4 x 4, 3/4 ton | | 121.40 | | 133.54 | 7.59 | 8.35 |
| 16 L.H., Daily Totals | | $693.80 | | $1006.34 | $43.36 | $62.90 |

| **Crew A-3F** | Hr. | Daily | Hr. | Daily | Bare Costs | Incl. O&P |
|---|---|---|---|---|---|---|
| 1 Equip. Oper. (crane) | $40.95 | $327.60 | $61.75 | $494.00 | $35.77 | $54.55 |
| 1 Truck Driver (heavy) | 30.60 | 244.80 | 47.35 | 378.80 | | |
| 1 Pickup truck, 4 x 4, 3/4 ton | | 121.40 | | 133.54 | | |
| 1 Truck Tractor, 6x4, 380 H.P. | | 453.60 | | 498.96 | | |
| 1 Lowbed Trailer, 75 Ton | | 193.40 | | 212.74 | 48.02 | 52.83 |
| 16 L.H., Daily Totals | | $1340.80 | | $1718.04 | $83.80 | $107.38 |

| Crew A-3G | Hr. | Daily | Hr. | Daily | Bare Costs | Incl. O&P |
|---|---|---|---|---|---|---|
| 1 Equip. Oper. (crane) | $40.95 | $327.60 | $61.75 | $494.00 | $35.77 | $54.55 |
| 1 Truck Driver (heavy) | 30.60 | 244.80 | 47.35 | 378.80 | | |
| 1 Pickup truck, 4 x 4, 3/4 ton | | 121.40 | | 133.54 | | |
| 1 Truck Tractor, 6x4, 450 H.P. | | 427.80 | | 470.58 | | |
| 1 Lowbed Trailer, 75 Ton | | 193.40 | | 212.74 | 46.41 | 51.05 |
| 16 L.H., Daily Totals | | $1315.00 | | $1689.66 | $82.19 | $105.60 |

| Crew A-3H | Hr. | Daily | Hr. | Daily | Bare Costs | Incl. O&P |
|---|---|---|---|---|---|---|
| 1 Equip. Oper. (crane) | $40.95 | $327.60 | $61.75 | $494.00 | $40.95 | $61.75 |
| 1 Hyd. crane, 12 Ton (daily) | | 967.00 | | 1063.70 | 120.88 | 132.96 |
| 8 L.H., Daily Totals | | $1294.60 | | $1557.70 | $161.82 | $194.71 |

| Crew A-3I | Hr. | Daily | Hr. | Daily | Bare Costs | Incl. O&P |
|---|---|---|---|---|---|---|
| 1 Equip. Oper. (crane) | $40.95 | $327.60 | $61.75 | $494.00 | $40.95 | $61.75 |
| 1 Hyd. crane, 25 Ton (daily) | | 988.60 | | 1087.46 | 123.58 | 135.93 |
| 8 L.H., Daily Totals | | $1316.20 | | $1581.46 | $164.53 | $197.68 |

| Crew A-3J | Hr. | Daily | Hr. | Daily | Bare Costs | Incl. O&P |
|---|---|---|---|---|---|---|
| 1 Equip. Oper. (crane) | $40.95 | $327.60 | $61.75 | $494.00 | $40.95 | $61.75 |
| 1 Hyd. crane, 40 Ton (daily) | | 987.60 | | 1086.36 | 123.45 | 135.79 |
| 8 L.H., Daily Totals | | $1315.20 | | $1580.36 | $164.40 | $197.54 |

| Crew A-3K | Hr. | Daily | Hr. | Daily | Bare Costs | Incl. O&P |
|---|---|---|---|---|---|---|
| 1 Equip. Oper. (crane) | $40.95 | $327.60 | $61.75 | $494.00 | $38.02 | $57.35 |
| 1 Equip. Oper. Oiler | 35.10 | 280.80 | 52.95 | 423.60 | | |
| 1 Hyd. crane, 55 Ton (daily) | | 1411.00 | | 1552.10 | | |
| 1 P/U Truck, 3/4 Ton (daily) | | 107.30 | | 118.03 | 94.89 | 104.38 |
| 16 L.H., Daily Totals | | $2126.70 | | $2587.73 | $132.92 | $161.73 |

| Crew A-3L | Hr. | Daily | Hr. | Daily | Bare Costs | Incl. O&P |
|---|---|---|---|---|---|---|
| 1 Equip. Oper. (crane) | $40.95 | $327.60 | $61.75 | $494.00 | $38.02 | $57.35 |
| 1 Equip. Oper. Oiler | 35.10 | 280.80 | 52.95 | 423.60 | | |
| 1 Hyd. crane, 80 Ton (daily) | | 1605.00 | | 1765.50 | | |
| 1 P/U Truck, 3/4 Ton (daily) | | 107.30 | | 118.03 | 107.02 | 117.72 |
| 16 L.H., Daily Totals | | $2320.70 | | $2801.13 | $145.04 | $175.07 |

| Crew A-3M | Hr. | Daily | Hr. | Daily | Bare Costs | Incl. O&P |
|---|---|---|---|---|---|---|
| 1 Equip. Oper. (crane) | $40.95 | $327.60 | $61.75 | $494.00 | $38.02 | $57.35 |
| 1 Equip. Oper. Oiler | 35.10 | 280.80 | 52.95 | 423.60 | | |
| 1 Hyd. crane, 100 Ton (daily) | | 3266.00 | | 3592.60 | | |
| 1 P/U Truck, 3/4 Ton (daily) | | 107.30 | | 118.03 | 210.83 | 231.91 |
| 16 L.H., Daily Totals | | $3981.70 | | $4628.23 | $248.86 | $289.26 |

| Crew A-3N | Hr. | Daily | Hr. | Daily | Bare Costs | Incl. O&P |
|---|---|---|---|---|---|---|
| 1 Equip. Oper. (crane) | $40.95 | $327.60 | $61.75 | $494.00 | $40.95 | $61.75 |
| 1 Tower crane (monthly) | | 982.00 | | 1080.20 | 122.75 | 135.03 |
| 8 L.H., Daily Totals | | $1309.60 | | $1574.20 | $163.70 | $196.78 |

| Crew A-3P | Hr. | Daily | Hr. | Daily | Bare Costs | Incl. O&P |
|---|---|---|---|---|---|---|
| 1 Equip. Oper., Light | $37.75 | $302.00 | $56.95 | $455.60 | $37.75 | $56.95 |
| 1 A.T. Forklift, 42' lift | | 434.60 | | 478.06 | 54.33 | 59.76 |
| 8 L.H., Daily Totals | | $736.60 | | $933.66 | $92.08 | $116.71 |

| Crew A-4 | Hr. | Daily | Hr. | Daily | Bare Costs | Incl. O&P |
|---|---|---|---|---|---|---|
| 2 Carpenters | $38.10 | $609.60 | $59.30 | $948.80 | $36.65 | $56.43 |
| 1 Painter, Ordinary | 33.75 | 270.00 | 50.70 | 405.60 | | |
| 24 L.H., Daily Totals | | $879.60 | | $1354.40 | $36.65 | $56.43 |

| Crew A-5 | Hr. | Daily | Hr. | Daily | Bare Costs | Incl. O&P |
|---|---|---|---|---|---|---|
| 2 Laborers | $30.25 | $484.00 | $47.05 | $752.80 | $30.16 | $46.88 |
| .25 Truck Driver (light) | 29.40 | 58.80 | 45.50 | 91.00 | | |
| .25 Flatbed Truck, Gas, 1.5 Ton | | 44.80 | | 49.28 | 2.49 | 2.74 |
| 18 L.H., Daily Totals | | $587.60 | | $893.08 | $32.64 | $49.62 |

| Crew A-6 | Hr. | Daily | Hr. | Daily | Bare Costs | Incl. O&P |
|---|---|---|---|---|---|---|
| 1 Instrument Man | $39.40 | $315.20 | $61.25 | $490.00 | $38.35 | $58.88 |
| 1 Rodman/Chainman | 37.30 | 298.40 | 56.50 | 452.00 | | |
| 1 Laser Transit/Level | | 68.90 | | 75.79 | 4.31 | 4.74 |
| 16 L.H., Daily Totals | | $682.50 | | $1017.79 | $42.66 | $63.61 |

| Crew A-7 | Hr. | Daily | Hr. | Daily | Bare Costs | Incl. O&P |
|---|---|---|---|---|---|---|
| 1 Chief Of Party | $48.65 | $389.20 | $75.05 | $600.40 | $41.78 | $64.27 |
| 1 Instrument Man | 39.40 | 315.20 | 61.25 | 490.00 | | |
| 1 Rodman/Chainman | 37.30 | 298.40 | 56.50 | 452.00 | | |
| 1 Laser Transit/Level | | 68.90 | | 75.79 | 2.87 | 3.16 |
| 24 L.H., Daily Totals | | $1071.70 | | $1618.19 | $44.65 | $67.42 |

| Crew A-8 | Hr. | Daily | Hr. | Daily | Bare Costs | Incl. O&P |
|---|---|---|---|---|---|---|
| 1 Chief of Party | $48.65 | $389.20 | $75.05 | $600.40 | $40.66 | $62.33 |
| 1 Instrument Man | 39.40 | 315.20 | 61.25 | 490.00 | | |
| 2 Rodmen/Chainmen | 37.30 | 596.80 | 56.50 | 904.00 | | |
| 1 Laser Transit/Level | | 68.90 | | 75.79 | 2.15 | 2.37 |
| 32 L.H., Daily Totals | | $1370.10 | | $2070.19 | $42.82 | $64.69 |

| Crew A-9 | Hr. | Daily | Hr. | Daily | Bare Costs | Incl. O&P |
|---|---|---|---|---|---|---|
| 1 Asbestos Foreman | $43.60 | $348.80 | $68.65 | $549.20 | $43.16 | $67.95 |
| 7 Asbestos Workers | 43.10 | 2413.60 | 67.85 | 3799.60 | | |
| 64 L.H., Daily Totals | | $2762.40 | | $4348.80 | $43.16 | $67.95 |

| Crew A-10 | Hr. | Daily | Hr. | Daily | Bare Costs | Incl. O&P |
|---|---|---|---|---|---|---|
| 1 Asbestos Foreman | $43.60 | $348.80 | $68.65 | $549.20 | $43.16 | $67.95 |
| 7 Asbestos Workers | 43.10 | 2413.60 | 67.85 | 3799.60 | | |
| 64 L.H., Daily Totals | | $2762.40 | | $4348.80 | $43.16 | $67.95 |

| Crew A-10A | Hr. | Daily | Hr. | Daily | Bare Costs | Incl. O&P |
|---|---|---|---|---|---|---|
| 1 Asbestos Foreman | $43.60 | $348.80 | $68.65 | $549.20 | $43.27 | $68.12 |
| 2 Asbestos Workers | 43.10 | 689.60 | 67.85 | 1085.60 | | |
| 24 L.H., Daily Totals | | $1038.40 | | $1634.80 | $43.27 | $68.12 |

| Crew A-10B | Hr. | Daily | Hr. | Daily | Bare Costs | Incl. O&P |
|---|---|---|---|---|---|---|
| 1 Asbestos Foreman | $43.60 | $348.80 | $68.65 | $549.20 | $43.23 | $68.05 |
| 3 Asbestos Workers | 43.10 | 1034.40 | 67.85 | 1628.40 | | |
| 32 L.H., Daily Totals | | $1383.20 | | $2177.60 | $43.23 | $68.05 |

| Crew A-10C | Hr. | Daily | Hr. | Daily | Bare Costs | Incl. O&P |
|---|---|---|---|---|---|---|
| 3 Asbestos Workers | $43.10 | $1034.40 | $67.85 | $1628.40 | $43.10 | $67.85 |
| 1 Flatbed Truck, Gas, 1.5 Ton | | 179.20 | | 197.12 | 7.47 | 8.21 |
| 24 L.H., Daily Totals | | $1213.60 | | $1825.52 | $50.57 | $76.06 |

| Crew A-10D | Hr. | Daily | Hr. | Daily | Bare Costs | Incl. O&P |
|---|---|---|---|---|---|---|
| 2 Asbestos Workers | $43.10 | $689.60 | $67.85 | $1085.60 | $40.56 | $62.60 |
| 1 Equip. Oper. (crane) | 40.95 | 327.60 | 61.75 | 494.00 | | |
| 1 Equip. Oper. Oiler | 35.10 | 280.80 | 52.95 | 423.60 | | |
| 1 Hydraulic Crane, 33 Ton | | 815.40 | | 896.94 | 25.48 | 28.03 |
| 32 L.H., Daily Totals | | $2113.40 | | $2900.14 | $66.04 | $90.63 |

## Crew A-11

| Crew No. | Bare Costs Hr. | Daily | Incl. Subs O&P Hr. | Daily | Bare Costs | Incl. O&P |
|---|---|---|---|---|---|---|
| 1 Asbestos Foreman | $43.60 | $348.80 | $68.65 | $549.20 | $43.16 | $67.95 |
| 7 Asbestos Workers | 43.10 | 2413.60 | 67.85 | 3799.60 | | |
| 2 Chipping Hammer, 12 Lb., Elec. | | 32.40 | | 35.64 | .51 | .56 |
| 64 L.H., Daily Totals | | $2794.80 | | $4384.44 | $43.67 | $68.51 |

## Crew A-12

| Crew No. | Bare Costs Hr. | Daily | Incl. Subs O&P Hr. | Daily | Bare Costs | Incl. O&P |
|---|---|---|---|---|---|---|
| 1 Asbestos Foreman | $43.60 | $348.80 | $68.65 | $549.20 | $43.16 | $67.95 |
| 7 Asbestos Workers | 43.10 | 2413.60 | 67.85 | 3799.60 | | |
| 1 Trk-mtd vac, 14 CY, 1500 Gal | | 525.05 | | 577.55 | | |
| 1 Flatbed Truck, 20,000 GVW | | 186.00 | | 204.60 | 11.11 | 12.22 |
| 64 L.H., Daily Totals | | $3473.45 | | $5130.95 | $54.27 | $80.17 |

## Crew A-13

| Crew No. | Bare Costs Hr. | Daily | Incl. Subs O&P Hr. | Daily | Bare Costs | Incl. O&P |
|---|---|---|---|---|---|---|
| 1 Equip. Oper. (light) | $37.75 | $302.00 | $56.95 | $455.60 | $37.75 | $56.95 |
| 1 Trk-mtd vac, 14 CY, 1500 Gal | | 525.05 | | 577.55 | | |
| 1 Flatbed Truck, 20,000 GVW | | 186.00 | | 204.60 | 88.88 | 97.77 |
| 8 L.H., Daily Totals | | $1013.05 | | $1237.76 | $126.63 | $154.72 |

## Crew B-1

| Crew No. | Bare Costs Hr. | Daily | Incl. Subs O&P Hr. | Daily | Bare Costs | Incl. O&P |
|---|---|---|---|---|---|---|
| 1 Labor Foreman (outside) | $32.25 | $258.00 | $50.20 | $401.60 | $30.92 | $48.10 |
| 2 Laborers | 30.25 | 484.00 | 47.05 | 752.80 | | |
| 24 L.H., Daily Totals | | $742.00 | | $1154.40 | $30.92 | $48.10 |

## Crew B-1A

| Crew No. | Bare Costs Hr. | Daily | Incl. Subs O&P Hr. | Daily | Bare Costs | Incl. O&P |
|---|---|---|---|---|---|---|
| 1 Laborer Foreman | $32.25 | $258.00 | $50.20 | $401.60 | $30.92 | $48.10 |
| 2 Laborers | 30.25 | 484.00 | 47.05 | 752.80 | | |
| 2 Cutting Torch | | 34.00 | | 37.40 | | |
| 2 Gases | | 144.00 | | 158.40 | 7.42 | 8.16 |
| 24 L.H., Daily Totals | | $920.00 | | $1350.20 | $38.33 | $56.26 |

## Crew B-1B

| Crew No. | Bare Costs Hr. | Daily | Incl. Subs O&P Hr. | Daily | Bare Costs | Incl. O&P |
|---|---|---|---|---|---|---|
| 1 Laborer Foreman | $32.25 | $258.00 | $50.20 | $401.60 | $33.42 | $51.51 |
| 2 Laborers | 30.25 | 484.00 | 47.05 | 752.80 | | |
| 1 Equip. Oper. (crane) | 40.95 | 327.60 | 61.75 | 494.00 | | |
| 2 Cutting Torch | | 34.00 | | 37.40 | | |
| 2 Gases | | 144.00 | | 158.40 | | |
| 1 Hyd. Crane, 12 Ton | | 766.40 | | 843.04 | 29.51 | 32.46 |
| 32 L.H., Daily Totals | | $2014.00 | | $2687.24 | $62.94 | $83.98 |

## Crew B-2

| Crew No. | Bare Costs Hr. | Daily | Incl. Subs O&P Hr. | Daily | Bare Costs | Incl. O&P |
|---|---|---|---|---|---|---|
| 1 Labor Foreman (outside) | $32.25 | $258.00 | $50.20 | $401.60 | $30.65 | $47.68 |
| 4 Laborers | 30.25 | 968.00 | 47.05 | 1505.60 | | |
| 40 L.H., Daily Totals | | $1226.00 | | $1907.20 | $30.65 | $47.68 |

## Crew B-3

| Crew No. | Bare Costs Hr. | Daily | Incl. Subs O&P Hr. | Daily | Bare Costs | Incl. O&P |
|---|---|---|---|---|---|---|
| 1 Labor Foreman (outside) | $32.25 | $258.00 | $50.20 | $401.60 | $32.30 | $49.85 |
| 2 Laborers | 30.25 | 484.00 | 47.05 | 752.80 | | |
| 1 Equip. Oper. (med.) | 39.85 | 318.80 | 60.10 | 480.80 | | |
| 2 Truck Drivers (heavy) | 30.60 | 489.60 | 47.35 | 757.60 | | |
| 1 Crawler Loader, 3 C.Y. | | 893.40 | | 982.74 | | |
| 2 Dump Truck, 12 C.Y., 400 H.P. | | 1005.60 | | 1106.16 | 39.56 | 43.52 |
| 48 L.H., Daily Totals | | $3449.40 | | $4481.70 | $71.86 | $93.37 |

## Crew B-3A

| Crew No. | Bare Costs Hr. | Daily | Incl. Subs O&P Hr. | Daily | Bare Costs | Incl. O&P |
|---|---|---|---|---|---|---|
| 4 Laborers | $30.25 | $968.00 | $47.05 | $1505.60 | $32.17 | $49.66 |
| 1 Equip. Oper. (med.) | 39.85 | 318.80 | 60.10 | 480.80 | | |
| 1 Hyd. Excavator, 1.5 C.Y. | | 830.00 | | 913.00 | 20.75 | 22.82 |
| 40 L.H., Daily Totals | | $2116.80 | | $2899.40 | $52.92 | $72.48 |

## Crew B-3B

| Crew No. | Bare Costs Hr. | Daily | Incl. Subs O&P Hr. | Daily | Bare Costs | Incl. O&P |
|---|---|---|---|---|---|---|
| 2 Laborers | $30.25 | $484.00 | $47.05 | $752.80 | $32.74 | $50.39 |
| 1 Equip. Oper. (med.) | 39.85 | 318.80 | 60.10 | 480.80 | | |
| 1 Truck Driver (heavy) | 30.60 | 244.80 | 47.35 | 378.80 | | |
| 1 Backhoe Loader, 80 H.P. | | 340.80 | | 374.88 | | |
| 1 Dump Truck, 12 C.Y., 400 H.P. | | 502.80 | | 553.08 | 26.36 | 29.00 |
| 32 L.H., Daily Totals | | $1891.20 | | $2540.36 | $59.10 | $79.39 |

## Crew B-3C

| Crew No. | Bare Costs Hr. | Daily | Incl. Subs O&P Hr. | Daily | Bare Costs | Incl. O&P |
|---|---|---|---|---|---|---|
| 3 Laborers | $30.25 | $726.00 | $47.05 | $1129.20 | $32.65 | $50.31 |
| 1 Equip. Oper. (med.) | 39.85 | 318.80 | 60.10 | 480.80 | | |
| 1 Crawler Loader, 4 C.Y. | | 1242.00 | | 1366.20 | 38.81 | 42.69 |
| 32 L.H., Daily Totals | | $2286.80 | | $2976.20 | $71.46 | $93.01 |

## Crew B-4

| Crew No. | Bare Costs Hr. | Daily | Incl. Subs O&P Hr. | Daily | Bare Costs | Incl. O&P |
|---|---|---|---|---|---|---|
| 1 Labor Foreman (outside) | $32.25 | $258.00 | $50.20 | $401.60 | $30.64 | $47.63 |
| 4 Laborers | 30.25 | 968.00 | 47.05 | 1505.60 | | |
| 1 Truck Driver (heavy) | 30.60 | 244.80 | 47.35 | 378.80 | | |
| 1 Truck Tractor, 220 H.P. | | 271.80 | | 298.98 | | |
| 1 Flatbed Trailer, 40 Ton | | 133.20 | | 146.52 | 8.44 | 9.28 |
| 48 L.H., Daily Totals | | $1875.80 | | $2731.50 | $39.08 | $56.91 |

## Crew B-5

| Crew No. | Bare Costs Hr. | Daily | Incl. Subs O&P Hr. | Daily | Bare Costs | Incl. O&P |
|---|---|---|---|---|---|---|
| 1 Labor Foreman (outside) | $32.25 | $258.00 | $50.20 | $401.60 | $33.28 | $51.23 |
| 4 Laborers | 30.25 | 968.00 | 47.05 | 1505.60 | | |
| 2 Equip. Oper. (med.) | 39.85 | 637.60 | 60.10 | 961.60 | | |
| 1 Air Compressor, 250 C.F.M. | | 161.80 | | 177.98 | | |
| 2 Breaker, Pavement, 60 lb. | | 17.20 | | 18.92 | | |
| 2 -50' Air Hose, 1.5" | | 12.60 | | 13.86 | | |
| 1 Crawler Loader, 3 C.Y. | | 893.40 | | 982.74 | 19.38 | 21.31 |
| 56 L.H., Daily Totals | | $2948.60 | | $4062.30 | $52.65 | $72.54 |

## Crew B-5A

| Crew No. | Bare Costs Hr. | Daily | Incl. Subs O&P Hr. | Daily | Bare Costs | Incl. O&P |
|---|---|---|---|---|---|---|
| 1 Foreman | $32.25 | $258.00 | $50.20 | $401.60 | $32.70 | $50.36 |
| 6 Laborers | 30.25 | 1452.00 | 47.05 | 2258.40 | | |
| 2 Equip. Oper. (med.) | 39.85 | 637.60 | 60.10 | 961.60 | | |
| 1 Equip. Oper. (light) | 37.75 | 302.00 | 56.95 | 455.60 | | |
| 2 Truck Drivers (heavy) | 30.60 | 489.60 | 47.35 | 757.60 | | |
| 1 Air Compressor, 365 C.F.M. | | 211.80 | | 232.98 | | |
| 2 Breaker, Pavement, 60 lb. | | 17.20 | | 18.92 | | |
| 8 -50' Air Hose, 1" | | 31.20 | | 34.32 | | |
| 2 Dump Truck, 8 C.Y., 220 H.P. | | 617.20 | | 678.92 | 9.14 | 10.05 |
| 96 L.H., Daily Totals | | $4016.60 | | $5799.94 | $41.84 | $60.42 |

## Crew B-5B

| Crew No. | Bare Costs Hr. | Daily | Incl. Subs O&P Hr. | Daily | Bare Costs | Incl. O&P |
|---|---|---|---|---|---|---|
| 1 Powderman | $39.40 | $315.20 | $61.25 | $490.00 | $35.15 | $53.92 |
| 2 Equip. Oper. (med.) | 39.85 | 637.60 | 60.10 | 961.60 | | |
| 3 Truck Drivers (heavy) | 30.60 | 734.40 | 47.35 | 1136.40 | | |
| 1 F.E. Loader, W.M., 2.5 C.Y. | | 386.40 | | 425.04 | | |
| 3 Dump Truck, 12 C.Y., 400 H.P. | | 1508.40 | | 1659.24 | | |
| 1 Air Compressor, 365 C.F.M. | | 211.80 | | 232.98 | 43.89 | 48.28 |
| 48 L.H., Daily Totals | | $3793.80 | | $4905.26 | $79.04 | $102.19 |

# Crews

## Crew B-5C

| | Bare Costs Hr. | Bare Costs Daily | Incl. Subs O&P Hr. | Incl. Subs O&P Daily | Cost Per Labor-Hour Bare Costs | Cost Per Labor-Hour Incl. O&P |
|---|---|---|---|---|---|---|
| 3 Laborers | $30.25 | $726.00 | $47.05 | $1129.20 | $33.48 | $51.33 |
| 1 Equip. Oper. (medium) | 39.85 | 318.80 | 60.10 | 480.80 | | |
| 2 Truck Drivers (heavy) | 30.60 | 489.60 | 47.35 | 757.60 | | |
| 1 Equip. Oper. (crane) | 40.95 | 327.60 | 61.75 | 494.00 | | |
| 1 Equip. Oper. Oiler | 35.10 | 280.80 | 52.95 | 423.60 | | |
| 2 Dump Truck, 12 C.Y., 400 H.P. | | 1005.60 | | 1106.16 | | |
| 1 Crawler Loader, 4 C.Y. | | 1242.00 | | 1366.20 | | |
| 1 S.P. Crane, 4x4, 25 Ton | | 701.80 | | 771.98 | 46.08 | 50.69 |
| 64 L.H., Daily Totals | | $5092.20 | | $6529.54 | $79.57 | $102.02 |

## Crew B-6

| | Bare Costs Hr. | Bare Costs Daily | Incl. Subs O&P Hr. | Incl. Subs O&P Daily | Cost Per Labor-Hour Bare Costs | Cost Per Labor-Hour Incl. O&P |
|---|---|---|---|---|---|---|
| 2 Laborers | $30.25 | $484.00 | $47.05 | $752.80 | $32.75 | $50.35 |
| 1 Equip. Oper. (light) | 37.75 | 302.00 | 56.95 | 455.60 | | |
| 1 Backhoe Loader, 48 H.P. | | 285.40 | | 313.94 | 11.89 | 13.08 |
| 24 L.H., Daily Totals | | $1071.40 | | $1522.34 | $44.64 | $63.43 |

## Crew B-6A

| | Bare Costs Hr. | Bare Costs Daily | Incl. Subs O&P Hr. | Incl. Subs O&P Daily | Cost Per Labor-Hour Bare Costs | Cost Per Labor-Hour Incl. O&P |
|---|---|---|---|---|---|---|
| .5 Labor Foreman (outside) | $32.25 | $129.00 | $50.20 | $200.80 | $34.49 | $52.90 |
| 1 Laborer | 30.25 | 242.00 | 47.05 | 376.40 | | |
| 1 Equip. Oper. (med.) | 39.85 | 318.80 | 60.10 | 480.80 | | |
| 1 Vacuum Trk.,5000 Gal. | | 361.20 | | 397.32 | 18.06 | 19.87 |
| 20 L.H., Daily Totals | | $1051.00 | | $1455.32 | $52.55 | $72.77 |

## Crew B-6B

| | Bare Costs Hr. | Bare Costs Daily | Incl. Subs O&P Hr. | Incl. Subs O&P Daily | Cost Per Labor-Hour Bare Costs | Cost Per Labor-Hour Incl. O&P |
|---|---|---|---|---|---|---|
| 2 Labor Foremen (out) | $32.25 | $516.00 | $50.20 | $803.20 | $30.92 | $48.10 |
| 4 Laborers | 30.25 | 968.00 | 47.05 | 1505.60 | | |
| 1 S.P. Crane, 4x4, 5 Ton | | 258.80 | | 284.68 | | |
| 1 Flatbed Truck, Gas, 1.5 Ton | | 179.20 | | 197.12 | | |
| 1 Butt Fusion Machine | | 257.60 | | 283.36 | 14.49 | 15.94 |
| 48 L.H., Daily Totals | | $2179.60 | | $3073.96 | $45.41 | $64.04 |

## Crew B-7

| | Bare Costs Hr. | Bare Costs Daily | Incl. Subs O&P Hr. | Incl. Subs O&P Daily | Cost Per Labor-Hour Bare Costs | Cost Per Labor-Hour Incl. O&P |
|---|---|---|---|---|---|---|
| 1 Labor Foreman (outside) | $32.25 | $258.00 | $50.20 | $401.60 | $32.18 | $49.75 |
| 4 Laborers | 30.25 | 968.00 | 47.05 | 1505.60 | | |
| 1 Equip. Oper. (med.) | 39.85 | 318.80 | 60.10 | 480.80 | | |
| 1 Brush Chipper, 12", 130 H.P. | | 215.60 | | 237.16 | | |
| 1 Crawler Loader, 3 C.Y. | | 893.40 | | 982.74 | | |
| 2 Chainsaw, Gas, 36" Long | | 73.60 | | 80.96 | 24.64 | 27.10 |
| 48 L.H., Daily Totals | | $2727.40 | | $3688.86 | $56.82 | $76.85 |

## Crew B-7A

| | Bare Costs Hr. | Bare Costs Daily | Incl. Subs O&P Hr. | Incl. Subs O&P Daily | Cost Per Labor-Hour Bare Costs | Cost Per Labor-Hour Incl. O&P |
|---|---|---|---|---|---|---|
| 2 Laborers | $30.25 | $484.00 | $47.05 | $752.80 | $32.75 | $50.35 |
| 1 Equip. Oper. (light) | 37.75 | 302.00 | 56.95 | 455.60 | | |
| 1 Rake w/Tractor | | 221.10 | | 243.21 | | |
| 2 Chain saw, gas, 18" | | 49.60 | | 54.56 | 11.28 | 12.41 |
| 24 L.H., Daily Totals | | $1056.70 | | $1506.17 | $44.03 | $62.76 |

## Crew B-8

| | Bare Costs Hr. | Bare Costs Daily | Incl. Subs O&P Hr. | Incl. Subs O&P Daily | Cost Per Labor-Hour Bare Costs | Cost Per Labor-Hour Incl. O&P |
|---|---|---|---|---|---|---|
| 1 Labor Foreman (outside) | $32.25 | $258.00 | $50.20 | $401.60 | $33.59 | $51.52 |
| 2 Laborers | 30.25 | 484.00 | 47.05 | 752.80 | | |
| 2 Equip. Oper. (med.) | 39.85 | 637.60 | 60.10 | 961.60 | | |
| 1 Equip. Oper. Oiler | 35.10 | 280.80 | 52.95 | 423.60 | | |
| 2 Truck Drivers (heavy) | 30.60 | 489.60 | 47.35 | 757.60 | | |
| 1 Hyd. Crane, 25 Ton | | 786.00 | | 864.60 | | |
| 1 Crawler Loader, 3 C.Y. | | 893.40 | | 982.74 | | |
| 2 Dump Truck, 12 C.Y., 400 H.P. | | 1005.60 | | 1106.16 | 41.95 | 46.15 |
| 64 L.H., Daily Totals | | $4835.00 | | $6250.70 | $75.55 | $97.67 |

## Crew B-9

| | Bare Costs Hr. | Bare Costs Daily | Incl. Subs O&P Hr. | Incl. Subs O&P Daily | Cost Per Labor-Hour Bare Costs | Cost Per Labor-Hour Incl. O&P |
|---|---|---|---|---|---|---|
| 1 Labor Foreman (outside) | $32.25 | $258.00 | $50.20 | $401.60 | $30.65 | $47.68 |
| 4 Laborers | 30.25 | 968.00 | 47.05 | 1505.60 | | |
| 1 Air Compressor, 250 C.F.M. | | 161.80 | | 177.98 | | |
| 2 Breaker, Pavement, 60 lb. | | 17.20 | | 18.92 | | |
| 2 -50' Air Hose, 1.5" | | 12.60 | | 13.86 | 4.79 | 5.27 |
| 40 L.H., Daily Totals | | $1417.60 | | $2117.96 | $35.44 | $52.95 |

## Crew B-9A

| | Bare Costs Hr. | Bare Costs Daily | Incl. Subs O&P Hr. | Incl. Subs O&P Daily | Cost Per Labor-Hour Bare Costs | Cost Per Labor-Hour Incl. O&P |
|---|---|---|---|---|---|---|
| 2 Laborers | $30.25 | $484.00 | $47.05 | $752.80 | $30.37 | $47.15 |
| 1 Truck Driver (heavy) | 30.60 | 244.80 | 47.35 | 378.80 | | |
| 1 Water Tanker, 5000 Gal. | | 129.60 | | 142.56 | | |
| 1 Truck Tractor, 220 H.P. | | 271.80 | | 298.98 | | |
| 2 -50' Discharge Hose, 3" | | 3.50 | | 3.85 | 16.87 | 18.56 |
| 24 L.H., Daily Totals | | $1133.70 | | $1576.99 | $47.24 | $65.71 |

## Crew B-9B

| | Bare Costs Hr. | Bare Costs Daily | Incl. Subs O&P Hr. | Incl. Subs O&P Daily | Cost Per Labor-Hour Bare Costs | Cost Per Labor-Hour Incl. O&P |
|---|---|---|---|---|---|---|
| 2 Laborers | $30.25 | $484.00 | $47.05 | $752.80 | $30.37 | $47.15 |
| 1 Truck Driver (heavy) | 30.60 | 244.80 | 47.35 | 378.80 | | |
| 2 -50' Discharge Hose, 3" | | 3.50 | | 3.85 | | |
| 1 Water Tanker, 5000 Gal. | | 129.60 | | 142.56 | | |
| 1 Truck Tractor, 220 H.P. | | 271.80 | | 298.98 | | |
| 1 Pressure Washer | | 60.00 | | 66.00 | 19.37 | 21.31 |
| 24 L.H., Daily Totals | | $1193.70 | | $1642.99 | $49.74 | $68.46 |

## Crew B-9C

| | Bare Costs Hr. | Bare Costs Daily | Incl. Subs O&P Hr. | Incl. Subs O&P Daily | Cost Per Labor-Hour Bare Costs | Cost Per Labor-Hour Incl. O&P |
|---|---|---|---|---|---|---|
| 1 Labor Foreman (outside) | $32.25 | $258.00 | $50.20 | $401.60 | $30.65 | $47.68 |
| 4 Laborers | 30.25 | 968.00 | 47.05 | 1505.60 | | |
| 1 Air Compressor, 250 C.F.M. | | 161.80 | | 177.98 | | |
| 2 -50' Air Hose, 1.5" | | 12.60 | | 13.86 | | |
| 2 Breaker, Pavement, 60 lb. | | 17.20 | | 18.92 | 4.79 | 5.27 |
| 40 L.H., Daily Totals | | $1417.60 | | $2117.96 | $35.44 | $52.95 |

## Crew B-9D

| | Bare Costs Hr. | Bare Costs Daily | Incl. Subs O&P Hr. | Incl. Subs O&P Daily | Cost Per Labor-Hour Bare Costs | Cost Per Labor-Hour Incl. O&P |
|---|---|---|---|---|---|---|
| 1 Labor Foreman (Outside) | $32.25 | $258.00 | $50.20 | $401.60 | $30.65 | $47.68 |
| 4 Common Laborers | 30.25 | 968.00 | 47.05 | 1505.60 | | |
| 1 Air Compressor, 250 C.F.M. | | 161.80 | | 177.98 | | |
| 2 -50' Air Hose, 1.5" | | 12.60 | | 13.86 | | |
| 2 Air Powered Tamper | | 46.10 | | 50.71 | 5.51 | 6.06 |
| 40 L.H., Daily Totals | | $1446.50 | | $2149.75 | $36.16 | $53.74 |

## Crew B-10

| | Bare Costs Hr. | Bare Costs Daily | Incl. Subs O&P Hr. | Incl. Subs O&P Daily | Cost Per Labor-Hour Bare Costs | Cost Per Labor-Hour Incl. O&P |
|---|---|---|---|---|---|---|
| 1 Equip. Oper. (med.) | $39.85 | $318.80 | $60.10 | $480.80 | $36.65 | $55.75 |
| .5 Laborer | 30.25 | 121.00 | 47.05 | 188.20 | | |
| 12 L.H., Daily Totals | | $439.80 | | $669.00 | $36.65 | $55.75 |

## Crew B-10A

| | Bare Costs Hr. | Bare Costs Daily | Incl. Subs O&P Hr. | Incl. Subs O&P Daily | Cost Per Labor-Hour Bare Costs | Cost Per Labor-Hour Incl. O&P |
|---|---|---|---|---|---|---|
| 1 Equip. Oper. (med.) | $39.85 | $318.80 | $60.10 | $480.80 | $36.65 | $55.75 |
| .5 Laborer | 30.25 | 121.00 | 47.05 | 188.20 | | |
| 1 Roller, 2-Drum, W.B., 7.5 HP | | 143.00 | | 157.30 | 11.92 | 13.11 |
| 12 L.H., Daily Totals | | $582.80 | | $826.30 | $48.57 | $68.86 |

## Crew B-10B

| | Bare Costs Hr. | Bare Costs Daily | Incl. Subs O&P Hr. | Incl. Subs O&P Daily | Cost Per Labor-Hour Bare Costs | Cost Per Labor-Hour Incl. O&P |
|---|---|---|---|---|---|---|
| 1 Equip. Oper. (med.) | $39.85 | $318.80 | $60.10 | $480.80 | $36.65 | $55.75 |
| .5 Laborer | 30.25 | 121.00 | 47.05 | 188.20 | | |
| 1 Dozer, 200 H.P. | | 1071.00 | | 1178.10 | 89.25 | 98.17 |
| 12 L.H., Daily Totals | | $1510.80 | | $1847.10 | $125.90 | $153.93 |

| Crew No. | Bare Costs | | Incl. Subs O & P | | Cost Per Labor-Hour | |

**Crew B-10C**

| | Hr. | Daily | Hr. | Daily | Bare Costs | Incl. O&P |
|---|---|---|---|---|---|---|
| 1 Equip. Oper. (med.) | $39.85 | $318.80 | $60.10 | $480.80 | $36.65 | $55.75 |
| .5 Laborer | 30.25 | 121.00 | 47.05 | 188.20 | | |
| 1 Dozer, 200 H.P. | | 1071.00 | | 1178.10 | | |
| 1 Vibratory Roller, Towed, 23 Ton | | 371.60 | | 408.76 | 120.22 | 132.24 |
| 12 L.H., Daily Totals | | $1882.40 | | $2255.86 | $156.87 | $187.99 |

**Crew B-10D**

| | Hr. | Daily | Hr. | Daily | Bare Costs | Incl. O&P |
|---|---|---|---|---|---|---|
| 1 Equip. Oper. (med.) | $39.85 | $318.80 | $60.10 | $480.80 | $36.65 | $55.75 |
| .5 Laborer | 30.25 | 121.00 | 47.05 | 188.20 | | |
| 1 Dozer, 200 H.P. | | 1071.00 | | 1178.10 | | |
| 1 Sheepsft. Roller, Towed | | 397.60 | | 437.36 | 122.38 | 134.62 |
| 12 L.H., Daily Totals | | $1908.40 | | $2284.46 | $159.03 | $190.37 |

**Crew B-10E**

| | Hr. | Daily | Hr. | Daily | Bare Costs | Incl. O&P |
|---|---|---|---|---|---|---|
| 1 Equip. Oper. (med.) | $39.85 | $318.80 | $60.10 | $480.80 | $36.65 | $55.75 |
| .5 Laborer | 30.25 | 121.00 | 47.05 | 188.20 | | |
| 1 Tandem Roller, 5 Ton | | 130.20 | | 143.22 | 10.85 | 11.94 |
| 12 L.H., Daily Totals | | $570.00 | | $812.22 | $47.50 | $67.69 |

**Crew B-10F**

| | Hr. | Daily | Hr. | Daily | Bare Costs | Incl. O&P |
|---|---|---|---|---|---|---|
| 1 Equip. Oper. (med.) | $39.85 | $318.80 | $60.10 | $480.80 | $36.65 | $55.75 |
| .5 Laborer | 30.25 | 121.00 | 47.05 | 188.20 | | |
| 1 Tandem Roller, 10 Ton | | 219.00 | | 240.90 | 18.25 | 20.07 |
| 12 L.H., Daily Totals | | $658.80 | | $909.90 | $54.90 | $75.83 |

**Crew B-10G**

| | Hr. | Daily | Hr. | Daily | Bare Costs | Incl. O&P |
|---|---|---|---|---|---|---|
| 1 Equip. Oper. (med.) | $39.85 | $318.80 | $60.10 | $480.80 | $36.65 | $55.75 |
| .5 Laborer | 30.25 | 121.00 | 47.05 | 188.20 | | |
| 1 Sheepsft. Roll., 130 H.P. | | 1006.00 | | 1106.60 | 83.83 | 92.22 |
| 12 L.H., Daily Totals | | $1445.80 | | $1775.60 | $120.48 | $147.97 |

**Crew B-10H**

| | Hr. | Daily | Hr. | Daily | Bare Costs | Incl. O&P |
|---|---|---|---|---|---|---|
| 1 Equip. Oper. (med.) | $39.85 | $318.80 | $60.10 | $480.80 | $36.65 | $55.75 |
| .5 Laborer | 30.25 | 121.00 | 47.05 | 188.20 | | |
| 1 Diaphragm Water Pump, 2" | | 61.40 | | 67.54 | | |
| 1 -20' Suction Hose, 2" | | 1.95 | | 2.15 | | |
| 2 -50' Discharge Hose, 2" | | 2.20 | | 2.42 | 5.46 | 6.01 |
| 12 L.H., Daily Totals | | $505.35 | | $741.11 | $42.11 | $61.76 |

**Crew B-10I**

| | Hr. | Daily | Hr. | Daily | Bare Costs | Incl. O&P |
|---|---|---|---|---|---|---|
| 1 Equip. Oper. (med.) | $39.85 | $318.80 | $60.10 | $480.80 | $36.65 | $55.75 |
| .5 Laborer | 30.25 | 121.00 | 47.05 | 188.20 | | |
| 1 Diaphragm Water Pump, 4" | | 84.40 | | 92.84 | | |
| 1 -20' Suction Hose, 4" | | 3.45 | | 3.79 | | |
| 2 -50' Discharge Hose, 4" | | 4.70 | | 5.17 | 7.71 | 8.48 |
| 12 L.H., Daily Totals | | $532.35 | | $770.80 | $44.36 | $64.23 |

**Crew B-10J**

| | Hr. | Daily | Hr. | Daily | Bare Costs | Incl. O&P |
|---|---|---|---|---|---|---|
| 1 Equip. Oper. (med.) | $39.85 | $318.80 | $60.10 | $480.80 | $36.65 | $55.75 |
| .5 Laborer | 30.25 | 121.00 | 47.05 | 188.20 | | |
| 1 Centrifugal Water Pump, 3" | | 67.60 | | 74.36 | | |
| 1 -20' Suction Hose, 3" | | 3.05 | | 3.36 | | |
| 2 -50' Discharge Hose, 3" | | 3.50 | | 3.85 | 6.18 | 6.80 |
| 12 L.H., Daily Totals | | $513.95 | | $750.57 | $42.83 | $62.55 |

| Crew No. | Bare Costs | | Incl. Subs O & P | | Cost Per Labor-Hour | |

**Crew B-10K**

| | Hr. | Daily | Hr. | Daily | Bare Costs | Incl. O&P |
|---|---|---|---|---|---|---|
| 1 Equip. Oper. (med.) | $39.85 | $318.80 | $60.10 | $480.80 | $36.65 | $55.75 |
| .5 Laborer | 30.25 | 121.00 | 47.05 | 188.20 | | |
| 1 Centr. Water Pump, 6" | | 305.20 | | 335.72 | | |
| 1 -20' Suction Hose, 6" | | 11.90 | | 13.09 | | |
| 2 -50' Discharge Hose, 6" | | 12.60 | | 13.86 | 27.48 | 30.22 |
| 12 L.H., Daily Totals | | $769.50 | | $1031.67 | $64.13 | $85.97 |

**Crew B-10L**

| | Hr. | Daily | Hr. | Daily | Bare Costs | Incl. O&P |
|---|---|---|---|---|---|---|
| 1 Equip. Oper. (med.) | $39.85 | $318.80 | $60.10 | $480.80 | $36.65 | $55.75 |
| .5 Laborer | 30.25 | 121.00 | 47.05 | 188.20 | | |
| 1 Dozer, 80 H.P. | | 379.40 | | 417.34 | 31.62 | 34.78 |
| 12 L.H., Daily Totals | | $819.20 | | $1086.34 | $68.27 | $90.53 |

**Crew B-10M**

| | Hr. | Daily | Hr. | Daily | Bare Costs | Incl. O&P |
|---|---|---|---|---|---|---|
| 1 Equip. Oper. (med.) | $39.85 | $318.80 | $60.10 | $480.80 | $36.65 | $55.75 |
| .5 Laborer | 30.25 | 121.00 | 47.05 | 188.20 | | |
| 1 Dozer, 300 H.P. | | 1388.00 | | 1526.80 | 115.67 | 127.23 |
| 12 L.H., Daily Totals | | $1827.80 | | $2195.80 | $152.32 | $182.98 |

**Crew B-10N**

| | Hr. | Daily | Hr. | Daily | Bare Costs | Incl. O&P |
|---|---|---|---|---|---|---|
| 1 Equip. Oper. (med.) | $39.85 | $318.80 | $60.10 | $480.80 | $36.65 | $55.75 |
| .5 Laborer | 30.25 | 121.00 | 47.05 | 188.20 | | |
| 1 F.E. Loader, T.M., 1.5 C.Y | | 357.20 | | 392.92 | 29.77 | 32.74 |
| 12 L.H., Daily Totals | | $797.00 | | $1061.92 | $66.42 | $88.49 |

**Crew B-10O**

| | Hr. | Daily | Hr. | Daily | Bare Costs | Incl. O&P |
|---|---|---|---|---|---|---|
| 1 Equip. Oper. (med.) | $39.85 | $318.80 | $60.10 | $480.80 | $36.65 | $55.75 |
| .5 Laborer | 30.25 | 121.00 | 47.05 | 188.20 | | |
| 1 F.E. Loader, T.M., 2.25 C.Y. | | 635.20 | | 698.72 | 52.93 | 58.23 |
| 12 L.H., Daily Totals | | $1075.00 | | $1367.72 | $89.58 | $113.98 |

**Crew B-10P**

| | Hr. | Daily | Hr. | Daily | Bare Costs | Incl. O&P |
|---|---|---|---|---|---|---|
| 1 Equip. Oper. (med.) | $39.85 | $318.80 | $60.10 | $480.80 | $36.65 | $55.75 |
| .5 Laborer | 30.25 | 121.00 | 47.05 | 188.20 | | |
| 1 Crawler Loader, 3 C.Y. | | 893.40 | | 982.74 | 74.45 | 81.89 |
| 12 L.H., Daily Totals | | $1333.20 | | $1651.74 | $111.10 | $137.65 |

**Crew B-10Q**

| | Hr. | Daily | Hr. | Daily | Bare Costs | Incl. O&P |
|---|---|---|---|---|---|---|
| 1 Equip. Oper. (med.) | $39.85 | $318.80 | $60.10 | $480.80 | $36.65 | $55.75 |
| .5 Laborer | 30.25 | 121.00 | 47.05 | 188.20 | | |
| 1 Crawler Loader, 4 C.Y. | | 1242.00 | | 1366.20 | 103.50 | 113.85 |
| 12 L.H., Daily Totals | | $1681.80 | | $2035.20 | $140.15 | $169.60 |

**Crew B-10R**

| | Hr. | Daily | Hr. | Daily | Bare Costs | Incl. O&P |
|---|---|---|---|---|---|---|
| 1 Equip. Oper. (med.) | $39.85 | $318.80 | $60.10 | $480.80 | $36.65 | $55.75 |
| .5 Laborer | 30.25 | 121.00 | 47.05 | 188.20 | | |
| 1 F.E. Loader, W.M., 1 C.Y. | | 226.40 | | 249.04 | 18.87 | 20.75 |
| 12 L.H., Daily Totals | | $666.20 | | $918.04 | $55.52 | $76.50 |

**Crew B-10S**

| | Hr. | Daily | Hr. | Daily | Bare Costs | Incl. O&P |
|---|---|---|---|---|---|---|
| 1 Equip. Oper. (med.) | $39.85 | $318.80 | $60.10 | $480.80 | $36.65 | $55.75 |
| .5 Laborer | 30.25 | 121.00 | 47.05 | 188.20 | | |
| 1 F.E. Loader, W.M., 1.5 C.Y. | | 302.80 | | 333.08 | 25.23 | 27.76 |
| 12 L.H., Daily Totals | | $742.60 | | $1002.08 | $61.88 | $83.51 |

**Crew B-10T**

| | Hr. | Daily | Hr. | Daily | Bare Costs | Incl. O&P |
|---|---|---|---|---|---|---|
| 1 Equip. Oper. (med.) | $39.85 | $318.80 | $60.10 | $480.80 | $36.65 | $55.75 |
| .5 Laborer | 30.25 | 121.00 | 47.05 | 188.20 | | |
| 1 F.E. Loader, W.M., 2.5 C.Y. | | 386.40 | | 425.04 | 32.20 | 35.42 |
| 12 L.H., Daily Totals | | $826.20 | | $1094.04 | $68.85 | $91.17 |

| Crew No. | Bare Costs | | Incl. Subs O & P | | Cost Per Labor-Hour | |
|---|---|---|---|---|---|---|

**Crew B-10U**

| Crew B-10U | Hr. | Daily | Hr. | Daily | Bare Costs | Incl. O&P |
|---|---|---|---|---|---|---|
| 1 Equip. Oper. (med.) | $39.85 | $318.80 | $60.10 | $480.80 | $36.65 | $55.75 |
| .5 Laborer | 30.25 | 121.00 | 47.05 | 188.20 | | |
| 1 F.E. Loader, W.M., 5.5 C.Y. | | 826.80 | | 909.48 | 68.90 | 75.79 |
| 12 L.H., Daily Totals | | $1266.60 | | $1578.48 | $105.55 | $131.54 |

| Crew B-10V | Hr. | Daily | Hr. | Daily | Bare Costs | Incl. O&P |
|---|---|---|---|---|---|---|
| 1 Equip. Oper. (med.) | $39.85 | $318.80 | $60.10 | $480.80 | $36.65 | $55.75 |
| .5 Laborer | 30.25 | 121.00 | 47.05 | 188.20 | | |
| 1 Dozer, 700 H.P. | | 3682.00 | | 4050.20 | 306.83 | 337.52 |
| 12 L.H., Daily Totals | | $4121.80 | | $4719.20 | $343.48 | $393.27 |

| Crew B-10W | Hr. | Daily | Hr. | Daily | Bare Costs | Incl. O&P |
|---|---|---|---|---|---|---|
| 1 Equip. Oper. (med.) | $39.85 | $318.80 | $60.10 | $480.80 | $36.65 | $55.75 |
| .5 Laborer | 30.25 | 121.00 | 47.05 | 188.20 | | |
| 1 Dozer, 105 H.P. | | 532.40 | | 585.64 | 44.37 | 48.80 |
| 12 L.H., Daily Totals | | $972.20 | | $1254.64 | $81.02 | $104.55 |

| Crew B-10X | Hr. | Daily | Hr. | Daily | Bare Costs | Incl. O&P |
|---|---|---|---|---|---|---|
| 1 Equip. Oper. (med.) | $39.85 | $318.80 | $60.10 | $480.80 | $36.65 | $55.75 |
| .5 Laborer | 30.25 | 121.00 | 47.05 | 188.20 | | |
| 1 Dozer, 410 H.P. | | 1817.00 | | 1998.70 | 151.42 | 166.56 |
| 12 L.H., Daily Totals | | $2256.80 | | $2667.70 | $188.07 | $222.31 |

| Crew B-10Y | Hr. | Daily | Hr. | Daily | Bare Costs | Incl. O&P |
|---|---|---|---|---|---|---|
| 1 Equip. Oper. (med.) | $39.85 | $318.80 | $60.10 | $480.80 | $36.65 | $55.75 |
| .5 Laborer | 30.25 | 121.00 | 47.05 | 188.20 | | |
| 1 Vibr. Roller, Towed, 12 Ton | | 470.40 | | 517.44 | 39.20 | 43.12 |
| 12 L.H., Daily Totals | | $910.20 | | $1186.44 | $75.85 | $98.87 |

| Crew B-11A | Hr. | Daily | Hr. | Daily | Bare Costs | Incl. O&P |
|---|---|---|---|---|---|---|
| 1 Equipment Oper. (med.) | $39.85 | $318.80 | $60.10 | $480.80 | $35.05 | $53.58 |
| 1 Laborer | 30.25 | 242.00 | 47.05 | 376.40 | | |
| 1 Dozer, 200 H.P. | | 1071.00 | | 1178.10 | 66.94 | 73.63 |
| 16 L.H., Daily Totals | | $1631.80 | | $2035.30 | $101.99 | $127.21 |

| Crew B-11B | Hr. | Daily | Hr. | Daily | Bare Costs | Incl. O&P |
|---|---|---|---|---|---|---|
| 1 Equipment Oper. (light) | $37.75 | $302.00 | $56.95 | $455.60 | $34.00 | $52.00 |
| 1 Laborer | 30.25 | 242.00 | 47.05 | 376.40 | | |
| 1 Air Powered Tamper | | 23.05 | | 25.36 | | |
| 1 Air Compressor, 365 C.F.M. | | 211.80 | | 232.98 | | |
| 2 -50' Air Hose, 1.5" | | 12.60 | | 13.86 | 15.47 | 17.01 |
| 16 L.H., Daily Totals | | $791.45 | | $1104.19 | $49.47 | $69.01 |

| Crew B-11C | Hr. | Daily | Hr. | Daily | Bare Costs | Incl. O&P |
|---|---|---|---|---|---|---|
| 1 Equipment Oper. (med.) | $39.85 | $318.80 | $60.10 | $480.80 | $35.05 | $53.58 |
| 1 Laborer | 30.25 | 242.00 | 47.05 | 376.40 | | |
| 1 Backhoe Loader, 48 H.P. | | 285.40 | | 313.94 | 17.84 | 19.62 |
| 16 L.H., Daily Totals | | $846.20 | | $1171.14 | $52.89 | $73.20 |

| Crew B-11J | Hr. | Daily | Hr. | Daily | Bare Costs | Incl. O&P |
|---|---|---|---|---|---|---|
| 1 Equipment Oper. (med.) | $39.85 | $318.80 | $60.10 | $480.80 | $35.05 | $53.58 |
| 1 Laborer | 30.25 | 242.00 | 47.05 | 376.40 | | |
| 1 Grader, 30,000 Lbs. | | 534.40 | | 587.84 | | |
| 1 Ripper, beam & 1 shank | | 77.80 | | 85.58 | 38.26 | 42.09 |
| 16 L.H., Daily Totals | | $1173.00 | | $1530.62 | $73.31 | $95.66 |

| Crew B-11K | Hr. | Daily | Hr. | Daily | Bare Costs | Incl. O&P |
|---|---|---|---|---|---|---|
| 1 Equipment Oper. (med.) | $39.85 | $318.80 | $60.10 | $480.80 | $35.05 | $53.58 |
| 1 Laborer | 30.25 | 242.00 | 47.05 | 376.40 | | |
| 1 Trencher, Chain Type, 8' D | | 1736.00 | | 1909.60 | 108.50 | 119.35 |
| 16 L.H., Daily Totals | | $2296.80 | | $2766.80 | $143.55 | $172.93 |

| Crew B-11L | Hr. | Daily | Hr. | Daily | Bare Costs | Incl. O&P |
|---|---|---|---|---|---|---|
| 1 Equipment Oper. (med.) | $39.85 | $318.80 | $60.10 | $480.80 | $35.05 | $53.58 |
| 1 Laborer | 30.25 | 242.00 | 47.05 | 376.40 | | |
| 1 Grader, 30,000 Lbs. | | 534.40 | | 587.84 | 33.40 | 36.74 |
| 16 L.H., Daily Totals | | $1095.20 | | $1445.04 | $68.45 | $90.31 |

| Crew B-11M | Hr. | Daily | Hr. | Daily | Bare Costs | Incl. O&P |
|---|---|---|---|---|---|---|
| 1 Equipment Oper. (med.) | $39.85 | $318.80 | $60.10 | $480.80 | $35.05 | $53.58 |
| 1 Laborer | 30.25 | 242.00 | 47.05 | 376.40 | | |
| 1 Backhoe Loader, 80 H.P. | | 340.80 | | 374.88 | 21.30 | 23.43 |
| 16 L.H., Daily Totals | | $901.60 | | $1232.08 | $56.35 | $77.00 |

| Crew B-11N | Hr. | Daily | Hr. | Daily | Bare Costs | Incl. O&P |
|---|---|---|---|---|---|---|
| 1 Labor Foreman | $32.25 | $258.00 | $50.20 | $401.60 | $32.84 | $50.50 |
| 2 Equipment Operators (med.) | 39.85 | 637.60 | 60.10 | 961.60 | | |
| 6 Truck Drivers (hvy.) | 30.60 | 1468.80 | 47.35 | 2272.80 | | |
| 1 F.E. Loader, W.M., 5.5 C.Y. | | 826.80 | | 909.48 | | |
| 1 Dozer, 410 H.P. | | 1817.00 | | 1998.70 | | |
| 6 Dump Truck, Off Hwy., 50 Ton | | 8556.00 | | 9411.60 | 155.55 | 171.11 |
| 72 L.H., Daily Totals | | $13564.20 | | $15955.78 | $188.39 | $221.61 |

| Crew B-11Q | Hr. | Daily | Hr. | Daily | Bare Costs | Incl. O&P |
|---|---|---|---|---|---|---|
| 1 Equipment Operator (med.) | $39.85 | $318.80 | $60.10 | $480.80 | $36.65 | $55.75 |
| .5 Laborer | 30.25 | 121.00 | 47.05 | 188.20 | | |
| 1 Dozer, 140 H.P. | | 664.40 | | 730.84 | 55.37 | 60.90 |
| 12 L.H., Daily Totals | | $1104.20 | | $1399.84 | $92.02 | $116.65 |

| Crew B-11R | Hr. | Daily | Hr. | Daily | Bare Costs | Incl. O&P |
|---|---|---|---|---|---|---|
| 1 Equipment Operator (med.) | $39.85 | $318.80 | $60.10 | $480.80 | $36.65 | $55.75 |
| .5 Laborer | 30.25 | 121.00 | 47.05 | 188.20 | | |
| 1 Dozer, 200 H.P. | | 1071.00 | | 1178.10 | 89.25 | 98.17 |
| 12 L.H., Daily Totals | | $1510.80 | | $1847.10 | $125.90 | $153.93 |

| Crew B-11S | Hr. | Daily | Hr. | Daily | Bare Costs | Incl. O&P |
|---|---|---|---|---|---|---|
| 1 Equipment Operator (med.) | $39.85 | $318.80 | $60.10 | $480.80 | $36.65 | $55.75 |
| .5 Laborer | 30.25 | 121.00 | 47.05 | 188.20 | | |
| 1 Dozer, 300 H.P. | | 1388.00 | | 1526.80 | | |
| 1 Ripper, beam & 1 shank | | 77.80 | | 85.58 | 122.15 | 134.37 |
| 12 L.H., Daily Totals | | $1905.60 | | $2281.38 | $158.80 | $190.12 |

| Crew B-11T | Hr. | Daily | Hr. | Daily | Bare Costs | Incl. O&P |
|---|---|---|---|---|---|---|
| 1 Equipment Operator (med.) | $39.85 | $318.80 | $60.10 | $480.80 | $36.65 | $55.75 |
| .5 Laborer | 30.25 | 121.00 | 47.05 | 188.20 | | |
| 1 Dozer, 410 H.P. | | 1817.00 | | 1998.70 | | |
| 1 Ripper, beam & 2 shanks | | 88.00 | | 96.80 | 158.75 | 174.63 |
| 12 L.H., Daily Totals | | $2344.80 | | $2764.50 | $195.40 | $230.38 |

| Crew B-11U | Hr. | Daily | Hr. | Daily | Bare Costs | Incl. O&P |
|---|---|---|---|---|---|---|
| 1 Equipment Operator (med.) | $39.85 | $318.80 | $60.10 | $480.80 | $36.65 | $55.75 |
| .5 Laborer | 30.25 | 121.00 | 47.05 | 188.20 | | |
| 1 Dozer, 520 H.P. | | 2430.00 | | 2673.00 | 202.50 | 222.75 |
| 12 L.H., Daily Totals | | $2869.80 | | $3342.00 | $239.15 | $278.50 |

# Crews

| Crew No. | Bare Costs | | Incl. Subs O & P | | Cost Per Labor-Hour | |
|---|---|---|---|---|---|---|

**Crew B-11V**

| | Hr. | Daily | Hr. | Daily | Bare Costs | Incl. O&P |
|---|---|---|---|---|---|---|
| 3 Laborers | $30.25 | $726.00 | $47.05 | $1129.20 | $30.25 | $47.05 |
| 1 Roller, 2-Drum, W.B., 7.5 HP | | 143.00 | | 157.30 | 5.96 | 6.55 |
| 24 L.H., Daily Totals | | $869.00 | | $1286.50 | $36.21 | $53.60 |

**Crew B-11W**

| | Hr. | Daily | Hr. | Daily | Bare Costs | Incl. O&P |
|---|---|---|---|---|---|---|
| 1 Equipment Operator (med.) | $39.85 | $318.80 | $60.10 | $480.80 | $31.34 | $48.39 |
| 1 Common Laborer | 30.25 | 242.00 | 47.05 | 376.40 | | |
| 10 Truck Drivers (hvy.) | 30.60 | 2448.00 | 47.35 | 3788.00 | | |
| 1 Dozer, 200 H.P. | | 1071.00 | | 1178.10 | | |
| 1 Vibratory Roller, Towed, 23 Ton | | 371.60 | | 408.76 | | |
| 10 Dump Truck, 8 C.Y., 220 H.P. | | 3086.00 | | 3394.60 | 47.17 | 51.89 |
| 96 L.H., Daily Totals | | $7537.40 | | $9626.66 | $78.51 | $100.28 |

**Crew B-11Y**

| | Hr. | Daily | Hr. | Daily | Bare Costs | Incl. O&P |
|---|---|---|---|---|---|---|
| 1 Labor Foreman (Outside) | $32.25 | $258.00 | $50.20 | $401.60 | $33.67 | $51.75 |
| 5 Common Laborers | 30.25 | 1210.00 | 47.05 | 1882.00 | | |
| 3 Equipment Operators (med.) | 39.85 | 956.40 | 60.10 | 1442.40 | | |
| 1 Dozer, 80 H.P. | | 379.40 | | 417.34 | | |
| 2 Roller, 2-Drum, W.B., 7.5 HP | | 286.00 | | 314.60 | | |
| 4 Vibratory Plate, Gas, 21" | | 153.60 | | 168.96 | 11.38 | 12.51 |
| 72 L.H., Daily Totals | | $3243.40 | | $4626.90 | $45.05 | $64.26 |

**Crew B-12A**

| | Hr. | Daily | Hr. | Daily | Bare Costs | Incl. O&P |
|---|---|---|---|---|---|---|
| 1 Equip. Oper. (crane) | $40.95 | $327.60 | $61.75 | $494.00 | $35.60 | $54.40 |
| 1 Laborer | 30.25 | 242.00 | 47.05 | 376.40 | | |
| 1 Hyd. Excavator, 1 C.Y. | | 646.60 | | 711.26 | 40.41 | 44.45 |
| 16 L.H., Daily Totals | | $1216.20 | | $1581.66 | $76.01 | $98.85 |

**Crew B-12B**

| | Hr. | Daily | Hr. | Daily | Bare Costs | Incl. O&P |
|---|---|---|---|---|---|---|
| 1 Equip. Oper. (crane) | $40.95 | $327.60 | $61.75 | $494.00 | $35.60 | $54.40 |
| 1 Laborer | 30.25 | 242.00 | 47.05 | 376.40 | | |
| 1 Hyd. Excavator, 1.5 C.Y. | | 830.00 | | 913.00 | 51.88 | 57.06 |
| 16 L.H., Daily Totals | | $1399.60 | | $1783.40 | $87.47 | $111.46 |

**Crew B-12C**

| | Hr. | Daily | Hr. | Daily | Bare Costs | Incl. O&P |
|---|---|---|---|---|---|---|
| 1 Equip. Oper. (crane) | $40.95 | $327.60 | $61.75 | $494.00 | $35.60 | $54.40 |
| 1 Laborer | 30.25 | 242.00 | 47.05 | 376.40 | | |
| 1 Hyd. Excavator, 2 C.Y. | | 1060.00 | | 1166.00 | 66.25 | 72.88 |
| 16 L.H., Daily Totals | | $1629.60 | | $2036.40 | $101.85 | $127.28 |

**Crew B-12D**

| | Hr. | Daily | Hr. | Daily | Bare Costs | Incl. O&P |
|---|---|---|---|---|---|---|
| 1 Equip. Oper. (crane) | $40.95 | $327.60 | $61.75 | $494.00 | $35.60 | $54.40 |
| 1 Laborer | 30.25 | 242.00 | 47.05 | 376.40 | | |
| 1 Hyd. Excavator, 3.5 C.Y. | | 2337.00 | | 2570.70 | 146.06 | 160.67 |
| 16 L.H., Daily Totals | | $2906.60 | | $3441.10 | $181.66 | $215.07 |

**Crew B-12E**

| | Hr. | Daily | Hr. | Daily | Bare Costs | Incl. O&P |
|---|---|---|---|---|---|---|
| 1 Equip. Oper. (crane) | $40.95 | $327.60 | $61.75 | $494.00 | $35.60 | $54.40 |
| 1 Laborer | 30.25 | 242.00 | 47.05 | 376.40 | | |
| 1 Hyd. Excavator, .5 C.Y. | | 382.00 | | 420.20 | 23.88 | 26.26 |
| 16 L.H., Daily Totals | | $951.60 | | $1290.60 | $59.48 | $80.66 |

**Crew B-12F**

| | Hr. | Daily | Hr. | Daily | Bare Costs | Incl. O&P |
|---|---|---|---|---|---|---|
| 1 Equip. Oper. (crane) | $40.95 | $327.60 | $61.75 | $494.00 | $35.60 | $54.40 |
| 1 Laborer | 30.25 | 242.00 | 47.05 | 376.40 | | |
| 1 Hyd. Excavator, .75 C.Y. | | 549.40 | | 604.34 | 34.34 | 37.77 |
| 16 L.H., Daily Totals | | $1119.00 | | $1474.74 | $69.94 | $92.17 |

**Crew B-12G**

| | Hr. | Daily | Hr. | Daily | Bare Costs | Incl. O&P |
|---|---|---|---|---|---|---|
| 1 Equip. Oper. (crane) | $40.95 | $327.60 | $61.75 | $494.00 | $35.60 | $54.40 |
| 1 Laborer | 30.25 | 242.00 | 47.05 | 376.40 | | |
| 1 Crawler Crane, 15 Ton | | 605.45 | | 666.00 | | |
| 1 Clamshell Bucket, .5 C.Y. | | 35.60 | | 39.16 | 40.07 | 44.07 |
| 16 L.H., Daily Totals | | $1210.65 | | $1575.56 | $75.67 | $98.47 |

**Crew B-12H**

| | Hr. | Daily | Hr. | Daily | Bare Costs | Incl. O&P |
|---|---|---|---|---|---|---|
| 1 Equip. Oper. (crane) | $40.95 | $327.60 | $61.75 | $494.00 | $35.60 | $54.40 |
| 1 Laborer | 30.25 | 242.00 | 47.05 | 376.40 | | |
| 1 Crawler Crane, 25 Ton | | 1033.00 | | 1136.30 | | |
| 1 Clamshell Bucket, 1 C.Y. | | 46.20 | | 50.82 | 67.45 | 74.19 |
| 16 L.H., Daily Totals | | $1648.80 | | $2057.52 | $103.05 | $128.60 |

**Crew B-12I**

| | Hr. | Daily | Hr. | Daily | Bare Costs | Incl. O&P |
|---|---|---|---|---|---|---|
| 1 Equip. Oper. (crane) | $40.95 | $327.60 | $61.75 | $494.00 | $35.60 | $54.40 |
| 1 Laborer | 30.25 | 242.00 | 47.05 | 376.40 | | |
| 1 Crawler Crane, 20 Ton | | 775.30 | | 852.83 | | |
| 1 Dragline Bucket, .75 C.Y. | | 19.80 | | 21.78 | 49.69 | 54.66 |
| 16 L.H., Daily Totals | | $1364.70 | | $1745.01 | $85.29 | $109.06 |

**Crew B-12J**

| | Hr. | Daily | Hr. | Daily | Bare Costs | Incl. O&P |
|---|---|---|---|---|---|---|
| 1 Equip. Oper. (crane) | $40.95 | $327.60 | $61.75 | $494.00 | $35.60 | $54.40 |
| 1 Laborer | 30.25 | 242.00 | 47.05 | 376.40 | | |
| 1 Gradall, 5/8 C.Y. | | 932.60 | | 1025.86 | 58.29 | 64.12 |
| 16 L.H., Daily Totals | | $1502.20 | | $1896.26 | $93.89 | $118.52 |

**Crew B-12K**

| | Hr. | Daily | Hr. | Daily | Bare Costs | Incl. O&P |
|---|---|---|---|---|---|---|
| 1 Equip. Oper. (crane) | $40.95 | $327.60 | $61.75 | $494.00 | $35.60 | $54.40 |
| 1 Laborer | 30.25 | 242.00 | 47.05 | 376.40 | | |
| 1 Gradall, 3 Ton, 1 C.Y. | | 1089.00 | | 1197.90 | 68.06 | 74.87 |
| 16 L.H., Daily Totals | | $1658.60 | | $2068.30 | $103.66 | $129.27 |

**Crew B-12L**

| | Hr. | Daily | Hr. | Daily | Bare Costs | Incl. O&P |
|---|---|---|---|---|---|---|
| 1 Equip. Oper. (crane) | $40.95 | $327.60 | $61.75 | $494.00 | $35.60 | $54.40 |
| 1 Laborer | 30.25 | 242.00 | 47.05 | 376.40 | | |
| 1 Crawler Crane, 15 Ton | | 605.45 | | 666.00 | | |
| 1 F.E. Attachment, .5 C.Y. | | 51.00 | | 56.10 | 41.03 | 45.13 |
| 16 L.H., Daily Totals | | $1226.05 | | $1592.49 | $76.63 | $99.53 |

**Crew B-12M**

| | Hr. | Daily | Hr. | Daily | Bare Costs | Incl. O&P |
|---|---|---|---|---|---|---|
| 1 Equip. Oper. (crane) | $40.95 | $327.60 | $61.75 | $494.00 | $35.60 | $54.40 |
| 1 Laborer | 30.25 | 242.00 | 47.05 | 376.40 | | |
| 1 Crawler Crane, 20 Ton | | 775.30 | | 852.83 | | |
| 1 F.E. Attachment, .75 C.Y. | | 56.40 | | 62.04 | 51.98 | 57.18 |
| 16 L.H., Daily Totals | | $1401.30 | | $1785.27 | $87.58 | $111.58 |

**Crew B-12N**

| | Hr. | Daily | Hr. | Daily | Bare Costs | Incl. O&P |
|---|---|---|---|---|---|---|
| 1 Equip. Oper. (crane) | $40.95 | $327.60 | $61.75 | $494.00 | $35.60 | $54.40 |
| 1 Laborer | 30.25 | 242.00 | 47.05 | 376.40 | | |
| 1 Crawler Crane, 25 Ton | | 1033.00 | | 1136.30 | | |
| 1 F.E. Attachment, 1 C.Y. | | 62.20 | | 68.42 | 68.45 | 75.30 |
| 16 L.H., Daily Totals | | $1664.80 | | $2075.12 | $104.05 | $129.69 |

**Crew B-12O**

| | Hr. | Daily | Hr. | Daily | Bare Costs | Incl. O&P |
|---|---|---|---|---|---|---|
| 1 Equip. Oper. (crane) | $40.95 | $327.60 | $61.75 | $494.00 | $35.60 | $54.40 |
| 1 Laborer | 30.25 | 242.00 | 47.05 | 376.40 | | |
| 1 Crawler Crane, 40 Ton | | 1054.00 | | 1159.40 | | |
| 1 F.E. Attachment, 1.5 C.Y. | | 71.40 | | 78.54 | 70.34 | 77.37 |
| 16 L.H., Daily Totals | | $1695.00 | | $2108.34 | $105.94 | $131.77 |

637

| Crew No. | Bare Costs | | Incl. Subs O & P | | Cost Per Labor-Hour | |
|---|---|---|---|---|---|---|
| | Hr. | Daily | Hr. | Daily | Bare Costs | Incl. O&P |
| **Crew B-12P** | | | | | | |
| 1 Equip. Oper. (crane) | $40.95 | $327.60 | $61.75 | $494.00 | $35.60 | $54.40 |
| 1 Laborer | 30.25 | 242.00 | 47.05 | 376.40 | | |
| 1 Crawler Crane, 40 Ton | | 1054.00 | | 1159.40 | | |
| 1 Dragline Bucket, 1.5 C.Y. | | 32.40 | | 35.64 | 67.90 | 74.69 |
| 16 L.H., Daily Totals | | $1656.00 | | $2065.44 | $103.50 | $129.09 |
| **Crew B-12Q** | | | | | Bare Costs | Incl. O&P |
| 1 Equip. Oper. (crane) | $40.95 | $327.60 | $61.75 | $494.00 | $35.60 | $54.40 |
| 1 Laborer | 30.25 | 242.00 | 47.05 | 376.40 | | |
| 1 Hyd. Excavator, 5/8 C.Y. | | 497.40 | | 547.14 | 31.09 | 34.20 |
| 16 L.H., Daily Totals | | $1067.00 | | $1417.54 | $66.69 | $88.60 |
| **Crew B-12R** | | | | | Bare Costs | Incl. O&P |
| 1 Equip. Oper. (crane) | $40.95 | $327.60 | $61.75 | $494.00 | $35.60 | $54.40 |
| 1 Laborer | 30.25 | 242.00 | 47.05 | 376.40 | | |
| 1 Hyd. Excavator, 1.5 C.Y. | | 830.00 | | 913.00 | 51.88 | 57.06 |
| 16 L.H., Daily Totals | | $1399.60 | | $1783.40 | $87.47 | $111.46 |
| **Crew B-12S** | | | | | Bare Costs | Incl. O&P |
| 1 Equip. Oper. (crane) | $40.95 | $327.60 | $61.75 | $494.00 | $35.60 | $54.40 |
| 1 Laborer | 30.25 | 242.00 | 47.05 | 376.40 | | |
| 1 Hyd. Excavator, 2.5 C.Y. | | 1466.00 | | 1612.60 | 91.63 | 100.79 |
| 16 L.H., Daily Totals | | $2035.60 | | $2483.00 | $127.22 | $155.19 |
| **Crew B-12T** | | | | | Bare Costs | Incl. O&P |
| 1 Equip. Oper. (crane) | $40.95 | $327.60 | $61.75 | $494.00 | $35.60 | $54.40 |
| 1 Laborer | 30.25 | 242.00 | 47.05 | 376.40 | | |
| 1 Crawler Crane, 75 Ton | | 1483.00 | | 1631.30 | | |
| 1 F.E. Attachment, 3 C.Y. | | 94.80 | | 104.28 | 98.61 | 108.47 |
| 16 L.H., Daily Totals | | $2147.40 | | $2605.98 | $134.21 | $162.87 |
| **Crew B-12V** | | | | | Bare Costs | Incl. O&P |
| 1 Equip. Oper. (crane) | $40.95 | $327.60 | $61.75 | $494.00 | $35.60 | $54.40 |
| 1 Laborer | 30.25 | 242.00 | 47.05 | 376.40 | | |
| 1 Crawler Crane, 75 Ton | | 1483.00 | | 1631.30 | | |
| 1 Dragline Bucket, 3 C.Y. | | 45.80 | | 50.38 | 95.55 | 105.11 |
| 16 L.H., Daily Totals | | $2098.40 | | $2552.08 | $131.15 | $159.51 |
| **Crew B-13** | | | | | Bare Costs | Incl. O&P |
| 1 Labor Foreman (outside) | $32.25 | $258.00 | $50.20 | $401.60 | $32.76 | $50.44 |
| 4 Laborers | 30.25 | 968.00 | 47.05 | 1505.60 | | |
| 1 Equip. Oper. (crane) | 40.95 | 327.60 | 61.75 | 494.00 | | |
| 1 Equip. Oper. Oiler | 35.10 | 280.80 | 52.95 | 423.60 | | |
| 1 Hyd. Crane, 25 Ton | | 786.00 | | 864.60 | 14.04 | 15.44 |
| 56 L.H., Daily Totals | | $2620.40 | | $3689.40 | $46.79 | $65.88 |
| **Crew B-13A** | | | | | Bare Costs | Incl. O&P |
| 1 Foreman | $32.25 | $258.00 | $50.20 | $401.60 | $33.38 | $51.31 |
| 2 Laborers | 30.25 | 484.00 | 47.05 | 752.80 | | |
| 2 Equipment Operators | 39.85 | 637.60 | 60.10 | 961.60 | | |
| 2 Truck Drivers (heavy) | 30.60 | 489.60 | 47.35 | 757.60 | | |
| 1 Crawler Crane, 75 Ton | | 1483.00 | | 1631.30 | | |
| 1 Crawler Loader, 4 C.Y. | | 1242.00 | | 1366.20 | | |
| 2 Dump Truck, 8 C.Y., 220 H.P. | | 617.20 | | 678.92 | 59.68 | 65.65 |
| 56 L.H., Daily Totals | | $5211.40 | | $6550.02 | $93.06 | $116.96 |

| Crew No. | Bare Costs | | Incl. Subs O & P | | Cost Per Labor-Hour | |
|---|---|---|---|---|---|---|
| | Hr. | Daily | Hr. | Daily | Bare Costs | Incl. O&P |
| **Crew B-13B** | | | | | | |
| 1 Labor Foreman (outside) | $32.25 | $258.00 | $50.20 | $401.60 | $32.76 | $50.44 |
| 4 Laborers | 30.25 | 968.00 | 47.05 | 1505.60 | | |
| 1 Equip. Oper. (crane) | 40.95 | 327.60 | 61.75 | 494.00 | | |
| 1 Equip. Oper. Oiler | 35.10 | 280.80 | 52.95 | 423.60 | | |
| 1 Hyd. Crane, 55 Ton | | 1119.00 | | 1230.90 | 19.98 | 21.98 |
| 56 L.H., Daily Totals | | $2953.40 | | $4055.70 | $52.74 | $72.42 |
| **Crew B-13C** | | | | | Bare Costs | Incl. O&P |
| 1 Labor Foreman (outside) | $32.25 | $258.00 | $50.20 | $401.60 | $32.76 | $50.44 |
| 4 Laborers | 30.25 | 968.00 | 47.05 | 1505.60 | | |
| 1 Equip. Oper. (crane) | 40.95 | 327.60 | 61.75 | 494.00 | | |
| 1 Equip. Oper. Oiler | 35.10 | 280.80 | 52.95 | 423.60 | | |
| 1 Crawler Crane, 100 Ton | | 1586.00 | | 1744.60 | 28.32 | 31.15 |
| 56 L.H., Daily Totals | | $3420.40 | | $4569.40 | $61.08 | $81.60 |
| **Crew B-13D** | | | | | Bare Costs | Incl. O&P |
| 1 Laborer | $30.25 | $242.00 | $47.05 | $376.40 | $35.60 | $54.40 |
| 1 Equip. Oper. (crane) | 40.95 | 327.60 | 61.75 | 494.00 | | |
| 1 Hyd. Excavator, 1 C.Y. | | 646.60 | | 711.26 | | |
| 1 Trench Box | | 113.40 | | 124.74 | 47.50 | 52.25 |
| 16 L.H., Daily Totals | | $1329.60 | | $1706.40 | $83.10 | $106.65 |
| **Crew B-13E** | | | | | Bare Costs | Incl. O&P |
| 1 Laborer | $30.25 | $242.00 | $47.05 | $376.40 | $35.60 | $54.40 |
| 1 Equip. Oper. (crane) | 40.95 | 327.60 | 61.75 | 494.00 | | |
| 1 Hyd. Excavator, 1.5 C.Y. | | 830.00 | | 913.00 | | |
| 1 Trench Box | | 113.40 | | 124.74 | 58.96 | 64.86 |
| 16 L.H., Daily Totals | | $1513.00 | | $1908.14 | $94.56 | $119.26 |
| **Crew B-13F** | | | | | Bare Costs | Incl. O&P |
| 1 Laborer | $30.25 | $242.00 | $47.05 | $376.40 | $35.60 | $54.40 |
| 1 Equip. Oper. (crane) | 40.95 | 327.60 | 61.75 | 494.00 | | |
| 1 Hyd. Excavator, 3.5 C.Y. | | 2337.00 | | 2570.70 | | |
| 1 Trench Box | | 113.40 | | 124.74 | 153.15 | 168.47 |
| 16 L.H., Daily Totals | | $3020.00 | | $3565.84 | $188.75 | $222.87 |
| **Crew B-13G** | | | | | Bare Costs | Incl. O&P |
| 1 Laborer | $30.25 | $242.00 | $47.05 | $376.40 | $35.60 | $54.40 |
| 1 Equip. Oper. (crane) | 40.95 | 327.60 | 61.75 | 494.00 | | |
| 1 Hyd. Excavator, .75 C.Y. | | 549.40 | | 604.34 | | |
| 1 Trench Box | | 113.40 | | 124.74 | 41.42 | 45.57 |
| 16 L.H., Daily Totals | | $1232.40 | | $1599.48 | $77.03 | $99.97 |
| **Crew B-13H** | | | | | Bare Costs | Incl. O&P |
| 1 Laborer | $30.25 | $242.00 | $47.05 | $376.40 | $35.60 | $54.40 |
| 1 Equip. Oper. (crane) | 40.95 | 327.60 | 61.75 | 494.00 | | |
| 1 Gradall, 5/8 C.Y. | | 932.60 | | 1025.86 | | |
| 1 Trench Box | | 113.40 | | 124.74 | 65.38 | 71.91 |
| 16 L.H., Daily Totals | | $1615.60 | | $2021.00 | $100.97 | $126.31 |
| **Crew B-13I** | | | | | Bare Costs | Incl. O&P |
| 1 Laborer | $30.25 | $242.00 | $47.05 | $376.40 | $35.60 | $54.40 |
| 1 Equip. Oper. (crane) | 40.95 | 327.60 | 61.75 | 494.00 | | |
| 1 Gradall, 3 Ton, 1 C.Y. | | 1089.00 | | 1197.90 | | |
| 1 Trench Box | | 113.40 | | 124.74 | 75.15 | 82.67 |
| 16 L.H., Daily Totals | | $1772.00 | | $2193.04 | $110.75 | $137.07 |

| Crew No. | Bare Costs | | Incl. Subs O & P | | Cost Per Labor-Hour | |
|---|---|---|---|---|---|---|
| **Crew B-13J** | Hr. | Daily | Hr. | Daily | Bare Costs | Incl. O&P |
| 1 Laborer | $30.25 | $242.00 | $47.05 | $376.40 | $35.60 | $54.40 |
| 1 Equip. Oper. (crane) | 40.95 | 327.60 | 61.75 | 494.00 | | |
| 1 Hyd. Excavator, 2.5 C.Y. | | 1466.00 | | 1612.60 | | |
| 1 Trench Box | | 113.40 | | 124.74 | 98.71 | 108.58 |
| 16 L.H., Daily Totals | | $2149.00 | | $2607.74 | $134.31 | $162.98 |

| **Crew B-14** | Hr. | Daily | Hr. | Daily | Bare Costs | Incl. O&P |
|---|---|---|---|---|---|---|
| 1 Labor Foreman (outside) | $32.25 | $258.00 | $50.20 | $401.60 | $31.83 | $49.23 |
| 4 Laborers | 30.25 | 968.00 | 47.05 | 1505.60 | | |
| 1 Equip. Oper. (light) | 37.75 | 302.00 | 56.95 | 455.60 | | |
| 1 Backhoe Loader, 48 H.P. | | 285.40 | | 313.94 | 5.95 | 6.54 |
| 48 L.H., Daily Totals | | $1813.40 | | $2676.74 | $37.78 | $55.77 |

| **Crew B-15** | Hr. | Daily | Hr. | Daily | Bare Costs | Incl. O&P |
|---|---|---|---|---|---|---|
| 1 Equipment Oper. (med) | $39.85 | $318.80 | $60.10 | $480.80 | $33.19 | $50.95 |
| .5 Laborer | 30.25 | 121.00 | 47.05 | 188.20 | | |
| 2 Truck Drivers (heavy) | 30.60 | 489.60 | 47.35 | 757.60 | | |
| 2 Dump Truck, 12 C.Y., 400 H.P. | | 1005.60 | | 1106.16 | | |
| 1 Dozer, 200 H.P. | | 1071.00 | | 1178.10 | 74.16 | 81.58 |
| 28 L.H., Daily Totals | | $3006.00 | | $3710.86 | $107.36 | $132.53 |

| **Crew B-16** | Hr. | Daily | Hr. | Daily | Bare Costs | Incl. O&P |
|---|---|---|---|---|---|---|
| 1 Labor Foreman (outside) | $32.25 | $258.00 | $50.20 | $401.60 | $30.84 | $47.91 |
| 2 Laborers | 30.25 | 484.00 | 47.05 | 752.80 | | |
| 1 Truck Driver (heavy) | 30.60 | 244.80 | 47.35 | 378.80 | | |
| 1 Dump Truck, 12 C.Y., 400 H.P. | | 502.80 | | 553.08 | 15.71 | 17.28 |
| 32 L.H., Daily Totals | | $1489.60 | | $2086.28 | $46.55 | $65.20 |

| **Crew B-17** | Hr. | Daily | Hr. | Daily | Bare Costs | Incl. O&P |
|---|---|---|---|---|---|---|
| 2 Laborers | $30.25 | $484.00 | $47.05 | $752.80 | $32.21 | $49.60 |
| 1 Equip. Oper. (light) | 37.75 | 302.00 | 56.95 | 455.60 | | |
| 1 Truck Driver (heavy) | 30.60 | 244.80 | 47.35 | 378.80 | | |
| 1 Backhoe Loader, 48 H.P. | | 285.40 | | 313.94 | | |
| 1 Dump Truck, 8 C.Y., 220 H.P. | | 308.60 | | 339.46 | 18.56 | 20.42 |
| 32 L.H., Daily Totals | | $1624.80 | | $2240.60 | $50.77 | $70.02 |

| **Crew B-17A** | Hr. | Daily | Hr. | Daily | Bare Costs | Incl. O&P |
|---|---|---|---|---|---|---|
| 2 Laborer Foremen | $32.25 | $516.00 | $50.20 | $803.20 | $32.68 | $50.84 |
| 6 Laborers | 30.25 | 1452.00 | 47.05 | 2258.40 | | |
| 1 Skilled Worker Foreman | 41.40 | 331.20 | 64.40 | 515.20 | | |
| 1 Skilled Worker | 39.40 | 315.20 | 61.25 | 490.00 | | |
| 80 L.H., Daily Totals | | $2614.40 | | $4066.80 | $32.68 | $50.84 |

| **Crew B-18** | Hr. | Daily | Hr. | Daily | Bare Costs | Incl. O&P |
|---|---|---|---|---|---|---|
| 1 Labor Foreman (outside) | $32.25 | $258.00 | $50.20 | $401.60 | $30.92 | $48.10 |
| 2 Laborers | 30.25 | 484.00 | 47.05 | 752.80 | | |
| 1 Vibratory Plate, Gas, 21" | | 38.40 | | 42.24 | 1.60 | 1.76 |
| 24 L.H., Daily Totals | | $780.40 | | $1196.64 | $32.52 | $49.86 |

| **Crew B-19** | Hr. | Daily | Hr. | Daily | Bare Costs | Incl. O&P |
|---|---|---|---|---|---|---|
| 1 Pile Driver Foreman | $39.15 | $313.20 | $64.15 | $513.20 | $38.09 | $60.50 |
| 4 Pile Drivers | 37.15 | 1188.80 | 60.85 | 1947.20 | | |
| 2 Equip. Oper. (crane) | 40.95 | 655.20 | 61.75 | 988.00 | | |
| 1 Equip. Oper. Oiler | 35.10 | 280.80 | 52.95 | 423.60 | | |
| 1 Crawler Crane, 40 Ton | | 1054.00 | | 1159.40 | | |
| 2 Leads, 30' long | | 110.80 | | 121.88 | | |
| 1 Hammer, Diesel, 22k Ft-Lb | | 577.80 | | 635.58 | 27.23 | 29.95 |
| 64 L.H., Daily Totals | | $4180.60 | | $5788.86 | $65.32 | $90.45 |

| **Crew B-19A** | Hr. | Daily | Hr. | Daily | Bare Costs | Incl. O&P |
|---|---|---|---|---|---|---|
| 1 Pile Driver Foreman | $39.15 | $313.20 | $64.15 | $513.20 | $38.09 | $60.50 |
| 4 Pile Drivers | 37.15 | 1188.80 | 60.85 | 1947.20 | | |
| 2 Equip. Oper. (crane) | 40.95 | 655.20 | 61.75 | 988.00 | | |
| 1 Equip. Oper. Oiler | 35.10 | 280.80 | 52.95 | 423.60 | | |
| 1 Crawler Crane, 75 Ton | | 1483.00 | | 1631.30 | | |
| 2 Leads, 30' long | | 110.80 | | 121.88 | | |
| 1 Hammer, Diesel, 41k Ft-Lb | | 661.20 | | 727.32 | 35.23 | 38.76 |
| 64 L.H., Daily Totals | | $4693.00 | | $6352.50 | $73.33 | $99.26 |

| **Crew B-20** | Hr. | Daily | Hr. | Daily | Bare Costs | Incl. O&P |
|---|---|---|---|---|---|---|
| 1 Labor Foreman (out) | $32.25 | $258.00 | $50.20 | $401.60 | $33.97 | $52.83 |
| 1 Skilled Worker | 39.40 | 315.20 | 61.25 | 490.00 | | |
| 1 Laborer | 30.25 | 242.00 | 47.05 | 376.40 | | |
| 24 L.H., Daily Totals | | $815.20 | | $1268.00 | $33.97 | $52.83 |

| **Crew B-20A** | Hr. | Daily | Hr. | Daily | Bare Costs | Incl. O&P |
|---|---|---|---|---|---|---|
| 1 Labor Foreman | $32.25 | $258.00 | $50.20 | $401.60 | $36.64 | $55.91 |
| 1 Laborer | 30.25 | 242.00 | 47.05 | 376.40 | | |
| 1 Plumber | 46.70 | 373.60 | 70.25 | 562.00 | | |
| 1 Plumber Apprentice | 37.35 | 298.80 | 56.15 | 449.20 | | |
| 32 L.H., Daily Totals | | $1172.40 | | $1789.20 | $36.64 | $55.91 |

| **Crew B-21** | Hr. | Daily | Hr. | Daily | Bare Costs | Incl. O&P |
|---|---|---|---|---|---|---|
| 1 Labor Foreman (out) | $32.25 | $258.00 | $50.20 | $401.60 | $34.96 | $54.11 |
| 1 Skilled Worker | 39.40 | 315.20 | 61.25 | 490.00 | | |
| 1 Laborer | 30.25 | 242.00 | 47.05 | 376.40 | | |
| .5 Equip. Oper. (crane) | 40.95 | 163.80 | 61.75 | 247.00 | | |
| .5 S.P. Crane, 4x4, 5 Ton | | 129.40 | | 142.34 | 4.62 | 5.08 |
| 28 L.H., Daily Totals | | $1108.40 | | $1657.34 | $39.59 | $59.19 |

| **Crew B-21A** | Hr. | Daily | Hr. | Daily | Bare Costs | Incl. O&P |
|---|---|---|---|---|---|---|
| 1 Labor Foreman | $32.25 | $258.00 | $50.20 | $401.60 | $37.50 | $57.08 |
| 1 Laborer | 30.25 | 242.00 | 47.05 | 376.40 | | |
| 1 Plumber | 46.70 | 373.60 | 70.25 | 562.00 | | |
| 1 Plumber Apprentice | 37.35 | 298.80 | 56.15 | 449.20 | | |
| 1 Equip. Oper. (crane) | 40.95 | 327.60 | 61.75 | 494.00 | | |
| 1 S.P. Crane, 4x4, 12 Ton | | 611.00 | | 672.10 | 15.28 | 16.80 |
| 40 L.H., Daily Totals | | $2111.00 | | $2955.30 | $52.77 | $73.88 |

| **Crew B-21B** | Hr. | Daily | Hr. | Daily | Bare Costs | Incl. O&P |
|---|---|---|---|---|---|---|
| 1 Laborer Foreman | $32.25 | $258.00 | $50.20 | $401.60 | $32.79 | $50.62 |
| 3 Laborers | 30.25 | 726.00 | 47.05 | 1129.20 | | |
| 1 Equip. Oper. (crane) | 40.95 | 327.60 | 61.75 | 494.00 | | |
| 1 Hyd. Crane, 12 Ton | | 766.40 | | 843.04 | 19.16 | 21.08 |
| 40 L.H., Daily Totals | | $2078.00 | | $2867.84 | $51.95 | $71.70 |

| **Crew B-21C** | Hr. | Daily | Hr. | Daily | Bare Costs | Incl. O&P |
|---|---|---|---|---|---|---|
| 1 Laborer Foreman | $32.25 | $258.00 | $50.20 | $401.60 | $32.76 | $50.44 |
| 4 Laborers | 30.25 | 968.00 | 47.05 | 1505.60 | | |
| 1 Equip. Oper. (crane) | 40.95 | 327.60 | 61.75 | 494.00 | | |
| 1 Equip. Oper. Oiler | 35.10 | 280.80 | 52.95 | 423.60 | | |
| 2 Cutting Torch | | 34.00 | | 37.40 | | |
| 2 Gases | | 144.00 | | 158.40 | | |
| 1 Lattice Boom Crane, 90 Ton | | 1567.00 | | 1723.70 | 31.16 | 34.28 |
| 56 L.H., Daily Totals | | $3579.40 | | $4744.30 | $63.92 | $84.72 |

| Crew No. | Bare Costs | | Incl. Subs O & P | | Cost Per Labor-Hour | |
|---|---|---|---|---|---|---|
| **Crew B-22** | Hr. | Daily | Hr. | Daily | Bare Costs | Incl. O&P |
| 1 Labor Foreman (out) | $32.25 | $258.00 | $50.20 | $401.60 | $35.36 | $54.62 |
| 1 Skilled Worker | 39.40 | 315.20 | 61.25 | 490.00 | | |
| 1 Laborer | 30.25 | 242.00 | 47.05 | 376.40 | | |
| .75 Equip. Oper. (crane) | 40.95 | 245.70 | 61.75 | 370.50 | | |
| .75 S.P. Crane, 4x4, 5 Ton | | 194.10 | | 213.51 | 6.47 | 7.12 |
| 30 L.H., Daily Totals | | $1255.00 | | $1852.01 | $41.83 | $61.73 |
| **Crew B-22A** | Hr. | Daily | Hr. | Daily | Bare Costs | Incl. O&P |
| 1 Labor Foreman (out) | $32.25 | $258.00 | $50.20 | $401.60 | $34.29 | $53.02 |
| 1 Skilled Worker | 39.40 | 315.20 | 61.25 | 490.00 | | |
| 2 Laborers | 30.25 | 484.00 | 47.05 | 752.80 | | |
| .75 Equipment Oper. (crane) | 40.95 | 245.70 | 61.75 | 370.50 | | |
| .75 S.P. Crane, 4x4, 5 Ton | | 194.10 | | 213.51 | | |
| 1 Generator, 5 KW | | 39.60 | | 43.56 | | |
| 1 Butt Fusion Machine | | 257.60 | | 283.36 | 12.93 | 14.22 |
| 38 L.H., Daily Totals | | $1794.20 | | $2555.33 | $47.22 | $67.25 |
| **Crew B-22B** | Hr. | Daily | Hr. | Daily | Bare Costs | Incl. O&P |
| 1 Skilled Worker | $39.40 | $315.20 | $61.25 | $490.00 | $34.83 | $54.15 |
| 1 Laborer | 30.25 | 242.00 | 47.05 | 376.40 | | |
| 1 Electro Fusion Machine | | 167.20 | | 183.92 | 10.45 | 11.49 |
| 16 L.H., Daily Totals | | $724.40 | | $1050.32 | $45.27 | $65.64 |
| **Crew B-23** | Hr. | Daily | Hr. | Daily | Bare Costs | Incl. O&P |
| 1 Labor Foreman (outside) | $32.25 | $258.00 | $50.20 | $401.60 | $30.65 | $47.68 |
| 4 Laborers | 30.25 | 968.00 | 47.05 | 1505.60 | | |
| 1 Drill Rig, Truck-Mounted | | 2530.00 | | 2783.00 | | |
| 1 Flatbed Truck, Gas, 3 Ton | | 224.00 | | 246.40 | 68.85 | 75.73 |
| 40 L.H., Daily Totals | | $3980.00 | | $4936.60 | $99.50 | $123.42 |
| **Crew B-23A** | Hr. | Daily | Hr. | Daily | Bare Costs | Incl. O&P |
| 1 Labor Foreman (outside) | $32.25 | $258.00 | $50.20 | $401.60 | $34.12 | $52.45 |
| 1 Laborer | 30.25 | 242.00 | 47.05 | 376.40 | | |
| 1 Equip. Operator (medium) | 39.85 | 318.80 | 60.10 | 480.80 | | |
| 1 Drill Rig, Truck-Mounted | | 2530.00 | | 2783.00 | | |
| 1 Pickup Truck, 3/4 Ton | | 109.00 | | 119.90 | 109.96 | 120.95 |
| 24 L.H., Daily Totals | | $3457.80 | | $4161.70 | $144.07 | $173.40 |
| **Crew B-23B** | Hr. | Daily | Hr. | Daily | Bare Costs | Incl. O&P |
| 1 Labor Foreman (outside) | $32.25 | $258.00 | $50.20 | $401.60 | $34.12 | $52.45 |
| 1 Laborer | 30.25 | 242.00 | 47.05 | 376.40 | | |
| 1 Equip. Operator (medium) | 39.85 | 318.80 | 60.10 | 480.80 | | |
| 1 Drill Rig, Truck-Mounted | | 2530.00 | | 2783.00 | | |
| 1 Pickup Truck, 3/4 Ton | | 109.00 | | 119.90 | | |
| 1 Centr. Water Pump, 6" | | 305.20 | | 335.72 | 122.68 | 134.94 |
| 24 L.H., Daily Totals | | $3763.00 | | $4497.42 | $156.79 | $187.39 |
| **Crew B-24** | Hr. | Daily | Hr. | Daily | Bare Costs | Incl. O&P |
| 1 Cement Finisher | $37.00 | $296.00 | $54.30 | $434.40 | $35.12 | $53.55 |
| 1 Laborer | 30.25 | 242.00 | 47.05 | 376.40 | | |
| 1 Carpenter | 38.10 | 304.80 | 59.30 | 474.40 | | |
| 24 L.H., Daily Totals | | $842.80 | | $1285.20 | $35.12 | $53.55 |
| **Crew B-25** | Hr. | Daily | Hr. | Daily | Bare Costs | Incl. O&P |
| 1 Labor Foreman | $32.25 | $258.00 | $50.20 | $401.60 | $33.05 | $50.90 |
| 7 Laborers | 30.25 | 1694.00 | 47.05 | 2634.80 | | |
| 3 Equip. Oper. (med.) | 39.85 | 956.40 | 60.10 | 1442.40 | | |
| 1 Asphalt Paver, 130 H.P. | | 1837.00 | | 2020.70 | | |
| 1 Tandem Roller, 10 Ton | | 219.00 | | 240.90 | | |
| 1 Roller, Pneum. Whl, 12 Ton | | 307.80 | | 338.58 | 26.86 | 29.55 |
| 88 L.H., Daily Totals | | $5272.20 | | $7078.98 | $59.91 | $80.44 |

| Crew No. | Bare Costs | | Incl. Subs O & P | | Cost Per Labor-Hour | |
|---|---|---|---|---|---|---|
| **Crew B-25B** | Hr. | Daily | Hr. | Daily | Bare Costs | Incl. O&P |
| 1 Labor Foreman | $32.25 | $258.00 | $50.20 | $401.60 | $33.62 | $51.66 |
| 7 Laborers | 30.25 | 1694.00 | 47.05 | 2634.80 | | |
| 4 Equip. Oper. (medium) | 39.85 | 1275.20 | 60.10 | 1923.20 | | |
| 1 Asphalt Paver, 130 H.P. | | 1837.00 | | 2020.70 | | |
| 2 Tandem Roller, 10 Ton | | 438.00 | | 481.80 | | |
| 1 Roller, Pneum. Whl, 12 Ton | | 307.80 | | 338.58 | 26.90 | 29.59 |
| 96 L.H., Daily Totals | | $5810.00 | | $7800.68 | $60.52 | $81.26 |
| **Crew B-25C** | Hr. | Daily | Hr. | Daily | Bare Costs | Incl. O&P |
| 1 Labor Foreman | $32.25 | $258.00 | $50.20 | $401.60 | $33.78 | $51.92 |
| 3 Laborers | 30.25 | 726.00 | 47.05 | 1129.20 | | |
| 2 Equip. Oper. (medium) | 39.85 | 637.60 | 60.10 | 961.60 | | |
| 1 Asphalt Paver, 130 H.P. | | 1837.00 | | 2020.70 | | |
| 1 Tandem Roller, 10 Ton | | 219.00 | | 240.90 | 42.83 | 47.12 |
| 48 L.H., Daily Totals | | $3677.60 | | $4754.00 | $76.62 | $99.04 |
| **Crew B-26** | Hr. | Daily | Hr. | Daily | Bare Costs | Incl. O&P |
| 1 Labor Foreman (outside) | $32.25 | $258.00 | $50.20 | $401.60 | $33.95 | $52.50 |
| 6 Laborers | 30.25 | 1452.00 | 47.05 | 2258.40 | | |
| 2 Equip. Oper. (med.) | 39.85 | 637.60 | 60.10 | 961.60 | | |
| 1 Rodman (reinf.) | 43.00 | 344.00 | 70.55 | 564.40 | | |
| 1 Cement Finisher | 37.00 | 296.00 | 54.30 | 434.40 | | |
| 1 Grader, 30,000 Lbs. | | 534.40 | | 587.84 | | |
| 1 Paving Mach. & Equip. | | 2447.00 | | 2691.70 | 33.88 | 37.27 |
| 88 L.H., Daily Totals | | $5969.00 | | $7899.94 | $67.83 | $89.77 |
| **Crew B-26A** | Hr. | Daily | Hr. | Daily | Bare Costs | Incl. O&P |
| 1 Labor Foreman (outside) | $32.25 | $258.00 | $50.20 | $401.60 | $33.95 | $52.50 |
| 6 Laborers | 30.25 | 1452.00 | 47.05 | 2258.40 | | |
| 2 Equip. Oper. (med.) | 39.85 | 637.60 | 60.10 | 961.60 | | |
| 1 Rodman (reinf.) | 43.00 | 344.00 | 70.55 | 564.40 | | |
| 1 Cement Finisher | 37.00 | 296.00 | 54.30 | 434.40 | | |
| 1 Grader, 30,000 Lbs. | | 534.40 | | 587.84 | | |
| 1 Paving Mach. & Equip. | | 2447.00 | | 2691.70 | | |
| 1 Concrete Saw | | 135.00 | | 148.50 | 35.41 | 38.95 |
| 88 L.H., Daily Totals | | $6104.00 | | $8048.44 | $69.36 | $91.46 |
| **Crew B-26B** | Hr. | Daily | Hr. | Daily | Bare Costs | Incl. O&P |
| 1 Labor Foreman (outside) | $32.25 | $258.00 | $50.20 | $401.60 | $34.44 | $53.14 |
| 6 Laborers | 30.25 | 1452.00 | 47.05 | 2258.40 | | |
| 3 Equip. Oper. (med.) | 39.85 | 956.40 | 60.10 | 1442.40 | | |
| 1 Rodman (reinf.) | 43.00 | 344.00 | 70.55 | 564.40 | | |
| 1 Cement Finisher | 37.00 | 296.00 | 54.30 | 434.40 | | |
| 1 Grader, 30,000 Lbs. | | 534.40 | | 587.84 | | |
| 1 Paving Mach. & Equip. | | 2447.00 | | 2691.70 | | |
| 1 Concrete Pump, 110' Boom | | 965.60 | | 1062.16 | 41.11 | 45.23 |
| 96 L.H., Daily Totals | | $7253.40 | | $9442.90 | $75.56 | $98.36 |
| **Crew B-27** | Hr. | Daily | Hr. | Daily | Bare Costs | Incl. O&P |
| 1 Labor Foreman (outside) | $32.25 | $258.00 | $50.20 | $401.60 | $30.75 | $47.84 |
| 3 Laborers | 30.25 | 726.00 | 47.05 | 1129.20 | | |
| 1 Berm Machine | | 262.60 | | 288.86 | 8.21 | 9.03 |
| 32 L.H., Daily Totals | | $1246.60 | | $1819.66 | $38.96 | $56.86 |
| **Crew B-28** | Hr. | Daily | Hr. | Daily | Bare Costs | Incl. O&P |
| 2 Carpenters | $38.10 | $609.60 | $59.30 | $948.80 | $35.48 | $55.22 |
| 1 Laborer | 30.25 | 242.00 | 47.05 | 376.40 | | |
| 24 L.H., Daily Totals | | $851.60 | | $1325.20 | $35.48 | $55.22 |

| Crew No. | Bare Costs | | Incl. Subs O & P | | Cost Per Labor-Hour | |
|---|---|---|---|---|---|---|
| **Crew B-29** | **Hr.** | **Daily** | **Hr.** | **Daily** | **Bare Costs** | **Incl. O&P** |
| 1 Labor Foreman (outside) | $32.25 | $258.00 | $50.20 | $401.60 | $32.76 | $50.44 |
| 4 Laborers | 30.25 | 968.00 | 47.05 | 1505.60 | | |
| 1 Equip. Oper. (crane) | 40.95 | 327.60 | 61.75 | 494.00 | | |
| 1 Equip. Oper. Oiler | 35.10 | 280.80 | 52.95 | 423.60 | | |
| 1 Gradall, 5/8 C.Y. | | 932.60 | | 1025.86 | 16.65 | 18.32 |
| 56 L.H., Daily Totals | | $2767.00 | | $3850.66 | $49.41 | $68.76 |
| **Crew B-30** | **Hr.** | **Daily** | **Hr.** | **Daily** | **Bare Costs** | **Incl. O&P** |
| 1 Equip. Oper. (med.) | $39.85 | $318.80 | $60.10 | $480.80 | $33.68 | $51.60 |
| 2 Truck Drivers (heavy) | 30.60 | 489.60 | 47.35 | 757.60 | | |
| 1 Hyd. Excavator, 1.5 C.Y. | | 830.00 | | 913.00 | | |
| 2 Dump Truck, 12 C.Y., 400 H.P. | | 1005.60 | | 1106.16 | 76.48 | 84.13 |
| 24 L.H., Daily Totals | | $2644.00 | | $3257.56 | $110.17 | $135.73 |
| **Crew B-31** | **Hr.** | **Daily** | **Hr.** | **Daily** | **Bare Costs** | **Incl. O&P** |
| 1 Labor Foreman (outside) | $32.25 | $258.00 | $50.20 | $401.60 | $32.22 | $50.13 |
| 3 Laborers | 30.25 | 726.00 | 47.05 | 1129.20 | | |
| 1 Carpenter | 38.10 | 304.80 | 59.30 | 474.40 | | |
| 1 Air Compressor, 250 C.F.M. | | 161.80 | | 177.98 | | |
| 1 Sheeting Driver | | 5.75 | | 6.33 | | |
| 2 -50' Air Hose, 1.5" | | 12.60 | | 13.86 | 4.50 | 4.95 |
| 40 L.H., Daily Totals | | $1468.95 | | $2203.36 | $36.72 | $55.08 |
| **Crew B-32** | **Hr.** | **Daily** | **Hr.** | **Daily** | **Bare Costs** | **Incl. O&P** |
| 1 Laborer | $30.25 | $242.00 | $47.05 | $376.40 | $37.45 | $56.84 |
| 3 Equip. Oper. (med.) | 39.85 | 956.40 | 60.10 | 1442.40 | | |
| 1 Grader, 30,000 Lbs. | | 534.40 | | 587.84 | | |
| 1 Tandem Roller, 10 Ton | | 219.00 | | 240.90 | | |
| 1 Dozer, 200 H.P. | | 1071.00 | | 1178.10 | 57.01 | 62.71 |
| 32 L.H., Daily Totals | | $3022.80 | | $3825.64 | $94.46 | $119.55 |
| **Crew B-32A** | **Hr.** | **Daily** | **Hr.** | **Daily** | **Bare Costs** | **Incl. O&P** |
| 1 Laborer | $30.25 | $242.00 | $47.05 | $376.40 | $36.65 | $55.75 |
| 2 Equip. Oper. (medium) | 39.85 | 637.60 | 60.10 | 961.60 | | |
| 1 Grader, 30,000 Lbs. | | 534.40 | | 587.84 | | |
| 1 Roller, Vibratory, 25 Ton | | 593.80 | | 653.18 | 47.01 | 51.71 |
| 24 L.H., Daily Totals | | $2007.80 | | $2579.02 | $83.66 | $107.46 |
| **Crew B-32B** | **Hr.** | **Daily** | **Hr.** | **Daily** | **Bare Costs** | **Incl. O&P** |
| 1 Laborer | $30.25 | $242.00 | $47.05 | $376.40 | $36.65 | $55.75 |
| 2 Equip. Oper. (medium) | 39.85 | 637.60 | 60.10 | 961.60 | | |
| 1 Dozer, 200 H.P. | | 1071.00 | | 1178.10 | | |
| 1 Roller, Vibratory, 25 Ton | | 593.80 | | 653.18 | 69.37 | 76.30 |
| 24 L.H., Daily Totals | | $2544.40 | | $3169.28 | $106.02 | $132.05 |
| **Crew B-32C** | **Hr.** | **Daily** | **Hr.** | **Daily** | **Bare Costs** | **Incl. O&P** |
| 1 Labor Foreman | $32.25 | $258.00 | $50.20 | $401.60 | $35.38 | $54.10 |
| 2 Laborers | 30.25 | 484.00 | 47.05 | 752.80 | | |
| 3 Equip. Oper. (medium) | 39.85 | 956.40 | 60.10 | 1442.40 | | |
| 1 Grader, 30,000 Lbs. | | 534.40 | | 587.84 | | |
| 1 Tandem Roller, 10 Ton | | 219.00 | | 240.90 | | |
| 1 Dozer, 200 H.P. | | 1071.00 | | 1178.10 | 38.01 | 41.81 |
| 48 L.H., Daily Totals | | $3522.80 | | $4603.64 | $73.39 | $95.91 |
| **Crew B-33A** | **Hr.** | **Daily** | **Hr.** | **Daily** | **Bare Costs** | **Incl. O&P** |
| 1 Equip. Oper. (med.) | $39.85 | $318.80 | $60.10 | $480.80 | $37.11 | $56.37 |
| .5 Laborer | 30.25 | 121.00 | 47.05 | 188.20 | | |
| .25 Equip. Oper. (med.) | 39.85 | 79.70 | 60.10 | 120.20 | | |
| 1 Scraper, Towed, 7 C.Y. | | 149.60 | | 164.56 | | |
| 1.25 Dozer, 300 H.P. | | 1735.00 | | 1908.50 | 134.61 | 148.08 |
| 14 L.H., Daily Totals | | $2404.10 | | $2862.26 | $171.72 | $204.45 |

| Crew No. | Bare Costs | | Incl. Subs O & P | | Cost Per Labor-Hour | |
|---|---|---|---|---|---|---|
| **Crew B-33B** | **Hr.** | **Daily** | **Hr.** | **Daily** | **Bare Costs** | **Incl. O&P** |
| 1 Equip. Oper. (med.) | $39.85 | $318.80 | $60.10 | $480.80 | $37.11 | $56.37 |
| .5 Laborer | 30.25 | 121.00 | 47.05 | 188.20 | | |
| .25 Equip. Oper. (med.) | 39.85 | 79.70 | 60.10 | 120.20 | | |
| 1 Scraper, Towed, 15 C.Y. | | 163.40 | | 179.74 | | |
| 1.25 Dozer, 300 H.P. | | 1735.00 | | 1908.50 | 135.60 | 149.16 |
| 14 L.H., Daily Totals | | $2417.90 | | $2877.44 | $172.71 | $205.53 |
| **Crew B-33C** | **Hr.** | **Daily** | **Hr.** | **Daily** | **Bare Costs** | **Incl. O&P** |
| 1 Equip. Oper. (med.) | $39.85 | $318.80 | $60.10 | $480.80 | $37.11 | $56.37 |
| .5 Laborer | 30.25 | 121.00 | 47.05 | 188.20 | | |
| .25 Equip. Oper. (med.) | 39.85 | 79.70 | 60.10 | 120.20 | | |
| 1 Scraper, Towed, 15 C.Y. | | 163.40 | | 179.74 | | |
| 1.25 Dozer, 300 H.P. | | 1735.00 | | 1908.50 | 135.60 | 149.16 |
| 14 L.H., Daily Totals | | $2417.90 | | $2877.44 | $172.71 | $205.53 |
| **Crew B-33D** | **Hr.** | **Daily** | **Hr.** | **Daily** | **Bare Costs** | **Incl. O&P** |
| 1 Equip. Oper. (med.) | $39.85 | $318.80 | $60.10 | $480.80 | $37.11 | $56.37 |
| .5 Laborer | 30.25 | 121.00 | 47.05 | 188.20 | | |
| .25 Equip. Oper. (med.) | 39.85 | 79.70 | 60.10 | 120.20 | | |
| 1 S.P. Scraper, 14 C.Y. | | 1882.00 | | 2070.20 | | |
| .25 Dozer, 300 H.P. | | 347.00 | | 381.70 | 159.21 | 175.14 |
| 14 L.H., Daily Totals | | $2748.50 | | $3241.10 | $196.32 | $231.51 |
| **Crew B-33E** | **Hr.** | **Daily** | **Hr.** | **Daily** | **Bare Costs** | **Incl. O&P** |
| 1 Equip. Oper. (med.) | $39.85 | $318.80 | $60.10 | $480.80 | $37.11 | $56.37 |
| .5 Laborer | 30.25 | 121.00 | 47.05 | 188.20 | | |
| .25 Equip. Oper. (med.) | 39.85 | 79.70 | 60.10 | 120.20 | | |
| 1 S.P. Scraper, 24 C.Y. | | 2829.00 | | 3111.90 | | |
| .25 Dozer, 300 H.P. | | 347.00 | | 381.70 | 226.86 | 249.54 |
| 14 L.H., Daily Totals | | $3695.50 | | $4282.80 | $263.96 | $305.91 |
| **Crew B-33F** | **Hr.** | **Daily** | **Hr.** | **Daily** | **Bare Costs** | **Incl. O&P** |
| 1 Equip. Oper. (med.) | $39.85 | $318.80 | $60.10 | $480.80 | $37.11 | $56.37 |
| .5 Laborer | 30.25 | 121.00 | 47.05 | 188.20 | | |
| .25 Equip. Oper. (med.) | 39.85 | 79.70 | 60.10 | 120.20 | | |
| 1 Elev. Scraper, 11 C.Y. | | 927.40 | | 1020.14 | | |
| .25 Dozer, 300 H.P. | | 347.00 | | 381.70 | 91.03 | 100.13 |
| 14 L.H., Daily Totals | | $1793.90 | | $2191.04 | $128.14 | $156.50 |
| **Crew B-33G** | **Hr.** | **Daily** | **Hr.** | **Daily** | **Bare Costs** | **Incl. O&P** |
| 1 Equip. Oper. (med.) | $39.85 | $318.80 | $60.10 | $480.80 | $37.11 | $56.37 |
| .5 Laborer | 30.25 | 121.00 | 47.05 | 188.20 | | |
| .25 Equip. Oper. (med.) | 39.85 | 79.70 | 60.10 | 120.20 | | |
| 1 Elev. Scraper, 20 C.Y. | | 1872.00 | | 2059.20 | | |
| .25 Dozer, 300 H.P. | | 347.00 | | 381.70 | 158.50 | 174.35 |
| 14 L.H., Daily Totals | | $2738.50 | | $3230.10 | $195.61 | $230.72 |
| **Crew B-33H** | **Hr.** | **Daily** | **Hr.** | **Daily** | **Bare Costs** | **Incl. O&P** |
| .25 Laborer | $30.25 | $60.50 | $47.05 | $94.10 | $38.19 | $57.85 |
| 1 Equipment Operator (med.) | 39.85 | 318.80 | 60.10 | 480.80 | | |
| .2 Equipment Operator (med.) | 39.85 | 63.76 | 60.10 | 96.16 | | |
| 1 Scraper, 32-44 C.Y. | | 3376.00 | | 3713.60 | | |
| .2 Dozer, 410 H.P. | | 363.40 | | 399.74 | 322.36 | 354.60 |
| 11.6 L.H., Daily Totals | | $4182.46 | | $4784.40 | $360.56 | $412.45 |
| **Crew B-33J** | **Hr.** | **Daily** | **Hr.** | **Daily** | **Bare Costs** | **Incl. O&P** |
| 1 Equipment Operator (med.) | $39.85 | $318.80 | $60.10 | $480.80 | $39.85 | $60.10 |
| 1 S.P. Scraper, 14 C.Y. | | 1882.00 | | 2070.20 | 235.25 | 258.77 |
| 8 L.H., Daily Totals | | $2200.80 | | $2551.00 | $275.10 | $318.88 |

| Crew No. | Bare Costs | | Incl. Subs O & P | | Cost Per Labor-Hour | |
|---|---|---|---|---|---|---|

## Crew B-34A

| | Hr. | Daily | Hr. | Daily | Bare Costs | Incl. O&P |
|---|---|---|---|---|---|---|
| 1 Truck Driver (heavy) | $30.60 | $244.80 | $47.35 | $378.80 | $30.60 | $47.35 |
| 1 Dump Truck, 8 C.Y., 220 H.P. | | 308.60 | | 339.46 | 38.58 | 42.43 |
| 8 L.H., Daily Totals | | $553.40 | | $718.26 | $69.17 | $89.78 |

## Crew B-34B

| | Hr. | Daily | Hr. | Daily | Bare Costs | Incl. O&P |
|---|---|---|---|---|---|---|
| 1 Truck Driver (heavy) | $30.60 | $244.80 | $47.35 | $378.80 | $30.60 | $47.35 |
| 1 Dump Truck, 12 C.Y., 400 H.P. | | 502.80 | | 553.08 | 62.85 | 69.14 |
| 8 L.H., Daily Totals | | $747.60 | | $931.88 | $93.45 | $116.49 |

## Crew B-34C

| | Hr. | Daily | Hr. | Daily | Bare Costs | Incl. O&P |
|---|---|---|---|---|---|---|
| 1 Truck Driver (heavy) | $30.60 | $244.80 | $47.35 | $378.80 | $30.60 | $47.35 |
| 1 Truck Tractor, 6x4, 380 H.P. | | 453.60 | | 498.96 | | |
| 1 Dump Trailer, 16.5 C.Y. | | 111.00 | | 122.10 | 70.58 | 77.63 |
| 8 L.H., Daily Totals | | $809.40 | | $999.86 | $101.18 | $124.98 |

## Crew B-34D

| | Hr. | Daily | Hr. | Daily | Bare Costs | Incl. O&P |
|---|---|---|---|---|---|---|
| 1 Truck Driver (heavy) | $30.60 | $244.80 | $47.35 | $378.80 | $30.60 | $47.35 |
| 1 Truck Tractor, 6x4, 380 H.P. | | 453.60 | | 498.96 | | |
| 1 Dump Trailer, 20 C.Y. | | 123.80 | | 136.18 | 72.17 | 79.39 |
| 8 L.H., Daily Totals | | $822.20 | | $1013.94 | $102.78 | $126.74 |

## Crew B-34E

| | Hr. | Daily | Hr. | Daily | Bare Costs | Incl. O&P |
|---|---|---|---|---|---|---|
| 1 Truck Driver (heavy) | $30.60 | $244.80 | $47.35 | $378.80 | $30.60 | $47.35 |
| 1 Dump Truck, Off Hwy., 25 Ton | | 1066.00 | | 1172.60 | 133.25 | 146.57 |
| 8 L.H., Daily Totals | | $1310.80 | | $1551.40 | $163.85 | $193.93 |

## Crew B-34F

| | Hr. | Daily | Hr. | Daily | Bare Costs | Incl. O&P |
|---|---|---|---|---|---|---|
| 1 Truck Driver (heavy) | $30.60 | $244.80 | $47.35 | $378.80 | $30.60 | $47.35 |
| 1 Dump Truck, Off Hwy., 35 Ton | | 1089.00 | | 1197.90 | 136.13 | 149.74 |
| 8 L.H., Daily Totals | | $1333.80 | | $1576.70 | $166.72 | $197.09 |

## Crew B-34G

| | Hr. | Daily | Hr. | Daily | Bare Costs | Incl. O&P |
|---|---|---|---|---|---|---|
| 1 Truck Driver (heavy) | $30.60 | $244.80 | $47.35 | $378.80 | $30.60 | $47.35 |
| 1 Dump Truck, Off Hwy., 50 Ton | | 1426.00 | | 1568.60 | 178.25 | 196.07 |
| 8 L.H., Daily Totals | | $1670.80 | | $1947.40 | $208.85 | $243.43 |

## Crew B-34H

| | Hr. | Daily | Hr. | Daily | Bare Costs | Incl. O&P |
|---|---|---|---|---|---|---|
| 1 Truck Driver (heavy) | $30.60 | $244.80 | $47.35 | $378.80 | $30.60 | $47.35 |
| 1 Dump Truck, Off Hwy., 65 Ton | | 1517.00 | | 1668.70 | 189.63 | 208.59 |
| 8 L.H., Daily Totals | | $1761.80 | | $2047.50 | $220.22 | $255.94 |

## Crew B-34J

| | Hr. | Daily | Hr. | Daily | Bare Costs | Incl. O&P |
|---|---|---|---|---|---|---|
| 1 Truck Driver (heavy) | $30.60 | $244.80 | $47.35 | $378.80 | $30.60 | $47.35 |
| 1 Dump Truck, Off Hwy., 100 Ton | | 1956.00 | | 2151.60 | 244.50 | 268.95 |
| 8 L.H., Daily Totals | | $2200.80 | | $2530.40 | $275.10 | $316.30 |

## Crew B-34K

| | Hr. | Daily | Hr. | Daily | Bare Costs | Incl. O&P |
|---|---|---|---|---|---|---|
| 1 Truck Driver (heavy) | $30.60 | $244.80 | $47.35 | $378.80 | $30.60 | $47.35 |
| 1 Truck Tractor, 6x4, 450 H.P. | | 427.80 | | 470.58 | | |
| 1 Lowbed Trailer, 75 Ton | | 193.40 | | 212.74 | 77.65 | 85.42 |
| 8 L.H., Daily Totals | | $866.00 | | $1062.12 | $108.25 | $132.76 |

## Crew B-34N

| | Hr. | Daily | Hr. | Daily | Bare Costs | Incl. O&P |
|---|---|---|---|---|---|---|
| 1 Truck Driver (heavy) | $30.60 | $244.80 | $47.35 | $378.80 | $30.60 | $47.35 |
| 1 Dump Truck, 8 C.Y., 220 H.P. | | 308.60 | | 339.46 | | |
| 1 Flatbed Trailer, 40 Ton | | 133.20 | | 146.52 | 55.23 | 60.75 |
| 8 L.H., Daily Totals | | $686.60 | | $864.78 | $85.83 | $108.10 |

## Crew B-34P

| | Hr. | Daily | Hr. | Daily | Bare Costs | Incl. O&P |
|---|---|---|---|---|---|---|
| 1 Pipe Fitter | $47.10 | $376.80 | $70.85 | $566.80 | $38.78 | $58.82 |
| 1 Truck Driver (light) | 29.40 | 235.20 | 45.50 | 364.00 | | |
| 1 Equip. Oper. (medium) | 39.85 | 318.80 | 60.10 | 480.80 | | |
| 1 Flatbed Truck, Gas, 3 Ton | | 224.00 | | 246.40 | | |
| 1 Backhoe Loader, 48 H.P. | | 285.40 | | 313.94 | 21.23 | 23.35 |
| 24 L.H., Daily Totals | | $1440.20 | | $1971.94 | $60.01 | $82.16 |

## Crew B-34Q

| | Hr. | Daily | Hr. | Daily | Bare Costs | Incl. O&P |
|---|---|---|---|---|---|---|
| 1 Pipe Fitter | $47.10 | $376.80 | $70.85 | $566.80 | $39.15 | $59.37 |
| 1 Truck Driver (light) | 29.40 | 235.20 | 45.50 | 364.00 | | |
| 1 Eqip. Oper. (crane) | 40.95 | 327.60 | 61.75 | 494.00 | | |
| 1 Flatbed Trailer, 25 Ton | | 97.00 | | 106.70 | | |
| 1 Dump Truck, 8 C.Y., 220 H.P. | | 308.60 | | 339.46 | | |
| 1 Hyd. Crane, 25 Ton | | 786.00 | | 864.60 | 49.65 | 54.62 |
| 24 L.H., Daily Totals | | $2131.20 | | $2735.56 | $88.80 | $113.98 |

## Crew B-34R

| | Hr. | Daily | Hr. | Daily | Bare Costs | Incl. O&P |
|---|---|---|---|---|---|---|
| 1 Pipe Fitter | $47.10 | $376.80 | $70.85 | $566.80 | $39.15 | $59.37 |
| 1 Truck Driver (light) | 29.40 | 235.20 | 45.50 | 364.00 | | |
| 1 Eqip. Oper. (crane) | 40.95 | 327.60 | 61.75 | 494.00 | | |
| 1 Flatbed Trailer, 25 Ton | | 97.00 | | 106.70 | | |
| 1 Dump Truck, 8 C.Y., 220 H.P. | | 308.60 | | 339.46 | | |
| 1 Hyd. Crane, 25 Ton | | 786.00 | | 864.60 | | |
| 1 Hyd. Excavator, 1 C.Y. | | 646.60 | | 711.26 | 76.59 | 84.25 |
| 24 L.H., Daily Totals | | $2777.80 | | $3446.82 | $115.74 | $143.62 |

## Crew B-34S

| | Hr. | Daily | Hr. | Daily | Bare Costs | Incl. O&P |
|---|---|---|---|---|---|---|
| 2 Pipe Fitters | $47.10 | $753.60 | $70.85 | $1133.60 | $41.44 | $62.70 |
| 1 Truck Driver (heavy) | 30.60 | 244.80 | 47.35 | 378.80 | | |
| 1 Eqip. Oper. (crane) | 40.95 | 327.60 | 61.75 | 494.00 | | |
| 1 Flatbed Trailer, 40 Ton | | 133.20 | | 146.52 | | |
| 1 Truck Tractor, 6x4, 380 H.P. | | 453.60 | | 498.96 | | |
| 1 Hyd. Crane, 80 Ton | | 1290.00 | | 1419.00 | | |
| 1 Hyd. Excavator, 2 C.Y. | | 1060.00 | | 1166.00 | 91.78 | 100.95 |
| 32 L.H., Daily Totals | | $4262.80 | | $5236.88 | $133.21 | $163.65 |

## Crew B-34T

| | Hr. | Daily | Hr. | Daily | Bare Costs | Incl. O&P |
|---|---|---|---|---|---|---|
| 2 Pipe Fitters | $47.10 | $753.60 | $70.85 | $1133.60 | $41.44 | $62.70 |
| 1 Truck Driver (heavy) | 30.60 | 244.80 | 47.35 | 378.80 | | |
| 1 Eqip. Oper. (crane) | 40.95 | 327.60 | 61.75 | 494.00 | | |
| 1 Flatbed Trailer, 40 Ton | | 133.20 | | 146.52 | | |
| 1 Truck Tractor, 6x4, 380 H.P. | | 453.60 | | 498.96 | | |
| 1 Hyd. Crane, 80 Ton | | 1290.00 | | 1419.00 | 58.65 | 64.52 |
| 32 L.H., Daily Totals | | $3202.80 | | $4070.88 | $100.09 | $127.22 |

## Crew B-35

| | Hr. | Daily | Hr. | Daily | Bare Costs | Incl. O&P |
|---|---|---|---|---|---|---|
| 1 Laborer Foreman (out) | $32.25 | $258.00 | $50.20 | $401.60 | $37.44 | $57.24 |
| 1 Skilled Worker | 39.40 | 315.20 | 61.25 | 490.00 | | |
| 1 Welder (plumber) | 46.70 | 373.60 | 70.25 | 562.00 | | |
| 1 Laborer | 30.25 | 242.00 | 47.05 | 376.40 | | |
| 1 Equip. Oper. (crane) | 40.95 | 327.60 | 61.75 | 494.00 | | |
| 1 Equip. Oper. Oiler | 35.10 | 280.80 | 52.95 | 423.60 | | |
| 1 Welder, electric, 300 amp | | 56.20 | | 61.82 | | |
| 1 Hyd. Excavator, .75 C.Y. | | 549.40 | | 604.34 | 12.62 | 13.88 |
| 48 L.H., Daily Totals | | $2402.80 | | $3413.76 | $50.06 | $71.12 |

| Crew No. | Bare Costs | | Incl. Subs O & P | | Cost Per Labor-Hour | |

**Crew B-35A**

| | Hr. | Daily | Hr. | Daily | Bare Costs | Incl. O&P |
|---|---|---|---|---|---|---|
| 1 Laborer Foreman (out) | $32.25 | $258.00 | $50.20 | $401.60 | $36.41 | $55.79 |
| 2 Laborers | 30.25 | 484.00 | 47.05 | 752.80 | | |
| 1 Skilled Worker | 39.40 | 315.20 | 61.25 | 490.00 | | |
| 1 Welder (plumber) | 46.70 | 373.60 | 70.25 | 562.00 | | |
| 1 Equip. Oper. (crane) | 40.95 | 327.60 | 61.75 | 494.00 | | |
| 1 Equip. Oper. Oiler | 35.10 | 280.80 | 52.95 | 423.60 | | |
| 1 Welder, gas engine, 300 amp | | 132.20 | | 145.42 | | |
| 1 Crawler Crane, 75 Ton | | 1483.00 | | 1631.30 | 28.84 | 31.73 |
| 56 L.H., Daily Totals | | $3654.40 | | $4900.72 | $65.26 | $87.51 |

**Crew B-36**

| | Hr. | Daily | Hr. | Daily | Bare Costs | Incl. O&P |
|---|---|---|---|---|---|---|
| 1 Labor Foreman (outside) | $32.25 | $258.00 | $50.20 | $401.60 | $34.49 | $52.90 |
| 2 Laborers | 30.25 | 484.00 | 47.05 | 752.80 | | |
| 2 Equip. Oper. (med.) | 39.85 | 637.60 | 60.10 | 961.60 | | |
| 1 Dozer, 200 H.P. | | 1071.00 | | 1178.10 | | |
| 1 Aggregate Spreader | | 33.60 | | 36.96 | | |
| 1 Tandem Roller, 10 Ton | | 219.00 | | 240.90 | 33.09 | 36.40 |
| 40 L.H., Daily Totals | | $2703.20 | | $3571.96 | $67.58 | $89.30 |

**Crew B-36A**

| | Hr. | Daily | Hr. | Daily | Bare Costs | Incl. O&P |
|---|---|---|---|---|---|---|
| 1 Labor Foreman (outside) | $32.25 | $258.00 | $50.20 | $401.60 | $36.02 | $54.96 |
| 2 Laborers | 30.25 | 484.00 | 47.05 | 752.80 | | |
| 4 Equip. Oper. (med.) | 39.85 | 1275.20 | 60.10 | 1923.20 | | |
| 1 Dozer, 200 H.P. | | 1071.00 | | 1178.10 | | |
| 1 Aggregate Spreader | | 33.60 | | 36.96 | | |
| 1 Tandem Roller, 10 Ton | | 219.00 | | 240.90 | | |
| 1 Roller, Pneum. Whl, 12 Ton | | 307.80 | | 338.58 | 29.13 | 32.05 |
| 56 L.H., Daily Totals | | $3648.60 | | $4872.14 | $65.15 | $87.00 |

**Crew B-36B**

| | Hr. | Daily | Hr. | Daily | Bare Costs | Incl. O&P |
|---|---|---|---|---|---|---|
| 1 Labor Foreman (outside) | $32.25 | $258.00 | $50.20 | $401.60 | $35.34 | $54.01 |
| 2 Laborers | 30.25 | 484.00 | 47.05 | 752.80 | | |
| 4 Equip. Oper. (medium) | 39.85 | 1275.20 | 60.10 | 1923.20 | | |
| 1 Truck Driver, Heavy | 30.60 | 244.80 | 47.35 | 378.80 | | |
| 1 Grader, 30,000 Lbs. | | 534.40 | | 587.84 | | |
| 1 F.E. Loader, crl, 1.5 C.Y. | | 438.60 | | 482.46 | | |
| 1 Dozer, 300 H.P. | | 1388.00 | | 1526.80 | | |
| 1 Roller, Vibratory, 25 Ton | | 593.80 | | 653.18 | | |
| 1 Truck Tractor, 6x4, 450 H.P. | | 427.80 | | 470.58 | | |
| 1 Water Tanker, 5000 Gal. | | 129.60 | | 142.56 | 54.88 | 60.37 |
| 64 L.H., Daily Totals | | $5774.20 | | $7319.82 | $90.22 | $114.37 |

**Crew B-36C**

| | Hr. | Daily | Hr. | Daily | Bare Costs | Incl. O&P |
|---|---|---|---|---|---|---|
| 1 Labor Foreman (outside) | $32.25 | $258.00 | $50.20 | $401.60 | $36.48 | $55.57 |
| 3 Equip. Oper. (medium) | 39.85 | 956.40 | 60.10 | 1442.40 | | |
| 1 Truck Driver, Heavy | 30.60 | 244.80 | 47.35 | 378.80 | | |
| 1 Grader, 30,000 Lbs. | | 534.40 | | 587.84 | | |
| 1 Dozer, 300 H.P. | | 1388.00 | | 1526.80 | | |
| 1 Roller, Vibratory, 25 Ton | | 593.80 | | 653.18 | | |
| 1 Truck Tractor, 6x4, 450 H.P. | | 427.80 | | 470.58 | | |
| 1 Water Tanker, 5000 Gal. | | 129.60 | | 142.56 | 76.84 | 84.52 |
| 40 L.H., Daily Totals | | $4532.80 | | $5603.76 | $113.32 | $140.09 |

**Crew B-37**

| | Hr. | Daily | Hr. | Daily | Bare Costs | Incl. O&P |
|---|---|---|---|---|---|---|
| 1 Labor Foreman (outside) | $32.25 | $258.00 | $50.20 | $401.60 | $31.83 | $49.23 |
| 4 Laborers | 30.25 | 968.00 | 47.05 | 1505.60 | | |
| 1 Equip. Oper. (light) | 37.75 | 302.00 | 56.95 | 455.60 | | |
| 1 Tandem Roller, 5 Ton | | 130.20 | | 143.22 | 2.71 | 2.98 |
| 48 L.H., Daily Totals | | $1658.20 | | $2506.02 | $34.55 | $52.21 |

**Crew B-38**

| | Hr. | Daily | Hr. | Daily | Bare Costs | Incl. O&P |
|---|---|---|---|---|---|---|
| 1 Labor Foreman (outside) | $32.25 | $258.00 | $50.20 | $401.60 | $34.07 | $52.27 |
| 2 Laborers | 30.25 | 484.00 | 47.05 | 752.80 | | |
| 1 Equip. Oper. (light) | 37.75 | 302.00 | 56.95 | 455.60 | | |
| 1 Equip. Oper. (medium) | 39.85 | 318.80 | 60.10 | 480.80 | | |
| 1 Backhoe Loader, 48 H.P. | | 285.40 | | 313.94 | | |
| 1 Hyd.Hammer, (1200 lb) | | 125.80 | | 138.38 | | |
| 1 F.E. Loader, W.M., 4 C.Y. | | 536.00 | | 589.60 | | |
| 1 Pavt. Rem. Bucket | | 55.00 | | 60.50 | 25.06 | 27.56 |
| 40 L.H., Daily Totals | | $2365.00 | | $3193.22 | $59.13 | $79.83 |

**Crew B-39**

| | Hr. | Daily | Hr. | Daily | Bare Costs | Incl. O&P |
|---|---|---|---|---|---|---|
| 1 Labor Foreman (outside) | $32.25 | $258.00 | $50.20 | $401.60 | $31.83 | $49.23 |
| 4 Laborers | 30.25 | 968.00 | 47.05 | 1505.60 | | |
| 1 Equip. Oper. (light) | 37.75 | 302.00 | 56.95 | 455.60 | | |
| 1 Air Compressor, 250 C.F.M. | | 161.80 | | 177.98 | | |
| 2 Breaker, Pavement, 60 lb. | | 17.20 | | 18.92 | | |
| 2 -50' Air Hose, 1.5" | | 12.60 | | 13.86 | 3.99 | 4.39 |
| 48 L.H., Daily Totals | | $1719.60 | | $2573.56 | $35.83 | $53.62 |

**Crew B-40**

| | Hr. | Daily | Hr. | Daily | Bare Costs | Incl. O&P |
|---|---|---|---|---|---|---|
| 1 Pile Driver Foreman (out) | $39.15 | $313.20 | $64.15 | $513.20 | $38.09 | $60.50 |
| 4 Pile Drivers | 37.15 | 1188.80 | 60.85 | 1947.20 | | |
| 2 Equip. Oper. (crane) | 40.95 | 655.20 | 61.75 | 988.00 | | |
| 1 Equip. Oper. Oiler | 35.10 | 280.80 | 52.95 | 423.60 | | |
| 1 Crawler Crane, 40 Ton | | 1054.00 | | 1159.40 | | |
| 1 Vibratory Hammer & Gen. | | 2178.00 | | 2395.80 | 50.50 | 55.55 |
| 64 L.H., Daily Totals | | $5670.00 | | $7427.20 | $88.59 | $116.05 |

**Crew B-40B**

| | Hr. | Daily | Hr. | Daily | Bare Costs | Incl. O&P |
|---|---|---|---|---|---|---|
| 1 Laborer Foreman | $32.25 | $258.00 | $50.20 | $401.60 | $33.17 | $51.01 |
| 3 Laborers | 30.25 | 726.00 | 47.05 | 1129.20 | | |
| 1 Equip. Oper. (crane) | 40.95 | 327.60 | 61.75 | 494.00 | | |
| 1 Equip. Oper. Oiler | 35.10 | 280.80 | 52.95 | 423.60 | | |
| 1 Lattice Boom Crane, 40 Ton | | 1225.00 | | 1347.50 | 25.52 | 28.07 |
| 48 L.H., Daily Totals | | $2817.40 | | $3795.90 | $58.70 | $79.08 |

**Crew B-41**

| | Hr. | Daily | Hr. | Daily | Bare Costs | Incl. O&P |
|---|---|---|---|---|---|---|
| 1 Labor Foreman (outside) | $32.25 | $258.00 | $50.20 | $401.60 | $31.32 | $48.56 |
| 4 Laborers | 30.25 | 968.00 | 47.05 | 1505.60 | | |
| .25 Equip. Oper. (crane) | 40.95 | 81.90 | 61.75 | 123.50 | | |
| .25 Equip. Oper. Oiler | 35.10 | 70.20 | 52.95 | 105.90 | | |
| .25 Crawler Crane, 40 Ton | | 263.50 | | 289.85 | 5.99 | 6.59 |
| 44 L.H., Daily Totals | | $1641.60 | | $2426.45 | $37.31 | $55.15 |

**Crew B-42**

| | Hr. | Daily | Hr. | Daily | Bare Costs | Incl. O&P |
|---|---|---|---|---|---|---|
| 1 Labor Foreman (outside) | $32.25 | $258.00 | $50.20 | $401.60 | $34.04 | $53.83 |
| 4 Laborers | 30.25 | 968.00 | 47.05 | 1505.60 | | |
| 1 Equip. Oper. (crane) | 40.95 | 327.60 | 61.75 | 494.00 | | |
| 1 Equip. Oper. Oiler | 35.10 | 280.80 | 52.95 | 423.60 | | |
| 1 Welder | 43.00 | 344.00 | 77.55 | 620.40 | | |
| 1 Hyd. Crane, 25 Ton | | 786.00 | | 864.60 | | |
| 1 Welder, gas engine, 300 amp | | 132.20 | | 145.42 | | |
| 1 Horz. Boring Csg. Mch. | | 441.20 | | 485.32 | 21.24 | 23.36 |
| 64 L.H., Daily Totals | | $3537.80 | | $4940.54 | $55.28 | $77.20 |

| Crew No. | Bare Costs Hr. | Daily | Incl. Subs O & P Hr. | Daily | Cost Per Labor-Hour Bare Costs | Incl. O&P |
|---|---|---|---|---|---|---|
| **Crew B-43** | Hr. | Daily | Hr. | Daily | Bare Costs | Incl. O&P |
| 1 Labor Foreman (outside) | $32.25 | $258.00 | $50.20 | $401.60 | $33.17 | $51.01 |
| 3 Laborers | 30.25 | 726.00 | 47.05 | 1129.20 | | |
| 1 Equip. Oper. (crane) | 40.95 | 327.60 | 61.75 | 494.00 | | |
| 1 Equip. Oper. Oiler | 35.10 | 280.80 | 52.95 | 423.60 | | |
| 1 Drill Rig, Truck-Mounted | | 2530.00 | | 2783.00 | 52.71 | 57.98 |
| 48 L.H., Daily Totals | | $4122.40 | | $5231.40 | $85.88 | $108.99 |
| **Crew B-44** | Hr. | Daily | Hr. | Daily | Bare Costs | Incl. O&P |
| 1 Pile Driver Foreman | $39.15 | $313.20 | $64.15 | $513.20 | $37.49 | $59.76 |
| 4 Pile Drivers | 37.15 | 1188.80 | 60.85 | 1947.20 | | |
| 2 Equip. Oper. (crane) | 40.95 | 655.20 | 61.75 | 988.00 | | |
| 1 Laborer | 30.25 | 242.00 | 47.05 | 376.40 | | |
| 1 Crawler Crane, 40 Ton | | 1054.00 | | 1159.40 | | |
| 2 Leads, 20' long | | 49.20 | | 54.12 | | |
| 1 Hammer, diesel, 15K Ft.-Lbs. | | 346.20 | | 380.82 | 22.65 | 24.91 |
| 64 L.H., Daily Totals | | $3848.60 | | $5419.14 | $60.13 | $84.67 |
| **Crew B-45** | Hr. | Daily | Hr. | Daily | Bare Costs | Incl. O&P |
| 1 Equip. Oper. (med.) | $39.85 | $318.80 | $60.10 | $480.80 | $35.23 | $53.73 |
| 1 Truck Driver (heavy) | 30.60 | 244.80 | 47.35 | 378.80 | | |
| 1 Dist. Tanker, 3000 Gallon | | 294.00 | | 323.40 | | |
| 1 Truck Tractor, 6x4, 380 H.P. | | 453.60 | | 498.96 | 46.73 | 51.40 |
| 16 L.H., Daily Totals | | $1311.20 | | $1681.96 | $81.95 | $105.12 |
| **Crew B-46** | Hr. | Daily | Hr. | Daily | Bare Costs | Incl. O&P |
| 1 Pile Driver Foreman | $39.15 | $313.20 | $64.15 | $513.20 | $34.03 | $54.50 |
| 2 Pile Drivers | 37.15 | 594.40 | 60.85 | 973.60 | | |
| 3 Laborers | 30.25 | 726.00 | 47.05 | 1129.20 | | |
| 1 Chainsaw, Gas, 36" Long | | 36.80 | | 40.48 | .77 | .84 |
| 48 L.H., Daily Totals | | $1670.40 | | $2656.48 | $34.80 | $55.34 |
| **Crew B-47** | Hr. | Daily | Hr. | Daily | Bare Costs | Incl. O&P |
| 1 Blast Foreman | $32.25 | $258.00 | $50.20 | $401.60 | $33.42 | $51.40 |
| 1 Driller | 30.25 | 242.00 | 47.05 | 376.40 | | |
| 1 Equip. Oper. (light) | 37.75 | 302.00 | 56.95 | 455.60 | | |
| 1 Air Track Drill, 4" | | 840.00 | | 924.00 | | |
| 1 Air Compressor, 600 C.F.M. | | 436.40 | | 480.04 | | |
| 2 -50' Air Hose, 3" | | 32.40 | | 35.64 | 54.53 | 59.99 |
| 24 L.H., Daily Totals | | $2110.80 | | $2673.28 | $87.95 | $111.39 |
| **Crew B-47A** | Hr. | Daily | Hr. | Daily | Bare Costs | Incl. O&P |
| 1 Drilling Foreman | $32.25 | $258.00 | $50.20 | $401.60 | $36.10 | $54.97 |
| 1 Equip. Oper. (heavy) | 40.95 | 327.60 | 61.75 | 494.00 | | |
| 1 Oiler | 35.10 | 280.80 | 52.95 | 423.60 | | |
| 1 Air Track Drill, 5" | | 964.60 | | 1061.06 | 40.19 | 44.21 |
| 24 L.H., Daily Totals | | $1831.00 | | $2380.26 | $76.29 | $99.18 |
| **Crew B-47C** | Hr. | Daily | Hr. | Daily | Bare Costs | Incl. O&P |
| 1 Laborer | $30.25 | $242.00 | $47.05 | $376.40 | $34.00 | $52.00 |
| 1 Equip. Oper. (light) | 37.75 | 302.00 | 56.95 | 455.60 | | |
| 1 Air Compressor, 750 C.F.M. | | 442.60 | | 486.86 | | |
| 2 -50' Air Hose, 3" | | 32.40 | | 35.64 | | |
| 1 Air Track Drill, 4" | | 840.00 | | 924.00 | 82.19 | 90.41 |
| 16 L.H., Daily Totals | | $1859.00 | | $2278.50 | $116.19 | $142.41 |
| **Crew B-47E** | Hr. | Daily | Hr. | Daily | Bare Costs | Incl. O&P |
| 1 Laborer Foreman | $32.25 | $258.00 | $50.20 | $401.60 | $30.75 | $47.84 |
| 3 Laborers | 30.25 | 726.00 | 47.05 | 1129.20 | | |
| 1 Flatbed Truck, Gas, 3 Ton | | 224.00 | | 246.40 | 7.00 | 7.70 |
| 32 L.H., Daily Totals | | $1208.00 | | $1777.20 | $37.75 | $55.54 |

| Crew No. | Bare Costs Hr. | Daily | Incl. Subs O & P Hr. | Daily | Cost Per Labor-Hour Bare Costs | Incl. O&P |
|---|---|---|---|---|---|---|
| **Crew B-47G** | Hr. | Daily | Hr. | Daily | Bare Costs | Incl. O&P |
| 1 Laborer Foreman | $32.25 | $258.00 | $50.20 | $401.60 | $32.63 | $50.31 |
| 2 Laborers | 30.25 | 484.00 | 47.05 | 752.80 | | |
| 1 Equip. Oper. (light) | 37.75 | 302.00 | 56.95 | 455.60 | | |
| 1 Air Track Drill, 4" | | 840.00 | | 924.00 | | |
| 1 Air Compressor, 600 C.F.M. | | 436.40 | | 480.04 | | |
| 2 -50' Air Hose, 3" | | 32.40 | | 35.64 | | |
| 1 Grout Pump | | 151.40 | | 166.54 | 45.63 | 50.19 |
| 32 L.H., Daily Totals | | $2504.20 | | $3216.22 | $78.26 | $100.51 |
| **Crew B-48** | Hr. | Daily | Hr. | Daily | Bare Costs | Incl. O&P |
| 1 Labor Foreman (outside) | $32.25 | $258.00 | $50.20 | $401.60 | $33.83 | $51.86 |
| 3 Laborers | 30.25 | 726.00 | 47.05 | 1129.20 | | |
| 1 Equip. Oper. (crane) | 40.95 | 327.60 | 61.75 | 494.00 | | |
| 1 Equip. Oper. Oiler | 35.10 | 280.80 | 52.95 | 423.60 | | |
| 1 Equip. Oper. (light) | 37.75 | 302.00 | 56.95 | 455.60 | | |
| 1 Centr. Water Pump, 6" | | 305.20 | | 335.72 | | |
| 1 -20' Suction Hose, 6" | | 11.90 | | 13.09 | | |
| 1 -50' Discharge Hose, 6" | | 6.30 | | 6.93 | | |
| 1 Drill Rig, Truck-Mounted | | 2530.00 | | 2783.00 | 50.95 | 56.05 |
| 56 L.H., Daily Totals | | $4747.80 | | $6042.74 | $84.78 | $107.91 |
| **Crew B-49** | Hr. | Daily | Hr. | Daily | Bare Costs | Incl. O&P |
| 1 Labor Foreman (outside) | $32.25 | $258.00 | $50.20 | $401.60 | $35.20 | $54.49 |
| 3 Laborers | 30.25 | 726.00 | 47.05 | 1129.20 | | |
| 2 Equip. Oper. (crane) | 40.95 | 655.20 | 61.75 | 988.00 | | |
| 2 Equip. Oper. Oilers | 35.10 | 561.60 | 52.95 | 847.20 | | |
| 1 Equip. Oper. (light) | 37.75 | 302.00 | 56.95 | 455.60 | | |
| 2 Pile Drivers | 37.15 | 594.40 | 60.85 | 973.60 | | |
| 1 Hyd. Crane, 25 Ton | | 786.00 | | 864.60 | | |
| 1 Centr. Water Pump, 6" | | 305.20 | | 335.72 | | |
| 1 -20' Suction Hose, 6" | | 11.90 | | 13.09 | | |
| 1 -50' Discharge Hose, 6" | | 6.30 | | 6.93 | | |
| 1 Drill Rig, Truck-Mounted | | 2530.00 | | 2783.00 | 41.36 | 45.49 |
| 88 L.H., Daily Totals | | $6736.60 | | $8798.54 | $76.55 | $99.98 |
| **Crew B-50** | Hr. | Daily | Hr. | Daily | Bare Costs | Incl. O&P |
| 2 Pile Driver Foremen | $39.15 | $626.40 | $64.15 | $1026.40 | $36.35 | $57.93 |
| 6 Pile Drivers | 37.15 | 1783.20 | 60.85 | 2920.80 | | |
| 2 Equip. Oper. (crane) | 40.95 | 655.20 | 61.75 | 988.00 | | |
| 1 Equip. Oper. Oiler | 35.10 | 280.80 | 52.95 | 423.60 | | |
| 3 Laborers | 30.25 | 726.00 | 47.05 | 1129.20 | | |
| 1 Crawler Crane, 40 Ton | | 1054.00 | | 1159.40 | | |
| 2 Leads, 20' long | | 49.20 | | 54.12 | | |
| 1 Hammer, diesel, 15K Ft.-Lbs. | | 346.20 | | 380.82 | | |
| 1 Air Compressor, 600 C.F.M. | | 436.40 | | 480.04 | | |
| 2 -50' Air Hose, 3" | | 32.40 | | 35.64 | | |
| 1 Chainsaw, Gas, 36" Long | | 36.80 | | 40.48 | 17.46 | 19.20 |
| 112 L.H., Daily Totals | | $6026.60 | | $8638.50 | $53.81 | $77.13 |
| **Crew B-51** | Hr. | Daily | Hr. | Daily | Bare Costs | Incl. O&P |
| 1 Labor Foreman (outside) | $32.25 | $258.00 | $50.20 | $401.60 | $30.44 | $47.32 |
| 4 Laborers | 30.25 | 968.00 | 47.05 | 1505.60 | | |
| 1 Truck Driver (light) | 29.40 | 235.20 | 45.50 | 364.00 | | |
| 1 Flatbed Truck, Gas, 1.5 Ton | | 179.20 | | 197.12 | 3.73 | 4.11 |
| 48 L.H., Daily Totals | | $1640.40 | | $2468.32 | $34.17 | $51.42 |

| Crew No. | Bare Costs | | Incl. Subs O & P | | Cost Per Labor-Hour | |
|---|---|---|---|---|---|---|

| Crew B-52 | Hr. | Daily | Hr. | Daily | Bare Costs | Incl. O&P |
|---|---|---|---|---|---|---|
| 1 Carpenter Foreman | $40.10 | $320.80 | $62.40 | $499.20 | $35.34 | $54.64 |
| 1 Carpenter | 38.10 | 304.80 | 59.30 | 474.40 | | |
| 3 Laborers | 30.25 | 726.00 | 47.05 | 1129.20 | | |
| 1 Cement Finisher | 37.00 | 296.00 | 54.30 | 434.40 | | |
| .5 Rodman (reinf.) | 43.00 | 172.00 | 70.55 | 282.20 | | |
| .5 Equip. Oper. (med.) | 39.85 | 159.40 | 60.10 | 240.40 | | |
| .5 Crawler Loader, 3 C.Y. | | 446.70 | | 491.37 | 7.98 | 8.77 |
| 56 L.H., Daily Totals | | $2425.70 | | $3551.17 | $43.32 | $63.41 |

| Crew B-53 | Hr. | Daily | Hr. | Daily | Bare Costs | Incl. O&P |
|---|---|---|---|---|---|---|
| 1 Equip. Oper. (light) | $37.75 | $302.00 | $56.95 | $455.60 | $37.75 | $56.95 |
| 1 Trencher, Chain, 12 H.P. | | 56.40 | | 62.04 | 7.05 | 7.75 |
| 8 L.H., Daily Totals | | $358.40 | | $517.64 | $44.80 | $64.70 |

| Crew B-54 | Hr. | Daily | Hr. | Daily | Bare Costs | Incl. O&P |
|---|---|---|---|---|---|---|
| 1 Equip. Oper. (light) | $37.75 | $302.00 | $56.95 | $455.60 | $37.75 | $56.95 |
| 1 Trencher, Chain, 40 H.P. | | 244.20 | | 268.62 | 30.52 | 33.58 |
| 8 L.H., Daily Totals | | $546.20 | | $724.22 | $68.28 | $90.53 |

| Crew B-54A | Hr. | Daily | Hr. | Daily | Bare Costs | Incl. O&P |
|---|---|---|---|---|---|---|
| .17 Labor Foreman (outside) | $32.25 | $43.86 | $50.20 | $68.27 | $38.75 | $58.66 |
| 1 Equipment Operator (med.) | 39.85 | 318.80 | 60.10 | 480.80 | | |
| 1 Wheel Trencher, 67 H.P. | | 967.40 | | 1064.14 | 103.35 | 113.69 |
| 9.36 L.H., Daily Totals | | $1330.06 | | $1613.21 | $142.10 | $172.35 |

| Crew B-54B | Hr. | Daily | Hr. | Daily | Bare Costs | Incl. O&P |
|---|---|---|---|---|---|---|
| .25 Labor Foreman (outside) | $32.25 | $64.50 | $50.20 | $100.40 | $38.33 | $58.12 |
| 1 Equipment Operator (med.) | 39.85 | 318.80 | 60.10 | 480.80 | | |
| 1 Wheel Trencher, 150 H.P. | | 1701.00 | | 1871.10 | 170.10 | 187.11 |
| 10 L.H., Daily Totals | | $2084.30 | | $2452.30 | $208.43 | $245.23 |

| Crew B-55 | Hr. | Daily | Hr. | Daily | Bare Costs | Incl. O&P |
|---|---|---|---|---|---|---|
| 2 Laborers | $30.25 | $484.00 | $47.05 | $752.80 | $29.97 | $46.53 |
| 1 Truck Driver (light) | 29.40 | 235.20 | 45.50 | 364.00 | | |
| 1 Truck-mounted earth auger | | 701.80 | | 771.98 | | |
| 1 Flatbed Truck, Gas, 3 Ton | | 224.00 | | 246.40 | 38.58 | 42.43 |
| 24 L.H., Daily Totals | | $1645.00 | | $2135.18 | $68.54 | $88.97 |

| Crew B-56 | Hr. | Daily | Hr. | Daily | Bare Costs | Incl. O&P |
|---|---|---|---|---|---|---|
| 1 Laborer | $30.25 | $242.00 | $47.05 | $376.40 | $34.00 | $52.00 |
| 1 Equip. Oper. (light) | 37.75 | 302.00 | 56.95 | 455.60 | | |
| 1 Air Track Drill, 4" | | 840.00 | | 924.00 | | |
| 1 Air Compressor, 600 C.F.M. | | 436.40 | | 480.04 | | |
| 1 -50' Air Hose, 3" | | 16.20 | | 17.82 | 80.79 | 88.87 |
| 16 L.H., Daily Totals | | $1836.60 | | $2253.86 | $114.79 | $140.87 |

| Crew B-57 | Hr. | Daily | Hr. | Daily | Bare Costs | Incl. O&P |
|---|---|---|---|---|---|---|
| 1 Labor Foreman (outside) | $32.25 | $258.00 | $50.20 | $401.60 | $34.42 | $52.66 |
| 2 Laborers | 30.25 | 484.00 | 47.05 | 752.80 | | |
| 1 Equip. Oper. (crane) | 40.95 | 327.60 | 61.75 | 494.00 | | |
| 1 Equip. Oper. (light) | 37.75 | 302.00 | 56.95 | 455.60 | | |
| 1 Equip. Oper. Oiler | 35.10 | 280.80 | 52.95 | 423.60 | | |
| 1 Crawler Crane, 25 Ton | | 1033.00 | | 1136.30 | | |
| 1 Clamshell Bucket, 1 C.Y. | | 46.20 | | 50.82 | | |
| 1 Centr. Water Pump, 6" | | 305.20 | | 335.72 | | |
| 1 -20' Suction Hose, 6" | | 11.90 | | 13.09 | | |
| 20 -50' Discharge Hose, 6" | | 126.00 | | 138.60 | 31.71 | 34.89 |
| 48 L.H., Daily Totals | | $3174.70 | | $4202.13 | $66.14 | $87.54 |

| Crew B-58 | Hr. | Daily | Hr. | Daily | Bare Costs | Incl. O&P |
|---|---|---|---|---|---|---|
| 2 Laborers | $30.25 | $484.00 | $47.05 | $752.80 | $32.75 | $50.35 |
| 1 Equip. Oper. (light) | 37.75 | 302.00 | 56.95 | 455.60 | | |
| 1 Backhoe Loader, 48 H.P. | | 285.40 | | 313.94 | | |
| 1 Small Helicopter, w/pilot | | 2433.00 | | 2676.30 | 113.27 | 124.59 |
| 24 L.H., Daily Totals | | $3504.40 | | $4198.64 | $146.02 | $174.94 |

| Crew B-59 | Hr. | Daily | Hr. | Daily | Bare Costs | Incl. O&P |
|---|---|---|---|---|---|---|
| 1 Truck Driver (heavy) | $30.60 | $244.80 | $47.35 | $378.80 | $30.60 | $47.35 |
| 1 Truck Tractor, 220 H.P. | | 271.80 | | 298.98 | | |
| 1 Water Tanker, 5000 Gal. | | 129.60 | | 142.56 | 50.17 | 55.19 |
| 8 L.H., Daily Totals | | $646.20 | | $820.34 | $80.78 | $102.54 |

| Crew B-59A | Hr. | Daily | Hr. | Daily | Bare Costs | Incl. O&P |
|---|---|---|---|---|---|---|
| 2 Laborers | $30.25 | $484.00 | $47.05 | $752.80 | $30.37 | $47.15 |
| 1 Truck Driver (heavy) | 30.60 | 244.80 | 47.35 | 378.80 | | |
| 1 Water Tanker, 5000 Gal. | | 129.60 | | 142.56 | | |
| 1 Truck Tractor, 220 H.P. | | 271.80 | | 298.98 | 16.73 | 18.40 |
| 24 L.H., Daily Totals | | $1130.20 | | $1573.14 | $47.09 | $65.55 |

| Crew B-60 | Hr. | Daily | Hr. | Daily | Bare Costs | Incl. O&P |
|---|---|---|---|---|---|---|
| 1 Labor Foreman (outside) | $32.25 | $258.00 | $50.20 | $401.60 | $34.90 | $53.27 |
| 2 Laborers | 30.25 | 484.00 | 47.05 | 752.80 | | |
| 1 Equip. Oper. (crane) | 40.95 | 327.60 | 61.75 | 494.00 | | |
| 2 Equip. Oper. (light) | 37.75 | 604.00 | 56.95 | 911.20 | | |
| 1 Equip. Oper. Oiler | 35.10 | 280.80 | 52.95 | 423.60 | | |
| 1 Crawler Crane, 40 Ton | | 1054.00 | | 1159.40 | | |
| 2 Leads, 20' long | | 49.20 | | 54.12 | | |
| 1 Hammer, diesel, 15K Ft.-Lbs. | | 346.20 | | 380.82 | | |
| 1 Backhoe Loader, 48 H.P. | | 285.40 | | 313.94 | 30.98 | 34.08 |
| 56 L.H., Daily Totals | | $3689.20 | | $4891.48 | $65.88 | $87.35 |

| Crew B-61 | Hr. | Daily | Hr. | Daily | Bare Costs | Incl. O&P |
|---|---|---|---|---|---|---|
| 1 Labor Foreman (outside) | $32.25 | $258.00 | $50.20 | $401.60 | $32.15 | $49.66 |
| 3 Laborers | 30.25 | 726.00 | 47.05 | 1129.20 | | |
| 1 Equip. Oper. (light) | 37.75 | 302.00 | 56.95 | 455.60 | | |
| 1 Cement Mixer, 2 C.Y. | | 184.20 | | 202.62 | | |
| 1 Air Compressor, 160 C.F.M. | | 137.60 | | 151.36 | 8.04 | 8.85 |
| 40 L.H., Daily Totals | | $1607.80 | | $2340.38 | $40.20 | $58.51 |

| Crew B-62 | Hr. | Daily | Hr. | Daily | Bare Costs | Incl. O&P |
|---|---|---|---|---|---|---|
| 2 Laborers | $30.25 | $484.00 | $47.05 | $752.80 | $32.75 | $50.35 |
| 1 Equip. Oper. (light) | 37.75 | 302.00 | 56.95 | 455.60 | | |
| 1 Loader, Skid Steer, 30 HP, gas | | 138.00 | | 151.80 | 5.75 | 6.33 |
| 24 L.H., Daily Totals | | $924.00 | | $1360.20 | $38.50 | $56.67 |

| Crew B-63 | Hr. | Daily | Hr. | Daily | Bare Costs | Incl. O&P |
|---|---|---|---|---|---|---|
| 4 Laborers | $30.25 | $968.00 | $47.05 | $1505.60 | $31.75 | $49.03 |
| 1 Equip. Oper. (light) | 37.75 | 302.00 | 56.95 | 455.60 | | |
| 1 Loader, Skid Steer, 30 HP, gas | | 138.00 | | 151.80 | 3.45 | 3.79 |
| 40 L.H., Daily Totals | | $1408.00 | | $2113.00 | $35.20 | $52.83 |

| Crew B-64 | Hr. | Daily | Hr. | Daily | Bare Costs | Incl. O&P |
|---|---|---|---|---|---|---|
| 1 Laborer | $30.25 | $242.00 | $47.05 | $376.40 | $29.82 | $46.27 |
| 1 Truck Driver (light) | 29.40 | 235.20 | 45.50 | 364.00 | | |
| 1 Power Mulcher (small) | | 131.20 | | 144.32 | | |
| 1 Flatbed Truck, Gas, 1.5 Ton | | 179.20 | | 197.12 | 19.40 | 21.34 |
| 16 L.H., Daily Totals | | $787.60 | | $1081.84 | $49.23 | $67.61 |

| Crew B-65 | Hr. | Daily | Hr. | Daily | Bare Costs | Incl. O&P |
|---|---|---|---|---|---|---|
| 1 Laborer | $30.25 | $242.00 | $47.05 | $376.40 | $29.82 | $46.27 |
| 1 Truck Driver (light) | 29.40 | 235.20 | 45.50 | 364.00 | | |
| 1 Power Mulcher (large) | | 261.00 | | 287.10 | | |
| 1 Flatbed Truck, Gas, 1.5 Ton | | 179.20 | | 197.12 | 27.51 | 30.26 |
| 16 L.H., Daily Totals | | $917.40 | | $1224.62 | $57.34 | $76.54 |

| Crew B-66 | Hr. | Daily | Hr. | Daily | Bare Costs | Incl. O&P |
|---|---|---|---|---|---|---|
| 1 Equip. Oper. (light) | $37.75 | $302.00 | $56.95 | $455.60 | $37.75 | $56.95 |
| 1 Loader-Backhoe | | 218.60 | | 240.46 | 27.32 | 30.06 |
| 8 L.H., Daily Totals | | $520.60 | | $696.06 | $65.08 | $87.01 |

| Crew B-67 | Hr. | Daily | Hr. | Daily | Bare Costs | Incl. O&P |
|---|---|---|---|---|---|---|
| 1 Millwright | $39.65 | $317.20 | $58.40 | $467.20 | $38.70 | $57.67 |
| 1 Equip. Oper. (light) | 37.75 | 302.00 | 56.95 | 455.60 | | |
| 1 Forklift, R/T, 4,000 Lb. | | 277.80 | | 305.58 | 17.36 | 19.10 |
| 16 L.H., Daily Totals | | $897.00 | | $1228.38 | $56.06 | $76.77 |

| Crew B-68 | Hr. | Daily | Hr. | Daily | Bare Costs | Incl. O&P |
|---|---|---|---|---|---|---|
| 2 Millwrights | $39.65 | $634.40 | $58.40 | $934.40 | $39.02 | $57.92 |
| 1 Equip. Oper. (light) | 37.75 | 302.00 | 56.95 | 455.60 | | |
| 1 Forklift, R/T, 4,000 Lb. | | 277.80 | | 305.58 | 11.57 | 12.73 |
| 24 L.H., Daily Totals | | $1214.20 | | $1695.58 | $50.59 | $70.65 |

| Crew B-69 | Hr. | Daily | Hr. | Daily | Bare Costs | Incl. O&P |
|---|---|---|---|---|---|---|
| 1 Labor Foreman (outside) | $32.25 | $258.00 | $50.20 | $401.60 | $33.17 | $51.01 |
| 3 Laborers | 30.25 | 726.00 | 47.05 | 1129.20 | | |
| 1 Equip Oper. (crane) | 40.95 | 327.60 | 61.75 | 494.00 | | |
| 1 Equip Oper. Oiler | 35.10 | 280.80 | 52.95 | 423.60 | | |
| 1 Hyd. Crane, 80 Ton | | 1290.00 | | 1419.00 | 26.88 | 29.56 |
| 48 L.H., Daily Totals | | $2882.40 | | $3867.40 | $60.05 | $80.57 |

| Crew B-69A | Hr. | Daily | Hr. | Daily | Bare Costs | Incl. O&P |
|---|---|---|---|---|---|---|
| 1 Labor Foreman | $32.25 | $258.00 | $50.20 | $401.60 | $33.31 | $50.96 |
| 3 Laborers | 30.25 | 726.00 | 47.05 | 1129.20 | | |
| 1 Equip. Oper. (medium) | 39.85 | 318.80 | 60.10 | 480.80 | | |
| 1 Concrete Finisher | 37.00 | 296.00 | 54.30 | 434.40 | | |
| 1 Curb/Gutter Paver, 2-Track | | 735.20 | | 808.72 | 15.32 | 16.85 |
| 48 L.H., Daily Totals | | $2334.00 | | $3254.72 | $48.63 | $67.81 |

| Crew B-69B | Hr. | Daily | Hr. | Daily | Bare Costs | Incl. O&P |
|---|---|---|---|---|---|---|
| 1 Labor Foreman | $32.25 | $258.00 | $50.20 | $401.60 | $33.31 | $50.96 |
| 3 Laborers | 30.25 | 726.00 | 47.05 | 1129.20 | | |
| 1 Equip. Oper. (medium) | 39.85 | 318.80 | 60.10 | 480.80 | | |
| 1 Cement Finisher | 37.00 | 296.00 | 54.30 | 434.40 | | |
| 1 Curb/Gutter Paver, 4-Track | | 830.40 | | 913.44 | 17.30 | 19.03 |
| 48 L.H., Daily Totals | | $2429.20 | | $3359.44 | $50.61 | $69.99 |

| Crew B-70 | Hr. | Daily | Hr. | Daily | Bare Costs | Incl. O&P |
|---|---|---|---|---|---|---|
| 1 Labor Foreman (outside) | $32.25 | $258.00 | $50.20 | $401.60 | $34.65 | $53.09 |
| 3 Laborers | 30.25 | 726.00 | 47.05 | 1129.20 | | |
| 3 Equip. Oper. (med.) | 39.85 | 956.40 | 60.10 | 1442.40 | | |
| 1 Grader, 30,000 Lbs. | | 534.40 | | 587.84 | | |
| 1 Ripper, beam & 1 shank | | 77.80 | | 85.58 | | |
| 1 Road Sweeper, SP, 8' wide | | 582.20 | | 640.42 | | |
| 1 F.E. Loader, W.M., 1.5 C.Y. | | 302.80 | | 333.08 | 26.74 | 29.41 |
| 56 L.H., Daily Totals | | $3437.60 | | $4620.12 | $61.39 | $82.50 |

| Crew B-71 | Hr. | Daily | Hr. | Daily | Bare Costs | Incl. O&P |
|---|---|---|---|---|---|---|
| 1 Labor Foreman (outside) | $32.25 | $258.00 | $50.20 | $401.60 | $34.65 | $53.09 |
| 3 Laborers | 30.25 | 726.00 | 47.05 | 1129.20 | | |
| 3 Equip. Oper. (med.) | 39.85 | 956.40 | 60.10 | 1442.40 | | |
| 1 Pvmt. Profiler, 750 H.P. | | 5445.00 | | 5989.50 | | |
| 1 Road Sweeper, SP, 8' wide | | 582.20 | | 640.42 | | |
| 1 F.E. Loader, W.M., 1.5 C.Y. | | 302.80 | | 333.08 | 113.04 | 124.34 |
| 56 L.H., Daily Totals | | $8270.40 | | $9936.20 | $147.69 | $177.43 |

| Crew B-72 | Hr. | Daily | Hr. | Daily | Bare Costs | Incl. O&P |
|---|---|---|---|---|---|---|
| 1 Labor Foreman (outside) | $32.25 | $258.00 | $50.20 | $401.60 | $35.30 | $53.97 |
| 3 Laborers | 30.25 | 726.00 | 47.05 | 1129.20 | | |
| 4 Equip. Oper. (med.) | 39.85 | 1275.20 | 60.10 | 1923.20 | | |
| 1 Pvmt. Profiler, 750 H.P. | | 5445.00 | | 5989.50 | | |
| 1 Hammermill, 250 H.P. | | 1582.00 | | 1740.20 | | |
| 1 Windrow Loader | | 910.80 | | 1001.88 | | |
| 1 Mix Paver 165 H.P. | | 1905.00 | | 2095.50 | | |
| 1 Roller, Pneum. Whl, 12 Ton | | 307.80 | | 338.58 | 158.60 | 174.46 |
| 64 L.H., Daily Totals | | $12409.80 | | $14619.66 | $193.90 | $228.43 |

| Crew B-73 | Hr. | Daily | Hr. | Daily | Bare Costs | Incl. O&P |
|---|---|---|---|---|---|---|
| 1 Labor Foreman (outside) | $32.25 | $258.00 | $50.20 | $401.60 | $36.50 | $55.60 |
| 2 Laborers | 30.25 | 484.00 | 47.05 | 752.80 | | |
| 5 Equip. Oper. (med.) | 39.85 | 1594.00 | 60.10 | 2404.00 | | |
| 1 Road Mixer, 310 H.P. | | 1884.00 | | 2072.40 | | |
| 1 Tandem Roller, 10 Ton | | 219.00 | | 240.90 | | |
| 1 Hammermill, 250 H.P. | | 1582.00 | | 1740.20 | | |
| 1 Grader, 30,000 Lbs. | | 534.40 | | 587.84 | | |
| .5 F.E. Loader, W.M., 1.5 C.Y. | | 151.40 | | 166.54 | | |
| .5 Truck Tractor, 220 H.P. | | 135.90 | | 149.49 | | |
| .5 Water Tanker, 5000 Gal. | | 64.80 | | 71.28 | 71.43 | 78.57 |
| 64 L.H., Daily Totals | | $6907.50 | | $8587.05 | $107.93 | $134.17 |

| Crew B-74 | Hr. | Daily | Hr. | Daily | Bare Costs | Incl. O&P |
|---|---|---|---|---|---|---|
| 1 Labor Foreman (outside) | $32.25 | $258.00 | $50.20 | $401.60 | $35.39 | $54.04 |
| 1 Laborer | 30.25 | 242.00 | 47.05 | 376.40 | | |
| 4 Equip. Oper. (med.) | 39.85 | 1275.20 | 60.10 | 1923.20 | | |
| 2 Truck Drivers (heavy) | 30.60 | 489.60 | 47.35 | 757.60 | | |
| 1 Grader, 30,000 Lbs. | | 534.40 | | 587.84 | | |
| 1 Ripper, beam & 1 shank | | 77.80 | | 85.58 | | |
| 2 Stabilizers, 310 H.P. | | 2674.00 | | 2941.40 | | |
| 1 Flatbed Truck, Gas, 3 Ton | | 224.00 | | 246.40 | | |
| 1 Chem. Spreader, Towed | | 46.80 | | 51.48 | | |
| 1 Roller, Vibratory, 25 Ton | | 593.80 | | 653.18 | | |
| 1 Water Tanker, 5000 Gal. | | 129.60 | | 142.56 | | |
| 1 Truck Tractor, 220 H.P. | | 271.80 | | 298.98 | 71.13 | 78.24 |
| 64 L.H., Daily Totals | | $6817.00 | | $8466.22 | $106.52 | $132.28 |

| Crew B-75 | Hr. | Daily | Hr. | Daily | Bare Costs | Incl. O&P |
|---|---|---|---|---|---|---|
| 1 Labor Foreman (outside) | $32.25 | $258.00 | $50.20 | $401.60 | $36.07 | $55.00 |
| 1 Laborer | 30.25 | 242.00 | 47.05 | 376.40 | | |
| 4 Equip. Oper. (med.) | 39.85 | 1275.20 | 60.10 | 1923.20 | | |
| 1 Truck Driver (heavy) | 30.60 | 244.80 | 47.35 | 378.80 | | |
| 1 Grader, 30,000 Lbs. | | 534.40 | | 587.84 | | |
| 1 Ripper, beam & 1 shank | | 77.80 | | 85.58 | | |
| 2 Stabilizers, 310 H.P. | | 2674.00 | | 2941.40 | | |
| 1 Dist. Tanker, 3000 Gallon | | 294.00 | | 323.40 | | |
| 1 Truck Tractor, 6x4, 380 H.P. | | 453.60 | | 498.96 | | |
| 1 Roller, Vibratory, 25 Ton | | 593.80 | | 653.18 | 82.64 | 90.90 |
| 56 L.H., Daily Totals | | $6647.60 | | $8170.36 | $118.71 | $145.90 |

| Crew No. | Bare Costs | | Incl. Subs O & P | | Cost Per Labor-Hour | |
|---|---|---|---|---|---|---|
| | Hr. | Daily | Hr. | Daily | Bare Costs | Incl. O&P |
| **Crew B-76** | Hr. | Daily | Hr. | Daily | Bare Costs | Incl. O&P |
| 1 Dock Builder Foreman | $39.15 | $313.20 | $64.15 | $513.20 | $37.99 | $60.54 |
| 5 Dock Builders | 37.15 | 1486.00 | 60.85 | 2434.00 | | |
| 2 Equip. Oper. (crane) | 40.95 | 655.20 | 61.75 | 988.00 | | |
| 1 Equip. Oper. Oiler | 35.10 | 280.80 | 52.95 | 423.60 | | |
| 1 Crawler Crane, 50 Ton | | 1098.00 | | 1207.80 | | |
| 1 Barge, 400 Ton | | 727.80 | | 800.58 | | |
| 1 Hammer, diesel, 15K Ft.-Lbs. | | 346.20 | | 380.82 | | |
| 2 Leads, 20' long | | 49.20 | | 54.12 | | |
| 1 Air Compressor, 600 C.F.M. | | 436.40 | | 480.04 | | |
| 2 -50' Air Hose, 3" | | 32.40 | | 35.64 | 37.36 | 41.10 |
| 72 L.H., Daily Totals | | $5425.20 | | $7317.80 | $75.35 | $101.64 |
| **Crew B-76A** | Hr. | Daily | Hr. | Daily | Bare Costs | Incl. O&P |
| 1 Laborer Foreman | $32.25 | $258.00 | $50.20 | $401.60 | $32.44 | $50.02 |
| 5 Laborers | 30.25 | 1210.00 | 47.05 | 1882.00 | | |
| 1 Equip. Oper. (crane) | 40.95 | 327.60 | 61.75 | 494.00 | | |
| 1 Equip. Oper. Oiler | 35.10 | 280.80 | 52.95 | 423.60 | | |
| 1 Crawler Crane, 50 Ton | | 1098.00 | | 1207.80 | | |
| 1 Barge, 400 Ton | | 727.80 | | 800.58 | 28.53 | 31.38 |
| 64 L.H., Daily Totals | | $3902.20 | | $5209.58 | $60.97 | $81.40 |
| **Crew B-77** | Hr. | Daily | Hr. | Daily | Bare Costs | Incl. O&P |
| 1 Labor Foreman | $32.25 | $258.00 | $50.20 | $401.60 | $30.48 | $47.37 |
| 3 Laborers | 30.25 | 726.00 | 47.05 | 1129.20 | | |
| 1 Truck Driver (light) | 29.40 | 235.20 | 45.50 | 364.00 | | |
| 1 Crack Cleaner, 25 H.P. | | 51.80 | | 56.98 | | |
| 1 Crack Filler, Trailer Mtd. | | 189.80 | | 208.78 | | |
| 1 Flatbed Truck, Gas, 3 Ton | | 224.00 | | 246.40 | 11.64 | 12.80 |
| 40 L.H., Daily Totals | | $1684.80 | | $2406.96 | $42.12 | $60.17 |
| **Crew B-78** | Hr. | Daily | Hr. | Daily | Bare Costs | Incl. O&P |
| 1 Labor Foreman | $32.25 | $258.00 | $50.20 | $401.60 | $30.44 | $47.32 |
| 4 Laborers | 30.25 | 968.00 | 47.05 | 1505.60 | | |
| 1 Truck Driver (light) | 29.40 | 235.20 | 45.50 | 364.00 | | |
| 1 Paint Striper, S.P. | | 144.00 | | 158.40 | | |
| 1 Flatbed Truck, Gas, 3 Ton | | 224.00 | | 246.40 | | |
| 1 Pickup Truck, 3/4 Ton | | 109.00 | | 119.90 | 9.94 | 10.93 |
| 48 L.H., Daily Totals | | $1938.20 | | $2795.90 | $40.38 | $58.25 |
| **Crew B-78A** | Hr. | Daily | Hr. | Daily | Bare Costs | Incl. O&P |
| 1 Equip. Oper. (light) | $37.75 | $302.00 | $56.95 | $455.60 | $37.75 | $56.95 |
| 1 Line Rem. (metal balls) 115 HP | | 890.80 | | 979.88 | 111.35 | 122.49 |
| 8 L.H., Daily Totals | | $1192.80 | | $1435.48 | $149.10 | $179.44 |
| **Crew B-78B** | Hr. | Daily | Hr. | Daily | Bare Costs | Incl. O&P |
| 2 Laborers | $30.25 | $484.00 | $47.05 | $752.80 | $31.08 | $48.15 |
| .25 Equip. Oper. (light) | 37.75 | 75.50 | 56.95 | 113.90 | | |
| 1 Pickup Truck, 3/4 Ton | | 109.00 | | 119.90 | | |
| 1 Line Rem., 11 HP, walk behind | | 51.40 | | 56.54 | | |
| .25 Road Sweeper, SP, 8' wide | | 145.55 | | 160.10 | 17.00 | 18.70 |
| 18 L.H., Daily Totals | | $865.45 | | $1203.24 | $48.08 | $66.85 |
| **Crew B-79** | Hr. | Daily | Hr. | Daily | Bare Costs | Incl. O&P |
| 1 Labor Foreman | $32.25 | $258.00 | $50.20 | $401.60 | $30.48 | $47.37 |
| 3 Laborers | 30.25 | 726.00 | 47.05 | 1129.20 | | |
| 1 Truck Driver (light) | 29.40 | 235.20 | 45.50 | 364.00 | | |
| 1 Thermo. Striper, T.M. | | 670.60 | | 737.66 | | |
| 1 Flatbed Truck, Gas, 3 Ton | | 224.00 | | 246.40 | | |
| 2 Pickup Truck, 3/4 Ton | | 218.00 | | 239.80 | 27.82 | 30.60 |
| 40 L.H., Daily Totals | | $2331.80 | | $3118.66 | $58.30 | $77.97 |

| Crew No. | Bare Costs | | Incl. Subs O & P | | Cost Per Labor-Hour | |
|---|---|---|---|---|---|---|
| | Hr. | Daily | Hr. | Daily | Bare Costs | Incl. O&P |
| **Crew B-79A** | Hr. | Daily | Hr. | Daily | Bare Costs | Incl. O&P |
| 1.5 Equip. Oper. (light) | $37.75 | $453.00 | $56.95 | $683.40 | $37.75 | $56.95 |
| .5 Line Remov. (grinder) 115 HP | | 434.50 | | 477.95 | | |
| 1 Line Rem. (metal balls) 115 HP | | 890.80 | | 979.88 | 110.44 | 121.49 |
| 12 L.H., Daily Totals | | $1778.30 | | $2141.23 | $148.19 | $178.44 |
| **Crew B-80** | Hr. | Daily | Hr. | Daily | Bare Costs | Incl. O&P |
| 1 Labor Foreman | $32.25 | $258.00 | $50.20 | $401.60 | $32.41 | $49.92 |
| 1 Laborer | 30.25 | 242.00 | 47.05 | 376.40 | | |
| 1 Truck Driver (light) | 29.40 | 235.20 | 45.50 | 364.00 | | |
| 1 Equip. Oper. (light) | 37.75 | 302.00 | 56.95 | 455.60 | | |
| 1 Flatbed Truck, Gas, 3 Ton | | 224.00 | | 246.40 | | |
| 1 Earth Auger, Truck-Mtd. | | 402.80 | | 443.08 | 19.59 | 21.55 |
| 32 L.H., Daily Totals | | $1664.00 | | $2287.08 | $52.00 | $71.47 |
| **Crew B-80A** | Hr. | Daily | Hr. | Daily | Bare Costs | Incl. O&P |
| 3 Laborers | $30.25 | $726.00 | $47.05 | $1129.20 | $30.25 | $47.05 |
| 1 Flatbed Truck, Gas, 3 Ton | | 224.00 | | 246.40 | 9.33 | 10.27 |
| 24 L.H., Daily Totals | | $950.00 | | $1375.60 | $39.58 | $57.32 |
| **Crew B-80B** | Hr. | Daily | Hr. | Daily | Bare Costs | Incl. O&P |
| 3 Laborers | $30.25 | $726.00 | $47.05 | $1129.20 | $32.13 | $49.52 |
| 1 Equip. Oper. (light) | 37.75 | 302.00 | 56.95 | 455.60 | | |
| 1 Crane, Flatbed Mounted, 3 Ton | | 224.60 | | 247.06 | 7.02 | 7.72 |
| 32 L.H., Daily Totals | | $1252.60 | | $1831.86 | $39.14 | $57.25 |
| **Crew B-80C** | Hr. | Daily | Hr. | Daily | Bare Costs | Incl. O&P |
| 2 Laborers | $30.25 | $484.00 | $47.05 | $752.80 | $29.97 | $46.53 |
| 1 Truck Driver (light) | 29.40 | 235.20 | 45.50 | 364.00 | | |
| 1 Flatbed Truck, Gas, 1.5 Ton | | 179.20 | | 197.12 | | |
| 1 Manual fence post auger, gas | | 6.80 | | 7.48 | 7.75 | 8.53 |
| 24 L.H., Daily Totals | | $905.20 | | $1321.40 | $37.72 | $55.06 |
| **Crew B-81** | Hr. | Daily | Hr. | Daily | Bare Costs | Incl. O&P |
| 1 Laborer | $30.25 | $242.00 | $47.05 | $376.40 | $33.57 | $51.50 |
| 1 Equip. Oper. (med.) | 39.85 | 318.80 | 60.10 | 480.80 | | |
| 1 Truck Driver (heavy) | 30.60 | 244.80 | 47.35 | 378.80 | | |
| 1 Hydromulcher, T.M. | | 281.60 | | 309.76 | | |
| 1 Truck Tractor, 220 H.P. | | 271.80 | | 298.98 | 23.06 | 25.36 |
| 24 L.H., Daily Totals | | $1359.00 | | $1844.74 | $56.63 | $76.86 |
| **Crew B-82** | Hr. | Daily | Hr. | Daily | Bare Costs | Incl. O&P |
| 1 Laborer | $30.25 | $242.00 | $47.05 | $376.40 | $34.00 | $52.00 |
| 1 Equip. Oper. (light) | 37.75 | 302.00 | 56.95 | 455.60 | | |
| 1 Horiz. Borer, 6 H.P. | | 76.40 | | 84.04 | 4.78 | 5.25 |
| 16 L.H., Daily Totals | | $620.40 | | $916.04 | $38.77 | $57.25 |
| **Crew B-82A** | Hr. | Daily | Hr. | Daily | Bare Costs | Incl. O&P |
| 1 Laborer | $30.25 | $242.00 | $47.05 | $376.40 | $34.00 | $52.00 |
| 1 Equip. Oper. (light) | 37.75 | 302.00 | 56.95 | 455.60 | | |
| 1 Flatbed Truck, Gas, 3 Ton | | 224.00 | | 246.40 | | |
| 1 Flatbed Trailer, 25 Ton | | 97.00 | | 106.70 | | |
| 1 Horiz. Dir. Drill, 20k lb thrust | | 603.00 | | 663.30 | 57.75 | 63.52 |
| 16 L.H., Daily Totals | | $1468.00 | | $1848.40 | $91.75 | $115.53 |

# Crews

| Crew B-82B | Hr. | Daily | Hr. | Daily | Bare Costs | Incl. O&P |
|---|---|---|---|---|---|---|
| 2 Laborers | $30.25 | $484.00 | $47.05 | $752.80 | $32.75 | $50.35 |
| 1 Equip. Oper. (light) | 37.75 | 302.00 | 56.95 | 455.60 | | |
| 1 Flatbed Truck, Gas, 3 Ton | | 224.00 | | 246.40 | | |
| 1 Flatbed Trailer, 25 Ton | | 97.00 | | 106.70 | | |
| 1 Horiz. Dir. Drill, 30k lb thrust | | 845.20 | | 929.72 | 48.59 | 53.45 |
| 24 L.H., Daily Totals | | $1952.20 | | $2491.22 | $81.34 | $103.80 |

| Crew B-82C | Hr. | Daily | Hr. | Daily | Bare Costs | Incl. O&P |
|---|---|---|---|---|---|---|
| 2 Laborers | $30.25 | $484.00 | $47.05 | $752.80 | $32.75 | $50.35 |
| 1 Equip. Oper. (light) | 37.75 | 302.00 | 56.95 | 455.60 | | |
| 1 Flatbed Truck, Gas, 3 Ton | | 224.00 | | 246.40 | | |
| 1 Flatbed Trailer, 25 Ton | | 97.00 | | 106.70 | | |
| 1 Horiz. Dir. Drill, 50k lb thrust | | 1117.00 | | 1228.70 | 59.92 | 65.91 |
| 24 L.H., Daily Totals | | $2224.00 | | $2790.20 | $92.67 | $116.26 |

| Crew B-82D | Hr. | Daily | Hr. | Daily | Bare Costs | Incl. O&P |
|---|---|---|---|---|---|---|
| 1 Equip. Oper. (light) | $37.75 | $302.00 | $56.95 | $455.60 | $37.75 | $56.95 |
| 1 Mud Trailer for HDD, 1500 gallon | | 267.00 | | 293.70 | 33.38 | 36.71 |
| 8 L.H., Daily Totals | | $569.00 | | $749.30 | $71.13 | $93.66 |

| Crew B-83 | Hr. | Daily | Hr. | Daily | Bare Costs | Incl. O&P |
|---|---|---|---|---|---|---|
| 1 Tugboat Captain | $39.85 | $318.80 | $60.10 | $480.80 | $35.05 | $53.58 |
| 1 Tugboat Hand | 30.25 | 242.00 | 47.05 | 376.40 | | |
| 1 Tugboat, 250 H.P. | | 624.00 | | 686.40 | 39.00 | 42.90 |
| 16 L.H., Daily Totals | | $1184.80 | | $1543.60 | $74.05 | $96.47 |

| Crew B-84 | Hr. | Daily | Hr. | Daily | Bare Costs | Incl. O&P |
|---|---|---|---|---|---|---|
| 1 Equip. Oper. (med.) | $39.85 | $318.80 | $60.10 | $480.80 | $39.85 | $60.10 |
| 1 Rotary Mower/Tractor | | 264.60 | | 291.06 | 33.08 | 36.38 |
| 8 L.H., Daily Totals | | $583.40 | | $771.86 | $72.92 | $96.48 |

| Crew B-85 | Hr. | Daily | Hr. | Daily | Bare Costs | Incl. O&P |
|---|---|---|---|---|---|---|
| 3 Laborers | $30.25 | $726.00 | $47.05 | $1129.20 | $32.24 | $49.72 |
| 1 Equip. Oper. (med.) | 39.85 | 318.80 | 60.10 | 480.80 | | |
| 1 Truck Driver (heavy) | 30.60 | 244.80 | 47.35 | 378.80 | | |
| 1 Aerial Lift Truck, 80' | | 614.60 | | 676.06 | | |
| 1 Brush Chipper, 12", 130 H.P. | | 215.60 | | 237.16 | | |
| 1 Pruning Saw, Rotary | | 7.45 | | 8.20 | 20.94 | 23.04 |
| 40 L.H., Daily Totals | | $2127.25 | | $2910.22 | $53.18 | $72.76 |

| Crew B-86 | Hr. | Daily | Hr. | Daily | Bare Costs | Incl. O&P |
|---|---|---|---|---|---|---|
| 1 Equip. Oper. (med.) | $39.85 | $318.80 | $60.10 | $480.80 | $39.85 | $60.10 |
| 1 Stump Chipper, S.P. | | 156.80 | | 172.48 | 19.60 | 21.56 |
| 8 L.H., Daily Totals | | $475.60 | | $653.28 | $59.45 | $81.66 |

| Crew B-86A | Hr. | Daily | Hr. | Daily | Bare Costs | Incl. O&P |
|---|---|---|---|---|---|---|
| 1 Equip. Oper. (medium) | $39.85 | $318.80 | $60.10 | $480.80 | $39.85 | $60.10 |
| 1 Grader, 30,000 Lbs. | | 534.40 | | 587.84 | 66.80 | 73.48 |
| 8 L.H., Daily Totals | | $853.20 | | $1068.64 | $106.65 | $133.58 |

| Crew B-86B | Hr. | Daily | Hr. | Daily | Bare Costs | Incl. O&P |
|---|---|---|---|---|---|---|
| 1 Equip. Oper. (medium) | $39.85 | $318.80 | $60.10 | $480.80 | $39.85 | $60.10 |
| 1 Dozer, 200 H.P. | | 1071.00 | | 1178.10 | 133.88 | 147.26 |
| 8 L.H., Daily Totals | | $1389.80 | | $1658.90 | $173.72 | $207.36 |

| Crew B-87 | Hr. | Daily | Hr. | Daily | Bare Costs | Incl. O&P |
|---|---|---|---|---|---|---|
| 1 Laborer | $30.25 | $242.00 | $47.05 | $376.40 | $37.93 | $57.49 |
| 4 Equip. Oper. (med.) | 39.85 | 1275.20 | 60.10 | 1923.20 | | |
| 2 Feller Buncher, 100 H.P. | | 1088.80 | | 1197.68 | | |
| 1 Log Chipper, 22" Tree | | 573.20 | | 630.52 | | |
| 1 Dozer, 105 H.P. | | 532.40 | | 585.64 | | |
| 1 Chainsaw, Gas, 36" Long | | 36.80 | | 40.48 | 55.78 | 61.36 |
| 40 L.H., Daily Totals | | $3748.40 | | $4753.92 | $93.71 | $118.85 |

| Crew B-88 | Hr. | Daily | Hr. | Daily | Bare Costs | Incl. O&P |
|---|---|---|---|---|---|---|
| 1 Laborer | $30.25 | $242.00 | $47.05 | $376.40 | $38.48 | $58.24 |
| 6 Equip. Oper. (med.) | 39.85 | 1912.80 | 60.10 | 2884.80 | | |
| 2 Feller Buncher, 100 H.P. | | 1088.80 | | 1197.68 | | |
| 1 Log Chipper, 22" Tree | | 573.20 | | 630.52 | | |
| 2 Log Skidders, 50 H.P. | | 1732.80 | | 1906.08 | | |
| 1 Dozer, 105 H.P. | | 532.40 | | 585.64 | | |
| 1 Chainsaw, Gas, 36" Long | | 36.80 | | 40.48 | 70.79 | 77.86 |
| 56 L.H., Daily Totals | | $6118.80 | | $7621.60 | $109.26 | $136.10 |

| Crew B-89 | Hr. | Daily | Hr. | Daily | Bare Costs | Incl. O&P |
|---|---|---|---|---|---|---|
| 1 Equip. Oper. (light) | $37.75 | $302.00 | $56.95 | $455.60 | $33.58 | $51.23 |
| 1 Truck Driver (light) | 29.40 | 235.20 | 45.50 | 364.00 | | |
| 1 Flatbed Truck, Gas, 3 Ton | | 224.00 | | 246.40 | | |
| 1 Concrete Saw | | 135.00 | | 148.50 | | |
| 1 Water Tank, 65 Gal. | | 18.45 | | 20.30 | 23.59 | 25.95 |
| 16 L.H., Daily Totals | | $914.65 | | $1234.80 | $57.17 | $77.17 |

| Crew B-89A | Hr. | Daily | Hr. | Daily | Bare Costs | Incl. O&P |
|---|---|---|---|---|---|---|
| 1 Skilled Worker | $39.40 | $315.20 | $61.25 | $490.00 | $34.83 | $54.15 |
| 1 Laborer | 30.25 | 242.00 | 47.05 | 376.40 | | |
| 1 Core Drill (large) | | 109.40 | | 120.34 | 6.84 | 7.52 |
| 16 L.H., Daily Totals | | $666.60 | | $986.74 | $41.66 | $61.67 |

| Crew B-89B | Hr. | Daily | Hr. | Daily | Bare Costs | Incl. O&P |
|---|---|---|---|---|---|---|
| 1 Equip. Oper. (light) | $37.75 | $302.00 | $56.95 | $455.60 | $33.58 | $51.23 |
| 1 Truck Driver, Light | 29.40 | 235.20 | 45.50 | 364.00 | | |
| 1 Wall Saw, Hydraulic, 10 H.P. | | 90.20 | | 99.22 | | |
| 1 Generator, Diesel, 100 KW | | 332.80 | | 366.08 | | |
| 1 Water Tank, 65 Gal. | | 18.45 | | 20.30 | | |
| 1 Flatbed Truck, Gas, 3 Ton | | 224.00 | | 246.40 | 41.59 | 45.75 |
| 16 L.H., Daily Totals | | $1202.65 | | $1551.60 | $75.17 | $96.97 |

| Crew B-90 | Hr. | Daily | Hr. | Daily | Bare Costs | Incl. O&P |
|---|---|---|---|---|---|---|
| 1 Labor Foreman (outside) | $32.25 | $258.00 | $50.20 | $401.60 | $32.46 | $49.99 |
| 3 Laborers | 30.25 | 726.00 | 47.05 | 1129.20 | | |
| 2 Equip. Oper. (light) | 37.75 | 604.00 | 56.95 | 911.20 | | |
| 2 Truck Drivers (heavy) | 30.60 | 489.60 | 47.35 | 757.60 | | |
| 1 Road Mixer, 310 H.P. | | 1884.00 | | 2072.40 | | |
| 1 Dist. Truck, 2000 Gal. | | 268.00 | | 294.80 | 33.63 | 36.99 |
| 64 L.H., Daily Totals | | $4229.60 | | $5566.80 | $66.09 | $86.98 |

| Crew B-90A | Hr. | Daily | Hr. | Daily | Bare Costs | Incl. O&P |
|---|---|---|---|---|---|---|
| 1 Labor Foreman | $32.25 | $258.00 | $50.20 | $401.60 | $36.02 | $54.96 |
| 2 Laborers | 30.25 | 484.00 | 47.05 | 752.80 | | |
| 4 Equip. Oper. (medium) | 39.85 | 1275.20 | 60.10 | 1923.20 | | |
| 2 Grader, 30,000 Lbs. | | 1068.80 | | 1175.68 | | |
| 1 Tandem Roller, 10 Ton | | 219.00 | | 240.90 | | |
| 1 Roller, Pneum. Whl, 12 Ton | | 307.80 | | 338.58 | 28.49 | 31.34 |
| 56 L.H., Daily Totals | | $3612.80 | | $4832.76 | $64.51 | $86.30 |

# Crews

| Crew No. | Bare Costs | | Incl. Subs O & P | | Cost Per Labor-Hour | |
|---|---|---|---|---|---|---|
| **Crew B-90B** | Hr. | Daily | Hr. | Daily | Bare Costs | Incl. O&P |
| 1 Labor Foreman | $32.25 | $258.00 | $50.20 | $401.60 | $35.38 | $54.10 |
| 2 Laborers | 30.25 | 484.00 | 47.05 | 752.80 | | |
| 3 Equip. Oper. (medium) | 39.85 | 956.40 | 60.10 | 1442.40 | | |
| 1 Tandem Roller, 10 Ton | | 219.00 | | 240.90 | | |
| 1 Roller, Pneum. Whl, 12 Ton | | 307.80 | | 338.58 | | |
| 1 Road Mixer, 310 H.P. | | 1884.00 | | 2072.40 | 50.23 | 55.25 |
| 48 L.H., Daily Totals | | $4109.20 | | $5248.68 | $85.61 | $109.35 |

| Crew No. | Bare Costs | | Incl. Subs O & P | | Cost Per Labor-Hour | |
|---|---|---|---|---|---|---|
| **Crew B-91** | Hr. | Daily | Hr. | Daily | Bare Costs | Incl. O&P |
| 1 Labor Foreman (outside) | $32.25 | $258.00 | $50.20 | $401.60 | $35.34 | $54.01 |
| 2 Laborers | 30.25 | 484.00 | 47.05 | 752.80 | | |
| 4 Equip. Oper. (med.) | 39.85 | 1275.20 | 60.10 | 1923.20 | | |
| 1 Truck Driver (heavy) | 30.60 | 244.80 | 47.35 | 378.80 | | |
| 1 Dist. Tanker, 3000 Gallon | | 294.00 | | 323.40 | | |
| 1 Truck Tractor, 6x4, 380 H.P. | | 453.60 | | 498.96 | | |
| 1 Aggreg. Spreader, S.P. | | 808.80 | | 889.68 | | |
| 1 Roller, Pneum. Whl, 12 Ton | | 307.80 | | 338.58 | | |
| 1 Tandem Roller, 10 Ton | | 219.00 | | 240.90 | 32.55 | 35.81 |
| 64 L.H., Daily Totals | | $4345.20 | | $5747.92 | $67.89 | $89.81 |

| Crew No. | Bare Costs | | Incl. Subs O & P | | Cost Per Labor-Hour | |
|---|---|---|---|---|---|---|
| **Crew B-92** | Hr. | Daily | Hr. | Daily | Bare Costs | Incl. O&P |
| 1 Labor Foreman (outside) | $32.25 | $258.00 | $50.20 | $401.60 | $30.75 | $47.84 |
| 3 Laborers | 30.25 | 726.00 | 47.05 | 1129.20 | | |
| 1 Crack Cleaner, 25 H.P. | | 51.80 | | 56.98 | | |
| 1 Air Compressor, 60 C.F.M. | | 120.40 | | 132.44 | | |
| 1 Tar Kettle, T.M. | | 70.70 | | 77.77 | | |
| 1 Flatbed Truck, Gas, 3 Ton | | 224.00 | | 246.40 | 14.59 | 16.05 |
| 32 L.H., Daily Totals | | $1450.90 | | $2044.39 | $45.34 | $63.89 |

| Crew No. | Bare Costs | | Incl. Subs O & P | | Cost Per Labor-Hour | |
|---|---|---|---|---|---|---|
| **Crew B-93** | Hr. | Daily | Hr. | Daily | Bare Costs | Incl. O&P |
| 1 Equip. Oper. (med.) | $39.85 | $318.80 | $60.10 | $480.80 | $39.85 | $60.10 |
| 1 Feller Buncher, 100 H.P. | | 544.40 | | 598.84 | 68.05 | 74.86 |
| 8 L.H., Daily Totals | | $863.20 | | $1079.64 | $107.90 | $134.96 |

| Crew No. | Bare Costs | | Incl. Subs O & P | | Cost Per Labor-Hour | |
|---|---|---|---|---|---|---|
| **Crew B-94A** | Hr. | Daily | Hr. | Daily | Bare Costs | Incl. O&P |
| 1 Laborer | $30.25 | $242.00 | $47.05 | $376.40 | $30.25 | $47.05 |
| 1 Diaphragm Water Pump, 2" | | 61.40 | | 67.54 | | |
| 1 -20' Suction Hose, 2" | | 1.95 | | 2.15 | | |
| 2 -50' Discharge Hose, 2" | | 2.20 | | 2.42 | 8.19 | 9.01 |
| 8 L.H., Daily Totals | | $307.55 | | $448.51 | $38.44 | $56.06 |

| Crew No. | Bare Costs | | Incl. Subs O & P | | Cost Per Labor-Hour | |
|---|---|---|---|---|---|---|
| **Crew B-94B** | Hr. | Daily | Hr. | Daily | Bare Costs | Incl. O&P |
| 1 Laborer | $30.25 | $242.00 | $47.05 | $376.40 | $30.25 | $47.05 |
| 1 Diaphragm Water Pump, 4" | | 84.40 | | 92.84 | | |
| 1 -20' Suction Hose, 4" | | 3.45 | | 3.79 | | |
| 2 -50' Discharge Hose, 4" | | 4.70 | | 5.17 | 11.57 | 12.73 |
| 8 L.H., Daily Totals | | $334.55 | | $478.20 | $41.82 | $59.78 |

| Crew No. | Bare Costs | | Incl. Subs O & P | | Cost Per Labor-Hour | |
|---|---|---|---|---|---|---|
| **Crew B-94C** | Hr. | Daily | Hr. | Daily | Bare Costs | Incl. O&P |
| 1 Laborer | $30.25 | $242.00 | $47.05 | $376.40 | $30.25 | $47.05 |
| 1 Centrifugal Water Pump, 3" | | 67.60 | | 74.36 | | |
| 1 -20' Suction Hose, 3" | | 3.05 | | 3.36 | | |
| 2 -50' Discharge Hose, 3" | | 3.50 | | 3.85 | 9.27 | 10.20 |
| 8 L.H., Daily Totals | | $316.15 | | $457.96 | $39.52 | $57.25 |

| Crew No. | Bare Costs | | Incl. Subs O & P | | Cost Per Labor-Hour | |
|---|---|---|---|---|---|---|
| **Crew B-94D** | Hr. | Daily | Hr. | Daily | Bare Costs | Incl. O&P |
| 1 Laborer | $30.25 | $242.00 | $47.05 | $376.40 | $30.25 | $47.05 |
| 1 Centr. Water Pump, 6" | | 305.20 | | 335.72 | | |
| 1 -20' Suction Hose, 6" | | 11.90 | | 13.09 | | |
| 2 -50' Discharge Hose, 6" | | 12.60 | | 13.86 | 41.21 | 45.33 |
| 8 L.H., Daily Totals | | $571.70 | | $739.07 | $71.46 | $92.38 |

| Crew No. | Bare Costs | | Incl. Subs O & P | | Cost Per Labor-Hour | |
|---|---|---|---|---|---|---|
| **Crew B-95A** | Hr. | Daily | Hr. | Daily | Bare Costs | Incl. O&P |
| 1 Equip. Oper. (crane) | $40.95 | $327.60 | $61.75 | $494.00 | $35.60 | $54.40 |
| 1 Laborer | 30.25 | 242.00 | 47.05 | 376.40 | | |
| 1 Hyd. Excavator, 5/8 C.Y. | | 497.40 | | 547.14 | 31.09 | 34.20 |
| 16 L.H., Daily Totals | | $1067.00 | | $1417.54 | $66.69 | $88.60 |

| Crew No. | Bare Costs | | Incl. Subs O & P | | Cost Per Labor-Hour | |
|---|---|---|---|---|---|---|
| **Crew B-95B** | Hr. | Daily | Hr. | Daily | Bare Costs | Incl. O&P |
| 1 Equip. Oper. (crane) | $40.95 | $327.60 | $61.75 | $494.00 | $35.60 | $54.40 |
| 1 Laborer | 30.25 | 242.00 | 47.05 | 376.40 | | |
| 1 Hyd. Excavator, 1.5 C.Y. | | 830.00 | | 913.00 | 51.88 | 57.06 |
| 16 L.H., Daily Totals | | $1399.60 | | $1783.40 | $87.47 | $111.46 |

| Crew No. | Bare Costs | | Incl. Subs O & P | | Cost Per Labor-Hour | |
|---|---|---|---|---|---|---|
| **Crew B-95C** | Hr. | Daily | Hr. | Daily | Bare Costs | Incl. O&P |
| 1 Equip. Oper. (crane) | $40.95 | $327.60 | $61.75 | $494.00 | $35.60 | $54.40 |
| 1 Laborer | 30.25 | 242.00 | 47.05 | 376.40 | | |
| 1 Hyd. Excavator, 2.5 C.Y. | | 1466.00 | | 1612.60 | 91.63 | 100.79 |
| 16 L.H., Daily Totals | | $2035.60 | | $2483.00 | $127.22 | $155.19 |

| Crew No. | Bare Costs | | Incl. Subs O & P | | Cost Per Labor-Hour | |
|---|---|---|---|---|---|---|
| **Crew C-1** | Hr. | Daily | Hr. | Daily | Bare Costs | Incl. O&P |
| 3 Carpenters | $38.10 | $914.40 | $59.30 | $1423.20 | $36.14 | $56.24 |
| 1 Laborer | 30.25 | 242.00 | 47.05 | 376.40 | | |
| 32 L.H., Daily Totals | | $1156.40 | | $1799.60 | $36.14 | $56.24 |

| Crew No. | Bare Costs | | Incl. Subs O & P | | Cost Per Labor-Hour | |
|---|---|---|---|---|---|---|
| **Crew C-2** | Hr. | Daily | Hr. | Daily | Bare Costs | Incl. O&P |
| 1 Carpenter Foreman (out) | $40.10 | $320.80 | $62.40 | $499.20 | $37.13 | $57.77 |
| 4 Carpenters | 38.10 | 1219.20 | 59.30 | 1897.60 | | |
| 1 Laborer | 30.25 | 242.00 | 47.05 | 376.40 | | |
| 48 L.H., Daily Totals | | $1782.00 | | $2773.20 | $37.13 | $57.77 |

| Crew No. | Bare Costs | | Incl. Subs O & P | | Cost Per Labor-Hour | |
|---|---|---|---|---|---|---|
| **Crew C-2A** | Hr. | Daily | Hr. | Daily | Bare Costs | Incl. O&P |
| 1 Carpenter Foreman (out) | $40.10 | $320.80 | $62.40 | $499.20 | $36.94 | $56.94 |
| 3 Carpenters | 38.10 | 914.40 | 59.30 | 1423.20 | | |
| 1 Cement Finisher | 37.00 | 296.00 | 54.30 | 434.40 | | |
| 1 Laborer | 30.25 | 242.00 | 47.05 | 376.40 | | |
| 48 L.H., Daily Totals | | $1773.20 | | $2733.20 | $36.94 | $56.94 |

| Crew No. | Bare Costs | | Incl. Subs O & P | | Cost Per Labor-Hour | |
|---|---|---|---|---|---|---|
| **Crew C-3** | Hr. | Daily | Hr. | Daily | Bare Costs | Incl. O&P |
| 1 Rodman Foreman | $45.00 | $360.00 | $73.85 | $590.80 | $39.41 | $63.39 |
| 4 Rodmen (reinf.) | 43.00 | 1376.00 | 70.55 | 2257.60 | | |
| 1 Equip. Oper. (light) | 37.75 | 302.00 | 56.95 | 455.60 | | |
| 2 Laborers | 30.25 | 484.00 | 47.05 | 752.80 | | |
| 3 Stressing Equipment | | 25.80 | | 28.38 | | |
| .5 Grouting Equipment | | 75.40 | | 82.94 | 1.58 | 1.74 |
| 64 L.H., Daily Totals | | $2623.20 | | $4168.12 | $40.99 | $65.13 |

| Crew No. | Bare Costs | | Incl. Subs O & P | | Cost Per Labor-Hour | |
|---|---|---|---|---|---|---|
| **Crew C-4** | Hr. | Daily | Hr. | Daily | Bare Costs | Incl. O&P |
| 1 Rodman Foreman | $45.00 | $360.00 | $73.85 | $590.80 | $43.50 | $71.38 |
| 3 Rodmen (reinf.) | 43.00 | 1032.00 | 70.55 | 1693.20 | | |
| 3 Stressing Equipment | | 25.80 | | 28.38 | .81 | .89 |
| 32 L.H., Daily Totals | | $1417.80 | | $2312.38 | $44.31 | $72.26 |

| Crew No. | Bare Costs | | Incl. Subs O & P | | Cost Per Labor-Hour | |
|---|---|---|---|---|---|---|
| **Crew C-5** | Hr. | Daily | Hr. | Daily | Bare Costs | Incl. O&P |
| 1 Rodman Foreman | $45.00 | $360.00 | $73.85 | $590.80 | $41.86 | $67.25 |
| 4 Rodmen (reinf.) | 43.00 | 1376.00 | 70.55 | 2257.60 | | |
| 1 Equip. Oper. (crane) | 40.95 | 327.60 | 61.75 | 494.00 | | |
| 1 Equip. Oper. Oiler | 35.10 | 280.80 | 52.95 | 423.60 | | |
| 1 Hyd. Crane, 25 Ton | | 786.00 | | 864.60 | 14.04 | 15.44 |
| 56 L.H., Daily Totals | | $3130.40 | | $4630.60 | $55.90 | $82.69 |

649

# Crews

| Crew C-6 | Hr. | Daily | Hr. | Daily | Bare Costs | Incl. O&P |
|---|---|---|---|---|---|---|
| 1 Labor Foreman (outside) | $32.25 | $258.00 | $50.20 | $401.60 | $31.71 | $48.78 |
| 4 Laborers | 30.25 | 968.00 | 47.05 | 1505.60 | | |
| 1 Cement Finisher | 37.00 | 296.00 | 54.30 | 434.40 | | |
| 2 Gas Engine Vibrator | | 49.60 | | 54.56 | 1.03 | 1.14 |
| 48 L.H., Daily Totals | | $1571.60 | | $2396.16 | $32.74 | $49.92 |

| Crew C-7 | Hr. | Daily | Hr. | Daily | Bare Costs | Incl. O&P |
|---|---|---|---|---|---|---|
| 1 Labor Foreman (outside) | $32.25 | $258.00 | $50.20 | $401.60 | $32.83 | $50.31 |
| 5 Laborers | 30.25 | 1210.00 | 47.05 | 1882.00 | | |
| 1 Cement Finisher | 37.00 | 296.00 | 54.30 | 434.40 | | |
| 1 Equip. Oper. (med.) | 39.85 | 318.80 | 60.10 | 480.80 | | |
| 1 Equip. Oper. (oiler) | 35.10 | 280.80 | 52.95 | 423.60 | | |
| 2 Gas Engine Vibrator | | 49.60 | | 54.56 | | |
| 1 Concrete Bucket, 1 C.Y. | | 19.60 | | 21.56 | | |
| 1 Hyd. Crane, 55 Ton | | 1119.00 | | 1230.90 | 16.50 | 18.15 |
| 72 L.H., Daily Totals | | $3551.80 | | $4929.42 | $49.33 | $68.46 |

| Crew C-7A | Hr. | Daily | Hr. | Daily | Bare Costs | Incl. O&P |
|---|---|---|---|---|---|---|
| 1 Labor Foreman (outside) | $32.25 | $258.00 | $50.20 | $401.60 | $30.59 | $47.52 |
| 5 Laborers | 30.25 | 1210.00 | 47.05 | 1882.00 | | |
| 2 Truck Drivers (Heavy) | 30.60 | 489.60 | 47.35 | 757.60 | | |
| 2 Conc. Transit Mixers | | 1713.60 | | 1884.96 | 26.77 | 29.45 |
| 64 L.H., Daily Totals | | $3671.20 | | $4926.16 | $57.36 | $76.97 |

| Crew C-7B | Hr. | Daily | Hr. | Daily | Bare Costs | Incl. O&P |
|---|---|---|---|---|---|---|
| 1 Labor Foreman (outside) | $32.25 | $258.00 | $50.20 | $401.60 | $32.44 | $50.02 |
| 5 Laborers | 30.25 | 1210.00 | 47.05 | 1882.00 | | |
| 1 Equipment Operator (heavy) | 40.95 | 327.60 | 61.75 | 494.00 | | |
| 1 Equipment Oiler | 35.10 | 280.80 | 52.95 | 423.60 | | |
| 1 Conc. Bucket, 2 C.Y. | | 30.60 | | 33.66 | | |
| 1 Lattice Boom Crane, 165 Ton | | 1992.00 | | 2191.20 | 31.60 | 34.76 |
| 64 L.H., Daily Totals | | $4099.00 | | $5426.06 | $64.05 | $84.78 |

| Crew C-7C | Hr. | Daily | Hr. | Daily | Bare Costs | Incl. O&P |
|---|---|---|---|---|---|---|
| 1 Labor Foreman (outside) | $32.25 | $258.00 | $50.20 | $401.60 | $32.90 | $50.71 |
| 5 Laborers | 30.25 | 1210.00 | 47.05 | 1882.00 | | |
| 2 Equipment Operator (medium) | 39.85 | 637.60 | 60.10 | 961.60 | | |
| 2 F.E. Loader, W.M., 4 C.Y. | | 1072.00 | | 1179.20 | 16.75 | 18.43 |
| 64 L.H., Daily Totals | | $3177.60 | | $4424.40 | $49.65 | $69.13 |

| Crew C-7D | Hr. | Daily | Hr. | Daily | Bare Costs | Incl. O&P |
|---|---|---|---|---|---|---|
| 1 Labor Foreman (outside) | $32.25 | $258.00 | $50.20 | $401.60 | $31.91 | $49.36 |
| 5 Laborers | 30.25 | 1210.00 | 47.05 | 1882.00 | | |
| 1 Equipment Operator (med.) | 39.85 | 318.80 | 60.10 | 480.80 | | |
| 1 Concrete Conveyer | | 172.80 | | 190.08 | 3.09 | 3.39 |
| 56 L.H., Daily Totals | | $1959.60 | | $2954.48 | $34.99 | $52.76 |

| Crew C-8 | Hr. | Daily | Hr. | Daily | Bare Costs | Incl. O&P |
|---|---|---|---|---|---|---|
| 1 Labor Foreman (outside) | $32.25 | $258.00 | $50.20 | $401.60 | $33.84 | $51.44 |
| 3 Laborers | 30.25 | 726.00 | 47.05 | 1129.20 | | |
| 2 Cement Finishers | 37.00 | 592.00 | 54.30 | 868.80 | | |
| 1 Equip. Oper. (med.) | 39.85 | 318.80 | 60.10 | 480.80 | | |
| 1 Concrete Pump (small) | | 728.20 | | 801.02 | 13.00 | 14.30 |
| 56 L.H., Daily Totals | | $2623.00 | | $3681.42 | $46.84 | $65.74 |

| Crew C-8A | Hr. | Daily | Hr. | Daily | Bare Costs | Incl. O&P |
|---|---|---|---|---|---|---|
| 1 Labor Foreman (outside) | $32.25 | $258.00 | $50.20 | $401.60 | $32.83 | $49.99 |
| 3 Laborers | 30.25 | 726.00 | 47.05 | 1129.20 | | |
| 2 Cement Finishers | 37.00 | 592.00 | 54.30 | 868.80 | | |
| 48 L.H., Daily Totals | | $1576.00 | | $2399.60 | $32.83 | $49.99 |

| Crew C-8B | Hr. | Daily | Hr. | Daily | Bare Costs | Incl. O&P |
|---|---|---|---|---|---|---|
| 1 Labor Foreman (outside) | $32.25 | $258.00 | $50.20 | $401.60 | $32.57 | $50.29 |
| 3 Laborers | 30.25 | 726.00 | 47.05 | 1129.20 | | |
| 1 Equipment Operator | 39.85 | 318.80 | 60.10 | 480.80 | | |
| 1 Vibrating Power Screed | | 65.95 | | 72.55 | | |
| 1 Roller, Vibratory, 25 Ton | | 593.80 | | 653.18 | | |
| 1 Dozer, 200 H.P. | | 1071.00 | | 1178.10 | 43.27 | 47.60 |
| 40 L.H., Daily Totals | | $3033.55 | | $3915.43 | $75.84 | $97.89 |

| Crew C-8C | Hr. | Daily | Hr. | Daily | Bare Costs | Incl. O&P |
|---|---|---|---|---|---|---|
| 1 Labor Foreman (outside) | $32.25 | $258.00 | $50.20 | $401.60 | $33.31 | $50.96 |
| 3 Laborers | 30.25 | 726.00 | 47.05 | 1129.20 | | |
| 1 Cement Finisher | 37.00 | 296.00 | 54.30 | 434.40 | | |
| 1 Equipment Operator (med.) | 39.85 | 318.80 | 60.10 | 480.80 | | |
| 1 Shotcrete Rig, 12 CY/hr | | 261.20 | | 287.32 | 5.44 | 5.99 |
| 48 L.H., Daily Totals | | $1860.00 | | $2733.32 | $38.75 | $56.94 |

| Crew C-8D | Hr. | Daily | Hr. | Daily | Bare Costs | Incl. O&P |
|---|---|---|---|---|---|---|
| 1 Labor Foreman (outside) | $32.25 | $258.00 | $50.20 | $401.60 | $34.31 | $52.13 |
| 1 Laborer | 30.25 | 242.00 | 47.05 | 376.40 | | |
| 1 Cement Finisher | 37.00 | 296.00 | 54.30 | 434.40 | | |
| 1 Equipment Operator (light) | 37.75 | 302.00 | 56.95 | 455.60 | | |
| 1 Air Compressor, 250 C.F.M. | | 161.80 | | 177.98 | | |
| 2 -50' Air Hose, 1" | | 7.80 | | 8.58 | 5.30 | 5.83 |
| 32 L.H., Daily Totals | | $1267.60 | | $1854.56 | $39.61 | $57.95 |

| Crew C-8E | Hr. | Daily | Hr. | Daily | Bare Costs | Incl. O&P |
|---|---|---|---|---|---|---|
| 1 Labor Foreman (outside) | $32.25 | $258.00 | $50.20 | $401.60 | $34.31 | $52.13 |
| 1 Laborer | 30.25 | 242.00 | 47.05 | 376.40 | | |
| 1 Cement Finisher | 37.00 | 296.00 | 54.30 | 434.40 | | |
| 1 Equipment Operator (light) | 37.75 | 302.00 | 56.95 | 455.60 | | |
| 1 Air Compressor, 250 C.F.M. | | 161.80 | | 177.98 | | |
| 2 -50' Air Hose, 1" | | 7.80 | | 8.58 | | |
| 1 Concrete Pump (small) | | 728.20 | | 801.02 | 28.06 | 30.86 |
| 32 L.H., Daily Totals | | $1995.80 | | $2655.58 | $62.37 | $82.99 |

| Crew C-10 | Hr. | Daily | Hr. | Daily | Bare Costs | Incl. O&P |
|---|---|---|---|---|---|---|
| 1 Laborer | $30.25 | $242.00 | $47.05 | $376.40 | $34.75 | $51.88 |
| 2 Cement Finishers | 37.00 | 592.00 | 54.30 | 868.80 | | |
| 24 L.H., Daily Totals | | $834.00 | | $1245.20 | $34.75 | $51.88 |

| Crew C-10B | Hr. | Daily | Hr. | Daily | Bare Costs | Incl. O&P |
|---|---|---|---|---|---|---|
| 3 Laborers | $30.25 | $726.00 | $47.05 | $1129.20 | $32.95 | $49.95 |
| 2 Cement Finishers | 37.00 | 592.00 | 54.30 | 868.80 | | |
| 1 Concrete Mixer, 10 CF | | 149.80 | | 164.78 | | |
| 2 Trowel, 48" Walk-Behind | | 79.60 | | 87.56 | 5.74 | 6.31 |
| 40 L.H., Daily Totals | | $1547.40 | | $2250.34 | $38.69 | $56.26 |

| Crew C-10C | Hr. | Daily | Hr. | Daily | Bare Costs | Incl. O&P |
|---|---|---|---|---|---|---|
| 1 Laborer | $30.25 | $242.00 | $47.05 | $376.40 | $34.75 | $51.88 |
| 2 Cement Finishers | 37.00 | 592.00 | 54.30 | 868.80 | | |
| 1 Trowel, 48" Walk-Behind | | 39.80 | | 43.78 | 1.66 | 1.82 |
| 24 L.H., Daily Totals | | $873.80 | | $1288.98 | $36.41 | $53.71 |

| Crew C-10D | Hr. | Daily | Hr. | Daily | Bare Costs | Incl. O&P |
|---|---|---|---|---|---|---|
| 1 Laborer | $30.25 | $242.00 | $47.05 | $376.40 | $34.75 | $51.88 |
| 2 Cement Finishers | 37.00 | 592.00 | 54.30 | 868.80 | | |
| 1 Vibrating Power Screed | | 65.95 | | 72.55 | | |
| 1 Trowel, 48" Walk-Behind | | 39.80 | | 43.78 | 4.41 | 4.85 |
| 24 L.H., Daily Totals | | $939.75 | | $1361.53 | $39.16 | $56.73 |

## Crew C-10E

| Crew C-10E | Bare Costs Hr. | Daily | Incl. Subs O & P Hr. | Daily | Cost Per Labor-Hour Bare Costs | Incl. O&P |
|---|---|---|---|---|---|---|
| 1 Laborer | $30.25 | $242.00 | $47.05 | $376.40 | $34.75 | $51.88 |
| 2 Cement Finishers | 37.00 | 592.00 | 54.30 | 868.80 | | |
| 1 Vibrating Power Screed | | 65.95 | | 72.55 | | |
| 1 Cement Trowel, 96" Ride-On | | 161.00 | | 177.10 | 9.46 | 10.40 |
| 24 L.H., Daily Totals | | $1060.95 | | $1494.85 | $44.21 | $62.29 |

## Crew C-11

| Crew C-11 | Bare Costs Hr. | Daily | Incl. Subs O & P Hr. | Daily | Cost Per Labor-Hour Bare Costs | Incl. O&P |
|---|---|---|---|---|---|---|
| 1 Struc. Steel Foreman | $45.00 | $360.00 | $81.20 | $649.60 | $42.12 | $73.47 |
| 6 Struc. Steel Workers | 43.00 | 2064.00 | 77.55 | 3722.40 | | |
| 1 Equip. Oper. (crane) | 40.95 | 327.60 | 61.75 | 494.00 | | |
| 1 Equip. Oper. Oiler | 35.10 | 280.80 | 52.95 | 423.60 | | |
| 1 Lattice Boom Crane, 150 Ton | | 1885.00 | | 2073.50 | 26.18 | 28.80 |
| 72 L.H., Daily Totals | | $4917.40 | | $7363.10 | $68.30 | $102.27 |

## Crew C-12

| Crew C-12 | Bare Costs Hr. | Daily | Incl. Subs O & P Hr. | Daily | Cost Per Labor-Hour Bare Costs | Incl. O&P |
|---|---|---|---|---|---|---|
| 1 Carpenter Foreman (out) | $40.10 | $320.80 | $62.40 | $499.20 | $37.60 | $58.18 |
| 3 Carpenters | 38.10 | 914.40 | 59.30 | 1423.20 | | |
| 1 Laborer | 30.25 | 242.00 | 47.05 | 376.40 | | |
| 1 Equip. Oper. (crane) | 40.95 | 327.60 | 61.75 | 494.00 | | |
| 1 Hyd. Crane, 12 Ton | | 766.40 | | 843.04 | 15.97 | 17.56 |
| 48 L.H., Daily Totals | | $2571.20 | | $3635.84 | $53.57 | $75.75 |

## Crew C-13

| Crew C-13 | Bare Costs Hr. | Daily | Incl. Subs O & P Hr. | Daily | Cost Per Labor-Hour Bare Costs | Incl. O&P |
|---|---|---|---|---|---|---|
| 1 Struc. Steel Worker | $43.00 | $344.00 | $77.55 | $620.40 | $41.37 | $71.47 |
| 1 Welder | 43.00 | 344.00 | 77.55 | 620.40 | | |
| 1 Carpenter | 38.10 | 304.80 | 59.30 | 474.40 | | |
| 1 Welder, gas engine, 300 amp | | 132.20 | | 145.42 | 5.51 | 6.06 |
| 24 L.H., Daily Totals | | $1125.00 | | $1860.62 | $46.88 | $77.53 |

## Crew C-14

| Crew C-14 | Bare Costs Hr. | Daily | Incl. Subs O & P Hr. | Daily | Cost Per Labor-Hour Bare Costs | Incl. O&P |
|---|---|---|---|---|---|---|
| 1 Carpenter Foreman (out) | $40.10 | $320.80 | $62.40 | $499.20 | $37.42 | $58.48 |
| 5 Carpenters | 38.10 | 1524.00 | 59.30 | 2372.00 | | |
| 4 Laborers | 30.25 | 968.00 | 47.05 | 1505.60 | | |
| 4 Rodmen (reinf.) | 43.00 | 1376.00 | 70.55 | 2257.60 | | |
| 2 Cement Finishers | 37.00 | 592.00 | 54.30 | 868.80 | | |
| 1 Equip. Oper. (crane) | 40.95 | 327.60 | 61.75 | 494.00 | | |
| 1 Equip. Oper. Oiler | 35.10 | 280.80 | 52.95 | 423.60 | | |
| 1 Hyd. Crane, 80 Ton | | 1290.00 | | 1419.00 | 8.96 | 9.85 |
| 144 L.H., Daily Totals | | $6679.20 | | $9839.80 | $46.38 | $68.33 |

## Crew C-14A

| Crew C-14A | Bare Costs Hr. | Daily | Incl. Subs O & P Hr. | Daily | Cost Per Labor-Hour Bare Costs | Incl. O&P |
|---|---|---|---|---|---|---|
| 1 Carpenter Foreman (out) | $40.10 | $320.80 | $62.40 | $499.20 | $38.36 | $60.08 |
| 16 Carpenters | 38.10 | 4876.80 | 59.30 | 7590.40 | | |
| 4 Rodmen (reinf.) | 43.00 | 1376.00 | 70.55 | 2257.60 | | |
| 2 Laborers | 30.25 | 484.00 | 47.05 | 752.80 | | |
| 1 Cement Finisher | 37.00 | 296.00 | 54.30 | 434.40 | | |
| 1 Equip. Oper. (med.) | 39.85 | 318.80 | 60.10 | 480.80 | | |
| 1 Gas Engine Vibrator | | 24.80 | | 27.28 | | |
| 1 Concrete Pump (small) | | 728.20 | | 801.02 | 3.77 | 4.14 |
| 200 L.H., Daily Totals | | $8425.40 | | $12843.50 | $42.13 | $64.22 |

## Crew C-14B

| Crew C-14B | Bare Costs Hr. | Daily | Incl. Subs O & P Hr. | Daily | Cost Per Labor-Hour Bare Costs | Incl. O&P |
|---|---|---|---|---|---|---|
| 1 Carpenter Foreman (out) | $40.10 | $320.80 | $62.40 | $499.20 | $38.31 | $59.85 |
| 16 Carpenters | 38.10 | 4876.80 | 59.30 | 7590.40 | | |
| 4 Rodmen (reinf.) | 43.00 | 1376.00 | 70.55 | 2257.60 | | |
| 2 Laborers | 30.25 | 484.00 | 47.05 | 752.80 | | |
| 2 Cement Finishers | 37.00 | 592.00 | 54.30 | 868.80 | | |
| 1 Equip. Oper. (med.) | 39.85 | 318.80 | 60.10 | 480.80 | | |
| 1 Gas Engine Vibrator | | 24.80 | | 27.28 | | |
| 1 Concrete Pump (small) | | 728.20 | | 801.02 | 3.62 | 3.98 |
| 208 L.H., Daily Totals | | $8721.40 | | $13277.90 | $41.93 | $63.84 |

## Crew C-14C

| Crew C-14C | Bare Costs Hr. | Daily | Incl. Subs O & P Hr. | Daily | Cost Per Labor-Hour Bare Costs | Incl. O&P |
|---|---|---|---|---|---|---|
| 1 Carpenter Foreman (out) | $40.10 | $320.80 | $62.40 | $499.20 | $36.62 | $57.27 |
| 6 Carpenters | 38.10 | 1828.80 | 59.30 | 2846.40 | | |
| 2 Rodmen (reinf.) | 43.00 | 688.00 | 70.55 | 1128.80 | | |
| 4 Laborers | 30.25 | 968.00 | 47.05 | 1505.60 | | |
| 1 Cement Finisher | 37.00 | 296.00 | 54.30 | 434.40 | | |
| 1 Gas Engine Vibrator | | 24.80 | | 27.28 | .22 | .24 |
| 112 L.H., Daily Totals | | $4126.40 | | $6441.68 | $36.84 | $57.52 |

## Crew C-14D

| Crew C-14D | Bare Costs Hr. | Daily | Incl. Subs O & P Hr. | Daily | Cost Per Labor-Hour Bare Costs | Incl. O&P |
|---|---|---|---|---|---|---|
| 1 Carpenter Foreman (out) | $40.10 | $320.80 | $62.40 | $499.20 | $37.97 | $59.18 |
| 18 Carpenters | 38.10 | 5486.40 | 59.30 | 8539.20 | | |
| 2 Rodmen (reinf.) | 43.00 | 688.00 | 70.55 | 1128.80 | | |
| 2 Laborers | 30.25 | 484.00 | 47.05 | 752.80 | | |
| 1 Cement Finisher | 37.00 | 296.00 | 54.30 | 434.40 | | |
| 1 Equip. Oper. (med.) | 39.85 | 318.80 | 60.10 | 480.80 | | |
| 1 Gas Engine Vibrator | | 24.80 | | 27.28 | | |
| 1 Concrete Pump (small) | | 728.20 | | 801.02 | 3.77 | 4.14 |
| 200 L.H., Daily Totals | | $8347.00 | | $12663.50 | $41.73 | $63.32 |

## Crew C-14E

| Crew C-14E | Bare Costs Hr. | Daily | Incl. Subs O & P Hr. | Daily | Cost Per Labor-Hour Bare Costs | Incl. O&P |
|---|---|---|---|---|---|---|
| 1 Carpenter Foreman (out) | $40.10 | $320.80 | $62.40 | $499.20 | $37.82 | $59.88 |
| 2 Carpenters | 38.10 | 609.60 | 59.30 | 948.80 | | |
| 4 Rodmen (reinf.) | 43.00 | 1376.00 | 70.55 | 2257.60 | | |
| 3 Laborers | 30.25 | 726.00 | 47.05 | 1129.20 | | |
| 1 Cement Finisher | 37.00 | 296.00 | 54.30 | 434.40 | | |
| 1 Gas Engine Vibrator | | 24.80 | | 27.28 | .28 | .31 |
| 88 L.H., Daily Totals | | $3353.20 | | $5296.48 | $38.10 | $60.19 |

## Crew C-14F

| Crew C-14F | Bare Costs Hr. | Daily | Incl. Subs O & P Hr. | Daily | Cost Per Labor-Hour Bare Costs | Incl. O&P |
|---|---|---|---|---|---|---|
| 1 Laborer Foreman (out) | $32.25 | $258.00 | $50.20 | $401.60 | $34.97 | $52.23 |
| 2 Laborers | 30.25 | 484.00 | 47.05 | 752.80 | | |
| 6 Cement Finishers | 37.00 | 1776.00 | 54.30 | 2606.40 | | |
| 1 Gas Engine Vibrator | | 24.80 | | 27.28 | .34 | .38 |
| 72 L.H., Daily Totals | | $2542.80 | | $3788.08 | $35.32 | $52.61 |

## Crew C-14G

| Crew C-14G | Bare Costs Hr. | Daily | Incl. Subs O & P Hr. | Daily | Cost Per Labor-Hour Bare Costs | Incl. O&P |
|---|---|---|---|---|---|---|
| 1 Laborer Foreman (out) | $32.25 | $258.00 | $50.20 | $401.60 | $34.39 | $51.64 |
| 2 Laborers | 30.25 | 484.00 | 47.05 | 752.80 | | |
| 4 Cement Finishers | 37.00 | 1184.00 | 54.30 | 1737.60 | | |
| 1 Gas Engine Vibrator | | 24.80 | | 27.28 | .44 | .49 |
| 56 L.H., Daily Totals | | $1950.80 | | $2919.28 | $34.84 | $52.13 |

## Crew C-14H

| Crew C-14H | Bare Costs Hr. | Daily | Incl. Subs O & P Hr. | Daily | Cost Per Labor-Hour Bare Costs | Incl. O&P |
|---|---|---|---|---|---|---|
| 1 Carpenter Foreman (out) | $40.10 | $320.80 | $62.40 | $499.20 | $37.76 | $58.82 |
| 2 Carpenters | 38.10 | 609.60 | 59.30 | 948.80 | | |
| 1 Rodman (reinf.) | 43.00 | 344.00 | 70.55 | 564.40 | | |
| 1 Laborer | 30.25 | 242.00 | 47.05 | 376.40 | | |
| 1 Cement Finisher | 37.00 | 296.00 | 54.30 | 434.40 | | |
| 1 Gas Engine Vibrator | | 24.80 | | 27.28 | .52 | .57 |
| 48 L.H., Daily Totals | | $1837.20 | | $2850.48 | $38.27 | $59.38 |

## Crew C-14L

| Crew C-14L | Bare Costs Hr. | Daily | Incl. Subs O & P Hr. | Daily | Cost Per Labor-Hour Bare Costs | Incl. O&P |
|---|---|---|---|---|---|---|
| 1 Carpenter Foreman (out) | $40.10 | $320.80 | $62.40 | $499.20 | $35.56 | $55.06 |
| 6 Carpenters | 38.10 | 1828.80 | 59.30 | 2846.40 | | |
| 4 Laborers | 30.25 | 968.00 | 47.05 | 1505.60 | | |
| 1 Cement Finisher | 37.00 | 296.00 | 54.30 | 434.40 | | |
| 1 Gas Engine Vibrator | | 24.80 | | 27.28 | .26 | .28 |
| 96 L.H., Daily Totals | | $3438.40 | | $5312.88 | $35.82 | $55.34 |

# Crews

| Crew No. | Bare Costs Hr. | Daily | Incl. Subs O & P Hr. | Daily | Cost Per Labor-Hour Bare Costs | Incl. O&P |
|---|---|---|---|---|---|---|
| **Crew C-15** | Hr. | Daily | Hr. | Daily | Bare Costs | Incl. O&P |
| 1 Carpenter Foreman (out) | $40.10 | $320.80 | $62.40 | $499.20 | $36.01 | $55.70 |
| 2 Carpenters | 38.10 | 609.60 | 59.30 | 948.80 | | |
| 3 Laborers | 30.25 | 726.00 | 47.05 | 1129.20 | | |
| 2 Cement Finishers | 37.00 | 592.00 | 54.30 | 868.80 | | |
| 1 Rodman (reinf.) | 43.00 | 344.00 | 70.55 | 564.40 | | |
| 72 L.H., Daily Totals | | $2592.40 | | $4010.40 | $36.01 | $55.70 |
| **Crew C-16** | Hr. | Daily | Hr. | Daily | Bare Costs | Incl. O&P |
| 1 Labor Foreman (outside) | $32.25 | $258.00 | $50.20 | $401.60 | $35.87 | $55.68 |
| 3 Laborers | 30.25 | 726.00 | 47.05 | 1129.20 | | |
| 2 Cement Finishers | 37.00 | 592.00 | 54.30 | 868.80 | | |
| 1 Equip. Oper. (med.) | 39.85 | 318.80 | 60.10 | 480.80 | | |
| 2 Rodmen (reinf.) | 43.00 | 688.00 | 70.55 | 1128.80 | | |
| 1 Concrete Pump (small) | | 728.20 | | 801.02 | 10.11 | 11.13 |
| 72 L.H., Daily Totals | | $3311.00 | | $4810.22 | $45.99 | $66.81 |
| **Crew C-17** | Hr. | Daily | Hr. | Daily | Bare Costs | Incl. O&P |
| 2 Skilled Worker Foremen | $41.40 | $662.40 | $64.40 | $1030.40 | $39.80 | $61.88 |
| 8 Skilled Workers | 39.40 | 2521.60 | 61.25 | 3920.00 | | |
| 80 L.H., Daily Totals | | $3184.00 | | $4950.40 | $39.80 | $61.88 |
| **Crew C-17A** | Hr. | Daily | Hr. | Daily | Bare Costs | Incl. O&P |
| 2 Skilled Worker Foremen | $41.40 | $662.40 | $64.40 | $1030.40 | $39.81 | $61.88 |
| 8 Skilled Workers | 39.40 | 2521.60 | 61.25 | 3920.00 | | |
| .125 Equip. Oper. (crane) | 40.95 | 40.95 | 61.75 | 61.75 | | |
| .125 Hyd. Crane, 80 Ton | | 161.25 | | 177.38 | 1.99 | 2.19 |
| 81 L.H., Daily Totals | | $3386.20 | | $5189.52 | $41.80 | $64.07 |
| **Crew C-17B** | Hr. | Daily | Hr. | Daily | Bare Costs | Incl. O&P |
| 2 Skilled Worker Foremen | $41.40 | $662.40 | $64.40 | $1030.40 | $39.83 | $61.88 |
| 8 Skilled Workers | 39.40 | 2521.60 | 61.25 | 3920.00 | | |
| .25 Equip. Oper. (crane) | 40.95 | 81.90 | 61.75 | 123.50 | | |
| .25 Hyd. Crane, 80 Ton | | 322.50 | | 354.75 | | |
| .25 Trowel, 48" Walk-Behind | | 9.95 | | 10.95 | 4.05 | 4.46 |
| 82 L.H., Daily Totals | | $3598.35 | | $5439.60 | $43.88 | $66.34 |
| **Crew C-17C** | Hr. | Daily | Hr. | Daily | Bare Costs | Incl. O&P |
| 2 Skilled Worker Foremen | $41.40 | $662.40 | $64.40 | $1030.40 | $39.84 | $61.88 |
| 8 Skilled Workers | 39.40 | 2521.60 | 61.25 | 3920.00 | | |
| .375 Equip. Oper. (crane) | 40.95 | 122.85 | 61.75 | 185.25 | | |
| .375 Hyd. Crane, 80 Ton | | 483.75 | | 532.13 | 5.83 | 6.41 |
| 83 L.H., Daily Totals | | $3790.60 | | $5667.77 | $45.67 | $68.29 |
| **Crew C-17D** | Hr. | Daily | Hr. | Daily | Bare Costs | Incl. O&P |
| 2 Skilled Worker Foremen | $41.40 | $662.40 | $64.40 | $1030.40 | $39.85 | $61.87 |
| 8 Skilled Workers | 39.40 | 2521.60 | 61.25 | 3920.00 | | |
| .5 Equip. Oper. (crane) | 40.95 | 163.80 | 61.75 | 247.00 | | |
| .5 Hyd. Crane, 80 Ton | | 645.00 | | 709.50 | 7.68 | 8.45 |
| 84 L.H., Daily Totals | | $3992.80 | | $5906.90 | $47.53 | $70.32 |
| **Crew C-17E** | Hr. | Daily | Hr. | Daily | Bare Costs | Incl. O&P |
| 2 Skilled Worker Foremen | $41.40 | $662.40 | $64.40 | $1030.40 | $39.80 | $61.88 |
| 8 Skilled Workers | 39.40 | 2521.60 | 61.25 | 3920.00 | | |
| 1 Hyd. Jack with Rods | | 84.00 | | 92.40 | 1.05 | 1.16 |
| 80 L.H., Daily Totals | | $3268.00 | | $5042.80 | $40.85 | $63.03 |
| **Crew C-18** | Hr. | Daily | Hr. | Daily | Bare Costs | Incl. O&P |
| .125 Labor Foreman (out) | $32.25 | $32.25 | $50.20 | $50.20 | $30.47 | $47.40 |
| 1 Laborer | 30.25 | 242.00 | 47.05 | 376.40 | | |
| 1 Concrete Cart, 10 C.F. | | 56.40 | | 62.04 | 6.27 | 6.89 |
| 9 L.H., Daily Totals | | $330.65 | | $488.64 | $36.74 | $54.29 |
| **Crew C-19** | Hr. | Daily | Hr. | Daily | Bare Costs | Incl. O&P |
| .125 Labor Foreman (out) | $32.25 | $32.25 | $50.20 | $50.20 | $30.47 | $47.40 |
| 1 Laborer | 30.25 | 242.00 | 47.05 | 376.40 | | |
| 1 Concrete Cart, 18 C.F. | | 84.40 | | 92.84 | 9.38 | 10.32 |
| 9 L.H., Daily Totals | | $358.65 | | $519.44 | $39.85 | $57.72 |
| **Crew C-20** | Hr. | Daily | Hr. | Daily | Bare Costs | Incl. O&P |
| 1 Labor Foreman (outside) | $32.25 | $258.00 | $50.20 | $401.60 | $32.54 | $49.98 |
| 5 Laborers | 30.25 | 1210.00 | 47.05 | 1882.00 | | |
| 1 Cement Finisher | 37.00 | 296.00 | 54.30 | 434.40 | | |
| 1 Equip. Oper. (med.) | 39.85 | 318.80 | 60.10 | 480.80 | | |
| 2 Gas Engine Vibrator | | 49.60 | | 54.56 | | |
| 1 Concrete Pump (small) | | 728.20 | | 801.02 | 12.15 | 13.37 |
| 64 L.H., Daily Totals | | $2860.60 | | $4054.38 | $44.70 | $63.35 |
| **Crew C-21** | Hr. | Daily | Hr. | Daily | Bare Costs | Incl. O&P |
| 1 Labor Foreman (outside) | $32.25 | $258.00 | $50.20 | $401.60 | $32.54 | $49.98 |
| 5 Laborers | 30.25 | 1210.00 | 47.05 | 1882.00 | | |
| 1 Cement Finisher | 37.00 | 296.00 | 54.30 | 434.40 | | |
| 1 Equip. Oper. (med.) | 39.85 | 318.80 | 60.10 | 480.80 | | |
| 2 Gas Engine Vibrator | | 49.60 | | 54.56 | | |
| 1 Concrete Conveyer | | 172.80 | | 190.08 | 3.48 | 3.82 |
| 64 L.H., Daily Totals | | $2305.20 | | $3443.44 | $36.02 | $53.80 |
| **Crew C-22** | Hr. | Daily | Hr. | Daily | Bare Costs | Incl. O&P |
| 1 Rodman Foreman | $45.00 | $360.00 | $73.85 | $590.80 | $43.14 | $70.55 |
| 4 Rodmen (reinf.) | 43.00 | 1376.00 | 70.55 | 2257.60 | | |
| .125 Equip. Oper. (crane) | 40.95 | 40.95 | 61.75 | 61.75 | | |
| .125 Equip. Oper. Oiler | 35.10 | 35.10 | 52.95 | 52.95 | | |
| .125 Hyd. Crane, 25 Ton | | 98.25 | | 108.08 | 2.34 | 2.57 |
| 42 L.H., Daily Totals | | $1910.30 | | $3071.18 | $45.48 | $73.12 |
| **Crew C-23** | Hr. | Daily | Hr. | Daily | Bare Costs | Incl. O&P |
| 2 Skilled Worker Foremen | $41.40 | $662.40 | $64.40 | $1030.40 | $39.52 | $61.10 |
| 6 Skilled Workers | 39.40 | 1891.20 | 61.25 | 2940.00 | | |
| 1 Equip. Oper. (crane) | 40.95 | 327.60 | 61.75 | 494.00 | | |
| 1 Equip. Oper. Oiler | 35.10 | 280.80 | 52.95 | 423.60 | | |
| 1 Lattice Boom Crane, 90 Ton | | 1567.00 | | 1723.70 | 19.59 | 21.55 |
| 80 L.H., Daily Totals | | $4729.00 | | $6611.70 | $59.11 | $82.65 |
| **Crew C-23A** | Hr. | Daily | Hr. | Daily | Bare Costs | Incl. O&P |
| 1 Labor Foreman (outside) | $32.25 | $258.00 | $50.20 | $401.60 | $33.76 | $51.80 |
| 2 Laborers | 30.25 | 484.00 | 47.05 | 752.80 | | |
| 1 Equip. Oper. (crane) | 40.95 | 327.60 | 61.75 | 494.00 | | |
| 1 Equip. Oper. Oiler | 35.10 | 280.80 | 52.95 | 423.60 | | |
| 1 Crawler Crane, 100 Ton | | 1586.00 | | 1744.60 | | |
| 3 Conc. bucket, 8 C.Y. | | 576.00 | | 633.60 | 54.05 | 59.45 |
| 40 L.H., Daily Totals | | $3512.40 | | $4450.20 | $87.81 | $111.26 |
| **Crew C-24** | Hr. | Daily | Hr. | Daily | Bare Costs | Incl. O&P |
| 2 Skilled Worker Foremen | $41.40 | $662.40 | $64.40 | $1030.40 | $39.52 | $61.10 |
| 6 Skilled Workers | 39.40 | 1891.20 | 61.25 | 2940.00 | | |
| 1 Equip. Oper. (crane) | 40.95 | 327.60 | 61.75 | 494.00 | | |
| 1 Equip. Oper. Oiler | 35.10 | 280.80 | 52.95 | 423.60 | | |
| 1 Lattice Boom Crane, 150 Ton | | 1885.00 | | 2073.50 | 23.56 | 25.92 |
| 80 L.H., Daily Totals | | $5047.00 | | $6961.50 | $63.09 | $87.02 |

# Crews

| Crew No. | Bare Costs Hr. | Daily | Incl. Subs O & P Hr. | Daily | Bare Costs | Incl. O&P |
|---|---|---|---|---|---|---|
| **Crew C-25** | Hr. | Daily | Hr. | Daily | Bare Costs | Incl. O&P |
| 2 Rodmen (reinf.) | $43.00 | $688.00 | $70.55 | $1128.80 | $33.80 | $56.20 |
| 2 Rodmen Helpers | 24.60 | 393.60 | 41.85 | 669.60 | | |
| 32 L.H., Daily Totals | | $1081.60 | | $1798.40 | $33.80 | $56.20 |

| **Crew C-27** | Hr. | Daily | Hr. | Daily | Bare Costs | Incl. O&P |
|---|---|---|---|---|---|---|
| 2 Cement Finishers | $37.00 | $592.00 | $54.30 | $868.80 | $37.00 | $54.30 |
| 1 Concrete Saw | | 135.00 | | 148.50 | 8.44 | 9.28 |
| 16 L.H., Daily Totals | | $727.00 | | $1017.30 | $45.44 | $63.58 |

| **Crew C-28** | Hr. | Daily | Hr. | Daily | Bare Costs | Incl. O&P |
|---|---|---|---|---|---|---|
| 1 Cement Finisher | $37.00 | $296.00 | $54.30 | $434.40 | $37.00 | $54.30 |
| 1 Portable Air Compressor, Gas | | 16.65 | | 18.32 | 2.08 | 2.29 |
| 8 L.H., Daily Totals | | $312.65 | | $452.71 | $39.08 | $56.59 |

| **Crew D-1** | Hr. | Daily | Hr. | Daily | Bare Costs | Incl. O&P |
|---|---|---|---|---|---|---|
| 1 Bricklayer | $39.15 | $313.20 | $59.55 | $476.40 | $34.88 | $53.05 |
| 1 Bricklayer Helper | 30.60 | 244.80 | 46.55 | 372.40 | | |
| 16 L.H., Daily Totals | | $558.00 | | $848.80 | $34.88 | $53.05 |

| **Crew D-2** | Hr. | Daily | Hr. | Daily | Bare Costs | Incl. O&P |
|---|---|---|---|---|---|---|
| 3 Bricklayers | $39.15 | $939.60 | $59.55 | $1429.20 | $35.95 | $54.80 |
| 2 Bricklayer Helpers | 30.60 | 489.60 | 46.55 | 744.80 | | |
| .5 Carpenter | 38.10 | 152.40 | 59.30 | 237.20 | | |
| 44 L.H., Daily Totals | | $1581.60 | | $2411.20 | $35.95 | $54.80 |

| **Crew D-3** | Hr. | Daily | Hr. | Daily | Bare Costs | Incl. O&P |
|---|---|---|---|---|---|---|
| 3 Bricklayers | $39.15 | $939.60 | $59.55 | $1429.20 | $35.84 | $54.59 |
| 2 Bricklayer Helpers | 30.60 | 489.60 | 46.55 | 744.80 | | |
| .25 Carpenter | 38.10 | 76.20 | 59.30 | 118.60 | | |
| 42 L.H., Daily Totals | | $1505.40 | | $2292.60 | $35.84 | $54.59 |

| **Crew D-4** | Hr. | Daily | Hr. | Daily | Bare Costs | Incl. O&P |
|---|---|---|---|---|---|---|
| 1 Bricklayer | $39.15 | $313.20 | $59.55 | $476.40 | $34.52 | $52.40 |
| 2 Bricklayer Helpers | 30.60 | 489.60 | 46.55 | 744.80 | | |
| 1 Equip. Oper. (light) | 37.75 | 302.00 | 56.95 | 455.60 | | |
| 1 Grout Pump, 50 C.F./hr | | 126.40 | | 139.04 | 3.95 | 4.34 |
| 32 L.H., Daily Totals | | $1231.20 | | $1815.84 | $38.48 | $56.74 |

| **Crew D-5** | Hr. | Daily | Hr. | Daily | Bare Costs | Incl. O&P |
|---|---|---|---|---|---|---|
| 1 Bricklayer | $39.15 | $313.20 | $59.55 | $476.40 | $39.15 | $59.55 |
| 8 L.H., Daily Totals | | $313.20 | | $476.40 | $39.15 | $59.55 |

| **Crew D-6** | Hr. | Daily | Hr. | Daily | Bare Costs | Incl. O&P |
|---|---|---|---|---|---|---|
| 3 Bricklayers | $39.15 | $939.60 | $59.55 | $1429.20 | $35.00 | $53.30 |
| 3 Bricklayer Helpers | 30.60 | 734.40 | 46.55 | 1117.20 | | |
| .25 Carpenter | 38.10 | 76.20 | 59.30 | 118.60 | | |
| 50 L.H., Daily Totals | | $1750.20 | | $2665.00 | $35.00 | $53.30 |

| **Crew D-7** | Hr. | Daily | Hr. | Daily | Bare Costs | Incl. O&P |
|---|---|---|---|---|---|---|
| 1 Tile Layer | $37.00 | $296.00 | $54.30 | $434.40 | $33.08 | $48.55 |
| 1 Tile Layer Helper | 29.15 | 233.20 | 42.80 | 342.40 | | |
| 16 L.H., Daily Totals | | $529.20 | | $776.80 | $33.08 | $48.55 |

| **Crew D-8** | Hr. | Daily | Hr. | Daily | Bare Costs | Incl. O&P |
|---|---|---|---|---|---|---|
| 3 Bricklayers | $39.15 | $939.60 | $59.55 | $1429.20 | $35.73 | $54.35 |
| 2 Bricklayer Helpers | 30.60 | 489.60 | 46.55 | 744.80 | | |
| 40 L.H., Daily Totals | | $1429.20 | | $2174.00 | $35.73 | $54.35 |

| **Crew D-9** | Hr. | Daily | Hr. | Daily | Bare Costs | Incl. O&P |
|---|---|---|---|---|---|---|
| 3 Bricklayers | $39.15 | $939.60 | $59.55 | $1429.20 | $34.88 | $53.05 |
| 3 Bricklayer Helpers | 30.60 | 734.40 | 46.55 | 1117.20 | | |
| 48 L.H., Daily Totals | | $1674.00 | | $2546.40 | $34.88 | $53.05 |

| **Crew D-10** | Hr. | Daily | Hr. | Daily | Bare Costs | Incl. O&P |
|---|---|---|---|---|---|---|
| 1 Bricklayer Foreman | $41.15 | $329.20 | $62.60 | $500.80 | $37.96 | $57.61 |
| 1 Bricklayer | 39.15 | 313.20 | 59.55 | 476.40 | | |
| 1 Bricklayer Helper | 30.60 | 244.80 | 46.55 | 372.40 | | |
| 1 Equip. Oper. (crane) | 40.95 | 327.60 | 61.75 | 494.00 | | |
| 1 S.P. Crane, 4x4, 12 Ton | | 611.00 | | 672.10 | 19.09 | 21.00 |
| 32 L.H., Daily Totals | | $1825.80 | | $2515.70 | $57.06 | $78.62 |

| **Crew D-11** | Hr. | Daily | Hr. | Daily | Bare Costs | Incl. O&P |
|---|---|---|---|---|---|---|
| 1 Bricklayer Foreman | $41.15 | $329.20 | $62.60 | $500.80 | $36.97 | $56.23 |
| 1 Bricklayer | 39.15 | 313.20 | 59.55 | 476.40 | | |
| 1 Bricklayer Helper | 30.60 | 244.80 | 46.55 | 372.40 | | |
| 24 L.H., Daily Totals | | $887.20 | | $1349.60 | $36.97 | $56.23 |

| **Crew D-12** | Hr. | Daily | Hr. | Daily | Bare Costs | Incl. O&P |
|---|---|---|---|---|---|---|
| 1 Bricklayer Foreman | $41.15 | $329.20 | $62.60 | $500.80 | $35.38 | $53.81 |
| 1 Bricklayer | 39.15 | 313.20 | 59.55 | 476.40 | | |
| 2 Bricklayer Helpers | 30.60 | 489.60 | 46.55 | 744.80 | | |
| 32 L.H., Daily Totals | | $1132.00 | | $1722.00 | $35.38 | $53.81 |

| **Crew D-13** | Hr. | Daily | Hr. | Daily | Bare Costs | Incl. O&P |
|---|---|---|---|---|---|---|
| 1 Bricklayer Foreman | $41.15 | $329.20 | $62.60 | $500.80 | $36.76 | $56.05 |
| 1 Bricklayer | 39.15 | 313.20 | 59.55 | 476.40 | | |
| 2 Bricklayer Helpers | 30.60 | 489.60 | 46.55 | 744.80 | | |
| 1 Carpenter | 38.10 | 304.80 | 59.30 | 474.40 | | |
| 1 Equip. Oper. (crane) | 40.95 | 327.60 | 61.75 | 494.00 | | |
| 1 S.P. Crane, 4x4, 12 Ton | | 611.00 | | 672.10 | 12.73 | 14.00 |
| 48 L.H., Daily Totals | | $2375.40 | | $3362.50 | $49.49 | $70.05 |

| **Crew E-1** | Hr. | Daily | Hr. | Daily | Bare Costs | Incl. O&P |
|---|---|---|---|---|---|---|
| 1 Welder Foreman | $45.00 | $360.00 | $81.20 | $649.60 | $41.92 | $71.90 |
| 1 Welder | 43.00 | 344.00 | 77.55 | 620.40 | | |
| 1 Equip. Oper. (light) | 37.75 | 302.00 | 56.95 | 455.60 | | |
| 1 Welder, gas engine, 300 amp | | 132.20 | | 145.42 | 5.51 | 6.06 |
| 24 L.H., Daily Totals | | $1138.20 | | $1871.02 | $47.42 | $77.96 |

| **Crew E-2** | Hr. | Daily | Hr. | Daily | Bare Costs | Incl. O&P |
|---|---|---|---|---|---|---|
| 1 Struc. Steel Foreman | $45.00 | $360.00 | $81.20 | $649.60 | $41.86 | $72.30 |
| 4 Struc. Steel Workers | 43.00 | 1376.00 | 77.55 | 2481.60 | | |
| 1 Equip. Oper. (crane) | 40.95 | 327.60 | 61.75 | 494.00 | | |
| 1 Equip. Oper. Oiler | 35.10 | 280.80 | 52.95 | 423.60 | | |
| 1 Lattice Boom Crane, 90 Ton | | 1567.00 | | 1723.70 | 27.98 | 30.78 |
| 56 L.H., Daily Totals | | $3911.40 | | $5772.50 | $69.85 | $103.08 |

| **Crew E-3** | Hr. | Daily | Hr. | Daily | Bare Costs | Incl. O&P |
|---|---|---|---|---|---|---|
| 1 Struc. Steel Foreman | $45.00 | $360.00 | $81.20 | $649.60 | $43.67 | $78.77 |
| 1 Struc. Steel Worker | 43.00 | 344.00 | 77.55 | 620.40 | | |
| 1 Welder | 43.00 | 344.00 | 77.55 | 620.40 | | |
| 1 Welder, gas engine, 300 amp | | 132.20 | | 145.42 | 5.51 | 6.06 |
| 24 L.H., Daily Totals | | $1180.20 | | $2035.82 | $49.17 | $84.83 |

| **Crew E-4** | Hr. | Daily | Hr. | Daily | Bare Costs | Incl. O&P |
|---|---|---|---|---|---|---|
| 1 Struc. Steel Foreman | $45.00 | $360.00 | $81.20 | $649.60 | $43.50 | $78.46 |
| 3 Struc. Steel Workers | 43.00 | 1032.00 | 77.55 | 1861.20 | | |
| 1 Welder, gas engine, 300 amp | | 132.20 | | 145.42 | 4.13 | 4.54 |
| 32 L.H., Daily Totals | | $1524.20 | | $2656.22 | $47.63 | $83.01 |

## Crew E-5

| Crew No. | Bare Costs Hr. | Bare Costs Daily | Incl. Subs O & P Hr. | Incl. Subs O & P Daily | Cost Per Labor-Hour Bare Costs | Cost Per Labor-Hour Incl. O&P |
|---|---|---|---|---|---|---|
| 2 Struc. Steel Foremen | $45.00 | $720.00 | $81.20 | $1299.20 | $42.41 | $74.24 |
| 5 Struc. Steel Workers | 43.00 | 1720.00 | 77.55 | 3102.00 | | |
| 1 Equip. Oper. (crane) | 40.95 | 327.60 | 61.75 | 494.00 | | |
| 1 Welder | 43.00 | 344.00 | 77.55 | 620.40 | | |
| 1 Equip. Oper. Oiler | 35.10 | 280.80 | 52.95 | 423.60 | | |
| 1 Lattice Boom Crane, 90 Ton | | 1567.00 | | 1723.70 | | |
| 1 Welder, gas engine, 300 amp | | 132.20 | | 145.42 | 21.24 | 23.36 |
| 80 L.H., Daily Totals | | $5091.60 | | $7808.32 | $63.65 | $97.60 |

## Crew E-6

| Crew No. | Bare Costs Hr. | Bare Costs Daily | Incl. Subs O & P Hr. | Incl. Subs O & P Daily | Cost Per Labor-Hour Bare Costs | Cost Per Labor-Hour Incl. O&P |
|---|---|---|---|---|---|---|
| 3 Struc. Steel Foremen | $45.00 | $1080.00 | $81.20 | $1948.80 | $42.42 | $74.42 |
| 9 Struc. Steel Workers | 43.00 | 3096.00 | 77.55 | 5583.60 | | |
| 1 Equip. Oper. (crane) | 40.95 | 327.60 | 61.75 | 494.00 | | |
| 1 Welder | 43.00 | 344.00 | 77.55 | 620.40 | | |
| 1 Equip. Oper. Oiler | 35.10 | 280.80 | 52.95 | 423.60 | | |
| 1 Equip. Oper. (light) | 37.75 | 302.00 | 56.95 | 455.60 | | |
| 1 Lattice Boom Crane, 90 Ton | | 1567.00 | | 1723.70 | | |
| 1 Welder, gas engine, 300 amp | | 132.20 | | 145.42 | | |
| 1 Air Compressor, 160 C.F.M. | | 137.60 | | 151.36 | | |
| 2 Impact Wrenches | | 30.40 | | 33.44 | 14.59 | 16.05 |
| 128 L.H., Daily Totals | | $7297.60 | | $11579.92 | $57.01 | $90.47 |

## Crew E-7

| Crew No. | Bare Costs Hr. | Bare Costs Daily | Incl. Subs O & P Hr. | Incl. Subs O & P Daily | Cost Per Labor-Hour Bare Costs | Cost Per Labor-Hour Incl. O&P |
|---|---|---|---|---|---|---|
| 1 Struc. Steel Foreman | $45.00 | $360.00 | $81.20 | $649.60 | $42.41 | $74.24 |
| 4 Struc. Steel Workers | 43.00 | 1376.00 | 77.55 | 2481.60 | | |
| 1 Equip. Oper. (crane) | 40.95 | 327.60 | 61.75 | 494.00 | | |
| 1 Equip. Oper. Oiler | 35.10 | 280.80 | 52.95 | 423.60 | | |
| 1 Welder Foreman | 45.00 | 360.00 | 81.20 | 649.60 | | |
| 2 Welders | 43.00 | 688.00 | 77.55 | 1240.80 | | |
| 1 Lattice Boom Crane, 90 Ton | | 1567.00 | | 1723.70 | | |
| 2 Welder, gas engine, 300 amp | | 264.40 | | 290.84 | 22.89 | 25.18 |
| 80 L.H., Daily Totals | | $5223.80 | | $7953.74 | $65.30 | $99.42 |

## Crew E-8

| Crew No. | Bare Costs Hr. | Bare Costs Daily | Incl. Subs O & P Hr. | Incl. Subs O & P Daily | Cost Per Labor-Hour Bare Costs | Cost Per Labor-Hour Incl. O&P |
|---|---|---|---|---|---|---|
| 1 Struc. Steel Foreman | $45.00 | $360.00 | $81.20 | $649.60 | $42.14 | $73.42 |
| 4 Struc. Steel Workers | 43.00 | 1376.00 | 77.55 | 2481.60 | | |
| 1 Welder Foreman | 45.00 | 360.00 | 81.20 | 649.60 | | |
| 4 Welders | 43.00 | 1376.00 | 77.55 | 2481.60 | | |
| 1 Equip. Oper. (crane) | 40.95 | 327.60 | 61.75 | 494.00 | | |
| 1 Equip. Oper. Oiler | 35.10 | 280.80 | 52.95 | 423.60 | | |
| 1 Equip. Oper. (light) | 37.75 | 302.00 | 56.95 | 455.60 | | |
| 1 Lattice Boom Crane, 90 Ton | | 1567.00 | | 1723.70 | | |
| 4 Welder, gas engine, 300 amp | | 528.80 | | 581.68 | 20.15 | 22.17 |
| 104 L.H., Daily Totals | | $6478.20 | | $9940.98 | $62.29 | $95.59 |

## Crew E-9

| Crew No. | Bare Costs Hr. | Bare Costs Daily | Incl. Subs O & P Hr. | Incl. Subs O & P Daily | Cost Per Labor-Hour Bare Costs | Cost Per Labor-Hour Incl. O&P |
|---|---|---|---|---|---|---|
| 2 Struc. Steel Foremen | $45.00 | $720.00 | $81.20 | $1299.20 | $42.42 | $74.42 |
| 5 Struc. Steel Workers | 43.00 | 1720.00 | 77.55 | 3102.00 | | |
| 1 Welder Foreman | 45.00 | 360.00 | 81.20 | 649.60 | | |
| 5 Welders | 43.00 | 1720.00 | 77.55 | 3102.00 | | |
| 1 Equip. Oper. (crane) | 40.95 | 327.60 | 61.75 | 494.00 | | |
| 1 Equip. Oper. Oiler | 35.10 | 280.80 | 52.95 | 423.60 | | |
| 1 Equip. Oper. (light) | 37.75 | 302.00 | 56.95 | 455.60 | | |
| 1 Lattice Boom Crane, 90 Ton | | 1567.00 | | 1723.70 | | |
| 5 Welder, gas engine, 300 amp | | 661.00 | | 727.10 | 17.41 | 19.15 |
| 128 L.H., Daily Totals | | $7658.40 | | $11976.80 | $59.83 | $93.57 |

## Crew E-10

| Crew No. | Bare Costs Hr. | Bare Costs Daily | Incl. Subs O & P Hr. | Incl. Subs O & P Daily | Cost Per Labor-Hour Bare Costs | Cost Per Labor-Hour Incl. O&P |
|---|---|---|---|---|---|---|
| 1 Welder Foreman | $45.00 | $360.00 | $81.20 | $649.60 | $44.00 | $79.38 |
| 1 Welder | 43.00 | 344.00 | 77.55 | 620.40 | | |
| 1 Welder, gas engine, 300 amp | | 132.20 | | 145.42 | | |
| 1 Flatbed Truck, Gas, 3 Ton | | 224.00 | | 246.40 | 22.26 | 24.49 |
| 16 L.H., Daily Totals | | $1060.20 | | $1661.82 | $66.26 | $103.86 |

## Crew E-11

| Crew No. | Bare Costs Hr. | Bare Costs Daily | Incl. Subs O & P Hr. | Incl. Subs O & P Daily | Cost Per Labor-Hour Bare Costs | Cost Per Labor-Hour Incl. O&P |
|---|---|---|---|---|---|---|
| 2 Painters, Struc. Steel | $34.40 | $550.40 | $62.15 | $994.40 | $34.20 | $57.08 |
| 1 Building Laborer | 30.25 | 242.00 | 47.05 | 376.40 | | |
| 1 Equip. Oper. (light) | 37.75 | 302.00 | 56.95 | 455.60 | | |
| 1 Air Compressor, 250 C.F.M. | | 161.80 | | 177.98 | | |
| 1 Sandblaster, portable, 3 C.F. | | 18.00 | | 19.80 | | |
| 1 Sand Blasting Accessories | | 12.55 | | 13.81 | 6.01 | 6.61 |
| 32 L.H., Daily Totals | | $1286.75 | | $2037.98 | $40.21 | $63.69 |

## Crew E-12

| Crew No. | Bare Costs Hr. | Bare Costs Daily | Incl. Subs O & P Hr. | Incl. Subs O & P Daily | Cost Per Labor-Hour Bare Costs | Cost Per Labor-Hour Incl. O&P |
|---|---|---|---|---|---|---|
| 1 Welder Foreman | $45.00 | $360.00 | $81.20 | $649.60 | $41.38 | $69.08 |
| 1 Equip. Oper. (light) | 37.75 | 302.00 | 56.95 | 455.60 | | |
| 1 Welder, gas engine, 300 amp | | 132.20 | | 145.42 | 8.26 | 9.09 |
| 16 L.H., Daily Totals | | $794.20 | | $1250.62 | $49.64 | $78.16 |

## Crew E-13

| Crew No. | Bare Costs Hr. | Bare Costs Daily | Incl. Subs O & P Hr. | Incl. Subs O & P Daily | Cost Per Labor-Hour Bare Costs | Cost Per Labor-Hour Incl. O&P |
|---|---|---|---|---|---|---|
| 1 Welder Foreman | $45.00 | $360.00 | $81.20 | $649.60 | $42.58 | $73.12 |
| .5 Equip. Oper. (light) | 37.75 | 151.00 | 56.95 | 227.80 | | |
| 1 Welder, gas engine, 300 amp | | 132.20 | | 145.42 | 11.02 | 12.12 |
| 12 L.H., Daily Totals | | $643.20 | | $1022.82 | $53.60 | $85.23 |

## Crew E-14

| Crew No. | Bare Costs Hr. | Bare Costs Daily | Incl. Subs O & P Hr. | Incl. Subs O & P Daily | Cost Per Labor-Hour Bare Costs | Cost Per Labor-Hour Incl. O&P |
|---|---|---|---|---|---|---|
| 1 Welder Foreman | $45.00 | $360.00 | $81.20 | $649.60 | $45.00 | $81.20 |
| 1 Welder, gas engine, 300 amp | | 132.20 | | 145.42 | 16.52 | 18.18 |
| 8 L.H., Daily Totals | | $492.20 | | $795.02 | $61.52 | $99.38 |

## Crew E-16

| Crew No. | Bare Costs Hr. | Bare Costs Daily | Incl. Subs O & P Hr. | Incl. Subs O & P Daily | Cost Per Labor-Hour Bare Costs | Cost Per Labor-Hour Incl. O&P |
|---|---|---|---|---|---|---|
| 1 Welder Foreman | $45.00 | $360.00 | $81.20 | $649.60 | $44.00 | $79.38 |
| 1 Welder | 43.00 | 344.00 | 77.55 | 620.40 | | |
| 1 Welder, gas engine, 300 amp | | 132.20 | | 145.42 | 8.26 | 9.09 |
| 16 L.H., Daily Totals | | $836.20 | | $1415.42 | $52.26 | $88.46 |

## Crew E-17

| Crew No. | Bare Costs Hr. | Bare Costs Daily | Incl. Subs O & P Hr. | Incl. Subs O & P Daily | Cost Per Labor-Hour Bare Costs | Cost Per Labor-Hour Incl. O&P |
|---|---|---|---|---|---|---|
| 1 Structural Steel Foreman | $45.00 | $360.00 | $81.20 | $649.60 | $44.00 | $79.38 |
| 1 Structural Steel Worker | 43.00 | 344.00 | 77.55 | 620.40 | | |
| 16 L.H., Daily Totals | | $704.00 | | $1270.00 | $44.00 | $79.38 |

## Crew E-18

| Crew No. | Bare Costs Hr. | Bare Costs Daily | Incl. Subs O & P Hr. | Incl. Subs O & P Daily | Cost Per Labor-Hour Bare Costs | Cost Per Labor-Hour Incl. O&P |
|---|---|---|---|---|---|---|
| 1 Structural Steel Foreman | $45.00 | $360.00 | $81.20 | $649.60 | $42.77 | $74.79 |
| 3 Structural Steel Workers | 43.00 | 1032.00 | 77.55 | 1861.20 | | |
| 1 Equipment Operator (med.) | 39.85 | 318.80 | 60.10 | 480.80 | | |
| 1 Lattice Boom Crane, 20 Ton | | 1005.00 | | 1105.50 | 25.13 | 27.64 |
| 40 L.H., Daily Totals | | $2715.80 | | $4097.10 | $67.89 | $102.43 |

## Crew E-19

| Crew No. | Bare Costs Hr. | Bare Costs Daily | Incl. Subs O & P Hr. | Incl. Subs O & P Daily | Cost Per Labor-Hour Bare Costs | Cost Per Labor-Hour Incl. O&P |
|---|---|---|---|---|---|---|
| 1 Structural Steel Worker | $43.00 | $344.00 | $77.55 | $620.40 | $41.92 | $71.90 |
| 1 Structural Steel Foreman | 45.00 | 360.00 | 81.20 | 649.60 | | |
| 1 Equip. Oper. (light) | 37.75 | 302.00 | 56.95 | 455.60 | | |
| 1 Lattice Boom Crane, 20 Ton | | 1005.00 | | 1105.50 | 41.88 | 46.06 |
| 24 L.H., Daily Totals | | $2011.00 | | $2831.10 | $83.79 | $117.96 |

# Crews

## Crew E-20

| Crew No. | Bare Costs Hr. | Bare Costs Daily | Incl. Subs O&P Hr. | Incl. Subs O&P Daily | Cost Per Labor-Hour Bare Costs | Cost Per Labor-Hour Incl. O&P |
|---|---|---|---|---|---|---|
| 1 Structural Steel Foreman | $45.00 | $360.00 | $81.20 | $649.60 | $42.01 | $72.96 |
| 5 Structural Steel Workers | 43.00 | 1720.00 | 77.55 | 3102.00 | | |
| 1 Equip. Oper. (crane) | 40.95 | 327.60 | 61.75 | 494.00 | | |
| 1 Oiler | 35.10 | 280.80 | 52.95 | 423.60 | | |
| 1 Lattice Boom Crane, 40 Ton | | 1225.00 | | 1347.50 | 19.14 | 21.05 |
| 64 L.H., Daily Totals | | $3913.40 | | $6016.70 | $61.15 | $94.01 |

## Crew E-22

| Crew No. | Bare Costs Hr. | Bare Costs Daily | Incl. Subs O&P Hr. | Incl. Subs O&P Daily | Cost Per Labor-Hour Bare Costs | Cost Per Labor-Hour Incl. O&P |
|---|---|---|---|---|---|---|
| 1 Skilled Worker Foreman | $41.40 | $331.20 | $64.40 | $515.20 | $40.07 | $62.30 |
| 2 Skilled Workers | 39.40 | 630.40 | 61.25 | 980.00 | | |
| 24 L.H., Daily Totals | | $961.60 | | $1495.20 | $40.07 | $62.30 |

## Crew E-24

| Crew No. | Bare Costs Hr. | Bare Costs Daily | Incl. Subs O&P Hr. | Incl. Subs O&P Daily | Cost Per Labor-Hour Bare Costs | Cost Per Labor-Hour Incl. O&P |
|---|---|---|---|---|---|---|
| 3 Structural Steel Workers | $43.00 | $1032.00 | $77.55 | $1861.20 | $42.21 | $73.19 |
| 1 Equipment Operator (medium) | 39.85 | 318.80 | 60.10 | 480.80 | | |
| 1 Hyd. Crane, 25 Ton | | 786.00 | | 864.60 | 24.56 | 27.02 |
| 32 L.H., Daily Totals | | $2136.80 | | $3206.60 | $66.78 | $100.21 |

## Crew E-25

| Crew No. | Bare Costs Hr. | Bare Costs Daily | Incl. Subs O&P Hr. | Incl. Subs O&P Daily | Cost Per Labor-Hour Bare Costs | Cost Per Labor-Hour Incl. O&P |
|---|---|---|---|---|---|---|
| 1 Welder Foreman | $45.00 | $360.00 | $81.20 | $649.60 | $45.00 | $81.20 |
| 1 Cutting Torch | | 17.00 | | 18.70 | | |
| 1 Gases | | 72.00 | | 79.20 | 11.13 | 12.24 |
| 8 L.H., Daily Totals | | $449.00 | | $747.50 | $56.13 | $93.44 |

## Crew F-3

| Crew No. | Bare Costs Hr. | Bare Costs Daily | Incl. Subs O&P Hr. | Incl. Subs O&P Daily | Cost Per Labor-Hour Bare Costs | Cost Per Labor-Hour Incl. O&P |
|---|---|---|---|---|---|---|
| 4 Carpenters | $38.10 | $1219.20 | $59.30 | $1897.60 | $38.67 | $59.79 |
| 1 Equip. Oper. (crane) | 40.95 | 327.60 | 61.75 | 494.00 | | |
| 1 Hyd. Crane, 12 Ton | | 766.40 | | 843.04 | 19.16 | 21.08 |
| 40 L.H., Daily Totals | | $2313.20 | | $3234.64 | $57.83 | $80.87 |

## Crew F-4

| Crew No. | Bare Costs Hr. | Bare Costs Daily | Incl. Subs O&P Hr. | Incl. Subs O&P Daily | Cost Per Labor-Hour Bare Costs | Cost Per Labor-Hour Incl. O&P |
|---|---|---|---|---|---|---|
| 4 Carpenters | $38.10 | $1219.20 | $59.30 | $1897.60 | $38.08 | $58.65 |
| 1 Equip. Oper. (crane) | 40.95 | 327.60 | 61.75 | 494.00 | | |
| 1 Equip. Oper. Oiler | 35.10 | 280.80 | 52.95 | 423.60 | | |
| 1 Hyd. Crane, 55 Ton | | 1119.00 | | 1230.90 | 23.31 | 25.64 |
| 48 L.H., Daily Totals | | $2946.60 | | $4046.10 | $61.39 | $84.29 |

## Crew F-5

| Crew No. | Bare Costs Hr. | Bare Costs Daily | Incl. Subs O&P Hr. | Incl. Subs O&P Daily | Cost Per Labor-Hour Bare Costs | Cost Per Labor-Hour Incl. O&P |
|---|---|---|---|---|---|---|
| 1 Carpenter Foreman | $40.10 | $320.80 | $62.40 | $499.20 | $38.60 | $60.08 |
| 3 Carpenters | 38.10 | 914.40 | 59.30 | 1423.20 | | |
| 32 L.H., Daily Totals | | $1235.20 | | $1922.40 | $38.60 | $60.08 |

## Crew F-6

| Crew No. | Bare Costs Hr. | Bare Costs Daily | Incl. Subs O&P Hr. | Incl. Subs O&P Daily | Cost Per Labor-Hour Bare Costs | Cost Per Labor-Hour Incl. O&P |
|---|---|---|---|---|---|---|
| 2 Carpenters | $38.10 | $609.60 | $59.30 | $948.80 | $35.53 | $54.89 |
| 2 Building Laborers | 30.25 | 484.00 | 47.05 | 752.80 | | |
| 1 Equip. Oper. (crane) | 40.95 | 327.60 | 61.75 | 494.00 | | |
| 1 Hyd. Crane, 12 Ton | | 766.40 | | 843.04 | 19.16 | 21.08 |
| 40 L.H., Daily Totals | | $2187.60 | | $3038.64 | $54.69 | $75.97 |

## Crew F-7

| Crew No. | Bare Costs Hr. | Bare Costs Daily | Incl. Subs O&P Hr. | Incl. Subs O&P Daily | Cost Per Labor-Hour Bare Costs | Cost Per Labor-Hour Incl. O&P |
|---|---|---|---|---|---|---|
| 2 Carpenters | $38.10 | $609.60 | $59.30 | $948.80 | $34.17 | $53.17 |
| 2 Building Laborers | 30.25 | 484.00 | 47.05 | 752.80 | | |
| 32 L.H., Daily Totals | | $1093.60 | | $1701.60 | $34.17 | $53.17 |

## Crew G-1

| Crew No. | Bare Costs Hr. | Bare Costs Daily | Incl. Subs O&P Hr. | Incl. Subs O&P Daily | Cost Per Labor-Hour Bare Costs | Cost Per Labor-Hour Incl. O&P |
|---|---|---|---|---|---|---|
| 1 Roofer Foreman | $35.00 | $280.00 | $59.55 | $476.40 | $30.89 | $52.55 |
| 4 Roofers, Composition | 33.00 | 1056.00 | 56.15 | 1796.80 | | |
| 2 Roofer Helpers | 24.60 | 393.60 | 41.85 | 669.60 | | |
| 1 Application Equipment | | 165.60 | | 182.16 | | |
| 1 Tar Kettle/Pot | | 86.10 | | 94.71 | | |
| 1 Crew Truck | | 160.40 | | 176.44 | 7.36 | 8.09 |
| 56 L.H., Daily Totals | | $2141.70 | | $3396.11 | $38.24 | $60.64 |

## Crew G-2

| Crew No. | Bare Costs Hr. | Bare Costs Daily | Incl. Subs O&P Hr. | Incl. Subs O&P Daily | Cost Per Labor-Hour Bare Costs | Cost Per Labor-Hour Incl. O&P |
|---|---|---|---|---|---|---|
| 1 Plasterer | $35.00 | $280.00 | $53.10 | $424.80 | $32.07 | $49.03 |
| 1 Plasterer Helper | 30.95 | 247.60 | 46.95 | 375.60 | | |
| 1 Building Laborer | 30.25 | 242.00 | 47.05 | 376.40 | | |
| 1 Grout Pump, 50 C.F./hr | | 126.40 | | 139.04 | 5.27 | 5.79 |
| 24 L.H., Daily Totals | | $896.00 | | $1315.84 | $37.33 | $54.83 |

## Crew G-2A

| Crew No. | Bare Costs Hr. | Bare Costs Daily | Incl. Subs O&P Hr. | Incl. Subs O&P Daily | Cost Per Labor-Hour Bare Costs | Cost Per Labor-Hour Incl. O&P |
|---|---|---|---|---|---|---|
| 1 Roofer, composition | $33.00 | $264.00 | $56.15 | $449.20 | $29.28 | $48.35 |
| 1 Roofer Helper | 24.60 | 196.80 | 41.85 | 334.80 | | |
| 1 Building Laborer | 30.25 | 242.00 | 47.05 | 376.40 | | |
| 1 Foam spray rig, trailer-mtd. | | 493.40 | | 542.74 | | |
| 1 Pickup Truck, 3/4 Ton | | 109.00 | | 119.90 | 25.10 | 27.61 |
| 24 L.H., Daily Totals | | $1305.20 | | $1823.04 | $54.38 | $75.96 |

## Crew G-3

| Crew No. | Bare Costs Hr. | Bare Costs Daily | Incl. Subs O&P Hr. | Incl. Subs O&P Daily | Cost Per Labor-Hour Bare Costs | Cost Per Labor-Hour Incl. O&P |
|---|---|---|---|---|---|---|
| 2 Sheet Metal Workers | $45.30 | $724.80 | $69.85 | $1117.60 | $37.77 | $58.45 |
| 2 Building Laborers | 30.25 | 484.00 | 47.05 | 752.80 | | |
| 32 L.H., Daily Totals | | $1208.80 | | $1870.40 | $37.77 | $58.45 |

## Crew G-4

| Crew No. | Bare Costs Hr. | Bare Costs Daily | Incl. Subs O&P Hr. | Incl. Subs O&P Daily | Cost Per Labor-Hour Bare Costs | Cost Per Labor-Hour Incl. O&P |
|---|---|---|---|---|---|---|
| 1 Labor Foreman (outside) | $32.25 | $258.00 | $50.20 | $401.60 | $30.92 | $48.10 |
| 2 Building Laborers | 30.25 | 484.00 | 47.05 | 752.80 | | |
| 1 Flatbed Truck, Gas, 1.5 Ton | | 179.20 | | 197.12 | | |
| 1 Air Compressor, 160 C.F.M. | | 137.60 | | 151.36 | 13.20 | 14.52 |
| 24 L.H., Daily Totals | | $1058.80 | | $1502.88 | $44.12 | $62.62 |

## Crew G-5

| Crew No. | Bare Costs Hr. | Bare Costs Daily | Incl. Subs O&P Hr. | Incl. Subs O&P Daily | Cost Per Labor-Hour Bare Costs | Cost Per Labor-Hour Incl. O&P |
|---|---|---|---|---|---|---|
| 1 Roofer Foreman | $35.00 | $280.00 | $59.55 | $476.40 | $30.04 | $51.11 |
| 2 Roofers, Composition | 33.00 | 528.00 | 56.15 | 898.40 | | |
| 2 Roofer Helpers | 24.60 | 393.60 | 41.85 | 669.60 | | |
| 1 Application Equipment | | 165.60 | | 182.16 | 4.14 | 4.55 |
| 40 L.H., Daily Totals | | $1367.20 | | $2226.56 | $34.18 | $55.66 |

## Crew G-6A

| Crew No. | Bare Costs Hr. | Bare Costs Daily | Incl. Subs O&P Hr. | Incl. Subs O&P Daily | Cost Per Labor-Hour Bare Costs | Cost Per Labor-Hour Incl. O&P |
|---|---|---|---|---|---|---|
| 2 Roofers Composition | $33.00 | $528.00 | $56.15 | $898.40 | $33.00 | $56.15 |
| 1 Small Compressor, Electric | | 10.70 | | 11.77 | | |
| 2 Pneumatic Nailer | | 43.20 | | 47.52 | 3.37 | 3.71 |
| 16 L.H., Daily Totals | | $581.90 | | $957.69 | $36.37 | $59.86 |

## Crew G-7

| Crew No. | Bare Costs Hr. | Bare Costs Daily | Incl. Subs O&P Hr. | Incl. Subs O&P Daily | Cost Per Labor-Hour Bare Costs | Cost Per Labor-Hour Incl. O&P |
|---|---|---|---|---|---|---|
| 1 Carpenter | $38.10 | $304.80 | $59.30 | $474.40 | $38.10 | $59.30 |
| 1 Small Compressor, Electric | | 10.70 | | 11.77 | | |
| 1 Pneumatic Nailer | | 21.60 | | 23.76 | 4.04 | 4.44 |
| 8 L.H., Daily Totals | | $337.10 | | $509.93 | $42.14 | $63.74 |

## Crew H-1

| Crew No. | Bare Costs Hr. | Bare Costs Daily | Incl. Subs O&P Hr. | Incl. Subs O&P Daily | Cost Per Labor-Hour Bare Costs | Cost Per Labor-Hour Incl. O&P |
|---|---|---|---|---|---|---|
| 2 Glaziers | $37.30 | $596.80 | $56.50 | $904.00 | $40.15 | $67.03 |
| 2 Struc. Steel Workers | 43.00 | 688.00 | 77.55 | 1240.80 | | |
| 32 L.H., Daily Totals | | $1284.80 | | $2144.80 | $40.15 | $67.03 |

# Crews

| Crew No. | Bare Costs Hr. | Daily | Incl. Subs O&P Hr. | Daily | Cost/LH Bare Costs | Incl. O&P |
|---|---|---|---|---|---|---|
| **Crew H-2** | | | | | | |
| 2 Glaziers | $37.30 | $596.80 | $56.50 | $904.00 | $34.95 | $53.35 |
| 1 Building Laborer | 30.25 | 242.00 | 47.05 | 376.40 | | |
| 24 L.H., Daily Totals | | $838.80 | | $1280.40 | $34.95 | $53.35 |
| **Crew H-3** | | | | | | |
| 1 Glazier | $37.30 | $298.40 | $56.50 | $452.00 | $33.20 | $50.85 |
| 1 Helper | 29.10 | 232.80 | 45.20 | 361.60 | | |
| 16 L.H., Daily Totals | | $531.20 | | $813.60 | $33.20 | $50.85 |
| **Crew J-1** | | | | | | |
| 3 Plasterers | $35.00 | $840.00 | $53.10 | $1274.40 | $33.38 | $50.64 |
| 2 Plasterer Helpers | 30.95 | 495.20 | 46.95 | 751.20 | | |
| 1 Mixing Machine, 6 C.F. | | 121.00 | | 133.10 | 3.02 | 3.33 |
| 40 L.H., Daily Totals | | $1456.20 | | $2158.70 | $36.41 | $53.97 |
| **Crew J-2** | | | | | | |
| 3 Plasterers | $35.00 | $840.00 | $53.10 | $1274.40 | $33.62 | $50.80 |
| 2 Plasterer Helpers | 30.95 | 495.20 | 46.95 | 751.20 | | |
| 1 Lather | 34.80 | 278.40 | 51.60 | 412.80 | | |
| 1 Mixing Machine, 6 C.F. | | 121.00 | | 133.10 | 2.52 | 2.77 |
| 48 L.H., Daily Totals | | $1734.60 | | $2571.50 | $36.14 | $53.57 |
| **Crew J-3** | | | | | | |
| 1 Terrazzo Worker | $36.80 | $294.40 | $54.00 | $432.00 | $33.48 | $49.13 |
| 1 Terrazzo Helper | 30.15 | 241.20 | 44.25 | 354.00 | | |
| 1 Terrazzo Grinder, Electric | | 81.45 | | 89.59 | | |
| 1 Terrazzo Mixer | | 166.20 | | 182.82 | 15.48 | 17.03 |
| 16 L.H., Daily Totals | | $783.25 | | $1058.42 | $48.95 | $66.15 |
| **Crew J-4** | | | | | | |
| 1 Tile Layer | $37.00 | $296.00 | $54.30 | $434.40 | $33.08 | $48.55 |
| 1 Tile Layer Helper | 29.15 | 233.20 | 42.80 | 342.40 | | |
| 16 L.H., Daily Totals | | $529.20 | | $776.80 | $33.08 | $48.55 |
| **Crew K-1** | | | | | | |
| 1 Carpenter | $38.10 | $304.80 | $59.30 | $474.40 | $33.75 | $52.40 |
| 1 Truck Driver (light) | 29.40 | 235.20 | 45.50 | 364.00 | | |
| 1 Flatbed Truck, Gas, 3 Ton | | 224.00 | | 246.40 | 14.00 | 15.40 |
| 16 L.H., Daily Totals | | $764.00 | | $1084.80 | $47.75 | $67.80 |
| **Crew K-2** | | | | | | |
| 1 Struc. Steel Foreman | $45.00 | $360.00 | $81.20 | $649.60 | $39.13 | $68.08 |
| 1 Struc. Steel Worker | 43.00 | 344.00 | 77.55 | 620.40 | | |
| 1 Truck Driver (light) | 29.40 | 235.20 | 45.50 | 364.00 | | |
| 1 Flatbed Truck, Gas, 3 Ton | | 224.00 | | 246.40 | 9.33 | 10.27 |
| 24 L.H., Daily Totals | | $1163.20 | | $1880.40 | $48.47 | $78.35 |
| **Crew L-1** | | | | | | |
| 1 Electrician | $45.55 | $364.40 | $67.85 | $542.80 | $46.13 | $69.05 |
| 1 Plumber | 46.70 | 373.60 | 70.25 | 562.00 | | |
| 16 L.H., Daily Totals | | $738.00 | | $1104.80 | $46.13 | $69.05 |
| **Crew L-2** | | | | | | |
| 1 Carpenter | $38.10 | $304.80 | $59.30 | $474.40 | $33.60 | $52.25 |
| 1 Carpenter Helper | 29.10 | 232.80 | 45.20 | 361.60 | | |
| 16 L.H., Daily Totals | | $537.60 | | $836.00 | $33.60 | $52.25 |

| Crew No. | Bare Costs Hr. | Daily | Incl. Subs O&P Hr. | Daily | Cost/LH Bare Costs | Incl. O&P |
|---|---|---|---|---|---|---|
| **Crew L-3** | | | | | | |
| 1 Carpenter | $38.10 | $304.80 | $59.30 | $474.40 | $41.76 | $64.08 |
| .5 Electrician | 45.55 | 182.20 | 67.85 | 271.40 | | |
| .5 Sheet Metal Worker | 45.30 | 181.20 | 69.85 | 279.40 | | |
| 16 L.H., Daily Totals | | $668.20 | | $1025.20 | $41.76 | $64.08 |
| **Crew L-3A** | | | | | | |
| 1 Carpenter Foreman (outside) | $40.10 | $320.80 | $62.40 | $499.20 | $41.83 | $64.88 |
| .5 Sheet Metal Worker | 45.30 | 181.20 | 69.85 | 279.40 | | |
| 12 L.H., Daily Totals | | $502.00 | | $778.60 | $41.83 | $64.88 |
| **Crew L-4** | | | | | | |
| 2 Skilled Workers | $39.40 | $630.40 | $61.25 | $980.00 | $35.97 | $55.90 |
| 1 Helper | 29.10 | 232.80 | 45.20 | 361.60 | | |
| 24 L.H., Daily Totals | | $863.20 | | $1341.60 | $35.97 | $55.90 |
| **Crew L-5** | | | | | | |
| 1 Struc. Steel Foreman | $45.00 | $360.00 | $81.20 | $649.60 | $42.99 | $75.81 |
| 5 Struc. Steel Workers | 43.00 | 1720.00 | 77.55 | 3102.00 | | |
| 1 Equip. Oper. (crane) | 40.95 | 327.60 | 61.75 | 494.00 | | |
| 1 Hyd. Crane, 25 Ton | | 786.00 | | 864.60 | 14.04 | 15.44 |
| 56 L.H., Daily Totals | | $3193.60 | | $5110.20 | $57.03 | $91.25 |
| **Crew L-5A** | | | | | | |
| 1 Structural Steel Foreman | $45.00 | $360.00 | $81.20 | $649.60 | $42.99 | $74.51 |
| 2 Structural Steel Workers | 43.00 | 688.00 | 77.55 | 1240.80 | | |
| 1 Equip. Oper. (crane) | 40.95 | 327.60 | 61.75 | 494.00 | | |
| 1 S.P. Crane, 4x4, 25 Ton | | 701.80 | | 771.98 | 21.93 | 24.12 |
| 32 L.H., Daily Totals | | $2077.40 | | $3156.38 | $64.92 | $98.64 |
| **Crew L-5B** | | | | | | |
| 1 Structural Steel Foreman | $45.00 | $360.00 | $81.20 | $649.60 | $43.59 | $69.82 |
| 2 Structural Steel Workers | 43.00 | 688.00 | 77.55 | 1240.80 | | |
| 2 Electricians | 45.55 | 728.80 | 67.85 | 1085.60 | | |
| 2 Steamfitters/Pipefitters | 47.10 | 753.60 | 70.85 | 1133.60 | | |
| 1 Equip. Oper. (crane) | 40.95 | 327.60 | 61.75 | 494.00 | | |
| 1 Equip. Oper. Oiler | 35.10 | 280.80 | 52.95 | 423.60 | | |
| 1 Hyd. Crane, 80 Ton | | 1290.00 | | 1419.00 | 17.92 | 19.71 |
| 72 L.H., Daily Totals | | $4428.80 | | $6446.20 | $61.51 | $89.53 |
| **Crew L-6** | | | | | | |
| 1 Plumber | $46.70 | $373.60 | $70.25 | $562.00 | $46.32 | $69.45 |
| .5 Electrician | 45.55 | 182.20 | 67.85 | 271.40 | | |
| 12 L.H., Daily Totals | | $555.80 | | $833.40 | $46.32 | $69.45 |
| **Crew L-7** | | | | | | |
| 2 Carpenters | $38.10 | $609.60 | $59.30 | $948.80 | $36.92 | $57.02 |
| 1 Building Laborer | 30.25 | 242.00 | 47.05 | 376.40 | | |
| .5 Electrician | 45.55 | 182.20 | 67.85 | 271.40 | | |
| 28 L.H., Daily Totals | | $1033.80 | | $1596.60 | $36.92 | $57.02 |
| **Crew L-8** | | | | | | |
| 2 Carpenters | $38.10 | $609.60 | $59.30 | $948.80 | $39.82 | $61.49 |
| .5 Plumber | 46.70 | 186.80 | 70.25 | 281.00 | | |
| 20 L.H., Daily Totals | | $796.40 | | $1229.80 | $39.82 | $61.49 |

# Crews

| Crew No. | Bare Costs | | Incl. Subs O & P | | Cost Per Labor-Hour | |
|---|---|---|---|---|---|---|

### Crew L-9

| | Hr. | Daily | Hr. | Daily | Bare Costs | Incl. O&P |
|---|---|---|---|---|---|---|
| 1 Labor Foreman (inside) | $30.75 | $246.00 | $47.85 | $382.80 | $34.89 | $56.32 |
| 2 Building Laborers | 30.25 | 484.00 | 47.05 | 752.80 | | |
| 1 Struc. Steel Worker | 43.00 | 344.00 | 77.55 | 620.40 | | |
| .5 Electrician | 45.55 | 182.20 | 67.85 | 271.40 | | |
| 36 L.H., Daily Totals | | $1256.20 | | $2027.40 | $34.89 | $56.32 |

### Crew L-10

| | Hr. | Daily | Hr. | Daily | Bare Costs | Incl. O&P |
|---|---|---|---|---|---|---|
| 1 Structural Steel Foreman | $45.00 | $360.00 | $81.20 | $649.60 | $42.98 | $73.50 |
| 1 Structural Steel Worker | 43.00 | 344.00 | 77.55 | 620.40 | | |
| 1 Equip. Oper. (crane) | 40.95 | 327.60 | 61.75 | 494.00 | | |
| 1 Hyd. Crane, 12 Ton | | 766.40 | | 843.04 | 31.93 | 35.13 |
| 24 L.H., Daily Totals | | $1798.00 | | $2607.04 | $74.92 | $108.63 |

### Crew L-11

| | Hr. | Daily | Hr. | Daily | Bare Costs | Incl. O&P |
|---|---|---|---|---|---|---|
| 2 Wreckers | $30.25 | $484.00 | $52.50 | $840.00 | $34.80 | $55.92 |
| 1 Equip. Oper. (crane) | 40.95 | 327.60 | 61.75 | 494.00 | | |
| 1 Equip. Oper. (light) | 37.75 | 302.00 | 56.95 | 455.60 | | |
| 1 Hyd. Excavator, 2.5 C.Y. | | 1466.00 | | 1612.60 | | |
| 1 Loader, Skid Steer, 78 HP | | 246.40 | | 271.04 | 53.51 | 58.86 |
| 32 L.H., Daily Totals | | $2826.00 | | $3673.24 | $88.31 | $114.79 |

### Crew M-1

| | Hr. | Daily | Hr. | Daily | Bare Costs | Incl. O&P |
|---|---|---|---|---|---|---|
| 3 Elevator Constructors | $55.10 | $1322.40 | $82.05 | $1969.20 | $52.35 | $77.95 |
| 1 Elevator Apprentice | 44.10 | 352.80 | 65.65 | 525.20 | | |
| 5 Hand Tools | | 50.00 | | 55.00 | 1.56 | 1.72 |
| 32 L.H., Daily Totals | | $1725.20 | | $2549.40 | $53.91 | $79.67 |

### Crew M-3

| | Hr. | Daily | Hr. | Daily | Bare Costs | Incl. O&P |
|---|---|---|---|---|---|---|
| 1 Electrician Foreman (out) | $47.55 | $380.40 | $70.85 | $566.80 | $43.99 | $66.03 |
| 1 Common Laborer | 30.25 | 242.00 | 47.05 | 376.40 | | |
| .25 Equipment Operator, Medium | 39.85 | 79.70 | 60.10 | 120.20 | | |
| 1 Elevator Constructor | 55.10 | 440.80 | 82.05 | 656.40 | | |
| 1 Elevator Apprentice | 44.10 | 352.80 | 65.65 | 525.20 | | |
| .25 S.P. Crane, 4x4, 20 Ton | | 171.25 | | 188.38 | 5.04 | 5.54 |
| 34 L.H., Daily Totals | | $1666.95 | | $2433.38 | $49.03 | $71.57 |

### Crew M-4

| | Hr. | Daily | Hr. | Daily | Bare Costs | Incl. O&P |
|---|---|---|---|---|---|---|
| 1 Electrician Foreman (out) | $47.55 | $380.40 | $70.85 | $566.80 | $43.56 | $65.39 |
| 1 Common Laborer | 30.25 | 242.00 | 47.05 | 376.40 | | |
| .25 Equipment Operator, Crane | 40.95 | 81.90 | 61.75 | 123.50 | | |
| .25 Equipment Operator, Oiler | 35.10 | 70.20 | 52.95 | 105.90 | | |
| 1 Elevator Constructor | 55.10 | 440.80 | 82.05 | 656.40 | | |
| 1 Elevator Apprentice | 44.10 | 352.80 | 65.65 | 525.20 | | |
| .25 S.P. Crane, 4x4, 40 Ton | | 229.10 | | 252.01 | 6.36 | 7.00 |
| 36 L.H., Daily Totals | | $1797.20 | | $2606.21 | $49.92 | $72.39 |

### Crew Q-1

| | Hr. | Daily | Hr. | Daily | Bare Costs | Incl. O&P |
|---|---|---|---|---|---|---|
| 1 Plumber | $46.70 | $373.60 | $70.25 | $562.00 | $42.02 | $63.20 |
| 1 Plumber Apprentice | 37.35 | 298.80 | 56.15 | 449.20 | | |
| 16 L.H., Daily Totals | | $672.40 | | $1011.20 | $42.02 | $63.20 |

### Crew Q-1A

| | Hr. | Daily | Hr. | Daily | Bare Costs | Incl. O&P |
|---|---|---|---|---|---|---|
| .25 Plumber | $48.70 | $97.40 | $73.25 | $146.50 | $47.10 | $70.85 |
| 1 Plumber | 46.70 | 373.60 | 70.25 | 562.00 | | |
| 10 L.H., Daily Totals | | $471.00 | | $708.50 | $47.10 | $70.85 |

### Crew Q-1C

| | Hr. | Daily | Hr. | Daily | Bare Costs | Incl. O&P |
|---|---|---|---|---|---|---|
| 1 Plumber | $46.70 | $373.60 | $70.25 | $562.00 | $41.30 | $62.17 |
| 1 Plumber Apprentice | 37.35 | 298.80 | 56.15 | 449.20 | | |
| 1 Equip. Oper. (medium) | 39.85 | 318.80 | 60.10 | 480.80 | | |
| 1 Trencher, Chain Type, 8' D | | 1736.00 | | 1909.60 | 72.33 | 79.57 |
| 24 L.H., Daily Totals | | $2727.20 | | $3401.60 | $113.63 | $141.73 |

### Crew Q-2

| | Hr. | Daily | Hr. | Daily | Bare Costs | Incl. O&P |
|---|---|---|---|---|---|---|
| 2 Plumbers | $46.70 | $747.20 | $70.25 | $1124.00 | $43.58 | $65.55 |
| 1 Plumber Apprentice | 37.35 | 298.80 | 56.15 | 449.20 | | |
| 24 L.H., Daily Totals | | $1046.00 | | $1573.20 | $43.58 | $65.55 |

### Crew Q-3

| | Hr. | Daily | Hr. | Daily | Bare Costs | Incl. O&P |
|---|---|---|---|---|---|---|
| 1 Plumber Foreman (inside) | $47.20 | $377.60 | $71.00 | $568.00 | $44.49 | $66.91 |
| 2 Plumbers | 46.70 | 747.20 | 70.25 | 1124.00 | | |
| 1 Plumber Apprentice | 37.35 | 298.80 | 56.15 | 449.20 | | |
| 32 L.H., Daily Totals | | $1423.60 | | $2141.20 | $44.49 | $66.91 |

### Crew Q-4

| | Hr. | Daily | Hr. | Daily | Bare Costs | Incl. O&P |
|---|---|---|---|---|---|---|
| 1 Plumber Foreman (inside) | $47.20 | $377.60 | $71.00 | $568.00 | $44.49 | $66.91 |
| 1 Plumber | 46.70 | 373.60 | 70.25 | 562.00 | | |
| 1 Welder (plumber) | 46.70 | 373.60 | 70.25 | 562.00 | | |
| 1 Plumber Apprentice | 37.35 | 298.80 | 56.15 | 449.20 | | |
| 1 Welder, electric, 300 amp | | 56.20 | | 61.82 | 1.76 | 1.93 |
| 32 L.H., Daily Totals | | $1479.80 | | $2203.02 | $46.24 | $68.84 |

### Crew Q-5

| | Hr. | Daily | Hr. | Daily | Bare Costs | Incl. O&P |
|---|---|---|---|---|---|---|
| 1 Steamfitter | $47.10 | $376.80 | $70.85 | $566.80 | $42.40 | $63.77 |
| 1 Steamfitter Apprentice | 37.70 | 301.60 | 56.70 | 453.60 | | |
| 16 L.H., Daily Totals | | $678.40 | | $1020.40 | $42.40 | $63.77 |

### Crew Q-6

| | Hr. | Daily | Hr. | Daily | Bare Costs | Incl. O&P |
|---|---|---|---|---|---|---|
| 2 Steamfitters | $47.10 | $753.60 | $70.85 | $1133.60 | $43.97 | $66.13 |
| 1 Steamfitter Apprentice | 37.70 | 301.60 | 56.70 | 453.60 | | |
| 24 L.H., Daily Totals | | $1055.20 | | $1587.20 | $43.97 | $66.13 |

### Crew Q-7

| | Hr. | Daily | Hr. | Daily | Bare Costs | Incl. O&P |
|---|---|---|---|---|---|---|
| 1 Steamfitter Foreman (inside) | $47.60 | $380.80 | $71.60 | $572.80 | $44.88 | $67.50 |
| 2 Steamfitters | 47.10 | 753.60 | 70.85 | 1133.60 | | |
| 1 Steamfitter Apprentice | 37.70 | 301.60 | 56.70 | 453.60 | | |
| 32 L.H., Daily Totals | | $1436.00 | | $2160.00 | $44.88 | $67.50 |

### Crew Q-8

| | Hr. | Daily | Hr. | Daily | Bare Costs | Incl. O&P |
|---|---|---|---|---|---|---|
| 1 Steamfitter Foreman (inside) | $47.60 | $380.80 | $71.60 | $572.80 | $44.88 | $67.50 |
| 1 Steamfitter | 47.10 | 376.80 | 70.85 | 566.80 | | |
| 1 Welder (steamfitter) | 47.10 | 376.80 | 70.85 | 566.80 | | |
| 1 Steamfitter Apprentice | 37.70 | 301.60 | 56.70 | 453.60 | | |
| 1 Welder, electric, 300 amp | | 56.20 | | 61.82 | 1.76 | 1.93 |
| 32 L.H., Daily Totals | | $1492.20 | | $2221.82 | $46.63 | $69.43 |

### Crew Q-9

| | Hr. | Daily | Hr. | Daily | Bare Costs | Incl. O&P |
|---|---|---|---|---|---|---|
| 1 Sheet Metal Worker | $45.30 | $362.40 | $69.85 | $558.80 | $40.77 | $62.88 |
| 1 Sheet Metal Apprentice | 36.25 | 290.00 | 55.90 | 447.20 | | |
| 16 L.H., Daily Totals | | $652.40 | | $1006.00 | $40.77 | $62.88 |

### Crew Q-10

| | Hr. | Daily | Hr. | Daily | Bare Costs | Incl. O&P |
|---|---|---|---|---|---|---|
| 2 Sheet Metal Workers | $45.30 | $724.80 | $69.85 | $1117.60 | $42.28 | $65.20 |
| 1 Sheet Metal Apprentice | 36.25 | 290.00 | 55.90 | 447.20 | | |
| 24 L.H., Daily Totals | | $1014.80 | | $1564.80 | $42.28 | $65.20 |

| Crew No. | Bare Costs | | | Incl. Subs O & P | Cost Per Labor-Hour | |
|---|---|---|---|---|---|---|
| **Crew Q-11** | Hr. | Daily | Hr. | Daily | Bare Costs | Incl. O&P |
| 1 Sheet Metal Foreman (inside) | $45.80 | $366.40 | $70.60 | $564.80 | $43.16 | $66.55 |
| 2 Sheet Metal Workers | 45.30 | 724.80 | 69.85 | 1117.60 | | |
| 1 Sheet Metal Apprentice | 36.25 | 290.00 | 55.90 | 447.20 | | |
| 32 L.H., Daily Totals | | $1381.20 | | $2129.60 | $43.16 | $66.55 |
| **Crew Q-12** | Hr. | Daily | Hr. | Daily | Bare Costs | Incl. O&P |
| 1 Sprinkler Installer | $46.65 | $373.20 | $70.25 | $562.00 | $41.98 | $63.20 |
| 1 Sprinkler Apprentice | 37.30 | 298.40 | 56.15 | 449.20 | | |
| 16 L.H., Daily Totals | | $671.60 | | $1011.20 | $41.98 | $63.20 |
| **Crew Q-13** | Hr. | Daily | Hr. | Daily | Bare Costs | Incl. O&P |
| 1 Sprinkler Foreman (inside) | $47.15 | $377.20 | $71.00 | $568.00 | $44.44 | $66.91 |
| 2 Sprinkler Installers | 46.65 | 746.40 | 70.25 | 1124.00 | | |
| 1 Sprinkler Apprentice | 37.30 | 298.40 | 56.15 | 449.20 | | |
| 32 L.H., Daily Totals | | $1422.00 | | $2141.20 | $44.44 | $66.91 |
| **Crew Q-14** | Hr. | Daily | Hr. | Daily | Bare Costs | Incl. O&P |
| 1 Asbestos Worker | $43.10 | $344.80 | $67.85 | $542.80 | $38.80 | $61.08 |
| 1 Asbestos Apprentice | 34.50 | 276.00 | 54.30 | 434.40 | | |
| 16 L.H., Daily Totals | | $620.80 | | $977.20 | $38.80 | $61.08 |
| **Crew Q-15** | Hr. | Daily | Hr. | Daily | Bare Costs | Incl. O&P |
| 1 Plumber | $46.70 | $373.60 | $70.25 | $562.00 | $42.02 | $63.20 |
| 1 Plumber Apprentice | 37.35 | 298.80 | 56.15 | 449.20 | | |
| 1 Welder, electric, 300 amp | | 56.20 | | 61.82 | 3.51 | 3.86 |
| 16 L.H., Daily Totals | | $728.60 | | $1073.02 | $45.54 | $67.06 |
| **Crew Q-16** | Hr. | Daily | Hr. | Daily | Bare Costs | Incl. O&P |
| 2 Plumbers | $46.70 | $747.20 | $70.25 | $1124.00 | $43.58 | $65.55 |
| 1 Plumber Apprentice | 37.35 | 298.80 | 56.15 | 449.20 | | |
| 1 Welder, electric, 300 amp | | 56.20 | | 61.82 | 2.34 | 2.58 |
| 24 L.H., Daily Totals | | $1102.20 | | $1635.02 | $45.92 | $68.13 |
| **Crew Q-17** | Hr. | Daily | Hr. | Daily | Bare Costs | Incl. O&P |
| 1 Steamfitter | $47.10 | $376.80 | $70.85 | $566.80 | $42.40 | $63.77 |
| 1 Steamfitter Apprentice | 37.70 | 301.60 | 56.70 | 453.60 | | |
| 1 Welder, electric, 300 amp | | 56.20 | | 61.82 | 3.51 | 3.86 |
| 16 L.H., Daily Totals | | $734.60 | | $1082.22 | $45.91 | $67.64 |
| **Crew Q-17A** | Hr. | Daily | Hr. | Daily | Bare Costs | Incl. O&P |
| 1 Steamfitter | $47.10 | $376.80 | $70.85 | $566.80 | $41.92 | $63.10 |
| 1 Steamfitter Apprentice | 37.70 | 301.60 | 56.70 | 453.60 | | |
| 1 Equip. Oper. (crane) | 40.95 | 327.60 | 61.75 | 494.00 | | |
| 1 Hyd. Crane, 12 Ton | | 766.40 | | 843.04 | | |
| 1 Welder, electric, 300 amp | | 56.20 | | 61.82 | 34.27 | 37.70 |
| 24 L.H., Daily Totals | | $1828.60 | | $2419.26 | $76.19 | $100.80 |
| **Crew Q-18** | Hr. | Daily | Hr. | Daily | Bare Costs | Incl. O&P |
| 2 Steamfitters | $47.10 | $753.60 | $70.85 | $1133.60 | $43.97 | $66.13 |
| 1 Steamfitter Apprentice | 37.70 | 301.60 | 56.70 | 453.60 | | |
| 1 Welder, electric, 300 amp | | 56.20 | | 61.82 | 2.34 | 2.58 |
| 24 L.H., Daily Totals | | $1111.40 | | $1649.02 | $46.31 | $68.71 |
| **Crew Q-19** | Hr. | Daily | Hr. | Daily | Bare Costs | Incl. O&P |
| 1 Steamfitter | $47.10 | $376.80 | $70.85 | $566.80 | $43.45 | $65.13 |
| 1 Steamfitter Apprentice | 37.70 | 301.60 | 56.70 | 453.60 | | |
| 1 Electrician | 45.55 | 364.40 | 67.85 | 542.80 | | |
| 24 L.H., Daily Totals | | $1042.80 | | $1563.20 | $43.45 | $65.13 |

| Crew No. | Bare Costs | | | Incl. Subs O & P | Cost Per Labor-Hour | |
|---|---|---|---|---|---|---|
| **Crew Q-20** | Hr. | Daily | Hr. | Daily | Bare Costs | Incl. O&P |
| 1 Sheet Metal Worker | $45.30 | $362.40 | $69.85 | $558.80 | $41.73 | $63.87 |
| 1 Sheet Metal Apprentice | 36.25 | 290.00 | 55.90 | 447.20 | | |
| .5 Electrician | 45.55 | 182.20 | 67.85 | 271.40 | | |
| 20 L.H., Daily Totals | | $834.60 | | $1277.40 | $41.73 | $63.87 |
| **Crew Q-21** | Hr. | Daily | Hr. | Daily | Bare Costs | Incl. O&P |
| 2 Steamfitters | $47.10 | $753.60 | $70.85 | $1133.60 | $44.36 | $66.56 |
| 1 Steamfitter Apprentice | 37.70 | 301.60 | 56.70 | 453.60 | | |
| 1 Electrician | 45.55 | 364.40 | 67.85 | 542.80 | | |
| 32 L.H., Daily Totals | | $1419.60 | | $2130.00 | $44.36 | $66.56 |
| **Crew Q-22** | Hr. | Daily | Hr. | Daily | Bare Costs | Incl. O&P |
| 1 Plumber | $46.70 | $373.60 | $70.25 | $562.00 | $42.02 | $63.20 |
| 1 Plumber Apprentice | 37.35 | 298.80 | 56.15 | 449.20 | | |
| 1 Hyd. Crane, 12 Ton | | 766.40 | | 843.04 | 47.90 | 52.69 |
| 16 L.H., Daily Totals | | $1438.80 | | $1854.24 | $89.92 | $115.89 |
| **Crew Q-22A** | Hr. | Daily | Hr. | Daily | Bare Costs | Incl. O&P |
| 1 Plumber | $46.70 | $373.60 | $70.25 | $562.00 | $38.81 | $58.80 |
| 1 Plumber Apprentice | 37.35 | 298.80 | 56.15 | 449.20 | | |
| 1 Laborer | 30.25 | 242.00 | 47.05 | 376.40 | | |
| 1 Equip. Oper. (crane) | 40.95 | 327.60 | 61.75 | 494.00 | | |
| 1 Hyd. Crane, 12 Ton | | 766.40 | | 843.04 | 23.95 | 26.34 |
| 32 L.H., Daily Totals | | $2008.40 | | $2724.64 | $62.76 | $85.14 |
| **Crew Q-23** | Hr. | Daily | Hr. | Daily | Bare Costs | Incl. O&P |
| 1 Plumber Foreman | $48.70 | $389.60 | $73.25 | $586.00 | $45.08 | $67.87 |
| 1 Plumber | 46.70 | 373.60 | 70.25 | 562.00 | | |
| 1 Equip. Oper. (medium) | 39.85 | 318.80 | 60.10 | 480.80 | | |
| 1 Lattice Boom Crane, 20 Ton | | 1005.00 | | 1105.50 | 41.88 | 46.06 |
| 24 L.H., Daily Totals | | $2087.00 | | $2734.30 | $86.96 | $113.93 |
| **Crew R-1** | Hr. | Daily | Hr. | Daily | Bare Costs | Incl. O&P |
| 1 Electrician Foreman | $46.05 | $368.40 | $68.60 | $548.80 | $40.15 | $60.42 |
| 3 Electricians | 45.55 | 1093.20 | 67.85 | 1628.40 | | |
| 2 Helpers | 29.10 | 465.60 | 45.20 | 723.20 | | |
| 48 L.H., Daily Totals | | $1927.20 | | $2900.40 | $40.15 | $60.42 |
| **Crew R-1A** | Hr. | Daily | Hr. | Daily | Bare Costs | Incl. O&P |
| 1 Electrician | $45.55 | $364.40 | $67.85 | $542.80 | $37.33 | $56.52 |
| 1 Helper | 29.10 | 232.80 | 45.20 | 361.60 | | |
| 16 L.H., Daily Totals | | $597.20 | | $904.40 | $37.33 | $56.52 |
| **Crew R-2** | Hr. | Daily | Hr. | Daily | Bare Costs | Incl. O&P |
| 1 Electrician Foreman | $46.05 | $368.40 | $68.60 | $548.80 | $40.26 | $60.61 |
| 3 Electricians | 45.55 | 1093.20 | 67.85 | 1628.40 | | |
| 2 Helpers | 29.10 | 465.60 | 45.20 | 723.20 | | |
| 1 Equip. Oper. (crane) | 40.95 | 327.60 | 61.75 | 494.00 | | |
| 1 S.P. Crane, 4x4, 5 Ton | | 258.80 | | 284.68 | 4.62 | 5.08 |
| 56 L.H., Daily Totals | | $2513.60 | | $3679.08 | $44.89 | $65.70 |
| **Crew R-3** | Hr. | Daily | Hr. | Daily | Bare Costs | Incl. O&P |
| 1 Electrician Foreman | $46.05 | $368.40 | $68.60 | $548.80 | $44.83 | $66.93 |
| 1 Electrician | 45.55 | 364.40 | 67.85 | 542.80 | | |
| .5 Equip. Oper. (crane) | 40.95 | 163.80 | 61.75 | 247.00 | | |
| .5 S.P. Crane, 4x4, 5 Ton | | 129.40 | | 142.34 | 6.47 | 7.12 |
| 20 L.H., Daily Totals | | $1026.00 | | $1480.94 | $51.30 | $74.05 |

| Crew No. | Bare Costs | | Incl. Subs O & P | | Cost Per Labor-Hour | |
|---|---|---|---|---|---|---|

| **Crew R-4** | Hr. | Daily | Hr. | Daily | Bare Costs | Incl. O&P |
|---|---|---|---|---|---|---|
| 1 Struc. Steel Foreman | $45.00 | $360.00 | $81.20 | $649.60 | $43.91 | $76.34 |
| 3 Struc. Steel Workers | 43.00 | 1032.00 | 77.55 | 1861.20 | | |
| 1 Electrician | 45.55 | 364.40 | 67.85 | 542.80 | | |
| 1 Welder, gas engine, 300 amp | | 132.20 | | 145.42 | 3.31 | 3.64 |
| 40 L.H., Daily Totals | | $1888.60 | | $3199.02 | $47.22 | $79.98 |

| **Crew R-5** | Hr. | Daily | Hr. | Daily | Bare Costs | Incl. O&P |
|---|---|---|---|---|---|---|
| 1 Electrician Foreman | $46.05 | $368.40 | $68.60 | $548.80 | $39.61 | $59.68 |
| 4 Electrician Linemen | 45.55 | 1457.60 | 67.85 | 2171.20 | | |
| 2 Electrician Operators | 45.55 | 728.80 | 67.85 | 1085.60 | | |
| 4 Electrician Groundmen | 29.10 | 931.20 | 45.20 | 1446.40 | | |
| 1 Crew Truck | | 160.40 | | 176.44 | | |
| 1 Flatbed Truck, 20,000 GVW | | 186.00 | | 204.60 | | |
| 1 Pickup Truck, 3/4 Ton | | 109.00 | | 119.90 | | |
| .2 Hyd. Crane, 55 Ton | | 223.80 | | 246.18 | | |
| .2 Hyd. Crane, 12 Ton | | 153.28 | | 168.61 | | |
| .2 Earth Auger, Truck-Mtd. | | 80.56 | | 88.62 | | |
| 1 Tractor w/Winch | | 336.40 | | 370.04 | 14.20 | 15.62 |
| 88 L.H., Daily Totals | | $4735.44 | | $6626.38 | $53.81 | $75.30 |

| **Crew R-6** | Hr. | Daily | Hr. | Daily | Bare Costs | Incl. O&P |
|---|---|---|---|---|---|---|
| 1 Electrician Foreman | $46.05 | $368.40 | $68.60 | $548.80 | $39.61 | $59.68 |
| 4 Electrician Linemen | 45.55 | 1457.60 | 67.85 | 2171.20 | | |
| 2 Electrician Operators | 45.55 | 728.80 | 67.85 | 1085.60 | | |
| 4 Electrician Groundmen | 29.10 | 931.20 | 45.20 | 1446.40 | | |
| 1 Crew Truck | | 160.40 | | 176.44 | | |
| 1 Flatbed Truck, 20,000 GVW | | 186.00 | | 204.60 | | |
| 1 Pickup Truck, 3/4 Ton | | 109.00 | | 119.90 | | |
| .2 Hyd. Crane, 55 Ton | | 223.80 | | 246.18 | | |
| .2 Hyd. Crane, 12 Ton | | 153.28 | | 168.61 | | |
| .2 Earth Auger, Truck-Mtd. | | 80.56 | | 88.62 | | |
| 1 Tractor w/Winch | | 336.40 | | 370.04 | | |
| 3 Cable Trailers | | 520.80 | | 572.88 | | |
| .5 Tensioning Rig | | 171.53 | | 188.68 | | |
| .5 Cable Pulling Rig | | 1011.00 | | 1112.10 | 33.55 | 36.91 |
| 88 L.H., Daily Totals | | $6438.77 | | $8500.04 | $73.17 | $96.59 |

| **Crew R-7** | Hr. | Daily | Hr. | Daily | Bare Costs | Incl. O&P |
|---|---|---|---|---|---|---|
| 1 Electrician Foreman | $46.05 | $368.40 | $68.60 | $548.80 | $31.93 | $49.10 |
| 5 Electrician Groundmen | 29.10 | 1164.00 | 45.20 | 1808.00 | | |
| 1 Crew Truck | | 160.40 | | 176.44 | 3.34 | 3.68 |
| 48 L.H., Daily Totals | | $1692.80 | | $2533.24 | $35.27 | $52.78 |

| **Crew R-8** | Hr. | Daily | Hr. | Daily | Bare Costs | Incl. O&P |
|---|---|---|---|---|---|---|
| 1 Electrician Foreman | $46.05 | $368.40 | $68.60 | $548.80 | $40.15 | $60.42 |
| 3 Electrician Linemen | 45.55 | 1093.20 | 67.85 | 1628.40 | | |
| 2 Electrician Groundmen | 29.10 | 465.60 | 45.20 | 723.20 | | |
| 1 Pickup Truck, 3/4 Ton | | 109.00 | | 119.90 | | |
| 1 Crew Truck | | 160.40 | | 176.44 | 5.61 | 6.17 |
| 48 L.H., Daily Totals | | $2196.60 | | $3196.74 | $45.76 | $66.60 |

| **Crew R-9** | Hr. | Daily | Hr. | Daily | Bare Costs | Incl. O&P |
|---|---|---|---|---|---|---|
| 1 Electrician Foreman | $46.05 | $368.40 | $68.60 | $548.80 | $37.39 | $56.62 |
| 1 Electrician Lineman | 45.55 | 364.40 | 67.85 | 542.80 | | |
| 2 Electrician Operators | 45.55 | 728.80 | 67.85 | 1085.60 | | |
| 4 Electrician Groundmen | 29.10 | 931.20 | 45.20 | 1446.40 | | |
| 1 Pickup Truck, 3/4 Ton | | 109.00 | | 119.90 | | |
| 1 Crew Truck | | 160.40 | | 176.44 | 4.21 | 4.63 |
| 64 L.H., Daily Totals | | $2662.20 | | $3919.94 | $41.60 | $61.25 |

| **Crew R-10** | Hr. | Daily | Hr. | Daily | Bare Costs | Incl. O&P |
|---|---|---|---|---|---|---|
| 1 Electrician Foreman | $46.05 | $368.40 | $68.60 | $548.80 | $42.89 | $64.20 |
| 4 Electrician Linemen | 45.55 | 1457.60 | 67.85 | 2171.20 | | |
| 1 Electrician Groundman | 29.10 | 232.80 | 45.20 | 361.60 | | |
| 1 Crew Truck | | 160.40 | | 176.44 | | |
| 3 Tram Cars | | 368.40 | | 405.24 | 11.02 | 12.12 |
| 48 L.H., Daily Totals | | $2587.60 | | $3663.28 | $53.91 | $76.32 |

| **Crew R-11** | Hr. | Daily | Hr. | Daily | Bare Costs | Incl. O&P |
|---|---|---|---|---|---|---|
| 1 Electrician Foreman | $46.05 | $368.40 | $68.60 | $548.80 | $42.78 | $64.11 |
| 4 Electricians | 45.55 | 1457.60 | 67.85 | 2171.20 | | |
| 1 Equip. Oper. (crane) | 40.95 | 327.60 | 61.75 | 494.00 | | |
| 1 Common Laborer | 30.25 | 242.00 | 47.05 | 376.40 | | |
| 1 Crew Truck | | 160.40 | | 176.44 | | |
| 1 Hyd. Crane, 12 Ton | | 766.40 | | 843.04 | 16.55 | 18.20 |
| 56 L.H., Daily Totals | | $3322.40 | | $4609.88 | $59.33 | $82.32 |

| **Crew R-12** | Hr. | Daily | Hr. | Daily | Bare Costs | Incl. O&P |
|---|---|---|---|---|---|---|
| 1 Carpenter Foreman | $38.60 | $308.80 | $60.05 | $480.40 | $35.90 | $56.65 |
| 4 Carpenters | 38.10 | 1219.20 | 59.30 | 1897.60 | | |
| 4 Common Laborers | 30.25 | 968.00 | 47.05 | 1505.60 | | |
| 1 Equip. Oper. (med.) | 39.85 | 318.80 | 60.10 | 480.80 | | |
| 1 Steel Worker | 43.00 | 344.00 | 77.55 | 620.40 | | |
| 1 Dozer, 200 H.P. | | 1071.00 | | 1178.10 | | |
| 1 Pickup Truck, 3/4 Ton | | 109.00 | | 119.90 | 13.41 | 14.75 |
| 88 L.H., Daily Totals | | $4338.80 | | $6282.80 | $49.30 | $71.40 |

| **Crew R-13** | Hr. | Daily | Hr. | Daily | Bare Costs | Incl. O&P |
|---|---|---|---|---|---|---|
| 1 Electrician Foreman | $46.05 | $368.40 | $68.60 | $548.80 | $43.44 | $64.86 |
| 3 Electricians | 45.55 | 1093.20 | 67.85 | 1628.40 | | |
| .25 Equip. Oper. (crane) | 40.95 | 81.90 | 61.75 | 123.50 | | |
| 1 Equipment Oiler | 35.10 | 280.80 | 52.95 | 423.60 | | |
| .25 Hydraulic Crane, 33 Ton | | 203.85 | | 224.24 | 4.85 | 5.34 |
| 42 L.H., Daily Totals | | $2028.15 | | $2948.53 | $48.29 | $70.20 |

| **Crew R-15** | Hr. | Daily | Hr. | Daily | Bare Costs | Incl. O&P |
|---|---|---|---|---|---|---|
| 1 Electrician Foreman | $46.05 | $368.40 | $68.60 | $548.80 | $44.33 | $66.16 |
| 4 Electricians | 45.55 | 1457.60 | 67.85 | 2171.20 | | |
| 1 Equipment Operator | 37.75 | 302.00 | 56.95 | 455.60 | | |
| 1 Aerial Lift Truck | | 319.00 | | 350.90 | 6.65 | 7.31 |
| 48 L.H., Daily Totals | | $2447.00 | | $3526.50 | $50.98 | $73.47 |

| **Crew R-18** | Hr. | Daily | Hr. | Daily | Bare Costs | Incl. O&P |
|---|---|---|---|---|---|---|
| .25 Electrician Foreman | $46.05 | $92.10 | $68.60 | $137.20 | $35.47 | $53.97 |
| 1 Electrician | 45.55 | 364.40 | 67.85 | 542.80 | | |
| 2 Helpers | 29.10 | 465.60 | 45.20 | 723.20 | | |
| 26 L.H., Daily Totals | | $922.10 | | $1403.20 | $35.47 | $53.97 |

| **Crew R-19** | Hr. | Daily | Hr. | Daily | Bare Costs | Incl. O&P |
|---|---|---|---|---|---|---|
| .5 Electrician Foreman | $46.05 | $184.20 | $68.60 | $274.40 | $45.65 | $68.00 |
| 2 Electricians | 45.55 | 728.80 | 67.85 | 1085.60 | | |
| 20 L.H., Daily Totals | | $913.00 | | $1360.00 | $45.65 | $68.00 |

| **Crew R-21** | Hr. | Daily | Hr. | Daily | Bare Costs | Incl. O&P |
|---|---|---|---|---|---|---|
| 1 Electrician Foreman | $46.05 | $368.40 | $68.60 | $548.80 | $45.53 | $67.84 |
| 3 Electricians | 45.55 | 1093.20 | 67.85 | 1628.40 | | |
| .1 Equip. Oper. (med.) | 39.85 | 31.88 | 60.10 | 48.08 | | |
| .1 S.P. Crane, 4x4, 25 Ton | | 70.18 | | 77.20 | 2.14 | 2.35 |
| 32.8 L.H., Daily Totals | | $1563.66 | | $2302.48 | $47.67 | $70.20 |

| Crew No. | Bare Costs | | Incl. Sub O & P | | Cost Per Labor-Hour | |
|---|---|---|---|---|---|---|
| **Crew R-22** | Hr. | Daily | Hr. | Daily | Bare Costs | Incl. O&P |
| .66 Electrician Foreman | $46.05 | $243.14 | $68.60 | $362.21 | $38.56 | $58.24 |
| 2 Helpers | 29.10 | 465.60 | 45.20 | 723.20 | | |
| 2 Electricians | 45.55 | 728.80 | 67.85 | 1085.60 | | |
| 37.28 L.H., Daily Totals | | $1437.54 | | $2171.01 | $38.56 | $58.24 |
| **Crew R-30** | Hr. | Daily | Hr. | Daily | Bare Costs | Incl. O&P |
| .25 Electrician Foreman (out) | $47.55 | $95.10 | $70.85 | $141.70 | $36.29 | $55.28 |
| 1 Electrician | 45.55 | 364.40 | 67.85 | 542.80 | | |
| 2 Laborers, (Semi-Skilled) | 30.25 | 484.00 | 47.05 | 752.80 | | |
| 26 L.H., Daily Totals | | $943.50 | | $1437.30 | $36.29 | $55.28 |
| **Crew R-31** | Hr. | Daily | Hr. | Daily | Bare Costs | Incl. O&P |
| 1 Electrician | $45.55 | $364.40 | $67.85 | $542.80 | $45.55 | $67.85 |
| 1 Core Drill, Elec, 2.5 HP | | 54.05 | | 59.45 | 6.76 | 7.43 |
| 8 L.H., Daily Totals | | $418.45 | | $602.26 | $52.31 | $75.28 |
| **Crew W-41E** | Hr. | Daily | Hr. | Daily | Bare Costs | Incl. O&P |
| 1 Laborers, (Semi-Skilled) | $30.25 | $242.00 | $47.05 | $376.40 | $40.52 | $61.57 |
| 1 Plumber | 46.70 | 373.60 | 70.25 | 562.00 | | |
| .5 Plumber | 48.70 | 194.80 | 73.25 | 293.00 | | |
| 20 L.H., Daily Totals | | $810.40 | | $1231.40 | $40.52 | $61.57 |

# Historical Cost Indexes

The table below lists both the RSMeans Historical Cost Index based on Jan. 1, 1993 = 100 as well as the computed value of an index based on Jan. 1, 2008 costs. Since the Jan. 1, 2008 figure is estimated, space is left to write in the actual index figures as they become available through either the quarterly "RSMeans Construction Cost Indexes" or as printed in the "Engineering News-Record." To compute the actual index based on Jan. 1, 2008 = 100, divide the Historical Cost Index for a particular year by the actual Jan. 1, 2008 Construction Cost Index. Space has been left to advance the index figures as the year progresses.

| Year | Historical Cost Index Jan. 1, 1993 = 100 Est. | Actual | Current Index Based on Jan. 1, 2008 = 100 Est. | Actual | Year | Historical Cost Index Jan. 1, 1993 = 100 Actual | Current Index Based on Jan. 1, 2008 = 100 Est. | Actual | Year | Historical Cost Index Jan. 1, 1993 = 100 Actual | Current Index Based on Jan. 1, 2008 = 100 Est. | Actual |
|---|---|---|---|---|---|---|---|---|---|---|---|---|
| Oct 2008 | | | | | July 1993 | 101.7 | 58.8 | | July 1975 | 44.8 | 25.9 | |
| July 2008 | | | | | 1992 | 99.4 | 57.5 | | 1974 | 41.4 | 23.9 | |
| April 2008 | | | | | 1991 | 96.8 | 56.0 | | 1973 | 37.7 | 21.8 | |
| Jan 2008 | 173.0 | | 100.0 | 100.0 | 1990 | 94.3 | 54.5 | | 1972 | 34.8 | 20.1 | |
| July 2007 | | 169.4 | 97.9 | | 1989 | 92.1 | 53.3 | | 1971 | 32.1 | 18.6 | |
| 2006 | | 162.0 | 93.6 | | 1988 | 89.9 | 51.9 | | 1970 | 28.7 | 16.6 | |
| 2005 | | 151.6 | 87.6 | | 1987 | 87.7 | 50.7 | | 1969 | 26.9 | 15.5 | |
| 2004 | | 143.7 | 83.1 | | 1986 | 84.2 | 48.7 | | 1968 | 24.9 | 14.4 | |
| 2003 | | 132.0 | 76.3 | | 1985 | 82.6 | 47.8 | | 1967 | 23.5 | 13.6 | |
| 2002 | | 128.7 | 74.4 | | 1984 | 82.0 | 47.4 | | 1966 | 22.7 | 13.1 | |
| 2001 | | 125.1 | 72.3 | | 1983 | 80.2 | 46.3 | | 1965 | 21.7 | 12.5 | |
| 2000 | | 120.9 | 69.9 | | 1982 | 76.1 | 44.0 | | 1964 | 21.2 | 12.3 | |
| 1999 | | 117.6 | 68.0 | | 1981 | 70.0 | 40.5 | | 1963 | 20.7 | 12.0 | |
| 1998 | | 115.1 | 66.5 | | 1980 | 62.9 | 36.4 | | 1962 | 20.2 | 11.7 | |
| 1997 | | 112.8 | 65.2 | | 1979 | 57.8 | 33.4 | | 1961 | 19.8 | 11.4 | |
| 1996 | | 110.2 | 63.7 | | 1978 | 53.5 | 30.9 | | 1960 | 19.7 | 11.4 | |
| 1995 | | 107.6 | 62.2 | | 1977 | 49.5 | 28.6 | | 1959 | 19.3 | 11.2 | |
| 1994 | | 104.4 | 60.3 | | 1976 | 46.9 | 27.1 | | 1958 | 18.8 | 10.9 | |

## Adjustments to Costs

The Historical Cost Index can be used to convert National Average building costs at a particular time to the approximate building costs for some other time.

## Example:

Estimate and compare construction costs for different years in the same city.

To estimate the National Average construction cost of a building in 1970, knowing that it cost $900,000 in 2008:

INDEX in 1970 = 28.7

INDEX in 2008 = 173.0

**Note:** The City Cost Indexes for Canada can be used to convert U.S. National averages to local costs in Canadian dollars.

**Time Adjustment using the Historical Cost Indexes:**

$$\frac{\text{Index for Year A}}{\text{Index for Year B}} \times \text{Cost in Year B} = \text{Cost in Year A}$$

$$\frac{\text{INDEX 1970}}{\text{INDEX 2008}} \times \text{Cost 2008} = \text{Cost 1970}$$

$$\frac{28.7}{173.0} \times \$900,000 = .173 \times \$900,000 = \$149,400$$

The construction cost of the building in 1970 is $149,400.

# How to Use the City Cost Indexes

## What you should know before you begin

RSMeans City Cost Indexes (CCI) are an extremely useful tool to use when you want to compare costs from city to city and region to region.

This publication contains average construction cost indexes for 731 U.S. and Canadian cities covering over 930 three-digit zip code locations, as listed directly under each city.

Keep in mind that a City Cost Index number is a percentage ratio of a specific city's cost to the national average cost of the same item at a stated time period.

In other words, these index figures represent relative construction factors (or, if you prefer, multipliers) for Material and Installation costs, as well as the weighted average for Total In Place costs for each CSI MasterFormat division. Installation costs include both labor and equipment rental costs. When estimating equipment rental rates only, for a specific location, use 015433 CONTRACTOR EQUIPMENT index.

The 30 City Average Index is the average of 30 major U.S. cities and serves as a National Average.

Index figures for both material and installation are based on the 30 major city average of 100 and represent the cost relationship as of July 1, 2007. The index for each division is computed from representative material and labor quantities for that division. The weighted average for each city is a weighted total of the components listed above it, but does not include relative productivity between trades or cities.

As changes occur in local material prices, labor rates and equipment rental rates, the impact of these changes should be accurately measured by the change in the City Cost Index for each particular city (as compared to the 30 City Average).

> Therefore, if you know (or have estimated) building costs in one city today, you can easily convert those costs to expected building costs in another city.

> In addition, by using the Historical Cost Index, you can easily convert National Average building costs at a particular time to the approximate building costs for some other time. The City Cost Indexes can then be applied to calculate the costs for a particular city.

## Quick Calculations

**Location Adjustment Using the City Cost Indexes:**

$$\frac{\text{Index for City A}}{\text{Index for City B}} \times \text{Cost in City B} = \text{Cost in City A}$$

**Time Adjustment for the National Average Using the Historical Cost Index:**

$$\frac{\text{Index for Year A}}{\text{Index for Year B}} \times \text{Cost in Year B} = \text{Cost in Year A}$$

**Adjustment from the National Average:**

$$\frac{\text{Index for City A}}{100} \times \text{National Average Cost} = \text{Cost in City A}$$

Since each of the other RSMeans publications contains many different items, any *one* item multiplied by the particular city index may give incorrect results. However, the larger the number of items compiled, the closer the results should be to actual costs for that particular city.

The City Cost Indexes for Canadian cities are calculated using Canadian material and equipment prices and labor rates, in Canadian dollars. Therefore, indexes for Canadian cities can be used to convert U.S. National Average prices to local costs in Canadian dollars.

## How to use this section

**1. Compare costs from city to city.**

In using the RSMeans Indexes, remember that an index number is not a fixed number but a ratio: It's a percentage ratio of a building component's cost at any stated time to the National Average cost of that same component at the same time period. Put in the form of an equation:

$$\frac{\text{Specific City Cost}}{\text{National Average Cost}} \times 100 = \text{City Index Number}$$

Therefore, when making cost comparisons between cities, do not subtract one city's index number from the index number of another city and read the result as a percentage difference. Instead, divide one city's index number by that of the other city. The resulting number may then be used as a multiplier to calculate cost differences from city to city.

The formula used to find cost differences between cities for the purpose of comparison is as follows:

$$\frac{\text{City A Index}}{\text{City B Index}} \times \text{City B Cost (Known)} = \text{City A Cost (Unknown)}$$

In addition, you can use RSMeans CCI to calculate and compare costs division by division between cities using the same basic formula. (Just be sure that you're comparing similar divisions.)

**2. Compare a specific city's construction costs with the National Average.**

When you're studying construction location feasibility, it's advisable to compare a prospective project's cost index with an index of the National Average cost.

For example, divide the weighted average index of construction costs of a specific city by that of the 30 City Average, which = 100.

$$\frac{\text{City Index}}{100} = \% \text{ of National Average}$$

**As a result, you get a ratio that indicates the relative cost of construction in that city in comparison with the National Average.**

**3. Convert U.S. National Average to actual costs in Canadian City.**

$$\frac{\text{Index for Canadian City}}{100} \times \text{National Average Cost} = \text{Cost in Canadian City in \$ CAN}$$

**4. Adjust construction cost data based on a National Average.**

When you use a source of construction cost data which is based on a National Average (such as RSMeans cost data publications), it is necessary to adjust those costs to a specific location.

$$\frac{\text{City Index}}{100} \times \frac{\text{"Book" Cost Based on}}{\text{National Average Costs}} = \frac{\text{City Cost}}{\text{(Unknown)}}$$

**5. When applying the City Cost Indexes to demolition projects, use the appropriate division installation index.** For example, for removal of existing doors and windows, use Division 8 (Openings) index.

# What you might like to know about how we developed the Indexes

The information presented in the CCI is organized according to the Construction Specifications Institute (CSI) MasterFormat 2004.

To create a reliable index, RSMeans researched the building type most often constructed in the United States and Canada. Because it was concluded that no one type of building completely represented the building construction industry, nine different types of buildings were combined to create a composite model.

The exact material, labor and equipment quantities are based on detailed analysis of these nine building types, then each quantity is weighted in proportion to expected usage. These various material items, labor hours, and equipment rental rates are thus combined to form a composite building representing as closely as possible the actual usage of materials, labor and equipment used in the North American Building Construction Industry.

The following structures were chosen to make up that composite model:

1. Factory, 1 story
2. Office, 2–4 story
3. Store, Retail
4. Town Hall, 2–3 story
5. High School, 2–3 story
6. Hospital, 4–8 story
7. Garage, Parking
8. Apartment, 1–3 story
9. Hotel/Motel, 2–3 story

For the purposes of ensuring the timeliness of the data, the components of the index for the composite model have been streamlined. They currently consist of:

- specific quantities of 66 commonly used construction materials;
- specific labor-hours for 21 building construction trades; and
- specific days of equipment rental for 6 types of construction equipment (normally used to install the 66 material items by the 21 trades.)

A sophisticated computer program handles the updating of all costs for each city on a quarterly basis. Material and equipment price quotations are gathered quarterly from 731 cities in the United States and Canada. These prices and the latest negotiated labor wage rates for 21 different building trades are used to compile the quarterly update of the City Cost Index.

The 30 major U.S. cities used to calculate the National Average are:

| | |
|---|---|
| Atlanta, GA | Memphis, TN |
| Baltimore, MD | Milwaukee, WI |
| Boston, MA | Minneapolis, MN |
| Buffalo, NY | Nashville, TN |
| Chicago, IL | New Orleans, LA |
| Cincinnati, OH | New York, NY |
| Cleveland, OH | Philadelphia, PA |
| Columbus, OH | Phoenix, AZ |
| Dallas, TX | Pittsburgh, PA |
| Denver, CO | St. Louis, MO |
| Detroit, MI | San Antonio, TX |
| Houston, TX | San Diego, CA |
| Indianapolis, IN | San Francisco, CA |
| Kansas City, MO | Seattle, WA |
| Los Angeles, CA | Washington, DC |

# What the CCI does not indicate

The weighted average for each city is a total of the divisional components weighted to reflect typical usage, but it does not include the productivity variations between trades or cities.

In addition, the CCI does not take into consideration factors such as the following:

- managerial efficiency
- competitive conditions
- automation
- restrictive union practices
- unique local requirements
- regional variations due to specific building codes

# City Cost Indexes

## UNITED STATES / ALABAMA

| DIVISION | | 30 CITY AVERAGE | | | ANNISTON 362 | | | BIRMINGHAM 350 - 352 | | | BUTLER 369 | | | DECATUR 356 | | | DOTHAN 363 | | |
|---|---|---|---|---|---|---|---|---|---|---|---|---|---|---|---|---|---|---|---|
| | | MAT. | INST. | TOTAL | MAT. | INST. | TOTAL | MAT. | INST. | TOTAL | MAT. | INST. | TOTAL | MAT. | INST. | TOTAL | MAT. | INST. | TOTAL |
| 015433 | CONTRACTOR EQUIPMENT | | 100.0 | 100.0 | | 101.6 | 101.6 | | 101.8 | 101.8 | | 98.2 | 98.2 | | 101.6 | 101.6 | | 98.2 | 98.2 |
| 0241, 31 - 34 | SITE & INFRASTRUCTURE, DEMOLITION | 100.0 | 100.0 | 100.0 | 87.5 | 92.3 | 90.9 | 83.7 | 93.8 | 90.7 | 101.5 | 86.0 | 90.7 | 80.5 | 91.9 | 88.4 | 98.9 | 85.9 | 89.9 |
| 0310 | Concrete Forming & Accessories | 100.0 | 100.0 | 100.0 | 91.1 | 50.4 | 56.0 | 91.5 | 75.6 | 77.8 | 87.2 | 50.8 | 55.8 | 95.6 | 53.6 | 59.4 | 96.5 | 50.0 | 56.5 |
| 0320 | Concrete Reinforcing | 100.0 | 100.0 | 100.0 | 89.0 | 81.7 | 85.5 | 89.0 | 83.2 | 86.2 | 94.0 | 55.6 | 75.5 | 89.0 | 52.6 | 71.4 | 94.0 | 54.7 | 75.1 |
| 0330 | Cast-in-Place Concrete | 100.0 | 100.0 | 100.0 | 91.6 | 47.6 | 75.3 | 100.5 | 72.0 | 89.9 | 89.3 | 60.9 | 78.8 | 91.1 | 58.5 | 79.0 | 89.3 | 50.2 | 74.8 |
| 03 | CONCRETE | 100.0 | 100.0 | 100.0 | 95.2 | 56.9 | 77.6 | 95.2 | 76.8 | 86.7 | 96.1 | 56.7 | 77.9 | 90.8 | 56.6 | 75.0 | 95.5 | 52.6 | 75.7 |
| 04 | MASONRY | 100.0 | 100.0 | 100.0 | 83.8 | 45.2 | 60.7 | 86.5 | 82.8 | 84.3 | 87.6 | 57.9 | 69.8 | 84.5 | 61.3 | 70.6 | 88.6 | 43.1 | 61.4 |
| 05 | METALS | 100.0 | 100.0 | 100.0 | 92.8 | 88.2 | 91.5 | 93.5 | 92.7 | 93.3 | 91.8 | 79.6 | 88.2 | 94.8 | 79.0 | 90.2 | 91.8 | 77.7 | 87.7 |
| 06 | WOOD, PLASTICS & COMPOSITES | 100.0 | 100.0 | 100.0 | 90.2 | 51.7 | 69.5 | 92.2 | 72.9 | 81.8 | 85.2 | 51.3 | 66.9 | 96.6 | 51.3 | 72.2 | 96.6 | 51.3 | 72.2 |
| 07 | THERMAL & MOISTURE PROTECTION | 100.0 | 100.0 | 100.0 | 95.3 | 49.9 | 77.6 | 97.2 | 87.2 | 93.3 | 95.4 | 64.2 | 83.2 | 95.1 | 64.7 | 83.3 | 95.4 | 56.9 | 80.4 |
| 08 | OPENINGS | 100.0 | 100.0 | 100.0 | 93.6 | 55.6 | 84.3 | 97.1 | 76.7 | 92.1 | 93.7 | 53.6 | 83.8 | 97.4 | 52.1 | 86.2 | 93.7 | 53.6 | 83.8 |
| 0920 | Plaster & Gypsum Board | 100.0 | 100.0 | 100.0 | 97.4 | 50.9 | 68.7 | 103.4 | 72.8 | 84.5 | 96.0 | 50.5 | 68.0 | 100.8 | 51.2 | 70.2 | 102.8 | 50.5 | 70.5 |
| 0950, 0980 | Ceilings & Acoustic Treatment | 100.0 | 100.0 | 100.0 | 95.9 | 50.9 | 68.3 | 98.7 | 72.8 | 82.8 | 95.9 | 50.5 | 68.0 | 100.2 | 51.2 | 70.1 | 95.9 | 50.5 | 68.0 |
| 0960 | Flooring | 100.0 | 100.0 | 100.0 | 101.1 | 32.0 | 82.3 | 104.1 | 69.6 | 94.7 | 107.4 | 64.7 | 95.8 | 104.1 | 47.1 | 88.6 | 115.4 | 31.8 | 92.7 |
| 0970, 0990 | Wall Finishes & Painting/Coating | 100.0 | 100.0 | 100.0 | 100.2 | 37.7 | 62.6 | 100.2 | 66.5 | 80.0 | 100.2 | 63.9 | 78.4 | 100.2 | 59.7 | 75.9 | 100.2 | 63.9 | 78.4 |
| 09 | FINISHES | 100.0 | 100.0 | 100.0 | 96.9 | 46.0 | 70.3 | 99.2 | 73.2 | 85.6 | 100.4 | 54.7 | 76.5 | 98.8 | 53.0 | 74.8 | 103.6 | 48.0 | 74.5 |
| COVERS | DIVS. 10 - 14, 25, 28, 41, 43, 44 | 100.0 | 52.0 | 90.2 | 100.0 | 52.0 | 90.2 | 100.0 | 89.5 | 97.8 | 100.0 | 52.1 | 90.2 | 100.0 | 54.5 | 90.7 | 100.0 | 52.1 | 90.2 |
| 21, 22, 23 | FIRE SUPPRESSION, PLUMBING & HVAC | 100.0 | 100.0 | 100.0 | 99.9 | 40.5 | 75.5 | 99.8 | 70.1 | 87.6 | 97.6 | 41.6 | 74.6 | 99.8 | 50.7 | 79.6 | 97.6 | 41.5 | 74.6 |
| 26, 27, 3370 | ELECTRICAL, COMMUNICATIONS & UTIL. | 100.0 | 100.0 | 100.0 | 96.4 | 40.7 | 69.1 | 99.4 | 61.8 | 81.0 | 98.4 | 48.2 | 73.8 | 98.1 | 63.4 | 81.1 | 97.2 | 48.2 | 73.2 |
| MF2004 | WEIGHTED AVERAGE | 100.0 | 100.0 | 100.0 | 95.6 | 54.0 | 77.8 | 96.6 | 76.9 | 88.2 | 96.0 | 56.6 | 79.2 | 95.9 | 61.3 | 81.1 | 96.2 | 53.3 | 77.8 |

## ALABAMA

| DIVISION | | EVERGREEN 364 | | | GADSDEN 359 | | | HUNTSVILLE 357 - 358 | | | JASPER 355 | | | MOBILE 365 - 366 | | | MONTGOMERY 360 - 361 | | |
|---|---|---|---|---|---|---|---|---|---|---|---|---|---|---|---|---|---|---|---|
| | | MAT. | INST. | TOTAL | MAT. | INST. | TOTAL | MAT. | INST. | TOTAL | MAT. | INST. | TOTAL | MAT. | INST. | TOTAL | MAT. | INST. | TOTAL |
| 015433 | CONTRACTOR EQUIPMENT | | 98.2 | 98.2 | | 101.6 | 101.6 | | 101.6 | 101.6 | | 101.6 | 101.6 | | 98.2 | 98.2 | | 98.2 | 98.2 |
| 0241, 31 - 34 | SITE & INFRASTRUCTURE, DEMOLITION | 102.0 | 86.3 | 91.1 | 86.1 | 92.5 | 90.6 | 80.2 | 93.2 | 89.3 | 85.7 | 92.3 | 90.3 | 93.4 | 87.0 | 88.9 | 91.7 | 87.0 | 88.4 |
| 0310 | Concrete Forming & Accessories | 83.5 | 52.9 | 57.1 | 87.4 | 49.0 | 54.3 | 95.6 | 69.5 | 73.1 | 93.1 | 40.2 | 47.5 | 95.8 | 61.2 | 66.0 | 93.2 | 51.4 | 57.2 |
| 0320 | Concrete Reinforcing | 94.0 | 55.6 | 75.5 | 94.2 | 82.2 | 88.4 | 89.0 | 79.1 | 84.2 | 89.0 | 81.9 | 85.6 | 91.8 | 54.7 | 74.0 | 91.8 | 81.8 | 87.0 |
| 0330 | Cast-in-Place Concrete | 89.3 | 64.0 | 80.0 | 91.1 | 53.7 | 77.3 | 88.7 | 68.8 | 81.3 | 100.9 | 47.6 | 81.2 | 93.6 | 64.3 | 82.8 | 98.3 | 50.9 | 80.7 |
| 03 | CONCRETE | 96.2 | 58.7 | 78.9 | 95.0 | 58.5 | 78.1 | 89.6 | 72.2 | 81.6 | 98.3 | 52.4 | 77.2 | 92.5 | 62.3 | 78.6 | 94.6 | 58.5 | 78.0 |
| 04 | MASONRY | 87.6 | 63.4 | 73.1 | 83.0 | 51.3 | 64.0 | 85.6 | 68.4 | 75.3 | 80.0 | 44.7 | 58.9 | 86.3 | 62.9 | 72.3 | 85.8 | 42.8 | 60.1 |
| 05 | METALS | 91.8 | 79.6 | 88.2 | 92.9 | 90.3 | 92.1 | 94.8 | 91.3 | 93.8 | 92.8 | 88.9 | 91.7 | 93.6 | 79.4 | 89.5 | 93.5 | 89.5 | 92.3 |
| 06 | WOOD, PLASTICS & COMPOSITES | 80.9 | 51.3 | 64.9 | 85.9 | 46.8 | 64.8 | 95.2 | 70.1 | 81.7 | 92.2 | 37.9 | 63.0 | 95.4 | 61.2 | 77.0 | 91.8 | 51.3 | 69.9 |
| 07 | THERMAL & MOISTURE PROTECTION | 95.3 | 65.6 | 83.8 | 95.2 | 71.6 | 86.0 | 94.8 | 79.6 | 88.9 | 95.3 | 52.3 | 78.5 | 94.8 | 78.8 | 88.6 | 94.3 | 69.1 | 84.5 |
| 08 | OPENINGS | 93.7 | 53.6 | 83.8 | 93.6 | 54.2 | 83.9 | 97.4 | 67.4 | 90.0 | 93.6 | 53.0 | 83.6 | 97.4 | 58.6 | 87.9 | 97.4 | 59.3 | 88.0 |
| 0920 | Plaster & Gypsum Board | 94.0 | 50.5 | 67.2 | 95.7 | 45.9 | 65.0 | 98.5 | 69.8 | 80.8 | 97.5 | 36.9 | 60.1 | 100.8 | 60.7 | 76.1 | 103.4 | 50.5 | 70.8 |
| 0950, 0980 | Ceilings & Acoustic Treatment | 95.9 | 50.5 | 68.0 | 95.9 | 45.9 | 65.2 | 102.1 | 69.8 | 82.3 | 95.1 | 36.9 | 59.3 | 102.1 | 60.7 | 76.7 | 98.7 | 50.5 | 69.1 |
| 0960 | Flooring | 104.6 | 64.7 | 93.7 | 98.9 | 52.0 | 86.1 | 104.1 | 62.4 | 92.8 | 102.1 | 30.8 | 82.7 | 114.3 | 64.7 | 100.8 | 112.5 | 34.2 | 91.2 |
| 0970, 0990 | Wall Finishes & Painting/Coating | 100.2 | 63.9 | 78.4 | 100.2 | 72.7 | 83.7 | 100.2 | 63.1 | 77.9 | 100.2 | 46.2 | 67.7 | 104.5 | 65.0 | 80.7 | 100.2 | 63.9 | 78.4 |
| 09 | FINISHES | 99.3 | 56.1 | 76.7 | 95.9 | 50.8 | 72.3 | 98.9 | 67.2 | 82.3 | 96.8 | 38.3 | 66.2 | 104.1 | 61.9 | 82.0 | 102.6 | 48.3 | 74.2 |
| COVERS | DIVS. 10 - 14, 25, 28, 41, 43, 44 | 100.0 | 54.1 | 90.6 | 100.0 | 80.3 | 96.0 | 100.0 | 85.5 | 97.0 | 100.0 | 49.7 | 89.7 | 100.0 | 83.1 | 96.5 | 100.0 | 80.2 | 95.9 |
| 21, 22, 23 | FIRE SUPPRESSION, PLUMBING & HVAC | 97.6 | 44.5 | 75.8 | 101.6 | 44.8 | 78.3 | 99.7 | 64.7 | 85.4 | 101.6 | 59.1 | 84.1 | 99.7 | 66.4 | 86.0 | 99.8 | 42.2 | 76.2 |
| 26, 27, 3370 | ELECTRICAL, COMMUNICATIONS & UTIL. | 95.8 | 48.2 | 72.4 | 98.2 | 61.8 | 80.3 | 99.3 | 67.4 | 83.6 | 97.6 | 34.7 | 66.7 | 99.3 | 60.1 | 80.0 | 98.5 | 70.6 | 84.8 |
| MF2004 | WEIGHTED AVERAGE | 95.6 | 58.4 | 79.7 | 95.9 | 60.8 | 80.9 | 96.0 | 72.8 | 86.0 | 96.2 | 55.1 | 78.6 | 97.0 | 67.4 | 84.3 | 96.9 | 60.0 | 81.1 |

## ALABAMA / ALASKA

| DIVISION | | PHENIX CITY 368 | | | SELMA 367 | | | TUSCALOOSA 354 | | | ANCHORAGE 995 - 996 | | | FAIRBANKS 997 | | | JUNEAU 998 | | |
|---|---|---|---|---|---|---|---|---|---|---|---|---|---|---|---|---|---|---|---|
| | | MAT. | INST. | TOTAL | MAT. | INST. | TOTAL | MAT. | INST. | TOTAL | MAT. | INST. | TOTAL | MAT. | INST. | TOTAL | MAT. | INST. | TOTAL |
| 015433 | CONTRACTOR EQUIPMENT | | 98.2 | 98.2 | | 98.2 | 98.2 | | 101.6 | 101.6 | | 118.4 | 118.4 | | 118.4 | 118.4 | | 118.4 | 118.4 |
| 0241, 31 - 34 | SITE & INFRASTRUCTURE, DEMOLITION | 106.0 | 87.1 | 92.8 | 98.8 | 87.0 | 90.6 | 80.7 | 92.7 | 89.1 | 142.1 | 133.6 | 136.2 | 127.7 | 133.6 | 131.8 | 137.2 | 133.5 | 134.7 |
| 0310 | Concrete Forming & Accessories | 91.0 | 45.5 | 51.8 | 88.6 | 50.6 | 55.9 | 95.5 | 55.5 | 61.1 | 130.1 | 115.8 | 117.8 | 135.9 | 118.4 | 120.8 | 131.6 | 115.6 | 117.9 |
| 0320 | Concrete Reinforcing | 93.9 | 74.3 | 84.5 | 94.0 | 81.7 | 88.1 | 89.0 | 82.2 | 85.7 | 144.4 | 107.6 | 126.7 | 147.1 | 107.7 | 128.1 | 110.7 | 107.6 | 109.2 |
| 0330 | Cast-in-Place Concrete | 89.3 | 51.7 | 75.4 | 89.3 | 50.8 | 75.1 | 92.4 | 53.7 | 78.1 | 178.3 | 114.8 | 154.8 | 148.7 | 115.2 | 136.3 | 179.3 | 114.7 | 155.4 |
| 03 | CONCRETE | 98.9 | 54.8 | 78.5 | 94.9 | 58.1 | 77.9 | 91.4 | 61.4 | 77.6 | 143.9 | 113.3 | 129.8 | 126.0 | 114.6 | 120.8 | 139.2 | 113.2 | 127.2 |
| 04 | MASONRY | 87.6 | 49.0 | 64.5 | 91.2 | 43.3 | 62.5 | 84.7 | 54.8 | 66.8 | 217.3 | 120.4 | 159.4 | 219.7 | 120.4 | 160.4 | 208.0 | 120.4 | 155.6 |
| 05 | METALS | 91.7 | 86.9 | 90.3 | 91.7 | 88.5 | 90.8 | 94.0 | 90.2 | 92.9 | 124.9 | 102.4 | 118.4 | 125.0 | 102.6 | 118.5 | 125.0 | 102.2 | 118.3 |
| 06 | WOOD, PLASTICS & COMPOSITES | 89.9 | 42.7 | 64.5 | 86.9 | 51.3 | 67.7 | 95.2 | 53.8 | 72.9 | 115.3 | 114.3 | 114.8 | 119.6 | 117.5 | 118.5 | 115.3 | 114.3 | 114.8 |
| 07 | THERMAL & MOISTURE PROTECTION | 95.7 | 70.1 | 85.7 | 95.2 | 57.9 | 80.7 | 95.1 | 73.3 | 86.6 | 175.2 | 114.7 | 151.6 | 172.6 | 116.9 | 150.9 | 173.3 | 114.6 | 150.4 |
| 08 | OPENINGS | 93.6 | 52.8 | 83.6 | 93.6 | 59.3 | 85.2 | 97.4 | 66.3 | 89.8 | 125.8 | 112.1 | 122.4 | 122.9 | 113.9 | 120.7 | 122.9 | 112.1 | 120.2 |
| 0920 | Plaster & Gypsum Board | 98.4 | 41.7 | 63.4 | 97.1 | 50.5 | 68.3 | 100.8 | 53.1 | 71.4 | 137.8 | 114.5 | 123.4 | 157.8 | 117.8 | 133.1 | 137.8 | 114.5 | 123.4 |
| 0950, 0980 | Ceilings & Acoustic Treatment | 95.9 | 41.7 | 62.6 | 95.9 | 50.5 | 68.0 | 102.1 | 53.1 | 72.0 | 125.3 | 114.5 | 118.7 | 130.5 | 117.8 | 122.7 | 125.3 | 114.5 | 118.7 |
| 0960 | Flooring | 110.4 | 34.2 | 89.7 | 108.2 | 25.3 | 85.7 | 104.1 | 43.3 | 87.6 | 163.6 | 124.4 | 153.0 | 163.6 | 124.4 | 153.0 | 163.6 | 124.4 | 153.0 |
| 0970, 0990 | Wall Finishes & Painting/Coating | 100.2 | 63.9 | 78.4 | 100.2 | 63.9 | 78.4 | 100.2 | 55.0 | 73.0 | 159.6 | 117.6 | 134.3 | 159.6 | 126.0 | 139.4 | 159.6 | 117.6 | 134.3 |
| 09 | FINISHES | 102.1 | 43.6 | 71.5 | 100.5 | 46.8 | 72.4 | 99.3 | 52.4 | 74.7 | 151.7 | 117.8 | 133.9 | 153.8 | 120.6 | 136.4 | 150.2 | 117.8 | 133.2 |
| COVERS | DIVS. 10 - 14, 25, 28, 41, 43, 44 | 100.0 | 79.7 | 95.8 | 100.0 | 52.1 | 90.2 | 100.0 | 82.6 | 96.4 | 100.0 | 112.8 | 102.6 | 100.0 | 113.1 | 102.7 | 100.0 | 112.8 | 102.6 |
| 21, 22, 23 | FIRE SUPPRESSION, PLUMBING & HVAC | 97.6 | 42.8 | 75.1 | 97.6 | 41.8 | 74.7 | 99.8 | 42.0 | 76.1 | 100.5 | 107.6 | 103.4 | 100.5 | 113.8 | 105.9 | 100.5 | 98.6 | 99.7 |
| 26, 27, 3370 | ELECTRICAL, COMMUNICATIONS & UTIL. | 97.9 | 80.8 | 89.5 | 96.9 | 48.2 | 73.0 | 98.8 | 61.8 | 80.6 | 148.7 | 112.6 | 131.0 | 150.2 | 112.6 | 131.7 | 150.2 | 112.6 | 131.7 |
| MF2004 | WEIGHTED AVERAGE | 96.6 | 60.5 | 81.2 | 95.9 | 55.3 | 78.5 | 96.0 | 61.9 | 81.4 | 131.4 | 114.0 | 124.0 | 129.0 | 116.1 | 123.5 | 130.0 | 112.1 | 122.3 |

## ALASKA / ARIZONA

| DIVISION | | ALASKA KETCHIKAN 999 MAT. | INST. | TOTAL | CHAMBERS 865 MAT. | INST. | TOTAL | FLAGSTAFF 860 MAT. | INST. | TOTAL | GLOBE 855 MAT. | INST. | TOTAL | KINGMAN 864 MAT. | INST. | TOTAL | MESA/TEMPE 852 MAT. | INST. | TOTAL |
|---|---|---|---|---|---|---|---|---|---|---|---|---|---|---|---|---|---|---|---|
| 015433 | CONTRACTOR EQUIPMENT | | 118.4 | 118.4 | | 94.5 | 94.5 | | 94.5 | 94.5 | | 98.0 | 98.0 | | 94.5 | 94.5 | | 98.0 | 98.0 |
| 0241, 31 - 34 | SITE & INFRASTRUCTURE, DEMOLITION | 194.1 | 133.5 | 151.9 | 64.0 | 98.6 | 88.1 | 81.6 | 99.8 | 94.2 | 101.2 | 102.5 | 102.1 | 63.9 | 100.2 | 89.2 | 90.3 | 103.0 | 99.1 |
| 0310 | Concrete Forming & Accessories | 126.8 | 115.6 | 117.1 | 96.8 | 51.3 | 57.6 | 102.2 | 67.4 | 72.2 | 97.6 | 51.1 | 57.6 | 94.8 | 65.7 | 69.5 | 100.6 | 62.0 | 67.4 |
| 0320 | Concrete Reinforcing | 115.4 | 107.6 | 111.6 | 100.8 | 76.7 | 89.2 | 100.7 | 77.5 | 89.5 | 103.9 | 76.7 | 90.8 | 100.9 | 77.5 | 89.7 | 104.6 | 77.5 | 91.6 |
| 0330 | Cast-in-Place Concrete | 301.4 | 114.7 | 232.3 | 95.5 | 58.8 | 81.9 | 95.6 | 73.3 | 87.4 | 104.2 | 59.1 | 87.5 | 95.2 | 59.9 | 82.1 | 105.0 | 65.7 | 90.5 |
| 03 | CONCRETE | 215.7 | 113.2 | 168.4 | 100.5 | 58.9 | 81.3 | 120.3 | 71.3 | 97.7 | 117.6 | 58.9 | 90.5 | 100.2 | 65.9 | 84.4 | 108.9 | 66.3 | 89.3 |
| 04 | MASONRY | 229.1 | 120.4 | 164.1 | 98.7 | 46.8 | 67.6 | 98.4 | 63.5 | 77.5 | 112.5 | 46.8 | 73.2 | 98.7 | 59.3 | 75.1 | 112.6 | 49.3 | 74.7 |
| 05 | METALS | 125.1 | 102.2 | 118.5 | 95.6 | 66.7 | 87.2 | 96.1 | 71.4 | 88.9 | 96.9 | 67.1 | 88.2 | 96.2 | 71.3 | 89.0 | 97.2 | 72.1 | 89.9 |
| 06 | WOOD, PLASTICS & COMPOSITES | 110.1 | 114.3 | 112.4 | 99.9 | 49.4 | 72.7 | 105.9 | 67.7 | 85.3 | 94.0 | 49.6 | 70.0 | 96.2 | 67.7 | 80.9 | 97.3 | 67.9 | 81.5 |
| 07 | THERMAL & MOISTURE PROTECTION | 175.7 | 114.6 | 151.9 | 95.9 | 57.2 | 80.8 | 97.8 | 68.0 | 86.2 | 103.9 | 54.7 | 84.7 | 95.8 | 63.2 | 83.1 | 103.0 | 60.0 | 86.2 |
| 08 | OPENINGS | 123.3 | 112.1 | 120.5 | 100.9 | 55.1 | 89.6 | 101.0 | 70.4 | 93.4 | 97.5 | 55.1 | 87.0 | 101.1 | 68.1 | 92.9 | 97.5 | 68.1 | 90.3 |
| 0920 | Plaster & Gypsum Board | 142.3 | 114.5 | 125.1 | 86.0 | 48.1 | 62.6 | 88.5 | 66.9 | 75.2 | 92.4 | 48.1 | 65.1 | 82.4 | 66.9 | 72.9 | 94.0 | 66.9 | 77.3 |
| 0950, 0980 | Ceilings & Acoustic Treatment | 123.8 | 114.5 | 118.1 | 109.0 | 48.1 | 71.6 | 109.9 | 66.9 | 83.5 | 97.1 | 48.1 | 67.0 | 109.9 | 66.9 | 83.5 | 97.1 | 66.9 | 78.6 |
| 0960 | Flooring | 163.6 | 124.4 | 153.0 | 97.1 | 45.7 | 83.1 | 99.8 | 45.9 | 85.1 | 101.4 | 45.7 | 86.2 | 96.1 | 62.0 | 86.8 | 102.9 | 57.2 | 90.5 |
| 0970, 0990 | Wall Finishes & Painting/Coating | 159.6 | 117.6 | 134.3 | 90.7 | 44.2 | 62.8 | 90.7 | 57.4 | 70.7 | 95.0 | 44.2 | 64.5 | 90.7 | 57.4 | 70.7 | 95.0 | 57.4 | 72.4 |
| 09 | FINISHES | 154.4 | 117.8 | 135.3 | 96.9 | 48.5 | 71.5 | 100.0 | 61.7 | 79.9 | 99.7 | 48.6 | 72.9 | 96.2 | 63.5 | 79.1 | 99.4 | 60.1 | 78.8 |
| COVERS | DIVS. 10 - 14, 25, 28, 41, 43, 44 | 100.0 | 112.8 | 102.6 | 100.0 | 79.3 | 95.8 | 100.0 | 83.0 | 96.5 | 100.0 | 79.7 | 95.8 | 100.0 | 81.5 | 96.2 | 100.0 | 78.1 | 95.5 |
| 21, 22, 23 | FIRE SUPPRESSION, PLUMBING & HVAC | 98.9 | 96.5 | 97.9 | 97.4 | 74.7 | 88.1 | 100.2 | 77.0 | 90.7 | 96.0 | 68.6 | 84.8 | 97.4 | 74.8 | 88.1 | 100.2 | 69.3 | 87.5 |
| 26, 27, 3370 | ELECTRICAL, COMMUNICATIONS & UTIL. | 150.2 | 112.6 | 131.7 | 100.4 | 71.8 | 86.4 | 99.3 | 63.0 | 81.5 | 96.9 | 68.3 | 82.9 | 100.4 | 63.0 | 82.0 | 93.6 | 63.0 | 78.6 |
| MF2004 | WEIGHTED AVERAGE | 141.8 | 111.7 | 128.9 | 97.4 | 65.8 | 83.9 | 101.2 | 71.9 | 88.7 | 100.8 | 64.3 | 85.2 | 97.4 | 70.2 | 85.8 | 100.1 | 67.8 | 86.3 |

## ARIZONA / ARKANSAS

| DIVISION | | PHOENIX 850,853 MAT. | INST. | TOTAL | PRESCOTT 863 MAT. | INST. | TOTAL | SHOW LOW 859 MAT. | INST. | TOTAL | TUCSON 856 - 857 MAT. | INST. | TOTAL | BATESVILLE 725 MAT. | INST. | TOTAL | CAMDEN 717 MAT. | INST. | TOTAL |
|---|---|---|---|---|---|---|---|---|---|---|---|---|---|---|---|---|---|---|---|
| 015433 | CONTRACTOR EQUIPMENT | | 98.6 | 98.6 | | 94.5 | 94.5 | | 98.0 | 98.0 | | 98.0 | 98.0 | | 86.6 | 86.6 | | 86.6 | 86.6 |
| 0241, 31 - 34 | SITE & INFRASTRUCTURE, DEMOLITION | 90.9 | 103.9 | 99.9 | 70.0 | 98.6 | 89.9 | 103.5 | 102.5 | 102.8 | 85.6 | 103.6 | 98.1 | 74.1 | 83.7 | 80.8 | 75.0 | 83.3 | 80.8 |
| 0310 | Concrete Forming & Accessories | 101.6 | 70.1 | 74.4 | 98.2 | 51.1 | 57.6 | 104.6 | 51.4 | 58.8 | 101.0 | 69.7 | 74.1 | 84.3 | 53.8 | 58.0 | 84.0 | 35.4 | 42.1 |
| 0320 | Concrete Reinforcing | 103.1 | 77.6 | 90.8 | 100.7 | 77.0 | 89.3 | 104.6 | 69.9 | 87.9 | 86.3 | 77.5 | 82.1 | 95.7 | 73.5 | 85.0 | 96.9 | 49.7 | 74.2 |
| 0330 | Cast-in-Place Concrete | 105.1 | 73.9 | 93.5 | 95.5 | 58.7 | 81.9 | 104.2 | 59.2 | 87.5 | 108.1 | 73.7 | 95.4 | 77.6 | 50.5 | 67.6 | 79.6 | 40.2 | 65.0 |
| 03 | CONCRETE | 108.6 | 72.7 | 92.0 | 105.9 | 58.8 | 84.1 | 119.9 | 57.8 | 91.2 | 107.4 | 72.5 | 91.3 | 81.8 | 56.9 | 69.4 | 81.8 | 40.7 | 62.8 |
| 04 | MASONRY | 99.3 | 63.7 | 78.0 | 98.7 | 52.7 | 71.2 | 112.5 | 48.5 | 74.2 | 97.2 | 63.4 | 77.0 | 99.8 | 48.9 | 69.4 | 108.5 | 37.1 | 65.8 |
| 05 | METALS | 98.8 | 73.0 | 91.3 | 96.1 | 66.9 | 87.6 | 96.7 | 64.7 | 87.4 | 98.0 | 72.0 | 90.4 | 98.6 | 68.9 | 90.0 | 98.7 | 59.3 | 87.2 |
| 06 | WOOD, PLASTICS & COMPOSITES | 98.3 | 71.1 | 83.7 | 101.4 | 49.4 | 73.4 | 101.8 | 49.6 | 73.7 | 97.6 | 71.1 | 83.3 | 86.3 | 55.1 | 69.5 | 86.1 | 35.6 | 58.9 |
| 07 | THERMAL & MOISTURE PROTECTION | 102.9 | 68.2 | 89.4 | 96.4 | 56.5 | 80.8 | 104.1 | 57.5 | 85.9 | 104.5 | 65.1 | 89.1 | 97.6 | 51.6 | 79.7 | 97.5 | 37.1 | 73.9 |
| 08 | OPENINGS | 98.7 | 72.2 | 92.2 | 101.0 | 55.1 | 89.7 | 96.6 | 53.4 | 85.9 | 93.9 | 72.2 | 88.5 | 96.2 | 53.3 | 85.6 | 92.4 | 41.4 | 79.8 |
| 0920 | Plaster & Gypsum Board | 96.0 | 70.2 | 80.1 | 86.1 | 48.1 | 62.7 | 95.7 | 48.1 | 66.4 | 99.0 | 70.2 | 81.3 | 83.6 | 54.5 | 65.7 | 83.6 | 34.5 | 53.3 |
| 0950, 0980 | Ceilings & Acoustic Treatment | 103.9 | 70.2 | 83.2 | 108.1 | 48.1 | 71.3 | 97.1 | 48.1 | 67.0 | 97.9 | 70.2 | 80.9 | 86.5 | 54.5 | 66.9 | 86.5 | 34.5 | 54.6 |
| 0960 | Flooring | 103.2 | 59.8 | 91.4 | 98.1 | 45.7 | 83.8 | 104.9 | 52.0 | 90.5 | 94.0 | 45.9 | 80.9 | 104.6 | 68.2 | 94.7 | 104.5 | 45.8 | 88.5 |
| 0970, 0990 | Wall Finishes & Painting/Coating | 95.0 | 57.4 | 72.4 | 90.7 | 44.2 | 62.8 | 95.0 | 44.2 | 64.5 | 94.8 | 57.4 | 72.3 | 98.2 | 49.3 | 68.8 | 98.2 | 53.8 | 71.5 |
| 09 | FINISHES | 101.4 | 66.3 | 83.0 | 97.5 | 48.5 | 71.8 | 101.4 | 49.7 | 74.3 | 97.6 | 63.7 | 79.8 | 91.6 | 56.0 | 73.0 | 91.6 | 39.1 | 64.1 |
| COVERS | DIVS. 10 - 14, 25, 28, 41, 43, 44 | 100.0 | 83.7 | 96.7 | 100.0 | 79.3 | 95.8 | 100.0 | 79.7 | 95.8 | 100.0 | 83.7 | 96.7 | 100.0 | 49.6 | 89.7 | 100.0 | 44.1 | 88.5 |
| 21, 22, 23 | FIRE SUPPRESSION, PLUMBING & HVAC | 100.2 | 77.0 | 90.7 | 100.2 | 74.3 | 89.6 | 96.0 | 74.6 | 87.3 | 100.1 | 71.3 | 88.3 | 95.9 | 42.5 | 74.0 | 95.9 | 34.5 | 70.7 |
| 26, 27, 3370 | ELECTRICAL, COMMUNICATIONS & UTIL. | 101.5 | 64.5 | 83.3 | 99.0 | 63.0 | 81.3 | 93.9 | 68.3 | 81.3 | 95.8 | 60.5 | 78.4 | 98.1 | 49.0 | 74.0 | 94.6 | 43.7 | 69.6 |
| MF2004 | WEIGHTED AVERAGE | 100.8 | 73.5 | 89.1 | 98.9 | 65.0 | 84.4 | 100.9 | 65.6 | 85.8 | 98.9 | 71.2 | 87.1 | 94.3 | 54.7 | 77.3 | 94.2 | 44.5 | 72.9 |

## ARKANSAS

| DIVISION | | FAYETTEVILLE 727 MAT. | INST. | TOTAL | FORT SMITH 729 MAT. | INST. | TOTAL | HARRISON 726 MAT. | INST. | TOTAL | HOT SPRINGS 719 MAT. | INST. | TOTAL | JONESBORO 724 MAT. | INST. | TOTAL | LITTLE ROCK 720 - 722 MAT. | INST. | TOTAL |
|---|---|---|---|---|---|---|---|---|---|---|---|---|---|---|---|---|---|---|---|
| 015433 | CONTRACTOR EQUIPMENT | | 86.6 | 86.6 | | 86.6 | 86.6 | | 86.6 | 86.6 | | 86.6 | 86.6 | | 108.5 | 108.5 | | 86.6 | 86.6 |
| 0241, 31 - 34 | SITE & INFRASTRUCTURE, DEMOLITION | 73.5 | 83.9 | 80.8 | 78.3 | 83.9 | 82.2 | 79.1 | 83.8 | 82.4 | 78.8 | 83.3 | 81.9 | 101.3 | 99.2 | 99.8 | 81.1 | 84.0 | 83.1 |
| 0310 | Concrete Forming & Accessories | 79.8 | 44.4 | 49.3 | 100.0 | 41.9 | 50.0 | 88.9 | 54.0 | 58.9 | 81.3 | 41.8 | 47.3 | 87.8 | 57.7 | 61.9 | 92.2 | 71.1 | 74.0 |
| 0320 | Concrete Reinforcing | 95.7 | 70.8 | 83.7 | 96.8 | 72.4 | 85.0 | 95.2 | 73.4 | 84.7 | 95.1 | 64.1 | 80.1 | 92.5 | 74.4 | 83.8 | 96.9 | 68.9 | 83.4 |
| 0330 | Cast-in-Place Concrete | 77.6 | 47.2 | 66.4 | 88.8 | 68.5 | 81.3 | 86.1 | 48.2 | 72.1 | 81.5 | 41.6 | 66.7 | 84.6 | 62.3 | 76.3 | 91.2 | 68.7 | 82.9 |
| 03 | CONCRETE | 79.9 | 51.1 | 66.6 | 87.7 | 57.6 | 73.8 | 86.9 | 56.2 | 72.7 | 84.8 | 46.8 | 67.2 | 84.5 | 63.7 | 74.9 | 88.5 | 70.0 | 79.9 |
| 04 | MASONRY | 89.9 | 45.7 | 63.5 | 95.6 | 59.1 | 73.7 | 100.2 | 46.9 | 68.3 | 81.0 | 30.7 | 50.9 | 91.3 | 50.3 | 66.8 | 94.2 | 59.1 | 73.2 |
| 05 | METALS | 98.6 | 68.2 | 89.8 | 100.7 | 70.6 | 92.0 | 99.7 | 68.9 | 90.7 | 98.6 | 64.7 | 88.8 | 94.9 | 84.0 | 91.7 | 96.5 | 69.9 | 88.8 |
| 06 | WOOD, PLASTICS & COMPOSITES | 81.9 | 42.8 | 60.8 | 104.1 | 37.3 | 68.1 | 92.0 | 55.1 | 72.1 | 83.0 | 43.0 | 61.5 | 89.9 | 58.6 | 73.0 | 98.0 | 76.1 | 86.2 |
| 07 | THERMAL & MOISTURE PROTECTION | 98.7 | 51.2 | 80.2 | 99.0 | 54.1 | 81.5 | 97.9 | 50.0 | 79.2 | 97.7 | 41.3 | 75.7 | 102.0 | 57.9 | 84.8 | 98.1 | 58.2 | 82.6 |
| 08 | OPENINGS | 96.2 | 50.7 | 85.0 | 97.0 | 46.1 | 84.4 | 97.0 | 54.1 | 86.4 | 92.4 | 47.2 | 81.2 | 98.7 | 62.7 | 89.8 | 97.0 | 67.7 | 89.8 |
| 0920 | Plaster & Gypsum Board | 81.9 | 41.9 | 57.2 | 88.0 | 36.3 | 56.1 | 87.0 | 54.5 | 67.0 | 82.6 | 42.1 | 57.6 | 98.4 | 57.7 | 73.3 | 84.5 | 76.1 | 79.3 |
| 0950, 0980 | Ceilings & Acoustic Treatment | 86.5 | 41.9 | 59.1 | 91.7 | 36.3 | 57.7 | 90.8 | 54.5 | 68.5 | 86.5 | 42.1 | 59.3 | 91.4 | 57.7 | 70.7 | 89.2 | 76.1 | 81.1 |
| 0960 | Flooring | 101.1 | 68.2 | 92.2 | 113.4 | 70.2 | 101.7 | 107.8 | 68.2 | 97.0 | 103.0 | 68.2 | 93.5 | 75.8 | 61.7 | 72.0 | 114.6 | 70.2 | 102.5 |
| 0970, 0990 | Wall Finishes & Painting/Coating | 98.2 | 34.4 | 59.9 | 98.2 | 64.4 | 77.9 | 98.2 | 49.3 | 68.8 | 98.2 | 42.7 | 64.9 | 86.8 | 57.9 | 69.4 | 98.2 | 66.1 | 78.9 |
| 09 | FINISHES | 90.3 | 46.9 | 67.6 | 96.3 | 48.6 | 71.3 | 94.3 | 56.1 | 74.3 | 91.3 | 46.5 | 67.8 | 89.2 | 58.2 | 73.0 | 95.7 | 71.4 | 83.0 |
| COVERS | DIVS. 10 - 14, 25, 28, 41, 43, 44 | 100.0 | 60.5 | 91.9 | 100.0 | 70.8 | 94.0 | 100.0 | 62.4 | 92.3 | 100.0 | 45.5 | 88.8 | 100.0 | 56.9 | 91.2 | 100.0 | 75.4 | 95.0 |
| 21, 22, 23 | FIRE SUPPRESSION, PLUMBING & HVAC | 95.9 | 47.1 | 75.9 | 100.1 | 50.1 | 79.6 | 95.9 | 49.2 | 76.7 | 95.9 | 39.6 | 72.8 | 100.3 | 50.1 | 79.7 | 100.0 | 69.2 | 87.4 |
| 26, 27, 3370 | ELECTRICAL, COMMUNICATIONS & UTIL. | 92.0 | 61.5 | 77.0 | 95.4 | 77.5 | 86.6 | 96.6 | 44.5 | 71.0 | 96.7 | 46.0 | 71.8 | 103.6 | 53.7 | 79.1 | 95.7 | 78.8 | 87.4 |
| MF2004 | WEIGHTED AVERAGE | 93.0 | 55.1 | 76.8 | 96.8 | 60.8 | 81.4 | 95.6 | 55.5 | 78.5 | 93.4 | 48.0 | 74.0 | 96.3 | 61.7 | 81.5 | 96.1 | 71.1 | 85.4 |

665

# City Cost Indexes

## ARKANSAS / CALIFORNIA

| | DIVISION | PINE BLUFF 716 | | | RUSSELLVILLE 728 | | | TEXARKANA 718 | | | WEST MEMPHIS 723 | | | ALHAMBRA 917 - 918 | | | ANAHEIM 928 | | |
|---|---|---|---|---|---|---|---|---|---|---|---|---|---|---|---|---|---|---|---|
| | | MAT. | INST. | TOTAL | MAT. | INST. | TOTAL | MAT. | INST. | TOTAL | MAT. | INST. | TOTAL | MAT. | INST. | TOTAL | MAT. | INST. | TOTAL |
| 015433 | CONTRACTOR EQUIPMENT | | 86.6 | 86.6 | | 86.6 | 86.6 | | 87.3 | 87.3 | | 108.5 | 108.5 | | 97.8 | 97.8 | | 102.1 | 102.1 |
| 0241, 31 - 34 | SITE & INFRASTRUCTURE, DEMOLITION | 80.6 | 84.0 | 82.9 | 75.5 | 83.8 | 81.3 | 96.0 | 84.5 | 88.0 | 109.4 | 99.3 | 102.4 | 105.9 | 109.9 | 108.7 | 103.4 | 109.7 | 107.5 |
| 0310 | Concrete Forming & Accessories | 80.9 | 70.8 | 72.2 | 85.1 | 56.2 | 60.2 | 88.1 | 47.5 | 53.1 | 93.5 | 57.6 | 62.6 | 115.6 | 116.4 | 116.3 | 106.0 | 126.2 | 123.4 |
| 0320 | Concrete Reinforcing | 96.9 | 68.9 | 83.4 | 96.3 | 66.1 | 81.7 | 96.4 | 72.3 | 84.8 | 92.5 | 65.7 | 79.6 | 99.6 | 116.2 | 107.6 | 98.4 | 116.3 | 107.0 |
| 0330 | Cast-in-Place Concrete | 81.5 | 68.6 | 76.7 | 81.4 | 50.5 | 69.9 | 88.8 | 47.8 | 73.6 | 88.7 | 62.2 | 78.9 | 104.1 | 119.7 | 109.9 | 101.7 | 122.7 | 109.5 |
| 03 | CONCRETE | 85.4 | 69.8 | 78.2 | 83.1 | 56.6 | 70.8 | 84.6 | 52.9 | 70.0 | 90.8 | 62.0 | 77.5 | 107.3 | 116.5 | 111.6 | 105.3 | 122.1 | 113.0 |
| 04 | MASONRY | 115.5 | 59.1 | 81.8 | 94.9 | 44.8 | 65.0 | 95.6 | 34.4 | 59.0 | 78.3 | 50.3 | 61.6 | 128.2 | 115.1 | 120.3 | 90.4 | 116.6 | 106.0 |
| 05 | METALS | 99.4 | 69.6 | 90.7 | 98.6 | 66.3 | 89.2 | 91.8 | 67.8 | 84.8 | 94.0 | 81.1 | 90.3 | 87.9 | 99.0 | 91.2 | 107.2 | 102.6 | 105.8 |
| 06 | WOOD, PLASTICS & COMPOSITES | 82.5 | 76.1 | 79.1 | 87.8 | 58.4 | 71.9 | 91.7 | 50.8 | 69.7 | 96.2 | 58.6 | 75.9 | 98.5 | 113.7 | 106.7 | 95.7 | 126.3 | 112.1 |
| 07 | THERMAL & MOISTURE PROTECTION | 97.7 | 58.2 | 82.3 | 98.9 | 50.1 | 79.9 | 98.7 | 46.9 | 78.5 | 102.4 | 57.9 | 85.1 | 96.5 | 111.5 | 102.3 | 100.5 | 117.9 | 107.3 |
| 08 | OPENINGS | 92.4 | 67.7 | 86.3 | 96.2 | 56.7 | 86.4 | 97.5 | 54.0 | 86.7 | 98.7 | 60.9 | 89.4 | 93.7 | 112.8 | 98.4 | 104.1 | 121.8 | 108.5 |
| 0920 | Plaster & Gypsum Board | 82.3 | 76.1 | 78.5 | 83.6 | 57.9 | 67.7 | 86.0 | 50.1 | 63.9 | 100.1 | 57.7 | 73.9 | 114.8 | 114.2 | 114.4 | 104.8 | 126.9 | 118.4 |
| 0950, 0980 | Ceilings & Acoustic Treatment | 87.5 | 76.1 | 80.5 | 86.5 | 57.9 | 68.9 | 93.5 | 50.1 | 66.8 | 89.5 | 57.7 | 70.0 | 99.7 | 114.2 | 108.6 | 113.5 | 126.9 | 121.7 |
| 0960 | Flooring | 102.8 | 70.2 | 93.9 | 104.2 | 68.2 | 94.4 | 105.4 | 58.9 | 92.8 | 78.6 | 61.7 | 74.0 | 104.8 | 103.0 | 104.3 | 117.2 | 110.9 | 115.5 |
| 0970, 0990 | Wall Finishes & Painting/Coating | 98.2 | 66.1 | 78.9 | 98.2 | 41.9 | 64.4 | 98.2 | 34.0 | 59.6 | 86.8 | 57.9 | 69.4 | 109.5 | 108.9 | 109.1 | 106.5 | 110.2 | 108.7 |
| 09 | FINISHES | 91.5 | 71.4 | 81.0 | 91.7 | 57.1 | 73.6 | 94.9 | 48.0 | 70.4 | 90.5 | 58.2 | 73.6 | 106.5 | 112.7 | 109.7 | 110.8 | 122.0 | 116.7 |
| COVERS | DIVS. 10 - 14, 25, 28, 41, 43, 44 | 100.0 | 75.4 | 95.0 | 100.0 | 50.0 | 89.7 | 100.0 | 40.5 | 87.8 | 100.0 | 56.9 | 91.2 | 100.0 | 111.7 | 102.4 | 100.0 | 113.6 | 102.8 |
| 21, 22, 23 | FIRE SUPPRESSION, PLUMBING & HVAC | 100.1 | 52.8 | 80.7 | 95.9 | 53.5 | 78.5 | 100.1 | 37.0 | 74.2 | 96.1 | 50.0 | 77.2 | 96.0 | 105.0 | 99.7 | 100.1 | 113.5 | 105.6 |
| 26, 27, 3370 | ELECTRICAL, COMMUNICATIONS & UTIL. | 94.7 | 78.8 | 86.9 | 95.4 | 53.6 | 74.9 | 96.6 | 43.2 | 70.4 | 105.2 | 53.7 | 79.9 | 118.6 | 107.6 | 113.2 | 92.7 | 108.2 | 100.3 |
| MF2004 | WEIGHTED AVERAGE | 96.2 | 67.6 | 84.0 | 94.2 | 57.2 | 78.4 | 95.4 | 49.2 | 75.6 | 95.9 | 61.2 | 81.1 | 101.5 | 109.6 | 105.0 | 101.9 | 114.6 | 107.4 |

## CALIFORNIA

| | DIVISION | BAKERSFIELD 932 - 933 | | | BERKELEY 947 | | | EUREKA 955 | | | FRESNO 936 - 938 | | | INGLEWOOD 903 - 905 | | | LONG BEACH 906 - 908 | | |
|---|---|---|---|---|---|---|---|---|---|---|---|---|---|---|---|---|---|---|---|
| | | MAT. | INST. | TOTAL | MAT. | INST. | TOTAL | MAT. | INST. | TOTAL | MAT. | INST. | TOTAL | MAT. | INST. | TOTAL | MAT. | INST. | TOTAL |
| 015433 | CONTRACTOR EQUIPMENT | | 99.6 | 99.6 | | 102.9 | 102.9 | | 99.2 | 99.2 | | 99.6 | 99.6 | | 96.8 | 96.8 | | 96.8 | 96.8 |
| 0241, 31 - 34 | SITE & INFRASTRUCTURE, DEMOLITION | 109.3 | 106.8 | 107.6 | 136.4 | 103.5 | 113.5 | 119.3 | 103.9 | 108.6 | 109.8 | 106.3 | 107.4 | 94.2 | 105.9 | 102.3 | 102.3 | 105.9 | 104.8 |
| 0310 | Concrete Forming & Accessories | 100.9 | 125.7 | 122.2 | 122.6 | 138.8 | 136.5 | 116.1 | 121.4 | 120.7 | 102.3 | 123.2 | 120.3 | 107.9 | 116.3 | 115.2 | 102.4 | 116.3 | 114.4 |
| 0320 | Concrete Reinforcing | 110.9 | 116.1 | 113.4 | 102.8 | 116.8 | 109.5 | 107.6 | 116.7 | 111.9 | 93.9 | 116.5 | 104.8 | 119.0 | 116.2 | 117.6 | 117.9 | 116.2 | 117.1 |
| 0330 | Cast-in-Place Concrete | 110.9 | 121.6 | 114.8 | 137.3 | 114.0 | 128.7 | 110.4 | 117.5 | 113.0 | 107.2 | 119.3 | 111.7 | 102.0 | 120.5 | 108.8 | 116.3 | 120.5 | 117.8 |
| 03 | CONCRETE | 109.2 | 121.4 | 114.9 | 123.0 | 124.9 | 123.9 | 116.4 | 118.2 | 117.2 | 107.1 | 119.6 | 112.9 | 104.7 | 116.9 | 110.3 | 115.3 | 116.9 | 116.0 |
| 04 | MASONRY | 113.2 | 113.8 | 113.6 | 154.4 | 116.3 | 131.6 | 119.9 | 118.0 | 118.8 | 114.8 | 115.6 | 115.3 | 81.9 | 115.2 | 101.8 | 91.2 | 115.2 | 105.6 |
| 05 | METALS | 102.2 | 101.5 | 102.0 | 107.3 | 105.8 | 106.9 | 106.9 | 101.4 | 105.3 | 107.4 | 102.0 | 105.9 | 100.2 | 100.4 | 100.3 | 100.1 | 100.4 | 100.2 |
| 06 | WOOD, PLASTICS & COMPOSITES | 88.2 | 126.4 | 108.7 | 122.1 | 144.2 | 134.0 | 109.3 | 123.9 | 117.2 | 100.4 | 123.9 | 113.1 | 91.8 | 113.6 | 103.6 | 85.3 | 113.6 | 100.5 |
| 07 | THERMAL & MOISTURE PROTECTION | 97.8 | 110.1 | 102.6 | 110.4 | 123.8 | 115.6 | 104.4 | 110.1 | 106.6 | 94.6 | 111.7 | 101.3 | 101.5 | 113.0 | 106.0 | 101.8 | 113.0 | 106.2 |
| 08 | OPENINGS | 101.7 | 119.1 | 106.0 | 104.6 | 132.6 | 111.5 | 102.9 | 108.9 | 104.4 | 103.5 | 116.8 | 106.7 | 90.5 | 112.8 | 96.0 | 90.5 | 112.8 | 96.0 |
| 0920 | Plaster & Gypsum Board | 100.6 | 126.9 | 116.8 | 113.8 | 144.8 | 132.9 | 108.9 | 124.4 | 118.4 | 100.9 | 124.4 | 115.4 | 101.6 | 114.2 | 109.4 | 98.9 | 114.2 | 108.3 |
| 0950, 0980 | Ceilings & Acoustic Treatment | 115.9 | 126.9 | 122.7 | 118.9 | 144.8 | 134.8 | 119.5 | 124.4 | 122.5 | 118.3 | 124.4 | 122.0 | 110.5 | 114.2 | 112.8 | 110.5 | 114.2 | 112.8 |
| 0960 | Flooring | 116.9 | 90.5 | 109.7 | 122.2 | 119.7 | 121.5 | 121.9 | 114.2 | 119.8 | 124.2 | 137.8 | 127.9 | 109.4 | 103.0 | 107.7 | 105.8 | 103.0 | 105.1 |
| 0970, 0990 | Wall Finishes & Painting/Coating | 107.7 | 102.1 | 104.3 | 108.7 | 133.6 | 123.6 | 107.1 | 55.4 | 76.0 | 126.9 | 104.6 | 113.5 | 97.5 | 108.9 | 104.4 | 97.5 | 108.9 | 104.4 |
| 09 | FINISHES | 112.6 | 117.4 | 115.1 | 119.2 | 136.2 | 128.1 | 117.2 | 114.2 | 115.6 | 116.8 | 124.7 | 120.9 | 106.4 | 112.7 | 109.7 | 105.4 | 112.7 | 109.2 |
| COVERS | DIVS. 10 - 14, 25, 28, 41, 43, 44 | 100.0 | 116.9 | 103.5 | 100.0 | 125.9 | 105.3 | 100.0 | 121.9 | 104.5 | 100.0 | 122.8 | 104.7 | 100.0 | 111.5 | 102.4 | 100.0 | 111.5 | 102.4 |
| 21, 22, 23 | FIRE SUPPRESSION, PLUMBING & HVAC | 100.1 | 102.5 | 101.1 | 96.2 | 130.8 | 110.4 | 96.0 | 108.1 | 101.0 | 100.3 | 112.4 | 105.3 | 96.1 | 104.9 | 99.7 | 96.1 | 104.9 | 99.7 |
| 26, 27, 3370 | ELECTRICAL, COMMUNICATIONS & UTIL. | 91.9 | 100.4 | 96.1 | 103.7 | 133.8 | 118.5 | 101.2 | 92.7 | 97.0 | 91.9 | 97.2 | 94.5 | 106.9 | 107.6 | 107.3 | 106.6 | 107.6 | 107.1 |
| MF2004 | WEIGHTED AVERAGE | 102.6 | 109.7 | 105.6 | 109.9 | 125.0 | 116.3 | 105.8 | 108.8 | 107.1 | 103.9 | 112.3 | 107.5 | 99.0 | 109.5 | 103.5 | 100.8 | 109.5 | 104.5 |

## CALIFORNIA

| | DIVISION | LOS ANGELES 900 - 902 | | | MARYSVILLE 959 | | | MODESTO 953 | | | MOJAVE 935 | | | OAKLAND 946 | | | OXNARD 930 | | |
|---|---|---|---|---|---|---|---|---|---|---|---|---|---|---|---|---|---|---|---|
| | | MAT. | INST. | TOTAL | MAT. | INST. | TOTAL | MAT. | INST. | TOTAL | MAT. | INST. | TOTAL | MAT. | INST. | TOTAL | MAT. | INST. | TOTAL |
| 015433 | CONTRACTOR EQUIPMENT | | 98.7 | 98.7 | | 99.2 | 99.2 | | 99.2 | 99.2 | | 99.6 | 99.6 | | 102.9 | 102.9 | | 98.2 | 98.2 |
| 0241, 31 - 34 | SITE & INFRASTRUCTURE, DEMOLITION | 101.3 | 108.6 | 106.4 | 114.9 | 105.0 | 108.0 | 108.1 | 105.8 | 106.5 | 102.4 | 106.8 | 105.5 | 143.9 | 103.8 | 116.0 | 110.2 | 104.5 | 106.3 |
| 0310 | Concrete Forming & Accessories | 105.1 | 126.0 | 123.1 | 104.8 | 121.9 | 119.5 | 100.4 | 123.1 | 120.0 | 112.9 | 115.1 | 114.8 | 109.6 | 141.8 | 137.4 | 104.9 | 126.1 | 123.2 |
| 0320 | Concrete Reinforcing | 119.0 | 116.4 | 117.7 | 107.6 | 116.1 | 111.7 | 111.5 | 116.2 | 113.7 | 112.9 | 116.0 | 114.4 | 105.1 | 116.8 | 110.8 | 110.9 | 116.0 | 113.4 |
| 0330 | Cast-in-Place Concrete | 111.2 | 120.9 | 114.8 | 123.4 | 117.4 | 121.2 | 110.4 | 119.4 | 113.7 | 92.7 | 121.4 | 103.3 | 130.2 | 124.6 | 128.1 | 108.0 | 121.9 | 113.1 |
| 03 | CONCRETE | 111.6 | 121.4 | 116.1 | 118.7 | 118.3 | 118.5 | 109.0 | 119.6 | 113.9 | 98.7 | 116.7 | 107.0 | 122.5 | 129.9 | 125.9 | 108.0 | 121.7 | 114.3 |
| 04 | MASONRY | 97.5 | 117.5 | 109.5 | 120.9 | 106.4 | 112.2 | 116.2 | 109.1 | 112.0 | 112.8 | 111.6 | 112.1 | 162.8 | 121.5 | 138.1 | 116.8 | 110.9 | 113.3 |
| 05 | METALS | 107.1 | 101.1 | 105.4 | 106.4 | 100.7 | 104.7 | 103.6 | 102.0 | 103.1 | 103.7 | 101.0 | 102.9 | 102.2 | 105.9 | 103.3 | 101.9 | 101.8 | 101.9 |
| 06 | WOOD, PLASTICS & COMPOSITES | 88.1 | 126.0 | 108.5 | 95.6 | 123.9 | 110.9 | 90.8 | 123.9 | 108.6 | 101.1 | 112.4 | 107.2 | 107.2 | 145.5 | 127.9 | 95.1 | 126.4 | 111.9 |
| 07 | THERMAL & MOISTURE PROTECTION | 101.8 | 116.9 | 107.7 | 103.9 | 110.0 | 106.3 | 103.4 | 111.0 | 106.4 | 99.0 | 107.6 | 102.3 | 107.8 | 126.2 | 115.0 | 103.5 | 113.5 | 107.4 |
| 08 | OPENINGS | 96.4 | 121.7 | 102.6 | 102.1 | 117.6 | 105.9 | 100.9 | 118.9 | 105.4 | 97.6 | 109.5 | 100.5 | 104.7 | 133.4 | 111.8 | 100.6 | 121.9 | 105.8 |
| 0920 | Plaster & Gypsum Board | 102.5 | 126.9 | 117.6 | 103.1 | 124.4 | 116.2 | 105.1 | 124.4 | 117.0 | 111.5 | 112.6 | 112.2 | 108.4 | 146.2 | 131.7 | 104.8 | 126.9 | 118.4 |
| 0950, 0980 | Ceilings & Acoustic Treatment | 121.6 | 126.9 | 124.8 | 117.8 | 124.4 | 121.8 | 113.5 | 124.4 | 120.2 | 117.8 | 112.6 | 114.6 | 122.5 | 146.2 | 137.0 | 120.2 | 126.9 | 124.3 |
| 0960 | Flooring | 107.5 | 110.9 | 108.4 | 116.3 | 112.9 | 115.4 | 116.9 | 108.6 | 114.6 | 124.5 | 90.5 | 115.3 | 116.4 | 119.7 | 117.3 | 115.4 | 110.9 | 114.1 |
| 0970, 0990 | Wall Finishes & Painting/Coating | 97.5 | 108.9 | 104.4 | 107.1 | 109.1 | 108.3 | 107.1 | 104.0 | 105.2 | 107.1 | 93.7 | 99.1 | 108.7 | 133.6 | 123.6 | 107.1 | 100.5 | 103.1 |
| 09 | FINISHES | 108.9 | 121.7 | 115.6 | 113.6 | 120.0 | 117.0 | 112.6 | 119.3 | 116.1 | 116.6 | 108.1 | 112.2 | 118.1 | 138.3 | 128.7 | 113.6 | 121.0 | 117.5 |
| COVERS | DIVS. 10 - 14, 25, 28, 41, 43, 44 | 100.0 | 113.0 | 102.7 | 100.0 | 121.9 | 104.5 | 100.0 | 122.9 | 104.7 | 100.0 | 115.2 | 103.1 | 100.0 | 128.0 | 105.7 | 100.0 | 113.8 | 102.8 |
| 21, 22, 23 | FIRE SUPPRESSION, PLUMBING & HVAC | 100.2 | 113.4 | 105.6 | 96.0 | 103.8 | 99.2 | 100.2 | 112.4 | 105.2 | 96.1 | 102.4 | 98.7 | 100.3 | 133.6 | 114.0 | 100.2 | 113.5 | 105.7 |
| 26, 27, 3370 | ELECTRICAL, COMMUNICATIONS & UTIL. | 103.8 | 113.7 | 108.7 | 97.7 | 110.8 | 104.1 | 100.4 | 101.8 | 101.1 | 90.6 | 94.3 | 92.4 | 102.9 | 133.8 | 118.1 | 97.6 | 102.4 | 99.9 |
| MF2004 | WEIGHTED AVERAGE | 103.3 | 115.1 | 108.3 | 105.1 | 110.4 | 107.3 | 104.0 | 111.6 | 107.3 | 100.4 | 106.0 | 102.8 | 110.2 | 127.3 | 117.5 | 103.5 | 112.4 | 107.3 |

| DIVISION | | CALIFORNIA | | | | | | | | | | | | | | | | |
|---|---|---|---|---|---|---|---|---|---|---|---|---|---|---|---|---|---|---|
| | | **PALM SPRINGS** 922 | | | **PALO ALTO** 943 | | | **PASADENA** 910 - 912 | | | **REDDING** 960 | | | **RICHMOND** 948 | | | **RIVERSIDE** 925 | | |
| | | MAT. | INST. | TOTAL | MAT. | INST. | TOTAL | MAT. | INST. | TOTAL | MAT. | INST. | TOTAL | MAT. | INST. | TOTAL | MAT. | INST. | TOTAL |
| 015433 | CONTRACTOR EQUIPMENT | | 100.7 | 100.7 | | 102.9 | 102.9 | | 97.8 | 97.8 | | 99.2 | 99.2 | | 102.9 | 102.9 | | 100.7 | 100.7 |
| 0241, 31 - 34 | SITE & INFRASTRUCTURE, DEMOLITION | 94.3 | 107.4 | 103.4 | 131.3 | 103.8 | 112.2 | 102.3 | 109.9 | 107.6 | 114.6 | 105.1 | 108.0 | 143.5 | 103.8 | 115.9 | 101.6 | 107.4 | 105.6 |
| 0310 | Concrete Forming & Accessories | 102.1 | 116.5 | 114.5 | 107.2 | 140.7 | 136.0 | 103.8 | 116.4 | 114.6 | 104.6 | 120.6 | 118.4 | 125.8 | 141.7 | 139.5 | 106.3 | 126.0 | 123.3 |
| 0320 | Concrete Reinforcing | 113.1 | 116.0 | 114.5 | 102.8 | 116.8 | 109.5 | 100.5 | 116.2 | 108.0 | 107.6 | 116.1 | 111.7 | 102.8 | 116.8 | 109.5 | 109.9 | 116.1 | 112.9 |
| 0330 | Cast-in-Place Concrete | 97.0 | 122.5 | 106.4 | 116.1 | 116.9 | 116.4 | 98.8 | 119.7 | 106.5 | 122.3 | 117.7 | 120.6 | 133.6 | 124.6 | 130.2 | 105.5 | 122.6 | 111.8 |
| 03 | CONCRETE | 100.3 | 117.7 | 108.3 | 110.3 | 126.8 | 117.9 | 102.4 | 116.5 | 108.9 | 117.6 | 117.8 | 117.7 | 124.8 | 129.8 | 127.1 | 106.7 | 122.0 | 113.8 |
| 04 | MASONRY | 88.0 | 111.8 | 102.3 | 127.3 | 121.5 | 123.8 | 109.6 | 115.1 | 112.9 | 120.9 | 106.6 | 112.3 | 154.1 | 121.5 | 134.6 | 89.0 | 111.8 | 102.7 |
| 05 | METALS | 108.0 | 101.7 | 106.1 | 99.8 | 105.8 | 101.6 | 88.0 | 99.0 | 91.2 | 106.7 | 101.0 | 105.1 | 99.9 | 105.8 | 101.6 | 107.5 | 102.0 | 105.9 |
| 06 | WOOD, PLASTICS & COMPOSITES | 90.3 | 113.9 | 103.0 | 104.3 | 144.2 | 125.8 | 84.9 | 113.7 | 100.4 | 95.3 | 122.2 | 109.8 | 126.4 | 145.5 | 136.7 | 95.7 | 126.3 | 112.1 |
| 07 | THERMAL & MOISTURE PROTECTION | 100.6 | 111.5 | 104.8 | 107.3 | 127.4 | 115.2 | 96.2 | 111.5 | 102.2 | 104.0 | 108.4 | 105.7 | 108.0 | 126.2 | 115.1 | 100.8 | 113.5 | 105.7 |
| 08 | OPENINGS | 99.6 | 112.9 | 102.9 | 104.7 | 132.6 | 111.6 | 93.7 | 112.8 | 98.4 | 103.1 | 116.7 | 106.5 | 104.7 | 133.4 | 111.8 | 102.6 | 121.8 | 107.4 |
| 0920 | Plaster & Gypsum Board | 101.3 | 114.2 | 109.3 | 107.1 | 144.8 | 130.3 | 110.4 | 114.2 | 112.7 | 103.5 | 122.6 | 115.3 | 115.2 | 146.2 | 134.3 | 104.4 | 126.9 | 118.3 |
| 0950, 0980 | Ceilings & Acoustic Treatment | 111.8 | 114.2 | 113.3 | 120.6 | 144.8 | 135.4 | 99.7 | 114.2 | 108.6 | 126.2 | 122.6 | 124.0 | 120.6 | 146.2 | 136.3 | 118.5 | 126.9 | 123.6 |
| 0960 | Flooring | 119.0 | 103.0 | 114.6 | 115.4 | 116.7 | 115.7 | 98.6 | 103.0 | 99.8 | 116.1 | 112.9 | 115.3 | 124.3 | 119.7 | 123.0 | 121.3 | 110.9 | 118.4 |
| 0970, 0990 | Wall Finishes & Painting/Coating | 104.4 | 133.2 | 121.7 | 108.7 | 133.6 | 123.6 | 109.5 | 108.9 | 109.1 | 107.1 | 109.1 | 108.3 | 108.7 | 133.6 | 123.6 | 104.4 | 110.2 | 107.9 |
| 09 | FINISHES | 109.6 | 115.6 | 112.8 | 116.3 | 137.0 | 127.1 | 103.7 | 112.7 | 108.4 | 115.5 | 119.1 | 117.4 | 121.1 | 138.3 | 130.1 | 112.7 | 122.0 | 117.6 |
| COVERS | DIVS. 10 - 14, 25, 28, 41, 43, 44 | 100.0 | 112.1 | 102.5 | 100.0 | 127.8 | 105.7 | 100.0 | 111.7 | 102.4 | 100.0 | 121.7 | 104.5 | 100.0 | 127.9 | 105.7 | 100.0 | 113.6 | 102.8 |
| 21, 22, 23 | FIRE SUPPRESSION, PLUMBING & HVAC | 96.0 | 105.0 | 99.7 | 96.2 | 132.6 | 111.1 | 96.0 | 105.0 | 99.7 | 100.2 | 103.9 | 101.7 | 96.2 | 129.7 | 110.0 | 100.1 | 113.4 | 105.6 |
| 26, 27, 3370 | ELECTRICAL, COMMUNICATIONS & UTIL. | 96.4 | 99.1 | 97.7 | 102.8 | 132.7 | 117.5 | 115.4 | 107.6 | 111.5 | 100.7 | 101.0 | 100.8 | 103.3 | 128.0 | 115.4 | 92.8 | 99.1 | 95.9 |
| MF2004 | WEIGHTED AVERAGE | 100.0 | 108.7 | 103.7 | 105.0 | 126.3 | 114.1 | 99.1 | 109.6 | 104.3 | 106.5 | 108.8 | 107.5 | 109.1 | 125.6 | 116.2 | 102.1 | 112.5 | 106.5 |

| DIVISION | | CALIFORNIA | | | | | | | | | | | | | | | | |
|---|---|---|---|---|---|---|---|---|---|---|---|---|---|---|---|---|---|---|
| | | **SACRAMENTO** 942,956 - 958 | | | **SALINAS** 939 | | | **SAN BERNARDINO** 923 - 924 | | | **SAN DIEGO** 919 - 921 | | | **SAN FRANCISCO** 940 - 941 | | | **SAN JOSE** 951 | | |
| | | MAT. | INST. | TOTAL | MAT. | INST. | TOTAL | MAT. | INST. | TOTAL | MAT. | INST. | TOTAL | MAT. | INST. | TOTAL | MAT. | INST. | TOTAL |
| 015433 | CONTRACTOR EQUIPMENT | | 102.3 | 102.3 | | 99.6 | 99.6 | | 100.7 | 100.7 | | 97.9 | 97.9 | | 108.1 | 108.1 | | 100.0 | 100.0 |
| 0241, 31 - 34 | SITE & INFRASTRUCTURE, DEMOLITION | 111.7 | 110.5 | 110.8 | 126.3 | 106.4 | 112.4 | 78.4 | 107.3 | 98.6 | 108.2 | 102.5 | 104.2 | 146.5 | 110.7 | 121.6 | 148.7 | 100.2 | 114.9 |
| 0310 | Concrete Forming & Accessories | 108.1 | 123.7 | 121.5 | 108.5 | 124.3 | 122.1 | 110.2 | 116.3 | 115.5 | 105.1 | 114.5 | 113.2 | 109.3 | 143.3 | 138.6 | 107.1 | 142.2 | 137.3 |
| 0320 | Concrete Reinforcing | 97.3 | 116.6 | 106.6 | 111.5 | 116.6 | 113.9 | 109.9 | 116.0 | 112.8 | 97.3 | 116.1 | 106.4 | 119.7 | 117.8 | 118.8 | 98.0 | 117.3 | 107.3 |
| 0330 | Cast-in-Place Concrete | 110.0 | 120.2 | 113.8 | 106.7 | 118.3 | 111.0 | 72.8 | 122.4 | 91.1 | 108.3 | 105.9 | 107.4 | 133.5 | 126.6 | 130.9 | 128.4 | 124.5 | 126.9 |
| 03 | CONCRETE | 111.1 | 120.1 | 115.2 | 117.6 | 119.8 | 118.6 | 79.6 | 117.6 | 97.1 | 108.4 | 111.1 | 109.6 | 126.4 | 131.4 | 128.7 | 116.3 | 130.2 | 122.7 |
| 04 | MASONRY | 129.6 | 115.6 | 121.2 | 112.4 | 113.1 | 112.8 | 95.6 | 111.8 | 105.3 | 101.1 | 111.4 | 107.2 | 163.4 | 134.7 | 146.3 | 152.0 | 128.2 | 137.7 |
| 05 | METALS | 97.8 | 102.1 | 99.1 | 106.6 | 103.0 | 105.5 | 107.4 | 101.5 | 105.7 | 104.5 | 101.3 | 103.6 | 108.1 | 109.6 | 108.5 | 101.4 | 108.9 | 103.6 |
| 06 | WOOD, PLASTICS & COMPOSITES | 101.3 | 124.1 | 113.6 | 100.1 | 126.0 | 114.0 | 99.9 | 113.9 | 107.4 | 98.3 | 112.4 | 105.9 | 107.2 | 145.8 | 128.0 | 102.6 | 145.3 | 125.6 |
| 07 | THERMAL & MOISTURE PROTECTION | 111.6 | 114.9 | 112.9 | 100.0 | 116.2 | 106.3 | 99.7 | 112.6 | 104.7 | 104.2 | 106.2 | 105.0 | 110.5 | 135.9 | 120.4 | 100.0 | 133.2 | 112.9 |
| 08 | OPENINGS | 117.9 | 119.0 | 118.2 | 101.9 | 122.8 | 107.1 | 99.6 | 112.9 | 102.9 | 101.4 | 111.8 | 104.0 | 109.1 | 136.0 | 115.7 | 93.7 | 134.5 | 103.7 |
| 0920 | Plaster & Gypsum Board | 104.0 | 124.4 | 116.6 | 105.8 | 126.5 | 118.5 | 105.8 | 114.2 | 111.0 | 115.4 | 112.5 | 113.6 | 110.6 | 146.2 | 132.6 | 100.7 | 146.2 | 128.8 |
| 0950, 0980 | Ceilings & Acoustic Treatment | 120.6 | 124.4 | 122.9 | 117.8 | 126.5 | 123.1 | 113.5 | 114.2 | 113.9 | 106.6 | 112.5 | 110.2 | 130.0 | 146.2 | 139.9 | 110.0 | 146.2 | 132.2 |
| 0960 | Flooring | 115.5 | 117.8 | 116.1 | 117.8 | 119.7 | 118.3 | 123.7 | 97.0 | 116.4 | 107.5 | 108.0 | 107.6 | 116.4 | 124.8 | 118.7 | 108.8 | 124.8 | 113.2 |
| 0970, 0990 | Wall Finishes & Painting/Coating | 105.5 | 119.1 | 113.7 | 108.1 | 139.7 | 127.1 | 104.4 | 106.4 | 105.6 | 106.5 | 108.9 | 107.9 | 108.7 | 157.2 | 137.8 | 107.9 | 139.7 | 127.0 |
| 09 | FINISHES | 114.6 | 123.0 | 119.0 | 115.8 | 125.9 | 121.1 | 110.8 | 111.4 | 111.1 | 109.5 | 112.7 | 111.2 | 120.3 | 142.4 | 131.9 | 110.5 | 139.9 | 125.9 |
| COVERS | DIVS. 10 - 14, 25, 28, 41, 43, 44 | 100.0 | 123.4 | 104.8 | 100.0 | 122.3 | 104.6 | 100.0 | 103.4 | 100.7 | 100.0 | 111.4 | 102.3 | 100.0 | 128.6 | 105.9 | 100.0 | 127.4 | 105.6 |
| 21, 22, 23 | FIRE SUPPRESSION, PLUMBING & HVAC | 100.1 | 110.2 | 104.3 | 96.1 | 111.3 | 102.3 | 96.0 | 105.0 | 99.7 | 100.2 | 112.2 | 105.1 | 100.4 | 150.3 | 120.9 | 100.2 | 139.3 | 116.3 |
| 26, 27, 3370 | ELECTRICAL, COMMUNICATIONS & UTIL. | 97.8 | 106.8 | 102.2 | 91.9 | 116.3 | 103.9 | 96.4 | 101.7 | 99.0 | 98.9 | 102.7 | 100.8 | 102.9 | 157.8 | 129.9 | 104.3 | 139.6 | 121.6 |
| MF2004 | WEIGHTED AVERAGE | 106.0 | 113.6 | 109.2 | 104.3 | 115.1 | 108.9 | 97.6 | 108.2 | 102.1 | 103.0 | 108.7 | 105.4 | 112.4 | 137.5 | 123.2 | 107.0 | 130.4 | 117.0 |

| DIVISION | | CALIFORNIA | | | | | | | | | | | | | | | | |
|---|---|---|---|---|---|---|---|---|---|---|---|---|---|---|---|---|---|---|
| | | **SAN LUIS OBISPO** 934 | | | **SAN MATEO** 944 | | | **SAN RAFAEL** 949 | | | **SANTA ANA** 926 - 927 | | | **SANTA BARBARA** 931 | | | **SANTA CRUZ** 950 | | |
| | | MAT. | INST. | TOTAL | MAT. | INST. | TOTAL | MAT. | INST. | TOTAL | MAT. | INST. | TOTAL | MAT. | INST. | TOTAL | MAT. | INST. | TOTAL |
| 015433 | CONTRACTOR EQUIPMENT | | 99.6 | 99.6 | | 102.9 | 102.9 | | 102.9 | 102.9 | | 100.7 | 100.7 | | 99.6 | 99.6 | | 100.0 | 100.0 |
| 0241, 31 - 34 | SITE & INFRASTRUCTURE, DEMOLITION | 116.9 | 106.8 | 109.8 | 140.3 | 103.8 | 114.9 | 127.1 | 110.0 | 115.2 | 92.3 | 107.3 | 102.8 | 110.1 | 106.8 | 107.8 | 148.0 | 99.8 | 114.4 |
| 0310 | Concrete Forming & Accessories | 114.9 | 116.3 | 116.1 | 114.3 | 141.9 | 138.1 | 119.9 | 141.5 | 138.5 | 110.9 | 116.4 | 115.7 | 105.6 | 125.5 | 123.1 | 107.1 | 124.5 | 122.1 |
| 0320 | Concrete Reinforcing | 112.9 | 115.9 | 114.4 | 102.8 | 117.0 | 109.6 | 103.4 | 117.0 | 109.9 | 113.6 | 116.0 | 114.8 | 110.9 | 116.0 | 113.4 | 121.4 | 116.6 | 119.1 |
| 0330 | Cast-in-Place Concrete | 114.7 | 121.4 | 117.2 | 129.3 | 124.7 | 127.6 | 150.6 | 123.2 | 140.5 | 93.0 | 122.4 | 103.9 | 107.6 | 121.7 | 112.8 | 127.5 | 120.3 | 124.8 |
| 03 | CONCRETE | 116.2 | 117.2 | 116.7 | 120.7 | 130.0 | 125.0 | 145.2 | 129.1 | 137.7 | 97.7 | 117.6 | 106.9 | 107.9 | 121.6 | 114.2 | 119.5 | 120.8 | 120.1 |
| 04 | MASONRY | 114.6 | 111.4 | 112.7 | 153.7 | 124.7 | 136.3 | 126.1 | 124.6 | 125.2 | 84.1 | 112.2 | 100.9 | 113.0 | 111.4 | 112.0 | 156.5 | 113.2 | 130.6 |
| 05 | METALS | 104.4 | 101.0 | 103.4 | 99.7 | 106.2 | 101.6 | 101.0 | 102.1 | 101.3 | 107.5 | 101.6 | 105.8 | 102.4 | 101.6 | 102.1 | 109.2 | 107.1 | 108.6 |
| 06 | WOOD, PLASTICS & COMPOSITES | 103.4 | 114.6 | 109.1 | 113.0 | 145.5 | 130.5 | 112.2 | 145.3 | 130.0 | 101.6 | 113.9 | 108.2 | 95.1 | 126.4 | 111.9 | 102.6 | 126.1 | 115.2 |
| 07 | THERMAL & MOISTURE PROTECTION | 99.9 | 108.4 | 103.2 | 107.8 | 128.8 | 116.0 | 113.2 | 125.3 | 117.9 | 100.9 | 111.6 | 105.1 | 99.3 | 110.5 | 103.7 | 99.8 | 118.2 | 106.9 |
| 08 | OPENINGS | 99.8 | 110.3 | 102.4 | 104.7 | 133.4 | 111.7 | 115.1 | 133.2 | 119.5 | 98.8 | 112.9 | 102.3 | 101.7 | 121.9 | 106.6 | 94.9 | 122.9 | 101.8 |
| 0920 | Plaster & Gypsum Board | 112.5 | 114.2 | 113.5 | 110.8 | 146.2 | 132.6 | 113.1 | 146.2 | 133.5 | 106.1 | 114.2 | 111.1 | 104.8 | 126.9 | 118.4 | 112.4 | 126.5 | 121.1 |
| 0950, 0980 | Ceilings & Acoustic Treatment | 117.8 | 114.2 | 115.6 | 120.6 | 146.2 | 136.3 | 128.3 | 146.2 | 139.3 | 113.5 | 114.2 | 113.9 | 120.2 | 126.9 | 124.3 | 115.2 | 126.5 | 122.1 |
| 0960 | Flooring | 125.8 | 90.5 | 116.2 | 118.5 | 119.7 | 118.9 | 129.8 | 116.7 | 126.3 | 124.4 | 103.0 | 118.5 | 116.9 | 90.5 | 109.7 | 113.6 | 119.7 | 115.2 |
| 0970, 0990 | Wall Finishes & Painting/Coating | 107.1 | 100.5 | 103.1 | 108.7 | 133.6 | 123.6 | 104.8 | 133.6 | 122.1 | 104.4 | 106.4 | 105.6 | 107.1 | 100.5 | 103.1 | 108.3 | 139.7 | 127.2 |
| 09 | FINISHES | 118.2 | 109.4 | 113.6 | 118.5 | 138.3 | 128.9 | 121.5 | 137.6 | 129.9 | 112.3 | 112.6 | 112.5 | 114.3 | 117.4 | 115.9 | 115.1 | 126.0 | 120.8 |
| COVERS | DIVS. 10 - 14, 25, 28, 41, 43, 44 | 100.0 | 115.4 | 102.4 | 100.0 | 128.0 | 105.7 | 100.0 | 127.2 | 105.6 | 100.0 | 112.1 | 102.5 | 100.0 | 113.8 | 102.8 | 100.0 | 122.6 | 104.6 |
| 21, 22, 23 | FIRE SUPPRESSION, PLUMBING & HVAC | 96.1 | 105.0 | 99.8 | 96.2 | 132.9 | 111.3 | 96.1 | 144.4 | 116.0 | 96.0 | 105.0 | 99.7 | 100.2 | 113.4 | 105.7 | 100.2 | 111.3 | 104.8 |
| 26, 27, 3370 | ELECTRICAL, COMMUNICATIONS & UTIL. | 90.6 | 95.6 | 93.1 | 102.8 | 136.1 | 119.1 | 98.0 | 110.7 | 104.3 | 96.4 | 101.2 | 98.7 | 89.5 | 103.2 | 96.3 | 103.3 | 116.3 | 109.7 |
| MF2004 | WEIGHTED AVERAGE | 103.5 | 107.1 | 105.0 | 108.1 | 127.9 | 116.6 | 110.3 | 126.5 | 117.3 | 99.6 | 108.6 | 103.5 | 102.5 | 112.2 | 106.7 | 109.2 | 115.2 | 111.8 |

# City Cost Indexes

## CALIFORNIA / COLORADO

| DIVISION | | SANTA ROSA 954 MAT. | INST. | TOTAL | STOCKTON 952 MAT. | INST. | TOTAL | SUSANVILLE 961 MAT. | INST. | TOTAL | VALLEJO 945 MAT. | INST. | TOTAL | VAN NUYS 913-916 MAT. | INST. | TOTAL | ALAMOSA 811 MAT. | INST. | TOTAL |
|---|---|---|---|---|---|---|---|---|---|---|---|---|---|---|---|---|---|---|---|
| 015433 | CONTRACTOR EQUIPMENT | | 99.9 | 99.9 | | 99.2 | 99.2 | | 99.2 | 99.2 | | 99.2 | 99.2 | | 102.9 | 102.9 | | 96.3 | 96.3 |
| 0241, 31-34 | SITE & INFRASTRUCTURE, DEMOLITION | 108.5 | 105.9 | 106.7 | 107.7 | 105.8 | 106.4 | 122.9 | 105.1 | 110.5 | 108.7 | 140.0 | 135.7 | 122.2 | 109.9 | 113.6 | 127.5 | 92.9 | 103.4 |
| 0310 | Concrete Forming & Accessories | 103.3 | 140.2 | 135.1 | 105.2 | 123.2 | 120.7 | 106.1 | 121.9 | 119.7 | 110.7 | 116.4 | 115.6 | 100.5 | 116.2 | 108.0 | 102.7 | 74.2 | 78.2 |
| 0320 | Concrete Reinforcing | 108.5 | 117.5 | 112.9 | 111.5 | 116.2 | 113.7 | 107.6 | 116.1 | 111.7 | 104.7 | 117.0 | 110.6 | 100.5 | 116.2 | 108.0 | 109.1 | 81.7 | 95.9 |
| 0330 | Cast-in-Place Concrete | 121.2 | 120.9 | 121.1 | 107.5 | 119.4 | 111.9 | 111.3 | 117.7 | 113.6 | 119.8 | 121.3 | 120.4 | 104.2 | 119.7 | 109.9 | 106.6 | 81.9 | 97.5 |
| 03 | CONCRETE | 118.3 | 128.0 | 122.8 | 107.9 | 119.6 | 113.3 | 118.3 | 118.4 | 118.4 | 117.2 | 127.8 | 122.1 | 116.7 | 116.5 | 116.6 | 120.2 | 78.5 | 101.0 |
| 04 | MASONRY | 117.8 | 130.7 | 125.5 | 116.4 | 109.1 | 112.0 | 119.9 | 106.6 | 111.9 | 91.8 | 120.7 | 109.1 | 128.2 | 115.1 | 120.3 | 132.5 | 76.5 | 99.0 |
| 05 | METALS | 107.8 | 105.4 | 107.1 | 103.8 | 102.0 | 103.2 | 105.8 | 101.1 | 104.4 | 101.0 | 103.4 | 101.7 | 87.1 | 99.0 | 90.6 | 97.9 | 83.2 | 93.6 |
| 06 | WOOD, PLASTICS & COMPOSITES | 91.6 | 145.1 | 120.4 | 97.0 | 123.9 | 111.5 | 97.4 | 123.9 | 111.7 | 99.3 | 145.3 | 124.1 | 93.2 | 113.7 | 104.2 | 98.8 | 76.2 | 86.6 |
| 07 | THERMAL & MOISTURE PROTECTION | 101.4 | 126.6 | 111.2 | 103.5 | 110.9 | 106.4 | 104.7 | 105.8 | 105.1 | 110.6 | 123.6 | 115.7 | 97.2 | 111.5 | 102.8 | 101.5 | 80.7 | 93.4 |
| 08 | OPENINGS | 100.6 | 135.6 | 109.2 | 100.9 | 118.9 | 105.4 | 103.0 | 117.6 | 106.6 | 117.4 | 135.8 | 122.0 | 93.5 | 112.8 | 98.3 | 92.4 | 82.2 | 89.9 |
| 0920 | Plaster & Gypsum Board | 102.1 | 146.2 | 129.3 | 105.1 | 124.4 | 117.0 | 104.1 | 124.4 | 116.6 | 108.3 | 146.2 | 131.7 | 113.2 | 114.2 | 113.8 | 80.1 | 75.3 | 77.1 |
| 0950, 0980 | Ceilings & Acoustic Treatment | 113.5 | 146.2 | 133.6 | 120.2 | 124.4 | 122.8 | 117.8 | 124.4 | 121.8 | 130.2 | 146.2 | 140.0 | 97.2 | 114.2 | 107.6 | 105.6 | 75.3 | 87.0 |
| 0960 | Flooring | 119.7 | 124.8 | 121.1 | 116.9 | 108.6 | 114.6 | 116.9 | 112.9 | 115.8 | 124.4 | 124.8 | 124.5 | 102.2 | 103.0 | 102.4 | 116.3 | 63.3 | 101.9 |
| 0970, 0990 | Wall Finishes & Painting/Coating | 104.4 | 133.6 | 121.9 | 107.1 | 109.5 | 108.5 | 107.1 | 123.2 | 116.7 | 105.6 | 133.6 | 122.4 | 109.5 | 108.9 | 109.1 | 110.0 | 28.3 | 60.9 |
| 09 | FINISHES | 111.3 | 138.2 | 125.4 | 114.1 | 120.0 | 117.2 | 114.8 | 121.6 | 118.4 | 118.0 | 138.3 | 128.6 | 105.9 | 112.7 | 109.5 | 105.9 | 67.1 | 85.6 |
| COVERS | DIVS. 10-14, 25, 28, 41, 43, 44 | 100.0 | 125.2 | 105.2 | 100.0 | 122.9 | 104.7 | 100.0 | 121.9 | 104.5 | 100.0 | 125.7 | 105.3 | 100.0 | 111.7 | 102.4 | 100.0 | 88.1 | 97.6 |
| 21, 22, 23 | FIRE SUPPRESSION, PLUMBING & HVAC | 96.0 | 142.0 | 114.9 | 100.2 | 105.4 | 102.3 | 96.1 | 103.9 | 99.3 | 100.3 | 119.8 | 108.3 | 96.0 | 105.0 | 99.7 | 95.8 | 70.6 | 85.5 |
| 26, 27, 3370 | ELECTRICAL, COMMUNICATIONS & UTIL. | 96.7 | 110.7 | 103.6 | 100.4 | 115.0 | 107.5 | 101.1 | 101.0 | 101.0 | 94.1 | 119.9 | 106.8 | 115.4 | 107.6 | 111.5 | 93.9 | 79.8 | 87.0 |
| MF2004 | WEIGHTED AVERAGE | 104.3 | 126.6 | 113.8 | 104.1 | 112.1 | 107.5 | 105.7 | 109.2 | 107.2 | 105.1 | 122.4 | 112.5 | 102.5 | 109.6 | 105.5 | 102.7 | 77.5 | 91.9 |

## COLORADO

| DIVISION | | BOULDER 803 MAT. | INST. | TOTAL | COLORADO SPRINGS 808-809 MAT. | INST. | TOTAL | DENVER 800-802 MAT. | INST. | TOTAL | DURANGO 813 MAT. | INST. | TOTAL | FORT COLLINS 805 MAT. | INST. | TOTAL | FORT MORGAN 807 MAT. | INST. | TOTAL |
|---|---|---|---|---|---|---|---|---|---|---|---|---|---|---|---|---|---|---|---|
| 015433 | CONTRACTOR EQUIPMENT | | 96.0 | 96.0 | | 94.4 | 94.4 | | 99.5 | 99.5 | | 96.3 | 96.3 | | 96.0 | 96.0 | | 96.0 | 96.0 |
| 0241, 31-34 | SITE & INFRASTRUCTURE, DEMOLITION | 85.4 | 97.6 | 93.9 | 87.0 | 94.8 | 92.4 | 86.2 | 104.0 | 98.6 | 121.3 | 92.9 | 101.5 | 96.2 | 97.3 | 97.0 | 87.9 | 97.4 | 94.5 |
| 0310 | Concrete Forming & Accessories | 102.3 | 79.4 | 82.5 | 92.4 | 84.0 | 85.1 | 99.2 | 80.3 | 82.9 | 108.7 | 74.4 | 79.1 | 99.8 | 77.6 | 80.6 | 102.7 | 78.8 | 82.1 |
| 0320 | Concrete Reinforcing | 103.6 | 81.9 | 93.1 | 102.8 | 82.6 | 93.0 | 102.8 | 82.6 | 93.0 | 109.1 | 81.7 | 95.9 | 103.7 | 80.6 | 92.6 | 103.8 | 81.7 | 93.2 |
| 0330 | Cast-in-Place Concrete | 98.0 | 81.7 | 92.0 | 100.7 | 82.4 | 93.9 | 95.3 | 83.0 | 90.7 | 122.6 | 82.0 | 107.6 | 110.6 | 79.3 | 99.1 | 96.1 | 80.7 | 90.4 |
| 03 | CONCRETE | 102.6 | 80.9 | 92.6 | 106.0 | 83.3 | 95.5 | 100.4 | 81.9 | 91.8 | 123.3 | 78.6 | 102.6 | 113.1 | 78.9 | 97.3 | 101.2 | 80.1 | 91.5 |
| 04 | MASONRY | 96.5 | 78.0 | 85.4 | 101.2 | 78.7 | 87.7 | 103.2 | 80.6 | 89.7 | 120.0 | 76.5 | 94.0 | 111.6 | 54.6 | 77.5 | 112.7 | 76.7 | 91.2 |
| 05 | METALS | 96.7 | 86.1 | 93.6 | 99.6 | 86.6 | 95.8 | 102.0 | 86.5 | 97.5 | 97.9 | 83.3 | 93.6 | 97.8 | 81.4 | 93.0 | 96.4 | 83.1 | 92.5 |
| 06 | WOOD, PLASTICS & COMPOSITES | 102.8 | 81.9 | 91.5 | 93.0 | 88.0 | 90.3 | 101.2 | 81.9 | 90.8 | 106.8 | 76.2 | 90.3 | 101.0 | 81.9 | 90.7 | 103.2 | 81.9 | 91.7 |
| 07 | THERMAL & MOISTURE PROTECTION | 99.4 | 81.6 | 92.4 | 100.1 | 82.9 | 93.4 | 99.0 | 77.9 | 90.8 | 101.3 | 80.7 | 93.3 | 99.8 | 66.4 | 86.8 | 99.3 | 76.8 | 90.6 |
| 08 | OPENINGS | 94.6 | 85.2 | 92.3 | 98.7 | 88.7 | 96.3 | 98.7 | 85.4 | 95.4 | 99.3 | 82.2 | 95.1 | 94.6 | 85.2 | 92.3 | 94.6 | 85.2 | 92.3 |
| 0920 | Plaster & Gypsum Board | 97.8 | 81.6 | 87.8 | 83.6 | 87.8 | 86.2 | 95.8 | 81.6 | 87.1 | 88.2 | 75.3 | 80.2 | 94.4 | 81.6 | 86.5 | 98.8 | 81.6 | 88.2 |
| 0950, 0980 | Ceilings & Acoustic Treatment | 99.7 | 81.6 | 88.6 | 106.6 | 87.8 | 95.0 | 105.7 | 81.6 | 90.9 | 105.6 | 75.3 | 87.0 | 99.7 | 81.6 | 88.6 | 99.7 | 81.6 | 88.6 |
| 0960 | Flooring | 116.2 | 89.4 | 108.9 | 106.8 | 78.8 | 99.2 | 112.0 | 89.4 | 105.9 | 121.7 | 63.3 | 105.8 | 111.9 | 63.3 | 98.7 | 116.7 | 63.3 | 102.2 |
| 0970, 0990 | Wall Finishes & Painting/Coating | 106.5 | 79.7 | 90.4 | 106.2 | 48.5 | 71.6 | 106.5 | 79.7 | 90.4 | 110.0 | 28.3 | 60.9 | 106.5 | 48.2 | 71.4 | 106.5 | 64.1 | 81.0 |
| 09 | FINISHES | 102.7 | 80.7 | 91.1 | 99.3 | 79.6 | 89.0 | 102.4 | 82.0 | 91.7 | 108.1 | 67.1 | 86.6 | 101.3 | 71.9 | 85.9 | 102.9 | 74.3 | 88.0 |
| COVERS | DIVS. 10-14, 25, 28, 41, 43, 44 | 100.0 | 87.6 | 97.5 | 100.0 | 88.8 | 97.7 | 100.0 | 88.3 | 97.6 | 100.0 | 88.1 | 97.6 | 100.0 | 86.7 | 97.3 | 100.0 | 87.6 | 97.5 |
| 21, 22, 23 | FIRE SUPPRESSION, PLUMBING & HVAC | 95.8 | 83.9 | 90.9 | 100.1 | 78.3 | 91.2 | 100.0 | 84.9 | 93.8 | 95.8 | 73.2 | 86.5 | 100.0 | 82.5 | 92.8 | 95.8 | 83.8 | 90.9 |
| 26, 27, 3370 | ELECTRICAL, COMMUNICATIONS & UTIL. | 95.8 | 87.8 | 91.9 | 99.3 | 85.7 | 92.6 | 101.0 | 87.8 | 94.5 | 93.3 | 81.0 | 87.2 | 95.7 | 87.8 | 91.9 | 96.1 | 87.8 | 92.0 |
| MF2004 | WEIGHTED AVERAGE | 97.5 | 84.5 | 91.9 | 100.1 | 83.4 | 92.9 | 100.3 | 85.8 | 94.1 | 103.1 | 78.2 | 92.4 | 100.8 | 79.5 | 91.7 | 98.3 | 83.0 | 91.7 |

## COLORADO

| DIVISION | | GLENWOOD SPRINGS 816 MAT. | INST. | TOTAL | GOLDEN 804 MAT. | INST. | TOTAL | GRAND JUNCTION 815 MAT. | INST. | TOTAL | GREELEY 806 MAT. | INST. | TOTAL | MONTROSE 814 MAT. | INST. | TOTAL | PUEBLO 810 MAT. | INST. | TOTAL |
|---|---|---|---|---|---|---|---|---|---|---|---|---|---|---|---|---|---|---|---|
| 015433 | CONTRACTOR EQUIPMENT | | 99.4 | 99.4 | | 96.0 | 96.0 | | 99.4 | 99.4 | | 96.0 | 96.0 | | 97.8 | 97.8 | | 96.3 | 96.3 |
| 0241, 31-34 | SITE & INFRASTRUCTURE, DEMOLITION | 136.3 | 100.6 | 111.5 | 96.3 | 97.7 | 97.3 | 120.6 | 100.2 | 106.4 | 84.5 | 96.0 | 92.5 | 130.0 | 96.4 | 106.6 | 112.2 | 94.5 | 99.9 |
| 0310 | Concrete Forming & Accessories | 99.7 | 78.6 | 81.5 | 95.1 | 78.7 | 81.0 | 107.6 | 77.9 | 82.0 | 97.6 | 48.6 | 55.4 | 99.2 | 78.4 | 81.3 | 104.8 | 84.2 | 87.0 |
| 0320 | Concrete Reinforcing | 108.0 | 81.7 | 95.3 | 103.8 | 81.7 | 93.2 | 108.3 | 80.5 | 94.9 | 103.6 | 80.0 | 92.3 | 107.9 | 81.6 | 95.2 | 104.4 | 82.5 | 93.8 |
| 0330 | Cast-in-Place Concrete | 106.5 | 81.2 | 97.1 | 96.2 | 80.8 | 90.5 | 118.0 | 80.3 | 104.0 | 92.4 | 55.5 | 78.8 | 106.6 | 81.1 | 97.1 | 105.7 | 83.6 | 97.5 |
| 03 | CONCRETE | 125.4 | 80.2 | 104.5 | 111.3 | 80.1 | 96.9 | 119.4 | 79.4 | 100.9 | 97.9 | 57.8 | 79.4 | 116.3 | 80.1 | 99.6 | 108.8 | 83.8 | 97.3 |
| 04 | MASONRY | 108.0 | 76.7 | 89.3 | 116.0 | 77.7 | 93.1 | 141.5 | 56.8 | 90.8 | 106.2 | 36.2 | 64.3 | 111.9 | 76.5 | 90.7 | 104.4 | 76.9 | 88.0 |
| 05 | METALS | 97.6 | 83.7 | 93.5 | 96.6 | 83.4 | 92.7 | 99.1 | 80.5 | 93.7 | 97.8 | 79.7 | 92.5 | 96.7 | 82.7 | 92.6 | 100.6 | 87.5 | 96.8 |
| 06 | WOOD, PLASTICS & COMPOSITES | 93.8 | 82.0 | 87.5 | 95.9 | 81.9 | 88.3 | 104.1 | 82.0 | 92.2 | 98.4 | 48.4 | 71.4 | 94.5 | 82.2 | 87.9 | 101.2 | 88.4 | 94.3 |
| 07 | THERMAL & MOISTURE PROTECTION | 101.2 | 76.1 | 91.5 | 100.4 | 74.6 | 90.3 | 100.1 | 62.9 | 85.6 | 99.2 | 55.5 | 82.2 | 101.4 | 81.3 | 93.6 | 99.7 | 82.2 | 92.9 |
| 08 | OPENINGS | 98.5 | 85.3 | 95.3 | 94.6 | 85.2 | 92.3 | 99.2 | 85.3 | 95.8 | 94.6 | 67.1 | 87.8 | 99.5 | 85.4 | 96.0 | 94.1 | 88.9 | 92.8 |
| 0920 | Plaster & Gypsum Board | 105.4 | 81.6 | 90.7 | 92.8 | 81.6 | 85.9 | 112.8 | 81.6 | 93.6 | 93.4 | 47.3 | 64.9 | 78.1 | 81.6 | 80.3 | 83.6 | 87.8 | 86.2 |
| 0950, 0980 | Ceilings & Acoustic Treatment | 103.9 | 81.6 | 90.2 | 99.7 | 81.6 | 88.6 | 103.9 | 81.6 | 90.2 | 99.7 | 47.3 | 67.5 | 105.6 | 81.6 | 90.9 | 115.0 | 87.8 | 98.3 |
| 0960 | Flooring | 115.3 | 58.3 | 99.8 | 109.3 | 63.3 | 96.8 | 121.1 | 63.3 | 105.4 | 110.5 | 63.3 | 97.7 | 118.8 | 52.4 | 100.8 | 117.3 | 89.4 | 109.7 |
| 0970, 0990 | Wall Finishes & Painting/Coating | 110.0 | 64.1 | 82.4 | 106.5 | 79.7 | 90.4 | 110.0 | 79.7 | 91.8 | 106.5 | 30.0 | 60.5 | 110.0 | 28.3 | 60.9 | 110.0 | 45.0 | 70.9 |
| 09 | FINISHES | 109.5 | 73.6 | 90.7 | 100.9 | 76.1 | 87.9 | 110.7 | 76.2 | 92.7 | 100.1 | 47.9 | 72.8 | 106.3 | 68.3 | 86.4 | 107.3 | 81.4 | 93.8 |
| COVERS | DIVS. 10-14, 25, 28, 41, 43, 44 | 100.0 | 88.0 | 97.5 | 100.0 | 87.6 | 97.5 | 100.0 | 87.9 | 97.5 | 100.0 | 79.2 | 95.7 | 100.0 | 88.3 | 97.6 | 100.0 | 89.6 | 97.9 |
| 21, 22, 23 | FIRE SUPPRESSION, PLUMBING & HVAC | 95.8 | 73.0 | 86.4 | 95.8 | 83.5 | 90.8 | 99.9 | 68.0 | 86.8 | 100.0 | 77.3 | 90.7 | 95.8 | 73.0 | 86.4 | 99.9 | 70.9 | 88.0 |
| 26, 27, 3370 | ELECTRICAL, COMMUNICATIONS & UTIL. | 90.6 | 81.0 | 85.9 | 96.1 | 87.8 | 92.0 | 92.9 | 63.5 | 78.5 | 95.7 | 87.8 | 91.8 | 92.9 | 63.5 | 78.5 | 93.9 | 79.9 | 87.0 |
| MF2004 | WEIGHTED AVERAGE | 102.7 | 80.0 | 93.0 | 99.7 | 83.2 | 92.7 | 104.9 | 74.0 | 91.7 | 98.3 | 68.7 | 85.6 | 101.6 | 76.5 | 90.9 | 101.1 | 81.2 | 92.6 |

# City Cost Indexes

| | | COLORADO | | | CONNECTICUT | | | | | | | | | | | | | | |
|---|---|---|---|---|---|---|---|---|---|---|---|---|---|---|---|---|---|---|---|
| | | SALIDA | | | BRIDGEPORT | | | BRISTOL | | | HARTFORD | | | MERIDEN | | | NEW BRITAIN | | |
| DIVISION | | 812 | | | 066 | | | 060 | | | 061 | | | 064 | | | 060 | | |
| | | MAT. | INST. | TOTAL | MAT. | INST. | TOTAL | MAT. | INST. | TOTAL | MAT. | INST. | TOTAL | MAT. | INST. | TOTAL | MAT. | INST. | TOTAL |
| 015433 | CONTRACTOR EQUIPMENT | | 97.8 | 97.8 | | 100.6 | 100.6 | | 100.6 | 100.6 | | 100.6 | 100.6 | | 101.1 | 101.1 | | 100.6 | 100.6 |
| 0241, 31 - 34 | SITE & INFRASTRUCTURE, DEMOLITION | 121.0 | 96.7 | 104.1 | 100.1 | 104.7 | 103.3 | 99.2 | 104.7 | 103.0 | 96.2 | 104.7 | 102.1 | 97.5 | 105.5 | 103.1 | 99.4 | 104.7 | 103.1 |
| 0310 | Concrete Forming & Accessories | 107.4 | 78.5 | 82.5 | 98.2 | 126.5 | 122.6 | 98.2 | 126.3 | 122.4 | 96.3 | 126.3 | 122.1 | 98.0 | 126.4 | 122.4 | 98.5 | 126.3 | 122.4 |
| 0320 | Concrete Reinforcing | 107.6 | 81.6 | 95.1 | 102.0 | 124.6 | 112.9 | 102.0 | 124.6 | 112.9 | 102.0 | 124.6 | 112.9 | 102.0 | 124.6 | 112.9 | 102.0 | 124.6 | 112.9 |
| 0330 | Cast-in-Place Concrete | 122.1 | 81.2 | 107.0 | 100.1 | 123.8 | 108.9 | 93.8 | 123.7 | 104.8 | 96.5 | 123.7 | 106.6 | 90.2 | 123.7 | 102.6 | 95.3 | 123.7 | 105.8 |
| 03 | CONCRETE | 118.3 | 80.1 | 100.7 | 108.3 | 124.9 | 116.0 | 105.2 | 124.8 | 114.2 | 106.4 | 124.8 | 114.9 | 103.4 | 124.8 | 113.3 | 106.0 | 124.8 | 114.7 |
| 04 | MASONRY | 142.6 | 76.5 | 103.0 | 106.4 | 132.2 | 121.8 | 98.7 | 132.2 | 118.7 | 98.9 | 132.2 | 118.8 | 98.5 | 132.2 | 118.6 | 100.8 | 132.2 | 119.6 |
| 05 | METALS | 96.4 | 82.8 | 92.5 | 94.4 | 124.8 | 103.3 | 94.4 | 124.5 | 103.2 | 99.0 | 124.5 | 106.4 | 92.1 | 124.6 | 101.5 | 91.3 | 124.5 | 100.9 |
| 06 | WOOD, PLASTICS & COMPOSITES | 102.6 | 82.2 | 91.6 | 98.9 | 125.2 | 113.1 | 98.9 | 125.2 | 113.1 | 97.4 | 125.2 | 112.4 | 98.9 | 125.2 | 113.1 | 98.9 | 125.2 | 113.1 |
| 07 | THERMAL & MOISTURE PROTECTION | 100.3 | 81.3 | 92.9 | 99.4 | 128.9 | 110.9 | 99.5 | 124.6 | 109.3 | 100.0 | 124.6 | 109.6 | 99.5 | 124.6 | 109.3 | 99.5 | 125.3 | 109.6 |
| 08 | OPENINGS | 92.5 | 85.4 | 90.7 | 105.3 | 132.8 | 112.1 | 105.3 | 130.7 | 111.6 | 105.9 | 130.7 | 112.0 | 107.8 | 132.8 | 114.0 | 105.3 | 130.7 | 111.6 |
| 0920 | Plaster & Gypsum Board | 79.7 | 81.6 | 80.9 | 104.4 | 125.1 | 117.2 | 104.4 | 125.1 | 117.2 | 105.6 | 125.1 | 117.6 | 106.0 | 125.1 | 117.8 | 104.4 | 125.1 | 117.2 |
| 0950, 0980 | Ceilings & Acoustic Treatment | 105.6 | 81.6 | 90.9 | 96.2 | 125.1 | 113.9 | 96.2 | 125.1 | 113.9 | 96.2 | 125.1 | 113.9 | 101.1 | 125.1 | 115.8 | 96.2 | 125.1 | 113.9 |
| 0960 | Flooring | 124.7 | 52.4 | 105.0 | 96.3 | 124.3 | 103.9 | 96.3 | 115.3 | 101.4 | 96.3 | 115.3 | 101.4 | 96.3 | 124.3 | 103.9 | 96.3 | 115.3 | 101.4 |
| 0970, 0990 | Wall Finishes & Painting/Coating | 110.0 | 28.3 | 60.9 | 91.6 | 116.5 | 106.5 | 91.6 | 121.6 | 109.6 | 91.6 | 121.6 | 109.6 | 91.6 | 116.5 | 106.5 | 91.6 | 121.6 | 109.6 |
| 09 | FINISHES | 107.4 | 68.3 | 86.9 | 101.5 | 125.0 | 113.8 | 101.5 | 124.1 | 113.3 | 101.2 | 124.1 | 113.2 | 102.9 | 125.0 | 114.5 | 101.5 | 124.1 | 113.3 |
| COVERS | DIVS. 10 - 14, 25, 28, 41, 43, 44 | 100.0 | 88.4 | 97.6 | 100.0 | 114.6 | 103.0 | 100.0 | 114.6 | 103.0 | 100.0 | 114.6 | 103.0 | 100.0 | 114.6 | 103.0 | 100.0 | 114.6 | 103.0 |
| 21, 22, 23 | FIRE SUPPRESSION, PLUMBING & HVAC | 95.8 | 70.6 | 85.4 | 100.1 | 118.6 | 107.7 | 100.1 | 118.6 | 107.7 | 100.0 | 118.6 | 107.7 | 96.0 | 118.6 | 105.3 | 100.1 | 118.6 | 107.7 |
| 26, 27, 3370 | ELECTRICAL, COMMUNICATIONS & UTIL. | 93.2 | 79.8 | 86.6 | 98.0 | 113.1 | 105.4 | 98.0 | 112.8 | 105.3 | 98.2 | 113.7 | 105.8 | 97.9 | 112.8 | 105.2 | 98.1 | 112.8 | 105.3 |
| MF2004 | WEIGHTED AVERAGE | 102.6 | 78.4 | 92.2 | 100.8 | 121.1 | 109.5 | 100.0 | 120.7 | 108.7 | 100.9 | 120.8 | 109.4 | 98.8 | 121.0 | 108.3 | 99.8 | 120.7 | 108.7 |

| | | CONNECTICUT | | | | | | | | | | | | | | | | | |
|---|---|---|---|---|---|---|---|---|---|---|---|---|---|---|---|---|---|---|---|
| | | NEW HAVEN | | | NEW LONDON | | | NORWALK | | | STAMFORD | | | WATERBURY | | | WILLIMANTIC | | |
| DIVISION | | 065 | | | 063 | | | 068 | | | 069 | | | 067 | | | 062 | | |
| | | MAT. | INST. | TOTAL | MAT. | INST. | TOTAL | MAT. | INST. | TOTAL | MAT. | INST. | TOTAL | MAT. | INST. | TOTAL | MAT. | INST. | TOTAL |
| 015433 | CONTRACTOR EQUIPMENT | | 101.1 | 101.1 | | 101.1 | 101.1 | | 100.6 | 100.6 | | 100.6 | 100.6 | | 100.6 | 100.6 | | 100.6 | 100.6 |
| 0241, 31 - 34 | SITE & INFRASTRUCTURE, DEMOLITION | 99.3 | 105.5 | 103.6 | 91.9 | 105.5 | 101.4 | 99.8 | 104.7 | 103.2 | 100.5 | 104.7 | 103.4 | 99.5 | 104.7 | 103.1 | 99.9 | 104.6 | 103.2 |
| 0310 | Concrete Forming & Accessories | 98.0 | 126.2 | 122.3 | 98.0 | 125.8 | 121.9 | 98.2 | 126.6 | 122.7 | 98.2 | 126.9 | 122.9 | 98.2 | 126.3 | 122.5 | 98.2 | 126.0 | 122.1 |
| 0320 | Concrete Reinforcing | 102.0 | 124.6 | 112.9 | 80.0 | 124.5 | 101.5 | 102.0 | 124.7 | 113.0 | 102.0 | 124.8 | 113.0 | 102.0 | 124.6 | 112.9 | 102.0 | 124.5 | 112.9 |
| 0330 | Cast-in-Place Concrete | 97.0 | 113.9 | 103.2 | 82.6 | 113.7 | 94.1 | 98.5 | 130.0 | 110.1 | 100.1 | 130.1 | 111.2 | 100.1 | 123.7 | 108.8 | 93.5 | 103.2 | 97.1 |
| 03 | CONCRETE | 122.2 | 121.4 | 121.8 | 93.0 | 121.1 | 106.0 | 107.5 | 127.1 | 116.6 | 108.3 | 127.3 | 117.1 | 108.3 | 124.8 | 115.9 | 105.0 | 117.6 | 110.9 |
| 04 | MASONRY | 99.0 | 132.2 | 118.8 | 97.4 | 132.2 | 118.2 | 98.4 | 133.9 | 119.6 | 99.2 | 133.9 | 120.0 | 99.2 | 132.2 | 118.9 | 98.7 | 132.2 | 118.7 |
| 05 | METALS | 91.5 | 124.4 | 101.0 | 91.2 | 124.0 | 100.7 | 94.4 | 125.0 | 103.3 | 94.4 | 125.3 | 103.4 | 94.4 | 124.6 | 103.2 | 94.2 | 124.2 | 102.9 |
| 06 | WOOD, PLASTICS & COMPOSITES | 98.9 | 125.2 | 113.1 | 98.9 | 125.2 | 113.1 | 98.9 | 125.2 | 113.1 | 98.9 | 125.2 | 113.1 | 98.9 | 125.2 | 113.1 | 98.9 | 125.2 | 113.1 |
| 07 | THERMAL & MOISTURE PROTECTION | 99.6 | 123.8 | 109.0 | 99.4 | 123.1 | 108.7 | 99.6 | 130.3 | 111.5 | 99.5 | 130.3 | 111.5 | 99.5 | 125.3 | 109.6 | 99.7 | 121.5 | 108.2 |
| 08 | OPENINGS | 105.3 | 132.8 | 112.1 | 108.4 | 120.8 | 111.5 | 105.3 | 132.8 | 112.1 | 105.3 | 132.8 | 112.1 | 105.3 | 132.8 | 112.1 | 108.5 | 132.8 | 114.5 |
| 0920 | Plaster & Gypsum Board | 104.4 | 125.1 | 117.2 | 104.4 | 125.1 | 117.2 | 104.4 | 125.1 | 117.2 | 104.4 | 125.1 | 117.2 | 104.4 | 125.1 | 117.2 | 104.4 | 125.1 | 117.2 |
| 0950, 0980 | Ceilings & Acoustic Treatment | 96.2 | 125.1 | 113.9 | 94.3 | 125.1 | 113.2 | 96.2 | 125.1 | 113.9 | 96.2 | 125.1 | 113.9 | 96.2 | 125.1 | 113.9 | 94.3 | 125.1 | 113.2 |
| 0960 | Flooring | 96.3 | 124.3 | 103.9 | 96.3 | 115.3 | 101.4 | 96.3 | 115.3 | 101.4 | 96.3 | 115.3 | 101.4 | 96.3 | 124.3 | 103.9 | 96.3 | 124.3 | 103.9 |
| 0970, 0990 | Wall Finishes & Painting/Coating | 91.6 | 116.5 | 106.5 | 91.6 | 116.5 | 106.5 | 91.6 | 116.5 | 106.5 | 91.6 | 116.5 | 106.5 | 91.6 | 116.5 | 106.5 | 91.6 | 116.5 | 106.5 |
| 09 | FINISHES | 101.5 | 125.0 | 113.8 | 100.5 | 123.5 | 112.5 | 101.5 | 123.5 | 113.0 | 101.6 | 123.5 | 113.0 | 101.4 | 125.0 | 113.8 | 101.2 | 125.0 | 113.7 |
| COVERS | DIVS. 10 - 14, 25, 28, 41, 43, 44 | 100.0 | 114.6 | 103.0 | 100.0 | 114.6 | 103.0 | 100.0 | 114.6 | 103.0 | 100.0 | 114.8 | 103.0 | 100.0 | 114.6 | 103.0 | 100.0 | 114.6 | 103.0 |
| 21, 22, 23 | FIRE SUPPRESSION, PLUMBING & HVAC | 100.1 | 118.6 | 107.7 | 96.0 | 118.5 | 105.2 | 100.1 | 118.6 | 107.7 | 100.1 | 118.7 | 107.7 | 100.1 | 118.6 | 107.7 | 100.1 | 118.6 | 107.7 |
| 26, 27, 3370 | ELECTRICAL, COMMUNICATIONS & UTIL. | 98.0 | 112.8 | 105.2 | 94.9 | 112.8 | 103.7 | 98.0 | 107.6 | 102.7 | 98.0 | 144.7 | 120.9 | 97.5 | 108.9 | 103.1 | 98.0 | 113.7 | 105.7 |
| MF2004 | WEIGHTED AVERAGE | 101.6 | 120.5 | 109.7 | 96.8 | 119.7 | 106.6 | 100.3 | 120.7 | 109.0 | 100.5 | 126.0 | 111.4 | 100.4 | 120.4 | 108.9 | 100.3 | 119.9 | 108.7 |

| | | D.C. | | | DELAWARE | | | | | | | | | FLORIDA | | | | | |
|---|---|---|---|---|---|---|---|---|---|---|---|---|---|---|---|---|---|---|---|
| | | WASHINGTON | | | DOVER | | | NEWARK | | | WILMINGTON | | | DAYTONA BEACH | | | FORT LAUDERDALE | | |
| DIVISION | | 200 - 205 | | | 199 | | | 197 | | | 198 | | | 321 | | | 333 | | |
| | | MAT. | INST. | TOTAL | MAT. | INST. | TOTAL | MAT. | INST. | TOTAL | MAT. | INST. | TOTAL | MAT. | INST. | TOTAL | MAT. | INST. | TOTAL |
| 015433 | CONTRACTOR EQUIPMENT | | 103.7 | 103.7 | | 118.9 | 118.9 | | 118.9 | 118.9 | | 119.1 | 119.1 | | 98.2 | 98.2 | | 89.7 | 89.7 |
| 0241, 31 - 34 | SITE & INFRASTRUCTURE, DEMOLITION | 112.7 | 91.6 | 98.0 | 103.5 | 112.6 | 109.9 | 103.3 | 112.6 | 109.8 | 90.8 | 112.9 | 106.2 | 113.2 | 88.7 | 96.1 | 98.8 | 75.2 | 82.4 |
| 0310 | Concrete Forming & Accessories | 99.5 | 82.3 | 84.7 | 96.5 | 107.0 | 105.5 | 98.8 | 107.0 | 105.8 | 100.3 | 107.0 | 106.0 | 96.5 | 80.7 | 82.9 | 94.6 | 70.4 | 73.8 |
| 0320 | Concrete Reinforcing | 102.1 | 90.2 | 96.4 | 102.2 | 103.6 | 102.9 | 103.1 | 103.6 | 103.4 | 103.1 | 103.6 | 103.4 | 91.8 | 82.9 | 87.5 | 91.8 | 72.8 | 82.7 |
| 0330 | Cast-in-Place Concrete | 125.5 | 88.0 | 111.6 | 106.9 | 90.8 | 100.9 | 97.0 | 90.8 | 94.7 | 101.4 | 90.8 | 97.4 | 90.9 | 76.7 | 85.6 | 95.3 | 75.2 | 87.9 |
| 03 | CONCRETE | 118.4 | 87.0 | 103.9 | 107.0 | 101.6 | 104.5 | 102.4 | 101.6 | 102.0 | 104.6 | 101.6 | 103.3 | 91.3 | 80.6 | 86.4 | 93.4 | 73.8 | 84.3 |
| 04 | MASONRY | 103.3 | 82.3 | 90.8 | 107.2 | 94.6 | 99.7 | 104.5 | 94.6 | 98.6 | 111.0 | 94.6 | 101.2 | 85.1 | 73.2 | 78.0 | 85.4 | 70.8 | 76.6 |
| 05 | METALS | 100.8 | 108.3 | 103.0 | 102.2 | 118.2 | 106.8 | 102.2 | 118.2 | 106.8 | 99.1 | 118.2 | 104.6 | 95.2 | 95.1 | 95.2 | 95.1 | 91.9 | 94.2 |
| 06 | WOOD, PLASTICS & COMPOSITES | 100.4 | 81.6 | 90.3 | 95.2 | 108.9 | 102.6 | 98.2 | 108.9 | 104.0 | 100.7 | 108.9 | 105.1 | 96.4 | 84.4 | 89.9 | 92.1 | 68.2 | 79.2 |
| 07 | THERMAL & MOISTURE PROTECTION | 107.6 | 83.9 | 98.3 | 101.2 | 105.1 | 102.7 | 100.9 | 105.1 | 102.5 | 101.6 | 105.1 | 103.0 | 97.7 | 81.7 | 91.5 | 97.7 | 85.0 | 92.8 |
| 08 | OPENINGS | 106.5 | 90.9 | 102.6 | 95.7 | 113.3 | 100.0 | 95.7 | 113.3 | 100.0 | 95.4 | 113.3 | 99.8 | 100.2 | 77.4 | 94.5 | 97.4 | 66.1 | 89.7 |
| 0920 | Plaster & Gypsum Board | 107.2 | 81.1 | 91.1 | 109.1 | 109.1 | 109.1 | 110.9 | 109.1 | 109.8 | 110.5 | 109.1 | 109.6 | 100.8 | 84.5 | 90.7 | 100.4 | 67.9 | 80.3 |
| 0950, 0980 | Ceilings & Acoustic Treatment | 105.0 | 81.1 | 90.3 | 100.4 | 109.1 | 105.7 | 103.8 | 109.1 | 107.0 | 96.0 | 109.1 | 104.0 | 102.1 | 84.5 | 91.3 | 102.1 | 67.9 | 81.1 |
| 0960 | Flooring | 120.9 | 101.9 | 115.7 | 82.1 | 101.1 | 87.3 | 82.3 | 101.1 | 87.4 | 81.9 | 101.1 | 87.1 | 118.1 | 79.6 | 107.6 | 118.1 | 67.4 | 104.3 |
| 0970, 0990 | Wall Finishes & Painting/Coating | 125.5 | 85.0 | 101.2 | 96.9 | 102.1 | 100.0 | 96.9 | 102.1 | 100.0 | 96.9 | 102.1 | 100.0 | 115.6 | 79.9 | 94.1 | 110.9 | 56.5 | 78.2 |
| 09 | FINISHES | 108.3 | 85.9 | 96.6 | 100.0 | 105.5 | 102.9 | 101.3 | 105.5 | 103.5 | 99.4 | 105.5 | 102.6 | 107.8 | 80.9 | 93.7 | 105.5 | 67.4 | 85.6 |
| COVERS | DIVS. 10 - 14, 25, 28, 41, 43, 44 | 100.0 | 97.4 | 99.5 | 100.0 | 100.9 | 100.2 | 100.0 | 100.9 | 100.2 | 100.0 | 100.9 | 100.2 | 100.0 | 85.3 | 97.0 | 100.0 | 88.2 | 97.6 |
| 21, 22, 23 | FIRE SUPPRESSION, PLUMBING & HVAC | 100.2 | 93.3 | 97.4 | 100.1 | 117.4 | 107.2 | 100.2 | 117.4 | 107.3 | 100.3 | 117.4 | 107.3 | 99.8 | 68.7 | 87.1 | 99.8 | 69.9 | 87.5 |
| 26, 27, 3370 | ELECTRICAL, COMMUNICATIONS & UTIL. | 101.7 | 97.0 | 99.4 | 102.7 | 106.4 | 104.5 | 102.7 | 106.4 | 104.5 | 102.7 | 106.4 | 104.5 | 97.9 | 62.9 | 80.7 | 97.9 | 75.1 | 86.7 |
| MF2004 | WEIGHTED AVERAGE | 104.7 | 91.7 | 99.1 | 101.6 | 108.4 | 104.5 | 101.0 | 108.4 | 104.2 | 100.6 | 108.5 | 104.0 | 98.1 | 77.0 | 89.1 | 97.5 | 74.1 | 87.5 |

# City Cost Indexes

## FLORIDA

| DIVISION | | FORT MYERS 339,341 | | | GAINESVILLE 326,344 | | | JACKSONVILLE 320,322 | | | LAKELAND 338 | | | MELBOURNE 329 | | | MIAMI 330 - 332,340 | | |
|---|---|---|---|---|---|---|---|---|---|---|---|---|---|---|---|---|---|---|---|---|
| | | MAT. | INST. | TOTAL | MAT. | INST. | TOTAL | MAT. | INST. | TOTAL | MAT. | INST. | TOTAL | MAT. | INST. | TOTAL | MAT. | INST. | TOTAL |
| 015433 | CONTRACTOR EQUIPMENT | | 98.2 | 98.2 | | 98.2 | 98.2 | | 98.2 | 98.2 | | 98.2 | 98.2 | | 98.2 | 98.2 | | 89.7 | 89.7 |
| 0241, 31 - 34 | SITE & INFRASTRUCTURE, DEMOLITION | 110.5 | 87.9 | 94.8 | 123.9 | 87.6 | 98.6 | 113.3 | 88.0 | 95.6 | 112.7 | 87.8 | 95.4 | 121.6 | 87.9 | 98.1 | 100.5 | 75.1 | 82.8 |
| 0310 | Concrete Forming & Accessories | 90.1 | 85.2 | 85.9 | 91.1 | 61.1 | 65.2 | 96.3 | 61.2 | 66.0 | 86.1 | 85.9 | 86.0 | 92.5 | 82.7 | 84.0 | 99.8 | 71.1 | 75.1 |
| 0320 | Concrete Reinforcing | 92.9 | 88.7 | 90.9 | 97.5 | 53.2 | 76.2 | 91.8 | 53.7 | 73.5 | 95.2 | 89.4 | 92.4 | 92.9 | 82.9 | 88.1 | 91.8 | 72.9 | 82.7 |
| 0330 | Cast-in-Place Concrete | 99.4 | 66.5 | 87.2 | 104.4 | 55.4 | 86.2 | 91.8 | 66.1 | 82.3 | 101.7 | 67.6 | 89.1 | 109.6 | 79.2 | 98.3 | 106.0 | 76.3 | 95.0 |
| 03 | CONCRETE | 94.2 | 80.3 | 87.8 | 102.4 | 59.1 | 82.4 | 91.7 | 62.9 | 78.4 | 96.2 | 81.1 | 89.2 | 103.0 | 82.4 | 93.5 | 99.0 | 74.4 | 87.6 |
| 04 | MASONRY | 79.2 | 64.2 | 70.2 | 98.1 | 51.7 | 70.4 | 84.9 | 60.8 | 70.5 | 94.3 | 75.7 | 83.1 | 83.2 | 77.4 | 79.7 | 84.5 | 74.5 | 78.5 |
| 05 | METALS | 97.4 | 97.2 | 97.4 | 94.2 | 80.0 | 90.1 | 93.8 | 80.8 | 90.0 | 97.3 | 97.3 | 97.3 | 103.6 | 95.6 | 101.2 | 100.1 | 91.2 | 97.5 |
| 06 | WOOD, PLASTICS & COMPOSITES | 89.0 | 90.2 | 89.6 | 90.1 | 60.0 | 73.9 | 96.4 | 60.0 | 76.8 | 84.5 | 90.2 | 87.5 | 91.8 | 84.4 | 87.8 | 98.4 | 68.2 | 82.1 |
| 07 | THERMAL & MOISTURE PROTECTION | 97.5 | 88.9 | 94.1 | 98.0 | 63.4 | 84.5 | 97.9 | 66.6 | 85.7 | 97.4 | 93.0 | 95.7 | 98.1 | 88.1 | 94.2 | 105.8 | 82.1 | 96.5 |
| 08 | OPENINGS | 98.9 | 80.4 | 94.3 | 98.3 | 53.4 | 87.2 | 100.2 | 54.0 | 88.8 | 98.8 | 78.5 | 93.8 | 99.4 | 83.7 | 95.5 | 97.4 | 66.4 | 89.8 |
| 0920 | Plaster & Gypsum Board | 97.1 | 90.4 | 93.0 | 97.2 | 59.5 | 73.9 | 100.8 | 59.5 | 75.3 | 95.2 | 90.4 | 92.2 | 97.4 | 84.5 | 89.5 | 96.7 | 67.9 | 78.9 |
| 0950, 0980 | Ceilings & Acoustic Treatment | 95.9 | 90.4 | 92.5 | 95.1 | 59.5 | 73.2 | 102.1 | 59.5 | 75.9 | 95.1 | 90.4 | 92.2 | 97.8 | 84.5 | 89.7 | 98.7 | 67.9 | 79.8 |
| 0960 | Flooring | 113.9 | 49.5 | 96.4 | 114.5 | 42.0 | 94.8 | 118.1 | 57.6 | 101.6 | 110.8 | 62.1 | 97.6 | 114.7 | 79.6 | 105.2 | 125.6 | 71.0 | 110.8 |
| 0970, 0990 | Wall Finishes & Painting/Coating | 115.6 | 64.2 | 84.7 | 115.6 | 46.3 | 74.0 | 115.6 | 51.7 | 77.2 | 115.6 | 64.2 | 84.7 | 115.6 | 110.1 | 112.3 | 110.9 | 56.5 | 78.2 |
| 09 | FINISHES | 104.3 | 77.0 | 90.0 | 105.5 | 55.3 | 79.2 | 107.8 | 59.1 | 82.3 | 103.0 | 79.6 | 90.8 | 105.9 | 85.3 | 95.1 | 106.3 | 68.6 | 86.6 |
| COVERS | DIVS. 10 - 14, 25, 28, 41, 43, 44 | 100.0 | 81.9 | 96.3 | 100.0 | 82.8 | 96.5 | 100.0 | 80.6 | 96.0 | 100.0 | 82.0 | 96.3 | 100.0 | 86.9 | 97.3 | 100.0 | 88.9 | 97.7 |
| 21, 22, 23 | FIRE SUPPRESSION, PLUMBING & HVAC | 97.6 | 62.4 | 83.2 | 98.8 | 68.8 | 86.5 | 99.8 | 50.0 | 79.4 | 97.6 | 93.1 | 95.8 | 99.8 | 71.0 | 88.0 | 99.8 | 73.8 | 89.1 |
| 26, 27, 3370 | ELECTRICAL, COMMUNICATIONS & UTIL. | 100.2 | 42.5 | 71.9 | 98.3 | 75.2 | 86.9 | 97.7 | 70.2 | 84.2 | 98.2 | 43.0 | 71.1 | 99.3 | 74.0 | 86.9 | 99.5 | 78.5 | 89.2 |
| MF2004 | WEIGHTED AVERAGE | 97.7 | 71.7 | 86.6 | 99.6 | 67.0 | 85.7 | 97.9 | 64.5 | 83.6 | 98.4 | 79.9 | 90.5 | 100.9 | 80.7 | 92.2 | 99.5 | 75.9 | 89.4 |

## FLORIDA

| DIVISION | | ORLANDO 327 - 328,347 | | | PANAMA CITY 324 | | | PENSACOLA 325 | | | SARASOTA 342 | | | ST. PETERSBURG 337 | | | TALLAHASSEE 323 | | |
|---|---|---|---|---|---|---|---|---|---|---|---|---|---|---|---|---|---|---|---|---|
| | | MAT. | INST. | TOTAL | MAT. | INST. | TOTAL | MAT. | INST. | TOTAL | MAT. | INST. | TOTAL | MAT. | INST. | TOTAL | MAT. | INST. | TOTAL |
| 015433 | CONTRACTOR EQUIPMENT | | 98.2 | 98.2 | | 98.2 | 98.2 | | 98.2 | 98.2 | | 98.2 | 98.2 | | 98.2 | 98.2 | | 98.2 | 98.2 |
| 0241, 31 - 34 | SITE & INFRASTRUCTURE, DEMOLITION | 115.7 | 87.6 | 96.1 | 127.9 | 85.7 | 98.5 | 127.6 | 87.2 | 99.4 | 114.8 | 87.7 | 95.9 | 114.1 | 87.1 | 95.3 | 111.0 | 86.8 | 94.2 |
| 0310 | Concrete Forming & Accessories | 96.2 | 82.4 | 84.3 | 95.5 | 44.8 | 51.8 | 93.4 | 57.7 | 62.7 | 96.5 | 85.3 | 86.9 | 94.3 | 51.5 | 57.4 | 98.0 | 47.2 | 54.2 |
| 0320 | Concrete Reinforcing | 91.8 | 79.6 | 85.9 | 95.9 | 50.5 | 74.0 | 98.3 | 50.5 | 75.3 | 91.8 | 89.3 | 90.6 | 95.2 | 57.4 | 76.9 | 91.8 | 53.5 | 73.4 |
| 0330 | Cast-in-Place Concrete | 111.6 | 76.4 | 98.6 | 96.4 | 44.7 | 77.3 | 119.2 | 62.5 | 98.2 | 104.0 | 67.4 | 90.4 | 102.8 | 61.6 | 87.5 | 100.7 | 53.4 | 83.2 |
| 03 | CONCRETE | 103.0 | 80.7 | 92.7 | 100.0 | 47.2 | 75.6 | 110.8 | 59.5 | 87.1 | 97.8 | 80.7 | 89.9 | 97.6 | 57.7 | 79.2 | 96.2 | 52.2 | 75.9 |
| 04 | MASONRY | 89.1 | 73.2 | 79.6 | 89.3 | 46.1 | 63.5 | 108.2 | 55.0 | 76.3 | 86.1 | 75.7 | 79.9 | 130.6 | 50.3 | 82.6 | 88.1 | 48.8 | 64.6 |
| 05 | METALS | 100.7 | 93.2 | 98.5 | 95.0 | 67.0 | 86.8 | 96.0 | 79.4 | 91.2 | 98.0 | 96.7 | 97.6 | 98.2 | 81.4 | 93.3 | 88.6 | 80.2 | 86.2 |
| 06 | WOOD, PLASTICS & COMPOSITES | 96.1 | 87.5 | 91.5 | 95.2 | 45.0 | 68.2 | 93.6 | 59.7 | 75.3 | 96.4 | 90.2 | 93.0 | 93.7 | 51.0 | 70.7 | 94.2 | 45.8 | 68.1 |
| 07 | THERMAL & MOISTURE PROTECTION | 98.8 | 82.1 | 92.3 | 98.2 | 48.5 | 78.8 | 98.1 | 60.8 | 83.6 | 97.7 | 93.0 | 95.8 | 97.6 | 57.1 | 81.8 | 103.1 | 76.5 | 92.7 |
| 08 | OPENINGS | 100.2 | 75.4 | 94.1 | 97.8 | 37.7 | 83.0 | 97.8 | 55.8 | 87.4 | 100.2 | 80.2 | 95.2 | 98.8 | 51.9 | 87.2 | 100.6 | 47.2 | 87.4 |
| 0920 | Plaster & Gypsum Board | 109.0 | 87.7 | 95.9 | 99.2 | 44.1 | 65.2 | 100.2 | 59.1 | 74.9 | 100.8 | 90.4 | 94.4 | 98.6 | 50.2 | 68.7 | 113.1 | 44.9 | 71.0 |
| 0950, 0980 | Ceilings & Acoustic Treatment | 102.1 | 87.7 | 93.3 | 97.0 | 44.1 | 64.5 | 97.8 | 59.1 | 74.1 | 100.2 | 90.4 | 94.2 | 97.0 | 50.2 | 68.3 | 102.1 | 44.9 | 67.0 |
| 0960 | Flooring | 118.3 | 79.6 | 107.8 | 117.5 | 48.4 | 98.7 | 111.6 | 61.2 | 97.9 | 118.1 | 59.2 | 102.1 | 116.4 | 62.1 | 101.7 | 118.1 | 51.8 | 100.1 |
| 0970, 0990 | Wall Finishes & Painting/Coating | 115.6 | 61.2 | 82.9 | 115.6 | 42.7 | 71.8 | 115.6 | 51.0 | 76.8 | 115.6 | 64.2 | 84.7 | 115.6 | 45.1 | 73.3 | 115.6 | 46.5 | 73.6 |
| 09 | FINISHES | 109.0 | 80.6 | 94.2 | 107.5 | 45.3 | 74.9 | 105.8 | 57.6 | 80.5 | 107.4 | 79.1 | 92.6 | 105.8 | 52.3 | 77.8 | 109.4 | 46.8 | 76.6 |
| COVERS | DIVS. 10 - 14, 25, 28, 41, 43, 44 | 100.0 | 85.6 | 97.0 | 100.0 | 46.6 | 89.1 | 100.0 | 47.7 | 89.3 | 100.0 | 81.9 | 96.3 | 100.0 | 57.0 | 91.2 | 100.0 | 72.8 | 94.4 |
| 21, 22, 23 | FIRE SUPPRESSION, PLUMBING & HVAC | 99.7 | 65.6 | 85.7 | 99.8 | 39.2 | 75.0 | 99.8 | 59.4 | 83.2 | 99.8 | 63.0 | 84.7 | 99.8 | 57.9 | 82.6 | 99.8 | 43.9 | 76.8 |
| 26, 27, 3370 | ELECTRICAL, COMMUNICATIONS & UTIL. | 99.6 | 41.5 | 71.1 | 96.6 | 43.0 | 70.3 | 100.7 | 59.9 | 80.6 | 97.9 | 38.4 | 68.7 | 98.2 | 48.3 | 73.7 | 99.7 | 37.7 | 69.2 |
| MF2004 | WEIGHTED AVERAGE | 101.0 | 73.0 | 89.0 | 99.3 | 49.2 | 77.9 | 102.0 | 62.5 | 85.1 | 99.4 | 72.8 | 88.0 | 101.4 | 59.2 | 83.4 | 98.2 | 53.8 | 79.2 |

## FLORIDA / GEORGIA

| DIVISION | | TAMPA 335 - 336,346 | | | WEST PALM BEACH 334,349 | | | ALBANY 317,398 | | | ATHENS 306 | | | ATLANTA 300 - 303,399 | | | AUGUSTA 308 - 309 | | |
|---|---|---|---|---|---|---|---|---|---|---|---|---|---|---|---|---|---|---|---|---|
| | | MAT. | INST. | TOTAL | MAT. | INST. | TOTAL | MAT. | INST. | TOTAL | MAT. | INST. | TOTAL | MAT. | INST. | TOTAL | MAT. | INST. | TOTAL |
| 015433 | CONTRACTOR EQUIPMENT | | 98.2 | 98.2 | | 89.7 | 89.7 | | 90.6 | 90.6 | | 91.6 | 91.6 | | 92.2 | 92.2 | | 91.6 | 91.6 |
| 0241, 31 - 34 | SITE & INFRASTRUCTURE, DEMOLITION | 114.5 | 87.7 | 95.8 | 95.5 | 75.3 | 81.4 | 99.1 | 76.9 | 83.7 | 105.2 | 91.4 | 95.6 | 101.0 | 94.2 | 96.3 | 97.4 | 91.5 | 93.3 |
| 0310 | Concrete Forming & Accessories | 97.5 | 86.1 | 87.7 | 98.1 | 69.8 | 73.7 | 95.6 | 50.7 | 56.9 | 94.5 | 47.7 | 54.2 | 98.3 | 75.2 | 78.4 | 95.7 | 56.8 | 62.2 |
| 0320 | Concrete Reinforcing | 91.8 | 89.4 | 90.7 | 94.4 | 72.6 | 83.9 | 91.5 | 88.4 | 90.0 | 91.5 | 87.3 | 89.5 | 91.0 | 90.3 | 90.6 | 91.8 | 71.8 | 82.2 |
| 0330 | Cast-in-Place Concrete | 100.5 | 67.7 | 88.3 | 90.6 | 64.0 | 80.8 | 97.1 | 50.1 | 79.7 | 112.4 | 53.0 | 90.4 | 112.4 | 71.6 | 97.3 | 106.2 | 52.5 | 86.3 |
| 03 | CONCRETE | 96.1 | 81.2 | 89.2 | 90.4 | 69.6 | 80.8 | 94.1 | 59.1 | 78.0 | 105.0 | 57.5 | 83.1 | 102.6 | 76.8 | 90.7 | 97.9 | 58.6 | 79.8 |
| 04 | MASONRY | 86.3 | 75.7 | 79.9 | 85.0 | 69.3 | 75.6 | 88.2 | 47.1 | 63.6 | 73.3 | 64.3 | 67.9 | 87.4 | 74.6 | 79.8 | 87.5 | 46.7 | 63.1 |
| 05 | METALS | 97.2 | 97.5 | 97.3 | 94.3 | 91.1 | 93.3 | 94.5 | 88.1 | 92.6 | 93.0 | 73.3 | 87.3 | 93.9 | 80.5 | 90.0 | 92.7 | 69.0 | 85.8 |
| 06 | WOOD, PLASTICS & COMPOSITES | 97.7 | 90.2 | 93.6 | 96.7 | 68.2 | 81.3 | 95.2 | 45.8 | 68.6 | 94.3 | 41.3 | 65.8 | 98.5 | 76.9 | 86.9 | 95.6 | 57.5 | 75.1 |
| 07 | THERMAL & MOISTURE PROTECTION | 97.9 | 93.0 | 96.0 | 97.4 | 72.7 | 87.8 | 94.8 | 60.9 | 81.1 | 95.7 | 58.1 | 81.1 | 98.5 | 77.0 | 88.5 | 95.3 | 56.7 | 80.3 |
| 08 | OPENINGS | 100.2 | 81.0 | 95.4 | 96.6 | 66.1 | 89.1 | 97.4 | 51.9 | 86.2 | 93.4 | 49.6 | 82.6 | 99.1 | 74.1 | 93.0 | 93.4 | 56.8 | 84.4 |
| 0920 | Plaster & Gypsum Board | 100.8 | 90.4 | 94.4 | 102.5 | 67.9 | 81.1 | 98.3 | 45.0 | 65.4 | 114.4 | 40.2 | 68.6 | 115.8 | 76.8 | 91.7 | 114.8 | 56.9 | 79.0 |
| 0950, 0980 | Ceilings & Acoustic Treatment | 102.1 | 90.4 | 94.9 | 95.9 | 67.9 | 78.7 | 101.2 | 45.0 | 66.7 | 115.3 | 40.2 | 69.2 | 115.3 | 76.8 | 91.6 | 116.3 | 56.9 | 79.8 |
| 0960 | Flooring | 118.1 | 62.1 | 102.9 | 120.8 | 65.0 | 105.6 | 118.1 | 35.7 | 95.7 | 88.7 | 62.3 | 81.5 | 90.4 | 71.2 | 85.1 | 89.2 | 45.4 | 77.3 |
| 0970, 0990 | Wall Finishes & Painting/Coating | 115.6 | 64.2 | 84.7 | 110.9 | 50.1 | 74.4 | 110.9 | 48.5 | 73.4 | 101.0 | 38.4 | 63.4 | 101.0 | 83.3 | 90.4 | 101.0 | 43.8 | 66.6 |
| 09 | FINISHES | 107.9 | 79.6 | 93.1 | 104.9 | 66.2 | 84.7 | 104.9 | 46.1 | 74.1 | 100.8 | 48.2 | 73.2 | 101.1 | 75.1 | 87.5 | 100.6 | 52.8 | 75.6 |
| COVERS | DIVS. 10 - 14, 25, 28, 41, 43, 44 | 100.0 | 86.6 | 97.3 | 100.0 | 88.1 | 97.6 | 100.0 | 80.6 | 96.0 | 100.0 | 48.8 | 89.5 | 100.0 | 84.0 | 96.7 | 100.0 | 59.8 | 91.8 |
| 21, 22, 23 | FIRE SUPPRESSION, PLUMBING & HVAC | 99.8 | 93.1 | 97.1 | 97.6 | 69.0 | 85.9 | 99.7 | 62.7 | 84.5 | 95.9 | 75.7 | 87.6 | 100.0 | 77.1 | 90.6 | 100.0 | 76.7 | 90.5 |
| 26, 27, 3370 | ELECTRICAL, COMMUNICATIONS & UTIL. | 97.9 | 48.3 | 73.6 | 99.3 | 55.7 | 77.9 | 93.2 | 59.9 | 76.9 | 96.5 | 78.6 | 87.7 | 96.1 | 76.1 | 86.3 | 97.1 | 65.2 | 81.4 |
| MF2004 | WEIGHTED AVERAGE | 99.1 | 80.9 | 91.3 | 96.4 | 69.9 | 85.1 | 96.9 | 61.4 | 81.7 | 96.2 | 67.3 | 83.8 | 98.1 | 78.2 | 89.6 | 96.8 | 65.0 | 83.2 |

| | | GEORGIA | | | | | | | | | | | | | | | | |
|---|---|---|---|---|---|---|---|---|---|---|---|---|---|---|---|---|---|---|
| | DIVISION | COLUMBUS | | | DALTON | | | GAINESVILLE | | | MACON | | | SAVANNAH | | | STATESBORO | | |
| | | 318 - 319 | | | 307 | | | 305 | | | 310 - 312 | | | 313 - 314 | | | 304 | | |
| | | MAT. | INST. | TOTAL | MAT. | INST. | TOTAL | MAT. | INST. | TOTAL | MAT. | INST. | TOTAL | MAT. | INST. | TOTAL | MAT. | INST. | TOTAL |
| 015433 | CONTRACTOR EQUIPMENT | | 90.6 | 90.6 | | 105.7 | 105.7 | | 91.6 | 91.6 | | 103.0 | 103.0 | | 91.7 | 91.7 | | 91.0 | 91.0 |
| 0241, 31 - 34 | SITE & INFRASTRUCTURE, DEMOLITION | 99.0 | 77.5 | 84.0 | 106.1 | 95.9 | 99.0 | 104.8 | 91.9 | 95.8 | 99.5 | 94.5 | 96.0 | 101.5 | 77.5 | 84.8 | 106.7 | 73.9 | 83.8 |
| 0310 | Concrete Forming & Accessories | 95.5 | 64.4 | 68.7 | 86.7 | 51.0 | 56.0 | 98.0 | 50.4 | 57.0 | 95.0 | 61.0 | 65.7 | 95.8 | 55.8 | 61.3 | 80.9 | 46.1 | 50.9 |
| 0320 | Concrete Reinforcing | 91.8 | 89.6 | 90.7 | 91.1 | 73.1 | 82.4 | 91.3 | 90.5 | 90.9 | 93.0 | 88.7 | 91.0 | 92.7 | 72.0 | 82.7 | 94.8 | 71.0 | 71.0 |
| 0330 | Cast-in-Place Concrete | 96.7 | 60.5 | 83.3 | 109.2 | 39.4 | 83.3 | 118.2 | 55.3 | 94.9 | 95.4 | 49.0 | 78.2 | 109.3 | 50.5 | 87.5 | 112.2 | 47.0 | 88.1 |
| 03 | CONCRETE | 94.0 | 69.0 | 82.4 | 103.8 | 52.2 | 80.0 | 107.0 | 59.9 | 85.3 | 93.5 | 63.4 | 79.6 | 100.4 | 58.4 | 81.0 | 104.3 | 48.7 | 78.6 |
| 04 | MASONRY | 87.2 | 66.3 | 74.7 | 75.5 | 38.1 | 53.2 | 82.9 | 39.6 | 57.0 | 100.4 | 44.7 | 67.1 | 87.2 | 56.1 | 68.6 | 76.1 | 46.9 | 58.6 |
| 05 | METALS | 94.0 | 92.0 | 93.4 | 94.1 | 69.9 | 87.0 | 92.2 | 68.3 | 85.3 | 90.0 | 90.7 | 90.2 | 90.3 | 82.7 | 88.1 | 97.6 | 71.2 | 89.9 |
| 06 | WOOD, PLASTICS & COMPOSITES | 95.2 | 63.3 | 78.0 | 77.3 | 54.2 | 64.8 | 98.3 | 45.7 | 70.0 | 103.7 | 62.1 | 81.3 | 109.1 | 54.2 | 79.5 | 70.0 | 47.5 | 57.9 |
| 07 | THERMAL & MOISTURE PROTECTION | 94.9 | 67.0 | 84.0 | 97.3 | 47.7 | 78.0 | 95.7 | 50.9 | 78.2 | 93.6 | 63.6 | 81.9 | 97.8 | 57.7 | 82.1 | 96.1 | 44.0 | 75.8 |
| 08 | OPENINGS | 97.4 | 63.6 | 89.1 | 95.0 | 40.5 | 81.6 | 93.4 | 43.7 | 81.1 | 95.5 | 61.8 | 87.2 | 98.5 | 52.4 | 87.2 | 95.8 | 38.0 | 81.5 |
| 0920 | Plaster & Gypsum Board | 100.6 | 62.9 | 77.3 | 101.6 | 53.5 | 71.9 | 115.8 | 44.7 | 71.9 | 107.8 | 61.6 | 79.3 | 97.5 | 53.5 | 70.4 | 122.1 | 46.6 | 67.9 |
| 0950, 0980 | Ceilings & Acoustic Treatment | 101.2 | 62.9 | 77.7 | 124.0 | 53.5 | 80.7 | 115.3 | 44.7 | 72.0 | 97.3 | 61.6 | 75.4 | 102.1 | 53.5 | 72.3 | 122.1 | 46.6 | 75.8 |
| 0960 | Flooring | 118.1 | 58.2 | 101.8 | 89.7 | 14.9 | 69.3 | 90.3 | 14.9 | 69.8 | 91.8 | 41.9 | 78.3 | 118.9 | 53.6 | 101.1 | 105.0 | 51.8 | 90.5 |
| 0970, 0990 | Wall Finishes & Painting/Coating | 110.9 | 57.1 | 78.6 | 91.2 | 46.1 | 64.1 | 101.0 | 40.2 | 64.5 | 113.1 | 54.0 | 77.6 | 112.9 | 54.7 | 78.0 | 99.0 | 39.3 | 63.1 |
| 09 | FINISHES | 105.2 | 61.7 | 82.4 | 107.2 | 44.1 | 74.2 | 101.3 | 41.2 | 69.8 | 94.1 | 55.9 | 74.1 | 105.6 | 55.0 | 79.1 | 110.4 | 47.0 | 77.2 |
| COVERS | DIVS. 10 - 14, 25, 28, 41, 43, 44 | 100.0 | 82.6 | 96.4 | 100.0 | 25.1 | 84.7 | 100.0 | 49.3 | 89.6 | 100.0 | 80.3 | 96.0 | 100.0 | 60.9 | 92.0 | 100.0 | 45.2 | 88.8 |
| 21, 22, 23 | FIRE SUPPRESSION, PLUMBING & HVAC | 99.8 | 58.0 | 82.7 | 95.9 | 39.5 | 72.8 | 95.9 | 81.2 | 89.9 | 99.8 | 65.4 | 85.7 | 99.9 | 61.2 | 84.0 | 96.3 | 40.4 | 73.4 |
| 26, 27, 3370 | ELECTRICAL, COMMUNICATIONS & UTIL. | 93.3 | 63.2 | 78.5 | 107.5 | 68.1 | 88.2 | 96.5 | 78.6 | 87.7 | 91.9 | 62.4 | 77.4 | 95.8 | 58.5 | 77.5 | 96.9 | 36.6 | 67.3 |
| MF2004 | WEIGHTED AVERAGE | 96.9 | 67.5 | 84.3 | 98.2 | 53.3 | 79.0 | 96.8 | 64.6 | 83.0 | 95.6 | 66.3 | 83.0 | 97.7 | 61.9 | 82.4 | 98.0 | 48.3 | 76.8 |

| | | GEORGIA | | | | | | HAWAII | | | | | | | | | IDAHO | | |
|---|---|---|---|---|---|---|---|---|---|---|---|---|---|---|---|---|---|---|---|
| | DIVISION | VALDOSTA | | | WAYCROSS | | | HILO | | | HONOLULU | | | STATES & POSS., GUAM | | | BOISE | | |
| | | 316 | | | 315 | | | 967 | | | 968 | | | 969 | | | 836 - 837 | | |
| | | MAT. | INST. | TOTAL | MAT. | INST. | TOTAL | MAT. | INST. | TOTAL | MAT. | INST. | TOTAL | MAT. | INST. | TOTAL | MAT. | INST. | TOTAL |
| 015433 | CONTRACTOR EQUIPMENT | | 90.6 | 90.6 | | 90.6 | 90.6 | | 99.4 | 99.4 | | 99.4 | 99.4 | | 175.9 | 175.9 | | 101.2 | 101.2 |
| 0241, 31 - 34 | SITE & INFRASTRUCTURE, DEMOLITION | 109.4 | 76.8 | 86.7 | 106.2 | 75.3 | 84.7 | 135.7 | 106.0 | 115.0 | 135.9 | 106.0 | 115.1 | 180.0 | 106.2 | 128.6 | 77.4 | 100.7 | 93.7 |
| 0310 | Concrete Forming & Accessories | 84.3 | 48.0 | 53.0 | 86.3 | 50.0 | 55.0 | 107.6 | 140.4 | 135.9 | 116.3 | 140.4 | 137.1 | 110.2 | 68.1 | 73.9 | 98.8 | 78.2 | 81.1 |
| 0320 | Concrete Reinforcing | 93.7 | 49.8 | 72.5 | 93.7 | 88.0 | 91.0 | 111.9 | 116.6 | 114.2 | 110.9 | 116.6 | 113.7 | 195.9 | 36.5 | 119.1 | 103.0 | 74.6 | 89.3 |
| 0330 | Cast-in-Place Concrete | 95.0 | 53.0 | 79.4 | 107.3 | 52.9 | 87.2 | 206.1 | 124.5 | 175.9 | 178.9 | 124.5 | 158.8 | 178.6 | 121.1 | 157.3 | 96.4 | 82.7 | 91.3 |
| 03 | CONCRETE | 98.2 | 51.6 | 76.7 | 102.2 | 59.3 | 82.4 | 157.1 | 129.2 | 144.2 | 144.0 | 129.2 | 137.2 | 156.8 | 80.7 | 121.7 | 104.8 | 79.0 | 92.9 |
| 04 | MASONRY | 93.1 | 50.7 | 67.8 | 94.1 | 46.8 | 65.8 | 138.6 | 130.1 | 133.5 | 130.9 | 130.1 | 130.4 | 195.3 | 52.1 | 109.7 | 130.6 | 66.8 | 92.4 |
| 05 | METALS | 93.7 | 74.2 | 88.0 | 92.8 | 81.5 | 89.5 | 114.9 | 107.5 | 112.7 | 138.8 | 107.5 | 129.7 | 148.7 | 83.9 | 129.9 | 101.8 | 74.6 | 93.9 |
| 06 | WOOD, PLASTICS & COMPOSITES | 82.0 | 44.7 | 61.9 | 84.7 | 51.2 | 66.7 | 98.9 | 145.6 | 124.0 | 111.2 | 145.6 | 129.7 | 111.1 | 69.6 | 88.8 | 93.6 | 79.4 | 85.9 |
| 07 | THERMAL & MOISTURE PROTECTION | 95.1 | 62.1 | 82.2 | 94.9 | 46.8 | 76.2 | 103.6 | 127.2 | 112.8 | 112.7 | 127.2 | 118.4 | 121.4 | 75.3 | 103.4 | 92.7 | 73.2 | 85.1 |
| 08 | OPENINGS | 93.0 | 42.1 | 80.4 | 93.0 | 49.6 | 82.3 | 100.5 | 135.1 | 109.0 | 105.7 | 135.1 | 113.0 | 105.2 | 59.0 | 93.8 | 93.0 | 74.1 | 88.3 |
| 0920 | Plaster & Gypsum Board | 93.8 | 43.8 | 63.0 | 95.5 | 50.5 | 67.7 | 105.2 | 146.6 | 130.7 | 135.3 | 146.6 | 142.3 | 204.3 | 56.4 | 113.1 | 84.2 | 78.6 | 80.8 |
| 0950, 0980 | Ceilings & Acoustic Treatment | 97.0 | 43.8 | 64.3 | 95.1 | 50.5 | 67.7 | 115.2 | 146.6 | 134.5 | 119.4 | 146.6 | 136.1 | 240.2 | 56.4 | 127.3 | 109.2 | 78.6 | 90.5 |
| 0960 | Flooring | 109.9 | 44.6 | 92.2 | 111.3 | 34.5 | 90.4 | 144.5 | 129.3 | 140.4 | 168.7 | 129.3 | 158.0 | 168.6 | 53.6 | 137.3 | 101.7 | 49.8 | 87.6 |
| 0970, 0990 | Wall Finishes & Painting/Coating | 110.9 | 38.6 | 67.5 | 110.9 | 47.8 | 73.0 | 100.5 | 145.0 | 127.2 | 105.0 | 145.0 | 129.0 | 107.1 | 43.0 | 68.6 | 92.7 | 70.1 | 84.1 |
| 09 | FINISHES | 101.5 | 45.8 | 72.3 | 101.4 | 46.5 | 72.7 | 122.5 | 140.4 | 131.9 | 136.3 | 140.4 | 138.4 | 203.0 | 63.4 | 129.9 | 99.5 | 70.1 | 84.1 |
| COVERS | DIVS. 10 - 14, 25, 28, 41, 43, 44 | 100.0 | 59.7 | 91.7 | 100.0 | 45.7 | 88.9 | 100.0 | 119.8 | 104.0 | 100.0 | 119.8 | 104.1 | 100.0 | 93.2 | 98.6 | 100.0 | 72.7 | 94.4 |
| 21, 22, 23 | FIRE SUPPRESSION, PLUMBING & HVAC | 99.8 | 41.5 | 75.9 | 97.2 | 50.5 | 78.0 | 100.2 | 112.0 | 105.1 | 100.2 | 112.0 | 105.0 | 103.1 | 46.7 | 79.9 | 99.9 | 72.1 | 88.5 |
| 26, 27, 3370 | ELECTRICAL, COMMUNICATIONS & UTIL. | 91.4 | 37.0 | 64.7 | 95.6 | 68.3 | 82.2 | 109.3 | 124.8 | 116.9 | 112.6 | 124.8 | 118.6 | 161.5 | 49.5 | 106.5 | 95.1 | 79.3 | 87.4 |
| MF2004 | WEIGHTED AVERAGE | 96.8 | 50.8 | 77.1 | 97.0 | 57.9 | 80.3 | 115.3 | 122.7 | 118.5 | 119.7 | 122.7 | 121.0 | 139.3 | 65.7 | 107.8 | 100.2 | 76.2 | 89.9 |

| | | IDAHO | | | | | | | | | | | | | | | ILLINOIS | | |
|---|---|---|---|---|---|---|---|---|---|---|---|---|---|---|---|---|---|---|---|
| | DIVISION | COEUR D'ALENE | | | IDAHO FALLS | | | LEWISTON | | | POCATELLO | | | TWIN FALLS | | | BLOOMINGTON | | |
| | | 838 | | | 834 | | | 835 | | | 832 | | | 833 | | | 617 | | |
| | | MAT. | INST. | TOTAL | MAT. | INST. | TOTAL | MAT. | INST. | TOTAL | MAT. | INST. | TOTAL | MAT. | INST. | TOTAL | MAT. | INST. | TOTAL |
| 015433 | CONTRACTOR EQUIPMENT | | 94.2 | 94.2 | | 101.2 | 101.2 | | 94.2 | 94.2 | | 101.2 | 101.2 | | 101.2 | 101.2 | | 101.4 | 101.4 |
| 0241, 31 - 34 | SITE & INFRASTRUCTURE, DEMOLITION | 78.5 | 95.3 | 90.2 | 75.8 | 99.7 | 92.5 | 84.8 | 95.7 | 92.4 | 78.9 | 100.7 | 94.1 | 85.5 | 98.7 | 94.7 | 95.2 | 95.0 | 95.1 |
| 0310 | Concrete Forming & Accessories | 109.3 | 64.0 | 70.3 | 92.6 | 46.7 | 53.0 | 114.7 | 65.5 | 72.3 | 99.0 | 77.8 | 80.7 | 99.7 | 32.8 | 42.1 | 86.6 | 109.1 | 106.0 |
| 0320 | Concrete Reinforcing | 110.3 | 98.9 | 104.8 | 104.9 | 73.4 | 89.7 | 110.3 | 99.2 | 104.9 | 103.3 | 74.1 | 89.3 | 105.2 | 73.8 | 90.1 | 97.0 | 96.7 | 96.9 |
| 0330 | Cast-in-Place Concrete | 104.3 | 90.6 | 99.2 | 91.8 | 56.3 | 78.6 | 108.4 | 91.7 | 102.2 | 99.1 | 82.5 | 93.0 | 101.7 | 41.7 | 79.5 | 98.3 | 97.1 | 97.8 |
| 03 | CONCRETE | 111.8 | 80.0 | 97.1 | 96.7 | 55.8 | 77.8 | 115.7 | 81.1 | 99.8 | 104.2 | 78.7 | 92.4 | 112.0 | 44.7 | 80.9 | 95.6 | 102.9 | 99.0 |
| 04 | MASONRY | 132.1 | 83.8 | 103.2 | 125.8 | 35.8 | 72.0 | 132.5 | 87.6 | 105.6 | 127.7 | 59.6 | 87.0 | 130.6 | 35.0 | 73.4 | 109.3 | 108.5 | 108.8 |
| 05 | METALS | 95.5 | 86.8 | 93.0 | 109.8 | 71.8 | 98.7 | 95.0 | 87.9 | 92.9 | 109.8 | 73.6 | 99.3 | 109.8 | 71.3 | 98.6 | 93.3 | 106.8 | 97.2 |
| 06 | WOOD, PLASTICS & COMPOSITES | 97.3 | 57.7 | 76.0 | 87.0 | 45.2 | 64.5 | 102.9 | 57.7 | 78.5 | 93.6 | 79.4 | 86.0 | 94.3 | 31.8 | 60.6 | 85.0 | 106.8 | 96.7 |
| 07 | THERMAL & MOISTURE PROTECTION | 139.1 | 76.6 | 114.7 | 92.2 | 49.1 | 75.4 | 139.3 | 80.2 | 116.3 | 92.8 | 64.6 | 81.8 | 93.6 | 42.6 | 73.7 | 98.9 | 106.1 | 101.7 |
| 08 | OPENINGS | 113.8 | 62.2 | 101.0 | 96.7 | 49.8 | 85.1 | 113.7 | 65.4 | 101.8 | 93.7 | 68.1 | 87.3 | 96.7 | 40.1 | 82.8 | 90.5 | 99.3 | 92.7 |
| 0920 | Plaster & Gypsum Board | 148.4 | 56.6 | 91.7 | 78.6 | 43.7 | 57.0 | 149.7 | 56.6 | 92.2 | 81.9 | 78.6 | 79.9 | 81.9 | 29.9 | 49.8 | 93.2 | 106.8 | 101.6 |
| 0950, 0980 | Ceilings & Acoustic Treatment | 141.7 | 56.6 | 89.4 | 106.4 | 43.7 | 67.9 | 141.7 | 56.6 | 89.4 | 115.0 | 78.6 | 92.7 | 109.0 | 29.9 | 60.4 | 87.9 | 106.8 | 99.5 |
| 0960 | Flooring | 140.8 | 53.0 | 116.9 | 101.1 | 49.8 | 87.2 | 144.1 | 92.4 | 130.1 | 104.9 | 49.8 | 89.9 | 106.3 | 49.8 | 90.9 | 90.5 | 111.6 | 96.2 |
| 0970, 0990 | Wall Finishes & Painting/Coating | 121.4 | 70.3 | 90.7 | 98.8 | 38.9 | 62.8 | 121.4 | 70.3 | 90.7 | 98.7 | 49.2 | 68.9 | 98.8 | 29.0 | 56.8 | 93.1 | 111.3 | 104.0 |
| 09 | FINISHES | 163.4 | 61.2 | 109.9 | 97.3 | 45.9 | 70.4 | 164.7 | 69.7 | 115.0 | 101.4 | 70.3 | 85.1 | 101.1 | 34.6 | 66.3 | 91.0 | 110.2 | 101.1 |
| COVERS | DIVS. 10 - 14, 25, 28, 41, 43, 44 | 100.0 | 60.1 | 91.8 | 100.0 | 45.8 | 88.9 | 100.0 | 75.7 | 95.0 | 100.0 | 72.6 | 94.4 | 100.0 | 40.7 | 87.9 | 100.0 | 99.0 | 99.8 |
| 21, 22, 23 | FIRE SUPPRESSION, PLUMBING & HVAC | 100.1 | 84.4 | 93.7 | 100.7 | 63.9 | 85.6 | 101.1 | 86.4 | 95.1 | 99.9 | 72.1 | 88.5 | 99.9 | 60.0 | 83.5 | 95.8 | 110.9 | 102.0 |
| 26, 27, 3370 | ELECTRICAL, COMMUNICATIONS & UTIL. | 85.2 | 80.3 | 82.8 | 85.1 | 73.8 | 79.5 | 83.3 | 80.3 | 81.8 | 91.9 | 74.9 | 83.6 | 86.5 | 65.4 | 76.1 | 93.7 | 80.5 | 87.2 |
| MF2004 | WEIGHTED AVERAGE | 108.2 | 79.2 | 95.8 | 99.5 | 61.0 | 83.0 | 108.9 | 82.0 | 97.4 | 101.2 | 74.2 | 89.7 | 102.2 | 55.0 | 82.0 | 95.2 | 102.5 | 98.3 |

# City Cost Indexes

## ILLINOIS

| DIVISION | | CARBONDALE 629 | | | CENTRALIA 628 | | | CHAMPAIGN 618 - 619 | | | CHICAGO 606 - 608 | | | DECATUR 625 | | | EAST ST. LOUIS 620 - 622 | | |
|---|---|---|---|---|---|---|---|---|---|---|---|---|---|---|---|---|---|---|---|
| | | MAT. | INST. | TOTAL | MAT. | INST. | TOTAL | MAT. | INST. | TOTAL | MAT. | INST. | TOTAL | MAT. | INST. | TOTAL | MAT. | INST. | TOTAL |
| 015433 | CONTRACTOR EQUIPMENT | | 108.9 | 108.9 | | 108.9 | 108.9 | | 102.2 | 102.2 | | 90.5 | 90.5 | | 102.2 | 102.2 | | 108.9 | 108.9 |
| 0241, 31 - 34 | SITE & INFRASTRUCTURE, DEMOLITION | 102.7 | 95.9 | 98.0 | 103.1 | 96.7 | 98.7 | 104.9 | 96.3 | 98.9 | 99.3 | 91.2 | 93.7 | 88.8 | 95.8 | 93.7 | 105.0 | 96.2 | 98.8 |
| 0310 | Concrete Forming & Accessories | 95.7 | 101.2 | 100.4 | 98.0 | 109.3 | 107.7 | 93.2 | 110.7 | 108.3 | 101.6 | 151.0 | 144.1 | 98.5 | 95.9 | 96.3 | 93.1 | 108.9 | 106.7 |
| 0320 | Concrete Reinforcing | 96.0 | 85.5 | 90.9 | 96.0 | 101.4 | 98.6 | 97.0 | 85.5 | 91.5 | 100.1 | 151.2 | 124.8 | 94.0 | 93.0 | 93.5 | 95.9 | 101.6 | 98.6 |
| 0330 | Cast-in-Place Concrete | 91.9 | 80.3 | 87.6 | 92.4 | 109.6 | 98.8 | 114.0 | 106.9 | 111.4 | 109.1 | 143.9 | 122.0 | 100.4 | 97.0 | 99.2 | 94.0 | 99.0 | 95.8 |
| 03 | CONCRETE | 86.8 | 92.0 | 89.2 | 87.3 | 108.7 | 97.2 | 108.0 | 104.8 | 106.5 | 104.8 | 147.5 | 124.5 | 97.0 | 96.2 | 96.6 | 88.2 | 104.9 | 95.9 |
| 04 | MASONRY | 73.5 | 96.6 | 87.3 | 73.5 | 113.9 | 97.7 | 132.2 | 88.4 | 106.0 | 93.8 | 149.9 | 127.4 | 70.1 | 104.6 | 90.7 | 73.7 | 108.6 | 94.6 |
| 05 | METALS | 92.5 | 108.8 | 97.3 | 92.6 | 118.3 | 100.0 | 93.3 | 99.5 | 95.1 | 95.3 | 129.8 | 105.3 | 95.8 | 103.4 | 98.0 | 93.6 | 118.2 | 100.8 |
| 06 | WOOD, PLASTICS & COMPOSITES | 99.8 | 103.4 | 101.7 | 102.5 | 107.3 | 105.1 | 92.3 | 111.1 | 102.5 | 104.5 | 150.4 | 129.2 | 100.4 | 92.4 | 96.1 | 97.0 | 110.7 | 104.4 |
| 07 | THERMAL & MOISTURE PROTECTION | 93.9 | 91.8 | 93.0 | 93.9 | 105.6 | 98.5 | 99.5 | 103.9 | 101.2 | 102.9 | 139.1 | 117.0 | 99.6 | 98.7 | 99.2 | 93.9 | 104.0 | 97.8 |
| 08 | OPENINGS | 86.6 | 105.2 | 91.2 | 86.6 | 108.6 | 92.1 | 91.2 | 103.1 | 94.3 | 102.0 | 152.0 | 114.3 | 97.0 | 95.4 | 96.6 | 86.7 | 113.5 | 93.3 |
| 0920 | Plaster & Gypsum Board | 96.9 | 103.4 | 100.9 | 97.9 | 107.4 | 103.8 | 95.5 | 111.3 | 105.2 | 93.6 | 151.7 | 129.4 | 99.3 | 92.1 | 94.8 | 96.2 | 110.9 | 105.3 |
| 0950, 0980 | Ceilings & Acoustic Treatment | 87.9 | 103.4 | 97.4 | 87.9 | 107.4 | 99.9 | 87.9 | 111.3 | 102.3 | 100.2 | 151.7 | 131.8 | 93.9 | 92.1 | 92.8 | 87.9 | 110.9 | 102.0 |
| 0960 | Flooring | 107.8 | 89.9 | 102.9 | 109.1 | 114.1 | 110.5 | 93.9 | 106.7 | 97.4 | 87.9 | 144.2 | 103.2 | 98.1 | 105.9 | 100.2 | 106.5 | 119.0 | 109.9 |
| 0970, 0990 | Wall Finishes & Painting/Coating | 100.8 | 95.0 | 97.3 | 100.8 | 103.3 | 102.3 | 93.1 | 107.3 | 101.6 | 86.1 | 144.1 | 121.0 | 93.1 | 103.1 | 99.1 | 100.8 | 103.8 | 102.6 |
| 09 | FINISHES | 94.9 | 99.1 | 97.1 | 95.5 | 109.7 | 102.9 | 93.0 | 110.6 | 102.2 | 91.5 | 149.8 | 122.0 | 95.6 | 98.6 | 97.2 | 94.5 | 109.1 | 102.1 |
| COVERS | DIVS. 10 - 14, 25, 28, 41, 43, 44 | 100.0 | 94.2 | 98.8 | 100.0 | 98.9 | 99.8 | 100.0 | 82.4 | 96.4 | 100.0 | 124.5 | 105.0 | 100.0 | 79.6 | 95.8 | 100.0 | 96.3 | 99.3 |
| 21, 22, 23 | FIRE SUPPRESSION, PLUMBING & HVAC | 95.7 | 92.9 | 94.6 | 95.7 | 95.3 | 95.5 | 95.8 | 104.0 | 99.1 | 99.9 | 134.1 | 113.9 | 99.9 | 98.1 | 99.2 | 99.9 | 92.8 | 97.0 |
| 26, 27, 3370 | ELECTRICAL, COMMUNICATIONS & UTIL. | 92.4 | 98.7 | 95.5 | 93.8 | 93.8 | 93.8 | 96.9 | 96.8 | 96.8 | 96.0 | 133.4 | 114.4 | 96.5 | 85.1 | 90.9 | 93.4 | 99.3 | 96.3 |
| MF2004 | WEIGHTED AVERAGE | 92.2 | 97.1 | 94.3 | 92.5 | 103.9 | 97.4 | 98.8 | 100.7 | 99.6 | 98.6 | 136.2 | 114.7 | 96.0 | 96.3 | 96.2 | 93.6 | 103.1 | 97.7 |

## ILLINOIS

| DIVISION | | EFFINGHAM 624 | | | GALESBURG 614 | | | JOLIET 604 | | | KANKAKEE 609 | | | LA SALLE 613 | | | NORTH SUBURBAN 600 - 603 | | |
|---|---|---|---|---|---|---|---|---|---|---|---|---|---|---|---|---|---|---|---|
| | | MAT. | INST. | TOTAL | MAT. | INST. | TOTAL | MAT. | INST. | TOTAL | MAT. | INST. | TOTAL | MAT. | INST. | TOTAL | MAT. | INST. | TOTAL |
| 015433 | CONTRACTOR EQUIPMENT | | 102.2 | 102.2 | | 101.4 | 101.4 | | 88.3 | 88.3 | | 88.3 | 88.3 | | 101.4 | 101.4 | | 88.3 | 88.3 |
| 0241, 31 - 34 | SITE & INFRASTRUCTURE, DEMOLITION | 96.4 | 95.9 | 96.1 | 97.6 | 95.0 | 95.8 | 99.2 | 88.8 | 92.0 | 93.0 | 88.5 | 89.9 | 97.0 | 95.6 | 96.1 | 98.4 | 89.3 | 92.0 |
| 0310 | Concrete Forming & Accessories | 103.0 | 107.7 | 107.1 | 93.1 | 112.5 | 109.8 | 103.6 | 130.0 | 126.3 | 96.3 | 105.1 | 103.8 | 107.5 | 116.5 | 115.3 | 102.8 | 127.3 | 123.9 |
| 0320 | Concrete Reinforcing | 97.0 | 95.2 | 96.2 | 96.6 | 96.8 | 96.7 | 100.1 | 125.6 | 112.4 | 100.9 | 103.9 | 102.3 | 96.7 | 107.0 | 101.7 | 100.1 | 136.2 | 117.5 |
| 0330 | Cast-in-Place Concrete | 100.1 | 103.7 | 101.4 | 101.2 | 98.6 | 100.2 | 109.1 | 120.8 | 113.4 | 101.7 | 116.5 | 107.1 | 101.1 | 106.7 | 103.2 | 109.1 | 132.0 | 117.6 |
| 03 | CONCRETE | 97.8 | 104.2 | 100.8 | 98.3 | 104.9 | 101.4 | 104.9 | 125.3 | 114.3 | 98.8 | 108.6 | 103.3 | 99.2 | 111.6 | 104.9 | 104.9 | 129.9 | 116.4 |
| 04 | MASONRY | 77.0 | 79.9 | 78.8 | 109.5 | 111.2 | 110.5 | 96.7 | 127.4 | 115.0 | 93.3 | 116.3 | 107.1 | 109.5 | 110.3 | 110.0 | 93.8 | 133.0 | 117.2 |
| 05 | METALS | 93.2 | 103.1 | 96.1 | 93.3 | 106.4 | 97.1 | 93.2 | 115.2 | 99.6 | 93.2 | 103.3 | 96.1 | 93.4 | 114.5 | 99.5 | 94.3 | 119.6 | 101.7 |
| 06 | WOOD, PLASTICS & COMPOSITES | 102.9 | 110.0 | 106.7 | 92.2 | 112.2 | 102.9 | 106.1 | 132.1 | 120.1 | 97.9 | 101.0 | 99.5 | 107.9 | 117.0 | 112.8 | 104.5 | 125.8 | 115.9 |
| 07 | THERMAL & MOISTURE PROTECTION | 99.2 | 96.4 | 98.1 | 99.0 | 103.8 | 100.9 | 102.7 | 126.8 | 112.1 | 101.9 | 119.3 | 108.7 | 99.2 | 108.9 | 103.0 | 103.2 | 127.2 | 112.6 |
| 08 | OPENINGS | 91.0 | 105.8 | 94.7 | 90.5 | 103.7 | 93.8 | 99.9 | 135.2 | 108.6 | 92.0 | 109.0 | 96.2 | 90.5 | 107.6 | 94.7 | 99.9 | 131.0 | 107.6 |
| 0920 | Plaster & Gypsum Board | 98.9 | 110.2 | 105.9 | 95.5 | 112.4 | 105.9 | 91.2 | 132.9 | 116.9 | 88.5 | 101.0 | 96.2 | 100.9 | 117.3 | 111.0 | 93.6 | 126.4 | 113.8 |
| 0950, 0980 | Ceilings & Acoustic Treatment | 87.9 | 110.2 | 101.6 | 87.9 | 112.4 | 102.9 | 100.2 | 132.9 | 120.3 | 100.2 | 101.0 | 100.7 | 87.9 | 117.3 | 106.0 | 100.2 | 126.4 | 116.3 |
| 0960 | Flooring | 99.5 | 106.7 | 101.5 | 93.9 | 108.7 | 97.9 | 87.5 | 133.9 | 100.4 | 84.4 | 98.8 | 88.3 | 101.9 | 110.1 | 104.2 | 87.9 | 133.9 | 100.4 |
| 0970, 0990 | Wall Finishes & Painting/Coating | 93.1 | 100.5 | 97.5 | 93.1 | 96.7 | 95.2 | 84.2 | 136.9 | 115.8 | 84.2 | 102.5 | 95.2 | 93.1 | 111.3 | 104.0 | 86.1 | 136.9 | 116.6 |
| 09 | FINISHES | 94.6 | 107.8 | 101.5 | 92.5 | 111.1 | 102.2 | 90.9 | 132.4 | 112.6 | 89.2 | 101.8 | 95.8 | 95.7 | 114.9 | 105.8 | 91.5 | 129.8 | 111.5 |
| COVERS | DIVS. 10 - 14, 25, 28, 41, 43, 44 | 100.0 | 80.2 | 96.0 | 100.0 | 99.5 | 99.9 | 100.0 | 116.0 | 103.3 | 100.0 | 92.1 | 98.4 | 100.0 | 99.3 | 99.9 | 100.0 | 105.2 | 101.1 |
| 21, 22, 23 | FIRE SUPPRESSION, PLUMBING & HVAC | 95.8 | 101.1 | 98.0 | 95.8 | 101.8 | 98.2 | 100.0 | 119.2 | 107.9 | 95.8 | 97.7 | 96.6 | 95.8 | 118.4 | 105.1 | 99.9 | 113.3 | 105.4 |
| 26, 27, 3370 | ELECTRICAL, COMMUNICATIONS & UTIL. | 94.4 | 98.7 | 96.5 | 94.6 | 77.4 | 86.2 | 94.9 | 95.7 | 95.3 | 89.8 | 128.0 | 108.5 | 91.7 | 92.5 | 92.1 | 94.8 | 120.3 | 107.3 |
| MF2004 | WEIGHTED AVERAGE | 94.5 | 99.2 | 96.5 | 95.9 | 100.9 | 98.1 | 98.1 | 117.2 | 106.3 | 94.5 | 106.6 | 99.7 | 96.1 | 109.0 | 101.6 | 98.1 | 120.2 | 107.6 |

## ILLINOIS

| DIVISION | | PEORIA 615 - 616 | | | QUINCY 623 | | | ROCK ISLAND 612 | | | ROCKFORD 610 - 611 | | | SOUTH SUBURBAN 605 | | | SPRINGFIELD 626 - 627 | | |
|---|---|---|---|---|---|---|---|---|---|---|---|---|---|---|---|---|---|---|---|
| | | MAT. | INST. | TOTAL | MAT. | INST. | TOTAL | MAT. | INST. | TOTAL | MAT. | INST. | TOTAL | MAT. | INST. | TOTAL | MAT. | INST. | TOTAL |
| 015433 | CONTRACTOR EQUIPMENT | | 101.4 | 101.4 | | 102.2 | 102.2 | | 101.4 | 101.4 | | 101.4 | 101.4 | | 88.3 | 88.3 | | 102.2 | 102.2 |
| 0241, 31 - 34 | SITE & INFRASTRUCTURE, DEMOLITION | 97.8 | 95.1 | 95.9 | 95.2 | 95.5 | 95.4 | 95.8 | 94.5 | 94.9 | 96.9 | 96.4 | 96.6 | 98.4 | 89.3 | 92.0 | 94.9 | 95.8 | 95.5 |
| 0310 | Concrete Forming & Accessories | 96.8 | 100.3 | 99.8 | 100.7 | 106.8 | 105.9 | 94.9 | 101.8 | 100.8 | 100.9 | 122.9 | 119.9 | 102.8 | 127.3 | 123.9 | 98.9 | 95.6 | 96.1 |
| 0320 | Concrete Reinforcing | 94.0 | 96.7 | 95.3 | 96.7 | 89.2 | 93.1 | 96.6 | 96.4 | 96.5 | 88.9 | 130.6 | 109.0 | 100.1 | 136.2 | 117.5 | 94.0 | 89.3 | 91.8 |
| 0330 | Cast-in-Place Concrete | 98.1 | 99.9 | 98.8 | 100.3 | 94.9 | 98.3 | 99.0 | 95.5 | 97.7 | 100.5 | 114.9 | 105.8 | 109.1 | 132.0 | 117.6 | 90.5 | 96.6 | 92.8 |
| 03 | CONCRETE | 95.7 | 99.9 | 97.7 | 97.4 | 99.6 | 98.4 | 96.6 | 99.0 | 97.7 | 96.3 | 121.7 | 108.0 | 104.9 | 129.9 | 116.4 | 92.0 | 95.3 | 93.5 |
| 04 | MASONRY | 110.3 | 109.6 | 109.9 | 95.8 | 96.9 | 96.5 | 109.3 | 99.4 | 103.4 | 85.6 | 104.9 | 97.2 | 93.8 | 133.0 | 117.2 | 74.0 | 104.1 | 92.0 |
| 05 | METALS | 95.8 | 106.8 | 99.0 | 93.2 | 101.5 | 95.6 | 93.3 | 105.3 | 96.8 | 95.8 | 124.6 | 104.2 | 94.3 | 119.6 | 101.7 | 98.2 | 101.8 | 99.3 |
| 06 | WOOD, PLASTICS & COMPOSITES | 100.4 | 94.4 | 97.2 | 100.3 | 110.0 | 105.5 | 94.2 | 101.3 | 98.0 | 100.4 | 123.3 | 112.7 | 104.5 | 125.8 | 115.9 | 101.1 | 92.4 | 96.4 |
| 07 | THERMAL & MOISTURE PROTECTION | 99.7 | 105.3 | 101.9 | 99.2 | 97.5 | 98.5 | 99.0 | 97.6 | 98.4 | 102.5 | 115.8 | 107.7 | 103.2 | 127.2 | 112.6 | 99.3 | 97.9 | 98.7 |
| 08 | OPENINGS | 97.1 | 97.3 | 97.1 | 91.8 | 103.9 | 94.8 | 90.5 | 97.8 | 92.3 | 97.1 | 123.0 | 103.5 | 99.9 | 131.0 | 107.6 | 98.1 | 94.4 | 97.2 |
| 0920 | Plaster & Gypsum Board | 99.3 | 94.1 | 96.1 | 97.9 | 110.2 | 105.5 | 96.2 | 101.2 | 99.3 | 99.3 | 123.8 | 114.4 | 93.6 | 126.4 | 113.8 | 96.0 | 92.1 | 93.6 |
| 0950, 0980 | Ceilings & Acoustic Treatment | 93.9 | 94.1 | 94.0 | 87.9 | 110.2 | 101.6 | 87.9 | 101.2 | 96.1 | 93.9 | 123.8 | 112.2 | 100.2 | 126.4 | 116.3 | 92.2 | 92.1 | 92.1 |
| 0960 | Flooring | 98.1 | 108.7 | 101.0 | 98.1 | 101.4 | 99.0 | 95.3 | 104.5 | 97.8 | 98.1 | 104.5 | 99.9 | 87.9 | 133.9 | 100.4 | 98.1 | 105.9 | 100.2 |
| 0970, 0990 | Wall Finishes & Painting/Coating | 93.1 | 105.4 | 100.5 | 93.1 | 103.1 | 99.1 | 93.1 | 96.7 | 95.2 | 93.1 | 119.4 | 108.9 | 86.1 | 136.9 | 116.6 | 93.1 | 103.1 | 99.1 |
| 09 | FINISHES | 95.7 | 101.9 | 99.0 | 94.0 | 106.7 | 100.7 | 92.9 | 102.3 | 97.8 | 95.7 | 119.4 | 108.1 | 91.5 | 129.8 | 111.5 | 94.6 | 98.5 | 96.7 |
| COVERS | DIVS. 10 - 14, 25, 28, 41, 43, 44 | 100.0 | 97.9 | 99.6 | 100.0 | 82.7 | 96.5 | 100.0 | 77.8 | 95.5 | 100.0 | 103.4 | 100.7 | 100.0 | 105.2 | 101.1 | 100.0 | 79.4 | 95.8 |
| 21, 22, 23 | FIRE SUPPRESSION, PLUMBING & HVAC | 99.9 | 105.3 | 102.1 | 95.8 | 96.4 | 96.0 | 95.8 | 98.5 | 96.9 | 95.9 | 110.2 | 104.2 | 99.9 | 113.3 | 105.4 | 99.8 | 93.4 | 97.2 |
| 26, 27, 3370 | ELECTRICAL, COMMUNICATIONS & UTIL. | 95.6 | 91.7 | 93.7 | 91.8 | 82.1 | 87.1 | 86.8 | 88.5 | 87.6 | 95.9 | 123.3 | 109.4 | 94.8 | 120.3 | 107.3 | 97.1 | 80.2 | 88.8 |
| MF2004 | WEIGHTED AVERAGE | 98.1 | 101.2 | 99.5 | 95.1 | 96.7 | 95.8 | 94.9 | 97.4 | 95.9 | 97.1 | 115.0 | 104.7 | 98.1 | 120.2 | 107.6 | 96.3 | 94.2 | 95.4 |

672

# City Cost Indexes

## INDIANA

| DIVISION | | ANDERSON 460 MAT. | INST. | TOTAL | BLOOMINGTON 474 MAT. | INST. | TOTAL | COLUMBUS 472 MAT. | INST. | TOTAL | EVANSVILLE 476 - 477 MAT. | INST. | TOTAL | FORT WAYNE 467 - 468 MAT. | INST. | TOTAL | GARY 463 - 464 MAT. | INST. | TOTAL |
|---|---|---|---|---|---|---|---|---|---|---|---|---|---|---|---|---|---|---|---|
| 015433 | CONTRACTOR EQUIPMENT | | 96.4 | 96.4 | | 85.4 | 85.4 | | 85.4 | 85.4 | | 120.6 | 120.6 | | 96.4 | 96.4 | | 96.4 | 96.4 |
| 0241, 31 - 34 | SITE & INFRASTRUCTURE, DEMOLITION | 83.7 | 94.6 | 91.3 | 73.9 | 94.6 | 88.3 | 71.1 | 94.4 | 87.3 | 78.6 | 128.6 | 113.4 | 84.8 | 94.6 | 91.6 | 84.3 | 97.5 | 93.5 |
| 0310 | Concrete Forming & Accessories | 94.1 | 78.7 | 80.9 | 99.5 | 79.1 | 82.0 | 93.9 | 76.6 | 79.0 | 93.2 | 81.0 | 82.7 | 92.8 | 76.9 | 79.1 | 94.2 | 110.6 | 108.3 |
| 0320 | Concrete Reinforcing | 95.9 | 79.3 | 87.9 | 89.6 | 79.3 | 84.6 | 90.0 | 78.9 | 84.6 | 98.1 | 76.2 | 87.6 | 95.9 | 78.6 | 87.5 | 95.9 | 95.2 | 95.5 |
| 0330 | Cast-in-Place Concrete | 91.6 | 80.3 | 87.4 | 96.1 | 77.6 | 89.2 | 95.6 | 72.4 | 87.0 | 91.8 | 88.6 | 90.6 | 97.4 | 79.4 | 90.7 | 95.7 | 109.9 | 101.0 |
| 03 | CONCRETE | 89.3 | 79.9 | 84.9 | 99.3 | 78.4 | 89.6 | 98.7 | 75.4 | 87.9 | 99.6 | 82.8 | 91.9 | 92.0 | 78.6 | 85.8 | 91.3 | 107.3 | 98.7 |
| 04 | MASONRY | 87.9 | 82.6 | 84.7 | 87.3 | 76.9 | 81.1 | 87.3 | 76.9 | 81.0 | 83.5 | 83.0 | 83.2 | 91.3 | 80.7 | 85.0 | 89.1 | 106.5 | 99.5 |
| 05 | METALS | 93.3 | 88.1 | 91.8 | 95.8 | 74.8 | 89.7 | 95.8 | 74.1 | 89.5 | 88.7 | 83.9 | 87.3 | 93.3 | 87.3 | 91.6 | 93.3 | 101.1 | 95.6 |
| 06 | WOOD, PLASTICS & COMPOSITES | 108.8 | 78.1 | 92.2 | 116.5 | 78.5 | 96.0 | 111.1 | 75.1 | 91.7 | 95.9 | 79.6 | 87.1 | 108.5 | 76.1 | 91.1 | 106.6 | 111.9 | 109.5 |
| 07 | THERMAL & MOISTURE PROTECTION | 96.2 | 80.7 | 90.2 | 91.7 | 81.6 | 87.8 | 91.4 | 81.2 | 87.4 | 95.6 | 85.5 | 91.7 | 96.0 | 83.9 | 91.3 | 95.3 | 105.3 | 99.2 |
| 08 | OPENINGS | 96.2 | 79.3 | 92.0 | 103.0 | 79.7 | 97.2 | 98.5 | 77.7 | 93.4 | 95.6 | 78.6 | 91.4 | 96.2 | 75.7 | 91.1 | 96.2 | 109.2 | 99.4 |
| 0920 | Plaster & Gypsum Board | 96.6 | 78.0 | 85.1 | 90.4 | 78.7 | 83.2 | 87.7 | 75.2 | 80.0 | 86.5 | 78.3 | 81.4 | 95.9 | 76.0 | 83.6 | 91.9 | 112.7 | 104.7 |
| 0950, 0980 | Ceilings & Acoustic Treatment | 97.2 | 78.0 | 85.4 | 81.9 | 78.7 | 79.9 | 81.9 | 75.2 | 77.8 | 87.5 | 78.3 | 81.9 | 97.2 | 76.0 | 84.2 | 97.2 | 112.7 | 106.7 |
| 0960 | Flooring | 91.0 | 89.7 | 90.6 | 104.1 | 86.7 | 99.4 | 98.5 | 86.7 | 95.3 | 97.6 | 85.1 | 94.2 | 91.0 | 78.5 | 87.6 | 91.0 | 115.9 | 97.8 |
| 0970, 0990 | Wall Finishes & Painting/Coating | 92.9 | 72.3 | 80.5 | 90.3 | 89.0 | 89.6 | 90.3 | 89.0 | 89.6 | 96.8 | 85.4 | 89.9 | 92.9 | 79.3 | 84.7 | 92.9 | 109.2 | 102.7 |
| 09 | FINISHES | 91.5 | 80.0 | 85.5 | 94.2 | 81.6 | 87.6 | 92.0 | 79.6 | 85.5 | 92.9 | 82.1 | 87.3 | 91.3 | 77.4 | 84.1 | 90.7 | 112.1 | 101.9 |
| COVERS | DIVS. 10 - 14, 25, 28, 41, 43, 44 | 100.0 | 90.1 | 98.0 | 100.0 | 81.9 | 96.3 | 100.0 | 81.6 | 96.2 | 100.0 | 86.3 | 97.2 | 100.0 | 81.0 | 96.1 | 100.0 | 87.5 | 97.4 |
| 21, 22, 23 | FIRE SUPPRESSION, PLUMBING & HVAC | 99.9 | 76.8 | 90.4 | 99.7 | 81.7 | 92.3 | 95.6 | 83.6 | 90.7 | 99.9 | 82.9 | 92.9 | 99.9 | 76.8 | 90.5 | 99.9 | 102.9 | 101.1 |
| 26, 27, 3370 | ELECTRICAL, COMMUNICATIONS & UTIL. | 85.9 | 90.1 | 88.0 | 99.0 | 81.1 | 90.2 | 98.2 | 90.1 | 94.2 | 94.3 | 86.0 | 90.2 | 86.8 | 79.6 | 83.2 | 99.2 | 100.3 | 99.8 |
| MF2004 | WEIGHTED AVERAGE | 93.9 | 83.2 | 89.3 | 97.3 | 81.0 | 90.4 | 95.5 | 81.8 | 89.6 | 94.8 | 87.1 | 91.5 | 94.5 | 80.6 | 88.6 | 95.5 | 104.0 | 99.2 |

## INDIANA

| DIVISION | | INDIANAPOLIS 461 - 462 MAT. | INST. | TOTAL | KOKOMO 469 MAT. | INST. | TOTAL | LAFAYETTE 479 MAT. | INST. | TOTAL | LAWRENCEBURG 470 MAT. | INST. | TOTAL | MUNCIE 473 MAT. | INST. | TOTAL | NEW ALBANY 471 MAT. | INST. | TOTAL |
|---|---|---|---|---|---|---|---|---|---|---|---|---|---|---|---|---|---|---|---|
| 015433 | CONTRACTOR EQUIPMENT | | 91.2 | 91.2 | | 96.4 | 96.4 | | 85.4 | 85.4 | | 107.4 | 107.4 | | 95.7 | 95.7 | | 95.4 | 95.4 |
| 0241, 31 - 34 | SITE & INFRASTRUCTURE, DEMOLITION | 83.5 | 98.6 | 94.0 | 80.9 | 94.6 | 90.4 | 72.0 | 94.3 | 87.6 | 70.2 | 113.8 | 100.6 | 74.0 | 94.8 | 88.5 | 67.1 | 98.2 | 88.8 |
| 0310 | Concrete Forming & Accessories | 94.6 | 86.9 | 88.0 | 97.0 | 78.4 | 81.0 | 91.6 | 81.5 | 82.9 | 90.3 | 75.9 | 77.9 | 91.4 | 78.4 | 80.2 | 88.6 | 73.6 | 75.6 |
| 0320 | Concrete Reinforcing | 95.2 | 83.6 | 89.6 | 86.7 | 77.3 | 82.2 | 89.6 | 77.1 | 83.6 | 88.7 | 79.7 | 84.4 | 99.1 | 79.3 | 89.6 | 90.2 | 80.0 | 85.3 |
| 0330 | Cast-in-Place Concrete | 88.2 | 87.5 | 87.9 | 90.7 | 82.9 | 87.8 | 96.2 | 82.0 | 90.9 | 89.9 | 73.9 | 84.0 | 101.0 | 79.4 | 93.0 | 92.8 | 73.1 | 85.5 |
| 03 | CONCRETE | 91.0 | 86.1 | 88.7 | 86.3 | 80.2 | 83.5 | 98.8 | 80.5 | 90.3 | 92.2 | 76.5 | 85.0 | 98.5 | 79.5 | 89.7 | 97.3 | 75.0 | 87.0 |
| 04 | MASONRY | 95.9 | 83.3 | 88.4 | 87.6 | 81.7 | 84.1 | 92.5 | 79.9 | 85.0 | 73.1 | 76.2 | 75.0 | 89.3 | 82.6 | 85.3 | 80.2 | 71.5 | 75.0 |
| 05 | METALS | 95.2 | 79.3 | 90.6 | 90.1 | 86.9 | 89.2 | 94.4 | 73.5 | 88.3 | 90.9 | 87.6 | 89.9 | 97.5 | 88.1 | 94.8 | 92.9 | 82.2 | 89.8 |
| 06 | WOOD, PLASTICS & COMPOSITES | 105.7 | 86.9 | 95.5 | 112.0 | 77.4 | 93.4 | 108.0 | 81.7 | 93.8 | 94.8 | 75.1 | 84.2 | 109.9 | 77.8 | 92.6 | 96.6 | 74.0 | 84.4 |
| 07 | THERMAL & MOISTURE PROTECTION | 94.5 | 85.8 | 91.2 | 95.9 | 80.7 | 89.9 | 91.3 | 80.0 | 86.9 | 93.2 | 78.3 | 87.4 | 94.0 | 80.7 | 88.8 | 85.0 | 71.4 | 79.7 |
| 08 | OPENINGS | 104.1 | 86.0 | 99.6 | 90.8 | 78.4 | 87.7 | 97.0 | 80.7 | 93.0 | 97.1 | 77.9 | 92.3 | 97.8 | 79.2 | 93.2 | 95.2 | 76.8 | 90.7 |
| 0920 | Plaster & Gypsum Board | 95.0 | 86.8 | 90.0 | 100.5 | 77.3 | 86.2 | 84.5 | 81.9 | 82.9 | 73.6 | 75.0 | 74.5 | 86.3 | 78.0 | 81.2 | 85.4 | 73.7 | 78.2 |
| 0950, 0980 | Ceilings & Acoustic Treatment | 101.4 | 86.8 | 92.5 | 96.3 | 77.3 | 84.7 | 75.1 | 81.9 | 79.3 | 91.7 | 75.0 | 81.4 | 82.8 | 78.0 | 79.8 | 87.5 | 73.7 | 79.0 |
| 0960 | Flooring | 90.8 | 91.0 | 90.8 | 95.4 | 88.5 | 93.5 | 97.3 | 91.3 | 95.6 | 72.6 | 89.7 | 77.2 | 96.7 | 89.7 | 94.8 | 95.6 | 67.3 | 87.9 |
| 0970, 0990 | Wall Finishes & Painting/Coating | 92.9 | 91.8 | 92.3 | 92.9 | 85.9 | 88.7 | 90.3 | 87.2 | 88.4 | 91.9 | 76.3 | 82.5 | 90.3 | 72.3 | 79.5 | 96.8 | 70.1 | 80.8 |
| 09 | FINISHES | 92.6 | 88.4 | 90.4 | 93.1 | 81.0 | 86.8 | 89.6 | 84.2 | 86.8 | 84.3 | 78.8 | 81.4 | 91.2 | 79.9 | 85.3 | 92.4 | 72.1 | 81.8 |
| COVERS | DIVS. 10 - 14, 25, 28, 41, 43, 44 | 100.0 | 92.7 | 98.5 | 100.0 | 82.4 | 96.4 | 100.0 | 90.1 | 98.0 | 100.0 | 50.8 | 89.9 | 100.0 | 89.5 | 97.9 | 100.0 | 50.4 | 89.8 |
| 21, 22, 23 | FIRE SUPPRESSION, PLUMBING & HVAC | 99.9 | 85.2 | 93.9 | 95.8 | 83.7 | 90.8 | 95.6 | 78.2 | 88.4 | 96.3 | 77.4 | 88.5 | 99.7 | 76.7 | 90.2 | 95.8 | 76.3 | 87.8 |
| 26, 27, 3370 | ELECTRICAL, COMMUNICATIONS & UTIL. | 102.0 | 90.1 | 96.1 | 90.5 | 81.4 | 86.0 | 97.7 | 83.2 | 90.6 | 92.0 | 69.4 | 80.9 | 89.6 | 80.5 | 85.1 | 92.8 | 77.2 | 85.1 |
| MF2004 | WEIGHTED AVERAGE | 97.3 | 87.1 | 93.0 | 92.1 | 83.2 | 88.3 | 95.1 | 81.6 | 89.4 | 91.8 | 79.5 | 86.5 | 95.9 | 81.8 | 89.8 | 93.2 | 76.7 | 86.2 |

## INDIANA / IOWA

| DIVISION | | SOUTH BEND 465 - 466 MAT. | INST. | TOTAL | TERRE HAUTE 478 MAT. | INST. | TOTAL | WASHINGTON 475 MAT. | INST. | TOTAL | BURLINGTON 526 MAT. | INST. | TOTAL | CARROLL 514 MAT. | INST. | TOTAL | CEDAR RAPIDS 522 - 524 MAT. | INST. | TOTAL |
|---|---|---|---|---|---|---|---|---|---|---|---|---|---|---|---|---|---|---|---|
| 015433 | CONTRACTOR EQUIPMENT | | 106.5 | 106.5 | | 120.6 | 120.6 | | 120.6 | 120.6 | | 100.1 | 100.1 | | 100.1 | 100.1 | | 96.0 | 96.0 |
| 0241, 31 - 34 | SITE & INFRASTRUCTURE, DEMOLITION | 84.9 | 95.0 | 92.0 | 80.1 | 128.4 | 113.8 | 80.3 | 126.8 | 112.7 | 92.2 | 96.0 | 94.8 | 81.3 | 93.6 | 89.9 | 94.1 | 95.7 | 95.2 |
| 0310 | Concrete Forming & Accessories | 95.8 | 80.6 | 82.7 | 94.4 | 80.8 | 82.6 | 95.1 | 80.0 | 82.1 | 95.6 | 70.8 | 74.2 | 83.1 | 46.4 | 51.5 | 101.2 | 80.3 | 83.2 |
| 0320 | Concrete Reinforcing | 95.9 | 75.6 | 86.1 | 98.1 | 82.0 | 90.3 | 90.7 | 58.7 | 75.3 | 95.1 | 79.5 | 87.6 | 95.9 | 47.7 | 72.7 | 95.9 | 83.6 | 90.0 |
| 0330 | Cast-in-Place Concrete | 88.1 | 83.8 | 86.5 | 88.9 | 89.0 | 88.9 | 96.7 | 91.9 | 94.9 | 105.3 | 50.5 | 85.0 | 105.3 | 54.8 | 86.6 | 105.5 | 80.4 | 96.2 |
| 03 | CONCRETE | 83.9 | 82.1 | 83.1 | 102.0 | 84.0 | 93.7 | 107.5 | 80.1 | 94.8 | 99.2 | 66.5 | 84.1 | 98.1 | 50.8 | 76.3 | 99.3 | 81.6 | 91.1 |
| 04 | MASONRY | 86.5 | 82.0 | 83.8 | 90.2 | 83.3 | 86.1 | 83.7 | 84.8 | 84.4 | 95.8 | 57.3 | 72.8 | 98.5 | 42.9 | 65.3 | 102.2 | 78.6 | 88.1 |
| 05 | METALS | 93.3 | 100.2 | 95.3 | 89.5 | 87.1 | 88.8 | 84.4 | 73.0 | 81.1 | 89.2 | 91.2 | 89.8 | 89.2 | 69.3 | 83.4 | 91.4 | 92.5 | 91.7 |
| 06 | WOOD, PLASTICS & COMPOSITES | 105.8 | 80.3 | 92.1 | 98.0 | 79.9 | 88.2 | 98.3 | 79.5 | 88.2 | 102.3 | 77.3 | 88.8 | 87.8 | 48.1 | 66.4 | 108.7 | 79.5 | 93.0 |
| 07 | THERMAL & MOISTURE PROTECTION | 91.3 | 85.0 | 88.9 | 95.7 | 82.9 | 90.7 | 95.8 | 83.8 | 91.1 | 100.7 | 61.9 | 85.5 | 101.0 | 50.0 | 81.1 | 101.6 | 80.1 | 93.2 |
| 08 | OPENINGS | 89.5 | 79.3 | 87.0 | 96.1 | 81.0 | 92.4 | 93.0 | 73.2 | 88.1 | 92.5 | 71.0 | 87.2 | 97.6 | 44.4 | 84.5 | 98.5 | 83.1 | 94.7 |
| 0920 | Plaster & Gypsum Board | 90.1 | 80.2 | 84.0 | 86.5 | 78.7 | 81.7 | 85.3 | 78.2 | 80.9 | 95.7 | 76.8 | 84.0 | 90.9 | 46.8 | 63.7 | 98.7 | 79.3 | 86.7 |
| 0950, 0980 | Ceilings & Acoustic Treatment | 92.9 | 80.2 | 85.1 | 87.5 | 78.7 | 82.1 | 78.1 | 78.2 | 78.2 | 109.3 | 76.8 | 89.3 | 109.3 | 46.8 | 71.0 | 113.6 | 79.3 | 92.5 |
| 0960 | Flooring | 89.4 | 86.0 | 88.5 | 97.6 | 89.9 | 95.5 | 98.7 | 88.3 | 95.9 | 111.4 | 43.7 | 93.0 | 104.1 | 38.4 | 86.3 | 128.9 | 51.5 | 107.9 |
| 0970, 0990 | Wall Finishes & Painting/Coating | 92.4 | 84.8 | 87.8 | 96.8 | 87.6 | 91.3 | 96.8 | 89.0 | 92.1 | 101.5 | 73.5 | 84.7 | 101.5 | 37.2 | 62.9 | 105.2 | 76.3 | 87.9 |
| 09 | FINISHES | 89.0 | 82.2 | 85.4 | 92.9 | 83.2 | 87.8 | 91.1 | 83.2 | 86.9 | 105.0 | 66.4 | 84.8 | 100.7 | 43.7 | 70.9 | 111.9 | 73.6 | 91.8 |
| COVERS | DIVS. 10 - 14, 25, 28, 41, 43, 44 | 100.0 | 81.9 | 96.3 | 100.0 | 93.2 | 98.6 | 100.0 | 86.3 | 97.2 | 100.0 | 80.6 | 96.0 | 100.0 | 76.2 | 95.1 | 100.0 | 86.6 | 97.3 |
| 21, 22, 23 | FIRE SUPPRESSION, PLUMBING & HVAC | 99.8 | 81.9 | 91.3 | 99.9 | 78.5 | 91.1 | 95.8 | 82.2 | 90.2 | 96.1 | 69.9 | 85.3 | 96.1 | 47.3 | 76.1 | 100.2 | 84.8 | 93.9 |
| 26, 27, 3370 | ELECTRICAL, COMMUNICATIONS & UTIL. | 97.3 | 85.1 | 91.3 | 92.6 | 81.2 | 87.0 | 93.1 | 86.0 | 89.6 | 98.3 | 73.6 | 86.2 | 99.0 | 37.8 | 69.0 | 96.0 | 80.8 | 88.5 |
| MF2004 | WEIGHTED AVERAGE | 93.4 | 84.4 | 89.5 | 95.5 | 86.4 | 91.6 | 93.7 | 85.5 | 90.2 | 96.4 | 72.6 | 86.2 | 96.2 | 52.2 | 77.4 | 99.1 | 83.2 | 92.3 |

# City Cost Indexes

## IOWA

| | DIVISION | COUNCIL BLUFFS 515 | | | CRESTON 508 | | | DAVENPORT 527 - 528 | | | DECORAH 521 | | | DES MOINES 500 - 503,509 | | | DUBUQUE 520 | | |
|---|---|---|---|---|---|---|---|---|---|---|---|---|---|---|---|---|---|---|---|
| | | MAT. | INST. | TOTAL | MAT. | INST. | TOTAL | MAT. | INST. | TOTAL | MAT. | INST. | TOTAL | MAT. | INST. | TOTAL | MAT. | INST. | TOTAL |
| 015433 | CONTRACTOR EQUIPMENT | | 95.7 | 95.7 | | 100.1 | 100.1 | | 100.1 | 100.1 | | 100.1 | 100.1 | | 102.0 | 102.0 | | 94.6 | 94.6 |
| 0241, 31 - 34 | SITE & INFRASTRUCTURE, DEMOLITION | 101.9 | 92.3 | 95.2 | 81.2 | 94.7 | 90.6 | 91.9 | 99.6 | 97.3 | 90.7 | 94.2 | 93.1 | 83.0 | 100.4 | 95.1 | 92.1 | 92.3 | 92.2 |
| 0310 | Concrete Forming & Accessories | 82.3 | 55.6 | 59.3 | 83.6 | 68.4 | 70.5 | 100.9 | 91.5 | 92.8 | 92.9 | 43.5 | 50.3 | 101.9 | 75.4 | 79.0 | 83.7 | 71.4 | 73.1 |
| 0320 | Concrete Reinforcing | 97.8 | 78.2 | 88.4 | 95.3 | 81.9 | 88.8 | 95.9 | 96.0 | 95.9 | 95.1 | 47.9 | 72.4 | 95.9 | 79.9 | 88.2 | 94.6 | 83.4 | 89.2 |
| 0330 | Cast-in-Place Concrete | 109.8 | 77.3 | 97.7 | 104.9 | 57.2 | 87.3 | 101.6 | 94.0 | 98.8 | 102.4 | 51.6 | 83.6 | 99.7 | 95.0 | 98.0 | 103.3 | 91.3 | 98.9 |
| 03 | CONCRETE | 101.6 | 68.5 | 86.4 | 97.9 | 67.9 | 84.0 | 97.4 | 93.7 | 95.7 | 97.2 | 48.4 | 74.6 | 95.4 | 83.7 | 90.0 | 96.1 | 81.3 | 89.3 |
| 04 | MASONRY | 102.7 | 77.4 | 87.6 | 98.4 | 46.6 | 67.4 | 98.3 | 88.0 | 92.1 | 116.6 | 39.9 | 70.7 | 95.6 | 72.0 | 81.5 | 103.1 | 69.8 | 83.2 |
| 05 | METALS | 96.9 | 89.5 | 94.8 | 89.1 | 85.8 | 88.2 | 91.4 | 102.4 | 94.6 | 89.3 | 68.8 | 83.3 | 91.6 | 92.0 | 91.7 | 90.1 | 91.9 | 90.7 |
| 06 | WOOD, PLASTICS & COMPOSITES | 86.6 | 49.3 | 66.5 | 88.3 | 75.1 | 81.2 | 108.7 | 90.3 | 98.8 | 99.1 | 44.7 | 69.8 | 108.6 | 75.1 | 90.5 | 88.5 | 71.1 | 79.1 |
| 07 | THERMAL & MOISTURE PROTECTION | 101.0 | 65.7 | 87.2 | 101.7 | 54.4 | 83.2 | 101.1 | 89.7 | 96.7 | 100.9 | 44.8 | 79.0 | 102.2 | 76.8 | 92.3 | 101.3 | 70.5 | 89.3 |
| 08 | OPENINGS | 97.6 | 65.6 | 89.7 | 110.0 | 73.1 | 100.9 | 98.5 | 93.2 | 97.2 | 95.9 | 46.3 | 83.7 | 98.5 | 80.1 | 94.0 | 97.6 | 80.6 | 93.4 |
| 0920 | Plaster & Gypsum Board | 90.9 | 48.3 | 64.7 | 90.9 | 74.5 | 80.8 | 98.7 | 90.1 | 93.4 | 94.6 | 43.3 | 63.0 | 90.0 | 74.5 | 80.4 | 91.3 | 70.7 | 78.6 |
| 0950, 0980 | Ceilings & Acoustic Treatment | 109.3 | 48.3 | 71.9 | 109.3 | 74.5 | 87.9 | 113.6 | 90.1 | 99.2 | 109.3 | 43.3 | 68.8 | 109.3 | 74.5 | 87.9 | 109.3 | 70.7 | 85.6 |
| 0960 | Flooring | 103.0 | 42.1 | 86.5 | 104.4 | 38.4 | 86.4 | 114.2 | 95.9 | 109.2 | 110.7 | 54.5 | 95.4 | 113.8 | 38.4 | 93.3 | 117.9 | 35.8 | 95.6 |
| 0970, 0990 | Wall Finishes & Painting/Coating | 97.7 | 73.2 | 83.0 | 101.5 | 46.0 | 68.1 | 101.5 | 92.2 | 95.9 | 101.5 | 39.4 | 64.2 | 101.5 | 79.6 | 88.3 | 104.2 | 76.3 | 87.4 |
| 09 | FINISHES | 101.5 | 52.8 | 76.0 | 100.8 | 61.3 | 80.1 | 107.3 | 92.3 | 99.4 | 104.6 | 45.3 | 73.6 | 103.6 | 68.0 | 85.0 | 106.2 | 64.2 | 84.2 |
| COVERS | DIVS. 10 - 14, 25, 28, 41, 43, 44 | 100.0 | 84.8 | 96.9 | 100.0 | 80.8 | 96.1 | 100.0 | 90.1 | 98.0 | 100.0 | 45.7 | 88.9 | 100.0 | 85.2 | 97.0 | 100.0 | 83.3 | 96.6 |
| 21, 22, 23 | FIRE SUPPRESSION, PLUMBING & HVAC | 100.2 | 80.4 | 92.1 | 96.1 | 49.4 | 76.9 | 100.2 | 91.8 | 96.8 | 96.1 | 41.0 | 73.5 | 100.1 | 73.5 | 89.2 | 100.2 | 76.1 | 90.3 |
| 26, 27, 3370 | ELECTRICAL, COMMUNICATIONS & UTIL. | 101.1 | 84.8 | 93.1 | 93.9 | 49.4 | 72.0 | 93.2 | 89.9 | 91.6 | 96.0 | 37.6 | 67.3 | 96.6 | 74.9 | 85.9 | 99.7 | 77.2 | 88.6 |
| MF2004 | WEIGHTED AVERAGE | 99.9 | 76.1 | 89.7 | 96.8 | 62.6 | 82.2 | 97.9 | 93.0 | 95.8 | 97.2 | 49.4 | 76.8 | 97.4 | 78.9 | 89.5 | 98.2 | 77.8 | 89.4 |

## IOWA

| | DIVISION | FORT DODGE 505 | | | MASON CITY 504 | | | OTTUMWA 525 | | | SHENANDOAH 516 | | | SIBLEY 512 | | | SIOUX CITY 510 - 511 | | |
|---|---|---|---|---|---|---|---|---|---|---|---|---|---|---|---|---|---|---|---|
| | | MAT. | INST. | TOTAL | MAT. | INST. | TOTAL | MAT. | INST. | TOTAL | MAT. | INST. | TOTAL | MAT. | INST. | TOTAL | MAT. | INST. | TOTAL |
| 015433 | CONTRACTOR EQUIPMENT | | 100.1 | 100.1 | | 100.1 | 100.1 | | 94.6 | 94.6 | | 95.7 | 95.7 | | 100.1 | 100.1 | | 100.1 | 100.1 |
| 0241, 31 - 34 | SITE & INFRASTRUCTURE, DEMOLITION | 87.9 | 93.9 | 92.0 | 87.9 | 94.2 | 92.3 | 92.8 | 90.5 | 91.2 | 100.0 | 89.3 | 92.5 | 101.7 | 93.6 | 96.1 | 102.7 | 95.9 | 98.0 |
| 0310 | Concrete Forming & Accessories | 84.3 | 51.1 | 55.7 | 89.0 | 44.6 | 50.7 | 91.0 | 59.0 | 63.5 | 84.1 | 56.7 | 60.5 | 84.6 | 39.7 | 45.9 | 101.2 | 64.3 | 69.4 |
| 0320 | Concrete Reinforcing | 95.3 | 47.7 | 72.4 | 95.1 | 61.4 | 78.9 | 95.1 | 82.3 | 89.0 | 97.8 | 76.2 | 87.4 | 97.8 | 60.8 | 80.0 | 95.9 | 63.0 | 80.0 |
| 0330 | Cast-in-Place Concrete | 98.5 | 46.6 | 79.3 | 98.5 | 52.0 | 81.3 | 106.0 | 58.4 | 88.3 | 106.1 | 47.3 | 84.3 | 104.0 | 47.4 | 83.0 | 104.6 | 53.2 | 85.6 |
| 03 | CONCRETE | 93.4 | 50.1 | 73.4 | 93.7 | 51.6 | 74.3 | 98.8 | 64.4 | 82.9 | 99.2 | 58.3 | 80.3 | 98.1 | 47.7 | 74.9 | 98.7 | 61.3 | 81.4 |
| 04 | MASONRY | 96.6 | 36.0 | 60.3 | 109.6 | 45.2 | 71.1 | 99.8 | 48.0 | 68.8 | 102.4 | 32.5 | 60.6 | 121.6 | 36.6 | 70.8 | 95.8 | 54.9 | 71.3 |
| 05 | METALS | 89.2 | 69.8 | 83.6 | 89.3 | 76.3 | 85.5 | 89.1 | 90.1 | 89.4 | 96.0 | 80.9 | 91.6 | 89.4 | 74.4 | 85.0 | 91.4 | 80.7 | 88.3 |
| 06 | WOOD, PLASTICS & COMPOSITES | 89.0 | 54.7 | 70.5 | 94.1 | 44.7 | 67.5 | 96.6 | 61.2 | 77.5 | 88.5 | 64.1 | 75.3 | 89.3 | 39.7 | 62.6 | 108.7 | 64.7 | 85.0 |
| 07 | THERMAL & MOISTURE PROTECTION | 101.1 | 37.0 | 76.1 | 100.6 | 46.0 | 79.3 | 101.4 | 56.3 | 83.8 | 100.4 | 42.3 | 77.7 | 100.7 | 47.4 | 79.9 | 101.1 | 53.5 | 82.6 |
| 08 | OPENINGS | 102.8 | 46.1 | 88.8 | 93.5 | 50.1 | 82.7 | 97.6 | 66.8 | 90.0 | 87.5 | 62.2 | 81.3 | 93.8 | 45.9 | 82.0 | 98.5 | 62.2 | 89.6 |
| 0920 | Plaster & Gypsum Board | 91.3 | 53.6 | 68.0 | 91.9 | 43.3 | 61.9 | 93.3 | 60.5 | 73.0 | 91.3 | 63.5 | 74.1 | 91.3 | 38.2 | 58.5 | 98.7 | 63.9 | 77.2 |
| 0950, 0980 | Ceilings & Acoustic Treatment | 109.3 | 53.6 | 75.1 | 109.3 | 43.3 | 68.8 | 109.3 | 60.5 | 79.3 | 109.3 | 63.5 | 81.2 | 109.3 | 38.2 | 65.7 | 113.6 | 63.9 | 83.1 |
| 0960 | Flooring | 106.2 | 54.5 | 92.1 | 109.0 | 54.5 | 94.1 | 121.8 | 58.0 | 104.4 | 103.9 | 39.6 | 86.4 | 105.2 | 39.3 | 87.3 | 114.7 | 54.3 | 98.3 |
| 0970, 0990 | Wall Finishes & Painting/Coating | 101.5 | 16.9 | 50.7 | 101.5 | 36.0 | 62.1 | 104.2 | 82.4 | 91.1 | 97.7 | 25.5 | 54.3 | 101.5 | 37.2 | 62.9 | 102.5 | 63.5 | 79.1 |
| 09 | FINISHES | 102.5 | 48.5 | 74.2 | 103.5 | 44.9 | 72.8 | 107.8 | 60.6 | 83.1 | 101.6 | 51.2 | 75.2 | 103.9 | 39.0 | 69.9 | 108.9 | 62.3 | 84.5 |
| COVERS | DIVS. 10 - 14, 25, 28, 41, 43, 44 | 100.0 | 76.9 | 95.3 | 100.0 | 46.6 | 89.1 | 100.0 | 77.9 | 95.5 | 100.0 | 76.5 | 95.2 | 100.0 | 56.3 | 91.1 | 100.0 | 82.2 | 96.4 |
| 21, 22, 23 | FIRE SUPPRESSION, PLUMBING & HVAC | 96.1 | 69.4 | 85.1 | 96.1 | 76.4 | 88.0 | 96.1 | 77.5 | 88.5 | 96.1 | 31.3 | 69.5 | 96.1 | 37.3 | 71.9 | 100.2 | 75.5 | 90.1 |
| 26, 27, 3370 | ELECTRICAL, COMMUNICATIONS & UTIL. | 100.7 | 50.2 | 75.9 | 99.7 | 66.8 | 83.5 | 98.2 | 73.6 | 86.1 | 96.0 | 30.0 | 63.5 | 96.0 | 37.8 | 67.4 | 96.0 | 73.6 | 85.0 |
| MF2004 | WEIGHTED AVERAGE | 96.6 | 58.2 | 80.2 | 96.4 | 62.8 | 82.0 | 97.3 | 71.0 | 86.0 | 96.9 | 50.1 | 76.9 | 97.6 | 48.2 | 76.5 | 98.7 | 70.6 | 86.7 |

## IOWA / KANSAS

| | DIVISION | IOWA SPENCER 513 | | | IOWA WATERLOO 506 - 507 | | | KANSAS BELLEVILLE 669 | | | KANSAS COLBY 677 | | | KANSAS DODGE CITY 678 | | | KANSAS EMPORIA 668 | | |
|---|---|---|---|---|---|---|---|---|---|---|---|---|---|---|---|---|---|---|---|
| | | MAT. | INST. | TOTAL | MAT. | INST. | TOTAL | MAT. | INST. | TOTAL | MAT. | INST. | TOTAL | MAT. | INST. | TOTAL | MAT. | INST. | TOTAL |
| 015433 | CONTRACTOR EQUIPMENT | | 100.1 | 100.1 | | 100.1 | 100.1 | | 103.3 | 103.3 | | 103.3 | 103.3 | | 103.3 | 103.3 | | 101.4 | 101.4 |
| 0241, 31 - 34 | SITE & INFRASTRUCTURE, DEMOLITION | 101.7 | 93.6 | 96.1 | 92.4 | 95.0 | 94.2 | 113.1 | 92.1 | 98.5 | 110.3 | 93.0 | 98.2 | 112.7 | 92.6 | 98.7 | 103.8 | 90.4 | 94.5 |
| 0310 | Concrete Forming & Accessories | 90.9 | 39.6 | 46.7 | 101.6 | 44.9 | 52.8 | 95.8 | 50.7 | 57.0 | 102.5 | 63.3 | 68.8 | 95.3 | 63.3 | 67.7 | 87.0 | 37.1 | 44.0 |
| 0320 | Concrete Reinforcing | 97.8 | 38.5 | 69.2 | 95.9 | 83.2 | 89.7 | 101.8 | 56.4 | 79.9 | 104.4 | 56.4 | 81.2 | 101.8 | 56.8 | 80.1 | 100.4 | 57.1 | 79.5 |
| 0330 | Cast-in-Place Concrete | 104.0 | 47.3 | 83.0 | 105.5 | 44.4 | 82.9 | 119.1 | 52.4 | 94.4 | 114.5 | 53.3 | 91.9 | 116.6 | 53.0 | 93.0 | 115.1 | 40.8 | 87.6 |
| 03 | CONCRETE | 98.5 | 43.4 | 73.1 | 99.4 | 53.5 | 78.2 | 115.5 | 53.7 | 87.0 | 112.8 | 59.8 | 88.3 | 113.9 | 59.6 | 88.9 | 108.3 | 43.9 | 78.6 |
| 04 | MASONRY | 121.6 | 36.6 | 70.8 | 97.2 | 57.7 | 73.6 | 94.7 | 46.7 | 66.0 | 95.8 | 45.6 | 65.8 | 102.5 | 53.2 | 73.0 | 99.9 | 56.3 | 73.8 |
| 05 | METALS | 89.3 | 64.1 | 82.0 | 91.4 | 90.1 | 91.0 | 91.6 | 76.1 | 87.1 | 91.9 | 79.2 | 88.2 | 93.3 | 78.6 | 89.0 | 91.3 | 80.2 | 88.1 |
| 06 | WOOD, PLASTICS & COMPOSITES | 96.4 | 39.7 | 65.9 | 109.3 | 44.7 | 74.5 | 94.2 | 53.8 | 72.4 | 101.6 | 70.4 | 84.8 | 93.5 | 70.4 | 81.1 | 85.2 | 36.0 | 58.7 |
| 07 | THERMAL & MOISTURE PROTECTION | 101.5 | 41.6 | 78.2 | 100.9 | 49.6 | 80.9 | 100.3 | 55.8 | 83.0 | 100.3 | 57.2 | 83.5 | 100.2 | 59.1 | 84.2 | 99.0 | 58.1 | 83.0 |
| 08 | OPENINGS | 106.8 | 39.3 | 90.1 | 94.4 | 58.3 | 85.5 | 96.8 | 51.1 | 85.5 | 96.9 | 60.1 | 87.8 | 96.9 | 60.1 | 87.8 | 94.5 | 41.5 | 81.4 |
| 0920 | Plaster & Gypsum Board | 93.3 | 38.2 | 59.3 | 98.7 | 43.3 | 64.5 | 97.2 | 52.5 | 69.6 | 100.5 | 69.5 | 81.4 | 96.5 | 69.5 | 79.9 | 93.8 | 34.2 | 57.0 |
| 0950, 0980 | Ceilings & Acoustic Treatment | 109.3 | 38.2 | 65.7 | 113.6 | 43.3 | 70.4 | 86.2 | 52.5 | 65.5 | 86.2 | 69.5 | 76.0 | 86.2 | 69.5 | 76.0 | 86.2 | 34.2 | 54.3 |
| 0960 | Flooring | 108.6 | 39.3 | 89.7 | 116.0 | 54.5 | 99.3 | 97.7 | 45.3 | 83.4 | 101.8 | 45.3 | 86.4 | 97.5 | 45.3 | 83.3 | 91.7 | 42.1 | 78.2 |
| 0970, 0990 | Wall Finishes & Painting/Coating | 101.5 | 37.2 | 62.9 | 102.5 | 33.3 | 61.0 | 93.1 | 46.6 | 65.1 | 93.1 | 46.6 | 65.1 | 93.1 | 46.6 | 65.1 | 93.1 | 46.6 | 65.1 |
| 09 | FINISHES | 105.2 | 39.0 | 70.5 | 107.9 | 44.6 | 74.8 | 94.6 | 49.2 | 70.8 | 96.2 | 58.9 | 76.7 | 94.4 | 58.9 | 75.8 | 91.4 | 37.6 | 63.2 |
| COVERS | DIVS. 10 - 14, 25, 28, 41, 43, 44 | 100.0 | 75.2 | 94.9 | 100.0 | 76.0 | 95.1 | 100.0 | 43.6 | 88.5 | 100.0 | 45.6 | 88.9 | 100.0 | 45.6 | 88.9 | 100.0 | 38.2 | 87.3 |
| 21, 22, 23 | FIRE SUPPRESSION, PLUMBING & HVAC | 96.1 | 47.4 | 72.0 | 100.2 | 41.5 | 76.1 | 95.8 | 69.4 | 85.0 | 95.8 | 61.9 | 81.9 | 99.9 | 61.9 | 84.3 | 95.8 | 68.5 | 84.6 |
| 26, 27, 3370 | ELECTRICAL, COMMUNICATIONS & UTIL. | 97.7 | 37.8 | 68.3 | 96.0 | 66.8 | 81.6 | 99.7 | 66.8 | 83.5 | 99.7 | 66.9 | 83.6 | 96.5 | 73.8 | 85.4 | 96.9 | 74.2 | 85.7 |
| MF2004 | WEIGHTED AVERAGE | 99.2 | 46.9 | 76.8 | 98.0 | 59.6 | 81.6 | 98.8 | 62.5 | 83.2 | 98.7 | 63.9 | 83.8 | 99.8 | 65.6 | 85.2 | 97.0 | 61.0 | 81.6 |

## KANSAS

| DIVISION | | FORT SCOTT 667 | | | HAYS 676 | | | HUTCHINSON 675 | | | INDEPENDENCE 673 | | | KANSAS CITY 660 - 662 | | | LIBERAL 679 | | |
|---|---|---|---|---|---|---|---|---|---|---|---|---|---|---|---|---|---|---|---|
| | | MAT. | INST. | TOTAL | MAT. | INST. | TOTAL | MAT. | INST. | TOTAL | MAT. | INST. | TOTAL | MAT. | INST. | TOTAL | MAT. | INST. | TOTAL |
| 015433 | CONTRACTOR EQUIPMENT | | 102.5 | 102.5 | | 103.3 | 103.3 | | 103.3 | 103.3 | | 103.3 | 103.3 | | 99.6 | 99.6 | | 103.3 | 103.3 |
| 0241, 31 - 34 | SITE & INFRASTRUCTURE, DEMOLITION | 100.2 | 91.6 | 94.2 | 116.2 | 93.0 | 100.0 | 92.5 | 92.9 | 92.8 | 114.0 | 93.0 | 99.4 | 92.3 | 91.3 | 91.6 | 116.4 | 92.9 | 100.0 |
| 0310 | Concrete Forming & Accessories | 103.8 | 80.4 | 83.6 | 100.0 | 63.3 | 68.4 | 89.6 | 61.6 | 65.4 | 111.8 | 56.1 | 63.8 | 100.2 | 99.3 | 99.4 | 95.8 | 61.6 | 66.3 |
| 0320 | Concrete Reinforcing | 99.8 | 90.4 | 95.2 | 101.8 | 56.5 | 80.0 | 101.8 | 56.7 | 80.1 | 101.2 | 59.5 | 81.1 | 96.7 | 91.8 | 94.3 | 103.3 | 56.7 | 80.9 |
| 0330 | Cast-in-Place Concrete | 106.8 | 57.0 | 88.3 | 90.2 | 53.3 | 76.6 | 83.6 | 39.3 | 67.2 | 117.1 | 40.1 | 88.6 | 91.4 | 92.2 | 91.7 | 90.2 | 39.3 | 71.4 |
| 03 | CONCRETE | 103.4 | 74.9 | 90.3 | 103.4 | 59.8 | 83.3 | 87.2 | 54.2 | 72.0 | 115.2 | 52.6 | 86.3 | 95.0 | 95.7 | 95.3 | 105.4 | 54.2 | 81.8 |
| 04 | MASONRY | 100.2 | 57.8 | 74.8 | 103.3 | 47.0 | 69.7 | 95.2 | 48.8 | 67.4 | 93.3 | 50.1 | 67.4 | 102.9 | 96.6 | 99.1 | 100.4 | 48.8 | 69.5 |
| 05 | METALS | 91.3 | 93.0 | 91.8 | 91.5 | 79.4 | 88.0 | 91.4 | 78.4 | 87.6 | 91.3 | 80.0 | 88.0 | 98.0 | 99.1 | 98.3 | 91.8 | 78.4 | 87.9 |
| 06 | WOOD, PLASTICS & COMPOSITES | 104.0 | 89.8 | 96.4 | 98.7 | 70.4 | 83.5 | 87.9 | 70.4 | 78.5 | 112.0 | 61.7 | 84.9 | 100.0 | 100.5 | 100.3 | 94.2 | 70.4 | 81.4 |
| 07 | THERMAL & MOISTURE PROTECTION | 99.7 | 71.8 | 88.8 | 100.5 | 57.6 | 83.8 | 99.3 | 55.6 | 82.3 | 100.3 | 64.3 | 86.3 | 98.6 | 98.6 | 98.6 | 100.7 | 55.6 | 83.1 |
| 08 | OPENINGS | 94.5 | 83.1 | 91.6 | 96.8 | 60.1 | 87.8 | 96.8 | 60.1 | 87.7 | 94.5 | 56.1 | 85.0 | 95.8 | 94.0 | 95.4 | 96.9 | 60.1 | 87.8 |
| 0920 | Plaster & Gypsum Board | 99.2 | 89.4 | 93.2 | 99.2 | 69.5 | 80.9 | 95.1 | 69.5 | 79.3 | 105.3 | 60.6 | 77.7 | 93.2 | 100.4 | 97.7 | 97.2 | 69.5 | 80.1 |
| 0950, 0980 | Ceilings & Acoustic Treatment | 86.2 | 89.4 | 88.2 | 86.2 | 69.5 | 76.0 | 86.2 | 69.5 | 76.0 | 86.2 | 60.6 | 70.5 | 87.1 | 100.4 | 95.3 | 86.2 | 69.5 | 76.0 |
| 0960 | Flooring | 108.2 | 45.5 | 91.2 | 100.5 | 45.3 | 85.5 | 93.9 | 45.3 | 80.7 | 107.1 | 45.3 | 90.3 | 88.2 | 97.9 | 90.8 | 97.7 | 45.3 | 83.4 |
| 0970, 0990 | Wall Finishes & Painting/Coating | 95.2 | 46.6 | 66.0 | 93.1 | 46.6 | 65.1 | 93.1 | 46.6 | 65.1 | 93.1 | 46.6 | 65.1 | 100.8 | 81.1 | 88.9 | 93.1 | 46.6 | 65.1 |
| 09 | FINISHES | 97.3 | 71.5 | 83.8 | 96.1 | 58.9 | 76.6 | 91.6 | 57.9 | 74.0 | 98.7 | 53.1 | 74.8 | 92.2 | 96.3 | 94.4 | 95.2 | 57.9 | 75.7 |
| COVERS | DIVS. 10 - 14, 25, 28, 41, 43, 44 | 100.0 | 54.1 | 90.6 | 100.0 | 45.6 | 88.9 | 100.0 | 44.1 | 88.6 | 100.0 | 43.5 | 88.4 | 100.0 | 74.6 | 94.8 | 100.0 | 44.1 | 88.6 |
| 21, 22, 23 | FIRE SUPPRESSION, PLUMBING & HVAC | 95.8 | 64.8 | 83.1 | 95.8 | 61.9 | 81.9 | 95.8 | 59.8 | 81.0 | 95.8 | 67.9 | 84.4 | 99.8 | 92.0 | 96.6 | 95.8 | 59.8 | 81.0 |
| 26, 27, 3370 | ELECTRICAL, COMMUNICATIONS & UTIL. | 96.1 | 74.2 | 85.4 | 98.6 | 66.9 | 83.0 | 93.5 | 66.8 | 80.4 | 95.7 | 74.2 | 85.2 | 101.8 | 99.9 | 100.9 | 96.5 | 73.8 | 85.4 |
| MF2004 | WEIGHTED AVERAGE | 96.9 | 73.4 | 86.8 | 97.9 | 64.1 | 83.4 | 93.8 | 62.7 | 80.5 | 98.5 | 64.9 | 84.1 | 98.1 | 95.1 | 96.8 | 97.7 | 63.7 | 83.2 |

## KANSAS / KENTUCKY

| DIVISION | | SALINA 674 | | | TOPEKA 664 - 666 | | | WICHITA 670 - 672 | | | ASHLAND 411 - 412 | | | BOWLING GREEN 421 - 422 | | | CAMPTON 413 - 414 | | |
|---|---|---|---|---|---|---|---|---|---|---|---|---|---|---|---|---|---|---|---|
| | | MAT. | INST. | TOTAL | MAT. | INST. | TOTAL | MAT. | INST. | TOTAL | MAT. | INST. | TOTAL | MAT. | INST. | TOTAL | MAT. | INST. | TOTAL |
| 015433 | CONTRACTOR EQUIPMENT | | 103.3 | 103.3 | | 101.4 | 101.4 | | 103.3 | 103.3 | | 98.4 | 98.4 | | 95.4 | 95.4 | | 102.9 | 102.9 |
| 0241, 31 - 34 | SITE & INFRASTRUCTURE, DEMOLITION | 102.1 | 93.0 | 95.8 | 93.8 | 90.4 | 91.4 | 94.6 | 92.8 | 93.3 | 99.1 | 85.5 | 89.7 | 67.0 | 99.3 | 89.5 | 75.1 | 100.2 | 92.6 |
| 0310 | Concrete Forming & Accessories | 91.6 | 50.9 | 56.6 | 99.1 | 47.4 | 54.6 | 98.8 | 52.5 | 58.9 | 86.9 | 99.6 | 97.8 | 84.7 | 83.1 | 83.3 | 88.1 | 54.3 | 58.9 |
| 0320 | Concrete Reinforcing | 101.2 | 73.2 | 87.7 | 94.0 | 94.9 | 94.5 | 94.0 | 75.7 | 85.2 | 91.8 | 102.1 | 96.8 | 88.9 | 91.4 | 90.1 | 89.8 | 73.0 | 81.7 |
| 0330 | Cast-in-Place Concrete | 101.1 | 45.3 | 80.5 | 93.7 | 50.1 | 77.6 | 87.3 | 54.1 | 75.0 | 84.5 | 101.2 | 90.7 | 83.8 | 111.1 | 93.9 | 93.5 | 64.3 | 82.7 |
| 03 | CONCRETE | 101.1 | 54.7 | 79.7 | 93.6 | 58.9 | 77.6 | 90.4 | 58.7 | 75.4 | 93.2 | 101.3 | 96.9 | 91.4 | 94.3 | 92.8 | 95.3 | 62.0 | 80.0 |
| 04 | MASONRY | 117.2 | 46.7 | 75.0 | 97.9 | 61.0 | 75.8 | 91.6 | 60.4 | 72.9 | 88.5 | 103.8 | 97.6 | 90.0 | 80.9 | 84.5 | 89.0 | 40.4 | 59.9 |
| 05 | METALS | 93.1 | 86.0 | 91.1 | 98.2 | 96.6 | 97.8 | 98.2 | 85.7 | 94.6 | 92.0 | 110.7 | 97.4 | 93.6 | 87.4 | 91.8 | 92.9 | 77.6 | 88.5 |
| 06 | WOOD, PLASTICS & COMPOSITES | 89.8 | 53.8 | 70.4 | 95.5 | 44.9 | 68.3 | 97.2 | 51.4 | 72.5 | 78.1 | 97.8 | 88.7 | 91.5 | 80.1 | 85.4 | 90.0 | 52.6 | 69.9 |
| 07 | THERMAL & MOISTURE PROTECTION | 99.8 | 54.5 | 82.1 | 100.7 | 66.6 | 87.4 | 99.3 | 61.0 | 84.4 | 87.4 | 98.5 | 91.7 | 84.9 | 89.9 | 86.8 | 96.0 | 54.9 | 79.9 |
| 08 | OPENINGS | 96.8 | 53.8 | 86.2 | 97.1 | 60.9 | 88.2 | 97.1 | 58.0 | 87.4 | 93.5 | 95.1 | 93.9 | 95.2 | 80.5 | 91.6 | 96.7 | 63.9 | 88.6 |
| 0920 | Plaster & Gypsum Board | 95.8 | 52.5 | 69.1 | 94.8 | 43.4 | 63.1 | 92.2 | 50.1 | 66.2 | 58.9 | 97.8 | 82.9 | 82.4 | 79.9 | 80.9 | 82.4 | 50.7 | 62.8 |
| 0950, 0980 | Ceilings & Acoustic Treatment | 86.2 | 52.5 | 65.5 | 87.1 | 43.4 | 60.3 | 85.4 | 50.1 | 63.7 | 81.8 | 97.8 | 91.6 | 87.5 | 79.9 | 82.8 | 87.5 | 50.7 | 64.9 |
| 0960 | Flooring | 95.4 | 33.1 | 78.4 | 99.1 | 42.1 | 83.6 | 98.0 | 72.9 | 91.1 | 77.9 | 100.9 | 84.2 | 93.2 | 87.6 | 91.7 | 94.8 | 47.6 | 82.0 |
| 0970, 0990 | Wall Finishes & Painting/Coating | 93.1 | 46.6 | 65.1 | 93.1 | 62.9 | 74.9 | 93.1 | 57.4 | 71.7 | 99.6 | 100.9 | 100.4 | 96.8 | 73.6 | 82.8 | 96.8 | 41.4 | 63.5 |
| 09 | FINISHES | 93.0 | 46.5 | 68.6 | 93.5 | 46.2 | 68.7 | 92.5 | 56.5 | 73.6 | 80.2 | 100.1 | 90.6 | 91.1 | 82.5 | 86.6 | 91.7 | 50.4 | 70.1 |
| COVERS | DIVS. 10 - 14, 25, 28, 41, 43, 44 | 100.0 | 56.4 | 91.1 | 100.0 | 59.7 | 91.7 | 100.0 | 58.8 | 91.6 | 100.0 | 88.0 | 97.5 | 100.0 | 70.8 | 94.0 | 100.0 | 61.8 | 92.2 |
| 21, 22, 23 | FIRE SUPPRESSION, PLUMBING & HVAC | 99.9 | 61.8 | 84.3 | 99.9 | 66.5 | 86.2 | 99.7 | 59.9 | 83.4 | 95.7 | 93.0 | 94.6 | 99.9 | 85.6 | 94.1 | 95.8 | 75.9 | 87.6 |
| 26, 27, 3370 | ELECTRICAL, COMMUNICATIONS & UTIL. | 96.2 | 73.8 | 85.2 | 101.4 | 74.2 | 88.1 | 99.3 | 73.8 | 86.8 | 90.5 | 94.4 | 92.4 | 93.3 | 79.5 | 86.5 | 90.7 | 79.4 | 85.1 |
| MF2004 | WEIGHTED AVERAGE | 98.5 | 63.1 | 83.4 | 98.0 | 67.4 | 84.9 | 96.9 | 66.2 | 83.8 | 92.3 | 97.4 | 94.5 | 94.0 | 85.8 | 90.5 | 93.9 | 68.1 | 82.8 |

## KENTUCKY

| DIVISION | | CORBIN 407 - 409 | | | COVINGTON 410 | | | ELIZABETHTOWN 427 | | | FRANKFORT 406 | | | HAZARD 417 - 418 | | | HENDERSON 424 | | |
|---|---|---|---|---|---|---|---|---|---|---|---|---|---|---|---|---|---|---|---|
| | | MAT. | INST. | TOTAL | MAT. | INST. | TOTAL | MAT. | INST. | TOTAL | MAT. | INST. | TOTAL | MAT. | INST. | TOTAL | MAT. | INST. | TOTAL |
| 015433 | CONTRACTOR EQUIPMENT | | 102.9 | 102.9 | | 107.4 | 107.4 | | 95.4 | 95.4 | | 102.9 | 102.9 | | 102.9 | 102.9 | | 120.6 | 120.6 |
| 0241, 31 - 34 | SITE & INFRASTRUCTURE, DEMOLITION | 72.7 | 100.2 | 91.8 | 71.5 | 116.6 | 102.9 | 62.4 | 98.7 | 87.7 | 74.8 | 101.0 | 93.3 | 73.3 | 102.0 | 93.3 | 70.0 | 128.1 | 110.5 |
| 0310 | Concrete Forming & Accessories | 85.2 | 53.8 | 58.1 | 84.1 | 109.9 | 106.3 | 79.9 | 80.1 | 80.1 | 96.2 | 66.0 | 70.2 | 85.2 | 46.7 | 52.0 | 91.4 | 81.9 | 83.3 |
| 0320 | Concrete Reinforcing | 89.4 | 73.0 | 81.5 | 88.3 | 101.2 | 94.5 | 89.4 | 91.5 | 90.4 | 90.6 | 89.4 | 90.0 | 90.2 | 73.7 | 82.3 | 89.0 | 89.5 | 89.3 |
| 0330 | Cast-in-Place Concrete | 88.5 | 64.1 | 79.5 | 89.5 | 97.6 | 92.5 | 75.8 | 76.1 | 75.9 | 85.4 | 71.9 | 80.4 | 89.9 | 95.5 | 92.0 | 74.0 | 95.0 | 81.8 |
| 03 | CONCRETE | 90.7 | 61.8 | 77.3 | 93.7 | 103.7 | 98.3 | 84.1 | 81.0 | 82.7 | 90.0 | 72.9 | 82.1 | 92.3 | 69.4 | 81.7 | 88.5 | 87.9 | 88.2 |
| 04 | MASONRY | 88.4 | 42.8 | 61.1 | 102.1 | 118.3 | 111.8 | 74.5 | 79.1 | 77.3 | 87.7 | 75.8 | 80.6 | 85.5 | 50.7 | 64.7 | 93.7 | 92.5 | 93.0 |
| 05 | METALS | 92.8 | 77.3 | 88.3 | 90.8 | 96.0 | 92.3 | 92.8 | 87.2 | 91.2 | 100.2 | 87.7 | 96.6 | 92.9 | 77.3 | 88.4 | 84.2 | 89.3 | 85.7 |
| 06 | WOOD, PLASTICS & COMPOSITES | 87.0 | 52.6 | 68.5 | 87.9 | 102.9 | 95.9 | 86.5 | 80.1 | 83.1 | 99.4 | 63.8 | 80.2 | 87.0 | 38.4 | 60.8 | 93.9 | 79.6 | 86.2 |
| 07 | THERMAL & MOISTURE PROTECTION | 95.8 | 56.6 | 80.5 | 93.4 | 103.3 | 97.3 | 84.5 | 80.9 | 83.1 | 95.9 | 75.9 | 88.1 | 95.9 | 54.2 | 79.6 | 95.3 | 94.0 | 94.8 |
| 08 | OPENINGS | 96.0 | 55.7 | 86.1 | 98.1 | 97.9 | 98.1 | 95.2 | 83.6 | 92.4 | 95.3 | 73.7 | 90.0 | 97.1 | 45.6 | 84.4 | 93.4 | 82.6 | 90.8 |
| 0920 | Plaster & Gypsum Board | 81.7 | 50.7 | 62.6 | 70.7 | 103.5 | 90.9 | 81.4 | 79.9 | 80.5 | 87.9 | 62.1 | 72.0 | 81.7 | 36.1 | 53.6 | 83.2 | 78.3 | 80.2 |
| 0950, 0980 | Ceilings & Acoustic Treatment | 87.5 | 50.7 | 64.9 | 89.2 | 103.5 | 98.0 | 87.5 | 79.9 | 82.8 | 88.3 | 62.1 | 72.2 | 87.5 | 36.1 | 55.9 | 78.1 | 78.3 | 78.2 |
| 0960 | Flooring | 92.9 | 47.6 | 80.6 | 70.0 | 93.3 | 76.3 | 90.3 | 69.8 | 84.7 | 98.0 | 62.9 | 88.4 | 92.9 | 42.2 | 79.1 | 96.7 | 90.8 | 95.1 |
| 0970, 0990 | Wall Finishes & Painting/Coating | 96.8 | 41.4 | 63.5 | 91.9 | 88.4 | 89.8 | 96.8 | 79.3 | 86.3 | 96.8 | 56.2 | 72.4 | 96.8 | 34.0 | 59.0 | 96.8 | 96.6 | 96.6 |
| 09 | FINISHES | 90.8 | 50.4 | 69.6 | 82.7 | 104.8 | 94.3 | 89.7 | 77.9 | 83.5 | 93.6 | 63.2 | 77.7 | 90.9 | 42.7 | 65.7 | 89.5 | 84.9 | 87.1 |
| COVERS | DIVS. 10 - 14, 25, 28, 41, 43, 44 | 100.0 | 55.5 | 90.9 | 100.0 | 109.2 | 101.9 | 100.0 | 85.1 | 96.9 | 100.0 | 76.5 | 95.2 | 100.0 | 63.9 | 92.6 | 100.0 | 78.2 | 95.5 |
| 21, 22, 23 | FIRE SUPPRESSION, PLUMBING & HVAC | 95.8 | 75.3 | 87.4 | 96.4 | 101.0 | 98.3 | 96.0 | 82.1 | 90.3 | 100.1 | 77.0 | 90.6 | 95.8 | 49.3 | 76.7 | 96.0 | 77.7 | 88.5 |
| 26, 27, 3370 | ELECTRICAL, COMMUNICATIONS & UTIL. | 90.9 | 79.4 | 85.2 | 94.3 | 82.2 | 88.3 | 90.5 | 79.5 | 85.1 | 93.4 | 104.6 | 98.9 | 90.7 | 60.3 | 75.7 | 92.7 | 82.7 | 87.8 |
| MF2004 | WEIGHTED AVERAGE | 93.0 | 67.6 | 82.2 | 93.7 | 102.0 | 97.2 | 90.7 | 82.7 | 87.3 | 95.7 | 81.1 | 89.5 | 93.2 | 60.1 | 79.0 | 91.5 | 88.3 | 90.1 |

## KENTUCKY

| DIVISION | | LEXINGTON 403-405 | | | LOUISVILLE 400-402 | | | OWENSBORO 423 | | | PADUCAH 420 | | | PIKEVILLE 415-416 | | | SOMERSET 425-426 | | |
|---|---|---|---|---|---|---|---|---|---|---|---|---|---|---|---|---|---|---|
| | | MAT. | INST. | TOTAL | MAT. | INST. | TOTAL | MAT. | INST. | TOTAL | MAT. | INST. | TOTAL | MAT. | INST. | TOTAL | MAT. | INST. | TOTAL |
| 015433 | CONTRACTOR EQUIPMENT | | 102.9 | 102.9 | | 95.4 | 95.4 | | 120.6 | 120.6 | | 120.6 | 120.6 | | 98.4 | 98.4 | | 102.9 | 102.9 |
| 0241, 31-34 | SITE & INFRASTRUCTURE, DEMOLITION | 74.3 | 101.7 | 93.4 | 65.2 | 98.8 | 88.6 | 78.5 | 129.1 | 113.7 | 72.5 | 128.5 | 111.5 | 108.7 | 85.3 | 92.4 | 67.0 | 100.8 | 90.5 |
| 0310 | Concrete Forming & Accessories | 97.4 | 73.8 | 77.0 | 93.2 | 80.3 | 82.1 | 89.7 | 77.7 | 79.4 | 87.6 | 82.1 | 82.8 | 95.7 | 75.3 | 78.1 | 85.9 | 52.1 | 56.8 |
| 0320 | Concrete Reinforcing | 98.1 | 91.3 | 94.8 | 98.1 | 91.5 | 94.9 | 89.0 | 88.8 | 88.9 | 89.6 | 86.0 | 87.9 | 92.3 | 98.6 | 95.4 | 89.4 | 88.3 | 88.8 |
| 0330 | Cast-in-Place Concrete | 90.5 | 84.0 | 88.1 | 92.7 | 76.1 | 86.6 | 86.4 | 106.1 | 93.7 | 78.9 | 94.5 | 84.7 | 92.9 | 100.8 | 95.8 | 74.0 | 111.6 | 88.0 |
| 03 | CONCRETE | 93.8 | 80.9 | 87.9 | 94.7 | 81.1 | 88.4 | 100.0 | 89.7 | 95.3 | 92.8 | 87.2 | 90.2 | 106.0 | 89.6 | 98.4 | 79.3 | 80.1 | 79.7 |
| 04 | MASONRY | 87.4 | 70.8 | 77.4 | 89.2 | 79.1 | 83.2 | 86.8 | 77.0 | 81.0 | 90.2 | 92.3 | 91.4 | 87.2 | 72.5 | 78.4 | 81.3 | 61.2 | 69.3 |
| 05 | METALS | 95.0 | 88.8 | 93.2 | 102.3 | 87.3 | 98.0 | 85.6 | 88.1 | 86.3 | 82.8 | 87.2 | 84.1 | 91.9 | 103.8 | 95.4 | 92.8 | 84.8 | 90.5 |
| 06 | WOOD, PLASTICS & COMPOSITES | 102.1 | 71.8 | 85.7 | 99.4 | 80.1 | 89.0 | 91.9 | 74.2 | 82.4 | 89.6 | 80.4 | 84.7 | 87.6 | 66.8 | 76.4 | 87.7 | 44.5 | 64.4 |
| 07 | THERMAL & MOISTURE PROTECTION | 96.0 | 91.1 | 94.1 | 90.0 | 81.0 | 86.5 | 95.7 | 80.4 | 89.7 | 95.4 | 86.1 | 91.8 | 88.1 | 65.6 | 79.3 | 95.3 | 60.7 | 81.8 |
| 08 | OPENINGS | 96.1 | 78.3 | 91.7 | 96.1 | 83.6 | 93.0 | 93.4 | 79.8 | 90.1 | 92.6 | 81.0 | 89.8 | 94.3 | 76.9 | 90.0 | 96.0 | 63.3 | 88.0 |
| 0920 | Plaster & Gypsum Board | 88.8 | 70.3 | 77.4 | 85.6 | 79.9 | 82.1 | 82.2 | 72.8 | 76.4 | 81.5 | 79.2 | 80.1 | 61.7 | 66.1 | 64.4 | 82.1 | 42.3 | 57.6 |
| 0950, 0980 | Ceilings & Acoustic Treatment | 91.7 | 70.3 | 78.6 | 88.3 | 79.9 | 83.2 | 78.1 | 72.8 | 74.8 | 78.1 | 79.2 | 78.8 | 81.8 | 66.1 | 72.2 | 87.5 | 42.3 | 59.8 |
| 0960 | Flooring | 98.3 | 64.1 | 89.0 | 96.8 | 69.8 | 89.4 | 95.8 | 87.6 | 93.6 | 94.5 | 68.6 | 87.5 | 82.9 | 56.7 | 75.8 | 93.2 | 47.6 | 80.8 |
| 0970, 0990 | Wall Finishes & Painting/Coating | 96.8 | 75.2 | 83.8 | 96.8 | 79.3 | 86.3 | 96.8 | 96.6 | 96.6 | 96.8 | 80.3 | 86.9 | 99.6 | 97.3 | 98.2 | 96.8 | 57.0 | 72.9 |
| 09 | FINISHES | 94.6 | 71.0 | 82.3 | 92.5 | 77.9 | 84.8 | 89.6 | 81.0 | 85.1 | 88.8 | 79.0 | 83.7 | 82.8 | 72.9 | 77.6 | 90.4 | 49.7 | 69.1 |
| COVERS | DIVS. 10-14, 25, 28, 41, 43, 44 | 100.0 | 95.1 | 99.0 | 100.0 | 94.3 | 98.8 | 100.0 | 91.5 | 98.3 | 100.0 | 74.8 | 94.8 | 100.0 | 67.1 | 93.3 | 100.0 | 66.3 | 93.1 |
| 21, 22, 23 | FIRE SUPPRESSION, PLUMBING & HVAC | 99.9 | 71.7 | 88.4 | 100.0 | 82.1 | 92.7 | 99.9 | 75.9 | 90.1 | 96.0 | 84.3 | 91.2 | 95.7 | 87.1 | 92.2 | 96.0 | 71.4 | 85.9 |
| 26, 27, 3370 | ELECTRICAL, COMMUNICATIONS & UTIL. | 93.8 | 78.8 | 86.4 | 94.2 | 79.5 | 87.0 | 92.8 | 82.7 | 87.8 | 95.1 | 84.4 | 89.8 | 93.4 | 88.1 | 90.8 | 91.1 | 78.8 | 85.1 |
| MF2004 | WEIGHTED AVERAGE | 95.5 | 79.4 | 88.6 | 96.2 | 83.0 | 90.6 | 93.9 | 85.8 | 90.4 | 91.8 | 88.4 | 90.3 | 94.8 | 83.8 | 90.0 | 91.2 | 72.4 | 83.2 |

## LOUISIANA

| DIVISION | | ALEXANDRIA 713-714 | | | BATON ROUGE 707-708 | | | HAMMOND 704 | | | LAFAYETTE 705 | | | LAKE CHARLES 706 | | | MONROE 712 | | |
|---|---|---|---|---|---|---|---|---|---|---|---|---|---|---|---|---|---|---|
| | | MAT. | INST. | TOTAL | MAT. | INST. | TOTAL | MAT. | INST. | TOTAL | MAT. | INST. | TOTAL | MAT. | INST. | TOTAL | MAT. | INST. | TOTAL |
| 015433 | CONTRACTOR EQUIPMENT | | 87.3 | 87.3 | | 87.4 | 87.4 | | 88.2 | 88.2 | | 88.2 | 88.2 | | 87.4 | 87.4 | | 87.3 | 87.3 |
| 0241, 31-34 | SITE & INFRASTRUCTURE, DEMOLITION | 103.6 | 85.1 | 90.7 | 114.0 | 85.1 | 93.9 | 113.6 | 86.6 | 94.8 | 114.2 | 86.5 | 94.9 | 114.8 | 84.9 | 94.0 | 103.6 | 84.7 | 90.4 |
| 0310 | Concrete Forming & Accessories | 83.4 | 40.6 | 46.5 | 99.4 | 65.9 | 70.5 | 82.8 | 54.9 | 58.8 | 102.1 | 50.6 | 57.7 | 103.1 | 55.8 | 62.4 | 82.9 | 41.3 | 47.1 |
| 0320 | Concrete Reinforcing | 98.3 | 60.9 | 80.3 | 100.1 | 62.6 | 82.0 | 98.8 | 63.2 | 81.6 | 100.1 | 62.3 | 81.9 | 100.1 | 62.5 | 82.0 | 97.2 | 61.1 | 79.8 |
| 0330 | Cast-in-Place Concrete | 92.8 | 40.8 | 73.5 | 82.8 | 62.5 | 75.3 | 85.1 | 47.7 | 71.2 | 84.7 | 48.1 | 71.1 | 89.1 | 62.6 | 79.3 | 92.8 | 60.5 | 80.8 |
| 03 | CONCRETE | 89.6 | 45.7 | 69.3 | 90.5 | 64.4 | 78.5 | 90.5 | 54.7 | 74.0 | 91.6 | 52.7 | 73.6 | 93.9 | 60.0 | 78.2 | 89.4 | 52.7 | 72.4 |
| 04 | MASONRY | 112.9 | 48.4 | 74.4 | 103.5 | 53.4 | 73.6 | 102.5 | 56.1 | 74.7 | 102.5 | 48.9 | 70.4 | 101.2 | 53.7 | 72.8 | 107.8 | 52.0 | 74.5 |
| 05 | METALS | 90.6 | 71.9 | 85.2 | 97.1 | 70.6 | 89.4 | 92.5 | 71.0 | 86.3 | 91.8 | 70.0 | 85.4 | 91.8 | 70.5 | 85.6 | 90.6 | 70.9 | 84.9 |
| 06 | WOOD, PLASTICS & COMPOSITES | 86.2 | 39.8 | 61.2 | 106.2 | 71.9 | 87.8 | 89.8 | 57.0 | 72.1 | 113.3 | 52.5 | 80.6 | 111.2 | 58.3 | 82.7 | 85.4 | 40.2 | 61.1 |
| 07 | THERMAL & MOISTURE PROTECTION | 99.1 | 50.3 | 80.1 | 100.1 | 60.1 | 84.5 | 101.6 | 60.9 | 85.7 | 102.2 | 54.4 | 83.6 | 101.4 | 58.1 | 84.5 | 99.1 | 54.9 | 81.9 |
| 08 | OPENINGS | 99.1 | 46.2 | 86.1 | 101.9 | 63.8 | 92.5 | 97.4 | 60.4 | 88.3 | 101.9 | 53.4 | 89.9 | 101.9 | 57.9 | 91.0 | 99.1 | 50.7 | 87.2 |
| 0920 | Plaster & Gypsum Board | 83.4 | 38.8 | 55.9 | 99.3 | 71.6 | 82.2 | 97.5 | 56.3 | 72.1 | 104.5 | 51.7 | 71.9 | 104.5 | 57.6 | 75.6 | 83.0 | 39.2 | 56.0 |
| 0950, 0980 | Ceilings & Acoustic Treatment | 90.9 | 38.8 | 58.9 | 96.8 | 71.6 | 81.3 | 96.7 | 56.3 | 71.9 | 95.0 | 51.7 | 68.4 | 95.9 | 57.6 | 72.4 | 90.9 | 39.2 | 59.2 |
| 0960 | Flooring | 103.0 | 61.0 | 91.6 | 110.6 | 66.0 | 98.4 | 100.0 | 53.5 | 87.4 | 110.8 | 40.1 | 91.5 | 110.8 | 66.0 | 98.6 | 102.5 | 66.0 | 92.6 |
| 0970, 0990 | Wall Finishes & Painting/Coating | 98.2 | 38.2 | 62.1 | 107.1 | 43.7 | 69.0 | 107.1 | 57.8 | 77.5 | 107.1 | 43.7 | 69.0 | 107.1 | 40.3 | 66.9 | 98.2 | 45.6 | 66.6 |
| 09 | FINISHES | 93.7 | 43.3 | 67.3 | 104.6 | 64.3 | 83.5 | 101.0 | 55.0 | 76.9 | 104.9 | 47.3 | 74.7 | 105.1 | 56.1 | 79.4 | 93.5 | 45.6 | 68.4 |
| COVERS | DIVS. 10-14, 25, 28, 41, 43, 44 | 100.0 | 59.8 | 91.8 | 100.0 | 78.3 | 95.6 | 100.0 | 57.3 | 91.3 | 100.0 | 75.7 | 95.0 | 100.0 | 76.8 | 95.2 | 100.0 | 54.7 | 90.7 |
| 21, 22, 23 | FIRE SUPPRESSION, PLUMBING & HVAC | 100.1 | 57.6 | 82.7 | 99.9 | 56.6 | 82.2 | 95.9 | 53.5 | 78.5 | 100.0 | 57.6 | 82.6 | 100.0 | 58.2 | 82.9 | 100.1 | 51.0 | 79.9 |
| 26, 27, 3370 | ELECTRICAL, COMMUNICATIONS & UTIL. | 93.1 | 57.2 | 75.5 | 95.4 | 62.7 | 79.3 | 94.0 | 53.9 | 74.3 | 95.2 | 62.9 | 79.3 | 94.7 | 62.9 | 79.1 | 95.0 | 58.4 | 77.0 |
| MF2004 | WEIGHTED AVERAGE | 96.5 | 55.9 | 79.2 | 99.1 | 64.1 | 84.1 | 96.4 | 59.2 | 80.5 | 98.5 | 59.2 | 81.7 | 98.6 | 62.3 | 83.1 | 96.4 | 56.4 | 79.3 |

## LOUISIANA / MAINE

| DIVISION | | NEW ORLEANS 700-701 | | | SHREVEPORT 710-711 | | | THIBODAUX 703 | | | AUGUSTA 043 | | | BANGOR 044 | | | BATH 045 | | |
|---|---|---|---|---|---|---|---|---|---|---|---|---|---|---|---|---|---|---|
| | | MAT. | INST. | TOTAL | MAT. | INST. | TOTAL | MAT. | INST. | TOTAL | MAT. | INST. | TOTAL | MAT. | INST. | TOTAL | MAT. | INST. | TOTAL |
| 015433 | CONTRACTOR EQUIPMENT | | 88.5 | 88.5 | | 87.3 | 87.3 | | 88.2 | 88.2 | | 100.6 | 100.6 | | 100.6 | 100.6 | | 100.6 | 100.6 |
| 0241, 31-34 | SITE & INFRASTRUCTURE, DEMOLITION | 118.2 | 87.7 | 96.9 | 102.4 | 84.5 | 89.9 | 116.5 | 86.5 | 95.6 | 82.1 | 101.3 | 95.5 | 81.6 | 99.1 | 93.8 | 87.7 | 101.3 | 94.8 |
| 0310 | Concrete Forming & Accessories | 103.8 | 68.6 | 73.5 | 99.3 | 43.6 | 51.3 | 96.0 | 63.9 | 68.3 | 96.9 | 92.1 | 92.8 | 91.9 | 87.1 | 87.7 | 87.7 | 92.3 | 91.6 |
| 0320 | Concrete Reinforcing | 100.1 | 63.8 | 82.6 | 96.8 | 61.0 | 79.5 | 98.8 | 63.2 | 81.6 | 83.4 | 102.7 | 92.7 | 83.1 | 102.9 | 92.6 | 82.1 | 102.7 | 92.0 |
| 0330 | Cast-in-Place Concrete | 88.2 | 72.6 | 82.4 | 86.0 | 47.6 | 71.8 | 91.4 | 51.2 | 76.5 | 80.2 | 57.9 | 71.9 | 77.5 | 58.9 | 70.6 | 77.5 | 58.0 | 70.3 |
| 03 | CONCRETE | 93.5 | 69.4 | 82.4 | 86.3 | 49.3 | 69.2 | 95.4 | 59.8 | 79.0 | 100.2 | 81.9 | 91.8 | 98.1 | 79.8 | 89.7 | 98.2 | 82.0 | 90.7 |
| 04 | MASONRY | 102.6 | 59.1 | 76.6 | 99.9 | 51.0 | 70.7 | 128.9 | 55.1 | 84.7 | 96.9 | 47.1 | 67.1 | 111.9 | 53.9 | 77.2 | 118.3 | 46.6 | 75.4 |
| 05 | METALS | 104.5 | 73.7 | 95.5 | 86.8 | 70.4 | 82.1 | 92.6 | 71.0 | 86.3 | 82.5 | 82.2 | 82.4 | 82.2 | 78.3 | 81.1 | 80.7 | 82.3 | 81.2 |
| 06 | WOOD, PLASTICS & COMPOSITES | 107.2 | 71.9 | 88.2 | 103.3 | 43.7 | 71.2 | 99.5 | 68.5 | 82.8 | 97.4 | 102.0 | 99.9 | 92.1 | 94.3 | 93.3 | 86.9 | 102.0 | 95.0 |
| 07 | THERMAL & MOISTURE PROTECTION | 102.3 | 63.4 | 87.1 | 98.5 | 53.0 | 80.7 | 102.1 | 58.8 | 85.2 | 99.3 | 55.1 | 82.0 | 99.7 | 55.8 | 82.6 | 99.7 | 59.0 | 83.8 |
| 08 | OPENINGS | 102.7 | 69.5 | 94.5 | 97.0 | 48.4 | 85.0 | 102.8 | 66.7 | 93.9 | 102.3 | 80.5 | 96.9 | 100.7 | 77.9 | 96.2 | 102.2 | 82.1 | 97.2 |
| 0920 | Plaster & Gypsum Board | 103.5 | 71.6 | 83.8 | 87.4 | 42.8 | 59.9 | 101.2 | 68.1 | 80.8 | 106.3 | 101.3 | 103.2 | 100.4 | 93.4 | 96.1 | 97.7 | 101.3 | 99.9 |
| 0950, 0980 | Ceilings & Acoustic Treatment | 95.0 | 71.6 | 80.6 | 89.2 | 42.8 | 60.7 | 96.7 | 68.1 | 79.1 | 86.8 | 101.3 | 95.7 | 87.7 | 93.4 | 91.2 | 85.8 | 101.3 | 95.3 |
| 0960 | Flooring | 111.2 | 66.0 | 98.9 | 112.8 | 66.0 | 100.1 | 107.3 | 50.9 | 92.0 | 96.3 | 38.8 | 80.6 | 93.9 | 48.5 | 81.6 | 91.9 | 38.8 | 77.5 |
| 0970, 0990 | Wall Finishes & Painting/Coating | 108.7 | 63.1 | 81.3 | 98.2 | 38.2 | 62.1 | 108.7 | 57.8 | 78.1 | 91.6 | 33.0 | 56.4 | 91.6 | 30.4 | 54.8 | 91.6 | 33.0 | 56.4 |
| 09 | FINISHES | 105.4 | 67.9 | 85.8 | 96.9 | 46.6 | 70.6 | 104.0 | 61.3 | 81.6 | 98.2 | 77.4 | 87.3 | 96.8 | 75.2 | 85.5 | 95.3 | 77.4 | 86.0 |
| COVERS | DIVS. 10-14, 25, 28, 41, 43, 44 | 100.0 | 80.3 | 96.0 | 100.0 | 70.0 | 93.9 | 100.0 | 78.6 | 95.6 | 100.0 | 58.5 | 91.5 | 100.0 | 71.4 | 94.1 | 100.0 | 58.5 | 91.5 |
| 21, 22, 23 | FIRE SUPPRESSION, PLUMBING & HVAC | 100.0 | 64.1 | 85.3 | 100.0 | 57.6 | 82.6 | 95.9 | 62.0 | 82.0 | 100.0 | 69.6 | 87.5 | 100.1 | 70.7 | 88.0 | 96.0 | 69.6 | 85.1 |
| 26, 27, 3370 | ELECTRICAL, COMMUNICATIONS & UTIL. | 95.5 | 67.2 | 81.6 | 94.1 | 68.4 | 81.4 | 92.6 | 65.3 | 79.2 | 97.9 | 81.0 | 89.6 | 96.2 | 79.4 | 87.9 | 94.3 | 81.0 | 87.8 |
| MF2004 | WEIGHTED AVERAGE | 101.0 | 68.9 | 87.2 | 95.1 | 59.0 | 79.6 | 99.1 | 64.9 | 84.5 | 96.3 | 75.5 | 87.4 | 96.5 | 75.3 | 87.4 | 95.2 | 75.7 | 86.8 |

# City Cost Indexes

## MAINE

| DIVISION | | HOULTON 047 | | | KITTERY 039 | | | LEWISTON 042 | | | MACHIAS 046 | | | PORTLAND 040 - 041 | | | ROCKLAND 048 | | |
|---|---|---|---|---|---|---|---|---|---|---|---|---|---|---|---|---|---|---|---|
| | | MAT. | INST. | TOTAL | MAT. | INST. | TOTAL | MAT. | INST. | TOTAL | MAT. | INST. | TOTAL | MAT. | INST. | TOTAL | MAT. | INST. | TOTAL |
| 015433 | CONTRACTOR EQUIPMENT | | 100.6 | 100.6 | | 100.6 | 100.6 | | 100.6 | 100.6 | | 100.6 | 100.6 | | 100.6 | 100.6 | | 100.6 | 100.6 |
| 0241, 31 - 34 | SITE & INFRASTRUCTURE, DEMOLITION | 81.5 | 101.3 | 95.3 | 76.3 | 101.3 | 93.7 | 78.9 | 99.1 | 93.0 | 80.9 | 101.3 | 95.1 | 80.5 | 99.1 | 93.4 | 77.6 | 101.3 | 94.1 |
| 0310 | Concrete Forming & Accessories | 95.2 | 92.3 | 92.7 | 88.2 | 92.3 | 91.7 | 97.1 | 87.1 | 88.5 | 92.6 | 92.1 | 92.2 | 96.1 | 87.1 | 88.3 | 93.5 | 92.2 | 92.4 |
| 0320 | Concrete Reinforcing | 83.1 | 102.7 | 92.5 | 81.6 | 102.7 | 91.8 | 102.0 | 102.9 | 102.4 | 83.1 | 102.6 | 92.5 | 102.0 | 102.9 | 102.4 | 83.1 | 102.7 | 92.5 |
| 0330 | Cast-in-Place Concrete | 77.5 | 58.0 | 70.3 | 77.5 | 58.0 | 70.3 | 79.1 | 58.9 | 71.6 | 77.5 | 57.9 | 70.3 | 103.7 | 58.9 | 87.1 | 79.1 | 57.9 | 71.3 |
| 03 | CONCRETE | 99.1 | 82.0 | 91.2 | 93.3 | 82.0 | 88.1 | 97.8 | 79.8 | 89.5 | 98.6 | 81.9 | 90.9 | 110.0 | 79.8 | 96.1 | 95.4 | 82.0 | 89.2 |
| 04 | MASONRY | 95.4 | 46.6 | 66.3 | 109.1 | 46.6 | 71.7 | 96.0 | 53.9 | 70.8 | 95.4 | 46.6 | 66.3 | 96.3 | 53.9 | 70.9 | 89.6 | 47.9 | 64.7 |
| 05 | METALS | 80.9 | 82.3 | 81.3 | 80.6 | 82.3 | 81.1 | 84.9 | 78.3 | 83.0 | 80.9 | 82.1 | 81.3 | 86.2 | 78.3 | 83.9 | 80.8 | 82.4 | 81.2 |
| 06 | WOOD, PLASTICS & COMPOSITES | 96.1 | 102.0 | 99.3 | 87.4 | 102.0 | 95.3 | 98.1 | 94.3 | 96.1 | 93.1 | 102.0 | 97.9 | 97.3 | 94.3 | 95.7 | 94.0 | 102.0 | 98.3 |
| 07 | THERMAL & MOISTURE PROTECTION | 99.8 | 59.0 | 83.9 | 99.3 | 59.0 | 83.6 | 99.5 | 55.8 | 82.5 | 99.7 | 59.0 | 83.9 | 102.2 | 55.8 | 84.1 | 99.4 | 59.4 | 83.8 |
| 08 | OPENINGS | 102.3 | 82.1 | 97.3 | 102.2 | 82.1 | 97.2 | 105.3 | 77.9 | 98.5 | 102.3 | 80.1 | 96.8 | 105.3 | 77.9 | 98.5 | 102.2 | 80.1 | 96.8 |
| 0920 | Plaster & Gypsum Board | 102.1 | 101.3 | 101.6 | 97.7 | 101.3 | 99.9 | 105.1 | 93.4 | 97.9 | 101.1 | 101.3 | 101.2 | 110.2 | 93.4 | 99.8 | 101.1 | 101.3 | 101.2 |
| 0950, 0980 | Ceilings & Acoustic Treatment | 85.8 | 101.3 | 95.3 | 85.8 | 101.3 | 95.3 | 96.2 | 93.4 | 94.5 | 85.8 | 101.3 | 95.3 | 93.7 | 93.4 | 93.5 | 85.8 | 101.3 | 95.3 |
| 0960 | Flooring | 95.2 | 38.8 | 79.9 | 92.2 | 38.8 | 77.7 | 97.0 | 48.5 | 83.8 | 94.3 | 19.1 | 73.8 | 96.3 | 48.5 | 83.3 | 94.6 | 38.8 | 79.4 |
| 0970, 0990 | Wall Finishes & Painting/Coating | 91.6 | 33.0 | 56.4 | 91.6 | 33.0 | 56.4 | 91.6 | 30.4 | 54.8 | 91.6 | 33.0 | 56.4 | 91.6 | 30.4 | 54.8 | 91.6 | 33.0 | 56.4 |
| 09 | FINISHES | 97.0 | 77.4 | 86.8 | 95.0 | 77.4 | 85.8 | 100.1 | 75.2 | 87.1 | 96.5 | 74.0 | 84.7 | 99.9 | 75.2 | 87.0 | 96.3 | 77.4 | 86.4 |
| COVERS | DIVS. 10 - 14, 25, 28, 41, 43, 44 | 100.0 | 58.5 | 91.5 | 100.0 | 58.5 | 91.5 | 100.0 | 71.4 | 94.1 | 100.0 | 58.5 | 91.5 | 100.0 | 71.4 | 94.1 | 100.0 | 58.5 | 91.5 |
| 21, 22, 23 | FIRE SUPPRESSION, PLUMBING & HVAC | 96.0 | 69.6 | 85.1 | 96.0 | 69.6 | 85.1 | 100.1 | 70.7 | 88.0 | 96.0 | 69.6 | 85.1 | 100.0 | 70.7 | 87.9 | 96.0 | 69.6 | 85.1 |
| 26, 27, 3370 | ELECTRICAL, COMMUNICATIONS & UTIL. | 98.1 | 81.0 | 89.7 | 94.3 | 81.0 | 87.8 | 98.1 | 79.4 | 88.9 | 98.1 | 81.0 | 89.7 | 99.4 | 79.4 | 89.6 | 98.0 | 81.0 | 89.7 |
| MF2004 | WEIGHTED AVERAGE | 94.9 | 75.7 | 86.7 | 94.0 | 75.7 | 86.2 | 96.8 | 75.3 | 87.6 | 94.7 | 75.1 | 86.3 | 98.7 | 75.3 | 88.7 | 93.9 | 75.7 | 86.1 |

| DIVISION | | MAINE WATERVILLE 049 | | | MARYLAND ANNAPOLIS 214 | | | BALTIMORE 210 - 212 | | | COLLEGE PARK 207 - 208 | | | CUMBERLAND 215 | | | EASTON 216 | | |
|---|---|---|---|---|---|---|---|---|---|---|---|---|---|---|---|---|---|---|---|
| | | MAT. | INST. | TOTAL | MAT. | INST. | TOTAL | MAT. | INST. | TOTAL | MAT. | INST. | TOTAL | MAT. | INST. | TOTAL | MAT. | INST. | TOTAL |
| 015433 | CONTRACTOR EQUIPMENT | | 100.6 | 100.6 | | 99.1 | 99.1 | | 103.3 | 103.3 | | 103.6 | 103.6 | | 99.1 | 99.1 | | 99.1 | 99.1 |
| 0241, 31 - 34 | SITE & INFRASTRUCTURE, DEMOLITION | 81.5 | 101.3 | 95.3 | 98.4 | 89.7 | 92.4 | 96.6 | 94.2 | 94.9 | 110.1 | 90.4 | 96.4 | 88.0 | 88.6 | 88.4 | 94.8 | 85.5 | 88.3 |
| 0310 | Concrete Forming & Accessories | 87.2 | 92.2 | 91.5 | 99.1 | 55.4 | 61.4 | 102.2 | 74.9 | 78.7 | 86.5 | 69.8 | 72.1 | 92.5 | 74.4 | 76.9 | 90.3 | 32.6 | 40.6 |
| 0320 | Concrete Reinforcing | 83.1 | 102.7 | 92.5 | 103.8 | 85.4 | 94.9 | 103.8 | 85.5 | 95.0 | 102.1 | 75.4 | 89.2 | 91.7 | 70.0 | 81.2 | 90.9 | 19.3 | 56.4 |
| 0330 | Cast-in-Place Concrete | 77.6 | 57.9 | 70.3 | 104.5 | 78.1 | 94.8 | 93.1 | 79.1 | 87.9 | 126.7 | 76.1 | 107.9 | 83.1 | 77.9 | 81.2 | 92.3 | 41.2 | 73.4 |
| 03 | CONCRETE | 99.9 | 81.9 | 91.6 | 107.3 | 70.4 | 90.3 | 101.8 | 79.4 | 91.5 | 118.4 | 74.4 | 98.1 | 90.9 | 75.8 | 83.9 | 98.5 | 35.0 | 69.2 |
| 04 | MASONRY | 105.0 | 47.1 | 70.4 | 96.2 | 71.1 | 81.2 | 97.7 | 71.1 | 81.8 | 117.3 | 69.4 | 88.6 | 95.4 | 72.3 | 81.6 | 110.0 | 34.8 | 65.0 |
| 05 | METALS | 80.9 | 82.3 | 81.3 | 94.0 | 96.7 | 94.8 | 94.9 | 97.7 | 95.7 | 87.5 | 95.4 | 89.8 | 91.4 | 89.8 | 90.9 | 91.6 | 60.0 | 82.4 |
| 06 | WOOD, PLASTICS & COMPOSITES | 86.3 | 102.0 | 94.8 | 96.0 | 49.5 | 71.0 | 99.2 | 75.7 | 86.5 | 84.9 | 71.5 | 77.7 | 88.8 | 73.7 | 80.7 | 86.0 | 32.8 | 57.4 |
| 07 | THERMAL & MOISTURE PROTECTION | 99.8 | 58.2 | 83.6 | 96.4 | 76.3 | 88.5 | 96.9 | 79.3 | 90.0 | 107.5 | 74.9 | 94.8 | 96.4 | 75.5 | 88.2 | 96.5 | 38.5 | 73.8 |
| 08 | OPENINGS | 102.3 | 80.5 | 96.9 | 90.8 | 67.0 | 84.9 | 92.8 | 83.1 | 90.4 | 100.7 | 75.2 | 94.4 | 91.9 | 77.8 | 88.4 | 90.1 | 29.9 | 75.3 |
| 0920 | Plaster & Gypsum Board | 97.7 | 101.3 | 99.9 | 102.9 | 48.6 | 69.4 | 104.5 | 75.3 | 86.5 | 99.6 | 70.8 | 81.8 | 101.1 | 73.4 | 84.0 | 99.8 | 31.5 | 57.7 |
| 0950, 0980 | Ceilings & Acoustic Treatment | 85.8 | 101.3 | 95.3 | 93.6 | 48.6 | 65.9 | 96.1 | 75.3 | 83.3 | 95.6 | 70.8 | 80.4 | 96.1 | 73.4 | 82.2 | 96.1 | 31.5 | 56.5 |
| 0960 | Flooring | 91.7 | 38.8 | 77.3 | 87.5 | 72.7 | 83.5 | 87.5 | 72.7 | 83.5 | 111.3 | 59.7 | 97.3 | 83.3 | 75.1 | 81.1 | 82.5 | 14.8 | 64.1 |
| 0970, 0990 | Wall Finishes & Painting/Coating | 91.6 | 33.0 | 56.4 | 92.9 | 81.9 | 86.3 | 92.9 | 81.9 | 86.3 | 125.5 | 80.3 | 98.6 | 92.9 | 58.0 | 72.0 | 92.9 | 24.3 | 51.7 |
| 09 | FINISHES | 95.4 | 77.4 | 86.0 | 92.9 | 59.1 | 75.2 | 93.8 | 74.5 | 83.7 | 102.0 | 68.6 | 84.5 | 91.4 | 72.4 | 81.5 | 91.4 | 29.2 | 58.8 |
| COVERS | DIVS. 10 - 14, 25, 28, 41, 43, 44 | 100.0 | 58.5 | 91.5 | 100.0 | 82.3 | 96.4 | 100.0 | 85.8 | 97.1 | 100.0 | 61.7 | 92.1 | 100.0 | 87.0 | 97.3 | 100.0 | 43.8 | 88.5 |
| 21, 22, 23 | FIRE SUPPRESSION, PLUMBING & HVAC | 96.0 | 69.6 | 85.1 | 99.8 | 88.2 | 95.1 | 99.9 | 88.3 | 95.1 | 96.0 | 82.6 | 90.5 | 95.8 | 72.1 | 86.0 | 95.8 | 25.6 | 67.0 |
| 26, 27, 3370 | ELECTRICAL, COMMUNICATIONS & UTIL. | 98.1 | 81.0 | 89.7 | 99.1 | 85.6 | 92.5 | 100.4 | 91.5 | 96.0 | 101.1 | 92.2 | 96.7 | 97.8 | 79.3 | 88.7 | 97.3 | 62.6 | 80.3 |
| MF2004 | WEIGHTED AVERAGE | 95.2 | 75.6 | 86.8 | 97.9 | 79.0 | 89.8 | 97.9 | 84.7 | 92.2 | 100.9 | 80.2 | 92.1 | 94.0 | 77.4 | 86.9 | 95.7 | 42.8 | 73.1 |

| DIVISION | | MARYLAND ELKTON 219 | | | HAGERSTOWN 217 | | | SALISBURY 218 | | | SILVER SPRING 209 | | | WALDORF 206 | | | MASSACHUSETTS BOSTON 020 - 022, 024 | | |
|---|---|---|---|---|---|---|---|---|---|---|---|---|---|---|---|---|---|---|---|
| | | MAT. | INST. | TOTAL | MAT. | INST. | TOTAL | MAT. | INST. | TOTAL | MAT. | INST. | TOTAL | MAT. | INST. | TOTAL | MAT. | INST. | TOTAL |
| 015433 | CONTRACTOR EQUIPMENT | | 99.1 | 99.1 | | 99.1 | 99.1 | | 99.1 | 99.1 | | 95.0 | 95.0 | | 95.0 | 95.0 | | 107.4 | 107.4 |
| 0241, 31 - 34 | SITE & INFRASTRUCTURE, DEMOLITION | 82.3 | 86.0 | 84.9 | 86.1 | 89.9 | 88.8 | 94.7 | 85.1 | 88.0 | 96.1 | 82.7 | 86.7 | 104.0 | 82.0 | 88.7 | 86.0 | 108.6 | 101.7 |
| 0310 | Concrete Forming & Accessories | 96.7 | 60.1 | 65.2 | 91.6 | 75.2 | 77.4 | 105.0 | 30.7 | 41.0 | 95.1 | 57.6 | 62.8 | 102.0 | 50.6 | 57.7 | 101.2 | 141.8 | 136.2 |
| 0320 | Concrete Reinforcing | 90.9 | 56.7 | 74.4 | 91.7 | 69.9 | 81.2 | 90.9 | 56.4 | 74.3 | 100.9 | 75.2 | 88.5 | 101.6 | 56.6 | 79.9 | 100.9 | 148.0 | 123.6 |
| 0330 | Cast-in-Place Concrete | 74.7 | 47.2 | 64.5 | 79.2 | 57.2 | 71.0 | 92.3 | 39.8 | 72.9 | 129.7 | 64.1 | 105.4 | 145.3 | 57.0 | 112.6 | 100.1 | 149.7 | 118.5 |
| 03 | CONCRETE | 83.7 | 55.9 | 70.9 | 87.2 | 69.1 | 78.9 | 99.4 | 40.0 | 72.0 | 116.4 | 64.6 | 92.5 | 128.3 | 55.3 | 94.6 | 111.4 | 144.8 | 126.8 |
| 04 | MASONRY | 96.0 | 38.0 | 61.3 | 101.8 | 72.3 | 84.1 | 109.2 | 32.3 | 63.2 | 115.8 | 66.0 | 86.1 | 99.2 | 62.3 | 77.2 | 114.9 | 157.1 | 140.1 |
| 05 | METALS | 91.6 | 69.8 | 85.3 | 91.5 | 89.1 | 90.8 | 91.6 | 61.4 | 82.8 | 91.7 | 90.9 | 91.5 | 91.7 | 77.1 | 87.4 | 96.3 | 130.4 | 106.2 |
| 06 | WOOD, PLASTICS & COMPOSITES | 93.4 | 66.6 | 79.0 | 87.5 | 75.5 | 81.0 | 103.2 | 29.1 | 63.3 | 91.8 | 57.2 | 73.2 | 99.2 | 51.2 | 73.4 | 101.8 | 142.1 | 123.5 |
| 07 | THERMAL & MOISTURE PROTECTION | 96.1 | 46.7 | 76.8 | 96.1 | 67.7 | 85.1 | 96.7 | 55.5 | 80.6 | 108.4 | 77.3 | 94.8 | 108.9 | 73.3 | 95.0 | 99.7 | 149.4 | 119.1 |
| 08 | OPENINGS | 90.1 | 54.5 | 81.3 | 90.1 | 75.5 | 86.5 | 90.4 | 25.0 | 74.2 | 93.8 | 66.9 | 87.2 | 94.7 | 49.9 | 83.6 | 101.2 | 139.7 | 110.7 |
| 0920 | Plaster & Gypsum Board | 102.5 | 66.2 | 80.1 | 100.1 | 75.3 | 84.8 | 106.2 | 27.6 | 57.7 | 105.2 | 57.1 | 75.5 | 107.6 | 50.9 | 72.6 | 107.3 | 142.4 | 129.0 |
| 0950, 0980 | Ceilings & Acoustic Treatment | 96.1 | 66.2 | 77.7 | 97.1 | 75.3 | 83.7 | 96.1 | 27.6 | 54.1 | 105.0 | 57.1 | 75.6 | 105.0 | 50.9 | 71.8 | 95.3 | 142.4 | 124.2 |
| 0960 | Flooring | 85.1 | 56.6 | 77.3 | 83.0 | 75.1 | 80.8 | 89.0 | 56.6 | 80.2 | 118.9 | 59.7 | 102.8 | 123.8 | 56.6 | 105.6 | 96.8 | 168.2 | 116.2 |
| 0970, 0990 | Wall Finishes & Painting/Coating | 92.9 | 80.8 | 85.6 | 92.9 | 37.2 | 59.5 | 92.9 | 27.5 | 53.6 | 131.9 | 80.8 | 101.2 | 131.9 | 64.1 | 91.2 | 94.3 | 154.4 | 130.4 |
| 09 | FINISHES | 91.8 | 62.7 | 76.6 | 91.2 | 71.1 | 80.7 | 94.3 | 34.3 | 62.9 | 103.4 | 59.2 | 80.3 | 105.5 | 52.3 | 77.7 | 100.1 | 148.8 | 125.6 |
| COVERS | DIVS. 10 - 14, 25, 28, 41, 43, 44 | 100.0 | 49.0 | 89.5 | 100.0 | 87.3 | 97.4 | 100.0 | 42.8 | 88.3 | 100.0 | 56.6 | 91.1 | 100.0 | 46.0 | 87.4 | 100.0 | 118.4 | 103.8 |
| 21, 22, 23 | FIRE SUPPRESSION, PLUMBING & HVAC | 95.8 | 72.9 | 86.4 | 99.9 | 82.4 | 92.7 | 95.8 | 56.5 | 79.6 | 96.0 | 80.4 | 89.6 | 96.0 | 78.5 | 88.8 | 100.1 | 131.7 | 113.3 |
| 26, 27, 3370 | ELECTRICAL, COMMUNICATIONS & UTIL. | 99.1 | 59.2 | 79.5 | 97.6 | 79.2 | 88.6 | 96.1 | 62.6 | 79.6 | 97.6 | 92.2 | 94.9 | 95.1 | 92.1 | 93.6 | 97.3 | 133.1 | 114.9 |
| MF2004 | WEIGHTED AVERAGE | 93.1 | 62.3 | 80.0 | 94.6 | 78.3 | 87.6 | 96.0 | 50.6 | 76.6 | 100.1 | 75.3 | 89.5 | 100.9 | 69.9 | 87.6 | 101.0 | 136.9 | 116.4 |

# City Cost Indexes

## MASSACHUSETTS

| DIVISION | | BROCKTON 023 MAT. | INST. | TOTAL | BUZZARDS BAY 025 MAT. | INST. | TOTAL | FALL RIVER 027 MAT. | INST. | TOTAL | FITCHBURG 014 MAT. | INST. | TOTAL | FRAMINGHAM 017 MAT. | INST. | TOTAL | GREENFIELD 013 MAT. | INST. | TOTAL |
|---|---|---|---|---|---|---|---|---|---|---|---|---|---|---|---|---|---|---|---|
| 015433 | CONTRACTOR EQUIPMENT | | 102.8 | 102.8 | | 102.8 | 102.8 | | 104.0 | 104.0 | | 100.6 | 100.6 | | 101.9 | 101.9 | | 100.6 | 100.6 |
| 0241, 31 - 34 | SITE & INFRASTRUCTURE, DEMOLITION | 83.7 | 104.3 | 98.1 | 75.1 | 104.3 | 95.4 | 82.8 | 104.4 | 97.9 | 76.5 | 104.2 | 95.8 | 73.3 | 103.9 | 94.6 | 79.8 | 102.8 | 95.8 |
| 0310 | Concrete Forming & Accessories | 101.6 | 123.7 | 120.6 | 99.0 | 123.2 | 119.9 | 101.6 | 123.6 | 120.5 | 93.3 | 129.3 | 124.3 | 100.1 | 123.6 | 120.4 | 91.5 | 103.1 | 101.5 |
| 0320 | Concrete Reinforcing | 102.0 | 147.7 | 124.0 | 81.8 | 122.4 | 101.4 | 102.0 | 123.5 | 112.4 | 81.8 | 129.6 | 104.8 | 81.8 | 147.7 | 113.5 | 85.5 | 112.8 | 98.7 |
| 0330 | Cast-in-Place Concrete | 95.3 | 143.7 | 113.2 | 79.1 | 147.9 | 104.6 | 92.2 | 148.6 | 113.0 | 83.0 | 143.4 | 105.3 | 83.0 | 139.0 | 103.7 | 85.3 | 120.6 | 98.4 |
| 03 | CONCRETE | 108.8 | 134.4 | 120.6 | 91.8 | 130.9 | 109.8 | 107.2 | 131.4 | 118.4 | 89.8 | 133.2 | 109.9 | 93.0 | 132.8 | 111.4 | 93.8 | 110.5 | 101.5 |
| 04 | MASONRY | 111.2 | 144.2 | 131.0 | 101.8 | 149.0 | 130.0 | 111.1 | 148.9 | 133.7 | 98.0 | 144.1 | 125.6 | 104.0 | 144.2 | 128.1 | 102.3 | 119.0 | 112.3 |
| 05 | METALS | 93.4 | 127.0 | 103.2 | 88.7 | 116.1 | 96.7 | 93.4 | 117.1 | 100.3 | 88.6 | 115.9 | 96.6 | 88.7 | 126.8 | 99.7 | 90.7 | 103.0 | 94.3 |
| 06 | WOOD, PLASTICS & COMPOSITES | 100.7 | 122.8 | 112.6 | 97.6 | 122.8 | 111.2 | 100.7 | 123.1 | 112.8 | 93.8 | 131.3 | 114.0 | 100.1 | 122.5 | 112.2 | 91.7 | 101.5 | 97.0 |
| 07 | THERMAL & MOISTURE PROTECTION | 99.8 | 140.7 | 115.8 | 99.1 | 138.4 | 114.5 | 99.8 | 137.6 | 114.5 | 99.2 | 135.2 | 113.2 | 99.2 | 141.1 | 115.6 | 99.2 | 111.7 | 104.1 |
| 08 | OPENINGS | 99.1 | 129.3 | 106.5 | 94.8 | 119.1 | 100.8 | 99.1 | 119.6 | 104.1 | 104.1 | 120.0 | 110.3 | 95.2 | 129.1 | 103.6 | 104.1 | 105.5 | 104.4 |
| 0920 | Plaster & Gypsum Board | 102.9 | 122.6 | 115.0 | 99.2 | 122.6 | 113.6 | 102.9 | 122.6 | 115.0 | 100.4 | 131.3 | 119.5 | 102.4 | 122.6 | 114.9 | 101.4 | 100.8 | 101.0 |
| 0950, 0980 | Ceilings & Acoustic Treatment | 97.2 | 122.6 | 112.8 | 86.7 | 122.6 | 108.7 | 97.2 | 122.6 | 112.8 | 85.8 | 131.3 | 113.7 | 85.8 | 122.6 | 108.4 | 94.3 | 100.8 | 98.3 |
| 0960 | Flooring | 97.3 | 168.2 | 116.6 | 95.9 | 168.2 | 115.5 | 97.1 | 168.2 | 116.4 | 93.9 | 168.2 | 114.2 | 95.7 | 168.2 | 115.5 | 93.1 | 131.6 | 103.6 |
| 0970, 0990 | Wall Finishes & Painting/Coating | 93.8 | 132.4 | 117.0 | 93.8 | 132.4 | 117.0 | 93.8 | 132.4 | 117.0 | 91.6 | 132.4 | 116.1 | 92.7 | 132.4 | 116.6 | 91.6 | 106.2 | 100.4 |
| 09 | FINISHES | 100.0 | 133.1 | 117.3 | 95.9 | 133.1 | 115.4 | 99.9 | 133.3 | 117.4 | 95.2 | 138.1 | 117.7 | 95.9 | 132.9 | 115.3 | 97.4 | 108.8 | 103.4 |
| COVERS | DIVS. 10 - 14, 25, 28, 41, 43, 44 | 100.0 | 113.2 | 102.7 | 100.0 | 113.2 | 102.7 | 100.0 | 113.9 | 102.9 | 100.0 | 102.4 | 100.5 | 100.0 | 112.5 | 102.6 | 100.0 | 96.9 | 99.4 |
| 21, 22, 23 | FIRE SUPPRESSION, PLUMBING & HVAC | 100.1 | 103.3 | 101.4 | 96.0 | 103.0 | 98.9 | 100.1 | 103.1 | 101.4 | 96.5 | 107.1 | 100.9 | 96.5 | 121.3 | 106.7 | 96.5 | 93.6 | 95.3 |
| 26, 27, 3370 | ELECTRICAL, COMMUNICATIONS & UTIL. | 96.4 | 98.9 | 97.6 | 93.8 | 98.9 | 96.3 | 96.2 | 98.9 | 97.5 | 98.5 | 98.5 | 98.5 | 95.3 | 111.0 | 103.0 | 98.5 | 91.6 | 95.1 |
| MF2004 | WEIGHTED AVERAGE | 99.6 | 119.7 | 108.2 | 94.1 | 118.2 | 104.4 | 99.4 | 118.4 | 107.5 | 95.2 | 119.5 | 105.6 | 94.7 | 124.9 | 107.6 | 96.5 | 103.0 | 99.2 |

## MASSACHUSETTS

| DIVISION | | HYANNIS 026 MAT. | INST. | TOTAL | LAWRENCE 019 MAT. | INST. | TOTAL | LOWELL 018 MAT. | INST. | TOTAL | NEW BEDFORD 027 MAT. | INST. | TOTAL | PITTSFIELD 012 MAT. | INST. | TOTAL | SPRINGFIELD 010 - 011 MAT. | INST. | TOTAL |
|---|---|---|---|---|---|---|---|---|---|---|---|---|---|---|---|---|---|---|---|
| 015433 | CONTRACTOR EQUIPMENT | | 102.8 | 102.8 | | 102.8 | 102.8 | | 100.6 | 100.6 | | 104.0 | 104.0 | | 100.6 | 100.6 | | 100.6 | 100.6 |
| 0241, 31 - 34 | SITE & INFRASTRUCTURE, DEMOLITION | 80.6 | 104.3 | 97.1 | 84.4 | 104.3 | 98.3 | 83.3 | 104.2 | 97.9 | 81.3 | 104.4 | 97.4 | 84.3 | 102.6 | 97.1 | 83.8 | 102.8 | 97.1 |
| 0310 | Concrete Forming & Accessories | 93.2 | 123.2 | 119.1 | 101.4 | 123.8 | 120.7 | 98.4 | 123.9 | 120.4 | 101.6 | 123.5 | 120.5 | 98.4 | 101.7 | 101.3 | 98.6 | 108.0 | 106.7 |
| 0320 | Concrete Reinforcing | 81.8 | 122.4 | 101.4 | 101.2 | 136.3 | 118.1 | 102.0 | 136.3 | 118.6 | 102.0 | 123.4 | 112.4 | 84.9 | 111.5 | 97.7 | 102.0 | 112.9 | 107.2 |
| 0330 | Cast-in-Place Concrete | 86.9 | 147.9 | 109.5 | 96.1 | 143.8 | 113.7 | 87.3 | 143.8 | 108.2 | 81.2 | 148.5 | 106.1 | 95.3 | 118.7 | 103.9 | 90.9 | 120.6 | 101.9 |
| 03 | CONCRETE | 98.8 | 130.9 | 113.6 | 109.0 | 132.4 | 119.8 | 99.5 | 132.3 | 114.6 | 101.7 | 131.4 | 115.4 | 100.8 | 109.0 | 104.5 | 101.3 | 112.7 | 106.5 |
| 04 | MASONRY | 110.1 | 149.0 | 133.4 | 110.6 | 144.2 | 130.7 | 96.7 | 144.1 | 125.0 | 110.1 | 148.9 | 133.3 | 97.3 | 115.7 | 108.3 | 96.9 | 119.0 | 110.1 |
| 05 | METALS | 90.1 | 116.1 | 97.7 | 91.1 | 122.3 | 100.2 | 91.1 | 119.6 | 99.4 | 93.4 | 117.0 | 100.3 | 90.9 | 102.4 | 94.2 | 93.4 | 103.0 | 96.2 |
| 06 | WOOD, PLASTICS & COMPOSITES | 91.1 | 122.8 | 108.2 | 100.7 | 122.8 | 112.6 | 100.0 | 122.8 | 112.2 | 100.7 | 123.1 | 112.8 | 100.0 | 101.5 | 100.8 | 100.0 | 108.2 | 104.4 |
| 07 | THERMAL & MOISTURE PROTECTION | 99.4 | 138.4 | 114.6 | 99.7 | 140.7 | 115.7 | 99.5 | 140.7 | 115.6 | 99.7 | 137.6 | 114.5 | 99.6 | 110.3 | 103.7 | 99.5 | 112.4 | 104.6 |
| 08 | OPENINGS | 95.4 | 119.1 | 101.3 | 99.1 | 126.2 | 105.8 | 105.3 | 126.2 | 110.4 | 99.1 | 119.6 | 104.1 | 105.3 | 105.2 | 105.3 | 105.3 | 109.2 | 106.2 |
| 0920 | Plaster & Gypsum Board | 96.5 | 122.6 | 112.6 | 105.1 | 122.6 | 115.9 | 105.1 | 122.6 | 115.9 | 102.9 | 122.6 | 115.0 | 105.1 | 100.8 | 102.4 | 105.1 | 107.7 | 106.7 |
| 0950, 0980 | Ceilings & Acoustic Treatment | 88.6 | 122.6 | 109.5 | 96.2 | 122.6 | 112.4 | 96.2 | 122.6 | 112.4 | 97.2 | 122.6 | 112.8 | 96.2 | 100.8 | 99.0 | 96.2 | 107.1 | 103.3 |
| 0960 | Flooring | 93.5 | 168.2 | 113.8 | 96.3 | 168.2 | 115.8 | 96.3 | 168.2 | 115.8 | 97.1 | 168.2 | 116.4 | 96.5 | 131.6 | 106.0 | 96.2 | 131.6 | 105.8 |
| 0970, 0990 | Wall Finishes & Painting/Coating | 93.8 | 132.4 | 117.0 | 91.7 | 132.4 | 116.1 | 91.6 | 132.4 | 116.1 | 93.8 | 129.1 | 115.0 | 91.6 | 106.2 | 100.4 | 93.2 | 106.2 | 101.0 |
| 09 | FINISHES | 95.6 | 133.1 | 115.2 | 99.6 | 133.1 | 117.1 | 99.6 | 133.1 | 117.1 | 99.8 | 132.9 | 117.2 | 99.7 | 108.0 | 104.0 | 99.7 | 112.7 | 106.5 |
| COVERS | DIVS. 10 - 14, 25, 28, 41, 43, 44 | 100.0 | 113.2 | 102.7 | 100.0 | 113.2 | 102.7 | 100.0 | 113.2 | 102.7 | 100.0 | 113.9 | 102.9 | 100.0 | 95.7 | 99.1 | 100.0 | 97.7 | 99.5 |
| 21, 22, 23 | FIRE SUPPRESSION, PLUMBING & HVAC | 100.1 | 103.0 | 101.3 | 100.1 | 110.9 | 104.6 | 100.1 | 118.9 | 107.9 | 100.1 | 103.1 | 101.4 | 100.1 | 90.2 | 96.1 | 100.1 | 93.6 | 97.5 |
| 26, 27, 3370 | ELECTRICAL, COMMUNICATIONS & UTIL. | 94.3 | 98.9 | 96.6 | 97.6 | 111.0 | 104.2 | 98.1 | 111.0 | 104.4 | 97.3 | 98.9 | 98.1 | 98.1 | 91.6 | 94.9 | 98.1 | 91.6 | 94.9 |
| MF2004 | WEIGHTED AVERAGE | 96.7 | 118.2 | 105.9 | 99.4 | 122.2 | 109.1 | 98.1 | 123.6 | 109.0 | 98.8 | 118.4 | 107.2 | 98.3 | 101.4 | 99.7 | 98.8 | 104.0 | 101.0 |

## MASSACHUSETTS / MICHIGAN

| DIVISION | | WORCESTER 015 - 016 MAT. | INST. | TOTAL | ANN ARBOR 481 MAT. | INST. | TOTAL | BATTLE CREEK 490 MAT. | INST. | TOTAL | BAY CITY 487 MAT. | INST. | TOTAL | DEARBORN 481 MAT. | INST. | TOTAL | DETROIT 482 MAT. | INST. | TOTAL |
|---|---|---|---|---|---|---|---|---|---|---|---|---|---|---|---|---|---|---|---|
| 015433 | CONTRACTOR EQUIPMENT | | 100.6 | 100.6 | | 112.8 | 112.8 | | 104.5 | 104.5 | | 112.8 | 112.8 | | 112.8 | 112.8 | | 98.3 | 98.3 |
| 0241, 31 - 34 | SITE & INFRASTRUCTURE, DEMOLITION | 83.7 | 104.2 | 98.0 | 75.7 | 96.1 | 89.9 | 78.9 | 87.1 | 84.6 | 68.0 | 94.5 | 86.5 | 75.5 | 96.3 | 89.9 | 89.5 | 98.0 | 95.4 |
| 0310 | Concrete Forming & Accessories | 99.0 | 129.5 | 125.3 | 97.9 | 113.8 | 111.6 | 97.0 | 85.5 | 87.1 | 98.0 | 90.4 | 91.4 | 97.7 | 116.4 | 113.8 | 98.9 | 116.5 | 114.0 |
| 0320 | Concrete Reinforcing | 102.0 | 146.8 | 123.6 | 99.2 | 129.8 | 113.9 | 98.1 | 89.0 | 93.7 | 99.2 | 128.9 | 113.5 | 99.2 | 130.2 | 114.1 | 98.5 | 130.1 | 113.7 |
| 0330 | Cast-in-Place Concrete | 90.4 | 143.4 | 110.0 | 84.8 | 117.4 | 96.9 | 90.4 | 108.2 | 97.0 | 81.2 | 96.2 | 86.7 | 82.9 | 117.2 | 95.6 | 91.1 | 117.2 | 100.7 |
| 03 | CONCRETE | 101.0 | 136.6 | 117.5 | 89.1 | 118.3 | 102.6 | 93.8 | 93.3 | 93.6 | 87.2 | 100.5 | 93.4 | 88.1 | 119.5 | 102.6 | 92.1 | 118.2 | 104.2 |
| 04 | MASONRY | 96.4 | 144.1 | 124.9 | 94.9 | 112.0 | 105.1 | 94.1 | 89.9 | 91.6 | 94.5 | 92.8 | 93.5 | 94.7 | 119.8 | 109.7 | 93.9 | 119.8 | 109.4 |
| 05 | METALS | 93.4 | 123.3 | 102.1 | 93.3 | 124.4 | 102.4 | 93.9 | 85.6 | 91.5 | 93.9 | 120.7 | 101.7 | 93.4 | 125.5 | 102.7 | 97.4 | 104.6 | 99.5 |
| 06 | WOOD, PLASTICS & COMPOSITES | 100.4 | 131.3 | 117.0 | 98.7 | 114.5 | 107.2 | 98.0 | 83.0 | 89.9 | 98.7 | 89.9 | 94.0 | 98.7 | 115.8 | 108.2 | 99.4 | 115.8 | 108.2 |
| 07 | THERMAL & MOISTURE PROTECTION | 99.5 | 135.2 | 113.5 | 101.9 | 113.2 | 106.3 | 91.4 | 88.7 | 90.4 | 99.6 | 91.0 | 96.3 | 100.6 | 121.2 | 108.7 | 98.6 | 121.2 | 107.4 |
| 08 | OPENINGS | 105.3 | 133.7 | 112.3 | 95.6 | 112.6 | 99.8 | 90.9 | 81.0 | 88.5 | 95.6 | 95.2 | 95.5 | 95.6 | 113.3 | 100.0 | 97.4 | 114.9 | 101.7 |
| 0920 | Plaster & Gypsum Board | 105.1 | 131.3 | 121.3 | 87.6 | 113.7 | 103.7 | 87.4 | 78.0 | 81.6 | 87.6 | 88.5 | 88.1 | 87.6 | 115.0 | 104.5 | 87.6 | 115.0 | 104.5 |
| 0950, 0980 | Ceilings & Acoustic Treatment | 96.2 | 131.3 | 117.8 | 89.0 | 113.7 | 104.2 | 91.7 | 78.0 | 83.3 | 89.9 | 88.5 | 89.0 | 89.0 | 115.0 | 105.0 | 89.9 | 115.0 | 105.3 |
| 0960 | Flooring | 96.3 | 163.7 | 114.6 | 92.6 | 118.7 | 99.7 | 97.2 | 98.0 | 97.4 | 92.4 | 82.3 | 89.7 | 92.3 | 130.0 | 102.5 | 92.3 | 130.0 | 102.6 |
| 0970, 0990 | Wall Finishes & Painting/Coating | 91.6 | 132.4 | 116.1 | 90.1 | 106.7 | 100.1 | 96.8 | 78.5 | 85.8 | 90.1 | 87.3 | 88.4 | 90.1 | 110.6 | 102.4 | 91.7 | 110.6 | 103.1 |
| 09 | FINISHES | 99.6 | 137.1 | 119.2 | 92.6 | 114.4 | 104.0 | 94.0 | 86.5 | 90.1 | 92.4 | 88.1 | 90.2 | 92.5 | 118.6 | 106.2 | 93.7 | 118.6 | 106.7 |
| COVERS | DIVS. 10 - 14, 25, 28, 41, 43, 44 | 100.0 | 102.4 | 100.5 | 100.0 | 108.7 | 101.8 | 100.0 | 100.4 | 99.9 | 100.0 | 93.9 | 98.8 | 100.0 | 109.9 | 102.0 | 100.0 | 109.9 | 102.0 |
| 21, 22, 23 | FIRE SUPPRESSION, PLUMBING & HVAC | 100.1 | 107.2 | 103.1 | 99.9 | 102.6 | 101.0 | 99.9 | 91.6 | 96.5 | 99.9 | 88.1 | 95.1 | 99.9 | 112.5 | 105.1 | 99.9 | 113.7 | 105.6 |
| 26, 27, 3370 | ELECTRICAL, COMMUNICATIONS & UTIL. | 98.1 | 98.5 | 98.3 | 93.2 | 79.1 | 86.3 | 93.3 | 85.3 | 89.4 | 92.0 | 74.9 | 83.6 | 93.2 | 114.1 | 103.5 | 94.4 | 114.1 | 104.0 |
| MF2004 | WEIGHTED AVERAGE | 98.7 | 120.8 | 108.1 | 94.9 | 106.3 | 99.8 | 94.9 | 88.8 | 92.3 | 94.4 | 92.4 | 93.5 | 94.8 | 115.2 | 103.5 | 96.6 | 113.6 | 103.9 |

# City Cost Indexes

## MICHIGAN

| DIVISION | | FLINT 484 - 485 | | | GAYLORD 497 | | | GRAND RAPIDS 493,495 | | | IRON MOUNTAIN 498 - 499 | | | JACKSON 492 | | | KALAMAZOO 491 | | |
|---|---|---|---|---|---|---|---|---|---|---|---|---|---|---|---|---|---|---|---|
| | | MAT. | INST. | TOTAL | MAT. | INST. | TOTAL | MAT. | INST. | TOTAL | MAT. | INST. | TOTAL | MAT. | INST. | TOTAL | MAT. | INST. | TOTAL |
| 015433 | CONTRACTOR EQUIPMENT | | 112.8 | 112.8 | | 107.2 | 107.2 | | 104.5 | 104.5 | | 93.8 | 93.8 | | 107.2 | 107.2 | | 104.5 | 104.5 |
| 0241, 31 - 34 | SITE & INFRASTRUCTURE, DEMOLITION | 66.1 | 95.5 | 86.6 | 75.3 | 84.9 | 82.0 | 79.1 | 86.5 | 84.2 | 81.9 | 94.5 | 90.7 | 93.7 | 86.5 | 88.7 | 79.2 | 87.1 | 84.7 |
| 0310 | Concrete Forming & Accessories | 101.0 | 92.5 | 93.7 | 94.2 | 58.9 | 63.8 | 97.5 | 71.8 | 75.3 | 88.1 | 84.3 | 84.8 | 91.9 | 90.4 | 90.6 | 97.0 | 85.2 | 86.8 |
| 0320 | Concrete Reinforcing | 99.2 | 129.1 | 113.6 | 91.5 | 105.5 | 98.2 | 98.1 | 86.8 | 92.7 | 91.3 | 100.3 | 95.6 | 88.8 | 129.2 | 108.3 | 98.1 | 88.9 | 93.7 |
| 0330 | Cast-in-Place Concrete | 85.4 | 100.9 | 91.2 | 90.2 | 71.8 | 83.4 | 91.7 | 91.6 | 91.6 | 106.9 | 91.4 | 101.1 | 90.1 | 96.2 | 92.3 | 92.3 | 108.1 | 98.1 |
| 03 | CONCRETE | 89.5 | 103.1 | 95.8 | 90.2 | 73.7 | 82.5 | 94.4 | 81.1 | 88.3 | 99.7 | 89.9 | 95.2 | 85.3 | 100.4 | 92.2 | 96.9 | 93.1 | 95.1 |
| 04 | MASONRY | 94.9 | 98.7 | 97.2 | 104.5 | 77.4 | 88.3 | 91.3 | 50.3 | 66.8 | 91.2 | 91.2 | 91.2 | 85.5 | 100.0 | 94.2 | 92.8 | 89.9 | 91.1 |
| 05 | METALS | 93.4 | 121.4 | 101.5 | 95.3 | 108.4 | 99.1 | 95.4 | 80.0 | 90.9 | 94.8 | 92.6 | 94.1 | 95.5 | 119.1 | 102.4 | 93.9 | 85.3 | 91.4 |
| 06 | WOOD, PLASTICS & COMPOSITES | 102.1 | 89.9 | 95.5 | 90.7 | 55.7 | 71.9 | 95.7 | 72.2 | 83.0 | 86.5 | 83.1 | 84.7 | 89.6 | 88.6 | 89.1 | 98.0 | 83.0 | 89.9 |
| 07 | THERMAL & MOISTURE PROTECTION | 99.7 | 94.5 | 97.7 | 90.1 | 66.9 | 81.1 | 93.0 | 56.7 | 78.8 | 93.3 | 82.1 | 88.9 | 89.5 | 98.7 | 93.1 | 91.4 | 88.7 | 90.4 |
| 08 | OPENINGS | 95.6 | 95.2 | 95.5 | 92.3 | 61.8 | 84.8 | 94.3 | 66.3 | 87.4 | 97.1 | 74.0 | 91.4 | 91.4 | 91.7 | 91.5 | 90.9 | 81.0 | 88.5 |
| 0920 | Plaster & Gypsum Board | 88.9 | 88.5 | 88.7 | 86.9 | 53.1 | 66.0 | 86.0 | 67.0 | 74.3 | 58.5 | 83.2 | 73.7 | 86.2 | 86.9 | 86.6 | 87.4 | 78.0 | 81.6 |
| 0950, 0980 | Ceilings & Acoustic Treatment | 89.0 | 88.5 | 88.7 | 89.2 | 53.1 | 67.0 | 90.0 | 67.0 | 75.9 | 89.8 | 83.2 | 85.8 | 90.9 | 86.9 | 88.4 | 91.7 | 78.0 | 83.3 |
| 0960 | Flooring | 92.4 | 85.0 | 90.4 | 90.4 | 55.6 | 80.9 | 97.4 | 39.1 | 81.5 | 109.5 | 96.3 | 105.9 | 88.7 | 76.6 | 85.4 | 97.2 | 76.5 | 91.5 |
| 0970, 0990 | Wall Finishes & Painting/Coating | 90.1 | 92.5 | 91.5 | 91.9 | 51.8 | 67.8 | 96.8 | 38.6 | 61.8 | 115.6 | 42.2 | 71.5 | 91.9 | 86.0 | 88.4 | 96.8 | 78.5 | 85.8 |
| 09 | FINISHES | 92.0 | 90.3 | 91.1 | 93.5 | 55.9 | 73.8 | 93.5 | 61.7 | 76.8 | 95.7 | 82.0 | 88.5 | 94.4 | 86.6 | 90.4 | 94.0 | 82.2 | 87.8 |
| COVERS | DIVS. 10 - 14, 25, 28, 41, 43, 44 | 100.0 | 95.6 | 99.1 | 100.0 | 86.5 | 97.2 | 100.0 | 96.2 | 99.2 | 100.0 | 89.6 | 97.9 | 100.0 | 95.3 | 99.0 | 100.0 | 100.4 | 100.1 |
| 21, 22, 23 | FIRE SUPPRESSION, PLUMBING & HVAC | 99.9 | 96.4 | 98.5 | 96.0 | 78.5 | 88.8 | 99.9 | 50.5 | 79.6 | 96.0 | 82.0 | 90.2 | 96.0 | 93.0 | 94.8 | 99.9 | 85.9 | 94.2 |
| 26, 27, 3370 | ELECTRICAL, COMMUNICATIONS & UTIL. | 93.2 | 102.2 | 97.6 | 91.5 | 55.3 | 73.7 | 94.7 | 55.2 | 75.3 | 97.8 | 80.0 | 89.0 | 95.2 | 79.1 | 87.3 | 93.1 | 81.8 | 87.5 |
| MF2004 | WEIGHTED AVERAGE | 94.6 | 99.5 | 96.7 | 94.1 | 73.7 | 85.4 | 95.6 | 64.8 | 82.4 | 96.0 | 85.6 | 91.6 | 93.5 | 93.8 | 93.6 | 95.2 | 86.5 | 91.5 |

## MICHIGAN / MINNESOTA

| DIVISION | | LANSING 488 - 489 | | | MUSKEGON 494 | | | ROYAL OAK 480,483 | | | SAGINAW 486 | | | TRAVERSE CITY 496 | | | BEMIDJI 566 | | |
|---|---|---|---|---|---|---|---|---|---|---|---|---|---|---|---|---|---|---|---|
| | | MAT. | INST. | TOTAL | MAT. | INST. | TOTAL | MAT. | INST. | TOTAL | MAT. | INST. | TOTAL | MAT. | INST. | TOTAL | MAT. | INST. | TOTAL |
| 015433 | CONTRACTOR EQUIPMENT | | 112.8 | 112.8 | | 104.5 | 104.5 | | 95.2 | 95.2 | | 112.8 | 112.8 | | 93.8 | 93.8 | | 98.7 | 98.7 |
| 0241, 31 - 34 | SITE & INFRASTRUCTURE, DEMOLITION | 82.8 | 94.7 | 91.1 | 77.0 | 87.0 | 84.0 | 79.2 | 95.3 | 90.4 | 68.9 | 94.5 | 86.8 | 69.4 | 93.7 | 86.3 | 89.7 | 98.9 | 96.1 |
| 0310 | Concrete Forming & Accessories | 101.6 | 91.8 | 93.1 | 97.6 | 84.3 | 86.1 | 94.2 | 111.2 | 108.8 | 97.9 | 90.3 | 91.4 | 88.1 | 56.8 | 61.1 | 85.9 | 94.9 | 93.6 |
| 0320 | Concrete Reinforcing | 99.2 | 129.1 | 113.6 | 98.7 | 88.1 | 93.6 | 89.9 | 107.1 | 98.2 | 99.2 | 128.9 | 113.5 | 92.8 | 87.9 | 90.4 | 97.9 | 105.1 | 101.4 |
| 0330 | Cast-in-Place Concrete | 87.9 | 95.3 | 90.6 | 90.1 | 101.9 | 94.5 | 74.2 | 115.2 | 89.4 | 83.8 | 96.1 | 88.4 | 83.3 | 62.8 | 75.7 | 99.9 | 104.8 | 101.7 |
| 03 | CONCRETE | 90.8 | 100.8 | 95.4 | 92.2 | 90.4 | 91.4 | 77.1 | 110.7 | 92.6 | 88.6 | 100.4 | 94.0 | 82.2 | 65.6 | 74.6 | 94.5 | 101.3 | 97.6 |
| 04 | MASONRY | 88.4 | 97.0 | 93.5 | 91.4 | 76.6 | 82.6 | 89.7 | 119.6 | 107.6 | 96.2 | 92.8 | 94.2 | 89.3 | 77.6 | 82.3 | 96.7 | 109.1 | 104.1 |
| 05 | METALS | 91.9 | 120.9 | 100.3 | 91.6 | 83.6 | 89.3 | 96.6 | 92.5 | 95.4 | 93.4 | 120.5 | 101.3 | 94.7 | 87.4 | 92.6 | 92.6 | 122.3 | 101.2 |
| 06 | WOOD, PLASTICS & COMPOSITES | 101.5 | 90.3 | 95.5 | 94.5 | 83.0 | 88.3 | 94.2 | 110.0 | 102.7 | 94.7 | 89.9 | 92.1 | 86.5 | 53.7 | 68.8 | 77.0 | 91.7 | 84.9 |
| 07 | THERMAL & MOISTURE PROTECTION | 100.5 | 94.3 | 98.1 | 90.6 | 77.1 | 85.3 | 98.2 | 114.8 | 104.7 | 100.3 | 91.2 | 96.8 | 92.4 | 65.0 | 81.7 | 102.5 | 95.0 | 99.6 |
| 08 | OPENINGS | 95.6 | 95.4 | 95.6 | 90.2 | 79.3 | 87.5 | 95.7 | 104.6 | 97.9 | 93.6 | 95.2 | 94.0 | 97.1 | 56.9 | 87.2 | 98.4 | 111.0 | 101.5 |
| 0920 | Plaster & Gypsum Board | 86.2 | 88.9 | 87.9 | 75.4 | 78.0 | 77.0 | 85.5 | 109.1 | 100.1 | 87.6 | 88.5 | 88.2 | 58.5 | 53.1 | 55.1 | 101.0 | 91.8 | 95.3 |
| 0950, 0980 | Ceilings & Acoustic Treatment | 87.3 | 88.9 | 88.3 | 93.5 | 78.0 | 84.0 | 88.2 | 109.1 | 101.0 | 89.0 | 88.5 | 88.7 | 89.8 | 53.1 | 67.3 | 132.9 | 91.8 | 107.7 |
| 0960 | Flooring | 102.4 | 90.6 | 99.2 | 96.3 | 72.1 | 89.7 | 89.9 | 117.2 | 97.3 | 92.6 | 82.3 | 89.8 | 109.4 | 55.6 | 94.8 | 107.6 | 125.9 | 112.6 |
| 0970, 0990 | Wall Finishes & Painting/Coating | 102.4 | 85.5 | 92.2 | 96.1 | 56.1 | 72.0 | 91.7 | 106.6 | 100.6 | 90.1 | 87.3 | 88.4 | 115.6 | 51.8 | 77.3 | 97.7 | 96.4 | 96.9 |
| 09 | FINISHES | 96.5 | 90.5 | 93.3 | 91.7 | 78.5 | 84.8 | 91.5 | 112.1 | 102.3 | 92.3 | 88.1 | 90.1 | 94.8 | 54.6 | 73.7 | 109.7 | 100.7 | 105.0 |
| COVERS | DIVS. 10 - 14, 25, 28, 41, 43, 44 | 100.0 | 94.9 | 98.9 | 100.0 | 100.1 | 100.0 | 100.0 | 109.1 | 101.9 | 100.0 | 93.9 | 98.8 | 100.0 | 81.6 | 96.2 | 100.0 | 91.9 | 98.3 |
| 21, 22, 23 | FIRE SUPPRESSION, PLUMBING & HVAC | 99.8 | 93.0 | 97.0 | 99.8 | 87.8 | 94.9 | 96.0 | 108.2 | 101.0 | 99.9 | 87.8 | 94.9 | 96.0 | 78.0 | 88.6 | 96.3 | 85.9 | 92.0 |
| 26, 27, 3370 | ELECTRICAL, COMMUNICATIONS & UTIL. | 92.1 | 79.4 | 85.9 | 93.7 | 76.1 | 85.1 | 95.2 | 106.3 | 100.6 | 90.5 | 74.9 | 82.9 | 93.2 | 54.6 | 74.3 | 102.4 | 91.4 | 97.0 |
| MF2004 | WEIGHTED AVERAGE | 94.9 | 95.0 | 95.0 | 93.9 | 83.4 | 89.4 | 93.0 | 107.5 | 99.2 | 94.2 | 92.3 | 93.4 | 92.9 | 70.7 | 83.4 | 97.7 | 98.9 | 98.2 |

## MINNESOTA

| DIVISION | | BRAINERD 564 | | | DETROIT LAKES 565 | | | DULUTH 556 - 558 | | | MANKATO 560 | | | MINNEAPOLIS 553 - 555 | | | ROCHESTER 559 | | |
|---|---|---|---|---|---|---|---|---|---|---|---|---|---|---|---|---|---|---|---|
| | | MAT. | INST. | TOTAL | MAT. | INST. | TOTAL | MAT. | INST. | TOTAL | MAT. | INST. | TOTAL | MAT. | INST. | TOTAL | MAT. | INST. | TOTAL |
| 015433 | CONTRACTOR EQUIPMENT | | 102.0 | 102.0 | | 98.7 | 98.7 | | 101.5 | 101.5 | | 102.0 | 102.0 | | 105.8 | 105.8 | | 101.5 | 101.5 |
| 0241, 31 - 34 | SITE & INFRASTRUCTURE, DEMOLITION | 87.7 | 104.4 | 99.3 | 87.9 | 99.3 | 95.8 | 89.6 | 102.6 | 98.6 | 84.1 | 103.8 | 97.8 | 90.0 | 108.6 | 103.0 | 89.0 | 101.7 | 97.8 |
| 0310 | Concrete Forming & Accessories | 88.1 | 97.2 | 95.9 | 83.0 | 98.9 | 96.7 | 98.0 | 119.4 | 116.5 | 96.2 | 108.0 | 106.4 | 100.5 | 137.4 | 132.3 | 100.9 | 109.4 | 108.2 |
| 0320 | Concrete Reinforcing | 96.7 | 105.1 | 100.8 | 97.9 | 105.1 | 101.4 | 94.6 | 105.5 | 99.9 | 96.6 | 122.0 | 108.9 | 94.8 | 122.5 | 108.2 | 94.6 | 122.3 | 107.9 |
| 0330 | Cast-in-Place Concrete | 108.7 | 109.1 | 108.8 | 97.0 | 108.2 | 101.2 | 105.6 | 108.4 | 106.7 | 100.0 | 112.4 | 104.6 | 112.3 | 122.0 | 115.9 | 110.2 | 104.5 | 108.0 |
| 03 | CONCRETE | 98.6 | 103.8 | 101.0 | 92.1 | 104.3 | 97.7 | 98.2 | 113.7 | 105.4 | 94.0 | 113.0 | 102.8 | 103.3 | 129.6 | 115.5 | 100.7 | 111.1 | 105.5 |
| 04 | MASONRY | 119.6 | 115.4 | 117.1 | 118.5 | 115.2 | 116.6 | 101.0 | 121.2 | 113.1 | 107.5 | 115.7 | 112.4 | 101.7 | 131.7 | 119.7 | 101.0 | 120.0 | 112.4 |
| 05 | METALS | 93.8 | 122.1 | 102.0 | 92.5 | 122.0 | 101.1 | 95.6 | 125.2 | 104.2 | 93.6 | 131.0 | 104.5 | 98.3 | 136.8 | 109.5 | 95.5 | 134.9 | 106.9 |
| 06 | WOOD, PLASTICS & COMPOSITES | 96.8 | 91.5 | 93.9 | 73.7 | 94.5 | 84.9 | 111.0 | 119.7 | 115.7 | 106.5 | 107.4 | 107.0 | 114.6 | 137.6 | 127.0 | 114.6 | 107.5 | 110.8 |
| 07 | THERMAL & MOISTURE PROTECTION | 100.9 | 107.0 | 103.3 | 102.4 | 99.5 | 101.2 | 101.3 | 119.6 | 108.4 | 101.2 | 99.1 | 100.4 | 101.5 | 134.8 | 114.5 | 101.6 | 106.0 | 103.3 |
| 08 | OPENINGS | 86.1 | 110.9 | 92.2 | 98.4 | 112.5 | 101.9 | 93.9 | 121.2 | 100.6 | 90.8 | 125.7 | 99.5 | 97.1 | 142.1 | 108.2 | 93.9 | 125.8 | 101.7 |
| 0920 | Plaster & Gypsum Board | 86.3 | 91.8 | 89.7 | 99.6 | 94.6 | 96.6 | 94.7 | 120.6 | 110.7 | 90.0 | 108.2 | 101.2 | 98.7 | 138.9 | 123.5 | 98.3 | 108.2 | 104.4 |
| 0950, 0980 | Ceilings & Acoustic Treatment | 69.9 | 91.8 | 83.4 | 132.9 | 94.6 | 109.4 | 93.6 | 120.6 | 110.2 | 69.9 | 108.2 | 93.4 | 97.0 | 138.9 | 122.7 | 95.3 | 108.2 | 103.2 |
| 0960 | Flooring | 106.4 | 125.9 | 111.7 | 106.2 | 125.9 | 111.6 | 107.1 | 127.4 | 112.6 | 108.8 | 125.9 | 113.4 | 104.9 | 125.9 | 110.6 | 107.3 | 95.3 | 104.0 |
| 0970, 0990 | Wall Finishes & Painting/Coating | 93.1 | 96.4 | 95.1 | 97.7 | 96.4 | 96.9 | 90.2 | 105.1 | 99.2 | 102.3 | 105.7 | 104.4 | 97.4 | 129.4 | 116.6 | 93.0 | 105.7 | 100.6 |
| 09 | FINISHES | 92.0 | 102.0 | 97.3 | 109.0 | 103.8 | 106.3 | 99.1 | 120.1 | 110.1 | 93.6 | 111.7 | 103.1 | 100.2 | 135.3 | 118.6 | 100.1 | 106.9 | 103.6 |
| COVERS | DIVS. 10 - 14, 25, 28, 41, 43, 44 | 100.0 | 93.8 | 98.7 | 100.0 | 94.4 | 98.9 | 100.0 | 97.9 | 99.5 | 100.0 | 94.4 | 98.9 | 100.0 | 104.3 | 100.9 | 100.0 | 96.2 | 99.2 |
| 21, 22, 23 | FIRE SUPPRESSION, PLUMBING & HVAC | 95.4 | 89.1 | 92.8 | 96.3 | 88.8 | 93.2 | 99.8 | 107.0 | 102.7 | 95.4 | 96.0 | 95.6 | 99.8 | 118.1 | 107.3 | 99.8 | 102.3 | 100.8 |
| 26, 27, 3370 | ELECTRICAL, COMMUNICATIONS & UTIL. | 100.2 | 99.7 | 100.0 | 102.2 | 64.7 | 83.7 | 101.0 | 99.7 | 100.4 | 106.7 | 88.2 | 97.6 | 102.3 | 114.3 | 108.2 | 101.0 | 88.2 | 94.7 |
| MF2004 | WEIGHTED AVERAGE | 96.5 | 102.7 | 99.1 | 98.3 | 97.5 | 98.0 | 98.4 | 112.1 | 104.2 | 96.6 | 106.4 | 100.8 | 100.0 | 124.9 | 110.7 | 98.7 | 107.7 | 102.6 |

## Table 1

| DIVISION | | MINNESOTA SAINT PAUL 550 - 551 | | | ST. CLOUD 563 | | | THIEF RIVER FALLS 567 | | | WILLMAR 562 | | | WINDOM 561 | | | MISSISSIPPI BILOXI 395 | | |
|---|---|---|---|---|---|---|---|---|---|---|---|---|---|---|---|---|---|---|---|---|
| | | MAT. | INST. | TOTAL | MAT. | INST. | TOTAL | MAT. | INST. | TOTAL | MAT. | INST. | TOTAL | MAT. | INST. | TOTAL | MAT. | INST. | TOTAL |
| 015433 | CONTRACTOR EQUIPMENT | | 101.5 | 101.5 | | 102.0 | 102.0 | | 98.7 | 98.7 | | 102.0 | 102.0 | | 102.0 | 102.0 | | 98.7 | 98.7 |
| 0241, 31 - 34 | SITE & INFRASTRUCTURE, DEMOLITION | 92.9 | 103.2 | 100.0 | 82.4 | 106.3 | 99.1 | 88.5 | 98.9 | 95.7 | 82.1 | 100.2 | 94.7 | 75.8 | 99.0 | 92.0 | 101.1 | 88.5 | 92.3 |
| 0310 | Concrete Forming & Accessories | 94.2 | 130.1 | 125.1 | 85.2 | 128.6 | 122.6 | 86.7 | 94.5 | 93.4 | 84.9 | 55.3 | 59.4 | 89.5 | 51.6 | 56.9 | 94.2 | 63.8 | 68.0 |
| 0320 | Concrete Reinforcing | 91.3 | 122.5 | 106.3 | 96.8 | 122.3 | 109.1 | 98.3 | 105.1 | 101.5 | 96.4 | 121.5 | 108.5 | 96.4 | 120.6 | 108.1 | 91.8 | 62.3 | 77.6 |
| 0330 | Cast-in-Place Concrete | 110.2 | 121.3 | 114.3 | 95.8 | 120.8 | 105.0 | 99.0 | 92.6 | 96.7 | 97.3 | 76.3 | 89.5 | 84.2 | 54.7 | 73.2 | 105.6 | 59.6 | 88.6 |
| 03 | CONCRETE | 103.5 | 126.1 | 113.9 | 90.0 | 125.2 | 106.2 | 93.3 | 97.0 | 95.0 | 90.1 | 76.9 | 84.0 | 81.2 | 67.7 | 75.0 | 98.4 | 63.5 | 82.3 |
| 04 | MASONRY | 110.4 | 131.7 | 123.2 | 104.8 | 128.9 | 119.2 | 96.6 | 109.1 | 104.1 | 108.2 | 91.1 | 98.0 | 118.3 | 67.1 | 87.7 | 87.5 | 51.8 | 66.2 |
| 05 | METALS | 95.1 | 136.4 | 107.1 | 94.4 | 134.1 | 105.9 | 92.7 | 121.9 | 101.2 | 93.6 | 123.0 | 102.2 | 93.5 | 121.8 | 101.7 | 91.2 | 86.2 | 89.7 |
| 06 | WOOD, PLASTICS & COMPOSITES | 106.8 | 128.1 | 118.3 | 93.6 | 126.5 | 111.3 | 78.1 | 91.7 | 85.4 | 93.3 | 52.4 | 71.3 | 98.1 | 52.4 | 73.5 | 95.3 | 68.2 | 80.7 |
| 07 | THERMAL & MOISTURE PROTECTION | 102.5 | 133.5 | 114.6 | 101.0 | 118.0 | 107.6 | 103.6 | 96.1 | 100.7 | 100.9 | 59.2 | 84.6 | 100.8 | 50.0 | 81.0 | 95.0 | 61.8 | 82.1 |
| 08 | OPENINGS | 91.6 | 136.9 | 102.8 | 90.8 | 136.1 | 102.0 | 98.4 | 111.0 | 101.5 | 88.4 | 77.1 | 85.6 | 92.6 | 77.1 | 88.8 | 97.4 | 67.9 | 90.1 |
| 0920 | Plaster & Gypsum Board | 92.4 | 129.3 | 115.1 | 85.6 | 127.8 | 111.6 | 100.6 | 91.8 | 95.2 | 85.6 | 51.8 | 64.7 | 86.3 | 51.8 | 65.0 | 103.5 | 67.9 | 81.5 |
| 0950, 0980 | Ceilings & Acoustic Treatment | 91.0 | 129.3 | 114.5 | 69.9 | 127.8 | 105.4 | 132.9 | 91.8 | 107.7 | 69.9 | 51.8 | 58.8 | 69.9 | 51.8 | 58.8 | 102.1 | 67.9 | 81.1 |
| 0960 | Flooring | 100.6 | 125.9 | 107.5 | 102.3 | 125.9 | 108.7 | 107.2 | 125.9 | 112.3 | 104.1 | 125.9 | 110.0 | 107.1 | 125.9 | 112.2 | 118.1 | 61.0 | 102.6 |
| 0970, 0990 | Wall Finishes & Painting/Coating | 97.4 | 124.8 | 113.9 | 102.3 | 129.4 | 118.6 | 97.7 | 96.4 | 96.9 | 97.7 | 96.4 | 96.9 | 97.7 | 105.7 | 102.5 | 110.9 | 52.0 | 75.5 |
| 09 | FINISHES | 96.9 | 129.2 | 113.8 | 90.9 | 128.8 | 110.7 | 109.5 | 100.7 | 104.9 | 91.2 | 69.8 | 80.0 | 91.6 | 68.6 | 79.6 | 105.9 | 62.4 | 83.1 |
| COVERS | DIVS. 10 - 14, 25, 28, 41, 43, 44 | 100.0 | 102.8 | 100.6 | 100.0 | 101.6 | 100.3 | 100.0 | 91.8 | 98.3 | 100.0 | 52.4 | 90.3 | 100.0 | 49.4 | 89.6 | 100.0 | 70.6 | 94.0 |
| 21, 22, 23 | FIRE SUPPRESSION, PLUMBING & HVAC | 99.7 | 116.2 | 106.5 | 99.5 | 117.9 | 107.1 | 96.3 | 85.6 | 91.9 | 95.4 | 93.1 | 94.4 | 95.4 | 78.5 | 88.4 | 99.8 | 52.0 | 80.2 |
| 26, 27, 3370 | ELECTRICAL, COMMUNICATIONS & UTIL. | 101.6 | 105.4 | 103.5 | 100.2 | 105.4 | 102.8 | 99.7 | 64.7 | 82.5 | 100.2 | 70.7 | 85.7 | 106.7 | 88.1 | 97.5 | 98.7 | 57.0 | 78.2 |
| MF2004 | WEIGHTED AVERAGE | 99.1 | 121.1 | 108.5 | 95.9 | 120.5 | 106.4 | 97.3 | 94.5 | 96.1 | 94.8 | 84.5 | 90.4 | 95.3 | 79.5 | 88.5 | 97.6 | 63.4 | 83.0 |

## Table 2

| DIVISION | | MISSISSIPPI CLARKSDALE 386 | | | COLUMBUS 397 | | | GREENVILLE 387 | | | GREENWOOD 389 | | | JACKSON 390 - 392 | | | LAUREL 394 | | |
|---|---|---|---|---|---|---|---|---|---|---|---|---|---|---|---|---|---|---|---|---|
| | | MAT. | INST. | TOTAL | MAT. | INST. | TOTAL | MAT. | INST. | TOTAL | MAT. | INST. | TOTAL | MAT. | INST. | TOTAL | MAT. | INST. | TOTAL |
| 015433 | CONTRACTOR EQUIPMENT | | 98.7 | 98.7 | | 98.7 | 98.7 | | 98.7 | 98.7 | | 98.7 | 98.7 | | 98.7 | 98.7 | | 98.7 | 98.7 |
| 0241, 31 - 34 | SITE & INFRASTRUCTURE, DEMOLITION | 98.5 | 87.7 | 91.0 | 99.9 | 88.1 | 91.7 | 104.9 | 88.1 | 93.2 | 101.8 | 87.5 | 91.9 | 96.3 | 88.1 | 90.6 | 106.5 | 87.6 | 93.3 |
| 0310 | Concrete Forming & Accessories | 84.5 | 49.5 | 54.4 | 82.5 | 53.9 | 57.9 | 80.9 | 66.5 | 68.5 | 94.1 | 50.0 | 56.1 | 93.5 | 61.7 | 66.1 | 82.6 | 54.0 | 58.0 |
| 0320 | Concrete Reinforcing | 98.9 | 42.1 | 71.5 | 98.3 | 51.3 | 75.7 | 99.5 | 73.1 | 86.8 | 98.9 | 63.7 | 81.9 | 91.8 | 63.8 | 78.3 | 98.9 | 47.3 | 74.0 |
| 0330 | Cast-in-Place Concrete | 103.0 | 58.7 | 86.6 | 107.7 | 60.7 | 90.3 | 106.1 | 61.6 | 89.6 | 110.7 | 58.5 | 91.4 | 100.5 | 61.6 | 86.1 | 105.3 | 60.1 | 88.6 |
| 03 | CONCRETE | 96.5 | 52.9 | 76.4 | 100.1 | 57.4 | 80.4 | 101.7 | 67.5 | 85.9 | 102.9 | 57.0 | 81.7 | 95.8 | 63.5 | 80.9 | 102.3 | 56.5 | 81.2 |
| 04 | MASONRY | 87.4 | 50.9 | 65.5 | 109.8 | 54.1 | 76.5 | 128.3 | 55.3 | 84.7 | 88.0 | 50.8 | 65.7 | 89.1 | 55.3 | 68.9 | 106.4 | 53.7 | 74.9 |
| 05 | METALS | 88.5 | 75.8 | 84.8 | 88.4 | 80.4 | 86.1 | 89.5 | 91.0 | 90.0 | 88.5 | 81.7 | 86.6 | 91.2 | 86.9 | 89.9 | 88.5 | 79.2 | 85.8 |
| 06 | WOOD, PLASTICS & COMPOSITES | 83.0 | 50.6 | 65.6 | 81.0 | 54.7 | 66.8 | 78.9 | 70.1 | 74.2 | 95.3 | 51.1 | 71.5 | 94.2 | 63.6 | 77.8 | 81.4 | 55.4 | 67.4 |
| 07 | THERMAL & MOISTURE PROTECTION | 94.8 | 51.6 | 78.0 | 95.0 | 53.1 | 78.6 | 95.1 | 64.3 | 83.1 | 95.2 | 49.7 | 77.4 | 96.8 | 63.6 | 83.9 | 95.1 | 55.3 | 79.6 |
| 08 | OPENINGS | 96.8 | 51.4 | 85.6 | 96.8 | 55.4 | 86.6 | 96.8 | 67.7 | 89.6 | 96.8 | 55.6 | 86.6 | 97.8 | 61.6 | 88.9 | 93.5 | 53.2 | 83.5 |
| 0920 | Plaster & Gypsum Board | 95.5 | 49.9 | 67.4 | 95.2 | 54.1 | 69.8 | 93.8 | 69.9 | 79.0 | 102.3 | 50.4 | 70.3 | 97.2 | 63.2 | 76.2 | 93.8 | 54.8 | 69.7 |
| 0950, 0980 | Ceilings & Acoustic Treatment | 95.1 | 49.9 | 67.3 | 95.1 | 54.1 | 69.9 | 97.0 | 69.9 | 80.3 | 95.1 | 50.4 | 67.6 | 98.7 | 63.2 | 76.9 | 95.1 | 54.8 | 70.3 |
| 0960 | Flooring | 110.9 | 61.0 | 97.3 | 109.6 | 61.0 | 96.4 | 108.6 | 61.0 | 95.7 | 118.1 | 61.0 | 102.6 | 111.6 | 61.0 | 102.9 | 107.4 | 61.0 | 94.8 |
| 0970, 0990 | Wall Finishes & Painting/Coating | 110.9 | 44.8 | 71.2 | 110.9 | 52.7 | 75.9 | 110.9 | 67.3 | 84.7 | 110.9 | 46.1 | 72.0 | 110.9 | 67.3 | 84.7 | 110.9 | 59.8 | 80.2 |
| 09 | FINISHES | 100.7 | 51.2 | 74.8 | 100.5 | 55.2 | 76.8 | 100.7 | 66.1 | 82.6 | 104.2 | 51.6 | 76.7 | 104.3 | 62.4 | 82.3 | 100.1 | 56.4 | 77.2 |
| COVERS | DIVS. 10 - 14, 25, 28, 41, 43, 44 | 100.0 | 68.6 | 93.6 | 100.0 | 70.2 | 93.9 | 100.0 | 72.2 | 94.3 | 100.0 | 68.6 | 93.6 | 100.0 | 71.4 | 94.1 | 100.0 | 44.0 | 88.5 |
| 21, 22, 23 | FIRE SUPPRESSION, PLUMBING & HVAC | 98.0 | 43.2 | 75.5 | 97.6 | 45.1 | 76.1 | 99.8 | 52.8 | 80.5 | 98.0 | 41.6 | 74.9 | 99.9 | 57.4 | 82.5 | 97.6 | 48.3 | 77.4 |
| 26, 27, 3370 | ELECTRICAL, COMMUNICATIONS & UTIL. | 98.0 | 47.4 | 73.1 | 96.1 | 50.4 | 73.7 | 98.0 | 65.0 | 81.8 | 98.0 | 44.9 | 71.9 | 99.9 | 65.0 | 82.7 | 97.6 | 54.4 | 76.4 |
| MF2004 | WEIGHTED AVERAGE | 95.8 | 55.0 | 78.4 | 97.1 | 58.0 | 80.4 | 99.2 | 66.6 | 85.3 | 97.1 | 55.5 | 79.3 | 97.4 | 65.8 | 83.9 | 97.2 | 58.3 | 80.5 |

## Table 3

| DIVISION | | MISSISSIPPI MCCOMB 396 | | | MERIDIAN 393 | | | TUPELO 388 | | | MISSOURI BOWLING GREEN 633 | | | CAPE GIRARDEAU 637 | | | CHILLICOTHE 646 | | |
|---|---|---|---|---|---|---|---|---|---|---|---|---|---|---|---|---|---|---|---|---|
| | | MAT. | INST. | TOTAL | MAT. | INST. | TOTAL | MAT. | INST. | TOTAL | MAT. | INST. | TOTAL | MAT. | INST. | TOTAL | MAT. | INST. | TOTAL |
| 015433 | CONTRACTOR EQUIPMENT | | 98.7 | 98.7 | | 98.7 | 98.7 | | 98.7 | 98.7 | | 108.5 | 108.5 | | 108.5 | 108.5 | | 103.3 | 103.3 |
| 0241, 31 - 34 | SITE & INFRASTRUCTURE, DEMOLITION | 92.0 | 88.4 | 89.5 | 96.2 | 88.3 | 90.7 | 96.2 | 87.7 | 90.2 | 92.2 | 93.3 | 93.0 | 93.3 | 93.8 | 93.6 | 105.0 | 90.8 | 95.1 |
| 0310 | Concrete Forming & Accessories | 82.5 | 62.0 | 64.8 | 79.6 | 65.7 | 67.7 | 81.5 | 52.6 | 56.6 | 93.2 | 90.4 | 90.8 | 86.3 | 77.1 | 78.4 | 91.6 | 90.7 | 90.8 |
| 0320 | Concrete Reinforcing | 99.5 | 49.8 | 75.6 | 98.3 | 63.8 | 81.7 | 96.8 | 63.7 | 80.9 | 93.6 | 96.7 | 95.1 | 94.8 | 86.2 | 90.6 | 98.5 | 87.5 | 93.2 |
| 0330 | Cast-in-Place Concrete | 93.5 | 60.4 | 81.2 | 100.0 | 63.7 | 86.6 | 103.0 | 60.2 | 87.1 | 93.1 | 81.1 | 88.6 | 92.1 | 85.7 | 89.7 | 94.5 | 67.8 | 84.6 |
| 03 | CONCRETE | 89.9 | 60.5 | 76.3 | 94.2 | 66.1 | 81.2 | 96.0 | 58.8 | 78.8 | 92.1 | 89.7 | 91.0 | 91.3 | 83.4 | 87.6 | 98.1 | 82.6 | 90.9 |
| 04 | MASONRY | 111.8 | 53.3 | 76.8 | 87.1 | 58.9 | 70.2 | 118.5 | 53.8 | 79.8 | 118.2 | 98.5 | 106.4 | 115.3 | 80.1 | 94.2 | 98.1 | 88.3 | 92.2 |
| 05 | METALS | 88.6 | 78.7 | 85.8 | 89.5 | 87.0 | 88.7 | 88.5 | 81.8 | 86.5 | 92.6 | 114.9 | 99.1 | 93.7 | 109.0 | 98.1 | 90.3 | 93.1 | 91.1 |
| 06 | WOOD, PLASTICS & COMPOSITES | 81.0 | 65.6 | 72.7 | 77.7 | 67.0 | 71.9 | 79.5 | 52.8 | 65.1 | 87.4 | 91.2 | 89.5 | 79.9 | 75.0 | 77.3 | 94.0 | 97.8 | 96.1 |
| 07 | THERMAL & MOISTURE PROTECTION | 94.6 | 54.8 | 79.0 | 94.7 | 65.5 | 83.3 | 94.8 | 56.6 | 79.9 | 101.5 | 99.1 | 100.5 | 101.4 | 80.7 | 93.3 | 96.3 | 81.8 | 90.6 |
| 08 | OPENINGS | 96.8 | 62.0 | 88.2 | 96.8 | 67.6 | 89.6 | 96.8 | 53.7 | 86.2 | 97.0 | 86.8 | 94.5 | 97.0 | 75.5 | 91.7 | 91.6 | 83.0 | 89.5 |
| 0920 | Plaster & Gypsum Board | 95.2 | 65.3 | 76.7 | 93.8 | 66.7 | 77.1 | 93.8 | 52.1 | 68.1 | 98.6 | 90.9 | 93.8 | 95.9 | 74.3 | 82.5 | 93.0 | 97.5 | 95.8 |
| 0950, 0980 | Ceilings & Acoustic Treatment | 95.1 | 65.3 | 76.8 | 97.0 | 66.7 | 78.4 | 95.1 | 52.1 | 68.7 | 84.7 | 90.9 | 88.5 | 84.7 | 74.3 | 78.3 | 87.5 | 97.5 | 93.7 |
| 0960 | Flooring | 109.6 | 61.0 | 96.4 | 107.3 | 61.0 | 94.7 | 108.9 | 61.0 | 95.9 | 91.7 | 69.2 | 85.6 | 87.5 | 69.2 | 82.5 | 94.2 | 49.7 | 82.1 |
| 0970, 0990 | Wall Finishes & Painting/Coating | 110.9 | 50.7 | 74.7 | 110.9 | 76.4 | 90.2 | 110.9 | 60.9 | 80.8 | 98.4 | 109.5 | 105.1 | 98.4 | 81.0 | 88.0 | 95.3 | 53.7 | 70.3 |
| 09 | FINISHES | 99.9 | 61.2 | 79.6 | 99.7 | 66.3 | 82.2 | 99.8 | 55.0 | 76.4 | 91.2 | 88.3 | 89.7 | 89.5 | 75.1 | 82.0 | 95.0 | 81.3 | 87.8 |
| COVERS | DIVS. 10 - 14, 25, 28, 41, 43, 44 | 100.0 | 75.6 | 95.0 | 100.0 | 73.1 | 94.5 | 100.0 | 70.0 | 93.8 | 100.0 | 63.7 | 92.6 | 100.0 | 61.1 | 92.0 | 100.0 | 61.4 | 92.1 |
| 21, 22, 23 | FIRE SUPPRESSION, PLUMBING & HVAC | 97.6 | 43.3 | 75.3 | 99.8 | 59.4 | 83.2 | 98.2 | 48.0 | 77.6 | 95.8 | 95.1 | 95.5 | 99.9 | 93.8 | 97.4 | 95.9 | 47.3 | 76.0 |
| 26, 27, 3370 | ELECTRICAL, COMMUNICATIONS & UTIL. | 94.6 | 59.4 | 77.3 | 97.6 | 60.6 | 79.4 | 97.7 | 50.1 | 74.3 | 100.6 | 87.8 | 94.3 | 100.6 | 111.5 | 105.9 | 94.0 | 39.4 | 67.2 |
| MF2004 | WEIGHTED AVERAGE | 95.6 | 60.5 | 80.6 | 95.9 | 67.2 | 83.6 | 97.2 | 58.8 | 80.8 | 96.6 | 93.2 | 95.2 | 97.3 | 90.1 | 94.2 | 95.3 | 70.8 | 84.8 |

## MISSOURI

| DIVISION | | COLUMBIA 652 MAT. | INST. | TOTAL | FLAT RIVER 636 MAT. | INST. | TOTAL | HANNIBAL 634 MAT. | INST. | TOTAL | HARRISONVILLE 647 MAT. | INST. | TOTAL | JEFFERSON CITY 650-651 MAT. | INST. | TOTAL | JOPLIN 648 MAT. | INST. | TOTAL |
|---|---|---|---|---|---|---|---|---|---|---|---|---|---|---|---|---|---|---|---|
| 015433 | CONTRACTOR EQUIPMENT | | 108.9 | 108.9 | | 108.5 | 108.5 | | 108.5 | 108.5 | | 103.3 | 103.3 | | 108.9 | 108.9 | | 107.3 | 107.3 |
| 0241, 31-34 | SITE & INFRASTRUCTURE, DEMOLITION | 103.1 | 94.8 | 97.3 | 95.0 | 93.9 | 94.2 | 89.5 | 92.6 | 91.6 | 96.0 | 95.3 | 95.5 | 103.9 | 94.2 | 97.2 | 104.9 | 99.1 | 100.9 |
| 0310 | Concrete Forming & Accessories | 87.9 | 69.0 | 71.6 | 99.1 | 86.3 | 88.1 | 91.5 | 66.1 | 69.6 | 88.4 | 103.0 | 101.0 | 98.7 | 61.2 | 66.4 | 103.8 | 71.9 | 76.3 |
| 0320 | Concrete Reinforcing | 97.8 | 113.3 | 105.3 | 94.8 | 106.9 | 100.6 | 93.2 | 82.9 | 88.2 | 98.1 | 108.9 | 103.3 | 96.5 | 111.1 | 103.5 | 101.6 | 73.5 | 88.1 |
| 0330 | Cast-in-Place Concrete | 89.9 | 86.9 | 88.8 | 96.1 | 80.8 | 90.4 | 88.1 | 74.1 | 82.9 | 96.8 | 101.3 | 98.4 | 91.2 | 69.3 | 83.1 | 102.3 | 70.5 | 90.5 |
| 03 | CONCRETE | 85.4 | 85.4 | 85.4 | 95.0 | 89.8 | 92.6 | 88.4 | 73.9 | 81.7 | 94.9 | 103.9 | 99.1 | 87.2 | 75.4 | 81.8 | 98.4 | 72.7 | 86.5 |
| 04 | MASONRY | 128.6 | 87.4 | 104.0 | 116.1 | 81.8 | 95.6 | 109.4 | 86.8 | 95.9 | 93.2 | 101.4 | 98.1 | 93.9 | 87.4 | 90.0 | 90.4 | 61.0 | 72.8 |
| 05 | METALS | 90.9 | 121.6 | 99.8 | 92.6 | 118.4 | 100.1 | 92.6 | 108.2 | 97.2 | 90.8 | 112.2 | 97.0 | 90.4 | 120.3 | 99.1 | 93.3 | 88.6 | 92.0 |
| 06 | WOOD, PLASTICS & COMPOSITES | 91.3 | 61.8 | 75.4 | 94.5 | 85.9 | 89.9 | 85.3 | 65.4 | 74.6 | 89.7 | 103.1 | 96.9 | 103.2 | 51.7 | 75.4 | 105.9 | 70.9 | 87.1 |
| 07 | THERMAL & MOISTURE PROTECTION | 94.0 | 84.2 | 90.2 | 101.6 | 94.0 | 98.7 | 101.3 | 86.3 | 95.5 | 95.5 | 102.8 | 98.4 | 93.8 | 80.7 | 88.7 | 96.5 | 66.8 | 84.9 |
| 08 | OPENINGS | 91.5 | 89.3 | 90.9 | 97.0 | 87.0 | 94.5 | 97.0 | 69.2 | 90.1 | 91.9 | 104.8 | 95.1 | 88.7 | 83.2 | 87.4 | 92.8 | 73.3 | 88.0 |
| 0920 | Plaster & Gypsum Board | 94.8 | 60.7 | 73.8 | 102.3 | 85.5 | 91.9 | 97.2 | 64.4 | 77.0 | 87.2 | 103.0 | 96.9 | 94.3 | 50.3 | 67.2 | 98.0 | 69.9 | 80.7 |
| 0950, 0980 | Ceilings & Acoustic Treatment | 87.9 | 60.7 | 71.2 | 84.7 | 85.5 | 85.2 | 84.7 | 64.4 | 72.3 | 87.5 | 103.0 | 97.0 | 84.5 | 50.3 | 63.5 | 90.0 | 69.9 | 77.7 |
| 0960 | Flooring | 103.2 | 91.2 | 100.0 | 95.3 | 69.2 | 88.2 | 90.6 | 69.2 | 84.8 | 89.9 | 100.0 | 92.6 | 111.9 | 91.2 | 106.2 | 118.7 | 46.5 | 99.0 |
| 0970, 0990 | Wall Finishes & Painting/Coating | 100.8 | 78.6 | 87.5 | 98.4 | 71.1 | 82.0 | 98.4 | 76.6 | 85.3 | 99.7 | 109.5 | 105.6 | 100.8 | 78.6 | 87.5 | 94.7 | 42.0 | 63.1 |
| 09 | FINISHES | 93.1 | 70.6 | 81.3 | 93.0 | 80.8 | 86.6 | 90.5 | 66.6 | 78.0 | 92.5 | 103.1 | 98.0 | 95.0 | 64.7 | 79.1 | 102.1 | 64.0 | 82.2 |
| COVERS | DIVS. 10-14, 25, 28, 41, 43, 44 | 100.0 | 93.8 | 98.7 | 100.0 | 63.0 | 92.4 | 100.0 | 56.3 | 91.0 | 100.0 | 91.7 | 98.3 | 100.0 | 92.6 | 98.5 | 100.0 | 70.6 | 94.0 |
| 21, 22, 23 | FIRE SUPPRESSION, PLUMBING & HVAC | 99.9 | 95.3 | 98.0 | 95.8 | 94.9 | 95.4 | 95.8 | 88.4 | 92.8 | 95.8 | 98.9 | 97.1 | 99.7 | 98.7 | 99.3 | 100.1 | 54.7 | 81.5 |
| 26, 27, 3370 | ELECTRICAL, COMMUNICATIONS & UTIL. | 95.6 | 87.8 | 91.8 | 105.3 | 111.5 | 108.3 | 99.3 | 80.7 | 90.2 | 100.4 | 104.1 | 102.2 | 97.5 | 87.8 | 92.7 | 91.9 | 70.8 | 81.5 |
| MF2004 | WEIGHTED AVERAGE | 96.2 | 90.2 | 93.6 | 97.6 | 94.1 | 96.1 | 95.4 | 82.5 | 89.9 | 94.9 | 102.2 | 98.0 | 94.7 | 88.2 | 91.9 | 96.9 | 69.8 | 85.3 |

## MISSOURI

| DIVISION | | KANSAS CITY 640-641 MAT. | INST. | TOTAL | KIRKSVILLE 635 MAT. | INST. | TOTAL | POPLAR BLUFF 639 MAT. | INST. | TOTAL | ROLLA 654-655 MAT. | INST. | TOTAL | SEDALIA 653 MAT. | INST. | TOTAL | SIKESTON 638 MAT. | INST. | TOTAL |
|---|---|---|---|---|---|---|---|---|---|---|---|---|---|---|---|---|---|---|---|
| 015433 | CONTRACTOR EQUIPMENT | | 104.8 | 104.8 | | 99.6 | 99.6 | | 102.2 | 102.2 | | 108.9 | 108.9 | | 99.6 | 99.6 | | 102.2 | 102.2 |
| 0241, 31-34 | SITE & INFRASTRUCTURE, DEMOLITION | 97.3 | 98.3 | 98.0 | 90.1 | 88.7 | 89.1 | 76.4 | 92.8 | 87.8 | 102.7 | 92.5 | 95.6 | 94.2 | 90.0 | 91.3 | 80.0 | 92.9 | 89.0 |
| 0310 | Concrete Forming & Accessories | 102.8 | 108.1 | 107.4 | 84.1 | 56.6 | 60.4 | 84.2 | 72.3 | 74.0 | 95.6 | 85.0 | 86.5 | 93.1 | 63.2 | 67.3 | 85.3 | 72.4 | 74.2 |
| 0320 | Concrete Reinforcing | 96.5 | 114.2 | 105.1 | 93.8 | 82.2 | 88.2 | 96.6 | 78.4 | 87.9 | 98.2 | 54.1 | 77.0 | 96.7 | 99.5 | 98.1 | 96.0 | 69.7 | 83.3 |
| 0330 | Cast-in-Place Concrete | 95.1 | 108.1 | 99.6 | 96.0 | 64.3 | 84.3 | 73.8 | 62.1 | 69.5 | 91.9 | 76.1 | 86.1 | 96.0 | 68.2 | 85.7 | 78.9 | 70.8 | 75.9 |
| 03 | CONCRETE | 94.3 | 109.6 | 101.3 | 104.9 | 65.6 | 86.8 | 81.6 | 71.1 | 76.8 | 87.2 | 77.3 | 82.6 | 98.6 | 73.2 | 86.9 | 85.2 | 72.5 | 79.4 |
| 04 | MASONRY | 95.5 | 107.1 | 102.4 | 121.6 | 73.5 | 92.8 | 113.9 | 58.4 | 80.7 | 106.4 | 46.5 | 70.6 | 112.1 | 55.8 | 78.4 | 113.7 | 63.8 | 83.8 |
| 05 | METALS | 100.4 | 115.7 | 104.9 | 92.3 | 97.0 | 93.6 | 92.8 | 94.5 | 93.3 | 90.4 | 86.4 | 89.2 | 88.9 | 103.7 | 93.2 | 93.1 | 90.2 | 92.3 |
| 06 | WOOD, PLASTICS & COMPOSITES | 105.2 | 108.1 | 106.7 | 73.7 | 55.0 | 63.6 | 72.9 | 75.0 | 74.1 | 99.6 | 97.2 | 98.3 | 92.5 | 55.6 | 72.6 | 74.2 | 75.0 | 74.6 |
| 07 | THERMAL & MOISTURE PROTECTION | 95.8 | 107.1 | 100.2 | 107.2 | 78.9 | 96.2 | 106.6 | 74.3 | 94.0 | 94.1 | 60.3 | 80.9 | 99.1 | 79.4 | 91.4 | 106.7 | 68.1 | 91.7 |
| 08 | OPENINGS | 98.8 | 110.6 | 101.7 | 100.9 | 63.7 | 91.7 | 101.9 | 76.0 | 95.5 | 91.5 | 73.1 | 86.9 | 94.9 | 76.3 | 90.3 | 101.9 | 66.2 | 93.1 |
| 0920 | Plaster & Gypsum Board | 94.9 | 108.1 | 103.0 | 92.2 | 53.7 | 68.5 | 92.8 | 74.3 | 81.4 | 96.9 | 97.0 | 97.0 | 90.7 | 54.3 | 68.2 | 93.8 | 74.3 | 81.8 |
| 0950, 0980 | Ceilings & Acoustic Treatment | 96.0 | 108.1 | 103.4 | 82.1 | 53.7 | 64.7 | 84.7 | 74.3 | 78.3 | 87.9 | 97.0 | 93.5 | 86.2 | 54.3 | 66.6 | 84.7 | 74.3 | 78.3 |
| 0960 | Flooring | 96.7 | 100.0 | 97.6 | 71.4 | 50.9 | 65.8 | 83.2 | 57.6 | 76.3 | 107.8 | 43.4 | 90.3 | 84.4 | 100.0 | 88.6 | 83.7 | 46.5 | 73.6 |
| 0970, 0990 | Wall Finishes & Painting/Coating | 99.7 | 120.4 | 112.1 | 94.0 | 42.0 | 62.8 | 93.5 | 92.0 | 92.6 | 100.8 | 109.5 | 106.0 | 93.5 | 60.4 | 73.6 | | | |
| 09 | FINISHES | 97.7 | 107.8 | 103.0 | 88.2 | 52.3 | 69.4 | 89.1 | 70.7 | 79.5 | 94.9 | 79.3 | 86.7 | 90.7 | 73.2 | 81.5 | 89.7 | 66.2 | 77.4 |
| COVERS | DIVS. 10-14, 25, 28, 41, 43, 44 | 100.0 | 101.0 | 100.2 | 100.0 | 52.0 | 90.2 | 100.0 | 55.2 | 90.8 | 100.0 | 57.6 | 91.3 | 100.0 | 82.6 | 96.4 | 100.0 | 56.1 | 91.0 |
| 21, 22, 23 | FIRE SUPPRESSION, PLUMBING & HVAC | 100.0 | 105.9 | 102.4 | 95.8 | 86.8 | 92.1 | 95.8 | 75.5 | 87.5 | 95.7 | 67.1 | 84.0 | 95.7 | 93.8 | 94.9 | 95.8 | 76.4 | 87.9 |
| 26, 27, 3370 | ELECTRICAL, COMMUNICATIONS & UTIL. | 102.5 | 104.8 | 103.6 | 99.2 | 80.7 | 90.1 | 99.6 | 111.5 | 105.4 | 94.1 | 87.7 | 91.0 | 95.2 | 104.1 | 99.6 | 98.7 | 111.5 | 104.9 |
| MF2004 | WEIGHTED AVERAGE | 98.9 | 106.9 | 102.4 | 98.2 | 75.8 | 88.6 | 95.0 | 80.2 | 88.7 | 94.3 | 74.9 | 86.0 | 95.6 | 84.6 | 90.9 | 95.5 | 79.6 | 88.7 |

## MISSOURI / MONTANA

| DIVISION | | SPRINGFIELD 656-658 MAT. | INST. | TOTAL | ST. JOSEPH 644-645 MAT. | INST. | TOTAL | ST. LOUIS 630-631 MAT. | INST. | TOTAL | BILLINGS 590-591 MAT. | INST. | TOTAL | BUTTE 597 MAT. | INST. | TOTAL | GREAT FALLS 594 MAT. | INST. | TOTAL |
|---|---|---|---|---|---|---|---|---|---|---|---|---|---|---|---|---|---|---|---|
| 015433 | CONTRACTOR EQUIPMENT | | 102.5 | 102.5 | | 103.3 | 103.3 | | 109.8 | 109.8 | | 99.0 | 99.0 | | 98.7 | 98.7 | | 98.7 | 98.7 |
| 0241, 31-34 | SITE & INFRASTRUCTURE, DEMOLITION | 96.4 | 93.4 | 94.3 | 98.8 | 94.1 | 95.5 | 93.1 | 97.4 | 96.1 | 90.1 | 97.1 | 95.0 | 99.8 | 95.9 | 97.1 | 103.6 | 96.5 | 98.6 |
| 0310 | Concrete Forming & Accessories | 101.5 | 74.4 | 78.1 | 102.6 | 82.5 | 85.3 | 99.2 | 108.8 | 107.5 | 97.8 | 65.8 | 70.3 | 85.6 | 67.9 | 70.3 | 97.8 | 67.8 | 72.0 |
| 0320 | Concrete Reinforcing | 94.0 | 113.0 | 103.2 | 95.4 | 108.6 | 101.7 | 86.7 | 112.1 | 99.0 | 95.8 | 73.1 | 84.9 | 104.0 | 73.2 | 89.1 | 95.9 | 73.0 | 84.8 |
| 0330 | Cast-in-Place Concrete | 97.6 | 62.8 | 84.7 | 95.0 | 104.4 | 98.5 | 92.1 | 113.5 | 100.0 | 109.0 | 66.8 | 93.4 | 119.9 | 71.0 | 101.8 | 126.8 | 66.2 | 104.3 |
| 03 | CONCRETE | 95.8 | 78.7 | 87.9 | 94.0 | 95.8 | 94.9 | 90.8 | 111.9 | 100.5 | 101.1 | 68.5 | 86.1 | 104.8 | 70.9 | 89.1 | 109.7 | 69.1 | 91.0 |
| 04 | MASONRY | 86.3 | 81.0 | 83.1 | 95.1 | 93.6 | 94.2 | 96.6 | 113.0 | 106.4 | 120.5 | 70.6 | 90.7 | 116.1 | 77.2 | 92.8 | 120.2 | 75.3 | 93.3 |
| 05 | METALS | 94.6 | 107.1 | 98.3 | 96.7 | 111.5 | 101.0 | 98.2 | 124.5 | 105.8 | 110.3 | 86.5 | 103.4 | 103.1 | 86.3 | 98.2 | 106.9 | 86.0 | 100.8 |
| 06 | WOOD, PLASTICS & COMPOSITES | 100.7 | 75.6 | 87.2 | 105.9 | 77.7 | 90.7 | 94.3 | 106.8 | 101.0 | 102.6 | 67.5 | 83.7 | 90.0 | 68.3 | 78.3 | 103.9 | 67.5 | 84.3 |
| 07 | THERMAL & MOISTURE PROTECTION | 98.6 | 75.7 | 89.7 | 96.2 | 95.3 | 95.8 | 101.3 | 109.9 | 104.6 | 101.2 | 65.7 | 87.4 | 101.1 | 69.3 | 88.7 | 101.6 | 66.2 | 87.8 |
| 08 | OPENINGS | 97.1 | 83.1 | 93.6 | 97.6 | 92.9 | 96.4 | 96.0 | 113.0 | 100.2 | 97.2 | 63.8 | 89.0 | 95.2 | 64.7 | 87.7 | 98.5 | 63.8 | 89.8 |
| 0920 | Plaster & Gypsum Board | 97.9 | 74.8 | 83.7 | 99.2 | 76.9 | 85.4 | 103.2 | 106.8 | 105.4 | 94.2 | 67.0 | 77.4 | 91.9 | 67.8 | 77.0 | 98.7 | 67.0 | 79.1 |
| 0950, 0980 | Ceilings & Acoustic Treatment | 87.9 | 74.8 | 79.9 | 95.2 | 76.9 | 84.0 | 89.8 | 106.8 | 100.3 | 106.9 | 67.0 | 82.4 | 111.9 | 67.8 | 84.8 | 113.6 | 67.0 | 85.0 |
| 0960 | Flooring | 106.8 | 46.5 | 90.4 | 99.4 | 100.0 | 99.6 | 95.0 | 99.2 | 96.2 | 107.7 | 45.3 | 90.8 | 104.1 | 36.1 | 85.6 | 112.8 | 49.0 | 95.4 |
| 0970, 0990 | Wall Finishes & Painting/Coating | 95.2 | 60.1 | 74.1 | 95.3 | 88.9 | 91.5 | 98.4 | 110.1 | 105.5 | 99.9 | 56.0 | 73.6 | 97.7 | 38.2 | 61.9 | 97.7 | 42.9 | 64.8 |
| 09 | FINISHES | 96.8 | 67.2 | 81.3 | 98.7 | 85.0 | 91.5 | 94.2 | 106.5 | 100.6 | 102.9 | 60.7 | 80.8 | 102.3 | 58.3 | 79.2 | 106.6 | 61.4 | 82.9 |
| COVERS | DIVS. 10-14, 25, 28, 41, 43, 44 | 100.0 | 91.3 | 98.2 | 100.0 | 95.3 | 99.0 | 100.0 | 103.7 | 100.8 | 100.0 | 61.0 | 92.0 | 100.0 | 62.8 | 92.4 | 100.0 | 63.2 | 92.5 |
| 21, 22, 23 | FIRE SUPPRESSION, PLUMBING & HVAC | 99.9 | 71.2 | 88.1 | 100.1 | 94.0 | 97.6 | 99.9 | 110.7 | 104.4 | 100.1 | 73.8 | 89.3 | 100.2 | 72.6 | 88.9 | 100.2 | 76.9 | 90.7 |
| 26, 27, 3370 | ELECTRICAL, COMMUNICATIONS & UTIL. | 99.6 | 75.2 | 87.6 | 100.4 | 86.4 | 93.5 | 103.3 | 113.9 | 108.5 | 94.7 | 74.8 | 85.0 | 102.1 | 72.2 | 87.4 | 94.9 | 67.6 | 81.5 |
| MF2004 | WEIGHTED AVERAGE | 97.2 | 79.6 | 89.7 | 98.1 | 93.4 | 96.1 | 97.7 | 110.9 | 103.4 | 102.1 | 73.2 | 89.7 | 101.8 | 73.4 | 89.7 | 103.4 | 73.5 | 90.6 |

# City Cost Indexes

## MONTANA

| DIVISION | | HAVRE 595 | | | HELENA 596 | | | KALISPELL 599 | | | MILES CITY 593 | | | MISSOULA 598 | | | WOLF POINT 592 | | |
|---|---|---|---|---|---|---|---|---|---|---|---|---|---|---|---|---|---|---|---|
| | | MAT. | INST. | TOTAL | MAT. | INST. | TOTAL | MAT. | INST. | TOTAL | MAT. | INST. | TOTAL | MAT. | INST. | TOTAL | MAT. | INST. | TOTAL |
| 015433 | CONTRACTOR EQUIPMENT | | 98.7 | 98.7 | | 98.7 | 98.7 | | 98.7 | 98.7 | | 98.7 | 98.7 | | 98.7 | 98.7 | | 98.7 | 98.7 |
| 0241, 31 - 34 | SITE & INFRASTRUCTURE, DEMOLITION | 108.6 | 95.4 | 99.4 | 101.3 | 95.6 | 97.4 | 89.3 | 94.8 | 93.1 | 96.5 | 95.4 | 95.7 | 80.8 | 94.8 | 90.5 | 116.4 | 95.4 | 101.8 |
| 0310 | Concrete Forming & Accessories | 78.5 | 56.5 | 59.5 | 98.1 | 66.8 | 71.1 | 88.7 | 53.4 | 58.3 | 96.0 | 56.5 | 62.0 | 88.7 | 53.6 | 58.5 | 88.7 | 55.2 | 59.9 |
| 0320 | Concrete Reinforcing | 104.8 | 58.9 | 82.7 | 99.2 | 58.3 | 79.5 | 106.8 | 82.0 | 94.8 | 104.4 | 58.9 | 82.5 | 105.8 | 82.9 | 94.8 | 105.9 | 58.9 | 83.2 |
| 0330 | Cast-in-Place Concrete | 129.2 | 57.7 | 102.8 | 109.5 | 62.4 | 92.1 | 104.1 | 59.1 | 87.4 | 114.0 | 57.5 | 93.1 | 88.3 | 59.2 | 77.5 | 127.7 | 53.4 | 100.2 |
| 03 | CONCRETE | 112.8 | 58.4 | 87.7 | 101.6 | 64.5 | 84.5 | 94.7 | 61.9 | 79.6 | 101.7 | 58.4 | 81.7 | 83.4 | 62.2 | 73.6 | 116.3 | 56.4 | 88.6 |
| 04 | MASONRY | 117.1 | 70.4 | 89.2 | 113.7 | 61.6 | 82.6 | 115.1 | 49.2 | 75.7 | 122.2 | 70.2 | 91.1 | 139.8 | 67.2 | 96.4 | 123.3 | 70.4 | 91.7 |
| 05 | METALS | 99.5 | 76.3 | 92.7 | 106.1 | 75.6 | 97.2 | 99.3 | 86.1 | 95.5 | 98.7 | 76.4 | 92.2 | 99.8 | 87.7 | 96.3 | 98.8 | 76.3 | 92.2 |
| 06 | WOOD, PLASTICS & COMPOSITES | 81.6 | 55.8 | 67.7 | 104.1 | 67.5 | 84.4 | 93.7 | 54.2 | 72.4 | 100.9 | 55.8 | 76.6 | 93.7 | 54.2 | 72.4 | 92.8 | 54.2 | 72.0 |
| 07 | THERMAL & MOISTURE PROTECTION | 101.4 | 60.9 | 85.6 | 101.3 | 64.3 | 86.9 | 100.7 | 61.0 | 85.2 | 101.1 | 64.7 | 86.9 | 100.4 | 67.5 | 87.6 | 101.9 | 61.6 | 86.2 |
| 08 | OPENINGS | 95.3 | 53.4 | 85.0 | 98.0 | 59.9 | 88.6 | 95.3 | 59.9 | 86.6 | 94.8 | 53.4 | 84.6 | 95.3 | 59.9 | 86.5 | 94.8 | 52.5 | 84.4 |
| 0920 | Plaster & Gypsum Board | 88.5 | 55.0 | 67.8 | 92.0 | 67.0 | 76.6 | 92.5 | 53.3 | 68.3 | 97.7 | 55.0 | 71.4 | 92.5 | 53.3 | 68.3 | 94.3 | 53.3 | 69.0 |
| 0950, 0980 | Ceilings & Acoustic Treatment | 111.9 | 55.0 | 77.0 | 108.4 | 67.0 | 83.0 | 111.9 | 53.3 | 75.9 | 109.3 | 55.0 | 76.0 | 111.9 | 53.3 | 75.9 | 109.3 | 53.3 | 74.9 |
| 0960 | Flooring | 100.7 | 39.7 | 84.1 | 112.8 | 47.4 | 95.0 | 106.3 | 56.4 | 92.7 | 112.6 | 44.5 | 94.1 | 106.3 | 56.4 | 92.7 | 108.0 | 39.7 | 89.4 |
| 0970, 0990 | Wall Finishes & Painting/Coating | 97.7 | 42.4 | 64.5 | 97.7 | 47.7 | 67.6 | 97.7 | 42.9 | 64.8 | 97.7 | 40.1 | 63.1 | 97.7 | 42.9 | 64.8 | 97.7 | 40.1 | 63.1 |
| 09 | FINISHES | 101.3 | 51.4 | 75.2 | 104.2 | 61.4 | 81.8 | 102.5 | 52.3 | 76.2 | 104.9 | 52.1 | 77.3 | 102.0 | 52.3 | 76.0 | 104.3 | 50.2 | 76.0 |
| COVERS | DIVS. 10 - 14, 25, 28, 41, 43, 44 | 100.0 | 48.6 | 89.5 | 100.0 | 51.4 | 90.0 | 100.0 | 46.1 | 89.0 | 100.0 | 48.5 | 89.5 | 100.0 | 46.1 | 89.0 | 100.0 | 48.4 | 89.4 |
| 21, 22, 23 | FIRE SUPPRESSION, PLUMBING & HVAC | 96.1 | 74.2 | 87.1 | 100.1 | 72.7 | 88.9 | 96.1 | 66.8 | 84.1 | 96.1 | 74.1 | 87.1 | 100.2 | 66.8 | 86.5 | 96.1 | 74.2 | 87.1 |
| 26, 27, 3370 | ELECTRICAL, COMMUNICATIONS & UTIL. | 94.9 | 56.9 | 76.2 | 94.9 | 72.1 | 83.7 | 98.9 | 78.8 | 89.1 | 94.9 | 58.9 | 77.2 | 100.0 | 78.8 | 89.6 | 94.9 | 58.9 | 77.2 |
| MF2004 | WEIGHTED AVERAGE | 100.7 | 66.1 | 85.9 | 101.6 | 69.7 | 88.0 | 98.5 | 67.1 | 85.1 | 99.6 | 66.6 | 85.4 | 99.2 | 69.3 | 86.4 | 101.8 | 65.9 | 86.5 |

## NEBRASKA

| DIVISION | | ALLIANCE 693 | | | COLUMBUS 686 | | | GRAND ISLAND 688 | | | HASTINGS 689 | | | LINCOLN 683 - 685 | | | MCCOOK 690 | | |
|---|---|---|---|---|---|---|---|---|---|---|---|---|---|---|---|---|---|---|---|
| | | MAT. | INST. | TOTAL | MAT. | INST. | TOTAL | MAT. | INST. | TOTAL | MAT. | INST. | TOTAL | MAT. | INST. | TOTAL | MAT. | INST. | TOTAL |
| 015433 | CONTRACTOR EQUIPMENT | | 96.4 | 96.4 | | 101.4 | 101.4 | | 101.4 | 101.4 | | 101.4 | 101.4 | | 101.4 | 101.4 | | 101.4 | 101.4 |
| 0241, 31 - 34 | SITE & INFRASTRUCTURE, DEMOLITION | 96.5 | 97.9 | 97.5 | 95.9 | 90.9 | 92.4 | 100.5 | 91.8 | 94.5 | 99.6 | 91.3 | 93.8 | 89.1 | 91.8 | 91.0 | 100.5 | 91.1 | 93.9 |
| 0310 | Concrete Forming & Accessories | 89.7 | 58.3 | 62.6 | 98.6 | 61.1 | 66.3 | 98.0 | 76.5 | 79.4 | 101.6 | 74.9 | 78.6 | 102.8 | 67.3 | 72.2 | 95.6 | 58.5 | 63.6 |
| 0320 | Concrete Reinforcing | 111.7 | 54.0 | 83.9 | 103.0 | 52.6 | 78.7 | 102.4 | 75.9 | 89.6 | 102.4 | 53.2 | 78.7 | 94.0 | 75.7 | 85.2 | 104.4 | 75.5 | 90.5 |
| 0330 | Cast-in-Place Concrete | 108.2 | 60.2 | 90.4 | 110.7 | 58.7 | 91.5 | 117.3 | 74.5 | 101.4 | 117.3 | 68.5 | 99.2 | 94.8 | 77.5 | 88.4 | 117.3 | 60.0 | 96.1 |
| 03 | CONCRETE | 116.9 | 58.5 | 89.9 | 103.5 | 59.7 | 83.3 | 108.1 | 76.4 | 93.4 | 108.3 | 69.3 | 90.3 | 94.4 | 73.3 | 84.7 | 108.2 | 63.3 | 87.5 |
| 04 | MASONRY | 106.9 | 68.9 | 84.2 | 112.0 | 73.6 | 89.0 | 105.2 | 81.1 | 90.8 | 113.8 | 89.1 | 99.0 | 94.8 | 75.8 | 83.4 | 102.5 | 68.8 | 82.3 |
| 05 | METALS | 97.1 | 65.6 | 87.9 | 89.3 | 77.9 | 86.0 | 91.0 | 87.6 | 90.0 | 91.8 | 79.4 | 88.2 | 95.8 | 87.3 | 93.4 | 92.0 | 85.9 | 90.3 |
| 06 | WOOD, PLASTICS & COMPOSITES | 86.2 | 56.8 | 70.4 | 97.9 | 61.9 | 78.5 | 97.2 | 76.4 | 86.0 | 101.1 | 76.4 | 87.8 | 100.2 | 63.8 | 80.6 | 95.0 | 56.9 | 74.5 |
| 07 | THERMAL & MOISTURE PROTECTION | 106.1 | 70.1 | 92.1 | 99.2 | 66.3 | 86.4 | 99.3 | 79.2 | 91.5 | 99.4 | 86.9 | 94.5 | 98.9 | 76.4 | 90.1 | 99.3 | 66.8 | 86.6 |
| 08 | OPENINGS | 91.3 | 54.7 | 82.2 | 90.8 | 60.6 | 83.4 | 90.9 | 73.1 | 86.5 | 90.9 | 68.4 | 85.3 | 96.3 | 63.3 | 88.1 | 90.9 | 60.5 | 83.4 |
| 0920 | Plaster & Gypsum Board | 89.2 | 55.7 | 68.5 | 96.1 | 60.8 | 74.3 | 95.8 | 75.7 | 83.4 | 97.2 | 75.7 | 83.9 | 92.8 | 62.8 | 74.3 | 95.8 | 55.7 | 71.1 |
| 0950, 0980 | Ceilings & Acoustic Treatment | 89.4 | 55.7 | 68.7 | 86.2 | 60.8 | 70.6 | 86.2 | 75.7 | 79.8 | 86.2 | 75.7 | 79.8 | 89.6 | 62.8 | 73.1 | 86.2 | 55.7 | 67.5 |
| 0960 | Flooring | 95.9 | 84.9 | 92.9 | 96.5 | 100.8 | 97.7 | 96.3 | 106.7 | 99.2 | 98.0 | 100.8 | 98.7 | 98.1 | 96.5 | 97.7 | 95.2 | 84.9 | 92.4 |
| 0970, 0990 | Wall Finishes & Painting/Coating | 155.5 | 59.3 | 97.7 | 93.1 | 76.3 | 83.0 | 93.1 | 70.4 | 79.5 | 93.1 | 76.3 | 83.0 | 93.1 | 93.3 | 93.2 | 93.1 | 53.0 | 69.0 |
| 09 | FINISHES | 95.1 | 62.3 | 77.9 | 93.3 | 69.0 | 80.6 | 93.5 | 80.4 | 86.6 | 94.2 | 79.0 | 86.3 | 94.0 | 75.0 | 84.1 | 93.1 | 61.4 | 76.5 |
| COVERS | DIVS. 10 - 14, 25, 28, 41, 43, 44 | 100.0 | 79.1 | 95.7 | 100.0 | 82.9 | 96.5 | 100.0 | 88.3 | 97.6 | 100.0 | 87.0 | 97.3 | 100.0 | 86.8 | 97.3 | 100.0 | 78.1 | 95.5 |
| 21, 22, 23 | FIRE SUPPRESSION, PLUMBING & HVAC | 95.9 | 63.8 | 82.7 | 95.8 | 76.7 | 88.0 | 99.9 | 82.7 | 92.9 | 95.8 | 80.3 | 89.4 | 99.8 | 82.7 | 92.8 | 95.8 | 78.5 | 88.7 |
| 26, 27, 3370 | ELECTRICAL, COMMUNICATIONS & UTIL. | 91.5 | 73.6 | 82.7 | 91.2 | 79.3 | 85.4 | 89.9 | 76.1 | 83.1 | 89.3 | 86.0 | 87.7 | 96.3 | 76.1 | 86.4 | 93.6 | 73.6 | 83.8 |
| MF2004 | WEIGHTED AVERAGE | 98.8 | 68.0 | 85.6 | 95.8 | 73.8 | 86.4 | 97.2 | 81.2 | 90.4 | 96.8 | 81.1 | 90.1 | 96.7 | 78.9 | 89.1 | 96.6 | 73.0 | 86.5 |

## NEBRASKA / NEVADA

| DIVISION | | NORFOLK 687 | | | NORTH PLATTE 691 | | | OMAHA 680 - 681 | | | VALENTINE 692 | | | CARSON CITY 897 | | | ELKO 898 | | |
|---|---|---|---|---|---|---|---|---|---|---|---|---|---|---|---|---|---|---|---|
| | | MAT. | INST. | TOTAL | MAT. | INST. | TOTAL | MAT. | INST. | TOTAL | MAT. | INST. | TOTAL | MAT. | INST. | TOTAL | MAT. | INST. | TOTAL |
| 015433 | CONTRACTOR EQUIPMENT | | 90.7 | 90.7 | | 101.4 | 101.4 | | 90.7 | 90.7 | | 94.0 | 94.0 | | 101.2 | 101.2 | | 101.2 | 101.2 |
| 0241, 31 - 34 | SITE & INFRASTRUCTURE, DEMOLITION | 79.5 | 90.2 | 86.9 | 101.4 | 91.3 | 94.4 | 79.5 | 90.6 | 87.2 | 84.2 | 94.7 | 91.5 | 67.1 | 102.6 | 95.9 | 106.7 | 82.9 | 88.5 |
| 0310 | Concrete Forming & Accessories | 84.8 | 74.2 | 75.7 | 97.9 | 74.7 | 77.9 | 94.8 | 74.6 | 77.4 | 86.0 | 57.5 | 61.5 | 99.4 | 95.3 | 95.9 | 106.7 | 82.9 | 86.2 |
| 0320 | Concrete Reinforcing | 103.1 | 56.0 | 80.4 | 103.8 | 76.5 | 90.6 | 98.5 | 75.9 | 87.6 | 104.4 | 52.3 | 79.3 | 108.3 | 117.4 | 112.7 | 110.0 | 104.7 | 107.5 |
| 0330 | Cast-in-Place Concrete | 111.4 | 67.7 | 95.3 | 117.3 | 67.2 | 98.7 | 101.6 | 79.6 | 93.4 | 103.2 | 58.9 | 86.8 | 111.2 | 93.2 | 104.6 | 102.1 | 76.0 | 92.4 |
| 03 | CONCRETE | 102.2 | 68.7 | 86.8 | 108.3 | 73.2 | 92.1 | 97.2 | 76.7 | 87.7 | 104.6 | 57.6 | 82.9 | 111.0 | 98.8 | 105.4 | 103.6 | 84.9 | 95.0 |
| 04 | MASONRY | 118.3 | 76.6 | 93.4 | 90.0 | 89.1 | 89.5 | 100.2 | 81.6 | 89.1 | 102.1 | 68.7 | 82.1 | 125.3 | 80.4 | 98.5 | 125.9 | 73.0 | 94.2 |
| 05 | METALS | 92.6 | 70.1 | 86.0 | 91.2 | 87.9 | 90.2 | 95.2 | 77.9 | 90.2 | 103.0 | 66.8 | 92.4 | 95.6 | 104.2 | 98.1 | 94.7 | 96.6 | 95.3 |
| 06 | WOOD, PLASTICS & COMPOSITES | 80.8 | 75.8 | 78.1 | 97.0 | 76.4 | 85.9 | 92.2 | 74.1 | 82.5 | 81.2 | 56.3 | 67.8 | 93.4 | 96.3 | 95.0 | 102.7 | 84.0 | 92.6 |
| 07 | THERMAL & MOISTURE PROTECTION | 98.0 | 78.8 | 90.5 | 99.3 | 82.6 | 92.8 | 94.7 | 85.0 | 90.9 | 98.7 | 69.2 | 87.2 | 97.2 | 86.8 | 93.1 | 98.5 | 75.6 | 89.5 |
| 08 | OPENINGS | 92.8 | 69.1 | 86.9 | 90.2 | 74.0 | 86.2 | 99.4 | 74.0 | 93.2 | 92.9 | 55.6 | 83.7 | 93.6 | 108.5 | 97.2 | 96.1 | 87.4 | 93.9 |
| 0920 | Plaster & Gypsum Board | 95.4 | 75.7 | 83.3 | 96.2 | 75.7 | 83.6 | 94.9 | 74.0 | 82.0 | 98.2 | 55.7 | 72.0 | 82.0 | 96.1 | 90.7 | 89.0 | 83.4 | 85.5 |
| 0950, 0980 | Ceilings & Acoustic Treatment | 102.0 | 75.7 | 85.8 | 87.9 | 75.7 | 80.4 | 102.8 | 74.0 | 85.1 | 105.1 | 55.7 | 74.8 | 105.6 | 96.1 | 99.7 | 109.0 | 83.4 | 93.3 |
| 0960 | Flooring | 118.5 | 100.8 | 113.7 | 96.3 | 100.8 | 97.5 | 124.1 | 56.1 | 105.6 | 121.4 | 83.0 | 110.9 | 106.3 | 59.1 | 93.4 | 112.4 | 59.1 | 97.9 |
| 0970, 0990 | Wall Finishes & Painting/Coating | 156.5 | 76.3 | 108.3 | 93.1 | 76.3 | 83.0 | 156.5 | 74.7 | 107.4 | 156.5 | 69.4 | 104.2 | 99.8 | 87.3 | 92.3 | 98.8 | 87.3 | 91.9 |
| 09 | FINISHES | 111.2 | 79.0 | 94.4 | 93.9 | 79.0 | 86.1 | 113.1 | 70.5 | 90.8 | 113.7 | 62.7 | 87.0 | 99.6 | 87.0 | 93.0 | 102.4 | 79.1 | 90.2 |
| COVERS | DIVS. 10 - 14, 25, 28, 41, 43, 44 | 100.0 | 85.5 | 97.0 | 100.0 | 77.2 | 95.3 | 100.0 | 86.7 | 97.3 | 100.0 | 71.4 | 94.1 | 100.0 | 112.7 | 102.6 | 100.0 | 76.2 | 95.1 |
| 21, 22, 23 | FIRE SUPPRESSION, PLUMBING & HVAC | 95.5 | 80.2 | 89.2 | 99.9 | 80.3 | 91.9 | 99.6 | 82.6 | 92.6 | 95.4 | 60.2 | 81.0 | 99.8 | 90.9 | 96.2 | 97.9 | 74.4 | 88.3 |
| 26, 27, 3370 | ELECTRICAL, COMMUNICATIONS & UTIL. | 90.1 | 93.3 | 91.6 | 91.8 | 79.3 | 85.7 | 93.6 | 85.6 | 89.7 | 88.9 | 89.1 | 89.0 | 94.0 | 102.2 | 98.1 | 92.0 | 63.1 | 77.8 |
| MF2004 | WEIGHTED AVERAGE | 97.4 | 79.5 | 89.7 | 96.7 | 81.2 | 90.0 | 98.4 | 80.6 | 90.8 | 98.8 | 69.0 | 86.0 | 99.5 | 95.5 | 97.8 | 98.2 | 79.8 | 90.3 |

# City Cost Indexes

| DIVISION | | NEVADA | | | | | | | | | NEW HAMPSHIRE | | | | | | | | |
|---|---|---|---|---|---|---|---|---|---|---|---|---|---|---|---|---|---|---|---|
| | | ELY 893 | | | LAS VEGAS 889 - 891 | | | RENO 894 - 895 | | | CHARLESTON 036 | | | CLAREMONT 037 | | | CONCORD 032 - 033 | | |
| | | MAT. | INST. | TOTAL | MAT. | INST. | TOTAL | MAT. | INST. | TOTAL | MAT. | INST. | TOTAL | MAT. | INST. | TOTAL | MAT. | INST. | TOTAL |
| 015433 | CONTRACTOR EQUIPMENT | | 101.2 | 101.2 | | 101.2 | 101.2 | | 101.2 | 101.2 | | 100.6 | 100.6 | | 100.6 | 100.6 | | 100.6 | 100.6 |
| 0241, 31 - 34 | SITE & INFRASTRUCTURE, DEMOLITION | 61.8 | 101.8 | 89.7 | 62.2 | 105.7 | 92.5 | 61.8 | 102.6 | 90.2 | 77.9 | 97.3 | 91.4 | 72.2 | 97.3 | 89.7 | 85.7 | 99.2 | 95.1 |
| 0310 | Concrete Forming & Accessories | 99.3 | 67.0 | 71.5 | 98.0 | 109.8 | 108.1 | 96.2 | 95.3 | 95.5 | 85.9 | 49.3 | 54.4 | 92.1 | 49.3 | 55.3 | 94.3 | 83.6 | 85.1 |
| 0320 | Concrete Reinforcing | 108.8 | 96.7 | 103.0 | 102.9 | 123.1 | 112.6 | 102.9 | 122.4 | 112.3 | 81.6 | 53.3 | 68.0 | 81.6 | 53.3 | 68.0 | 81.6 | 93.0 | 87.4 |
| 0330 | Cast-in-Place Concrete | 109.7 | 73.6 | 96.3 | 105.2 | 115.5 | 109.0 | 116.0 | 93.2 | 107.6 | 92.8 | 53.7 | 78.4 | 85.3 | 53.7 | 73.6 | 97.5 | 95.6 | 96.8 |
| 03 | CONCRETE | 112.5 | 75.5 | 95.4 | 107.1 | 113.9 | 110.3 | 112.3 | 99.7 | 106.5 | 103.0 | 52.2 | 79.5 | 94.4 | 52.2 | 74.9 | 103.6 | 89.5 | 97.1 |
| 04 | MASONRY | 131.4 | 65.2 | 91.8 | 119.3 | 101.1 | 108.4 | 125.0 | 80.4 | 98.3 | 91.4 | 43.0 | 62.4 | 91.7 | 43.0 | 62.6 | 95.2 | 91.1 | 92.7 |
| 05 | METALS | 94.7 | 93.0 | 94.2 | 96.2 | 110.3 | 100.3 | 96.1 | 106.4 | 99.1 | 88.0 | 63.4 | 80.9 | 88.0 | 63.4 | 80.9 | 88.7 | 88.9 | 88.8 |
| 06 | WOOD, PLASTICS & COMPOSITES | 93.3 | 66.6 | 78.9 | 93.1 | 107.8 | 101.0 | 89.4 | 96.3 | 93.1 | 85.4 | 51.2 | 67.0 | 92.3 | 51.2 | 70.1 | 96.5 | 83.8 | 89.6 |
| 07 | THERMAL & MOISTURE PROTECTION | 99.2 | 70.4 | 88.0 | 104.1 | 101.9 | 103.3 | 98.6 | 86.8 | 94.0 | 98.9 | 45.9 | 78.2 | 98.7 | 45.9 | 78.1 | 97.6 | 90.3 | 94.7 |
| 08 | OPENINGS | 96.0 | 75.9 | 91.0 | 95.1 | 116.0 | 100.2 | 93.9 | 108.7 | 97.6 | 102.1 | 46.4 | 88.4 | 103.3 | 46.4 | 89.3 | 103.3 | 79.7 | 97.5 |
| 0920 | Plaster & Gypsum Board | 85.6 | 65.6 | 73.3 | 85.3 | 107.9 | 99.2 | 81.9 | 96.1 | 90.7 | 97.4 | 49.1 | 67.6 | 99.4 | 49.1 | 68.4 | 101.6 | 82.6 | 89.9 |
| 0950, 0980 | Ceilings & Acoustic Treatment | 109.0 | 65.6 | 82.3 | 113.3 | 107.9 | 109.9 | 115.0 | 96.1 | 103.4 | 85.8 | 49.1 | 63.3 | 85.8 | 49.1 | 63.3 | 85.8 | 82.6 | 83.8 |
| 0960 | Flooring | 109.8 | 66.1 | 97.9 | 99.9 | 96.2 | 98.9 | 105.9 | 59.1 | 93.1 | 90.5 | 37.1 | 76.0 | 93.3 | 37.1 | 78.0 | 90.7 | 103.4 | 94.2 |
| 0970, 0990 | Wall Finishes & Painting/Coating | 98.8 | 89.8 | 93.4 | 101.0 | 119.5 | 112.1 | 98.8 | 87.3 | 91.9 | 91.6 | 54.7 | 69.5 | 91.6 | 54.7 | 69.5 | 91.6 | 98.5 | 95.7 |
| 09 | FINISHES | 101.6 | 68.7 | 84.4 | 99.5 | 107.9 | 103.9 | 101.0 | 87.0 | 93.7 | 93.6 | 47.9 | 69.7 | 94.3 | 47.9 | 70.0 | 95.4 | 89.1 | 92.1 |
| COVERS | DIVS. 10 - 14, 25, 28, 41, 43, 44 | 100.0 | 63.4 | 92.5 | 100.0 | 106.2 | 101.3 | 100.0 | 112.7 | 102.6 | 100.0 | 44.5 | 88.6 | 100.0 | 44.5 | 88.6 | 100.0 | 70.8 | 94.0 |
| 21, 22, 23 | FIRE SUPPRESSION, PLUMBING & HVAC | 97.9 | 70.2 | 86.5 | 99.9 | 110.0 | 104.0 | 99.9 | 90.9 | 96.2 | 96.0 | 45.9 | 75.4 | 96.0 | 45.9 | 75.4 | 100.0 | 85.8 | 94.2 |
| 26, 27, 3370 | ELECTRICAL, COMMUNICATIONS & UTIL. | 92.3 | 63.1 | 77.9 | 94.6 | 112.4 | 103.3 | 92.6 | 102.2 | 97.4 | 95.6 | 38.5 | 67.6 | 95.6 | 38.5 | 67.6 | 98.0 | 67.1 | 82.8 |
| MF2004 | WEIGHTED AVERAGE | 99.5 | 73.9 | 88.6 | 99.1 | 109.2 | 103.4 | 99.6 | 95.8 | 98.0 | 95.5 | 51.6 | 76.7 | 94.6 | 51.6 | 76.2 | 97.5 | 85.4 | 92.4 |

| DIVISION | | NEW HAMPSHIRE | | | | | | | | | | | | | | | NEW JERSEY | | |
|---|---|---|---|---|---|---|---|---|---|---|---|---|---|---|---|---|---|---|---|
| | | KEENE 034 | | | LITTLETON 035 | | | MANCHESTER 031 | | | NASHUA 030 | | | PORTSMOUTH 038 | | | ATLANTIC CITY 082,084 | | |
| | | MAT. | INST. | TOTAL | MAT. | INST. | TOTAL | MAT. | INST. | TOTAL | MAT. | INST. | TOTAL | MAT. | INST. | TOTAL | MAT. | INST. | TOTAL |
| 015433 | CONTRACTOR EQUIPMENT | | 100.6 | 100.6 | | 100.6 | 100.6 | | 100.6 | 100.6 | | 100.6 | 100.6 | | 100.6 | 100.6 | | 98.4 | 98.4 |
| 0241, 31 - 34 | SITE & INFRASTRUCTURE, DEMOLITION | 84.9 | 97.4 | 93.7 | 72.2 | 97.0 | 89.4 | 83.2 | 99.3 | 94.4 | 85.7 | 99.3 | 95.1 | 80.0 | 100.4 | 94.2 | 88.2 | 104.2 | 99.3 |
| 0310 | Concrete Forming & Accessories | 90.7 | 47.1 | 53.2 | 101.1 | 52.6 | 59.3 | 96.2 | 84.3 | 85.9 | 98.6 | 84.3 | 86.3 | 87.3 | 86.8 | 86.8 | 107.3 | 125.5 | 123.0 |
| 0320 | Concrete Reinforcing | 81.6 | 63.5 | 72.9 | 82.4 | 38.1 | 61.1 | 102.0 | 93.7 | 98.0 | 102.0 | 93.7 | 98.0 | 81.6 | 93.8 | 87.5 | 77.8 | 107.9 | 92.3 |
| 0330 | Cast-in-Place Concrete | 93.3 | 55.4 | 79.3 | 83.7 | 56.2 | 73.5 | 102.7 | 121.3 | 109.6 | 88.3 | 121.3 | 100.5 | 83.7 | 125.2 | 99.1 | 79.1 | 126.8 | 96.8 |
| 03 | CONCRETE | 102.7 | 53.7 | 80.1 | 93.7 | 51.6 | 74.2 | 109.5 | 98.6 | 104.5 | 102.5 | 98.6 | 100.7 | 93.8 | 101.2 | 97.2 | 95.9 | 121.5 | 107.7 |
| 04 | MASONRY | 95.5 | 45.4 | 65.5 | 104.4 | 42.7 | 67.5 | 97.5 | 91.1 | 93.7 | 97.3 | 91.1 | 93.6 | 92.9 | 96.5 | 95.0 | 99.3 | 121.4 | 112.5 |
| 05 | METALS | 88.7 | 68.4 | 82.8 | 88.7 | 56.4 | 79.3 | 93.4 | 89.6 | 92.3 | 93.4 | 89.6 | 92.3 | 90.1 | 92.9 | 90.9 | 88.5 | 101.1 | 92.1 |
| 06 | WOOD, PLASTICS & COMPOSITES | 90.6 | 45.6 | 66.3 | 101.7 | 52.3 | 75.1 | 96.3 | 83.8 | 89.6 | 100.0 | 83.8 | 91.2 | 86.7 | 83.8 | 85.1 | 110.8 | 126.5 | 119.2 |
| 07 | THERMAL & MOISTURE PROTECTION | 99.4 | 48.2 | 79.4 | 98.8 | 50.1 | 79.8 | 99.0 | 94.1 | 97.1 | 99.7 | 94.1 | 97.5 | 99.3 | 114.1 | 105.1 | 99.4 | 123.2 | 108.7 |
| 08 | OPENINGS | 100.6 | 51.9 | 88.6 | 104.4 | 44.0 | 89.5 | 105.3 | 79.7 | 99.0 | 105.3 | 79.7 | 99.0 | 106.1 | 74.3 | 98.2 | 103.0 | 119.9 | 107.2 |
| 0920 | Plaster & Gypsum Board | 98.7 | 43.4 | 64.6 | 109.5 | 50.3 | 73.0 | 107.9 | 82.6 | 92.3 | 105.1 | 82.6 | 91.2 | 97.4 | 82.6 | 88.2 | 107.8 | 126.4 | 119.3 |
| 0950, 0980 | Ceilings & Acoustic Treatment | 85.8 | 43.4 | 59.7 | 85.8 | 50.3 | 64.0 | 93.7 | 82.6 | 86.9 | 96.2 | 82.6 | 87.8 | 87.7 | 82.6 | 84.5 | 85.8 | 126.4 | 110.7 |
| 0960 | Flooring | 92.7 | 60.8 | 84.0 | 102.7 | 37.1 | 84.8 | 97.3 | 103.4 | 98.9 | 96.3 | 103.4 | 98.2 | 91.1 | 103.4 | 94.4 | 100.3 | 135.1 | 109.8 |
| 0970, 0990 | Wall Finishes & Painting/Coating | 91.6 | 54.7 | 69.5 | 91.6 | 71.8 | 79.7 | 91.6 | 98.5 | 95.7 | 91.6 | 98.5 | 95.7 | 91.6 | 98.5 | 95.7 | 91.6 | 125.6 | 112.0 |
| 09 | FINISHES | 95.6 | 50.2 | 71.8 | 98.7 | 51.8 | 74.1 | 99.6 | 89.1 | 94.1 | 100.1 | 89.1 | 94.3 | 94.9 | 90.4 | 92.5 | 99.7 | 128.5 | 114.8 |
| COVERS | DIVS. 10 - 14, 25, 28, 41, 43, 44 | 100.0 | 61.9 | 92.2 | 100.0 | 46.7 | 89.1 | 100.0 | 70.8 | 94.0 | 100.0 | 70.8 | 94.0 | 100.0 | 72.7 | 94.4 | 100.0 | 113.4 | 102.8 |
| 21, 22, 23 | FIRE SUPPRESSION, PLUMBING & HVAC | 96.0 | 48.4 | 76.4 | 96.0 | 76.8 | 88.1 | 100.0 | 85.9 | 94.2 | 100.1 | 85.9 | 94.3 | 100.1 | 88.7 | 95.4 | 99.8 | 118.9 | 107.7 |
| 26, 27, 3370 | ELECTRICAL, COMMUNICATIONS & UTIL. | 95.6 | 38.5 | 67.6 | 96.7 | 67.0 | 82.1 | 97.9 | 84.4 | 91.3 | 98.0 | 84.4 | 91.3 | 96.1 | 84.5 | 90.4 | 93.7 | 122.9 | 108.0 |
| MF2004 | WEIGHTED AVERAGE | 96.0 | 54.1 | 78.1 | 95.9 | 61.9 | 81.4 | 99.6 | 89.3 | 95.2 | 99.0 | 89.3 | 94.9 | 96.4 | 91.8 | 94.4 | 96.9 | 118.6 | 106.2 |

| DIVISION | | NEW JERSEY | | | | | | | | | | | | | | | | | |
|---|---|---|---|---|---|---|---|---|---|---|---|---|---|---|---|---|---|---|---|
| | | CAMDEN 081 | | | DOVER 078 | | | ELIZABETH 072 | | | HACKENSACK 076 | | | JERSEY CITY 073 | | | LONG BRANCH 077 | | |
| | | MAT. | INST. | TOTAL | MAT. | INST. | TOTAL | MAT. | INST. | TOTAL | MAT. | INST. | TOTAL | MAT. | INST. | TOTAL | MAT. | INST. | TOTAL |
| 015433 | CONTRACTOR EQUIPMENT | | 98.4 | 98.4 | | 100.6 | 100.6 | | 100.6 | 100.6 | | 100.6 | 100.6 | | 98.4 | 98.4 | | 97.9 | 97.9 |
| 0241, 31 - 34 | SITE & INFRASTRUCTURE, DEMOLITION | 88.9 | 104.4 | 99.7 | 98.1 | 105.3 | 103.1 | 101.9 | 105.3 | 104.2 | 98.7 | 105.4 | 103.3 | 88.9 | 105.3 | 100.3 | 93.8 | 105.2 | 101.7 |
| 0310 | Concrete Forming & Accessories | 98.6 | 125.5 | 121.8 | 95.2 | 123.2 | 119.3 | 107.2 | 123.1 | 120.9 | 95.2 | 123.1 | 119.2 | 98.6 | 123.2 | 119.8 | 99.2 | 125.9 | 122.2 |
| 0320 | Concrete Reinforcing | 102.0 | 118.2 | 109.8 | 78.6 | 119.0 | 98.1 | 78.6 | 119.0 | 98.1 | 78.6 | 119.0 | 98.1 | 102.0 | 119.0 | 110.2 | 78.6 | 118.9 | 98.0 |
| 0330 | Cast-in-Place Concrete | 76.7 | 123.8 | 94.1 | 98.4 | 126.1 | 108.7 | 84.5 | 126.1 | 99.9 | 96.2 | 126.1 | 107.3 | 76.7 | 126.1 | 95.0 | 85.3 | 126.6 | 100.6 |
| 03 | CONCRETE | 96.7 | 122.5 | 108.6 | 103.7 | 122.6 | 112.4 | 99.3 | 122.5 | 110.0 | 101.7 | 122.5 | 111.3 | 96.7 | 122.4 | 108.6 | 101.5 | 123.8 | 111.8 |
| 04 | MASONRY | 90.9 | 121.4 | 109.1 | 94.4 | 121.9 | 110.8 | 110.7 | 121.9 | 117.4 | 98.5 | 121.9 | 112.5 | 88.2 | 121.9 | 108.4 | 103.1 | 121.4 | 114.0 |
| 05 | METALS | 93.2 | 104.5 | 96.5 | 88.5 | 110.1 | 94.7 | 89.9 | 110.0 | 95.7 | 88.5 | 110.0 | 94.8 | 93.3 | 107.3 | 97.4 | 88.5 | 106.8 | 93.9 |
| 06 | WOOD, PLASTICS & COMPOSITES | 100.0 | 126.5 | 114.2 | 99.1 | 122.4 | 111.6 | 114.3 | 122.4 | 118.6 | 99.1 | 122.4 | 111.6 | 100.0 | 122.4 | 112.0 | 101.1 | 126.4 | 114.7 |
| 07 | THERMAL & MOISTURE PROTECTION | 99.3 | 123.5 | 108.7 | 99.8 | 127.8 | 110.7 | 100.0 | 127.8 | 110.7 | 99.6 | 121.6 | 108.2 | 99.2 | 127.8 | 110.4 | 99.4 | 121.8 | 110.6 |
| 08 | OPENINGS | 105.3 | 122.1 | 109.4 | 108.8 | 119.0 | 111.3 | 106.8 | 119.0 | 109.8 | 106.0 | 119.0 | 109.2 | 105.3 | 119.0 | 108.7 | 101.4 | 121.2 | 106.3 |
| 0920 | Plaster & Gypsum Board | 105.1 | 126.4 | 118.2 | 102.1 | 122.2 | 114.5 | 108.5 | 122.2 | 116.9 | 102.1 | 122.2 | 114.5 | 105.1 | 122.2 | 115.6 | 103.8 | 126.4 | 117.7 |
| 0950, 0980 | Ceilings & Acoustic Treatment | 96.2 | 126.4 | 114.7 | 85.8 | 122.2 | 108.1 | 87.7 | 122.2 | 108.8 | 85.8 | 122.2 | 108.1 | 96.2 | 122.2 | 112.1 | 85.8 | 126.4 | 110.7 |
| 0960 | Flooring | 96.3 | 135.1 | 106.8 | 95.1 | 156.4 | 111.8 | 100.7 | 156.4 | 115.9 | 95.1 | 156.4 | 111.8 | 96.3 | 156.4 | 112.6 | 96.5 | 129.1 | 105.4 |
| 0970, 0990 | Wall Finishes & Painting/Coating | 91.6 | 125.6 | 112.0 | 91.5 | 125.6 | 112.0 | 91.5 | 125.6 | 112.0 | 91.5 | 125.6 | 112.0 | 91.6 | 125.6 | 112.0 | 91.6 | 125.6 | 112.0 |
| 09 | FINISHES | 100.4 | 128.5 | 115.1 | 97.4 | 129.8 | 114.4 | 101.1 | 129.8 | 116.1 | 97.3 | 129.8 | 114.3 | 100.4 | 129.8 | 115.8 | 98.4 | 127.4 | 113.6 |
| COVERS | DIVS. 10 - 14, 25, 28, 41, 43, 44 | 100.0 | 113.4 | 102.8 | 100.0 | 116.7 | 103.4 | 100.0 | 116.7 | 103.4 | 100.0 | 116.7 | 103.4 | 100.0 | 116.7 | 103.4 | 100.0 | 113.3 | 102.7 |
| 21, 22, 23 | FIRE SUPPRESSION, PLUMBING & HVAC | 100.1 | 118.8 | 107.8 | 99.9 | 126.7 | 110.9 | 100.1 | 123.0 | 109.5 | 99.9 | 126.7 | 111.0 | 100.1 | 126.7 | 111.1 | 99.9 | 124.9 | 110.2 |
| 26, 27, 3370 | ELECTRICAL, COMMUNICATIONS & UTIL. | 98.5 | 122.9 | 110.5 | 95.2 | 141.5 | 117.9 | 95.8 | 141.5 | 118.2 | 95.2 | 145.2 | 119.8 | 99.7 | 145.2 | 122.0 | 94.9 | 133.0 | 113.6 |
| MF2004 | WEIGHTED AVERAGE | 98.1 | 119.1 | 107.1 | 98.3 | 124.2 | 109.4 | 99.3 | 123.4 | 109.6 | 98.0 | 124.5 | 109.3 | 98.1 | 124.5 | 109.4 | 97.7 | 122.2 | 108.2 |

## NEW JERSEY

| DIVISION | | NEW BRUNSWICK 088-089 | | | NEWARK 070-071 | | | PATERSON 074-075 | | | POINT PLEASANT 087 | | | SUMMIT 079 | | | TRENTON 085-086 | | |
|---|---|---|---|---|---|---|---|---|---|---|---|---|---|---|---|---|---|---|---|
| | | MAT. | INST. | TOTAL | MAT. | INST. | TOTAL | MAT. | INST. | TOTAL | MAT. | INST. | TOTAL | MAT. | INST. | TOTAL | MAT. | INST. | TOTAL |
| 015433 | CONTRACTOR EQUIPMENT | | 97.9 | 97.9 | | 100.6 | 100.6 | | 100.6 | 100.6 | | 97.9 | 97.9 | | 100.6 | 100.6 | | 97.9 | 97.9 |
| 0241, 31 - 34 | SITE & INFRASTRUCTURE, DEMOLITION | 101.3 | 105.2 | 104.0 | 104.0 | 105.3 | 104.9 | 100.2 | 105.3 | 103.8 | 102.8 | 105.2 | 104.5 | 99.6 | 105.3 | 103.5 | 89.1 | 105.2 | 100.3 |
| 0310 | Concrete Forming & Accessories | 101.7 | 123.1 | 120.1 | 95.0 | 123.1 | 119.2 | 97.4 | 123.0 | 119.5 | 96.2 | 125.9 | 121.8 | 98.2 | 123.1 | 119.6 | 95.7 | 125.9 | 121.7 |
| 0320 | Concrete Reinforcing | 78.6 | 119.0 | 98.1 | 102.0 | 119.0 | 110.2 | 102.0 | 119.0 | 110.2 | 78.6 | 118.9 | 98.0 | 78.6 | 119.0 | 98.1 | 102.0 | 117.2 | 109.4 |
| 0330 | Cast-in-Place Concrete | 97.8 | 126.7 | 108.5 | 93.5 | 126.1 | 105.5 | 97.9 | 126.1 | 108.3 | 97.8 | 126.6 | 108.5 | 81.7 | 126.1 | 98.1 | 89.3 | 126.7 | 103.1 |
| 03 | CONCRETE | 114.0 | 122.6 | 118.0 | 104.9 | 122.6 | 113.0 | 107.2 | 122.5 | 114.3 | 113.7 | 123.8 | 118.3 | 96.1 | 122.5 | 108.3 | 102.8 | 123.4 | 112.3 |
| 04 | MASONRY | 97.4 | 121.4 | 111.8 | 99.2 | 121.9 | 112.8 | 94.9 | 121.9 | 111.0 | 88.5 | 121.4 | 108.2 | 97.0 | 121.9 | 111.9 | 87.8 | 121.4 | 107.9 |
| 05 | METALS | 88.5 | 107.1 | 93.9 | 93.3 | 110.0 | 98.1 | 88.6 | 110.0 | 94.8 | 88.5 | 106.8 | 93.8 | 88.5 | 110.0 | 94.7 | 88.5 | 104.4 | 93.2 |
| 06 | WOOD, PLASTICS & COMPOSITES | 104.2 | 122.3 | 114.0 | 98.4 | 122.4 | 111.3 | 101.7 | 122.4 | 112.8 | 97.4 | 126.4 | 113.1 | 102.9 | 122.4 | 113.4 | 96.8 | 126.4 | 112.7 |
| 07 | THERMAL & MOISTURE PROTECTION | 99.6 | 127.4 | 110.5 | 99.5 | 127.8 | 110.5 | 99.8 | 121.6 | 108.3 | 99.7 | 128.1 | 110.7 | 100.2 | 127.8 | 110.9 | 95.2 | 123.0 | 106.0 |
| 08 | OPENINGS | 97.6 | 119.0 | 102.9 | 111.5 | 119.0 | 113.4 | 111.5 | 119.0 | 113.4 | 99.6 | 123.3 | 105.4 | 113.9 | 119.0 | 115.1 | 105.8 | 119.7 | 109.3 |
| 0920 | Plaster & Gypsum Board | 105.1 | 122.2 | 115.6 | 107.9 | 122.2 | 116.7 | 105.1 | 122.2 | 115.6 | 102.1 | 126.4 | 117.1 | 103.8 | 122.2 | 115.1 | 107.9 | 126.4 | 119.3 |
| 0950, 0980 | Ceilings & Acoustic Treatment | 85.8 | 122.2 | 108.1 | 93.7 | 122.2 | 111.2 | 96.2 | 122.2 | 112.1 | 85.8 | 126.4 | 110.7 | 85.8 | 122.2 | 108.1 | 93.7 | 126.4 | 113.8 |
| 0960 | Flooring | 97.9 | 156.4 | 113.8 | 96.5 | 156.4 | 112.8 | 96.3 | 156.4 | 112.6 | 95.1 | 135.1 | 106.0 | 96.6 | 156.4 | 112.8 | 96.7 | 156.4 | 112.9 |
| 0970, 0990 | Wall Finishes & Painting/Coating | 91.6 | 125.6 | 112.0 | 91.5 | 125.6 | 112.0 | 91.5 | 125.6 | 112.0 | 91.6 | 125.6 | 112.0 | 91.5 | 125.6 | 112.0 | 91.6 | 125.6 | 112.0 |
| 09 | FINISHES | 99.8 | 129.7 | 115.5 | 100.6 | 129.8 | 115.9 | 100.6 | 129.8 | 115.9 | 98.5 | 128.4 | 114.2 | 98.4 | 129.8 | 114.9 | 100.2 | 132.1 | 116.9 |
| COVERS | DIVS. 10 - 14, 25, 28, 41, 43, 44 | 100.0 | 116.5 | 103.4 | 100.0 | 116.7 | 103.4 | 100.0 | 116.7 | 103.4 | 100.0 | 104.3 | 100.9 | 100.0 | 116.7 | 103.4 | 100.0 | 113.4 | 102.7 |
| 21, 22, 23 | FIRE SUPPRESSION, PLUMBING & HVAC | 99.8 | 125.0 | 110.1 | 100.2 | 123.0 | 109.6 | 100.1 | 126.7 | 111.1 | 99.8 | 124.9 | 110.1 | 99.9 | 123.0 | 109.4 | 100.2 | 124.9 | 110.4 |
| 26, 27, 3370 | ELECTRICAL, COMMUNICATIONS & UTIL. | 94.4 | 141.2 | 117.4 | 98.7 | 145.2 | 121.5 | 99.7 | 141.5 | 120.2 | 93.7 | 133.0 | 113.0 | 95.8 | 141.5 | 118.2 | 96.8 | 136.9 | 116.5 |
| MF2004 | WEIGHTED AVERAGE | 98.8 | 123.9 | 109.3 | 100.6 | 123.9 | 110.6 | 99.9 | 124.0 | 110.2 | 98.3 | 122.2 | 108.5 | 98.2 | 123.4 | 109.0 | 97.6 | 122.9 | 108.4 |

## NEW JERSEY / NEW MEXICO

| DIVISION | | NEW JERSEY VINELAND 080,083 | | | ALBUQUERQUE 870-872 | | | CARRIZOZO 883 | | | CLOVIS 881 | | | FARMINGTON 874 | | | GALLUP 873 | | |
|---|---|---|---|---|---|---|---|---|---|---|---|---|---|---|---|---|---|---|---|
| | | MAT. | INST. | TOTAL | MAT. | INST. | TOTAL | MAT. | INST. | TOTAL | MAT. | INST. | TOTAL | MAT. | INST. | TOTAL | MAT. | INST. | TOTAL |
| 015433 | CONTRACTOR EQUIPMENT | | 98.4 | 98.4 | | 115.7 | 115.7 | | 115.7 | 115.7 | | 115.7 | 115.7 | | 115.7 | 115.7 | | 115.7 | 115.7 |
| 0241, 31 - 34 | SITE & INFRASTRUCTURE, DEMOLITION | 92.7 | 104.4 | 100.8 | 78.6 | 110.3 | 100.7 | 99.5 | 110.3 | 107.0 | 87.5 | 110.3 | 103.4 | 84.9 | 110.3 | 102.6 | 92.7 | 110.3 | 105.0 |
| 0310 | Concrete Forming & Accessories | 93.7 | 125.5 | 121.1 | 97.4 | 69.1 | 73.1 | 97.5 | 69.1 | 73.1 | 97.5 | 68.8 | 72.7 | 97.5 | 69.1 | 73.1 | 97.5 | 69.1 | 73.1 |
| 0320 | Concrete Reinforcing | 77.8 | 107.9 | 92.3 | 103.6 | 70.3 | 87.5 | 111.0 | 70.3 | 91.4 | 112.3 | 52.7 | 83.6 | 113.1 | 70.3 | 92.5 | 108.3 | 70.3 | 90.0 |
| 0330 | Cast-in-Place Concrete | 85.3 | 126.8 | 100.7 | 108.5 | 75.0 | 96.1 | 100.9 | 75.0 | 91.3 | 100.8 | 74.9 | 91.2 | 109.5 | 75.0 | 96.7 | 103.0 | 75.0 | 92.6 |
| 03 | CONCRETE | 101.1 | 121.5 | 110.5 | 108.8 | 72.4 | 92.0 | 123.6 | 72.4 | 100.0 | 111.9 | 68.8 | 92.0 | 112.7 | 72.4 | 94.1 | 118.7 | 72.4 | 97.3 |
| 04 | MASONRY | 87.2 | 121.4 | 107.7 | 114.9 | 66.1 | 85.7 | 112.4 | 66.1 | 84.7 | 112.4 | 66.1 | 84.7 | 121.3 | 66.1 | 88.3 | 112.5 | 66.1 | 84.7 |
| 05 | METALS | 88.4 | 101.1 | 92.1 | 102.3 | 89.2 | 98.5 | 99.1 | 89.2 | 96.2 | 98.8 | 80.1 | 93.4 | 100.0 | 89.2 | 96.9 | 99.2 | 89.2 | 96.3 |
| 06 | WOOD, PLASTICS & COMPOSITES | 94.5 | 126.5 | 111.7 | 93.5 | 69.9 | 80.8 | 93.6 | 69.9 | 80.9 | 93.6 | 69.9 | 80.9 | 93.6 | 69.9 | 80.9 | 93.6 | 69.9 | 80.9 |
| 07 | THERMAL & MOISTURE PROTECTION | 99.2 | 123.2 | 108.6 | 98.1 | 75.0 | 89.1 | 100.0 | 75.0 | 90.2 | 98.6 | 75.0 | 89.4 | 98.4 | 75.0 | 89.3 | 99.6 | 75.0 | 90.0 |
| 08 | OPENINGS | 99.1 | 119.9 | 104.2 | 93.7 | 72.4 | 88.5 | 92.5 | 72.4 | 87.6 | 92.7 | 66.9 | 86.3 | 96.3 | 72.4 | 90.4 | 96.3 | 72.4 | 90.4 |
| 0920 | Plaster & Gypsum Board | 101.1 | 126.4 | 116.7 | 86.0 | 68.6 | 75.3 | 79.7 | 68.6 | 72.9 | 79.7 | 68.6 | 72.9 | 79.7 | 68.6 | 72.9 | 79.7 | 68.6 | 72.9 |
| 0950, 0980 | Ceilings & Acoustic Treatment | 85.8 | 126.4 | 110.7 | 109.4 | 68.6 | 84.4 | 105.6 | 68.6 | 82.9 | 105.6 | 68.6 | 82.9 | 105.6 | 68.6 | 82.9 | 105.6 | 68.6 | 82.9 |
| 0960 | Flooring | 94.2 | 135.1 | 105.3 | 103.5 | 71.1 | 94.7 | 105.9 | 71.1 | 96.4 | 105.9 | 71.1 | 96.4 | 105.9 | 71.1 | 96.4 | 105.9 | 71.1 | 96.4 |
| 0970, 0990 | Wall Finishes & Painting/Coating | 91.6 | 125.6 | 112.0 | 103.2 | 57.2 | 75.6 | 98.8 | 57.2 | 73.8 | 98.8 | 57.2 | 73.8 | 98.8 | 57.2 | 73.8 | 98.8 | 57.2 | 73.8 |
| 09 | FINISHES | 97.3 | 128.5 | 113.6 | 100.4 | 68.1 | 83.5 | 100.8 | 68.1 | 83.7 | 99.6 | 68.1 | 83.1 | 99.2 | 68.1 | 82.9 | 100.2 | 68.1 | 83.4 |
| COVERS | DIVS. 10 - 14, 25, 28, 41, 43, 44 | 100.0 | 113.4 | 102.8 | 100.0 | 75.6 | 95.0 | 100.0 | 75.6 | 95.0 | 100.0 | 75.6 | 95.0 | 100.0 | 75.6 | 95.0 | 100.0 | 75.6 | 95.0 |
| 21, 22, 23 | FIRE SUPPRESSION, PLUMBING & HVAC | 99.8 | 118.9 | 107.7 | 100.0 | 70.3 | 87.8 | 97.5 | 70.3 | 86.3 | 97.5 | 69.8 | 86.1 | 99.9 | 70.3 | 87.8 | 97.4 | 70.3 | 86.3 |
| 26, 27, 3370 | ELECTRICAL, COMMUNICATIONS & UTIL. | 93.7 | 122.9 | 108.0 | 87.1 | 76.0 | 81.6 | 87.1 | 76.0 | 81.6 | 84.7 | 76.0 | 80.4 | 85.3 | 76.0 | 80.7 | 84.5 | 76.0 | 80.3 |
| MF2004 | WEIGHTED AVERAGE | 96.3 | 118.6 | 105.8 | 99.5 | 76.1 | 89.5 | 100.6 | 76.1 | 90.1 | 98.4 | 74.5 | 88.2 | 100.0 | 76.1 | 89.8 | 99.8 | 76.1 | 89.7 |

## NEW MEXICO

| DIVISION | | LAS CRUCES 880 | | | LAS VEGAS 877 | | | ROSWELL 882 | | | SANTA FE 875 | | | SOCORRO 878 | | | TRUTH/CONSEQUENCES 879 | | |
|---|---|---|---|---|---|---|---|---|---|---|---|---|---|---|---|---|---|---|---|
| | | MAT. | INST. | TOTAL | MAT. | INST. | TOTAL | MAT. | INST. | TOTAL | MAT. | INST. | TOTAL | MAT. | INST. | TOTAL | MAT. | INST. | TOTAL |
| 015433 | CONTRACTOR EQUIPMENT | | 86.4 | 86.4 | | 115.7 | 115.7 | | 115.7 | 115.7 | | 115.7 | 115.7 | | 115.7 | 115.7 | | 86.4 | 86.4 |
| 0241, 31 - 34 | SITE & INFRASTRUCTURE, DEMOLITION | 90.0 | 86.0 | 87.3 | 84.5 | 110.3 | 102.4 | 89.4 | 110.3 | 103.9 | 79.8 | 110.3 | 101.0 | 80.8 | 110.3 | 101.3 | 101.7 | 86.1 | 90.8 |
| 0310 | Concrete Forming & Accessories | 94.8 | 67.3 | 71.1 | 97.5 | 69.1 | 73.0 | 97.5 | 68.9 | 72.9 | 96.5 | 69.1 | 72.9 | 97.5 | 69.1 | 73.1 | 94.8 | 67.5 | 71.2 |
| 0320 | Concrete Reinforcing | 107.2 | 52.4 | 80.8 | 110.1 | 70.2 | 90.8 | 112.3 | 52.7 | 83.6 | 111.0 | 70.3 | 91.4 | 112.3 | 70.3 | 92.0 | 105.9 | 52.4 | 80.1 |
| 0330 | Cast-in-Place Concrete | 95.2 | 66.0 | 84.4 | 106.5 | 75.0 | 94.8 | 100.8 | 74.9 | 91.2 | 109.1 | 75.0 | 96.5 | 104.3 | 75.0 | 93.5 | 114.4 | 66.0 | 96.5 |
| 03 | CONCRETE | 89.9 | 64.7 | 78.3 | 109.8 | 72.3 | 92.5 | 112.8 | 68.9 | 92.5 | 110.2 | 72.4 | 92.7 | 108.5 | 72.4 | 91.8 | 102.6 | 64.8 | 85.1 |
| 04 | MASONRY | 108.4 | 63.4 | 81.5 | 112.8 | 63.8 | 83.5 | 123.0 | 66.1 | 89.0 | 116.5 | 66.1 | 86.4 | 112.7 | 66.1 | 84.8 | 109.9 | 63.4 | 82.1 |
| 05 | METALS | 99.9 | 72.0 | 91.8 | 98.9 | 89.0 | 96.0 | 100.0 | 80.2 | 94.2 | 100.0 | 89.2 | 96.8 | 99.2 | 89.2 | 96.3 | 98.8 | 72.1 | 91.0 |
| 06 | WOOD, PLASTICS & COMPOSITES | 85.0 | 68.6 | 76.1 | 93.6 | 69.9 | 80.9 | 93.6 | 69.9 | 80.9 | 92.9 | 69.9 | 80.5 | 93.6 | 69.9 | 80.9 | 85.0 | 68.6 | 76.1 |
| 07 | THERMAL & MOISTURE PROTECTION | 84.3 | 69.1 | 78.3 | 98.1 | 74.4 | 88.8 | 98.7 | 75.0 | 89.4 | 97.9 | 75.0 | 89.0 | 98.0 | 75.0 | 89.0 | 84.8 | 69.1 | 78.7 |
| 08 | OPENINGS | 86.1 | 66.1 | 81.2 | 92.7 | 72.4 | 87.7 | 92.5 | 66.9 | 86.2 | 92.7 | 72.4 | 87.7 | 92.5 | 72.4 | 87.6 | 86.1 | 66.1 | 81.2 |
| 0920 | Plaster & Gypsum Board | 81.5 | 68.6 | 73.6 | 79.7 | 68.6 | 72.9 | 79.7 | 68.6 | 72.9 | 87.4 | 68.6 | 75.8 | 79.7 | 68.6 | 72.9 | 81.5 | 68.6 | 73.6 |
| 0950, 0980 | Ceilings & Acoustic Treatment | 98.0 | 68.6 | 79.9 | 105.6 | 68.6 | 82.9 | 105.6 | 68.6 | 82.9 | 105.6 | 68.6 | 82.9 | 105.6 | 68.6 | 82.9 | 98.0 | 68.6 | 79.9 |
| 0960 | Flooring | 140.1 | 67.2 | 120.2 | 105.9 | 71.1 | 96.4 | 105.9 | 71.1 | 96.4 | 105.9 | 71.1 | 96.4 | 105.9 | 71.1 | 96.4 | 140.1 | 67.2 | 120.2 |
| 0970, 0990 | Wall Finishes & Painting/Coating | 91.9 | 57.2 | 71.1 | 98.8 | 57.2 | 73.8 | 98.8 | 57.2 | 73.8 | 98.8 | 57.2 | 73.8 | 98.8 | 57.2 | 73.8 | 91.9 | 57.2 | 71.1 |
| 09 | FINISHES | 112.9 | 66.3 | 88.5 | 99.1 | 68.1 | 82.9 | 99.7 | 68.1 | 83.2 | 100.3 | 68.1 | 83.5 | 99.0 | 68.1 | 82.9 | 113.5 | 66.3 | 88.8 |
| COVERS | DIVS. 10 - 14, 25, 28, 41, 43, 44 | 100.0 | 72.1 | 94.3 | 100.0 | 75.6 | 95.0 | 100.0 | 75.6 | 95.0 | 100.0 | 75.6 | 95.0 | 100.0 | 75.6 | 95.0 | 100.0 | 72.2 | 94.3 |
| 21, 22, 23 | FIRE SUPPRESSION, PLUMBING & HVAC | 100.2 | 69.8 | 87.7 | 97.4 | 70.3 | 86.3 | 99.9 | 70.1 | 87.7 | 99.9 | 70.3 | 87.8 | 97.4 | 70.3 | 86.3 | 97.3 | 69.8 | 86.0 |
| 26, 27, 3370 | ELECTRICAL, COMMUNICATIONS & UTIL. | 86.3 | 58.7 | 72.8 | 87.1 | 76.0 | 81.6 | 86.1 | 76.0 | 81.1 | 94.0 | 76.0 | 85.1 | 85.0 | 76.0 | 80.6 | 89.2 | 75.9 | 82.7 |
| MF2004 | WEIGHTED AVERAGE | 96.6 | 67.9 | 84.3 | 98.3 | 75.9 | 88.7 | 100.0 | 74.6 | 89.1 | 100.0 | 76.1 | 89.8 | 97.8 | 76.1 | 88.6 | 98.1 | 70.4 | 86.2 |

## NEW MEXICO / NEW YORK

| DIVISION | | TUCUMCARI 884 MAT. | INST. | TOTAL | ALBANY 120-122 MAT. | INST. | TOTAL | BINGHAMTON 137-139 MAT. | INST. | TOTAL | BRONX 104 MAT. | INST. | TOTAL | BROOKLYN 112 MAT. | INST. | TOTAL | BUFFALO 140-142 MAT. | INST. | TOTAL |
|---|---|---|---|---|---|---|---|---|---|---|---|---|---|---|---|---|---|---|---|
| 015433 | CONTRACTOR EQUIPMENT | | 115.7 | 115.7 | | 115.6 | 115.6 | | 115.9 | 115.9 | | 115.7 | 115.7 | | 116.9 | 116.9 | | 94.5 | 94.5 |
| 0241, 31 - 34 | SITE & INFRASTRUCTURE, DEMOLITION | 87.2 | 110.3 | 103.3 | 72.5 | 106.5 | 96.2 | 94.4 | 90.1 | 91.4 | 123.1 | 126.1 | 125.2 | 120.6 | 130.5 | 127.5 | 93.9 | 95.7 | 95.1 |
| 0310 | Concrete Forming & Accessories | 97.5 | 68.8 | 72.7 | 96.9 | 90.2 | 91.2 | 102.1 | 81.7 | 84.5 | 104.1 | 170.5 | 161.3 | 108.6 | 170.1 | 161.6 | 97.8 | 110.9 | 109.1 |
| 0320 | Concrete Reinforcing | 110.1 | 52.7 | 82.4 | 99.9 | 94.5 | 97.3 | 98.9 | 91.6 | 95.4 | 106.1 | 189.1 | 146.1 | 100.3 | 189.1 | 143.0 | 95.2 | 102.8 | 98.9 |
| 0330 | Cast-in-Place Concrete | 100.8 | 74.9 | 91.2 | 85.8 | 102.1 | 91.9 | 104.4 | 91.9 | 99.8 | 95.1 | 157.7 | 118.3 | 106.3 | 155.8 | 124.7 | 114.1 | 114.9 | 114.4 |
| 03 | CONCRETE | 111.2 | 68.8 | 91.6 | 99.5 | 96.0 | 97.9 | 100.3 | 88.9 | 95.0 | 100.9 | 167.9 | 131.8 | 112.4 | 167.1 | 137.6 | 108.5 | 110.0 | 109.2 |
| 04 | MASONRY | 126.8 | 66.1 | 90.5 | 89.9 | 100.1 | 96.0 | 107.2 | 84.0 | 93.3 | 96.3 | 158.7 | 133.7 | 116.8 | 158.7 | 141.8 | 108.6 | 115.6 | 112.7 |
| 05 | METALS | 98.8 | 80.1 | 93.4 | 96.2 | 106.5 | 99.2 | 92.8 | 116.3 | 99.6 | 93.9 | 144.3 | 108.6 | 101.3 | 143.4 | 113.6 | 101.2 | 94.5 | 99.2 |
| 06 | WOOD, PLASTICS & COMPOSITES | 93.6 | 69.9 | 80.9 | 94.6 | 88.1 | 91.1 | 105.0 | 83.0 | 93.2 | 101.8 | 176.5 | 142.0 | 107.3 | 176.1 | 144.3 | 99.3 | 110.6 | 105.4 |
| 07 | THERMAL & MOISTURE PROTECTION | 98.6 | 75.0 | 89.4 | 90.7 | 90.8 | 90.7 | 103.7 | 83.1 | 95.7 | 109.9 | 156.3 | 128.0 | 108.2 | 155.8 | 126.7 | 101.3 | 107.3 | 103.6 |
| 08 | OPENINGS | 92.5 | 66.9 | 86.2 | 96.5 | 84.9 | 93.7 | 91.5 | 80.0 | 88.7 | 91.8 | 167.7 | 110.5 | 90.9 | 167.0 | 109.7 | 95.7 | 100.4 | 96.9 |
| 0920 | Plaster & Gypsum Board | 79.7 | 68.6 | 72.9 | 107.3 | 87.6 | 95.1 | 118.2 | 82.1 | 95.9 | 118.5 | 178.0 | 155.2 | 113.0 | 178.0 | 153.1 | 95.3 | 110.6 | 104.7 |
| 0950, 0980 | Ceilings & Acoustic Treatment | 105.6 | 68.6 | 82.9 | 92.9 | 87.6 | 89.6 | 97.2 | 82.1 | 87.9 | 87.0 | 178.0 | 142.9 | 79.4 | 178.0 | 139.9 | 92.3 | 110.6 | 103.5 |
| 0960 | Flooring | 105.9 | 71.1 | 96.4 | 84.5 | 89.3 | 85.8 | 94.9 | 84.4 | 92.0 | 91.8 | 169.6 | 112.9 | 101.3 | 169.6 | 119.9 | 94.1 | 114.4 | 99.6 |
| 0970, 0990 | Wall Finishes & Painting/Coating | 98.8 | 57.2 | 73.8 | 83.0 | 79.9 | 81.2 | 87.7 | 84.2 | 85.6 | 91.1 | 142.1 | 121.8 | 111.1 | 142.1 | 129.8 | 86.8 | 111.2 | 101.5 |
| 09 | FINISHES | 99.5 | 68.1 | 83.1 | 94.0 | 88.8 | 91.3 | 97.3 | 82.4 | 89.5 | 100.4 | 168.3 | 136.0 | 106.8 | 168.0 | 138.8 | 91.5 | 112.3 | 102.4 |
| COVERS | DIVS. 10 - 14, 25, 28, 41, 43, 44 | 100.0 | 75.6 | 95.0 | 100.0 | 87.7 | 97.5 | 100.0 | 84.0 | 96.7 | 100.0 | 136.0 | 107.4 | 100.0 | 135.0 | 107.2 | 100.0 | 106.2 | 101.3 |
| 21, 22, 23 | FIRE SUPPRESSION, PLUMBING & HVAC | 97.5 | 69.8 | 86.1 | 100.0 | 87.0 | 94.7 | 100.5 | 79.8 | 92.0 | 100.3 | 163.5 | 126.3 | 99.7 | 163.4 | 125.9 | 99.8 | 94.6 | 97.6 |
| 26, 27, 3370 | ELECTRICAL, COMMUNICATIONS & UTIL. | 87.1 | 76.0 | 81.6 | 104.1 | 86.8 | 95.6 | 102.8 | 80.6 | 91.9 | 100.3 | 164.9 | 132.0 | 103.7 | 164.9 | 133.7 | 99.4 | 97.3 | 98.4 |
| MF2004 | WEIGHTED AVERAGE | 99.3 | 74.5 | 88.7 | 97.3 | 93.2 | 95.5 | 98.6 | 86.3 | 93.3 | 99.3 | 158.9 | 124.8 | 103.5 | 158.9 | 127.2 | 100.2 | 102.7 | 101.3 |

## NEW YORK

| DIVISION | | ELMIRA 148-149 MAT. | INST. | TOTAL | FAR ROCKAWAY 116 MAT. | INST. | TOTAL | FLUSHING 113 MAT. | INST. | TOTAL | GLENS FALLS 128 MAT. | INST. | TOTAL | HICKSVILLE 115,117,118 MAT. | INST. | TOTAL | JAMAICA 114 MAT. | INST. | TOTAL |
|---|---|---|---|---|---|---|---|---|---|---|---|---|---|---|---|---|---|---|---|
| 015433 | CONTRACTOR EQUIPMENT | | 117.6 | 117.6 | | 116.9 | 116.9 | | 116.9 | 116.9 | | 115.6 | 115.6 | | 116.9 | 116.9 | | 116.9 | 116.9 |
| 0241, 31 - 34 | SITE & INFRASTRUCTURE, DEMOLITION | 89.5 | 90.5 | 90.2 | 125.0 | 130.5 | 128.9 | 125.1 | 130.5 | 128.9 | 62.6 | 105.9 | 92.8 | 113.0 | 130.2 | 125.0 | 118.5 | 130.5 | 126.9 |
| 0310 | Concrete Forming & Accessories | 82.3 | 69.2 | 71.0 | 94.3 | 170.1 | 159.6 | 98.3 | 170.1 | 160.2 | 84.7 | 83.5 | 83.7 | 90.6 | 148.0 | 140.0 | 98.3 | 170.1 | 160.2 |
| 0320 | Concrete Reinforcing | 96.4 | 87.9 | 92.3 | 100.3 | 189.1 | 143.0 | 102.0 | 189.1 | 144.0 | 99.6 | 94.4 | 97.1 | 100.3 | 188.5 | 142.8 | 100.3 | 189.1 | 143.0 |
| 0330 | Cast-in-Place Concrete | 106.6 | 74.1 | 94.6 | 115.0 | 155.8 | 130.1 | 115.0 | 155.8 | 130.1 | 79.3 | 98.3 | 86.4 | 97.6 | 155.8 | 119.1 | 106.3 | 155.8 | 124.7 |
| 03 | CONCRETE | 102.0 | 76.8 | 90.4 | 118.9 | 167.1 | 141.2 | 119.5 | 167.1 | 141.4 | 89.9 | 91.7 | 90.7 | 103.8 | 157.1 | 128.4 | 111.7 | 167.1 | 137.3 |
| 04 | MASONRY | 104.8 | 66.0 | 81.6 | 121.1 | 158.7 | 143.6 | 114.7 | 158.7 | 141.0 | 92.7 | 93.6 | 93.3 | 111.1 | 155.6 | 137.7 | 118.9 | 158.7 | 142.7 |
| 05 | METALS | 96.6 | 116.8 | 102.5 | 101.4 | 143.4 | 113.6 | 101.4 | 143.4 | 113.6 | 92.6 | 106.1 | 96.5 | 102.8 | 140.8 | 113.8 | 101.4 | 143.4 | 113.6 |
| 06 | WOOD, PLASTICS & COMPOSITES | 82.8 | 67.5 | 74.6 | 90.6 | 176.1 | 136.6 | 95.4 | 176.1 | 138.8 | 81.2 | 82.7 | 82.0 | 86.8 | 147.5 | 119.5 | 95.4 | 176.1 | 138.8 |
| 07 | THERMAL & MOISTURE PROTECTION | 101.7 | 73.8 | 90.8 | 108.0 | 155.8 | 126.7 | 108.1 | 155.8 | 126.7 | 90.2 | 87.4 | 89.2 | 107.7 | 142.8 | 121.3 | 107.9 | 155.8 | 126.6 |
| 08 | OPENINGS | 96.7 | 71.0 | 90.4 | 89.3 | 167.0 | 108.5 | 89.3 | 167.0 | 108.5 | 90.1 | 82.0 | 88.1 | 89.3 | 152.8 | 104.9 | 89.3 | 167.0 | 108.5 |
| 0920 | Plaster & Gypsum Board | 90.9 | 66.4 | 75.8 | 107.2 | 178.0 | 150.9 | 108.9 | 178.0 | 151.5 | 105.2 | 82.1 | 90.9 | 106.5 | 148.7 | 132.6 | 108.9 | 178.0 | 151.5 |
| 0950, 0980 | Ceilings & Acoustic Treatment | 88.9 | 66.4 | 75.1 | 79.4 | 178.0 | 139.9 | 79.4 | 178.0 | 139.9 | 90.5 | 82.1 | 85.3 | 78.4 | 148.7 | 121.6 | 79.4 | 178.0 | 139.9 |
| 0960 | Flooring | 84.0 | 68.6 | 79.8 | 95.7 | 169.6 | 115.8 | 97.3 | 169.6 | 117.0 | 75.8 | 89.3 | 79.4 | 94.3 | 79.8 | 90.4 | 97.3 | 169.6 | 117.0 |
| 0970, 0990 | Wall Finishes & Painting/Coating | 85.2 | 82.6 | 83.6 | 111.1 | 142.1 | 129.8 | 111.1 | 142.1 | 129.8 | 83.0 | 79.9 | 81.2 | 111.1 | 142.1 | 129.8 | 111.1 | 142.1 | 129.8 |
| 09 | FINISHES | 86.7 | 69.6 | 77.8 | 104.6 | 168.0 | 137.8 | 105.4 | 168.0 | 138.2 | 89.7 | 84.0 | 86.7 | 103.0 | 133.2 | 118.8 | 104.9 | 168.0 | 138.0 |
| COVERS | DIVS. 10 - 14, 25, 28, 41, 43, 44 | 100.0 | 81.3 | 96.2 | 100.0 | 135.0 | 107.2 | 100.0 | 135.0 | 107.2 | 100.0 | 59.5 | 91.7 | 100.0 | 132.3 | 106.6 | 100.0 | 135.0 | 107.2 |
| 21, 22, 23 | FIRE SUPPRESSION, PLUMBING & HVAC | 95.8 | 79.2 | 89.0 | 95.6 | 163.4 | 123.4 | 95.6 | 163.4 | 123.4 | 96.2 | 83.4 | 90.9 | 99.7 | 143.7 | 117.8 | 95.6 | 163.4 | 123.4 |
| 26, 27, 3370 | ELECTRICAL, COMMUNICATIONS & UTIL. | 98.2 | 90.8 | 94.6 | 110.8 | 164.9 | 137.4 | 110.8 | 164.9 | 137.4 | 98.3 | 86.8 | 92.6 | 102.8 | 148.1 | 125.1 | 101.8 | 164.9 | 132.8 |
| MF2004 | WEIGHTED AVERAGE | 97.0 | 81.7 | 90.4 | 104.0 | 158.9 | 127.5 | 103.8 | 158.9 | 127.4 | 92.8 | 89.4 | 91.4 | 101.4 | 144.7 | 119.9 | 101.9 | 158.9 | 126.3 |

## NEW YORK

| DIVISION | | JAMESTOWN 147 MAT. | INST. | TOTAL | KINGSTON 124 MAT. | INST. | TOTAL | LONG ISLAND CITY 111 MAT. | INST. | TOTAL | MONTICELLO 127 MAT. | INST. | TOTAL | MOUNT VERNON 105 MAT. | INST. | TOTAL | NEW ROCHELLE 108 MAT. | INST. | TOTAL |
|---|---|---|---|---|---|---|---|---|---|---|---|---|---|---|---|---|---|---|---|
| 015433 | CONTRACTOR EQUIPMENT | | 90.8 | 90.8 | | 116.9 | 116.9 | | 116.9 | 116.9 | | 116.9 | 116.9 | | 115.7 | 115.7 | | 115.7 | 115.7 |
| 0241, 31 - 34 | SITE & INFRASTRUCTURE, DEMOLITION | 90.8 | 94.0 | 92.6 | 120.5 | 127.6 | 125.4 | 122.1 | 130.5 | 128.0 | 115.4 | 127.7 | 124.0 | 133.0 | 122.4 | 125.6 | 131.3 | 122.4 | 125.1 |
| 0310 | Concrete Forming & Accessories | 82.4 | 81.2 | 81.4 | 86.4 | 106.4 | 103.6 | 102.9 | 170.1 | 160.8 | 93.8 | 107.4 | 105.5 | 93.9 | 134.0 | 130.6 | 109.4 | 134.0 | 130.6 |
| 0320 | Concrete Reinforcing | 96.5 | 83.1 | 90.1 | 99.9 | 122.6 | 110.8 | 100.3 | 189.1 | 143.0 | 99.2 | 122.6 | 110.5 | 105.0 | 188.0 | 145.0 | 105.2 | 188.0 | 145.1 |
| 0330 | Cast-in-Place Concrete | 110.6 | 103.3 | 107.9 | 107.1 | 131.9 | 116.3 | 109.7 | 155.8 | 126.8 | 100.3 | 133.2 | 112.4 | 106.4 | 133.5 | 116.4 | 106.4 | 133.5 | 116.4 |
| 03 | CONCRETE | 105.3 | 89.1 | 97.8 | 112.8 | 118.0 | 115.2 | 115.2 | 167.1 | 139.1 | 107.2 | 118.9 | 112.6 | 110.9 | 143.1 | 125.7 | 110.3 | 143.1 | 125.4 |
| 04 | MASONRY | 113.5 | 89.2 | 99.0 | 108.3 | 134.5 | 124.0 | 113.6 | 158.7 | 140.6 | 101.3 | 136.5 | 122.4 | 102.6 | 132.0 | 120.2 | 102.6 | 132.0 | 120.2 |
| 05 | METALS | 93.8 | 81.6 | 90.3 | 101.3 | 111.4 | 104.3 | 101.3 | 143.4 | 113.6 | 101.3 | 111.7 | 104.3 | 93.7 | 138.2 | 106.6 | 94.0 | 138.2 | 106.8 |
| 06 | WOOD, PLASTICS & COMPOSITES | 81.6 | 76.3 | 78.7 | 82.5 | 100.8 | 92.4 | 101.1 | 176.1 | 141.5 | 91.0 | 100.8 | 96.3 | 90.8 | 135.3 | 114.8 | 109.0 | 135.3 | 123.2 |
| 07 | THERMAL & MOISTURE PROTECTION | 101.3 | 87.9 | 96.0 | 109.8 | 135.0 | 119.6 | 108.0 | 155.8 | 126.7 | 109.5 | 135.9 | 119.8 | 110.8 | 139.6 | 122.0 | 110.9 | 139.6 | 122.1 |
| 08 | OPENINGS | 96.5 | 77.1 | 91.7 | 94.6 | 112.7 | 99.1 | 89.3 | 167.0 | 108.4 | 89.3 | 112.7 | 95.1 | 91.8 | 146.2 | 105.2 | 91.9 | 146.2 | 105.3 |
| 0920 | Plaster & Gypsum Board | 86.9 | 75.5 | 79.8 | 103.8 | 100.8 | 102.0 | 111.6 | 178.0 | 152.6 | 106.2 | 100.8 | 102.9 | 114.1 | 135.9 | 127.6 | 123.6 | 135.9 | 131.2 |
| 0950, 0980 | Ceilings & Acoustic Treatment | 85.5 | 75.5 | 79.3 | 75.1 | 100.8 | 90.9 | 79.4 | 178.0 | 139.9 | 75.1 | 100.8 | 90.9 | 84.5 | 135.9 | 116.0 | 84.5 | 135.9 | 116.0 |
| 0960 | Flooring | 86.7 | 82.1 | 85.5 | 88.4 | 83.8 | 87.1 | 99.0 | 169.6 | 118.2 | 91.4 | 83.8 | 89.3 | 83.6 | 164.0 | 105.5 | 91.8 | 164.0 | 111.5 |
| 0970, 0990 | Wall Finishes & Painting/Coating | 86.8 | 81.4 | 83.6 | 109.0 | 116.8 | 113.7 | 111.1 | 142.1 | 129.8 | 109.0 | 103.0 | 105.4 | 89.0 | 142.1 | 120.9 | 89.0 | 142.1 | 120.9 |
| 09 | FINISHES | 86.3 | 80.7 | 83.4 | 100.5 | 101.2 | 100.9 | 106.0 | 168.0 | 138.5 | 101.4 | 100.2 | 100.8 | 97.5 | 140.6 | 120.0 | 101.2 | 140.6 | 121.8 |
| COVERS | DIVS. 10 - 14, 25, 28, 41, 43, 44 | 100.0 | 90.5 | 98.0 | 100.0 | 113.0 | 102.7 | 100.0 | 135.0 | 107.2 | 100.0 | 113.7 | 102.8 | 100.0 | 126.9 | 105.5 | 100.0 | 126.9 | 105.5 |
| 21, 22, 23 | FIRE SUPPRESSION, PLUMBING & HVAC | 95.6 | 73.8 | 86.7 | 96.1 | 98.8 | 97.2 | 99.7 | 163.4 | 125.9 | 96.1 | 117.0 | 104.7 | 96.3 | 125.6 | 108.3 | 96.3 | 125.6 | 108.3 |
| 26, 27, 3370 | ELECTRICAL, COMMUNICATIONS & UTIL. | 96.9 | 83.5 | 90.3 | 100.1 | 115.9 | 107.9 | 102.3 | 164.9 | 133.1 | 100.1 | 115.9 | 107.9 | 97.8 | 141.5 | 119.3 | 97.8 | 141.5 | 119.3 |
| MF2004 | WEIGHTED AVERAGE | 97.1 | 82.9 | 91.0 | 101.6 | 113.4 | 106.6 | 103.3 | 158.9 | 127.1 | 100.0 | 117.5 | 107.5 | 99.5 | 135.0 | 114.7 | 99.9 | 135.0 | 114.9 |

## NEW YORK

| DIVISION | | NEW YORK 100-102 MAT. | INST. | TOTAL | NIAGARA FALLS 143 MAT. | INST. | TOTAL | PLATTSBURGH 129 MAT. | INST. | TOTAL | POUGHKEEPSIE 125-126 MAT. | INST. | TOTAL | QUEENS 110 MAT. | INST. | TOTAL | RIVERHEAD 119 MAT. | INST. | TOTAL |
|---|---|---|---|---|---|---|---|---|---|---|---|---|---|---|---|---|---|---|---|
| 015433 | CONTRACTOR EQUIPMENT | | 116.1 | 116.1 | | 90.8 | 90.8 | | 97.8 | 97.8 | | 116.9 | 116.9 | | 116.9 | 116.9 | | 116.9 | 116.9 |
| 0241, 31-34 | SITE & INFRASTRUCTURE, DEMOLITION | 133.2 | 127.3 | 129.0 | 93.1 | 92.6 | 92.7 | 85.4 | 102.6 | 97.4 | 116.4 | 127.8 | 124.3 | 116.6 | 130.5 | 126.3 | 113.8 | 130.2 | 125.3 |
| 0310 | Concrete Forming & Accessories | 108.7 | 176.7 | 167.2 | 82.3 | 110.6 | 106.7 | 89.3 | 78.8 | 80.3 | 86.4 | 114.0 | 110.2 | 90.8 | 170.1 | 159.1 | 95.5 | 148.0 | 140.7 |
| 0320 | Concrete Reinforcing | 112.3 | 191.4 | 150.4 | 95.2 | 98.9 | 97.0 | 104.1 | 94.1 | 99.2 | 99.9 | 122.8 | 110.9 | 102.0 | 189.1 | 144.0 | 102.2 | 188.5 | 143.8 |
| 0330 | Cast-in-Place Concrete | 107.1 | 169.6 | 130.2 | 114.5 | 108.5 | 112.3 | 97.0 | 94.4 | 96.0 | 103.7 | 133.5 | 114.7 | 101.0 | 155.8 | 121.3 | 99.2 | 155.8 | 120.2 |
| 03 | CONCRETE | 111.7 | 175.1 | 140.9 | 107.8 | 106.8 | 107.4 | 103.9 | 86.8 | 96.0 | 109.7 | 122.0 | 115.3 | 107.2 | 167.1 | 134.9 | 104.6 | 157.1 | 128.8 |
| 04 | MASONRY | 107.2 | 171.7 | 145.7 | 122.0 | 113.3 | 116.8 | 88.8 | 87.5 | 88.0 | 101.5 | 136.5 | 122.4 | 107.8 | 158.7 | 138.3 | 116.8 | 155.6 | 140.0 |
| 05 | METALS | 105.6 | 144.9 | 117.0 | 96.6 | 89.8 | 94.6 | 97.2 | 83.7 | 93.2 | 101.4 | 112.7 | 104.7 | 101.3 | 143.4 | 113.6 | 103.2 | 140.8 | 114.1 |
| 06 | WOOD, PLASTICS & COMPOSITES | 106.4 | 177.3 | 144.6 | 81.5 | 109.8 | 96.8 | 88.6 | 76.5 | 82.1 | 82.5 | 108.6 | 96.6 | 87.0 | 176.1 | 135.0 | 92.4 | 147.5 | 122.1 |
| 07 | THERMAL & MOISTURE PROTECTION | 110.2 | 165.8 | 131.9 | 101.3 | 104.1 | 102.4 | 101.9 | 82.2 | 94.2 | 109.8 | 136.7 | 120.3 | 107.7 | 155.8 | 126.5 | 108.3 | 142.8 | 121.7 |
| 08 | OPENINGS | 97.1 | 172.1 | 115.6 | 96.5 | 98.1 | 96.9 | 99.6 | 78.6 | 94.5 | 94.6 | 116.9 | 100.1 | 96.3 | 167.0 | 108.4 | 89.3 | 152.8 | 105.0 |
| 0920 | Plaster & Gypsum Board | 126.3 | 178.9 | 158.8 | 86.9 | 109.9 | 101.1 | 121.6 | 75.1 | 92.9 | 103.8 | 108.8 | 106.9 | 106.5 | 178.0 | 150.6 | 108.7 | 148.7 | 133.4 |
| 0950, 0980 | Ceilings & Acoustic Treatment | 111.8 | 178.9 | 153.0 | 85.5 | 109.9 | 100.4 | 100.0 | 75.1 | 84.7 | 75.1 | 108.8 | 95.8 | 79.4 | 178.0 | 139.9 | 81.8 | 148.7 | 122.9 |
| 0960 | Flooring | 93.3 | 169.6 | 114.0 | 86.6 | 107.8 | 92.4 | 97.4 | 89.3 | 95.2 | 88.4 | 143.3 | 103.3 | 94.3 | 169.6 | 114.8 | 95.7 | 79.8 | 91.3 |
| 0970, 0990 | Wall Finishes & Painting/Coating | 91.1 | 158.9 | 131.8 | 86.8 | 104.7 | 97.6 | 103.1 | 79.9 | 89.2 | 109.0 | 103.0 | 105.4 | 111.1 | 142.1 | 129.8 | 111.1 | 142.1 | 129.8 |
| 09 | FINISHES | 108.6 | 174.0 | 142.8 | 86.4 | 110.2 | 98.9 | 98.9 | 80.5 | 89.3 | 100.3 | 117.2 | 109.2 | 103.4 | 168.0 | 137.2 | 104.5 | 133.2 | 119.5 |
| COVERS | DIVS. 10-14, 25, 28, 41, 43, 44 | 100.0 | 140.9 | 108.4 | 100.0 | 97.4 | 99.5 | 100.0 | 54.4 | 90.7 | 100.0 | 114.7 | 103.0 | 100.0 | 135.0 | 107.2 | 100.0 | 132.3 | 106.6 |
| 21, 22, 23 | FIRE SUPPRESSION, PLUMBING & HVAC | 100.3 | 170.4 | 129.1 | 95.6 | 95.4 | 95.5 | 96.1 | 83.3 | 90.8 | 96.1 | 101.0 | 98.1 | 99.7 | 163.4 | 125.9 | 99.9 | 143.7 | 117.9 |
| 26, 27, 3370 | ELECTRICAL, COMMUNICATIONS & UTIL. | 108.0 | 178.2 | 142.5 | 95.5 | 93.3 | 94.4 | 94.5 | 84.3 | 89.5 | 100.1 | 115.9 | 107.9 | 102.8 | 164.9 | 133.3 | 104.5 | 148.1 | 125.9 |
| MF2004 | WEIGHTED AVERAGE | 105.4 | 166.0 | 131.3 | 98.2 | 100.2 | 99.1 | 97.4 | 84.5 | 91.9 | 100.7 | 117.1 | 107.7 | 101.6 | 158.9 | 126.1 | 102.3 | 144.7 | 120.4 |

## NEW YORK

| DIVISION | | ROCHESTER 144-146 MAT. | INST. | TOTAL | SCHENECTADY 123 MAT. | INST. | TOTAL | STATEN ISLAND 103 MAT. | INST. | TOTAL | SUFFERN 109 MAT. | INST. | TOTAL | SYRACUSE 130-132 MAT. | INST. | TOTAL | UTICA 133-135 MAT. | INST. | TOTAL |
|---|---|---|---|---|---|---|---|---|---|---|---|---|---|---|---|---|---|---|---|
| 015433 | CONTRACTOR EQUIPMENT | | 118.4 | 118.4 | | 115.6 | 115.6 | | 115.7 | 115.7 | | 115.7 | 115.7 | | 115.6 | 115.6 | | 115.6 | 115.6 |
| 0241, 31-34 | SITE & INFRASTRUCTURE, DEMOLITION | 70.4 | 109.4 | 97.6 | 72.3 | 106.4 | 96.0 | 138.1 | 125.8 | 129.6 | 127.6 | 122.7 | 124.2 | 93.2 | 106.5 | 102.5 | 70.5 | 104.8 | 94.4 |
| 0310 | Concrete Forming & Accessories | 98.7 | 96.0 | 96.4 | 101.7 | 89.6 | 91.3 | 93.3 | 169.0 | 158.5 | 102.9 | 128.8 | 125.2 | 101.0 | 88.9 | 90.6 | 102.3 | 81.0 | 83.9 |
| 0320 | Concrete Reinforcing | 96.1 | 89.2 | 92.8 | 98.5 | 94.5 | 96.6 | 106.1 | 189.1 | 146.1 | 105.2 | 122.7 | 113.6 | 99.9 | 88.7 | 94.5 | 99.9 | 88.4 | 94.3 |
| 0330 | Cast-in-Place Concrete | 102.5 | 99.3 | 101.3 | 95.9 | 101.2 | 97.9 | 106.4 | 155.4 | 124.5 | 103.1 | 129.6 | 112.9 | 96.9 | 95.3 | 96.3 | 88.6 | 89.6 | 89.0 |
| 03 | CONCRETE | 111.7 | 96.8 | 104.8 | 104.5 | 95.4 | 100.3 | 112.6 | 166.4 | 137.5 | 107.2 | 127.1 | 116.4 | 103.4 | 92.0 | 98.1 | 101.2 | 86.4 | 94.4 |
| 04 | MASONRY | 105.5 | 96.9 | 100.3 | 91.1 | 98.5 | 95.5 | 110.4 | 154.8 | 136.9 | 102.6 | 127.0 | 117.2 | 98.2 | 97.8 | 98.0 | 89.7 | 88.8 | 89.2 |
| 05 | METALS | 97.7 | 107.2 | 100.4 | 96.3 | 106.5 | 99.2 | 91.9 | 144.3 | 107.1 | 91.9 | 111.8 | 97.7 | 96.1 | 103.3 | 98.2 | 94.4 | 102.7 | 96.8 |
| 06 | WOOD, PLASTICS & COMPOSITES | 96.3 | 96.8 | 96.6 | 101.5 | 88.1 | 94.3 | 89.3 | 176.5 | 136.2 | 101.3 | 134.1 | 118.9 | 101.5 | 87.7 | 94.0 | 101.5 | 81.3 | 90.6 |
| 07 | THERMAL & MOISTURE PROTECTION | 97.1 | 96.6 | 96.9 | 91.4 | 90.1 | 90.9 | 110.2 | 154.6 | 127.5 | 110.8 | 132.4 | 119.2 | 101.2 | 94.4 | 98.5 | 91.2 | 90.0 | 90.8 |
| 08 | OPENINGS | 99.1 | 89.0 | 96.6 | 96.5 | 84.9 | 93.7 | 91.8 | 167.7 | 110.5 | 91.9 | 130.7 | 101.5 | 94.5 | 81.6 | 91.3 | 96.5 | 80.4 | 92.5 |
| 0920 | Plaster & Gypsum Board | 94.5 | 96.8 | 95.9 | 113.8 | 87.6 | 97.6 | 114.4 | 178.0 | 153.7 | 117.5 | 134.6 | 128.0 | 113.8 | 87.1 | 97.3 | 113.8 | 80.6 | 93.3 |
| 0950, 0980 | Ceilings & Acoustic Treatment | 91.5 | 96.8 | 94.8 | 97.2 | 87.6 | 91.3 | 87.0 | 178.0 | 142.9 | 84.5 | 134.6 | 115.2 | 97.2 | 87.1 | 91.0 | 97.2 | 80.6 | 87.0 |
| 0960 | Flooring | 83.8 | 104.2 | 89.3 | 84.1 | 89.3 | 85.5 | 87.2 | 169.6 | 109.6 | 87.5 | 55.5 | 78.8 | 85.9 | 88.7 | 86.6 | 84.1 | 83.8 | 84.0 |
| 0970, 0990 | Wall Finishes & Painting/Coating | 85.0 | 100.0 | 94.0 | 83.0 | 79.9 | 81.2 | 91.1 | 142.1 | 121.8 | 89.0 | 108.8 | 100.9 | 88.6 | 82.8 | 85.1 | 83.0 | 81.1 | 81.8 |
| 09 | FINISHES | 90.6 | 98.4 | 94.7 | 95.7 | 88.4 | 91.8 | 99.7 | 167.3 | 135.1 | 98.7 | 112.3 | 105.8 | 97.2 | 88.1 | 92.4 | 95.7 | 81.2 | 88.1 |
| COVERS | DIVS. 10-14, 25, 28, 41, 43, 44 | 100.0 | 90.3 | 98.0 | 100.0 | 87.2 | 97.4 | 100.0 | 134.5 | 107.1 | 100.0 | 124.9 | 105.1 | 100.0 | 94.8 | 98.9 | 100.0 | 83.2 | 96.6 |
| 21, 22, 23 | FIRE SUPPRESSION, PLUMBING & HVAC | 99.8 | 90.3 | 95.9 | 100.2 | 86.2 | 94.5 | 100.3 | 161.4 | 125.4 | 96.3 | 115.5 | 104.2 | 100.2 | 84.6 | 93.8 | 100.2 | 79.9 | 91.9 |
| 26, 27, 3370 | ELECTRICAL, COMMUNICATIONS & UTIL. | 102.0 | 88.7 | 95.5 | 102.9 | 86.8 | 95.0 | 100.3 | 164.9 | 132.0 | 105.5 | 125.1 | 115.1 | 102.9 | 89.6 | 96.3 | 100.4 | 89.3 | 94.9 |
| MF2004 | WEIGHTED AVERAGE | 99.6 | 96.0 | 98.1 | 98.1 | 92.7 | 95.8 | 101.3 | 157.6 | 125.4 | 99.7 | 121.1 | 108.9 | 99.1 | 92.1 | 96.1 | 97.0 | 87.8 | 93.0 |

## NEW YORK / NORTH CAROLINA

| DIVISION | | WATERTOWN 136 MAT. | INST. | TOTAL | WHITE PLAINS 106 MAT. | INST. | TOTAL | YONKERS 107 MAT. | INST. | TOTAL | ASHEVILLE 287-288 MAT. | INST. | TOTAL | CHARLOTTE 281-282 MAT. | INST. | TOTAL | DURHAM 277 MAT. | INST. | TOTAL |
|---|---|---|---|---|---|---|---|---|---|---|---|---|---|---|---|---|---|---|---|
| 015433 | CONTRACTOR EQUIPMENT | | 115.6 | 115.6 | | 115.7 | 115.7 | | 115.7 | 115.7 | | 93.8 | 93.8 | | 93.8 | 93.8 | | 100.3 | 100.3 |
| 0241, 31-34 | SITE & INFRASTRUCTURE, DEMOLITION | 79.0 | 106.8 | 98.3 | 122.6 | 122.4 | 122.5 | 132.5 | 122.2 | 125.3 | 108.2 | 73.0 | 83.7 | 109.8 | 73.0 | 84.2 | 108.3 | 82.8 | 90.5 |
| 0310 | Concrete Forming & Accessories | 86.4 | 84.2 | 84.5 | 108.2 | 134.0 | 130.4 | 108.4 | 134.1 | 130.5 | 95.9 | 42.4 | 49.8 | 100.6 | 44.5 | 52.3 | 98.3 | 42.9 | 50.6 |
| 0320 | Concrete Reinforcing | 100.5 | 78.4 | 89.9 | 105.2 | 188.0 | 145.1 | 109.3 | 188.0 | 147.2 | 97.1 | 46.8 | 72.9 | 97.6 | 43.7 | 71.6 | 98.7 | 54.7 | 77.5 |
| 0330 | Cast-in-Place Concrete | 103.2 | 77.9 | 93.8 | 94.4 | 133.5 | 108.9 | 105.7 | 133.5 | 116.0 | 101.3 | 48.1 | 81.6 | 109.0 | 50.4 | 87.3 | 102.9 | 48.4 | 82.7 |
| 03 | CONCRETE | 114.4 | 82.0 | 99.5 | 100.4 | 143.1 | 120.1 | 110.6 | 143.1 | 125.6 | 105.2 | 47.0 | 78.4 | 108.7 | 48.1 | 80.7 | 105.7 | 48.8 | 79.5 |
| 04 | MASONRY | 90.8 | 87.1 | 88.6 | 101.9 | 132.0 | 119.9 | 106.7 | 132.0 | 121.8 | 86.1 | 43.4 | 60.6 | 93.3 | 47.5 | 65.9 | 91.8 | 39.1 | 60.3 |
| 05 | METALS | 94.4 | 98.0 | 95.5 | 93.4 | 138.2 | 106.4 | 101.9 | 138.2 | 112.5 | 88.7 | 76.3 | 85.1 | 92.8 | 75.2 | 87.7 | 102.3 | 79.8 | 95.7 |
| 06 | WOOD, PLASTICS & COMPOSITES | 83.1 | 86.3 | 84.8 | 107.4 | 135.3 | 122.5 | 107.3 | 135.3 | 122.4 | 96.7 | 41.8 | 67.1 | 102.1 | 44.2 | 70.9 | 99.2 | 43.5 | 69.2 |
| 07 | THERMAL & MOISTURE PROTECTION | 91.5 | 86.8 | 89.7 | 110.6 | 139.6 | 121.9 | 110.9 | 139.6 | 122.1 | 103.1 | 46.2 | 80.9 | 100.5 | 47.9 | 80.0 | 103.9 | 48.4 | 82.3 |
| 08 | OPENINGS | 96.5 | 75.4 | 91.3 | 91.9 | 146.2 | 105.3 | 95.2 | 148.9 | 108.4 | 93.6 | 41.8 | 80.9 | 97.6 | 43.5 | 84.3 | 97.6 | 46.3 | 85.0 |
| 0920 | Plaster & Gypsum Board | 107.3 | 85.8 | 94.0 | 120.2 | 135.9 | 129.9 | 125.9 | 135.9 | 132.0 | 105.8 | 40.2 | 65.3 | 105.0 | 42.6 | 66.5 | 109.5 | 41.9 | 67.8 |
| 0950, 0980 | Ceilings & Acoustic Treatment | 97.2 | 85.8 | 90.2 | 84.5 | 135.9 | 116.0 | 110.1 | 135.9 | 125.9 | 91.5 | 40.2 | 60.0 | 94.1 | 42.6 | 62.5 | 96.7 | 41.9 | 63.0 |
| 0960 | Flooring | 76.4 | 83.8 | 78.4 | 89.8 | 164.0 | 110.0 | 89.3 | 164.0 | 109.7 | 102.6 | 48.2 | 87.8 | 106.1 | 48.3 | 90.4 | 106.7 | 48.2 | 90.8 |
| 0970, 0990 | Wall Finishes & Painting/Coating | 83.0 | 66.5 | 73.1 | 89.0 | 142.1 | 120.9 | 89.0 | 142.1 | 120.9 | 113.6 | 38.3 | 68.4 | 113.6 | 43.8 | 71.7 | 113.6 | 40.2 | 69.5 |
| 09 | FINISHES | 93.1 | 82.1 | 87.3 | 99.3 | 140.6 | 120.9 | 106.8 | 140.6 | 124.5 | 99.4 | 42.7 | 69.7 | 100.7 | 44.9 | 71.5 | 102.4 | 43.3 | 71.4 |
| COVERS | DIVS. 10-14, 25, 28, 41, 43, 44 | 100.0 | 70.2 | 93.9 | 100.0 | 126.9 | 105.5 | 100.0 | 126.9 | 105.5 | 100.0 | 76.3 | 95.1 | 100.0 | 76.9 | 95.3 | 100.0 | 71.2 | 94.1 |
| 21, 22, 23 | FIRE SUPPRESSION, PLUMBING & HVAC | 100.2 | 67.8 | 86.9 | 100.5 | 125.6 | 110.8 | 100.5 | 125.6 | 110.8 | 100.2 | 43.1 | 76.8 | 100.0 | 43.3 | 76.7 | 100.3 | 41.7 | 76.3 |
| 26, 27, 3370 | ELECTRICAL, COMMUNICATIONS & UTIL. | 102.9 | 84.3 | 93.8 | 97.8 | 141.5 | 119.3 | 105.5 | 141.5 | 123.2 | 97.9 | 41.3 | 70.1 | 100.2 | 53.8 | 77.4 | 98.8 | 52.3 | 76.0 |
| MF2004 | WEIGHTED AVERAGE | 98.8 | 83.0 | 92.0 | 99.2 | 135.0 | 114.5 | 104.1 | 135.1 | 117.4 | 97.5 | 49.8 | 77.1 | 99.7 | 52.6 | 79.5 | 100.9 | 52.2 | 80.1 |

## NORTH CAROLINA

| | DIVISION | ELIZABETH CITY 279 | | | FAYETTEVILLE 283 | | | GASTONIA 280 | | | GREENSBORO 270,272 - 274 | | | HICKORY 286 | | | KINSTON 285 | | |
|---|---|---|---|---|---|---|---|---|---|---|---|---|---|---|---|---|---|---|---|
| | | MAT. | INST. | TOTAL | MAT. | INST. | TOTAL | MAT. | INST. | TOTAL | MAT. | INST. | TOTAL | MAT. | INST. | TOTAL | MAT. | INST. | TOTAL |
| 015433 | CONTRACTOR EQUIPMENT | | 105.3 | 105.3 | | 100.3 | 100.3 | | 93.8 | 93.8 | | 100.3 | 100.3 | | 100.3 | 100.3 | | 100.3 | 100.3 |
| 0241, 31 - 34 | SITE & INFRASTRUCTURE, DEMOLITION | 114.2 | 84.0 | 93.2 | 107.0 | 82.9 | 90.2 | 107.7 | 73.0 | 83.5 | 108.2 | 82.9 | 90.6 | 107.4 | 82.9 | 90.3 | 106.0 | 82.6 | 89.7 |
| 0310 | Concrete Forming & Accessories | 83.9 | 36.7 | 43.2 | 95.3 | 43.7 | 50.9 | 102.8 | 43.5 | 51.7 | 98.0 | 43.7 | 51.2 | 91.5 | 41.4 | 48.3 | 87.8 | 34.8 | 42.1 |
| 0320 | Concrete Reinforcing | 96.6 | 45.5 | 72.0 | 100.9 | 54.9 | 78.7 | 97.6 | 46.7 | 73.1 | 97.6 | 54.6 | 76.9 | 97.1 | 21.2 | 60.5 | 96.6 | 20.5 | 60.0 |
| 0330 | Cast-in-Place Concrete | 103.1 | 35.2 | 78.0 | 106.2 | 51.7 | 86.0 | 99.0 | 56.4 | 83.2 | 102.2 | 49.8 | 82.8 | 101.2 | 49.4 | 82.0 | 97.7 | 38.7 | 75.9 |
| 03 | CONCRETE | 106.1 | 39.8 | 75.5 | 107.1 | 50.4 | 80.9 | 103.9 | 50.3 | 79.2 | 105.2 | 49.6 | 79.5 | 105.0 | 42.3 | 76.0 | 101.7 | 35.6 | 71.2 |
| 04 | MASONRY | 103.8 | 28.8 | 58.9 | 89.4 | 44.5 | 62.5 | 90.8 | 41.0 | 61.1 | 89.6 | 39.8 | 59.8 | 75.5 | 44.7 | 57.1 | 82.2 | 31.4 | 51.8 |
| 05 | METALS | 90.4 | 75.1 | 85.9 | 106.7 | 79.9 | 98.9 | 89.3 | 76.2 | 85.5 | 95.9 | 79.5 | 91.1 | 88.7 | 68.4 | 82.8 | 87.7 | 67.0 | 81.7 |
| 06 | WOOD, PLASTICS & COMPOSITES | 82.3 | 38.6 | 58.8 | 95.4 | 43.5 | 67.4 | 105.4 | 43.4 | 72.0 | 98.9 | 43.4 | 69.0 | 90.9 | 41.6 | 64.3 | 87.0 | 35.2 | 59.1 |
| 07 | THERMAL & MOISTURE PROTECTION | 103.2 | 33.5 | 76.0 | 103.0 | 46.8 | 81.1 | 103.4 | 46.5 | 81.2 | 103.6 | 45.8 | 81.1 | 103.4 | 45.0 | 80.6 | 103.3 | 34.0 | 76.3 |
| 08 | OPENINGS | 94.6 | 35.4 | 80.0 | 97.6 | 43.6 | 84.3 | 97.6 | 43.6 | 84.3 | 97.6 | 46.3 | 85.0 | 93.7 | 33.3 | 78.8 | 93.8 | 30.2 | 78.1 |
| 0920 | Plaster & Gypsum Board | 103.3 | 36.1 | 61.9 | 108.9 | 41.8 | 67.5 | 111.1 | 41.8 | 68.3 | 111.1 | 41.8 | 68.3 | 105.8 | 39.9 | 65.2 | 105.1 | 33.3 | 60.8 |
| 0950, 0980 | Ceilings & Acoustic Treatment | 96.7 | 36.1 | 59.5 | 92.4 | 41.8 | 61.4 | 96.7 | 41.8 | 63.0 | 96.7 | 41.8 | 63.0 | 91.5 | 39.9 | 59.8 | 95.8 | 33.3 | 57.5 |
| 0960 | Flooring | 96.1 | 15.5 | 74.2 | 102.7 | 48.2 | 87.9 | 106.7 | 48.2 | 90.8 | 106.7 | 44.5 | 89.8 | 102.4 | 37.1 | 84.6 | 99.2 | 21.2 | 78.0 |
| 0970, 0990 | Wall Finishes & Painting/Coating | 113.6 | 49.5 | 75.1 | 113.6 | 38.3 | 68.4 | 113.6 | 44.0 | 71.8 | 113.6 | 37.3 | 67.8 | 113.6 | 37.3 | 67.8 | 113.6 | 34.0 | 65.8 |
| 09 | FINISHES | 98.6 | 33.9 | 64.7 | 100.0 | 43.7 | 70.5 | 102.5 | 44.1 | 71.9 | 102.7 | 42.9 | 71.4 | 99.5 | 39.5 | 68.1 | 99.2 | 32.1 | 64.1 |
| COVERS | DIVS. 10 - 14, 25, 28, 41, 43, 44 | 100.0 | 75.1 | 94.9 | 100.0 | 72.1 | 94.3 | 100.0 | 76.3 | 95.1 | 100.0 | 76.5 | 95.2 | 100.0 | 76.2 | 95.1 | 100.0 | 69.9 | 93.8 |
| 21, 22, 23 | FIRE SUPPRESSION, PLUMBING & HVAC | 96.1 | 33.5 | 70.4 | 100.1 | 43.1 | 76.7 | 100.2 | 42.7 | 76.6 | 100.2 | 43.1 | 76.8 | 96.1 | 35.4 | 71.2 | 96.1 | 28.5 | 68.4 |
| 26, 27, 3370 | ELECTRICAL, COMMUNICATIONS & UTIL. | 98.4 | 32.8 | 66.2 | 97.4 | 47.5 | 72.9 | 97.3 | 38.4 | 68.4 | 97.8 | 41.5 | 70.1 | 95.4 | 34.8 | 65.6 | 95.2 | 54.2 | 75.1 |
| MF2004 | WEIGHTED AVERAGE | 98.0 | 43.2 | 74.6 | 100.8 | 52.6 | 80.2 | 98.4 | 49.8 | 77.6 | 99.6 | 51.2 | 78.9 | 95.7 | 46.1 | 74.5 | 95.4 | 43.4 | 73.1 |

## NORTH CAROLINA / NORTH DAKOTA

| | DIVISION | MURPHY 289 | | | RALEIGH 275 - 276 | | | ROCKY MOUNT 278 | | | WILMINGTON 284 | | | WINSTON-SALEM 271 | | | BISMARCK 585 | | |
|---|---|---|---|---|---|---|---|---|---|---|---|---|---|---|---|---|---|---|---|
| | | MAT. | INST. | TOTAL | MAT. | INST. | TOTAL | MAT. | INST. | TOTAL | MAT. | INST. | TOTAL | MAT. | INST. | TOTAL | MAT. | INST. | TOTAL |
| 015433 | CONTRACTOR EQUIPMENT | | 93.8 | 93.8 | | 100.3 | 100.3 | | 100.3 | 100.3 | | 93.8 | 93.8 | | 100.3 | 100.3 | | 98.7 | 98.7 |
| 0241, 31 - 34 | SITE & INFRASTRUCTURE, DEMOLITION | 110.0 | 72.7 | 84.0 | 109.7 | 83.0 | 91.1 | 112.0 | 82.4 | 91.4 | 109.3 | 73.0 | 84.0 | 108.5 | 82.9 | 90.6 | 93.5 | 97.2 | 96.1 |
| 0310 | Concrete Forming & Accessories | 103.3 | 26.6 | 37.2 | 98.5 | 44.6 | 52.1 | 90.5 | 31.6 | 39.7 | 97.3 | 42.9 | 50.4 | 99.2 | 42.7 | 50.5 | 95.6 | 46.8 | 53.5 |
| 0320 | Concrete Reinforcing | 96.7 | 20.3 | 59.9 | 97.6 | 54.9 | 77.0 | 96.6 | 29.9 | 64.5 | 97.9 | 52.9 | 76.2 | 97.6 | 43.4 | 71.5 | 104.0 | 72.2 | 88.7 |
| 0330 | Cast-in-Place Concrete | 104.7 | 34.7 | 78.8 | 112.2 | 55.7 | 91.2 | 100.8 | 31.8 | 75.3 | 100.8 | 49.5 | 81.8 | 104.7 | 47.0 | 83.3 | 100.8 | 52.1 | 82.8 |
| 03 | CONCRETE | 108.4 | 30.5 | 72.4 | 110.2 | 52.1 | 83.4 | 106.9 | 33.4 | 73.0 | 105.1 | 48.8 | 79.2 | 106.5 | 46.1 | 78.6 | 97.9 | 54.7 | 78.0 |
| 04 | MASONRY | 77.8 | 28.9 | 48.5 | 92.2 | 45.4 | 64.2 | 82.5 | 28.0 | 49.9 | 75.5 | 41.2 | 55.0 | 89.8 | 40.9 | 60.6 | 100.7 | 60.1 | 76.4 |
| 05 | METALS | 86.7 | 66.4 | 80.8 | 93.5 | 79.9 | 89.5 | 89.6 | 67.1 | 83.1 | 88.3 | 78.8 | 85.6 | 93.5 | 74.6 | 88.0 | 96.4 | 80.5 | 91.8 |
| 06 | WOOD, PLASTICS & COMPOSITES | 106.1 | 24.6 | 62.2 | 98.9 | 44.2 | 69.4 | 89.8 | 32.5 | 58.9 | 98.4 | 42.7 | 68.4 | 98.9 | 42.7 | 68.6 | 87.6 | 41.8 | 62.9 |
| 07 | THERMAL & MOISTURE PROTECTION | 103.4 | 32.4 | 75.7 | 102.8 | 47.1 | 81.1 | 103.7 | 29.2 | 74.6 | 103.1 | 46.2 | 80.9 | 103.6 | 45.4 | 80.9 | 101.5 | 51.9 | 82.2 |
| 08 | OPENINGS | 93.6 | 27.8 | 77.4 | 94.5 | 46.4 | 82.6 | 93.8 | 27.9 | 77.5 | 93.8 | 44.7 | 81.7 | 97.6 | 42.8 | 84.1 | 98.7 | 48.1 | 86.2 |
| 0920 | Plaster & Gypsum Board | 109.9 | 22.5 | 56.0 | 107.2 | 42.6 | 67.4 | 104.7 | 30.6 | 59.0 | 106.7 | 41.1 | 66.2 | 111.1 | 41.0 | 67.9 | 99.3 | 40.6 | 63.1 |
| 0950, 0980 | Ceilings & Acoustic Treatment | 91.5 | 22.5 | 49.1 | 94.1 | 42.6 | 62.5 | 92.4 | 30.6 | 54.5 | 92.4 | 41.1 | 60.9 | 96.7 | 41.0 | 62.5 | 139.7 | 40.6 | 78.9 |
| 0960 | Flooring | 107.1 | 22.7 | 84.1 | 106.7 | 48.2 | 90.8 | 106.9 | 15.0 | 77.3 | 103.5 | 48.2 | 88.5 | 106.7 | 48.2 | 90.8 | 113.3 | 69.4 | 101.4 |
| 0970, 0990 | Wall Finishes & Painting/Coating | 113.6 | 17.4 | 55.8 | 113.6 | 42.3 | 70.8 | 113.6 | 36.0 | 67.0 | 113.6 | 37.2 | 67.7 | 113.6 | 39.1 | 68.9 | 97.7 | 35.2 | 60.2 |
| 09 | FINISHES | 101.5 | 24.2 | 61.0 | 101.5 | 44.8 | 71.8 | 99.3 | 28.8 | 62.4 | 100.0 | 43.0 | 70.1 | 102.7 | 43.1 | 71.5 | 113.0 | 48.4 | 79.1 |
| COVERS | DIVS. 10 - 14, 25, 28, 41, 43, 44 | 100.0 | 72.9 | 94.5 | 100.0 | 72.6 | 94.4 | 100.0 | 68.3 | 93.5 | 100.0 | 71.8 | 94.2 | 100.0 | 76.2 | 95.1 | 100.0 | 81.7 | 96.2 |
| 21, 22, 23 | FIRE SUPPRESSION, PLUMBING & HVAC | 96.1 | 21.1 | 65.3 | 100.0 | 41.1 | 75.9 | 96.1 | 36.6 | 71.7 | 100.2 | 42.8 | 76.7 | 100.2 | 41.6 | 76.2 | 100.3 | 63.5 | 85.2 |
| 26, 27, 3370 | ELECTRICAL, COMMUNICATIONS & UTIL. | 98.8 | 29.0 | 64.5 | 98.2 | 41.2 | 70.2 | 100.5 | 39.5 | 70.5 | 98.2 | 39.9 | 69.6 | 97.8 | 45.3 | 72.0 | 94.2 | 68.2 | 81.4 |
| MF2004 | WEIGHTED AVERAGE | 96.7 | 35.2 | 70.4 | 99.5 | 51.9 | 79.1 | 97.1 | 41.6 | 73.4 | 97.1 | 49.8 | 76.9 | 99.3 | 50.5 | 78.4 | 99.4 | 64.3 | 84.4 |

## NORTH DAKOTA

| | DIVISION | DEVILS LAKE 583 | | | DICKINSON 586 | | | FARGO 580 - 581 | | | GRAND FORKS 582 | | | JAMESTOWN 584 | | | MINOT 587 | | |
|---|---|---|---|---|---|---|---|---|---|---|---|---|---|---|---|---|---|---|---|
| | | MAT. | INST. | TOTAL | MAT. | INST. | TOTAL | MAT. | INST. | TOTAL | MAT. | INST. | TOTAL | MAT. | INST. | TOTAL | MAT. | INST. | TOTAL |
| 015433 | CONTRACTOR EQUIPMENT | | 98.7 | 98.7 | | 98.7 | 98.7 | | 98.7 | 98.7 | | 98.7 | 98.7 | | 98.7 | 98.7 | | 98.7 | 98.7 |
| 0241, 31 - 34 | SITE & INFRASTRUCTURE, DEMOLITION | 100.2 | 95.5 | 96.9 | 109.3 | 94.3 | 98.9 | 94.0 | 97.2 | 96.3 | 104.3 | 94.3 | 97.3 | 99.2 | 94.3 | 95.8 | 101.5 | 97.2 | 98.5 |
| 0310 | Concrete Forming & Accessories | 99.0 | 41.2 | 49.2 | 88.4 | 40.6 | 47.3 | 96.5 | 47.2 | 54.0 | 92.4 | 40.4 | 47.6 | 90.0 | 40.3 | 47.2 | 88.1 | 62.7 | 66.2 |
| 0320 | Concrete Reinforcing | 104.0 | 72.8 | 88.9 | 105.0 | 47.7 | 77.4 | 95.9 | 71.4 | 84.1 | 102.4 | 72.6 | 88.1 | 104.6 | 56.8 | 81.6 | 105.9 | 72.7 | 89.9 |
| 0330 | Cast-in-Place Concrete | 116.2 | 50.7 | 92.0 | 105.1 | 49.4 | 84.5 | 99.8 | 54.1 | 82.9 | 105.1 | 49.3 | 84.5 | 114.8 | 49.3 | 90.5 | 105.1 | 50.9 | 85.0 |
| 03 | CONCRETE | 108.4 | 51.8 | 82.3 | 107.7 | 46.2 | 79.3 | 105.3 | 55.4 | 82.2 | 104.8 | 50.7 | 79.8 | 107.0 | 47.7 | 79.6 | 103.5 | 61.4 | 84.1 |
| 04 | MASONRY | 108.1 | 68.0 | 84.1 | 110.7 | 61.9 | 81.5 | 102.5 | 45.0 | 68.1 | 102.4 | 67.5 | 81.6 | 120.6 | 39.4 | 72.0 | 102.7 | 67.6 | 81.7 |
| 05 | METALS | 96.5 | 80.3 | 91.8 | 96.4 | 66.5 | 87.7 | 98.8 | 79.3 | 93.1 | 96.4 | 76.0 | 90.5 | 96.4 | 68.3 | 88.3 | 96.7 | 81.4 | 92.3 |
| 06 | WOOD, PLASTICS & COMPOSITES | 91.5 | 38.4 | 62.9 | 79.8 | 38.4 | 57.5 | 87.4 | 42.4 | 63.2 | 84.1 | 38.4 | 59.5 | 81.7 | 38.4 | 58.4 | 79.5 | 63.1 | 70.6 |
| 07 | THERMAL & MOISTURE PROTECTION | 102.3 | 54.0 | 83.5 | 102.8 | 51.6 | 82.8 | 100.3 | 49.5 | 80.5 | 102.5 | 54.2 | 83.6 | 102.1 | 46.8 | 80.5 | 102.2 | 55.9 | 84.2 |
| 08 | OPENINGS | 98.7 | 42.3 | 84.8 | 98.7 | 36.4 | 83.3 | 98.7 | 48.4 | 86.3 | 98.7 | 42.3 | 84.8 | 98.7 | 38.9 | 83.9 | 98.9 | 56.9 | 89.2 |
| 0920 | Plaster & Gypsum Board | 111.6 | 37.2 | 65.7 | 104.5 | 37.2 | 63.0 | 101.5 | 41.3 | 64.3 | 105.9 | 37.2 | 63.5 | 105.5 | 37.2 | 63.4 | 104.5 | 62.4 | 78.6 |
| 0950, 0980 | Ceilings & Acoustic Treatment | 142.3 | 37.2 | 77.7 | 142.3 | 37.2 | 77.7 | 139.7 | 41.3 | 79.3 | 142.3 | 37.2 | 77.7 | 142.3 | 37.2 | 77.7 | 142.3 | 62.4 | 93.2 |
| 0960 | Flooring | 117.6 | 41.5 | 96.9 | 109.0 | 41.5 | 90.6 | 112.9 | 41.5 | 93.5 | 111.5 | 41.5 | 92.5 | 110.2 | 41.5 | 91.5 | 108.8 | 83.2 | 101.9 |
| 0970, 0990 | Wall Finishes & Painting/Coating | 97.7 | 26.9 | 55.2 | 97.7 | 26.9 | 55.2 | 97.7 | 72.6 | 82.6 | 97.7 | 26.9 | 55.2 | 97.7 | 26.9 | 55.2 | 97.7 | 29.5 | 56.7 |
| 09 | FINISHES | 117.2 | 38.4 | 75.9 | 114.4 | 38.4 | 74.6 | 113.3 | 47.2 | 78.7 | 114.9 | 38.4 | 74.8 | 114.0 | 38.4 | 74.4 | 113.7 | 63.0 | 87.1 |
| COVERS | DIVS. 10 - 14, 25, 28, 41, 43, 44 | 100.0 | 40.2 | 87.7 | 100.0 | 40.3 | 87.8 | 100.0 | 81.7 | 96.3 | 100.0 | 40.3 | 87.8 | 100.0 | 79.2 | 95.7 | 100.0 | 84.2 | 96.8 |
| 21, 22, 23 | FIRE SUPPRESSION, PLUMBING & HVAC | 96.3 | 63.9 | 83.0 | 96.3 | 74.6 | 87.3 | 100.3 | 67.4 | 86.8 | 100.4 | 41.4 | 76.2 | 96.3 | 41.2 | 73.7 | 100.4 | 62.9 | 85.0 |
| 26, 27, 3370 | ELECTRICAL, COMMUNICATIONS & UTIL. | 93.6 | 42.9 | 68.7 | 102.1 | 69.3 | 86.0 | 97.4 | 68.2 | 83.1 | 97.0 | 64.3 | 80.9 | 93.6 | 42.9 | 68.7 | 100.2 | 69.4 | 85.0 |
| MF2004 | WEIGHTED AVERAGE | 100.7 | 58.4 | 82.6 | 101.6 | 61.4 | 84.4 | 101.1 | 63.4 | 85.0 | 101.1 | 56.1 | 81.8 | 100.7 | 49.8 | 79.0 | 101.1 | 68.9 | 87.4 |

| DIVISION | | NORTH DAKOTA | | | OHIO | | | | | | | | | | | | | | | | |
|---|---|---|---|---|---|---|---|---|---|---|---|---|---|---|---|---|---|---|---|---|---|
| | | WILLISTON | | | AKRON | | | ATHENS | | | CANTON | | | CHILLICOTHE | | | CINCINNATI | | | | |
| | | 588 | | | 442 - 443 | | | 457 | | | 446 - 447 | | | 456 | | | 451 - 452 | | | | |
| | | MAT. | INST. | TOTAL | MAT. | INST. | TOTAL | MAT. | INST. | TOTAL | MAT. | INST. | TOTAL | MAT. | INST. | TOTAL | MAT. | INST. | TOTAL | | |
| 015433 | CONTRACTOR EQUIPMENT | | 98.7 | 98.7 | | 96.4 | 96.4 | | 90.0 | 90.0 | | 96.4 | 96.4 | | 102.1 | 102.1 | | 101.8 | 101.8 | | |
| 0241, 31 - 34 | SITE & INFRASTRUCTURE, DEMOLITION | 102.4 | 94.3 | 96.8 | 89.2 | 105.2 | 100.3 | 86.1 | 92.5 | 90.6 | 89.3 | 105.2 | 100.4 | 75.8 | 107.9 | 98.2 | 73.3 | 107.2 | 96.9 | | |
| 0310 | Concrete Forming & Accessories | 94.1 | 40.6 | 48.0 | 99.4 | 98.0 | 98.2 | 92.9 | 90.9 | 91.2 | 99.4 | 86.9 | 88.7 | 94.9 | 96.8 | 96.5 | 96.9 | 85.0 | 86.7 | | |
| 0320 | Concrete Reinforcing | 107.0 | 47.7 | 78.4 | 101.3 | 94.2 | 97.8 | 92.0 | 84.1 | 88.2 | 101.3 | 79.9 | 91.0 | 89.2 | 86.1 | 87.7 | 94.6 | 87.8 | 91.3 | | |
| 0330 | Cast-in-Place Concrete | 105.1 | 49.4 | 84.5 | 94.0 | 102.3 | 97.1 | 99.5 | 100.4 | 99.8 | 94.9 | 99.8 | 96.7 | 90.2 | 93.2 | 91.3 | 83.1 | 87.0 | 84.6 | | |
| 03 | CONCRETE | 104.8 | 46.2 | 77.8 | 95.1 | 97.8 | 96.4 | 101.5 | 92.0 | 97.1 | 95.6 | 89.3 | 92.7 | 96.2 | 93.4 | 94.9 | 90.9 | 86.3 | 88.8 | | |
| 04 | MASONRY | 97.5 | 61.9 | 76.2 | 88.6 | 98.2 | 94.3 | 69.3 | 96.0 | 85.2 | 89.3 | 90.2 | 89.8 | 76.8 | 97.8 | 89.3 | 76.3 | 92.8 | 86.2 | | |
| 05 | METALS | 96.6 | 66.5 | 87.8 | 92.6 | 81.1 | 89.2 | 105.2 | 72.0 | 95.5 | 92.6 | 74.3 | 87.2 | 96.6 | 87.5 | 94.0 | 98.8 | 88.0 | 95.6 | | |
| 06 | WOOD, PLASTICS & COMPOSITES | 85.5 | 38.4 | 60.2 | 94.3 | 98.0 | 96.3 | 81.4 | 91.0 | 86.6 | 94.6 | 86.5 | 90.2 | 93.3 | 95.6 | 94.5 | 95.6 | 82.1 | 88.3 | | |
| 07 | THERMAL & MOISTURE PROTECTION | 102.4 | 51.6 | 82.6 | 101.6 | 100.0 | 101.0 | 98.6 | 97.8 | 98.3 | 102.4 | 96.1 | 99.9 | 99.4 | 96.7 | 98.3 | 97.4 | 94.8 | 96.4 | | |
| 08 | OPENINGS | 98.8 | 36.4 | 83.4 | 106.4 | 97.3 | 104.2 | 98.2 | 78.9 | 93.4 | 100.7 | 76.8 | 94.8 | 90.0 | 90.0 | 90.0 | 97.7 | 83.6 | 94.2 | | |
| 0920 | Plaster & Gypsum Board | 105.9 | 37.2 | 63.5 | 92.4 | 97.6 | 95.6 | 90.8 | 90.3 | 90.5 | 93.1 | 85.8 | 88.6 | 91.9 | 95.8 | 94.3 | 93.1 | 81.9 | 86.2 | | |
| 0950, 0980 | Ceilings & Acoustic Treatment | 142.3 | 37.2 | 77.7 | 94.5 | 97.6 | 96.4 | 102.1 | 90.3 | 94.9 | 94.5 | 85.8 | 89.1 | 96.5 | 95.8 | 96.1 | 97.4 | 81.9 | 87.9 | | |
| 0960 | Flooring | 112.7 | 41.5 | 93.3 | 99.9 | 90.9 | 97.5 | 127.7 | 97.7 | 119.6 | 100.1 | 83.3 | 95.5 | 105.5 | 96.8 | 103.1 | 106.7 | 96.5 | 103.9 | | |
| 0970, 0990 | Wall Finishes & Painting/Coating | 97.7 | 26.9 | 55.2 | 104.6 | 112.5 | 109.4 | 109.0 | 49.9 | 73.5 | 104.6 | 84.8 | 92.7 | 105.8 | 96.4 | 100.1 | 105.8 | 90.5 | 96.6 | | |
| 09 | FINISHES | 115.2 | 38.4 | 74.9 | 98.9 | 98.3 | 98.6 | 101.2 | 88.8 | 94.7 | 99.0 | 86.0 | 92.2 | 97.2 | 97.1 | 97.1 | 97.8 | 87.2 | 92.2 | | |
| COVERS | DIVS. 10 - 14, 25, 28, 41, 43, 44 | 100.0 | 40.3 | 87.8 | 100.0 | 90.6 | 98.1 | 100.0 | 64.2 | 92.7 | 100.0 | 68.8 | 93.6 | 100.0 | 87.5 | 97.4 | 100.0 | 93.2 | 98.6 | | |
| 21, 22, 23 | FIRE SUPPRESSION, PLUMBING & HVAC | 96.3 | 74.6 | 87.3 | 100.0 | 99.6 | 99.8 | 95.9 | 63.9 | 82.8 | 100.0 | 84.9 | 93.8 | 96.6 | 94.0 | 95.5 | 100.1 | 87.5 | 94.9 | | |
| 26, 27, 3370 | ELECTRICAL, COMMUNICATIONS & UTIL. | 97.4 | 69.3 | 83.6 | 97.4 | 90.2 | 93.9 | 99.1 | 52.6 | 76.3 | 96.7 | 90.8 | 93.8 | 97.7 | 87.9 | 92.9 | 96.9 | 82.3 | 89.7 | | |
| MF2004 | WEIGHTED AVERAGE | 100.0 | 61.4 | 83.5 | 97.6 | 96.2 | 97.0 | 97.8 | 77.6 | 89.2 | 97.1 | 87.3 | 92.9 | 94.8 | 94.2 | 94.6 | 95.9 | 89.0 | 92.9 | | |

| DIVISION | | OHIO | | | | | | | | | | | | | | | | |
|---|---|---|---|---|---|---|---|---|---|---|---|---|---|---|---|---|---|---|
| | | CLEVELAND | | | COLUMBUS | | | DAYTON | | | HAMILTON | | | LIMA | | | LORAIN | | |
| | | 441 | | | 430 - 432 | | | 453 - 454 | | | 450 | | | 458 | | | 440 | | |
| | | MAT. | INST. | TOTAL | MAT. | INST. | TOTAL | MAT. | INST. | TOTAL | MAT. | INST. | TOTAL | MAT. | INST. | TOTAL | MAT. | INST. | TOTAL |
| 015433 | CONTRACTOR EQUIPMENT | | 96.8 | 96.8 | | 95.2 | 95.2 | | 96.1 | 96.1 | | 102.1 | 102.1 | | 93.0 | 93.0 | | 96.4 | 96.4 |
| 0241, 31 - 34 | SITE & INFRASTRUCTURE, DEMOLITION | 89.2 | 105.7 | 100.7 | 85.7 | 101.0 | 96.4 | 72.3 | 107.3 | 96.7 | 72.4 | 107.5 | 96.9 | 81.2 | 93.8 | 90.0 | 88.6 | 104.5 | 99.7 |
| 0310 | Concrete Forming & Accessories | 99.5 | 104.7 | 104.0 | 98.0 | 86.2 | 87.8 | 96.8 | 83.9 | 85.7 | 96.9 | 84.4 | 86.2 | 92.9 | 86.7 | 87.6 | 99.4 | 98.4 | 98.6 |
| 0320 | Concrete Reinforcing | 101.9 | 94.5 | 98.3 | 99.7 | 86.1 | 93.1 | 94.6 | 83.5 | 89.2 | 94.6 | 87.8 | 91.3 | 92.0 | 83.5 | 87.9 | 101.3 | 94.4 | 98.0 |
| 0330 | Cast-in-Place Concrete | 92.2 | 111.2 | 99.2 | 91.2 | 91.1 | 91.1 | 77.3 | 89.5 | 81.8 | 82.9 | 86.0 | 84.0 | 91.4 | 100.0 | 94.6 | 89.5 | 106.6 | 95.8 |
| 03 | CONCRETE | 94.3 | 104.0 | 98.8 | 93.8 | 87.5 | 90.9 | 88.0 | 85.3 | 86.8 | 90.8 | 85.7 | 88.5 | 94.7 | 90.4 | 92.7 | 92.9 | 99.6 | 96.0 |
| 04 | MASONRY | 93.1 | 108.1 | 102.0 | 93.0 | 91.0 | 91.8 | 75.9 | 91.3 | 85.1 | 76.3 | 91.5 | 85.4 | 94.4 | 88.9 | 91.1 | 85.3 | 101.7 | 95.1 |
| 05 | METALS | 94.1 | 84.5 | 91.3 | 97.6 | 81.6 | 92.9 | 98.0 | 78.5 | 92.3 | 98.1 | 87.9 | 95.1 | 105.2 | 81.9 | 98.4 | 93.2 | 82.4 | 90.0 |
| 06 | WOOD, PLASTICS & COMPOSITES | 93.4 | 102.2 | 98.1 | 98.9 | 84.6 | 91.2 | 96.8 | 81.4 | 88.5 | 95.6 | 82.1 | 88.3 | 81.3 | 85.0 | 83.3 | 94.3 | 98.0 | 96.3 |
| 07 | THERMAL & MOISTURE PROTECTION | 100.4 | 112.3 | 105.0 | 98.8 | 94.7 | 97.2 | 103.1 | 92.4 | 99.0 | 99.4 | 94.1 | 97.4 | 98.2 | 101.2 | 99.4 | 102.3 | 106.2 | 103.8 |
| 08 | OPENINGS | 97.0 | 99.5 | 97.6 | 99.6 | 84.1 | 95.8 | 97.9 | 81.5 | 93.8 | 95.4 | 83.6 | 92.5 | 98.2 | 82.7 | 94.4 | 100.7 | 97.3 | 99.8 |
| 0920 | Plaster & Gypsum Board | 91.7 | 101.8 | 97.9 | 88.9 | 84.2 | 86.0 | 93.1 | 81.2 | 85.8 | 93.1 | 81.9 | 86.2 | 90.8 | 84.2 | 86.7 | 92.4 | 97.6 | 95.6 |
| 0950, 0980 | Ceilings & Acoustic Treatment | 92.8 | 101.8 | 98.3 | 95.3 | 84.2 | 88.5 | 98.3 | 81.2 | 87.8 | 97.4 | 81.9 | 87.9 | 101.1 | 84.2 | 90.7 | 94.5 | 97.6 | 96.4 |
| 0960 | Flooring | 99.7 | 106.4 | 101.5 | 94.4 | 88.0 | 92.7 | 109.3 | 88.8 | 103.8 | 106.7 | 93.3 | 103.0 | 126.9 | 93.1 | 117.7 | 100.1 | 108.8 | 102.5 |
| 0970, 0990 | Wall Finishes & Painting/Coating | 104.6 | 115.1 | 110.9 | 98.5 | 96.4 | 97.2 | 105.8 | 89.1 | 95.8 | 105.8 | 90.5 | 96.6 | 109.0 | 86.7 | 95.6 | 104.6 | 115.1 | 110.9 |
| 09 | FINISHES | 98.4 | 106.0 | 102.3 | 96.7 | 87.2 | 91.7 | 98.9 | 84.8 | 91.4 | 97.7 | 86.3 | 91.7 | 100.4 | 87.4 | 93.6 | 98.9 | 102.3 | 100.7 |
| COVERS | DIVS. 10 - 14, 25, 28, 41, 43, 44 | 100.0 | 105.6 | 101.1 | 100.0 | 93.5 | 98.7 | 100.0 | 92.8 | 98.5 | 100.0 | 92.7 | 98.5 | 100.0 | 89.3 | 97.8 | 100.0 | 102.6 | 100.5 |
| 21, 22, 23 | FIRE SUPPRESSION, PLUMBING & HVAC | 100.0 | 106.7 | 102.7 | 99.7 | 92.1 | 96.6 | 101.2 | 88.9 | 96.2 | 100.7 | 86.8 | 95.0 | 95.9 | 88.3 | 92.8 | 100.0 | 87.0 | 94.7 |
| 26, 27, 3370 | ELECTRICAL, COMMUNICATIONS & UTIL. | 97.1 | 107.2 | 102.1 | 97.0 | 84.6 | 90.9 | 95.2 | 85.7 | 90.6 | 95.6 | 72.0 | 84.0 | 99.4 | 82.6 | 91.2 | 96.9 | 91.0 | 94.0 |
| MF2004 | WEIGHTED AVERAGE | 96.9 | 104.2 | 100.0 | 97.4 | 89.2 | 93.9 | 95.8 | 88.1 | 92.5 | 95.6 | 87.0 | 91.9 | 98.1 | 87.7 | 93.7 | 96.6 | 95.4 | 96.1 |

| DIVISION | | OHIO | | | | | | | | | | | | | | | | |
|---|---|---|---|---|---|---|---|---|---|---|---|---|---|---|---|---|---|---|
| | | MANSFIELD | | | MARION | | | SPRINGFIELD | | | STEUBENVILLE | | | TOLEDO | | | YOUNGSTOWN | | |
| | | 448 - 449 | | | 433 | | | 455 | | | 439 | | | 434 - 436 | | | 444 - 445 | | |
| | | MAT. | INST. | TOTAL | MAT. | INST. | TOTAL | MAT. | INST. | TOTAL | MAT. | INST. | TOTAL | MAT. | INST. | TOTAL | MAT. | INST. | TOTAL |
| 015433 | CONTRACTOR EQUIPMENT | | 96.4 | 96.4 | | 94.8 | 94.8 | | 96.1 | 96.1 | | 100.4 | 100.4 | | 98.2 | 98.2 | | 96.4 | 96.4 |
| 0241, 31 - 34 | SITE & INFRASTRUCTURE, DEMOLITION | 85.3 | 105.7 | 99.5 | 81.6 | 100.2 | 94.5 | 72.6 | 105.7 | 95.7 | 122.1 | 110.5 | 114.0 | 85.0 | 101.2 | 96.3 | 89.1 | 105.7 | 100.7 |
| 0310 | Concrete Forming & Accessories | 89.1 | 96.8 | 95.8 | 94.5 | 82.0 | 83.7 | 96.8 | 85.5 | 87.1 | 95.6 | 90.9 | 91.6 | 98.0 | 101.8 | 101.2 | 99.4 | 91.1 | 92.3 |
| 0320 | Concrete Reinforcing | 92.1 | 80.4 | 86.5 | 91.9 | 86.2 | 89.1 | 94.6 | 86.0 | 90.4 | 89.2 | 87.3 | 88.3 | 99.7 | 91.1 | 95.5 | 101.3 | 91.5 | 96.6 |
| 0330 | Cast-in-Place Concrete | 87.0 | 88.8 | 87.7 | 83.3 | 84.7 | 83.8 | 79.4 | 88.9 | 82.9 | 90.5 | 96.4 | 92.7 | 91.2 | 108.0 | 97.4 | 93.1 | 103.4 | 96.9 |
| 03 | CONCRETE | 87.7 | 90.1 | 88.8 | 86.1 | 83.3 | 84.8 | 89.1 | 86.4 | 87.8 | 89.9 | 91.4 | 90.6 | 93.8 | 101.3 | 97.3 | 94.7 | 94.6 | 94.7 |
| 04 | MASONRY | 87.8 | 98.4 | 94.2 | 95.2 | 94.1 | 94.6 | 76.0 | 90.5 | 84.7 | 81.8 | 93.6 | 88.8 | 102.2 | 101.2 | 101.6 | 88.9 | 96.0 | 93.1 |
| 05 | METALS | 93.3 | 76.2 | 88.3 | 96.6 | 78.4 | 91.3 | 98.0 | 79.2 | 92.5 | 93.0 | 78.8 | 88.8 | 97.4 | 87.8 | 94.6 | 92.6 | 80.1 | 89.0 |
| 06 | WOOD, PLASTICS & COMPOSITES | 82.6 | 98.0 | 90.9 | 95.0 | 81.9 | 87.9 | 98.1 | 84.3 | 90.7 | 91.0 | 89.9 | 90.4 | 98.9 | 102.5 | 100.8 | 94.3 | 89.7 | 91.8 |
| 07 | THERMAL & MOISTURE PROTECTION | 101.8 | 98.3 | 100.4 | 98.3 | 87.9 | 94.2 | 103.0 | 92.4 | 98.9 | 110.1 | 95.6 | 104.5 | 100.6 | 108.6 | 103.7 | 102.5 | 97.4 | 100.5 |
| 08 | OPENINGS | 100.0 | 88.9 | 97.3 | 94.0 | 81.7 | 91.0 | 95.8 | 83.7 | 92.8 | 94.6 | 87.6 | 92.8 | 97.6 | 99.7 | 97.6 | 100.7 | 92.0 | 98.5 |
| 0920 | Plaster & Gypsum Board | 88.3 | 97.6 | 94.0 | 87.6 | 81.4 | 83.7 | 93.1 | 84.2 | 87.6 | 88.3 | 89.1 | 88.8 | 88.9 | 102.5 | 97.3 | 92.4 | 89.1 | 90.4 |
| 0950, 0980 | Ceilings & Acoustic Treatment | 97.1 | 97.6 | 97.4 | 95.3 | 81.4 | 86.7 | 98.3 | 84.2 | 89.7 | 92.3 | 89.1 | 90.3 | 95.3 | 102.5 | 99.7 | 94.5 | 89.1 | 91.2 |
| 0960 | Flooring | 95.0 | 106.7 | 98.2 | 92.6 | 80.6 | 89.4 | 109.3 | 88.8 | 103.8 | 120.6 | 91.9 | 112.8 | 93.6 | 101.8 | 95.8 | 100.1 | 92.0 | 97.9 |
| 0970, 0990 | Wall Finishes & Painting/Coating | 104.6 | 92.0 | 97.0 | 98.5 | 56.9 | 73.5 | 105.8 | 89.1 | 95.8 | 114.6 | 98.4 | 104.9 | 98.5 | 108.9 | 104.7 | 104.6 | 97.7 | 100.4 |
| 09 | FINISHES | 97.1 | 98.8 | 98.0 | 95.6 | 78.9 | 86.9 | 98.8 | 86.3 | 92.2 | 112.8 | 91.6 | 101.7 | 96.4 | 102.7 | 99.7 | 99.0 | 91.6 | 95.1 |
| COVERS | DIVS. 10 - 14, 25, 28, 41, 43, 44 | 100.0 | 94.3 | 98.8 | 100.0 | 63.9 | 92.6 | 100.0 | 92.8 | 98.5 | 100.0 | 93.7 | 98.7 | 100.0 | 91.9 | 98.3 | 100.0 | 89.0 | 97.8 |
| 21, 22, 23 | FIRE SUPPRESSION, PLUMBING & HVAC | 95.8 | 85.5 | 91.6 | 95.6 | 88.8 | 92.8 | 101.2 | 88.5 | 96.0 | 95.8 | 87.8 | 92.5 | 99.7 | 101.1 | 100.3 | 100.0 | 89.2 | 95.6 |
| 26, 27, 3370 | ELECTRICAL, COMMUNICATIONS & UTIL. | 94.6 | 83.0 | 88.9 | 91.0 | 82.2 | 86.7 | 95.2 | 84.6 | 90.0 | 85.3 | 106.4 | 95.7 | 97.0 | 108.0 | 102.4 | 96.9 | 88.5 | 92.8 |
| MF2004 | WEIGHTED AVERAGE | 94.6 | 90.6 | 92.9 | 94.0 | 85.3 | 90.3 | 95.7 | 88.2 | 92.5 | 95.7 | 93.5 | 94.7 | 97.6 | 101.0 | 99.1 | 97.0 | 91.8 | 94.8 |

| DIVISION | | OHIO ZANESVILLE 437 - 438 | | | OKLAHOMA ARDMORE 734 | | | CLINTON 736 | | | DURANT 747 | | | ENID 737 | | | GUYMON 739 | | |
|---|---|---|---|---|---|---|---|---|---|---|---|---|---|---|---|---|---|---|---|
| | | MAT. | INST. | TOTAL | MAT. | INST. | TOTAL | MAT. | INST. | TOTAL | MAT. | INST. | TOTAL | MAT. | INST. | TOTAL | MAT. | INST. | TOTAL |
| 015433 | CONTRACTOR EQUIPMENT | | 94.8 | 94.8 | | 78.6 | 78.6 | | 77.6 | 77.6 | | 77.6 | 77.6 | | 77.6 | 77.6 | | 77.6 | 77.6 |
| 0241, 31 - 34 | SITE & INFRASTRUCTURE, DEMOLITION | 84.2 | 101.6 | 96.3 | 106.9 | 90.6 | 95.5 | 108.6 | 89.0 | 94.9 | 101.0 | 88.7 | 92.5 | 110.1 | 89.0 | 95.4 | 114.0 | 87.4 | 95.5 |
| 0310 | Concrete Forming & Accessories | 91.4 | 83.0 | 84.2 | 93.8 | 44.1 | 51.0 | 92.6 | 37.9 | 45.5 | 85.0 | 44.3 | 49.9 | 96.3 | 37.2 | 45.4 | 100.3 | 23.1 | 33.8 |
| 0320 | Concrete Reinforcing | 91.3 | 86.9 | 89.2 | 96.6 | 80.0 | 88.6 | 97.2 | 80.0 | 88.9 | 97.5 | 62.4 | 80.6 | 96.5 | 80.0 | 88.6 | 97.2 | 31.0 | 65.3 |
| 0330 | Cast-in-Place Concrete | 87.8 | 91.1 | 89.0 | 94.7 | 45.2 | 76.4 | 91.6 | 45.1 | 74.4 | 88.5 | 45.1 | 72.5 | 91.6 | 47.9 | 75.4 | 91.6 | 30.1 | 68.8 |
| 03 | CONCRETE | 89.5 | 86.2 | 88.0 | 91.3 | 51.5 | 72.9 | 90.5 | 48.7 | 71.2 | 86.2 | 48.2 | 68.7 | 91.0 | 49.4 | 71.8 | 93.4 | 27.5 | 63.0 |
| 04 | MASONRY | 91.9 | 85.3 | 88.0 | 93.0 | 57.6 | 71.8 | 119.1 | 57.6 | 82.3 | 91.5 | 72.3 | 80.0 | 101.2 | 57.6 | 75.1 | 95.7 | 22.6 | 52.0 |
| 05 | METALS | 98.1 | 80.1 | 92.9 | 92.7 | 67.8 | 85.4 | 92.8 | 67.7 | 85.5 | 92.7 | 60.8 | 83.4 | 94.1 | 67.7 | 86.4 | 93.2 | 37.7 | 77.1 |
| 06 | WOOD, PLASTICS & COMPOSITES | 91.2 | 81.9 | 86.2 | 98.0 | 43.4 | 68.6 | 96.9 | 35.0 | 63.6 | 88.1 | 43.4 | 64.0 | 101.0 | 34.1 | 65.0 | 105.2 | 22.3 | 60.6 |
| 07 | THERMAL & MOISTURE PROTECTION | 98.4 | 93.4 | 96.4 | 99.1 | 59.8 | 83.8 | 99.2 | 58.9 | 83.5 | 98.8 | 61.8 | 84.4 | 99.3 | 58.8 | 83.5 | 99.6 | 28.2 | 71.8 |
| 08 | OPENINGS | 94.0 | 82.8 | 91.3 | 95.4 | 53.4 | 85.0 | 95.4 | 48.9 | 84.0 | 95.4 | 48.9 | 83.9 | 95.4 | 48.1 | 83.8 | 95.6 | 24.2 | 77.9 |
| 0920 | Plaster & Gypsum Board | 85.9 | 81.4 | 83.1 | 85.3 | 42.6 | 59.0 | 85.0 | 34.1 | 53.6 | 82.3 | 42.6 | 57.8 | 86.0 | 33.1 | 53.3 | 86.6 | 21.0 | 46.1 |
| 0950, 0980 | Ceilings & Acoustic Treatment | 95.3 | 81.4 | 86.7 | 82.2 | 42.6 | 57.9 | 82.2 | 34.1 | 52.7 | 82.2 | 42.6 | 57.9 | 83.2 | 33.1 | 52.4 | 84.8 | 21.0 | 45.6 |
| 0960 | Flooring | 90.6 | 84.9 | 89.0 | 109.9 | 49.9 | 93.6 | 108.2 | 47.5 | 91.7 | 103.9 | 68.0 | 94.1 | 110.6 | 47.5 | 93.5 | 113.0 | 28.1 | 89.9 |
| 0970, 0990 | Wall Finishes & Painting/Coating | 98.5 | 81.0 | 88.0 | 98.2 | 61.4 | 76.1 | 98.2 | 61.4 | 76.1 | 98.2 | 61.4 | 76.1 | 98.2 | 61.4 | 76.1 | 98.2 | 18.2 | 50.1 |
| 09 | FINISHES | 94.9 | 82.7 | 88.5 | 94.6 | 45.6 | 68.9 | 94.2 | 40.3 | 66.0 | 91.9 | 49.5 | 69.7 | 95.4 | 39.6 | 66.2 | 97.0 | 23.4 | 58.4 |
| COVERS | DIVS. 10 - 14, 25, 28, 41, 43, 44 | 100.0 | 83.3 | 96.6 | 100.0 | 66.9 | 93.2 | 100.0 | 65.9 | 93.0 | 100.0 | 67.1 | 93.3 | 100.0 | 65.8 | 93.0 | 100.0 | 62.5 | 92.3 |
| 21, 22, 23 | FIRE SUPPRESSION, PLUMBING & HVAC | 95.6 | 83.7 | 90.7 | 95.9 | 60.0 | 81.2 | 95.9 | 60.0 | 81.2 | 95.9 | 60.1 | 81.2 | 100.1 | 60.0 | 83.6 | 95.9 | 25.5 | 67.0 |
| 26, 27, 3370 | ELECTRICAL, COMMUNICATIONS & UTIL. | 91.4 | 76.8 | 84.3 | 94.1 | 68.5 | 81.6 | 95.2 | 68.5 | 82.1 | 96.8 | 58.4 | 77.9 | 95.2 | 68.5 | 82.1 | 96.8 | 18.5 | 58.3 |
| MF2004 | WEIGHTED AVERAGE | 94.5 | 84.5 | 90.2 | 95.1 | 61.0 | 80.5 | 96.5 | 59.4 | 80.6 | 94.3 | 60.2 | 79.7 | 97.0 | 59.4 | 80.9 | 96.4 | 31.6 | 68.7 |

| DIVISION | | OKLAHOMA LAWTON 735 | | | MCALESTER 745 | | | MIAMI 743 | | | MUSKOGEE 744 | | | OKLAHOMA CITY 730 - 731 | | | PONCA CITY 746 | | |
|---|---|---|---|---|---|---|---|---|---|---|---|---|---|---|---|---|---|---|---|
| | | MAT. | INST. | TOTAL | MAT. | INST. | TOTAL | MAT. | INST. | TOTAL | MAT. | INST. | TOTAL | MAT. | INST. | TOTAL | MAT. | INST. | TOTAL |
| 015433 | CONTRACTOR EQUIPMENT | | 78.6 | 78.6 | | 77.6 | 77.6 | | 87.3 | 87.3 | | 87.3 | 87.3 | | 78.9 | 78.9 | | 77.6 | 77.6 |
| 0241, 31 - 34 | SITE & INFRASTRUCTURE, DEMOLITION | 105.0 | 90.6 | 95.0 | 93.0 | 89.1 | 90.3 | 95.0 | 86.0 | 88.7 | 95.1 | 84.6 | 87.8 | 103.4 | 91.2 | 94.9 | 101.8 | 89.0 | 92.9 |
| 0310 | Concrete Forming & Accessories | 99.9 | 50.6 | 57.5 | 82.8 | 46.0 | 51.1 | 96.5 | 54.5 | 60.3 | 101.2 | 33.3 | 42.7 | 99.0 | 43.7 | 51.4 | 91.7 | 44.6 | 51.1 |
| 0320 | Concrete Reinforcing | 96.8 | 80.0 | 88.7 | 97.2 | 46.4 | 72.7 | 95.7 | 80.1 | 88.2 | 96.5 | 35.5 | 67.1 | 96.8 | 80.0 | 88.7 | 96.5 | 80.0 | 88.5 |
| 0330 | Cast-in-Place Concrete | 88.6 | 47.9 | 73.5 | 77.6 | 48.1 | 66.7 | 81.4 | 47.1 | 68.7 | 82.3 | 36.6 | 65.4 | 88.1 | 51.0 | 74.4 | 90.9 | 39.7 | 72.0 |
| 03 | CONCRETE | 87.6 | 55.4 | 72.7 | 77.7 | 47.0 | 63.5 | 81.8 | 57.7 | 70.6 | 83.4 | 36.0 | 61.5 | 87.3 | 53.3 | 71.6 | 88.1 | 49.8 | 70.4 |
| 04 | MASONRY | 95.6 | 57.6 | 72.9 | 109.3 | 58.3 | 78.8 | 94.2 | 58.9 | 73.1 | 110.8 | 50.7 | 74.8 | 96.6 | 59.6 | 74.5 | 86.1 | 58.2 | 69.4 |
| 05 | METALS | 97.6 | 67.8 | 88.9 | 92.7 | 52.7 | 81.1 | 92.6 | 82.3 | 89.6 | 94.1 | 56.6 | 83.2 | 99.5 | 67.8 | 90.3 | 92.6 | 67.5 | 85.3 |
| 06 | WOOD, PLASTICS & COMPOSITES | 104.1 | 52.2 | 76.2 | 85.4 | 47.1 | 64.8 | 100.9 | 56.5 | 77.0 | 106.3 | 33.7 | 67.2 | 103.3 | 41.9 | 70.2 | 96.1 | 44.0 | 68.1 |
| 07 | THERMAL & MOISTURE PROTECTION | 99.1 | 60.7 | 84.1 | 98.5 | 59.0 | 83.1 | 98.9 | 60.8 | 84.0 | 98.9 | 44.7 | 77.8 | 97.2 | 60.5 | 82.9 | 99.0 | 58.8 | 83.3 |
| 08 | OPENINGS | 97.0 | 58.0 | 87.4 | 95.4 | 45.9 | 83.2 | 95.4 | 61.1 | 86.9 | 95.4 | 33.0 | 80.0 | 97.0 | 52.4 | 86.0 | 95.4 | 53.7 | 85.1 |
| 0920 | Plaster & Gypsum Board | 88.0 | 51.7 | 65.6 | 81.3 | 46.5 | 59.8 | 86.0 | 56.0 | 67.5 | 89.3 | 32.5 | 54.3 | 84.5 | 41.1 | 57.7 | 85.0 | 43.3 | 59.3 |
| 0950, 0980 | Ceilings & Acoustic Treatment | 91.7 | 51.7 | 67.2 | 82.2 | 46.5 | 60.3 | 82.2 | 56.0 | 66.1 | 91.7 | 32.5 | 55.4 | 89.2 | 41.1 | 59.7 | 82.2 | 43.3 | 58.3 |
| 0960 | Flooring | 113.4 | 47.5 | 95.5 | 102.5 | 47.5 | 87.6 | 111.6 | 68.0 | 99.7 | 114.6 | 38.3 | 93.9 | 113.4 | 47.5 | 95.5 | 107.8 | 47.5 | 91.4 |
| 0970, 0990 | Wall Finishes & Painting/Coating | 98.2 | 61.4 | 76.1 | 98.2 | 46.5 | 66.4 | 98.2 | 79.3 | 86.8 | 98.2 | 32.9 | 58.9 | 98.2 | 61.4 | 76.1 | 98.2 | 61.4 | 76.1 |
| 09 | FINISHES | 98.0 | 50.2 | 73.0 | 90.8 | 45.6 | 67.1 | 94.1 | 59.3 | 75.9 | 97.8 | 34.5 | 64.7 | 96.7 | 44.7 | 69.5 | 93.6 | 45.7 | 68.5 |
| COVERS | DIVS. 10 - 14, 25, 28, 41, 43, 44 | 100.0 | 68.0 | 93.4 | 100.0 | 67.6 | 93.4 | 100.0 | 69.3 | 93.7 | 100.0 | 65.0 | 92.8 | 100.0 | 67.4 | 93.3 | 100.0 | 67.2 | 93.3 |
| 21, 22, 23 | FIRE SUPPRESSION, PLUMBING & HVAC | 100.1 | 60.0 | 83.6 | 95.9 | 35.1 | 71.0 | 95.9 | 64.4 | 83.0 | 100.1 | 26.7 | 70.0 | 100.0 | 61.0 | 84.0 | 95.9 | 64.0 | 82.8 |
| 26, 27, 3370 | ELECTRICAL, COMMUNICATIONS & UTIL. | 96.8 | 68.5 | 82.9 | 95.2 | 65.8 | 80.8 | 96.6 | 65.9 | 81.5 | 94.8 | 31.6 | 63.8 | 96.2 | 68.5 | 82.6 | 94.8 | 68.4 | 81.8 |
| MF2004 | WEIGHTED AVERAGE | 97.3 | 62.4 | 82.4 | 93.6 | 53.1 | 76.3 | 94.0 | 65.7 | 81.9 | 96.3 | 41.6 | 72.9 | 97.3 | 61.5 | 82.0 | 94.2 | 61.5 | 80.2 |

| DIVISION | | OKLAHOMA POTEAU 749 | | | SHAWNEE 748 | | | TULSA 740 - 741 | | | WOODWARD 738 | | | OREGON BEND 977 | | | EUGENE 974 | | |
|---|---|---|---|---|---|---|---|---|---|---|---|---|---|---|---|---|---|---|---|
| | | MAT. | INST. | TOTAL | MAT. | INST. | TOTAL | MAT. | INST. | TOTAL | MAT. | INST. | TOTAL | MAT. | INST. | TOTAL | MAT. | INST. | TOTAL |
| 015433 | CONTRACTOR EQUIPMENT | | 86.6 | 86.6 | | 77.6 | 77.6 | | 87.3 | 87.3 | | 77.6 | 77.6 | | 99.6 | 99.6 | | 99.6 | 99.6 |
| 0241, 31 - 34 | SITE & INFRASTRUCTURE, DEMOLITION | 76.6 | 84.5 | 82.1 | 105.2 | 88.9 | 93.8 | 101.9 | 86.0 | 90.8 | 109.1 | 89.0 | 95.1 | 122.3 | 104.6 | 109.9 | 109.0 | 104.6 | 105.9 |
| 0310 | Concrete Forming & Accessories | 89.3 | 47.2 | 53.1 | 84.8 | 43.0 | 48.8 | 100.9 | 43.9 | 51.8 | 92.7 | 37.8 | 45.4 | 108.7 | 104.3 | 104.9 | 104.8 | 104.2 | 104.3 |
| 0320 | Concrete Reinforcing | 97.7 | 80.1 | 89.2 | 96.5 | 50.9 | 74.6 | 96.8 | 79.9 | 88.7 | 96.5 | 80.0 | 88.6 | 103.6 | 97.1 | 100.5 | 108.0 | 97.1 | 102.8 |
| 0330 | Cast-in-Place Concrete | 81.4 | 46.7 | 68.5 | 93.9 | 44.6 | 75.6 | 89.7 | 46.8 | 73.8 | 91.6 | 45.1 | 74.4 | 108.8 | 105.8 | 107.7 | 105.4 | 105.8 | 105.5 |
| 03 | CONCRETE | 83.5 | 54.3 | 70.0 | 89.8 | 45.3 | 69.3 | 88.3 | 52.9 | 71.9 | 90.8 | 48.7 | 71.4 | 115.2 | 103.1 | 109.6 | 106.3 | 103.1 | 104.8 |
| 04 | MASONRY | 94.9 | 58.3 | 73.0 | 110.6 | 56.9 | 78.5 | 95.0 | 59.6 | 73.8 | 89.8 | 57.6 | 70.5 | 119.2 | 101.8 | 108.8 | 116.5 | 101.8 | 107.7 |
| 05 | METALS | 92.7 | 82.1 | 89.6 | 92.6 | 54.4 | 81.5 | 96.9 | 81.3 | 92.4 | 92.8 | 67.7 | 85.5 | 91.4 | 96.2 | 92.8 | 92.1 | 96.1 | 93.2 |
| 06 | WOOD, PLASTICS & COMPOSITES | 93.0 | 47.3 | 68.3 | 88.0 | 43.1 | 63.8 | 104.8 | 43.1 | 71.6 | 97.0 | 34.9 | 63.6 | 99.5 | 104.4 | 102.1 | 95.0 | 104.4 | 100.0 |
| 07 | THERMAL & MOISTURE PROTECTION | 99.0 | 59.3 | 83.5 | 99.0 | 59.5 | 83.6 | 98.9 | 57.6 | 82.8 | 99.3 | 58.9 | 83.5 | 103.9 | 96.5 | 101.1 | 103.1 | 94.6 | 99.8 |
| 08 | OPENINGS | 95.4 | 56.1 | 85.7 | 95.4 | 42.7 | 82.4 | 97.0 | 52.6 | 86.0 | 95.5 | 48.8 | 83.9 | 98.5 | 105.0 | 100.1 | 98.9 | 105.0 | 100.4 |
| 0920 | Plaster & Gypsum Board | 84.3 | 46.5 | 61.0 | 82.3 | 42.4 | 57.7 | 88.0 | 42.2 | 59.8 | 85.6 | 34.0 | 53.7 | 103.9 | 104.3 | 104.2 | 102.2 | 104.3 | 103.5 |
| 0950, 0980 | Ceilings & Acoustic Treatment | 82.2 | 46.5 | 60.3 | 82.2 | 42.4 | 57.8 | 91.7 | 42.2 | 61.4 | 84.8 | 34.0 | 53.6 | 102.4 | 104.3 | 103.6 | 103.4 | 104.3 | 104.0 |
| 0960 | Flooring | 106.9 | 68.0 | 96.3 | 103.7 | 37.8 | 85.8 | 113.2 | 49.5 | 95.9 | 108.3 | 49.9 | 92.4 | 117.1 | 102.0 | 113.0 | 115.1 | 102.0 | 111.6 |
| 0970, 0990 | Wall Finishes & Painting/Coating | 98.2 | 61.4 | 76.1 | 98.2 | 40.9 | 63.7 | 98.2 | 48.5 | 68.3 | 98.2 | 61.4 | 76.1 | 111.9 | 70.6 | 87.1 | 111.9 | 70.6 | 87.1 |
| 09 | FINISHES | 91.6 | 51.7 | 70.7 | 92.2 | 40.7 | 65.2 | 97.4 | 44.4 | 69.6 | 95.0 | 40.6 | 66.5 | 111.3 | 100.4 | 105.6 | 109.5 | 100.4 | 104.7 |
| COVERS | DIVS. 10 - 14, 25, 28, 41, 43, 44 | 100.0 | 67.9 | 93.4 | 100.0 | 66.6 | 93.2 | 100.0 | 67.8 | 93.4 | 100.0 | 65.9 | 93.0 | 100.0 | 104.0 | 100.8 | 100.0 | 104.0 | 100.8 |
| 21, 22, 23 | FIRE SUPPRESSION, PLUMBING & HVAC | 95.9 | 64.1 | 82.9 | 95.9 | 59.2 | 80.9 | 100.1 | 55.2 | 81.7 | 95.9 | 60.0 | 81.2 | 96.0 | 103.9 | 99.3 | 100.2 | 103.9 | 101.7 |
| 26, 27, 3370 | ELECTRICAL, COMMUNICATIONS & UTIL. | 94.9 | 65.9 | 80.6 | 96.9 | 68.5 | 82.9 | 96.8 | 41.2 | 69.5 | 96.7 | 68.5 | 82.8 | 102.0 | 97.9 | 99.9 | 100.6 | 97.9 | 99.2 |
| MF2004 | WEIGHTED AVERAGE | 93.2 | 63.6 | 80.6 | 95.8 | 57.5 | 79.4 | 97.1 | 57.1 | 80.0 | 95.3 | 59.5 | 80.0 | 102.3 | 101.5 | 101.9 | 101.4 | 101.4 | 101.4 |

## OREGON

| DIVISION | | KLAMATH FALLS 976 | | | MEDFORD 975 | | | PENDLETON 978 | | | PORTLAND 970 - 972 | | | SALEM 973 | | | VALE 979 | | |
|---|---|---|---|---|---|---|---|---|---|---|---|---|---|---|---|---|---|---|---|
| | | MAT. | INST. | TOTAL | MAT. | INST. | TOTAL | MAT. | INST. | TOTAL | MAT. | INST. | TOTAL | MAT. | INST. | TOTAL | MAT. | INST. | TOTAL |
| 015433 | CONTRACTOR EQUIPMENT | | 99.6 | 99.6 | | 99.6 | 99.6 | | 96.5 | 96.5 | | 99.6 | 99.6 | | 99.6 | 99.6 | | 96.5 | 96.5 |
| 0241, 31 - 34 | SITE & INFRASTRUCTURE, DEMOLITION | 127.5 | 104.6 | 111.5 | 118.8 | 104.6 | 108.9 | 115.0 | 97.2 | 102.6 | 111.8 | 104.6 | 106.8 | 106.0 | 104.6 | 105.0 | 100.2 | 97.1 | 98.1 |
| 0310 | Concrete Forming & Accessories | 101.3 | 104.2 | 103.8 | 100.3 | 104.2 | 103.7 | 102.5 | 104.5 | 104.2 | 106.3 | 104.6 | 104.8 | 103.6 | 104.3 | 104.2 | 109.3 | 103.5 | 104.3 |
| 0320 | Concrete Reinforcing | 103.6 | 97.1 | 100.5 | 105.3 | 97.1 | 101.4 | 108.7 | 97.4 | 100.2 | 108.8 | 97.4 | 103.3 | 109.0 | 97.4 | 103.4 | 100.3 | 97.3 | 98.8 |
| 0330 | Cast-in-Place Concrete | 108.8 | 104.0 | 107.0 | 108.8 | 105.8 | 107.7 | 109.6 | 105.5 | 108.1 | 108.3 | 105.9 | 107.4 | 97.0 | 105.8 | 100.3 | 86.2 | 105.1 | 93.2 |
| 03 | CONCRETE | 118.1 | 102.4 | 110.8 | 112.6 | 103.1 | 108.2 | 98.6 | 103.2 | 100.7 | 107.9 | 103.3 | 105.8 | 102.2 | 103.2 | 102.7 | 82.5 | 102.6 | 91.7 |
| 04 | MASONRY | 136.5 | 101.8 | 115.7 | 113.9 | 101.8 | 106.7 | 124.8 | 107.1 | 114.2 | 117.9 | 107.0 | 111.4 | 121.1 | 107.0 | 112.7 | 122.9 | 107.1 | 113.4 |
| 05 | METALS | 91.4 | 96.1 | 92.8 | 91.7 | 96.1 | 93.0 | 98.2 | 97.2 | 97.9 | 93.1 | 96.9 | 94.2 | 92.5 | 96.7 | 93.7 | 98.1 | 96.2 | 97.5 |
| 06 | WOOD, PLASTICS & COMPOSITES | 90.2 | 104.4 | 97.9 | 89.0 | 104.4 | 97.3 | 92.6 | 104.5 | 99.0 | 96.3 | 104.4 | 100.7 | 92.4 | 104.4 | 98.8 | 101.5 | 104.5 | 103.1 |
| 07 | THERMAL & MOISTURE PROTECTION | 104.2 | 96.7 | 101.3 | 103.8 | 96.7 | 101.0 | 94.1 | 98.2 | 95.7 | 102.9 | 102.4 | 102.7 | 100.4 | 97.9 | 99.4 | 93.5 | 95.6 | 94.3 |
| 08 | OPENINGS | 98.5 | 105.0 | 100.1 | 101.5 | 105.0 | 102.3 | 94.3 | 105.1 | 96.9 | 96.5 | 105.0 | 98.6 | 98.3 | 105.0 | 100.0 | 94.2 | 98.4 | 95.2 |
| 0920 | Plaster & Gypsum Board | 101.3 | 104.3 | 103.2 | 100.7 | 104.3 | 102.9 | 82.6 | 104.3 | 96.0 | 107.2 | 104.3 | 105.4 | 95.9 | 104.3 | 101.1 | 87.3 | 104.3 | 97.8 |
| 0950, 0980 | Ceilings & Acoustic Treatment | 111.8 | 104.3 | 107.2 | 118.5 | 104.3 | 109.8 | 69.8 | 104.3 | 91.0 | 107.2 | 104.3 | 105.4 | 104.8 | 104.3 | 104.5 | 69.8 | 104.3 | 91.0 |
| 0960 | Flooring | 113.4 | 102.0 | 110.3 | 112.6 | 102.0 | 109.7 | 79.9 | 102.0 | 85.9 | 112.6 | 102.0 | 109.7 | 115.3 | 102.0 | 111.7 | 82.1 | 102.0 | 87.5 |
| 0970, 0990 | Wall Finishes & Painting/Coating | 111.9 | 64.7 | 83.6 | 111.9 | 64.7 | 83.6 | 95.1 | 75.8 | 83.5 | 111.4 | 75.8 | 90.0 | 111.9 | 70.6 | 87.1 | 95.1 | 70.6 | 80.4 |
| 09 | FINISHES | 112.5 | 99.7 | 105.8 | 112.9 | 99.7 | 106.0 | 76.9 | 101.0 | 89.5 | 110.5 | 100.9 | 105.5 | 108.7 | 100.4 | 104.3 | 77.2 | 100.5 | 89.4 |
| COVERS | DIVS. 10 - 14, 25, 28, 41, 43, 44 | 100.0 | 103.9 | 100.8 | 100.0 | 103.9 | 100.8 | 100.0 | 104.1 | 100.8 | 100.0 | 104.0 | 100.8 | 100.0 | 104.0 | 100.8 | 100.0 | 104.3 | 100.9 |
| 21, 22, 23 | FIRE SUPPRESSION, PLUMBING & HVAC | 96.0 | 102.9 | 98.9 | 100.2 | 103.9 | 101.7 | 97.4 | 106.4 | 101.1 | 100.1 | 108.9 | 103.7 | 100.0 | 103.9 | 101.6 | 97.4 | 79.2 | 89.9 |
| 26, 27, 3370 | ELECTRICAL, COMMUNICATIONS & UTIL. | 100.7 | 87.5 | 94.2 | 104.1 | 87.5 | 96.0 | 92.1 | 95.5 | 93.8 | 100.9 | 102.7 | 101.8 | 101.6 | 97.9 | 99.8 | 92.1 | 75.0 | 83.7 |
| MF2004 | WEIGHTED AVERAGE | 103.5 | 99.6 | 101.9 | 103.1 | 99.9 | 101.8 | 97.0 | 101.8 | 99.1 | 101.8 | 104.1 | 102.8 | 101.0 | 102.1 | 101.5 | 94.6 | 92.6 | 93.8 |

## PENNSYLVANIA

| DIVISION | | ALLENTOWN 181 | | | ALTOONA 166 | | | BEDFORD 155 | | | BRADFORD 167 | | | BUTLER 160 | | | CHAMBERSBURG 172 | | |
|---|---|---|---|---|---|---|---|---|---|---|---|---|---|---|---|---|---|---|---|
| | | MAT. | INST. | TOTAL | MAT. | INST. | TOTAL | MAT. | INST. | TOTAL | MAT. | INST. | TOTAL | MAT. | INST. | TOTAL | MAT. | INST. | TOTAL |
| 015433 | CONTRACTOR EQUIPMENT | | 115.6 | 115.6 | | 115.6 | 115.6 | | 112.9 | 112.9 | | 115.6 | 115.6 | | 115.6 | 115.6 | | 114.7 | 114.7 |
| 0241, 31 - 34 | SITE & INFRASTRUCTURE, DEMOLITION | 91.9 | 106.5 | 102.1 | 96.8 | 106.3 | 103.4 | 102.7 | 103.5 | 103.3 | 91.5 | 105.8 | 101.5 | 87.6 | 107.2 | 101.2 | 86.2 | 103.8 | 98.5 |
| 0310 | Concrete Forming & Accessories | 100.3 | 115.0 | 113.0 | 84.6 | 81.5 | 81.9 | 85.7 | 83.5 | 83.8 | 87.1 | 81.2 | 82.0 | 86.2 | 92.4 | 91.6 | 85.7 | 82.8 | 83.2 |
| 0320 | Concrete Reinforcing | 99.9 | 104.0 | 101.9 | 96.9 | 86.3 | 91.8 | 92.9 | 77.6 | 85.5 | 98.9 | 86.3 | 92.9 | 97.5 | 104.4 | 100.9 | 97.3 | 94.8 | 96.1 |
| 0330 | Cast-in-Place Concrete | 87.7 | 103.2 | 93.5 | 97.8 | 85.7 | 93.3 | 100.8 | 77.2 | 92.1 | 93.4 | 88.1 | 91.5 | 86.4 | 92.0 | 88.4 | 94.9 | 76.9 | 88.2 |
| 03 | CONCRETE | 97.8 | 109.7 | 103.3 | 93.4 | 85.3 | 89.6 | 98.9 | 81.6 | 90.9 | 99.8 | 86.0 | 93.4 | 85.0 | 95.9 | 90.0 | 105.7 | 84.6 | 96.0 |
| 04 | MASONRY | 94.9 | 103.2 | 99.9 | 97.0 | 77.3 | 85.2 | 95.3 | 85.5 | 89.4 | 93.9 | 82.8 | 87.3 | 99.1 | 91.3 | 94.4 | 95.2 | 87.4 | 90.5 |
| 05 | METALS | 96.7 | 122.4 | 104.2 | 90.6 | 110.9 | 96.5 | 95.1 | 104.8 | 97.9 | 94.8 | 111.0 | 99.5 | 90.3 | 122.1 | 99.6 | 94.7 | 113.8 | 100.3 |
| 06 | WOOD, PLASTICS & COMPOSITES | 100.8 | 118.8 | 110.5 | 79.2 | 83.7 | 81.6 | 80.0 | 83.6 | 82.0 | 85.6 | 80.3 | 82.7 | 80.9 | 92.1 | 86.9 | 89.1 | 83.7 | 86.2 |
| 07 | THERMAL & MOISTURE PROTECTION | 101.2 | 117.1 | 107.4 | 100.3 | 89.2 | 96.0 | 101.1 | 87.3 | 95.7 | 101.2 | 90.8 | 97.1 | 100.0 | 96.9 | 98.8 | 100.5 | 75.6 | 90.8 |
| 08 | OPENINGS | 94.5 | 113.3 | 99.1 | 88.9 | 87.6 | 88.6 | 91.4 | 85.4 | 89.9 | 95.0 | 90.0 | 93.7 | 88.9 | 102.2 | 92.2 | 91.3 | 83.8 | 89.5 |
| 0920 | Plaster & Gypsum Board | 111.6 | 119.0 | 116.2 | 105.8 | 83.0 | 91.7 | 91.7 | 83.0 | 86.3 | 106.6 | 79.5 | 89.9 | 106.1 | 91.7 | 97.2 | 109.3 | 83.0 | 93.1 |
| 0950, 0980 | Ceilings & Acoustic Treatment | 87.8 | 119.0 | 107.0 | 92.1 | 83.0 | 86.5 | 88.5 | 83.0 | 85.1 | 90.5 | 79.5 | 83.8 | 93.0 | 91.7 | 92.2 | 90.5 | 83.0 | 85.9 |
| 0960 | Flooring | 85.9 | 93.3 | 87.9 | 79.7 | 52.7 | 72.4 | 87.3 | 53.5 | 78.1 | 79.3 | 98.3 | 84.4 | 80.6 | 93.6 | 84.2 | 83.2 | 53.5 | 75.1 |
| 0970, 0990 | Wall Finishes & Painting/Coating | 88.6 | 84.5 | 86.1 | 84.4 | 106.4 | 97.6 | 96.5 | 81.0 | 87.2 | 88.6 | 91.6 | 90.4 | 84.4 | 106.3 | 97.5 | 88.6 | 69.2 | 76.9 |
| 09 | FINISHES | 94.7 | 107.5 | 101.4 | 93.3 | 77.8 | 85.2 | 93.2 | 76.8 | 84.6 | 92.6 | 84.0 | 88.1 | 93.3 | 93.1 | 93.2 | 93.3 | 75.6 | 84.0 |
| COVERS | DIVS. 10 - 14, 25, 28, 41, 43, 44 | 100.0 | 103.7 | 100.8 | 100.0 | 96.0 | 99.2 | 100.0 | 98.6 | 99.7 | 100.0 | 97.6 | 99.5 | 100.0 | 100.5 | 100.1 | 100.0 | 90.3 | 98.0 |
| 21, 22, 23 | FIRE SUPPRESSION, PLUMBING & HVAC | 100.2 | 111.7 | 105.0 | 99.7 | 82.9 | 92.8 | 95.7 | 86.5 | 91.9 | 96.1 | 86.0 | 92.0 | 95.6 | 89.0 | 92.9 | 96.2 | 91.3 | 94.2 |
| 26, 27, 3370 | ELECTRICAL, COMMUNICATIONS & UTIL. | 101.9 | 91.8 | 96.9 | 91.1 | 100.8 | 95.9 | 94.9 | 100.8 | 97.8 | 95.5 | 100.8 | 98.1 | 91.7 | 97.5 | 94.6 | 94.0 | 80.0 | 87.1 |
| MF2004 | WEIGHTED AVERAGE | 98.0 | 107.8 | 102.2 | 94.6 | 89.8 | 92.5 | 95.9 | 89.9 | 93.3 | 96.0 | 92.0 | 94.3 | 92.6 | 97.5 | 94.7 | 96.2 | 88.6 | 92.9 |

## PENNSYLVANIA

| DIVISION | | DOYLESTOWN 189 | | | DUBOIS 158 | | | ERIE 164 - 165 | | | GREENSBURG 156 | | | HARRISBURG 170 - 171 | | | HAZLETON 182 | | |
|---|---|---|---|---|---|---|---|---|---|---|---|---|---|---|---|---|---|---|---|
| | | MAT. | INST. | TOTAL | MAT. | INST. | TOTAL | MAT. | INST. | TOTAL | MAT. | INST. | TOTAL | MAT. | INST. | TOTAL | MAT. | INST. | TOTAL |
| 015433 | CONTRACTOR EQUIPMENT | | 92.5 | 92.5 | | 112.9 | 112.9 | | 115.6 | 115.6 | | 112.9 | 112.9 | | 114.7 | 114.7 | | 115.6 | 115.6 |
| 0241, 31 - 34 | SITE & INFRASTRUCTURE, DEMOLITION | 105.5 | 89.5 | 94.4 | 108.0 | 103.7 | 105.0 | 93.2 | 106.8 | 102.7 | 98.4 | 105.0 | 103.0 | 83.4 | 104.9 | 98.4 | 85.0 | 106.2 | 99.8 |
| 0310 | Concrete Forming & Accessories | 83.6 | 129.6 | 123.2 | 85.1 | 84.6 | 84.7 | 99.7 | 89.4 | 90.8 | 92.5 | 94.3 | 94.1 | 93.3 | 84.5 | 85.7 | 81.3 | 85.3 | 84.7 |
| 0320 | Concrete Reinforcing | 96.6 | 120.6 | 108.2 | 92.3 | 86.5 | 89.5 | 98.9 | 83.8 | 91.6 | 92.3 | 104.2 | 98.1 | 99.9 | 96.4 | 98.2 | 97.0 | 108.4 | 102.5 |
| 0330 | Cast-in-Place Concrete | 82.9 | 93.2 | 86.7 | 97.2 | 89.6 | 94.4 | 96.2 | 78.9 | 89.8 | 93.5 | 91.7 | 92.8 | 96.7 | 90.3 | 94.3 | 82.9 | 87.4 | 84.6 |
| 03 | CONCRETE | 93.3 | 115.0 | 103.3 | 100.2 | 88.0 | 94.6 | 92.3 | 86.1 | 89.4 | 94.0 | 96.5 | 95.2 | 100.0 | 90.2 | 95.5 | 90.3 | 91.9 | 91.0 |
| 04 | MASONRY | 98.1 | 127.2 | 115.5 | 95.3 | 86.4 | 90.0 | 87.1 | 90.5 | 89.2 | 105.2 | 87.0 | 94.3 | 95.5 | 85.8 | 89.7 | 107.2 | 92.2 | 98.2 |
| 05 | METALS | 94.2 | 117.3 | 101.0 | 95.1 | 110.2 | 99.5 | 90.7 | 109.9 | 96.3 | 95.0 | 120.5 | 102.4 | 98.5 | 117.7 | 104.1 | 96.5 | 123.0 | 104.2 |
| 06 | WOOD, PLASTICS & COMPOSITES | 80.9 | 132.6 | 108.8 | 79.0 | 83.6 | 81.5 | 97.1 | 89.1 | 92.8 | 87.5 | 94.7 | 91.4 | 94.4 | 83.9 | 88.7 | 79.4 | 83.8 | 81.8 |
| 07 | THERMAL & MOISTURE PROTECTION | 99.6 | 127.4 | 110.4 | 101.4 | 94.0 | 98.5 | 100.4 | 94.2 | 98.0 | 101.0 | 95.6 | 98.9 | 105.9 | 105.2 | 105.6 | 100.7 | 101.8 | 101.1 |
| 08 | OPENINGS | 96.2 | 133.0 | 105.2 | 91.4 | 91.8 | 91.5 | 89.1 | 87.8 | 88.7 | 91.3 | 103.5 | 94.4 | 94.5 | 90.8 | 93.6 | 95.2 | 94.5 | 95.0 |
| 0920 | Plaster & Gypsum Board | 104.4 | 133.2 | 122.2 | 91.1 | 83.0 | 86.1 | 111.6 | 88.6 | 97.4 | 93.2 | 94.3 | 93.9 | 108.9 | 83.2 | 93.1 | 104.8 | 83.2 | 91.5 |
| 0950, 0980 | Ceilings & Acoustic Treatment | 87.1 | 133.2 | 115.4 | 88.5 | 83.0 | 85.1 | 87.8 | 88.6 | 88.3 | 87.6 | 94.3 | 91.7 | 90.4 | 83.2 | 86.0 | 88.8 | 83.2 | 85.3 |
| 0960 | Flooring | 69.9 | 95.8 | 76.9 | 86.9 | 98.3 | 90.0 | 88.0 | 78.4 | 85.4 | 90.8 | 78.6 | 87.5 | 86.4 | 88.5 | 87.0 | 76.3 | 91.8 | 80.5 |
| 0970, 0990 | Wall Finishes & Painting/Coating | 88.1 | 82.6 | 84.8 | 96.5 | 106.3 | 102.4 | 95.1 | 88.7 | 91.3 | 96.5 | 106.3 | 102.4 | 88.6 | 83.9 | 85.8 | 88.6 | 95.7 | 92.9 |
| 09 | FINISHES | 86.1 | 118.8 | 103.2 | 93.4 | 87.5 | 90.3 | 96.2 | 86.9 | 91.3 | 94.0 | 92.7 | 93.3 | 93.8 | 84.7 | 89.1 | 90.5 | 86.0 | 88.2 |
| COVERS | DIVS. 10 - 14, 25, 28, 41, 43, 44 | 100.0 | 83.4 | 96.6 | 100.0 | 98.6 | 99.7 | 100.0 | 100.4 | 100.1 | 100.0 | 100.8 | 100.2 | 100.0 | 89.7 | 97.9 | 100.0 | 95.1 | 99.0 |
| 21, 22, 23 | FIRE SUPPRESSION, PLUMBING & HVAC | 95.6 | 125.7 | 108.0 | 95.7 | 86.7 | 92.0 | 99.7 | 88.9 | 95.3 | 95.7 | 88.2 | 92.6 | 100.1 | 91.1 | 96.4 | 96.1 | 86.9 | 92.0 |
| 26, 27, 3370 | ELECTRICAL, COMMUNICATIONS & UTIL. | 94.6 | 114.1 | 104.2 | 95.4 | 100.8 | 98.1 | 93.0 | 88.0 | 90.6 | 95.4 | 100.8 | 98.1 | 101.0 | 80.1 | 90.7 | 96.4 | 84.6 | 90.6 |
| MF2004 | WEIGHTED AVERAGE | 95.0 | 117.3 | 104.6 | 96.2 | 93.2 | 94.9 | 94.5 | 92.1 | 93.5 | 95.8 | 97.2 | 96.4 | 98.3 | 91.9 | 95.6 | 95.6 | 93.3 | 94.6 |

## PENNSYLVANIA

| DIVISION | | INDIANA 157 | | | JOHNSTOWN 159 | | | KITTANNING 162 | | | LANCASTER 175 - 176 | | | LEHIGH VALLEY 180 | | | MONTROSE 188 | | |
|---|---|---|---|---|---|---|---|---|---|---|---|---|---|---|---|---|---|---|---|
| | | MAT. | INST. | TOTAL | MAT. | INST. | TOTAL | MAT. | INST. | TOTAL | MAT. | INST. | TOTAL | MAT. | INST. | TOTAL | MAT. | INST. | TOTAL |
| 015433 | CONTRACTOR EQUIPMENT | | 112.9 | 112.9 | | 112.9 | 112.9 | | 115.6 | 115.6 | | 114.7 | 114.7 | | 115.6 | 115.6 | | 115.6 | 115.6 |
| 0241, 31 - 34 | SITE & INFRASTRUCTURE, DEMOLITION | 96.5 | 104.3 | 101.9 | 103.3 | 104.5 | 104.1 | 90.3 | 107.3 | 102.2 | 77.8 | 104.9 | 96.6 | 89.4 | 106.2 | 101.1 | 88.2 | 104.7 | 99.7 |
| 0310 | Concrete Forming & Accessories | 86.4 | 86.0 | 86.1 | 85.1 | 84.8 | 84.8 | 86.2 | 94.5 | 93.4 | 87.7 | 83.9 | 84.4 | 93.6 | 111.4 | 108.9 | 82.2 | 85.3 | 84.8 |
| 0320 | Concrete Reinforcing | 91.6 | 104.5 | 97.8 | 92.9 | 104.1 | 98.3 | 97.5 | 104.6 | 100.9 | 97.0 | 96.3 | 96.7 | 97.0 | 102.8 | 99.8 | 101.6 | 108.2 | 104.8 |
| 0330 | Cast-in-Place Concrete | 91.7 | 91.6 | 91.7 | 101.7 | 89.9 | 97.3 | 89.8 | 92.1 | 90.6 | 80.7 | 90.0 | 84.1 | 89.7 | 97.7 | 92.7 | 88.0 | 85.1 | 86.9 |
| 03 | CONCRETE | 91.7 | 92.9 | 92.3 | 99.7 | 91.6 | 96.0 | 87.6 | 96.9 | 91.9 | 92.8 | 89.9 | 91.4 | 96.9 | 106.0 | 101.1 | 95.5 | 90.9 | 93.4 |
| 04 | MASONRY | 91.7 | 92.9 | 92.4 | 92.5 | 85.9 | 88.6 | 102.9 | 92.9 | 96.9 | 100.6 | 85.8 | 91.7 | 95.0 | 94.7 | 94.8 | 94.9 | 92.8 | 93.6 |
| 05 | METALS | 95.1 | 120.9 | 102.6 | 95.1 | 118.7 | 102.0 | 90.4 | 122.5 | 99.7 | 94.7 | 117.1 | 101.2 | 96.4 | 121.6 | 103.8 | 94.9 | 118.8 | 101.8 |
| 06 | WOOD, PLASTICS & COMPOSITES | 80.9 | 83.6 | 82.4 | 79.0 | 83.6 | 81.5 | 80.9 | 94.7 | 88.3 | 91.9 | 83.9 | 87.6 | 92.9 | 116.5 | 105.6 | 80.2 | 84.4 | 82.5 |
| 07 | THERMAL & MOISTURE PROTECTION | 100.9 | 94.8 | 98.5 | 101.1 | 92.7 | 97.8 | 100.1 | 97.6 | 99.1 | 100.1 | 98.6 | 99.5 | 101.1 | 105.3 | 102.7 | 100.7 | 92.6 | 97.5 |
| 08 | OPENINGS | 91.4 | 97.3 | 92.8 | 91.4 | 93.0 | 91.8 | 88.9 | 103.3 | 92.5 | 91.3 | 92.2 | 91.5 | 95.2 | 111.8 | 99.3 | 91.5 | 94.7 | 92.0 |
| 0920 | Plaster & Gypsum Board | 92.1 | 83.0 | 86.5 | 90.9 | 83.0 | 86.0 | 106.1 | 94.3 | 98.9 | 111.0 | 83.2 | 93.9 | 107.9 | 116.7 | 113.3 | 105.2 | 83.8 | 92.0 |
| 0950, 0980 | Ceilings & Acoustic Treatment | 88.5 | 83.0 | 85.1 | 87.6 | 83.0 | 84.8 | 93.0 | 94.3 | 93.8 | 90.5 | 83.2 | 86.0 | 88.8 | 116.7 | 105.9 | 90.5 | 83.8 | 86.4 |
| 0960 | Flooring | 87.7 | 99.9 | 91.0 | 86.9 | 67.1 | 81.5 | 80.6 | 99.9 | 85.9 | 84.3 | 88.5 | 85.5 | 82.1 | 93.3 | 85.2 | 77.0 | 66.9 | 74.3 |
| 0970, 0990 | Wall Finishes & Painting/Coating | 96.5 | 106.3 | 102.4 | 96.5 | 106.4 | 102.4 | 84.4 | 106.3 | 97.5 | 88.6 | 68.4 | 76.5 | 88.6 | 79.6 | 83.2 | 88.6 | 95.7 | 92.9 |
| 09 | FINISHES | 93.0 | 89.4 | 91.1 | 92.8 | 82.7 | 87.5 | 93.4 | 95.9 | 94.7 | 93.4 | 81.3 | 87.0 | 93.1 | 104.4 | 99.0 | 91.4 | 82.5 | 86.8 |
| COVERS | DIVS. 10 - 14, 25, 28, 41, 43, 44 | 100.0 | 99.4 | 99.9 | 100.0 | 98.8 | 99.7 | 100.0 | 100.8 | 100.2 | 100.0 | 89.5 | 97.9 | 100.0 | 100.0 | 100.0 | 100.0 | 95.6 | 99.1 |
| 21, 22, 23 | FIRE SUPPRESSION, PLUMBING & HVAC | 95.7 | 88.2 | 92.6 | 95.7 | 87.1 | 92.2 | 95.6 | 95.3 | 95.5 | 96.2 | 91.0 | 94.1 | 96.1 | 109.0 | 101.4 | 96.1 | 91.0 | 94.0 |
| 26, 27, 3370 | ELECTRICAL, COMMUNICATIONS & UTIL. | 95.4 | 100.8 | 98.1 | 95.4 | 100.8 | 98.1 | 91.1 | 100.8 | 95.9 | 95.4 | 52.8 | 74.5 | 96.4 | 138.5 | 117.1 | 95.5 | 93.3 | 94.4 |
| MF2004 | WEIGHTED AVERAGE | 94.7 | 96.4 | 95.4 | 95.8 | 94.0 | 95.0 | 93.1 | 100.1 | 96.1 | 94.9 | 87.3 | 91.6 | 96.2 | 111.4 | 102.7 | 95.0 | 94.3 | 94.7 |

## PENNSYLVANIA

| DIVISION | | NEW CASTLE 161 | | | NORRISTOWN 194 | | | OIL CITY 163 | | | PHILADELPHIA 190 - 191 | | | PITTSBURGH 150 - 152 | | | POTTSVILLE 179 | | |
|---|---|---|---|---|---|---|---|---|---|---|---|---|---|---|---|---|---|---|---|
| | | MAT. | INST. | TOTAL | MAT. | INST. | TOTAL | MAT. | INST. | TOTAL | MAT. | INST. | TOTAL | MAT. | INST. | TOTAL | MAT. | INST. | TOTAL |
| 015433 | CONTRACTOR EQUIPMENT | | 115.6 | 115.6 | | 95.9 | 95.9 | | 115.6 | 115.6 | | 95.2 | 95.2 | | 114.4 | 114.4 | | 114.7 | 114.7 |
| 0241, 31 - 34 | SITE & INFRASTRUCTURE, DEMOLITION | 88.1 | 107.3 | 101.5 | 96.1 | 97.1 | 96.8 | 86.4 | 106.1 | 100.2 | 103.4 | 96.5 | 98.6 | 101.8 | 107.5 | 105.8 | 80.9 | 104.7 | 97.5 |
| 0310 | Concrete Forming & Accessories | 86.2 | 94.0 | 92.9 | 84.2 | 132.2 | 125.6 | 86.2 | 83.3 | 83.7 | 101.4 | 141.9 | 136.3 | 100.6 | 94.6 | 95.5 | 79.2 | 84.3 | 83.6 |
| 0320 | Concrete Reinforcing | 96.3 | 98.6 | 97.4 | 101.7 | 138.1 | 119.2 | 97.5 | 98.4 | 97.9 | 104.9 | 138.8 | 121.2 | 93.4 | 104.7 | 98.9 | 96.2 | 100.8 | 98.4 |
| 0330 | Cast-in-Place Concrete | 87.2 | 91.8 | 88.9 | 91.6 | 122.3 | 103.0 | 84.7 | 94.2 | 88.2 | 112.5 | 132.7 | 119.9 | 97.2 | 91.8 | 95.2 | 85.9 | 79.9 | 83.7 |
| 03 | CONCRETE | 85.4 | 95.4 | 90.0 | 96.7 | 129.6 | 111.9 | 83.7 | 91.4 | 87.3 | 110.5 | 137.5 | 123.0 | 97.3 | 96.8 | 97.1 | 96.8 | 87.5 | 92.5 |
| 04 | MASONRY | 98.2 | 91.3 | 94.1 | 111.7 | 127.3 | 121.0 | 98.8 | 90.1 | 93.6 | 98.4 | 136.2 | 121.0 | 86.8 | 95.8 | 92.2 | 94.7 | 86.3 | 89.7 |
| 05 | METALS | 90.4 | 118.9 | 98.7 | 98.1 | 128.7 | 107.0 | 90.4 | 117.0 | 98.1 | 101.5 | 130.9 | 110.0 | 96.4 | 121.5 | 103.7 | 94.9 | 119.1 | 102.0 |
| 06 | WOOD, PLASTICS & COMPOSITES | 80.9 | 94.7 | 88.3 | 81.3 | 132.5 | 108.9 | 80.9 | 80.3 | 80.5 | 100.9 | 143.8 | 124.0 | 97.4 | 94.7 | 95.9 | 82.0 | 83.8 | 83.0 |
| 07 | THERMAL & MOISTURE PROTECTION | 100.0 | 96.5 | 98.7 | 100.7 | 132.1 | 112.9 | 99.9 | 94.1 | 97.7 | 101.4 | 137.6 | 115.5 | 101.3 | 98.0 | 100.0 | 100.1 | 100.6 | 100.3 |
| 08 | OPENINGS | 88.9 | 101.3 | 91.9 | 89.7 | 138.1 | 101.7 | 88.9 | 84.6 | 87.8 | 97.8 | 145.7 | 109.6 | 94.0 | 104.3 | 96.5 | 91.4 | 92.1 | 91.5 |
| 0920 | Plaster & Gypsum Board | 106.1 | 94.3 | 98.9 | 97.6 | 133.2 | 119.6 | 106.1 | 79.5 | 89.7 | 104.0 | 144.8 | 129.2 | 97.8 | 94.3 | 95.7 | 106.6 | 83.2 | 92.3 |
| 0950, 0980 | Ceilings & Acoustic Treatment | 93.0 | 94.3 | 93.8 | 97.8 | 133.2 | 119.6 | 93.0 | 79.5 | 84.7 | 97.8 | 144.8 | 126.7 | 88.5 | 94.3 | 92.1 | 90.5 | 83.2 | 86.0 |
| 0960 | Flooring | 80.6 | 66.4 | 76.8 | 75.6 | 134.4 | 91.6 | 80.6 | 98.3 | 85.4 | 84.0 | 140.8 | 99.4 | 95.0 | 101.6 | 96.8 | 80.1 | 84.4 | 81.2 |
| 0970, 0990 | Wall Finishes & Painting/Coating | 84.4 | 106.3 | 97.5 | 98.5 | 144.3 | 126.0 | 84.4 | 106.3 | 97.5 | 98.5 | 144.3 | 126.0 | 96.5 | 106.5 | 102.5 | 88.6 | 95.7 | 92.9 |
| 09 | FINISHES | 93.3 | 89.5 | 91.3 | 95.4 | 134.2 | 115.7 | 93.2 | 86.6 | 89.7 | 99.2 | 142.5 | 121.9 | 96.3 | 96.5 | 96.4 | 91.7 | 85.4 | 88.4 |
| COVERS | DIVS. 10 - 14, 25, 28, 41, 43, 44 | 100.0 | 100.8 | 100.2 | 100.0 | 112.3 | 102.5 | 100.0 | 99.6 | 99.9 | 100.0 | 124.2 | 105.0 | 100.0 | 100.8 | 100.2 | 100.0 | 89.8 | 97.9 |
| 21, 22, 23 | FIRE SUPPRESSION, PLUMBING & HVAC | 95.6 | 88.8 | 92.8 | 95.9 | 130.0 | 109.9 | 95.6 | 89.2 | 93.0 | 100.1 | 133.1 | 113.6 | 99.9 | 95.5 | 98.1 | 96.2 | 89.3 | 93.4 |
| 26, 27, 3370 | ELECTRICAL, COMMUNICATIONS & UTIL. | 91.7 | 97.7 | 94.6 | 97.1 | 133.8 | 115.1 | 93.7 | 97.5 | 95.6 | 101.7 | 141.5 | 121.3 | 97.8 | 100.8 | 99.3 | 93.6 | 90.5 | 92.1 |
| MF2004 | WEIGHTED AVERAGE | 92.6 | 96.7 | 94.4 | 97.0 | 127.8 | 110.2 | 92.6 | 94.5 | 93.4 | 101.5 | 133.6 | 115.2 | 97.3 | 100.5 | 98.7 | 94.7 | 92.8 | 93.9 |

## PENNSYLVANIA

| DIVISION | | READING 195 - 196 | | | SCRANTON 184 - 185 | | | STATE COLLEGE 168 | | | STROUDSBURG 183 | | | SUNBURY 178 | | | UNIONTOWN 154 | | |
|---|---|---|---|---|---|---|---|---|---|---|---|---|---|---|---|---|---|---|---|
| | | MAT. | INST. | TOTAL | MAT. | INST. | TOTAL | MAT. | INST. | TOTAL | MAT. | INST. | TOTAL | MAT. | INST. | TOTAL | MAT. | INST. | TOTAL |
| 015433 | CONTRACTOR EQUIPMENT | | 118.9 | 118.9 | | 115.6 | 115.6 | | 114.7 | 114.7 | | 115.6 | 115.6 | | 115.6 | 115.6 | | 112.9 | 112.9 |
| 0241, 31 - 34 | SITE & INFRASTRUCTURE, DEMOLITION | 100.4 | 111.8 | 108.3 | 92.5 | 106.3 | 102.1 | 83.1 | 105.0 | 98.4 | 86.9 | 104.6 | 99.2 | 91.2 | 105.9 | 101.5 | 97.1 | 104.9 | 102.6 |
| 0310 | Concrete Forming & Accessories | 100.9 | 84.8 | 87.0 | 100.5 | 85.2 | 87.3 | 84.8 | 81.4 | 81.9 | 87.9 | 85.4 | 85.8 | 91.4 | 83.3 | 84.4 | 79.1 | 94.1 | 92.0 |
| 0320 | Concrete Reinforcing | 103.1 | 96.6 | 99.9 | 99.9 | 108.4 | 104.0 | 98.1 | 86.5 | 92.5 | 100.2 | 103.4 | 101.8 | 98.9 | 95.1 | 97.1 | 92.3 | 103.9 | 97.9 |
| 0330 | Cast-in-Place Concrete | 82.1 | 94.8 | 86.8 | 91.7 | 88.5 | 90.5 | 88.4 | 73.6 | 82.9 | 86.3 | 75.7 | 82.4 | 94.0 | 89.8 | 92.4 | 91.7 | 91.6 | 91.6 |
| 03 | CONCRETE | 95.1 | 92.0 | 93.7 | 99.7 | 92.3 | 96.3 | 99.8 | 81.2 | 91.2 | 94.2 | 86.9 | 90.8 | 100.5 | 89.3 | 95.3 | 91.4 | 96.3 | 93.7 |
| 04 | MASONRY | 99.6 | 88.2 | 92.8 | 95.3 | 94.1 | 94.6 | 100.6 | 81.0 | 88.9 | 91.7 | 94.3 | 93.3 | 94.0 | 85.9 | 89.2 | 107.2 | 81.5 | 91.8 |
| 05 | METALS | 98.3 | 118.3 | 104.1 | 98.6 | 123.5 | 105.8 | 94.6 | 111.1 | 99.4 | 96.5 | 116.1 | 102.2 | 94.7 | 116.1 | 100.9 | 94.9 | 119.8 | 102.1 |
| 06 | WOOD, PLASTICS & COMPOSITES | 101.0 | 83.0 | 91.3 | 100.8 | 82.1 | 90.7 | 88.0 | 83.7 | 85.7 | 86.6 | 85.1 | 85.8 | 90.3 | 83.0 | 86.4 | 71.9 | 94.7 | 84.2 |
| 07 | THERMAL & MOISTURE PROTECTION | 100.9 | 108.0 | 103.7 | 101.1 | 98.0 | 99.9 | 100.3 | 92.7 | 97.4 | 100.9 | 80.8 | 93.1 | 101.0 | 99.6 | 100.5 | 100.8 | 94.2 | 98.2 |
| 08 | OPENINGS | 95.4 | 91.8 | 94.5 | 94.5 | 93.6 | 94.3 | 91.3 | 87.6 | 90.4 | 95.2 | 85.5 | 92.8 | 91.5 | 89.9 | 91.1 | 91.3 | 103.5 | 94.3 |
| 0920 | Plaster & Gypsum Board | 107.3 | 82.4 | 91.9 | 113.8 | 81.4 | 93.8 | 108.0 | 83.0 | 92.6 | 106.1 | 84.5 | 92.7 | 107.0 | 82.3 | 91.8 | 88.2 | 94.3 | 92.0 |
| 0950, 0980 | Ceilings & Acoustic Treatment | 87.5 | 82.4 | 84.4 | 97.2 | 81.4 | 87.5 | 87.9 | 83.0 | 84.9 | 87.1 | 84.5 | 85.5 | 87.9 | 82.3 | 84.5 | 87.6 | 94.3 | 91.7 |
| 0960 | Flooring | 82.3 | 94.0 | 85.5 | 85.9 | 105.7 | 91.3 | 82.7 | 57.5 | 75.8 | 79.8 | 59.3 | 74.2 | 81.1 | 49.1 | 72.4 | 83.9 | 74.0 | 81.2 |
| 0970, 0990 | Wall Finishes & Painting/Coating | 96.9 | 96.8 | 96.9 | 88.6 | 95.7 | 92.9 | 88.6 | 106.4 | 99.3 | 88.6 | 77.3 | 81.9 | 88.6 | 95.7 | 92.9 | 96.5 | 106.3 | 102.4 |
| 09 | FINISHES | 96.8 | 86.6 | 91.4 | 97.2 | 89.5 | 93.1 | 92.1 | 78.9 | 85.2 | 91.5 | 79.5 | 85.2 | 92.6 | 78.7 | 85.3 | 91.0 | 91.0 | 91.0 |
| COVERS | DIVS. 10 - 14, 25, 28, 41, 43, 44 | 100.0 | 95.7 | 99.1 | 100.0 | 95.9 | 99.1 | 100.0 | 87.7 | 97.5 | 100.0 | 71.8 | 94.2 | 100.0 | 89.6 | 97.9 | 100.0 | 100.8 | 100.2 |
| 21, 22, 23 | FIRE SUPPRESSION, PLUMBING & HVAC | 100.2 | 106.5 | 102.8 | 100.2 | 92.0 | 96.9 | 96.2 | 88.0 | 92.8 | 96.1 | 91.4 | 94.2 | 96.1 | 90.9 | 94.0 | 95.7 | 88.2 | 92.6 |
| 26, 27, 3370 | ELECTRICAL, COMMUNICATIONS & UTIL. | 104.0 | 90.5 | 97.4 | 101.9 | 93.3 | 97.7 | 94.5 | 100.8 | 97.6 | 96.4 | 147.2 | 121.4 | 94.1 | 85.2 | 89.7 | 92.4 | 100.8 | 96.5 |
| MF2004 | WEIGHTED AVERAGE | 99.0 | 98.2 | 98.6 | 98.8 | 96.4 | 97.8 | 95.6 | 90.6 | 93.5 | 95.4 | 99.6 | 97.2 | 95.6 | 91.4 | 93.8 | 94.8 | 96.3 | 95.4 |

## PENNSYLVANIA

| DIVISION | | WASHINGTON 153 | | | WELLSBORO 169 | | | WESTCHESTER 193 | | | WILKES-BARRE 186 - 187 | | | WILLIAMSPORT 177 | | | YORK 173 - 174 | | |
|---|---|---|---|---|---|---|---|---|---|---|---|---|---|---|---|---|---|---|---|
| | | MAT. | INST. | TOTAL | MAT. | INST. | TOTAL | MAT. | INST. | TOTAL | MAT. | INST. | TOTAL | MAT. | INST. | TOTAL | MAT. | INST. | TOTAL |
| 015433 | CONTRACTOR EQUIPMENT | | 112.9 | 112.9 | | 115.6 | 115.6 | | 95.9 | 95.9 | | 115.6 | 115.6 | | 115.6 | 115.6 | | 114.7 | 114.7 |
| 0241, 31 - 34 | SITE & INFRASTRUCTURE, DEMOLITION | 97.1 | 105.0 | 102.6 | 95.7 | 104.5 | 101.8 | 102.9 | 95.2 | 97.6 | 84.8 | 106.2 | 99.7 | 82.0 | 104.5 | 97.7 | 81.4 | 104.9 | 97.8 |
| 0310 | Concrete Forming & Accessories | 86.6 | 94.5 | 93.4 | 86.5 | 79.3 | 80.3 | 91.3 | 130.4 | 125.0 | 90.5 | 86.2 | 86.8 | 87.8 | 63.6 | 67.0 | 82.7 | 84.5 | 84.2 |
| 0320 | Concrete Reinforcing | 92.3 | 104.6 | 98.2 | 98.1 | 108.1 | 102.9 | 100.7 | 105.0 | 102.8 | 98.9 | 108.4 | 103.5 | 98.1 | 77.4 | 88.1 | 98.9 | 96.4 | 97.7 |
| 0330 | Cast-in-Place Concrete | 91.7 | 91.7 | 91.7 | 92.6 | 83.1 | 89.1 | 101.5 | 126.4 | 110.7 | 82.9 | 88.0 | 84.8 | 79.5 | 72.5 | 76.9 | 86.4 | 90.3 | 87.8 |
| 03 | CONCRETE | 91.8 | 96.7 | 94.1 | 102.2 | 87.6 | 95.5 | 105.1 | 123.8 | 113.7 | 91.2 | 92.6 | 91.8 | 87.9 | 71.3 | 80.2 | 98.0 | 90.2 | 94.4 |
| 04 | MASONRY | 91.8 | 92.9 | 92.4 | 100.2 | 84.8 | 91.0 | 106.0 | 127.4 | 118.8 | 107.9 | 93.1 | 99.1 | 86.2 | 79.3 | 82.1 | 95.0 | 85.8 | 89.5 |
| 05 | METALS | 94.8 | 121.2 | 102.5 | 94.7 | 119.2 | 101.8 | 98.1 | 112.2 | 102.2 | 94.8 | 123.3 | 103.1 | 94.7 | 106.7 | 98.2 | 96.3 | 117.7 | 102.5 |
| 06 | WOOD, PLASTICS & COMPOSITES | 80.9 | 94.7 | 88.3 | 85.0 | 79.7 | 82.1 | 89.3 | 132.5 | 112.6 | 89.3 | 84.3 | 86.6 | 86.6 | 61.9 | 73.3 | 85.9 | 83.9 | 84.8 |
| 07 | THERMAL & MOISTURE PROTECTION | 100.9 | 97.2 | 99.5 | 101.4 | 88.9 | 96.5 | 101.0 | 127.3 | 111.3 | 100.7 | 102.2 | 101.3 | 100.6 | 93.2 | 97.7 | 100.2 | 105.2 | 102.2 |
| 08 | OPENINGS | 91.3 | 103.5 | 94.3 | 94.9 | 92.1 | 94.2 | 89.7 | 110.8 | 94.9 | 91.5 | 96.3 | 92.7 | 91.5 | 65.0 | 85.0 | 91.3 | 90.8 | 91.2 |
| 0920 | Plaster & Gypsum Board | 91.9 | 94.3 | 93.4 | 106.0 | 78.9 | 89.3 | 99.6 | 133.2 | 120.4 | 107.2 | 83.6 | 92.7 | 106.9 | 60.7 | 78.4 | 108.3 | 83.2 | 92.8 |
| 0950, 0980 | Ceilings & Acoustic Treatment | 87.6 | 94.3 | 91.7 | 87.9 | 78.9 | 82.4 | 97.8 | 133.2 | 119.6 | 90.5 | 83.6 | 86.3 | 90.5 | 60.7 | 72.2 | 89.5 | 83.2 | 85.7 |
| 0960 | Flooring | 87.8 | 99.9 | 91.1 | 79.0 | 58.7 | 73.5 | 79.3 | 134.4 | 94.3 | 80.8 | 91.8 | 83.8 | 79.8 | 57.5 | 73.7 | 81.6 | 88.5 | 83.5 |
| 0970, 0990 | Wall Finishes & Painting/Coating | 96.5 | 106.3 | 102.4 | 88.6 | 95.7 | 92.9 | 98.5 | 144.3 | 126.0 | 88.6 | 95.7 | 92.9 | 88.6 | 95.7 | 92.9 | 88.6 | 83.9 | 85.8 |
| 09 | FINISHES | 92.8 | 96.0 | 94.4 | 92.2 | 76.5 | 84.0 | 97.3 | 132.4 | 115.7 | 92.7 | 87.6 | 90.0 | 92.1 | 64.5 | 77.7 | 92.1 | 84.7 | 88.3 |
| COVERS | DIVS. 10 - 14, 25, 28, 41, 43, 44 | 100.0 | 100.8 | 100.2 | 100.0 | 88.6 | 97.7 | 100.0 | 112.1 | 102.5 | 100.0 | 95.5 | 99.1 | 100.0 | 84.2 | 96.8 | 100.0 | 89.7 | 97.9 |
| 21, 22, 23 | FIRE SUPPRESSION, PLUMBING & HVAC | 95.7 | 95.5 | 95.6 | 96.1 | 89.8 | 93.5 | 95.9 | 127.4 | 108.9 | 96.1 | 86.7 | 92.3 | 96.1 | 81.8 | 90.3 | 100.2 | 91.1 | 96.5 |
| 26, 27, 3370 | ELECTRICAL, COMMUNICATIONS & UTIL. | 94.8 | 100.8 | 97.8 | 95.5 | 83.3 | 89.5 | 97.0 | 105.1 | 101.0 | 96.4 | 84.6 | 90.6 | 94.6 | 55.9 | 75.6 | 95.4 | 80.1 | 87.9 |
| MF2004 | WEIGHTED AVERAGE | 94.6 | 99.8 | 96.8 | 96.7 | 90.2 | 93.9 | 98.2 | 119.2 | 107.2 | 95.3 | 93.9 | 94.7 | 93.5 | 77.9 | 86.8 | 96.3 | 91.9 | 94.4 |

| DIVISION | | PUERTO RICO / SAN JUAN 009 | | | RHODE ISLAND / NEWPORT 028 | | | PROVIDENCE 029 | | | SOUTH CAROLINA / AIKEN 298 | | | BEAUFORT 299 | | | CHARLESTON 294 | | |
|---|---|---|---|---|---|---|---|---|---|---|---|---|---|---|---|---|---|---|---|
| | | MAT. | INST. | TOTAL | MAT. | INST. | TOTAL | MAT. | INST. | TOTAL | MAT. | INST. | TOTAL | MAT. | INST. | TOTAL | MAT. | INST. | TOTAL |
| 015433 | CONTRACTOR EQUIPMENT | | 88.2 | 88.2 | | 102.5 | 102.5 | | 102.5 | 102.5 | | 99.9 | 99.9 | | 99.9 | 99.9 | | 99.9 | 99.9 |
| 0241, 31 - 34 | SITE & INFRASTRUCTURE, DEMOLITION | 118.0 | 90.6 | 98.9 | 79.1 | 102.7 | 95.6 | 80.9 | 103.0 | 96.3 | 129.9 | 84.1 | 98.0 | 124.1 | 83.5 | 95.8 | 103.9 | 83.0 | 89.3 |
| 0310 | Concrete Forming & Accessories | 91.8 | 18.1 | 28.3 | 101.5 | 115.9 | 113.9 | 100.4 | 115.9 | 113.8 | 100.2 | 69.7 | 74.0 | 98.8 | 44.7 | 52.2 | 97.8 | 46.6 | 53.7 |
| 0320 | Concrete Reinforcing | 183.3 | 11.1 | 100.3 | 102.0 | 114.6 | 108.1 | 102.0 | 114.6 | 108.1 | 98.7 | 67.5 | 83.7 | 97.8 | 31.1 | 65.7 | 97.6 | 67.3 | 83.0 |
| 0330 | Cast-in-Place Concrete | 100.0 | 28.3 | 73.4 | 77.5 | 120.2 | 93.3 | 90.4 | 120.2 | 101.4 | 79.9 | 70.5 | 76.4 | 79.9 | 52.4 | 69.7 | 93.7 | 53.1 | 78.7 |
| 03 | CONCRETE | 111.7 | 21.0 | 69.8 | 99.9 | 116.7 | 107.6 | 106.2 | 116.7 | 111.1 | 110.5 | 70.7 | 92.1 | 107.4 | 46.7 | 79.4 | 101.0 | 54.3 | 79.4 |
| 04 | MASONRY | 86.3 | 15.5 | 44.0 | 103.4 | 123.2 | 115.2 | 106.8 | 123.2 | 116.6 | 80.2 | 61.3 | 68.9 | 96.3 | 39.5 | 62.3 | 97.8 | 44.1 | 65.7 |
| 05 | METALS | 106.7 | 29.2 | 84.2 | 93.4 | 109.7 | 98.1 | 93.4 | 109.7 | 98.1 | 87.4 | 86.2 | 87.1 | 87.4 | 72.6 | 83.1 | 89.2 | 81.7 | 87.0 |
| 06 | WOOD, PLASTICS & COMPOSITES | 91.5 | 18.4 | 52.2 | 100.6 | 115.1 | 108.4 | 99.7 | 115.1 | 108.0 | 102.2 | 71.2 | 85.5 | 100.2 | 45.6 | 70.8 | 98.9 | 45.6 | 70.2 |
| 07 | THERMAL & MOISTURE PROTECTION | 137.3 | 21.5 | 92.2 | 99.7 | 115.5 | 105.8 | 97.8 | 115.5 | 104.7 | 104.4 | 68.3 | 90.3 | 104.1 | 42.2 | 80.0 | 103.3 | 47.4 | 81.5 |
| 08 | OPENINGS | 151.4 | 15.4 | 117.8 | 99.1 | 115.1 | 103.0 | 99.7 | 115.1 | 103.5 | 93.7 | 68.1 | 87.4 | 93.7 | 44.3 | 81.5 | 97.6 | 50.0 | 85.9 |
| 0920 | Plaster & Gypsum Board | 117.7 | 16.2 | 55.1 | 102.5 | 114.8 | 110.1 | 103.1 | 114.8 | 110.3 | 108.5 | 70.3 | 84.9 | 111.8 | 44.0 | 69.9 | 113.3 | 44.0 | 70.5 |
| 0950, 0980 | Ceilings & Acoustic Treatment | 210.9 | 16.2 | 91.4 | 93.6 | 114.8 | 106.6 | 92.9 | 114.8 | 106.3 | 91.5 | 70.3 | 78.5 | 96.7 | 44.0 | 64.3 | 96.7 | 44.0 | 64.3 |
| 0960 | Flooring | 199.7 | 15.2 | 149.5 | 97.1 | 125.3 | 104.8 | 96.7 | 125.3 | 104.5 | 105.4 | 66.2 | 94.8 | 107.2 | 59.2 | 94.2 | 106.7 | 67.3 | 96.0 |
| 0970, 0990 | Wall Finishes & Painting/Coating | 198.8 | 14.3 | 88.0 | 93.8 | 120.0 | 109.5 | 93.8 | 120.0 | 109.5 | 113.6 | 72.4 | 88.8 | 113.6 | 41.5 | 70.3 | 113.6 | 46.9 | 73.5 |
| 09 | FINISHES | 198.6 | 17.4 | 103.7 | 99.0 | 118.5 | 109.3 | 98.9 | 118.5 | 109.2 | 103.6 | 69.7 | 85.8 | 105.4 | 47.5 | 75.0 | 103.4 | 50.1 | 75.5 |
| COVERS | DIVS. 10 - 14, 25, 28, 41, 43, 44 | 100.0 | 17.5 | 83.1 | 100.0 | 100.1 | 100.0 | 100.0 | 100.1 | 100.0 | 100.0 | 75.2 | 94.9 | 100.0 | 54.5 | 90.7 | 100.0 | 69.8 | 93.8 |
| 21, 22, 23 | FIRE SUPPRESSION, PLUMBING & HVAC | 104.3 | 14.0 | 67.2 | 100.1 | 110.8 | 104.5 | 100.0 | 110.8 | 104.4 | 96.1 | 69.4 | 85.1 | 96.1 | 29.6 | 68.8 | 100.2 | 46.6 | 78.2 |
| 26, 27, 3370 | ELECTRICAL, COMMUNICATIONS & UTIL. | 124.4 | 14.1 | 70.3 | 97.3 | 97.2 | 97.3 | 95.4 | 97.2 | 96.3 | 95.5 | 68.6 | 82.3 | 98.9 | 36.3 | 68.2 | 97.5 | 106.6 | 102.0 |
| MF2004 | WEIGHTED AVERAGE | 120.5 | 23.8 | 79.1 | 98.1 | 111.2 | 103.7 | 98.8 | 111.2 | 104.1 | 97.5 | 71.5 | 86.4 | 98.3 | 46.4 | 76.1 | 98.3 | 63.3 | 83.3 |

## SOUTH CAROLINA / SOUTH DAKOTA

| DIVISION | | COLUMBIA 290 - 292 | | | FLORENCE 295 | | | GREENVILLE 296 | | | ROCK HILL 297 | | | SPARTANBURG 293 | | | ABERDEEN 574 | | |
|---|---|---|---|---|---|---|---|---|---|---|---|---|---|---|---|---|---|---|---|
| | | MAT. | INST. | TOTAL | MAT. | INST. | TOTAL | MAT. | INST. | TOTAL | MAT. | INST. | TOTAL | MAT. | INST. | TOTAL | MAT. | INST. | TOTAL |
| 015433 | CONTRACTOR EQUIPMENT | | 99.9 | 99.9 | | 99.9 | 99.9 | | 99.9 | 99.9 | | 99.9 | 99.9 | | 99.9 | 99.9 | | 98.7 | 98.7 |
| 0241, 31 - 34 | SITE & INFRASTRUCTURE, DEMOLITION | 102.4 | 82.9 | 88.8 | 116.3 | 82.9 | 93.1 | 110.4 | 82.5 | 91.0 | 107.7 | 82.4 | 90.1 | 110.2 | 82.5 | 90.9 | 90.2 | 94.3 | 93.1 |
| 0310 | Concrete Forming & Accessories | 99.9 | 45.5 | 53.0 | 85.0 | 45.7 | 51.1 | 97.5 | 45.5 | 52.7 | 96.0 | 42.8 | 50.2 | 100.9 | 45.5 | 53.2 | 95.7 | 43.8 | 51.0 |
| 0320 | Concrete Reinforcing | 97.6 | 67.0 | 82.9 | 97.2 | 67.2 | 82.8 | 97.1 | 53.6 | 76.1 | 98.0 | 53.3 | 76.5 | 97.1 | 53.6 | 76.1 | 102.6 | 45.4 | 75.0 |
| 0330 | Cast-in-Place Concrete | 90.9 | 53.7 | 77.1 | 79.8 | 52.8 | 69.9 | 79.8 | 52.8 | 69.8 | 79.8 | 47.0 | 67.7 | 79.8 | 52.8 | 69.8 | 100.2 | 48.5 | 81.1 |
| 03 | CONCRETE | 99.7 | 54.0 | 78.6 | 101.3 | 53.8 | 79.3 | 99.6 | 51.1 | 77.2 | 97.5 | 47.9 | 74.6 | 99.8 | 51.1 | 77.3 | 98.0 | 46.9 | 74.4 |
| 04 | MASONRY | 92.5 | 41.8 | 62.2 | 80.2 | 44.1 | 58.7 | 78.1 | 44.1 | 57.8 | 104.3 | 38.7 | 65.1 | 80.2 | 44.1 | 58.7 | 103.9 | 62.6 | 79.2 |
| 05 | METALS | 89.2 | 80.8 | 86.7 | 88.2 | 81.1 | 86.1 | 88.2 | 75.9 | 84.6 | 87.4 | 75.3 | 83.9 | 88.2 | 75.9 | 84.6 | 103.0 | 68.1 | 92.8 |
| 06 | WOOD, PLASTICS & COMPOSITES | 101.3 | 45.0 | 71.0 | 83.6 | 45.0 | 62.8 | 98.7 | 45.0 | 69.8 | 96.8 | 42.8 | 67.7 | 102.9 | 45.0 | 71.7 | 101.5 | 43.4 | 70.2 |
| 07 | THERMAL & MOISTURE PROTECTION | 102.3 | 46.0 | 80.3 | 103.6 | 47.3 | 81.7 | 103.5 | 47.3 | 81.6 | 103.4 | 44.6 | 80.5 | 103.6 | 47.3 | 81.6 | 101.0 | 54.2 | 82.7 |
| 08 | OPENINGS | 97.6 | 49.8 | 85.8 | 93.7 | 49.8 | 82.9 | 93.7 | 46.5 | 82.0 | 93.7 | 45.4 | 81.8 | 93.7 | 46.5 | 82.1 | 94.5 | 44.5 | 82.1 |
| 0920 | Plaster & Gypsum Board | 105.0 | 43.4 | 67.0 | 102.3 | 43.4 | 66.0 | 107.2 | 43.4 | 67.9 | 106.5 | 41.1 | 66.2 | 108.9 | 43.4 | 68.5 | 100.1 | 42.2 | 64.4 |
| 0950, 0980 | Ceilings & Acoustic Treatment | 94.1 | 43.4 | 63.0 | 92.4 | 43.4 | 62.3 | 91.5 | 43.4 | 62.0 | 91.5 | 41.1 | 60.6 | 91.5 | 43.4 | 62.0 | 111.5 | 42.2 | 69.0 |
| 0960 | Flooring | 103.2 | 50.4 | 88.9 | 96.7 | 50.4 | 84.1 | 103.9 | 66.0 | 93.6 | 102.9 | 51.4 | 88.9 | 105.6 | 66.0 | 94.8 | 113.6 | 55.0 | 97.7 |
| 0970, 0990 | Wall Finishes & Painting/Coating | 111.0 | 46.9 | 72.5 | 113.6 | 46.9 | 73.5 | 113.6 | 46.9 | 73.5 | 113.6 | 46.9 | 73.5 | 113.6 | 46.9 | 73.5 | 97.7 | 37.7 | 61.6 |
| 09 | FINISHES | 100.1 | 46.3 | 71.9 | 99.0 | 46.9 | 71.7 | 101.2 | 49.6 | 74.2 | 100.5 | 44.5 | 71.2 | 102.0 | 49.6 | 74.6 | 106.1 | 45.0 | 74.1 |
| COVERS | DIVS. 10 - 14, 25, 28, 41, 43, 44 | 100.0 | 69.5 | 93.7 | 100.0 | 69.5 | 93.7 | 100.0 | 69.5 | 93.7 | 100.0 | 68.5 | 93.5 | 100.0 | 69.5 | 93.7 | 100.0 | 50.9 | 90.0 |
| 21, 22, 23 | FIRE SUPPRESSION, PLUMBING & HVAC | 100.0 | 41.2 | 75.8 | 100.2 | 41.2 | 76.0 | 100.2 | 39.5 | 75.3 | 96.1 | 38.4 | 72.4 | 100.2 | 39.5 | 75.3 | 100.1 | 41.7 | 76.2 |
| 26, 27, 3370 | ELECTRICAL, COMMUNICATIONS & UTIL. | 97.5 | 54.5 | 76.4 | 95.4 | 51.9 | 74.0 | 97.5 | 56.0 | 77.1 | 97.5 | 56.0 | 77.1 | 97.5 | 56.0 | 77.1 | 97.5 | 61.4 | 79.8 |
| MF2004 | WEIGHTED AVERAGE | 97.5 | 53.9 | 78.9 | 96.5 | 53.9 | 78.3 | 96.6 | 53.5 | 78.2 | 96.5 | 51.4 | 77.2 | 96.8 | 53.5 | 78.3 | 100.0 | 55.3 | 80.9 |

## SOUTH DAKOTA

| DIVISION | | MITCHELL 573 | | | MOBRIDGE 576 | | | PIERRE 575 | | | RAPID CITY 577 | | | SIOUX FALLS 570 - 571 | | | WATERTOWN 572 | | |
|---|---|---|---|---|---|---|---|---|---|---|---|---|---|---|---|---|---|---|---|
| | | MAT. | INST. | TOTAL | MAT. | INST. | TOTAL | MAT. | INST. | TOTAL | MAT. | INST. | TOTAL | MAT. | INST. | TOTAL | MAT. | INST. | TOTAL |
| 015433 | CONTRACTOR EQUIPMENT | | 98.7 | 98.7 | | 98.7 | 98.7 | | 98.7 | 98.7 | | 98.7 | 98.7 | | 99.9 | 99.9 | | 98.7 | 98.7 |
| 0241, 31 - 34 | SITE & INFRASTRUCTURE, DEMOLITION | 87.3 | 94.3 | 92.2 | 87.3 | 94.3 | 92.2 | 88.6 | 94.3 | 92.6 | 88.4 | 94.0 | 92.3 | 90.0 | 96.2 | 94.3 | 87.2 | 94.3 | 92.1 |
| 0310 | Concrete Forming & Accessories | 94.9 | 42.3 | 49.6 | 85.9 | 40.4 | 46.7 | 94.3 | 41.2 | 48.6 | 102.4 | 36.7 | 45.8 | 95.1 | 44.0 | 51.1 | 82.4 | 40.2 | 46.0 |
| 0320 | Concrete Reinforcing | 102.0 | 55.9 | 79.8 | 104.6 | 45.9 | 76.3 | 102.1 | 57.7 | 80.7 | 95.9 | 57.7 | 77.5 | 95.9 | 57.9 | 77.6 | 99.2 | 45.9 | 73.5 |
| 0330 | Cast-in-Place Concrete | 97.3 | 46.9 | 78.7 | 97.3 | 48.4 | 79.2 | 94.3 | 45.4 | 76.2 | 96.6 | 42.3 | 76.5 | 94.3 | 47.5 | 77.0 | 97.3 | 48.4 | 79.2 |
| 03 | CONCRETE | 95.8 | 47.5 | 73.5 | 95.7 | 45.5 | 72.5 | 94.3 | 47.1 | 72.5 | 95.0 | 44.1 | 71.5 | 92.3 | 49.1 | 72.4 | 94.6 | 45.4 | 71.9 |
| 04 | MASONRY | 92.5 | 59.5 | 72.8 | 100.8 | 62.6 | 78.0 | 100.6 | 59.7 | 76.1 | 100.9 | 51.3 | 71.2 | 97.9 | 60.2 | 75.4 | 125.5 | 62.3 | 87.7 |
| 05 | METALS | 102.1 | 67.9 | 92.1 | 102.1 | 67.7 | 92.1 | 103.0 | 73.6 | 94.4 | 104.7 | 73.8 | 95.7 | 104.9 | 74.4 | 96.0 | 102.1 | 68.1 | 92.2 |
| 06 | WOOD, PLASTICS & COMPOSITES | 100.4 | 41.7 | 68.8 | 89.8 | 39.2 | 62.5 | 99.2 | 39.7 | 67.2 | 105.4 | 36.0 | 68.0 | 100.2 | 42.5 | 69.1 | 86.0 | 38.9 | 60.6 |
| 07 | THERMAL & MOISTURE PROTECTION | 100.8 | 51.2 | 81.5 | 100.8 | 53.8 | 82.5 | 100.7 | 51.3 | 81.4 | 101.4 | 50.8 | 81.6 | 102.3 | 55.5 | 84.0 | 100.6 | 53.6 | 82.3 |
| 08 | OPENINGS | 93.0 | 41.9 | 80.3 | 95.8 | 40.2 | 82.1 | 97.6 | 44.7 | 84.5 | 98.5 | 42.7 | 84.8 | 98.8 | 46.2 | 85.8 | 93.0 | 40.3 | 80.0 |
| 0920 | Plaster & Gypsum Board | 99.0 | 40.6 | 63.0 | 94.7 | 37.9 | 59.7 | 94.8 | 38.5 | 60.1 | 100.1 | 34.6 | 59.7 | 99.9 | 41.3 | 63.8 | 92.9 | 37.7 | 58.8 |
| 0950, 0980 | Ceilings & Acoustic Treatment | 109.7 | 40.6 | 67.3 | 111.5 | 37.9 | 66.3 | 107.2 | 38.5 | 65.0 | 115.7 | 34.6 | 65.9 | 109.7 | 41.3 | 67.8 | 109.7 | 37.7 | 65.5 |
| 0960 | Flooring | 113.1 | 58.1 | 98.2 | 107.4 | 55.0 | 93.2 | 112.8 | 39.2 | 92.8 | 112.8 | 73.2 | 102.0 | 112.8 | 79.0 | 103.6 | 105.7 | 55.0 | 91.9 |
| 0970, 0990 | Wall Finishes & Painting/Coating | 97.7 | 44.9 | 66.0 | 97.7 | 38.1 | 61.9 | 97.7 | 45.2 | 66.2 | 97.7 | 45.2 | 66.2 | 97.7 | 45.2 | 66.2 | 97.7 | 37.7 | 61.6 |
| 09 | FINISHES | 105.3 | 45.4 | 73.9 | 103.3 | 42.6 | 71.5 | 104.0 | 40.5 | 70.8 | 106.8 | 43.9 | 73.9 | 105.6 | 50.4 | 76.7 | 102.1 | 42.4 | 70.8 |
| COVERS | DIVS. 10 - 14, 25, 28, 41, 43, 44 | 100.0 | 46.0 | 88.9 | 100.0 | 50.4 | 89.8 | 100.0 | 76.7 | 95.2 | 100.0 | 74.2 | 94.7 | 100.0 | 77.1 | 95.3 | 100.0 | 49.5 | 89.6 |
| 21, 22, 23 | FIRE SUPPRESSION, PLUMBING & HVAC | 96.0 | 37.3 | 71.9 | 96.0 | 40.8 | 73.3 | 100.0 | 38.4 | 74.7 | 100.1 | 35.4 | 73.6 | 100.0 | 37.4 | 74.3 | 96.0 | 41.3 | 73.5 |
| 26, 27, 3370 | ELECTRICAL, COMMUNICATIONS & UTIL. | 95.9 | 47.0 | 71.9 | 97.5 | 40.8 | 69.7 | 94.9 | 53.3 | 74.4 | 94.2 | 53.3 | 74.1 | 94.2 | 71.1 | 82.9 | 95.1 | 40.8 | 68.4 |
| MF2004 | WEIGHTED AVERAGE | 97.6 | 51.8 | 78.0 | 98.2 | 51.4 | 78.2 | 99.1 | 53.7 | 79.7 | 99.8 | 52.1 | 79.4 | 99.3 | 58.1 | 81.7 | 98.6 | 51.5 | 78.4 |

## TENNESSEE

| DIVISION | | CHATTANOOGA 373 - 374 | | | COLUMBIA 384 | | | COOKEVILLE 385 | | | JACKSON 383 | | | JOHNSON CITY 376 | | | KNOXVILLE 377 - 379 | | |
|---|---|---|---|---|---|---|---|---|---|---|---|---|---|---|---|---|---|---|---|
| | | MAT. | INST. | TOTAL | MAT. | INST. | TOTAL | MAT. | INST. | TOTAL | MAT. | INST. | TOTAL | MAT. | INST. | TOTAL | MAT. | INST. | TOTAL |
| 015433 | CONTRACTOR EQUIPMENT | | 105.5 | 105.5 | | 98.2 | 98.2 | | 98.2 | 98.2 | | 105.4 | 105.4 | | 98.2 | 98.2 | | 98.2 | 98.2 |
| 0241, 31 - 34 | SITE & INFRASTRUCTURE, DEMOLITION | 99.7 | 97.2 | 98.0 | 89.7 | 86.0 | 87.1 | 96.2 | 86.1 | 89.2 | 98.2 | 95.6 | 96.4 | 109.1 | 85.9 | 93.0 | 86.0 | 86.0 | 86.0 |
| 0310 | Concrete Forming & Accessories | 95.3 | 43.1 | 50.3 | 81.4 | 48.4 | 53.0 | 81.6 | 41.2 | 46.8 | 88.4 | 34.6 | 42.1 | 82.2 | 43.8 | 49.1 | 94.3 | 43.8 | 50.8 |
| 0320 | Concrete Reinforcing | 87.2 | 61.8 | 74.9 | 86.7 | 62.4 | 75.0 | 86.7 | 62.4 | 75.0 | 86.7 | 39.2 | 63.8 | 87.8 | 60.7 | 74.7 | 87.2 | 60.7 | 74.4 |
| 0330 | Cast-in-Place Concrete | 95.3 | 45.1 | 76.8 | 91.8 | 50.1 | 76.4 | 104.1 | 47.6 | 83.2 | 101.6 | 38.9 | 78.4 | 76.7 | 49.4 | 66.6 | 89.6 | 45.3 | 73.2 |
| 03 | CONCRETE | 92.0 | 49.3 | 72.3 | 93.9 | 53.6 | 75.3 | 103.8 | 49.5 | 78.7 | 95.3 | 39.0 | 69.3 | 98.2 | 50.8 | 76.3 | 89.3 | 49.4 | 70.9 |
| 04 | MASONRY | 96.3 | 39.8 | 62.5 | 108.4 | 50.2 | 73.6 | 104.0 | 50.6 | 72.1 | 108.7 | 30.9 | 62.2 | 107.7 | 39.6 | 67.0 | 73.7 | 39.6 | 53.3 |
| 05 | METALS | 93.5 | 84.0 | 90.8 | 89.6 | 88.9 | 89.4 | 89.7 | 88.0 | 89.2 | 91.8 | 71.0 | 85.7 | 90.9 | 83.6 | 88.8 | 94.0 | 83.8 | 91.1 |
| 06 | WOOD, PLASTICS & COMPOSITES | 99.4 | 43.5 | 69.3 | 70.6 | 50.4 | 59.7 | 70.8 | 40.5 | 54.5 | 86.3 | 34.6 | 58.5 | 74.1 | 44.6 | 58.2 | 88.0 | 44.6 | 64.6 |
| 07 | THERMAL & MOISTURE PROTECTION | 98.7 | 56.1 | 82.1 | 92.2 | 57.0 | 78.5 | 92.6 | 51.3 | 76.5 | 94.3 | 36.9 | 71.9 | 93.2 | 56.1 | 78.7 | 91.3 | 55.7 | 77.4 |
| 08 | OPENINGS | 99.9 | 50.1 | 87.6 | 92.0 | 51.2 | 81.9 | 92.0 | 47.6 | 81.0 | 100.8 | 36.5 | 84.9 | 95.9 | 51.1 | 84.9 | 92.7 | 51.1 | 82.4 |
| 0920 | Plaster & Gypsum Board | 84.0 | 42.6 | 58.5 | 91.9 | 49.6 | 65.8 | 91.9 | 39.5 | 59.6 | 91.8 | 33.5 | 55.8 | 96.7 | 43.7 | 64.0 | 102.3 | 43.7 | 66.1 |
| 0950, 0980 | Ceilings & Acoustic Treatment | 96.8 | 42.6 | 63.6 | 88.2 | 49.6 | 64.5 | 88.2 | 39.5 | 58.3 | 97.5 | 33.5 | 58.2 | 93.1 | 43.7 | 62.8 | 94.0 | 43.7 | 63.1 |
| 0960 | Flooring | 100.7 | 45.7 | 85.7 | 91.3 | 23.7 | 72.9 | 91.5 | 22.1 | 72.6 | 92.5 | 22.1 | 73.3 | 94.1 | 47.0 | 81.3 | 99.7 | 47.0 | 85.4 |
| 0970, 0990 | Wall Finishes & Painting/Coating | 110.3 | 43.0 | 69.9 | 99.4 | 40.0 | 63.7 | 99.4 | 43.7 | 65.9 | 100.7 | 29.1 | 57.7 | 107.7 | 50.4 | 73.3 | 107.7 | 50.4 | 73.3 |
| 09 | FINISHES | 96.0 | 43.1 | 68.3 | 94.7 | 42.7 | 67.5 | 95.2 | 36.5 | 64.5 | 95.7 | 31.7 | 62.2 | 97.6 | 44.6 | 69.9 | 92.6 | 44.6 | 67.5 |
| COVERS | DIVS. 10 - 14, 25, 28, 41, 43, 44 | 100.0 | 46.3 | 89.0 | 100.0 | 52.4 | 90.2 | 100.0 | 51.5 | 90.1 | 100.0 | 50.2 | 89.8 | 100.0 | 53.1 | 90.4 | 100.0 | 53.1 | 90.4 |
| 21, 22, 23 | FIRE SUPPRESSION, PLUMBING & HVAC | 100.0 | 41.3 | 75.9 | 97.6 | 48.4 | 77.4 | 97.6 | 62.6 | 83.2 | 99.9 | 50.8 | 79.7 | 99.7 | 54.3 | 81.1 | 99.7 | 54.3 | 81.1 |
| 26, 27, 3370 | ELECTRICAL, COMMUNICATIONS & UTIL. | 105.9 | 71.3 | 88.9 | 94.8 | 64.0 | 79.7 | 96.5 | 64.0 | 80.5 | 102.8 | 47.1 | 75.4 | 94.4 | 55.4 | 75.3 | 100.3 | 59.9 | 80.5 |
| MF2004 | WEIGHTED AVERAGE | 98.0 | 56.2 | 80.1 | 94.9 | 58.1 | 79.1 | 96.3 | 59.2 | 80.4 | 98.2 | 48.6 | 77.0 | 97.2 | 56.3 | 79.7 | 94.3 | 56.8 | 78.2 |

## TENNESSEE / TEXAS

| DIVISION | | TENNESSEE — MCKENZIE 382 | | | MEMPHIS 375, 380 - 381 | | | NASHVILLE 370 - 372 | | | TEXAS — ABILENE 795 - 796 | | | AMARILLO 790 - 791 | | | AUSTIN 786 - 787 | | |
|---|---|---|---|---|---|---|---|---|---|---|---|---|---|---|---|---|---|---|---|
| | | MAT. | INST. | TOTAL | MAT. | INST. | TOTAL | MAT. | INST. | TOTAL | MAT. | INST. | TOTAL | MAT. | INST. | TOTAL | MAT. | INST. | TOTAL |
| 015433 | CONTRACTOR EQUIPMENT | | 98.2 | 98.2 | | 103.1 | 103.1 | | 106.5 | 106.5 | | 87.3 | 87.3 | | 87.3 | 87.3 | | 86.7 | 86.7 |
| 0241, 31 - 34 | SITE & INFRASTRUCTURE, DEMOLITION | 95.5 | 85.8 | 88.8 | 89.2 | 92.5 | 91.5 | 94.0 | 99.8 | 98.0 | 102.2 | 84.9 | 90.2 | 102.7 | 85.8 | 90.9 | 91.5 | 85.2 | 87.1 |
| 0310 | Concrete Forming & Accessories | 89.8 | 34.5 | 42.2 | 96.2 | 62.6 | 67.2 | 93.9 | 61.4 | 65.9 | 97.9 | 40.0 | 48.0 | 98.1 | 50.6 | 57.2 | 91.8 | 55.8 | 60.8 |
| 0320 | Concrete Reinforcing | 86.8 | 32.5 | 60.6 | 92.8 | 65.4 | 79.6 | 94.6 | 64.5 | 80.1 | 94.0 | 48.5 | 72.1 | 94.0 | 49.7 | 72.6 | 84.8 | 47.9 | 67.0 |
| 0330 | Cast-in-Place Concrete | 101.8 | 41.9 | 79.6 | 83.2 | 66.8 | 77.1 | 90.2 | 65.8 | 81.2 | 93.1 | 40.2 | 73.5 | 94.3 | 45.9 | 76.4 | 85.1 | 46.7 | 70.9 |
| 03 | CONCRETE | 102.3 | 38.9 | 73.0 | 87.1 | 66.1 | 77.4 | 91.2 | 65.0 | 79.1 | 89.3 | 42.8 | 67.8 | 89.9 | 49.7 | 71.3 | 78.4 | 51.8 | 66.1 |
| 04 | MASONRY | 106.9 | 49.5 | 72.6 | 87.5 | 70.5 | 77.3 | 81.1 | 62.1 | 69.7 | 98.5 | 52.0 | 70.7 | 99.9 | 47.4 | 68.5 | 87.4 | 50.5 | 65.4 |
| 05 | METALS | 89.7 | 74.0 | 85.1 | 95.9 | 91.4 | 94.6 | 94.0 | 88.9 | 92.5 | 100.7 | 64.7 | 90.3 | 100.7 | 65.3 | 90.4 | 98.5 | 62.4 | 88.0 |
| 06 | WOOD, PLASTICS & COMPOSITES | 80.3 | 32.5 | 54.6 | 92.9 | 63.4 | 77.0 | 96.4 | 61.9 | 77.8 | 100.7 | 39.3 | 67.7 | 99.1 | 53.4 | 74.5 | 95.2 | 60.2 | 76.3 |
| 07 | THERMAL & MOISTURE PROTECTION | 92.6 | 48.7 | 75.5 | 93.7 | 69.6 | 84.3 | 96.0 | 64.3 | 83.1 | 99.0 | 47.3 | 78.9 | 99.1 | 46.1 | 78.5 | 87.4 | 52.7 | 73.8 |
| 08 | OPENINGS | 92.0 | 32.9 | 77.4 | 99.6 | 65.0 | 91.1 | 97.4 | 63.2 | 89.0 | 92.8 | 42.0 | 80.3 | 92.8 | 47.9 | 81.7 | 100.0 | 56.7 | 89.3 |
| 0920 | Plaster & Gypsum Board | 95.3 | 31.3 | 55.8 | 91.7 | 62.9 | 73.9 | 98.7 | 61.3 | 75.6 | 88.0 | 38.3 | 57.4 | 84.1 | 52.8 | 64.8 | 90.7 | 59.8 | 71.6 |
| 0950, 0980 | Ceilings & Acoustic Treatment | 88.2 | 31.3 | 53.3 | 104.0 | 62.9 | 78.8 | 91.3 | 61.3 | 72.9 | 91.7 | 38.3 | 59.0 | 89.2 | 52.8 | 66.8 | 86.0 | 59.8 | 69.9 |
| 0960 | Flooring | 95.1 | 45.4 | 81.6 | 93.4 | 41.7 | 79.3 | 103.9 | 71.5 | 95.1 | 113.4 | 66.7 | 100.7 | 113.2 | 59.0 | 98.5 | 96.4 | 45.3 | 82.5 |
| 0970, 0990 | Wall Finishes & Painting/Coating | 99.4 | 50.9 | 70.2 | 102.6 | 59.4 | 76.6 | 110.1 | 65.4 | 83.2 | 96.9 | 51.3 | 69.5 | 96.9 | 35.5 | 60.0 | 93.6 | 39.9 | 61.3 |
| 09 | FINISHES | 96.7 | 37.2 | 65.6 | 93.6 | 57.7 | 74.8 | 100.9 | 63.5 | 81.4 | 97.4 | 45.8 | 70.4 | 96.3 | 50.6 | 72.4 | 90.7 | 52.3 | 70.6 |
| COVERS | DIVS. 10 - 14, 25, 28, 41, 43, 44 | 100.0 | 30.7 | 85.8 | 100.0 | 80.7 | 96.0 | 100.0 | 80.3 | 96.0 | 100.0 | 74.6 | 94.8 | 100.0 | 67.3 | 93.3 | 100.0 | 67.9 | 93.4 |
| 21, 22, 23 | FIRE SUPPRESSION, PLUMBING & HVAC | 97.6 | 66.6 | 84.8 | 99.9 | 69.4 | 87.4 | 99.8 | 78.0 | 90.8 | 100.1 | 41.4 | 76.0 | 100.0 | 50.2 | 79.6 | 99.9 | 57.7 | 82.6 |
| 26, 27, 3370 | ELECTRICAL, COMMUNICATIONS & UTIL. | 96.3 | 65.3 | 81.1 | 102.3 | 70.7 | 86.8 | 102.7 | 65.3 | 84.3 | 96.9 | 45.0 | 71.4 | 98.6 | 70.6 | 84.9 | 100.8 | 69.6 | 85.5 |
| MF2004 | WEIGHTED AVERAGE | 96.4 | 56.1 | 79.2 | 96.2 | 71.8 | 85.8 | 96.8 | 72.6 | 86.4 | 97.6 | 50.6 | 77.5 | 97.8 | 57.5 | 80.5 | 95.1 | 60.1 | 80.1 |

# City Cost Indexes

## TEXAS

| DIVISION | | BEAUMONT 776-777 MAT. | INST. | TOTAL | BROWNWOOD 768 MAT. | INST. | TOTAL | BRYAN 778 MAT. | INST. | TOTAL | CHILDRESS 792 MAT. | INST. | TOTAL | CORPUS CHRISTI 783-784 MAT. | INST. | TOTAL | DALLAS 752-753 MAT. | INST. | TOTAL |
|---|---|---|---|---|---|---|---|---|---|---|---|---|---|---|---|---|---|---|---|
| 015433 | CONTRACTOR EQUIPMENT | | 88.4 | 88.4 | | 87.3 | 87.3 | | 88.4 | 88.4 | | 87.3 | 87.3 | | 95.4 | 95.4 | | 98.4 | 98.4 |
| 0241, 31 - 34 | SITE & INFRASTRUCTURE, DEMOLITION | 99.7 | 85.2 | 89.6 | 109.6 | 83.6 | 91.5 | 89.3 | 86.7 | 87.5 | 115.5 | 84.2 | 93.7 | 125.7 | 80.5 | 94.2 | 123.3 | 86.4 | 97.6 |
| 0310 | Concrete Forming & Accessories | 105.4 | 49.5 | 57.3 | 96.1 | 26.9 | 36.4 | 83.3 | 40.6 | 46.5 | 96.3 | 48.9 | 55.5 | 98.0 | 36.3 | 44.9 | 95.0 | 56.0 | 61.4 |
| 0320 | Concrete Reinforcing | 99.1 | 40.8 | 71.0 | 94.3 | 24.3 | 60.6 | 101.8 | 47.9 | 75.8 | 94.1 | 38.0 | 67.1 | 84.1 | 46.3 | 65.9 | 97.3 | 52.9 | 75.9 |
| 0330 | Cast-in-Place Concrete | 92.3 | 51.5 | 77.2 | 100.4 | 35.6 | 76.4 | 73.9 | 67.4 | 71.5 | 95.5 | 44.1 | 76.5 | 100.6 | 43.4 | 79.4 | 93.1 | 53.2 | 78.4 |
| 03 | CONCRETE | 91.9 | 49.4 | 72.3 | 96.2 | 30.6 | 65.9 | 77.3 | 52.3 | 65.8 | 96.8 | 45.9 | 73.3 | 88.3 | 42.6 | 67.2 | 88.5 | 56.0 | 73.5 |
| 04 | MASONRY | 101.5 | 58.1 | 75.5 | 125.7 | 45.9 | 77.9 | 137.4 | 59.1 | 90.6 | 102.8 | 45.8 | 68.7 | 79.9 | 50.2 | 62.2 | 101.6 | 58.6 | 75.9 |
| 05 | METALS | 105.6 | 62.8 | 93.1 | 98.6 | 49.2 | 84.2 | 105.8 | 66.8 | 94.5 | 98.4 | 57.1 | 86.4 | 98.0 | 75.1 | 91.4 | 98.9 | 80.4 | 93.5 |
| 06 | WOOD, PLASTICS & COMPOSITES | 112.8 | 49.9 | 78.9 | 99.2 | 25.9 | 59.7 | 78.6 | 33.3 | 54.2 | 100.1 | 53.4 | 75.0 | 112.9 | 35.7 | 71.3 | 97.1 | 56.4 | 75.2 |
| 07 | THERMAL & MOISTURE PROTECTION | 104.7 | 56.7 | 86.0 | 99.2 | 38.7 | 75.6 | 98.3 | 57.0 | 82.2 | 99.7 | 43.3 | 77.7 | 95.2 | 45.3 | 75.8 | 94.2 | 62.8 | 81.9 |
| 08 | OPENINGS | 95.3 | 45.8 | 83.1 | 88.9 | 26.6 | 73.5 | 97.3 | 43.2 | 83.9 | 89.9 | 45.5 | 78.9 | 107.5 | 37.2 | 90.2 | 104.3 | 52.3 | 91.5 |
| 0920 | Plaster & Gypsum Board | 96.3 | 49.2 | 67.3 | 87.0 | 24.5 | 48.4 | 87.2 | 32.2 | 53.2 | 87.0 | 52.8 | 65.9 | 94.3 | 34.4 | 57.4 | 90.9 | 55.8 | 69.2 |
| 0950, 0980 | Ceilings & Acoustic Treatment | 100.9 | 49.2 | 69.2 | 86.5 | 24.5 | 48.5 | 93.8 | 32.2 | 55.9 | 86.5 | 52.8 | 65.8 | 87.7 | 34.4 | 55.0 | 94.1 | 55.8 | 70.6 |
| 0960 | Flooring | 112.0 | 73.0 | 101.4 | 112.1 | 37.6 | 91.9 | 83.0 | 60.5 | 76.9 | 111.0 | 39.4 | 91.6 | 108.9 | 44.8 | 91.4 | 99.9 | 54.9 | 87.6 |
| 0970, 0990 | Wall Finishes & Painting/Coating | 94.0 | 47.9 | 66.3 | 96.9 | 28.6 | 55.8 | 89.0 | 59.8 | 71.5 | 96.9 | 37.7 | 61.3 | 106.7 | 55.7 | 76.1 | 100.6 | 55.3 | 73.4 |
| 09 | FINISHES | 95.5 | 53.5 | 73.5 | 96.2 | 28.7 | 60.9 | 82.9 | 44.6 | 62.8 | 96.6 | 46.5 | 70.4 | 97.9 | 39.2 | 67.2 | 96.9 | 55.4 | 75.2 |
| COVERS | DIVS. 10 - 14, 25, 28, 41, 43, 44 | 100.0 | 78.1 | 95.5 | 100.0 | 39.8 | 87.7 | 100.0 | 68.4 | 93.5 | 100.0 | 66.7 | 93.2 | 100.0 | 75.3 | 94.9 | 100.0 | 79.4 | 95.8 |
| 21, 22, 23 | FIRE SUPPRESSION, PLUMBING & HVAC | 100.0 | 61.5 | 84.2 | 95.9 | 27.2 | 67.7 | 95.9 | 69.4 | 85.0 | 95.9 | 49.1 | 76.7 | 99.8 | 42.2 | 76.2 | 99.8 | 65.3 | 85.6 |
| 26, 27, 3370 | ELECTRICAL, COMMUNICATIONS & UTIL. | 93.8 | 66.9 | 80.6 | 93.1 | 26.4 | 60.3 | 92.4 | 68.2 | 80.5 | 96.9 | 36.1 | 67.0 | 98.4 | 51.5 | 75.4 | 97.2 | 71.2 | 84.4 |
| MF2004 | WEIGHTED AVERAGE | 98.8 | 60.9 | 82.6 | 97.8 | 37.0 | 71.8 | 96.2 | 62.0 | 81.6 | 97.4 | 50.1 | 77.2 | 98.3 | 50.9 | 78.0 | 98.8 | 65.8 | 84.6 |

## TEXAS

| DIVISION | | DEL RIO 788 MAT. | INST. | TOTAL | DENTON 762 MAT. | INST. | TOTAL | EASTLAND 764 MAT. | INST. | TOTAL | EL PASO 798 - 799,885 MAT. | INST. | TOTAL | FORT WORTH 760 - 761 MAT. | INST. | TOTAL | GALVESTON 775 MAT. | INST. | TOTAL |
|---|---|---|---|---|---|---|---|---|---|---|---|---|---|---|---|---|---|---|---|
| 015433 | CONTRACTOR EQUIPMENT | | 86.7 | 86.7 | | 94.5 | 94.5 | | 87.3 | 87.3 | | 87.3 | 87.3 | | 87.3 | 87.3 | | 99.2 | 99.2 |
| 0241, 31 - 34 | SITE & INFRASTRUCTURE, DEMOLITION | 111.7 | 83.1 | 91.8 | 109.7 | 77.2 | 87.0 | 113.1 | 83.7 | 92.6 | 100.7 | 84.5 | 89.4 | 102.4 | 85.3 | 90.5 | 128.5 | 84.3 | 97.7 |
| 0310 | Concrete Forming & Accessories | 92.5 | 23.6 | 33.1 | 103.2 | 35.5 | 44.9 | 97.1 | 31.6 | 40.6 | 97.3 | 44.4 | 51.7 | 93.5 | 55.2 | 60.5 | 92.2 | 64.0 | 67.9 |
| 0320 | Concrete Reinforcing | 84.8 | 17.1 | 52.2 | 95.8 | 48.4 | 73.0 | 94.6 | 39.4 | 68.0 | 94.0 | 45.1 | 70.4 | 94.0 | 52.8 | 74.1 | 101.2 | 60.1 | 81.4 |
| 0330 | Cast-in-Place Concrete | 108.4 | 30.9 | 79.7 | 77.6 | 46.8 | 66.2 | 106.1 | 36.2 | 80.3 | 87.0 | 39.0 | 69.3 | 95.4 | 49.0 | 78.2 | 98.2 | 68.7 | 87.3 |
| 03 | CONCRETE | 102.5 | 26.1 | 67.3 | 102.6 | 43.8 | 61.5 | 100.5 | 35.6 | 70.5 | 86.3 | 43.5 | 66.5 | 90.2 | 53.3 | 73.2 | 93.6 | 66.1 | 81.1 |
| 04 | MASONRY | 93.3 | 41.4 | 62.3 | 133.6 | 49.5 | 83.3 | 97.0 | 45.0 | 65.9 | 96.6 | 47.9 | 67.5 | 94.2 | 58.5 | 72.9 | 96.7 | 59.2 | 74.2 |
| 05 | METALS | 97.0 | 44.5 | 81.8 | 98.2 | 76.0 | 91.8 | 98.4 | 51.9 | 84.9 | 100.5 | 60.2 | 88.8 | 97.4 | 66.6 | 88.5 | 107.6 | 87.8 | 101.9 |
| 06 | WOOD, PLASTICS & COMPOSITES | 94.5 | 24.0 | 56.5 | 110.5 | 35.8 | 70.3 | 106.0 | 32.4 | 66.4 | 100.3 | 47.2 | 71.7 | 100.8 | 56.3 | 76.9 | 95.4 | 64.4 | 78.7 |
| 07 | THERMAL & MOISTURE PROTECTION | 92.4 | 32.3 | 69.0 | 98.3 | 45.4 | 77.7 | 99.5 | 39.0 | 75.9 | 95.7 | 53.8 | 79.4 | 100.2 | 51.9 | 81.4 | 97.7 | 63.8 | 84.5 |
| 08 | OPENINGS | 100.8 | 20.4 | 81.0 | 104.8 | 40.0 | 88.8 | 77.4 | 29.7 | 65.7 | 92.8 | 42.7 | 80.4 | 86.9 | 52.2 | 78.3 | 102.7 | 63.2 | 92.9 |
| 0920 | Plaster & Gypsum Board | 90.8 | 22.6 | 48.8 | 90.9 | 34.6 | 56.1 | 87.0 | 31.2 | 52.6 | 86.4 | 46.4 | 61.7 | 87.3 | 55.8 | 67.8 | 92.7 | 63.9 | 74.9 |
| 0950, 0980 | Ceilings & Acoustic Treatment | 84.3 | 22.6 | 46.4 | 91.6 | 34.6 | 56.6 | 86.5 | 31.2 | 52.6 | 89.2 | 46.4 | 62.9 | 91.7 | 55.8 | 69.6 | 97.2 | 63.9 | 76.8 |
| 0960 | Flooring | 93.4 | 18.0 | 72.9 | 104.3 | 43.9 | 87.8 | 145.7 | 27.1 | 113.4 | 113.4 | 64.3 | 100.1 | 147.1 | 43.9 | 119.1 | 97.7 | 66.0 | 87.7 |
| 0970, 0990 | Wall Finishes & Painting/Coating | 93.6 | 25.1 | 52.5 | 107.8 | 28.9 | 60.4 | 98.2 | 29.8 | 57.1 | 96.9 | 34.1 | 59.2 | 98.2 | 50.7 | 69.6 | 101.7 | 60.7 | 77.0 |
| 09 | FINISHES | 90.9 | 23.1 | 55.4 | 93.4 | 35.9 | 63.3 | 106.6 | 30.8 | 66.9 | 96.4 | 47.4 | 70.7 | 107.5 | 52.5 | 78.7 | 93.3 | 62.8 | 77.4 |
| COVERS | DIVS. 10 - 14, 25, 28, 41, 43, 44 | 100.0 | 37.4 | 87.2 | 100.0 | 41.4 | 88.0 | 100.0 | 40.2 | 87.8 | 100.0 | 65.7 | 93.0 | 100.0 | 79.0 | 95.7 | 100.0 | 83.1 | 96.5 |
| 21, 22, 23 | FIRE SUPPRESSION, PLUMBING & HVAC | 95.6 | 17.7 | 63.6 | 95.9 | 43.5 | 74.4 | 95.9 | 27.5 | 67.8 | 100.0 | 36.2 | 73.8 | 100.0 | 54.6 | 81.4 | 95.8 | 69.2 | 84.9 |
| 26, 27, 3370 | ELECTRICAL, COMMUNICATIONS & UTIL. | 99.9 | 18.8 | 60.1 | 95.9 | 42.9 | 69.8 | 92.9 | 33.0 | 63.5 | 95.1 | 53.4 | 74.6 | 97.2 | 62.1 | 79.9 | 93.8 | 63.3 | 78.8 |
| MF2004 | WEIGHTED AVERAGE | 97.8 | 31.2 | 69.3 | 97.5 | 48.6 | 76.6 | 96.7 | 39.4 | 72.2 | 96.6 | 50.2 | 76.8 | 97.3 | 59.9 | 81.3 | 99.1 | 69.0 | 86.2 |

## TEXAS

| DIVISION | | GIDDINGS 789 MAT. | INST. | TOTAL | GREENVILLE 754 MAT. | INST. | TOTAL | HOUSTON 770 - 772 MAT. | INST. | TOTAL | HUNTSVILLE 773 MAT. | INST. | TOTAL | LAREDO 780 MAT. | INST. | TOTAL | LONGVIEW 756 MAT. | INST. | TOTAL |
|---|---|---|---|---|---|---|---|---|---|---|---|---|---|---|---|---|---|---|---|
| 015433 | CONTRACTOR EQUIPMENT | | 86.7 | 86.7 | | 95.6 | 95.6 | | 99.1 | 99.1 | | 88.4 | 88.4 | | 86.7 | 86.7 | | 89.2 | 89.2 |
| 0241, 31 - 34 | SITE & INFRASTRUCTURE, DEMOLITION | 97.5 | 83.5 | 87.8 | 114.8 | 81.1 | 91.4 | 125.8 | 84.0 | 96.7 | 110.0 | 84.0 | 91.9 | 91.0 | 85.0 | 86.8 | 109.6 | 89.3 | 95.5 |
| 0310 | Concrete Forming & Accessories | 90.8 | 31.6 | 39.8 | 86.7 | 26.7 | 35.0 | 94.4 | 64.1 | 68.3 | 90.9 | 32.8 | 40.9 | 92.5 | 36.6 | 44.3 | 83.0 | 27.5 | 35.2 |
| 0320 | Concrete Reinforcing | 85.3 | 40.2 | 63.6 | 97.9 | 24.6 | 62.6 | 101.0 | 60.2 | 81.3 | 102.1 | 26.8 | 65.8 | 84.8 | 46.3 | 66.3 | 96.7 | 22.4 | 60.9 |
| 0330 | Cast-in-Place Concrete | 91.8 | 36.3 | 71.3 | 84.8 | 35.4 | 66.5 | 95.2 | 68.7 | 85.4 | 101.7 | 42.9 | 79.9 | 77.5 | 59.5 | 70.8 | 98.6 | 32.8 | 74.2 |
| 03 | CONCRETE | 84.2 | 35.8 | 61.9 | 82.0 | 31.3 | 58.6 | 91.4 | 66.5 | 79.9 | 99.0 | 36.3 | 70.1 | 78.6 | 47.3 | 64.2 | 95.2 | 29.5 | 64.9 |
| 04 | MASONRY | 99.9 | 46.8 | 68.1 | 159.7 | 48.3 | 93.1 | 96.5 | 60.9 | 75.2 | 137.4 | 31.4 | 74.0 | 87.5 | 49.7 | 64.9 | 155.3 | 43.0 | 88.1 |
| 05 | METALS | 96.6 | 51.8 | 83.6 | 96.4 | 62.3 | 86.5 | 110.3 | 87.9 | 103.8 | 105.7 | 51.8 | 90.1 | 99.4 | 61.3 | 88.3 | 89.7 | 48.1 | 77.6 |
| 06 | WOOD, PLASTICS & COMPOSITES | 93.6 | 32.4 | 60.6 | 88.1 | 25.9 | 54.6 | 97.9 | 64.4 | 79.8 | 88.0 | 34.5 | 59.2 | 94.5 | 35.5 | 62.7 | 81.7 | 28.0 | 52.8 |
| 07 | THERMAL & MOISTURE PROTECTION | 93.0 | 39.7 | 72.2 | 94.0 | 40.1 | 73.0 | 97.6 | 64.1 | 84.5 | 99.3 | 36.8 | 74.9 | 91.5 | 50.2 | 75.4 | 94.2 | 34.3 | 70.9 |
| 08 | OPENINGS | 100.0 | 29.7 | 82.7 | 103.0 | 26.6 | 84.1 | 105.0 | 63.2 | 94.7 | 97.3 | 29.5 | 80.6 | 100.7 | 37.8 | 85.2 | 92.7 | 25.6 | 76.1 |
| 0920 | Plaster & Gypsum Board | 89.6 | 31.2 | 53.6 | 87.4 | 24.5 | 48.6 | 94.7 | 63.9 | 75.7 | 90.9 | 33.5 | 55.4 | 91.6 | 34.4 | 56.3 | 84.7 | 26.8 | 49.0 |
| 0950, 0980 | Ceilings & Acoustic Treatment | 83.4 | 31.2 | 51.4 | 90.7 | 24.5 | 50.1 | 101.4 | 63.9 | 78.4 | 93.8 | 33.5 | 56.7 | 87.7 | 34.4 | 55.0 | 86.4 | 26.8 | 49.8 |
| 0960 | Flooring | 93.0 | 27.1 | 75.0 | 95.0 | 43.9 | 81.1 | 99.1 | 60.5 | 88.6 | 87.0 | 27.1 | 70.7 | 93.3 | 44.8 | 80.1 | 101.2 | 38.6 | 84.2 |
| 0970, 0990 | Wall Finishes & Painting/Coating | 93.6 | 29.8 | 55.3 | 100.6 | 24.6 | 54.9 | 101.7 | 59.8 | 76.5 | 89.0 | 30.6 | 53.9 | 93.6 | 52.1 | 68.7 | 92.7 | 32.7 | 56.7 |
| 09 | FINISHES | 89.5 | 30.6 | 58.7 | 93.6 | 29.4 | 60.0 | 100.0 | 62.7 | 80.5 | 85.8 | 31.9 | 57.6 | 90.5 | 38.7 | 63.4 | 97.6 | 30.1 | 62.2 |
| COVERS | DIVS. 10 - 14, 25, 28, 41, 43, 44 | 100.0 | 38.7 | 87.4 | 100.0 | 39.5 | 87.6 | 100.0 | 83.1 | 96.5 | 100.0 | 38.7 | 87.4 | 100.0 | 72.9 | 94.5 | 100.0 | 21.8 | 84.0 |
| 21, 22, 23 | FIRE SUPPRESSION, PLUMBING & HVAC | 95.7 | 27.4 | 67.7 | 95.6 | 26.7 | 67.3 | 100.0 | 69.7 | 87.5 | 95.9 | 25.9 | 67.1 | 99.8 | 38.0 | 74.4 | 95.6 | 26.1 | 67.9 |
| 26, 27, 3370 | ELECTRICAL, COMMUNICATIONS & UTIL. | 96.8 | 33.0 | 65.4 | 93.7 | 26.5 | 60.7 | 95.8 | 68.2 | 82.3 | 92.4 | 32.3 | 62.9 | 100.1 | 64.8 | 82.8 | 93.6 | 51.5 | 72.9 |
| MF2004 | WEIGHTED AVERAGE | 95.0 | 39.5 | 71.3 | 98.5 | 38.4 | 72.8 | 101.1 | 70.0 | 87.8 | 99.6 | 37.7 | 73.2 | 95.4 | 51.7 | 76.7 | 97.9 | 39.9 | 73.1 |

## TEXAS

| DIVISION | | LUBBOCK 793 - 794 | | | LUFKIN 759 | | | MCALLEN 785 | | | MCKINNEY 750 | | | MIDLAND 797 | | | ODESSA 797 | | |
|---|---|---|---|---|---|---|---|---|---|---|---|---|---|---|---|---|---|---|---|---|
| | | MAT. | INST. | TOTAL | MAT. | INST. | TOTAL | MAT. | INST. | TOTAL | MAT. | INST. | TOTAL | MAT. | INST. | TOTAL | MAT. | INST. | TOTAL |
| 015433 | CONTRACTOR EQUIPMENT | | 97.6 | 97.6 | | 89.2 | 89.2 | | 95.4 | 95.4 | | 95.6 | 95.6 | | 97.6 | 97.6 | | 87.3 | 87.3 |
| 0241, 31 - 34 | SITE & INFRASTRUCTURE, DEMOLITION | 132.0 | 83.1 | 97.9 | 103.3 | 89.4 | 93.6 | 130.4 | 80.5 | 95.6 | 110.0 | 81.9 | 90.5 | 136.2 | 83.0 | 99.1 | 102.4 | 85.3 | 90.5 |
| 0310 | Concrete Forming & Accessories | 97.2 | 39.3 | 47.3 | 86.2 | 38.6 | 45.2 | 96.9 | 34.3 | 42.9 | 85.7 | 40.6 | 46.9 | 101.2 | 37.5 | 46.3 | 97.8 | 37.3 | 45.7 |
| 0320 | Concrete Reinforcing | 95.3 | 48.3 | 72.6 | 98.3 | 29.9 | 65.4 | 84.3 | 46.3 | 66.0 | 97.9 | 48.4 | 74.1 | 96.4 | 48.2 | 73.2 | 94.0 | 48.2 | 71.9 |
| 0330 | Cast-in-Place Concrete | 93.2 | 46.0 | 75.8 | 88.2 | 37.9 | 69.6 | 109.4 | 41.8 | 84.4 | 79.5 | 47.8 | 67.8 | 99.1 | 43.3 | 78.4 | 93.1 | 42.1 | 74.2 |
| 03 | CONCRETE | 88.4 | 45.3 | 68.5 | 88.3 | 37.8 | 65.0 | 93.8 | 41.1 | 69.5 | 78.0 | 46.3 | 63.4 | 92.7 | 43.6 | 70.0 | 89.3 | 42.2 | 67.6 |
| 04 | MASONRY | 97.8 | 46.0 | 66.8 | 118.7 | 36.7 | 69.7 | 92.9 | 50.2 | 67.4 | 171.9 | 52.6 | 100.5 | 115.3 | 46.3 | 74.0 | 98.5 | 46.2 | 67.2 |
| 05 | METALS | 104.4 | 78.5 | 96.9 | 96.5 | 55.3 | 84.5 | 96.9 | 74.8 | 90.5 | 96.3 | 74.6 | 90.0 | 102.8 | 78.0 | 95.6 | 100.1 | 63.6 | 89.5 |
| 06 | WOOD, PLASTICS & COMPOSITES | 100.8 | 39.4 | 67.8 | 90.0 | 40.2 | 63.1 | 111.4 | 33.2 | 69.3 | 86.7 | 40.9 | 62.0 | 106.2 | 37.5 | 69.2 | 100.7 | 37.4 | 66.6 |
| 07 | THERMAL & MOISTURE PROTECTION | 90.4 | 47.9 | 73.8 | 94.1 | 39.2 | 72.7 | 95.2 | 44.3 | 75.3 | 93.8 | 48.7 | 76.2 | 90.6 | 44.3 | 72.6 | 99.0 | 43.4 | 77.3 |
| 08 | OPENINGS | 104.2 | 40.3 | 88.4 | 74.3 | 36.9 | 65.1 | 105.9 | 36.4 | 88.7 | 103.0 | 42.8 | 88.1 | 103.1 | 38.9 | 87.3 | 92.8 | 38.9 | 79.5 |
| 0920 | Plaster & Gypsum Board | 88.4 | 38.3 | 57.5 | 84.6 | 39.3 | 56.6 | 94.3 | 31.9 | 55.8 | 86.3 | 39.9 | 57.7 | 90.5 | 36.3 | 57.1 | 88.0 | 36.3 | 56.1 |
| 0950, 0980 | Ceilings & Acoustic Treatment | 93.5 | 38.3 | 59.6 | 78.7 | 39.3 | 54.5 | 87.7 | 31.9 | 53.5 | 90.7 | 39.9 | 59.5 | 89.9 | 36.3 | 57.0 | 91.7 | 36.3 | 57.7 |
| 0960 | Flooring | 105.1 | 37.2 | 86.6 | 135.6 | 36.1 | 108.5 | 108.2 | 66.7 | 96.9 | 94.6 | 43.9 | 80.8 | 106.8 | 36.8 | 87.7 | 113.4 | 36.8 | 92.6 |
| 0970, 0990 | Wall Finishes & Painting/Coating | 108.4 | 31.9 | 62.4 | 92.7 | 36.9 | 59.2 | 106.7 | 28.2 | 59.5 | 100.6 | 46.0 | 67.8 | 108.4 | 31.5 | 62.2 | 96.9 | 31.9 | 57.8 |
| 09 | FINISHES | 99.7 | 37.2 | 66.9 | 105.6 | 37.9 | 70.2 | 98.0 | 39.2 | 67.2 | 93.0 | 41.6 | 66.1 | 100.1 | 36.0 | 66.5 | 97.4 | 35.9 | 65.2 |
| COVERS | DIVS. 10 - 14, 25, 28, 41, 43, 44 | 100.0 | 74.3 | 94.7 | 100.0 | 66.3 | 93.1 | 100.0 | 72.8 | 94.4 | 100.0 | 42.9 | 88.3 | 100.0 | 65.2 | 92.9 | 100.0 | 64.9 | 92.8 |
| 21, 22, 23 | FIRE SUPPRESSION, PLUMBING & HVAC | 99.6 | 47.6 | 78.3 | 95.6 | 30.7 | 68.9 | 95.7 | 29.8 | 68.6 | 95.6 | 45.1 | 74.9 | 95.5 | 34.6 | 70.5 | 100.1 | 34.6 | 73.2 |
| 26, 27, 3370 | ELECTRICAL, COMMUNICATIONS & UTIL. | 95.5 | 42.3 | 69.4 | 94.9 | 45.2 | 70.5 | 97.6 | 33.4 | 66.1 | 93.8 | 51.5 | 73.0 | 95.5 | 39.5 | 67.9 | 97.1 | 39.4 | 68.8 |
| MF2004 | WEIGHTED AVERAGE | 99.6 | 51.2 | 78.9 | 95.3 | 44.1 | 73.4 | 98.3 | 45.4 | 75.7 | 98.5 | 52.1 | 78.6 | 99.9 | 47.2 | 77.4 | 97.5 | 45.9 | 75.4 |

## TEXAS

| DIVISION | | PALESTINE 758 | | | SAN ANGELO 769 | | | SAN ANTONIO 781 - 782 | | | TEMPLE 765 | | | TEXARKANA 755 | | | TYLER 757 | | |
|---|---|---|---|---|---|---|---|---|---|---|---|---|---|---|---|---|---|---|---|---|
| | | MAT. | INST. | TOTAL | MAT. | INST. | TOTAL | MAT. | INST. | TOTAL | MAT. | INST. | TOTAL | MAT. | INST. | TOTAL | MAT. | INST. | TOTAL |
| 015433 | CONTRACTOR EQUIPMENT | | 89.2 | 89.2 | | 87.3 | 87.3 | | 89.6 | 89.6 | | 87.3 | 87.3 | | 89.2 | 89.2 | | 89.2 | 89.2 |
| 0241, 31 - 34 | SITE & INFRASTRUCTURE, DEMOLITION | 112.3 | 88.9 | 96.0 | 105.2 | 85.6 | 91.5 | 90.7 | 90.0 | 90.2 | 91.7 | 84.3 | 86.5 | 96.2 | 89.9 | 91.8 | 109.1 | 89.9 | 95.8 |
| 0310 | Concrete Forming & Accessories | 77.7 | 31.6 | 37.9 | 96.5 | 35.4 | 43.8 | 92.5 | 55.2 | 60.4 | 100.1 | 33.7 | 42.9 | 93.2 | 33.3 | 42.0 | 87.9 | 32.8 | 40.4 |
| 0320 | Concrete Reinforcing | 96.0 | 40.1 | 69.0 | 94.2 | 48.2 | 72.0 | 90.6 | 49.7 | 70.9 | 94.4 | 47.1 | 71.6 | 95.8 | 52.5 | 75.0 | 96.7 | 52.8 | 75.5 |
| 0330 | Cast-in-Place Concrete | 80.6 | 35.5 | 63.9 | 94.7 | 40.5 | 74.6 | 76.0 | 67.4 | 72.8 | 77.6 | 45.9 | 65.9 | 81.2 | 41.6 | 66.5 | 96.9 | 40.5 | 76.0 |
| 03 | CONCRETE | 88.3 | 35.4 | 63.9 | 91.7 | 40.6 | 68.1 | 78.8 | 59.0 | 69.7 | 78.8 | 41.6 | 61.6 | 82.4 | 41.2 | 63.4 | 94.7 | 40.4 | 69.7 |
| 04 | MASONRY | 114.1 | 44.4 | 72.4 | 122.4 | 45.8 | 76.6 | 87.3 | 60.3 | 71.2 | 132.8 | 48.7 | 82.5 | 176.4 | 46.3 | 98.6 | 165.5 | 50.3 | 96.6 |
| 05 | METALS | 96.3 | 50.8 | 83.1 | 98.8 | 61.0 | 87.8 | 100.1 | 66.4 | 90.3 | 98.5 | 60.6 | 87.5 | 89.6 | 65.0 | 82.4 | 96.2 | 65.7 | 87.3 |
| 06 | WOOD, PLASTICS & COMPOSITES | 80.1 | 32.3 | 54.4 | 99.5 | 35.7 | 65.1 | 94.5 | 53.6 | 72.5 | 109.3 | 32.4 | 67.9 | 93.1 | 31.9 | 60.1 | 91.6 | 30.1 | 58.4 |
| 07 | THERMAL & MOISTURE PROTECTION | 94.5 | 40.1 | 73.3 | 99.0 | 41.7 | 76.7 | 91.5 | 63.6 | 80.6 | 98.6 | 44.3 | 77.4 | 93.9 | 48.8 | 76.3 | 94.3 | 54.3 | 78.7 |
| 08 | OPENINGS | 74.3 | 30.3 | 63.4 | 88.9 | 37.9 | 76.3 | 102.6 | 53.6 | 90.6 | 75.3 | 34.8 | 65.3 | 92.7 | 37.8 | 79.1 | 74.2 | 36.8 | 65.0 |
| 0920 | Plaster & Gypsum Board | 80.8 | 31.2 | 50.2 | 87.0 | 34.6 | 54.7 | 91.6 | 52.9 | 67.7 | 88.3 | 31.2 | 53.1 | 87.9 | 30.8 | 52.6 | 84.6 | 28.9 | 50.2 |
| 0950, 0980 | Ceilings & Acoustic Treatment | 78.7 | 31.2 | 49.6 | 86.5 | 34.6 | 54.7 | 87.7 | 52.9 | 66.3 | 86.5 | 31.2 | 52.6 | 85.6 | 30.8 | 51.9 | 78.7 | 28.9 | 48.1 |
| 0960 | Flooring | 125.6 | 27.1 | 98.8 | 112.3 | 32.8 | 90.7 | 93.3 | 68.5 | 86.6 | 148.7 | 45.1 | 120.5 | 110.4 | 60.1 | 96.7 | 137.6 | 40.0 | 111.1 |
| 0970, 0990 | Wall Finishes & Painting/Coating | 92.7 | 29.8 | 54.9 | 96.9 | 32.9 | 58.4 | 93.6 | 52.1 | 68.7 | 98.2 | 32.9 | 58.9 | 92.7 | 38.4 | 60.1 | 92.7 | 38.4 | 60.1 |
| 09 | FINISHES | 102.8 | 30.4 | 64.9 | 96.0 | 33.9 | 63.5 | 90.5 | 56.3 | 72.6 | 106.4 | 34.9 | 68.9 | 99.9 | 38.2 | 67.6 | 106.6 | 33.0 | 68.0 |
| COVERS | DIVS. 10 - 14, 25, 28, 41, 43, 44 | 100.0 | 40.0 | 87.7 | 100.0 | 63.8 | 92.6 | 100.0 | 79.1 | 95.7 | 100.0 | 40.2 | 87.7 | 100.0 | 72.9 | 94.5 | 100.0 | 72.7 | 94.4 |
| 21, 22, 23 | FIRE SUPPRESSION, PLUMBING & HVAC | 95.6 | 27.5 | 67.6 | 95.9 | 39.9 | 72.9 | 99.8 | 67.1 | 86.4 | 95.9 | 32.7 | 70.0 | 95.6 | 36.1 | 71.2 | 95.6 | 60.9 | 81.3 |
| 26, 27, 3370 | ELECTRICAL, COMMUNICATIONS & UTIL. | 91.1 | 37.3 | 64.7 | 96.9 | 31.4 | 64.7 | 100.6 | 64.8 | 83.0 | 94.1 | 73.9 | 84.2 | 94.8 | 66.9 | 81.1 | 93.6 | 57.6 | 75.9 |
| MF2004 | WEIGHTED AVERAGE | 94.5 | 40.2 | 71.3 | 97.4 | 45.0 | 75.0 | 95.7 | 65.0 | 82.6 | 95.3 | 49.1 | 75.6 | 97.5 | 51.0 | 77.6 | 98.5 | 54.7 | 79.7 |

## TEXAS / UTAH

| DIVISION | | VICTORIA 779 | | | WACO 766 - 767 | | | WAXAHACHIE 751 | | | WHARTON 774 | | | WICHITA FALLS 763 | | | LOGAN 843 | | |
|---|---|---|---|---|---|---|---|---|---|---|---|---|---|---|---|---|---|---|---|---|
| | | MAT. | INST. | TOTAL | MAT. | INST. | TOTAL | MAT. | INST. | TOTAL | MAT. | INST. | TOTAL | MAT. | INST. | TOTAL | MAT. | INST. | TOTAL |
| 015433 | CONTRACTOR EQUIPMENT | | 97.9 | 97.9 | | 87.3 | 87.3 | | 95.6 | 95.6 | | 99.2 | 99.2 | | 87.3 | 87.3 | | 100.2 | 100.2 |
| 0241, 31 - 34 | SITE & INFRASTRUCTURE, DEMOLITION | 134.9 | 79.8 | 96.5 | 101.0 | 85.3 | 90.1 | 112.8 | 82.3 | 91.6 | 143.0 | 81.6 | 100.2 | 101.8 | 85.0 | 90.1 | 89.2 | 99.2 | 96.2 |
| 0310 | Concrete Forming & Accessories | 92.9 | 38.6 | 46.1 | 98.5 | 38.8 | 47.1 | 85.7 | 45.5 | 51.1 | 86.8 | 35.3 | 42.4 | 98.5 | 40.4 | 48.5 | 102.5 | 57.1 | 63.4 |
| 0320 | Concrete Reinforcing | 97.1 | 29.9 | 64.7 | 94.0 | 47.7 | 71.7 | 97.9 | 48.5 | 74.1 | 101.1 | 58.3 | 80.5 | 94.0 | 48.9 | 72.3 | 103.3 | 72.1 | 88.3 |
| 0330 | Cast-in-Place Concrete | 110.3 | 39.7 | 84.1 | 84.0 | 50.5 | 71.6 | 83.9 | 39.8 | 67.6 | 113.3 | 47.0 | 88.8 | 89.7 | 45.6 | 73.4 | 91.9 | 72.0 | 84.5 |
| 03 | CONCRETE | 100.8 | 39.6 | 72.5 | 84.8 | 45.6 | 66.7 | 81.2 | 45.9 | 64.9 | 104.6 | 45.7 | 77.4 | 87.7 | 44.9 | 67.9 | 111.8 | 65.5 | 90.5 |
| 04 | MASONRY | 112.5 | 36.9 | 67.3 | 95.2 | 55.2 | 71.3 | 160.3 | 50.8 | 94.8 | 97.9 | 32.3 | 58.6 | 95.7 | 58.2 | 73.3 | 114.4 | 60.1 | 81.9 |
| 05 | METALS | 105.8 | 73.5 | 96.4 | 100.6 | 64.0 | 90.0 | 96.4 | 76.5 | 90.6 | 107.6 | 80.1 | 99.6 | 100.6 | 65.7 | 90.4 | 101.6 | 72.5 | 93.2 |
| 06 | WOOD, PLASTICS & COMPOSITES | 99.4 | 40.3 | 67.6 | 106.9 | 34.7 | 68.0 | 86.7 | 48.3 | 66.0 | 89.1 | 36.5 | 60.8 | 106.9 | 39.3 | 70.5 | 85.7 | 54.1 | 68.6 |
| 07 | THERMAL & MOISTURE PROTECTION | 100.7 | 41.0 | 77.4 | 99.5 | 47.4 | 79.2 | 93.9 | 45.9 | 75.2 | 98.0 | 47.2 | 78.2 | 99.5 | 52.3 | 81.1 | 97.7 | 65.8 | 85.3 |
| 08 | OPENINGS | 102.5 | 38.6 | 86.7 | 86.9 | 36.1 | 74.4 | 103.0 | 46.8 | 89.1 | 102.7 | 40.9 | 87.4 | 86.9 | 41.9 | 75.8 | 88.6 | 55.7 | 80.5 |
| 0920 | Plaster & Gypsum Board | 91.5 | 39.3 | 59.3 | 88.0 | 33.6 | 54.4 | 86.5 | 47.4 | 62.4 | 90.0 | 35.4 | 56.3 | 88.0 | 38.3 | 57.3 | 79.9 | 52.7 | 63.1 |
| 0950, 0980 | Ceilings & Acoustic Treatment | 98.0 | 39.3 | 62.0 | 91.7 | 33.6 | 56.1 | 91.5 | 47.4 | 64.5 | 97.2 | 35.4 | 59.2 | 91.7 | 38.3 | 58.9 | 106.4 | 52.7 | 73.4 |
| 0960 | Flooring | 96.3 | 36.1 | 79.9 | 147.1 | 34.1 | 116.4 | 94.6 | 36.1 | 78.7 | 94.7 | 27.1 | 76.3 | 148.4 | 77.3 | 129.0 | 105.9 | 55.1 | 92.1 |
| 0970, 0990 | Wall Finishes & Painting/Coating | 101.9 | 36.9 | 62.8 | 98.2 | 32.9 | 58.9 | 100.6 | 36.9 | 62.3 | 101.7 | 30.6 | 59.0 | 101.9 | 52.1 | 72.0 | 98.8 | 44.9 | 66.4 |
| 09 | FINISHES | 91.7 | 38.1 | 63.6 | 107.6 | 35.9 | 70.0 | 93.5 | 43.0 | 67.0 | 93.0 | 33.2 | 61.7 | 108.2 | 48.0 | 76.7 | 100.3 | 54.7 | 76.4 |
| COVERS | DIVS. 10 - 14, 25, 28, 41, 43, 44 | 100.0 | 42.6 | 88.2 | 100.0 | 76.5 | 95.2 | 100.0 | 44.1 | 88.5 | 100.0 | 41.2 | 88.0 | 100.0 | 65.7 | 93.0 | 100.0 | 64.7 | 92.8 |
| 21, 22, 23 | FIRE SUPPRESSION, PLUMBING & HVAC | 95.9 | 30.7 | 69.1 | 100.1 | 55.3 | 81.7 | 95.6 | 44.1 | 74.5 | 95.8 | 25.5 | 67.0 | 100.1 | 47.4 | 78.5 | 99.9 | 67.4 | 86.5 |
| 26, 27, 3370 | ELECTRICAL, COMMUNICATIONS & UTIL. | 98.7 | 45.2 | 72.5 | 97.1 | 74.0 | 85.7 | 93.8 | 71.2 | 82.7 | 97.4 | 32.4 | 65.5 | 99.3 | 62.4 | 81.2 | 92.7 | 68.7 | 80.9 |
| MF2004 | WEIGHTED AVERAGE | 101.1 | 44.6 | 76.9 | 97.2 | 56.8 | 79.9 | 98.4 | 55.1 | 79.9 | 101.1 | 42.4 | 76.0 | 97.9 | 55.5 | 79.8 | 100.0 | 67.3 | 86.0 |

## UTAH / VERMONT

| DIVISION | | OGDEN 842,844 MAT. | INST. | TOTAL | PRICE 845 MAT. | INST. | TOTAL | PROVO 846-847 MAT. | INST. | TOTAL | SALT LAKE CITY 840-841 MAT. | INST. | TOTAL | BELLOWS FALLS 051 MAT. | INST. | TOTAL | BENNINGTON 052 MAT. | INST. | TOTAL |
|---|---|---|---|---|---|---|---|---|---|---|---|---|---|---|---|---|---|---|---|
| 015433 | CONTRACTOR EQUIPMENT | | 100.2 | 100.2 | | 99.0 | 99.0 | | 99.0 | 99.0 | | 100.2 | 100.2 | | 100.6 | 100.6 | | 100.6 | 100.6 |
| 0241,31-34 | SITE & INFRASTRUCTURE, DEMOLITION | 77.9 | 99.2 | 92.8 | 87.1 | 95.9 | 93.3 | 85.8 | 97.3 | 93.8 | 77.7 | 99.2 | 92.7 | 74.7 | 97.7 | 90.7 | 74.1 | 98.5 | 91.1 |
| 0310 | Concrete Forming & Accessories | 102.5 | 57.1 | 63.4 | 104.7 | 30.5 | 40.8 | 103.8 | 57.3 | 63.7 | 102.3 | 57.3 | 63.5 | 98.4 | 44.7 | 52.1 | 95.9 | 56.5 | 61.9 |
| 0320 | Concrete Reinforcing | 103.0 | 72.1 | 88.1 | 110.8 | 71.7 | 92.0 | 111.8 | 72.2 | 92.7 | 105.4 | 72.2 | 89.4 | 81.6 | 72.3 | 77.1 | 81.6 | 72.3 | 77.1 |
| 0330 | Cast-in-Place Concrete | 93.3 | 72.0 | 85.4 | 92.0 | 43.8 | 74.2 | 92.0 | 72.0 | 84.6 | 102.0 | 72.0 | 90.9 | 90.0 | 62.7 | 79.9 | 90.0 | 69.0 | 82.2 |
| 03 | CONCRETE | 101.5 | 65.5 | 84.9 | 113.2 | 44.0 | 81.2 | 111.7 | 65.6 | 90.4 | 121.2 | 65.6 | 95.6 | 99.0 | 56.8 | 79.5 | 98.8 | 64.1 | 82.8 |
| 04 | MASONRY | 107.9 | 60.1 | 79.3 | 119.7 | 38.5 | 71.1 | 119.7 | 60.1 | 84.0 | 122.1 | 60.1 | 85.0 | 95.2 | 35.5 | 59.5 | 104.5 | 53.2 | 73.8 |
| 05 | METALS | 102.1 | 72.5 | 93.5 | 99.0 | 70.6 | 90.7 | 99.9 | 72.6 | 92.0 | 106.5 | 72.6 | 96.7 | 88.3 | 71.3 | 83.3 | 88.2 | 70.3 | 83.0 |
| 06 | WOOD, PLASTICS & COMPOSITES | 85.7 | 54.1 | 68.6 | 88.4 | 28.5 | 56.1 | 87.1 | 54.1 | 69.3 | 87.5 | 54.1 | 69.5 | 99.9 | 43.6 | 69.6 | 96.9 | 51.1 | 72.2 |
| 07 | THERMAL & MOISTURE PROTECTION | 96.4 | 65.8 | 84.5 | 99.6 | 51.7 | 80.9 | 99.6 | 65.8 | 86.4 | 99.7 | 65.8 | 86.5 | 98.8 | 53.2 | 81.0 | 98.8 | 53.9 | 81.3 |
| 08 | OPENINGS | 88.6 | 55.7 | 80.5 | 92.6 | 40.6 | 79.8 | 92.6 | 55.7 | 83.5 | 90.4 | 55.7 | 81.9 | 102.1 | 47.0 | 88.3 | 102.2 | 48.7 | 89.0 |
| 0920 | Plaster & Gypsum Board | 79.9 | 52.7 | 63.1 | 81.3 | 26.4 | 47.5 | 80.3 | 52.7 | 63.3 | 82.2 | 52.7 | 64.0 | 103.1 | 41.3 | 65.0 | 101.4 | 49.0 | 69.1 |
| 0950, 0980 | Ceilings & Acoustic Treatment | 106.4 | 52.7 | 73.4 | 106.4 | 26.4 | 57.3 | 106.4 | 52.7 | 73.4 | 100.7 | 52.7 | 71.2 | 85.8 | 41.3 | 58.5 | 85.8 | 49.0 | 63.2 |
| 0960 | Flooring | 103.6 | 55.1 | 90.4 | 107.1 | 41.0 | 89.2 | 106.7 | 55.1 | 92.7 | 104.8 | 55.1 | 91.3 | 96.3 | 35.2 | 79.7 | 95.0 | 35.2 | 78.7 |
| 0970, 0990 | Wall Finishes & Painting/Coating | 98.8 | 44.9 | 66.4 | 98.8 | 44.9 | 66.4 | 98.8 | 63.3 | 77.4 | 101.3 | 63.3 | 78.5 | 91.6 | 32.0 | 55.8 | 91.6 | 32.0 | 55.8 |
| 09 | FINISHES | 98.5 | 54.7 | 75.6 | 101.5 | 32.6 | 65.4 | 101.1 | 56.7 | 77.9 | 98.6 | 56.7 | 76.7 | 95.9 | 40.2 | 66.7 | 95.3 | 49.0 | 71.1 |
| COVERS | DIVS. 10 - 14, 25, 28, 41, 43, 44 | 100.0 | 64.7 | 92.8 | 100.0 | 47.8 | 89.3 | 100.0 | 64.7 | 92.8 | 100.0 | 64.7 | 92.8 | 100.0 | 43.4 | 88.4 | 100.0 | 50.8 | 89.9 |
| 21, 22, 23 | FIRE SUPPRESSION, PLUMBING & HVAC | 99.9 | 67.4 | 86.5 | 97.8 | 37.0 | 72.8 | 99.9 | 67.4 | 86.5 | 100.0 | 67.4 | 86.6 | 96.0 | 81.7 | 90.1 | 96.0 | 89.4 | 93.3 |
| 26, 27, 3370 | ELECTRICAL, COMMUNICATIONS & UTIL. | 93.0 | 68.7 | 81.1 | 98.2 | 40.8 | 70.0 | 93.3 | 71.7 | 82.7 | 96.2 | 71.7 | 84.2 | 97.8 | 85.5 | 91.8 | 97.8 | 64.6 | 81.5 |
| MF2004 | WEIGHTED AVERAGE | 98.1 | 67.3 | 84.9 | 100.7 | 46.8 | 77.6 | 100.5 | 67.9 | 86.5 | 102.5 | 68.0 | 87.8 | 95.7 | 65.5 | 82.8 | 96.1 | 68.4 | 84.2 |

## VERMONT

| DIVISION | | BRATTLEBORO 053 MAT. | INST. | TOTAL | BURLINGTON 054 MAT. | INST. | TOTAL | GUILDHALL 059 MAT. | INST. | TOTAL | MONTPELIER 056 MAT. | INST. | TOTAL | RUTLAND 057 MAT. | INST. | TOTAL | ST. JOHNSBURY 058 MAT. | INST. | TOTAL |
|---|---|---|---|---|---|---|---|---|---|---|---|---|---|---|---|---|---|---|---|
| 015433 | CONTRACTOR EQUIPMENT | | 100.6 | 100.6 | | 100.6 | 100.6 | | 100.6 | 100.6 | | 100.6 | 100.6 | | 100.6 | 100.6 | | 100.6 | 100.6 |
| 0241,31-34 | SITE & INFRASTRUCTURE, DEMOLITION | 75.5 | 98.7 | 91.7 | 77.3 | 97.8 | 91.6 | 73.8 | 97.0 | 90.0 | 78.5 | 97.8 | 91.9 | 77.2 | 97.8 | 91.6 | 73.9 | 97.2 | 90.1 |
| 0310 | Concrete Forming & Accessories | 98.7 | 51.3 | 57.8 | 95.2 | 57.5 | 62.7 | 95.8 | 49.3 | 55.7 | 100.0 | 58.1 | 63.9 | 98.9 | 58.1 | 63.8 | 93.8 | 49.4 | 55.5 |
| 0320 | Concrete Reinforcing | 80.8 | 72.3 | 76.7 | 102.0 | 84.1 | 93.4 | 82.4 | 42.7 | 63.3 | 81.2 | 84.1 | 82.6 | 102.0 | 84.1 | 93.4 | 80.8 | 48.7 | 65.4 |
| 0330 | Cast-in-Place Concrete | 92.8 | 69.4 | 84.2 | 95.5 | 110.5 | 101.0 | 87.2 | 59.0 | 76.8 | 99.5 | 110.7 | 103.7 | 88.1 | 110.7 | 96.5 | 87.2 | 59.4 | 76.9 |
| 03 | CONCRETE | 101.4 | 62.0 | 83.2 | 105.9 | 81.0 | 94.4 | 96.5 | 51.9 | 75.9 | 104.9 | 81.4 | 94.0 | 102.4 | 81.4 | 92.7 | 130.3 | 53.1 | 76.3 |
| 04 | MASONRY | 104.5 | 53.3 | 73.9 | 104.7 | 55.7 | 75.4 | 104.7 | 40.5 | 66.3 | 89.3 | 55.7 | 69.2 | 85.5 | 55.7 | 67.7 | 88.3 | 58.7 | 79.7 |
| 05 | METALS | 88.2 | 71.1 | 83.3 | 94.9 | 78.6 | 90.2 | 88.3 | 58.2 | 79.5 | 88.2 | 79.2 | 85.6 | 93.4 | 79.2 | 89.2 | 88.3 | 58.7 | 79.7 |
| 06 | WOOD, PLASTICS & COMPOSITES | 100.3 | 43.6 | 69.7 | 94.7 | 57.9 | 74.9 | 96.0 | 51.1 | 71.8 | 99.1 | 57.9 | 76.9 | 100.4 | 57.9 | 77.5 | 92.0 | 51.1 | 69.9 |
| 07 | THERMAL & MOISTURE PROTECTION | 98.9 | 54.0 | 81.4 | 99.0 | 56.0 | 82.2 | 98.7 | 43.4 | 77.1 | 98.4 | 64.8 | 85.3 | 99.0 | 64.8 | 85.7 | 98.6 | 43.4 | 77.1 |
| 08 | OPENINGS | 102.2 | 47.0 | 88.5 | 105.3 | 57.5 | 93.5 | 102.2 | 43.5 | 87.7 | 102.2 | 57.5 | 91.1 | 105.3 | 57.5 | 93.5 | 102.2 | 43.5 | 87.7 |
| 0920 | Plaster & Gypsum Board | 103.1 | 41.3 | 65.0 | 104.7 | 56.0 | 74.7 | 107.5 | 49.0 | 71.4 | 113.0 | 56.0 | 77.8 | 103.7 | 56.0 | 74.3 | 110.5 | 49.0 | 72.6 |
| 0950, 0980 | Ceilings & Acoustic Treatment | 85.8 | 41.3 | 58.5 | 89.4 | 56.0 | 68.9 | 85.8 | 49.0 | 63.2 | 85.8 | 56.0 | 67.5 | 90.2 | 56.0 | 69.2 | 85.8 | 49.0 | 63.2 |
| 0960 | Flooring | 96.4 | 35.2 | 79.8 | 96.5 | 63.7 | 87.6 | 99.7 | 35.2 | 82.2 | 103.6 | 63.7 | 92.8 | 96.3 | 63.7 | 87.4 | 103.6 | 35.2 | 85.0 |
| 0970, 0990 | Wall Finishes & Painting/Coating | 91.6 | 32.0 | 55.8 | 91.6 | 37.2 | 58.9 | 91.6 | 24.8 | 51.5 | 91.6 | 37.2 | 58.9 | 91.6 | 37.2 | 58.9 | 91.6 | 26.0 | 52.2 |
| 09 | FINISHES | 96.1 | 44.6 | 69.1 | 97.3 | 55.8 | 75.6 | 97.6 | 43.9 | 69.5 | 99.9 | 55.8 | 76.8 | 97.2 | 55.8 | 75.5 | 99.2 | 44.1 | 70.3 |
| COVERS | DIVS. 10 - 14, 25, 28, 41, 43, 44 | 100.0 | 50.0 | 89.8 | 100.0 | 83.6 | 96.6 | 100.0 | 44.5 | 88.6 | 100.0 | 83.6 | 96.6 | 100.0 | 83.6 | 96.6 | 100.0 | 44.5 | 88.6 |
| 21, 22, 23 | FIRE SUPPRESSION, PLUMBING & HVAC | 96.0 | 91.0 | 94.0 | 100.0 | 65.6 | 85.9 | 96.0 | 63.7 | 82.7 | 95.8 | 65.6 | 83.4 | 100.1 | 65.6 | 86.0 | 96.0 | 63.7 | 82.7 |
| 26, 27, 3370 | ELECTRICAL, COMMUNICATIONS & UTIL. | 97.8 | 85.5 | 91.8 | 98.2 | 64.6 | 81.7 | 97.8 | 64.6 | 81.5 | 97.4 | 64.7 | 81.3 | 97.8 | 64.7 | 81.5 | 97.8 | 64.6 | 81.5 |
| MF2004 | WEIGHTED AVERAGE | 96.5 | 70.8 | 85.5 | 99.5 | 69.0 | 86.4 | 96.0 | 57.6 | 79.6 | 96.5 | 69.4 | 84.9 | 97.9 | 69.4 | 85.7 | 97.4 | 57.8 | 80.5 |

## VERMONT / VIRGINIA

| DIVISION | | WHITE RIVER JCT. 050 MAT. | INST. | TOTAL | ALEXANDRIA 223 MAT. | INST. | TOTAL | ARLINGTON 222 MAT. | INST. | TOTAL | BRISTOL 242 MAT. | INST. | TOTAL | CHARLOTTESVILLE 229 MAT. | INST. | TOTAL | CULPEPER 227 MAT. | INST. | TOTAL |
|---|---|---|---|---|---|---|---|---|---|---|---|---|---|---|---|---|---|---|---|
| 015433 | CONTRACTOR EQUIPMENT | | 100.6 | 100.6 | | 101.8 | 101.8 | | 100.3 | 100.3 | | 100.3 | 100.3 | | 105.4 | 105.4 | | 100.3 | 100.3 |
| 0241,31-34 | SITE & INFRASTRUCTURE, DEMOLITION | 77.6 | 97.1 | 91.2 | 117.9 | 87.1 | 96.5 | 130.3 | 84.1 | 98.1 | 113.9 | 83.5 | 92.7 | 119.2 | 85.6 | 95.8 | 116.3 | 84.6 | 94.2 |
| 0310 | Concrete Forming & Accessories | 93.3 | 47.4 | 53.8 | 93.4 | 76.5 | 78.8 | 92.5 | 74.6 | 77.0 | 88.0 | 49.7 | 55.0 | 86.3 | 56.8 | 60.9 | 83.7 | 73.7 | 75.1 |
| 0320 | Concrete Reinforcing | 81.6 | 42.9 | 62.9 | 86.7 | 82.2 | 84.5 | 97.8 | 81.5 | 90.0 | 97.9 | 67.2 | 83.1 | 97.2 | 69.8 | 84.0 | 97.8 | 75.1 | 86.9 |
| 0330 | Cast-in-Place Concrete | 92.8 | 58.7 | 80.2 | 104.7 | 82.2 | 96.4 | 101.9 | 79.8 | 93.7 | 101.5 | 52.3 | 83.3 | 105.6 | 61.6 | 89.3 | 104.4 | 73.1 | 92.8 |
| 03 | CONCRETE | 103.4 | 51.1 | 79.3 | 107.9 | 80.5 | 95.2 | 113.0 | 78.3 | 97.0 | 108.9 | 55.6 | 84.3 | 109.6 | 62.4 | 87.8 | 106.2 | 74.6 | 91.6 |
| 04 | MASONRY | 116.7 | 42.9 | 72.6 | 92.7 | 74.9 | 82.1 | 106.1 | 71.8 | 85.6 | 93.9 | 47.1 | 65.9 | 120.0 | 54.4 | 80.8 | 108.6 | 70.3 | 85.7 |
| 05 | METALS | 88.3 | 58.7 | 79.7 | 97.4 | 94.9 | 96.7 | 96.1 | 86.5 | 93.3 | 95.0 | 86.5 | 92.6 | 95.3 | 89.6 | 93.6 | 95.3 | 86.1 | 92.7 |
| 06 | WOOD, PLASTICS & COMPOSITES | 93.8 | 49.1 | 69.7 | 98.0 | 76.0 | 86.1 | 94.6 | 76.0 | 84.6 | 86.8 | 48.2 | 66.0 | 84.9 | 55.1 | 68.8 | 83.7 | 76.0 | 79.5 |
| 07 | THERMAL & MOISTURE PROTECTION | 99.0 | 38.8 | 75.5 | 102.3 | 80.4 | 93.8 | 104.1 | 73.3 | 92.1 | 103.6 | 54.1 | 84.3 | 103.3 | 60.3 | 86.5 | 103.4 | 69.0 | 90.0 |
| 08 | OPENINGS | 102.2 | 45.0 | 88.1 | 97.6 | 76.8 | 92.5 | 95.6 | 71.8 | 89.7 | 98.9 | 52.7 | 87.5 | 96.9 | 58.6 | 87.5 | 97.3 | 69.5 | 90.4 |
| 0920 | Plaster & Gypsum Board | 100.4 | 47.0 | 67.5 | 111.1 | 75.2 | 88.9 | 108.1 | 75.2 | 87.8 | 104.5 | 46.7 | 68.8 | 103.8 | 53.0 | 72.4 | 104.3 | 75.2 | 86.3 |
| 0950, 0980 | Ceilings & Acoustic Treatment | 85.8 | 47.0 | 62.0 | 96.7 | 75.2 | 83.5 | 92.4 | 75.2 | 81.8 | 91.5 | 46.7 | 64.0 | 91.5 | 53.0 | 67.9 | 92.4 | 75.2 | 81.8 |
| 0960 | Flooring | 93.9 | 35.2 | 78.0 | 106.7 | 90.3 | 102.2 | 104.8 | 63.6 | 93.6 | 100.4 | 43.2 | 84.8 | 98.8 | 51.0 | 85.8 | 98.8 | 63.6 | 89.2 |
| 0970, 0990 | Wall Finishes & Painting/Coating | 91.6 | 19.8 | 48.4 | 126.3 | 83.2 | 100.4 | 126.3 | 80.4 | 98.7 | 113.6 | 49.8 | 75.3 | 113.6 | 70.4 | 87.7 | 126.3 | 62.6 | 88.0 |
| 09 | FINISHES | 95.1 | 42.0 | 67.3 | 103.4 | 79.5 | 90.9 | 102.6 | 73.8 | 87.5 | 99.1 | 47.9 | 72.3 | 98.5 | 56.5 | 76.5 | 99.1 | 71.6 | 84.7 |
| COVERS | DIVS. 10 - 14, 25, 28, 41, 43, 44 | 100.0 | 44.0 | 88.5 | 100.0 | 87.6 | 97.5 | 100.0 | 82.0 | 96.3 | 100.0 | 68.8 | 93.6 | 100.0 | 80.1 | 95.9 | 100.0 | 69.3 | 93.7 |
| 21, 22, 23 | FIRE SUPPRESSION, PLUMBING & HVAC | 96.0 | 63.2 | 82.5 | 100.2 | 88.0 | 95.2 | 100.2 | 83.1 | 93.2 | 96.1 | 57.0 | 80.0 | 96.1 | 66.5 | 83.9 | 96.1 | 73.5 | 86.8 |
| 26, 27, 3370 | ELECTRICAL, COMMUNICATIONS & UTIL. | 97.8 | 64.6 | 81.5 | 97.8 | 93.9 | 95.9 | 95.3 | 87.8 | 91.7 | 97.4 | 42.5 | 70.4 | 97.3 | 68.8 | 83.3 | 99.8 | 62.6 | 81.5 |
| MF2004 | WEIGHTED AVERAGE | 97.3 | 57.3 | 80.2 | 100.6 | 85.1 | 94.0 | 101.5 | 80.3 | 92.4 | 99.0 | 57.4 | 81.2 | 100.3 | 67.2 | 86.1 | 99.6 | 73.2 | 88.3 |

## VIRGINIA

| DIVISION | | FAIRFAX 220 - 221 | | | FARMVILLE 239 | | | FREDERICKSBURG 224 - 225 | | | GRUNDY 246 | | | HARRISONBURG 228 | | | LYNCHBURG 245 | | |
|---|---|---|---|---|---|---|---|---|---|---|---|---|---|---|---|---|---|---|---|
| | | MAT. | INST. | TOTAL | MAT. | INST. | TOTAL | MAT. | INST. | TOTAL | MAT. | INST. | TOTAL | MAT. | INST. | TOTAL | MAT. | INST. | TOTAL |
| 015433 | CONTRACTOR EQUIPMENT | | 100.3 | 100.3 | | 105.4 | 105.4 | | 100.3 | 100.3 | | 100.3 | 100.3 | | 100.3 | 100.3 | | 100.3 | 100.3 |
| 0241, 31 - 34 | SITE & INFRASTRUCTURE, DEMOLITION | 129.3 | 84.5 | 98.1 | 114.7 | 85.2 | 94.2 | 115.7 | 84.5 | 93.9 | 111.4 | 82.4 | 91.2 | 125.7 | 83.8 | 96.5 | 112.2 | 83.6 | 92.3 |
| 0310 | Concrete Forming & Accessories | 86.5 | 74.8 | 76.4 | 98.8 | 52.0 | 58.5 | 86.5 | 56.1 | 60.3 | 91.2 | 43.2 | 49.9 | 82.5 | 50.0 | 54.5 | 88.0 | 71.9 | 74.1 |
| 0320 | Concrete Reinforcing | 97.8 | 79.1 | 88.8 | 97.9 | 60.5 | 79.8 | 98.6 | 78.2 | 88.8 | 96.6 | 61.1 | 79.5 | 97.8 | 54.9 | 77.2 | 97.2 | 68.0 | 83.2 |
| 0330 | Cast-in-Place Concrete | 101.9 | 77.0 | 92.7 | 105.6 | 59.8 | 88.6 | 103.5 | 57.7 | 86.5 | 101.5 | 53.1 | 83.6 | 101.9 | 65.6 | 88.5 | 101.5 | 65.2 | 88.1 |
| 03 | CONCRETE | 112.6 | 77.4 | 96.4 | 108.5 | 57.8 | 85.1 | 105.9 | 62.4 | 85.8 | 107.5 | 51.4 | 81.6 | 110.2 | 58.2 | 86.2 | 107.4 | 70.0 | 90.2 |
| 04 | MASONRY | 106.0 | 71.9 | 85.6 | 103.6 | 53.8 | 73.8 | 107.2 | 52.2 | 74.3 | 98.0 | 56.9 | 73.4 | 104.5 | 59.2 | 77.4 | 112.5 | 61.5 | 82.0 |
| 05 | METALS | 95.4 | 94.8 | 95.2 | 95.3 | 82.4 | 91.5 | 95.4 | 92.6 | 94.6 | 95.0 | 75.1 | 89.2 | 95.3 | 89.6 | 93.7 | 95.2 | 88.3 | 93.2 |
| 06 | WOOD, PLASTICS & COMPOSITES | 86.8 | 76.0 | 80.9 | 100.1 | 53.2 | 74.8 | 86.8 | 54.3 | 69.3 | 90.1 | 42.1 | 64.3 | 82.5 | 47.0 | 63.4 | 86.8 | 76.2 | 81.1 |
| 07 | THERMAL & MOISTURE PROTECTION | 104.0 | 74.3 | 92.4 | 103.3 | 54.5 | 84.3 | 103.4 | 57.2 | 85.4 | 103.6 | 53.8 | 84.2 | 103.8 | 68.3 | 89.9 | 103.5 | 62.8 | 87.6 |
| 08 | OPENINGS | 95.6 | 76.4 | 90.9 | 97.3 | 52.1 | 86.1 | 96.9 | 60.3 | 87.9 | 98.9 | 41.6 | 84.8 | 97.3 | 59.4 | 87.9 | 97.2 | 67.8 | 90.0 |
| 0920 | Plaster & Gypsum Board | 104.7 | 75.2 | 86.5 | 109.9 | 51.0 | 73.6 | 104.7 | 53.0 | 72.8 | 105.2 | 40.5 | 65.3 | 103.8 | 45.5 | 67.8 | 104.5 | 75.4 | 86.5 |
| 0950, 0980 | Ceilings & Acoustic Treatment | 92.4 | 75.2 | 81.8 | 91.5 | 51.0 | 66.7 | 92.4 | 53.0 | 68.2 | 91.5 | 40.5 | 60.2 | 91.5 | 45.5 | 63.2 | 91.5 | 75.4 | 81.6 |
| 0960 | Flooring | 100.7 | 63.6 | 90.6 | 106.7 | 69.6 | 96.6 | 100.7 | 85.5 | 96.6 | 102.1 | 38.9 | 84.9 | 98.3 | 85.5 | 94.8 | 100.4 | 48.2 | 86.2 |
| 0970, 0990 | Wall Finishes & Painting/Coating | 126.3 | 80.4 | 98.7 | 113.6 | 46.4 | 73.2 | 126.3 | 76.9 | 96.6 | 113.6 | 42.0 | 70.6 | 126.3 | 60.8 | 86.9 | 113.6 | 49.8 | 75.3 |
| 09 | FINISHES | 100.9 | 73.8 | 86.7 | 101.5 | 55.1 | 77.2 | 99.7 | 63.2 | 80.6 | 99.5 | 41.9 | 69.3 | 99.4 | 56.8 | 77.1 | 98.9 | 65.7 | 81.5 |
| COVERS | DIVS. 10 - 14, 25, 28, 41, 43, 44 | 100.0 | 82.0 | 96.3 | 100.0 | 57.4 | 91.3 | 100.0 | 69.8 | 93.8 | 100.0 | 55.0 | 90.8 | 100.0 | 68.5 | 93.5 | 100.0 | 73.0 | 94.5 |
| 21, 22, 23 | FIRE SUPPRESSION, PLUMBING & HVAC | 96.1 | 83.3 | 90.8 | 96.1 | 42.8 | 74.2 | 96.1 | 80.3 | 89.6 | 96.1 | 48.1 | 76.4 | 96.1 | 62.8 | 82.4 | 96.1 | 65.8 | 83.7 |
| 26, 27, 3370 | ELECTRICAL, COMMUNICATIONS & UTIL. | 98.5 | 89.5 | 94.1 | 94.6 | 56.3 | 75.8 | 95.5 | 93.9 | 94.7 | 97.4 | 53.5 | 75.8 | 97.6 | 81.2 | 89.5 | 98.4 | 63.2 | 81.1 |
| MF2004 | WEIGHTED AVERAGE | 100.5 | 81.5 | 92.4 | 99.3 | 57.8 | 81.6 | 99.1 | 74.1 | 88.4 | 99.0 | 54.7 | 80.1 | 99.9 | 67.8 | 86.2 | 99.7 | 69.4 | 86.7 |

## VIRGINIA

| DIVISION | | NEWPORT NEWS 236 | | | NORFOLK 233 - 235 | | | PETERSBURG 238 | | | PORTSMOUTH 237 | | | PULASKI 243 | | | RICHMOND 230 - 232 | | |
|---|---|---|---|---|---|---|---|---|---|---|---|---|---|---|---|---|---|---|---|
| | | MAT. | INST. | TOTAL | MAT. | INST. | TOTAL | MAT. | INST. | TOTAL | MAT. | INST. | TOTAL | MAT. | INST. | TOTAL | MAT. | INST. | TOTAL |
| 015433 | CONTRACTOR EQUIPMENT | | 105.4 | 105.4 | | 106.2 | 106.2 | | 105.4 | 105.4 | | 105.3 | 105.3 | | 100.3 | 100.3 | | 105.4 | 105.4 |
| 0241, 31 - 34 | SITE & INFRASTRUCTURE, DEMOLITION | 112.6 | 86.2 | 94.2 | 109.3 | 87.3 | 94.0 | 117.6 | 86.8 | 96.1 | 111.2 | 85.6 | 93.4 | 110.7 | 82.4 | 91.0 | 109.8 | 86.7 | 93.7 |
| 0310 | Concrete Forming & Accessories | 98.0 | 74.1 | 77.4 | 99.7 | 74.1 | 77.7 | 91.3 | 67.7 | 71.0 | 87.2 | 60.4 | 64.1 | 91.2 | 43.4 | 50.0 | 97.4 | 67.7 | 71.8 |
| 0320 | Concrete Reinforcing | 97.6 | 69.0 | 83.8 | 97.6 | 69.1 | 83.8 | 97.2 | 70.6 | 84.4 | 97.2 | 68.9 | 83.6 | 96.6 | 61.1 | 79.5 | 97.6 | 70.6 | 84.6 |
| 0330 | Cast-in-Place Concrete | 102.6 | 63.8 | 88.2 | 105.7 | 63.9 | 90.2 | 109.0 | 59.5 | 90.6 | 101.6 | 63.4 | 87.5 | 101.5 | 53.2 | 83.6 | 102.6 | 59.5 | 86.6 |
| 03 | CONCRETE | 105.4 | 70.7 | 89.4 | 107.0 | 70.7 | 90.3 | 111.1 | 66.7 | 90.6 | 104.2 | 64.4 | 85.8 | 107.5 | 51.5 | 81.7 | 105.3 | 66.7 | 87.5 |
| 04 | MASONRY | 98.7 | 57.9 | 74.3 | 105.1 | 57.9 | 76.9 | 111.5 | 63.1 | 82.5 | 103.7 | 56.1 | 75.2 | 90.5 | 56.9 | 70.4 | 97.0 | 63.1 | 76.7 |
| 05 | METALS | 97.4 | 90.0 | 95.3 | 96.5 | 90.1 | 94.6 | 95.3 | 91.4 | 94.2 | 96.4 | 88.3 | 94.1 | 95.1 | 75.3 | 89.3 | 99.4 | 91.4 | 97.1 |
| 06 | WOOD, PLASTICS & COMPOSITES | 98.9 | 80.6 | 89.0 | 100.9 | 80.6 | 89.9 | 90.6 | 71.1 | 80.1 | 86.3 | 62.3 | 73.4 | 90.1 | 42.1 | 64.3 | 97.6 | 71.1 | 83.3 |
| 07 | THERMAL & MOISTURE PROTECTION | 103.3 | 61.9 | 87.1 | 100.6 | 61.9 | 85.5 | 103.3 | 63.6 | 87.8 | 103.3 | 58.8 | 86.0 | 103.6 | 53.8 | 84.2 | 102.2 | 63.5 | 87.2 |
| 08 | OPENINGS | 97.6 | 71.0 | 91.1 | 97.6 | 71.0 | 91.1 | 96.9 | 67.3 | 89.6 | 97.7 | 61.2 | 88.7 | 98.9 | 41.6 | 84.8 | 97.6 | 67.3 | 90.1 |
| 0920 | Plaster & Gypsum Board | 111.1 | 79.1 | 91.4 | 107.8 | 79.1 | 90.1 | 105.4 | 69.4 | 83.2 | 104.7 | 60.4 | 77.4 | 105.2 | 40.5 | 65.3 | 115.3 | 69.4 | 87.0 |
| 0950, 0980 | Ceilings & Acoustic Treatment | 96.7 | 79.1 | 85.9 | 96.7 | 79.1 | 85.9 | 92.4 | 69.4 | 78.3 | 96.7 | 60.4 | 74.4 | 91.5 | 40.5 | 60.2 | 100.1 | 69.4 | 81.3 |
| 0960 | Flooring | 106.7 | 58.4 | 93.6 | 106.1 | 58.4 | 93.1 | 101.7 | 82.3 | 96.4 | 97.8 | 73.8 | 91.3 | 102.1 | 38.9 | 84.9 | 106.1 | 82.3 | 99.6 |
| 0970, 0990 | Wall Finishes & Painting/Coating | 113.6 | 50.3 | 75.6 | 113.6 | 60.9 | 81.9 | 113.6 | 70.4 | 87.7 | 113.6 | 60.9 | 81.9 | 113.6 | 42.0 | 70.6 | 113.6 | 70.4 | 87.7 |
| 09 | FINISHES | 102.7 | 69.4 | 85.3 | 101.7 | 70.6 | 85.4 | 99.7 | 71.2 | 84.8 | 99.1 | 62.7 | 80.0 | 99.5 | 41.9 | 69.3 | 103.6 | 71.2 | 86.6 |
| COVERS | DIVS. 10 - 14, 25, 28, 41, 43, 44 | 100.0 | 81.4 | 96.2 | 100.0 | 81.4 | 96.2 | 100.0 | 80.4 | 96.0 | 100.0 | 72.0 | 94.3 | 100.0 | 55.0 | 90.8 | 100.0 | 80.4 | 96.0 |
| 21, 22, 23 | FIRE SUPPRESSION, PLUMBING & HVAC | 100.2 | 62.9 | 84.9 | 100.0 | 64.9 | 85.6 | 96.1 | 64.3 | 83.0 | 100.2 | 64.9 | 85.7 | 96.1 | 48.4 | 76.5 | 100.1 | 64.3 | 85.4 |
| 26, 27, 3370 | ELECTRICAL, COMMUNICATIONS & UTIL. | 97.4 | 65.6 | 81.8 | 96.7 | 60.5 | 78.9 | 97.6 | 68.8 | 83.4 | 95.7 | 60.4 | 78.4 | 97.4 | 57.8 | 77.9 | 100.8 | 68.8 | 85.1 |
| MF2004 | WEIGHTED AVERAGE | 100.4 | 70.1 | 87.4 | 100.4 | 70.1 | 87.4 | 100.2 | 71.0 | 87.7 | 99.7 | 66.7 | 85.6 | 98.6 | 55.4 | 80.2 | 100.9 | 71.0 | 88.1 |

| DIVISION | | VIRGINIA | | | | | | | | | WASHINGTON | | | | | | | | |
|---|---|---|---|---|---|---|---|---|---|---|---|---|---|---|---|---|---|---|---|
| | | ROANOKE 240 - 241 | | | STAUNTON 244 | | | WINCHESTER 226 | | | CLARKSTON 994 | | | EVERETT 982 | | | OLYMPIA 985 | | |
| | | MAT. | INST. | TOTAL | MAT. | INST. | TOTAL | MAT. | INST. | TOTAL | MAT. | INST. | TOTAL | MAT. | INST. | TOTAL | MAT. | INST. | TOTAL |
| 015433 | CONTRACTOR EQUIPMENT | | 100.2 | 100.2 | | 105.4 | 105.4 | | 100.3 | 100.3 | | 90.1 | 90.1 | | 103.7 | 103.7 | | 103.7 | 103.7 |
| 0241, 31 - 34 | SITE & INFRASTRUCTURE, DEMOLITION | 109.9 | 83.6 | 91.6 | 115.3 | 85.8 | 94.8 | 124.1 | 83.9 | 96.1 | 104.7 | 88.4 | 93.3 | 99.9 | 114.3 | 109.9 | 102.7 | 114.4 | 110.8 |
| 0310 | Concrete Forming & Accessories | 97.8 | 71.5 | 75.2 | 90.8 | 59.6 | 64.0 | 85.0 | 55.8 | 59.8 | 115.8 | 79.1 | 84.2 | 110.3 | 97.7 | 99.5 | 99.5 | 98.0 | 98.2 |
| 0320 | Concrete Reinforcing | 97.6 | 68.1 | 83.4 | 97.2 | 59.3 | 78.9 | 97.2 | 81.3 | 89.6 | 109.4 | 89.3 | 99.7 | 116.2 | 96.7 | 106.8 | 116.8 | 96.7 | 107.1 |
| 0330 | Cast-in-Place Concrete | 115.4 | 65.1 | 96.7 | 105.6 | 57.7 | 87.9 | 101.9 | 61.2 | 86.8 | 111.5 | 82.5 | 100.7 | 102.3 | 103.8 | 102.8 | 97.3 | 104.3 | 99.9 |
| 03 | CONCRETE | 111.7 | 69.8 | 92.4 | 108.6 | 60.5 | 86.4 | 109.5 | 63.9 | 88.4 | 104.3 | 82.1 | 94.1 | 97.8 | 99.1 | 98.4 | 95.9 | 99.4 | 97.5 |
| 04 | MASONRY | 99.2 | 63.4 | 77.8 | 109.4 | 61.8 | 80.9 | 101.8 | 52.0 | 72.0 | 118.1 | 83.3 | 97.3 | 139.9 | 99.9 | 116.0 | 131.0 | 100.6 | 112.8 |
| 05 | METALS | 97.2 | 88.1 | 94.5 | 95.3 | 88.1 | 93.2 | 95.4 | 91.6 | 94.3 | 91.6 | 82.2 | 88.9 | 105.2 | 88.8 | 100.4 | 99.8 | 88.9 | 96.6 |
| 06 | WOOD, PLASTICS & COMPOSITES | 98.9 | 76.2 | 86.7 | 90.1 | 60.4 | 74.1 | 85.2 | 54.3 | 68.6 | 96.9 | 77.7 | 86.5 | 102.1 | 97.2 | 99.5 | 88.5 | 97.2 | 93.2 |
| 07 | THERMAL & MOISTURE PROTECTION | 103.2 | 61.7 | 87.0 | 103.2 | 58.9 | 85.9 | 103.9 | 64.2 | 88.4 | 142.7 | 79.8 | 118.2 | 102.5 | 95.5 | 99.8 | 102.0 | 95.3 | 99.4 |
| 08 | OPENINGS | 97.6 | 67.8 | 90.3 | 97.3 | 58.4 | 87.7 | 99.0 | 61.1 | 89.6 | 111.3 | 79.9 | 103.6 | 102.3 | 96.9 | 101.0 | 102.2 | 96.9 | 100.9 |
| 0920 | Plaster & Gypsum Board | 111.1 | 75.4 | 89.1 | 105.2 | 58.4 | 76.3 | 104.7 | 53.0 | 72.8 | 143.0 | 76.9 | 102.2 | 111.2 | 97.1 | 102.5 | 107.3 | 97.1 | 101.0 |
| 0950, 0980 | Ceilings & Acoustic Treatment | 96.7 | 75.4 | 83.6 | 91.5 | 58.4 | 71.2 | 92.4 | 53.0 | 68.2 | 104.1 | 76.9 | 87.4 | 104.4 | 97.1 | 99.9 | 97.4 | 97.1 | 97.2 |
| 0960 | Flooring | 106.7 | 45.2 | 90.0 | 101.4 | 45.6 | 86.2 | 100.0 | 85.5 | 96.0 | 109.5 | 54.5 | 94.5 | 127.0 | 105.8 | 121.3 | 119.2 | 106.0 | 115.6 |
| 0970, 0990 | Wall Finishes & Painting/Coating | 113.6 | 49.8 | 75.3 | 113.6 | 34.7 | 66.2 | 126.3 | 53.5 | 82.5 | 109.7 | 70.1 | 85.9 | 111.0 | 85.0 | 95.4 | 111.0 | 86.6 | 96.3 |
| 09 | FINISHES | 102.5 | 65.2 | 83.0 | 99.3 | 55.0 | 76.1 | 100.2 | 60.6 | 79.4 | 123.5 | 73.0 | 97.1 | 113.7 | 97.8 | 105.4 | 109.4 | 98.2 | 103.5 |
| COVERS | DIVS. 10 - 14, 25, 28, 41, 43, 44 | 100.0 | 73.0 | 94.4 | 100.0 | 72.6 | 94.4 | 100.0 | 64.8 | 92.8 | 100.0 | 95.8 | 99.1 | 100.0 | 99.6 | 99.9 | 100.0 | 101.6 | 100.3 |
| 21, 22, 23 | FIRE SUPPRESSION, PLUMBING & HVAC | 100.2 | 55.3 | 81.8 | 96.1 | 64.8 | 83.2 | 96.1 | 78.8 | 89.0 | 96.4 | 85.0 | 91.7 | 100.2 | 100.6 | 100.4 | 100.1 | 100.9 | 100.4 |
| 26, 27, 3370 | ELECTRICAL, COMMUNICATIONS & UTIL. | 97.4 | 45.7 | 72.0 | 96.2 | 49.6 | 73.3 | 96.0 | 51.5 | 74.1 | 101.6 | 93.4 | 97.5 | 105.9 | 93.0 | 99.6 | 110.6 | 98.3 | 104.6 |
| MF2004 | WEIGHTED AVERAGE | 101.0 | 64.8 | 85.5 | 99.6 | 64.1 | 84.4 | 99.7 | 67.6 | 86.0 | 104.1 | 84.0 | 95.5 | 104.8 | 98.6 | 102.2 | 103.3 | 99.7 | 101.8 |

697

| | | WASHINGTON | | | | | | | | | | | | | | | | | |
|---|---|---|---|---|---|---|---|---|---|---|---|---|---|---|---|---|---|---|---|
| | DIVISION | RICHLAND | | | SEATTLE | | | SPOKANE | | | TACOMA | | | VANCOUVER | | | WENATCHEE | | |
| | | 993 | | | 980 - 981,987 | | | 990 - 992 | | | 983 - 984 | | | 986 | | | 988 | | |
| | | MAT. | INST. | TOTAL | MAT. | INST. | TOTAL | MAT. | INST. | TOTAL | MAT. | INST. | TOTAL | MAT. | INST. | TOTAL | MAT. | INST. | TOTAL |
| 015433 | CONTRACTOR EQUIPMENT | | 90.1 | 90.1 | | 103.5 | 103.5 | | 90.1 | 90.1 | | 103.7 | 103.7 | | 97.0 | 97.0 | | 103.7 | 103.7 |
| 0241, 31 - 34 | SITE & INFRASTRUCTURE, DEMOLITION | 105.8 | 89.5 | 94.4 | 104.4 | 112.2 | 109.8 | 105.2 | 89.5 | 94.3 | 103.4 | 114.4 | 111.0 | 116.6 | 100.2 | 105.1 | 116.2 | 113.3 | 114.2 |
| 0310 | Concrete Forming & Accessories | 115.5 | 80.4 | 85.2 | 101.5 | 98.3 | 98.7 | 121.5 | 80.4 | 86.1 | 101.5 | 98.1 | 98.6 | 102.3 | 95.4 | 96.4 | 102.8 | 78.7 | 82.0 |
| 0320 | Concrete Reinforcing | 105.0 | 89.3 | 97.4 | 114.9 | 96.8 | 106.2 | 105.7 | 89.4 | 97.9 | 114.9 | 96.7 | 106.2 | 115.8 | 96.4 | 106.4 | 115.7 | 89.3 | 103.0 |
| 0330 | Cast-in-Place Concrete | 111.7 | 84.8 | 101.8 | 107.3 | 104.4 | 106.3 | 116.1 | 84.8 | 104.5 | 105.2 | 104.4 | 104.9 | 117.5 | 100.7 | 111.3 | 107.4 | 83.9 | 98.7 |
| 03 | CONCRETE | 103.8 | 83.5 | 94.4 | 100.7 | 99.7 | 100.2 | 106.5 | 83.5 | 95.9 | 99.7 | 99.5 | 99.6 | 109.5 | 97.1 | 103.8 | 106.7 | 82.5 | 95.5 |
| 04 | MASONRY | 118.0 | 83.4 | 97.3 | 132.8 | 100.6 | 113.5 | 118.7 | 85.8 | 99.0 | 132.6 | 100.6 | 113.4 | 133.5 | 96.4 | 111.3 | 136.0 | 81.3 | 103.3 |
| 05 | METALS | 92.0 | 82.7 | 89.3 | 106.8 | 90.7 | 102.2 | 94.4 | 82.9 | 91.1 | 106.8 | 89.0 | 101.7 | 104.1 | 90.1 | 100.0 | 104.4 | 83.5 | 98.4 |
| 06 | WOOD, PLASTICS & COMPOSITES | 97.1 | 79.2 | 87.4 | 92.7 | 97.2 | 95.1 | 106.3 | 79.2 | 91.7 | 91.7 | 97.2 | 94.7 | 85.2 | 95.6 | 90.8 | 92.6 | 77.4 | 84.4 |
| 07 | THERMAL & MOISTURE PROTECTION | 143.9 | 81.7 | 119.6 | 102.5 | 97.5 | 100.5 | 141.0 | 82.4 | 118.2 | 102.2 | 97.0 | 100.2 | 103.4 | 88.7 | 97.6 | 102.7 | 79.3 | 93.6 |
| 08 | OPENINGS | 111.9 | 75.6 | 103.0 | 104.6 | 96.9 | 102.7 | 112.5 | 75.6 | 103.4 | 103.0 | 96.9 | 101.5 | 100.4 | 95.3 | 99.1 | 102.5 | 74.5 | 95.6 |
| 0920 | Plaster & Gypsum Board | 143.0 | 78.5 | 103.2 | 106.3 | 97.1 | 100.6 | 135.9 | 78.5 | 100.5 | 108.4 | 97.1 | 101.4 | 106.7 | 95.7 | 99.9 | 109.3 | 76.8 | 89.2 |
| 0950, 0980 | Ceilings & Acoustic Treatment | 110.8 | 78.5 | 91.0 | 107.6 | 97.1 | 101.1 | 106.0 | 78.5 | 89.1 | 107.8 | 97.1 | 101.2 | 102.8 | 95.7 | 98.5 | 100.8 | 76.8 | 86.1 |
| 0960 | Flooring | 109.7 | 40.0 | 90.7 | 119.0 | 106.0 | 115.5 | 110.2 | 72.4 | 99.9 | 119.6 | 106.0 | 115.9 | 125.5 | 73.6 | 111.4 | 122.9 | 72.4 | 109.2 |
| 0970, 0990 | Wall Finishes & Painting/Coating | 109.7 | 70.1 | 85.9 | 111.0 | 86.6 | 96.3 | 109.6 | 70.1 | 85.9 | 111.0 | 86.6 | 96.3 | 118.0 | 66.8 | 87.2 | 111.0 | 70.1 | 86.4 |
| 09 | FINISHES | 125.2 | 70.9 | 96.8 | 111.6 | 98.2 | 104.6 | 123.2 | 77.6 | 99.3 | 112.1 | 98.2 | 104.8 | 110.5 | 88.0 | 98.7 | 112.6 | 75.9 | 93.4 |
| COVERS | DIVS. 10 - 14, 25, 28, 41, 43, 44 | 100.0 | 76.5 | 95.2 | 100.0 | 101.6 | 100.3 | 100.0 | 76.4 | 95.2 | 100.0 | 101.6 | 100.3 | 100.0 | 73.4 | 94.5 | 100.0 | 94.7 | 98.9 |
| 21, 22, 23 | FIRE SUPPRESSION, PLUMBING & HVAC | 100.6 | 100.0 | 100.4 | 100.2 | 106.5 | 102.8 | 100.5 | 85.0 | 94.1 | 100.2 | 100.9 | 100.5 | 100.3 | 105.4 | 102.4 | 96.1 | 80.6 | 89.8 |
| 26, 27, 3370 | ELECTRICAL, COMMUNICATIONS & UTIL. | 98.2 | 93.4 | 95.8 | 105.7 | 102.2 | 104.0 | 96.5 | 78.5 | 87.7 | 105.7 | 98.3 | 102.1 | 112.3 | 100.4 | 106.5 | 106.6 | 84.2 | 95.6 |
| MF2004 | WEIGHTED AVERAGE | 104.9 | 86.5 | 97.1 | 105.1 | 101.5 | 103.6 | 105.3 | 82.4 | 95.5 | 104.8 | 99.0 | 102.7 | 106.3 | 96.7 | 102.2 | 105.0 | 84.0 | 96.0 |

| | | WASHINGTON | | | WEST VIRGINIA | | | | | | | | | | | | | | |
|---|---|---|---|---|---|---|---|---|---|---|---|---|---|---|---|---|---|---|---|
| | DIVISION | YAKIMA | | | BECKLEY | | | BLUEFIELD | | | BUCKHANNON | | | CHARLESTON | | | CLARKSBURG | | |
| | | 989 | | | 258 - 259 | | | 247 - 248 | | | 262 | | | 250 - 253 | | | 263 - 264 | | |
| | | MAT. | INST. | TOTAL | MAT. | INST. | TOTAL | MAT. | INST. | TOTAL | MAT. | INST. | TOTAL | MAT. | INST. | TOTAL | MAT. | INST. | TOTAL |
| 015433 | CONTRACTOR EQUIPMENT | | 103.7 | 103.7 | | 100.3 | 100.3 | | 100.3 | 100.3 | | 100.3 | 100.3 | | 100.3 | 100.3 | | 100.3 | 100.3 |
| 0241, 31 - 34 | SITE & INFRASTRUCTURE, DEMOLITION | 106.6 | 113.0 | 111.0 | 104.8 | 85.6 | 91.4 | 104.5 | 85.5 | 91.3 | 111.6 | 85.3 | 93.3 | 105.5 | 86.7 | 92.4 | 112.2 | 85.3 | 93.4 |
| 0310 | Concrete Forming & Accessories | 101.9 | 91.7 | 93.1 | 86.8 | 84.6 | 84.9 | 88.2 | 83.6 | 84.2 | 87.5 | 85.3 | 85.6 | 103.8 | 86.0 | 88.4 | 85.0 | 85.2 | 85.2 |
| 0320 | Concrete Reinforcing | 115.4 | 88.8 | 102.6 | 96.2 | 80.3 | 88.5 | 96.2 | 64.2 | 80.8 | 96.7 | 85.6 | 91.4 | 97.6 | 80.5 | 89.3 | 96.7 | 85.4 | 91.2 |
| 0330 | Cast-in-Place Concrete | 112.4 | 80.7 | 100.7 | 99.3 | 100.6 | 99.8 | 99.3 | 100.4 | 99.7 | 99.0 | 96.9 | 98.2 | 100.5 | 102.0 | 101.0 | 108.5 | 96.9 | 104.2 |
| 03 | CONCRETE | 104.5 | 87.1 | 96.4 | 102.8 | 90.1 | 96.9 | 102.9 | 86.5 | 95.3 | 106.4 | 90.1 | 98.9 | 104.7 | 91.2 | 98.5 | 110.4 | 90.0 | 101.0 |
| 04 | MASONRY | 124.9 | 65.7 | 89.5 | 97.4 | 87.8 | 91.7 | 92.1 | 87.8 | 89.5 | 104.1 | 83.5 | 91.8 | 96.2 | 89.7 | 92.3 | 105.8 | 83.5 | 92.5 |
| 05 | METALS | 105.1 | 83.7 | 98.8 | 95.3 | 95.5 | 95.3 | 95.3 | 88.6 | 93.3 | 95.4 | 98.0 | 96.2 | 97.4 | 96.5 | 97.2 | 95.4 | 97.9 | 96.1 |
| 06 | WOOD, PLASTICS & COMPOSITES | 92.0 | 97.2 | 94.8 | 86.7 | 84.9 | 85.8 | 88.4 | 84.9 | 86.5 | 87.7 | 84.7 | 86.0 | 105.2 | 84.5 | 94.1 | 84.4 | 84.7 | 84.5 |
| 07 | THERMAL & MOISTURE PROTECTION | 102.3 | 77.8 | 92.7 | 103.3 | 86.6 | 96.8 | 103.4 | 81.3 | 94.8 | 103.7 | 84.5 | 96.2 | 100.5 | 87.3 | 95.4 | 103.6 | 84.5 | 96.1 |
| 08 | OPENINGS | 102.5 | 82.9 | 97.6 | 98.3 | 79.1 | 93.6 | 99.1 | 75.4 | 93.3 | 99.2 | 80.2 | 94.5 | 98.8 | 78.9 | 93.9 | 99.2 | 84.2 | 95.5 |
| 0920 | Plaster & Gypsum Board | 107.9 | 97.1 | 101.2 | 102.5 | 84.4 | 91.3 | 102.9 | 84.4 | 91.5 | 103.3 | 84.1 | 91.4 | 104.8 | 84.0 | 92.0 | 101.9 | 84.1 | 90.9 |
| 0950, 0980 | Ceilings & Acoustic Treatment | 102.7 | 97.1 | 99.2 | 89.0 | 84.4 | 86.1 | 89.0 | 84.4 | 86.1 | 90.7 | 84.1 | 86.6 | 93.2 | 84.0 | 87.6 | 90.7 | 84.1 | 86.6 |
| 0960 | Flooring | 120.9 | 60.1 | 104.4 | 97.2 | 104.0 | 99.0 | 97.3 | 104.0 | 99.5 | 97.4 | 95.7 | 96.9 | 106.7 | 104.0 | 106.0 | 96.1 | 95.7 | 96.0 |
| 0970, 0990 | Wall Finishes & Painting/Coating | 111.0 | 70.1 | 86.4 | 113.6 | 41.9 | 70.5 | 113.6 | 41.9 | 70.5 | 113.6 | 95.1 | 102.5 | 113.6 | 90.0 | 99.5 | 113.6 | 95.1 | 102.5 |
| 09 | FINISHES | 111.4 | 83.8 | 96.9 | 96.6 | 84.1 | 90.1 | 96.9 | 84.1 | 90.2 | 97.7 | 88.3 | 92.8 | 100.7 | 89.8 | 95.0 | 97.0 | 88.3 | 92.4 |
| COVERS | DIVS. 10 - 14, 25, 28, 41, 43, 44 | 100.0 | 97.0 | 99.4 | 100.0 | 63.7 | 92.6 | 100.0 | 63.6 | 92.6 | 100.0 | 84.5 | 96.8 | 100.0 | 85.2 | 97.0 | 100.0 | 84.5 | 96.8 |
| 21, 22, 23 | FIRE SUPPRESSION, PLUMBING & HVAC | 100.2 | 97.0 | 98.9 | 96.1 | 81.5 | 90.1 | 96.1 | 61.4 | 81.9 | 96.1 | 92.3 | 94.5 | 100.0 | 83.3 | 93.2 | 96.1 | 87.4 | 92.5 |
| 26, 27, 3370 | ELECTRICAL, COMMUNICATIONS & UTIL. | 108.8 | 93.4 | 101.2 | 93.7 | 90.5 | 92.2 | 96.3 | 71.0 | 83.9 | 97.7 | 92.2 | 95.0 | 95.8 | 90.6 | 93.2 | 97.7 | 92.2 | 95.0 |
| MF2004 | WEIGHTED AVERAGE | 105.0 | 89.3 | 98.3 | 97.6 | 86.1 | 92.6 | 97.7 | 77.7 | 89.1 | 99.2 | 89.5 | 95.0 | 99.6 | 88.3 | 94.8 | 99.7 | 88.6 | 94.9 |

| | | WEST VIRGINIA | | | | | | | | | | | | | | | | | |
|---|---|---|---|---|---|---|---|---|---|---|---|---|---|---|---|---|---|---|---|
| | DIVISION | GASSAWAY | | | HUNTINGTON | | | LEWISBURG | | | MARTINSBURG | | | MORGANTOWN | | | PARKERSBURG | | |
| | | 266 | | | 255 - 257 | | | 249 | | | 254 | | | 265 | | | 261 | | |
| | | MAT. | INST. | TOTAL | MAT. | INST. | TOTAL | MAT. | INST. | TOTAL | MAT. | INST. | TOTAL | MAT. | INST. | TOTAL | MAT. | INST. | TOTAL |
| 015433 | CONTRACTOR EQUIPMENT | | 100.3 | 100.3 | | 100.3 | 100.3 | | 100.3 | 100.3 | | 100.3 | 100.3 | | 100.3 | 100.3 | | 100.3 | 100.3 |
| 0241, 31 - 34 | SITE & INFRASTRUCTURE, DEMOLITION | 108.5 | 85.8 | 92.7 | 109.0 | 87.5 | 94.0 | 122.9 | 85.6 | 96.9 | 108.8 | 83.4 | 91.1 | 105.5 | 85.6 | 91.6 | 114.5 | 86.6 | 95.1 |
| 0310 | Concrete Forming & Accessories | 86.9 | 85.5 | 85.7 | 98.9 | 89.7 | 91.0 | 85.4 | 84.3 | 84.4 | 86.8 | 75.7 | 77.2 | 85.4 | 85.3 | 85.3 | 89.4 | 85.7 | 86.2 |
| 0320 | Concrete Reinforcing | 96.7 | 80.5 | 88.9 | 97.6 | 86.6 | 92.3 | 96.7 | 64.4 | 81.1 | 96.2 | 70.0 | 83.5 | 96.7 | 85.4 | 91.2 | 96.2 | 85.6 | 91.1 |
| 0330 | Cast-in-Place Concrete | 103.6 | 101.1 | 102.7 | 108.3 | 105.7 | 107.3 | 99.3 | 100.4 | 99.7 | 104.0 | 91.3 | 99.3 | 99.0 | 96.9 | 98.2 | 101.2 | 96.1 | 99.3 |
| 03 | CONCRETE | 106.5 | 90.7 | 99.2 | 108.3 | 95.3 | 102.3 | 113.7 | 86.9 | 101.3 | 106.7 | 80.7 | 94.7 | 102.7 | 90.1 | 96.9 | 108.4 | 90.0 | 99.9 |
| 04 | MASONRY | 107.0 | 87.9 | 95.6 | 98.6 | 87.2 | 91.8 | 97.4 | 87.8 | 91.7 | 99.6 | 73.9 | 84.2 | 126.8 | 83.5 | 100.9 | 82.5 | 84.3 | 83.6 |
| 05 | METALS | 95.4 | 96.7 | 95.8 | 97.5 | 98.8 | 97.8 | 95.3 | 89.3 | 93.6 | 95.6 | 84.6 | 92.4 | 95.5 | 97.9 | 96.2 | 96.1 | 98.0 | 96.6 |
| 06 | WOOD, PLASTICS & COMPOSITES | 86.9 | 84.7 | 85.7 | 98.9 | 88.6 | 93.3 | 84.7 | 84.9 | 84.8 | 86.7 | 77.6 | 81.8 | 84.7 | 84.7 | 84.7 | 88.3 | 84.7 | 86.3 |
| 07 | THERMAL & MOISTURE PROTECTION | 103.4 | 86.9 | 96.9 | 103.5 | 87.9 | 97.4 | 104.2 | 86.6 | 97.3 | 103.6 | 67.2 | 89.4 | 103.4 | 84.5 | 96.0 | 103.3 | 85.2 | 96.2 |
| 08 | OPENINGS | 97.1 | 79.0 | 92.7 | 97.6 | 82.6 | 93.9 | 99.2 | 75.4 | 93.3 | 100.5 | 66.9 | 92.2 | 100.5 | 84.2 | 96.5 | 98.2 | 80.2 | 93.8 |
| 0920 | Plaster & Gypsum Board | 102.9 | 84.1 | 91.3 | 109.9 | 88.1 | 96.4 | 101.9 | 84.4 | 91.1 | 102.9 | 76.8 | 86.8 | 101.9 | 84.1 | 90.9 | 104.6 | 84.1 | 91.9 |
| 0950, 0980 | Ceilings & Acoustic Treatment | 90.7 | 84.1 | 86.6 | 91.5 | 88.1 | 89.4 | 90.7 | 84.4 | 86.8 | 90.7 | 76.8 | 82.2 | 90.7 | 84.1 | 86.6 | 90.7 | 84.1 | 86.6 |
| 0960 | Flooring | 97.2 | 104.0 | 99.1 | 106.5 | 96.5 | 103.8 | 96.2 | 104.0 | 98.3 | 97.2 | 62.0 | 87.6 | 96.2 | 95.7 | 96.1 | 101.0 | 95.2 | 99.4 |
| 0970, 0990 | Wall Finishes & Painting/Coating | 113.6 | 90.0 | 99.5 | 113.6 | 89.4 | 99.1 | 113.6 | 41.9 | 70.5 | 113.6 | 49.5 | 75.1 | 113.6 | 95.1 | 102.5 | 113.6 | 90.7 | 99.9 |
| 09 | FINISHES | 97.3 | 89.4 | 93.2 | 101.1 | 90.9 | 95.7 | 98.1 | 84.1 | 90.8 | 97.3 | 71.0 | 83.5 | 96.6 | 88.3 | 92.2 | 99.1 | 87.9 | 93.2 |
| COVERS | DIVS. 10 - 14, 25, 28, 41, 43, 44 | 100.0 | 84.5 | 96.8 | 100.0 | 86.3 | 97.2 | 100.0 | 63.6 | 92.6 | 100.0 | 61.3 | 92.1 | 100.0 | 75.6 | 95.0 | 100.0 | 85.0 | 96.9 |
| 21, 22, 23 | FIRE SUPPRESSION, PLUMBING & HVAC | 96.1 | 95.4 | 95.8 | 100.2 | 84.5 | 93.8 | 96.1 | 81.3 | 90.0 | 96.1 | 73.7 | 86.9 | 96.1 | 92.2 | 94.5 | 100.1 | 84.9 | 93.9 |
| 26, 27, 3370 | ELECTRICAL, COMMUNICATIONS & UTIL. | 97.7 | 90.6 | 94.2 | 97.4 | 98.5 | 98.0 | 93.7 | 71.0 | 82.6 | 99.5 | 80.5 | 90.2 | 97.9 | 92.2 | 95.1 | 97.8 | 93.8 | 95.9 |
| MF2004 | WEIGHTED AVERAGE | 99.0 | 90.5 | 95.3 | 100.5 | 90.7 | 96.3 | 99.6 | 82.1 | 92.1 | 99.2 | 76.3 | 89.4 | 99.8 | 89.3 | 95.3 | 99.4 | 88.3 | 94.7 |

# City Cost Indexes

## WEST VIRGINIA / WISCONSIN

| | DIVISION | PETERSBURG 268 MAT. | INST. | TOTAL | ROMNEY 267 MAT. | INST. | TOTAL | WHEELING 260 MAT. | INST. | TOTAL | BELOIT 535 MAT. | INST. | TOTAL | EAU CLAIRE 547 MAT. | INST. | TOTAL | GREEN BAY 541 - 543 MAT. | INST. | TOTAL |
|---|---|---|---|---|---|---|---|---|---|---|---|---|---|---|---|---|---|---|---|
| 015433 | CONTRACTOR EQUIPMENT | | 100.3 | 100.3 | | 100.3 | 100.3 | | 100.3 | 100.3 | | 101.5 | 101.5 | | 101.1 | 101.1 | | 98.7 | 98.7 |
| 0241, 31 - 34 | SITE & INFRASTRUCTURE, DEMOLITION | 104.8 | 86.0 | 91.7 | 108.0 | 86.0 | 92.6 | 115.2 | 86.3 | 95.0 | 91.6 | 107.3 | 102.5 | 90.4 | 103.6 | 99.6 | 93.6 | 99.4 | 97.7 |
| 0310 | Concrete Forming & Accessories | 88.6 | 79.4 | 80.6 | 84.6 | 79.0 | 79.8 | 91.2 | 85.5 | 86.3 | 97.8 | 97.8 | 97.8 | 97.9 | 98.4 | 98.3 | 106.7 | 97.6 | 98.9 |
| 0320 | Concrete Reinforcing | 96.2 | 74.3 | 85.6 | 96.7 | 66.8 | 82.3 | 95.5 | 85.4 | 90.6 | 95.2 | 111.7 | 103.1 | 94.5 | 103.8 | 99.0 | 92.7 | 88.8 | 90.8 |
| 0330 | Cast-in-Place Concrete | 99.0 | 96.7 | 98.1 | 103.6 | 96.5 | 101.0 | 101.2 | 97.1 | 99.7 | 99.4 | 97.9 | 98.8 | 98.0 | 97.1 | 97.7 | 101.4 | 99.0 | 100.5 |
| 03 | CONCRETE | 102.8 | 85.3 | 94.7 | 106.4 | 83.6 | 95.9 | 108.4 | 90.2 | 100.0 | 96.6 | 100.6 | 98.4 | 96.2 | 99.2 | 97.6 | 97.1 | 96.7 | 96.9 |
| 04 | MASONRY | 99.9 | 83.5 | 90.1 | 97.8 | 70.0 | 81.1 | 107.2 | 83.5 | 93.0 | 102.0 | 98.4 | 99.9 | 88.9 | 98.6 | 94.7 | 119.3 | 97.7 | 106.4 |
| 05 | METALS | 95.5 | 93.2 | 94.8 | 95.6 | 89.3 | 93.7 | 96.2 | 98.2 | 96.8 | 99.9 | 106.7 | 101.9 | 95.8 | 104.9 | 98.5 | 97.9 | 97.9 | 97.9 |
| 06 | WOOD, PLASTICS & COMPOSITES | 88.7 | 77.6 | 82.7 | 83.7 | 77.6 | 80.4 | 90.1 | 84.7 | 87.2 | 110.3 | 99.0 | 104.2 | 113.2 | 99.1 | 105.6 | 116.6 | 99.1 | 107.2 |
| 07 | THERMAL & MOISTURE PROTECTION | 103.5 | 74.0 | 92.0 | 103.5 | 70.9 | 90.8 | 103.7 | 85.4 | 96.5 | 100.3 | 97.0 | 99.0 | 100.0 | 88.1 | 95.4 | 102.0 | 86.3 | 95.9 |
| 08 | OPENINGS | 100.6 | 73.8 | 94.0 | 100.5 | 72.2 | 93.5 | 99.1 | 84.2 | 95.4 | 103.2 | 103.6 | 103.3 | 100.3 | 97.5 | 99.6 | 98.3 | 95.7 | 97.7 |
| 0920 | Plaster & Gypsum Board | 103.3 | 76.8 | 87.0 | 101.2 | 76.8 | 86.2 | 105.0 | 84.1 | 92.1 | 96.5 | 99.3 | 98.3 | 100.5 | 99.3 | 99.8 | 93.4 | 99.3 | 97.1 |
| 0950, 0980 | Ceilings & Acoustic Treatment | 90.7 | 76.8 | 82.2 | 90.7 | 76.8 | 82.2 | 90.7 | 84.1 | 86.6 | 85.7 | 99.3 | 94.1 | 99.9 | 99.3 | 99.6 | 92.3 | 99.3 | 96.6 |
| 0960 | Flooring | 98.3 | 95.7 | 97.6 | 95.9 | 69.9 | 88.9 | 102.1 | 95.7 | 100.4 | 100.5 | 115.0 | 104.4 | 95.0 | 110.0 | 99.1 | 114.0 | 110.0 | 112.9 |
| 0970, 0990 | Wall Finishes & Painting/Coating | 113.6 | 89.1 | 98.9 | 113.6 | 89.1 | 98.9 | 113.6 | 95.1 | 102.5 | 93.5 | 97.4 | 95.8 | 88.6 | 95.7 | 92.8 | 100.4 | 77.6 | 86.7 |
| 09 | FINISHES | 97.5 | 83.5 | 90.1 | 96.7 | 78.1 | 87.0 | 99.4 | 88.3 | 93.6 | 94.9 | 101.3 | 98.3 | 97.4 | 100.7 | 99.2 | 101.5 | 98.5 | 99.9 |
| COVERS | DIVS. 10 - 14, 25, 28, 41, 43, 44 | 100.0 | 74.7 | 94.8 | 100.0 | 83.7 | 96.7 | 100.0 | 91.6 | 98.3 | 100.0 | 87.9 | 97.5 | 100.0 | 89.4 | 97.8 | 100.0 | 88.6 | 97.7 |
| 21, 22, 23 | FIRE SUPPRESSION, PLUMBING & HVAC | 96.1 | 88.6 | 93.0 | 96.1 | 88.4 | 92.9 | 100.2 | 92.2 | 96.9 | 99.9 | 92.1 | 96.7 | 100.1 | 83.5 | 93.3 | 100.4 | 87.4 | 95.1 |
| 26, 27, 3370 | ELECTRICAL, COMMUNICATIONS & UTIL. | 101.0 | 80.6 | 91.0 | 100.3 | 80.6 | 90.6 | 95.0 | 92.3 | 93.7 | 96.7 | 88.4 | 92.6 | 101.3 | 90.2 | 95.8 | 96.1 | 85.8 | 91.0 |
| MF2004 | WEIGHTED AVERAGE | 98.8 | 84.5 | 92.7 | 99.0 | 81.9 | 91.7 | 100.6 | 89.9 | 96.0 | 99.0 | 97.7 | 98.5 | 98.1 | 95.0 | 96.8 | 100.0 | 93.3 | 97.1 |

## WISCONSIN

| | DIVISION | KENOSHA 531 MAT. | INST. | TOTAL | LA CROSSE 546 MAT. | INST. | TOTAL | LANCASTER 538 MAT. | INST. | TOTAL | MADISON 537 MAT. | INST. | TOTAL | MILWAUKEE 530,532 MAT. | INST. | TOTAL | NEW RICHMOND 540 MAT. | INST. | TOTAL |
|---|---|---|---|---|---|---|---|---|---|---|---|---|---|---|---|---|---|---|---|
| 015433 | CONTRACTOR EQUIPMENT | | 99.1 | 99.1 | | 101.1 | 101.1 | | 101.5 | 101.5 | | 101.5 | 101.5 | | 87.4 | 87.4 | | 102.0 | 102.0 |
| 0241, 31 - 34 | SITE & INFRASTRUCTURE, DEMOLITION | 97.4 | 104.3 | 102.2 | 83.9 | 103.7 | 97.7 | 90.9 | 107.5 | 102.4 | 91.5 | 107.6 | 102.7 | 92.2 | 96.1 | 94.9 | 84.9 | 104.6 | 98.6 |
| 0310 | Concrete Forming & Accessories | 105.8 | 108.8 | 108.3 | 84.5 | 98.9 | 96.9 | 97.0 | 98.2 | 98.0 | 96.5 | 99.7 | 99.3 | 100.5 | 116.9 | 114.6 | 92.5 | 108.3 | 106.1 |
| 0320 | Concrete Reinforcing | 95.0 | 101.9 | 98.3 | 94.2 | 91.4 | 92.9 | 96.5 | 91.5 | 94.1 | 95.2 | 91.9 | 93.6 | 95.2 | 102.2 | 98.6 | 91.8 | 103.7 | 97.5 |
| 0330 | Cast-in-Place Concrete | 108.2 | 103.3 | 106.4 | 88.1 | 97.2 | 91.5 | 98.8 | 100.5 | 99.4 | 99.2 | 101.1 | 99.9 | 97.1 | 112.0 | 102.6 | 102.0 | 89.2 | 97.3 |
| 03 | CONCRETE | 101.4 | 105.5 | 103.3 | 87.8 | 97.1 | 92.1 | 96.3 | 97.8 | 97.0 | 96.4 | 98.8 | 97.5 | 95.8 | 111.5 | 103.1 | 94.3 | 100.9 | 97.4 |
| 04 | MASONRY | 99.0 | 111.7 | 106.6 | 88.1 | 101.6 | 96.2 | 102.0 | 104.2 | 103.4 | 102.5 | 107.8 | 105.7 | 101.8 | 118.8 | 112.0 | 113.8 | 98.8 | 104.8 |
| 05 | METALS | 100.6 | 103.5 | 101.4 | 95.7 | 98.8 | 96.6 | 97.6 | 95.9 | 97.1 | 102.6 | 97.9 | 101.2 | 103.3 | 95.5 | 101.1 | 95.8 | 104.0 | 98.2 |
| 06 | WOOD, PLASTICS & COMPOSITES | 113.4 | 108.6 | 110.8 | 97.3 | 99.1 | 98.3 | 109.5 | 99.0 | 103.8 | 107.1 | 99.0 | 102.7 | 112.7 | 116.9 | 115.0 | 101.7 | 113.2 | 107.9 |
| 07 | THERMAL & MOISTURE PROTECTION | 100.7 | 100.8 | 100.7 | 99.5 | 88.1 | 95.1 | 100.1 | 83.9 | 93.8 | 96.3 | 96.2 | 96.3 | 98.7 | 112.9 | 104.2 | 101.0 | 98.3 | 100.0 |
| 08 | OPENINGS | 98.3 | 108.3 | 100.8 | 100.3 | 86.3 | 96.8 | 98.4 | 87.3 | 95.7 | 103.2 | 99.2 | 102.2 | 105.5 | 112.8 | 107.3 | 88.1 | 105.1 | 92.3 |
| 0920 | Plaster & Gypsum Board | 86.9 | 109.2 | 100.7 | 95.3 | 99.3 | 97.8 | 95.3 | 99.3 | 97.8 | 93.3 | 99.3 | 97.0 | 97.3 | 117.6 | 109.8 | 87.1 | 114.1 | 103.7 |
| 0950, 0980 | Ceilings & Acoustic Treatment | 84.8 | 109.2 | 99.8 | 98.2 | 99.3 | 98.9 | 80.5 | 99.3 | 92.1 | 87.6 | 99.3 | 94.8 | 89.1 | 117.6 | 106.6 | 67.3 | 114.1 | 96.0 |
| 0960 | Flooring | 117.8 | 115.6 | 117.2 | 87.5 | 110.0 | 93.6 | 99.7 | 108.2 | 102.0 | 95.0 | 108.2 | 98.6 | 103.2 | 116.6 | 106.9 | 106.3 | 110.0 | 107.3 |
| 0970, 0990 | Wall Finishes & Painting/Coating | 103.1 | 106.1 | 104.9 | 88.6 | 74.5 | 80.1 | 93.5 | 79.5 | 85.1 | 93.5 | 97.4 | 95.8 | 95.6 | 112.0 | 105.5 | 102.3 | 95.7 | 98.3 |
| 09 | FINISHES | 99.1 | 110.4 | 105.0 | 93.6 | 99.1 | 96.5 | 93.3 | 97.7 | 95.6 | 93.2 | 101.5 | 97.6 | 96.8 | 117.0 | 107.4 | 91.9 | 107.1 | 99.9 |
| COVERS | DIVS. 10 - 14, 25, 28, 41, 43, 44 | 100.0 | 101.5 | 100.3 | 100.0 | 90.5 | 98.1 | 100.0 | 57.1 | 91.2 | 100.0 | 90.1 | 98.0 | 100.0 | 104.2 | 100.9 | 100.0 | 90.5 | 98.1 |
| 21, 22, 23 | FIRE SUPPRESSION, PLUMBING & HVAC | 100.1 | 92.2 | 96.9 | 100.1 | 84.8 | 93.8 | 95.8 | 84.6 | 91.2 | 99.7 | 93.2 | 97.0 | 99.9 | 104.1 | 101.6 | 95.4 | 83.0 | 90.3 |
| 26, 27, 3370 | ELECTRICAL, COMMUNICATIONS & UTIL. | 97.1 | 95.6 | 96.4 | 101.6 | 90.2 | 96.0 | 96.4 | 90.2 | 93.3 | 96.9 | 91.5 | 94.3 | 98.1 | 103.5 | 100.8 | 99.6 | 90.2 | 95.0 |
| MF2004 | WEIGHTED AVERAGE | 99.7 | 102.2 | 100.8 | 96.4 | 94.1 | 95.4 | 97.0 | 93.3 | 95.4 | 99.1 | 98.2 | 98.7 | 100.0 | 107.5 | 103.2 | 96.1 | 96.8 | 96.4 |

## WISCONSIN

| | DIVISION | OSHKOSH 549 MAT. | INST. | TOTAL | PORTAGE 539 MAT. | INST. | TOTAL | RACINE 534 MAT. | INST. | TOTAL | RHINELANDER 545 MAT. | INST. | TOTAL | SUPERIOR 548 MAT. | INST. | TOTAL | WAUSAU 544 MAT. | INST. | TOTAL |
|---|---|---|---|---|---|---|---|---|---|---|---|---|---|---|---|---|---|---|---|
| 015433 | CONTRACTOR EQUIPMENT | | 98.7 | 98.7 | | 101.5 | 101.5 | | 101.5 | 101.5 | | 98.7 | 98.7 | | 102.0 | 102.0 | | 98.7 | 98.7 |
| 0241, 31 - 34 | SITE & INFRASTRUCTURE, DEMOLITION | 85.4 | 99.4 | 95.2 | 81.4 | 107.5 | 99.6 | 91.3 | 108.2 | 103.1 | 98.5 | 99.5 | 99.2 | 81.5 | 104.7 | 97.7 | 81.1 | 99.4 | 93.9 |
| 0310 | Concrete Forming & Accessories | 89.9 | 97.3 | 96.3 | 89.8 | 99.2 | 97.9 | 98.2 | 109.0 | 107.5 | 87.4 | 97.9 | 96.4 | 91.0 | 98.2 | 97.2 | 89.3 | 97.2 | 96.1 |
| 0320 | Concrete Reinforcing | 92.8 | 88.8 | 90.9 | 96.6 | 91.6 | 94.2 | 95.2 | 101.9 | 98.4 | 93.0 | 89.4 | 91.2 | 91.8 | 90.2 | 91.0 | 93.0 | 91.4 | 92.2 |
| 0330 | Cast-in-Place Concrete | 94.0 | 98.8 | 95.8 | 84.8 | 103.6 | 91.7 | 97.5 | 103.1 | 99.5 | 106.6 | 98.0 | 103.4 | 96.2 | 98.7 | 97.1 | 87.6 | 98.8 | 91.7 |
| 03 | CONCRETE | 89.4 | 96.5 | 92.7 | 84.7 | 99.3 | 91.5 | 95.7 | 105.5 | 100.2 | 101.2 | 96.5 | 99.0 | 89.0 | 97.1 | 92.7 | 84.6 | 96.9 | 90.3 |
| 04 | MASONRY | 101.1 | 97.7 | 99.1 | 100.9 | 104.7 | 103.2 | 101.9 | 111.7 | 107.7 | 118.6 | 98.3 | 106.4 | 113.1 | 107.8 | 110.0 | 100.6 | 97.7 | 98.9 |
| 05 | METALS | 96.0 | 97.5 | 96.5 | 98.2 | 97.1 | 97.9 | 101.6 | 103.7 | 102.2 | 95.9 | 97.1 | 96.3 | 96.7 | 99.4 | 97.5 | 95.8 | 98.6 | 96.6 |
| 06 | WOOD, PLASTICS & COMPOSITES | 96.7 | 99.1 | 98.0 | 100.5 | 99.9 | 99.7 | 110.6 | 108.6 | 109.5 | 93.8 | 99.1 | 96.6 | 100.0 | 98.0 | 98.9 | 96.0 | 99.1 | 97.6 |
| 07 | THERMAL & MOISTURE PROTECTION | 101.2 | 87.8 | 96.0 | 99.6 | 94.3 | 97.5 | 100.3 | 102.1 | 101.0 | 101.9 | 83.0 | 94.6 | 100.8 | 98.9 | 100.1 | 101.0 | 81.1 | 93.2 |
| 08 | OPENINGS | 93.8 | 95.7 | 94.2 | 98.6 | 95.3 | 97.8 | 103.2 | 108.3 | 104.4 | 93.8 | 88.5 | 92.5 | 88.0 | 94.7 | 89.6 | 94.0 | 96.4 | 94.6 |
| 0920 | Plaster & Gypsum Board | 85.3 | 99.3 | 94.0 | 91.4 | 99.3 | 96.3 | 96.5 | 109.2 | 104.3 | 84.6 | 99.3 | 93.7 | 86.9 | 98.5 | 94.1 | 85.0 | 99.3 | 93.8 |
| 0950, 0980 | Ceilings & Acoustic Treatment | 92.3 | 99.3 | 96.6 | 81.4 | 99.3 | 92.4 | 85.7 | 109.2 | 100.1 | 92.3 | 99.3 | 96.6 | 68.2 | 98.5 | 86.8 | 92.3 | 99.3 | 96.5 |
| 0960 | Flooring | 104.1 | 110.0 | 105.7 | 95.7 | 115.5 | 101.1 | 100.5 | 115.6 | 104.6 | 103.2 | 105.5 | 103.8 | 107.7 | 124.8 | 112.3 | 104.0 | 110.0 | 105.6 |
| 0970, 0990 | Wall Finishes & Painting/Coating | 97.7 | 77.6 | 85.7 | 93.5 | 79.5 | 85.1 | 93.4 | 106.1 | 101.0 | 97.7 | 72.3 | 82.4 | 93.1 | 105.9 | 100.8 | 97.7 | 77.6 | 85.7 |
| 09 | FINISHES | 96.6 | 97.1 | 96.8 | 91.1 | 100.1 | 95.8 | 94.9 | 110.4 | 103.0 | 97.2 | 97.2 | 97.2 | 91.6 | 104.5 | 98.4 | 96.2 | 98.5 | 97.4 |
| COVERS | DIVS. 10 - 14, 25, 28, 41, 43, 44 | 100.0 | 75.8 | 94.9 | 100.0 | 75.3 | 94.9 | 100.0 | 101.5 | 100.3 | 100.0 | 64.2 | 92.7 | 100.0 | 89.0 | 97.8 | 100.0 | 88.6 | 97.7 |
| 21, 22, 23 | FIRE SUPPRESSION, PLUMBING & HVAC | 96.3 | 87.4 | 92.6 | 95.8 | 93.0 | 94.6 | 99.9 | 97.7 | 99.0 | 96.3 | 89.2 | 93.3 | 95.4 | 97.8 | 96.4 | 96.3 | 82.2 | 90.5 |
| 26, 27, 3370 | ELECTRICAL, COMMUNICATIONS & UTIL. | 100.1 | 86.1 | 93.2 | 100.2 | 94.9 | 97.6 | 96.5 | 98.9 | 97.7 | 99.5 | 79.7 | 89.8 | 104.4 | 90.8 | 97.7 | 101.2 | 79.7 | 90.7 |
| MF2004 | WEIGHTED AVERAGE | 96.1 | 92.8 | 94.7 | 95.6 | 97.5 | 96.4 | 99.2 | 104.2 | 101.3 | 98.7 | 91.5 | 95.6 | 95.9 | 99.0 | 97.2 | 95.4 | 91.4 | 93.7 |

## WYOMING

| DIVISION | | CASPER 826 | | | CHEYENNE 820 | | | NEWCASTLE 827 | | | RAWLINS 823 | | | RIVERTON 825 | | | ROCK SPRINGS 829 - 831 | | |
|---|---|---|---|---|---|---|---|---|---|---|---|---|---|---|---|---|---|---|---|
| | | MAT. | INST. | TOTAL | MAT. | INST. | TOTAL | MAT. | INST. | TOTAL | MAT. | INST. | TOTAL | MAT. | INST. | TOTAL | MAT. | INST. | TOTAL |
| 015433 | CONTRACTOR EQUIPMENT | | 101.2 | 101.2 | | 101.2 | 101.2 | | 101.2 | 101.2 | | 101.2 | 101.2 | | 101.2 | 101.2 | | 101.2 | 101.2 |
| 0241, 31 - 34 | SITE & INFRASTRUCTURE, DEMOLITION | 92.0 | 99.8 | 97.4 | 86.4 | 99.8 | 95.7 | 79.2 | 98.5 | 92.7 | 93.5 | 98.5 | 97.0 | 86.8 | 98.5 | 95.0 | 82.6 | 98.5 | 93.7 |
| 0310 | Concrete Forming & Accessories | 101.9 | 46.3 | 54.0 | 103.6 | 63.4 | 68.9 | 93.6 | 41.4 | 48.7 | 98.0 | 41.4 | 49.3 | 92.4 | 41.4 | 48.4 | 99.6 | 41.4 | 49.4 |
| 0320 | Concrete Reinforcing | 110.1 | 47.6 | 80.0 | 103.9 | 48.5 | 77.2 | 111.7 | 48.3 | 81.2 | 111.3 | 48.3 | 81.0 | 112.3 | 48.3 | 81.5 | 112.3 | 48.3 | 81.5 |
| 0330 | Cast-in-Place Concrete | 100.8 | 77.2 | 92.1 | 97.6 | 77.4 | 90.1 | 98.6 | 56.2 | 82.9 | 98.7 | 56.2 | 83.0 | 98.7 | 56.2 | 83.0 | 98.6 | 56.2 | 82.9 |
| 03 | CONCRETE | 106.3 | 57.9 | 83.9 | 104.3 | 65.7 | 86.5 | 104.9 | 48.6 | 78.9 | 118.6 | 48.6 | 86.3 | 113.0 | 48.5 | 83.3 | 105.4 | 48.5 | 79.1 |
| 04 | MASONRY | 107.6 | 40.7 | 67.6 | 104.8 | 56.2 | 75.7 | 101.7 | 50.4 | 71.0 | 101.7 | 50.4 | 71.0 | 101.7 | 50.4 | 71.0 | 165.1 | 50.4 | 96.5 |
| 05 | METALS | 99.0 | 61.6 | 88.2 | 100.2 | 63.4 | 89.5 | 95.5 | 61.0 | 85.5 | 95.6 | 61.0 | 85.5 | 95.6 | 60.9 | 85.5 | 96.3 | 60.9 | 86.0 |
| 06 | WOOD, PLASTICS & COMPOSITES | 97.9 | 43.6 | 68.7 | 99.6 | 66.2 | 81.6 | 88.9 | 40.1 | 62.6 | 93.5 | 40.1 | 64.7 | 87.8 | 40.1 | 62.1 | 96.2 | 40.1 | 66.0 |
| 07 | THERMAL & MOISTURE PROTECTION | 95.3 | 53.3 | 78.9 | 97.5 | 59.7 | 82.8 | 98.5 | 51.1 | 80.0 | 100.3 | 51.1 | 81.1 | 99.6 | 51.2 | 80.7 | 98.5 | 51.1 | 80.1 |
| 08 | OPENINGS | 93.0 | 43.3 | 80.8 | 90.5 | 55.5 | 85.3 | 98.7 | 41.4 | 84.6 | 98.4 | 41.4 | 84.4 | 98.6 | 41.4 | 84.5 | 99.1 | 41.4 | 84.9 |
| 0920 | Plaster & Gypsum Board | 93.9 | 42.0 | 61.9 | 85.2 | 65.1 | 72.8 | 80.6 | 38.4 | 54.6 | 82.0 | 38.4 | 55.1 | 80.6 | 38.4 | 54.6 | 87.0 | 38.4 | 57.0 |
| 0950, 0980 | Ceilings & Acoustic Treatment | 110.0 | 42.0 | 68.2 | 103.7 | 65.1 | 80.0 | 106.5 | 38.4 | 64.7 | 106.5 | 38.4 | 64.7 | 106.5 | 38.4 | 64.7 | 106.5 | 38.4 | 64.7 |
| 0960 | Flooring | 104.9 | 38.1 | 86.7 | 109.5 | 61.2 | 96.4 | 102.8 | 53.9 | 89.5 | 105.9 | 53.9 | 91.8 | 102.0 | 53.9 | 88.9 | 108.6 | 53.9 | 93.7 |
| 0970, 0990 | Wall Finishes & Painting/Coating | 98.5 | 51.6 | 70.3 | 101.7 | 51.6 | 71.6 | 97.9 | 33.0 | 58.9 | 97.9 | 33.0 | 58.9 | 97.9 | 33.0 | 58.9 | 97.9 | 33.0 | 58.9 |
| 09 | FINISHES | 104.3 | 44.2 | 72.8 | 103.4 | 62.1 | 81.8 | 98.5 | 41.6 | 68.7 | 101.2 | 41.6 | 70.0 | 99.2 | 41.6 | 69.0 | 101.3 | 41.6 | 70.0 |
| COVERS | DIVS. 10 - 14, 25, 28, 41, 43, 44 | 100.0 | 81.0 | 96.1 | 100.0 | 83.7 | 96.7 | 100.0 | 66.2 | 93.1 | 100.0 | 66.2 | 93.1 | 100.0 | 66.1 | 93.1 | 100.0 | 66.1 | 93.1 |
| 21, 22, 23 | FIRE SUPPRESSION, PLUMBING & HVAC | 100.0 | 63.2 | 84.9 | 99.9 | 57.9 | 82.7 | 97.8 | 59.7 | 82.1 | 97.8 | 59.7 | 82.1 | 97.8 | 59.7 | 82.1 | 99.9 | 59.7 | 83.4 |
| 26, 27, 3370 | ELECTRICAL, COMMUNICATIONS & UTIL. | 94.5 | 61.0 | 78.1 | 95.7 | 74.8 | 85.5 | 93.2 | 75.5 | 84.5 | 93.2 | 75.5 | 84.5 | 93.2 | 62.1 | 78.0 | 91.5 | 62.1 | 77.1 |
| MF2004 | WEIGHTED AVERAGE | 99.7 | 59.6 | 82.5 | 99.7 | 66.5 | 85.5 | 97.7 | 59.5 | 81.4 | 100.0 | 59.5 | 82.7 | 99.0 | 57.6 | 81.3 | 101.9 | 57.6 | 82.9 |

## WYOMING / CANADA

| DIVISION | | SHERIDAN 828 | | | WHEATLAND 822 | | | WORLAND 824 | | | YELLOWSTONE NAT'L PA 821 | | | BARRIE, ONTARIO | | | BATHURST, NEW BRUNSWICK | | |
|---|---|---|---|---|---|---|---|---|---|---|---|---|---|---|---|---|---|---|---|
| | | MAT. | INST. | TOTAL | MAT. | INST. | TOTAL | MAT. | INST. | TOTAL | MAT. | INST. | TOTAL | MAT. | INST. | TOTAL | MAT. | INST. | TOTAL |
| 015433 | CONTRACTOR EQUIPMENT | | 101.2 | 101.2 | | 101.2 | 101.2 | | 101.2 | 101.2 | | 101.2 | 101.2 | | 100.4 | 100.4 | | 98.6 | 98.6 |
| 0241, 31 - 34 | SITE & INFRASTRUCTURE, DEMOLITION | 86.9 | 99.8 | 95.9 | 83.5 | 98.6 | 94.0 | 81.0 | 98.5 | 93.2 | 81.1 | 98.9 | 93.5 | 123.4 | 91.0 | 95.5 | 96.3 | 95.2 | 95.5 |
| 0310 | Concrete Forming & Accessories | 101.8 | 46.5 | 54.2 | 95.7 | 41.8 | 49.3 | 95.7 | 41.4 | 48.9 | 95.8 | 43.9 | 51.1 | 123.3 | 98.7 | 102.1 | 101.2 | 64.5 | 69.6 |
| 0320 | Concrete Reinforcing | 112.3 | 48.5 | 81.5 | 111.7 | 48.3 | 81.2 | 112.3 | 48.3 | 81.5 | 114.3 | 48.3 | 82.5 | 179.9 | 87.8 | 135.5 | 148.3 | 59.2 | 105.4 |
| 0330 | Cast-in-Place Concrete | 102.0 | 77.3 | 92.8 | 103.0 | 56.8 | 85.9 | 98.6 | 56.2 | 82.9 | 98.6 | 60.0 | 84.3 | 167.7 | 88.2 | 138.3 | 138.3 | 60.5 | 109.5 |
| 03 | CONCRETE | 113.2 | 58.2 | 87.8 | 109.9 | 49.0 | 81.8 | 105.1 | 48.5 | 79.0 | 105.5 | 51.0 | 80.3 | 153.3 | 89.5 | 123.8 | 135.6 | 62.7 | 101.9 |
| 04 | MASONRY | 102.0 | 55.5 | 74.2 | 102.0 | 51.4 | 71.7 | 101.7 | 50.4 | 71.0 | 101.7 | 57.1 | 75.1 | 169.3 | 99.5 | 127.6 | 159.8 | 66.0 | 103.7 |
| 05 | METALS | 99.0 | 63.1 | 88.6 | 95.5 | 61.0 | 85.4 | 95.6 | 60.9 | 85.5 | 96.2 | 60.9 | 86.0 | 107.7 | 90.4 | 102.6 | 105.2 | 69.9 | 95.0 |
| 06 | WOOD, PLASTICS & COMPOSITES | 101.0 | 43.6 | 70.1 | 90.8 | 40.1 | 63.5 | 90.9 | 40.1 | 63.5 | 90.9 | 40.1 | 63.5 | 118.7 | 89.4 | 102.9 | 93.7 | 64.6 | 78.0 |
| 07 | THERMAL & MOISTURE PROTECTION | 99.6 | 57.2 | 83.0 | 98.8 | 52.2 | 80.6 | 98.5 | 51.1 | 80.0 | 98.1 | 54.7 | 81.2 | 110.5 | 90.5 | 102.7 | 104.1 | 63.2 | 88.2 |
| 08 | OPENINGS | 99.3 | 44.4 | 85.8 | 97.4 | 41.4 | 83.6 | 98.9 | 41.4 | 84.7 | 92.6 | 41.4 | 80.0 | 90.7 | 87.9 | 90.1 | 86.0 | 56.6 | 78.8 |
| 0920 | Plaster & Gypsum Board | 101.8 | 42.0 | 64.9 | 80.6 | 38.4 | 54.6 | 80.6 | 38.4 | 54.6 | 81.0 | 38.4 | 54.7 | 153.5 | 89.2 | 113.8 | 168.9 | 63.8 | 104.0 |
| 0950, 0980 | Ceilings & Acoustic Treatment | 109.4 | 42.0 | 68.0 | 106.5 | 38.4 | 64.7 | 106.5 | 38.4 | 64.7 | 108.2 | 38.4 | 65.4 | 95.3 | 89.2 | 91.5 | 96.1 | 63.8 | 76.3 |
| 0960 | Flooring | 105.1 | 53.9 | 91.1 | 104.4 | 53.9 | 90.6 | 104.4 | 53.9 | 90.6 | 104.4 | 53.9 | 90.6 | 132.6 | 97.7 | 123.1 | 113.7 | 46.6 | 95.5 |
| 0970, 0990 | Wall Finishes & Painting/Coating | 99.8 | 51.6 | 70.8 | 97.9 | 33.0 | 58.9 | 97.9 | 33.0 | 58.9 | 97.9 | 33.0 | 58.9 | 110.2 | 90.4 | 98.3 | 109.4 | 51.9 | 74.9 |
| 09 | FINISHES | 105.8 | 47.1 | 75.1 | 99.3 | 41.8 | 69.2 | 99.0 | 41.6 | 68.9 | 99.5 | 43.3 | 70.0 | 119.8 | 92.3 | 105.4 | 115.3 | 59.8 | 86.2 |
| COVERS | DIVS. 10 - 14, 25, 28, 41, 43, 44 | 100.0 | 81.0 | 96.1 | 100.0 | 66.6 | 93.1 | 100.0 | 66.1 | 93.1 | 100.0 | 68.6 | 93.6 | 140.0 | 81.3 | 128.0 | 140.0 | 71.0 | 125.9 |
| 21, 22, 23 | FIRE SUPPRESSION, PLUMBING & HVAC | 97.8 | 62.4 | 83.2 | 97.8 | 60.3 | 82.4 | 97.8 | 59.7 | 82.1 | 97.8 | 63.3 | 83.6 | 104.2 | 105.5 | 104.7 | 104.0 | 74.1 | 91.7 |
| 26, 27, 3370 | ELECTRICAL, COMMUNICATIONS & UTIL. | 95.8 | 62.1 | 79.3 | 93.2 | 74.8 | 84.2 | 93.2 | 62.1 | 78.0 | 92.2 | 62.1 | 77.4 | 123.0 | 95.4 | 109.4 | 126.4 | 65.2 | 96.3 |
| MF2004 | WEIGHTED AVERAGE | 100.6 | 61.8 | 84.0 | 98.4 | 59.8 | 81.9 | 97.9 | 57.6 | 80.7 | 97.3 | 59.8 | 81.3 | 119.6 | 95.7 | 109.4 | 115.2 | 68.8 | 95.4 |

## CANADA

| DIVISION | | BRANDON, MANITOBA | | | BRANTFORD, ONTARIO | | | BRIDGEWATER, NOVA SCOTIA | | | CALGARY, ALBERTA | | | CAP-DE-LA-MADELEINE, QUEBEC | | | CHARLESBOURG, QUEBEC | | |
|---|---|---|---|---|---|---|---|---|---|---|---|---|---|---|---|---|---|---|---|
| | | MAT. | INST. | TOTAL | MAT. | INST. | TOTAL | MAT. | INST. | TOTAL | MAT. | INST. | TOTAL | MAT. | INST. | TOTAL | MAT. | INST. | TOTAL |
| 015433 | CONTRACTOR EQUIPMENT | | 102.8 | 102.8 | | 100.4 | 100.4 | | 98.6 | 98.6 | | 106.9 | 106.9 | | 99.2 | 99.2 | | 99.2 | 99.2 |
| 0241, 31 - 34 | SITE & INFRASTRUCTURE, DEMOLITION | 112.2 | 99.2 | 103.1 | 114.6 | 100.6 | 104.9 | 99.2 | 96.9 | 97.6 | 117.5 | 106.0 | 109.5 | 94.3 | 98.3 | 97.1 | 94.3 | 98.3 | 97.1 |
| 0310 | Concrete Forming & Accessories | 122.6 | 73.6 | 80.4 | 123.3 | 98.7 | 102.1 | 94.9 | 72.7 | 75.8 | 127.5 | 93.9 | 98.5 | 129.5 | 89.4 | 95.0 | 129.5 | 89.4 | 95.0 |
| 0320 | Concrete Reinforcing | 161.5 | 55.7 | 110.5 | 174.7 | 86.5 | 132.2 | 148.3 | 48.9 | 100.4 | 161.5 | 65.5 | 115.2 | 148.3 | 82.6 | 116.7 | 148.3 | 82.6 | 116.7 |
| 0330 | Cast-in-Place Concrete | 151.2 | 76.0 | 123.4 | 163.7 | 110.1 | 143.8 | 168.2 | 71.1 | 132.3 | 189.2 | 103.7 | 157.6 | 132.0 | 97.0 | 119.0 | 132.0 | 97.0 | 119.0 |
| 03 | CONCRETE | 135.5 | 71.6 | 106.0 | 150.4 | 100.2 | 127.2 | 148.1 | 68.2 | 111.2 | 161.3 | 92.1 | 129.4 | 130.9 | 90.8 | 112.4 | 130.9 | 90.8 | 112.4 |
| 04 | MASONRY | 164.1 | 68.7 | 107.1 | 166.0 | 104.2 | 129.1 | 160.9 | 73.1 | 108.3 | 179.6 | 94.8 | 128.9 | 160.9 | 88.5 | 117.6 | 160.9 | 88.5 | 117.6 |
| 05 | METALS | 107.8 | 76.4 | 98.7 | 107.0 | 91.7 | 102.6 | 106.2 | 72.9 | 96.5 | 134.6 | 87.7 | 120.9 | 105.5 | 87.1 | 100.1 | 105.5 | 87.1 | 100.1 |
| 06 | WOOD, PLASTICS & COMPOSITES | 114.5 | 74.4 | 92.9 | 116.8 | 97.1 | 106.2 | 85.4 | 71.9 | 78.1 | 114.6 | 93.3 | 103.1 | 128.9 | 89.1 | 107.5 | 128.9 | 89.1 | 107.5 |
| 07 | THERMAL & MOISTURE PROTECTION | 104.4 | 72.9 | 92.1 | 110.3 | 96.0 | 104.7 | 105.3 | 71.0 | 91.9 | 127.0 | 90.8 | 112.9 | 104.5 | 91.1 | 99.3 | 104.5 | 91.1 | 99.3 |
| 08 | OPENINGS | 91.8 | 65.8 | 85.4 | 90.6 | 94.2 | 91.5 | 82.7 | 65.7 | 78.5 | 91.8 | 83.1 | 89.6 | 91.8 | 82.3 | 89.5 | 91.8 | 82.3 | 89.5 |
| 0920 | Plaster & Gypsum Board | 124.1 | 73.4 | 92.8 | 153.5 | 97.1 | 118.7 | 163.6 | 71.2 | 106.6 | 141.0 | 92.7 | 111.2 | 188.3 | 88.8 | 126.9 | 188.3 | 88.8 | 126.9 |
| 0950, 0980 | Ceilings & Acoustic Treatment | 95.3 | 73.4 | 81.8 | 95.3 | 97.1 | 96.4 | 95.3 | 71.2 | 80.5 | 108.9 | 92.7 | 98.9 | 95.3 | 88.8 | 91.3 | 95.3 | 88.8 | 91.3 |
| 0960 | Flooring | 132.5 | 69.4 | 115.3 | 132.5 | 97.7 | 123.0 | 109.7 | 66.5 | 97.9 | 134.8 | 91.5 | 123.0 | 132.5 | 98.3 | 123.2 | 132.5 | 98.3 | 123.2 |
| 0970, 0990 | Wall Finishes & Painting/Coating | 109.5 | 59.1 | 79.2 | 109.4 | 99.3 | 103.3 | 109.4 | 64.5 | 82.4 | 109.4 | 104.9 | 106.7 | 109.4 | 92.3 | 99.1 | 109.4 | 92.3 | 99.1 |
| 09 | FINISHES | 114.3 | 71.5 | 91.9 | 118.7 | 98.8 | 108.2 | 112.8 | 70.6 | 90.7 | 121.1 | 95.2 | 107.5 | 123.4 | 91.5 | 106.7 | 123.4 | 91.5 | 106.7 |
| COVERS | DIVS. 10 - 14, 25, 28, 41, 43, 44 | 140.0 | 73.7 | 126.4 | 140.0 | 83.6 | 128.4 | 140.0 | 72.4 | 126.1 | 140.0 | 105.0 | 132.8 | 140.0 | 93.2 | 130.4 | 140.0 | 93.2 | 130.4 |
| 21, 22, 23 | FIRE SUPPRESSION, PLUMBING & HVAC | 104.0 | 89.4 | 98.0 | 104.0 | 108.7 | 105.9 | 104.0 | 89.7 | 98.2 | 101.7 | 91.4 | 97.5 | 104.7 | 96.7 | 101.4 | 104.7 | 96.7 | 101.4 |
| 26, 27, 3370 | ELECTRICAL, COMMUNICATIONS & UTIL. | 125.6 | 73.4 | 100.0 | 123.0 | 94.9 | 109.2 | 129.0 | 67.9 | 99.0 | 122.5 | 87.2 | 105.1 | 122.1 | 76.6 | 99.7 | 122.1 | 76.6 | 99.7 |
| MF2004 | WEIGHTED AVERAGE | 116.8 | 77.9 | 100.2 | 118.8 | 99.8 | 110.7 | 116.7 | 76.4 | 99.5 | 125.6 | 92.7 | 111.5 | 115.9 | 89.9 | 104.8 | 115.9 | 89.9 | 104.8 |

# City Cost Indexes

## CANADA

| DIVISION | | CHARLOTTETOWN, PRINCE EDWARD ISLAND | | | CHICOUTIMI, QUEBEC | | | CORNER BROOK, NEWFOUNDLAND | | | CORNWALL, ONTARIO | | | DALHOUSIE, NEW BRUNSWICK | | | DARTMOUTH, NOVA SCOTIA | | |
|---|---|---|---|---|---|---|---|---|---|---|---|---|---|---|---|---|---|---|---|
| | | MAT. | INST. | TOTAL | MAT. | INST. | TOTAL | MAT. | INST. | TOTAL | MAT. | INST. | TOTAL | MAT. | INST. | TOTAL | MAT. | INST. | TOTAL |
| 015433 | CONTRACTOR EQUIPMENT | | 98.6 | 98.6 | | 99.2 | 99.2 | | 98.6 | 98.6 | | 100.4 | 100.4 | | 98.6 | 98.6 | | 98.6 | 98.6 |
| 0241, 31 - 34 | SITE & INFRASTRUCTURE, DEMOLITION | 107.3 | 94.5 | 98.4 | 93.6 | 97.9 | 96.6 | 115.6 | 94.9 | 101.2 | 112.4 | 100.1 | 103.9 | 96.3 | 95.2 | 95.5 | 107.3 | 96.9 | 100.1 |
| 0310 | Concrete Forming & Accessories | 95.1 | 58.9 | 63.9 | 129.5 | 97.1 | 101.6 | 102.9 | 62.4 | 68.0 | 120.9 | 91.1 | 95.2 | 101.2 | 64.5 | 69.6 | 94.9 | 72.7 | 75.8 |
| 0320 | Concrete Reinforcing | 158.5 | 49.0 | 105.7 | 111.9 | 97.4 | 104.9 | 148.3 | 50.8 | 101.4 | 174.7 | 86.2 | 132.1 | 148.3 | 59.2 | 105.4 | 154.9 | 48.9 | 103.8 |
| 0330 | Cast-in-Place Concrete | 159.4 | 59.8 | 122.6 | 130.2 | 102.4 | 119.9 | 172.4 | 69.1 | 134.2 | 147.2 | 100.2 | 129.8 | 138.3 | 60.5 | 109.5 | 170.0 | 71.1 | 133.4 |
| 03 | CONCRETE | 153.7 | 58.0 | 109.5 | 124.3 | 98.8 | 112.5 | 162.2 | 63.2 | 116.5 | 142.1 | 93.3 | 119.6 | 135.6 | 62.7 | 101.9 | 150.0 | 68.2 | 112.3 |
| 04 | MASONRY | 161.2 | 63.7 | 102.9 | 161.2 | 97.1 | 122.8 | 161.2 | 65.2 | 103.8 | 164.7 | 95.6 | 123.4 | 157.8 | 66.0 | 102.9 | 172.3 | 73.1 | 112.9 |
| 05 | METALS | 106.2 | 65.8 | 94.5 | 105.0 | 93.0 | 101.5 | 108.2 | 70.8 | 97.3 | 107.0 | 90.1 | 102.1 | 105.2 | 69.9 | 95.0 | 108.3 | 72.9 | 98.0 |
| 06 | WOOD, PLASTICS & COMPOSITES | 85.7 | 58.3 | 71.0 | 128.9 | 96.7 | 112.0 | 94.8 | 61.3 | 76.8 | 111.4 | 90.3 | 101.9 | 93.7 | 64.6 | 78.0 | 85.4 | 71.9 | 78.1 |
| 07 | THERMAL & MOISTURE PROTECTION | 105.1 | 60.7 | 87.8 | 104.5 | 99.5 | 102.6 | 107.3 | 62.7 | 89.9 | 110.1 | 89.4 | 102.0 | 107.4 | 63.2 | 90.1 | 105.3 | 71.0 | 91.9 |
| 08 | OPENINGS | 94.0 | 50.6 | 83.3 | 91.4 | 83.5 | 89.4 | 97.9 | 57.8 | 88.0 | 91.8 | 87.6 | 90.8 | 86.0 | 56.6 | 78.8 | 82.7 | 65.7 | 78.5 |
| 0920 | Plaster & Gypsum Board | 167.3 | 57.3 | 99.4 | 188.3 | 97.5 | 132.2 | 169.1 | 60.3 | 102.0 | 230.4 | 90.1 | 143.8 | 168.9 | 63.8 | 104.0 | 166.2 | 71.2 | 107.6 |
| 0950, 0980 | Ceilings & Acoustic Treatment | 109.8 | 57.3 | 77.6 | 95.3 | 97.5 | 96.6 | 97.0 | 60.3 | 74.5 | 98.7 | 90.1 | 93.4 | 96.1 | 63.8 | 76.3 | 106.4 | 71.2 | 84.8 |
| 0960 | Flooring | 109.8 | 62.1 | 96.8 | 132.5 | 98.3 | 123.2 | 114.6 | 56.6 | 98.8 | 132.5 | 96.3 | 122.6 | 113.7 | 46.6 | 95.5 | 109.7 | 66.5 | 97.9 |
| 0970, 0990 | Wall Finishes & Painting/Coating | 109.4 | 43.2 | 69.7 | 109.4 | 108.5 | 108.9 | 109.4 | 62.2 | 81.0 | 109.4 | 92.5 | 99.3 | 109.4 | 51.9 | 74.9 | 109.4 | 64.5 | 82.4 |
| 09 | FINISHES | 117.7 | 58.1 | 86.5 | 123.4 | 99.3 | 110.8 | 116.7 | 61.1 | 87.6 | 131.5 | 92.4 | 111.0 | 115.3 | 59.8 | 86.2 | 115.8 | 70.6 | 92.2 |
| COVERS | DIVS. 10 - 14, 25, 28, 41, 43, 44 | 140.0 | 70.5 | 125.8 | 140.0 | 95.2 | 130.8 | 140.0 | 71.2 | 125.9 | 140.0 | 80.8 | 127.9 | 140.0 | 71.0 | 125.9 | 140.0 | 72.4 | 126.1 |
| 21, 22, 23 | FIRE SUPPRESSION, PLUMBING & HVAC | 104.0 | 67.7 | 89.1 | 104.0 | 98.4 | 101.7 | 104.0 | 76.3 | 92.6 | 104.7 | 106.4 | 105.4 | 104.0 | 74.1 | 91.7 | 104.0 | 89.7 | 98.2 |
| 26, 27, 3370 | ELECTRICAL, COMMUNICATIONS & UTIL. | 123.0 | 55.2 | 89.7 | 122.1 | 88.6 | 105.6 | 122.1 | 61.4 | 92.3 | 123.9 | 95.9 | 110.1 | 125.6 | 65.2 | 95.9 | 126.8 | 67.9 | 97.9 |
| MF2004 | WEIGHTED AVERAGE | 118.4 | 64.1 | 95.2 | 114.9 | 95.8 | 106.7 | 120.3 | 69.0 | 98.4 | 119.1 | 96.1 | 109.3 | 115.1 | 68.8 | 95.3 | 118.1 | 76.4 | 100.3 |

## CANADA

| DIVISION | | EDMONTON, ALBERTA | | | FORT MCMURRAY, ALBERTA | | | FREDERICTON, NEW BRUNSWICK | | | GATINEAU, QUEBEC | | | GRANBY, QUEBEC | | | HALIFAX, NOVA SCOTIA | | |
|---|---|---|---|---|---|---|---|---|---|---|---|---|---|---|---|---|---|---|---|
| | | MAT. | INST. | TOTAL | MAT. | INST. | TOTAL | MAT. | INST. | TOTAL | MAT. | INST. | TOTAL | MAT. | INST. | TOTAL | MAT. | INST. | TOTAL |
| 015433 | CONTRACTOR EQUIPMENT | | 106.9 | 106.9 | | 103.7 | 103.7 | | 98.6 | 98.6 | | 99.2 | 99.2 | | 99.2 | 99.2 | | 98.6 | 98.6 |
| 0241, 31 - 34 | SITE & INFRASTRUCTURE, DEMOLITION | 125.6 | 106.0 | 111.9 | 120.5 | 102.4 | 107.9 | 95.7 | 95.2 | 95.3 | 94.0 | 98.3 | 97.0 | 94.6 | 98.3 | 97.2 | 99.5 | 96.8 | 97.6 |
| 0310 | Concrete Forming & Accessories | 125.5 | 93.8 | 98.2 | 120.9 | 94.0 | 97.7 | 121.0 | 64.8 | 72.6 | 129.5 | 89.3 | 94.9 | 129.5 | 89.2 | 94.8 | 95.1 | 79.1 | 81.4 |
| 0320 | Concrete Reinforcing | 161.5 | 65.5 | 115.2 | 161.5 | 65.5 | 115.2 | 149.3 | 59.4 | 106.0 | 157.0 | 82.6 | 121.2 | 157.0 | 82.6 | 121.2 | 154.9 | 63.4 | 110.8 |
| 0330 | Cast-in-Place Concrete | 198.3 | 103.7 | 163.3 | 217.5 | 102.8 | 175.1 | 131.6 | 60.6 | 105.3 | 130.2 | 97.0 | 117.9 | 134.5 | 96.9 | 120.6 | 171.3 | 75.5 | 135.9 |
| 03 | CONCRETE | 165.7 | 92.1 | 131.7 | 175.0 | 91.9 | 136.6 | 133.8 | 62.8 | 101.0 | 131.4 | 90.7 | 112.6 | 133.5 | 90.7 | 113.7 | 150.7 | 75.3 | 115.9 |
| 04 | MASONRY | 175.8 | 94.8 | 127.3 | 205.6 | 94.7 | 139.3 | 157.3 | 67.6 | 103.6 | 160.7 | 88.5 | 117.5 | 161.1 | 88.5 | 117.7 | 173.9 | 85.9 | 121.3 |
| 05 | METALS | 135.4 | 87.7 | 121.5 | 133.1 | 87.7 | 119.9 | 105.1 | 70.5 | 95.1 | 105.5 | 87.0 | 100.1 | 105.5 | 86.9 | 100.1 | 120.2 | 78.2 | 108.0 |
| 06 | WOOD, PLASTICS & COMPOSITES | 111.2 | 93.3 | 101.6 | 111.2 | 93.2 | 101.5 | 117.6 | 64.6 | 89.1 | 128.9 | 89.1 | 107.5 | 128.9 | 89.1 | 107.5 | 85.4 | 78.3 | 81.6 |
| 07 | THERMAL & MOISTURE PROTECTION | 125.8 | 90.8 | 112.2 | 119.3 | 90.0 | 107.9 | 107.6 | 64.2 | 90.7 | 104.5 | 91.1 | 99.3 | 104.5 | 89.5 | 98.6 | 105.5 | 78.5 | 95.0 |
| 08 | OPENINGS | 91.8 | 83.1 | 89.6 | 91.8 | 83.0 | 89.6 | 85.9 | 55.5 | 78.4 | 91.8 | 77.5 | 88.3 | 91.8 | 77.5 | 88.3 | 82.7 | 71.5 | 80.0 |
| 0920 | Plaster & Gypsum Board | 146.9 | 92.7 | 113.4 | 154.2 | 92.7 | 116.2 | 183.5 | 63.8 | 109.6 | 137.1 | 88.8 | 107.3 | 139.4 | 88.8 | 108.2 | 166.2 | 77.8 | 111.7 |
| 0950, 0980 | Ceilings & Acoustic Treatment | 122.6 | 92.7 | 104.2 | 106.4 | 92.7 | 98.0 | 103.8 | 63.8 | 79.2 | 95.3 | 88.8 | 91.3 | 95.3 | 88.8 | 91.3 | 106.4 | 77.8 | 88.8 |
| 0960 | Flooring | 134.8 | 91.5 | 123.0 | 132.5 | 91.5 | 121.4 | 127.6 | 46.6 | 105.6 | 132.5 | 98.3 | 123.2 | 132.5 | 98.3 | 123.2 | 109.7 | 66.5 | 97.9 |
| 0970, 0990 | Wall Finishes & Painting/Coating | 109.5 | 96.1 | 101.4 | 109.5 | 96.1 | 101.4 | 109.4 | 66.2 | 83.5 | 109.4 | 92.3 | 99.1 | 109.4 | 92.3 | 99.1 | 109.4 | 77.5 | 90.2 |
| 09 | FINISHES | 126.0 | 94.2 | 109.4 | 122.8 | 94.1 | 107.8 | 123.5 | 61.4 | 91.0 | 115.3 | 91.5 | 102.9 | 115.7 | 91.5 | 103.0 | 115.8 | 76.8 | 95.4 |
| COVERS | DIVS. 10 - 14, 25, 28, 41, 43, 44 | 140.0 | 105.0 | 132.8 | 140.0 | 104.7 | 132.8 | 140.0 | 71.0 | 125.9 | 140.0 | 93.2 | 130.4 | 140.0 | 93.2 | 130.4 | 140.0 | 74.5 | 126.6 |
| 21, 22, 23 | FIRE SUPPRESSION, PLUMBING & HVAC | 101.8 | 91.4 | 97.5 | 104.7 | 105.0 | 104.8 | 104.0 | 84.3 | 95.9 | 104.7 | 96.7 | 101.4 | 104.0 | 96.7 | 101.0 | 101.1 | 79.3 | 92.1 |
| 26, 27, 3370 | ELECTRICAL, COMMUNICATIONS & UTIL. | 122.4 | 87.2 | 105.1 | 115.8 | 90.1 | 103.2 | 134.6 | 81.3 | 108.4 | 122.1 | 76.6 | 99.7 | 123.0 | 76.6 | 100.2 | 128.7 | 76.7 | 103.2 |
| MF2004 | WEIGHTED AVERAGE | 126.7 | 92.6 | 112.1 | 128.2 | 95.4 | 114.2 | 116.7 | 73.6 | 98.3 | 115.3 | 89.7 | 104.3 | 115.5 | 89.6 | 104.4 | 119.5 | 79.6 | 102.5 |

## CANADA

| DIVISION | | HAMILTON, ONTARIO | | | HULL, QUEBEC | | | JOLIETTE, QUEBEC | | | KAMLOOPS, BRITISH COLUMBIA | | | KINGSTON, ONTARIO | | | KITCHENER, ONTARIO | | |
|---|---|---|---|---|---|---|---|---|---|---|---|---|---|---|---|---|---|---|---|
| | | MAT. | INST. | TOTAL | MAT. | INST. | TOTAL | MAT. | INST. | TOTAL | MAT. | INST. | TOTAL | MAT. | INST. | TOTAL | MAT. | INST. | TOTAL |
| 015433 | CONTRACTOR EQUIPMENT | | 103.1 | 103.1 | | 99.2 | 99.2 | | 99.2 | 99.2 | | 103.4 | 103.4 | | 103.1 | 103.1 | | 102.9 | 102.9 |
| 0241, 31 - 34 | SITE & INFRASTRUCTURE, DEMOLITION | 115.2 | 105.7 | 108.6 | 94.0 | 98.3 | 97.0 | 94.7 | 98.3 | 97.2 | 117.8 | 102.4 | 107.1 | 112.4 | 104.4 | 106.8 | 101.6 | 105.3 | 104.2 |
| 0310 | Concrete Forming & Accessories | 122.4 | 99.3 | 102.5 | 129.5 | 89.3 | 94.9 | 129.5 | 89.4 | 95.0 | 120.0 | 92.4 | 96.2 | 121.0 | 91.2 | 95.3 | 117.2 | 91.3 | 94.9 |
| 0320 | Concrete Reinforcing | 175.4 | 93.6 | 136.0 | 157.0 | 82.6 | 121.2 | 148.3 | 82.6 | 116.7 | 116.5 | 80.4 | 99.1 | 174.7 | 86.2 | 132.1 | 110.4 | 93.5 | 102.3 |
| 0330 | Cast-in-Place Concrete | 154.0 | 103.9 | 135.5 | 130.2 | 97.0 | 117.9 | 135.6 | 97.0 | 121.3 | 117.3 | 101.2 | 111.3 | 147.2 | 100.2 | 129.8 | 140.8 | 83.5 | 119.6 |
| 03 | CONCRETE | 145.7 | 99.7 | 124.4 | 131.4 | 90.7 | 112.6 | 132.7 | 90.8 | 113.3 | 137.8 | 93.1 | 117.2 | 142.1 | 93.3 | 119.6 | 122.4 | 89.1 | 107.0 |
| 04 | MASONRY | 167.3 | 105.3 | 130.2 | 160.7 | 88.5 | 117.5 | 161.2 | 88.5 | 117.7 | 167.6 | 96.5 | 125.1 | 171.1 | 95.6 | 126.0 | 162.6 | 101.4 | 126.0 |
| 05 | METALS | 138.2 | 94.3 | 125.4 | 105.5 | 87.0 | 100.1 | 105.5 | 87.1 | 100.1 | 107.6 | 87.3 | 101.7 | 108.6 | 90.1 | 103.2 | 116.0 | 93.8 | 109.5 |
| 06 | WOOD, PLASTICS & COMPOSITES | 115.9 | 98.6 | 106.6 | 128.9 | 89.1 | 107.5 | 128.9 | 89.1 | 107.5 | 98.1 | 90.6 | 94.0 | 115.4 | 90.4 | 102.0 | 109.6 | 89.7 | 98.9 |
| 07 | THERMAL & MOISTURE PROTECTION | 110.8 | 99.8 | 106.5 | 104.5 | 91.1 | 99.3 | 104.5 | 91.1 | 99.3 | 120.3 | 88.1 | 107.7 | 110.9 | 90.5 | 102.4 | 109.4 | 96.4 | 104.3 |
| 08 | OPENINGS | 91.8 | 95.2 | 92.6 | 91.8 | 77.5 | 88.3 | 91.8 | 82.3 | 89.5 | 87.7 | 87.0 | 87.6 | 91.8 | 87.3 | 90.7 | 83.2 | 88.7 | 84.5 |
| 0920 | Plaster & Gypsum Board | 185.2 | 98.6 | 131.8 | 137.1 | 88.8 | 107.3 | 188.3 | 88.8 | 126.9 | 138.7 | 90.0 | 108.7 | 233.7 | 90.2 | 145.2 | 152.4 | 89.4 | 113.5 |
| 0950, 0980 | Ceilings & Acoustic Treatment | 112.4 | 98.6 | 103.9 | 95.3 | 88.8 | 91.3 | 95.3 | 88.8 | 91.3 | 95.3 | 90.0 | 92.0 | 113.2 | 90.2 | 99.1 | 106.4 | 89.4 | 96.0 |
| 0960 | Flooring | 132.5 | 97.7 | 123.0 | 132.5 | 98.3 | 123.2 | 132.5 | 98.3 | 123.2 | 129.9 | 54.9 | 109.5 | 132.5 | 96.3 | 122.6 | 128.1 | 97.7 | 119.8 |
| 0970, 0990 | Wall Finishes & Painting/Coating | 109.4 | 104.7 | 106.6 | 109.4 | 92.3 | 99.1 | 109.4 | 92.3 | 99.1 | 109.4 | 84.5 | 94.4 | 109.4 | 85.5 | 95.0 | 109.4 | 93.5 | 99.9 |
| 09 | FINISHES | 127.8 | 99.6 | 113.1 | 115.3 | 91.5 | 102.9 | 123.4 | 91.5 | 106.7 | 117.6 | 84.7 | 100.3 | 135.4 | 91.6 | 112.5 | 119.0 | 92.4 | 105.1 |
| COVERS | DIVS. 10 - 14, 25, 28, 41, 43, 44 | 140.0 | 109.4 | 133.7 | 140.0 | 93.2 | 130.4 | 140.0 | 93.2 | 130.4 | 140.0 | 104.9 | 132.8 | 140.0 | 80.8 | 127.9 | 140.0 | 107.2 | 133.3 |
| 21, 22, 23 | FIRE SUPPRESSION, PLUMBING & HVAC | 101.6 | 95.9 | 99.2 | 104.0 | 96.7 | 101.0 | 104.0 | 96.1 | 100.8 | 104.0 | 100.3 | 102.5 | 104.7 | 106.6 | 105.4 | 101.1 | 92.8 | 97.6 |
| 26, 27, 3370 | ELECTRICAL, COMMUNICATIONS & UTIL. | 129.9 | 98.9 | 114.6 | 124.7 | 76.6 | 101.1 | 123.0 | 76.6 | 100.2 | 127.3 | 86.4 | 107.2 | 123.9 | 94.5 | 109.4 | 124.1 | 96.1 | 110.3 |
| MF2004 | WEIGHTED AVERAGE | 124.5 | 99.4 | 113.8 | 115.4 | 89.7 | 104.4 | 116.1 | 89.9 | 104.9 | 117.9 | 93.1 | 107.3 | 120.0 | 96.2 | 109.8 | 115.1 | 95.0 | 106.5 |

| | CANADA | | | | | | | | | | | | | | | | |
|---|---|---|---|---|---|---|---|---|---|---|---|---|---|---|---|---|---|
| DIVISION | LAVAL, QUEBEC | | | LETHBRIDGE, ALBERTA | | | LLOYDMINSTER, ALBERTA | | | LONDON, ONTARIO | | | MEDICINE HAT, ALBERTA | | | MONCTON, NEW BRUNSWICK | | |
| | MAT. | INST. | TOTAL | MAT. | INST. | TOTAL | MAT. | INST. | TOTAL | MAT. | INST. | TOTAL | MAT. | INST. | TOTAL | MAT. | INST. | TOTAL |
| 015433 CONTRACTOR EQUIPMENT | | 99.2 | 99.2 | | 103.7 | 103.7 | | 103.7 | 103.7 | | 103.2 | 103.2 | | 103.7 | 103.7 | | 98.6 | 98.6 |
| 0241, 31 - 34 SITE & INFRASTRUCTURE, DEMOLITION | 94.6 | 98.3 | 97.2 | 112.1 | 102.4 | 105.4 | 111.9 | 101.9 | 104.9 | 116.1 | 105.5 | 108.7 | 110.5 | 101.9 | 104.5 | 95.6 | 95.4 | 95.4 |
| 0310 Concrete Forming & Accessories | 129.7 | 89.3 | 94.9 | 122.4 | 94.0 | 97.9 | 120.4 | 83.9 | 89.0 | 128.1 | 92.5 | 97.5 | 122.4 | 83.9 | 89.2 | 101.2 | 64.9 | 69.9 |
| 0320 Concrete Reinforcing | 157.0 | 82.6 | 121.2 | 161.5 | 65.5 | 115.2 | 161.5 | 65.5 | 115.2 | 135.3 | 92.2 | 114.5 | 161.5 | 65.5 | 115.2 | 148.3 | 62.4 | 106.9 |
| 0330 Cast-in-Place Concrete | 134.5 | 97.0 | 120.6 | 163.0 | 102.8 | 140.7 | 151.2 | 99.0 | 131.9 | 150.8 | 101.8 | 132.7 | 151.2 | 99.0 | 131.9 | 133.1 | 60.9 | 106.4 |
| 03 CONCRETE | 133.5 | 90.7 | 113.8 | 148.0 | 91.8 | 122.1 | 142.0 | 86.1 | 116.2 | 138.1 | 95.6 | 118.5 | 142.1 | 86.1 | 116.2 | 133.1 | 63.6 | 101.0 |
| 04 MASONRY | 161.1 | 88.5 | 117.7 | 178.4 | 94.7 | 128.4 | 161.2 | 88.2 | 117.5 | 166.8 | 102.8 | 128.5 | 161.2 | 88.2 | 117.5 | 159.4 | 66.1 | 103.6 |
| 05 METALS | 105.5 | 87.0 | 100.1 | 127.1 | 87.7 | 115.7 | 107.8 | 87.5 | 101.9 | 123.8 | 91.9 | 114.5 | 107.8 | 87.5 | 101.9 | 105.2 | 73.5 | 96.0 |
| 06 WOOD, PLASTICS & COMPOSITES | 128.9 | 89.1 | 107.5 | 114.6 | 93.2 | 103.1 | 111.2 | 83.2 | 96.1 | 115.9 | 90.6 | 102.3 | 114.6 | 83.2 | 97.7 | 93.7 | 64.6 | 78.0 |
| 07 THERMAL & MOISTURE PROTECTION | 104.8 | 91.1 | 99.4 | 116.4 | 90.0 | 106.1 | 113.4 | 85.6 | 102.6 | 113.2 | 96.4 | 106.7 | 118.3 | 85.6 | 105.6 | 107.4 | 65.1 | 90.9 |
| 08 OPENINGS | 91.8 | 77.5 | 88.3 | 91.8 | 83.0 | 89.6 | 91.8 | 77.6 | 88.3 | 92.9 | 88.9 | 91.9 | 91.8 | 77.6 | 88.3 | 86.0 | 58.3 | 79.2 |
| 0920 Plaster & Gypsum Board | 141.6 | 88.8 | 109.0 | 133.5 | 92.7 | 108.3 | 129.4 | 82.4 | 100.4 | 185.4 | 90.4 | 126.8 | 131.1 | 82.4 | 101.0 | 168.9 | 63.8 | 104.0 |
| 0950, 0980 Ceilings & Acoustic Treatment | 95.3 | 88.8 | 91.3 | 105.5 | 92.7 | 97.6 | 95.3 | 82.4 | 87.4 | 113.2 | 90.4 | 99.2 | 95.3 | 82.4 | 87.4 | 96.1 | 63.8 | 76.3 |
| 0960 Flooring | 132.5 | 98.3 | 123.2 | 132.5 | 91.5 | 121.4 | 132.5 | 91.5 | 121.4 | 134.8 | 97.7 | 124.7 | 132.5 | 91.5 | 121.4 | 113.7 | 57.4 | 98.4 |
| 0970, 0990 Wall Finishes & Painting/Coating | 109.4 | 92.3 | 99.1 | 109.4 | 104.9 | 106.7 | 109.5 | 81.7 | 92.8 | 109.4 | 101.0 | 104.4 | 109.4 | 81.7 | 92.8 | 109.4 | 51.9 | 74.9 |
| 09 FINISHES | 116.0 | 91.5 | 103.2 | 118.4 | 95.1 | 106.2 | 115.4 | 85.0 | 99.5 | 128.9 | 94.1 | 110.7 | 115.5 | 85.0 | 99.6 | 115.3 | 62.0 | 87.4 |
| COVERS DIVS. 10 - 14, 25, 28, 41, 43, 44 | 140.0 | 93.2 | 130.4 | 140.0 | 104.7 | 132.8 | 140.0 | 101.1 | 132.0 | 140.0 | 107.9 | 133.4 | 140.0 | 101.1 | 132.0 | 140.0 | 71.0 | 125.9 |
| 21, 22, 23 FIRE SUPPRESSION, PLUMBING & HVAC | 101.1 | 96.7 | 99.3 | 104.4 | 101.5 | 103.2 | 104.7 | 101.5 | 103.4 | 101.6 | 92.8 | 98.0 | 104.0 | 98.0 | 101.6 | 104.0 | 74.2 | 91.8 |
| 26, 27, 3370 ELECTRICAL, COMMUNICATIONS & UTIL. | 123.9 | 76.6 | 100.7 | 117.7 | 90.1 | 104.2 | 114.5 | 90.1 | 102.5 | 130.2 | 96.2 | 113.5 | 114.5 | 90.1 | 102.5 | 131.1 | 65.2 | 98.7 |
| MF2004 WEIGHTED AVERAGE | 115.0 | 89.7 | 104.2 | 122.1 | 94.8 | 110.4 | 116.7 | 91.5 | 105.9 | 121.6 | 96.2 | 110.7 | 116.8 | 90.7 | 105.6 | 115.5 | 69.7 | 95.9 |

| | CANADA | | | | | | | | | | | | | | | | |
|---|---|---|---|---|---|---|---|---|---|---|---|---|---|---|---|---|---|
| DIVISION | MONTREAL, QUEBEC | | | MOOSE JAW, SASKATCHEWAN | | | NEW GLASGOW, NOVA SCOTIA | | | NEWCASTLE, NEW BRUNSWICK | | | NORTH BAY, ONTARIO | | | OSHAWA, ONTARIO | | |
| | MAT. | INST. | TOTAL | MAT. | INST. | TOTAL | MAT. | INST. | TOTAL | MAT. | INST. | TOTAL | MAT. | INST. | TOTAL | MAT. | INST. | TOTAL |
| 015433 CONTRACTOR EQUIPMENT | | 101.0 | 101.0 | | 98.6 | 98.6 | | 98.6 | 98.6 | | 98.6 | 98.6 | | 100.4 | 100.4 | | 102.9 | 102.9 |
| 0241, 31 - 34 SITE & INFRASTRUCTURE, DEMOLITION | 96.4 | 98.2 | 97.6 | 111.9 | 95.5 | 100.5 | 99.4 | 96.9 | 97.7 | 96.3 | 95.2 | 95.5 | 114.6 | 99.7 | 104.2 | 114.5 | 104.6 | 107.6 |
| 0310 Concrete Forming & Accessories | 130.0 | 97.4 | 101.9 | 105.1 | 61.4 | 67.5 | 94.9 | 72.7 | 75.8 | 101.2 | 64.5 | 69.6 | 123.3 | 88.6 | 93.4 | 123.4 | 91.2 | 95.7 |
| 0320 Concrete Reinforcing | 159.6 | 97.4 | 129.7 | 114.0 | 64.8 | 90.3 | 148.3 | 48.9 | 100.4 | 148.3 | 59.2 | 105.4 | 174.7 | 85.7 | 131.9 | 174.7 | 88.5 | 133.2 |
| 0330 Cast-in-Place Concrete | 132.0 | 103.9 | 121.6 | 146.7 | 70.2 | 118.4 | 170.0 | 71.1 | 133.4 | 138.3 | 60.5 | 109.5 | 163.7 | 86.5 | 135.1 | 162.9 | 88.3 | 135.3 |
| 03 CONCRETE | 132.7 | 99.4 | 117.3 | 125.0 | 65.7 | 97.6 | 149.0 | 68.2 | 111.7 | 135.6 | 62.7 | 101.9 | 150.4 | 87.5 | 121.4 | 150.1 | 89.8 | 122.2 |
| 04 MASONRY | 165.5 | 97.1 | 124.6 | 159.7 | 65.4 | 103.3 | 161.0 | 73.1 | 108.4 | 159.8 | 66.0 | 103.7 | 166.0 | 91.5 | 121.4 | 165.7 | 97.3 | 124.8 |
| 05 METALS | 124.3 | 93.5 | 115.4 | 104.4 | 73.4 | 95.4 | 106.2 | 72.9 | 96.5 | 105.2 | 69.5 | 95.0 | 107.0 | 89.9 | 102.1 | 107.1 | 92.5 | 102.9 |
| 06 WOOD, PLASTICS & COMPOSITES | 128.9 | 97.8 | 112.1 | 95.4 | 59.7 | 76.2 | 85.4 | 71.9 | 78.1 | 93.7 | 64.6 | 78.0 | 116.8 | 88.8 | 101.7 | 116.8 | 89.4 | 102.0 |
| 07 THERMAL & MOISTURE PROTECTION | 105.5 | 100.1 | 103.4 | 103.9 | 65.2 | 88.8 | 105.3 | 71.0 | 91.9 | 107.4 | 63.2 | 90.1 | 110.3 | 86.9 | 101.1 | 110.4 | 89.2 | 102.1 |
| 08 OPENINGS | 91.8 | 85.4 | 90.2 | 86.8 | 57.6 | 79.6 | 82.7 | 65.7 | 78.5 | 86.0 | 56.6 | 78.8 | 90.6 | 85.1 | 89.2 | 90.6 | 89.3 | 90.3 |
| 0920 Plaster & Gypsum Board | 144.2 | 97.5 | 115.4 | 133.1 | 58.7 | 87.2 | 163.6 | 71.2 | 106.6 | 168.9 | 63.8 | 104.0 | 153.5 | 88.6 | 113.5 | 154.5 | 89.2 | 114.2 |
| 0950, 0980 Ceilings & Acoustic Treatment | 106.4 | 97.5 | 100.9 | 95.3 | 58.7 | 72.8 | 95.3 | 71.2 | 80.5 | 96.1 | 63.8 | 76.3 | 95.3 | 88.6 | 91.2 | 99.5 | 89.2 | 93.2 |
| 0960 Flooring | 132.5 | 98.3 | 123.2 | 119.8 | 62.5 | 104.2 | 109.7 | 66.5 | 97.9 | 113.7 | 46.6 | 95.5 | 132.5 | 96.3 | 122.6 | 132.5 | 100.2 | 123.7 |
| 0970, 0990 Wall Finishes & Painting/Coating | 109.4 | 108.5 | 108.9 | 109.4 | 67.2 | 84.1 | 109.4 | 64.5 | 82.4 | 109.4 | 51.9 | 74.9 | 109.4 | 91.8 | 98.8 | 109.4 | 109.3 | 109.3 |
| 09 FINISHES | 119.3 | 99.5 | 108.9 | 112.1 | 61.8 | 85.7 | 112.8 | 70.6 | 90.7 | 115.3 | 59.8 | 86.2 | 118.7 | 90.0 | 104.0 | 119.8 | 94.6 | 106.6 |
| COVERS DIVS. 10 - 14, 25, 28, 41, 43, 44 | 140.0 | 95.9 | 131.0 | 140.0 | 70.4 | 125.7 | 140.0 | 72.4 | 126.1 | 140.0 | 71.0 | 125.9 | 140.0 | 79.4 | 127.6 | 140.0 | 107.4 | 133.3 |
| 21, 22, 23 FIRE SUPPRESSION, PLUMBING & HVAC | 101.6 | 98.5 | 100.3 | 104.7 | 80.9 | 94.9 | 104.0 | 89.7 | 98.2 | 104.0 | 74.1 | 91.7 | 104.0 | 104.3 | 104.2 | 101.1 | 107.7 | 103.8 |
| 26, 27, 3370 ELECTRICAL, COMMUNICATIONS & UTIL. | 132.3 | 88.6 | 110.8 | 126.0 | 66.2 | 96.6 | 122.5 | 67.9 | 95.7 | 125.6 | 65.2 | 95.9 | 123.0 | 95.8 | 109.6 | 125.3 | 95.4 | 110.6 |
| MF2004 WEIGHTED AVERAGE | 119.6 | 96.1 | 109.6 | 114.1 | 71.3 | 95.8 | 116.1 | 76.4 | 99.1 | 115.2 | 68.8 | 95.4 | 118.8 | 93.9 | 108.2 | 118.4 | 97.7 | 109.6 |

| | CANADA | | | | | | | | | | | | | | | | |
|---|---|---|---|---|---|---|---|---|---|---|---|---|---|---|---|---|---|
| DIVISION | OTTAWA, ONTARIO | | | OWEN SOUND, ONTARIO | | | PETERBOROUGH, ONTARIO | | | PORTAGE LA PRAIRIE, MANITOBA | | | PRINCE ALBERT, SASKATCHEWAN | | | PRINCE GEORGE, BRITISH COLUMBIA | | |
| | MAT. | INST. | TOTAL | MAT. | INST. | TOTAL | MAT. | INST. | TOTAL | MAT. | INST. | TOTAL | MAT. | INST. | TOTAL | MAT. | INST. | TOTAL |
| 015433 CONTRACTOR EQUIPMENT | | 102.9 | 102.9 | | 100.4 | 100.4 | | 100.4 | 100.4 | | 102.8 | 102.8 | | 98.6 | 98.6 | | 103.4 | 103.4 |
| 0241, 31 - 34 SITE & INFRASTRUCTURE, DEMOLITION | 113.4 | 105.2 | 107.7 | 116.9 | 99.9 | 105.1 | 114.6 | 100.1 | 104.5 | 112.7 | 99.2 | 103.3 | 106.5 | 95.6 | 99.0 | 121.8 | 102.4 | 108.3 |
| 0310 Concrete Forming & Accessories | 121.2 | 95.4 | 99.0 | 123.4 | 87.0 | 92.0 | 123.3 | 89.6 | 94.3 | 122.6 | 73.6 | 80.4 | 105.1 | 61.2 | 67.3 | 110.5 | 92.4 | 94.9 |
| 0320 Concrete Reinforcing | 173.8 | 92.1 | 134.5 | 179.9 | 87.8 | 135.5 | 174.7 | 86.3 | 132.1 | 161.5 | 55.7 | 110.5 | 119.1 | 64.8 | 92.9 | 116.5 | 80.4 | 99.1 |
| 0330 Cast-in-Place Concrete | 155.1 | 100.7 | 135.0 | 167.7 | 82.1 | 136.1 | 163.7 | 88.2 | 135.7 | 151.2 | 76.0 | 123.4 | 132.8 | 70.1 | 109.6 | 147.2 | 101.2 | 130.2 |
| 03 CONCRETE | 145.9 | 96.6 | 123.1 | 153.3 | 85.6 | 122.0 | 150.4 | 88.6 | 121.9 | 135.5 | 71.6 | 106.0 | 118.9 | 65.5 | 94.3 | 152.1 | 93.1 | 124.9 |
| 04 MASONRY | 160.1 | 100.8 | 124.7 | 169.3 | 97.1 | 126.1 | 166.0 | 98.3 | 125.5 | 164.1 | 68.7 | 107.1 | 158.7 | 65.4 | 102.9 | 170.0 | 96.5 | 126.0 |
| 05 METALS | 116.0 | 93.7 | 109.5 | 107.7 | 90.2 | 102.6 | 107.0 | 90.4 | 102.2 | 107.8 | 76.3 | 98.6 | 104.5 | 73.2 | 95.4 | 107.6 | 87.3 | 101.7 |
| 06 WOOD, PLASTICS & COMPOSITES | 115.4 | 94.8 | 104.3 | 118.7 | 85.5 | 100.8 | 116.8 | 87.5 | 101.0 | 114.5 | 74.4 | 92.9 | 95.4 | 59.7 | 76.2 | 98.1 | 90.6 | 94.0 |
| 07 THERMAL & MOISTURE PROTECTION | 111.0 | 95.8 | 105.1 | 110.5 | 87.7 | 101.6 | 110.3 | 92.5 | 103.3 | 104.4 | 72.9 | 92.1 | 103.9 | 64.0 | 88.3 | 115.5 | 88.1 | 104.8 |
| 08 OPENINGS | 91.8 | 92.0 | 91.8 | 90.7 | 84.4 | 89.2 | 90.6 | 86.9 | 89.7 | 91.8 | 65.8 | 85.4 | 85.4 | 57.6 | 78.6 | 87.7 | 87.0 | 87.6 |
| 0920 Plaster & Gypsum Board | 232.0 | 94.7 | 147.3 | 153.5 | 85.1 | 111.3 | 153.5 | 87.2 | 112.6 | 124.1 | 73.4 | 92.8 | 133.1 | 58.7 | 87.2 | 136.5 | 90.0 | 107.8 |
| 0950, 0980 Ceilings & Acoustic Treatment | 105.5 | 94.7 | 98.9 | 95.3 | 85.1 | 89.0 | 95.3 | 87.2 | 90.3 | 95.3 | 73.4 | 81.8 | 95.3 | 58.7 | 72.8 | 95.3 | 90.0 | 92.0 |
| 0960 Flooring | 132.5 | 96.3 | 122.6 | 132.6 | 97.7 | 123.1 | 132.5 | 96.3 | 122.6 | 132.5 | 69.4 | 115.3 | 119.8 | 62.5 | 104.2 | 126.8 | 54.9 | 107.3 |
| 0970, 0990 Wall Finishes & Painting/Coating | 109.4 | 95.2 | 100.9 | 110.2 | 90.4 | 98.3 | 109.4 | 94.1 | 100.2 | 109.5 | 59.1 | 79.2 | 109.4 | 57.3 | 78.1 | 109.4 | 84.5 | 94.4 |
| 09 FINISHES | 133.3 | 95.5 | 113.5 | 119.8 | 89.4 | 103.8 | 118.7 | 91.3 | 104.3 | 114.4 | 71.5 | 91.9 | 112.1 | 60.7 | 85.2 | 116.3 | 84.7 | 99.7 |
| COVERS DIVS. 10 - 14, 25, 28, 41, 43, 44 | 140.0 | 105.7 | 133.0 | 140.0 | 79.9 | 127.7 | 140.0 | 81.0 | 127.9 | 140.0 | 73.7 | 126.4 | 140.0 | 70.4 | 125.7 | 140.0 | 104.9 | 132.8 |
| 21, 22, 23 FIRE SUPPRESSION, PLUMBING & HVAC | 101.6 | 93.2 | 98.2 | 104.2 | 104.2 | 104.2 | 104.0 | 108.1 | 105.7 | 104.0 | 89.4 | 98.0 | 104.7 | 72.9 | 91.6 | 104.0 | 100.3 | 102.5 |
| 26, 27, 3370 ELECTRICAL, COMMUNICATIONS & UTIL. | 123.9 | 97.1 | 110.8 | 124.6 | 94.5 | 109.8 | 123.0 | 95.4 | 109.4 | 125.6 | 63.3 | 95.0 | 126.0 | 66.2 | 96.6 | 123.1 | 86.4 | 105.1 |
| MF2004 WEIGHTED AVERAGE | 120.4 | 96.8 | 110.3 | 119.8 | 93.9 | 108.7 | 118.8 | 95.9 | 109.0 | 116.8 | 76.5 | 99.6 | 113.1 | 69.5 | 94.4 | 119.1 | 93.1 | 108.0 |

# City Cost Indexes

## CANADA

| DIVISION | | QUEBEC, QUEBEC | | | RED DEER, ALBERTA | | | REGINA, SASKATCHEWAN | | | RIMOUSKI, QUEBEC | | | ROUYN-NORANDA, QUEBEC | | | SAINT HYACINTHE, QUEBEC | | |
|---|---|---|---|---|---|---|---|---|---|---|---|---|---|---|---|---|---|---|---|
| | | MAT. | INST. | TOTAL | MAT. | INST. | TOTAL | MAT. | INST. | TOTAL | MAT. | INST. | TOTAL | MAT. | INST. | TOTAL | MAT. | INST. | TOTAL |
| 015433 | CONTRACTOR EQUIPMENT | | 101.4 | 101.4 | | 103.7 | 103.7 | | 98.6 | 98.6 | | 99.2 | 99.2 | | 99.2 | 99.2 | | 99.2 | 99.2 |
| 0241, 31 - 34 | SITE & INFRASTRUCTURE, DEMOLITION | 96.1 | 98.3 | 97.6 | 110.5 | 101.9 | 104.5 | 113.3 | 95.5 | 100.9 | 94.5 | 97.9 | 96.9 | 94.0 | 98.3 | 97.0 | 94.6 | 98.3 | 97.2 |
| 0310 | Concrete Forming & Accessories | 129.9 | 97.7 | 102.1 | 136.2 | 83.9 | 91.1 | 105.2 | 61.4 | 67.5 | 129.5 | 97.1 | 101.6 | 129.5 | 89.3 | 94.9 | 129.5 | 89.3 | 94.9 |
| 0320 | Concrete Reinforcing | 148.3 | 97.4 | 123.8 | 161.5 | 65.5 | 115.2 | 126.1 | 64.9 | 96.6 | 111.9 | 97.4 | 104.9 | 157.0 | 82.6 | 121.2 | 157.0 | 82.6 | 121.2 |
| 0330 | Cast-in-Place Concrete | 145.5 | 104.3 | 130.2 | 151.2 | 99.0 | 131.9 | 156.3 | 70.2 | 124.4 | 137.0 | 102.4 | 124.2 | 130.2 | 97.0 | 117.9 | 134.5 | 97.0 | 120.6 |
| 03 | CONCRETE | 137.6 | 99.7 | 120.1 | 142.9 | 86.1 | 116.7 | 131.7 | 65.7 | 101.2 | 127.7 | 98.8 | 114.3 | 131.4 | 90.7 | 112.6 | 133.5 | 90.7 | 113.8 |
| 04 | MASONRY | 167.7 | 97.1 | 125.5 | 161.2 | 88.2 | 117.5 | 166.8 | 65.9 | 106.5 | 160.4 | 97.1 | 122.5 | 160.7 | 88.5 | 117.5 | 161.0 | 88.5 | 117.7 |
| 05 | METALS | 120.1 | 93.8 | 112.5 | 107.8 | 87.5 | 101.9 | 105.4 | 73.5 | 96.1 | 105.0 | 93.0 | 101.5 | 105.5 | 87.0 | 100.1 | 105.5 | 87.0 | 100.1 |
| 06 | WOOD, PLASTICS & COMPOSITES | 129.5 | 97.9 | 112.5 | 114.6 | 83.2 | 97.7 | 95.4 | 59.7 | 76.2 | 128.9 | 97.5 | 112.0 | 128.9 | 89.1 | 107.5 | 128.9 | 89.1 | 107.5 |
| 07 | THERMAL & MOISTURE PROTECTION | 105.1 | 100.3 | 103.3 | 126.2 | 85.6 | 110.4 | 105.8 | 65.3 | 90.0 | 104.5 | 99.5 | 102.6 | 104.5 | 91.1 | 99.3 | 104.8 | 91.1 | 99.4 |
| 08 | OPENINGS | 91.8 | 93.2 | 92.1 | 91.8 | 77.6 | 88.3 | 86.8 | 57.6 | 79.6 | 91.4 | 83.5 | 89.4 | 91.8 | 77.5 | 88.3 | 91.8 | 77.5 | 88.3 |
| 0920 | Plaster & Gypsum Board | 190.0 | 97.5 | 132.9 | 131.1 | 82.4 | 101.0 | 165.6 | 58.7 | 99.7 | 187.7 | 97.5 | 132.0 | 136.5 | 88.8 | 107.1 | 141.0 | 88.8 | 108.8 |
| 0950, 0980 | Ceilings & Acoustic Treatment | 97.0 | 97.5 | 97.3 | 95.3 | 82.4 | 87.4 | 120.0 | 58.7 | 82.4 | 92.7 | 97.5 | 95.6 | 92.7 | 88.8 | 90.3 | 92.7 | 88.8 | 90.3 |
| 0960 | Flooring | 132.5 | 98.3 | 123.2 | 134.8 | 91.5 | 123.0 | 119.8 | 62.5 | 104.2 | 132.5 | 98.3 | 123.2 | 132.5 | 98.3 | 123.2 | 132.5 | 98.3 | 123.2 |
| 0970, 0990 | Wall Finishes & Painting/Coating | 110.0 | 108.5 | 109.1 | 109.4 | 81.7 | 92.8 | 109.4 | 67.2 | 84.1 | 109.4 | 108.5 | 108.9 | 109.4 | 92.3 | 99.1 | 109.4 | 92.3 | 99.1 |
| 09 | FINISHES | 124.1 | 99.5 | 111.2 | 116.2 | 85.0 | 99.9 | 123.2 | 61.8 | 91.1 | 122.7 | 99.3 | 110.4 | 114.6 | 91.5 | 102.5 | 115.3 | 91.5 | 102.9 |
| COVERS | DIVS. 10 - 14, 25, 28, 41, 43, 44 | 140.0 | 96.0 | 131.0 | 140.0 | 101.1 | 132.0 | 140.0 | 70.4 | 125.7 | 140.0 | 95.2 | 130.8 | 140.0 | 93.2 | 130.4 | 140.0 | 93.2 | 130.4 |
| 21, 22, 23 | FIRE SUPPRESSION, PLUMBING & HVAC | 101.5 | 98.5 | 100.3 | 104.0 | 98.0 | 101.6 | 101.3 | 80.9 | 92.9 | 104.0 | 98.4 | 101.7 | 104.0 | 96.7 | 101.0 | 99.6 | 96.7 | 98.4 |
| 26, 27, 3370 | ELECTRICAL, COMMUNICATIONS & UTIL. | 128.2 | 88.6 | 108.7 | 114.5 | 90.1 | 102.5 | 127.0 | 66.2 | 97.1 | 123.0 | 88.6 | 106.1 | 123.0 | 76.6 | 100.2 | 123.9 | 76.6 | 100.7 |
| MF2004 | WEIGHTED AVERAGE | 119.5 | 96.6 | 109.7 | 117.2 | 90.7 | 105.9 | 115.9 | 71.4 | 96.8 | 115.3 | 95.8 | 107.0 | 115.1 | 89.7 | 104.2 | 114.6 | 89.7 | 103.9 |

## CANADA

| DIVISION | | SAINT JOHN, NEW BRUNSWICK | | | SARNIA, ONTARIO | | | SASKATOON, SASKATCHEWAN | | | SAULT STE MARIE, ONTARIO | | | SHERBROOKE, QUEBEC | | | SOREL, QUEBEC | | |
|---|---|---|---|---|---|---|---|---|---|---|---|---|---|---|---|---|---|---|---|
| | | MAT. | INST. | TOTAL | MAT. | INST. | TOTAL | MAT. | INST. | TOTAL | MAT. | INST. | TOTAL | MAT. | INST. | TOTAL | MAT. | INST. | TOTAL |
| 015433 | CONTRACTOR EQUIPMENT | | 98.6 | 98.6 | | 100.4 | 100.4 | | 98.6 | 98.6 | | 100.4 | 100.4 | | 99.2 | 99.2 | | 99.2 | 99.2 |
| 0241, 31 - 34 | SITE & INFRASTRUCTURE, DEMOLITION | 96.4 | 96.1 | 96.2 | 112.9 | 100.2 | 104.0 | 107.7 | 95.7 | 99.3 | 102.5 | 99.8 | 100.6 | 94.6 | 98.3 | 97.2 | 94.7 | 98.3 | 97.2 |
| 0310 | Concrete Forming & Accessories | 121.0 | 64.2 | 72.0 | 121.9 | 97.0 | 100.4 | 105.2 | 61.3 | 67.4 | 110.9 | 90.6 | 93.4 | 129.5 | 89.3 | 94.9 | 129.5 | 89.4 | 95.0 |
| 0320 | Concrete Reinforcing | 148.3 | 62.5 | 107.0 | 123.6 | 87.7 | 106.3 | 119.1 | 64.8 | 92.9 | 112.3 | 86.1 | 99.7 | 157.0 | 82.6 | 121.2 | 148.3 | 82.6 | 116.7 |
| 0330 | Cast-in-Place Concrete | 136.2 | 60.9 | 108.3 | 151.0 | 101.8 | 132.8 | 142.0 | 70.2 | 115.4 | 135.6 | 86.6 | 117.5 | 134.5 | 97.0 | 120.6 | 135.6 | 97.0 | 121.3 |
| 03 | CONCRETE | 136.0 | 63.3 | 102.4 | 136.0 | 96.7 | 117.9 | 123.5 | 65.6 | 96.8 | 119.7 | 88.5 | 105.3 | 133.5 | 90.7 | 113.8 | 132.7 | 90.8 | 113.3 |
| 04 | MASONRY | 177.6 | 67.8 | 111.9 | 176.4 | 101.1 | 131.4 | 166.5 | 65.9 | 106.3 | 162.4 | 97.3 | 123.5 | 161.1 | 88.5 | 117.7 | 161.1 | 88.5 | 117.7 |
| 05 | METALS | 105.1 | 74.0 | 96.1 | 107.0 | 90.8 | 102.3 | 105.4 | 73.4 | 96.1 | 106.2 | 91.7 | 102.0 | 105.5 | 87.0 | 100.1 | 105.5 | 87.1 | 100.1 |
| 06 | WOOD, PLASTICS & COMPOSITES | 117.6 | 63.3 | 88.3 | 115.9 | 96.0 | 105.2 | 93.9 | 59.7 | 75.5 | 102.7 | 91.0 | 96.4 | 128.9 | 89.1 | 107.5 | 128.9 | 89.1 | 107.5 |
| 07 | THERMAL & MOISTURE PROTECTION | 107.6 | 64.9 | 91.0 | 110.3 | 96.1 | 104.8 | 104.6 | 64.2 | 88.8 | 109.1 | 90.2 | 101.7 | 104.5 | 91.1 | 99.3 | 104.5 | 91.1 | 99.3 |
| 08 | OPENINGS | 85.9 | 56.4 | 78.6 | 92.9 | 90.8 | 92.4 | 85.9 | 57.6 | 78.9 | 83.6 | 88.2 | 84.7 | 91.8 | 77.5 | 88.3 | 91.8 | 82.3 | 89.5 |
| 0920 | Plaster & Gypsum Board | 183.5 | 62.4 | 108.8 | 182.2 | 96.0 | 129.0 | 145.6 | 58.7 | 92.0 | 142.3 | 90.9 | 110.5 | 138.8 | 88.8 | 108.0 | 187.7 | 88.8 | 126.7 |
| 0950, 0980 | Ceilings & Acoustic Treatment | 103.8 | 62.4 | 78.4 | 99.5 | 96.0 | 97.4 | 120.0 | 58.7 | 82.4 | 95.3 | 90.9 | 92.6 | 92.7 | 88.8 | 90.3 | 92.7 | 88.8 | 90.3 |
| 0960 | Flooring | 127.6 | 57.4 | 108.5 | 132.5 | 101.7 | 124.1 | 119.8 | 62.5 | 104.2 | 123.4 | 96.3 | 116.0 | 132.5 | 98.3 | 123.2 | 132.5 | 98.3 | 123.2 |
| 0970, 0990 | Wall Finishes & Painting/Coating | 109.4 | 72.0 | 87.0 | 109.4 | 106.4 | 107.6 | 109.4 | 57.3 | 78.1 | 109.4 | 98.5 | 102.9 | 109.4 | 92.3 | 99.1 | 109.4 | 92.3 | 99.1 |
| 09 | FINISHES | 123.5 | 63.4 | 92.1 | 124.2 | 99.2 | 111.1 | 119.8 | 60.7 | 88.9 | 113.5 | 92.6 | 102.6 | 115.0 | 91.5 | 102.7 | 122.7 | 91.5 | 106.4 |
| COVERS | DIVS. 10 - 14, 25, 28, 41, 43, 44 | 140.0 | 70.8 | 125.8 | 140.0 | 82.6 | 128.2 | 140.0 | 70.4 | 125.7 | 140.0 | 106.2 | 133.1 | 140.0 | 93.2 | 130.4 | 140.0 | 93.2 | 130.4 |
| 21, 22, 23 | FIRE SUPPRESSION, PLUMBING & HVAC | 104.0 | 80.5 | 94.4 | 104.0 | 114.6 | 108.4 | 101.2 | 80.9 | 92.9 | 104.0 | 100.8 | 102.7 | 104.7 | 96.7 | 101.4 | 104.0 | 96.7 | 101.0 |
| 26, 27, 3370 | ELECTRICAL, COMMUNICATIONS & UTIL. | 134.2 | 81.1 | 108.1 | 126.9 | 97.8 | 112.6 | 127.3 | 66.2 | 97.3 | 125.2 | 95.8 | 110.7 | 123.0 | 76.6 | 100.2 | 123.0 | 76.6 | 100.2 |
| MF2004 | WEIGHTED AVERAGE | 118.0 | 73.6 | 99.0 | 118.7 | 100.4 | 110.9 | 114.3 | 71.2 | 95.9 | 113.5 | 95.3 | 105.7 | 115.6 | 89.7 | 104.5 | 116.0 | 89.9 | 104.8 |

## CANADA

| DIVISION | | ST CATHARINES, ONTARIO | | | ST JEROME, QUEBEC | | | ST JOHNS, NEWFOUNDLAND | | | SUDBURY, ONTARIO | | | SUMMERSIDE, PRINCE EDWARD ISLAND | | | SYDNEY, NOVA SCOTIA | | |
|---|---|---|---|---|---|---|---|---|---|---|---|---|---|---|---|---|---|---|---|
| | | MAT. | INST. | TOTAL | MAT. | INST. | TOTAL | MAT. | INST. | TOTAL | MAT. | INST. | TOTAL | MAT. | INST. | TOTAL | MAT. | INST. | TOTAL |
| 015433 | CONTRACTOR EQUIPMENT | | 100.4 | 100.4 | | 99.2 | 99.2 | | 98.6 | 98.6 | | 100.4 | 100.4 | | 98.6 | 98.6 | | 98.6 | 98.6 |
| 0241, 31 - 34 | SITE & INFRASTRUCTURE, DEMOLITION | 102.4 | 101.4 | 101.7 | 94.0 | 98.3 | 97.0 | 116.1 | 95.9 | 102.1 | 102.5 | 101.0 | 101.4 | 107.6 | 94.5 | 98.5 | 94.3 | 96.9 | 96.1 |
| 0310 | Concrete Forming & Accessories | 115.1 | 96.4 | 99.0 | 129.5 | 89.3 | 94.9 | 102.9 | 66.2 | 71.3 | 110.9 | 92.0 | 94.6 | 95.1 | 58.9 | 63.9 | 94.9 | 72.7 | 75.8 |
| 0320 | Concrete Reinforcing | 111.3 | 93.6 | 102.8 | 157.0 | 82.6 | 121.2 | 164.9 | 59.7 | 114.2 | 112.3 | 91.8 | 102.4 | 148.3 | 49.0 | 100.5 | 148.3 | 48.9 | 100.4 |
| 0330 | Cast-in-Place Concrete | 134.5 | 103.7 | 123.1 | 130.2 | 97.0 | 117.9 | 172.4 | 77.1 | 137.1 | 135.6 | 99.8 | 122.3 | 161.3 | 59.8 | 123.7 | 130.9 | 71.1 | 108.8 |
| 03 | CONCRETE | 119.3 | 98.3 | 109.6 | 131.4 | 90.7 | 112.6 | 164.8 | 69.3 | 120.7 | 119.7 | 94.7 | 108.2 | 153.0 | 58.0 | 109.2 | 129.6 | 68.2 | 101.3 |
| 04 | MASONRY | 162.0 | 105.3 | 128.1 | 160.7 | 88.5 | 117.5 | 164.2 | 67.5 | 106.4 | 162.1 | 100.2 | 125.1 | 160.3 | 63.7 | 102.5 | 157.9 | 73.1 | 107.2 |
| 05 | METALS | 106.3 | 93.7 | 102.6 | 105.5 | 87.0 | 100.1 | 108.2 | 74.2 | 98.3 | 106.2 | 93.4 | 102.5 | 106.2 | 65.8 | 94.5 | 106.2 | 72.9 | 96.5 |
| 06 | WOOD, PLASTICS & COMPOSITES | 107.1 | 95.4 | 100.8 | 128.9 | 89.1 | 107.5 | 94.8 | 66.4 | 79.5 | 102.7 | 91.0 | 96.4 | 85.7 | 58.3 | 71.0 | 85.4 | 71.9 | 78.1 |
| 07 | THERMAL & MOISTURE PROTECTION | 109.4 | 96.5 | 104.4 | 104.5 | 91.1 | 99.3 | 108.9 | 65.0 | 91.8 | 109.1 | 94.3 | 103.3 | 105.1 | 60.7 | 87.8 | 105.3 | 71.0 | 91.9 |
| 08 | OPENINGS | 82.7 | 92.1 | 85.0 | 91.8 | 77.5 | 88.3 | 97.9 | 62.4 | 89.1 | 83.6 | 88.2 | 84.7 | 94.0 | 50.6 | 83.3 | 82.7 | 65.7 | 78.5 |
| 0920 | Plaster & Gypsum Board | 136.1 | 95.3 | 110.9 | 136.5 | 88.8 | 107.1 | 171.1 | 65.5 | 106.0 | 142.3 | 90.9 | 110.5 | 163.9 | 57.3 | 98.1 | 163.6 | 71.2 | 106.6 |
| 0950, 0980 | Ceilings & Acoustic Treatment | 99.5 | 95.3 | 96.9 | 92.7 | 88.8 | 90.3 | 105.5 | 65.5 | 81.0 | 95.3 | 90.9 | 92.6 | 95.3 | 57.3 | 72.0 | 95.3 | 71.2 | 80.5 |
| 0960 | Flooring | 126.3 | 97.7 | 118.5 | 132.5 | 98.3 | 123.2 | 114.6 | 56.6 | 98.8 | 123.4 | 96.3 | 116.0 | 109.8 | 62.1 | 96.8 | 109.7 | 66.5 | 97.9 |
| 0970, 0990 | Wall Finishes & Painting/Coating | 109.4 | 104.7 | 106.6 | 109.4 | 92.3 | 99.1 | 109.4 | 67.2 | 84.1 | 109.4 | 94.6 | 100.5 | 109.4 | 43.2 | 69.7 | 109.4 | 64.5 | 82.4 |
| 09 | FINISHES | 114.3 | 97.7 | 105.5 | 114.6 | 91.5 | 102.5 | 119.0 | 64.4 | 90.4 | 113.5 | 92.9 | 102.7 | 113.7 | 58.1 | 84.6 | 112.8 | 70.6 | 90.7 |
| COVERS | DIVS. 10 - 14, 25, 28, 41, 43, 44 | 140.0 | 82.6 | 128.2 | 140.0 | 93.2 | 130.4 | 140.0 | 71.4 | 126.0 | 140.0 | 107.2 | 133.3 | 140.0 | 70.5 | 125.8 | 140.0 | 72.4 | 126.1 |
| 21, 22, 23 | FIRE SUPPRESSION, PLUMBING & HVAC | 101.1 | 94.5 | 98.4 | 104.0 | 96.7 | 101.0 | 101.5 | 66.8 | 87.3 | 104.2 | 93.7 | 99.9 | 104.0 | 67.7 | 89.1 | 104.0 | 89.7 | 98.2 |
| 26, 27, 3370 | ELECTRICAL, COMMUNICATIONS & UTIL. | 126.3 | 97.2 | 112.0 | 123.8 | 76.6 | 100.6 | 123.3 | 67.7 | 96.0 | 123.0 | 97.2 | 110.3 | 121.2 | 55.2 | 88.8 | 122.5 | 67.9 | 95.7 |
| MF2004 | WEIGHTED AVERAGE | 112.9 | 97.0 | 106.1 | 115.2 | 89.7 | 104.3 | 120.6 | 70.1 | 99.0 | 113.3 | 95.6 | 105.7 | 117.8 | 64.1 | 94.8 | 113.5 | 76.4 | 97.7 |

# City Cost Indexes

## CANADA

| DIVISION | | THUNDER BAY, ONTARIO | | | TIMMINS, ONTARIO | | | TORONTO, ONTARIO | | | TROIS RIVIERES, QUEBEC | | | TRURO, NOVA SCOTIA | | | VANCOUVER, BRITISH COLUMBIA | | |
|---|---|---|---|---|---|---|---|---|---|---|---|---|---|---|---|---|---|---|---|
| | | MAT. | INST. | TOTAL | MAT. | INST. | TOTAL | MAT. | INST. | TOTAL | MAT. | INST. | TOTAL | MAT. | INST. | TOTAL | MAT. | INST. | TOTAL |
| 015433 | CONTRACTOR EQUIPMENT | | 100.4 | 100.4 | | 100.4 | 100.4 | | 103.2 | 103.2 | | 99.2 | 99.2 | | 98.6 | 98.6 | | 111.3 | 111.3 |
| 0241, 31 - 34 | SITE & INFRASTRUCTURE, DEMOLITION | 108.0 | 101.3 | 103.4 | 114.6 | 99.7 | 104.2 | 115.9 | 106.1 | 109.0 | 94.7 | 98.3 | 97.2 | 99.4 | 96.9 | 97.7 | 119.6 | 107.2 | 111.0 |
| 0310 | Concrete Forming & Accessories | 123.4 | 96.7 | 100.4 | 123.3 | 88.6 | 93.4 | 123.8 | 104.9 | 107.5 | 129.5 | 89.4 | 95.0 | 94.9 | 72.7 | 75.8 | 123.9 | 80.8 | 86.8 |
| 0320 | Concrete Reinforcing | 99.5 | 93.0 | 96.3 | 174.7 | 85.7 | 131.9 | 170.9 | 94.3 | 134.0 | 148.3 | 82.6 | 116.7 | 148.3 | 48.9 | 100.4 | 173.3 | 74.9 | 125.9 |
| 0330 | Cast-in-Place Concrete | 148.1 | 102.2 | 131.1 | 163.7 | 86.5 | 135.1 | 149.4 | 112.7 | 135.8 | 135.6 | 97.0 | 121.3 | 170.0 | 71.1 | 133.4 | 151.9 | 93.4 | 130.2 |
| 03 | CONCRETE | 127.9 | 97.8 | 114.0 | 150.4 | 87.5 | 121.4 | 142.8 | 105.3 | 125.5 | 132.7 | 90.8 | 113.3 | 149.0 | 68.2 | 111.7 | 150.1 | 84.5 | 119.8 |
| 04 | MASONRY | 162.8 | 105.1 | 128.3 | 166.0 | 91.5 | 121.4 | 175.4 | 110.7 | 136.7 | 161.1 | 88.5 | 117.7 | 161.0 | 73.1 | 108.4 | 168.5 | 84.1 | 118.0 |
| 05 | METALS | 106.1 | 92.5 | 102.1 | 107.0 | 89.9 | 102.1 | 128.4 | 95.1 | 118.7 | 105.5 | 87.1 | 100.1 | 106.2 | 73.0 | 96.6 | 143.4 | 87.2 | 127.1 |
| 06 | WOOD, PLASTICS & COMPOSITES | 116.8 | 95.5 | 105.3 | 116.8 | 88.8 | 101.7 | 116.8 | 103.7 | 109.7 | 128.9 | 89.1 | 107.5 | 85.4 | 71.9 | 78.1 | 113.9 | 78.0 | 94.6 |
| 07 | THERMAL & MOISTURE PROTECTION | 109.6 | 98.1 | 105.1 | 110.3 | 86.9 | 101.1 | 111.5 | 104.7 | 108.8 | 104.5 | 91.1 | 99.3 | 105.3 | 71.0 | 91.9 | 133.6 | 84.6 | 114.5 |
| 08 | OPENINGS | 81.7 | 91.5 | 84.1 | 90.6 | 85.1 | 89.2 | 90.6 | 100.0 | 92.9 | 91.8 | 82.3 | 89.5 | 82.7 | 65.7 | 78.5 | 93.5 | 78.8 | 89.8 |
| 0920 | Plaster & Gypsum Board | 166.8 | 95.5 | 122.8 | 153.5 | 88.6 | 113.5 | 165.7 | 103.9 | 127.6 | 187.7 | 88.8 | 126.7 | 163.6 | 71.2 | 106.6 | 145.3 | 76.9 | 103.1 |
| 0950, 0980 | Ceilings & Acoustic Treatment | 95.3 | 95.5 | 95.4 | 95.3 | 88.6 | 91.2 | 119.2 | 103.9 | 109.8 | 92.7 | 88.8 | 90.3 | 95.3 | 71.2 | 80.5 | 109.8 | 76.9 | 89.6 |
| 0960 | Flooring | 132.5 | 56.2 | 111.8 | 132.5 | 96.3 | 122.6 | 132.5 | 103.5 | 124.6 | 132.5 | 98.3 | 123.2 | 109.7 | 66.5 | 97.9 | 134.8 | 94.8 | 123.9 |
| 0970, 0990 | Wall Finishes & Painting/Coating | 109.4 | 97.1 | 102.0 | 109.4 | 91.8 | 98.8 | 111.2 | 109.3 | 110.1 | 109.4 | 92.3 | 99.1 | 109.4 | 64.5 | 82.4 | 109.4 | 92.4 | 99.2 |
| 09 | FINISHES | 120.4 | 90.0 | 104.5 | 118.7 | 90.6 | 104.0 | 126.9 | 105.3 | 115.6 | 122.7 | 91.5 | 106.4 | 112.8 | 70.6 | 90.7 | 122.7 | 84.2 | 102.5 |
| COVERS | DIVS. 10 - 14, 25, 28, 41, 43, 44 | 140.0 | 83.0 | 128.3 | 140.0 | 79.4 | 127.6 | 140.0 | 111.4 | 134.1 | 140.0 | 93.2 | 130.4 | 140.0 | 72.4 | 126.1 | 140.0 | 102.1 | 132.2 |
| 21, 22, 23 | FIRE SUPPRESSION, PLUMBING & HVAC | 101.1 | 94.6 | 98.4 | 104.0 | 104.3 | 104.2 | 101.6 | 100.1 | 101.0 | 104.0 | 96.7 | 101.0 | 104.0 | 89.7 | 98.2 | 101.5 | 76.4 | 91.2 |
| 26, 27, 3370 | ELECTRICAL, COMMUNICATIONS & UTIL. | 124.1 | 95.4 | 110.0 | 125.2 | 95.8 | 110.7 | 128.9 | 99.6 | 114.5 | 123.0 | 76.6 | 100.2 | 122.5 | 67.9 | 95.7 | 131.6 | 77.2 | 104.9 |
| MF2004 | WEIGHTED AVERAGE | 114.4 | 95.7 | 106.4 | 119.1 | 93.9 | 108.3 | 122.7 | 103.0 | 114.3 | 116.0 | 89.9 | 104.8 | 116.1 | 76.5 | 99.1 | 126.7 | 84.0 | 108.5 |

## CANADA

| DIVISION | | VICTORIA, BRITISH COLUMBIA | | | WHITEHORSE, YUKON | | | WINDSOR, ONTARIO | | | WINNIPEG, MANITOBA | | | YARMOUTH, NOVA SCOTIA | | | YELLOWKNIFE, NWT | | |
|---|---|---|---|---|---|---|---|---|---|---|---|---|---|---|---|---|---|---|---|
| | | MAT. | INST. | TOTAL | MAT. | INST. | TOTAL | MAT. | INST. | TOTAL | MAT. | INST. | TOTAL | MAT. | INST. | TOTAL | MAT. | INST. | TOTAL |
| 015433 | CONTRACTOR EQUIPMENT | | 107.2 | 107.2 | | 99.2 | 99.2 | | 100.4 | 100.4 | | 105.2 | 105.2 | | 98.6 | 98.6 | | 98.7 | 98.7 |
| 0241, 31 - 34 | SITE & INFRASTRUCTURE, DEMOLITION | 121.7 | 106.6 | 111.2 | 108.3 | 95.7 | 99.5 | 97.4 | 101.0 | 99.9 | 115.7 | 100.8 | 105.3 | 99.2 | 96.9 | 97.6 | 121.0 | 99.9 | 106.3 |
| 0310 | Concrete Forming & Accessories | 110.5 | 79.9 | 84.2 | 105.2 | 60.4 | 66.6 | 123.4 | 93.6 | 97.7 | 123.1 | 67.7 | 75.4 | 94.9 | 72.7 | 75.8 | 105.3 | 82.9 | 86.0 |
| 0320 | Concrete Reinforcing | 116.5 | 74.8 | 96.4 | 119.1 | 62.9 | 92.0 | 109.1 | 92.2 | 100.9 | 161.5 | 58.0 | 111.6 | 148.3 | 48.9 | 100.4 | 119.1 | 66.8 | 93.9 |
| 0330 | Cast-in-Place Concrete | 147.2 | 92.5 | 126.9 | 146.7 | 69.2 | 118.0 | 137.7 | 103.2 | 125.0 | 174.4 | 72.3 | 136.6 | 168.2 | 71.1 | 132.3 | 243.6 | 88.4 | 186.1 |
| 03 | CONCRETE | 152.1 | 83.5 | 120.4 | 125.8 | 64.5 | 97.5 | 121.1 | 96.6 | 109.8 | 153.5 | 68.1 | 114.0 | 148.1 | 68.2 | 111.2 | 174.0 | 81.9 | 131.5 |
| 04 | MASONRY | 169.2 | 84.1 | 118.3 | 159.1 | 63.8 | 102.1 | 162.2 | 103.6 | 127.1 | 178.6 | 64.4 | 110.3 | 160.9 | 73.1 | 108.3 | 167.5 | 77.4 | 113.6 |
| 05 | METALS | 107.6 | 82.1 | 100.2 | 105.6 | 72.5 | 96.0 | 106.1 | 93.3 | 102.4 | 138.1 | 75.9 | 120.0 | 106.2 | 72.9 | 96.5 | 106.3 | 78.9 | 98.4 |
| 06 | WOOD, PLASTICS & COMPOSITES | 98.1 | 77.9 | 87.2 | 95.4 | 58.9 | 75.7 | 116.8 | 92.0 | 103.4 | 114.5 | 68.4 | 89.7 | 85.4 | 71.9 | 78.1 | 95.4 | 84.3 | 89.4 |
| 07 | THERMAL & MOISTURE PROTECTION | 115.5 | 82.8 | 102.7 | 103.8 | 63.0 | 87.9 | 109.4 | 96.8 | 104.5 | 105.6 | 69.2 | 91.4 | 105.3 | 71.0 | 91.9 | 105.5 | 80.7 | 95.8 |
| 08 | OPENINGS | 87.7 | 75.0 | 84.6 | 85.4 | 56.3 | 78.2 | 81.4 | 90.1 | 83.6 | 91.8 | 63.0 | 84.7 | 82.7 | 65.7 | 78.5 | 85.4 | 71.3 | 81.9 |
| 0920 | Plaster & Gypsum Board | 136.5 | 76.9 | 99.8 | 115.3 | 57.8 | 79.8 | 155.7 | 91.8 | 116.3 | 148.9 | 67.1 | 98.4 | 163.6 | 71.2 | 106.6 | 146.4 | 83.9 | 107.9 |
| 0950, 0980 | Ceilings & Acoustic Treatment | 95.3 | 76.9 | 84.0 | 95.3 | 57.8 | 72.2 | 95.3 | 91.8 | 93.2 | 106.4 | 67.1 | 82.3 | 95.3 | 71.2 | 80.5 | 95.3 | 83.9 | 88.3 |
| 0960 | Flooring | 126.8 | 45.8 | 104.8 | 119.8 | 60.6 | 103.7 | 132.5 | 98.4 | 123.2 | 132.5 | 69.4 | 115.3 | 109.7 | 66.5 | 97.9 | 119.8 | 93.0 | 112.5 |
| 0970, 0990 | Wall Finishes & Painting/Coating | 109.4 | 78.8 | 91.0 | 109.4 | 56.4 | 77.6 | 109.4 | 96.7 | 101.8 | 109.5 | 50.1 | 73.8 | 109.4 | 64.5 | 82.4 | 109.4 | 82.2 | 93.0 |
| 09 | FINISHES | 116.3 | 73.9 | 94.1 | 109.3 | 59.6 | 83.3 | 118.3 | 94.8 | 106.0 | 121.1 | 66.4 | 92.5 | 112.8 | 70.6 | 90.7 | 114.2 | 83.9 | 98.3 |
| COVERS | DIVS. 10 - 14, 25, 28, 41, 43, 44 | 140.0 | 75.7 | 126.8 | 140.0 | 69.5 | 125.6 | 140.0 | 81.9 | 128.1 | 140.0 | 72.4 | 126.2 | 140.0 | 72.4 | 126.1 | 140.0 | 74.1 | 126.5 |
| 21, 22, 23 | FIRE SUPPRESSION, PLUMBING & HVAC | 104.0 | 74.4 | 91.9 | 104.0 | 79.5 | 94.0 | 101.1 | 94.1 | 98.2 | 101.5 | 68.4 | 87.9 | 104.0 | 89.7 | 98.2 | 104.0 | 101.6 | 103.1 |
| 26, 27, 3370 | ELECTRICAL, COMMUNICATIONS & UTIL. | 123.7 | 76.9 | 100.7 | 126.0 | 65.6 | 96.3 | 129.9 | 97.2 | 113.8 | 132.7 | 68.9 | 101.4 | 122.5 | 67.9 | 95.7 | 126.9 | 91.4 | 109.5 |
| MF2004 | WEIGHTED AVERAGE | 119.1 | 80.7 | 102.7 | 113.8 | 70.1 | 95.1 | 113.7 | 96.0 | 106.1 | 125.5 | 71.1 | 102.2 | 116.0 | 76.4 | 99.1 | 121.0 | 87.7 | 106.8 |

# Location Factors

Costs shown in *RSMeans cost data publications* are based on National Averages for materials and installation. To adjust these costs to a specific location, simply multiply the base cost by the factor and divide by 100 for that city. The data is arranged alphabetically by state and postal zip code numbers. For a city not listed, use the factor for a nearby city with similar economic characteristics.

| STATE/ZIP | CITY | MAT. | INST. | TOTAL |
|---|---|---|---|---|
| **ALABAMA** | | | | |
| 350-352 | Birmingham | 96.6 | 76.9 | 88.2 |
| 354 | Tuscaloosa | 96.0 | 61.9 | 81.4 |
| 355 | Jasper | 96.2 | 55.1 | 78.6 |
| 356 | Decatur | 95.9 | 61.3 | 81.1 |
| 357-358 | Huntsville | 96.0 | 72.8 | 86.0 |
| 359 | Gadsden | 95.9 | 60.8 | 80.9 |
| 360-361 | Montgomery | 96.9 | 60.0 | 81.1 |
| 362 | Anniston | 95.6 | 54.0 | 77.8 |
| 363 | Dothan | 96.2 | 53.3 | 77.8 |
| 364 | Evergreen | 95.6 | 58.4 | 79.7 |
| 365-366 | Mobile | 97.0 | 67.4 | 84.3 |
| 367 | Selma | 95.9 | 55.3 | 78.5 |
| 368 | Phenix City | 96.6 | 60.5 | 81.2 |
| 369 | Butler | 96.0 | 56.6 | 79.2 |
| **ALASKA** | | | | |
| 995-996 | Anchorage | 131.4 | 114.0 | 124.0 |
| 997 | Fairbanks | 129.0 | 116.1 | 123.5 |
| 998 | Juneau | 130.0 | 112.1 | 122.3 |
| 999 | Ketchikan | 141.8 | 111.7 | 128.9 |
| **ARIZONA** | | | | |
| 850,853 | Phoenix | 100.8 | 73.5 | 89.1 |
| 852 | Mesa/Tempe | 100.1 | 67.8 | 86.3 |
| 855 | Globe | 100.8 | 64.3 | 85.2 |
| 856-857 | Tucson | 98.9 | 71.2 | 87.1 |
| 859 | Show Low | 100.9 | 65.6 | 85.8 |
| 860 | Flagstaff | 101.2 | 71.9 | 88.7 |
| 863 | Prescott | 98.9 | 65.0 | 84.4 |
| 864 | Kingman | 97.4 | 70.2 | 85.8 |
| 865 | Chambers | 97.4 | 65.8 | 83.9 |
| **ARKANSAS** | | | | |
| 716 | Pine Bluff | 96.2 | 67.6 | 84.0 |
| 717 | Camden | 94.2 | 44.5 | 72.9 |
| 718 | Texarkana | 95.4 | 49.2 | 75.6 |
| 719 | Hot Springs | 93.4 | 48.0 | 74.0 |
| 720-722 | Little Rock | 96.1 | 71.1 | 85.4 |
| 723 | West Memphis | 95.9 | 61.2 | 81.1 |
| 724 | Jonesboro | 96.3 | 61.7 | 81.5 |
| 725 | Batesville | 94.3 | 54.7 | 77.3 |
| 726 | Harrison | 95.6 | 55.5 | 78.5 |
| 727 | Fayetteville | 93.0 | 55.1 | 76.8 |
| 728 | Russellville | 94.2 | 57.2 | 78.4 |
| 729 | Fort Smith | 96.8 | 60.8 | 81.4 |
| **CALIFORNIA** | | | | |
| 900-902 | Los Angeles | 103.3 | 115.1 | 108.3 |
| 903-905 | Inglewood | 99.0 | 109.5 | 103.5 |
| 906-908 | Long Beach | 100.8 | 109.5 | 104.5 |
| 910-912 | Pasadena | 99.1 | 109.6 | 103.6 |
| 913-916 | Van Nuys | 102.5 | 109.6 | 105.5 |
| 917-918 | Alhambra | 101.5 | 109.6 | 105.0 |
| 919-921 | San Diego | 103.0 | 108.7 | 105.4 |
| 922 | Palm Springs | 100.0 | 108.7 | 103.7 |
| 923-924 | San Bernardino | 97.6 | 108.2 | 102.1 |
| 925 | Riverside | 102.1 | 112.5 | 106.5 |
| 926-927 | Santa Ana | 99.6 | 108.6 | 103.5 |
| 928 | Anaheim | 101.9 | 114.6 | 107.4 |
| 930 | Oxnard | 103.5 | 112.4 | 107.3 |
| 931 | Santa Barbara | 102.5 | 112.2 | 106.7 |
| 932-933 | Bakersfield | 102.6 | 109.7 | 105.6 |
| 934 | San Luis Obispo | 103.5 | 107.1 | 105.0 |
| 935 | Mojave | 100.4 | 106.0 | 102.8 |
| 936-938 | Fresno | 103.9 | 112.3 | 107.5 |
| 939 | Salinas | 104.3 | 115.1 | 108.9 |
| 940-941 | San Francisco | 112.4 | 137.5 | 123.2 |
| 942,956-958 | Sacramento | 106.0 | 113.6 | 109.2 |
| 943 | Palo Alto | 105.0 | 126.3 | 114.1 |
| 944 | San Mateo | 108.1 | 127.9 | 116.6 |
| 945 | Vallejo | 105.1 | 122.4 | 112.5 |
| 946 | Oakland | 110.2 | 127.3 | 117.5 |
| 947 | Berkeley | 109.9 | 125.0 | 116.3 |
| 948 | Richmond | 109.1 | 125.6 | 116.2 |
| 949 | San Rafael | 110.3 | 126.5 | 117.3 |
| 950 | Santa Cruz | 109.2 | 115.2 | 111.8 |

| STATE/ZIP | CITY | MAT. | INST. | TOTAL |
|---|---|---|---|---|
| **CALIFORNIA (CONT'D)** | | | | |
| 951 | San Jose | 107.0 | 130.4 | 117.0 |
| 952 | Stockton | 104.1 | 112.1 | 107.5 |
| 953 | Modesto | 104.0 | 111.6 | 107.3 |
| 954 | Santa Rosa | 104.3 | 126.6 | 113.8 |
| 955 | Eureka | 105.8 | 108.8 | 107.1 |
| 959 | Marysville | 105.1 | 110.4 | 107.3 |
| 960 | Redding | 106.5 | 108.8 | 107.5 |
| 961 | Susanville | 105.7 | 109.2 | 107.2 |
| **COLORADO** | | | | |
| 800-802 | Denver | 100.3 | 85.8 | 94.1 |
| 803 | Boulder | 97.5 | 84.5 | 91.9 |
| 804 | Golden | 99.7 | 83.2 | 92.7 |
| 805 | Fort Collins | 100.8 | 79.5 | 91.7 |
| 806 | Greeley | 98.3 | 68.7 | 85.6 |
| 807 | Fort Morgan | 98.3 | 83.0 | 91.7 |
| 808-809 | Colorado Springs | 100.1 | 83.4 | 92.9 |
| 810 | Pueblo | 101.1 | 81.2 | 92.6 |
| 811 | Alamosa | 102.7 | 77.5 | 91.9 |
| 812 | Salida | 102.6 | 78.4 | 92.2 |
| 813 | Durango | 103.1 | 78.2 | 92.4 |
| 814 | Montrose | 101.6 | 76.5 | 90.9 |
| 815 | Grand Junction | 104.9 | 74.0 | 91.7 |
| 816 | Glenwood Springs | 102.7 | 80.0 | 93.0 |
| **CONNECTICUT** | | | | |
| 060 | New Britain | 99.8 | 120.7 | 108.7 |
| 061 | Hartford | 100.9 | 120.8 | 109.4 |
| 062 | Willimantic | 100.3 | 119.9 | 108.7 |
| 063 | New London | 96.8 | 119.7 | 106.6 |
| 064 | Meriden | 98.8 | 121.0 | 108.3 |
| 065 | New Haven | 101.6 | 120.5 | 109.7 |
| 066 | Bridgeport | 100.8 | 121.1 | 109.5 |
| 067 | Waterbury | 100.4 | 120.4 | 108.9 |
| 068 | Norwalk | 100.3 | 120.7 | 109.0 |
| 069 | Stamford | 100.5 | 126.0 | 111.4 |
| **D.C.** | | | | |
| 200-205 | Washington | 104.7 | 91.7 | 99.1 |
| **DELAWARE** | | | | |
| 197 | Newark | 101.0 | 108.4 | 104.2 |
| 198 | Wilmington | 100.6 | 108.5 | 104.0 |
| 199 | Dover | 101.6 | 108.4 | 104.5 |
| **FLORIDA** | | | | |
| 320,322 | Jacksonville | 97.9 | 64.5 | 83.6 |
| 321 | Daytona Beach | 98.1 | 77.0 | 89.1 |
| 323 | Tallahassee | 98.2 | 53.8 | 79.2 |
| 324 | Panama City | 99.3 | 49.2 | 77.9 |
| 325 | Pensacola | 102.0 | 62.5 | 85.1 |
| 326,344 | Gainesville | 99.6 | 67.0 | 85.7 |
| 327-328,347 | Orlando | 101.0 | 73.0 | 89.0 |
| 329 | Melbourne | 100.9 | 80.7 | 92.2 |
| 330-332,340 | Miami | 99.5 | 75.9 | 89.4 |
| 333 | Fort Lauderdale | 97.5 | 74.1 | 87.5 |
| 334,349 | West Palm Beach | 96.4 | 69.9 | 85.1 |
| 335-336,346 | Tampa | 99.1 | 80.9 | 91.3 |
| 337 | St. Petersburg | 101.4 | 59.2 | 83.4 |
| 338 | Lakeland | 98.4 | 79.9 | 90.5 |
| 339,341 | Fort Myers | 97.7 | 71.7 | 86.6 |
| 342 | Sarasota | 99.4 | 72.8 | 88.0 |
| **GEORGIA** | | | | |
| 300-303,399 | Atlanta | 98.1 | 78.2 | 89.6 |
| 304 | Statesboro | 98.0 | 48.3 | 76.8 |
| 305 | Gainesville | 96.8 | 64.6 | 83.0 |
| 306 | Athens | 96.2 | 67.3 | 83.8 |
| 307 | Dalton | 98.2 | 53.3 | 79.0 |
| 308-309 | Augusta | 96.8 | 65.0 | 83.2 |
| 310-312 | Macon | 95.6 | 66.3 | 83.0 |
| 313-314 | Savannah | 97.7 | 61.9 | 82.4 |
| 315 | Waycross | 97.0 | 57.9 | 80.3 |
| 316 | Valdosta | 96.8 | 50.8 | 77.1 |
| 317,398 | Albany | 96.9 | 61.4 | 81.7 |
| 318-319 | Columbus | 96.9 | 67.5 | 84.3 |

# Location Factors

| STATE/ZIP | CITY | MAT. | INST. | TOTAL |
|---|---|---|---|---|
| **HAWAII** | | | | |
| 967 | Hilo | 115.3 | 122.7 | 118.5 |
| 968 | Honolulu | 119.7 | 122.7 | 121.0 |
| **STATES & POSS.** | | | | |
| 969 | Guam | 139.3 | 65.7 | 107.8 |
| **IDAHO** | | | | |
| 832 | Pocatello | 101.2 | 74.2 | 89.7 |
| 833 | Twin Falls | 102.2 | 55.0 | 82.0 |
| 834 | Idaho Falls | 99.5 | 61.0 | 83.0 |
| 835 | Lewiston | 108.9 | 82.0 | 97.4 |
| 836-837 | Boise | 100.2 | 76.2 | 89.9 |
| 838 | Coeur d'Alene | 108.2 | 79.2 | 95.8 |
| **ILLINOIS** | | | | |
| 600-603 | North Suburban | 98.1 | 120.2 | 107.6 |
| 604 | Joliet | 98.1 | 117.2 | 106.3 |
| 605 | South Suburban | 98.1 | 120.2 | 107.6 |
| 606-608 | Chicago | 98.6 | 136.2 | 114.7 |
| 609 | Kankakee | 94.5 | 106.6 | 99.7 |
| 610-611 | Rockford | 97.1 | 115.0 | 104.7 |
| 612 | Rock Island | 94.9 | 97.4 | 95.9 |
| 613 | La Salle | 96.1 | 109.0 | 101.6 |
| 614 | Galesburg | 95.9 | 100.9 | 98.1 |
| 615-616 | Peoria | 98.1 | 101.2 | 99.5 |
| 617 | Bloomington | 95.2 | 102.5 | 98.3 |
| 618-619 | Champaign | 98.8 | 100.7 | 99.6 |
| 620-622 | East St. Louis | 93.6 | 103.1 | 97.7 |
| 623 | Quincy | 95.1 | 96.7 | 95.8 |
| 624 | Effingham | 94.5 | 99.2 | 96.5 |
| 625 | Decatur | 96.0 | 96.3 | 96.2 |
| 626-627 | Springfield | 96.3 | 94.2 | 95.4 |
| 628 | Centralia | 92.5 | 103.9 | 97.4 |
| 629 | Carbondale | 92.2 | 97.1 | 94.3 |
| **INDIANA** | | | | |
| 460 | Anderson | 93.9 | 83.2 | 89.3 |
| 461-462 | Indianapolis | 97.3 | 87.1 | 93.0 |
| 463-464 | Gary | 95.5 | 104.0 | 99.2 |
| 465-466 | South Bend | 93.4 | 84.4 | 89.5 |
| 467-468 | Fort Wayne | 94.5 | 80.6 | 88.6 |
| 469 | Kokomo | 92.1 | 83.2 | 88.3 |
| 470 | Lawrenceburg | 91.8 | 79.5 | 86.5 |
| 471 | New Albany | 93.2 | 76.7 | 86.2 |
| 472 | Columbus | 95.5 | 81.8 | 89.6 |
| 473 | Muncie | 95.9 | 81.8 | 89.8 |
| 474 | Bloomington | 97.3 | 81.0 | 90.4 |
| 475 | Washington | 93.7 | 85.5 | 90.2 |
| 476-477 | Evansville | 94.8 | 87.1 | 91.5 |
| 478 | Terre Haute | 95.5 | 86.4 | 91.6 |
| 479 | Lafayette | 95.1 | 81.6 | 89.4 |
| **IOWA** | | | | |
| 500-503,509 | Des Moines | 97.4 | 78.9 | 89.5 |
| 504 | Mason City | 96.4 | 62.8 | 82.0 |
| 505 | Fort Dodge | 96.6 | 58.2 | 80.2 |
| 506-507 | Waterloo | 98.0 | 59.6 | 81.6 |
| 508 | Creston | 96.8 | 62.6 | 82.2 |
| 510-511 | Sioux City | 98.7 | 70.6 | 86.7 |
| 512 | Sibley | 97.6 | 48.2 | 76.5 |
| 513 | Spencer | 99.2 | 46.9 | 76.8 |
| 514 | Carroll | 96.2 | 52.2 | 77.4 |
| 515 | Council Bluffs | 99.9 | 76.1 | 89.7 |
| 516 | Shenandoah | 96.9 | 50.1 | 76.9 |
| 520 | Dubuque | 98.2 | 77.8 | 89.4 |
| 521 | Decorah | 97.2 | 49.4 | 76.8 |
| 522-524 | Cedar Rapids | 99.1 | 83.2 | 92.3 |
| 525 | Ottumwa | 97.3 | 71.0 | 86.0 |
| 526 | Burlington | 96.4 | 72.6 | 86.2 |
| 527-528 | Davenport | 97.9 | 93.0 | 95.8 |
| **KANSAS** | | | | |
| 660-662 | Kansas City | 98.1 | 95.1 | 96.8 |
| 664-666 | Topeka | 98.0 | 67.4 | 84.9 |
| 667 | Fort Scott | 96.9 | 73.4 | 86.8 |
| 668 | Emporia | 97.0 | 61.0 | 81.6 |
| 669 | Belleville | 98.8 | 62.5 | 83.2 |
| 670-672 | Wichita | 96.9 | 66.2 | 83.8 |
| 673 | Independence | 98.5 | 64.9 | 84.1 |
| 674 | Salina | 98.5 | 63.1 | 83.4 |
| 675 | Hutchinson | 93.8 | 62.7 | 80.5 |
| 676 | Hays | 97.9 | 64.1 | 83.4 |
| 677 | Colby | 98.7 | 63.9 | 83.8 |

| STATE/ZIP | CITY | MAT. | INST. | TOTAL |
|---|---|---|---|---|
| **KANSAS (CONT'D)** | | | | |
| 678 | Dodge City | 99.8 | 65.6 | 85.2 |
| 679 | Liberal | 97.7 | 63.7 | 83.2 |
| **KENTUCKY** | | | | |
| 400-402 | Louisville | 96.2 | 83.0 | 90.6 |
| 403-405 | Lexington | 95.5 | 79.4 | 88.6 |
| 406 | Frankfort | 95.7 | 81.1 | 89.5 |
| 407-409 | Corbin | 93.0 | 67.6 | 82.2 |
| 410 | Covington | 93.7 | 102.0 | 97.2 |
| 411-412 | Ashland | 92.3 | 97.4 | 94.5 |
| 413-414 | Campton | 93.9 | 68.1 | 82.8 |
| 415-416 | Pikeville | 94.8 | 83.8 | 90.0 |
| 417-418 | Hazard | 93.2 | 60.1 | 79.0 |
| 420 | Paducah | 91.8 | 88.4 | 90.3 |
| 421-422 | Bowling Green | 94.0 | 85.8 | 90.5 |
| 423 | Owensboro | 93.9 | 85.8 | 90.4 |
| 424 | Henderson | 91.5 | 88.3 | 90.1 |
| 425-426 | Somerset | 91.2 | 72.4 | 83.2 |
| 427 | Elizabethtown | 90.7 | 82.7 | 87.3 |
| **LOUISIANA** | | | | |
| 700-701 | New Orleans | 101.0 | 68.9 | 87.2 |
| 703 | Thibodaux | 99.1 | 64.9 | 84.5 |
| 704 | Hammond | 96.4 | 59.2 | 80.5 |
| 705 | Lafayette | 98.5 | 59.2 | 81.7 |
| 706 | Lake Charles | 98.6 | 62.3 | 83.1 |
| 707-708 | Baton Rouge | 99.1 | 64.1 | 84.1 |
| 710-711 | Shreveport | 95.1 | 59.0 | 79.6 |
| 712 | Monroe | 96.4 | 56.4 | 79.3 |
| 713-714 | Alexandria | 96.5 | 55.9 | 79.2 |
| **MAINE** | | | | |
| 039 | Kittery | 94.0 | 75.7 | 86.2 |
| 040-041 | Portland | 98.7 | 75.3 | 88.7 |
| 042 | Lewiston | 96.8 | 75.3 | 87.6 |
| 043 | Augusta | 96.3 | 75.5 | 87.4 |
| 044 | Bangor | 96.5 | 75.3 | 87.4 |
| 045 | Bath | 95.2 | 75.7 | 86.8 |
| 046 | Machias | 94.7 | 75.1 | 86.3 |
| 047 | Houlton | 94.9 | 75.7 | 86.7 |
| 048 | Rockland | 93.9 | 75.7 | 86.1 |
| 049 | Waterville | 95.2 | 75.6 | 86.8 |
| **MARYLAND** | | | | |
| 206 | Waldorf | 100.9 | 69.9 | 87.6 |
| 207-208 | College Park | 100.9 | 80.2 | 92.1 |
| 209 | Silver Spring | 100.1 | 75.3 | 89.5 |
| 210-212 | Baltimore | 97.9 | 84.7 | 92.2 |
| 214 | Annapolis | 97.9 | 79.0 | 89.8 |
| 215 | Cumberland | 94.0 | 77.4 | 86.9 |
| 216 | Easton | 95.7 | 42.8 | 73.1 |
| 217 | Hagerstown | 94.6 | 78.3 | 87.6 |
| 218 | Salisbury | 96.0 | 50.6 | 76.6 |
| 219 | Elkton | 93.1 | 62.3 | 80.0 |
| **MASSACHUSETTS** | | | | |
| 010-011 | Springfield | 98.8 | 104.0 | 101.0 |
| 012 | Pittsfield | 98.3 | 101.4 | 99.7 |
| 013 | Greenfield | 96.5 | 103.0 | 99.2 |
| 014 | Fitchburg | 95.2 | 119.5 | 105.6 |
| 015-016 | Worcester | 98.7 | 120.8 | 108.1 |
| 017 | Framingham | 94.7 | 124.9 | 107.6 |
| 018 | Lowell | 98.1 | 123.6 | 109.0 |
| 019 | Lawrence | 99.4 | 122.2 | 109.1 |
| 020-022, 024 | Boston | 101.0 | 136.9 | 116.4 |
| 023 | Brockton | 99.6 | 119.7 | 108.2 |
| 025 | Buzzards Bay | 94.1 | 118.2 | 104.4 |
| 026 | Hyannis | 96.7 | 118.2 | 105.9 |
| 027 | New Bedford | 98.8 | 118.4 | 107.2 |
| **MICHIGAN** | | | | |
| 480,483 | Royal Oak | 93.0 | 107.5 | 99.2 |
| 481 | Ann Arbor | 94.9 | 106.3 | 99.8 |
| 482 | Detroit | 96.6 | 113.6 | 103.9 |
| 484-485 | Flint | 94.6 | 99.5 | 96.7 |
| 486 | Saginaw | 94.2 | 92.3 | 93.4 |
| 487 | Bay City | 94.4 | 92.4 | 93.5 |
| 488-489 | Lansing | 94.9 | 95.0 | 95.0 |
| 490 | Battle Creek | 94.9 | 88.8 | 92.3 |
| 491 | Kalamazoo | 95.2 | 86.5 | 91.5 |
| 492 | Jackson | 93.5 | 93.8 | 93.6 |
| 493,495 | Grand Rapids | 95.6 | 64.8 | 82.4 |
| 494 | Muskegon | 93.9 | 83.4 | 89.4 |

| STATE/ZIP | CITY | MAT. | INST. | TOTAL |
|---|---|---|---|---|
| **MICHIGAN (CONT'D)** | | | | |
| 496 | Traverse City | 92.9 | 70.7 | 83.4 |
| 497 | Gaylord | 94.1 | 73.7 | 85.4 |
| 498-499 | Iron mountain | 96.0 | 85.6 | 91.6 |
| **MINNESOTA** | | | | |
| 550-551 | Saint Paul | 99.1 | 121.1 | 108.5 |
| 553-555 | Minneapolis | 100.0 | 124.9 | 110.7 |
| 556-558 | Duluth | 98.4 | 112.1 | 104.2 |
| 559 | Rochester | 98.7 | 107.7 | 102.6 |
| 560 | Mankato | 96.6 | 106.4 | 100.8 |
| 561 | Windom | 95.3 | 79.5 | 88.5 |
| 562 | Willmar | 94.8 | 84.5 | 90.4 |
| 563 | St. Cloud | 95.9 | 120.5 | 106.4 |
| 564 | Brainerd | 96.5 | 102.7 | 99.1 |
| 565 | Detroit Lakes | 98.3 | 97.5 | 98.0 |
| 566 | Bemidji | 97.7 | 98.9 | 98.2 |
| 567 | Thief River Falls | 97.3 | 94.5 | 96.1 |
| **MISSISSIPPI** | | | | |
| 386 | Clarksdale | 95.8 | 55.0 | 78.4 |
| 387 | Greenville | 99.2 | 66.6 | 85.3 |
| 388 | Tupelo | 97.2 | 58.8 | 80.8 |
| 389 | Greenwood | 97.1 | 55.5 | 79.3 |
| 390-392 | Jackson | 97.4 | 65.8 | 83.9 |
| 393 | Meridian | 95.9 | 67.2 | 83.6 |
| 394 | Laurel | 97.2 | 58.3 | 80.5 |
| 395 | Biloxi | 97.6 | 63.4 | 83.0 |
| 396 | Mccomb | 95.6 | 60.5 | 80.6 |
| 397 | Columbus | 97.1 | 58.0 | 80.4 |
| **MISSOURI** | | | | |
| 630-631 | St. Louis | 97.7 | 110.9 | 103.4 |
| 633 | Bowling Green | 96.6 | 93.2 | 95.2 |
| 634 | Hannibal | 95.4 | 82.5 | 89.9 |
| 635 | Kirksville | 98.2 | 75.8 | 88.6 |
| 636 | Flat River | 97.6 | 94.1 | 96.1 |
| 637 | Cape Girardeau | 97.3 | 90.1 | 94.2 |
| 638 | Sikeston | 95.5 | 79.6 | 88.7 |
| 639 | Poplar Bluff | 95.0 | 80.2 | 88.7 |
| 640-641 | Kansas City | 98.9 | 106.9 | 102.4 |
| 644-645 | St. Joseph | 98.1 | 93.4 | 96.1 |
| 646 | Chillicothe | 95.3 | 70.8 | 84.8 |
| 647 | Harrisonville | 94.9 | 102.2 | 98.0 |
| 648 | Joplin | 96.9 | 69.8 | 85.3 |
| 650-651 | Jefferson City | 94.7 | 88.2 | 91.9 |
| 652 | Columbia | 96.2 | 90.2 | 93.6 |
| 653 | Sedalia | 95.6 | 84.6 | 90.9 |
| 654-655 | Rolla | 94.3 | 74.9 | 86.0 |
| 656-658 | Springfield | 97.2 | 79.6 | 89.7 |
| **MONTANA** | | | | |
| 590-591 | Billings | 102.1 | 73.2 | 89.7 |
| 592 | Wolf Point | 101.8 | 65.9 | 86.5 |
| 593 | Miles City | 99.6 | 66.6 | 85.4 |
| 594 | Great Falls | 103.4 | 73.5 | 90.6 |
| 595 | Havre | 100.7 | 66.1 | 85.9 |
| 596 | Helena | 101.6 | 69.7 | 88.0 |
| 597 | Butte | 101.8 | 73.4 | 89.7 |
| 598 | Missoula | 99.2 | 69.3 | 86.4 |
| 599 | Kalispell | 98.5 | 67.1 | 85.1 |
| **NEBRASKA** | | | | |
| 680-681 | Omaha | 98.4 | 80.6 | 90.8 |
| 683-685 | Lincoln | 96.7 | 78.9 | 89.1 |
| 686 | Columbus | 95.8 | 73.8 | 86.4 |
| 687 | Norfolk | 97.4 | 79.5 | 89.7 |
| 688 | Grand Island | 97.2 | 81.2 | 90.4 |
| 689 | Hastings | 96.8 | 81.1 | 90.1 |
| 690 | Mccook | 96.6 | 73.0 | 86.5 |
| 691 | North Platte | 96.7 | 81.2 | 90.0 |
| 692 | Valentine | 98.8 | 69.0 | 86.0 |
| 693 | Alliance | 98.8 | 68.0 | 85.6 |
| **NEVADA** | | | | |
| 889-891 | Las Vegas | 99.1 | 109.2 | 103.4 |
| 893 | Ely | 99.5 | 73.9 | 88.6 |
| 894-895 | Reno | 99.6 | 95.8 | 98.0 |
| 897 | Carson City | 99.5 | 95.5 | 97.8 |
| 898 | Elko | 98.2 | 79.8 | 90.3 |
| **NEW HAMPSHIRE** | | | | |
| 030 | Nashua | 99.0 | 89.3 | 94.9 |
| 031 | Manchester | 99.6 | 89.3 | 95.2 |

| STATE/ZIP | CITY | MAT. | INST. | TOTAL |
|---|---|---|---|---|
| **NEW HAMPSHIRE (CONT'D)** | | | | |
| 032-033 | Concord | 97.5 | 85.4 | 92.4 |
| 034 | Keene | 96.0 | 54.1 | 78.1 |
| 035 | Littleton | 95.9 | 61.9 | 81.4 |
| 036 | Charleston | 95.5 | 51.6 | 76.7 |
| 037 | Claremont | 94.6 | 51.6 | 76.2 |
| 038 | Portsmouth | 96.4 | 91.8 | 94.4 |
| **NEW JERSEY** | | | | |
| 070-071 | Newark | 100.6 | 123.9 | 110.6 |
| 072 | Elizabeth | 99.3 | 123.4 | 109.6 |
| 073 | Jersey City | 98.1 | 124.5 | 109.4 |
| 074-075 | Paterson | 99.9 | 124.0 | 110.2 |
| 076 | Hackensack | 98.0 | 124.5 | 109.3 |
| 077 | Long Branch | 97.7 | 122.2 | 108.2 |
| 078 | Dover | 98.3 | 124.2 | 109.4 |
| 079 | Summit | 98.2 | 123.4 | 109.0 |
| 080,083 | Vineland | 96.3 | 118.6 | 105.8 |
| 081 | Camden | 98.1 | 119.1 | 107.1 |
| 082,084 | Atlantic City | 96.9 | 118.6 | 106.2 |
| 085-086 | Trenton | 97.6 | 122.9 | 108.4 |
| 087 | Point Pleasant | 98.3 | 122.2 | 108.5 |
| 088-089 | New Brunswick | 98.8 | 123.4 | 109.3 |
| **NEW MEXICO** | | | | |
| 870-872 | Albuquerque | 99.5 | 76.1 | 89.5 |
| 873 | Gallup | 99.8 | 76.1 | 89.7 |
| 874 | Farmington | 100.0 | 76.1 | 89.8 |
| 875 | Santa Fe | 100.0 | 76.1 | 89.8 |
| 877 | Las Vegas | 98.3 | 75.9 | 88.7 |
| 878 | Socorro | 97.8 | 76.1 | 88.6 |
| 879 | Truth/Consequences | 98.1 | 70.4 | 86.2 |
| 880 | Las Cruces | 96.6 | 67.9 | 84.3 |
| 881 | Clovis | 98.4 | 74.5 | 88.2 |
| 882 | Roswell | 100.0 | 74.6 | 89.1 |
| 883 | Carrizozo | 100.6 | 76.1 | 90.1 |
| 884 | Tucumcari | 99.3 | 74.5 | 88.7 |
| **NEW YORK** | | | | |
| 100-102 | New York | 105.4 | 166.0 | 131.3 |
| 103 | Staten Island | 101.3 | 157.6 | 125.4 |
| 104 | Bronx | 99.3 | 158.9 | 124.8 |
| 105 | Mount Vernon | 99.5 | 135.0 | 114.7 |
| 106 | White Plains | 99.2 | 135.0 | 114.5 |
| 107 | Yonkers | 104.1 | 135.1 | 117.4 |
| 108 | New Rochelle | 99.9 | 135.0 | 114.9 |
| 109 | Suffern | 99.7 | 121.1 | 108.9 |
| 110 | Queens | 101.6 | 158.9 | 126.1 |
| 111 | Long Island City | 103.3 | 158.9 | 127.1 |
| 112 | Brooklyn | 103.5 | 158.9 | 127.2 |
| 113 | Flushing | 103.8 | 158.9 | 127.4 |
| 114 | Jamaica | 101.9 | 158.9 | 126.3 |
| 115,117,118 | Hicksville | 104.4 | 144.7 | 119.9 |
| 116 | Far Rockaway | 104.0 | 158.9 | 127.5 |
| 119 | Riverhead | 102.3 | 144.7 | 120.4 |
| 120-122 | Albany | 97.3 | 93.2 | 95.5 |
| 123 | Schenectady | 98.1 | 92.7 | 95.8 |
| 124 | Kingston | 101.6 | 113.4 | 106.6 |
| 125-126 | Poughkeepsie | 100.7 | 117.1 | 107.7 |
| 127 | Monticello | 100.0 | 117.5 | 107.5 |
| 128 | Glens Falls | 92.8 | 89.4 | 91.4 |
| 129 | Plattsburgh | 97.4 | 84.5 | 91.9 |
| 130-132 | Syracuse | 99.1 | 92.1 | 96.1 |
| 133-135 | Utica | 97.0 | 87.8 | 93.0 |
| 136 | Watertown | 98.8 | 83.0 | 92.0 |
| 137-139 | Binghamton | 98.6 | 86.3 | 93.3 |
| 140-142 | Buffalo | 100.2 | 102.7 | 101.3 |
| 143 | Niagara Falls | 98.2 | 100.2 | 99.1 |
| 144-146 | Rochester | 99.6 | 96.0 | 98.1 |
| 147 | Jamestown | 97.1 | 82.9 | 91.0 |
| 148-149 | Elmira | 97.0 | 81.7 | 90.4 |
| **NORTH CAROLINA** | | | | |
| 270,272-274 | Greensboro | 99.6 | 51.2 | 78.9 |
| 271 | Winston-Salem | 99.3 | 50.5 | 78.4 |
| 275-276 | Raleigh | 99.5 | 51.9 | 79.1 |
| 277 | Durham | 100.9 | 52.2 | 80.1 |
| 278 | Rocky Mount | 97.1 | 41.6 | 73.4 |
| 279 | Elizabeth City | 98.0 | 43.2 | 74.6 |
| 280 | Gastonia | 98.4 | 49.8 | 77.6 |
| 281-282 | Charlotte | 99.7 | 52.6 | 79.5 |
| 283 | Fayetteville | 100.8 | 52.6 | 80.2 |
| 284 | Wilmington | 97.1 | 49.8 | 76.9 |
| 285 | Kinston | 95.4 | 43.4 | 73.1 |

# Location Factors

| STATE/ZIP | CITY | MAT. | INST. | TOTAL |
|---|---|---|---|---|
| **NORTH CAROLINA (CONT'D)** | | | | |
| 286 | Hickory | 95.7 | 46.1 | 74.5 |
| 287-288 | Asheville | 97.5 | 49.8 | 77.1 |
| 289 | Murphy | 96.7 | 35.2 | 70.4 |
| **NORTH DAKOTA** | | | | |
| 580-581 | Fargo | 101.1 | 63.4 | 85.0 |
| 582 | Grand Forks | 101.1 | 56.1 | 81.8 |
| 583 | Devils Lake | 100.7 | 58.4 | 82.6 |
| 584 | Jamestown | 100.7 | 49.8 | 79.0 |
| 585 | Bismarck | 99.4 | 64.3 | 84.4 |
| 586 | Dickinson | 101.6 | 61.4 | 84.4 |
| 587 | Minot | 101.1 | 68.9 | 87.4 |
| 588 | Williston | 100.0 | 61.4 | 83.5 |
| **OHIO** | | | | |
| 430-432 | Columbus | 97.4 | 89.2 | 93.9 |
| 433 | Marion | 94.0 | 85.3 | 90.3 |
| 434-436 | Toledo | 97.6 | 101.0 | 99.1 |
| 437-438 | Zanesville | 94.5 | 84.5 | 90.2 |
| 439 | Steubenville | 95.7 | 93.5 | 94.7 |
| 440 | Lorain | 96.6 | 95.4 | 96.1 |
| 441 | Cleveland | 96.9 | 104.2 | 100.0 |
| 442-443 | Akron | 97.6 | 96.2 | 97.0 |
| 444-445 | Youngstown | 97.0 | 91.8 | 94.8 |
| 446-447 | Canton | 97.1 | 87.3 | 92.9 |
| 448-449 | Mansfield | 94.6 | 90.6 | 92.9 |
| 450 | Hamilton | 95.6 | 87.0 | 91.9 |
| 451-452 | Cincinnati | 95.9 | 89.0 | 92.9 |
| 453-454 | Dayton | 95.8 | 88.1 | 92.5 |
| 455 | Springfield | 95.7 | 88.2 | 92.5 |
| 456 | Chillicothe | 94.8 | 94.2 | 94.6 |
| 457 | Athens | 97.8 | 77.6 | 89.2 |
| 458 | Lima | 98.1 | 87.7 | 93.7 |
| **OKLAHOMA** | | | | |
| 730-731 | Oklahoma City | 97.3 | 61.5 | 82.0 |
| 734 | Ardmore | 95.1 | 61.0 | 80.5 |
| 735 | Lawton | 97.3 | 62.4 | 82.4 |
| 736 | Clinton | 96.5 | 59.4 | 80.6 |
| 737 | Enid | 97.0 | 59.4 | 80.9 |
| 738 | Woodward | 95.3 | 59.5 | 80.0 |
| 739 | Guymon | 96.4 | 31.6 | 68.7 |
| 740-741 | Tulsa | 97.1 | 57.1 | 80.0 |
| 743 | Miami | 94.0 | 65.7 | 81.9 |
| 744 | Muskogee | 96.3 | 41.6 | 72.9 |
| 745 | Mcalester | 93.6 | 53.1 | 76.3 |
| 746 | Ponca City | 94.2 | 61.5 | 80.2 |
| 747 | Durant | 94.3 | 60.2 | 79.7 |
| 748 | Shawnee | 95.8 | 57.5 | 79.4 |
| 749 | Poteau | 93.2 | 63.6 | 80.6 |
| **OREGON** | | | | |
| 970-972 | Portland | 101.8 | 104.1 | 102.8 |
| 973 | Salem | 101.0 | 102.1 | 101.5 |
| 974 | Eugene | 101.4 | 101.4 | 101.4 |
| 975 | Medford | 103.1 | 99.9 | 101.8 |
| 976 | Klamath Falls | 103.5 | 99.6 | 101.9 |
| 977 | Bend | 102.3 | 101.5 | 101.9 |
| 978 | Pendleton | 97.0 | 101.8 | 99.1 |
| 979 | Vale | 94.6 | 92.6 | 93.8 |
| **PENNSYLVANIA** | | | | |
| 150-152 | Pittsburgh | 97.3 | 100.5 | 98.7 |
| 153 | Washington | 94.6 | 99.8 | 96.8 |
| 154 | Uniontown | 94.8 | 96.3 | 95.4 |
| 155 | Bedford | 95.9 | 89.9 | 93.3 |
| 156 | Greensburg | 95.8 | 97.2 | 96.4 |
| 157 | Indiana | 94.7 | 96.4 | 95.4 |
| 158 | Dubois | 96.2 | 93.2 | 94.9 |
| 159 | Johnstown | 95.8 | 94.0 | 95.0 |
| 160 | Butler | 92.6 | 97.5 | 94.7 |
| 161 | New Castle | 92.6 | 96.7 | 94.4 |
| 162 | Kittanning | 93.1 | 100.1 | 96.1 |
| 163 | Oil City | 92.6 | 94.5 | 93.4 |
| 164-165 | Erie | 94.5 | 92.1 | 93.5 |
| 166 | Altoona | 94.6 | 89.8 | 92.5 |
| 167 | Bradford | 96.0 | 92.0 | 94.3 |
| 168 | State College | 95.6 | 90.6 | 93.5 |
| 169 | Wellsboro | 96.7 | 90.2 | 93.9 |
| 170-171 | Harrisburg | 98.3 | 91.9 | 95.6 |
| 172 | Chambersburg | 96.2 | 88.6 | 92.9 |
| 173-174 | York | 96.3 | 91.9 | 94.4 |
| 175-176 | Lancaster | 94.9 | 87.3 | 91.6 |
| **PENNSYLVANIA (CONT'D)** | | | | |
| 177 | Williamsport | 93.5 | 77.9 | 86.8 |
| 178 | Sunbury | 95.6 | 91.4 | 93.8 |
| 179 | Pottsville | 94.7 | 92.8 | 93.9 |
| 180 | Lehigh Valley | 96.2 | 111.4 | 102.7 |
| 181 | Allentown | 98.0 | 107.8 | 102.2 |
| 182 | Hazleton | 95.6 | 93.3 | 94.6 |
| 183 | Stroudsburg | 95.4 | 99.6 | 97.2 |
| 184-185 | Scranton | 98.8 | 96.4 | 97.8 |
| 186-187 | Wilkes-Barre | 95.3 | 93.9 | 94.7 |
| 188 | Montrose | 95.0 | 94.3 | 94.7 |
| 189 | Doylestown | 95.0 | 117.3 | 104.6 |
| 190-191 | Philadelphia | 101.5 | 133.6 | 115.2 |
| 193 | Westchester | 98.2 | 119.2 | 107.2 |
| 194 | Norristown | 97.0 | 127.8 | 110.2 |
| 195-196 | Reading | 99.0 | 98.2 | 98.6 |
| **PUERTO RICO** | | | | |
| 009 | San Juan | 120.5 | 23.8 | 79.1 |
| **RHODE ISLAND** | | | | |
| 028 | Newport | 98.1 | 111.2 | 103.7 |
| 029 | Providence | 98.8 | 111.2 | 104.1 |
| **SOUTH CAROLINA** | | | | |
| 290-292 | Columbia | 97.5 | 53.9 | 78.9 |
| 293 | Spartanburg | 96.8 | 53.5 | 78.3 |
| 294 | Charleston | 98.3 | 63.3 | 83.3 |
| 295 | Florence | 96.5 | 53.9 | 78.3 |
| 296 | Greenville | 96.6 | 53.5 | 78.2 |
| 297 | Rock Hill | 96.5 | 51.4 | 77.2 |
| 298 | Aiken | 97.5 | 71.5 | 86.4 |
| 299 | Beaufort | 98.3 | 46.4 | 76.1 |
| **SOUTH DAKOTA** | | | | |
| 570-571 | Sioux Falls | 99.3 | 58.1 | 81.7 |
| 572 | Watertown | 98.6 | 51.5 | 78.4 |
| 573 | Mitchell | 97.6 | 51.8 | 78.0 |
| 574 | Aberdeen | 100.0 | 55.3 | 80.9 |
| 575 | Pierre | 99.1 | 53.7 | 79.7 |
| 576 | Mobridge | 98.2 | 51.4 | 78.2 |
| 577 | Rapid City | 99.8 | 52.1 | 79.4 |
| **TENNESSEE** | | | | |
| 370-372 | Nashville | 96.8 | 72.6 | 86.4 |
| 373-374 | Chattanooga | 98.0 | 56.2 | 80.1 |
| 375,380-381 | Memphis | 96.2 | 71.8 | 85.8 |
| 376 | Johnson City | 97.2 | 56.3 | 79.7 |
| 377-379 | Knoxville | 94.3 | 56.8 | 78.2 |
| 382 | Mckenzie | 96.4 | 56.1 | 79.2 |
| 383 | Jackson | 98.2 | 48.6 | 77.0 |
| 384 | Columbia | 94.9 | 58.1 | 79.1 |
| 385 | Cookeville | 96.3 | 59.2 | 80.4 |
| **TEXAS** | | | | |
| 750 | Mckinney | 98.5 | 52.1 | 78.6 |
| 751 | Waxahachie | 98.4 | 55.1 | 79.9 |
| 752-753 | Dallas | 98.8 | 65.8 | 84.6 |
| 754 | Greenville | 98.5 | 38.4 | 72.8 |
| 755 | Texarkana | 97.5 | 51.0 | 77.6 |
| 756 | Longview | 97.9 | 39.9 | 73.1 |
| 757 | Tyler | 98.5 | 54.7 | 79.7 |
| 758 | Palestine | 94.5 | 40.2 | 71.3 |
| 759 | Lufkin | 95.3 | 44.1 | 73.4 |
| 760-761 | Fort Worth | 97.3 | 59.9 | 81.3 |
| 762 | Denton | 97.5 | 48.6 | 76.6 |
| 763 | Wichita Falls | 97.9 | 55.5 | 79.8 |
| 764 | Eastland | 96.7 | 39.4 | 72.2 |
| 765 | Temple | 95.3 | 49.1 | 75.6 |
| 766-767 | Waco | 97.2 | 56.8 | 79.9 |
| 768 | Brownwood | 97.8 | 37.0 | 71.8 |
| 769 | San Angelo | 97.4 | 45.0 | 75.0 |
| 770-772 | Houston | 101.1 | 70.0 | 87.8 |
| 773 | Huntsville | 99.6 | 37.7 | 73.2 |
| 774 | Wharton | 101.1 | 42.4 | 76.0 |
| 775 | Galveston | 99.1 | 69.0 | 86.2 |
| 776-777 | Beaumont | 98.8 | 60.9 | 82.6 |
| 778 | Bryan | 96.2 | 62.0 | 81.6 |
| 779 | Victoria | 101.1 | 44.6 | 76.9 |
| 780 | Laredo | 95.4 | 51.7 | 76.7 |
| 781-782 | San Antonio | 95.7 | 65.0 | 82.6 |
| 783-784 | Corpus Christi | 98.3 | 50.9 | 78.0 |
| 785 | Mc Allen | 98.3 | 45.4 | 75.7 |
| 786-787 | Austin | 95.1 | 60.1 | 80.1 |

# Location Factors

| STATE/ZIP | CITY | MAT. | INST. | TOTAL | STATE/ZIP | CITY | MAT. | INST. | TOTAL |
|---|---|---|---|---|---|---|---|---|---|
| **TEXAS (CONT'D)** | | | | | **WISCONSIN (CONT'D)** | | | | |
| 788 | Del Rio | 97.8 | 31.2 | 69.3 | 538 | Lancaster | 97.0 | 93.3 | 95.4 |
| 789 | Giddings | 95.0 | 39.5 | 71.3 | 539 | Portage | 95.6 | 97.5 | 96.4 |
| 790-791 | Amarillo | 97.8 | 57.5 | 80.5 | 540 | New Richmond | 96.1 | 96.8 | 96.4 |
| 792 | Childress | 97.4 | 50.1 | 77.2 | 541-543 | Green Bay | 100.0 | 93.3 | 97.1 |
| 793-794 | Lubbock | 99.6 | 51.2 | 78.9 | 544 | Wausau | 95.4 | 91.4 | 93.7 |
| 795-796 | Abilene | 97.6 | 50.6 | 77.5 | 545 | Rhinelander | 98.7 | 91.5 | 95.6 |
| 797 | Midland | 99.9 | 47.2 | 77.4 | 546 | La Crosse | 96.4 | 94.1 | 95.4 |
| 798-799,885 | El Paso | 96.6 | 50.2 | 76.8 | 547 | Eau Claire | 98.1 | 95.0 | 96.8 |
| | | | | | 548 | Superior | 95.9 | 99.0 | 97.2 |
| **UTAH** | | | | | 549 | Oshkosh | 96.1 | 92.8 | 94.7 |
| 840-841 | Salt Lake City | 102.5 | 68.0 | 87.8 | | | | | |
| 842,844 | Ogden | 98.1 | 67.3 | 84.9 | **WYOMING** | | | | |
| 843 | Logan | 100.0 | 67.3 | 86.0 | 820 | Cheyenne | 99.7 | 66.5 | 85.5 |
| 845 | Price | 100.7 | 46.8 | 77.6 | 821 | Yellowstone Nat'l Park | 97.3 | 59.8 | 81.3 |
| 846-847 | Provo | 100.5 | 67.9 | 86.5 | 822 | Wheatland | 98.4 | 59.8 | 81.9 |
| | | | | | 823 | Rawlins | 100.0 | 59.5 | 82.7 |
| **VERMONT** | | | | | 824 | Worland | 97.9 | 57.6 | 80.7 |
| 050 | White River Jct. | 97.3 | 57.3 | 80.2 | 825 | Riverton | 99.0 | 57.6 | 81.3 |
| 051 | Bellows Falls | 95.7 | 65.5 | 82.8 | 826 | Casper | 99.7 | 59.6 | 82.5 |
| 052 | Bennington | 96.1 | 68.4 | 84.2 | 827 | Newcastle | 97.7 | 59.5 | 81.4 |
| 053 | Brattleboro | 96.5 | 70.8 | 85.5 | 828 | Sheridan | 100.6 | 61.8 | 84.0 |
| 054 | Burlington | 99.5 | 69.0 | 86.4 | 829-831 | Rock Springs | 101.9 | 57.6 | 82.9 |
| 056 | Montpelier | 96.5 | 69.4 | 84.9 | | | | | |
| 057 | Rutland | 97.9 | 69.4 | 85.7 | **CANADIAN FACTORS (reflect Canadian currency)** | | | | |
| 058 | St. Johnsbury | 97.4 | 57.8 | 80.5 | | | | | |
| 059 | Guildhall | 96.0 | 57.6 | 79.6 | **ALBERTA** | | | | |
| | | | | | | Calgary | 125.6 | 92.7 | 111.5 |
| **VIRGINIA** | | | | | | Edmonton | 126.7 | 92.6 | 112.1 |
| 220-221 | Fairfax | 100.5 | 81.5 | 92.4 | | Fort McMurray | 128.2 | 95.4 | 114.2 |
| 222 | Arlington | 101.5 | 80.3 | 92.4 | | Lethbridge | 122.1 | 94.8 | 110.4 |
| 223 | Alexandria | 100.6 | 85.1 | 94.0 | | Lloydminster | 116.7 | 91.5 | 105.9 |
| 224-225 | Fredericksburg | 99.1 | 74.1 | 88.4 | | Medicine Hat | 116.8 | 90.7 | 105.6 |
| 226 | Winchester | 99.7 | 67.6 | 86.0 | | Red Deer | 117.2 | 90.7 | 105.9 |
| 227 | Culpeper | 99.6 | 73.2 | 88.3 | | | | | |
| 228 | Harrisonburg | 99.9 | 67.8 | 86.2 | **BRITISH COLUMBIA** | | | | |
| 229 | Charlottesville | 100.3 | 67.2 | 86.1 | | Kamloops | 117.9 | 93.1 | 107.3 |
| 230-232 | Richmond | 100.9 | 71.0 | 88.1 | | Prince George | 119.1 | 93.1 | 108.0 |
| 233-235 | Norfolk | 100.4 | 70.1 | 87.4 | | Vancouver | 126.7 | 84.0 | 108.5 |
| 236 | Newport News | 100.4 | 70.1 | 87.4 | | Victoria | 119.1 | 80.7 | 102.7 |
| 237 | Portsmouth | 99.7 | 66.7 | 85.6 | | | | | |
| 238 | Petersburg | 100.2 | 71.0 | 87.7 | **MANITOBA** | | | | |
| 239 | Farmville | 99.3 | 57.8 | 81.6 | | Brandon | 116.8 | 77.9 | 100.2 |
| 240-241 | Roanoke | 101.0 | 64.8 | 85.5 | | Portage la Prairie | 116.8 | 76.5 | 99.6 |
| 242 | Bristol | 99.0 | 57.4 | 81.2 | | Winnipeg | 125.5 | 71.1 | 102.2 |
| 243 | Pulaski | 98.6 | 55.4 | 80.2 | | | | | |
| 244 | Staunton | 99.6 | 64.1 | 84.4 | **NEW BRUNSWICK** | | | | |
| 245 | Lynchburg | 99.7 | 69.4 | 86.7 | | Bathurst | 115.2 | 68.8 | 95.4 |
| 246 | Grundy | 99.0 | 54.7 | 80.1 | | Dalhousie | 115.1 | 68.8 | 95.3 |
| | | | | | | Fredericton | 116.7 | 73.6 | 98.3 |
| **WASHINGTON** | | | | | | Moncton | 115.5 | 69.7 | 95.9 |
| 980-981,987 | Seattle | 105.1 | 101.5 | 103.6 | | Newcastle | 115.2 | 68.8 | 95.4 |
| 982 | Everett | 104.8 | 98.6 | 102.2 | | St. John | 118.0 | 73.6 | 99.0 |
| 983-984 | Tacoma | 104.8 | 99.8 | 102.7 | | | | | |
| 985 | Olympia | 103.3 | 99.7 | 101.8 | **NEWFOUNDLAND** | | | | |
| 986 | Vancouver | 106.3 | 96.7 | 102.2 | | Corner Brook | 120.3 | 69.0 | 98.4 |
| 988 | Wenatchee | 105.0 | 84.0 | 96.0 | | St Johns | 120.6 | 70.1 | 99.0 |
| 989 | Yakima | 105.0 | 89.3 | 98.3 | | | | | |
| 990-992 | Spokane | 105.3 | 82.4 | 95.5 | **NORTHWEST TERRITORIES** | | | | |
| 993 | Richland | 104.9 | 86.5 | 97.1 | | Yellowknife | 121.0 | 87.7 | 106.8 |
| 994 | Clarkston | 104.1 | 84.0 | 95.5 | | | | | |
| | | | | | **NOVA SCOTIA** | | | | |
| **WEST VIRGINIA** | | | | | | Bridgewater | 116.7 | 76.4 | 99.5 |
| 247-248 | Bluefield | 97.7 | 77.7 | 89.1 | | Dartmouth | 118.1 | 76.4 | 100.3 |
| 249 | Lewisburg | 99.6 | 82.1 | 92.1 | | Halifax | 119.5 | 79.6 | 102.5 |
| 250-253 | Charleston | 99.6 | 88.3 | 94.8 | | New Glasgow | 116.1 | 76.4 | 99.1 |
| 254 | Martinsburg | 99.2 | 76.3 | 89.4 | | Sydney | 113.5 | 76.4 | 97.7 |
| 255-257 | Huntington | 100.5 | 90.7 | 96.3 | | Truro | 116.1 | 76.5 | 99.1 |
| 258-259 | Beckley | 97.6 | 86.1 | 92.6 | | Yarmouth | 116.0 | 76.4 | 99.1 |
| 260 | Wheeling | 100.6 | 89.9 | 96.0 | | | | | |
| 261 | Parkersburg | 99.4 | 88.3 | 94.7 | **ONTARIO** | | | | |
| 262 | Buckhannon | 99.2 | 89.5 | 95.0 | | Barrie | 119.6 | 95.7 | 109.4 |
| 263-264 | Clarksburg | 99.7 | 88.6 | 94.9 | | Brantford | 118.8 | 99.8 | 110.7 |
| 265 | Morgantown | 99.8 | 89.3 | 95.3 | | Cornwall | 119.1 | 96.1 | 109.3 |
| 266 | Gassaway | 99.0 | 90.5 | 95.3 | | Hamilton | 124.5 | 99.4 | 113.8 |
| 267 | Romney | 99.0 | 81.9 | 91.7 | | Kingston | 120.0 | 96.2 | 109.8 |
| 268 | Petersburg | 98.8 | 84.5 | 92.7 | | Kitchener | 115.1 | 95.0 | 106.5 |
| | | | | | | London | 121.6 | 96.2 | 110.7 |
| **WISCONSIN** | | | | | | North Bay | 118.8 | 93.9 | 108.2 |
| 530,532 | Milwaukee | 100.0 | 107.5 | 103.2 | | Oshawa | 118.4 | 97.7 | 109.6 |
| 531 | Kenosha | 99.7 | 102.2 | 100.8 | | Ottawa | 120.4 | 96.8 | 110.3 |
| 534 | Racine | 99.2 | 104.2 | 101.3 | | Owen Sound | 119.8 | 93.9 | 108.7 |
| 535 | Beloit | 99.0 | 97.7 | 98.5 | | Peterborough | 118.8 | 95.9 | 109.0 |
| 537 | Madison | 99.1 | 98.2 | 98.7 | | Sarnia | 118.7 | 100.4 | 110.9 |
| | | | | | | Sault Ste Marie | 113.5 | 95.3 | 105.7 |

# Location Factors

| STATE/ZIP | CITY | MAT. | INST. | TOTAL |
|---|---|---|---|---|
| **ONTARIO (CONT'D)** | | | | |
| | St. Catharines | 112.9 | 97.0 | 106.1 |
| | Sudbury | 113.3 | 95.6 | 105.7 |
| | Thunder Bay | 114.4 | 95.7 | 106.4 |
| | Timmins | 119.1 | 93.9 | 108.3 |
| | Toronto | 122.7 | 103.0 | 114.3 |
| | Windsor | 113.7 | 96.0 | 106.1 |
| **PRINCE EDWARD ISLAND** | | | | |
| | Charlottetown | 118.4 | 64.1 | 95.2 |
| | Summerside | 117.8 | 64.1 | 94.8 |
| **QUEBEC** | | | | |
| | Cap-de-la-Madeleine | 115.9 | 89.9 | 104.8 |
| | Charlesbourg | 115.9 | 89.9 | 104.8 |
| | Chicoutimi | 114.9 | 95.8 | 106.7 |
| | Gatineau | 115.3 | 89.7 | 104.3 |
| | Granby | 115.5 | 89.6 | 104.4 |
| | Hull | 115.4 | 89.7 | 104.4 |
| | Joliette | 116.1 | 89.9 | 104.9 |
| | Laval | 115.0 | 89.7 | 104.2 |
| | Montreal | 119.6 | 96.1 | 109.6 |
| | Quebec | 119.5 | 96.6 | 109.7 |
| | Rimouski | 115.3 | 95.8 | 107.0 |
| | Rouyn-Noranda | 115.1 | 89.7 | 104.2 |
| | Saint Hyacinthe | 114.6 | 89.7 | 103.9 |
| | Sherbrooke | 115.6 | 89.7 | 104.5 |
| | Sorel | 116.0 | 89.9 | 104.8 |
| | St Jerome | 115.2 | 89.7 | 104.3 |
| | Trois Rivieres | 116.0 | 89.9 | 104.8 |
| **SASKATCHEWAN** | | | | |
| | Moose Jaw | 114.1 | 71.3 | 95.8 |
| | Prince Albert | 113.1 | 69.5 | 94.4 |
| | Regina | 115.9 | 71.4 | 96.8 |
| | Saskatoon | 114.3 | 71.2 | 95.9 |
| **YUKON** | | | | |
| | Whitehorse | 113.8 | 70.1 | 95.1 |

## R011105-05  Tips for Accurate Estimating

1. Use pre-printed or columnar forms for orderly sequence of dimensions and locations and for recording telephone quotations.

2. Use only the front side of each paper or form except for certain pre-printed summary forms.

3. Be consistent in listing dimensions: For example, length x width x height. This helps in rechecking to ensure that, the total length of partitions is appropriate for the building area.

4. Use printed (rather than measured) dimensions where given.

5. Add up multiple printed dimensions for a single entry where possible.

6. Measure all other dimensions carefully.

7. Use each set of dimensions to calculate multiple related quantities.

8. Convert foot and inch measurements to decimal feet when listing. Memorize decimal equivalents to .01 parts of a foot (1/8″ equals approximately .01′).

9. Do not "round off" quantities until the final summary.

10. Mark drawings with different colors as items are taken off.

11. Keep similar items together, different items separate.

12. Identify location and drawing numbers to aid in future checking for completeness.

13. Measure or list everything on the drawings or mentioned in the specifications.

14. It may be necessary to list items not called for to make the job complete.

15. Be alert for: Notes on plans such as N.T.S. (not to scale); changes in scale throughout the drawings; reduced size drawings; discrepancies between the specifications and the drawings.

16. Develop a consistent pattern of performing an estimate. For example:
    a. Start the quantity takeoff at the lower floor and move to the next higher floor.
    b. Proceed from the main section of the building to the wings.
    c. Proceed from south to north or vice versa, clockwise or counterclockwise.
    d. Take off floor plan quantities first, elevations next, then detail drawings.

17. List all gross dimensions that can be either used again for different quantities, or used as a rough check of other quantities for verification (exterior perimeter, gross floor area, individual floor areas, etc.).

18. Utilize design symmetry or repetition (repetitive floors, repetitive wings, symmetrical design around a center line, similar room layouts, etc.). Note: Extreme caution is needed here so as not to omit or duplicate an area.

19. Do not convert units until the final total is obtained. For instance, when estimating concrete work, keep all units to the nearest cubic foot, then summarize and convert to cubic yards.

20. When figuring alternatives, it is best to total all items involved in the basic system, then total all items involved in the alternates. Therefore you work with positive numbers in all cases. When adds and deducts are used, it is often confusing whether to add or subtract a portion of an item; especially on a complicated or involved alternate.

## R011110-10  Architectural Fees

Tabulated below are typical percentage fees by project size, for good professional architectural service. Fees may vary from those listed depending upon degree of design difficulty and economic conditions in any particular area.

Rates can be interpolated horizontally and vertically. Various portions of the same project requiring different rates should be adjusted proportionately. For alterations, add 50% to the fee for the first $500,000 of project cost and add 25% to the fee for project cost over $500,000.

Architectural fees tabulated below include Structural, Mechanical and Electrical Engineering Fees. They do not include the fees for special consultants such as kitchen planning, security, acoustical, interior design, etc.

Civil Engineering fees are included in the Architectural fee for project sites requiring minimal design such as city sites. However, separate Civil Engineering fees must be added when utility connections require design, drainage calculations are needed, stepped foundations are required, or provisions are required to protect adjacent wetlands.

| Building Types | Total Project Size in Thousands of Dollars | | | | | | |
|---|---|---|---|---|---|---|---|
| | 100 | 250 | 500 | 1,000 | 5,000 | 10,000 | 50,000 |
| Factories, garages, warehouses, repetitive housing | 9.0% | 8.0% | 7.0% | 6.2% | 5.3% | 4.9% | 4.5% |
| Apartments, banks, schools, libraries, offices, municipal buildings | 12.2 | 12.3 | 9.2 | 8.0 | 7.0 | 6.6 | 6.2 |
| Churches, hospitals, homes, laboratories, museums, research | 15.0 | 13.6 | 12.7 | 11.9 | 9.5 | 8.8 | 8.0 |
| Memorials, monumental work, decorative furnishings | — | 16.0 | 14.5 | 13.1 | 10.0 | 9.0 | 8.3 |

# General Requirements | R0111 Summary of Work

## R011110-30  Engineering Fees

Typical **Structural Engineering Fees** based on type of construction and total project size. These fees are included in Architectural Fees.

| Type of Construction | Total Project Size (in thousands of dollars) | | | |
|---|---|---|---|---|
| | $500 | $500-$1,000 | $1,000-$5,000 | Over $5000 |
| Industrial buildings, factories & warehouses | Technical payroll times 2.0 to 2.5 | 1.60% | 1.25% | 1.00% |
| Hotels, apartments, offices, dormitories, hospitals, public buildings, food stores | | 2.00% | 1.70% | 1.20% |
| Museums, banks, churches and cathedrals | | 2.00% | 1.75% | 1.25% |
| Thin shells, prestressed concrete, earthquake resistive | | 2.00% | 1.75% | 1.50% |
| Parking ramps, auditoriums, stadiums, convention halls, hangars & boiler houses | | 2.50% | 2.00% | 1.75% |
| Special buildings, major alterations, underpinning & future expansion | | Add to above 0.5% | Add to above 0.5% | Add to above 0.5% |

For complex reinforced concrete or unusually complicated structures, add 20% to 50%.

Typical **Mechanical and Electrical Engineering Fees** are based on the size of the subcontract. The fee structure for both are shown below. These fees are included in Architectural Fees.

| Type of Construction | Subcontract Size | | | | | | | |
|---|---|---|---|---|---|---|---|---|
| | $25,000 | $50,000 | $100,000 | $225,000 | $350,000 | $500,000 | $750,000 | $1,000,000 |
| Simple structures | 6.4% | 5.7% | 4.8% | 4.5% | 4.4% | 4.3% | 4.2% | 4.1% |
| Intermediate structures | 8.0 | 7.3 | 6.5 | 5.6 | 5.1 | 5.0 | 4.9 | 4.8 |
| Complex structures | 10.1 | 9.0 | 9.0 | 8.0 | 7.5 | 7.5 | 7.0 | 7.0 |

For renovations, add 15% to 25% to applicable fee.

# General Requirements | R0121 Allowances

## R012157-20  Construction Time Requirements

Table at left is average construction time in months for different types of building projects. Table at right is the construction time in months for different size projects. Design time runs 25% to 40% of construction time.

| Type Building | Construction Time | Project Value | Construction Time |
|---|---|---|---|
| Industrial Buildings | 12 Months | Under $1,400,000 | 10 Months |
| Commercial Buildings | 15 Months | Up to $3,800,000 | 15 Months |
| Research & Development | 18 Months | Up to $19,000,000 | 21 Months |
| Institutional Buildings | 20 Months | over $19,000,000 | 28 Months |

## R012909-80   Sales Tax by State

State sales tax on materials is tabulated below (5 states have no sales tax). Many states allow local jurisdictions, such as a county or city, to levy additional sales tax.

Some projects may be sales tax exempt, particularly those constructed with public funds.

| State | Tax (%) | State | Tax (%) | State | Tax (%) | State | Tax (%) |
|---|---|---|---|---|---|---|---|
| Alabama | 4 | Illinois | 6.25 | Montana | 0 | Rhode Island | 7 |
| Alaska | 0 | Indiana | 6 | Nebraska | 5.5 | South Carolina | 5 |
| Arizona | 5.6 | Iowa | 5 | Nevada | 6.5 | South Dakota | 4 |
| Arkansas | 6 | Kansas | 5.3 | New Hampshire | 0 | Tennessee | 7 |
| California | 7.25 | Kentucky | 6 | New Jersey | 7 | Texas | 6.25 |
| Colorado | 2.9 | Louisiana | 4 | New Mexico | 5 | Utah | 4.75 |
| Connecticut | 6 | Maine | 5 | New York | 4 | Vermont | 6 |
| Delaware | 0 | Maryland | 5 | North Carolina | 4.25 | Virginia | 5 |
| District of Columbia | 5.75 | Massachusetts | 5 | North Dakota | 5 | Washington | 6.5 |
| Florida | 6 | Michigan | 6 | Ohio | 5.5 | West Virginia | 6 |
| Georgia | 4 | Minnesota | 6.5 | Oklahoma | 4.5 | Wisconsin | 5 |
| Hawaii | 4 | Mississippi | 7 | Oregon | 0 | Wyoming | 4 |
| Idaho | 5 | Missouri | 4.225 | Pennsylvania | 6 | Average | 4.87% |

## Sales Tax by Province (Canada)

GST - a value-added tax, which the government imposes on most goods and services provided in or imported into Canada. PST - a retail sales tax, which five of the provinces impose on the price of most goods and some

services. QST - a value-added tax, similar to the federal GST, which Quebec imposes. HST - Three provinces have combined their retail sales tax with the federal GST into one harmonized tax.

| Province | PST (%) | QST (%) | GST(%) | HST(%) |
|---|---|---|---|---|
| Alberta | 0 | 0 | 6 | 0 |
| British Columbia | 7 | 0 | 6 | 0 |
| Manitoba | 7 | 0 | 6 | 0 |
| New Brunswick | 0 | 0 | 0 | 14 |
| Newfoundland | 0 | 0 | 0 | 14 |
| Northwest Territories | 0 | 0 | 6 | 0 |
| Nova Scotia | 0 | 0 | 0 | 14 |
| Ontario | 8 | 0 | 6 | 0 |
| Prince Edward Island | 10 | 0 | 6 | 0 |
| Quebec | 0 | 7.5 | 6 | 0 |
| Saskatchewan | 5 | 0 | 6 | 0 |
| Yukon | 0 | 0 | 6 | 0 |

### R012909-85 Unemployment Taxes and Social Security Taxes

State Unemployment Tax rates vary not only from state to state, but also with the experience rating of the contractor. The Federal Unemployment Tax rate is 6.2% of the first $7,000 of wages. This is reduced by a credit of up to 5.4% for timely payment to the state. The minimum Federal Unemployment Tax is 0.8% after all credits.

Social Security (FICA) for 2008 is estimated at time of publication to be 7.65% of wages up to $97,500.

### R012909-90 Overtime

One way to improve the completion date of a project or eliminate negative float from a schedule is to compress activity duration times. This can be achieved by increasing the crew size or working overtime with the proposed crew.

To determine the costs of working overtime to compress activity duration times, consider the following examples. Below is an overtime efficiency and cost chart based on a five, six, or seven day week with an eight through twelve hour day. Payroll percentage increases for time and one half and double time are shown for the various working days.

| Days per Week | Hours per Day | Production Efficiency | | | | | Payroll Cost Factors | |
|---|---|---|---|---|---|---|---|---|
| | | 1st Week | 2nd Week | 3rd Week | 4th Week | Average 4 Weeks | @ 1-1/2 Times | @ 2 Times |
| 5 | 8 | 100% | 100% | 100% | 100% | 100 % | 100 % | 100 % |
| | 9 | 100 | 100 | 95 | 90 | 96.25 | 105.6 | 111.1 |
| | 10 | 100 | 95 | 90 | 85 | 91.25 | 110.0 | 120.0 |
| | 11 | 95 | 90 | 75 | 65 | 81.25 | 113.6 | 127.3 |
| | 12 | 90 | 85 | 70 | 60 | 76.25 | 116.7 | 133.3 |
| 6 | 8 | 100 | 100 | 95 | 90 | 96.25 | 108.3 | 116.7 |
| | 9 | 100 | 95 | 90 | 85 | 92.50 | 113.0 | 125.9 |
| | 10 | 95 | 90 | 85 | 80 | 87.50 | 116.7 | 133.3 |
| | 11 | 95 | 85 | 70 | 65 | 78.75 | 119.7 | 139.4 |
| | 12 | 90 | 80 | 65 | 60 | 73.75 | 122.2 | 144.4 |
| 7 | 8 | 100 | 95 | 85 | 75 | 88.75 | 114.3 | 128.6 |
| | 9 | 95 | 90 | 80 | 70 | 83.75 | 118.3 | 136.5 |
| | 10 | 90 | 85 | 75 | 65 | 78.75 | 121.4 | 142.9 |
| | 11 | 85 | 80 | 65 | 60 | 72.50 | 124.0 | 148.1 |
| | 12 | 85 | 75 | 60 | 55 | 68.75 | 126.2 | 152.4 |

### R013113-40 Builder's Risk Insurance

Builder's Risk Insurance is insurance on a building during construction. Premiums are paid by the owner or the contractor. Blasting, collapse and underground insurance would raise total insurance costs above those listed. Floater policy for materials delivered to the job runs $.75 to $1.25 per $100 value. Contractor equipment insurance runs $.50 to $1.50 per $100 value. Insurance for miscellaneous tools to $1,500 value runs from $3.00 to $7.50 per $100 value.

Tabulated below are New England Builder's Risk insurance rates in dollars per $100 value for $1,000 deductible. For $25,000 deductible, rates can be reduced 13% to 34%. On contracts over $1,000,000, rates may be lower than those tabulated. Policies are written annually for the total completed value in place. For "all risk" insurance (excluding flood, earthquake and certain other perils) add $.025 to total rates below.

| Coverage | Frame Construction (Class 1) | | | Brick Construction (Class 4) | | | Fire Resistive (Class 6) | | |
|---|---|---|---|---|---|---|---|---|---|
| | Range | | Average | Range | | Average | Range | | Average |
| Fire Insurance | $.350 to | $ .850 | $.600 | $.158 to | $.189 | $.174 | $.052 to | $.080 | $.070 |
| Extended Coverage | .115 to | .200 | .158 | .080 to | .105 | .101 | .081 to | .105 | .100 |
| Vandalism | .012 to | .016 | .014 | .008 to | .011 | .011 | .008 to | .011 | .010 |
| Total Annual Rate | $.477 to | $1.066 | $.772 | $.246 to | $.305 | $.286 | $.141 to | $.196 | $.180 |

# R013113-50    General Contractor's Overhead

There are two distinct types of overhead on a construction project: Project Overhead and Main Office Overhead. Project Overhead includes those costs at a construction site not directly associated with the installation of construction materials. Examples of Project Overhead costs include the following:

1. Superintendent
2. Construction office and storage trailers
3. Temporary sanitary facilities
4. Temporary utilities
5. Security fencing
6. Photographs
7. Clean up
8. Performance and payment bonds

The above Project Overhead items are also referred to as General Requirements and therefore are estimated in Division 1. Division 1 is the first division listed in the CSI MasterFormat but it is usually the last division estimated. The sum of the costs in Divisions 1 through 49 is referred to as the sum of the direct costs.

All construction projects also include indirect costs. The primary components of indirect costs are the contractor's Main Office Overhead and profit. The amount of the Main Office Overhead expense varies depending on the following:

1. Owner's compensation
2. Project managers and estimator's wages
3. Clerical support wages
4. Office rent and utilities
5. Corporate legal and accounting costs
6. Advertising
7. Automobile expenses
8. Association dues
9. Travel and entertainment expenses

These costs are usually calculated as a percentage of annual sales volume. This percentage can range from 35% for a small contractor doing less than $500,000 to 5% for a large contractor with sales in excess of $100 million.

## R013113-60 Workers' Compensation Insurance Rates by Trade

The table below tabulates the national averages for Workers' Compensation insurance rates by trade and type of building. The average "Insurance Rate" is multiplied by the "% of Building Cost" for each trade. This produces the "Workers' Compensation Cost" by % of total labor cost, to be added for each trade by building type to determine the weighted average Workers' Compensation rate for the building types analyzed.

| Trade | Insurance Rate (% Labor Cost) Range | | | Average | % of Building Cost Office Bldgs. | Schools & Apts. | Mfg. | Workers' Compensation Office Bldgs. | Schools & Apts. | Mfg. |
|---|---|---|---|---|---|---|---|---|---|---|
| Excavation, Grading, etc. | 4.5 % | to | 10.5% | 10.5% | 4.8% | 4.9% | 4.5% | .50% | .51% | .47% |
| Piles & Foundations | 8.9 | to | 42.9 | 21.5 | 7.1 | 5.2 | 8.7 | 1.53 | 1.12 | 1.87 |
| Concrete | 5.1 | to | 29.8 | 15.2 | 5.0 | 14.8 | 3.7 | .76 | 2.25 | .56 |
| Masonry | 5.4 | to | 34.5 | 14.8 | 6.9 | 7.5 | 1.9 | 1.02 | 1.11 | .28 |
| Structural Steel | 8.6 | to | 104.1 | 40.1 | 10.7 | 3.9 | 17.6 | 4.29 | 1.56 | 7.06 |
| Miscellaneous & Ornamental Metals | 5.2 | to | 22.6 | 11.4 | 2.8 | 4.0 | 3.6 | .32 | .46 | .41 |
| Carpentry & Millwork | 7.6 | to | 53.2 | 18.3 | 3.7 | 4.0 | 0.5 | .68 | .73 | .09 |
| Metal or Composition Siding | 6.8 | to | 34.1 | 16.9 | 2.3 | 0.3 | 4.3 | .39 | .05 | .73 |
| Roofing | 8.4 | to | 77.1 | 32.9 | 2.3 | 2.6 | 3.1 | .76 | .86 | 1.02 |
| Doors & Hardware | 5 | to | 24.9 | 11.7 | 0.9 | 1.4 | 0.4 | .11 | .16 | .05 |
| Sash & Glazing | 5.6 | to | 28.9 | 14.2 | 3.5 | 4.0 | 1.0 | .50 | .57 | .14 |
| Lath & Plaster | 3.1 | to | 35.4 | 14.4 | 3.3 | 6.9 | 0.8 | .48 | .99 | .12 |
| Tile, Marble & Floors | 2 | to | 29.4 | 9.5 | 2.6 | 3.0 | 0.5 | .25 | .29 | .05 |
| Acoustical Ceilings | 2.3 | to | 50.2 | 11.0 | 2.4 | 0.2 | 0.3 | .26 | .02 | .03 |
| Painting | 4.9 | to | 29.6 | 12.9 | 1.5 | 1.6 | 1.6 | .19 | .21 | .21 |
| Interior Partitions | 7.6 | to | 53.2 | 18.3 | 3.9 | 4.3 | 4.4 | .71 | .79 | .81 |
| Miscellaneous Items | 2.3 | to | 197.9 | 16.3 | 5.2 | 3.7 | 9.7 | .85 | .60 | 1.59 |
| Elevators | 2.9 | to | 13.7 | 6.6 | 2.1 | 1.1 | 2.2 | .14 | .07 | .15 |
| Sprinklers | 2.8 | to | 15.3 | 8.3 | 0.5 | — | 2.0 | .04 | — | .17 |
| Plumbing | 2.9 | to | 14.2 | 8.1 | 4.9 | 7.2 | 5.2 | .40 | .58 | .42 |
| Heat., Vent., Air Conditioning | 4.6 | to | 24.8 | 11.9 | 13.5 | 11.0 | 12.9 | 1.61 | 1.31 | 1.54 |
| Electrical | 2.7 | to | 13.6 | 6.7 | 10.1 | 8.4 | 11.1 | .68 | .56 | .74 |
| Total | 2 % | to | 197.9% | — | 100.0% | 100.0% | 100.0% | 16.47% | 14.80% | 18.51% |
| | | | | | | | Overall Weighted Average | 16.59% | | |

## Workers' Compensation Insurance Rates by States

The table below lists the weighted average Workers' Compensation base rate for each state with a factor comparing this with the national average of 16.2%.

| State | Weighted Average | Factor | State | Weighted Average | Factor | State | Weighted Average | Factor |
|---|---|---|---|---|---|---|---|---|
| Alabama | 28.3% | 175 | Kentucky | 19.1% | 118 | North Dakota | 13.7% | 85 |
| Alaska | 22.8 | 141 | Louisiana | 28.3 | 175 | Ohio | 13.8 | 85 |
| Arizona | 8.3 | 51 | Maine | 18.3 | 113 | Oklahoma | 14.6 | 90 |
| Arkansas | 12.8 | 79 | Maryland | 18.4 | 114 | Oregon | 13.5 | 83 |
| California | 20.3 | 125 | Massachusetts | 15.0 | 93 | Pennsylvania | 14.8 | 91 |
| Colorado | 13.3 | 82 | Michigan | 17.3 | 107 | Rhode Island | 21.3 | 131 |
| Connecticut | 21.9 | 135 | Minnesota | 25.7 | 159 | South Carolina | 18.3 | 113 |
| Delaware | 19.2 | 119 | Mississippi | 19.5 | 120 | South Dakota | 18.8 | 116 |
| District of Columbia | 15.3 | 94 | Missouri | 17.3 | 107 | Tennessee | 15.4 | 95 |
| Florida | 17.2 | 106 | Montana | 17.9 | 110 | Texas | 13.0 | 80 |
| Georgia | 23.2 | 143 | Nebraska | 24.0 | 148 | Utah | 13.2 | 81 |
| Hawaii | 17.0 | 105 | Nevada | 13.0 | 80 | Vermont | 21.2 | 131 |
| Idaho | 11.1 | 69 | New Hampshire | 21.7 | 134 | Virginia | 11.1 | 69 |
| Illinois | 20.7 | 128 | New Jersey | 13.1 | 81 | Washington | 10.4 | 64 |
| Indiana | 6.2 | 38 | New Mexico | 20.4 | 126 | West Virginia | 8.9 | 55 |
| Iowa | 11.9 | 73 | New York | 13.5 | 83 | Wisconsin | 15.2 | 94 |
| Kansas | 8.9 | 55 | North Carolina | 17.8 | 110 | Wyoming | 10.2 | 63 |
| | | | Weighted Average for U.S. is | 16.6% of payroll = 100% | | | | |

Rates in the following table are the base or manual costs per $100 of payroll for Workers' Compensation in each state. Rates are usually applied to straight time wages only and not to premium time wages and bonuses.

The weighted average skilled worker rate for 35 trades is 16.2%. For bidding purposes, apply the full value of Workers' Compensation directly to total labor costs, or if labor is 38%, materials 42% and overhead and profit 20% of total cost, carry 38/80 x 16.2% =7.7% of cost (before overhead and profit) into overhead. Rates vary not only from state to state but also with the experience rating of the contractor.

Rates are the most current available at the time of publication.

## R013113-60 Workers' Compensation Insurance Rates by Trade and State (cont.)

| State | Carpentry — 3 stories or less | Carpentry — interior cab. work | Carpentry — general | Concrete Work — NOC | Concrete Work — flat (flr., sdwk.) | Electrical Wiring — inside | Excavation — earth NOC | Excavation — rock | Glaziers | Insulation Work | Lathing | Masonry | Painting & Decorating | Pile Driving | Plastering | Plumbing | Roofing | Sheet Metal Work (HVAC) | Steel Erection — door & sash | Steel Erection — inter., ornam. | Steel Erection — structure | Steel Erection — NOC | Tile Work — (interior ceramic) | Waterproofing | Wrecking |
|---|---|---|---|---|---|---|---|---|---|---|---|---|---|---|---|---|---|---|---|---|---|---|---|---|---|
| | 5651 | 5437 | 5403 | 5213 | 5221 | 5190 | 6217 | 6217 | 5462 | 5479 | 5443 | 5022 | 5474 | 6003 | 5480 | 5183 | 5551 | 5538 | 5102 | 5102 | 5040 | 5057 | 5348 | 9014 | 5701 |
| AL | 40.80 | 23.71 | 39.67 | 15.88 | 11.76 | 11.45 | 15.46 | 15.46 | 21.18 | 16.77 | 12.85 | 26.47 | 25.34 | 45.31 | 25.32 | 12.03 | 70.69 | 22.96 | 15.27 | 15.27 | 75.41 | 35.22 | 13.06 | 6.56 | 75.41 |
| AK | 17.96 | 12.90 | 17.09 | 14.57 | 12.77 | 11.33 | 14.84 | 14.84 | 28.65 | 28.48 | 10.17 | 40.02 | 27.82 | 33.80 | 38.82 | 11.44 | 31.10 | 11.07 | 10.79 | 10.79 | 48.59 | 29.22 | 8.08 | 8.25 | 48.59 |
| AZ | 9.10 | 5.52 | 12.36 | 6.39 | 3.34 | 4.01 | 4.22 | 4.22 | 10.29 | 4.56 | 5.79 | 5.94 | 10.69 | 5.06 | 3.97 | | 12.30 | 7.38 | 9.60 | 9.60 | 22.01 | 11.91 | 2.29 | 2.72 | 22.01 |
| AR | 14.53 | 7.23 | 15.84 | 11.83 | 6.28 | 4.89 | 7.50 | 7.50 | 9.56 | 15.90 | 5.73 | 9.69 | 11.19 | 15.93 | 15.55 | 5.00 | 22.50 | 13.09 | 6.55 | 6.55 | 30.66 | 25.06 | 5.88 | 3.65 | 30.66 |
| CA | 30.29 | 30.29 | 30.29 | 11.42 | 11.42 | 7.84 | 13.27 | 13.27 | 17.86 | 12.98 | 11.79 | 17.53 | 15.03 | 27.23 | 12.47 | | 51.93 | 18.17 | 14.14 | 14.14 | 17.31 | 20.57 | 8.69 | 16.24 | 20.57 |
| CO | 16.28 | 8.03 | 12.76 | 13.19 | 7.46 | 5.18 | 10.35 | 10.35 | 9.79 | 13.91 | 6.03 | 14.30 | 10.29 | 15.08 | 9.00 | 8.45 | 23.95 | 11.46 | 8.38 | 8.38 | 35.52 | 15.85 | 8.60 | 5.74 | 15.85 |
| CT | 16.21 | 15.95 | 30.34 | 21.48 | 10.72 | 8.22 | 11.70 | 11.70 | 22.78 | 14.71 | 27.22 | 23.29 | 16.45 | 28.37 | 17.45 | 10.34 | 44.86 | 15.61 | 19.02 | 19.02 | 47.14 | 25.53 | 9.66 | 5.83 | 47.14 |
| DE | 19.94 | 19.94 | 14.95 | 15.05 | 12.41 | 7.94 | 12.34 | 12.34 | 14.19 | 17.39 | 17.20 | 16.39 | 20.46 | 24.99 | 17.20 | 10.28 | 35.23 | 12.73 | 16.38 | 16.38 | 35.93 | 16.38 | 12.36 | 16.39 | 35.93 |
| DC | 10.17 | 12.06 | 10.82 | 9.43 | 12.00 | 6.35 | 12.14 | 12.14 | 17.96 | 9.67 | 12.83 | 15.03 | 8.37 | 14.12 | 12.98 | 11.77 | 21.47 | 8.93 | 12.87 | 12.87 | 43.78 | 18.27 | 21.67 | 4.05 | 43.78 |
| FL | 17.61 | 13.01 | 18.25 | 18.38 | 8.91 | 7.48 | 9.33 | 9.33 | 14.41 | 11.19 | 9.35 | 13.96 | 13.51 | 38.24 | 25.08 | 8.13 | 28.05 | 12.68 | 10.60 | 10.60 | 35.41 | 23.49 | 8.34 | 6.22 | 35.41 |
| GA | 33.47 | 16.81 | 24.91 | 14.49 | 10.83 | 9.87 | 17.01 | 17.01 | 15.94 | 22.44 | 14.78 | 19.68 | 18.93 | 26.79 | 18.55 | 10.89 | 44.56 | 20.76 | 16.29 | 16.29 | 52.69 | 41.28 | 10.07 | 8.65 | 52.69 |
| HI | 17.38 | 11.62 | 28.20 | 13.74 | 12.27 | 7.10 | 7.73 | 7.73 | 20.55 | 21.19 | 10.94 | 17.87 | 11.33 | 20.15 | 15.61 | 6.06 | 33.24 | 8.02 | 11.11 | 11.11 | 31.71 | 21.70 | 9.78 | 11.54 | 31.71 |
| ID | 9.62 | 5.65 | 11.41 | 10.52 | 6.09 | 4.32 | 6.17 | 6.17 | 9.27 | 7.82 | 7.38 | 8.34 | 7.94 | 14.23 | 11.05 | 5.39 | 31.77 | 8.89 | 6.57 | 6.57 | 31.36 | 11.34 | 8.50 | 4.30 | 31.36 |
| IL | 20.85 | 13.88 | 19.97 | 26.08 | 12.01 | 9.40 | 10.02 | 10.02 | 19.20 | 16.47 | 11.95 | 18.27 | 11.33 | 39.43 | 16.99 | 9.74 | 30.89 | 14.96 | 14.76 | 14.76 | 66.73 | 21.46 | 13.86 | 4.61 | 66.73 |
| IN | 7.72 | 4.92 | 7.45 | 5.04 | 3.48 | 2.74 | 4.62 | 4.62 | 5.59 | 6.77 | 2.23 | 5.15 | 4.77 | 8.47 | 3.83 | 2.85 | 11.36 | 4.45 | 4.07 | 4.07 | 15.75 | 7.98 | 3.09 | 2.27 | 15.75 |
| IA | 13.19 | 7.87 | 10.60 | 11.45 | 7.24 | 4.45 | 5.84 | 5.84 | 11.14 | 7.92 | 4.92 | 9.36 | 7.30 | 10.55 | 8.57 | 5.27 | 17.75 | 7.52 | 6.79 | 6.79 | 36.84 | 40.70 | 6.84 | 3.87 | 40.70 |
| KS | 9.38 | 8.13 | 10.53 | 7.48 | 5.92 | 3.42 | 4.60 | 4.60 | 8.43 | 7.50 | 3.74 | 7.30 | 6.04 | 11.65 | 6.62 | 5.24 | 15.66 | 7.14 | 5.80 | 5.80 | 25.44 | 12.23 | 6.41 | 3.22 | 12.23 |
| KY | 21.02 | 14.00 | 22.00 | 15.75 | 8.00 | 6.00 | 10.40 | 10.40 | 20.44 | 20.69 | 13.22 | 9.50 | 12.50 | 25.37 | 15.33 | 7.00 | 45.00 | 19.58 | 14.49 | 14.49 | 46.98 | 23.88 | 11.89 | 6.75 | 46.98 |
| LA | 22.02 | 24.93 | 53.17 | 26.43 | 15.61 | 9.88 | 17.49 | 17.49 | 20.14 | 21.43 | 24.51 | 28.33 | 29.58 | 31.25 | 22.37 | 8.64 | 77.12 | 21.20 | 18.98 | 18.98 | 51.76 | 24.21 | 13.77 | 13.78 | 66.41 |
| ME | 11.61 | 11.35 | 29.57 | 25.29 | 7.24 | 5.50 | 10.72 | 10.72 | 22.58 | 14.64 | 8.18 | 20.78 | 16.11 | 17.92 | 14.62 | 10.89 | 32.20 | 11.61 | 11.06 | 11.06 | 42.25 | 32.55 | 8.28 | 8.53 | 38.53 |
| MD | 15.64 | 12.36 | 15.78 | 15.60 | 7.45 | 8.72 | 10.70 | 10.70 | 23.29 | 17.47 | 9.75 | 10.78 | 7.77 | 21.74 | 17.05 | 7.11 | 40.29 | 13.54 | 11.06 | 11.06 | 65.62 | 31.35 | 7.57 | 6.14 | 35.74 |
| MA | 9.03 | 6.88 | 16.48 | 22.32 | 9.18 | 4.18 | 6.08 | 6.08 | 9.25 | 14.59 | 5.89 | 15.67 | 6.85 | 15.92 | 6.62 | 4.80 | 47.57 | 6.62 | 11.04 | 11.04 | 43.69 | 34.06 | 8.78 | 2.65 | 24.03 |
| MI | 18.40 | 11.39 | 20.64 | 19.45 | 8.95 | 4.72 | 10.20 | 10.20 | 12.41 | 14.75 | 13.59 | 15.54 | 13.64 | 40.27 | 15.18 | 6.84 | 30.67 | 10.00 | 10.16 | 10.16 | 40.27 | 22.21 | 11.11 | 4.87 | 40.27 |
| MN | 19.53 | 19.80 | 41.48 | 14.65 | 15.73 | 7.53 | 14.95 | 14.95 | 15.68 | 11.90 | 22.05 | 19.18 | 16.95 | 24.63 | 22.05 | 10.88 | 70.18 | 14.23 | 10.58 | 10.58 | 104.13 | 33.30 | 14.55 | 6.68 | 36.03 |
| MS | 19.48 | 11.54 | 24.97 | 13.61 | 9.12 | 6.46 | 11.75 | 11.75 | 14.36 | 17.03 | 7.58 | 12.08 | 15.10 | 31.16 | 33.48 | 9.97 | 42.58 | 16.91 | 16.37 | 16.37 | 36.73 | 27.37 | 10.79 | 4.89 | 36.73 |
| MO | 21.35 | 11.97 | 15.74 | 17.31 | 11.10 | 7.55 | 9.14 | 9.14 | 11.37 | 17.18 | 9.41 | 14.98 | 13.98 | 20.15 | 15.98 | 9.74 | 32.47 | 13.07 | 11.70 | 11.70 | 39.79 | 34.69 | 10.52 | 5.66 | 39.79 |
| MT | 16.07 | 12.88 | 21.13 | 12.84 | 11.28 | 7.97 | 14.85 | 14.85 | 11.94 | 30.09 | 15.86 | 13.71 | 9.70 | 33.39 | 11.78 | 10.03 | 39.71 | 11.20 | 9.70 | 9.70 | 36.35 | 18.79 | 7.76 | 6.04 | 36.35 |
| NE | 23.75 | 13.88 | 23.27 | 29.72 | 14.88 | 10.42 | 18.22 | 18.22 | 25.88 | 34.32 | 11.60 | 21.35 | 21.77 | 24.40 | 20.13 | 11.13 | 35.72 | 19.42 | 15.60 | 15.60 | 59.72 | 30.63 | 12.10 | 7.40 | 45.82 |
| NV | 18.33 | 7.62 | 10.82 | 11.51 | 7.31 | 6.58 | 10.55 | 10.55 | 12.77 | 9.51 | 6.99 | 8.48 | 9.80 | 14.95 | 9.51 | 7.15 | 15.73 | 18.10 | 10.21 | 10.21 | 23.22 | 29.75 | 6.53 | 6.31 | 29.75 |
| NH | 34.33 | 11.93 | 22.16 | 30.97 | 15.95 | 7.31 | 18.29 | 18.29 | 11.81 | 23.02 | 9.10 | 24.86 | 14.96 | 21.22 | 15.45 | 10.52 | 54.28 | 13.59 | 13.30 | 13.30 | 47.69 | 18.84 | 11.31 | 6.52 | 47.69 |
| NJ | 13.69 | 8.84 | 13.69 | 15.18 | 9.47 | 4.42 | 7.83 | 7.83 | 7.43 | 13.14 | 11.63 | 12.42 | 11.61 | 15.28 | 11.63 | 6.25 | 35.61 | 6.75 | 9.69 | 9.69 | 26.18 | 13.33 | 6.06 | 5.21 | 21.99 |
| NM | 21.98 | 7.32 | 23.36 | 20.96 | 11.05 | 7.32 | 12.61 | 12.61 | 20.74 | 15.13 | 10.05 | 16.90 | 15.74 | 25.65 | 14.22 | 10.24 | 38.57 | 13.47 | 16.37 | 16.37 | 59.26 | 36.67 | 7.63 | 8.01 | 59.26 |
| NY | 14.21 | 6.29 | 12.39 | 17.19 | 11.26 | 6.69 | 8.37 | 8.37 | 10.18 | 9.91 | 11.27 | 15.70 | 10.41 | 15.68 | 9.04 | 7.33 | 33.39 | 12.79 | 9.59 | 9.59 | 21.77 | 15.20 | 8.72 | 6.92 | 10.56 |
| NC | 15.94 | 13.64 | 15.69 | 17.06 | 7.70 | 10.65 | 11.76 | 11.76 | 11.60 | 15.96 | 18.26 | 11.35 | 12.32 | 17.27 | 15.99 | 8.98 | 25.08 | 14.16 | 9.82 | 9.82 | 75.62 | 22.09 | 7.45 | 5.71 | 75.62 |
| ND | 11.17 | 11.13 | 11.17 | 6.42 | 6.42 | 3.63 | 6.64 | 6.64 | 11.17 | 11.17 | 7.51 | 7.71 | 6.61 | 22.78 | 7.51 | 5.22 | 23.53 | 5.22 | 22.78 | 22.78 | 22.78 | 22.78 | 11.17 | 23.53 | 10.90 |
| OH | 8.73 | 7.85 | 10.23 | 12.12 | 10.40 | 6.01 | 8.47 | 8.47 | 6.46 | 17.17 | 35.11 | 11.70 | 11.47 | 24.62 | 2.52 | 6.91 | 30.15 | 9.71 | 8.53 | 8.53 | 23.80 | 13.86 | 10.86 | 6.09 | 13.86 |
| OK | 13.42 | 9.17 | 11.76 | 11.76 | 6.34 | 5.73 | 10.83 | 10.83 | 16.07 | 19.47 | 8.45 | 10.02 | 8.47 | 20.25 | 12.19 | 7.09 | 21.13 | 9.05 | 13.76 | 13.76 | 39.72 | 23.97 | 6.50 | 5.71 | 39.72 |
| OR | 15.43 | 8.10 | 15.69 | 14.22 | 8.97 | 5.14 | 9.33 | 9.33 | 15.22 | 11.80 | 7.60 | 14.07 | 10.63 | 16.17 | 12.73 | 5.50 | 26.30 | 9.41 | 7.93 | 7.93 | 26.94 | 18.78 | 11.04 | 4.54 | 26.94 |
| PA | 14.09 | 14.09 | 12.54 | 15.08 | 11.02 | 6.39 | 8.88 | 8.88 | 10.45 | 12.15 | 12.56 | 12.80 | 14.34 | 17.16 | 12.56 | 7.91 | 29.73 | 8.42 | 15.59 | 15.59 | 23.44 | 15.59 | 8.68 | 12.80 | 23.44 |
| RI | 19.53 | 11.65 | 18.07 | 18.23 | 16.24 | 4.43 | 10.38 | 10.38 | 12.85 | 22.78 | 11.97 | 25.11 | 24.13 | 37.66 | 17.25 | 8.52 | 33.92 | 10.29 | 14.07 | 14.07 | 59.49 | 37.50 | 14.36 | 7.70 | 59.49 |
| SC | 22.54 | 15.41 | 20.91 | 14.80 | 7.92 | 10.92 | 13.16 | 13.16 | 16.12 | 14.69 | 11.32 | 12.88 | 16.52 | 19.48 | 16.02 | 11.47 | 45.24 | 12.95 | 12.99 | 12.99 | 32.57 | 26.39 | 9.62 | 6.68 | 47.05 |
| SD | 22.94 | 7.74 | 24.42 | 28.24 | 8.33 | 5.60 | 12.27 | 12.27 | 11.43 | 12.46 | 8.11 | 9.46 | 10.34 | 21.36 | 12.74 | 12.97 | 19.88 | 12.48 | 8.97 | 8.97 | 89.39 | 33.82 | 8.80 | 4.25 | 89.39 |
| TN | 17.22 | 13.12 | 20.60 | 15.01 | 8.79 | 7.29 | 11.93 | 11.93 | 14.45 | 12.33 | 8.81 | 15.81 | 11.24 | 22.08 | 15.35 | 8.19 | 24.12 | 12.77 | 8.23 | 8.23 | 30.18 | 19.75 | 10.76 | 5.36 | 30.18 |
| TX | 12.39 | 9.47 | 12.39 | 9.42 | 8.01 | 7.04 | 8.91 | 8.91 | 10.57 | 12.55 | 6.81 | 12.21 | 9.37 | 23.99 | 9.37 | 6.87 | 21.07 | 13.20 | 9.92 | 9.92 | 28.93 | 15.23 | 7.84 | 7.53 | 11.78 |
| UT | 15.42 | 8.98 | 11.45 | 8.90 | 8.20 | 5.29 | 10.07 | 10.07 | 15.37 | 11.06 | 8.22 | 13.59 | 12.95 | 8.60 | 6.16 | | 28.05 | 12.64 | 8.94 | 8.94 | 30.58 | 21.05 | 7.39 | 3.87 | 21.05 |
| VT | 20.39 | 10.61 | 16.24 | 22.43 | 9.35 | 7.23 | 14.94 | 14.94 | 19.81 | 20.65 | 8.70 | 17.13 | 13.55 | 19.85 | 12.78 | 9.77 | 47.32 | 11.59 | 13.83 | 13.83 | 58.40 | 55.60 | 10.52 | 8.60 | 58.40 |
| VA | 11.28 | 6.97 | 8.14 | 9.88 | 4.74 | 5.22 | 6.50 | 6.50 | 8.08 | 10.04 | 14.64 | 8.94 | 8.49 | 10.97 | 10.39 | 5.69 | 19.52 | 7.65 | 8.55 | 8.55 | 34.22 | 18.16 | 4.84 | 3.04 | 34.22 |
| WA | 8.93 | 8.93 | 8.93 | 7.76 | 7.76 | 3.16 | 7.52 | 7.52 | 12.29 | 10.59 | 8.93 | 10.21 | 10.26 | 17.07 | 10.98 | 4.31 | 17.46 | 4.39 | 7.53 | 7.53 | 7.53 | 7.53 | 10.05 | 17.46 | 7.53 |
| WV | 9.43 | 6.66 | 9.78 | 7.89 | 4.05 | 4.38 | 5.65 | 5.65 | 6.78 | 6.91 | 5.90 | 9.79 | 7.03 | 12.20 | 7.74 | 4.63 | 16.46 | 7.63 | 5.35 | 5.35 | 24.13 | 12.06 | 4.95 | 2.65 | 17.53 |
| WI | 10.98 | 12.78 | 14.88 | 12.73 | 8.80 | 5.46 | 7.75 | 7.75 | 11.03 | 14.06 | 7.05 | 7.22 | 12.96 | 18.78 | 10.72 | 6.77 | 43.79 | 7.44 | 9.27 | 9.27 | 31.67 | 36.80 | 14.65 | 5.76 | 31.67 |
| WY | 8.93 | 8.93 | 8.93 | 8.93 | 8.93 | 8.93 | 8.93 | 8.93 | 8.93 | 8.93 | 8.93 | 16.00 | 8.93 | 8.93 | 8.93 | 8.93 | 8.93 | 8.93 | 8.93 | 8.93 | 8.93 | 8.93 | 8.93 | 8.93 | 8.93 |
| AVG. | 16.94 | 11.68 | 18.31 | 15.22 | 9.42 | 6.66 | 10.46 | 10.46 | 14.15 | 15.12 | 11.04 | 14.80 | 12.86 | 21.48 | 14.39 | 8.11 | 32.94 | 11.88 | 11.45 | 11.45 | 40.12 | 23.82 | 9.47 | 7.07 | 36.28 |

## R013113-60  Workers' Compensation (cont.) (Canada in Canadian dollars)

| Province | | Alberta | British Columbia | Manitoba | Ontario | New Brunswick | Newfndld. & Labrador | Northwest Territories | Nova Scotia | Prince Edward Island | Quebec | Saskatchewan | Yukon |
|---|---|---|---|---|---|---|---|---|---|---|---|---|---|
| Carpentry—3 stories or less | Rate | 7.32 | 4.74 | 4.36 | 4.35 | 3.79 | 10.08 | 3.84 | 7.82 | 5.96 | 15.05 | 6.23 | 8.89 |
| | Code | 42143 | 721028 | 40102 | 723 | 4226 | 4226 | 4-41 | 4226 | 401 | 80110 | B1317 | 202 |
| Carpentry—interior cab. work | Rate | 2.18 | 4.90 | 4.36 | 4.35 | 4.40 | 4.69 | 3.84 | 4.52 | 3.71 | 15.05 | 3.51 | 8.89 |
| | Code | 42133 | 721021 | 40102 | 723 | 4279 | 4270 | 4-41 | 4274 | 402 | 80110 | B11-27 | 202 |
| CARPENTRY—general | Rate | 7.32 | 4.74 | 4.36 | 4.35 | 3.79 | 4.69 | 3.84 | 7.82 | 5.96 | 15.05 | 6.23 | 8.89 |
| | Code | 42143 | 721028 | 40102 | 723 | 4226 | 4299 | 4-41 | 4226 | 401 | 80110 | B1317 | 202 |
| CONCRETE WORK—NOC | Rate | 4.41 | 4.81 | 7.46 | 16.02 | 3.79 | 10.08 | 3.84 | 4.52 | 5.96 | 17.99 | 6.24 | 4.67 |
| | Code | 42104 | 721010 | 40110 | 748 | 4224 | 4224 | 4-41 | 4224 | 401 | 80100 | B13-14 | 203 |
| CONCRETE WORK—flat (flr. sidewalk) | Rate | 4.41 | 4.81 | 7.46 | 16.02 | 3.79 | 10.08 | 3.84 | 4.52 | 5.96 | 17.99 | 6.24 | 4.67 |
| | Code | 42104 | 721010 | 40110 | 748 | 4224 | 4224 | 4-41 | 4224 | 401 | 80100 | B13-14 | 203 |
| ELECTRICAL Wiring—inside | Rate | 2.13 | 1.77 | 2.51 | 3.79 | 2.17 | 3.01 | 3.52 | 2.31 | 3.71 | 6.12 | 3.51 | 4.67 |
| | Code | 42124 | 721019 | 40203 | 704 | 4261 | 4261 | 4-46 | 4261 | 402 | 80170 | B11-05 | 206 |
| EXCAVATION—earth NOC | Rate | 2.51 | 3.56 | 3.76 | 4.55 | 2.62 | 4.37 | 3.64 | 3.34 | 3.82 | 7.13 | 3.93 | 4.67 |
| | Code | 40604 | 721031 | 40706 | 711 | 4214 | 4214 | 4-43 | 4214 | 404 | 80030 | R11-06 | 207 |
| EXCAVATION—rock | Rate | 2.51 | 3.56 | 3.76 | 4.55 | 2.62 | 4.37 | 3.64 | 3.34 | 3.82 | 7.13 | 3.93 | 4.67 |
| | Code | 40604 | 721031 | 40706 | 711 | 4214 | 4214 | 4-43 | 4214 | 404 | 80030 | R11-06 | 207 |
| GLAZIERS | Rate | 3.16 | 3.62 | 4.36 | 8.90 | 4.55 | 6.81 | 3.84 | 5.21 | 3.71 | 17.08 | 6.23 | 4.67 |
| | Code | 42121 | 715020 | 40109 | 751 | 4233 | 4233 | 4-41 | 4233 | 402 | 80150 | B13-04 | 212 |
| INSULATION WORK | Rate | 2.57 | 8.42 | 4.36 | 8.90 | 4.55 | 6.81 | 3.84 | 5.21 | 5.96 | 15.05 | 5.98 | 8.89 |
| | Code | 42184 | 721029 | 40102 | 751 | 4234 | 4234 | 4-41 | 4234 | 401 | 80110 | B12-07 | 202 |
| LATHING | Rate | 5.59 | 6.78 | 4.36 | 4.35 | 4.40 | 4.69 | 3.84 | 4.52 | 3.71 | 15.05 | 6.23 | 8.89 |
| | Code | 42135 | 721033 | 40102 | 723 | 4273 | 4279 | 4-41 | 4271 | 402 | 80110 | B13-16 | 202 |
| MASONRY | Rate | 4.41 | 6.78 | 4.36 | 11.15 | 4.55 | 6.81 | 3.84 | 5.21 | 5.96 | 17.99 | 6.23 | 8.89 |
| | Code | 42102 | 721037 | 40102 | 741 | 4231 | 4231 | 4-41 | 4231 | 401 | 80100 | B13-18 | 202 |
| PAINTING & DECORATING | Rate | 4.35 | 4.94 | 3.18 | 6.75 | 4.40 | 4.69 | 3.84 | 4.52 | 3.71 | 15.05 | 5.98 | 8.89 |
| | Code | 42111 | 721041 | 40105 | 719 | 4275 | 4275 | 4-41 | 4275 | 402 | 80110 | B12-01 | 202 |
| PILE DRIVING | Rate | 4.41 | 5.18 | 3.76 | 6.34 | 3.79 | 9.78 | 3.64 | 4.64 | 5.96 | 7.13 | 6.23 | 8.89 |
| | Code | 42159 | 722004 | 40706 | 732 | 4221 | 4221 | 4-43 | 4221 | 401 | 80030 | B13-10 | 202 |
| PLASTERING | Rate | 5.59 | 6.78 | 5.08 | 6.75 | 4.40 | 4.69 | 3.84 | 4.52 | 3.71 | 15.05 | 5.98 | 8.89 |
| | Code | 42135 | 721042 | 40108 | 719 | 4271 | 4271 | 4-41 | 4271 | 402 | 80110 | B12-21 | 202 |
| PLUMBING | Rate | 2.13 | 3.11 | 3.05 | 4.02 | 2.32 | 3.37 | 3.52 | 2.43 | 3.71 | 6.93 | 3.51 | 4.67 |
| | Code | 42122 | 721043 | 40204 | 707 | 4241 | 4241 | 4-46 | 4241 | 402 | 80160 | B11-01 | 214 |
| ROOFING | Rate | 8.12 | 8.68 | 7.02 | 12.98 | 4.55 | 10.08 | 3.84 | 10.57 | 5.96 | 23.01 | 6.23 | 8.89 |
| | Code | 42118 | 721036 | 40403 | 728 | 4236 | 4236 | 4-41 | 4236 | 401 | 80130 | B13-20 | 202 |
| SHEET METAL WORK (HVAC) | Rate | 2.13 | 3.11 | 7.02 | 4.02 | 2.32 | 3.37 | 3.52 | 2.43 | 3.71 | 6.93 | 3.51 | 4.67 |
| | Code | 42117 | 721043 | 40402 | 707 | 4244 | 4244 | 4-46 | 4244 | 402 | 80160 | B11-07 | 208 |
| STEEL ERECTION—door & sash | Rate | 2.57 | 14.07 | 11.32 | 16.02 | 3.79 | 10.08 | 3.84 | 5.21 | 5.96 | 25.32 | 6.23 | 8.89 |
| | Code | 42106 | 722005 | 40502 | 748 | 4227 | 4227 | 4-41 | 4227 | 401 | 80080 | B13-22 | 202 |
| STEEL ERECTION—inter., ornam. | Rate | 2.57 | 14.07 | 11.32 | 16.02 | 3.79 | 10.08 | 3.84 | 5.21 | 5.96 | 25.32 | 6.23 | 8.89 |
| | Code | 42106 | 722005 | 40502 | 748 | 4227 | 4227 | 4-41 | 4227 | 401 | 80080 | B13-22 | 202 |
| STEEL ERECTION—structure | Rate | 2.57 | 14.07 | 11.32 | 16.02 | 3.79 | 10.08 | 3.84 | 5.21 | 5.96 | 25.32 | 6.23 | 8.89 |
| | Code | 42106 | 722005 | 40502 | 748 | 4227 | 4227 | 4-41 | 4227 | 401 | 80080 | B13-22 | 202 |
| STEEL ERECTION—NOC | Rate | 2.57 | 14.07 | 11.32 | 16.02 | 3.79 | 10.08 | 3.84 | 5.21 | 5.96 | 25.32 | 6.23 | 8.89 |
| | Code | 42106 | 722005 | 40502 | 748 | 4227 | 4227 | 4-41 | 4227 | 401 | 80080 | B13-22 | 202 |
| TILE WORK—inter. (ceramic) | Rate | 3.63 | 5.62 | 1.97 | 6.75 | 4.40 | 10.08 | 3.84 | 4.52 | 3.71 | 15.05 | 6.23 | 8.89 |
| | Code | 42113 | 721054 | 40103 | 719 | 4276 | 4276 | 4-41 | 4276 | 402 | 80110 | B13-01 | 202 |
| WATERPROOFING | Rate | 4.35 | 4.93 | 4.36 | 4.35 | 4.55 | 4.69 | 3.84 | 5.21 | 3.71 | 23.01 | 5.98 | 8.89 |
| | Code | 42139 | 721016 | 40102 | 723 | 4239 | 4299 | 4-41 | 4239 | 402 | 80130 | B12-17 | 202 |
| WRECKING | Rate | 2.51 | 4.59 | 6.59 | 16.02 | 2.62 | 4.39 | 3.64 | 3.34 | 5.96 | 15.05 | 6.23 | 8.89 |
| | Code | 40604 | 721005 | 40106 | 748 | 4211 | 4211 | 4-43 | 4211 | 401 | 80110 | B13-09 | 202 |

## R013113-80   Performance Bond

This table shows the cost of a Performance Bond for a construction job scheduled to be completed in 12 months. Add 1% of the premium cost per month for jobs requiring more than 12 months to complete. The rates are "standard" rates offered to contractors that the bonding company considers financially sound and capable of doing the work. Preferred rates are offered by some bonding companies based upon financial strength of the contractor. Actual rates vary from contractor to contractor and from bonding company to bonding company. Contractors should prequalify through a bonding agency before submitting a bid on a contract that requires a bond.

| Contract Amount | Building Construction Class B Projects | | | Highways & Bridges | | | | | |
|---|---|---|---|---|---|---|---|---|---|
| | | | | Class A New Construction | | | Class A-1 Highway Resurfacing | | |
| First $ 100,000 bid | $25.00 per M | | | $15.00 per M | | | $9.40 per M | | |
| Next 400,000 bid | $ 2,500 | plus | $15.00 per M | $ 1,500 | plus | $10.00 per M | $ 940 | plus | $7.20 per M |
| Next 2,000,000 bid | 8,500 | plus | 10.00 per M | 5,500 | plus | 7.00 per M | 3,820 | plus | 5.00 per M |
| Next 2,500,000 bid | 28,500 | plus | 7.50 per M | 19,500 | plus | 5.50 per M | 15,820 | plus | 4.50 per M |
| Next 2,500,000 bid | 47,250 | plus | 7.00 per M | 33,250 | plus | 5.00 per M | 28,320 | plus | 4.50 per M |
| Over 7,500,000 bid | 64,750 | plus | 6.00 per M | 45,750 | plus | 4.50 per M | 39,570 | plus | 4.00 per M |

## R015113-65   Temporary Power Equipment

Cost data for the temporary equipment was developed utilizing the following information.

1) Re-usable material-services, transformers, equipment and cords are based on new purchase and prorated to three projects.
2) PVC feeder includes trench and backfill.
3) Connections include disconnects and fuses.
4) Labor units include an allowance for removal.
5) No utility company charges or fees are included.
6) Concrete pads or vaults are not included.
7) Utility company conduits not included.

## R015423-10   Steel Tubular Scaffolding

On new construction, tubular scaffolding is efficient up to 60' high or five stories. Above this it is usually better to use a hung scaffolding if construction permits. Swing scaffolding operations may interfere with tenants. In this case, the tubular is more practical at all heights.

In repairing or cleaning the front of an existing building the cost of tubular scaffolding per S.F. of building front increases as the height increases above the first tier. The first tier cost is relatively high due to leveling and alignment.

The minimum efficient crew for erecting and dismantling is three workers. They can set up and remove 18 frame sections per day up to 5 stories high. For 6 to 12 stories high, a crew of four is most efficient. Use two or more on top and two on the bottom for handing up or hoisting. They can

also set up and remove 18 frame sections per day. At 7' horizontal spacing, this will run about 800 S.F. per day of erecting and dismantling. Time for placing and removing planks must be added to the above. A crew of three can place and remove 72 planks per day up to 5 stories. For over 5 stories, a crew of four can place and remove 80 planks per day.

The table below shows the number of pieces required to erect tubular steel scaffolding for 1000 S.F. of building frontage. This area is made up of a scaffolding system that is 12 frames (11 bays) long by 2 frames high.

For jobs under twenty-five frames, add 50% to rental cost. Rental rates will be lower for jobs over three months duration. Large quantities for long periods can reduce rental rates by 20%.

| Description of Component | Number of Pieces for 1000 S.F. of Building Front | Unit |
|---|---|---|
| 5' Wide Standard Frame, 6'-4" High | 24 | Ea. |
| Leveling Jack & Plate | 24 | |
| Cross Brace | 44 | |
| Side Arm Bracket, 21" | 12 | |
| Guardrail Post | 12 | |
| Guardrail, 7' section | 22 | |
| Stairway Section | 2 | |
| Stairway Starter Bar | 1 | |
| Stairway Inside Handrail | 2 | |
| Stairway Outside Handrail | 2 | |
| Walk-Thru Frame Guardrail | 2 | |

Scaffolding is often used as falsework over 15' high during construction of cast-in-place concrete beams and slabs. Two foot wide scaffolding is generally used for heavy beam construction. The span between frames depends upon the load to be carried with a maximum span of 5'.

Heavy duty shoring frames with a capacity of 10,000#/leg can be spaced up to 10' O.C. depending upon form support design and loading.

Scaffolding used as horizontal shoring requires less than half the material required with conventional shoring.

On new construction, erection is done by carpenters.

Rolling towers supporting horizontal shores can reduce labor and speed the job. For maintenance work, catwalks with spans up to 70' can be supported by the rolling towers.

## R015423-20   Pump Staging

Pump staging is generally not available for rent. The table below shows the number of pieces required to erect pump staging for 2400 S.F. of building frontage. This area is made up of a pump jack system that is 3 poles (2 bays) wide by 2 poles high.

| Item | Number of Pieces for 2400 S.F. of Building Front | Unit |
|---|---|---|
| Aluminum pole section, 24' long | 6 | Ea. |
| Aluminum splice joint, 6' long | 3 | |
| Aluminum foldable brace | 3 | |
| Aluminum pump jack | 3 | |
| Aluminum support for workbench/back safety rail | 3 | |
| Aluminum scaffold plank/workbench, 14" wide x 24' long | 4 | |
| Safety net, 22' long | 2 | |
| Aluminum plank end safety rail | 2 | |

The cost in place for this 2400 S.F. will depend on how many uses are realized during the life of the equipment.

## R015433-10    Contractor Equipment

**Rental Rates** shown elsewhere in the book pertain to late model high quality machines in excellent working condition, rented from equipment dealers. Rental rates from contractors may be substantially lower than the rental rates from equipment dealers depending upon economic conditions; for older, less productive machines, reduce rates by a maximum of 15%. Any overtime must be added to the base rates. For shift work, rates are lower. Usual rule of thumb is 150% of one shift rate for two shifts; 200% for three shifts.

For periods of less than one week, operated equipment is usually more economical to rent than renting bare equipment and hiring an operator.

Costs to move equipment to a job site (mobilization) or from a job site (demobilization) are not included in rental rates, nor in any Equipment costs on any Unit Price line items or crew listings. These costs can be found elsewhere. If a piece of equipment is already at a job site, it is not appropriate to utilize mob/demob costs in an estimate again.

Rental rates vary throughout the country with larger cities generally having lower rates. Lease plans for new equipment are available for periods in excess of six months with a percentage of payments applying toward purchase.

Monthly rental rates vary from 2% to 5% of the cost of the equipment depending on the anticipated life of the equipment and its wearing parts. Weekly rates are about 1/3 the monthly rates and daily rental rates about 1/3 the weekly rate.

The hourly operating costs for each piece of equipment include costs to the user such as fuel, oil, lubrication, normal expendables for the equipment, and a percentage of mechanic's wages chargeable to maintenance. The hourly operating costs listed do not include the operator's wages.

The daily cost for equipment used in the standard crews is figured by dividing the weekly rate by five, then adding eight times the hourly operating cost to give the total daily equipment cost, not including the operator. This figure is in the right hand column of the Equipment listings under Crew Equipment Cost/Day.

**Pile Driving** rates shown for pile hammer and extractor do not include leads, crane, boiler or compressor. Vibratory pile driving requires an added field specialist during set-up and pile driving operation for the electric model. The hydraulic model requires a field specialist for set-up only. Up to 125 reuses of sheet piling are possible using vibratory drivers. For normal conditions, crane capacity for hammer type and size are as follows.

| Crane Capacity | Hammer Type and Size | | |
|---|---|---|---|
| | Air or Steam | Diesel | Vibratory |
| 25 ton | to 8,750 ft.-lb. | | 70 H.P. |
| 40 ton | 15,000 ft.-lb. | to 32,000 ft.-lb. | 170 H.P. |
| 60 ton | 25,000 ft.-lb. | | 300 H.P. |
| 100 ton | | 112,000 ft.-lb. | |

**Cranes** should be specified for the job by size, building and site characteristics, availability, performance characteristics, and duration of time required.

**Backhoes & Shovels** rent for about the same as equivalent size cranes but maintenance and operating expense is higher. Crane operators rate must be adjusted for high boom heights. Average adjustments: for 150' boom add 2% per hour; over 185', add 4% per hour; over 210', add 6% per hour; over 250', add 8% per hour and over 295', add 12% per hour.

**Tower Cranes** of the climbing or static type have jibs from 50' to 200' and capacities at maximum reach range from 4,000 to 14,000 pounds. Lifting capacities increase up to maximum load as the hook radius decreases.

Typical rental rates, based on purchase price are about 2% to 3% per month.

Erection and dismantling runs between 500 and 2000 labor hours. Climbing operation takes 10 labor hours per 20' climb. Crane dead time is about 5 hours per 40' climb. If crane is bolted to side of the building add cost of ties and extra mast sections. Climbing cranes have from 80' to 180' of mast while static cranes have 80' to 800' of mast.

**Truck Cranes** can be converted to tower cranes by using tower attachments. Mast heights over 400' have been used.

A single 100' high material **Hoist and Tower** can be erected and dismantled in about 400 labor hours; a double 100' high hoist and tower in about 600 labor hours. Erection times for additional heights are 3 and 4 labor hours per vertical foot respectively up to 150', and 4 to 5 labor hours per vertical foot over 150' high. A 40' high portable Buck hoist takes about 160 labor hours to erect and dismantle. Additional heights take 2 labor hours per vertical foot to 80' and 3 labor hours per vertical foot for the next 100'. Most material hoists do not meet local code requirements for carrying personnel.

A 150' high **Personnel Hoist** requires about 500 to 800 labor hours to erect and dismantle. Budget erection time at 5 labor hours per vertical foot for all trades. Local code requirements or labor scarcity requiring overtime can add up to 50% to any of the above erection costs.

**Earthmoving Equipment**: The selection of earthmoving equipment depends upon the type and quantity of material, moisture content, haul distance, haul road, time available, and equipment available. Short haul cut and fill operations may require dozers only, while another operation may require excavators, a fleet of trucks, and spreading and compaction equipment. Stockpiled material and granular material are easily excavated with front end loaders. Scrapers are most economically used with hauls between 300' and 1-1/2 miles if adequate haul roads can be maintained. Shovels are often used for blasted rock and any material where a vertical face of 8' or more can be excavated. Special conditions may dictate the use of draglines, clamshells, or backhoes. Spreading and compaction equipment must be matched to the soil characteristics, the compaction required and the rate the fill is being supplied.

## R015433-15    Heavy Lifting

### Hydraulic Climbing Jacks

The use of hydraulic heavy lift systems is an alternative to conventional type crane equipment. The lifting, lowering, pushing, or pulling mechanism is a hydraulic climbing jack moving on a square steel jackrod from 1-5/8" to 4" square, or a steel cable. The jackrod or cable can be vertical or horizontal, stationary or movable, depending on the individual application. When the jackrod is stationary, the climbing jack will climb the rod and push or pull the load along with itself. When the climbing jack is stationary, the jackrod is movable with the load attached to the end and the climbing jack will lift or lower the jackrod with the attached load. The heavy lift system is normally operated by a single control lever located at the hydraulic pump.

The system is flexible in that one or more climbing jacks can be applied wherever a load support point is required, and the rate of lift synchronized.

Economic benefits have been demonstrated on projects such as: erection of ground assembled roofs and floors, complete bridge spans, girders and trusses, towers, chimney liners and steel vessels, storage tanks, and heavy machinery. Other uses are raising and lowering offshore work platforms, caissons, tunnel sections and pipelines.

### R024119-10   Demolition Defined

**Whole Building Demolition** - Demolition of the whole building with no concern for any particular building element, component, or material type being demolished. This type of demolition is accomplished with large pieces of construction equipment that break up the structure, load it into trucks and haul it to a disposal site, but disposal or dump fees are not included. Demolition of below-grade foundation elements, such as footings, foundation walls, grade beams, slabs on grade, etc., is not included. Certain mechanical equipment containing flammable liquids or ozone-depleting refrigerants, electric lighting elements, communication equipment components, and other building elements may contain hazardous waste, and must be removed, either selectively or carefully, as hazardous waste before the building can be demolished.

**Foundation Demolition** - Demolition of below-grade foundation footings, foundation walls, grade beams, and slabs on grade. This type of demolition is accomplished by hand or pneumatic hand tools, and does not include saw cutting, or handling, loading, hauling, or disposal of the debris.

**Gutting** - Removal of building interior finishes and electrical/mechanical systems down to the load-bearing and sub-floor elements of the rough building frame, with no concern for any particular building element, component, or material type being demolished. This type of demolition is accomplished by hand or pneumatic hand tools, and includes loading into trucks, but not hauling, disposal or dump fees, scaffolding, or shoring. Certain mechanical equipment containing flammable liquids or ozone-depleting refrigerants, electric lighting elements, communication equipment components, and other building elements may contain hazardous waste, and must be removed, either selectively or carefully, as hazardous waste, before the building is gutted.

**Selective Demolition** - Demolition of a selected building element, component, or finish, with some concern for surrounding or adjacent elements, components, or finishes (see the first Subdivision (s) at the beginning of appropriate Divisions). This type of demolition is accomplished by hand or pneumatic hand tools, and does not include handling, loading,

storing, hauling, or disposal of the debris, scaffolding, or shoring. "Gutting" methods may be used in order to save time, but damage that is caused to surrounding or adjacent elements, components, or finishes may have to be repaired at a later time.

**Careful Removal** - Removal of a piece of service equipment, building element or component, or material type, with great concern for both the removed item and surrounding or adjacent elements, components or finishes. The purpose of careful removal may be to protect the removed item for later re-use, preserve a higher salvage value of the removed item, or replace an item while taking care to protect surrounding or adjacent elements, components, connections, or finishes from cosmetic and/or structural damage. An approximation of the time required to perform this type of removal is 1/3 to 1/2 the time it would take to install a new item of like kind (see Reference Number R220105-10). This type of removal is accomplished by hand or pneumatic hand tools, and does not include loading, hauling, or storing the removed item, scaffolding, shoring, or lifting equipment.

**Cutout Demolition** - Demolition of a small quantity of floor, wall, roof, or other assembly, with concern for the appearance and structural integrity of the surrounding materials. This type of demolition is accomplished by hand or pneumatic hand tools, and does not include saw cutting, handling, loading, hauling, or disposal of debris, scaffolding, or shoring.

**Rubbish Handling** - Work activities that involve handling, loading or hauling of debris. Generally, the cost of rubbish handling must be added to the cost of all types of demolition, with the exception of whole building demolition.

**Minor Site Demolition** - Demolition of site elements outside the footprint of a building. This type of demolition is accomplished by hand or pneumatic hand tools, or with larger pieces of construction equipment, and may include loading a removed item onto a truck (check the Crew for equipment used). It does not include saw cutting, hauling or disposal of debris, and, sometimes, handling or loading.

### R024119-20   Dumpsters

Dumpster rental costs on construction sites are presented in two ways.

The cost per week rental includes the delivery of the dumpster; it's pulling or emptying once per week, and its final removal. The assumption is made that the dumpster contractor could choose to empty a dumpster by simply brining in an empty unit and removing the full one. These costs also include the disposal of the materials in the dumpster.

The Alternate Pricing can be used when actual planned conditions are not approximated by the weekly numbers. For example, these lines can be used when a dumpster is needed for 4 weeks and will need to be emptied 2 or 3 times per week. Conversely the Alternate Pricing lines can be used when a dumpster will be rented for several weeks or months but need to be emptied only a few times over this period.

### R026510-20   Underground Storage Tank Removal

Underground Storage Tank Removal can be divided into two categories: Non-Leaking and Leaking. Prior to removing an underground storage tank, tests should be made, with the proper authorities present, to determine whether a tank has been leaking or the surrounding soil has been contaminated.

To safely remove Liquid Underground Storage Tanks:

1. Excavate to the top of the tank.
2. Disconnect all piping.
3. Open all tank vents and access ports.

4. Remove all liquids and/or sludge.
5. Purge the tank with an inert gas.
6. Provide access to the inside of the tank and clean out the interior using proper personal protective equipment (PPE).
7. Excavate soil surrounding the tank using proper PPE for on-site personnel.
8. Pull and properly dispose of the tank.
9. Clean up the site of all contaminated material.
10. Install new tanks or close the excavation.

## Existing Conditions          R0282 Asbestos Remediation

### R028213-20     Asbestos Removal Process

Asbestos removal is accomplished by a specialty contractor who understands the federal and state regulations regarding the handling and disposal of the material. The process of asbestos removal is divided into many individual steps. An accurate estimate can be calculated only after all the steps have been priced.

The steps are generally as follows:
1. Obtain an asbestos abatement plan from an industrial hygienist.
2. Monitor the air quality in and around the removal area and along the path of travel between the removal area and transport area. This establishes the background contamination.
3. Construct a two part decontamination chamber at entrance to removal area.
4. Install a HEPA filter to create a negative pressure in the removal area.
5. Install wall, floor and ceiling protection as required by the plan, usually 2 layers of fireproof 6 mil polyethylene.
6. Industrial hygienist visually inspects work area to verify compliance with plan.
7. Provide temporary supports for conduit and piping affected by the removal process.
8. Proceed with asbestos removal and bagging process. Monitor air quality as described in Step #2. Discontinue operations when contaminate levels exceed applicable standards.
9. Document the legal disposal of materials in accordance with EPA standards.
10. Thoroughly clean removal area including all ledges, crevices and surfaces.
11. Post abatement inspection by industrial hygienist to verify plan compliance.
12. Provide a certificate from a licensed industrial hygienist attesting that contaminate levels are within acceptable standards before returning area to regular use.

## Existing Conditions          R0283 Lead Remediation

### R028319-60     Lead Paint Remediation Methods

Lead paint remediation can be accomplished by the following methods.
1. Abrasive blast
2. Chemical stripping
3. Power tool cleaning with vacuum collection system
4. Encapsulation
5. Remove and replace
6. Enclosure

Each of these methods has strengths and weakness depending on the specific circumstances of the project. The following is an overview of each method.

1. **Abrasive blasting** is usually accomplished with sand or recyclable metallic blast. Before work can begin, the area must be contained to ensure the blast material with lead does not escape to the atmosphere. The use of vacuum blast greatly reduces the containment requirements. Lead abatement equipment that may be associated with this work includes a negative air machine. In addition, it is necessary to have an industrial hygienist monitor the project on a continual basis. When the work is complete, the spent blast sand with lead must be disposed of as a hazardous material. If metallic shot was used, the lead is separated from the shot and disposed of as hazardous material. Worker protection includes disposable clothing and respiratory protection.

2. **Chemical stripping** requires strong chemicals be applied to the surface to remove the lead paint. Before the work can begin, the area under/adjacent to the work area must be covered to catch the chemical and removed lead. After the chemical is applied to the painted surface it is usually covered with paper. The chemical is left in place for the specified period, then the paper with lead paint is pulled or scraped off. The process may require several chemical applications. The paper with chemicals and lead paint adhered to it, plus the containment and loose scrapings collected by a HEPA (High Efficiency Particulate Air Filter) vac, must be disposed of as a hazardous material. The chemical stripping process usually requires a neutralizing agent and several wash downs after the paint is removed. Worker protection includes a neoprene or other compatible protective clothing and respiratory protection with face shield. An industrial hygienist is required intermittently during the process.

3. **Power tool cleaning** is accomplished using shrouded needle blasting guns. The shrouding with different end configurations is held up against the surface to be cleaned. The area is blasted with hardened needles and the shroud captures the lead with a HEPA vac and deposits it in a holding tank. An industrial hygienist monitors the project, protective clothing and a respirator is required until air samples prove otherwise. When the work is complete the lead must be disposed of as a hazardous material.

4. **Encapsulation** is a method that leaves the well bonded lead paint in place after the peeling paint has been removed. Before the work can begin, the area under/adjacent to the work must be covered to catch the scrapings. The scraped surface is then washed with a detergent and rinsed. The prepared surface is covered with approximately 10 mils of paint. A reinforcing fabric can also be embedded in the paint covering. The scraped paint and containment must be disposed of as a hazardous material. Workers must wear protective clothing and respirators.

5. **Remove and replace** is an effective way to remove lead paint from windows, gypsum walls and concrete masonry surfaces. The painted materials are removed and new materials are installed. Workers should wear a respirator and tyvek suit. The demolished materials must be disposed of as hazardous waste if it fails the TCLP (Toxicity Characteristic Leachate Process) test.

6. **Enclosure** is the process that permanently seals lead painted materials in place. This process has many applications such as covering lead painted drywall with new drywall, covering exterior construction with tyvek paper then residing, or covering lead painted structural members with aluminum or plastic. The seams on all enclosing materials must be securely sealed. An industrial hygienist monitors the project, and protective clothing and a respirator is required until air samples prove otherwise.

All the processes require clearance monitoring and wipe testing as required by the hygienist.

## R031113-10    Wall Form Materials

### Aluminum Forms

Approximate weight is 3 lbs. per S.F.C.A. Standard widths are available from 4″ to 36″ with 36″ most common. Standard lengths of 2′, 4′, 6′ to 8′ are available. Forms are lightweight and fewer ties are needed with the wider widths. The form face is either smooth or textured.

### Metal Framed Plywood Forms

Manufacturers claim over 75 reuses of plywood and over 300 reuses of steel frames. Many specials such as corners, fillers, pilasters, etc. are available. Monthly rental is generally about 15% of purchase price for first month and 9% per month thereafter with 90% of rental applied to purchase for the first month and decreasing percentages thereafter. Aluminum framed forms cost 25% to 30% more than steel framed.

After the first month, extra days may be prorated from the monthly charge. Rental rates do not include ties, accessories, cleaning, loss of hardware or freight in and out. Approximate weight is 5 lbs. per S.F. for steel; 3 lbs. per S.F. for aluminum.

Forms can be rented with option to buy.

### Plywood Forms, Job Fabricated

There are two types of plywood used for concrete forms.

1. Exterior plyform which is completely waterproof. This is face oiled to facilitate stripping. Ten reuses can be expected with this type with 25 reuses possible.
2. An overlaid type consists of a resin fiber fused to exterior plyform. No oiling is required except to facilitate cleaning. This is available in both high density (HDO) and medium density overlaid (MDO). Using HDO, 50 reuses can be expected with 200 possible.

Plyform is available in 5/8″ and 3/4″ thickness. High density overlaid is available in 3/8″, 1/2″, 5/8″ and 3/4″ thickness.

5/8″ thick is sufficient for most building forms, while 3/4″ is best on heavy construction.

### Plywood Forms, Modular, Prefabricated

There are many plywood forming systems without frames. Most of these are manufactured from 1-1/8″ (HDO) plywood and have some hardware attached. These are used principally for foundation walls 8′ or less high. With care and maintenance, 100 reuses can be attained with decreasing quality of surface finish.

### Steel Forms

Approximate weight is 6-1/2 lbs. per S.F.C.A. including accessories. Standard widths are available from 2″ to 24″, with 24″ most common. Standard lengths are from 2′ to 8′, with 4′ the most common. Forms are easily ganged into modular units.

Forms are usually leased for 15% of the purchase price per month prorated daily over 30 days.

Rental may be applied to sale price, and usually rental forms are bought. With careful handling and cleaning 200 to 400 reuses are possible.

Straight wall gang forms up to 12′ x 20′ or 8′ x 30′ can be fabricated. These crane handled forms usually lease for approx. 9% per month.

Individual job analysis is available from the manufacturer at no charge.

## R031113-30    Slipforms

The slipform method of forming may be used for forming circular silo and multi-celled storage bin type structures over 30′ high, and building core shear walls over eight stories high. The shear walls, usually enclose elevator shafts, stairwells, mechanical spaces, and toilet rooms. Reuse of the form on duplicate structures will reduce the height necessary and spread the cost of building the form. Slipform systems can be used to cast chimneys, towers, piers, dams, underground shafts or other structures capable of being extruded.

Slipforms are usually 4′ high and are raised semi-continuously by jacks climbing on rods which are embedded in the concrete. The jacks are powered by a hydraulic, pneumatic, or electric source and are available in 3, 6, and 22 ton capacities. Interior work decks and exterior scaffolds must be provided for placing inserts, embedded items, reinforcing steel, and

concrete. Scaffolds below the form for finishers may be required. The interior work decks are often used as roof slab forms on silos and bin work. Form raising rates will range from 6″ to 20″ per hour for silos; 6″ to 30″ per hour for buildings; and 6″ to 48″ per hour for shaft work.

Reinforcing bars and stressing strands are usually hoisted by crane or gin pole, and the concrete material can be hoisted by crane, winch-powered skip, or pumps. The slipform system is operated on a continuous 24-hour day when a monolithic structure is desired. For least cost, the system is operated only during normal working hours.

Placing concrete will range from 0.5 to 1.5 labor-hours per C.Y. Bucks, blockouts, keyways, weldplates, etc. are extra.

## R031113-40  Forms for Reinforced Concrete

### Design Economy

Avoid many sizes in proportioning beams and columns.

From story to story avoid changing column dimensions. Gain strength by adding steel or using a richer mix. If a change in size of column is necessary, vary one dimension only to minimize form alterations. Keep beams and columns the same width.

From floor to floor in a multi-story building vary beam depth, not width, as that will leave slab panel form unchanged. It is cheaper to vary the strength of a beam from floor to floor by means of steel area than by 2" changes in either width or depth.

### Cost Factors

Material includes the cost of lumber, cost of rent for metal pans or forms if used, nails, form ties, form oil, bolts and accessories.

Labor includes the cost of carpenters to make up, erect, remove and repair, plus common labor to clean and move. Having carpenters remove forms minimizes repairs.

Improper alignment and condition of forms will increase finishing cost. When forms are heavily oiled, concrete surfaces must be neutralized before finishing. Special curing compounds will cause spillages to spall off in first frost. Gang forming methods will reduce costs on large projects.

### Materials Used

Boards are seldom used unless their architectural finish is required. Generally, steel, fiberglass and plywood are used for contact surfaces. Labor on plywood is 10% less than with boards. The plywood is backed up with

2 x 4's at 12" to 32" O.C. Walers are generally 2 - 2 x 4's. Column forms are held together with steel yokes or bands. Shoring is with adjustable shoring or scaffolding for high ceilings.

### Reuse

Floor and column forms can be reused four or possibly five times without excessive repair. Remember to allow for 10% waste on each reuse.

When modular sized wall forms are made, up to twenty uses can be expected with exterior plyform.

When forms are reused, the cost to erect, strip, clean and move will not be affected. 10% replacement of lumber should be included and about one hour of carpenter time for repairs on each reuse per 100 S.F.

The reuse cost for certain accessory items normally rented on a monthly basis will be lower than the cost for the first use.

After fifth use, new material required plus time needed for repair prevent form cost from dropping further and it may go up. Much depends on care in stripping, the number of special bays, changes in beam or column sizes and other factors.

**Costs for multiple use of formwork may be developed as follows:**

| 2 Uses | 3 Uses | 4 Uses |
|---|---|---|
| $\dfrac{\text{(1st Use + Reuse)}}{2} = \text{avg. cost/2 uses}$ | $\dfrac{\text{(1st Use + 2 Reuse)}}{3} = \text{avg. cost/3 uses}$ | $\dfrac{\text{(1st use + 3 Reuse)}}{4} = \text{avg. cost/4 uses}$ |

## R031113-60  Formwork Labor-Hours

| Item | Unit | Hours Required | | | Total Hours | Multiple Use | | |
|---|---|---|---|---|---|---|---|---|
| | | Fabricate | Erect & Strip | Clean & Move | 1 Use | 2 Use | 3 Use | 4 Use |
| Beam and Girder, interior beams, 12" wide | 100 S.F. | 6.4 | 8.3 | 1.3 | 16.0 | 13.3 | 12.4 | 12.0 |
|   Hung from steel beams | | 5.8 | 7.7 | 1.3 | 14.8 | 12.4 | 11.6 | 11.2 |
|   Beam sides only, 36" high | | 5.8 | 7.2 | 1.3 | 14.3 | 11.9 | 11.1 | 10.7 |
|   Beam bottoms only, 24" wide | | 6.6 | 13.0 | 1.3 | 20.9 | 18.1 | 17.2 | 16.7 |
| Box out for openings | | 9.9 | 10.0 | 1.1 | 21.0 | 16.6 | 15.1 | 14.3 |
| Buttress forms, to 8' high | | 6.0 | 6.5 | 1.2 | 13.7 | 11.2 | 10.4 | 10.0 |
| Centering, steel, 3/4" rib lath | | | 1.0 | | 1.0 | | | |
|   3/8" rib lath or slab form | | | 0.9 | | 0.9 | | | |
| Chamfer strip or keyway | 100 L.F. | | 1.5 | | 1.5 | 1.5 | 1.5 | 1.5 |
| Columns, fiber tube 8" diameter | | | 20.6 | | 20.6 | | | |
|   12" | | | 21.3 | | 21.3 | | | |
|   16" | | | 22.9 | | 22.9 | | | |
|   20" | | | 23.7 | | 23.7 | | | |
|   24" | | | 24.6 | | 24.6 | | | |
|   30" | | | 25.6 | | 25.6 | | | |
| Columns, round steel, 12" diameter | | | 22.0 | | 22.0 | 22.0 | 22.0 | 22.0 |
|   16" | | | 25.6 | | 25.6 | 25.6 | 25.6 | 25.6 |
|   20" | | | 30.5 | | 30.5 | 30.5 | 30.5 | 30.5 |
|   24" | | | 37.7 | | 37.7 | 37.7 | 37.7 | 37.7 |
| Columns, plywood 8" x 8" | 100 S.F. | 7.0 | 11.0 | 1.2 | 19.2 | 16.2 | 15.2 | 14.7 |
|   12" x 12" | | 6.0 | 10.5 | 1.2 | 17.7 | 15.2 | 14.4 | 14.0 |
|   16" x 16" | | 5.9 | 10.0 | 1.2 | 17.1 | 14.7 | 13.8 | 13.4 |
|   24" x 24" | | 5.8 | 9.8 | 1.2 | 16.8 | 14.4 | 13.6 | 13.2 |
| Columns, steel framed plywood 8" x 8" | | | 10.0 | 1.0 | 11.0 | 11.0 | 11.0 | 11.0 |
|   12" x 12" | | | 9.3 | 1.0 | 10.3 | 10.3 | 10.3 | 10.3 |
|   16" x 16" | | | 8.5 | 1.0 | 9.5 | 9.5 | 9.5 | 9.5 |
|   24" x 24" | | | 7.8 | 1.0 | 8.8 | 8.8 | 8.8 | 8.8 |
| Drop head forms, plywood | | 9.0 | 12.5 | 1.5 | 23.0 | 19.0 | 17.7 | 17.0 |
| Coping forms | | 8.5 | 15.0 | 1.5 | 25.0 | 21.3 | 20.0 | 19.4 |
| Culvert, box | | | 14.5 | 4.3 | 18.8 | 18.8 | 18.8 | 18.8 |
| Curb forms, 6" to 12" high, on grade | | 5.0 | 8.5 | 1.2 | 14.7 | 12.7 | 12.1 | 11.7 |
|   On elevated slabs | | 6.0 | 10.8 | 1.2 | 18.0 | 15.5 | 14.7 | 14.3 |
| Edge forms to 6" high, on grade | 100 L.F. | 2.0 | 3.5 | 0.6 | 6.1 | 5.6 | 5.4 | 5.3 |
|   7" to 12" high | 100 S.F. | 2.5 | 5.0 | 1.0 | 8.5 | 7.8 | 7.5 | 7.4 |
| Equipment foundations | | 10.0 | 18.0 | 2.0 | 30.0 | 25.5 | 24.0 | 23.3 |
| Flat slabs, including drops | | 3.5 | 6.0 | 1.2 | 10.7 | 9.5 | 9.0 | 8.8 |
|   Hung from steel | | 3.0 | 5.5 | 1.2 | 9.7 | 8.7 | 8.4 | 8.2 |
|   Closed deck for domes | | 3.0 | 5.8 | 1.2 | 10.0 | 9.0 | 8.7 | 8.5 |
|   Open deck for pans | | 2.2 | 5.3 | 1.0 | 8.5 | 7.9 | 7.7 | 7.6 |
| Footings, continuous, 12" high | | 3.5 | 3.5 | 1.5 | 8.5 | 7.3 | 6.8 | 6.6 |
|   Spread, 12" high | | 4.7 | 4.2 | 1.6 | 10.5 | 8.7 | 8.0 | 7.7 |
|   Pile caps, square or rectangular | | 4.5 | 5.0 | 1.5 | 11.0 | 9.3 | 8.7 | 8.4 |
| Grade beams, 24" deep | | 2.5 | 5.3 | 1.2 | 9.0 | 8.3 | 8.0 | 7.9 |
| Lintel or Sill forms | | 8.0 | 17.0 | 2.0 | 27.0 | 23.5 | 22.3 | 21.8 |
| Spandrel beams, 12" wide | | 9.0 | 11.2 | 1.3 | 21.5 | 17.5 | 16.2 | 15.5 |
| Stairs | | | 25.0 | 4.0 | 29.0 | 29.0 | 29.0 | 29.0 |
| Trench forms in floor | | 4.5 | 14.0 | 1.5 | 20.0 | 18.3 | 17.7 | 17.4 |
| Walls, Plywood, at grade, to 8' high | | 5.0 | 6.5 | 1.5 | 13.0 | 11.0 | 9.7 | 9.5 |
|   8' to 16' | | 7.5 | 8.0 | 1.5 | 17.0 | 13.8 | 12.7 | 12.1 |
|   16' to 20' | | 9.0 | 10.0 | 1.5 | 20.5 | 16.5 | 15.2 | 14.5 |
| Foundation walls, to 8' high | | 4.5 | 6.5 | 1.0 | 12.0 | 10.3 | 9.7 | 9.4 |
|   8' to 16' high | | 5.5 | 7.5 | 1.0 | 14.0 | 11.8 | 11.0 | 10.6 |
| Retaining wall to 12' high, battered | | 6.0 | 8.5 | 1.5 | 16.0 | 13.5 | 12.7 | 12.3 |
| Radial walls to 12' high, smooth | | 8.0 | 9.5 | 2.0 | 19.5 | 16.0 | 14.8 | 14.3 |
|   2' chords | | 7.0 | 8.0 | 1.5 | 16.5 | 13.5 | 12.5 | 12.0 |
| Prefabricated modular, to 8' high | | — | 4.3 | 1.0 | 5.3 | 5.3 | 5.3 | 5.3 |
| Steel, to 8' high | | — | 6.8 | 1.2 | 8.0 | 8.0 | 8.0 | 8.0 |
|   8' to 16' high | | — | 9.1 | 1.5 | 10.6 | 10.3 | 10.2 | 10.2 |
| Steel framed plywood to 8' high | | — | 6.8 | 1.2 | 8.0 | 7.5 | 7.3 | 7.2 |
|   8' to 16' high | | — | 9.3 | 1.2 | 10.5 | 9.5 | 9.2 | 9.0 |

## R032110-10　Reinforcing Steel Weights and Measures

| Bar Designation No.** | Nominal Weight Lb./Ft. | U.S. Customary Units Nominal Dimensions* | | | SI Units Nominal Dimensions* | | | |
|---|---|---|---|---|---|---|---|---|
| | | Diameter in. | Cross Sectional Area, in.² | Perimeter in. | Nominal Weight kg/m | Diameter mm | Cross Sectional Area, cm² | Perimeter mm |
| 3 | .376 | .375 | .11 | 1.178 | .560 | 9.52 | .71 | 29.9 |
| 4 | .668 | .500 | .20 | 1.571 | .994 | 12.70 | 1.29 | 39.9 |
| 5 | 1.043 | .625 | .31 | 1.963 | 1.552 | 15.88 | 2.00 | 49.9 |
| 6 | 1.502 | .750 | .44 | 2.356 | 2.235 | 19.05 | 2.84 | 59.8 |
| 7 | 2.044 | .875 | .60 | 2.749 | 3.042 | 22.22 | 3.87 | 69.8 |
| 8 | 2.670 | 1.000 | .79 | 3.142 | 3.973 | 25.40 | 5.10 | 79.8 |
| 9 | 3.400 | 1.128 | 1.00 | 3.544 | 5.059 | 28.65 | 6.45 | 90.0 |
| 10 | 4.303 | 1.270 | 1.27 | 3.990 | 6.403 | 32.26 | 8.19 | 101.4 |
| 11 | 5.313 | 1.410 | 1.56 | 4.430 | 7.906 | 35.81 | 10.06 | 112.5 |
| 14 | 7.650 | 1.693 | 2.25 | 5.320 | 11.384 | 43.00 | 14.52 | 135.1 |
| 18 | 13.600 | 2.257 | 4.00 | 7.090 | 20.238 | 57.33 | 25.81 | 180.1 |

* The nominal dimensions of a deformed bar are equivalent to those of a plain round bar having the same weight per foot as the deformed bar.
** Bar numbers are based on the number of eighths of an inch included in the nominal diameter of the bars.

## R032110-20　Metric Rebar Specification - ASTM A615-81

| Grade 300 (300 MPa* = 43,560 psi; +8.7% vs. Grade 40) | | | | |
|---|---|---|---|---|
| Grade 400 (400 MPa* = 58,000 psi; −3.4% vs. Grade 60) | | | | |
| Bar No. | Diameter mm | Area mm² | Equivalent in.² | Comparison with U.S. Customary Bars |
| 10M | 11.3 | 100 | .16 | Between #3 & #4 |
| 15M | 16.0 | 200 | .31 | #5 (.31 in.²) |
| 20M | 19.5 | 300 | .47 | #6 (.44 in.²) |
| 25M | 25.2 | 500 | .78 | #8 (.79 in.²) |
| 30M | 29.9 | 700 | 1.09 | #9 (1.00 in.²) |
| 35M | 35.7 | 1000 | 1.55 | #11 (1.56 in.²) |
| 45M | 43.7 | 1500 | 2.33 | #14 (2.25 in.²) |
| 55M | 56.4 | 2500 | 3.88 | #18 (4.00 in.²) |

* MPa = megapascals

### R032110-40    Weight of Steel Reinforcing Per Square Foot of Wall (PSF)

Reinforced Weights: The table below suggests the weights per square foot for reinforcing steel in walls. Weights are approximate and will be the same for all grades of steel bars. For bars in two directions, add weights for each size and spacing.

| C/C Spacing in Inches | Bar Size | | | | | | | | |
|---|---|---|---|---|---|---|---|---|---|
| | #3 Wt. (PSF) | #4 Wt. (PSF) | #5 Wt. (PSF) | #6 Wt. (PSF) | #7 Wt. (PSF) | #8 Wt. (PSF) | #9 Wt. (PSF) | #10 Wt. (PSF) | #11 Wt. (PSF) |
| 2" | 2.26 | 4.01 | 6.26 | 9.01 | 12.27 | | | | |
| 3" | 1.50 | 2.67 | 4.17 | 6.01 | 8.18 | 10.68 | 13.60 | 17.21 | 21.25 |
| 4" | 1.13 | 2.01 | 3.13 | 4.51 | 6.13 | 8.10 | 10.20 | 12.91 | 15.94 |
| 5" | .90 | 1.60 | 2.50 | 3.60 | 4.91 | 6.41 | 8.16 | 10.33 | 12.75 |
| 6" | .752 | 1.34 | 2.09 | 3.00 | 4.09 | 5.34 | 6.80 | 8.61 | 10.63 |
| 8" | .564 | 1.00 | 1.57 | 2.25 | 3.07 | 4.01 | 5.10 | 6.46 | 7.97 |
| 10" | .451 | .802 | 1.25 | 1.80 | 2.45 | 3.20 | 4.08 | 5.16 | 6.38 |
| 12" | .376 | .668 | 1.04 | 1.50 | 2.04 | 2.67 | 3.40 | 4.30 | 5.31 |
| 18" | .251 | .445 | .695 | 1.00 | 1.32 | 1.78 | 2.27 | 2.86 | 3.54 |
| 24" | .188 | .334 | .522 | .751 | 1.02 | 1.34 | 1.70 | 2.15 | 2.66 |
| 30" | .150 | .267 | .417 | .600 | .817 | 1.07 | 1.36 | 1.72 | 2.13 |
| 36" | .125 | .223 | .348 | .501 | .681 | .890 | 1.13 | 1.43 | 1.77 |
| 42" | .107 | .191 | .298 | .429 | .584 | .753 | .97 | 1.17 | 1.52 |
| 48" | .094 | .167 | .261 | .376 | .511 | .668 | .85 | 1.08 | 1.33 |

### R032110-50    Minimum Wall Reinforcement Weight (PSF)

This table lists the approximate minimum wall reinforcement weights per S.F. according to the specification of .12% of gross area for vertical bars and .20% of gross area for horizontal bars.

| Location | Wall Thickness | Bar Size | Horizontal Steel Spacing C/C | Sq. In. Req'd per S.F. | Total Wt. per S.F. | Bar Size | Vertical Steel Spacing C/C | Sq. In. Req'd per S.F. | Total Wt. per S.F. | Horizontal & Vertical Steel Total Weight per S.F. |
|---|---|---|---|---|---|---|---|---|---|---|
| Both Faces | 10" | #4 | 18" | .24 | .89# | #3 | 18" | .14 | .50# | 1.39# |
| | 12" | #4 | 16" | .29 | 1.00 | #3 | 16" | .17 | .60 | 1.60 |
| | 14" | #4 | 14" | .34 | 1.14 | #3 | 13" | .20 | .69 | 1.84 |
| | 16" | #4 | 12" | .38 | 1.34 | #3 | 11" | .23 | .82 | 2.16 |
| | 18" | #5 | 17" | .43 | 1.47 | #4 | 18" | .26 | .89 | 2.36 |
| One Face | 6" | #3 | 9" | .15 | .50 | #3 | 18" | .09 | .25 | .75 |
| | 8" | #4 | 12" | .19 | .67 | #3 | 11" | .12 | .41 | 1.08 |
| | 10" | #5 | 15" | .24 | .83 | #4 | 16" | .14 | .50 | 1.34 |

### R032110-70    Bend, Place and Tie Reinforcing

Placing and tying by rodmen for footings and slabs runs from nine hrs. per ton for heavy bars to fifteen hrs. per ton for light bars. For beams, columns, and walls, production runs from eight hrs. per ton for heavy bars to twenty hrs. per ton for light bars. Overall average for typical reinforced concrete buildings is about fourteen hrs. per ton. These production figures include the time for placing of accessories and usual inserts, but not their material cost (allow 15% of the cost of delivered bent rods). Equipment handling is necessary for the larger-sized bars so that installation costs for the very heavy bars will not decrease proportionately.

Installation costs for splicing reinforcing bars include allowance for equipment to hold the bars in place while splicing as well as necessary scaffolding for iron workers.

### R032110-80    Shop-Fabricated Reinforcing Steel

The material prices for reinforcing, shown in the unit cost sections of the book, are for 50 tons or more of shop-fabricated reinforcing steel and include:

1. Mill base price of reinforcing steel
2. Mill grade/size/length extras
3. Mill delivery to the fabrication shop
4. Shop storage and handling
5. Shop drafting/detailing
6. Shop shearing and bending
7. Shop listing
8. Shop delivery to the job site

Both material and installation costs can be considerably higher for small jobs consisting primarily of smaller bars, while material costs may be slightly lower for larger jobs.

## R032205-30   Common Stock Styles of Welded Wire Fabric

This table provides some of the basic specifications, sizes, and weights of welded wire fabric used for reinforcing concrete.

| New Designation | | Old Designation | | Steel Area per Foot | | | | Approximate Weight per 100 S.F. | |
|---|---|---|---|---|---|---|---|---|---|
| Spacing — Cross Sectional Area (in.) — (Sq. in. 100) | | Spacing — Wire Gauge (in.) — (AS & W) | | Longitudinal | | Transverse | | | |
| | | | | in. | cm | in. | cm | lbs | kg |
| Rolls | 6 x 6 — W1.4 x W1.4 | 6 x 6 — 10 x 10 | | .028 | .071 | .028 | .071 | 21 | 9.53 |
| | 6 x 6 — W2.0 x W2.0 | 6 x 6 — 8 x 8 | 1 | .040 | .102 | .040 | .102 | 29 | 13.15 |
| | 6 x 6 — W2.9 x W2.9 | 6 x 6 — 6 x 6 | | .058 | .147 | .058 | .147 | 42 | 19.05 |
| | 6 x 6 — W4.0 x W4.0 | 6 x 6 — 4 x 4 | | .080 | .203 | .080 | .203 | 58 | 26.91 |
| | 4 x 4 — W1.4 x W1.4 | 4 x 4 — 10 x 10 | | .042 | .107 | .042 | .107 | 31 | 14.06 |
| | 4 x 4 — W2.0 x W2.0 | 4 x 4 — 8 x 8 | 1 | .060 | .152 | .060 | .152 | 43 | 19.50 |
| | 4 x 4 — W2.9 x W2.9 | 4 x 4 — 6 x 6 | | .087 | .227 | .087 | .227 | 62 | 28.12 |
| | 4 x 4 — W4.0 x W4.0 | 4 x 4 — 4 x 4 | | .120 | .305 | .120 | .305 | 85 | 38.56 |
| Sheets | 6 x 6 — W2.9 x W2.9 | 6 x 6 — 6 x 6 | | .058 | .147 | .058 | .147 | 42 | 19.05 |
| | 6 x 6 — W4.0 x W4.0 | 6 x 6 — 4 x 4 | | .080 | .203 | .080 | .203 | 58 | 26.31 |
| | 6 x 6 — W5.5 x W5.5 | 6 x 6 — 2 x 2 | 2 | .110 | .279 | .110 | .279 | 80 | 36.29 |
| | 4 x 4 — W1.4 x W1.4 | 4 x 4 — 4 x 4 | | .120 | .305 | .120 | .305 | 85 | 38.56 |

NOTES: 1. Exact W—number size for 8 gauge is W2.1
     2. Exact W—number size for 2 gauge is W5.4

## R033053-50   Industrial Chimneys

Foundation requirements in C.Y. of concrete for various sized chimneys.

| Size Chimney | 2 Ton Soil | 3 Ton Soil | Size Chimney | 2 Ton Soil | 3 Ton Soil | Size Chimney | 2 Ton Soil | 3 Ton Soil |
|---|---|---|---|---|---|---|---|---|
| 75' x 3'-0" | 13   C.Y. | 11   C.Y. | 160' x 6'-6" | 86   C.Y. | 76   C.Y. | 300' x 10'-0" | 325   C.Y. | 245   C.Y. |
| 85' x 5'-6" | 19 | 16 | 175' x 7'-0" | 108 | 95 | 350' x 12'-0" | 422 | 320 |
| 100' x 5'-0" | 24 | 20 | 200' x 6'-0" | 125 | 105 | 400' x 14'-0" | 520 | 400 |
| 125' x 5'-6" | 43 | 36 | 250' x 8'-0" | 230 | 175 | 500' x 18'-0" | 725 | 575 |

## R033105-10  Proportionate Quantities

The tables below show both quantities per S.F. of floor areas as well as form and reinforcing quantities per C.Y. Unusual structural requirements would increase the ratios below. High strength reinforcing would reduce the steel weights. Figures are for 3000 psi concrete and 60,000 psi reinforcing unless specified otherwise.

| Type of Construction | Live Load | Span | Per S.F. of Floor Area | | | | Per C.Y. of Concrete | | |
|---|---|---|---|---|---|---|---|---|---|
| | | | Concrete | Forms | Reinf. | Pans | Forms | Reinf. | Pans |
| Flat Plate | 50 psf | 15 Ft. | .46 C.F. | 1.06 S.F. | 1.71 lb. | | 62 S.F. | 101 lb. | |
| | | 20 | .63 | 1.02 | 2.40 | | 44 | 104 | |
| | | 25 | .79 | 1.02 | 3.03 | | 35 | 104 | |
| | 100 | 15 | .46 | 1.04 | 2.14 | | 61 | 126 | |
| | | 20 | .71 | 1.02 | 2.72 | | 39 | 104 | |
| | | 25 | .83 | 1.01 | 3.47 | | 33 | 113 | |
| Flat Plate (waffle construction) 20" domes | 50 | 20 | .43 | 1.00 | 2.10 | .84 S.F. | 63 | 135 | 53 S.F. |
| | | 25 | .52 | 1.00 | 2.90 | .89 | 52 | 150 | 46 |
| | | 30 | .64 | 1.00 | 3.70 | .87 | 42 | 155 | 37 |
| | 100 | 20 | .51 | 1.00 | 2.30 | .84 | 53 | 125 | 45 |
| | | 25 | .64 | 1.00 | 3.20 | .83 | 42 | 135 | 35 |
| | | 30 | .76 | 1.00 | 4.40 | .81 | 36 | 160 | 29 |
| Waffle Construction 30" domes | 50 | 25 | .69 | 1.06 | 1.83 | .68 | 42 | 72 | 40 |
| | | 30 | .74 | 1.06 | 2.39 | .69 | 39 | 87 | 39 |
| | | 35 | .86 | 1.05 | 2.71 | .69 | 33 | 85 | 39 |
| | | 40 | .78 | 1.00 | 4.80 | .68 | 35 | 165 | 40 |
| Flat Slab (two way with drop panels) | 50 | 20 | .62 | 1.03 | 2.34 | | 45 | 102 | |
| | | 25 | .77 | 1.03 | 2.99 | | 36 | 105 | |
| | | 30 | .95 | 1.03 | 4.09 | | 29 | 116 | |
| | 100 | 20 | .64 | 1.03 | 2.83 | | 43 | 119 | |
| | | 25 | .79 | 1.03 | 3.88 | | 35 | 133 | |
| | | 30 | .96 | 1.03 | 4.66 | | 29 | 131 | |
| | 200 | 20 | .73 | 1.03 | 3.03 | | 38 | 112 | |
| | | 25 | .86 | 1.03 | 4.23 | | 32 | 133 | |
| | | 30 | 1.06 | 1.03 | 5.30 | | 26 | 135 | |
| One Way Joists 20" Pans | 50 | 15 | .36 | 1.04 | 1.40 | .93 | 78 | 105 | 70 |
| | | 20 | .42 | 1.05 | 1.80 | .94 | 67 | 120 | 60 |
| | | 25 | .47 | 1.05 | 2.60 | .94 | 60 | 150 | 54 |
| | 100 | 15 | .38 | 1.07 | 1.90 | .93 | 77 | 140 | 66 |
| | | 20 | .44 | 1.08 | 2.40 | .94 | 67 | 150 | 58 |
| | | 25 | .52 | 1.07 | 3.50 | .94 | 55 | 185 | 49 |
| One Way Joists 8" x 16" filler blocks | 50 | 15 | .34 | 1.06 | 1.80 | .81 Ea. | 84 | 145 | 64 Ea. |
| | | 20 | .40 | 1.08 | 2.20 | .82 | 73 | 145 | 55 |
| | | 25 | .46 | 1.07 | 3.20 | .83 | 63 | 190 | 49 |
| | 100 | 15 | .39 | 1.07 | 1.90 | .81 | 74 | 130 | 56 |
| | | 20 | .46 | 1.09 | 2.80 | .82 | 64 | 160 | 48 |
| | | 25 | .53 | 1.10 | 3.60 | .83 | 56 | 190 | 42 |
| One Way Beam & Slab | 50 | 15 | .42 | 1.30 | 1.73 | | 84 | 111 | |
| | | 20 | .51 | 1.28 | 2.61 | | 68 | 138 | |
| | | 25 | .64 | 1.25 | 2.78 | | 53 | 117 | |
| | 100 | 15 | .42 | 1.30 | 1.90 | | 84 | 122 | |
| | | 20 | .54 | 1.35 | 2.69 | | 68 | 154 | |
| | | 25 | .69 | 1.37 | 3.93 | | 54 | 145 | |
| | 200 | 15 | .44 | 1.31 | 2.24 | | 80 | 137 | |
| | | 20 | .58 | 1.40 | 3.30 | | 65 | 163 | |
| | | 25 | .69 | 1.42 | 4.89 | | 53 | 183 | |
| Two Way Beam & Slab | 100 | 15 | .47 | 1.20 | 2.26 | | 69 | 130 | |
| | | 20 | .63 | 1.29 | 3.06 | | 55 | 131 | |
| | | 25 | .83 | 1.33 | 3.79 | | 43 | 123 | |
| | 200 | 15 | .49 | 1.25 | 2.70 | | 41 | 149 | |
| | | 20 | .66 | 1.32 | 4.04 | | 54 | 165 | |
| | | 25 | .88 | 1.32 | 6.08 | | 41 | 187 | |

**Concrete** | **R0331 Structural Concrete**

Reference Tables

## R033105-10  Proportionate Quantities (cont.)

| 4000 psi Concrete and 60,000 psi Reinforcing—Form and Reinforcing Quantities per C.Y. | | | | | |
|---|---|---|---|---|---|
| Item | Size | Forms | Reinforcing | Minimum | Maximum |
| Columns (square tied) | 10" x 10" | 130 S.F.C.A. | #5 to #11 | 220 lbs. | 875 lbs. |
| | 12" x 12" | 108 | #6 to #14 | 200 | 955 |
| | 14" x 14" | 92 | #7 to #14 | 190 | 900 |
| | 16" x 16" | 81 | #6 to #14 | 187 | 1082 |
| | 18" x 18" | 72 | #6 to #14 | 170 | 906 |
| | 20" x 20" | 65 | #7 to #18 | 150 | 1080 |
| | 22" x 22" | 59 | #8 to #18 | 153 | 902 |
| | 24" x 24" | 54 | #8 to #18 | 164 | 884 |
| | 26" x 26" | 50 | #9 to #18 | 169 | 994 |
| | 28" x 28" | 46 | #9 to #18 | 147 | 864 |
| | 30" x 30" | 43 | #10 to #18 | 146 | 983 |
| | 32" x 32" | 40 | #10 to #18 | 175 | 866 |
| | 34" x 34" | 38 | #10 to #18 | 157 | 772 |
| | 36" x 36" | 36 | #10 to #18 | 175 | 852 |
| | 38" x 38" | 34 | #10 to #18 | 158 | 765 |
| | 40" x 40" | 32 | #10 to #18 | 143 | 692 |

| Item | Size | Form | Spiral | Reinforcing | Minimum | Maximum |
|---|---|---|---|---|---|---|
| Columns (spirally reinforced) | 12" diameter | 34.5 L.F. | 190 lbs. | #4 to #11 | 165 lbs. | 1505 lb. |
| | | 34.5 | 190 | #14 & #18 | — | 1100 |
| | 14" | 25 | 170 | #4 to #11 | 150 | 970 |
| | | 25 | 170 | #14 & #18 | 800 | 1000 |
| | 16" | 19 | 160 | #4 to #11 | 160 | 950 |
| | | 19 | 160 | #14 & #18 | 605 | 1080 |
| | 18" | 15 | 150 | #4 to #11 | 160 | 915 |
| | | 15 | 150 | #14 & #18 | 480 | 1075 |
| | 20" | 12 | 130 | #4 to #11 | 155 | 865 |
| | | 12 | 130 | #14 & #18 | 385 | 1020 |
| | 22" | 10 | 125 | #4 to #11 | 165 | 775 |
| | | 10 | 125 | #14 & #18 | 320 | 995 |
| | 24" | 9 | 120 | #4 to #11 | 195 | 800 |
| | | 9 | 120 | #14 & #18 | 290 | 1150 |
| | 26" | 7.3 | 100 | #4 to #11 | 200 | 729 |
| | | 7.3 | 100 | #14 & #18 | 235 | 1035 |
| | 28" | 6.3 | 95 | #4 to #11 | 175 | 700 |
| | | 6.3 | 95 | #14 & #18 | 200 | 1075 |
| | 30" | 5.5 | 90 | #4 to #11 | 180 | 670 |
| | | 5.5 | 90 | #14 & #18 | 175 | 1015 |
| | 32" | 4.8 | 85 | #4 to #11 | 185 | 615 |
| | | 4.8 | 85 | #14 & #18 | 155 | 955 |
| | 34" | 4.3 | 80 | #4 to #11 | 180 | 600 |
| | | 4.3 | 80 | #14 & #18 | 170 | 855 |
| | 36" | 3.8 | 75 | #4 to #11 | 165 | 570 |
| | | 3.8 | 75 | #14 & #18 | 155 | 865 |
| | 40" | 3.0 | 70 | #4 to #11 | 165 | 500 |
| | | 3.0 | 70 | #14 & #18 | 145 | 765 |

## R033105-10 Proportionate Quantities (cont.)

| 3000 psi Concrete and 60,000 psi Reinforcing—Form and Reinforcing Quantities per C.Y. | | | | | | |
|---|---|---|---|---|---|---|
| Item | Type | Loading | Height | C.Y./L.F. | Forms/C.Y. | Reinf./C.Y. |
| Retaining Walls | Cantilever | Level Backfill | 4 Ft. | 0.2 C.Y. | 49 S.F. | 35 lbs. |
| | | | 8 | 0.5 | 42 | 45 |
| | | | 12 | 0.8 | 35 | 70 |
| | | | 16 | 1.1 | 32 | 85 |
| | | | 20 | 1.6 | 28 | 105 |
| | | Highway Surcharge | 4 | 0.3 | 41 | 35 |
| | | | 8 | 0.5 | 36 | 55 |
| | | | 12 | 0.8 | 33 | 90 |
| | | | 16 | 1.2 | 30 | 120 |
| | | | 20 | 1.7 | 27 | 155 |
| | | Railroad Surcharge | 4 | 0.4 | 28 | 45 |
| | | | 8 | 0.8 | 25 | 65 |
| | | | 12 | 1.3 | 22 | 90 |
| | | | 16 | 1.9 | 20 | 100 |
| | | | 20 | 2.6 | 18 | 120 |
| | Gravity, with Vertical Face | Level Backfill | 4 | 0.4 | 37 | None |
| | | | 7 | 0.6 | 27 | ↓ |
| | | | 10 | 1.2 | 20 | |
| | | Sloping Backfill | 4 | 0.3 | 31 | |
| | | | 7 | 0.8 | 21 | |
| | | | 10 | 1.6 | 15 | ▼ |

| | | Live Load in Kips per Linear Foot | | | | | | |
|---|---|---|---|---|---|---|---|---|
| | Span | Under 1 Kip | | 2 to 3 Kips | | 4 to 5 Kips | | 6 to 7 Kips | |
| | | Forms | Reinf. | Forms | Reinf. | Forms | Reinf. | Forms | Reinf. |
| Beams | 10 Ft. | — | — | 90 S.F. | 170 # | 85 S.F. | 175 # | 75 S.F. | 185 # |
| | 16 | 130 S.F. | 165 # | 85 | 180 | 75 | 180 | 65 | 225 |
| | 20 | 110 | 170 | 75 | 185 | 62 | 200 | 51 | 200 |
| | 26 | 90 | 170 | 65 | 215 | 62 | 215 | — | — |
| | 30 | 85 | 175 | 60 | 200 | — | — | — | — |

| Item | Size | Type | Forms per C.Y. | Reinforcing per C.Y. |
|---|---|---|---|---|
| Spread Footings | Under 1 C.Y. | 1,000 psf soil | 24 S.F. | 44 lbs. |
| | | 5,000 | 24 | 42 |
| | | 10,000 | 24 | 52 |
| | 1 C.Y. to 5 C.Y. | 1,000 | 14 | 49 |
| | | 5,000 | 14 | 50 |
| | | 10,000 | 14 | 50 |
| | Over 5 C.Y. | 1,000 | 9 | 54 |
| | | 5,000 | 9 | 52 |
| | | 10,000 | 9 | 56 |
| Pile Caps (30 Ton Concrete Piles) | Under 5 C.Y. | shallow caps | 20 | 65 |
| | | medium | 20 | 50 |
| | | deep | 20 | 40 |
| | 5 C.Y. to 10 C.Y. | shallow | 14 | 55 |
| | | medium | 15 | 45 |
| | | deep | 15 | 40 |
| | 10 C.Y. to 20 C.Y. | shallow | 11 | 60 |
| | | medium | 11 | 45 |
| | | deep | 12 | 35 |
| | Over 20 C.Y. | shallow | 9 | 60 |
| | | medium | 9 | 45 |
| | | deep | 10 | 40 |

## R033105-10   Proportionate Quantities (cont.)

| 3000 psi Concrete and 60,000 psi Reinforcing — Form and Reinforcing Quantities per C.Y. | | | | | | | |
|---|---|---|---|---|---|---|---|
| Item | Size | Pile Spacing | 50 T Pile | 100 T Pile | 50 T Pile | 100 T Pile | |
| Pile Caps (Steel H Piles) | Under 5 C.Y. | 24" O.C. | 24 S.F. | 24 S.F. | 75 lbs. | 90 lbs. | |
| | | 30" | 25 | 25 | 80 | 100 | |
| | | 36" | 24 | 24 | 80 | 110 | |
| | 5 C.Y. to 10 C.Y. | 24" | 15 | 15 | 80 | 110 | |
| | | 30" | 15 | 15 | 85 | 110 | |
| | | 36" | 15 | 15 | 75 | 90 | |
| | Over 10 C.Y. | 24" | 13 | 13 | 85 | 90 | |
| | | 30" | 11 | 11 | 85 | 95 | |
| | | 36" | 10 | 10 | 85 | 90 | |

| | | 8" Thick | | 10" Thick | | 12" Thick | | 15" Thick | |
|---|---|---|---|---|---|---|---|---|---|
| | Height | Forms | Reinf. | Forms | Reinf. | Forms | Reinf. | Forms | Reinf. |
| Basement Walls | 7 Ft. | 81 S.F. | 44 lbs. | 65 S.F. | 45 lbs. | 54 S.F. | 44 lbs. | 41 S.F. | 43 lbs. |
| | 8 | | 44 | | 45 | | 44 | | 43 |
| | 9 | | 46 | | 45 | | 44 | | 43 |
| | 10 | | 57 | | 45 | | 44 | | 43 |
| | 12 | | 83 | | 50 | | 52 | | 43 |
| | 14 | | 116 | | 65 | | 64 | | 51 |
| | 16 | | | | 86 | | 90 | | 65 |
| | 18 | ↓ | | ↓ | | ↓ | 106 | ↓ | 70 |

## R033105-20   Materials for One C.Y. of Concrete

This is an approximate method of figuring quantities of cement, sand and coarse aggregate for a field mix with waste allowance included.

With crushed gravel as coarse aggregate, to determine barrels of cement required, divide 10 by total mix; that is, for 1:2:4 mix, 10 divided by 7 = 1-3/7 barrels. If the coarse aggregate is crushed stone, use 10-1/2 instead of 10 as given for gravel.

To determine tons of sand required, multiply barrels of cement by parts of sand and then by 0.2; that is, for the 1:2:4 mix, as above, 1-3/7 x 2 x .2 = .57 tons.

Tons of crushed gravel are in the same ratio to tons of sand as parts in the mix, or 4/2 x .57 = 1.14 tons.

1 bag cement = 94#        1 C.Y. sand or crushed gravel = 2700#        1 C.Y. crushed stone = 2575#
4 bags = 1 barrel        1 ton sand or crushed gravel = 20 C.F.        1 ton crushed stone = 21 C.F.

Average carload of cement is 692 bags; of sand or gravel is 56 tons.

Do not stack stored cement over 10 bags high.

## R033105-30   Metric Equivalents of Cement Content for Concrete Mixes

| 94 Pound Bags per Cubic Yard | Kilograms per Cubic Meter | 94 Pound Bags per Cubic Yard | Kilograms per Cubic Meter |
|---|---|---|---|
| 1.0 | 55.77 | 7.0 | 390.4 |
| 1.5 | 83.65 | 7.5 | 418.3 |
| 2.0 | 111.5 | 8.0 | 446.2 |
| 2.5 | 139.4 | 8.5 | 474.0 |
| 3.0 | 167.3 | 9.0 | 501.9 |
| 3.5 | 195.2 | 9.5 | 529.8 |
| 4.0 | 223.1 | 10.0 | 557.7 |
| 4.5 | 251.0 | 10.5 | 585.6 |
| 5.0 | 278.8 | 11.0 | 613.5 |
| 5.5 | 306.7 | 11.5 | 641.3 |
| 6.0 | 334.6 | 12.0 | 669.2 |
| 6.5 | 362.5 | 12.5 | 697.1 |

a. If you know the cement content in pounds per cubic yard,
   multiply by .5933 to obtain kilograms per cubic meter.

b. If you know the cement content in 94 pound bags per cubic yard,
   multiply by 55.77 to obtain kilograms per cubic meter.

## R033105-40 Metric Equivalents of Common Concrete Strengths
### (to convert other psi values to megapascals, multiply by 0.006895)

| U.S. Values psi | SI Value Megapascals | Non-SI Metric Value kgf/cm²* |
|---|---|---|
| 2000 | 14 | 140 |
| 2500 | 17 | 175 |
| 3000 | 21 | 210 |
| 3500 | 24 | 245 |
| 4000 | 28 | 280 |
| 4500 | 31 | 315 |
| 5000 | 34 | 350 |
| 6000 | 41 | 420 |
| 7000 | 48 | 490 |
| 8000 | 55 | 560 |
| 9000 | 62 | 630 |
| 10,000 | 69 | 705 |

* kilograms force per square centimeter

## R033105-50 Quantities of Cement, Sand and Stone for One C.Y. of Concrete per Various Mixes

This table can be used to determine the quantities of the ingredients for smaller quantities of site mixed concrete.

| Concrete (C.Y.) | Mix = 1:1:1-3/4 | | | Mix = 1:2:2.25 | | | Mix = 1:2.25:3 | | | Mix = 1:3:4 | | |
|---|---|---|---|---|---|---|---|---|---|---|---|---|
| | Cement (sacks) | Sand (C.Y.) | Stone (C.Y.) | Cement (sacks) | Sand (C.Y.) | Stone (C.Y.) | Cement (sacks) | Sand (C.Y.) | Stone (C.Y.) | Cement (sacks) | Sand (C.Y.) | Stone (C.Y.) |
| 1 | 10 | .37 | .63 | 7.75 | .56 | .65 | 6.25 | .52 | .70 | 5 | .56 | .74 |
| 2 | 20 | .74 | 1.26 | 15.50 | 1.12 | 1.30 | 12.50 | 1.04 | 1.40 | 10 | 1.12 | 1.48 |
| 3 | 30 | 1.11 | 1.89 | 23.25 | 1.68 | 1.95 | 18.75 | 1.56 | 2.10 | 15 | 1.68 | 2.22 |
| 4 | 40 | 1.48 | 2.52 | 31.00 | 2.24 | 2.60 | 25.00 | 2.08 | 2.80 | 20 | 2.24 | 2.96 |
| 5 | 50 | 1.85 | 3.15 | 38.75 | 2.80 | 3.25 | 31.25 | 2.60 | 3.50 | 25 | 2.80 | 3.70 |
| 6 | 60 | 2.22 | 3.78 | 46.50 | 3.36 | 3.90 | 37.50 | 3.12 | 4.20 | 30 | 3.36 | 4.44 |
| 7 | 70 | 2.59 | 4.41 | 54.25 | 3.92 | 4.55 | 43.75 | 3.64 | 4.90 | 35 | 3.92 | 5.18 |
| 8 | 80 | 2.96 | 5.04 | 62.00 | 4.48 | 5.20 | 50.00 | 4.16 | 5.60 | 40 | 4.48 | 5.92 |
| 9 | 90 | 3.33 | 5.67 | 69.75 | 5.04 | 5.85 | 56.25 | 4.68 | 6.30 | 45 | 5.04 | 6.66 |
| 10 | 100 | 3.70 | 6.30 | 77.50 | 5.60 | 6.50 | 62.50 | 5.20 | 7.00 | 50 | 5.60 | 7.40 |
| 11 | 110 | 4.07 | 6.93 | 85.25 | 6.16 | 7.15 | 68.75 | 5.72 | 7.70 | 55 | 6.16 | 8.14 |
| 12 | 120 | 4.44 | 7.56 | 93.00 | 6.72 | 7.80 | 75.00 | 6.24 | 8.40 | 60 | 6.72 | 8.88 |
| 13 | 130 | 4.82 | 8.20 | 100.76 | 7.28 | 8.46 | 81.26 | 6.76 | 9.10 | 65 | 7.28 | 9.62 |
| 14 | 140 | 5.18 | 8.82 | 108.50 | 7.84 | 9.10 | 87.50 | 7.28 | 9.80 | 70 | 7.84 | 10.36 |
| 15 | 150 | 5.56 | 9.46 | 116.26 | 8.40 | 9.76 | 93.76 | 7.80 | 10.50 | 75 | 8.40 | 11.10 |
| 16 | 160 | 5.92 | 10.08 | 124.00 | 8.96 | 10.40 | 100.00 | 8.32 | 11.20 | 80 | 8.96 | 11.84 |
| 17 | 170 | 6.30 | 10.72 | 131.76 | 9.52 | 11.06 | 106.26 | 8.84 | 11.90 | 85 | 9.52 | 12.58 |
| 18 | 180 | 6.66 | 11.34 | 139.50 | 10.08 | 11.70 | 112.50 | 9.36 | 12.60 | 90 | 10.08 | 13.32 |
| 19 | 190 | 7.04 | 11.98 | 147.26 | 10.64 | 12.36 | 118.76 | 9.84 | 13.30 | 95 | 10.64 | 14.06 |
| 20 | 200 | 7.40 | 12.60 | 155.00 | 11.20 | 13.00 | 125.00 | 10.40 | 14.00 | 100 | 11.20 | 14.80 |
| 21 | 210 | 7.77 | 13.23 | 162.75 | 11.76 | 13.65 | 131.25 | 10.92 | 14.70 | 105 | 11.76 | 15.54 |
| 22 | 220 | 8.14 | 13.86 | 170.05 | 12.32 | 14.30 | 137.50 | 11.44 | 15.40 | 110 | 12.32 | 16.28 |
| 23 | 230 | 8.51 | 14.49 | 178.25 | 12.88 | 14.95 | 143.75 | 11.96 | 16.10 | 115 | 12.88 | 17.02 |
| 24 | 240 | 8.88 | 15.12 | 186.00 | 13.44 | 15.60 | 150.00 | 12.48 | 16.80 | 120 | 13.44 | 17.76 |
| 25 | 250 | 9.25 | 15.75 | 193.75 | 14.00 | 16.25 | 156.25 | 13.00 | 17.50 | 125 | 14.00 | 18.50 |
| 26 | 260 | 9.64 | 16.40 | 201.52 | 14.56 | 16.92 | 162.52 | 13.52 | 18.20 | 130 | 14.56 | 19.24 |
| 27 | 270 | 10.00 | 17.00 | 209.26 | 15.12 | 17.56 | 168.76 | 14.04 | 18.90 | 135 | 15.02 | 20.00 |
| 28 | 280 | 10.36 | 17.64 | 217.00 | 15.68 | 18.20 | 175.00 | 14.56 | 19.60 | 140 | 15.68 | 20.72 |
| 29 | 290 | 10.74 | 18.28 | 224.76 | 16.24 | 18.86 | 181.26 | 15.08 | 20.30 | 145 | 16.24 | 21.46 |

R0331 Structural Concrete

## R033105-65   Field-Mix Concrete

Presently most building jobs are built with ready-mixed concrete except at isolated locations and some larger jobs requiring over 10,000 C.Y. where land is readily available for setting up a temporary batch plant.

The most economical mix is a controlled mix using local aggregate proportioned by trial to give the required strength with the least cost of material.

## R033105-70   Placing Ready-Mixed Concrete

For ground pours allow for 5% waste when figuring quantities.

Prices in the front of the book assume normal deliveries. If deliveries are made before 8 A.M. or after 5 P.M. or on Saturday afternoons add 30%. Negotiated discounts for large volumes are not included in prices in front of book.

For the lower floors without truck access, concrete may be wheeled in rubber-tired buggies, conveyer handled, crane handled or pumped. Pumping is economical if there is top steel. Conveyers are more efficient for thick slabs.

At higher floors the rubber-tired buggies may be hoisted by a hoisting tower and wheeled to location. Placement by a conveyer is limited to three floors

and is best for high-volume pours. Pumped concrete is best when building has no crane access. Concrete may be pumped directly as high as thirty-six stories using special pumping techniques. Normal maximum height is about fifteen stories.

Best pumping aggregate is screened and graded bank gravel rather than crushed stone.

Pumping downward is more difficult than pumping upward. Horizontal distance from pump to pour may increase preparation time prior to pour. Placing by cranes, either mobile, climbing or tower types, continues as the most efficient method for high-rise concrete buildings.

## R033105-85   Lift Slabs

The cost advantage of the lift slab method is due to placing all concrete, reinforcing steel, inserts and electrical conduit at ground level and in reduction of formwork. Minimum economical project size is about 30,000 S.F. Slabs may be tilted for parking garage ramps.

It is now used in all types of buildings and has gone up to 22 stories high in apartment buildings. Current trend is to use post-tensioned flat plate slabs with spans from 22' to 35'. Cylindrical void forms are used when deep slabs are required. One pound of prestressing steel is about equal to seven pounds of conventional reinforcing.

To be considered cured for stressing and lifting, a slab must have attained 75% of design strength. Seven days are usually sufficient with four to five days possible if high early strength cement is used. Slabs can be stacked using two coats of a non-bonding agent to insure that slabs do not stick to each other. Lifting is done by companies specializing in this work. Lift rate is 5' to 15' per hour with an average of 10' per hour. Total areas up to 33,000 S.F. have been lifted at one time. 24 to 36 jacking columns are common. Most economical bay sizes are 24' to 28' with four to fourteen stories most efficient. Continuous design reduces reinforcing steel cost. Use of post-tensioned slabs allows larger bay sizes.

## R034105-30  Prestressed Precast Concrete Structural Units

| Type | Location | Depth | Span in Ft. | | Live Load Lb. per S.F. |
|---|---|---|---|---|---|
| **Double Tee** 8' to 10' | Floor | 28" to 34" | 60 to 80 | | 50 to 80 |
| | Roof | 12" to 24" | 30 to 50 | | 40 |
| | Wall | Width 8' | Up to 55' high | | Wind |
| **Multiple Tee** 8' | Roof | 8" to 12" | 15 to 40 | | 40 |
| | Floor | 8" to 12" | 15 to 30 | | 100 |
| **Plank** or | Roof or Floor | | Roof | Floor | 40 for Roof |
| | | 4" | 13 | 12 | |
| | | 6" | 22 | 18 | |
| | | 8" | 26 | 25 | |
| | | 10" | 33 | 29 | 100 for Floor |
| | | 12" | 42 | 32 | |
| **Single Tee** 8' to 10' | Roof | 28" | 40 | | |
| | | 32" | 80 | | |
| | | 36" | 100 | | 40 |
| | | 48" | 120 | | |
| **AASHTO Girder** | Bridges | Type 4 | 100 | | |
| | | 5 | 110 | | Highway |
| | | 6 | 125 | | |
| **Box Beam** 4' | Bridges | 15" 27" 33" | 40 to 100 | | Highway |

The majority of precast projects today utilize double tees rather than single tees because of speed and ease of installation. As a result casting beds at manufacturing plants are normally formed for double tees. Single tee projects will therefore require an initial set up charge to be spread over the individual single tee costs.

For floors, a 2" to 3" topping is field cast over the shapes. For roofs, insulating concrete or rigid insulation is placed over the shapes.

Member lengths up to 40' are standard haul, 40' to 60' require special permits and lengths over 60' must be escorted. Over width and/or over length can add up to 100% on hauling costs.

Large heavy members may require two cranes for lifting which would increase erection costs by about 45%. An eight man crew can install 12 to 20 double tees, or 45 to 70 quad tees or planks per day.

Grouting of connections must also be included.

Several system buildings utilizing precast members are available. Heights can go up to 22 stories for apartment buildings. Optimum design ratio is 3 S.F. of surface to 1 S.F. of floor area.

## R034136-90   Prestressed Concrete, Post-Tensioned

In post-tensioned concrete the steel tendons are tensioned after the concrete has reached about 3/4 of its ultimate strength. The cableways are grouted after tensioning to provide bond between the steel and concrete. If bond is to be prevented, the tendons are coated with a corrosion-preventative grease and wrapped with waterproofed paper or plastic. Bonded tendons are usually used when ultimate strength (beams & girders) are controlling factors.

High strength concrete is used to fully utilize the steel, thereby reducing the size and weight of the member. A plasticizing agent may be added to reduce water content. Maximum size aggregate ranges from 1/2" to 1-1/2" depending on the spacing of the tendons.

The types of steel commonly used are bars and strands. Job conditions determine which is best suited. Bars are best for vertical prestresses since they are easy to support. The trend is for steel manufacturers to supply a finished package, cut to length, which reduces field preparation to a minimum.

Bars vary from 3/4" to 1-3/8" diameter. Table below gives time in labor-hours per tendon for placing, tensioning and grouting (if required) a 75' beam. Tendons used in buildings are not usually grouted; tendons for bridges usually are grouted. For strands the table indicates the labor-hours per pound for typical prestressed units 100' long. Simple span beams usually require one-end stressing regardless of lengths. Continuous beams are usually stressed from two ends. Long slabs are poured from the center outward and stressed in 75' increments after the initial 150' center pour.

| | 100' Beam | | 75' Beam | | 100' Slab | |
|---|---|---|---|---|---|---|
| **Length** | Strand | | Bars | | Strand | |
| **Type Steel** | | | | | | |
| **Diameter** | 0.5" | | 3/4" | 1-3/8" | 0.5" | 0.6" |
| **Number** | 4 | 12 | 1 | 1 | 1 | 1 |
| **Force in Kips** | 100 | 300 | 42 | 143 | 25 | 35 |
| Preparation & Placing Cables | 3.6 | 7.4 | 0.9 | 2.9 | 0.9 | 1.1 |
| Stressing Cables | 2.0 | 2.4 | 0.8 | 1.6 | 0.5 | 0.5 |
| Grouting, if required | 2.5 | 3.0 | 0.6 | 1.3 | | |
| Total Labor Hours | 8.1 | 12.8 | 2.3 | 5.8 | 1.4 | 1.6 |
| Prestressing Steel Weights (Lbs.) | 215 | 640 | 115 | 380 | 53 | 74 |
| Labor-hours per Lb. Bonded | 0.038 | 0.020 | 0.020 | 0.015 | | |
| Non-bonded | | | | | 0.026 | 0.022 |

Flat Slab construction — 4000 psi concrete with span-to-depth ratio between 36 and 44. Two way post-tensioned steel averages 1.0 lb. per S.F. for 24' to 28' bays (usually strand) and additional reinforcing steel averages .5 lb. per S.F.

Pan and Joist construction — 4000 psi concrete with span-to-depth ratio 28 to 30. Post-tensioned steel averages .8 lb. per S.F. and reinforcing steel about 1.0 lb. per S.F. Placing and stressing averages 40 hours per ton of total material.

Beam construction — 4000 to 5000 psi concrete. Steel weights vary greatly.

Labor cost per pound goes down as the size and length of the tendon increase. The primary economic consideration is the cost per kip for the member.

Post-tensioning becomes feasible for beams and girders over 30' long; for continuous two-way slabs over 20' clear; also in transferring upper building loads over longer spans at lower levels. Post-tension suppliers will provide engineering services at no cost to the user. Substantial economies are possible by using post-tensioned Lift Slabs.

### R034513-10    Precast Concrete Wall Panels

Panels are either solid or insulated with plain, colored or textured finishes. Transportation is an important cost factor. Prices shown in the unit cost section of the book are based on delivery within 50 miles of a plant including fabricators' overhead and profit. Engineering data is available from fabricators to assist with construction details. Usual minimum job size for economical use of panels is about 5000 S.F. Small jobs can double the prices shown. For large, highly repetitive jobs, deduct up to 15% from the prices shown.

2" thick panels cost about the same as 3" thick panels, and maximum panel size is less. For building panels faced with granite, marble or stone, add the material prices from those unit cost sections to the plain panel price shown. There is a growing trend toward aggregate facings and broken rib finish rather than plain gray concrete panels.

No allowance has been made in the unit cost section for supporting steel framework. On one story buildings, panels may rest on grade beams and require only wind bracing and fasteners. On multi-story buildings panels can span from column to column and floor to floor. Plastic-designed steel-framed structures may have large deflections which slow down erection and raise costs.

Large panels are more economical than small panels on a S.F. basis. When figuring areas include all protrusions, returns, etc. Overhangs can triple erection costs. Panels over 45' have been produced. Larger flat units should be prestressed. Vacuum lifting of smooth finish panels eliminates inserts and can speed erection.

### R034713-20    Tilt Up Concrete Panels

The advantage of tilt up construction is in the low cost of forms and the placing of concrete and reinforcing. Panels up to 75' high and 5-1/2" thick have been tilted using strongbacks. Tilt up has been used for one to five story buildings and is well-suited for warehouses, stores, offices, schools and residences.

The panels are cast in forms on the floor slab. Most jobs use 5-1/2" thick solid reinforced concrete panels. Sandwich panels with a layer of insulating materials are also used. Where dampness is a factor, lightweight aggregate is used. Optimum panel size is 300 to 500 S.F.

Slabs are usually poured with 3000 psi concrete which permits tilting seven days after pouring. Slabs may be stacked on top of each other and are separated from each other by either two coats of bond breaker or a film of polyethylene. Use of high early-strength cement allows tilting two days after a pour. Tilting up is done with a roller outrigger crane with a capacity of at least 1-1/2 times the weight of the panel at the required reach. Exterior precast columns can be set at the same time as the panels; interior precast columns can be set first and the panels clipped directly to them. The use of cast-in-place concrete columns is diminishing due to shrinkage problems. Structural steel columns are sometimes used if crane rails are planned. Panels can be clipped to the columns or lowered between the flanges. Steel channels with anchors may be used as edge forms for the slab. When the panels are lifted the channels form an integral steel column to take structural loads. Roof loads can be carried directly by the panels for wall heights to 14'.

Requirements of local building codes may be a limiting factor and should be checked. Building floor slabs should be poured first and should be a minimum of 5" thick with 100% compaction of soil or 6" thick with less than 100% compaction.

Setting times as fast as nine minutes per panel have been observed, but a safer expectation would be four panels per hour with a crane and a four-man setting crew. If crane erects from inside building, some provision must be made to get crane out after walls are erected. Good yarding procedure is important to minimize delays. Equalizing three-point lifting beams and self-releasing pick-up hooks speed erection. If panels must be carried to their final location, setting time per panel will be increased and erection costs may approach the erection cost range of architectural precast wall panels. Placing panels into slots formed in continuous footers will speed erection.

Reinforcing should be with #5 bars with vertical bars on the bottom. If surface is to be sandblasted, stainless steel chairs should be used to prevent rust staining.

Use of a broom finish is popular since the unavoidable surface blemishes are concealed.

Precast columns run from three to five times the C.Y. price of the panels only.

### R035216-10    Lightweight Concrete

Lightweight aggregate concrete is usually purchased ready mixed, but it can also be field mixed.

Vermiculite or Perlite comes in bags of 4 C.F. under various trade names. Weight is about 8 lbs. per C.F. For insulating roof fill use 1:6 mix. For structural deck use 1:4 mix over gypsum boards, steeltex, steel centering, etc., supported by closely spaced joists or bulb trees. For structural slabs use 1:3:2 vermiculite sand concrete over steeltex, metal lath, steel centering, etc., on joists spaced 2'-0" O.C. for maximum L.L. of 80 P.S.F. Use same mix

for slab base fill over steel flooring or regular reinforced concrete slab when tile, terrazzo or other finish is to be laid over.

For slabs on grade use 1:3:2 mix when tile, etc., finish is to be laid over. If radiant heating units are installed use a 1:6 mix for a base. After coils are in place, cover with a regular granolithic finish (mix 1:3:2) to a minimum depth of 1-1/2" over top of units.

Reinforce all slabs with 6 x 6 or 10 x 10 welded wire mesh.

## R040130-10    Cleaning Face Brick

On smooth brick a person can clean 70 S.F. an hour; on rough brick 50 S.F. per hour. Use one gallon muriatic acid to 20 gallons of water for 1000

S.F. Do not use acid solution until wall is at least seven days old, but a mild soap solution may be used after two days.

Time has been allowed for clean-up in brick prices.

## R040513-10    Cement Mortar (material only)

Type N - 1:1:6 mix by volume. Use everywhere above grade except as noted below. - 1:3 mix using conventional masonry cement which saves handling two separate bagged materials.

Type M - 1:1/4:3 mix by volume, or 1 part cement, 1/4 (10% by wt.) lime, 3 parts sand. Use for heavy loads and where earthquakes or hurricanes may occur. Also for reinforced brick, sewers, manholes and everywhere below grade.

Mix Proportions by Volume and Compressive Strength of Mortar

| Where Used | Allowable Proportions by Volume | | | | | Compressive Strength @ 28 days |
|---|---|---|---|---|---|---|
| | Mortar Type | Portland Cement | Masonry Cement | Hydrated Lime | Masonry Sand | |
| Plain Masonry | M | 1 | 1 | — | 6 | 2500 psi |
| | | 1 | — | 1/4 | 3 | |
| | S | 1/2 | 1 | — | 4 | 1800 psi |
| | | 1 | — | 1/4 to 1/2 | 4 | |
| | N | — | 1 | — | 3 | 750 psi |
| | | 1 | — | 1/2 to 1-1/4 | 6 | |
| | O | — | 1 | — | 3 | 350 psi |
| | | 1 | — | 1-1/4 to 2-1/2 | 9 | |
| | K | 1 | — | 2-1/2 to 4 | 12 | 75 psi |
| Reinforced Masonry | PM | 1 | 1 | — | 6 | 2500 psi |
| | PL | 1 | — | 1/4 to 1/2 | 4 | 2500 psi |

Note: The total aggregate should be between 2.25 to 3 times the sum of the cement and lime used.

The labor cost to mix the mortar is included in the productivity and labor cost of unit price lines in unit cost sections for brickwork, blockwork and stonework.

The material cost of mixed mortar is included in the material cost of those same unit price lines and includes the cost of renting and operating a 10 C.F. mixer at the rate of 200 C.F. per day.

There are two types of mortar color used. One type is the inert additive type with about 100 lbs. per M brick as the typical quantity required. These colors are also available in smaller-batch-sized bags (1 lb. to 15 lb.) which can be placed directly into the mixer without measuring. The other type is premixed and replaces the masonry cement. Dark green color has the highest cost.

## R040519-50    Masonry Reinforcing

Horizontal joint reinforcing helps prevent wall cracks where wall movement may occur and in many locations is required by code. Horizontal joint reinforcing is generally not considered to be structural reinforcing and an unreinforced wall may still contain joint reinforcing.

Reinforcing strips come in 10' and 12' lengths and in truss and ladder shapes, with and without drips. Field labor runs between 2.7 to 5.3 hours per 1000 L.F. for wall thicknesses up to 12".

The wire meets ASTM A82 for cold drawn steel wire and the typical size is 9 ga. sides and ties with 3/16" diameter also available. Typical finish is mill galvanized with zinc coating at .10 oz. per S.F. Class I (.40 oz. per S.F.) and Class III (.80 oz per S.F.) are also available, as is hot dipped galvanizing at 1.50 oz. per S.F.

## R042110-10 Economy in Bricklaying

Have adequate supervision. Be sure bricklayers are always supplied with materials so there is no waiting. Place best bricklayers at corners and openings.

Use only screened sand for mortar. Otherwise, labor time will be wasted picking out pebbles. Use seamless metal tubs for mortar as they do not leak or catch the trowel. Locate stack and mortar for easy wheeling.

Have brick delivered for stacking. This makes for faster handling, reduces chipping and breakage, and requires less storage space. Many dealers will deliver select common in 2' x 3' x 4' pallets or face brick packaged. This affords quick handling with a crane or forklift and easy tonging in units of ten, which reduces waste.

Use wider bricks for one wythe wall construction. Keep scaffolding away from wall to allow mortar to fall clear and not stain wall.

On large jobs develop specialized crews for each type of masonry unit.

Consider designing for prefabricated panel construction on high rise projects.

Avoid excessive corners or openings. Each opening adds about 50% to labor cost for area of opening.

Bolting stone panels and using window frames as stops reduces labor costs and speeds up erection.

## R042110-20 Common and Face Brick

Common building brick manufactured according to ASTM C62 and facing brick manufactured according to ASTM C216 are the two standard bricks available for general building use.

Building brick is made in three grades; SW, where high resistance to damage caused by cyclic freezing is required; MW, where moderate resistance to cyclic freezing is needed; and NW, where little resistance to cyclic freezing is needed. Facing brick is made in only the two grades SW and MW. Additionally, facing brick is available in three types; FBS, for general use; FBX, for general use where a higher degree of precision and lower permissible variation in size than FBS is needed; and FBA, for general use to produce characteristic architectural effects resulting from non-uniformity in size and texture of the units.

In figuring the material cost of brickwork, an allowance of 25% mortar waste and 3% brick breakage was included. If bricks are delivered palletized

with 280 to 300 per pallet, or packaged, allow only 1-1/2% for breakage. Packaged or palletized delivery is practical when a job is big enough to have a crane or other equipment available to handle a package of brick. This is so on all industrial work but not always true on small commercial buildings.

The use of buff and gray face is increasing, and there is a continuing trend to the Norman, Roman, Jumbo and SCR brick.

Common red clay brick for backup is not used that often. Concrete block is the most usual backup material with occasional use of sand lime or cement brick. Building brick is commonly used in solid walls for strength and as a fire stop.

Brick panels built on the ground and then crane erected to the upper floors have proven to be economical. This allows the work to be done under cover and without scaffolding.

## R042110-50 Brick, Block & Mortar Quantities

| Type Brick | Nominal Size (incl. mortar) L | H | W | Modular Coursing | Number of Brick per S.F. | C.F. of Mortar per M Bricks, Waste Included 3/8" Joint | 1/2" Joint |
|---|---|---|---|---|---|---|---|
| Standard | 8 x 2-2/3 x 4 | | | 3C=8" | 6.75 | 10.3 | 12.9 |
| Economy | 8 x 4 x 4 | | | 1C=4" | 4.50 | 11.4 | 14.6 |
| Engineer | 8 x 3-1/5 x 4 | | | 5C=16" | 5.63 | 10.6 | 13.6 |
| Fire | 9 x 2-1/2 x 4-1/2 | | | 2C=5" | 6.40 | 550 # Fireclay | — |
| Jumbo | 12 x 4 x 6 or 8 | | | 1C=4" | 3.00 | 23.8 | 30.8 |
| Norman | 12 x 2-2/3 x 4 | | | 3C=8" | 4.50 | 14.0 | 17.9 |
| Norwegian | 12 x 3-1/5 x 4 | | | 5C=16" | 3.75 | 14.6 | 18.6 |
| Roman | 12 x 2 x 4 | | | 2C=4" | 6.00 | 13.4 | 17.0 |
| SCR | 12 x 2-2/3 x 6 | | | 3C=8" | 4.50 | 21.8 | 28.0 |
| Utility | 12 x 4 x 4 | | | 1C=4" | 3.00 | 15.4 | 19.6 |

**Running Bond** — Number of Brick per S.F. of Wall - Single Wythe with 3/8" Joints

**For Other Bonds Standard Size — Add to S.F. Quantities in Table to Left**

| Bond Type | Description | Factor |
|---|---|---|
| Common | full header every fifth course | +20% |
| | full header every sixth course | +16.7% |
| English | full header every second course | +50% |
| Flemish | alternate headers every course | +33.3% |
| | every sixth course | +5.6% |
| Header = W x H exposed | | +100% |
| Rowlock = H x W exposed | | +100% |
| Rowlock stretcher = L x W exposed | | +33.3% |
| Soldier = H x L exposed | | — |
| Sailor = W x L exposed | | -33.3% |

| Concrete Blocks Nominal Size | Approximate Weight per S.F. Standard | Lightweight | Blocks per 100 S.F. | Mortar per M block, waste included Partitions | Back up |
|---|---|---|---|---|---|
| 2"      x 8" x 16" | 20    PSF | 15    PSF | 113 | 27    C.F. | 36    C.F. |
| 4" | 30 | 20 | | 41 | 51 |
| 6" | 42 | 30 | | 56 | 66 |
| 8" | 55 | 38 | | 72 | 82 |
| 10" | 70 | 47 | | 87 | 97 |
| 12" | 85 | 55 | | 102 | 112 |

Reference Tables

## R042210-20 Concrete Block

The material cost of special block such as corner, jamb and head block can be figured at the same price as ordinary block of same size. Labor on specials is about the same as equal-sized regular block.

Bond beam and 16″ high lintel blocks are more expensive than regular units of equal size. Lintel blocks are 8″ long and either 8″ or 16″ high.

Use of motorized mortar spreader box will speed construction of continuous walls.

Hollow non-load-bearing units are made according to ASTM C129 and hollow load-bearing units according to ASTM C90.

## R050516-30 Coating Structural Steel

On field-welded jobs, the shop-applied primer coat is necessarily omitted. All painting must be done in the field and usually consists of red oxide rust inhibitive paint or an aluminum paint. The table below shows paint coverage and daily production for field painting.

See Division 09 97 13.23 for hot-dipped galvanizing and for field-applied cold galvanizing and other paints and protective coatings.

See Division 05 01 10.51 for steel surface preparation treatments such as wire brushing, pressure washing and sand blasting.

| Type Construction | Surface Area per Ton | Coat | One Gallon Covers | | In 8 Hrs. Person Covers | | Average per Ton Spray | |
|---|---|---|---|---|---|---|---|---|
| | | | Brush | Spray | Brush | Spray | Gallons | Labor-hours |
| Light Structural | 300 S.F. to 500 S.F. | 1st | 500 S.F. | 455 S.F. | 640 S.F. | 2000 S.F. | 0.9 gals. | 1.6 L.H. |
| | | 2nd | 450 | 410 | 800 | 2400 | 1.0 | 1.3 |
| | | 3rd | 450 | 410 | 960 | 3200 | 1.0 | 1.0 |
| Medium | 150 S.F. to 300 S.F. | All | 400 | 365 | 1600 | 3200 | 0.6 | 0.6 |
| Heavy Structural | 50 S.F. to 150 S.F. | 1st | 400 | 365 | 1920 | 4000 | 0.2 | 0.2 |
| | | 2nd | 400 | 365 | 2000 | 4000 | 0.2 | 0.2 |
| | | 3rd | 400 | 365 | 2000 | 4000 | 0.2 | 0.2 |
| Weighted Average | 225 S.F. | All | 400 | 365 | 1350 | 3000 | 0.6 | 0.6 |

## R050521-20 Welded Structural Steel

Usual weight reductions with welded design run 10% to 20% compared with bolted or riveted connections. This amounts to about the same total cost compared with bolted structures since field welding is more expensive than bolts. For normal spans of 18′ to 24′ figure 6 to 7 connections per ton.

Trusses — For welded trusses add 4% to weight of main members for connections. Up to 15% less steel can be expected in a welded truss compared to one that is shop bolted. Cost of erection is the same whether shop bolted or welded.

General — Typical electrodes for structural steel welding are E6010, E6011, E60T and E70T. Typical buildings vary between 2# to 8# of weld rod per

ton of steel. Buildings utilizing continuous design require about three times as much welding as conventional welded structures. In estimating field erection by welding, it is best to use the average linear feet of weld per ton to arrive at the welding cost per ton. The type, size and position of the weld will have a direct bearing on the cost per linear foot. A typical field welder will deposit 1.8# to 2# of weld rod per hour manually. Using semiautomatic methods can increase production by as much as 50% to 75%.

## R050523-10 High Strength Bolts

Common bolts (A307) are usually used in secondary connections (see Division 05 05 23.10).

High strength bolts (A325 and A490) are usually specified for primary connections such as column splices, beam and girder connections to columns, column bracing, connections for supports of operating equipment or of other live loads which produce impact or reversal of stress, and in structures carrying cranes of over 5-ton capacity.

Allow 20 field bolts per ton of steel for a 6 story office building, apartment house or light industrial building. For 6 to 12 stories allow 25 bolts per ton, and above 12 stories, 30 bolts per ton. On power stations, 20 to 25 bolts per ton are needed.

## R051223-10    Structural Steel

The bare material prices for structural steel, shown in the unit cost sections of the book, are for 100 tons of shop-fabricated structural steel and include:

1. Mill base price of structural steel
2. Mill scrap/grade/size/length extras
3. Mill delivery to a metals service center (warehouse)
4. Service center storage and handling
5. Service center delivery to a fabrication shop
6. Shop storage and handling
7. Shop drafting/detailing
8. Shop fabrication
9. Shop coat of primer paint
10. Shop listing
11. Shop delivery to the job site

In unit cost sections of the book that contain items for field fabrication of steel components, the bare material cost of steel includes:

1. Mill base price of structural steel
2. Mill scrap/grade/size/length extras
3. Mill delivery to a metals service center (warehouse)
4. Service center storage and handling
5. Service center delivery to the job site

## R051223-20    Steel Estimating Quantities

One estimate on erection is that a crane can handle 35 to 60 pieces per day. Say the average is 45. With usual sizes of beams, girders, and columns, this would amount to about 20 tons per day. The type of connection greatly affects the speed of erection. Moment connections for continuous design slow down production and increase erection costs.

Short open web bar joists can be set at the rate of 75 to 80 per day, with 50 per day being the average for setting long span joists.

After main members are calculated, add the following for usual allowances: base plates 2% to 3%; column splices 4% to 5%; and miscellaneous details 4% to 5%, for a total of 10% to 13% in addition to main members.

The ratio of column to beam tonnage varies depending on type of steels used, typical spans, story heights and live loads.

It is more economical to keep the column size constant and to vary the strength of the column by using high strength steels. This also saves floor space. Buildings have recently gone as high as ten stories with 8″ high strength columns. For light columns under W8X31 lb. sections, concrete filled steel columns are economical.

High strength steels may be used in columns and beams to save floor space and to meet head room requirements. High strength steels in some sizes sometimes require long lead times.

Round, square and rectangular columns, both plain and concrete filled, are readily available and save floor area, but are higher in cost per pound than rolled columns. For high unbraced columns, tube columns may be less expensive.

Below are average minimum figures for the weights of the structural steel frame for different types of buildings using A36 steel, rolled shapes and simple joints. For economy in domes, rise to span ratio = .13. Open web joist framing systems will reduce weights by 10% to 40%. Composite design can reduce steel weight by up to 25% but additional concrete floor slab thickness may be required. Continuous design can reduce the weights up to 20%. There are many building codes with different live load requirements and different structural requirements, such as hurricane and earthquake loadings which can alter the figures.

| Structural Steel Weights per S.F. of Floor Area | | | | | | | | | |
|---|---|---|---|---|---|---|---|---|---|
| Type of Building | No. of Stories | Avg. Spans | L.L. #/S.F. | Lbs. Per S.F. | Type of Building | No. of Stories | Avg. Spans | L.L. #/S.F. | Lbs. Per S.F. |
| Steel Frame Mfg. | 1 | 20'x20' | 40 | 8 | Apartments | 2-8 | 20'x20' | 40 | 8 |
| | | 30'x30' | | 13 | | 9-25 | | | 14 |
| | | 40'x40' | | 18 | Office | to 10 | Various | 80 | 10 |
| Parking garage | 4 | Various | 80 | 8.5 | | 20 | | | 18 |
| Domes (Schwedler)* | 1 | 200' | 30 | 10 | | 30 | | | 26 |
| | | 300' | | 15 | | over 50 | | | 35 |

## R051223-25  Common Structural Steel Specifications

ASTM A992 (formerly A36, then A572 Grade 50) is the all-purpose carbon grade steel widely used in building and bridge construction.

The other high-strength steels listed below may each have certain advantages over ASTM A992 stuctural carbon steel, depending on the application. They have proven to be economical choices where, due to lighter members, the reduction of dead load and the associated savings in shipping cost can be significant.

ASTM A588 atmospheric weathering, high-strength low-alloy steels can be used in the bare (uncoated) condition, where exposure to normal atmosphere causes a tightly adherant oxide to form on the surface protecting the steel from further oxidation. ASTM A242 corrosion-resistant, high-strength low-alloy steels have enhanced atmospheric corrosion resistance of at least two times that of carbon structural steels with copper, or four times that of carbon structural steels without copper. The reduction or elimination of maintenance resulting from the use of these steels often offsets their higher initial cost.

| Steel Type | ASTM Designation | Minimum Yield Stress in KSI | Shapes Available |
|---|---|---|---|
| Carbon | A36 | 36 | All structural shape groups, and plates & bars up thru 8" thick |
| | A529 | 42 | Structural shape group 1, and plates & bars up thru 1/2" thick |
| High-Strength Low-Alloy Manganese-Vanadium | A441 | 40 | Plates & bars over 4" up thru 8" thick |
| | | 42 | Structural shape groups 4 & 5, and plates & bars over 1-1/2" up thru 4" thick |
| | | 46 | Structural shape group 3, and plates & bars over 3/4" up thru 1-1/2" thick |
| | | 50 | Structural shape groups 1 & 2, and plates & bars up thru 3/4" thick |
| High-Strength Low-Alloy Columbium-Vanadium | A572 | 42 | All structural shape groups, and plates & bars up thru 6" thick |
| | | 50 | All structural shape groups, and plates & bars up thru 4" thick |
| | | 60 | Structural shape groups 1 & 2, and plates & bars up thru 1-1/4" thick |
| | | 65 | Structural shape group 1, and plates & bars up thru 1-1/4" thick |
| High-Strength Low-Alloy Columbium-Vanadium | A992 | 50 | All structural shape groups |
| Corrosion-Resistant High-Strength Low-Alloy | A242 | 42 | Structural shape groups 4 & 5, and plates & bars over 1-1/2" up thru 4" thick |
| | | 46 | Structural shape group 3, and plates & bars over 3/4" up thru 1-1/2" thick |
| | | 50 | Structural shape groups 1 & 2, and plates & bars up thru 3/4" thick |
| Weathering High-Strength Low-Alloy | A588 | 42 | Plates & bars over 5" up thru 8" thick |
| | | 46 | Plates & bars over 4" up thru 5" thick |
| | | 50 | All structural shape groups, and plates & bars up thru 4" thick |
| Quenched and Tempered Low-Alloy | A852 | 70 | Plates & bars up thru 4" thick |
| Quenched and Tempered Alloy | A514 | 90 | Plates & bars over 2-1/2" up thru 6" thick |
| | | 100 | Plates & bars up thru 2-1/2" thick |

## R051223-30  High Strength Steels

The mill price of high strength steels may be higher than A992 carbon steel but their proper use can achieve overall savings thru total reduced weights. For columns with L/r over 100, A992 steel is best; under 100, high strength steels are economical. For heavy columns, high strength steels are economical when cover plates are eliminated. There is no economy using high strength steels for clip angles or supports or for beams where deflection governs. Thinner members are more economical than thick.

The per ton erection and fabricating costs of the high strength steels will be higher than for A992 since the same number of pieces, but less weight, will be installed.

## R051223-35   Common Steel Sections

The upper portion of this table shows the name, shape, common designation and basic characteristics of commonly used steel sections. The lower portion explains how to read the designations used for the above illustrated common sections.

| Shape & Designation | Name & Characteristics | Shape & Designation | Name & Characteristics |
|---|---|---|---|
| W | W Shape<br><br>Parallel flange surfaces | MC | Miscellaneous Channel<br><br>Infrequently rolled by some producers |
| S | American Standard Beam (I Beam)<br><br>Sloped inner flange | L | Angle<br><br>Equal or unequal legs, constant thickness |
| M | Miscellaneous Beams<br><br>Cannot be classified as W, HP or S; infrequently rolled by some producers | T | Structural Tee<br><br>Cut from W, M or S on center of web |
| C | American Standard Channel<br><br>Sloped inner flange | HP | Bearing Pile<br><br>Parallel flanges and equal flange and web thickness |

Common drawing designations follow:

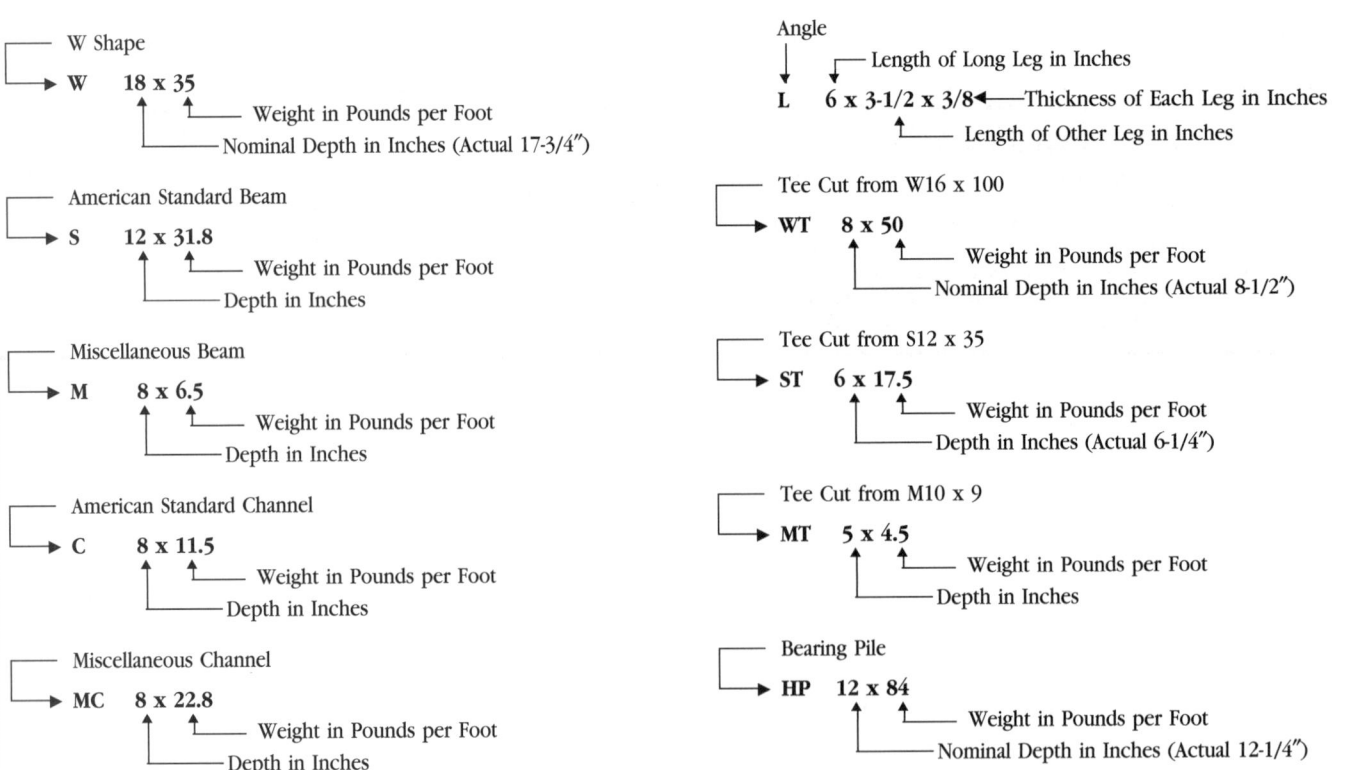

W Shape
W  18 x 35
— Weight in Pounds per Foot
— Nominal Depth in Inches (Actual 17-3/4")

American Standard Beam
S  12 x 31.8
— Weight in Pounds per Foot
— Depth in Inches

Miscellaneous Beam
M  8 x 6.5
— Weight in Pounds per Foot
— Depth in Inches

American Standard Channel
C  8 x 11.5
— Weight in Pounds per Foot
— Depth in Inches

Miscellaneous Channel
MC  8 x 22.8
— Weight in Pounds per Foot
— Depth in Inches

Angle
L  6 x 3-1/2 x 3/8 — Length of Long Leg in Inches / Thickness of Each Leg in Inches / Length of Other Leg in Inches

Tee Cut from W16 x 100
WT  8 x 50
— Weight in Pounds per Foot
— Nominal Depth in Inches (Actual 8-1/2")

Tee Cut from S12 x 35
ST  6 x 17.5
— Weight in Pounds per Foot
— Depth in Inches (Actual 6-1/4")

Tee Cut from M10 x 9
MT  5 x 4.5
— Weight in Pounds per Foot
— Depth in Inches

Bearing Pile
HP  12 x 84
— Weight in Pounds per Foot
— Nominal Depth in Inches (Actual 12-1/4")

## R051223-45    Installation Time for Structural Steel Building Components

The following tables show the expected average installation times for various structural steel shapes. Table A presents installation times for columns, Table B for beams, Table C for light framing and bolts, and Table D for structural steel for various project types.

### Table A

| Description | Labor-Hours | Unit |
|---|---|---|
| Columns | | |
| Steel, Concrete Filled | | |
| 3-1/2" Diameter | .933 | Ea. |
| 6-5/8" Diameter | 1.120 | Ea. |
| Steel Pipe | | |
| 3" Diameter | .933 | Ea. |
| 8" Diameter | 1.120 | Ea. |
| 12" Diameter | 1.244 | Ea. |
| Structural Tubing | | |
| 4" x 4" | .966 | Ea. |
| 8" x 8" | 1.120 | Ea. |
| 12" x 8" | 1.167 | Ea. |
| W Shape 2 Tier | | |
| W8 x 31 | .052 | L.F. |
| W8 x 67 | .057 | L.F. |
| W10 x 45 | .054 | L.F. |
| W10 x 112 | .058 | L.F. |
| W12 x 50 | .054 | L.F. |
| W12 x 190 | .061 | L.F. |
| W14 x 74 | .057 | L.F. |
| W14 x 176 | .061 | L.F. |

### Table B

| Description | Labor-Hours | Unit | Labor-Hours | Unit |
|---|---|---|---|---|
| Beams, W Shape | | | | |
| W6 x 9 | .949 | Ea. | .093 | L.F. |
| W10 x 22 | 1.037 | Ea. | .085 | L.F. |
| W12 x 26 | 1.037 | Ea. | .064 | L.F. |
| W14 x 34 | 1.333 | Ea. | .069 | L.F. |
| W16 x 31 | 1.333 | Ea. | .062 | L.F. |
| W18 x 50 | 2.162 | Ea. | .088 | L.F. |
| W21 x 62 | 2.222 | Ea. | .077 | L.F. |
| W24 x 76 | 2.353 | Ea. | .072 | L.F. |
| W27 x 94 | 2.581 | Ea. | .067 | L.F. |
| W30 x 108 | 2.857 | Ea. | .067 | L.F. |
| W33 x 130 | 3.200 | Ea. | .071 | L.F. |
| W36 x 300 | 3.810 | Ea. | .077 | L.F. |

### Table C

| Description | Labor-Hours | Unit |
|---|---|---|
| Light Framing | | |
| Angles 4" and Larger | .055 | lbs. |
| Less than 4" | .091 | lbs. |
| Channels 8" and Larger | .048 | lbs. |
| Less than 8" | .072 | lbs. |
| Cross Bracing Angles | .055 | lbs. |
| Rods | .034 | lbs. |
| Hanging Lintels | .069 | lbs. |
| High Strength Bolts in Place | | |
| 3/4" Bolts | .070 | Ea. |
| 7/8" Bolts | .076 | Ea. |

### Table D

| Description | Labor-Hours | Unit | Labor-Hours | Unit |
|---|---|---|---|---|
| Apartments, Nursing Homes, etc. | | | | |
| 1-2 Stories | 4.211 | Piece | 7.767 | Ton |
| 3-6 Stories | 4.444 | Piece | 7.921 | Ton |
| 7-15 Stories | 4.923 | Piece | 9.014 | Ton |
| Over 15 Stories | 5.333 | Piece | 9.209 | Ton |
| Offices, Hospitals, etc. | | | | |
| 1-2 Stories | 4.211 | Piece | 7.767 | Ton |
| 3-6 Stories | 4.741 | Piece | 8.889 | Ton |
| 7-15 Stories | 4.923 | Piece | 9.014 | Ton |
| Over 15 Stories | 5.120 | Piece | 9.209 | Ton |
| Industrial Buildings | | | | |
| 1 Story | 3.478 | Piece | 6.202 | Ton |

## R051223-50    Subpurlins

Bulb tee subpurlins are structural members designed to support and reinforce a variety of roof deck systems such as precast cement fiber roof deck tiles, monolithic roof deck systems, and gypsum or lightweight concrete over formboard. Other uses include interstitial service ceiling systems, wall panel systems, and joist anchoring in bond beams. See Unit Price section for pricing on a square foot basis at 32-5/8" O.C. Maximum span is based on a 3-span condition with a total allowable vertical load of 40 psf.

## R051223-80  Dimensions and Weights of Sheet Steel

| Gauge No. | Inches (in fractions) Wrought Iron | Inches (in decimal parts) Wrought Iron | Steel | Millimeters Steel | per S.F. in Ounces | per S.F. in Lbs. | per Square Meter in Kg. |
|---|---|---|---|---|---|---|---|
| 0000000 | 1/2" | .5 | .4782 | 12.146 | 320 | 20.000 | 97.650 |
| 000000 | 15/32" | .46875 | .4484 | 11.389 | 300 | 18.750 | 91.550 |
| 00000 | 7/16" | .4375 | .4185 | 10.630 | 280 | 17.500 | 85.440 |
| 0000 | 13/32" | .40625 | .3886 | 9.870 | 260 | 16.250 | 79.330 |
| 000 | 3/8" | .375 | .3587 | 9.111 | 240 | 15.000 | 73.240 |
| 00 | 11/32" | .34375 | .3288 | 8.352 | 220 | 13.750 | 67.130 |
| 0 | 5/16" | .3125 | .2989 | 7.592 | 200 | 12.500 | 61.030 |
| 1 | 9/32" | .28125 | .2690 | 6.833 | 180 | 11.250 | 54.930 |
| 2 | 17/64" | .265625 | .2541 | 6.454 | 170 | 10.625 | 51.880 |
| 3 | 1/4" | .25 | .2391 | 6.073 | 160 | 10.000 | 48.820 |
| 4 | 15/64" | .234375 | .2242 | 5.695 | 150 | 9.375 | 45.770 |
| 5 | 7/32" | .21875 | .2092 | 5.314 | 140 | 8.750 | 42.720 |
| 6 | 13/64" | .203125 | .1943 | 4.935 | 130 | 8.125 | 39.670 |
| 7 | 3/16" | .1875 | .1793 | 4.554 | 120 | 7.500 | 36.320 |
| 8 | 11/64" | .171875 | .1644 | 4.176 | 110 | 6.875 | 33.570 |
| 9 | 5/32" | .15625 | .1495 | 3.797 | 100 | 6.250 | 30.520 |
| 10 | 9/64" | .140625 | .1345 | 3.416 | 90 | 5.625 | 27.460 |
| 11 | 1/8" | .125 | .1196 | 3.038 | 80 | 5.000 | 24.410 |
| 12 | 7/64" | .109375 | .1046 | 2.657 | 70 | 4.375 | 21.360 |
| 13 | 3/32" | .09375 | .0897 | 2.278 | 60 | 3.750 | 18.310 |
| 14 | 5/64" | .078125 | .0747 | 1.897 | 50 | 3.125 | 15.260 |
| 15 | 9/128" | .0713125 | .0673 | 1.709 | 45 | 2.813 | 13.730 |
| 16 | 1/16" | .0625 | .0598 | 1.519 | 40 | 2.500 | 12.210 |
| 17 | 9/160" | .05625 | .0538 | 1.367 | 36 | 2.250 | 10.990 |
| 18 | 1/20" | .05 | .0478 | 1.214 | 32 | 2.000 | 9.765 |
| 19 | 7/160" | .04375 | .0418 | 1.062 | 28 | 1.750 | 8.544 |
| 20 | 3/80" | .0375 | .0359 | .912 | 24 | 1.500 | 7.324 |
| 21 | 11/320" | .034375 | .0329 | .836 | 22 | 1.375 | 6.713 |
| 22 | 1/32" | .03125 | .0299 | .759 | 20 | 1.250 | 6.103 |
| 23 | 9/320" | .028125 | .0269 | .683 | 18 | 1.125 | 5.490 |
| 24 | 1/40" | .025 | .0239 | .607 | 16 | 1.000 | 4.882 |
| 25 | 7/320" | .021875 | .0209 | .531 | 14 | .875 | 4.272 |
| 26 | 3/160" | .01875 | .0179 | .455 | 12 | .750 | 3.662 |
| 27 | 11/640" | .0171875 | .0164 | .417 | 11 | .688 | 3.357 |
| 28 | 1/64" | .015625 | .0149 | .378 | 10 | .625 | 3.052 |

## R053100-10  Decking Descriptions

### General - All Deck Products

Steel deck is made by cold forming structural grade sheet steel into a repeating pattern of parallel ribs. The strength and stiffness of the panels are the result of the ribs and the material properties of the steel. Deck lengths can be varied to suit job conditions, but because of shipping considerations, are usually less than 40 feet. Standard deck width varies with the product used but full sheets are usually 12″, 18″, 24″, 30″, or 36″. Deck is typically furnished in a standard width with the ends cut square. Any cutting for width, such as at openings or for angular fit, is done at the job site.

Deck is typically attached to the building frame with arc puddle welds, self-drilling screws, or powder or pneumatically driven pins. Sheet to sheet fastening is done with screws, button punching (crimping), or welds.

### Composite Floor Deck

After installation and adequate fastening, floor deck serves several purposes. It (a) acts as a working platform, (b) stabilizes the frame, (c) serves as a concrete form for the slab, and (d) reinforces the slab to carry the design loads applied during the life of the building. Composite decks are distinguished by the presence of shear connector devices as part of the deck. These devices are designed to mechanically lock the concrete and deck together so that the concrete and the deck work together to carry subsequent floor loads. These shear connector devices can be rolled-in embossments, lugs, holes, or wires welded to the panels. The deck profile can also be used to interlock concrete and steel.

Composite deck finishes are either galvanized (zinc coated) or phosphatized/painted. Galvanized deck has a zinc coating on both the top and bottom surfaces. The phosphatized/painted deck has a bare (phosphatized) top surface that will come into contact with the concrete. This bare top surface can be expected to develop rust before the concrete is placed. The bottom side of the deck has a primer coat of paint.

Composite floor deck is normally installed so the panel ends do not overlap on the supporting beams. Shear lugs or panel profile shape often prevent a tight metal to metal fit if the panel ends overlap; the air gap caused by overlapping will prevent proper fusion with the structural steel supports when the panel end laps are shear stud welded.

Adequate end bearing of the deck must be obtained as shown on the drawings. If bearing is actually less in the field than shown on the drawings, further investigation is required.

### Roof Deck

Roof deck is not designed to act compositely with other materials. Roof deck acts alone in transferring horizontal and vertical loads into the building frame. Roof deck rib openings are usually narrower than floor deck rib openings. This provides adequate support of rigid thermal insulation board.

Roof deck is typically installed to endlap approximately 2″ over supports. However, it can be butted (or lapped more than 2″) to solve field fit problems. Since designers frequently use the installed deck system as part of the horizontal bracing system (the deck as a diaphragm), any fastening substitution or change should be approved by the designer. Continuous perimeter support of the deck is necessary to limit edge deflection in the finished roof and may be required for diaphragm shear transfer.

Standard roof deck finishes are galvanized or primer painted. The standard factory applied paint for roof deck is a primer paint and is not intended to weather for extended periods of time. Field painting or touching up of abrasions and deterioration of the primer coat or other protective finishes is the responsibility of the contractor.

### Cellular Deck

Cellular deck is made by attaching a bottom steel sheet to a roof deck or composite floor deck panel. Cellular deck can be used in the same manner as floor deck. Electrical, telephone, and data wires are easily run through the chase created between the deck panel and the bottom sheet.

When used as part of the electrical distribution system, the cellular deck must be installed so that the ribs line up and create a smooth cell transition at abutting ends. The joint that occurs at butting cell ends must be taped or otherwise sealed to prevent wet concrete from seeping into the cell. Cell interiors must be free of welding burrs, or other sharp intrusions, to prevent damage to wires.

When used as a roof deck, the bottom flat plate is usually left exposed to view. Care must be maintained during erection to keep good alignment and prevent damage.

Cellular deck is sometimes used with the flat plate on the top side to provide a flat working surface. Installation of the deck for this purpose requires special methods for attachment to the frame because the flat plate, now on the top, can prevent direct access to the deck material that is bearing on the structural steel. It may be advisable to treat the flat top surface to prevent slipping.

Cellular deck is always furnished galvanized or painted over galvanized.

### Form Deck

Form deck can be any floor or roof deck product used as a concrete form. Connections to the frame are by the same methods used to anchor floor and roof deck. Welding washers are recommended when welding deck that is less than 20 gauge thickness.

Form deck is furnished galvanized, prime painted, or uncoated. Galvanized deck must be used for those roof deck systems where form deck is used to carry a lightweight insulating concrete fill.

## Wood, Plastics & Comp. | R0611 Wood Framing

### R061110-30 Lumber Product Material Prices

The price of forest products fluctuates widely from location to location and from season to season depending upon economic conditions. The bare material prices in the unit cost sections of the book show the National Average material prices in effect Jan. 1 of this book year. It must be noted that lumber prices in general may change significantly during the year.

Availability of certain items depends upon geographic location and must be checked prior to firm-price bidding.

## Wood, Plastics & Comp. | R0616 Sheathing

### R061636-20 Plywood

There are two types of plywood used in construction: interior, which is moisture-resistant but not waterproofed, and exterior, which is waterproofed.

The grade of the exterior surface of the plywood sheets is designated by the first letter: A, for smooth surface with patches allowed; B, for solid surface with patches and plugs allowed; C, which may be surface plugged or may have knot holes up to 1″ wide; and D, which is used only for interior type plywood and may have knot holes up to 2-1/2″ wide. "Structural Grade" is specifically designed for engineered applications such as box beams. All CC & DD grades have roof and floor spans marked on them.

Underlayment-grade plywood runs from 1/4″ to 1-1/4″ thick. Thicknesses 5/8″ and over have optional tongue and groove joints which eliminate the need for blocking the edges. Underlayment 19/32″ and over may be referred to as Sturd-i-Floor.

The price of plywood can fluctuate widely due to geographic and economic conditions.

Typical uses for various plywood grades are as follows:

AA-AD Interior — cupboards, shelving, paneling, furniture

BB Plyform — concrete form plywood

CDX — wall and roof sheathing

Structural — box beams, girders, stressed skin panels

AA-AC Exterior — fences, signs, siding, soffits, etc.

Underlayment — base for resilient floor coverings

Overlaid HDO — high density for concrete forms & highway signs

Overlaid MDO — medium density for painting, siding, soffits & signs

303 Siding — exterior siding, textured, striated, embossed, etc.

## Thermal & Moist. Protec. | R0731 Shingles & Shakes

### R073126-20 Roof Slate

16″, 18″ and 20″ are standard lengths, and slate usually comes in random widths. For standard 3/16″ thickness use 1-1/2″ copper nails. Allow for 3% breakage.

## Thermal & Moist. Protec. | R0751 Built-Up Bituminous Roofing

### R075113-20 Built-Up Roofing

Asphalt is available in kegs of 100 lbs. each; coal tar pitch in 560 lb. kegs. Prepared roofing felts are available in a wide range of sizes, weights and characteristics. However, the most commonly used are #15 (432 S.F. per roll, 13 lbs. per square) and #30 (216 S.F. per roll, 27 lbs. per square).

Inter-ply bitumen varies from 24 lbs. per sq. (asphalt) to 30 lbs. per sq. (coal tar) per ply, MF4@ 25%. Flood coat bitumen also varies from 60 lbs. per sq. (asphalt) to 75 lbs. per sq. (coal tar), MF4@ 25%. Expendable equipment (mops, brooms, screeds, etc.) runs about 16% of the bitumen cost. For new, inexperienced crews this factor may be much higher.

Rigid insulation board is typically applied in two layers. The first is mechanically attached to nailable decks or spot or solid mopped to non-nailable decks; the second layer is then spot or solid mopped to the first layer. Membrane application follows the insulation, except in protected membrane roofs, where the membrane goes down first and the insulation on top, followed with ballast (stone or concrete pavers). Insulation and related labor costs are NOT included in prices for built-up roofing.

## Thermal & Moist. Protec. | R0752 Modified Bituminous Membrane Roofing

### R075213-30    Modified Bitumen Roofing

The cost of modified bitumen roofing is highly dependent on the type of installation that is planned. Installation is based on the type of modifier used in the bitumen. The two most popular modifiers are atactic polypropylene (APP) and styrene butadiene styrene (SBS). The modifiers are added to heated bitumen during the manufacturing process to change its characteristics. A polyethylene, polyester or fiberglass reinforcing sheet is then sandwiched between layers of this bitumen. When completed, the result is a pre-assembled, built-up roof that has increased elasticity and weatherablility. Some manufacturers include a surfacing material such as ceramic or mineral granules, metal particles or sand.

The preferred method of adhering SBS-modified bitumen roofing to the substrate is with hot-mopped asphalt (much the same as built-up roofing). This installation method requires a tar kettle/pot to heat the asphalt, as well as the labor, tools and equipment necessary to distribute and spread the hot asphalt.

The alternative method for applying APP and SBS modified bitumen is as follows. A skilled installer uses a torch to melt a small pool of bitumen off the membrane. This pool must form across the entire roll for proper adhesion. The installer must unroll the roofing at a pace slow enough to melt the bitumen, but fast enough to prevent damage to the rest of the membrane.

Modified bitumen roofing provides the advantages of both built-up and single-ply roofing. Labor costs are reduced over those of built-up roofing because only a single ply is necessary. The elasticity of single-ply roofing is attained with the reinforcing sheet and polymer modifiers. Modifieds have some self-healing characteristics and because of their multi-layer construction, they offer the reliability and safety of built-up roofing.

## Thermal & Moist. Protec. | R0784 Firestopping

### R078413-30    Firestopping

Firestopping is the sealing of structural, mechanical, electrical and other penetrations through fire-rated assemblies. The basic components of firestop systems are safing insulation and firestop sealant on both sides of wall penetrations and the top side of floor penetrations.

Pipe penetrations are assumed to be through concrete, grout, or joint compound and can be sleeved or unsleeved. Costs for the penetrations and sleeves are not included. An annular space of 1″ is assumed. Escutcheons are not included.

Metallic pipe is assumed to be copper, aluminum, cast iron or similar metallic material. Insulated metallic pipe is assumed to be covered with a thermal insulating jacket of varying thickness and materials.

Non-metallic pipe is assumed to be PVC, CPVC, FR Polypropylene or similar plastic piping material. Intumescent firestop sealant or wrap strips are included. Collars on both sides of wall penetrations and a sheet metal plate on the underside of floor penetrations are included.

Ductwork is assumed to be sheet metal, stainless steel or similar metallic material. Duct penetrations are assumed to be through concrete, grout or joint compound. Costs for penetrations and sleeves are not included. An annular space of 1/2″ is assumed.

Multi-trade openings include costs for sheet metal forms, firestop mortar, wrap strips, collars and sealants as necessary.

Structural penetrations joints are assumed to be 1/2″ or less. CMU walls are assumed to be within 1-1/2″ of metal deck. Drywall walls are assumed to be tight to the underside of metal decking.

Metal panel, glass or curtain wall systems include a spandrel area of 5′ filled with mineral wool foil-faced insulation. Fasteners and stiffeners are included.

## Openings · R0813 Metal Doors

### R081313-20  Steel Door Selection Guide

Standard steel doors are classified into four levels, as recommended by the Steel Door Institute in the chart below. Each of the four levels offers a range of construction models and designs, to meet architectural requirements for preference and appearance, including full flush, seamless, and stile & rail. Recommended minimum gauge requirements are also included.

For complete standard steel door construction specifications and available sizes, refer to the Steel Door Institute Technical Data Series, ANSI A250.8-98 (SDI-100), and ANSI A250.4-94 Test Procedure and Acceptance Criteria for Physical Endurance of Steel Door and Hardware Reinforcements.

| Level | | Model | Construction | For Full Flush or Seamless | | |
|---|---|---|---|---|---|---|
| | | | | Min. Gauge | Thickness (in) | Thickness (mm) |
| I | Standard Duty | 1 | Full Flush | | | |
| | | 2 | Seamless | 20 | 0.032 | 0.8 |
| II | Heavy Duty | 1 | Full Flush | | | |
| | | 2 | Seamless | 18 | 0.042 | 1.0 |
| III | Extra Heavy Duty | 1 | Full Flush | | | |
| | | 2 | Seamless | | | |
| | | 3 | *Stile & Rail | 16 | 0.053 | 1.3 |
| IV | Maximum Duty | 1 | Full Flush | | | |
| | | 2 | Seamless | 14 | 0.067 | 1.6 |

*Stiles & rails are 16 gauge; flush panels, when specified, are 18 gauge

## Openings · R0851 Metal Windows

### R085123-10  Steel Sash

Ironworker crew will erect 25 S.F. or 1.3 sash unit per hour, whichever is less.

Mechanic will point 30 L.F. per hour.

Painter will paint 90 S.F. per coat per hour.

Glazier production depends on light size.

Allow 1 lb. special steel sash putty per 16″ x 20″ light.

## Openings · R0852 Wood Windows

### R085216-10  Window Estimates

To ensure a complete window estimate, be sure to include the material and labor costs for each window, as well as the material and labor costs for an interior wood trim set.

## Openings      R0871 Door Hardware

### R087120-10    Hinges

All closer equipped doors should have ball bearing hinges. Lead lined or extremely heavy doors require special strength hinges. Usually 1-1/2 pair of hinges are used per door up to 7'-6" high openings. Table below shows typical hinge requirements.

| Use Frequency | Type Hinge Required | Type of Opening | Type of Structure |
|---|---|---|---|
| High | Heavy weight ball bearing | Entrances | Banks, Office buildings, Schools, Stores & Theaters |
| | | Toilet Rooms | Office buildings and Schools |
| Average | Standard weight ball bearing | Entrances | Dwellings |
| | | Corridors | Office buildings and Schools |
| | | Toilet Rooms | Stores |
| Low | Plain bearing | Interior | Dwellings |

| Door Thickness | Weight of Doors in Pounds per Square Foot | | | | |
|---|---|---|---|---|---|
| | White Pine | Oak | Hollow Core | Solid Core | Hollow Metal |
| 1-3/8" | 3psf | 6psf | 1-1/2psf | 3-1/2 — 4psf | 6-1/2psf |
| 1-3/4" | 3-1/2 | 7 | 2-1/2 | 4-1/2 — 5-1/4 | 6-1/2 |
| 2-1/4" | 4-1/2 | 9 | — | 5-1/2 — 6-3/4 | 6-1/2 |

## Openings      R0881 Glass Glazing

### R088110-10    Glazing Productivity

Some glass sizes are estimated by the "united inch" (height + width). The table below shows the number of lights glazed in an eight-hour period by the crew size indicated, for glass up to 1/4" thick. Square or nearly square lights are more economical on a S.F. basis. Long slender lights will have a high S.F. installation cost. For insulated glass reduce production by 33%. For 1/2" float glass reduce production by 50%. Production time for glazing with two glaziers per day averages: 1/4" float glass 120 S.F.; 1/2" float glass 55 S.F.; 1/2" insulated glass 95 S.F.; 3/4" insulated glass 75 S.F.

| Glazing Method | United Inches per Light | | | | | | | |
|---|---|---|---|---|---|---|---|---|
| | 40" | 60" | 80" | 100" | 135" | 165" | 200" | 240" |
| Number of Men in Crew | 1 | 1 | 1 | 1 | 2 | 3 | 3 | 4 |
| Industrial sash, putty | 60 | 45 | 24 | 15 | 18 | — | — | — |
| With stops, putty bed | 50 | 36 | 21 | 12 | 16 | 8 | 4 | 3 |
| Wood stops, rubber | 40 | 27 | 15 | 9 | 11 | 6 | 3 | 2 |
| Metal stops, rubber | 30 | 24 | 14 | 9 | 9 | 6 | 3 | 2 |
| Structural glass | 10 | 7 | 4 | 3 | — | — | — | — |
| Corrugated glass | 12 | 9 | 7 | 4 | 4 | 4 | 3 | — |
| Storefronts | 16 | 15 | 13 | 11 | 7 | 6 | 4 | 4 |
| Skylights, putty glass | 60 | 36 | 21 | 12 | 16 | — | — | — |
| Thiokol set | 15 | 15 | 11 | 9 | 9 | 6 | 3 | 2 |
| Vinyl set, snap on | 18 | 18 | 13 | 12 | 12 | 7 | 5 | 4 |
| Maximum area per light | 2.8 S.F. | 6.3 S.F. | 11.1 S.F. | 17.4 S.F. | 31.6 S.F. | 47 S.F. | 69 S.F. | 100 S.F. |

## R092000-50   Lath, Plaster and Gypsum Board

**Gypsum board lath** is available in 3/8″ thick x 16″ wide x 4′ long sheets as a base material for multi-layer plaster applications. It is also available as a base for either multi-layer or veneer plaster applications in 1/2″ and 5/8″ thick–4′ wide x 8′, 10′ or 12′ long sheets. Fasteners are screws or blued ring shank nails for wood framing and screws for metal framing.

**Metal lath** is available in diamond mesh pattern with flat or self-furring profiles. Paper backing is available for applications where excessive plaster waste needs to be avoided. A slotted mesh ribbed lath should be used in areas where the span between structural supports is greater than normal. Most metal lath comes in 27″ x 96″ sheets. Diamond mesh weighs 1.75, 2.5 or 3.4 pounds per square yard, slotted mesh lath weighs 2.75 or 3.4 pounds per square yard. Metal lath can be nailed, screwed or tied in place.

Many **accessories** are available. Corner beads, flat reinforcing strips, casing beads, control and expansion joints, furring brackets and channels are some examples. Note that accessories are not included in plaster or stucco line items.

**Plaster** is defined as a material or combination of materials that when mixed with a suitable amount of water, forms a plastic mass or paste. When applied to a surface, the paste adheres to it and subsequently hardens, preserving in a rigid state the form or texture imposed during the period of elasticity.

**Gypsum plaster** is made from ground calcined gypsum. It is mixed with aggregates and water for use as a base coat plaster.

**Vermiculite plaster** is a fire-retardant plaster covering used on steel beams, concrete slabs and other heavy construction materials. Vermiculite is a group name for certain clay minerals, hydrous silicates or aluminum, magnesium and iron that have been expanded by heat.

**Perlite plaster** is a plaster using perlite as an aggregate instead of sand. Perlite is a volcanic glass that has been expanded by heat.

**Gauging plaster** is a mix of gypsum plaster and lime putty that when applied produces a quick drying finish coat.

**Veneer plaster** is a one or two component gypsum plaster used as a thin finish coat over special gypsum board.

**Keenes cement** is a white cementitious material manufactured from gypsum that has been burned at a high temperature and ground to a fine powder. Alum is added to accelerate the set. The resulting plaster is hard and strong and accepts and maintains a high polish, hence it is used as a finishing plaster.

**Stucco** is a Portland cement based plaster used primarily as an exterior finish.

Plaster is used on both interior and exterior surfaces. Generally it is applied in multiple-coat systems. A three-coat system uses the terms scratch, brown and finish to identify each coat. A two-coat system uses base and finish to describe each coat. Each type of plaster and application system has attributes that are chosen by the designer to best fit the intended use.

| Gypsum Plaster<br>Quantities for 100 S.Y. | 2 Coat, 5/8″ Thick | | 3 Coat, 3/4″ Thick | | |
|---|---|---|---|---|---|
| | Base | Finish | Scratch | Brown | Finish |
| | 1:3 Mix | 2:1 Mix | 1:2 Mix | 1:3 Mix | 2:1 Mix |
| Gypsum plaster | 1,300 lb. | | 1,350 lb. | 650 lb. | |
| Sand | 1.75 C.Y. | | 1.85 C.Y. | 1.35 C.Y. | |
| Finish hydrated lime | | 340 lb. | | | 340 lb. |
| Gauging plaster | | 170 lb. | | | 170 lb. |

| Vermiculite or Perlite Plaster<br>Quantities for 100 S.Y. | 2 Coat, 5/8″ Thick | | 3 Coat, 3/4″ Thick | | |
|---|---|---|---|---|---|
| | Base | Finish | Scratch | Brown | Finish |
| Gypsum plaster | 1,250 lb. | | 1,450 lb. | 800 lb. | |
| Vermiculite or perlite | 7.8 bags | | 8.0 bags | 3.3 bags | |
| Finish hydrated lime | | 340 lb. | | | 340 lb. |
| Gauging plaster | | 170 lb. | | | 170 lb. |

| Stucco–Three-Coat System<br>Quantities for 100 S.Y. | On Wood<br>Frame | On<br>Masonry |
|---|---|---|
| Portland cement | 29 bags | 21 bags |
| Sand | 2.6 C.Y. | 2.0 C.Y. |
| Hydrated lime | 180 lb. | 120 lb. |

## R092910-10   Levels of Gypsum Drywall Finish

In the past, contract documents often used phrases such as "industry standard" and "workmanlike finish" to specify the expected quality of gypsum board wall and ceiling installations. The vagueness of these descriptions led to unacceptable work and disputes.

In order to resolve this problem, four major trade associations concerned with the manufacture, erection, finish and decoration of gypsum board wall and ceiling systems have developed an industry-wide *Recommended Levels of Gypsum Board Finish*.

The finish of gypsum board walls and ceilings for specific final decoration is dependent on a number of factors. A primary consideration is the location of the surface and the degree of decorative treatment desired. Painted and unpainted surfaces in warehouses and other areas where appearance is normally not critical may simply require the taping of wallboard joints and 'spotting' of fastener heads. Blemish-free, smooth, monolithic surfaces often intended for painted and decorated walls and ceilings in habitated structures, ranging from single-family dwellings through monumental buildings, require additional finishing prior to the application of the final decoration.

Other factors to be considered in determining the level of finish of the gypsum board surface are (1) the type of angle of surface illumination (both natural and artificial lighting), and (2) the paint and method of application or the type and finish of wallcovering specified as the final decoration. Critical lighting conditions, gloss paints, and thin wallcoverings require a higher level of gypsum board finish than do heavily textured surfaces which are subsequently painted or surfaces which are to be decorated with heavy grade wallcoverings.

The following descriptions were developed jointly by the Association of the Wall and Ceiling Industries-International (AWCI), Ceiling & Interior Systems Construction Association (CISCA), Gypsum Association (GA), and Painting and Decorating Contractors of America (PDCA) as a guide.

**Level 0: No taping, finishing, or accessories required.** This level of finish may be useful in temporary construction or whenever the final decoration has not been determined.

**Level 1: All joints and interior angles shall have tape set in joint compound. Surface shall be free of excess joint compound. Tool marks and ridges are acceptable.** Frequently specified in plenum areas above ceilings, in attics, in areas where the assembly would generally be concealed or in building service corridors, and other areas not normally open to public view.

**Level 2: All joints and interior angles shall have tape embedded in joint compound and wiped with a joint knife leaving a thin coating of joint compound over all joints and interior angles. Fastener heads and accessories shall be covered with a coat of joint compound. Surface shall be free of excess joint compound. Tool marks and ridges are acceptable. Joint compound applied over the body of the tape at the time of tape embedment shall be considered a separate coat of joint compound and shall satisfy the conditions of this level.** Specified where water-resistant gypsum backing board is used as a substrate for tile; may be specified in garages, warehouse storage, or other similar areas where surface appearance is not of primary concern.

**Level 3: All joints and interior angles shall have tape embedded in joint compound and one additional coat of joint compound applied over all joints and interior angles. Fastener heads and accessories shall be covered with two separate coats of joint compound. All joint compound shall be smooth and free of tool marks and ridges.** Typically specified in appearance areas which are to receive heavy- or medium-texture (spray or hand applied) finishes before final painting, or where heavy-grade wallcoverings are to be applied as the final decoration. This level of finish is not recommended where smooth painted surfaces or light to medium wallcoverings are specified.

**Level 4: All joints and interior angles shall have tape embedded in joint compound and two separate coats of joint compound applied over all flat joints and one separate coat of joint compound applied over interior angles. Fastener heads and accessories shall be covered with three separate coats of joint compound. All joint compound shall be smooth and free of tool marks and ridges.** This level should be specified where flat paints, light textures, or wallcoverings are to be applied. In critical lighting areas, flat paints applied over light textures tend to reduce joint photographing. Gloss, semi-gloss, and enamel paints are not recommended over this level of finish. The weight, texture, and sheen level of wallcoverings applied over this level of finish should be carefully evaluated. Joints and fasteners must be adequately concealed if the wallcovering material is lightweight, contains limited pattern, has a gloss finish, or any combination of these finishes is present. Unbacked vinyl wallcoverings are not recommended over this level of finish.

**Level 5: All joints and interior angles shall have tape embedded in joint compound and two separate coats of joint compound applied over all flat joints and one separate coat of joint compound applied over interior angles. Fastener heads and accessories shall be covered with three separate coats of joint compound. A thin skim coat of joint compound or a material manufactured especially for this purpose, shall be applied to the entire surface. The surface shall be smooth and free of tool marks and ridges.** This level of finish is highly recommended where gloss, semi-gloss, enamel, or nontextured flat paints are specified or where severe lighting conditions occur. This highest quality finish is the most effective method to provide a uniform surface and minimize the possibility of joint photographing and of fasteners showing through the final decoration.

## Finishes                    R0966 Terrazzo Flooring

### R096613-10    Terrazzo Floor

The table below lists quantities required for 100 S.F. of 5/8" terrazzo topping, either bonded or not bonded.

| Description | Bonded to Concrete 1-1/8" Bed, 1:4 Mix | Not Bonded 2-1/8" Bed and 1/4" Sand |
|---|---|---|
| Portland cement, 94 lb. Bag | 6 bags | 8 bags |
| Sand | 10 C.F. | 20 C.F. |
| Divider strips, 4' squares | 50 L.F. | 50 L.F. |
| Terrazzo fill, 50 lb. Bag | 12 bags | 12 bags |
| 15 Lb. tarred felt | | 1 C.S.F. |
| Mesh 2 x 2 #14 galvanized | | 1 C.S.F. |
| Crew J-3 | 0.77 days | 0.87 days |

2' x 2' panels require 1.00 L.F. divider strip per S.F.

3' x 3' panels require 0.67 L.F. divider strip per S.F.

4' x 4' panels require 0.50 L.F. divider strip per S.F.

5' x 5' panels require 0.40 L.F. divider strip per S.F.

6' x 6' panels require 0.33 L.F. divider strip per S.F.

## Finishes                    R0972 Wall Coverings

### R097223-10    Wall Covering

The table below lists the quantities required for 100 S.F. of wall covering.

| Description | Medium-Priced Paper | Expensive Paper |
|---|---|---|
| Paper | 1.6 dbl. rolls | 1.6 dbl. rolls |
| Wall sizing | 0.25 gallon | 0.25 gallon |
| Vinyl wall paste | 0.6 gallon | 0.6 gallon |
| Apply sizing | 0.3 hour | 0.3 hour |
| Apply paper | 1.2 hours | 1.5 hours |

Most wallpapers now come in double rolls only.

To remove old paper, allow 1.3 hours per 100 S.F.

## R099100-10    Painting Estimating Techniques

Proper estimating methodology is needed to obtain an accurate painting estimate. There is no known reliable shortcut or square foot method. The following steps should be followed:

- List all surfaces to be painted, with an accurate quantity (area) of each. Items having similar surface condition, finish, application method and accessibility may be grouped together.
- List all the tasks required for each surface to be painted, including surface preparation, masking, and protection of adjacent surfaces. Surface preparation may include minor repairs, washing, sanding and puttying.
- Select the proper Means line for each task. Review and consider all adjustments to labor and materials for type of paint and location of work. Apply the height adjustment carefully. For instance, when applying the adjustment for work over 8' high to a wall that is 12' high, apply the adjustment only to the area between 8' and 12' high, and not to the entire wall.

When applying more than one percent (%) adjustment, apply each to the base cost of the data, rather than applying one percentage adjustment on top of the other.

When estimating the cost of painting walls and ceilings remember to add the brushwork for all cut-ins at inside corners and around windows and doors as a LF measure. One linear foot of cut-in with brush equals one square foot of painting.

All items for spray painting include the labor for roll-back.

Deduct for openings greater than 100 SF, or openings that extend from floor to ceiling and are greater than 5' wide. Do not deduct small openings.

The cost of brushes, rollers, ladders and spray equipment are considered to be part of a painting contractor's overhead, and should not be added to the estimate. The cost of rented equipment such as scaffolding and swing staging should be added to the estimate.

## R099100-20    Painting

| Item | Coat | One Gallon Covers | | | In 8 Hours a Laborer Covers | | | Labor-Hours per 100 S.F. | | |
|------|------|-------|--------|-------|-------|--------|-------|-------|--------|-------|
| | | Brush | Roller | Spray | Brush | Roller | Spray | Brush | Roller | Spray |
| Paint wood siding | prime | 250 S.F. | 225 S.F. | 290 S.F. | 1150 S.F. | 1300 S.F. | 2275 S.F. | .695 | .615 | .351 |
| | others | 270 | 250 | 290 | 1300 | 1625 | 2600 | .615 | .492 | .307 |
| Paint exterior trim | prime | 400 | — | — | 650 | — | — | 1.230 | — | — |
| | 1st | 475 | — | — | 800 | — | — | 1.000 | — | — |
| | 2nd | 520 | — | — | 975 | — | — | .820 | — | — |
| Paint shingle siding | prime | 270 | 255 | 300 | 650 | 975 | 1950 | 1.230 | .820 | .410 |
| | others | 360 | 340 | 380 | 800 | 1150 | 2275 | 1.000 | .695 | .351 |
| Stain shingle siding | 1st | 180 | 170 | 200 | 750 | 1125 | 2250 | 1.068 | .711 | .355 |
| | 2nd | 270 | 250 | 290 | 900 | 1325 | 2600 | .888 | .603 | .307 |
| Paint brick masonry | prime | 180 | 135 | 160 | 750 | 800 | 1800 | 1.066 | 1.000 | .444 |
| | 1st | 270 | 225 | 290 | 815 | 975 | 2275 | .981 | .820 | .351 |
| | 2nd | 340 | 305 | 360 | 815 | 1150 | 2925 | .981 | .695 | .273 |
| Paint interior plaster or drywall | prime | 400 | 380 | 495 | 1150 | 2000 | 3250 | .695 | .400 | .246 |
| | others | 450 | 425 | 495 | 1300 | 2300 | 4000 | .615 | .347 | .200 |
| Paint interior doors and windows | prime | 400 | — | — | 650 | — | — | 1.230 | — | — |
| | 1st | 425 | — | — | 800 | — | — | 1.000 | — | — |
| | 2nd | 450 | — | — | 975 | — | — | .820 | — | — |

**Special Construction** **R1311 Swimming Pools**

## R131113-20    Swimming Pools

Pool prices given per square foot of surface area include pool structure, filter and chlorination equipment, pumps, related piping, ladders/steps, maintenance kit, skimmer and vacuum system. Decks and electrical service to equipment are not included.

Residential in-ground pool construction can be divided into two categories: vinyl lined and gunite. Vinyl lined pool walls are constructed of different materials including wood, concrete, plastic or metal. The bottom is often graded with sand over which the vinyl liner is installed. Vermiculite or soil cement bottoms may be substituted for an added cost.

Gunite pool construction is used both in residential and municipal installations. These structures are steel reinforced for strength and finished with a white cement limestone plaster.

Municipal pools will have a higher cost because plumbing codes require more expensive materials, chlorination equipment and higher filtration rates.

Municipal pools greater than 1,800 S.F. require gutter systems to control waves. This gutter may be formed into the concrete wall. Often a vinyl/stainless steel gutter or gutter/wall system is specified, which will raise the pool cost.

Competition pools usually require tile bottoms and sides with contrasting lane striping, which will also raise the pool cost.

## Special Construction    R1331 Fabric Structures

### R133113-10    Air Supported Structures

Air supported structures are made from fabrics that can be classified into two groups: temporary and permanent. Temporary fabrics include nylon, woven polyethylene, vinyl film, and vinyl coated dacron. These have lifespans that range from five to fifteen plus years. The cost per square foot includes a fabric shell, tension cables, primary and back-up inflation systems and doors. The lower cost structures are used for construction shelters, bulk storage and pond covers. The more expensive are used for recreational structures and warehouses.

Permanent fabrics are teflon coated fiberglass. The life of this structure is twenty plus years. The high cost limits its application to architectural designed structures which call for a clear span covered area, such as stadiums and convention centers. Both temporary and permanent structures are available in translucent fabrics which eliminates the need for daytime lighting.

Areas to be covered vary from 10,000 S.F. to any area up to 1000 foot wide by any length. Height restrictions range from a maximum of 1/2 of

width to a minimum of 1/6 of the width. Erection of even the largest of the temporary structures requires no more than a week.

Centrifugal fans provide the inflation necessary to support the structure during application of live loads. Airlocks are usually used at large entrances to prevent loss of static pressure. Some manufacturers employ propeller fans which generate sufficient airflow (30,000 CFM) to eliminate the need for airlocks. These fans may also be automatically controlled to resist high wind conditions, regulate humidity (air changes), and provide cooling and heat.

Insulation can be provided with the addition of a second or even third interior liner, creating a dead air space with an "R" value of four to nine. Some structures allow for the liner to be collapsed into the outer shell to enable the internal heat to melt accumulated snow. For cooling or air conditioning, the exterior face of the liner can be aluminized to reflect the sun's heat.

### R133113-90    Seismic Bracing

Sometimes referred to as anti-sway bracing, this support system is required in earthquake areas. The individual components must be assembled to

make a required system.

| Example | | | Additionally, height factors must be taken into account. Add the following percentages to labor for elevated installations: | |
|---|---|---|---|---|
| | C-Clamp 3/8" rod | 2 ea. | 15' to 20' high | 10% |
| | Rod, continuous thread 3/8" | 10 L.F. | 21' to 25' high | 20% |
| | Field, weld 1" | 2 ea. | 26' to 30' high | 30% |
| | | | 31' to 35' high | 40% |
| | | | 36' to 40' high | 50% |
| | | | 41' to 50' high | 60% |

## Special Construction    R1334 Fabricated Engineered Structures

### R133419-10    Pre-Engineered Steel Buildings

These buildings are manufactured by many companies and normally erected by franchised dealers throughout the U.S. The four basic types are: Rigid Frames, Truss type, Post and Beam and the Sloped Beam type. Most popular roof slope is low pitch of 1" in 12". The minimum economical area of these buildings is about 3000 S.F. of floor area. Bay sizes are usually 20' to 24' but can go as high as 30' with heavier girts and purlins. Eave heights are usually 12' to 24' with 18' to 20' most typical.

Material prices shown in the Unit Price section are bare costs for the building shell only and do not include floors, foundations, anchor bolts, interior finishes or utilities. Costs assume at least three bays of 24' each, a 1" in 12" roof slope, and they are based on 30 psf roof load and 20 psf wind load

(wind load is a function of wind speed, building height, and terrain characteristics; this should be determined by a Registered Structural Engineer) and no unusual requirements. Costs include the structural frame, 26 ga. non-insulated colored corrugated or ribbed roofing and siding panels, fasteners, closures, trim and flashing but no allowance for insulation, doors, windows, skylights, gutters or downspouts. Very large projects would generally cost less for materials than the prices shown. For roof panel substitutions and wall panel substitutions, see appropriate Unit Price sections.

Conditions at the site, weather, shape and size of the building, and labor availability will affect the erection cost of the building.

### R133423-30    Dome Structures

**Steel** — The four types are Lamella, Schwedler, Arch and Geodesic. For maximum economy, rise should be about 15 to 20% of diameter. Most common diameters are in the 200' to 300' range. Lamella domes weigh about 5 P.S.F. of floor area less than Schwedler domes. Schwedler dome weight in lbs. per S.F. approaches .046 times the diameter. Domes below 125' diameter weigh .07 times diameter and the cost per ton of steel is higher. See R051223-20 for estimating weight.

**Wood** — Small domes are of sawn lumber, larger ones are laminated. In larger sizes, triaxial and triangular cost about the same; radial domes cost more. Radial domes are economical in the 60' to 70' diameter range. Most economical range of all types is 80' to 200' diameters. Diameters can

run over 400'. All costs are quoted above the foundation. Prices include 2" decking and a tension tie ring in place.

**Plywood** — Stock prefab geodesic domes are available with diameters from 24' to 60'.

**Fiberglass** — Aluminum framed translucent sandwich panels with spans from 5' to 45' are commercially available.

**Aluminum** — Stressed skin aluminum panels form geodesic domes with spans ranging from 82' to 232'. An aluminum space truss, triangulated or nontriangulated, with aluminum or clear acrylic closure panels can be used for clear spans of 40' to 415'.

## R142000-10    Freight Elevators

Capacities run from 2,000 lbs. to over 100,000 lbs. with 3,000 lbs. to 10,000 lbs. most common. Travel speeds are generally lower and control less intricate than on passenger elevators. Costs in the Unit Price sections are for hydraulic and geared elevators.

## R142000-20    Elevator Selective Costs    See R142000-40 for cost development.

| A. Base Unit | Passenger | | Freight | | Hospital | |
|---|---|---|---|---|---|---|
| | **Hydraulic** | **Electric** | **Hydraulic** | **Electric** | **Hydraulic** | **Electric** |
| Capacity | 1,500 lb. | 2,000 lb. | 2,000 lb. | 4,000 lb. | 4,000 lb. | 4,000 lb. |
| Speed | 100 F.P.M. | 200 F.P.M. | 100 F.P.M. | 200 F.P.M. | 100 F.P.M. | 200 F.P.M. |
| #Stops/Travel Ft. | 2/12 | 4/40 | 2/20 | 4/40 | 2/20 | 4/40 |
| Push Button Oper. | Yes | Yes | Yes | Yes | Yes | Yes |
| Telephone Box & Wire | " | " | " | " | " | " |
| Emergency Lighting | " | " | No | No | " | " |
| Cab | Plastic Lam. Walls | Plastic Lam. Walls | Painted Steel | Painted Steel | Plastic Lam. Walls | Plastic Lam. Walls |
| Cove Lighting | Yes | Yes | No | No | Yes | Yes |
| Floor | V.C.T. | V.C.T. | Wood w/Safety Treads | Wood w/Safety Treads | V.C.T. | V.C.T. |
| Doors, & Speedside Slide | Yes | Yes | Yes | Yes | Yes | Yes |
| Gates, Manual | No | No | No | No | No | No |
| Signals, Lighted Buttons | Car and Hall | Car and Hall | Car and Hall | Car and Hall | Car and Hall | Car and Hall |
| O.H. Geared Machine | N.A. | Yes | N.A. | Yes | N.A. | Yes |
| Variable Voltage Contr. | " | " | N.A. | " | " | " |
| Emergency Alarm | Yes | " | Yes | " | Yes | " |
| Class "A" Loading | N.A. | N.A. | " | " | N.A. | N.A. |

## R142000-30    Passenger Elevators

Electric elevators are used generally but hydraulic elevators can be used for lifts up to 70' and where large capacities are required. Hydraulic speeds are limited to 200 F.P.M. but cars are self leveling at the stops. On low rises, hydraulic installation runs about 15% less than standard electric types but on higher rises this installation cost advantage is reduced. Maintenance of hydraulic elevators is about the same as electric type but underground portion is not included in the maintenance contract.

In electric elevators there are several control systems available, the choice of which will be based upon elevator use, size, speed and cost criteria. The two types of drives are geared for low speeds and gearless for 450 F.P.M. and over.

The tables on the preceding pages illustrate typical installed costs of the various types of elevators available.

## R142000-40    Elevator Cost Development

To price a new car or truck from the factory, you must start with the manufacturer's basic model, then add or exchange optional equipment and features. The same is true for pricing elevators.

**Example:**

Requirement: One-passenger elevator, five-story hydraulic, 2,500 lb. capacity, 12' floor to floor, speed 150 F.P.M., emergency power switching and maintenance contract.

| Description | Adjustment |
|---|---|
| A. Base Elevator: Hydraulic Passenger, 1500 lb. Capacity, 100 fpm, 2 Stops, Standard Finish | 1 Ea. |
| B. Capacity Adjustment (2,500 lb.) | 1 Ea. |
| C. Excess Travel Adjustment: 48' Total Travel (4 x 12') minus 12' Base Unit Travel = | 36 V.L.F. |
| D. Stops Adjustment: 5 Total Stops minus 2 Stops (Base Unit) = | 3 Stops |
| E. Speed Adjustment (150 F.P.M.) | 1 Ea. |
| F. Options: | |
| 1. Intercom Service | 1 Ea. |
| 2. Emergency Power Switching, Automatic | 1 Ea. |
| 3. Stainless Steel Entrance Doors | 5 Ea. |
| 4. Maintenance Contract (12 Months) | 1 Ea. |
| 5. Position Indicator for main floor level (none indicated in Base Unit) | 1 Ea. |

## R143110-10    Escalators

Moving stairs can be used for buildings where 600 or more people are to be carried to the second floor or beyond. Freight cannot be carried on escalators and at least one elevator must be available for this function.

Carrying capacity is 5,000 to 8,000 people per hour. Power requirement is 2 to 3 KW per hour and incline angle is 30°.

## R143210-20    Moving Ramps and Walks

These are a specialized form of conveyor 3′ to 6′ wide with capacities of 3,600 to 18,000 persons per hour. Maximum speed is 140 F.P.M. and normal incline is 0° to 15°.

Local codes will determine the maximum angle. Outdoor units would require additional weather protection.

## R220105-10    Demolition (Selective vs. Removal for Replacement)

Demolition can be divided into two basic categories.

One type of demolition involves the removal of material with no concern for its replacement. The labor-hours to estimate this work are found under "Selective Demolition" in the Fire Protection, Plumbing and HVAC Divisions. It is selective in that individual items or all the material installed as a system or trade grouping such as plumbing or heating systems are removed. This may be accomplished by the easiest way possible, such as sawing, torch cutting, or sledge hammer as well as simple unbolting.

The second type of demolition is the removal of some item for repair or replacement. This removal may involve careful draining, opening of unions,

disconnecting and tagging of electrical connections, capping of pipes/ducts to prevent entry of debris or leakage of the material contained as well as transport of the item away from its in-place location to a truck/dumpster. An approximation of the time required to accomplish this type of demolition is to use half of the time indicated as necessary to install a new unit. For example; installation of a new pump might be listed as requiring 6 labor-hours so if we had to estimate the removal of the old pump we would allow an additional 3 hours for a total of 9 hours. That is, the complete replacement of a defective pump with a new pump would be estimated to take 9 labor-hours.

## R221113-50    Pipe Material Considerations

1. Malleable fittings should be used for gas service.
2. Malleable fittings are used where there are stresses/strains due to expansion and vibration.
3. Cast fittings may be broken as an aid to disassembling of heating lines frozen by long use, temperature and minerals.
4. Cast iron pipe is extensively used for underground and submerged service.
5. Type M (light wall) copper tubing is available in hard temper only and is used for nonpressure and less severe applications than K and L.

6. Type L (medium wall) copper tubing, available hard or soft for interior service.
7. Type K (heavy wall) copper tubing, available in hard or soft temper for use where conditions are severe. For underground and interior service.
8. Hard drawn tubing requires fewer hangers or supports but should not be bent. Silver brazed fittings are recommended, however soft solder is normally used.
9. Type DMV (very light wall) copper tubing designed for drainage, waste and vent plus other non-critical pressure services.

### Domestic/Imported Pipe and Fittings Cost

The prices shown in this publication for steel/cast iron pipe and steel, cast iron, malleable iron fittings are based on domestic production sold at the normal trade discounts. The above listed items of foreign manufacture may be available at prices of 1/3 to 1/2 those shown. Some imported items after minor machining or finishing operations are being sold as domestic to further complicate the system.

**Caution:** Most pipe prices in this book also include a coupling and pipe hangers which for the larger sizes can add significantly to the per foot cost and should be taken into account when comparing "book cost" with quoted supplier's cost.

## R224000-40   Plumbing Fixture Installation Time

| Item | Rough-In | Set | Total Hours | Item | Rough-In | Set | Total Hours |
|---|---|---|---|---|---|---|---|
| Bathtub | 5 | 5 | 10 | Shower head only | 2 | 1 | 3 |
| Bathtub and shower, cast iron | 6 | 6 | 12 | Shower drain | 3 | 1 | 4 |
| Fire hose reel and cabinet | 4 | 2 | 6 | Shower stall, slate | | 15 | 15 |
| Floor drain to 4 inch diameter | 3 | 1 | 4 | Slop sink | 5 | 3 | 8 |
| Grease trap, single, cast iron | 5 | 3 | 8 | Test 6 fixtures | | | 14 |
| Kitchen gas range | | 4 | 4 | Urinal, wall | 6 | 2 | 8 |
| Kitchen sink, single | 4 | 4 | 8 | Urinal, pedestal or floor | 6 | 4 | 10 |
| Kitchen sink, double | 6 | 6 | 12 | Water closet and tank | 4 | 3 | 7 |
| Laundry tubs | 4 | 2 | 6 | Water closet and tank, wall hung | 5 | 3 | 8 |
| Lavatory wall hung | 5 | 3 | 8 | Water heater, 45 gals. gas, automatic | 5 | 2 | 7 |
| Lavatory pedestal | 5 | 3 | 8 | Water heaters, 65 gals. gas, automatic | 5 | 2 | 7 |
| Shower and stall | 6 | 4 | 10 | Water heaters, electric, plumbing only | 4 | 2 | 6 |

Fixture prices in front of book are based on the cost per fixture set in place. The rough-in cost, which must be added for each fixture, includes carrier, if required, some supply, waste and vent pipe connecting fittings and stops. The lengths of rough-in pipe are nominal runs which would connect to the larger runs and stacks. The supply runs and DWV runs and stacks must be accounted for in separate entries. In the eastern half of the United States it is common for the plumber to carry these to a point 5' outside the building.

## R224000-50   Water Cooler Application

| Type of Service | Requirement |
|---|---|
| Office, School or Hospital | 12 persons per gallon per hour |
| Office, Lobby or Department Store | 4 or 5 gallons per hour per fountain |
| Light manufacturing | 7 persons per gallon per hour |
| Heavy manufacturing | 5 persons per gallon per hour |
| Hot heavy manufacturing | 4 persons per gallon per hour |
| Hotel | .08 gallons per hour per room |
| Theatre | 1 gallon per hour per 100 seats |

# Heating, Ventilating & A.C.   R2331 HVAC Ducts & Casings

## R233100-20   Ductwork

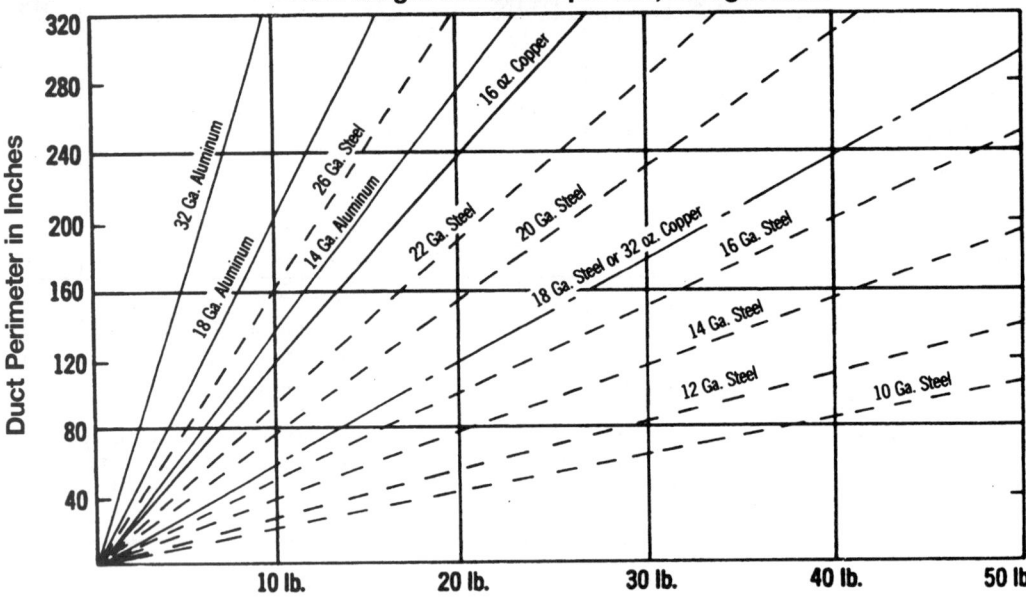

**Duct Weight in Pounds per L.F., Straight Runs**

Add to the above for fittings; 90° elbow is 3 L.F.; 45° elbow is 2.5 L.F.; offset is 4 L.F.; transition offset is 6 L.F.; square-to-round transition is 4 L.F.; 90° reducing elbow is 5 L.F. For bracing and waste, add 20% to aluminum and copper, 15% to steel.

# Heating, Ventilating & A.C.   R2334 HVAC Fans

## R233400-10   Recommended Ventilation Air Changes

Table below lists range of time in minutes per change for various types of facilities.

| | | | | | |
|---|---|---|---|---|---|
| Assembly Halls | 2-10 | Dance Halls | 2-10 | Laundries | 1-3 |
| Auditoriums | 2-10 | Dining Rooms | 3-10 | Markets | 2-10 |
| Bakeries | 2-3 | Dry Cleaners | 1-5 | Offices | 2-10 |
| Banks | 3-10 | Factories | 2-5 | Pool Rooms | 2-5 |
| Bars | 2-5 | Garages | 2-10 | Recreation Rooms | 2-10 |
| Beauty Parlors | 2-5 | Generator Rooms | 2-5 | Sales Rooms | 2-10 |
| Boiler Rooms | 1-5 | Gymnasiums | 2-10 | Theaters | 2-8 |
| Bowling Alleys | 2-10 | Kitchens-Hospitals | 2-5 | Toilets | 2-5 |
| Churches | 5-10 | Kitchens-Restaurant | 1-3 | Transformer Rooms | 1-5 |

CFM air required for changes = Volume of room in cubic feet ÷ Minutes per change.

# Heating, Ventilating & A.C.   R2350 Central Heating Equipment

## R235000-35   Heating (42° degrees latitude)

$$\text{Approximate S.F. radiation} = \frac{\text{S.F. sash}}{2} + \frac{\text{S.F. wall + roof} - \text{sash}}{20} + \frac{\text{C.F. building}}{200}$$

## R235000-50  Factor for Determining Heat Loss for Various Types of Buildings

**General:** While the most accurate estimates of heating requirements would naturally be based on detailed information about the building being considered, it is possible to arrive at a reasonable approximation using the following procedure:

1. Calculate the cubic volume of the room or building.
2. Select the appropriate factor from Table 1 below. Note that the factors apply only to inside temperatures listed in the first column and to 0° F outside temperature.
3. If the building has bad north and west exposures, multiply the heat loss factor by 1.1.
4. If the outside design temperature is other than 0° F, multiply the factor from Table 1 by the factor from Table 2.
5. Multiply the cubic volume by the factor selected from Table 1. This will give the estimated BTUH heat loss which must be made up to maintain inside temperature.

| Table 1 — Building Type | Conditions | Qualifications | Loss Factor* |
|---|---|---|---|
| Factories & Industrial Plants General Office Areas at 70° F | One Story | Skylight in Roof | 6.2 |
| | | No Skylight in Roof | 5.7 |
| | Multiple Story | Two Story | 4.6 |
| | | Three Story | 4.3 |
| | | Four Story | 4.1 |
| | | Five Story | 3.9 |
| | | Six Story | 3.6 |
| | All Walls Exposed | Flat Roof | 6.9 |
| | | Heated Space Above | 5.2 |
| | One Long Warm Common Wall | Flat Roof | 6.3 |
| | | Heated Space Above | 4.7 |
| | Warm Common Walls on Both Long Sides | Flat Roof | 5.8 |
| | | Heated Space Above | 4.1 |
| Warehouses at 60° F | All Walls Exposed | Skylights in Roof | 5.5 |
| | | No Skylight in Roof | 5.1 |
| | | Heated Space Above | 4.0 |
| | One Long Warm Common Wall | Skylight in Roof | 5.0 |
| | | No Skylight in Roof | 4.9 |
| | | Heated Space Above | 3.4 |
| | Warm Common Walls on Both Long Sides | Skylight in Roof | 4.7 |
| | | No Skylight in Roof | 4.4 |
| | | Heated Space Above | 3.0 |

*Note: This table tends to be conservative particularly for new buildings designed for minimum energy consumption.

| Table 2 — Outside Design Temperature Correction Factor (for Degrees Fahrenheit) | | | | | | | | | |
|---|---|---|---|---|---|---|---|---|---|
| Outside Design Temperature | 50 | 40 | 30 | 20 | 10 | 0 | -10 | -20 | -30 |
| Correction Factor | .29 | .43 | .57 | .72 | .86 | 1.00 | 1.14 | 1.28 | 1.43 |

## R235616-60    Solar Heating (Space and Hot Water)

Collectors should face as close to due South as possible, however, variations of up to 20 degrees on either side of true South are acceptable. Local climate and collector type may influence the choice between east or west deviations. Obviously they should be located so they are not shaded from the sun's rays. Incline collectors at a slope of latitude minus 5 degrees for domestic hot water and latitude plus 15 degrees for space heating.

Flat plate collectors consist of a number of components as follows: Insulation to reduce heat loss through the bottom and sides of the collector. The enclosure which contains all the components in this assembly is usually weatherproof and prevents dust, wind and water from coming in contact with the absorber plate. The cover plate usually consists of one or more layers of a variety of glass or plastic and reduces the reradiation by creating an air space which traps the heat between the cover and the absorber plates.

The absorber plate must have a good thermal bond with the fluid passages. The absorber plate is usually metallic and treated with a surface coating which improves absorptivity. Black or dark paints or selective coatings are used for this purpose, and the design of this passage and plate combination helps determine a solar system's effectiveness.

Heat transfer fluid passage tubes are attached above and below or integral with an absorber plate for the purpose of transferring thermal energy from the absorber plate to a heat transfer medium. The heat exchanger is a device for transferring thermal energy from one fluid to another.

Piping and storage tanks should be well insulated to minimize heat losses.

Size domestic water heating storage tanks to hold 20 gallons of water per user, minimum, plus 10 gallons per dishwasher or washing machine. For domestic water heating an optimum collector size is approximately 3/4 square foot of area per gallon of water storage. For space heating of residences and small commercial applications the collector is commonly sized between 30% and 50% of the internal floor area. For space heating of large commercial applications, collector areas less than 30% of the internal floor area can still provide significant heat reductions.

A supplementary heat source is recommended for Northern states for December through February.

The solar energy transmission per square foot of collector surface varies greatly with the material used. Initial cost, heat transmittance and useful life are obviously interrelated.

## R236000-20    Air Conditioning Requirements

BTU's per hour per S.F. of floor area and S.F. per ton of air conditioning.

| Type of Building | BTU per S.F. | S.F. per Ton | Type of Building | BTU per S.F. | S.F. per Ton | Type of Building | BTU per S.F. | S.F. per Ton |
|---|---|---|---|---|---|---|---|---|
| Apartments, Individual | 26 | 450 | Dormitory, Rooms | 40 | 300 | Libraries | 50 | 240 |
| Corridors | 22 | 550 | Corridors | 30 | 400 | Low Rise Office, Exterior | 38 | 320 |
| Auditoriums & Theaters | 40 | 300/18* | Dress Shops | 43 | 280 | Interior | 33 | 360 |
| Banks | 50 | 240 | Drug Stores | 80 | 150 | Medical Centers | 28 | 425 |
| Barber Shops | 48 | 250 | Factories | 40 | 300 | Motels | 28 | 425 |
| Bars & Taverns | 133 | 90 | High Rise Office—Ext. Rms. | 46 | 263 | Office (small suite) | 43 | 280 |
| Beauty Parlors | 66 | 180 | Interior Rooms | 37 | 325 | Post Office, Individual Office | 42 | 285 |
| Bowling Alleys | 68 | 175 | Hospitals, Core | 43 | 280 | Central Area | 46 | 260 |
| Churches | 36 | 330/20* | Perimeter | 46 | 260 | Residences | 20 | 600 |
| Cocktail Lounges | 68 | 175 | Hotel, Guest Rooms | 44 | 275 | Restaurants | 60 | 200 |
| Computer Rooms | 141 | 85 | Corridors | 30 | 400 | Schools & Colleges | 46 | 260 |
| Dental Offices | 52 | 230 | Public Spaces | 55 | 220 | Shoe Stores | 55 | 220 |
| Dept. Stores, Basement | 34 | 350 | Industrial Plants, Offices | 38 | 320 | Shop'g. Ctrs., Supermarkets | 34 | 350 |
| Main Floor | 40 | 300 | General Offices | 34 | 350 | Retail Stores | 48 | 250 |
| Upper Floor | 30 | 400 | Plant Areas | 40 | 300 | Specialty | 60 | 200 |

*Persons per ton

12,000 BTU = 1 ton of air conditioning

## R260519-92   Minimum Copper and Aluminum Wire Size Allowed for Various Types of Insulation

| | Minimum Wire Sizes | | | | | | | | |
| | Copper | | Aluminum | | | Copper | | Aluminum | |
| Amperes | THW THWN or XHHW | THHN XHHW * | THW XHHW | THHN XHHW * | Amperes | THW THWN or XHHW | THHN XHHW * | THW XHHW | THHN XHHW * |
|---|---|---|---|---|---|---|---|---|---|
| 15A | #14 | #14 | #12 | #12 | 195 | 3/0 | 2/0 | 250kcmil | 4/0 |
| 20 | #12 | #12 | #10 | #10 | 200 | 3/0 | 3/0 | 250kcmil | 4/0 |
| 25 | #10 | #10 | #10 | #10 | 205 | 4/0 | 3/0 | 250kcmil | 4/0 |
| 30 | #10 | #10 | #8 | #8 | 225 | 4/0 | 3/0 | 300kcmil | 250kcmil |
| 40 | #8 | #8 | #8 | #8 | 230 | 4/0 | 4/0 | 300kcmil | 250kcmil |
| 45 | #8 | #8 | #6 | #8 | 250 | 250kcmil | 4/0 | 350kcmil | 300kcmil |
| 50 | #8 | #8 | #6 | #6 | 255 | 250kcmil | 4/0 | 400kcmil | 300kcmil |
| 55 | #6 | #8 | #4 | #6 | 260 | 300kcmil | 4/0 | 400kcmil | 350kcmil |
| 60 | #6 | #6 | #4 | #6 | 270 | 300kcmil | 250kcmil | 400kcmil | 350kcmil |
| 65 | #6 | #6 | #4 | #4 | 280 | 300kcmil | 250kcmil | 500kcmil | 350kcmil |
| 75 | #4 | #6 | #3 | #4 | 285 | 300kcmil | 250kcmil | 500kcmil | 400kcmil |
| 85 | #4 | #4 | #2 | #3 | 290 | 350kcmil | 250kcmil | 500kcmil | 400kcmil |
| 90 | #3 | #4 | #2 | #2 | 305 | 350kcmil | 300kcmil | 500kcmil | 400kcmil |
| 95 | #3 | #4 | #1 | #2 | 310 | 350kcmil | 300kcmil | 500kcmil | 500kcmil |
| 100 | #3 | #3 | #1 | #2 | 320 | 400kcmil | 300kcmil | 600kcmil | 500kcmil |
| 110 | #2 | #3 | 1/0 | #1 | 335 | 400kcmil | 350kcmil | 600kcmil | 500kcmil |
| 115 | #2 | #2 | 1/0 | #1 | 340 | 500kcmil | 350kcmil | 600kcmil | 500kcmil |
| 120 | #1 | #2 | 1/0 | 1/0 | 350 | 500kcmil | 350kcmil | 700kcmil | 500kcmil |
| 130 | #1 | #2 | 2/0 | 1/0 | 375 | 500kcmil | 400kcmil | 700kcmil | 600kcmil |
| 135 | 1/0 | #1 | 2/0 | 1/0 | 380 | 500kcmil | 400kcmil | 750kcmil | 600kcmil |
| 150 | 1/0 | #1 | 3/0 | 2/0 | 385 | 600kcmil | 500kcmil | 750kcmil | 600kcmil |
| 155 | 2/0 | 1/0 | 3/0 | 3/0 | 420 | 600kcmil | 500kcmil | | 700kcmil |
| 170 | 2/0 | 1/0 | 4/0 | 3/0 | 430 | | 500kcmil | | 750kcmil |
| 175 | 2/0 | 2/0 | 4/0 | 3/0 | 435 | | 600kcmil | | 750kcmil |
| 180 | 3/0 | 2/0 | 4/0 | 4/0 | 475 | | 600kcmil | | |

*Dry Locations Only

**Notes:**
1. Size #14 to 4/0 is in AWG units (American Wire Gauge).
2. Size 250 to 750 is in kcmil units (Thousand Circular Mils).
3. Use next higher ampere value if exact value is not listed in table.
4. For loads that operate continuously increase ampere value by 25% to obtain proper wire size.
5. Refer to Table R260519-91 for the maximum circuit length for the various size wires.
6. Table R260519-92 has been written for estimating purpose only, based on ambient temperature of 30°C (86° F); for ambient temperature other than 30°C (86° F), ampacity correction factors will be applied.

Reference Tables

## R260533-22 Conductors in Conduit

Table below lists maximum number of conductors for various sized conduit using THW, TW or THWN insulations.

| Copper Wire Size | 1/2" | | | 3/4" | | | 1" | | | 1-1/4" | | | 1-1/2" | | | 2" | | | 2-1/2" | | | 3" | | 3-1/2" | | 4" | |
|---|---|---|---|---|---|---|---|---|---|---|---|---|---|---|---|---|---|---|---|---|---|---|---|---|---|---|---|
| | TW | THW | THWN | TW | THW | THWN | TW | THW | THWN | TW | THW | THWN | TW | THW | THWN | TW | THW | THWN | TW | THW | THWN | THW | THWN | THW | THWN | THW | THWN |
| #14 | 9 | 6 | 13 | 15 | 10 | 24 | 25 | 16 | 39 | 44 | 29 | 69 | 60 | 40 | 94 | 99 | 65 | 154 | 142 | 93 | | 143 | | 192 | | | |
| #12 | 7 | 4 | 10 | 12 | 8 | 18 | 19 | 13 | 29 | 35 | 24 | 51 | 47 | 32 | 70 | 78 | 53 | 114 | 111 | 76 | 164 | 117 | | 157 | | | |
| #10 | 5 | 4 | 6 | 9 | 6 | 11 | 15 | 11 | 18 | 26 | 19 | 32 | 36 | 26 | 44 | 60 | 43 | 73 | 85 | 61 | 104 | 95 | 160 | 127 | | 163 | |
| #8 | 2 | 1 | 3 | 4 | 3 | 5 | 7 | 5 | 9 | 12 | 10 | 16 | 17 | 13 | 22 | 28 | 22 | 36 | 40 | 32 | 51 | 49 | 79 | 66 | 106 | 85 | 136 |
| #6 | | 1 | 1 | | 2 | 4 | | 4 | 6 | | 7 | 11 | | 10 | 15 | | 16 | 26 | | 23 | 37 | 36 | 57 | 48 | 76 | 62 | 98 |
| #4 | | 1 | 1 | | 1 | 2 | | 3 | 4 | | 5 | 7 | | 7 | 9 | | 12 | 16 | | 17 | 22 | 27 | 35 | 36 | 47 | 47 | 60 |
| #3 | | 1 | 1 | | 1 | 1 | | 2 | 3 | | 4 | 6 | | 6 | 8 | | 10 | 13 | | 15 | 19 | 23 | 29 | 31 | 39 | 40 | 51 |
| #2 | | 1 | 1 | | 1 | 1 | | 2 | 3 | | 4 | 5 | | 5 | 7 | | 9 | 11 | | 13 | 16 | 20 | 25 | 27 | 33 | 34 | 43 |
| #1 | | | | | 1 | 1 | | 1 | 1 | | 3 | 3 | | 4 | 5 | | 6 | 8 | | 9 | 12 | 14 | 18 | 19 | 25 | 25 | 32 |
| 1/0 | | | | | 1 | 1 | | 1 | 1 | | 2 | 3 | | 3 | 4 | | 5 | 7 | | 8 | 10 | 12 | 15 | 16 | 21 | 21 | 27 |
| 2/0 | | | | | 1 | 1 | | 1 | 1 | | 1 | 2 | | 3 | 3 | | 5 | 6 | | 7 | 8 | 10 | 13 | 14 | 17 | 18 | 22 |
| 3/0 | | | | | 1 | 1 | | 1 | 1 | | 1 | 1 | | 2 | 3 | | 4 | 5 | | 6 | 7 | 9 | 11 | 12 | 14 | 15 | 18 |
| 4/0 | | | | | | 1 | | 1 | 1 | | 1 | 1 | | 1 | 2 | | 3 | 4 | | 5 | 6 | 7 | 9 | 10 | 12 | 13 | 15 |
| 250 kcmil | | | | | | | | 1 | 1 | | 1 | 1 | | 1 | 1 | | 2 | 3 | | 4 | 4 | 6 | 7 | 8 | 10 | 10 | 12 |
| 300 | | | | | | | | 1 | 1 | | 1 | 1 | | 1 | 1 | | 2 | 3 | | 3 | 4 | 5 | 6 | 7 | 8 | 9 | 11 |
| 350 | | | | | | | | | 1 | | 1 | 1 | | 1 | 1 | | 1 | 2 | | 3 | 3 | 4 | 5 | 6 | 7 | 8 | 9 |
| 400 | | | | | | | | | | | 1 | 1 | | 1 | 1 | | 1 | 1 | | 2 | 3 | 4 | 5 | 5 | 6 | 7 | 8 |
| 500 | | | | | | | | | | | 1 | 1 | | 1 | 1 | | 1 | 1 | | 1 | 2 | 3 | 4 | 4 | 5 | 6 | 7 |
| 600 | | | | | | | | | | | | 1 | | 1 | 1 | | 1 | 1 | | 1 | 1 | 3 | 3 | 4 | 4 | 5 | 5 |
| 700 | | | | | | | | | | | | | | 1 | 1 | | 1 | 1 | | 1 | 1 | 2 | 3 | 3 | 4 | 4 | 5 |
| 750 | | | | | | | | | | | | | | 1 | 1 | | 1 | 1 | | 1 | 1 | 2 | 2 | 3 | 3 | 4 | 4 |

## R312316-40 Excavating

The selection of equipment used for structural excavation and bulk excavation or for grading is determined by the following factors.

1. Quantity of material
2. Type of material
3. Depth or height of cut
4. Length of haul
5. Condition of haul road
6. Accessibility of site
7. Moisture content and dewatering requirements
8. Availability of excavating and hauling equipment

Some additional costs must be allowed for hand trimming the sides and bottom of concrete pours and other excavation below the general excavation.

Number of B.C.Y. per truck = 1.5 C.Y. bucket x 8 passes = 12 loose C.Y.

$$= 12 \times \frac{100}{118} = 10.2 \text{ B.C.Y. per truck}$$

Truck Haul Cycle:

| | | |
|---|---|---|
| Load truck, 8 passes | = | 4 minutes |
| Haul distance, 1 mile | = | 9 minutes |
| Dump time | = | 2 minutes |
| Return, 1 mile | = | 7 minutes |
| Spot under machine | = | 1 minute |
| | | 23 minute cycle |

Add the mobilization and demobilization costs to the total excavation costs. When equipment is rented for more than three days, there is often no mobilization charge by the equipment dealer. On larger jobs outside of urban areas, scrapers can move earth economically provided a dump site or fill area and adequate haul roads are available. Excavation within sheeting bracing or cofferdam bracing is usually done with a clamshell and production

When planning excavation and fill, the following should also be considered.

1. Swell factor
2. Compaction factor
3. Moisture content
4. Density requirements

A typical example for scheduling and estimating the cost of excavation of a 15' deep basement on a dry site when the material must be hauled off the site is outlined below.

Assumptions:

1. Swell factor, 18%
2. No mobilization or demobilization
3. Allowance included for idle time and moving on job
4. No dewatering, sheeting, or bracing
5. No truck spotter or hand trimming

Fleet Haul Production per day in B.C.Y.

$$4 \text{ trucks} \times \frac{50 \text{ min. hour}}{23 \text{ min. haul cycle}} \times 8 \text{ hrs.} \times 10.2 \text{ B.C.Y.}$$

$$= 4 \times 2.2 \times 8 \times 10.2 = 718 \text{ B.C.Y./day}$$

is low, since the clamshell may have to be guided by hand between the bracing. When excavating or filling an area enclosed with a wellpoint system, add 10% to 15% to the cost to allow for restricted access. When estimating earth excavation quantities for structures, allow work space outside the building footprint for construction of the foundation and a slope of 1:1 unless sheeting is used.

### R312316-45  Excavating Equipment

The table below lists THEORETICAL hourly production in C.Y./hr. bank measure for some typical excavation equipment. Figures assume 50 minute hours, 83% job efficiency, 100% operator efficiency, 90° swing and properly sized hauling units, which must be modified for adverse digging and loading conditions. Actual production costs in the front of the book average about 50% of the theoretical values listed here.

| Equipment | Soil Type | B.C.Y. Weight | % Swell | 1 C.Y. | 1-1/2 C.Y. | 2 C.Y. | 2-1/2 C.Y. | 3 C.Y. | 3-1/2 C.Y. | 4 C.Y. |
|---|---|---|---|---|---|---|---|---|---|---|
| Hydraulic Excavator "Backhoe" 15' Deep Cut | Moist loam, sandy clay | 3400 lb. | 40% | 165 | 195 | 200 | 275 | 330 | 385 | 440 |
| | Sand and gravel | 3100 | 18 | 140 | 170 | 225 | 240 | 285 | 330 | 380 |
| | Common earth | 2800 | 30 | 150 | 180 | 230 | 250 | 300 | 350 | 400 |
| | Clay, hard, dense | 3000 | 33 | 120 | 140 | 190 | 200 | 240 | 260 | 320 |
| Power Shovel Optimum Cut (Ft.) | Moist loam, sandy clay | 3400 | 40 | 170 (6.0) | 245 (7.0) | 295 (7.8) | 335 (8.4) | 385 (8.8) | 435 (9.1) | 475 (9.4) |
| | Sand and gravel | 3100 | 18 | 165 (6.0) | 225 (7.0) | 275 (7.8) | 325 (8.4) | 375 (8.8) | 420 (9.1) | 460 (9.4) |
| | Common earth | 2800 | 30 | 145 (7.8) | 200 (9.2) | 250 (10.2) | 295 (11.2) | 335 (12.1) | 375 (13.0) | 425 (13.8) |
| | Clay, hard, dense | 3000 | 33 | 120 (9.0) | 175 (10.7) | 220 (12.2) | 255 (13.3) | 300 (14.2) | 335 (15.1) | 375 (16.0) |
| Drag Line Optimum Cut (Ft.) | Moist loam, sandy clay | 3400 | 40 | 130 (6.6) | 180 (7.4) | 220 (8.0) | 250 (8.5) | 290 (9.0) | 325 (9.5) | 385 (10.0) |
| | Sand and gravel | 3100 | 18 | 130 (6.6) | 175 (7.4) | 210 (8.0) | 245 (8.5) | 280 (9.0) | 315 (9.5) | 375 (10.0) |
| | Common earth | 2800 | 30 | 110 (8.0) | 160 (9.0) | 190 (9.9) | 220 (10.5) | 250 (11.0) | 280 (11.5) | 310 (12.0) |
| | Clay, hard, dense | 3000 | 33 | 90 (9.3) | 130 (10.7) | 160 (11.8) | 190 (12.3) | 225 (12.8) | 250 (13.3) | 280 (12.0) |

|  |  |  |  | Wheel Loaders | | | | Track Loaders | | |
|---|---|---|---|---|---|---|---|---|---|---|
|  |  |  |  | 3 C.Y. | 4 C.Y. | 6 C.Y. | 8 C.Y. | 2-1/4 C.Y. | 3 C.Y. | 4 C.Y. |
| Loading Tractors | Moist loam, sandy clay | 3400 | 40 | 260 | 340 | 510 | 690 | 135 | 180 | 250 |
| | Sand and gravel | 3100 | 18 | 245 | 320 | 480 | 650 | 130 | 170 | 235 |
| | Common earth | 2800 | 30 | 230 | 300 | 460 | 620 | 120 | 155 | 220 |
| | Clay, hard, dense | 3000 | 33 | 200 | 270 | 415 | 560 | 110 | 145 | 200 |
| | Rock, well-blasted | 4000 | 50 | 180 | 245 | 380 | 520 | 100 | 130 | 180 |

## R312319-90    Wellpoints

A single stage wellpoint system is usually limited to dewatering an average 15' depth below normal ground water level. Multi-stage systems are employed for greater depth with the pumping equipment installed only at the lowest header level. Ejectors with unlimited lift capacity can be economical when two or more stages of wellpoints can be replaced or when horizontal clearance is restricted, such as in deep trenches or tunneling projects, and where low water flows are expected. Wellpoints are usually spaced on 2-1/2' to 10' centers along a header pipe. Wellpoint spacing, header size, and pump size are all determined by the expected flow as dictated by soil conditions.

In almost all soils encountered in wellpoint dewatering, the wellpoints may be jetted into place. Cemented soils and stiff clays may require sand wicks about 12" in diameter around each wellpoint to increase efficiency and eliminate weeping into the excavation. These sand wicks require 1/2 to 3 C.Y. of washed filter sand and are installed by using a 12" diameter steel casing and hole puncher jetted into the ground 2' deeper than the wellpoint. Rock may require predrilled holes.

Labor required for the complete installation and removal of a single stage wellpoint system is in the range of 3/4 to 2 labor-hours per linear foot of header, depending upon jetting conditions, wellpoint spacing, etc.

Continuous pumping is necessary except in some free draining soil where temporary flooding is permissible (as in trenches which are backfilled after each day's work). Good practice requires provision of a stand-by pump during the continuous pumping operation.

Systems for continuous trenching below the water table should be installed three to four times the length of expected daily progress to ensure uninterrupted digging, and header pipe size should not be changed during the job.

For pervious free draining soils, deep wells in place of wellpoints may be economical because of lower installation and maintenance costs. Daily production ranges between two to three wells per day, for 25' to 40' depths, to one well per day for depths over 50'.

Detailed analysis and estimating for any dewatering problem is available at no cost from wellpoint manufacturers. Major firms will quote "sufficient equipment" quotes or their affiliates offer lump sum proposals to cover complete dewatering responsibility.

| Description for 200' System with 8" Header | | Quantities |
|---|---|---|
| Equipment & Material | Wellpoints 25' long, 2" diameter @ 5' O.C. | 40 Each |
| | Header pipe, 8" diameter | 200 L.F. |
| | Discharge pipe, 8" diameter | 100 L.F. |
| | 8" valves | 3 Each |
| | Combination jetting & wellpoint pump (standby) | 1 Each |
| | Wellpoint pump, 8" diameter | 1 Each |
| | Transportation to and from site | 1 Day |
| | Fuel for 30 days x 60 gal./day | 1800 Gallons |
| | Lubricants for 30 days x 16 lbs./day | 480 Lbs. |
| | Sand for points | 40 C.Y. |
| Labor | Technician to supervise installation | 1 Week |
| | Labor for installation and removal of system | 300 Labor-hours |
| | 4 Operators straight time 40 hrs./wk. for 4.33 wks. | 693 Hrs. |
| | 4 Operators overtime 2 hrs./wk. for 4.33 wks. | 35 Hrs. |

## R312323-30    Compacting Backfill

Compaction of fill in embankments, around structures, in trenches, and under slabs is important to control settlement. Factors affecting compaction are:

1. Soil gradation
2. Moisture content
3. Equipment used
4. Depth of fill per lift
5. Density required

Production Rate:

$$\frac{1.75' \text{ plate width x 50 F.P.M. x 50 min./hr. x .67' lift}}{27 \text{ C.F. per C.Y.}} = 108.5 \text{ C.Y./hr.}$$

Production Rate for 4 Passes:

$$\frac{108.5 \text{ C.Y.}}{4 \text{ passes}} = 27.125 \text{ C.Y./hr. x 8 hrs.} = 217 \text{ C.Y./day}$$

**Example:**

Compact granular fill around a building foundation using a 21" wide x 24" vibratory plate in 8" lifts. Operator moves at 50 F.P.M. working a 50 minute hour to develop 95% Modified Proctor Density with 4 passes.

# Earthwork | R3141 Shoring

## R314116-40  Wood Sheet Piling

Wood sheet piling may be used for depths to 20′ where there is no ground water. If moderate ground water is encountered Tongue & Groove sheeting will help to keep it out. When considerable ground water is present, steel sheeting must be used.

### For estimating purposes on trench excavation, sizes are as follows:

| Depth | Sheeting | Wales | Braces | B.F. per S.F. |
|---|---|---|---|---|
| To 8′ | 3 x 12′s | 6 x 8′s, 2 line | 6 x 8′s, @ 10′ | 4.0 @ 8′ |
| 8′ x 12′ | 3 x 12′s | 10 x 10′s, 2 line | 10 x 10′s, @ 9′ | 5.0 average |
| 12′ to 20′ | 3 x 12′s | 12 x 12′s, 3 line | 12 x 12′s, @ 8′ | 7.0 average |

Sheeting to be toed in at least 2′ depending upon soil conditions. A five person crew with an air compressor and sheeting driver can drive and brace 440 SF/day at 8′ deep, 360 SF/day at 12′ deep, and 320 SF/day at 16′ deep.

For normal soils, piling can be pulled in 1/3 the time to install. Pulling difficulty increases with the time in the ground. Production can be increased by high pressure jetting.

## R314116-45  Steel Sheet Piling

Limiting weights are 22 to 38#/S.F. of wall surface with 27#/S.F. average for usual types and sizes. (Weights of piles themselves are from 30.7#/L.F. to 57#/L.F. but they are 15″ to 21″ wide.) Lightweight sections 12″ to 28″ wide from 3 ga. to 12 ga. thick are also available for shallow excavations. Piles may be driven two at a time with an impact or vibratory hammer (use vibratory to pull) hung from a crane without leads. A reasonable estimate of the life of steel sheet piling is 10 uses with up to 125 uses possible if a vibratory hammer is used. Used piling costs from 50% to 80% of new piling depending on location and market conditions. Sheet piling and H piles can be rented for about 30% of the delivered mill price for the first month and 5% per month thereafter. Allow 1 labor-hour per pile for cleaning and trimming after driving. These costs increase with depth and hydrostatic head. Vibratory drivers are faster in wet granular soils and are excellent for pile extraction. Pulling difficulty increases with the time in the ground and may cost more than driving. It is often economical to abandon the sheet piling, especially if it can be used as the outer wall form. Allow about 1/3 additional length or more for toeing into ground. Add bracing, waler and strut costs. Waler costs can equal the cost per ton of sheeting.

# Earthwork | R3145 Vibroflotation & Densification

## R314513-90  Vibroflotation and Vibro Replacement Soil Compaction

**Vibroflotation** is a proprietary system of compacting sandy soils in place to increase relative density to about 70%. Typical bearing capacities attained will be 6000 psf for saturated sand and 12,000 psf for dry sand. Usual range is 4000 to 8000 psf capacity. Costs in the front of the book are for a vertical foot of compacted cylinder 6′ to 10′ in diameter.

**Vibro replacement** is a proprietary system of improving cohesive soils in place to increase bearing capacity. Most silts and clays above or below the water table can be strengthened by installation of stone columns.

The process consists of radial displacement of the soil by vibration. The created hole is then backfilled in stages with coarse granular fill which is thoroughly compacted and displaced into the surrounding soil in the form of a column.

The total project cost would depend on the number and depth of the compacted cylinders. The installing company guarantees relative soil density of the sand cylinders after compaction and the bearing capacity of the soil after the replacement process. Detailed estimating information is available from the installer at no cost.

# Earthwork — R3163 Drilled Caissons

## R316326-60　Caissons

The three principal types of cassions are:

**(1) Belled Caissons,** which except for shallow depths and poor soil conditions, are generally recommended. They provide more bearing than shaft area. Because of its conical shape, no horizontal reinforcement of the bell is required.

**(2) Straight Shaft Caissons** are used where relatively light loads are to be supported by caissons that rest on high value bearing strata. While the shaft is larger in diameter than for belled types this is more than offset by the saving in time and labor.

**(3) Keyed Caissons** are used when extremely heavy loads are to be carried. A keyed or socketed caisson transfers its load into rock by a combination of end-bearing and shear reinforcing of the shaft. The most economical shaft often consists of a steel casing, a steel wide flange core and concrete. Allowable compressive stresses of .225 f'c for concrete, 16,000 psi for the wide flange core, and 9,000 psi for the steel casing are commonly used. The usual range of shaft diameter is 18″ to 84″. The number of sizes specified for any one project should be limited due to the problems of casing and auger storage. When hand work is to be performed, shaft diameters should not be less than 32″. When inspection of borings is required a minimum shaft diameter of 30″ is recommended. Concrete caissons are intended to be poured against earth excavation so permanent forms which add to cost should not be used if the excavation is clean and the earth sufficiently impervious to prevent excessive loss of concrete.

### Soil Conditions for Belling

| Good | Requires Handwork | Not Recommended |
|---|---|---|
| Clay | Hard Shale | Silt |
| Sandy Clay | Limestone | Sand |
| Silty Clay | Sandstone | Gravel |
| Clayey Silt | Weathered Mica | Igneous Rock |
| Hard-pan | | |
| Soft Shale | | |
| Decomposed Rock | | |

# Exterior Improvements — R3292 Turf & Grasses

## R329219-50　Seeding

The type of grass is determined by light, shade and moisture content of soil plus intended use. Fertilizer should be disked 4″ before seeding. For steep slopes disk five tons of mulch and lay two tons of hay or straw on surface per acre after seeding. Surface mulch can be staked, lightly disked or tar emulsion sprayed. Material for mulch can be wood chips, peat moss, partially rotted hay or straw, wood fibers and sprayed emulsions. Hemp seed blankets with fertilizer are also available. For spring seeding, watering is necessary. Late fall seeding may have to be reseeded in the spring. Hydraulic seeding, power mulching, and aerial seeding can be used on large areas.

### R331113-80    Piping Designations

There are several systems currently in use to describe pipe and fittings. The following paragraphs will help to identify and clarify classifications of piping systems used for water distribution.

Piping may be classified by schedule. Piping schedules include 5S, 10S, 10, 20, 30, Standard, 40, 60, Extra Strong, 80, 100, 120, 140, 160 and Double Extra Strong. These schedules are dependent upon the pipe wall thickness. The wall thickness of a particular schedule may vary with pipe size.

**Ductile iron pipe** for water distribution is classified by Pressure Classes such as Class 150, 200, 250, 300 and 350. These classes are actually the rated water working pressure of the pipe in pounds per square inch (psi). The pipe in these pressure classes is designed to withstand the rated water working pressure plus a surge allowance of 100 psi.

The American Water Works Association (AWWA) provides standards for various types of **plastic pipe.** C-900 is the specification for polyvinyl chloride (PVC) piping used for water distribution in sizes ranging from 4" through 12". C-901 is the specification for polyethylene (PE) pressure pipe, tubing and fittings used for water distribution in sizes ranging from 1/2" through 3". C-905 is the specification for PVC piping sizes 14" and greater.

**PVC pressure-rated pipe** is identified using the standard dimensional ratio (SDR) method. This method is defined by the American Society for Testing and Materials (ASTM) Standard D 2241. This pipe is available in SDR numbers 64, 41, 32.5, 26, 21, 17, and 13.5. Pipe with an SDR of 64 will have the thinnest wall while pipe with an SDR of 13.5 will have the thickest wall. When the pressure rating (PR) of a pipe is given in psi, it is based on a line supplying water at 73 degrees F.

The National Sanitation Foundation (NSF) seal of approval is applied to products that can be used with potable water. These products have been tested to ANSI/NSF Standard 14.

**Valves and strainers** are classified by American National Standards Institute (ANSI) Classes. These Classes are 125, 150, 200, 250, 300, 400, 600, 900, 1500 and 2500. Within each class there is an operating pressure range dependent upon temperature. Design parameters should be compared to the appropriate material dependent, pressure-temperature rating chart for accurate valve selection.

### R347216-10    Single Track R.R. Siding

The costs for a single track RR siding in the Unit Price section include the components shown in the table below.

| Description of Component | Qty. per L.F. of Track | Unit |
|---|---|---|
| Ballast, 1-1/2" crushed stone | .667 | C.Y. |
| 6" x 8" x 8'-6" Treated timber ties, 22" O.C. | .545 | Ea. |
| Tie plates, 2 per tie | 1.091 | Ea. |
| Track rail | 2.000 | L.F. |
| Spikes, 6", 4 per tie | 2.182 | Ea. |
| Splice bars w/ bolts, lock washers & nuts, @ 33' O.C. | .061 | Pair |
| Crew B-14 @ 57 L.F./Day | .018 | Day |

### R347216-20    Single Track, Steel Ties, Concrete Bed

The costs for a R.R. siding with steel ties and a concrete bed in the Unit Price section include the components shown in the table below.

| Description of Component | Qty. per L.F. of Track | Unit |
|---|---|---|
| Concrete bed, 9' wide, 10" thick | .278 | C.Y. |
| Ties, W6x16 x 6'-6" long, @ 30" O.C. | .400 | Ea. |
| Tie plates, 4 per tie | 1.600 | Ea. |
| Track rail | 2.000 | L.F. |
| Tie plate bolts, 1", 8 per tie | 3.200 | Ea. |
| Splice bars w/bolts, lock washers & nuts, @ 33' O.C. | .061 | Pair |
| Crew B-14 @ 22 L.F./Day | .045 | Day |

# Change Orders

## Change Order Considerations

A Change Order is a written document, usually prepared by the design professional, and signed by the owner, the architect/engineer and the contractor. A change order states the agreement of the parties to: an addition, deletion, or revision in the work; an adjustment in the contract sum, if any; or an adjustment in the contract time, if any. Change orders, or "extras" in the construction process occur after execution of the construction contract and impact architects/engineers, contractors and owners.

Change orders that are properly recognized and managed can ensure orderly, professional and profitable progress for all who are involved in the project. There are many causes for change orders and change order requests. In all cases, change orders or change order requests should be addressed promptly and in a precise and prescribed manner. The following paragraphs include information regarding change order pricing and procedures.

## The Causes of Change Orders

Reasons for issuing change orders include:

- Unforeseen field conditions that require a change in the work
- Correction of design discrepancies, errors or omissions in the contract documents
- Owner-requested changes, either by design criteria, scope of work, or project objectives
- Completion date changes for reasons unrelated to the construction process
- Changes in building code interpretations, or other public authority requirements that require a change in the work
- Changes in availability of existing or new materials and products

## Procedures

Properly written contract documents must include the correct change order procedures for all parties—owners, design professionals and contractors—to follow in order to avoid costly delays and litigation.

Being "in the right" is not always a sufficient or acceptable defense. The contract provisions requiring notification and documentation must be adhered to within a defined or reasonable time frame.

The appropriate method of handling change orders is by a written proposal and acceptance by all parties involved. Prior to starting work on a project, all parties should identify their authorized agents who may sign and accept change orders, as well as any limits placed on their authority.

Time may be a critical factor when the need for a change arises. For such cases, the contractor might be directed to proceed on a "time and materials" basis, rather than wait for all paperwork to be processed—a delay that could impede progress. In this situation, the contractor must still follow the prescribed change order procedures, including but not limited to, notification and documentation.

All forms used for change orders should be dated and signed by the proper authority. Lack of documentation can be very costly, especially if legal judgments are to be made and if certain field personnel are no longer available. For time and material change orders, the contractor should keep accurate daily records of all labor and material allocated to the change. Forms that can be used to document change order work are available in *Means Forms for Building Construction Professionals.*

Owners or awarding authorities who do considerable and continual building construction (such as the federal government) realize the inevitability of change orders for numerous reasons, both predictable and unpredictable. As a result, the federal government, the American Institute of Architects (AIA), the Engineers Joint Contract Documents Committee (EJCDC) and other contractor, legal and technical organizations have developed standards and procedures to be followed by all parties to achieve contract continuance and timely completion, while being financially fair to all concerned.

In addition to the change order standards put forth by industry associations, there are also many books available on the subject.

## Pricing Change Orders

When pricing change orders, regardless of their cause, the most significant factor is when the change occurs. The need for a change may be perceived in the field or requested by the architect/engineer *before* any of the actual installation has begun, or may evolve or appear *during* construction when the item of work in question is partially installed. In the latter cases, the original sequence of construction is disrupted, along with all contiguous and supporting systems. Change orders cause the greatest impact when they occur *after* the installation has been completed and must be uncovered, or even replaced. Post-completion changes may be caused by necessary design changes, product failure, or changes in the owner's requirements that are not discovered until the building or the systems begin to function.

Specified procedures of notification and record keeping must be adhered to and enforced regardless of the stage of construction: *before, during,* or *after* installation. Some bidding documents anticipate change orders by requiring that unit prices including overhead and profit percentages—for additional as well as deductible changes—be listed. Generally these unit prices do not fully take into account the ripple effect, or impact on other trades, and should be used for general guidance only.

When pricing change orders, it is important to classify the time frame in which the change occurs. There are two basic time frames for change orders: *pre-installation change orders,* which occur before the start of construction, and *post-installation change orders,* which involve reworking after the original installation. Change orders that occur between these stages may be priced according to the extent of work completed using a combination of techniques developed for pricing *pre-* and *post-installation* changes.

The following factors are the basis for a check list to use when preparing a change order estimate.

## Factors To Consider When Pricing Change Orders

As an estimator begins to prepare a change order, the following questions should be reviewed to determine their impact on the final price.

### General

- Is the change order work *pre-installation* or *post-installation*?

  Change order work costs vary according to how much of the installation has been completed. Once workers have the project scoped in their mind, even though they have not started, it can be difficult to refocus.

Consequently they may spend more than the normal amount of time understanding the change. Also, modifications to work in place such as trimming or refitting usually take more time than was initially estimated. The greater the amount of work in place, the more reluctant workers are to change it. Psychologically they may resent the change and as a result the rework takes longer than normal. Post-installation change order estimates must include demolition of existing work as required to accomplish the change. If the work is performed at a later time, additional obstacles such as building finishes may be present which must be protected. Regardless of whether the change

occurs pre-installation or post-installation, attempt to isolate the identifiable factors and price them separately. For example, add shipping costs that may be required pre-installation or any demolition required post-installation. Then analyze the potential impact on productivity of psychological and/or learning curve factors and adjust the output rates accordingly. One approach is to break down the typical workday into segments and quantify the impact on each segment. The following chart may be useful as a guide:

| | Activities (Productivity) Expressed as Percentages of a Workday | | |
|---|---|---|---|
| **Task** | **Means Mechanical Cost Data (for New Construction)** | **Pre-Installation Change Orders** | **Post-Installation Change Orders** |
| 1. Study plans | 3% | 6% | 6% |
| 2. Material procurement | 3% | 3% | 3% |
| 3. Receiving and storing | 3% | 3% | 3% |
| 4. Mobilization | 5% | 5% | 5% |
| 5. Site movement | 5% | 5% | 8% |
| 6. Layout and marking | 8% | 10% | 12% |
| 7. Actual installation | 64% | 59% | 54% |
| 8. Clean-up | 3% | 3% | 3% |
| 9. Breaks—non-productive | 6% | 6% | 6% |
| Total | 100% | 100% | 100% |

### Change Order Installation Efficiency

The labor-hours expressed (for new construction) are based on average installation time, using an efficiency level of approximately 60-65%. For change order situations, adjustments to this efficiency level should reflect the daily labor-hour allocation for that particular occurrence.

If any of the specific percentages expressed in the above chart do not apply to a particular project situation, then those percentage points should be reallocated to the appropriate task(s). Example: Using data for new construction, assume there is no new material being utilized. The percentages for Tasks 2 and 3 would therefore be reallocated to other tasks. If the time required for Tasks 2 and 3 can now be applied to installation, we can add the time allocated for *Material Procurement* and *Receiving and Storing* to the *Actual Installation* time for new construction, thereby increasing the Actual Installation percentage.

This chart shows that, due to reduced productivity, labor costs will be higher than those for new construction by 5% to 15% for pre-installation change orders and by 15% to 25% for post-installation change orders. Each job and change order is unique and must be examined individually. Many factors, covered elsewhere in this section, can each have a significant impact on productivity and change order costs. All such factors should be considered in every case.

- Will the change substantially delay the original completion date?

  A significant change in the project may cause the original completion date to be extended. The extended schedule may subject the contractor to new wage rates dictated by relevant labor contracts. Project supervision and other project overhead must also be extended beyond the original completion date. The schedule extension may also put installation into a new weather season. For example, underground piping scheduled for October installation was delayed until January. As a result, frost penetrated the trench area, thereby changing the degree of difficulty of the task. Changes and delays may have a ripple effect throughout the project. This effect must be analyzed and negotiated with the owner.

- What is the net effect of a deduct change order?

  In most cases, change orders resulting in a deduction or credit reflect only bare costs. The contractor may retain the overhead and profit based on the original bid.

## Materials

- Will you have to pay more or less for the new material, required by the change order, than you paid for the original purchase?

  The same material prices or discounts will usually apply to materials purchased for change orders as new construction. In some instances, however, the contractor may forfeit the advantages of competitive pricing for change orders. Consider the following example:

  A contractor purchased over $20,000 worth of fan coil units for an installation, and obtained the maximum discount. Some time later it was determined the project required an additional matching unit. The contractor has to purchase this unit from the original supplier to ensure a match. The supplier at this time may not discount the unit because of the small quantity, and the fact that he is no longer in a competitive situation. The impact of quantity on purchase can add between 0% and 25% to material prices and/or subcontractor quotes.

- If materials have been ordered or delivered to the job site, will they be subject to a cancellation charge or restocking fee?

  Check with the supplier to determine if ordered materials are subject to a cancellation charge. Delivered materials not used as result of a change order may be subject to a restocking fee if returned to the supplier. Common restocking charges run between 20% and 40%. Also, delivery charges to return the goods to the supplier must be added.

## Labor

- How efficient is the existing crew at the actual installation?

  Is the same crew that performed the initial work going to do the change order? Possibly the change consists of the installation of a unit identical to one already installed; therefore the change should take less time. Be sure to consider this potential productivity increase and modify the productivity rates accordingly.

- If the crew size is increased, what impact will that have on supervision requirements?

  Under most bargaining agreements or management practices, there is a point at which a working foreman is replaced by a nonworking foreman. This replacement increases project overhead by adding a nonproductive worker. If additional workers are added to accelerate the project or to perform changes while maintaining the schedule, be sure to add additional supervision time if warranted. Calculate the hours involved and the additional cost directly if possible.

- What are the other impacts of increased crew size?

  The larger the crew, the greater the potential for productivity to decrease. Some of the factors that cause this productivity loss are: overcrowding (producing restrictive conditions in the working space), and possibly a shortage of any special tools and equipment required. Such factors affect not only the crew working on the elements directly involved in the change order, but other crews whose movement may also be hampered.

  As the crew increases, check its basic composition for changes by the addition or deletion of apprentices or nonworking foreman and quantify the potential effects of equipment shortages or other logistical factors.

- As new crews, unfamiliar with the project, are brought onto the site, how long will it take them to become oriented to the project requirements?

  The orientation time for a new crew to become 100% effective varies with the site and type of project. Orientation is easiest at a new construction site, and most difficult at existing, very restrictive renovation sites. The type of work also affects orientation time. When all elements of the work are exposed, such as concrete or masonry work, orientation is decreased. When the work is concealed or less visible, such as existing electrical systems, orientation takes longer. Usually orientation can be accomplished in one day or less. Costs for added orientation should be itemized and added to the total estimated cost.

- How much actual production can be gained by working overtime?

  Short term overtime can be used effectively to accomplish more work in a day. However, as overtime is scheduled to run beyond several weeks, studies have shown marked decreases in output. The following chart shows the effect of long term overtime on worker efficiency. If the anticipated change requires extended overtime to keep the job on schedule, these factors can be used as a guide to predict the impact on time and cost. Add project overhead, particularly supervision, that may also be incurred.

| Days per Week | Hours per Day | Production Efficiency | | | | | Payroll Cost Factors | |
|---|---|---|---|---|---|---|---|---|
| | | 1 Week | 2 Weeks | 3 Weeks | 4 Weeks | Average 4 Weeks | @ 1-1/2 Times | @ 2 Times |
| 5 | 8 | 100% | 100% | 100% | 100% | 100% | 100% | 100% |
| | 9 | 100 | 100 | 95 | 90 | 96.25 | 105.6 | 111.1 |
| | 10 | 100 | 95 | 90 | 85 | 91.25 | 110.0 | 120.0 |
| | 11 | 95 | 90 | 75 | 65 | 81.25 | 113.6 | 127.3 |
| | 12 | 90 | 85 | 70 | 60 | 76.25 | 116.7 | 133.3 |
| 6 | 8 | 100 | 100 | 95 | 90 | 96.25 | 108.3 | 116.7 |
| | 9 | 100 | 95 | 90 | 85 | 92.50 | 113.0 | 125.9 |
| | 10 | 95 | 90 | 85 | 80 | 87.50 | 116.7 | 133.3 |
| | 11 | 95 | 85 | 70 | 65 | 78.75 | 119.7 | 139.4 |
| | 12 | 90 | 80 | 65 | 60 | 73.75 | 122.2 | 144.4 |
| 7 | 8 | 100 | 95 | 85 | 75 | 88.75 | 114.3 | 128.6 |
| | 9 | 95 | 90 | 80 | 70 | 83.75 | 118.3 | 136.5 |
| | 10 | 90 | 85 | 75 | 65 | 78.75 | 121.4 | 142.9 |
| | 11 | 85 | 80 | 65 | 60 | 72.50 | 124.0 | 148.1 |
| | 12 | 85 | 75 | 60 | 55 | 68.75 | 126.2 | 152.4 |

## Effects of Overtime

Caution: Under many labor agreements, Sundays and holidays are paid at a higher premium than the normal overtime rate.

The use of long-term overtime is counterproductive on almost any construction job; that is, the longer the period of overtime, the lower the actual production rate. Numerous studies have been conducted, and while they have resulted in slightly different numbers, all reach the same conclusion. The figure above tabulates the effects of overtime work on efficiency.

As illustrated, there can be a difference between the *actual* payroll cost per hour and the *effective* cost per hour for overtime work. This is due to the reduced production efficiency with the increase in weekly hours beyond 40. This difference between actual and effective cost results from overtime work over a prolonged period. Short-term overtime work does not result in as great a reduction in efficiency, and in such cases, effective cost may not vary significantly from the actual payroll cost. As the total hours per week are increased on a regular basis, more time is lost because of fatigue, lowered morale, and an increased accident rate.

As an example, assume a project where workers are working 6 days a week, 10 hours per day. From the figure above (based on productivity studies), the average effective productive hours over a four-week period are:

$$0.875 \times 60 = 52.5$$

Depending upon the locale and day of week, overtime hours may be paid at time and a half or double time. For time and a half, the overall (average) *actual* payroll cost (including regular and overtime hours) is determined as follows:

$$\frac{40 \text{ reg. hrs.} + (20 \text{ overtime hrs.} \times 1.5)}{60 \text{ hrs.}} = 1.167$$

Based on 60 hours, the payroll cost per hour will be 116.7% of the normal rate at 40 hours per week. However, because the effective production (efficiency) for 60 hours is reduced to the equivalent of 52.5 hours, the effective cost of overtime is calculated as follows:

For time and a half:

$$\frac{40 \text{ reg. hrs.} + (20 \text{ overtime hrs.} \times 1.5)}{52.5 \text{ hrs.}} = 1.33$$

Installed cost will be 133% of the normal rate (for labor).

Thus, when figuring overtime, the actual cost per unit of work will be higher than the apparent overtime payroll dollar increase, due to the reduced productivity of the longer workweek. These efficiency calculations are true only for those cost factors determined by hours worked. Costs that are applied weekly or monthly, such as equipment rentals, will not be similarly affected.

## Equipment

- What equipment is required to complete the change order?

Change orders may require extending the rental period of equipment already on the job site, or the addition of special equipment brought in to accomplish the change work. In either case, the additional rental charges and operator labor charges must be added.

## Summary

The preceding considerations and others you deem appropriate should be analyzed and applied to a change order estimate. The impact of each should be quantified and listed on the estimate to form an audit trail.

Change orders that are properly identified, documented, and managed help to ensure the orderly, professional and profitable progress of the work. They also minimize potential claims or disputes at the end of the project.

# Estimating Tips

- The cost figures in this Square Foot Cost section were derived from approximately 11,200 projects contained in the RSMeans database of completed construction projects. They include the contractor's overhead and profit, but do not generally include architectural fees or land costs. The figures have been adjusted to January of the current year. New projects are added to our files each year, and outdated projects are discarded. For this reason, certain costs may not show a uniform annual progression. In no case are all subdivisions of a project listed.

- These projects were located throughout the U.S. and reflect a tremendous variation in square foot (S.F.) and cubic foot (C.F.) costs. This is due to differences, not only in labor and material costs, but also in individual owners' requirements. For instance, a bank in a large city would have different features than one in a rural area. This is true of all the different types of buildings analyzed. Therefore, caution should be exercised when using these Square Foot costs. For example, for court houses, costs in the database are local court house costs and will not apply to the larger, more elaborate federal court houses. As a general rule, the projects in the 1/4 column do not include any site work or equipment, while the projects in the 3/4 column may include both equipment and site work. The median figures do not generally include site work.

- None of the figures "go with" any others. All individual cost items were computed and tabulated separately. Thus, the sum of the median figures for Plumbing, HVAC and Electrical will not normally total up to the total Mechanical and Electrical costs arrived at by separate analysis and tabulation of the projects.

- Each building was analyzed as to total and component costs and percentages. The figures were arranged in ascending order with the results tabulated as shown. The 1/4 column shows that 25% of the projects had lower costs and 75% had higher. The 3/4 column shows that 75% of the projects had lower costs and 25% had higher. The median column shows that 50% of the projects had lower costs and 50% had higher.

- There are two times when square foot costs are useful. The first is in the conceptual stage when no details are available. Then square foot costs make a useful starting point. The second is after the bids are in and the costs can be worked back into their appropriate units for information purposes. As soon as details become available in the project design, the square foot approach should be discontinued and the project priced as to its particular components. When more precision is required, or for estimating the replacement cost of specific buildings, the current edition of *RSMeans Square Foot Costs* should be used.

- In using the figures in this section, it is recommended that the median column be used for preliminary figures if no additional information is available. The median figures, when multiplied by the total city construction cost index figures (see City Cost Indexes) and then multiplied by the project size modifier at the end of this section, should present a fairly accurate base figure, which would then have to be adjusted in view of the estimator's experience, local economic conditions, code requirements, and the owner's particular requirements. There is no need to factor the percentage figures, as these should remain constant from city to city. All tabulations mentioning air conditioning had at least partial air conditioning.

- The editors of this book would greatly appreciate receiving cost figures on one or more of your recent projects, which would then be included in the averages for next year. All cost figures received will be kept confidential, except that they will be averaged with other similar projects to arrive at Square Foot cost figures for next year's book. See the last page of the book for details and the discount available for submitting one or more of your projects.

| 50 17 00 \| S.F. Costs | | UNIT | UNIT COSTS | | | % OF TOTAL | | | |
|---|---|---|---|---|---|---|---|---|---|
| | | | 1/4 | MEDIAN | 3/4 | 1/4 | MEDIAN | 3/4 | |
| **01** 0010 | **APARTMENTS Low Rise (1 to 3 story)** | S.F. | 62.50 | 78.50 | 105 | | | | **01** |
| 0020 | Total project cost | C.F. | 5.60 | 7.40 | 9.15 | | | | |
| 0100 | Site work | S.F. | 5.35 | 7.30 | 12.80 | 6.05% | 10.55% | 14.05% | |
| 0500 | Masonry | | 1.23 | 2.86 | 4.94 | 1.54% | 3.67% | 6.35% | |
| 1500 | Finishes | | 6.65 | 9.10 | 11.25 | 9.05% | 10.75% | 12.85% | |
| 1800 | Equipment | | 2.04 | 3.09 | 4.60 | 2.73% | 4.03% | 5.95% | |
| 2720 | Plumbing | | 4.86 | 6.25 | 7.95 | 6.65% | 8.95% | 10.05% | |
| 2770 | Heating, ventilating, air conditioning | | 3.10 | 3.81 | 5.60 | 4.20% | 5.60% | 7.60% | |
| 2900 | Electrical | | 3.61 | 4.79 | 6.45 | 5.20% | 6.65% | 8.40% | |
| 3100 | Total: Mechanical & Electrical | | 12.50 | 15.95 | 19.90 | 15.90% | 18.05% | 23% | |
| 9000 | Per apartment unit, total cost | Apt. | 58,000 | 89,000 | 131,000 | | | | |
| 9500 | Total: Mechanical & Electrical | " | 11,000 | 17,300 | 22,600 | | | | |
| **02** 0010 | **APARTMENTS Mid Rise (4 to 7 story)** | S.F. | 83 | 100 | 124 | | | | **02** |
| 0020 | Total project costs | C.F. | 6.45 | 8.90 | 12.20 | | | | |
| 0100 | Site work | S.F. | 3.31 | 6.55 | 11.80 | 5.25% | 6.70% | 9.15% | |
| 0500 | Masonry | | 5.50 | 7.60 | 10.80 | 5.10% | 7.25% | 10.50% | |
| 1500 | Finishes | | 10.40 | 14.50 | 17.10 | 10.55% | 13.45% | 17.70% | |
| 1800 | Equipment | | 2.51 | 3.88 | 4.94 | 2.54% | 3.48% | 4.31% | |
| 2500 | Conveying equipment | | 1.87 | 2.27 | 2.75 | 1.94% | 2.27% | 2.69% | |
| 2720 | Plumbing | | 4.85 | 7.80 | 8.60 | 5.70% | 7.20% | 8.95% | |
| 2900 | Electrical | | 5.45 | 7.80 | 9 | 6.65% | 7.20% | 8.95% | |
| 3100 | Total: Mechanical & Electrical | | 17.45 | 22 | 26.50 | 18.50% | 21% | 23% | |
| 9000 | Per apartment unit, total cost | Apt. | 93,500 | 110,500 | 183,000 | | | | |
| 9500 | Total: Mechanical & Electrical | " | 17,700 | 20,400 | 25,800 | | | | |
| **03** 0010 | **APARTMENTS High Rise (8 to 24 story)** | S.F. | 94 | 114 | 138 | | | | **03** |
| 0020 | Total project costs | C.F. | 9.10 | 11.15 | 13.55 | | | | |
| 0100 | Site work | S.F. | 3.40 | 5.50 | 7.70 | 2.58% | 4.84% | 6.15% | |
| 0500 | Masonry | | 5.45 | 9.90 | 12.30 | 4.74% | 9.65% | 11.05% | |
| 1500 | Finishes | | 10.40 | 13 | 15.35 | 9.75% | 11.80% | 13.70% | |
| 1800 | Equipment | | 3.02 | 3.71 | 4.91 | 2.78% | 3.49% | 4.35% | |
| 2500 | Conveying equipment | | 2.13 | 3.24 | 4.40 | 2.23% | 2.78% | 3.37% | |
| 2720 | Plumbing | | 6.90 | 8.15 | 11.40 | 6.80% | 7.20% | 10.45% | |
| 2900 | Electrical | | 6.45 | 8.15 | 11 | 6.45% | 7.65% | 8.80% | |
| 3100 | Total: Mechanical & Electrical | | 19.30 | 24.50 | 29.50 | 17.95% | 22.50% | 24.50% | |
| 9000 | Per apartment unit, total cost | Apt. | 97,500 | 107,500 | 149,000 | | | | |
| 9500 | Total: Mechanical & Electrical | " | 21,100 | 24,100 | 25,500 | | | | |
| **04** 0010 | **AUDITORIUMS** | S.F. | 96.50 | 132 | 189 | | | | **04** |
| 0020 | Total project costs | C.F. | 6.10 | 8.50 | 12.20 | | | | |
| 2720 | Plumbing | S.F. | 6.15 | 8.55 | 10.80 | 5.85% | 7.20% | 8.70% | |
| 2900 | Electrical | | 7.55 | 10.90 | 14.65 | 6.80% | 8.95% | 11.30% | |
| 3100 | Total: Mechanical & Electrical | | 21.50 | 38 | 52 | 24.50% | 30.50% | 31.50% | |
| **05** 0010 | **AUTOMOTIVE SALES** | S.F. | 72 | 98 | 121 | | | | **05** |
| 0020 | Total project costs | C.F. | 4.75 | 5.70 | 7.40 | | | | |
| 2720 | Plumbing | S.F. | 3.29 | 5.70 | 6.25 | 2.89% | 6.05% | 6.50% | |
| 2770 | Heating, ventilating, air conditioning | | 5.10 | 7.75 | 8.40 | 4.61% | 10% | 10.35% | |
| 2900 | Electrical | | 5.80 | 8.95 | 12.15 | 7.30% | 9.80% | 12.15% | |
| 3100 | Total: Mechanical & Electrical | | 18.20 | 26 | 31 | 20.50% | 21.50% | 26% | |
| **06** 0010 | **BANKS** | S.F. | 141 | 176 | 223 | | | | **06** |
| 0020 | Total project costs | C.F. | 10.10 | 13.75 | 18.15 | | | | |
| 0100 | Site work | S.F. | 16.15 | 24.50 | 35 | 7.75% | 12.95% | 17% | |
| 0500 | Masonry | | 7.35 | 14.10 | 25 | 3.36% | 7.65% | 10.35% | |
| 1500 | Finishes | | 12.50 | 17.10 | 22 | 5.80% | 8.35% | 11.05% | |
| 1800 | Equipment | | 5.55 | 11.70 | 25 | 1.34% | 5.95% | 10.65% | |
| 2720 | Plumbing | | 4.43 | 6.35 | 9.25 | 2.82% | 3.90% | 4.93% | |
| 2770 | Heating, ventilating, air conditioning | | 8.45 | 11.25 | 15 | 4.86% | 7.15% | 8.50% | |
| 2900 | Electrical | | 13.35 | 17.85 | 23.50 | 8.20% | 10.20% | 12.20% | |
| 3100 | Total: Mechanical & Electrical | | 31.50 | 42.50 | 51 | 16.55% | 19.45% | 23% | |
| 3500 | See also division 11020 & 11030 (MF2004 11 16 00 & 11 17 00) | | | | | | | | |

| | | | UNIT | UNIT COSTS | | | % OF TOTAL | | |
|---|---|---|---|---|---|---|---|---|---|
| | **50 17 00 \| S.F. Costs** | | | 1/4 | MEDIAN | 3/4 | 1/4 | MEDIAN | 3/4 |
| 13 | 0010 | **CHURCHES** | S.F. | 95 | 121 | 156 | | | |
| | 0020 | Total project costs | C.F. | 5.90 | 7.45 | 9.85 | | | |
| | 1800 | Equipment | S.F. | 1.14 | 2.72 | 5.80 | .95% | 2.24% | 4.50% |
| | 2720 | Plumbing | | 3.71 | 5.20 | 7.65 | 3.51% | 4.96% | 6.25% |
| | 2770 | Heating, ventilating, air conditioning | | 8.70 | 11.30 | 16 | 7.50% | 10% | 12% |
| | 2900 | Electrical | | 8 | 11 | 14.70 | 7.35% | 8.75% | 10.95% |
| | 3100 | Total: Mechanical & Electrical | ↓ | 25 | 31.50 | 43 | 18.30% | 21.50% | 24% |
| | 3500 | See also division 11040 (MF2004 11 91 00) | | | | | | | |
| 15 | 0010 | **CLUBS, COUNTRY** | S.F. | 102 | 123 | 155 | | | |
| | 0020 | Total project costs | C.F. | 8.25 | 10.05 | 13.85 | | | |
| | 2720 | Plumbing | S.F. | 6.35 | 9.15 | 21 | 5.60% | 7.90% | 10% |
| | 2900 | Electrical | | 8.05 | 11 | 14.35 | 7% | 8.95% | 11% |
| | 3100 | Total: Mechanical & Electrical | ↓ | 42.50 | 53.50 | 56.50 | 19% | 26.50% | 29.50% |
| 17 | 0010 | **CLUBS, SOCIAL Fraternal** | S.F. | 81.50 | 117 | 157 | | | |
| | 0020 | Total project costs | C.F. | 5.10 | 7.75 | 9.20 | | | |
| | 2720 | Plumbing | S.F. | 5.15 | 6.40 | 9.65 | 5.60% | 6.90% | 8.55% |
| | 2770 | Heating, ventilating, air conditioning | | 7.40 | 8.95 | 11.50 | 8.20% | 9.25% | 14.40% |
| | 2900 | Electrical | | 6.50 | 10.10 | 12.20 | 6.50% | 9.50% | 10.55% |
| | 3100 | Total: Mechanical & Electrical | ↓ | 18.10 | 34.50 | 43.50 | 21% | 23% | 23.50% |
| 18 | 0010 | **CLUBS, Y.M.C.A.** | S.F. | 102 | 138 | 167 | | | |
| | 0020 | Total project costs | C.F. | 4.72 | 7.90 | 11.75 | | | |
| | 2720 | Plumbing | S.F. | 6.45 | 12.90 | 14.45 | 5.65% | 7.60% | 10.85% |
| | 2900 | Electrical | | 8.20 | 10.60 | 14.10 | 6.05% | 7.60% | 9.25% |
| | 3100 | Total: Mechanical & Electrical | ↓ | 31.50 | 35 | 48 | 18.40% | 21.50% | 28.50% |
| 19 | 0010 | **COLLEGES Classrooms & Administration** | S.F. | 110 | 149 | 198 | | | |
| | 0020 | Total project costs | C.F. | 8.05 | 11.40 | 18.05 | | | |
| | 0500 | Masonry | S.F. | 7.60 | 14.30 | 17.55 | 5.65% | 8.25% | 10.50% |
| | 2720 | Plumbing | | 5.60 | 10.95 | 19.55 | 5.10% | 6.60% | 8.95% |
| | 2900 | Electrical | | 9.15 | 13.80 | 17.85 | 7.70% | 9.85% | 12% |
| | 3100 | Total: Mechanical & Electrical | ↓ | 34.50 | 48 | 57 | 24% | 28% | 31.50% |
| 21 | 0010 | **COLLEGES Science, Engineering, Laboratories** | S.F. | 192 | 225 | 274 | | | |
| | 0020 | Total project costs | C.F. | 11.05 | 16.10 | 18.25 | | | |
| | 1800 | Equipment | S.F. | 10.70 | 24.50 | 26.50 | 2% | 6.45% | 12.65% |
| | 2900 | Electrical | | 15.85 | 21.50 | 34.50 | 7.10% | 9.40% | 12.10% |
| | 3100 | Total: Mechanical & Electrical | ↓ | 59 | 70 | 108 | 28.50% | 31.50% | 41% |
| | 3500 | See also division 11600 (MF2004 11 53 00) | | | | | | | |
| 23 | 0010 | **COLLEGES Student Unions** | S.F. | 123 | 172 | 201 | | | |
| | 0020 | Total project costs | C.F. | 6.85 | 8.95 | 11.55 | | | |
| | 3100 | Total: Mechanical & Electrical | S.F. | 46 | 50 | 59 | 23.50% | 26% | 29% |
| 25 | 0010 | **COMMUNITY CENTERS** | S.F. | 100 | 125 | 166 | | | |
| | 0020 | Total project costs | C.F. | 6.60 | 9.45 | 12.25 | | | |
| | 1800 | Equipment | S.F. | 2.54 | 4.33 | 6.60 | 1.69% | 3.12% | 5.60% |
| | 2720 | Plumbing | | 4.80 | 8.40 | 11.60 | 4.85% | 7% | 8.95% |
| | 2770 | Heating, ventilating, air conditioning | | 8.10 | 11.65 | 16 | 6.80% | 10.35% | 12.90% |
| | 2900 | Electrical | | 8.30 | 11.05 | 16.10 | 7.35% | 9.10% | 10.85% |
| | 3100 | Total: Mechanical & Electrical | ↓ | 30 | 35.50 | 51.50 | 20.50% | 25.50% | 32.50% |
| 28 | 0010 | **COURT HOUSES** | S.F. | 146 | 168 | 217 | | | |
| | 0020 | Total project costs | C.F. | 11.20 | 13.40 | 16.90 | | | |
| | 2720 | Plumbing | S.F. | 6.95 | 9.70 | 13.95 | 5.95% | 7.45% | 8.20% |
| | 2900 | Electrical | | 15.50 | 17.25 | 25.50 | 8.90% | 10.45% | 11.55% |
| | 3100 | Total: Mechanical & Electrical | ↓ | 39.50 | 54 | 60 | 22.50% | 27.50% | 30.50% |
| 30 | 0010 | **DEPARTMENT STORES** | S.F. | 54 | 73 | 92.50 | | | |
| | 0020 | Total project costs | C.F. | 2.90 | 3.75 | 5.10 | | | |
| | 2720 | Plumbing | S.F. | 1.68 | 2.13 | 3.22 | 1.82% | 4.21% | 5.90% |
| | 2770 | Heating, ventilating, air conditioning | ↓ | 4.91 | 7.60 | 11.40 | 8.20% | 9.10% | 14.80% |

| | | 50 17 00 \| S.F. Costs | UNIT | UNIT COSTS | | | % OF TOTAL | | |
|---|---|---|---|---|---|---|---|---|---|
| | | | | 1/4 | MEDIAN | 3/4 | 1/4 | MEDIAN | 3/4 |
| 30 | 2900 | Electrical | S.F. | 6.20 | 8.50 | 10.05 | 9.05% | 12.15% | 14.95% | 30 |
| | 3100 | Total: Mechanical & Electrical | ↓ | 10.90 | 13.95 | 24.50 | 13.20% | 21.50% | 50% | |
| 31 | 0010 | **DORMITORIES Low Rise (1 to 3 story)** | S.F. | 101 | 133 | 172 | | | | 31 |
| | 0020 | Total project costs | C.F. | 6.10 | 9.35 | 14 | | | | |
| | 2720 | Plumbing | S.F. | 6.15 | 8.25 | 10.40 | 8.05% | 9% | 9.65% | |
| | 2770 | Heating, ventilating, air conditioning | | 6.50 | 7.80 | 10.40 | 4.61% | 8.05% | 10% | |
| | 2900 | Electrical | | 6.65 | 10.20 | 13.80 | 6.25% | 8.65% | 9.50% | |
| | 3100 | Total: Mechanical & Electrical | ↓ | 34 | 37.50 | 59 | 21.50% | 24% | 27% | |
| | 9000 | Per bed, total cost | Bed | 43,400 | 48,200 | 103,500 | | | | |
| 32 | 0010 | **DORMITORIES Mid Rise (4 to 8 story)** | S.F. | 126 | 164 | 203 | | | | 32 |
| | 0020 | Total project costs | C.F. | 13.85 | 15.25 | 18.25 | | | | |
| | 2900 | Electrical | S.F. | 13.35 | 15.20 | 20.50 | 8.20% | 10.20% | 11.95% | |
| | 3100 | Total: Mechanical & Electrical | " | 37.50 | 39 | 76 | 25.50% | 34.50% | 37.50% | |
| | 9000 | Per bed, total cost | Bed | 17,900 | 40,900 | 103,500 | | | | |
| 34 | 0010 | **FACTORIES** | S.F. | 47.50 | 71 | 109 | | | | 34 |
| | 0020 | Total project costs | C.F. | 3.05 | 4.56 | 7.55 | | | | |
| | 0100 | Site work | S.F. | 5.45 | 9.90 | 15.70 | 6.95% | 11.45% | 17.95% | |
| | 2720 | Plumbing | | 2.57 | 4.78 | 7.90 | 3.73% | 6.05% | 8.10% | |
| | 2770 | Heating, ventilating, air conditioning | | 5 | 7.15 | 9.65 | 5.25% | 8.45% | 11.35% | |
| | 2900 | Electrical | | 5.90 | 9.35 | 14.30 | 8.10% | 10.50% | 14.20% | |
| | 3100 | Total: Mechanical & Electrical | ↓ | 16.90 | 22.50 | 34.50 | 21% | 28.50% | 35.50% | |
| 36 | 0010 | **FIRE STATIONS** | S.F. | 94.50 | 129 | 169 | | | | 36 |
| | 0020 | Total project costs | C.F. | 5.50 | 7.60 | 10.10 | | | | |
| | 0500 | Masonry | S.F. | 13.85 | 25 | 32 | 8.60% | 12.40% | 16.45% | |
| | 1140 | Roofing | | 3.08 | 8.35 | 9.50 | 1.90% | 4.94% | 5.05% | |
| | 1580 | Painting | | 2.53 | 3.57 | 3.65 | 1.37% | 1.57% | 2.07% | |
| | 1800 | Equipment | | 1.99 | 2.83 | 6.80 | .76% | 2.11% | 3.69% | |
| | 2720 | Plumbing | | 6 | 8.80 | 12.95 | 5.85% | 7.35% | 9.45% | |
| | 2770 | Heating, ventilating, air conditioning | | 5.25 | 8.50 | 13.10 | 5.15% | 7.40% | 9.40% | |
| | 2900 | Electrical | | 6.70 | 11.65 | 15.65 | 6.85% | 8.65% | 10.60% | |
| | 3100 | Total: Mechanical & Electrical | ↓ | 33 | 41 | 47 | 19.60% | 23% | 26% | |
| 37 | 0010 | **FRATERNITY HOUSES & Sorority Houses** | S.F. | 94.50 | 122 | 166 | | | | 37 |
| | 0020 | Total project costs | C.F. | 9.40 | 9.80 | 12.55 | | | | |
| | 2720 | Plumbing | S.F. | 7.15 | 8.20 | 14.95 | 6.80% | 8% | 10.85% | |
| | 2900 | Electrical | | 6.25 | 13.45 | 16.50 | 6.60% | 9.90% | 10.65% | |
| | 3100 | Total: Mechanical & Electrical | ↓ | 16.70 | 24 | 29 | 14.60% | 15.10% | 15.90% | |
| 38 | 0010 | **FUNERAL HOMES** | S.F. | 99.50 | 136 | 247 | | | | 38 |
| | 0020 | Total project costs | C.F. | 10.15 | 11.30 | 21.50 | | | | |
| | 2900 | Electrical | S.F. | 4.40 | 8.05 | 8.85 | 3.58% | 4.44% | 5.95% | |
| | 3100 | Total: Mechanical & Electrical | ↓ | 15.60 | 23 | 32 | 12.90% | 12.90% | 12.90% | |
| 39 | 0010 | **GARAGES, COMMERCIAL (Service)** | S.F. | 58 | 87 | 120 | | | | 39 |
| | 0020 | Total project costs | C.F. | 3.79 | 5.50 | 8 | | | | |
| | 1800 | Equipment | S.F. | 3.18 | 7.15 | 11.10 | 2.69% | 4.62% | 6.80% | |
| | 2720 | Plumbing | | 3.91 | 6 | 11 | 5.45% | 7.85% | 10.65% | |
| | 2730 | Heating & ventilating | | 5.15 | 7 | 9.65 | 5.25% | 6.85% | 8.20% | |
| | 2900 | Electrical | | 5.35 | 8.20 | 11.80 | 7.15% | 9.20% | 10.75% | |
| | 3100 | Total: Mechanical & Electrical | ↓ | 12.20 | 22.50 | 33.50 | 12.35% | 16.50% | 26% | |
| 40 | 0010 | **GARAGES, MUNICIPAL (Repair)** | S.F. | 83 | 110 | 156 | | | | 40 |
| | 0020 | Total project costs | C.F. | 5.20 | 6.55 | 11.30 | | | | |
| | 0500 | Masonry | S.F. | 7.80 | 15.20 | 23.50 | 5.60% | 9.15% | 12.50% | |
| | 2720 | Plumbing | | 3.72 | 7.15 | 13.45 | 3.59% | 6.70% | 7.95% | |
| | 2730 | Heating & ventilating | | 6.35 | 9.20 | 17.75 | 6.15% | 7.45% | 13.50% | |
| | 2900 | Electrical | | 6.15 | 9.65 | 13.90 | 6.65% | 8.15% | 11.15% | |
| | 3100 | Total: Mechanical & Electrical | ↓ | 28.50 | 39.50 | 57 | 21.50% | 25.50% | 28.50% | |

| | | 50 17 00 \| S.F. Costs | UNIT | UNIT COSTS | | | % OF TOTAL | | |
|---|---|---|---|---|---|---|---|---|---|
| | | | | 1/4 | MEDIAN | 3/4 | 1/4 | MEDIAN | 3/4 |
| 41 | 0010 | **GARAGES, PARKING** | S.F. | 32 | 47 | 81 | | | |
| | 0020 | Total project costs | C.F. | 3.03 | 4.12 | 6 | | | |
| | 2720 | Plumbing | S.F. | .91 | 1.42 | 2.19 | 1.72% | 2.70% | 3.85% |
| | 2900 | Electrical | | 1.77 | 2.17 | 3.41 | 4.33% | 5.20% | 6.30% |
| | 3100 | Total: Mechanical & Electrical | ↓ | 3.62 | 5.05 | 6.30 | 7% | 8.90% | 11.05% |
| | 3200 | | | | | | | | |
| | 9000 | Per car, total cost | Car | 13,600 | 17,100 | 21,800 | | | |
| 43 | 0010 | **GYMNASIUMS** | S.F. | 90 | 120 | 158 | | | |
| | 0020 | Total project costs | C.F. | 4.47 | 6.05 | 7.45 | | | |
| | 1800 | Equipment | S.F. | 2.13 | 4 | 7.65 | 2.03% | 3.35% | 6.70% |
| | 2720 | Plumbing | | 5.70 | 7 | 8.70 | 4.65% | 6.40% | 7.75% |
| | 2770 | Heating, ventilating, air conditioning | | 6.10 | 9.30 | 18.65 | 5.15% | 9.05% | 11.10% |
| | 2900 | Electrical | | 6.90 | 9.40 | 12.40 | 6.60% | 8.50% | 10.30% |
| | 3100 | Total: Mechanical & Electrical | ↓ | 24.50 | 33.50 | 39.50 | 19.60% | 23.50% | 29% |
| | 3500 | See also division 11480 (MF2004 11 67 00) | | | | | | | |
| 46 | 0010 | **HOSPITALS** | S.F. | 172 | 212 | 310 | | | |
| | 0020 | Total project costs | C.F. | 13.05 | 16.25 | 23.50 | | | |
| | 1800 | Equipment | S.F. | 4.37 | 8.40 | 14.50 | .96% | 2.63% | 5% |
| | 2720 | Plumbing | | 14.85 | 20.50 | 26.50 | 7.60% | 9.10% | 10.85% |
| | 2770 | Heating, ventilating, air conditioning | | 22 | 28 | 37.50 | 7.80% | 12.95% | 16.65% |
| | 2900 | Electrical | | 18.80 | 24.50 | 38 | 9.85% | 11.55% | 13.90% |
| | 3100 | Total: Mechanical & Electrical | ↓ | 53 | 76 | 115 | 27% | 33.50% | 36.50% |
| | 9000 | Per bed or person, total cost | Bed | 199,500 | 275,000 | 316,500 | | | |
| | 9900 | See also division 11700 (MF2004 11 71 00) | | | | | | | |
| 48 | 0010 | **HOUSING For the Elderly** | S.F. | 84.50 | 107 | 132 | | | |
| | 0020 | Total project costs | C.F. | 6.05 | 8.40 | 10.70 | | | |
| | 0100 | Site work | S.F. | 6.30 | 9.15 | 13.40 | 5.05% | 7.90% | 12.10% |
| | 0500 | Masonry | | 2.58 | 9.65 | 14.10 | 1.30% | 6.05% | 11% |
| | 1800 | Equipment | | 2.05 | 2.82 | 4.49 | 1.88% | 3.23% | 4.43% |
| | 2510 | Conveying systems | | 2.06 | 2.77 | 3.75 | 1.78% | 2.20% | 2.81% |
| | 2720 | Plumbing | | 6.30 | 8 | 10.10 | 8.15% | 9.55% | 10.50% |
| | 2730 | Heating, ventilating, air conditioning | | 3.23 | 4.57 | 6.85 | 3.30% | 5.60% | 7.25% |
| | 2900 | Electrical | | 6.30 | 8.55 | 11 | 7.30% | 8.50% | 10.25% |
| | 3100 | Total: Mechanical & Electrical | ↓ | 21.50 | 26 | 34.50 | 18.10% | 22.50% | 29% |
| | 9000 | Per rental unit, total cost | Unit | 79,000 | 92,000 | 102,500 | | | |
| | 9500 | Total: Mechanical & Electrical | " | 17,500 | 20,200 | 23,600 | | | |
| 50 | 0010 | **HOUSING Public (Low Rise)** | S.F. | 71.50 | 99 | 129 | | | |
| | 0020 | Total project costs | C.F. | 6.35 | 7.90 | 9.85 | | | |
| | 0100 | Site work | S.F. | 9.05 | 13.05 | 21 | 8.35% | 11.75% | 16.50% |
| | 1800 | Equipment | | 1.94 | 3.16 | 4.81 | 2.26% | 3.03% | 4.24% |
| | 2720 | Plumbing | | 5.15 | 6.80 | 8.60 | 7.15% | 9.05% | 11.60% |
| | 2730 | Heating, ventilating, air conditioning | | 2.58 | 5 | 5.50 | 4.26% | 6.05% | 6.45% |
| | 2900 | Electrical | | 4.31 | 6.40 | 8.90 | 5.10% | 6.55% | 8.25% |
| | 3100 | Total: Mechanical & Electrical | ↓ | 20.50 | 26.50 | 29.50 | 14.50% | 17.55% | 26.50% |
| | 9000 | Per apartment, total cost | Apt. | 78,000 | 89,000 | 111,500 | | | |
| | 9500 | Total: Mechanical & Electrical | " | 16,700 | 20,600 | 22,800 | | | |
| 51 | 0010 | **ICE SKATING RINKS** | S.F. | 61 | 142 | 156 | | | |
| | 0020 | Total project costs | C.F. | 4.47 | 4.58 | 5.30 | | | |
| | 2720 | Plumbing | S.F. | 2.27 | 4.26 | 4.36 | 3.12% | 3.23% | 5.65% |
| | 2900 | Electrical | | 6.50 | 10 | 10.60 | 6.30% | 10.15% | 15.05% |
| | 3100 | Total: Mechanical & Electrical | ↓ | 10.85 | 15.35 | 19.20 | 18.95% | 18.95% | 18.95% |
| 52 | 0010 | **JAILS** | S.F. | 185 | 239 | 310 | | | |
| | 0020 | Total project costs | C.F. | 16.70 | 23.50 | 28.50 | | | |
| | 1800 | Equipment | S.F. | 7.25 | 21.50 | 36.50 | 2.80% | 5.55% | 11.90% |
| | 2720 | Plumbing | | 18.85 | 24 | 31.50 | 7% | 8.90% | 13.35% |
| | 2770 | Heating, ventilating, air conditioning | | 16.70 | 22.50 | 43 | 7.50% | 9.45% | 17.75% |
| | 2900 | Electrical | ↓ | 19.30 | 25.50 | 32 | 8.20% | 11.55% | 14.70% |

| | | 50 17 00 \| S.F. Costs | UNIT | UNIT COSTS | | | % OF TOTAL | | | |
|---|---|---|---|---|---|---|---|---|---|---|
| | | | | 1/4 | MEDIAN | 3/4 | 1/4 | MEDIAN | 3/4 | |
| 52 | 3100 | Total: Mechanical & Electrical | S.F. | 49 | 92.50 | 109 | 27.50% | 30% | 34% | 52 |
| 53 | 0010 | **LIBRARIES** | S.F. | 117 | 148 | 195 | | | | 53 |
| | 0020 | Total project costs | C.F. | 8 | 10.05 | 12.80 | | | | |
| | 0500 | Masonry | S.F. | 9.15 | 16.20 | 27 | 5.80% | 7.60% | 11.80% | |
| | 1800 | Equipment | | 1.60 | 4.31 | 6.50 | .37% | 1.50% | 4.16% | |
| | 2720 | Plumbing | | 4.32 | 6.30 | 8.55 | 3.38% | 4.60% | 5.70% | |
| | 2770 | Heating, ventilating, air conditioning | | 9.55 | 16.20 | 21 | 7.80% | 10.95% | 12.80% | |
| | 2900 | Electrical | | 11.95 | 15.45 | 19.70 | 8.30% | 10.30% | 11.95% | |
| | 3100 | Total: Mechanical & Electrical | | 35 | 44.50 | 54.50 | 19.65% | 22.50% | 26.50% | |
| 54 | 0010 | **LIVING, ASSISTED** | S.F. | 108 | 128 | 150 | | | | 54 |
| | 0020 | Total project costs | C.F. | 9.10 | 10.65 | 12.10 | | | | |
| | 0500 | Masonry | S.F. | 3.18 | 3.79 | 4.46 | 2.37% | 3.16% | 3.86% | |
| | 1800 | Equipment | | 2.46 | 2.86 | 3.67 | 2.12% | 2.45% | 2.66% | |
| | 2720 | Plumbing | | 9.10 | 12.15 | 12.60 | 6.05% | 8.15% | 10.60% | |
| | 2770 | Heating, ventilating, air conditioning | | 10.80 | 11.25 | 12.35 | 7.95% | 9.35% | 9.70% | |
| | 2900 | Electrical | | 10.60 | 11.75 | 13.55 | 9% | 10% | 10.70% | |
| | 3100 | Total: Mechanical & Electrical | | 29.50 | 34.50 | 40 | 26% | 29% | 31.50% | |
| 55 | 0010 | **MEDICAL CLINICS** | S.F. | 110 | 136 | 172 | | | | 55 |
| | 0020 | Total project costs | C.F. | 8.10 | 10.45 | 13.90 | | | | |
| | 1800 | Equipment | S.F. | 2.98 | 6.25 | 9.75 | 1.05% | 2.94% | 6.35% | |
| | 2720 | Plumbing | | 7.30 | 10.30 | 13.80 | 6.15% | 8.40% | 10.10% | |
| | 2770 | Heating, ventilating, air conditioning | | 8.75 | 11.45 | 16.80 | 6.65% | 8.85% | 11.35% | |
| | 2900 | Electrical | | 9.45 | 13.45 | 17.60 | 8.10% | 10% | 12.25% | |
| | 3100 | Total: Mechanical & Electrical | | 30 | 41 | 56.50 | 22.50% | 27% | 33.50% | |
| | 3500 | See also division 11700 (MF2004 11 71 00) | | | | | | | | |
| 57 | 0010 | **MEDICAL OFFICES** | S.F. | 104 | 128 | 157 | | | | 57 |
| | 0020 | Total project costs | C.F. | 7.75 | 10.50 | 14.20 | | | | |
| | 1800 | Equipment | S.F. | 3.51 | 6.75 | 9.60 | .98% | 5.10% | 7.05% | |
| | 2720 | Plumbing | | 5.75 | 8.80 | 11.90 | 5.60% | 6.80% | 8.50% | |
| | 2770 | Heating, ventilating, air conditioning | | 6.90 | 10 | 13.20 | 6.10% | 8% | 9.70% | |
| | 2900 | Electrical | | 8.30 | 12.05 | 16.85 | 7.60% | 9.80% | 11.70% | |
| | 3100 | Total: Mechanical & Electrical | | 22.50 | 32 | 48 | 19.30% | 23% | 29% | |
| 59 | 0010 | **MOTELS** | S.F. | 65.50 | 95 | 124 | | | | 59 |
| | 0020 | Total project costs | C.F. | 5.80 | 7.80 | 12.75 | | | | |
| | 2720 | Plumbing | S.F. | 6.65 | 8.45 | 10.05 | 9.45% | 10.60% | 12.55% | |
| | 2770 | Heating, ventilating, air conditioning | | 4.04 | 6.05 | 10.80 | 5.60% | 5.60% | 10% | |
| | 2900 | Electrical | | 6.20 | 7.80 | 9.75 | 7.45% | 9.05% | 10.45% | |
| | 3100 | Total: Mechanical & Electrical | | 21 | 26.50 | 45 | 18.50% | 24% | 25.50% | |
| | 5000 | | | | | | | | | |
| | 9000 | Per rental unit, total cost | Unit | 33,300 | 63,500 | 68,500 | | | | |
| | 9500 | Total: Mechanical & Electrical | " | 6,500 | 9,825 | 11,400 | | | | |
| 60 | 0010 | **NURSING HOMES** | S.F. | 103 | 132 | 162 | | | | 60 |
| | 0020 | Total project costs | C.F. | 8.05 | 10.05 | 13.75 | | | | |
| | 1800 | Equipment | S.F. | 3.23 | 4.28 | 7.15 | 2.02% | 3.62% | 4.99% | |
| | 2720 | Plumbing | | 8.80 | 13.30 | 16.05 | 8.75% | 10.10% | 12.70% | |
| | 2770 | Heating, ventilating, air conditioning | | 9.25 | 14.05 | 18.60 | 9.70% | 11.45% | 11.80% | |
| | 2900 | Electrical | | 10.15 | 12.70 | 17.25 | 9.40% | 10.55% | 12.45% | |
| | 3100 | Total: Mechanical & Electrical | | 24 | 34 | 57 | 26% | 29.50% | 30.50% | |
| | 9000 | Per bed or person, total cost | Bed | 45,500 | 57,000 | 73,500 | | | | |
| 61 | 0010 | **OFFICES Low Rise (1 to 4 story)** | S.F. | 86.50 | 111 | 144 | | | | 61 |
| | 0020 | Total project costs | C.F. | 6.15 | 8.50 | 11.20 | | | | |
| | 0100 | Site work | S.F. | 6.90 | 11.70 | 17.55 | 6.20% | 9.70% | 13.60% | |
| | 0500 | Masonry | | 2.97 | 6.75 | 12.25 | 2.62% | 5.50% | 8.45% | |
| | 1800 | Equipment | | .92 | 1.80 | 4.90 | .68% | 1.50% | 3.63% | |
| | 2720 | Plumbing | | 3.09 | 4.77 | 7 | 3.66% | 4.50% | 6.10% | |
| | 2770 | Heating, ventilating, air conditioning | | 6.85 | 9.50 | 13.95 | 7.20% | 10.30% | 11.70% | |
| | 2900 | Electrical | | 7.05 | 10 | 14.15 | 7.45% | 9.60% | 11.35% | |

# 50 17 | Square Foot Costs

| | | | UNIT | UNIT COSTS | | | % OF TOTAL | | | |
|---|---|---|---|---|---|---|---|---|---|---|
| | **50 17 00 \| S.F. Costs** | | UNIT | 1/4 | MEDIAN | 3/4 | 1/4 | MEDIAN | 3/4 | |
| 61 | 3100 | Total: Mechanical & Electrical | S.F. | 19.20 | 25.50 | 38 | 18% | 22% | 27% | 61 |
| 62 | 0010 | **OFFICES Mid Rise (5 to 10 story)** | S.F. | 91.50 | 111 | 147 | | | | 62 |
| | 0020 | Total project costs | C.F. | 6.50 | 8.25 | 11.75 | | | | |
| | 2720 | Plumbing | S.F. | 2.77 | 4.29 | 6.15 | 2.83% | 3.74% | 4.50% | |
| | 2770 | Heating, ventilating, air conditioning | | 6.95 | 9.95 | 15.85 | 7.65% | 9.40% | 11% | |
| | 2900 | Electrical | | 6.80 | 8.70 | 12.05 | 6.35% | 7.80% | 10% | |
| | 3100 | Total: Mechanical & Electrical | | 17.60 | 22.50 | 43 | 19.15% | 21.50% | 27.50% | |
| 63 | 0010 | **OFFICES High Rise (11 to 20 story)** | S.F. | 112 | 142 | 174 | | | | 63 |
| | 0020 | Total project costs | C.F. | 7.85 | 9.80 | 14.10 | | | | |
| | 2900 | Electrical | S.F. | 6.85 | 8.35 | 12.35 | 5.80% | 7.85% | 10.50% | |
| | 3100 | Total: Mechanical & Electrical | | 22 | 29.50 | 49.50 | 16.90% | 23.50% | 34% | |
| 64 | 0010 | **POLICE STATIONS** | S.F. | 135 | 173 | 220 | | | | 64 |
| | 0020 | Total project costs | C.F. | 10.75 | 13.15 | 18 | | | | |
| | 0500 | Masonry | S.F. | 12.65 | 22.50 | 28 | 6.70% | 10.55% | 11.35% | |
| | 1800 | Equipment | | 2.14 | 9.40 | 14.90 | 1.43% | 4.07% | 6.70% | |
| | 2720 | Plumbing | | 7.55 | 15 | 18.70 | 5.65% | 6.90% | 10.75% | |
| | 2770 | Heating, ventilating, air conditioning | | 11.80 | 15.65 | 21.50 | 5.85% | 10.55% | 11.70% | |
| | 2900 | Electrical | | 14.70 | 21 | 28 | 9.80% | 11.85% | 14.80% | |
| | 3100 | Total: Mechanical & Electrical | | 48.50 | 58 | 78.50 | 28.50% | 32% | 32.50% | |
| 65 | 0010 | **POST OFFICES** | S.F. | 106 | 131 | 168 | | | | 65 |
| | 0020 | Total project costs | C.F. | 6.40 | 8.10 | 9.20 | | | | |
| | 2720 | Plumbing | S.F. | 4.79 | 5.95 | 7.50 | 4.24% | 5.30% | 5.60% | |
| | 2770 | Heating, ventilating, air conditioning | | 7.50 | 9.25 | 10.30 | 6.65% | 7.15% | 9.35% | |
| | 2900 | Electrical | | 8.75 | 12.35 | 14.65 | 7.25% | 9% | 11% | |
| | 3100 | Total: Mechanical & Electrical | | 25.50 | 33 | 37.50 | 16.25% | 18.80% | 22% | |
| 66 | 0010 | **POWER PLANTS** | S.F. | 740 | 975 | 1,800 | | | | 66 |
| | 0020 | Total project costs | C.F. | 20.50 | 44.50 | 95 | | | | |
| | 2900 | Electrical | S.F. | 52 | 111 | 165 | 9.30% | 12.75% | 21.50% | |
| | 8100 | Total: Mechanical & Electrical | | 130 | 425 | 945 | 32.50% | 32.50% | 52.50% | |
| 67 | 0010 | **RELIGIOUS EDUCATION** | S.F. | 86 | 112 | 138 | | | | 67 |
| | 0020 | Total project costs | C.F. | 4.76 | 6.80 | 8.55 | | | | |
| | 2720 | Plumbing | S.F. | 3.58 | 5.10 | 7.15 | 4.40% | 5.30% | 7.10% | |
| | 2770 | Heating, ventilating, air conditioning | | 9.05 | 10.25 | 14.50 | 10.05% | 11.45% | 12.35% | |
| | 2900 | Electrical | | 6.80 | 9.60 | 12.70 | 7.60% | 9.05% | 10.35% | |
| | 3100 | Total: Mechanical & Electrical | | 27.50 | 36.50 | 44.50 | 22% | 23% | 27% | |
| 69 | 0010 | **RESEARCH Laboratories & Facilities** | S.F. | 128 | 184 | 268 | | | | 69 |
| | 0020 | Total project costs | C.F. | 10.05 | 19.30 | 22.50 | | | | |
| | 1800 | Equipment | S.F. | 5.70 | 11.20 | 27.50 | .90% | 4.58% | 8.80% | |
| | 2720 | Plumbing | | 12.90 | 16.45 | 26.50 | 6.15% | 8.30% | 10.80% | |
| | 2770 | Heating, ventilating, air conditioning | | 11.55 | 39 | 46 | 7.25% | 16.50% | 17.50% | |
| | 2900 | Electrical | | 14.80 | 25 | 42 | 9.45% | 11.15% | 15.40% | |
| | 3100 | Total: Mechanical & Electrical | | 45.50 | 86.50 | 123 | 29.50% | 37% | 45.50% | |
| 70 | 0010 | **RESTAURANTS** | S.F. | 123 | 159 | 209 | | | | 70 |
| | 0020 | Total project costs | C.F. | 10.45 | 13.70 | 18 | | | | |
| | 1800 | Equipment | S.F. | 8.05 | 19.75 | 30 | 6.10% | 13% | 15.65% | |
| | 2720 | Plumbing | | 9.85 | 11.95 | 15.70 | 6.10% | 8.15% | 9% | |
| | 2770 | Heating, ventilating, air conditioning | | 12.50 | 17.30 | 22.50 | 9.20% | 12% | 12.40% | |
| | 2900 | Electrical | | 13.20 | 16.20 | 21 | 8.35% | 10.55% | 11.55% | |
| | 3100 | Total: Mechanical & Electrical | | 41 | 43.50 | 56.50 | 21% | 24.50% | 30% | |
| | 9000 | Per seat unit, total cost | Seat | 4,575 | 6,075 | 7,200 | | | | |
| | 9500 | Total: Mechanical & Electrical | " | 1,150 | 1,525 | 1,800 | | | | |
| 72 | 0010 | **RETAIL STORES** | S.F. | 58 | 78 | 103 | | | | 72 |
| | 0020 | Total project costs | C.F. | 3.94 | 5.60 | 7.80 | | | | |
| | 2720 | Plumbing | S.F. | 2.11 | 3.52 | 6 | 3.26% | 4.60% | 6.80% | |
| | 2770 | Heating, ventilating, air conditioning | | 4.55 | 6.25 | 9.35 | 6.75% | 8.75% | 10.15% | |
| | 2900 | Electrical | | 5.20 | 7.15 | 10.35 | 7.25% | 9.90% | 11.65% | |
| | 3100 | Total: Mechanical & Electrical | | 13.35 | 17.80 | 24 | 17.05% | 21% | 23.50% | |

| | | **50 17 00 \| S.F. Costs** | UNIT | UNIT COSTS | | | % OF TOTAL | | |
|---|---|---|---|---|---|---|---|---|---|
| | | | | 1/4 | MEDIAN | 3/4 | 1/4 | MEDIAN | 3/4 |
| **74** | 0010 | **SCHOOLS Elementary** | S.F. | 93.50 | 116 | 143 | | | |
| | 0020 | Total project costs | C.F. | 6.20 | 7.95 | 10.25 | | | |
| | 0500 | Masonry | S.F. | 8.35 | 14 | 21.50 | 5.45% | 10.65% | 14.95% |
| | 1800 | Equipment | | 2.68 | 4.49 | 8.65 | 1.89% | 3.33% | 4.78% |
| | 2720 | Plumbing | | 5.45 | 7.70 | 10.30 | 5.70% | 7.15% | 9.35% |
| | 2730 | Heating, ventilating, air conditioning | | 8.20 | 13 | 18.15 | 8.15% | 10.80% | 14.90% |
| | 2900 | Electrical | | 8.90 | 11.65 | 14.80 | 8.45% | 10.05% | 11.80% |
| | 3100 | Total: Mechanical & Electrical | ↓ | 31.50 | 40 | 48.50 | 25% | 27.50% | 30% |
| | 9000 | Per pupil, total cost | Ea. | 10,900 | 16,200 | 48,000 | | | |
| | 9500 | Total: Mechanical & Electrical | " | 3,075 | 3,900 | 13,900 | | | |
| **76** | 0010 | **SCHOOLS Junior High & Middle** | S.F. | 96 | 120 | 146 | | | |
| | 0020 | Total project costs | C.F. | 6.20 | 8.05 | 9 | | | |
| | 0500 | Masonry | S.F. | 12.20 | 15.70 | 18.40 | 8% | 11.40% | 14.30% |
| | 1800 | Equipment | | 3.12 | 5.05 | 7.60 | 1.81% | 3.26% | 4.86% |
| | 2720 | Plumbing | | 5.70 | 7 | 9.10 | 5.30% | 6.80% | 7.25% |
| | 2770 | Heating, ventilating, air conditioning | | 11.35 | 13.85 | 24.50 | 8.90% | 11.55% | 14.20% |
| | 2900 | Electrical | | 9.60 | 11.55 | 14.85 | 7.90% | 9.35% | 10.60% |
| | 3100 | Total: Mechanical & Electrical | ↓ | 31 | 40 | 49 | 23.50% | 27% | 29.50% |
| | 9000 | Per pupil, total cost | Ea. | 12,400 | 16,300 | 21,900 | | | |
| **78** | 0010 | **SCHOOLS Senior High** | S.F. | 101 | 123 | 156 | | | |
| | 0020 | Total project costs | C.F. | 6.15 | 9.05 | 14.55 | | | |
| | 1800 | Equipment | S.F. | 2.67 | 6.50 | 9.30 | 1.86% | 2.98% | 4.80% |
| | 2720 | Plumbing | | 5.70 | 8.55 | 15.65 | 5.60% | 6.90% | 8.30% |
| | 2770 | Heating, ventilating, air conditioning | | 11.65 | 13.35 | 25.50 | 8.95% | 11.60% | 15% |
| | 2900 | Electrical | | 10.20 | 13.25 | 20 | 8.65% | 10.15% | 12.35% |
| | 3100 | Total: Mechanical & Electrical | ↓ | 34 | 39.50 | 66.50 | 23.50% | 26.50% | 28.50% |
| | 9000 | Per pupil, total cost | Ea. | 9,575 | 19,500 | 24,400 | | | |
| **80** | 0010 | **SCHOOLS Vocational** | S.F. | 82 | 117 | 146 | | | |
| | 0020 | Total project costs | C.F. | 5.10 | 7.35 | 10.15 | | | |
| | 0500 | Masonry | S.F. | 4.83 | 11.95 | 18.25 | 3.53% | 4.61% | 10.95% |
| | 1800 | Equipment | | 2.46 | 3.39 | 8.85 | 1.24% | 3.13% | 4.68% |
| | 2720 | Plumbing | | 5.25 | 7.85 | 11.55 | 5.40% | 6.90% | 8.55% |
| | 2770 | Heating, ventilating, air conditioning | | 7.35 | 13.70 | 23 | 8.60% | 11.90% | 14.65% |
| | 2900 | Electrical | | 8.60 | 11.25 | 16.05 | 8.45% | 10.95% | 13.20% |
| | 3100 | Total: Mechanical & Electrical | ↓ | 29.50 | 33 | 56.50 | 23.50% | 29.50% | 31% |
| | 9000 | Per pupil, total cost | Ea. | 11,500 | 30,700 | 45,800 | | | |
| **83** | 0010 | **SPORTS ARENAS** | S.F. | 72 | 96 | 148 | | | |
| | 0020 | Total project costs | C.F. | 3.91 | 7 | 9 | | | |
| | 2720 | Plumbing | S.F. | 4.17 | 6.35 | 13.35 | 4.35% | 6.35% | 9.40% |
| | 2770 | Heating, ventilating, air conditioning | | 9 | 10.65 | 14.75 | 8.80% | 10.20% | 13.55% |
| | 2900 | Electrical | | 7.50 | 10.20 | 13.15 | 8.60% | 9.90% | 12.25% |
| | 3100 | Total: Mechanical & Electrical | ↓ | 18.65 | 33 | 44 | 21.50% | 25% | 27.50% |
| **85** | 0010 | **SUPERMARKETS** | S.F. | 66.50 | 77 | 90.50 | | | |
| | 0020 | Total project costs | C.F. | 3.70 | 4.48 | 6.80 | | | |
| | 2720 | Plumbing | S.F. | 3.71 | 4.68 | 5.45 | 5.40% | 6% | 7.45% |
| | 2770 | Heating, ventilating, air conditioning | | 5.45 | 7.25 | 8.85 | 8.60% | 8.65% | 9.60% |
| | 2900 | Electrical | | 8.30 | 9.55 | 11.30 | 10.40% | 12.45% | 13.60% |
| | 3100 | Total: Mechanical & Electrical | ↓ | 21.50 | 23 | 30.50 | 20.50% | 26.50% | 31% |
| **86** | 0010 | **SWIMMING POOLS** | S.F. | 108 | 180 | 385 | | | |
| | 0020 | Total project costs | C.F. | 8.65 | 10.75 | 11.75 | | | |
| | 2720 | Plumbing | S.F. | 9.95 | 11.35 | 15.50 | 4.80% | 9.70% | 20.50% |
| | 2900 | Electrical | | 8.10 | 13.10 | 19.10 | 5.75% | 6.95% | 7.60% |
| | 3100 | Total: Mechanical & Electrical | ↓ | 19.75 | 51 | 68.50 | 11.15% | 14.10% | 23.50% |
| **87** | 0010 | **TELEPHONE EXCHANGES** | S.F. | 143 | 209 | 265 | | | |
| | 0020 | Total project costs | C.F. | 8.90 | 14.25 | 19.65 | | | |
| | 2720 | Plumbing | S.F. | 6.05 | 9.55 | 13.65 | 4.52% | 5.80% | 6.90% |
| | 2770 | Heating, ventilating, air conditioning | ↓ | 14 | 28 | 35 | 11.80% | 16.05% | 18.40% |

# 50 17 | Square Foot Costs

| | | 50 17 00 \| S.F. Costs | UNIT | UNIT COSTS | | | % OF TOTAL | | |
|---|---|---|---|---|---|---|---|---|---|
| | | | | 1/4 | MEDIAN | 3/4 | 1/4 | MEDIAN | 3/4 |
| 87 | 2900 | Electrical | S.F. | 14.55 | 23 | 41 | 10.90% | 14% | 17.85% | 
| | 3100 | Total: Mechanical & Electrical | ↓ | 43 | 81.50 | 115 | 29.50% | 33.50% | 44.50% |
| 91 | 0010 | **THEATERS** | S.F. | 90 | 112 | 170 | | | |
| | 0020 | Total project costs | C.F. | 4.15 | 6.15 | 9 | | | |
| | 2720 | Plumbing | S.F. | 3 | 3.25 | 13.25 | 2.92% | 4.70% | 6.80% |
| | 2770 | Heating, ventilating, air conditioning | | 8.75 | 10.55 | 13.10 | 8% | 12.25% | 13.40% |
| | 2900 | Electrical | | 7.85 | 10.60 | 21.50 | 8.05% | 9.95% | 12.25% |
| | 3100 | Total: Mechanical & Electrical | ↓ | 20 | 30 | 62 | 23% | 26.50% | 27.50% |
| 94 | 0010 | **TOWN HALLS City Halls & Municipal Buildings** | S.F. | 102 | 132 | 166 | | | |
| | 0020 | Total project costs | C.F. | 9.15 | 11 | 15.45 | | | |
| | 2720 | Plumbing | S.F. | 4.19 | 7.85 | 14.40 | 4.31% | 5.95% | 7.95% |
| | 2770 | Heating, ventilating, air conditioning | | 7.55 | 15.05 | 22 | 7.05% | 9.05% | 13.45% |
| | 2900 | Electrical | | 9.50 | 13.90 | 18.55 | 8.05% | 9.45% | 11.65% |
| | 3100 | Total: Mechanical & Electrical | ↓ | 33 | 42 | 64 | 22% | 26.50% | 31% |
| 97 | 0010 | **WAREHOUSES & Storage Buildings** | S.F. | 38 | 56 | 80 | | | |
| | 0020 | Total project costs | C.F. | 1.96 | 3.07 | 5.10 | | | |
| | 0100 | Site work | S.F. | 3.87 | 7.70 | 11.60 | 6.05% | 12.95% | 19.85% |
| | 0500 | Masonry | | 2.34 | 5.30 | 11.50 | 3.73% | 7.40% | 12.30% |
| | 1800 | Equipment | | .60 | 1.30 | 7.25 | .91% | 1.82% | 5.55% |
| | 2720 | Plumbing | | 1.25 | 2.24 | 4.19 | 2.90% | 4.80% | 6.55% |
| | 2730 | Heating, ventilating, air conditioning | | 1.43 | 4.02 | 5.40 | 2.41% | 5% | 8.90% |
| | 2900 | Electrical | | 2.22 | 4.17 | 6.90 | 5.15% | 7.20% | 10.10% |
| | 3100 | Total: Mechanical & Electrical | ↓ | 6.20 | 9.50 | 18.70 | 12.75% | 18.90% | 26% |
| 99 | 0010 | **WAREHOUSE & OFFICES Combination** | S.F. | 46 | 61.50 | 82.50 | | | |
| | 0020 | Total project costs | C.F. | 2.36 | 3.42 | 5.05 | | | |
| | 1800 | Equipment | S.F. | .80 | 1.54 | 2.30 | .52% | 1.21% | 2.40% |
| | 2720 | Plumbing | | 1.78 | 3.15 | 4.61 | 3.74% | 4.76% | 6.30% |
| | 2770 | Heating, ventilating, air conditioning | | 2.81 | 4.39 | 6.15 | 5% | 5.65% | 10.05% |
| | 2900 | Electrical | | 3.08 | 4.58 | 7.20 | 5.85% | 8% | 10% |
| | 3100 | Total: Mechanical & Electrical | S.F. | 8.60 | 13.10 | 21 | 14.40% | 19.95% | 24.50% |

783

# Square Foot Project Size Modifier

One factor that affects the S.F. cost of a particular building is the size. In general, for buildings built to the same specifications in the same locality, the larger building will have the lower S.F. cost. This is due mainly to the decreasing contribution of the exterior walls plus the economy of scale usually achievable in larger buildings. The Area Conversion Scale shown below will give a factor to convert costs for the typical size building to an adjusted cost for the particular project.

The Square Foot Base Size lists the median costs, most typical project size in our accumulated data, and the range in size of the projects.

The Size Factor for your project is determined by dividing your project area in S.F. by the typical project size for the particular Building Type. With this factor, enter the Area Conversion Scale at the appropriate Size Factor and determine the appropriate cost multiplier for your building size.

**Example:** Determine the cost per S.F. for a 100,000 S.F. Mid-rise apartment building.

$$\frac{\text{Proposed building area} = 100,000 \text{ S.F.}}{\text{Typical size from below} = 50,000 \text{ S.F.}} = 2.00$$

Enter Area Conversion scale at 2.0, intersect curve, read horizontally the appropriate cost multiplier of .94. Size adjusted cost becomes .94 x $100.00 = $94.00 based on national average costs.

Note: For Size Factors less than .50, the Cost Multiplier is 1.1
For Size Factors greater than 3.5, the Cost Multiplier is .90

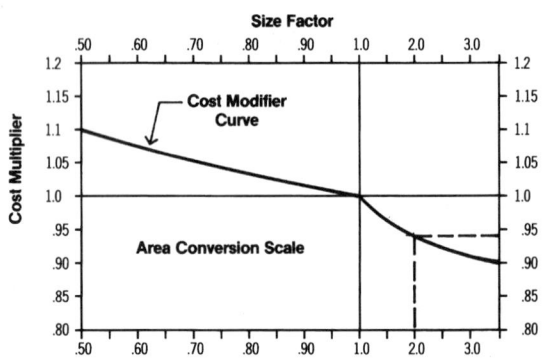

| Building Type | Median Cost per S.F. | Typical Size Gross S.F. | Typical Range Gross S.F. | Building Type | Median Cost per S.F. | Typical Size Gross S.F. | Typical Range Gross S.F. |
|---|---|---|---|---|---|---|---|
| Apartments, Low Rise | $ 78.50 | 21,000 | 9,700 - 37,200 | Jails | $239.00 | 40,000 | 5,500 - 145,000 |
| Apartments, Mid Rise | 100.00 | 50,000 | 32,000 - 100,000 | Libraries | 148.00 | 12,000 | 7,000 - 31,000 |
| Apartments, High Rise | 114.00 | 145,000 | 95,000 - 600,000 | Living, Assisted | 128.00 | 32,300 | 23,500 - 50,300 |
| Auditoriums | 132.00 | 25,000 | 7,600 - 39,000 | Medical Clinics | 136.00 | 7,200 | 4,200 - 15,700 |
| Auto Sales | 98.00 | 20,000 | 10,800 - 28,600 | Medical Offices | 128.00 | 6,000 | 4,000 - 15,000 |
| Banks | 176.00 | 4,200 | 2,500 - 7,500 | Motels | 95.00 | 40,000 | 15,800 - 120,000 |
| Churches | 121.00 | 17,000 | 2,000 - 42,000 | Nursing Homes | 132.00 | 23,000 | 15,000 - 37,000 |
| Clubs, Country | 123.00 | 6,500 | 4,500 - 15,000 | Offices, Low Rise | 111.00 | 20,000 | 5,000 - 80,000 |
| Clubs, Social | 117.00 | 10,000 | 6,000 - 13,500 | Offices, Mid Rise | 111.00 | 120,000 | 20,000 - 300,000 |
| Clubs, YMCA | 138.00 | 28,300 | 12,800 - 39,400 | Offices, High Rise | 142.00 | 260,000 | 120,000 - 800,000 |
| Colleges (Class) | 149.00 | 50,000 | 15,000 - 150,000 | Police Stations | 173.00 | 10,500 | 4,000 - 19,000 |
| Colleges (Science Lab) | 225.00 | 45,600 | 16,600 - 80,000 | Post Offices | 131.00 | 12,400 | 6,800 - 30,000 |
| College (Student Union) | 172.00 | 33,400 | 16,000 - 85,000 | Power Plants | 975.00 | 7,500 | 1,000 - 20,000 |
| Community Center | 125.00 | 9,400 | 5,300 - 16,700 | Religious Education | 112.00 | 9,000 | 6,000 - 12,000 |
| Court Houses | 168.00 | 32,400 | 17,800 - 106,000 | Research | 184.00 | 19,000 | 6,300 - 45,000 |
| Dept. Stores | 73.00 | 90,000 | 44,000 - 122,000 | Restaurants | 159.00 | 4,400 | 2,800 - 6,000 |
| Dormitories, Low Rise | 133.00 | 25,000 | 10,000 - 95,000 | Retail Stores | 78.00 | 7,200 | 4,000 - 17,600 |
| Dormitories, Mid Rise | 164.00 | 85,000 | 20,000 - 200,000 | Schools, Elementary | 116.00 | 41,000 | 24,500 - 55,000 |
| Factories | 71.00 | 26,400 | 12,900 - 50,000 | Schools, Jr. High | 120.00 | 92,000 | 52,000 - 119,000 |
| Fire Stations | 129.00 | 5,800 | 4,000 - 8,700 | Schools, Sr. High | 123.00 | 101,000 | 50,500 - 175,000 |
| Fraternity Houses | 122.00 | 12,500 | 8,200 - 14,800 | Schools, Vocational | 117.00 | 37,000 | 20,500 - 82,000 |
| Funeral Homes | 136.00 | 10,000 | 4,000 - 20,000 | Sports Arenas | 96.00 | 15,000 | 5,000 - 40,000 |
| Garages, Commercial | 87.00 | 9,300 | 5,000 - 13,600 | Supermarkets | 77.00 | 44,000 | 12,000 - 60,000 |
| Garages, Municipal | 110.00 | 8,300 | 4,500 - 12,600 | Swimming Pools | 180.00 | 20,000 | 10,000 - 32,000 |
| Garages, Parking | 47.00 | 163,000 | 76,400 - 225,300 | Telephone Exchange | 209.00 | 4,500 | 1,200 - 10,600 |
| Gymnasiums | 120.00 | 19,200 | 11,600 - 41,000 | Theaters | 112.00 | 10,500 | 8,800 - 17,500 |
| Hospitals | 212.00 | 55,000 | 27,200 - 125,000 | Town Halls | 132.00 | 10,800 | 4,800 - 23,400 |
| House (Elderly) | 107.00 | 37,000 | 21,000 - 66,000 | Warehouses | 56.00 | 25,000 | 8,000 - 72,000 |
| Housing (Public) | 99.00 | 36,000 | 14,400 - 74,400 | Warehouse & Office | 61.50 | 25,000 | 8,000 - 72,000 |
| Ice Rinks | 142.00 | 29,000 | 27,200 - 33,600 | | | | |

| | | | |
|---|---|---|---|
| A | Area Square Feet; Ampere | Cab. | Cabinet |
| ABS | Acrylonitrile Butadiene Stryrene; Asbestos Bonded Steel | Cair. | Air Tool Laborer |
| A.C. | Alternating Current; Air-Conditioning; Asbestos Cement; Plywood Grade A & C | Calc | Calculated |
| | | Cap. | Capacity |
| | | Carp. | Carpenter |
| | | C.B. | Circuit Breaker |
| A.C.I. | American Concrete Institute | C.C.A. | Chromate Copper Arsenate |
| AD | Plywood, Grade A & D | C.C.F. | Hundred Cubic Feet |
| Addit. | Additional | cd | Candela |
| Adj. | Adjustable | cd/sf | Candela per Square Foot |
| af | Audio-frequency | CD | Grade of Plywood Face & Back |
| A.G.A. | American Gas Association | CDX | Plywood, Grade C & D, exterior glue |
| Agg. | Aggregate | | |
| A.H. | Ampere Hours | Cefi. | Cement Finisher |
| A hr. | Ampere-hour | Cem. | Cement |
| A.H.U. | Air Handling Unit | CF | Hundred Feet |
| A.I.A. | American Institute of Architects | C.F. | Cubic Feet |
| AIC | Ampere Interrupting Capacity | CFM | Cubic Feet per Minute |
| Allow. | Allowance | c.g. | Center of Gravity |
| alt. | Altitude | CHW | Chilled Water; Commercial Hot Water |
| Alum. | Aluminum | | |
| a.m. | Ante Meridiem | C.I. | Cast Iron |
| Amp. | Ampere | C.I.P. | Cast in Place |
| Anod. | Anodized | Circ. | Circuit |
| Approx. | Approximate | C.L. | Carload Lot |
| Apt. | Apartment | Clab. | Common Laborer |
| Asb. | Asbestos | Clam | Common maintenance laborer |
| A.S.B.C. | American Standard Building Code | C.L.F. | Hundred Linear Feet |
| Asbe. | Asbestos Worker | CLF | Current Limiting Fuse |
| A.S.H.R.A.E. | American Society of Heating, Refrig. & AC Engineers | CLP | Cross Linked Polyethylene |
| | | cm | Centimeter |
| A.S.M.E. | American Society of Mechanical Engineers | CMP | Corr. Metal Pipe |
| | | C.M.U. | Concrete Masonry Unit |
| A.S.T.M. | American Society for Testing and Materials | CN | Change Notice |
| | | Col. | Column |
| Attchmt. | Attachment | CO2 | Carbon Dioxide |
| Avg. | Average | Comb. | Combination |
| A.W.G. | American Wire Gauge | Compr. | Compressor |
| AWWA | American Water Works Assoc. | Conc. | Concrete |
| Bbl. | Barrel | Cont. | Continuous; Continued |
| B&B | Grade B and Better; Balled & Burlapped | Corr. | Corrugated |
| | | Cos | Cosine |
| B.&S. | Bell and Spigot | Cot | Cotangent |
| B.&W. | Black and White | Cov. | Cover |
| b.c.c. | Body-centered Cubic | C/P | Cedar on Paneling |
| B.C.Y. | Bank Cubic Yards | CPA | Control Point Adjustment |
| BE | Bevel End | Cplg. | Coupling |
| B.F. | Board Feet | C.P.M. | Critical Path Method |
| Bg. cem. | Bag of Cement | CPVC | Chlorinated Polyvinyl Chloride |
| BHP | Boiler Horsepower; Brake Horsepower | C.Pr. | Hundred Pair |
| | | CRC | Cold Rolled Channel |
| B.I. | Black Iron | Creos. | Creosote |
| Bit.; Bitum. | Bituminous | Crpt. | Carpet & Linoleum Layer |
| Bk. | Backed | CRT | Cathode-ray Tube |
| Bkrs. | Breakers | CS | Carbon Steel, Constant Shear Bar Joist |
| Bldg. | Building | | |
| Blk. | Block | Csc | Cosecant |
| Bm. | Beam | C.S.F. | Hundred Square Feet |
| Boil. | Boilermaker | CSI | Construction Specifications Institute |
| B.P.M. | Blows per Minute | | |
| BR | Bedroom | C.T. | Current Transformer |
| Brg. | Bearing | CTS | Copper Tube Size |
| Brhe. | Bricklayer Helper | Cu | Copper, Cubic |
| Bric. | Bricklayer | Cu. Ft. | Cubic Foot |
| Brk. | Brick | cw | Continuous Wave |
| Brng. | Bearing | C.W. | Cool White; Cold Water |
| Brs. | Brass | Cwt. | 100 Pounds |
| Brz. | Bronze | C.W.X. | Cool White Deluxe |
| Bsn. | Basin | C.Y. | Cubic Yard (27 cubic feet) |
| Btr. | Better | C.Y./Hr. | Cubic Yard per Hour |
| BTU | British Thermal Unit | Cyl. | Cylinder |
| BTUH | BTU per Hour | d | Penny (nail size) |
| B.U.R. | Built-up Roofing | D | Deep; Depth; Discharge |
| BX | Interlocked Armored Cable | Dis.;Disch. | Discharge |
| c | Conductivity, Copper Sweat | Db. | Decibel |
| C | Hundred; Centigrade | Dbl. | Double |
| C/C | Center to Center, Cedar on Cedar | DC | Direct Current |
| | | DDC | Direct Digital Control |
| | | Demob. | Demobilization |

| | |
|---|---|
| d.f.u. | Drainage Fixture Units |
| D.H. | Double Hung |
| DHW | Domestic Hot Water |
| Diag. | Diagonal |
| Diam. | Diameter |
| Distrib. | Distribution |
| Div. | Division |
| Dk. | Deck |
| D.L. | Dead Load; Diesel |
| DLH | Deep Long Span Bar Joist |
| Do. | Ditto |
| Dp. | Depth |
| D.P.S.T. | Double Pole, Single Throw |
| Dr. | Driver |
| Drink. | Drinking |
| D.S. | Double Strength |
| D.S.A. | Double Strength A Grade |
| D.S.B. | Double Strength B Grade |
| Dty. | Duty |
| DWV | Drain Waste Vent |
| DX | Deluxe White, Direct Expansion |
| dyn | Dyne |
| e | Eccentricity |
| E | Equipment Only; East |
| Ea. | Each |
| E.B. | Encased Burial |
| Econ. | Economy |
| E.C.Y | Embankment Cubic Yards |
| EDP | Electronic Data Processing |
| EIFS | Exterior Insulation Finish System |
| E.D.R. | Equiv. Direct Radiation |
| Eq. | Equation |
| Elec. | Electrician; Electrical |
| Elev. | Elevator; Elevating |
| EMT | Electrical Metallic Conduit; Thin Wall Conduit |
| Eng. | Engine, Engineered |
| EPDM | Ethylene Propylene Diene Monomer |
| EPS | Expanded Polystyrene |
| Eqhv. | Equip. Oper., Heavy |
| Eqlt. | Equip. Oper., Light |
| Eqmd. | Equip. Oper., Medium |
| Eqmm. | Equip. Oper., Master Mechanic |
| Eqol. | Equip. Oper., Oilers |
| Equip. | Equipment |
| ERW | Electric Resistance Welded |
| E.S. | Energy Saver |
| Est. | Estimated |
| esu | Electrostatic Units |
| E.W. | Each Way |
| EWT | Entering Water Temperature |
| Excav. | Excavation |
| Exp. | Expansion, Exposure |
| Ext. | Exterior |
| Extru. | Extrusion |
| f. | Fiber stress |
| F | Fahrenheit; Female; Fill |
| Fab. | Fabricated |
| FBGS | Fiberglass |
| F.C. | Footcandles |
| f.c.c. | Face-centered Cubic |
| f'c. | Compressive Stress in Concrete; Extreme Compressive Stress |
| F.E. | Front End |
| FEP | Fluorinated Ethylene Propylene (Teflon) |
| F.G. | Flat Grain |
| F.H.A. | Federal Housing Administration |
| Fig. | Figure |
| Fin. | Finished |
| Fixt. | Fixture |
| Fl. Oz. | Fluid Ounces |
| Flr. | Floor |
| F.M. | Frequency Modulation; Factory Mutual |
| Fmg. | Framing |
| Fndtn. | Foundation |
| Fori. | Foreman, Inside |

# Abbreviations

| | | | | | |
|---|---|---|---|---|---|
| Foro. | Foreman, Outside | J.I.C. | Joint Industrial Council | M.C.P. | Motor Circuit Protector |
| Fount. | Fountain | K | Thousand; Thousand Pounds; | MD | Medium Duty |
| FPM | Feet per Minute | | Heavy Wall Copper Tubing, Kelvin | M.D.O. | Medium Density Overlaid |
| FPT | Female Pipe Thread | K.A.H. | Thousand Amp. Hours | Med. | Medium |
| Fr. | Frame | KCMIL | Thousand Circular Mils | MF | Thousand Feet |
| F.R. | Fire Rating | KD | Knock Down | M.F.B.M. | Thousand Feet Board Measure |
| FRK | Foil Reinforced Kraft | K.D.A.T. | Kiln Dried After Treatment | Mfg. | Manufacturing |
| FRP | Fiberglass Reinforced Plastic | kg | Kilogram | Mfrs. | Manufacturers |
| FS | Forged Steel | kG | Kilogauss | mg | Milligram |
| FSC | Cast Body; Cast Switch Box | kgf | Kilogram Force | MGD | Million Gallons per Day |
| Ft. | Foot; Feet | kHz | Kilohertz | MGPH | Thousand Gallons per Hour |
| Ftng. | Fitting | Kip. | 1000 Pounds | MH, M.H. | Manhole; Metal Halide; Man-Hour |
| Ftg. | Footing | KJ | Kiljoule | MHz | Megahertz |
| Ft. Lb. | Foot Pound | K.L. | Effective Length Factor | Mi. | Mile |
| Furn. | Furniture | K.L.F. | Kips per Linear Foot | MI | Malleable Iron; Mineral Insulated |
| FVNR | Full Voltage Non-Reversing | Km | Kilometer | mm | Millimeter |
| FXM | Female by Male | K.S.F. | Kips per Square Foot | Mill. | Millwright |
| Fy. | Minimum Yield Stress of Steel | K.S.I. | Kips per Square Inch | Min., min. | Minimum, minute |
| g | Gram | kV | Kilovolt | Misc. | Miscellaneous |
| G | Gauss | kVA | Kilovolt Ampere | ml | Milliliter, Mainline |
| Ga. | Gauge | K.V.A.R. | Kilovar (Reactance) | M.L.F. | Thousand Linear Feet |
| Gal. | Gallon | KW | Kilowatt | Mo. | Month |
| Gal./Min. | Gallon per Minute | KWh | Kilowatt-hour | Mobil. | Mobilization |
| Galv. | Galvanized | L | Labor Only; Length; Long; | Mog. | Mogul Base |
| Gen. | General | | Medium Wall Copper Tubing | MPH | Miles per Hour |
| G.F.I. | Ground Fault Interrupter | Lab. | Labor | MPT | Male Pipe Thread |
| Glaz. | Glazier | lat | Latitude | MRT | Mile Round Trip |
| GPD | Gallons per Day | Lath. | Lather | ms | Millisecond |
| GPH | Gallons per Hour | Lav. | Lavatory | M.S.F. | Thousand Square Feet |
| GPM | Gallons per Minute | lb.; # | Pound | Mstz. | Mosaic & Terrazzo Worker |
| GR | Grade | L.B. | Load Bearing; L Conduit Body | M.S.Y. | Thousand Square Yards |
| Gran. | Granular | L. & E. | Labor & Equipment | Mtd. | Mounted |
| Grnd. | Ground | lb./hr. | Pounds per Hour | Mthe. | Mosaic & Terrazzo Helper |
| H | High; High Strength Bar Joist; | lb./L.F. | Pounds per Linear Foot | Mtng. | Mounting |
| | Henry | lbf/sq.in. | Pound-force per Square Inch | Mult. | Multi; Multiply |
| H.C. | High Capacity | L.C.L. | Less than Carload Lot | M.V.A. | Million Volt Amperes |
| H.D. | Heavy Duty; High Density | L.C.Y. | Loose Cubic Yard | M.V.A.R. | Million Volt Amperes Reactance |
| H.D.O. | High Density Overlaid | Ld. | Load | MV | Megavolt |
| Hdr. | Header | LE | Lead Equivalent | MW | Megawatt |
| Hdwe. | Hardware | LED | Light Emitting Diode | MXM | Male by Male |
| Help. | Helper Average | L.F. | Linear Foot | MYD | Thousand Yards |
| HEPA | High Efficiency Particulate Air | Lg. | Long; Length; Large | N | Natural; North |
| | Filter | L & H | Light and Heat | nA | Nanoampere |
| Hg | Mercury | LH | Long Span Bar Joist | NA | Not Available; Not Applicable |
| HIC | High Interrupting Capacity | L.H. | Labor Hours | N.B.C. | National Building Code |
| HM | Hollow Metal | L.L. | Live Load | NC | Normally Closed |
| H.O. | High Output | L.L.D. | Lamp Lumen Depreciation | N.E.M.A. | National Electrical Manufacturers |
| Horiz. | Horizontal | lm | Lumen | | Assoc. |
| H.P. | Horsepower; High Pressure | lm/sf | Lumen per Square Foot | NEHB | Bolted Circuit Breaker to 600V. |
| H.P.F. | High Power Factor | lm/W | Lumen per Watt | N.L.B. | Non-Load-Bearing |
| Hr. | Hour | L.O.A. | Length Over All | NM | Non-Metallic Cable |
| Hrs./Day | Hours per Day | log | Logarithm | nm | Nanometer |
| HSC | High Short Circuit | L-O-L | Lateralolet | No. | Number |
| Ht. | Height | L.P. | Liquefied Petroleum; Low Pressure | NO | Normally Open |
| Htg. | Heating | L.P.F. | Low Power Factor | N.O.C. | Not Otherwise Classified |
| Htrs. | Heaters | LR | Long Radius | Nose. | Nosing |
| HVAC | Heating, Ventilation & Air- | L.S. | Lump Sum | N.P.T. | National Pipe Thread |
| | Conditioning | Lt. | Light | NQOD | Combination Plug-on/Bolt on |
| Hvy. | Heavy | Lt. Ga. | Light Gauge | | Circuit Breaker to 240V. |
| HW | Hot Water | L.T.L. | Less than Truckload Lot | N.R.C. | Noise Reduction Coefficient |
| Hyd.;Hydr. | Hydraulic | Lt. Wt. | Lightweight | N.R.S. | Non Rising Stem |
| Hz. | Hertz (cycles) | L.V. | Low Voltage | ns | Nanosecond |
| I. | Moment of Inertia | M | Thousand; Material; Male; | nW | Nanowatt |
| I.C. | Interrupting Capacity | | Light Wall Copper Tubing | OB | Opposing Blade |
| ID | Inside Diameter | M²CA | Meters Squared Contact Area | OC | On Center |
| I.D. | Inside Dimension; Identification | m/hr; M.H. | Man-hour | OD | Outside Diameter |
| I.F. | Inside Frosted | mA | Milliampere | O.D. | Outside Dimension |
| I.M.C. | Intermediate Metal Conduit | Mach. | Machine | ODS | Overhead Distribution System |
| In. | Inch | Mag. Str. | Magnetic Starter | O.G. | Ogee |
| Incan. | Incandescent | Maint. | Maintenance | O.H. | Overhead |
| Incl. | Included; Including | Marb. | Marble Setter | O&P | Overhead and Profit |
| Int. | Interior | Mat; Mat'l. | Material | Oper. | Operator |
| Inst. | Installation | Max. | Maximum | Opng. | Opening |
| Insul. | Insulation/Insulated | MBF | Thousand Board Feet | Orna. | Ornamental |
| I.P. | Iron Pipe | MBH | Thousand BTU's per hr. | OSB | Oriented Strand Board |
| I.P.S. | Iron Pipe Size | MC | Metal Clad Cable | O.S.&Y. | Outside Screw and Yoke |
| I.P.T. | Iron Pipe Threaded | M.C.F. | Thousand Cubic Feet | Ovhd. | Overhead |
| I.W. | Indirect Waste | M.C.F.M. | Thousand Cubic Feet per Minute | OWG | Oil, Water or Gas |
| J | Joule | M.C.M. | Thousand Circular Mils | Oz. | Ounce |

# Abbreviations

| | |
|---|---|
| P. | Pole; Applied Load; Projection |
| p. | Page |
| Pape. | Paperhanger |
| P.A.P.R. | Powered Air Purifying Respirator |
| PAR | Parabolic Reflector |
| Pc., Pcs. | Piece, Pieces |
| P.C. | Portland Cement; Power Connector |
| P.C.F. | Pounds per Cubic Foot |
| P.C.M. | Phase Contrast Microscopy |
| P.E. | Professional Engineer; Porcelain Enamel; Polyethylene; Plain End |
| Perf. | Perforated |
| Ph. | Phase |
| P.I. | Pressure Injected |
| Pile. | Pile Driver |
| Pkg. | Package |
| Pl. | Plate |
| Plah. | Plasterer Helper |
| Plas. | Plasterer |
| Pluh. | Plumbers Helper |
| Plum. | Plumber |
| Ply. | Plywood |
| p.m. | Post Meridiem |
| Pntd. | Painted |
| Pord. | Painter, Ordinary |
| pp | Pages |
| PP; PPL | Polypropylene |
| P.P.M. | Parts per Million |
| Pr. | Pair |
| P.E.S.B. | Pre-engineered Steel Building |
| Prefab. | Prefabricated |
| Prefin. | Prefinished |
| Prop. | Propelled |
| PSF; psf | Pounds per Square Foot |
| PSI; psi | Pounds per Square Inch |
| PSIG | Pounds per Square Inch Gauge |
| PSP | Plastic Sewer Pipe |
| Pspr. | Painter, Spray |
| Psst. | Painter, Structural Steel |
| P.T. | Potential Transformer |
| P. & T. | Pressure & Temperature |
| Ptd. | Painted |
| Ptns. | Partitions |
| Pu | Ultimate Load |
| PVC | Polyvinyl Chloride |
| Pvmt. | Pavement |
| Pwr. | Power |
| Q | Quantity Heat Flow |
| Quan.; Qty. | Quantity |
| Q.C. | Quick Coupling |
| r | Radius of Gyration |
| R | Resistance |
| R.C.P. | Reinforced Concrete Pipe |
| Rect. | Rectangle |
| Reg. | Regular |
| Reinf. | Reinforced |
| Req'd. | Required |
| Res. | Resistant |
| Resi. | Residential |
| Rgh. | Rough |
| RGS | Rigid Galvanized Steel |
| R.H.W. | Rubber, Heat & Water Resistant; Residential Hot Water |
| rms | Root Mean Square |
| Rnd. | Round |
| Rodm. | Rodman |
| Rofc. | Roofer, Composition |
| Rofp. | Roofer, Precast |
| Rohe. | Roofer Helpers (Composition) |
| Rots. | Roofer, Tile & Slate |
| R.O.W. | Right of Way |
| RPM | Revolutions per Minute |
| R.S. | Rapid Start |
| Rsr | Riser |
| RT | Round Trip |
| S. | Suction; Single Entrance; South |
| SC | Screw Cover |
| SCFM | Standard Cubic Feet per Minute |
| Scaf. | Scaffold |
| Sch.; Sched. | Schedule |
| S.C.R. | Modular Brick |
| S.D. | Sound Deadening |
| S.D.R. | Standard Dimension Ratio |
| S.E. | Surfaced Edge |
| Sel. | Select |
| S.E.R.; S.E.U. | Service Entrance Cable |
| S.F. | Square Foot |
| S.F.C.A. | Square Foot Contact Area |
| S.F. Flr. | Square Foot of Floor |
| S.F.G. | Square Foot of Ground |
| S.F. Hor. | Square Foot Horizontal |
| S.F.R. | Square Feet of Radiation |
| S.F. Shlf. | Square Foot of Shelf |
| S4S | Surface 4 Sides |
| Shee. | Sheet Metal Worker |
| Sin. | Sine |
| Skwk. | Skilled Worker |
| SL | Saran Lined |
| S.L. | Slimline |
| Sldr. | Solder |
| SLH | Super Long Span Bar Joist |
| S.N. | Solid Neutral |
| S-O-L | Socketolet |
| sp | Standpipe |
| S.P. | Static Pressure; Single Pole; Self-Propelled |
| Spri. | Sprinkler Installer |
| spwg | Static Pressure Water Gauge |
| S.P.D.T. | Single Pole, Double Throw |
| SPF | Spruce Pine Fir |
| S.P.S.T. | Single Pole, Single Throw |
| SPT | Standard Pipe Thread |
| Sq. | Square; 100 Square Feet |
| Sq. Hd. | Square Head |
| Sq. In. | Square Inch |
| S.S. | Single Strength; Stainless Steel |
| S.S.B. | Single Strength B Grade |
| sst | Stainless Steel |
| Sswk. | Structural Steel Worker |
| Sswl. | Structural Steel Welder |
| St.; Stl. | Steel |
| S.T.C. | Sound Transmission Coefficient |
| Std. | Standard |
| STK | Select Tight Knot |
| STP | Standard Temperature & Pressure |
| Stpi. | Steamfitter, Pipefitter |
| Str. | Strength; Starter; Straight |
| Strd. | Stranded |
| Struct. | Structural |
| Sty. | Story |
| Subj. | Subject |
| Subs. | Subcontractors |
| Surf. | Surface |
| Sw. | Switch |
| Swbd. | Switchboard |
| S.Y. | Square Yard |
| Syn. | Synthetic |
| S.Y.P. | Southern Yellow Pine |
| Sys. | System |
| t. | Thickness |
| T | Temperature; Ton |
| Tan | Tangent |
| T.C. | Terra Cotta |
| T & C | Threaded and Coupled |
| T.D. | Temperature Difference |
| Tdd | Telecommunications Device for the Deaf |
| T.E.M. | Transmission Electron Microscopy |
| TFE | Tetrafluoroethylene (Teflon) |
| T. & G. | Tongue & Groove; Tar & Gravel |
| Th.; Thk. | Thick |
| Thn. | Thin |
| Thrded | Threaded |
| Tilf. | Tile Layer, Floor |
| Tilh. | Tile Layer, Helper |
| THHN | Nylon Jacketed Wire |
| THW. | Insulated Strand Wire |
| THWN; | Nylon Jacketed Wire |
| T.L. | Truckload |
| T.M. | Track Mounted |
| Tot. | Total |
| T-O-L | Threadolet |
| T.S. | Trigger Start |
| Tr. | Trade |
| Transf. | Transformer |
| Trhv. | Truck Driver, Heavy |
| Trlr | Trailer |
| Trlt. | Truck Driver, Light |
| TTY | Teletypewriter |
| TV | Television |
| T.W. | Thermoplastic Water Resistant Wire |
| UCI | Uniform Construction Index |
| UF | Underground Feeder |
| UGND | Underground Feeder |
| U.H.F. | Ultra High Frequency |
| U.L. | Underwriters Laboratory |
| Uld. | unloading |
| Unfin. | Unfinished |
| URD | Underground Residential Distribution |
| US | United States |
| USP | United States Primed |
| UTP | Unshielded Twisted Pair |
| V | Volt |
| V.A. | Volt Amperes |
| V.C.T. | Vinyl Composition Tile |
| VAV | Variable Air Volume |
| VC | Veneer Core |
| Vent. | Ventilation |
| Vert. | Vertical |
| V.F. | Vinyl Faced |
| V.G. | Vertical Grain |
| V.H.F. | Very High Frequency |
| VHO | Very High Output |
| Vib. | Vibrating |
| V.L.F. | Vertical Linear Foot |
| Vol. | Volume |
| VRP | Vinyl Reinforced Polyester |
| W | Wire; Watt; Wide; West |
| w/ | With |
| W.C. | Water Column; Water Closet |
| W.F. | Wide Flange |
| W.G. | Water Gauge |
| Wldg. | Welding |
| W. Mile | Wire Mile |
| W-O-L | Weldolet |
| W.R. | Water Resistant |
| Wrck. | Wrecker |
| W.S.P. | Water, Steam, Petroleum |
| WT., Wt. | Weight |
| WWF | Welded Wire Fabric |
| XFER | Transfer |
| XFMR | Transformer |
| XHD | Extra Heavy Duty |
| XHHW; XLPE | Cross-Linked Polyethylene Wire Insulation |
| XLP | Cross-linked Polyethylene |
| Y | Wye |
| yd | Yard |
| yr | Year |
| Δ | Delta |
| % | Percent |
| ~ | Approximately |
| Ø | Phase |
| @ | At |
| # | Pound; Number |
| < | Less Than |
| > | Greater Than |

# Index

# Index

# Index

# Index

798

# Index

800

# Index

# Notes

819

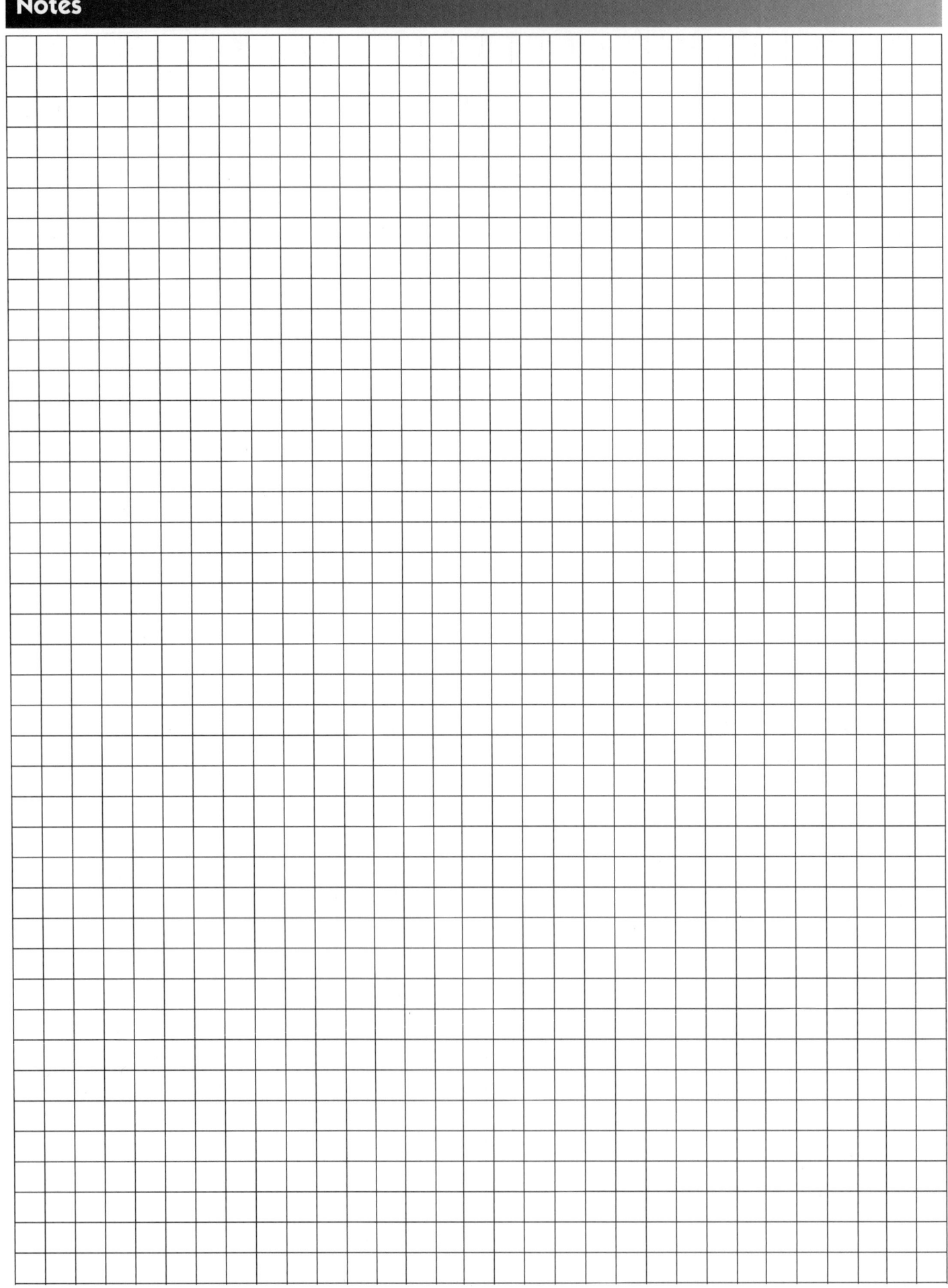

**Table of Contents**
Annual Cost Guides
Reference Books
Seminars
Electronic Data
New Titles
Order Form

# Reed Construction Data/RSMeans... a tradition of excellence in construction cost information and services since 1942.

**For more information visit the RSMeans Website at www.rsmeans.com**

## Book Selection Guide
The following table provides definitive information on the content of each cost data publication. The number of lines of data provided in each unit price or assemblies division, as well as the number of reference tables and crews, is listed for each book. The presence of other elements such as equipment rental costs, historical cost indexes, city cost indexes, square foot models, or cross-referenced indexes is also indicated. You can use the table to help select the RSMeans book that has the quantity and type of information you most need in your work.

| Unit Cost Divisions | Building Construction Costs | Mechanical | Electrical | Repair & Remodel | Square Foot | Site Work Landsc. | Assemblies | Interior | Concrete Masonry | Open Shop | Heavy Construc. | Light Commercial | Facil. Construc. | Plumbing | Western Construction Costs | Residential |
|---|---|---|---|---|---|---|---|---|---|---|---|---|---|---|---|---|
| 1 | 545 | 364 | 385 | 474 | | 489 | | 301 | 437 | 544 | 483 | 212 | 960 | 386 | 544 | 157 |
| 2 | 533 | 236 | 58 | 528 | | 761 | | 330 | 183 | 532 | 659 | 409 | 1000 | 259 | 533 | 218 |
| 3 | 1476 | 189 | 175 | 814 | | 1325 | | 273 | 1829 | 1470 | 1482 | 261 | 1398 | 158 | 1471 | 294 |
| 4 | 873 | 24 | 0 | 674 | | 686 | | 557 | 1084 | 849 | 579 | 452 | 1123 | 0 | 859 | 379 |
| 5 | 1821 | 205 | 159 | 960 | | 776 | | 987 | 725 | 1789 | 1014 | 796 | 1810 | 283 | 1758 | 729 |
| 6 | 1481 | 78 | 78 | 1434 | | 482 | | 1204 | 318 | 1459 | 417 | 1540 | 1460 | 22 | 1818 | 1687 |
| 7 | 1341 | 167 | 71 | 1358 | | 512 | | 522 | 438 | 1340 | 0 | 1011 | 1403 | 176 | 1340 | 788 |
| 8 | 1928 | 61 | 10 | 1944 | | 301 | | 1679 | 671 | 1895 | 0 | 1337 | 2123 | 0 | 1878 | 1279 |
| 9 | 1679 | 72 | 26 | 1486 | | 255 | | 1766 | 373 | 1643 | 0 | 1390 | 1894 | 54 | 1667 | 1265 |
| 10 | 906 | 17 | 10 | 508 | | 226 | | 799 | 156 | 908 | 29 | 396 | 997 | 233 | 906 | 212 |
| 11 | 987 | 211 | 160 | 463 | | 126 | | 837 | 28 | 972 | 0 | 212 | 1001 | 172 | 964 | 100 |
| 12 | 557 | 0 | 2 | 299 | | 267 | | 1701 | 31 | 546 | 19 | 343 | 1751 | 23 | 548 | 316 |
| 13 | 701 | 119 | 111 | 244 | | 339 | | 255 | 69 | 693 | 240 | 77 | 716 | 74 | 685 | 76 |
| 14 | 281 | 36 | 0 | 230 | | 28 | | 260 | 0 | 280 | 0 | 12 | 300 | 21 | 281 | 6 |
| 21 | 78 | 0 | 16 | 25 | | | | 244 | 0 | 78 | 0 | 59 | 362 | 367 | 77 | 0 |
| 22 | 1028 | 7030 | 154 | 1053 | | 1442 | | 595 | 20 | 1032 | 1655 | 735 | 6887 | 8747 | 1078 | 520 |
| 23 | 1109 | 7115 | 610 | 774 | | 159 | | 659 | 38 | 1092 | 110 | 576 | 5144 | 1854 | 1073 | 346 |
| 26 | 1241 | 493 | 9810 | 988 | | 734 | | 1049 | 55 | 1229 | 526 | 1045 | 9744 | 438 | 1201 | 556 |
| 27 | 75 | 0 | 200 | 34 | | 9 | | 67 | 0 | 75 | 35 | 48 | 197 | 0 | 66 | 4 |
| 28 | 87 | 59 | 94 | 64 | | 0 | | 69 | 0 | 72 | 0 | 42 | 108 | 45 | 87 | 27 |
| 31 | 1298 | 538 | 406 | 600 | | 1896 | | 7 | 1020 | 1244 | 1991 | 393 | 1361 | 460 | 1293 | 400 |
| 32 | 736 | 46 | 0 | 601 | | 3839 | | 360 | 271 | 710 | 1357 | 353 | 1368 | 158 | 722 | 412 |
| 33 | 517 | 1019 | 429 | 199 | | 1926 | | 0 | 225 | 520 | 1896 | 94 | 1561 | 1179 | 514 | 92 |
| 34 | 99 | 0 | 20 | 4 | | 134 | | 0 | 31 | 55 | 113 | 0 | 119 | 0 | 99 | 0 |
| 35 | 18 | 0 | 0 | 0 | | 166 | | 0 | 0 | 18 | 166 | 0 | 83 | 0 | 18 | 0 |
| 41 | 52 | 0 | 0 | 24 | | 7 | | 22 | 0 | 52 | 30 | 0 | 59 | 14 | 52 | 0 |
| 44 | 98 | 90 | 0 | 0 | | 32 | | 0 | 0 | 23 | 32 | 0 | 98 | 105 | 23 | 0 |
| **Totals** | 21545 | 18169 | 12984 | 15782 | | 16917 | | 14543 | 8002 | 21120 | 12835 | 11793 | 45027 | 15228 | 21555 | 9863 |

| Assembly Divisions | Building Construction Costs | Mechanical | Electrical | Repair & Remodel | Square Foot | Site Work Landsc. | Assemblies | Interior | Concrete Masonry | Open Shop | Heavy Construc. | Light Commercial | Facil. Construc. | Plumbing | Western Construction Costs | Asm Div | Residential |
|---|---|---|---|---|---|---|---|---|---|---|---|---|---|---|---|---|---|
| A | | 19 | 0 | 192 | 150 | 540 | 612 | 0 | 550 | | 580 | 153 | 24 | 0 | | 1 | 374 |
| B | | 0 | 0 | 808 | 2467 | 0 | 5581 | 329 | 1914 | | 368 | 2010 | 143 | 0 | | 2 | 217 |
| C | | 0 | 0 | 635 | 862 | 0 | 1224 | 1565 | 146 | | 0 | 763 | 238 | 0 | | 3 | 587 |
| D | | 1014 | 803 | 693 | 1780 | 0 | 2412 | 757 | 0 | | 0 | 1266 | 1015 | 889 | | 4 | 861 |
| E | | 0 | 0 | 85 | 257 | 0 | 294 | 5 | 0 | | 0 | 257 | 5 | 0 | | 5 | 392 |
| F | | 0 | 0 | 0 | 123 | 0 | 124 | 0 | 0 | | 0 | 123 | 3 | 0 | | 6 | 358 |
| G | | 548 | 293 | 331 | 202 | 2162 | 667 | 0 | 535 | | 1154 | 200 | 292 | 680 | | 7 | 299 |
| | | | | | | | | | | | | | | | | 8 | 760 |
| | | | | | | | | | | | | | | | | 9 | 80 |
| | | | | | | | | | | | | | | | | 10 | 0 |
| | | | | | | | | | | | | | | | | 11 | 0 |
| | | | | | | | | | | | | | | | | 12 | 0 |
| **Totals** | | 1581 | 1096 | 2744 | 5841 | 2702 | 10914 | 2656 | 3145 | | 2102 | 4772 | 1720 | 1569 | | | 3930 |

| Reference Section | Building Construction Costs | Mechanical | Electrical | Repair & Remodel | Square Foot | Site Work Landsc. | Assemblies | Interior | Concrete Masonry | Open Shop | Heavy Construc. | Light Commercial | Facil. Construc. | Plumbing | Western Construction Costs | Residential |
|---|---|---|---|---|---|---|---|---|---|---|---|---|---|---|---|---|
| Reference Tables | yes | yes | yes | yes | no | yes | yes | yes | yes | yes | yes | yes | yes | yes | yes | yes |
| Models | | | | | 105 | | | | | | | 46 | | | | 32 |
| Crews | 479 | 479 | 479 | 461 | | 479 | | 479 | 479 | 458 | 479 | 458 | 461 | 479 | 479 | 458 |
| Equipment Rental Costs | yes | yes | yes | yes | | yes | | yes | yes | yes | yes | yes | yes | yes | yes | yes |
| Historical Cost Indexes | yes | yes | yes | yes | | yes | yes | yes | yes | yes | yes | yes | yes | yes | yes | no |
| City Cost Indexes | yes | yes | yes | yes | yes | yes | yes | yes | yes | yes | yes | yes | yes | yes | yes | yes |

# Annual Cost Guides

**For more information
visit the RSMeans Website
at www.rsmeans.com**

## RSMeans Building Construction Cost Data 2008

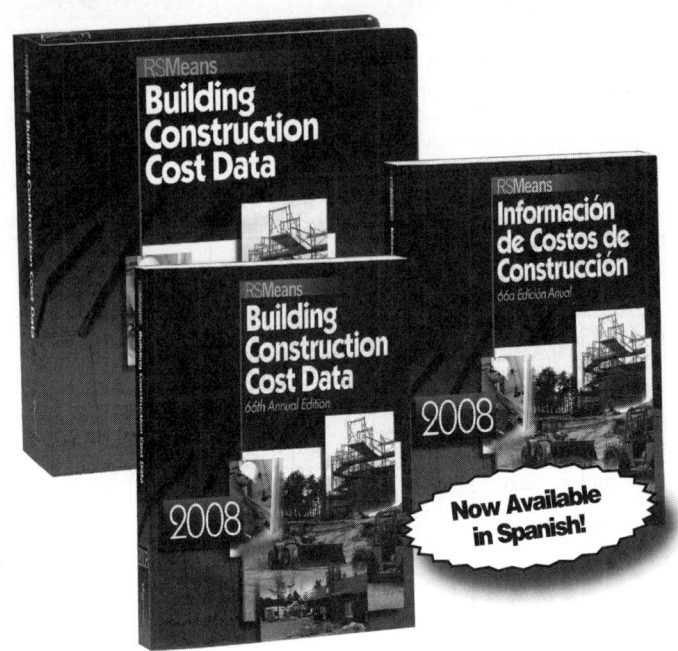

**Now Available in Spanish!**

### Available in Softbound, Looseleaf, and Spanish Versions

Many customers enjoy the convenience and flexibility of the looseleaf binder, which increases the usefulness of *RSMeans Building Construction Cost Data 2008* by making it easy to add and remove pages. You can insert your own cost information pages, so everything is in one place. Copying pages for faxing is easier also. Whichever edition you prefer—softbound, looseleaf, or the new Spanish version—you'll be eligible to receive *RSMeans Quarterly Update Service* FREE. Current subscribers can receive *RSMeans Quarterly Update Service* via e-mail.

**Unit prices now updated to MasterFormat 2004!**

**$149.95 per copy (English or Spanish)
Catalog no. 60018 (English) Available Oct. 2007
Catalog no. 60718 (Spanish) Available Dec. 2007**

**$187.95 per copy, looseleaf
Available Oct. 2007
Catalog no. 61018**

---

## RSMeans Building Construction Cost Data 2008

**Now available in Spanish!**

Offers you unchallenged unit price reliability in an easy-to-use arrangement. Whether used for complete, finished estimates or for periodic checks, it supplies more cost facts better and faster than any comparable source. Over 20,000 unit prices for 2008. The City Cost Indexes and Location Factors cover over 930 areas, for indexing to any project location in North America. Order and get *RSMeans Quarterly Update Service* FREE. You'll have year-long access to the RSMeans Estimating **HOTLINE** FREE with your subscription. Expert assistance when using RSMeans data is just a phone call away.

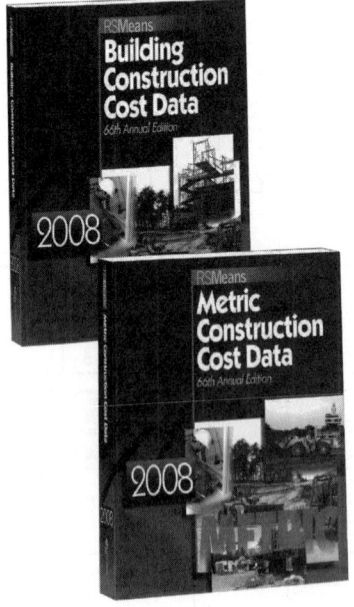

**$149.95 per copy (English or Spanish)
Catalog no. 60018 (English) Available Oct. 2007
Catalog no. 60718 (Spanish) Available Dec. 2007**

**Unit prices now updated to
MasterFormat 2004!**

## RSMeans Metric Construction Cost Data 2008

A massive compendium of all the data from both the *RSMeans Building Construction Cost Data* AND *Heavy Construction Cost Data*, in **metric** format! Access all of this vital information from one complete source. It contains more than 600 pages of unit costs and 40 pages of assemblies costs. The Reference Section contains over 200 pages of tables, charts, and other estimating aids. A great way to stay in step with today's construction trends and rapidly changing costs.

**$179.95 per copy
Available Dec. 2007
Catalog no. 63018**

# Annual Cost Guides

## RSMeans Mechanical Cost Data 2008

- **HVAC**
- **Controls**

Total unit and systems price guidance for mechanical construction. . . materials, parts, fittings, and complete labor cost information. Includes prices for piping, heating, air conditioning, ventilation, and all related construction.

Plus new 2008 unit costs for:

- Over 2,500 installed HVAC/controls assemblies components
- "On-site" Location Factors for over 930 cities and towns in the U.S. and Canada
- Crews, labor, and equipment

**$149.95 per copy**
**Available Oct. 2007**
**Catalog no. 60028**

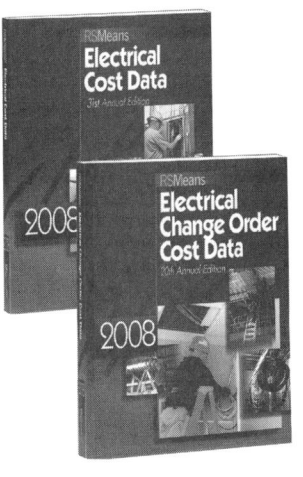

**Unit prices now updated to
MasterFormat 2004!**

## RSMeans Plumbing Cost Data 2008

Comprehensive unit prices and assemblies for plumbing, irrigation systems, commercial and residential fire protection, point-of-use water heaters, and the latest approved materials. This publication and its companion, *RSMeans Mechanical Cost Data*, provide full-range cost estimating coverage for all the mechanical trades.

Now contains more lines of no-hub CI soil pipe fittings, more flange-type escutcheons, fiberglass pipe insulation in a full range of sizes for 2-1/2" and 3" wall thicknesses, 220 lines of grease duct, and much more.

**$149.95 per copy**
**Available Oct. 2007**
**Catalog no. 60218**

## RSMeans Electrical Cost Data 2008

Pricing information for every part of electrical cost planning. More than 13,000 unit and systems costs with design tables; clear specifications and drawings; engineering guides; illustrated estimating procedures; complete labor-hour and materials costs for better scheduling and procurement; and the latest electrical products and construction methods.

- A variety of special electrical systems including cathodic protection
- Costs for maintenance, demolition, HVAC/ mechanical, specialties, equipment, and more

**$149.95 per copy**
**Available Oct. 2007**
**Catalog no. 60038**

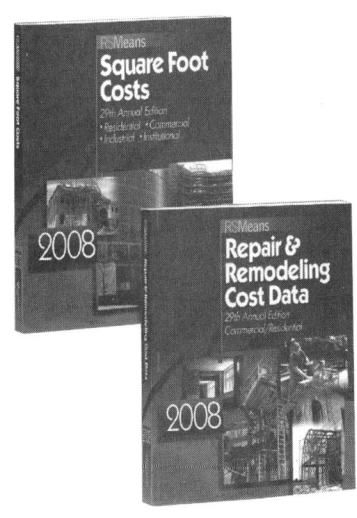

**Unit prices now updated to
MasterFormat 2004!**

## RSMeans Electrical Change Order Cost Data 2008

*RSMeans Electrical Change Order Cost Data* provides you with electrical unit prices exclusively for pricing change orders—based on the recent, direct experience of contractors and suppliers. Analyze and check your own change order estimates against the experience others have had doing the same work. It also covers productivity analysis and change order cost justifications. With useful information for calculating the effects of change orders and dealing with their administration.

**$149.95 per copy**
**Available Nov. 2007**
**Catalog no. 60238**

## RSMeans Square Foot Costs 2008

*It's Accurate and Easy To Use!*

- **Updated price information** based on nationwide figures from suppliers, estimators, labor experts, and contractors
- "How-to-Use" sections, with **clear examples** of commercial, residential, industrial, and institutional structures
- Realistic graphics, offering true-to-life illustrations of building projects
- Extensive information on using square foot cost data, including sample estimates and alternate pricing methods

**$163.95 per copy**
**Available Nov. 2007**
**Catalog no. 60058**

## RSMeans Repair & Remodeling Cost Data 2008

**Commercial/Residential**

Use this valuable tool to estimate commercial and residential renovation and remodeling.

**Includes: New costs for hundreds of unique methods, materials, and conditions that only come up in repair and remodeling, PLUS:**

- Unit costs for over 15,000 construction components
- Installed costs for over 90 assemblies
- Over 930 "on-site" localization factors for the U.S. and Canada.

**Unit prices now updated to MasterFormat 2004!**

**$128.95 per copy**
**Available Nov. 2007**
**Catalog no. 60048**

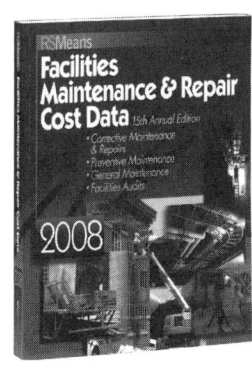

# Reference Books

For more information
visit the RSMeans Website
at www.rsmeans.com

## Value Engineering: Practical Applications

*For Design, Construction, Maintenance & Operations*

**by Alphonse Dell'Isola, PE**

A tool for immediate application—for engineers, architects, facility managers, owners, and contractors. Includes making the case for VE—the management briefing; integrating VE into planning, budgeting, and design; conducting life cycle costing; using VE methodology in design review and consultant selection; case studies; VE workbook; and a life cycle costing program on disk.

$79.95 per copy
Over 450 pages, illustrated, softcover
Catalog no. 67319A

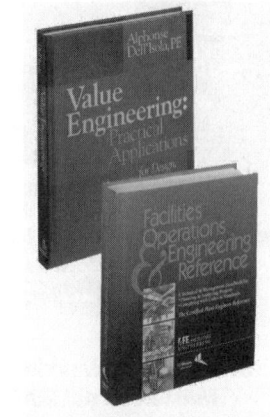

## Facilities Operations & Engineering Reference

**by the Association for Facilities Engineering and RSMeans**

An all-in-one technical reference for planning and managing facility projects and solving day-to-day operations problems. Selected as the official certified plant engineer reference, this handbook covers financial analysis, maintenance, HVAC and energy efficiency, and more.

$54.98 per copy
Over 700 pages, illustrated, hardcover
Catalog no. 67318

## The Building Professional's Guide to Contract Documents

**3rd Edition**

**by Waller S. Poage, AIA, CSI, CVS**

A comprehensive reference for owners, design professionals, contractors, and students

- Structure your documents for maximum efficiency.
- Effectively communicate construction requirements.
- Understand the roles and responsibilities of construction professionals.
- Improve methods of project delivery.

$32.48 per copy, 400 pages
Diagrams and construction forms, hardcover
Catalog no. 67261A

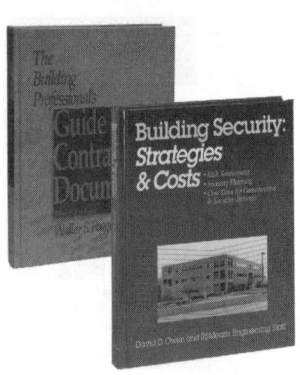

## Building Security: Strategies & Costs

**by David Owen**

This comprehensive resource will help you evaluate your facility's security needs, and design and budget for the materials and devices needed to fulfill them.

Includes over 130 pages of RSMeans cost data for installation of security systems and materials, plus a review of more than 50 security devices and construction solutions.

$44.98 per copy
350 pages, illustrated, hardcover
Catalog no. 67339

## Cost Planning & Estimating for Facilities Maintenance

In this unique book, a team of facilities management authorities shares their expertise on:

- Evaluating and budgeting maintenance operations
- Maintaining and repairing key building components
- Applying *RSMeans Facilities Maintenance & Repair Cost Data* to your estimating

Covers special maintenance requirements of the ten major building types.

$89.95 per copy
Over 475 pages, hardcover
Catalog no. 67314

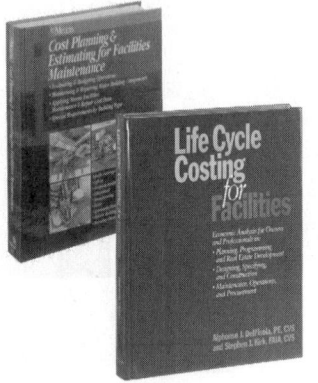

## Life Cycle Costing for Facilities

**by Alphonse Dell'Isola and Dr. Steven Kirk**

Guidance for achieving higher quality design and construction projects at lower costs! Cost-cutting efforts often sacrifice quality to yield the cheapest product. Life cycle costing enables building designers and owners to achieve both. The authors of this book show how LCC can work for a variety of projects — from roads to HVAC upgrades to different types of buildings.

$99.95 per copy
450 pages, hardcover
Catalog no. 67341

## Planning & Managing Interior Projects 2nd Edition

**by Carol E. Farren, CFM**

*Expert guidance on managing renovation & relocation projects.*

This book guides you through every step in relocating to a new space or renovating an old one. From initial meeting through design and construction, to post-project administration, it helps you get the most for your company or client. Includes sample forms, spec lists, agreements, drawings, and much more!

$34.98 per copy
200 pages, softcover
Catalog no. 67245A

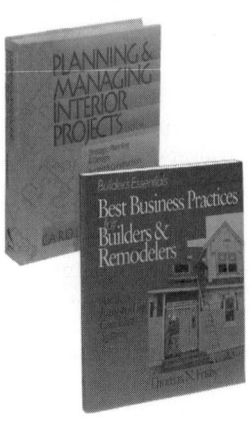

## Builder's Essentials: Best Business Practices for Builders & Remodelers

*An Easy-to-Use Checklist System*

**by Thomas N. Frisby**

A comprehensive guide covering all aspects of running a construction business, with more than 40 user-friendly checklists. Provides expert guidance on increasing your revenue and keeping more of your profit, planning for long-term growth, keeping good employees, and managing subcontractors.

$29.95 per copy
Over 220 pages, softcover
Catalog no. 67329

For more information
visit the RSMeans Website
at www.rsmeans.com

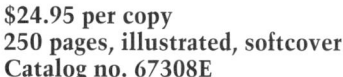

# Reference Books

## Interior Home Improvement Costs 9th Edition

Updated estimates for the most popular remodeling and repair projects—from small, do-it-yourself jobs to major renovations and new construction. Includes: kitchens & baths; new living space from your attic, basement, or garage; new floors, paint, and wallpaper; tearing out or building new walls; closets, stairs, and fireplaces; new energy-saving improvements, home theaters, and more!

$24.95 per copy
250 pages, illustrated, softcover
Catalog no. 67308E

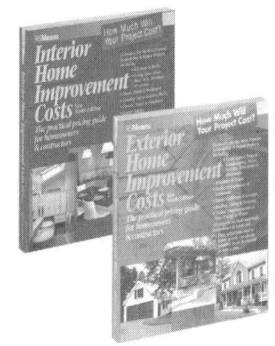

## Exterior Home Improvement Costs 9th Edition

Updated estimates for the most popular remodeling and repair projects—from small, do-it-yourself jobs, to major renovations and new construction. Includes: curb appeal projects—landscaping, patios, porches, driveways, and walkways; new windows and doors; decks, greenhouses, and sunrooms; room additions and garages; roofing, siding, and painting; "green" improvements to save energy & water.

$24.95 per copy
Over 275 pages, illustrated, softcover
Catalog no. 67309E

## Builder's Essentials: Plan Reading & Material Takeoff

*For Residential and Light Commercial Construction*

### by Wayne J. DelPico

A valuable tool for understanding plans and specs, and accurately calculating material quantities. Step-by-step instructions and takeoff procedures based on a full set of working drawings.

$35.95 per copy
Over 420 pages, softcover
Catalog no. 67307

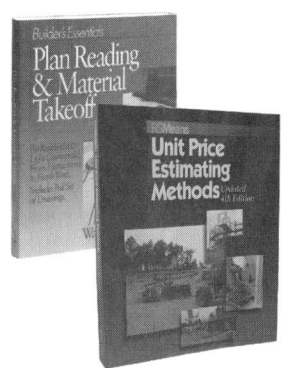

## Means Unit Price Estimating Methods

### New 4th Edition

This new edition includes up-to-date cost data and estimating examples, updated to reflect changes to the CSI numbering system and new features of RSMeans cost data. It describes the most productive, universally accepted ways to estimate, and uses checklists and forms to illustrate shortcuts and timesavers. A model estimate demonstrates procedures. A new chapter explores computer estimating alternatives.

$59.95 per copy
Over 350 pages, illustrated, softcover
Catalog no. 67303B

## Total Productive Facilities Management

### by Richard W. Sievert, Jr.

Today, facilities are viewed as strategic resources. . . elevating the facility manager to the role of asset manager supporting the organization's overall business goals. Now, Richard Sievert Jr., in this well-articulated guidebook, sets forth a new operational standard for the facility manager's emerging role. . . a comprehensive program for managing facilities as a true profit center.

$29.98 per copy
275 pages, softcover
Catalog no. 67321

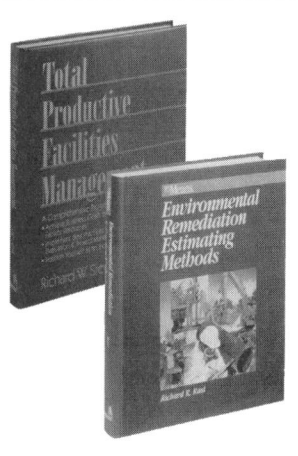

## Means Environmental Remediation Estimating Methods 2nd Edition

### by Richard R. Rast

Guidelines for estimating 50 standard remediation technologies. Use it to prepare preliminary budgets, develop estimates, compare costs and solutions, estimate liability, review quotes, negotiate settlements.

$49.98 per copy
Over 750 pages, illustrated, hardcover
Catalog no. 64777A

## Concrete Repair and Maintenance Illustrated

### by Peter Emmons

Hundreds of illustrations show users how to analyze, repair, clean, and maintain concrete structures for optimal performance and cost effectiveness. From parking garages to roads and bridges to structural concrete, this comprehensive book describes the causes, effects, and remedies for concrete wear and failure. Invaluable for planning jobs, selecting materials, and training employees, this book is a must-have for concrete specialists, general contractors, facility managers, civil and structural engineers, and architects.

$69.95 per copy
300 pages, illustrated, softcover
Catalog no. 67146

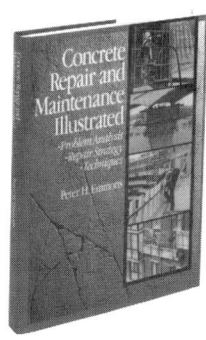

# Reference Books

For more information
visit the RSMeans Website
at www.rsmeans.com

## Means Illustrated Construction Dictionary Condensed, 2nd Edition

The best portable dictionary for office or field use—an essential tool for contractors, architects, insurance and real estate personnel, facility managers, homeowners, and anyone who needs quick, clear definitions for construction terms. The second edition has been further enhanced with updates and hundreds of new terms and illustrations . . . in keeping with the most recent developments in the construction industry.

Now with a quick-reference Spanish section. Includes tools and equipment, materials, tasks, and more!

**$59.95 per copy**
**Over 500 pages, softcover**
**Catalog no. 67282A**

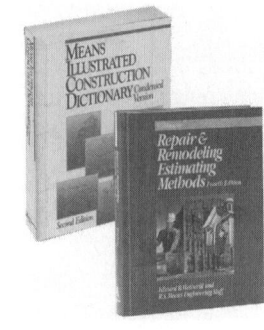

## Means Repair & Remodeling Estimating New 4th Edition
### By Edward B. Wetherill and RSMeans

This important reference focuses on the unique problems of estimating renovations of existing structures, and helps you determine the true costs of remodeling through careful evaluation of architectural details and a site visit.

*New section on disaster restoration costs.*

**$69.95 per copy**
**Over 450 pages, illustrated, hardcover**
**Catalog no. 67265B**

## Facilities Planning & Relocation
### by David D. Owen

A complete system for planning space needs and managing relocations. Includes step-by-step manual, over 50 forms, and extensive reference section on materials and furnishings.

*New lower price and user-friendly format.*

**$89.95 per copy**
**Over 450 pages, softcover**
**Catalog no. 67301**

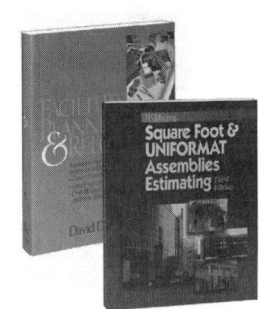

## Means Square Foot & UNIFORMAT Assemblies Estimating Methods 3rd Edition

Develop realistic square foot and assemblies costs for budgeting and construction funding. The new edition features updated guidance on square foot and assemblies estimating using UNIFORMAT II. An essential reference for anyone who performs conceptual estimates.

**$69.95 per copy**
**Over 300 pages, illustrated, softcover**
**Catalog no. 67145B**

## Means Electrical Estimating Methods 3rd Edition

Expanded edition includes sample estimates and cost information in keeping with the latest version of the CSI MasterFormat and UNIFORMAT II. Complete coverage of fiber optic and uninterruptible power supply electrical systems, broken down by components, and explained in detail. Includes a new chapter on computerized estimating methods. A practical companion to *RSMeans Electrical Cost Data.*

**$64.95 per copy**
**Over 325 pages, hardcover**
**Catalog no. 67230B**

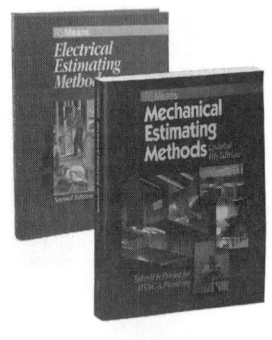

## Means Mechanical Estimating Methods 4th Edition

Completely updated, this guide assists you in making a review of plans, specs, and bid packages, with suggestions for takeoff procedures, listings, substitutions, and pre-bid scheduling for all components of HVAC. Includes suggestions for budgeting labor and equipment usage. Compares materials and construction methods to allow you to select the best option.

**$64.95 per copy**
**Over 350 pages, illustrated, softcover**
**Catalog no. 67294B**

## Means ADA Compliance Pricing Guide New 2nd Edition
### by Adaptive Environments and RSMeans

Completely updated and revised to the new 2004 *Americans with Disabilities Act Accessibility Guidelines,* this book features more than 70 of the most commonly needed modifications for ADA compliance. Projects range from installing ramps and walkways, widening doorways and entryways, and installing and refitting elevators, to relocating light switches and signage.

**$79.95 per copy**
**Over 350 pages, illustrated, softcover**
**Catalog no. 67310A**

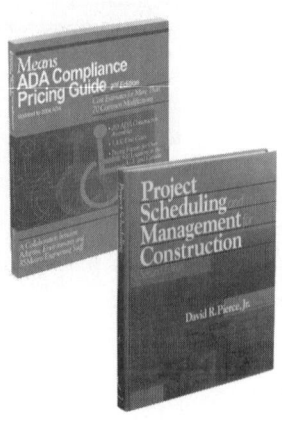

## Project Scheduling & Management for Construction
### New 3rd Edition
### by David R. Pierce, Jr.

A comprehensive yet easy-to-follow guide to construction project scheduling and control—from vital project management principles through the latest scheduling, tracking, and controlling techniques. The author is a leading authority on scheduling, with years of field and teaching experience at leading academic institutions. Spend a few hours with this book and come away with a solid understanding of this essential management topic.

**$64.95 per copy**
**Over 300 pages, illustrated, hardcover**
**Catalog no. 67247B**

**For more information
visit the RSMeans Website
at www.rsmeans.com**

# Reference Books

## The Practice of Cost Segregation Analysis

**by Bruce A. Desrosiers and
Wayne J. DelPico**

This expert guide walks you through the practice of cost segregation analysis, which enables property owners to defer taxes and benefit from "accelerated cost recovery" through depreciation deductions on assets that are properly identified and classified.

With a glossary of terms, sample cost segregation estimates for various building types, key information resources, and updates via a dedicated Web site, this book is a critical resource for anyone involved in cost segregation analysis.

**$99.95 per copy
Over 225 pages
Catalog no. 67345**

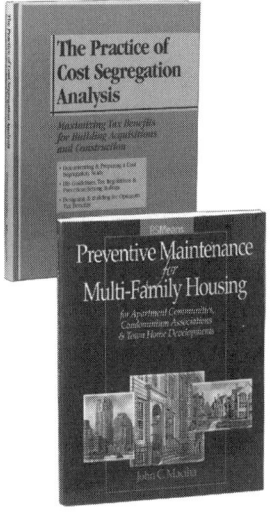

## Preventive Maintenance for Multi-Family Housing

**by John C. Maciha**

Prepared by one of the nation's leading experts on multi-family housing.

This complete PM system for apartment and condominium communities features expert guidance, checklists for buildings and grounds maintenance tasks and their frequencies, a reusable wall chart to track maintenance, and a dedicated Web site featuring customizable electronic forms. A must-have for anyone involved with multi-family housing maintenance and upkeep.

**$89.95 per copy
225 pages
Catalog no. 67346**

## How to Estimate with Means Data & CostWorks

**New 3rd Edition**

**by RSMeans and
Saleh A. Mubarak, Ph.D.**

New 3rd Edition—fully updated with new chapters, plus new CD with updated *CostWorks* cost data and MasterFormat organization. Includes all major construction items—with more than 300 exercises and two sets of plans that show how to estimate for a broad range of construction items and systems—including general conditions and equipment costs.

**$59.95 per copy
272 pages, softcover
Includes CostWorks CD
Catalog no. 67324B**

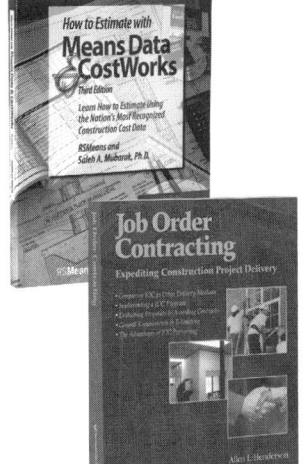

## Job Order Contracting

*Expediting Construction
Project Delivery*

**by Allen Henderson**

Expert guidance to help you implement JOC—fast becoming the preferred project delivery method for repair and renovation, minor new construction, and maintenance projects in the public sector and in many states and municipalities. The author, a leading JOC expert and practitioner, shows how to:

• Establish a JOC program

• Evaluate proposals and award contracts

• Handle general requirements and estimating

• Partner for maximum benefits

**$89.95 per copy
192 pages, illustrated, hardcover
Catalog no. 67348**

## Builder's Essentials: Estimating Building Costs

*For the Residential & Light
Commercial Contractor*

**by Wayne J. DelPico**

Step-by-step estimating methods for residential and light commercial contractors. Includes a detailed look at every construction specialty—explaining all the components, takeoff units, and labor needed for well-organized, complete estimates. Covers correctly interpreting plans and specifications, and developing accurate and complete labor and material costs.

**$29.95 per copy
Over 400 pages, illustrated, softcover
Catalog no. 67343**

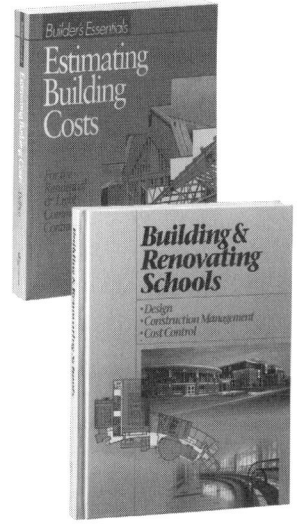

## Building & Renovating Schools

This all-inclusive guide covers every step of the school construction process—from initial planning, needs assessment, and design, right through moving into the new facility. A must-have resource for anyone concerned with new school construction or renovation. With square foot cost models for elementary, middle, and high school facilities, and real-life case studies of recently completed school projects.

The contributors to this book—architects, construction project managers, contractors, and estimators who specialize in school construction—provide start-to-finish, expert guidance on the process.

**$99.95 per copy
Over 425 pages, hardcover
Catalog no. 67342**

# Reference Books

For more information
visit the RSMeans Website
at www.rsmeans.com

## Residential & Light Commercial Construction Standards 2nd Edition

### by RSMeans and contributing authors

This book provides authoritative requirements and recommendations compiled from the nation's leading professional associations, industry publications, and building code organizations.

It's an all-in-one reference for establishing a standard for workmanship, quickly resolving disputes, and avoiding defect claims.

**$59.95 per copy**
**600 pages, illustrated, softcover**
**Catalog no. 67322A**

## Means Illustrated Construction Dictionary

### Unabridged 3rd Edition, with CD-ROM

Long regarded as the industry's finest, *Means Illustrated Construction Dictionary* is now even better. With the addition of over 1,000 new terms and hundreds of new illustrations, it is the clear choice for the most comprehensive and current information. The companion CD-ROM that comes with this new edition adds many extra features: larger graphics, expanded definitions, and links to both CSI MasterFormat numbers and product information.

**$99.95 per copy**
**Over 790 pages, illustrated, hardcover**
**Catalog no. 67292A**

## Designing & Building with the IBC 2nd Edition

### by Rolf Jensen & Associates, Inc.

This updated, comprehensive guide helps building professionals make the transition to the 2003 International Building Code®. Includes a side-by-side code comparison of the IBC 2003 to the IBC 2000 and the three primary model codes, a quick-find index, and professional code commentary. With illustrations, abbreviations key, and an extensive Resource section.

**$99.95 per copy**
**Over 875 pages, softcover**
**Catalog no. 67328A**

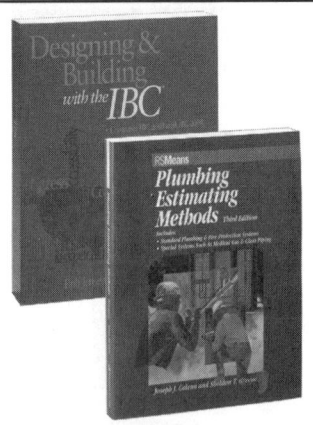

## Means Plumbing Estimating Methods 3rd Edition

### by Joseph Galeno and Sheldon Greene

Updated and revised! This practical guide walks you through a plumbing estimate, from basic materials and installation methods through change order analysis. *Plumbing Estimating Methods* covers residential, commercial, industrial, and medical systems, and features sample takeoff and estimate forms and detailed illustrations of systems and components.

**$29.98 per copy**
**330+ pages, softcover**
**Catalog no. 67283B**

## Understanding & Negotiating Construction Contracts

### by Kit Werremeyer

Take advantage of the author's 30 years' experience in small-to-large (including international) construction projects. Learn how to identify, understand, and evaluate high risk terms and conditions typically found in all construction contracts—then negotiate to lower or eliminate the risk, improve terms of payment, and reduce exposure to claims and disputes. The author avoids "legalese" and gives real-life examples from actual projects.

**$69.95 per copy**
**300 pages, softcover**
**Catalog no. 67350**

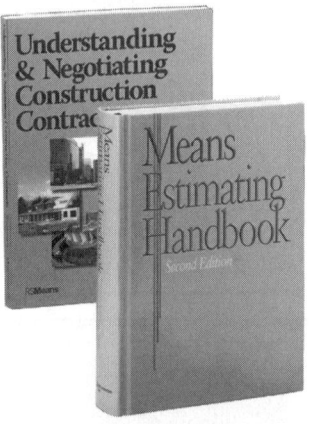

## Means Estimating Handbook

### 2nd Edition

Updated Second Edition answers virtually any estimating technical question—all organized by CSI MasterFormat. This comprehensive reference covers the full spectrum of technical data required to estimate construction costs. The book includes information on sizing, productivity, equipment requirements, code-mandated specifications, design standards, and engineering factors.

**$99.95 per copy**
**Over 900 pages, hardcover**
**Catalog no. 67276A**

## Means Spanish/English Construction Dictionary 2nd Edition

### by RSMeans and the International Code Council

This expanded edition features thousands of the most common words and useful phrases in the construction industry with easy-to-follow pronunciations in both Spanish and English. Over 800 new terms, phrases, and illustrations have been added. It also features a new stand-alone "Safety & Emergencies" section, with colored pages for quick access.

Unique to this dictionary are the systems illustrations showing the relationship of components in the most common building systems for all major trades.

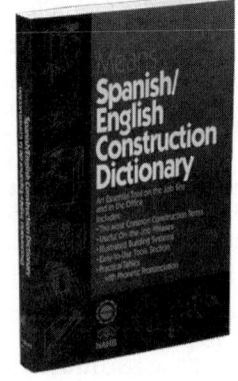

**$23.95 per copy**
**Over 400 pages**
**Catalog no. 67327A**

For more information
visit the RSMeans Website
at www.rsmeans.com

# Seminars

## Means CostWorks® Training

This *one-day* seminar has been designed with the intention of assisting both new and existing users to become more familiar with the *Means CostWorks* program. The class is broken into two unique sections: (1) A one-half day presentation on the function of each icon; and each student will be shown how to use the software to develop a cost estimate. (2) Hands-on estimating exercises that will ensure that each student thoroughly understands how to use *CostWorks*. You must bring your own laptop computer to this course.

**Means CostWorks Benefits/Features:**
- Estimate in your own spreadsheet format
- Power of RSMeans National Database
- Database automatically regionalized
- Save time with keyword searches
- Save time by establishing common estimate items in "Bookmark" files
- Customize your spreadsheet template
- Hot Key to Product Manufacturers' listings and specs
- Merge capability for networking environments
- View crews and assembly components
- AutoSave capability
- Enhanced sorting capability

## Unit Price Estimating

This interactive *two-day* seminar teaches attendees how to interpret project information and process it into final, detailed estimates with the greatest accuracy level.

The single most important credential an estimator can take to the job is the ability to visualize construction in the mind's eye, and thereby estimate accurately.

**Some of what you'll learn:**
- Interpreting the design in terms of cost
- The most detailed, time-tested methodology for accurate "pricing"
- Key cost drivers—material, labor, equipment, staging, and subcontracts
- Understanding direct and indirect costs for accurate job cost accounting and change order management

**Who should attend:** Corporate and government estimators and purchasers, architects, engineers... and others needing to produce accurate project estimates.

## Square Foot and Assemblies Estimating

This *two-day* course teaches attendees how to quickly deliver accurate square foot estimates using limited budget and design information.

**Some of what you'll learn:**
- How square foot costing gets the estimate done faster
- Taking advantage of a "systems" or "assemblies" format
- The RSMeans "building assemblies/square foot cost approach"
- How to create a very reliable preliminary and systems estimate using bare-bones design information

**Who should attend:** Facilities managers, facilities engineers, estimators, planners, developers, construction finance professionals... and others needing to make quick, accurate construction cost estimates at commercial, government, educational, and medical facilities.

## Repair and Remodeling Estimating

This *two-day* seminar emphasizes all the underlying considerations unique to repair/remodeling estimating and presents the correct methods for generating accurate, reliable R&R project costs using the unit price and assemblies methods.

**Some of what you'll learn:**
- Estimating considerations—like labor-hours, building code compliance, working within existing structures, purchasing materials in smaller quantities, unforeseen deficiencies
- Identifying problems and providing solutions to estimating building alterations
- Rules for factoring in minimum labor costs, accurate productivity estimates, and allowances for project contingencies
- R&R estimating examples calculated using unit price and assemblies data

**Who should attend:** Facilities managers, plant engineers, architects, contractors, estimators, builders... and others who are concerned with the proper preparation and/or evaluation of repair and remodeling estimates.

## Mechanical and Electrical Estimating

This *two-day* course teaches attendees how to prepare more accurate and complete mechanical/electrical estimates, avoiding the pitfalls of omission and double-counting, while understanding the composition and rationale within the RSMeans Mechanical/Electrical database.

**Some of what you'll learn:**
- The unique way mechanical and electrical systems are interrelated
- M&E estimates–conceptual, planning, budgeting, and bidding stages
- Order of magnitude, square foot, assemblies, and unit price estimating
- Comparative cost analysis of equipment and design alternatives

**Who should attend:** Architects, engineers, facilities managers, mechanical and electrical contractors... and others needing a highly reliable method for developing, understanding, and evaluating mechanical and electrical contracts.

## Green Building Planning & Construction

In this *two-day* course, learn about tailoring a building and its placement on the site to the local climate, site conditions, culture, and community. Includes information to reduce resource consumption and augment resource supply.

**Some of what you'll learn:**
- Green technologies, materials, systems, and standards
- Energy efficiencies with energy modeling tools
- Cost vs. value of green products over their life cycle
- Low-cost strategies and economic incentives and funding
- Health, comfort, and productivity goals and techniques

**Who should attend:** Contractors, project managers, building owners, building officials, healthcare and insurance professionals.

## Facilities Maintenance and Repair Estimating

This *two-day* course teaches attendees how to plan, budget, and estimate the cost of ongoing and preventive maintenance and repair for existing buildings and grounds.

**Some of what you'll learn:**
- The most financially favorable maintenance, repair, and replacement scheduling and estimating
- Auditing and value engineering facilities
- Preventive planning and facilities upgrading
- Determining both in-house and contract-out service costs
- Annual, asset-protecting M&R plan

**Who should attend:** Facility managers, maintenance supervisors, buildings and grounds superintendents, plant managers, planners, estimators... and others involved in facilities planning and budgeting.

## Practical Project Management for Construction Professionals

In this *two-day* course, acquire the essential knowledge and develop the skills to effectively and efficiently execute the day-to-day responsibilities of the construction project manager.

**Covers:**
- General conditions of the construction contract
- Contract modifications: change orders and construction change directives
- Negotiations with subcontractors and vendors
- Effective writing: notification and communications
- Dispute resolution: claims and liens

**Who should attend:** Architects, engineers, owner's representatives, project managers.

## Life Cycle Costing for Facilities

This *two-day* course teaches attendees how to plan and conduct life cycle cost analysis studies.

**Some of what you'll learn:**
- Initial project feasibility
- Developing guidelines for LCC studies and their accomplishment
- Selecting the best design
- Applying the latest economic models for energy conservation and greening of the environment

**Who should attend:** Professionals involved in planning, programming, real estate development, maintenance, operation, procurement, design, specifying, and construction.

# Seminars

For more information
visit the RSMeans Website
at www.rsmeans.com

## Scheduling and Project Management

This *two-day* course teaches attendees the most current and proven scheduling and management techniques needed to bring projects in on time and on budget.

### Some of what you'll learn:
- Crucial phases of planning and scheduling
- How to establish project priorities and develop realistic schedules and management techniques
- Critical Path and Precedence Methods
- Special emphasis on cost control

**Who should attend:** Construction project managers, supervisors, engineers, estimators, contractors... and others who want to improve their project planning, scheduling, and management skills.

## Understanding & Negotiating Construction Contracts

In this *two-day* course, learn how to protect the assets of your company by justifying or eliminating commercial risk through negotiation of a contract's terms and conditions.

### Some of what you'll learn:
- Myths and paradigms of contracts
- Scope of work, terms of payment and scheduling
- Dispute resolution
- Why clients love CLAIMS!
- Negotiating issues and much more

**Who should attend:** Contractors & subcontractors, material suppliers, project managers, risk & insurance managers, procurement managers, owners and facility managers, corporate executives.

## Site Work & Heavy Construction Estimating

This *two-day* course teaches attendees how to estimate earthwork, site utilities, foundations, and site improvements, using the assemblies and the unit price methods.

### Some of what you'll learn:
- Basic site work and heavy construction estimating skills
- Estimating foundations, utilities, earthwork, and site improvements
- Correct equipment usage, quality control, and site investigation for estimating purposes

**Who should attend:** Project managers, design engineers, estimators, and contractors doing site work and heavy construction.

## Assessing Scope of Work for Facility Construction Estimating

This *two-day* course is a practical training program that addresses the vital importance of understanding the SCOPE of projects in order to produce accurate cost estimates in a facility repair and remodeling environment.

### Some of what you'll learn:
- Discussions on site visits, plans/specs, record drawings of facilities, and site-specific lists
- Review of CSI divisions, including means, methods, materials, and the challenges of scoping each topic
- Exercises in SCOPE identification and SCOPE writing for accurate estimating of projects
- Hands-on exercises that require SCOPE, take-off, and pricing

**Who should attend:** Corporate and government estimators, planners, facility managers, and others who need to produce accurate project estimates.

# 2008 RSMeans Seminar Schedule

Note: Call for exact dates and details.

| Location | Dates |
| --- | --- |
| Las Vegas, NV | March |
| Washington, DC | April |
| Denver, CO | May |
| San Francisco, CA | June |
| Washington, DC | September |
| Dallas, TX | September |
| Las Vegas, NV | October |
| Orlando, FL | November |
| Atlantic City, NJ | October |
| San Diego, CA | December |

## 1-800-334-3509, ext. 5115

For more information
visit the RSMeans Website
at www.rsmeans.com

# Registration Information

**Register early... Save up to $100!** Register 30 days before the start date of a seminar and save $100 off your total fee. *Note: This discount can be applied only once per order. It cannot be applied to team discount registrations or any other special offer.*

**How to register** Register by phone today! The RSMeans toll-free number for making reservations is **1-800-334-3509, ext. 5115.**

**Individual seminar registration fee - $935.** *Means CostWorks®* **training registration fee - $375.** To register by mail, complete the registration form and return, with your full fee, to: Seminar Division, Reed Construction Data, RSMeans Seminars, 63 Smiths Lane, Kingston, MA 02364.

**Federal government pricing** All federal government employees save 25% off the regular seminar price. Other promotional discounts cannot be combined with the federal government discount.

**Team discount program** for two to four seminar registrations. Call for pricing: 1-800-334-3509, ext. 5115

**Multiple course discounts** When signing up for two or more courses, call for pricing.

**Refund policy** Cancellations will be accepted up to ten days prior to the seminar start. There are no refunds for cancellations received later than ten working days prior to the first day of the seminar. A $150 processing fee will be applied for all cancellations. Written notice of cancellation is required. Substitutions can be made at any time before the session starts. **No-shows are subject to the full seminar fee.**

**AACE approved courses** Many seminars described and offered here have been approved for 14 hours (1.4 recertification credits) of credit by the AACE

International Certification Board toward meeting the continuing education requirements for recertification as a Certified Cost Engineer/Certified Cost Consultant.

**AIA Continuing Education** We are registered with the AIA Continuing Education System (AIA/CES) and are committed to developing quality learning activities in accordance with the CES criteria. Many seminars meet the AIA/CES criteria for Quality Level 2. AIA members may receive (14) learning units (LUs) for each two-day RSMeans course.

**NASBA CPE sponsor credits** We are part of the National Registry of CPE sponsors. Attendees may be eligible for (16) CPE credits.

**Daily course schedule** The first day of each seminar session begins at 8:30 a.m. and ends at 4:30 p.m. The second day begins at 8:00 a.m. and ends at 4:00 p.m. Participants are urged to bring a hand-held calculator, since many actual problems will be worked out in each session.

**Continental breakfast** Your registration includes the cost of a continental breakfast, a morning coffee break, and an afternoon break. These informal segments will allow you to discuss topics of mutual interest with other members of the seminar. (You are free to make your own lunch and dinner arrangements.)

**Hotel/transportation arrangements** RSMeans has arranged to hold a block of rooms at most host hotels. To take advantage of special group rates when making your reservation, be sure to mention that you are attending the RSMeans seminar. You are, of course, free to stay at the lodging place of your choice. (**Hotel reservations and transportation arrangements should be made directly by seminar attendees.**)

**Important** Class sizes are limited, so please register as soon as possible.

*Note: Pricing subject to change.*

# Registration Form

**Call 1-800-334-3509, ext. 5115 to register or FAX 1-800-632-6732. Visit our Web site: www.rsmeans.com**

Please register the following people for the RSMeans construction seminars as shown here. We understand that we must make our own hotel reservations if overnight stays are necessary.

☐ Full payment of $_____ enclosed.

☐ Bill me

Name of registrant(s)

(To appear on certificate of completion)

_____

_____

_____

_____

P.O. #: _____
GOVERNMENT AGENCIES MUST SUPPLY PURCHASE ORDER NUMBER OR
TRAINING FORM.

Firm name_____

Address_____

City/State/Zip_____

Telephone no._____ Fax no._____

E-mail address_____

Charge our registration(s) to: ☐ MasterCard ☐ VISA ☐ American Express ☐ Discover

Account no._____ Exp. date_____

Cardholder's signature_____

Seminar name_____

City _____ Dates _____

**Please mail check to: Seminar Division, Reed Construction Data, RSMeans Seminars, 63 Smiths Lane, P.O. Box 800, Kingston, MA 02364 USA**

# MeansData™

## CONSTRUCTION COSTS FOR SOFTWARE APPLICATIONS
### Your construction estimating software is only as good as your cost data.

A proven construction cost database is a mandatory part of any estimating package. The following list of software providers can offer you MeansData™ as an added feature for their estimating systems. See the table below for what types of products and services they offer (match their numbers). Visit online at **www.rsmeans.com/demosource/** for more information and free demos. Or call their numbers listed below.

1. **3D International**
   713-871-7000
   venegas@3di.com

2. **4Clicks-Solutions, LLC**
   719-574-7721
   mbrown@4clicks-solutions.com

3. **ArenaSoft Estimating**
   888-370-8806
   info@arenasoft.com

4. **Beck Technology**
   214-303-6293
   stewartcarroll@beckgroup.com

5. **BSD - Building Systems Design, Inc.**
   888-273-7638
   bsd@bsdsoftlink.com

6. **Building Explorer LLC**
   949-500-9773
   info@buildingexplorer.com

7. **CMS - Computerized Micro Solutions**
   800-255-7407
   cms@proest.com

8. **Corecon Technologies, Inc.**
   714-895-7222
   sales@corecon.com

9. **CorVet Systems**
   301-622-9069
   sales@corvetsys.com

10. **Digital Alchemy**
    206-779-6308
    info@DigitalAlchemyPro.com

11. **Earth Tech**
    303-771-3103
    kyle.knudson@earthtech.com

12. **Estimating Systems, Inc.**
    800-967-8572
    esipulsar@adelphia.net

13. **MC² - Management Computer**
    800-225-5622
    vkeys@mc2-ice.com

14. **Maximus Asset Solutions**
    800-659-9001
    assetsolutions@maximus.com

15. **PrioSoft**
    888-394-0252
    sales@priosoft.com

16. **Sage Timberline Office**
    800-628-6583
    productinfo.timberline@sage.com

17. **SchoolDude.com**
    877-868-3833
    info@schooldude.com

18. **US Cost, Inc.**
    800-372-4003
    sales@uscost.com

19. **Vanderweil Facility Advisors**
    617-451-5100
    info@VFA.com

20. **WinEstimator, Inc.**
    800-950-2374
    sales@winest.com

| TYPE | 1 | 2 | 3 | 4 | 5 | 6 | 7 | 8 | 9 | 10 | 11 | 12 | 13 | 14 | 15 | 16 | 17 | 18 | 19 | 20 |
|---|---|---|---|---|---|---|---|---|---|---|---|---|---|---|---|---|---|---|---|---|
| BID | | | • | | • | | • | | • | | | | • | | | • | | | | • |
| Estimating | | • | • | • | • | | • | • | • | | • | • | • | | • | • | | • | | • |
| DOC/JOC/SABER | | • | • | | • | | | | • | | | • | | • | | • | | | | • |
| ID/IQ | | • | | | | | | | • | | | • | | • | | | | | | • |
| Asset Mgmt. | | | | | | | | | | | | | | • | | | • | | • | • |
| Facility Mgmt. | • | | | | | | | | | | | | | • | | | • | | • | |
| Project Mgmt. | • | • | | | | | | • | • | | | | | • | • | | | | | |
| TAKE-OFF | | | • | | | | • | • | | | • | | • | | | • | | • | | |
| EARTHWORK | | | | | | | | • | | | • | | • | | | | | | | |
| Pipe Flow | | | | | | | | | | | | | | | | | | | | |
| HVAC/Plumbing | | | • | | | | • | | • | | | | | | | | | | | |
| Roofing | | | • | | | | • | | • | | | | | | | | | | | |
| Design | • | | • | • | | | | | | | • | | | | | • | | | | • |
| **Other Offers/Links:** | | | | | | | | | | | | | | | | | | | | |
| Accounting/HR | | • | • | | | | | | | | | | • | | | • | | | | |
| Scheduling | | | • | | | | | | | | | | | | | • | | • | | • |
| CAD | | | | • | | • | | | | • | | | | | | • | | | | |
| PDA | | | | | | | | | | | | | | | | • | | • | | • |
| Lt. Versions | | • | | | | | • | | | | | | | | | • | | • | | |
| Consulting | • | • | • | • | | | • | | • | | • | | • | | | • | • | • | • | • |
| Training | | • | • | • | • | • | • | • | • | • | • | • | • | • | | • | • | • | • | • |

**Qualified re-seller applications now being accepted. Call Carol Polio, ext. 5107.**

# FOR MORE INFORMATION
## CALL 1-800-448-8182, EXT. 5107 OR FAX 1-800-632-6732

For more information
visit the RSMeans Website
at www.rsmeans.com

# New Titles

## How Your House Works
### by Charlie Wing

A must-have reference for every homeowner, handyman, and contractor—for repair, remodeling, and new construction. This book uncovers the mysteries behind just about every major appliance and building element in your house—from electrical, heating and AC, to plumbing, framing, foundations and appliances. Clear, "exploded" drawings show exactly how things should be put together and how they function—what to check if they don't work, and what you can do that might save you having to call in a professional.

$21.95 per copy
160 pages, softcover
Catalog no. 67351

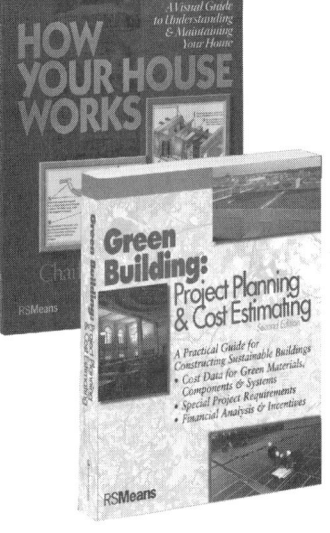

## Green Building: Project Planning & Cost Estimating 2nd Edition

This new edition has been completely updated with the latest in green building technologies, design concepts, standards, and costs. Now includes a 2008 Green Building *CostWorks* CD with more than 300 green building assemblies and over 5,000 unit price line items for sustainable building. The new edition is also full-color with all new case studies—plus a new chapter on deconstruction, a key aspect of green building.

$129.95 per copy
350 pages, softcover
Catalog no. 67338A

## Complete Book of Framing
### by Scot Simpson

This straightforward, easy-to-learn method will help framers, carpenters, and handy homeowners build their skills in rough carpentry and framing. Shows how to frame all the parts of a house: floors, walls, roofs, door & window openings, and stairs—with hundreds of color photographs and drawings that show every detail.
The book gives beginners all the basics they need to go from zero framing knowledge to a journeyman level. And it provides valuable tips and tables for the experienced carpenter—plus "framer-friendly" tips and a dedicated Website to access framing formulas.

$29.95 per copy
352 pages, softcover
Catalog no. 67353

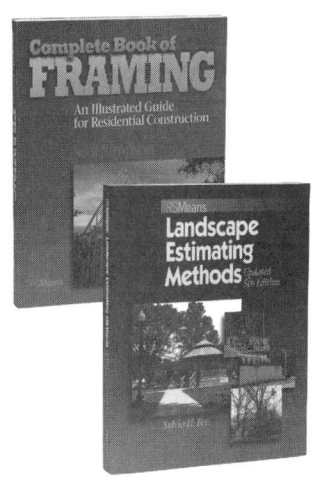

## Means Landscape Estimating Methods
### New 5th Edition

Answers questions about preparing competitive landscape construction estimates, with up-to-date cost estimates and the new MasterFormat classification system. Expanded and revised to address the latest materials and methods, including new coverage on approaches to green building that save water, reduce maintenance costs, and provide other benefits. Includes:

- Step-by-step explanation of the estimating process and a sample estimate for a major project.
- Sample forms and worksheets that save time and prevent errors—now available on a new companion Website.

$64.95 per copy
Over 350 pages, softcover
Catalog no. 67295C

## Construction Business Management
### by Nick Ganaway

Only 43% of construction firms stay in business after four years. Make sure your company thrives with valuable guidance from a pro with 25 years of success as a commercial contractor. Find out what it takes to build all aspects of a business that is profitable, enjoyable, and enduring. With a bonus chapter on retail construction.

$49.95 per copy
200 pages, softcover
Catalog no. 67352

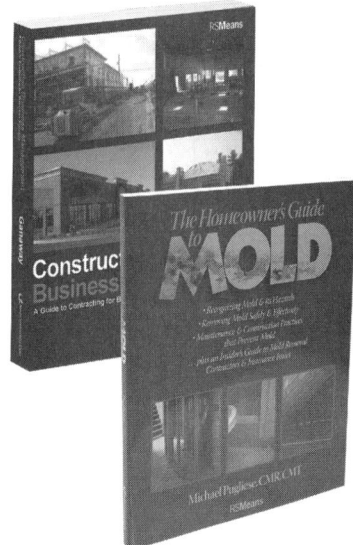

## The Homeowner's Guide to Mold By Michael Pugliese

Expert guidance to protect your health and your home.

Mold, whether caused by leaks, humidity or flooding, is a real health and financial issue—for homeowners and contractors. This full-color book explains:

- Construction and maintenance practices to prevent mold
- How to inspect for and remove mold
- Mold remediation procedures and costs
- What to do after a flood
- How to deal with insurance companies if you're thinking of submitting a mold damages claim

$21.95 per copy
144 pages, softcover
Catalog no. 67344

# 2008 Order Form

| Qty. | Book no. | COST ESTIMATING BOOKS | Unit Price | Total |
|---|---|---|---|---|
| | 60068 | Assemblies Cost Data 2008 | $245.95 | |
| | 60018 | Building Construction Cost Data 2008 | 149.95 | |
| | 61018 | Building Const. Cost Data–Looseleaf Ed. 2008 | 187.95 | |
| | 60718 | Building Const. Cost Data–Spanish 2008 | 149.95 | |
| | 60228 | Building Const. Cost Data–Western Ed. 2008 | 149.95 | |
| | 60118 | Concrete & Masonry Cost Data 2008 | 136.95 | |
| | 50148 | Construction Cost Indexes 2008 (subscription) | 325.00 | |
| | 60148A | Construction Cost Index–January 2008 | 81.25 | |
| | 60148B | Construction Cost Index–April 2008 | 81.25 | |
| | 60148C | Construction Cost Index–July 2008 | 81.25 | |
| | 60148D | Construction Cost Index–October 2008 | 81.25 | |
| | 60348 | Contr. Pricing Guide: Resid. R & R Costs 2008 | 39.95 | |
| | 60338 | Contr. Pricing Guide: Resid. Detailed 2008 | 39.95 | |
| | 60328 | Contr. Pricing Guide: Resid. Sq. Ft. 2008 | 39.95 | |
| | 60238 | Electrical Change Order Cost Data 2008 | 149.95 | |
| | 60038 | Electrical Cost Data 2008 | 149.95 | |
| | 60208 | Facilities Construction Cost Data 2008 | 357.95 | |
| | 60308 | Facilities Maintenance & Repair Cost Data 2008 | 326.95 | |
| | 60168 | Heavy Construction Cost Data 2008 | 149.95 | |
| | 60098 | Interior Cost Data 2008 | 149.95 | |
| | 60128 | Labor Rates for the Const. Industry 2008 | 326.95 | |
| | 60188 | Light Commercial Cost Data 2008 | 128.95 | |
| | 60028 | Mechanical Cost Data 2008 | 149.95 | |
| | 63018 | Metric Construction Cost Data 2008 | 179.95 | |
| | 60158 | Open Shop Building Const. Cost Data 2008 | 149.95 | |
| | 60218 | Plumbing Cost Data 2008 | 149.95 | |
| | 60048 | Repair and Remodeling Cost Data 2008 | 128.95 | |
| | 60178 | Residential Cost Data 2008 | 128.95 | |
| | 60288 | Site Work & Landscape Cost Data 2008 | 149.95 | |
| | 60058 | Square Foot Costs 2008 | 163.95 | |
| | 62018 | Yardsticks for Costing (2008) | 149.95 | |
| | 62017 | Yardsticks for Costing (2007) | 136.95 | |
| | | **REFERENCE BOOKS** | | |
| | 67310A | ADA Compliance Pricing Guide, 2nd Ed. | 79.95 | |
| | 67330 | Bldrs Essentials: Adv. Framing Methods | 12.98 | |
| | 67329 | Bldrs Essentials: Best Bus. Practices for Bldrs | 29.95 | |
| | 67298A | Bldrs Essentials: Framing/Carpentry 2nd Ed. | 24.95 | |
| | 67298AS | Bldrs Essentials: Framing/Carpentry Spanish | 24.95 | |
| | 67307 | Bldrs Essentials: Plan Reading & Takeoff | 35.95 | |
| | 67342 | Building & Renovating Schools | 99.95 | |
| | 67339 | Building Security: Strategies & Costs | 44.98 | |
| | 67353 | Complete Book of Framing | 29.95 | |
| | 67146 | Concrete Repair & Maintenance Illustrated | 69.95 | |
| | 67352 | Construction Business Management | 49.95 | |
| | 67314 | Cost Planning & Est. for Facil. Maint. | 89.95 | |
| | 67328A | Designing & Building with the IBC, 2nd Ed. | 99.95 | |
| | 67230B | Electrical Estimating Methods, 3rd Ed. | 64.95 | |
| | 64777A | Environmental Remediation Est. Methods, 2nd Ed. | 49.98 | |
| | 67343 | Estimating Bldg. Costs for Resi. & Lt. Comm. | 29.95 | |

| Qty. | Book no. | REFERENCE BOOKS (Cont.) | Unit Price | Total |
|---|---|---|---|---|
| | 67276A | Estimating Handbook, 2nd Ed. | $99.95 | |
| | 67318 | Facilities Operations & Engineering Reference | 54.98 | |
| | 67301 | Facilities Planning & Relocation | 89.95 | |
| | 67338A | Green Building: Proj. Planning & Cost Est., 2nd Ed. | 129.95 | |
| | 67349 | Home Addition & Renovation Project Costs | 29.95 | |
| | 67308E | Home Improvement Costs–Int. Projects, 9th Ed. | 24.95 | |
| | 67309E | Home Improvement Costs–Ext. Projects, 9th Ed. | 24.95 | |
| | 67344 | Homeowner's Guide to Mold | 21.95 | |
| | 67324B | How to Est.w/Means Data & CostWorks, 3rd Ed. | 59.95 | |
| | 67351 | How Your House Works | 21.95 | |
| | 67282A | Illustrated Const. Dictionary, Condensed, 2nd Ed. | 59.95 | |
| | 67292A | Illustrated Const. Dictionary, w/CD-ROM, 3rd Ed. | 99.95 | |
| | 67348 | Job Order Contracting | 89.95 | |
| | 67347 | Kitchen & Bath Project Costs | 29.95 | |
| | 67295C | Landscape Estimating Methods, 5th Ed. | 64.95 | |
| | 67341 | Life Cycle Costing for Facilities | 99.95 | |
| | 67294B | Mechanical Estimating Methods, 4th Ed. | 64.95 | |
| | 67245A | Planning & Managing Interior Projects, 2nd Ed. | 34.98 | |
| | 67283B | Plumbing Estimating Methods, 3rd Ed. | 29.98 | |
| | 67345 | Practice of Cost Segregation Analysis | 99.95 | |
| | 67337 | Preventive Maint. for Higher Education Facilities | 149.95 | |
| | 67346 | Preventive Maint. for Multi-Family Housing | 89.95 | |
| | 67326 | Preventive Maint. Guidelines for School Facil. | 149.95 | |
| | 67247B | Project Scheduling & Management for Constr. 3rd Ed. | 64.95 | |
| | 67265B | Repair & Remodeling Estimating Methods, 4th Ed. | 69.95 | |
| | 67322A | Resi. & Light Commercial Const. Stds., 2nd Ed. | 59.95 | |
| | 67327A | Spanish/English Construction Dictionary, 2nd Ed. | 23.95 | |
| | 67145B | Sq. Ft. & Assem. Estimating Methods, 3rd Ed. | 69.95 | |
| | 67321 | Total Productive Facilities Management | 29.98 | |
| | 67350 | Understanding and Negotiating Const. Contracts | 69.95 | |
| | 67303B | Unit Price Estimating Methods, 4th Ed. | 59.95 | |
| | 67319A | Value Engineering: Practical Applications | 79.95 | |

| | | |
|---|---|---|
| MA residents add 5% state sales tax | | |
| Shipping & Handling** | | |
| Total (U.S. Funds)* | | |

Prices are subject to change and are for U.S. delivery only. *Canadian customers may call for current prices. **Shipping & handling charges: Add 7% of total order for check and credit card payments. Add 9% of total order for invoiced orders.

**Send order to:**                                    **ADDV-1000**

Name (please print) _____

Company _____

☐ **Company**

☐ **Home  Address** _____

_____

City/State/Zip _____

Phone # _____ P.O. # _____

(Must accompany all orders being billed)

# Reed Construction Data, Inc.

**Reed Construction Data, Inc.** is a leading worldwide provider of total construction information solutions. The company's portfolio of information products and services is designed specifically to help construction industry professionals advance their businesses with timely, accurate, and actionable project, product, and cost data. Reed Construction Data is a division of Reed Business Information, a member of the Reed Elsevier PLC group of companies.

## Cost Information

RSMeans, the undisputed market leader in construction costs, provides current cost and estimating information through its innovative MeansCostworks.com® web-based solution. In addition, RSMeans publishes annual cost books, estimating software, and a rich library of reference books. RSMeans also conducts a series of professional seminars and provides construction cost consulting for owners, manufacturers, designers, and contractors to sharpen personal skills and maximize the effective use of cost estimating and management tools.

## Project Data

Reed Construction Data assembles one of the largest databases of public and private project data for use by contractors, distributors, and building product manufacturers in the U.S. and Canadian markets. In addition, Reed Construction Data is the North American construction community's premier resource for project leads and bid documents. Reed Bulletin and Reed CONNECT™ provide project leads and project data through all stages of construction for many of the country's largest public sector, commercial, industrial, and multi-family residential projects.

## Building Product Information

Reed First Source™ in the U.S. and BuildCore in Canada are the only integrated building product information systems offered to the commercial construction industry for searching, selecting, and specifying building products. Written by industry professionals and organized using CSI MasterFormat™ 2004 criteria, the design and construction community uses this information to make better, more informed design decisions.

## Research and Analytics

Reed Construction Data's forecasting tools cover most aspects of the construction business in the U.S. and Canada. Our vast network of resources makes us uniquely qualified to give you the information you need to keep your business profitable.

## Associated Construction Publications (ACP)

Reed Construction Data's regional construction magazines cover the nation through a network of 14 regional magazines. Serving the construction market for more than 100 years, our magazines are a trusted source of news and information in the local and national construction communities.

For more information, please visit our website at www.reedconstructiondata.com

Reed Construction Data, Inc.
30 Technology Parkway South
Norcross, GA 30092-2912
(800) 322-6996
(800) 895-8661 (fax)
Email: info@reedbusiness.com

**Reed Construction Data**®

# RSMeans Project Cost Report

By filling out this report, your project data will contribute to the database that supports the RSMeans Project Cost Square Foot Data. When you fill out this form, RSMeans will provide a $30 discount off one of the RSMeans products advertised in the preceding pages. Please complete the form including all items where you have cost data, and all the items marked (✔).

> ## *$30.00 Discount per product for each report you submit.*

## Project Description (No remodeling projects, please.)

✔ Building Use (Office, School...) _____

✔ Address (City, State) _____

_____

✔ Building Area (SF) _____

✔ Frame (Wood, Steel...) _____

✔ Exterior Wall (Brick, Tilt-up...) _____

✔ Basement: (check one)  ☐ Full  ☐ Partial  ☐ None

✔ Number Stories _____

✔ Floor-to-Floor Height _____

✔ Volume (C.F.) _____

% Air Conditioned _____ Tons _____

**Total Project Cost**　　　$ _____

Owner _____

Architect _____

General Contractor _____

✔ Bid Date _____

✔ Typical Bay Size _____

✔ Capacity _____

✔ Labor Force: _____ % Union _____ % Non-Union

✔ Project Description (Circle one number in each line)

1. Economy  2. Average　　3. Custom  4. Luxury
1. Square　　2. Rectangular  3. Irregular  4. Very Irregular

Comments _____

| A | ✔ General Conditions | $ |
|---|---|---|
| B | ✔ Site Work | $ |
| C | ✔ Concrete | $ |
| D | ✔ Masonry | $ |
| E | ✔ Metals | $ |
| F | ✔ Wood & Plastics | $ |
| G | ✔ Thermal & Moisture Protection | $ |
| GR | Roofing & Flashing | $ |
| H | ✔ Doors and Windows | $ |
| J | ✔ Finishes | $ |
| JP | Painting & Wall Covering | $ |

| K | ✔ Specialties | $ |
|---|---|---|
| L | ✔ Equipment | $ |
| M | ✔ Furnishings | $ |
| N | ✔ Special Construction | $ |
| P | ✔ Conveying Systems | $ |
| Q | ✔ Mechanical | $ |
| QP | Plumbing | $ |
| QB | HVAC | $ |
| R | ✔ Electrical | $ |
| S | ✔ Mech./Elec. Combined | $ |

Please specify the RSMeans product you wish to receive. Complete the address information.

Product Name _____

Product Number _____

Your Name _____

Title _____

Company _____

☐ Company
☐ Home　　Street Address _____

City, State, Zip _____

Method of Payment:

Credit Card # _____

Expiration Date _____

Check _____

Purchase Order _____

**Reed Construction Data/RSMeans**
Square Foot Costs Department
P.O. Box 800
Kingston, MA 02364-9988

Return by mail or Fax 888-492-6770.